*The Art of the Short Story*

# The Art of the Short Story

## Stories and Authors in Historical Context

**Wendy Martin**
Claremont Graduate University

with

**Danielle Hinrichs**
University of Southern California

and

**Sharon Becker**
Claremont Graduate University

Houghton Mifflin Company
Boston    New York

*Publisher:* Patricia Coryell
*Executive Editor:* Suzanne Phelps Weir
*Associate Editor:* Bruce Cantley
*Editorial Assistant:* Lindsey Gentel
*Senior Project Editor:* Rosemary Winfield
*Editorial Assistant:* Jake Perry
*Design Manager:* Gary Crespo
*Art and Design Coordinator:* Jill Haber
*Photo Editor:* Jennifer Meyer Dare
*Composition Buyer:* Chuck Dutton
*Manufacturing Coordinator:* Karen Banks
*Marketing Manager:* Cindy Graff Cohen
*Marketing Associate:* Wendy Thayer

Cover: *Cataluña* by Joaquin Sorolla y Bastida. Courtesy of The Hispanic Society of America, New York.

Credits continue on page C-1, which constitutes an extension of the copyright page.

Printed in the U.S.A.
Library of Congress Catalog Card Number 2004112191

ISBN 0-618-15575-9

2 3 4 5 6 7 8 9 – DOC – 08 07 06

# Brief Contents

# Brief Contents

# Contents

xii • Contents

## PART 2 Reading, Writing, Discussing 1411

### Reading: The Critical Essays 1413

## Writing: Crafting the Short Story 1529

## Discussing: Writers Talk about Their Work 1569

## PART 3  Appendixes  1625

# Preface

Like our most imaginative sculpture, inventive painting, and evocative music, the best short stories are works of art that live on, becoming part of our cultural and historical legacy. An extraordinary short story, like any great work of art, can be revisited again and again, each reading or viewing revealing new layers of meaning and raising new questions. Like a series of brush strokes or a lyrical melody, a compelling metaphor can evoke a quick and palpable response while opening a path to new interpretations. In this innovative anthology, stories by many of the world's most gifted writers of short fiction will enhance the intellect and stir emotions. Above all, *The Art of the Short Story* will engage your imagination, challenge your mind, and, finally, entertain.

A good short story captures an extraordinary richness of character and setting— a world in microcosm. In this anthology, you will find that each story embodies a compact, yet complete, literary experience. In the classroom setting, students can experience the work of a great writer and analyze the full expression of a theme or plot in a few class sessions rather than in the longer period it takes to read and discuss a novel. The historical and literary context of a story can profoundly deepen its meaning; therefore, in *The Art of the Short Story*, we have placed stories in dialogue with each other, helping readers to see how the characters and plots within a story respond to their historical moment.

This anthology encourages a variety of approaches to teaching literature:

- The organization into time periods accommodates a historical approach to literature and culture.

- The critical essays support emphasis on literary criticism and analysis and on writing about short stories.

- The essays by authors give students insight into the creative process of writing.

- The interviews offer the opportunity to join a literary discussion and to think about literature as dialogue.

- The thematic and historical clusters help to focus analysis.

Taken together, all of these aspects of the anthology foster creative approaches to teaching the short story, and literature as a whole, that will be different in every classroom.

Nevertheless, the various aspects of the anthology only enhance its true heart: stories that are engaging, thought-provoking, and meaningful; stories that we remember long after reading them and that offer new, illuminating insights with each re-reading. In the end, the anthology honors the stories themselves.

## HISTORICAL ORGANIZATION

The most striking innovation of *The Art of the Short Story* is its historical organization, an organizational scheme not found in other college-level short story anthologies, which are typically arranged alphabetically or thematically. This fresh organizational scheme enables readers to understand the evolution of the genre from the precursors of the short story, such as parables, myths, oral narratives, and fables, to the contemporary short stories we read today.

The anthology is organized into four distinct historical periods—Precursors to the Short Story, The Nineteenth-Century Short Story, The Modern Short Story (1900 to 1969), and the Contemporary Short Story (1970 to the present). An in-depth introduction, interweaving both historical/cultural trends and developments in the art of the short story, precedes each section. Thus, in this collection, the text is always placed in context.

Within each time period, a thematic cluster includes a group of stories and critical essays related to a specific historical theme. Within the larger context of nineteenth-century literature, students can embark on an in-depth exploration of various depictions of domestic space in stories by Charlotte Perkins Gilman, Mary Wilkins Freeman, and Kate Chopin; in the modern section, students experience the Harlem Renaissance in writings by Arna Bontemps, Langston Hughes, and Zora Neale Hurston; and in the contemporary section, students get a glimpse of the postcolonial in the works of Ama Ata Aidoo, Peter Carey, Hanif Kureishi, and Salman Rushdie. The clusters also include critical essays that provide complex and meaningful terms and ideas to enhance students' understanding of these compelling stories.

Art and photo montages reinforce and extend the contextual support of historical introductions and thematic clusters by offering a visual array of people and events important within each historical period. These images frame the stories, evoking intertextual meaning and encouraging reading practices that move both within and outside of individual stories.

Finally, readers are encouraged to visit *The Art of the Short Story* companion Web site, where they will find eight distinct timelines, highlighting key historical and cultural events from the invention of the printing press in 1450 to the present. These timelines give readers an additional framework for the anthology's stories, creating a broad and lively overview of interesting events that can serve as a springboard for research paper topics.

## INTRODUCTION: THE ELEMENTS OF THE SHORT STORY

This general introduction to *The Art of the Short Story* speaks directly to the student reader and provides essential, practical background information about formal elements of fiction such as plot, character, setting, and point of view. The chapter allows students to evaluate and appreciate the literary craft of storytelling. Clear definitions of literary terms are followed by a discussion of how students can intelligently and thoughtfully approach the short story via active reading, annotating a text, keeping a reading notebook, generating ideas via free writing and clustering, and writing a provisional thesis statement. In this section, students are guided through an analysis of Chinua Achebe's "Dead Men's Path" and asked to embrace a process-oriented and critical approach to reading and writing about fiction.

## Part One: Stories

The 126 stories and novella (Henry James's *Daisy Miller*) chosen for *The Art of the Short Story* constitute a comprehensive anthology of "the best of the best"—the most compelling classic stories as well as the most relevant and engaging modern and contemporary stories, both American and international. The collection emphasizes stories that are well crafted as well as emotionally resonant. Selections from such diverse writers as Aesop, Marie de France, Geoffrey Chaucer, Anton Chekhov, Sarah Orne Jewett, Guy de Maupassant, Edith Wharton, Henry James, Zora Neale Hurston, Ernest Hemingway, Jorge Luis Borges, Flannery O'Connor, Yukio Mishima, Isabel Allende, Jhumpa Lahiri, and Ama Ata Aidoo encompass a universe of experience in powerfully written narratives that speak to readers on the deepest levels. These are stories that readers love and want to return to again and again.

### Special Features

- **Historical section introductions**   Each historical unit is preceded by an informative essay, tracing the evolution of the short story during that era in tandem with pivotal historical events and thus demonstrating how literature and history are vitally interconnected.

- **Author headnotes**   Each author's work in the anthology is preceded by a brief biographical headnote. The author headnotes are designed to be informative without being prescriptive, allowing students to freshly read an author's work free of preconceived notions about that author.

- **Thematic clusters**   The book's three thematic clusters encourage deeper exploration of the historical themes through a combination of interrelated short stories and critical essays. The thematic clusters are "Domestic Fictions" in the Nineteenth-Century Short Story section, "The Harlem Renaissance" in the Modern Short Story section, and "Postcolonial Literature" in the Contemporary Short Story section.

## PRECURSORS TO THE SHORT STORY

While most short story anthologies begin with early nineteenth-century innovators of the form, such as Washington Irving, Mary Shelley, Nathaniel Hawthorne, and Edgar Allan Poe, the first historical unit in this anthology, "Precursors to the Short Story," enables readers to understand and appreciate the genesis of this genre as well as its evolution in history. From Aesop's fables, to creation stories drawn from a range of cultures, to fairy tales and parables, we can appreciate the persistent human desire to learn about and interpret human behavior in a range of historical moments and cultural contexts. Several of the entries in this section introduce characters and themes that appear in later stories, providing engaging examples of stories in dialogue throughout history.

## THE NINETEENTH-CENTURY SHORT STORY

An informative introduction to this pivotal era in the development of the short story discusses the importance of the magazine industry in the development of the short story as we know it today and considers the way that increased global communication and travel have shaped the short story internationally. The stories anthologized in this section include such international innovators as Edgar Allan Poe, Anton Chekhov, Guy de Maupassant, and Nikolai Gogol. An illuminating thematic unit entitled "Domestic Fictions" collects stories by three of the most influential women writers of the era—Charlotte Perkins Gilman, Kate Chopin, and Mary Wilkins Freeman—which, along with related critical essays, provide a unique opportunity to discuss how domesticity shaped the lives and writings of many nineteenth-century women.

## THE MODERN SHORT STORY

Focusing on the period from 1900 to 1969, the introduction to this section suggests that the social upheavals of the industrial revolution, two World Wars, and the atomic age gave rise to corresponding radical changes in the short story form. Short stories in this section include a wide variety of important authors, from James Joyce, Franz Kafka, Katherine Mansfield, and F. Scott Fitzgerald in the early part of the century, to Jorge Luis Borges, Flannery O'Connor, Jean-Paul Sartre, and Tillie Olsen in midcentury. This section's thematic unit, "The Harlem Renaissance," contains a selection of stories by Langston Hughes, Zora Neale Hurston, and Arna Bontemps, as well as critical essays, thus providing an excellent opportunity to explore in depth this historically unprecedented explosion of African American arts and letters.

## THE CONTEMPORARY SHORT STORY

This section focuses on literature from 1970 to the present, a time in which developments in the women's movement, the end of colonial rule in much of the world, and a dramatic growth of awareness and pride in cultural and individual identities have given us such diverse authors as Toni Morrison, Leslie Marmon Silko, David Leavitt, Sandra Cisneros, R. K. Narayan, and Maxine Hong Kingston. This anthology emphasizes dialogue between and juxtapositions of writers from various countries and traditions. As part of this focus on cross-cultural experience, this section's thematic unit, "Postcolonial Literature," spotlights writers such as Salman Rushdie, Ama Ata Aidoo, and Peter Carey, from formerly colonized countries.

## PART TWO: READING, WRITING, DISCUSSING

Part Two of *The Art of the Short Story,* "Reading, Writing, Discussing," contains three distinct sections that provide further context and conversation for exploring the art of the short story. In these additional articles, students can experience fruitful discussions that surround the short story and create a deeper understanding of its themes and practices. The essays and interviews within these three sections are cross-referenced in the short story table of contents, where applicable, enabling instructors to create groups or pairings of readings for unique and in-depth assignments.

- **Reading: The Critical Essays** contains essays that either discuss the art of the short story in general or respond directly to particular short stories or authors in this collection. Examples include a critique by Edgar Allan Poe of Nathaniel Hawthorne's collection of stories *Twice Told Tales,* Pancho Savery's "Baldwin, Bebop, and 'Sonny's Blues,'" and Margaret Atwood's self-referential essay, "Reading Blind."

- **Writing: Crafting the Story** is particularly helpful to those using *The Art of the Short Story* in a creative fiction writing course. Here, six authors—Raymond Carver, Henry James, Jhumpa Lahiri, Alice Munro, Flannery O'Connor, and Joyce Carol Oates—provide readers with an intimate glimpse into their aesthetic preoccupations and literary values.

- In **Discussing: Writers Talk about Their Work,** interviews show writers in dialogue with their readers, offering firsthand perspectives on writing practices and important themes. The section includes interviews with Isabel Allende, Ernest Hemingway, Louise Erdrich, Richard Ford, Leslie Marmon Silko, and Luisa Valenzuela.

## PART THREE: APPENDIXES

Five appendixes round out this rich anthology, making it a comprehensive tool for classroom learning:

- The **Glossary of Literary Terms** features a wealth of short story–related literary terms, clearly and succinctly defined.

- The **MLA Documentation** appendix provides information on the basics of documentation, note-taking, quoting sources, and avoiding plagiarism and includes sample MLA-style citations.

- The **Film Bibliography** contains an extensive list of film adaptations of short stories collected in *The Art of the Short Story,* with director, cast, and running time information, as well as video release information. An imbedded bibliography, "Essays about Film Adaptations of Short Stories," also provides textual sources for exploring the topic of literature to film adaptation.

- Both the **Chronological Table of Contents** and the **Thematic Table of Contents** allow for multiple ways of structuring a course based on this collection.

## SUPPLEMENTS

### INSTRUCTOR'S RESOURCE MANUAL (AVAILABLE ONLINE AT HTTP:// ENGLISH.COLLEGE.HMCO.COM/INSTRUCTORS)

An unusually rich Instructor's Resource Manual, by Danielle Hinrichs of the University of Southern California, includes a wealth of teaching materials. For every story collected in the student text, the Instructor's Resource Manual provides a brief analysis of the story, discussion questions, writing assignments, a class activity, and an extensive bibliography for further reading and research. In addition, the manual contains sample syllabi to help facilitate organizing a course based on *The Art of the Short Story,* advice on grading, and multiple handouts useful for facilitating classroom activities, assignments, and discussions.

### STUDENT WEB SITE (AVAILABLE AT HTTP://ENGLISH.COLLEGE.HMCO.COM/ STUDENTS)

Using *The Art of the Short Story* student Web site is an excellent way to enhance the student text, containing a number of features appropriate for a Web environment:

- **Annotated author links** are organized alphabetically by the author's last name and include every author in the student text. These annotated links can be used as a springboard for further research into any author's work.

- **Timelines** are broken into eight user-friendly parts and provide a detailed context for the stories. Events like the invention of the printing press, the steam engine, electricity, and the radio and movie camera shape the stories we tell as surely as do wars, famines, and other disasters or triumphs. These timelines also provide correlations with other art forms, enabling readers to consider parallels in music and the visual arts for a given story or cluster of stories.

- **Short story walkthroughs** (one of Charles Chesnutt's "The Goophered Grapevine" and one of Mary Wilkins Freeman's "The Revolt of 'Mother'") allow readers to interact with these two stories on multiple levels. Each walkthrough features a general contextual introduction. By choosing a topic (such as Plot and Structure, Character and Dialogue, or Symbolism), readers explore the story in those terms—highlighted passages and pop-up windows guide readers as they go.

- **Sample student papers** provide excellent models of student essays in response to reading short fiction.

## PEDAGOGICAL POSSIBILITIES

The historical approach of this anthology allows for flexibility and honors and enables various approaches to teaching literature. The accompanying "Reading" section of critical essays is useful for instructors who want to emphasize a history of literary criticism and the way we analyze and write about short stories. The "Writing" section, including authors discussing writing practices, allows instructors to speak to the creative practices of writing. The "Discussing" section, including author interviews, gives instructors the opportunity to ask students to join a literary discussion and to think about literature as dialogue. In addition, the clusters work well for a thematic approach to literature, and the unique way that the stories are organized by chronological time period enables a historical approach to literature and culture. Finally, the number and quality of stories in this anthology accommodate instructors who prefer to skip around through the text, choosing a stunning group of powerful stories. All of the ancillary sections, materials, and organizational aspects are merely ways of enhancing the true heart of the anthology: stories that are engaging, thought-provoking, and meaningful. The stories are ones that we remember long after reading them and that offer new, life-sized insights with each rereading.

## ACKNOWLEDGMENTS

The editors of this anthology would like to thank the following people for their contributions: Lisa Colletta, Tim Geaghan, Tanja Laden, Susan Pramschuffer, Jan Roselle, and Michelle Wester. Their research skills, story suggestions, and general goodwill have contributed much to this effort. Thank you also to the students of Claremont Graduate University, Claremont McKenna College, and Edgewood College for reading and evaluating the numerous drafts and permutations of this project. Special thanks to Bonnie Millhollin-Bane and Denisa Chapman-Riley for extensive contributions to the headnotes and timelines and to Maureen O'Connor and Sarah Fields for their invaluable help with the introductions.

Much appreciation also to Gayle Greene, Beverly Gross, Susan Fox, Leslie Martin, Frances Starn, Donald Stone, and Elaine Showalter for their many excellent suggestions for short stories and for their support throughout this project.

As always, we would like to express ongoing gratitude to our families: Laurel Martin-Harris, Jed Harris, Pamela Doolan, Lark, Stephen, Daniel, and Scot Doolan, Sheryl Cavales, Daniel Martin, Berenice deLuca Palmer, Claude and Teresa Palmer, Christopher Gaalaas, Bruce Hinrichs, Nancy Hinrichs, Robert and Lois Becker, and Rob Show. And in memory of Earl E. Martin and Teresa deLuca Martin.

Our reviewers nationwide have provided valuable advice on all aspects of the anthology:

Lee Abbott, Ohio State University; John Aber, College of Mount St. Joseph; Cora Agatucci, Central Oregon Community College; Jocelyn Bartkevicius, University of Central Florida; Bert Bender, Arizona State University; Sandy Camillo, Finger Lakes Community College; John Patrick Clifford, University of North Carolina at Wilmington; Isabella DiBari, Diablo Valley College; Robert Dunne, Central Connecticut State University; Patrick M. Ellingham, Broward Community College; Preston Fambrough, Baker University; Eileen Ferritti, Kingsborough Community College; Suzanne Forster, University of Alaska at Anchorage; James Gill, Southern Illinois University at Carbondale; Lisa Goddard, Orange Coast College; Daniel Gonzalez, Louisiana State University; Lucy Graca, Arapahoe Community College; Paul Hagood, Linn-Benton Community College; Jack Hicks, University of California at Davis; Lawrence Kinsman, New Hampshire College; Gale K. Larson, California State University at Northridge; Andrew E. Mathis, Temple University; Kathryn McKinley, Florida International University; Ruth Moose, University of North Carolina at Chapel Hill; Virginia Nelson, Johnson County Community College; Christopher Rieger, Louisiana State University; Lavina D. Shankar, Bates College ; Sheryl St. Germain, Iowa State University; Andrew Stauffer, Boston University; Marc Thompson, Parkland College; Jessica Treadway, Emerson College; Michael White, Community College of Southern Nevada; and Judy A. Worman, Dartmouth College

Finally, we would like to thank Bruce Cantley, Patricia Coryell, Michael Gillespie, Rosemary Winfield, Jake Perry, Cindy Graff Cohen, and Suzanne Phelps Weir for their enthusiasm for this project.

# The Art of the Short Story

# Elements of the Short Story

## Guidelines for Reading and Writing

*I think that everything is true, that fiction is just a way of saying something truthful from the very beginning. What is fiction? A bunch of lies, but it wouldn't work if these lies didn't come from a very honest truthful place inside you.*

—ISABEL ALLENDE

*Read widely, read enthusiastically, be guided by instinct and not design. For if you read, you need not become a writer; but if you hope to become a writer, you must read.*

—JOYCE CAROL OATES

In the first epigraph of this chapter, Isabel Allende, a Latin American novelist and short story writer, suggests that fiction can convey fundamental truths about life. Nevertheless, we commonly discuss fiction as a story—long or short or somewhere in between—that comes primarily from the imagination of the author and does not strictly adhere to history or fact. A quick glance at the short stories included in this anthology demonstrates that successful fiction takes a variety of paths to reach the same goal: entertaining the reader. Short stories (as well as novels and novellas) are shaped by the unique vision and skills of an author and can be funny, serious, romantic, surreal, or a combination of all of these fundamentals, but most stories employ **formal elements of fiction.** Understanding the definitions of these elements will help you better comprehend the complexity of a story and how its meaning extends beyond its own boundaries.

## PLOT

Plot, the most obvious element of fiction, is simply what happens in a story. Plot consists of a series of actions and events that take place over the course of a text. These actions and events usually involve a main character who faces an external or internal conflict that drives his or her choices and decisions. In turn, these choices and decisions shape the action and the direction of the plot.

The plot can unfold in a myriad of ways; an author can tell a story from point A to point B with a straightforward and chronological sequence of events (a linear plot) or move back and forth in time, jumping between past and present within one story. How the author chooses to depict the action, though, usually includes basic components of plot: **conflict, rising action, climax, falling action,** and **conclusion.** A successful story does not necessarily have all these elements, but most good stories have at least a few. The **conflict** in a story gives the main character a problem or situation to wrestle with and perhaps resolve. The **rising action** in a story is the substance of the text, a deepening of the drama as the main character faces complications while pursuing a resolution to the conflict. The **climax** of the story is the resolution, either positive or negative, of the main character's conflict. The **falling action** is the subsiding of the drama and often brings together various narrative threads, preparing the reader for the **conclusion,** or ending, to the story.

## CHARACTER

The plot of a story would not be particularly interesting if it did not include characters, or representations of humans (or animals, creatures, robots, etc.), who help move the story forward with their actions, thoughts, and feelings. Characters can be "brought to life" through numerous means, including biographical information; the way they look, walk, or talk; and what they think or feel about other characters in the text.

There are as many characters as there are authors and stories, but there are a few accepted categories into which most characters in a story fall. The main character, or **protagonist,** draws a reader through the beginning, middle, and end of a story. The **antagonist** is usually a source of tension or conflict for the protagonist and someone the reader opposes. It is important to note, however, that protagonists are not always likeable and antagonists are not necessarily mean or unlikeable. A **round** character is complex and well defined and usually provokes an emotional response from the reader, whereas a **flat** character is minimally described and does not play a central role in the story.

## SETTING

The setting is where the story happens and includes everything from time and place to the social, cultural, and historical context in which the story occurs. Thus, a story's setting can include details as simple as the color of a character's living room couch or as far-reaching as underlying tensions between whites and African Americans in a small southern town in June of 1956. The setting allows the author to create a meaningful mood by placing characters within detailed and significant places and times. The setting is not only a backdrop, but also a richly interactive context that can direct, explain, subvert, or circumscribe a character's thoughts and actions. At times, the setting becomes the focal point of plot or a presence as lively as a character in its interactions with other characters in the story.

## POINT OF VIEW

An author conveys plot, characters, and setting through a voice that may or may not belong to a character in the story. Point of view describes the voice the author uses to tell the story; it is the "eyes" through which the reader watches the action unfold. The point of view is ascribed to two different kinds of narrators: **third-person** and **first-person.** In a **third-person narrative,** the narrator is outside of the story and reports on the actions of the characters. In a **first-person narrative,** the narrator is the "I" of the story and participates in the story, although this participation is sometimes limited or minimal.

The third-person point of view can further be divided into two separate categories: **omniscient** point of view and **limited** point of view. The **omniscient** narrator knows and sees everything and has equal access to all characters' actions, thoughts, feelings, and motivations. This type of narrator can be **intrusive,** expressing personal feelings about the characters and their actions, or **unintrusive,** simply reporting the action without judgment. In the **limited** point of view, the narrator has access only to the heart, mind, and actions of one character.

The first-person point of view limits the reader's access to the story by presenting what only one character thinks and feels. A reader finds out about other characters only through interactions with the narrator, who either directly witnesses or participates in the main events or is a minor participant or peripheral player in the story as a whole. Thus the first-person point of view challenges a reader to decide if the narrator is a **reliable** or accurate reporter of events.

## THEME

The **theme** is the reverberating meaning or concept a reader is left with at the conclusion of the story. It is the meaning of the story that exists beyond the understanding of what actually happens in the plot. Although an author might be straightforward with his or her intentions, the theme is rarely directly stated and must be understood by carefully examining all of the above-discussed elements of fiction. In fact, many authors actively work to obscure their theme with the hopes that readers will feel free to interpret the story in a myriad of ways, making the story's message meaningful within a variety of cultural and social settings.

## ACTIVE READING

The important elements of a story and their significance are identified through critical reading and writing. Critical thinkers read carefully, ask questions about stories, and uncover multiple meanings. Engaging in active reading practices will help you fully understand, remember, and think deeply about the details of stories.

## ANNOTATING

Annotating a text, or writing notes on the story itself, helps readers to remember and generate ideas about stories. As you read, write questions or words in the margins about the elements of fiction, noting the point of view of a story, whether its narrator is reliable or its plot linear, or which details of the setting help to explain the characters' motivations. Here are a few other types of notes that will help you respond to stories in a thoughtful way:

- Circle unfamiliar or particularly complex words and write a brief definition in the margin.

- Underline important sentences in the story. Underlining too much can make this exercise useless, so be sure to use underlining for the most central passages in the story.

- Write questions in the margins about characters, setting, plot, theme, or point of view. For example, brief notes might ask, "Why does this character have this name?" or "Why does the author shift the point of view in the middle of the story?"

- Trace possible themes in the story by writing a key word wherever the author returns to an important idea. For example, you might realize that an author refers to a particular color many times throughout the story. Writing the word *blue* in the margin wherever it appears will help you keep track of how often and in what context this color is used. Similarly, you might decide that the idea of freedom or justice is important in the story, and you can use these words to identify portions of the story that explore these concepts.

- If you find yourself confused, write a question mark in the margin to remind yourself that there is something you didn't understand in that part of the story. Keep reading, and return to the confusing passage in a second reading or in class discussion.

- Often, something in a story will remind readers of an image, character, or theme from another story. Circle or underline this part of the story and write the title of the other story in the margin. If you're asked to write a comparison of two stories or to trace a theme through several stories, this will be an important insight.

Writing such notes on your story will make you a more active participant in class discussion and a better writer. Before you go to class, skim the story to remind yourself of major themes, and consider offering questions from your margins in class. If a part of the story confused you, it probably confused other students as well, and your instructor will be grateful for your question. Most important, your annotations will be invaluable as you write essays. If your instructor gives you a flexible topic, review your annotations to recall themes in the story that interested you. If you wrote a question in the margin about characterization, plot, or style, you might begin an essay by trying to answer your own question.

## KEEPING A READING NOTEBOOK

Dedicating a small notebook to reflections on stories helps readers gain unique insights about narrative elements and ideas. For each story you read, make a separate entry in your notebook with the author's name and the title and date of the story. After you finish reading the short story, write down your immediate thoughts, referring to the following list if you need some prompting:

- What is the author trying to communicate to readers?

- What is the central theme of this story?

- Have you read other stories by this author? If so, how is this story similar or different?

- How does this story compare with the last short story you read?

- Do you recognize images, themes, or characters that are similar to those in other literature that you've read? What are the similarities and differences?

A reading notebook is a place to record your initial response to each of your readings. It will be a fertile starting place for papers, exam questions, and discussion.

## A SAMPLE ANALYSIS: CHINUA ACHEBE'S "DEAD MEN'S PATH"

Although each reader's annotations reveal that reader's unique interests and insights, the following annotated story by Chinua Achebe offers an example of the types of notes readers make in a text.

# Chinua Achebe

> From the headnote, I know that Achebe is from Nigeria and draws on oral traditions.

## Dead Men's Path

1953

Michael Obi's hopes were fulfilled much earlier than he had expected. He was appointed headmaster of Ndume Central School in January 1949. It had always been an unprogressive school, so the Mission authorities decided to send a young and energetic man to run it. Obi accepted this responsibility with enthusiasm. He had many wonderful ideas and this was an opportunity to put them into practice. He had had sound secondary school education which designated him a "pivotal teacher" in the official records and set him apart from the other headmasters in the mission field. He was outspoken in his condemnation of the narrow views of these older and often less-educated ones.

> Signif. of date?

> Old v. new, educated v. uneducated

"We shall make a good job of it, shan't we?" he asked his young wife when they first heard the joyful news of his promotion.

"We shall do our best," she replied. "We shall have such beautiful gardens and everything will be just *modern* and delightful. . . ." In their two years of married life she had become completely infected by his passion for "modern methods" and his denigration of "these old and superannuated people in the teaching field who would be better employed as traders in the Onitsha market." She began to see herself already as the admired wife of the young headmaster, the queen of the school.

> Superannuated means retired but also obsolete

The wives of the other teachers would envy her position. She would set the fashion in everything. . . . Then, suddenly, it occurred to her that there might not be other wives. Wavering between hope and fear, she asked her husband, looking anxiously at him.

> Wife concerned with status

"All our colleagues are young and unmarried," he said with enthusiasm which for once she did not share. "Which is a good thing," he continued.

"Why?"

"Why? They will give all their time and energy to the school."

Nancy was downcast. For a few minutes she became skeptical about the new school; but it was only for a few minutes. Her little personal misfortune could not blind her to her husband's happy prospects. She looked at him as he sat folded up in a chair. He was stoop-shouldered and looked frail. But he sometimes surprised people with sudden bursts of physical energy. In his present posture, however, all his bodily strength seems to have retired behind his deep-set eyes, giving them an extraordinary power of penetration. He was only twenty-six, but looked thirty or more. On the whole, he was not unhandsome.

> Youth v. elderly

"A penny for your thoughts, Mike," said Nancy after a while, imitating the woman's magazine she read.

> Magazine: symbol of modernity

"I was thinking what a grand opportunity we've got at last to show these people how a school should be run."

Ndume School was backward in every sense of the word. Mr. Obi put his whole life into the work, and his wife hers too. He had two aims. A high standard of teaching was insisted upon, and the school compound was to be turned into a place of beauty. Nancy's dream-gardens came to life with the coming of the rains, and blossomed. Beautiful hibiscus and allamanda hedges in brilliant red and yellow marked out the carefully tended school compound from the rank neighborhood bushes.

> Hedges = barrier between school and community

One evening as Obi was admiring his work he was scandalized to see an old woman from the village hobble right across the compound, through a marigold flower-bed and the hedges. On going up there he found faint signs of an almost disused path from the village across the school compound to the bush on the other side.

> New v. old

"It amazes me," said Obi to one of his teachers who had been three years in the school, "that you people allowed the villagers to make use of this footpath. It is simply incredible." He shook his head.

> Incredible: Obi can't imagine a point of view other than his own.

"The path," said the teacher apologetically, "appears to be very important to them. Although it is hardly used, it connects the village shrine with their place of burial."

> Tradition and community connected themes

"And what has that got to do with the school?" asked the headmaster.

"Well, I don't know," replied the other with a shrug of the shoulders. "But I remember there was a big row some time ago when we attempted to close it."

"That was some time ago. But it will not be used now," said Obi as he walked away. "What will the Government Education Officer think of this when he comes to inspect the school next week? The villagers might, for all I know, decide to use the schoolroom for a pagan ritual during the inspection."

Heavy sticks were planted closely across the path at the two places where it entered and left the school premises. These were further strengthened with barbed wire.

Three days later the village priest of Ani called on the headmaster. He was an old man and walked with a slight stoop. He carried a stout walking-stick which he usually tapped on the floor, by way of emphasis, each time he made a new point in his argument.

> The path is a "footpath" for walking. The priest carries walking stick: symbolic of importance of walking on path. Walking connected to communication: uses walking stick to emphasize ideas in speech.

"I have heard," he said after the usual exchange of cordialities, "that our ancestral footpath has recently been closed. . . ."

"Yes," replied Mr. Obi. "We cannot allow people to make a highway of our school compound."

"Look here, my son," said the priest bringing down his walking-stick, "this path was here before you were born and before your father was born. The whole life of this village depends on it. Our dead relatives depart by it and our ancestors visit us by it. But most important, it is the path of children coming in to be born. . . ."

Mr. Obi listened with a satisfied smile on his face.

> What is the purpose/ duty of education?

"The whole purpose of our school," he said finally, "is to eradicate just such beliefs as that. Dead men do not require footpaths. The whole idea is just fantastic. Our duty is to teach your children to laugh at such ideas."

> Modern = get rid of past, tradition

"What you say may be true," replied the priest, "but we follow the practices of our fathers. If you reopen the path we shall have nothing to quarrel about. What I always say is: let the hawk perch and let the eagle perch." He rose to go.

> ?

"I am sorry," said the young headmaster. "But the school compound cannot be a thoroughfare. It is against our regulations. I would suggest your constructing another path, skirting our premises. We can even get our boys to help in building it. I don't suppose the ancestors will find the little detour too burdensome."

> Old v. new

"I have no more words to say," said the old priest, already outside.

> Old v. new

> Old v. new

Two days later a young woman in the village died in childbed. A diviner was immediately consulted and he prescribed heavy sacrifices to propitiate ancestors insulted by the fence.

> Symbolic: what is being torn down?

Obi woke up next morning among the ruins of his work. The beautiful hedges were torn up not just near the path but right round the school, the flowers trampled to death and one of the school buildings pulled down. . . . That day, the white Supervisor came to inspect the school and wrote a nasty report on the state of the premises but more seriously about the "tribal-war situation developing between the school and the village, arising in part from the misguided zeal of the new headmaster."

> How is race important in this story?

## GENERATING IDEAS

Readers identify important themes in a story by reviewing their marginal comments, but they also use strategies like free-writing, listing, and clustering to more deeply examine the story's meanings. In free-writing, writers write without structuring or revising their thoughts in order to record many ideas as quickly as possible. Set a time limit of five to ten minutes and write constantly about the story without censoring your thoughts or worrying about structure, grammar, or punctuation. Although much of free-writing is not appropriate for a paper or exam, you will often find the beginning of a useful idea in this informal exercise. Listing is similar, but it involves recording important themes as key words and phrases rather than as whole sentences. A list of themes addressed in Achebe's story might look something like this:

### Achebe's "Dead Men's Path"

| | |
|---|---|
| Education | Power |
| Modernity | Respect |
| Age | Marriage |
| Community | Walking/Paths |
| Tradition | Childbirth |
| Generations/Ancestors | Gardens |
| Communication | Status |
| Hierarchies | Oral Traditions/Language |
| Race | |

Return to your list to refine the focus of your essay and to make connections between the many themes in the story. Using a cluster diagram, sometimes called a mind-map, helps a reader define key ideas and explore connections between multiple themes. A student who read Achebe's story came up with a diagram that identifies three main themes and comments on the connections between them.

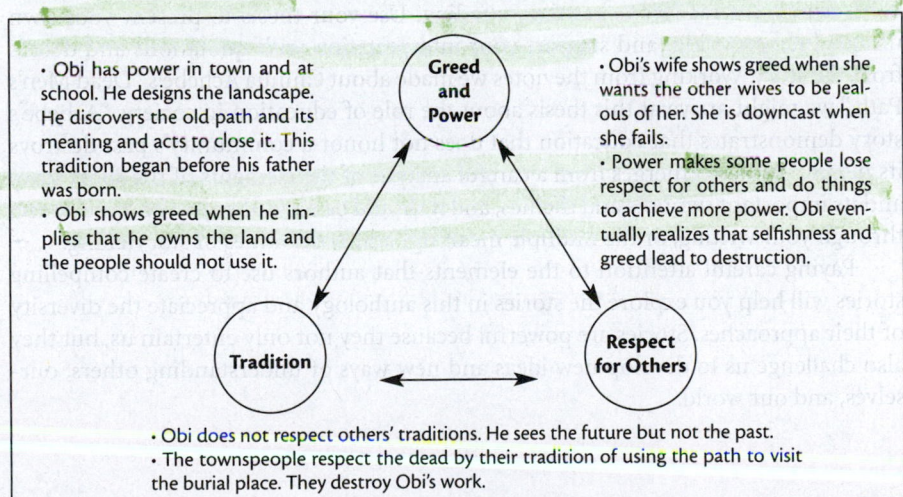

- Obi has power in town and at school. He designs the landscape. He discovers the old path and its meaning and acts to close it. This tradition began before his father was born.
- Obi shows greed when he implies that he owns the land and the people should not use it.

**Greed and Power**

- Obi's wife shows greed when she wants the other wives to be jealous of her. She is downcast when she fails.
- Power makes some people lose respect for others and do things to achieve more power. Obi eventually realizes that selfishness and greed lead to destruction.

**Tradition**

**Respect for Others**

- Obi does not respect others' traditions. He sees the future but not the past.
- The townspeople respect the dead by their tradition of using the path to visit the burial place. They destroy Obi's work.

## DEVELOPING IDEAS

Because themes like modernity, tradition, community, and education are substantial concepts with complicated meanings, critical readers must ask themselves how Achebe defines each of these terms in the story and how they are related to each other. Obi obviously associates education with modernity and believes that one of its purposes is to convince community members to discard traditional ways in favor of more modern ideas. What, though, constitutes modernity in this story? Let us turn to the marginal notes above for help. The magazine that Nancy reads is noted as a symbol of modernity, and from it comes her phrase "A penny for your thoughts." Because a penny is an American type of money, the magazine suggests ideas that are both modern and Western (not African). Thus, the couple's goal of teaching modernity means instructing students to replace their traditional African beliefs with "modern," European-American ideals. The school is destroyed, in a physical and symbolic sense, because Obi's form of education does not respect or respond to the traditions of the school's community.

## A THESIS STATEMENT

A thesis statement helps writers to clarify ideas and articulate the main point of an essay. A thesis can be more than one sentence, but it should be both concise and specific. For most writers, a statement conveying the overall point of the essay will appear at the end of the first paragraph, early in the essay but after background on the topic of the paper. You will need to revise your thesis statement as your paper develops, and each revision will make your thesis more clear, arguable, and specific. Determine whether your thesis is arguable by asking whether someone who has read the story carefully could support an alternate interpretation. If your thesis is too obvious, there is no reason for readers to continue reading. Use your thesis to present your own unique interpretation, and support your interpretation with quotations and details from the story. Working from the notes we made about Chinua Achebe's "Dead Men's Path," we might arrive at this thesis about the role of education in society: "Achebe's story demonstrates that education that does not honor a community's past destroys its future." A thesis emerges from a careful analysis of the elements of the short story and its important symbols and themes, and it should be revised as you become aware, through your writing, of the multiple meanings and possibilities of storytelling.

Paying careful attention to the elements that authors use to create compelling stories will help you explore the stories in this anthology and appreciate the diversity of their approaches. Stories are powerful because they not only entertain us, but they also challenge us to develop new ideas and new ways of understanding others, ourselves, and our world.

# Part 1

# Stories

# Precursors to the Short Story

1. The Creation, *frontispiece from the Luther Bible, 1534*
2. *Bust of Plato, Sala delle Muse, undated*
3. *Aesop,* The Fox and the Grapes, *illustration by Herrick, 1879*
4. *Calligraphy, letter written on a snowy day, 4th century Chinese*
5. *The Mausoleum at Halicarnassus, one of the seven wonders of the ancient world, 353 B.C.*
6. *Han Kan,* Two Horses and a Groom, *painting, 8th century Chinese*

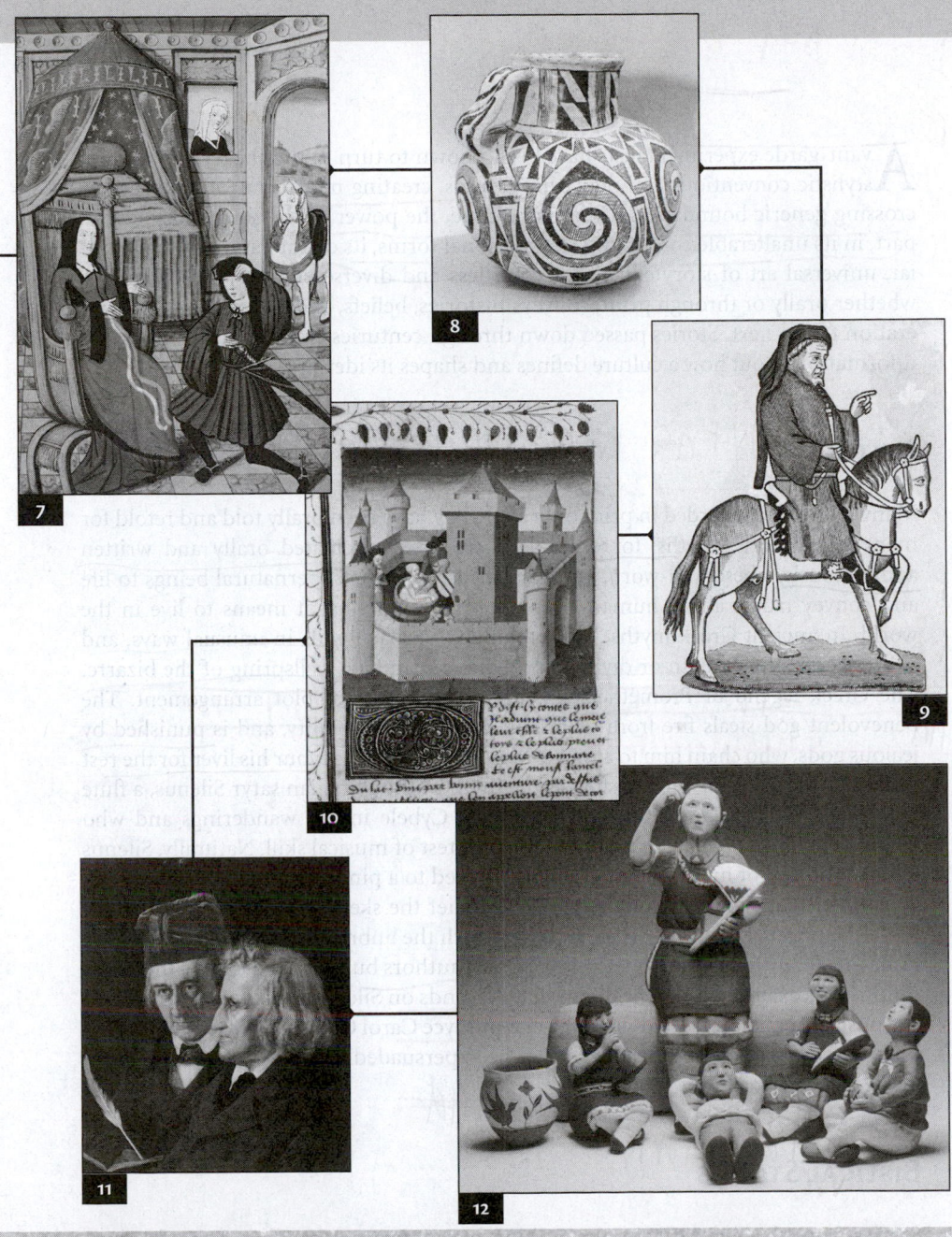

7. *A knight visiting his lady, manuscript illustration, 1475*
8. *Pitcher with a spiral design, Mogollon/Anasazi culture, United States, c. 1100*
9. *Geoffrey Chaucer riding a horse, woodcut, undated*
10. *Bath scene in the courtyard of a castle, manuscript illustration, 15th century French*
11. *Anna Maria Elisabeth Jerichau-Baumann,* **The Brothers Grimm,** *oil painting, 1855*
12. *Joe Cajero, Jr., Storyteller, sculpture, 1994*

A vant-garde experimentalists have been known to turn to the short story to flout stylistic conventions and defy expectations, creating new forms of literature by crossing generic boundaries. At the same time, the power of the short story lies, in part, in its unalterable connection to traditional forms, its continuation of the familiar, universal art of storytelling. For countless and diverse cultures, telling stories, whether orally or through print, conveys histories, beliefs, and hopes from one generation to the next. Stories passed down through centuries communicate important information about how a culture defines and shapes its identity.

## MYTHS

*Myths were wrote anonymously*

Many stories are recorded in print only after they have been orally told and retold for many generations. Myths, for example, were often circulated orally and written anonymously. These well-worn, familiar narratives bring supernatural beings to life and convey truths about human existence, exploring what it means to live in the world. In ancient Greek myths, humans often approach gods in unusual ways, and consequences for human or divine disobedience can be a wellspring of the bizarre. The Greek legend of Prometheus exemplifies this sort of plot arrangement. The benevolent god steals fire from Olympus, gives it to humanity, and is punished by jealous gods, who chain him to a rock where vultures daily devour his liver for the rest of time. Another such ancient story is the myth of the Phrygian satyr Silenus, a flute player who accompanies the harvest goddess Cybele in her wanderings and who comes to grief after challenging Apollo to a contest of musical skill. Naturally, Silenus loses to the god of music and is subsequently tied to a pine tree and dismembered.

In these ancient tales, one sees in bold relief the skeleton of the contemporary loss-of-innocence, coming-of-age story, in which the hubris of a particular innocence leads inevitably to destruction. Contemporary authors build on and extend these traditions. For example, the same doom that descends on Silenus envelops Connie when she pushes open the screen door at the end of Joyce Carol Oates's "Where Are You Going, Where Have You Been?" after she has been persuaded to walk out of the house of her teenage invincibility.

*comtempary authors build on & extend traditions*

## BIBLICAL STORIES

*Judeo christian have huge affect on short story*

Stories from the Judeo-Christian tradition have enormously affected the development of the short story throughout the Western world. Although biblical tales take part in a larger narrative, many stand on their own as self-contained stories that convey cultural beliefs and attempt to explain human life. "The Creation of the World" from Genesis demonstrates this important act of storytelling as it defines the role of the divine and the purpose and responsibility of human existence. Similarly, the "Book of Job" is undeniably also a compact story with unique characters. The God and the Satan associated with Job are not quite the same in other books of the Bible. The story of Job is perhaps one of the most autonomous parts of Scripture and has influenced the nature of European storytelling.

Traditionally written in Latin and oriented toward a small, highly educated readership, such biblical stories, along with other religious literature, were among the first texts to be translated and made available to a general population of readers. Called hagiography, some of the earliest short narratives recounted the lives of saints. At the end of the twelfth century, writers began translating these accounts into the vernacular, making them accessible to a wider audience. People who did not study Latin were now able to read saints' stories, sermons, and other religious literature, widening the influence and scope of short narrative.

## LAIS

Lais, lyrical compositions often sung with instrumental accompaniment, found their largest audience in France, Scandinavia, and England. Marie de France, the first Western European woman to employ the vernacular in narrative, wrote a series of lais in the late twelfth century about knights employed by a heroic Briton king. De France's lais tell of valiant knights and their romantic adventures. Inevitably, in these short, courtly tales, the divine universe rewards goodness and punishes evil, taking part in a courtly tradition focused on romance and the lives of the elite. In "Guigemar," for example, the devotion of a mistreated princess and valiant knight is rewarded when they rediscover each other after a long separation. The lais were inspired not only by popular tradition, but also, probably, by Geoffrey of Monmouth's seminal fiction *Prophecies of Merlin,* written around 1136, for which he borrowed freely from Welsh legend, the Roman historian Nennius, and Buddhist parable. It is important to note that authors borrowed freely from each other and from well-known oral stories in the medieval tradition, reworking and revising familiar material into creative new narratives. For medieval readers, the connection of a new tale to a familiar one increased the value of the new work.

## FABLIAUX AND FABLES

Marie de France also wrote fabliaux: short, coarse, verse tales named by the French and immortalized by Chaucer. Although the fabliau resembles the lay in length and form, it is traditionally very different in content. Lais address the elevated lives of knights, queens, and kings, whereas fabliaux tell comic and bawdy stories that parody courtly literature. The ancient fables of Aesop are probably the oldest and most famous form of fabliaux. Often populated with animal characters possessing human emotions and abilities, fables reveal the foibles and frailties of humanity. Most importantly, fables are didactic, presenting the reader with a clear and specific moral message. Thus, the classic fable of the fox and the grapes teaches us that it's easy to despise what we cannot attain. Such characteristics are found as well in the traditional beast fable whose hero is a fox, named Reynard by the French but present in various other languages as well. This story is influenced by the picaresque tradition (in which likeable, lowly characters encounter a series of adventures) and by the many incarnations of the trickster archetype found in folklore, mythology, and religious literatures.

Chinese fables and parables that predate the short story form include "The Removal of Mountains" and "Why Tsen Sheng Killed the Pig." Such comic stories also appear in Hindu (the Panca Tantra collection) and Arabic (Book of Kalilah and Dimnah), as well as in the more romantically oriented work of Christine de Pizan, who counted the *Metamorphoses* of Ovid among her influences.

## FOLKTALES AND FAIRY TALES

The phantasmagorical character of the Headless Horseman in Washington Irving's "Legend of Sleepy Hollow" harks back to the familiarly ludicrous universe of folk narrative or fairy tale. Fairy tales, fantastical stories with whimsical characters, are integral parts of cultural histories, repeated and revised by successive generations of storytellers. One Norwegian story of this type concerns an adventure of a youngest son by the name of Ashiepattle, a kind of male version of "Cinderella." It recounts the fate of the enterprising lad who, in the space of a scant four pages, enlists the help of a sly princess to discover and destroy the heart of a wicked giant, which turns out to be hidden in an unlaid duck egg inside a duck who sits at the bottom of a well in the nave of a church on an island in the middle of a distant lake. The equally fantastical Russian tales of the witch Baba Yaga feature an old woman who lives in a hut with chickens' feet; in one story, the woman pursues the child heroine in a flying mortar powered by a grinding pestle, and the girl escapes by throwing a comb to the ground that, on impact, turns into an impenetrable forest.

The hideous head of Irving's horseman hits the earth and is revealed to be a pumpkin, whereas Baba Yaga continues flying through the air indefinitely, yet the journeys seem related in their estrangement from the everyday. The marks of oral tradition are evident in characters as smoothed-over as river stones, their individuality sanded away to reveal the archetypal through the touch of many generations. And it is difficult not to see these stories nestled within modern works, like eggs containing the hearts of far-off giants.

## INFLUENCES

Although nineteenth-century writers and readers would come to define the short story by its readable length, detailed characters, and developed plot, the genre continues to demonstrate the flexible path of its vibrant precursors. The patterns and possibilities of the oral tradition lay beneath the surface of each short story, creating a genre amazingly amenable to new versions and interpretations. Short stories continue to raise fundamental questions about the universalities of human life while also allowing each writer to explore the unique literary forms and traditions of distinct cultures. For example, many modern writers of the Japanese short story incorporate characteristics of the haiku, an ancient Japanese literary form. Native American short story writers, like Louise Erdrich, rewrite traditional Native American legends in a modern context. Other authors—like Franz Kafka in Germany, Angela Carter in England, Italo Calvino in Italy, and Jorge Luis Borges in Argentina—convey the substance of modern and contemporary life while reviving the stuff of fairy tale, folktale, parable, legend, and fable. Although perhaps not as explicitly as their medieval predecessors, all of the authors represented in this anthology borrow from and build on diverse narratives, creating exciting new stories that help readers explore and define themselves and their world.

# Aesop

## (C. 620–560 B.C.)

Few facts are known about the man called Aesop. In *The Book of Xanthus the Philosopher and His Slave Aesop,* he is described as a deformed, mute slave. According to the book, when he is kind to an attendant of the goddess Isis, Aesop receives the ability to speak and craft fables. As Xanthus's slave, Aesop is credited with many adventures and obscene episodes found implausible by historians. Other stories tell of Aesop gaining his freedom, traveling through Asia Minor and Egypt, and becoming a member of the court of Croesus, King of Lydia. Aesop was sent with an embassy to Delphi, where he so offended the inhabitants with his sarcasms that they hurled him from a cliff to his death. His history may be altogether legendary.

## The Fox and the Grapes                                         6th century B.C.

TRANSLATED BY V. S. VERNON JONES

A hungry Fox saw some fine bunches of Grapes hanging from a vine that was trained along a high trellis, and did his best to reach them by jumping as high as he could into the air. But it was all in vain, for they were just out of reach: so he gave up trying, and walked away with an air of dignity and unconcern, remarking, "I thought those Grapes were ripe, but I see now they are quite sour."

## The Town Mouse and the Country Mouse
*6th century* B.C.

TRANSLATED BY V. S. VERNON JONES

A Town Mouse and a Country Mouse were acquaintances, and the Country Mouse one day invited his friend to come and see him at his home in the fields. The Town Mouse came, and they sat down to a dinner of barleycorns and roots, the latter of which had a distinctly earthy flavour. The fare was not much to the taste of the guest, and presently he broke out with "My poor dear friend, you live here no better than the ants. Now, you should just see how I fare! My larder is a regular horn of plenty. You must come and stay with me, and I promise you you shall live on the fat of the land." So when he returned to town he took the Country Mouse with him, and showed him into a larder containing flour and oatmeal and figs and honey and dates. The Country Mouse had never seen anything like it, and sat down to enjoy the luxuries his friend provided: but before they had well begun, the door of the larder opened and some one came in. The two Mice scampered off and hid themselves in a narrow and exceedingly uncomfortable hole. Presently, when all was quiet, they ventured out again; but some one else came in, and off they scuttled again. This was too much for the visitor. "Good-bye," said he, "I'm off. You live in the lap of luxury, I can see, but you are surrounded by dangers; whereas at home I can enjoy my simple dinner of roots and corn in peace."

*[handwritten annotation: —two acquaintances enjoy the luxury of lard]*

## The King James Bible

(1611)

*[handwritten annotation left margin: Have enormous influence on literary tradition]*

Biblical plots and language have had an enormous influence on literary traditions, particularly in the West. Like other cultural explanations of human origin, the Christian creation story has assumed many textual and oral forms. The most influential version is probably from the King James Bible, which contains such well-known expressions as "And God said, 'Let there be light': and there was light." During the reign of Elizabeth (1558–1603), a request was made for an act of Parliament to create a new version of the Bible to reduce the diversity of bibles available at the time. Although no action was taken during Elizabeth's time, King James I called the Hampton Court Conference in 1604 to address church issues. At that meeting, Dr. John Reynolds, leader of the Puritan Party, made a motion to retranslate the Bible. The majority of the conference attendees were against it. Nevertheless, the king found it worthy. Fifty-four biblical scholars were divided into six groups, three groups designated for work on the Old Testament and three for the New Testament. The translation began in 1607 and was completed in 1610. It was made available to the public in 1611.

*[handwritten annotation right margin: request was made for an newer version]*

*[handwritten annotation bottom: -55 scholars divided into 6 groups *3 for old testament *3 for new testament]*

# The Creation of the World
## (Genesis 1:1–2:3)

*10th–2nd centuries* B.C.

In the beginning God created the heaven and the earth. And the earth was without form, and void; and darkness was upon the face of the deep. And the Spirit of God moved upon the face of the waters. And God said, "Let there be light": and there was light. And God saw the light, that it was good: and God divided the light from the darkness. And God called the light Day, and the darkness he called Night. And the evening and the morning were the first day.

*[margin: earth w/out form & void.]*

And God said, "Let there be a firmament in the midst of the waters, and let it divide the waters from the waters." And God made the firmament, and divided the waters which were under the firmament from the waters which were above the firmament: and it was so. And God called the firmament Heaven. And the evening and the morning were the second day.

And God said, "Let the waters under the heaven be gathered together unto one place, and let the dry land appear": and it was so. And God called the dry land Earth; and the gathering together of the waters called he Seas: and God saw that it was good. And God said, "Let the earth bring forth grass, the herb yielding seed, and the fruit tree yielding fruit after his kind, whose seed is in itself, upon the earth": and it was so. And the earth brought forth grass, and herb yielding seed after his kind, and the tree yielding fruit, whose seed was in itself, after his kind: and God saw that it was good. And the evening and the morning were the third day.

*[margin: god saw it was good.]*

And God said: "Let there be lights in the firmament of the heaven to divide the day from the night; and let them be for signs, and for seasons, and for days, and years; and let them be for lights in the firmament of the heaven to give light upon the earth." And it was so. And God made two great lights; the greater light to rule the day, and the lesser light to rule the night: he made the stars also. And God set them in the firmament of the heaven to give light upon the earth. And to rule over the day and over the night, and to divide the light from the darkness: and God saw that it was good. And the evening and the morning were the fourth day.

*[margin: god created all living creatures]*

And God said, "Let the waters bring forth abundantly the moving creature that hath life, and fowl that may fly above the earth in the open firmament of heaven." And God created great whales, and every living creature that moveth, which the waters brought forth abundantly, after their kind, and every winged fowl after his kind: and God saw that it was good. And God blessed them, saying, "Be fruitful, and multiply, and fill the waters in the seas, and let fowl multiply in the earth." And the evening and the morning were the fifth day.

And God said, "Let the earth bring forth the living creature after his kind, cattle, and creeping thing, and beast of the earth after his kind": and it was so. And God made the beast of the earth after his kind, and cattle after their kind, and every thing that creepeth upon the earth after his kind: and God saw that it was good.

And God said, "Let us make man in our image, after our likeness: and let them have dominion over the fish of the sea, and over the fowl of the air, and over the cattle, and over all the earth, and over every creeping thing that creepeth upon the earth."

So God created man in his own image, in the image of God created he him; male and female created he them. And God blessed them, and God said unto them, "Be fruitful, and multiply, and replenish the earth, and subdue it: and have dominion over the fish of the sea, and over the fowl of the air, and over every living thing that moveth upon the earth." And God said, "Behold, I have given you every herb bearing seed, which is upon the face of all the earth, and every tree, in the which is the fruit of a tree yielding seed; to you it shall be for meat. And to every beast of the earth, and to every fowl of the air, and to every thing that creepeth upon the earth, wherein there is life, I have given every green herb for meat." And it was so. And God saw every thing that he had made, and, behold, it was very good. And the evening and the morning were the sixth day.

Thus the heavens and the earth were finished, and all the host of them. And on the seventh day God ended his work which he had made; and he rested on the seventh day from all his work which he had made. And God blessed the seventh day, and sanctified it: because that in it he had rested from all his work which God created and made.

# Chuang Tzu

## (C. 369–268 B.C.)

Chuang Tzu used parables and anecdotes to set forth the early ideas of what would become the Taoist school. He believed that only by understanding Tao (the Way of Nature) and dwelling in unity can man achieve happiness and be truly free. *The Inner Chapters,* edited by A. C. Graham, and *Chuang Tzu* include translations of Chuang Tzu's writing.

## A Butterfly's Dream
3rd century B.C.

RETOLD BY CHEO-KANG SIE

Twang Tsen, the well-known Taoist philosopher, related a dream of his as follows:

He dreamt that he was a butterfly. At the beginning he felt somewhat awkward, since it was the first time he had been such a creature. Soon other butterflies gave him a friendly welcome and one after the other said:

Why do you stay in a corner like a little girl?
The gods created nature for us.
And the sweetness of flowers, too.
Love is delicious.
The sun calls us.
Come with us.

With such words in his ears, he behaved then as befitted his appearance and, bit by bit, really became a butterfly. He flitted alone or with others from flower to flower. He quenched his thirst with the dew from the rose. He challenged the variegated chameleons with his multicolored body; and the perfume of the lily, the jasmine, and the honeysuckle inebriated him.

When he remembered he was a male, he courted female butterflies, who not only allowed themselves to be charmed but delighted in his fascination, some even provoking him.

All the butterflies seemed to live from minute to minute. Unlike animals and still less like human beings, the butterflies did not appear to him to have a warlike nature, worries of life, fears of death, and complicated feelings such as jealousy.

So it happened that one male butterfly told him joyfully:

"Come, I'll show you an adorable female to whom I have just made love. I think she may have 70, 68, 84, and comma 98!"

"What on earth do you mean by those figures?"

"That's a convention of ours. The first number means the percentage for looks, the second for colors, the third for perfume, and after the comma for sex appeal."

"Then show her to me at once. She must surely be a dream."

In truth, this marvel was charm itself. Attracted, he began to make love to her, while his friend and the others flew round the couple very pleased. The happiness of the two was so great and wild that he woke up.

Himself once more, he was bitterly tormented. Butterfly life was so carefree, and human life . . .

Finally, after reflection, he said to himself: There is nothing to worry about. Who knows, maybe *my* life is only a *butterfly's* dream.

# from *Discussion on Making All Things Equal*

3rd century B.C.

TRANSLATED BY BURTON WATSON

"Suppose you and I have had an argument. If you have beaten me instead of my beating you, then are you necessarily right and am I necessarily wrong? If I have beaten you instead of your beating me, then am I necessarily right and are you necessarily wrong? Is one of us right and the other wrong? Are both of us right or are both of us wrong? If you and I don't know the answer, then other people are bound to be even more in the dark. Whom shall we get to decide what is right? Shall we get someone who agrees with you to decide? But if he already agrees with you, how can he decide fairly? Shall we get someone who agrees with me? But if he already agrees with me, how can he decide? Shall we get someone who disagrees with both of us? But if he already disagrees with both of us, how can he decide? Shall we get someone who agrees with both of us? But if he already agrees with both of us, how can he decide? Obviously, then, neither you nor I nor anyone else can decide for each other. Shall we wait for still another person?

"But waiting for one shifting voice [to pass judgment on] another is the same as waiting for none of them. Harmonize them all with the Heavenly Equality, leave them

*[handwritten: no need for argument.]*

to their endless changes, and so live out your years. What do I mean by harmonizing them with the Heavenly Equality? Right is not right; so is not so. If right were really right, it would differ so clearly from not right that there would be no need for argument. If so were really so, it would differ so clearly from not so that there would be no need for argument. Forget the years; forget distinctions. Leap into the boundless and make it your home!" ...

Once Chuang Chou dreamt he was a butterfly, a butterfly flitting and fluttering around, happy with himself and doing as he pleased. He didn't know he was Chuang Chou. Suddenly he woke up and there he was, solid and unmistakable Chuang Chou. But he didn't know if he was Chuang Chou who had dreamt he was a butterfly or a butterfly dreaming he was Chuang Chou. Between Chuang Chou and a butterfly there must be *some* distinction! This is called the transformation of things.

*[handwritten: It is Tranformation of things]*

# Geoffrey Chaucer

## (C. 1342–1400)

Born in London, Geoffrey Chaucer was the son of a prosperous wine merchant and deputy to the king's butler. Although little is known about Chaucer's education, he was capable of reading French, Latin, and Italian. In 1359, Chaucer went to France with Edward III's army during the Hundred Years' War and was captured in the Ardennes. He was returned for a sum of £16. Sometime between 1361 and 1366, he likely married Philippa Roet, the sister of John Gaunt's wife. She died in 1387. Chaucer enjoyed Gaunt's patronage for the rest of his life.

Chaucer's *Book of the Duchess* was published c. 1370, and in 1374 he became a government official at the port of London. During that time he was charged with rape, but the charge was later withdrawn after Chaucer offered to pay his accuser. He lost his position in 1385 but was elected to Parliament. In the same year, he published *Troilus and Cressida*. In 1389, Chaucer reentered the service of the crown under Richard II as Clerk of the King's Works. From 1378 to 1400, the year of his death, Chaucer labored over *The Canterbury Tales*. He died before completing the work.

## *The Wife of Bath's Tale*                1392–1395

**TRANSLATED BY THEODORE MORRISON**

In the old days when King Arthur ruled the nation,
Whom Welshmen speak of with such veneration,
This realm we live in was a fairy land.
The fairy queen danced with her jolly band

On the green meadows where they held dominion.
This was, as I have read, the old opinion;
I speak of many hundred years ago.
But no one sees an elf now, as you know,
For in our time the charity and prayers
And all the begging of these holy friars
Who swarm through every nook and every stream
Thicker than motes of dust in a sunbeam,
Blessing our chambers, kitchens, halls, and bowers,
Our cities, towns, and castles, our high towers,
Our villages, our stables, barns, and dairies,
They keep us all from seeing any fairies,
For where you might have come upon an elf
There now you find the holy friar himself
Working his district on industrious legs
And saying his devotions while he begs.
Women are safe now under every tree.
No incubus is there unless it's he,
And all they have to fear from him is shame.
  It chanced that Arthur had a knight who came
Lustily riding home one day from hawking,
And in his path he saw a maiden walking
Before him, stark alone, right in his course.
This young knight took her maidenhead by force,
A crime at which the outcry was so keen
It would have cost his neck, but that the queen,
With other ladies, begged the king so long
That Arthur spared his life, for right or wrong.
And gave him to the queen, at her own will,
According to her choice, to save or kill.
  She thanked the king, and later told this knight,
Choosing her time, "You are still in such a plight
Your very life has no security.
I grant your life, if you can answer me
This question: what is the thing that most of all
Women desire? Think, or your neck will fall
Under the ax! If you cannot let me know
Immediately, I give you leave to go
A twelvemonth and a day, no more, in quest
Of such an answer as will meet the test.
But you must pledge your honor to return
And yield your body, whatever you may learn."
  The knight sighed; he was rueful beyond measure.
But what! He could not follow his own pleasure.
He chose at last upon his way to ride

And with such answer as God might provide
To come back when the year was at the close.
And so he takes his leave, and off he goes.
  He seeks out every house and every place
Where he has any hope, by luck or grace,
Of learning what thing women covet most.
But it seemed he could not light on any coast
Where on this point two people would agree,
For some said wealth and some said jollity,
Some said position, some said sport in bed
And often to be widowed, often wed;
Some said that to a woman's heart what mattered
Above all else was to be pleased and flattered.
That shaft, to tell the truth, was a close hit.
Men win us best by flattery, I admit,
And by attention. Some say our greatest ease
Is to be free and do just as we please,
And not to have our faults thrown in our eyes,
But always to be praised for being wise.
And true enough, there's not one of us all
Who will not kick if you rub us on a gall.
Whatever vices we may have within,
We won't be taxed with any fault or sin.
  Some say that women are delighted well
If it is thought that they will never tell
A secret they are trusted with, or scandal.
But that tale isn't worth an old rake handle!
We women, for a fact, can never hold
A secret. Will you hear a story told?
Then witness Midas! For it can be read
In Ovid that he had upon his head
Two ass's ears that he kept out of sight
Beneath his long hair with such skill and sleight
That no one else besides his wife could guess.
He loved her well, and trusted her no less.
He begged her not to make his blemish known,
But keep her knowledge to herself alone.
She swore that never, though to save her skin,
Would she be guilty of so mean a sin,
And yet it seemed to her she nearly died
Keeping a secret locked so long inside.
It swelled about her heart so hard and deep
She was afraid some word was bound to leap
Out of her mouth, and since there was no man

She dared to tell, down to a swamp she ran—
Her heart, until she got there, all agog—
And like a bittern booming in the bog
She put her mouth close to the watery ground:
"Water, do not betray me with your sound!
I speak to you, and you alone," she said.
"Two ass's ears grow on my husband's head!
And now my heart is whole, now it is out.
I'd burst if I held it longer, past all doubt."
Safely, you see, awhile you may confide
In us, but it will out; we cannot hide
A secret. Look in Ovid if you care
To learn what followed; the whole tale is there.
   This knight, when he perceived he could not find
What women covet most, was low in mind;
But the day had come when homeward he must ride,
And as he crossed a wooded countryside
Some four and twenty ladies there by chance
He saw, all circling in a woodland dance,
And toward this dance he eagerly drew near
In hope of any counsel he might hear.
But the truth was, he had not reached the place
When dance and all, they vanished into space.
No living soul remained there to be seen
Save an old woman sitting on the green,
As ugly a witch as fancy could devise.
As he approached her she began to rise
And said, "Sir knight, here runs no thoroughfare.
What are you seeking with such anxious air?
Tell me! The better may your fortune be.
We old folk know a lot of things," said she.
   "Good mother," said the knight, "my life's to pay,
That's all too certain, if I cannot say
What women covet most. If you could tell
That secret to me, I'd requite you well."
   "Give me your hand," she answered. "Swear me true
That whatsoever I next ask of you,
You'll do it if it lies within your might
And I'll enlighten you before the night."
   "Granted, upon my honor," he replied.
   "Then I dare boast, and with no empty pride,
Your life is safe," she told him. "Let me die
If the queen herself won't say the same as I.
Let's learn if the haughtiest of all who wear

A net or coverchief upon their hair
Will be so forward as to answer 'no'
To what I'll teach you. No more; let us go."
With that she whispered something in his ear,
And told him to be glad and have no fear.
   When they had reached the court, the knight declared
That he had kept his day, and was prepared
To give his answer, standing for his life.
Many the wise widow, many the wife,
Many the maid who rallied to the scene,
And at the head as justice sat the queen.
Then silence was enjoined; the knight was told
In open court to say what women hold
Precious above all else. He did not stand
Dumb like a beast, but spoke up at command
And plainly offered them his answering word
In manly voice, so that the whole court heard.
   "My liege and lady, most of all," said he,
"Women desire to have the sovereignty
And sit in rule and government above
Their husbands, and to have their way in love.
That is what most you want. Spare me or kill
As you may like; I stand here by your will."
   No widow, wife, or maid gave any token
Of contradicting what the knight had spoken.
He should not die; he should be spared instead;
He was worthy of his life, the whole court said.
   The old woman whom the knight met on the green
Sprang up at this. "My sovereign lady queen,
Before your court has risen, do me right!
It was I who taught this answer to the knight,
For which he pledged his honor in my hand,
Solemnly, that the first thing I demand,
He would do it, if it lay within his might.
Before the court I ask you, then, sir knight,
To take me," said the woman, "as your wife,
For well you know that I have saved your life.
Deny me, on your honor, if you can."
   "Alas," replied this miserable man,
"That was my promise, it must be confessed.
For the love of God, though, choose a new request!
Take all my wealth, and let my body be."
   "If that's your tune, then curse both you and me,"
She said. "Though I am ugly, old, and poor,

I'll have, for all the metal and the ore
That under earth is hidden or lies above,
Nothing, except to be your wife and love."
  "My love? No, my damnation, if you can!
Alas," he said, "that any of my clan
Should be so miserably misallied!"
  All to no good; force overruled his pride,
And in the end he is constrained to wed,
And marries his old wife and goes to bed.
  Now some will charge me with an oversight
In failing to describe the day's delight,
The merriment, the food, the dress at least.
But I reply, there was no joy nor feast;
There was only sorrow and sharp misery.
He married her in private, secretly,
And all day after, such was his distress,
Hid like an owl from his wife's ugliness.
  Great was the woe this knight had in his head
When in due time they both were brought to bed.
He shuddered, tossed, and turned, and all the while
His old wife lay and waited with a smile.
"Is every knight so backward with a spouse?
Is it," she said, "a law in Arthur's house?
I am your love, your own, your wedded wife,
I am the woman who has saved your life.
I have never done you anything but right.
Why do you treat me this way the first night?
You must be mad, the way that you behave!
Tell me my fault, and as God's love can save,
I will amend it, truly, if I can."
  "Amend it?" answered this unhappy man.
"It can never be amended, truth to tell.
You are so loathsome and so old as well,
And your low birth besides is such a cross
It is no wonder that I turn and toss.
God take my woeful spirit from my breast!"
  "Is this," she said, "the cause of your unrest?"
  "No wonder!" said the knight. "It truly is."
  "Now sir," she said, "I could amend all this
Within three days, if it should please me to,
And if you deal with me as you should do.
  "But since you speak of that nobility
That comes from ancient wealth and pedigree,
As if *that* constituted gentlemen,

I hold such arrogance not worth a hen!
The man whose virtue is pre-eminent,
In public and alone, always intent
On doing every generous act he can,
Take him—he is the greatest gentleman!
Christ wills that we should claim nobility
From him, not from old wealth or family.
Our elders left us all that they were worth
And through their wealth and blood we claim high birth,
But never, since it was beyond their giving,
Could they bequeath to us their virtuous living;
Although it first conferred on them the name
Of gentlemen, they could not leave that claim!
   "Dante the Florentine on this was wise:
'Erail is the branch on which man's virtues rise'—
Thus runs his rhyme—'God's goodness wills that we
Should claim from him alone nobility.'
Thus from our elders we can only claim
Such temporal things as men may hurt and maim.
   "It is clear enough that true nobility
Is not bequeathed along with property,
For many a lord's son does a deed of shame
And yet, God knows, enjoys his noble name.
But though descended from a noble house
And elders who were wise and virtuous,
If he will not follow his elders, who are dead,
But leads, himself, a shameful life instead,
He is not noble, be he duke or earl.
It is the churlish deed that makes the churl.
And therefore, my dear husband, I conclude
That though my ancestors were rough and rude,
Yet may Almighty God confer on me
The grace to live, as I hope, virtuously.
Call me of noble blood when I begin
To live in virtue and to cast out sin.
   "As for my poverty, at which you grieve,
Almighty God in whom we all believe
In willful poverty chose to lead his life,
And surely every man and maid and wife
Can understand that Jesus, heaven's king,
Would never choose a low or vicious thing.
A poor and cheerful life is nobly led;
So Seneca and others have well said.

The man so poor he doesn't have a stitch,
If he thinks himself repaid, I count him rich.
He that is covetous, he is the poor man,
Pining to have the things he never can.
It is of cheerful mind, true poverty.
Juvenal says about it happily:
'The poor man as he goes along his way
And passes thieves is free to sing and play.'
Poverty is a good we loathe, a great
Reliever of our busy worldly state,
A great amender also of our minds
As he that patiently will bear it finds.
And poverty, for all it seems distressed,
Is a possession no one will contest.
Poverty, too, by bringing a man low,
Helps him the better both God and self to know.
Poverty is a glass where we can see
Which are our true friends, as it seems to me.
So, sir, I do not wrong you on this score;
Reproach me with my poverty no more.

  "Now, sir, you tax me with my age; but, sir,
You gentlemen of breeding all aver
That men should not despise old age, but rather
Grant an old man respect, and call him 'father.'

  "If I am old and ugly, as you have said,
You have less fear of being cuckolded,
For ugliness and age, as all agree,
Are notable guardians of chastity.
But since I know in what you take delight,
I'll gratify your worldly appetite.

  "Choose now, which of two courses you will try:
To have me old and ugly till I die
But evermore your true and humble wife,
Never displeasing you in all my life,
Or will you have me rather young and fair
And take your chances on who may repair
Either to your house on account of me
Or to some other place, it well may be.
Now make your choice, whichever you prefer."

  The knight took thought, and sighed, and said to her
At last, "My love and lady, my dear wife,
In your wise government I put my life.
Choose for yourself which course will best agree

With pleasure and honor, both for you and me.
I do not care, choose either of the two;
I am content, whatever pleases you."
  "Then have I won from you the sovereignty,
Since I may choose and rule at will?" said she.
  He answered, "That is best, I think, dear wife."
  "Kiss me," she said. "Now we are done with strife,
For on my word, I will be both to you,
That is to say, fair, yes, and faithful too.
May I die mad unless I am as true
As ever wife was since the world was new.
Unless I am as lovely to be seen
By morning as an empress or a queen
Or any lady between east and west,
Do with my life or death as you think best.
Lift up the curtain, see what you may see."
  And when the knight saw what had come to be
And knew her as she was, so young, so fair,
His joy was such that it was past compare.
He took her in his arms and gave her kisses
A thousand times on end; he bathed in blisses.
And she obeyed him also in full measure
In everything that tended to his pleasure.
  And so they lived in full joy to the end.
And now to all us women may Christ send
Submissive husbands, full of youth in bed,
And grace to outlive all the men we wed.
And I pray Jesus to cut short the lives
Of those who won't be governed by their wives;
And old, ill-tempered niggards who hate expense,
God promptly bring them down with pestilence!

# Marie de France

## (C. 1150)

Marie de France was a native of Normandy. She lived during the second half of
the twelfth century and was most likely a contemporary of Chrétien de Troyes
and the court of troubadours during Henry II's reign. De France wrote *Ysopet*, a
collection of 103 fables, and *Purgatory of Saint Patrick*, in which the narrator
tells of the adventures of an Irish knight who, in order to atone for his sins, de-

scends into a cavern where he witnesses the torments of the sinners and the happiness of the just.

## Guigemar

*12th century*

TRANSLATED BY GLYN S. BURGESS AND KEITH BUSBY

Whoever has good material for a story is grieved if the tale is not well told. Hear, my lords, the words of Marie, who, when she has the opportunity, does not squander her talents. Those who gain a good reputation should be commended, but when there exists in a country a man or woman of great renown, people who are envious of their abilities frequently speak insultingly of them in order to damage this reputation. Thus they start acting like a vicious, cowardly, treacherous dog which will bite others out of malice. But just because spiteful tittle-tattlers attempt to find fault with me I do not intend to give up. They have a right to make slanderous remarks.

I shall relate briefly to you stories which I know to be true and from which the Bretons have composed their lays. After these opening words I shall recount to you, just as it has been set down in writing, an adventure which happened in Brittany long ago.

At that time Hoilas ruled the land, which was as often at war as at peace. The king had a baron who was lord of Liun. His name was Oridial and he enjoyed the confidence of his lord. He was a brave and valiant knight and his wife had borne him two children, a son and a beautiful daughter. The girl's name was Noguent and the boy was called Guigemar. There was no more handsome young man in the kingdom. His mother cherished him greatly and his father loved him dearly. As soon as he could bear to part with the boy, his father placed him in the service of another king. The young man was wise, brave and loved by everyone. When the time came that he had reached the right age and maturity of mind, the king dubbed him nobly and gave him whatever armour he desired. He left the court, dispensing lavish gifts before he departed, and went off to Flanders, where one could always find war and strife, in search of renown. At that time no one could find his equal as a knight, be it in Lorraine, Burgundy, Anjou or Gascony. But Nature had done him such a grievous wrong that he never displayed the slightest interest in love. There was no lady or maiden on earth, however noble or beautiful, who would not have been happy to accept him as her lover, if he had sought her love. Women frequently made advances to him, but he was indifferent to them. He showed no visible interest in love and was thus considered a lost cause by stranger and friend alike.

At the height of his fame this noble knight returned to his homeland to see his father and his lord, his loving mother and his sister, who had all longed for his return. He had spent a month with them, I think, when the fancy took him to go hunting. That evening he summoned his knights, his hunters and his beaters, and in the morning went off into the forest, for hunting brought him great pleasure. They gathered in pursuit of a large stag and the hounds were unleashed. The hunters ran in front and the young man lingered behind. A servant carried his bow, his hunting-knife and his quiver. If the opportunity arose, he wished to be ready to shoot an arrow, before the animal had stirred. In the heart of a large bush he saw a hind with its fawn; the beast was completely white with the antlers of a stag on its head. When the dog barked, it darted forth and Guigemar stretched his bow, fired his arrow and struck the animal in its forehead. Immediately the hind fell to the ground, but the arrow rebounded, hitting Guigemar in the thigh and going right through into the horse's flesh. He was forced to dismount and fell back on the thick grass beside the hind he had struck. The animal, wounded and in great pain, lamented in these words: "Alas! I am mortally wounded. Vassal, you who have wounded me, let this be your fate. May you never find a cure, nor may any herb, root, doctor or potion ever heal the wound you have in your thigh until you are cured by a woman who will suffer for your love more pain and anguish than any other woman has ever known, and you will suffer likewise for her, so much so that all those who are in love, who have known love or are yet to experience it, will marvel at it. Be gone from here and leave me in peace."

Guigemar was seriously wounded and dismayed by what he had heard. He wondered where he could go to find a cure for his wound, for he did not intend to allow himself to die. He knew full well, and said to himself, that he had never seen any woman whom he could love or who could cure him of his suffering. He called to his squire: "My friend, ride quickly and bring my companions back, for I should like to speak with them." The young man rode off and Guigemar remained behind, lamenting his suffering. He bound his wound firmly and tightly with his shirt, then mounted his horse and departed. He was keen to get away, for he did not want any of his followers to come and hinder him, or attempt to detain him. A green path traversed the wood which led him out into an open space. There on the plain he saw a cliff and a mountain and from a stream which ran below a creek was formed. On it lay a harbour, in which there was a single ship whose sail Guigemar could see. The ship was fully prepared for departure, caulked inside and out in such a way that it was impossible to detect any joints. There was no peg or deck-rail which was not made of ebony. No gold on earth was worth more and the sail was made entirely of silk, very beautiful when unfurled.

The knight was perturbed, as he had never heard say that ships could dock there. He rode forward, dismounted and in great pain climbed aboard expecting to find men in charge. But the ship was deserted and he saw no one. In the centre of the ship he discovered a bed whose posts and side-pieces were wrought after the fashion of Solomon, engraved with inlaid gold and made of cypress wood and white ivory. The quilt which lay upon it was of silk woven with gold. I could not set a price on the other bedclothes, but I can tell you this much about the pillow: no one who had lain his head on it would ever have white hair. The sable-skin coverlet was lined with Alexandrian silk, and on the prow of the ship stood two pure gold candelabra (even the less valuable of the two was worth a fortune) in which were lighted candles. Guigemar marvelled at all this and in great pain from his wound reclined on the bed to rest. Then he rose intending to leave the ship, but he could not go back, as the ship was al-

*[handwritten: was going to a city to get cured in the morning]*

ready on the high seas, speeding quickly away with him, the wind favourable and blowing gently. There was no question of his returning to land and he was grief-stricken, not knowing what to do. No wonder he was dismayed, for his wound was causing him great suffering. But he had to accept his fate and he prayed to God to take care of him, to bring him, if at all possible, to a safe harbour and protect him from death. He lay down on the bed and slept, but by now the worst was over and before evening he would reach the place where he would be cured, below an ancient city, capital of its realm.

The lord who ruled over the city was a very old man whose wife was a lady of high birth. She was noble, courtly, beautiful and wise, and he was exceedingly jealous, as befitted his nature, for all old men are jealous and hate to be cuckolded. Such is the perversity of age. He did not take lightly the task of guarding her. In a garden at the foot of the keep was an enclosure, with a thick, high wall made of green marble. There was only a single point of entry, guarded day and night. The sea enclosed it on the other side, so it was impossible to get in or out, except by boat, should the need arise in the castle. As a secure place for his wife, the lord had constructed within the enclosure a chamber of incomparable beauty, at the entrance of which stood a chapel. The walls of the chamber were covered in paintings in which Venus, the goddess of love, was skilfully depicted together with the nature and obligations of love; how it should be observed with loyalty and good service. In the painting Venus was shown as casting into a blazing fire the book in which Ovid teaches the art of controlling love and as excommunicating all those who read this book or adopted its teachings. In this room the lady was imprisoned. To serve her the lord had provided her with a noble and intelligent maiden, who was his niece, his sister's daughter. The two loved each other dearly, and when the husband was away, the girl remained with her until his return. No one, man or woman, could have gained access to this spot, or escaped from this walled enclosure. An old priest with hoary-white hair guarded the key to the gate; he had lost his lower members, otherwise he would not have been trusted. He recited the divine service and served her at table. *[handwritten: old priest guarded gate to castle]*

That very day, in the early afternoon, the lady had made her way into the garden. She had fallen asleep after her meal, and then gone with her maiden in search of recreation. They looked down towards the shore and saw the ship rising on the waves as it sailed into the harbour, but they could not see how it was being steered. The lady wanted to turn and run: no wonder she was afraid. Her face became quite flushed. But the maiden, who was wise and of bolder disposition, comforted and reassured her. They hastened towards the ship, and taking off her coat, the girl boarded the beautiful vessel. She found there no living thing apart from the sleeping knight. Seeing how pale he was the girl assumed he was dead. She stopped and looked at him, then returned, called hastily to her lady and gave her a true account. She lamented the dead man she had seen and the lady replied: "Let us go together, and, if he is dead, we shall bury him. Our priest will help us. But if I find him alive, he will speak to us." They made their way without delay, the lady leading and the maiden following. When she entered the ship, the lady paused before the bed; she looked at the knight and grieved deeply over his handsome body, which filled her with sorrow. She deplored the loss of

*[handwritten: lady thought he was dead]*

*[handwritten margin note: tells lady he had been shot & wounded]*

this young life. Placing her hand on his chest, she discovered that it was warm and his heart sound, beating beneath his ribs. The knight who was sleeping awoke and saw her. Joyfully he greeted her, knowing full well that he had reached the shore. The lady, tearful and perturbed, responded to him politely and inquired how he came to be there, and from what land he was, and whether he had been exiled through war. "My lady," he said, "that is not the case. But if you wish me to tell you the truth, I shall do so and withhold nothing from you. I have come from Brittany and today I went hunting in a wood, where I shot a white hind. The arrow rebounded, giving me such a wound in the thigh that I think a cure is impossible. The hind lamented and spoke to me, cursing me and swearing that my only cure would be at the hands of a damsel. I do not know where she is to be found. But when I heard my fate I hurriedly left the wood, saw this ship in a harbour and foolishly got on board. The ship quickly sailed away with me in it. I do not know where I am or what this city is called. Fair lady, I beg you in God's name, please help me, for I do not know where to go, or how to steer the ship." She replied: "My dear lord, I shall gladly help you: this city belongs to my husband, as does all the surrounding country. He is a rich man of high lineage, but he is very old and fearfully jealous. On my honour, he has imprisoned me in this enclosure. There is only a single entrance and an old priest guards the gate: may God grant that he be consumed by hell-fire! I am shut in here day and night, and not once would I dare leave without his permission or unless my lord asked for me. My bedchamber and my chapel are here and this maiden is with me. If you wish to remain until you can travel more easily, we shall be pleased to shelter you and will serve you wholeheartedly." When he heard these words, Guigemar thanked the lady politely and said he would stay with her. He raised himself up off the bed and they supported him with some difficulty. The lady took the young man to her chamber, where he was placed on the maiden's bed, behind a canopy which served as a curtain in the bedroom. They brought water in golden basins, washed his wounded thigh, then removed the surrounding blood with a fine piece of white linen and bound it tightly. They treated him with loving care, and when their evening meal arrived the maiden retained sufficient for the knight's needs, so that he was well supplied with food and drink. But love had now pierced him to the quick and his heart was greatly disturbed. For the lady had wounded him so deeply that he had completely forgotten his homeland. He felt no pain from the wound in his thigh, yet he sighed in great anguish and asked the maiden serving him to let him sleep. As he had dismissed her, she returned to her mistress, who was, like Guigemar, affected by the ardour which had kindled within her heart.

The knight remained alone, mournful and downcast. He did not yet realize the cause, but at least he knew that, if he were not cured by the lady, his death would be assured. "Alas," he said, "what shall I do? I shall go and ask her to have mercy and pity on this forlorn wretch. If she refuses my request and is arrogant or harsh, then I must die of grief and languish forever from this ill." Then he sighed, but soon a new thought struck him: he told himself that suffering was inevitable, for there was no alternative. He spent a sleepless night, sighing in anguish. In his mind he constantly recalled her speech, her appearance, her sparkling eyes and beautiful mouth: the pain

*[handwritten margin notes: He thought wound was impossible to cure. / Felt no pain in his thigh. / He fell in love w/ white]*

she caused reached deep into his heart. In a whisper he begged her for mercy and almost called her his beloved. If he had only known her feelings and how love was afflicting her, he would, I think, have been happy. A little comfort would have gone some way towards assuaging the suffering which had drained his face of colour. But if he was feeling anguish for love of her, the lady had no reason to feel superior. Next morning, before daybreak, she rose, bewailing the fact that she had spent the night awake. Love, which was torturing her, was the cause. The maiden, who was with her, could see from her appearance that she was in love with the knight who was lodging in her chamber for his cure. But the lady did not know whether or not he loved her. When she entered the chapel, the maiden went to the knight.

She sat down by the bed and he addressed her in these words: "My friend, where has my lady gone? Why did she rise so early?" Then he fell silent and sighed. The maiden replied: "My lord, you are in love: mind you do not conceal the fact too long. Your love may well have found a true home. The man who wishes to love my lady must keep her constantly in his thoughts and, if you remain faithful to each other, the love between you will be right and proper. You are handsome and she is beautiful." He replied to the damsel: "I am inflamed with such love that, if I do not receive succour, I shall be in a sorry plight. Help me, my sweet friend. What shall I do with this love?" The maiden comforted him most tenderly, and assured him of her assistance and good offices, wherever possible: she was most courtly and noble.

When the lady had heard mass, she returned, aware of her obligations. She wished to know what the knight was doing, if he was awake or asleep. The love for him which had entered her heart had not abated. The maiden summoned her to approach the knight. She would have ample time to explain her feelings to him, no matter what the consequences. He greeted her and she him. They were both suffering great distress, but he did not dare ask anything of her, as he was a stranger from a foreign land. He was afraid that, if he spoke to her of his emotions, she would hate him and send him away. But he who does not let his infirmity be known can scarcely expect to receive a cure. Love is an invisible wound within the body, and, since it has its source in nature, it is a long-lasting ill. For many it is the butt of jokes, as for those ignoble courtiers who philander around the world and then boast of their deeds. That is not love, but rather foolishness, wickedness and debauchery. A loyal partner, once discovered, should be served, loved and obeyed.

Guigemar was very much in love and either had to receive relief or be forced to live a life of misery. Love emboldened him to reveal his feelings to her. "My lady," he said, "I am dying because of you; my heart is giving me great pain. If you are not willing to cure me, then it must all end in my death. I am asking for your love. Fair one, do not refuse me." When she heard his words, she replied fittingly, and said lightly: "Friend, such a decision would be over-hasty: I am not accustomed to such requests." "My lady," he replied, "in God's name, have mercy on me! Do not be distressed if I say this: a woman who is always fickle likes to extend courtship in order to enhance her own esteem and so that the man will not realize that she has experienced the pleasure of love. But the well-intentioned lady, who is worthy and wise, should not be too harsh towards a man, if she finds him to her liking; she should rather love him and

*The lady gave in*

enjoy his love. Before anyone discovers or hears of their love, they will greatly profit from it. Fair lady, let us put an end to this discussion." The lady recognized the truth of his words and granted him her love without delay. He kissed her and henceforth was at peace. They lay together and talked, kissing and embracing. May the final act, which others are accustomed to enjoy, give them pleasure.

Guigemar was with her for a year and a half, I believe, and their life gave them great delight. But fortune, never unmindful of her duties, can soon turn her wheel. One man takes a fall, another rises; so it was in their case, for they were soon discovered.

*Both made pledges to each other*

One summer morning the lady lay next to the young man. She kissed his mouth and his face, then said: "My fair, sweet friend, my heart tells me I am about to lose you: we are going to be discovered. If you die, I too wish to die; and if you manage to escape, you will find another love and I shall remain here, grief-stricken." "My lady," he replied, "do not say such things! May I have no peace or joy, if I ever turn to another woman. Do not be afraid." "Beloved, give me assurance of this. Hand me your shirt and I shall tie a knot in the tailpiece. I give you leave, wherever you may be, to love the woman who can undo the knot and untie it." He gave it to her, made his pledge and she tied the knot in such a way that no woman could undo it, without the help of scissors or a knife. She gave him back the shirt and he took it on the understanding that she would make a similar pledge to him, by means of a belt which she would gird about her bare flesh and draw tightly around her loins. He encouraged her to love any man who could open the buckle without tearing or severing it. Then he kissed her and let the matter drop.

*They were discovered*

That day they were perceived, discovered, found and seen by a cunning chamberlain sent by her husband. He wished to speak to the lady, but could not gain access to the chamber. Seeing them through a window, he reported the matter to his lord. When the lord heard him, it gave him more pain than he had ever known. Summoning three trustworthy men, he went forthwith to the chamber, had the door broken down and discovered the knight, whereupon in great anger he ordered him to be killed. Guigemar stood up, quite unafraid. He seized a large fir-wood pole, used for hanging clothes, and waited for them, intending to make someone suffer: before any of his adversaries had got near him, he would have maimed them one and all. The lord looked at him intently, asked who he was, where he was from and how he had entered. Guigemar explained how he had arrived, how the lady had retained him, and all about the prophecy of the wounded hind, about the ship and his wound. Now he was entirely in the lord's power. The lord replied that he did not believe him, but that if things were as he stated and he could find the ship, he would then put him out to sea. If he survived, he would be sorry, and if he drowned, he would be delighted. When the lord had given this assurance, they went together to the harbour, where they found the ship and put him aboard. The ship set sail, taking him back to his own country, and got under way without delay while the knight sighed and wept, lamenting the lady frequently and praying to Almighty God to let him die a quick death without ever reaching land, if he could not see again his beloved whom he desired more than his life. His grief was unabated until the ship arrived in the harbour where it had first been discovered, very close to his homeland. Guigemar disembarked as

*He made it back safely*

quickly as possible and recognized a young man whom he had raised and who was leading a charger for a knight he was following. Guigemar called to the youth, who looked round, saw his lord and dismounted. He offered him the horse, and they rode off together. All his friends were full of joy that he had been found. But although Guigemar was highly regarded in his land, he was constantly sad and downcast. They wanted him to take a wife, but he would not hear of the idea. Never would he take a wife, for love or money, unless she could undo his shirt without tearing it. The news travelled throughout Brittany and there was no lady or maiden who did not make the attempt, but they were never successful.

I must tell you about the lady whom Guigemar loved so much. On the advice of one of his barons her husband imprisoned her in a tower of dark-hued marble. She suffered during the day and at night it was worse. No man on earth could describe the great pain, agony, anguish and grief which the lady experienced in the tower, where she spent, I think, over two years. She knew no joy or pleasure and frequently mourned for her beloved: "Guigemar, lord, how sad that I met you! I prefer to die a speedy death rather than suffer this misfortune too long. Beloved, if I could escape, I should drown myself just where you were put to sea!" Then she rose: distraught, she went to the door and found no key or bolt. Thus she had the chance to escape, and no one at all hindered her. She went to the harbour where she found the ship. It was attached to the rock where she intended to drown herself. Seeing it, she went aboard. But she had only one thing on her mind: it was there that her beloved must have drowned. Suddenly she could not remain upright. If she could have reached the side, she would have thrown herself overboard, so great was the anguish she was suffering. The ship set sail, carrying her quickly away, and reached port in Brittany, beneath a fine, strong castle. The lord of the castle, whose name was Meriaduc, was waging war against a neighbour, and for that purpose he had risen early, intending to send his men forth to inflict losses on his enemy. Standing at a window, he saw the ship arrive. He went down some steps and summoned a chamberlain; they went quickly towards the ship, climbed the ladder and boarded it; there they found the lady who was as lovely as a fairy. Taking her by the mantle, the lord took her off to his castle, delighted by his discovery, as the lady was extremely beautiful. He knew full well that, whatever the reason for her being on the ship, she was of a noble lineage, and he conceived a love for her greater than for any other woman. He had a very beautiful, young sister in his chamber, to whom he entrusted the lady. She was well served and honoured, richly dressed and attired, but she was always sad and downcast. The lord often went to speak to her, for he loved her with all his heart. He begged her for her love, but she remained indifferent to his pleas. Instead she showed him the belt: she would love only the man who could undo the knot without tearing it. When he heard her, he replied angrily: "There is also in this land a knight of very great renown who refuses in similar fashion to take a wife because of a shirt with its right flap knotted. It cannot be untied, except by using scissors or a knife. I think it was you who tied that knot." When she heard this, she sighed and almost fainted. He took her in his arms, cut the lacing of her tunic, and endeavoured to open the belt, but to no avail. Afterwards all the knights in the land were summoned to make the attempt.

Thus things remained for a long while until the occasion of a tournament which Meriaduc proclaimed against his enemy. He summoned knights and retained them, confident that Guigemar would come. He asked for Guigemar's presence as a friend and companion, promising him recompense and beseeching him not to fail him in his hour of need, but to come to his assistance. Guigemar arrived, richly attired, bringing with him more than a hundred knights. Meriaduc lodged him in his tower with great honour, then called for his sister to greet him, sending two knights with orders that she should adorn herself and come forward, bringing the lady whom he loved so much. She obeyed his commands, and richly attired, the two entered the hall hand in hand. The lady was sad and pale, and hearing Guigemar's name she lost her balance. If the sister had not held her, she would have fallen to the ground. The knight rose to greet them; he saw the lady and looked at her appearance and bearing. Stepping back a pace, he said: "Is this my sweet friend, my hope, my heart, my life, my beautiful lady who loved me? Where has she come from? Who brought her here? But I have been indulging in very foolish thoughts. I know it is not she; women look very much alike. My mind has been disturbed for nothing, but since she resembles the woman for whom my heart sighs and trembles I shall gladly speak to her." Then the knight went forward, kissed her and sat her down beside him; he spoke no other word than his request for her to be seated. Meriaduc looked at them, very unhappy at the way things appeared. He called laughingly to Guigemar: "Lord, if you wish, this maiden will see if she can manage to undo your shirt." Guigemar replied: "I accept," and he summoned a chamberlain who looked after the shirt, ordering it to be brought to him. It was given to the maiden, but she did not untie it. She recognized the knot easily, but her heart was too full of anguish; she would have been willing to try, if she could and if she dared. Meriaduc realized this and it grieved him. All he could do was to say: "Lady, try to undo it." When she heard the command, she took the flap of the shirt and, to the knight's astonishment, untied it easily. He recognized her, but nevertheless he was not completely convinced. He addressed her in these words: "Beloved, sweet creature, tell me the truth: let me see your body and the belt with which I girded you." He placed his hands on her hips and found the belt. "Beloved," he said, "how fortunate that I have discovered you like this! Who brought you here?" She related to him the grief, the great suffering and the dreariness of the prison in which she had been, and how things had turned out, how she escaped with the intention of drowning herself, but had found the ship, gone on board and arrived at this port; and how the knight had retained her and looked after her with great honour, but had constantly made advances to her. Now she was once more full of joy: "Beloved, take your sweetheart away!" Guigemar rose. "My lords," he said, "listen to me! I have discovered a friend whom I thought I had lost forever. I implore Meriaduc in his mercy to restore her to me. I shall become his vassal and serve him for two or three years with a hundred knights or more." Then Meriaduc replied: "Guigemar, I am not in sufficiently dire straits or so troubled by war that you should request this of me. I found her and I shall keep her and defend her against you."

When Guigemar heard this, he quickly commanded his men to mount. He departed, issuing a challenge to Meriaduc. It grieved him very much to leave his beloved. He took with him every knight in the town who had come for the tournament. Each one pledged his support: they would accompany him wherever he went: the man who failed him now would be disgraced. That night they arrived at the castle of Meriaduc's opponent. The lord lodged them and was happy to have Guigemar and his assistance. He realized the war was over. Next day they rose early and everyone in the lodgings equipped himself, whereupon they made a noisy exit from the town with Guigemar out in front. They reached the castle and attacked it, but it was strong and they could not take it. Guigemar besieged the town and would not leave until it was captured. His friends and followers increased in number so much that he starved all those inside. He captured and destroyed the castle and killed the lord within. With great joy he took away his beloved. Now his tribulations were over.

The lay of *Guigemar*, which is performed on harp and rote, was composed from the tale you have heard. The melody is pleasing to the ear.

# Jakob and Wilhelm Grimm

### (1785–1863 AND 1786–1859)

Brothers Jakob and Wilhelm Grimm were the oldest of nine children. Their father died in 1796 and, two years later, they were sent to Kassel, their mother's home city, to begin secondary school. They both studied law at the University of Marburg. When their mother died in 1808, Jakob and then Wilhelm took positions as librarians in Kassel. In 1812, the brothers published *Grimm's Fairy Tales* and *Children's and Household Tales*. They continued to collect and publish folklore and fairy tales throughout their lives. In 1814, they published a popular second volume of *Children's and Household Tales*. Both brothers received honorary degrees from the University of Marburg in 1819. In 1822, Jakob formulated Grimm's Law, a principle of relationship in Indo-European language. He also published *German Mythology* (1835) and *German Grammar* (1837). Jakob and Wilhelm resigned their positions as librarians in 1830 and accepted jobs at the University of Göttingen.

## Godfather Death

*1822, from the oral tradition*

TRANSLATED BY LORE SEGAL

A poor man had twelve children and worked night and day just to get enough bread for them to eat. Now when the thirteenth came into the world, he did not know what to do and in his misery ran out onto the great highway to ask the first person he met to be godfather. The first to come along was God, and he already knew what it was that weighed on the man's mind and said, "Poor man, I pity you. I will hold your child at the font and I will look after it and make it happy upon earth." "Who are you?" asked the man. "I am God." "Then I don't want you for a godfather," the man said.

"You give to the rich and let the poor go hungry." That was how the man talked because he did not understand how wisely God shares out wealth and poverty, and thus he turned from the Lord and walked on. Next came the Devil and said, "What is it you want? If you let me be godfather to your child, I will give him gold as much as he can use, and all the pleasures of the world besides." "Who are you?" asked the man. "I am the Devil." "Then I don't want you for a godfather," said the man. "You deceive and mislead mankind." He walked on and along came spindle-legged Death striding toward him and said, "Take me as godfather." The man asked, "Who are you?" "I am Death who makes all men equal." Said the man, "Then you're the one for me; you take rich and poor without distinction. You shall be godfather." Answered Death, "I will make your child rich and famous, because the one who has me for a friend shall want for nothing." The man said, "Next Sunday is the baptism. Be there in good time." Death appeared as he had promised and made a perfectly fine godfather.

When the boy was of age, the godfather walked in one day, told him to come along, and led him out into the woods. He showed him an herb which grew there and said, "This is your christening gift. I shall make you into a famous doctor. When you are called to a patient's bedside I will appear and if I stand at the sick man's head you can boldly say that you will cure him and if you give him some of this herb he will recover. But if I stand at the sick man's feet, then he is mine, and you must say there is no help for him and no doctor on this earth could save him. But take care not to use the herb against my will or it could be the worse for you."

It wasn't long before the young man had become the most famous doctor in the whole world. "He looks at a patient and right away he knows how things stand, whether he will get better or if he's going to die." That is what they said about him, and from near and far the people came, took him to see the sick, and gave him so much money he became a rich man. Now it happened that the king fell ill. The doctor was summoned to say if he was going to get well. When he came to the bed, there stood Death at the feet of the sick man, so that no herb on earth could have done him any good. If I could only just this once outwit Death! thought the doctor. He'll be annoyed, I know, but I am his godchild and he's sure to turn a blind eye. I'll take my chance. And so he lifted the sick man and laid him the other way around so that Death was standing at his head. Then he gave him some of the herb and the king began to feel better and was soon in perfect health. But Death came toward the doctor, his face dark and angry, threatened him with raised forefinger, and said, "You have tricked me. This time I will let it pass because you are my godchild, but if you ever dare do such a thing again, you put your own head in the noose and it is you I shall carry away with me."

Soon after that, the king's daughter lapsed into a deep illness. She was his only child, he wept day and night until his eyes failed him and he let it be known that whoever saved the princess from death should become her husband and inherit the crown. When the doctor came to the sick girl's bed, he saw Death at her feet. He ought to have remembered his godfather's warning, but the great beauty of the princess and the happiness of becoming her husband so bedazzled him that he threw caution to the winds, nor did he see Death's angry glances and how he lifted his hand in the air and threatened him with his bony fist. He picked the sick girl up and laid her head *death wanted Revenge.*

where her feet had lain, then he gave her some of the herb and at once her cheeks reddened and life stirred anew.

When Death saw himself cheated of his property the second time, he strode toward *saw* the doctor on his long legs and said, "It is all up with you, and now it is your turn," *doctor* grasped him harshly with his ice-cold hand so that the doctor could not resist, and led *cheat* him to an underground cave, and here he saw thousands upon thousands of lights burn- *himself* ing in rows without end, some big, some middle-sized, others small. Every moment *again.* some went out and others lit up so that the little flames seemed to be jumping here and there in perpetual exchange. "Look," said Death, "these are the life lights of mankind. The big ones belong to children, the middle-sized ones to married couples in their best years, the little ones belong to very old people. Yet children and the young often have only little lights." "Show me my life light," said the doctor, imagining that it must be one of the big ones. Death pointed to a little stub threatening to go out and said, "Here it is." "Ah, dear godfather," said the terrified doctor, "light me a new one, do it, for my sake, so that I may enjoy my life and become king and marry the beautiful princess." "I cannot," answered Death. "A light must go out before a new one lights up." "Then set the old on top of a new one so it can go on burning when the first is finished," begged the doctor. Death made as if to grant his wish, reached for a tall new taper, but because he wanted revenge he purposely fumbled and the little stub fell over and went out. Thereupon the doctor sank to the ground and had himself fallen into the hands of death.

*He blew out the candle & Doctor fell into death's hands.*

# Delia Oshogay

(1900S?)

Although many of the details of Delia Oshogay's life are unknown, she belonged to the Wisconsin Chippewa tribe and was a storyteller whose traditional tale, "Oshkikwe's Baby," was first recorded by anthropologist Ernestine Friedl in 1942. The Chippewa lived a primarily sedentary life of hunting, fishing, and harvesting wild rice around the shores of Lake Superior and eventually expanded their lands from the Turtle Mountains in North Dakota to the eastern shore of Lake Huron in Michigan. Today the Chippewa are the third largest group of Native Americans living in the United States. They are also known as the Ojibwa, Anishinabe, Anishaabe, Ojibwe, Ojibway, or Chippeway. The Chippewa number over 100,000 tribal members and live in a region stretching from Michigan to Montana.

*Oshkikwe's Baby*                                    *Traditional, first published 1942*

INTERPRETED BY MAGGIE LAMORIE *get taken by witch*

Matchikwewis and Oshkikwe were out picking cranberries and staying by themselves. One day Oshkikwe found a tiny pipe with a little face on it. The eyes were looking at her and would wink at her. She showed it to her older sister and said, "Look at this little pipe! I guess we're not really alone in the world. There must be somebody else in the world."

Matchikwewis said that they had once lived in a village and that their father had been the head man. When he died, she took Oshkikwe away, because she didn't want her to be abused by the people.

Matchikwewis knew that her sister was going to give birth to a child because of the pipe. One time, when they woke up, they saw a *tikinagan* (cradleboard) with wraps and everything set for a baby, including a little bow and arrow. Oshkikwe took sick and found a little boy and a little pup.

Matchikwewis took good care of her sister, and everything was going fine. One day Matchikwewis told her sister that she'd had a dream which told her not to leave the baby out of her sight for ten days but always stay with him, for otherwise an old witch would come for him. Once Oshkikwe just went outside to get a stick of wood, and when she came back she could see the swing moving. The pup used to guard the little cradleboard. While she went out, she heard the pup barking. When she got back, both the baby and the pup were gone. All that remained was a piece of the hindquarters of the witch which the dog must have bitten off and a little piece of the *tikinagan* which the pup must have got too.

As soon as she saw this, she said that she'd get ready to look for the child and the pup. She told her sister she'd be gone for ten days. The sister told her to work on her breasts, so they wouldn't run dry. She had been nursing the baby on one breast and the pup on the other. The sister also said that the further the witch went with the child, the bigger he'd get, and soon he'd become a man.

The mother started walking, and she crossed a deer trail. She kept on going and came to another trail: a man's tracks, deer tracks, and a dog's tracks. This was her son's tracks, because the witch had so much power that it didn't take the child long to grow up. Finally, Oshkikwe came to a wigwam. Outside of it, she saw a man who must have been her son already grown up.

The man went into the wigwam to tell his "mother" what he had seen. He told her that he had seen a young woman. But the witch said, "Don't you dare look at that woman, because she's just a dirty old witch. As soon as you look at her, you'll become ugly."

The young man said, "Well, I don't like to see her trying to build a wigwam of old birchbark and things. Why don't you give her some nice birchbark, so it won't rain on her?"

The witch didn't like to do it, but she had to. Whenever this old witch knew that there was a new-born boy, she'd kidnap him, and as soon as they got into her territory, the boy would grow up and go hunting and work for her, so she got all the profit out of it.

This man of Oshkikwe's got home early one afternoon, because he had to make arrows before it got dark. Just as he went by Oshkikwe's wigwam, she had her breasts open. The pup was hanging around Oshkikwe, because he remembered her.

While the young man was whittling his arrows, the first thing he knew Oshkikwe was sitting on a woodpile, showing her breasts to her son. He knew that there was something he couldn't remember, but he couldn't remember what it was. He suspected something, though. In his dream he made a wish that his "mother" would sleep soundly, so that he could go over and visit this young woman whom his "mother" called an old witch. So his "mother" slept soundly that night. He went to see the young woman, accompanied by the pup. When the pup got there, he went to nurse at the woman's left breast. Oshkikwe said to him, "You are my son, and here is the milk you lived on before this old witch got hold of you."

He couldn't remember, but she told him, and she brought a piece of his cradleboard made of cedar and shells, and also a piece of the old witch's hindquarters, and showed them to her son. He asked his mother how she managed to live and whether the old witch gave her anything to eat. Oshkikwe said, "When she gives me something, she brings only the livers and dirties them on the way." Then the man told his mother he'd go back with her, but not for a while. The minute he'd go back to her, he'd turn right into a baby. At the same time, though, he had to find out the real facts about who his mother was.

That night he pretended to be sick and started to moan. His "mother" asked him what was the matter, and he said he was dying and that the only thing that would save him would be the sight of his old cradleboard. The old lady went out and got a very old cradleboard, but he said that wasn't his. Then she got his real one, with the pretty shells, and he saw that part of it was missing, and he knew then that Oshkikwe was right, since she had the missing part. Then he started to moan again. His "mother" asked him what the matter was. He said he had to taste the milk he used to nurse on. She pulled out her own breast and squeezed out some old yellow stuff and gave it to him to taste. He thought it was funny that he'd ever grown up with such awful stuff for food. He had to find out one more thing. He said, "The only way I can live is if you pull up your skirts high and dance around a little." So she danced for him and lifted up her buckskin dress. He called out, "Higher, ma!" Then he knew that Oshkikwe was right. The old witch went to sleep after that.

The man went back to his mother and told her that he'd go hunting the next morning. He planned to kill a deer and hang it high up on a tree, and then come back and tell the old witch to go and bring it back because his feet were all blistered.

The next morning he came back and told the witch that he'd killed two deer, one near and one far. He told the witch to send Oshkikwe to go and get the more distant deer, and she should get the other one. They both set out, but instead of going on, Oshkikwe came right back.

The old witch had two children. The man banged them both on the head with a club and killed them. Then he stuck two sugar cookies in their mouths and made it look as though they were still alive.

Then he and his mother picked up one stake of the wigwam and went down into that hole a long ways. The man and the puppy got smaller and smaller. By the time the old witch got home, her boy was gone, and here were her two children with sugar cookies in their mouths. She yelled at the kids, because they were eating something she was saving for their brother; but when she got closer to them, she saw that they were dead.

Then she spoke aloud to her son: "Huh! What do you think? This world is too small for you to get away from me!" She found the hole they had gone down and followed them. By this time the man and the puppy had become very small. He told his mother to put him in the cradleboard which she'd brought along. The last thing he managed to tell his mother was that she should make a big mark with his arrow, and there the earth would split. She took the arrow and marked the ground just as the witch came along. Then the witch fell into the split, and that was the end of her. When Oshkikwe got home, she found her sister all dressed up and her hair oiled. She said that if Oshkikwe hadn't arrived that night, she would have gone after her the next day.

# Plato

## (C. 427–347 B.C.)

Plato was born in Athens into an aristocratic family. A student of Socrates, he was deeply influenced by Anaxagoras, Parmenides, and Pythagoras, whose notions of numerical harmony shaped Plato's notion of the "forms." Plato founded the Academy, one of the earliest known organized schools in Western civilization. It operated until A.D. 529, when Justinian I of Byzantium closed it. Plato recorded his philosophy in the form of dialogues in which several characters discuss a topic by asking questions. His works include *The Republic, The Trial and Death of Socrates, Apology,* and *Symposium.* Plato is the father of "Platonism," a philosophy that divides the world into two distinct aspects: the intelligible world of "forms" and the perceptual world we see around us. Plato believed that the perceptual world was full of imperfect copies of the intelligible forms or idea. According to Plato, the perfect forms are comprehensible only through the intellect.

## The Parable of the Cave                                    3rd century B.C.

TRANSLATED BY BENJAMIN JOWETT

And now, I said, let me show in a figure how far our nature is enlightened or unenlightened:—Behold! human beings living in an underground den, which has a mouth open towards the light and reaching all along the den; here they have been from their childhood, and have their legs and necks chained so that they cannot move, and can only see before them, being prevented by the chains from turning round their heads. Above and behind them a fire is blazing at a distance, and between the fire and the prisoners there is a raised way; and you will see, if you look, a low wall built along the way, like the screen which marionette players have in front of them, over which they show the puppets.

I see.

And do you see, I said, men passing along the wall carrying all sorts of vessels, and statues and figures of animals made of wood and stone and various materials, which appear over the wall? Some of them are talking, others silent.

You have shown me a strange image, and they are strange prisoners.

Like ourselves, I replied; and they see only their own shadows, or the shadows of one another, which the fire throws on the opposite wall of the cave?

True, he said; how could they see anything but the shadows if they were never allowed to move their heads?

And of the objects which are being carried in like manner they would only see the shadows?

Yes, he said.

And if they were able to converse with one another, would they not suppose that they were naming what was actually before them?

Very true.

And suppose further that the prison had an echo which came from the other side, would they not be sure to fancy when one of the passers-by spoke that the voice which they heard came from the passing shadow?

No question, he replied.

To them, I said, the truth would be literally nothing but the shadows of the images.

That is certain.

And now look again, and see what will naturally follow if the prisoners are released and disabused of their error. At first, when any of them is liberated and compelled suddenly to stand up and turn his neck round and walk and look towards the light, he will suffer sharp pains; the glare will distress him, and he will be unable to see the realities of which in his former state he had seen the shadows; and then conceive some one saying to him, that what he saw before was an illusion, but that now, when he is approaching nearer to being and his eye is turned towards more real existence, he has a clearer vision,—what will be his reply? And you may further imagine that his instructor is pointing to the objects as they pass and requiring him to name them,— will he not be perplexed? Will he not fancy that the shadows which he formerly saw are truer than the objects which are now shown to him?

Far truer.

And if he is compelled to look straight at the light, will he not have a pain in his eyes which will make him turn away to take refuge in the objects of vision which he can see, and which he will conceive to be in reality clearer than the things which are now being shown to him?

True, he said.

And suppose once more, that he is reluctantly dragged up a steep and rugged ascent, and held fast until he is forced into the presence of the sun himself, is he not likely to be pained and irritated? When he approaches the light his eyes will be dazzled, and he will not be able to see anything at all of what are now called realities.

Not all in a moment, he said.

He will require to grow accustomed to the sight of the upper world. And first he will see the shadows best, next the reflections of men and other objects in the water, and then the objects themselves; then he will gaze upon the light of the moon and the stars and the spangled heaven; and he will see the sky and the stars by night better than the sun or the light of the sun by day?

Certainly.

Last of all he will be able to see the sun, and not mere reflections of him in the water, but he will see him in his own proper place, and not in another; and he will contemplate him as he is.

Certainly.

He will then proceed to argue that this is he who gives the season and the years, and is the guardian of all that is in the visible world, and in a certain way the cause of all things which he and his fellows have been accustomed to behold?

Clearly, he said, he would first see the sun and then reason about him.

And when he remembered his old habitation, and the wisdom of the den and his fellow-prisoners, do you not suppose that he would felicitate himself on the change, and pity them?

Certainly, he would.

And if they were in the habit of conferring honors among themselves on those who were quickest to observe the passing shadows and to remark which of them went before, and which followed after, and which were together; and who were therefore best able to draw conclusions as to the future, do you think that he would care for such honors and glories, or envy the possessors of them? Would he not say with Homer,

> "Better to be the poor servant of a poor master,"

and to endure anything, rather than think as they do and live after their manner?

Yes, he said, I think that he would rather suffer anything than entertain these false notions and live in this miserable manner.

Imagine once more, I said, such an one coming suddenly out of the sun to be replaced in his old situation; would he not be certain to have his eyes full of darkness?

To be sure, he said.

And if there were a contest, and he had to compete in measuring the shadows with the prisoners who had never moved out of the den, while his sight was still weak, and before his eyes had become steady (and the time which would be needed to acquire this new habit of sight might be very considerable), would he not be ridiculous? Men would say of him that up he went and down he came without his eyes; and that it was better not even to think of ascending; and if any one tried to loose another and lead him up to the light, let them only catch the offender, and they would put him to death.

No question, he said.

This entire allegory, I said, you may now append, dear Glaucon, to the previous argument; the prison-house is the world of sight, the light of the fire is the sun, and you will not misapprehend me if you interpret the journey upwards to be the ascent of the soul into the intellectual world according to my poor belief, which, at your desire, I have expressed—whether rightly or wrongly God knows. But, whether true or false, my opinion is that in the world of knowledge the idea of good appears last of all, and is seen only with an effort; and, when seen, is also inferred to be the universal author of all things beautiful and right, parent of light and of the lord of light in this visible world, and the immediate source of reason and truth in the intellectual; and that this is the power upon which he who would act rationally either in public or private life must have his eye fixed.

I agree, he said, as far as I am able to understand you.

Moreover, I said, you must not wonder that those who attain to this beatific vision are unwilling to descend to human affairs; for their souls are ever hastening into the upper world where they desire to dwell; which desire of theirs is very natural, if our allegory may be trusted.

Yes, very natural.

And is there anything surprising in one who passes from divine contemplations to the evil state of man, misbehaving himself in a ridiculous manner; if, while his eyes are blinking and before he has become accustomed to the surrounding darkness, he is compelled to fight in courts of law, or in other places, about the images or the shadows of images of justice, and is endeavoring to meet the conceptions of those who have never yet seen absolute justice?

Anything but surprising, he replied.

Any one who has common sense will remember that the bewilderments of the eyes are of two kinds, and arise from two causes, either from coming out of the light or from going into the light, which is true of the mind's eye, quite as much as of the bodily eye; and he who remembers this when he sees any one whose vision is perplexed and weak, will not be too ready to laugh; he will first ask whether that soul of man has come out of the brighter life, and is unable to see because unaccustomed to the dark, or having turned from darkness to the day is dazzled by the excess of light. And he will count the one happy in his condition and state of being, and he will pity the other; or, if he have a mind to laugh at the soul which comes from below into the light, there will be more reason in this than in the laugh which greets him who returns from above out of the light into the den.

That, he said, is a very just distinction.

But then, if I am right, certain professors of education must be wrong when they say that they can put a knowledge into the soul which was not there before, like sight into blind eyes.

They undoubtedly say this, he replied.

Whereas, our argument shows that the power and capacity of learning exists in the soul already; and that just as the eye was unable to turn from darkness to light without the whole body, so too the instrument of knowledge can only by the movement of the whole soul be turned from the world of becoming into that of being, and learn by degrees to endure the sight of being, and of the brightest and best of being, or in other words, of the good.

# The Nineteenth-Century Short Story

*1800 to 1899*

1. *Mary Wollstonecraft, oil painting, undated*
2. *Nathaniel Currier and James Merritt Ives,* **Westward the Course of Empire Takes Its Way,**
   *lithograph, 1886*
3. *Nikolai Gogol, 1841*
4. *Francisco de Goya y Lucientes,* **The Clothed Maja,** *oil painting, c. 1800*
5. *Nathanial Hawthorne, 1800s*
6. *George Catlin,* **Six, Chief of the Plains Ojibwa,** *oil painting, 1832*

7. *Four generations of a slave family, Beaufort, South Carolina, photograph, 1862*
8. *Edgar Allan Poe, photograph, 1848*
9. *Ilya Repin,* The Boatmen of the Volga, *oil painting, 1873*
10. *A Civil War soldier in battle dress, photograph, 1862*
11. *Anton Chekhov, photograph, undated*
12. *The Avenue d'Opera, Paris, with the Opera house in the distance, photograph, late nineteenth century*

13. *Victoria, Queen of the United Kingdom and Ireland, Empress of India, photograph, 1886*
14. *Kate Chopin, photograph, c. 1870–1875*
15. *Ku Klux Klan induction ceremony for new members, photograph, 1915*
16. James Abbott McNeil Whistler, *Arrangement in Gray and Black No. 1: Portrait of the Artist's Mother, oil painting, 1871*
17. Jacques Emile Blanche, *Henry James, Author, oil painting, 1908*
18. *Bishops Palace in Galveston, Texas, photograph, c. 1887–1893*

19. Woman and two children digging potatoes during the Irish famine
20. Frank Edwin Larson, Mark Twain, Author, *oil painting, 1935*
21. Head of the Statue of Liberty on display in a public garden in Paris before being sent to New York, *photograph, undated*
22. Vincent van Gogh, The Starry Night, *oil painting, 1889*
23. Charlotte Perkins Gilman, *photograph, undated*
24. Shoe factory worker in Lynn, Massachusetts, *photograph, c. 1895*

L ais, myths, and fabliaux influenced tales, sketches, and short stories, forming a vast web of storytelling. The continuity of the tradition is evident in Washington Irving's "Rip Van Winkle" and "The Legend of Sleepy Hollow," the plots of which come directly from German folktales. Nevertheless, most histories of the short story begin in the nineteenth century, when publishing short narratives became increasingly common and when storywriting began to move toward a more deliberate and compact execution of plot and character. In contrast to the fable or parable, the nineteenth-century short story often presents readers with highly developed characters interacting in detailed, realistic social worlds. The popularity of short fiction grew in tandem with the expansion of the magazine industry and the development of technologies that made it possible to print and circulate short works among a large and diverse population of readers. At the same time, amidst considerable cultural controversy, popular tastes shifted away from philosophical, political, and religious essays and toward novels and other works of fiction, creating a desire and demand for the emerging genre.

## THE MAGAZINE INDUSTRY

As railroad tracks spanned the landscape and new technologies revolutionized the printing industry, weekly and monthly periodicals occupied an increasingly significant place in literary culture. Eighteenth-century periodicals contained little that fits today's definition of the short story. Such magazines included brief sketches, fables, or anecdotes alongside political essays, biographical sketches, and travel narratives, all of which sought not just to entertain but also to educate readers with political, religious, or moral lessons. Readers expected literature to be useful and instructive.

Particularly in the United States, editors envisioned magazines as part of a democratic movement, a medium that would equalize access to information. In its first issue in 1798, the *Philadelphia Monthly Magazine* brazenly declared, "In America, periodical publications may be properly termed the *literature of the people*" (5). Over fifty years later, the popular *Harper's New Monthly Magazine* expressed this democratic notion in very similar terms. In its advertisement on the first page of Volume 1, editors explain that the magazine "was projected and commenced in the belief, that it might be made the means of bringing within the reach of the great mass of the American people, an immense amount of useful and entertaining reading matter" (1). Although the short story today has shed much of its focus on literary lessons for the people, many short stories carry on this educative tradition in their attempts to communicate important observations about culture, history, and humanity.

The magazine industry grew particularly quickly in the United States, where American novelists could not compete with the popular British market (lax copyright laws made the distribution of British works in the United States inexpensive). Between 1885 and 1905, the number of periodicals in the United States increased from 3,300 to 10,800 (Levy 31), a boom fueled in part by new technologies that drastically reduced publication costs. The late eighteenth and early nineteenth centuries nurtured the rise of the short story as Americans struggled with their postrevolutionary identity, the burdens of a new political and social order, and the uncertain yet idealistic visions of a new nation. As the magazine industry flourished, it called on American citizens to contribute to magazines in order to advance the status of the new nation. Eighteenth-century journals published political, philosophical, and religious essays, poetry, biographical sketches, and travel narratives, while fictional material often took the form of brief anecdotes or Native American tales considered informative and instructional. A July 1774 issue of the *Royal American Magazine* published, for example, "The Bees, a Fable." Like many early American stories, the tale conveys a brief instructive message about the importance of the public good. As fable developed into story, however, the primary function of short fiction began to shift from instruction to entertainment.

## THE RISE OF FICTION

As readers increasingly turned from nonfiction, instructive essays to fiction, many magazines began to publish serials, multiple installments that continued stories from one issue to the next. In a format not unlike some television shows today, authors like Sarah Orne Jewett and Charles Dickens published their stories in several episodes, writing suspenseful endings that kept readers waiting eagerly for the next installment. These narratives entertained readers with lively stories, suspenseful plots, and mysterious characters.

Controversy accompanied the increasing popularity of such fictional works. Critics lamented the movement away from the moral tendencies of religious, philosophical, and descriptive writing. As women became, more frequently, writers and readers of fiction, creators and consumers of imaginative tales, one critic exclaimed, "How many thousands [of women] have, by a free use of such books, corrupted their principles, inflamed their imagination, and vitiated their taste, without balancing the account by any solid advantage?" (Davidson 47). Because they believed in literature's powerful ability to influence and instruct readers, many feared that stories without a moral purpose would corrupt readers by allowing them to escape into a world of fantasy. The admonishments of these critics, however, could not abate the steady rise of fiction.

## EDGAR ALLAN POE

Most histories of the short story genre locate one of its crystallizing moments in Poe's 1842 review of Nathaniel Hawthorne's *Twice Told Tales,* an essay that amounted to a kind of manifesto broadcasting the birth of a revolutionary, radically modern form of fiction. Poe's pronouncements about the short story, which he still calls a "tale" in the Hawthorne review, were almost exclusively concerned with the technology of the form—the tale's style and its effects—and less so with content. Influenced by the British and German romantics, Poe popularized the idea of unity in the short story and suggested that a short story should be read in one sitting. He wrote, "In the whole composition there should be no word written, of which the tendency, direct or indirect, is not to the one pre-established design" (657). Poe's influence on Continental, especially French, practitioners of the genre was considerable, and the efflorescence of the form in Britain late in the century was, in turn, influenced by what had been happening on the Continent.

## THE REALIST SHORT STORY OF THE NINETEENTH CENTURY

Throughout Poe's influential review of Hawthorne's collection, he refers to the short works as "tales." Traditionally, tales are short narratives that contain fantastical elements. The supernatural suspense of Irving's headless horseman, the mystery of Poe's "The Cask of Amontillado," and the fantastical forest of Hawthorne's "Young Goodman Brown" all convey the magical and mysterious worlds associated with tales. Because the short story derived from such fantastical forms as the fairytale or fabliaux, influential writers like Hawthorne, Gogol, and Poe developed a powerful new genre by combining realist and magical subject matter. Although many authors were inspired by Poe's preoccupation with the bizarre and supernatural, the prevailing trend in nineteenth-century short fiction was realism, which found its subject matter in the everyday lives of ordinary lower-class and working-class people struggling to survive in a newly industrialized, urban world that was crowded, noisy, dirty, and in constant motion. Novels became filled with the gritty minutiae of realistic life, and short stories began to revolve around these details as well.

In lais, fables, and religious literature, careful description of the everyday lives of middle- and lower-class people seemed an unworthy topic, but in the nineteenth century, the short story turned its attention to the significance and interest of realistic characters. Writers crafted detailed portrayals of social life, including rich descriptions of setting and the nuanced dialogue of carefully delineated characters. Throughout Europe, as well as in Russia, the evolution of the modern short story often accompanied a revolt against the philosophies and precepts of romanticism, its outdated pastoral visions and humanist ideals. In France in the latter part of the century, two related movements animated the short stories written there: realism, practiced by writers like Gustave Flaubert and Guy de Maupassant, and naturalism, a more relentlessly materialistic and scientific approach to realism practiced by writers like Stephen Crane and Jack London. Italian literature saw a corresponding *verisimo* movement in the 1870s, and the "natural" school of Russian fiction of mid-century included Leo Tolstoy, Fyodor Dostoevsky, Nikolai Gogol, and Ivan Turgenev, seminal forces in the development of short fiction. In Latin America as well, the short story became popular in the nineteenth century with such accomplished writers as Joaquim Maria Machado de Assis, but it would become most influential in the twentieth when writers from Argentina, Mexico, Colombia, and Brazil became central figures in a new movement called magical realism.

## THE CHANGING READERSHIP

The democratic potential of the short story was, to some degree, realized as women and minorities increasingly published stories in magazines. In 1849, Amelia Bloomer launched *The Lily,* a magazine devoted to women's rights and temperance. The rise in women's authorship seemed to go hand-in-hand with the rights being demanded in other aspects of women's social, political, and economic lives. In 1850, the same year in which *Harper's Monthly* began publication, U.S. stores employed female clerks for the first time, and women gathered in Worcester, Massachusetts, for the National Women's Rights Convention. By 1857, the editor of the newly established *Atlantic Monthly* declared that the magazine would emphasize fiction by women writers. By 1872, women were writing 75 percent of the books published in the United States (Tebbel 179). Rebecca Harding Davis, Sarah Orne Jewett, and Mary Wilkins Freeman grew to prominence in magazines throughout the nineteenth century.

The relative accessibility of short story publication allowed for the development of diverse traditions in short story writing. Thanks to widespread education reform and increased freedoms and rights granted to women and the lower classes in the industrial world, literacy and leisure increased, creating a vast, new, and newly diverse readership. Larger and larger segments of a once rural population lived in a new urban landscape where the old diurnal rhythms of the countryside were shattered by the time clock, the train schedule, and the factory night shift, which was lit by gaslight and then, by the late 1880s, electricity. Borrowing from the conventions of journalism, alongside which it often appeared, the short story frequently spoke to its readers in their own language, employing a breathless, telegraphic, colloquial style, written, it seemed, in its vibrant immediacy, at the very pace of modern life.

## GLOBAL LITERARY CONNECTIONS

Technological changes throughout the nineteenth century began creating a network of communication and travel between diverse regions and nations, facilitating international exchange and influence. Throughout the century, landmarks in transportation quickened the pace of life and created a more mobile world. In 1816, for example, regular clipper service enabled more convenient travel between New York and Liverpool. The growing transportation network facilitated the circulation of magazines as well as the movement of people: England constructed its first railroad in 1825, the United States followed suit in 1826, and the American transcontinental railroad was completed in 1869. By the century's end, the United States had opened its first subway line in Boston. The short story genre accommodated and prospered in the midst of these changes, often depicting characters grappling with psychological and social transformation.

At the same time, colonies in the Americas were beginning to shake off colonial influence and develop distinct new literatures. In 1816, Argentina declared its independence from Spain. In 1821, Nicaragua, Peru, Guatemala, Honduras, Costa Rica, and Panama also gained independence from Spain. And in 1822, Brazil achieved independence from Portugal. These countries began to develop rich examples of the short story that drew on traditional stories and depicted cultural change.

## AN INTERNATIONAL FORM

The most influential writers of the nineteenth century came from diverse countries and practiced many types of short story writing. Writers like Nikolai Gogol, Sir Walter Scott, Edgar Allan Poe, Charles Dickens, Rudyard Kipling, Washington Irving, Sarah Orne Jewett, Ivan Turgenev, Guy de Maupassant, Anton Chekhov, and Elizabeth Gaskell shaped the short story tradition and had an enormous impact on later writers. Gogol, for example, combined Ukrainian folklore and social realism in stories that influenced authors throughout the world. Charles May quotes a well-used phrase when he suggests that "it has been said that all modern Russian fiction springs from under Gogol's 'Overcoat'" (23). Indeed, writers of many countries have donned Gogol's overcoat. The traditions of various countries developed concurrently and emphasized distinctive styles and methods. While American writers like Poe and Hawthorne developed stories in a romantic style with a highly condensed structure, French writers like Mérimée, Gautier, and Balzac concentrated on the development of plot. At the same time, English writers Dickens, Thackeray, Gaskell, and Hardy published narratives shorter than the novel but longer than the short stories of their international contemporaries. In the 1840s, while Poe wrote tales of the extraordinary, Turgenev crafted sketches of Russian serfs. All of these diverse traditions influenced later writers, creating a genre populated by manifold and distinctive voices.

## FRENCH AND RUSSIAN WRITERS OF THE SHORT STORY

In *The Writing of Fiction*, Edith Wharton discusses the extent to which French and Russian writers, in particular, shaped the early development of the short story tradition, "giving to the short story . . . great closeness of texture with profundity of form. Instead of a loose web spread over the surface of life they have made it, at its best, a shaft driven straight into the heart of human experience." In 1888, Henry James published a biographical essay on Maupassant, prompting further translations of Maupassant's stories and dramatically widening the reach of the writer's influence. By the early twentieth century, Guy de Maupassant and Anton Chekhov would be considered, arguably, the most influential writers of short stories. Stephen Crane, Frank Norris, O. Henry, and Kate Chopin were all influenced by Maupassant's complex and economical prose. The influences and correspondences of these writers grew as the genre did.

## The Short Story and Technology

Nearly all the countries taking part in this revolution in literary form were prosperous beneficiaries of the triumphs of the Industrial Revolution that had begun in the late eighteenth century. Often they were also vigorous, colonizing powers in a century marked by colonial expansion and exploitation. Most of the world's property was in the hands of relatively few countries in the nineteenth century, and so the wealth, resources, technology, and literacy necessary for successful mass literary production were still restricted to a small part of the globe. In Europe, Britain, and Russia, as in the United States, the explosion of the short story form in the middle decades of the nineteenth century was enabled by a concomitant explosion in the production of periodicals: journals, magazines, literary reviews, and newspapers. Advances in the production of paper that made it cheaper to produce, along with the development of the rotary press and new processes of photoengraving that made graphic reproduction speedier and more economical, contributed to this explosion, which continued for several decades into the next century. The technologically innovative popular press of the nineteenth century, churning out material at breakneck speed for mass consumption, responded to and reflected the increasingly mechanized, fast-paced lives of individuals in an industrialized world.

## The Short Story at the End of the Century

Near the end of the century, resistance to realism in the arts and a growing awareness of art's vexed relationship to the marketplace gave rise to the aesthetic and symbolist movements, loosely affiliated under the credo of "art for art's sake," in Russia, in Britain, and in Europe, from France to Romania. Recalling Poe's midcentury tales, the decadent and symbolist artists of the period turned to the mysterious and the occult. They rejected the materialism of high Victorian culture, insisting on the superiority of mood and emotion over scientifically recorded and rationalized information. Richard Wagner's theory of *Gesamptkunstwerk,* or the total artwork, urged the demolition of barriers separating music, literature, dance, and other arts. Charles Algernon Swinburne, Dante Gabriel Rossetti, and Oscar Wilde in England, and J. K. Huysmans, Stéphane Mallarmé, and Charles Baudelaire in France wrote poetry and fiction with strong connections to both music and the visual arts, and their works are frequently cited examples of this late-century phenomenon. Not only do these works defy conventional modes of representation and perception, but they also roam far outside of realism's bounds, returning to myth, horror, the supernatural, the depraved, and the perverse.

The short story, a locus for experimentation from its beginnings, presented an ideal format for the theories informing the aesthetic movements in circulation from the 1880s into the early twentieth century. The genre's liberating format allowed for a shift from concerns with plot and character to more immediate effects such as image and rhythm, qualities more often associated with music or poetry. As the century turned, the ease with which the form suited various genres guaranteed its prominent place in the literature of the twentieth century.

## WORKS CITED

Davidson, Cathy N. *Revolution and the Word: The Rise of the Novel in America.* New York: Oxford UP, 1986.

Harper's Monthly. Advertisement. *Harper's New Monthly Magazine.* June 1850: 1.

Levy, Andrew. *The Culture and Commerce of the American Short Story.* New York: Cambridge UP, 1993.

May, Charles E. *The Short Story: The Reality of Artifice.* New York: Routledge, 2002.

Philadelphia Monthly Magazine. Preface. *The Philadelphia Monthly Magazine.* January 1798: 1-5.

Poe, Edgar Allan. "The Importance of the Single Effect in a Prose Tale." [First published 1842]. Rpt. *Literature and Its Writers: A Compact Introduction to Fiction, Poetry, and Drama.* Ed. Ann Charters. Boston: Bedford/St. Martin's, 2004. 656–658.

Tebbel, John. *A History of Book Publishing in the United States.* Vol. I. New York: Bowker, 1972.

Wharton, Edith. *The Writing of Fiction.* New York: Scribner, 1925.

# Emilia Pardo Bazan

## (1851–1921)

Emilia Pardo Bazán was born in La Coruña, in the Galician region of Spain, in 1851. Married at the age of eighteen, Pardo Bazán took a great interest in the politics of her region and is thought to have participated in a campaign against the Amadeo of Savoy. In 1876 she won a literary contest with an essay about a Benedictine monk, Benito Jernimo Feijo. She followed with several other articles in regional newspapers, but quickly turned to fiction. Pardo Bazán is best known for introducing Spanish readers to French naturalism, both in her controversial essay about French writer Zola and in her own work, beginning with her novel, *Un Viaje de novios* (1881). The novel caused a sensation in Spain and led Pardo Bazán to answer her critics in a sharp-tongued essay entitled, *La Cuestion palpante* (1883). Pardo Bazán's novels and short stories most often describe social decay in her native Galicia but also contain a poetic rendering of the Galician countryside. Pardo Bazán's other publications include *El Cisne de Vilamorta* (1885; tr. *The Swan of Vilamorta,* 1891); *Los Pazos de Ulloa* (1886); and its sequel, *La Madre naturaleza* (1887), the novel generally considered to be her masterpiece. Pardo Bazán is also the author of numerous short stories and the play *Verdad* (1905).

## The Heart Lover                                                    1898

TRANSLATED BY EDWARD AND ELIZABETH HUBERMAN

### I

That mill in the village of Tornelos, in Galicia, would have charmed any landscape painter. It was built on the slope of a small mountain, where a dam fed its wheel, and formed a lovely natural pool garlanded with reeds. Like a hand mirror on a green skirt, the pool was set in the velvet of a meadow where golden buttercups grew, and where, in autumn, the elegant purple iris opened their corollas. On the other side of the dam, a path was worn by the feet of men and the hoofs of donkeys who went out and returned laden with sacks. To the mill came corn, wheat, and rye; out of the mill came flour—dark, white or golden. And how well, crowning the crude mill and the miller's wretched hut, did the large chestnut tree, with its horizontal branches and its leafy top, fit with the landscape! Covered in summer with pale and shaggy flowers, in October with prickly, bursting burrs, how bravely and majestically it stood out against the bluish crest of the hill! Except, that is, when it was half hidden by the gray curtain of smoke that came out, not through the chimney—since the miller's shack had none, nor do many farm houses in Galicia, even today—but from all directions, the doors, windows, cracks in the roof, and chinks in the dilapidated walls!

To round out the picture, there was a girl of thirteen or fourteen who used to lead a cow to pasture on those fresh, flowery slopes, even in the heat of summer, when cattle languish for lack of grass. A strange child, full of poetry, worthy of an idyllic painting by some congenial artist, Minia was the very model of a shepherdess in that she harmonized with the background. In the village they called her blonde, since her hair was the color of the flax she used to spin. It was a pale and faded blonde which, like a wavering glow of light, surrounded her little face, oval and sunburned, where only her eyes shone with a sky-blue light, like the blue that sometimes shines through the mists of the mountain clouds. Minia was dressed in a reddish skirt, faded and worn; a coarse cloth shift hid her breasts, still scarcely formed. She was barefoot, her short hair was tangled and unkempt, and at times mixed with blades of straw or shoots of grass she had picked up for the cow on the edge of the pastureland. And yet she was pretty, pretty as an angel, or, better said, pretty as the patron saint of the nearby shrine to whom—so people said—she bore a singular resemblance.

The celebrated patron saint, an object of fervent devotion for the villagers in the area, was a *cuerpo santo*, brought from Rome by a certain hard-working Galician, who had come, by chance, into the service of a Roman cardinal. When his master died, the man asked for no other reward for his ten years of good and loyal service than the glass case and image which had adorned the Cardinal's oratory. They were given to him, and he brought them to his village, not without some ostentation. Using his savings, supplemented by some help from the Archbishop, he erected a modest chapel. Within a few years after his death, the alms of the faithful, enlarged by the sudden devotion aroused for some distance around, transformed the chapel into a rich shrine, complete with baroque church and a good living for the caretaker. This office the parish priest promptly assumed: the forgotten mountain parish had turned into a profitable benefice. It was not easy to determine with strict historical accuracy, not even by relying on authentic and incontrovertible documents, to whom the little bone from a human cranium, incrusted in the wax head of the Saint, had belonged. Only a yellowing paper, written in a minute but steady hand, and attached to the back of the glass case, affirmed that these were the relics of the blessed Herminia, a noble virgin who suffered martyrdom under Diocletian. It seems useless to look in the *Lives of the Martyrs* for the name of the blessed Herminia or the manner of her death. Nor did the villagers raise these questions, or show any desire to concern themselves with such profundities. For them, this was not a wax statue of their Saint, but her very body, chaste and uncorrupted. The martyr's Germanic name they changed to the graceful and familiar *Minia;* and, the better to appropriate her to themselves, they added to hers the name of the parish, calling her Santa Minia of Tornelos. The how and the when of their Saint mattered little to the devout mountain folk; in her they worshipped innocence and martyrdom, the sublime heroism of weakness.

The young mill girl had been named Minia at the baptismal font. Every year, on her Saint's day, she kneeled in front of the glass case, so enraptured with contemplation of the Saint, that she barely managed to move her lips in prayer. The effigy fascinated her, for to her also it was a real body, flesh that had lived and breathed. The fact is that the Saint was beautiful—and terrifying at the same time. The wax figure represented a young girl of about fifteen, with perfect pale features. Through her eyelids, almost but not entirely closed by death, could be seen her crystal eyes shining with a mysterious brilliance. Her lips, half open too, were livid, and the enamel of her teeth showed through. On the blond hair of her head, which rested on a red silk pillow covered by tarnished gold lace, she wore a crown of silver roses. And her position permitted one to see perfectly the wound on her throat, copied with clinical accuracy: her severed arteries, her larynx, her blood, some drops of which appeared black on her neck. The Saint was wearing a vestment of green brocade over a caramel-colored taffeta tunic, clothing somewhat more theatrical than Roman, ornamented by a profusion of sequins and gold thread. Her hands, pale and most delicately molded, were crossed on the palm leaf which signified the triumph of her martyrdom. Through the panes of the glass case, where the wax tapers were reflected, the dusty image, its clothing faded by the passage of time, acquired a supernatural life. It almost seemed that the wound was going to shed fresh blood.

The young girl always returned from church absorbed and entranced. She was naturally a child of few words; but a month after the Saint's holiday, she would break her silence only with difficulty. Nor could one see a smile on her lips, unless the neighbors told her "she looked very much like the Saint."

The villagers are not tenderhearted; on the contrary, their hearts are as hard and as callous as the palms of their hands. But when their own interest is not at stake, they possess a certain instinct for justice which impels them to take the part of the weak oppressed by the strong. For this reason they looked at Minia with deep pity. An orphan, the child lived with her uncle and aunt. Her father, a miller, had died of intermittent fever, a frequent disease among those in his occupation. Her mother followed him to the grave, not because of grief, which in a country woman would have been a strange kind of death, but because of a pain in the side which attacked her as she emerged, perspiring, after baking her bread. At the age of one and a half, only recently weaned, Minia was alone in the world. Her uncle, Juan Ramón, who earned a difficult living as a bricklayer—since he was not fond of farming—entered the mill as if it were his own house. Finding a going business, an established clientele, and work that was pleasant and amusing, he rose to the position of miller. And in the village, to be the miller was to be a person of importance. It wasn't long before he was married to his lady friend, by whom he already had two unlawfully begotten children, a boy and a girl. Minia and these little ones grew up together, without much difference among them, except that the miller's children called their parents "Papa" and "Mamma," while Minia, although nobody could have taught her this, never called them anything but "Uncle" and "Aunt."

A closer look at the family situation showed more serious differences. Minia was reduced to the condition of maidservant or chore-girl. Not that her cousins didn't work too, for no one is exempt from work in a peasant's home; but the most unpleasant jobs, the hardest tasks were saved for Minia. Her cousin Melia, destined by her mother to be a seamstress, an aristocratic profession among peasant women, used to sit on a little chair to do her sewing. At the same time she had fun listening to the barbarous flirtations and pranks of the young people who used to gather at the mill and spend the night there in fun and merriment, with notorious advantage to the devil, and not without frequent and illegal augmentation of our species. Minia was the one who would help load the cart with furze; the one who, with her tiny hands, used to knead the dough for bread; the one who fed the calf, the pig and the hens; the one who led the cow out to pasture and, bent over and tired, brought the bundle of firewood down from the mountain, or the sack of chestnuts from the thicket, or the basket of greens from the meadow. Andrés, her cousin, wasn't much help to her: he spent his time in the mill, assisting with the grinding and with the collection of tolls; or else he was out on a spree, singing and shaking his tambourine with the other young sports. In this early school of corruption the boy learned filthy words and expressions, and low tricks which often bothered Minia, although she neither knew why, nor tried to understand.

For many years the mill produced enough to permit the family to live in some comfort. Juan Ramón took an interest in the business: he was always on hand to wait on customers; he was industrious, vigilant, and punctual. But little by little the pleasures of this uneventful life began to wear thin; Juan Ramón's old inclination to laziness and luxury revived; he began to neglect the mill, then let it slip toward complete ruin.

That word, luxury! Of how little it consists for a peasant: a bit more bacon and fat in the pot, meat from time to time, wheat bread if one wants it, milk curdled or fresh—this is enough to distinguish the well-to-do farmer from the destitute farmer. The next step is the luxury of clothing: a good velvet suit, leggings of fine backstitch, an embroidered shirt, a sash adorned with silk flowers, a flashy handkerchief, and silver buttons on a red vest. Juan Ramón now needed these things; yet perhaps it was neither food nor clothing which unbalanced his budget, but the merry habit, which became ever more deeply rooted, of "bending the elbow" at the Canela tavern. At first he did this only on Sundays, then on holy days, and finally on a great many days when Holy Mother Church does not require the faithful to go to mass. After these libations, the miller returned to his mill, at one moment bubbling over with joy, at another, gloomy and sullen, cursing his luck and eager to beat somebody up. Melia, when she saw him come home this way, would run and hide. Andrés, the first time his father tried to strike him with the door bar, turned on him like a wild animal, subdued him, and left him without desire for further aggressions. Pepona, the miller's wife, whose big frame carried more strength and weight than her husband's, was also capable of paying back a punch in the face. There remained only Minia, a constant, long-suffering victim. The girl received the blows stoically, turning pale at times when she felt acute pain— when, for example, the tip of a wooden shoe struck her in the shin or in the hip—but never weeping. The parish was not unaware of these doings, and some of the local women were very sorry for Minia. At the church door, after mass; at cornhusking; in the crowds at the shrine on holy days; or at the market fairs, whispers began to be heard that the miller was going into debt. Worse yet, said the whispers, the mill business was collapsing; and the miller, in collecting his tolls, was robbing without fear of God: before long, the mill-wheel would stop, and the bailiffs would come in to seize the very shirt the miller wore on his back.

One person struggled against the growing disorganization of that humble industry, the poor home. It was Pepona, the miller's wife, a stingy, grasping, penny-pinching woman; stubborn, forceful and brusque. Tireless in her labor, she rose before the sun; and she was always to be seen, now bending over to cultivate the earth, now haggling over tolls in the mill, or now trotting, barefoot, along the road to Santiago, with a basket of eggs, poultry and vegetables on her head, to be sold in the market. But what use is the care and zeal, the miserable frugality, of a woman, against the vice and laziness of two men? In one morning, Juan Ramón could drink up, and in one night of license Andrés could waste, the fruit of a whole week of Pepona's labor.

The business of the house was bad indeed, and worse still was the disposition of the miller's wife, when an evil year arrived, to make matters worst of all—a year of misery and drought; a year when, because the harvest of corn and wheat was lost, the people lived on spoiled black beans, poor, rachitic garden greens, and some worm-eaten, moldy rye from the last year's harvest.

The most shrunken and constricted thing that can be imagined in the world does not serve to give any idea of the shrinkage undergone by the stomach of a Galician peasant, nor of the emptiness of his belly in years such as this. Cabbage thickened with flour and greased with a rind of rancid bacon—this was his food day after day, without the nourishment of any meat, without a drop of wine to strengthen a little the vital spirits and to restore vigor to the body. The potato—the bread of the poor— was then hardly known, for I am not sure if I explained that what I am telling happened in the first decades of the nineteenth century.

Think how, in such a season, the mill of Juan Ramón would be doing. With the harvest lost, the millstone naturally was at rest. The water wheel, silent, sad and motionless, was like the arm of a paralytic. The starving rats, furious not to find grain to eat, shrieked in shrill tones around the stone. Andrés, bored by the lack of the usual crowd at the mill, plunged himself more and more into dances and amorous adventures, from which he returned home like his father, exhausted and irritable, with hands that itched to beat something. He beat Minia, with a mixture of rustic gallantry and brutality, and he bared his teeth at his mother because the rations were so scarce and unsavory. Now a vagabond by profession, he wandered from fair to fair in search of dice games, quarrels and drinks. Fortunately in the spring he was drafted as a soldier and set off with his musket en route to the city. To tell the hard truth, we must confess that the greatest satisfaction he could give his mother was to take himself out of her sight; he never brought a piece of bread to the house, and while he lived there he did nothing but waste everything, and grumble in the bargain. Thus he confirmed the proverb, "Where there is no food, there is hate."

The propitiatory victim, the one who suffered for all the worries and disappointments of Pepona was . . . who else? Pepona had always treated Minia with cold hostility, but now she turned on the child the furious hatred of an impious stepmother. For Minia the rags, for Melia the scarlet skirts; for Minia the pallet on the hard earth, for Melia a little bed like her parents'; to Minia was thrown the crust of moldy corn bread, while the rest of the family dined on hot broth and cold pork. Minia never complained. She was a little more faded and continually absorbed, and her head at times inclined languidly on her shoulder, so that her likeness to the Saint increased. Silent, outwardly impassive, the child suffered secretly a mortal anguish, strange fits of nausea, a passion to weep, sorrow in the very depths of her being, mysterious pain, and, above all, constant longings to die, to go to heaven and rest. . . . And yet if a landscape painter or poet passed by the mill and saw the leafy chestnut, the dam with its sleeping water, fringed by reeds, and the pensive little blond shepherdess who let her cow eat its fill along the flowered banks, then he might dream of idylls and compose an enchanting, peaceful description of the unhappy child, beaten, starved and made half idiot by the hate and cruelty she had suffered.

**II**

One day the greatest terror of all struck the miller's cottage: the date had arrived when the rent must be paid. The term of grace had expired, and now either they paid the landlord or they would be evicted, with no roof to cover them, nor any land on which to grow cabbage for their soup. And both the lazy Juan Ramón and the diligent Pepona professed for that plot of land a deeper affection than any they bore to a child sprung from their own loins. To leave that land seemed to them worse than going to the grave: every mortal, after all must die, whereas only those who have the blackest luck lose their land. But where would they find money? In the entire district, probably, there did not exist the two gold coins needed to pay the rent of the place. During that miserable year—Pepona calculated—two such coins were to be found only in the poor-box of Santa Minia. The priest very likely had two, and more besides, sewn in his mattress or buried in his garden. . . . This likelihood was the subject of conversation between the couple, one night, as they talked in their bed, a kind of box, or bunk, padded with corn leaves and a worn-out blanket. In deference to truth, one must point out that Juan Ramón, still a bit tipsy from the four drinks he had taken that evening to comfort his almost empty stomach, had never given a thought to the priest's gold until his wife, like a true Eve, suggested it to him; and it is only fair to observe also that he responded to the temptation very prudently, not at all as if the spirit of the wild wine were speaking through his mouth.

"Listen, Juan Ramón, the parson must be loaded with what we need. . . . I'll bet he's sitting on a great pile of gold. Are you snoring, or are you listening to me, or what?"

"The devil you say! Suppose he has money, what in blazes is that to us! He doesn't have to give it to us."

"Naturally, he won't give it to us. But a little loan?"

"Nonsense! You'll see how he'll lend it to you."

"I mean a loan of a different kind—one he's forced to make. . . . Damnation! . . . You're not a man; there's nothing of a man about you but your talk. . . . If my son Andrés were here . . . one day after dark . . ."

"If you mention that once more, I swear I'll knock your teeth out!"

"Cowardly pig! Even we women have more guts!"

"Shut up, you she-wolf! You want to lose me? The priest has a gun . . . and what's more, you want Santa Minia to send lightning after us, to mash us to a pulp."

"So it's the fear of Santa Minia that's eating you!"

"Take that! You wicked woman!"

"Drunkard! Souse!"

At a short distance from her uncle and aunt lay Minia, stretched out on a pile of straw, in that easy promiscuity of the Galician cabin, where men and beasts, parents and children lie mingled indiscriminately one with the other. Stiff with cold under her clothing, which she had heaped up as a covering (for only in heaven would she have a blanket), she heard vaguely some suspicious but indistinct phrases, the muffled incitements of the woman, the grunts and drunken jests of the man. They were talking about the Saint. . . . But the girl did not understand. Nevertheless, it sounded bad to her; it smacked of some offense which, if she had had any idea of what such a word meant, she would have called disrespect. She moved her lips to repeat the only prayer she knew, and thus, praying, she fell asleep.

Scarcely was she asleep when a golden blue light filled the whole hut. In the midst of that light, or forming that light, was the Saint herself, looking something like the "Lady of Fire" displayed by the master of fireworks on fiesta day. No longer lying down, but erect, she brandished her palm branch as if it were a terrible weapon. Minia thought she distinctly heard these words: "You see? I'm killing them." And looking toward the bed of her aunt and uncle, she saw two corpses, black and charred, with their mouths twisted and the tongues hanging out. . . . At that moment the cock crowed his morning song; in the stable the calf bleated, demanding his mother's milk. . . . It was day.

If the child could have had her way, she would have remained huddled in the straw that morning after her vision. Her bones ached. She trembled all over, and she had a burning thirst. But they pulled her by the hair, called her lazy, and made her get up. Besides, as usual, she had to take out the cow. With her customary apathy, she made no answer to their insults; she merely took hold of the rope and set out for the field. As for Pepona, after she had washed first her feet and then her face in the nearest puddle to the mill dam, and put on the cape and the apron reserved for important days, plus—unheard of luxury—her shoes, she placed in a basket about two dozen apples, a lump of butter wrapped in a cabbage leaf, some eggs, and the best laying hen. Then, with the basket on her head, she left the mill and set out, with a resolute air, on the road to Compostela. She was going to beg, to plead, for a delay, an extension, a pardon of the rent—something that would enable them to get through that terrible year without abandoning their beloved land, fertilized by their own sweat. . . . Of course, there *were* two gold coins that would pay the rent. . . . But no! They would stay, as they were, in the poor-box of Santa Minia or in the priest's mattress, because Juan Ramón was a weakling, and Andrés was never at home. And she—she went on wearing petticoats instead of taking over the breeches her husband couldn't fill.

Pepona nourished no great hope of obtaining the slightest concession, the tiniest breathing spell. Thus she informed her neighbor and friend, Jacoba de Alberte, whom she met at the crossroads, where she learned they were both about to make the same trip to town. For Jacoba had to bring back medicine for her husband, who was ill with a devilish asthma that all night kept him from lying down, and in the morning almost kept him from breathing.

The two gossips decided to travel together, as a protection against wolves or ghosts, especially if it should be dark when they returned. Side by side, then, they started on their way, busily chattering and praying devoutly, from time to time, that it would not rain. For Pepona was carrying practically all her worldly goods in the basket on her head.

"What worries me," said Pepona, "is that I won't be able to talk face to face with the Marquis, but instead I'll have to kneel down to his attorney. The gentlemen of highest rank are always the most merciful to the poor. The worst are those, like Don Mauricio, the attorney, who have had to fight to become gentlemen; their hearts are hard as stones, and they treat you worse than the sole of a shoe. I tell you, I'm going there like a steer to the slaughterhouse."

Jacoba, a little woman with red eyelids, yellow, wrinkled features, and two brick-red spots on her cheeks, answered in a mournful voice:

"Ah, my friend! I'd gladly go a hundred times where you're going, but never once where I must go. Santa Minia be with us. God knows that it's my husband's health that takes me there, for health is worth more than riches. If it weren't for the sake of health, who would be brave enough to enter the drug store of Don Custodio?"

At the sound of this name, a lively expression of curiosity showed on Pepona's face, and she wrinkled her low, flat forehead until her thick eyebrows came to a finger's breadth from her hairline.

"Ah, yes indeed! . . . I never was there. I don't even like to walk in front of that shop. All sorts of stories are going around, about how the druggist is a sorcerer."

"You're right, it's not good even to walk there, but when one has a man's health on one's hands. . . . Health is worth more than all the goods of this world; a poor fellow lacks everything if he lacks health, and what would he not do to get it? . . . I'd be willing to go right down to hell and ask the devil himself for a good ointment for my husband. We've already spent so much money on drugs this year, with no results. He might just as well have been drinking water from the fountain. It's almost a sin to waste money that way, when there isn't even a crust of bread in the house. So last night my husband, who was coughing so much he almost burst, said to me: 'Look, Jacoba,' he said, 'either you go and ask Don Custodio for some of that ointment, or I'm going to die. Never mind the doctor; and pay no attention to Christ our Lord, either, even if he makes a special appearance for you. It's Don Custodio you need to deal with. If he wants to, he can relieve me of all this trouble with only two little spoonfuls of that medicine he knows how to make. And never mind the money, woman, unless you want to be left a widow.'"

With an air of mystery, Jacoba now placed her hand on her bosom, and drew from it a very small object, wrapped in a piece of paper:

"So that's why I'm carrying here the heart of our treasure—a gold doubloon! It's killing me—I was going to use it to buy clothing, for I'm going around almost naked. But the life of my man comes first, my friend. So I'm taking it to that robber of a Don Custodio. May Jesus forgive me!"

Pepona started to think, dazzled by the sight of the doubloon and feeling in her soul an emotion of covetousness so strong that it almost choked her.

"But tell me, my friend," she whispered ardently, clenching her large, horse-like teeth, her eyes sparkling. "Tell me, what does Don Custodio do to make so much money? Do you know the stories they tell around here? That this year he bought several properties from the Marquis. The most valuable properties. They say he already has the income from hundreds of acres of wheat."

"Ah, my friend! Why shouldn't this man make money, since he can cure any disease the good Lord ever invented? It's terrifying to go into that place. But when you come out with health in your hand . . . Listen: who do you think cured the priest at Morlán of his rheumatism? He'd been five years in bed, crippled, no good for anything at all. . . . And suddenly one day he gets up, all better, walking around like you and me. Well, what did it? The ointment they rubbed into his hips, the ointment that cost him half a gold coin at Don Custodio's. And old man Gorio, the innkeeper at Silleda? That was a real miracle. They'd already given him the last rites, when somebody brought him a white liquid from Don Custodio. It was just as if he rose from the dead."

"The wonders God works."

"God?" answered Jacoba. "We'll see whether it's God or the devil. . . . Pepona, I beg you, please, to come with me when I go into that shop."

"I'll do it."

Preoccupied with their prattling, the two gossips found their journey an easy one, and arrived at Compostela in time to hear the bells of the cathedral and of several churches ring out for mass. They entered Las Animas, a church favored by the country people, and consequently filthy and malodorous. Having heard mass, they crossed the Plaza of Pan, which was crowded with peasants and horses, and with women selling muffins or earthen pots. The two friends walked under the arcade, supported by columns with Byzantine capitals, and soon reached the fearful lair of Don Custodio.

The entrance was two steps below the surface of the street. And since the arcade shut out much of the light, the shop was almost always submerged in a wavering shadow. The red, blue, and green glass windows, then a startling novelty, made the shadow even deeper. On the shelves were still displayed those colorful jars, today valued as objects of art, bearing in Gothic letters inscriptions resembling formulas of alchemy: *Rad. Polip. Q., Ra. Su. Eboris, Stirac. Cala,* and other labels of no less sinister appearance. In a leather armchair, now glossy with use, before a table where an open volume of great bulk rested upon a lectern, was the druggist himself. He was reading when the two country women entered and as soon as he saw them he rose. He seemed a man of some forty-odd years, with lean features, sunken eyes, hollowed-out cheeks, and a pointed gray beard. His bald spot, already shiny, was surrounded with long hairs which were beginning to turn gray. His thin, rather pleasant head resembled that of a penitent saint, or of a German scholar cloistered in his laboratory. As he stood before the two women, with the reflection from one of the blue window panes falling on his face, he could easily have been taken for an effigy in sculpture. He spoke no word, contenting himself with looking fixedly at the women. Jacoba trembled as if quicksilver were running through her veins; it was Pepona, more daring, who burst out with the story of the asthma, the ointment, the sick husband, and the doubloon. With a grave nod of his head, Don Custodio seemed to assent. He disappeared for three minutes behind the red serge curtain which covered the entrance to his back room, then returned with a little flask carefully sealed with wax. He took the doubloon, dropped it into the table drawer, and, returning a silver peso to Jacoba, said to her: "Rub this salve into his chest morning and night." Without another word, he returned to his book. The two women stared at each other and then left the apothecary's shop as if the devil were after them. Once outside, Jacoba crossed herself.

It must have been about three in the afternoon when they again met at the tavern, near the entrance to the highway. To a snack consisting of bread and a crust of hard cheese they added the consolation of two small glasses of brandy. Presently they started on the return journey. Jacoba was bubbling over with joy; she had the medicine for her husband, she had made a good bargain for her half measure beans, and, by mercy of Don Custodio, a peso still remained of her treasured doubloon. Pepona, on the other hand, had a hoarse voice and burning eyes; her eyebrows knit closer together than ever; when she walked, her large, clumsy body bent over double, as if she had suffered a severe cudgeling. No sooner had they reached the highway, than she gave bitter voice to her afflictions: the rascally Don Mauricio had behaved as if he were born deaf, as if his mission in life were to scourge the unfortunate.

"Pay the rent or leave the place!" he had shouted.

"Jacoba, I wept. I screamed, I got down on my knees, I tore my hair. I begged him, by the soul of his mother, and of anyone else he claimed in the world beyond. . . . He didn't budge. 'Pay, or get out! This isn't the only year you've been behind in your payments, nor can you put the blame on a bad harvest. . . . Your husband drinks and your son dances too much. . . . The Marquis would say the same thing to you. . . . He has no more patience with you. He doesn't like drunkards on his property.' I answered him: 'Señor, we'll sell our oxen and our cow. . . . But then, how will we work the farm? We'll sell ourselves as slaves. . . .' 'Pay up, I tell you . . . or get out!' And that was all he would say. Before I knew it, he had pushed me out the door. Poor me! You do well to take care of your husband, Jacoba. . . . A man who doesn't drink! That sot of mine will send me to my grave. . . . If he fell ill, he wouldn't get well from the medicine I'd buy him."

Since the dark comes early in winter, the two gossips took a short-cut toward the mountain, through some thick pine groves. From a distant belfry they heard the sound of the Angelus; and the mist, rising from the river, made it difficult to distinguish ordinary objects. Pine trees and brambles faded away into a vague ghostly grayness. It was hard for them to find the path.

"In God's name," the worried Jacoba suddenly observed, "I beg you to say nothing in the village about that ointment. . . ."

"Don't worry, my friend. . . . My mouth is a deep well."

"For if the priest knew about it, he might censure us at mass. . . ."

"But what concern is it of his?"

"Well, since they say this salve is made of . . ."

"Of what?"

"Good heavens, my friend!" whispered Jacoba, stopping, and lowering her voice, as if the pine trees might hear her and inform on her: "Don't you really know? I'm amazed. At market this very day the women talked about nothing else, and the young girls said they would rather be torn to pieces than go near the arcade. As for me, if I went in there, it's because I'm no longer a girl; but old as I am, if you hadn't been with me, I should not have set foot in that shop. May the glorious Santa Minia protect us!"

"Honestly, Jacoba, I know nothing about this. Tell me. I'll be as silent as if I were dead."

"But, Pepona, there's no more to say! Beloved Jesus! These miraculous remedies, which restore the dead to life, Don Custodio makes them with *maidens' hearts*."

"Maidens' hearts . . . ?"

"The hearts of unwed maids, of girls who are ripe, ready for marriage. With a knife he cuts out their hearts, and then, the devil knows how, he prepares his medications. He used to have two young servant girls, and nobody knows what became of them, unless the earth swallowed them, for they disappeared and nobody ever saw them again. They say that no human being ever enters the back room of that shop and comes out again alive. For he has a trap door there, and any girl who enters and puts her foot on the trap door . . . Wham! She falls into a deep pit, so terribly deep you can't measure how deep it is . . . and there the apothecary cuts out her heart."

Perhaps Jacoba should have been asked how many fathoms below ground that ghoulish laboratory was located. But since Pepona's analytical faculties were not so deep as the pit, she limited herself to asking, anxiously:

"And does he use the hearts of *young* girls only?"

"That's right. We old women are no use to him."

Pepona remained silent. The moist fog of that hilly place was changing into a light drizzle, which fell almost imperceptibly on the two companions. Both women were numb from the cold and terrified by the darkness. As they made their way through the bare wasteland which lies just this side of the lovely Tornelos valley and from which, far off, the tower of the shrine may be seen, Jacoba murmured in a faint voice:

"My friend . . . isn't that a wolf over there?"

"A wolf?" said Pepona, shaking.

"There, behind those rocks. I hear they've been eating a lot of people these days. They ate a young boy at Morlán, everything except his head and his shoes. Jesus!"

The wolf scare was repeated two or three times before the women came within sight of their village. Nevertheless, nothing confirmed their fears; no wolf came upon them. They said good-by at the door of Jacoba's hut, and Pepona went on alone to her own wretched hearth. The first thing she stumbled upon at her threshold was the body of Juan Ramón, drunk as a lord; while he cursed and blasphemed, he had to be lifted bodily and carried to his bed. At about midnight, the sot emerged from his stupor, and proceeded, in words of the gutter, to ask his wife about the rent. After this distressing question, and Pepona's still more distressing reply, followed recriminations, threats, blasphemies, and a strange, heated, angered whispering.

Minia, lying on the straw, could not help overhearing; her heart throbbed; her chest pained her; she scarcely breathed. But in a moment Pepona, rushing out of bed, ordered her to move to the other side of the cabin, where the animals slept. Minia picked up her armful of straw, carried it across the room, and wrapped herself up in it again not far from the stable, where she shivered with fear and cold. She was very tired that day; because of Pepona's absence she had been obliged to take care of everything, to prepare the soup, to gather herbs, to do the washing, to perform whatever tasks the house required. . . . Yet, exhausted as she was, and tormented by that strange unrest she so often felt, that anxiety, that nameless oppression, still no sleep came to her eyelids, nor rest to her spirit. She prayed mechanically; she thought of the Saint, and said to herself, without moving her lips: "Beloved Santa Minia, take me soon to heaven, soon, soon." At last, if she wasn't exactly asleep, she was at least in that confused, trance-like state which leads to visions, revelations, and even physical changes. Then it seemed to her, as it had the night before, that she could see the figure of the martyr. Yet, marvelous to say, it was not the Saint: it was herself, the poor young girl, bereft of all protection, who was stretched out there in church, in the glass case surrounded by candles. It was she herself who wore the crown of roses; the green brocade vestment covered her shoulders; her cold, pale hands grasped the palm leaf; in her own throat the bleeding wound was opened; and through it, sweetly and insensibly, her life was slipping away, in soft little waves of blood. And as her blood ebbed, it left her tranquil, happy, ecstatic. . . . A sigh escaped from the little girl's breast, her eyes went blank, she shuddered . . . and was motionless. Her last, confused impression was that she had arrived in heaven, accompanied by her Patron Saint.

## III

In that room behind the apothecary's shop where, according to the assurances of Jacoba de Alberte, no human being ever entered, a Canon of the Holy Metropolitan Church came almost every evening to have a friendly chat with Don Custodio. He had been a fellow-student with the Don, and he was now a seasoned, pleasant-faced man, dry as tinder, and a great lover of tobacco. As the loyal friend and intimate confidant of Don Custodio, no one was more suited to keep the secret of the apothecary's crimes—if the abominations attributed to him by the common folk were true—than the Canon Don Lucas Llorente, who seemed to the lay public the very quintessence of mystery, and of reserve. Silence, the most absolute taciturnity, assumed in Llorente the proportions and characteristics of a mania. He allowed nothing of his own life and activities, even the slightest and most innocent, to show through to other people. The Canon's motto was: "Let no one know anything at all about you," and he even added (in the intimacy of the back room): "Whatever people learn about what we do or think, they'll turn into deadly malice. It is better for them to invent their own stories than for us to give them facts to build on."

Because Llorente was this kind of person, and because of their long friendship, Don Custodio's trust in him was complete. Only with him did the Don talk on certain serious matters; only from him did he take advice on difficult or dangerous cases. One night, for example, during a violent downpour punctuated by intervals of lightning and thunder, Llorente found the apothecary excited, nervous, almost in convulsions. As the Canon entered, Don Custodio rushed toward him, grasped his hands, and pulled him to the back room—that famous back room, where instead of the frightful trap door and the bottomless pit, there were bookshelves, chests, a sofa, and other equally inoffensive furnishings. There, the apothecary said in an anguished voice:

"Alas, my friend Llorente! How sorry I am that I've always followed your advice, that I've fed the babblings of fools! From the very first day I should really have given the lie to those absurd stories. I should have squelched those stupid rumors. . . . You advised me, didn't you, to do nothing, absolutely nothing, to change the impression the common people had about me? Of course I knew I seemed strange to them, because I'm a bachelor and live a solitary life, because I take journeys abroad to learn about advances in my profession, and because there was that accursed accident" (here the apothecary hesitated a bit) "that two maids . . . young ones . . . had to leave this house secretly, without telling anyone. But why the devil should their reasons matter to the public anyway, will you please tell me? And you kept saying to me, 'Friend Custodio, let things run their course; don't insist on trying to undeceive the fools, for they're going to remain foolish anyway. What's more, they're bound to misunderstand any efforts you make to overcome their prejudices. Let them go on believing that you make your ointment out of human hearts, and that they must therefore pay more for it; let them talk nonsense if they will. Continue to sell them your good medicines, new ones, one of the modern pharmacopoeia, which you say is very advanced in the foreign countries you visited. Cure their illnesses, and let the imbeciles believe you do it by magic. The greatest asininity of all those which the cursed liberals are to-day inventing and trying to spread is the one about *enlightening the multitudes.* May God enlighten you, my friend! But you can't enlighten the common people; they're a lot of simpletons, and they always will be, a herd of asses. If you confront them with natural, rational ideas, they won't believe you. They long for what's strange, freakish, miraculous, and impossible. The bigger the lie, the sooner they'll believe it. So then, friend Custodio, let the parade march by, and, if you can, steal the flag. . . . This world is a dance. . . .'"

"Certainly," interrupted the Canon, taking out his snuffbox and torturing the powder between his fingertips, "I have said those things to you. But after all, has my advice really been so bad for you? Hasn't the shop's cash box been overflowing with money, and haven't you recently purchased some very attractive property in Valeiro?"

"Yes, yes, I bought it, but I'm unhappy about it, too!" exclaimed the pharmacist. "Oh, if I were to tell you what happened to me today! Go on, guess! What do you think happened to me? No matter how hard you try to think of the most extreme out-rage . . . it won't be any use. You'll never guess what this is, nor would three like you."

"What was it?"

"You'll see, you'll see! This takes the prize. A village woman came into my shop today, at a moment when no one else was there. She had been in a few days before, with a friend who asked me for an asthma remedy. This was a tall woman, with a hard face, eyebrows knit together, a protruding jaw, a flat forehead, and a pair of eyes like two pieces of charcoal. Believe me, she was an impressive character. She tells me she wants to talk to me privately, and when she sees that she's alone with me and can talk safely, it turns out . . . Here's the amazing part of it! It turns out she's there to offer me the heart of a young girl, a niece of hers! The girl was marriageable, virgin, fair, and thus met all the conditions supposedly required for her heart to be usable in the med-icines I manufacture. . . . What do you say to that, Canon? That's what we've come to. In these parts it's common knowledge that I take the heart out of young girls, and use them to compound these miraculous remedies—ugh!—capable even of bringing the dead back to life. The woman assured me of every word of this. Do you see what's happened? Do you understand the stigma that has fallen upon me? I am the terror of the villages, the murderer of young girls, and the most loathsome and nasty creature the imagination can conjure up."

A low, distant thunder accompanied the apothecary's last few words. The Canon laughed, rubbing his dry hands and merrily shaking his head. It seemed that he had achieved a great and much desired triumph.

"Just what I said! Can't you understand, man? Don't you see that these creatures are more beastly, ignorant, and baboonish than even I ever thought? Don't you see how they always think of the greatest cruelty, the grossest folly, the sheerest stupidity? Just because you're the mildest, best natured, most harmless man on earth; just be-cause you have, as you do, such a soft heart that you worry over everyone else's prob-lems, whether they concern you or not; and just because you couldn't kill a fly, and you think only of your books and your studies and your chemicals, that's the very reason why all these hopeless savages consider you a horrible monster, a murderer, guilty of every possible crime and abomination."

"But who could have invented these slanders, Llorente?"

"Who? Universal stupidity, supported by universal malice. The beast of the Apocalypse . . . which is the common mob, believe me, even though Saint John may not have stated it so clearly."

"All right, then! So be it! But in future I shall not permit myself to be slandered any further. No sir; I won't have it. Look at the fix I'm in! If I'm not careful, a young girl may die because of me! And that wild beast of a woman, so ready to strike her dead! Just imagine what she said to me: 'I'll kill her, then I'll leave her on the mountain, and I'll say that the wolves ate her; there are lots of them around at this time of year. And you'll see how it is—the next day she'll certainly look as if she'd been eaten.' Well, Canon, you should have seen how hard I worked to convince that old warhorse that I never cut out anyone's heart, nor did I ever dream of such a thing! Time after time I told her, 'This is a stupid story that's going around, an atrocity, a piece of foolish knavery; and when I find out who's been spreading it, that's the fellow whose heart I really will cut out!' Yet the woman remained obstinate, firm as a post: 'Señor, only two pieces of gold. . . . We'll keep it a secret: nobody will say a word about it. . . . For two coins you may have the heart. No one else will make you such a good proposition.' What an evil viper! The furies of hell must have a face like hers. . . . I tell you I was barely able to persuade her. She wouldn't go away. Soon I had to chase her out with a cudgel."

"Oh, how I hope you *did* convince her!" exclaimed the Canon, suddenly worried and disturbed. He kept turning the snuffbox around between his fingers. "I'm afraid you've made matters worse instead of better. Alas, Custodio! You have misled her; I'll take an oath right now that you have misled her."

"What are you saying, man? Or Canon, or devil?" exclaimed the apothecary, alarmed, and practically jumping out of his seat.

"I tell you, you've misled her, and you've committed a major foolishness in imagining, as you always do, that there's a spark of natural reason in these brutes, and that it's proper or worthwhile to tell them the truth, and to argue with them and try to enlighten them. By now the girl is probably in heaven, as dead as my grandmother. . . . Tomorrow morning, or the next day, they'll bring you her heart wrapped in a rag. . . . You'll see!"

"Quiet! Quiet! I can't bear to hear it! No human mind could possibly conceive of any such thing. . . . What should I have done? For God's sake, don't drive me crazy!"

"What should you have done? The contrary of what is right or rational, the opposite of what you'd have done with me or any other person capable of reason, and although perhaps just as bad as the mob, somewhat less beastly. . . . You should have said yes, you'd buy the heart for two gold coins, or three, or a hundred . . ."

"But then . . ."

"Wait. Let me finish. . . . But that the heart removed by anyone else would be of no use at all; that since you yourself would have to perform the operation, they must bring the girl to you fresh and healthy. . . . And when you had her safe in your hands, then we could call upon the law to apprehend and punish the evildoers. . . . Don't you see that this is apparently a person they want to get rid of, someone who's in their way, either because she makes one more mouth to feed, or she possesses something they're eager to fall heir to. Hasn't it occurred to you that although an atrocity of this kind may be decided upon in one day, it must have been fermenting in the mind for a good many years? The girl is sentenced to death. That's all. Believe me, right at this moment . . ." And the Canon brandished his snuffbox in a murderous gesture.

"Canon, you'll be the death of me! Who can sleep tonight! I'll saddle the mare this minute, and set out for Tornelos. . . ."

A frightening thunderclap, very close by, told the apothecary that his resolution was impractical. The wind roared, and the rain broke loose furiously, beating against the windows.

"And do you really think," asked Don Custodio in a discouraged tone, "that they'd be capable of such iniquity?"

"By the means. And of inventing many more crimes not yet known. Ignorance cannot be overcome, and ignorance is the source of crime."

"But what you're doing," argued the pharmacist, "is to claim that ignorance will last forever."

"Alas, my friend!" answered the Canon. "Ignorance is an evil, but a necessary and eternal evil, here in this rascally world. Neither from evil nor from death shall we ever succeed in freeing ourselves."

What a night for that honest apothecary, who was thought by the people to be such a horrible monster! Two centuries earlier, perhaps, they might even have apprehended him on charges of witchcraft!

At dawn he saddled the white mare he usually rode on his trips to the countryside, and set out on the road to Tornelos. The mill would serve as a signpost to help him find, very quickly, what he was seeking.

The sun was beginning to climb higher into the sky, now brilliantly clear and cloudless after the storm. The rain that had covered the grass was now soaked into the ground, and the tears that the night had shed on the brambles were all dried. The clear, transparent air, not too cold, was fragrant with the light aroma of the drenched pines. A magpie, marked in black and white, took flight almost at the feet of Don Custodio's horse. A frightened hare peered out of the underbrush, then gracefully jumped across the apothecary's path. Everything announced one of those splendid, calm winter days, which in Galicia so often follow nights of storm. The apothecary, filled with the delight of that atmosphere, was beginning to believe that the whole affair of the preceding evening was a delusion, a tragic nightmare, or some extravagant invention of the Canon's. How could one person assassinate another, and in such a barbarous and inhuman way? A madness, a foolishness, an absurdity of Llorente's imagination, nothing more. Bah! In the mill, at this time of day, surely they would be preparing to grind the grain. From the sanctuary of Santa Minia there came, borne by the breeze, the silvery ring of the bell, calling people to first mass. In the countryside, everything was peace, love and serenity. . . . Don Custodio felt exhilarated, happy as a child, and his thoughts changed course. If the girl whose heart had been offered him was pretty and modest . . . he might take her home with him, rescuing her from the unhappy slavery, danger and neglect in which she was living. And if she turned out to be a good, loyal, plain, decent girl, not like those two wild ones, one of whom had run away to Zamora with a sergeant, while the other got into trouble with a student, so that she had to find a hiding-place elsewhere . . . Well, if the little mill girl wasn't like this, but rather of a gentle type dreamed of from time to time by the obstinate old bachelor . . . then . . . Who knows, Custodio? You're not really so old that . . .

Intrigued by thoughts such as these, he gave free rein to the mare . . . and he did not observe that they were getting farther and farther up the mountain, to its darkest and roughest slopes. He noticed it only after he'd already covered a good stretch of road. Turning his horse around, he went back the way he had come, but without much luck, for he became even more lost, in a wild and rocky area. A strange heaviness oppressed his heart, he could not tell why. Suddenly, there in front of him, under the rays of the sun, the happy, glorious sun which reconciles human beings with themselves and with existence, he descried a form, a dead body, that of a girl. . . . Her head, bent back, revealed the enormous wound on her neck; a coarse apron covered her mutilated breast; blood, diluted now by the rain, stained the grass all around; and the turf and shrubbery were trampled. Round about, the high hills and the solitary pine groves kept their silence. . . .

## IV

Pepona was hanged in La Coruña. Juan Ramón was sentenced to the penitentiary. But the apothecary's intervention in this legal drama sufficed to convince the mass of local people that he was more of a murderer than before, one who could make honest men pay for the wrongs of sinners, one who accused others of the transgressions he committed himself. Luckily there was no popular disturbance then in Compostela; had there been, someone might have set fire to his shop. This, of course, would have given Canon Llorente cause to rub his hands in satisfaction as he saw his belief confirmed, that stupidity is universal and irremediable.

# Ambrose Bierce

## (1842–C. 1914)

With only one year of formal education, Ambrose Bierce earned his living in San Francisco and then London as one of the most famous journalists of his time. He was nicknamed "Bitter Bierce" for his condemnations of corruption and pomposity, and he published the completed version of a characteristically satirical book, *The Devil's Dictionary*, in 1906, wherein he defined *birth* as "the first and direst of all disasters," and *brute* with "n., See HUSBAND." A drummer boy in the Civil War decorated for rescuing a comrade (who died anyway) from the battlefield, Bierce created the most memorable tale of a public hanging ever written in "An Occurrence at Owl Creek Bridge." Other stories from his war experiences were collected in the 1891 *Tales of Soldiers and Civilians* and the 1893 *Can Such Things Be?* He was a friend of the American writer Bret Harte and contributed a set of diatribes called "The Grizzly Papers" to Harte's publication, *The Overland Monthly.* His other nonfiction essay collections include *The Fiend's Delight* and *Cobwebs from an Empty Skull.* Bierce aspired stylistically to emulate Edgar Allan Poe, and he was preoccupied with the tragic and fatal. The exact circumstances of Bierce's own death are unknown: in 1913 he set off for Mexico to meet Pancho Villa and, after one last letter in late December of the same year, was never heard from again. Both the mysteriousness of his death and his literary use of stream of consciousness may have contributed to making him an object of fascination for such later writers as Borges, Cortazar, and Fuentes, whose novel *The Old Gringo* considers the fate of Bierce.

## An Occurrence at Owl Creek Bridge     1891

I

A man stood upon a railroad bridge in northern Alabama, looking down into the swift water twenty feet below. The man's hands were behind his back, the wrists bound with a cord. A rope closely encircled his neck. It was attached to a stout crosstimber above his head and the slack fell to the level of his knees. Some loose boards laid upon the sleepers supporting the metals of the railway supplied a footing for him and his executioners—two private soldiers of the Federal army, directed by a sergeant who in civil life may have been a deputy sheriff. At a short remove upon the same temporary platform was an officer in the uniform of his rank, armed. He was a captain. A sentinel at each end of the bridge stood with his rifle in the position known as "support," that is to say, vertical in front of the left shoulder, the hammer resting on the forearm thrown straight across the chest—a formal and unnatural position, enforcing an erect carriage of the body. It did not appear to be the duty of these two men to know what was occurring at the center of the bridge; they merely blockaded the two ends of the foot planking that traversed it.

Beyond one of the sentinels nobody was in sight; the railroad ran straight away into a forest for a hundred yards, then, curving, was lost to view. Doubtless there was an outpost farther along. The other bank of the stream was open ground—a gentle acclivity topped with a stockade of vertical tree trunks, loopholed for rifles, with a single embrasure through which protruded the muzzle of a brass cannon commanding the bridge. Midway of the slope between bridge and fort were the spectators—a single company of infantry in line, at "parade rest," the butts of the rifles on the ground, the barrels inclining slightly backward against the right shoulder, the hands crossed upon the stock. A lieutenant stood at the right of the line, the point of his sword upon the ground, his left hand resting upon his right. Excepting the group of four at the center of the bridge, not a man moved. The company faced the bridge, staring stonily, motionless. The sentinels, facing the banks of the stream, might have been statues to adorn the bridge. The captain stood with folded arms, silent, observing the work of his subordinates, but making no sign. Death is a dignitary who when he comes announced is to be received with formal manifestations of respect, even by those most familiar with him. In the code of military etiquette silence and fixity are forms of deference.

The man who was engaged in being hanged was apparently about thirty-five years of age. He was a civilian, if one might judge from his habit, which was that of a planter. His features were good—a straight nose, firm mouth, broad forehead, from which his long, dark hair was combed straight back, falling behind his ears to the collar of his well-fitting frock-coat. He wore a mustache and pointed beard, but no whiskers; his eyes were large and dark gray, and had a kindly expression which one would hardly have expected in one whose neck was in the hemp. Evidently this was no vulgar assassin. The liberal military code makes provision for hanging many kinds of persons, and gentlemen are not excluded.

The preparations being complete, the two private soldiers stepped aside and each drew away the plank upon which he had been standing. The sergeant turned to the captain, saluted, and placed himself immediately behind that officer, who in turn moved apart one pace. These movements left the condemned man and the sergeant standing on the two ends of the same plank, which spanned three of the cross-ties of the bridge. The end upon which the civilian stood almost, but not quite, reached a fourth. This plank had been held in place by the weight of the captain; it was now held by that of the sergeant. At a signal from the former the latter would step aside, the plank would tilt and the condemned man go down between two ties. The arrangement commended itself to his judgment as simple and effective. His face had not been covered nor his eyes bandaged. He looked a moment at his "unsteadfast footing," then let his gaze wander to the swirling water of the stream racing madly beneath his feet. A piece of dancing driftwood caught his attention and his eyes followed it down the current. How slowly it appeared to move! What a sluggish stream!

He closed his eyes in order to fix his last thoughts upon his wife and children. The water, touched to gold by the early sun, the brooding mists under the banks at some distance down the stream, the fort, the soldiers, the piece of drift—all had distracted him. And now he became conscious of a new disturbance. Striking through the thought of his dear ones was a sound which he could neither ignore nor understand, a sharp, distinct, metallic percussion like the stroke of a blacksmith's hammer upon the anvil; it had the same ringing quality. He wondered what it was, and whether immeasurably distant or nearby—it seemed both. Its recurrence was regular, but as slow as the tolling of a death knell. He awaited each stroke with impatience and—he knew not why—apprehension. The intervals of silence grew progressively longer; the delays became maddening. With their greater infrequency the sounds increased in strength and sharpness. They hurt his ear like the thrust of a knife; he feared he would shriek. What he heard was the ticking of his watch.

He unclosed his eyes and saw again the water below him. "If I could free my hands," he thought, "I might throw off the noose and spring into the stream. By diving I could evade the bullets and, swimming vigorously, reach the bank, take to the woods and get away home. My home, thank God, is as yet outside their lines; my wife and little ones are still beyond the invader's farthest advance."

As these thoughts, which have here to be set down in words, were flashed into the doomed man's brain rather than evolved from it the captain nodded to the sergeant. The sergeant stepped aside.

## II

Peyton Farquhar was a well-to-do planter, of an old and highly respected Alabama family. Being a slave owner and like other slave owners a politician he was naturally an original secessionist and ardently devoted to the Southern cause. Circumstances of an imperious nature, which it is unnecessary to relate here, had prevented him from taking service with the gallant army that had fought the disastrous campaigns ending with the fall of Corinth, and he chafed under the inglorious restraint, longing for the release of his energies, the larger life of the soldier, the opportunity for distinction. That opportunity, he felt, would come, as it comes to all in wartime. Meanwhile he did what he could. No service was too humble for him to perform in aid of the South, no adventure too perilous for him to undertake if consistent with the character of a civilian who was at heart a soldier, and who in good faith and without too much qualification assented to at least a part of the frankly villainous dictum that all is fair in love and war.

One evening while Farquhar and his wife were sitting on a rustic bench near the entrance to his grounds, a gray-clad soldier rode up to the gate and asked for a drink of water. Mrs. Farquhar was only too happy to serve him with her own white hands. While she was fetching the water her husband approached the dusty horseman and inquired eagerly for news from the front.

"The Yanks are repairing the railroads," said the man, "and are getting ready for another advance. They have reached the Owl Creek bridge, put it in order, and built a stockade on the north bank. The commandant has issued an order, which is posted everywhere, declaring that any civilian caught interfering with the railroad, its bridges, tunnels or trains will be summarily hanged. I saw the order."

"How far is it to the Owl Creek bridge?" Farquhar asked.

"About thirty miles."

"Is there no force on this side the creek?"

"Only a picket post half a mile out, on the railroad, and a single sentinel at this end of the bridge."

"Suppose a man—a civilian and student of hanging—should elude the picket post and perhaps get the better of the sentinel," said Farquhar, smiling, "what could he accomplish?"

The soldier reflected. "I was there a month ago," he replied. "I observed that the flood of last winter had lodged a great quantity of driftwood against the wooden pier at this end of the bridge. It is now dry and would burn like tow."

The lady had now brought the water, which the soldier drank. He thanked her ceremoniously, bowed to her husband and rode away. An hour later, after nightfall, he repassed the plantation, going northward in the direction from which he had come. He was a Federal scout.

## III

As Peyton Farquhar fell straight downward through the bridge he lost consciousness and was as one already dead. From this state he was awakened—ages later, it seemed to him—by the pain of a sharp pressure upon his throat, followed by a sense of suffocation. Keen, poignant agonies seemed to shoot from his neck downward through every fiber of his body and limbs. These pains appeared to flash along well-defined lines of ramification and to beat with an inconceivably rapid periodicity. They seemed like streams of pulsating fire heating him to an intolerable temperature. As to his head, he was conscious of nothing but a feeling of fullness—of congestion. These sensations were unaccompanied by thought. The intellectual part of his nature was already effaced; he had power only to feel, and feeling was torment. He was conscious of motion. Encompassed in a luminous cloud, of which he was now merely the fiery heart, without material substance, he swung through unthinkable arcs of oscillation, like a vast pendulum. Then all at once, with terrible suddenness, the light about him shot upward with the noise of a loud plash; a frightful roaring was in his ears, and all was cold and dark. The power of thought was restored; he knew that the rope had broken and he had fallen into the stream. There was no additional strangulation; the noose about his neck was already suffocating him and kept the water from his lungs. To die of hanging at the bottom of a river!—the idea seemed to him ludicrous. He opened his eyes in the darkness and saw above him a gleam of light, but how distant, how inaccessible! He was still sinking, for the light became fainter and fainter until it was a mere glimmer. Then it began to grow and brighten, and he knew that he was rising toward the surface—knew it with reluctance, for he was now very comfortable. "To be hanged and drowned," he thought, "that is not so bad, but I do not wish to be shot. No, I will not be shot. That is not fair."

He was not conscious of an effort, but a sharp pain in his wrist apprised him that he was trying to free his hands. He gave the struggle his attention, as an idler might observe the feat of a juggler, without interest in the outcome. What splendid effort! What magnificent, what superhuman strength! Ah, that was a fine endeavor! Bravo! The cord fell away; his arms parted and floated upward, the hands dimly seen on each side in the growing light. He watched them with a new interest as first one and then the other pounced upon the noose at his neck. They tore it away and thrust it fiercely aside, its undulations resembling those of a water snake. "Put it back, put it back!" He thought he shouted these words to his hands, for the undoing of the noose had been succeeded by the direst pang that he had yet experienced. His neck ached horribly; his brain was on fire; his heart, which had been fluttering faintly, gave a great leap, trying to force itself out at his mouth. His whole body was racked and wrenched with an insupportable anguish! But his disobedient hands gave no heed to the command. They beat the water vigorously with quick, downward strokes, forcing him to the surface. He felt his head emerge; his eyes were blinded by the sunlight; his chest expanded convulsively, and with a supreme and crowning agony his lungs engulfed a great draught of air, which instantly he expelled in a shriek!

He was now in full possession of his physical senses. They were, indeed, preternaturally keen and alert. Something in the awful disturbance of his organic system had so exalted and defined them that they made record of things never before perceived. He felt the ripples upon his face and heard their separate sounds as they struck. He looked at the forest on the bank of the stream, saw the individual trees, the leaves and the veining of each leaf—saw the very insects upon them: the locusts, the brilliant-bodied flies, the gray spiders stretching their webs from twig to twig. He noted the prismatic colors in all the dewdrops upon a million blades of grass. The humming of the gnats that danced above the eddies of the stream, the beating of the dragonflies' wings, the strokes of the water spiders' legs, like oars which had lifted their boat—all these made audible music. A fish slid along beneath his eyes and he heard the rush of its body parting the water.

He had come to the surface facing down the stream; in a moment the visible world seemed to wheel slowly round, himself the pivotal point, and he saw the bridge, the fort, the soldiers upon the bridge, the captain, the sergeant, the two privates, his executioners. They were in silhouette against the blue sky. They shouted and gesticulated, pointing at him. The captain had drawn his pistol, but did not fire; the others were unarmed. Their movements were grotesque and horrible, their forms gigantic.

Suddenly he heard a sharp report and something struck the water smartly within a few inches of his head, spattering his face with spray. He heard a second report, and saw one of the sentinels with his rifle at his shoulder, a light cloud of blue smoke rising from the muzzle. The man in the water saw the eye of the man on the bridge gazing into his own through the sights of the rifle. He observed that it was a gray eye and remembered having read that gray eyes were keenest, and that all famous marksmen had them. Nevertheless, this one had missed.

A counter-swirl had caught Farquhar and turned him half round; he was again looking into the forest on the bank opposite the fort. The sound of a clear, high voice in a monotonous singsong now rang out behind him and came across the water with a distinctness that pierced and subdued all other sounds, even the beating of the ripples in his ears. Although no soldier, he had frequented camps enough to know the dread significance of that deliberate, drawling aspirated chant; the lieutenant on shore was taking a part in the morning's work. How coldly and pitilessly—with what an even, calm intonation, presaging, and enforcing tranquillity in the men—with what accurately measured intervals fell those cruel words:

"Attention, company! . . . Shoulder arms! . . . Ready! . . . Aim! . . . Fire!"

Farquhar dived—dived as deeply as he could. The water roared in his ears like the voice of Niagara, yet he heard the dulled thunder of the volley and, rising again toward the surface, met shining bits of metal, singularly flattened, oscillating slowly downward. Some of them touched him on the face and hands, then fell away, continuing their descent. One lodged between his collar and neck; it was uncomfortably warm and he snatched it out.

As he rose to the surface, gasping for breath, he saw that he had been a long time under water; he was perceptibly farther downstream—nearer to safety. The soldiers had almost finished reloading; the metal ramrods flashed all at once in the sunshine as they were drawn from the barrels, turned in the air, and thrust into their sockets. The two sentinels fired again, independently and ineffectually.

The hunted man saw all this over his shoulder; he was now swimming vigorously with the current. His brain was as energetic as his arms and legs; he thought with the rapidity of lightning.

"The officer," he reasoned, "will not make that martinet's error a second time. It is as easy to dodge a volley as a single shot. He has probably already given the command to fire at will. God help me, I cannot dodge them all!"

An appalling plash within two yards of him was followed by a loud, rushing sound, *diminuendo,* which seemed to travel back through the air to the fort and died in an explosion which stirred the very river to its deeps! A rising sheet of water curved over him, fell down upon him, blinded him, strangled him! The cannon had taken a hand in the game. As he shook his head free from the commotion of the smitten water he heard the deflected shot humming through the air ahead, and in an instant it was cracking and smashing the branches in the forest beyond.

"They will not do that again," he thought. "The next time they will use a charge of grape. I must keep my eye upon the gun. The smoke will apprise me—the report arrives too late; it lags behind the missile. That is a good gun."

Suddenly he felt himself whirled round and round—spinning like a top. The water, the banks, the forests, the now distant bridge, fort and men—all were commingled and blurred. Objects were represented by their colors only; circular horizontal streaks of color—that was all he saw. He had been caught in a vortex and was being whirled on with a velocity of advance and gyration that made him giddy and sick. In a few moments he was flung upon the gravel at the foot of the left bank of the stream—the southern bank—and behind a projecting point which concealed him from his enemies. The sudden arrest of his motion, the abrasion of one of his hands on the gravel, restored him, and he wept with delight. He dug his fingers into the sand, threw it over himself in handfuls and audibly blessed it. It looked like diamonds, rubies, emeralds; he could think of nothing beautiful which it did not resemble. The trees upon the bank were giant garden plants; he noted a definite order in their arrangement, inhaled the fragrance of their blooms. A strange, roseate light shone through the spaces among their trunks and the wind made in their branches the music of aeolian harps. He had no wish to perfect his escape—was content to remain in that enchanting spot until retaken.

A whiz and rattle of grapeshot among the branches high above his head roused him from his dream. The baffled cannoneer had fired him a random farewell. He sprang to his feet, rushed up the sloping bank, and plunged into the forest.

All that day he traveled, laying his course by the rounding sun. The forest seemed interminable; nowhere did he discover a break in it, not even a woodman's road. He had not known that he lived in so wild a region. There was something uncanny in the revelation.

By nightfall he was fatigued, footsore, famishing. The thought of his wife and children urged him on. At last he found a road which led him in what he knew to be the right direction. It was as wide and straight as a city street, yet it seemed untraveled. No fields bordered it, no dwelling anywhere. Not so much as the barking of a dog suggested human habitation. The black bodies of the trees formed a straight wall on both sides, terminating on the horizon in a point, like a diagram in a lesson in perspective. Overhead, as he looked up through this rift in the wood, shone great golden stars looking unfamiliar and grouped in strange constellations. He was sure they were arranged in some order which had a secret and malign significance. The wood on either side was full of singular noises, among which—once, twice, and again—he distinctly heard whispers in an unknown tongue.

His neck was in pain and lifting his hand to it he found it horribly swollen. He knew that it had a circle of black where the rope had bruised it. His eyes felt congested; he could no longer close them. His tongue was swollen with thirst; he relieved its fever by thrusting it forward from between his teeth into the cold air. How softly the turf had carpeted the untraveled avenue—he could no longer feel the roadway beneath his feet!

Doubtless, despite his suffering, he had fallen asleep while walking, for now he sees another scene—perhaps he has merely recovered from a delirium. He stands at the gate of his own home. All is as he left it, and all bright and beautiful in the morning sunshine. He must have traveled the entire night. As he pushes open the gate and passes up the wide white walk, he sees a flutter of female garments; his wife, looking fresh and cool and sweet, steps down from the veranda to meet him. At the bottom of the steps she stands waiting, with a smile of ineffable joy, an attitude of matchless grace and dignity. Ah, how beautiful she is! He springs forward with extended arms. As he is about to clasp her he feels a stunning blow upon the back of the neck; a blinding white light blazes all about him with a sound like the shock of a cannon—then all is darkness and silence!

Peyton Farquhar was dead; his body, with a broken neck, swung gently from side to side beneath the timbers of the Owl Creek bridge.

# Anton Chekhov

## (1860–1904)

For many modern readers, the late-nineteenth-century Russian writer Anton Chekhov is better known for his dramatic work than for his short fiction. Nevertheless, Chekhov, though a part-time physician, made his living primarily as a writer of stories. His style has been described as "comfortable pessimism," an attitude perhaps symptomatic of his own chronic ill health and his existence amidst a social upheaval that began with the 1861 emancipation of the peasant class. Of Chekhov's dramas about shifting class identities and dying traditions, *The Cherry Orchard* is perhaps the most familiar to contemporary audiences; the author himself always insisted that this work, usually interpreted as deeply serious and often as an enactment of the end of aristocratic repression, is a comedy. Addressing his own so-called authorial realism, Chekhov wrote, "You abuse me for objectivity, calling it indifference to good and evil. . . . You would have me, when I describe horse-thieves, say: 'Stealing horses is an evil.' But that has been known for ages without my saying so. . . . it's my job simply to show . . . that horse-stealing is not simply theft but a passion." Chekhov's other most enduring plays include *The Sea Gull, Uncle Vanya*, and *The Three Sisters*. Among Chekhov's numerous short stories are "The Darling," "Perpetuum Mobile," "The Examining Magistrate," "Late-Blooming Flowers," "Hydrophobia," "The Head Gardener's Story," "Happiness," "In Exile," "The Man in a Case," and "The Lady with the Dog."

## The Darling                                                                      1899

TRANSLATED BY CONSTANCE GARNETT

Olenka, the daughter of the retired collegiate assessor, Plemyanniakov, was sitting in her back porch, lost in thought. I was hot, the flies were persistent and teasing, and it was pleasant to reflect that it would soon be evening. Dark rainclouds were gathering from the east, and bringing from time to time a breath of moisture in the air.

Kukin, who was the manager of an open-air theatre called the Tivoli, and who lived in the lodge, was standing in the middle of the garden looking at the sky.

"Again!" he observed despairingly. "It's going to rain again! Rain every day, as though to spite me. I might as well hang myself ! It's ruin! Fearful losses every day."

He flung up his hands, and went on, addressing Olenka:

"There! That's the life we lead, Olga Semyonovna. It's enough to make one cry. One works and does one's utmost; one wears oneself out, getting no sleep at night, and racks one's brain what to do for the best. And then what happens? To begin with, one's public is ignorant, boorish. I give them the very best operetta, a dainty masque, first rate music-hall artists. But do you suppose that's what they want! They don't understand anything of that sort. They want a clown; what they ask for is vulgarity. And then look at the weather! Almost every evening it rains. It started on the tenth of May, and it's kept it up all May and June. It's simply awful! The public doesn't come, but I've to pay the rent just the same, and pay the artists."

The next evening the clouds would gather again, and Kukin would say with an hysterical laugh:

"Well, rain away, then! Flood the garden, drown me! Damn my luck in this world and the next! Let the artists have me up! Send me to prison!—to Siberia!—the scaffold! Ha, ha, ha!"

And next day the same thing.

Olenka listened to Kukin with silent gravity, and sometimes tears came into her eyes. In the end his misfortunes touched her; she grew to love him. He was a small thin man, with a yellow face, and curls combed forward on his forehead. He spoke in a thin tenor; as he talked his mouth worked on one side, and there was always an expression of despair on his face; yet he aroused a deep and genuine affection in her. She was always fond of some one, and could not exist without loving. In earlier days she had loved her papa, who now sat in a darkened room, breathing with difficulty; she had loved her aunt who used to come every other year from Bryansk; and before that, when she was at school, she had loved her French master. She was a gentle, softhearted, compassionate girl, with mild, tender eyes and very good health. At the sight of her full rosy cheeks, her soft white neck with a little dark mole on it, and the kind, naïve smile, which came into her face when she listened to anything pleasant, men thought, "Yes, not half bad," and smiled too, while lady visitors could not refrain from seizing her hand in the middle of a conversation, exclaiming in a gush of delight, "You darling!"

The house in which she had lived from her birth upwards, and which was left her in her father's will, was at the extreme end of the town, not far from the Tivoli. In the evenings and at night she could hear the band playing, and the crackling and banging of fireworks, and it seemed to her that it was Kukin struggling with his destiny, storming the entrenchments of his chief foe, the indifferent public; there was a sweet thrill at her heart, she had no desire to sleep, and when he returned home at daybreak, she tapped softly at her bedroom window, and showing him only her face and one shoulder through the curtain, she gave him a friendly smile. . . .

He proposed to her, and they were married. And when he had a closer view of her neck and her plump, fine shoulders, he threw up his hands, and said:

"You darling!"

He was happy, but as it rained on the day and night of his wedding, his face still retained an expression of despair.

They got on very well together. She used to sit in his office, to look after things in the Tivoli, to put down the accounts and pay the wages. And her rosy cheeks, her sweet, naïve, radiant smile, were to be seen now at the office window, now in the refreshment bar or behind the scenes of the theatre. And already she used to say to her acquaintances that the theatre was the chief and most important thing in life, and that it was only through the drama that one could derive true enjoyment and become cultivated and humane.

"But do you suppose the public understands that?" she used to say. "What they want is a clown. Yesterday we gave 'Fraust Inside Out,' and almost all the boxes were empty; but if Vanitchka and I had been producing some vulgar thing, I assure you the theatre would have been packed. Tomorrow Vanitchka and I are doing 'Orpheus in Hell.'[1] Do come."

And what Kukin said about the theatre and the actors she repeated. Like him she despised the public for their ignorance and their indifference to art; she took part in the rehearsals, she corrected the actors, she kept an eye on the behaviour of the musicians, and when there was an unfavourable notice in the local paper, she shed tears, and then went to the editor's office to set things right.

The actors were fond of her and used to call her "Vanitchka and I," and "the darling"; she was sorry for them and used to lend them small sums of money, and if they deceived her, she used to shed a few tears in private, but did not complain to her husband.

They got on well in the winter too. They took the theatre in the town for the whole winter, and let it for short terms to a Little Russian[2] company, or to a conjurer, or to a local dramatic society. Olenka grew stouter, and was always beaming with satisfaction, while Kukin grew thinner and yellower, and continually complained of their terrible losses, although he had done badly all the winter. He used to cough at night, and she used to give him hot raspberry tea or lime-flower water, to rub him with eau-de-Cologne and to wrap him in her warm shawls.

"You're such a sweet pet!" she used to say with perfect sincerity, stroking his hair. "You're such a pretty dear!"

Towards Lent he went to Moscow to collect a new troupe, and without him she could not sleep, but sat all night at her window, looking at the stars, and she compared herself with the hens, who are awake all night and uneasy when the cock is not in the hen-house. Kukin was detained in Moscow, and wrote that he would be back at Easter, adding some instructions about the Tivoli. But on the Sunday before Easter, late in the evening, came a sudden ominous knock at the gate; some one was hammering on the gate as though on a barrel—boom, boom, boom! The drowsy cook went flopping with her bare feet through the puddles, as she ran to open the gate.

"Please open," said some one outside in a thick bass. "There is a telegram for you."

Olenka had received telegrams from her husband before, but this time for some reason she felt numb with terror. With shaking hands she opened the telegram and read as follows:

> "Ivan Petrovitch died suddenly to-day. Awaiting immate instructions fufuneral Tuesday."

That was how it was written in the telegram—"fufuneral," and the utterly incomprehensible word "immate." It was signed by the stage manager of the operatic company.

---

1 *Orpheus in Hell:* Comic operetta by Jacques Offenbach (1819–1880).
2 **Little Russian:** Someone who lives in the Ukraine or adjacent territories in southwest Russia.

"My darling!" sobbed Olenka. "Vanitchka, my precious, my darling! Why did I ever meet you! Why did I know you and love you! Your poor heart-broken Olenka is all alone without you!"

Kukin's funeral took place on Tuesday in Moscow, Olenka returned home on Wednesday, and as soon as she got indoors she threw herself on her bed and sobbed so loudly that it could be heard next door, and in the street.

"Poor darling!" the neighbours said, as they crossed themselves. "Olga Semyonovna, poor darling! How she does take on!"

Three months later Olenka was coming home from mass, melancholy and in deep mourning. It happened that one of her neighbours, Vassily Andreitch Pustovalov, returning home from church, walked back beside her. He was the manager of Babakayev's, the timber merchant's. He wore a straw hat, a white waistcoat, and a gold watch-chain, and looked more like a country gentleman than a man in trade.

"Everything happens as it is ordained, Olga Semyonovna," he said gravely, with a sympathetic note in his voice; "and if any of our dear ones die, it must be because it is the will of God, so we ought to have fortitude and bear it submissively."

After seeing Olenka to her gate, he said good-bye and went on. All day afterwards she heard his sedately dignified voice, and whenever she shut her eyes she saw his dark beard. She liked him very much. And apparently she had made an impression on him too, for not long afterwards an elderly lady, with whom she was only slightly acquainted, came to drink coffee with her, and as soon as she was seated at table began to talk about Pustovalov, saying that he was an excellent man whom one could thoroughly depend upon, and that any girl would be glad to marry him. Three days later Pustovalov came himself. He did not stay long, only about ten minutes, and he did not say much, but when he left, Olenka loved him—loved him so much that she lay awake all night in a perfect fever, and in the morning she sent for the elderly lady. The match was quickly arranged, and then came the wedding.

Pustovalov and Olenka got on very well together when they were married.

Usually he sat in the office till dinner-time, then he went out on business, while Olenka took his place, and sat in the office till evening, making up accounts and booking orders.

"Timber gets dearer every year; the price rises twenty per cent," she would say to her customers and friends. "Only fancy we used to sell local timber, and now Vassitchka always has to go for wood to the Mogilev district. And the freight!" she would add, covering her cheeks with her hands in horror. "The freight!"

It seemed to her that she had been in the timber trade for ages and ages, and that the most important and necessary thing in life was timber; and there was something intimate and touching to her in the very sound of words such as "baulk," "post," "beam," "pole," "scantling," "batten," "lath," "plank," etc.

At night when she was asleep she dreamed of perfect mountains of planks and boards, and long strings of wagons, carting timber somewhere far away. She dreamed that a whole regiment of six-inch beams forty feet high, standing on end, was marching upon the timber-yard; that logs, beams, and boards knocked together with the resounding crash of dry wood, kept falling and getting up again, piling themselves on each other. Olenka cried out in her sleep, and Pustovalov said to her tenderly: "Olenka, what's the matter, darling? Cross yourself!"

Her husband's ideas were hers. If he thought the room was too hot, or that business was slack, she thought the same. Her husband did not care for entertainments, and on holidays he stayed at home. She did likewise.

"You are always at home or in the office," her friends said to her. "You should go to the theatre, darling, or to the circus."

"Vassitchka and I have no time to go to the theatres," she would answer sedately. "We have no time for nonsense. What's the use of these theatres?"

On Saturdays Pustovalov and she used to go to the evening service; on holidays to early mass, and they walked side by side with softened faces as they came home from church. There was a pleasant fragrance about them both, and her silk dress rustled agreeably. At home they drank tea, with fancy bread and jams of various kinds, and afterwards they ate pie. Every day at twelve o'clock there was a savoury smell of beet-root soup and of mutton or duck in their yard, and on fast-days of fish, and no one could pass the gate without feeling hungry. In the office the samovar was always boiling, and customers were regaled with tea and cracknels. Once a week the couple went to the baths and returned side by side, both red in the face.

"Yes, we have nothing to complain of, thank God," Olenka used to say to her acquaintances. "I wish every one were as well off as Vassitchka and I."

When Pustovalov went away to buy wood in the Mogilev district, she missed him dreadfully, lay awake and cried. A young veterinary surgeon in the army, called Smirnin, to whom they had let their lodge, used sometimes to come in in the evening. He used to talk to her and play cards with her, and this entertained her in her husband's absence. She was particularly interested in what he told her of his home life. He was married and had a little boy, but was separated from his wife because she had been unfaithful to him, and now he hated her and used to send her forty roubles a month for the maintenance of their son. And hearing of all this, Olenka sighed and shook her head. She was sorry for him.

"Well, God keep you," she used to say to him at parting, as she lighted him down the stairs with a candle. "Thank you for coming to cheer me up, and may the Mother of God give you health."

And she always expressed herself with the same sedateness and dignity, the same reasonableness, in imitation of her husband. As the veterinary surgeon was disappearing behind the door below, she would say:

"You know, Vladimir Platonitch, you'd better make it up with your wife. You should forgive her for the sake of your son. You may be sure the little fellow understands."

And when Pustovalov came back, she told him in a low voice about the veterinary surgeon and his unhappy home life, and both sighed and shook their heads and talked about the boy, who, no doubt, missed his father, and by some strange connection of ideas, they went up to the holy ikons, bowed to the ground before them and prayed that God would give them children.

And so the Pustovalovs lived for six years quietly and peaceably in love and complete harmony.

But behold! One winter day after drinking hot tea in the office, Vassily Andreitch went out into the yard without his cap on to see about sending off some timber, caught cold and was taken ill. He had the best doctors, but he grew worse and died after four months' illness. And Olenka was a widow once more.

"I've nobody, now you've left me, my darling," she sobbed, after her husband's funeral. "How can I live without you, in wretchedness and misery! Pity me, good people, all alone in the world!"

She went about dressed in black with long "weepers,"[3] and gave up wearing hat and gloves for good. She hardly ever went out, except to church, or to her husband's grave, and led the life of a nun. It was not till six months later that she took off the weepers and opened the shutters of the windows. She was sometimes seen in the mornings, going with her cook to market for provisions, but what went on in her house and how she lived now could only be surmised. People guessed, from seeing her drinking tea in her garden with the veterinary surgeon, who read the newspaper aloud to her, and from the fact that, meeting a lady she knew at the post-office, she said to her:

"There is no proper veterinary inspection in our town, and that's the cause of all sorts of epidemics. One is always hearing of people's getting infection from the milk supply, or catching diseases from horses and cows. The health of domestic animals ought to be as well cared for as the health of human beings."

She repeated the veterinary surgeon's words, and was of the same opinion as he about everything. It was evident that she could not live a year without some attachment, and had found new happiness in the lodge. In any one else this would have been censured, but no one could think ill of Olenka; everything she did was so natural. Neither she nor the veterinary surgeon said anything to other people of the change in their relations, and tried, indeed, to conceal it, but without success, for Olenka could not keep a secret. When he had visitors, men serving in his regiment, and she poured out tea or served the supper, she would begin talking of the cattle plague, of the foot and mouth disease, and of the municipal slaughter-houses. He was dreadfully embarrassed, and when the guests had gone, he would seize her by the hand and hiss angrily:

"I've asked you before not to talk about what you don't understand. When we veterinary surgeons are talking among ourselves, please don't put your word in. It's really annoying."

And she would look at him with astonishment and dismay, and ask him in alarm: "But, Voloditchka, what *am* I to talk about?"

And with tears in her eyes she would embrace him, begging him not to be angry, and they were both happy.

But this happiness did not last long. The veterinary surgeon departed, departed

---

3 **weepers:** Streamers or ribbons that designate a person in mourning.

for ever with his regiment, when it was transferred to a distant place—to Siberia, it may be. And Olenka was left alone.

Now she was absolutely alone. Her father had long been dead, and his armchair lay in the attic, covered with dust and lame of one leg. She got thinner and plainer, and when people met her in the street they did not look at her as they used to, and did not smile to her; evidently her best years were over and left behind, and now a new sort of life had begun for her, which did not bear thinking about. In the evening Olenka sat in the porch, and heard the band playing and the fireworks popping in the Tivoli, but now the sound stirred no response. She looked into her yard without interest, thought of nothing, wished for nothing, and afterwards, when night came on she went to bed and dreamed of her empty yard. She ate and drank as it were unwillingly.

And what was worst of all, she had no opinions of any sort. She saw the objects about her and understood what she saw, but could not form any opinion about them, and did not know what to talk about. And how awful it is not to have any opinions! One sees a bottle, for instance, or the rain, or a peasant driving in his cart, but what the bottle is for, or the rain, or the peasant, and what is the meaning of it, one can't say, and could not even for a thousand roubles. When she had Kukin, or Pustovalov, or the veterinary surgeon, Olenka could explain everything, and give her opinion about anything you like, but now there was the same emptiness in her brain and in her heart as there was in her yard outside. And it was as harsh and as bitter as wormwood in the mouth.

Little by little the town grew in all directions. The road became a street, and where the Tivoli and the timber-yard had been, there were new turnings and houses. How rapidly time passes! Olenka's house grew dingy, the roof got rusty, the shed sank on one side, and the whole yard was overgrown with docks and stinging-nettles. Olenka herself had grown plain and elderly; in summer she sat in the porch, and her soul, as before, was empty and dreary and full of bitterness. In winter she sat at her window and looked at the snow. When she caught the scent of spring, or heard the chime of the church bells, a sudden rush of memories from the past came over her, there was a tender ache in her heart, and her eyes brimmed over with tears; but this was only for a minute, and then came emptiness again and the sense of the futility of life. The black kitten, Briska, rubbed against her and purred softly, but Olenka was not touched by these feline caresses. That was not what she needed. She wanted a love that would absorb her whole being, her whole soul and reason—that would give her ideas and an object in life, and would warm her old blood. And she would shake the kitten off her skirt and say with vexation:

"Get along; I don't want you!"

And so it was, day after day and year after year, and no joy, and no opinions. Whatever Mavra, the cook, said she accepted.

One hot July day, towards evening, just as the cattle were being driven away, and the whole yard was full of dust, some one suddenly knocked at the gate. Olenka went to open it herself and was dumbfounded when she looked out: she saw Smirnin, the veterinary surgeon, grey-headed, and dressed as a civilian. She suddenly remembered everything. She could not help crying and letting her head fall on his breast without uttering a word, and in the violence of her feeling she did not notice how they both walked into the house and sat down to tea.

"My dear Vladimir Platonitch! What fate has brought you?" she muttered, trembling with joy.

"I want to settle here for good, Olga Semyonovna," he told her. "I have resigned my post, and have come to settle down and try my luck on my own account. Besides, it's time for my boy to go to school. He's a big boy. I am reconciled with my wife, you know."

"Where is she?" asked Olenka.

"She's at the hotel with the boy, and I'm looking for lodgings."

"Good gracious, my dear soul! Lodgings? Why not have my house? Why shouldn't that suit you? Why, my goodness, I wouldn't take any rent!" cried Olenka in a flutter, beginning to cry again. "You live here, and the lodge will do nicely for me. Oh dear! how glad I am!"

Next day the roof was painted and the walls were whitewashed, and Olenka, with her arms akimbo, walked about the yard giving directions. Her face was beaming with her old smile, and she was brisk and alert as though she had waked from a long sleep. The veterinary's wife arrived—a thin, plain lady, with short hair and a peevish expression. With her was her little Sasha, a boy of ten, small for his age, blue-eyed, chubby, with dimples in his cheeks. And scarcely had the boy walked into the yard when he ran after the cat, and at once there was the sound of his gay, joyous laugh.

"Is that your puss, auntie?" he asked Olenka. "When she has little ones, do give us a kitten. Mamma is awfully afraid of mice."

Olenka talked to him, and gave him tea. Her heart warmed and there was a sweet ache in her bosom, as though the boy had been her own child. And when he sat at the table in the evening, going over his lessons, she looked at him with deep tenderness and pity as she murmured to herself:

"You pretty pet! . . . my precious! . . . Such a fair little thing, and so clever."

"'An island is a piece of land which is entirely surrounded by water,'" he read aloud.

"An island is a piece of land," she repeated, and this was the first opinion to which she gave utterance with positive conviction after so many years of silence and dearth of ideas.

Now she had opinions of her own, and at supper she talked to Sasha's parents, saying how difficult the lessons were at the high schools, but that yet the high-school was better than a commercial one, since with a high-school education all careers were open to one, such as being a doctor or an engineer.

Sasha began going to the high school. His mother departed to Harkov to her sister's and did not return; his father used to go off every day to inspect cattle, and would often be away from home for three days together, and it seemed to Olenka as though Sasha was entirely abandoned, that he was not wanted at home, that he was being starved, and she carried him off to her lodge and gave him a little room there.

And for six months Sasha had lived in the lodge with her. Every morning Olenka came into his bedroom and found him fast asleep, sleeping noiselessly with his hand under his cheek. She was sorry to wake him.

"Sashenka," she would say mournfully, "get up, darling. It's time for school."

He would get up, dress and say his prayers, and then sit down to breakfast, drink three glasses of tea, and eat two large cracknels and half a buttered roll. All this time he was hardly awake and a little ill-humoured in consequence.

"You don't quite know your fable, Sashenka," Olenka would say, looking at him as though he were about to set off on a long journey. "What a lot of trouble I have with you! You must work and do your best, darling, and obey your teachers."

"Oh, do leave me alone!" Sasha would say.

Then he would go down the street to school, a little figure, wearing a big cap and carrying a satchel on his shoulder. Olenka would follow him noiselessly.

"Sashenka!" she would call after him, and she would pop into his hand a date or a caramel. When he reached the street where the school was, he would feel ashamed of being followed by a tall, stout woman; he would turn round and say:

"You'd better go home, auntie. I can go the rest of the way alone."

She would stand still and look after him fixedly till he had disappeared at the school-gate.

Ah, how she loved him! Of her former attachments not one had been so deep; never had her soul surrendered to any feeling so spontaneously, so disinterestedly, and so joyously as now that her maternal instincts were aroused. For this little boy with the dimple in his cheek and the big school cap, she would have given her whole life, she would have given it with joy and tears of tenderness. Why? Who can tell why?

When she had seen the last of Sasha, she returned home, contented and serene, brimming over with love; her face, which had grown younger during the last six months, smiled and beamed; people meeting her looked at her with pleasure.

"Good-morning, Olga Semyonovna, darling. How are you, darling?"

"The lessons at the high school are very difficult now," she would relate at the market. "It's too much; in the first class yesterday they gave him a fable to learn by heart, and a Latin translation and a problem. You know it's too much for a little chap."

And she would begin talking about the teachers, the lessons, and the school books, saying just what Sasha said.

At three o'clock they had dinner together: in the evening they learned their lessons together and cried. When she put him to bed, she would stay a long time making the Cross over him and murmuring a prayer; then she would go to bed and dream of that far-away misty future when Sasha would finish his studies and become a doctor or an engineer, would have a big house of his own with horses and a carriage, would get married and have children. . . . She would fall asleep still thinking of the same thing, and tears would run down her cheeks from her closed eyes, while the black cat lay purring beside her: "Mrr, mrr, mrr."

Suddenly there would come a loud knock at the gate.

Olenka would wake up breathless with alarm, her heart throbbing. Half a minute later would come another knock.

"It must be a telegram from Harkov," she would think, beginning to tremble from head to foot. "Sasha's mother is sending for him from Harkov. . . . Oh, mercy on us!"

She was in despair. Her head, her hands, and her feet would turn chill, and she would feel that she was the most unhappy woman in the world. But another minute would pass, voices would be heard: it would turn out to be the veterinary surgeon coming home from the club.

"Well, thank God!" she would think.

And gradually the load in her heart would pass off, and she would feel at ease. She would go back to bed thinking of Sasha, who lay sound asleep in the next room, sometimes crying out in his sleep:

"I'll give it you! Get away! Shut up!"

## The Lady with the Dog                                                    1899

TRANSLATED BY CONSTANCE GARNETT

**I**

It was said that a new person had appeared on the sea-front: a lady with a little dog. Dmitri Dmitritch Gurov, who had by then been a fortnight at Yalta,[1] and so was fairly at home there, had begun to take an interest in new arrivals. Sitting in Verney's pavilion, he saw, walking on the sea-front, a fair-haired young lady of medium height, wearing a *béret;* a white Pomeranian dog was running behind her.

And afterwards he met her in the public gardens and in the square several times a day. She was walking alone, always wearing the same *béret,* and always with the same white dog; no one knew who she was, and every one called her simply "the lady with the dog."

"If she is here alone without a husband or friends, it wouldn't be amiss to make her acquaintance," Gurov reflected.

He was under forty, but he had a daughter already twelve years old, and two sons at school. He had been married young, when he was a student in his second year, and by now his wife seemed half as old again as he. She was a tall, erect woman with dark eyebrows, staid and dignified, and, as she said of herself, intellectual. She read a great deal, used phonetic spelling, called her husband, not Dmitri, but Dimitri, and he secretly considered her unintelligent, narrow, inelegant, was afraid of her, and did not like to be at home. He had begun being unfaithful to her long ago—had been unfaithful to her often, and, probably on that account, almost always spoke ill of women, and when they were talked about in his presence, used to call them "the lower race."

It seemed to him that he had been so schooled by bitter experience that he might call them what he liked, and yet he could not get on for two days together without

---

1 **Yalta:** Russian city on the Black Sea, a popular resort town.

"the lower race." In the society of men he was bored and not himself, with them he was cold and uncommunicative; but when he was in the company of women he felt free, and knew what to say to them and how to behave; and he was at ease with them even when he was silent. In his appearance, in his character, in his whole nature, there was something attractive and elusive which allured women and disposed them in his favour; he knew that, and some force seemed to draw him, too, to them.

Experience often repeated, truly bitter experience, had taught him long ago that with decent people, especially Moscow people—always slow to move and irresolute— every intimacy, which at first so agreeably diversifies life and appears a light and charming adventure, inevitably grows into a regular problem of extreme intricacy, and in the long run the situation becomes unbearable. But at every fresh meeting with an interesting woman this experience seemed to slip out of his memory, and he was eager for life, and everything seemed simple and amusing.

One evening he was dining in the gardens, and the lady in the *béret* came up slowly to take the next table. Her expression, her gait, her dress, and the way she did her hair told him that she was a lady, that she was married, that she was in Yalta for the first time alone, and that she was dull there. . . . The stories told of the immorality in such places as Yalta are to a great extent untrue; he despised them, and knew that such stories were for the most part made up by persons who would themselves have been glad to sin if they had been able; but when the lady sat down at the next table three paces from him, he remembered these tales of easy conquests, of trips to the mountains, and the tempting thought of a swift, fleeting love affair, a romance with an unknown woman, whose name he did not know, suddenly took possession of him.

He beckoned coaxingly to the Pomeranian, and when the dog came up to him he shook his finger at it. The Pomeranian growled: Gurov shook his finger at it again.

The lady looked at him and at once dropped her eyes.

"He doesn't bite," she said, and blushed.

"May I give him a bone?" he asked; and when she nodded he asked courteously, "Have you been long in Yalta?"

"Five days."

"And I have already dragged out a fortnight here."

There was a brief silence.

"Time goes fast, and yet it is so dull here!" she said, not looking at him.

"That's only the fashion to say it is dull here. A provincial will live in Belyov or Zhidra and not be dull, and when he comes here it's 'Oh, the dullness! Oh, the dust!' One would think he came from Grenada."[2]

She laughed. Then both continued eating in silence, like strangers, but after dinner they walked side by side; and there sprang up between them the light jesting conversation of people who are free and satisfied, to whom it does not matter where they go or what they talk about. They walked and talked of the strange light on the sea: the water was of a soft warm lilac hue, and there was a golden streak from the moon upon it. They talked of how sultry it was after a hot day. Gurov told her that he came from

---

2 **Granada:** A city in southern Spain.

Moscow, that he had taken his degree in Arts, but had a post in a bank; that he had trained as an opera-singer, but had given it up, that he owned two houses in Moscow. . . . And from her he learnt that she had grown up in Petersburg, but had lived in S—— since her marriage two years before, that she was staying another month in Yalta, and that her husband, who needed a holiday too, might perhaps come and fetch her. She was not sure whether her husband had a post in a Crown Department or under the Provincial Council—and was amused by her own ignorance. And Gurov learnt, too, that she was called Anna Sergeyevna.

Afterwards he thought about her in his room at the hotel—thought she would certainly meet him next day; it would be sure to happen. As he got into bed he thought how lately she had been a girl at school, doing lessons like his own daughter; he recalled the diffidence, the angularity, that was still manifest in her laugh and her manner of talking with a stranger. This must have been the first time in her life she had been alone in surroundings in which she was followed, looked at, and spoken to merely from a secret motive which she could hardly fail to guess. He recalled her slender, delicate neck, her lovely grey eyes.

"There's something pathetic about her, anyway," he thought, and fell asleep.

## II

A week had passed since they had made acquaintance. It was a holiday. It was sultry indoors, while in the street the wind whirled the dust round and round, and blew people's hats off. It was a thirsty day, and Gurov often went into the pavilion, and pressed Anna Sergeyevna to have syrup and water or an ice. One did not know what to do with oneself.

In the evening when the wind had dropped a little, they went out on the groyne to see the steamer come in. There were a great many people walking about the harbour; they had gathered to welcome some one, bringing bouquets. And two peculiarities of a well-dressed Yalta crowd were very conspicuous: the elderly ladies were dressed like young ones, and there were great numbers of generals.

Owing to the roughness of the sea, the steamer arrived late, after the sun had set, and it was a long time turning about before it reached the groyne. Anna Sergeyevna looked through her lorgnette at the steamer and the passengers as though looking for acquaintances, and when she turned to Gurov her eyes were shining. She talked a great deal and asked disconnected questions, forgetting next moment what she had asked; then she dropped her lorgnette in the crush.

The festive crowd began to disperse; it was too dark to see people's faces. The wind had completely dropped, but Gurov and Anna Sergeyevna still stood as though waiting to see some one else come from the steamer. Anna Sergeyevna was silent now, and sniffed the flowers without looking at Gurov.

"The weather is better this evening," he said. "Where shall we go now? Shall we drive somewhere?"

She made no answer.

Then he looked at her intently, and all at once put his arm round her and kissed her on the lips, and breathed in the moisture and the fragrance of the flowers; and he immediately looked round him, anxiously wondering whether any one had seen them.

"Let us go to your hotel," he said softly. And both walked quickly.

The room was close and smelt of the scent she had bought at the Japanese shop. Gurov looked at her and thought: "What different people one meets in the world!" From the past he preserved memories of careless, good-natured women, who loved cheerfully and were grateful to him for the happiness he gave them, however brief it might be; and of women like his wife who loved without any genuine feeling, with superfluous phrases, affectedly, hysterically, with an expression that suggested that it was not love nor passion, but something more significant; and of two or three others, very beautiful, cold women, on whose faces he had caught a glimpse of a rapacious expression—an obstinate desire to snatch from life more than it could give, and these were capricious, unreflecting, domineering, unintelligent women not in their first youth, and when Gurov grew cold to them their beauty excited his hatred, and the lace on their linen seemed to him like scales.

But in this case there was still the diffidence, the angularity of inexperienced youth, an awkward feeling; and there was a sense of consternation as though some one had suddenly knocked at the door. The attitude of Anna Sergeyevna—"the lady with the dog"—to what had happened was somehow peculiar, very grave, as though it were her fall—so it seemed, and it was strange and inappropriate. Her face dropped and faded, and on both sides of it her long hair hung down mournfully; she mused in a dejected attitude like "the woman who was a sinner" in an old-fashioned picture.

"It's wrong," she said. "You will be the first to despise me now."

There was a water-melon on the table. Gurov cut himself a slice and began eating it without haste. There followed at least half an hour of silence.

Anna Sergeyevna was touching; there was about her the purity of a good, simple woman who had seen little of life. The solitary candle burning on the table threw a faint light on her face, yet it was clear that she was very unhappy.

"How could I despise you?" asked Gurov. "You don't know what you are saying."

"God forgive me," she said, and her eyes filled with tears. "It's awful."

"You seem to feel you need to be forgiven."

"Forgiven? No. I am a bad, low woman; I despise myself and don't attempt to justify myself. It's not my husband but myself I have deceived. And not only just now; I have been deceiving myself for a long time. My husband may be a good, honest man, but he is a flunkey! I don't know what he does there, what his work is, but I know he is a flunkey! I was twenty when I was married to him. I have been tormented by curiosity; I wanted something better. 'There must be a different sort of life,' I said to myself. I wanted to live! To live, to live! . . . I was fired by curiosity . . . you don't understand it, but, I swear to God, I could not control myself; something happened to me: I could not be restrained. I told my husband I was ill, and came here. . . . And here I have been walking about as though I were dazed, like a mad creature; . . . and now I have become a vulgar, contemptible woman whom any one may despise."

Gurov felt bored already, listening to her. He was irritated by the naïve tone, by this remorse, so unexpected and inopportune; but for the tears in her eyes, he might have thought she was jesting or playing a part.

"I don't understand," he said softly. "What is it you want?"

She hid her face on his breast and pressed close to him.

"Believe me, believe me, I beseech you . . ." she said. "I love a pure, honest life, and sin is loathsome to me. I don't know what I am doing. Simple people say: 'The Evil One has beguiled me.' And I may say of myself now that the Evil One has beguiled me."

"Hush, hush! . . ." he muttered.

He looked at her fixed, scared eyes, kissed her, talked softly and affectionately, and by degrees she was comforted, and her gaiety returned; they both began laughing.

Afterwards when they went out there was not a soul on the sea-front. The town with its cypresses had quite a deathlike air, but the sea still broke noisily on the shore; a single barge was rocking on the waves, and a lantern was blinking sleepily on it.

They found a cab and drove to Oreanda.

"I found out your surname in the hall just now: it was written on the board—Von Diderits," said Gurov. "Is your husband a German?"

"No; I believe his grandfather was a German, but he is an Orthodox Russian himself."

At Oreanda they sat on a seat not far from the church, looked down at the sea, and were silent. Yalta was hardly visible through the morning mist; white clouds stood motionless on the mountain-tops. The leaves did not stir on the trees, grasshoppers chirruped, and the monotonous hollow sound of the sea rising up from below, spoke of the peace, of the eternal sleep awaiting us. So it must have sounded when there was no Yalta, no Oreanda here; so it sounds now, and it will sound as indifferently and monotonously when we are all no more. And in this constancy, in this complete indifference to the life and death of each of us, there lies hid, perhaps, a pledge of our eternal salvation, of the unceasing movement of life upon earth, of unceasing progress toward perfection. Sitting beside a young woman who in the dawn seemed so lovely, soothed and spellbound in these magical surroundings—the sea, mountains, clouds, the open sky—Gurov thought how in reality everything is beautiful in this world when one reflects: everything except what we think or do ourselves when we forget our human dignity and the higher aims of our existence.

A man walked up to them—probably a keeper—looked at them and walked away. And this detail seemed mysterious and beautiful, too. They saw a steamer come from Theodosia, with its lights out in the glow of dawn.

"There is dew on the grass," said Anna Sergeyevna, after a silence.

"Yes. It's time to go home."

They went back to the town.

Then they met every day at twelve o'clock on the sea-front, lunched and dined together, went for walks, admired the sea. She complained that she slept badly, that her heart throbbed violently; asked the same questions, troubled now by jealousy and now by the fear that he did not respect her sufficiently. And often in the square or gardens, when there was no one near them, he suddenly drew her to him and kissed her passionately. Complete idleness, these kisses in broad daylight while he looked round in dread of some one's seeing them, the heat, the smell of the sea, and the continual passing to and fro before him of idle, well-dressed, well-fed people, made a new man of him; he told Anna Sergeyevna how beautiful she was, how fascinating. He was impatiently passionate, he would not move a step away from her, while she was often pensive and continually urged him to confess that he did not respect her, did not love her in the least, and thought of her as nothing but a common woman. Rather late almost every evening they drove somewhere out of town, to Oreanda or to the waterfall; and the expedition was always a success, the scenery invariably impressed them as grand and beautiful.

They were expecting her husband to come, but a letter came from him, saying that there was something wrong with his eyes, and he entreated his wife to come home as quickly as possible. Anna Sergeyevna made haste to go.

"It's a good thing I am going away," she said to Gurov. "It's the finger of destiny!"

She went by coach and he went with her. They were driving the whole day. When she had got into a compartment of the express, and when the second bell had rung, she said:

"Let me look at you once more . . . look at you once again. That's right."

She did not shed tears, but was so sad that she seemed ill, and her face was quivering.

"I shall remember you . . . think of you," she said. "God be with you; be happy. Don't remember evil against me. We are parting forever—it must be so, for we ought never to have met. Well, God be with you."

The train moved off rapidly, its lights soon vanished from sight, and a minute later there was no sound of it, as though everything had conspired together to end as quickly as possible that sweet delirium, that madness. Left alone on the platform, and gazing into the dark distance, Gurov listened to the chirrup of the grasshoppers and the hum of the telegraph wires, feeling as though he had only just waked up. And he thought, musing, that there had been another episode or adventure in his life, and it, too, was at an end, and nothing was left of it but a memory. . . . He was moved, sad, and conscious of a slight remorse. This young woman whom he would never meet again had not been happy with him; he was genuinely warm and affectionate with her, but yet in his manner, his tone, and his caresses there had been a shade of light irony, the coarse condescension of a happy man who was, besides, almost twice her age. All the time she had called him kind, exceptional, lofty; obviously he had seemed to her different from what he really was, so he had unintentionally deceived her. . . .

Here at the station was already a scent of autumn; it was a cold evening.

"It's time for me to go north," thought Gurov as he left the platform. "High time!"

### III

At home in Moscow everything was in its winter routine; the stoves were heated, and in the morning it was still dark when the children were having breakfast and getting ready for school, and the nurse would light the lamp for a short time. The frosts had begun already. When the first snow has fallen, on the first day of sledge-driving it is pleasant to see the white earth, the white roofs, to draw soft, delicious breath, and the season brings back the days of one's youth. The old limes and birches, white with hoar-frost, have a good-natured expression; they are nearer to one's heart than cypresses and palms, and near them one doesn't want to be thinking of the sea and the mountains.

Gurov was Moscow born; he arrived in Moscow on a fine frosty day, and when he put on his fur coat and warm gloves, and walked along Petrovka, and when on Saturday evening he heard the ringing of the bells, his recent trip and the places he had seen lost all charm for him. Little by little he became absorbed in Moscow life, greedily read three newspapers a day, and declared he did not read the Moscow papers on principle! He already felt a longing to go to restaurants, clubs, dinner-parties, anniversary celebrations, and he felt flattered at entertaining distinguished lawyers and artists, and at playing cards with a professor at the doctors' club. He could already eat a whole plateful of salt fish and cabbage. . . .

In another month, he fancied, the image of Anna Sergeyevna would be shrouded in a mist in his memory, and only from time to time would visit him in his dreams with a touching smile as others did. But more than a month passed, real winter had come, and everything was still clear in his memory as though he had parted with Anna Sergeyevna only the day before. And his memories glowed more and more vividly. When in the evening stillness he heard from his study the voices of his children, preparing their lessons, or when he listened to a song or the organ at the restaurant, or the storm howled in the chimney, suddenly everything would rise up in his memory: what had happened on the groyne, and the early morning with the mist on the mountains, and the steamer coming from Theodosia, and the kisses. He would pace a long time about his room, remembering it all and smiling; then his memories passed into dreams, and in his fancy the past was mingled with what was to come. Anna Sergeyevna did not visit him in dreams, but followed him about everywhere like a shadow and haunted him. When he shut his eyes he saw her as though she were living before him, and she seemed to him lovelier, younger, tenderer than she was; and he imagined himself finer than he had been in Yalta. In the evenings she peeped out at him from the bookcase, from the fireplace, from the corner—he heard her breathing, the caressing rustle of her dress. In the street he watched the women, looking for some one like her.

He was tormented by an intense desire to confide his memories to some one. But in his home it was impossible to talk of his love, and he had no one outside; he could not talk to his tenants nor to any one at the bank. And what had he to talk of? Had he been in love, then? Had there been anything beautiful, poetical, or edifying or simply interesting in his relations with Anna Sergeyevna? And there was nothing for him but to talk vaguely of love, of woman, and no one guessed what it meant; only his wife twitched her black eyebrows, and said: "The part of a lady-killer does not suit you at all, Dimitri."

One evening, coming out of the doctors' club with an official with whom he had been playing cards, he could not resist saying:

"If only you knew what a fascinating woman I made the acquaintance of in Yalta!"

The official got into his sledge and was driving away, but turned suddenly and shouted:

"Dmitri Dmitritch!"

"What?"

"You were right this evening: the sturgeon was a bit too strong!"[3]

Those words, so ordinary, for some reason moved Gurov to indignation, and struck him as degrading and unclean. What savage manners, what people! What senseless nights, what uninteresting, uneventful days! The rage for card-playing, the gluttony, the drunkenness, the continual talk always about the same thing. Useless pursuits and conversations always about the same things absorb the better part of one's time, the better part of one's strength, and in the end there is left a life grovelling and curtailed, worthless and trivial, and there is no escaping or getting away from it— just as though one were in a madhouse or a prison.

Gurov did not sleep all night, and was filled with indignation. And he had a headache all next day. And the next night he slept badly; he sat up in bed, thinking, or paced up and down his room. He was sick of his children, sick of the bank; he had no desire to go anywhere or to talk of anything.

In the holidays in December he prepared for a journey, and told his wife he was going to Petersburg to do something in the interests of a young friend—and he set off for S——. What for? He did not very well know himself. He wanted to see Anna Sergeyevna and to talk with her—to arrange a meeting, if possible.

He reached S—— in the morning, and took the best room at the hotel, in which the floor was covered with grey army cloth, and on the table was an inkstand, grey with dust and adorned with a figure on horseback, with its hat in its hand and its head broken off. The hotel porter gave him the necessary information; Von Diderits lived in a house of his own in Old Gontcharny Street—it was not far from the hotel: he was rich and lived in good style, and had his own horses; every one in the town knew him. The porter pronounced the name "Dridirits."

Gurov went without haste to Old Gontcharny Street and found the house. Just opposite the house stretched a long grey fence adorned with nails.

"One would run away from a fence like that," thought Gurov, looking from the fence to the windows of the house and back again.

He considered: to-day was a holiday, and the husband would probably be at home. And in any case it would be tactless to go into the house and upset her. If he were to send her a note it might fall into her husband's hands, and then it might ruin everything. The best thing was to trust to chance. And he kept walking up and down the street by the fence, waiting for the chance. He saw a beggar go in at the gate and dogs fly at him; then an hour later he heard a piano, and the sounds were faint and indistinct. Probably it was Anna Sergeyevna playing. The front door suddenly opened, and an old woman came out, followed by the familiar white Pomeranian. Gurov was

---

3 **was a bit too strong:** Tasted spoiled.

on the point of calling to the dog, but his heart began beating violently, and in his excitement he could not remember the dog's name.

He walked up and down, and loathed the grey fence more and more, and by now he thought irritably that Anna Sergeyevna had forgotten him, and was perhaps already amusing herself with some one else, and that that was very natural in a young woman who had nothing to look at from morning till night but that confounded fence. He went back to his hotel room and sat for a long while on the sofa, not knowing what to do, then he had dinner and a long nap.

"How stupid and worrying it is!" he thought when he woke and looked at the dark windows: it was already evening. "Here I've had a good sleep for some reason. What shall I do in the night?"

He sat on the bed, which was covered by a cheap grey blanket, such as one sees in hospitals, and he taunted himself in his vexation:

"So much for the lady with the dog . . . so much for the adventure. . . . You're in a nice fix. . . ."

That morning at the station a poster in large letters had caught his eye. "The Geisha" was to be performed for the first time. He thought of this and went to the theatre.

"It's quite possible she may go to the first performance," he thought.

The theatre was full. As in all provincial theatres, there was a fog above the chandelier, the gallery was noisy and restless; in the front row the local dandies were standing up before the beginning of the performance, with their hands behind them; in the Governor's box the Governor's daughter, wearing a boa, was sitting in the front seat, while the Governor himself lurked modestly behind the curtain with only his hands visible; the orchestra was a long time tuning up; the stage curtain swayed. All the time the audience were coming in and taking their seats Gurov looked at them eagerly.

Anna Sergeyevna, too, came in. She sat down in the third row, and when Gurov looked at her his heart contracted, and he understood clearly that for him there was in the whole world no creature so near, so precious, and so important to him; she, this little woman, in no way remarkable, lost in a provincial crowd, with a vulgar lorgnette in her hand, filled his whole life now, was his sorrow and his joy, the one happiness that he now desired for himself, and to the sounds of the inferior orchestra, of the wretched provincial violins, he thought how lovely she was. He thought and dreamed.

A young man with small side-whiskers, tall and stooping, came in with Anna Sergeyevna and sat down beside her; he bent his head at every step and seemed to be continually bowing. Most likely this was the husband whom at Yalta, in a rush of bitter feeling, she had called a flunkey. And there really was in his long figure, his side-whiskers, and the small bald patch on his head, something of the flunkey's obsequiousness; his smile was sugary, and in his buttonhole there was some badge of distinction like the number on a waiter.

During the first interval the husband went away to smoke; she remained alone in her stall. Gurov, who was sitting in the stalls, too, went up to her and said in a trembling voice, with a forced smile:

"Good-evening."

She glanced at him and turned pale, then glanced again with horror, unable to believe her eyes, and tightly gripped the fan and the lorgnette in her hands, evidently struggling with herself not to faint. Both were silent. She was sitting, he was standing, frightened by her confusion and not venturing to sit down beside her. The violins and the flute began tuning up. He felt suddenly frightened; it seemed as though all the people in the boxes were looking at them. She got up and went quickly to the door; he followed her, and both walked senselessly along passages, and up and down stairs, and figures in legal, scholastic, and civil service uniforms, all wearing badges, flitted before their eyes. They caught glimpses of ladies, of fur coats hanging on pegs; the draughts blew on them, bringing a smell of stale tobacco. And Gurov, whose heart was beating violently, thought:

"Oh, heavens! Why are these people here and this orchestra! . . ."

And at that instant he recalled how when he had seen Anna Sergeyevna off at the station he had thought that everything was over and they would never meet again. But how far they were still from the end!

On the narrow, gloomy staircase over which was written "To the Amphitheatre," she stopped.

"How you have frightened me!" she said, breathing hard, still pale and over-whelmed. "Oh, how you have frightened me! I am half dead. Why have you come? Why?"

"But do understand, Anna, do understand . . ." he said hastily in a low voice. "I entreat you to understand. . . ."

She looked at him with dread, with entreaty, with love; she looked at him intently, to keep his features more distinctly in her memory.

"I am so unhappy," she went on, not heeding him. "I have thought of nothing but you all the time; I live only in the thought of you. And I wanted to forget, to forget you; but why, oh, why, have you come?"

On the landing above them two schoolboys were smoking and looking down, but that was nothing to Gurov; he drew Anna Sergeyevna to him, and began kissing her face, her cheeks, and her hands.

"What are you doing, what are you doing!" she cried in horror, pushing him away. "We are mad. Go away to-day; go away at once. . . . I beseech you by all that is sacred, I implore you. . . . There are people coming this way!"

Some one was coming up the stairs.

"You must go away," Anna Sergeyevna went on in a whisper. "Do you hear, Dmitri Dmitritch? I will come and see you in Moscow. I have never been happy; I am miserable now, and I never, never shall be happy, never! Don't make me suffer still more! I swear I'll come to Moscow. But now let us part. My precious, good, dear one, we must part!"

She pressed his hand and began rapidly going downstairs, looking round at him, and from her eyes he could see that she really was unhappy. Gurov stood for a little while, listened, then, when all sound had died away, he found his coat and left the theatre.

## IV

And Anna Sergeyevna began coming to see him in Moscow. Once in two or three months she left S——, telling her husband that she was going to consult a doctor about an internal complaint—and her husband believed her, and did not believe her. In Moscow she stayed at the Slaviansky Bazaar hotel, and at once sent a man in a red cap to Gurov. Gurov went to see her, and no one in Moscow knew of it.

Once he was going to see her in this way on a winter morning (the messenger had come the evening before when he was out). With him walked his daughter, whom he wanted to take to school; it was on the way. Snow was falling in big wet flakes.

"It's three degrees above freezing-point, and yet it is snowing," said Gurov to his daughter. "The thaw is only on the surface of the earth; there is quite a different temperature at a greater height in the atmosphere."

"And why are there no thunderstorms in the winter, father?"

He explained that, too. He talked, thinking all the while that he was going to see *her,* and no living soul knew of it, and probably never would know. He had two lives: one, open, seen and known by all who cared to know, full of relative truth and of relative falsehood, exactly like the lives of his friends and acquaintances; and another life running its course in secret. And through some strange, perhaps accidental, conjunction of circumstances, everything that was essential, of interest and of value to him, everything in which he was sincere and did not deceive himself, everything that made the kernel of his life, was hidden from other people; and all that was false in him, the sheath in which he hid himself to conceal the truth—such, for instance, as his work in the bank, his discussions at the club, his "lower race," his presence with his wife at anniversary festivities—all that was open. And he judged of others by himself, not believing in what he saw, and always believing that every man had his real, most interesting life under the cover of secrecy and under the cover of night. All personal life rested on secrecy, and possibly it was partly on that account that civilised man was so nervously anxious that personal privacy should be respected.

After leaving his daughter at school, Gurov went on to the Slaviansky Bazaar. He took off his fur coat below, went upstairs, and softly knocked at the door. Anna Sergeyevna, wearing his favourite grey dress, exhausted by the journey and the suspense, had been expecting him since the evening before. She was pale; she looked at him, and did not smile, and he had hardly come in when she fell on his breast. Their kiss was slow and prolonged, as though they had not met for two years.

"Well, how are you getting on there?" he asked. "What news?"

"Wait; I'll tell you directly. . . . I can't talk."

She could not speak; she was crying. She turned away from him, and pressed her handkerchief to her eyes.

"Let her have her cry out. I'll sit down and wait," he thought, and he sat down in an arm-chair.

Then he rang and asked for tea to be brought him, and while he drank his tea she remained standing at the window with her back to him. She was crying from emotion, from the miserable consciousness that their life was so hard for them; they could only meet in secret, hiding themselves from people, like thieves! Was not their life shattered?

"Come, do stop!" he said.

It was evident to him that this love of theirs would not soon be over, that he could not see the end of it. Anna Sergeyevna grew more and more attached to him. She adored him, and it was unthinkable to say to her that it was bound to have an end some day; besides, she would not have believed it!

He went up to her and took her by the shoulders to say something affectionate and cheering, and at that moment he saw himself in the looking-glass.

His hair was already beginning to turn grey. And it seemed strange to him that he had grown so much older, so much plainer during the last few years. The shoulders on which his hands rested were warm and quivering. He felt compassion for this life, still so warm and lovely, but probably already not far from beginning to fade and wither like his own. Why did she love him so much? He always seemed to women different from what he was, and they loved in him not himself, but the man created by their imagination, whom they had been eagerly seeking all their lives; and afterwards, when they noticed their mistake, they loved him all the same. And not one of them had been happy with him. Time passed, he had made their acquaintance, got on with them, parted, but he had never once loved; it was anything you like, but not love.

And only now when his head was grey he had fallen properly, really in love—for the first time in his life.

Anna Sergeyevna and he loved each other like people very close and akin, like husband and wife, like tender friends; it seemed to them that fate itself had meant them for one another, and they could not understand why he had a wife and she a husband; and it was as though they were a pair of birds of passage, caught and forced to live in different cages. They forgave each other for what they were ashamed of in their past, they forgave everything in the present, and felt that this love of theirs had changed them both.

In moments of depression in the past he had comforted himself with any arguments that came into his mind, but now he no longer cared for arguments; he felt profound compassion, he wanted to be sincere and tender. . . .

"Don't cry, my darling," he said. "You've had your cry; that's enough. . . . Let us talk now, let us think of some plan."

Then they spent a long while taking counsel together, talked of how to avoid the necessity for secrecy, for deception, for living in different towns and not seeing each other for long at a time. How could they be free from this intolerable bondage?

"How? How?" he asked, clutching his head. "How?"

And it seemed as though in a little while the solution would be found, and then a new and splendid life would begin; and it was clear to both of them that they had still a long, long road before them, and that the most complicated and difficult part of it was only just beginning.

# Stephen Crane

## (1871–1900)

His mother had been a writer for the *New York Tribune* and the *Philadelphia Press,* and so Stephen Crane had only to follow in the footsteps of this woman, who through journalism alone had supported a family of fourteen. Crane began reporting while still in his teens, and his novel *Maggie, A Girl of the Streets* was inspired by his observations while on the beat in New York City's Bowery slums. The book, published on Crane's own dime and not an immediate popular success, earned him the respect and friendship of William Dean Howells. Crane gained fame as an author with the 1895 serial publication of his tale of the Civil War, *The Red Badge of Courage.* He wrote for newspapers throughout his life, transforming his own personal survival of a shipwreck on New Year's Day, 1897, into a newspaper account and short story in "The Sinking of the Commodore" and "The Open Boat." His other stories include "The Bride Comes to Yellow Sky" and "The Blue Hotel," both published in 1898. Stylistically, Crane preserved the stamp of the journalist and utilized the best parts of realism and sensationalism in his fiction. He published collections of poetry as well, among them *War Is Kind* in 1900. He traveled extensively, reporting on the war between Greece and Turkey and on the internecine strife in Cuba. Crane also lived next door to both Henry James and Joseph Conrad in England for the few years before his death from tuberculosis at the age of twenty-nine.

## *The Open Boat*                                                                                  1897

### I

None of them knew the color of the sky. Their eyes glanced level, and were fastened upon the waves that swept toward them. These waves were of the hue of slate, save for the tops, which were of foaming white, and all of the men knew the colors of the sea. The horizon narrowed and widened, and dipped and rose, and at all times its edge was jagged with waves that seemed thrust up in points like rocks.

Many a man ought to have a bath-tub larger than the boat which here rode upon the sea. These waves were most wrongfully and barbarously abrupt and tall, and each froth-top was a problem in small boat navigation.

The cook squatted in the bottom and looked with both eyes at the six inches of gunwale which separated him from the ocean. His sleeves were rolled over his fat forearms, and the two flaps of his unbuttoned vest dangled as he bent to bail out the boat. Often he said: "Gawd! That was a narrow clip." As he remarked it he invariably gazed eastward over the broken sea.

The oiler, steering with one of the two oars in the boat, sometimes raised himself suddenly to keep clear of water that swirled in over the stern. It was a thin little oar and it seemed often ready to snap.

The correspondent, pulling at the other oar, watched the waves and wondered why he was there.

The injured captain, lying in the bow, was at this time buried in that profound dejection and indifference which comes, temporarily at least, to even the bravest and most enduring when, willy nilly, the firm fails, the army loses, the ship goes down. The mind of the master of a vessel is rooted deep in the timbers of her, though he command for a day or a decade, and this captain had on him the stern impression of a scene in the grays of dawn of seven turned faces, and later a stump of a top-mast with a white ball on it that slashed to and fro at the waves, went low and lower, and down. Thereafter there was something strange in his voice. Although steady, it was deep with mourning, and of a quality beyond oration or tears.

"Keep 'er a little more south, Billie," said he.

"'A little more south,' sir," said the oiler in the stern.

A seat in this boat was not unlike a seat upon a bucking broncho, and, by the same token, a broncho is not much smaller. The craft pranced and reared, and plunged like an animal. As each wave came, and she rose for it, she seemed like a horse making at a fence outrageously high. The manner of her scramble over these walls of water is a mystic thing, and, moreover, at the top of them were ordinarily these problems in white water, the foam racing down from the summit of each wave, requiring a new leap, and a leap from the air. Then, after scornfully bumping a crest, she would slide, and race, and splash down a long incline, and arrive bobbing and nodding in front of the next menace.

A singular disadvantage of the sea lies in the fact that after successfully surmounting one wave you discover that there is another behind it just as important and just as nervously anxious to do something effective in the way of swamping boats. In a ten-foot dingey one can get an idea of the resources of the sea in the line of waves that is not probable to the average experience which is never at sea in a dingey. As each slaty wall of water approached, it shut all else from the view of the men in the boat, and it was not difficult to imagine that this particular wave was the final outburst of the ocean, the last effort of the grim water. There was a terrible grace in the move of the waves, and they came in silence, save for the snarling of the crests.

In the wan light, the faces of the men must have been gray. Their eyes must have glinted in strange ways as they gazed steadily astern. Viewed from a balcony, the whole thing would doubtless have been weirdly picturesque. But the men in the boat had no time to see it, and if they had had leisure there were other things to occupy their minds. The sun swung steadily up the sky, and they knew it was broad day because the color of the sea changed from slate to emerald-green, streaked with amber lights, and the foam was like tumbling snow. The process of the breaking day was unknown to them. They were aware only of this effect upon the color of the waves that rolled toward them.

In disjointed sentences the cook and the correspondent argued as to the difference between a life-saving station and a house of refuge. The cook had said: "There's a house of refuge just north of the Mosquito Inlet Light, and as soon as they see us, they'll come off in their boat and pick us up."

"As soon as who see us?" said the correspondent.

"The crew," said the cook.

"Houses of refuge don't have crews," said the correspondent. "As I understand them, they are only places where clothes and grub are stored for the benefit of shipwrecked people. They don't carry crews."

"Oh, yes, they do," said the cook.

"No, they don't," said the correspondent.

"Well, we're not there yet, anyhow," said the oiler, in the stern.

"Well," said the cook, "perhaps it's not a house of refuge that I'm thinking of as being near Mosquito Inlet Light. Perhaps it's a life-saving station."

"We're not there yet," said the oiler, in the stern.

## II

As the boat bounced from the top of each wave, the wind tore through the hair of the hatless men, and as the craft plopped her stern down again the spray slashed past them. The crest of each of these waves was a hill, from the top of which the men surveyed, for a moment, a broad tumultuous expanse, shining and wind-riven. It was probably splendid. It was probably glorious, this play of the free sea, wild with lights of emerald and white and amber.

"Bully good thing it's an on-shore wind," said the cook. "If not, where would we be? Wouldn't have a show."

"That's right," said the correspondent.

The busy oiler nodded his assent.

Then the captain, in the bow, chuckled in a way that expressed humor, contempt, tragedy, all in one. "Do you think we've got much of a show now, boys?" said he.

Whereupon the three were silent, save for a trifle of hemming and hawing. To express any particular optimism at this time they felt to be childish and stupid, but they all doubtless possessed this sense of the situation in their mind. A young man thinks doggedly at such times. On the other hand, the ethics of their condition was decidedly against any open suggestion of hopelessness. So they were silent.

"Oh, well," said the captain, soothing his children, "we'll get ashore all right."

But there was that in his tone which made them think, so the oiler quoth: "Yes! If this wind holds!"

The cook was bailing: "Yes! If we don't catch hell in the surf."

Canton flannel gulls flew near and far. Sometimes they sat down on the sea, near patches of brown seaweed that rolled over the waves with a movement like carpets on a line in a gale. The birds sat comfortably in groups, and they were envied by some in the dingey, for the wrath of the sea was no more to them than it was to a covey of prairie chickens a thousand miles inland. Often they came very close and stared at the men with black bead-like eyes. At these times they were uncanny and sinister in their unblinking scrutiny, and the men hooted angrily at them, telling them to be gone. One came, and evidently decided to alight on the top of the captain's head. The bird flew parallel to the boat and did not circle, but made short sidelong jumps in the air in chicken-fashion. His black eyes were wistfully fixed upon the captain's head. "Ugly brute," said the oiler to the bird. "You look as if you were made with a jack-knife." The cook and the correspondent swore darkly at the creature. The captain naturally wished to knock it away with the end of the heavy painter;[1] but he did not dare do it, because anything resembling an emphatic gesture would have capsized this freighted boat, and so with his open hand, the captain gently and carefully waved the gull away. After it had been discouraged from the pursuit the captain breathed easier on account of his hair, and others breathed easier because the bird struck their minds at this time as being somehow gruesome and ominous.

In the meantime the oiler and the correspondent rowed. And also they rowed. They sat together in the same seat, and each rowed an oar. Then the oiler took both oars; then the correspondent took both oars; then the oiler; then the correspondent. They rowed and they rowed. The very ticklish part of the business was when the time came for the reclining one in the stern to take his turn at the oars. By the very last star of truth, it is easier to steal eggs from under a hen than it was to change seats in the dingey. First the man in the stern slid his hand along the thwart and moved with care, as if he were of Sèvres.[2] Then the man in the rowing seat slid his hand along the other thwart. It was all done with the most extraordinary care. As the two sidled past each other, the whole party kept watchful eyes on the coming wave, and the captain cried: "Look out now! Steady there!"

The brown mats of seaweed that appeared from time to time were like islands, bits of earth. They were travelling, apparently, neither one way nor the other. They were, to all intents, stationary. They informed the men in the boat that it was making progress slowly toward the land.

The captain, rearing cautiously in the bow, after the dingey soared on a great swell, said that he had seen the lighthouse at Mosquito Inlet. Presently the cook remarked that he had seen it. The correspondent was at the oars then, and for some reason he too wished to look at the lighthouse, but his back was toward the far shore and the waves were important, and for some time he could not seize an opportunity to turn his head. But at last there came a wave more gentle than the others, and when at the crest of it he swiftly scoured the western horizon.

"See it?" said the captain.

"No," said the correspondent slowly. "I didn't see anything."

"Look again," said the captain. He pointed. "It's exactly in that direction."

At the top of another wave, the correspondent did as he was bid, and this time his

---

1 **painter:** A rope attached to the bow to secure the boat to a pier or to tow another boat.
2 **Sèvres:** Elaborately decorated fine porcelain made in Sèvres, France.

eyes chanced on a small still thing on the edge of the swaying horizon. It was precisely like the point of a pin. It took an anxious eye to find a lighthouse so tiny.

"Think we'll make it, captain?"

"If this wind holds and the boat don't swamp, we can't do much else," said the captain.

The little boat, lifted by each towering sea, and splashed viciously by the crests, made progress that in the absence of seaweed was not apparent to those in her. She seemed just a wee thing wallowing, miraculously top up, at the mercy of five oceans. Occasionally, a great spread of water, like white flames, swarmed into her.

"Bail her, cook," said the captain serenely.

"All right, captain," said the cheerful cook.

## III

It would be difficult to describe the subtle brotherhood of men that was here established on the seas. No one said that it was so. No one mentioned it. But it dwelt in the boat, and each man felt it warm him. They were a captain, an oiler, a cook, and a correspondent, and they were friends, friends in a more curiously iron-bound degree than may be common. The hurt captain, lying against the water-jar in the bow, spoke always in a low voice and calmly, but he could never command a more ready and swiftly obedient crew than the motley three of the dingey. It was more than a mere recognition of what was best for the common safety. There was surely in it a quality that was personal and heartfelt. And after this devotion to the commander of the boat there was this comradeship that the correspondent, for instance, who had been taught to be cynical of men, knew even at the time was the best experience of his life. But no one said that it was so. No one mentioned it.

"I wish we had a sail," remarked the captain. "We might try my overcoat on the end of an oar and give you two boys a chance to rest." So the cook and the correspondent held the mast and spread wide the overcoat. The oiler steered, and the little boat made good way with her new rig. Sometimes the oiler had to scull sharply to keep a sea from breaking into the boat, but otherwise sailing was a success.

Meanwhile the lighthouse had been growing slowly larger. It had now almost assumed color, and appeared like a little gray shadow on the sky. The man at the oars could not be prevented from turning his head rather often to try for a glimpse of this little gray shadow.

At last, from the top of each wave the men in the tossing boat could see land. Even as the lighthouse was an upright shadow on the sky, this land seemed but a long black shadow on the sea. It certainly was thinner than paper. "We must be about opposite New Smyrna," said the cook, who had coasted this shore often in schooners. "Captain, by the way, I believe they abandoned that life-saving station there about a year ago."

"Did they?" said the captain.

The wind slowly died away. The cook and the correspondent were not now obliged to slave in order to hold high the oar. But the waves continued their old impetuous swooping at the dingey, and the little craft, no longer under way, struggled woundily over them. The oiler or the correspondent took the oars again.

Shipwrecks are *apropos* of nothing. If men could only train for them and have them occur when the men had reached pink condition, there would be less drowning at sea. Of the four in the dingey none had slept any time worth mentioning for two days and two nights previous to embarking in the dingey, and in the excitement of clambering about the deck of a foundering ship they had also forgotten to eat heartily.

For these reasons, and for others, neither the oiler nor the correspondent was fond of rowing at this time. The correspondent wondered ingenuously how in the name of all that was sane could there be people who thought it amusing to row a boat. It was not an amusement; it was a diabolical punishment, and even a genius of mental aberrations could never conclude that it was anything but a horror to the muscles and a crime against the back. He mentioned to the boat in general how the amusement of rowing struck him, and the weary-faced oiler smiled in full sympathy. Previously to the foundering, by the way, the oiler had worked double-watch in the engine-room of the ship.

"Take her easy, now, boys," said the captain. "Don't spend yourselves. If we have to run a surf you'll need all your strength, because we'll sure have to swim for it. Take your time."

Slowly the land arose from the sea. From a black line it became a line of black and a line of white, trees and sand. Finally, the captain said that he could make out a house on the shore. "That's the house of refuge, sure," said the cook. "They'll see us before long, and come out after us."

The distant lighthouse reared high. "The keeper ought to be able to make us out now, if he's looking through a glass," said the captain. "He'll notify the life-saving people."

"None of those other boats could have got ashore to give word of the wreck," said the oiler, in a low voice. "Else the life-boat would be out hunting us."

Slowly and beautifully the land loomed out of the sea. The wind came again. It had veered from the north-east to the south-east. Finally, a new sound struck the ears of the men in the boat. It was the low thunder of the surf on the shore. "We'll never be able to make the lighthouse now," said the captain. "Swing her head a little more north, Billie."

"'A little more north,' sir," said the oiler.

Whereupon the little boat turned her nose once more down the wind, and all but the oarsman watched the shore grow. Under the influence of this expansion doubt and direful apprehension was leaving the minds of the men. The management of the boat was still most absorbing, but it could not prevent a quiet cheerfulness. In an hour, perhaps, they would be ashore.

Their backbones had become thoroughly used to balancing in the boat, and they now rode this wild colt of a dingey like circus men. The correspondent thought that he had been drenched to the skin, but happening to feel in the top pocket of his coat, he found therein eight cigars. Four of them were soaked with sea-water; four were perfectly scatheless. After a search, somebody produced three dry matches, and thereupon the four waifs rode in their little boat, and with an assurance of an impending rescue shining in their eyes, puffed at the big cigars and judged well and ill of all men. Everybody took a drink of water.

## IV

"Cook," remarked the captain, "there don't seem to be any signs of life about your house of refuge."

"No," replied the cook. "Funny they don't see us!"

A broad stretch of lowly coast lay before the eyes of the men. It was of low dunes topped with dark vegetation. The roar of the surf was plain, and sometimes they could see the white lip of a wave as it spun up the beach. A tiny house was blocked out black upon the sky. Southward, the slim lighthouse lifted its little gray length.

Tide, wind, and waves were swinging the dingey northward. "Funny they don't see us," said the men.

The surf's roar was here dulled, but its tone was, nevertheless, thunderous and mighty. As the boat swam over the great rollers, the men sat listening to this roar. "We'll swamp sure," said everybody.

It is fair to say here that there was not a life-saving station within twenty miles in either direction, but the men did not know this fact, and in consequence they made dark and opprobrious remarks concerning the eyesight of the nation's lifesavers. Four scowling men sat in the dingey and surpassed records in the invention of epithets.

"Funny they don't see us."

The light-heartedness of a former time had completely faded. To their sharpened minds it was easy to conjure pictures of all kinds of incompetency and blindness and, indeed, cowardice. There was the shore of the populous land, and it was bitter and bitter to them that from it came no sign.

"Well," said the captain, ultimately, "I suppose we'll have to make a try for ourselves. If we stay out here too long, we'll none of us have strength left to swim after the boat swamps."

And so the oiler, who was at the oars, turned the boat straight for the shore. There was a sudden tightening of muscles. There was some thinking.

"If we don't all get ashore—" said the captain. "If we don't all get ashore, I suppose you fellows know where to send news of my finish?"

They then briefly exchanged some addresses and admonitions. As for the reflections of the men, there was a great deal of rage in them. Perchance they might be formulated thus: "If I am going to be drowned—if I am going to be drowned—if I am going to be drowned, why, in the name of the seven mad gods who rule the sea, was I allowed to come thus far and contemplate sand and trees? Was I brought here merely to have my nose dragged away as I was about to nibble the sacred cheese of life? It is preposterous. If this old ninny-woman, Fate, cannot do better than this, she should be deprived of the management of men's fortunes. She is an old hen who knows not her intention. If she has decided to drown me, why did she not do it in the beginning and save me all this trouble? The whole affair is absurd. . . . But no, she cannot mean to drown me. She dare not drown me. She cannot drown me. Not after all this work." Afterward the man might have had an impulse to shake his fist at the clouds: "Just you drown me, now, and then hear what I call you!"

The billows that came at this time were more formidable. They seemed always just about to break and roll over the little boat in a turmoil of foam. There was a preparatory and long growl in the speech of them. No mind unused to the sea would have concluded that the dingey could ascend these sheer heights in time. The shore was still afar. The oiler was a wily surfman. "Boys," he said swiftly, "she won't live three minutes more, and we're too far out to swim. Shall I take her to sea again, captain?"

"Yes! go ahead!" said the captain.

This oiler, by a series of quick miracles, and fast and steady oarsmanship, turned the boat in the middle of the surf and took her safely to sea again.

There was a considerable silence as the boat bumped over the furrowed sea to deeper water. Then somebody in gloom spoke. "Well, anyhow, they must have seen us from the shore by now."

The gulls went in slanting flight up the wind toward the gray desolate east. A squall, marked by dingy clouds, and clouds brick-red, like smoke from a burning building, appeared from the south-east.

"What do you think of those life-saving people? Ain't they peaches?"

"Funny they haven't seen us."

"Maybe they think we're out here for sport! Maybe they think we're fishin'. Maybe they think we're damned fools."

It was a long afternoon. A changed tide tried to force them southward, but wind and wave said northward. Far ahead, where coastline, sea, and sky formed their mighty angle, there were little dots which seemed to indicate a city on the shore.

"St. Augustine?"

The captain shook his head. "Too near Mosquito Inlet."

And the oiler rowed, and then the correspondent rowed. Then the oiler rowed. It was a weary business. The human back can become the seat of more aches and pains than are registered in books for the composite anatomy of a regiment. It is a limited area, but it can become the theater of innumerable muscular conflicts, tangles, wrenches, knots, and other comforts.

"Did you ever like to row, Billie?" asked the correspondent.

"No," said the oiler. "Hang it!"

When one exchanged the rowing-seat for a place in the bottom of the boat, he suffered a bodily depression that caused him to be careless of everything save an obligation to wiggle one finger. There was cold sea-water swashing to and fro in the boat, and he lay in it. His head, pillowed on a thwart, was within an inch of the swirl of a wave crest, and sometimes a particularly obstreperous sea came inboard and drenched him once more. But these matters did not annoy him. It is almost certain that if the boat had capsized he would have tumbled comfortably out upon the ocean as if he felt sure that it was a great soft mattress.

"Look! There's a man on the shore!"

"Where?"

"There! See 'im? See 'im?"

"Yes, sure! He's walking along."

"Now he's stopped. Look! He's facing us!"

"He's waving at us!"

"So he is! By thunder!"

"Ah, now we're all right! Now we're all right! There'll be a boat out here for us in half an hour."

"He's going on. He's running. He's going up to that house there."

The remote beach seemed lower than the sea, and it required a searching glance to discern the little black figure. The captain saw a floating stick and they rowed to it. A bath-towel was by some weird chance in the boat, and tying this on the stick, the captain waved it. The oarsman did not dare turn his head, so he was obliged to ask questions.

"What's he doing now?"

"He's standing still again. He's looking. I think. . . . There he goes again. Toward the house. . . . Now he's stopped again."

"Is he waving at us?"

"No, not now! he was, though."

"Look! There comes another man!"

"He's running."

"Look at him go, would you."

"Why, he's on a bicycle. Now he's met the other man. They're both waving at us. Look!"

"There comes something up the beach."

"What the devil is that thing?"

"Why, it looks like a boat."

"Why, certainly it's a boat."

"No, it's on wheels."

"Yes, so it is. Well, that must be the life-boat. They drag them along shore on a wagon."

"That's the life-boat, sure."

"No, by—, it's—it's an omnibus."

"I tell you it's a life-boat."

"It is not! It's an omnibus. I can see it plain. See? One of these big hotel omnibuses."

"By thunder, you're right. It's an omnibus, sure as fate. What do you suppose they are doing with an omnibus? Maybe they are going around collecting the life-crew, hey?"

"That's it, likely. Look! There's a fellow waving a little black flag. He's standing on the steps of the omnibus. There come those other two fellows. Now they're all talking together. Look at the fellow with the flag. Maybe he ain't waving it."

"That ain't a flag, is it? That's his coat. Why, certainly, that's his coat."

"So it is. It's his coat. He's taken it off and is waving it around his head. But would you look at him swing it."

"Oh, say, there isn't any life-saving station there. That's just a winter resort hotel omnibus that has brought over some of the boarders to see us drown."

"What's that idiot with the coat mean? What's he signaling, anyhow?"

"It looks as if he were trying to tell us to go north. There must be a life-saving station up there."

"No! He thinks we're fishing. Just giving us a merry hand. See? Ah, there, Willie."

"Well, I wish I could make something out of those signals. What do you suppose he means?"

"He don't mean anything. He's just playing."

"Well, if he'd just signal us to try the surf again, or to go to sea and wait, or go north, or go south, or go to hell—there would be some reason in it. But look at him. He just stands there and keeps his coat revolving like a wheel. The ass!"

"There come more people."

"Now there's quite a mob. Look! Isn't that a boat?"

"Where? Oh, I see where you mean. No, that's no boat."

"That fellow is still waving his coat."

"He must think we like to see him do that. Why don't he quit it? It don't mean anything."

"I don't know. I think he is trying to make us go north. It must be that there's a life-saving station there somewhere."

"Say, he ain't tired yet. Look at 'im wave."

"Wonder how long he can keep that up. He's been revolving his coat ever since he caught sight of us. He's an idiot. Why aren't they getting men to bring a boat out? A fishing boat—one of those big yawls—could come out here all right. Why don't he do something?"

"Oh, it's all right, now."

"They'll have a boat out here for us in less than no time, now that they've seen us."

A faint yellow tone came into the sky over the low land. The shadows on the sea slowly deepened. The wind bore coldness with it, and the men began to shiver.

"Holy smoke!" said one, allowing his voice to express his impious mood, "if we keep on monkeying out here! If we've got to flounder out here all night!"

"Oh, we'll never have to stay here all night! Don't you worry. They've seen us now, and it won't be long before they'll come chasing out after us."

The shore grew dusky. The man waving a coat blended gradually into this gloom, and it swallowed in the same manner the omnibus and the group of people. The spray, when it dashed uproariously over the side, made the voyagers shrink and swear like men who were being branded.

"I'd like to catch the chump who waved the coat. I feel like soaking him one, just for luck."

"Why? What did he do?"

"Oh, nothing, but then he seemed so damned cheerful."

In the meantime the oiler rowed, and then the correspondent rowed, and then the oiler rowed. Gray-faced and bowed forward, they mechanically, turn by turn, plied the leaden oars. The form of the lighthouse had vanished from the southern horizon, but finally a pale star appeared, just lifting from the sea. The streaked saffron in the west passed before the all-merging darkness, and the sea to the east was black. The land had vanished, and was expressed only by the low and drear thunder of the surf.

"If I am going to be drowned—if I am going to be drowned—if I am going to be drowned, why, in the name of the seven mad gods who rule the sea, was I allowed to come thus far and contemplate sand and trees? Was I brought here merely to have my nose dragged away as I was about to nibble the sacred cheese of life?"

The patient captain, dropped over the water-jar, was sometimes obliged to speak to the oarsman.

"Keep her head up! Keep her head up!"

"'Keep her head up,' sir." The voices were weary and low.

This was surely a quiet evening. All save the oarsman lay heavily and listlessly in the boat's bottom. As for him, his eyes were just capable of noting the tall black waves that swept forward in a most sinister silence, save for an occasional subdued growl of a crest.

The cook's head was on a thwart, and he looked without interest at the water under his nose. He was deep in other scenes. Finally he spoke. "Billie," he murmured, dreamfully, "what kind of pie do you like best?"

## V

"Pie," said the oiler and the correspondent, agitatedly. "Don't talk about those things, blast you!"

"Well," said the cook, "I was just thinking about ham sandwiches, and—"

A night on the sea in an open boat is a long night. As darkness settled finally, the shine of the light, lifting from the sea in the south, changed to full gold. On the northern horizon a new light appeared, a small bluish gleam on the edge of the waters. These two lights were the furniture of the world. Otherwise there was nothing but waves.

Two men huddled in the stern, and distances were so magnificent in the dingey that the rower was enabled to keep his feet partly warmed by thrusting them under his companions. Their legs indeed extended far under the rowing-seat until they touched the feet of the captain forward. Sometimes, despite the efforts of the tired oarsman, a wave came piling into the boat, an icy wave of the night, and the chilling water soaked them anew. They would twist their bodies for a moment and groan, and sleep the dead sleep once more, while the water in the boat gurgled about them as the craft rocked.

The plan of the oiler and the correspondent was for one to row until he lost the ability, and then arouse the other from his sea-water couch in the bottom of the boat.

The oiler plied the oars until his head drooped forward, and the overpowering sleep blinded him. And he rowed yet afterward. Then he touched a man in the bottom of the boat, and called his name. "Will you spell me for a little while?" he said, meekly.

"Sure, Billie," said the correspondent, awakening and dragging himself to a sitting position. They exchanged places carefully, and the oiler, cuddling down in the sea-water at the cook's side, seemed to go to sleep instantly.

The particular violence of the sea had ceased. The waves came without snarling. The obligation of the man at the oars was to keep the boat headed so that the tilt of the rollers would not capsize her, and to preserve her from filling when the crests rushed past. The black waves were silent and hard to be seen in the darkness. Often one was almost upon the boat before the oarsman was aware.

In a low voice the correspondent addressed the captain. He was not sure that the captain was awake, although this iron man seemed to be always awake. "Captain, shall I keep her making for that light north, sir?"

The same steady voice answered him. "Yes. Keep it about two points off the port bow."

The cook had tied a life-belt around himself in order to get even the warmth which this clumsy cork contrivance could donate, and he seemed almost stove-like when a rower, whose teeth invariably chattered wildly as soon as he ceased his labor, dropped down to sleep.

The correspondent, as he rowed, looked down at the two men sleeping underfoot. The cook's arm was around the oiler's shoulders, and, with their fragmentary clothing and haggard faces, they were the babes of the sea, a grotesque rendering of the old babes in the wood.

Later he must have grown stupid at his work, for suddenly there was a growling of water, and a crest came with a roar and a swash into the boat, and it was a wonder that it did not set the cook afloat in his life-belt. The cook continued to sleep, but the oiler sat up, blinking his eyes and shaking with the new cold.

"Oh, I'm awfully sorry, Billie," said the correspondent, contritely.

"That's all right, old boy," said the oiler, and lay down again and was asleep.

Presently it seemed that even the captain dozed, and the correspondent thought that he was the one man afloat on all the oceans. The wind had a voice as it came over the waves, and it was sadder than the end.

There was a long, loud swishing astern of the boat, and a gleaming trail of phosphorescence, like blue flame, was furrowed on the black waters. It might have been made by a monstrous knife.

Then there came a stillness, while the correspondent breathed with the open mouth and looked at the sea.

Suddenly there was another swish and another long flash of bluish light, and this time it was alongside the boat, and might almost have been reached with an oar. The correspondent saw an enormous fin speed like a shadow through the water, hurling the crystalline spray and leaving the long glowing trail.

The correspondent looked over his shoulder at the captain. His face was hidden, and he seemed to be asleep. He looked at the babes of the sea. They certainly were asleep. So, being bereft of sympathy, he leaned a little way to one side and swore softly into the sea.

But the thing did not then leave the vicinity of the boat. Ahead or astern, on one side or the other, at intervals long or short, fled the long sparkling streak, and there was to be heard the *whiroo* of the dark fin. The speed and power of the thing was greatly to be admired. It cut the water like a gigantic and keen projectile.

The presence of this biding thing did not affect the man with the same horror that it would if he had been a picnicker. He simply looked at the sea dully and swore in an undertone.

Nevertheless, it is true that he did not wish to be alone. He wished one of his companions to awaken by chance and keep him company with it. But the captain hung motionless over the water-jar, and the oiler and the cook in the bottom of the boat were plunged in slumber.

## VI

"If I am going to be drowned—if I am going to be drowned—if I am going to be drowned, why, in the name of the seven mad gods who rule the sea, was I allowed to come thus far and contemplate sand and trees?"

During this dismal night, it may be remarked that a man would conclude that it was really the intention of the seven mad gods to drown him, despite the abominable injustice of it. For it was certainly an abominable injustice to drown a man who had worked so hard, so hard. The man felt it would be a crime most unnatural. Other people had drowned at sea since galleys swarmed with painted sails, but still—

When it occurs to a man that nature does not regard him as important, and that she feels she would not maim the universe by disposing of him, he at first wishes to throw bricks at the temple, and he hates deeply the fact that there are no bricks and no temples. Any visible expression of nature would surely be pelleted with his jeers.

Then, if there be no tangible thing to hoot he feels, perhaps, the desire to confront a personification and indulge in pleas, bowed to one knee, and with hands supplicant, saying: "Yes, but I love myself."

A high cold star on a winter's night is the word he feels that she says to him. Thereafter he knows the pathos of his situation.

The men in the dingey had not discussed these matters, but each had, no doubt, reflected upon them in silence and according to his mind. There was seldom any expression upon their faces save the general one of complete weariness. Speech was devoted to the business of the boat.

To chime the notes of his emotion, a verse mysteriously entered the correspondent's head. He had even forgotten that he had forgotten this verse, but it suddenly was in his mind.

> A soldier of the Legion lay dying in Algiers,
> There was lack of woman's nursing, there was dearth of woman's tears;
> But a comrade stood beside him, and he took that comrade's hand,
> And he said: "I shall never see my own, my native land."[3]

In his childhood, the correspondent had been made acquainted with the fact that a soldier of the Legion lay dying in Algiers, but he had never regarded the fact as important. Myriads of his school-fellows had informed him of the soldier's plight, but the dinning had naturally ended by making him perfectly indifferent. He had never considered it his affair that a soldier of the Legion lay dying in Algiers, nor had it appeared to him as a matter for sorrow. It was less to him than the breaking of a pencil's point.

Now, however, it quaintly came to him as a human, living thing. It was no longer merely a picture of a few throes in the breast of a poet, meanwhile drinking tea and warming his feet at the grate; it was an actuality—stern, mournful, and fine.

The correspondent plainly saw the soldier. He lay on the sand with his feet out straight and still. While his pale left hand was upon his chest in an attempt to thwart the going of his life, the blood came between his fingers. In the far Algerian distance, a city of low square forms was set against a sky that was faint with the last sunset hues. The correspondent, plying the oars and dreaming of the slow and slower movements of the lips of the soldier, was moved by a profound and perfectly impersonal comprehension. He was sorry for the soldier of the Legion who lay dying in Algiers.

The thing which had followed the boat and waited had evidently grown bored at the delay. There was no longer to be heard the slash of the cut water, and there was no longer the flame of the long trail. The light in the north still glimmered, but it was apparently no nearer to the boat. Sometimes the boom of the surf rang in the correspondent's ears, and he turned the craft seaward then and rowed harder. Southward, someone had evidently built a watch-fire on the beach. It was too low and too far to be seen, but it made a shimmering, roseate reflection upon the bluff back of it, and this could be discerned from the boat. The wind came stronger, and sometimes a wave suddenly raged out like a mountain-cat, and there was to be seen the sheen and sparkle of a broken crest.

The captain, in the bow, moved on his water-jar and sat erect. "Pretty long night," he observed to the correspondent. He looked at the shore. "Those life-saving people take their time."

"Did you see that shark playing around?"

"Yes, I saw him. He was a big fellow, all right."

"Wish I had known you were awake."

Later the correspondent spoke into the bottom of the boat.

"Billie!" There was a slow and gradual disentanglement. "Billie, will you spell me?"

---

3 **A soldier . . . my native land:** From the poem "Bingen on the Rhine" (1883) by Caroline E. S. Norton.

"Sure," said the oiler.

As soon as the correspondent touched the cold comfortable seater in the bottom of the boat, and had huddled close to the cook's life-belt he was deep in sleep, despite the fact that his teeth played all the popular airs. This sleep was so good to him that it was but a moment before he heard a voice call his name in a tone that demonstrated the last stages of exhaustion. "Will you spell me?"

"Sure, Billie."

The light in the north had mysteriously vanished, but the correspondent took his course from the wide-awake captain.

Later in the night they took the boat farther out to sea, and the captain directed the cook to take one oar at the stern and keep the boat facing the seas. He was to call out if he should hear the thunder of the surf. This plan enabled the oiler and the correspondent to get respite together. "We'll give those boys a chance to get into shape again," said the captain. They curled down and, after a few preliminary chatterings and trembles, slept once more the dead sleep. Neither knew they had bequeathed to the cook the company of another shark, or perhaps the same shark.

As the boat caroused on the waves, spray occasionally bumped over the side and gave them a fresh soaking, but this had no power to break their repose. The ominous slash of the wind and the water affected them as it would have affected mummies.

"Boys," said the cook, with the notes of every reluctance in his voice, "she's drifted in pretty close. I guess one of you had better take her to sea again." The correspondent, aroused, heard the crash of the toppled crests.

As he was rowing, the captain gave him some whiskey-and-water, and this steadied the chills out of him. "If I ever get ashore and anybody shows me even a photograph of an oar—"

At last there was a short conversation.

"Billie . . . Billie, will you spell me?"

"Sure," said the oiler.

## VII

When the correspondent again opened his eyes, the sea and the sky were each of the gray hue of the dawning. Later, carmine and gold was painted upon the waters. The morning appeared finally, in its splendor, with a sky of pure blue, and the sunlight flamed on the tips of the waves.

On the distant dunes were set many little black cottages, and a tall white windmill reared above them. No man, nor dog, nor bicycle appeared on the beach. The cottages might have formed a deserted village.

The voyagers scanned the shore. A conference was held in the boat. "Well," said the captain, "if no help is coming, we might better try a run through the surf right away. If we stay out here much longer we will be too weak to do anything for ourselves at all." The others silently acquiesced in this reasoning. The boat was headed for the beach. The correspondent wondered if none ever ascended the tall wind-tower, and if then they never looked seaward. This tower was a giant, standing with its back to the plight of the ants. It represented in a degree, to the correspondent, the serenity of nature amid the struggles of the individual—nature in the wind, and nature in the vision of men. She did not seem cruel to him then, nor beneficent, nor treacherous, nor wise. But she was indifferent, flatly indifferent. It is, perhaps, plausible that a man in this situation, impressed with the unconcern of the universe, should see the innumerable flaws of his life, and have them taste wickedly in his mind and wish for another chance. A distinction between right and wrong seems absurdly clear to him, then, in this new ignorance of the grave-edge, and he understands that if he were given another opportunity he would mend his conduct and his words, and be better and brighter during an introduction or at a tea.

"Now, boys," said the captain, "she is going to swamp sure. All we can do is to work her in as far as possible, and then when she swamps, pile out and scramble for the beach. Keep cool now, and don't jump until she swamps sure."

The oiler took the oars. Over his shoulders he scanned the surf. "Captain," he said, "I think I'd better bring her about, and keep her head-on to the seas and back her in."

"All right, Billie," said the captain. "Back her in." The oiler swung the boat then and, seated in the stern, the cook and the correspondent were obliged to look over their shoulders to contemplate the lonely and indifferent shore.

The monstrous in-shore rollers heaved the boat high until the men were again enabled to see the white sheets of water scudding up the slanted beach. "We won't get in very close," said the captain. Each time a man could wrest his attention from the rollers, he turned his glance toward the shore, and in the expression of the eyes during this contemplation there was a singular quality. The correspondent, observing the others, knew that they were not afraid, but the full meaning of their glances was shrouded.

As for himself, he was too tired to grapple fundamentally with the fact. He tried to coerce his mind into thinking of it, but the mind was dominated at this time by the muscles, and the muscles said they did not care. It merely occurred to him that if he should drown it would be a shame.

There were no hurried words, no pallor, no plain agitation. The men simply looked at the shore. "Now, remember to get well clear of the boat when you jump," said the captain.

Seaward the crest of a roller suddenly fell with a thunderous crash, and the long white comber came roaring down upon the boat.

"Steady now," said the captain. The men were silent. They turned their eyes from the shore to the comber and waited. The boat slid up the incline, leaped at the furious top, bounced over it, and swung down the long back of the waves. Some water had been shipped and the cook bailed it out.

But the next crest crashed also. The tumbling, boiling flood of white water caught the boat and whirled it almost perpendicular. Water swarmed in from all sides. The correspondent had his hands on the gunwale at this time, and when the water entered at that place he swiftly withdrew his fingers, as if he objected to wetting them.

The little boat, drunken with this weight of water, reeled and snuggled deeper into the sea.

"Bail her out, cook! Bail her out," said the captain.

"All right, captain," said the cook.

"Now, boys, the next one will do for us, sure," said the oiler. "Mind to jump clear of the boat."

The third wave moved forward, huge, furious, implacable. It fairly swallowed the dingey, and almost simultaneously the men tumbled into the sea. A piece of life-belt had lain in the bottom of the boat, and as the correspondent went overboard he held this to his chest with his left hand.

The January water was icy, and he reflected immediately that it was colder than he had expected to find it off the coast of Florida. This appeared to his dazed mind as a fact important enough to be noted at the time. The coldness of the water was sad; it was tragic. This fact was somehow so mixed and confused with his opinion of his own situation that it seemed almost a proper reason for tears. The water was cold.

When he came to the surface he was conscious of little but the noisy water. Afterward he saw his companions in the sea. The oiler was ahead in the race. He was swimming strongly and rapidly. Off to the correspondent's left, the cook's great white and corked back bulged out of the water, and in the rear the captain was hanging with his one good hand to the keel of the overturned dingey.

There is a certain immovable quality to a shore, and the correspondent wondered at it amid the confusion of the sea.

It seemed also very attractive, but the correspondent knew that it was a long journey, and he paddled leisurely. The piece of life-preserver lay under him, and sometimes he whirled down the incline of a wave as if he were on a hand-sled.

But finally he arrived at a place in the sea where travel was beset with difficulty. He did not pause swimming to inquire what manner of current had caught him, but there his progress ceased. The shore was set before him like a bit of scenery on a stage, and he looked at it and understood with his eyes each detail of it.

As the cook passed, much farther to the left, the captain was calling to him, "Turn over on your back, cook! Turn over on your back and use the oar."

"All right, sir." The cook turned on his back, and, paddling with an oar, went ahead as if he were a canoe.

Presently the boat also passed to the left of the correspondent with the captain clinging with one hand to the keel. He would have appeared like a man raising himself to look over a board fence, if it were not for the extraordinary gymnastics of the boat. The correspondent marvelled that the captain could still hold to it.

They passed on, nearer to shore—the oiler, the cook, the captain—and following them went the water-jar, bouncing gaily over the seas.

The correspondent remained in the grip of this strange new enemy—a current. The shore, with its white slope of sand and its green bluff, topped with little silent cottages, was spread like a picture before him. It was very near to him then, but he was impressed as one who in a gallery looks at a scene from Brittany or Algiers.

He thought: "I am going to drown? Can it be possible? Can it be possible? Can it be possible?" Perhaps an individual must consider his own death to be the final phenomenon of nature.

But later a wave perhaps whirled him out of this small deadly current, for he found suddenly that he could again make progress toward the shore. Later still, he was aware that the captain, clinging with one hand to the keel of the dingey, had his face turned away from the shore and toward him, and was calling his name. "Come to the boat! Come to the boat!"

In his struggle to reach the captain and the boat, he reflected that when one gets properly wearied, drowning must really be a comfortable arrangement, a cessation of hostilities accompanied by a large degree of relief, and he was glad of it, for the main thing in his mind for some moments had been horror of the temporary agony. He did not wish to be hurt.

Presently he saw a man running along the shore. He was undressing with most remarkable speed. Coat, trousers, shirt, everything flew magically off him.

"Come to the boat," called the captain.

"All right, captain." As the correspondent paddled, he saw the captain let himself down to bottom and leave the boat. Then the correspondent performed his one little marvel of the voyage. A large wave caught him and flung him with ease and supreme speed completely over the boat and far beyond it. It struck him even then as an event in gymnastics, and a true miracle of the sea. An overturned boat in the surf is not a plaything to a swimming man.

The correspondent arrived in water that reached only to his waist but his condition did not enable him to stand for more than a moment. Each wave knocked him into a heap, and the under-tow pulled at him.

Then he saw the man who had been running and undressing, and undressing and running, come bounding into the water. He dragged ashore the cook, and then waded toward the captain, but the captain waved him away, and sent him to the correspondent. He was naked, naked as a tree in winter, but a halo was about his head, and he shone like a saint. He gave a strong pull, and a long drag, and a bully heave at the correspondent's hand. The correspondent schooled in the minor formulae, said: "Thanks, old man." But suddenly the man cried: "What's that?" He pointed a swift finger. The correspondent said: "Go."

In the shallows, face downward, lay the oiler. His forehead touched sand that was periodically, between each wave, clear of the sea.

The correspondent did not know all that transpired afterward. When he achieved safe ground he fell, striking the sand with each particular part of his body. It was as if he had dropped from a roof but the thud was grateful to him.

It seems that instantly the beach was populated with men, with blankets, clothes, and flasks, and women with coffee-pots and all the remedies sacred to their minds. The welcome of the land to the men from the sea was warm and generous, but a still and dripping shape was carried slowly up the beach, and the land's welcome for it could only be the different and sinister hospitality of the grave.

When it came night, the white waves paced to and fro in the moonlight, and the wind brought the sound of the great sea's voice to the men on shore, and they felt that they could then be interpreters.

# Fyodor Dostoevsky

## (1821–1881)

The preeminent Russian novelist Fyodor Dostoevsky managed to produce only two novels, *Poor People* and *The Double,* before being condemned to death by Czar Nicholas I for belonging to an underground socialist society known as the Petrashevsky Circle. Reprieved as he stood before the firing squad, Dostoevsky was instead sent to Siberia for ten years; upon his 1859 return to St. Petersburg, he began to publish a periodical, *Time,* which was suppressed shortly thereafter despite its expression of conservative, nationalist views. In 1864, his satirical stories *Notes from Underground* were published, followed by *Crime and Punishment* and the autobiographical *The Gambler,* both novels written during the winter of 1866. Fleeing the country to escape his creditors, having acquired many gambling debts, Dostoevsky lived in Switzerland, Italy, and Germany before eventually completing *The Possessed,* the success of which allowed him to return to St. Petersburg in 1871. There, Dostoevsky wrote his hugely popular final novel, *The Brothers Karamazov;* one year later, he died. Dostoevsky infused much of his writing with a kind of Christian mysticism. Throughout his life, he suffered from epilepsy and believed that his seizures conferred upon him ecstatic and holy revelations. His writing is both idealistic and satirical, his characters both angelic and deranged. Dostoevsky's work is not a realist's portrait of the Russian people, but he used what he saw of Russia and its people to describe his knowledge of the human soul.

## The Dream of a Ridiculous Man

1877

TRANSLATED BY DAVID MAGARSHACK

I am a ridiculous man. They call me a madman now. That would be a distinct rise in my social position were it not that they still regard me as being as ridiculous as ever. But that does not make me angry any more. They are all dear to me now even while they laugh at me—yes, even then they are for some reason particularly dear to me. I shouldn't have minded laughing with them—not at myself, of course, but because I love them—had I not felt so sad as I looked at them. I feel sad because they do not know the truth, whereas I know it. Oh, how hard it is to be the only man to know the truth! But they won't understand that. No, they will not understand.

And yet in the past I used to be terribly distressed at appearing to be ridiculous. No, not appearing to be, but being. I've always cut a ridiculous figure. I suppose I must have known it from the day I was born. At any rate, I've known for certain that I was ridiculous ever since I was seven years old. Afterwards I went to school, then to the university, and—well—the more I learned, the more conscious did I become of the fact that I was ridiculous. So that for me my years of hard work at the university seem in the end to have existed for the sole purpose of demonstrating and proving to me, the more deeply engrossed I became in my studies, that I was an utterly absurd person. And as during my studies, so all my life. Every year the same consciousness that I was ridiculous in every way strengthened and intensified in my mind. They always laughed at me. But not one of them knew or suspected that if there were one man on earth who knew better than anyone else that he was ridiculous, that man was I. And this—I mean, the fact that they did not know it—was the bitterest pill for me to swallow. But there I was myself at fault. I was always so proud that I never wanted to confess it to anyone. No, I wouldn't do that for anything in the world. As the years passed, this pride increased in me so that I do believe that if ever I had by chance confessed it to any one I should have blown my brains out the same evening. Oh, how I suffered in the days of my youth from the thought that I might not myself resist the impulse to confess it to my schoolfellows. But ever since I became a man I grew for some unknown reason a little more composed in my mind, though I was more and more conscious of that awful characteristic of mine. Yes, most decidedly for some unknown reason, for to this day I have not been able to find out why that was so. Perhaps it was because I was becoming terribly disheartened owing to one circumstance which was beyond my power to control, namely, the conviction which was gaining upon me that nothing in the whole world *made any difference*. I had long felt it dawning upon me, but I was fully convinced of it only last year, and that, too, all of a sudden, as it were. I suddenly felt that it made *no* difference to me whether the world existed or whether nothing existed anywhere at all. I began to be acutely conscious that *nothing existed in my own lifetime*. At first I couldn't help feeling that at any rate in the past many things had existed; but later on I came to the conclusion that there had not been anything even in the past, but that for some reason it had merely seemed to have been. Little by little I became convinced that there would be nothing in the future, either. It was then that I suddenly ceased to be angry with people and almost stopped noticing them. This indeed disclosed itself in the smallest trifles. For instance, I would knock against people while walking in the street. And not because I was lost in thought—I had nothing to think about—I had stopped thinking about anything at that time: it made no difference to me. Not that I had found an answer to all the questions. Oh, I had not settled a single question, and there were thousands of them! But *it made no difference to me*, and all the questions disappeared.

And, well, it was only after that that I learnt the truth. I learnt the truth last November, on the third of November, to be precise, and every moment since then has been imprinted indelibly on my mind. It happened on a dismal evening, as dismal an evening as could be imagined. I was returning home at about eleven o'clock and I remember thinking all the time that there could not be a more dismal evening. Even the weather was foul. It had been pouring all day, and the rain too was the coldest and most dismal rain that ever was, a sort of menacing rain—I remember that—a rain with a distinct animosity towards people. But about eleven o'clock it had stopped suddenly, and a horrible dampness descended upon everything, and it became much damper and colder than when it had been raining. And a sort of steam was rising from everything, from every cobble in the street, and from every side-street if you peered closely into it from the street as far as the eye could reach. I could not help feeling that if the gaslight had been extinguished everywhere, everything would have seemed much more cheerful, and that the gaslight oppressed the heart so much just because it shed a light upon it all. I had had scarcely any dinner that day. I had been spending the whole evening with an engineer who had two more friends visiting him. I never opened my mouth, and I expect I must have got on their nerves. They were discussing some highly controversial subject, and suddenly got very excited over it. But it really did not make any difference to them. I could see that. I knew that their excitement was not genuine. So I suddenly blurted it out. "My dear fellows," I said, "you don't really care a damn about it, do you?" They were not in the least offended, but they all burst out laughing at me. That was because I had said it without meaning to rebuke them, but simply because it made no difference to me. Well, they realised that it made no difference to me, and they felt happy.

When I was thinking about the gaslight in the streets, I looked up at the sky. The sky was awfully dark, but I could clearly distinguish the torn wisps of cloud and between them fathomless dark patches. All of a sudden I became aware of a little star in one of those patches and I began looking at it intently. That was because the little star gave me an idea: I made up my mind to kill myself that night. I had made up my mind to kill myself already two months before and, poor as I am, I bought myself an excellent revolver and loaded it the same day. But two months had elapsed and it was still lying in the drawer. I was so utterly indifferent to everything that I was anxious to wait for the moment when I would not be so indifferent and then kill myself. Why—I don't know. And so every night during these two months I thought of shooting myself as I was going home. I was only waiting for the right moment. And now the little star gave me an idea, and I made up my mind then and there that it should *most certainly* be that night. But why the little star gave me the idea—I don't know.

And just as I was looking at the sky, this little girl suddenly grasped me by the elbow. The street was already deserted and there was scarcely a soul to be seen. In the distance a cabman was fast asleep on his box. The girl was about eight years old. She had a kerchief on her head, and she wore only an old, shabby little dress. She was soaked to the skin, but what stuck in my memory was her little torn wet boots. I still remember them. They caught my eye especially. She suddenly began tugging at my elbow and calling me. She was not crying, but saying something in a loud, jerky sort of voice, something that did not make sense, for she was trembling all over and her teeth were chattering from cold. She seemed to be terrified of something and she was crying desperately, "Mummy! Mummy!" I turned round to look at her, but did not utter a word and went on walking. But she ran after me and kept tugging at my clothes, and there was a sound in her voice which in very frightened children signifies despair. I know that sound. Though her words sounded as if they were choking her, I realised that her mother must be dying somewhere very near, or that something similar was happening to her, and that she had run out to call someone, to find someone who would help her mother. But I did not go with her; on the contrary, something made me drive her away. At first I told her to go and find a policeman. But she suddenly clasped her hands and, whimpering and gasping for breath, kept running at my side and would not leave me. It was then that I stamped my foot and shouted at her. She just cried, "Sir! Sir! . . ." and then she left me suddenly and rushed headlong across the road: another man appeared there and she evidently rushed from me to him.

I climbed to the fifth floor. I live apart from my landlord. We all have separate rooms as in an hotel. My room is very small and poor. My window is a semicircular skylight. I have a sofa covered with American cloth, a table with books on it, two chairs and a comfortable armchair, a very old armchair indeed, but low-seated and with a high back serving as a head-rest. I sat down in the armchair, lighted the candle, and began thinking. Next door in the other room behind the partition, the usual bedlam was going on. It had been going on since the day before yesterday. A retired army captain lived there, and he had visitors—six merry gentlemen who drank vodka and played faro with an old pack of cards. Last night they had a fight and I know that two of them were for a long time pulling each other about by the hair. The landlady wanted to complain, but she is dreadfully afraid of the captain. We had only one more lodger in our rooms, a thin little lady, the wife of an army officer, on a visit to Petersburg with her three little children who had all been taken ill since their arrival at our house. She and her children were simply terrified of the captain and they lay shivering and crossing themselves all night long, and the youngest child had a sort of nervous attack from fright. This captain (I know that for a fact) sometimes stops people on Nevsky Avenue and asks them for a few coppers, telling them he is very poor. He can't get a job in the Civil Service, but the strange thing is (and that's why I am telling you this) that the captain had never once during the month he had been living with us made me feel in the least irritated. From the very first, of course, I would not have anything to do with him, and he himself was bored with me the very first time we met. But however big a noise they raised behind their partition and however many of them there were in the captain's room, it makes no difference to me. I sit up all night and, I assure you, I don't hear them at all—so completely do I forget about them. You see, I stay awake all night till daybreak, and that has been going on for a whole year now. I sit up all night in the armchair at the table—doing nothing. I read books only in the daytime. At night I sit like that without even thinking about anything in particular: some thoughts wander in and out of my mind, and I let them come and go as they please. In the night the candle burns out completely.

I sat down at the table, took the gun out of the drawer, and put it down in front of me. I remember asking myself as I put it down, "Is it to be then?" and I replied with complete certainty, "It is!" That is to say, I was going to shoot myself. I knew I should shoot myself that night for certain. What I did not know was how much longer I should go on sitting at the table till I shot myself. And I should of course have shot myself, had it not been for the little girl.

**II**

You see, though nothing made any difference to me, I could feel pain, for instance, couldn't I? If anyone had struck me, I should have felt pain. The same was true so far as my moral perceptions were concerned. If anything happened to arouse my pity, I should have felt pity, just as I used to do at the time when things did make a difference to me. So I had felt pity that night: I should most decidedly have helped a child. Why then did I not help the little girl? Because of a thought that had occurred to me at the time: when she was pulling at me and calling me, a question suddenly arose in my mind and I could not settle it. It was an idle question, but it made me angry. What made me angry was the conclusion I drew from the reflection that if I had really decided to do away with myself that night, everything in the world should have been more indifferent to me than ever. Why then should I have suddenly felt that I was not indifferent and be sorry for the little girl? I remember that I was very sorry for her, so much so that I felt a strange pang which was quite incomprehensible in my position. I'm afraid I am unable better to convey that fleeting sensation of mine, but it persisted with me at home when I was sitting at the table, and I was very much irritated. I had not been so irritated for a long time past. One train of thought followed another. It was clear to me that so long as I was still a human being and not a meaningless cipher, and till I became a cipher, I was alive, and consequently able to suffer, be angry, and feel shame at my actions. Very well. But if, on the other hand, I were going to kill myself in say, two hours, what did that little girl matter to me and what did I care for shame or anything else in the world? I was going to turn into a cipher, into an absolute cipher. And surely the realisation that I should soon cease to exist *altogether*, and hence everything would cease to exist, ought to have had some slight effect on my feeling of pity for the little girl or on my feeling of shame after so mean an action. Why after all did I stamp and shout so fiercely at the little girl? I did it because I thought that not only did I feel no pity, but that it wouldn't matter now if I were guilty of the most inhuman baseness, since in another two hours everything would become extinct. Do you believe me when I tell you that that was the only reason why I shouted like that? I am almost convinced of it now. It seemed clear to me that life and the world in some way or other depended on me now. It might almost be said that the world seemed to be created for me alone. If I were to shoot myself, the world would cease to exist—for me at any rate. To say nothing of the possibility that nothing would in fact exist for anyone after me and the whole world would dissolve as soon as my consciousness became extinct, would disappear in a twinkling like a phantom, like some integral part of my consciousness, and vanish without leaving a trace behind, for all this world and all these people exist perhaps only in my consciousness.

I remember that as I sat and meditated, I began to examine all these questions which thronged in my mind one after another from quite a different angle, and thought of something quite new. For instance, the strange notion occurred to me that if I had lived before on the moon or on Mars and had committed there the most shameful and dishonourable action that can be imagined, and had been so disgraced and dishonoured there as can be imagined and experienced only occasionally in a dream, a nightmare, and if, finding myself afterwards on earth, I had retained the memory of what I had done on the other planet, and moreover knew that I should never in any circumstances go back there—if that were to have happened, should I or should I not have felt, as I looked from the earth upon the moon, that *it made no difference* to me? Should I or should I not have felt ashamed of that action? The questions were idle and useless, for the gun was already lying before me and there was not a shadow of doubt in my mind that *it* was going to take place for certain, but they excited and maddened me. It seemed to me that I could not die now without having settled something first. The little girl, in fact, had saved me, for by these questions I put off my own execution.

Meanwhile things had grown more quiet in the captain's room: they had finished their card game and were getting ready to turn in for the night, and now were only grumbling and swearing at each other in a halfhearted sort of way. It was at that moment that I suddenly fell asleep in my armchair at the table, a thing that had never happened to me before.

I fell asleep without being aware of it at all. Dreams, as we all know, are very curious things: certain incidents in them are presented with quite uncanny vividness, each detail executed with the finishing touch of a jeweller, while others you leap across as though entirely unaware of, for instance, space and time. Dreams seem to be induced not by reason but by desire, not by the head but by the heart, and yet what clever tricks my reason has sometimes played on me in dreams! And furthermore what incomprehensible things happen to it in a dream. My brother, for instance, died five years ago. I sometimes dream about him: he takes a keen interest in my affairs, we are both very interested, and yet I know very well all through my dream that my brother is dead and buried. How is it that I am not surprised that, though dead, he is here beside me, doing his best to help me? Why does my reason accept all this without the slightest hesitation? But enough. Let me tell you about my dream. Yes, I dreamed that dream that night. My dream of the third of November. They are making fun of me now by saying that it was only a dream. But what does it matter whether it was a dream or not, so long as that dream revealed the Truth to me? For once you have recognised the truth and seen it, you know it is the one and only truth and that there can be no other, whether you are asleep or awake. But never mind. Let it be a dream, but remember that I had intended to cut short by suicide the life that means so much to us, and that my dream—my dream—oh, it revealed to me a new, grand, regenerated, strong life!

Listen.

## III

I have said that I fell asleep imperceptibly and even while I seemed to be revolving the same thoughts again in my mind. Suddenly I dreamed that I picked up the gun and, sitting in my armchair, pointed it straight at my heart—at my heart, and not at my head. For I had firmly resolved to shoot myself through the head, through the right temple, to be precise. Having aimed the gun at my breast, I paused for a second or two, and suddenly my candle, the table and the wall began moving and swaying before me. I fired quickly.

In a dream you sometimes fall from a great height, or you are being murdered or beaten, but you never feel any pain unless you really manage somehow or other to hurt yourself in bed, when you feel pain and almost always wake up from it. So it was in my dream: I did not feel any pain, but it seemed as though with my shot everything within me was shaken and everything was suddenly extinguished, and a terrible darkness descended all around me. I seemed to have become blind and dumb. I was lying on something hard, stretched out full length on my back. I saw nothing and could not make the slightest movement. All round me people were walking and shouting. The captain was yelling in his deep bass voice, the landlady was screaming and—suddenly another hiatus, and I was being carried in a closed coffin. I could feel the coffin swaying and I was thinking about it, and for the first time the idea flashed through my mind that I was dead, dead as a doornail, that I knew it, that there was not the least doubt about it, that I could neither see nor move, and yet I could feel and reason. But I was soon reconciled to that and, as usually happens in dreams, I accepted the facts without questioning them.

And now I was buried in the earth. They all went away, and I was left alone, entirely alone. I did not move. Whenever before I imagined how I should be buried in a grave, there was only one sensation I actually associated with the grave, namely, that of damp and cold. And so it was now. I felt that I was very cold, especially in the tips of my toes, but I felt nothing else.

I lay in my grave and, strange to say, I did not expect anything, accepting the idea that a dead man had nothing to expect as an incontestable fact. But it was damp. I don't know how long a time passed, whether an hour, or several days, or many days. But suddenly a drop of water, which had seeped through the lid of the coffin, fell on my closed left eye. It was followed by another drop a minute later, then after another minute by another drop, and so on. One drop every minute. All at once deep indignation blazed up in my heart, and I suddenly felt a twinge of physical pain in it. "That's my wound," I thought. "It's the shot I fired. There's a bullet there. . . ." And drop after drop still kept falling every minute on my closed eyelid. And suddenly I called (not with my voice, for I was motionless, but with the whole of my being) upon Him who was responsible for all that was happening to me:

"Whoever Thou art, and if anything more rational exists than what is happening here, let it, I pray Thee, come to pass here too. But if Thou art revenging Thyself for my senseless act of self-destruction by the infamy and absurdity of life after death, then know that no torture that may be inflicted upon me can ever equal the contempt which I shall go on feeling in silence, though my martyrdom last for aeons upon aeons!"

I made this appeal and was silent. The dead silence went on for almost a minute, and one more drop fell on my closed eyelid, but I knew, I knew and believed infinitely and unshakably that everything would without a doubt change immediately. And then my grave was opened. I don't know, that is, whether it was opened or dug open, but I was seized by some dark and unknown being and we found ourselves in space. I suddenly regained my sight. It was a pitch-black night. Never, never had there been such darkness! We were flying through space at a terrific speed and we had already left the earth behind us. I did not question the being who was carrying me. I was proud and waited. I was telling myself that I was not afraid, and I was filled with admiration at the thought that I was not afraid. I cannot remember how long we were flying, nor can I give you an idea of the time; it all happened as it always does happen in dreams when you leap over space and time and the laws of nature and reason, and only pause at the points which are especially dear to your heart. All I remember is that I suddenly beheld a little star in the darkness.

"Is that Sirius?" I asked, feeling suddenly unable to restrain myself, for I had made up my mind not to ask any questions.

"No," answered the being who was carrying me, "that is the same star you saw between the clouds when you were coming home."

I knew that its face bore some resemblance to a human face. It is a strange fact but I did not like that being, and I even felt an intense aversion for it. I had expected complete non-existence and that was why I had shot myself through the heart. And yet there I was in the hands of a being, not human of course, but which *was,* which existed. "So there is life beyond the grave!" I thought with the curious irrelevance of a dream, but at heart I remained essentially unchanged. "If I must *be* again," I thought, "and live again at someone's unalterable behest, I won't be defeated and humiliated!"

"You know I'm afraid of you and that's why you despise me," I said suddenly to my companion, unable to refrain from the humiliating remark with its implied admission, and feeling my own humiliation in my heart like the sharp prick of a needle.

He did not answer me, but I suddenly felt that I was not despised, that no one was laughing at me, that no one was even pitying me, and that our journey had a purpose, an unknown and mysterious purpose that concerned only me. Fear was steadily growing in my heart. Something was communicated to me from my silent companion—mutely but agonisingly—and it seemed to permeate my whole being. We were speeding through dark and unknown regions of space. I had long since lost sight of the constellations familiar to me. I knew that there were stars in the heavenly spaces whose light took thousands of millions of years to reach the earth. Possibly we were already flying through those spaces. I expected something in the terrible anguish that wrung my heart. And suddenly a strangely familiar and incredibly nostalgic feeling shook me to the very core: I suddenly caught sight of our sun! I knew that it could not possibly be *our* sun that gave birth to our earth, and that we were millions of miles away from our sun, but for some unknown reason I recognized with every fibre of my being that it was precisely the same sun as ours, its exact copy and twin. A sweet, nostalgic feeling filled my heart with rapture: the old familiar power of the same light which had given me life stirred an echo in my heart and revived it, and I felt the same life stirring within me for the first time since I had been in the grave.

"But if it is the sun, if it's exactly the same sun as ours," I cried, "then where is the earth?"

And my companion pointed to a little star twinkling in the darkness with an emerald light. We were making straight for it.

"But are such repetitions possible in the universe? Can that be nature's law? And if that is an earth there, is it the same earth as ours? Just the same poor, unhappy, but dear, dear earth, and beloved for ever and ever? Arousing like our earth the same poignant love for herself even in the most ungrateful of her children?" I kept crying, deeply moved by an uncontrollable, rapturous love for the dear old earth I had left behind.

The face of the poor little girl I had treated so badly flashed through my mind.

"You shall see it all," answered my companion, and a strange sadness sounded in his voice.

But we were rapidly approaching the planet. It was growing before my eyes. I could already distinguish the ocean, the outlines of Europe, and suddenly a strange feeling of some great and sacred jealously blazed up in my heart.

"How is such a repetition possible and why? I love, I can only love the earth I've left behind, stained with my blood when, ungrateful wretch that I am, I extinguished my life by shooting myself through the heart. But never, never have I ceased to love that earth, and even on the night I parted from it I loved it perhaps more poignantly than ever. Is there suffering on this new earth? On our earth we can truly love only with suffering and through suffering! We know not how to love otherwise. We know no other love. I want suffering in order to love. I want and thirst this very minute to kiss, with tears streaming down my cheeks, the one and only earth I have left behind. I don't want, I won't accept life on any other! . . ."

But my companion had already left me. Suddenly, and without as it were being aware of it myself, I stood on this other earth in the bright light of a sunny day, fair and beautiful as paradise. I believe I was standing on one of the islands which on our earth form the Greek archipelago, or somewhere on the coast of the mainland close to this archipelago. Oh, everything was just as it is with us, except that everything seemed to be bathed in the radiance of some public festival and of some great and holy triumph attained at last. The gentle emerald sea softly lapped the shore and kissed it with manifest, visible, almost conscious love. Tall, beautiful trees stood in all the glory of their green luxuriant foliage, and their innumerable leaves (I am sure of that) welcomed me with their soft, tender rustle, and seemed to utter sweet words of love. The lush grass blazed with bright and fragrant flowers. Birds were flying in flocks through the air and, without being afraid of me, alighted on my shoulders and hands and joyfully beat against me with their sweet fluttering wings. And at last I saw and came to know the people of this blessed earth. They came to me themselves. They surrounded me. They kissed me. Children of the sun, children of their sun—oh, how beautiful they were! Never on our earth had I beheld such beauty in man. Only perhaps in our children during the very first years of their life could one have found a remote, though faint, reflection of this beauty. The eyes of these happy people shone with a bright lustre. Their faces were radiant with understanding and a serenity of mind that had reached its greatest fulfillment. Those faces were joyous; in the words and voices of these people there was a child-like gladness. Oh, at the first glance at their faces I at once understood all, all! It was an earth unstained by the Fall, inhabited by people who had not sinned and who lived in the same paradise as that in which, according to the legends of mankind, our first parents lived before they sinned, with the only difference that all the earth here was everywhere the same paradise. These people, laughing happily, thronged round me and overwhelmed me with their caresses; they took me home with them, and each of them was anxious to set my mind at peace. Oh, they asked me no questions, but seemed to know everything already (that was the impression I got), and they longed to remove every trace of suffering from my face as soon as possible.

## IV

Well, you see, again let me repeat: All right, let us assume it was only a dream! But the sensation of the love of those innocent and beautiful people has remained with me for ever, and I can feel that their love is even now flowing out to me from over there. I have seen them myself. I have known them thoroughly and been convinced. I loved them and I suffered for them afterwards. Oh, I knew at once even all the time that there were many things about them I should never be able to understand. To me, a modern Russian progressive and a despicable citizen of Petersburg, it seemed inexplicable that, knowing so much, they knew nothing of our science, for instance. But I soon realised that their knowledge was derived from, and fostered by emotions other than those to which we were accustomed on earth, and that their aspirations, too, were quite different. They desired nothing. They were at peace with themselves. They did not strive to gain knowledge of life as we strive to understand it because their lives were full. But their knowledge was higher and deeper than the knowledge we derive from our science; for our science seeks to explain what life is and strives to understand it in order to teach others how to live, while they knew how to live without science. I understood that, but I couldn't understand their knowledge. They pointed out their trees to me, and I could not understand the intense love with which they looked on them; it was as though they were talking with beings like themselves. And, you know, I don't think I am exaggerating in saying that they talked with them! Yes, they had discovered their language, and I am sure the trees understood them. They looked upon all nature like that—the animals which lived peaceably with them and did not attack them, but loved them, conquered by their love for them. They pointed out the stars to me and talked to me about them in a way that I could not understand, but I am certain that in some curious way they communed with the stars in the heavens, not only in thought, but in some actual, living way. Oh, these people were not concerned whether I understood them or not; they loved me without it. But I too knew that they would never be able to understand me, and for that reason I hardly ever spoke to them about our earth. I merely kissed the earth on which they lived in their presence, and worshipped them without any words. And they saw that and let me worship them without being ashamed that I was worshipping them, for they themselves loved much. They did not suffer for me when, weeping, I sometimes kissed their feet, for in their hearts they were joyfully aware of the strong affection with which they would return my love. At times I asked myself in amazement how they had managed never to offend a person like me and not once arouse in a person like me a feeling of jealousy and envy. Many times I asked myself how I—a braggart and a liar—could refrain from telling them all I knew of science and philosophy, of which of course they had no idea? How it had never occurred to me to impress them with my store of learning, or impart my learning to them out of the love I bore them?

They were playful and high-spirited like children. They wandered about their beautiful woods and groves, they sang their beautiful songs, they lived on simple food—the fruits of their trees, the honey from their woods, and the milk of the animals that loved them. To obtain their food and clothes, they did not work very hard or long. They knew love and they begot children, but I never noticed in them those outbursts of *cruel* sensuality which overtake almost everybody on our earth, whether man or woman, and are the only source of almost every sin of our human race. They rejoiced in their new-born children as new sharers in their bliss. There were no quarrels or jealousy among them, and they did not even know what the words meant. Their children were the children of them all, for they were all one family. There was scarcely any illness among them, though there was death; but their old people died peacefully, as though falling asleep, surrounded by the people who took leave of them, blessing them and smiling at them, and themselves receiving with bright smiles the farewell wishes of their friends. I never saw grief or tears on those occasions. What I did see was love that seemed to reach the point of rapture, but it was a gentle, self-sufficient, and contemplative rapture. There was reason to believe that they communicated with the departed after death, and that their earthly union was not cut short by death. They found it almost impossible to understand me when I questioned them about life eternal, but apparently they were so convinced of it in their minds that for them it was no question at all. They had no places of worship, but they had a certain awareness of a constant, uninterrupted, and living union with the Universe at large. They had no specific religions, but instead they had a certain knowledge that when their earthly joy had reached the limits imposed upon it by nature, they—both the living and the dead—would reach a state of still closer communion with the Universe at large. They looked forward to that moment with joy, but without haste and without pining for it, as though already possessing it in the vague stirrings of their hearts, which they communicated to each other.

In the evening, before going to sleep, they were fond of gathering together and singing in melodious and harmonious choirs. In their songs they expressed all the sensations the parting day had given them. They praised it and bade it farewell. They praised nature, the earth, the sea, and the woods. They were also fond of composing songs about one another, and they praised each other like children. Their songs were very simple, but they sprang straight from the heart and they touched the heart. And not only in their songs alone, but they seemed to spend all their lives in perpetual praise of one another. It seemed to be a universal and all-embracing love for each other. Some of their songs were solemn and ecstatic, and I was scarcely able to understand them at all. While understanding the words, I could never entirely fathom their meaning. It remained somehow beyond the grasp of my reason, and yet it sank unconsciously deeper and deeper into my heart. I often told them that I had had a presentiment of it years ago and that all that joy and glory had been perceived by me while I was still on our earth as a nostalgic yearning, bordering at times on unendurably poignant sorrow; that I had had a presentiment of them all and of their glory in the dreams of my heart and in the reveries of my soul; that often on our earth I could not look at the setting sun without tears. . . . That there always was a sharp pang of anguish in my hatred of the men of our earth; why could I not hate them without loving them too? why could I not forgive them? And in my love for them, too, there was a sharp pang of anguish: why could I not love them without hating them? They listened to me, and I could tell that they did not know what I was talking about. But I was not sorry to have spoken to them of it, for I knew that they appreciated how much and how anxiously I yearned for those I had forsaken. Oh yes, when they looked at me with their dear eyes full of love, when I realized that in their presence my heart, too, became as innocent and truthful as theirs, I did not regret my inability to understand them, either. The sensation of the fullness of life left me breathless, and I worshipped them in silence.

Oh, everyone laughs in my face now and everyone assures me that I could not possibly have seen and felt anything so definite, but was merely conscious of a sensation that arose in my own feverish heart, and that I invented all those details myself when I woke up. And when I told them that they were probably right, good Lord, what mirth that admission of mine caused and how they laughed at me! Why, of course, I was overpowered by the mere sensation of that dream and it alone survived in my sorely wounded heart. But none the less the real shapes and forms of my dream, that is, those I actually saw at the very time of my dream, were filled with such harmony and were so enchanting and beautiful, and so intensely true, that on awakening I was indeed unable to clothe them in our feeble words so that they were bound as it were to become blurred in my mind; so is it any wonder that perhaps unconsciously I was myself afterwards driven to make up the details which I could not help distorting, particularly in view of my passionate desire to convey some of them at least as quickly as I could. But that does not mean that I have no right to believe that it all did happen. As a matter of fact, it was quite possibly a thousand times better, brighter, and more joyful than I describe it. What if it was only a dream? All that couldn't possibly not have been. And do you know, I think I'll tell you a secret: perhaps it was no dream at all! For what happened afterwards was so awful, so horribly true, that it couldn't possibly have been a mere coinage of my brain seen in a dream. Granted that my heart was responsible for my dream, but could my heart alone have been responsible for the awful truth of what happened to me afterwards? Surely my paltry heart and my vacillating and trivial mind could not have risen to such a revelation of truth! Oh, judge for yourselves: I have been concealing it all the time, but now I will tell you the whole truth. The fact is, I—corrupted them all!

## V

Yes, yes, it ended in my corrupting them all! How it could have happened I do not know, but I remember it clearly. The dream encompassed thousands of years and left in me only a vague sensation of the whole. I only know that the cause of the Fall was I. Like a horrible trichina, like the germ of the plague infecting whole kingdoms, so did I infect with myself all that happy earth that knew no sin before me. They learnt to lie, and they grew to appreciate the beauty of a lie. Oh, perhaps, it all began *innocently*, with a jest, with a desire to show off, with amorous play, and perhaps indeed only with a germ, but this germ made its way into their hearts and they liked it. The voluptuousness was soon born, voluptuousness begot jealousy, and jealousy—cruelty. . . . Oh, I don't know, I can't remember, but soon, very soon the first blood was shed; they were shocked and horrified, and they began to separate and to shun one another. They formed alliances but it was one against another. Recriminations began, reproaches. They came to know shame, and they made shame into a virtue. The conception of honour was born, and every alliance raised its own standard. They began torturing animals, and the animals ran away from them into the forests and became their enemies. A struggle began for separation, for isolation, for personality, for mine and thine. They began talking in different languages. They came to know sorrow, and they loved sorrow. They thirsted for suffering, and they said that Truth could only be attained through suffering. It was then that science made its appearance among them. When they became wicked, they began talking of brotherhood and humanity and understood the meaning of those ideas. When they became guilty of crimes, they invented justice, and drew up whole codes of law, and to ensure the carrying out of their laws they erected a guillotine. They only vaguely remembered what they had lost, and they would not believe that they ever were happy and innocent. They even laughed at the possibility of their former happiness and called it a dream. They could not even imagine it in any definite shape or form, but the strange and wonderful thing was that though they had lost faith in their former state of happiness and called it a fairy-tale, they longed so much to be happy and innocent once more that, like children, they succumbed to the desire of their hearts, glorified this desire, built temples, and began offering up prayers to their own idea, their own "desire," and at the same time firmly believed that it could not be realised and brought about, though they still worshipped it and adored it with tears. And yet if they could have in one way or another returned to the state of happy innocence they had lost, and if someone had shown it to them again and had asked them whether they desired to go back to it, they would certainly have refused. The answer they gave me was, "What if we are dishonest, cruel, and unjust? We *know* it and we are sorry for it, and we torment ourselves for it, and inflict pain upon ourselves, and punish ourselves more perhaps than the merciful Judge who will judge us and whose name we do not know. But we have science and with its aid we shall again discover truth, though we shall accept it only when we perceive it with our reason. Knowledge is higher than feeling, and the consciousness of life is higher than life. Science will give us wisdom. Wisdom will reveal to us the laws. And the knowledge of the laws of happiness is higher than happiness." That is what they said to me, and having uttered those words, each of them began to love himself better than anyone else, and indeed they could not do otherwise. Every one of them became so jealous of his own personality that he strove with might and main to belittle and humble it in others; and therein he saw the whole purpose of his life. Slavery made its appearance, even voluntary slavery: the weak eagerly submitted themselves to the will of the strong on condition that the strong helped them to oppress those who were weaker than themselves. Saints made their appearance, saints who came to these people with tears and told them of their pride, of their loss of proportion and harmony, of their loss of shame. They were laughed to scorn and stoned to death. Their sacred blood was spilt on the threshold of the temples. But then men arose who began to wonder how they could all be united again, so that everybody should, without ceasing to love himself best of all, not interfere with everybody else and so that all of them should live together in a society which would at least seem to be founded on mutual understanding. Whole wars were fought over this idea. All the combatants at one and the same time firmly believed that science, wisdom, and the instinct of self-preservation would in the end force mankind to unite into a harmonious and intelligent society, and therefore, to hasten matters, the "very wise" did their best to exterminate as rapidly as possible the "not so wise" who did not understand their idea, so as to prevent them from interfering with its triumph. But the instinct of self-preservation began to weaken rapidly. Proud and voluptuous men appeared who frankly demanded all or nothing. In order to obtain everything they did not hesitate to resort to violence, and if it failed—to suicide. Religions were founded to propagate the cult of non-existence and self-destruction for the sake of the everlasting peace in nothingness. At last these people grew weary of their senseless labours and suffering appeared on their faces, and these people proclaimed that suffering was beauty, for in suffering alone was there thought. They glorified suffering in their songs. I walked among them, wringing my hands and weeping over them, but I loved them perhaps more than before when there was no sign of suffering in their faces and when they were innocent and—oh, so beautiful! I loved the earth they had polluted even more than when it had been a paradise, and only because sorrow had made its appearance on it. Alas, I always loved sorrow and affliction, but only for myself, only for myself; for them I wept now, for I pitied them. I stretched out my hands to them, accusing, cursing, and despising myself. I told them that I alone was responsible for it all—I alone; that it was I who had brought them corruption, contamination, and lies! I implored them to crucify me, and I taught them how to make the cross. I could not kill myself; I had not the courage to do it; but I longed to receive martyrdom at their hands. I thirsted for martyrdom, I yearned for my blood to be shed to the last drop in torment and suffering. But they only laughed at me, and in the end they began looking upon me as a madman. They justified me. They said that they had got what they themselves wanted and that what was now could not have been otherwise. At last they told me I was becoming dangerous to them and that they would lock me up in a lunatic asylum if I did not hold my peace. Then sorrow entered my soul with such force that my heart was wrung and I felt as though I were dying, and then—well, then I awoke.

It was morning, that is, the sun had not risen yet, but it was about six o'clock. When I came to, I found myself in the same armchair, my candle had burnt out, in the captain's room they were asleep, and silence, so rare in our house, reigned around. The first thing I did was to jump up in great amazement. Nothing like this had ever happened to me before, not even so far as the most trivial details were concerned.

Never, for instance, had I fallen asleep like this in my armchair. Then, suddenly, as I was standing and coming to myself, I caught sight of my gun lying there ready and loaded. But I pushed it away from me at once! Oh, how I longed for life, life! I lifted up my hands and called upon eternal Truth—no, not called upon it, but wept. Rapture, infinite and boundless rapture intoxicated me. Yes, life and—preaching! I made up my mind to preach from that very moment and, of course, to go on preaching all my life. I am going to preach, I want to preach. What? Why, truth. For I have beheld truth, I have beheld it with mine own eyes, I have beheld it in all its glory!

And since then I have been preaching. Moreover, I love all who laugh at me more than all the rest. Why that is so, I don't know and I cannot explain, but let it be so. They say that even now I often get muddled and confused and that if I am getting muddled and confused now, what will be later on? It is perfectly true. I do get muddles and confused and it is quite possible that I shall be getting worse later. And, of course, I shall get muddled several times before I find out how to preach, that is, what words to use and what deeds to perform, for that is all very difficult! All this is even now as clear to me as daylight, but, pray, tell me who does not get muddled and confused? And yet all follow the same path, at least all strive to achieve the same thing, from the philosopher to the lowest criminal, only by different roads. It is an old truth, but this is what is new: I cannot even get very much muddled and confused. For I have beheld the Truth. I have beheld it and I know that people can be happy and beautiful without losing their ability to live on earth. I will not and I cannot believe that evil is the normal condition among men. And yet they all laugh at this faith of mine. But how can I help believing it? I have beheld it—the Truth—it is not as though I had invented it with my mind: I have beheld it, I have beheld it, and the *living image* of it has filled my soul for ever. I have beheld it in all its glory and I cannot believe that it cannot exist among men. So how can I grow muddled and confused? I shall of course lose my way and I'm afraid that now and again I may speak with words that are not my own, but not for long: the living image of what I beheld will always be with me and it will always correct me and lead me back on to the right path. Oh, I'm in fine fettle, and I am of good cheer. I will go on and on for a thousand years, if need be. Do you know, at first I did not mean to tell you that I corrupted them, but that was a mistake—there you have my first mistake! But Truth whispered to me that I was *lying*, and so preserved me and set me on the right path. But I'm afraid I do not know how to establish a heaven on earth, for I do not know how to put it into words. After my dream I lost the knack of putting things into words. At least, onto the most necessary and most important words. But never mind, I shall go on and I shall keep on talking, for I have indeed beheld it with my own eyes, though I cannot describe what I saw. It is this the scoffers do not understand. "He had a dream," they say, "a vision, a hallucination!" Oh dear, is this all they have to say? Do they really think that is very clever? And how proud they are! A dream! What is a dream? And what about our life? Is that not a dream too? I will say more: even—yes, even if this never comes to pass, even if there never is a heaven on earth (that, at any rate, I can see very well!), even then I shall go on preaching. And really how simple it all is: in one day, *in one hour,* everything could be arranged at once! The main thing is to love your neighbour as yourself—that is the main thing, and that is everything, for nothing else matters. Once you do that, you will discover at once how everything can be arranged. And yet it is an old truth, a truth that has been told over and over again, but in spite of that it finds no place among men! "The consciousness of life is higher than life, the knowledge of happiness is higher than happiness"—that is what we have to fight against! And I shall, I shall fight against it! If only we all wanted it, everything could be arranged immediately.

And—I did find that little girl. . . . And I shall go on! I shall go on!

# Arthur Conan Doyle

## (1859–1930)

Though best known for creating Sherlock Holmes, Sir Arthur Conan Doyle spent a great deal of his life obsessed with spiritualism and the occult. Doyle first chose to follow a career in medicine and attended the University of Edinburgh. He received his degree in 1880 and soon opened his own practice. In 1885 he married Louisa Hawkins and, three years later, published *A Study in Scarlet* (1888), his first novel to feature Sherlock Holmes. Though Doyle preferred his next novel, *Micah Clark* (1889), the creation of Holmes was what catapulted him to fame. Doyle considered the detective stories to be, at best, "commercial." When he killed Holmes off in "The Final Problem" (1893), 20,000 subscribers of *The Strand* magazine canceled their subscriptions and wore mourning bands. As his wife's health began to deteriorate because of tuberculosis, Doyle became increasingly fascinated with "life beyond the veil." In 1901 Holmes resurfaced in *The Hound of the Baskervilles*, which Doyle advertised as a previously untold story, and the detective was resurrected in "The Empty House" (1903).

Louisa died in 1906, and Doyle suffered from depression for several months afterwards. In 1907 he married Jean Leckie, whom he had been seeing since 1897. Doyle attempted several plays, but he continued to lose money on them. Only after writing *The Speckled Band* (1912), which featured Holmes, did Doyle make any money from his "stage work." Both Doyle and Leckie became increasingly fascinated with the occult, particularly after the death of Doyle's son Kingsley in World War I. Doyle published several books on fairies, including *The Evidence for Fairies* (1921) and *Fairies Photographed* (1921). He continued to explore the realms of spiritualism until his death in 1930.

## A Scandal in Bohemia

To Sherlock Holmes she is always the woman. I have seldom heard him mention her under any other name. In his eyes she eclipses and predominates the whole of her sex. It was not that he felt any emotion akin to love for Irene Adler. All emotions, and that one particularly, were abhorrent to his cold, precise but admirably balanced mind. He was, I take it, the most perfect reasoning and observing machine that the world had seen, but as a lover he would have placed himself in a false position. He never spoke of the softer passions, save with a gibe and a sneer. They were admirable things for the observer—excellent for drawing the veil from men's motives and actions. But for the trained reasoner to admit such intrusions into his own delicate and finely adjusted temperament was to introduce a distracting factor which might throw a doubt upon all his mental results. Grit in a sensitive instrument, or a crack in one of his own high-power lenses, would not be more disturbing than a strong emotion in a nature such as his. And yet there was but one woman to him, and that woman was the late Irene Adler, of dubious and questionable memory.

I had seen little of Holmes lately. My marriage had drifted us away from each other. My own complete happiness, and the home-centred interests which rise up around the man who first finds himself master of his own establishment, were sufficient to absorb all my attention, while Holmes, who loathed every form of society with his whole Bohemian soul, remained in our lodgings in Baker Street, buried among his old books, and alternating from week to week between cocaine and ambition, the drowsiness of the drug, and the fierce energy of his own keen nature. He was still, as ever, deeply attracted by the study of crime, and occupied his immense faculties and extraordinary powers of observation in following out those clues, and clearing up those mysteries which had been abandoned as hopeless by the official police. From time to time I heard some vague account of his doings: of his summons to Odessa in the case of the Trepoff murder, of his clearing up of the singular tragedy of the Atkinson brothers at Trincomalee, and finally of the mission which he had accomplished so delicately and successfully for the reigning family of Holland. Beyond these signs of his activity, however, which I merely shared with all the readers of the daily press, I knew little of my former friend and companion.

One night—it was on the twentieth of March, 1888—I was returning from a journey to a patient (for I had now returned to civil practice), when my way led me through Baker Street. As I passed the well-remembered door, which must always be associated in my mind with my wooing, and with the dark incidents of the Study in Scarlet, I was seized with a keen desire to see Holmes again, and to know how he was employing his extraordinary powers. His rooms were brilliantly lit, and, even as I looked up, I saw his tall, spare figure pass twice in a dark silhouette against the blind. He was pacing the room swiftly, eagerly, with his head sunk upon his chest and his hands clasped behind him. To me, who knew his every mood and habit, his attitude and manner told their own story. He was at work again. He had risen out of his drug-created dreams and was hot upon the scent of some new problem. I rang the bell and was shown up to the chamber which had formerly been in part my own.

His manner was not effusive. It seldom was; but he was glad, I think, to see me. With hardly a word spoken, but with a kindly eye, he waved me to an armchair, threw across his case of cigars, and indicated a spirit case and a gasogene in the corner. Then he stood before the fire and looked me over in his singular introspective fashion.

"Wedlock suits you," he remarked. "I think, Watson, that you have put on seven and a half pounds since I saw you."

"Seven!" I answered.

"Indeed, I should have thought a little more. Just a trifle more, I fancy, Watson. And in practice again, I observe. You did not tell me that you intended to go into harness."

"Then, how do you know?"

"I see it, I deduce it. How do I know that you have been getting yourself very wet lately, and that you have a most clumsy and careless servant girl?"

"My dear Holmes," said I, "this is too much. You would certainly have been burned, had you lived a few centuries ago. It is true that I had a country walk on Thursday and came home in a dreadful mess, but as I have changed my clothes I can't imagine how you deduce it. As to Mary Jane, she is incorrigible, and my wife has given her notice, but there, again, I fail to see how you work it out."

He chuckled to himself and rubbed his long, nervous hands together.

"It is simplicity itself," said he; "my eyes tell me that on the inside of your left shoe, just where the firelight strikes it, the leather is scored by six almost parallel cuts. Obviously they have been caused by someone who has very carelessly scraped round the edges of the sole in order to remove crusted mud from it. Hence, you see, my double deduction that you had been out in vile weather, and that you had a particularly malignant boot-slitting specimen of the London slavey. As to your practice, if a gentleman walks into my rooms smelling of iodoform, with a black mark of nitrate of silver upon his right forefinger, and a bulge on the right side of his top-hat to show where he has secreted his stethoscope, I must be dull, indeed, if I do not pronounce him to be an active member of the medical profession."

I could not help laughing at the ease with which he explained his process of deduction. "When I hear you give your reasons," I remarked, "the thing always appears to me to be so ridiculously simple that I could easily do it myself, though at each successive instance of your reasoning I am baffled until you explain your process. And yet I believe that my eyes are as good as yours."

"Quite so," he answered, lighting a cigarette, and throwing himself down into an armchair. "You see, but you do not observe. The distinction is clear. For example, you have frequently seen the steps which lead up from the hall to this room."

"Frequently."

"How often?"

"Well, some hundreds of times."

"Then how many are there?"

"How many? I don't know."

"Quite so! You have not observed. And yet you have seen. That is just my point. Now, I know that there are seventeen steps, because I have both seen and observed. By the way, since you are interested in these little problems, and since you are good enough to chronicle one or two of my trifling experiences, you may be interested in this." He threw over a sheet of thick, pink-tinted note-paper which had been lying open upon the table. "It came by the last post," said he. "Read it aloud."

The note was undated, and without either signature or address.

> "There will call upon you to-night, at a quarter to eight o'clock [it said], a gentleman who desires to consult you upon a matter of the very deepest moment. Your recent services to one of the royal houses of Europe have shown that you are one who may safely be trusted with matters which are of an importance which can hardly be exaggerated. This account of you we have from all quarters received. Be in your chamber then at that hour, and do not take it amiss if your visitor wear a mask.

"This is indeed a mystery," I remarked. "What do you imagine that it means?"

"I have no data yet. It is a capital mistake to theorize before one has data. Insensibly one begins to twist facts to suit theories, instead of theories to suit facts. But the note itself. What do you deduce from it?"

I carefully examined the writing, and the paper upon which it was written.

"The man who wrote it was presumably well to do," I remarked, endeavouring to imitate my companion's processes. "Such paper could not be bought under half a crown a packet. It is peculiarly strong and stiff."

"Peculiar—that is the very word," said Holmes. "It is not an English paper at all. Hold it up to the light."

I did so, and saw a large "E" with a small "g" a "P," and a large "G" with a small "f" woven into the texture of the paper.

"What do you make of that?" asked Holmes.

"The name of the maker, no doubt; or his monogram, rather."

"Not at all. The 'G' with the small 't' stands for 'Gesellschaft,' which is the German for 'Company.' It is a customary contraction like our 'Co.' 'P,' of course, stands for 'Papier.' Now for the 'Eg.' Let us glance at our Continental Gazetteer." He took down a heavy brown volume from his shelves. "Eglow, Eglonitz—here we are, Egria. It is in a German-speaking country—in Bohemia, not far from Carlsbad. 'Remarkable as being the scene of the death of Wallenstein, and for its numerous glass-factories and paper-mills.' Ha, ha, my boy, what do you make of that?" His eyes sparkled, and he sent up a great blue triumphant cloud from his cigarette.

"The paper was made in Bohemia," I said.

"Precisely. And the man who wrote the note is a German. Do you note the peculiar construction of the sentence—'This account of you we have from all quarters received.' A Frenchman or Russian could not have written that. It is the German who is so uncourteous to his verbs. It only remains, therefore, to discover what is wanted by this German who writes upon Bohemian paper and prefers wearing a mask to showing his face. And here he comes, if I am not mistaken, to resolve all our doubts."

As he spoke there was the sharp sound of horses' hoofs and grating wheels against the curb, followed by a sharp pull at the bell. Holmes whistled.

"A pair, by the sound," said he. "Yes," he continued, glancing out of the window. "A nice little brougham and a pair of beauties. A hundred and fifty guineas apiece. There's money in this case, Watson, if there is nothing else."

"I think that I had better go, Holmes."

"Not a bit, Doctor. Stay where you are. I am lost without my Boswell. And this promises to be interesting. It would be a pity to miss it."

"But your client—"

"Never mind him. I may want your help, and so may he. Here he comes. Sit down in that armchair, Doctor, and give us your best attention."

A slow and heavy step, which had been heard upon the stairs and in the passage, paused immediately outside the door. Then there was a loud and authoritative tap.

"Come in!" said Holmes.

A man entered who could hardly have been less than six feet six inches in height, with the chest and limbs of Hercules. His dress was rich with a richness which would, in England, be looked upon as akin to bad taste. Heavy bands of astrakhan were slashed across the sleeves and fronts of his double-breasted coat, while the deep blue cloak which was thrown over his shoulders was lined with flame-coloured silk and secured at the neck with a brooch which consisted of a single flaming beryl. Boots which extended halfway up his calves, and which were trimmed at the tops with rich brown fur, completed the impression of barbaric opulence which was suggested by his whole appearance. He carried a broad-brimmed hat in his hand, while he wore across the upper part of his face, extending down past the cheekbones, a black vizard mask, which he had apparently adjusted that very moment, for his hand was still raised to it as he entered. From the lower part of the face he appeared to be a man of strong character, with a thick, hanging lip, and a long, straight chin suggestive of resolution pushed to the length of obstinacy.

"You had my note?" he asked with a deep harsh voice and a strongly marked German accent. "I told you that I would call." He looked from one to the other of us, as if uncertain which to address.

"Pray take a seat," said Holmes. "This is my friend and colleague, Dr. Watson, who is occasionally good enough to help me in my cases. Whom have I the honour to address?"

"You may address me as the Count Von Kramm, a Bohemian nobleman. I understand that this gentleman, your friend, is a man of honour and discretion, whom I may trust with a matter of the most extreme importance. If not, I should much prefer to communicate with you alone."

I rose to go, but Holmes caught me by the wrist and pushed me back into my chair. "It is both, or none," said he. "You may say before the gentleman anything which you may say to me."

The Count shrugged his broad shoulders. "Then I must begin," said he, "by binding you both to absolute secrecy for two years; at the end of that time the matter will be of no importance. At present it is not too much to say that it is of such weight it may have an influence upon European history."

"I promise," said Holmes.

"And I."

"You will excuse this mask," continued our strange visitor. "The august person who employs me wishes his agent to be unknown to you, and I may confess at once that the title by which I have just called myself is not exactly my own."

"I was aware of it," said Holmes drily.

"The circumstances are of great delicacy, and every precaution has to be taken to quench what might grow to be an immense scandal and seriously compromise one of the reigning families of Europe. To speak plainly, the matter implicates the great House of Ormstein, hereditary kings of Bohemia."

"I was also aware of that," murmured Holmes, settling himself down in his armchair and closing his eyes.

Our visitor glanced with some apparent surprise at the languid, lounging figure of the man who had been no doubt depicted to him as the most incisive reasoner and most energetic agent in Europe. Holmes reopened his eyes and looked impatiently at his gigantic client.

"If your Majesty would condescend to state your case," he remarked, "I should be better able to advise you."

The man sprang from his chair and paced up and down the room in uncontrollable agitation. Then, with a gesture of desperation, he tore the mask from his face and hurled it upon the ground. "You are right," he cried; "I am the King. Why should I attempt to conceal it?"

"Why, indeed?" murmured Holmes. "Your Majesty had not spoken before I was aware that I was addressing Wilhelm Gottsreich Sigismond von Ormstein, Grand Duke of CasselFelstein, and hereditary King of Bohemia."

"But you can understand," said our strange visitor, sitting down once more and passing his hand over his high white forehead, "you can understand that I am not accustomed to doing such business in my own person. Yet the matter was so delicate that I could not confide it to an agent without putting myself in his power. I have come incognito from Prague for the purpose of consulting you."

"Then, pray consult," said Holmes, shutting his eyes once more.

"The facts are briefly these: Some five years ago, during a lengthy visit to Warsaw, I made the acquaintance of the well known adventuress, Irene Adler. The name is no doubt familiar to you."

"Kindly look her up in my index, Doctor," murmured Holmes without opening his eyes. For many years he had adopted a system of docketing all paragraphs concerning men and things, so that it was difficult to name a subject or a person on which he could not at once furnish information. In this case I found her biography sandwiched in between that of a Hebrew rabbi and that of a staff-commander who had written a monograph upon the deep-sea fishes.

"Let me see!" said Holmes. "Hum! Born in New Jersey in the year 1858. Contralto—

hum! La Scala, hum! Prima donna Imperial Opera of Warsaw—yes! Retired from operatic stage—ha! Living in London—quite so! Your Majesty, as I understand, became entangled with this young person, wrote her some compromising letters, and is now desirous of getting those letters back."

"Precisely so. But how—"

"Was there a secret marriage?"

"None."

"No legal papers or certificates?"

"None."

"Then I fail to follow your Majesty. If this young person should produce her letters for blackmailing or other purposes, how is she to prove their authenticity?"

"There is the writing."

"Pooh, pooh! Forgery."

"My private note-paper."

"Stolen."

"My own seal."

"Imitated."

"My photograph."

"Bought."

"We were both in the photograph."

"Oh, dear! That is very bad! Your Majesty has indeed committed an indiscretion."

"I was mad—insane."

"You have compromised yourself seriously."

"It must be recovered."

"We have tried and failed."

"Your Majesty must pay. It must be bought."

"She will not sell."

"Stolen, then."

"Five attempts have been made. Twice burglars in my pay ransacked her house. Once we diverted her luggage when she traveled. Twice she has been waylaid. There has been no result."

"No sign of it?"

"Absolutely none."

Holmes laughed. "It is quite a pretty little problem," said he.

"But a very serious one to me," returned the King reproachfully.

"Very, indeed. And what does she propose to do with the photograph?"

"To ruin me."

"But how?"

"I am about to be married."

"So I have heard."

"To Clotilde Lothman von Saxe-Meningen, second daughter of the King of Scandinavia. You may know the strict principles of her family. She is herself the very soul of delicacy. A shadow of a doubt as to my conduct would bring the matter to an end."

"And Irene Adler?"

"Threatens to send them the photograph. And she will do it. I know that she will do it. You do not know her, but she has a soul of steel. She has the face of the most beautiful of women, and the mind of the most resolute of men. Rather than I should marry another woman, there are no lengths to which she would not go—none."

"You are sure that she has not sent it yet?"

"I am sure."

"And why?"

"Because she has said that she would send it on the day when the betrothal was publicly proclaimed. That will be next Monday."

"Oh, then we have three days yet," said Holmes with a yawn. "That is very fortunate, as I have one or two matters of importance to look into just at present. Your Majesty will, of course, stay in London for the present?"

"Certainly. You will find me at the Langham under the name of the Count Von Kramm."

"Then I shall drop you a line to let you know how we progress."

"Pray do so. I shall be all anxiety."

"Then, as to money?"

"You have carte blanche."

"Absolutely?"

"I tell you that I would give one of the provinces of my kingdom to have that photograph."

"And for present expenses?"

The King took a heavy chamois leather bag from under his cloak and laid it on the table.

"There are three hundred pounds in gold and seven hundred in notes," he said.

Holmes scribbled a receipt upon a sheet of his note-book and handed it to him.

"And Mademoiselle's address?" he asked.

"Is Briony Lodge, Serpentine Avenue, St. John's Wood."

Holmes took a note of it. "One other question," said he. "Was the photograph a cabinet?"

"It was."

"Then, good-night, your Majesty, and I trust that we shall soon have some good news for you. And good-night, Watson," he added, as the wheels of the royal brougham rolled down the street. "If you will be good enough to call to-morrow afternoon at three o'clock I should like to chat this little matter over with you."

At three o'clock precisely I was at Baker Street, but Holmes had not yet returned. The landlady informed me that he had left the house shortly after eight o'clock in the morning. I sat down beside the fire, however, with the intention of awaiting him, however long he might be. I was already deeply interested in his inquiry, for, though it was surrounded by none of the grim and strange features which were associated with the two crimes which I have already recorded, still, the nature of the case and the exalted station of his client gave it a character of its own. Indeed, apart from the nature of the investigation which my friend had on hand, there was something in his masterly grasp of a situation, and his keen, incisive reasoning, which made it a pleasure to me to study his system of work, and to follow the quick, subtle methods by which he disentangled the most inextricable mysteries. So accustomed was I to his invariable success that the very possibility of his failing had ceased to enter into my head.

It was close upon four before the door opened, and a drunken-looking groom, ill-kempt and side-whiskered, with an inflamed face and disreputable clothes, walked into the room. Accustomed as I was to my friend's amazing powers in the use of disguises, I had to look three times before I was certain that it was indeed he. With a nod he vanished into the bedroom, whence he emerged in five minutes tweed-suited and respectable, as of old. Putting his hand into his pockets, he stretched out his legs in front of the fire and laughed heartily for some minutes.

"Well, really!" he cried, and then he choked and laughed again until he was obliged to lie back, limp and helpless, in the chair.

"What is it?"

"It's quite too funny. I am sure you could never guess how I employed my morning, or what I ended by doing."

"I can't imagine. I suppose that you have been watching the habits, and perhaps the house, of Miss Irene Adler."

"Quite so; but the sequel was rather unusual. I will tell you, however. I left the house a little after eight o'clock this morning in the character of a groom out of work. There is a wonderful sympathy and freemasonry among horsy men. Be one of them, and you will know all that there is to know. I soon found Briony Lodge. It is a bijou villa, with a garden at the back, but built out in front right up to the road, two stories. Chubb lock to the door. Large sitting-room on the right side, well furnished, with long windows almost to the floor, and those preposterous English window fasteners which a child could open. Behind there was nothing remarkable, save that the passage window could be reached from the top of the coach-house. I walked round it and examined it closely from every point of view, but without noting anything else of interest.

"I then lounged down the street and found, as I expected, that there was a mews in a lane which runs down by one wall of the garden. I lent the ostlers a hand in rubbing down their horses, and received in exchange twopence, a glass of half and half, two fills of shag tobacco, and as much information as I could desire about Miss Adler, to say nothing of half a dozen other people in the neighbourhood in whom I was not in the least interested, but whose biographies I was compelled to listen to."

"And what of Irene Adler?" I asked.

"Oh, she has turned all the men's heads down in that part. She is the daintiest thing under a bonnet on this planet. So say the Serpentine-mews, to a man. She lives quietly, sings at concerts, drives out at five every day, and returns at seven sharp for dinner. Seldom goes out at other times, except when she sings. Has only one male visitor, but a good deal of him. He is dark, handsome, and dashing, never calls less than once a day, and often twice. He is a Mr. Godfrey Norton, of the Inner Temple. See the advantages of a cabman as a confidant. They had driven him home a dozen times from Serpentine-mews, and knew all about him. When I had listened to all they had to tell, I began to walk up and down near Briony Lodge once more, and to think over my plan of campaign.

"This Godfrey Norton was evidently an important factor in the matter. He was a lawyer. That sounded ominous. What was the relation between them, and what the object of his repeated visits? Was she his client, his friend, or his mistress? If the former, she had probably transferred the photograph to his keeping. If the latter, it was less likely. On the issue of this question depended whether I should continue my work at Briony Lodge, or turn my attention to the gentleman's chambers in the Temple. It was a delicate point, and it widened the field of my inquiry. I fear that I bore you with these details, but I have to let you see my little difficulties, if you are to understand the situation."

"I am following you closely," I answered.

"I was still balancing the matter in my mind when a hansom cab drove up to Briony Lodge, and a gentleman sprang out. He was a remarkably handsome man, dark, aquiline, and moustached—evidently the man of whom I had heard. He appeared to be in a great hurry, shouted to the cabman to wait, and brushed past the maid who opened the door with the air of a man who was thoroughly at home.

"He was in the house about half an hour, and I could catch glimpses of him in the windows of the sitting-room, pacing up and down, talking excitedly, and waving his arms. Of her I could see nothing. Presently he emerged, looking even more flurried than before. As he stepped up to the cab, he pulled a gold watch from his pocket and looked at it earnestly, 'Drive like the devil,' he shouted, 'first to Gross & Hankey's in Regent Street, and then to the Church of St. Monica in the Edgeware Road. Half a guinea if you do it in twenty minutes!'

"Away they went, and I was just wondering whether I should not do well to follow them when up the lane came a neat little landau, the coachman with his coat only half-buttoned, and his tie under his ear, while all the tags of his harness were sticking out of the buckles. It hadn't pulled up before she shot out of the hall door and into it. I only caught a glimpse of her at the moment, but she was a lovely woman, with a face that a man might die for.

"'The Church of St. Monica, John,' she cried, 'and half a sovereign if you reach it in twenty minutes.'

"This was quite too good to lose, Watson. I was just balancing whether I should run for it, or whether I should perch behind her landau when a cab came through the street. The driver looked twice at such a shabby fare, but I jumped in before he could object. 'The Church of St. Monica,' said I, 'and half a sovereign if you reach it in twenty minutes.' It was twenty-five minutes to twelve, and of course it was clear enough what was in the wind.

"My cabby drove fast. I don't think I ever drove faster, but the others were there before us. The cab and the landau with their steaming horses were in front of the door when I arrived. I paid the man and hurried into the church. There was not a soul there save the two whom I had followed and a surpliced clergyman, who seemed to be expostulating with them. They were all three standing in a knot in front of the altar. I lounged up the side aisle like any other idler who has dropped into a church. Suddenly, to my surprise, the three at the altar faced round to me, and Godfrey Norton came running as hard as he could towards me.

"'Thank God,' he cried. 'You'll do. Come! Come!'

"'What then?' I asked.

"'Come, man, come, only three minutes, or it won't be legal.'

"I was half-dragged up to the altar, and before I knew where I was I found myself mumbling responses which were whispered in my ear, and vouching for things of which I knew nothing, and generally assisting in the secure tying up of Irene Adler, spinster, to Godfrey Norton, bachelor. It was all done in an instant, and there was the gentleman thanking me on the one side and the lady on the other, while the clergyman beamed on me in front. It was the most preposterous position in which I ever found myself in my life, and it was the thought of it that started me laughing just now. It seems that there had been some informality about their license, that the clergyman absolutely refused to marry them without a witness of some sort, and that my lucky appearance saved the bridegroom from having to sally out into the streets in search of a best man. The bride gave me a sovereign, and I mean to wear it on my watch-chain in memory of the occasion."

"This is a very unexpected turn of affairs," said I; "and what then?"

"Well, I found my plans very seriously menaced. It looked as if the pair might take an immediate departure, and so necessitate very prompt and energetic measures on my part. At the church door, however, they separated, he driving back to the Temple, and she to her own house. 'I shall drive out in the park at five as usual,' she said as she left him. I heard no more. They drove away in different directions, and I went off to make my own arrangements."

"Which are?"

"Some cold beef and a glass of beer," he answered, ringing the bell. "I have been too busy to think of food, and I am likely to be busier still this evening. By the way, Doctor, I shall want your cooperation."

"I shall be delighted."

"You don't mind breaking the law?"

"Not in the least."

"Nor running a chance of arrest?"

"Not in a good cause."

"Oh, the cause is excellent!"

"Then I am your man."

"I was sure that I might rely on you."

"But what is it you wish?"

"When Mrs. Turner has brought in the tray I will make it clear to you. Now," he said as he turned hungrily on the simple fare that our landlady had provided, "I must discuss it while I eat, for I have not much time. It is nearly five now. In two hours we must be on the scene of action. Miss Irene, or Madame, rather, returns from her drive at seven. We must be at Briony Lodge to meet her."

"And what then?"

"You must leave that to me. I have already arranged what is to occur. There is only one point on which I must insist. You must not interfere, come what may. You understand?"

"I am to be neutral?"

"To do nothing whatever. There will probably be some small unpleasantness. Do not join in it. It will end in my being conveyed into the house. Four or five minutes afterwards the sitting-room window will open. You are to station yourself close to that open window."

"You are to watch me, for I will be visible to you."

"Yes."

"And when I raise my hand—so—you will throw into the room what I give you to throw, and will, at the same time, raise the cry of fire. You quite follow me?"

"Entirely."

"It is nothing very formidable," he said, taking a long cigarshaped roll from his pocket. "It is an ordinary plumber's smokerocket, fitted with a cap at either end to make it self-lighting. Your task is confined to that. When you raise your cry of fire, it will be taken up by quite a number of people. You may then walk to the end of the street, and I will rejoin you in ten minutes. I hope that I have made myself clear?"

"I am to remain neutral, to get near the window, to watch you, and at the signal to throw in this object, then to raise the cry of fire, and to wait you at the corner of the street."

"Precisely."

"Then you may entirely rely on me."

"That is excellent. I think, perhaps, it is almost time that I prepare for the new role I have to play."

He disappeared into his bedroom and returned in a few minutes in the character of an amiable and simple-minded Nonconformist clergyman. His broad black hat, his baggy trousers, his white tie, his sympathetic smile, and general look of peering and benevolent curiosity were such as Mr. John Hare alone could have equalled. It was not merely that Holmes changed his costume. His expression, his manner, his very soul seemed to vary with every fresh part that he assumed. The stage lost a fine actor, even as science lost an acute reasoner, when he became a specialist in crime.

It was a quarter past six when we left Baker Street, and it still wanted ten minutes to the hour when we found ourselves in Serpentine Avenue. It was already dusk, and the lamps were just being lighted as we paced up and down in front of Briony Lodge, waiting for the coming of its occupant. The house was just such as I had pictured it from Sherlock Holmes's succinct description, but the locality appeared to be less private than I expected. On the contrary, for a small street in a quiet neighbourhood, it was remarkably animated. There was a group of shabbily dressed men smoking and laughing in a corner, a scissors-grinder with his wheel, two guardsmen who were flirting with a nurse-girl, and several well-dressed young men who were lounging up and down with cigars in their mouths.

"You see," remarked Holmes, as we paced to and fro in front of the house, "this marriage rather simplifies matters. The photograph becomes a double-edged weapon now. The chances are that she would be as averse to its being seen by Mr. Godfrey

Norton, as our client is to its coming to the eyes of his princess. Now the question is, Where are we to find the photograph?"

"Where, indeed?"

"It is most unlikely that she carries it about with her. It is cabinet size. Too large for easy concealment about a woman's dress. She knows that the King is capable of having her waylaid and searched. Two attempts of the sort have already been made. We may take it, then, that she does not carry it about with her."

"Where, then?"

"Her banker or her lawyer. There is that double possibility. But I am inclined to think neither. Women are naturally secretive, and they like to do their own secreting. Why should she hand it over to anyone else? She could trust her own guardianship, but she could not tell what indirect or political influence might be brought to bear upon a business man. Besides, remember that she had resolved to use it within a few days. It must be where she can lay her hands upon it. It must be in her own house."

"But it has twice been burgled."

"Pshaw! They did not know how to look."

"But how will you look?"

"I will not look."

"What then?"

"I will get her to show me."

"But she will refuse."

"She will not be able to. But I hear the rumble of wheels. It is her carriage. Now carry out my orders to the letter."

As he spoke the gleam of the side-lights of a carriage came round the curve of the avenue. It was a smart little landau which rattled up to the door of Briony Lodge. As it pulled up, one of the loafing men at the corner dashed forward to open the door in the hope of earning a copper, but was elbowed away by another loafer, who had rushed up with the same intention. A fierce quarrel broke out, which was increased by the two guardsmen, who took sides with one of the loungers, and by the scissors-grinder, who was equally hot upon the other side. A blow was struck, and in an instant the lady, who had stepped from her carriage, was the centre of a little knot of flushed and struggling men, who struck savagely at each other with their fists and sticks. Holmes dashed into the crowd to protect the lady; but just as he reached her he gave a cry and dropped to the ground, with the blood running freely down his face. At his fall the guardsmen took to their heels in one direction and the loungers in the other, while a number of better-dressed people, who had watched the scuffle without taking part in it, crowded in to help the lady and to attend to the injured man. Irene Adler, as I will still call her, had hurried up the steps; but she stood at the top with her superb figure outlined against the lights of the hall, looking back into the street.

"Is the poor gentleman much hurt?" she asked.

"He is dead," cried several voices.

"No, no, there's life in him!" shouted another. "But he'll be gone before you can get him to hospital."

"He's a brave fellow," said a woman. "They would have had the lady's purse and watch if it hadn't been for him. They were a gang, and a rough one, too. Ah, he's breathing now."

"He can't lie in the street. May we bring him in, marm?"

"Surely. Bring him into the sitting room. There is a comfortable sofa. This way, please!"

Slowly and solemnly he was borne into Briony Lodge and laid out in the principal room, while I still observed the proceedings from my post by the window. The lamps had been lit, but the blinds had not been drawn, so that I could see Holmes as he lay upon the couch. I do not know whether he was seized with compunction at that moment for the part he was playing, but I know that I never felt more heartily ashamed of myself in my life than when I saw the beautiful creature against whom I was conspiring, or the grace and kindliness with which she waited upon the injured man. And yet it would be the blackest treachery to Holmes to draw back now from the part which he had intrusted to me. I hardened my heart, and took the smoke-rocket from under my ulster. After all, I thought, we are not injuring her. We are but preventing her from injuring another.

Holmes had sat up upon the couch, and I saw him motion like a man who is in need of air. A maid rushed across and threw open the window. At the same instant I saw him raise his hand and at the signal I tossed my rocket into the room with a cry of "Fire!" The word was no sooner out of my mouth than the whole crowd of spectators, well dressed and ill—gentlemen, ostlers, and servant-maids—joined in a general shriek of "Fire!" Thick clouds of smoke curled through the room and out at the open window. I caught a glimpse of rushing figures, and a moment later the voice of Holmes from within assuring them that it was a false alarm. Slipping through the shouting crowd I made my way to the corner of the street, and in ten minutes was rejoiced to find my friend's arm in mine, and to get away from the scene of uproar. He walked swiftly and in silence for some few minutes until we had turned down one of the quiet streets which lead towards the Edgeware Road.

"You did it very nicely, Doctor," he remarked. "Nothing could have been better. It is all right."

"You have the photograph?"

"I know where it is."

"And how did you find out?"

"She showed me, as I told you she would."

"I am still in the dark."

"I do not wish to make a mystery," said he, laughing. "The matter was perfectly simple. You, of course, saw that everyone in the street was an accomplice. They were all engaged for the evening."

"I guessed as much."

"Then, when the row broke out, I had a little moist red paint in the palm of my hand. I rushed forward, fell down, clapped my hand to my face, and became a piteous spectacle. It is an old trick."

"That also I could fathom."

"Then they carried me in. She was bound to have me in. What else could she do? And into her sitting-room, which was the very room which I suspected. It lay between that and her bedroom, and I was determined to see which. They laid me on a couch, I motioned for air, they were compelled to open the window, and you had your chance."

"How did that help you?"

"It was all-important. When a woman thinks that her house is on fire, her instinct is at once to rush to the thing which she values most. It is a perfectly overpowering impulse, and I have more than once taken advantage of it. In the case of the Darlington substitution scandal it was of use to me, and also in the Arnsworth Castle business. A married woman grabs at her baby; an unmarried one reaches for her jewel-box. Now it was clear to me that our lady of to-day had nothing in the house more precious to her than what we are in quest of. She would rush to secure it. The alarm of fire was admirably done. The smoke and shouting were enough to shake nerves of steel. She responded beautifully. The photograph is in a recess behind a sliding panel just above the right bell-pull. She was there in an instant, and I caught a glimpse of it as she half-drew it out. When I cried out that it was a false alarm, she replaced it, glanced at the rocket, rushed from the room, and I have not seen her since. I rose, and, making my excuses, escaped from the house. I hesitated whether to attempt to secure the photograph at once; but the coachman had come in, and as he was watching me narrowly it seemed safer to wait. A little over-precipitance may ruin all."

"And now?" I asked.

"Our quest is practically finished. I shall call with the King to-morrow, and with you, if you care to come with us. We will be shown into the sitting-room to wait for the lady; but it is probable that when she comes she may find neither us nor the photograph. It might be a satisfaction to his Majesty to regain it with his own hands."

"And when will you call?"

"At eight in the morning. She will not be up, so that we shall have a clear field. Besides, we must be prompt, for this marriage may mean a complete change in her life and habits. I must wire to the King without delay."

We had reached Baker Street and had stopped at the door. He was searching his pockets for the key when someone passing said:

"Good-night, Mister Sherlock Holmes."

There were several people on the pavement at the time, but the greeting appeared to come from a slim youth in an ulster who had hurried by.

"I've heard that voice before," said Holmes, staring down the dimly lit street. "Now, I wonder who the deuce that could have been."

I slept at Baker Street that night, and we were engaged upon our toast and coffee in the morning when the King of Bohemia rushed into the room.

"You have really got it!" he cried, grasping Sherlock Holmes by either shoulder and looking eagerly into his face.

"Not yet."

"But you have hopes?"

"I have hopes."

"Then, come. I am all impatience to be gone."

"We must have a cab."

"No, my brougham is waiting."

"Then that will simplify matters." We descended and started off once more for Briony Lodge.

"Irene Adler is married," remarked Holmes.

"Married! When?"

"Yesterday."

"But to whom?"

"To an English lawyer named Norton."

"But she could not love him."

"I am in hopes that she does."

"And why in hopes?"

"Because it would spare your Majesty all fear of future annoyance. If the lady loves her husband, she does not love your Majesty. If she does not love your Majesty, there is no reason why she should interfere with your Majesty's plan."

"It is true. And yet Well! I wish she had been of my own station! What a queen she would have made!" He relapsed into a moody silence, which was not broken until we drew up in Serpentine Avenue.

The door of Briony Lodge was open, and an elderly woman stood upon the steps. She watched us with a sardonic eye as we stepped from the brougham.

"Mr. Sherlock Holmes, I believe?" said she.

"I am Mr. Holmes," answered my companion, looking at her with a questioning and rather startled gaze.

"Indeed! My mistress told me that you were likely to call. She left this morning with her husband by the 5:15 train from Charing Cross for the Continent."

"What!" Sherlock Holmes staggered back, white with chagrin and surprise. "Do you mean that she has left England?"

"Never to return."

"And the papers?" asked the King hoarsely. "All is lost."

"We shall see." He pushed past the servant and rushed into the drawing-room followed by the King and myself. The furniture was scattered about in every direction, with dismantled shelves and open drawers, as if the lady had hurriedly ransacked them before her flight. Holmes rushed at the bell-pull, tore back a small sliding shutter, and, plunging in his hand, pulled out a photograph and a letter. The photograph was of Irene Adler herself in evening dress, the letter was superscribed to "Sherlock Holmes, Esq. To be left till called for." My friend tore it open and we all three read it together. It was dated at midnight of the preceding night and ran in this way:

MY DEAR MR. SHERLOCK HOLMES:

You really did it very well. You took me in completely. Until after the alarm of fire, I had not a suspicion. But then, when I found how I had betrayed myself, I began to think. I had been warned against you months ago. I had been told that if the King employed an agent it would certainly be you. And your address had been given me. Yet, with all this, you made me reveal what you wanted to know. Even after I became suspicious, I found it hard to think evil of such a dear, kind old clergyman. But, you know, I have been trained as an actress myself. Male costume is nothing new to me. I often take advantage of the freedom which it gives. I sent John, the coachman, to watch you, ran up stairs, got into my walking-clothes, as I call them, and came down just as you departed.

Well, I followed you to your door, and so made sure that I was really an object of interest to the celebrated Mr. Sherlock Holmes. Then I, rather imprudently, wished you good-night, and started for the Temple to see my husband.

We both thought the best resource was flight, when pursued by so formidable an antagonist; so you will find the nest empty when you call to-morrow. As to the photograph, your client may rest in peace. I love and am loved by a better man than he. The King may do what he will without hindrance from one whom he has cruelly wronged. I keep it only to safeguard myself, and to preserve a weapon which will always secure me from any steps which he might take in the future. I leave a photograph which he might care to possess; and I remain, dear Mr. Sherlock Holmes,

Very truly yours,<br>
Irene Norton, nee ADLER.

"What a woman—oh, what a woman!" cried the King of Bohemia, when we had all three read this epistle. "Did I not tell you how quick and resolute she was? Would she not have made an admirable queen? Is it not a pity that she was not on my level?"

"From what I have seen of the lady she seems indeed to be on a very different level to your Majesty," said Holmes coldly. "I am sorry that I have not been able to bring your Majesty's business to a more successful conclusion."

"On the contrary, my dear sir," cried the King; "nothing could be more successful. I know that her word is inviolate. The photograph is now safe as if it were in the fire."

"I am glad to hear your Majesty say so."

"I am immensely indebted to you. Pray tell me in what way I can reward you. This ring— —" He slipped an emerald snake ring from his finger and held it out upon the palm of his hand.

"Your Majesty has something which I should value even more highly," said Holmes.

"You have but to name it."

"This photograph!"

The King stared at him in amazement.

"Irene's photograph!" he cried. "Certainly, if you wish it."

"I thank your Majesty. Then there is no more to be done in the matter. I have the honour to wish you a very good-morning." He bowed, and, turning away without observing the hand which the King had stretched out to him, he set off in my company for his chambers.

And that was how a great scandal threatened to affect the kingdom of Bohemia, and how the best plans of Mr. Sherlock Holmes were beaten by a woman's wit. He used to make merry over the cleverness of women, but I have not heard him do it of late. And when he speaks of Irene Adler, or when he refers to her photograph, it is always under the honourable title of *the* woman.

# Nikolai Gogol

## (1809–1852)

The phrase "We all came out from under Gogol's 'Overcoat'" has been attributed variously to Turgenev, Dostoevsky, and Tolstoy. It is agreed, however, that Nikolai Gogol should be considered the inventor of Russian realism. Although he himself believed his novel *Dead Souls,* a humorous portrayal of life in Russia during his time, to be his most significant work, it was Gogol's short story "The Overcoat" that set the tone for Russian writers during the rest of the nineteenth century. It is, in brief, the compassionately told tale of an unheroic protagonist who must deal with apathetic bureaucrats and who leads an essentially lonely and absurd existence. The tragically absurd, the absurdity even of logic itself, "was Gogol's favorite muse," according to Vladimir Nabokov; indeed, he said of Gogol that "whenever he tried to . . . treat rational ideas in a logical way, he lost all trace of talent." This might be thought an overstatement were it not for the fact that Gogol died insane. Clearly, he was not cut out for the plodding life of the bureaucrats whom he satirized in his play of 1836, *The Inspector General;* though he attempted to lead the life of a civil servant, he was unhappy in the profession and managed to transcend this only by befriending the great poet Alexander Pushkin, his literary mentor. The prevailing powers ridiculed in *The Inspector General* were considered so offensive that Gogol was exiled to Rome, where he lived out the rest of his life; but his work and its influence were to remain an ineradicable part of Russia.

---

## The Overcoat                                                                    1840

TRANSLATED BY CONSTANCE GARNETT AND REVISED BY LEONARD J. KENT

In the department of . . . but I had better not mention which department. There is nothing in the world more touchy than a department, a regiment, a government office, and, in fact, any sort of official body. Nowadays every private individual considers all society insulted in his person. I have been told that very lately a complaint was lodged by a police inspector of which town I don't remember, and that in this complaint he set forth clearly that the institutions of the State were in danger and that his sacred name was being taken in vain; and, in proof thereof, he appended to his complaint an enormously long volume of some romantic work in which a police inspector appeared on every tenth page, occasionally, indeed, in an intoxicated condition. And so, to avoid any unpleasantness, we had better call the department of which we are speaking "a certain department."

And so, in a *certain department* there was a *certain clerk;* a clerk of whom it cannot be said that he was very remarkable; he was short, somewhat pock-marked, with rather reddish hair and rather dim, bleary eyes, with a small bald patch on the top of his head, with wrinkles on both sides of his cheeks and the sort of complexion which is usually described as hemorrhoidal . . . nothing can be done about that, it is the Petersburg climate. As for his grade in the civil service (for among us a man's rank is what must be established first) he was what is called a perpetual titular councilor, a class at which, as we all know, various writers who indulge in the praiseworthy habit of attacking those who cannot defend themselves jeer and jibe to their hearts' content. This clerk's surname was Bashmachkin. From the very name it is clear that it must have been derived from a shoe (*bashmak*); but when and under what circumstances it was derived from a shoe, it is impossible to say. Both his father and his grandfather and even his brother-in-law, and all the Bashmachkins without exception wore boots, which they simply resoled two or three times a year. His name was Akaky Akakievich. Perhaps it may strike the reader as a rather strange and contrived name, but I can assure him that it was not contrived at all, that the circumstances were such that it was quite out of the question to give him any other name. Akaky Akakievich was born toward nightfall, if my memory does not deceive me, on the twenty-third of March. His mother, the wife of a government clerk, a very good woman, made arrangements in due course to christen the child. She was still lying in bed, facing the door, while on her right hand stood the godfather, an excellent man called Ivan Ivanovich Yeroshkin, one of the head clerks in the Senate, and the godmother, the wife of a police official and a woman of rare qualities, Arina Semeonovna Belobriushkova. Three names were offered to the happy mother for selection—Mokky, Sossy, or the name of the martyr Khozdazat. "No," thought the poor lady, "they are all such names!" To satisfy her, they opened the calendar at another page, and the names which turned up were: Trifily, Dula, Varakhasy. "What an infliction!" said the mother. "What names they all are! I really never heard such names. Varadat or Varukh would be bad enough, but Trifily and Varakhasy!" They turned over another page and the names were: Pavsikakhy and Vakhisy. "Well, I see," said the mother, "it is clear that it is his fate. Since that is how it is, he had better be named after his father; his father is Akaky; let the son be Akaky, too." This was how he came to be Akaky Akakievich. The baby was christened and cried and made sour faces during the ceremony, as though he foresaw that he would be a titular councilor. So that was how it all came to pass. We have reported it here so that the reader may see for himself that it happened quite inevitably and that to give him any other name was out of the question.

No one has been able to remember when and how long ago he entered the department, nor who gave him the job. Regardless of how many directors and higher officials of all sorts came and went, he was always seen in the same place, in the same position, at the very same duty, precisely the same copying clerk, so that they used to declare that he must have been born a copying clerk, uniform, bald patch, and all. No respect at all was shown him in the department. The porters, far from getting up from their seats when he came in, took no more notice of him than if a simple fly had flown across the reception room. His superiors treated him with a sort of despotic aloofness. The head clerk's assistant used to throw papers under his nose without even saying "Copy this" or "Here is an interesting, nice little case" or some agreeable remark of the sort, as is usually done in well-bred offices. And he would take it, gazing only at the paper without looking to see who had put it there and whether he had the right to do so; he would take it and at once begin copying it. The young clerks jeered and made jokes at him to the best of their clerkly wit, and told before his face all sorts of stories of their own invention about him; they would say of his landlady, an old woman of seventy, that she beat him, would ask when the wedding was to take place, and would scatter bits of paper on his head, calling them snow. Akaky Akakievich never answered a word, however, but behaved as though there were no one there. It had no influence on his work; in the midst of all this teasing, he never made a single mistake in his copying. It was only when the jokes became too unbearable, when they jolted his arm, and prevented him from going on with his work, that he would say: "Leave me alone! Why do you insult me?" and there was something touching in the words and in the voice in which they were uttered. There was a note in it of something that aroused compassion, so that one young man, new to the office, who, following the example of the rest, had allowed himself to tease him, suddenly stopped as though cut to the heart, and from that time on, everything was, as it were, changed and appeared in a different light to him. Some unseen force seemed to repel him from the companions with whom he had become acquainted because he thought they were well-bred and decent men. And long afterward, during moments of the greatest gaiety, the figure of the humble little clerk with a bald patch on his head appeared before him with his heart-rending words: "Leave me alone! Why do you insult me?" and within those moving words he heard others: "I am your brother." And the poor young man hid his face in his hands, and many times afterward in his life he shuddered, seeing how much inhumanity there is in man, how much savage brutality lies hidden under refined, cultured politeness, and, my God! even in a man whom the world accepts as a gentleman and a man of honor. . . .

It would be hard to find a man who lived for his work as did Akaky Akakievich. To say that he was zealous in his work is not enough; no, he loved his work. In it, in that copying, he found an interesting and pleasant world of his own. There was a look of enjoyment on his face; certain letters were favorites with him, and when he came to them he was delighted; he chuckled to himself and winked and moved his lips, so that it seemed as though every letter his pen was forming could be read in his face. If rewards had been given according to the measure of zeal in the service, he might to his amazement have even found himself a civil councilor; but all he gained in the service, as the wits, his fellow clerks, expressed it, was a button in his buttonhole and hemorrhoids where he sat. It cannot be said, however, that no notice had ever been taken of him. One director, being a good-natured man and anxious to reward him for his long service, sent him something a little more important than his ordinary copying; he was instructed to make some sort of report from a finished document for another office; the work consisted only of altering the headings and in places changing the first person into the third. This cost him so much effort that he was covered with perspiration: he mopped his brow and said at last, "No, I'd rather copy something."

From that time on they left him to his copying forever. It seemed as though nothing in the world existed for him except his copying. He gave no thought at all to his clothes; his uniform was—well, not green but some sort of rusty, muddy color. His collar was very low and narrow, so that, although his neck was not particularly long, yet, standing out of the collar, it looked as immensely long as those of the dozens of plaster kittens with nodding heads which foreigners carry about on their heads and peddle in Russia. And there were always things sticking to his uniform, either bits of hay or threads; moreover, he had a special knack of passing under a window at the very moment when various garbage was being flung out into the street, and so was continually carrying off bits of melon rind and similar litter on his hat. He had never once in his life noticed what was being done and what was going on in the street, all those things at which, as we all know, his colleagues, the young clerks, always stare, utilizing their keen sight so well that they notice anyone on the other side of the street with a trouser strap hanging loose—an observation which always calls forth a sly grin. Whatever Akaky Akakievich looked at, he saw nothing but his clear, evenly written lines, and it was only perhaps when a horse suddenly appeared from nowhere and placed its head on his shoulder, and with its nostrils blew a real gale upon his cheek, that he would notice that he was not in the middle of his writing, but rather in the middle of the street.

On reaching home, he would sit down at once at the table, hurriedly eat his soup and a piece of beef with an onion; he did not notice the taste at all but ate it all with the flies and anything else that Providence happened to send him. When he felt that his stomach was beginning to be full, he would get up from the table, take out a bottle of ink and begin copying the papers he had brought home with him. When he had none to do, he would make a copy especially for his own pleasure, particularly if the document were remarkable not for the beauty of its style but because it was addressed to some new or distinguished person.

Even at those hours when the gray Petersburg sky is completely overcast and the whole population of clerks have dined and eaten their fill, each as best he can, according to the salary he receives and his personal tastes; when they are all resting after the scratching of pens and bustle of the office, their own necessary work and other people's, and all the tasks that an overzealous man voluntarily sets himself even beyond what is necessary; when the clerks are hastening to devote what is left of their time to pleasure; some more enterprising are flying to the theater, others to the street to spend their leisure staring at women's hats, some to spend the evening paying compliments to some attractive girl, the star of a little official circle, while some—and this is the most frequent of all—go simply to a fellow clerk's apartment on the third or fourth story, two little rooms with a hall or a kitchen, with some pretensions to style, with a lamp or some such article that has cost many sacrifices of dinners and excursions—at the time when all the clerks are scattered about the apartments of their friends, playing a stormy game of whist, sipping tea out of glasses, eating cheap biscuits, sucking in smoke from long pipes, telling, as the cards are dealt, some scandal that has floated down from higher circles, a pleasure which the Russian can never by any possibility deny himself, or, when there is nothing better to talk about, repeating the everlasting anecdote of the commanding officer who was told that the tail had been cut off the horse on the Falconet monument—in short, even when everyone was eagerly seeking entertainment, Akaky Akakievich did not indulge in any amusement. No one could say that they had ever seen him at an evening party. After working to his heart's content, he would go to bed, smiling at the thought of the next day and wondering what God would send him to copy. So flowed on the peaceful life of a man who knew how to be content with his fate on a salary of four hundred rubles, and so perhaps it would have flowed on to extreme old age, had it not been for the various disasters strewn along the road of life, not only of titular, but even of privy, actual court, and all other councilors, even those who neither give counsel to others nor accept it themselves.

There is in Petersburg a mighty foe of all who receive a salary of about four hundred rubles. That foe is none other than our northern frost, although it is said to be very good for the health. Between eight and nine in the morning, precisely at the hour when the streets are filled with clerks going to their departments, the frost begins indiscriminately giving such sharp and stinging nips at all their noses that the poor fellows don't know what to do with them. At that time, when even those in the higher grade have a pain in their brows and tears in their eyes from the frost, the poor titular councilors are sometimes almost defenseless. Their only protection lies in running as fast as they can through five or six streets in a wretched, thin little overcoat and then warming their feet thoroughly in the porter's room, till all their faculties and talents for their various duties thaw out again after having been frozen on the way. Akaky Akakievich had for some time been feeling that his back and shoulders were particularly nipped by the cold, although he did try to run the regular distance as fast as he could. He wondered at last whether there were any defects in his overcoat. After examining it thoroughly in the privacy of his home, he discovered that in two or three places, on the back and the shoulders, it had become a regular sieve; the cloth was so worn that you could see through it and the lining was coming out. I must note that Akaky Akakievich's overcoat had also served as a butt for the jokes of the clerks. It had even been deprived of the honorable name of overcoat and had been referred to as the "dressing gown." It was indeed of rather a peculiar make. Its collar had been growing smaller year by year as it served to patch the other parts. The patches were not good specimens of the tailor's art, and they certainly looked clumsy and ugly. On seeing what was wrong, Akaky Akakievich decided that he would have to take the overcoat to Petrovich, a tailor who lived on the fourth floor up a back staircase, and, in spite of having only one eye and being pockmarked all over his face, was rather successful in repairing the trousers and coats of clerks and others—that is, when he was sober, be it understood, and had no other enterprise in his mind. Of this tailor I ought not, of course, say much, but since it is now the rule that the character of every person in a novel must be completely described, well, there's nothing I can do but describe Petrovich too. At first he was called simply Grigory, and was a serf belonging to some gentleman or other. He began to be called Petrovich from the time that he got his freedom and began to drink rather heavily on every holiday, at first only on the main holidays, but afterward, on all church holidays indiscriminately, wherever there was a cross in the calendar. In this he was true to the customs of his forefathers, and when he quarreled with his wife he used to call her a worldly woman and a German. Since we have now mentioned the wife, it will be necessary to say a few words about her, too, but unfortunately not much is known about her, except indeed that Petrovich had a wife and that she wore a cap and not a kerchief, but apparently she could not boast of beauty; anyway, none but soldiers of the guard peered under her cap when they met her, and they twitched their mustaches and gave vent to a rather peculiar sound.

As he climbed the stairs leading to Petrovich's—which, to do them justice, were all soaked with water and slops and saturated through and through with that smell of ammonia which makes the eyes smart, and is, as we all know, inseparable from the backstairs of Petersburg houses—Akaky Akakievich was already wondering how much Petrovich would ask for the job, and inwardly resolving not to give more than two rubles. The door was open, because Petrovich's wife was frying some fish and had so filled the kitchen with smoke that you could not even see the cockroaches. Akaky Akakievich crossed the kitchen unnoticed by the good woman, and walked at last into a room where he saw Petrovich sitting on a big, wooden, unpainted table with his legs tucked under him like a Turkish pasha. The feet, as is usual with tailors when they sit at work, were bare; and the first object that caught Akaky Akakievich's eye was the big toe, with which he was already familiar, with a misshapen nail as thick and strong as the shell of a tortoise. Around Petrovich's neck hung a skein of silk and another of thread and on his knees was a rag of some sort. He had for the last three minutes been trying to thread his needle, but could not get the thread into the eye and so was very angry with the darkness and indeed with the thread itself, muttering in an undertone: "She won't go in, the savage! You wear me out, you bitch." Akaky Akakievich was unhappy that he had come just at the minute when Petrovich was in a bad humor; he liked to give him an order when he was a little "elevated," or, as his wife expressed it, "had fortified himself with vodka, the one-eyed devil." In such circumstances Petrovich was as a rule very ready to give way and agree, and invariably bowed and thanked him. Afterward, it is true, his wife would come wailing that her husband had been drunk and so had asked too little, but adding a single ten-kopek piece would settle that. But on this occasion Petrovich was apparently sober and consequently curt, unwilling to bargain, and the devil knows what price he would be ready to demand. Akaky Akakievich realized this, and was, as the saying is, beating a retreat, but things had gone too far, for Petrovich was screwing up his solitary eye very attentively at him and Akaky Akakievich involuntarily said: "Good day, Petrovich!"

"I wish you a good day, sir," said Petrovich, and squinted at Akaky Akakievich's hands, trying to discover what sort of goods he had brought.

"Here I have come to you, Petrovich, do you see . . . !"

It must be noticed that Akaky Akakievich for the most part explained himself by apologies, vague phrases, and meaningless parts of speech which have absolutely no significance whatever. If the subject were a very difficult one, it was his habit indeed to leave his sentences quite unfinished, so that very often after a sentence had begun with the words, "It really is, don't you know . . ." nothing at all would follow and he himself would be quite oblivious to the fact that he had not finished his thought, supposing he had said all that was necessary.

"What is it?" said Petrovich, and at the same time with his solitary eye he scrutinized his whole uniform from the collar to the sleeves, the back, the skirts, the buttonholes—with all of which he was very familiar since they were all his own work. Such scrutiny is habitual with tailors; it is the first thing they do on meeting one.

"It's like this, Petrovich . . . the overcoat, the cloth . . . you see everywhere else it is quite strong; it's a little dusty and looks as though it were old, but it is new and it is only in one place just a little . . . on the back, and just a little worn on one shoulder and on this shoulder, too, a little . . . do you see? that's all, and it's not much work . . ."

Petrovich took the "dressing gown," first spread it out over the table, examined it for a long time, shook his head, and put his hand out to the window sill for a round snuffbox with a portrait on the lid of some general—which general I can't exactly say, for a finger had been thrust through the spot where a face should have been, and the hole had been pasted over with a square piece of paper. After taking a pinch of snuff, Petrovich held the "dressing gown" up in his hands and looked at it against the light, and again he shook his head; then he turned it with the lining upward and once more shook his head; again he took off the lid with the general pasted up with paper and stuffed a pinch into his nose, shut the box, put it away, and at last said: "No, it can't be repaired; a wretched garment!" Akaky Akakievich's heart sank at those words.

"Why can't it, Petrovich?" he said, almost in the imploring voice of a child. "Why, the only thing is, it is a bit worn on the shoulders; why, you have got some little pieces . . ."

"Yes, the pieces will be found all right," said Petrovich, "but it can't be patched, the stuff is rotten; if you put a needle in it, it would give way."

"Let it give way, but you just put a patch on it."

"There is nothing to put a patch on. There is nothing for it to hold on to; there is a great strain on it; it is not worth calling cloth; it would fly away at a breath of wind."

"Well, then, strengthen it with something—I'm sure, really, this is . . . !"

"No," said Petrovich resolutely, "there is nothing that can be done, the thing is no good at all. You had far better, when the cold winter weather comes, make yourself leg wrappings out of it, for there is no warmth in stockings; the Germans invented them just to make money." (Petrovich enjoyed a dig at the Germans occasionally.) "And as for the overcoat, it is obvious that you will have to have a new one."

At the word "new" there was a mist before Akaky Akakievich's eyes, and everything in the room seemed blurred. He could see nothing clearly but the general with the piece of paper over his face on the lid of Petrovich's snuffbox.

"A new one?" he said, still feeling as though he were in a dream; "why, I haven't the money for it."

"Yes, a new one," Petrovich repeated with barbarous composure.

"Well, and if I did have a new one, how much would it . . . ?"

"You mean what will it cost?"

"Yes."

"Well, at least one hundred and fifty rubles," said Petrovich, and he compressed his lips meaningfully. He was very fond of making an effect; he was fond of suddenly disconcerting a man completely and then squinting sideways to see what sort of a face he made.

"A hundred and fifty rubles for an overcoat!" screamed poor Akaky Akakievich—it was perhaps the first time he had screamed in his life, for he was always distinguished by the softness of his voice.

"Yes," said Petrovich, "and even then it depends on the coat. If I were to put marten on the collar, and add a hood with silk linings, it would come to two hundred."

"Petrovich, please," said Akaky Akakievich in an imploring voice, not hearing and not trying to hear what Petrovich said, and missing all his effects, "repair it somehow, so that it will serve a little longer."

"No, that would be wasting work and spending money for nothing," said Petrovich, and after that Akaky Akakievich went away completely crushed, and when he had gone Petrovich remained standing for a long time with his lips pursed up meaningfully before he began his work again, feeling pleased that he had not demeaned himself or lowered the dignity of the tailor's art.

When he got into the street, Akaky Akakievich felt as though he was in a dream. "So that is how it is," he said to himself. "I really did not think it would be this way . . ." and then after a pause he added, "So that's it! So that's how it is at last! and I really could never have supposed it would be this way. And there . . ." There followed another long silence, after which he said: "So that's it! well, it really is so utterly unexpected . . . who would have thought . . . what a circumstance . . ." Saying this, instead of going home he walked off in quite the opposite direction without suspecting what he was doing. On the way a clumsy chimney sweep brushed the whole of his sooty side against him and blackened his entire shoulder; a whole hatful of plaster scattered upon him from the top of a house that was being built. He noticed nothing of this, and only after he had jostled against a policeman who had set his halberd down beside him and was shaking some snuff out of his horn into his rough fist, he came to himself a little and then only because the policeman said: "Why are you poking yourself right in one's face, haven't you enough room on the street?" This made him look around and turn homeward; only there he began to collect his thoughts, to see his position in a clear and true light, and began talking to himself no longer incoherently but reasonably and openly as with a sensible friend with whom one can discuss the most intimate and vital matters. "No," said Akaky Akakievich, "it is no use talking to Petrovich now; just now he really is . . . his wife must have been giving it to him. I had better go to him on Sunday morning; after Saturday night he will have a crossed eye and be sleepy, so he'll want a little drink and his wife won't give him a kopek. I'll slip ten kopeks into his hand and then he will be more accommodating and maybe take the overcoat . . ."

So reasoning with himself, Akaky Akakievich cheered up and waited until the next Sunday; then, seeing from a distance Petrovich's wife leaving the house, he went straight in. Petrovich certainly had a crossed eye after Saturday. He could hardly hold his head up and was very drowsy; but, despite all that, as soon as he heard what Akaky Akakievich was speaking about, it seemed as though the devil had nudged him. "I can't," he said, "you must order a new one." Akaky Akakievich at once slipped a ten-kopek piece into his hand. "I thank you, sir, I will have just a drop to your health, but don't trouble yourself about the overcoat; it is no good for anything. I'll make you a fine new coat; you can have faith in me for that."

Akaky Akakievich would have said more about repairs, but Petrovich, without listening, said: "A new one I'll make you without fail; you can rely on that; I'll do my best. It could even be like the fashion that is popular, with the collar to fasten with silver-plated hooks under a flap."

Then Akaky Akakievich saw that there was no escape from a new overcoat and he was utterly depressed. How indeed, for what, with what money could he get it? Of course he could to some extent rely on the bonus for the coming holiday, but that money had long ago been appropriated and its use determined beforehand. It was needed for new trousers and to pay the cobbler an old debt for putting some new tops on some old boots, and he had to order three shirts from a seamstress as well as two items of undergarments which it is indecent to mention in print; in short, all that money absolutely must be spent, and even if the director were to be so gracious as to give him a holiday bonus of forty-five or even fifty, instead of forty rubles, there would be still left a mere trifle, which would be but a drop in the ocean compared to the fortune needed for an overcoat. Though, of course, he knew that Petrovich had a strange craze for suddenly demanding the devil knows what enormous price, so that at times his own wife could not help crying out: "Why, you are out of your wits, you idiot! Another time he'll undertake a job for nothing, and here the devil has be-witched him to ask more than he is worth himself." Though, of course, he knew that Petrovich would undertake to make it for eighty rubles, still where would he get those eighty rubles? He might manage half of that sum; half of it could be found, perhaps even a little more; but where could he get the other half? . . . But, first of all, the reader ought to know where that first half was to be found. Akaky Akakievich had the habit every time he spent a ruble of putting aside two kopeks in a little box which he kept locked, with a slit in the lid for dropping in the money. At the end of every six months he would inspect the pile of coppers there and change them for small silver. He had done this for a long time, and in the course of many years the sum had mounted up to forty rubles and so he had half the money in his hands, but where was he to get the other half; where was he to get another forty rubles? Akaky Akakievich thought and thought and decided at last that he would have to diminish his ordinary expenses, at least for a year; give up burning candles in the evening, and if he had to do any work he must go into the landlady's room and work by her candle; that as he walked along the streets he must walk as lightly and carefully as possible, almost on tiptoe, on the cobbles and flagstones, so that his soles might last a little longer than usual; that he must send his linen to the wash less frequently, and that, to preserve it from being worn, he must take it off every day when he came home and sit in a thin cotton dress-ing gown, a very ancient garment which Time itself had spared. To tell the truth, he found it at first rather difficult to get used to these privations, but after a while it be-came a habit and went smoothly enough—he even became quite accustomed to be-ing hungry in the evening; on the other hand, he had spiritual nourishment, for he carried ever in his thoughts the idea of his future overcoat. His whole existence had in a sense become fuller, as though he had married, as though some other person were present with him, as though he were no longer alone but an agreeable companion had consented to walk the path of life hand in hand with him, and that companion was none other than the new overcoat with its thick padding and its strong, durable lining. He became, as it were, more alive, even more strong-willed, like a man who has set before himself a definite goal. Uncertainty, indecision, in fact all the hesitating and vague characteristics, vanished from his face and his manners. At times there was a gleam in his eyes; indeed, the most bold and audacious ideas flashed through his mind. Why not really have marten on the collar? Meditation on the subject always made him absent-minded. On one occasion when he was copying a document, he very nearly made a mistake, so that he almost cried out "ough" aloud and crossed himself. At least once every month he went to Petrovich to talk about the overcoat: where it would be best to buy the cloth, and what color it should be, and what price; and, though he returned home a little anxious, he was always pleased at the thought that at last the time was at hand when everything would be bought and the overcoat would be made. Things moved even faster than he had anticipated. Contrary to all expectations, the director bestowed on Akaky Akakievich a bonus of no less than sixty rubles. Whether it was that he had an inkling that Akaky Akakievich needed a coat, or whether it happened by luck, owing to this he found he had twenty rubles extra. This circumstance hastened the course of affairs. Another two or three months of partial starvation and Akaky Akakievich had actually saved up nearly eighty rubles. His heart, as a rule very tranquil, began to throb.

The very first day he set out with Petrovich for the shops. They bought some very good cloth, and no wonder, since they had been thinking of it for more than six months, and scarcely a month had passed without their going out to the shop to compare prices; now Petrovich himself declared that there was no better cloth to be had. For the lining they chose calico, but of such good quality, that in Petrovich's words it was even better than silk, and actually as strong and handsome to look at. Marten they did not buy, because it was too expensive, but instead they chose cat fur, the best to be found in the shop—cat which in the distance might almost be taken for marten. Petrovich was busy making the coat for two weeks, because there was a great deal of quilting; otherwise it would have been ready sooner. Petrovich charged twelve rubles for the work; less than that it hardly could have been; everything was sewn with silk, with fine double seams, and Petrovich went over every seam afterwards with his own teeth, imprinting various patterns with them. It was . . . it is hard to say precisely on what day, but probably on the most triumphant day in the life of Akaky Akakievich, that Petrovich at last brought the overcoat. He brought it in the morning, just before it was time to set off for the department. The overcoat could not have arrived at a more opportune time, because severe frosts were just beginning and seemed threatening to become even harsher. Petrovich brought the coat himself as a good tailor should. There was an expression of importance on his face, such as Akaky Akakievich had never seen there before. He seemed fully conscious of having completed a work of no little importance and of having shown by his own example the gulf that separates tailors who only put in linings and do repairs from those who make new coats. He took the coat out of the huge handkerchief in which he had brought it (the hand-kerchief had just come home from the wash); he then folded it up and put it in his pocket for future use. After taking out the overcoat, he looked at it with much pride and holding it in both hands, threw it very deftly over Akaky Akakievich's shoulders, then pulled it down and smoothed it out behind with his hands; then draped it about Akaky Akakievich somewhat jauntily. Akaky Akakievich, a practical man, wanted to try it with his arms in the sleeves. Petrovich helped him to put it on, and it looked splendid with his arms in the sleeves, too. In fact, it turned out that the overcoat was completely and entirely successful. Petrovich did not let slip the occasion for observing that it was only because he lived in a small street and had no signboard, and because he had known Akaky Akakievich so long, that he had done it so cheaply, and that on Nevsky Prospekt they would have asked him seventy-five rubles for the tailoring alone. Akaky Akakievich had no inclination to discuss this with Petrovich; besides he was frightened of the big sums that Petrovich was fond of flinging airily about in conversation. He paid him, thanked him, and went off, with his new overcoat on, to the department. Petrovich followed him out and stopped in the street, staring for a long time at the coat from a distance and then purposely turned off and, taking a short cut through a side street, came back into the street, and got another view of the coat from the other side, that is, from the front.

Meanwhile Akaky Akakievich walked along in a gay holiday mood. Every second he was conscious that he had a new overcoat on his shoulders, and several times he actually laughed from inward satisfaction. Indeed, it had two advantages: one that it was warm and the other that it was good. He did not notice how far he had walked at all and he suddenly found himself in the department; in the porter's room he took off the overcoat, looked it over, and entrusted it to the porter's special care. I cannot tell how it happened, but all at once everyone in the department learned that Akaky Akakievich had a new overcoat and that the "dressing gown" no longer existed. They all ran out at once into the cloakroom to look at Akaky Akakievich's new overcoat; they began welcoming him and congratulating him so that at first he could do nothing but smile and then felt positively embarrassed. When, coming up to him, they all began saying that he must "sprinkle" the new overcoat and that he ought at least to buy them all a supper, Akaky Akakievich lost his head completely and did not know what to do, how to get out of it, nor what to answer. A few minutes later, flushing crimson, he even began assuring them with great simplicity that it was not a new overcoat at all, that it wasn't much, that it was an old overcoat. At last one of the clerks, indeed the assistant of the head clerk of the room, probably in order to show that he wasn't too proud to mingle with those beneath him, said: "So be it, I'll give a party instead of Akaky Akakievich and invite you all to tea with me this evening; as luck would have it, it is my birthday." The clerks naturally congratulated the assistant head clerk and eagerly accepted the invitation. Akaky Akakievich was beginning to make excuses, but they all declared that it was uncivil of him, that it would be simply a shame and a disgrace and that he could not possibly refuse. So, he finally relented, and later felt pleased about it when he remembered that through this he would have the opportunity of going out in the evening, too, in his new overcoat. That whole day was for Akaky Akakievich the most triumphant and festive day in his life. He returned home in the happiest frame of mind, took off the overcoat, and hung it carefully on the wall, admiring the cloth and lining once more, and then pulled out his old "dressing gown," now completely falling apart, and put it next to his new overcoat to compare the two. He glanced at it and laughed: the difference was enormous! And long afterwards he went on laughing at dinner, as the position in which the "dressing gown" was placed recurred to his mind. He dined in excellent spirits and after dinner wrote nothing, no papers at all, but just relaxed for a little while on his bed, till it got dark; then, without putting things off, he dressed, put on his overcoat, and went out into the street. Where precisely the clerk who had invited him lived we regret to say we cannot tell; our memory is beginning to fail sadly, and everything there in Petersburg, all the streets and houses, are so blurred and muddled in our head that it is a very difficult business to put anything in orderly fashion. Regardless of that, there is no doubt that the clerk lived in the better part of the town and consequently a very long distance from Akaky Akakievich. At first Akaky Akakievich had to walk through deserted streets, scantily lighted, but as he approached his destination the streets became more lively, more full of people, and more brightly lighted; passers-by began to be more frequent, ladies began to appear, here and there beautifully dressed, and beaver collars were to be seen on the men. Cabmen with wooden, railed sledges, studded with brass-topped nails, were less frequently seen; on the other hand, jaunty drivers in raspberry-colored velvet caps, with lacquered sledges and bearskin rugs, appeared and carriages with decorated boxes dashed along the streets, their wheels crunching through the snow.

Akaky Akakievich looked at all this as a novelty; for several years he had not gone out into the streets in the evening. He stopped with curiosity before a lighted shop window to look at a picture in which a beautiful woman was represented in the act of taking off her shoe and displaying as she did so the whole of a very shapely leg, while behind her back a gentleman with whiskers and a handsome imperial on his chin was sticking his head in at the door. Akaky Akakievich shook his head and smiled and then went on his way. Why did he smile? Was it because he had come across something quite unfamiliar to him, though every man retains some instinctive feeling on the subject, or was it that he reflected, like many other clerks, as follows: "Well, those Frenchmen! It's beyond anything! If they go in for anything of the sort, it really is . . . !" Though possibly he did not even think that; there is no creeping into a man's soul and finding out all that he thinks. At last he reached the house in which the assistant head clerk lived in fine style; there was a lamp burning on the stairs, and the apartment was on the second floor. As he went into the hall Akaky Akakievich saw rows of galoshes. Among them in the middle of the room stood a hissing samovar puffing clouds of steam. On the walls hung coats and cloaks among which some actually had beaver collars or velvet lapels. From the other side of the wall there came noise and talk, which suddenly became clear and loud when the door opened and the footman came out with a tray full of empty glasses, a jug of cream, and a basket of biscuits. It was evident that the clerks had arrived long before and had already drunk their first glass of tea. Akaky Akakievich, after hanging up his coat with his own hands, went into the room, and at the same moment there flashed before his eyes a vision of candles, clerks, pipes, and card tables, together with the confused sounds of conversation rising up on all sides and the noise of moving chairs. He stopped very awkwardly in the middle of the room, looking about and trying to think of what to do, but he was noticed and received with a shout and they all went at once into the hall and again took a look at his overcoat. Though Akaky Akakievich was somewhat embarrassed, yet, being a simplehearted man, he could not help being pleased at seeing how they all admired his coat. Then of course they all abandoned him and his coat, and turned their attention as usual to the tables set for whist. All this—the noise, the talk, and the crowd of people—was strange and wonderful to Akaky Akakievich. He simply did not know how to behave, what to do with his arms and legs and his whole body; at last he sat down beside the players, looked at the cards, stared first at one and then at another of the faces, and in a little while, feeling bored, began to yawn—especially since it was long past the time at which he usually went to bed. He tried to say goodbye to his hosts, but they would not let him go, saying that he absolutely must have a glass of champagne in honor of the new coat. An hour later supper was served, consisting of salad, cold veal, pastry and pies from the bakery, and champagne. They made Akaky Akakievich drink two glasses, after which he felt that things were much more cheerful, though he could not forget that it was twelve o'clock, and that he ought to have been home long ago. That his host might not take it into his head to detain him, he slipped out of the room, hunted in the hall for his coat, which he found, not without regret, lying on the floor, shook it, removed some fluff from it, put it on, and went down the stairs into the street. It was still light in the streets. Some little grocery shops, those perpetual clubs for servants and all sorts of people, were open; others which were closed showed, however, a long streak of light at every crack of the door, proving that they were not yet deserted, and probably maids and menservants were still finishing their conversation and discussion, driving their masters to utter perplexity as to their whereabouts. Akaky Akakievich walked along in a cheerful state of mind; he was even on the point of running, goodness knows why, after a lady of some sort who passed by like lightning with every part of her frame in violent motion. He checked himself at once, however, and again walked along very gently, feeling positively surprised at the inexplicable impulse that had seized him. Soon the deserted streets, which are not particularly cheerful by day and even less so in the evening, stretched before him. Now they were still more dead and deserted; the light of street lamps was scantier, the oil evidently running low; then came wooden houses and fences; not a soul anywhere; only the snow gleamed on the streets and the low-pitched slumbering hovels looked black and gloomy with their closed shutters. He approached the spot where the street was intersected by an endless square, which looked like a fearful desert with its houses scarcely visible on the far side.

In the distance, goodness knows where, there was a gleam of light from some sentry box which seemed to be at the end of the world. Akaky Akakievich's lightheartedness faded. He stepped into the square, not without uneasiness, as though his heart had a premonition of evil. He looked behind him and to both sides—it was as though the sea were all around him. "No, better not look," he thought, and walked on, shutting his eyes, and when he opened them to see whether the end of the square was near, he suddenly saw standing before him, almost under his very nose, some men with mustaches; just what they were like he could not even distinguish. There was a mist before his eyes, and a throbbing in his chest. "Why, that overcoat is mine!" said one of them in a voice like a clap of thunder, seizing him by the collar. Akaky Akakievich was on the point of shouting "Help" when another put a fist the size of a clerk's head against his lips, saying: "You just shout now." Akaky Akakievich felt only that they took the overcoat off, and gave him a kick with their knees, and he fell on his face in the snow and was conscious of nothing more. A few minutes later he recovered consciousness and got up on his feet, but there was no one there. He felt that it was cold on the ground and that he had no overcoat, and began screaming, but it seemed as though his voice would not carry to the end of the square. Overwhelmed with despair and continuing to scream, he ran across the square straight to the sentry box beside which stood a policeman leaning on his halberd and, so it seemed, looking with curiosity to see who the devil the man was who was screaming and running toward him from the distance. As Akaky Akakievich reached him, he began breathlessly shouting that he was asleep and not looking after his duty not to see that a man was being robbed. The policeman answered that he had seen nothing, that he had only seen him stopped in the middle of the square by two men, and supposed that they were his friends, and that, instead of abusing him for nothing, he had better go the next day to the police inspector, who would certainly find out who had taken the overcoat. Akaky Akakievich ran home in a terrible state: his hair, which was still comparatively abundant on his temples and the back of his head, was completely disheveled; his sides and chest and his trousers were all covered with snow. When his old landlady heard a fearful knock at the door, she jumped hurriedly out of bed and, with only one slipper on, ran to open it, modestly holding her chemise over her bosom; but when she opened it she stepped back, seeing in what a state Akaky Akakievich was. When he told her what had happened, she clasped her hands in horror and said that he must go straight to the district commissioner, because the local police inspector would deceive him, make promises, and lead him a dance; that it would be best of all to go to the district commissioner, and that she knew him, because Anna, the Finnish girl who was once her cook, was now in service as a nurse at the commissioner's; and that she often saw him himself when he passed by their house, and that he used to be every Sunday at church too, saying his prayers and at the same time looking good-humoredly at everyone, and that therefore by every token he must be a kind-hearted man. After listening to this advice, Akaky Akakievich made his way very gloomily to his room, and how he spent that night I leave to the imagination of those who are in the least able to picture the position of others.

Early in the morning he set off to the police commissioner's but was told that he was asleep. He came at ten o'clock, he was told again that he was asleep; he came at eleven and was told that the commissioner was not at home; he came at dinnertime, but the clerks in the anteroom would not let him in, and insisted on knowing what was the matter and what business had brought him and exactly what had happened; so that at last Akaky Akakievich for the first time in his life tried to show the strength of his character and said curtly that he must see the commissioner himself, that they dare not refuse to admit him, that he had come from the department on government business, and that if he made complaint of them they would see. The clerks dared say nothing to this, and one of them went to summon the commissioner. The latter received his story of being robbed of his overcoat in an extremely peculiar manner. Instead of attending to the main point, he began asking Akaky Akakievich questions: why had he been coming home so late? wasn't he going, or hadn't he been, to some bawdy house? so that Akaky Akakievich was overwhelmed with confusion, and went away without knowing whether or not the proper measures would be taken regarding his overcoat. He was absent from the office all that day (the only time that it had happened in his life). Next day he appeared with a pale face, wearing his old "dressing gown" which had become a still more pitiful sight. The news of the theft of the overcoat—though there were clerks who did not let even this chance slip of jeering at Akaky Akakievich—touched many of them. They decided on the spot to get up a collection for him, but collected only a very trifling sum, because the clerks had already spent a good deal contributing to the director's portrait and on the purchase of a book, at the suggestion of the head of their department, who was a friend of the author, and so the total realized was very insignificant. One of the clerks, moved by compassion, ventured at any rate to assist Akaky Akakievich with good advice, telling him not to go to the local police inspector, because, though it might happen that the latter might succeed in finding his overcoat because he wanted to impress his superiors, it would remain in the possession of the police unless he presented legal proofs that it belonged to him; he urged that by far the best thing would be to appeal to a Person of Consequence; that the Person of Consequence, by writing and getting into communication with the proper authorities, could push the matter through more successfully. There was nothing else to do. Akaky Akakievich made up his mind to go to the Person of Consequence. What precisely was the nature of the functions of the Person of Consequence has remained a matter of uncertainty. It must be noted that this Person of Consequence had only lately become a person of consequence, and until recently had been a person of no consequence. Though, indeed, his position even now was not reckoned of consequence in comparison with others of still greater consequence. But there is always to be found a circle of persons to whom a person of little consequence in the eyes of others is a person of consequence. It is true that he did his utmost to increase the consequence of his position in various ways, for instance by insisting that his subordinates should come out onto the stairs to meet him when he arrived at his office; that no one should venture to approach him directly but all proceedings should follow the strictest chain of command; that a collegiate registrar should report the matter to the governmental secretary; and the governmental secretary to the titular councilor or whomsoever it might be, and that business should only reach him through this channel. Everyone in Holy Russia has a craze for imitation; everyone apes and mimics his superiors. I have actually been told that a titular councilor who was put in charge of a small separate office, immediately partitioned off a special room for himself, calling it the head office, and posted lackeys at the door with red collars and gold braid, who took hold of the handle of the door and opened it for everyone who went in, though the "head office" was so tiny that it was with difficulty that an ordinary writing desk could be put into it. The manners and habits of the Person of Consequence were dignified and majestic, but hardly subtle. The chief foundation of his system was strictness; "strictness, strictness, and—strictness!" he used to say, and at the last word he would look very significantly at the person he was addressing, though, indeed, he had no reason to do so, for the dozen clerks who made up the whole administrative mechanism of his office stood in appropriate awe of him; any clerk who saw him in the distance would leave his work and remain standing at attention till his superior had left the room. His conversation with his subordinates was usually marked by severity and almost confined to three phrases: "How dare you? Do you know to whom you are speaking? Do you understand who I am?" He was, however, at heart a good-natured man, pleasant and obliging with his colleagues; but his advancement to a high rank had completely turned his head. When he received it, he was perplexed, thrown off his balance, and quite at a loss as to how to behave. If he chanced to be with his equals, he was still quite a decent man, a very gentlemanly man, in fact, and in many ways even an intelligent man; but as soon as he was in company with men who were even one grade below him, there was simply no doing anything with him: he sat silent and his position excited compassion, the more so as he himself felt that he might have been spending his time to so much more advantage. At times there could be seen in his eyes an intense desire to join in some interesting conversation, but he was restrained by the doubt whether it would not be too much on his part, whether it would not be too great a familiarity and lowering of his dignity, and in consequence of these reflections he remained everlastingly in the same mute condition, only uttering from time to time monosyllabic sounds, and in this way he gained the reputation of being a terrible bore.

So this was the Person of Consequence to whom our friend Akaky Akakievich appealed, and he appealed to him at a most unpropitious moment, very unfortunate for himself, though fortunate, indeed, for the Person of Consequence. The latter happened to be in his study, talking in the very best of spirits with an old friend of his childhood who had only just arrived and whom he had not seen for several years. It was at this moment that he was informed that a man called Bashmachkin was asking to see him. He asked abruptly, "What sort of man is he?" and received the answer, "A government clerk." "Ah! he can wait. I haven't time now," said the Person of Consequence. Here I must observe that this was a complete lie on the part of the Person of Consequence; he had time; his friend and he had long ago said all they had to say to each other and their conversation had begun to be broken by very long pauses during which they merely slapped each other on the knee, saying, "So that's how things are, Ivan Abramovich!"—"So that's it, Stepan Varlamovich!" but, despite that, he told the clerk to wait in order to show his friend, who had left the civil service some years before and was living at home in the country, how long clerks had to wait for him. At last, after they had talked or rather been silent, to their heart's content and had smoked a cigar in very comfortable armchairs with sloping backs, he seemed suddenly to recollect, and said to the secretary, who was standing at the door with papers for his signature: "Oh, by the way, there is a clerk waiting, isn't there? tell him he can come in." When he saw Akaky Akakievich's meek appearance and old uniform, he turned to him at once and said: "What do you want?" in a firm and abrupt voice, which he had purposely rehearsed in his own room in solitude before the mirror for a week before receiving his present post and the grade of a general. Akaky Akakievich, who was overwhelmed with appropriate awe beforehand, was somewhat confused and, as far as his tongue would allow him, explained to the best of his powers, with even more frequent "ers" than usual, that he had had a perfectly new overcoat and now he had been robbed of it in the most inhuman way, and that now he had come to beg him by his intervention either to correspond with his honor, the head police commissioner, or anybody else, and find the overcoat. This mode of proceeding struck the general for some reason as too familiar. "What next, sir?" he went on abruptly. "Don't you know the way to proceed? To whom are you addressing yourself? Don't you know how things are done? You ought first to have handed in a petition to the office; it would have gone to the head clerk of the room, and to the head clerk of the section; then it would have been handed to the secretary and the secretary would have brought it to me . . ."

"But, your Excellency," said Akaky Akakievich, trying to gather the drop of courage he possessed and feeling at the same time that he was perspiring all over, "I ventured, your Excellency, to trouble you because secretaries . . . er . . . are people you can't depend on . . ."

"What? what? what?" said the Person of Consequence, "where did you get hold of that attitude? where did you pick up such ideas? What insubordination is spreading among young men against their superiors and their chiefs!" The Person of Consequence did not apparently observe that Akaky Akakievich was well over fifty, and therefore if he could have been called a young man it would only have been in comparison with a man of seventy. "Do you know to whom you are speaking? Do you understand who I am? Do you understand that, I ask you?" At this point he stamped, and raised his voice to such a powerful note that Akaky Akakievich was not the only one to be terrified. Akaky Akakievich was positively petrified; he staggered, trembling all over, and could not stand; if the porters had not run up to support him, he would have flopped on the floor; he was led out almost unconscious. The Person of Consequence, pleased that the effect had surpassed his expectations and enchanted at the idea that his words could even deprive a man of consciousness, stole a sideway glance at his friend to see how he was taking it, and perceived not without satisfaction that his friend was feeling very uncertain and even beginning to be a little terrified himself.

How he got downstairs, how he went out into the street—of all that Akaky Akakievich remembered nothing; he had no feeling in his arms or his legs. In all his life he had never been so severely reprimanded by a general, and this was by one of another department, too. He went out into the snowstorm that was whistling through the streets, with his mouth open, and as he went he stumbled off the pavement; the wind, as its way is in Petersburg, blew upon him from all points of the compass and from every side street. In an instant it had blown a quinsy into his throat, and when he got home he was not able to utter a word; he went to bed with a swollen face and throat. That's how violent the effects of an appropriate reprimand can be!

Next day he was in a high fever. Thanks to the gracious assistance of the Petersburg climate, the disease made more rapid progress than could have been expected, and when the doctor came, after feeling his pulse he could find nothing to do but prescribe a poultice, and that simply so that the patient might not be left without the benefit of medical assistance; however, two days later he informed him that his end was at hand, after which he turned to Akaky Akakievich's landlady and said: "And you had better lose no time, my good woman, but order him now a pine coffin, for an oak one will be too expensive for him." Whether Akaky Akakievich heard these fateful words or not, whether they produced a shattering effect upon him, and whether he regretted his pitiful life, no one can tell, for he was constantly in delirium and fever. Apparitions, each stranger than the one before, were continually haunting him: first he saw Petrovich and was ordering him to make an overcoat trimmed with some sort of traps for robbers, who were, he believed, continually under the bed, and he was calling his landlady every minute to pull out a thief who had even got under the quilt; then he kept asking why his old "dressing gown" was hanging before him when he had a new overcoat; then he thought he was standing before the general listening to the appropriate reprimand and saying, "I am sorry, your Excellency"; then finally he became abusive, uttering the most awful language, so that his old landlady positively crossed herself, having never heard anything of the kind from him before, and the more horrified because these dreadful words followed immediately upon the phrase "your Excellency." Later on, his talk was merely a medley of nonsense, so that it was quite unintelligible; all that was evident was that his incoherent words and thoughts were concerned with nothing but the overcoat. At last poor Akaky Akakievich gave up the ghost. No seal was put upon his room nor upon his things, because, in the first place, he had no heirs and, in the second, the property left was very small, to wit, a bundle of quills, a quire of white government paper, three pairs of socks, two or three buttons that had come off his trousers, and the "dressing gown" with which the reader is already familiar. Who came into all this wealth God only knows; even I who tell the tale must admit that I have not bothered to inquire. And Petersburg carried on without Akaky Akakievich, as though, indeed, he had never been in the city. A creature had vanished and departed whose cause no one had championed, who was dear to no one, of interest to no one, who never attracted the attention of a naturalist, though the latter does not disdain to fix a common fly upon a pin and look at him under the microscope—a creature who bore patiently the jeers of the office and for no particular reason went to his grave, though even he at the very end of his life was visited by an exalted guest in the form of an overcoat that for one instant brought color into his poor, drab life—a creature on whom disease fell as it falls upon the heads of the mighty ones of this world . . . !

Several days after his death, a messenger from the department was sent to his lodgings with instructions that he should go at once to the office, for his chief was asking for him; but the messenger was obliged to return without him, explaining that he could not come, and to the inquiry "Why?" he added, "Well, you see, the fact is he is dead; he was buried three days ago." This was how they learned at the office of the death of Akaky Akakievich, and the next day there was sitting in his seat a new clerk who was very much taller and who wrote not in the same straight handwriting but made his letters more slanting and crooked.

But who could have imagined that this was not all there was to tell about Akaky Akakievich, that he was destined for a few days to make his presence felt in the world after his death, as though to make up for his life having been unnoticed by anyone? But so it happened, and our little story unexpectedly finishes with a fantastic ending.

Rumors were suddenly floating about Petersburg that in the neighborhood of the Kalinkin Bridge and for a little distance beyond, a corpse had begun appearing at night in the form of a clerk looking for a stolen overcoat, and stripping from the shoulders of all passers-by, regardless of grade and calling, overcoats of all descriptions—trimmed with cat fur or beaver or padded, lined with raccoon, fox, and bear—made, in fact of all sorts of skin which men have adapted for the covering of their own. One of the clerks of the department saw the corpse with his own eyes and at once recognized it as Akaky Akakievich; but it excited in him such terror that he ran away as fast as his legs could carry him and so could not get a very clear view of him, and only saw him hold up his finger threateningly in the distance.

From all sides complaints were continually coming that backs and shoulders, not of mere titular councilors, but even of upper court councilors, had been exposed to catching cold, as a result of being stripped of their overcoats. Orders were given to the police to catch the corpse regardless of trouble or expense, dead or alive, and to punish him severely, as an example to others, and, indeed, they very nearly succeeded in doing so. The policeman of one district in Kiryushkin Alley snatched a corpse by the collar on the spot of the crime in the very act of attempting to snatch a frieze overcoat from a retired musician, who used, in his day, to play the flute. Having caught him by the collar, he shouted until he had brought two other policemen whom he ordered to hold the corpse while he felt just a minute in his boot to get out a snuffbox in order to revive his nose which had six times in his life been frostbitten, but the snuff was probably so strong that not even a dead man could stand it. The policeman had hardly had time to put his finger over his right nostril and draw up some snuff in the left when the corpse sneezed violently right into the eyes of all three. While they were putting their fists up to wipe their eyes, the corpse completely vanished, so that they were not even sure whether he had actually been in their hands. From that time forward, the policemen had such a horror of the dead that they were even afraid to seize the living and confined themselves to shouting from the distance: "Hey, you! Move on!" and the clerk's body began to appear even on the other side of the Kalinkin Bridge, terrorizing all timid people.

We have, however, quite neglected the Person of Consequence, who may in reality almost be said to be the cause of the fantastic ending of this perfectly true story. To begin with, my duty requires me to do justice to the Person of Consequence by recording that soon after poor Akaky Akakievich had gone away crushed to powder, he felt something not unlike regret. Sympathy was a feeling not unknown to him; his heart was open to many kindly impulses, although his exalted grade very often prevented them from being shown. As soon as his friend had gone out of his study, he even began brooding over poor Akaky Akakievich, and from that time forward, he was almost every day haunted by the image of the poor clerk who had been unable to survive the official reprimand. The thought of the man so worried him that a week later he actually decided to send a clerk to find out how he was and whether he really could help him in any way. And when they brought him word that Akaky Akakievich had died suddenly in delirium and fever, it made a great impression on him; his conscience reproached him and he was depressed all day. Anxious to distract his mind and to forget the unpleasant incident, he went to spend the evening with one of his friends, where he found respectable company, and what was best of all, almost everyone was of the same grade so that he was able to be quite uninhibited. This had a wonderful effect on his spirits. He let himself go, became affable and genial—in short, spent a very agreeable evening. At supper he drank a couple of glasses of champagne—a proceeding which we all know is not a bad recipe for cheerfulness. The champagne made him inclined to do something unusual, and he decided not to go home yet but to visit a lady of his acquaintance, a certain Karolina Ivanovna—a lady apparently of German extraction, for whom he entertained extremely friendly feelings. It must be noted that the Person of Consequence was a man no longer young. He was an excellent husband, and the respectable father of a family. He had two sons, one already serving in an office, and a nice-looking daughter of sixteen with a rather turned-up, pretty little nose, who used to come every morning to kiss his hand, saying: "*Bon jour, Papa.*" His wife, who was still blooming and decidedly good-looking, indeed, used first to give him her hand to kiss and then turning his hand over would kiss it. But though the Person of Consequence was perfectly satisfied with the pleasant amenities of his domestic life, he thought it proper to have a lady friend in another quarter of the town. This lady friend was not a bit better looking nor younger than his wife, but these puzzling things exist in the world and it is not our business to criticize them. And so the Person of Consequence went downstairs, got into his sledge, and said to his coachman, "To Karolina Ivanovna." While luxuriously wrapped in his warm fur coat he remained in that agreeable frame of mind sweeter to a Russian than anything that could be invented, that is, when one thinks of nothing while thoughts come into the mind by themselves, one pleasanter than the other, without your having to bother following them or looking for them. Full of satisfaction, he recalled all the amusing moments of the evening he had spent, all the phrases that had started the intimate circle of friends laughing; many of them he repeated in an undertone and found them as amusing as before, and so, very naturally, laughed very heartily at them again. From time to time, however, he was disturbed by a gust of wind which, blowing suddenly, God knows why or where from, cut him in the face, pelting him with flakes of snow, puffing out his coat collar like a sail, or suddenly flinging it with unnatural force over his head and giving him endless trouble to extricate himself from it. All at once, the Person of Consequence felt that someone had clutched him very tightly by the collar. Turning around he saw a short man in a shabby old uniform, and not without horror recognized him as Akaky Akakievich. The clerk's face was white as snow and looked like that of a corpse, but the horror of the Person of Consequence was beyond all bounds when he saw the mouth of the corpse distorted into speech, and breathing upon him the chill of the grave, it uttered the following words: "Ah, so here you are at last! At last I've . . . er . . . caught you by the collar. It's your overcoat I want; you refused to help me and abused me into the bargain! So now give me yours!" The poor Person of Consequence very nearly dropped dead. Resolute and determined as he was in his office and before subordinates in general, and though anyone looking at his manly air and figure would have said: "Oh, what a man of character!" yet in this situation he felt, like very many persons of heroic appearance, such terror that not without reason he began to be afraid he would have some sort of fit. He actually flung his overcoat off his shoulders as far as he could and shouted to his coachman in an unnatural voice: "Drive home! Let's get out of here!" The coachman, hearing the tone which he had only heard in critical moments and then accompanied by something even more tangible, hunched his shoulders up to his ears in case of worse following, swung his whip, and flew on like an arrow. In a little over six minutes, the Person of Consequence was at the entrance of his own house. Pale, panic-stricken, and without his overcoat, he arrived home instead of at Karolina Ivanovna's, dragged himself to his own room, and spent the night in great distress, so that next morning his daughter said to him at breakfast, "You look very pale today, Papa"; but her papa remained mute and said not a word to anyone of what had happened to him, where he had been, and where he had been going. The incident made a great impression upon him. Indeed, it happened far more rarely that he said to his subordinates, "How dare you? Do you understand who I am?" and he never uttered those words at all until he had first heard all the facts of the case.

What was even more remarkable is that from that time on the apparition of the dead clerk ceased entirely; apparently the general's overcoat had fitted him perfectly; anyway nothing more was heard of overcoats being snatched from anyone. Many restless and anxious people refused, however, to be pacified, and still maintained that in remote parts of the town the dead clerk went on appearing. One policeman, in Kolomna, for instance, saw with his own eyes an apparition appear from behind a house; but, being by natural constitution somewhat frail—so much so that on one occasion an ordinary grown-up suckling pig, making a sudden dash out of some private building, knocked him off his feet to the great amusement of the cabmen standing around, whom he fined two kopeks each for snuff for such disrespect—he did not dare to stop it, and so followed it in the dark until the apparition suddenly looked around and, stopping, asked him: "What do you want?" displaying a huge fist such as you never see among the living. The policeman said: "Nothing," and turned back on the spot. This apparition, however, was considerably taller and adorned with immense mustaches, and, directing its steps apparently toward Obukhov Bridge, vanished into the darkness of the night.

# Nathaniel Hawthorne

## (1804–1864)

Contemporary and rival writer Edgar Allan Poe introduced Nathaniel Hawthorne's *Twice-Told Tales* by remarking, "There is, perhaps, a somewhat too general or prevalent . . . tone of melancholy and mysticism. The subjects are insufficiently varied." This out of the way, Poe tacked in the other direction, continuing, "But beyond these trivial exceptions we have really none to make. The style is purity itself. Force abounds. High imagination gleams from every page. Mr. Hawthorne is a man of the truest genius." Whether or not his writing is truly "purity itself," Hawthorne undoubtedly cultivated a style all his own. Hawthorne wrote while residing in the notorious city of his birth, Salem, Massachusetts. His fiction is set against the backdrop of colonial America and, appropriately, pursues questions of morality. He had a passion for allegory, demonstrated in his second book of stories, *Mosses from an Old Manse,* in his well-known pieces "My Kinsman, Major Molineux" and "Young Goodman Brown," and in the 1850 novel that has now been immortalized in the high school classroom, *The Scarlet Letter.* Hawthorne's most apt observation about the writing process was probably his early comment about working in the family stagecoach office while preparing for college: "No Man can be a Poet and a Book-Keeper at the same time."

## *Rappaccini's Daughter* 1844

A young man, named Giovanni Guasconti, came, very long ago, from the more southern region of Italy, to pursue his studies at the University of Padua. Giovanni, who had but a scanty supply of gold ducats in his pocket, took lodgings in a high and gloomy chamber of an old edifice, which looked not unworthy to have been the palace of a Paduan noble, and which, in fact, exhibited over its entrance the armorial bearings of a family long since extinct. The young stranger, who was not unstudied in the great poem of his country, recollected that one of the ancestors of this family, and perhaps an occupant of this very mansion, had been pictured by Dante as a partaker of the immortal agonies of his Inferno. These reminiscences and associations, together with the tendency to heart-break natural to a young man for the first time out of his native sphere, caused Giovanni to sigh heavily, as he looked around the desolate and ill-furnished apartment.

"Holy Virgin, Signor," cried old dame Lisabetta, who, won by the youth's remarkable beauty of person, was kindly endeavoring to give the chamber a habitable air, "what a sigh was that to come out of a young man's heart! Do you find this old mansion gloomy? For the love of heaven, then, put your head out of the window, and you will see as bright sunshine as you have left in Naples."

Guasconti mechanically did as the old woman advised, but could not quite agree with her that the Paduan sunshine was as cheerful as that of southern Italy. Such as it was, however, it fell upon a garden beneath the window, and expended its fostering influences on a variety of plants, which seemed to have been cultivated with exceeding care.

"Does this garden belong to the house?" asked Giovanni.

"Heaven forbid, Signor!—unless it were fruitful of better pot-herbs than any that grow there now," answered old Lisabetta. "No; that garden is cultivated by the own hands of Signor Giacomo Rappaccini, the famous Doctor, who, I warrant him, has been heard of as far as Naples. It is said that he distils these plants into medicines that are as potent as a charm. Oftentimes you may see the Signor Doctor at work, and perchance the Signora his daughter, too, gathering the strange flowers that grow in the garden."

The old woman had now done what she could for the aspect of the chamber, and, commending the young man to the protection of the saints, took her departure.

Giovanni still found no better occupation than to look down into the garden beneath his window. From its appearance, he judged it to be one of those botanic gardens, which were of earlier date in Padua than elsewhere in Italy, or in the world. Or, not improbably, it might once have been the pleasure-place of an opulent family; for there was the ruin of a marble fountain in the centre, sculptured with rare art, but so wofully shattered that it was impossible to trace the original design from the chaos of remaining fragments. The water, however, continued to gush and sparkle into the sunbeams as cheerfully as ever. A little gurgling sound ascended to the young man's window, and made him feel as if the fountain were an immortal spirit, that sung its song unceasingly, and without heeding the vicissitudes around it; while one century embodied it in marble, and another scattered the perishable garniture on the soil. All about the pool into which the water subsided, grew various plants, that seemed to require a plentiful supply of moisture for the nourishment of gigantic leaves, and, in some instances, flowers gorgeously magnificent. There was one shrub in particular, set in a marble vase in the midst of the pool, that bore a profusion of purple blossoms, each of which had the lustre and richness of a gem; and the whole together made a show so resplendent that it seemed enough to illuminate the garden, even had there been no sunshine. Every portion of the soil was peopled with plants and herbs, which, if less beautiful, still bore tokens of assiduous care; as if all had their individual virtues, known to the scientific mind that fostered them. Some were placed in urns, rich with old carving, and others in common garden-pots; some crept serpent-like along the ground, or climbed on high, using whatever means of ascent was offered them. One plant had wreathed itself round a statue of Vertumnus,[1] which was thus quite veiled and shrouded in a drapery of hanging foliage, so happily arranged that it might have served a sculptor for a study.

While Giovanni stood at the window, he heard a rustling behind a screen of leaves, and became aware that a person was at work in the garden. His figure soon emerged into view, and showed itself to be that of no common laborer, but a tall,

---

1 **Vertumnus:** The Roman god of the seasons and of the vegetation produced in those seasons.

emaciated, sallow, and sickly-looking man, dressed in a scholar's garb of black. He was beyond the middle term of life, with grey hair, a thin grey beard, and a face singularly marked with intellect and cultivation, but which could never, even in his more youthful days, have expressed much warmth of heart.

Nothing could exceed the intentness with which this scientific gardener examined every shrub which grew in his path; it seemed as if he was looking into their inmost nature, making observations in regard to their creative essence, and discovering why one leaf grew in this shape, and another in that, and wherefore such and such flowers differed among themselves in hue and perfume. Nevertheless, in spite of this deep intelligence on his part, there was no approach to intimacy between himself and these vegetable existences. On the contrary, he avoided their actual touch, or the direct inhaling of their odors, with a caution that impressed Giovanni most disagreeably; for the man's demeanor was that of one walking among malignant influences, such as savage beasts, or deadly snakes, or evil spirits, which, should he allow them one moment of license, would wreak upon him some terrible fatality. It was strangely frightful to the young man's imagination, to see this air of insecurity in a person cultivating a garden, that most simple and innocent of human toils, and which had been alike the joy and labor of the unfallen parents of the race. Was this garden, then, the Eden of the present world?—and this man, with such a perception of harm in what his own hands caused to grow, was he the Adam?

The distrustful gardener, while plucking away the dead leaves or pruning the too luxuriant growth of the shrubs, defended his hands with a pair of thick gloves. Nor were these his only armor. When, in his walk through the garden, he came to the magnificent plant that hung its purple gems beside the marble fountain, he placed a kind of mask over his mouth and nostrils, as if all this beauty did but conceal a deadlier malice. But finding his task still too dangerous, he drew back, removed the mask, and called loudly, but in the infirm voice of a person affected with inward disease:

"Beatrice!—Beatrice!"

"Here am I, my father! What would you?" cried a rich and youthful voice from the window of the opposite house; a voice as rich as a tropical sunset, and which made Giovanni, though he knew not why, think of deep hues of purple or crimson, and of perfumes heavily delectable.—"Are you in the garden?"

"Yes, Beatrice," answered the gardener, "and I need your help."

Soon there emerged from under a sculptured portal the figure of a young girl, arrayed with as much richness of taste as the most splendid of the flowers, beautiful as the day, and with a bloom so deep and vivid that one shade more would have been too much. She looked redundant with life, health, and energy; all of which attributes were bound down and compressed, as it were, and girdled tensely, in their luxuriance, by her virgin zone.[2] Yet Giovanni's fancy must have grown morbid, while he looked down into the garden; for the impression which the fair stranger made upon him was as if here were another flower, the human sister of those vegetable ones, as beautiful as they—more beautiful than the richest of them—but still to be touched only with a

---

2 **virgin zone:** Wide belt worn by unmarried women.

glove, nor to be approached without a mask. As Beatrice came down the garden path, it was observable that she handled and inhaled the odor of several of the plants, which her father had most sedulously avoided.

"Here, Beatrice," said the latter,—"see how many needful offices require to be done to our chief treasure. Yet, shattered as I am, my life might pay the penalty of approaching it so closely as circumstances demand. Henceforth, I fear, this plant must be consigned to your sole charge."

"And gladly will I undertake it," cried again the rich tones of the young lady, as she bent towards the magnificent plant, and opened her arms as if to embrace it. "Yes, my sister, my splendor, it shall be Beatrice's task to nurse and serve thee; and thou shalt reward her with thy kisses and perfumed breath, which to her is as the breath of life!"

Then, with all the tenderness in her manner that was so strikingly expressed in her words, she busied herself with such attentions as the plant seemed to require; and Giovanni, at his lofty window, rubbed his eyes, and almost doubted whether it were a girl tending her favorite flower, or one sister performing the duties of affection to another. The scene soon terminated. Whether Doctor Rappaccini had finished his labors in the garden, or that his watchful eye had caught the stranger's face, he now took his daughter's arm and retired. Night was already closing in; oppressive exhalations seemed to proceed from the plants, and steal upward past the open window; and Giovanni, closing the lattice, went to his couch, and dreamed of a rich flower and beautiful girl. Flower and maiden were different and yet the same, and fraught with some strange peril in either shape.

But there is an influence in the light of morning that tends to rectify whatever errors of fancy, or even of judgment, we may have incurred during the sun's decline, or among the shadows of the night, or in the less wholesome glow of moonshine. Giovanni's first movement on starting from sleep, was to throw open the window, and gaze down into the garden which his dreams had made so fertile of mysteries. He was surprised, and a little ashamed, to find how real and matter-of-fact an affair it proved to be, in the first rays of the sun, which gilded the dew-drops that hung upon leaf and blossom, and, while giving a brighter beauty to each rare flower, brought everything within the limits of ordinary experience. The young man rejoiced, that, in the heart of the barren city, he had the privilege of overlooking this spot of lovely and luxuriant vegetation. It would serve, he said to himself, as a symbolic language, to keep him in communion with Nature. Neither the sickly and thought-worn Doctor Giacomo Rappaccini, it is true, nor his brilliant daughter, were now visible; so that Giovanni could not determine how much of the singularity which he attributed to both, was due to their own qualities, and how much to his wonder-working fancy. But he was inclined to take a most rational view of the whole matter.

In the course of the day, he paid his respects to Signor Pietro Baglioni, professor of medicine in the University, a physician of eminent repute, to whom Giovanni had brought a letter of introduction. The Professor was an elderly personage, apparently of genial nature, and habits that might almost be called jovial; he kept the young man to dinner, and made himself very agreeable by the freedom and liveliness of his conversation, especially when warmed by a flask or two of Tuscan wine. Giovanni, conceiving that men of science, inhabitants of the same city, must needs be on familiar terms with one another, took an opportunity to mention the name of Doctor Rappaccini. But the Professor did not respond with so much cordiality as he had anticipated.

"Ill would it become a teacher of the divine art of medicine," said Professor Pietro Baglioni, in answer to a question of Giovanni, "to withhold due and well-considered praise of a physician so eminently skilled as Rappaccini. But, on the other hand, I should answer it but scantily to my conscience, were I to permit a worthy youth like yourself, Signor Giovanni, the son of an ancient friend, to imbibe erroneous ideas respecting a man who might hereafter chance to hold your life and death in his hands. The truth is, our worshipful Doctor Rappaccini has as much science as any member of the faculty—with perhaps one single exception—in Padua, or all Italy. But there are certain grave objections to his professional character."

"And what are they?" asked the young man.

"Has my friend Giovanni any disease of body or heart, that he is so inquisitive about physicians?" said the Professor, with a smile. "But as for Rappaccini, it is said of him—and I, who know the man well, can answer for its truth—that he cares infinitely more for science than for mankind. His patients are interesting to him only as subjects for some new experiment. He would sacrifice human life, his own among the rest, or whatever else was dearest to him, for the sake of adding so much as a grain of mustard-seed to the great heap of his accumulated knowledge."

"Methinks he is an awful man, indeed," remarked Guasconti, mentally recalling the cold and purely intellectual aspect of Rappaccini. "And yet, worshipful Professor, is it not a noble spirit? Are there many men capable of so spiritual a love of science?"

"God forbid," answered the Professor, somewhat testily—"at least, unless they take sounder views of the healing art than those adopted by Rappaccini. It is his theory, that all medicinal virtues are comprised within those substances which we term vegetable poisons. These he cultivates with his own hands, and is said even to have produced new varieties of poison, more horribly deleterious than Nature, without the assistance of this learned person, would ever have plagued the world withal. That the Signor Doctor does less mischief than might be expected, with such dangerous substances, is undeniable. Now and then, it must be owned, he has effected—or seemed to effect—a marvellous cure. But, to tell you my private mind, Signor Giovanni, he should receive little credit for such instances of success—they being probably the work of chance—but should be held strictly accountable for his failures, which may justly be considered his own work."

The youth might have taken Baglioni's opinions with many grains of allowance, had he known that there was a professional warfare of long continuance between him and Doctor Rappaccini, in which the latter was generally thought to have gained the advantage. If the reader be inclined to judge for himself, we refer him to certain black-letter tracts on both sides, preserved in the medical department of the University of Padua.

"I know not, most learned Professor," returned Giovanni, after musing on what had been said of Rappaccini's exclusive zeal for science—"I know not how dearly this physician may love his art; but surely there is one object more dear to him. He has a daughter."

"Aha!" cried the Professor with a laugh. "So now our friend Giovanni's secret is out. You have heard of this daughter, whom all the young men in Padua are wild about, though not half a dozen have ever had the good hap to see her face. I know little of the Signora Beatrice, save that Rappaccini is said to have instructed her deeply in his science, and that, young and beautiful as fame reports her, she is already qualified to fill a professor's chair. Perchance her father destines her for mine! Other absurd rumors there be, not worth talking about, or listening to. So now, Signor Giovanni, drink off your glass of Lacryma."[3]

Guasconti returned to his lodgings somewhat heated with the wine he had quaffed, and which caused his brain to swim with strange fantasies in reference to Doctor Rappaccini and the beautiful Beatrice. On his way, happening to pass by a florist's, he bought a fresh bouquet of flowers.

Ascending to his chamber, he seated himself near the window, but within the shadow thrown by the depth of the wall, so that he could look down into the garden with little risk of being discovered. All beneath his eye was a solitude. The strange plants were basking in the sunshine, and now and then nodding gently to one another, as if in acknowledgment of sympathy and kindred. In the midst, by the shattered fountain, grew the magnificent shrub, with its purple gems clustering all over it; they glowed in the air, and gleamed back again out of the depths of the pool, which thus seemed to overflow with colored radiance from the rich reflection that was steeped in it. At first, as we have said, the garden was a solitude. Soon, however,—as Giovanni had half-hoped, half-feared, would be the case,—a figure appeared beneath the antique sculptured portal, and came down between the rows of plants, inhaling their various perfumes, as if she were one of those beings of old classic fable, that lived upon sweet odors. On again beholding Beatrice, the young man was even startled to perceive how much her beauty exceeded his recollection of it; so brilliant, so vivid was its character, that she glowed amid the sunlight, and, as Giovanni whispered to himself, positively illuminated the more shadowy intervals of the garden path. Her face being now more revealed than on the former occasion, he was struck by its expression of simplicity and sweetness; qualities that had not entered into his idea of her character, and which made him ask anew, what manner of mortal she might be. Nor did he fail again to observe, or imagine, an analogy between the beautiful girl and the gorgeous shrub that hung its gem-like flowers over the fountain; a resemblance which Beatrice seemed to have indulged a fantastic humor in heightening, both by the arrangement of her dress and the selection of its hues.

Approaching the shrub, she threw open her arms, as with a passionate ardor, and drew its branches into an intimate embrace; so intimate, that her features were hidden in its leafy bosom, and her glistening ringlets all intermingled with the flowers.

"Give me thy breath, my sister," exclaimed Beatrice; "for I am faint with common

---

3 **lachryma:** Italian white wine.

air! And give me this flower of thine, which I separate with gentlest fingers from the stem, and place it close beside my heart."

With these words, the beautiful daughter of Rappaccini plucked one of the richest blossoms of the shrub, and was about to fasten it in her bosom. But now, unless Giovanni's draughts of wine had bewildered his senses, a singular incident occurred. A small orange-colored reptile, of the lizard or chameleon species, chanced to be creeping along the path, just at the feet of Beatrice. It appeared to Giovanni—but, at the distance from which he gazed, he could scarcely have seen anything so minute—it appeared to him, however, that a drop or two of moisture from the broken stem of the flower descended upon the lizard's head. For an instant, the reptile contorted itself violently, and then lay motionless in the sunshine. Beatrice observed this remarkable phenomenon, and crossed herself, sadly, but without surprise; nor did she therefore hesitate to arrange the fatal flower in her bosom. There it blushed, and almost glimmered with the dazzling effect of a precious stone, adding to her dress and aspect the one appropriate charm, which nothing else in the world could have supplied. But Giovanni, out of the shadow of his window, bent forward and shrank back, and murmured and trembled.

"Am I awake? Have I my senses?" said he to himself. "What is this being?—beautiful, shall I call her?—or inexpressibly terrible?"

Beatrice now strayed carelessly through the garden, approaching closer beneath Giovanni's window, so that he was compelled to thrust his head quite out of its concealment in order to gratify the intense and painful curiosity which she excited. At this moment, there came a beautiful insect over the garden wall; it had perhaps wandered through the city and found no flowers nor verdure among those antique haunts of men, until the heavy perfumes of Doctor Rappaccini's shrubs had lured it from afar. Without alighting on the flowers, this winged brightness seemed to be attracted by Beatrice, and lingered in the air and fluttered about her head. Now, here it could not be but that Giovanni Guasconti's eyes deceived him. Be that as it might, he fancied that while Beatrice was gazing at the insect with childish delight, it grew faint and fell at her feet;—its bright wings shivered; it was dead—from no cause that he could discern, unless it were the atmosphere of her breath. Again Beatrice crossed herself and sighed heavily, as she bent over the dead insect.

An impulsive movement of Giovanni drew her eyes to the window. There she beheld the beautiful head of the young man—rather a Grecian than an Italian head, with fair, regular features, and a glistening of gold among his ringlets—gazing down upon her like a being that hovered in midair. Scarcely knowing what he did, Giovanni threw down the bouquet which he had hitherto held in his hand.

"Signora," said he, "there are pure and healthful flowers. Wear them for the sake of Giovanni Guasconti!"

"Thanks, Signor," replied Beatrice, with her rich voice, that came forth as it were like a gush of music; and with a mirthful expression half childish and half womanlike. "I accept your gift, and would fain recompense it with this precious purple flower; but if I toss it into the air, it will not reach you. So Signor Guasconti must even content himself with my thanks."

She lifted the bouquet from the ground, and then as if inwardly ashamed at having stepped aside from her maidenly reserve to respond to a stranger's greeting, passed swiftly homeward through the garden. But, few as the moments were, it seemed to Giovanni when she was on the point of vanishing beneath the sculptured portal, that his beautiful bouquet was already beginning to wither in her grasp. It was an idle thought; there could be no possibility of distinguishing a faded flower from a fresh one at so great a distance.

For many days after this incident, the young man avoided the window that looked into Doctor Rappaccini's garden, as if something ugly and monstrous would have blasted his eyesight, had he been betrayed into a glance. He felt conscious of having put himself, to a certain extent, within the influence of an unintelligible power, by the communication which he had opened with Beatrice. The wisest course would have been, if his heart were in any real danger, to quit his lodgings and Padua itself, at once; the next wiser, to have accustomed himself, as far as possible, to the familiar and day-light view of Beatrice; thus bringing her rigidly and systematically within the limits of ordinary experience. Least of all, while avoiding her sight, ought Giovanni to have remained so near this extraordinary being, that the proximity and possibility even of intercourse, should give a kind of substance and reality to the wild vagaries which his imagination ran riot continually in producing. Guasconti had not a deep heart—or at all events, its depths were not sounded now—but he had a quick fancy, and an ardent southern temperament, which rose every instant to a higher fever-pitch. Whether or no Beatrice possessed those terrible attributes—that fatal breath—the affinity with those so beautiful and deadly flowers—which were indicated by what Giovanni had witnessed, she had at least instilled a fierce and subtle poison into his system. It was not love, although her rich beauty was a madness to him; nor horror, even while he fancied her spirit to be imbued with the same baneful essence that seemed to pervade her physical frame; but a wild offspring of both love and horror that had each parent in it, and burned like one and shivered like the other. Giovanni knew not what to dread; still less did he know what to hope; yet hope and dread kept a continual warfare in his breast, alternately vanquishing one another and starting up afresh to renew the contest. Blessed are all simple emotions, be they dark or bright! It is the lurid intermixture of the two that produces the illuminating blaze of the infernal regions.

Sometimes he endeavored to assuage the fever of his spirit by a rapid walk through the streets of Padua, or beyond its gates; his footsteps kept time with the throbbings of his brain, so that the walk was apt to accelerate itself to a race. One day, he found himself arrested; his arm was seized by a portly personage who had turned back on recognizing the young man, and expended much breath in overtaking him.

"Signor Giovanni!—stay, my young friend!" cried he. "Have you forgotten me? That might well be the case, if I were as much altered as yourself."

It was Baglioni, whom Giovanni had avoided, ever since their first meeting, from a doubt that the Professor's sagacity would look too deeply into his secrets. Endeavoring to recover himself, he stared forth wildly from his inner world into the outer one, and spoke like a man in a dream:

"Yes; I am Giovanni Guasconti. You are Professor Pietro Baglioni. Now let me pass!"

"Not yet—not yet, Signor Giovanni Guasconti," said the Professor, smiling, but at the same time scrutinizing the youth with an earnest glance.—"What; did I grow up side by side with your father, and shall his son pass me like a stranger, in these old streets of Padua? Stand still, Signor Giovanni; for we must have a word or two, before we part."

"Speedily, then, most worshipful Professor, speedily!" said Giovanni, with feverish impatience. "Does not your worship see that I am in haste?"

Now, while he was speaking, there came a man in black along the street, stooping and moving feebly, like a person in inferior health. His face was all overspread with a most sickly and sallow hue, but yet so pervaded with an expression of piercing and active intellect, that an observer might easily have overlooked the merely physical attributes, and have seen only this wonderful energy. As he passed, this person exchanged a cold and distant salutation with Baglioni, but fixed his eyes upon Giovanni with an intentness that seemed to bring out whatever was within him worthy of notice. Nevertheless, there was a peculiar quietness in the look, as if taking merely a speculative, not a human, interest in the young man.

"It is Doctor Rappaccini!" whispered the Professor, when the stranger had passed.—"Has he ever seen your face before?"

"Not that I know," answered Giovanni, starting at the name.

"He *has* seen you!—he must have seen you!" said Baglioni, hastily. "For some purpose or other, this man of science is making a study of you. I know that look of his! It is the same that coldly illuminates his face, as he bends over a bird, a mouse, or a butterfly, which, in pursuance of some experiment, he has killed by the perfume of a flower;—a look as deep as nature itself, but without Nature's warmth of love. Signor Giovanni, I will stake my life upon it, you are the subject of one of Rappaccini's experiments!"

"Will you make a fool of me?" cried Giovanni, passionately. "*That*, Signor Professor, were an untoward experiment."

"Patience, patience!" replied the imperturbable Professor.—"I tell thee, my poor Giovanni, that Rappaccini has a scientific interest in thee. Thou hast fallen into fearful hands! And the Signora Beatrice? What part does she act in this mystery?"

But Guasconti, finding Baglioni's pertinacity intolerable, here broke away, and was gone before the Professor could again seize his arm. He looked after the young man intently, and shook his head.

"This must not be," said Baglioni to himself. "The youth is the son of my old friend, and shall not come to any harm from which the arcana of medical science can preserve him. Besides, it is too insufferable an impertinence in Rappaccini, thus to snatch the lad out of my own hands, as I may say, and make use of him for his infernal experiments. This daughter of his! It shall be looked to. Perchance, most learned Rappaccini, I may foil you where you little dream of it!"

Meanwhile, Giovanni had pursued a circuitous route, and at length found himself at the door of his lodgings. As he crossed the threshold, he was met by old Lisabetta, who smirked and smiled, and was evidently desirous to attract his attention; vainly, however, as the ebullition of his feelings had momentarily subsided into a cold and dull vacuity. He turned his eyes full upon the withered face that was puckering itself into a smile, but seemed to behold it not. The old dame, therefore, laid her grasp upon his cloak.

"Signor!—Signor!" whispered she, still with a smile over the whole breadth of her visage, so that it looked not unlike a grotesque carving in wood, darkened by centuries—"Listen, Signor! There is a private entrance into the garden!"

"What do you say?" exclaimed Giovanni, turning quickly about, as if an inanimate thing should start into feverish life.—"A private entrance into Doctor Rappaccini's garden!"

"Hush! hush!—not so loud!" whispered Lisabetta, putting her hand over his mouth. "Yes; into the worshipful Doctor's garden, where you may see all his fine shrubbery. Many a young man in Padua would give gold to be admitted among those flowers."

Giovanni put a piece of gold into her hand.

"Show me the way," said he.

A surmise, probably excited by his conversation with Baglioni, crossed his mind, that this interposition of old Lisabetta might perchance be connected with the intrigue, whatever were its nature, in which the Professor seemed to suppose that Doctor Rappaccini was involving him. But such a suspicion, though it disturbed Giovanni, was inadequate to restrain him. The instant that he was aware of the possibility of approaching Beatrice, it seemed an absolute necessity of his existence to do so. It mattered not whether she were angel or demon; he was irrevocably within her sphere, and must obey the law that whirled him onward, in ever lessening circles, towards a result which he did not attempt to foreshadow. And yet, strange to say, there came across him a sudden doubt, whether this intense interest on his part were not delusory—whether it were really of so deep and positive a nature as to justify him in now thrusting himself into an incalculable position—whether it were not merely the fantasy of a young man's brain, only slightly, or not at all, connected with his heart!

He paused—hesitated—turned half about—but again went on. His withered guide led him along several obscure passages, and finally undid a door, through which, as it was opened, there came the sight and sound of rustling leaves, with the broken sunshine glimmering among them. Giovanni stepped forth, and forcing himself through the entanglement of a shrub that wreathed its tendrils over the hidden entrance, he stood beneath his own window, in the open area of Doctor Rappaccini's garden.

How often is it the case, that, when impossibilities have come to pass, and dreams have condensed their misty substance into tangible realities, we find ourselves calm, and even coldly self-possessed, amid circumstances which it would have been a delirium of joy or agony to anticipate! Fate delights to thwart us thus. Passion will choose his own time to rush upon the scene, and lingers sluggishly behind, when an appropriate adjustment of events would seem to summon his appearance. So was it now with Giovanni. Day after day, his pulses had throbbed with feverish blood, at the improbable idea of an interview with Beatrice, and of standing with her, face to face, in this very garden, basking in the Oriental sunshine of her beauty, and snatching from her full gaze the mystery which he deemed the riddle of his own existence. But now there was a singular and untimely equanimity within his breast. He threw a glance around the garden to discover if Beatrice or her father were present, and perceiving that he was alone, began a critical observation of the plants.

The aspect of one and all of them dissatisfied him; their gorgeousness seemed fierce, passionate, and even unnatural. There was hardly an individual shrub which a wanderer, straying by himself through a forest, would not have been startled to find growing wild, as if an unearthly face had glared at him out of the thicket. Several, also, would have shocked a delicate instinct by an appearance of artificialness, indicating that there had been such commixture, and, as it were, adultery of various vegetable species, that the production was no longer of God's making, but the monstrous offspring of man's depraved fancy, glowing with only an evil mockery of beauty. They were probably the result of experiment, which, in one or two cases, had succeeded in mingling plants individually lovely into a compound possessing the questionable and ominous character that distinguished the whole growth of the garden. In fine, Giovanni recognized but two or three plants in the collection, and those of a kind that he well knew to be poisonous. While busy with these contemplations, he heard the rustling of a silken garment, and turning, beheld Beatrice emerging from beneath the sculptured portal.

Giovanni had not considered with himself what should be his deportment; whether he should apologize for his intrusion into the garden, or assume that he was there with the privity, at least, if not by the desire, of Doctor Rappaccini or his daughter. But Beatrice's manner placed him at his ease, though leaving him still in doubt by what agency he had gained admittance. She came lightly along the path, and met him near the broken fountain. There was surprise in her face, but brightened by a simple and kind expression of pleasure.

"You are a connoisseur in flowers, Signor," said Beatrice with a smile, alluding to the bouquet which he had flung her from the window. "It is no marvel, therefore, if the sight of my father's rare collection has tempted you to take a nearer view. If he were here, he could tell you many strange and interesting facts as to the nature and habits of these shrubs, for he has spent a life-time in such studies, and this garden is his world."

"And yourself, lady"—observed Giovanni—"if fame says true—you, likewise, are deeply skilled in the virtues indicated by these rich blossoms, and these spicy perfumes. Would you deign to be my instructress, I should prove an apter scholar than if taught by Signor Rappaccini himself."

"Are there such idle rumors?" asked Beatrice, with the music of a pleasant laugh. "Do people say that I am skilled in my father's science of plants? What a jest is there! No; though I have grown up among these flowers, I know no more of them than their hues and perfume; and sometimes, methinks I would fain rid myself of even that small knowledge. There are many flowers here, and those not the least brilliant, that shock and offend me, when they meet my eye. But, pray, Signor, do not believe these stories about my science. Believe nothing of me save what you see with your own eyes."

"And must I believe all that I have seen with my own eyes?" asked Giovanni pointedly, while the recollection of former scenes made him shrink. "No, Signora, you demand too little of me. Bid me believe nothing, save what comes from your own lips."

It would appear that Beatrice understood him. There came a deep flush to her cheek; but she looked full into Giovanni's eyes, and responded to his gaze of uneasy suspicion with a queen-like haughtiness.

"I do so bid you, Signor!" she replied. "Forget whatever you may have fancied in regard to me. If true to the outward senses, still it may be false in its essence. But the words of Beatrice Rappaccini's lips are true from the depths of the heart outward. Those you may believe!"

A fervor glowed in her whole aspect, and beamed upon Giovanni's consciousness like the light of truth itself. But while she spoke, there was a fragrance in the atmosphere around her, rich and delightful, though evanescent, yet which the young man, from an indefinable reluctance, scarcely dared to draw into his lungs. It might be the odor of the flowers. Could it be Beatrice's breath, which thus embalmed her words with a strange richness, as if by steeping them in her heart? A faintness passed like a shadow over Giovanni, and flitted away; he seemed to gaze through the beautiful girl's eyes into her transparent soul, and felt no more doubt or fear.

The tinge of passion that had colored Beatrice's manner vanished; she became gay, and appeared to derive a pure delight from her communion with the youth, not unlike what the maiden of a lonely island might have felt, conversing with a voyager from the civilized world. Evidently her experience of life had been confined within the limits of that garden. She talked now about matters as simple as the day-light or summer-clouds, and now asked questions in reference to the city, or Giovanni's distant home, his friends, his mother, and his sisters; questions indicating such seclusion, and such lack of familiarity with modes and forms, that Giovanni responded as if to an infant. Her spirit gushed out before him like a fresh rill, that was just catching its first glimpse of the sunlight, and wondering at the reflections of earth and sky which were flung into its bosom. There came thoughts, too, from a deep source, and fantasies of a gem-like brilliancy, as if diamonds and rubies sparkled upward among the bubbles of the fountain. Ever and anon, there gleamed across the young man's mind a sense of wonder, that he should be walking side by side with the being who had so wrought upon his imagination—whom he had idealized in such hues of terror—in whom he had positively witnessed such manifestations of dreadful attributes—that he should be conversing with Beatrice like a brother, and should find her so human and so maiden-like. But such reflections were only momentary; the effect of her character was too real, not to make itself familiar at once.

In this free intercourse, they had strayed through the garden, and now, after many turns among its avenues, were come to the shattered fountain, beside which grew the magnificent shrub with its treasury of glowing blossoms. A fragrance was diffused from it, which Giovanni recognized as identical with that which he had attributed to Beatrice's breath, but incomparably more powerful. As her eyes fell upon it, Giovanni beheld her press her hand to her bosom, as if her heart were throbbing suddenly and painfully.

"For the first time in my life," murmured she, addressing the shrub, "I had forgotten thee!"

"I remember, Signora," said Giovanni, "that you once promised to reward me with one of these living gems for the bouquet, which I had the happy boldness to fling to your feet. Permit me now to pluck it as a memorial of this interview."

He made a step towards the shrub, with extended hand. But Beatrice darted forward, uttering a shriek that went through his heart like a dagger. She caught his hand, and drew it back with the whole force of her slender figure. Giovanni felt her touch thrilling through his fibres.

"Touch it not!" exclaimed she, in a voice of agony. "Not for thy life! It is fatal!"

Then, hiding her face, she fled from him, and vanished beneath the sculptured portal. As Giovanni followed her with his eyes, he beheld the emaciated figure and pale intelligence of Doctor Rappaccini, who had been watching the scene, he knew not how long, within the shadow of the entrance.

No sooner was Guasconti alone in his chamber, than the image of Beatrice came back to his passionate musings, invested with all the witchery that had been gathering around it ever since his first glimpse of her, and now likewise imbued with a tender warmth of girlish womanhood. She was human: her nature was endowed with all gentle and feminine qualities; she was worthiest to be worshipped; she was capable, surely, on her part, of the height and heroism of love. Those tokens, which he had hitherto considered as proofs of a frightful peculiarity in her physical and moral system, were now either forgotten, or, by the subtle sophistry of passion, transmuted into a golden crown of enchantment, rendering Beatrice the more admirable, by so much as she was the more unique. Whatever had looked ugly, was now beautiful; or, if incapable of such a change, it stole away and hid itself among those shapeless half-ideas, which throng the dim region beyond the daylight of our perfect consciousness. Thus did he spend the night, nor fell asleep, until the dawn had begun to awake the slumbering flowers in Doctor Rappaccini's garden, whither Giovanni's dreams doubtless led him. Up rose the sun in his due season, and flinging his beams upon the young man's eyelids, awoke him to a sense of pain. When thoroughly aroused, he became sensible of a burning and tingling agony in his hand—in his right hand—the very hand which Beatrice had grasped in her own, when he was on the point of plucking one of the gem-like flowers. On the back of that hand there was now a purple print, like that of four small fingers, and the likeness of a slender thumb upon his wrist.

Oh, how stubbornly does love—or even that cunning semblance of love which flourishes in the imagination, but strikes no depth of root into the heart—how stubbornly does it hold its faith, until the moment come, when it is doomed to vanish into thin mist! Giovanni wrapt a handkerchief about his hand, and wondered what evil thing had stung him, and soon forgot his pain in a reverie of Beatrice.

After the first interview, a second was in the inevitable course of what we call fate. A third; a fourth; and a meeting with Beatrice in the garden was no longer an incident in Giovanni's daily life, but the whole space in which he might be said to live; for the anticipation and memory of that ecstatic hour made up the remainder. Nor was it otherwise with the daughter of Rappaccini. She watched for the youth's appearance, and flew to his side with confidence as unreserved as if they had been playmates from early infancy—as if they were such playmates still. If, by any unwonted chance, he failed to come at the appointed moment, she stood beneath the window, and sent up the rich sweetness of her tones to float around him in his chamber, and echo and reverberate throughout his heart—"Giovanni! Giovanni! Why tarriest thou? Come down!"—And down he hastened into that Eden of poisonous flowers.

But, with all this intimate familiarity, there was still a reserve in Beatrice's demeanor, so rigidly and invariably sustained, that the idea of infringing it scarcely occurred to his imagination. By all appreciable signs, they loved; they had looked love, with eyes that conveyed the holy secret from the depths of one soul into the depths of the other, as if it were too sacred to be whispered by the way; they had even spoken love, in those gushes of passion when their spirits darted forth in articulated breath, like tongues of long-hidden flame; and yet there had been no seal of lips, no clasp of hands, nor any slightest caress, such as love claims and hallows. He had never touched one of the gleaming ringlets of her hair; her garment—so marked was the physical barrier between them—had never been waved against him by a breeze. On the few occasions when Giovanni had seemed tempted to overstep the limit, Beatrice grew so sad, so stern, and withal wore such a look of desolate separation, shuddering at itself, that not a spoken word was requisite to repel him. At such times, he was startled at the horrible suspicions that rose, monster-like, out of the caverns of his heart, and stared him in the face; his love grew thin and faint as the morning-mist; his doubts alone had substance. But when Beatrice's face brightened again, after the momentary shadow, she was transformed at once from the mysterious, questionable being, whom he had watched with so much awe and horror; she was now the beautiful and unsophisticated girl, whom he felt that his spirit knew with a certainty beyond all other knowledge.

A considerable time had now passed since Giovanni's last meeting with Baglioni. One morning, however, he was disagreeably surprised by a visit from the Professor, whom he had scarcely thought of for whole weeks, and would willingly have forgotten still longer. Given up, as he had long been, to a pervading excitement, he could tolerate no companions, except upon condition of their perfect sympathy with his present state of feeling. Such sympathy was not to be expected from Professor Baglioni.

The visitor chatted carelessly, for a few moments, about the gossip of the city and the University, and then took up another topic.

"I have been reading an old classic author lately," said he, "and met with a story that strangely interested me. Possibly you may remember it. It is of an Indian prince, who sent a beautiful woman as a present to Alexander the Great. She was as lovely as the dawn, and gorgeous as the sunset; but what especially distinguished her was a certain rich perfume in her breath—richer than a garden of Persian roses. Alexander, as was natural to a youthful conqueror, fell in love at first sight with this magnificent stranger. But a certain sage physician, happening to be present, discovered a terrible secret in regard to her."

"And what was that?" asked Giovanni, turning his eyes downward to avoid those of the Professor.

"That this lovely woman," continued Baglioni, with emphasis, "had been nourished with poisons from her birth upward, until her whole nature was so imbued with them, that she herself had become the deadliest poison in existence. Poison was her element of life. With that rich perfume of her breath, she blasted the very air. Her love would have been poison!—her embrace death! Is not this a marvelous tale?"

"A childish fable," answered Giovanni, nervously starting from his chair. "I marvel how your worship finds time to read such nonsense, among your graver studies."

"By the bye," said the Professor, looking uneasily about him, "what singular fragrance is this in your apartment? Is it the perfume of your gloves? It is faint, but delicious, and yet, after all, by no means agreeable. Were I to breathe it long, methinks it would make me ill. It is like the breath of a flower—but I see no flowers in the chamber."

"Nor are there any," replied Giovanni, who had turned pale as the Professor spoke; "nor, I think, is there any fragrance, except in your worship's imagination. Odors, being a sort of element combined of the sensual and the spiritual, are apt to deceive us in this manner. The recollection of a perfume—the bare idea of it—may easily be mistaken for a present reality."

"Aye; but my sober imagination does not often play such tricks," said Baglioni; "and were I to fancy any kind of odor, it would be that of some vile apothecary drug, wherewith my fingers are likely enough to be imbued. Our worshipful friend Rappaccini, as I have heard, tinctures his medicaments with odors richer than those of Araby. Doubtless, likewise, the fair and learned Signora Beatrice would minister to her patients with draughts as sweet as a maiden's breath. But wo to him that sips them!"

Giovanni's face evinced many contending emotions. The tone in which the Professor alluded to the pure and lovely daughter of Rappaccini was a torture to his soul; and yet, the intimation of a view of her character, opposite to his own, gave instantaneous distinctness to a thousand dim suspicions, which now grinned at him like so many demons. But he strove hard to quell them, and to respond to Baglioni with a true lover's perfect faith.

"Signor Professor," said he, "you were my father's friend—perchance, too, it is your purpose to act a friendly part towards his son. I would fain feel nothing towards you, save respect and deference. But I pray you to observe, Signor, that there is one subject on which we must not speak. You know not the Signora Beatrice. You cannot, therefore, estimate the wrong—the blasphemy, I may even say—that is offered to her character by a light or injurious word."

"Giovanni!—my poor Giovanni!" answered the Professor, with a calm expression of pity, "I know this wretched girl far better than yourself. You shall hear the truth in respect to the poisoner Rappaccini, and his poisonous daughter. Yes; poisonous as she is beautiful! Listen; for even should you do violence to my grey hairs, it shall not silence me. That old fable of the Indian woman has become a truth, by the deep and deadly science of Rappaccini, and in the person of the lovely Beatrice!"

Giovanni groaned and hid his face.

"Her father," continued Baglioni, "was not restrained by natural affection from offering up his child, in this horrible manner, as the victim of his insane zeal for science. For—let us do him justice—he is as true a man of science as ever distilled his own heart in an alembic. What, then, will be your fate? Beyond a doubt, you are selected as the material of some new experiment. Perhaps the result is to be death—perhaps a fate more awful still! Rappaccini, with what he calls the interest of science before his eyes, will hesitate at nothing."

"It is a dream!" muttered Giovanni to himself, "surely it is a dream!"

"But," resumed the Professor, "be of good cheer, son of my friend! It is not yet too late for the rescue. Possibly, we may even succeed in bringing back this miserable child within the limits of ordinary nature, from which her father's madness has estranged her. Behold this little silver vase! It was wrought by the hands of the renowned Benvenuto Cellini,[4] and is well worthy to be a love-gift to the fairest dame in Italy. But its contents are invaluable. One little sip of this antidote would have rendered the most virulent poisons of the Borgias[5] innocuous. Doubt not that it will be as efficacious against those of Rappaccini. Bestow the vase, and the precious liquid within it, on your Beatrice, and hopefully await the result."

Baglioni laid a small, exquisitely wrought silver phial on the table, and withdrew, leaving what he had said to produce its effect upon the young man's mind.

"We will thwart Rappaccini yet!" thought he, chuckling to himself, as he descended the stairs. "But, let us confess the truth of him, he is a wonderful man!—a wonderful man indeed! A vile empiric, however, in his practice, and therefore not to be tolerated by those who respect the good old rules of the medical profession!"

Throughout Giovanni's whole acquaintance with Beatrice, he had occasionally, as we have said, been haunted by dark surmises as to her character. Yet, so thoroughly had she made herself felt by him as a simple, natural, most affectionate and guileless creature, that the image now held up by Professor Baglioni, looked as strange and incredible, as if it were not in accordance with his own original conception. True, there were ugly recollections connected with his first glimpses of the beautiful girl; he could not quite forget the bouquet that withered in her grasp, and the insect that perished amid the sunny air, by no ostensible agency, save the fragrance of her breath. These incidents, however, dissolving in the pure light of her character, had no longer the efficacy of facts, but were acknowledged as mistaken fantasies, by whatever testimony of the senses they might appear to be substantiated. There is something truer and more real, than what we can see with the eyes, and touch with the finger. On such better evidence, had Giovanni founded his confidence in Beatrice, though rather by the necessary force of her high attributes, than by any deep and generous faith, on his part. But, now, his spirit was incapable of sustaining itself at the height to which the early en-

---

4 **Benvenuto Cellini:** Italian goldsmith, sculptor, and writer (1500–1571).
5 **Borgias:** Italian Renaissance family notorious for its cruel and licentious behavior.

thusiasm of passion had exalted it; he fell down, grovelling among earthly doubts, and defiled therewith the pure whiteness of Beatrice's image. Not that he gave her up; he did but distrust. He resolved to institute some decisive test that should satisfy him, once for all, whether there were those dreadful peculiarities in her physical nature, which could not be supposed to exist without some corresponding monstrosity of soul. His eyes, gazing down afar, might have deceived him as to the lizard, the insect, and the flowers. But if he could witness, at the distance of a few paces, the sudden blight of one fresh and healthful flower in Beatrice's hand, there would be room for no further question. With this idea, he hastened to the florist's, and purchased a bouquet that was still gemmed with the morning dew-drops.

It was now the customary hour of his daily interview with Beatrice. Before descending into the garden, Giovanni failed not to look at his figure in the mirror; a vanity to be expected in a beautiful young man, yet, as displaying itself at that troubled and feverish moment, the token of a certain shallowness of feeling and insincerity of character. He did gaze, however, and said to himself, that his features had never before possessed so rich a grace, nor his eyes such vivacity, nor his cheeks so warm a hue of superabundant life.

"At least," thought he, "her poison has not yet insinuated itself into my system. I am no flower to perish in her grasp!"

With that thought, he turned his eyes on the bouquet, which he had never once laid aside from his hand. A thrill of indefinable horror shot through his frame, on perceiving that those dewy flowers were already beginning to droop; they wore the aspect of things that had been fresh and lovely, yesterday. Giovanni grew white as marble, and stood motionless before the mirror, staring at his own reflection there, as at the likeness of something frightful. He remembered Baglioni's remark about the fragrance that seemed to pervade the chamber. It must have been the poison in his breath! Then he shuddered—shuddered at himself! Recovering from his stupor, he began to watch, with curious eye, a spider that was busily at work, hanging its web from the antique cornice of the apartment, crossing and re-crossing the artful system of interwoven lines, as vigorous and active a spider as ever dangled from an old ceiling. Giovanni bent towards the insect, and emitted a deep, long breath. The spider suddenly ceased its toil; the web vibrated with a tremor originating in the body of the small artisan. Again Giovanni sent forth a breath, deeper, longer, and imbued with a venomous feeling out of his heart; he knew not whether he were wicked or only desperate. The spider made a convulsive gripe with his limbs, and hung dead across the window.

"Accursed! Accursed!" muttered Giovanni, addressing himself. "Hast thou grown so poisonous, that this deadly insect perishes by thy breath?"

At that moment, a rich, sweet voice came floating up from the garden:—

"Giovanni! Giovanni! It is past the hour! Why tarriest thou! Come down!"

"Yes," muttered Giovanni again. "She is the only being whom my breath may not slay! Would that it might!"

He rushed down, and in an instant, was standing before the bright and loving eyes of Beatrice. A moment ago, his wrath and despair had been so fierce that he could have desired nothing so much as to wither her by a glance. But, with her actual presence, there came influences which had too real an existence to be at once shaken off; recollections of the delicate and benign power of her feminine nature, which had so often enveloped him in a religious calm; recollections of many a holy and passionate outgush of her heart, when the pure fountain had been unsealed from its depths, and made visible in its transparency to his mental eye; recollections which, had Giovanni known how to estimate them, would have assured him that all this ugly mystery was but an earthly illusion, and that, whatever mist of evil might seem to have gathered over her, the real Beatrice was a heavenly angel. Incapable as he was of such high faith, still her presence had not utterly lost its magic. Giovanni's rage was quelled into an aspect of sullen insensibility. Beatrice, with a quick spiritual sense, immediately felt that there was a gulf of blackness between them, which neither he nor she could pass. They walked on together, sad and silent, and came thus to the marble fountain, and to its pool of water on the ground, in the midst of which grew the shrub that bore gem-like blossoms. Giovanni was affrighted at the eager enjoyment—the appetite, as it were—with which he found himself inhaling the fragrance of the flowers.

"Beatrice," asked he abruptly, "whence came this shrub?"

"My father created it," answered she, with simplicity.

"Created it! created it!" repeated Giovanni. "What mean you, Beatrice?"

"He is a man fearfully acquainted with the secrets of nature," replied Beatrice; "and, at the hour when I first drew breath, this plant sprang from the soil, the offspring of his science, of his intellect, while I was but his earthly child. Approach it not!" continued she, observing with terror that Giovanni was drawing nearer to the shrub. "It has qualities that you little dream of. But I, dearest Giovanni,—I grew up and blossomed with the plant, and was nourished with its breath. It was my sister, and I loved it with a human affection: for—alas! hast thou not suspected it? there was an awful doom."

Here Giovanni frowned so darkly upon her that Beatrice paused and trembled. But her faith in his tenderness reassured her, and made her blush that she had doubted for an instant.

"There was an awful doom," she continued,—"the effect of my father's fatal love of science—which estranged me from all society of my kind. Until Heaven sent thee, dearest Giovanni, Oh! how lonely was thy poor Beatrice!"

"Was it a hard doom?" asked Giovanni, fixing his eyes upon her.

"Only of late have I known how hard it was," answered she tenderly. "Oh, yes; but my heart was torpid, and therefore quiet."

Giovanni's rage broke forth from his sullen gloom like a lightning-flash out of a dark cloud.

"Accursed one!" cried he, with venomous scorn and anger. "And finding thy solitude wearisome, thou hast severed me, likewise, from all the warmth of life, and enticed me into thy region of unspeakable horror!"

"Giovanni!" exclaimed Beatrice, turning her large bright eyes upon his face. The force of his words had not found its way into her mind; she was merely thunder-struck.

"Yes, poisonous thing!" repeated Giovanni, beside himself with passion. "Thou hast done it! Thou hast blasted me! Thou hast filled my veins with poison! Thou hast made me as hateful, as ugly, as loathsome and deadly a creature as thyself,—a world's wonder of hideous monstrosity! Now—if our breath be happily as fatal to ourselves as to all others—let us join our lips in one kiss of unutterable hatred, and so die!"

"What has befallen me?" murmured Beatrice, with a low moan out of her heart. "Holy Virgin pity me, a poor heart-broken child!"

"Thou! Dost thou pray?" cried Giovanni, still with the same fiendish scorn. "Thy very prayers, as they come from thy lips, taint the atmosphere with death. Yes, yes; let us pray! Let us to church, and dip our fingers in the holy water at the portal! They that come after us will perish as by a pestilence. Let us sign crosses in the air! It will be scattering curses abroad in the likeness of holy symbols!"

"Giovanni," said Beatrice calmly, for her grief was beyond passion, "why dost thou join thyself with me thus in those terrible words? I, it is true, am the horrible thing thou namest me. But thou!—what hast thou to do, save with one other shudder at my hideous misery, to go forth out of the garden and mingle with thy race, and forget that there ever crawled on earth such a monster as poor Beatrice?"

"Dost thou pretend ignorance?" asked Giovanni, scowling upon her. "Behold! This power have I gained from the pure daughter of Rappaccini!"

There was a swarm of summer-insects flitting through the air, in search of the food promised by the flower-odors of the fatal garden. They circled round Giovanni's head, and were evidently attracted towards him by the same influence which had drawn them, for an instant, within the sphere of several of the shrubs. He sent forth a breath among them, and smiled bitterly at Beatrice, as at least a score of the insects fell dead upon the ground.

"I see it! I see it!" shrieked Beatrice. "It is my father's fatal science! No, no, Giovanni; it was not I! Never, never! I dreamed only to love thee, and be with thee a little time, and so to let thee pass away, leaving but thine image in mine heart. For, Giovanni—believe it—though my body be nourished with poison, my spirit is God's creature, and craves love as its daily food. But my father!—he has united us in this fearful sympathy. Yes; spurn me!—tread upon me!—kill me! Oh, what is death, after such words as thine? But it was not I! Not for a world of bliss would I have done it!"

Giovanni's passion had exhausted itself in its outburst from his lips. There now came across him a sense, mournful, and not without tenderness, of the intimate and peculiar relationship between Beatrice and himself. They stood, as it were, in an utter solitude, which would be made none the less solitary by the densest throng of human life. Ought not, then, the desert of humanity around them to press this insulated pair closer together? If they should be cruel to one another, who was there to be kind to them? Besides, thought Giovanni, might there not still be a hope of his returning within the limits of ordinary nature, and leading Beatrice—the redeemed Beatrice—by the hand? Oh, weak, and selfish, and unworthy spirit, that could dream of an earthly union and earthly happiness as possible, after such deep love had been so bitterly wronged as was Beatrice's love by Giovanni's blighting words! No, no; there could be no such hope. She must pass heavily, with that broken heart, across the borders of Time—she must bathe her hurts in some fount of Paradise, and forget her grief in the light of immortality—and *there* be well!

But Giovanni did not know it.

"Dear Beatrice," said he, approaching her, while she shrank away, as always at his approach, but now with a different impulse—"dearest Beatrice, our fate is not yet so desperate. Behold! There is a medicine, potent, as a wise physician has assured me, and almost divine in its efficacy. It is composed of ingredients the most opposite to those by which thy awful father has brought this calamity upon thee and me. It is distilled of blessed herbs. Shall we not quaff it together, and thus be purified from evil?"

"Give it me!" said Beatrice, extending her hand to receive the little silver phial which Giovanni took from his bosom. She added, with a peculiar emphasis: "I will drink—but do thou await the result."

She put Baglioni's antidote to her lips; and, at the same moment, the figure of Rappaccini emerged from the portal, and came slowly towards the marble fountain. As he drew near, the pale man of science seemed to gaze with a triumphant expression at the beautiful youth and maiden, as might an artist who should spend his life in achieving a picture or a group of statuary, and finally be satisfied with his success. He paused—his bent form grew erect with conscious power, he spread out his hands over them, in the attitude of a father imploring a blessing upon his children. But those were the same hands that had thrown poison into the stream of their lives! Giovanni trembled. Beatrice shuddered nervously, and pressed her hand upon her heart.

"My daughter," said Rappaccini, "thou art no longer lonely in the world! Pluck one of those precious gems from thy sister shrub, and bid thy bridegroom wear it in his bosom. It will not harm him now! My science, and the sympathy between thee and him, have so wrought within his system, that he now stands apart from common men, as thou dost, daughter of my pride and triumph, from ordinary women. Pass on, then, through the world, most dear to one another, and dreadful to all besides!"

"My father," said Beatrice, feebly—and still, as she spoke, she kept her hand upon her heart—"wherefore didst thou inflict this miserable doom upon thy child?"

"Miserable!" exclaimed Rappaccini. "What mean you, foolish girl? Dost thou deem it misery to be endowed with marvellous gifts, against which no power nor strength could avail an enemy? Misery, to be able to quell the mightiest with a breath? Misery, to be as terrible as thou art beautiful? Wouldst thou, then, have preferred the condition of a weak woman, exposed to all evil, and capable of none?"

"I would fain have been loved, not feared," murmured Beatrice, sinking down upon the ground.—"But now it matters not; I am going, father, where the evil, which thou hast striven to mingle with my being, will pass away like a dream—like the fragrance of these poisonous flowers, which will no longer taint my breath among the flowers of Eden. Farewell, Giovanni! Thy words of hatred are like lead within my heart—but they, too, will fall away as I ascend. Oh, was there not, from the first, more poison in thy nature than in mine?"

To Beatrice—so radically had her earthly part been wrought upon by Rappaccini's skill—as poison had been life, so the powerful antidote was death. And thus the poor victim of man's ingenuity and of thwarted nature, and of the fatality that attends all such efforts of perverted wisdom, perished there, at the feet of her father and Giovanni. Just at that moment, Professor Pietro Baglioni looked forth from the window, and called loudly, in a tone of triumph mixed with horror, to the thunder-stricken man of science:

"Rappaccini! Rappaccini! And is *this* the upshot of your experiment?"

## Young Goodman Brown                                                    1835

Young Goodman[1] Brown came forth, at sunset, into the street of Salem village, but put his head back, after crossing the threshold, to exchange a parting kiss with his young wife. And Faith, as the wife was aptly named, thrust her own pretty head into the street, letting the wind play with the pink ribbons of her cap, while she called to Goodman Brown.

[handwritten margin note: PINK RIBBONS REPRESENT INNOCENCE]

"Dearest heart," whispered she, softly and rather sadly, when her lips were close to his ear, "pr'y thee, put off your journey until sunrise, and sleep in your own bed tonight. A lone woman is troubled with such dreams and such thoughts, that she's afeard of herself, sometimes. Pray, tarry with me this night, dear husband, of all nights in the year!"

"My love and my Faith," replied young Goodman Brown, "of all nights in the year, this one night must I tarry away from thee. My journey, as thou callest it, forth and back again, must needs be done 'twixt now and sunrise. What, my sweet, pretty wife, dost thou doubt me already, and we but three months married!"

"Then, God bless you!" said Faith, with the pink ribbons, "and may you find all well, when you come back."

"Amen!" cried Goodman Brown. "Say thy prayers, dear Faith, and go to bed at dusk, and no harm will come to thee."

So they parted; and the young man pursued his way, until, being about to turn the corner by the meeting-house, he looked back, and saw the head of Faith still peeping after him, with a melancholy air, in spite of her pink ribbons.

"Poor little Faith!" thought he, for his heart smote him. "What a wretch am I, to leave her on such an errand! She talks of dreams, too. Methought, as she spoke, there was trouble in her face, as if a dream had warned her what work is to be done tonight. But, no, no! 'twould kill her to think it. Well; she's a blessed angel on earth; and after this one night, I'll cling to her skirts and follow her to Heaven."

With this excellent resolve for the future, Goodman Brown felt himself justified in making more haste on his present evil purpose. He had taken a dreary road, darkened by all the gloomiest trees of the forest, which barely stood aside to let the narrow path creep through, and closed immediately behind. It was all as lonely as could be; and there is this peculiarity in such a solitude, that the traveller knows not who may be concealed by the innumerable trunks and the thick boughs overhead; so that, with lonely footsteps, he may yet be passing through an unseen multitude.

1 **Young Goodman:** A polite term of address.

"There may be a devilish Indian behind every tree," said Goodman Brown, to himself; and he glanced fearfully behind him, as he added, "What if the devil himself should be at my very elbow!"

His head being turned back, he passed a crook of the road, and looking forward again, beheld the figure of a man, in grave and decent attire, seated at the foot of an old tree. He arose, at Goodman Brown's approach, and walked onward, side by side with him.

"You are late, Goodman Brown," said he. "The clock of the Old South was striking as I came through Boston; and that is full fifteen minutes agone."

"Faith kept me back awhile," replied the young man, with a tremor in his voice, caused by the sudden appearance of his companion, though not wholly unexpected.

It was now deep dusk in the forest, and deepest in that part of it where these two were journeying. As nearly as could be discerned, the second traveller was about fifty years old, apparently in the same rank of life as Goodman Brown, and bearing a considerable resemblance to him, though perhaps more in expression than features. Still, they might have been taken for father and son. And yet, though the elder person was as simply clad as the younger, and as simple in manner too, he had an indescribable air of one who knew the world, and would not have felt abashed at the governor's dinner-table, or in King William's court,[2] were it possible that his affairs should call him thither. But the only thing about him, that could be fixed upon as remarkable, was his staff, which bore the likeness of a great black snake, so curiously wrought, that it might almost be seen to twist and wriggle itself, like a living serpent. This, of course, must have been an ocular deception, assisted by the uncertain light.

"Come, Goodman Brown!" cried his fellow-traveller, "this is a dull pace for the beginning of a journey. Take my staff, if you are so soon weary."

"Friend," said the other, exchanging his slow pace for a full stop, "having kept covenant by meeting thee here, it is my purpose now to return whence I came. I have scruples, touching the matter thou wot'st of."

"Sayest thou so?" replied he of the serpent, smiling apart. "Let us walk on, nevertheless, reasoning as we go, and if I convince thee not, thou shalt turn back. We are but a little way in the forest, yet."

"Too far, too far!" exclaimed the goodman, unconsciously resuming his walk. "My father never went into the woods on such an errand, nor his father before him. We have been a race of honest men and good Christians, since the days of the martyrs.[3] And shall I be the first of the name of Brown, that ever took this path, and kept—"

"Such company, thou wouldst say," observed the elder person, interpreting his pause. "Well said, Goodman Brown! I have been as well acquainted with your family as with ever a one among the Puritans; and that's no trifle to say. I helped your grandfather, the constable, when he lashed the Quaker woman so smartly through the streets of Salem. And it was I that brought your father a pitch-pine knot, kindled at

2 **King William's court:** William of Orange and his wife Queen Mary II ruled England from 1689 to 1702.
3 **martyrs:** Reference to the murder of Protestants during the reign of Catholic Mary Tudor (Bloody Mary) of England (1553–1558).

my own hearth, to set fire to an Indian village, in King Philip's war.[4] They were my good friends, both; and many a pleasant walk have we had along this path, and returned merrily after midnight. I would fain be friends with you, for their sake."

"If it be as thou sayest," replied Goodman Brown, "I marvel they never spoke of these matters. Or, verily, I marvel not, seeing that the least rumor of the sort would have driven them from New-England. We are a people of prayer, and good works, to boot, and abide no such wickedness."

"Wickedness or not," said the traveller with the twisted staff, "I have a very general acquaintance here in New-England. The deacons of many a church have drunk the communion wine with me; the selectmen, of divers towns, make me their chairman; and a majority of the Great and General Court[5] are firm supporters of my interest. The governor and I, too—but these are state-secrets."

"Can this be so!" cried Goodman Brown, with a stare of amazement at his undisturbed companion. "Howbeit, I have nothing to do with the governor and council; they have their own ways, and are no rule for a simple husbandman,[6] like me. But, were I to go on with thee, how should I meet the eye of that good old man, our minister, at Salem village? Oh, his voice would make me tremble, both Sabbath-day and lecture-day!"[7]

Thus far, the elder traveller had listened with due gravity, but now burst into a fit of irrepressible mirth, shaking himself so violently, that his snake-like staff actually seemed to wriggle in sympathy.

"Ha! ha! ha!" shouted he, again and again; then composing himself, "Well, go on, Goodman Brown, go on; but pr'y thee, don't kill me with laughing!"

"Well, then, to end the matter at once," said Goodman Brown, considerably nettled, "there is my wife, Faith. It would break her dear little heart; and I'd rather break my own!"

"Nay, if that be the case," answered the other, "e'en go thy ways, Goodman Brown. I would not, for twenty old women like the one hobbling before us, that Faith should come to any harm."

As he spoke, he pointed his staff at a female figure on the path, in whom Goodman Brown recognized a very pious and exemplary dame, who had taught him his catechism, in youth, and was still his moral and spiritual adviser, jointly with the minister and Deacon Gookin.

"A marvel, truly, that Goody[8] Cloyse should be so far in the wilderness, at nightfall!" said he. "But, with your leave, friend, I shall take a cut through the woods, until we have left this Christian woman behind. Bring a stranger to you, she might ask whom I was consorting with, and whither I was going."

4 **King Philip's war:** King Philip was the leader of the Wampanoag tribe who fought the colonists (1675–1676).
5 **General Court:** Legislature.
6 **husbandman:** Farmer.
7 **lecture-day:** Midweek sermon day.
8 **Goody:** Short for *goodwife,* a polite term for married women of humble rank.

"Be it so," said his fellow-traveller. "Betake you to the woods, and let me keep the path."

Accordingly, the young man turned aside, but took care to watch his companion, who advanced softly along the road, until he had come within a staff's length of the old dame. She, meanwhile, was making the best of her way, with singular speed for so aged a woman, and mumbling some indistinct words, a prayer, doubtless, as she went. The traveller put forth his staff, and touched her withered neck with what seemed the serpent's tail.

"The devil!" screamed the pious old lady.

"Then Goody Cloyse knows her old friend?" observed the traveller, confronting her, and leaning on his writhing stick.

"Ah, forsooth, and is it your worship, indeed?" cried the good dame. "Yea, truly is it, and in the very image of my old gossip, Goodman Brown, the grandfather of the silly fellow that now is. But—would your worship believe it?—my broomstick hath strangely disappeared, stolen, as I suspect, by that unhanged witch, Goody Cory, and that, too, when I was all anointed with the juice of smallage and cinque-foil and wolf's-bane—"

"Mingled with fine wheat and the fat of a new-born babe," said the shape of old Goodman Brown.

"Ah, your worship knows the receipt," cried the old lady, cackling aloud. "So, as I was saying, being all ready for the meeting, and no horse to ride on, I made up my mind to foot it; for they tell me, there is a nice young man to be taken into communion to-night. But now your good worship will lend me your arm, and we shall be there in a twinkling."

"That can hardly be," answered her friend. "I may not spare you my arm, Goody Cloyse, but here is my staff, if you will."

So saying, he threw it down at her feet, where, perhaps, it assumed life, being one of the rods which its owner had formerly lent to the Egyptian Magi.[9] Of this fact, however, Goodman Brown could not take cognizance. He had cast up his eyes in astonishment, and looking down again, beheld neither Goody Cloyse nor the serpentine staff, but his fellow-traveller alone, who waited for him as calmly as if nothing had happened.

"That old woman taught me my catechism!" said the young man; and there was a world of meaning in this simple comment.

They continued to walk onward, while the elder traveller exhorted his companion to make good speed and persevere in the path, discoursing so aptly, that his arguments seemed rather to spring up in the bosom of his auditor, than to be suggested by himself. As they went, he plucked a branch of maple, to serve for a walking-stick, and began to strip it of the twigs and little boughs, which were wet with evening dew. The moment his fingers touched them, they became strangely withered and dried up, as with a week's sunshine. Thus the pair proceeded, at a good free pace, until

9 **Egyptian Magi:** See Exodus 7:11. Magicians of Egypt duplicated Aaron's feat of throwing down a rod and turning it into a serpent.

suddenly, in a gloomy hollow of the road, Goodman Brown sat himself down on the stump of a tree, and refused to go any farther.

"Friend," said he, stubbornly, "my mind is made up. Not another step will I budge on this errand. What if a wretched old woman do choose to go to the devil, when I thought she was going to Heaven! Is that any reason why I should quit my dear Faith, and go after her?"

"You will think better of this, by-and-by," said his acquaintance, composedly. "Sit here and rest yourself awhile; and when you feel like moving again, there is my staff to help you along."

Without more words, he threw his companion the maple stick, and was as speedily out of sight, as if he had vanished into the deepening gloom. The young man sat a few moments, by the road-side, applauding himself greatly, and thinking with how clear a conscience he should meet the minister, in his morning-walk, nor shrink from the eye of good old Deacon Gookin. And what calm sleep would be his, that very night, which was to have been spent so wickedly, but purely and sweetly now, in the arms of Faith! Amidst these pleasant and praiseworthy meditations, Goodman Brown heard the tramp of horses along the road, and deemed it advisable to conceal himself within the verge of the forest, conscious of the guilty purpose that had brought him thither, though now so happily turned from it.

On came the hoof-tramps and the voices of the riders, two grave old voices, conversing soberly as they drew near. These mingled sounds appeared to pass along the road, within a few yards of the young man's hiding-place; but owing, doubtless, to the depth of the gloom, at that particular spot, neither the travellers nor their steeds were visible. Though their figures brushed the small boughs by the way-side, it could not be seen that they intercepted, even for a moment, the faint gleam from the strip of bright sky, athwart which they must have passed. Goodman Brown alternately crouched and stood on tip-toe, pulling aside the branches, and thrusting forth his head as far as he durst, without discerning so much as a shadow. It vexed him the more, because he could have sworn, were such a thing possible, that he recognized the voices of the minister and Deacon Gookin, jogging along quietly, as they were wont to do, when bound to some ordination or ecclesiastical council. While yet within hearing, one of the riders stopped to pluck a switch.

"Of the two, reverend Sir," said the voice like the deacon's, "I had rather miss an ordination-dinner than to-night's meeting. They tell me that some of our community are to be here from Falmouth and beyond, and others from Connecticut and Rhode-Island; besides several of the Indian powows,[10] who, after their fashion, know almost as much deviltry as the best of us. Moreover, there is a goodly young woman to be taken into communion."

"Mighty well, Deacon Gookin!" replied the solemn old tones of the minister. "Spur up, or we shall be late. Nothing can be done, you know, until I get on the ground."

The hoofs clattered again, and the voices, talking so strangely in the empty air,

10 **powwows:** Medicine men.

passed on through the forest, where no church had ever been gathered, nor solitary Christian prayed. Whither, then, could these holy men be journeying, so deep into the heathen wilderness? Young Goodman Brown caught hold of a tree, for support, being ready to sink down on the ground, faint and overburthened with the heavy sickness of his heart. He looked up to the sky, doubting whether there really was a Heaven above him. Yet, there was the blue arch, and the stars brightening in it.

"With Heaven above, and Faith below, I will yet stand firm against the devil!" cried Goodman Brown.

While he still gazed upward, into the deep arch of the firmament, and had lifted his hands to pray, a cloud, though no wind was stirring, hurried across the zenith, and hid the brightening stars. The blue sky was still visible, except directly overhead, where this black mass of cloud was sweeping swiftly northward. Aloft in the air, as if from the depths of the cloud, came a confused and doubtful sound of voices. Once, the listener fancied that he could distinguish the accents of town's-people of his own, men and women, both pious and ungodly, many of whom he had met at the communion-table, and had seen others rioting at the tavern. The next moment, so indistinct were the sounds, he doubted whether he had heard aught but the murmur of the old forest, whispering without a wind. Then came a stronger swell of those familiar tones, heard daily in the sunshine, at Salem village, but never, until now, from a cloud of night. There was one voice, of a young woman, uttering lamentations, yet with an uncertain sorrow, and entreating for some favor, which, perhaps, it would grieve her to obtain. And all the unseen multitude, both saints and sinners, seemed to encourage her onward.

"Faith!" shouted Goodman Brown, in a voice of agony and desperation; and the echoes of the forest mocked him, crying—"Faith! Faith!" as if bewildered wretches were seeking her, all through the wilderness.

The cry of grief, rage, and terror, was yet piercing the night, when the unhappy husband held his breath for a response. There was a scream, drowned immediately in a louder murmur of voices, fading into far-off laughter, as the dark cloud swept away, leaving the clear and silent sky above Goodman Brown. But something fluttered lightly down through the air, and caught on the branch of a tree. The young man seized it, and beheld a pink ribbon.

"My Faith is gone!" cried he, after one stupefied moment. "There is no good on earth; and sin is but a name. Come, devil! for to thee is this world given."

And maddened with despair, so that he laughed loud and long, did Goodman Brown grasp his staff and set forth again, at such a rate, that he seemed to fly along the forest-path, rather than to walk or run. The road grew wilder and drearier, and more faintly traced, and vanished at length, leaving him in the heart of the dark wilderness, still rushing onward, with the instinct that guides mortal man to evil. The whole forest was peopled with frightful sounds; the creaking of the trees, the howling of wild beasts, and the yell of Indians; while, sometimes, the wind tolled like a distant churchbell, and sometimes gave a broad roar around the traveller, as if all Nature were laughing him to scorn. But he was himself the chief horror of the scene, and shrank not from its other horrors.

"Ha! ha! ha!" roared Goodman Brown, when the wind laughed at him. "Let us hear which will laugh loudest! Think not to frighten me with your deviltry! Come witch, come wizard, come Indian powow, come devil himself! and here comes Goodman Brown. You may as well fear him as he fear you!"

In truth, all through the haunted forest, there could be nothing more frightful than the figure of Goodman Brown. On he flew, among the black pines, brandishing his staff with frenzied gestures, now giving vent to an inspiration of horrid blasphemy, and now shouting forth such laughter, as set all the echoes of the forest laughing like demons around him. The fiend in his own shape is less hideous, than when he rages in the breast of man. Thus sped the demoniac on his course, until, quivering among the trees, he saw a red light before him, as when the felled trunks and branches of a clearing have been set on fire, and throw up their lurid blaze against the sky, at the hour of midnight. He paused, in a lull of the tempest that had driven him onward, and heard the swell of what seemed a hymn, rolling solemnly from a distance, with the weight of many voices. He knew the tune; it was a familiar one in the choir of the village meeting-house. The verse died heavily away, and was lengthened by a chorus, not of human voices, but of all the sounds of the benighted wilderness, pealing in awful harmony together. Goodman Brown cried out; and his cry was lost to his own ear, by its unison with the cry of the desert.

In the interval of silence, he stole forward, until the light glared full upon his eyes. At one extremity of an open space, hemmed in by the dark wall of the forest, arose a rock, bearing some rude, natural resemblance either to an altar or a pulpit, and surrounded by four blazing pines, their tops aflame, their stems untouched, like candles at an evening meeting. The mass of foliage, that had overgrown the summit of the rock, was all on fire, blazing high into the night, and fitfully illuminating the whole field. Each pendent twig and leafy festoon was in a blaze. As the red light arose and fell, a numerous congregation alternately shone forth, then disappeared in shadow, and again grew, as it were, out of the darkness, peopling the heart of the solitary woods at once.

"A grave and dark-clad company!" quoth Goodman Brown.

In truth, they were such. Among them, quivering to-and-fro, between gloom and splendor, appeared faces that would be seen, next day, at the council-board of the province, and others which, Sabbath after Sabbath, looked devoutly heavenward, and benignantly over the crowded pews, from the holiest pulpits in the land. Some affirm, that the lady of the governor was there. At least, there were high dames well known to her, and wives of honored husbands, and widows, a great multitude, and ancient maidens, all of excellent repute, and fair young girls, who trembled, lest their mothers should espy them. Either the sudden gleams of light, flashing over the obscure field, bedazzled Goodman Brown, or he recognized a score of the church-members of Salem village, famous for their especial sanctity. Good old Deacon Gookin had arrived, and waited at the skirts of that venerable saint, his revered pastor. But, irreverently consorting with these grave, reputable, and pious people, these elders of the church, these chaste dames and dewy virgins, there were men of dissolute lives and women of spotted fame, wretches given over to all mean and filthy vice, and suspected even of horrid crimes. It was strange to see, that the good shrank not from the wicked, nor were the sinners abashed by the saints. Scattered, also, among their pale-faced enemies, were the Indian priests, or powows, who had often scared their native forest with more hideous incantations than any known to English witchcraft.

"But, where is Faith?" thought Goodman Brown; and, as hope came into his heart, he trembled.

Another verse of the hymn arose, a slow and mournful strain, such as the pious love, but joined to words which expressed all that our nature can conceive of sin, and darkly hinted at far more. Unfathomable to mere mortals is the lore of fiends. Verse after verse was sung, and still the chorus of the desert swelled between, like the deepest tone of a mighty organ. And, with the final peal of that dreadful anthem, there came a sound, as if the roaring wind, the rushing streams, the howling beasts, and every other voice of the unconverted wilderness, were mingling and according with the voice of guilty man, in homage to the prince of all. The four blazing pines threw up a loftier flame, and obscurely discovered shapes and visages of horror on the smoke-wreaths, above the impious assembly. At the same moment, the fire on the rock shot redly forth, and formed a glowing arch above its base, where now appeared a figure. With reverence be it spoken, the figure bore no slight similitude, both in garb and manner, to some grave divine of the New-England churches.

"Bring forth the converts!" cried a voice, that echoed through the field and rolled into the forest.

At the word, Goodman Brown stept forth from the shadow of the trees, and approached the congregation, with whom he felt a loathful brotherhood, by the sympathy of all that was wicked in his heart. He could have well nigh sworn, that the shape of his own dead father beckoned him to advance, looking downward from a smoke-wreath, while a woman, with dim features of despair, threw out her hand to warn him back. Was it his mother? But he had no power to retreat one step, nor to resist, even in thought, when the minister and good old Deacon Gookin seized his arms, and led him to the blazing rock. Thither came also the slender form of a veiled female, led between Goody Cloyse, that pious teacher of the catechism, and Martha Carrier, who had received the devil's promise to be queen of hell. A rampant hag was she! And there stood the proselytes, beneath the canopy of fire.

"Welcome, my children," said the dark figure, "to the communion of your race! Ye have found, thus young, your nature and your destiny. My children, look behind you!"

They turned; and flashing forth, as it were, in a sheet of flame, the fiend-worshippers were seen; the smile of welcome gleamed darkly on every visage.

"There," resumed the sable form, "are all whom ye have reverenced from youth. Ye deemed them holier than yourselves, and shrank from your own sin, contrasting it with their lives of righteousness, and prayerful aspirations heavenward. Yet, here are they all, in my worshipping assembly! This night it shall be granted you to know their secret deeds; how hoary-bearded elders of the church have whispered wanton words to the young maids of their households; how many a woman, eager for widow's weeds, has given her husband a drink at bedtime, and let him sleep his last sleep in her bosom; how beardless youths have made haste to inherit their fathers' wealth; and how fair damsels—blush not, sweet ones!—have dug little graves in the garden, and bidden me, the sole guest, to an infant's funeral. By the sympathy of your human hearts for sin, ye shall scent out all the places—whether in church, bed-chamber, street, field, or forest—where crime has been committed, and shall exult to behold the whole earth one stain of guilt, one mighty blood-spot. Far more than this! It shall be yours to penetrate, in every bosom, the deep mystery of sin, the fountain of all wicked arts, and which inexhaustibly supplies more evil impulses than human power—than my power, at its utmost!—can make manifest in deeds. And now, my children, look upon each other."

They did so; and, by the blaze of the hell-kindled torches, the wretched man beheld his Faith, and the wife her husband, trembling before that unhallowed altar.

"Lo! there ye stand, my children," said the figure, in a deep and solemn tone, almost sad, with its despairing awfulness, as if his once angelic nature could yet mourn for our miserable race. "Depending upon one another's hearts, ye had still hoped, that virtue were not all a dream. Now are ye undeceived! Evil is the nature of mankind. Evil must be your only happiness. Welcome, again, my children, to the communion of your race!"

"Welcome!" repeated the fiend-worshippers, in one cry of despair and triumph.

And there they stood, the only pair, as it seemed, who were yet hesitating on the verge of wickedness, in this dark world. A basin was hollowed, naturally, in the rock. Did it contain water, reddened by the lurid light? or was it blood? or, perchance, a liquid flame? Herein did the Shape of Evil dip his hand, and prepare to lay the mark of baptism upon their foreheads, that they might be partakers of the mystery of sin, more conscious of the secret guilt of others, both in deed and thought, than they could now be of their own. The husband cast one look at his pale wife, and Faith at him. What polluted wretches would the next glance shew them to each other, shuddering alike at what they disclosed and what they saw!

"Faith! Faith!" cried the husband. "Look up to Heaven, and resist the Wicked One!"

Whether Faith obeyed, he knew not. Hardly had he spoken, when he found himself amid calm night and solitude, listening to a roar of the wind, which died heavily away through the forest. He staggered against the rock and felt it chill and damp, while a hanging twig, that had been all on fire, besprinkled his cheek with the coldest dew.

The next morning, young Goodman Brown came slowly into the street of Salem village, staring around him like a bewildered man. The good old minister was taking a walk along the grave-yard, to get an appetite for breakfast and meditate his sermon, and bestowed a blessing, as he passed, on Goodman Brown. He shrank from the venerable saint, as if to avoid an anathema. Old Deacon Gookin was at domestic worship, and the holy words of his prayer were heard through the open window. "What God doth the wizard pray to?" quoth Goodman Brown. Goody Cloyse, that excellent old Christian, stood in the early sunshine, at her own lattice, catechising a little girl, who had brought her a pint of morning's milk. Goodman Brown snatched away the child, as from the grasp of the fiend himself. Turning the corner by the meeting-house, he spied the head of Faith, with the pink ribbons, gazing anxiously forth, and bursting into such joy at sight of him, that she skipt along the street, and almost kissed her husband before the whole village. But, Goodman Brown looked sternly and sadly into her face, and passed on without a greeting.

Had Goodman Brown fallen asleep in the forest, and only dreamed a wild dream of a witch-meeting?

Be it so, if you will. But, alas! it was a dream of evil omen for young Goodman Brown. A stern, a sad, a darkly meditative, a distrustful, if not a desperate man, did he become, from the night of that fearful dream. On the Sabbath-day, when the congregation were singing a holy psalm, he could not listen, because an anthem of sin rushed loudly upon his ear, and drowned all the blessed strain. When the minister spoke from the pulpit, with power and fervid eloquence, and, with his hand on the open Bible, of the sacred truths of our religion, and of saint-like lives and triumphant deaths, and of future bliss or misery unutterable, then did Goodman Brown turn pale, dreading, lest the roof should thunder down upon the gray blasphemer and his hearers. Often, awakening suddenly at midnight, he shrank from the bosom of Faith, and at morning or eventide, when the family knelt down at prayer, he scowled, and muttered to himself, and gazed sternly at his wife, and turned away. And when he had lived long, and was borne to his grave, a hoary corpse, followed by Faith, an aged woman, and children and grand-children, a goodly procession, besides neighbors, not a few, they carved no hopeful verse upon his tomb-stone; for his dying hour was gloom.

# Washington Irving

## (1783–1859)

Washington Irving was born in New York City in 1783, the youngest of eleven children in a newly minted America. Irving's approach to employment seemed to equal the restless spirit of the growing nation. He practiced law for a few years before joining two brothers in a hardware business, leaving in 1812 to become an editor of the *Analectic Magazine,* which he subsequently left to become an officer in the War of 1812. In 1815 he left America for Europe, where he remained until 1832. After returning to America for ten years, Irving went to Spain, where he served as a United States minister. In 1846 he returned to the United States and lived there until his death in 1859. Irving's travels and exploratory approach to employment did not supersede his interest in literature and writing. He began his career as a writer in journals and newspapers, contributing to the *Morning Chronicle* (1802–1803), a magazine edited by his brother Peter, and publishing *Salmagundi* (1807–1808), a collection of satirical papers written with other Knickerbocker wits (a group of writers based in New

York City who imitated English and European styles of popular literature). In 1809, Irving's comic history of the Dutch regime in New York, *A History of New York*, by the imaginary Dutch-American scholar Diedrich Knickerbocker, was published with great success. He followed this work with two collections of stories, *The Sketch Book of Geoffrey Crayon, Gent.* (1819–1820), and *The Sketch Book, Bracebridge Hall* (1822). Irving also tried his hand at history, writing books on Christopher Columbus, George Washington, and westward travel.

Irving's most important contribution to American letters, however, is his exploration of the short story. He often created multiple narrators who are saddled with eccentricities and forced to face supernatural horrors. Irving also developed a particularly American voice in his storytelling: easy, flexible, and conversational. His themes set the tone for American literature as his characters pursue love, wealth, and happiness and attempt to escape disillusion, disappointment, and conflict. Thus, for Irving, the American landscape itself is a model of freedom: open, searchable, and mutable. Irving's experimentation and his "moment in time" brand of storytelling enabled future writers of the American short story to explore endless literary possibilities.

## Rip Van Winkle

1819

### A Posthumous Writing of Diedrich Knickerbocker

> "By Woden,[1] God of Saxons,
> From whence comes Wensday, that is Wodensday,
> Truth is a thing that ever I will keep
> Until thylke day in which I creep into
> My sepulchre—"
>
> —CARTWRIGHT[2]

[The following Tale was found among the papers of the late Diedrich Knickerbocker, an old gentleman of New York, who was very curious, in the Dutch History of the province, and the manners of the descendants from its primitive settlers. His historical researches, however, did not lie so much among books as among men; for the former are lamentably scanty on his favorite topics; whereas he found the old burghers, and still more, their wives, rich in that legendary lore, so invaluable to true history. Whenever, therefore, he happened upon a genuine Dutch family, snugly shut up in its low-roofed farmhouse under a spreading sycamore, he looked upon it as a little clasped volume of black-letter, and studied it with the zeal of a bookworm.

The result of all these researches was a history of the province during the reign of the Dutch governors, which he published some years since. There have been various

---

1 **Woden:** the Norse god of war.
2 **Cartwright:** English playwright (1611–1643). This quotation is from his play, *The Ordinary*.

opinions as to the literary character of his work, and, to tell the truth, it is not a whit better than it should be. Its chief merit is its scrupulous accuracy, which, indeed, was a little questioned on its first appearance, but has since been completely established; and it is now admitted into all historical collections as a book of unquestionable authority.

The old gentleman died shortly after the publication of his work, and, now that he is dead and gone, it cannot do much harm to his memory to say that his time might have been much better employed in weightier labors. He, however, was apt to ride his hobby his own way; and though it did now and then kick up the dust a little in the eyes of his neighbors, and grieve the spirit of some friends for whom he felt the truest deference and affection, yet his errors and follies are remembered "more in sorrow than in anger,"[3] and it begins to be suspected that he never intended to injure or offend. But however his memory may be appreciated by critics, it is still held dear among many folk, whose good opinion is well worth having; particularly by certain biscuit bakers, who have gone so far as to imprint his likeness on their new year cakes, and have thus given him a chance for immortality almost equal to the being stamped on a Waterloo medal, or a Queen Anne's farthing.][4]

Whoever has made a voyage up the Hudson must remember the Kaatskill mountains. They are a dismembered branch of the great Appalachian family, and are seen away to the west of the river, swelling up to a noble height, and lording it over the surrounding country. Every change of season, every change of weather, indeed every hour of the day, produces some change in the magical hues and shapes of these mountains; and they are regarded by all the good wives, far and near, as perfect barometers. When the weather is fair and settled they are clothed in blue and purple, and print their bold outlines on the clear evening sky; but sometimes, when the rest of the landscape is cloudless, they will gather a hood of gray vapors about their summits, which, in the last rays of the setting sun, will glow and light up like a crown of glory.

At the foot of these fairy mountains the voyager may have descried the light smoke curling up from a village, whose shingle roofs gleam among the trees just where the blue tints of the upland melt away into the fresh green of the nearer landscape. It is a little village of great antiquity, having been founded by some of the Dutch colonists, in the early times of the province, just about the beginning of the government of the good Peter Stuyvesant (may he rest in peace!), and there were some of the houses of the original settlers standing within a few years, built of small yellow bricks brought from Holland, having latticed windows and gable fronts, surmounted with weathercocks.

In that same village, and in one of these very houses (which, to tell the precise truth, was sadly time-worn and weather-beaten), there lived many years since, while the country was yet a province of Great Britain, a simple, good-natured fellow, of the

---

3 **"more in sorrow than in anger"**: From Shakespeare's *Hamlet* I:ii.
4 **Waterloo medal, or a Queen Anne's farthing**: Both medals and coins were frequently minted. In other words, neither was scarce.

name of Rip Van Winkle. He was a descendant of the Van Winkles who figure so gallantly in the chivalrous days of Peter Stuyvesant[5] and accompanied him to the siege of Fort Christina. He inherited, however, but little of the martial character of his ancestors. I have observed that he was a simple, good-natured man; he was moreover a kind neighbor, and an obedient henpecked husband. Indeed, to the latter circumstance might be owing that meekness of spirit which gained him such universal popularity; for those men are most apt to be obsequious and conciliating abroad who are under the discipline of shrews at home. Their tempers, doubtless, are rendered pliant and malleable in the fiery furnace of domestic tribulation, and a curtain lecture is worth all the sermons in the world for teaching the virtues of patience and long-suffering. A termagant wife may, therefore, in some respects, be considered a tolerable blessing; and, if so, Rip Van Winkle was thrice blessed.

Certain it is that he was a great favorite among all the good wives of the village, who, as usual with the amiable sex, took his part in all family squabbles, and never failed, whenever they talked those matters over in their evening gossipings, to lay all the blame on Dame Van Winkle. The children of the village, too, would shout with joy whenever he approached. He assisted at their sports, made their playthings, taught them to fly kites and shoot marbles, and told them long stories of ghosts, witches, and Indians. Whenever he went dodging about the village, he was surrounded by a troop of them hanging on his skirts, clambering on his back, and playing a thousand tricks on him with impunity; and not a dog would bark at him throughout the neighborhood.

The great error in Rip's composition was an insuperable aversion to all kinds of profitable labor. It could not be from the want of assiduity or perseverance; for he would sit on a wet rock, with a rod as long and heavy as a Tartar's lance, and fish all day without a murmur, even though he should not be encouraged by a single nibble. He would carry a fowling-piece on his shoulder, for hours together, trudging through woods and swamps, and up hill and down dale, to shoot a few squirrels or wild pigeons. He would never refuse to assist a neighbor even in the roughest toil, and was a foremost man at all country frolics for husking Indian corn, or building stone fences. The women of the village, too, used to employ him to run their errands, and to do such little odd jobs as their less obliging husbands would not do for them—in a word, Rip was ready to attend to anybody's business but his own; but as to doing family duty, and keeping his farm in order, he found it impossible.

In fact, he declared it was of no use to work on his farm; it was the most pestilent little piece of ground in the whole country; everything about it went wrong, and would go wrong in spite of him. His fences were continually falling to pieces; his cow would either go astray, or get among the cabbages; weeds were sure to grow quicker in his fields than anywhere else; the rain always made a point of setting in just as he had some outdoor work to do; so that, though his patrimonial estate had dwindled away under his management, acre by acre, until there was little more left than a mere patch of Indian corn and potatoes, yet it was the worst conditioned farm in the neighborhood.

---

5 **Peter Stuyvesant:** Last governor of New Netherlands (1592–1672).

His children, too, were as ragged and wild as if they belonged to nobody. His son Rip, an urchin begotten in his own likeness, promised to inherit the habits, with the old clothes of his father. He was generally seen trooping like a colt at his mother's heels, equipped in a pair of his father's cast-off galligaskins, which he had much ado to hold up with one hand, as a fine lady does her train in bad weather.

Rip Van Winkle, however, was one of those happy mortals, of foolish, well-oiled dispositions, who take the world easy, eat white bread or brown, whichever can be got with least thought or trouble, and would rather starve on a penny than work for a pound. If left to himself, he would have whistled life away, in perfect contentment; but his wife kept continually dinning in his ears about his idleness, his carelessness, and the ruin he was bringing on his family. Morning, noon, and night, her tongue was incessantly going, and everything he said or did was sure to produce a torrent of household eloquence. Rip had but one way of replying to all lectures of the kind, and that, by frequent use, had grown into a habit. He shrugged his shoulders, shook his head, cast up his eyes, but said nothing. This, however, always provoked a fresh volley from his wife, so that he was fain to draw off his forces, and take to the outside of the house—the only side which, in truth, belongs to a henpecked husband.

Rip's sole domestic adherent was his dog Wolf, who was as much henpecked as his master; for Dame Van Winkle regarded them as companions in idleness, and even looked upon Wolf with an evil eye, as the cause of his master's going so often astray. True it is, in all points of spirit befitting an honorable dog, he was as courageous an animal as ever scoured the woods—but what courage can withstand the ever-during and all-besetting terrors of a woman's tongue? The moment Wolf entered the house, his crest fell, his tail drooped to the ground, or curled between his legs, he sneaked about with a gallows air, casting many a sidelong glance at Dame Van Winkle, and at the least flourish of a broomstick or ladle he would fly to the door with yelping precipitation.

Times grew worse and worse with Rip Van Winkle, as years of matrimony rolled on: a tart temper never mellows with age, and a sharp tongue is the only edge tool that grows keener with constant use. For a long while he used to console himself, when driven from home, by frequenting a kind of perpetual club of the sages, philosophers, and other idle personages of the village, which held its sessions on a bench before a small inn, designated by a rubicund portrait of his Majesty George the Third. Here they used to sit in the shade, of a long lazy summer's day, talking listlessly over village gossip, or telling endless sleepy stories about nothing. But it would have been worth any statesman's money to have heard the profound discussions which sometimes took place, when by chance an old newspaper fell into their hands from some passing traveler. How solemnly they would listen to the contents, as drawled out by Derrick Van Bummel, the schoolmaster, a dapper learned little man, who was not to be daunted by the most gigantic word in the dictionary; and how sagely they would deliberate upon public events some months after they had taken place.

The opinions of this junto were completely controlled by Nicholas Vedder, a patriarch of the village, and landlord of the inn, at the door of which he took his seat from morning till night, just moving sufficiently to avoid the sun, and keep in the shade of a large tree; so that the neighbors could tell the hour by his movements as accurately as by a sun-dial. It is true, he was rarely heard to speak, but smoked his pipe incessantly. His adherents, however (for every great man has his adherents), perfectly understood him, and knew how to gather his opinions. When anything that was read or related displeased him, he was observed to smoke his pipe vehemently, and to send forth short, frequent, and angry puffs; but when pleased, he would inhale the smoke slowly and tranquilly, and emit it in light and placid clouds, and sometimes taking the pipe from his mouth, and letting the fragrant vapor curl about his nose, would gravely nod his head in token of perfect approbation.

From even this stronghold the unlucky Rip was at length routed by his termagant wife, who would suddenly break in upon the tranquillity of the assemblage, and call the members all to naught; nor was that august personage, Nicholas Vedder himself, sacred from the daring tongue of this terrible virago, who charged him outright with encouraging her husband in habits of idleness.

Poor Rip was at last reduced almost to despair, and his only alternative to escape from the labor of the farm and the clamor of his wife was to take gun in hand and stroll away into the woods. Here he would sometimes seat himself at the foot of a tree, and share the contents of his wallet with Wolf, with whom he sympathized as a fellow-sufferer in persecution. "Poor Wolf," he would say, "thy mistress leads thee a dog's life of it; but never mind, my lad, while I live thou shalt never want a friend to stand by thee!" Wolf would wag his tail, look wistfully in his master's face, and if dogs can feel pity, I verily believe he reciprocated the sentiment with all his heart.

In a long ramble of the kind, on a fine autumnal day, Rip had unconsciously scrambled to one of the highest parts of the Kaatskill mountains. He was after his favorite sport of squirrel-shooting, and the still solitudes had echoed and re-echoed with the reports of his gun. Panting and fatigued, he threw himself, late in the afternoon, on a green knoll covered with mountain herbage that crowned the brow of a precipice. From an opening between the trees, he could overlook all the lower country for many a mile of rich woodland. He saw at a distance the lordly Hudson, far, far below him, moving on its silent but majestic course, with the reflection of a purple cloud, or the sail of a lagging bark, here and there sleeping on its glassy bosom, and at last losing itself in the blue highlands.

On the other side he looked down into a deep mountain glen, wild, lonely, and shagged, the bottom filled with fragments from the impending cliffs, and scarcely lighted by the reflected rays of the setting sun. For some time Rip lay musing on this scene; evening was gradually advancing; the mountains began to throw their long blue shadows over the valleys; he saw that it would be dark long before he could reach the village; and he heaved a heavy sigh when he thought of encountering the terrors of Dame Van Winkle.

As he was about to descend he heard a voice from a distance hallooing, "Rip Van Winkle! Rip Van Winkle!" He looked around, but could see nothing but a crow winging its solitary flight across the mountain. He thought his fancy must have deceived him, and turned again to descend, when he heard the same cry ring through the still evening air, "Rip Van Winkle! Rip Van Winkle!"—at the same time Wolf bristled up his back, and giving a low growl, skulked to his master's side, looking fearfully down into the glen. Rip now felt a vague apprehension stealing over him: he looked anxiously in the same direction, and perceived a strange figure slowly toiling up the rocks, and bending under the weight of something he carried on his back. He was surprised to see any human being in this lonely and unfrequented place, but supposing it to be some one of the neighborhood in need of his assistance, he hastened down to yield it.

On nearer approach, he was still more surprised at the singularity of the stranger's appearance. He was a short square built old fellow, with thick bushy hair, and a grizzled beard. His dress was of the antique Dutch fashion—a cloth jerkin strapped round the waist—several pair of breeches, the outer one of ample volume, decorated with rows of buttons down the sides, and bunches at the knees. He bore on his shoulders a stout keg, that seemed full of liquor, and made signs for Rip to approach and assist him with the load. Though rather shy and distrustful of this new acquaintance, Rip complied with his usual alacrity, and, mutually relieving each other, they clambered up a narrow gully, apparently the dry bed of a mountain torrent. As they ascended, Rip every now and then heard long rolling peals, like distant thunder, that seemed to issue out of a deep ravine, or rather cleft, between lofty rocks, toward which their rugged path conducted. He paused for an instant, but supposing it to be the muttering of one of those transient thunder-showers which often take place in mountain heights, he proceeded. Passing through the ravine, they came to a hollow, like a small amphitheater, surrounded by perpendicular precipices, over the brinks of which impending trees shot their branches, so that you only caught glimpses of the azure sky, and the bright evening cloud. During the whole time, Rip and his companion had labored on in silence; for though the former marveled greatly what could be the object of carrying a keg of liquor up this wild mountain, yet there was something strange and incomprehensible about the unknown that inspired awe, and checked familiarity.

On entering the amphitheater, new objects of wonder presented themselves. On a level spot in the center was a company of odd-looking personages playing at nine-pins. They were dressed in a quaint outlandish fashion: some wore short doublets, others jerkins, with long knives in their belts, and most of them had enormous breeches, of similar style with that of the guide's. Their visages, too, were peculiar: one had a large head, broad face, and small piggish eyes; the face of another seemed to consist entirely of nose, and was surmounted by a white sugar-loaf hat, set off with a little red cock's tail. They all had beards, of various shapes and colors. There was one who seemed to be the commander. He was a stout old gentleman, with a weather-beaten countenance; he wore a laced doublet, broad belt and hanger,[6] high-crowned hat and feather, red stockings, and high-heeled shoes, with roses in them. The whole group reminded Rip of the figures in an old Flemish painting, in the parlor of Dominie Van Schaick, the village parson, and which had been brought over from Holland at the time of the settlement.

6 **hanger:** Short sword.

What seemed particularly odd to Rip, was, that though these folks were evidently amusing themselves, yet they maintained the gravest faces, the most mysterious silence, and were, withal, the most melancholy party of pleasure he had ever witnessed. Nothing interrupted the stillness of the scene but the noise of the balls, which, whenever they rolled, echoed along the mountains like rumbling peals of thunder.

As Rip and his companion approached them, they suddenly desisted from their play, and stared at him with such a fixed statue-like gaze, and such strange, uncouth, lackluster countenances, that his heart turned within him, and his knees smote together. His companion now emptied the contents of the keg into large flagons, and made signs to him to wait upon the company. He obeyed with fear and trembling; they quaffed the liquor in profound silence, and then returned to their game.

By degrees Rip's awe and apprehension subsided. He even ventured, when no eye was fixed upon him, to taste the beverage, which he found had much of the flavor of excellent Hollands. He was naturally a thirsty soul, and was soon tempted to repeat the draught. One taste provoked another, and he reiterated his visits to the flagon so often that at length his senses were overpowered, his eyes swam in his head, his head gradually declined, and he fell into a deep sleep.

On waking, he found himself on the green knoll from whence he had first seen the old man of the glen. He rubbed his eyes—it was a bright sunny morning. The birds were hopping and twittering among the bushes, and the eagle was wheeling aloft, and breasting the pure mountain breeze. "Surely," thought Rip, "I have not slept here all night." He recalled the occurrences before he fell asleep. The strange man with the keg of liquor—the mountain ravine—the wild retreat among the rocks—the woe-begone party at nine-pins—the flagon—"Oh! that wicked flagon!" thought Rip—"what excuse shall I make to Dame Van Winkle?"

He looked round for his gun, but in place of the clean, well-oiled fowling-piece, he found an old firelock lying by him, the barrel incrusted with rust, the lock falling off, and the stock worm-eaten. He now suspected that the grave roisterers of the mountain had put a trick upon him, and having dosed him with liquor, had robbed him of his gun. Wolf, too, had disappeared, but he might have strayed away after a squirrel or partridge. He whistled after him, and shouted his name, but all in vain; the echoes repeated his whistle and shout, but no dog was to be seen.

He determined to revisit the scene of the last evening's gambol, and if he met with any of the party, to demand his dog and gun. As he rose to walk, he found himself stiff in the joints, and wanting in his usual activity. "These mountain beds do not agree with me," thought Rip, "and if this frolic should lay me up with a fit of the rheumatism, I shall have a blessed time with Dame Van Winkle." With some difficulty he got down into the glen; he found the gully up which he and his companion had ascended the preceding evening; but to his astonishment a mountain stream was now foaming down it, leaping from rock to rock, and filling the glen with babbling murmurs. He, however, made shift to scramble up its sides, working his toilsome way through thickets of birch, sassafras, and witch-hazel; and sometimes tripped up or entangled by the wild grape-vines that twisted their coils and tendrils from tree to tree, and spread a kind of network in his path.

At length he reached to where the ravine had opened through the cliffs to the amphitheater; but no traces of such opening remained. The rocks presented a high impenetrable wall, over which the torrent came tumbling in a sheet of feathery foam, and fell into a broad deep basin, black from the shadows of the surrounding forest. Here, then, poor Rip was brought to a stand. He again called and whistled after his dog; he was only answered by the cawing of a flock of idle crows, sporting high in air about a dry tree that overhung a sunny precipice; and who, secure in their elevation, seemed to look down and scoff at the poor man's perplexities. What was to be done? The morning was passing away, and Rip felt famished for want of his breakfast. He grieved to give up his dog and gun; he dreaded to meet his wife; but it would not do to starve among the mountains. He shook his head, shouldered the rusty firelock, and, with a heart full of trouble and anxiety, turned his steps homeward.

As he approached the village, he met a number of people, but none whom he knew, which somewhat surprised him, for he had thought himself acquainted with every one in the country round. Their dress, too, was of a different fashion from that to which he was accustomed. They all stared at him with equal marks of surprise, and whenever they cast eyes upon him, invariably stroked their chins. The constant recurrence of this gesture induced Rip, involuntarily, to do the same, when, to his astonishment, he found his beard had grown a foot long.

He had now entered the skirts of the village. A troop of strange children ran at his heels, hooting after him, and pointing at his gray beard. The dogs, too, not one of which he recognized for an old acquaintance, barked at him as he passed. The very village was altered: it was larger and more populous. There were rows of houses which he had never seen before, and those which had been his familiar haunts had disappeared. Strange names were over the doors—strange faces at the windows—everything was strange. His mind now misgave him; he began to doubt whether both he and the world around him were not bewitched. Surely this was his native village, which he had left but a day before. There stood the Kaatskill mountains—there ran the silver Hudson at a distance—there was every hill and dale precisely as it had always been—Rip was sorely perplexed—"That flagon last night," thought he, "has addled my poor head sadly!"

It was with some difficulty that he found the way to his own house, which he approached with silent awe, expecting every moment to hear the shrill voice of Dame Van Winkle. He found the house gone to decay—the roof fallen in, the windows shattered, and the doors off the hinges. A half-starved dog, that looked like Wolf, was skulking about it. Rip called him by name, but the cur snarled, showed his teeth, and passed on. This was an unkind cut indeed.—"My very dog," sighed poor Rip, "has forgotten me!"

He entered the house, which, to tell the truth, Dame Van Winkle had always kept in neat order. It was empty, forlorn, and apparently abandoned. This desolateness overcame all his connubial fears—he called loudly for his wife and children—the lonely chambers rang for a moment with his voice, and then all again was silence.

He now hurried forth, and hastened to his old resort, the village inn—but it too was gone. A large rickety wooden building stood in its place, with great gaping windows, some of them broken, and mended with old hats and petticoats, and over the door was painted, "The Union Hotel, by Jonathan Doolittle." Instead of the great tree that used to shelter the quiet little Dutch inn of yore, there now was reared a tall naked pole, with something on the top that looked like a red night-cap,[7] and from it was fluttering a flag, on which was a singular assemblage of stars and stripes—all this was strange and incomprehensible. He recognized on the sign, however, the ruby face of King George, under which he had smoked so many a peaceful pipe, but even this was singularly metamorphosed. The red coat was changed for one of blue and buff, a sword was held in the hand instead of a scepter, the head was decorated with a cocked hat, and underneath was painted in large characters, General Washington.

There was, as usual, a crowd of folk about the door, but none that Rip recollected. The very character of the people seemed changed. There was a busy, bustling, disputatious tone about it, instead of the accustomed phlegm and drowsy tranquillity. He looked in vain for the sage Nicholas Vedder, with his broad face, double chin, and fair long pipe, uttering clouds of tobacco smoke, instead of idle speeches; or Van Bummel, the schoolmaster, doling forth the contents of an ancient newspaper. In place of these, a lean, bilious-looking fellow, with his pockets full of handbills, was haranguing vehemently about rights of citizens—election—members of Congress—liberty—Bunker's hill—heroes of seventy-six—and other words, that were a perfect Babylonish[8] jargon to the bewildered Van Winkle.

The appearance of Rip, with his long, grizzled beard, his rusty fowling-piece, his uncouth dress, and the army of women and children that had gathered at his heels, soon attracted the attention of the tavern politicians. They crowded round him, eying him from head to foot, with great curiosity. The orator bustled up to him, and drawing him partly aside, inquired, "on which side he voted?" Rip stared in vacant stupidity. Another short but busy little fellow pulled him by the arm, and rising on tiptoe, inquired in his ear, "whether he was Federal or Democrat." Rip was equally at a loss to comprehend the question; when a knowing, self-important old gentleman, in a sharp cocked hat, made his way through the crowd, putting them to the right and left with his elbows as he passed, and planting himself before Van Winkle, with one arm akimbo, the other resting on his cane, his keen eyes and sharp hat penetrating, as it were, into his very soul, demanded in an austere tone, "what brought him to the election with a gun on his shoulder, and a mob at his heels, and whether he meant to breed a riot in the village?"

"Alas! gentlemen," cried Rip, somewhat dismayed, "I am a poor, quiet man, a native of the place, and a loyal subject of the King, God bless him!"

Here a general shout burst from the bystanders—"a Tory! a Tory! a spy! a refugee! hustle him! away with him!"

It was with great difficulty that the self-important man in the cocked hat restored order; and having assumed a tenfold austerity of brow, demanded again of the un-

---

7 **pole:** Liberty pole, symbol used in the American Revolution. **red night-cap:** Liberty cap, worn during the French Revolution.
8 **Babylonish:** Reference to the Tower of Babel.

known culprit, what he came there for, and whom he was seeking. The poor man humbly assured him that he meant no harm, but merely came there in search of some of his neighbors, who used to keep about the tavern.

"Well—who are they?—name them."

Rip bethought himself a moment, and inquired, "Where's Nicholas Vedder?"

There was a silence for a little while, when an old man replied, in a thin, piping voice, "Nicholas Vedder? why, he is dead and gone these eighteen years! There was a wooden tombstone in the churchyard that used to tell all about him, but that's rotten and gone too."

"Where's Brom Dutcher?"

"Oh, he went off to the army in the beginning of the war; some say he was killed at the storming of Stony-Point—others say he was drowned in the squall, at the foot of Anthony's Nose. I don't know—he never came back again."

"Where's Van Bummel, the schoolmaster?"

"He went off to the wars, too; was a great militia general, and is now in Congress."

Rip's heart died away at hearing of these sad changes in his home and friends, and finding himself thus alone in the world. Every answer puzzled him, too, by treating of such enormous lapses of time, and of matters which he could not understand: war—Congress—Stony-Point!—he had no courage to ask after any more friends, but cried out in despair, "Does nobody here know Rip Van Winkle?"

"Oh, Rip Van Winkle!" exclaimed two or three. "Oh, to be sure! that's Rip Van Winkle yonder, leaning against the tree."

Rip looked, and beheld a precise counterpart of himself as he went up the mountain; apparently as lazy, and certainly as ragged. The poor fellow was now completely confounded. He doubted his own identity, and whether he was himself or another man. In the midst of his bewilderment, the man in the cocked hat demanded who he was, and what was his name?

"God knows," exclaimed he, at his wit's end; "I'm not myself—I'm somebody else—that's me yonder—no—that's somebody else, got into my shoes—I was myself last night, but I fell asleep on the mountain, and they've changed my gun, and everything's changed, and I'm changed, and I can't tell what's my name, or who I am!"

The bystanders began now to look at each other, nod, wink significantly, and tap their fingers against their foreheads. There was a whisper, also, about securing the gun, and keeping the old fellow from doing mischief; at the very suggestion of which, the self-important man with the cocked hat retired with some precipitation. At this critical moment a fresh comely woman passed through the throng to get a peep at the gray-bearded man. She had a chubby child in her arms, which, frightened at his looks, began to cry. "Hush, Rip," cried she, "hush, you little fool; the old man won't hurt you." The name of the child, the air of the mother, the tone of her voice, all awakened a train of recollections in his mind.

"What is your name, my good woman?" asked he.

"Judith Gardenier."

"And your father's name?"

"Ah, poor man, his name was Rip Van Winkle; it's twenty years since he went away from home with his gun, and never has been heard of since—his dog came home without him; but whether he shot himself, or was carried away by the Indians, nobody can tell. I was then but a little girl."

Rip had but one question more to ask; but he put it with a faltering voice: "Where's your mother?"

Oh, she too had died but a short time since: she broke a blood-vessel in a fit of passion at a New England peddler.

There was a drop of comfort, at least, in this intelligence. The honest man could contain himself no longer. He caught his daughter and her child in his arms. "I am your father!" cried he—"young Rip Van Winkle once—old Rip Van Winkle now!— Does nobody know poor Rip Van Winkle?"

All stood amazed, until an old woman, tottering out from among the crowd, put her hand to her brow, and peering under it in his face for a moment, exclaimed, "Sure enough! it is Rip Van Winkle—it is himself. Welcome home again, old neighbor. Why, where have you been these twenty long years?"

Rip's story was soon told, for the whole twenty years had been to him but as one night. The neighbors stared when they heard it; some were seen to wink at each other, and put their tongues in their cheeks; and the self-important man in the cocked hat, who, when the alarm was over, had returned to the field, screwed down the corners of his mouth, and shook his head—upon which there was a general shaking of the head throughout the assemblage.

It was determined, however, to take the opinion of old Peter Vanderdonk, who was seen slowly advancing up the road. He was a descendant of the historian of that name, who wrote one of the earliest accounts of the province. Peter was the most ancient inhabitant of the village, and well versed in all the wonderful events and traditions of the neighborhood. He recollected Rip at once, and corroborated his story in the most satisfactory manner. He assured the company that it was a fact, handed down from his ancestor the historian, that the Kaatskill mountains had always been haunted by strange beings. That it was affirmed that the great Hendrick Hudson, the first discoverer of the river and country, kept a kind of vigil there every twenty years, with his crew of the "Half Moon," being permitted in this way to revisit the scenes of his enterprise, and keep a guardian eye upon the river and the great city called by his name. That his father had once seen them in their old Dutch dresses playing at nine-pins in a hollow of the mountain; and that he himself had heard, one summer afternoon, the sound of their balls, like distant peals of thunder.

To make a long story short, the company broke up, and returned to the more important concerns of the election. Rip's daughter took him home to live with her; she had a snug, well-furnished house, and a stout cheery farmer for a husband, whom Rip recollected for one of the urchins that used to climb upon his back. As to Rip's son and heir, who was the ditto of himself, seen leaning against the tree, he was employed to work on the farm; but evinced a hereditary disposition to attend to anything else but his business.

Rip now resumed his old walks and habits; he soon found many of his former cronies, though all rather the worse for the wear and tear of time; and preferred making friends among the rising generation, with whom he soon grew into great favor.

Having nothing to do at home, and being arrived at that happy age when a man can do nothing with impunity, he took his place once more on the bench, at the inn door, and was reverenced as one of the patriarchs of the village, and a chronicle of the old times "before the war." It was some time before he could get into the regular track of gossip, or could be made to comprehend the strange events that had taken place during his torpor. How that there had been a revolutionary war—that the country had thrown off the yoke of old England—and that, instead of being a subject of his Majesty George the Third, he was now a free citizen of the United States. Rip, in fact, was no politician; the changes of states and empires made but little impression on him; but there was one species of despotism under which he had long groaned, and that was—petticoat government. Happily that was at an end; he had got his neck out of the yoke of matrimony, and could go in and out whenever he pleased, without dreading the tyranny of Dame Van Winkle. Whenever her name was mentioned, however, he shook his head, shrugged his shoulders, and cast up his eyes; which might pass either for an expression of resignation to his fate, or joy at his deliverance.

He used to tell his story to every stranger that arrived at Mr. Doolittle's hotel. He was observed, at first, to vary on some points every time he told it, which was doubtless owing to his having so recently awaked. It at last settled down precisely to the tale I have related, and not a man, woman, or child in the neighborhood but knew it by heart. Some always pretended to doubt the reality of it, and insisted that Rip had been out of his head, and that this was one point on which he always remained flighty. The old Dutch inhabitants, however, almost universally gave it full credit. Even to this day, they never hear a thunderstorm of a summer afternoon about the Kaatskill, but they say Hendrick Hudson and his crew are at their game of nine-pins; and it is a common wish of all henpecked husbands in the neighborhood, when life hangs heavy on their hands, that they might have a quieting draught out of Rip Van Winkle's flagon.

## Note

The foregoing tale, one would suspect, had been suggested to Mr. Knickerbocker by a little German superstition about the Emperor Frederick *der Rothbart*[9] and the Kypphauser mountain; the subjoined note, however, which he had appended to the tale, shows that it is an absolute fact, narrated with his usual fidelity.

"The story of Rip Van Winkle may seem incredible to many, but nevertheless I give it my full belief, for I know the vicinity of our old Dutch settlements to have been very subject to marvelous events and appearances. Indeed, I have heard many stranger stories than this, in the villages along the Hudson, all of which were too well authenticated to admit of a doubt. I have even talked with Rip Van Winkle myself,

9 **Frederick *der Rothbart*:** Frederick I (1152–1190), according to legend, lay asleep in a mountain cave and would reemerge only when Germany rose as the most powerful nation in the world.

who, when last I saw him, was a very venerable old man, and so perfectly rational and consistent on every other point that I think no conscientious person could refuse to take this into the bargain; nay, I have seen a certificate on the subject taken before a country justice, and signed with a cross, in the justice's own handwriting. The story, therefore, is beyond the possibility of doubt." —"D.K."

# Henry James

## (1843–1916)

Having moved permanently from New York City to England at the age of twenty-eight, Henry James became acquainted with many European writers, including Flaubert and Maupassant. His subject often concerns emotional entanglement, his writing style is highly symbolic, and his characters' situations are charged with ambiguity. His novels include *Portrait of a Lady*, *The Bostonians*, *The Wings of the Dove* (perhaps inspired by the early death of a doting young cousin), *The Ambassadors*, and *The Golden Bowl*. Over the course of his lifetime, James completed more than seventy short stories. In his essay "The Art of Fiction," James discusses his respect for someone he identifies only as "an English novelist"; he admires her for "the power to guess the seen from the unseen, to trace the implication of things, to judge the whole piece by the pattern, the condition of feeling life in general so completely that you are well on your way to knowing any particular corner of it—this cluster of gifts may almost be said to constitute experience, and they occur in country and in town, and in the most differing stages of education. . . . [I would say to a novice writer], 'Try to be one of the people on whom nothing is lost!'"

## *Daisy Miller: A Study* 1878

At the little town of Vevey, in Switzerland, there is a particularly comfortable hotel. There are, indeed, many hotels; for the entertainment of tourists is the business of the place, which, as many travellers will remember, is seated upon the edge of a remarkably blue lake—a lake that it behoves every tourist to visit. The shore of the lake presents an unbroken array of establishments of this order, of every category, from the "grand hotel" of the newest fashion, with a chalk-white front, a hundred balconies, and a dozen flags flying from its roof, to the little Swiss *pension* of an elder day, with its name inscribed in German-looking lettering upon a pink or yellow wall, and an awkward summer-house in the angle of the garden. One of the hotels at Vevey, however, is famous, even classical, being distinguished from many of its upstart neighbours by an air both of luxury and of maturity. In this region, in the month of June, American travellers are extremely numerous; it may be said, indeed, that Vevey assumes at this period some of the characteristics of an American watering-place. There are sights and sounds which evoke a vision, an echo, of Newport and Saratoga.[1] There is a flitting hither and thither of "stylish" young girls, a rustling of muslin flounces, a rattle of dance-music in the morning hours, a sound of high-pitched voices at all times. You receive an impression of these things at the excellent inn of the "Trois Couronnes," and are transported in fancy to the Ocean House or to Congress Hall.[2] But at the "Trois Couronnes," it must be added, there are other features that are much at variance with these suggestions: neat German waiters, who look like secretaries of legation; Russian princesses sitting in the garden; little Polish boys walking about, held by the hand, with their governors; a view of the snowy crest of the Dent du Midi[3] and the picturesque towers of the Castle of Chillon.

I hardly know whether it was the analogies or the differences that were uppermost in the mind of a young American, who, two or three years ago, sat in the garden of the "Trois Couronnes," looking about him, rather idly, at some of the graceful objects I have mentioned. It was a beautiful summer morning, and in whatever fashion the young American looked at things, they must have seemed to him charming. He had come from Geneva the day before, by the little steamer, to see his aunt, who was staying at the hotel—Geneva having been for a long time his place of residence. But his aunt had a headache—his aunt had almost always a headache—and now she was shut up in her room, smelling camphor, so that he was at liberty to wander about. He was some seven-and-twenty years of age; when his friends spoke of him, they usually said that he was at Geneva, "studying." When his enemies spoke of him they said—but, after all, he had no enemies; he was an extremely amiable fellow, and universally liked. What I should say is, simply, that when certain persons spoke of him they affirmed that the reason of his spending so much time at Geneva was that he was extremely devoted to a lady who lived there—a foreign lady—a person older than himself. Very few Americans—indeed I think none—had ever seen this lady, about whom there were some singular stories. But Winterbourne had an old attachment for the little metropolis of Calvinism; he had been put to school there as a boy, and he had afterwards gone to college there—circumstances which had led to his forming a great many youthful friendships. Many of these he had kept, and they were a source of great satisfaction to him.

After knocking at his aunt's door and learning that she was indisposed, he had taken a walk about the town, and then he had come in to his breakfast. He had now finished his breakfast; but he was drinking a small cup of coffee, which had been

---

1 **Newport and Saratoga:** Resort towns in Rhode Island and New York, respectively. Particularly popular with the upper class in the late nineteenth century.

2 **Ocean House . . . Congress Hall:** Newport and Saratoga hotels. Ocean House was built in Newport in 1840 and was one of the area's first large hotels. Congress Hall was built in Saratoga in Congress Park by Gideon Putnam in 1806.

3 **Dent du Midi:** Swiss mountain peak. Tourism became popular in this region in 1857 with the opening of the Grand Hotel de Dent du Midi.

served to him on a little table in the garden by one of the waiters who looked like an *attaché*. At last he finished his coffee and lit a cigarette. Presently a small boy came walking along the path—an urchin of nine or ten. The child, who was diminutive for his years, had an aged expression of countenance, a pale complexion, and sharp little features. He was dressed in knickerbockers, with red stockings, which displayed his poor little spindleshanks; he also wore a brilliant red cravat. He carried in his hand a long alpenstock, the sharp point of which he thrust into everything that he approached—the flower-beds, the garden-benches, the trains of the ladies' dresses. In front of Winterbourne he paused, looking at him with a pair of bright, penetrating little eyes.

"Will you give me a lump of sugar?" he asked, in a sharp, hard little voice—a voice immature, and yet, somehow, not young.

Winterbourne glanced at the small table near him, on which his coffee-service rested, and saw that several morsels of sugar remained. "Yes, you may take one," he answered; "but I don't think sugar is good for little boys."

This little boy stepped forward and carefully selected three of the coveted fragments, two of which he buried in the pocket of his knickerbockers, depositing the other as promptly in another place. He poked his alpenstock, lance-fashion, into Winterbourne's bench, and tried to crack the lump of sugar with his teeth.

"Oh, blazes; it's har-r-d!" he exclaimed, pronouncing the adjective in a peculiar manner.

Winterbourne had immediately perceived that he might have the honour of claiming him as a fellow-countryman. "Take care you don't hurt your teeth," he said, paternally.

"I haven't got any teeth to hurt. They have all come out. I have only got seven teeth. My mother counted them last night, and one came out right afterwards. She said she'd slap me if any more came out. I can't help it. It's this old Europe. It's the climate that makes them come out. In America they didn't come out. It's these hotels."

Winterbourne was much amused. "If you eat three lumps of sugar, your mother will certainly slap you," he said.

"She's got to give me some candy, then," rejoined his young interlocutor. "I can't get any candy here—any American candy. American candy's the best candy."

"And are American little boys the best little boys?" asked Winterbourne.

"I don't know. I'm an American boy," said the child.

"I see you are one of the best!" laughed Winterbourne.

"Are you an American man?" pursued this vivacious infant. And then, on Winterbourne's affirmative reply—"American men are the best," he declared.

His companion thanked him for the compliment; and the child, who had now got astride of his alpenstock, stood looking about him, while he attacked a second lump of sugar. Winterbourne wondered if he himself had been like this in his infancy, for he had been brought to Europe at about this age.

"Here comes my sister!" cried the child, in a moment. "She's an American girl."

Winterbourne looked along the path and saw a beautiful young lady advancing. "American girls are the best girls," he said, cheerfully, to his young companion.

"My sister ain't the best!" the child declared. "She's always blowing at me."

"I imagine that is your fault, not hers," said Winterbourne. The young lady meanwhile had drawn near. She was dressed in white muslin, with a hundred frills and flounces, and knots of pale-coloured ribbon. She was bare-headed; but she balanced in her hand a large parasol, with a deep border of embroidery; and she was strikingly, admirably pretty. "How pretty they are!" thought Winterbourne, straightening himself in his seat, as if he were prepared to rise.

The young lady paused in front of his bench, near the parapet of the garden, which overlooked the lake. The little boy had now converted his alpenstock into a vaulting-pole, by the aid of which he was springing about in the gravel, and kicking it up not a little.

"Randolph," said the young lady, "what *are* you doing?"

"I'm going up the Alps," replied Randolph. "This is the way!" And he gave another little jump, scattering the pebbles about Winterbourne's ears.

"That's the way they come down," said Winterbourne.

"He's an American man!" cried Randolph, in his little hard voice.

The young lady gave no heed to this announcement, but looked straight at her brother. "Well, I guess you had better be quiet," she simply observed.

It seemed to Winterbourne that he had been in a manner presented. He got up and stepped slowly towards the young girl, throwing away his cigarette. "This little boy and I have made acquaintance," he said, with great civility. In Geneva, as he had been perfectly aware, a young man was not at liberty to speak to a young unmarried lady except under certain rarely-occurring conditions; but here at Vevey, what conditions could be better than these?—a pretty American girl coming and standing in front of you in a garden. This pretty American girl, however, on hearing Winterbourne's observation, simply glanced at him; she then turned her head and looked over the parapet, at the lake and the opposite mountains. He wondered whether he had gone too far; but he decided that he must advance farther, rather than retreat. While he was thinking of something else to say, the young lady turned to the little boy again. "I should like to know where you got that pole," she said.

"I bought it!" responded Randolph.

"You don't mean to say you're going to take it to Italy?"

"Yes, I am going to take it to Italy!" the child declared.

The young girl glanced over the front of her dress, and smoothed out a knot or two of ribbon. Then she rested her eyes upon the prospect again. "Well, I guess you had better leave it somewhere," she said, after a moment.

"Are you going to Italy?" Winterbourne inquired, in a tone of great respect.

The young lady glanced at him again. "Yes, sir," she replied. And she said nothing more.

"Are you—a—going over the Simplon?"[4] Winterbourne pursued, a little embarrassed.

---

4 **Simplon:** The Simplon Pass connects Valais, Switzerland, to northern Italy via a route through the Alps.

"I don't know," she said. "I suppose it's some mountain. Randolph, what mountain are we going over?"

"Going where?" the child demanded.

"To Italy," Winterbourne explained.

"I don't know," said Randolph. "I don't want to go to Italy. I want to go to America."

"Oh, Italy is a beautiful place!" rejoined the young man.

"Can you get candy there?" Randolph loudly inquired.

"I hope not," said his sister. "I guess you have had enough candy, and mother thinks so too."

"I haven't had any for ever so long—for a hundred weeks!" cried the boy, still jumping about.

The young lady inspected her flounces and smoothed her ribbons again; and Winterbourne presently risked an observation upon the beauty of the view. He was ceasing to be embarrassed, for he had begun to perceive that she was not in the least embarrassed herself. There had not been the slightest alteration in her charming complexion; she was evidently neither offended nor fluttered. If she looked another way when he spoke to her, and seemed not particularly to hear him, this was simply her habit, her manner. Yet, as he talked a little more and pointed out some of the objects of interest in the view, with which she appeared quite unacquainted, she gradually gave him more of the benefit of her glance; and then he saw that this glance was perfectly direct and unshrinking. It was not, however, what would have been called an immodest glance, for the young girl's eyes were singularly honest and fresh. They were wonderfully pretty eyes; and, indeed, Winterbourne had not seen for a long time anything prettier than his fair countrywoman's various features—her complexion, her nose, her ears, her teeth. He had a great relish for feminine beauty; he was addicted to observing and analyzing it; and as regards this young lady's face he made several observations. It was not at all insipid, but it was not exactly expressive; and though it was eminently delicate, Winterbourne mentally accused it—very forgivingly—of a want of finish. He thought it very possible that Master Randolph's sister was a coquette; he was sure she had a spirit of her own; but in her bright, sweet, superficial little visage there was no mockery, no irony. Before long it became obvious that she was much disposed towards conversation. She told him that they were going to Rome for the winter—she and her mother and Randolph. She asked him if he was a "real American;" she wouldn't have taken him for one; he seemed more like a German—this was said after a little hesitation—especially when he spoke. Winterbourne, laughing, answered that he had met Germans who spoke like Americans, but that he had not, so far as he remembered, met an American who spoke like a German. Then he asked her if she would not be more comfortable in sitting upon the bench which he had just quitted. She answered that she liked standing up and walking about; but she presently sat down. She told him she was from New York State—"if you know where that is." Winterbourne learned more about her by catching hold of her small, slippery brother and making him stand a few minutes by his side.

"Tell me your name, my boy," he said.

"Randolph C. Miller," said the boy, sharply. "And I'll tell you her name;" and he levelled his alpenstock at his sister.

"You had better wait till you are asked!" said this young lady, calmly.

"I should like very much to know your name," said Winterbourne.

"Her name is Daisy Miller!" cried the child. "But that isn't her real name; that isn't her name on her cards."

"It's a pity you haven't got one of my cards!" said Miss Miller.

"Her real name is Annie P. Miller," the boy went on.

"Ask him *his* name," said his sister, indicating Winterbourne.

But on this point Randolph seemed perfectly indifferent; he continued to supply information with regard to his own family. "My father's name is Ezra B. Miller," he announced. "My father ain't in Europe; my father's in a better place than Europe."

Winterbourne imagined for a moment that this was the manner in which the child had been taught to intimate that Mr. Miller had been removed to the sphere of celestial rewards. But Randolph immediately added, "My father's in Schenectady. He's got a big business. My father's rich, you bet."

"Well!" ejaculated Miss Miller, lowering her parasol and looking at the embroidered border. Winterbourne presently released the child, who departed, dragging his alpenstock along the path. "He doesn't like Europe," said the young girl. "He wants to go back."

"To Schenectady, you mean?"

"Yes; he wants to go right home. He hasn't got any boys here. There is one boy here, but he always goes round with a teacher; they won't let him play."

"And your brother hasn't any teacher?" Winterbourne inquired.

"Mother thought of getting him one, to travel round with us. There was a lady told her of a very good teacher; an American lady—perhaps you know her—Mrs. Sanders. I think she came from Boston. She told her of this teacher, and we thought of getting him to travel round with us. But Randolph said he didn't want a teacher travelling round with us. He said he wouldn't have lessons when he was in the cars. And we *are* in the cars about half the time. There was an English lady we met in the cars—I think her name was Miss Featherstone; perhaps you know her. She wanted to know why I didn't give Randolph lessons—give him 'instruction,' she called it. I guess he could give me more instruction than I could give him. He's very smart."

"Yes," said Winterbourne; "he seems very smart."

"Mother's going to get a teacher for him as soon as we get to Italy. Can you get good teachers in Italy?"

"Very good, I should think," said Winterbourne.

"Or else she's going to find some school. He ought to learn some more. He's only nine. He's going to college." And in this way Miss Miller continued to converse upon the affairs of her family, and upon other topics. She sat there with her extremely pretty hands, ornamented with very brilliant rings, folded in her lap, and with her pretty eyes now resting upon those of Winterbourne, now wandering over the garden, the people who passed by, and the beautiful view. She talked to Winterbourne as if she had known him a long time. He found it very pleasant. It was many years since he had heard a young girl talk so much. It might have been said of this unknown young lady, who had come and sat down beside him upon a bench, that she chattered. She was very quiet, she sat in a charming tranquil attitude; but her lips and her eyes were constantly moving. She had a soft, slender, agreeable voice, and her tone was decidedly sociable. She gave Winterbourne a history of her movements and intentions, and those of her mother and brother, in Europe, and enumerated, in particular, the various hotels at which they had stopped. "That English lady in the cars," she said— "Miss Featherstone—asked me if we didn't all live in hotels in America. I told her I had never been in so many hotels in my life as since I came to Europe. I have never seen so many—it's nothing but hotels." But Miss Miller did not make this remark with a querulous accent; she appeared to be in the best humour with everything. She declared that the hotels were very good, when once you got used to their ways, and that Europe was perfectly sweet. She was not disappointed—not a bit. Perhaps it was because she had heard so much about it before. She had ever so many intimate friends that had been there ever so many times. And then she had had ever so many dresses and things from Paris. Whenever she put on a Paris dress she felt as if she were in Europe.

"It was a kind of a wishing-cap," said Winterbourne.

"Yes," said Miss Miller, without examining this analogy; "it always made me wish I was here. But I needn't have done that for dresses. I am sure they send all the pretty ones to America; you see the most frightful things here. The only thing I don't like," she proceeded, "is the society. There isn't any society; or, if there is, I don't know where it keeps itself. Do you? I suppose there is some society somewhere, but I haven't seen anything of it. I'm very fond of society, and I have always had a great deal of it. I don't mean only in Schenectady, but in New York. I used to go to New York every winter. In New York I had lots of society. Last winter I had seventeen dinners given me; and three of them were by gentlemen," added Daisy Miller. "I have more friends in New York than in Schenectady—more gentlemen friends; and more young lady friends too," she resumed in a moment. She paused again for an instant; she was looking at Winterbourne with all her prettiness in her lively eyes and in her light, slightly monotonous smile. "I have always had," she said, "a great deal of gentlemen's society."

Poor Winterbourne was amused, perplexed, and decidedly charmed. He had never yet heard a young girl express herself in just this fashion; never, at least, save in cases where to say such things seemed a kind of demonstrative evidence of a certain laxity of deportment. And yet was he to accuse Miss Daisy Miller of actual or potential *inconduite*,[5] as they said at Geneva? He felt that he had lived at Geneva so long that he had lost a good deal; he had become dishabituated to the American tone. Never, indeed, since he had grown old enough to appreciate things, had he encountered a young American girl of so pronounced a type as this. Certainly she was very charming; but how deucedly sociable! Was she simply a pretty girl from New York State— were they all like that, the pretty girls who had a good deal of gentlemen's society? Or was she also a designing, an audacious, an unscrupulous young person? Winter-

---

5 *inconduite*: French. Misconduct.

bourne had lost his instinct in this matter, and his reason could not help him. Miss Daisy Miller looked extremely innocent. Some people had told him that, after all, American girls were exceedingly innocent; and others had told him that, after all, they were not. He was inclined to think Miss Daisy Miller was a flirt—a pretty American flirt. He had never, as yet, had any relations with young ladies of this category. He had known, here in Europe, two or three women—persons older than Miss Daisy Miller, and provided, for respectability's sake, with husbands—who were great coquettes—dangerous, terrible women, with whom one's relations were liable to take a serious turn. But this young girl was not a coquette in that sense; she was very unsophisticated; she was only a pretty American flirt. Winterbourne was almost grateful for having found the formula that applied to Miss Daisy Miller. He leaned back in his seat; he remarked to himself that she had the most charming nose he had ever seen; he wondered what were the regular conditions and limitations of one's intercourse with a pretty American flirt. It presently became apparent that he was on the way to learn.

"Have you been to that old castle?" asked the young girl, pointing with her parasol to the far-gleaming walls of the Château de Chillon.

"Yes, formerly, more than once," said Winterbourne. "You too, I suppose, have seen it?"

"No; we haven't been there. I want to go there dreadfully. Of course I mean to go there. I wouldn't go away from here without having seen that old castle."

"It's a very pretty excursion," said Winterbourne, "and very easy to make. You can drive, you know, or you can go by the little steamer."

"You can go in the cars," said Miss Miller.

"Yes; you can go in the cars," Winterbourne assented.

"Our courier says they take you right up to the castle," the young girl continued. "We were going last week; but my mother gave out. She suffers dreadfully from dyspepsia. She said she couldn't go. Randolph wouldn't go either; he says he doesn't think much of old castles. But I guess we'll go this week, if we can get Randolph."

"Your brother is not interested in ancient monuments?" Winterbourne inquired, smiling.

"He says he don't care much about old castles. He's only nine. He wants to stay at the hotel. Mother's afraid to leave him alone, and the courier won't stay with him; so we haven't been to many places. But it will be too bad if we don't go up there." And Miss Miller pointed again at the Château de Chillon.

"I should think it might be arranged," said Winterbourne. "Couldn't you get some one to stay—for the afternoon—with Randolph?"

Miss Miller looked at him a moment; and then, very placidly—"I wish *you* would stay with him!" she said.

Winterbourne hesitated a moment. "I would much rather go to Chillon with you."

"With me?" asked the young girl, with the same placidity.

She didn't rise, blushing, as a young girl at Geneva would have done; and yet Winterbourne, conscious that he had been very bold, thought it possible she was offended. "With your mother," he answered very respectfully.

But it seemed that both his audacity and his respect were lost upon Miss Daisy Miller. "I guess my mother won't go, after all," she said. "She don't like to ride round in the afternoon. But did you really mean what you said just now; that you would like to go up there?"

"Most earnestly," Winterbourne declared.

"Then we may arrange it. If mother will stay with Randolph, I guess Eugenio will."

"Eugenio?" the young man inquired.

"Eugenio's our courier. He doesn't like to stay with Randolph; he's the most fastidious man I ever saw. But he's a splendid courier. I guess he'll stay at home with Randolph if mother does, and then we can go to the castle."

Winterbourne reflected for an instant as lucidly as possible—"we" could only mean Miss Daisy Miller and himself. This programme seemed almost too agreeable for credence; he felt as if he ought to kiss the young lady's hand. Possibly he would have done so—and quite spoiled the project; but at this moment another person—presumably Eugenio—appeared. A tall, handsome man, with superb whiskers, wearing a velvet morning-coat and a brilliant watch-chain, approached Miss Miller, looking sharply at her companion. "Oh, Eugenio!" said Miss Miller, with the friendliest accent.

Eugenio had looked at Winterbourne from head to foot; he now bowed gravely to the young lady. "I have the honour to inform mademoiselle that luncheon is upon the table."

Miss Miller slowly rose. "See here, Eugenio," she said. "I'm going to that old castle, any way."

"To the Château de Chillon, mademoiselle?" the courier inquired. "Mademoiselle has made arrangements?" he added, in a tone which struck Winterbourne as very impertinent.

Eugenio's tone apparently threw, even to Miss Miller's own apprehension, a slightly ironical light upon the young girl's situation. She turned to Winterbourne, blushing a little—a very little. "You won't back out?" she said.

"I shall not be happy till we go!" he protested.

"And you are staying in this hotel?" she went on. "And you are really an American?"

The courier stood looking at Winterbourne, offensively. The young man, at least, thought his manner of looking an offence to Miss Miller; it conveyed an imputation that she "picked up" acquaintances. "I shall have the honour of presenting to you a person who will tell you all about me," he said smiling, and referring to his aunt.

"Oh, well, we'll go some day," said Miss Miller. And she gave him a smile and turned away. She put up her parasol and walked back to the inn beside Eugenio. Winterbourne stood looking after her; and as she moved away, drawing her muslin furbelows over the gravel, said to himself that she had the *tournure*[6] of a princess.

6 ***tournure***: French. Look, appearance.

## II

He had, however, engaged to do more than proved feasible, in promising to present his aunt, Mrs. Costello, to Miss Daisy Miller. As soon as the former lady had got better of her headache he waited upon her in her apartment; and, after the proper inquiries in regard to her health, he asked her if she had observed, in the hotel, an American family—a mamma, a daughter, and a little boy.

"And a courier?" said Mrs. Costello. "Oh, yes, I have observed them. Seen them—heard them—and kept out of their way." Mrs. Costello was a widow with a fortune; a person of much distinction, who frequently intimated that, if she were not so dreadfully liable to sick-headaches, she would probably have left a deeper impress upon her time. She had a long pale face, a high nose, and a great deal of very striking white hair, which she wore in large puffs and *rouleaux*[7] over the top of her head. She had two sons married in New York, and another who was now in Europe. This young man was amusing himself at Homburg,[8] and, though he was on his travels, was rarely perceived to visit any particular city at the moment selected by his mother for her own appearance there. Her nephew, who had come up to Vevey expressly to see her, was therefore more attentive than those who, as she said, were nearer to her. He had imbibed at Geneva the idea that one must always be attentive to one's aunt. Mrs. Costello had not seen him for many years, and she was greatly pleased with him, manifesting her approbation by initiating him into many of the secrets of that social sway which, as she gave him to understand, she exerted in the American capital. She admitted that she was very exclusive; but, if he were acquainted with New York, he would see that one had to be. And her picture of the minutely hierarchical constitution of the society of that city, which she presented to him in many different lights, was, to Winterbourne's imagination, almost oppressively striking.

He immediately perceived, from her tone, that Miss Daisy Miller's place in the social scale was low. "I am afraid you don't approve of them," he said.

"They are very common," Mrs. Costello declared. "They are the sort of Americans that one does one's duty by not—not accepting."

"Ah, you don't accept them?" said the young man.

"I can't, my dear Frederick. I would if I could, but I can't."

"The young girl is very pretty," said Winterbourne, in a moment.

"Of course she's pretty. But she is very common."

"I see what you mean, of course," said Winterbourne, after another pause.

"She has that charming look that they all have," his aunt resumed. "I can't think where they pick it up; and she dresses in perfection—no, you don't know how well she dresses. I can't think where they get their taste."

"But, my dear aunt, she is not, after all, a Comanche savage."

---

7 *rouleaux:* French. Rolls.
8 **Homburg:** German resort town famous for curative spas and waters.

"She is a young lady," said Mrs. Costello, "who has an intimacy with her mamma's courier?"

"An intimacy with the courier?" the young man demanded.

"Oh, the mother is just as bad! They treat the courier like a familiar friend—like a gentleman. I shouldn't wonder if he dines with them. Very likely they have never seen a man with such good manners, such fine clothes, so like a gentleman. He probably corresponds to the young lady's idea of a Count. He sits with them in the garden, in the evening. I think he smokes."

Winterbourne listened with interest to these disclosures; they helped him to make up his mind about Miss Daisy. Evidently she was rather wild. "Well," he said, "I am not a courier, and yet she was very charming to me."

"You had better have said at first," said Mrs. Costello with dignity, "that you had made her acquaintance."

"We simply met in the garden, and we talked a bit."

"*Tout bonnement!*⁹ And pray what did you say?"

"I said I should take the liberty of introducing her to my admirable aunt."

"I am much obliged to you."

"It was to guarantee my respectability," said Winterbourne.

"And pray who is to guarantee hers?"

"Ah, you are cruel!" said the young man. "She's a very nice girl."

"You don't say that as if you believed it," Mrs. Costello observed.

"She is completely uncultivated," Winterbourne went on. "But she is wonderfully pretty, and, in short, she is very nice. To prove that I believe it, I am going to take her to the Château de Chillon."

"You two are going off there together? I should say it proved just the contrary. How long had you known her, may I ask, when this interesting project was formed? You haven't been twenty-four hours in the house."

"I had known her half-an-hour!" said Winterbourne, smiling.

"Dear me!" cried Mrs. Costello. "What a dreadful girl!"

Her nephew was silent for some moments. "You really think, then," he began, earnestly, and with a desire for trustworthy information—"you really think that——" But he paused again.

"Think what, sir?" said his aunt.

"That she is the sort of young lady who expects a man—sooner or later—to carry her off?"

"I haven't the least idea what such young ladies expect a man to do. But I really think that you had better not meddle with little American girls that are uncultivated, as you call them. You have lived too long out of the country. You will be sure to make some great mistake. You are too innocent."

"My dear aunt, I am not so innocent," said Winterbourne, smiling and curling his moustache.

---

9 *Tout bonnement!*: French. Quite simply!

"You are too guilty, then!"

Winterbourne continued to curl his moustache, meditatively. "You won't let the poor girl know you then?" he asked at last.

"Is it literally true that she is going to the Château de Chillon with you?"

"I think that she fully intends it."

"Then, my dear Frederick," said Mrs. Costello, "I must decline the honour of her acquaintance. I am an old woman, but I am not too old—thank Heaven—to be shocked!"

"But don't they all do these things—the young girls in America?" Winterbourne inquired.

Mrs. Costello stared a moment. "I should like to see my granddaughters do them!" she declared, grimly.

This seemed to throw some light upon the matter, for Winterbourne remembered to have heard that his pretty cousins in New York were "tremendous flirts." If, therefore, Miss Daisy Miller exceeded the liberal license allowed to these young ladies, it was probable that anything might be expected of her. Winterbourne was impatient to see her again, and he was vexed with himself that, by instinct, he should not appreciate her justly.

Though he was impatient to see her, he hardly knew what he should say to her about his aunt's refusal to become acquainted with her; but he discovered, promptly enough, that with Miss Daisy Miller there was no great need of walking on tiptoe. He found her that evening in the garden, wandering about in the warm starlight, like an indolent sylph, and swinging to and fro the largest fan he had ever beheld. It was ten o'clock. He had dined with his aunt, had been sitting with her since dinner, and had just taken leave of her till the morrow. Miss Daisy Miller seemed very glad to see him; she declared it was the longest evening she had ever passed.

"Have you been all alone?" he asked.

"I have been walking round with mother. But mother gets tired walking round," she answered.

"Has she gone to bed?"

"No; she doesn't like to go to bed," said the young girl. "She doesn't sleep—not three hours. She says she doesn't know how she lives. She's dreadfully nervous. I guess she sleeps more than she thinks. She's gone somewhere after Randolph; she wants to try to get him to go to bed. He doesn't like to go to bed."

"Let us hope she will persuade him," observed Winterbourne.

"She will talk to him all she can; but he doesn't like her to talk to him," said Miss Daisy, opening her fan. "She's going to try to get Eugenio to talk to him. But he isn't afraid of Eugenio. Eugenio's a splendid courier, but he can't make much impression on Randolph! I don't believe he'll go to bed before eleven." It appeared that Randolph's vigil was in fact triumphantly prolonged, for Winterbourne strolled about with the young girl for some time without meeting her mother. "I have been looking round for that lady you want to introduce me to," his companion resumed. "She's your aunt." Then, on Winterbourne's admitting the fact, and expressing some curiosity as to how she had learned it, she said she had heard all about Mrs. Costello from the chambermaid. She was very quiet and very *comme il faut;*[10] she wore white puffs; she spoke to no one, and she never dined at the *table d'hôte.*[11] Every two days she had a headache. "I think that's a lovely description, headache and all!" said Miss Daisy, chattering along in her thin, gay voice. "I want to know her ever so much. I know just what *your* aunt would be; I know I should like her. She would be very exclusive. I like a lady to be exclusive; I'm dying to be exclusive myself. Well, we *are* exclusive, mother and I. We don't speak to every one—or they don't speak to us. I suppose it's about the same thing. Any way, I shall be ever so glad to know your aunt."

Winterbourne was embarrassed. "She would be most happy," he said; "but I am afraid those headaches will interfere."

The young girl looked at him through the dusk. "But I suppose she doesn't have a headache every day," she said, sympathetically.

Winterbourne was silent a moment. "She tells me she does," he answered at last—not knowing what to say.

Miss Daisy Miller stopped and stood looking at him. Her prettiness was still visible in the darkness; she was opening and closing her enormous fan. "She doesn't want to know me!" she said, suddenly. "Why don't you say so? You needn't be afraid. I'm not afraid!" And she gave a little laugh.

Winterbourne fancied there was a tremor in her voice; he was touched, shocked, mortified by it. "My dear young lady," he protested, "she knows no one. It's her wretched health."

The young girl walked on a few steps, laughing still. "You needn't be afraid," she repeated. "Why should she want to know me?" Then she paused again; she was close to the parapet of the garden, and in front of her was the starlit lake. There was a vague sheen upon its surface, and in the distance were dimly-seen mountain forms. Daisy Miller looked out upon the mysterious prospect, and then she gave another little laugh. "Gracious! she *is* exclusive!" she said. Winterbourne wondered whether she was seriously wounded, and for a moment almost wished that her sense of injury might be such as to make it becoming in him to attempt to reassure and comfort her. He had a pleasant sense that she would be very approachable for consolatory purposes. He felt then, for the instant, quite ready to sacrifice his aunt, conversationally; to admit that she was a proud, rude woman, and to declare that they needn't mind her. But before he had time to commit himself to this perilous mixture of gallantry and impiety, the young lady, resuming her walk, gave an exclamation in quite another tone. "Well; here's mother! I guess she hasn't got Randolph to go to bed." The figure of a lady appeared, at a distance, very indistinct in the darkness, and advancing with a slow and wavering movement. Suddenly it seemed to pause.

"Are you sure it is your mother? Can you distinguish her in this thick dusk?" Winterbourne asked.

10  ***comme il faut:*** French. Proper, well mannered.
11  ***table d'hôte:*** French. A common table for guests.

"Well!" cried Miss Daisy Miller, with a laugh, "I guess I know my own mother. And when she has got on my shawl, too! She is always wearing my things."

The lady in question, ceasing to advance, hovered vaguely about the spot at which she had checked her steps.

"I am afraid your mother doesn't see you," said Winterbourne. "Or perhaps," he added—thinking, with Miss Miller, the joke permissible—"perhaps she feels guilty about your shawl."

"Oh, it's a fearful old thing!" the young girl replied, serenely. "I told her she could wear it. She won't come here, because she sees you."

"Ah, then," said Winterbourne, "I had better leave you."

"Oh no; come on!" urged Miss Daisy Miller.

"I'm afraid your mother doesn't approve of my walking with you."

Miss Miller gave him a serious glance. "It isn't for me; it's for you—that is, it's for *her*. Well; I don't know who it's for! But mother doesn't like any of my gentlemen friends. She's right down timid. She always makes a fuss if I introduce a gentleman. But I *do* introduce them—almost always. If I didn't introduce my gentlemen friends to mother," the young girl added, in her little soft, flat monotone, "I shouldn't think I was natural."

"To introduce me," said Winterbourne, "you must know my name." And he proceeded to pronounce it.

"Oh, dear; I can't say all that!" said his companion, with a laugh. But by this time they had come up to Mrs. Miller, who, as they drew near, walked to the parapet of the garden and leaned upon it, looking intently at the lake and turning her back upon them. "Mother!" said the young girl, in a tone of decision. Upon this the elder lady turned round. "Mr. Winterbourne," said Miss Daisy Miller, introducing the young man very frankly and prettily. "Common," she was, as Mrs. Costello had pronounced her; yet it was a wonder to Winterbourne that, with her commonness, she had a singularly delicate grace.

Her mother was a small, spare, light person, with a wandering eye, a very exiguous nose, and a large forehead, decorated with a certain amount of thin, much-frizzled hair. Like her daughter, Mrs. Miller was dressed with extreme elegance; she had enormous diamonds in her ears. So far as Winterbourne could observe, she gave him no greeting—she certainly was not looking at him. Daisy was near her, pulling her shawl straight. "What are you doing, poking round here?" this young lady inquired; but by no means with that harshness of accent which her choice of words may imply.

"I don't know," said her mother, turning towards the lake again.

"I shouldn't think you'd want that shawl!" Daisy exclaimed.

"Well—I do!" her mother answered, with a little laugh.

"Did you get Randolph to go to bed?" asked the young girl.

"No; I couldn't induce him," said Mrs. Miller, very gently. "He wants to talk to the waiter. He likes to talk to that waiter."

"I was telling Mr. Winterbourne," the young girl went on; and to the young man's ear her tone might have indicated that she had been uttering his name all her life.

"Oh, yes!" said Winterbourne; "I have the pleasure of knowing your son."

Randolph's mamma was silent; she turned her attention to the lake. But at last she spoke. "Well, I don't see how he lives!"

"Anyhow, it isn't so bad as it was at Dover," said Daisy Miller.

"And what occurred at Dover?" Winterbourne asked.

"He wouldn't go to bed at all. I guess he sat up all night—in the public parlour. He wasn't in bed at twelve o'clock: I know that."

"It was half-past twelve," declared Mrs. Miller, with mild emphasis.

"Does he sleep much during the day?" Winterbourne demanded.

"I guess he doesn't sleep much," Daisy rejoined.

"I wish he would!" said her mother. "It seems as if he couldn't."

"I think he's real tiresome," Daisy pursued.

Then, for some moments, there was silence. "Well, Daisy Miller," said the elder lady, presently, "I shouldn't think you'd want to talk against your own brother!"

"Well, he is tiresome, mother," said Daisy, quite without the asperity of a retort.

"He's only nine," urged Mrs. Miller.

"Well, he wouldn't go to that castle," said the young girl. "I'm going there with Mr. Winterbourne."

To this announcement, very placidly made, Daisy's mamma offered no response. Winterbourne took for granted that she deeply disapproved of the projected excursion; but he said to himself that she was a simple, easily-managed person, and that a few deferential protestations would take the edge from her displeasure. "Yes," he began; "your daughter has kindly allowed me the honour of being her guide."

Mrs. Miller's wandering eyes attached themselves, with a sort of appealing air, to Daisy, who, however, strolled a few steps farther, gently humming to herself. "I presume you will go in the cars," said her mother.

"Yes; or in the boat," said Winterbourne.

"Well, of course, I don't know," Mrs. Miller rejoined. "I have never been to that castle."

"It is a pity you shouldn't go," said Winterbourne, beginning to feel reassured as to her opposition. And yet he was quite prepared to find that, as a matter of course, she meant to accompany her daughter.

"We've been thinking ever so much about going," she pursued; "but it seems as if we couldn't. Of course Daisy—she wants to go round. But there's a lady here—I don't know her name—she says she shouldn't think we'd want to go to see castles here; she should think we'd want to wait till we got to Italy. It seems as if there would be so many there," continued Mrs. Miller, with an air of increasing confidence. "Of course, we only want to see the principal ones. We visited several in England," she presently added.

"Ah, yes! in England there are beautiful castles," said Winterbourne. "But Chillon, here, is very well worth seeing."

"Well, if Daisy feels up to it——," said Mrs. Miller, in a tone impregnated with a sense of the magnitude of the enterprise. "It seems as if there was nothing she wouldn't undertake."

"Oh, I think she'll enjoy it!" Winterbourne declared. And he desired more and more to make it a certainty that he was to have the privilege of a *tête-à-tête* with the young lady, who was still strolling along in front of them, softly vocalising. "You are not disposed, madam," he inquired, "to undertake it yourself?"

Daisy's mother looked at him, an instant, askance, and then walked forward in silence. Then—"I guess she had better go alone," she said, simply.

Winterbourne observed to himself that this was a very different type of maternity from that of the vigilant matrons who massed themselves in the forefront of social intercourse in the dark old city at the other end of the lake. But his meditations were interrupted by hearing his name very distinctly pronounced by Mrs. Miller's unprotected daughter.

"Mr. Winterbourne!" murmured Daisy.

"Mademoiselle!" said the young man.

"Don't you want to take me out in a boat?"

"At present?" he asked.

"Of course!" said Daisy.

"Well, Annie Miller!" exclaimed her mother.

"I beg you, madam, to let her go," said Winterbourne, ardently; for he had never yet enjoyed the sensation of guiding through the summer starlight a skiff freighted with a fresh and beautiful young girl.

"I shouldn't think she'd want to," said her mother. "I should think she'd rather go indoors."

"I'm sure Mr. Winterbourne wants to take me," Daisy declared. "He's so awfully devoted!"

"I will row you over to Chillon, in the starlight."

"I don't believe it!" said Daisy.

"Well!" ejaculated the elder lady again.

"You haven't spoken to me for half-an-hour," her daughter went on.

"I have been having some very pleasant conversation with your mother," said Winterbourne.

"Well; I want you to take me out in a boat!" Daisy repeated. They had all stopped, and she had turned round and was looking at Winterbourne. Her face wore a charming smile, her pretty eyes were gleaming, she was swinging her great fan about. No; it's impossible to be prettier than that, thought Winterbourne.

"There are half-a-dozen boats moored at that landing-place," he said, pointing to certain steps which descended from the garden to the lake. "If you will do me the honour to accept my arm, we will go and select one of them."

Daisy stood there smiling; she threw back her head and gave a little light laugh. "I like a gentleman to be formal!" she declared.

"I assure you it's a formal offer."

"I was bound I would make you say something," Daisy went on.

"You see it's not very difficult," said Winterbourne. "But I am afraid you are chaffing me."

"I think not, sir," remarked Mrs. Miller, very gently.

"Do, then, let me give you a row," he said to the young girl.

"It's quite lovely, the way you say that!" cried Daisy.

"It will be still more lovely to do it."

"Yes, it would be lovely!" said Daisy. But she made no movement to accompany him; she only stood there laughing.

"I should think you had better find out what time it is," interposed her mother.

"It is eleven o'clock, madam," said a voice, with a foreign accent, out of the neighbouring darkness; and Winterbourne, turning, perceived the florid personage who was in attendance upon the two ladies. He had apparently just approached.

"Oh, Eugenio," said Daisy, "I am going out in a boat!"

Eugenio bowed. "At eleven o'clock, mademoiselle?"

"I am going with Mr. Winterbourne. This very minute."

"Do tell her she can't," said Mrs. Miller to the courier.

"I think you had better not go out in a boat, mademoiselle," Eugenio declared.

Winterbourne wished to Heaven this pretty girl were not so familiar with her courier; but he said nothing.

"I suppose you don't think it's proper!" Daisy exclaimed. "Eugenio doesn't think anything's proper."

"I am at your service," said Winterbourne.

"Does mademoiselle propose to go alone?" asked Eugenio of Mrs. Miller.

"Oh, no; with this gentleman!" answered Daisy's mamma.

The courier looked for a moment at Winterbourne—the latter thought he was smiling—and then, solemnly, with a bow, "As mademoiselle pleases!" he said.

"Oh, I hoped you would make a fuss!" said Daisy. "I don't care to go now."

"I myself shall make a fuss if you don't go," said Winterbourne.

"That's all I want—a little fuss!" And the young girl began to laugh again.

"Mr. Randolph has gone to bed!" the courier announced, frigidly.

"Oh, Daisy; now we can go!" said Mrs. Miller.

Daisy turned away from Winterbourne, looking at him, smiling and fanning herself. "Good night," she said; "I hope you are disappointed, or disgusted, or something!"

He looked at her, taking the hand she offered him. "I am puzzled," he answered.

"Well; I hope it won't keep you awake!" she said, very smartly; and, under the escort of the privileged Eugenio, the two ladies passed towards the house.

Winterbourne stood looking after them; he was indeed puzzled. He lingered beside the lake for a quarter of an hour, turning over the mystery of the young girl's sudden familiarities and caprices. But the only very definite conclusion he came to was that he should enjoy deucedly "going off" with her somewhere.

Two days afterwards he went off with her to the Castle of Chillon. He waited for her in the large hall of the hotel, where the couriers, the servants, the foreign tourists were lounging about and staring. It was not the place he would have chosen, but she had appointed it. She came tripping downstairs, buttoning her long gloves, squeezing her folded parasol against her pretty figure, dressed in the perfection of a soberly elegant travelling-costume. Winterbourne was a man of imagination and, as our ancestors used to say, of sensibility; as he looked at her dress and, on the great staircase, her little rapid, confiding step, he felt as if there were something romantic going forward. He could have believed he was going to elope with her. He passed out with her among all the idle people that were assembled there; they were all looking at her very hard; she had begun to chatter as soon as she joined him. Winterbourne's preference had been that they should be conveyed to Chillon in a carriage; but she expressed a lively wish to go in the little steamer; she declared that she had a passion for steamboats. There was always such a lovely breeze upon the water, and you saw such lots of people. The sail was not long, but Winterbourne's companion found time to say a great many things. To the young man himself their little excursion was so much of an escapade—an adventure—that, even allowing for her habitual sense of freedom, he had some expectation of seeing her regard it in the same way. But it must be confessed that, in this particular, he was disappointed. Daisy Miller was extremely animated, she was in charming spirits; but she was apparently not at all excited; she was not fluttered; she avoided neither his eyes nor those of any one else; she blushed neither when she looked at him nor when she saw that people were looking at her. People continued to look at her a great deal, and Winterbourne took much satisfaction in his pretty companion's distinguished air. He had been a little afraid that she would talk loud, laugh overmuch, and even, perhaps, desire to move about the boat a good deal. But he quite forgot his fears; he sat smiling, with his eyes upon her face, while, without moving from her place, she delivered herself of a great number of original reflections. It was the most charming garrulity he had ever heard. He had assented to the idea that she was "common;" but was she so, after all, or was he simply getting used to her commonness? Her conversation was chiefly of what metaphysicians term the objective cast; but every now and then it took a subjective turn.

"What on *earth* are you so grave about?" she suddenly demanded, fixing her agreeable eyes upon Winterbourne's.

"Am I grave?" he asked. "I had an idea I was grinning from ear to ear."

"You look as if you were taking me to a funeral. If that's a grin, your ears are very near together."

"Should you like me to dance a hornpipe on the deck?"

"Pray do, and I'll carry round your hat. It will pay the expenses of our journey."

"I never was better pleased in my life," murmured Winterbourne.

She looked at him a moment, and then burst into a little laugh. "I like to make you say those things! You're a queer mixture!"

In the castle, after they had landed, the subjective element decidedly prevailed. Daisy tripped about the vaulted chambers, rustled her skirts in the corkscrew staircases, flirted back with a pretty little cry and a shudder from the edge of the *oubliettes*,[12] and turned a singularly well-shaped ear to everything that Winterbourne told her about the place. But he saw that she cared very little for feudal antiquities, and that the dusky traditions of Chillon made but a slight impression upon her. They had the good fortune to have been able to walk about without other companionship than

---

12  **oubliettes:** French. From *oublier*, "to forget." Dungeons with a trapdoor in the ceiling as the only means of entrance or exit.

that of the custodian; and Winterbourne arranged with this functionary that they should not be hurried—that they should linger and pause wherever they chose. The custodian interpreted the bargain generously—Winterbourne, on his side, had been generous—and ended by leaving them quite to themselves. Miss Miller's observations were not remarkable for logical consistency; for anything she wanted to say she was sure to find a pretext. She found a great many pretexts in the rugged embrasures of Chillon for asking Winterbourne sudden questions about himself—his family, his previous history, his tastes, his habits, his intentions—and for supplying information upon corresponding points in her own personality. Of her own tastes, habits and intentions Miss Miller was prepared to give the most definite, and indeed the most favourable, account.

"Well; I hope you know enough!" she said to her companion, after he had told her the history of the unhappy Bonivard.[13] "I never saw a man that knew so much!" The history of Bonivard had evidently, as they say, gone into one ear and out of the other. But Daisy went on to say that she wished Winterbourne would travel with them and "go round" with them; they might know something, in that case. "Don't you want to come and teach Randolph?" she asked. Winterbourne said that nothing could possibly please him so much; but that he had unfortunately other occupations. "Other occupations? I don't believe it!" said Miss Daisy. "What do you mean? You are not in business." The young man admitted that he was not in business; but he had engagements which, even within a day or two, would force him to go back to Geneva. "Oh, bother!" she said, "I don't believe it!" and she began to talk about something else. But a few moments later, when he was pointing out to her the pretty design of an antique fireplace, she broke out irrelevantly, "You don't mean to say you are going back to Geneva?"

"It is a melancholy fact that I shall have to return to Geneva to-morrow."

"Well, Mr. Winterbourne," said Daisy; "I think you're horrid!"

"Oh, don't say such dreadful things!" said Winterbourne—"just at the last."

"The last!" cried the young girl; "I call it the first. I have half a mind to leave you here and go straight back to the hotel alone." And for the next ten minutes she did nothing but call him horrid. Poor Winterbourne was fairly bewildered; no young lady had as yet done him the honour to be so agitated by the announcement of his movements. His companion, after this, ceased to pay any attention to the curiosities of Chillon or the beauties of the lake; she opened fire upon the mysterious charmer in Geneva, whom she appeared to have instantly taken it for granted that he was hurrying back to see. How did Miss Daisy Miller know that there was a charmer in Geneva? Winterbourne, who denied the existence of such a person, was quite unable to discover; and he was divided between amazement at the rapidity of her induction and amusement at the frankness of her *persiflage.*[14] She seemed to him, in all this, an extraordinary mixture of innocence and crudity. "Does she never allow you more than

13  **Bonivard:** Leader of Genevan resistance who was imprisoned in the Castle of Chillon from 1530 to 1536. Lord Byron idealized Bonivard's rejection of the Geneven duke and his subsequent imprisonment in the poem "The Prisoner of Chillon" (1816).

14  *persiflage:* French. Frivolous, bantering talk or mockery.

three days at a time?" asked Daisy, ironically. "Doesn't she give you a vacation in summer? There's no one so hard worked but they can get leave to go off somewhere at this season. I suppose, if you stay another day, she'll come after you in the boat. Do wait over till Friday, and I will go down to the landing to see her arrive!" Winterbourne began to think he had been wrong to feel disappointed in the temper in which the young lady had embarked. If he had missed the personal accent, the personal accent was now making its appearance. It sounded very distinctly, at last, in her telling him she would stop "teasing" him if he would promise her solemnly to come down to Rome in the winter.

"That's not a difficult promise to make," said Winterbourne. "My aunt has taken an apartment in Rome for the winter, and has already asked me to come and see her."

"I don't want you to come for your aunt," said Daisy; "I want you to come for me." And this was the only allusion that the young man was ever to hear her make to his invidious kinswoman. He declared that, at any rate, he would certainly come. After this Daisy stopped teasing. Winterbourne took a carriage, and they drove back to Vevey in the dusk; the young girl was very quiet.

In the evening Winterbourne mentioned to Mrs. Costello that he had spent the afternoon at Chillon, with Miss Daisy Miller.

"The Americans—of the courier?" asked this lady.

"Ah, happily," said Winterbourne, "the courier stayed at home."

"She went with you all alone?"

"All alone."

Mrs. Costello sniffed a little at her smelling-bottle. "And that," she exclaimed, "is the young person you wanted me to know!"

### III

Winterbourne, who had returned to Geneva the day after his excursion to Chillon, went to Rome towards the end of January. His aunt had been established there for several weeks, and he had received a couple of letters from her. "Those people you were so devoted to last summer at Vevey have turned up here, courier and all," she wrote. "They seem to have made several acquaintances, but the courier continues to be the most *intime*. The young lady, however, is also very intimate with some third-rate Italians, with whom she rackets about in a way that makes much talk. Bring me that pretty novel of Cherbuliez's—'Paule Méré'[15]—and don't come later than the 23rd."

In the natural course of events, Winterbourne, on arriving in Rome, would presently have ascertained Mrs. Miller's address at the American banker's and have gone to pay his compliments to Miss Daisy. "After what happened at Vevey I certainly think I may call upon them," he said to Mrs. Costello.

---

15 **Paule Méré:** Published in 1865, Cherbuliez's novel follows an innocent girl whose reputation is destroyed by gossip.

"If, after what happens—at Vevey and everywhere—you desire to keep up the acquaintance, you are very welcome. Of course a man may know every one. Men are welcome to the privilege!"

"Pray what is it that happens—here, for instance?" Winterbourne demanded.

"The girl goes about alone with her foreigners. As to what happens farther, you must apply elsewhere for information. She has picked up half-a-dozen of the regular Roman fortune-hunters, and she takes them about to people's houses. When she comes to a party she brings with her a gentleman with a good deal of manner and a wonderful moustache."

"And where is the mother?"

"I haven't the least idea. They are very dreadful people."

Winterbourne meditated a moment. "They are very ignorant—very innocent only. Depend upon it they are not bad."

"They are hopelessly vulgar," said Mrs. Costello. "Whether or not being hopelessly vulgar is being 'bad' is a question for the metaphysicians. They are bad enough to dislike, at any rate; and for this short life that is quite enough."

The news that Daisy Miller was surrounded by half-a-dozen wonderful moustaches checked Winterbourne's impulse to go straightway to see her. He had perhaps not definitely flattered himself that he had made an ineffaceable impression upon her heart, but he was annoyed at hearing of a state of affairs so little in harmony with an image that had lately flitted in and out of his own meditations; the image of a very pretty girl looking out of an old Roman window and asking herself urgently when Mr. Winterbourne would arrive. If, however, he determined to wait a little before reminding Miss Miller of his claims to her consideration, he went very soon to call upon two or three other friends. One of these friends was an American lady who had spent several winters at Geneva, where she had placed her children at school. She was a very accomplished woman and she lived in the Via Gregoriana. Winterbourne found her in a little crimson drawing-room, on a third-floor; the room was filled with southern sunshine. He had not been there ten minutes when the servant came in, announcing "Madame Mila!" This announcement was presently followed by the entrance of little Randolph Miller, who stopped in the middle of the room and stood staring at Winterbourne. An instant later his pretty sister crossed the threshold; and then, after a considerable interval, Mrs. Miller slowly advanced.

"I know you!" said Randolph.

"I'm sure you know a great many things," exclaimed Winterbourne, taking him by the hand. "How is your education coming on?"

Daisy was exchanging greetings very prettily with her hostess; but when she heard Winterbourne's voice she quickly turned her head. "Well, I declare!" she said.

"I told you I should come, you know," Winterbourne rejoined, smiling.

"Well—I didn't believe it," said Miss Daisy.

"I am much obliged to you," laughed the young man.

"You might have come to see me!" said Daisy.

"I arrived only yesterday."

"I don't believe that!" the young girl declared.

Winterbourne turned with a protesting smile to her mother; but this lady evaded his glance, and seating herself, fixed her eyes upon her son. "We've got a bigger place than this," said Randolph. "It's all gold on the walls."

Mrs. Miller turned uneasily in her chair. "I told you if I were to bring you, you would say something!" she murmured.

"I told *you!*" Randolph exclaimed. "I tell *you*, sir!" he added jocosely, giving Winterbourne a thump on the knee. "It *is* bigger, too!"

Daisy had entered upon a lively conversation with her hostess; Winterbourne judged it becoming to address a few words to her mother. "I hope you have been well since we parted at Vevey," he said.

Mrs. Miller now certainly looked at him—at his chin. "Not very well, sir," she answered.

"She's got the dyspepsia," said Randolph. "I've got it too. Father's got it. I've got it worst!"

This announcement, instead of embarrassing Mrs. Miller, seemed to relieve her. "I suffer from the liver," she said. "I think it's this climate; it's less bracing than Schenectady, especially in the winter season. I don't know whether you know we reside at Schenectady. I was saying to Daisy that I certainly hadn't found any one like Dr. Davis, and I didn't believe I should. Oh, at Schenectady, he stands first; they think everything of him. He has so much to do, and yet there was nothing he wouldn't do for me. He said he never saw anything like my dyspepsia, but he was bound to cure it. I'm sure there was nothing he wouldn't try. He was just going to try something new when we came off. Mr. Miller wanted Daisy to see Europe for herself. But I wrote to Mr. Miller that it seems as if I couldn't get on without Dr. Davis. At Schenectady he stands at the very top; and there's a great deal of sickness there, too. It affects my sleep."

Winterbourne had a good deal of pathological gossip with Dr. Davis's patient, during which Daisy chattered unremittingly to her own companion. The young man asked Mrs. Miller how she was pleased with Rome. "Well, I must say I am disappointed," she answered. "We had heard so much about it; I suppose we had heard too much. But we couldn't help that. We had been led to expect something different."

"Ah, wait a little, and you will become very fond of it," said Winterbourne.

"I hate it worse and worse every day!" cried Randolph.

"You are like the infant Hannibal," said Winterbourne.

"No, I ain't!" Randolph declared, at a venture.

"You are not much like an infant," said his mother. "But we have seen places," she resumed, "that I should put a long way before Rome." And in reply to Winterbourne's interrogation, "There's Zurich," she observed; "I think Zurich is lovely; and we hadn't heard half so much about it."

"The best place we've seen is the City of Richmond!" said Randolph.

"He means the ship," his mother explained. "We crossed in that ship. Randolph had a good time on the City of Richmond."

"It's the best place I've seen," the child repeated. "Only it was turned the wrong way."

"Well, we've got to turn the right way some time," said Mrs. Miller, with a little laugh. Winterbourne expressed the hope that her daughter at least found some gratification in Rome, and she declared that Daisy was quite carried away. "It's on account of the society—the society's splendid. She goes round everywhere; she has made a great number of acquaintances. Of course she goes round more than I do. I must say they have been very sociable; they have taken her right in. And then she knows a great many gentlemen. Oh, she thinks there's nothing like Rome. Of course, it's a great deal pleasanter for a young lady if she knows plenty of gentlemen."

By this time Daisy had turned her attention again to Winterbourne. "I've been telling Mrs. Walker how mean you were!" the young girl announced.

"And what is the evidence you have offered?" asked Winterbourne, rather annoyed at Miss Miller's want of appreciation of the zeal of an admirer who on his way down to Rome had stopped neither at Bologna nor at Florence, simply because of a certain sentimental impatience. He remembered that a cynical compatriot had once told him that American women—the pretty ones, and this gave a largeness to the axiom—were at once the most exacting in the world and the least endowed with a sense of indebtedness.

"Why, you were awfully mean at Vevey," said Daisy. "You wouldn't do anything. You wouldn't stay there when I asked you."

"My dearest young lady," cried Winterbourne, with eloquence, "have I come all the way to Rome to encounter your reproaches?"

"Just hear him say that!" said Daisy to her hostess, giving a twist to a bow on this lady's dress. "Did you ever hear anything so quaint?"

"So quaint, my dear?" murmured Mrs. Walker, in the tone of a partisan of Winterbourne.

"Well, I don't know," said Daisy, fingering Mrs. Walker's ribbons. "Mrs. Walker, I want to tell you something."

"Mother," interposed Randolph, with his rough ends to his words, "I tell you you've got to go. Eugenio'll raise something!"

"I'm not afraid of Eugenio," said Daisy, with a toss of her head. "Look here, Mrs. Walker," she went on, "you know I'm coming to your party."

"I am delighted to hear it."

"I've got a lovely dress."

"I am very sure of that."

"But I want to ask a favour—permission to bring a friend."

"I shall be happy to see any of your friends," said Mrs. Walker, turning with a smile to Mrs. Miller.

"Oh, they are not my friends," answered Daisy's mamma, smiling shyly, in her own fashion. "I never spoke to them!"

"It's an intimate friend of mine—Mr. Giovanelli," said Daisy, without a tremor in her clear little voice or a shadow on her brilliant little face.

Mrs. Walker was silent a moment, she gave a rapid glance at Winterbourne. "I shall be glad to see Mr. Giovanelli," she then said.

"He's an Italian," Daisy pursued, with the prettiest serenity. "He's a great friend of mine—he's the handsomest man in the world—except Mr. Winterbourne! He knows plenty of Italians, but he wants to know some Americans. He thinks ever so much of Americans. He's tremendously clever. He's perfectly lovely!"

It was settled that this brilliant personage should be brought to Mrs. Walker's party, and then Mrs. Miller prepared to take her leave. "I guess we'll go back to the hotel," she said.

"You may go back to the hotel, mother, but I'm going to take a walk," said Daisy.

"She's going to walk with Mr. Giovanelli," Randolph proclaimed.

"I am going to the Pincio,"[16] said Daisy, smiling.

"Alone, my dear—at this hour?" Mrs. Walker asked. The afternoon was drawing to a close—it was the hour for the throng of carriages and of contemplative pedestrians. "I don't think it's safe, my dear," said Mrs. Walker.

"Neither do I," subjoined Mrs. Miller. "You'll get the fever as sure as you live. Remember what Dr. Davis told you!"

"Give her some medicine before she goes," said Randolph.

The company had risen to its feet; Daisy, still showing her pretty teeth, bent over and kissed her hostess. "Mrs. Walker, you are too perfect," she said. "I'm not going alone; I am going to meet a friend."

"Your friend won't keep you from getting the fever,"[17] Mrs. Miller observed.

"Is it Mr. Giovanelli?" asked the hostess.

Winterbourne was watching the young girl; at this question his attention quickened. She stood there smiling and smoothing her bonnet-ribbons; she glanced at Winterbourne. Then, while she glanced and smiled, she answered without a shade of hesitation, "Mr. Giovanelli—the beautiful Giovanelli."

"My dear young friend," said Mrs. Walker, taking her hand, pleadingly, "don't walk off to the Pincio at this hour to meet a beautiful Italian."

"Well, he speaks English," said Mrs. Miller.

"Gracious me!" Daisy exclaimed, "I don't want to do anything improper. There's an easy way to settle it." She continued to glance at Winterbourne. "The Pincio is only a hundred yards distant, and if Mr. Winterbourne were as polite as he pretends he would offer to walk with me!"

Winterbourne's politeness hastened to affirm itself, and the young girl gave him gracious leave to accompany her. They passed down-stairs before her mother, and at the door Winterbourne perceived Mrs. Miller's carriage drawn up, with the ornamental courier whose acquaintance he had made at Vevey seated within. "Good-bye, Eugenio!" cried Daisy, "I'm going to take a walk." The distance from the Via Gregoriana to the beautiful garden at the other end of the Pincian Hill is, in fact, rapidly traversed. As the day was splendid, however, and the concourse of vehicles, walkers, and loungers numerous, the young Americans found their progress much delayed. This fact was highly agreeable to Winterbourne, in spite of his consciousness of his singular situation. The slow-moving, idly-gazing Roman crowd bestowed much attention

---

16  **Pincio:** Originally a garden belonging to a nearby convent, the Pincio was developed into a public garden by Giuseppe Valadier for Napoleon in 1818.
17  **fever:** Malaria, known also as Roman fever.

upon the extremely pretty young foreign lady who was passing through it upon his arm; and he wondered what on earth had been in Daisy's mind when she proposed to expose herself, unattended, to its appreciation. His own mission, to her sense, apparently, was to consign her to the hands of Mr. Giovanelli; but Winterbourne, at once annoyed and gratified, resolved that he would do no such thing.

"Why haven't you been to see me?" asked Daisy. "You can't get out of that."

"I have had the honour of telling you that I have only just stepped out of the train."

"You must have stayed in the train a good while after it stopped!" cried the young girl, with her little laugh. "I suppose you were asleep. You have had time to go to see Mrs. Walker."

"I knew Mrs. Walker—" Winterbourne began to explain.

"I knew where you knew her. You knew her at Geneva. She told me so. Well, you knew me at Vevey. That's just as good. So you ought to have come." She asked him no other question than this; she began to prattle about her own affairs. "We've got splendid rooms at the hotel; Eugenio says they're the best rooms in Rome. We are going to stay all winter—if we don't die of the fever; and I guess we'll stay then. It's a great deal nicer than I thought; I thought it would be fearfully quiet; I was sure it would be awfully poky. I was sure we should be going round all the time with one of those dreadful old men that explain about the pictures and things. But we only had about a week of that, and now I'm enjoying myself. I know ever so many people, and they are all so charming. The society's extremely select. There are all kinds—English, and Germans, and Italians. I think I like the English best. I like their style of conversation. But there are some lovely Americans. I never saw anything so hospitable. There's something or other every day. There's not much dancing; but I must say I never thought dancing was everything. I was always fond of conversation. I guess I shall have plenty at Mrs. Walker's—her rooms are so small." When they had passed the gate of the Pincian Gardens, Miss Miller began to wonder where Mr. Giovanelli might be. "We had better go straight to that place in front," she said, "where you look at the view."

"I certainly shall not help you to find him," Winterbourne declared.

"Then I shall find him without you," said Miss Daisy.

"You certainly won't leave me!" cried Winterbourne.

She burst into her little laugh. "Are you afraid you'll get lost—or run over? But there's Giovanelli, leaning against that tree. He's staring at the women in the carriages: did you ever see anything so cool?"

Winterbourne perceived at some distance a little man standing with folded arms, nursing his cane. He had a handsome face, an artfully poised hat, a glass in one eye and a nosegay in his button-hole. Winterbourne looked at him a moment and then said, "Do you mean to speak to that man?"

"Do I mean to speak to him? Why, you don't suppose I mean to communicate by signs?"

"Pray understand, then," said Winterbourne, "that I intend to remain with you."

Daisy stopped and looked at him, without a sign of troubled consciousness in her face; with nothing but the presence of her charming eyes and her happy dimples. "Well, she's a cool one!" thought the young man.

"I don't like the way you say that," said Daisy. "It's too imperious."

"I beg your pardon if I say it wrong. The main point is to give you an idea of my meaning."

The young girl looked at him more gravely, but with eyes that were prettier than ever. "I have never allowed a gentleman to dictate to me, or to interfere with anything I do."

"I think you have made a mistake," said Winterbourne. "You should sometimes listen to a gentleman—the right one?"

Daisy began to laugh again. "I do nothing but listen to gentlemen!" she exclaimed. "Tell me if Mr. Giovanelli is the right one?"

The gentleman with the nosegay in his bosom had now perceived our two friends, and was approaching the young girl with obsequious rapidity. He bowed to Winterbourne as well as to the latter's companion; he had a brilliant smile, an intelligent eye; Winterbourne thought him not a bad-looking fellow. But he nevertheless said to Daisy—"No, he's not the right one."

Daisy evidently had a natural talent for performing introductions; she mentioned the name of each of her companions to the other. She strolled along with one of them on each side of her; Mr. Giovanelli, who spoke English very cleverly—Winterbourne afterwards learned that he had practised the idiom upon a great many American heiresses—addressed her a great deal of very polite nonsense; he was extremely urbane, and the young American, who said nothing, reflected upon that profundity of Italian cleverness which enables people to appear more gracious in proportion as they are more acutely disappointed. Giovanelli, of course, had counted upon something more intimate; he had not bargained for a party of three. But he kept his temper in a manner which suggested far-stretching intentions. Winterbourne flattered himself that he had taken his measure. "He is not a gentleman," said the young American; "he is only a clever imitation of one. He is a music-master, or a penny-a-liner, or a third-rate artist. Damn his good looks!" Mr. Giovanelli had certainly a very pretty face; but Winterbourne felt a superior indignation at his own lovely fellow-country-woman's not knowing the difference between a spurious gentleman and a real one. Giovanelli chattered and jested and made himself wonderfully agreeable. It was true that if he was an imitation the imitation was very skilful. "Nevertheless," Winterbourne said to himself, "a nice girl ought to know!" And then he came back to the question whether this was in fact a nice girl. Would a nice girl—even allowing for her being a little American flirt—make a rendezvous with a presumably low-lived foreigner? The rendezvous in this case, indeed, had been in broad daylight, and in the most crowded corner of Rome; but was it not impossible to regard the choice of these circumstances as a proof of extreme cynicism? Singular though it may seem, Winterbourne was vexed that the young girl, in joining her *amoroso,* should not appear more impatient of his own company, and he was vexed because of his inclination. It was impossible to regard her as a perfectly well-conducted young lady; she was wanting in a certain indispensable delicacy. It would therefore simplify matters greatly to be able to treat her as the object of one of those sentiments which are called by romancers "lawless passions." That she should seem to wish to get rid of him would help him to think more lightly of her, and to be able to think more lightly of her would make her much less perplexing. But Daisy, on this occasion, continued to present herself as an inscrutable combination of audacity and innocence.

She had been walking some quarter of an hour, attended by her two cavaliers, and responding in a tone of very childish gaiety, as it seemed to Winterbourne, to the pretty speeches of Mr. Giovanelli, when a carriage that had detached itself from the revolving train drew up beside the path. At the same moment Winterbourne perceived that his friend Mrs. Walker—the lady whose house he had lately left—was seated in the vehicle and was beckoning to him. Leaving Miss Miller's side, he hastened to obey her summons. Mrs. Walker was flushed; she wore an excited air. "It is really too dreadful," she said. "That girl must not do this sort of thing. She must not walk here with you two men. Fifty people have noticed her."

Winterbourne raised his eyebrows. "I think it's a pity to make too much fuss about it."

"It's a pity to let the girl ruin herself!"

"She is very innocent," said Winterbourne.

"She's very crazy!" cried Mrs. Walker. "Did you ever see anything so imbecile as her mother? After you had all left me, just now, I could not sit still for thinking of it. It seemed too pitiful, not even to attempt to save her. I ordered the carriage and put on my bonnet, and came here as quickly as possible. Thank heaven I have found you!"

"What do you propose to do with us?" asked Winterbourne, smiling.

"To ask her to get in, to drive her about here for half-an-hour, so that the world may see she is not running absolutely wild, and then to take her safely home."

"I don't think it's a very happy thought," said Winterbourne; "but you can try."

Mrs. Walker tried. The young man went in pursuit of Miss Miller, who had simply nodded and smiled at his interlocutrix in the carriage and had gone her way with her own companion. Daisy, on learning that Mrs. Walker wished to speak to her, retraced her steps with a perfect good grace and with Mr. Giovanelli at her side. She declared that she was delighted to have a chance to present this gentleman to Mrs. Walker. She immediately achieved the introduction, and declared that she had never in her life seen anything so lovely as Mrs. Walker's carriage-rug.

"I am glad you admire it," said this lady, smiling sweetly. "Will you get in and let me put it over you?"

"Oh, no, thank you," said Daisy. "I shall admire it much more as I see you driving round with it."

"Do get in and drive with me," said Mrs. Walker.

"That would be charming, but it's so enchanting just as I am!" and Daisy gave a brilliant glance at the gentlemen on either side of her.

"It may be enchanting, dear child, but it is not the custom here," urged Mrs. Walker, leaning forward in her victoria[18] with her hands devoutly clasped.

"Well, it ought to be, then!" said Daisy. "If I didn't walk I should expire."

"You should walk with your mother, dear," cried the lady from Geneva, losing patience.

18  **victoria:** Open-passenger, four-wheeled carriage for two with an elevated seat for the driver.

"With my mother dear!" exclaimed the young girl. Winterbourne saw that she scented interference. "My mother never walked ten steps in her life. And then, you know," she added with a laugh, "I am more than five years old."

"You are old enough to be more reasonable. You are old enough, dear Miss Miller, to be talked about."

Daisy looked at Mrs. Walker, smiling intensely. "Talked about? What do you mean?"

"Come into my carriage and I will tell you."

Daisy turned her quickened glance again from one of the gentlemen beside her to the other. Mr. Giovanelli was bowing to and fro, rubbing down his gloves and laughing very agreeably; Winterbourne thought it a most unpleasant scene. "I don't think I want to know what you mean," said Daisy presently. "I don't think I should like it."

Winterbourne wished that Mrs. Walker would tuck in her carriage-rug and drive away; but this lady did not enjoy being defied, as she afterwards told him. "Should you prefer being thought a very reckless girl?" she demanded.

"Gracious me!" exclaimed Daisy. She looked again at Mr. Giovanelli, then she turned to Winterbourne. There was a little pink flush in her cheek; she was tremendously pretty. "Does Mr. Winterbourne think," she asked slowly, smiling, throwing back her head and glancing at him from head to foot, "that—to save my reputation—I ought to get into the carriage?"

Winterbourne coloured; for an instant he hesitated greatly. It seemed so strange to hear her speak that way of her "reputation." But he himself, in fact, must speak in accordance with gallantry. The finest gallantry, here, was simply to tell her the truth; and the truth, for Winterbourne, as the few indications I have been able to give have made him known to the reader, was that Daisy Miller should take Mrs. Walker's advice. He looked at her exquisite prettiness; and then he said very gently, "I think you should get into the carriage."

Daisy gave a violent laugh. "I never heard anything so stiff! If this is improper, Mrs. Walker," she pursued, "then I am all improper, and you must give me up. Good-bye; I hope you'll have a lovely ride!" and, with Mr. Giovanelli, who made a triumphantly obsequious salute, she turned away.

Mrs. Walker sat looking after her, and there were tears in Mrs. Walker's eyes. "Get in here, sir," she said to Winterbourne, indicating the place beside her. The young man answered that he felt bound to accompany Miss Miller; whereupon Mrs. Walker declared that if he refused her this favour she would never speak to him again. She was evidently in earnest. Winterbourne overtook Daisy and her companion and, offering the young girl his hand, told her that Mrs. Walker had made an imperious claim upon his society. He expected that in answer she would say something rather free, something to commit herself still farther to that "recklessness" from which Mrs. Walker had so charitably endeavoured to dissuade her. But she only shook his hand, hardly looking at him, while Mr. Giovanelli bade him farewell with a too emphatic flourish of the hat.

Winterbourne was not in the best possible humour as he took his seat in Mrs.

Walker's victoria. "That was not clever of you," he said candidly, while the vehicle mingled again with the throng of carriages.

"In such a case," his companion answered, "I don't wish to be clever, I wish to be *earnest!*"

"Well, your earnestness has only offended her and put her off."

"It has happened very well," said Mrs. Walker. "If she is so perfectly determined to compromise herself, the sooner one knows it the better; one can act accordingly."

"I suspect she meant no harm," Winterbourne rejoined.

"So I thought a month ago. But she has been going too far."

"What has she been doing?"

"Everything that is not done here. Flirting with any man she could pick up; sitting in corners with mysterious Italians; dancing all the evening with the same partners; receiving visits at eleven o'clock at night. Her mother goes away when visitors come."

"But her brother," said Winterbourne, laughing, "sits up till midnight."

"He must be edified by what he sees. I'm told that at their hotel every one is talking about her, and that a smile goes round among the servants when a gentleman comes and asks for Miss Miller."

"The servants be hanged!" said Winterbourne angrily. "The poor girl's only fault," he presently added, "is that she is very uncultivated."

"She is naturally indelicate," Mrs. Walker declared. "Take that example this morning. How long had you known her at Vevey?"

"A couple of days."

"Fancy, then, her making it a personal matter that you should have left the place!"

Winterbourne was silent for some moments; then he said, "I suspect, Mrs. Walker, that you and I have lived too long at Geneva!" And he added a request that she should inform him with what particular design she had made him enter her carriage.

"I wished to beg you to cease your relations with Miss Miller—not to flirt with her—to give her no farther opportunity to expose herself—to let her alone, in short."

"I'm afraid I can't do that," said Winterbourne. "I like her extremely."

"All the more reason that you shouldn't help her to make a scandal."

"There shall be nothing scandalous in my attentions to her."

"There certainly will be in the way she takes them. But I have said what I had on my conscience," Mrs. Walker pursued. "If you wish to rejoin the young lady I will put you down. Here, by-the-way, you have a chance."

The carriage was traversing that part of the Pincian Garden which overhangs the wall of Rome and overlooks the beautiful Villa Borghese.[19] It is bordered by a large parapet, near which there are several seats. One of the seats, at a distance, was occupied by a gentleman and a lady, towards whom Mrs. Walker gave a toss of her head. At the same moment these persons rose and walked towards the parapet. Winter-

---

19  **Villa Borghese:** Originally built in the seventeenth century, the Villa Borghese became an art museum in the nineteenth century, and the owners added a zoo to the grounds in 1911.

bourne had asked the coachman to stop; he now descended from the carriage. His companion looked at him a moment in silence; then, while he raised his hat, she drove majestically away. Winterbourne stood there; he had turned his eyes towards Daisy and her cavalier. They evidently saw no one; they were too deeply occupied with each other. When they reached the low garden-wall they stood a moment looking off at the great flat-topped pine-clusters of the Villa Borghese; then Giovanelli seated himself familiarly upon the broad ledge of the wall. The western sun in the opposite sky sent out a brilliant shaft through a couple of cloud-bars; whereupon Daisy's companion took her parasol out of her hands and opened it. She came a little nearer and he held the parasol over her; then, still holding it, he let it rest upon her shoulder, so that both of their heads were hidden from Winterbourne. This young man lingered a moment, then he began to walk. But he walked—not towards the couple with the parasol; towards the residence of his aunt, Mrs. Costello.

## IV

He flattered himself on the following day that there was no smiling among the servants when he, at least, asked for Mrs. Miller at her hotel. This lady and her daughter, however, were not at home; and on the next day after, repeating his visit, Winterbourne again had the misfortune not to find them. Mrs. Walker's party took place on the evening of the third day, and in spite of the frigidity of his last interview with the hostess Winterbourne was among the guests. Mrs. Walker was one of those American ladies who, while residing abroad, make a point, in their own phrase, of studying European society; and she had on this occasion collected several specimens of her diversely-born fellow-mortals to serve, as it were, as text-books. When Winterbourne arrived Daisy Miller was not there; but in a few moments he saw her mother come in alone, very shyly and ruefully. Mrs. Miller's hair, above her exposed-looking temples, was more frizzled than ever. As she approached Mrs. Walker, Winterbourne also drew near.

"You see I've come all alone," said poor Mrs. Miller. "I'm so frightened; I don't know what to do; it's the first time I've ever been to a party alone—especially in this country. I wanted to bring Randolph or Eugenio, or some one, but Daisy just pushed me off by myself. I ain't used to going round alone."

"And does not your daughter intend to favour us with her society?" demanded Mrs. Walker, impressively.

"Well, Daisy's all dressed," said Mrs. Miller, with that accent of the dispassionate, if not of the philosophic, historian with which she always recorded the current incidents of her daughter's career. "She got dressed on purpose before dinner. But she's got a friend of hers there; that gentleman—the Italian—that she wanted to bring. They've got going at the piano; it seems as if they couldn't leave off. Mr. Giovanelli sings splendidly. But I guess they'll come before very long," concluded Mrs. Miller hopefully.

"I'm sorry she should come—in that way," said Mrs. Walker.

"Well, I told her that there was no use in her getting dressed before dinner if she was going to wait three hours," responded Daisy's mamma. "I didn't see the use of her putting on such a dress as that to sit round with Mr. Giovanelli."

"This is most horrible!" said Mrs. Walker, turning away and addressing herself to Winterbourne. "*Elle s'affiche.*[20] It's her revenge for my having ventured to remonstrate with her. When she comes I shall not speak to her."

Daisy came after eleven o'clock, but she was not, on such an occasion, a young lady to wait to be spoken to. She rustled forward in radiant loveliness, smiling and chattering, carrying a large bouquet and attended by Mr. Giovanelli. Every one stopped talking, and turned and looked at her. She came straight to Mrs. Walker. "I'm afraid you thought I never was coming, so I sent mother off to tell you. I wanted to make Mr. Giovanelli practise some things before he came; you know he sings beautifully, and I want you to ask him to sing. This is Mr. Giovanelli; you know I introduced him to you; he's got the most lovely voice and he knows the most charming set of songs. I made him go over them this evening, on purpose; we had the greatest time at the hotel." Of all this Daisy delivered herself with the sweetest, brightest audibleness, looking now at her hostess and now round the room, while she gave a series of little pats, round her shoulders, to the edges of her dress. "Is there any one I know?" she asked.

"I think every one knows you!" said Mrs. Walker pregnantly, and she gave a very cursory greeting to Mr. Giovanelli. This gentleman bore himself gallantly. He smiled and bowed and showed his white teeth, he curled his moustaches and rolled his eyes, and performed all the proper functions of a handsome Italian at an evening party. He sang, very prettily, half-a-dozen songs, though Mrs. Walker afterwards declared that she had been quite unable to find out who asked him. It was apparently not Daisy who had given him his orders. Daisy sat at a distance from the piano, and though she had publicly, as it were, professed a high admiration for his singing, talked, not inaudibly, while it was going on.

"It's a pity these rooms are so small; we can't dance," she said to Winterbourne, as if she had seen him five minutes before.

"I am not sorry we can't dance," Winterbourne answered; "I don't dance."

"Of course you don't dance; you're too stiff," said Miss Daisy. "I hope you enjoyed your drive with Mrs. Walker."

"No, I didn't enjoy it; I preferred walking with you."

"We paired off, that was much better," said Daisy. "But did you ever hear anything so cool as Mrs. Walker's wanting me to get into her carriage and drop poor Mr. Giovanelli; and under the pretext that it was proper? People have different ideas! It would have been most unkind; he had been talking about that walk for ten days."

"He should not have talked about it at all," said Winterbourne; "he would never have proposed to a young lady of this country to walk about the streets with him."

"About the streets?" cried Daisy, with her pretty stare. "Where then would he have proposed to her to walk? The Pincio is not the streets, either; and I, thank goodness,

---

20 *Elle s'affiche:* French. She is making a spectacle of herself; she's showing off.

am not a young lady of this country. The young ladies of this country have a dreadfully poky time of it, so far as I can learn; I don't see why I should change my habits for *them*."

"I am afraid your habits are those of a flirt," said Winterbourne gravely.

"Of course they are," she cried, giving him her little smiling stare again. "I'm a fearful, frightful flirt! Did you ever hear of a nice girl that was not? But I suppose you will tell me now that I am not a nice girl."

"You're a very nice girl, but I wish you would flirt with me, and me only," said Winterbourne.

"Ah! thank you, thank you very much; you are the last man I should think of flirting with. As I have had the pleasure of informing you, you are too stiff."

"You say that too often," said Winterbourne.

Daisy gave a delighted laugh. "If I could have the sweet hope of making you angry, I would say it again."

"Don't do that; when I am angry I'm stiffer than ever. But if you won't flirt with me, do cease at least to flirt with your friend at the piano; they don't understand that sort of thing here."

"I thought they understood nothing else!" exclaimed Daisy.

"Not in young unmarried women."

"It seems to me much more proper in young unmarried women than in old married ones," Daisy declared.

"Well," said Winterbourne, "when you deal with natives you must go by the custom of the place. Flirting is a purely American custom; it doesn't exist here. So when you show yourself in public with Mr. Giovanelli and without your mother——"

"Gracious! poor mother!" interposed Daisy.

"Though you may be flirting, Mr. Giovanelli is not; he means something else."

"He isn't preaching, at any rate," said Daisy with vivacity. "And if you want very much to know, we are neither of us flirting; we are too good friends for that; we are very intimate friends."

"Ah!" rejoined Winterbourne, "if you are in love with each other it is another affair."

She had allowed him up to this point to talk so frankly that he had no expectation of shocking her by this ejaculation; but she immediately got up, blushing visibly, and leaving him to exclaim mentally that little American flirts were the queerest creatures in the world. "Mr. Giovanelli, at least," she said, giving her interlocutor a single glance, "never says such very disagreeable things to me."

Winterbourne was bewildered; he stood staring. Mr. Giovanelli had finished singing; he left the piano and came over to Daisy. "Won't you come into the other room and have some tea?" he asked, bending before her with his decorative smile.

Daisy turned to Winterbourne, beginning to smile again. He was still more perplexed, for this inconsequent smile made nothing clear, though it seemed to prove, indeed, that she had a sweetness and softness that reverted instinctively to the pardon of offences. "It has never occurred to Mr. Winterbourne to offer me any tea," she said, with her little tormenting manner.

"I have offered you advice," Winterbourne rejoined.

"I prefer weak tea!" cried Daisy, and she went off with the brilliant Giovanelli. She sat with him in the adjoining room, in the embrasure of the window, for the rest of the evening. There was an interesting performance at the piano, but neither of these young people gave heed to it. When Daisy came to take leave of Mrs. Walker, this lady conscientiously repaired the weakness of which she had been guilty at the moment of the young girl's arrival. She turned her back straight upon Miss Miller and left her to depart with what grace she might. Winterbourne was standing near the door; he saw it all. Daisy turned very pale and looked at her mother, but Mrs. Miller was humbly unconscious of any violation of the usual social forms. She appeared, indeed, to have felt an incongruous impulse to draw attention to her own striking observance of them. "Good night, Mrs. Walker," she said; "we've had a beautiful evening. You see if I let Daisy come to parties without me, I don't want her to go away without me." Daisy turned away, looking with a pale, grave face at the circle near the door; Winterbourne saw that, for the first moment, she was too much shocked and puzzled even for indignation. He on his side was greatly touched.

"That was very cruel," he said to Mrs. Walker.

"She never enters my drawing-room again," replied his hostess.

Since Winterbourne was not to meet her in Mrs. Walker's drawing-room, he went as often as possible to Mrs. Miller's hotel. The ladies were rarely at home, but when he found them the devoted Giovanelli was always present. Very often the polished little Roman was in the drawing-room with Daisy alone, Mrs. Miller being apparently constantly of the opinion that discretion is the better part of surveillance. Winterbourne noted, at first with surprise, that Daisy on these occasions was never embarrassed or annoyed by his own entrance; but he very presently began to feel that she had no more surprises for him; the unexpected in her behaviour was the only thing to expect. She showed no displeasure at her *tête-à-tête* with Giovanelli being interrupted; she could chatter as freshly and freely with two gentlemen as with one; there was always in her conversation, the same odd mixture of audacity and puerility. Winterbourne remarked to himself that if she was seriously interested in Giovanelli it was very singular that she should not take more trouble to preserve the sanctity of their interviews, and he liked her the more for her innocent-looking indifference and her apparently inexhaustible good humour. He could hardly have said why, but she seemed to him a girl who would never be jealous. At the risk of exciting a somewhat derisive smile on the reader's part, I may affirm that with regard to the women who had hitherto interested him it very often seemed to Winterbourne among the possibilities that, given certain contingencies, he should be afraid—literally afraid—of these ladies. He had a pleasant sense that he should never be afraid of Daisy Miller. It must be added that this sentiment was not altogether flattering to Daisy; it was part of his conviction, or rather of his apprehension, that she would prove a very light young person.

But she was evidently very much interested in Giovanelli. She looked at him whenever he spoke; she was perpetually telling him to do this and to do that; she was constantly "chaffing" and abusing him. She appeared completely to have forgotten that Winterbourne had said anything to displease her at Mrs. Walker's little party. One Sunday afternoon, having gone to St. Peter's[21] with his aunt, Winterbourne perceived Daisy strolling about the great church in company with the inevitable Giovanelli. Presently he pointed out the young girl and her cavalier to Mrs. Costello. This lady looked at them a moment through her eyeglass, and then she said:

"That's what makes you so pensive in these days, eh?"

"I had not the least idea I was pensive," said the young man.

"You are very much pre-occupied, you are thinking of something."

"And what is it," he asked, "that you accuse me of thinking of?"

"Of that young lady's—Miss Baker's, Miss Chandler's—what's her name?—Miss Miller's intrigue with that little barber's block."

"Do you call it an intrigue," Winterbourne asked—"an affair that goes on with such peculiar publicity?"

"That's their folly," said Mrs. Costello, "it's not their merit."

"No," rejoined Winterbourne, with something of that pensiveness to which his aunt had alluded. "I don't believe that there is anything to be called an intrigue."

"I have heard a dozen people speak of it; they say she is quite carried away by him."

"They are certainly very intimate," said Winterbourne.

Mrs. Costello inspected the young couple again with her optical instrument. "He is very handsome. One easily sees how it is. She thinks him the most elegant man in the world, the finest gentleman. She has never seen anything like him; he is better even than the courier. It was the courier probably who introduced him, and if he succeeds in marrying the young lady, the courier will come in for a magnificent commission."

"I don't believe she thinks of marrying him," said Winterbourne, "and I don't believe he hopes to marry her."

"You may be very sure she thinks of nothing. She goes on from day to day, from hour to hour, as they did in the Golden Age. I can imagine nothing more vulgar. And at the same time," added Mrs. Costello, "depend upon it that she may tell you any moment that she is 'engaged.'"

"I think that is more than Giovanelli expects," said Winterbourne.

"Who is Giovanelli?"

"The little Italian. I have asked questions about him and learned something. He is apparently a perfectly respectable little man. I believe he is in a small way a *cavaliere avvocato*.[22] But he doesn't move in what are called the first circles. I think it is really not absolutely impossible that the courier introduced him. He is evidently immensely charmed with Miss Miller. If she thinks him the finest gentleman in the world, he, on his side, has never found himself in personal contact with such splendour, such opulence, such expensiveness, as this young lady's. And then she must seem to him wonderfully pretty and interesting. I rather doubt whether he dreams of marrying her.

---

21  **St. Peter's:** Located in Vatican City, St. Peter's Basilica is a holy center for the Roman Catholic church and the location of St. Peter's tomb.

22  *cavaliere avvocato:* Italian. Literally "knight lawyer," a lawyer given an honorary knighthood.

That must appear to him too impossible a piece of luck. He has nothing but his handsome face to offer, and there is a substantial Mr. Miller in that mysterious land of dollars. Giovanelli knows that he hasn't a title to offer. If he were only a count or a *marchese!* He must wonder at his luck at the way they have taken him up."

"He accounts for it by his handsome face, and thinks Miss Miller a young lady *qui se passe ses fantaisies!*"[23] said Mrs. Costello.

"It is very true," Winterbourne pursued, "that Daisy and her mamma have not yet risen to that stage of—what shall I call it?—of culture, at which the idea of catching a count or a *marchese* begins. I believe that they are intellectually incapable of that conception."

"Ah! but the *cavaliere* can't believe it," said Mrs. Costello.

Of the observation excited by Daisy's "intrigue," Winterbourne gathered that day at St. Peter's sufficient evidence. A dozen of the American colonists in Rome came to talk with Mrs. Costello, who sat on a little portable stool at the base of one of the great pilasters. The vesper-service was going forward in splendid chants and organ-tones in the adjacent choir, and meanwhile, between Mrs. Costello and her friends, there was a great deal said about poor little Miss Miller's going really "too far." Winterbourne was not pleased with what he heard; but when, coming out upon the great steps of the church, he saw Daisy, who had emerged before him, get into an open cab with her accomplice and roll away through the cynical streets of Rome, he could not deny to himself that she was going very far indeed. He felt very sorry for her—not exactly that he believed that she had completely lost her head, but because it was painful to hear so much that was pretty and undefended and natural assigned to a vulgar place among the categories of disorder. He made an attempt after this to give a hint to Mrs. Miller. He met one day in the Corso[24] a friend—a tourist like himself—who had just come out of the Doria Palace,[25] where he had been walking through the beautiful gallery. His friend talked for a moment about the superb portrait of Innocent X. by Velasquez, which hangs in one of the cabinets of the palace, and then said, "And in the same cabinet, by-the-way, I had the pleasure of contemplating a picture of a different kind—that pretty American girl whom you pointed out to me last week." In answer to Winterbourne's inquiries, his friend narrated that the pretty American girl—prettier than ever—was seated with a companion in the secluded nook in which the great papal portrait is enshrined.

"Who was her companion?" asked Winterbourne.

"A little Italian with a bouquet in his button-hole. The girl is delightfully pretty, but I thought I understood from you the other day that she was a young lady *du meilleur monde.*"[26]

"So she is!" answered Winterbourne; and having assured himself that his in-

---

23   *qui se passe ses fantaisies:* French. Who is indulging her fantasies, whims.
24   **Corso:** Fashionable street.
25   **Doria Palace:** With over 1,000 rooms, Doria Pamphili Palace is one of Rome's largest palaces. The Pamphili family private art collection contains over six hundred paintings, including masterpieces by Velazquez, Titian, and Caravaggio.
26   *du meilleur monde:* French. Literally, "of a better world," or of the better society.

formant had seen Daisy and her companion but five minutes before, he jumped into a cab and went to call on Mrs. Miller. She was at home; but she apologised to him for receiving him in Daisy's absence.

"She's gone out somewhere with Mr. Giovanelli," said Mrs. Miller. "She's always going round with Mr. Giovanelli."

"I have noticed that they are very intimate," Winterbourne observed.

"Oh! it seems as if they couldn't live without each other!" said Mrs. Miller. "Well, he's a real gentleman, anyhow. I keep telling Daisy she's engaged!"

"And what does Daisy say?"

"Oh, she says she isn't engaged. But she might as well be!" this impartial parent resumed. "She goes on as if she was. But I've made Mr. Giovanelli promise to tell me, if *she* doesn't. I should want to write to Mr. Miller about it—shouldn't you?"

Winterbourne replied that he certainly should; and the state of mind of Daisy's mamma struck him as so unprecedented in the annals of parental vigilance that he gave up as utterly irrelevant the attempt to place her upon her guard.

After this Daisy was never at home, and Winterbourne ceased to meet her at the houses of their common acquaintance, because, as he perceived, these shrewd people had quite made up their minds that she was going too far. They ceased to invite her, and they intimated that they desired to express to observant Europeans the great truth that, though Miss Daisy Miller was a young American lady, her behaviour was not representative—was regarded by her compatriots as abnormal. Winterbourne wondered how she felt about all the cold shoulders that were turned towards her, and sometimes it annoyed him to suspect that she did not feel at all. He said to himself that she was too light and childish, too uncultivated and unreasoning, too provincial, to have reflected upon her ostracism or even to have perceived it. Then at other moments he believed that she carried about in her elegant and irresponsible little organism a defiant, passionate, perfectly observant consciousness of the impression she produced. He asked himself whether Daisy's defiance came from the consciousness of innocence or from her being, essentially, a young person of the reckless class. It must be admitted that holding oneself to a belief in Daisy's "innocence" came to seem to Winterbourne more and more a matter of fine-spun gallantry. As I have already had occasion to relate, he was angry at finding himself reduced to chopping logic about this young lady; he was vexed at his want of instinctive certitude as to how far her eccentricities were generic, national, and how far they were personal. From either view of them he had somehow missed her, and now it was too late. She was "carried away" by Mr. Giovanelli.

A few days after his brief interview with her mother, he encountered her in that beautiful abode of flowering desolation known as the Palace of the Caesars. The early Roman spring had filled the air with bloom and perfume, and the rugged surface of the Palatine[27] was muffled with tender verdure. Daisy was strolling along the top of one of those great mounds of ruin that are embanked with mossy marble and paved

---

27  **Palatine:** A plateau between the Tiber and the Forum. It was here that Romulus erected the first walls of the city. During the Roman Empire, the Palatine was an exclusive residential area.

with monumental inscriptions. It seemed to him that Rome had never been so lovely as just then. He stood looking off at the enchanting harmony of line and colour that remotely encircles the city, inhaling the softly humid odours and feeling the freshness of the year and the antiquity of the place reaffirm themselves in mysterious interfusion. It seemed to him also that Daisy had never looked so pretty; but this had been an observation of his whenever he met her. Giovanelli was at her side, and Giovanelli, too, wore an aspect of even unwonted brilliancy.

"Well," said Daisy, "I should think you would be lonesome!"

"Lonesome?" asked Winterbourne.

"You are always going round by yourself. Can't you get any one to walk with you?"

"I am not so fortunate," said Winterbourne, "as your companion."

Giovanelli, from the first, had treated Winterbourne with distinguished politeness; he listened with a deferential air to his remarks; he laughed, punctiliously, at his pleasantries; he seemed disposed to testify to his belief that Winterbourne was a superior young man. He carried himself in no degree like a jealous wooer; he had obviously a great deal of tact; he had no objection to your expecting a little humility of him. It even seemed to Winterbourne at times that Giovanelli would find a certain mental relief in being able to have a private understanding with him—to say to him, as an intelligent man, that, bless you, *he* knew how extraordinary was this young lady, and didn't flatter himself with delusive—or at least *too* delusive—hopes of matrimony and dollars. On this occasion he strolled away from his companion to pluck a sprig of almond blossom, which he carefully arranged in his button-hole.

"I know why you say that," said Daisy, watching Giovanelli. "Because you think I go round too much with *him!*" And she nodded at her attendant.

"Every one thinks so—if you care to know," said Winterbourne.

"Of course I care to know!" Daisy exclaimed seriously. "But I don't believe it. They are only pretending to be shocked. They don't really care a straw what I do. Besides, I don't go round so much."

"I think you will find they do care. They will show it—disagreeably."

Daisy looked at him a moment. "How—disagreeably?"

"Haven't you noticed anything?" Winterbourne asked.

"I have noticed you. But I noticed you were as stiff as an umbrella the first time I saw you."

"You will find I am not so stiff as several others," said Winterbourne, smiling.

"How shall I find it?"

"By going to see the others."

"What will they do to me?"

"They will give you the cold shoulder. Do you know what that means?"

Daisy was looking at him intently; she began to colour. "Do you mean as Mrs. Walker did the other night?"

"Exactly!" said Winterbourne.

She looked away at Giovanelli, who was decorating himself with his almond-blossom. Then looking back at Winterbourne—"I shouldn't think you would let people be so unkind!" she said.

"How can I help it?" he asked.

"I should think you would say something."

"I do say something;" and he paused a moment. "I say that your mother tells me that she believes you are engaged."

"Well, she does," said Daisy very simply.

Winterbourne began to laugh. "And does Randolph believe it?" he asked.

"I guess Randolph doesn't believe anything," said Daisy. Randolph's scepticism excited Winterbourne to farther hilarity, and he observed that Giovanelli was coming back to them. Daisy, observing it too, addressed herself again to her countryman. "Since you have mentioned it," she said, "I *am* engaged." . . . Winterbourne looked at her; he had stopped laughing. "You don't believe it!" she added.

He was silent a moment; and then, "Yes, I believe it!" he said.

"Oh, no, you don't," she answered. "Well, then—I am not!"

The young girl and her cicerone were on their way to the gate of the enclosure, so that Winterbourne, who had but lately entered, presently took leave of them. A week afterwards he went to dine at a beautiful villa on the Cælian Hill,[28] and, on arriving, dismissed his hired vehicle. The evening was charming, and he promised himself the satisfaction of walking home beneath the Arch of Constantine[29] and past the vaguely-lighted monuments of the Forum.[30] There was a waning moon in the sky, and her radiance was not brilliant, but she was veiled in a thin cloud-curtain which seemed to diffuse and equalise it. When, on his return from the villa (it was eleven o'clock), Winterbourne approached the dusky circle of the Colosseum,[31] it occurred to him, as a lover of the picturesque, that the interior, in the pale moonshine, would be well worth a glance. He turned aside and walked to one of the empty arches, near which, as he observed, an open carriage—one of the little Roman street-cabs—was stationed. Then he passed in among the cavernous shadows of the great structure, and emerged upon the clear and silent arena. The place had never seemed to him more impressive. One-half of the gigantic circus was in deep shade; the other was sleeping in the luminous dusk. As he stood there he began to murmur Byron's famous lines, out of "Manfred"; but before he had finished his quotation he remembered that if nocturnal meditations in the Colosseum are recommended by the poets, they are deprecated by the doctors. The historic atmosphere was there, certainly; but the historic atmosphere, scientifically considered, was no better than a villainous miasma. Winterbourne walked to the middle of the arena, to take a more general glance, intending thereafter to make a hasty retreat. The great cross in the centre was covered with shadow; it was only as he drew near it that he made it out distinctly. Then he saw that two persons were stationed upon the low steps which formed its base. One of these was a woman, seated; her companion was standing in front of her.

28 **Caelian Hill:** Home to the San Giovanni neighborhood in southern Italy.
29 **Arch of Constantine:** Erected in 315 to commemorate Constantine I's victory over Maxentius. Located between Palentine Hill and the Colosseum.
30 **Forum:** Site of Roman civic life for over five hundred years.
31 **Colosseum:** The best-known monument in ancient Rome, the site where gladiators and Christians clashed. It was built by the Flavian emperors between A.D. 70 and 80.

Presently the sound of the woman's voice came to him distinctly in the warm night-air. "Well, he looks at us as one of the old lions or tigers may have looked at the Christian martyrs!" These were the words he heard, in the familiar accent of Miss Daisy Miller.

"Let us hope he is not very hungry," responded the ingenious Giovanelli. "He will have to take me first; you will serve for dessert!"

Winterbourne stopped, with a sort of horror; and, it must be added, with a sort of relief. It was as if a sudden illumination had been flashed upon the ambiguity of Daisy's behaviour and the riddle had become easy to read. She was a young lady whom a gentleman need no longer be at pains to respect. He stood there looking at her—looking at her companion, and not reflecting that though he saw them vaguely, he himself must have been more brightly visible. He felt angry with himself that he had bothered so much about the right way of regarding Miss Daisy Miller. Then, as he was going to advance again, he checked himself; not from the fear that he was doing her injustice, but from a sense of the danger of appearing unbecomingly exhilarated by this sudden revulsion from cautious criticism. He turned away towards the entrance of the place; but as he did so he heard Daisy speak again.

"Why, it was Mr. Winterbourne! He saw me—and he cuts me!"

What a clever little reprobate she was, and how smartly she played an injured innocence! But he wouldn't cut her. Winterbourne came forward again, and went towards the great cross. Daisy had got up; Giovanelli lifted his hat. Winterbourne had now begun to think simply of the craziness, from a sanitary point of view, of a delicate young girl lounging away the evening in this nest of malaria. What if she *were* a clever little reprobate? that was no reason for her dying of the *perniciosa*.[32] "How long have you been here?" he asked, almost brutally.

Daisy, lovely in the flattering moonlight, looked at him a moment. Then—"All the evening," she answered gently. . . . "I never saw anything so pretty."

"I am afraid," said Winterbourne, "that you will not think Roman fever very pretty. This is the way people catch it. I wonder," he added, turning to Giovanelli, "that you, a native Roman, should countenance such a terrible indiscretion."

"Ah," said the handsome native, "for myself, I am not afraid."

"Neither am I—for you! I am speaking for this young lady."

Giovanelli lifted his well-shaped eyebrows and showed his brilliant teeth. But he took Winterbourne's rebuke with docility. "I told the Signorina it was a grave indiscretion; but when was the Signorina ever prudent?"

"I never was sick, and I don't mean to be!" the Signorina declared. "I don't look like much, but I'm healthy! I was bound to see the Colosseum by moonlight; I shouldn't have wanted to go home without that; and we have had the most beautiful time, haven't we, Mr. Giovanelli? If there has been any danger, Eugenio can give me some pills. He has got some splendid pills."

"I should advise you," said Winterbourne, "to drive home as fast as possible and take one!"

---

32  *perniciosa:* Italian. Pernicious malaria.

"What you say is very wise," Giovanelli rejoined. "I will go and make sure the carriage is at hand." And he went forward rapidly.

Daisy followed with Winterbourne. He kept looking at her; she seemed not in the least embarrassed. Winterbourne said nothing; Daisy chattered about the beauty of the place. "Well, I *have* seen the Colosseum by moonlight!" she exclaimed. "That's one good thing." Then, noticing Winterbourne's silence, she asked him why he didn't speak. He made no answer; he only began to laugh. They passed under one of the dark archways; Giovanelli was in front with the carriage. Here Daisy stopped a moment, looking at the young American. "*Did* you believe I was engaged the other day?" she asked.

"It doesn't matter what I believed the other day," said Winterbourne, still laughing.

"Well, what do you believe now?"

"I believe that it makes very little difference whether you are engaged or not!"

He felt the young girl's pretty eyes fixed upon him through the thick gloom of the archway; she was apparently going to answer. But Giovanelli hurried her forward. "Quick, quick," he said; "if we get in by midnight we are quite safe."

Daisy took her seat in the carriage, and the fortunate Italian placed himself beside her. "Don't forget Eugenio's pills!" said Winterbourne, as he lifted his hat.

"I don't care," said Daisy, in a little strange tone, "whether I have Roman fever or not!" Upon this the cab-driver cracked his whip, and they rolled away over the desultory patches of the antique pavement.

Winterbourne—to do him justice, as it were—mentioned to no one that he had encountered Miss Miller, at midnight, in the Colosseum with a gentleman; but nevertheless, a couple of days later, the fact of her having been there under these circumstances was known to every member of the little American circle, and commented accordingly. Winterbourne reflected that they had of course known it at the hotel, and that, after Daisy's return, there had been an exchange of jokes between the porter and the cab-driver. But the young man was conscious at the same moment that it had ceased to be a matter of serious regret to him that the little American flirt should be "talked about" by low-minded menials. These people, a day or two later, had serious information to give: the little American flirt was alarmingly ill. Winterbourne, when the rumour came to him, immediately went to the hotel for more news. He found that two or three charitable friends had preceded him, and that they were being entertained in Mrs. Miller's salon by Randolph.

"It's going round at night," said Randolph—"that's what made her sick. She's always going round at night. I shouldn't think she'd want to—it's so plaguey dark. You can't see anything here at night, except when there's a moon. In America there's always a moon!" Mrs. Miller was invisible; she was now, at least, giving her daughter the advantage of her society. It was evident that Daisy was dangerously ill.

Winterbourne went often to ask for news of her, and once he saw Mrs. Miller, who, though deeply alarmed, was—rather to his surprise—perfectly composed, and, as it appeared, a most efficient and judicious nurse. She talked a good deal about Dr. Davis, but Winterbourne paid her the compliment of saying to himself that she was not, after all, such a monstrous goose. "Daisy spoke of you the other day," she said to him. "Half the time she doesn't know what she's saying, but that time I think she did. She gave me a message; she told me to tell you. She told me to tell you that she never was engaged to that handsome Italian. I am sure I am very glad; Mr. Giovanelli hasn't been near us since she was taken ill. I thought he was so much of a gentleman; but I don't call that very polite! A lady told me that he was afraid I was angry with him for taking Daisy round at night. Well, so I am; but I suppose he knows I'm a lady. I would scorn to scold him. Any way, she says she's not engaged. I don't know why she wanted you to know; but she said to me three times—'Mind you tell Mr. Winterbourne.' And then she told me to ask if you remembered the time you went to that castle, in Switzerland. But I said I wouldn't give any such messages as that. Only, if she is not engaged, I'm sure I'm glad to know it."

But, as Winterbourne had said, it mattered very little. A week after this the poor girl died; it had been a terrible case of the fever. Daisy's grave was in the little Protestant cemetery, in an angle of the wall of imperial Rome, beneath the cypresses and the thick spring-flowers. Winterbourne stood there beside it, with a number of other mourners; a number larger than the scandal excited by the young lady's career would have led you to expect. Near him stood Giovanelli, who came nearer still before Winterbourne turned away. Giovanelli was very pale; on this occasion he had no flower in his button-hole; he seemed to wish to say something. At last he said, "She was the most beautiful young lady I ever saw, and the most amiable." And then he added in a moment, "And she was the most innocent."

Winterbourne looked at him, and presently repeated his words, "And the most innocent?"

"The most innocent!"

Winterbourne felt sore and angry. "Why the devil," he asked, "did you take her to that fatal place?"

Mr. Giovanelli's urbanity was apparently imperturbable. He looked on the ground a moment, and then he said, "For myself, I had no fear; and she wanted to go."

"That was no reason!" Winterbourne declared.

The subtle Roman again dropped his eyes. "If she had lived, I should have got nothing. She would never have married me, I am sure."

"She would never have married you?"

"For a moment I hoped so. But no. I am sure."

Winterbourne listened to him; he stood staring at the raw protuberance among the April daisies. When he turned away again Mr. Giovanelli, with his light slow step, had retired.

Winterbourne almost immediately left Rome; but the following summer he again met his aunt, Mrs. Costello, at Vevey. Mrs. Costello was fond of Vevey. In the interval Winterbourne had often thought of Daisy Miller and her mystifying manners. One day he spoke of her to his aunt—said it was on his conscience that he had done her injustice.

"I am sure I don't know," said Mrs. Costello. "How did your injustice affect her?"

"She sent me a message before her death which I didn't understand at the time. But I have understood it since. She would have appreciated one's esteem."

"Is that a modest way," asked Mrs. Costello, "of saying that she would have reciprocated one's affection?"

Winterbourne offered no answer to this question; but he presently said, "You were right in that remark that you made last summer. I was booked to make a mistake. I have lived too long in foreign parts."

Nevertheless, he went back to live at Geneva, whence there continue to come the most contradictory accounts of his motives of sojourn: a report that he is "studying" hard—an intimation that he is much interested in a very clever foreign lady.

# Sarah Orne Jewett

## (1849–1909)

Sarah Orne Jewett developed an eye for human experience and an ear for provincial dialect when her physician father took her along on his countryside visits to the ailing. In literature, Jewett found her earliest inspiration in the fiction of Harriet Beecher Stowe, and she was later influenced by Henry James and Gustave Flaubert, among others. At least part of this admiration was mutual, for of New England writers, Henry James found Jewett to be second only to Hawthorne. She also influenced the writing of her friend Willa Cather, whom she advised to abandon a job in publishing and become a full-time writer. Cather dedicated her novel *O Pioneers!* to Jewett. In addition, Kate Chopin and Edith Wharton came under her influence. Jewett published her first story at age eighteen; many of her stories appear in her 1886 collection, *The White Heron and Other Stories. The Country of the Pointed Firs*, set in rural Maine, was published in 1896. On writing, Jewett commented in "Looking Back on Girlhood": "My first thought flies back to those who taught me to observe, and to know the deep pleasures of simple things; and to be interested in the lives of people about me."

## *A White Heron*                                                                                     1886

### I

The woods were already filled with shadows one June evening, just before eight o'clock, though a bright sunset still glimmered faintly among the trunks of the trees. A little girl was driving home her cow, a plodding, dilatory, provoking creature in her behavior, but a valued companion for all that. They were going away from whatever light there was, and striking deep into the woods, but their feet were familiar with the path, and it was no matter whether their eyes could see it or not.

There was hardly a night the summer through when the old cow could be found waiting at the pasture bars; on the contrary, it was her greatest pleasure to hide herself away among the huckleberry bushes, and though she wore a loud bell she had made the discovery that if one stood perfectly still it would not ring. So Sylvia had to hunt for her until she found her, and call Co'! Co'! with never an answering Moo, until her childish patience was quite spent. If the creature had not given good milk and plenty of it, the case would have seemed very different to her owners. Besides, Sylvia had all the time there was, and very little use to make of it. Sometimes in pleasant weather it was a consolation to look upon the cow's pranks as an intelligent attempt to play hide and seek, and as the child had no playmates she lent herself to this amusement with a good deal of zest. Though this chase had been so long that the wary animal herself had given an unusual signal of her whereabouts, Sylvia had only laughed when she came upon Mistress Moolly at the swampside, and urged her affectionately home-ward with a twig of birch leaves. The old cow was not inclined to wander farther, she even turned in the right direction for once as they left the pasture, and stepped along the road at a good pace. She was quite ready to be milked now, and seldom stopped to browse. Sylvia wondered what her grandmother would say because they were so late. It was a great while since she had left home at half-past five o'clock, but everybody knew the difficulty of making this errand a short one. Mrs. Tilley had chased the hornéd torment too many summer evenings herself to blame any one else for linger-ing, and was only thankful as she waited that she had Sylvia, nowadays, to give such valuable assistance. The good woman suspected that Sylvia loitered occasionally on her own account; there never was such a child for straying about out-of-doors since the world was made! Everybody said that it was a good change for a little maid who had tried to grow for eight years in a crowded manufacturing town, but, as for Sylvia herself, it seemed as if she never had been alive at all before she came to live at the farm. She thought often with wistful compassion of a wretched geranium that be-longed to a town neighbor.

"'Afraid of folks,'" old Mrs. Tilley said to herself, with a smile, after she had made the unlikely choice of Sylvia from her daughter's houseful of children, and was re-turning to the farm. "'Afraid of folks,' they said! I guess she won't be troubled no great with 'em up to the old place!" When they reached the door of the lonely house and stopped to unlock it, and the cat came to purr loudly, and rub against them, a de-serted pussy, indeed, but fat with young robins, Sylvia whispered that this was a beau-tiful place to live in, and she never should wish to go home.

The companions followed the shady woodroad, the cow taking slow steps and the child very fast ones. The cow stopped long at the brook to drink, as if the pasture were not half a swamp, and Sylvia stood still and waited, letting her bare feet cool themselves in the shoal water, while the great twilight moths struck softly against her. She waded on through the brook as the cow moved away, and listened to the thrushes with a heart that beat fast with pleasure. There was a stirring in the great boughs overhead. They were full of little birds and beasts that seemed to be wide awake, and going about their world, or else saying good-night to each other in sleepy twitters. Sylvia herself felt sleepy as she walked along. However, it was not much farther to the house, and the air was soft and sweet. She was not often in the woods so late as this, and it made her feel as if she were a part of the gray shadows and the moving leaves. She was just thinking how long it seemed since she first came to the farm a year ago, and wondering if everything went on in the noisy town just the same as when she was there; the thought of the great red-faced boy who used to chase and frighten her made her hurry along the path to escape from the shadow of the trees.

Suddenly this little woods-girl is horror-stricken to hear a clear whistle not very far away. Not a bird's-whistle, which would have a sort of friendliness, but a boy's whistle, determined, and somewhat aggressive. Sylvia left the cow to whatever sad fate might await her, and stepped discreetly aside into the bushes, but she was just too late. The enemy had discovered her, and called out in a very cheerful and persuasive tone, "Halloa, little girl, how far is it to the road?" and trembling Sylvia answered almost inaudibly, "A good ways."

She did not dare to look boldly at the tall young man, who carried a gun over his shoulder, but she came out of her bush and again followed the cow, while he walked alongside.

"I have been hunting for some birds," the stranger said kindly, "and I have lost my way, and need a friend very much. Don't be afraid," he added gallantly. "Speak up and tell me what your name is, and whether you think I can spend the night at your house, and go out gunning early in the morning."

Sylvia was more alarmed than before. Would not her grandmother consider her much to blame? But who could have foreseen such an accident as this? It did not seem to be her fault, and she hung her head as if the stem of it were broken, but managed to answer "Sylvy," with much effort when her companion again asked her name.

Mrs. Tilley was standing in the doorway when the trio came into view. The cow gave a loud moo by way of explanation.

"Yes, you'd better speak up for yourself, you old trial! Where'd she tucked herself away this time, Sylvy?" But Sylvia kept an awed silence; she knew by instinct that her grandmother did not comprehend the gravity of the situation. She must be mistaking the stranger for one of the farmer-lads of the region.

The young man stood his gun beside the door, and dropped a lumpy game-bag beside it; then he bade Mrs. Tilley good-evening, and repeated his wayfarer's story, and asked if he could have a night's lodging.

"Put me anywhere you like," he said. "I must be off early in the morning, before day; but I am very hungry, indeed. You can give me some milk at any rate, that's plain."

"Dear sakes, yes," responded the hostess, whose long slumbering hospitality seemed to be easily awakened. "You might fare better if you went out to the main road a mile or so, but you're welcome to what we've got. I'll milk right off, and you make yourself at home. You can sleep on husks or feathers," she proffered graciously. "I raised them all myself. There's good pasturing for geese just below here towards the ma'sh. Now step round and set a plate for the gentleman, Sylvy!" And Sylvia promptly stepped. She was glad to have something to do, and she was hungry herself.

It was a surprise to find so clean and comfortable a little dwelling in this New England wilderness. The young man had known the horrors of its most primitive housekeeping, and the dreary squalor of that level of society which does not rebel at the companionship of hens. This was the best thrift of an old-fashioned farmstead, though on such a small scale that it seemed like a hermitage. He listened eagerly to the old woman's quaint talk, he watched Sylvia's pale face and shining gray eyes with ever growing enthusiasm, and insisted that this was the best supper he had eaten for a month, and afterward the new-made friends sat down in the door-way together while the moon came up.

Soon it would be berry-time, and Sylvia was a great help at picking. The cow was a good milker, though a plaguy thing to keep track of, the hostess gossiped frankly, adding presently that she had buried four children, so Sylvia's mother, and a son (who might be dead) in California were all the children she had left. "Dan, my boy, was a great hand to go gunning," she explained sadly. "I never wanted for pa'tridges or gray squer'ls while he was to home. He's been a great wand'rer, I expect, and he's no hand to write letters. There, I don't blame him, I'd ha' seen the world myself if it had been so I could."

"Sylvia takes after him," the grandmother continued affectionately, after a minute's pause. "There ain't a foot o' ground she don't know her way over, and the wild creaturs counts her one o' themselves. Squer'ls she'll tame to come an' feed right out o' her hands, and all sorts o' birds. Last winter she got the jaybirds to bangeing[1] here, and I believe she'd 'a' scanted herself of her own meals to have plenty to throw out amongst 'em, if I had n't kep' watch. Anything but crows, I tell her, I'm willin' to help support—though Dan he had a tamed one o' them that did seem to have reason same as folks. It was round here a good spell after he went away. Dan an' his father they did n't hitch,—but he never held up his head ag'in after Dan had dared him an' gone off."

The guest did not notice this hint of family sorrows in his eager interest in something else.

"So Sylvy knows all about birds, does she?" he exclaimed, as he looked round at the little girl who sat, very demure but increasingly sleepy, in the moonlight. "I am making a collection of birds myself. I have been at it ever since I was a boy." (Mrs. Tilley smiled.) "There are two or three very rare ones I have been hunting for these five years. I mean to get them on my own ground if they can be found."

"Do you cage 'em up?" asked Mrs. Tilley doubtfully, in response to this enthusiastic announcement.

"Oh no, they're stuffed and preserved, dozens and dozens of them," said the ornithologist, "and I have shot or snared every one myself. I caught a glimpse of a white heron a few miles from here on Saturday, and I have followed it in this direction. They

---

1 **bangeing:** New England term: loafing, lounging.

have never been found in this district at all. The little white heron, it is," and he turned again to look at Sylvia with the hope of discovering that the rare bird was one of her acquaintances.

But Sylvia was watching a hop-toad in the narrow footpath.

"You would know the heron if you saw it," the stranger continued eagerly. "A queer tall white bird with soft feathers and long thin legs. And it would have a nest perhaps in the top of a high tree, made of sticks, something like a hawk's nest."

Sylvia's heart gave a wild beat; she knew that strange white bird, and had once stolen softly near where it stood in some bright green swamp grass, away over at the other side of the woods. There was an open place where the sunshine always seemed strangely yellow and hot, where tall, nodding rushes grew, and her grandmother had warned her that she might sink in the soft black mud underneath and never be heard of more. Not far beyond were the salt marshes just this side the sea itself, which Sylvia wondered and dreamed much about, but never had seen, whose great voice could sometimes be heard above the noise of the woods on stormy nights.

"I can't think of anything I should like so much as to find that heron's nest," the handsome stranger was saying. "I would give ten dollars to anybody who could show it to me," he added desperately, "and I mean to spend my whole vacation hunting for it if need be. Perhaps it was only migrating, or had been chased out of its own region by some bird of prey."

Mrs. Tilley gave amazed attention to all this, but Sylvia still watched the toad, not divining, as she might have done at some calmer time, that the creature wished to get to its hole under the door-step, and was much hindered by the unusual spectators at that hour of the evening. No amount of thought, that night, could decide how many wished-for treasures the ten dollars, so lightly spoken of, would buy.

The next day the young sportsman hovered about the woods, and Sylvia kept him company, having lost her first fear of the friendly lad, who proved to be most kind and sympathetic. He told her many things about the birds and what they knew and where they lived and what they did with themselves. And he gave her a jack-knife, which she thought as great a treasure as if she were a desert-islander. All day long he did not once make her troubled or afraid except when he brought down some unsuspecting singing creature from its bough. Sylvia would have liked him vastly better without his gun; she could not understand why he killed the very birds he seemed to like so much. But as the day waned, Sylvia still watched the young man with loving admiration. She had never seen anybody so charming and delightful; the woman's heart, asleep in the child, was vaguely thrilled by a dream of love. Some premonition of that great power stirred and swayed these young creatures who traversed the solemn woodlands with soft-footed silent care. They stopped to listen to a bird's song; they pressed forward again eagerly, parting the branches—speaking to each other rarely and in whispers; the young man going first and Sylvia following, fascinated, a few steps behind, with her gray eyes dark with excitement.

She grieved because the longed-for white heron was elusive, but she did not lead the guest, she only followed, and there was no such thing as speaking first. The sound of her own unquestioned voice would have terrified her—it was hard enough to answer yes or no when there was need of that. At last evening began to fall, and they drove the cow home together, and Sylvia smiled with pleasure when they came to the place where she heard the whistle and was afraid only the night before.

## II

Half a mile from home, at the farther edge of the woods, where the land was highest, a great pine-tree stood, the last of its generation. Whether it was left for a boundary mark, or for what reason, no one could say; the wood-choppers who had felled its mates were dead and gone long ago, and a whole forest of sturdy trees, pines and oaks and maples, had grown again. But the stately head of this old pine towered above them all and made a landmark for sea and shore miles and miles away. Sylvia knew it well. She had always believed that whoever climbed to the top of it could see the ocean; and the little girl had often laid her hand on the great rough trunk and looked up wistfully at those dark boughs that the wind always stirred, no matter how hot and still the air might be below. Now she thought of the tree with a new excitement, for why, if one climbed it at break of day could not one see all the world, and easily discover from whence the white heron flew, and mark the place, and find the hidden nest?

What a spirit of adventure, what wild ambition! What fancied triumph and delight and glory for the later morning when she could make known the secret! It was almost too real and too great for the childish heart to bear.

All night the door of the little house stood open and the whippoorwills came and sang upon the very step. The young sportsman and his old hostess were sound asleep, but Sylvia's great design kept her broad awake and watching. She forgot to think of sleep. The short summer night seemed as long as the winter darkness, and at last when the whippoorwills ceased, and she was afraid the morning would after all come too soon, she stole out of the house and followed the pasture path through the woods, hastening toward the open ground beyond, listening with a sense of comfort and companionship to the drowsy twitter of a half-awakened bird, whose perch she had jarred in passing. Alas, if the great wave of human interest which flooded for the first time this dull little life should sweep away the satisfactions of an existence heart to heart with nature and the dumb life of the forest!

There was the huge tree asleep yet in the paling moonlight, and small and silly Sylvia began with utmost bravery to mount to the top of it, with tingling, eager blood coursing the channels of her whole frame, with her bare feet and fingers, that pinched and held like bird's claws to the monstrous ladder reaching up, up, almost to the sky itself. First she must mount the white oak tree that grew alongside, where she was almost lost among the dark branches and the green leaves heavy and wet with dew; a bird fluttered off its nest, and a red squirrel ran to and fro and scolded pettishly at the harmless housebreaker. Sylvia felt her way easily. She had often climbed there, and knew that higher still one of the oak's upper branches chafed against the pine trunk, just where its lower boughs were set close together. There, when she made the dangerous pass from one tree to the other, the great enterprise would really begin.

She crept out along the swaying oak limb at last, and took the daring step across into the old pine-tree. The way was harder than she thought; she must reach far and hold fast, the sharp dry twigs caught and held her and scratched her like angry talons, the pitch made her thin little fingers clumsy and stiff as she went round and round the tree's great stem, higher and higher upward. The sparrows and robins in the woods below were beginning to wake and twitter to the dawn, yet it seemed much lighter there aloft in the pine-tree, and the child knew she must hurry if her project were to be of any use.

The tree seemed to lengthen itself out as she went up, and to reach farther and farther upward. It was like a great main-mast to the voyaging earth; it must truly have been amazed that morning through all its ponderous frame as it felt this determined spark of human spirit wending its way from higher branch to branch. Who knows how steadily the least twigs held themselves to advantage this light, weak creature on her way! The old pine must have loved his new dependent. More than all the hawks, and bats, and moths, and even the sweet voiced thrushes, was the brave, beating heart of the solitary gray-eyed child. And the tree stood still and frowned away the winds that June morning while the dawn grew bright in the east.

Sylvia's face was like a pale star, if one had seen it from the ground, when the last thorny bough was past, and she stood trembling and tired but wholly triumphant, high in the treetop. Yes, there was the sea with the dawning sun making a golden dazzle over it, and toward that glorious east flew two hawks with slow-moving pinions. How low they looked in the air from that height when one had only seen them before far up, and dark against the blue sky. Their gray feathers were as soft as moths; they seemed only a little way from the tree, and Sylvia felt as if she too could go flying away among the clouds. Westward, the woodlands and farms reached miles and miles into the distance; here and there were church steeples, and white villages, truly it was a vast and awesome world!

The birds sang louder and louder. At last the sun came up bewilderingly bright. Sylvia could see the white sails of ships out at sea, and the clouds that were purple and rose-colored and yellow at first began to fade away. Where was the white heron's nest in the sea of green branches, and was this wonderful sight and pageant of the world the only reward for having climbed to such a giddy height? Now look down again, Sylvia, where the green marsh is set among the shining birches and dark hemlocks; there where you saw the white heron once you will see him again; look, look! a white spot of him like a single floating feather comes up from the dead hemlock and grows larger, and rises, and comes close at last, and goes by the landmark pine with steady sweep of wing and outstretched slender neck and crested head. And wait! wait! do not move a foot or a finger, little girl, do not send an arrow of light and consciousness from your two eager eyes, for the heron has perched on a pine bough not far beyond yours, and cries back to his mate on the nest and plumes his feathers for the new day!

The child gives a long sigh a minute later when a company of shouting cat-birds comes also to the tree, and vexed by their fluttering and lawlessness the solemn heron goes away. She knows his secret now, the wild, light, slender bird that floats and wavers, and goes back like an arrow presently to his home in the green world beneath. Then Sylvia, well satisfied, makes her perilous way down again, not daring to look far below the branch she stands on, ready to cry sometimes because her fingers ache and her lamed feet slip. Wondering over and over again what the stranger would say to her, and what he would think when she told him how to find his way straight to the heron's nest.

"Sylvy, Sylvy!" called the busy old grandmother again and again, but nobody answered, and the small husk bed was empty and Sylvia had disappeared.

The guest waked from a dream, and remembering his day's pleasure hurried to dress himself that might it sooner begin. He was sure from the way the shy little girl looked once or twice yesterday that she had at least seen the white heron, and now she must really be made to tell. Here she comes now, paler than ever, and her worn old frock is torn and tattered, and smeared with pine pitch. The grandmother and the sportsman stand in the door together and question her, and the splendid moment has come to speak of the dead hemlock-tree by the green marsh.

But Sylvia does not speak after all, though the old grandmother fretfully rebukes her, and the young man's kind, appealing eyes are looking straight in her own. He can make them rich with money; he has promised it, and they are poor now. He is so well worth making happy, and he waits to hear the story she can tell.

No, she must keep silence! What is it that suddenly forbids her and makes her dumb? Has she been nine years growing and now, when the great world for the first time puts out a hand to her, must she thrust it aside for a bird's sake? The murmur of the pine's green branches is in her ears, she remembers how the white heron came flying through the golden air and how they watched the sea and the morning together, and Sylvia cannot speak; she cannot tell the heron's secret and give its life away.

Dear loyalty, that suffered a sharp pang as the guest went away disappointed later in the day, that could have served and followed him and loved him as a dog loves! Many a night Sylvia heard the echo of his whistle haunting the pasture path as she came home with the loitering cow. She forgot even her sorrow at the sharp report of his gun and the sight of thrushes and sparrows dropping silent to the ground, their songs hushed and their pretty feathers stained and wet with blood. Were the birds better friends than their hunter might have been,—who can tell? Whatever treasures were lost to her, woodlands and summer-time, remember! Bring your gifts and graces and tell your secrets to this lonely country child!

# Guy de Maupassant

## (1850–1893)

"Life . . . is composed of the most unpredictable, disparate, and contradictory elements. It is brutal, inconsequential, and disconnected, full of inexplicable, illogical catastrophes. . . . [but] the writer . . . will take from this . . . only the details useful to his subject, and omit all the others." So said the French writer Guy de Maupassant in his preface to his 1888 novel, *Pierre et Jean*. A distant relative of Gustave Flaubert, he became this luminary's student at the age of twenty-two and learned from him to search for the hitherto unseen and unknown in ordinary existence. Compared with the fiction of his predecessors, the stories of Maupassant are technically concise and in subject amoral. In works like "The Necklace," Maupassant is concerned with the way the slightest mistake, like a twig turning the course of a stream, may alter the direction of a lifetime. Maupassant was influenced by a Parisian group of writers that included Emile Zola and Ivan Turgenev. His first short story, an 1880 instant sensation, focused on prostitution and hypocrisy and was picturesquely entitled "Ball of Fat." Maupassant wrote roughly three hundred short stories, the most well known published in the collections *La Maison Tellier*, *Mademoiselle Fifi*, *Contes de la Becasse*, *Contes et Nouvelles*, and *L'Inutile Beauté*. All were published during the single decade following the year 1880, when Flaubert, after seven years of tutelage, finally allowed Maupassant to publish under his own name.

## The Necklace                                                          1884

TRANSLATED BY BRANDER MATTHEWS

She was one of those pretty and charming girls, born by a blunder of destiny in a family of employees. She had no dowry, no expectations, no means of being known, understood, loved, married by a man rich and distinguished; and she let them make a match for her with a little clerk in the Department of Education.

She was simple since she could not be adorned; but she was unhappy as though kept out of her own class; for women have no caste and no descent, their beauty, their grace, and their charm serving them instead of birth and fortune. Their native keenness, their instinctive elegance, their flexibility of mind, are their only hierarchy; and these make the daughters of the people the equals of the most lofty dames.

She suffered intensely, feeling herself born for every delicacy and every luxury. She suffered from the poverty of her dwelling, from the worn walls, the abraded chairs, the ugliness of the stuffs. All these things, which another woman of her caste would not even have noticed, tortured her and made her indignant. The sight of the little girl from Brittany who did her humble housework awake in her desolated regrets and distracted dreams. She let her mind dwell on the quiet vestibules, hung with Oriental tapestries, lighted by tall lamps of bronze, and on the two tall footmen in knee breeches who dozed in the large armchairs, made drowsy by the heat of the furnace. She let her mind dwell on the large parlors, decked with old silk, with their delicate furniture, supporting precious bric-a-brac, and on the coquettish little rooms, perfumed, prepared for the five o'clock chat with the most intimate friends, men well known and sought after, whose attentions all women envied and desired.

When she sat down to dine, before a tablecloth three days old, in front of her husband, who lifted the cover of the tureen, declaring with an air of satisfaction, "Ah, the good *pot-au-feu*. I don't know anything better than that," she was thinking of delicate repasts, with glittering silver, with tapestries peopling the walls with ancient figures and with strange birds in a fairy-like forest; she was thinking of exquisite dishes, served in marvelous platters, of compliment whispered and heard with a sphinx-like smile, while she was eating the rosy flesh of a trout or the wings of a quail.

She had no dresses, no jewelry, nothing. And she loved nothing else; she felt herself made for that only. She would so much have liked to please, to be envied, to be seductive and sought after.

She had a rich friend, a comrade of her convent days, whom she did not want to go and see any more, so much did she suffer as she came away. And she wept all day long, from chagrin, from regret, from despair, and from distress.

But one evening her husband came in with a proud air, holding in his hand a large envelope.

"There," said he, "there's something for you."

She quickly tore the paper and took out of it a printed card which bore these words:—

"The Minister of Education and Mme. Georges Rampouneau beg M. and Mme. Loisel to do them the honor to pass the evening with them at the palace of the Ministry, on Monday, January 18."

Instead of being delighted, as her husband hoped, she threw the invitation on the table with annoyance, murmuring—

"What do you want me to do with that?"

"But, my dear, I thought you would be pleased. You never go out, and here's a chance, a fine one. I had the hardest work to get it. Everybody is after them; they are greatly sought for and not many are given to the clerks. You will see there all the official world."

She looked at him with an irritated eye and she declared with impatience:—

"What do you want me to put on my back to go there?"

He had not thought of that; he hesitated:—

"But the dress in which you go to the theater. That looks very well to me—"

He shut up, astonished and distracted at seeing that his wife was weeping. Two big tears were descending slowly from the corners of the eyes to the corners of the mouth. He stuttered:—

"What's the matter? What's the matter?"

But by a violent effort she had conquered her trouble, and she replied in a calm voice as she wiped her damp cheeks:—

"Nothing. Only I have no clothes, and in consequence I cannot go to this party. Give your card to some colleague whose wife has a better outfit than I."

He was disconsolate. He began again:—

"See here, Mathilde, how much would this cost, a proper dress, which would do on other occasions; something very simple?"

She reflected a few seconds, going over her calculations, and thinking also of the sum which she might ask without meeting an immediate refusal and a frightened exclamation from the frugal clerk.

At last, she answered hesitatingly:—

"I don't know exactly, but it seems to me that with four hundred francs I might do it."

He grew a little pale, for he was reserving just that sum to buy a gun and treat himself to a little shooting, the next summer, on the plain of Nanterre, with some friends who used to shoot larks there on Sundays.

But he said:—

"All right. I will give you four hundred francs. But take care to have a pretty dress."

The day of the party drew near, and Mme. Loisel seemed sad, restless, anxious. Yet her dress was ready. One evening her husband said to her:—

"What's the matter? Come, now, you have been quite queer these last three days."

And she answered:—

"It annoys me not to have a jewel, not a single stone, to put on. I shall look like distress. I would almost rather not go to this party."

He answered:—

"You will wear some natural flowers. They are very stylish this time of the year. For ten francs you will have two or three magnificent roses."

But she was not convinced.

"No; there's nothing more humiliating than to look poor among a lot of rich women."

But her husband cried:—

"What a goose you are! Go find your friend, Mme. Forester, and ask her to lend you some jewelry. You know her well enough to do that."

She gave a cry of joy:—

"That's true. I had not thought of it."

The next day she went to her friend's and told her about her distress.

Mme. Forester went to her mirrored wardrobe, took out a large casket, brought it, opened it, and said to Mme. Loisel:—

"Choose, my dear."

She saw at first bracelets, then a necklace of pearls, then a Venetian cross of gold set with precious stones of an admirable workmanship. She tried on the ornaments before the glass, hesitated, and could not decide to take them off and to give them up. She kept on asking:—

"You haven't anything else?"

"Yes, yes. Look. I do not know what will happen to please you."

All at once she discovered, in a box of black satin, a superb necklace of diamonds, and her heart began to beat with boundless desire. Her hands trembled in taking it up. She fastened it round her throat, on her high dress, and remained in ecstasy before herself.

Then, she asked, hesitating, full of anxiety:—

"Can you lend me this, only this?"

"Yes, yes, certainly."

She sprang to her friend's neck, kissed her with ardor, and then escaped with her treasure.

The day of the party arrived. Mme. Loisel was a success. She was the prettiest of them all, elegant, gracious, smiling, and mad with joy. All the men were looking at her, inquiring her name, asking to be introduced. All the attaches of the Cabinet wanted to dance with her. The Minister took notice of her.

She danced with delight, with passion, intoxicated with pleasure, thinking of nothing, in the triumph of her beauty, in the glory of her success, in a sort of cloud of happiness made up of all these tributes, of all the admirations, of all these awakened desires, of this victory so complete and so sweet to a woman's heart.

She went away about four in the morning. Since midnight—her husband has been dozing in a little anteroom with three other men whose wives were having a good time.

He threw over her shoulders the wraps he had brought to go home in, modest garments of every-day life, the poverty of which was out of keeping with the elegance of the ball dress. She felt this, and wanted to fly so as not to be noticed by the other women, who were wrapping themselves in rich furs.

Loisel kept her back—

"Wait a minute; you will catch cold outside; I'll call a cab."

But she did not listen to him, and went downstairs rapidly. When they were in the street, they could not find a carriage, and they set out in search of one, hailing the drivers whom they saw passing in the distance.

They went down toward the Seine, disgusted, shivering. Finally, they found on the Quai one of those old night-hawk cabs which one sees in Paris only after night has fallen, as though they are ashamed of their misery in the daytime.

It brought them to their door, rue des Martyrs; and they went up their own stairs sadly. For her it was finished. And he was thinking that he would have to be at the Ministry at ten o'clock.

She took off the wraps with which she had covered her shoulders, before the mirror, so as to see herself once more in her glory. But suddenly she gave a cry. She no longer had the necklace around her throat!

Her husband, half undressed already, asked—

"What is the matter with you?"

She turned to him, terror-stricken:—

"I—I—I have not Mme. Forester's diamond necklace!"

He jumped up, frightened—

"What? How? It is not possible!"

And they searched in the folds of the dress, in the folds of the wrap, in the pockets, everywhere. They did not find it.

He asked:—

"Are you sure you still had it when you left the ball?"

"Yes, I touched it in the vestibule of the Ministry."

"But if you had lost it in the street, we should have heard it fall. It must be in the cab."

"Yes. That is probable. Did you take the number?"

"No. And you—you did not even look at it?"

"No."

They gazed at each other, crushed. At last Loisel dressed himself again.

"I'm going," he said, "back the whole distance we came on foot, to see if I cannot find it."

And he went out. She stayed there, in her ball dress, without strength to go to bed, overwhelmed, on a chair, without a fire, without a thought.

Her husband came back about seven o'clock. He had found nothing.

Then he went to police headquarters, to the newspapers to offer a reward, to the cab company; he did everything, in fact, that a trace of hope could urge him to.

She waited all day, in the same dazed state in face of this horrible disaster.

Loisel came back in the evening, with his face worn and white; he had discovered nothing.

"You must write to your friend," he said, "that you have broken the clasp of her necklace and that you are having it repaired. That will give us time to turn around."

She wrote as he dictated.

At the end of a week they had lost all hope. And Loisel, aged by five years, declared:—

"We must see how we can replace those jewels."

The next day they took the case which had held them to the jeweler whose name was in the cover. He consulted his books.

"It was not I, madam, who sold this necklace. I only supplied the case."

Then they went from jeweler to jeweler, looking for a necklace like the other, consulting their memory,—sick both of them with grief and anxiety.

In a shop in the Palais Royal, they found a diamond necklace that seemed to them absolutely like the one they were seeking. It was priced forty thousand francs. They could have it for thirty-six.

They begged the jeweler not to sell it for three days. And they made a bargain that he should take it back for thirty-four thousand, if the first was found before the end of February.

Loisel possessed eighteen thousand francs which his father had left him. He had to borrow the remainder.

He borrowed, asking a thousand francs from one, five hundred from another, five here, three louis there. He gave promissory notes, made ruinous agreements, dealt with usurers, with all kinds of lenders. He compromised the end of his life, risked his signature without even knowing whether it could be honored; and frightened by all the anguish of the future, by the black misery which was about to settle down on him, by the perspective of all sorts of physical deprivations and of all sorts of moral tortures, he went to buy the new diamond necklace, laying down on the jeweler's counter thirty-six thousand francs.

When Mme. Loisel took back the necklace to Mme. Forester, the latter said, with an irritated air:—

"You ought to have brought it back sooner, for I might have needed it."

She did not open the case, which her friend had been fearing. If she had noticed the substitution, what would she have thought? What would she have said? Might she not have been taken for a thief?

Mme. Loisel learned the horrible life of the needy She made the best of it, moreover, frankly, heroically. The frightful debt must be paid. She would pay it. They dismissed the servant; they changed their rooms; they took an attic under the roof.

She learned the rough work of the household, the odious labors of the kitchen. She washed the dishes, wearing out her pink nails on the greasy pots and the bottoms of the pans. She washed the dirty linen, the shirts and the towels, which she dried on a rope; she carried down the garbage to the street every morning, and she carried up the water, pausing for breath on every floor. And, dressed like a woman of the people, she went to the fruiterer, the grocer, the butcher, a basket on her arm, bargaining, insulted, fighting for her wretched money, sou by sou.

Every month they had to pay notes, to renew others to gain time.

The husband worked in the evening keeping up the books of a shopkeeper, and at night often he did copying at five sous the page.

And this life lasted ten years.

At the end of ten years they had paid everything back, everything, with the rates of usury and all the accumulation of heaped-up interest.

Mme. Loisel seemed aged now. She had become the robust woman, hard and rough, of a poor household. Badly combed, with her skirts awry and her hands red, her voice was loud, and she washed the floor with splashing water.

But sometimes, when her husband was at the office, she sat down by the window and she thought of that evening long ago, of that ball, where she had been so beautiful and so admired.

What would have happened if she had not lost that necklace? Who knows? Who knows? How singular life is, how changeable! What a little thing it takes to save you or to lose you.

Then, one Sunday, as she was taking a turn in the Champs Elysées, as a recreation after the labors of the week, she perceived suddenly a woman walking with a child. It was Mme. Forester, still young, still beautiful, still seductive.

Mme. Loisel felt moved.  Should she speak to her? Yes, certainly. And now that she had paid up, she would tell her all. Why not?

She drew near.

"Good morning, Jeanne."

The other did not recognize her, astonished to be hailed thus familiarly by this woman of the people. She hesitated—

"But—madam—I don't know—are you not making a mistake?"

"No. I am Mathilde Loisel."

Her friend gave a cry—

"Oh!—My poor Mathilde, how you are changed."

"Yes, I have had hard days since I saw you, and many troubles,—and that because of you."

"Of me?—How so?"

"You remember that diamond necklace that you lent me to go to the ball at the Ministry?"

"Yes. And then?"

"Well, I lost it."

"How can that be?—since you brought it back to me?"

"I brought you back another just like it. And now for ten years we have been paying for it. You will understand that it was not easy for us, who had nothing. At last, it is done, and I am mighty glad."

Mme. Forester had guessed.

"You say that you bought a diamond necklace to replace mine?"

"Yes. You did not notice it, even, did you? They were exactly alike?"

And she smiled with proud and naïve joy.

Mme. Forester, much moved, took her by both hands:—

"Oh, my poor Mathilde. But mine were false. At most they were worth five hundred francs!"

# Herman Melville

## (1819–1891)

Melville began his career by chronicling his experiences at sea, recorded in a series of novels written between 1845 and 1851. The most famous, *Moby-Dick*, was conceived and completed under the influence of Melville's contemporary, Nathaniel Hawthorne (with whom Melville shared the experience of working in a New England customs house). The work following *Moby-Dick*, entitled *Pierre*, was difficult for critics to comprehend and not generally well received, and so

Melville turned to writing short stories. Of writing and in particular of Hawthorne's short stories, Melville wrote, "In certain moods, no man can weigh this world, without throwing in something, somehow like Original Sin, to strike the uneven balance." His own spirituality and dark vision are evident in short stories such as "Bartleby the Scrivener" and "Benito Cereno" and in the short novel *Billy Budd*. His style reflects the encounter between nineteenth-century American romanticism and New England realism.

---

## Bartleby, the Scrivener                                                          1853

### A Story of Wall-Street

I am a rather elderly man. The nature of my avocations, for the last thirty years, has brought me into more than ordinary contact with what would seem an interesting and somewhat singular set of men, of whom, as yet, nothing, that I know of, has ever been written—I mean, the law-copyists, or scriveners. I have known very many of them, professionally and privately, and, if I pleased, could relate divers histories, at which good-natured gentlemen might smile, and sentimental souls might weep. But I waive the biographies of all other scriveners, for a few passages in the life of Bartleby, who was a scrivener, the strangest I ever saw, or heard of. While, of other law-copyists, I might write the complete life, of Bartleby nothing of that sort can be done. I believe that no materials exist, for a full and satisfactory biography of this man. It is an irreparable loss to literature. Bartleby was one of those beings of whom nothing is ascertainable, except from the original sources, and, in his case, those are very small. What my own astonished eyes saw of Bartleby, *that* is all I know of him, except, indeed, one vague report, which will appear in the sequel.

Ere introducing the scrivener, as he first appeared to me, it is fit I make some mention of myself, my *employés,* my business, my chambers, and general surroundings; because some such description is indispensable to an adequate understanding of the chief character about to be presented. Imprimis: I am a man who, from his youth upwards, has been filled with a profound conviction that the easiest way of life is the best. Hence, though I belong to a profession proverbially energetic and nervous, even to turbulence, at times, yet nothing of that sort have I ever suffered to invade my peace. I am one of those unambitious lawyers who never address a jury, or in any way draw down public applause; but, in the cool tranquillity of a snug retreat, do a snug business among rich men's bonds, and mortgages, and title-deeds. All who know me, consider me an eminently *safe* man. The late John Jacob Astor,[1] a personage little given to poetic enthusiasm, had no hesitation in pronouncing my first grand point to be prudence; my next, method. I do not speak it in vanity, but simply record the fact,

---

1 **John Jacob Astor:** American millionaire (1763–1848). Born in Germany, Astor made his fortune in the fur trades and real estate. Famous but unpopular in the nineteenth century, Astor was often singled out as a symbol of corrupt big business.

that I was not unemployed in my profession by the late John Jacob Astor; a name which, I admit, I love to repeat; for it hath a rounded and orbicular sound to it, and rings like unto bullion. I will freely add, that I was not insensible to the late John Jacob Astor's good opinion.

Some time prior to the period at which this little history begins, my avocations had been largely increased. The good old office, now extinct in the State of New York, of a Master in Chancery,[2] had been conferred upon me. It was not a very arduous office, but very pleasantly remunerative. I seldom lose my temper; much more seldom indulge in dangerous indignation at wrongs and outrages; but I must be permitted to be rash here and declare, that I consider the sudden and violent abrogation of the office of Master in Chancery, by the new Constitution, as a ———premature act; inasmuch as I had counted upon a life-lease of the profits, whereas I only received those of a few short years. But this is by the way.

My chambers were up stairs, at No.——Wall Street. At one end, they looked upon the white wall of the interior of a spacious sky-light shaft, penetrating the building from top to bottom.

This view might have been considered rather tame than otherwise, deficient in what landscape painters call "life." But, if so, the view from the other end of my chambers offered, at least, a contrast, if nothing more. In that direction, my windows commanded an unobstructed view of a lofty brick wall, black by age and everlasting shade; which wall required no spy-glass to bring out its lurking beauties, but, for the benefit of all near-sighted spectators, was pushed up to within ten feet of my windowpanes. Owing to the great height of the surrounding buildings, and my chambers being on the second floor, the interval between this wall and mine not a little resembled a huge square cistern.

At the period just preceding the advent of Bartleby, I had two persons as copyists in my employment, and a promising lad as an office-boy. First, Turkey; second, Nippers; third, Ginger Nut. These may seem names, the like of which are not usually found in the Directory. In truth, they were nicknames, mutually conferred upon each other by my three clerks, and were deemed expressive of their respective persons or characters. Turkey was a short, pursy[3] Englishman, of about my own age—that is, somewhere not far from sixty. In the morning, one might say, his face was of a fine florid hue, but after twelve o'clock, meridian—his dinner hour—it blazed like a grate full of Christmas coals; and continued blazing—but, as it were, with a gradual wane—till six o'clock, P.M., or thereabouts; after which, I saw no more of the proprietor of the face, which, gaining its meridian with the sun, seemed to set with it, to rise, culminate, and decline the following day, with the like regularity and undiminished glory. There are many singular coincidences I have known in the course of my life, not the least among which was the fact, that, exactly when Turkey displayed his fullest

2 **Master in Chancery:** A lawyer who is guaranteed fees regardless of the outcome of the case. The deletion of the position was due to a change in New York property laws, which were once held to a standard of natural rights and now were held to a standard of written law.
3 **pursy:** Short-winded because of obesity.

beams from his red and radiant countenance, just then, too, at that critical moment, began the daily period when I considered his business capacities as seriously disturbed for the remainder of the twenty-four hours. Not that he was absolutely idle, or averse to business then; far from it. The difficulty was, he was apt to be altogether too energetic. There was a strange, inflamed, flurried, flighty recklessness of activity about him. He would be incautious in dipping his pen into his inkstand. All his blots upon my documents were dropped there after twelve o'clock, meridian. Indeed, not only would he be reckless, and sadly given to making blots in the afternoon, but, some days, he went further, and was rather noisy. At such times, too, his face flamed with augmented blazonry, as if cannel coal had been heaped on anthracite. He made an unpleasant racket with his chair; spilled his sand-box; in mending his pens, impatiently split them all to pieces, and threw them on the floor in a sudden passion; stood up, and leaned over his table, boxing his papers about in a most indecorous manner, very sad to behold in an elderly man like him. Nevertheless, as he was in many ways a most valuable person to me, and all the time before twelve o'clock, meridian, was the quickest, steadiest creature, too, accomplishing a great deal of work in a style not easily to be matched—for these reasons, I was willing to overlook his eccentricities, though, indeed, occasionally, I remonstrated with him. I did this very gently, however, because, though the civilest, nay, the blandest and most reverential of men in the morning, yet, in the afternoon, he was disposed, upon provocation, to be slightly rash with his tongue—in fact, insolent. Now, valuing his morning services as I did, and resolved not to lose them—yet, at the same time, made uncomfortable by his inflamed ways after twelve o'clock—and being a man of peace, unwilling by my admonitions to call forth unseemly retorts from him, I took upon me, one Saturday noon (he was always worse on Saturdays) to hint to him, very kindly, that, perhaps, now that he was growing old, it might be well to abridge his labors; in short, he need not come to my chambers after twelve o'clock, but, dinner over, had best go home to his lodgings, and rest himself till tea-time. But no; he insisted upon his afternoon devotions. His countenance became intolerably fervid, as he oratorically assured me—gesticulating with a long ruler at the other end of the room—that if his services in the morning were useful, how indispensable, then, in the afternoon?

"With submission, sir," said Turkey, on this occasion, "I consider myself your right-hand man. In the morning I but marshal and deploy my columns; but in the afternoon I put myself at their head, and gallantly charge the foe, thus"—and he made a violent thrust with the ruler.

"But the blots, Turkey," intimated I.

"True; but, with submission, sir, behold these hairs! I am getting old. Surely, sir, a blot or two of a warm afternoon is not to be severely urged against gray hairs. Old age—even if it blot the page—is honorable. With submission, sir, we *both* are getting old."

This appeal to my fellow-feeling was hardly to be resisted. At all events, I saw that go he would not. So, I made up my mind to let him stay, resolving, nevertheless, to see to it that, during the afternoon, he had to do with my less important papers.

Nippers, the second on my list, was a whiskered, sallow, and, upon the whole, rather piratical-looking young man, of about five-and-twenty. I always deemed him the victim of two evil powers—ambition and indigestion. The ambition was evinced by a certain impatience of the duties of a mere copyist, an unwarrantable usurpation of strictly professional affairs, such as the original drawing up of legal documents. The indigestion seemed betokened in an occasional nervous testiness and grinning irritability, causing the teeth to audibly grind together over mistakes committed in copying; unnecessary maledictions, hissed, rather than spoken, in the heat of business; and especially by a continual discontent with the height of the table where he worked. Though of a very ingenious mechanical turn, Nippers could never get this table to suit him. He put chips under it, blocks of various sorts, bits of pasteboard, and at last went so far as to attempt an exquisite adjustment, by final pieces of folded blotting-paper. But no invention would answer. If, for the sake of easing his back, he brought the table-lid at a sharp angle well up towards his chin, and wrote there like a man using the steep roof of a Dutch house for his desk, then he declared that it stopped the circulation in his arms. If now he lowered the table to his waistbands, and stooped over it in writing, then there was a sore aching in his back. In short, the truth of the matter was, Nippers knew not what he wanted. Or, if he wanted anything, it was to be rid of a scrivener's table altogether. Among the manifestations of his diseased ambition was a fondness he had for receiving visits from certain ambiguous-looking fellows in seedy coats, whom he called his clients. Indeed, I was aware that not only was he, at times, considerable of a ward-politician, but he occasionally did a little business at the Justices' courts, and was not unknown on the steps of the Tombs.[4] I have good reason to believe, however, that one individual who called upon him at my chambers, and who, with a grand air, he insisted was his client, was no other than a dun,[5] and the alleged titledeed, a bill. But, with all his failings, and the annoyances he caused me, Nippers, like his compatriot Turkey, was a very useful man to me; wrote a neat, swift hand; and, when he chose, was not deficient in a gentlemanly sort of deportment. Added to this, he always dressed in a gentlemanly sort of way; and so, incidentally, reflected credit upon my chambers. Whereas, with respect to Turkey, I had much ado to keep him from being a reproach to me. His clothes were apt to look oily, and smell of eating-houses. He wore his pantaloons very loose and baggy in summer. His coats were execrable; his hat not to be handled. But while the hat was a thing of indifference to me, inasmuch as his natural civility and deference, as a dependent Englishman, always led him to doff it the moment he entered the room, yet his coat was another matter. Concerning his coats, I reasoned with him; but with no effect. The truth was, I suppose, that a man with so small an income could not afford to sport such a lustrous face and a lustrous coat at one and the same time. As Nippers once observed, Turkey's money went chiefly for red ink. One winter day, I presented Turkey with a highly respectable-looking coat of my own—a padded gray coat, of a most comfortable warmth, and which buttoned straight up from the knee to the neck. I thought Turkey would appreciate the favor, and abate his rashness and

4 **Tombs:** New York prison. Nippers is perhaps arranging bail for prisoners.
5 **dun:** Persistent bill collector.

obstreperousness of afternoons. But no; I verily believe that buttoning himself up in so downy and blanket-like a coat had a pernicious effect upon him—upon the same principle that too much oats are bad for horses. In fact, precisely as a rash, restive horse is said to feel his oats, so Turkey felt his coat. It made him insolent. He was a man whom prosperity harmed.

Though, concerning the self-indulgent habits of Turkey, I had my own private surmises, yet, touching Nippers, I was well persuaded that, whatever might be his faults in other respects, he was, at least, a temperate young man. But, indeed, nature herself seemed to have been his vintner, and, at his birth, charged him so thoroughly with an irritable, brandy-like disposition, that all subsequent potations were needless. When I consider how, amid the stillness of my chambers, Nippers would sometimes impatiently rise from his seat, and stooping over his table, spread his arms wide apart, seize the whole desk, and move it, and jerk it, with a grim, grinding motion on the floor, as if the table were a perverse voluntary agent, intent on thwarting and vexing him, I plainly perceive that, for Nippers, brandy-and-water were altogether superfluous.

It was fortunate for me that, owing to its peculiar cause—indigestion—the irritability and consequent nervousness of Nippers were mainly observable in the morning, while in the afternoon he was comparatively mild. So that, Turkey's paroxysms only coming on about twelve o'clock, I never had to do with their eccentricities at one time. Their fits relieved each other, like guards. When Nippers's was on, Turkey's was off; and *vice versa*. This was a good natural arrangement, under the circumstances.

Ginger Nut, the third on my list, was a lad, some twelve years old. His father was a carman, ambitious of seeing his son on the bench instead of a cart, before he died. So he sent him to my office, as student at law, errand-boy, cleaner and sweeper, at the rate of one dollar a week. He had a little desk to himself, but he did not use it much. Upon inspection, the drawer exhibited a great array of the shells of various sorts of nuts. Indeed, to this quick-witted youth, the whole noble science of the law was contained in a nut-shell. Not the least among the employments of Ginger Nut, as well as one which he discharged with the most alacrity, was his duty as cake and apple purveyor for Turkey and Nippers. Copying law-papers being proverbially a dry, husky sort of business, my two scriveners were fain to moisten their mouths very often with Spitzenbergs,[6] to be had at the numerous stalls nigh the Custom House and Post Office. Also, they sent Ginger Nut very frequently for that peculiar cake—small, flat, round, and very spicy—after which he had been named by them. Of a cold morning, when business was but dull, Turkey would gobble up scores of these cakes, as if they were mere wafers—indeed, they sell them at the rate of six or eight for a penny—the scrape of his pen blending with the crunching of the crisp particles in his mouth. Of all the fiery afternoon blunders and flurried rashnesses of Turkey, was his once moistening a ginger-cake between his lips, and clapping it on to a mortgage, for a seal. I came within an ace of dismissing him then. But he mollified me by making an oriental bow, and saying—

6 **Spitzenbergs:** Variety of apple.

"With submission, sir, it was generous of me to find you in stationery on my own account."

Now my original business—that of a conveyancer[7] and title hunter, and drawer-up of recondite documents of all sorts—was considerably increased by receiving the Master's office. There was now great work for scriveners. Not only must I push the clerks already with me, but I must have additional help.

In answer to my advertisement, a motionless young man one morning stood upon my office threshold, the door being open, for it was summer. I can see that figure now—pallidly neat, pitiably respectable, incurably forlorn! It was Bartleby.

After a few words touching his qualifications, I engaged him, glad to have among my corps of copyists a man of so singularly sedate an aspect, which I thought might operate beneficially upon the flighty temper of Turkey, and the fiery one of Nippers.

I should have stated before that ground-glass folding-doors divided my premises into two parts, one of which was occupied by my scriveners, the other by myself. According to my humor, I threw open these doors, or closed them. I resolved to assign Bartleby a corner by the folding-doors, but on my side of them, so as to have this quiet man within easy call, in case any trifling thing was to be done. I placed his desk close up to a small side-window in that part of the room, a window which originally had afforded a lateral view of certain grimy backyards and bricks, but which, owing to subsequent erections, commanded at present no view at all, though it gave some light. Within three feet of the panes was a wall, and the light came down from far above, between two lofty buildings, as from a very small opening in a dome. Still further to a satisfactory arrangement, I procured a high green folding screen, which might entirely isolate Bartleby from my sight, though not remove him from my voice. And thus, in a manner, privacy and society were conjoined.

At first, Bartleby did an extraordinary quantity of writing. As if long famishing for something to copy, he seemed to gorge himself on my documents. There was no pause for digestion. He ran a day and night line, copying by sunlight and by candle-light. I should have been quite delighted with his application, had he been cheerfully industrious. But he wrote on silently, palely, mechanically.

It is, of course, an indispensable part of a scrivener's business to verify the accuracy of his copy, word by word. Where there are two or more scriveners in an office, they assist each other in this examination, one reading from the copy, the other holding the original. It is a very dull, wearisome, and lethargic affair. I can readily imagine that, to some sanguine temperaments, it would be altogether intolerable. For example, I cannot credit that the mettlesome poet, Byron, would have contentedly sat down with Bartleby to examine a law document of, say five hundred pages, closely written in a crimpy hand.

Now and then, in the haste of business, it had been my habit to assist in comparing some brief document myself, calling Turkey or Nippers for this purpose. One object I had, in placing Bartleby so handy to me behind the screen, was, to avail myself of his services on such trivial occasions. It was on the third day, I think, of his being

---

7 **conveyancer:** Lawyer specializing in cases involving the transfer of title to property.

with me, and before any necessity had arisen for having his own writing examined, that, being much hurried to complete a small affair I had in hand, I abruptly called to Bartleby. In my haste and natural expectancy of instant compliance, I sat with my head bent over the original on my desk, and my right hand sideways, and somewhat nervously extended with the copy, so that, immediately upon emerging from his retreat, Bartleby might snatch it and proceed to business without the least delay.

In this very attitude did I sit when I called to him, rapidly stating what it was I wanted him to do—namely, to examine a small paper with me. Imagine my surprise, nay, my consternation, when, without moving from his privacy, Bartleby, in a singularly mild, firm voice, replied, "I would prefer not to."

I sat awhile in perfect silence, rallying my stunned faculties. Immediately it occurred to me that my ears had deceived me, or Bartleby had entirely misunderstood my meaning. I repeated my request in the clearest tone I could assume; but in quite as clear a one came the previous reply, "I would prefer not to."

"Prefer not to," echoed I, rising in high excitement, and crossing the room with a stride. "What do you mean? Are you moon-struck? I want you to help me compare this sheet here—take it," and I thrust it towards him.

"I would prefer not to," said he.

I looked at him steadfastly. His face was leanly composed; his gray eye dimly calm. Not a wrinkle of agitation rippled him. Had there been the least uneasiness, anger, impatience or impertinence in his manner; in other words, had there been anything ordinarily human about him, doubtless I should have violently dismissed him from the premises. But as it was, I should have as soon thought of turning my pale plaster-of-paris bust of Cicero out of doors. I stood gazing at him awhile, as he went on with his own writing, and then reseated myself at my desk. This is very strange, thought I. What had one best do? But my business hurried me. I concluded to forget the matter for the present, reserving it for my future leisure. So, calling Nippers from the other room, the paper was speedily examined.

A few days after this, Bartleby concluded four lengthy documents, being quadruplicates of a week's testimony taken before me in my High Court of Chancery. It became necessary to examine them. It was an important suit, and great accuracy was imperative. Having all things arranged, I called Turkey, Nippers and Ginger Nut, from the next room, meaning to place the four copies in the hands of my four clerks, while I should read from the original. Accordingly, Turkey, Nippers, and Ginger Nut had taken their seats in a row, each with his document in his hand, when I called to Bartleby to join this interesting group.

"Bartleby! quick, I am waiting."

I heard a slow scrape of his chair legs on the uncarpeted floor, and soon he appeared standing at the entrance of his hermitage.

"What is wanted?" said he, mildly.

"The copies, the copies," said I, hurriedly. "We are going to examine them. There"—and I held towards him the fourth quadruplicate.

"I would prefer not to," he said, and gently disappeared behind the screen.

For a few moments I was turned into a pillar of salt, standing at the head of my seated column of clerks. Recovering myself, I advanced towards the screen, and demanded the reason for such extraordinary conduct.

"*Why* do you refuse?"

"I would prefer not to."

With any other man I should have flown outright into a dreadful passion, scorned all further words, and thrust him ignominiously from my presence. But there was something about Bartleby that not only strangely disarmed me, but, in a wonderful manner, touched and disconcerted me. I began to reason with him.

"These are your own copies we are about to examine. It is labor saving to you, because one examination will answer for your four papers. It is common usage. Every copyist is bound to help examine his copy. Is it not so? Will you not speak? Answer!"

"I prefer not to," he replied in a flute-like tone. It seemed to me that, while I had been addressing him, he carefully revolved every statement that I made; fully comprehended the meaning; could not gainsay the irresistible conclusion; but, at the same time, some paramount consideration prevailed with him to reply as he did.

"You are decided, then, not to comply with my request—a request made according to common usage and common sense?"

He briefly gave me to understand, that on that point my judgment was sound. Yes: his decision was irreversible.

It is not seldom the case that, when a man is browbeaten in some unprecedented and violently unreasonable way, he begins to stagger in his own plainest faith. He begins, as it were, vaguely to surmise that, wonderful as it may be, all the justice and all the reason is on the other side. Accordingly, if any disinterested persons are present, he turns to them for some reinforcement for his own faltering mind.

"Turkey," said I, "what do you think of this? Am I not right?"

"With submission, sir," said Turkey, in his blandest tone, "I think that you are."

"Nippers," said I, "what do *you* think of it?"

"I think I should kick him out of the office."

(The reader of nice perceptions will here perceive that, it being morning, Turkey's answer is couched in polite and tranquil terms, but Nippers replies in ill-tempered ones. Or, to repeat a previous sentence, Nippers's ugly mood was on duty, and Turkey's off.)

"Ginger Nut," said I, willing to enlist the smallest suffrage in my behalf, "what do *you* think of it?"

"I think sir, he's a little *luny*," replied Ginger Nut, with a grin.

"You hear what they say," said I, turning towards the screen, "come forth and do your duty."

But he vouchsafed no reply. I pondered a moment in sore perplexity. But once more business hurried me. I determined again to postpone the consideration of this dilemma to my future leisure. With a little trouble we made out to examine the papers without Bartleby, though at every page or two Turkey deferentially dropped his opinion, that this proceeding was quite out of the common; while Nippers, twitching in his chair with a dyspeptic nervousness, ground out, between his set teeth, occasional hissing maledictions against the stubborn oaf behind the screen. And for his

(Nippers's) part, this was the first and the last time he would do another man's business without pay.

Meanwhile Bartleby sat in his hermitage, oblivious to everything but his own peculiar business there.

Some days passed, the scrivener being employed upon another lengthy work. His late remarkable conduct led me to regard his ways narrowly. I observed that he never went to dinner; indeed, that he never went anywhere. As yet I had never, of my personal knowledge, known him to be outside of my office. He was a perpetual sentry in the corner. At about eleven o'clock though, in the morning, I noticed that Ginger Nut would advance toward the opening in Bartleby's screen, as if silently beckoned thither by a gesture invisible to me where I sat. The boy would then leave the office, jingling a few pence, and reappear with a handful of ginger-nuts, which he delivered in the hermitage, receiving two of the cakes for his trouble.

He lives, then, on ginger-nuts, thought I; never eats a dinner, properly speaking; he must be a vegetarian, then; but no; he never eats even vegetables, he eats nothing but ginger-nuts. My mind then ran on in reveries concerning the probable effects upon the human constitution of living entirely on ginger-nuts. Ginger-nuts are so called, because they contain ginger as one of their peculiar constituents, and the final flavoring one. Now, what was ginger? A hot, spicy thing. Was Bartleby hot and spicy? Not at all. Ginger, then, had no effect upon Bartleby. Probably he preferred it should have none.

Nothing so aggravates an earnest person as a passive resistance. If the individual so resisted be of a not inhumane temper, and the resisting one perfectly harmless in his passivity, then, in the better moods of the former, he will endeavor charitably to construe to his imagination what proves impossible to be solved by his judgment. Even so, for the most part, I regarded Bartleby and his ways. Poor fellow! thought I, he means no mischief; it is plain he intends no insolence; his aspect sufficiently evinces that his eccentricities are involuntary. He is useful to me. I can get along with him. If I turn him away, the chances are he will fall in with some less indulgent employer, and then he will be rudely treated, and perhaps driven forth miserably to starve. Yes, Here I can cheaply purchase a delicious self-approval. To befriend Bartleby; to humor him in his strange wilfulness, will cost me little or nothing, while I lay up in my soul what will eventually prove a sweet morsel for my conscience. But this mood was not invariable with me. The passiveness of Bartleby sometimes irritated me. I felt strangely goaded on to encounter him in new opposition—to elicit some angry spark from him answerable to my own. But, indeed, I might as well have essayed to strike fire with my knuckles against a bit of Windsor soap. But one afternoon the evil impulse in me mastered me, and the following little scene ensued:

"Bartleby," said I, "when those papers are all copied, I will compare them with you."

"I would prefer not to."

"How? Surely you do not mean to persist in that mulish vagary?"

No answer.

I threw open the folding-doors near by, and, turning upon Turkey and Nippers, exclaimed in an excited manner—

"He says, a second time, he won't examine his papers. What do you think of it, Turkey?"

It was afternoon, be it remembered. Turkey sat glowing like a brass boiler; his bald head steaming; his hands reeling among his blotted papers.

"Think of it?" roared Turkey. "I think I'll just step behind his screen, and black his eyes for him!"

So saying, Turkey rose to his feet and threw his arms into a pugilistic position. He was hurrying away to make good his promise, when I detained him, alarmed at the effect of incautiously rousing Turkey's combativeness after dinner.

"Sit down, Turkey," said I, "and hear what Nippers has to say. What do you think of it, Nippers? Would I not be justified in immediately dismissing Bartleby?"

"Excuse me, that is for you to decide, sir. I think his conduct quite unusual, and, indeed, unjust, as regards Turkey and myself. But it may only be a passing whim."

"Ah," exclaimed I, "you have strangely changed your mind, then—you speak very gently of him now."

"All beer," cried Turkey; "gentleness is effects of beer—Nippers and I dined together to-day. You see how gentle *I* am, sir. Shall I go and black his eyes?"

"You refer to Bartleby, I suppose. No, not to-day, Turkey," I replied; "pray, put up your fists."

I closed the doors, and again advanced towards Bartleby. I felt additional incentives tempting me to my fate. I burned to be rebelled against again. I remembered that Bartleby never left the office.

"Bartleby," said I, "Ginger Nut is away; just step around to the Post Office, won't you?" (it was but a three minutes' walk) "and see if there is anything for me."

"I would prefer not to."

"You *will* not?"

"I *prefer* not."

I staggered to my desk, and sat there in a deep study. My blind inveteracy returned. Was there any other thing in which I could procure myself to be ignominiously repulsed by this lean, penniless wight?—my hired clerk? What added thing is there, perfectly reasonable, that he will be sure to refuse to do?

"Bartleby!"

No answer.

"Bartleby," in a louder tone.

No answer.

"Bartleby," I roared.

Like a very ghost, agreeably to the laws of magical invocation, at the third summons, he appeared at the entrance of his hermitage.

"Go to the next room, and tell Nippers to come to me."

"I prefer not to," he respectfully and slowly said, and mildly disappeared.

"Very good, Bartleby," said I, in a quiet sort of serenely-severe self-possessed tone, intimating the unalterable purpose of some terrible retribution very close at hand. At the moment I half intended something of the kind. But upon the whole, as it was drawing towards my dinner-hour, I thought it best to put on my hat and walk home for the day, suffering much from perplexity and distress of mind.

Shall I acknowledge it? The conclusion of this whole business was, that it soon became a fixed fact of my chambers, that a pale young scrivener, by the name of Bartleby, had a desk there; that he copied for me at the usual rate of four cents a folio (one hundred words); but he was permanently exempt from examining the work done by him, that duty being transferred to Turkey and Nippers, out of compliment, doubtless, to their superior acuteness; moreover, said Bartleby was never, on any account, to be dispatched on the most trivial errand of any sort; and that even if entreated to take upon him such a matter, it was generally understood that he would "prefer not to"—in other words, that he would refuse point-blank.

As days passed on, I became considerably reconciled to Bartleby. His steadiness, his freedom from all dissipation, his incessant industry (except when he chose to throw himself into a standing revery behind his screen), his great stillness, his unalterableness of demeanor under all circumstances, made him a valuable acquisition. One prime thing was this—*he was always there*—first in the morning, continually through the day, and the last at night. I had a singular confidence in his honesty. I felt my most precious papers perfectly safe in his hands. Sometimes, to be sure, I could not, for the very soul of me, avoid falling into sudden spasmodic passions with him. For it was exceeding difficult to bear in mind all the time those strange peculiarities, privileges, and unheard-of exemptions, forming the tacit stipulations on Bartleby's part under which he remained in my office. Now and then, in the eagerness of dispatching pressing business, I would inadvertently summon Bartleby, in a short, rapid tone, to put his finger, say, on the incipient tie of a bit of red tape with which I was about compressing some papers. Of course, from behind the screen the usual answer, "I prefer not to," was sure to come; and then, how could a human creature, with the common infirmities of our nature, refrain from bitterly exclaiming upon such perverseness—such unreasonableness? However, every added repulse of this sort which I received only tended to lessen the probability of my repeating the inadvertence.

Here it must be said, that, according to the custom of most legal gentlemen occupying chambers in densely-populated law buildings, there were several keys to my door. One was kept by a woman residing in the attic, which person weekly scrubbed and daily swept and dusted my apartments. Another was kept by Turkey for convenience sake. The third I sometimes carried in my own pocket. The fourth I knew not who had.

Now, one Sunday morning I happened to go to Trinity Church, to hear a celebrated preacher, and finding myself rather early on the ground I thought I would walk round to my chambers for a while. Luckily I had my key with me; but upon applying it to the lock, I found it resisted by something inserted from the inside. Quite surprised, I called out; when to my consternation a key was turned from within; and thrusting his lean visage at me, and holding the door ajar, the apparition of Bartleby appeared, in his shirt-sleeves, and otherwise in a strangely tattered deshabille, saying quietly that he was sorry, but he was deeply engaged just then, and—preferred not admitting me at present. In a brief word or two, he moreover added, that perhaps I had better walk round the block two or three times, and by that time he would probably have concluded his affairs.

Now, the utterly unsurmised appearance of Bartleby, tenanting my law-chambers of a Sunday morning, with his cadaverously gentlemanly *nonchalance,* yet withal firm and self-possessed, had such a strange effect upon me, that incontinently I slunk away from my own door, and did as desired. But not without sundry twinges of impotent rebellion against the mild effrontery of this unaccountable scrivener. Indeed, it was his wonderful mildness chiefly, which not only disarmed me, but unmanned me, as it were. For I consider that one, for the time, is a sort of unmanned when he tranquilly permits his hired clerk to dictate to him, and order him away from his own premises. Furthermore, I was full of uneasiness as to what Bartleby could possibly be doing in my office in his shirt-sleeves, and in an otherwise dismantled condition of a Sunday morning. Was anything amiss going on? Nay, that was out of the question. It was not to be thought of for a moment that Bartleby was an immoral person. But what could he be doing there?—copying? Nay again, whatever might be his eccentricities, Bartleby was an eminently decorous person. He would be the last man to sit down to his desk in any state approaching to nudity. Besides, it was Sunday; and there was something about Bartleby that forbade the supposition that he would by any secular occupation violate the proprieties of the day

Nevertheless, my mind was not pacified; and full of a restless curiosity, at last I returned to the door. Without hindrance I inserted my key, opened it, and entered. Bartleby was not to be seen. I looked round anxiously, peeped behind his screen; but it was very plain that he was gone. Upon more closely examining the place, I surmised that for an indefinite period Bartleby must have ate, dressed, and slept in my office, and that too without plate, mirror, or bed. The cushioned seat of a rickety old sofa in one corner bore the faint impress of a lean, reclining form. Rolled away under his desk, I found a blanket; under the empty grate, a blacking box and brush; on a chair, a tin basin, with soap and a ragged towel; in a newspaper a few crumbs of ginger-nuts and a morsel of cheese. Yes, thought I, it is evident enough that Bartleby has been making his home here, keeping bachelor's hall all by himself. Immediately then the thought came sweeping across me, what miserable friendlessness and loneliness are here revealed! His poverty is great; but his solitude, how horrible! Think of it. Of a Sunday, Wall Street is deserted as Petra;[8] and every night of every day it is an emptiness. This building, too, which of week-days hums with industry and life, at nightfall echoes with sheer vacancy, and all through Sunday is forlorn. And here Bartleby makes his home; sole spectator of a solitude which he has seen all populous—a sort of innocent and transformed Marius[9] brooding among the ruins of Carthage!

For the first time in my life a feeling of overpowering stinging melancholy seized me. Before, I had never experienced aught but a not unpleasing sadness. The bond of a common humanity now drew me irresistibly to gloom. A fraternal melancholy! For both I and Bartleby were sons of Adam. I remembered the bright silks and sparkling

8 **Petra:** An ancient ruined city in the Edom desert, located in present-day southwest Jordan.
9 **Marius:** Gaius Marius (157–86 B.C.), Roman general who returned to power after exile in Africa.

faces I had seen that day, in gala trim, swan-like sailing down the Mississippi of Broadway; and I contrasted them with the pallid copyist, and thought to myself, Ah, happiness courts the light, so we deem the world is gay; but misery hides aloof, so we deem that misery there is none. These sad fancyings—chimeras, doubtless, of a sick and silly brain—led on to other and more special thoughts, concerning the eccentricities of Bartleby. Presentiments of strange discoveries hovered round me. The scrivener's pale form appeared to me laid out, among uncaring strangers, in its shivering winding-sheet.

Suddenly I was attracted by Bartleby's closed desk, the key in open sight left in the lock.

I mean no mischief, seek the gratification of no heartless curiosity, thought I; besides, the desk is mine, and its contents, too, so I will make bold to look within. Everything was methodically arranged, the papers smoothly placed. The pigeon-holes were deep, and removing the files of documents, I groped into their recesses. Presently I felt something there, and dragged it out. It was an old bandanna handkerchief, heavy and knotted. I opened it, and saw it was a saving's bank.

I now recalled all the quiet mysteries which I had noted in the man. I remembered that he never spoke but to answer; that, though at intervals he had considerable time to himself, yet I had never seen him reading—no, not even a newspaper; that for long periods he would stand looking out, at his pale window behind the screen, upon the dead brick wall; I was quite sure he never visited any refectory or eating-house; while his pale face clearly indicated that he never drank beer like Turkey, or tea and coffee even, like other men; that he never went anywhere in particular that I could learn; never went out for a walk, unless, indeed, that was the case at present; that he had declined telling who he was, or whence he came, or whether he had any relatives in the world; that though so thin and pale, he never complained of ill-health. And more than all, I remembered a certain unconscious air of pallid—how shall I call it?—of pallid haughtiness, say, or rather an austere reserve about him, which had positively awed me into my tame compliance with his eccentricities, when I had feared to ask him to do the slightest incidental thing for me, even though I might know, from his long-continued motionlessness, that behind his screen he must be standing in one of those dead-wall reveries of his.

Revolving all these things, and coupling them with the recently discovered fact, that he made my office his constant abiding place and home, and not forgetful of his morbid moodiness; revolving all these things, a prudential feeling began to steal over me. My first emotions had been those of pure melancholy and sincerest pity; but just in proportion as the forlornness of Bartleby grew and grew to my imagination, did that same melancholy merge into fear, that pity into repulsion. So true it is, and so terrible, too, that up to a certain point the thought or sight of misery enlists our best affections; but, in certain special cases, beyond that point it does not. They err who would assert that invariably this is owing to the inherent selfishness of the human heart. It rather proceeds from a certain hopelessness of remedying excessive and organic ill. To a sensitive being, pity is not seldom pain. And when at last it is perceived that such pity cannot lead to effectual succor, common sense bids the soul be rid of it.

What I saw that morning persuaded me that the scrivener was the victim of innate and incurable disorder. I might give alms to his body; but his body did not pain him; it was his soul that suffered, and his soul I could not reach.

I did not accomplish the purpose of going to Trinity Church that morning. Somehow, the things I had seen disqualified me for the time from church-going. I walked homeward, thinking what I would do with Bartleby. Finally, I resolved upon this—I would put certain calm questions to him the next morning, touching his history, etc., and if he declined to answer them openly and unreservedly (and I supposed he would prefer not), then to give him a twenty dollar bill over and above whatever I might owe him, and tell him his services were no longer required; but that if in any other way I could assist him, I would be happy to do so, especially if he desired to return to his native place, wherever that might be, I would willingly help to defray the expenses. Moreover, if, after reaching home, he found himself at any time in want of aid, a letter from him would be sure of a reply.

The next morning came.

"Bartleby," said I, gently calling to him behind his screen.

No reply.

"Bartleby," said I, in a still gentler tone, "come here; I am not going to ask you to do anything you would prefer not to do—I simply wish to speak to you."

Upon this he noiselessly slid into view.

"Will you tell me, Bartleby, where you were born?"

"I would prefer not to."

"Will you tell me *anything* about yourself?"

"I would prefer not to."

"But what reasonable objection can you have to speak to me? I feel friendly towards you."

He did not look at me while I spoke, but kept his glance fixed upon my bust of Cicero, which, as I then sat, was directly behind me, some six inches above my head.

"What is your answer, Bartleby?" said I, after waiting a considerable time for a reply, during which his countenance remained immovable, only there was the faintest conceivable tremor of the white attenuated mouth.

"At present I prefer to give no answer," he said, and retired into his hermitage.

It was rather weak in me I confess, but his manner, on this occasion, nettled me. Not only did there seem to lurk in it a certain calm disdain, but his perverseness seemed ungrateful, considering the undeniable good usage and indulgence he had received from me.

Again I sat ruminating what I should do. Mortified as I was at his behavior, and resolved as I had been to dismiss him when I entered my office, nevertheless I strangely felt something superstitious knocking at my heart, and forbidding me to carry out my purpose, and denouncing me for a villain if I dared to breathe one bitter word against this forlornest of mankind. At last, familiarly drawing my chair behind his screen, I sat down and said: "Bartleby, never mind, then, about revealing your history; but let me entreat you, as a friend, to comply as far as may be with the usages of this office. Say now, you will help to examine papers to-morrow or next day: in short, say now, that in a day or two you will begin to be a little reasonable:—say so, Bartleby."

"At present I would prefer not to be a little reasonable," was his mildly cadaverous reply.

Just then the folding-doors opened, and Nippers approached. He seemed suffering from an unusually bad night's rest, induced by severer indigestion than common. He overheard those final words of Bartleby.

"*Prefer not,* eh?" gritted Nippers—"I'd *prefer* him, if I were you, sir," addressing me—"I'd *prefer* him; I'd give him preferences, the stubborn mule! What is it, sir, pray, that he *prefers* not to do now?"

Bartleby moved not a limb.

"Mr. Nippers," said I, "I'd prefer that you would withdraw for the present."

Somehow, of late, I had got into the way of involuntarily using this word "prefer" upon all sorts of not exactly suitable occasions. And I trembled to think that my contact with the scrivener had already and seriously affected me in a mental way. And what further and deeper aberration might it not yet produce? This apprehension had not been without efficacy in determining me to summary measures.

As Nippers, looking very sour and sulky, was departing, Turkey blandly and deferentially approached.

"With submission, sir," said he, "yesterday I was thinking about Bartleby here, and I think that if he would but prefer to take a quart of good ale every day, it would do much towards mending him, and enabling him to assist in examining his papers."

"So you have got the word, too," said I, slightly excited.

"With submission, what word, sir?" asked Turkey, respectfully crowding himself into the contracted space behind the screen, and by so doing, making me jostle the scrivener. "What word, sir?"

"I would prefer to be left alone here," said Bartleby, as if offended at being mobbed in his privacy.

"*That's* the word, Turkey," said I—"*that's* it."

"Oh, *prefer?* oh yes—queer word. I never use it myself. But, sir, as I was saying, if he would but prefer—"

"Turkey," interrupted I, "you will please withdraw."

"Oh certainly, sir, if you prefer that I should."

As he opened the folding-door to retire, Nippers at his desk caught a glimpse of me, and asked whether I would prefer to have a certain paper copied on blue paper or white. He did not in the least roguishly accent the word "prefer." It was plain that it involuntarily rolled from his tongue. I thought to myself, surely I must get rid of a demented man, who already has in some degree turned the tongues, if not the heads of myself and clerks. But I thought it prudent not to break the dismission at once.

The next day I noticed that Bartleby did nothing but stand at his window in his dead-wall revery. Upon asking him why he did not write, he said that he had decided upon doing no more writing.

"Why, how now? what next?" exclaimed I, "do no more writing?"

"No more."

"And what is the reason?"

"Do you not see the reason for yourself?" he indifferently replied.

I looked steadfastly at him, and perceived that his eyes looked dull and glazed. Instantly it occurred to me, that his unexampled diligence in copying by his dim window for the first few weeks of his stay with me might have temporarily impaired his vision.

I was touched. I said something in condolence with him. I hinted that of course he did wisely in abstaining from writing for a while; and urged him to embrace that opportunity of taking wholesome exercise in the open air. This, however, he did not do. A few days after this, my other clerks being absent, and being in a great hurry to dispatch certain letters by the mail, I thought that, having nothing else earthly to do, Bartleby would surely be less inflexible than usual, and carry these letters to the post-office. But he blankly declined. So, much to my inconvenience, I went myself.

Still added days went by. Whether Bartleby's eyes improved or not, I could not say. To all appearance, I thought they did. But when I asked him if they did, he vouchsafed no answer. At all events, he would do no copying. At last, in reply to my urgings, he informed me that he had permanently given up copying.

"What!" exclaimed I; "suppose your eyes should get entirely well—better than ever before—would you not copy then?"

"I have given up copying," he answered, and slid aside.

He remained as ever, a fixture in my chamber. Nay—if that were possible—he became still more of a fixture than before. What was to be done? He would do nothing in the office; why should he stay there? In plain fact, he had now become a millstone to me, not only useless as a necklace, but afflictive to bear. Yet I was sorry for him. I speak less than truth when I say that, on his own account, he occasioned me uneasiness. If he would but have named a single relative or friend, I would instantly have written, and urged their taking the poor fellow away to some convenient retreat. But he seemed alone, absolutely alone in the universe. A bit of wreck in the mid-Atlantic. At length, necessities connected with my business tyrannized over all other considerations. Decently as I could, I told Bartleby that in six days' time he must unconditionally leave the office. I warned him to take measures, in the interval, for procuring some other abode. I offered to assist him in this endeavor, if he himself would but take the first step towards a removal. "And when you finally quit me, Bartleby," added I, "I shall see that you go not away entirely unprovided. Six days from this hour, remember."

At the expiration of that period, I peeped behind the screen, and lo! Bartleby was there.

I buttoned up my coat, balanced myself; advanced slowly towards him, touched his shoulder, and said, "The time has come; you must quit this place; I am sorry for you; here is money; but you must go."

"I would prefer not," he replied, with his back still towards me.

"You *must*."

He remained silent.

Now I had an unbounded confidence in this man's common honesty. He had frequently restored to me sixpences and shillings carelessly dropped upon the floor, for

I am apt to be very reckless in such shirt-button affairs. The proceeding, then, which followed will not be deemed extraordinary.

"Bartleby," said I, "I owe you twelve dollars on account; here are thirty-two; the odd twenty are yours—Will you take it?" and I handed the bills towards him.

But he made no motion.

"I will leave them here, then," putting them under a weight on the table. Then taking my hat and cane and going to the door, I tranquilly turned and added—"After you have removed your things from these offices, Bartleby, you will of course lock the door—since every one is now gone for the day but you—and if you please, slip your key underneath the mat, so that I may have it in the morning. I shall not see you again; so good-bye to you. If, hereafter, in your new place of abode, I can be of any service to you, do not fail to advise me by letter. Good-bye, Bartleby, and fare you well."

But he answered not a word; like the last column of some ruined temple, he remained standing mute and solitary in the middle of the otherwise deserted room.

As I walked home in a pensive mood, my vanity got the better of my pity. I could not but highly plume myself on my masterly management in getting rid of Bartleby. Masterly I call it, and such it must appear to any dispassionate thinker. The beauty of my procedure seemed to consist in its perfect quietness. There was no vulgar bullying, no bravado of any sort, no choleric hectoring, and striding to and fro across the apartment, jerking out vehement commands for Bartleby to bundle himself off with his beggarly traps. Nothing of the kind. Without loudly bidding Bartleby depart—as an inferior genius might have done—I *assumed* the ground that depart he must; and upon that assumption built all I had to say. The more I thought over my procedure, the more I was charmed with it. Nevertheless, next morning, upon awakening, I had my doubts—I had somehow slept off the fumes of vanity. One of the coolest and wisest hours a man has, is just after he awakes in the morning. My procedure seemed as sagacious as ever—but only in theory. How it would prove in practice—there was the rub. It was truly a beautiful thought to have assumed Bartleby's departure; but, after all, that assumption was simply my own, and none of Bartleby's. The great point was, not whether I had assumed that he would quit me, but whether he would prefer so to do. He was more a man of preferences than assumptions.

After breakfast, I walked down town, arguing the probabilities *pro* and *con.* One moment I thought it would prove a miserable failure, and Bartleby would be found all alive at my office as usual; the next moment it seemed certain that I should find his chair empty. And so I kept veering about. At the corner of Broadway and Canal Street, I saw quite an excited group of people standing in earnest conversation.

"I'll take odds he doesn't," said a voice as I passed.

"Doesn't go?—done!" said I, "put up your money."

I was instinctively putting my hand in my pocket to produce my own, when I remembered that this was an election day. The words I had overheard bore no reference to Bartleby, but to the success or non-success of some candidate for the mayoralty. In my intent frame of mind, I had, as it were, imagined that all Broadway shared in my excitement, and were debating the same question with me. I passed on, very thankful that the uproar of the street screened my momentary absent-mindedness.

As I had intended, I was earlier than usual at my office door. I stood listening for a moment. All was still. He must be gone. I tried the knob. The door was locked. Yes, my procedure had worked to a charm; he indeed must be vanished. Yet a certain melancholy mixed with this: I was almost sorry for my brilliant success. I was fumbling under the door mat for the key, which Bartleby was to have left there for me, when accidentally my knee knocked against a panel, producing a summoning sound, and in response a voice came to me from within—"Not yet; I am occupied."

It was Bartleby.

I was thunderstruck. For an instant I stood like the man who, pipe in mouth, was killed one cloudless afternoon long ago in Virginia, by summer lightning; at his own warm open window he was killed, and remained leaning out there upon the dreamy afternoon, till some one touched him, when he fell.

"Not gone!" I murmured at last. But again obeying that wondrous ascendancy which the inscrutable scrivener had over me, and from which ascendancy, for all my chafing, I could not completely escape, I slowly went down stairs and out into the street, and while walking round the block, considered what I should next do in this unheard-of perplexity. Turn the man out by an actual thrusting I could not; to drive him away by calling him hard names would not do; calling in the police was an unpleasant idea; and yet, permit him to enjoy his cadaverous triumph over me—this, too, I could not think of. What was to be done? or, if nothing could be done, was there anything further that I could *assume* in the matter? Yes, as before I had prospectively assumed that Bartleby would depart, so now I might retrospectively assume that departed he was. In the legitimate carrying out of this assumption, I might enter my office in a great hurry, and pretending not to see Bartleby at all, walk straight against him as if he were air. Such a proceeding would in a singular degree have the appearance of a home-thrust. It was hardly possible that Bartleby could withstand such an application of the doctrine of assumptions. But upon second thoughts the success of the plan seemed rather dubious. I resolved to argue the matter over with him again.

"Bartleby," said I, entering the office, with a quietly severe expression, "I am seriously displeased. I am pained, Bartleby. I had thought better of you. I had imagined you of such a gentlemanly organization, that in any delicate dilemma a slight hint would suffice—in short, an assumption. But it appears I am deceived. Why," I added, unaffectedly starting, "you have not even touched that money yet," pointing to it, just where I had left it the evening previous.

He answered nothing.

"Will you, or will you not, quit me?" I now demanded in a sudden passion, advancing close to him.

"I would prefer *not* to quit you," he replied, gently emphasizing the *not*.

"What earthly right have you to stay here? Do you pay any rent? Do you pay my taxes? Or is this property yours?"

He answered nothing.

"Are you ready to go on and write now? Are your eyes recovered? Could you copy a small paper for me this morning? or help examine a few lines? or step round to the post-office? In a word, will you do anything at all, to give a coloring to your refusal to depart the premises?"

He silently retired into his hermitage.

I was now in such a state of nervous resentment that I thought it but prudent to check myself at present from further demonstrations. Bartleby and I were alone. I remembered the tragedy of the unfortunate Adams and the still more unfortunate Colt[10] in the solitary office of the latter; and how poor Colt, being dreadfully incensed by Adams, and imprudently permitting himself to get wildly excited, was at unawares hurried into his fatal act—an act which certainly no man could possibly deplore more than the actor himself. Often it had occurred to me in my ponderings upon the subject that had that altercation taken place in the public street, or at a private residence, it would not have terminated as it did. It was the circumstance of being alone in a solitary office, up stairs, of a building entirely unhallowed by humanizing domestic associations—an uncarpeted office, doubtless, of a dusty, haggard sort of appearance—that it must have been, which greatly helped to enhance the irritable desperation of the hapless Colt.

But when this old Adam of resentment rose in me and tempted me concerning Bartleby, I grappled him and threw him. How? Why, simply by recalling the divine injunction: "A new commandment give I unto you, that ye love one another." Yes, this it was that saved me. Aside from higher considerations, charity often operates as a vastly wise and prudent principle—a great safeguard to its possessor. Men have committed murder for jealousy's sake, and anger's sake, and hatred's sake, and selfishness' sake, and spiritual pride's sake; but no man, that ever I heard of, ever committed a diabolical murder for sweet charity's sake. Mere self-interest, then, if no better motive can be enlisted, should, especially with high-tempered men, prompt all beings to charity and philanthropy. At any rate, upon the occasion in question, I strove to drown my exasperated feelings towards the scrivener by benevolently construing his conduct. Poor fellow, poor fellow! thought I, he don't mean anything; and besides, he has seen hard times, and ought to be indulged.

I endeavored, also, immediately to occupy myself, and at the same time to comfort my despondency. I tried to fancy, that in the course of the morning, at such time as might prove agreeable to him, Bartleby, of his own free accord, would emerge from his hermitage and take up some decided line of march in the direction of the door. But no. Half-past twelve o'clock came; Turkey began to glow in the face, overturn his inkstand, and become generally obstreperous; Nippers abated down into quietude and courtesy; Ginger Nut munched his noon apple; and Bartleby remained standing at his window in one of his profoundest dead-wall reveries. Will it be credited? Ought I to acknowledge it? That afternoon I left the office without saying one further word to him.

---

10 **Adams and . . . Colt:** A notorious nineteenth-century murder case involving John Colt, brother of the inventor of the Colt revolver, and a printer named Samuel Adams. Adams visited Colt to collect on a debt and was murdered by Colt. Colt killed Adams with a hatchet and salted and crated the body for shipment to New Orleans. Colt was sentenced to hang for the murder in November 1842 but died in jail from stab wounds. His death was initially ruled a suicide, but the wounds were then assumed to be inflicted on Colt by his mistress, who visited Colt in jail before he was to be hanged.

Some days now passed, during which, at leisure intervals I looked a little into "Edwards on the Will," and "Priestley on Necessity."[11] Under the circumstances, those books induced a salutary feeling. Gradually I slid into the persuasion that these troubles of mine, touching the scrivener, had been all predestined from eternity, and Bartleby was billeted upon me for some mysterious purpose of an all-wise Providence, which it was not for a mere mortal like me to fathom. Yes, Bartleby, stay there behind your screen, thought I; I shall persecute you no more; you are harmless and noiseless as any of these old chairs; in short, I never feel so private as when I know you are here. At last I see it, I feel it; I penetrate to the predestinated purpose of my life. I am content. Others may have loftier parts to enact; but my mission in this world, Bartleby, is to furnish you with office-room for such period as you may see fit to remain.

I believe that this wise and blessed frame of mind would have continued with me, had it not been for the unsolicited and uncharitable remarks obtruded upon me by my professional friends who visited the rooms. But thus it often is, that the constant friction of illiberal minds wears out at last the best resolves of the more generous. Though to be sure, when I reflected upon it, it was not strange that people entering my office should be struck by the peculiar aspect of the unaccountable Bartleby, and so be tempted to throw out some sinister observations concerning him. Sometimes an attorney, having business with me, and calling at my office, and finding no one but the scrivener there, would undertake to obtain some sort of precise information from him touching my whereabouts; but without heeding his idle talk, Bartleby would remain standing immovable in the middle of the room. So after contemplating him in that position for a time, the attorney would depart, no wiser than he came.

Also, when a reference[12] was going on, and the room full of lawyers and witnesses, and business driving fast, some deeply-occupied legal gentleman present, seeing Bartleby wholly unemployed, would request him to run round to his (the legal gentleman's) office and fetch some papers for him. Thereupon, Bartleby would tranquilly decline, and yet remain idle as before. Then the lawyer would give a great stare, and turn to me. And what could I say? At last I was made aware that all through the circle of my professional acquaintance, a whisper of wonder was running round, having reference to the strange creature I kept at my office. This worried me very much. And as the idea came upon me of his possibly turning out a long-lived man, and keep occupying my chambers, and denying my authority; and perplexing my visitors; and scandalizing my professional reputation; and casting a general gloom over the premises; keeping soul and body together to the last upon his savings (for doubtless he spent but half a dime a day), and in the end perhaps outlive me, and claim possession of my office by right of his perpetual occupancy: as all these dark anticipations crowded upon me more and more, and my friends continually intruded their relentless remarks upon the apparition in my room; a great change was wrought in me. I

---

11  **"Edwards on the Will" and "Priestley on Necessity":** Jonathan Edwards's *Freedom of the Will* (1754) and Joseph Priestley's *Doctrine of Philosophical Necessity Illustrated* (1777). Edwards, a colonial minister, and Priestley, an English scientist, both argue that human will is not free and that human lives are preordained.

12  **reference:** A dispute moderated by a referee.

resolved to gather all my faculties together, and forever rid me of this intolerable incubus.

Ere revolving any complicated project, however, adapted to this end, I first simply suggested to Bartleby the propriety of his permanent departure. In a calm and serious tone, I commended the idea to his careful and mature consideration. But, having taken three days to meditate upon it, he apprised me, that his original determination remained the same; in short, that he still preferred to abide with me.

What shall I do? I now said to myself, buttoning up my coat to the last button. What shall I do? what ought I to do? what does conscience say I *should* do with this man, or, rather, ghost. Rid myself of him, I must; go, he shall. But how? You will not thrust him, the poor, pale, passive mortal—you will not thrust such a helpless creature out of your door? you will not dishonor yourself by such cruelty? No, I will not, I cannot do that. Rather would I let him live and die here, and then mason up his remains in the wall. What, then, will you do? For all your coaxing, he will not budge. Bribes he leaves under your own paper-weight on your table; in short, it is quite plain that he prefers to cling to you.

Then something severe, something unusual must be done. What! surely you will not have him collared by a constable, and commit his innocent pallor to the common jail? And upon what ground could you procure such a thing to be done?—a vagrant, is he? What! he a vagrant, a wanderer, who refuses to budge? It is because he will *not* be a vagrant, then, that you seek to count him *as* a vagrant. That is too absurd. No visible means of support: there I have him. Wrong again: for indubitably he *does* support himself, and that is the only unanswerable proof that any man can show of his possessing the means so to do. No more, then. Since he will not quit me, I must quit him. I will change my offices; I will move elsewhere, and give him fair notice, that if I find him on my new premises I will then proceed against him as a common trespasser.

Acting accordingly, next day I thus addressed him: "I find these chambers too far from the City Hall; the air is unwholesome. In a word, I propose to remove my offices next week, and shall no longer require your services. I tell you this now, in order that you may seek another place."

He made no reply, and nothing more was said.

On the appointed day I engaged carts and men, proceeded to my chambers, and, having but little furniture, everything was removed in a few hours. Throughout, the scrivener remained standing behind the screen, which I directed to be removed the last thing. It was withdrawn; and, being folded up like a huge folio, left him the motionless occupant of a naked room. I stood in the entry watching him a moment, while something from within me upbraided me.

I re-entered, with my hand in my pocket—and—and my heart in my mouth.

"Good-bye, Bartleby; I am going—good-bye, and God some way bless you; and take that," slipping something in his hand. But it dropped upon the floor, and then—strange to say—I tore myself from him whom I had so longed to be rid of.

Established in my new quarters, for a day or two I kept the door locked, and started at every footfall in the passages. When I returned to my rooms, after any little absence, I would pause at the threshold for an instant, and attentively listen, ere applying my key. But these fears were needless. Bartleby never came nigh me.

I thought all was going well, when a perturbed-looking stranger visited me, inquiring whether I was the person who had recently occupied rooms at No.———— Wall Street.

Full of forebodings, I replied that I was.

"Then, sir," said the stranger, who proved a lawyer, "you are responsible for the man you left there. He refuses to do any copying; he refuses to do anything; he says he prefers not to; and he refuses to quit the premises."

"I am very sorry, sir," said I, with assumed tranquillity, but an inward tremor, "but, really, the man you allude to is nothing to me—he is no relation or apprentice of mine, that you should hold me responsible for him."

"In mercy's name, who is he?"

"I certainly cannot inform you. I know nothing about him. Formerly I employed him as a copyist; but he has done nothing for me now for some time past."

"I shall settle him, then—good morning, sir."

Several days passed, and I heard nothing more; and, though I often felt a charitable prompting to call at the place and see poor Bartleby, yet a certain squeamishness, of I know not what, withheld me.

All is over with him, by this time, thought I, at last, when, through another week, no further intelligence reached me. But, coming to my room the day after, I found several persons waiting at my door in a high state of nervous excitement.

"That's the man—here he comes," cried the foremost one, whom I recognized as the lawyer who had previously called upon me alone.

"You must take him away, sir, at once," cried a portly person among them, advancing upon me, and whom I knew to be the landlord of No.————Wall Street. "These gentlemen, my tenants, cannot stand it any longer; Mr. B————," pointing to the lawyer, "has turned him out of his room, and he now persists in haunting the building generally, sitting upon the banisters of the stairs by day, and sleeping in the entry by night. Everybody is concerned; clients are leaving the offices; some fears are entertained of a mob; something you must do, and that without delay."

Aghast at this torrent, I fell back before it, and would fain have locked myself in my new quarters. In vain I persisted that Bartleby was nothing to me—no more than to any one else. In vain—I was the last person known to have anything to do with him, and they held me to the terrible account. Fearful, then, of being exposed in the papers (as one person present obscurely threatened), I considered the matter, and, at length, said, that if the lawyer would give me a confidential interview with the scrivener, in his (the lawyer's) own room, I would, that afternoon, strive my best to rid them of the nuisance they complained of.

Going up stairs to my old haunt, there was Bartleby silently sitting upon the banister at the landing.

"What are you doing here, Bartleby?" said I.

"Sitting upon the banister," he mildly replied.

I motioned him into the lawyer's room, who then left us.

"Bartleby," said I, "are you aware that you are the cause of great tribulation to me, by persisting in occupying the entry after being dismissed from the office?"

No answer.

"Now one of two things must take place. Either you must do something, or something must be done to you. Now what sort of business would you like to engage in? Would you like to re-engage in copying for some one?"

"No; I would prefer not to make any change."

"Would you like a clerkship in a dry-goods store?"

"There is too much confinement about that. No, I would not like a clerkship; but I am not particular."

"Too much confinement," I cried, "why, you keep yourself confined all the time!"

"I would prefer not to take a clerkship," he rejoined, as if to settle that little item at once.

"How would a bar-tender's business suit you? There is no trying of the eye-sight in that."

"I would not like it at all; though, as I said before, I am not particular."

His unwonted wordiness inspirited me. I returned to the charge.

"Well, then, would you like to travel through the country collecting bills for the merchants? That would improve your health."

"No, I would prefer to be doing something else."

"How, then, would going as a companion to Europe, to entertain some young gentleman with your conversation—how would that suit you?"

"Not at all. It does not strike me that there is anything definite about that. I like to be stationary. But I am not particular."

"Stationary you shall be, then," I cried, now losing all patience, and, for the first time in all my exasperating connection with him, fairly flying into a passion. "If you do not go away from these premises before night, I shall feel bound—indeed, I *am* bound—to—to—to quit the premises myself!" I rather absurdly concluded, knowing not with what possible threat to try to frighten his immobility into compliance. Despairing of all further efforts, I was precipitately leaving him, when a final thought occurred to me—one which had not been wholly unindulged before.

"Bartleby," said I, in the kindest tone I could assume under such exciting circumstances, "will you go home with me now—not to my office, but my dwelling—and remain there till we can conclude upon some convenient arrangement for you at our leisure? Come, let us start now, right away."

"No: at present I would prefer not to make any change at all."

I answered nothing; but, effectually dodging every one by the suddenness and rapidity of my flight, rushed from the building, ran up Wall Street towards Broadway, and, jumping into the first omnibus, was soon removed from pursuit. As soon as tranquillity returned, I distinctly perceived that I had now done all that I possibly could, both in respect to the demands of the landlord and his tenants, and with regard to my own desire and sense of duty, to benefit Bartleby, and shield him from rude persecution. I now strove to be entirely care-free and quiescent; and my conscience justified me in the attempt; though, indeed, it was not so successful as I could have wished. So fearful was I of being again hunted out by the incensed landlord and his exasperated tenants, that, surrendering my business to Nippers, for a few days, I drove about the upper part of the town and through the suburbs, in my rockaway;[13] crossed over to Jersey City and Hoboken, and paid fugitive visits to Manhattanville and Astoria. In fact, I almost lived in my rockaway for the time.

When again I entered my office, lo, a note from the landlord lay upon the desk. I opened it with trembling hands. It informed me that the writer had sent to the police, and had Bartleby removed to the Tombs as a vagrant. Moreover, since I knew more about him than any one else, he wished me to appear at that place, and make a suitable statement of the facts. These tidings had a conflicting effect upon me. At first I was indignant; but at last, almost approved. The landlord's energetic, summary disposition, had led him to adopt a procedure which I do not think I would have decided upon myself; and yet, as a last resort, under such peculiar circumstances, it seemed the only plan.

As I afterwards learned, the poor scrivener, when told that he must be conducted to the Tombs, offered not the slightest obstacle, but, in his pale, unmoving way, silently acquiesced.

Some of the compassionate and curious by-standers joined the party; and headed by one of the constables arm-in-arm with Bartleby, the silent procession filed its way through all the noise, and heat, and joy of the roaring thoroughfares at noon.

The same day I received the note, I went to the Tombs, or, to speak more properly, the Halls of Justice. Seeking the right officer, I stated the purpose of my call, and was informed that the individual I described was, indeed, within. I then assured the functionary that Bartleby was a perfectly honest man, and greatly to be compassionated, however unaccountably eccentric. I narrated all I knew, and closed by suggesting the idea of letting him remain in as indulgent confinement as possible, till something less harsh might be done—though, indeed, I hardly knew what. At all events, if nothing else could be decided upon, the alms-house must receive him. I then begged to have an interview.

Being under no disgraceful charge, and quite serene and harmless in all his ways, they had permitted him freely to wander about the prison, and, especially, in the inclosed grass-platted yards thereof. And so I found him there, standing all alone in the quietest of the yards, his face towards a high wall, while all around, from the narrow slits of the jail windows, I thought I saw peering out upon him the eyes of murderers and thieves.

"Bartleby!"

"I know you," he said, without looking round—"and I want nothing to say to you."

"It was not I that brought you here, Bartleby," said I, keenly pained at his implied suspicion. "And to you, this should not be so vile a place. Nothing reproachful attaches to you by being here. And see, it is not so sad a place as one might think. Look, there is the sky, and here is the grass."

13  **rockaway:** Low carriage with open sides and a covered top.

"I know where I am," he replied, but would say nothing more, and so I left him.

As I entered the corridor again, a broad meat-like man, in an apron, accosted me, and, jerking his thumb over his shoulder, said—"Is that your friend?"

"Yes."

"Does he want to starve? If he does, let him live on the prison fare, that's all."

"Who are you?" asked I, not knowing what to make of such an unofficially speaking person in such a place.

"I am the grub-man. Such gentlemen as have friends here, hire me to provide them with something good to eat."

"Is this so?" said I, turning to the turnkey.

He said it was.

"Well, then," said I, slipping some silver into the grub-man's hands (for so they called him), "I want you to give particular attention to my friend there; let him have the best dinner you can get. And you must be as polite to him as possible."

"Introduce me, will you?" said the grub-man, looking at me with an expression which seemed to say he was all impatience for an opportunity to give a specimen of his breeding.

Thinking it would prove of benefit to the scrivener, I acquiesced; and, asking the grub-man his name, went up with him to Bartleby.

"Bartleby, this is a friend; you will find him very useful to you."

"Your sarvant, sir, your sarvant," said the grub-man, making a low salutation behind his apron. "Hope you find it pleasant here, sir; nice grounds—cool apartments—hope you'll stay with us some time—try to make it agreeable. What will you have for dinner to-day?"

"I prefer not to dine to-day," said Bartleby, turning away. "It would disagree with me; I am unused to dinners." So saying, he slowly moved to the other side of the inclosure, and took up a position fronting the dead-wall.

"How's this?" said the grub-man, addressing me with a stare of astonishment. "He's odd, ain't he?"

"I think he is a little deranged," said I, sadly.

"Deranged? deranged is it? Well, now, upon my word, I thought that friend of yourn was a gentleman forger; they are always pale and genteel-like, them forgers. I can't help pity 'em—can't help it, sir. Did you know Monroe Edwards?"[14] he added, touchingly, and paused. Then, laying his hand piteously on my shoulder, sighed, "he died of consumption at Sing-Sing.[15] So you weren't acquainted with Monroe?"

"No, I was never socially acquainted with any forgers. But I cannot stop longer. Look to my friend yonder. You will not lose by it. I will see you again."

Some few days after this, I again obtained admission to the Tombs, and went through the corridors in quest of Bartleby; but without finding him.

14  **Monroe Edwards:** Colonel Monroe Edwards (1808–1847), a financier convicted of swindling two businesses out of $25,000 each.
15  **Sing-Sing:** A New York prison.

"I saw him coming from his cell not long ago," said a turnkey, "may be he's gone to loiter in the yards."

So I went in that direction.

"Are you looking for the silent man?" said another turnkey, passing me. "Yonder he lies—sleeping in the yard there. 'Tis not twenty minutes since I saw him lie down."

The yard was entirely quiet. It was not accessible to the common prisoners. The surrounding walls, of amazing thickness, kept off all sounds behind them. The Egyptian character of the masonry weighed upon me with its gloom. But a soft imprisoned turf grew under foot. The heart of the eternal pyramids, it seemed, wherein, by some strange magic, through the clefts, grass-seed, dropped by birds, had sprung.

Strangely huddled at the base of the wall, his knees drawn up, and lying on his side, his head touching the cold stones, I saw the wasted Bartleby. But nothing stirred. I paused; then went close up to him; stooped over, and saw that his dim eyes were open; otherwise he seemed profoundly sleeping. Something prompted me to touch him. I felt his hand, when a tingling shiver ran up my arm and down my spine to my feet.

The round face of the grub-man peered upon me now. "His dinner is ready. Won't he dine to-day, either? Or does he live without dining?"

"Lives without dining," said I, and closed the eyes.

"Eh!—He's asleep, ain't he?"

"With kings and counselors," murmured I.

There would seem little need for proceeding further in this history. Imagination will readily supply the meagre recital of poor Bartleby's interment. But, ere parting with the reader, let me say, that if this little narrative has sufficently interested him, to awaken curiosity as to who Bartleby was, and what manner of life he led prior to the present narrator's making his acquaintance, I can only reply, that in such curiosity I fully share, but am wholly unable to gratify it. Yet here I hardly know whether I should divulge one little item of rumor, which came to my ear a few months after the scrivener's decease. Upon what basis it rested, I could never ascertain; and hence, how true it is I cannot now tell. But, inasmuch as this vague report has not been without a certain suggestive interest to me, however sad, it may prove the same with some others; and so I will briefly mention it. The report was this: that Bartleby had been a subordinate clerk in the Dead Letter Office at Washington, from which he had been suddenly removed by a change in the administration. When I think over this rumor, hardly can I express the emotions which seize me. Dead letters! does it not sound like dead men? Conceive a man by nature and misfortune prone to a pallid hopelessness, can any business seem more fitted to heighten it than that of continually handling these dead letters, and assorting them for the flames? For by the cart-load they are annually burned. Sometimes from out the folded paper the pale clerk takes a ring—the finger it was meant for, perhaps, moulders in the grave; a bank-note sent in swiftest charity—he whom it would relieve, nor eats nor hungers any more; pardon for those who died despairing; hope for those who died unhoping; good tidings for those who died stifled by unrelieved calamities. On errands of life, these letters speed to death.

Ah Bartleby! Ah humanity!

# Edgar Allan Poe

## (1809–1849)

Born in Boston to the talented actress Eliza Arnold and the struggling actor David Poe, Edgar Allan Poe began his life in near destitution, a state in which he would often find himself until his mysterious, purportedly alcohol-induced death on October 7, 1849. Orphaned at a young age, Poe was raised by the affluent Allan family. He grew up to lead the life of a wanderer, moving from a thwarted career as a student at the University of Virginia to the army, which he later left to attend West Point. His ultimate expulsion from the academy destroyed his relationship with his wealthy adopted father, who grew tired of supporting Poe's wandering lifestyle. Poe attempted to support himself through writing, working as an editor on several newspapers, and eventually becoming a successful literary critic. He also wrote and published many poems and short stories in which he took fragments of autobiographical material, such as the loss of his young cousin and wife, Virginia Clemm, and wove them into tales morbidly obsessed with death.

Poe's short stories confronting the nightmarish and grotesque influenced the development of science fiction and the detective story. Although he had already published prolifically, beginning with *Tamerlane and Other Poems* in 1827, it was only after the popular reception of *The Raven and Other Poems* in 1845, three years before his death, that he began to achieve any literary success. His other works include *The Narrative of Arthur Gordon Pym*, *The Conchologist's First Book*, *Tales of the Grotesque and Arabesque*, *Prose Romances*, *Tales*, and *Eureka: A Prose Poem*.

## The Cask of Amontillado

1846

The thousand injuries of Fortunato I had borne as I best could, but when he ventured upon insult, I vowed revenge. You, who so well know the nature of my soul, will not suppose, however, that I gave utterance to a threat. *At length* I would be avenged; this was a point definitely settled—but the very definitiveness with which it was resolved, precluded the idea of risk. I must not only punish, but punish with impunity. A wrong is unredressed when retribution overtakes its redresser. It is equally unredressed when the avenger fails to make himself felt as such to him who has done the wrong.

It must be understood that neither by word nor deed had I given Fortunato cause to doubt my good will. I continued as was my wont, to smile in his face, and he did not perceive that my smile *now* was at the thought of his immolation.

He had a weak point—this Fortunato—although in other regards he was a man to be respected and even feared. He prided himself on his connoisseurship in wine. Few Italians have the true virtuoso spirit. For the most part their enthusiasm is adapted to suit the time and opportunity—to practice imposture upon the British and Austrian *millionaires*. In painting and gemmary Fortunato, like his country men, was a quack—but in the matter of old wines he was sincere. In this respect I did not differ from him materially: I was skilful in the Italian vintages myself, and bought largely whenever I could.

It was about dusk, one evening during the supreme madness of the carnival season, that I encountered my friend. He accosted me with excessive warmth, for he had been drinking much. The man wore motley.[1] He had on a tight-fitting parti-striped dress, and his head was surmounted by the conical cap and bells. I was so pleased to see him, that I thought I should never have done wringing his hand.

I said to him: "My dear Fortunato, you are luckily met. How remarkably well you are looking to-day! But I have received a pipe of what passes for Amontillado,[2] and I have my doubts."

"How?" said he. "Amontillado? A pipe? Impossible! And in the middle of the carnival!"

"I have my doubts," I replied; "and I was silly enough to pay the full Amontillado price without consulting you in the matter. You were not to be found, and I was fearful of losing a bargain."

"Amontillado!"

"I have my doubts."

"Amontillado!"

"And I must satisfy them."

"Amontillado!"

"As you are engaged, I am on my way to Luchesi. If any one has a critical turn, it is he. He will tell me—"

"Luchesi cannot tell Amontillado from Sherry."

"And yet some fools will have it that his taste is a match for your own."

"Come, let us go."

"Whither?"

"To your vaults."

"My friend, no; I will not impose upon your good nature. I perceive you have an engagement. Luchesi——"

"I have no engagement;—come."

"My friend, no. It is not the engagement, but the severe cold with which I perceive you are afflicted. The vaults are insufferably damp. They are encrusted with nitre."

"Let us go, nevertheless. The cold is merely nothing. Amontillado! You have been imposed upon. And as for Luchesi, he cannot distinguish Sherry from Amontillado."

1 **motley:** Multicolored costume associated with the Fool.
2 **Amontillado:** A pale dry sherry made in Montilla, Spain.

Thus speaking, Fortunato possessed himself of my arm. Putting on a mask of black silk, and drawing a *roquelaire*[3] closely about my person, I suffered him to hurry me to my palazzo.

There were no attendants at home; they had absconded to make merry in honor of the time. I had told them that I should not return until the morning, and had given them explicit orders not to stir from the house. These orders were sufficient, I well knew, to insure their immediate disappearance, one and all, as soon as my back was turned.

I took from their sconces two flambeaux, and giving one to Fortunato, bowed him through several suites of rooms to the archway that led into the vaults. I passed down a long and winding staircase, requesting him to be cautious as he followed. We came at length to the foot of the descent, and stood together on the damp ground of the catacombs of the Montresors.

The gait of my friend was unsteady, and the bells upon his cap jingled as he strode.

"The pipe?" said he.

"It is farther on," said I; "but observe the white web-work which gleams from these cavern walls."

He turned toward me, and looked into my eyes with two filmy orbs that distilled the rheum of intoxication.

"Nitre?" he asked, at length.

"Nitre," I replied. "How long have you had that cough?"

"Ugh! ugh! ugh!—ugh! ugh! ugh!—ugh! ugh! ugh!—ugh! ugh! ugh!—ugh! ugh! ugh!"

My poor friend found it impossible to reply for many minutes.

"It is nothing," he said, at last.

"Come," I said, with decision, "we will go back; your health is precious. You are rich, respected, admired, beloved; you are happy, as once I was. You are a man to be missed. For me it is no matter. We will go back; you will be ill, and I cannot be responsible. Besides, there is Luchesi——"

"Enough," he said; "the cough is a mere nothing; it will not kill me. I shall not die of a cough."

"True—true," I replied; "and, indeed, I had no intention of alarming you unnecessarily—but you should use all proper caution. A draught of this Medoc[4] will defend us from the damps."

Here I knocked off the neck of a bottle which I drew from a long row of its fellows that lay upon the mould.

"Drink," I said, presenting him the wine.

He raised it to his lips with a leer. He paused and nodded to me familiarly, while his bells jingled.

"I drink," he said, "to the buried that repose around us."

3 *roquelaire:* French. Knee-length cloak.
4 **Medoc:** A dry red wine from Bordeaux.

"And I to your long life."

He again took my arm, and we proceeded.

"These vaults," he said, "are extensive."

"The Montresors," I replied, "were a great and numerous family."

"I forget your arms."[5]

"A huge human foot d'or, in a field azure; the foot crushes a serpent rampant whose fangs are imbedded in the heel."

"And the motto?"

"*Nemo me impune lacessit.*"[6]

"Good!" he said.

The wine sparkled in his eyes and the bells jingled. My own fancy grew warm with the Medoc. We had passed through walls of piled bones, with casks and puncheons intermingling, into the inmost recesses of the catacombs. I paused again, and this time I made bold to seize Fortunato by an arm above the elbow.

"The nitre!" I said; "see, it increases. It hangs like moss upon the vaults. We are below the river's bed. The drops of moisture trickle among the bones. Come, we will go back ere it is too late. Your cough——"

"It is nothing," he said; "let us go on. But first, another draught of the Medoc."

I broke and reached him a flagon of De Grave.[7] He emptied it at a breath. His eyes flashed with a fierce light. He laughed and threw the bottle upward with a gesticulation I did not understand.

I looked at him in surprise. He repeated the movement—a grotesque one.

"You do not comprehend?" he said.

"Not I," I replied.

"Then you are not of the brotherhood."

"How?"

"You are not of the masons."

"Yes, yes," I said; "yes, yes."

"You? Impossible! A mason?"

"A mason," I replied.

"A sign," he said.

"It is this," I answered, producing a trowel from beneath the folds of my *roquelaire.*

"You just," he exclaimed, recoiling a few paces. "But let us proceed to the Amontillado."

"Be it so," I said, replacing the tool beneath the cloak, and again offering my arm. He leaned upon it heavily. We continued our route in search of the Amontillado. We passed through a range of low arches, descended, passed on, and descending again, arrived at a deep crypt, in which the foulness of the air caused our flambeaux rather to glow than flame.

5 **arms:** A coat of arms or a shield with heraldic symbols indicating ancestry.
6 *Nemo me impune lacessit:* Latin. "No one insults me with impunity."
7 **De Grave:** White wine.

At the most remote end of the crypt there appeared another less spacious. Its walls had been lined with human remains, piled to the vault overhead, in the fashion of the great catacombs of Paris. Three sides of this interior crypt were still ornamented in this manner. From the fourth the bones had been thrown down, and lay promiscuously upon the earth, forming at one point a mount of some size. Within the wall thus exposed by the displacing of the bones, we perceived a still interior recess, in depth about four feet, in width three, in height six or seven. It seemed to have been constructed for no especial use within itself, but formed merely the interval between two of the colossal supports of the roof of the catacombs, and was backed by one of their circumscribing walls of solid granite.

It was in vain that Fortunato, uplifting his dull torch, endeavored to pry into the depth of the recess. Its termination the feeble light did not enable us to see.

"Proceed," I said; "herein is the Amontillado. As for Luchesi——"

"He is an ignoramus," interrupted my friend, as he stepped unsteadily forward, while I followed immediately at his heels. In an instant he had reached the extremity of the niche, and finding his progress arrested by the rock, stood stupidly bewildered. A moment more and I had fettered him to the granite. In its surface were two iron staples, distant from each other about two feet, horizontally. From one of these depended a short chain, from the other a padlock. Throwing the links about his waist, it was but the work of a few seconds to secure it. He was too much astounded to resist. Withdrawing the key I stepped back from the recess.

"Pass your hand," I said, "over the wall; you cannot help feeling the nitre. Indeed it is *very* damp. Once more let me *implore* you to return. No? Then I must positively leave you. But I must first render you all the little attentions in my power."

"The Amontillado!" ejaculated my friend, not yet recovered from his astonishment.

"True," I replied; "the Amontillado."

As I said these words I busied myself among the pile of bones of which I have before spoken. Throwing them aside, I soon uncovered a quantity of building stone and mortar. With these materials and with the aid of my trowel, I began vigorously to wall up the entrance of the niche.

I had scarcely laid the first tier of the masonry when I discovered that the intoxication of Fortunato had in a great measure worn off. The earliest indication I had of this was a low moaning cry from the depth of the recess. It was *not* the cry of a drunken man. There was then a long and obstinate silence. I laid the second tier, and the third, and the fourth; and then I heard the furious vibrations of the chain. The noise lasted for several minutes, during which, that I might hearken to it with the more satisfaction, I ceased my labors and sat down upon the bones. When at last the clanking subsided, I resumed the trowel, and finished without interruption the fifth, the sixth, and the seventh tier. The wall was now nearly upon a level with my breast. I again paused, and holding the flambeaux over the mason-work, threw a few feeble rays upon the figure within.

A succession of loud and shrill screams, bursting suddenly from the throat of the chained form, seemed to thrust me violently back. For a brief moment I hesitated—I trembled. Unsheathing my rapier, I began to grope with it about the recess; but the thought of an instant reassured me. I placed my hand upon the solid fabric of the catacombs, and felt satisfied. I reapproached the wall. I replied to the yells of him who clamored. I re-echoed—I aided—I surpassed them in volume and in strength. I did this, and the clamorer grew still.

It was now midnight, and my task was drawing to a close. I had completed the eighth, the ninth, and the tenth tier. I had finished a portion of the last and the eleventh; there remained but a single stone to be fitted and plastered in. I struggled with its weight; I placed it partially in its destined position. But now there came from out the niche a low laugh that erected the hairs upon my head. It was succeeded by a sad voice, which I had difficulty in recognizing as that of the noble Fortunato. The voice said—

"Ha! ha! ha!—he! he!—a very good joke indeed—an excellent jest. We will have many a rich laugh about it at the palazzo—he! he! he!—over our wine—he! he! he!"

"The Amontillado!" I said.

"He! he! he!—he! he! he!—yes, the Amontillado. But is it not getting late? Will not they be awaiting us at the palazzo, the Lady Fortunato and the rest? Let us be gone."

"Yes," I said, "let us be gone."

*"For the love of God, Montresor!"*

"Yes," I said, "for the love of God!"

But to these words I hearkened in vain for a reply. I grew impatient. I called aloud;

"Fortunato!"

No answer. I called again;

"Fortunato!"

No answer still. I thrust a torch through the remaining aperture and let it fall within. There came forth in return only a jingling of the bells. My heart grew sick—on account of the dampness of the catacombs. I hastened to make an end of my labor. I forced the last stone into its position; I plastered it up. Against the new masonry I reerected the old rampart of bones. For the half of a century no mortal has disturbed them. *In pace requiescat!*[8]

## The Purloined Letter                                                                     1845

*Nil sapientiæ odiosius acumine nimio.*[1]

—SENECA

At Paris, just after dark one gusty evening in the autumn of 18——, I was enjoying the twofold luxury of meditation and a meerschaum, in company with my friend

---

8 *In pace requiescat!:* Latin. May he rest in peace!
1 *Nil sapientiae odiosius acumine nimio:* Latin. Nothing is more distasteful to good sense than too much cunning. Although Poe attributes the quote to the Roman philosopher Seneca (4 B.C.–65 A.D.), the source is the English philosopher, essayist, and politician Francis Bacon (1561–1626).

C. Auguste Dupin, in his little back library, or book-closet, *au troisième*,[2] No. 33, *Rue Dunôt, Faubourg St. Germain*. For one hour at least we had maintained a profound silence; while each, to any casual observer, might have seemed intently and exclusively occupied with the curling eddies of smoke that oppressed the atmosphere of the chamber. For myself, however, I was mentally discussing certain topics which had formed matter for conversation between us at an earlier period of the evening; I mean the affair of the Rue Morgue, and the mystery attending the murder of Marie Rogêt. I looked upon it, therefore, as something of a coincidence, when the door of our apartment was thrown open and admitted our old acquaintance, Monsieur G——, the Prefect of the Parisian police.

We gave him a hearty welcome; for there was nearly half as much of the entertaining as of the contemptible about the man, and we had not seen him for several years. We had been sitting in the dark, and Dupin now arose for the purpose of lighting a lamp, but sat down again, without doing so, upon G.'s saying that he had called to consult us, or rather to ask the opinion of my friend, about some official business which had occasioned a great deal of trouble.

"If it is any point requiring reflection," observed Dupin, as he forbore to enkindle the wick, "we shall examine it to better purpose in the dark."

"That is another of your odd notions," said the Prefect, who had a fashion of calling every thing "odd" that was beyond his comprehension, and thus lived amid an absolute legion of "oddities."

"Very true," said Dupin, as he supplied his visitor with a pipe, and rolled towards him a comfortable chair.

"And what is the difficulty now?" I asked. "Nothing more in the assassination way, I hope?"

"Oh no; nothing of that nature. The fact is, the business is *very* simple indeed, and I make no doubt that we can manage it sufficiently well ourselves; but then I thought Dupin would like to hear the details of it, because it is so excessively *odd*."

"Simple and odd," said Dupin.

"Why, yes; and not exactly that either. The fact is, we have all been a good deal puzzled because the affair *is* so simple, and yet baffles us altogether."

"Perhaps it is the very simplicity of the thing which puts you at fault," said my friend.

"What nonsense you *do* talk!" replied the Prefect, laughing heartily.

"Perhaps the mystery is a little *too* plain," said Dupin.

"Oh, good heavens! who ever heard of such an idea?"

"A little *too* self-evident."

"Ha! ha! ha!—ha! ha! ha!—ho! ho! ho!"—roared our visitor, profoundly amused, "oh, Dupin, you will be the death of me yet!"

"And what, after all, *is* the matter on hand?" I asked.

"Why, I will tell you," replied the Prefect, as he gave a long, steady, and contem-

---

2 *au troisième:* French. On the third (floor). The French do not count the first floor, so Americans would refer to this floor as the fourth.

plative puff, and settled himself in his chair. "I will tell you in a few words; but, before I begin, let me caution you that this is an affair demanding the greatest secrecy, and that I should most probably lose the position I now hold, were it known that I confided it to any one."

"Proceed," said I.

"Or not," said Dupin.

"Well, then; I have received personal information, from a very high quarter, that a certain document of the last importance has been purloined from the royal apartments. The individual who purloined it is known; this beyond a doubt; he was seen to take it. It is known, also, that it still remains in his possession."

"How is this known?" asked Dupin.

"It is clearly inferred," replied the Prefect, "from the nature of the document, and from the non-appearance of certain results which would at once arise from its passing *out* of the robber's possession;—that is to say, from his employing it as he must design in the end to employ it."

"Be a little more explicit," I said.

"Well, I may venture so far as to say that the paper gives its holder a certain power in a certain quarter where such power is immensely valuable." The Prefect was fond of the cant of diplomacy.

"Still I do not quite understand," said Dupin.

"No? Well; the disclosure of the document to a third person, who shall be nameless, would bring in question the honour of a personage of most exalted station; and this fact gives the holder of the document an ascendancy over the illustrious personage whose honour and peace are so jeopardized."

"But this ascendancy," I interposed, "would depend upon the robber's knowledge of the loser's knowledge of the robber. Who would dare—"

"The thief," said G., "is the Minister D——, who dares all things, those unbecoming as well as those becoming a man. The method of the theft was not less ingenious than bold. The document in question—a letter, to be frank—had been received by the personage robbed while alone in the royal *boudoir*. During its perusal she was suddenly interrupted by the entrance of the other exalted personage from whom especially it was her wish to conceal it. After a hurried and vain endeavour to thrust it in a drawer, she was forced to place it, open it was, upon a table. The address, however, was uppermost, and, the contents thus unexposed, the letter escaped notice. At this juncture enters the Minister D——. His lynx eye immediately perceives the paper, recognizes the handwriting of the address, observes the confusion of the personage addressed, and fathoms her secret. After some business transactions, hurried through in his ordinary manner, he produces a letter somewhat similar to the one in question, opens it, pretends to read it, and then places it in close juxtaposition to the other. Again he converses, for some fifteen minutes, upon the public affairs. At length, in taking leave, he takes also from the table the letter to which he had no claim. Its rightful owner saw, but, of course, dared not call attention to the act, in the presence of the third personage who stood at her elbow. The minister decamped; leaving his own letter—one of no importance—upon the table."

"Here, then," said Dupin to me, "you have precisely what you demand to make the ascendancy complete—the robber's knowledge of the loser's knowledge of the robber."

"Yes," replied the Prefect; "and the power thus attained has, for some months past, been wielded, for political purposes, to a very dangerous extent. The personage robbed is more thoroughly convinced, every day, of the necessity of reclaiming her letter. But this, of course, cannot be done openly. In fine, driven to despair, she has committed the matter to me."

"Than whom," said Dupin, amid a perfect whirlwind of smoke, "no more sagacious agent could, I suppose, be desired, or even imagined."

"You flatter me," replied the Prefect; "but it is possible that some such opinion may have been entertained."

"It is clear," said I, "as you observe, that the letter is still in the possession of the minister; since it is this possession, and not any employment of the letter, which bestows the power. With the employment the power departs."

"True," said G.; "and upon this conviction I proceeded. My first care was to make thorough search of the minister's hotel; and here my chief embarrassment lay in the necessity of searching without his knowledge. Beyond all things, I have been warned of the danger which would result from giving him reason to suspect our design."

"But," said I, "you are quite *au fait*[3] in these investigations. The Parisian police have done this thing often before."

"O yes; and for this reason I did not despair. The habits of the minister gave me, too, a great advantage. He is frequently absent from home all night. His servants are by no means numerous. They sleep at a distance from their master's apartment, and being chiefly Neapolitans, are readily made drunk. I have keys, as you know, with which I can open any chamber or cabinet in Paris. For three months a night has not passed, during the greater part of which I have not been engaged, personally, in ransacking the D—— Hôtel. My honour is interested, and, to mention a great secret, the reward is enormous. So I did not abandon the search until I had become fully satisfied that the thief is a more astute man than myself. I fancy that I have investigated every nook and corner of the premises in which it is possible that the paper can be concealed."

"But is it not possible," I suggested, "that although the letter may be in the possession of the minister, as it unquestionably is, he may have concealed it elsewhere than upon his own premises?"

"This is barely possible," said Dupin. "The present peculiar condition of affairs at court, and especially of those intrigues in which D—— is known to be involved, would render the instant availability of the document—its susceptibility of being produced at a moment's notice—a point of nearly equal importance with its possession."

"Its susceptibility of being produced?" said I.

"That is to say, of being *destroyed*," said Dupin.

3 *au fait:* French. Expert, well informed.

"True," I observed; "the paper is clearly then upon the premises. As for its being upon the person of the minister, we may consider that as out of the question."

"Entirely," said the Prefect. "He had been twice waylaid, as if by footpads,[4] and his person rigorously searched under my own inspection."

"You might have spared yourself this trouble," said Dupin. "D——, I presume, is not altogether a fool, and, if not, must have anticipated these waylayings, as a matter of course."

"Not *altogether* a fool," said G., "but then he is a poet, which I take to be only one remove from a fool."

"True," said Dupin, after a long and thoughtful whiff from his meerschaum, "although I have been guilty of certain doggerel myself."

"Suppose you detail," said I, "the particulars of your search."

"Why the fact is, we took our time, and we searched *every where*. I have had long experience in these affairs. I took the entire building, room by room; devoting the nights of a whole week to each. We examined, first, the furniture of each apartment. We opened every possible drawer; and I presume you know that, to a properly trained police agent, such a thing as a *secret* drawer is impossible. Any man is a dolt who permits a 'secret' drawer to escape him in a search of this kind. The thing is *so* plain. There is a certain amount of bulk—of space—to be accounted for in every cabinet. Then we have accurate rules. The fiftieth part of a line could not escape us. After the cabinets we took the chairs. The cushions we probed with the fine long needles you have seen me employ. From the tables we removed the tops."

"Why so?"

"Sometimes the top of a table, or other similarly arranged piece of furniture, is removed by the person wishing to conceal an article; then the leg is excavated, the article deposited within the cavity, and the top replaced. The bottoms and tops of bedposts are employed in the same way."

"But could not the cavity be detected by sounding?" I asked.

"By no means, if, when the article is deposited, a sufficient wadding of cotton be placed around it. Besides, in our case, we were obliged to proceed without noise."

"But you could not have removed—you could not have taken to pieces *all* articles of furniture in which it would have been possible to make a deposit in the manner you mention. A letter may be compressed into a thin spiral roll, not differing much in shape or bulk from a large knitting-needle, and in this form it might be inserted into the rung of a chair, for example. You did not take to pieces all the chairs?"

"Certainly not; but we did better—we examined the rungs of every chair in the hotel, and indeed the jointings of every description of furniture, by the aid of a most powerful microscope.[5] Had there been any traces of recent disturbance we should not have failed to detect it instantly. A single grain of gimlet-dust, for example, would have been as obvious as an apple. Any disorder in the glueing—any unusual gaping in the joints—would have sufficed to insure detection."

---

4 **footpads:** Highwaymen on foot.
5 **microscope:** Magnifying glass.

"I presume you looked to the mirrors, between the boards and the plates, and you probed the beds and the bed-clothes, as well as the curtains and carpets."

"That of course; and when we had absolutely completed every particle of the furniture in this way, then we examined the house itself. We divided its entire surface into compartments, which we numbered, so that none might be missed; then we scrutinized each individual square inch throughout the premises, including the two houses immediately adjoining, with the microscope as before."

"The two houses adjoining!" I exclaimed; "you must have had a great deal of trouble."

"We had; but the reward offered is prodigious."

"You include the *grounds* about the houses?"

"All the grounds are paved with brick. They gave us comparatively little trouble. We examined the moss between the bricks, and found it undisturbed."

"You looked among D——'s papers, of course, and into the books of the library?"

"Certainly; we opened every package and parcel; we not only opened every book, but we turned over every leaf in each volume, not contenting ourselves with a mere shake, according to the fashion of some of our police officers. We also measured the thickness of every book-*cover*, with the most accurate admeasurement, and applied to each the most jealous scrutiny of the microscope. Had any of the bindings been recently meddled with, it would have been utterly impossible that the fact should have escaped observation. Some five or six volumes, just from the hands of the binder, we carefully probed, longitudinally, with the needles."

"You explored the floors beneath the carpets?"

"Beyond doubt. We removed every carpet, and examined the boards with the microscope."

"And the paper on the walls?"

"Yes."

"You looked into the cellars?"

"We did."

"Then," I said, "you have been making a miscalculation, and the letter is *not* upon the premises as you suppose."

"I fear you are right there," said the Prefect. "And now, Dupin, what would you advise me to do?"

"To make a thorough re-search of the premises."

"That is absolutely needless," replied G——. "I am not more sure that I breathe than I am that the letter is not at the Hôtel."

"I have no better advice to give you," said Dupin. "You have, of course, an accurate description of the letter?"

"Oh, yes!"—And here the Prefect, producing a memorandum-book, proceeded to read aloud a minute account of the internal, and especially of the external, appearance of the missing document. Soon after finishing the perusal of this description, he took his departure, more entirely depressed in spirits than I had ever known the good gentleman before.

In about a month afterward he paid us another visit, and found us occupied very nearly as before. He took a pipe and a chair and entered into some ordinary conversation. At length I said;—

"Well, but G——, what of the purloined letter? I presume you have at last made up your mind that there is no such thing as overreaching the Minister?"

"Confound him, say I—yes; I made the re-examination, however, as Dupin suggested—but it was all labour lost, as I knew it would be."

"How much was the reward offered, did you say?" asked Dupin.

"Why, a very great deal—a *very* liberal reward—I don't like to say how much, precisely; but one thing I *will* say, that I wouldn't mind giving my individual check for fifty thousand francs to any one who could obtain me that letter. The fact is, it is becoming of more and more importance every day; and the reward has been lately doubled. If it were trebled, however, I could do no more than I have done."

"Why, yes," said Dupin, drawlingly, between the whiffs of his meerschaum, "I really—think, G——, you have not exerted yourself—to the utmost in this matter. You might—do a little more, I think, eh?"

"How?—in what way?"

"Why—puff, puff,—you might—puff, puff—employ counsel in the matter, eh?—puff, puff, puff. Do you remember the story they tell of Abernethy?"

"No; hang Abernethy!"

"To be sure! hang him and welcome. But, once upon a time, a certain rich miser conceived the design of spunging upon this Abernethy for a medical opinion. Getting up, for this purpose, an ordinary conversation in a private company, he insinuated his case to the physician, as that of an imaginary individual."

"'We will suppose,' said the miser, 'that his symptoms are such and such; now, doctor, what would *you* have directed him to take?'"

"'Take!' said Abernethy, 'why, take *advice*, to be sure.'"

"But," said the Prefect, a little discomposed, "I am *perfectly* willing to take advice, and to pay for it. I would *really* give fifty thousand francs to any one who would aid me in the matter."

"In that case," replied Dupin, opening a drawer, and producing a check-book, "you may as well fill me up a check for the amount you mentioned. When you have signed it, I will hand you the letter."

I was astounded. The Prefect appeared absolutely thunderstricken. For some minutes he remained speechless and motionless, looking incredulously at my friend with open mouth, and eyes that seemed starting from their sockets; then, apparently recovering himself in some measure, he seized a pen, and after several pauses and vacant stares, finally filled up and signed a check for fifty thousand francs, and handed it across the table to Dupin. The latter examined it carefully and deposited it in his pocket-book; then, unlocking an *escritoire*,[6] took thence a letter and gave it to the Prefect. This functionary grasped it in a perfect agony of joy, opened it with a trembling hand, cast a rapid glance at its contents, and then, scrambling and struggling to the

---

6 *escritoire:* French. Writing desk.

door, rushed at length unceremoniously from the room and from the house, without having uttered a syllable since Dupin had requested him to fill up the check.

When he had gone, my friend entered into some explanations.

"The Parisian police," he said, "are exceedingly able in their way. They are persevering, ingenious, cunning, and thoroughly versed in the knowledge which their duties seem chiefly to demand. Thus, when G—— detailed to us his mode of searching the premises at the Hôtel D——, I felt entire confidence in his having made a satisfactory investigation—so far as his labours extended."

"So far as his labours extended?" said I.

"Yes," said Dupin. "The measures adopted were not only the best of their kind, but carried out to absolute perfection. Had the letter been deposited within the range of their search, these fellows would, beyond a question, have found it."

I merely laughed—but he seemed quite serious in all that he said.

"The measures, then," he continued, "were good in their kind, and well executed; their defect lay in their being inapplicable to the case, and to the man. A certain set of highly ingenious resources are, with the Prefect, a sort of Procrustean bed,[7] to which he forcibly adapts his designs. But he perpetually errs by being too deep or too shallow, for the matter in hand; and many a schoolboy is a better reasoner than he. I knew one about eight years of age, whose success at guessing in the game of 'even and odd' attracted universal admiration. This game is simple, and is played with marbles. One player holds in his hand a number of these toys, and demands of another whether that number is even or odd. If the guess is right, the guesser wins one; if wrong, he loses one. The boy to whom I allude won all the marbles of the school. Of course he had some principle of guessing; and this lay in mere observation and admeasurement of the astuteness of his opponents. For example, an arrant simpleton is his opponent, and, holding up his closed hand, asks: 'Are they even or odd?' Our schoolboy replies, 'Odd,' and loses; but upon the second trial he wins, for he then says to himself, 'The simpleton had them even upon the first trial, and his amount of cunning is just sufficient to make him have them odd upon the second; I will therefore guess odd';—he guesses odd, and wins. Now, with a simpleton a degree above the first, he would have reasoned thus: 'This fellow finds that in the first instance I guessed odd, and, in the second, he will propose to himself upon the first impulse, a simple variation from even to odd, as did the first simpleton; but then a second thought will suggest that this is too simple a variation, and finally he will decide upon putting it even as before. I will therefore guess even';—he guesses even, and wins. Now this mode of reasoning in the schoolboy, whom his fellows termed 'lucky,'—what, in its last analysis, is it?"

"It is merely," I said, "an identification of the reasoner's intellect with that of his opponent."

"It is," said Dupin; "and, upon inquiring of the boy by what means he effected the *thorough* identification in which his success consisted, I received answer as follows: 'When I wish to find out how wise, or how stupid, or how good, or how wicked is any

---

7 **Procrustean bed:** Procrustes (Greek mythology) was a giant who bound his victims to a bed, lopping off their limbs or stretching them to fit its length.

one, or what are his thoughts at the moment, I fashion the expression on my face, as accurately as possible, in accordance with the expression of his, and then wait to see what thoughts or sentiments arise in my mind or heart, as if to match or correspond with the expression.' This response of the schoolboy lies at the bottom of all the spurious profundity which has been attributed to Rochefoucault, to La Bougive, to Machiavelli, and to Campanella."[8]

"And the identification," I said, "of the reasoner's intellect with that of his opponent, depends, if I understand you aright, upon the accuracy with which the opponent's intellect is admeasured."

"For its practical value it depends upon this," replied Dupin; "and the Prefect and his cohort fail so frequently, first, by default of this identification, and secondly, by ill-admeasurement, or rather through non-admeasurement, of the intellect with which they are engaged. They consider only their *own* ideas of ingenuity; and, in searching for anything hidden, advert only to the modes in which *they* would have hidden it. They are right in this much—that their own ingenuity is a faithful representative of that of *the mass;* but when the cunning of the individual felon is diverse in character from their own, the felon foils them, of course. This always happens when it is above their own, and very usually when it is below. They have no variation of principle in their investigations; at best, when urged by some unusual emergency—by some extraordinary reward—they extend or exaggerate their old modes of *practice,* without touching their principles. What, for example, in this case of D——, has been done to vary the principle of action? What is all this boring, and probing, and sounding, and scrutinizing with the microscope, and dividing the surface of the building into registered square inches—what is it all but an exaggeration *of the application* of one principle or set of principles of search, which are based upon the one set of notions regarding human ingenuity, to which the Prefect, in the long routine of his duty, has been accustomed? Do you not see he has taken it for granted that *all* men proceed to conceal a letter,—not exactly in a gimlet-hole bored in a chair-leg—but, at least, in *some* out-of-the-way hole or corner suggested by the same tenor or thought which would urge a man to secret a letter in a gimlet-hole bored in a chair-leg? And do you not see also, that such *recherchés*[9] nooks for concealment are adapted only for ordinary occasions, and would be adopted only by ordinary intellects; for, in all cases of concealment, a disposal of the article concealed—a disposal of it in this *recherché* manner—is, in the very first instance, presumable and presumed; and thus its discovery depends, not at all upon the acumen, but altogether upon the mere care, patience, and determination of the seekers; and where the case is of importance—or, what amounts to the same thing in the political eyes, when the reward is of magnitude,—the qualities in question have *never* been known to fail. You will now understand what I meant in suggesting that, had the purloined letter been hidden anywhere within the limits of the Prefect's examination—in other words, had the principle of its concealment

8 **François Duc de la Rochefoucauld (1613–1680), to La Bougive, to Niccolo Machiavelli (1469–1527), and to Tommaso Campanella (1568–1639):** Philosophers and moralists.
9 *recherchés:* French. Rare, out of the ordinary.

been comprehended within the principles of the Prefect—its discovery would have been a matter altogether beyond question. This functionary, however, has been thoroughly mystified; and the remote source of his defeat lies in the supposition that the Minister is a fool, because he has acquired renown as a poet. All fools are poets; this the Prefect *feels;* and he is merely guilty of a *non distributio medii*[10] in thence inferring that all poets are fools."

"But is this really the poet?" I asked. "There are two brothers, I know; and both have attained reputation in letters. The Minister I believe has written learnedly on the Differential Calculus. He is a mathematician, and no poet."

"You are mistaken; I know him well: he is both. As poet *and* mathematician, he would reason well; as mere mathematician, he could not have reasoned at all, and thus would have been at the mercy of the Prefect."

"You surprise me," I said, "by these opinions, which have been contradicted by the voice of the world. You do not mean to set at naught the well-digested idea of centuries. The mathematical reason has long been regarded as *the* reason *par excellence.*"

"*'Il y a à parier,'*" replied Dupin, quoting from Chamfort, "*'que toute idée publique, toute convention reçue, est une sottise, car elle a convenu au plus grand nombre.'*[11] The mathematicians, I grant you, have done their best to promulgate the popular error to which you allude, and which is none the less an error for its promulgation as truth. With an art worthy a better cause, for example, they have insinuated the term 'analysis' into application to algebra. The French are the originators of this particular deception; but if a term is of any importance—if words derive any value from applicability—then 'analysis' conveys 'algebra' about as much as, in Latin, *'ambitus'* implies 'ambition,' *'religio'* 'religion,' or *'homines honesti,'* a set of honourable men."

"You have a quarrel on hand, I see," said I, "with some of the algebraists of Paris; but proceed."

"I dispute the availability, and thus the value, of that reason which is cultivated in any especial form other than the abstractly logical. I dispute, in particular, the reason educed by mathematical study. The mathematics are the science of form and quantity; mathematical reasoning is merely logic applied to observation upon form and quantity. The great error lies in supposing that even the truths of what is called *pure* algebra, are abstract or general truths. And this error is so egregious that I am confounded at the universality with which it has been received. Mathematical axioms are *not* axioms of general truth. What is true of *relation*—of form and quantity—is often grossly false in regard to morals, for example. In this latter science it is very usually *un*true that the aggregated parts are equal to the whole. In chemistry also the axiom fails. In the consideration of motive it fails; for two motives, each of a given value, have not, necessarily, a value when united, equal to the sum of their values apart. There are numerous other mathematical truths which are only truths within the lim-

10  *non distributio medii:* Latin. A fallacy in logic in which the premises do not justify the conclusion.
11  *'Il y a à parier . . . que toute idée publique, tout convention reçue, est une sottise, car elle a convenue au plus grand nombre':* French. The odds are that every accepted notion is nonsense because it has been accepted by the majority. Sebastian Roch Nicolas Chamfort (1741–1794), French author.

its of *relation*. But the mathematician argues from his *finite truths,* through habit, as if they were of an absolutely general applicability—as the world indeed imagines them to be. Bryant, in his very learned 'Mythology,'[12] mentions an analogous source of error, when he says that 'although the Pagan fables are not believed, yet we forget ourselves continually, and make inferences from them as existing realities.' With the algebraists, however, who are Pagans themselves, the 'Pagan fables' *are* believed, and the inferences are made, not so much through lapse of memory as through an unaccountable addling of the brains. In short, I never yet encountered the mere mathematician who could be trusted out of equal roots, or one who did not clandestinely hold it as a point of his faith that $x^2 + px$ was absolutely and unconditionally equal to $q$. Say to one of these gentlemen, by way of experiment, if you please, that you believe occasions may occur where $x^2 + px$ is *not* altogether equal to $q$, and having made him understand what you mean, get out of his reach as speedily as convenient, for, beyond doubt, he will endeavour to knock you down."

"I mean to say," continued Dupin, while I merely laughed at his last observations, "that if the Minister had been no more than a mathematician, the Prefect would have been under no necessity of giving me this check. I knew him, however, as both mathematician and poet, and my measures were adapted to his capacity, with reference to the circumstances by which he was surrounded. I knew him as a courtier, too, and as a bold *intriguant*. Such a man, I considered, could not fail to be aware of the ordinary political modes of action. He could not have failed to anticipate—and events have proved that he did not fail to anticipate—the waylayings to which he was subjected. He must have foreseen, I reflected, the secret investigations of his premises. His frequent absences from home at night, which were hailed by the Prefect as certain aids to his success, I regarded only as *ruses,* to afford opportunity for thorough search to the police, and thus the sooner to impress them with the conviction to which G——, in fact, did finally arrive—the conviction that the letter was not upon the premises. I felt, also, that the whole train of thought, which I was at some pains in detailing to you just now, concerning the invariable principle of political action in searches for articles concealed—I felt that this whole train of thought would necessarily pass through the mind of the Minister. It would imperatively lead him to despise all the ordinary *nooks* of concealment. *He* could not, I reflected, be so weak as not to see that the most intricate and remote recess of his hotel would be as open as his commonest closets to the eyes, to the probes, to the gimlets, and to the microscopes of the Prefect. I saw, in fine, that he would be driven, as a matter of course, to simplicity, if not deliberately induced to it as a matter of choice. You will remember, perhaps, how desperately the Prefect laughed when I suggested, upon our first interview, that it was just possible this mystery troubled him so much on account of its being so *very* self-evident."

"Yes," said I, "I remember his merriment well. I really thought he would have fallen into convulsions."

---

12 **Bryant:** Jacob Bryant (1715–1804), author of *A New System, or an Analysis of Ancient Mythology* (1774–1776). Bryant believed that all of mythology connected to a Christian understanding of the world.

"The material world," continued Dupin, "abounds with very strict analogies to the immaterial; and thus some color of truth has been given to the rhetorical dogma, that metaphor, or simile, may be made to strengthen an argument as well as to embellish a description. The principle of the *vis inertiae*,[13] for example, seems to be identical in physics and metaphysics. It is not more true in the former, that a large body is with more difficulty set in motion than a smaller one, and that its subsequent *momentum* is commensurate with this difficulty, than it is, in the latter, that intellects of the vaster capacity, while more forcible, more constant, and more eventful in their movements than those of inferior grade, are yet the less readily moved, and more embarrassed and full of hesitation in the first few steps of their progress. Again: have you ever noticed which of the street signs, over the shop doors, are the most attractive of attention?"

"I have never given the matter a thought," I said.

"There is a game of puzzles," he resumed, "which is played upon a map. One party playing requires another to find a given word—the name of town, river, state, or empire—any word, in short, upon the motley and perplexed surface of the chart. A novice in the game generally seeks to embarrass his opponents by giving them the most minutely lettered names; but the adept selects such words as stretch, in large characters, from one end of the chart to the other. These, like the over-largely lettered signs and placards of the street, escape observation by the dint of being excessively obvious; and here the physical oversight is precisely analogous with the moral inapprehension by which the intellect suffers to pass unnoticed those considerations which are too obtrusively and too palpably self-evident. But this is a point, it appears, somewhat above or beneath the understanding of the Prefect. He never once thought it probable, or possible, that the Minister had deposited the letter immediately beneath the nose of the whole world, by way of best preventing any portion of that world from perceiving it."

"But the more I reflected upon the daring, dashing, and discriminating ingenuity of D——; upon the fact that the document must always have been *at hand,* if he intended to use it to good purpose; and upon the decisive evidence, obtained by the Prefect, that it was not hidden within the limits of that dignitary's ordinary search— the more satisfied I became that, to conceal this letter, the Minister had resorted to the comprehensive and sagacious expedient of not attempting to conceal it at all."

"Full of these ideas, I prepared myself with a pair of green spectacles, and called one fine morning, quite by accident, at the Ministerial hotel. I found D—— at home, yawning, lounging, and dawdling, as usual, and pretending to be in the last extremity of *ennui*. He is, perhaps, the most really energetic human being now alive—but that is only when nobody sees him."

"To be even with him, I complained of my weak eyes, and lamented the necessity of the spectacles, under cover of which I cautiously and thoroughly surveyed the whole apartment, while seemingly intent only upon the conversation of my host."

"I paid especial attention to a large writing-table near which he sat, and upon which lay confusedly, some miscellaneous letters and other papers, with one or two

---

13 *vis inertiae:* Power of inertia.

musical instruments and a few books. Here, however, after a long and very deliberate scrutiny, I saw nothing to excite particular suspicion."

"At length my eyes, in going the circuit of the room, fell upon a trumpery filigree card-rack of pasteboard, that hung dangling by a dirty blue ribbon, from a little brass knob just beneath the middle of the mantel-piece. In this rack, which had three or four compartments, were five or six visiting cards and a solitary letter. This last was much soiled and crumpled. It was torn nearly in two, across the middle—as if a design, in the first instance, to tear it entirely up as worthless, had been altered, or stayed, in the second. It had a large black seal, bearing the D—— cipher *very* conspicuously, and was addressed, in a diminutive female hand, to D——, the minister, himself. It was thrust carelessly, and even, as it seemed, contemptuously, into one of the upper divisions of the rack."

"No sooner had I glanced at this letter than I concluded it to be that of which I was in search. To be sure, it was, to all appearance, radically different from the one of which the Prefect had read us so minute a description. Here the seal was large and black, with the D—— cipher; there it was small and red, with the ducal arms of the S—— family. Here, the address, to the Minister, was diminutive and feminine; there the superscription, to a certain royal personage, was markedly bold and decided; the size alone formed a point of correspondence. But, then, the *radicalness* of these differences, which was excessive; the dirt; the soiled and torn condition of the paper, so inconsistent with the *true* methodical habits of D——, and so suggestive of a design to delude the beholder into an idea of the worthlessness of the document; these things, together with the hyperobtrusive situation of this document, full in the view of every visitor, and thus exactly in accordance with the conclusions to which I had previously arrived; these things, I say, were strongly corroborative of suspicion, in one who came with the intention to suspect."

"I protracted my visit as long as possible, and, while I maintained a most animated discussion with the Minister, upon a topic which I knew well had never failed to interest and excite him, I kept my attention really riveted upon the letter. In this examination, I committed to memory its external appearance and arrangement in the rack; and also fell, at length, upon a discovery which set at rest whatever trivial doubt I might have entertained. In scrutinizing the edges of the paper, I observed them to be more *chafed* than seemed necessary. They presented the *broken* appearance which is manifested when a stiff paper, having been once folded and pressed with a folder, is refolded in a reversed direction, in the same creases or edges which had formed the original fold. This discovery was sufficient. It was clear to me that the letter had been turned, as a glove, inside out, re-directed, and re-sealed. I bade the Minister good morning, and took my departure at once, leaving a gold snuff-box upon the table."

"The next morning I called for the snuff-box, when we resumed, quite eagerly, the conversation of the preceding day. While thus engaged, however, a loud report, as if of a pistol, was heard immediately beneath the windows of the hotel, and was succeeded by a series of fearful screams, and the shoutings of a mob. D—— rushed to a casement, threw it open, and looked out. In the meantime I stepped to the card-rack, took the letter, put it in my pocket, and replaced it by a *facsimile,* (so far as regards externals) which I had carefully prepared at my lodgings; imitating the D—— cipher, very readily, by means of a seal formed of bread."

"The disturbance in the street had been occasioned by the frantic behaviour of a man with a musket. He had fired it among a crowd of women and children. It proved, however, to have been without ball, and the fellow was suffered to go his way as a lunatic or a drunkard. When he had gone, D—— came from the window, whither I had followed him immediately upon securing the object in view. Soon afterward I bade him farewell. The pretended lunatic was a man in my own pay."

"But what purpose had you," I asked, "in replacing the letter by a *facsimile?* Would it not have been better, at the first visit, to have seized it openly, and departed?"

"D——," replied Dupin, "is a desperate man, and a man of nerve. His hotel, too, is not without attendants devoted to his interests. Had I made the wild attempt you suggest, I might never have left the Ministerial presence alive. The good people of Paris might have heard of me no more. But I had an object apart from these considerations. You know my political prepossessions. In this matter, I act as a partisan of the lady concerned. For eighteen months the Minister has had her in his power. She has now him in hers; since, being unaware that the letter is not in his possession, he will proceed with his exactions as if it was. Thus will he inevitably commit himself, at once, to his political destruction. His downfall, too, will not be more precipitate than awkward. It is all very well to talk about the *facilis descensus Averni;*[14] but in all kinds of climbing, as Catalani[15] said of singing, it is far more easy to get up than to come down. In the present instance I have no sympathy—at least no pity—for him who descends. He is that *monstrum horrendum,*[16] an unprincipled man of genius. I confess, however, that I should like very well to know the precise character of his thoughts, when, being defied by her whom the Prefect terms 'a certain personage,' he is reduced to opening the letter which I left for him in the card-rack."

"How? did you put any thing particular in it?"

"Why—it did not seem altogether right to leave the interior blank—that would have been insulting. D——, at Vienna once, did me an evil turn, which I told him, quite good-humouredly, that I should remember. So, as I knew he would feel some curiosity in regard to the identity of the person who had outwitted him, I thought it a pity not to give him a clue. He is well acquainted with my MS., and I just copied into the middle of the blank sheet the words—

——Un dessein si funeste,
S'il n'est digne d'Atrée, est digne de Thyeste.[17]

They are to be found in Crébillon's 'Atrée.'"

14  *facilis descensus Averni:* Latin. "The easy descent to Hell," quoted from Virgil's *Aeneid.*
15  **Catalani:** Angelica Catalani (1780–1849), Italian opera singer.
16  *monstrum horrendum:* Latin. "Horrible monster" or "dreadful monstrosity." Also from Virgil.
17  **"Un dessein si funeste, S'il n'est digne d'Atrée, est digne de Thyeste":** French. "So deadly a scheme, if not worthy of Atreus is worthy of Thyestes." From the play *Atrée et Thyeste* (1707) by French playwright Crébillon. In the play, Thyestes seduces the wife of his brother Atreus. In revenge, Atreus kills Thyestes' sons and serves them to their father for dinner.

# Mary Shelley

## (1797–1851)

Mary Shelley was born in Somers Town, Great Britain, in 1797 to author Mary Wollstonecraft, an influential feminist, and philosopher William Godwin. Her mother died shortly after giving birth and Mary's father raised her. She was educated at home with two sisters and two brothers, and little distinction was made in their education based on gender. The children were often exposed to acquaintances of Godwin's, ranging from Samuel Taylor Coleridge to scientists like Humphry Davy and William Nicholson. These men in particular would become influences for *Frankenstein* (1818). Another acquaintance of Godwin's was the young Percy Bysshe Shelley. At the age of sixteen, Mary eloped with Percy, despite the fact that he was already married. The two kept a journal of their elopement, which Mary later published as *History of a Six Weeks' Tour* (1817). Upon their return to England, the couple found themselves shunned because of their transgression; Godwin refused to even see Percy. The two were finally married in late December 1816, just two weeks after Percy's wife Harriet committed suicide.

The couple left England for Italy in 1818 to escape persecution, but they found trouble there as well. In 1819, Mary became depressed after the death of her second child (her first died in 1817). Her depression was only partially relieved by the birth of Percy, their only surviving child. In 1822, her husband drowned during a sailing trip and Mary, lacking the financial support to continue living in Italy, was forced to return to England a year later, where she devoted herself to raising her son. In the following years she published *The Life and Adventures of Castruccio, Prince of Lucca* (1823), *The Last Man* (1826), *The Fortunes of Perkin Warbeck* (1830), *Lodore* (1835), and *Falkner* (1837).

## The Mortal Immortal                                                    1834

### A Tale

July 16, 1833.—This is a memorable anniversary for me; on it I complete my three hundred and twenty-third year!

The Wandering Jew?—certainly not. More than eighteen centuries have passed over his head. In comparison with him, I am a very young Immortal.

Am I, then, immortal? This is a question which I have asked myself, by day and night, for now three hundred and three years, and yet cannot answer it. I detected a gray hair amidst my brown locks this very day—that surely signifies decay. Yet it may have remained concealed there for three hundred years—for some persons have become entirely white-headed before twenty years of age.

I will tell my story, and my reader shall judge for me. I will tell my story, and so contrive to pass some few hours of a long eternity, become so wearisome to me. For ever! Can it be? to live for ever! I have heard of enchantments, in which the victims were plunged into a deep sleep, to wake, after a hundred years, as fresh as ever: I have heard of the Seven Sleepers—thus to be immortal would not be so burthensome: but, oh! the weight of never-ending time—the tedious passage of the still-succeeding hours! How happy was the fabled Nourjahad!——But to my task.

All the world has heard of Cornelius Agrippa. His memory is as immortal as his arts have made me. All the world has also heard of his scholar, who, unawares, raised the foul fiend during his master's absence, and was destroyed by him. The report, true or false, of this accident, was attended with many inconveniences to the renowned philosopher. All his scholars at once deserted him—his servants disappeared. He had no one near him to put coals on his ever-burning fires while he slept, or to attend to the changeful colours of his medicines while he studied. Experiment after experiment failed, because one pair of hands was insufficient to complete them: the dark spirits laughed at him for not being able to retain a single mortal in his service.

I was then very young—very poor—and very much in love. I had been for about a year the pupil of Cornelius, though I was absent when this accident took place. On my return, my friends implored me not to return to the alchymist's abode. I trembled as I listened to the dire tale they told; I required no second warning; and when Cornelius came and offered me a purse of gold if I would remain under his roof, I felt as if Satan himself tempted me. My teeth chattered—my hair stood on end:—I ran off as fast as my trembling knees would permit.

My failing steps were directed whither for two years they had every evening been attracted,—a gently bubbling spring of pure living waters, beside which lingered a dark-haired girl, whose beaming eyes were fixed on the path I was accustomed each night to tread. I cannot remember the hour when I did not love Bertha; we had been neighbours and playmates from infancy—her parents, like mine, were of humble life, yet respectable—our attachment had been a source of pleasure to them. In an evil hour, a malignant fever carried off both her father and mother, and Bertha became an orphan. She would have found a home beneath my paternal roof, but, unfortunately, the old lady of the near castle, rich, childless, and solitary, declared her intention to adopt her. Henceforth Bertha was clad in silk—inhabited a marble palace—and was looked on as being highly favoured by fortune. But in her new situation among her new associates, Bertha remained true to the friend of her humbler days; she often visited the cottage of my father, and when forbidden to go thither, she would stray towards the neighbouring wood, and meet me beside its shady fountain.

She often declared that she owed no duty to her new protectress equal in sanctity to that which bound us. Yet still I was too poor to marry, and she grew weary of being tormented on my account. She had a haughty but an impatient spirit, and grew angry at the obstacles that prevented our union. We met now after an absence, and she had been sorely beset while I was away; she complained bitterly, and almost reproached me for being poor. I replied hastily,—

"I am honest, if I am poor!—were I not, I might soon become rich!"

This exclamation produced a thousand questions. I feared to shock her by owning the truth, but she drew it from me; and then, casting a look of disdain on me, she said—

"You pretend to love, and you fear to face the Devil for my sake!"

I protested that I had only dreaded to offend her;—while she dwelt on the magnitude of the reward that I should receive. Thus encouraged—shamed by her—led on by love and hope, laughing at my late fears, with quick steps and a light heart, I returned to accept the offers of the alchymist, and was instantly installed in my office.

A year passed away. I became possessed of no insignificant sum of money. Custom had banished my fears. In spite of the most painful vigilance, I had never detected the trace of a cloven foot; nor was the studious silence of our abode ever disturbed by demoniac howls. I still continued my stolen interviews with Bertha, and Hope dawned on me—Hope—but not perfect joy; for Bertha fancied that love and security were enemies, and her pleasure was to divide them in my bosom. Though true of heart, she was somewhat of a coquette in manner; and I was jealous as a Turk. She slighted me in a thousand ways, yet would never acknowledge herself to be in the wrong. She would drive me mad with anger, and then force me to beg her pardon. Sometimes she fancied that I was not sufficiently submissive, and then she had some story of a rival, favoured by her protectress. She was surrounded by silk-clad youths— the rich and gay—What chance had the sad-robed scholar of Cornelius compared with these?

On one occasion, the philosopher made such large demands upon my time, that I was unable to meet her as I was wont. He was engaged in some mighty work, and I was forced to remain, day and night, feeding his furnaces and watching his chemical preparations. Bertha waited for me in vain at the fountain. Her haughty spirit fired at this neglect; and when at last I stole out during the few short minutes allotted to me for slumber, and hoped to be consoled by her, she received me with disdain, dismissed me in scorn, and vowed that any man should possess her hand rather than he who could not be in two places at once for her sake. She would be revenged!—And truly she was. In my dingy retreat I heard that she had been hunting, attended by Albert Hoffer. Albert Hoffer was favoured by her protectress, and the three passed in cavalcade before my smoky window. Methought that they mentioned my name—it was followed by a laugh of derision, as her dark eyes glanced contemptuously towards my abode.

Jealousy, with all its venom, and all its misery, entered my breast. Now I shed a torrent of tears, to think that I should never call her mine; and, anon, I imprecated a thousand curses on her inconstancy. Yet, still I must stir the fires of the alchymist, still attend on the changes of his unintelligible medicines.

Cornelius had watched for three days and nights, nor closed his eyes. The progress of his alembics was slower than he expected: in spite of his anxiety, sleep weighed upon his eyelids. Again and again he threw off drowsiness with more than human energy; again and again it stole away his senses. He eyed his crucibles wistfully. "Not ready yet," he murmured; "will another night pass before the work is accomplished? Winzy, you are vigilant—you are faithful—you have slept, my boy—you slept last night. Look at that glass vessel. The liquid it contains is of a soft rose-colour:

the moment it begins to change its hue, awaken me—till then I may close my eyes. First, it will turn white, and then emit golden flashes; but wait not till then; when the rose-colour fades, rouse me." I scarcely heard the last words, muttered, as they were, in sleep. Even then he did not quite yield to nature. "Winzy, my boy," he again said, "do not touch the vessel—do not put it to your lips; it is a philter—a philter to cure love; you would not cease to love your Bertha—beware to drink!"

And he slept. His venerable head sunk on his breast, and I scarce heard his regular breathing. For a few minutes I watched the vessel—the rosy hue of the liquid remained unchanged. Then my thoughts wandered—they visited the fountain, and dwelt on a thousand charming scenes never to be renewed—never! Serpents and adders were in my heart as the word "Never!" half formed itself on my lips. False girl!—false and cruel! Never more would she smile on me as that evening she smiled on Albert. Worthless, detested woman! I would not remain unrevenged—she should see Albert expire at her feet—she should die beneath my vengeance. She had smiled in disdain and triumph—she knew my wretchedness and her power. Yet what power had she?—the power of exciting my hate—my utter scorn—my—oh, all but indifference! Could I attain that—could I regard her with careless eyes, transferring my rejected love to one fairer and more true, that were indeed a victory!

A bright flash darted before my eyes. I had forgotten the medicine of the adept; I gazed on it with wonder: flashes of admirable beauty, more bright than those which the diamond emits when the sun's rays are on it, glanced from the surface of the liquid; an odour the most fragrant and grateful stole over my sense; the vessel seemed one globe of living radiance, lovely to the eye, and most inviting to the taste. The first thought, instinctively inspired by the grosser sense, was, I will—I must drink. I raised the vessel to my lips. "It will cure me of love—of torture!" Already I had quaffed half of the most delicious liquor ever tasted by the palate of man, when the philosopher stirred. I started—I dropped the glass—the fluid flamed and glanced along the floor, while I felt Cornelius's grip at my throat, as he shrieked aloud, "Wretch! you have destroyed the labour of my life!"

The philosopher was totally unaware that I had drunk any portion of his drug. His idea was, and I gave a tacit assent to it, that I had raised the vessel from curiosity, and that, frighted at its brightness, and the flashes of intense light it gave forth, I had let it fall. I never undeceived him. The fire of the medicine was quenched—the fragrance died away—he grew calm, as a philosopher should under the heaviest trials, and dismissed me to rest.

I will not attempt to describe the sleep of glory and bliss which bathed my soul in paradise during the remaining hours of that memorable night. Words would be faint and shallow types of my enjoyment, or of the gladness that possessed my bosom when I woke. I trod air—my thoughts were in heaven. Earth appeared heaven, and my inheritance upon it was to be one trance of delight. "This it is to be cured of love," I thought; "I will see Bertha this day, and she will find her lover cold and regardless; too happy to be disdainful, yet how utterly indifferent to her!"

The hours danced away. The philosopher, secure that he had once succeeded, and believing that he might again, began to concoct the same medicine once more. He

was shut up with his books and drugs, and I had a holiday. I dressed myself with care; I looked in an old but polished shield, which served me for a mirror; methought my good looks had wonderfully improved. I hurried beyond the precincts of the town, joy in my soul, the beauty of heaven and earth around me. I turned my steps towards the castle—I could look on its lofty turrets with lightness of heart, for I was cured of love. My Bertha saw me afar off, as I came up the avenue. I know not what sudden impulse animated her bosom, but at the sight, she sprung with a light fawn-like bound down the marble steps, and was hastening towards me. But I had been perceived by another person. The old high-born hag, who called herself her protectress, and was her tyrant, had seen me, also; she hobbled, panting, up the terrace; a page, as ugly as herself, held up her train, and fanned her as she hurried along, and stopped my fair girl with a "How, now, my bold mistress? whither so fast? Back to your cage—hawks are abroad!"

Bertha clasped her hands—her eyes were still bent on my approaching figure. I saw the contest. How I abhorred the old crone who checked the kind impulses of my Bertha's softening heart. Hitherto, respect for her rank had caused me to avoid the lady of the castle; now I disdained such trivial considerations. I was cured of love, and lifted above all human fears; I hastened forwards, and soon reached the terrace. How lovely Bertha looked! her eyes flashing fire, her cheeks glowing with impatience and anger, she was a thousand times more graceful and charming than ever—I no longer loved—Oh! no, I adored—worshipped—idolized her!

She had that morning been persecuted, with more than usual vehemence, to consent to an immediate marriage with my rival. She was reproached with the encouragement that she had shown him—she was threatened with being turned out of doors with disgrace and shame. Her proud spirit rose in arms at the threat; but when she remembered the scorn that she had heaped upon me, and how, perhaps, she had thus lost one whom she now regarded as her only friend, she wept with remorse and rage. At that moment I appeared. "O, Winzy!" she exclaimed, "take me to your mother's cot; swiftly let me leave the detested luxuries and wretchedness of this noble dwelling—take me to poverty and happiness."

I clasped her in my arms with transport. The old lady was speechless with fury, and broke forth into invective only when we were far on our road to my natal cottage. My mother received the fair fugitive, escaped from a gilt cage to nature and liberty, with tenderness and joy; my father, who loved her, welcomed her heartily; it was a day of rejoicing, which did not need the addition of the celestial potion of the alchymist to steep me in delight.

Soon after this eventful day, I became the husband of Bertha. I ceased to be the scholar of Cornelius, but I continued his friend. I always felt grateful to him for having, unawares, procured me that delicious draught of a divine elixir, which, instead of curing me of love (sad cure! solitary and joyless remedy for evils which seem blessings to the memory), had inspired me with courage and resolution, thus winning for me an inestimable treasure in my Bertha.

I often called to mind that period of trance-like inebriation with wonder. The drink of Cornelius had not fulfilled the task for which he affirmed that it had been prepared, but its effects were more potent and blissful than words can express. They had faded by degrees, yet they lingered long—and painted life in hues of splendour. Bertha often wondered at my lightness of heart and unaccustomed gaiety; for, before, I had been rather serious, or even sad, in my disposition. She loved me the better for my cheerful temper, and our days were winged by joy.

Five years afterwards I was suddenly summoned to the bedside of the dying Cornelius. He had sent for me in haste, conjuring my instant presence. I found him stretched on his pallet, enfeebled even to death; all of life that yet remained animated his piercing eyes, and they were fixed on a glass vessel, full of a roseate liquid.

"Behold," he said, in a broken and inward voice, "the vanity of human wishes! a second time my hopes are about to be crowned, a second time they are destroyed. Look at that liquor—you remember five years ago I had prepared the same, with the same success;—then, as now, my thirsting lips expected to taste the immortal elixir— you dashed it from me! and at present it is too late."

He spoke with difficulty, and fell back on his pillow. I could not help saying,—

"How, revered master, can a cure for love restore you to life?"

A faint smile gleamed across his face as I listened earnestly to his scarcely intelligible answer.

"A cure for love and for all things—the Elixir of Immortality. Ah! if now I might drink, I should live for ever!"

As he spoke, a golden flash gleamed from the fluid; a well-remembered fragrance stole over the air; he raised himself, all weak as he was—strength seemed miraculously to re-enter his frame—he stretched forth his hand—a loud explosion startled me—a ray of fire shot up from the elixir, and the glass vessel which contained it was shivered to atoms! I turned my eyes towards the philosopher; he had fallen back—his eyes were glassy—his features rigid—he was dead!

But I lived, and was to live for ever! So said the unfortunate alchymist, and for a few days I believed his words. I remembered the glorious drunkenness that had followed my stolen draught. I reflected on the change I had felt in my frame—in my soul. The bounding elasticity of the one—the buoyant lightness of the other. I surveyed myself in a mirror, and could perceive no change in my features during the space of the five years which had elapsed. I remembered the radiant hues and grateful scent of that delicious beverage—worthy the gift it was capable of bestowing—I was, then, IMMORTAL!

A few days after I laughed at my credulity. The old proverb, that "a prophet is least regarded in his own country," was true with respect to me and my defunct master. I loved him as a man—I respected him as a sage—but I derided the notion that he could command the powers of darkness, and laughed at the superstitious fears with which he was regarded by the vulgar. He was a wise philosopher, but had no acquaintance with any spirits but those clad in flesh and blood. His science was simply human; and human science, I soon persuaded myself, could never conquer nature's laws so far as to imprison the soul for ever within its carnal habitation. Cornelius had brewed a soul-refreshing drink—more inebriating than wine—sweeter and more fragrant than any fruit: it possessed probably strong medicinal powers, imparting gladness to the heart and vigor to the limbs; but its effects would wear out; already were they diminished in my frame. I was a lucky fellow to have quaffed health and joyous spirits, and perhaps long life, at my master's hands; but my good fortune ended there: longevity was far different from immortality.

I continued to entertain this belief for many years. Sometimes a thought stole across me—Was the alchymist indeed deceived? But my habitual credence was, that I should meet the fate of all the children of Adam at my appointed time—a little late, but still at a natural age. Yet it was certain that I retained a wonderfully youthful look. I was laughed at for my vanity in consulting the mirror so often, but I consulted it in vain—my brow was untrenched—my cheeks—my eyes—my whole person continued as untarnished as in my twentieth year.

I was troubled. I looked at the faded beauty of Bertha—I seemed more like her son. By degrees our neighbours began to make similar observations, and I found at last that I went by the name of the Scholar bewitched. Bertha herself grew uneasy. She became jealous and peevish, and at length she began to question me. We had no children; we were all in all to each other; and though, as she grew older, her vivacious spirit became a little allied to ill-temper, and her beauty sadly diminished, I cherished her in my heart as the mistress I had idolized, the wife I had sought and won with such perfect love.

At last our situation became intolerable: Bertha was fifty—I twenty years of age. I had, in very shame, in some measure adopted the habits of a more advanced age; I no longer mingled in the dance among the young and gay, but my heart bounded along with them while I restrained my feet; and a sorry figure I cut among the Nestors of our village. But before the time I mention, things were altered—we were universally shunned; we were—at least, I was—reported to have kept up an iniquitous acquaintance with some of my former master's supposed friends. Poor Bertha was pitied, but deserted. I was regarded with horror and detestation.

What was to be done? we sat by our winter fire—poverty had made itself felt, for none would buy the produce of my farm; and often I had been forced to journey twenty miles, to some place where I was not known, to dispose of our property. It is true we had saved something for an evil day—that day was come.

We sat by our lone fireside—the old-hearted youth and his antiquated wife. Again Bertha insisted on knowing the truth; she recapitulated all she had ever heard said about me, and added her own observations. She conjured me to cast off the spell; she described how much more comely gray hairs were than my chestnut locks; she descanted on the reverence and respect due to age—how preferable to the slight regard paid to mere children: could I imagine that the despicable gifts of youth and good looks outweighed disgrace, hatred, and scorn? Nay, in the end I should be burnt as a dealer in the black art, while she, to whom I had not deigned to communicate any portion of my good fortune, might be stoned as my accomplice. At length she insinuated that I must share my secret with her, and bestow on her like benefits to those I myself enjoyed, or she would denounce me—and then she burst into tears.

Thus beset, methought it was the best way to tell the truth. I revealed it as tenderly as I could, and spoke only of a *very long life,* not of immortality—which representation, indeed, coincided best with my own ideas. When I ended, I rose and said,

"And now, my Bertha, will you denounce the lover of your youth?—You will not, I know. But it is too hard, my poor wife, that you should suffer from my ill-luck and the accursed arts of Cornelius. I will leave you—you have wealth enough, and friends will return in my absence. I will go; young as I seem, and strong as I am, I can work and gain my bread among strangers, unsuspected and unknown. I loved you in youth; God is my witness that I would not desert you in age, but that your safety and happiness require it."

I took my cap and moved towards the door; in a moment Bertha's arms were round my neck, and her lips were pressed to mine. "No, my husband, my Winzy," she said, "you shall not go alone—take me with you; we will remove from this place, and, as you say, among strangers we shall be unsuspected and safe. I am not so very old as quite to shame you, my Winzy; and I dare say the charm will soon wear off, and, with the blessing of God, you will become more elderly-looking, as is fitting; you shall not leave me."

I returned the good soul's embrace heartily. "I will not, my Bertha; but for your sake I had not thought of such a thing. I will be your true, faithful husband while you are spared to me, and do my duty by you to the last."

The next day we prepared secretly for our emigration. We were obliged to make great pecuniary sacrifices—it could not be helped. We realised a sum sufficient, at least, to maintain us while Bertha lived; and, without saying adieu to any one, quitted our native country to take refuge in a remote part of western France.

It was a cruel thing to transport poor Bertha from her native village, and the friends of her youth, to a new country, new language, new customs. The strange secret of my destiny rendered this removal immaterial to me; but I compassionated her deeply, and was glad to perceive that she found compensation for her misfortunes in a variety of little ridiculous circumstances. Away from all tell-tale chroniclers, she sought to decrease the apparent disparity of our ages by a thousand feminine arts—rouge, youthful dress, and assumed juvenility of manner. I could not be angry—Did not I myself wear a mask? Why quarrel with hers, because it was less successful? I grieved deeply when I remembered that this was my Bertha, whom I had loved so fondly, and won with such transport—the dark-eyed, dark-haired girl, with smiles of enchanting archness and a step like a fawn—this mincing, simpering, jealous old woman. I should have revered her gray locks and withered cheeks; but thus!——It was my work, I knew; but I did not the less deplore this type of human weakness.

Her jealousy never slept. Her chief occupation was to discover that, in spite of outward appearances, I was myself growing old. I verily believe that the poor soul loved me truly in her heart, but never had woman so tormenting a mode of displaying fondness. She would discern wrinkles in my face and decrepitude in my walk, while I bounded along in youthful vigour, the youngest looking of twenty youths. I never dared address another woman: on one occasion, fancying that the belle of the village regarded me with favouring eyes, she bought me a gray wig. Her constant discourse among her acquaintances was, that though I looked so young, there was ruin at work within my frame; and she affirmed that the worst symptom about me was my apparent health. My youth was a disease, she said, and I ought at all times to prepare, if not for a sudden and awful death, at least to wake some morning white-headed, and bowed down with the marks of advanced years. I let her talk—I often joined in her conjectures. Her warnings chimed in with my never-ceasing speculations concerning my state, and I took an earnest, though painful, interest in listening to all that her quick wit and excited imagination could say on the subject.

Why dwell on these minute circumstances? We lived on for many long years. Bertha became bed-rid and paralytic: I nursed her as a mother might a child. She grew peevish, and still harped upon one string—of how long I should survive her. It has ever been a source of consolation to me, that I performed my duty scrupulously towards her. She had been mine in youth, she was mine in age, and at last, when I heaped the sod over her corpse, I wept to feel that I had lost all that really bound me to humanity.

Since then how many have been my cares and woes, how few and empty my enjoyments! I pause here in my history—I will pursue it no further. A sailor without rudder or compass, tossed on a stormy sea—a traveller lost on a wide-spread heath, without landmark or star to guide him—such have I been: more lost, more helpless than either. A nearing ship, a gleam from some far cot, may save them; but I have no beacon except the hope of death.

Death! mysterious, ill-visaged friend of weak humanity! Why alone of all mortals have you cast me from your sheltering fold? O, for the peace of the grave! the deep silence of the iron-bound tomb! that thought would cease to work in my brain, and my heart beat no more with emotions varied only by new forms of sadness!

Am I immortal? I return to my first question. In the first place, is it not more probable that the beverage of the alchymist was fraught rather with longevity than eternal life? Such is my hope. And then be it remembered, that I only drank *half* of the portion prepared by him. Was not the whole necessary to complete the charm? To have drained half the Elixir of Immortality is but to be half immortal—my For-ever is thus truncated and null.

But again, who shall number the years of the half of eternity? I often try to imagine by what rule the infinite may be divided. Sometimes I fancy age advancing upon me. One gray hair I have found. Fool! do I lament? Yes, the fear of age and death often creeps coldly into my heart; and the more I live, the more I dread death, even while I abhor life. Such an enigma is man—born to perish—when he wars, as I do, against the established laws of his nature.

But for this anomaly of feeling surely I might die: the medicine of the alchymist would not be proof against fire—sword—and the strangling waters. I have gazed upon the blue depths of many a placid lake, and the tumultuous rushing of many a mighty river, and have said, peace inhabits those waters; yet I have turned my steps away, to live yet another day. I have asked myself, whether suicide would be a crime in one to whom thus only the portals of the other world could be opened. I have done all, except presenting myself as a soldier or duellist, an object of destruction to my—

no, *not* my fellow-mortals, and therefore I have shrunk away. They are not my fellows. The inextinguishable power of life in my frame, and their ephemeral existence, place us wide as the poles asunder. I could not raise a hand against the meanest or the most powerful among them.

Thus I have lived on for many a year—alone, and weary of myself—desirous of death, yet never dying—a mortal immortal. Neither ambition nor avarice can enter my mind, and the ardent love that gnaws at my heart, never to be returned—never to find an equal on which to expend itself—lives there only to torment me.

This very day I conceived a design by which I may end all—without self-slaughter, without making another man a Cain—an expedition, which mortal frame can never survive, even endued with the youth and strength that inhabits mine. Thus I shall put my immortality to the test, and rest for ever—or return, the wonder and benefactor of the human species.

Before I go, a miserable vanity has caused me to pen these pages. I would not die, and leave no name behind. Three centuries have passed since I quaffed the fatal beverage: another year shall not elapse before, encountering gigantic dangers—warring with the powers of frost in their home—beset by famine, toil, and tempest—I yield this body, too tenacious a cage for a soul which thirsts for freedom, to the destructive elements of air and water—or, if I survive, my name shall be recorded as one of the most famous among the sons of men; and, my task achieved, I shall adopt more resolute means, and, by scattering and annihilating the atoms that compose my frame, set at liberty the life imprisoned within, and so cruelly prevented from soaring from this dim earth to a sphere more congenial to its immortal essence.

# Leo Tolstoy

## (1828–1910)

Leo Tolstoy was born at Yasnaya Polyana, his parents' estate near Tula Province. Orphaned at the age of nine, he was raised by his aunts and privately tutored. In 1844, Tolstoy began studying law and oriental language at the University of Kazan, but he became bored with university life and left without a degree. After contracting heavy gambling debts, Tolstoy followed his brother into army service in 1851. In 1854 he participated in the defense of Sevastopol and published descriptions of the event in the journal *The Contemporary*. During this time, Tolstoy read Plato, Rousseau, Dickens, Sterne, Goethe, Stendhal, Thackeray, and George Eliot. After leaving the army in 1855, he visited France, Switzerland, and Germany to learn more about society and how to reform it. He believed that education is the key to changing society, so he investigated educational theory and practice and published magazines and textbooks on the subject. After his travels, Tolstoy returned to his family's estate and opened a school for peasant children. In 1862 he married Sophia Anderyevna Bers, who bore thirteen children. In the following years, Tolstoy wrote *The Cossacks* (1863), *War and Peace* (1869), and *Anna Karenina* (1875–1877). In "The Hedgehog and The Fox," Isaiah Berlin says of Tolstoy, "No one has ever excelled Tolstoy in expressing the specific flavour, the exact quality of a feeling—the degree of its 'oscillation,' the ebb and flow, the minute movements . . . the inner and outer texture and 'feel' of a look, a thought, a pang of sentiment, no less than of a specific situation, of an entire period, of the lives of individuals, families, communities, entire nations."

In 1876, Tolstoy denounced his earlier works and dedicated himself to his new faith, based heavily on the Sermon on the Mount. He preached nonviolence and considered all organizations based on force to be wrong, including the government and the church. He was excommunicated by the Russian church in 1901. His works during these years include *Confession* (1879), *A Short Exposition of the Gospels* (1881), *What I Believe In* (1882), *The Power of Darkness* (1886), *The Kreutzer Sonata* (1889), *What Is Art?* (1897–1898), and *Resurrection* (1899–1900). In 1910, at the age of eighty-three, Tolstoy left home to live as a wandering ascetic. He died of pneumonia at the railroad stationmaster's house at Astapovo.

---

## The Death of Ivan Ilych                                                1886

TRANSLATED BY LOUISE AND AYLMER MAUDE AND REVISED
BY MICHAEL R. KATZ

**I**

During an interval in the Melvinsky trial in the large building of the Law Court the members and public prosecutor met in Ivan Egorovich Shebek's private room, where the conversation turned to the celebrated Krasovsky case. Fedor Vasilievich fervently declared that it was not subject to their jurisdiction, Ivan Egorovich maintained the contrary, while Peter Ivanovich, not having entered into the discussion at the start, took no part in it, but looked through the *Gazette* which he had just been handed.

"Gentlemen," he said, "Ivan Ilych has died!"

"You don't say so!"

"Here, read it yourself," replied Peter Ivanovich, handing Fedor Vasilievich the paper still damp from the press. Surrounded by a black border were the words: "Praskovya Fedorovna Golovina, with profound sorrow, informs relatives and friends of the demise of her beloved husband Ivan Ilych Golovin, Member of the Court of Justice, which occurred on February the 4th of this year 1882. The funeral will take place on Friday at one o'clock in the afternoon."

Ivan Ilych had been a colleague of the gentlemen present and was liked by them all. He had been ill for some weeks with an illness said to be incurable. His post had been kept open for him, but there had been conjectures that in case of his death Alexeev might receive his appointment, and that either Vinnikov or Shtabel would succeed Alexeev. So on receiving the news of Ivan Ilych's death the first thought of each of the gentlemen present in that private room was about the changes and promotions it might occasion among themselves or their acquaintances.

"I shall be sure to get Shtabel's place or Vinnikov's," thought Fedor Vasilievich. "I was promised that long ago, and the promotion means an extra eight hundred rubles a year for me besides the allowance."

"Now I must apply for my brother-in-law's transfer from Kaluga," thought Peter Ivanovich. "My wife will be very pleased, and then she won't be able to say that I never do anything for her relatives."

"I thought he would never leave his bed again," said Peter Ivanovich aloud. "It's very sad."

"But what was really the matter with him?"

"The doctors couldn't say—at least they could, but each of them said something different. When last I saw him I thought he was getting better."

"I haven't been to see him since the holidays. I always meant to go."

"Did he have any property?"

"I think his wife had a little—but it was quite unimportant."

"We shall have to go to see her, but they live so terribly far away."

"Far from you, you mean. Everything's far away from your place."

"You see, he never can forgive my living on the other side of the river," said Peter Ivanovich, smiling at Shebek. Then, still talking of the distances between different parts of the city, they returned to the Court.

Besides considerations as to possible transfers and promotions likely to result from Ivan Ilych's death, the mere fact of the death of a near acquaintance aroused, as usual, in all who heard of it the complacent feeling that, "it's he who is dead and not I."

Each one thought or felt, "Well, he's dead but I'm alive!" But the more intimate of Ivan Ilych's acquaintances, his so-called friends, could not help also thinking that now they would have to fulfil the very tiresome demands of propriety by attending the funeral service and paying a condolence call on the widow.

Fedor Vasilievich and Peter Ivanovich had been his nearest acquaintances. Peter Ivanovich had studied law with Ivan Ilych and had considered himself to be under obligations to him.

Having told his wife at dinner of Ivan Ilych's death, and of his conjecture that it might be possible to get her brother transferred to their circuit,[1] Peter Ivanovich sacrificed his usual nap, put on his evening clothes and drove to Ivan Ilych's house.

At the entrance stood a carriage and two cabs. Leaning against the wall in the hall downstairs near the coat-stand was a coffin-lid covered with cloth of gold, ornamented with gold cord and tassels, that had been polished with metal powder. Two ladies in black were taking off their fur cloaks. Peter Ivanovich recognized one

---

1 **circuit:** District to which a judge is assigned.

of them as Ivan Ilych's sister, but the other was a stranger to him. His colleague Schwartz was just coming downstairs, but on seeing Peter Ivanovich enter he stopped and winked at him, as if to say: "Ivan Ilych has made a mess of things—not like you and me."

Schwartz's face with his Piccadilly whiskers, and his slim figure in evening dress, as usual had an air of elegant solemnity which contrasted with the playfulness of his character and had a special piquancy here, or so it seemed to Peter Ivanovich.

Peter Ivanovich allowed the ladies to precede him and slowly followed them up-stairs. Schwartz did not come down but remained where he was, and Peter Ivanovich understood that he wanted to arrange where they should play bridge that evening. The ladies went upstairs to the widow's room, and Schwartz with seriously com-pressed lips but a playful look in his eyes, indicated by a twist of his eyebrows the room to the right where the body lay.

Peter Ivanovich, like everyone else on such occasions, entered feeling uncertain what he would have to do. All he knew was that at such times it is always safe to cross oneself. But he was not quite sure whether one should bow while doing so. He there-fore adopted a middle course. On entering the room he began crossing himself and made a slight movement resembling a bow. At the same time, as far as the motion of his head and arm allowed, he surveyed the room. Two young men—apparently nephews, one of whom was a high-school pupil—were leaving the room, crossing themselves as they did so. An old woman was standing motionless, and a lady with strangely arched eyebrows was saying something to her in a whisper. A vigorous, res-olute Church Reader, in a frock-coat, was reading something in a loud voice with an expression that precluded any contradiction. The butler's assistant, Gerasim, stepping lightly in front of Peter Ivanovich, was strewing something on the floor. Noticing this, Peter Ivanovich was immediately aware of a faint odor of a decomposing body.

The last time he had called on Ivan Ilych, Peter Ivanovich had seen Gerasim in the study. Ivan Ilych had been particularly fond of him and he was performing the duty of a sick nurse.

Peter Ivanovich continued to make the sign of the cross slightly inclining his head in an intermediate direction between the coffin, the Reader, and the icons on the table in a corner of the room. Afterwards, when it seemed to him that this movement of his arm in crossing himself had gone on too long, he stopped and began to look at the corpse.

The dead man lay, as dead men always lie, in a specially heavy way, his rigid limbs sunk in the soft cushions of the coffin, with the head forever bowed on the pillow. His yellow waxen brow with bald patches over his sunken temples was thrust up in the way peculiar to the dead, the protruding nose seeming to press on the upper lip. He was much changed and had grown even thinner since Peter Ivanovich had last seen him, but, as is always the case with the dead, his face was handsomer and above all more dignified than when he was alive. The expression on the face said that what was necessary had been accomplished, and accomplished rightly. Besides this there was in that expression a reproach and a warning to the living. This warning seemed out of place to Peter Ivanovich, or at least not applicable to him. He felt a certain discomfort and so he hurriedly crossed himself once more, turned and went out the door—too hurriedly and regardless of propriety, as he himself was aware.

Schwartz was waiting for him in the adjoining room with legs spread wide apart and both hands toying with his top-hat behind his back. The mere sight of that playful, well-groomed, and elegant figure restored Peter Ivanovich. He felt that Schwartz stood above all these happenings and would not surrender to any depressing influences. His very look said that this incident of a church service for Ivan Ilych could not be a sufficient reason for infringing the order of the session—in other words, that it would certainly not prevent his unwrapping a new pack of cards and shuffling them that evening while a footman placed four fresh candles on the table: in fact, that there was no reason for supposing that this incident would hinder their spending the evening agreeably. Indeed he said this in a whisper as Peter Ivanovich passed him, proposing that they should meet for a game at Fedor Vasilievich's. But apparently Peter Ivanovich was not destined to play bridge that evening. Praskovya Fedorovna (a short, fat woman who despite all efforts to the contrary had continued to broaden steadily from her shoulders downwards and who had the same extraordinarily arched eyebrows as the lady who had been standing by the coffin), dressed all in black, her head covered with lace, came out of her own room with some other ladies, conducted them to the room where the dead body lay, and said: "The service will begin immediately. Please go in."

Schwartz, making an indefinite bow, stood still, evidently neither accepting nor declining this invitation. Praskovya Fedorovna recognizing Peter Ivanovich, sighed, went up close to him, took his hand, and said: "I know you were a true friend to Ivan Ilych . . ." and looked at him awaiting some suitable response. And Peter Ivanovich knew that, just as it had been the right thing to cross himself in that room, what he had to do here was press her hand, sigh, and say, "Believe me . . ." So he did all this and as he did it felt that the desired result had been achieved: both he and she were touched.

"Come with me. I want to speak to you before it begins," said the widow. "Give me your arm."

Peter Ivanovich gave her his arm and they went to the inner rooms, passing Schwartz who winked at Peter Ivanovich compassionately.

"That does it for our bridge! Don't object if we find another player. Perhaps you can cut in when you do escape," said his playful look.

Peter Ivanovich sighed still more deeply and despondently, and Praskovya Fedorovna pressed his arm gratefully. When they reached the drawing-room, upholstered in pink cretonne and lighted by a dim lamp, they sat down at the table—she on a sofa and Peter Ivanovich on a low pouffe, the springs of which yielded spasmodically under his weight. Praskovya Fedorovna had been on the point of warning him to take another seat, but felt that such a warning was out of keeping with her present condition and so she changed her mind. As he sat down on the pouffe Peter Ivanovich recalled how Ivan Ilych had arranged this room and had consulted him regarding this pink cretonne with green leaves. The whole room was full of furniture and knick-knacks, and on her way to the sofa the lace of the widow's black shawl caught on the carved edge of the table. Peter Ivanovich rose to detach it, and the springs of the pouffe, relieved of his weight, rose also and gave him a push. The widow began detaching her shawl herself, and Peter Ivanovich again sat down, suppressing the rebellious springs of the pouffe under him. But the widow had not quite freed herself and Peter Ivanovich got up again, and again the pouffe rebelled and even creaked. When this was all over she took out a clean cambric handkerchief and began to weep. The episode with the shawl and the struggle with the pouffe had cooled Peter Ivanovich's emotions and he sat there with a sullen look on his face. This awkward situation was interrupted by Sokolov, Ivan Ilych's butler, who came in to report that the plot in the cemetery that Praskovya Fedorovna had chosen would cost two hundred rubles. She stopped weeping and, looking at Peter Ivanovich with the air of a victim, remarked in French that it was very hard for her. Peter Ivanovich made a silent gesture signifying his full conviction that it must indeed be so.

"You may smoke," she said in a magnanimous yet crushed voice, and turned to discuss the price of the plot for the grave with Sokolov.

While lighting his cigarette Peter Ivanovich heard her inquiring very circumstantially into the prices of different plots in the cemetery and finally decide which one she would take. When that was done she gave instructions about engaging the choir. Sokolov then left the room.

"I look after everything myself," she told Peter Ivanovich, shifting the albums that lay on the table; and noticing that the table was endangered by his cigarette-ash, she immediately passed him an ash-tray, saying as she did so: "I consider it an affectation to say that my grief prevents me from attending to practical affairs. On the contrary, if anything can—I won't say console me, but—distract me, it is seeing to everything concerning him." Once again she took out her handkerchief as if preparing to cry, but suddenly, as if mastering her feeling, shook herself and began to speak calmly. "But there is something I want to talk to you about."

Peter Ivanovich bowed, keeping control of the springs of the pouffe, which immediately began quivering under him.

"He suffered terribly during the last few days."

"Did he?" said Peter Ivanovich.

"Oh, terribly! He screamed unceasingly, not for minutes but for hours. For the last three days he screamed incessantly. It was unendurable. I cannot understand how I stood it; you could hear him three rooms away. Oh, what I have suffered!"

"Is it possible that he was conscious all that time?" asked Peter Ivanovich.

"Yes," she whispered. "To the last moment. He took leave of us a quarter of an hour before he died, and asked us to take Volodya away."

The thought of the suffering of this man whom he had known so intimately, first as a cheerful little boy, then as a schoolmate, and later as a grown-up colleague, suddenly struck Peter Ivanovich with horror, despite an unpleasant consciousness of his own and this woman's dissimulation. He saw that brow again, and that nose pressing down on the lip, and he felt afraid for himself.

"Three days of frightful suffering and then the death! Why, that might suddenly, at any time, happen to me," he thought, and for a moment felt terrified. But—he did not know how—the customary reflection at once occurred to him that this terrible thing had happened to Ivan Ilych and not to him, and that it should not and could not happen to him, and that to think that it could would be yielding to depression which he ought not to do, as Schwartz's expression plainly showed. After this reflection Peter Ivanovich felt reassured, and began to ask with interest about the details of Ivan Ilych's death, as though death was an accident natural to Ivan Ilych but certainly not to himself.

After many details of the really dreadful physical sufferings Ivan Ilych had endured (which details he learned only from the effect those sufferings had produced on Praskovya Fedorovna's nerves) the widow apparently found it necessary to get down to business.

"Oh, Peter Ivanovich, how hard it is! How terribly, terribly hard!" and she began to weep again.

Peter Ivanovich sighed and waited for her to finish blowing her nose. When she had done so he said, "Believe me . . ." and again she began talking and brought out what was evidently her chief concern with him—namely, to question him as to how she could obtain a grant from the government on the occasion of her husband's death. She made it appear that she was asking Peter Ivanovich's advice about her pension, but he soon saw that she already knew about that to the minutest detail, more even than he did himself. She knew how much could be procured from the government in consequence of her husband's death, but wanted to find out whether she could possibly extract some more. Peter Ivanovich tried to think of some means of doing so, but after reflecting for a while and, out of propriety, condemning the government for its niggardliness, said he thought that nothing more could be got. Then she sighed and evidently began to devise some means of getting rid of her visitor. Noticing this, he put out his cigarette, rose, pressed her hand, and went out into the anteroom.

In the dining-room where the clock stood that Ivan Ilych had liked so much and had bought at an antique shop, Peter Ivanovich met a priest and a few acquaintances who had come to attend the service, and he recognized Ivan Ilych's daughter, a handsome young woman. She was dressed in black and her slim figure appeared slimmer than ever. She had a gloomy, determined, almost angry expression, and bowed to Peter Ivanovich as though he were in some way to blame. Behind her, with the same offended look, stood a wealthy young man, an examining magistrate, whom Peter Ivanovich also knew and who was her fiancé, as he had heard. He bowed mournfully to them and was about to pass into the death-chamber, when from under the stairs appeared the figure of Ivan Ilych's schoolboy son, who looked extremely like his father. He seemed a little Ivan Ilych, such as Peter Ivanovich remembered when they studied law together. His tear-stained eyes had in them the look that is seen in the eyes of boys of thirteen or fourteen who are not pure-minded. When he saw Peter Ivanovich he scowled morosely and shamefacedly. Peter Ivanovich nodded to him and entered the death-chamber. The service began: candles, groans, incense, tears, and sobs. Peter Ivanovich stood looking gloomily down at his feet. He did not look at the dead man once, did not yield to any depressing influence, and was one of the first to leave the room. There was no one in the anteroom, but Gerasim darted out of the dead man's room, rummaged with his strong hands among the fur coats to find Peter Ivanovich's, and helped him on with it.

"Well, friend Gerasim," said Peter Ivanovich, so as to say something. "It's a sad affair, isn't it?"

"It's God's will. We shall all come to it some day," said Gerasim, displaying his teeth—the even, white teeth of a healthy peasant—and, like a man in the thick of urgent work, he briskly opened the front door, called the coachman, helped Peter Ivanovich into the sledge, and sprang back to the porch as if in readiness for what he had to do next.

Peter Ivanovich found the fresh air particularly pleasant after the smell of incense, the dead body, and carbolic acid.

"Where to, sir?" asked the coachman.

"It's still not too late . . . I'll call Fedor Vasilievich."

Accordingly he drove there and found them just finishing the first rubber,[2] so that it was quite convenient for him to cut in.

## II

Ivan Ilych's life had been most simple and most ordinary and therefore most terrible.

He had been a member of the Court of Justice, and died at the age of forty-five. His father had been an official who after serving in various ministries and departments in Petersburg had made the sort of career which brings men to positions from which by reason of their long service they cannot be dismissed, though they are obviously unfit to hold any responsible position, and for whom therefore posts are specially created, which though fictitious carry salaries of from six to ten thousand rubles that are not fictitious, in receipt of which they live on to a great age.

Such was the Privy Councillor and superfluous member of various superfluous institutions, Ilya Epimovich Golovin.

He had three sons, of whom Ivan Ilych was the second. The eldest son was following in his father's footsteps only in another department, and was already approaching that stage in the service at which a similar sinecure would be reached. The third son was a failure. He had ruined his prospects in a number of positions and was now serving in the railway department. His father and brothers, and still more their wives, not merely disliked meeting him, but avoided remembering his existence unless compelled to do so. His sister had married Baron Greff, a Petersburg official of her father's type. Ivan Ilych was *le phénix de la famille*[3] as people said. He was neither as cold and formal as his elder brother nor as wild as the younger; he was a happy mean between them—an intelligent, polished, lively and agreeable man. He had studied with his younger brother at the School of Law, but the latter had failed to complete

---

2 **rubber:** Round of hands in bridge.
3 *le phénix de la famille:* French. The pride of the family.

the course and was expelled when he was in his fifth year. Ivan Ilych finished the course well. Even when he was at the School of Law he was just what he remained for the rest of his life: a capable, cheerful, good-natured, and sociable man, though strict in the fulfilment of what he considered to be his duty. And he considered his duty to be what was so considered by those in authority. Neither as a boy nor as a man was he a toady, but from early youth he was by nature attracted to people of high station as a fly is drawn to the light, assimilating their ways and views of life and establishing friendly relations with them. All the enthusiasms of childhood and youth passed without leaving much trace on him; he succumbed to sensuality, to vanity, and recently among the highest classes to liberalism, but always within limits which his instinct unfailingly indicated to him as correct.

At school he had done things which had formerly seemed to him very horrid and made him feel disgusted with himself when he did them; but later on when he saw that such actions were done by people of good position and that they did not regard them as wrong, he was not exactly able to regard them as right, but to forget about them entirely or not be troubled at all by remembering them.

Having graduated from the School of Law and qualified for the tenth rank of the civil service, and having received money from his father for his equipment, Ivan Ilych ordered himself clothes at Scharmer's, the fashionable tailor, hung a medallion inscribed *respice finem*[4] on his watch-chain, took leave of his professor and the prince who was patron of the school, had a farewell dinner with his comrades at Donon's first-class restaurant, and with his new and fashionable portmanteau, linen, clothes, shaving and other toilet articles, and a travelling rug, all purchased at the best shops, he set off for one of the provinces where, through his father's influence, he had been attached to the governor as an official for special service.

In the province Ivan Ilych soon arranged as easy and agreeable a position for himself as he had enjoyed at the School of Law. He performed his official tasks, established his career, and at the same time amused himself pleasantly and decorously. Occasionally he paid official visits to country districts where he behaved with dignity both to his superiors and inferiors, and performed the duties entrusted to him, which related chiefly to the schismatics, with an exactness and incorruptible honesty of which he could not but feel proud.

In official matters, despite his youth and taste for frivolous gaiety, he was exceedingly reserved, punctilious, and even severe; but in society he was often amusing and witty, always good-natured, correct in his manner, and *bon enfant*,[5] as the governor and his wife—with whom he was like one of the family—used to say of him.

In the province he had an affair with a lady who made advances to the elegant young lawyer, and there was also a milliner; and there were carousals with aides-de-camp who visited the district, and after-supper visits to a certain outlying street of doubtful reputation; and there was also some obsequiousness to his chief and even to his chief's wife, but all this was done with such a tone of good breeding that no harsh

4 *respice finem:* Latin. Consider your end.
5 *bon enfant:* French. Good boy, or one of the boys.

names could be applied to it. It all came under the heading of the French saying: "*Il faut que jeunesse se passe*."[6] It was all done with clean hands, in clean linen, with French phrases, and above all among people of the best society and consequently with the approval of people of rank.

So Ivan Ilych served for five years and then came a change in his official life. The new and reformed judicial institutions were introduced, and new men were needed. Ivan Ilych became such a new man. He was offered the post of examining magistrate, and he accepted it though the post was in another province and required him to give up the connections he had formed and to make new ones. His friends met to give him a send-off; they had a group-photograph taken and presented him with a silver cigarette-case, and he set off to his new post.

As examining magistrate Ivan Ilych was just as *comme il faut*[7] and decorous a man, inspiring general respect and capable of separating his official duties from his private life, as he had been when acting as an official on special service. His duties now as examining magistrate were far more interesting and attractive than before. In his former position it had been pleasant to wear an everyday uniform made by Scharmer, and to pass through the crowd of petitioners and officials who were timorously awaiting an audience with the governor, and who envied him as with a free and easy gait he went straight into his chief's private room to have a cup of tea and a cigarette with him. But not many people had then been directly dependent on him—only police officials and the sectarians when he went on special missions—and he liked to treat them politely, almost as comrades, as if he were letting them feel that he who had the power to crush them was treating them in this simple, friendly way. Then there were only a few such people. But now, as an examining magistrate, Ivan Ilych felt that everyone without exception, even the most important and self-satisfied, was in his power, and that he need only write a few words on a sheet of paper with a certain heading, and this or that important, self-satisfied person would be brought before him in the role of an accused party or a witness, and if he did not choose to allow him to sit down, would have to stand before him and answer his questions. Ivan Ilych never abused his power; on the contrary he tried to soften its expression, but the consciousness of it and the possibility of softening its effect, supplied the chief interest and attraction of his office. In his work itself, especially in his examinations, he soon acquired a method of eliminating all considerations irrelevant to the legal aspect of the case, and reducing even the most complicated case to a form in which it would be presented on paper only in its externals, completely excluding his personal opinion of the matter, while above all observing every prescribed formality. The work was new and Ivan Ilych was one of the first men to apply the new Code of 1864.[8]

On taking up the post of examining magistrate in a new town, he made new acquaintances and connections, placed himself on a new footing, and assumed a somewhat different tone. He took up an attitude of rather dignified aloofness towards the

---

6 *Il faut que jeunesse se passe:* French. "Youth will have its day."
7 *comme il faut:* French. In good taste, as it should be.
8 **Code of 1864:** Reform of judicial proceedings in Russia; followed the freeing of serfs in 1861.

provincial authorities, but picked out the best circle of legal gentlemen and wealthy gentry living in town and assumed a tone of slight dissatisfaction with the government, of moderate liberalism, and of enlightened citizenship. At the same time, without at all altering the elegance of his toilet, he ceased shaving his chin and allowed his beard to grow as it pleased.

Ivan Ilych settled down very pleasantly in this new town. The society there, which inclined towards opposition to the governor, was friendly, his salary was larger, and he began to play *vint,*[9] which he found added considerably to the pleasure of life, for he had a capacity for cards, played good-humoredly, and calculated rapidly and astutely, so that he usually won.

After living there for two years he met his future wife, Praskovya Fedorovna Mikhel, who was the most attractive, clever, and brilliant girl of the set in which he moved, and among other amusements and relaxations from his labors as examining magistrate, Ivan Ilych established light and playful relations with her.

While he had been an official on special service he had been accustomed to dance, but as an examining magistrate it was exceptional for him to do so. If he danced now, he did it as if to show that though he served under the reformed order of things, and had reached the fifth official rank, still when it came to dancing he could do it better than most people. So at the end of an evening he sometimes danced with Praskovya Fedorovna, and it was chiefly during these dances that he captivated her. She fell in love with him. At first Ivan Ilych had no definite intention of marrying, but when the girl fell in love with him he said to himself: "Really, why shouldn't I marry?"

Praskovya Fedorovna came from a good family, was not bad looking, and had a bit of property. Ivan Ilych might have aspired to a more brilliant match, but even this was good. He had his salary, and she, he hoped, would have an equal income. She was well connected, and was a sweet, pretty, thoroughly correct young woman. To say that Ivan Ilych married because he fell in love with Praskovya Fedorovna and found that she sympathized with his views of life would be as incorrect as to say that he married because his social circle approved of the match. He was swayed by both these considerations: the marriage gave him personal satisfaction, and at the same time it was considered the right thing to do by the most highly placed of his associates.

So Ivan Ilych got married.

The preparations for marriage and the beginning of married life, with its conjugal caresses, new furniture, new crockery, and new linen, were very pleasant until his wife became pregnant—so that Ivan Ilych had begun to think that marriage would not impair the easy, agreeable, pleasant and always decorous character of his life, approved of by society and regarded by himself as natural, but would even improve it. But from the first months of his wife's pregnancy, something new, unpleasant, depressing, and unseemly, from which there was no way of escape, unexpectedly showed itself.

9 **vint:** A form of bridge.

His wife, without any reason—*de gaieté de cœur*[10] as Ivan Ilych expressed it to himself—began to disturb the pleasure and propriety of their life. She began to be jealous without cause, expected him to devote his whole attention to her; she found fault with everything, and made coarse and ill-mannered scenes.

At first Ivan Ilych hoped to escape from the unpleasantness of this state of affairs by the same easy and decorous relation to life that had served him heretofore: he tried to ignore his wife's disagreeable moods, continued to live in his usual easy and pleasant way, invited friends to his house for a game of cards, and also tried going out to his club or spending his evenings with friends. But one day his wife began upbraiding him so vigorously, using such coarse words, and continued to abuse him every time he did not fulfil her demands, so resolutely and with such evident determination not to give way till he submitted—that is, till he stayed at home and was bored just as she was—that he became alarmed. He now realized that matrimony—at any rate with Praskovya Fedorovna—was not always conducive to the pleasures and amenities of life, but on the contrary often infringed both comfort and propriety, and that he must therefore entrench himself against such infringement. And Ivan Ilych began to seek means of doing so. His official duties were the one thing that imposed upon Praskovya Fedorovna, and by means of his official work and the duties attached to it he began struggling with his wife to secure his own independence.

With the birth of their child, attempts to feed it and various failures in doing so, and with the real and imaginary illnesses of mother and child, in which Ivan Ilych's sympathy was demanded but about which he understood nothing, the need of securing for himself an existence outside his family life became still more imperative.

As his wife grew more irritable and exacting and Ivan Ilych transferred the center of gravity of his life more and more to his official work, so did he grow to like his work better and became more ambitious than before.

Very soon, within a year of his wedding, Ivan Ilych had realized that marriage, though it may add some comforts to life, is in fact a very intricate and difficult affair towards which in order to perform one's duty, that is, to lead a decorous life approved of by society, one must adopt a definite attitude, just as towards one's official duties.

And Ivan Ilych evolved such an attitude towards married life. He only required of it those conveniences—dinner at home, housewife, and bed—which it could give him, and above all that propriety of external forms required by public opinion. For the rest he looked for light-hearted pleasure and propriety, and was very thankful when he found them, but if he met with antagonism and querulousness he retired at once into his separate fenced-off world of official duties, where he found satisfaction.

Ivan Ilych was esteemed a good official, and after three years was made Assistant Public Prosecutor. His new duties, their importance, the possibility of indicting and imprisoning anyone he chose, the publicity his speeches received, and the success he had in all these things, made his work still more attractive.

More children came. His wife became more and more querulous and ill-tempered,

10  *de gaieté de coeur:* French. From cheerfulness of heart. From sheer exuberance.

but the attitude Ivan Ilych had adopted towards his home life rendered him almost impervious to her grumbling.

After seven years' service in that town he was transferred to another province as Public Prosecutor. They moved, but were short of money and his wife did not like the place they moved to. Though the salary was higher the cost of living was greater, besides which two of their children died and family life became still more unpleasant for him.

Praskovya Fedorovna blamed her husband for every inconvenience they encountered in their new home. Most of the conversations between husband and wife, especially as to the children's education, led to topics which recalled former disputes, and these disputes were apt to flare up again at any moment. There remained only those rare periods of amorousness which still came to them at times but did not last long. These were islets at which they anchored for a while and then again set out upon that ocean of veiled hostility which showed itself in their aloofness from one another. This aloofness might have grieved Ivan Ilych had he considered that it ought not to exist, but now he regarded the position as normal, and even made it the goal at which he aimed in family life. His aim was to free himself more and more from those unpleasantnesses and to give them a semblance of harmlessness and propriety. He attained this by spending less and less time with his family, and when obliged to be at home he tried to safeguard his position by the presence of outsiders. The chief thing however was that he had his official duties. The whole interest of his life now centered in the official world and that interest absorbed him. The consciousness of his power, being able to ruin anybody he wished to ruin, the importance, even the external dignity of his entry into court, or meetings with his subordinates, his success with superiors and inferiors, and above all his masterly handling of cases, of which he was conscious—all this gave him pleasure and filled his life, together with chats with his colleagues, dinners, and bridge. So that on the whole Ivan Ilych's life continued to flow as he considered it should do—pleasantly and properly.

So things continued for another seven years. His eldest daughter was already sixteen, another child had died, and only one son was left, a schoolboy and a subject of dissension. Ivan Ilych wanted to put him in the School of Law, but to spite him Praskovya Fedorovna entered him at the High School.[11] The daughter had been educated at home and had turned out well: the boy did not learn badly either.

## III

So Ivan Ilych lived for seventeen years after his marriage. He was already a Public Prosecutor of long standing, and had declined several proposed transfers while awaiting a more desirable post, when an unanticipated and unpleasant occurrence quite upset the peaceful course of his life. He was expecting to be offered the post of pre-

---

11  **School of Law . . . High School:** Schools of equal level at this time period.

siding judge in a University town, but Happe somehow came to the front and obtained the appointment instead. Ivan Ilych became irritable, reproached Happe, and quarrelled both with him and with his immediate superiors—who became colder to him and again passed him over when other appointments were made.

This was in 1880, the hardest year of Ivan Ilych's life. It was then that it became evident on the one hand that his salary was insufficient for them to live on, and on the other that he had been forgotten, and not only that; what was for him the greatest and most cruel injustice appeared to others as quite an ordinary occurrence. Even his father did not consider it his duty to help him. Ivan Ilych felt himself abandoned by everyone; they regarded his position with a salary of 3,500 rubles as quite normal and even fortunate. He alone knew that with the consciousness of the injustices done him, with his wife's incessant nagging, and with the debts he had contracted by living beyond his means, his position was far from normal.

In order to save money that summer he obtained a leave of absence and went away with his wife to live in the country at her brother's place.

There, without his work, he experienced boredom for the first time in his life, and not only boredom but intolerable depression. He decided it was impossible to go on living this way, and that it was necessary to take energetic measures.

Having passed a sleepless night pacing up and down the veranda, he decided to go to Petersburg and bestir himself, in order to punish those who had failed to appreciate him and to get transferred to another ministry.

Next day, despite many protests from his wife and her brother, he started for Petersburg with the sole object of obtaining a post with a salary of five thousand rubles a year. He was no longer bent on any particular department, or tendency, or kind of activity. Now all he wanted was an appointment to another post with a salary of five thousand rubles, either in the administration, in the banks, with the railways in one of the Empress Marya's Institutions,[12] or even in customs—but it had to provide a salary of five thousand rubles and be in a ministry other than the one in which they had failed to appreciate him.

And this quest of Ivan Ilych's was crowned with remarkable and unexpected success. At Kursk an acquaintance of his, F. I. Ilyin, got into the first-class carriage, sat down beside Ivan Ilych, and told him about a telegram just received by the governor of Kursk announcing that a change was about to take place in the ministry: Peter Ivanovich was to be superseded by Ivan Semenovich.

The proposed change, apart from its significance for Russia, had a special significance for Ivan Ilych, because by bringing forward a new man, Peter Petrovich, and consequently his friend Zakhar Ivanovich, it was highly favorable for Ivan Ilych, since Zakhar Ivanovich was a friend and colleague of his.

In Moscow this news was confirmed, and on reaching Petersburg Ivan Ilych found Zakhar Ivanovich and received a definite promise of an appointment in his former Department of Justice.

---

12 **Empress Marya's Institutions:** Orphanages founded by the wife of Tsar Paul I, who ruled from 1796 to 1801.

A week later he telegraphed his wife: "Zakhar in Miller's place. I shall receive appointment on presentation of report."

Thanks to this change of personnel, Ivan Ilych had unexpectedly obtained an appointment in his former ministry which placed him two stages above his former colleagues besides giving him five thousand rubles salary and three thousand five hundred rubles for expenses connected with his transfer. All his ill humor towards his former enemies and the whole department vanished, and Ivan Ilych was completely happy.

He returned to the country more cheerful and contented than he had been for a long time. Praskovya Fedorovna also cheered up and a truce was arranged between them. Ivan Ilych told of how he had been fêted by everybody in Petersburg, how all those who had been his enemies were put to shame and now fawned on him, how envious they were of his appointment, and how much everybody in Petersburg had liked him.

Praskovya Fedorovna listened to all this and appeared to believe it. She did not contradict anything, but only made plans for their life in the town to which they were going. Ivan Ilych saw with delight that these plans were his plans, that he and his wife agreed, and that, after a stumble, his life was regaining its due and natural character of pleasant lightheartedness and decorum.

Ivan Ilych had come back for a short time only, for he had to take up his new duties on the 10th of September. Moreover, he needed time to settle into the new place, to move all his belongings from the province, and to buy and order many additional things: in a word, to make arrangements as he had resolved on, which were almost exactly what Praskovya Fedorovna had also decided on.

Now that everything had happened so fortunately, and he and his wife were at one in their aims and moreover saw so little of one another, they got on together better than they had done since the first years of their marriage. Ivan Ilych had thought of taking his family away with him at once, but the insistence of his wife's brother and her sister-in-law, who had suddenly become particularly amiable and friendly to him and his family, induced him to depart alone.

So he left, and the cheerful state of mind induced by his success and by the harmony between his wife and himself, the one intensifying the other, did not desert him. He found a delightful house, just the thing both he and his wife had dreamt about. Spacious, lofty reception rooms in the old style, a convenient and dignified study, rooms for his wife and daughter, a study for his son—it might have been made to order for them. Ivan Ilych himself oversaw all the arrangements, chose the wallpapers, supplemented the furniture (preferably with antiques which he considered particularly *comme il faut*), and supervised the upholstering. Everything progressed and approached the ideal he had set himself: even when things were only half completed they exceeded his expectations. He saw what a refined and elegant character, free from vulgarity, it would all have when it was ready. On falling asleep he pictured to himself how the reception-room would look. Looking at the yet unfinished drawing-room he could see the fireplace, the screen, the bookcase, the little chairs dotted here and there, the dishes and plates on the walls, and the bronzes, as they would be when everything was in place. He was pleased by the thought of how his wife and daughter, who shared his taste in this matter, would be impressed by it. They were certainly not expecting as much. He had been particularly successful in finding, and buying cheaply, antiques which gave a particularly aristocratic character to the whole place. But in his letters he intentionally understated everything in order to be able to surprise them. All this so absorbed him that his new duties—though he liked his official work—interested him less than he had expected. Sometimes he even had moments of absent-mindedness during the court sessions, and would consider whether he should have straight or curved cornices for his curtains. He was so interested in it all that he often did things himself, rearranging the furniture, or rehanging the curtains. Once when mounting a stepladder to show the upholsterer, who did not understand, how he wanted the hangings draped, he made a false step and slipped, but being a strong and agile man he clung on and only knocked his side against the knob of the window frame. The bruised place was painful but the pain soon passed, and he felt particularly bright and well just then. He wrote: "I feel fifteen years younger." He thought he would have everything ready by September, but it dragged on till mid-October. The result was charming not only in his eyes but to everyone who saw it.

In reality it was just what is usually seen in the houses of people of moderate means who want to appear rich, and therefore succeed only in resembling others like themselves: there were damasks, dark wood, plants, rugs, dull and polished bronzes— all the things people of a certain class have in order to resemble other people of that class. His house was so like others that it would never have been noticed, but to him it all seemed to be quite exceptional. He was very happy when he met his family at the station and brought them to the newly furnished house all lit up, where a footman in a white tie opened the door into the hall decorated with plants, and when they went on into the drawing-room and the study uttering exclamations of delight. He conducted them everywhere, drank in their praises eagerly, and beamed with delight. At tea that evening, when Praskovya Fedorovna among other things asked him about his fall, he laughed, and showed them how he had gone flying and had frightened the upholsterer.

"It's a good thing I'm a bit of an athlete. Another man might have been killed, but I merely knocked myself, just here; it hurts when it's touched, but it's passing already—it's only a bruise."

So they began living in their new home—in which, as always happens, when they got thoroughly settled in they found they were just one room short—and with the increased income, which as always was just a little (about five hundred rubles) too little, but it was all very nice.

Things went particularly well at first, before everything was finally arranged and while something still had to be done: this thing bought, that thing ordered, another thing moved, and something else adjusted. Though there were some disputes between husband and wife, they were both so well satisfied and had so much to do that it all passed off without any serious quarrels. When nothing was left to arrange it became rather dull and something seemed to be lacking, but then they were making acquaintances, forming habits, and life was growing fuller.

Ivan Ilych spent his mornings at the law court and came home to dinner; at first he was generally in a good humor, though he occasionally became irritable just on account of his house. (Every spot on the tablecloth or the upholstery, and every broken window-blind string, irritated him. He had devoted so much trouble to arranging it all that every disturbance distressed him.) But on the whole his life ran its course as he believed life should do: easily, pleasantly, and decorously.

He got up at nine, drank his coffee, read the paper, and then put on his uniform and went to the law courts. There the harness in which he worked had already been stretched to fit him and he donned it without a hitch: petitioners, inquiries at the chancery, the chancery itself, and the sittings, both public and administrative. In all this the thing was to exclude everything fresh and vital, which always disturbs the regular course of official business, and to admit only official relations with people, and then only on official grounds. A man would come, for instance, wanting some information. Ivan Ilych, as one in whose sphere the matter did not lie, would have nothing to do with him: but if the man had some business with him in his official capacity, something that could be expressed on officially stamped paper, he would do everything, positively everything he could within the limits of such relations, and in so doing would maintain the semblance of friendly human relations, that is, would observe the courtesies of life. As soon as the official relations ended, so did everything else. Ivan Ilych possessed this capacity to separate his real life from the official side of affairs and not mix the two, in the highest degree, and by long practice and natural aptitude had brought it to such a pitch that sometimes, in the manner of a virtuoso, he would even allow himself to let the human and official relations mingle. He let himself do this just because he felt that at any time he could resume the strictly official attitude again and drop the human relations. And he did it all easily, pleasantly, correctly, even artistically. In the intervals between sessions he smoked, drank tea, chatted a little about politics, a little about general topics, a little about cards, but most of all about official appointments. Tired, but feeling like a virtuoso—one of the first violins who has played his part in an orchestra with precision—he would return home to find that his wife and daughter had been out paying calls, or had a visitor, and that his son had been to school, had done his homework with his tutor, and was duly learning what is taught at High Schools. Everything was as it should be. After dinner, if they had no visitors, Ivan Ilych sometimes read a book that was being widely discussed at the time, and in the evening settled down to work, that is, read official papers, compared the depositions of witnesses, and noted paragraphs of the Code applying to them. This was neither dull nor amusing. It was dull when he might have been playing bridge, but if no bridge was available it was certainly better than doing nothing or sitting with his wife. Ivan Ilych's chief pleasure was giving little dinners to which he invited men and women of good social position, and just as his drawing-room resembled all other drawing-rooms, so did his enjoyable little parties resemble all other parties.

Once they even gave a dance. Ivan Ilych enjoyed it and everything went off well, except that it led to a violent quarrel with his wife about the cakes and sweets. Praskovya Fedorovna had made her own plans, but Ivan Ilych insisted on getting everything from an expensive confectioner and ordered too many cakes. The quarrel occurred because some of those cakes were left over and the confectioner's bill came to forty-five rubles. It was a great and disagreeable quarrel. Praskovya Fedorovna called him "a fool and an imbecile," and he clutched at his head and made angry allusions to divorce.

But the dance itself had been enjoyable. The best people were there, and Ivan Ilych had danced with Princess Trufonova, a sister of the distinguished founder of the Society "Bear My Grief."

The pleasures connected with his work were pleasures of ambition; his social pleasures were those of vanity; but Ivan Ilych's greatest pleasure was playing bridge. He acknowledged that whatever disagreeable incident happened in his life, the pleasure that beamed like a ray of sunshine above everything else was to sit down to bridge with good players, not noisy partners, and of course to four-handed bridge (with five players it was annoying to have to stand out, though one pretended not to mind), to play a clever and serious game (when the cards allowed it) and then to have supper and drink a glass of wine. After a game of bridge, especially if he had won a little (to win a large sum was unpleasant), Ivan Ilych went to bed in specially good humor.

So they lived. They formed a circle of acquaintances among the best people and were visited by people of importance and by young folk. In their views as to their acquaintances, husband, wife and daughter were entirely agreed, and tacitly and unanimously kept at arm's length and shook off various shabby friends and relations who, with much show of affection, gushed into the drawing-room with its Japanese plates on the walls. Soon these shabby friends ceased to obtrude themselves and only the best people remained in the Golovins' set.

Young men courted Lisa, and Petrishchev, an examining magistrate and Dmitri Ivanovich Petrishchev's son and sole heir, began to be so attentive to her that Ivan Ilych had already spoken to Praskovya Fedorovna about it, and considered whether they should not arrange a party for them, or organize some private theatricals.

So they lived, and all went well, without change, and life flowed pleasantly.

## IV

They were all in good health. It could not be called ill health if Ivan Ilych sometimes said that he had a queer taste in his mouth and felt some discomfort in his left side.

But this discomfort increased and, though not exactly painful, grew into a sense of pressure in his side accompanied by ill humor. His irritability became worse and worse and began to mar the agreeable, easy, and correct life that had established itself in the Golovin family. Quarrels between husband and wife became more and more frequent, and soon the ease and amenity disappeared and even the decorum was barely maintained. Once again scenes became frequent, and very few issues remained on which husband and wife could meet without an explosion. Praskovya Fedorovna now had good reason to say that her husband's temper was trying. With characteristic exaggeration she said he had always had a dreadful temper, and that it had needed all her good nature to put up with it for twenty years. It was true that now their quarrels were started by him. His bursts of temper always came just before dinner, often just as he began to eat his soup. Sometimes he noticed that a plate or dish was chipped, or the food was not right, or his son put his elbow on the table, or his daughter's hair was not done as he liked it, and for all this he blamed Praskovya Fedorovna. At first she retorted and said disagreeable things to him, but once or twice he fell into such a rage at the beginning of dinner that she realized it was due to some physical derangement brought on by taking food, and so she restrained herself and did not answer, but only hurried to get through dinner. She regarded this self-restraint as highly praiseworthy. Having come to the conclusion that her husband had a dreadful temper and made her life miserable, she began to feel sorry for herself; the more she pitied herself the more she hated her husband. She began to wish he would die; yet she did not want him to die because then his salary would cease. And this irritated her still more. She considered herself dreadfully unhappy just because not even his death could save her, and though she concealed her exasperation, that hidden emotion of hers increased his irritation as well.

After one scene in which Ivan Ilych had been particularly unfair and after which he had said in explanation that he certainly was irritable but that it was due to his not being well, she said that if he was ill it should be attended to, and insisted on his going to see a celebrated doctor.

He went. Everything took place as he had expected and as it always does. There was the usual waiting and the important air assumed by the doctor, with which he was so familiar (resembling that which he himself assumed in court), and the sounding and listening, and the questions which called for answers that were foregone conclusions and were evidently unnecessary, and the look of importance which implied that "if only you put yourself in our hands we will arrange everything—we know indubitably how it has to be done, always the same for everybody." It was all just as it was in the law courts. The doctor put on just the same air towards him as he himself put on towards an accused person.

The doctor said that so-and-so indicated that there was such-and-such inside the patient, but if the investigation of so-and-so did not confirm this, then he must assume this and that. If he assumed this and that, then . . . and so on. To Ivan Ilych only one question was important: was his case serious or not? But the doctor ignored that inappropriate question. From his point of view it was not the one under consideration; the real question was to decide between a floating kidney, chronic catarrh, or appendicitis. It was not a question of Ivan Ilych's life or death, but one between a floating kidney and appendicitis. And that question the doctor solved brilliantly, as it seemed to Ivan Ilych, in favor of the appendix, with the reservation that should an examination of his urine give fresh indications, the matter would be reconsidered. All this was just what Ivan Ilych had himself brilliantly accomplished a thousand times in dealing with men on trial. The doctor summed it up just as brilliantly, looking over his spectacles triumphantly and even gaily at the accused. From the doctor's summation Ivan Ilych concluded that things were bad, but that for the doctor, and perhaps for everybody else, it was a matter of indifference, though for him it was bad. This conclusion struck him painfully, arousing in him a great feeling of pity for himself and of bitterness towards the doctor's indifference to a matter of such importance.

He said nothing about it, but rose, placed the doctor's fee on the table, and remarked with a sigh: "We sick people probably pose inappropriate questions frequently. But tell me, doctor, in general, is this complaint dangerous, or not? . . ."

The doctor looked at him sternly over his spectacles with one eye, as if to say: "Prisoner, if you will not keep to the questions put to you, I shall be obliged to have you removed from the court."

"I have already told you what I consider necessary and proper. The analysis may show something more." And the doctor bowed.

Ivan Ilych went out slowly, seated himself disconsolately in his sleigh, and drove home. All the way home he was going over what the doctor had said, trying to translate those complicated, obscure, scientific phrases into plain language and find in them an answer to the question: "Is my condition bad? Is it very bad? Or is there still nothing much wrong?" It seemed to him that the meaning of what the doctor had said was that it was very bad. Everything in the streets seemed depressing. The cabmen, the houses, the passers-by, and the shops, were dismal. His ache, this dull gnawing ache that never ceased for a moment, seemed to have acquired a new and more serious significance from the doctor's dubious remarks. Ivan Ilych now watched it with a new and oppressive feeling.

He reached home and began to tell his wife about it. She listened, but in the middle of his account his daughter came in with her hat on, ready to go out with her mother. She sat down reluctantly to listen to his tedious story, but could not stand it for very long, and her mother too did not hear him out to the end.

"Well, I'm very glad," she said. "Mind now to take your medicine regularly. Give me the prescription and I'll send Gerasim out to the pharmacy." And she went to get ready to go out.

While she was in the room Ivan Ilych had hardly taken time to breathe, but he sighed deeply when she left.

"Well," he thought, "perhaps it isn't so bad after all."

He began taking his medicine and following his doctor's orders, which had been altered after the examination of his urine. But then it seemed that there was a contradiction between the indications drawn from the examination of his urine and the symptoms that showed themselves. It turned out that what was happening differed from what the doctor had told him, and that he had either forgotten, or blundered, or hidden something from him. He could not, however, be blamed for that, and Ivan Ilych still obeyed his orders implicitly and at first derived some comfort from doing so.

From the time of his visit to the doctor, Ivan Ilych's chief occupation was the exact fulfillment of his doctor's instructions regarding hygiene and the taking of medicine, and the observation of his pain and his excretions. His chief interests came to be people's ailments and their health. When sickness, deaths, or recoveries were mentioned in his presence, especially when the illness resembled his own, he listened with considerable agitation which he tried to conceal, asked questions, and applied what he heard to his own case.

The pain did not diminish, but Ivan Ilych made efforts to force himself to think that he was better. He could do this so long as nothing agitated him. But as soon as he had any unpleasantness with his wife, any lack of success in his official work, or held bad cards at bridge, he was at once acutely aware of his disease. He had formerly borne such mishaps, hoping soon to adjust what was wrong, to master it and attain success, or make a grand slam. But now every mishap upset him and plunged him into despair. He would say to himself: "There now, just as I was beginning to get better and the medicine had begun to take effect, comes this accursed misfortune, or unpleasantness . . ." And he was furious with the mishap, or with the people who were causing the unpleasantness, for he felt that this fury was killing him but he could not restrain it. One would have thought that it should have been clear to him that this exasperation with circumstances and people aggravated his illness, and that therefore he ought to ignore unpleasant occurrences. But he drew the very opposite conclusion: he said that he needed peace, and he watched for everything that might disturb it and became irritable at the slightest infringement. His condition was rendered worse by the fact that he read medical books and consulted doctors. The progress of his disease was so gradual that he could deceive himself when comparing one day with another—the difference was so slight. But when he consulted the doctors it seemed to him that he was getting worse, even very rapidly. Yet despite this he was continually consulting them.

That month he went to see another celebrity, who told him almost the same as the first had done, but put his questions rather differently, and the interview with this celebrity only increased Ivan Ilych's doubts and fears. A friend of a friend of his, a very good doctor, diagnosed his illness again quite differently from the others, and though he predicted recovery, his questions and suppositions bewildered Ivan Ilych still more and increased his doubts. A homeopathist diagnosed the disease in yet another way, and prescribed medicine which Ivan Ilych took secretly for a week. But after this week, not feeling any improvement and having lost confidence both in the former doctor's treatment and in this one's, he became still more despondent. One day a lady acquaintance mentioned a cure effected by a wonder-working icon. Ivan Ilych caught himself listening attentively and beginning to believe that it had occurred. This incident alarmed him. "Has my mind really weakened to such an extent?" he asked himself. "Nonsense! It's all rubbish. I mustn't give way to nervous fears; having chosen a doctor I must keep strictly to his treatment. That is what I will do. Now it's all settled. I won't think about it, but will follow the treatment seriously till summer, and then we shall see. From now on there must be no more wavering!" This was easy to say but impossible to carry out. The pain in his side oppressed him and seemed to grow worse and more incessant, while the taste in his mouth grew stranger and stranger. It seemed to him that his breath had a disgusting smell, and he was conscious of a loss of appetite and strength. There was no deceiving himself: something terrible, new, and more important than anything before in his life, was taking place within him of which he alone was aware. Those about him did not understand or would not understand it, but thought everything in the world was going on as usual. That tormented Ivan Ilych more than anything. He saw that his household, especially his wife and daughter who were in a perfect whirl of visiting, did not understand anything about it and were annoyed that he was so depressed and so exacting, as if he were to blame. Though they tried to disguise it he saw that he was an obstacle in their path, and that his wife had adopted a definite line in regard to his illness and kept to it regardless of anything he said or did. Her attitude was this: "You know," she would say to her friends, "Ivan Ilych can't do as other people do, and keep to the treatment prescribed for him. One day he takes his drops and keeps strictly to his diet and goes to bed in good time, but the next day unless I watch him, he suddenly forgets his medicine, eats sturgeon—which is forbidden—and sits up playing cards till one in the morning."

"Oh, come, when was that?" Ivan Ilych would ask in vexation. "Only once at Peter Ivanovich's."

"And yesterday with Shebek."

"Well, even if I hadn't stayed up, the pain would have kept me awake."

"Be that as it may you'll never get well like that, but you'll always make us wretched."

Praskovya Fedorovna's attitude to Ivan Ilych's illness, as she expressed it both to others and to him, was that it was all his own fault and was yet another of the annoyances he caused her. Ivan Ilych felt that this opinion escaped her involuntarily—but that did not make it any easier for him.

At the law courts too, Ivan Ilych noticed, or thought he noticed, a strange attitude towards himself. It sometimes seemed that people were watching him inquisitively as a man whose place might soon become vacant. Then again, his friends would suddenly begin to tease him in a friendly way about his low spirits, as if the awful, horrible, and unheard-of thing that was going on within him, incessantly gnawing at him and irresistibly drawing him away, was a very agreeable subject for jests. Schwartz particular irritated him by his jocularity, vivacity, and *savoir-faire,* which reminded him of what he himself had been ten years ago.

Friends came to make up a set and they sat down to cards. They dealt, bending the new cards to soften them, and he sorted the diamonds in his hand and found he had seven. His partner said "No trumps" and supported him with two diamonds. What more could be wished for? It ought to be jolly and lively. They would make a grand slam. But suddenly Ivan Ilych was conscious of that gnawing pain, that taste in his mouth, and it seemed ridiculous that in such circumstances he should be pleased to make a grand slam.

He looked at his partner Mikhail Mikhailovich, who rapped the table with his strong hand and instead of snatching up the tricks pushed the cards courteously and indulgently towards Ivan Ilych that he might have the pleasure of gathering them up without the trouble of stretching out his hand for them. "Does he think I'm too weak to stretch out my arm?" thought Ivan Ilych, and forgetting what he was doing he over-trumped his partner, missing the grand slam by three tricks. And what was most awful of all was that he saw how Mikhail Mikhailovich was about it, but he himself did not care. And it was dreadful to realize why he did not care.

They all saw that he was suffering, and said: "We can stop if you're tired. Take a rest." Lie down? No, he was not tired at all, and finished the rubber. All were gloomy and silent. Ivan Ilych felt that he had diffused this gloom over them and was unable to dispel it. They had supper and went away; Ivan Ilych was left alone with the consciousness that his life was poisoned and was poisoning the lives of others, and that this poison did not lessen but penetrated more and more deeply into his whole being.

With this consciousness, and with physical pain besides the terror, he must go to bed, often to lie awake the greater part of the night. The next morning he had to get up again, dress, go to the law courts, speak, and write; or if he did not go out, spend those twenty-four hours a day at home each of which was a torture. And he had to live thus all alone on the brink of an abyss, with no one who understood him or pitied him.

## V

So one month passed and then another. Just before the New Year his brother-in-law came to town and stayed at their house. Ivan Ilych was at the law courts and Praskovya Fedorovna had gone shopping. When Ivan Ilych came home and entered his study he found his brother-in-law there—a healthy, florid man—unpacking his bag himself. He raised his head on hearing Ivan Ilych's footsteps and looked up at him for a moment without a word. That stare told Ivan Ilych everything. His brother-in-law opened his mouth to utter an exclamation of surprise but checked himself, and that action confirmed it all.

"I've changed, eh?"

"Yes, there's been a change."

After that, try as he would to get his brother-in-law to return to the subject of his looks, the latter would say nothing about it. Praskovya Fedorovna came home and her brother went out to her. Ivan Ilych locked the door and began to examine himself in the glass, first full face, then in profile. He took up a portrait of himself taken with his wife, and compared it with what he saw in the mirror. The change was immense. Then he bared his arms to the elbow, looked at them, drew the sleeves down again, sat down on an ottoman, and grew blacker than night.

"No, no, this won't do!" he said to himself, and jumped up, went to the table, took up some law papers and began to read them, but he could not continue. He unlocked the door and went into the reception-room. The door leading to the drawing-room was shut. He approached it on tiptoe and listened.

"No, you're exaggerating!" Praskovya Fedorovna was saying.

"Exaggerating! Don't you see it? Why, he's a dead man! Look at his eyes—there's no light in them. But what's wrong with him?"

"No one knows. Nikolaevich (that was another doctor) said something, but I don't know what. And Leshchetitsky (this was the celebrated specialist) said quite the opposite . . ."

Ivan Ilych walked away, went to his own room, lay down, and began musing: "A kidney, a floating kidney." He recalled all the doctors had told him about how it detached itself and swayed about. By an effort of imagination he tried to catch that kidney and arrest it and support it. So little was needed for this, it seemed to him. "No, I'll go see Peter Ivanovich again." (That was the friend whose friend was a doctor.) He rang, ordered the carriage, and got ready to go.

"Where are you going, Jean?"[13] asked his wife, with a specially sad and exceptionally kind look.

This exceptionally kind look irritated him. He looked at her morosely.

"I must go see Peter Ivanovich."

He went to see Peter Ivanovich, and together they went to see his friend, the doctor. He was in, and Ivan Ilych had a long talk with him.

Reviewing the anatomical and physiological details of what in the doctor's opinion was going on inside him, he understood it all.

There was something, a small thing, in the vermiform appendix. It might be all right. Only stimulate the energy of one organ and check the activity of another, then absorption would take place and everything would be all right. He got home rather late, ate his dinner, and conversed cheerfully, but for a long time he could not bring himself to go back to work in his room. At last, however, he went to his study and did what was necessary, but the consciousness that he had put something aside—an important, intimate matter which he would revert to when his work was done—never left him. When he had finished his work he remembered that this intimate matter was the thought of his vermiform appendix. But he did not give himself up to it, and went to the drawing-room for tea. There were callers there, including the examining magistrate who was a desirable match for his daughter, and they were conversing, playing the piano, and singing. Ivan Ilych, as Praskovya Fedorovna remarked, spent that evening more cheerfully than usual, but he never forgot for a moment that he had postponed the important matter of his appendix. At eleven o'clock he said goodnight and went to his bedroom. Since his illness he had slept alone in a small room next to his study. He undressed and took up a novel by Zola,[14] but instead of reading it he fell into thought, and in his imagination that desired improvement in the vermiform appendix occurred. There took place the absorption and evacuation and the re-establishment of normal activity. "Yes, that's it!" he said to himself. "One need only assist nature, that's all." He remembered his medicine, got up, took it, and lay down on his back waiting for the beneficent action of the medicine and for it to lessen the pain. "I need only take it regularly and avoid all injurious influences. I'm feeling better already, much better." He began touching his side: it was not painful to the touch. "There, I really don't feel it. It's much better already." He put out the light and turned over on his side . . . "My appendix is getting better, absorption is occurring." Suddenly he felt the old, familiar, dull, gnawing pain, stubborn and serious. There was the same familiar loathsome taste in his mouth. His heart sank and he felt dazed. "My God! My God!" he muttered. "Again, again! It will never cease." Suddenly the matter presented itself in quite a different aspect. "Vermiform appendix! Kidney!" he said to

---

13  **Jean:** French equivalent for Ivan.
14  **Zola:** Émile Zola (1840–1902), French novelist known for his realistic style.

himself. "It's not a question of my appendix or my kidney, but of life and . . . death. Yes, life was there and now it is going, going and I cannot stop it. Yes. Why deceive myself? Isn't it obvious to everyone but me that I'm dying, and that it's only a question of weeks, days . . . it may happen any moment. There was light and now there's darkness. I was here and now I'm going there! Where?" A chill came over him, his breathing ceased, and he felt only the throbbing of his heart.

"When I'm not, what will there be? There'll be nothing. Then where will I be when I'm no more? Can this be dying? No, I don't want to!" He jumped up and tried to light the candle, felt for it with his trembling hands, dropped both candle and candlestick on the floor, and fell back on his pillow.

"What's the use? It makes no difference," he said to himself, staring with wide-open eyes into the darkness. "Death. Yes, death. And none of them knows or wishes to know it, and they have no pity for me. Now they are singing and playing." (He heard through the door the distant sound of a song and its accompaniment.) "It's all the same to them, but they'll die too! Fools! First me, and later them, but it'll be the same for them. And now they're merry . . . the beasts!"

Anger choked him and he was agonizingly, unbearably miserable. "It's impossible that all men have been doomed to suffer this awful horror!" He raised himself up.

"Something must be wrong. I must calm myself—I must think it all over from the beginning." He began thinking again. "Yes, the beginning of my illness: I bumped my side, but I was still quite well that day and the next. It hurt a little, then rather more. I saw doctors, there followed despondency and anguish, more doctors, and I drew nearer to the abyss. My strength grew less and I kept coming nearer and nearer; now I have wasted away and there is no light left in my eyes. I think about my appendix—but this is really death! I think of mending my appendix, and all the while here comes death! Can it really be death?" Terror seized him again and he gasped for breath. He leant down and began feeling for the matches, pressing on the stand beside the bed with his elbow. It was in his way and it hurt him, he grew furious with it, pressed on it still harder, and upset it. Breathless and in despair he fell on his back, expecting death to come immediately.

Meanwhile the visitors were leaving. Praskovya Fedorovna was seeing them off. She heard something fall and came in.

"What happened?"

"Nothing. I knocked it over accidentally."

She went out and returned with a candle. He lay there panting heavily, like a man who's run a thousand yards, and stared at her with a fixed look.

"What is it, Jean?"

"No . . . o . . . thing. I knocked it over." ("Why speak about it? She won't understand," he thought.)

Indeed she did not understand. She picked up the stand, lit his candle, and hurried away to see another visitor off. When she came back he still lay on his back, looking upwards.

"What is it? Do you feel worse?"

"Yes."

She shook her head and sat down.

"Do you know, Jean, I think we must ask Leshchetitsky to come and see you here."

This meant calling in the famous specialist, regardless of expense. He smiled malignantly and said "No." She stayed a little longer and then went up to him and kissed his forehead.

While she was kissing him he hated her from the bottom of his heart and refrained with difficulty from pushing her away.

"Good-night. I pray to God you'll get some sleep."

"Yes."

## VI

Ivan Ilych saw that he was dying, and he was in continual despair.

In the depth of his heart he knew he was dying, but not only was he unaccustomed to the thought, he simply did not and could not grasp it.

The syllogism he had learnt from Kiesewetter's Logic:[15] "Caius is a man, men are mortal, therefore Caius is mortal," had always seemed to him correct as applied to Caius, but it certainly didn't apply to himself. That Caius—man in the abstract—was mortal, was perfectly correct, but he was not Caius, not an abstract man, but a creature quite separate from all others. He had been little Vanya, with a mamma and a papa, with Mitya and Volodya, with toys, a coachman and a nanny, afterwards with Katenka and with all the joys, griefs, and delights of childhood, boyhood, and youth. What did Caius know of the smell of that striped leather ball Vanya had been so fond of? Had Caius kissed his mother's hand like that, and did the silk of her dress rustle for Caius? Had he rioted like that at school when the pastry was bad? Had Caius been in love like that? Could Caius preside at a session as he did? "Caius really was mortal, and it was right for him to die; but as for me, little Vanya, Ivan Ilych, with all my thoughts and emotions, it's altogether a different matter. It cannot be that I ought to die. That would be too terrible."

Such was his feeling.

"If I had to die like Caius I should have known it. An inner voice would have told me so, but there was nothing of the sort in me; I and all my friends felt that our case was quite different from that of Caius. And now here it is!" he said to himself. "It can't be. It's impossible! But here it is. How's this? How's one to understand it?"

He could not understand it, and tried to drive away this false, incorrect, morbid thought and to replace it by other proper, healthy thoughts. But that thought, and not only the thought but the reality itself, seemed to come and confront him.

To replace that thought he called up a succession of others, hoping to find some support in them. He tried to get back into the former current of thoughts that had

---

15 **Kiesewetter's Logic:** *The Outline of Logic According to Kantian Principles* by Klaus Kiesewetter (1766–1819).

once screened the thought of death from him. But strange to say, all that had formerly shut off, hidden, and destroyed his consciousness of death, no longer had that effect. Ivan Ilych now spent most of his time attempting to re-establish that old current. He would say to himself: "I will take up my duties again—after all I used to live by them." Banishing all doubts he would go to the law courts, enter into conversation with his colleagues, and sit carelessly as was his wont, scanning the crowd with a thoughtful look and leaning both his emaciated arms on the arms of his oak chair; bending over as usual to a colleague and drawing his papers nearer he would exchange whispers with him, and then suddenly raising his eyes and sitting erect would pronounce certain words and open the proceedings. But suddenly in the midst of those proceedings the pain in his side, regardless of the stage the proceedings had reached, would begin its own gnawing work. Ivan Ilych would turn his attention to it and try to drive the thought of it away, but without success. *It* would come and stand before him and look at him, and he would be petrified. The light would die out in his eyes, and he would begin asking himself again whether *It* alone was true. His colleagues and subordinates would notice with surprise and distress that he, the brilliant and subtle judge, was becoming confused and making mistakes. He would shake himself, try to pull himself together, somehow manage to bring the session to a close, and return home with the sorrowful consciousness that his judicial labors could no longer hide from him what he wanted them to hide, and could not deliver him from *It*. And what was worst of all was that *It* drew his attention to itself not in order to make him take some action, but only so that he should look at *It*, look it straight in the face: look at it and without doing anything, suffer inexpressibly.

To save himself from this condition Ivan Ilych looked for consolations—new screens—and they were found and for a while seemed to save him, but then they immediately fell to pieces or rather became transparent, as if *It* penetrated them and nothing could veil *It*.

During these last few days he would go into the drawing-room he had arranged—that drawing-room where he had fallen and for the sake of which (how bitterly ridiculous it seemed) he had sacrificed his life—for he knew that his illness originated with that knock. He would enter and see that something had scratched the polished table. He would look for the cause and find that it was the bronze ornament on an album, that had got bent. He would take up the expensive album which he had lovingly arranged, and feel vexed with his daughter and her friends for their untidiness—the album was torn here and there and some of the photographs were turned upside down. He would put it carefully in order and bend the ornament back into position. Then it would occur to him to place all those things in another corner of the room, near the plants. He would call the footman, but his daughter or wife would come to help him. They wouldn't agree, and his wife would contradict him; he would dispute and grow angry. But that was all right, for then he didn't think about *It*. *It* was invisible.

But then, when he was moving something himself, his wife would say: "Let the servants do it. You'll hurt yourself again." Suddenly *It* would flash through the screen and he would see it. It was just a flash, and he hoped it would disappear, but involuntarily he would pay attention to his side. "It just sits there as before, gnawing just the same!" He could no longer forget *It*, but could see it distinctly looking at him from behind the flowers. "What's it all for?"

"It really is so! I lost my life over that curtain as I might have done storming a fort. Is that possible? How terrible and how stupid. It can't be true! It can't, but it is."

He would go to his study, lie down, and be alone again with *It*: face to face with *It*. Nothing could be done with *It* except to look at it and shudder.

## VII

How it happened it is impossible to say because it came about step by step, unnoticed, but in the third month of Ivan Ilych's illness, his wife, his daughter, his son, his acquaintances, the doctors, the servants, and above all he himself, were aware that the whole interest he had for other people was whether he would soon vacate his place, and at last release the living from the discomfort caused by his presence and be released himself from his sufferings.

He slept less and less. He was given opium and hypodermic injections of morphine, but this did not relieve his pain. The dull depression he experienced in a somnolent condition at first gave him a little relief, but only as something new; afterwards it became as distressing as the pain itself or even more so.

Special foods were prepared for him on the doctors' orders, but all those foods became increasingly distasteful and disgusting to him.

For his excretions special arrangements had to be made, and this was a torment to him every time—a torment from the uncleanliness, the unseemliness, and the smell, and from knowing that another person had to take part in it.

But it was just through this most unpleasant matter, that Ivan Ilych obtained some comfort. Gerasim, the butler's young assistant, always came to carry things out. Gerasim was a clean, fresh peasant lad, grown stout on town food, always cheerful and bright. At first the sight of him, in his clean Russian peasant costume, engaged on such a disgusting task embarrassed Ivan Ilych.

Once when he got up from the commode too weak to draw up his own trousers, he dropped into a soft armchair and looked with horror at his bare, enfeebled thighs with the muscles so sharply marked on them.

Gerasim with a firm light tread, his heavy boots emitting a pleasant smell of tar and fresh winter air, came in wearing a clean Hessian apron, the sleeves of his print shirt tucked up over his strong bare young arms; refraining from looking at his sick master out of consideration for his feelings, and restraining the joy of life that beamed from his face, he went up to the commode.

"Gerasim!" said Ivan Ilych in a weak voice.

Gerasim started, evidently afraid he might have committed some blunder, and with a rapid movement turned his fresh, kind, simple young face which just showed the first downy signs of a beard.

"Yes, sir?"

"That must be very unpleasant for you. You must forgive me. I am helpless."

"Oh, why, sir," Gerasim's eyes beamed and he showed his glistening white teeth, "what's a little trouble? It's a case of illness with you, sir."

His deft strong hands did their accustomed task, and he went out of the room stepping lightly. Five minutes later he returned as lightly.

Ivan Ilych was still sitting in the same position in the armchair.

"Gerasim," he said when the latter had replaced the freshly-washed item. "Please come here and help me." Gerasim went up to him. "Lift me up. It is hard for me to get up, and I have sent Dmitri away."

Gerasim went up to him, grasped his master with his strong arms deftly but gently, in the same way that he moved—lifted him, supported him with one hand, and with the other drew up his trousers and would have set him down again, but Ivan Ilych asked to be led to the sofa. Gerasim, without effort and without apparent pressure, led him, almost lifting him, to the sofa and placed him on it.

"Thank you. How easily and well you do it all!"

Gerasim smiled again and turned to leave the room. But Ivan Ilych felt his presence such a comfort that he did not want to let him go.

"One thing more, please move up that chair. No, the other one—under my feet. It's easier for me when my feet are raised."

Gerasim brought the chair, set it down gently in place, and raised Ivan Ilych's legs on to it. It seemed to Ivan Ilych that he felt better while Gerasim was holding up his legs.

"It's better when my legs are higher," he said. "Place that cushion under them."

Gerasim did so. Again he lifted the legs and placed them, and again Ivan Ilych felt better while Gerasim held his legs. When he set them down Ivan Ilych fancied he felt worse.

"Gerasim," he said. "Are you busy now?"

"Not at all, sir," said Gerasim, who had learnt from townspeople how to speak to gentlefolk.

"What have you still to do?"

"What have I to do? I've done everything except chop the logs for tomorrow."

"Then hold my legs up a bit higher, will you?"

"Of course I will. Why not?" Gerasim raised his master's legs higher and Ivan Ilych thought that in that position he did not feel any pain at all.

"How about the logs?"

"Don't worry about that, sir. There's plenty of time."

Ivan Ilych told Gerasim to sit down and hold his legs, and began to talk to him. Strange to say it seemed that he felt better while Gerasim held his legs up.

After that Ivan Ilych would sometimes call Gerasim and get him to hold his legs on his shoulders, and he liked talking to him. Gerasim did it all easily, willingly, simply, and with good humor that touched Ivan Ilych. Health, strength, and vitality in other people were offensive to him, but Gerasim's strength and vitality did not mortify, but soothed him.

What tormented Ivan Ilych most was the deception, the lie, which for some reason they all accepted, that he was not dying but was simply ill, and that he need only keep still and undergo treatment and then something very good would result. He knew however that do what they would nothing would come of it, only still more agonizing suffering and death. This deception tortured him—their not wishing to admit what they all knew and what he knew, but wanting to lie to him concerning his terrible condition, and wishing and forcing him to participate in that lie. Those lies—enacted over him on the eve of his death and destined to degrade this awful, solemn act to the level of their visits, their curtains, their sturgeon for dinner—were a terrible agony for Ivan Ilych. And strangely enough, many times when they were going through their antics over him he had been within a hairbreadth of calling out to them: "Stop lying! You know and I know that I'm dying. Then at least stop lying about it!" But he had never the courage to do it. The awful, terrible act of his dying was, he could see, reduced by those around him to the level of a casual, unpleasant, almost indecorous incident (as if someone entered a drawing-room diffusing an unpleasant odor) and this was done by that very decorum which he had served his whole life long. He saw that no one felt for him, because no one even wished to grasp his position. Only Gerasim recognized it and pitied him. And so Ivan Ilych felt at ease only with him. He felt comforted when Gerasim supported his legs (sometimes all night long) and refused to go to bed, saying: "Don't you worry, Ivan Ilych. I'll get sleep enough later on," or when he suddenly became familiar and exclaimed: "If you weren't sick it would be another matter, but as it is, why should I grudge a little trouble?" Only Gerasim did not lie; everything showed that he alone understood the facts of the case and did not consider it necessary to disguise them, but simply felt sorry for his emaciated and enfeebled master. Once when Ivan Ilych was sending him away he even said straight out: "We shall all die, so why should I grudge a little trouble?"—expressing the fact that he did not consider his work burdensome, because he was doing it for a dying man and hoped someone would do the same for him when his time came.

Apart from this lying, or because of it, what tormented Ivan Ilych most was that no one pitied him as he wished to be pitied. At certain moments after prolonged suffering he wished most of all (though he would have been ashamed to confess it) for someone to pity him as a sick child is pitied. He longed to be petted and comforted. He knew he was an important functionary, that his beard was turning grey, and that therefore what he longed for was impossible, but still he longed for it. In Gerasim's attitude towards him there was something akin to what he wished for, and so that attitude comforted him. Ivan Ilych wanted to weep, wanted to be petted and cried over; then his colleague Shebek would come, and instead of weeping and being petted, Ivan Ilych would assume a serious, severe, and profound air. By force of habit he would express his opinion on a decision of the Court of Cassation[16] and would stubbornly insist on that view. This falsity around him and within him did more than anything else to poison his last days.

---

16  **Court of Cassation:** The highest court of appeal.

## VIII

It was morning. He knew it was morning because Gerasim had gone, and Peter the footman had come in and put out the candles, drawn back one of the curtains, and quietly begun to tidy up. Whether it was morning or evening, Friday or Sunday, made no difference, it was all just the same: the gnawing, unmitigated, agonizing pain, never ceasing for an instant, the consciousness of life inexorably waning but not yet extinguished, the approach of that ever dreaded and hateful Death which was the only reality, and always the same falsity. What were days, weeks, hours, in such a case?

"Will you have some tea, sir?"

"He wants things to be regular, and wishes the gentlefolk to drink tea in the morning," thought Ivan Ilych, and only said "No."

"Wouldn't you like to move onto the sofa, sir?"

"He wants to tidy up the room, and I'm in the way. I am uncleanliness and disorder," he thought, and said only:

"No, leave me alone."

The man went on bustling about. Ivan Ilych stretched out his hand. Peter came up, ready to help.

"What is it, sir?"

"My watch."

Peter took the watch which was close at hand and gave it to his master.

"Half-past eight. Are they up?"

"No sir, except Vladimir Ivanich" (the son) "who has gone to school. Praskovya Fedorovna ordered me to wake her if you asked for her. Shall I do so?"

"No, there's no need to." "Perhaps I'd better have some tea," he thought, and added aloud: "Yes, bring me some tea."

Peter went to the door, but Ivan Ilych dreaded being left alone. "How can I keep him here? Oh yes, my medicine." "Peter, give me my medicine." "Why not? Perhaps it may still do me some good." He took a spoonful and swallowed it. "No, it won't help. It's all foolishness, all deception," he decided as soon as he became aware of the familiar, sickly, hopeless taste. "No, I can't believe in it any longer. But the pain, why this pain? If it would only cease just for a moment!" And he moaned. Peter turned towards him. "It's all right. Go and fetch me some tea."

Peter went out. Left alone Ivan Ilych groaned not so much with pain, terrible though that was, as from mental anguish. Always and forever the same, always these endless days and nights. If only it would come quicker! If only *what* would come quicker? Death, darkness? . . . No, no! Anything rather than death!

When Peter returned with the tea on a tray, Ivan Ilych stared at him for a time in perplexity, not realizing who and what he was. Peter was disconcerted by that look and his embarrassment brought Ivan Ilych to himself.

"Oh, tea! All right, put it down. Only help me wash and put on a clean shirt."

Ivan Ilych began to wash. With pauses for rest, he washed his hands and then his face, cleaned his teeth, brushed his hair, and looked in the mirror. He was terrified by what he saw, especially by the limp way in which his hair clung to his pallid forehead.

While his shirt was being changed he knew that he would be still more frightened at the sight of his body, so he avoided looking at it. Finally he was ready. He drew on a dressing-gown, wrapped himself in a plaid, and sat down in the armchair to take his tea. For a moment he felt refreshed, but as soon as he began to drink the tea he was again aware of the same taste, and the pain returned too. He finished it with an effort, and then lay down stretching out his legs, and dismissed Peter.

Always the same. Now a spark of hope flashes up, then a sea of despair rages, and always pain; always pain, always despair, and always the same. When alone he had a dreadful and distressing desire to call someone, but he knew beforehand that with others present it would be still worse. "Another dose of morphine—to lose consciousness. I'll tell him, the doctor, that he must think of something else. It's impossible, impossible, to go on like this."

An hour and another pass like that. But now there's a ring at the door bell. Perhaps it's the doctor? It is. He comes in fresh, hearty, plump, and cheerful, with that look on his face that seems to say: "There now, you're in a panic about something, but we'll arrange it all for you at once!" The doctor knows this expression is out of place here, but he has put it on once and for all and can't take it off—like a man who has put on a frock-coat in the morning to pay a round of calls.

The doctor rubs his hands vigorously and reassuringly.

"Brr! How cold it is! There's such a sharp frost; just let me warm myself!" he says, as if it were only a matter of waiting till he was warm, and then he would put everything right.

"Well now, how are you?"

Ivan Ilych feels the doctor would like to say: "Well, how are our affairs?" but that even he feels this would not do, and says instead: "What sort of a night did you have?"

Ivan Ilych looks at him as if to say: "Are you really never ashamed of lying?" But the doctor does not wish to understand this question, and Ivan Ilych says: "Just as terrible as ever. The pain never leaves me and never subsides. If only something . . ."

"Yes, you sick people are always like that. . . . There, now I think I'm warm enough. Even Praskovya Fedorovna, who's so particular, could find no fault with my temperature. Well, now I can say good-morning," and the doctor presses his patient's hand.

Then, dropping his former playfulness, he begins with a most serious face to examine the patient, feeling his pulse and taking his temperature, and then begins the sounding and auscultation.

Ivan Ilych knows quite well and definitely that this is all nonsense and pure deception, but when the doctor, getting down on his knee, leans over him, putting his ear first higher then lower, and performs various gymnastic movements over him with a significant expression on his face, Ivan Ilych submits to it all just as he used to submit to the speeches of the lawyers, though he knew very well that they were all lying and knew why they were lying.

The doctor, kneeling on the sofa, is still sounding him when Praskovya Fedorovna's silk dress rustles at the door and she's heard scolding Peter for not having let her know of the doctor's arrival.

She comes in, kisses her husband, and at once proceeds to prove that she has been up a long time, and owing only to a misunderstanding failed to be there when the doctor arrived.

Ivan Ilych looks at her, scans her all over, sets against her the whiteness, plumpness, and cleanness of her hands and neck, the gloss of her hair, and the sparkle of her vivacious eyes. He hates her with his whole soul. The thrill of hatred he feels for her makes him suffer from her touch.

Her attitude towards him and his disease is still the same. Just as the doctor had adopted a certain relation to his patient which he could not abandon, so had she formed one towards him—that he was not doing something he ought to do and was himself to blame, and she reproached him lovingly for this—and now she could not change that attitude.

"You see he doesn't listen to me and doesn't take his medicine at the proper time. Above all he lies in a position that's no doubt bad for him—with his legs up."

She described how he made Gerasim hold his legs up.

The doctor smiled with a contemptuous affability that said: "What's to be done? These sick people do have foolish fancies of that kind, but we must forgive them."

When the examination was over the doctor looked at his watch, and then Praskovya Fedorovna announced to Ivan Ilych that it was of course as he pleased, but she had sent to-day for a celebrated specialist who would examine him and have a consultation with Mikhail Danilovich (their regular doctor).

"Please don't raise any objections. I'm doing this for my own sake," she said ironically, letting it be felt that she was doing it all for his sake and only said this to leave him no right to refuse. He remained silent, knitting his brows. He felt that he was surrounded and involved in such a mesh of falsity that it was hard to unravel anything.

Everything she did for him was entirely for her own sake; she told him she was doing for herself what she actually was doing for herself, as if that was so incredible he must understand the opposite.

At half-past eleven the celebrated specialist arrived. Again the sounding began and the significant conversations in his presence and in another room, about his kidneys and appendix, and the questions and answers, with such an air of importance that again, instead of the real question of life and death which now alone confronted him, the question arose of his kidney and appendix which were not behaving as they ought to and would now be attacked by Mikhail Danilovich and the specialist and forced to mend their ways.

The celebrated specialist took leave of him with a serious though not hopeless look, and in reply to the timid question Ivan Ilych, eyes glistening with fear and hope, put to him as to whether there was any chance of recovery, said that he could not vouch for it but there was a possibility. The look of hope with which Ivan Ilych watched the doctor out was so pathetic that Praskovya Fedorovna, seeing it, even wept as she left the room to hand the doctor his fee.

The gleam of hope kindled by the doctor's encouragement did not last long. The same room, the same pictures, curtains, wall-paper, medicine bottles, were all there, and the same aching suffering body, and Ivan Ilych began to moan. They gave him a subcutaneous injection and he sank into oblivion.

It was twilight when he came to. They brought him his dinner and he swallowed some beef broth with difficulty; then everything was the same again and night was coming on.

After dinner, at seven o'clock, Praskovya Fedorovna came into the room in evening dress, her full bosom pushed up by her corset, and with traces of powder on her face. She had reminded him in the morning that they were going to the theater. Sarah Bernhardt[17] was visiting town and they had a box, which he had insisted on their taking. Now he had forgotten about it and her toilet offended him, but he concealed his vexation when he remembered that he had himself insisted on their securing a box and going because it would be an instructive and aesthetic pleasure for the children.

Praskovya Fedorovna came in, self-satisfied but with a rather guilty air. She sat down and asked how he was, but, as he saw, only for the sake of asking and not in order to learn about it, knowing that there was nothing to learn. Then she went on to what she really wanted to say: she would not on any account have gone but the box had been taken and Helen and their daughter were going, as well as Petrishchev (the examining magistrate, their daughter's fiancé) and that it was out of the question to let them go alone. She would have much preferred to sit with him for a while; he must be sure to follow the doctor's orders while she was away.

"Oh, and Fedor Petrovich" (the fiancé) "would like to come in. May he? And Lisa?"

"All right."

Their daughter came in in full evening dress, her fresh young flesh exposed (making a show of that very flesh which in his own case caused so much suffering), strong, healthy, evidently in love, and impatient with his illness, suffering, and death, because they interfered with her happiness.

Fedor Petrovich came in too, in evening dress, his hair curled *à la Capoul*,[18] a tight stiff collar around his long sinewy neck, an enormous white shirt-front and narrow black trousers tightly stretched over his strong thighs. He had one white glove tightly drawn on, and was holding his opera hat in his hand.

Following him the schoolboy crept in unnoticed, in a new uniform, poor little fellow, and wearing gloves. Terribly dark shadows showed under his eyes, the meaning of which Ivan Ilych knew well.

His son had always seemed pathetic to him, and now it was dreadful to see the boy's frightened look of pity. It seemed to Ivan Ilych that Vasya was the only one besides Gerasim who understood and pitied him.

They all sat down and again asked how he was. A silence followed. Lisa asked her

---

17 **Sarah Bernhardt:** French actress (1844–1923) who was a sensation in the nineteenth century.
18 *à la Capoul:* Elaborate man's hairstyle. Capoul was a popular French singer of the time.

mother about the opera-glasses, and there was an altercation between mother and daughter as to who had taken them and where they had been put. This occasioned some unpleasantness.

Fedor Petrovich inquired of Ivan Ilych whether he had ever seen Sarah Bernhardt. Ivan Ilych did not at first catch the question, but then replied: "No, have you seen her before?"

"Yes, in *Adrienne Lecouvreur*."[19]

Praskovya Fedorovna mentioned some roles in which Sarah Bernhardt was particularly good. Her daughter disagreed. Conversation sprang up as to the elegance and realism of her acting—the sort of conversation that is always repeated and is always the same.

In the midst of the conversation Fedor Petrovich glanced at Ivan Ilych and became silent. The others also looked at him and grew silent. Ivan Ilych was staring with glittering eyes straight before him, evidently indignant with them. This had to be rectified, but it was impossible to do so. The silence had to be broken, but for a time no one dared break it and they all became afraid that the conventional deception would suddenly become obvious and the truth become plain to all. Lisa was the first to pluck up her courage and break that silence, but by trying to hide what everybody was feeling, she betrayed it.

"Well, if we're going it's time to start," she said, looking at her watch, a present from her father, with a faint, significant smile at Fedor Petrovich relating to something known only to them. She got up with a rustle of her dress.

They all rose, said good-night, and went away.

When they had gone it seemed to Ivan Ilych that he felt better; the falsity had gone away with them. But the pain remained—the same pain and the same fear that made everything monotonously alike, nothing harder and nothing easier. Everything was worse.

Again minute followed minute and hour followed hour. Everything remained the same; there was no cessation. The inevitable end of it all became more and more terrible.

"Yes, send Gerasim in here," he replied to a question Peter asked.

## IX

His wife returned late at night. She came in on tip-toe, but he heard her, opened his eyes, and made haste to close them again. She wished to send Gerasim away and sit with him herself, but he opened his eyes and said: "No, go away."

"Are you in great pain?"

"Always the same."

"Take some opium."

---

19 *Adrienne Lecouvreur:* Comedic play (1849) by Eugène Scribe (1791–1861) and Ernest Legouvé (1807–1903).

He agreed and took some. She went away.

Till about three in the morning he was in a state of stupefied misery. It seemed to him that he and his pain were being thrust into a narrow, deep black sack, and though they were being pushed further and further in they could not be pushed to the bottom. And this, terrible enough in itself, was accompanied by suffering. He was frightened, yet wanted to fall through the sack; he struggled yet co-operated. Suddenly he broke through, fell, and regained consciousness. Gerasim was sitting at the foot of the bed dozing quietly and patiently, while he himself lay with his emaciated stockinged legs resting on Gerasim's shoulders; the same shaded candle stood there and the same unceasing pain.

"Go away, Gerasim," he whispered.

"It's all right, sir. I'll stay a while."

"No. Go away."

He removed his legs from Gerasim's shoulders, turned sideways onto his arm, and felt sorry for himself. He only waited till Gerasim had gone into the next room and then restrained himself no longer but wept like a child. He wept on account of his helplessness, his terrible loneliness, the cruelty of man, the cruelty of God, and the absence of God.

"Why hast Thou done all this? Why hast Thou brought me here? Why, why dost Thou torment me so terribly?"

He did not expect an answer and wept because there was no answer and could be none. The pain grew more acute again, but he did not stir and did not call. He said to himself: "Go on! Strike me! But what is it for? What have I done to Thee? What is it for?"

Then he grew quiet and not only ceased weeping, but even held his breath and became all attention. It was as though he were listening not to an audible voice, but to the voice of his soul, to the current of thoughts arising within him.

"What do you want?" was the first clear conception capable of being expressed in words, that he heard.

"What do you want? What do you want?" he repeated to himself.

"What do I want? To live and not to suffer," he answered.

Again he listened with such concentrated attention that even his pain did not distract him.

"To live? How?" asked his inner voice.

"Why, to live as I used to—well and pleasantly."

"As you lived before, well and pleasantly?" the voice repeated.

And in his imagination he began to recall the best moments of his pleasant life. But strange to say none of those best moments of his pleasant life now seemed at all what they had seemed then—none of them except his first recollections of childhood. There, in childhood, there had been something really pleasant with which it would be possible to live, if it could return. But the child who had experienced that happiness no longer existed, it was like a recollection of somebody else.

As soon as the period began which had produced the present Ivan Ilych, all that had then seemed joys now melted away before his sight and turned into something trivial and often nasty.

The further he departed from childhood and the nearer he came to the present the more worthless and doubtful were the joys. This began with the School of Law. A little that was really good was still to be found there—there was light-heartedness, friendship, and hope. But in the upper classes there had already been fewer good moments. Then during the first years of his official career, when he was in the service of the governor, some pleasant moments occurred again: they were the memories of his love for a woman. Then all became confused and there was still less of what was good; later on again there was even less that was good, and the further he went the less there was. His marriage, a mere accident, then the disenchantment that followed it, his wife's bad breath and her sensuality and hypocrisy: then that deadly official life and those preoccupations about money, a year of it, two, ten, twenty, and always the same thing. The longer it lasted the more deadly it became. "It is as if I had been going downhill while I imagined I was going up. And that's really what it was. I was going up in public opinion, but to the same extent life was ebbing away from me. And now it's all over and there's only death.

"Then what does it mean? Why? It can't be that life is so senseless and horrible. But if it really has been so horrible and senseless, why must I die and die in agony? There's something wrong!

"Maybe I didn't live as I ought to have done," it suddenly occurred to him. "But how could that be, when I did everything properly?" he replied, and immediately dismissed from his mind this, the sole solution of all the riddles of life and death, as something quite impossible.

"Then what do you want now? To live? Live how? Live as you lived in the law courts when the usher proclaimed 'The judge is coming!' The judge is coming, the judge!" he repeated to himself. "Here he is, the judge. But I'm not guilty!" he exclaimed angrily. "What is it for?" And he ceased crying, but turning his face to the wall continued to ponder the same question: Why, and for what purpose, is there all this horror? But however much he pondered, he found no answer. And whenever the thought occurred to him, as it often did, that it all resulted from his not having lived as he ought to have done, he recalled at once the correctness of his whole life and dismissed so strange an idea.

# X

Another fortnight passed. Ivan Ilych now no longer left his sofa. He would not lie in bed but lay on the sofa, facing the wall nearly all the time. He suffered the same unceasing agonies and in his loneliness pondered the same insoluble question: "What is this? Can it be that it is Death?" And the inner voice answered: "Yes, it is Death."

"Why these sufferings?" And the voice answered, "For no reason—just so." Beyond and besides this, there was nothing.

From the very beginning of his illness, ever since he had first been to see the doctor, Ivan Ilych's life had been divided between two contrary and alternating moods: either despair and the expectation of this uncomprehended and terrible death, or hope and an intently interested observation of the functioning of his organs. Before his eyes there was either a kidney or an intestine that temporarily evaded its duty, or that incomprehensible and dreadful death from which it was impossible to escape.

These two states of mind had alternated from the very beginning of his illness, but the further it progressed, the more doubtful and fantastic became the conception of his kidney, and the more real the sense of impending death.

He had but to recall what he had been three months before and what he was now, to recall with what regularity he had been going downhill, for every possibility of hope to be shattered.

Lately during that loneliness in which he found himself as he lay facing the back of the sofa, a loneliness in the mist of a populous town, surrounded by numerous acquaintances and relations, but that could not have been more complete anywhere—either at the bottom of the sea or under the earth—during that terrible loneliness Ivan Ilych had lived only in memories of the past. Pictures of his past rose before him one after another. They always began with what was nearest in time and then went back to what was most remote—to his childhood—and stopped there. If he thought of the stewed prunes that had been offered him that day, his mind went back to the raw shrivelled French plums of his childhood, their peculiar flavor and the flow of saliva when he sucked their pits; along with the memory of that taste came a whole series of memories of those days: his nanny, his brother, and their toys. "No, I mustn't think of that. . . . It's too painful," Ivan Ilych said to himself, and brought himself back to the present—to the button on the back of the sofa and the creases in its morocco. "Morocco is expensive, but it doesn't wear well: there had been a quarrel about it. It was a different kind of quarrel and a different kind of morocco that time when we tore father's portfolio and were punished, and mamma brought us some tarts. . . ." Once again his thoughts dwelt on childhood; again it was painful and he tried to banish them and fix his mind on something else.

Then together with that chain of memories another series passed through his mind—of how his illness had progressed and grown worse. There too the further back he looked, the more life there was. There had been more of what was good in life and more of life itself. The two merged. "Just as the pain went on getting worse and worse, so my life grew worse and worse," he thought. "There's one bright spot there at the back, at the beginning of life, and afterwards all becomes blacker and blacker and proceeds more and more rapidly—in inverse ratio to the square of the distance from death," thought Ivan Ilych. And the example of a stone falling downwards with increasing velocity entered his mind. Life, a series of increasing sufferings, flies further and further towards its end—the most terrible suffering. "I'm flying. . . ." He shuddered, shifted himself, and tried to resist, but was already aware that resistance was impossible, and again with eyes tired of gazing but unable to cease seeing what was before them, he stared at the back of the sofa and waited—awaiting that dreadful fall and shock and destruction.

"Resistance is impossible!" he said to himself. "If I could only understand what it's all for! But that too is impossible. An explanation would be possible if it could be said that I've not lived as I ought to. But it's impossible to say that," and he remembered all the legality, correctitude, and propriety of his life. "At any rate that can certainly not be admitted," he thought, and his lips smiled ironically as if someone could see that smile and be taken in by it. "There's no explanation! Agony, death. . . . What for?"

## XI

Another two weeks went by in this way and during that time an event occurred that Ivan Ilych and his wife had desired. Petrishchev formally proposed. It happened in the evening. The next day Praskovya Fedorovna came into her husband's room considering how best to inform him of it, but that very night there had been a change for the worse in his condition. She found him still lying on the sofa but in a different position. He lay on his back, groaning and staring fixedly straight in front of him.

She began to remind him about his medicines, but he turned his eyes towards her with such a look that she did not finish what she was saying; so great an animosity, to her in particular, did that look express.

"For Christ's sake let me die in peace!" he said.

She would have gone away, but just then their daughter came in and went to say good morning. He looked at her as he had his wife, and in reply to her inquiry about his health said dryly that he would soon free them all of himself. They were both silent and after sitting with him for a while went away.

"Is it our fault?" Lisa asked her mother. "It's as if we were to blame! I'm sorry for papa, but why should we be tortured?"

The doctor came at his usual time. Ivan Ilych answered "Yes" and "No," never taking his angry eyes from him, and said at last: "You know you can do nothing for me, so leave me alone."

"We can ease your sufferings."

"You can't even do that. Let me be."

The doctor went into the drawing-room and told Praskovya Fedorovna that the situation was very serious and that the only resource left was opium to allay her husband's sufferings, which must be terrible.

It was true, as the doctor said, Ivan Ilych's physical sufferings were terrible, but worse than the physical sufferings were his mental sufferings which were his chief torture.

His mental sufferings were due to the fact that that night, as he looked at Gerasim's sleepy, good-natured face with its prominent cheek-bones, the question suddenly occurred to him: "What if my whole life has been wrong?"

It occurred to him that what had appeared perfectly impossible before, namely that he had not spent his life as he should have done, might be true after all. It occurred to him that his scarcely perceptible attempts to struggle against what was considered good by the most highly placed people, those scarcely noticeable impulses which he had immediately suppressed, might have been the real thing, and all the rest false. His professional duties and the whole arrangement of his life and his family, all his social and official interests, might all have been false. He tried to defend all those things to himself and suddenly felt the weakness of what he was defending. There was nothing to defend.

"But if that's so," he said to himself, "and I'm leaving this life with the consciousness that I've lost all that was given me and it's impossible to rectify it—what then?"

He lay on his back and began to pass his life in review in quite a new way. In the morning when he first saw his footman, then his wife, then his daughter, and then the doctor, their every word and movement confirmed the awful truth that had been revealed to him during the night. In them he saw himself—all that for which he had lived—and saw clearly that it was not real at all, but a terrible and huge deception which had hidden both life and death. This consciousness intensified his physical suffering tenfold. He groaned, tossed about, and pulled at his clothing which choked and stifled him. And he hated them on that account.

He was given a large dose of opium and became unconscious, but at noon his sufferings began again. He drove everybody away and tossed from side to side.

His wife came to him and said:

"Jean, my dear, do this for me. It can't do any harm and it often helps. Healthy people often do it."

He opened his eyes wide.

"What? Take communion? Why? It's unnecessary! However . . ."

She began to cry.

"Yes, do, my dear. I'll send for our priest. He's such a nice man."

"All right. Very well," he muttered.

When the priest came and heard his confession, Ivan Ilych was softened and seemed to feel some relief from his doubts and consequently from his sufferings, and for a moment there came a ray of hope. Again he began to think of his vermiform appendix and the possibility of correcting it. He received the sacrament with tears in his eyes.

When they laid him down again afterwards he felt a moment's peace, and the hope that he might live awoke in him once again. He began to think of the operation that had been suggested to him. "To live! I want to live!" he said to himself.

His wife came in to congratulate him after his communion, and when uttering the usual conventional words she added:

"You feel better, don't you?"

Without looking at her he said "Yes."

Her dress, her figure, the expression of her face, the tone of her voice, all revealed the same thing. "This is wrong, it's not as it should be. All you've lived for and still live for is falsehood and deception, hiding life and death from you." As soon as he admitted that thought, his hatred and agonizing physical suffering increased again, and with that suffering a consciousness of the unavoidable, approaching end. And to this was added a new sensation of grinding, shooting pain and a feeling of suffocation.

The expression of his face when he uttered that "Yes" was dreadful. Having uttered it, he looked her straight in the eye, turned his face away with a rapidity extraordinary in his weak state and shouted:

"Go away! Go away and leave me alone!"

## XII

From that moment the screaming began that continued for three days, and was so terrible that one could not hear it through two closed doors without horror. At the moment he answered his wife he realized that he was lost, that there was no return, that the end had come, the very end, and his doubts were still unsolved and remained doubts.

"Oh! Oh! Oh!" he cried in various intonations. He had begun by screaming "I won't!" and continued screaming on the letter "O."

For three whole days, during which time did not exist for him, he struggled in that black sack into which he was being thrust by an invisible, irresistible force. He struggled as a man condemned to death struggles in the hands of the executioner, knowing that he cannot save himself. Every moment he felt that despite all his efforts he was drawing nearer and nearer to what terrified him. He felt that his agony was due to his being thrust into that black hole and still more to his not being able to get right into it. He was hindered from getting into it by his conviction that his life had been a good one. That very justification of his life held him fast and prevented his moving forward, and it caused him the most torment of all.

Suddenly some force struck him in the chest and side, making it even harder to breathe, and he fell through the hole and there at the bottom was a light. What had happened to him was like the sensation one sometimes experiences in a railway carriage when one thinks one is going backwards while one is really going forwards and suddenly becomes aware of the real direction.

"Yes, it was all not the right thing," he said to himself, "but that doesn't matter. The 'right thing' can still be done. But what *is* the right thing?" he asked himself, and suddenly grew quiet.

This occurred at the end of the third day, two hours before his death. Just then his schoolboy son had crept in softly and gone up to the bedside. The dying man was still screaming desperately and waving his arms. His hand fell on the boy's head, and the boy caught it, pressed it to his lips, and began to cry.

At that very moment Ivan Ilych fell through and caught sight of the light, and it was revealed to him that though his life had not been what it should have been, it could still be rectified. He asked himself, "What *is* the right thing?" and grew still, listening. Then he felt that someone was kissing his hand. He opened his eyes, looked at his son, and felt sorry for him. His wife came up to him and he glanced at her. She was gazing at him open-mouthed, with undried tears on her nose and cheek and a despairing look on her face. He felt sorry for her too.

"Yes, I am making them all wretched," he thought. "They're sorry, but it'll be better for them when I die." He wished to say this, but didn't have the strength to utter it. "Besides, why speak? I must act," he thought. With a look at his wife he indicated his son and said:

"Take him away . . . sorry for him . . . and for you too. . . ." He tried to add, "Forgive me," but said "Let me through" and waved his hand, knowing that He whose understanding mattered would understand.

Suddenly it grew clear to him that what had been oppressing him and would not leave him was all dropping away at once from two sides, from ten sides, from all sides. He was sorry for them, he must act so as not to hurt them: release them and free himself from these sufferings. "How good and how simple!" he thought. "And the pain?" he asked himself. "What has become of it? Where are you, pain?"

He turned his attention to it.

"Yes, here it is. Well, what of it? Let it be."

"And death . . . where is it?"

He looked for his former accustomed fear of death and did not find it. "Where is it? What death?" There was no fear because there was no death.

In place of death there was light.

"So that's what it is!" he suddenly exclaimed aloud. "What joy!"

To him all this happened in a single instant, and the meaning of that instant did not change. For those present his agony continued for another two hours. Something rattled in his throat, his emaciated body twitched, then the gasping and rattle became less and less frequent.

"It is finished!" said someone near him.

He heard these words and repeated them in his soul.

"Death is finished," he said to himself. "It is no more!"

He drew in a breath, stopped in the midst of a sigh, stretched out, and died.

# Mark Twain

## (1835–1910)

Joseph Twichell, a friend of Mark Twain, described the writer as "ever profoundly affected with the feeling of the pathos of life. Contemplating its heritage of inevitable pain and tears, he would question if to anyone it was a good gift." Twain, born Samuel Clemens, survived his wife and children and suffered from heavy financial debts. He came from modest beginnings, growing up in the Mississippi River town of Hannibal. His father died in 1847, and Clemens left school to work as an apprentice to a printer. Between 1857 and 1861, Clemens worked as a Mississippi riverboat pilot, but the Civil War put an end to this career. He joined an unorganized Confederate unit but resigned two weeks later to travel with his older brother to Nevada. This journey inspired *Roughing It* (1872). In the summer of 1862, Clemens began working for the Virginia City *Territorial Enterprise,* and it was here that he first used the name Mark Twain (adopted from his days as a riverboat pilot and meaning two fathoms). He left two years later to work as a reporter in San Francisco while also working, unsuccessfully, as a miner. However, at Angel's camp, Twain first heard the story that would eventually become "The Celebrated Jumping Frog of Calaveras County" (1865).

After a successful journey on the *Quaker City* steamer, Clemens became well known for his "travel literature." He married Olivia "Livy" Langdon in 1870, but sickness and disease haunted their marriage. Twain published many successful books, among them *The Adventures of Tom Sawyer* (1876), *The Prince and the Pauper* (1881), *Life on the Mississippi* (1883), *The Adventures of Huckleberry Finn* (1884), *A Connecticut Yankee in King Arthur's Court* (1889), and *Puddn'head Wilson* (1894). However, he continued to lose money on financial gambles, investments, and his own publishing company. In the 1890s, to recover his finances, Twain began touring the world. While he was on tour, his daughter Susy died (1894). Livy, Twain's wife and editor, died in 1904. In 1909, the day before Christmas, his daughter Jean also died. Twain passed away less than a year later.

## Jim Baker's Blue-Jay Yarn                                                    *1880*

Animals talk to each other, of course. There can be no question about that; but I suppose there are very few people who can understand them. I never knew but one man who could. I knew he could, however, because he told me so himself. He was a middle-aged, simple-hearted miner who had lived in a lonely corner of California, among the woods and mountains, a good many years, and had studied the ways of his only neighbors, the beasts and the birds, until he believed he could accurately translate any remark which they made. This was Jim Baker. According to Jim Baker, some animals have only a limited education, and some use only simple words, and scarcely ever a comparison or a flowery figure; whereas, certain other animals have a large vocabulary, a fine command of language and a ready and fluent delivery; consequently these latter talk a great deal; they like it; they are so conscious of their talent, and they enjoy "showing off." Baker said, that after long and careful observation, he had come to the conclusion that the bluejays were the best talkers he had found among birds and beasts. Said he:

"There's more *to* a bluejay than any other creature. He has got more moods, and more different kinds of feelings than other creatures; and, mind you, whatever a bluejay feels, he can put into language. And no mere commonplace language, either, but rattling, out-and-out book-talk—and bristling with metaphor, too—just bristling! And as for command of language—why *you* never see a bluejay get stuck for a word. No man ever did. They just boil out of him! And another thing: I've noticed a good deal, and there's no bird, or cow, or anything that uses as good grammar as a bluejay. You may say a cat uses good grammar. Well, a cat does—but you let a cat get excited once; you let a cat get to pulling fur with another cat on a shed, nights, and you'll hear grammar that will give you the lockjaw. Ignorant people think it's the *noise* which fighting cats make that is so aggravating, but it ain't so; it's the sickening grammar they use. Now I've never heard a jay use bad grammar but very seldom; and when they do, they are as ashamed as a human; they shut right down and leave.

"You may call a jay a bird. Well, so he is, in a measure—but he's got feathers on him, and don't belong to no church, perhaps; but otherwise he is just as much human as you be. And I'll tell you for why. A jaw's gifts, and instincts, and feelings, and interests, cover the whole ground. A jay hasn't got any more principle than a Congressman. A jay will lie, a jay will steal, a jay will deceive, a jay will betray; and four times out of five, a jay will go back on his solemnest promise. The sacredness of an obligation is such a thing which you can't cram into no bluejay's head. Now, on top of all this, there's another thing; a jay can out-swear any gentleman in the mines. You think a cat can swear. Well, a cat can; but you give a bluejay a subject that calls for his reserve-powers, and where is your cat? Don't talk to *me*—I know too much about this thing; in the one little particular scolding—just good, clean, out-and-out scolding—a bluejay can lay over anything, human or divine. Yes, sir, a jay is everything that a man is. A jay can cry, a jay can laugh, a jay can feel shame, a jay can reason and plan and discuss, a jay likes gossip and scandal, a jay has got a sense of humor, a jay knows when he is an ass just as well as you do—maybe better. If a jay ain't human, he better take in his sign, that's all. Now I'm going to tell you a perfectly true fact about some bluejays.

## Baker's Blue-Jay Yarn

"When I first begun to understand jay language correctly, there was a little incident happened here. Seven years ago, the last man in this region but me moved away. There stands his house—been empty ever since; a log house, with a plank roof—just one big room, and no more; no ceiling—nothing between the rafters and the floor. Well, one Sunday morning I was sitting out here in front of my cabin, with my cat, taking the sun, and looking at the blue hills, and listening to the leaves rustling so lonely in the trees, and thinking of the home away yonder in the states, that I hadn't heard from in thirteen years, when a bluejay lit on that house, with an acorn in his mouth, and says, 'Hello, I reckon I've struck something.' When he spoke, the acorn dropped out of his mouth and rolled down the roof, of course, but he didn't care; his mind was all on the thing he had struck. It was a knot-hole in the roof. He cocked his head to one side, shut one eye and put the other one to the hole, like a possum looking down a jug; then he glanced up with his bright eyes, gave a wink or two with his wings—which signifies gratification, you understand—and says, 'It looks like a hole, it's located like a hole—blamed if I don't believe it *is* a hole!'

"Then he cocked his head down and took another look; he glances up perfectly joyful, this time; winks his wings and his tail both, and says, 'Oh, no, this ain't no fat thing, I reckon! If I ain't in luck!—Why it's a perfectly elegant hole!' So he flew down and got that acorn, and fetched it up and dropped it in, and was just tilting his head back, with the heavenliest smile on his face, when all of a sudden he was paralyzed into a listening attitude and that smile faded gradually out of his countenance like breath off'n a razor, and the queerest look of surprise took its place. Then he says,

'Why, I didn't hear it fall!' He cocked his eye at the hole again, and took a long look; raised up and shook his head; stepped around to the other side of the hole and took another look from that side; shook his head again. He studied a while, then he just went into the *de*tails—walked round and round the hole and spied into it from every point of the compass. No use. Now he took a thinking attitude on the comb of the roof and scratched the back of his head with his right foot a minute, and finally says, 'Well, it's too many for *me*, that's certain; must be a mighty long hole; however, I ain't got no time to fool around here, I got to "tend to business"; I reckon it's all right— chance it, anyway."

"So he flew off and fetched another acorn and dropped it in, and tried to flirt his eye to the hole quick enough to see what become of it, but he was too late. He held his eye there as much as a minute; then he raised up and sighed, and says, 'Confound it, I don't seem to understand this thing, no way; however, I'll tackle her again.' He fetched another acorn, and done his level best to see what become of it, but he couldn't. He says, 'Well, I never struck no such a hole as this before; I'm of the opinion it's a totally new kind of a hole.' Then he begun to get mad. He held in for a spell, walking up and down the comb of the roof and shaking his head and muttering to himself; but his feelings got the upper hand of him, presently, and he broke loose and cussed himself black in the face. I never see a bird take on so about a little thing. When he got through he walks to the hole and looks in again for a half a minute; then he says, 'Well, you're a long hole, and a deep hole, and a mighty singular hole altogether—but I've started in to fill you, and I'm damned if I *don't* fill you, if it takes a hundred years!'

"And with that, away he went. You never see a bird work so since you was born. He laid into his work like a nigger, and the way he hove acorns into that hole for about two hours and a half was one of the most exciting and astonishing spectacles I ever struck. He never stopped to take a look anymore—he just hove 'em in and went for more. Well, at last he could hardly flop his wings, he was so tuckered out. He comes a-dropping down, once more, sweating like an ice-pitcher, dropped his acorn in and says, '*Now* I guess I've got the bulge on you by this time!' So he bent down for a look. If you'll believe me, when his head come up again he was just pale with rage. He says, 'I've shoveled acorns enough in there to keep the family thirty years, and if I can see a sign of one of 'em I wish I may land in a museum with a belly full of sawdust in two minutes!'

"He just had strength enough to crawl up on to the comb and lean his back agin the chimbly, and then he collected his impressions and begun to free his mind. I see in a second that what I had mistook for profanity in the mines was only just the rudiments, as you may say.

"Another jay was going by, and heard him doing his devotions, and stops to inquire what was up. The sufferer told him the whole circumstance, and says, 'Now yonder's the hole, and if you don't believe me, go and look for yourself.' So this fellow went and looked, and comes back and says, 'How many did you say you put in there?' 'Not any less than two tons,' says the sufferer. The other jay went and looked again. He couldn't seem to make it out, so he raised a yell, and three more jays come. They all examined the hole, they all made the sufferer tell it over again, then they all discussed it, and got off as many leather-headed opinions about it as an average crowd of humans could have done.

"They called in more jays; then more and more, till pretty soon this whole region 'peared to have a blue flush about it. There must have been five thousand of them; and such another jawing and disputing and ripping and cussing, you never heard. Every jay in the whole lot put his eye to the hole and delivered a more chuckle-headed opinion about the mystery than the jay that went there before him. They examined the house all over, too. The door was standing half open, and at last one old jay happened to go and light on it and look in. Of course, that knocked the mystery galley-west in a second. There lay the acorns, scattered all over the floor . . . He flopped his wings and raised a whoop. 'Come here!' he says, 'Come here, everybody; hang'd if this fool hasn't been trying to fill up a house with acorns!' They all came a-swooping down like a blue cloud, and as each fellow lit on the door and took a glance, the whole absurdity of the contract that that first jay had tackled hit him home and he fell over backward suffocating with laughter, and the next jay took his place and done the same.

"Well, sir, they roosted around here on the housetop and the trees for an hour, and guffawed over that thing like human beings. It ain't any use to tell me a bluejay hasn't got a sense of humor, because I know better. And memory, too. They brought jays here from all over the United States to look down that hole, every summer for three years. Other birds, too. And they could all see the point except an owl that come from Nova Scotia to visit the Yo Semite, and he took this thing in on his way back. He said he couldn't see anything funny in it. But then he was a good deal disappointed about Yo Semite, too." Humor, a jay knows when he is an ass just as well as you do—maybe better. If a jay ain't human, he better take in his sign, that's all. Now I'm going to tell you a perfectly true fact about some bluejays."

## The Celebrated Jumping Frog of Calaveras County    1865

In compliance with the request of a friend of mine, who wrote me from the East, I called on good-natured, garrulous old Simon Wheeler, and inquired after my friend's friend, Leonidas W. Smiley, as requested to do, and I hereunto append the result. I have a lurking suspicion that *Leonidas W.* Smiley is a myth; that my friend never knew such a personage; and that he only conjectured that if I asked old Wheeler about him, it would remind him of his infamous *Jim* Smiley, and he would go to work and bore me to death with some exasperating reminiscence of him as long and as tedious as it should be useless to me. If that was the design, it succeeded.

I found Simon Wheeler dozing comfortably by the barroom stove of the dilapidated tavern in the decayed mining camp of Angel's, and I noticed that he was fat and bald-headed, and had an expression of winning gentleness and simplicity upon his tranquil countenance. He roused up, and gave me good-day. I told him a friend of mine had commissioned me to make some inquiries about a cherished companion of his boyhood named *Leonidas W.* Smiley—*Rev. Leonidas W.* Smiley, a young minister of the Gospel, who he had heard was at one time a resident of Angel's Camp. I added that if Mr. Wheeler could tell me anything about this Rev. Leonidas W. Smiley, I would feel under many obligations to him.

Simon Wheeler backed me into a corner and blockaded me there with his chair, and then sat down and reeled off the monotonous narrative which follows this paragraph. He never smiled, he never frowned, he never changed his voice from the gentle-flowing key to which he tuned his initial sentence, he never betrayed the slightest suspicion of enthusiasm; but all through the interminable narrative there ran a vein of impressive earnestness and sincerity, which showed me plainly that, so far from his imagining that there was anything ridiculous or funny about his story, he regarded it as a really important matter, and admired its two heroes as men of transcendent genius in *finesse*. I let him go on in his own way, and never interrupted him once.

"Rev. Leonidas W. H'm, Reverend Le—well, there was a feller here once by the name of *Jim* Smiley, in the winter of '49—or may be it was the spring of '50—I don't recollect exactly, somehow, though what makes me think it was one or the other is because I remember the big flume warn't finished when he first come to the camp; but any way, he was the curiosest man about always betting on anything that turned up you ever see, if he could get anybody to bet on the other side; and if couldn't he'd change sides. Any way that suited the other man would suit *him*—any way just so's he got a bet, *he* was satisfied. But still he was lucky, uncommon lucky; he most always come out winner. He was always ready and laying for a chance; there couldn't be no solit'ry thing mentioned but that feller'd offer to bet on it, and take ary side you please, as I was just telling you. If there was a horse-race, you'd find him flush or you'd find him busted at the end of it; if there was a dog-fight, he'd bet on it; if there was a cat-fight, he'd bet on it; if there was a chicken-fight, he'd bet on it; why, if there was two birds setting on a fence, he would bet you which one would fly first; or if there was a camp-meeting, he would be there reg'lar to bet on Parson Walker, which he judged to be the best exhorter about here, and so he was too, and a good man. If he even see a straddle-bug start to go anywheres, he would bet you how long it would take him to get to—to wherever he was going to, and if you took him up, he would foller that straddle-bug to Mexico but what he would find out where he was bound for and how long he was on the road. Lots of the boys here has seen that Smiley, and can tell you about him. Why, it never made no difference to *him*—he'd bet on *any* thing—the dangest feller. Parson Walker's wife laid very sick once, for a good while, and it seemed as if they warn't going to save her; but one morning he come in, and Smiley up and asked him how she was, and he said she was considerable better—thank the Lord for his inf'nite mercy—and coming on so smart that with the blessing of Prov'dence she'd get well yet; and Smiley, before he thought, says, "Well, I'll resk two-and-a-half she don't anyway."

Thish-yer Smiley had a mare—the boys called her the fifteen-minute nag, but that was only in fun, you know, because of course she was faster than that—and he used to win money on that horse, for all she was so slow and always had the asthma, or the distemper, or the consumption, or something of that kind. They used to give her two or three hundred yards start, and then pass her under way; but always at the

fag end of the race she'd get excited and desperate like, and come cavorting and straddling up, and scattering her legs around limber, sometimes in the air, and sometimes
out to one side among the fences, and kicking up m-o-r-e dust and raising m-o-r-e
racket with her coughing and sneezing and blowing her nose—and *always* fetch up at
the stand just about a neck ahead, as near as you could cipher it down.

And he had a little small bull-pup, that to look at him you'd think he warn't worth
a cent but to set around and look ornery and lay for a chance to steal something. But
as soon as money was up on him he was a different dog; his under-jaw'd begin to stick
out like the fo'castle of a steamboat, and his teeth would uncover and shine like the
furnaces. And a dog might tackle him and bully-rag him, and bite him, and throw him
over his shoulder two or three times, and Andrew Jackson—which was the name of the
pup—Andrew Jackson would never let on but what *he* was satisfied, and hadn't expected nothing else—and the bets being doubled and doubled on the other side all the
time, till the money was all up; and then all of a sudden he would grab the other dog
jest by the j'int of his hind leg and freeze to it—not chaw, you understand, but only just
grip and hang on till they throwed up the sponge, if it was a year. Smiley always come
out winner on that pup, till he harnessed a dog once that didn't have no hind legs, because they'd been sawed off in a circular saw, and when the thing had gone along far
enough, and the money was all up, and he come to make a snatch for his pet holt, he
see in a minute how he'd been imposed on, and how the other dog had him in the
door, so to speak, and he 'peared surprised, and then he looked sorter discouraged-
like, and didn't try no more to win the fight, and so he got shucked out bad. He gave
Smiley a look, as much as to say his heart was broke, and it was *his* fault, for putting up
a dog that hadn't no hind legs for him to take holt of, which was his main dependence
in a fight, and then he limped off a piece and laid down and died. It was a good pup,
was that Andrew Jackson, and would have made a name for hisself if he'd lived, for the
stuff was in him and he had genius—I know it, because he hadn't no opportunities to
speak of, and it don't stand to reason that a dog could make such a fight as he could under them circumstances if he hadn't no talent. It always makes me feel sorry when I
think of that last fight of his'n, and the way it turned out.

Well, thish-yer Smiley had rat-tarriers, and chicken cocks, and tomcats and all
them kind of things, till you couldn't rest, and you couldn't fetch nothing for him to
bet on but he'd match you. He ketched a frog one day, and took him home, and said
he cal'lated to educate him; and so he never done nothing for three months but set in
his back yard and learn that frog to jump. And you bet you he *did* learn him, too. He'd
give him a little pinch behind, and the next minute you'd see that frog whirling in the
air like a doughnut—see him turn one summerset, or may be a couple, if he got a
good start, and come down flat-footed and all right, like a cat. He got him up so in the
matter of ketching flies, and kep' him in practice so constant, that he'd nail a fly every
time as fur as he could see him. Smiley said all a frog wanted was education, and he
could do 'most anything—and I believe him. Why, I've seen him set Dan'l Webster
down here on this floor—Dan'l Webster was the name of the frog—and sing out,
"Flies, Dan'l, flies!" and quicker'n you could wink he'd spring straight up and snake a
fly off'n the counter there, and flop down on the floor ag'in as solid as a gob of mud,

and fall to scratching the side of his head with his hind foot as indifferent as if he hadn't no idea he'd been doin' any more'n any frog might do. You never see a frog so modest and straightfor'ard as he was, for all he was so gifted. And when it come to fair and square jumping on a dead level, he could get over more ground at one straddle than any animal of his breed you ever see. Jumping on a dead level was his strong suit, you understand; and when it come to that, Smiley would ante up money on him as long as he had a red. Smiley was monstrous proud of his frog, and well he might be, for fellers that had traveled and been everywheres all said he laid over any frog that ever *they* see.

Well, Smiley kep' the beast in a little lattice box, and he used to fetch him down town sometimes and lay for a bet. One day a feller—a stranger in the camp, he was—come acrost him with his box, and says:

"What might it be that you've got in the box?"

And Smiley says, sorter indifferent-like, "It might be a parrot, or it might be a canary, maybe, but it ain't—it's only just a frog."

And the feller took it, and looked at it careful, and turned it round this way and that, and says, "H'm—so 'tis. Well, what's *he* good for?"

"Well," Smiley says, easy and careless, "he's good enough for *one* thing, I should judge—he can outjump any frog in Calaveras county."

The feller took the box again, and took another long, particular look, and give it back to Smiley, and says, very deliberate, "Well," he says, "I don't see no p'ints about that frog that's any better'n any other frog."

"Maybe you don't," Smiley says. "Maybe you understand frogs and maybe you don't understand 'em; maybe you've had experience, and maybe you ain't only a amature, as it were. Anyways, I've got *my* opinion, and I'll resk forty dollars that he can outjump any frog in Calaveras county."

And the feller studied a minute, and then says, kinder sad like, "Well, I'm only a stranger here, and I ain't got no frog; but if I had a frog, I'd bet you."

And then Smiley says, "That's all right—that's all right—if you'll hold my box a minute, I'll go and get you a frog." And so the feller took the box, and put up his forty dollars along with Smiley's, and set down to wait.

So he set there a good while thinking and thinking to hisself, and then he got the frog out and prized his mouth open and took a teaspoon and filled him full of quail shot—filled him pretty near up to his chin—and set him on the floor. Smiley he went to the swamp and slopped around in the mud for a long time, and finally he ketched a frog, and fetched him in, and give him to this feller, and says:

"Now, if you're ready, set him alongside of Dan'l, with his forepaws just even with Dan'l's, and I'll give the word." Then he says, "One—two—three—*git!*" and him and the feller touched up the frogs from behind, and the new frog hopped off lively, but Dan'l give a heave, and hysted up his shoulders—so—like a Frenchman, but it warn't no use—he couldn't budge; he was planted as solid as a church, and he couldn't no more stir than if he was anchored out. Smiley was a good deal surprised, and he was disgusted too, but he didn't have no idea what the matter was, of course.

The feller took the money and started away; and when he was going out at the door, he sorter jerked his thumb over his shoulder—so—at Dan'l, and says again, very deliberate, "Well," he says, "*I* don't see no p'ints about that frog that's any better'n any other frog."

Smiley stood scratching his head and looking down at Dan'l a long time, and at last he says, "I do wonder what in the nation that frog throw'd off for—I wonder if there ain't something the matter with him—he 'pears to look mighty baggy, some-how." And he ketched Dan'l by the nap of the neck, and hefted him, and says, "Why blame my cats if he don't weigh five pound!" and turned him upside down and he belched out a double handful of shot. And then he see how it was, and he was the maddest man—he set the frog down and took out after that feller, but he never ketched him. And—"

Here Simon Wheeler heard his name called from the front yard, and got up to see what was wanted. And turning to me as he moved away, he said: "Just set where you are, stranger, and rest easy—I ain't going to be gone a second."

But, by your leave, I did not think that a continuation of the history of the enter-prising vagabond *Jim* Smiley would likely to afford me much information concerning the Rev. *Leonidas W.* Smiley, and so I started away.

At the door I met the sociable Wheeler returning, and he buttonholed me and re-commenced:

"Well, thish-yer Smiley had a yaller one-eyed cow that didn't have no tail, only just a short stump like a bannanner, and—"

However, lacking both time and inclination, I did not wait to hear about the af-flicted cow, but took my leave.

## The War Prayer                                                                    1905

It was a time of great and exalting excitement. The country was up in arms, the war was on, in every breast burned the holy fire of patriotism; the drums were beating, the bands playing, the toy pistols popping, the bunched firecrackers hissing and splutter-ing; on every hand and far down the receding and fading spread of roofs and bal-conies a fluttering wilderness of flags flashed in the sun; daily the young volunteers marched down the wide avenue gay and fine in their new uniforms, the proud fathers and mothers and sisters and sweethearts cheering them with voices choked with happy emotion as they swung by; nightly the packed mass meetings listened, panting, to patriot oratory which stirred the deepest deeps of their hearts, and which they in-terrupted at briefest intervals with cyclones of applause, the tears running down their cheeks the while; in the churches the pastors preached devotion to flag and country, and invoked the God of Battles, beseeching His aid in our good cause in outpouring of fervid eloquence which moved every listener. It was indeed a glad and gracious time, and the half dozen rash spirits that ventured to disapprove of the war and cast a doubt upon its righteousness straightway got such a stern and angry warning that for their personal safety's sake they quickly shrank out of sight and offended no more in that way.

Sunday morning came—next day the battalions would leave for the front; the church was filled; the volunteers were there, their young faces alight with martial dreams—visions of the stern advance, the gathering momentum, the rushing charge, the flashing sabers, the flight of the foe, the tumult, the enveloping smoke, the fierce pursuit, and surrender!—then home from the war, bronzed heroes, welcomed, adored, submerged in golden seas of glory! With the volunteers sat their dear ones, proud, happy, and envied by the neighbors and friends who had no sons and brothers to send forth to the field of honor, there to win for the flag, or, failing, die the noblest of noble deaths. The service proceeded; a war chapter from the Old Testament was read; the first prayer was said; it was followed by an organ burst that shook the building, and with one impulse the house rose, with glowing eyes and beating hearts, and poured out that tremendous invocation—

> "God the all-terrible! Thou who ordainest,
> Thunder thy clarion and lightning thy sword!"

Then came the "long" prayer. None could remember the like of it for passionate pleading and moving and beautiful language. The burden of its supplication was, that an ever-merciful and benignant Father of us all would watch over our noble young soldiers, and aid, comfort, and encourage them in their patriotic work; bless them, shield them in the day of battle and the hour of peril, bear them in His mighty hand, make them strong and confident, invincible in the bloody onset; help them to crush the foe, grant to them and to their flag and country imperishable honor and glory—

An aged stranger entered and moved with slow and noiseless step up the main aisle, his eyes fixed upon the minister, his long body clothed in a robe that reached to his feet, his head bare, his white hair descending in a frothy cataract to his shoulders, his seamy face unnaturally pale, pale even to ghastliness. With all eyes following him and wondering, he made his silent way; without pausing, he ascended to the preacher's side and stood there, waiting. With shut lids the preacher, unconscious of his presence, continued his moving prayer, and at last finished it with the words, uttered in fervent appeal, "Bless our arms, grant us the victory, O Lord our God, Father and Protector of our land and flag!"

The stranger touched his arm, motioned him to step aside—which the startled minister did—and took his place. During some moments he surveyed the spellbound audience with solemn eyes, in which burned an uncanny light; then in a deep voice he said:

"I come from the Throne—bearing a message from Almighty God!" The words smote the house with a shock; if the stranger perceived it he gave no attention. "He has heard the prayer of His servant your shepherd, and will grant it if such shall be your desire after I, His messenger, shall have explained to you its import—that is to say, its full import. For it is like unto many of the prayers of men, in that it asks for more than he who utters it is aware of—except he pause and think.

"God's servant and yours has prayed his prayer. Has he paused and taken thought? Is it one prayer? No, it is two—one uttered, the other not. Both have reached the ear of Him Who heareth all supplications, the spoken and the unspoken. Ponder this—keep it in mind. If you would beseech a blessing upon yourself, beware! lest without intent you invoke a curse upon a neighbor at the same time. If you pray for the blessing of rain upon your crop which needs it, by that act you are possibly praying for a curse upon some neighbor's crop which may not need rain and can be injured by it.

"You have heard your servant's prayer—the uttered part of it. I am commissioned of God to put into words the other part of it—that part which the pastor—and also you in your hearts—fervently prayed silently. And ignorantly and unthinkingly? God grant that it was so! You heard these words: 'Grant us the victory, O Lord our God!' That is sufficient. The *whole* of the uttered prayer is compact into those pregnant words. Elaborations were not necessary. When you have prayed for victory you have prayed for many unmentioned results which follow victory—*must* follow it, cannot help but follow it. Upon the listening spirit of God the Father fell also the unspoken part of the prayer. He commandeth me to put it into words. Listen!

"O Lord our Father, our young patriots, idols of our hearts, go forth to battle—be Thou near them! With them—in spirit—we also go forth from the sweet peace of our beloved firesides to smite the foe. O Lord our God, help us to tear their soldiers to bloody shreds with our shells; help us to cover their smiling fields with the pale forms of their patriot dead; help us to drown the thunder of the guns with the shrieks of their wounded, writhing in pain; help us to lay waste their humble homes with a hurricane of fire; help us to wring the hearts of their unoffending widows with unavailing grief; help us to turn them out roofless with their little children to wander unfriended the wastes of their desolated land in rags and hunger and thirst, sports of the sun flames of summer and the icy winds of winter, broken in spirit, worn with travail, imploring Thee for the refuge of the grave and denied it—for our sakes who adore Thee, Lord, blast their hopes, blight their lives, protract their bitter pilgrimage, make heavy their steps, water their way with their tears, stain the white snow with the blood of their wounded feet! We ask it, in the spirit of love, or Him Who is the Source of Love, and Who is the ever-faithful refuge and friend of all that are sore beset and seek His aid with humble and contrite hearts. Amen."

(*After a pause.*) "Ye have prayed it; if ye still desire it, speak! The messenger of the Most High waits."

It was believed afterward that the man was a lunatic, because there was no sense in what he said.

# Oscar Wilde

## (1854–1900)

Born Oscar Fingal O'Flahertie Wills Wilde in 1854, Oscar Wilde was the second of three children. His mother, Jane Francesca Elgee, was a poet and journalist, and his father, Sir William Wilde, was a writer and specialist in diseases of the eye and ear. Wilde proved to be an exceptional student, winning a scholarship to attend Trinity College in Dublin in 1871. He excelled in his classics courses and placed first in his examinations. In 1874 he won the college's Berkeley Gold Medal for Greek and was awarded a Demyship scholarship to Magdalen College in Oxford. It was there that Wilde took to heart the teaching of English writers John Ruskin and Walter Pater about the central importance of art in life. In 1881, Wilde published his first collection of poetry to mixed reviews and sailed to New York to deliver a series of lectures on aestheticism, the late-nineteenth-century movement advocating art for art's sake. The tour, scheduled to last four months, stretched out to nearly a year. In that time, Wilde met with Henry Longfellow, Oliver Wendell Holmes, and Walt Whitman.

In 1844, Wilde married Constance Lloyd, an independent and outspoken woman who was well read and spoke several languages. They had two sons, Cyril and Vyvyan. In the following years, Wilde published *The Happy Prince and Other Tales* (1888), *The House of Pomegranates* (1892), and *The Picture of Dorian Gray* (1891). *Dorian Gray*'s implicit homoerotic theme would come back to haunt Wilde as evidence used against him during his later legal trials. His first play, *Lady Windermere's Fan* (1892), met with financial and critical success. He continued to write for the theater, producing plays such as *A Woman of No Importance* (1893), *An Ideal Husband* (1895), and *The Importance of Being Earnest* (1895). In 1891, Wilde met Lord Alfred "Bosie" Douglas, third son of the Marquis of Queensberry. The two became lovers. The Marquis, who did not approve of Wilde, accused him of homosexuality in 1895. Wilde sued Bosie's father for libel, but the case went badly for him. He was arrested and convicted of gross indecency and sentenced to two years hard labor. Constance took the children to Switzerland and reverted to an old family name, "Holland." Upon his release, Wilde wrote *The Ballad of Reading Gaol* (1898) under the pseudonym Sebastian Melmoth. It was a response to the agony he experienced in prison. He and Bosie briefly reunited, but Wilde spent the last three years of his life wandering through Europe, where he died of meningitis.

# Lord Arthur Savile's Crime                                                          1891

## A Study of Duty

### 1

It was Lady Windermere's last reception before Easter, and Bentinck House was even more crowded than usual. Six Cabinet Ministers had come on from the Speaker's Levée in their stars and ribands, all the pretty women wore their smartest dresses, and at the end of the picture-gallery stood the Princess Sophia of Carlsrühe, a heavy Tartar-looking lady, with tiny black eyes and wonderful emeralds, talking bad French at the top of her voice, and laughing immoderately at everything that was said to her. It was certainly a wonderful medley of people. Gorgeous peeresses chatted affably to violent Radicals, popular preachers brushed coat-tails with eminent sceptics, a perfect bevy of bishops kept following a stout prima-donna from room to room, on the staircase stood several Royal Academicians, disguised as artists, and it was said that at one time the supper-room was absolutely crammed with geniuses. In fact, it was one of Lady Windermere's best nights, and the Princess stayed till nearly half-past eleven.

As soon as she had gone, Lady Windermere returned to the picture-gallery, where a celebrated political economist was solemnly explaining the scientific theory of music to an indignant virtuoso from Hungary, and began to talk to the Duchess of Paisley. She looked wonderfully beautiful with her grand ivory throat, her large blue forget-me-not eyes, and her heavy coils of golden hair. *Or pur* they were—not that pale straw colour that nowadays usurps the gracious name of gold, but such gold as is woven into sunbeams or hidden in strange amber; and they gave to her face something of the frame of a saint, with not a little of the fascination of a sinner. She was a curious psychological study. Early in life she had discovered the important truth that nothing looks so like innocence as an indiscretion; and by a series of reckless escapades, half of them quite harmless, she had acquired all the privileges of a personality. She had more than once changed her husband; indeed, Debrett credits her with three marriages; but as she had never changed her lover, the world had long ago ceased to talk scandal about her. She was now forty years of age, childless, and with that inordinate passion for pleasure which is the secret of remaining young.

Suddenly she looked eagerly round the room, and said, in her clear contralto voice, "Where is my chiromantist?"

"Your what, Gladys?" exclaimed the Duchess, giving an involuntary start.

"My chiromantist, Duchess; I can't live without him at present."

"Dear Gladys! you are always so original," murmured the Duchess, trying to remember what a chiromantist really was, and hoping it was not the same as a chiropodist.

"He comes to see my hand twice a week regularly," continued Lady Windermere, "and is most interesting about it."

"Good heavens!" said the Duchess to herself, "he is a sort of chiropodist after all. How very dreadful. I hope he is a foreigner at any rate. It wouldn't be quite so bad then."

"I must certainly introduce him to you."

"Introduce him!" cried the Duchess; "you don't mean to say he is here?" and she began looking about for a small tortoise-shell fan and a very tattered lace shawl, so as to be ready to go at a moment's notice.

"Of course he is here; I would not dream of giving a party without him. He tells me I have a pure psychic hand, and that if my thumb had been the least little bit shorter, I should have been a confirmed pessimist, and gone into a convent."

"Oh, I see!" said the Duchess, feeling very much relieved; "he tells fortunes, I suppose?"

"And misfortunes, too," answered Lady Windermere, "any amount of them. Next year, for instance, I am in great danger, both by land and sea, so I am going to live in a balloon, and draw up my dinner in a basket every evening. It is all written down on my little finger, or on the palm of my hand, I forget which."

"But surely that is tempting Providence, Gladys."

"My dear Duchess, surely Providence can resist temptation by this time. I think every one should have their hands told once a month so as to know what not to do. Of course, one does it all the same, but it is so pleasant to be warned. Now if some one doesn't go and fetch Mr. Podgers at once, I shall have to go myself."

"Let me go, Lady Windermere," said a tall handsome young man, who was standing by, listening to the conversation with an amused smile.

"Thanks so much, Lord Arthur; but I am afraid you wouldn't recognise him."

"If he is as wonderful as you say, Lady Windermere, I couldn't well miss him. Tell me what he is like, and I'll bring him to you at once."

"Well, he is not a bit like a chiromantist. I mean he is not mysterious, or esoteric, or romantic-looking. He is a little, stout man, with a funny, bald head, and great gold-rimmed spectacles; something between a family doctor and a country attorney. I'm really very sorry, but it is not my fault. People are so annoying. All my pianists look exactly like poets; and all my poets look exactly like pianists; and I remember last season asking a most dreadful conspirator to dinner, a man who had blown up ever so many people, and always wore a coat of mail, and carried a dagger up his shirt-sleeve; and do you know that when he came he looked just like a nice old clergyman, and cracked jokes all the evening? Of course, he was very amusing, and all that, but I was awfully disappointed; and when I asked him about the coat of mail, he only laughed, and said it was far too cold to wear in England. Ah, here is Mr. Podgers! Now, Mr. Podgers, I want you to tell the Duchess of Paisley's hand. Duchess, you must take your glove off. No, not the left hand, the other."

"Dear Gladys, I really don't think it is quite right," said the Duchess, feebly unbuttoning a rather soiled kid glove.

"Nothing interesting ever is," said Lady Windermere: "*on a fait le monde ainsi.* But I must introduce you. Duchess, this is Mr. Podgers, my pet chiromantist. Mr. Podgers, this is the Duchess of Paisley, and if you say that she has a larger mountain of the moon than I have, I will never believe in you again."

"I am sure, Gladys, there is nothing of the kind in my hand," said the Duchess gravely.

"Your Grace is quite right," said Mr. Podgers, glancing at the little fat hand with its short square fingers, "the mountain of the moon is not developed. The line of life, however, is excellent. Kindly bend the wrist. Thank you. Three distinct lines on the *rascette!* You will live to a great age, Duchess, and be extremely happy. Ambition—very moderate, line of intellect not exaggerated, line of heart—"

"Now, do be indiscreet, Mr. Podgers," cried Lady Windermere.

"Nothing would give me greater pleasure," said Mr. Podgers, bowing, "if the Duchess ever had been, but I am sorry to say that I see great permanence of affection, combined with a strong sense of duty."

"Pray go on, Mr. Podgers," said the Duchess, looking quite pleased.

"Economy is not the least of your Grace's virtues," continued Mr. Podgers, and Lady Windermere went off into fits of laughter.

"Economy is a very good thing," remarked the Duchess complacently; "when I married Paisley he had eleven castles, and not a single house fit to live in."

"And now he has twelve houses, and not a single castle," cried Lady Windermere.

"Well, my dear," said the Duchess, "I like—"

"Comfort," said Mr. Podgers, "and modern improvements, and hot water laid on in every bedroom. Your Grace is quite right. Comfort is the only thing our civilisation can give us."

"You have told the Duchess's character admirably, Mr. Podgers, and now you must tell Lady Flora's"; and in answer to a nod from the smiling hostess, a tall girl, with sandy Scotch hair, and high shoulder-blades, stepped awkwardly from behind the sofa, and held out a long, bony hand with spatulate fingers.

"Ah, a pianist! I see," said Mr. Podgers, "an excellent pianist, but perhaps hardly a musician. Very reserved, very honest, and with a great love of animals."

"Quite true!" exclaimed the Duchess, turning to Lady Windermere, "absolutely true! Flora keeps two dozen collie dogs at Macloskie, and would turn our town house into a menagerie if her father would let her."

"Well, that is just what I do with my house every Thursday evening," cried Lady Windermere, laughing, "only I like lions better than collie dogs."

"Your one mistake, Lady Windermere," said Mr. Podgers, with a pompous bow.

"If a woman can't make her mistakes charming, she is only a female," was the answer. "But you must read some more hands for us. Come, Sir Thomas, show Mr. Podgers yours;" and a genial-looking old gentleman, in a white waistcoat, came forward, and held out a thick rugged hand, with a very long third finger.

"An adventurous nature; four long voyages in the past, and one to come. Been shipwrecked three times. No, only twice, but in danger of a shipwreck your next journey. A strong Conservative, very punctual and with a passion for collecting curiosities. Had a severe illness between the ages of sixteen and eighteen. Was left a fortune when about thirty. Great aversion to cats and Radicals."

"Extraordinary!" exclaimed Sir Thomas: "you must really tell my wife's hand, too."

"Your second wife's," said Mr. Podgers quietly, still keeping Sir Thomas's hand in his. "Your second wife's. I shall be charmed"; but Lady Marvel, a melancholy-looking woman, with brown hair and sentimental eyelashes, entirely declined to have her past or her future exposed; and nothing that Lady Windermere could do would induce Monsieur de Koloff, the Russian Ambassador, even to take his gloves off. In fact, many people seemed afraid to face the odd little man with his stereotyped smile, his gold spectacles, and his bright, beady eyes; and when he told poor Lady Fermor right out before every one, that she did not care a bit for music, but was extremely fond of musicians, it was generally felt that chiromancy was a most dangerous science, and one that ought not to be encouraged, except in a *tête-à-tête*.

Lord Arthur Savile, however, who did not know anything about Lady Fermor's unfortunate story, and who had been watching Mr. Podgers with a great deal of interest, was filled with an immense curiosity to have his own hand read, and feeling somewhat shy about putting himself forward, crossed over the room to where Lady

Windermere was sitting, and, with a charming blush, asked her if she thought Mr. Podgers would mind.

"Of course he won't mind," said Lady Windermere, "that is what he is here for. All my lions, Lord Arthur, are performing lions, and jump through hoops whenever I ask them. But I must warn you beforehand that I shall tell Sybil everything. She is coming to lunch with me to-morrow, to talk about bonnets, and if Mr. Podgers finds out that you have a bad temper, or a tendency to gout, or a wife living in Bayswater, I shall certainly let her know all about it."

Lord Arthur smiled, and shook his head. "I am not afraid," he answered. "Sybil knows me as well as I know her."

"Ah! I am a little sorry to hear you say that. The proper basis for marriage is a mutual misunderstanding. No, I am not at all cynical, I have merely got experience, which, however, is very much the same thing. Mr. Podgers, Lord Arthur Savile is dying to have his hand read. Don't tell him that he is engaged to one of the most beautiful girls in London, because that appeared in the *Morning Post* a month ago."

"Dear Lady Windermere," cried the Marchioness of Jedburgh, "do let Mr. Podgers stay here a little longer. He has just told me I should go on the stage, and I am so interested."

"If he has told you that, Lady Jedburgh, I shall certainly take him away. Come over at once, Mr. Podgers, and read Lord Arthur's hand."

"Well," said Lady Jedburgh, making a little *moue* as she rose from the sofa, "if I am not to be allowed to go on the stage, I must be allowed to be part of the audience at any rate."

"Of course; we are all going to be part of the audience," said Lady Windermere; "and now, Mr. Podgers, be sure and tell us something nice. Lord Arthur is one of my special favourites."

But when Mr. Podgers saw Lord Arthur's hand he grew curiously pale, and said nothing. A shudder seemed to pass through him, and his great bushy eyebrows twitched convulsively, in an odd, irritating way they had when he was puzzled. Then some huge beads of perspiration broke out on his yellow forehead, like a poisonous dew, and his fat fingers grew cold and clammy.

Lord Arthur did not fail to notice these strange signs of agitation, and, for the first time in his life, he himself felt fear. His impulse was to rush from the room, but he restrained himself. It was better to know the worst, whatever it was, than to be left in this hideous uncertainty.

"I am waiting, Mr. Podgers," he said.

"We are all waiting," cried Lady Windermere, in her quick, impatient manner, but the chiromantist made no reply.

"I believe Arthur is going on the stage," said Lady Jedburgh, "and that, after your scolding, Mr. Podgers is afraid to tell him so."

Suddenly Mr. Podgers dropped Lord Arthur's right hand, and seized hold of his left, bending down so low to examine it that the gold rims of his spectacles seemed almost to touch the palm. For a moment his face became a white mask of horror, but he soon recovered his *sang-froid,* and looking up at Lady Windermere, said with a forced smile, "It is the hand of a charming young man."

"Of course it is!" answered Lady Windermere, "but will he be a charming husband? That is what I want to know."

"All charming young men are," said Mr. Podgers.

"I don't think a husband should be too fascinating," murmured Lady Jedburgh pensively, "it is so dangerous."

"My dear child, they never are too fascinating," cried Lady Windermere. "But what I want are details. Details are the only things that interest. What is going to happen to Lord Arthur?"

"Well, within the next few months Lord Arthur will go on a voyage—"

"Oh yes, his honeymoon, of course!"

"And lose a relative."

"Not his sister, I hope?" said Lady Jedburgh, in a piteous tone of voice.

"Certainly not his sister," answered Mr. Podgers, with a deprecating wave of the hand, "a distant relative merely."

"Well, I am dreadfully disappointed," said Lady Windermere. "I have absolutely nothing to tell Sybil to-morrow. No one cares about distant relatives nowadays. They went out of fashion years ago. However, I suppose she had better have a black silk by her; it always does for church, you know. And now let us go to supper. They are sure to have eaten everything up, but we may find some hot soup. François used to make excellent soup once, but he is so agitated about politics at present, that I never feel quite certain about him. I do wish General Boulanger would keep quiet. Duchess, I am sure you are tired?"

"Not at all, dear Gladys," answered the Duchess, waddling towards the door. "I have enjoyed myself immensely, and the chiropodist, I mean the chiromantist, is most interesting. Flora, where can my tortoise-shell fan be? Oh, thank you, Sir Thomas, so much. And my lace shawl, Flora? Oh, thank you, Sir Thomas, very kind, I'm sure"; and the worthy creature finally managed to get downstairs without dropping her scent-bottle more than twice.

All this time Lord Arthur Savile had remained standing by the fireplace, with the same feeling of dread over him, the same sickening sense of coming evil. He smiled sadly at his sister, as she swept past him on Lord Plymdale's arm, looking lovely in her pink brocade and pearls, and he hardly heard Lady Windermere when she called to him to follow her. He thought of Sybil Merton, and the idea that anything could come between them made his eyes dim with tears.

Looking at him, one would have said that Nemesis had stolen the shield of Pallas, and shown him the Gorgon's head. He seemed turned to stone, and his face was like marble in its melancholy. He had lived the delicate and luxurious life of a young man of birth and fortune, a life exquisite in its freedom from sordid care, its beautiful boyish insouciance; and now for the first time he had become conscious of the terrible mystery of Destiny, of the awful meaning of Doom.

How mad and monstrous it all seemed! Could it be that written on his hand, in characters that he could not read himself, but that another could decipher, was some fearful secret of sin, some blood-red sign of crime? Was there no escape possible? Were we no better than chessmen, moved by an unseen power, vessels the potter fashions at his fancy, for honour or for shame? His reason revolted against it, and yet he felt that some tragedy was hanging over him, and that he had been suddenly called upon to bear an intolerable burden. Actors are so fortunate. They can choose whether they will appear in tragedy or in comedy, whether they will suffer or make merry, laugh or shed tears. But in real life it is different. Most men and women are forced to perform parts for which they have no qualifications. Our Guildensterns play Hamlet for us, and our Hamlets have to jest like Prince Hal. The world is a stage, but the play is badly cast.

Suddenly Mr. Podgers entered the room. When he saw Lord Arthur he started, and his coarse, fat face became a sort of greenish-yellow colour. The two men's eyes met, and for a moment there was silence.

"The Duchess has left one of her gloves here, Lord Arthur, and has asked me to bring it to her," said Mr. Podgers finally. "Ah, I see it on the sofa! Good evening."

"Mr. Podgers, I must insist on your giving me a straightforward answer to a question I am going to put to you."

"Another time, Lord Arthur, but the Duchess is anxious. I am afraid I must go."

"You shall not go. The Duchess is in no hurry."

"Ladies should not be kept waiting, Lord Arthur," said Mr. Podgers, with his sickly smile. "The fair sex is apt to be impatient."

Lord Arthur's finely-chiselled lips curled in petulant disdain. The poor Duchess seemed to him of very little importance at that moment. He walked across the room to where Mr. Podgers was standing, and held his hand out.

"Tell me what you saw there," he said. "Tell me the truth. I must know it. I am not a child."

Mr. Podger's eyes blinked behind his gold-rimmed spectacles, and he moved uneasily from one foot to the other, while his fingers played nervously with a flash watch-chain.

"What makes you think that I saw anything in your hand, Lord Arthur, more than I told you?"

"I know you did, and I insist on your telling me what it was. I will pay you. I will give you a cheque for a hundred pounds."

The green eyes flashed for a moment, and then became dull again.

"Guineas?" said Mr. Podgers at last, in a low voice.

"Certainly. I will send you a cheque to-morrow. What is your club?"

"I have no club. That is to say, not just at present. My address is——, but allow me to give you my card"; and producing a bit of gilt-edge pasteboard from his waistcoat pocket, Mr. Podgers handed it, with a low bow, to Lord Arthur, who read on it, "*Mr. Septimus R. Podgers, Professional Chiromantist, 1030 West Moon Street.*"

"My hours are from ten to four," murmured Mr. Podgers mechanically, "and I make a reduction for families."

"Be quick," cried Lord Arthur, looking very pale, and holding his hand out.

Mr. Podgers glanced nervously round, and drew the heavy *portière* across the door.

"It will take a little time, Lord Arthur, you had better sit down."

"Be quick, sir," cried Lord Arthur again, stamping his foot angrily on the polished floor.

Mr. Podgers smiled, drew from his breast-pocket a small magnifying glass, and wiped it carefully with his handkerchief.

"I am quite ready," he said.

## 2

Ten minutes later, with face blanched by terror and eyes wild with grief, Lord Arthur Savile rushed from Bentinck House, crushing his way through the crowd of fur-coated footmen that stood round the large striped awning, and seeming not to see or hear anything. The night was bitter cold, and the gas-lamps round the square flared and flickered in the keen wind; but his hands were hot with fever, and his forehead burned like fire. On and on he went, almost with the gait of a drunken man. A policeman looked curiously at him as he passed, and a beggar, who slouched from an archway to ask for alms, grew frightened, seeing misery greater than his own. Once he stopped under a lamp, and looked at his hands. He thought he could detect the stain of blood already upon them, and a faint cry broke from his trembling lips.

Murder! that is what the chiromantist had seen there. Murder! The very night seemed to know it, and the desolate wind to howl it in his ear. The dark corners of the streets were full of it. It grinned at him from the roofs of the houses.

First he came to the Park, whose sombre woodland seemed to fascinate him. He leaned wearily up against the railings, cooling his brow against the wet metal, and listening to the tremulous silence of the trees. "Murder! murder!" he kept repeating, as though iteration could dim the horror of the word. The sound of his own voice made him shudder, yet he almost hoped that Echo might hear him, and wake the slumbering city from its dreams. He felt a mad desire to stop the casual passer-by, and tell him everything.

Then he wandered across Oxford Street into narrow, shameful alleys. Two women with painted faces mocked at him as he went by. From a dark courtyard came a sound of oaths and blows, followed by shrill screams, and, huddled upon a damp door-step, he saw the crooked-back forms of poverty and eld. A strange pity came over him. Were these children of sin and misery predestined to their end, as he to his? Were they, like him, merely the puppets of a monstrous show?

And yet it was not the mystery, but the comedy of suffering that struck him; its absolute uselessness, its grotesque want of meaning. How incoherent everything seemed! How lacking in all harmony! He was amazed at the discord between the shallow optimism of the day, and the real facts of existence. He was still very young.

After a time he found himself in front of Marylebone Church. The silent roadway looked like a long riband of polished silver, flecked here and there by the dark arabesques of waving shadows. Far into the distance curved the line of flickering gas-lamps, and outside a little walled-in house stood a solitary hansom, the driver asleep inside. He walked hastily in the direction of Portland Place, now and then looking round, as though he feared that he was being followed. At the corner of Rich Street stood two men, reading a small bill upon a hoarding. An odd feeling of curiosity stirred him, and he crossed over. As he came near, the word "Murder," printed in black letters, met his eye. He started, and a deep flush came into his cheek. It was an advertisement offering a reward for any information leading to the arrest of a man of medium height, between thirty and forty years of age, wearing a billycock hat, a black coat, and check trousers, and with a scar upon his right cheek. He read it over and over again, and wondered if the wretched man would be caught, and how he had been scarred. Perhaps, some day, his own name might be placarded on the walls of London. Some day, perhaps, a price would be set on his head also.

The thought made him sick with horror. He turned on his heel, and hurried into the night.

Where he went he hardly knew. He had a dim memory of wandering through a labyrinth of sordid houses, and it was bright dawn when he found himself at last in Piccadilly Circus. As he strolled home towards Belgrave Square, he met the great waggons on their way to Covent Garden. The white-smocked carters, with their pleasant sunburnt faces and coarse curly hair, strode sturdily on, cracking their whips, and calling out now and then to each other; on the back of a huge grey horse, the leader of a jangling team, sat a chubby boy, with a bunch of primroses in his battered hat, keeping tight hold of the mane with his little hands, and laughing; and the great piles of vegetables looked like masses of jade against the morning sky, like masses of green jade against the pink petals of some marvellous rose. Lord Arthur felt curiously affected, he could not tell why. There was something in the dawn's delicate loveliness that seemed to him inexpressibly pathetic, and he thought of all the days that break in beauty, and that set in storm. These rustics, too, with their rough, good-humoured voices, and their nonchalant ways, what a strange London they saw! A London free from the sin of night and the smoke of day, a pallid, ghost-like city, a desolate town of tombs! He wondered what they thought of it, and whether they knew anything of its splendour and its shame, of its fierce, fiery-coloured joys, and its horrible hunger, of all it makes and mars from morn to eve. Probably it was to them merely a mart where they brought their fruit to sell, and where they tarried for a few hours at most, leaving the streets still silent, the houses still asleep. It gave him pleasure to watch them as they went by. Rude as they were, with their heavy, hob-nailed shoes, and their awkward gait, they brought a little of Arcady with them. He felt that they had lived with Nature, and that she had taught them peace. He envied them all that they did not know.

By the time he had reached Belgrave Square the sky was a faint blue, and the birds were beginning to twitter in the gardens.

## 3

When Lord Arthur woke it was twelve o'clock, and the midday sun was streaming through the ivory-silk curtains of his room. He got up and looked out of the window. A dim haze of heat was hanging over the great city, and the roofs of the houses were like dull silver. In the flickering green of the square below some children were flitting about like white butterflies, and the pavement was crowded with people on their way to the Park. Never had life seemed lovelier to him, never had the things of evil seemed more remote.

Then his valet brought him a cup of chocolate on a tray. After he had drunk it, he drew aside a heavy *portière* of peach-coloured plush, and passed into the bathroom. The light stole softly from above, through thin slabs of transparent onyx, and the water in the marble tank glimmered like a moonstone. He plunged hastily in, till the cool ripples touched throat and hair, and then dipped his head right under, as though he would have wiped away the stain of some shameful memory. When he stepped out he felt almost at peace. The exquisite physical conditions of the moment had dominated him, as indeed often happens in the case of very finely-wrought natures, for the senses, like fire, can purify as well as destroy.

After breakfast, he flung himself down on a divan and lit a cigarette. On the mantelshelf, framed in dainty old brocade, stood a large photograph of Sybil Merton, as he had seen her first at Lady Noel's ball. The small, exquisitely-shaped head drooped slightly to one side, as though the thin, reed-like throat could hardly bear the burden of so much beauty; the lips were slightly parted, and seemed made for sweet music; and all the tender purity of girlhood looked out in wonder from the dreaming eyes. With her soft, clinging dress of *crêpe de chine,* and her large leaf-shaped fan, she looked like one of those delicate little figures men find in the olive-woods near Tanagra; and there was a touch of Greek grace in her pose and attitude. Yet she was not *petite.* She was simply perfectly proportioned—a rare thing in an age when so many women are either over life-size or insignificant.

Now as Lord Arthur looked at her, he was filled with the terrible pity that is born of love. He felt that to marry her, with the doom of murder hanging over his head, would be a betrayal like that of Judas, a sin worse than any the Borgia had ever dreamed of. What happiness could there be for them, when at any moment he might be called upon to carry out the awful prophecy written in his hand? What manner of life would be theirs while Fate still held this fearful fortune in the scales? The marriage must be postponed, at all costs. Of this he was quite resolved. Ardently though he loved the girl, and the mere touch of her fingers, when they sat together, made each nerve of his body thrill with exquisite joy, he recognised none the less clearly where his duty lay, and was fully conscious of the fact that he had no right to marry until he had committed the murder. This done, he could stand before the altar with Sybil Merton, and give his life into her hands without terror of wrongdoing. This done, he could take her to his arms, knowing that she would never have to blush for him, never have to hang her head in shame. But done it must be first; and the sooner the better for both.

Many men in his position would have preferred the primrose path of dalliance to the steep heights of duty; but Lord Arthur was too conscientious to set pleasure above principle. There was more than mere passion in his love; and Sybil was to him a symbol of all that is good and noble. For a moment he had a natural repugnance against what he was asked to do, but it soon passed away. His heart told him that it was not a sin, but a sacrifice; his reason reminded him that there was no other course open. He had to choose between living for himself and living for others, and terrible though the task laid upon him undoubtedly was, yet he knew that he must not suffer selfishness to triumph over love. Sooner or later we are all called upon to decide on the same issue—of us all the same question is asked. To Lord Arthur it came early in life— before his nature had been spoiled by the calculating cynicism of middle-age, or his heart corroded by the shallow, fashionable egotism of our day, and he felt no hesitation about doing his duty. Fortunately also, for him, he was no mere dreamer, or idle dilettante. Had he been so, he would have hesitated, like Hamlet, and let irresolution mar his purpose. But he was esentially practical. Life to him meant action, rather than thought. He had that rarest of all things, common sense.

The wild, turbid feelings of the previous night had by this time completely passed away, and it was almost with a sense of shame that he looked back upon his mad wanderings from street to street, his fierce emotional agony. The very sincerity of his sufferings made them seem unreal to him now. He wondered how he could have been so foolish as to rant and rave about the inevitable. The only question that seemed to trouble him was, whom to make away with; for he was not blind to the fact that murder, like the religions of the Pagan world, requires a victim as well as a priest. Not being a genius, he had no enemies, and indeed he felt that this was not the time for the gratification of any personal pique or dislike, the mission in which he was engaged being one of great and grave solemnity. He accordingly made out a list of his friends and relatives on a sheet of notepaper, and after careful consideration, decided in favour of Lady Clementina Beauchamp, a dear old lady who lived in Curzon Street, and was his own second cousin by his mother's side. He had always been very fond of Lady Clem, as every one called her, and as he was very wealthy himself, having come into all Lord Rugby's property when he came of age, there was no possibility of his deriving any vulgar monetary advantage by her death. In fact, the more he thought over the matter, the more she seemed to him to be just the right person, and, feeling that any delay would be unfair to Sybil, he determined to make his arrangements at once.

The first thing to be done was, of course, to settle with the chiromantist; so he sat down at a small Sheraton writing-table that stood near the window, drew a cheque for £105, payable to the order of Mr. Septimus Podgers, and, enclosing it in an envelope, told his valet to take it to West Moon Street. He then telephoned to the stables for his hansom, and dressed to go out. As he was leaving the room he looked back at Sybil Merton's photograph, and swore that, come what may, he would never let her know what he was doing for her sake, but would keep the secret of his self-sacrifice hidden always in his heart.

On his way to the Buckingham, he stopped at a florist's, and sent Sybil a beautiful basket of narcissi, with lovely white petals and staring pheasants' eyes, and on arriving at the club went straight to the library, rang the bell, and ordered the waiter to bring him a lemon-and-soda, and a book on Toxicology. He had fully decided that poison was the best means to adopt in this troublesome business. Anything like personal violence was extremely distasteful to him, and besides, he was very anxious not to murder Lady Clementina in any way that might attract public attention, as he hated the idea of being lionised at Lady Windermere's, or seeing his name figuring in the paragraphs of vulgar society-newspapers. He had also to think of Sybil's father and mother, who were rather old-fashioned people, and might possibly object to the marriage if there was anything like a scandal, though he felt certain that if he told them the whole facts of the case they would be the very first to appreciate the motives that had actuated him. He had every reason, then, to decide in favour of poison. It was safe, sure, and quiet, and did away with any necessity for painful scenes, to which, like most Englishmen, he had a rooted objection.

Of the science of poisons, however, he knew absolutely nothing, and as the waiter seemed quite unable to find anything in the library but *Ruff's Guide* and *Bailey's Magazine* he examined the book-shelves himself, and finally came across a handsomely-bound edition of the *Pharmacopœia,* and a copy of Erskine's *Toxicology,* edited by Sir Mathew Reid, the President of the Royal College of Physicians, and one of the oldest members of the Buckingham, having been elected in mistake for somebody else; a *contretemps* that so enraged the Committee, that when the real man came up they black-balled him unanimously. Lord Arthur was a good deal puzzled at the technical terms used in both books, and had begun to regret that he had not paid more attention to his classics at Oxford, when in the second volume of Erskine, he found a very interesting and complete account of the properties of aconitine, written in fairly clear English. It seemed to him to be exactly the poison he wanted. It was swift—indeed, almost immediate, in its effect—perfectly painless, and when taken in the form of a gelatine capsule, the mode recommended by Sir Mathew, not by any means unpalatable. He accordingly made a note, upon his shirt-cuff, of the amount necessary for a fatal dose, put the books back in their places, and strolled up St. James's Street, to Pestle and Humbey's, the great chemists. Mr. Pestle, who always attended personally on the aristocracy, was a good deal surprised at the order, and in a very deferential manner murmured something about a medical certificate being necessary. However, as soon as Lord Arthur explained to him that it was for a large Norwegian mastiff that he was obliged to get rid of, as it showed signs of incipient rabies, and had already bitten the coachman twice in the calf of the leg, he expressed himself as being perfectly satisfied, complimented Lord Arthur on his wonderful knowledge of Toxicology, and had the prescription made up immediately.

Lord Arthur put the capsule into a pretty little silver *bonbonnière* that he saw in a shop window in Bond Street, threw away Pestle and Humbey's ugly pill-box, and drove off at once to Lady Clementina's.

"Well, *monsieur le mauvais sujet,*" cried the old lady, as he entered the room, "why haven't you been to see me all this time?"

"My dear Lady Clem, I never have a moment to myself," said Lord Arthur, smiling.

"I suppose you mean that you go about all day long with Miss Sybil Merton, buying *chiffons* and talking nonsense? I cannot understand why people make such a fuss about being married. In my day we never dreamed of billing and cooing in public, or in private for that matter."

"I assure you I have not seen Sybil for twenty-four hours, Lady Clem. As far as I can make out, she belongs entirely to her milliners."

"Of course; that is the only reason you come to see an ugly old woman like myself. I wonder you men don't take warning. *On a fait des folies pour moi,* and here I am, a poor rheumatic creature, with a false front and a bad temper. Why, if it were not for dear Lady Jansen, who sends me all the worst French novels she can find, I don't think I could get through the day. Doctors are no use at all, except to get fees out of one. They can't even cure my heartburn."

"I have brought you a cure for that, Lady Clem," said Lord Arthur gravely. "It is a wonderful thing, invented by an American."

"I don't think I like American inventions, Arthur. I am quite sure I don't. I read some American novels lately, and they were quite nonsensical."

"Oh, but there is no nonsense at all about this, Lady Clem! I assure you it is a perfect cure. You must promise to try it"; and Lord Arthur brought the little box out of his pocket, and handed it to her.

"Well, the box is charming, Arthur. Is it really a present? That is very sweet of you. And is this the wonderful medicine? It looks like a *bonbon*. I'll take it at once."

"Good heavens! Lady Clem," cried Lord Arthur, catching hold of her hand, "you mustn't do anything of the kind. It is a homoeopathic medicine, and if you take it without having heartburn, it might do you no end of harm. Wait till you have an attack, and take it then. You will be astonished at the result."

"I should like to take it now," said Lady Clementina, holding up to the light the little transparent capsule, with its floating bubble of liquid aconitine. "I am sure it is delicious. The fact is that, though I hate doctors, I love medicines. However, I'll keep it till my next attack."

"And when will that be?" asked Lord Arthur eagerly. "Will it be soon?"

"I hope not for a week. I had a very bad time yesterday morning with it. But one never knows."

"You are sure to have one before the end of the month then, Lady Clem?"

"I am afraid so. But how sympathetic you are to-day, Arthur! Really, Sybil has done you a great deal of good. And now you must run away, for I am dining with some very dull people, who won't talk scandal, and I know that if I don't get my sleep now I shall never be able to keep awake during dinner. Good-bye, Arthur, give my love to Sybil, and thank you so much for the American medicine."

"You won't forget to take it, Lady Clem, will you?" said Lord Arthur, rising from his seat.

"Of course I won't, you silly boy. I think it is most kind of you to think of me, and I shall write and tell you if I want any more."

Lord Arthur left the house in high spirits, and with a feeling of immense relief.

That night he had an interview with Sybil Merton. He told her how he had been suddenly placed in a position of terrible difficulty, from which neither honour nor duty would allow him to recede. He told her that the marriage must be put off for the present, as until he had got rid of his fearful entanglements, he was not a free man. He implored her to trust him, and not to have any doubts about the future. Everything would come right, but patience was necessary.

The scene took place in the conservatory of Mr. Merton's house, in Park Lane, where Lord Arthur had dined as usual. Sybil had never seemed more happy, and for a moment Lord Arthur had been tempted to play the coward's part, to write to Lady

Clementina for the pill, and to let the marriage go on as if there was no such person as Mr. Podgers in the world. His better nature, however, soon asserted itself, and even when Sybil flung herself weeping into his arms, he did not falter. The beauty that stirred his senses had touched his conscience also. He felt that to wreck so fair a life for the sake of a few months' pleasure would be a wrong thing to do.

He stayed with Sibyl till nearly midnight, comforting her and being comforted in turn, and early the next morning he left for Venice, after writing a manly, firm letter to Mr. Merton about the necessary postponement of the marriage.

## 4

In Venice he met his brother, Lord Surbiton, who happened to have come over from Corfu in his yacht. The two young men spent a delightful fortnight together. In the morning they rode on the Lido, or glided up and down the green canal in their long black gondola; in the afternoon they usually entertained visitors on the yacht; and in the evening they dined at Florian's, and smoked innumerable cigarettes on the Piazza. Yet somehow Lord Arthur was not happy. Every day he studied the obituary column in the *Times,* expecting to see a notice of Lady Clementina's death, but every day he was disappointed. He began to be afraid that some accident had happened to her, and often regretted that he had prevented her taking the aconitine when she had been so anxious to try its effect. Sybil's letters, too, though full of love, and trust, and tenderness, were often very sad in their tone, and sometimes he used to think that he was parted from her for ever.

After a fortnight Lord Surbiton got bored with Venice, and determined to run down the coast to Ravenna, as he heard that there was some capital cock-shooting in the Pinetum. Lord Arthur at first refused absolutely to come, but Surbiton, of whom he was extremely fond, finally persuaded him that if he stayed at Danielli's by himself he would be moped to death, and on the morning of the 15th they started, with a strong nor'east wind blowing, and a rather choppy sea. The sport was excellent, and the free, open-air life brought the colour back to Lord Arthur's cheek, but about the 22nd he became anxious about Lady Clementina, and, in spite of Surbiton's remonstrances, came back to Venice by train.

As he stepped out of his gondola on to the hotel steps, the proprietor came forward to meet him with a sheaf of telegrams. Lord Arthur snatched them out of his hand, and tore them open. Everything had been quite successful. Lady Clementina had died quite suddenly on the night of the 17th!

His first thought was for Sybil, and he sent her off a telegram announcing his immediate return to London. He then ordered his valet to pack his things for the night mail, sent his gondoliers about five times their proper fare, and ran up to his sitting-room with a light step and a buoyant heart. There he found three letters waiting for him. One was from Sybil herself, full of sympathy and condolence. The others were from his mother, and from Lady Clementina's solicitor. It seemed that the old lady had dined with the Duchess that very night, had delighted every one by her wit and *esprit,* but had gone home somewhat early, complaining of heartburn. In the morning she was found dead in her bed, having apparently suffered no pain. Sir Mathew Reid had been sent for at once, but, of course, there was nothing to be done, and she was to be buried on the 22nd at Beauchamp Chalcote. A few days before she died she had made her will, and left Lord Arthur her little house in Curzon Street, and all her furniture, personal effects, and pictures, with the exception of her collection of miniatures, which was to go to her sister, Lady Margaret Rufford, and her amethyst necklace, which Sybil Merton was to have. The property was not of much value; but Mr. Mansfield, the solicitor, was extremely anxious for Lord Arthur to return at once, if possible, as there were a great many bills to be paid, and Lady Clementina had never kept any regular accounts.

Lord Arthur was very much touched by Lady Clementina's kind remembrance of him, and felt that Mr. Podgers had a great deal to answer for. His love of Sybil, however, dominated every other emotion, and the consciousness that he had done his duty gave him peace and comfort. When he arrived at Charing Cross, he felt perfectly happy.

The Mertons received him very kindly. Sybil made him promise that he would never again allow anything to come between them, and the marriage was fixed for the 7th June. Life seemed to him once more bright and beautiful, and all his old gladness came back to him again.

One day, however, as he was going over the house in Curzon Street, in company with Lady Clementina's solicitor and Sybil herself, burning packages of faded letters and turning out drawers of odd rubbish, the young girl suddenly gave a cry of delight.

"What have you found, Sybil?" said Lord Arthur, looking up from his work, and smiling.

"This lovely little silver *bonbonnière,* Arthur. Isn't it quaint and Dutch? Do give it to me! I know amethysts won't become me till I am over eighty."

It was the box that had held the aconitine.

Lord Arthur started, and a faint blush came into his cheek. He had almost entirely forgotten what he had done, and it seemed to him a curious coincidence that Sybil, for whose sake he had gone through all that terrible anxiety, should have been the first to remind him of it.

"Of course you can have it, Sybil. I gave it to poor Lady Clem myself."

"Oh! thank you, Arthur; and may I have the *bonbon* too? I had no notion that Lady Clementina liked sweets. I thought she was far too intellectual."

Lord Arthur grew deadly pale, and a horrible idea crossed his mind.

"*Bonbon,* Sybil? What do you mean?" he said in a slow, hoarse voice.

"There is one in it, that is all. It looks quite old and dusty, and I have not the slightest intention of eating it. What is the matter, Arthur? How white you look!"

Lord Arthur rushed across the room, and seized the box. Inside it was the amber-coloured capsule, with its poison-bubble. Lady Clementina had died a natural death after all!

The shock of the discovery was almost too much for him. He flung the capsule into the fire, and sank on the sofa with a cry of despair.

**5**

Mr. Merton was a good deal distressed at the second postponement of the marriage, and Lady Julia, who had already ordered her dress for the wedding, did all in her power to make Sybil break off the match. Dearly, however, as Sybil loved her mother, she had given her whole life into Lord Arthur's hands, and nothing that Lady Julia could say could make her waver in her faith. As for Lord Arthur himself, it took him days to get over his terrible disappointment, and for a time his nerves were completely unstrung. His excellent common sense, however, soon asserted itself, and his sound, practical mind did not leave him long in doubt about what to do. Poison having proved a complete failure, dynamite, or some other form of explosive, was obviously the proper thing to try.

He accordingly looked again over the list of his friends and relatives, and, after careful consideration, determined to blow up his uncle, the Dean of Chichester. The Dean, who was a man of great culture and learning, was extremely fond of clocks, and had a wonderful collection of timepieces, ranging from the fifteenth century to the present day, and it seemed to Lord Arthur that this hobby of the good Dean's offered him an excellent opportunity for carrying out his scheme. Where to procure an explosive machine was, of course, quite another matter. The London Directory gave him no information on the point, and he felt that there was very little use in going to Scotland Yard about it, as they never seemed to know anything about the movements of the dynamite faction till after an explosion had taken place, and not much even then.

Suddenly he thought of his friend Rouvaloff, a young Russian of very revolutionary tendencies, whom he had met at Lady Windermere's in the winter. Count Rouvaloff was supposed to be writing a life of Peter the Great, and to have come over to England for the purpose of studying the documents relating to that Tsar's residence in this country as a ship carpenter; but it was generally suspected that he was a Nihilist agent, and there was no doubt that the Russian Embassy did not look with any favour upon his presence in London. Lord Arthur felt that he was just the man for his purpose, and drove down one morning to his lodgings in Bloomsbury, to ask his advice and assistance.

"So you are taking up politics seriously?" said Count Rouvaloff, when Lord Arthur had told him the object of his mission; but Lord Arthur, who hated swagger of any kind, felt bound to admit to him that he had not the slightest interest in social questions, and simply wanted the explosive machine for a purely family matter, in which no one was concerned but himself.

Count Rouvaloff looked at him for some moments in amazement, and then seeing that he was quite serious, wrote an address on a piece of paper, initialled it, and handed it to him across the table.

"Scotland Yard would give a good deal to know this address, my dear fellow."

"They shan't have it," cried Lord Arthur, laughing; and after shaking the young Russian warmly by the hand he ran downstairs, examined the paper, and told the coachman to drive to Soho Square.

There he dismissed him, and strolled down Greek Street, till he came to a place called Bayle's Court. He passed under the archway, and found himself in a curious *cul-de-sac,* that was apparently occupied by a French laundry, as a perfect network of clothes-lines was stretched across from house to house, and there was a flutter of white linen in the morning air. He walked right to the end, and knocked at a little green house. After some delay, during which every window became a blurred mass of peering faces, the door was opened by a rather rough-looking foreigner, who asked him in very bad English what his business was. Lord Arthur handed him the paper Count Rouvaloff had given him. When the man saw it he bowed, and invited Lord Arthur into a very shabby front parlour on the ground floor, and in a few moments Herr Winckelkopf, as he was called in England, bustled into the room, with a very wine-stained napkin round his neck, and a fork in his left hand.

"Count Rouvaloff has given me an introduction to you," said Lord Arthur, bowing, "and I am anxious to have a short interview with you on a matter of business. My name is Smith, Mr. Robert Smith, and I want you to supply me with an explosive clock."

"Charmed to meet you, Lord Arthur," said the genial little German, laughing. "Don't look so alarmed, it is my duty to know everybody, and I remember seeing you one evening at Lady Windermere's. I hope her ladyship is quite well. Do you mind sitting with me while I finish my breakfast? There is an excellent *paté,* and my friends are kind enough to say that my Rhine wine is better than any they get at the German Embassy," and before Lord Arthur had got over his surprise at being recognised, he found himself seated in the back-room, sipping the most delicious Marcobrünner out of a pale yellow hock-glass marked with the Imperial monogram, and chatting in the friendliest manner possible to the famous conspirator.

"Explosive clocks," said Herr Winckelkopf, "are not very good things for foreign exploration, as, even if they succeed in passing the Custom House, the train service is so irregular, that they usually go off before they have reached their proper destination. If, however, you want one for home use, I can supply you with an excellent article, and guarantee that you will be satisfied with the result. May I ask for whom it is intended? If it is for the police, or for any one connected with Scotland Yard, I am afraid I cannot do anything for you. The English detectives are really our best friends, and I have always found that by relying on their stupidity, we can do exactly what we like. I could not spare one of them."

"I assure you," said Lord Arthur, "that it has nothing to do with the police at all. In fact, the clock is intended for the Dean of Chichester."

"Dear me! I had no idea that you felt so strongly about religion, Lord Arthur. Few young men do nowadays."

"I am afraid you overrate me, Herr Winckelkopf," said Lord Arthur, blushing. "The fact is, I really know nothing about theology."

"It is a purely private matter then?"

"Purely private."

Herr Winckelkopf shrugged his shoulders, and left the room, returning in a few minutes with a round cake of dynamite about the size of a penny, and a pretty little

French clock, surmounted by an ormolu figure of Liberty trampling on the hydra of Despotism.

Lord Arthur's face brightened up when he saw it. "That is just what I want," he cried, "and now tell me how it goes off."

"Ah! there is my secret," answered Herr Winckelkopf, contemplating his invention with a justifiable look of pride; "let me know when you wish it to explode, and I will set the machine to the moment."

"Well, to-day is Tuesday, and if you could send it off at once—"

"That is impossible; I have a great deal of important work on hand for some friends of mine in Moscow. Still, I might send it off to-morrow."

"Oh, it will be quite time enough!" said Lord Arthur politely, "if it is delivered to-morrow night or Thursday morning. For the moment of the explosion, say Friday at noon exactly. The Dean is always at home at that hour."

"Friday, at noon," repeated Herr Winckelkopf, and he made a note to that effect in a large ledger that was lying on a bureau near the fireplace.

"And now," said Lord Arthur, rising from his seat, "pray let me know how much I am in your debt."

"It is such a small matter, Lord Arthur, that I do not care to make any charge. The dynamite comes to seven and sixpence, the clock will be three pounds ten, and the carriage about five shillings. I am only too pleased to oblige any friend of Count Rouvaloff's."

"But your trouble, Herr Winckelkopf?"

"Oh, that is nothing! It is a pleasure to me. I do not work for money; I live entirely for my art."

Lord Arthur laid down £4.2s.6d on the table, thanked the little German for his kindness, and, having succeeded in declining an invitation to meet some Anarchists at a meat-tea on the following Saturday, left the house and went off to the Park.

For the next two days he was in a state of the greatest excitement, and on Friday at twelve o'clock he drove down to the Buckingham to wait for news. All the afternoon the stolid hall-porter kept posting up telegrams from various parts of the country giving the results of horse-races, the verdicts in divorce suits, the state of the weather, and the like, while the tape ticked out wearisome details about an all-night sitting in the House of Commons, and a small panic on the Stock Exchange. At four o'clock the evening papers came in, and Lord Arthur disappeared into the library with the *Pall Mall*, the *St. James's*, the *Globe*, and the *Echo*, to the immense indignation of Colonel Goodchild, who wanted to read the reports of a speech he had delivered that morning at the Mansion House, on the subject of South African Missions, and the advisability of having black Bishops in every province, and for some reason or other had a strong prejudice against the *Evening News*. None of the papers, however, contained even the slightest allusion to Chichester, and Lord Arthur felt that the attempt must have failed. It was a terrible blow to him, and for a time he was quite unnerved. Herr Winckelkopf, whom he went to see the next day, was full of elaborate apologies, and offered to supply him with another clock free of charge, or with a case of nitro-glycerine bombs at cost price. But he had lost all faith in explosives, and Herr

Winckelkopf himself acknowledged that everything is so adulterated nowadays, that even dynamite can hardly be got in a pure condition. The little German, however, while admitting that something must have gone wrong with the machinery, was not without hope that the clock might still go off, and instanced the case of a barometer that he had once sent to the military Governor at Odessa, which, though timed to explode in ten days, had not done so for something like three months. It was quite true that when it did go off, it merely succeeded in blowing a housemaid to atoms, the Governor having gone out of town six weeks before, but at least it showed that dynamite, as a destructive force, was, when under the control of machinery, a powerful, though somewhat unpunctual agent. Lord Arthur was a little consoled by this reflection, but even here he was destined to disappointment, for two days afterwards, as he was going upstairs, the Duchess called him into her boudoir, and showed him a letter she had just received from the Deanery.

"Jane writes charming letters," said the Duchess; "you must really read her last. It is quite as good as the novels Mudie sends us."

Lord Arthur seized the letter from her hand. It ran as follows:—

THE DEANERY, CHICHESTER,
27th May.

My dearest Aunt,

Thank you so much for the flannel for the Dorcas Society, and also for the gingham. I quite agree with you that it is nonsense their wanting to wear pretty things, but everybody is so Radical and irreligious nowadays, that it is difficult to make them see that they should not try and dress like the upper classes. I am sure I don't know what we are coming to. As papa has often said in his sermons, we live in an age of unbelief.

We have had great fun over a clock that an unknown admirer sent papa last Thursday. It arrived in a wooden box from London, carriage paid; and papa feels it must have been sent by some one who had read his remarkable sermon, "Is Licence Liberty?" for on the top of the clock was a figure of a woman, with what papa said was the cap of Liberty on her head. I don't think it very becoming myself, but papa said it was historical, so I suppose it is all right. Parker unpacked it, and papa put it on the mantelpiece in the library, and we were all sitting there on Friday morning, when just as the clock struck twelve, we heard a whirring noise, a little puff of smoke came from the pedestal of the figure, and the goddess of Liberty fell off, and broke her nose on the fender! Maria was quite alarmed, but it looked so ridiculous, that James and I went off into fits of laughter, and even papa was amused. When we examined it, we found it was a sort of alarm clock, and that, if you set it to a particular hour, and put some gunpowder and a cap under a little hammer, it went off whenever you wanted. Papa said it must not remain in the library, as it made a noise, so Reggie carried it away to the schoolroom, and does nothing but have small explosions all day long. Do you think Arthur would like one for a wedding present? I suppose they are quite fashionable in London. Papa says they should do a great deal of good, as they show that Liberty can't last, but must fall down. Papa says Liberty was invented at the time of the French Revolution. How awful it seems!

I have now to go to the Dorcas, where I will read your most instructive letter. How true, dear aunt, your idea is, that in their rank of life they should wear what is unbecoming. I must say it is absurd, their anxiety about dress, when there are so many more important things in this world, and in the next. I am so glad your flowered poplin turned out so well, and that your lace was not torn. I am wearing my yellow satin, that you so kindly gave me, at the Bishop's on Wednesday, and think it will look all right. Would you have bows or not? Jennings says that every one wears bows now, and that the underskirt should be frilled. Reggie has just had another explosion, and papa has ordered the clock to be sent to the stables. I don't think papa likes it so much as he did at first, through he is very flattered at being sent such a pretty and ingenious toy. It shows that people read his sermons, and profit by them.

Papa sends his love, in which James, and Reggie, and Maria all unite, and, hoping that Uncle Cecil's gout is better, believe me, dear aunt, ever your affectionate niece,

Jane Percy.

PS.—Do tell me about the bows. Jennings insists they are the fashion.

Lord Arthur looked so serious and unhappy over the letter, that the Duchess went into fits of laughter.

"My dear Arthur," she cried, "I shall never show you a young lady's letter again! But what shall I say about the clock? I think it is a capital invention and I should like to have one myself."

"I don't think much of them," said Lord Arthur, with a sad smile, and, after kissing his mother, he left the room.

When he got upstairs, he flung himself on a sofa, and his eyes filled with tears. He had done his best to commit this murder, but on both occasions he had failed, and through no fault of his own. He had tried to do his duty, but it seemed as if Destiny herself had turned traitor. He was oppressed with the sense of the barrenness of good intentions, of the futility of trying to be fine. Perhaps it would be better to break off the marriage altogether. Sybil would suffer, it is true, but suffering could not really mar a nature so noble as hers. As for himself, what did it matter? There is always some war in which a man can die, some cause to which a man can give his life, and as life had no pleasure for him, so death had no terror. Let Destiny work out his doom. He would not stir to help her.

At half-past seven he dressed, and went down to the club. Surbiton was there with a party of young men, and he was obliged to dine with them. Their trivial conversation and idle jests did not interest him, and as soon as coffee was brought he left them, inventing some engagement in order to get away. As he was going out of the club, the hall-porter handed him a letter. It was from Herr Winckelkopf, asking him to call down the next evening, and look at an explosive umbrella, that went off as soon as it was opened. It was the very latest invention, and had just arrived from Geneva. He tore the letter up into fragments. He had made up his mind not to try any more experiments. Then wandered down to the Thames Embankment, and sat for hours by the river. The moon peered through a mane of tawny clouds, as if it were a lion's eye, and innumerable stars spangled the hollow vault, like gold dust powdered on a purple dome. Now and then a barge swung out into the turbid stream, and floated away with the tide, and the railway signals changed from green to scarlet as the trains ran shrieking across the bridge. After some time, twelve o'clock boomed from the tall tower at Westminster, and at each stroke of the sonorous bell the night seemed to tremble. Then the railway lights went out, one solitary lamp left gleaming like a large ruby on a giant mast, and the roar of the city became fainter.

At two o'clock he got up, and strolled towards Blackfriars. How unreal everything looked! How like a strange dream! The houses on the other side of the river seemed built out of darkness. One would have said that silver and shadow had fashioned the world anew. The huge dome of St. Paul's loomed like a bubble through the dusky air.

As he approached Cleopatra's Needle he saw a man leaning over the parapet, and as he came nearer the man looked up, the gas-light falling full upon his face.

It was Mr. Podgers, the chiromantist! No one could mistake the fat, flabby face, the gold-rimmed spectacles, the sickly feeble smile, the sensual mouth.

Lord Arthur stopped. A brilliant idea flashed across him, and he stole softly up behind. In a moment he had seized Mr. Podgers by the legs, and flung him into the Thames. There was a coarse oath, a heavy splash, and all was still. Lord Arthur looked anxiously over, but could see nothing of the chiromantist but a tall hat, pirouetting in an eddy of moonlit water. After a time it also sank, and no trace of Mr. Podgers was visible. Once he thought that he caught sight of the bulky misshapen figure striking out for the staircase by the bridge, and a horrible feeling of failure came over him but it turned out to be merely a reflection, and when the moon shone out from behind a cloud it passed away. At last he seemed to have realised the decree of Destiny. He heaved a deep sigh of relief, and Sybil's name came to his lips.

"Have you dropped anything, sir?" said a voice behind him suddenly.

He turned round, and saw a policeman with a bull's-eye lantern.

"Nothing of importance, sergeant," he answered, smiling, and hailing a passing hansom, he jumped in, and told the man to drive to Belgrave Square.

For the next few days he alternated between hope and fear. There were moments when he almost expected Mr. Podgers to walk into the room, and yet at other times he felt that Fate could not be so unjust to him. Twice he went to the chiromantist's address in West Moon Street, but he could not bring himself to ring the bell. He longed for certainty, and was afraid of it.

Finally it came. He was sitting in the smoking-room of the club having tea, and listening rather wearily to Surbiton's account of the last comic song at the Gaiety, when the waiter came in with the evening papers. He took up the *St. James's,* and was listlessly turning over its pages, when this strange heading caught his eye:

"SUICIDE OF A CHIROMANTIST."

He turned pale with excitement, and began to read. The paragraph ran as follows:

"Yesterday morning, at seven o'clock, the body of Mr. Septimus R. Podgers, the eminent chiromantist, was washed on shore at Greenwich, just in front of the Ship Hotel. The unfortunate gentleman had been missing for some days, and considerable anxiety for his safety had been felt in chiromantic circles. It is supposed that he committed suicide under the influence of a temporary mental derangement, caused by overwork, and a verdict to that effect was returned this afternoon by the coroner's jury. Mr. Podgers had just completed an elaborate treatise on the subject of the Human Hand, that will shortly be published, when it will no doubt attract much attention. The deceased was sixty-five years of age, and does not seem to have left any relations."

Lord Arthur rushed out of the club with the paper still in his hand, to the immense amazement of the hall-porter, who tried in vain to stop him, and drove at once to Park Lane. Sybil saw him from the window, and something told her that he was the bearer of good news. She ran down to meet him, and, when she saw his face, she knew that all was well.

"My dear Sybil," cried Lord Arthur, "let us be married to-morrow!"

"You foolish boy! Why, the cake is not even ordered!" said Sybil, laughing through her tears.

# 6

When the wedding took place, some three weeks later, St. Peter's was crowded with a perfect mob of smart people. The service was read in the most impressive manner by the Dean of Chichester, and everybody agreed that they had never seen a handsomer couple than the bride and bridegroom. They were more than handsome, however—they were happy. Never for a single moment did Lord Arthur regret all that he had suffered for Sybil's sake, while she, on her side, gave him the best things a woman can give to any man—worship, tenderness, and love. For them romance was not killed by reality. They always felt young.

Some years afterwards, when two beautiful children had been born to them, Lady Windermere came down on a visit to Alton Priory, a lovely old place, that had been the Duke's wedding present to his son; and one afternoon as she was sitting with Lady Arthur under a lime-tree in the garden, watching the little boy and girl as they played up and down the rose-walk, like fitful sunbeams, she suddenly took her hostess's hand in hers, and said, "Are you happy, Sybil?"

"Dear Lady Windermere, of course I am happy. Aren't you?"

"I have no time to be happy, Sybil. I always like the last person who is introduced to me; but, as a rule, as soon as I know people I get tired of them."

"Don't your lions satisfy you, Lady Windermere?"

"Oh dear, no! lions are only good for one season. As soon as their manes are cut, they are the dullest creatures going. Besides, they behave very badly, if you are really nice to them. Do you remember that horrid Mr. Podgers? He was a dreadful impostor.

Of course, I didn't mind that at all, and even when he wanted to borrow money I forgave him, but I could not stand his making love to me. He has really made me hate chiromancy. I go in for telepathy now. It is much more amusing."

"You mustn't say anything against chiromancy here, Lady Windermere; it is the only subject that Arthur does not like people to chaff about. I assure you he is quite serious over it."

"You don't mean to say that he believes in it, Sybil?"

"Ask him, Lady Windermere, here he is"; and Lord Arthur came up the garden with a large bunch of yellow roses in his hand, and his two children dancing round him.

"Lord Arthur?"

"Yes, Lady Windermere."

"You don't mean to say that you believe in chiromancy?"

"Of course I do," said the young man, smiling.

"But why?"

"Because I owe to it all the happiness of my life," he murmured, throwing himself into a wicker chair.

"My dear Lord Arthur, what do you owe to it?"

"Sybil," he answered, handing his wife the roses, and looking into her violet eyes.

"What nonsense!" cried Lady Windermere. "I never heard such nonsense in all my life."

# Nineteenth-Century Cluster:

## Domestic Fictions

Partly because of the increasing luxuries within the middle class and professional opportunities outside the home, nineteenth-century norms aligned men with the public sphere of the workplace, the marketplace, travel, and politics, and women with the private sphere, including homebound activities such as childrearing, cooking, cleaning, and decorating. The public sphere was considered too rough and dangerous for the delicate sensibilities of women, and, instead, wives were charged to create a domestic haven to attract and shelter their husbands from the hectic work world. Documents of popular culture like magazines and advice books touted the "cult of domesticity," a new view of womanhood professing the importance of the womanly virtues of piety, purity, submissiveness, and domesticity. Trapped by expectations of passivity, submission, and increasing isolation from community, many women sought ways to escape their domestic lives.

By writing about houses and women's relationships to them, nineteenth-century authors investigated gender roles—their definitions, consequences, and limitations. Confined to the house by both convention and force, women characters like the narrator of "The Yellow Wall-Paper" recognize the physical, emotional, and intellectual limitations of a life lived within walls. The house becomes the structural manifestation of all of society's restrictions on women's ideas, speech, and actions. Nevertheless, characters like Sarah Penn in "The Revolt of 'Mother'" show us that domestic space can also be a site of power and subversion in which women resist the social forces that imprison them; and Louisa, in "A New England Nun," blurs the distinction between the spheres by making her home a workplace.

The life of nineteenth-century domesticity, with its limitations and privileges, did not extend to women of the lower classes, who continued to work outside the home to support their families. In this sense, the gendered world of the home also conveys socioeconomic status and can be an expression of individual or familial identity. Within houses, characters continually collide with prescribed boundaries that reflect their hopes and dreams as well as their often limited choices.

# Kate Chopin

## (1851–1904)

Born in St. Louis, Missouri, and raised by the family of her Creole mother, Kate Chopin moved to New Orleans, Louisiana, after her 1870 marriage to a cotton broker. After the death of her husband in 1882, she returned to her birthplace and, at the age of forty, began to write. She finished her first novel, *At Fault*, in 1890, and between 1894 and 1897 she published two short story collections, *Bayou Folk* and *A Night in Acadie*. Among her most famous stories are "A Pair of Silk Stockings" and "The Story of an Hour," which explore the psychological pitfalls of traditional feminine roles, and "Désirée's Baby," which addresses cultural biases about miscegenation. Her third and most famous novel, *The Awakening*, so shocked the nation with its sympathetic portrayal of female adultery that it was removed from libraries; Chopin was subsequently shunned by certain literary societies, and her third collection of short stories was refused publication. Chopin observed that the moralistic nature of the general American intellect is sometimes destructive to the full expression of its artistic talents. The writer whom she most admired and took as her model was Maupassant, whose work she believed was "life, not fiction."

## *Désirée's Baby*                                             1893

As the day was pleasant, Madame Valmondé drove over to L'Abri to see Désirée and the baby.

It made her laugh to think of Désirée with a baby. Why, it seemed but yesterday that Désirée was little more than a baby herself; when Monsieur in riding through the gateway of Valmondé had found her lying asleep in the shadow of the big stone pillar.

The little one awoke in his arms and began to cry for "Dada." That was as much as she could do or say. Some people thought she might have strayed there of her own accord, for she was of the toddling age. The prevailing belief was that she had been purposely left by a party of Texans, whose canvas-covered wagon, late in the day, had crossed the ferry that Coton Maïs kept, just below the plantation. In time Madame Valmondé abandoned every speculation but the one that Désirée had been sent to her by a beneficent Providence to be the child of her affection, seeing that she was without child of the flesh. For the girl grew to be beautiful and gentle, affectionate and sincere,—the idol of Valmondé.

It was no wonder, when she stood one day against the stone pillar in whose shadow she had lain asleep, eighteen years before, that Armand Aubigny riding by and seeing her there, had fallen in love with her. That was the way all the Aubignys fell in love, as if struck by a pistol shot. The wonder was that he had not loved her before; for he had known her since his father brought him home from Paris, a boy of eight, after his mother died there. The passion that awoke in him that day, when he saw her at the gate, swept along like an avalanche, or like a prairie fire, or like anything that drives headlong over all obstacles.

*fell in love w/ the girl*

Monsieur Valmondé grew practical and wanted things well considered: that is, the girl's obscure origin. Armand looked into her eyes and did not care. He was reminded that she was nameless. What did it matter about a name when he could give her one of the oldest and proudest in Louisiana? He ordered the *corbeille*[1] from Paris, and contained himself with what patience he could until it arrived; then they were married.

Madame Valmondé had not seen Désirée and the baby for four weeks. When she reached L'Abri she shuddered at the first sight of it, as she always did. It was a sad looking place, which for many years had not known the gentle presence of a mistress, old Monsieur Aubigny having married and buried his wife in France, and she having loved her own land too well ever to leave it. The roof came down steep and black like a cowl, reaching out beyond the wide galleries that encircled the yellow stuccoed house. Big, solemn oaks grew close to it, and their thick-leaved, far-reaching branches shadowed it like a pall. Young Aubigny's rule was a strict one, too, and under it his negroes had forgotten how to be gay, as they had been during the old master's easy-going and indulgent lifetime.

The young mother was recovering slowly, and lay full length, in her soft white muslins and laces, upon a couch. The baby was beside her, upon her arm, where he had fallen asleep, at her breast. The yellow nurse woman sat beside a window fanning herself.

Madame Valmondé bent her portly figure over Désirée and kissed her, holding her an instant tenderly in her arms. Then she turned to the child.

"This is not the baby!" she exclaimed, in startled tones. French was the language spoken at Valmondé in those days.

"I knew you would be astonished," laughed Désirée, "at the way he has grown. The little *cochon de lait!*[2] Look at his legs, mamma, and his hands and finger-nails,— real finger-nails. Zandrine had to cut them this morning. Isn't it true, Zandrine?"

The woman bowed her turbaned head majestically, "Mais si,[3] Madame."

"And the way he cries," went on Désirée, "is deafening. Armand heard him the other day as far away as La Blanche's cabin."

Madame Valmondé had never removed her eyes from the child. She lifted it and walked with it over to the window that was lightest. She scanned the baby narrowly, then looked as searchingly at Zandrine, whose face was turned to gaze across the fields.

"Yes, the child has grown, has changed;" said Madame Valmondé, slowly, as she replaced it beside its mother. "What does Armand say?"

Désirée's face became suffused with a glow that was happiness itself.

---

1 *corbeille:* French. Wedding gifts.
2 *cochon de lait!:* French. Suckling pig!
3 **Mais si:** French. Yes, indeed.

"Oh, Armand is the proudest father in the parish, I believe, chiefly because it is a boy, to bear his name; though he says not,—that he would have loved a girl as well. But I know it isn't true. I know he says that to please me. And mamma," she added, drawing Madame Valmondé's head down to her, and speaking in a whisper, "he hasn't punished one of them—not one of them—since baby is born. Even Négrillon, who pretended to have burnt his leg that he might rest from work—he only laughed, and said Négrillon was a great scamp. Oh, mamma, I'm so happy; it frightens me."

What Désirée said was true. Marriage, and later the birth of his son, had softened Armand Aubigny's imperious and exacting nature greatly. This was what made the gentle Désirée so happy, for she loved him desperately. When he frowned she trembled, but loved him. When he smiled, she asked no greater blessing of God. But Armand's dark, handsome face had not often been disfigured by frowns since the day he fell in love with her.

When the baby was about three months old, Désirée awoke one day to the conviction that there was something in the air menacing her peace. It was at first too subtle to grasp. It had only been a disquieting suggestion; an air of mystery among the blacks; unexpected visits from far-off neighbors who could hardly account for their coming. Then a strange, an awful change in her husband's manner, which she dared not ask him to explain. When he spoke to her, it was with averted eyes, from which the old love-light seemed to have gone out. He absented himself from home; and when there, avoided her presence and that of her child, without excuse. And the very spirit of Satan seemed suddenly to take hold of him in his dealings with the slaves. Désirée was miserable enough to die.

She sat in her room, one hot afternoon, in her *peignoir*,[4] listlessly drawing through her fingers the strands of her long, silky brown hair that hung about her shoulders. The baby, half naked, lay asleep upon her own great mahogany bed, that was like a sumptuous throne, with its satin-lined half-canopy. One of La Blanche's little quadroon boys—half naked too—stood fanning the child slowly with a fan of peacock feathers. Désirée's eyes had been fixed absently and sadly upon the baby, while she was striving to penetrate the threatening mist that she felt closing about her. She looked from her child to the boy who stood beside him, and back again; over and over. "Ah!" It was a cry that she could not help; which she was not conscious of having uttered. The blood turned like ice in her veins, and a clammy moisture gathered upon her face.

She tried to speak to the little quadroon boy; but no sound would come, at first. When he heard his name uttered, he looked up, and his mistress was pointing to the door. He laid aside the great, soft fan, and obediently stole away, over the polished floor, on his bare tiptoes.

She stayed motionless, with gaze riveted upon her child, and her face the picture of fright.

Presently her husband entered the room, and without noticing her, went to a table and began to search among some papers which covered it.

---

4 *peignoir*: French. Dressing gown.

"Armand," she called to him, in a voice which must have stabbed him, if he was human. But he did not notice. "Armand," she said again. Then she rose and tottered towards him. "Armand," she panted once more, clutching his arm, "look at our child. What does it mean? tell me."

He coldly but gently loosened her fingers from about his arm and thrust the hand away from him. "Tell me what it means!" she cried despairingly.

"It means," he answered lightly, "that the child is not white; it means that you are not white."

A quick conception of all that this accusation meant for her nerved her with unwonted courage to deny it. "It is a lie; it is not true, I am white! Look at my hair, it is brown; and my eyes are gray, Armand, you know they are gray. And my skin is fair," seizing his wrist. "Look at my hand; whiter than yours, Armand," she laughed hysterically.

"As white as La Blanche's," he returned cruelly; and went away leaving her alone with their child.

When she could hold a pen in her hand, she sent a despairing letter to Madame Valmondé.

"My mother, they tell me I am not white. Armand has told me I am not white. For God's sake tell them it is not true. You must know it is not true. I shall die. I must die. I cannot be so unhappy, and live."

The answer that came was as brief:

"My own Désirée: Come home to Valmondé; back to your mother who loves you. Come with your child."

When the letter reached Désirée she went with it to her husband's study, and laid it open upon the desk before which he sat. She was like a stone image: silent, white, motionless after she placed it there.

In silence he ran his cold eyes over the written words. He said nothing. "Shall I go, Armand?" she asked in tones sharp with agonized suspense.

"Yes, go."

"Do you want me to go?"

"Yes, I want you to go."

He thought Almighty God had dealt cruelly and unjustly with him; and felt, somehow, that he was paying Him back in kind when he stabbed thus into his wife's soul. Moreover he no longer loved her, because of the unconscious injury she had brought upon his home and his name.

She turned away like one stunned by a blow, and walked slowly towards the door, hoping he would call her back.

"Good-by, Armand," she moaned.

He did not answer her. That was his last blow at fate.

Désirée went in search of her child. Zandrine was pacing the sombre gallery with it. She took the little one from the nurse's arms with no word of explanation, and descending the steps, walked away, under the live-oak branches.

It was an October afternoon; the sun was just sinking. Out in the still fields the negroes were picking cotton.

Désirée had not changed the thin white garment nor the slippers which she wore. Her hair was uncovered and the sun's rays brought a golden gleam from its brown meshes. She did not take the broad, beaten road which led to the far-off plantation of Valmondé. She walked across a deserted field, where the stubble bruised her tender feet, so delicately shod, and tore her thin gown to shreds.

She disappeared among the reeds and willows that grew thick along the banks of the deep, sluggish bayou; and she did not come back again.

*Mother in kitchen peeling potato and talking to child, photograph, 1895*

Some weeks later there was a curious scene enacted at L'Abri. In the centre of the smoothly swept back yard was a great bonfire. Armand Aubigny sat in the wide hallway that commanded a view of the spectacle; and it was he who dealt out to a half dozen negroes the material which kept this fire ablaze.

A graceful cradle of willow, with all its dainty furbishings, was laid upon the pyre, which had already been fed with the richness of a priceless *layette*.[5] Then there were silk gowns, and velvet and satin ones added to these; laces, too, and embroideries; bonnets and gloves; for the *corbeille* had been of rare quality.

The last thing to go was a tiny bundle of letters; innocent little scribblings that Désirée had sent to him during the days of their espousal. There was the remnant of one back in the drawer from which he took them. But it was not Désirée's; it was part of an old letter from his mother to his father. He read it. She was thanking God for the blessing of her husband's love:—

"But, above all," she wrote, "night and day, I thank the good God for having so arranged our lives that our dear Armand will never know that his mother, who adores him, belongs to the race that is cursed with the brand of slavery."

## The Story of an Hour
1894

Knowing that Mrs. Mallard was afflicted with a heart trouble, great care was taken to break to her as gently as possible the news of her husband's death.

It was her sister Josephine who told her, in broken sentences; veiled hints that revealed in half concealing. Her husband's friend Richards was there, too, near her. It was he who had been in the newspaper office when intelligence of the railroad disas-

5 *layette*: Outfit for a newborn baby, including bedding.

ter was received, with Brently Mallard's name leading the list of "killed." He had only taken the time to assure himself of its truth by a second telegram, and had hastened to forestall any less careful, less tender friend in bearing the sad message.

She did not hear the story as many women have heard the same, with a paralyzed inability to accept its significance. She wept at once, with sudden, wild abandonment, in her sister's arms. When the storm of grief had spent itself she went away to her room alone. She would have no one follow her.

There stood, facing the open window, a comfortable, roomy armchair. Into this she sank, pressed down by a physical exhaustion that haunted her body and seemed to reach into her soul.

She could see in the open square before her house the tops of trees that were all aquiver with the new spring life. The delicious breath of rain was in the air. In the street below a peddler was crying his wares. The notes of a distant song which some one was singing reached her faintly, and countless sparrows were twittering in the eaves.

There were patches of blue sky showing here and there through the clouds that had met and piled one above the other in the west facing her window.

She sat with her head thrown back upon the cushion of the chair, quite motion-less, except when a sob came up into her throat and shook her, as a child who has cried itself to sleep continues to sob in its dreams.

She was young, with a fair, calm face, whose lines bespoke repression and even a certain strength. But now there was a dull stare in her eyes, whose gaze was fixed away off yonder on one of those patches of blue sky. It was not a glance of reflection, but rather indicated a suspension of intelligent thought.

There was something coming to her and she was waiting for it, fearfully. What was it? She did not know; it was too subtle and elusive to name. But she felt it, creep-ing out of the sky, reaching toward her through the sounds, the scents, the color that filled the air.

Now her bosom rose and fell tumultuously. She was beginning to recognize this thing that was approaching to possess her, and she was striving to beat it back with her will—as powerless as her two white slender hands would have been.

When she abandoned herself a little whispered word escaped her slightly parted lips. She said it over and over under her breath: "free, free, free!" The vacant stare and the look of terror that had followed it went from her eyes. They stayed keen and bright. Her pulses beat fast, and the coursing blood warmed and relaxed every inch of her body.

She did not stop to ask if it were or were not a monstrous joy that held her. A clear and exalted perception enabled her to dismiss the suggestion as trivial.

She knew that she would weep again when she saw the kind, tender hands folded in death; the face that had never looked save with love upon her, fixed and gray and dead. But she saw beyond that bitter moment a long procession of years to come that would belong to her absolutely. And she opened and spread her arms out to them in welcome.

There would be no one to live for her during those coming years; she would live for herself. There would be no powerful will bending hers in that blind persistence with which men and women believe they have a right to impose a private will upon a fellow-creature. A kind intention or a cruel intention made the act seem no less a crime as she looked upon it in that brief moment of illumination.

And yet she had loved him—sometimes. Often she had not. What did it matter! What could love, the unsolved mystery, count for in face of this possession of self-assertion which she suddenly recognized as the strongest impulse of her being!

"Free! Body and soul free!" she kept whispering.

Josephine was kneeling before the closed door with her lips to the keyhole, imploring for admission. "Louise, open the door! I beg; open the door—you will make yourself ill. What are you doing, Louise? For heaven's sake open the door."

"Go away. I am not making myself ill." No; she was drinking in a very elixir of life through that open window.

Her fancy was running riot along those days ahead of her. Spring days, and summer days, and all sorts of days that would be her own. She breathed a quick prayer that life might be long. It was only yesterday she had thought with a shudder that life might be long.

She arose at length and opened the door to her sister's importunities. There was a feverish triumph in her eyes, and she carried herself unwittingly like a goddess of Victory. She clasped her sister's waist, and together they descended the stairs. Richards stood waiting for them at the bottom.

Some one was opening the front door with a latchkey. It was Brently Mallard who entered, a little travel-stained, composedly carrying his grip-sack and umbrella. He had been far from the scene of accident, and did not even know there had been one. He stood amazed at Josephine's piercing cry; at Richards' quick motion to screen him from the view of his wife.

But Richards was too late.

When the doctors came they said she had died of heart disease—of joy that kills.

# Mary Wilkins Freeman

## (1852–1930)

Although her most widely read short story, "The Revolt of 'Mother,'" depicts an independent and assertive heroine, Mary Wilkins Freeman did not declare herself a feminist; in fact, she was annoyed when she learned that President Theodore Roosevelt had held up Sarah Penn, the eponymous character of Freeman's tale, as a role model for American women. Nevertheless, the female New Englanders portrayed in Freeman's enduring stories triumph over the stifling powers in their lives, and Freeman's work continues to be a favorite among feminist readers. Coincidentally, she, like Emily Dickinson, dropped out of Mount Holyoke College after a brief time and then spent a number of years living and writing in someone else's attic. Freeman claimed that she wrote simply for the money, and toward this end over the course of her lifetime she produced more than fifteen collections of short stories, in addition to writing children's fiction, poetry, and novels. With Elizabeth Stuart Phelps, William Dean Howells, Henry James, and other novelists, she participated in the creation of a multiply authored volume entitled *The Whole Family* and was one of the two first women (the other being Edith Wharton) to be granted membership in the National Institute of Arts and Letters, in 1926.

---

## A New England Nun · 1891

It was late in the afternoon, and the light was waning. There was a difference in the look of the tree shadows out in the yard. Somewhere in the distance cows were lowing and a little bell was tinkling; now and then a farm-wagon tilted by, and the dust flew; some blue-shirted laborers with shovels over their shoulders plodded past; little swarms of flies were dancing up and down before the peoples' faces in the soft air. There seemed to be a gentle stir arising over everything for the mere sake of subsidence—a very premonition of rest and hush and night.

This soft diurnal commotion was over Louisa Ellis also. She had been peacefully sewing at her sitting-room window all the afternoon. Now she quilted her needle carefully into her work, which she folded precisely, and laid in a basket with her thimble and thread and scissors. Louisa Ellis could not remember that ever in her life she had mislaid one of these little feminine appurtenances, which had become, from long use and constant association, a very part of her personality.

Louisa tied a green apron round her waist, and got out a flat straw hat with a green ribbon. Then she went into the garden with a little blue crockery bowl, to pick some currants for her tea. After the currants were picked she sat on the back doorstep and stemmed them, collecting the stems carefully in her apron, and afterwards throwing them into the hen-coop. She looked sharply at the grass beside the step to see if any had fallen there.

Louisa was slow and still in her movements; it took her a long time to prepare her tea; but when ready it was set forth with as much grace as if she had been a veritable guest to her own self. The little square table stood exactly in the centre of the kitchen, and was covered with a starched linen cloth whose border pattern of flowers glistened. Louisa had a damask napkin on her tea-tray, where were arranged a cut-glass tumbler full of teaspoons, a silver cream-pitcher, a china sugar-bowl, and one pink china cup and saucer. Louisa used china every day—something which none of her neighbors did. They whispered about it among themselves. Their daily tables were laid with common crockery, their sets of best china stayed in the parlor closet, and Louisa Ellis was no richer nor better bred than they. Still she would use the china. She had for her supper a glass dish full of sugared currants, a plate of little cakes, and one of light white biscuits. Also a leaf or two of lettuce, which she cut up daintily. Louisa was very fond of lettuce, which she raised to perfection in her little garden. She ate quite heartily, though in a delicate, pecking way; it seemed almost surprising that any considerable bulk of the food should vanish.

After tea she filled a plate with nicely baked thin corn-cakes, and carried them out into the back-yard.

"Caesar!" she called. "Caesar! Caesar!"

There was a little rush, and the clank of a chain, and a large yellow-and-white dog appeared at the door of his tiny hut, which was half hidden among the tall grasses and flowers. Louisa patted him and gave him the corn-cakes. Then she returned to the house and washed the tea-things, polishing the china carefully. The twilight had deepened; the chorus of the frogs floated in at the open window wonderfully loud and shrill, and once in a while a long sharp drone from a tree-toad pierced it. Louisa took off her green gingham apron, disclosing a shorter one of pink and white print. She lighted her lamp, and sat down again with her sewing.

In about half an hour Joe Dagget came. She heard his heavy step on the walk, and rose and took off her pink-and-white apron. Under that was still another—white linen with a little cambric edging on the bottom; that was Louisa's company apron. She never wore it without her calico sewing apron over it unless she had a guest. She had barely folded the pink and white one with methodical haste and laid it in a table drawer when the door opened and Joe Dagget entered.

He seemed to fill up the whole room. A little yellow canary that had been asleep in his green cage at the south window woke up and fluttered wildly, beating his little yellow wings against the wires. He always did so when Joe Dagget came into the room.

"Good-evening," said Louisa. She extended her hand with a kind of solemn cordiality.

"Good-evening, Louisa," returned the man, in a loud voice.

She placed a chair for him, and they sat facing each other, with the table between them. He sat bolt-upright, toeing out his heavy feet squarely, glancing with a good-humored uneasiness around the room. She sat gently erect, folding her slender hands in her white-linen lap.

"Been a pleasant day," remarked Dagget.

"Real pleasant," Louisa assented, softly. "Have you been haying?" she asked, after a little while.

"Yes, I've been haying all day, down in the ten-acre lot. Pretty hot work."

"It must be."

"Yes, it's pretty hot work in the sun."

"Is your mother well to-day?"

"Yes, mother's pretty well."

"I suppose Lily Dyer's with her now?"

Dagget colored. "Yes, she's with her," he answered, slowly.

He was not very young, but there was a boyish look about his large face. Louisa was not quite as old as he, her face was fairer and smoother, but she gave people the impression of being older.

"I suppose she's a good deal of help to your mother," she said, further.

"I guess she is; I don't know how mother'd get along without her," said Dagget, with a sort of embarrassed warmth.

"She looks like a real capable girl. She's pretty-looking too," remarked Louisa.

"Yes, she is pretty fair looking."

Presently Dagget began fingering the books on the table. There was a square red autograph album, and a Young Lady's Gift-Book which had belonged to Louisa's mother. He took them up one after the other and opened them; then laid them down again, the album on the Gift-Book.

Louisa kept eyeing them with mild uneasiness. Finally she rose and changed the position of the books, putting the album underneath. That was the way they had been arranged in the first place.

Dagget gave an awkward little laugh. "Now what difference did it make which book was on top?" said he.

Louisa looked at him with a deprecating smile. "I always keep them that way," murmured she.

"You do beat everything," said Dagget, trying to laugh again. His large face was flushed.

He remained about an hour longer, then rose to take leave. Going out, he stumbled over a rug, and trying to recover himself, hit Louisa's work-basket on the table and knocked it on the floor.

He looked at Louisa, then at the rolling spools; he ducked himself awkwardly toward them, but she stopped him. "Never mind," said she; "I'll pick them up after you're gone."

She spoke with a mild stiffness. Either she was a little disturbed, or his nervousness affected her, and made her seem constrained in her effort to reassure him.

When Joe Dagget was outside he drew in the sweet evening air with a sigh, and felt much as an innocent and perfectly well-intentioned bear might after his exit from a china shop.

Louisa, on her part, felt much as the kind-hearted, long-suffering owner of the china shop might have done after the exit of the bear.

She tied on the pink, then the green apron, picked up all the scattered treasures and replaced them in her work-basket, and straightened the rug. Then she set the lamp on the floor, and began sharply examining the carpet. She even rubbed her fingers over it, and looked at them.

"He's tracked in a good deal of dust," she murmured. "I thought he must have."

Louisa got a dust-pan and brush, and swept Joe Dagget's track carefully.

If he could have known it, it would have increased his perplexity and uneasiness, although it would not have disturbed his loyalty in the least. He came twice a week to see Louisa Ellis, and every time, sitting there in her delicately sweet room, he felt as if surrounded by a hedge of lace. He was afraid to stir lest he should put a clumsy foot or hand through the fairy web, and he had always the consciousness that Louisa was watching fearfully lest he should.

Still the lace and Louisa commanded perforce his perfect respect and patience and loyalty. They were to be married in a month, after a singular courtship which had lasted for a matter of fifteen years. For fourteen out of the fifteen years the two had not once seen each other, and they had seldom exchanged letters. Joe had been all those years in Australia, where he had gone to make his fortune, and where he had stayed until he made it. He would have stayed fifty years if it had taken so long, and come home feeble and tottering, or never come home at all, to marry Louisa.

But the fortune had been made in the fourteen years, and he had come home now to marry the woman who had been patiently and unquestioningly waiting for him all that time.

Shortly after they were engaged he had announced to Louisa his determination to strike out into new fields, and secure a competency before they should be married. She had listened and assented with the sweet serenity which never failed her, not even when her lover set forth on that long and uncertain journey. Joe, buoyed up as he was by his sturdy determination, broke down a little at the last, but Louisa kissed him with a mild blush, and said good-by.

"It won't be for long," poor Joe had said, huskily; but it was for fourteen years.

In that length of time much had happened. Louisa's mother and brother had died, and she was all alone in the world. But greatest happening of all—a subtle happening which both were too simple to understand—Louisa's feet had turned into a path, smooth maybe under a calm, serene sky, but so straight and unswerving that it could only meet a check at her grave, and so narrow that there was no room for any one at her side.

Louisa's first emotion when Joe Dagget came home (he had not apprised her of his coming) was consternation, although she would not admit it to herself, and he never dreamed of it. Fifteen years ago she had been in love with him—at least she considered herself to be. Just at that time, gently acquiescing with and falling into the natural drift of girlhood, she had seen marriage ahead as a reasonable feature and a probable desirability of life. She had listened with calm docility to her mother's views upon the subject. Her mother was remarkable for her cool sense and sweet, even temperament. She talked wisely to her daughter when Joe Dagget presented himself, and Louisa accepted him with no hesitation. He was the first lover she had ever had.

She had been faithful to him all these years. She had never dreamed of the possibility of marrying any one else. Her life, especially for the last seven years, had been full of a pleasant peace, she had never felt discontented nor impatient over her lover's absence; still she had always looked forward to his return and their marriage as the inevitable conclusion of things. However, she had fallen into a way of placing it so far in the future that it was almost equal to placing it over the boundaries of another life.

When Joe came she had been expecting him, and expecting to be married for fourteen years, but she was as much surprised and taken aback as if she had never thought of it.

Joe's consternation came later. He eyed Louisa with an instant confirmation of his old admiration. She had changed but little. She still kept her pretty manner and soft grace, and was, he considered, every whit as attractive as ever. As for himself, his stent was done; he had turned his face away from fortune-seeking, and the old winds of romance whistled as loud and sweet as ever through his ears. All the song which he had been wont to hear in them was Louisa; he had for a long time a loyal belief that he heard it still, but finally it seemed to him that although the winds sang always that one song, it had another name. But for Louisa the wind had never more than murmured; now it had gone down, and everything was still. She listened for a little while with half-wistful attention; then she turned quietly away and went to work on her wedding clothes.

Joe had made some extensive and quite magnificent alterations to his house. It was the old homestead; the newly-married couple would live there, for Joe could not desert his mother, who refused to leave her old home. So Louisa must leave hers. Every morning, rising and going about among her neat maidenly possessions, she felt as one looking her last upon the faces of dear friends. It was true that in a measure she could take them with her, but, robbed of their old environments, they would appear in such new guises that they would almost cease to be themselves. Then there were some peculiar features of her happy solitary life which she would probably be obliged to relinquish altogether. Sterner tasks than these graceful but half-needless ones would probably devolve upon her. There would be a large house to care for; there would be company to entertain; there would be Joe's rigorous and feeble old mother to wait upon; and it would be contrary to all thrifty village traditions for her to keep more than one servant. Louisa had a little still, and she used to occupy herself pleasantly in summer weather with distilling the sweet and aromatic essences from roses and peppermint and spearmint. By-and-by her still must be laid away. Her store of essences was already considerable, and there would be no time for her to distil for the mere pleasure of it. Then Joe's mother would think it foolishness; she had already hinted her opinion in the matter. Louisa dearly loved to sew a linen seam, not always for use, but for the simple, mild pleasure which she took in it. She would have been loath to confess how more than once she had ripped a seam for the mere delight of sewing it together again. Sitting at her window during long sweet afternoons, drawing her needle gently through the dainty fabric, she was peace itself. But there was small chance of such foolish comfort in the future. Joe's mother, domineering, shrewd old matron that she was even in her old age, and very likely even Joe himself, with his honest masculine rudeness, would laugh and frown down all these pretty but senseless old maiden ways.

Louisa had almost the enthusiasm of an artist over the mere order and cleanliness of her solitary home. She had throbs of genuine triumph at the sight of the window-panes which she had polished until they shone like jewels. She gloated gently over her orderly bureau-drawers, with their exquisitely folded contents redolent with lavender and sweet clover and very purity. Could she be sure of the endurance of even this? She had visions, so startling that she half repudiated them as indelicate, of coarse masculine belongings strewn about in endless litter; of dust and disorder arising necessarily from a coarse masculine presence in the midst of all this delicate harmony.

Among her forebodings of disturbance, not the least was with regard to Caesar. Caesar was a veritable hermit of a dog. For the greater part of his life he had dwelt in his secluded hut, shut out from the society of his kind and all innocent canine joys. Never had Caesar since his early youth watched at a woodchuck's hole; never had he known the delights of a stray bone at a neighbor's kitchen door. And it was all on account of a sin committed when hardly out of his puppyhood. No one knew the possible depth of remorse of which this mild-visaged, altogether innocent-looking old dog might be capable; but whether or not he had encountered remorse, he had encountered a full measure of righteous retribution. Old Caesar seldom lifted up his voice in a growl or a bark; he was fat and sleepy; there were yellow rings which looked like spectacles around his dim old eyes; but there was a neighbor who bore on his hand the imprint of several of Caesar's sharp white youthful teeth, and for that he had lived at the end of a chain, all alone in a little hut, for fourteen years. The neighbor, who was choleric and smarting with the pain of his wound, had demanded either Caesar's death or complete ostracism. So Louisa's brother, to whom the dog had belonged, had built him his little kennel and tied him up. It was now fourteen years since, in a flood of youthful spirits, he had inflicted that memorable bite, and with the exception of short excursions, always at the end of the chain, under the strict guardianship of his master or Louisa, the old dog had remained a close prisoner. It is doubtful if, with his limited ambition, he took much pride in the fact, but it is certain that he was possessed of considerable cheap fame. He was regarded by all the children in the village and by many adults as a very monster of ferocity. St. George's dragon could hardly have surpassed in evil repute Louisa Ellis's old yellow dog. Mothers charged their children with solemn emphasis not to go too near to him, and the children listened and believed greedily, with a fascinated appetite for terror, and ran by Louisa's house stealthily, with many sidelong and backward glances at the terrible dog. If perchance he sounded a hoarse bark, there was a panic. Wayfarers chancing into Louisa's yard eyed him with respect, and inquired if the chain were stout. Caesar at large might have seemed a very ordinary dog, and excited no comment whatever; chained, his reputation overshadowed him, so that he lost his own proper outlines and looked darkly vague and enormous. Joe Dagget, however, with his good-humored sense and shrewdness, saw him as he was. He strode valiantly up to him and patted him on the head, in spite of Louisa's soft clamor of warning, and even attempted to set him loose. Louisa grew so alarmed that he desisted, but kept announcing his opinion in the matter quite forcibly at intervals. "There ain't a better-natured dog in town," he would say, "and it's downright cruel to keep him tied up there. Some day I'm going to take him out."

Louisa had very little hope he would not, one of these days, when their interests and possessions should be more completely fused in one. She pictured to herself Caesar on the rampage through the quiet and unguarded village. She saw innocent children bleeding in his path. She was herself very fond of the old dog, because he had belonged to her dead brother, and he was always very gentle with her; still she had great faith in his ferocity. She always warned people not to go too near him. She fed him on ascetic fare of corn-mush and cakes, and never fired his dangerous temper with heating and sanguinary diet of flesh and bones. Louisa looked at the old dog munching his simple fare, and thought of her approaching marriage and trembled. Still no anticipation of disorder and confusion in lieu of sweet peace and harmony, no forebodings of Caesar on the rampage, no wild fluttering of her little yellow canary, were sufficient to turn her a hair's-breadth. Joe Dagget had been fond of her and working for her all these years. It was not for her, whatever came to pass, to prove untrue and break his heart. She put the exquisite little stitches into her wedding-garments, and time went on until it was only a week before her wedding-day. It was a Tuesday evening, and the wedding was to be a week from Wednesday.

There was a full moon that night. About nine o'clock Louisa strolled down the road a little way. There were harvest-fields on either hand, bordered by low stone walls. Luxuriant clumps of bushes grew beside the wall, and trees—wild cherry and old apple-trees—at intervals. Presently Louisa sat down on the wall and looked about her with mildly sorrowful reflectiveness. Tall shrubs of blueberry and meadow-sweet, all woven together and tangled with blackberry vines and horsebriers, shut her in on either side. She had a little clear space between them. Opposite her, on the other side of the road, was a spreading tree; the moon shone between its boughs, and the leaves twinkled like silver. The road was bespread with a beautiful shifting dapple of silver and shadow; the air was full of a mysterious sweetness. "I wonder if it's wild grapes?" murmured Louisa. She sat there some time. She was just thinking of rising, when she heard footsteps and low voices, and remained quiet. It was a lonely place, and she felt a little timid. She thought she would keep still in the shadow and let the persons, whoever they might be, pass her.

But just before they reached her the voices ceased, and the footsteps. She understood that their owners had also found seats upon the stone wall. She was wondering if she could not steal away unobserved, when the voice broke the stillness. It was Joe Dagget's. She sat still and listened.

The voice was announced by a loud sigh, which was as familiar as itself. "Well," said Dagget, "you've made up your mind, then, I suppose?"

"Yes," returned another voice; "I'm going day after to-morrow."

"That's Lily Dyer," thought Louisa to herself. The voice embodied itself in her mind. She saw a girl tall and full-figured, with a firm, fair face, looking fairer and firmer in the moonlight, her strong yellow hair braided in a close knot. A girl full of a calm, rustic strength and bloom, with a masterful way which might have beseemed a princess. Lily Dyer was a favorite with the village folk; she had just the qualities to arouse the admiration. She was good and handsome and smart. Louisa had often heard her praises sounded.

"Well," said Joe Dagget. "I ain't got a word to say."

"I don't know what you could say," returned Lily Dyer.

"Not a word to say," repeated Joe, drawing out the words heavily. Then there was a silence. "I ain't sorry," he began at last, "that that happened yesterday—that we kind of let on how we felt to each other. I guess it's just as well we knew. Of course I can't do anything different. I'm going right on an' get married next week. I ain't going back on a woman that's waited for me fourteen years, an' break her heart."

"If you should jilt her to-morrow, I wouldn't have you," spoke up the girl, with sudden vehemence.

"Well, I ain't going to give you the chance," said he; "but I don't believe you would, either."

"You'd see I wouldn't. Honor's honor, an' right's right. An' I'd never think any-thing of any man that went against 'em for me or any other girl; you'd find that out, Joe Dagget."

"Well, you'll find out fast enough that I ain't going against 'em for you or any other girl," returned he. Their voices sounded almost as if they were angry with each other. Louisa was listening eagerly.

"I'm sorry you feel as if you must go away," said Joe, "but I don't know but it's best."

"Of course it's best. I hope you and I have got common-sense."

"Well, I suppose you're right." Suddenly Joe's voice got an undertone of tender-ness. "Say, Lily," said he, "I'll get along well enough myself, but I can't bear to think— You don't suppose you're going to fret much over it?"

"I guess you'll find out I sha'n't fret much over a married man."

"Well, I hope you won't—I hope you won't, Lily. God knows I do. And—I hope—one of these days—you'll—come across somebody else—"

"I don't see any reason why I shouldn't." Suddenly her tone changed. She spoke in a sweet, clear voice, so loud that she could have been heard across the street. "No, Joe Dagget," said she, "I'll never marry any other man as long as I live. I've got good sense, an' I ain't going to break my heart nor make a fool of myself; but I'm never going to be married, you can be sure of that. I ain't that sort of a girl to feel this way twice."

Louisa heard an exclamation and a soft commotion behind the bushes; then Lily spoke again,—the voice sounded as if she had risen. "This must be put a stop to," said she. "We've stayed here long enough. I'm going home."

Louisa sat there in a daze, listening to their retreating steps. After a while she got up and slunk softly home herself. The next day she did her housework methodically; that was as much a matter of course as breathing; but she did not sew on her wedding-clothes. She sat at her window and meditated. In the evening Joe came. Louisa Ellis had never known that she had any diplomacy in her, but when she came to look for it that night she found it, although meek of its kind, among her little fem-inine weapons. Even now she could hardly believe that she had heard aright, and that she would not do Joe a terrible injury should she break her troth-plight. She wanted to sound him without betraying too soon her own inclinations in the matter. She did it successfully, and they finally came to an understanding; but it was a difficult thing, for he was as afraid of betraying himself as she.

She never mentioned Lily Dyer. She simply said that while she had no cause of complaint against him, she had lived so long in one way that she shrank from making a change.

"Well, I never shrank, Louisa," said Dagget. "I'm going to be honest enough to say that I think maybe it's better this way; but if you'd wanted to keep on, I'd have stuck to you till my dying day. I hope you know that."

"Yes, I do," said she.

That night she and Joe parted more tenderly than they had done for a long time. Standing in the door, holding each other's hands, a last great wave of regretful mem-ory swept over them.

"Well, this ain't the way we've thought it was all going to end, is it, Louisa?" said Joe.

She shook her head. There was a little quiver on her placid face.

"You let me know if there's ever anything I can do for you," said he. "I ain't ever going to forget you, Louisa." Then he kissed her, and went down the path.

Louisa, all alone by herself that night, wept a little, she hardly knew why; but the next morning, on waking, she felt like a queen who, after fearing lest her domain be wrested away from her, sees it firmly insured in her possession.

Now the tall weeds and grasses might cluster around Caesar's little hermit hut, the snow might fall on its roof year in and year out, but he never would go on a rampage through the unguarded village. Now the little canary might turn itself into a peaceful yellow ball night after night, and have no need to wake and flutter with wild terror against its bars. Louisa could sew linen seams, and distil roses, and dust and polish and fold away in lavender, as long as she listed. That afternoon she sat with her needle-work at the window, and felt fairly steeped in peace. Lily Dyer, tall and erect and blooming, went past; but she felt no qualm. If Louisa Ellis had sold her birthright she did not know it, the taste of the pottage was so delicious, and had been her sole satisfaction for so long. Serenity and placid narrowness had become to her as the birthright itself. She gazed ahead through a long reach of future days strung together like pearls in a rosary, every one like the others, and all smooth and flawless and innocent, and her heart went up in thankfulness. Outside was the fervid summer afternoon; the air was filled with the sounds of the busy harvest of men and birds and bees; there were halloos, metallic clatterings, sweet calls, and long hummings. Louisa sat, prayerfully numbering her days, like an uncloistered nun.

## The Revolt of "Mother" 1891

"**F**ather!"

"What is it?"

"What are them men diggin' over there in the field for?"

There was a sudden dropping and enlarging of the lower part of the old man's face, as if some heavy weight had settled therein; he shut his mouth tight, and went on harnessing the great bay mare. He hustled the collar on to her neck with a jerk.

"Father!"

The old man slapped the saddle upon the mare's back.

"Look here, father, I want to know what them men are diggin' over in the field for, an' I'm goin' to know."

"I wish you'd go into the house, mother, an' 'tend to your own affairs," the old man said then. He ran his words together, and his speech was almost as inarticulate as a growl.

But the woman understood; it was her most native tongue. "I ain't goin' into the house till you tell me what them men are doin' over there in the field," said she.

Then she stood waiting. She was a small woman, short and straight-waisted like a child in her brown cotton gown. Her forehead was mild and benevolent between the smooth curves of gray hair; there were meek downward lines about her nose and mouth; but her eyes, fixed upon the old man, looked as if the meekness had been the result of her own will, never of the will of another.

They were in the barn, standing before the wide open doors. The spring air, full of the smell of growing grass and unseen blossoms, came in their faces. The deep yard in front was littered with farm wagons and piles of wood; on the edges, close to the fence and the house, the grass was a vivid green, and there were some dandelions.

The old man glanced doggedly at his wife as he tightened the last buckles on the harness. She looked as immovable to him as one of the rocks in his pasture-land, bound to the earth with generations of blackberry vines. He slapped the reins over the horse, and started forth from the barn.

"*Father!*" said she.

The old man pulled up. "What is it?"

"I want to know what them men are diggin' over there in that field for."

"They're diggin' a cellar, I s'pose, if you've got to know."

"A cellar for what?"

"A barn."

"A barn? You ain't goin' to build a barn over there where we was goin' to have a house, father?"

The old man said not another word. He hurried the horse into the farm wagon, and clattered out of the yard, jouncing as sturdily on his seat as a boy.

The woman stood a moment looking after him, then she went out of the barn across a corner of the yard to the house. The house, standing at right angles with the great barn and a long reach of sheds and out-buildings, was infinitesimal compared with them. It was scarcely as commodious for people as the little boxes under the barn eaves were for doves.

A pretty girl's face, pink and delicate as a flower, was looking out of one of the house windows. She was watching three men who were digging over in the field which bounded the yard near the road line. She turned quietly when the woman entered.

"What are they digging for, mother?" said she. "Did he tell you?"

"They're diggin' for—a cellar for a new barn."

"Oh, mother, he ain't going to build another barn?"

"That's what he says."

A boy stood before the kitchen glass combing his hair. He combed slowly and painstakingly, arranging his brown hair in a smooth hillock over his forehead. He did not seem to pay any attention to the conversation.

"Sammy, did you know father was going to build a new barn?" asked the girl.

The boy combed assiduously.

"Sammy!"

He turned, and showed a face like his father's under his smooth crest of hair. "Yes, I s'pose I did," he said, reluctantly.

"How long have you known it?" asked his mother.

"'Bout three months, I guess."

"Why didn't you tell of it?"

"Didn't think 'twould do no good."

"I don't see what father wants another barn for," said the girl, in her sweet, slow voice. She turned again to the window, and stared out at the digging men in the field. Her tender, sweet face was full of a gentle distress. Her forehead was as bald and innocent as a baby's, with the light hair strained back from it in a row of curl-papers. She was quite large, but her soft curves did not look as if they covered muscles.

Her mother looked sternly at the boy. "Is he goin' to buy more cows?" said she.

The boy did not reply; he was tying his shoes.

"Sammy, I want you to tell me if he's goin' to buy more cows."

"I s'pose he is."

"How many?"

"Four, I guess."

His mother said nothing more. She went into the pantry, and there was a clatter of dishes. The boy got his cap from a nail behind the door, took an old arithmetic from the shelf, and started for school. He was lightly built, but clumsy. He went out of the yard with a curious spring in the hips, that made his loose homemade jacket tilt up in the rear.

The girl went to the sink, and began to wash the dishes that were piled up there. Her mother came promptly out of the pantry, and shoved her aside. "You wipe 'em," said she; "I'll wash. There's a good many this mornin'."

The mother plunged her hands vigorously into the water, the girl wiped the plates slowly and dreamily. "Mother," said she, "don't you think it's too bad father's going to build that new barn, much as we need a decent house to live in?"

Her mother scrubbed a dish fiercely. "You ain't found out yet we're women-folks, Nanny Penn," said she. "You ain't seen enough of men-folks yet to. One of these days you'll find it out, an' then you'll know that we know only what men-folks think we do, so far as any use of it goes, an' how we'd ought to reckon men-folks in with Providence, an' not complain of what they do any more than we do of the weather."

"I don't care; I don't believe George is anything like that, anyhow," said Nanny. Her delicate face flushed pink, her lips pouted softly, as if she were going to cry.

"You wait an' see. I guess George Eastman ain't no better than other men. You hadn't ought to judge father, though. He can't help it, 'cause he don't look at things jest the way we do. An' we've been pretty comfortable here, after all. The roof don't leak—ain't never but once—that's one thing. Father's kept it shingled right up."

"I do wish we had a parlor."

"I guess it won't hurt George Eastman any to come to see you in a nice clean kitchen. I guess a good many girls don't have as good a place as this. Nobody's ever heard me complain."

"I ain't complained either, mother."

"Well, I don't think you'd better, a good father an' a good home as you've got. S'pose your father made you go out an' work for your livin'? Lots of girls have to that ain't no stronger an' better able to than you be."

Sarah Penn washed the frying-pan with a conclusive air. She scrubbed the outside of it as faithfully as the inside. She was a masterly keeper of her box of a house. Her one living-room never seemed to have in it any of the dust which the friction of life with inanimate matter produces. She swept, and there seemed to be no dirt to go before the broom; she cleaned, and one could see no difference. She was like an artist so perfect that he has apparently no art. To-day she got out a mixing bowl and a board, and rolled some pies, and there was no more flour upon her than upon her daughter who was doing finer work. Nanny was to be married in the fall, and she was sewing on some white cambric and embroidery. She sewed industriously while her mother cooked, her soft milk-white hands and wrists showed whiter than her delicate work.

"We must have the stove moved out in the shed before long," said Mrs. Penn. "Talk about not havin' things, it's been a real blessin' to be able to put a stove up in that shed in hot weather. Father did one good thing when he fixed that stove-pipe out there."

Sarah Penn's face as she rolled her pies had that expression of meek vigor which might have characterized one of the New Testament saints. She was making mince-pies. Her husband, Adoniram Penn, liked them better than any other kind. She baked twice a week. Adoniram often liked a piece of pie between meals. She hurried this morning. It had been later than usual when she began, and she wanted to have a pie baked for dinner. However deep a resentment she might be forced to hold against her husband, she would never fail in sedulous attention to his wants.

Nobility of character manifests itself at loop-holes when it is not provided with large doors. Sarah Penn's showed itself to-day in flaky dishes of pastry. So she made the pies faithfully, while across the table she could see, when she glanced up from her work, the sight that rankled in her patient and steadfast soul—the digging of the cellar of the new barn in the place where Adoniram forty years ago had promised her their new house should stand.

The pies were done for dinner. Adoniram and Sammy were home a few minutes after twelve o'clock. The dinner was eaten with serious haste. There was never much conversation at the table in the Penn family. Adoniram asked a blessing, and they ate promptly, then rose up and went about their work.

Sammy went back to school, taking soft sly lopes out of the yard like a rabbit. He wanted a game of marbles before school, and feared his father would give him some chores to do. Adoniram hastened to the door and called after him, but he was out of sight.

"I don't see what you let him go for, mother," said he. "I wanted him to help me unload that wood."

Adoniram went to work out in the yard unloading wood from the wagon. Sarah put away the dinner dishes, while Nanny took down her curl-papers and changed her dress. She was going down to the store to buy some more embroidery and thread.

When Nanny was gone, Mrs. Penn went to the door. "Father!" she called.

"Well, what is it!"

"I want to see you jest a minute, father."

"I can't leave this wood nohow. I've got to git it unloaded an' go for a load of gravel afore two o'clock. Sammy had ought to helped me. You hadn't ought to let him go to school so early."

"I want to see you jest a minute."

"I tell ye I can't, nohow, mother."

"Father, you come here." Sarah Penn stood in the door like a queen; she held her head as if it bore a crown; there was the patience which makes authority royal in her voice. Adoniram went.

Mrs. Penn led the way into the kitchen, and pointed to a chair. "Sit down, father," said she; "I've got somethin' I want to say to you."

He sat down heavily; his face was quite stolid, but he looked at her with restive eyes. "Well, what is it, mother?"

"I want to know what you're buildin' that new barn for, father?"

"I ain't got nothin' to say about it."

"It can't be you think you need another barn?"

"I tell ye I ain't got nothin' to say about it, mother; an' I ain't goin' to say nothin'."

"Be you goin' to buy more cows?"

Adoniram did not reply; he shut his mouth tight.

"I know you be, as well as I want to. Now, father, look here"—Sarah Penn had not sat down; she stood before her husband in the humble fashion of a Scripture woman—"I'm goin' to talk real plain to you; I never have sence I married you, but I'm goin' to now. I ain't never complained, an' I ain't goin' to complain now, but I'm goin' to talk plain. You see this room here, father; you look at it well. You see there ain't no carpet on the floor, an' you see the paper is all dirty, an' droppin' off the walls. We ain't had no new paper on it for ten year, an' then I put it on myself, an' it didn't cost but ninepence a roll. You see this room, father; it's all the one I've had to work in an' eat in an' sit in sence we was married. There ain't another woman in the whole town whose husband ain't got half the means you have but what's got better. It's all the room Nanny's got to have her company in; an' there ain't one of her mates but what's got better, an' their fathers not so able as hers is. It's all the room she'll have to be married in. What would you have thought, father, if we had had our weddin' in a room no better than this? I was married in my mother's parlor, with a carpet on the floor, an' stuffed furniture, an' a mahogany card-table. An' this is all the room my daughter will have to be married in. Look here, father!"

Sarah Penn went across the room as though it were a tragic stage. She flung open a door and disclosed a tiny bedroom, only large enough for a bed and bureau, with a path between. "There, father," said she—"there's all the room I've had to sleep in forty year. All my children were born there—the two that died, an' the two that's livin'. I was sick with a fever there."

She stepped to another door and opened it. It led into the small, ill-lighted pantry. "Here," said she, "is all the buttery I've got—every place I've got for my dishes, to set away my victuals in, an' to keep my milk-pans in. Father, I've been takin' care of the milk of six cows in this place, an' now you're goin' to build a new barn, an' keep more cows, an' give me more to do in it."

She threw open another door. A narrow crooked flight of stairs wound upward from it. "There, father," said she, "I want you to look at the stairs that go up to them two unfinished chambers that are all the places our son an' daughter have had to sleep in all their lives. There ain't a prettier girl in town nor a more ladylike one than Nanny, an' that's the place she has to sleep in. It ain't so good as your horse's stall; it ain't so warm an' tight."

Sarah Penn went back and stood before her husband. "Now, father," said she, "I want to know if you think you're doin' right an' accordin' to what you profess. Here, when we was married, forty year ago, you promised me faithful that we should have a new house built in that lot over in the field before the year was out. You said you had money enough, an' you wouldn't ask me to live in no such place as this. It is forty year now, an' you've been makin' more money, an' I've been savin' of it for you ever since, an' you ain't built no house yet. You've built sheds an' cow-houses an' one new barn, an' now you're goin' to build another. Father, I want to know if you think it's right. You're lodgin' your dumb beasts better than you are your own flesh an' blood. I want to know if you think it's right."

"I ain't got nothin' to say."

"You can't say nothin' without ownin' it ain't right, father. An' there's another thing—I ain't complained; I've got along forty year, an' I s'pose I should forty more, if it wa'n't for that—if we don't have another house. Nanny she can't live with us after she's married. She'll have to go somewheres else to live away from us, an' it don't seem as if I could have it so, noways, father. She wa'n't ever strong. She's got considerable color, but there wa'n't ever any backbone to her. I've always took the heft of everything off her, an' she ain't fit to keep house an' do everything herself. She'll be all worn out inside of a year. Think of her doin' all the washin' an' ironin' an' bakin' with them soft white hands an' arms, an' sweepin'! I can't have it so, noways, father."

Mrs. Penn's face was burning; her mild eyes gleamed. She had pleaded her little cause like a Webster;[1] she had ranged from severity to pathos; but her opponent employed that obstinate silence which makes eloquence futile with mocking echoes. Adoniram arose clumsily.

"Father, ain't you got nothin' to say?" said Mrs. Penn.

"I've got to go off after that load of gravel. I can't stan' here talkin' all day."

"Father, won't you think it over, an' have a house built there instead of a barn?"

"I ain't got nothin' to say."

Adoniram shuffled out. Mrs. Penn went into her bedroom. When she came out, her eyes were red. She had a roll of unbleached cotton cloth. She spread it out on the kitchen table, and began cutting out some shirts for her husband. The men over in the field had a team to help them this afternoon; she could hear their halloos. She had a scanty pattern for the shirts; she had to plan and piece the sleeves.

Nanny came home with her embroidery, and sat down with her needlework. She had taken down her curl-papers, and there was a soft roll of fair hair like an aureole over her forehead; her face was as delicately fine and clear as porcelain. Suddenly she looked up, and the tender red flamed all over her face and neck. "Mother," said she.

"What say?"

---

1 **Webster:** Reference to Daniel Webster (1782–1852), American senator and orator.

"I've been thinking—I don't see how we're goin' to have any—wedding in this room. I'd be ashamed to have his folks come if we didn't have anybody else."

"Mebbe we can have some new paper before then; I can put it on. I guess you won't have no call to be ashamed of your belongin's."

"We might have the wedding in the new barn," said Nanny, with gentle pettishness. "Why, mother, what makes you look so?"

Mrs. Penn had started, and was staring at her with a curious expression. She turned again to her work, and spread out a pattern carefully on the cloth. "Nothin'," said she.

Presently Adoniram clattered out of the yard in his two-wheeled dump cart, standing as proudly upright as a Roman charioteer. Mrs. Penn opened the door and stood there a minute looking out; the halloos of the men sounded louder.

It seemed to her all through the spring months that she heard nothing but the halloos and the noises of saws and hammers. The new barn grew fast. It was a fine edifice for this little village. Men came on pleasant Sundays, in their meeting suits and clean shirt bosoms, and stood around it admiringly. Mrs. Penn did not speak of it, and Adoniram did not mention it to her, although sometimes, upon a return from inspecting it, he bore himself with injured dignity.

"It's a strange thing how your mother feels about the new barn," he said, confidentially, to Sammy one day.

Sammy only grunted after an odd fashion for a boy; he had learned it from his father.

The barn was all completed ready for use by the third week in July. Adoniram had planned to move his stock in on Wednesday; on Tuesday he received a letter which changed his plans. He came in with it early in the morning. "Sammy's been to the post-office," said he, "an' I've got a letter from Hiram." Hiram was Mrs. Penn's brother, who lived in Vermont.

"Well," said Mrs. Penn, "what does he say about the folks?"

"I guess they're all right. He says he thinks if I come up country right off there's a chance to buy jest the kind of a horse I want." He stared reflectively out of the window at the new barn.

Mrs. Penn was making pies. She went on clapping the rolling-pin into the crust, although she was very pale, and her heart beat loudly.

"I dun' know but what I'd better go," said Adoniram. "I hate to go off jest now, right in the midst of hayin', but the ten-acre lot's cut, an' I guess Rufus an' the others can git along without me three or four days. I can't get a horse round here to suit me, nohow, an' I've got to have another for all that wood-haulin' in the fall. I told Hiram to watch out, an' if he got wind of a good horse to let me know. I guess I'd better go."

"I'll get out your clean shirt an' collar," said Mrs. Penn calmly.

She laid out Adoniram's Sunday suit and his clean clothes on the bed in the little bedroom. She got his shaving-water and razor ready. At last she buttoned on his collar and fastened his black cravat.

Adoniram never wore his collar and cravat except on extra occasions. He held his head high, with a rasped dignity. When he was all ready, with his coat and hat brushed, and a lunch of pie and cheese in a paper bag, he hesitated on the threshold of the door. He looked at his wife, and his manner was defiantly apologetic. "*If* them cows come to-day, Sammy can drive 'em into the new barn," said he; "an' when they bring the hay up, they can pitch it in there."

"Well," replied Mrs. Penn.

Adoniram set his shaven face ahead and started. When he had cleared the door-step, he turned and looked back with a kind of nervous solemnity. "I shall be back by Saturday if nothin' happens," said he.

"Do be careful, father," returned his wife.

She stood in the door with Nanny at her elbow and watched him out of sight. Her eyes had a strange, doubtful expression in them; her peaceful forehead was contracted. She went in, and about her baking again. Nanny sat sewing. Her wedding-day was drawing nearer, and she was getting pale and thin with her steady sewing. Her mother kept glancing at her.

"Have you got that pain in your side this mornin'?" she asked.

"A little."

Mrs. Penn's face, as she worked, changed, her perplexed forehead smoothed, her eyes were steady, her lips firmly set. She formed a maxim for herself, although incoherently with her unlettered thoughts. "Unsolicited opportunities are the guide-posts of the Lord to the new roads of life," she repeated in effect, and she made up her mind to her course of action.

"S'posin' I *had* wrote to Hiram," she muttered once, when she was in the pantry—"s'posin' I had wrote, an' asked him if he knew of any horse? But I didn't, an' father's goin' wa'n't none of my doin'. It looks like a providence." Her voice rang out quite loud at the last.

"What you talkin' about, mother?" called Nanny.

"Nothin'."

Mrs. Penn hurried her baking; at eleven o'clock it was all done. The load of hay from the west field came slowly down the cart track, and drew up at the new barn. Mrs. Penn ran out. "Stop!" she screamed—"stop!"

The men stopped and looked; Sammy upreared from the top of the load, and stared at his mother.

"Stop!" she cried out again. "Don't you put the hay in that barn; put it in the old one."

"Why, he said to put it in here," returned one of the hay-makers, wonderingly. He was a young man, a neighbor's son, whom Adoniram hired by the year to help on the farm.

"Don't you put the hay in the new barn; there's room enough in the old one, ain't there?" said Mrs. Penn.

"Room enough," returned the hired man, in his thick, rustic tones. "Didn't need the new barn, nohow, far as room's concerned. Well, I s'pose he changed his mind." He took hold of the horses' bridles.

Mrs. Penn went back to the house. Soon the kitchen windows were darkened, and a fragrance like warm honey came into the room.

Nanny laid down her work. "I thought father wanted them to put the hay into the new barn?" she said, wonderingly.

"It's all right," replied her mother.

Sammy slid down from the load of hay, and came in to see if dinner was ready.

"I ain't goin' to get a regular dinner to-day, as long as father's gone," said his mother. "I've let the fire go out. You can have some bread an' milk an' pie. I thought we could get along." She set out some bowls of milk, some bread and a pie on the kitchen table. "You'd better eat your dinner now," said she. "You might jest as well get through with it. I want you to help me afterward."

Nanny and Sammy stared at each other. There was something strange in their mother's manner. Mrs. Penn did not eat anything herself. She went into the pantry, and they heard her moving dishes while they ate. Presently she came out with a pile of plates. She got the clothes-basket out of the shed, and packed them in it. Nanny and Sammy watched. She brought out cups and saucers, and put them in with the plates.

"What you goin' to do, mother?" inquired Nanny, in a timid voice. A sense of something unusual made her tremble, as if it were a ghost. Sammy rolled his eyes over his pie.

"You'll see what I'm goin' to do," replied Mrs. Penn. "If you're through, Nanny, I want you to go up-stairs an' pack up your things; an' I want you, Sammy, to help me take down the bed in the bedroom."

"Oh, mother, what for?" gasped Nanny.

"You'll see."

During the next few hours a feat was performed by this simple, pious New England mother which was equal in its way to Wolfe's[2] storming of the Heights of Abraham. It took no more genius and audacity of bravery for Wolfe to cheer his wondering soldiers up those steep precipices, under the sleeping eyes of the enemy, than for Sarah Penn, at the head of her children, to move all their little household goods into the new barn while her husband was away.

Nanny and Sammy followed their mother's instructions without a murmur; indeed, they were overawed. There is a certain uncanny and superhuman quality about all such purely original undertakings as their mother's was to them. Nanny went back and forth with her light loads, and Sammy tugged with sober energy.

At five o'clock in the afternoon the little house in which the Penns had lived for forty years had emptied itself into the new barn.

Every builder builds somewhat for unknown purposes, and is in a measure a prophet. The architect of Adoniram Penn's barn, while he designed it for the comfort of four-footed animals, had planned better than he knew for the comfort of humans. Sarah Penn saw at a glance its possibilities. These great box-stalls, with quilts hung before them, would make better bedrooms than the one she had occupied for forty years, and there was a tight carriage-room. The harness-room, with its chimney and shelves, would make a kitchen of her dreams. The great middle space would make a

2 **Wolfe:** James Wolfe (1727–1759), British general involved in the Seven Years War (1756–1763). Died a hero after scoring a decisive victory against Quebec.

parlor, by-and-by, fit for a palace. Up-stairs there was as much room as down. With partitions and windows, what a house would there be! Sarah looked at the row of stanchions before the allotted space for cows, and reflected that she would have her front entry there.

At six o'clock the stove was up in the harness-room, the kettle was boiling, and the table set for tea. It looked almost as home-like as the abandoned house across the yard had ever done. The young hired man milked, and Sarah directed him calmly to bring the milk to the new barn. He came gaping, dropping little blots of foam from the brimming pails on the grass. Before the next morning he had spread the story of Adoniram Penn's wife moving into the new barn all over the little village. Men assembled in the store and talked it over, women with shawls over their heads scuttled into each other's houses before their work was done. Any deviation from the ordinary course of life in this quiet town was enough to stop all progress in it. Everybody paused to look at the staid, independent figure on the side track. There was a difference of opinion with regard to her. Some held her to be insane; some, of a lawless and rebellious spirit.

Friday the minister went to see her. It was in the forenoon, and she was at the barn door shelling pease for dinner. She looked up and returned his salutation with dignity, then she went on with her work. She did not invite him in. The saintly expression of her face remained fixed, but there was an angry flush over it.

The minister stood awkwardly before her, and talked. She handled the pease as if they were bullets. At last she looked up, and her eyes showed the spirit that her meek front had covered for a lifetime.

"There ain't no use talkin', Mr. Hersey," said she. "I've thought it all over an' over, an' I believe I'm doin' what's right. I've made it the subject of prayer, an' it's betwixt me an' the Lord an' Adoniram. There ain't no call for nobody else to worry about it."

"Well, of course, if you have brought it to the Lord in prayer, and feel satisfied that you are doing right, Mrs. Penn," said the minister, helplessly. His thin gray-bearded face was pathetic. He was a sickly man; his youthful confidence had cooled; he had to scourge himself up to some of his pastoral duties as relentlessly as a Catholic ascetic, and then he was prostrated by the smart.

"I think it's right jest as much as I think it was right for our forefathers to come over from the old country 'cause they didn't have what belonged to 'em," said Mrs. Penn. She arose. The barn threshold might have been Plymouth Rock from her bearing. "I don't doubt you mean well, Mr. Hersey," said she, "but there are things people hadn't ought to interfere with. I've been a member of the church for over forty year. I've got my own mind an' my own feet, an' I'm goin' to think my own thoughts an' go my own ways, an' nobody but the Lord is goin' to dictate to me unless I've a mind to have him. Won't you come in an' set down? How is Mis' Hersey?"

"She is well, I thank you," replied the minister. He added some more perplexed apologetic remarks; then he retreated.

He could expound the intricacies of every character study in the Scriptures, he was competent to grasp the Pilgrim Fathers and all historical innovators, but Sarah Penn was beyond him. He could deal with primal cases, but parallel ones worsted him. But, after all, although it was aside from his province, he wondered more how Adoniram Penn would deal with his wife than how the Lord would. Everybody shared the wonder. When Adoniram's four new cows arrived, Sarah ordered three to be put in the old barn, the other in the house shed where the cooking-stove had stood. That added to the excitement. It was whispered that all four cows were domiciled in the house.

Towards sunset on Saturday, when Adoniram was expected home, there was a knot of men in the road near the new barn. The hired man had milked, but he still hung around the premises. Sarah Penn had supper all ready. There were brown-bread and baked beans and a custard pie; it was the supper Adoniram loved on a Saturday night. She had a clean calico, and she bore herself imperturbably. Nanny and Sammy kept close at her heels. Their eyes were large, and Nanny was full of nervous tremors. Still there was to them more pleasant excitement than anything else. An inborn confidence in their mother over their father asserted itself.

Sammy looked out of the harness-room window. "There he is," he announced, in an awed whisper. He and Nanny peeped around the casing. Mrs. Penn kept on about her work. The children watched Adoniram leave the new horse standing in the drive while he went to the house door. It was fastened. Then he went around to the shed. That door was seldom locked, even when the family was away. The thought how her father would be confronted by the cow flashed upon Nanny. There was a hysterical sob in her throat. Adoniram emerged from the shed and stood looking about in a dazed fashion. His lips moved; he was saying something, but they could not hear what it was. The hired man was peeping around a corner of the old barn, but nobody saw him.

Adoniram took the new horse by the bridle and led him across the yard to the new barn. Nanny and Sammy slunk close to their mother. The barn doors rolled back, and there stood Adoniram, with the long mild face of the great Canadian farm horse looking over his shoulder.

Nanny kept behind her mother, but Sammy stepped suddenly forward, and stood in front of her.

Adoniram stared at the group. "What on airth you all down here for?" said he. "What's the matter over to the house?"

"We've come here to live, father," said Sammy. His shrill voice quavered out bravely.

"What"—Adoniram sniffed—"what is it smells like cookin'?" said he. He stepped forward and looked in the open door of the harness-room. Then he turned to his wife. His old bristling face was pale and frightened. "What on airth does this mean, mother?" he gasped.

"You come in here, father," said Sarah. She led the way into the harness-room and shut the door. "Now, father," said she, "you needn't be scared. I ain't crazy. There ain't nothin' to be upset over. But we've come here to live, an' we're goin' to live here. We've got jest as good a right here as new horses an' cows. The house wa'n't fit for us to live in any longer, an' I made up my mind I wa'n't goin' to stay there. I've done my duty by you forty year, an' I'm goin' to do it now; but I'm goin' to live here. You've got to put in some windows and partitions; an' you'll have to buy some furniture."

"Why, mother!" the old man gasped.

"You'd better take your coat off an' get washed—there's the wash-basin—an' then we'll have supper."

"Why, mother!"

Sammy went past the window, leading the new horse to the old barn. The old man saw him, and shook his head speechlessly. He tried to take off his coat, but his arms seemed to lack the power. His wife helped him. She poured some water into the tin basin, and put in a piece of soap. She got the comb and brush, and smoothed his thin gray hair after he had washed. Then she put the beans, hot bread, and tea on the table. Sammy came in, and the family drew up. Adoniram sat looking dazedly at his plate, and they waited.

"Ain't you goin' to ask a blessin', father?" said Sarah.

And the old man bent his head and mumbled.

All through the meal he stopped eating at intervals, and stared furtively at his wife; but he ate well. The home food tasted good to him, and his old frame was too sturdily healthy to be affected by his mind. But after supper he went out, and sat down on the step of the smaller door at the right of the barn, through which he had meant his Jerseys to pass in stately file, but which Sarah designed for her front house door, and he leaned his head on his hands.

After the supper dishes were cleared away and the milk-pans washed, Sarah went out to him. The twilight was deepening. There was a clear green glow in the sky. Before them stretched the smooth level of field; in the distance was a cluster of haystacks like the huts of a village; the air was very cool and calm and sweet. The landscape might have been an ideal one of peace.

Sarah bent over and touched her husband on one of his thin, sinewy shoulders. "Father!"

The old man's shoulders heaved: he was weeping.

"Why, don't do so, father," said Sarah.

"I'll—put up the—partitions, an'—everything you—want, mother."

Sarah put her apron up to her face; she was overcome by her own triumph.

Adoniram was like a fortress whose walls had no active resistance, and went down the instant the right besieging tools were used. "Why, mother," he said, hoarsely, "I hadn't no idee you was so set on't as all this comes to."

# Charlotte Perkins Gilman

## (1860–1935)

The great-niece of Harriet Beecher Stowe, Charlotte Perkins Gilman is perhaps the seminal American feminist short story writer. "The Yellow Wall-Paper," written shortly after Gilman's 1890 partial recovery from a nervous breakdown (which can now be diagnosed as postpartum psychosis), borrowed stylistically from "women's fiction," or gothic romance, of the time, and was highly autobiographical. Sandra Gilbert and Susan Gubar wrote of the story that "the anxiety-inducing connections between what women writers tend to see as their parallel confinements in texts, houses, and maternal female bodies—Charlotte Perkins Gilman brought them all together in 1890." Gilman published a number of nonfiction works, such as *Women and Economics* (1898) and *The Man-Made World* (1911), arguing that enabling women's financial independence was a crucial step toward improving society as a whole. From 1910 to 1916, she published a periodical called *The Forerunner* to which she herself was the sole contributor of poetry, short stories, editorials, and other articles. In 1935, suffering from cancer, Gilman committed suicide. Gilman's most telling remark about the purpose of her writing may be the one she made upon hearing that the doctor who treated her postpartum depression had changed his methods after reading "The Yellow Wall-Paper": "If that is a fact, I have not lived in vain."

## The Yellow Wall-Paper
1892

It is very seldom that mere ordinary people like John and myself secure ancestral halls for the summer.

A colonial mansion, a hereditary estate, I would say a haunted house, and reach the height of romantic felicity—but that would be asking too much of fate!

Still I will proudly declare that there is something queer about it.

Else, why should it be let so cheaply? And why have stood so long untenanted?

John laughs at me, of course, but one expects that in marriage.

John is practical in the extreme. He has no patience with faith, an intense horror of superstition, and he scoffs openly at any talk of things not to be felt and seen and put down in figures.

John is a physician, and *perhaps*—(I would not say it to a living soul, of course, but this is dead paper and a great relief to my mind)—*perhaps* that is one reason I do not get well faster.

You see he does not believe I am sick!

And what can one do?

If a physician of high standing, and one's own husband, assures friends and relatives that there is really nothing the matter with one but temporary nervous depression—a slight hysterical tendency—what is one to do?

My brother is also a physician, and also of high standing, and he says the same thing.

So I take phosphates or phosphites—whichever it is, and tonics, and journeys, and air, and exercise, and am absolutely forbidden to "work" until I am well again.

Personally, I disagree with their ideas.

Personally, I believe that congenial work, with excitement and change, would do me good.

But what is one to do?

I did write for a while in spite of them; but it *does* exhaust me a good deal—having to be so sly about it, or else meet with heavy opposition.

I sometimes fancy that in my condition if I had less opposition and more society and stimulus—but John says the very worst thing I can do is to think about my condition, and I confess it always makes me feel bad.

So I will let it alone and talk about the house.

The most beautiful place! It is quite alone, standing well back from the road, quite three miles from the village. It makes me think of English places that you read about, for there are hedges and walls and gates that lock, and lots of separate little houses for the gardeners and people.

There is a *delicious* garden! I never saw such a garden—large and shady, full of box-bordered paths, and lined with long grape-covered arbors with seats under them.

There were greenhouses, too, but they are all broken now.

There was some legal trouble, I believe, something about the heirs and coheirs; anyhow, the place has been empty for years.

That spoils my ghostliness, I am afraid, but I don't care—there is something strange about the house—I can feel it.

I even said so to John one moonlight evening, but he said what I felt was a *draught,* and shut the window.

I get unreasonably angry with John sometimes. I'm sure I never used to be so sensitive. I think it is due to this nervous condition.

But John says if I feel so, I shall neglect proper self-control; so I take pains to control myself—before him, at least, and that makes me very tired.

I don't like our room a bit. I wanted one downstairs that opened on the piazza and had roses all over the window, and such pretty old-fashioned chintz hangings! but John would not hear of it.

He said there was only one window and not room for two beds, and no near room for him if he took another.

He is very careful and loving, and hardly lets me stir without special direction.

I have a schedule prescription for each hour in the day; he takes all care from me, and so I feel basely ungrateful not to value it more.

He said we came here solely on my account, that I was to have perfect rest and all the air I could get. "Your exercise depends on your strength, my dear," said he, "and your food somewhat on your appetite; but air you can absorb all the time." So we took the nursery at the top of the house.

It is a big, airy room, the whole floor nearly, with windows that look all ways, and air and sunshine galore. It was nursery first and then playroom and gymnasium, I should judge; for the windows are barred for little children, and there are rings and things in the walls.

The paint and paper look as if a boys' school had used it. It is stripped off—the paper—in great patches all around the head of my bed, about as far as I can reach, and in a great place on the other side of the room low down. I never saw a worse paper in my life.

One of those sprawling flamboyant patterns committing every artistic sin.

It is dull enough to confuse the eye in following, pronounced enough to constantly irritate and provoke study, and when you follow the lame uncertain curves for a little distance they suddenly commit suicide—plunge off at outrageous angles, destroy themselves in unheard of contradictions.

The color is repellent, almost revolting; a smouldering unclean yellow, strangely faded by the slow-turning sunlight.

It is a dull yet lurid orange in some places, a sickly sulphur tint in others.

No wonder the children hated it! I should hate it myself if I had to live in this room long.

There comes John, and I must put this away,—he hates to have me write a word.

We have been here two weeks, and I haven't felt like writing before, since that first day.

I am sitting by the window now, up in this atrocious nursery, and there is nothing to hinder my writing as much as I please, save lack of strength.

John is away all day, and even some nights when his cases are serious.

I am glad my case is not serious!

But these nervous troubles are dreadfully depressing.

John does not know how much I really suffer. He knows there is no *reason* to suffer, and that satisfies him.

Of course it is only nervousness. It does weigh on me so not to do my duty in any way!

I meant to be such a help to John, such a real rest and comfort, and here I am a comparative burden already!

Nobody would believe what an effort it is to do what little I am able,—to dress and entertain, and order things.

It is fortunate Mary is so good with the baby. Such a dear baby!

And yet I *cannot* be with him, it makes me so nervous.

I suppose John never was nervous in his life. He laughs at me so about this wall-paper!

At first he meant to repaper the room, but afterwards he said that I was letting it get the better of me, and that nothing was worse for a nervous patient than to give way to such fancies.

He said that after the wall-paper was changed it would be the heavy bedstead, and then the barred windows, and then that gate at the head of the stairs, and so on.

"You know the place is doing you good," he said, "and really, dear, I don't care to renovate the house just for a three months' rental."

"Then do let us go downstairs," I said, "there are such pretty rooms there."

Then he took me in his arms and called me a blessed little goose, and said he would go down to the cellar, if I wished, and have it whitewashed into the bargain.

But he is right enough about the beds and windows and things.

It is an airy and comfortable room as any one need wish, and, of course, I would not be so silly as to make him uncomfortable just for a whim.

I'm really getting quite fond of the big room, all but that horrid paper.

Out of one window I can see the garden, those mysterious deep-shaded arbors, the riotous old-fashioned flowers, and bushes and gnarly trees.

Out of another I get a lovely view of the bay and a little private wharf belonging to the estate. There is a beautiful shaded lane that runs down there from the house. I always fancy I see people walking in these numerous paths and arbors, but John has cautioned me not to give way to fancy in the least. He says that with my imaginative power and habit of story-making, a nervous weakness like mine is sure to lead to all manner of excited fancies, and that I ought to use my will and good sense to check the tendency. So I try.

I think sometimes that if I were only well enough to write a little it would relieve the press of ideas and rest me.

But I find I get pretty tired when I try.

It is so discouraging not to have any advice and companionship about my work. When I get really well, John says we will ask Cousin Henry and Julia down for a long visit; but he says he would as soon put fireworks in my pillow-case as to let me have those stimulating people about now.

I wish I could get well faster.

But I must not think about that. This paper looks to me as if it *knew* what a vicious influence it had!

There is a recurrent spot where the pattern lolls like a broken neck and two bulbous eyes stare at you upside down.

I get positively angry with the impertinence of it and the everlastingness. Up and down and sideways they crawl, and those absurd, unblinking eyes are everywhere. There is one place where two breadths didn't match, and the eyes go all up and down the line, one a little higher than the other.

I never saw so much expression in an inanimate thing before, and we all know how much expression they have! I used to lie awake as a child and get more entertainment and terror out of blank walls and plain furniture than most children could find in a toy-store.

I remember what a kindly wink the knobs of our big, old bureau used to have, and there was one chair that always seemed like a strong friend.

I used to feel that if any of the other things looked too fierce I could always hop into that chair and be safe.

The furniture in this room is no worse than inharmonious, however, for we had to bring it all from downstairs. I suppose when this was used as a playroom they had to take the nursery things out, and no wonder! I never saw such ravages as the children have made here.

The wall-paper, as I said before, is torn off in spots, and it sticketh closer than a brother—they must have had perseverance as well as hatred.

Then the floor is scratched and gouged and splintered, the plaster itself is dug out here and there, and this great heavy bed which is all we found in the room, looks as if it had been through the wars.

But I don't mind it a bit—only the paper.

There comes John's sister. Such a dear girl as she is, and so careful of me! I must not let her find me writing.

She is a perfect and enthusiastic housekeeper, and hopes for no better profession. I verily believe she thinks it is the writing which made me sick!

But I can write when she is out, and see her a long way off from these windows.

There is one that commands the road, a lovely shaded winding road, and one that just looks off over the country. A lovely country, too, full of great elms and velvet meadows.

This wall-paper has a kind of sub-pattern in a different shade, a particularly irritating one, for you can only see it in certain lights, and not clearly then.

But in the places where it isn't faded and where the sun is just so—I can see a strange, provoking, formless sort of figure, that seems to skulk about behind that silly and conspicuous front design.

There's sister on the stairs!

Well, the Fourth of July is over! The people are all gone and I am tired out. John thought it might do me good to see a little company, so we just had mother and Nellie and the children down for a week.

Of course I didn't do a thing. Jennie sees to everything now.

But it tired me all the same.

John says if I don't pick up faster he shall send me to Weir Mitchell[1] in the fall.

But I don't want to go there at all. I had a friend who was in his hands once, and she says he is just like John and my brother, only more so!

Besides, it is such an undertaking to go so far.

I don't feel as if it was worth while to turn my hand over for anything, and I'm getting dreadfully fretful and querulous.

I cry at nothing, and cry most of the time.

Of course I don't when John is here, or anybody else, but when I am alone.

And I am alone a good deal just now. John is kept in town very often by serious cases, and Jennie is good and lets me alone when I want her to.

So I walk a little in the garden or down that lovely lane, sit on the porch under the roses, and lie down up here a good deal.

I'm getting really fond of the room in spite of the wall-paper. Perhaps *because* of the wall-paper.

It dwells in my mind so!

I lie here on this great immovable bed—it is nailed down, I believe—and follow that pattern about by the hour. It is as good as gymnastics, I assure you. I start, we'll say, at the bottom, down in the corner over there where it has not been touched, and I determine for the thousandth time that I *will* follow that pointless pattern to some sort of a conclusion.

I know a little of the principle of design, and I know this thing was not arranged

---

1 **Weir Mitchell:** Dr. Silas Weir Mitchell (1829–1914), American physician known for prescribing the "rest cure."

on any laws of radiation, or alternation, or repetition, or symmetry, or anything else that I ever heard of.

It is repeated, of course, by the breadths, but not otherwise.

Looked at in one way each breadth stands alone, the bloated curves and flourishes—a kind of "debased Romanesque"[2] with *delirium tremens*—go waddling up and down in isolated columns of fatuity.

But, on the other hand, they connect diagonally, and the sprawling outlines run off in great slanting waves of optic horror, like a lot of wallowing seaweeds in full chase.

The whole thing goes horizontally, too, at least it seems so, and I exhaust myself in trying to distinguish the order of its going in that direction.

They have used a horizontal breadth for a frieze,[3] and that adds wonderfully to the confusion.

There is one end of the room where it is almost intact, and there, when the crosslights fade and the low sun shines directly upon it, I can almost fancy radiation after all,—the interminable grotesques seem to form around a common centre and rush off in headlong plunges of equal distraction.

It makes me tired to follow it. I will take a nap I guess.

I don't know why I should write this.

I don't want to.

I don't feel able.

And I know John would think it absurd. But I *must* say what I feel and think in some way—it is such a relief!

But the effort is getting to be greater than the relief.

Half the time now I am awfully lazy, and lie down ever so much.

John says I mustn't lose my strength, and has me take cod liver oil and lots of tonics and things, to say nothing of ale and wine and rare meat.

Dear John! He loves me very dearly, and hates to have me sick. I tried to have a real earnest reasonable talk with him the other day, and tell him how I wish he would let me go and make a visit to Cousin Henry and Julia.

But he said I wasn't able to go, nor able to stand it after I got there; and I did not make out a very good case for myself, for I was crying before I had finished.

It is getting to be a great effort for me to think straight. Just this nervous weakness I suppose.

And dear John gathered me up in his arms, and just carried me upstairs and laid me on the bed, and sat by me and read to me till it tired my head.

He said I was his darling and his comfort and all he had, and that I must take care of myself for his sake, and keep well.

He says no one but myself can help me out of it, that I must use my will and self-control and not let any silly fancies run away with me.

There's one comfort, the baby is well and happy, and does not have to occupy this nursery with the horrid wall-paper.

---

2 **Romanesque:** A style of European architecture containing Roman and Byzantine elements. Known mostly for its profuse ornamentation.

3 **frieze:** A decorative horizontal band along the upper part of a wall in a room.

If we had not used it, that blessed child would have! What a fortunate escape! Why, I wouldn't have a child of mine, an impressionable little thing, live in such a room for worlds.

I never thought of it before, but it is lucky that John kept me here after all, I can stand it so much easier than a baby, you see.

Of course I never mention it to them any more—I am too wise,—but I keep watch of it all the same.

There are things in that paper that nobody knows but me, or ever will.

Behind that outside pattern the dim shapes get clearer every day.

It is always the same shape, only very numerous.

And it is like a woman stooping down and creeping about behind that pattern. I don't like it a bit. I wonder—I begin to think—I wish John would take me away from here!

It is so hard to talk with John about my case, because he is so wise, and because he loves me so.

But I tried it last night.

It was moonlight. The moon shines in all around just as the sun does.

I hate to see it sometimes, it creeps so slowly, and always comes in by one window or another.

John was asleep and I hated to waken him, so I kept still and watched the moonlight on that undulating wall-paper till I felt creepy.

The faint figure behind seemed to shake the pattern, just as if she wanted to get out.

I got up softly and went to feel and see if the paper *did* move, and when I came back John was awake.

"What is it, little girl?" he said. "Don't go walking about like that—you'll get cold."

I thought it was a good time to talk, so I told him that I really was not gaining here, and that I wished he would take me away.

"Why darling!" said he, "our lease will be up in three weeks, and I can't see how to leave before.

"The repairs are not done at home, and I cannot possibly leave town just now. Of course if you were in any danger, I could and would, but you really are better, dear, whether you can see it or not. I am a doctor, dear, and I know. You are gaining flesh and color, your appetite is better, I feel really much easier about you."

"I don't weigh a bit more," said I, "nor as much; and my appetite may be better in the evening when you are here, but it is worse in the morning when you are away!"

"Bless her little heart!" said he with a big hug, "she shall be as sick as she pleases! But now let's improve the shining hours by going to sleep, and talk about it in the morning!"

"And you won't go away?" I asked gloomily.

"Why, how can I, dear? It is only three weeks more and then we will take a nice little trip of a few days while Jennie is getting the house ready. Really dear you are better!"

"Better in body perhaps—" I began, and stopped short, for he sat up straight and looked at me with such a stern, reproachful look that I could not say another word.

"My darling," said he, "I beg of you, for my sake and for our child's sake, as well as for your own, that you will never for one instant let that idea enter your mind! There is nothing so dangerous, so fascinating, to a temperament like yours. It is a false and foolish fancy. Can you not trust me as a physician when I tell you so?"

So of course I said no more on that score, and we went to sleep before long. He thought I was asleep first, but I wasn't, and lay there for hours trying to decide whether that front pattern and the back pattern really did move together or separately.

On a pattern like this, by daylight, there is a lack of sequence, a defiance of law, that is a constant irritant to a normal mind.

The color is hideous enough, and unreliable enough, and infuriating enough, but the pattern is torturing.

You think you have mastered it, but just as you get well underway in following, it turns a back-somersault and there you are. It slaps you in the face, knocks you down, and tramples upon you. It is like a bad dream.

The outside pattern is a florid arabesque, reminding one of a fungus. If you can imagine a toadstool in joints, an interminable string of toadstools, budding and sprouting in endless convolutions—why, that is something like it.

That is, sometimes!

There is one marked peculiarity about this paper, a thing nobody seems to notice but myself, and that is that it changes as the light changes.

When the sun shoots in through the east window—I always watch for that first long, straight ray—it changes so quickly that I never can quite believe it.

That is why I watch it always.

By moonlight—the moon shines in all night when there is a moon—I wouldn't know it was the same paper.

At night in any kind of light, in twilight, candle light, lamplight, and worst of all by moonlight, it becomes bars! The outside pattern I mean, and the woman behind it is as plain as can be.

I didn't realize for a long time what the thing was that showed behind, that dim sub-pattern, but now I am quite sure it is a woman.

By daylight she is subdued, quiet. I fancy it is the pattern that keeps her so still. It is so puzzling. It keeps me quiet by the hour.

I lie down ever so much now. John says it is good for me, and to sleep all I can.

Indeed he started the habit by making me lie down for an hour after each meal.

It is a very bad habit I am convinced, for you see I don't sleep.

And that cultivates deceit, for I don't tell them I'm awake—O no!

The fact is I am getting a little afraid of John.

He seems very queer sometimes, and even Jennie has an inexplicable look.

It strikes me occasionally, just as a scientific hypothesis,—that perhaps it is the paper!

I have watched John when he did not know I was looking, and come into the room suddenly on the most innocent excuses, and I've caught him several times *looking at the paper!* And Jennie too. I caught Jennie with her hand on it once.

She didn't know I was in the room, and when I asked her in a quiet, a very quiet voice, with the most restrained manner possible, what she was doing with the paper—she turned around as if she had been caught stealing, and looked quite angry—asked me why I should frighten her so!

Then she said that the paper stained everything it touched, that she had found yellow smooches on all my clothes and John's, and she wished we would be more careful!

Did not that sound innocent? But I know she was studying that pattern, and I am determined that nobody shall find it out but myself!

Life is very much more exciting now than it used to be. You see I have something more to expect, to look forward to, to watch. I really do eat better, and am more quiet than I was.

John is so pleased to see me improve! He laughed a little the other day, and said I seemed to be flourishing in spite of my wall-paper.

I turned it off with a laugh. I had no intention of telling him it was *because* of the wall-paper—he would make fun of me. He might even want to take me away.

I don't want to leave now until I have found it out. There is a week more, and I think that will be enough.

I'm feeling ever so much better! I don't sleep much at night, for it is so interesting to watch developments; but I sleep a good deal in the daytime.

In the daytime it is tiresome and perplexing.

There are always new shoots on the fungus, and new shades of yellow all over it. I cannot keep count of them, though I have tried conscientiously.

It is the strangest yellow, that wall-paper! It makes me think of all the yellow things I ever saw—not beautiful ones like buttercups, but old foul, bad yellow things.

But there is something else about that paper—the smell! I noticed it the moment we came into the room, but with so much air and sun it was not bad. Now we have had a week of fog and rain, and whether the windows are open or not, the smell is here.

It creeps all over the house.

I find it hovering in the dining-room, skulking in the parlor, hiding in the hall, lying in wait for me on the stairs.

It gets into my hair.

Even when I go to ride, if I turn my head suddenly and surprise it—there is that smell!

Such a peculiar odor, too! I have spent hours in trying to analyze it, to find what it smelled like.

It is not bad—at first, and very gentle, but quite the subtlest, most enduring odor I ever met.

In this damp weather it is awful, I wake up in the night and find it hanging over me.

It used to disturb me at first. I thought seriously of burning the house—to reach the smell.

But now I am used to it. The only thing I can think of that it is like is the *color* of the paper! A yellow smell.

There is a very funny mark on this wall, low down, near the mopboard. A streak that runs round the room. It goes behind every piece of furniture, except the bed, a long, straight, even *smooch,* as if it had been rubbed over and over.

I wonder how it was done and who did it, and what they did it for. Round and round and round—round and round and round—it makes me dizzy!

I really have discovered something at last.

Through watching so much at night, when it changes so, I have finally found out.

The front pattern *does* move—and no wonder! The woman behind shakes it!

Sometimes I think there are a great many women behind, and sometimes only one, and she crawls around fast, and her crawling shakes it all over.

Then in the very bright spots she keeps still, and in the very shady spots she just takes hold of the bars and shakes them hard.

And she is all the time trying to climb through. But nobody could climb through that pattern—it strangles so; I think that is why it has so many heads.

They get through, and then the pattern strangles them off and turns them upside down, and makes their eyes white!

If those heads were covered or taken off it would not be half so bad.

I think that woman gets out in the daytime!

And I'll tell you why—privately—I've seen her!

I can see her out of every one of my windows!

It is the same woman, I know, for she is always creeping, and most women do not creep by daylight.

I see her on that long road under the trees, creeping along, and when a carriage comes she hides under the blackberry vines.

I don't blame her a bit. It must be very humiliating to be caught creeping by daylight!

I always lock the door when I creep by daylight. I can't do it at night, for I know John would suspect something at once.

And John is so queer now, that I don't want to irritate him. I wish he would take another room! Besides, I don't want anybody to get that woman out at night but myself.

I often wonder if I could see her out of all the windows at once.

But, turn as fast as I can, I can only see out of one at one time.

And though I always see her, she *may* be able to creep faster than I can turn!

I have watched her sometimes away off in the open country, creeping as fast as a cloud shadow in a high wind.

If only that top pattern could be gotten off from the under one! I mean to try it, little by little.

I have found out another funny thing, but I shan't tell it this time! It does not do to trust people too much.

There are only two more days to get this paper off, and I believe John is beginning to notice. I don't like the look in his eyes.

And I heard him ask Jennie a lot of professional questions about me. She had a very good report to give.

She said I slept a good deal in the daytime.

John knows I don't sleep very well at night, for all I'm so quiet!

He asked me all sorts of questions, too, and pretended to be very loving and kind.

As if I couldn't see through him!

Still, I don't wonder he acts so, sleeping under this paper for three months.

It only interests me, but I feel sure John and Jennie are secretly affected by it.

Hurrah! This is the last day, but it is enough. John is to stay in town over night, and won't be out until this evening.

Jennie wanted to sleep with me—the sly thing! but I told her I should undoubtedly rest better for a night all alone.

That was clever, for really I wasn't alone a bit! As soon as it was moonlight and that poor thing began to crawl and shake the pattern, I got up and ran to help her.

I pulled and she shook, I shook and she pulled, and before morning we had peeled off yards of that paper.

A strip about as high as my head and half around the room.

And then when the sun came and that awful pattern began to laugh at me, I declared I would finish it to-day!

We go away to-morrow, and they are moving all my furniture down again to leave things as they were before.

Jennie looked at the wall in amazement, but I told her merrily that I did it out of pure spite at the vicious thing.

She laughed and said she wouldn't mind doing it herself, but I must not get tired.

How she betrayed herself that time!

But I am here, and no person touches this paper but me,—not *alive!*

She tried to get me out of the room—it was too patent! But I said it was so quiet and empty and clean now that I believed I would lie down again and sleep all I could; and not to wake me even for dinner—I would call when I woke.

So now she is gone, and the servants are gone, and the things are gone, and there is nothing left but that great bedstead nailed down, with the canvas mattress we found on it.

We shall sleep downstairs to-night, and take the boat home to-morrow.

I quite enjoy the room, now it is bare again.

How those children did tear about here!

This bedstead is fairly gnawed!

But I must get to work.

I have locked the door and thrown the key down into the front path.

I don't want to go out, and I don't want to have anybody come in, till John comes.

I want to astonish him.

I've got a rope up here that even Jennie did not find. If that woman does get out, and tries to get away, I can tie her!

But I forgot I could not reach far without anything to stand on!

This bed will *not* move!

I tried to lift and push it until I was lame, and then I got so angry I bit off a little piece at one corner—but it hurt my teeth.

Then I peeled off all the paper I could reach standing on the floor. It sticks horribly and the pattern just enjoys it! All those strangled heads and bulbous eyes and waddling fungus growths just shriek with derision!

I am getting angry enough to do something desperate. To jump out of the window would be admirable exercise, but the bars are too strong even to try.

Besides I wouldn't do it. Of course not. I know well enough that a step like that is improper and might be misconstrued.

I don't like to *look* out of the windows even—there are so many of those creeping women, and they creep so fast.

I wonder if they all come out of that wall-paper as I did?

But I am securely fastened now by my well-hidden rope—you don't get *me* out in the road there!

I suppose I shall have to get back behind the pattern when it comes night, and that is hard!

It is so pleasant to be out in this great room and creep around as I please!

I don't want to go outside. I won't, even if Jennie asks me to.

For outside you have to creep on the ground, and everything is green instead of yellow.

But here I can creep smoothly on the floor, and my shoulder just fits in that long smooch around the wall, so I cannot lose my way.

Why there's John at the door!

It is no use, young man, you can't open it!

How he does call and pound!

Now he's crying for an axe.

It would be a shame to break down that beautiful door!

"John dear!" said I in the gentlest voice, "the key is down by the front steps, under a plantain leaf!"

That silenced him for a few moments.

Then he said—very quietly indeed, "Open the door, my darling!"

"I can't," said I. "The key is down by the front door under a plantain leaf!"

And then I said it again, several times, very gently and slowly, and said it so often that he had to go and see, and he got it of course, and came in. He stopped short by the door.

"What is the matter?" he cried. "For God's sake, what are you doing!"

I kept on creeping just the same, but I looked at him over my shoulder.

"I've got out at last," said I, "in spite of you and Jane. And I've pulled off most of the paper, so you can't put me back!"

Now why should that man have fainted? But he did, and right across my path by the wall, so that I had to creep over him every time!

# Martha J. Cutter

## Frontiers of Language: Engendering Discourse in "The Revolt of 'Mother'"

Sarah Penn, the heroine of Mary E. Wilkins Freeman's well-known short story "The Revolt of 'Mother,'" wants a comfortable home for her family.[1] But her husband, although well off, insists on building more barns and buying more cattle, thereby confining his family to their meager, run-down hovel of a home. So while Father is away, Sarah takes control of the situation, subverting her husband's intentions by moving her family and all their possessions into Father's newest barn. When Father returns, Sarah tells him: "we've come here to live, an' we're goin' to live here. We've got jest as good a right here as new horses an' cows."[2] And Father tearfully agrees.

On the surface, this domestic drama may seem comic, and indeed some critics have called it funny.[3] Behind this folksy humor, however, there is a serious subtext. Sarah Penn is forced repeatedly to understand her powerless status, a status that stems from her position in a patriarchal, frontier society more oriented towards animals than people, a society that through its focus on conquest and colonization often excludes feminine values. Yet Sarah Penn lacks more than just a home for her family, more than just a place to maintain what Carol Gilligan would call a web of relationship between individuals.[4] Sarah Penn also lacks a language; she cannot become a speaking subject. The story shows language to be patriarchal, and it illustrates that women, marginalized by frontier values, are also marginalized in this other sense: they cannot speak; they are excluded from a discourse that is patriarchal in intent and meaning. The story, then, in many ways, is not about actual frontier values; it is not about whether people or animals, nurturing or conquering, are more important. The real focus of the story is Sarah Penn's struggle to redefine a linguistic frontier which has excluded her as a speaking subject. In order to escape from the binary system of silent women/speaking men which entraps her, she must engender a new linguistic

1 A version of this paper was presented at the Tufts University Conference on "Frontiers and Literature" in October 1989. My thanks to Professor Ellen Rooney of Brown University for her comments on an earlier draft of this essay.

2 "The Revolt of 'Mother,'" in *A New England Nun and Other Stories* (New York: Harper, 1891), p. 467. All page numbers will be cited parenthetically.

3 See, for example, Charles Miner Thompson's statement that "The Revolt of 'Mother,'" is "the most distinctly humorous of [Freeman's] stories" (p. 668) in "Miss Wilkins: An Idealist in Masquerade," *Atlantic Monthly,* 83 (1899), 665–75. But for alternative views of the story's "comic" quality, see Alice Glarden Brand, "Mary Wilkins Freeman: Misanthropy as Propaganda," *New England Quarterly,* 50 (1977), 91; or Victoria Aarons, "A Community of Women: Surviving Marriage in the Wilderness," in *Portraits of Marriage in Literature,* ed. Anne Hargrove and Maurine Magliocco (Macomb: Western Illinois Univ. Press, 1984), p. 143.

4 See *In a Different Voice: Psychological Theory and Women's Development* (Cambridge: Harvard Univ. Press, 1982).

frontier which merges the conflicting value systems of Father's and Mother's frontiers through a radical restructuring of the process of signification itself.

Recently, criticism of Freeman's writing has focused on her portrayal of women characters whose choices of autonomy and self-definition can be interpreted using feminist paradigms.[5] An example of this is Sarah Penn who, according to Marjorie Pryse, "establishes domestic power and vision as a countervailing force to the theme of flight from domesticity that appears throughout nineteenth-century fiction."[6] In Freeman's fiction, however, domestic power and vision are intertwined with the issue of language. Men and women do have differing visions of the worlds they inhabit; as Mother says of Father to her daughter Nanny, "He can't help it, 'cause he don't look at things jest the way we do" (p. 452). And yet, it is not this literal difference of world vision that "The Revolt of 'Mother'" seeks to exploit. Rather, what Freeman indicates is that when these two frontiers clash a new linguistic frontier must be created or engendered in order to make communication possible.

To understand why communication fails, however, we must begin by examining the different psychological orientations which Mother's and Father's visions of the frontier reveal. Father values building barns, but what does this mean in terms of his view of the frontier and of the world itself? From the outset, Father's vision seems peculiarly overdetermined; the story emphasizes that he already has more than enough barns, more than enough cows, to provide an adequate source of income for his family. As Mother says: "You've built sheds an' cow-houses an' one new barn, an' now you're goin' to build another. . . . You're lodgin' your dumb beasts better than you are your own flesh an' blood. I want to know if you think it's right" (p. 457). To Mother's question, Father's "response" is only, "I ain't got nothin' to say"—a non-response he repeats three times in rapid succession when Mother asks him about the purpose of the new barn:

> "I want to know what you're buildin' that new barn for, father?"
> "I ain't got nothin' to say about it."
> "It can't be you think you need another barn?"
> "I tell ye I ain't got nothin' to say about it, mother; an' I ain't goin' to say nothin'"
> (p. 455).

Father will not explain his reasons for building the new barn. Father is concerned only with making more money for the sake of the money itself. Like the logic of his speech, his version of capitalism is peculiarly circular: he translates the wilderness into cattle, the cattle into money, and then the money into more barns to house more cattle.

---

5 Feminist analysis of Freeman's works have recently been provided by, among others, Leah Blatt Glasser's "Mary E. Wilkins Freeman: The Stranger in the Mirror," *Massachusetts Review*, 25 (1984), 323–39; and Barbara John's "'Love Cracked': Spinsters as Subversives in 'Anna Malann,' 'Christmas Jenny,' and 'An Object of Love,'" *Colby Library Quarterly*, 23 (1987), 4–15. No critics, however, have applied feminist theories about language to "The Revolt of 'Mother,'" although Victoria Aarons does briefly mention the story's linguistic battle (pp. 143–44).

6 *Selected Stories of Mary E. Wilkins Freeman*, ed. Marjorie Pryse (New York: Norton, 1983), pp. viii–ix.

Father's main symbol of success is his barn, and it is in opposition to the symbolic realm of the barn that Mother counterpoises the actual and symbolic realm of the home. Mother values the home not as a symbol of wealth or social status but rather as a place in which the generation and regeneration of human life can occur. The Penns' daughter Nanny is engaged, and Sarah believes that her daughter will not be able to live with the Penns after her marriage unless the Penns live in a larger house. Mother is concerned partially because she wants to keep her small, limited community together. But, more important, Sarah also believes Nanny's life to be threatened: "She wa'n't ever strong. She's got considerable color, but there wa'n't never any backbone to her. I've always took the heft of everything off her, an' she ain't fit to keep house an' do everything herself. She'll be all worn out inside of a year. . . . I can't have it so, noways, father" (p. 457). Sarah has endured the psychic restriction of her box of a house for forty years, but with Nanny's upcoming marriage the need for the new house becomes dire.[7] Without the new house, Nanny's life may not continue.

As Alice Glarden Brand has argued, "The Revolt of 'Mother'" indicates distinctly gendered priorities: "By contrasting father as antagonist with mother as protagonist, Freeman points to [skewed] priorities; father's are for animals; mother's are for the human and relational."[8] These different priorities may be related to socialization practices described by nineteenth-century historians. For example, children's books from this time period taught young boys to value competition, material success, and achievement, whereas young girls were taught to value cooperation and relationships.[9] We can perhaps trace the different psychological profiles depicted by Freeman to such gendered socialization practices, practices which encouraged nineteenth-century women to be oriented towards the relational and the personal.[10] Mother clearly does demonstrate the affiliation motivation, centering her concept of morality on preserving human relationships in the family. Father is more interested in achievement, in getting ahead, in becoming wealthy and materially successful. Across and against these gender differences, Mother must find a way to communicate her values to Father.

However, ordinary language does not provide Sarah Penn with a tool for communication, since patriarchal discourse systematically excludes women as speakers. We do not need Lacan's idea that the Name-of-the-Father acts as a linguistic enforcement of patriarchy to see patriarchal discourse at work in Freeman's fiction. In Freeman's "The Revolt of 'Mother'" we have, literally, the name of the father—"Father"

7 For more about the relationship between psychic and spatial defiance, see Marilyn Davis DeEulis, "'Her Box of a House': Spatial Restriction as Psychic Signpost in Mary Wilkins Freeman's 'The Revolt of 'Mother,'" *Markham Review,* 8 (1979), 51–52.

8 See "Mary Wilkins Freeman: Misanthropy as Propaganda," p. 91.

9 Nancy Cott describes these books in *The Bonds of Womanhood: "Woman's Sphere" in New England, 1780–1835* (New Haven: Yale Univ. Press, 1977), p. 72, as does Bernard Wishy in *The Child and The Republic* (Philadelphia: Univ. of Pennsylvania Press, 1968), pp. 57–58.

10 Nineteenth-century historians have extensively documented women's relational psychological orientation. See, for example, Cott, pp. 71–72; or Carroll Smith-Rosenberg, "The Female World of Love and Ritual: Relations Between Women in Nineteenth-Century America," *Disorderly Conduct: Visions of Gender in Victorian America* (New York: Oxford Univ. Press, 1985), pp. 53–76.

who controls the discourse of the family, who jealously and vigorously guards control of language so that "there was never much conversation at the table in the Penn family. Adoniram asked a blessing, and they ate promptly, then rose up and went about their work" (pp. 453–54). This description of the family's daily dining habits makes clear that Father is the only one allowed to speak on any sort of regular basis, and it also makes clear Father's habitually rigid and miserly control over the flow of conversation. Similarly, Father can refuse to speak, if he wants, as he repeatedly does at the opening of the story: "The old man said not another word" (p. 449), "he shut his mouth tight," "He ran his words together, and his speech was almost as inarticulate as a growl" (p. 448). Through his words, Father can order that more barns be built, for he controls not only language but also commerce and commercial power; and yet he also frequently refuses to answer even the most simple question. Furthermore, he never has to explain himself; he merely does what he wants and responds when questioned about his actions: "I ain't got nothin' to say" (which he says repeatedly throughout the story).

It should be emphasized that though Adoniram Penn is terse, his terseness comes from a linguistic control, a repression of discourse, rather than the inability to speak. Father's mouth, literally, becomes full with the discourse he is repressing so that "there was a sudden dropping and *enlarging* of the lower part of the old man's face, as if some heavy weight had settled therein; he shut his mouth tight" (p. 448, my emphasis). Father's refusal to speak, then, comes not from a lack of speech but rather is a deliberate act of volition, a deliberate repression of speech, and it is part of the stranglehold he keeps on language: "he shut his mouth tight, and went on harnessing the great bay mare. He hustled the collar on to her neck with a jerk" (p. 448). It is no coincidence that Father is harnessing an old mare, that he is hustling a collar onto her neck with force. Adoniram treats his wife like a dumb beast, in refusing to engage in any meaningful discourse with her, and he treats the dumb beast like his wife, in collaring, jerking, forcibly repressing any power the mare might have.

Worse yet, Adoniram has taught his son Sammy to behave in like manner with discourse—to guard it jealously and to refuse women's access to it. The story thus shows a distinctly gendered pattern of discourse. According to this pattern, Sarah and her daughter Nanny question the men but are not allowed to engage in discourse; and the men—Sammy and Adoniram—carefully guard access to the citadel of power and knowledge: language. Even specific topics of conversation are replicated in this gendered, generational pattern. For example, Sammy and Nanny have a conversation about the new barn which replicates Sarah and Adoniram's earlier conversation about the same subject. When Nanny asks whether Sammy knew about the barn, Sammy does not answer, only continuing to comb his hair assiduously. When questioned again, Sammy turns, showing "a face like his father's" and responds "reluctantly" and tersely, "Yes, I s'pose I did" (p. 450). Like his father, Sammy will only reluctantly and sporadically give information to females, and he will barely agree to engage in discourse with them at all. No wonder he has "a face like his father's." Both literally and symbolically, he replicates the old man, the Father.

Sammy and Adoniram's commitment to repressing female discourse, and to denying women's right to subjectivity, is crucial to their own patriarchal status. For, as Luce Irigaray has argued, representation and discourse are irremediably founded on the repression of women's subjectivity: "Subjectivity denied to woman: indisputably this provides the financial backing for every irreducible constitution as an object: of representation, of discourse, of desire. Once imagine that woman imagines and the object loses its fixed, obsessional character. As a bench mark that is ultimately more crucial than the subject, for he can sustain himself only by bouncing back off some objectiveness, some objective."[11] Denial of subjectivity to Nanny and Mother is crucial to Sammy and Adoniram's power over them. The men guard speech and knowledge jealously, sharing it with each other but only reluctantly allowing women to possess any knowledge. Sammy, it seems, has known about Father's proposed new barn for three months; but he has kept this information from his mother since he "didn't think 'twould do no good" to tell her (p. 450).

And indeed, it might not; Sarah is locked out of language and power, and to change this status would be difficult. But Sarah does try to empower herself. She takes the key to the citadel—language—and attempts to unlock the door to change. Sarah does something she has not done before; as she says: "I'm goin' to talk real plain to you; I never have sence I married you, but I'm goin' to now. I ain't never complained, an' I ain't goin' to complain now, but I'm goin' to talk plain" (p. 455). Sarah, further, adopts male discourse; she "pleaded her little cause like a Webster; she . . . ranged from severity to pathos" (p. 457).[12] Yet in adopting a male discourse pattern, in adopting male models like Daniel Webster and plain speech, she falls into patriarchal discourse. And this ultimately renders her silent. As Adrienne Munich explains, "discourse—linear, logical and theoretical—is masculine. When women speak, therefore, they cannot help but enter male-dominated discourse; speaking women are silent as women."[13] And indeed, it is as if all of Sarah's eloquence is silent, unheard; Adoniram merely responds "I ain't got nothin' to say" (p. 457) and goes out to get a load of gravel. In assuming that she can speak like a man, Sarah presents no challenge to Father's rule, for Father knows very well that she is not a man. Sarah does not enunciate or initiate a challenge to Father's structuring of the universe; instead she merely reflects the pattern of male dominance since, as Stephen Heath has argued, "any discourse which fails to take account of the problem of sexual difference in its enunciation and address will be, within a patriarchal order, precisely indifferent, a reflection of male domination."[14] Father is indifferent to Sarah's plea because the plea, itself, is indifferent, undifferent, undifferentiated; it fails to take account of sexual difference.

Mother's fall into patriarchal discourse ultimately only serves to reinscribe her silent and powerless status, a status she acknowledges earlier in the story when she

---

11  Luce Irigaray, *Speculum of the Other Woman,* trans. Gillian C. Gill (Ithaca: Cornell Univ. Press, 1985) p. 133.

12  DeEulis has also noted that Sarah Penn adopts masculine discourse (p. 52), but seems to suggest that it is Sarah's adoption of the role of masculine speaker which creates change.

13  "Notorious signs, feminist criticism and literary tradition," in *Making a Difference: Feminist Literary Criticism,* ed. Gayle Greene and Coppélia Kahn (New York: Routledge, 1985), p. 239.

14  Stephen Heath, "Difference," *Screen,* 19 (1978), 53.

disparagingly tells her daughter "You ain't found out yet we're women-folks. . . . One of these days you'll find it out, an' then you'll know that we know only what men-folks think we do, so far as any use of it goes" (p. 451). When Sarah tries to be a speaking subject, to adopt male discourse, she fails, since, as Irigaray argues, "any theory of the subject has always been appropriated by the 'masculine.' " Sarah momentarily loses touch with her female focus and loses, in Irigaray's terms, "the specificity of her own relationship to the imaginary."[15] Sarah's access into patriarchal discourse, then, is a fall into powerlessness, defeatism, and a loss of the imaginary. Denying the validity of her own knowledge, of her own relationship with the world and with the imaginary, Mother momentarily reverts to the belief that women know "only what men-folks think we do."

Interestingly, Sarah makes this disparaging statement about men to her daughter when Nanny herself will soon become a part of the institution of marriage. This overt criticism of marriage and men may reflect Sarah Penn's understanding of marriage as a constricting patriarchal institution which denies women subjectivity. For marriage, in and of itself, is also a structure of patriarchy, as Nelly Furman argues: "Marriage produces a single social unit wherein differences among individuals are seemingly dissolved under one name, the name of the father. Thus . . . we cannot escape the structure it imposes, the patriarchal society it sustains."[16] Nanny, of course, believes that her fiancé is different from all other men and that her marriage will not be a part of the patriarchy; as she says in response to her mother's remarks, "I don't care; I don't believe George is anything like that, anyhow" (p. 452). Sarah's response reflects the mother's knowledge of the omnipresence of the patriarchy: "You wait an' see. I guess George Eastman ain't no better than other men."

Mother's inability to communicate, then, stems from her inscription within the patriarchal institutions of marriage and discourse. And yet, the problem may lie even deeper than this, in the fact that her signification system itself is different from Father's. To Father, value resides in money, commerce, and getting ahead, and all this is symbolized by one thing for him: barns. Father's transcendental signifier is figured forth by "Barn," and by all that "Barn" represents to him. To Mother, however, value resides in people, family, generativity—all of the values symbolized for her by the transcendental signifier "Home." For both Mother and Father, value resides in different spatial locations and in different symbolic realms or registers. No wonder Mother cannot convey her meaning to Father. It is not just that he does not understand what she values but that the terms of her value equation themselves are different; Mother's and Father's linguistic universes are structured around entirely opposed and mutually inaccessible notions of value. And Mother has no way into Father's universe of signification.

But, if there is a language of "The Father" in this story, there is also a language of "The Mother." It is not a fall into patriarchal discourse but rather a language of the

---

15  *Speculum*, p. 133.
16  "The politics of language: beyond the gender principle?" in *Making a Difference: Feminist Literary Criticism*, p. 76. Much of my thinking about language and gender has been influenced by this article.

mother that reenacts and revises the garden of Eden typology in feminine terms. For feminist critics like Josephine Donovan, Freeman's world presents only two options for female characters: "either they may remain in the prepatriarchal world of the Mother (the world of nature), which means they remain silent, or they enter the patriarchal world of language (culture) and are forced to submit to its misogynist exigencies." So, Freeman's women, if we agree with this line of reasoning, have only two alternatives: silence or capitulation.[17] I would argue, however, that Freeman tries to elude this binary system of male/female discourse, of speaking men/silent women, of oedipal discourse/pre-oedipal silence. Through actions which speak, through spatial reinscription, and through a renaming of objects, Mother revises, reassigns, the fundamental oppositions which structure her and Father's systems of signification, thereby developing a system of discourse in which she can be a speaking subject.

Since Mother cannot tell Father what it is that she wants, she creates a "language"—a system of signs—based on interpretable actions, actions which can function as words, actions which speak. She moves the house into the barn, she empties "all their little household goods into the new barn" (p. 463). She dumps all the "value" of "Home" into "Barn," and she thereby takes an action which indicates that to her "Home" is as important, if not more important, than "Barn." And Adoniram finally understands; where words cannot communicate, gestures succeed. Seeing Sarah's action, Adoniram says: "Why, mother . . . I hadn't no idee you was so set on't as all this comes to" (p. 468). Mother finds an action, in short, which can speak louder than words but which can also *be* words. She takes an action that speaks, a speaking action, an action which communicates to Father "all this comes to." Mother creates a sort of sign language in which actions speak as words and bridge the gap between different systems of signification.

Second, Sarah also uses space itself as a communicative tool. She thus creates a physical expression of her system of value. Mother manages to speak to her husband by co-opting his "barnyard" terminology. Thus, where Father sees "box-stalls," Mother sees "better bedrooms than the one she had occupied for forty years" (p. 463); where Father had planned to have a harness room, Mother "would make a kitchen of her dreams." She physically co-opts the space and plan for his new barn: "Sarah looked at the row of stanchions before the allotted space for cows, and reflected that she would have her front entry there." Ultimately, it is Sarah's architectural design for the barn as home, not Adoniram's plan for the barn as barn, that is enforced by the story's ending and that reduces Father to tears: " . . . after supper he went out, and sat down on the step of the smaller door at the right of the barn, through which he had meant his Jerseys to pass in stately file, but which Sarah *designed* for her front house door, and he leaned his head on his hands" (p. 468, my emphasis). By architecturally redesigning the barn so that it is a home, Sarah imposes the muted culture of the home onto, and over, the dominant culture of the barn. In spatially and physically

17 "Silence or Capitulation: Prepatriarchal 'Mothers' Gardens' in Jewett and Freeman," *Studies in Short Fiction*, 23 (1986), 44. Although Donovan applies these terms only to Freeman's "Evelina's Garden," her analysis of the linguistic issues in Freeman's work has greatly clarified my thinking on this subject.

imposing this muted feminine realm onto the previously dominant masculine sphere of the barn, Sarah forces Adoniram, quite literally, to see houses where he has previously seen only barns. And it is this change in vision, in envisioning, that causes Father to weep but that finally allows him to understand what it is that Sarah really wants. Father finally stammers out: "I'll—put up the—partitions, an'—everything you—want, mother."

Finally, Mother also achieves a radical renaming that underscores the arbitrary nature of naming itself. Sarah, like Adam in the Garden of Eden, points and names. Adam, pointing to a green growing thing, said "Tree," and so it became a tree. Sarah, pointing to a barn says "Home," and so it becomes a home. But Sarah's action is more complex than this; where Adam sees one tree, with one name, Sarah sees something that has been called "Barn" and renames it as its opposite: "Home." This revolutionary linguistic act emphasizes the arbitrary nature of signification itself and also seeks to undermine the fundamental oppositions which Father has used to structure his system of discourse, as well as his entire universe. In breaking the established pattern of discourse, Sarah undermines, breaches, the Law-of-the-Father, disrupting patriarchy itself, for as Nelly Furman explains: "a linguistic intervention which ruptures accepted (acceptable) discursive practices reverts us to the constitution of the social subject which is predicated on the repression of the maternal. Through disruption of the symbolic function of language, we are able to give expression to the repressed, or to detect traces of repression, but in so doing we are, even if only momentarily, in breach of the Law-of-the-Father."[18] So Sarah breaches the Law-of-the-Father through her house/barn. Indeed, Mother's renaming is so revolutionary in its breaking of the established pattern of discourse that the villagers see her as either "insane" or "of a lawless and rebellious spirit" (p. 464). Further, Adoniram's own amazed reaction to Sarah's actions testifies to the undermining of his authority Mother has achieved; he turns to Sarah in a "dazed fashion" (p. 466), exhibiting "his old bristling face [which] was pale and frightened" (p. 467). As well it should be, for Sarah has managed to subvert the authority he has kept tightly in his control for the last forty years.

Sarah resignifies, reinscribes in order to create a new discourse in which she can be a speaking subject. In so doing, she breaks the stranglehold of "The Father" on language and, in fact, renders the father inarticulate. When Father first sees the new house/barn, he is reduced to speech without sound; watching him, the family sees that "his lips moved; he was saying something, but they could not hear what it was" (p. 466). Later, Adoniram is still speechless—so much so that Mother must remind him to say prayers: "'Ain't you goin' to ask a blessin', father?' said Sarah" (p. 468). This last scene forms a striking contrast to Adoniram's early recitation of prayers, as well as to the earlier scenes where he was silent. His silence, earlier, was the silence of the possessor of knowledge, the possessor of discourse. Now, he is literally speechless ("the old man . . . shook his head speechlessly" p. 467) or gasping for words ("'Why, Mother!' the old man gasped"). His silence comes from being, literally, without words, from being at a loss for words. For the first time in the story, *Father* asks *Mother* to explain, to

18  Furman, p. 74.

interpret, the meaning of events: "'What on airth does this mean, mother?' he gasped." And, Sarah tells him: "we've come here to live, an' we're goin' to live here." Sammy backs up Sarah on this point, speaking out "bravely" and further demonstrating that the father's miserly and gendered control of language has been lost. And once Adoniram is without speech and Sarah is with it, Adoniram's jealous guarding of the citadel of knowledge also collapses: "Adoniram was like a fortress whose walls had no active resistance, and went down the instant the right besieging tools were used" (p. 468). Speech is the key to the tumbling fortress; but Sarah must redefine language itself, and break the stranglehold of the father on language before she can speak it.

*Poster for the Improved Genuine Alaska Down Bustle, 1890*

And yet, it is not just that Sarah has wrested control of language from her husband and placed it in her own hands. The compromise Freeman works out is potentially more sophisticated than this. Adoniram is silent, or he weeps, because he finally understands what it is that Sarah now wants. She succeeds in communicating that her system of values, her focus on home, nurturance, connectivity, and generativity is valid. Sarah succeeds in engendering a language that expresses the values of her gender but that can also be understood by Father. And so her husband capitulates to her demands; weeping, he says "I'll—put up the—partitions, an'—everything you—want, mother." But he does so because he now understands her demands; he understands what she is "set on," as he says: "Why, mother, . . . I hadn't no idee you was so set on't as all this comes to." And so, a temporary truce is reached; a temporary moment of understanding and true communication occurs.

Through a physical act of revolt, through actions which speak, and through revolutionary renaming, Sarah *merges* these two conflicting value systems and gains the power to be a speaking subject. But it is a compromise that Sarah has reached; she has reclaimed language not only for herself but also so that her husband and family can now speak in a more meaningful and open way. And, as if to indicate this truce, the landscape at the end of the story becomes peaceful and possibly utopian: "The twilight was deepening. There was a clear green glow in the sky. Before them stretched the smooth level of field; in the distance was a cluster of hay-stacks like the huts of a village; the air was very cool and calm and sweet. *The landscape might have been an ideal one of peace*" (my emphasis). This story, then, might enact a truce, a temporary act of communication that is successful, that invents a system of discourse which slips free from the binary system of sexual difference, of patriarchal or non-patriarchal language, of speaking men or silent women, of barn versus home. Like Derrida, Freeman perhaps imagines a world beyond binary oppositions, a world that could approach "the area of a relationship to the other where the code of sexual marks would no longer be discriminating."[19] When the barn becomes the home, and the home the barn, when men and women *both* engage in discourse, Freeman suggests that the chance for peace—linguistically and sexually—might also exist. Perhaps.

# Sandra M. Gilbert and Susan Gubar

## from *The Madwoman in the Attic*

Many nineteenth-century male writers also, of course, used imagery of enclosure and escape to make deeply felt points about the relationship of the individual and society. Dickens and Poe, for instance, on opposite sides of the Atlantic, wrote of prisons, cages, tombs, and cellars in similar ways and for similar reasons. Still, the male writer is so much more comfortable with his literary role that he can usually elaborate upon his visionary theme more consciously and objectively than the female writer can. The distinction between male and female images of imprisonment is—and always has been—a distinction between, on the one hand, that which is both metaphysical and metaphorical, and on the other hand, that which is social and actual. Sleeping in his coffin, the seventeenth-century poet John Donne was piously rehearsing the constraints of the grave in advance, but the nineteenth-century poet Emily Dickinson, in purdah in her white dress, was anxiously living those constraints in the present. Imagining himself buried alive in tombs and cellars, Edgar Allan Poe was letting his mind poetically wander into the deepest recesses if his own psyche, but Dickinson, reporting that "I do not cross my Father's ground to any house in town," was recording a real, self-willed, self-burial. Similarly, when Byron's Prisoner of Chillon notes that "my very chains and I grew friends," the poet himself is making an epistemological point about the nature of the human mind, as well as a political point about the tyranny of the state. But when Rose Yorke in *Shirley* describes Caroline Helstone as living the life of a toad enclosed in a block of marble, Charlotte Brontë is speaking through her about her own deprived and constricted life, and its real conditions.

Thus, though most male metaphors of imprisonment have obvious implications in common (and many can be traced back to traditional images used by, say, Shakespeare and Plato), such metaphors may have very different aesthetic functions and philosophical messages in different male literary works. Wordsworth's prison-house in the "Intimations" ode serves a purpose quite unlike that served by the jails in Dickens's novels. Coleridge's twice-five miles of visionary greenery ought not to be confused with Keats's vale of soul-making, and the escape of Tennyson's Art from her Palace should not be identified with the resurrection of Poe's Ligeia. Women authors, however, reflect the literal reality of their own confinement in the constraints they de-

19  Jacques Derrida and Christie V. McDonald, "Choreographies," *Diacritics*, 12 (1982), 76.

pict, and so all at least begin with the same unconscious or conscious purpose in employing such spatial imagery. Recording their own distinctively female experience, they are secretly working through and within the conventions of literary texts to define their own lives.

While some male authors also use such imagery for implicitly or explicitly confessional projects, women seem forced to live more intimately with the metaphors they have created to solve the "problem" of their fall. At least one critic does deal not only with such images but with their psychological meaning as they accrue around houses. Noting in *The Poetics of Space* that "the house image would appear to have become the topography of our inmost being," Gaston Bachelard shows the ways in which houses, nests, shells, and wardrobes are in us as much as we are in them. What is significant from our point of view, however, is the extraordinary discrepancy between the almost consistently "felicitous space" he discusses and the negative space we have found. Clearly, for Bachelard the protective asylum of the house is closely associated with its maternal features, and to this extent he is following the work done on dream symbolism by Freud and on female inner space by Erikson. It seems clear too, however, that such symbolism must inevitably have very different implications for male critics and for female authors.

Women themselves have often, of course, been described or imagined as houses. Most recently Erik Erikson advanced his controversial theory of female "inner space" in an effort to account for little girls' interest in domestic enclosures. But in medieval times, as if to anticipate Erikson, statues of the Madonna were made to open up and reveal the holy family hidden in the Virgin's inner space. The female womb has certainly, always and everywhere, been a child's first and most satisfying house, a source of food and dark security, and therefore a mythic paradise imaged over and over again in sacred caves, secret shrines, consecrated huts. Yet for many a woman writer these ancient associations of house and self seem mainly to have strengthened the anxiety about enclosure which she projected into her art. Disturbed by the real physiological prospect of enclosing an unknown part of herself that is somehow also not herself, the female artist may, like Mary Shelley, conflate anxieties about maternity with anxieties about literary creativity. Alternatively, troubled by the anatomical "emptiness" of spinsterhood, she may, like Emily Dickinson, fear the inhabitations of nothingness and death, the transformation of womb into tomb. Moreover, conditioned to believe that as a house she is herself owned (and ought to be inhabited) by a man, she may once again but for yet another reason see herself as inescapably an object. In other words, even if she does not experience her womb as a kind of tomb or perceive her child's occupation of her house/body as depersonalizing, she may recognize that in an essential way she has been defined simply by her purely biological usefulness to her species.

To become literally a house, after all, is to be denied the hope of that spiritual transcendence of the body which, as Simone de Beauvoir has argued, is what makes humanity distinctively human. Thus, to be confined in childbirth (and significantly "confinement" was the key nineteenth-century term for what we would now, just as significantly, call "delivery") is in a way just as problematical as to be confined in a house or prison. Indeed, it might well seem to the literary woman that, just as on-togeny may be said to recapitulate phylogeny, the confinement of pregnancy repli-cates the confinement of society. For even if she is only metaphorically denied transcendence, the woman writer who perceives the implications of the house/body equation must unconsciously realize that such a trope does not just "place" her in a glass coffin; it transforms her into a version of the glass coffin herself. There is a sense, therefore, in which, confined in such a network of metaphors, what Adrienne Rich has called a "thinking woman" might inevitably feel that now she has been impris-oned within her own alien and loathsome body. Once again, in other words, she has become not only a prisoner but a monster.

As if to comment on the unity of all these points—on, that is, the anxiety-inducing connections between what women writers tend to see as their parallel confinements in texts, houses, and maternal female bodies—Charlotte Perkins Gilman brought them all together in 1890 in a striking story of female confinement and escape, a par-adigmatic tale which (like *Jane Eyre*) seems to tell *the* story that all literary women would tell if they could speak their "speechless woe." "The Yellow Wallpaper," which Gilman herself called "a description of a case of nervous breakdown," recounts in the first person the experiences of a woman who is evidently suffering from a severe post-partum psychosis. Her husband, a censorious and paternalistic physician, is treating her according to methods by which S. Weir Mitchell, a famous "nerve specialist," treated Gilman herself for a similar problem. He has confined her to a large garret room in an "ancestral hall" he has rented, and he has forbidden her to touch pen to paper until she is well again, for he feels, says the narrator, "that with my imaginative power and habit of story-making, a nervous weakness like mine is sure to lead to all manner of excited fancies, and that I ought to use my will and good sense to check the tendency."

The cure, of course, is worse than the disease, for the sick woman's mental con-dition deteriorates rapidly. "I think sometimes that if I were only well enough to write a little it would relieve the press of ideas and rest me," she remarks, but literally confined in a room she thinks is a one-time nursery because it has "rings and things" in the walls, she is literally locked away from creativity. The "rings and things," al-though reminiscent of children's gymnastic equipment, are really the paraphernalia of confinement, like the gate at the head of the stairs, instruments that definitively indicate her imprisonment. Even more tormenting, however, is the room's wallpaper: a sulphurous yellow paper, torn off in spots, and patterned with "lame uncertain curves" that "plunge off at outrageous angles" and "destroy themselves in unheard of contradictions." Ancient, smoldering, "unclean" as the oppressive structures of the society in which she finds herself, this paper surrounds the narrator like an inexplica-ble text, censorious and overwhelming as her physician husband, haunting as the "hereditary estate" in which she is trying to survive. Inevitably she studies its suicidal implications—and inevitably, because of her "imaginative power and habit of story-making," she revises it, projecting her own passion for escape into its otherwise incomprehensible hieroglyphics. "This wall-paper," she decides, at a key point in her story,

> has a kind of sub-pattern in a different shade, a particularly irritating one,
> for you can only see it in certain lights, and not clearly then.
>     But in the places where it isn't faded and where the sun is just so—I
> can see a strange, provoking, formless sort of figure, that seems to skulk
> about behind that silly and conspicuous front design.

As time passes, this figure concealed behind what corresponds (in terms of what we have been discussing) to the facade of the patriarchal text becomes clearer and clearer. By moonlight the pattern of the wallpaper "becomes bars! The outside pattern I mean, and the woman behind it is as plain as can be." And eventually, as the narrator sinks more deeply into what the world calls madness, the terrifying implications of both the paper and the figure imprisoned behind the paper begin to permeate—that is, to *haunt*—the rented ancestral mansion in which she and her husband are immured. The "yellow smell" of the paper "creeps all over the house," drenching every room in its subtle aroma of decay. And the woman creeps too—through the house, in the house, and out of the house, in the garden and "on that long road under the trees." Sometimes, indeed, the narrator confesses, "I think there are a great many women" both behind the paper and creeping in the garden,

> and sometimes only one, and she crawls around fast, and her crawling
> shakes [the paper] all over. . . . And she is all the time trying to climb
> through. But nobody could climb through that pattern—it strangles so; I
> think that is why it has so many heads.

Eventually it becomes obvious to both reader and narrator that the figure creeping through and behind the wallpaper is both the narrator and the narrator's double. By the end of the story, moreover, the narrator has enabled this double to escape from her textual/architectural confinement: "I pulled and she shook, I shook and she pulled, and before morning we had peeled off yards of that paper." Is the message of the tale's conclusion mere madness? Certainly the righteous Doctor John—whose name links him to the anti-hero of Charlotte Brontë's *Villette*—has been temporarily defeated, or at least momentarily stunned. "Now why should that man have fainted?" the narrator ironically asks as she creeps around her attic. But John's unmasculine swoon of surprise is the least of the triumphs Gilman imagines for her madwoman. More significant are the madwoman's own imaginings and creations, mirages of health and freedom with which her author endows her like a fairy godmother showering gold on a sleeping heroine. The woman from behind the wallpaper creeps away, for instance, creeps fast and far on the long road, in broad daylight. "I have watched her sometimes away off in the open country," says the narrator, "creeping as fast as a cloud shadow in a high wind."

Indistinct and yet rapid, barely perceptible but inexorable, the progress of that cloud shadow is not unlike the progress of nineteenth-century literary women out of the texts defined by patriarchal poetics into the open spaces of their own authority. That such an escape from the numb world behind the patterned walls of the text was a flight from dis-ease into health was quite clear to Gilman herself. When "The Yellow

Wallpaper" was published she sent it to Weir Mitchell, whose strictures had kept her from attempting the pen during her own breakdown, thereby aggravating her illness, and she was delighted to learn, years later, that "he had changed his treatment of nervous prostration since reading" her story. "If that is a fact," she declared, "I have not lived in vain." Because she was a rebellious feminist besides being a medical iconoclast, we can be sure that Gilman did not think of this triumph of hers in narrowly therapeutic terms. Because she knew, with Emily Dickinson, that "Infection in the sentence breeds," she knew that the cure for female despair must be spiritual as well as physical, aesthetic as well as social. What "The Yellow Wallpaper" shows she knew, too, is that even when a supposedly "mad" woman has been sentenced to imprisonment in the "infected" house of her own body, she may discover that, as Sylvia Plath was to put it seventy years later, she has "a self to recover, a queen."

# Leah Blatt Glasser

## from *In a Closet Hidden*

In light of her mother's mixture of disappointment in married life and pride in her domestic arts, Freeman's story about a rebellious mother, "The Revolt of 'Mother,'" is intriguing. Soon after her sister Anna died in 1876, Freeman's parents were forced to give up their little cottage because her father's financial position had worsened. In 1877, the family moved into the home of the Reverend Mr. Tyler, the father of Hanson Tyler, Freeman's unrequited love. Freeman's mother was hired to serve as housekeeper for the invalid minister and his wife. It is easy to imagine Freeman's response to her mother's suddenly subservient position. In addition to the dream of the elegant home never built, Eleanor had also now lost the little she actually had. As Michele Clark explains in her afterword to *The Revolt of 'Mother' and Other Stories,* "Eleanor, the wife, the mother, was now deprived of the very things which made a woman proud—her own kitchen, furniture, family china; and she had lost the one place in which it was acceptable for her to be powerful: her home." Certainly Sarah Penn's desperate determination to win a decent work environment in the form of a fine kitchen reflects the need Freeman must have sensed in her own mother. The spirit of the story conveys the pleasure Freeman took in transforming her mother's subservience into revolt and creating the home her mother never had. In a rare moment of candid self-expression, Freeman mentioned that she wished her parents "might have been spared" to her, that she "longed to make some return to them for their love and care, but that now as they were gone" she would have "to pass it on to someone else." This story was Freeman's vehicle for "passing it on." Freeman was able to invest her fictional mother with the spirit, self-determination, and self-knowledge that her own mother never openly exhibited. Perhaps the mother she created is the mother she wished she could have had. In a letter of 1893, about a decade after her mother's death and two years after she wrote "The Revolt of 'Mother,'" Freeman expressed a longing to go to a "land where there are no circumstances." In this story, she created such a land by granting "Mother" the right to overthrow those circumstances that most oppress.

Freeman's loving depiction of Sarah Penn as the "masterly keeper of her box of a house" was a way of acknowledging her mother's unacknowledged gifts, a delayed response to her mother's life story:

> Sarah Penn washed the frying-pan with a conclusive air. She scrubbed the outside of it as faithfully as the inside. She was a masterly keeper of her box of a house. Her one living-room never seemed to have in it any of the dust which the friction of life with inanimate matter produces. She swept, and there seemed to be no dirt to go before the broom; she cleaned, and one could see no difference. She was like an artist so perfect that he has apparently no art. Today she got out a mixing bowl and a board, and rolled some pies, and there was no more flour upon her than upon her daughter who was doing finer work.

The passage stresses the seriousness with which Sarah approaches her job. She has created an art out of daily chores.

It is interesting that just after this description of Sarah as artist, Freeman inserts commentary which reflects her ambivalence about the source of her mother's art. Much as Sarah Penn is an artful creator of pies, the pies are designed to please her husband, Adoniram, although he fails to acknowledge the value of his wife's work:

> She was making mince-pies. Her husband, Adoniram Penn, liked them better than any other kind. She baked twice a week. Adoniram often liked a piece of pie between meals. She hurried this morning. It had been later than usual when she began, and she wanted to have a pie baked for dinner. However deep a resentment she might be forced to hold against her husband, she would never fail in sedulous attention to his wants.

As the story makes clear, her "attention to his wants" is not reciprocated, hence a "deep resentment" builds until it fires the central action of the story, Sarah Penn's revolt.

"The Revolt of 'Mother'" is one of Freeman's most frequently anthologized stories. It reflects Freeman's understanding of her mother's world as much as it does her disappointment in its limitations. Her family had moved to Brattleboro because of her father's needs, and the move failed to bring her mother the one thing she had hoped it would achieve: a better home in which to assert her creative energies, energies that of necessity had been channeled into mothering and homemaking. Freeman's fictive mother in the story, Sarah Penn, has a similar experience as she watches her husband build a new barn for the animals and witnesses his refusal to build a much needed new home instead. Sarah's response is the positive response Freeman must have wished her mother could have made. Sarah defiantly moves into the barn and creatively redesigns it. By the end of her intensive labor, the barn is virtually a work of art—a comfortable new residence for Sarah Penn and her family. The spirit and determination of Sarah's actions capture the rhythm of domestic revolt with such energy that students reading the story today are moved by its power and see it as a feminist tale for women of any period.

Freeman's representation of gender communication in this story suggests her understandable resistance to leaving the comforts of Eleanor's nurturing to become someone's wife. Sarah's battle to be heard was one Freeman preferred to wage symbolically in the context of her writing. In her fiction she was assured an audience and could create an Adoniram who, in the end, had to hear and see his wife's art. Even after her battle, however, Sarah has won the right to a space in which she can serve Adoniram more effectively. Freeman honored the fight but recognized this irony and avoided such a fate by resisting marriage for many years.

In presenting Sarah Penn's rebellion, Freeman manages to break through most of the barriers of gender differences in the domestic realm. She creates, in effect, a utopia in which the work of women must be recognized, valued, and embraced by men. Even the landscape is utopian at the end of the story, "an ideal one of peace," where "the air was very cool and calm and sweet." Peace comes when Adoniram sees the meaning and power of Sarah's creativity, her capacity to envision and then transform the barn he had built into the home she had wanted so that she might better nurture those she loves. Adoniram embraces feminine values by the end of the story and his muttering has changed to weeping. He becomes a "fortress whose walls had no active resistance, and went down the instant the right besieging tools were used." "Besieging tools" were available to Freeman's fictive heroine. They were tools her mother never used. The lessons Freeman learned from her mother are more like those voiced by Sarah in an early speech to her daughter, Nanny:

> "You ain't found out yet we're women-folks, Nancy Penn," said she. "You ain't seen enough of men-folks yet to. One of these days you'll find it out, an' then you'll know that we know only what men-folks think we do, so far as any use of it goes, an' how we'd ought to reckon men-folks in with Providence, an' not complain of what they do any more than we do of the weather."

Sarah's fight for self-determination and for recognition of the value of her work begins verbally. Sarah "talks plain" to Adoniram as Freeman's mother never did to Warren Wilkins, and Freeman gives voice to her mother's unexpressed rage:

> "You see this room father; it's all the one I've had to work in an' eat in an' sit in sence we was married. . . . I want to know if you think you're doin right an accordin' to what you profess. Here when we was married, forty year ago, you promised me faithful that we should have a new house built in that lot over in the field before the year was out. . . . Father, I want to know if you think it's right. You're lodgin' your dumb beasts better than you are your own Flesh an' blood."

Freeman's magnification of Sarah's revolt is what tempted her early biographers to call this simply a "comic folk tale." Freeman has Sarah Penn march "across the room as though it were a tragic stage." If not classic tragedy, the drama was one familiar to most New England women. As Sarah pleads her case, Freeman equates the power of her speech and its shift "from severity to pathos" with the eloquence of Daniel Webster;

in this sense, she redefines oratory and heroism in women's terms. Exposing the inadequacy of her working headquarters, a small ill-lighted pantry, Sarah's "little" argument becomes larger than life. She shows that this "is all the buttery I've got—every place I've got for my dishes, to set away my victuals in an' to keep my milk-pans in." The passion of Sarah's argument is a passion about work that has value. "Father, I've been takin' care of the milk of six cows in this place an' now you're goin' to build a new barn an' keep more cows, an' give me more to do in it."

Adoniram's response captures the dilemma of gender communication. Women's words are lost on Adoniram: "I've got to go off after that load of gravel. I can't stan' here talkin' all day." "Talkin'" then is not a means for transformation. As Martha Cutter stresses, the failure of language to open communication between the sexes is an important element in the story.

The aggressive actions, actions that are described in terms of male battlefields, but that have at their center female rather than male values, become the source for breaking through the barrier and enabling a genuine "talk" between Sarah and her husband at the end of the story.

> During the next few hours a feat was performed by this simple pious New England mother which was equal in its way to Wolfe's storming of the Heights of Abraham. It took no more genius and audacity of bravery for Wolfe to cheer his wondering soldiers up those steep precipices under the sleeping eyes of the enemy, than for Sarah Penn, at the head of her children, to move all of their little household goods into the new barn while her husband was away.

Comparing Sarah's actions to those of heroic males, Freeman redefines heroism, equating Sarah with Wolfe on the marital battlefield. Had Freeman seen such a battle when her family moved to Brattleboro, had such a battle been realizable in the New England she knew, she might have considered the possibility of an early marriage. Through her fiction, she could win the battle, write stories about seemingly small battles and determine a female victory. As a woman writer in a tiny New England village, Freeman shared in Sarah's battle. Just as Sarah struggles to have her work recognized, Freeman fought to be taken seriously as a writer. For decades, critics categorized her subject matter as small, insignificant. Yet like Sarah Penn's vision of great possibility in ordinary things—a barn, for example—Freeman's work explores the largest questions through small incidents. Freeman's description of Sarah's artistic architectural feat is a symbol for her own work as an artist. When Sarah looks at the large barn, "she saw at a glance its possibilities."

> Those great box-stalls, with quilts hung before them, would make better bedrooms than the one she had occupied for forty years, and there was a tight carriage room. The harness room, with its chimney and shelves, would make a kitchen of her dreams. The great middle space would make a parlor, by the by, fit for a palace. . . . With partitions and windows, what a house would there be! Sarah looked at the row of stanchions before

the allotted space for cows, and reflected that she would have her front entry there.

Sarah's creativity, generally lost or unexpressed in the endless tasks that occupy her days, is at last given full voice with this opportunity for rebellion. Her visions of possibilities hint at what Freeman must have felt as architect of her stories. In one day, the barn is transformed to match Sarah's artistic visions.

The village reaction to Sarah's aggression becomes an index for the courage her rebellion requires. "Some held her to be insane, some, of a lawless and rebellious spirit." Female rebellion and madness were commonly equated in Freeman's time. But Sarah's response to the local minister strengthens her capacity now to combine gesture and language, to be heard in a male world. She insists upon the justice of her actions:

> "I think it's right jest as much as I think it was right for our forefathers to come over from the old country because they didn't have what belonged to 'em," said Mrs. Penn. She arose. The barn threshold might have been Plymouth Rock from her bearing. . . . "I've got my own mind an' my own feet, an' I'm goin' to think my own thoughts an' go my own ways, an' nobody but the Lord is goin' to dictate to me unless I've a mind to have him."

Sarah's revolutionary language invests creative domesticity with a sense of purpose and strength. As it builds in power and as she translates her words into actions which are now visible to the male eye, her language must be heard, can no longer be met with patriarchal silence. Sarah turns to physical action to overthrow the ideas of "men-folks," to defy the patriarchal system of valuing commodities over a woman's capacity for love and creativity.

"The Revolt of 'Mother'" offers, as Martha Cutter suggests, a vision of gender and language. Cutter's analysis of Sarah's initial dilemma is useful: "Sarah Penn lacks more than just a home for her family, more than just a place to maintain what Carol Gilligan would call a web of relationship between individuals. Sarah Penn also lacks a language; she cannot become a speaking subject." From the very start of the story, Adoniram's inability to hear Sarah stems from the degree to which "language is patriarchal, and it illustrates that women, marginalized by frontier values, are also marginalized in this other sense: they cannot speak; they are excluded from a discourse that is patriarchal in intent and meaning." Sarah Penn's most poignant battle was the battle Freeman was fighting in her fiction as she struggled to "redefine a linguistic frontier which has excluded her as a speaking subject." Domestic power can only be recognized in Freeman's story when Sarah finds a language with which to communicate that power to her husband. The story then explores conflicting value systems. Adoniram wants to build another barn because he values the fact that the barn provides for cattle, cattle provides money, and money provides the opportunity to build another barn.

Sarah Penn's value system is clear in her conversations with her daughter. As Freeman's mother must have wished, Sarah longed to have a home large enough to accommodate Nanny and the man she is about to marry, along with their future offspring—a desire then to ensure familial closeness and continued nurturance. This was never possible for Freeman's mother; Freeman's marriage would have required a parting from home. Sarah's desire to continue to protect Nanny, however, does resemble Eleanor's protection of Mary. Sarah says of Nanny "She wa'n't ever strong. She's got considerable color, but there wa'n't never any backbone to her. I've always took the heft of everything off her an' she ain't fit to keep house an' do everything herself. She'll be all worn out inside of a year. I can't have it so, noways, father." Interestingly, then, Sarah's motivation for revolt is continued protection of her daughter. The conflicting priorities of mother and father, are clearly drawn: "father's are for animals; mother's are for the human and relational."

Freeman's story begins to create a new means for communicating differing gender values so that long overlooked feminine principles can begin to receive some recognition. It is only when Mother "creates a system of signs," in place of earlier attempts to "tell" Father, that the breakthrough begins. Moving the house into the barn "she dumps all the 'value' of 'Home' into 'Barn,' and thereby takes an action which indicates that to her 'Home' is as important if not more important than 'Barn.' And Adoniram finally understands; where words cannot communicate, gestures succeed." Cutter calls this moment "renaming," for it is Sarah's gesture to rename the "barn" as "home" and hence to shift the values by which Adoniram will live.

The feminizing of Adoniram in the end is poignant. He becomes "pale and frightened," parts with authority, agrees to put up the partitions, and genuinely pleads for explanation from Mother: "'What on airth does this mean mother?' he gasped." When Sarah tells him that "we've come here to live, an' we're going to live here," Adoniram must recognize a new form of living with a new source at its center, the power of his wife, Sarah Penn. What Sarah wins in the end is recognition that "her focus on home nurturance, connectivity and generativity is valid."

Had Freeman believed such a revolutionary breakthrough in language between the sexes were possible, her own choices might have been different. Sarah's impassioned description of the importance of her work and the inadequacy of her work space was a speech Freeman's father never heard, one that most likely her mother never had the opportunity to make. Furthermore, Eleanor was never able to move into the home Warren planned to build when they first moved to Brattleboro. Perhaps when Freeman harshly rejected the story years later, she was remembering these discrepancies between her own mother and the one she clearly took such pleasure in creating:

> In the first place all fiction ought to be true and "The Revolt of 'Mother'"
> is not true . . . there never was in New England a woman like Mother. If
> there had been she certainly would have lacked the nerve. She would also
> have lacked the imagination. New England women of the period coincided
> with their husbands in thinking that the source of wealth should be better
> housed than the consumers.

Not "lacking the imagination," Freeman's story creates an alternative to her choice as an unmarried writer: rebellion within the context of conventional marriage. Yet her own rejection of the story helps explain the choice she made in her twenties to bury her longings for sexual fulfillment, to resist the pressure to marry, and to begin a career in writing. By observing her mother's world during her own early stages of sexual development, Freeman could see that heterosexuality and marriage constituted a threat to autonomy. From the start, the idea of entering heterosexual relationships carried the association of parting with the love of women, the community in which she had flourished in her mother's kitchen in Randolph and in the home of Mary Wales. While Sarah Penn's rebellion was, after all, to create a home in which to better serve her family, Freeman's choice was to thrive in the "female world of love and ritual" and to inhabit a home in which she would serve herself through her writing.

# The Modern Short Story

*1900 to 1969*

1. *Women riding in a Ford Model T car, photograph, 1919*
2. *Edith Wharton, photograph, 1905*
3. *Gustav Klimt,* Judith with the Head of Holofernes, *1901*
4. *White Star Line poster advertising the* Titanic, *1912*
5. *James Joyce, photograph, 1938*
6. *Pablo Picasso,* Les Demoiselles d'Avignon, *oil painting, 1907*

7. *Women's suffrage march, New York, photograph, 1915*

8. *Franz Kafka, photograph, undated*

9. *Scene from* **The Cabinet of Dr. Caligari**, *photograph, 1920*

10. *Zora Neale Hurston, photograph, c. 1950s*

11. *English and French troops in a defensive line in World War I, photograph, 1918*

12. *Man and woman doing the Charleston, photograph, c. 1920*

13. Georgia O'Keeffe, Jimson Weed, *oil painting, 1932*

14. Dorothea Lange, Migrant Mother, *photograph, 1936*

15. Katherine Anne Porter, *photograph, 1947*

16. *The damaged USS* California *and the partially capsized USS* Oklahoma *during the Japanese attack on Pearl Harbor, photograph, December 7, 1941*

17. Jorge Luis Borges, *photograph, 1977*

18. *Mushroom cloud over Hiroshima, photograph, August 6, 1945*

19. *Frida Kahlo,* Self-Portrait with Cropped Hair, *oil painting, 1940*
20. *Flannery O'Connor, photograph, 1950s*
21. *Girl watching television, photograph, 1956*
22. *James Baldwin, photograph, 1975*
23. *Andy Warhol,* Campbell's Soup Can (Tomato), *synthetic polymer paint and silkscreen, 1965*
24. *Martin Luther King Jr. giving his* I Have a Dream *speech in Washington, D.C., photograph,*
*1963*

As the world entered the twentieth century, its citizens felt they were on the brink of a true modernity. Though every generation is, in essence, *modern,* the generation traveling into the twentieth century expressed a particular need to reclassify their lives as modern lives. The industrial revolution of the nineteenth century changed the way in which Americans and Europeans defined their work life and profoundly altered the structure of their home and social lives. This alteration was borne out in the twentieth century as practitioners of a new school of architecture called "modernist" redefined the family home as well as public buildings. Men and women had to rethink their relationship to public and private spaces, from crowded rooms favored in the Victorian era to the clean, uncluttered spaces advocated by modernists. The skylines of major cities became majestic as skyscrapers were erected, and elegant hotels boasting every modern comfort spread along whole blocks of city streets. The department store flourished, offering an array of goods and services appealing to citizens of the twentieth century who increasingly wanted to define themselves as modern sophisticates.

For writers and other artists at the turn of the twentieth century, the divide between the 1800s and the 1900s was not a simple matter of turning a calendar page. The twentieth century felt like a thunderous blast, rendering the world into two discrete and permanently separated parts: the past and *now.* This exhilarating uncertainty spawned numerous artistic and theoretical movements in America, Britain, France, and Russia as thinkers and artists suddenly felt disconnected from the artistic innovators of the past. Avant-garde artistic and literary movements prevalent in the years before World War I, such as cubism, vorticism, constructivism, and futurism, dismissed the bourgeois values of Victorianism with vigor, humor, and daring. In philosophy and the sciences, turn-of-the-century thinkers like Henri Bergson, Karl Marx, Sigmund Freud, and Albert Einstein encouraged a vision of the world stripped of tradition, barriers, and limitations, including those imposed by time and space. The future seemed to promise that technology would abolish physical labor and class differences, creating unlimited prosperity and equality. With the advent of the First World War, however, destruction of the old thoughts, practices, and ways of living was accomplished in a way not even the most revolutionary thinkers had anticipated or imagined. The effects of the "war to end all wars" on the arts were radical and profound.

## THE DIVIDING LINE: WORLD WAR I

The period between World War I and World War II is often referred to as the traumatic "coming of age" for the United States. Although American life had already begun to alter in the first decade of the twentieth century, World War I (1914–1918) became the true dividing line between the nineteenth century and modern America. The war was billed as a way to "Keep Free in Freedom," but the ferocious, bloody battles brought about a spirit of resistance and political activism in American writers and artists. Modernity in literature and the arts became synonymous with a rejection of a warring and violent America. Writers, painters, actors, and political activists set out to create new forms of expression as traditional artistic forms could no longer embody the loss of innocence they wished to portray.

Simultaneous with this artistic reformation, a modern revolution was occurring in other segments of American society. The young soldiers from rural American towns returning home from the war yearned for the modern, urban life they experienced in the great cities of Europe. Innovation in farm machinery drastically reduced the demand for farm jobs, causing more families to leave small towns for the promised prosperity of the big city. In the postwar "Big Boom," American business flourished, and those lucky enough to be successful experienced prosperity beyond anything they could have imagined. College enrollment exploded in the 1920s, and the middle class grew in numbers. Many Americans purchased the two ultimate status symbols of American success: the automobile and the single-family home. This new urban American home often glowed with electric lights and buzzed with the radio and telephone, which increasingly connected families to a larger world.

The landscape of early-twentieth-century literature was varied, as the traditions of realism, naturalism, and popular fiction were still being published for an eager audience. However, writers who defined themselves as "modernists" began to rebel against these older traditions of storytelling in a unique brand of literature and poetics. The cultural wave of modernism, which emerged in Europe before the turn of the century and swept the United States in the early years of the twentieth century, rejected past traditions of writing as insufficient for portraying the rhythms and meanings of modern life. Modernists sought a sharp break from the literary past, as well as from Western civilization's classical traditions. Modern life was, indeed, radically different from life in the nineteenth century, in part because science, technology, mechanization, and the beat of city life outstripped the quiet rhythm of country living.

Modernist literature and the culture growing up around modernist writers, artists, and political activists indicated a distinctive break from claustrophobic Victorian morality. Modernists broke from the nineteenth-century understanding of life and presented instead a profoundly pessimistic picture of a culture in disarray. As modernists sought to put modern life into words, they threw off the aesthetic burden of the realist novel, which purported to reflect life as it really was. Modernists purposefully disrupted the linear flow of narrative, fought against the expected notion of a final moralistic lesson, and refused conventional expectations concerning a united, coherent plot and straightforward character development, instead introducing characters who remain morally ambiguous throughout the story. By challenging stylistic forms, modernist writers sought to portray the simple moments of ordinary lives made extraordinary by their expression.

The horrors of a war that was conducted on an unprecedented scale and that incorporated a terrifying array of modern weaponry tempered many modernist writers' enthusiasm for technology and disdain for the past. History came to occupy a crucial position in the modernist literature produced by those countries involved in World War I. The past as subject influenced the stylistic innovations in writing during the early twentieth century, a time when history was constantly being unraveled, fragmented, and interrupted on the battlefield, on city streets, and in dwindling country towns. For modernists, the past lived in the present, and so a "tradition of the new" in literature was born. Myths, ancient storytelling forms, and traditional tales from other cultures made their way into modernist texts as authors pieced together the fragments of a war-shattered world. Through literature, writers could knit the unraveled world back together, but the final product was purposefully inexact and imprecise, a state reflective of the instability and insecurity of modern life. The short story conveys this experience of discontinuity and rupture, as the seamless whole of the nineteenth-century novel gave way to smaller, varied texts, and the experience of reading itself was broken into pieces. Nevertheless, a fragmented world facilitated a modern pursuit of new countries, cultures, and experiences as modernists began to stretch their legs in worlds far beyond ordinary borders. Writers and artists in America, Europe, Latin America, and Africa began to explore modernism within and without their own continents and cultures.

## Restless Modernity

Modernism was not the only literary movement in the era between the two world wars that allowed writers to pursue a story through unique means. The Harlem Renaissance, a genre of writing created by African American male and female writers between the teens and the 1920s, came of age in this new era of artistic exploration. The movement began in New York City, specifically Harlem, as blacks left the South for the North in the Reconstruction era. Members of the Harlem Renaissance like Langston Hughes, Zora Neale Hurston, and Arna Bontemps wrote stories, essays, and poems reflecting vibrant creativity and plumbing the concerns of the African American community.

In the 1920s, novels and short stories that examined and challenged racial divides reflected the Jazz Age that was holding the world in its thrall. In both America and Europe, writers looked to the heady environs of Paris as a place perfectly constructed for modern tastes. Ernest Hemingway, Sherwood Anderson, Henry Miller, Djuna Barnes, and Anaïs Nin all moved to Paris in the 1920s and 1930s, establishing literary salons where cosmopolitan writers and artists met, argued, ate, and danced the nights away. Jazz became the musical language that everyone tried to speak, and the flapper, with her bobbed hair and fringed dresses, entered the literary, artistic, and pop culture lexicon. The stock market crash of 1929, however, brought the bubbly Jazz Age to an abrupt end. As the money that had buoyed up the 1920s circled down the drain, citizens of both America and Europe questioned capitalism and its ability to protect and serve the people of the world.

International crises in the 1930s, the Great Depression and the Dust Bowl in America, rampant inflation in Germany, and failing businesses and starving families in England represented the failure of a money system that, at first, seemed poised to solve the problems inherited after World War I. Political unrest began to take hold in cities such as London, Chicago, and New York as citizens agitated for governments and leaders who addressed the people's concerns. Economic and political discontent on the Continent led to the rise of Benito Mussolini, established as ruler of Italy in 1922, and Adolf Hitler, who held an absolute dictatorship over Germany by 1933. Totalitarian regimes also rose in Japan and Russia as Hirohito became emperor of Japan in 1926 and cast an eye toward international expansion, and Joseph Stalin commandeered the Soviet Union. Citizens of many countries found themselves at the mercy of brutal governments that attempted to control every aspect of their lives.

The wounds of World War I were still fresh and raw when the unthinkable occurred. In 1939, another world war erupted that would last until 1945. This war was truly modern, with countries as diverse as Germany, Poland, France, England, and Japan involved in active conflict. Though Russia was an ally to the West in both world wars, in 1917, in the very midst of World War I, the country underwent a series of revolutions that ended imperialist czarist rule and established the communist Soviet state, making it a de facto enemy to its former allies by midcentury. The dropping of atomic bombs on Japan by the United States not only ended the conflict but also began the arms race, as the Soviets built their own postwar nuclear arsenal. World War II inaugurated the invasion and annexation by the Soviet Union (the USSR) of nations around the world, especially in Eastern Europe and Central Asia, even as the war's ravages contributed to the dissolution of Western colonialism's hold over much of the globe. The war's further fracturing of the world thus brought expected pain, as well as the sweetness of freedom.

## THE LITERATURE OF CHANGE

In the 1930s, amidst the dreary hardship of the Depression, American writers returned to a form of writing known traditionally as naturalism in order to push literary modernity into a discussion of social class, wealth, and disparity of power. Novels such as Henry Roth's *Call It Sleep* and John Steinbeck's Dust Bowl exposé *The Grapes of Wrath* brought realism in touch with modernist sensibilities. Far from simple melodramas, these novels provoked a thoughtful analysis of the psychological damage inflicted on the powerless victims of capitalism.

European and American writers, in an attempt to understand the world that seemed to have slipped off its axis, explored perceptions of time and space in fiction's many forms. Freud's groundbreaking text, *The Interpretation of Dreams*, appeared in its first translations from the original German just before World War I; modernist writers' inward turning and their preoccupation with personality and inner psychological processes reflect Freud's early theories of the unconscious. The short story's rapid plunge into plot and character development, its exaggerated tension, and the intensified readerly attention it could command made it a vehicle for interrogating the modern world. A distinguishing feature of much twentieth-century fiction beginning with modernism, the stream-of-consciousness technique of narration reflects not only a growing interest in psychology and a person's inner voice, but also the modern experience of incoherence and instability, as language itself fractures and dissolves under the pressures of modernity.

In the twentieth-century short story, the previous century's concern with creating socially responsible readers gave way to modernism's preoccupations with style and the development of individual personality. Modernism is often accused of being elitist and socially disengaged, but the bonds of trust and belief broken by war made human connection an enterprise fraught with tension. The material hardship and psychological trauma that lingered after the war threatened to obliterate the exhilaration and daring that had marked the turn of the century, and reactionary rumblings for a return to safe and stifling Victorian values in the 1940s and 1950s continued to infuse the short story with subversive potential.

After the mechanized mayhem of World War I and its continuation in World War II, a casual view of modern technology was no longer possible for any of the world's citizens. The telegram, the telephone, and the radio had in their own ways contributed to the horror of war. The voice over the wire, whether relaying a directive from headquarters or an intercepted enemy message, was faceless, impersonal, and potentially untrustworthy. The dream of overcoming barriers of time and space proved itself a nightmare; new possibilities in human connection created instead a breakdown in communication, as the disembodied voice further fragmented and alienated humans from the world and each other. These technologies, along with related developments in entertainment like radio and movies, entered modern literature. The techniques of the cinema, such as montage, time lapse, and juxtaposition, as well as abbreviated bursts of narrative, the incorporation of advertising jingles, and the elliptical, silence-filled dialogue typical of telephone conversations, began to appear on fiction's pages. Again, these elements not only reflected the episodic nature of twentieth-century life; in their self-reflexive irony, these literary devices also commented on the quality of that life, which was increasingly shaped by the technology that once promised freedom and expansion.

## THE WORLD EXPANDS

The literature of the 1940s and 1950s pushed away from the politically leftist leanings of the 1930s and instead tried to dismantle the facade of the perfect American family constructed in the pages of women's magazines and in television shows like *Leave It to Beaver*. Stories such as John Cheever's "The Enormous Radio" and the grotesques that populate the strangely humorous stories of Flannery O'Connor are indicative of a growing awareness that the American family did not protect Americans from corruption; it corrupted them outright. Philosophical movements, such as existentialism, which posited that humans must act only for themselves, rose in opposition to the prepackaged world of perfection shaped by advertising in the 1950s. Writers also reacted against the confines of 1950s America. Novels such as Sloan Wilson's *The Man in the Grey Flannel Suit* (1955), an examination of a World War II soldier's difficulty with returning to a "normal" life at home; sociological studies such as David Reisman's *The Lonely Crowd* (1961), a critique of suburbia; and William H. Whyle Jr.'s *The Organization Man* (1956), which took contemporary business practices to task, were counterattacks on the post–World War II, media-constructed version of perfect suburban lives.

With the exception of the United States, the "first world" victors of World War II suffered decades of hardship following the conclusion of the conflict. Once powerful empires lost control of countries they had held with an iron fist, and young new nations—most of which were simultaneously ancient cultures—struggled for independence and equality with the industrialized world that had left them behind. By midcentury, European writers felt exhausted as they struggled with the legacy of modernism's literary "giants," whose work no longer seemed to speak for the postwar world. In Russia, Josef Stalin's culturally and politically repressive regime restricted literary expression to those texts that adhered to the rules of Soviet realism. As Isaac Babel, a Russian short story writer active during this period, remarked, he had to become, like other writers in his country, "a master of a new literary genre, the genre of silence."

In 1945 the United Nations was established, signaling that the notion of nations existing in isolation from each other was beginning to disintegrate. India, aided by Mohandas Gandhi, won its independence from Britain in 1947. In 1948, both Burma and Israel were established as independent states. The 1950s and 1960s were decades of change for a number of African states, as Ghana, Nigeria, and Kenya were freed from British rule, and Chad, the Congo Republic, Mali, and Senegal were permanently separated from France. Writers from these new nations set about recovering lost traditions while exposing the truths of their suddenly free and contemporary lives. Chinua Achebe, Amos Tutuola, Kamala Das, and Ama Ata Aidoo expressed the tenuous position of a culture in conflict—caught between the past and the future—and the particular struggles of people left in the aftermath of a country recently dominated by the ruling power's traditions, cultural norms, and forms of expression.

It is in formerly colonized nations asserting their newly assumed independence that the most vibrant and innovative short stories of the midcentury emerge, particularly in magical realist fiction by Latin American writers like Jorge Luis Borges, Jorge Amado, Alejo Carpentier, and Gabriel García Márquez. Centuries of Spanish and Portuguese colonialism in Central and South America ended in the early nineteenth century, a hundred years before much of Asia, Africa, and the Caribbean experienced their modern liberation. Most Latin American countries, however, didn't experience the promise of independence, as fascist dictators, coups, revolutions, counterrevolutions, repressive military regimes, and territorial struggles among neighboring countries destabilized the region. Latin America, then, hovered between the colonized past and the modernized present, and its people found themselves, like citizens in Africa, feeling as if they had no culture that was wholly theirs. In this context, magical realism arose as an imaginative technique that bridged the seemingly irreconcilable realities of indigenous folkways with modern life. Magical realist fiction creates a fantasy of seamless interaction between two opposing worlds of experience, the natural and supernatural. In the midst of ordinary life, the supernatural arises without surprise, and fantasy and realism exist side by side, much the way the past and present were superimposed in modernist texts. Like modernism, magical realism incorporates a fragmented reality that at once builds on and leaves behind established literary traditions.

## THE WORLD EXPLODES

In the decades after World War II, nations appeared and disappeared with unprecedented rapidity; some gained new names, some were dissolved—their old borders lost, their names erased—and the globe became largely divided between two ideologies based on economic theories: communism and capitalism. Neither system could claim the undivided loyalty of those living under it, and even in the so-called "free world," or "first world" of Western capitalism, the middle decades of the century were marked by unrest and violent protest, often in the name of the oppressed and disenfranchised. From the 1950s through the early 1970s, the civil rights movement, the antiwar movement protesting the action in Vietnam, and the assassinations of John F. Kennedy, Martin Luther King, and Robert Kennedy roiled the United States. The year 1958 saw the notorious Notting Hill race riots in London, when whites fought emigrated West-Indian blacks for over a week. In Paris in May of 1968, college students, inspired by American war protests and sympathy for revolutionaries in Latin America, rioted in the streets, inciting a bloody confrontation with police, while in October of that year, similar student protests in Mexico City were suppressed with violent force. In that same fateful year, on the other side of the "Iron Curtain"—as Winston Churchill in 1946 famously referred to the postwar division between the Western powers and Soviet territories—Czechoslovakia's "Prague Spring," a short-lived reform movement and resistance of Soviet domination, was swiftly quelled by troops and tanks.

One of the figures idolized by the period's rioting youth was the Argentinean Che Guevara, a revolutionary communist leader specializing in guerrilla warfare who was instrumental in the Cuban Revolution at the end of the 1950s and who went on to work with insurgent groups throughout Latin America, as well as in the Congo. The Cuban Revolution, which allied the island nation off the coast of Florida with the increasingly powerful Soviet Union, along with the Warsaw Pact of 1955, a defense treaty that brought together the communist countries of Albania, Bulgaria, Czechoslovakia, East Germany, Hungary, Poland, Romania, and the USSR, constituted some of the first moves in the Cold War between Soviet Bloc countries and the United States and its Western allies, a standoff lasting into the 1980s. Other significant events in this ideological division among world powers include the Cuban missile crisis of 1962, when the Soviet installation of nuclear missiles in Cuba conveyed the threat of war; China's communist Cultural Revolution, which began under Mao Zedong in 1966; and the erection of the Berlin Wall in 1961, which divided communist East Germany from "free" West Germany. Korea and Vietnam were also separated along similar ideological lines in the latter half of the century; they followed their own devastating civil wars, abetted by the intervention of the world's coldly warring "superpowers."

The civil rights movement in the early 1960s brought the writing of African Americans to the fore of American culture, much the way the Jazz Age of the 1920s brought writers of the Harlem Renaissance to the attention of the world. At the same time, another group of writers emerged known as the *beats,* a term that writer Jack Kerouac coined by joining the words *beaten* and *beatified* to express the writers' alliance with jazz and black culture and their existence on the margins of traditional American life. Allen Ginsberg's groundbreaking poem, "Howl," exemplified the beats' status: "I saw the best minds of my generation destroyed by madness, starving hysterical naked, dragging themselves through the negro streets at dawn looking for an angry fix." Their writing was representative of the current elements of America in the 1960s: protest, activism, and the eventual mainstreaming of outsider culture.

Students on college campuses across America left their classrooms to protest not only U.S. involvement in the Vietnam War but also censorship, inequality between the races, lack of women's rights, and the destruction of the environment. Soon, the beats of the early 1960s became the hippies of the late 1960s. The twin thrust of hippies and the political protests of students and American citizens everywhere inevitably had an effect on arts and literature. Comedians such as Lenny Bruce and Woody Allen pushed the boundaries of what was once considered acceptable nightclub material, and their brand of "black humor" surfaced in American writing as well. Donald Barthleme, Thomas Pynchon, and Terry Southern wrote novels and stories that fractured taboos with raucous humor and disjointed, fantastical narratives. The pointed humor of Jewish American writers Philip Roth, Grace Paley, Saul Bellow, Bernard Malamud, Cynthia Ozick, and John Updike exposed not only the struggles of Jewish characters living in a largely Christian America, but also the tension between men and women in the 1960s. These novels were matched by the sharp texts of English writers Kingsley Amis and Iris Murdoch, while novels of social criticism by Doris Lessing and Margaret Drabble illuminated the world of 1960s English womanhood. The emergence of these disparate and various voices was indicative of the direction the world was traveling. The divisions between nations and cultures were dissolving, and countries like England and the United States were fast becoming collections of differing ethnicities and religions. As borders became more porous, the literature of the world suddenly broke open—available to everybody in every corner on every continent.

## CRASHING INTO CONTEMPORARY LITERATURE

After World War II, national borders lost their rigidity, partly because of the collateral effects of war, such as the proliferation, affordability, and accessibility of modern technologies of communication and transportation. Contingents of formerly colonized populations migrated from the peripheries of once occupied territories to the metropolitan centers that had dominated the world and that were still considered centers of culture, knowledge, prestige, and power. Magical realism's imaginative and celebratory accommodation of diverse traditions and perspectives, its vision of peaceful negotiation among jarring realities, provided a literary model for a confusing world of disparate languages and cultures. Magical realism was a significant influence on regional literatures emerging worldwide in the latter half of the century, as well as on postmodern fiction in general. It is of central importance to the development of postcolonial literature in late-twentieth-century Africa, the Afro-Caribbean, and Asia, especially in the fiction produced by pioneering Indian writers like Salman Rushdie and Anita Desai, who in turn became significant models for postmodern fiction in the Western world, reversing colonialism's centuries-long cultural influence.

# Chinua Achebe

## (B. 1930)

His satire and keen ear for the spoken word have made Chinua Achebe one of the most highly esteemed African writers. Born in Ogidi, Nigeria, to Protestant parents who named him Albert after Queen Victoria's husband, Achebe adopted his indigenous name while studying at the University College of Ibadan. He graduated in 1953 and, a year later, joined the Nigerian Broadcasting Company in Lagos. His first novel, *Things Fall Apart,* was published in 1958. During the Nigerian Civil War (1967–1970), Achebe was in the Biafran government service and taught at U.S. and Nigerian universities. Over his lifetime, he has taught at the University of Massachusetts, the University of Nigeria, and Bard College. His works include *No Longer at Ease* (1960), *Arrow of God* (1964), *A Man of the People* (1966), *Beware, Soul Brother* (1971), and *Anthills of the Savannah* (1987). In 1990, Achebe was paralyzed from the waist down in a serious car accident.

## Dead Men's Path
1953

Michael Obi's hopes were fulfilled much earlier than he had expected. He was appointed headmaster of Ndume Central School in January 1949. It had always been an unprogressive school, so the Mission authorities decided to send a young and energetic man to run it. Obi accepted this responsibility with enthusiasm. He had many wonderful ideas and this was an opportunity to put them into practice. He had had sound secondary school education which designated him a "pivotal teacher" in the official records and set him apart from the other headmasters in the mission field. He was outspoken in his condemnation of the narrow views of these older and often less-educated ones.

"We shall make a good job of it, shan't we?" he asked his young wife when they first heard the joyful news of his promotion.

"We shall do our best," she replied. "We shall have such beautiful gardens and everything will be just *modern* and delightful . . ." In their two years of married life she had become completely infected by his passion for "modern methods" and his denigration of "these old and superannuated people in the teaching field who would be better employed as traders in the Onitsha market." She began to see herself already as the admired wife of the young headmaster, the queen of the school.

The wives of the other teachers would envy her position. She would set the fashion in everything . . . Then, suddenly, it occurred to her that there might not be other wives. Wavering between hope and fear, she asked her husband, looking anxiously at him.

"All our colleagues are young and unmarried," he said with enthusiasm which for once she did not share. "Which is a good thing," he continued.

"Why?"

"Why? They will give all their time and energy to the school."

Nancy was downcast. For a few minutes she became sceptical about the new school; but it was only for a few minutes. Her little personal misfortune could not blind her to her husband's happy prospects. She looked at him as he sat folded up in a chair. He was stoop-shouldered and looked frail. But he sometimes surprised people with sudden bursts of physical energy. In his present posture, however, all his bodily strength seemed to have retired behind his deep-set eyes, giving them an extraordinary power of penetration. He was only twenty-six, but looked thirty or more. On the whole, he was not unhandsome.

"A penny for your thoughts, Mike," said Nancy after a while, imitating the woman's magazine she read.

"I was thinking what a grand opportunity we've got at last to show these people how a school should be run."

Ndume School was backward in every sense of the word. Mr. Obi put his whole life into the work, and his wife hers too. He had two aims. A high standard of teaching was insisted upon, and the school compound was to be turned into a place of beauty. Nancy's dream-gardens came to life with the coming of the rains, and blossomed. Beautiful hibiscus and allamanda hedges in brilliant red and yellow marked out the carefully tended school compound from the rank neighbourhood bushes.

One evening as Obi was admiring his work he was scandalized to see an old woman from the village hobble right across the compound, through a marigold flower-bed and the hedges. On going up there he found faint signs of an almost disused path from the village across the school compound to the bush on the other side.

"It amazes me," said Obi to one of his teachers who had been three years in the school, "that you people allowed the villagers to make use of this footpath. It is simply incredible." He shook his head.

"The path," said the teacher apologetically, "appears to be very important to them. Although it is hardly used, it connects the village shrine with their place of burial."

"And what has that got to do with the school?" asked the headmaster.

"Well, I don't know," replied the other with a shrug of the shoulders. "But I remember there was a big row some time ago when we attempted to close it."

"That was some time ago. But it will not be used now," said Obi as he walked away. "What will the Government Education Officer think of this when he comes to inspect the school next week? The villagers might, for all I know, decide to use the schoolroom for a pagan ritual during the inspection."

Heavy sticks were planted closely across the path at the two places where it entered and left the school premises. These were further strengthened with barbed wire.

Three days later the village priest of *Ani* called on the headmaster. He was an old man and walked with a slight stoop. He carried a stout walking-stick which he usually tapped on the floor, by way of emphasis, each time he made a new point in his argument.

"I have heard," he said after the usual exchange of cordialities, "that our ancestral footpath has recently been closed . . ."

"Yes," replied Mr. Obi. "We cannot allow people to make a highway of our school compound."

"Look here, my son," said the priest bringing down his walking-stick, "this path was here before you were born and before your father was born. The whole life of this village depends on it. Our dead relatives depart by it and our ancestors visit us by it. But most important, it is the path of children coming in to be born . . ."

Mr. Obi listened with a satisfied smile on his face.

"The whole purpose of our school," he said finally, "is to eradicate just such beliefs as that. Dead men do not require footpaths. The whole idea is just fantastic. Our duty is to teach your children to laugh at such ideas."

"What you say may be true," replied the priest, "but we follow the practices of our fathers. If you reopen the path we shall have nothing to quarrel about. What I always say is: let the hawk perch and let the eagle perch." He rose to go.

"I am sorry," said the young headmaster. "But the school compound cannot be a thoroughfare. It is against our regulations. I would suggest your constructing another path, skirting our premises. We can even get our boys to help in building it. I don't suppose the ancestors will find the little detour too burdensome."

"I have no more words to say," said the old priest, already outside.

Two days later a young woman in the village died in childbed. A diviner was immediately consulted and he prescribed heavy sacrifices to propitiate ancestors insulted by the fence.

Obi woke up next morning among the ruins of his work. The beautiful hedges were torn up not just near the path but right round the school, the flowers trampled to death and one of the school buildings pulled down . . . That day, the white Supervisor came to inspect the school and wrote a nasty report on the state of the premises but more seriously about the "tribal-war situation developing between the school and the village, arising in part from the misguided zeal of the new headmaster."

# Sherwood Anderson

## (1876–1941)

Inspired by the fiction of Gertrude Stein and his friendship with Chicago authors like the poet Carl Sandburg, Sherwood Anderson began writing later than most and published his first book after the age of forty. His first successful novel was the 1919 *Winesburg, Ohio*; after this came *Poor White* (1920), *The Triumph of the Egg* (1921), *Horses and Men* (1923), and *Death in the Woods and Other Stories* (1933). Between 1895 and 1900, Anderson fought in the Spanish-American War before turning his hand to advertising in Chicago. Several years later he returned to Ohio to start a paint business, but the enterprise failed as Anderson became increasingly obsessed with writing, and he finally devoted himself to literature in 1912.

Anderson's writing style is distinctive for its disregard of plot and close attention to a significant moment, and he is credited with being the first American writer to use a story cycle format. He met and influenced a number of the great writers of his time, including Ernest Hemingway, William Faulkner, Erskine Caldwell, F. Scott Fitzgerald, and Jean Toomer. Faulkner said of Anderson, "He was the father of my whole generation of writers." In "Form, Not Plot, in the Short Story," Anderson sees himself as an American writer trying to break free of the British literary tradition by creating fiction that is authentically true to life. He wrote, "Form [grows] out of the materials of the tale and the teller's reaction to them. It [is] the tale trying to take form that kick[s] about inside the tale-teller. . . . Words [are] the surfaces, the clothes of the tale."

## The Triumph of the Egg

1920

My father was, I am sure, intended by nature to be a cheerful, kindly man. Until he was thirty-four years old he worked as a farmhand for a man named Thomas Butterworth whose place lay near the town of Bidwell, Ohio. He had then a horse of his own, and on Saturday evenings drove into town to spend a few hours in social intercourse with other farmhands. In town he drank several glasses of beer and stood about in Ben Head's saloon—crowded on Saturday evenings with visiting farmhands. Songs were sung and glasses thumped on the bar. At ten o'clock father drove home along a lonely country road, made his horse comfortable for the night, and himself went to bed, quite happy in his position in life. He had at that time no notion of trying to rise in the world.

It was in the spring of his thirty-fifth year that father married my mother, then a country schoolteacher, and in the following spring I came wriggling and crying into the world. Something happened to the two people. They became ambitious. The American passion for getting up in the world took possession of them.

It may have been that mother was responsible. Being a schoolteacher she had no doubt read books and magazines. She had, I presume, read of how Garfield, Fin coin, and other Americans rose from poverty to fame and greatness, and as I lay beside her—in the days of her lying-in—she may have dreamed that I would some day rule men and cities. At any rate she induced father to give up his place as a farmhand, sell his horse, and embark on an independent enterprise of his own. She was a tall silent woman with a long nose and troubled gray eyes. For herself she wanted nothing. For father and myself she was incurably ambitious.

The first venture into which these two people went turned out badly. They rented ten acres of poor stony land on Grigg's Road, eight miles from Bidwell, and launched into chicken-raising. I grew into boyhood on the place and got my first impressions of life there. From the beginning they were impressions of disaster, and if, in my turn, I am a gloomy man inclined to see the darker side of life, I attribute it to the fact that what should have been for me the happy joyous days of childhood were spent on a chicken farm.

One unversed in such matters can have no notion of the many and tragic things that can happen to a chicken. It is born out of an egg, lives for a few weeks as a tiny fluffy thing such as you will see pictured on Easter cards, then becomes hideously naked, eats quantities of corn and meal bought by the sweat of your father's brow, gets diseases called pip, cholera, and other names, stands looking with stupid eyes at the sun, becomes sick and dies. A few hens and now and then a rooster, intended to serve God's mysterious ends, struggle through to maturity. The hens lay eggs out of which come other chickens and the dreadful cycle is thus made complete. It is all unbelievably complex. Most philosophers must have been raised on chicken farms. One hopes for so much from a chicken and is so dreadfully disillusioned. Small chickens, just setting out on the journey of life, look so bright and alert and they are in fact so dreadfully stupid. They are so much like people they mix one up in one's judgments of life. If disease does not kill them, they wait until your expectations are thoroughly aroused and then walk under the wheels of a wagon—to go squashed and dead back to their maker. Vermin infest their youth, and fortunes must be spent for curative powders. In later life I have seen how a literature has been built up on the subject of fortunes to be made out of the raising of chickens. It is intended to be read by the gods who have just eaten of the tree of the knowledge of good and evil. It is a hopeful literature and declares that much may be done by simple ambitious people who own a few hens. Do not be led astray by it. It was not written for you. Go hunt for gold on the frozen hills of Alaska, put your faith in the honesty of a politician, believe if you will that the world is daily growing better and that good will triumph over evil, but do not read and believe the literature that is written concerning the hen. It was not written for you.

I, however, digress. My tale does not primarily concern itself with the hen. If correctly told it will center on the egg. For ten years my father and mother struggled to make our chicken farm pay and then they gave up their struggle and began another. They moved into the town of Bidwell, Ohio, and embarked in the restaurant business.

After ten years of worry with incubators that did not hatch, and with tiny—and in their own way lovely—balls of fluff that passed on into semi-naked pullethood and from that into dead henhood, we threw all aside and, packing our belongings on a wagon, drove down Grigg's Road toward Bidwell, a tiny caravan of hope looking for a new place from which to start on our upward journey through life.

We must have been a sad-looking lot, not, I fancy, unlike refugees fleeing from a battlefield. Mother and I walked in the road. The wagon that contained our goods had been borrowed for the day from Mr. Albert Griggs, a neighbor. Out of its side stuck the legs of cheap chairs, and at the back of the pile of beds, tables, and boxes filled with kitchen utensils was a crate of live chickens, and on top of that the baby carriage in which I had been wheeled about in my infancy. Why we stuck to the baby carriage I don't know. It was unlikely other children would be born and the wheels were broken. People who have few possessions cling tightly to those they have. That is one of the facts that make life so discouraging.

Father rode on top of the wagon. He was then a baldheaded man of forty-five, a little fat, and from long association with mother and the chickens he had become habitually silent and discouraged. All during our ten years on the chicken farm he had worked as a laborer on neighboring farms and most of the money he had earned had been spent on remedies to cure chicken diseases, on Wilmer's White Wonder Cholera Cure or Professor Bidlow's Egg Producer or some other preparations that mother found advertised in the poultry papers. There were two little patches of hair on father's head just above his ears. I remember that as a child I used to sit looking at him when he had gone to sleep in a chair before the stove, on Sunday afternoons in the winter. I had at that time already begun to read books and have notions of my own, and the bald path that led over the top of his head was, I fancied, something like a broad road, such a road as Caesar might have made on which to lead his legions out of Rome and into the wonders of an unknown world. The tufts of hair that grew above father's ears were, I thought, like forests. I fell into a half sleeping, half waking state and dreamed I was a tiny thing going along the road into a far beautiful place where there were no chicken farms and where life was a happy eggless affair.

One might write a book concerning our flight from the chicken farm into town. Mother and I walked the entire eight miles—she to be sure that nothing fell from the wagon and I to see the wonders of the world. On the seat of the wagon beside father was his greatest treasure. I will tell you of that.

On a chicken farm, where hundreds and even thousands of chickens come out of eggs, surprising things sometimes happen. Grotesques are born out of eggs as out of people. The accident does not often occur—perhaps once in a thousand births. A chicken is, you see, born that has four legs, two pairs of wings, two heads, or what not. The things do not live. They go quickly back to the hand of their maker that has for a moment trembled. The fact that the poor little things could not live was one of the tragedies of life to father. He had some sort of notion that if he could but bring into henhood or roosterhood a five-legged hen or a two-headed rooster his fortune would be made. He dreamed of taking the wonder about the county fairs and of growing rich by exhibiting it to other farmhands.

At any rate, he saved all the little monstrous things that had been born on our chicken farm. They were preserved in alcohol and put each in its own glass bottle. These he had carefully put into a box, and on our journey into town it was carried on the wagon seat beside him. He drove the horses with one hand and with the other clung to the box. When we got to our destination, the box was taken down at once and the bottles removed. All during our days as keepers of a restaurant in the town of Bidwell, Ohio, the grotesques in their little glass bottles sat on a shelf back of the counter. Mother sometimes protested, but father was a rock on the subject of his treasure. The grotesques were, he declared, valuable. People, he said, liked to look at strange and wonderful things.

Did I say that we embarked in the restaurant business in the town of Bidwell, Ohio? I exaggerated a little. The town itself lay at the foot of a low hill and on the shore of a small river. The railroad did not run through the town and the station was a mile away to the north at a place called Pickleville. There had been a cider mill and pickle factory at the station, but before the time of our coming they had both gone out of business. In the morning and in the evening buses came down to the station along a road called Turner's Pike from the hotel on the main street of Bidwell. Our going to the out-of-the-way place to embark in the restaurant business was mother's idea. She talked of it for a year and then one day went off and rented an empty store building opposite the railroad station. It was her idea that the restaurant would be profitable. Traveling men, she said, would be always waiting around to take trains out of town and town people would come to the station to await incoming trains. They would come to the restaurant to buy pieces of pie and drink coffee. Now that I am older I know that she had another motive in going. She was ambitious for me. She wanted me to rise in the world, to get into a town school and become a man of the towns.

At Pickleville father and mother worked hard, as they always had done. At first there was the necessity of putting our place into shape to be a restaurant. That took a month. Father built a shelf on which he put tins of vegetables. He painted a sign on which he put his name in large red letters. Below his name was the sharp command—"EAT HERE"—that was so seldom obeyed. A showcase was bought and filled with cigars and tobacco. Mother scrubbed the floors and the walls of the room. I went to school in the town and was glad to be away from the farm, from the presence of the discouraged, sad-looking chickens. Still I was not very joyous. In the evening I walked home from school along Turner's Pike and remembered the children I had seen playing in the town school yard. A troop of little girls had gone hopping about and singing. I tried that. Down along the frozen road I went hopping solemnly on one leg. "Hippity Hop To The Barber Shop," I sang shrilly. Then I stopped and looked doubtfully about. I was afraid of being seen in my gay mood. It must have seemed to me that I was doing a thing that should not be done by one who, like myself, had been raised on a chicken farm where death was a daily visitor.

Mother decided that our restaurant should remain open at night. At ten in the evening a passenger train went north past our door followed by a local freight. The freight crew had switching to do in Pickleville, and when the work was done they came to our restaurant for hot coffee and food. Sometimes one of them ordered a fried egg. In the morning at four they resumed northbound and again visited us. A little trade began to grow up. Mother slept at night and during the day tended the restaurant and fed our boarders while father slept. He slept in the same bed mother had occupied during the night and I went off to the town of Bidwell and to school. During the long nights, while mother and I slept, father cooked meats that were to go into sandwiches for the lunch baskets of our boarders. Then an idea in regard to getting up in the world came into his head. The American spirit took hold of him. He also became ambitious.

In the long nights when there was little to do, father had time to think. That was his undoing. He decided that he had in the past been an unsuccessful man because he had not been cheerful enough and that in the future he would adopt a cheerful outlook on life. In the early morning he came upstairs and got into bed with mother. She woke and the two talked. From my bed in the corner I listened.

It was father's idea that both he and mother should try to entertain the people who came to eat at our restaurant. I cannot now remember his words, but he gave the impression of one about to become in some obscure way a kind of public entertainer. When people, particularly young people from the town of Bidwell, came into our place, as on very rare occasions they did, bright entertaining conversation was to be made. From father's words I gathered that something of the jolly innkeeper effect was to be sought. Mother must have been doubtful from the first, but she said nothing discouraging. It was father's notion that a passion for the company of himself and mother would spring up in the breasts of the younger people of the town of Bidwell. In the evening bright happy groups would come singing down Turner's Pike. They would troop shouting with joy and laughter into our place. There would be song and festivity. I do not mean to give the impression that father spoke so elaborately of the matter. He was, as I have said, an uncommunicative man. "They want some place to go. I tell you they want some place to go," he said over and over. That was as far as he got. My own imagination has filled in the blanks.

For two or three weeks this notion of father's invaded our house. We did not talk much, but in our daily lives tried earnestly to make smiles take the place of glum looks. Mother smiled at the boarders and I, catching the infection, smiled at our cat. Father became a little feverish in his anxiety to please. There was, no doubt, lurking somewhere in him, a touch of the spirit of the showman. He did not waste much of his ammunition on the railroad men he served at night, but seemed to be waiting for a young man or woman from Bidwell to come in to show what he could do. On the counter in the restaurant there was a wire basket kept always filled with eggs, and it must have been before his eyes when the idea of being entertaining was born in his brain. There was something pre-natal about the way eggs kept themselves connected with the development of his idea. At any rate, an egg ruined his new impulse in life. Late one night I was awakened by a roar of anger coming from father's throat. Both mother and I sat upright in our beds. With trembling hands she lighted a lamp that stood on a table by her head. Downstairs the front door of our restaurant went shut with a bang and in a few minutes father tramped up the stairs. He held an egg in his hand and his hand trembled as though he were having a chill. There was a half-insane light in his eyes. As he stood glaring at us I was sure he intended throwing the egg at either mother or me. Then he laid it gently on the table beside the lamp and dropped on his knees beside mother's bed. He began to cry like a boy, and I, carried away by his grief, cried with him. The two of us filled the little upstairs room with our wailing voices. It is ridiculous, but of the picture we made I can remember only the fact that mother's hand continually stroked the bald path that ran across the top of his head. I have forgotten what mother said to him and how she induced him to tell her of what had happened downstairs. His explanation also has gone out of my mind. I remember only my own grief and fright and the shiny path over father's head glowing in the lamplight as he knelt by the bed.

As to what happened downstairs. For some unexplainable reason I know the story as well as though I had been a witness to my father's discomfiture. One in time gets to know many unexplainable things. On that evening young Joe Kane, son of a merchant of Bidwell, came to Pickleville to meet his father, who was expected on the ten-o'clock evening train from the South. The train was three hours late and Joe came into our place to loaf about and to wait for its arrival. The local freight train came in and the freight crew were fed. Joe was left alone in the restaurant with father.

From the moment he came into our place the Bidwell young man must have been puzzled by my father's actions. It was his notion that father was angry at him for hanging around. He noticed that the restaurant-keeper was apparently disturbed by his presence and he thought of going out. However, it began to rain and he did not fancy the long walk to town and back. He bought a five-cent cigar and ordered a cup of coffee. He had a newspaper in his pocket and took it out and began to read. "I'm waiting for the evening train. It's late," he said apologetically.

For a long time father, whom Joe Kane had never seen before, remained silently gazing at his visitor. He was no doubt suffering from an attack of stage fright. As so often happens in life he had thought so much and so often of the situation that now confronted him that he was somewhat nervous in its presence.

For one thing, he did not know what to do with his hands. He thrust one of them nervously over the counter and shook hands with Joe Kane. "How-de-do," he said. Joe Kane put his newspaper down and stared at him. Father's eyes lighted on the basket of eggs that sat on the counter and he began to talk. "Well," he began hesitatingly, "Well, you have heard of Christopher Columbus, eh?" He seemed to be angry. "That Christopher Columbus was a cheat," he declared emphatically. "He talked of making an egg stand on its end. He talked, he did, and then he went and broke the end of the egg."

My father seemed to his visitor to be beside himself at the duplicity of Christopher Columbus. He muttered and swore. He declared it was wrong to teach children that Christopher Columbus was a great man when, after all, he cheated at the critical moment. He had declared he would make an egg stand on end and then, when his bluff had been called, he had done a trick. Still grumbling at Columbus, father took an egg from the basket on the counter and began to walk up and down. He rolled the egg between the palms of his hands. He smiled genially. He began to mumble words regarding the effect to be produced on an egg by the electricity that comes out of the human body. He declared that, without breaking its shell and by virtue of rolling back and forth in his hands, he could stand the egg on its head. He explained that the warmth of his hands and the gentle rolling movement he gave the egg created a new center of gravity, and Joe Kane was mildly interested. "I have handled thousands of eggs," father said. "No one knows more about eggs than I do."

He stood the egg on the counter and it fell on its side. He tried the trick again and again, each time rolling the egg between the palms of his hands and saying the words regarding the wonders of electricity and the laws of gravity. When after a half hour's effort he did succeed in making the egg stand for a moment, he looked up to find that his visitor was no longer watching. By the time he had succeeded in calling Joe Kane's attention to the success of his effort, the egg had again rolled over and lay on its side.

Afire with the showman's passion and at the same time a good deal disconcerted by the failure of his first effort, father now took the bottles containing the poultry monstrosities down from their place on the shelf and began to show them to his visitor. "How would you like to have seven legs and two heads like this fellow?" he asked, exhibiting the most remarkable of his treasures. A cheerful smile played over his face. He reached over the counter and tried to slap Joe Kane on the shoulder as he had seen men do in Ben Head's saloon when he was a young farmhand and drove to town on Saturday evenings. His visitor was made a little ill by the sight of the body of the terribly deformed bird floating in the alcohol in the bottle and got up to go. Coming from behind the counter, father took hold of the young man's arm and led him back to his seat. He grew a little angry and for a moment had to turn his face away and force himself to smile. Then he put the bottles back on the shelf. In an outburst of generosity he fairly compelled Joe Kane to have a fresh cup of coffee and another cigar at his expense. Then he took a pan and filling it with vinegar, taken from a jug that sat beneath the counter, he declared himself about to do a new trick. "I will heat this egg in this pan of vinegar," he said. "Then I will put it through the neck of a bottle without breaking the shell. When the egg is inside the bottle it will resume its normal shape and the shell will become hard again. Then I will give the bottle with the egg in it to you. You can take it about with you wherever you go. People will want to know how you got the egg in the bottle. Don't tell them. Keep them guessing. That is the way to have fun with this trick."

Father grinned and winked at his visitor. Joe Kane decided that the man who confronted him was mildly insane but harmless. He drank the cup of coffee that had been given him and began to read his paper again. When the egg had been heated in vinegar, father carried it on a spoon to the counter and going into a back room got an empty bottle. He was angry because his visitor did not watch him as he began to do his trick, but nevertheless went cheerfully to work. For a long time he struggled, trying to get the egg to go through the neck of the bottle. He put the pan of vinegar back on the stove, intending to reheat the egg, then picked it up and burned his fingers. After a second bath in the hot vinegar, the shell of the egg had been softened a little, but not enough for his purpose. He worked and worked and a spirit of desperate determination took possession of him. When he thought that at last the trick was about to be consummated, the delayed train came in at the station and Joe Kane started to go nonchalantly out at the door. Father made a last desperate effort to conquer the egg and make it do the thing that would establish his reputation as one who knew how to entertain guests who came into his restaurant. He worried the egg. He attempted to be somewhat rough with it. He swore and the sweat stood out on his forehead. The egg broke under his hand. When the contents spurted over his clothes, Joe Kane, who had stopped at the door, turned and laughed.

A roar of anger rose from my father's throat. He danced and shouted a string of inarticulate words. Grabbing another egg from the basket on the counter, he threw it, just missing the head of the young man as he dodged through the door and escaped.

Father came upstairs to mother and me with an egg in his hand. I do not know what he intended to do. I imagine he had some idea of destroying it, of destroying all eggs, and that he intended to let mother and me see him begin. When, however, he got into the presence of mother, something happened to him. He laid the egg gently on the table and dropped on his knees by the bed as I have already explained. He later decided to close the restaurant for the night and to come upstairs and get into bed. When he did so, he blew out the light and after much muttered conversation both he and mother went to sleep. I suppose I went to sleep also, but my sleep was troubled. I awoke at dawn and for a long time looked at the egg that lay on the table. I wondered why eggs had to be and why from the egg came the hen who again laid the egg. The question got into my blood. It has stayed there, I imagine, because I am the son of my father. At any rate, the problem remains unsolved in my mind. And that, I conclude, is but another evidence of the complete and final triumph of the egg—at least as far as my family is concerned.

# James Baldwin

## (1924–1987)

Although his single-minded father wanted him to become a preacher, James Baldwin made this calling his own for scarcely three years before, at age seventeen, he underwent a conversion from public speaker to would-be professional writer. Baldwin was born in Harlem and, while helping to raise seven siblings, read voraciously. His favorite books as a child were Dickens's *A Tale of Two Cities* and Stowe's *Uncle Tom's Cabin.* After leaving home and moving to Greenwich Village in 1941, Baldwin began work on a novel, supporting himself by writing book reviews. At age nineteen, he met Richard Wright, who was so impressed with Baldwin's work-in-progress that he helped him earn a Saxton Fellowship, which funded his work on the book for a year. At age twenty-four, Baldwin lived in France while finishing his successful novel *Go Tell It on the Mountain.* "Any writer, I suppose," writes Baldwin in *Autobiographical Notes,* "feels that the world into which he was born is nothing less than a conspiracy against the cultivation of his talent—which attitude certainly has a great deal to support it. On the other hand, it is only because the world looks on . . . with such a frightening indifference that the artist is compelled to make his talent important."

Baldwin went on to write numerous works addressing the relationships between fathers and sons and drawing on his own problematic childhood as the stepson of an alcoholic religious fanatic. He became controversial for producing such books as *Giovanni's Room* in 1956 and *Another Country* in 1962, which centered on issues of homosexuality. He was a vital literary figure for the civil rights movement of the 1960s, and he published a collection of short stories in 1965, *Going to Meet the Man*, including stories like "Sonny's Blues," whose characters are African Americans experiencing the psychological disruptions and repercussions of entrenched racism. As a spokesman for civil rights, Baldwin also wrote collections of essays and authored several plays, including *Blues for Mister Charlie*, a drama based on the Emmett Till case in Mississippi. Baldwin's most well-known work is probably the novel *Notes of a Native Son*, published in 1955.

## Sonny's Blues                                                      1957

I read about it in the paper, in the subway, on my way to work. I read it, and I couldn't believe it, and I read it again. Then perhaps I just stared at it, at the newsprint spelling out his name, spelling out the story. I stared at it in the swinging lights of the subway car, and in the faces and bodies of the people, and in my own face, trapped in the darkness which roared outside.

It was not to be believed and I kept telling myself that as I walked from the subway station to the high school. And at the same time I couldn't doubt it. I was scared, scared for Sonny. He became real to me again. A great block of ice got settled in my belly and kept melting there slowly all day long, while I taught my classes algebra. It was a special kind of ice. It kept melting, sending trickles of ice water all up and down my veins, but it never got less. Sometimes it hardened and seemed to expand until I felt my guts were going to come spilling out or that I was going to choke or scream. This would always be at a moment when I was remembering some specific thing Sonny had once said or done.

When he was about as old as the boys in my classes his face had been bright and open, there was a lot of copper in it; and he'd had wonderfully direct brown eyes, and great gentleness and privacy. I wondered what he looked like now. He had been picked up, the evening before, in a raid on an apartment downtown, for peddling and using heroin.

I couldn't believe it: but what I mean by that is that I couldn't find any room for it anywhere inside me. I had kept it outside me for a long time. I hadn't wanted to know. I had had suspicions, but I didn't name them, I kept putting them away. I told myself that Sonny was wild, but he wasn't crazy. And he'd always been a good boy, he hadn't ever turned hard or evil or disrespectful, the way kids can, so quick, so quick, especially in Harlem. I didn't want to believe that I'd ever see my brother going down, coming to nothing, all that light in his face gone out, in the condition I'd already seen so many others. Yet it had happened and here I was, talking about algebra to a lot of boys who might, every one of them for all I knew, be popping off needles every time they went to the head. Maybe it did more for them than algebra could.

I was sure that the first time Sonny had ever had horse,[1] he couldn't have been much older than these boys were now. These boys, now, were living as we'd been living then, they were growing up with a rush and their heads bumped abruptly against the low ceiling of their actual possibilities. They were filled with rage. All they really knew were two darknesses, the darkness of their lives, which was now closing in on them, and the darkness of the movies, which had blinded them to that other darkness, and in which they now, vindictively, dreamed, at once more together than they were at any other time, and more alone.

When the last bell rang, the last class ended, I let out my breath. It seemed I'd been holding it for all that time. My clothes were wet—I may have looked as though I'd been sitting in a steam bath, all dressed up, all afternoon. I sat alone in the classroom a long time. I listened to the boys outside, downstairs, shouting and cursing and laughing. Their laughter struck me for perhaps the first time. It was not the joyous laughter which—God knows why—one associates with children. It was mocking and insular, its intent was to denigrate. It was disenchanted, and in this, also, lay the authority of their curses. Perhaps I was listening to them because I was thinking about my brother and in them I heard my brother. And myself.

One boy was whistling a tune, at once very complicated and very simple, it seemed to be pouring out of him as though he were a bird, and it sounded very cool and moving through all that harsh, bright air, only just holding its own through all those other sounds.

I stood up and walked over to the window and looked down into the courtyard. It was the beginning of the spring and the sap was rising in the boys. A teacher passed through them every now and again, quickly, as though he or she couldn't wait to get out of that courtyard, to get those boys out of their sight and off their minds. I started collecting my stuff. I thought I'd better get home and talk to Isabel.

The courtyard was almost deserted by the time I got downstairs. I saw this boy standing in the shadow of a doorway, looking just like Sonny. I almost called his name. Then I saw that it wasn't Sonny, but somebody we used to know, a boy from around our block. He'd been Sonny's friend. He'd never been mine, having been too young for me, and, anyway, I'd never liked him. And now, even though he was a grown-up man, he still hung around that block, still spent hours on the street corner, was always high and raggy. I used to run into him from time to time and he'd often work around to asking me for a quarter or fifty cents. He always had some real good excuse, too, and I always gave it to him, I don't know why.

But now, abruptly, I hated him. I couldn't stand the way he looked at me, partly like a dog, partly like a cunning child. I wanted to ask him what the hell he was doing in the school courtyard.

1 **horse:** Heroin.

He sort of shuffled over to me, and he said, "I see you got the papers. So you already know about it."

"You mean about Sonny? Yes, I already know about it. How come they didn't get you?"

He grinned. It made him repulsive and it also brought to mind what he'd looked like as a kid. "I wasn't there. I stay away from them people."

"Good for you." I offered him a cigarette and I watched him through the smoke. "You come all the way down here just to tell me about Sonny?"

"That's right." He was sort of shaking his head and his eyes looked strange, as though they were about to cross. The bright sun deadened his damp dark brown skin and it made his eyes look yellow and showed up the dirt in his conked hair. He smelled funky. I moved a little away from him and I said, "Well, thanks. But I already know about it and I got to get home."

"I'll walk you a little ways," he said. We started walking. There were a couple of kids still loitering in the courtyard and one of them said good night to me and looked strangely at the boy beside me.

"What're you going to do?" he asked me. "I mean, about Sonny?"

"Look. I haven't seen Sonny for over a year, I'm not sure I'm going to do anything. Anyway, what the hell *can* I do?"

"That's right," he said quickly, "ain't nothing you can do. Can't much help old Sonny no more, I guess."

It was what I was thinking and so it seemed to me he had no right to say it.

"I'm surprised at Sonny, though," he went on—he had a funny way of talking, he looked straight ahead as though he were talking to himself—"I thought Sonny was a smart boy, I thought he was too smart to get hung."

"I guess he thought so too," I said sharply, "and that's how he got hung. And how about you? You're pretty goddamn smart, I bet."

Then he looked directly at me, just for a minute. "I ain't smart," he said. "If I was smart, I'd have reached for a pistol a long time ago."

"Look. Don't tell *me* your sad story, if it was up to me, I'd give you one." Then I felt guilty—guilty, probably, for never having supposed that the poor bastard *had* a story of his own, much less a sad one, and I asked, quickly, "What's going to happen to him now?"

He didn't answer this. He was off by himself some place. "Funny thing," he said, and from his tone we might have been discussing the quickest way to get to Brooklyn, "when I saw the papers this morning, the first thing I asked myself was if I had anything to do with it. I felt sort of responsible."

I began to listen more carefully. The subway station was on the corner, just before us, and I stopped. He stopped, too. We were in front of a bar and he ducked slightly, peering in, but whoever he was looking for didn't seem to be there. The juke box was blasting away with something black and bouncy and I half watched the barmaid as she danced her way from the juke box to her place behind the bar. And I watched her face as she laughingly responded to something someone said to her, still keeping time to the music. When she smiled one saw the little girl, one sensed the doomed, still-struggling woman beneath the battered face of the semi-whore.

"I never *give* Sonny nothing," the boy said finally, "but a long time ago I come to school high and Sonny asked me how it felt." He paused, I couldn't bear to watch him, I watched the barmaid, and I listened to the music which seemed to be causing the pavement to shake. "I told him it felt great." The music stopped, the barmaid paused and watched the juke box until the music began again. "It did."

All this was carrying me some place I didn't want to go. I certainly didn't want to know how it felt. It filled everything, the people, the houses, the music, the dark, quicksilver barmaid, with menace; and this menace was their reality.

"What's going to happen to him now?" I asked again.

"They'll send him away some place and they'll try to cure him." He shook his head. "Maybe he'll even think he's kicked the habit. Then they'll let him loose"—he gestured, throwing his cigarette into the gutter. "That's all."

"What do you mean, that's *all?*"

But I knew what he meant.

"I *mean,* that's *all.*" He turned his head and looked at me, pulling down the corners of his mouth. "Don't you know what I mean?" he asked softly.

"How the hell *would* I know what you mean?" I almost whispered it, I don't know why.

"That's right," he said to the air, "how would *he* know what I mean?" He turned toward me again, patient and calm, and yet I somehow felt him shaking, shaking as though he were going to fall apart. I felt that ice in my guts again, the dread I'd felt all afternoon; and again I watched the barmaid, moving about the bar, washing glasses, and singing. "Listen. They'll let him out and then it'll just start all over again. That's what I mean."

"You mean—they'll let him out. And then he'll just start working his way back in again. You mean he'll never kick the habit. Is that what you mean?"

"That's right," he said, cheerfully. "*You* see what I mean."

"Tell me," I said at last, "why does he want to die? He must want to die, he's killing himself, why does he want to die?"

He looked at me in surprise. He licked his lips. "He don't want to die. He wants to live. Don't nobody want to die, ever."

Then I wanted to ask him—too many things. He could not have answered, or if he had, I could not have borne the answers. I started walking. "Well, I guess it's none of my business."

"It's going to be rough on old Sonny," he said. We reached the subway station. "This is your station?" he asked. I nodded. I took one step down. "Damn!" he said, suddenly. I looked up at him. He grinned again. "Damn if I didn't leave all my money home. You ain't got a dollar on you, have you? Just for a couple of days, is all."

All at once something inside gave and threatened to come pouring out of me. I didn't hate him any more. I felt that in another moment I'd start crying like a child.

"Sure," I said. "Don't sweat." I looked in my wallet and didn't have a dollar, I only had a five. "Here," I said. "That hold you?"

He didn't look at it—he didn't want to look at it. A terrible, closed look came over his face, as though he were keeping the number on the bill a secret from him and me. "Thanks," he said, and now he was dying to see me go. "Don't worry about Sonny. Maybe I'll write him or something."

"Sure," I said. "You do that. So long."

"Be seeing you," he said. I went on down the steps.

And I didn't write Sonny or send him anything for a long time. When I finally did, it was just after my little girl died, he wrote me back a letter which made me feel like a bastard.

Here's what he said:

> Dear Brother,
>
> You don't know how much I needed to hear from you. I wanted to write you many a time but I dug how much I must have hurt you and so I didn't write. But now I feel like a man who's been trying to climb up out of some deep, real deep and funky hole and just saw the sun up there, outside. I got to get outside.
>
> I can't tell you much about how I got here. I mean I don't know how to tell you. I guess I was afraid of something or I was trying to escape from something and you know I have never been very strong in the head (smile). I'm glad Mama and Daddy are dead and can't see what's happened to their son and I swear if I'd known what I was doing I would never have hurt you so, you and a lot of other fine people who were nice to me and who believed in me.
>
> I don't want you to think it had anything to do with me being a musician. It's more than that. Or maybe less than that. I can't get anything straight in my head down here and I try not to think about what's going to happen to me when I get outside again. Sometime I think I'm going to flip and *never* get outside and sometime I think I'll come straight back. I tell you one thing, though, I'd rather blow my brains out than go through this again. But that's what they all say, so they tell me. If I tell you when I'm coming to New York and if you could meet me, I sure would appreciate it. Give my love to Isabel and the kids and I was sorry to hear about little Gracie. I wish I could be like Mama and say the Lord's will be done, but I don't know it seems to me that trouble is the one thing that never does get stopped and I don't know what good it does to blame it on the Lord. But maybe it does some good if you believe it.
>
> Your brother,
> SONNY

Then I kept in constant touch with him and I sent him whatever I could and I went to meet him when he came back to New York. When I saw him many things I thought I had forgotten came flooding back to me. This was because I had begun, finally, to wonder about Sonny, about the life that Sonny lived inside. This life, whatever it was, had made him older and thinner and it had deepened the distant stillness in which he had always moved. He looked very unlike my baby brother. Yet, when he smiled, when we shook hands, the baby brother I'd never known looked out from the depths of his private life, like an animal waiting to be coaxed into the light.

"How you been keeping?" he asked me.

"All right. And you?"

"Just fine." He was smiling all over his face. "It's good to see you again."

"It's good to see you."

The seven years' difference in our ages lay between us like a chasm: I wondered if these years would ever operate between us as a bridge. I was remembering, and it made it hard to catch my breath, that I had been there when he was born; and I had heard the first words he had ever spoken. When he started to walk, he walked from our mother straight to me. I caught him just before he fell when he took the first steps he ever took in this world.

"How's Isabel?"

"Just fine. She's dying to see you."

"And the boys?"

"They're fine, too. They're anxious to see their uncle."

"Oh, come on. You know they don't remember me."

"Are you kidding? Of course they remember you."

He grinned again. We got into a taxi. We had a lot to say to each other, far too much to know how to begin.

As the taxi began to move, I asked, "You still want to go to India?"

He laughed. "You still remember that. Hell, no. This place is Indian enough for me."

"It used to belong to them," I said.

And he laughed again. "They damn sure knew what they were doing when they got rid of it."

Years ago, when he was around fourteen, he'd been all hipped on the idea of going to India. He read books about people sitting on rocks, naked, in all kinds of weather, but mostly bad, naturally, and walking barefoot through hot coals and arriving at wisdom. I used to say that it sounded to me as though they were getting away from wisdom as fast as they could. I think he sort of looked down on me for that.

"Do you mind," he asked, "if we have the driver drive alongside the park? On the west side—I haven't seen the city in so long."

"Of course not," I said. I was afraid that I might sound as though I were humoring him, but I hoped he wouldn't take it that way.

So we drove along, between the green of the park and the stony, lifeless elegance of hotels and apartment buildings, toward the vivid, killing streets of our childhood. These streets hadn't changed, though housing projects jutted up out of them now like rocks in the middle of a boiling sea. Most of the houses in which we had grown up had vanished, as had the stores from which we had stolen, the basements in which we had first tried sex, the rooftops from which we had hurled tin cans and bricks. But houses exactly like the houses of our past yet dominated the landscape, boys exactly like the boys we once had been found themselves smothering in these houses, came down into the streets for light and air and found themselves encircled by disaster. Some escaped the trap, most didn't. Those who got out always left something of themselves behind, as some animals amputate a leg and leave it in the trap. It might be said, perhaps, that I had escaped, after all, I was a school teacher; or that Sonny had, he hadn't lived in Harlem for years. Yet, as the cab moved uptown through streets which seemed, with a rush, to darken with dark people, and as I covertly studied Sonny's face, it came to me that what we both were seeking through our separate cab windows was that part of ourselves which had been left behind. It's always at the hour of trouble and confrontation that the missing member aches.

We hit 110th Street and started rolling up Lenox Avenue. And I'd known this avenue all my life, but it seemed to me again, as it had seemed on the day I'd first heard about Sonny's trouble, filled with a hidden menace which was its very breath of life.

"We almost there," said Sonny.

"Almost." We were both too nervous to say anything more.

We live in a housing project. It hasn't been up long. A few days after it was up it seemed uninhabitably new, now, of course, it's already run-down. It looks like a parody of the good, clean, faceless life—God knows the people who live in it do their best to make it a parody. The beat-looking grass lying around isn't enough to make their lives green, the hedges will never hold out the streets, and they know it. The big windows fool no one, they aren't big enough to make space out of no space. They don't bother with the windows, they watch the TV screen instead. The playground is most popular with the children who don't play at jacks, or skip rope, or roller skate, or swing, and they can be found in it after dark. We moved in partly because it's not too far from where I teach, and partly for the kids; but it's really just like the houses in which Sonny and I grew up. The same things happen, they'll have the same things to remember. The moment Sonny and I started into the house I had the feeling that I was simply bringing him back into the danger he had almost died trying to escape.

Sonny has never been talkative. So I don't know why I was sure he'd be dying to talk to me when supper was over the first night. Everything went fine, the oldest boy remembered him, and the youngest boy liked him, and Sonny had remembered to bring something for each of them; and Isabel, who is really much nicer than I am, more open and giving, had gone to a lot of trouble about dinner and was genuinely glad to see him. And she's always been able to tease Sonny in a way that I haven't. It was nice to see her face so vivid again and to hear her laugh and watch her make Sonny laugh. She wasn't, or, anyway, she didn't seem to be, at all uneasy or embarrassed. She chatted as though there were no subject which had to be avoided and she got Sonny past his first, faint stiffness. And thank God she was there, for I was filled with that icy dread again. Everything I did seemed awkward to me, and everything I said sounded freighted with hidden meaning. I was trying to remember everything I'd heard about dope addiction and I couldn't help watching Sonny for signs. I wasn't doing it out of malice. I was trying to find out something about my brother. I was dying to hear him tell me he was safe.

"Safe!" my father grunted, whenever Mama suggested trying to move to a neighborhood which might be safer for children. "Safe, hell! Ain't no place safe for kids, nor nobody."

He always went on like this, but he wasn't, ever, really as bad as he sounded, not even on weekends, when he got drunk. As a matter of fact, he was always on the lookout for "something a little better," but he died before he found it. He died suddenly, during a drunken weekend in the middle of the war, when Sonny was fifteen. He and Sonny hadn't ever got on too well. And this was partly because Sonny was the apple of his father's eye. It was because he loved Sonny so much and was frightened for him, that he was always fighting with him. It doesn't do any good to fight with Sonny. Sonny just moves back, inside himself, where he can't be reached. But the principal reason that they never hit it off is that they were so much alike. Daddy was big and rough and loud-talking, just the opposite of Sonny, but they both had—that same privacy.

Mama tried to tell me something about this, just after Daddy died. I was home on leave from the army.

This was the last time I ever saw my mother alive. Just the same, this picture gets all mixed up in my mind with pictures I had of her when she was younger. The way I always see her is the way she used to be on a Sunday afternoon, say, when the old folks were talking after the big Sunday dinner. I always see her wearing pale blue. She'd be sitting on the sofa. And my father would be sitting in the easy chair, not far from her. And the living room would be full of church folks and relatives. There they sit, in chairs all around the living room, and the night is creeping up outside, but nobody knows it yet. You can see the darkness growing against the window-panes and you hear the street noises every now and again, or maybe the jangling beat of a tambourine from one of the churches close by, but it's real quiet in the room. For a moment nobody's talking, but every face looks darkening, like the sky outside. And my mother rocks a little from the waist, and my father's eyes are closed. Everyone is looking at something a child can't see. For a minute they've forgotten the children. Maybe a kid is lying on the rug half asleep. Maybe somebody's got a kid on his lap and is absent-mindedly stroking the kid's head. Maybe there's a kid, quiet and big-eyed, curled up in a big chair in the corner. The silence, the darkness coming, and the darkness in the faces frightens the child obscurely. He hopes that the hand which strokes his forehead will never stop—will never die. He hopes that there will never come a time when the old folks won't be sitting around the living room, talking about where they've come from, and what they've seen, and what's happened to them and their kinfolk.

But something deep and watchful in the child knows that this is bound to end, is already ending. In a moment someone will get up and turn on the light. Then the old folks will remember the children and they won't talk any more that day. And when light fills the room, the child is filled with darkness. He knows that every time this happens he's moved just a little closer to that darkness outside. The darkness outside is what the old folks have been talking about. It's what they've come from. It's what they endure. The child knows that they won't talk any more because if he knows too much about what's happened to *them*, he'll know too much too soon, about what's going to happen to *him*.

The last time I talked to my mother, I remember I was restless. I wanted to get out and see Isabel. We weren't married then and we had a lot to straighten out between us.

There Mama sat, in black, by the window. She was humming an old church song, *Lord, you brought me from a long ways off.* Sonny was out somewhere. Mama kept watching the streets.

"I don't know," she said, "if I'll ever see you again, after you go off from here. But I hope you'll remember the things I tried to teach you."

"Don't talk like that," I said, and smiled. "You'll be here a long time yet."

She smiled, too, but she said nothing. She was quiet for a long time. And I said, "Mama, don't you worry about nothing. I'll be writing all the time, and you be getting the checks. . . ."

"I want to talk to you about your brother," she said, suddenly. "If anything happens to me he ain't going to have nobody to look out for him."

"Mama," I said, "ain't nothing going to happen to you *or* Sonny. Sonny's all right. He's a good boy and he's got good sense."

"It ain't a question of his being a good boy," Mama said, "nor of his having good sense. It ain't only the bad ones, nor yet the dumb ones that gets sucked under." She stopped, looking at me. "Your Daddy once had a brother," she said, and she smiled in a way that made me feel she was in pain. "You didn't never know that, did you?"

"No," I said, "I never knew that," and I watched her face.

"Oh, yes," she said, "your Daddy had a brother." She looked out of the window again. "I know you never saw your Daddy cry. But *I* did—many a time, through all these years."

I asked her, "What happened to his brother? How come nobody's ever talked about him?"

This was the first time I ever saw my mother look old.

"His brother got killed," she said, "when he was just a little younger than you are now. I knew him. He was a fine boy. He was maybe a little full of the devil, but he didn't mean nobody no harm."

Then she stopped and the room was silent, exactly as it had sometimes been on those Sunday afternoons. Mama kept looking out into the streets.

"He used to have a job in the mill," she said, "and, like all young folks, he just liked to perform on Saturday nights. Saturday nights, him and your father would drift around to different places, go to dances and things like that, or just sit around with people they knew, and your father's brother would sing, he had a fine voice, and play along with himself on his guitar. Well, this particular Saturday night, him and your father was coming home from some place, and they were both a little drunk and there was a moon that night, it was bright like day. Your father's brother was feeling kind of good, and he was whistling to himself, and he had his guitar slung over his shoulder. They was coming down a hill and beneath them was a road that turned off from the highway. Well, your father's brother, being always kind of frisky, decided to run down this hill, and he did, with that guitar banging and clanging behind him, and he ran across the road, and he was making water behind a tree. And your father was sort of amused at him and he was still coming down the hill, kind of slow. Then he heard a car motor and that same minute his brother stepped from behind the tree, into the road, in the moonlight. And he started to cross the road. And your father started to run down the hill, he says he don't know why. This car was full of white men. They was all drunk, and when they seen your father's brother they let out a great whoop and holler and they aimed the car straight at him. They was having fun, they just wanted to scare him, the way they do sometimes, you know. But they was drunk. And I guess the boy, being drunk, too, and scared, kind of lost his head. By the time he jumped it was too late. Your father says he heard his brother scream when the car rolled over him, and he heard the wood of that guitar when it give, and he heard them strings go flying, and he heard them white men shouting, and the car kept on a-going and it ain't stopped till this day. And, time your father got down the hill, his brother weren't nothing but blood and pulp."

Tears were gleaming on my mother's face. There wasn't anything I could say.

"He never mentioned it," she said, "because I never let him mention it before you children. Your Daddy was like a crazy man that night and for many a night thereafter. He says he never in his life seen anything as dark as that road after the lights of that car had gone away. Weren't nothing, weren't nobody on that road, just your Daddy and his brother and that busted guitar. Oh, yes. Your Daddy never did really get right again. Till the day he died he weren't sure but that every white man he saw was the man that killed his brother."

She stopped and took out her handkerchief and dried her eyes and looked at me.

"I ain't telling you all this," she said, "to make you scared or bitter or to make you hate nobody. I'm telling you this because you got a brother. And the world ain't changed."

I guess I didn't want to believe this. I guess she saw this in my face. She turned away from me, toward the window again, searching those streets.

"But I praise my Redeemer," she said at last, "that He called your Daddy home before me. I ain't saying it to throw no flowers at myself, but, I declare, it keeps me from feeling too cast down to know I helped your father get safely through this world. Your father always acted like he was the roughest, strongest man on earth. And everybody took him to be like that. But if he hadn't had *me* there—to see his tears!"

She was crying again. Still, I couldn't move. I said, "Lord, Lord, Mama, I didn't know it was like that."

"Oh, honey," she said, "there's a lot that you don't know. But you are going to find it out." She stood up from the window and came over to me. "You got to hold on to your brother," she said, "and don't let him fall, no matter what it looks like is happening to him and no matter how evil you gets with him. You going to be evil with him many a time. But don't you forget what I told you, you hear?"

"I won't forget," I said. "Don't you worry, I won't forget. I won't let nothing happen to Sonny."

My mother smiled as though she were amused at something she saw in my face. Then, "You may not be able to stop nothing from happening. But you got to let him know you's *there.*"

Two days later I was married, and then I was gone. And I had a lot of things on my mind and I pretty well forgot my promise to Mama until I got shipped home on a special furlough for her funeral.

And, after the funeral, with just Sonny and me alone in the empty kitchen, I tried to find out something about him.

"What do you want to do?" I asked him.

"I'm going to be a musician," he said.

For he had graduated, in the time I had been away, from dancing to the juke box to finding out who was playing what, and what they were doing with it, and he had bought himself a set of drums.

"You mean, you want to be a drummer?" I somehow had the feeling that being a drummer might be all right for other people but not for my brother Sonny.

"I don't think," he said, looking at me very gravely, "that I'll ever be a good drummer. But I think I can play a piano."

I frowned. I'd never played the role of the older brother quite so seriously before, had scarcely ever, in fact, *asked* Sonny a damn thing. I sensed myself in the presence of something I didn't really know how to handle, didn't understand. So I made my frown a little deeper as I asked: "What kind of musician do you want to be?"

He grinned. "How many kinds do you think there are?"

"Be *serious*," I said.

He laughed, throwing his head back, and then looked at me. "I *am* serious."

"Well, then, for Christ's sake, stop kidding around and answer a serious question. I mean, do you want to be a concert pianist, you want to play classical music and all that, or—or what?" Long before I finished he was laughing again. "For Christ's *sake*, Sonny!"

He sobered, but with difficulty. "I'm sorry. But you sound so—*scared!*" and he was off again.

"Well, you may think it's funny now, baby, but it's not going to be so funny when you have to make your living at it, let me tell you *that*." I was furious because I knew he was laughing at me and I didn't know why.

"No," he said, very sober now, and afraid, perhaps, that he'd hurt me, "I don't want to be a classical pianist. That isn't what interests me. I mean"—he paused, looking hard at me, as though his eyes would help me to understand, and then gestured helplessly, as though perhaps his hand would help—"I mean, I'll have a lot of studying to do, and I'll have to study *everything*, but I mean, I want to play *with*—jazz musicians." He stopped. "I want to play jazz," he said.

Well, the word had never before sounded as heavy, as real, as it sounded that afternoon in Sonny's mouth. I just looked at him and I was probably frowning a real frown by this time. I simply couldn't see why on earth he'd want to spend his time hanging around night clubs, clowning around on bandstands, while people pushed each other around a dance floor. It seemed—beneath him, somehow. I had never thought about it before, had never been forced to, but I suppose I had always put jazz musicians in a class with what Daddy called "good-time people."

"Are you *serious*?"

"Hell, *yes*, I'm serious."

He looked more helpless than ever, and annoyed, and deeply hurt.

I suggested, helpfully: "You mean—like Louis Armstrong?"

His face closed as though I'd struck him. "No. I'm not talking about none of that old-time, down home crap."

"Well, look, Sonny, I'm sorry, don't get mad. I just don't altogether get it, that's all. Name somebody—you know, a jazz musician you admire."

"Bird."

"Who?"

"Bird! Charlie Parker! Don't they teach you nothing in the goddamn army?"

I lit a cigarette. I was surprised and then a little amused to discover that I was trembling. "I've been out of touch," I said. "You'll have to be patient with me. Now. Who's this Parker character?"

"He's just one of the greatest jazz musicians alive," said Sonny, sullenly, his hands in his pockets, his back to me. "Maybe *the* greatest," he added, bitterly, "that's probably why *you* never heard of him."

"All right," I said. "I'm ignorant. I'm sorry. I'll go out and buy all the cat's records right away, all right?"

"It don't," said Sonny, with dignity, "make any difference to me. I don't care what you listen to. Don't do me no favors."

I was beginning to realize that I'd never seen him so upset before. With another part of my mind I was thinking that this would probably turn out to be one of those things kids go through and that I shouldn't make it seem important by pushing it too hard. Still, I didn't think it would do any harm to ask: "Doesn't all this take a lot of time? Can you make a living at it?"

He turned back to me and half leaned, half sat, on the kitchen table. "Everything takes time," he said, "and—well, yes, sure, I can make a living at it. But what I don't seem to be able to make you understand is that it's the only thing I want to do."

"Well Sonny," I said, gently, "you know people can't always do exactly what they *want* to do—"

"*No,* I don't know that," said Sonny, surprising me. "I think people *ought* to do what they want to do, what else are they alive for?"

"You getting to be a big boy," I said desperately, "it's time you started thinking about your future."

"I'm thinking about my future," said Sonny, grimly. "I think about it all the time."

I gave up. I decided, if he didn't change his mind, that we could always talk about it later. "In the meantime," I said, "you got to finish school." We had already decided that he'd have to move in with Isabel and her folks. I knew this wasn't the ideal arrangement because Isabel's folks are inclined to be dicty² and they hadn't especially wanted Isabel to marry me. But I didn't know what else to do. "And we have to get you fixed up at Isabel's."

There was a long silence. He moved from the kitchen table to the window. "That's a terrible idea. You know it yourself."

"Do you have a *better* idea?"

He just walked up and down the kitchen for a minute. He was as tall as I was. He had started to shave. I suddenly had the feeling that I didn't know him at all.

2 **dicty:** Snobbish.

He stopped at the kitchen table and picked up my cigarettes. Looking at me with a kind of mocking, amused defiance, he put one between his lips. "You mind?"

"You smoking already?"

He lit the cigarette and nodded, watching me through the smoke. "I just wanted to see if I'd have the courage to smoke in front of you." He grinned and blew a great cloud of smoke to the ceiling. "It was easy." He looked at my face. "Come on, now. I bet you was smoking at my age, tell the truth."

I didn't say anything but the truth was on my face, and he laughed. But now there was something very strained in his laugh. "Sure. And I bet that ain't all you was doing."

He was frightening me a little. "Cut the crap," I said. "We already decided that you was going to go and live at Isabel's. Now what's got into you all of a sudden?"

"*You* decided it," he pointed out. "*I* didn't decide nothing." He stopped in front of me, leaning against the stove, arms loosely folded. "Look, brother. I don't want to stay in Harlem no more, I really don't." He was very earnest. He looked at me, then over toward the kitchen window. There was something in his eyes I'd never seen before, some thoughtfulness, some worry all his own. He rubbed the muscle of one arm. "It's time I was getting out of here."

"Where do you want to *go,* Sonny?"

"I want to join the army. Or the navy, I don't care. If I say I'm old enough they'll believe me."

Then I got mad. It was because I was so scared. "You must be crazy. You goddamn fool, what the hell do you want to go and join the *army* for?"

"I just told you. To get out of Harlem."

"Sonny, you haven't even finished *school.* And if you really want to be a musician, how do you expect to study if you're in the *army?*"

He looked at me, trapped, and in anguish. "There's ways. I might be able to work out some kind of deal. Anyway, I'll have the G.I. Bill when I come out."

"*If* you come out." We stared at each other. "Sonny, please. Be reasonable. I know the setup is far from perfect. But we got to do the best we can."

"I ain't learning nothing in school," he said. "Even when I go." He turned away from me and opened the window and threw his cigarette out into the narrow alley. I watched his back. "At least, I ain't learning nothing you'd want me to learn." He slammed the window so hard I thought the glass would fly out, and turned back to me. "And I'm sick of the stink of these garbage cans!"

"Sonny," I said, "I know how you feel. But if you don't finish school now, you're going to be sorry later that you didn't." I grabbed him by the shoulders. "And you only got another year. It ain't so bad. And I'll come back and I swear I'll help you do *whatever* you want to do. Just try to put up with it till I come back. Will you please do that? For me?"

He didn't answer and he wouldn't look at me.

"Sonny. You hear me?"

He pulled away. "I hear you. But you never hear anything *I* say."

I didn't know what to say to that. He looked out of the window and then back at me. "OK," he said, and sighed. "I'll try."

Then I said, trying to cheer him up a little, "They got a piano at Isabel's. You can practice on it."

And as a matter of fact, it did cheer him up for a minute. "That's right," he said to himself. "I forgot that." His face relaxed a little. But the worry, the thoughtfulness, played on it still, the way shadows play on a face which is staring into the fire.

But I thought I'd never hear the end of that piano. At first, Isabel would write me, saying how nice it was that Sonny was so serious about his music and how, as soon as he came in from school, or wherever he had been when he was supposed to be at school, he went straight to that piano and stayed there until suppertime. And, after supper, he went back to that piano and stayed there until everybody went to bed. He was at the piano all day Saturday and all day Sunday. Then he bought a record player and started playing records. He'd play one record over and over again, all day long sometimes, and he'd improvise along with it on the piano. Or he'd play one section of the record, one chord, one change, one progression, then he'd do it on the piano. Then back to the record. Then back to the piano.

Well, I really don't know how they stood it. Isabel finally confessed that it wasn't like living with a person at all, it was like living with sound. And the sound didn't make any sense to her, didn't make any sense to any of them—naturally. They began, in a way, to be afflicted by this presence that was living in their home. It was as though Sonny were some sort of god, or monster. He moved in an atmosphere which wasn't like theirs at all. They fed him and he ate, he washed himself, he walked in and out of their door; he certainly wasn't nasty or unpleasant or rude, Sonny isn't any of those things; but it was as though he were all wrapped up in some cloud, some fire, some vision all his own; and there wasn't any way to reach him.

At the same time, he wasn't really a man yet, he was still a child, and they had to watch out for him in all kinds of ways. They certainly couldn't throw him out. Neither did they dare to make a great scene about that piano because even they dimly sensed, as I sensed, from so many thousands of miles away, that Sonny was at that piano playing for his life.

But he hadn't been going to school. One day a letter came from the school board and Isabel's mother got it—there had, apparently, been other letters but Sonny had torn them up. This day, when Sonny came in, Isabel's mother showed him the letter and asked where he'd been spending his time. And she finally got it out of him that he'd been down in Greenwich Village, with musicians and other characters, in a white girl's apartment. And this scared her and she started to scream at him and what came up, once she began—though she denies it to this day—was what sacrifices they were making to give Sonny a decent home and how little he appreciated it.

Sonny didn't play the piano that day. By evening, Isabel's mother had calmed down but then there was the old man to deal with, and Isabel herself. Isabel says she did her best to be calm but she broke down and started crying. She says she just watched Sonny's face. She could tell, by watching him, what was happening with him.

And what was happening was that they penetrated his cloud, they had reached him. Even if their fingers had been a thousand times more gentle than human fingers ever are, he could hardly help feeling that they had stripped him naked and were spitting on that nakedness. For he also had to see that his presence, that music, which was life or death to him, had been torture for them and that they had endured it, not at all for his sake, but only for mine. And Sonny couldn't take that. He can take it a little better today than he could then but he's still not very good at it and, frankly, I don't know anybody who is.

The silence of the next few days must have been louder than the sound of all the music ever played since time began. One morning, before she went to work, Isabel was in his room for something and she suddenly realized that all of his records were gone. And she knew for certain that he was gone. And he was. He went as far as the navy would carry him. He finally sent me a postcard from some place in Greece and that was the first I knew that Sonny was still alive. I didn't see him any more until we were both back in New York and the war had long been over.

He was a man by then, of course, but I wasn't willing to see it. He came by the house from time to time, but we fought almost every time we met. I didn't like the way he carried himself, loose and dreamlike all the time, and I didn't like his friends, and his music seemed to be merely an excuse for the life he led. It sounded just that weird and disordered.

Then we had a fight, a pretty awful fight, and I didn't see him for months. By and by I looked him up, where he was living, in a furnished room in the Village, and I tried to make it up. But there were lots of other people in the room and Sonny just lay on his bed, and he wouldn't come downstairs with me, and he treated these other people as though they were his family and I weren't. So I got mad and then he got mad, and then I told him that he might just as well be dead as live the way he was living. Then he stood up and he told me not to worry about him any more in life, that he *was* dead as far as I was concerned. Then he pushed me to the door and the other people looked on as though nothing were happening, and he slammed the door behind me. I stood in the hallway, staring at the door. I heard somebody laugh in the room and then the tears came to my eyes. I started down the steps, whistling to keep from crying, I kept whistling to myself, *You going to need me, baby, one of these cold, rainy days.*

I read about Sonny's trouble in the spring. Little Grace died in the fall. She was a beautiful little girl. But she only lived a little over two years. She died of polio and she suffered. She had a slight fever for a couple of days, but it didn't seem like anything and we just kept her in bed. And we would certainly have called the doctor, but the fever dropped, she seemed to be all right. So we thought it had just been a cold. Then, one day, she was up, playing; Isabel was in the kitchen fixing lunch for the two boys when they'd come in from school, and she heard Grace fall down in the living room. When you have a lot of children you don't always start running when one of them falls, unless they start screaming or something. And, this time, Grace was quiet. Yet, Isabel says that when she heard that *thump* and then that silence, something happened in her to make her afraid. And she ran to the living room and there was little Grace on the floor, all twisted up and the reason she hadn't screamed was that she couldn't get her breath. And when she did scream, it was the worst sound, Isabel says, that she'd ever heard in all her life, and she still hears it sometimes in her dreams. Isabel will sometimes wake me up with a low, moaning, strangled sound and I have to be quick to awaken her and hold her to me and where Isabel is weeping against me seems a mortal wound.

I think I may have written Sonny the very day that little Grace was buried. I was sitting in the living room in the dark, by myself, and I suddenly thought of Sonny. My trouble made his real.

One Saturday afternoon, when Sonny had been living with us, or, anyway, been in our house, for nearly two weeks, I found myself wandering aimlessly about the living room, drinking from a can of beer, and trying to work up the courage to search Sonny's room. He was out, he was usually out whenever I was home, and Isabel had taken the children to see their grandparents. Suddenly I was standing still in front of the living room window, watching Seventh Avenue. The idea of searching Sonny's room made me still. I scarcely dared to admit to myself what I'd be searching for. I didn't know what I'd do if I found it. Or if I didn't.

On the sidewalk across from me, near the entrance to a barbecue joint, some people were holding an old-fashioned revival meeting. The barbecue cook, wearing a dirty white apron, his conked[3] hair reddish and metallic in the pale sun and a cigarette between his lips, stood in the doorway, watching them. Kids and older people paused in their errands and stood there, along with some older men and a couple of very tough-looking women who watched everything that happened on the avenue, as though they owned it, or were maybe owned by it. Well, they were watching this, too. The revival was being carried on by three sisters in black, and a brother. All they had were their voices and their Bibles and a tambourine. The brother was testifying and while he testified two of the sisters stood together, seeming to say, Amen, and the third sister walked around with the tambourine outstretched and a couple of people dropped coins into it. Then the brother's testimony ended and the sister who had been taking up the collection dumped the coins into her palm and transferred them to the pocket of her long black robe. Then she raised both hands, striking the tambourine against the air, and then against one hand, and she started to sing. And the two other sisters and the brother joined in.

It was strange, suddenly, to watch, though I had been seeing these street meetings all my life. So, of course, had everybody else down there. Yet, they paused and watched and listened and I stood still at the window. *"Tis the old ship of Zion,"* they sang, and the sister with the tambourine kept a steady, jangling beat, *"It has rescued many a thousand!"* Not a soul under the sound of their voices was hearing this song for the first time, not one of them had been rescued. Nor had they seen much in the way of rescue work being done around them. Neither did they especially believe in the holiness of the three sisters and the brother, they knew too much about them, knew where

3 **conked:** Straightened.

they lived, and how. The woman with the tambourine, whose voice dominated the air, whose face was bright with joy, was divided by very little from the woman who stood watching her, a cigarette between her heavy, chapped lips, her hair a cuckoo's nest, her face scarred and swollen from many beatings, and her black eyes glittering like coal. Perhaps they both knew this, which was why, when, as rarely, they addressed each other, they addressed each other as Sister. As the singing filled the air the watching, listening faces underwent a change, the eyes focusing on something within; the music seemed to soothe a poison out of them; and time seemed, nearly, to fall away from the sullen, belligerent, battered faces, as though they were fleeing back to their first condition, while dreaming of their last. The barbecue cook half shook his head and smiled, and dropped his cigarette and disappeared into his joint. A man fumbled in his pockets for change and stood holding it in his hand impatiently, as though he had just remembered a pressing appointment further up the avenue. He looked furious. Then I saw Sonny, standing on the edge of the crowd. He was carrying a wide, flat notebook with a green cover, and it made him look, from where I was standing, almost like a schoolboy. The coppery sun brought out the copper in his skin, he was very faintly smiling, standing very still. Then the singing stopped, the tambourine turned into a collection plate again. The furious man dropped in his coins and vanished, so did a couple of the women, and Sonny dropped some change in the plate, looking directly at the woman with a little smile. He started across the avenue, toward the house. He has a slow, loping walk, something like the way Harlem hipsters walk, only he's imposed on this his own halfbeat. I had never really noticed it before.

I stayed at the window, both relieved and apprehensive. As Sonny disappeared from my sight, they began singing again. And they were still singing when his key turned in the lock.

"Hey," he said.

"Hey, yourself. You want some beer?"

"No. Well, maybe." But he came up to the window and stood beside me, looking out. "What a warm voice," he said.

They were singing *If I could only hear my mother pray again!*

"Yes," I said, "and she can sure beat that tambourine."

"But what a terrible song," he said, and laughed. He dropped his notebook on the sofa and disappeared into the kitchen. "Where's Isabel and the kids?"

"I think they went to see their grandparents. You hungry?"

"No." He came back into the living room with his can of beer. "You want to come some place with me tonight?"

I sensed, I don't know how, that I couldn't possibly say No. "Sure. Where?"

He sat down on the sofa and picked up his notebook and started leafing through it. "I'm going to sit in with some fellows in a joint in the Village."

"You mean, you're going to play, tonight?"

"That's right." He took a swallow of his beer and moved back to the window. He gave me a sidelong look. "If you can stand it."

"I'll try," I said.

He smiled to himself and we both watched as the meeting across the way broke up. The three sisters and the brother, heads bowed, were singing *God be with you till we meet again*. The faces around them were very quiet. Then the song ended. The small crowd dispersed. We watched the three women and the lone man walk slowly up the avenue.

"When she was singing before," said Sonny, abruptly, "her voice reminded me for a minute of what heroin feels like sometimes—when it's in your veins. It makes you feel sort of warm and cool at the same time. And distant. And—and sure." He sipped his beer, very deliberately not looking at me. I watched his face. "It makes you feel—in control. Sometimes you've got to have that feeling."

"Do you?" I sat down slowly in the easy chair.

"Sometimes." He went to the sofa and picked up his notebook again. "Some people do."

"In order," I asked, "to play?" And my voice was very ugly, full of contempt and anger.

"Well"—he looked at me with great, troubled eyes, as though, in fact, he hoped his eyes would tell me things he could never otherwise say—"they *think* so. And *if* they think so—!"

"And what do *you* think?" I asked.

He sat on the sofa and put his can of beer on the floor. "I don't know," he said, and I couldn't be sure if he were answering my question or pursuing his thoughts. His face didn't tell me. "It's not so much to *play*. It's to *stand* it, to be able to make it at all. On any level." He frowned and smiled: "In order to keep from shaking to pieces."

"But these friends of yours," I said, "they seem to shake themselves to pieces pretty goddamn fast."

"Maybe." He played with the notebook. And something told me that I should curb my tongue, that Sonny was doing his best to talk, that I should listen. "But of course you only know the ones that've gone to pieces. Some don't—or at least they haven't *yet* and that's just about all *any* of us can say." He paused. "And then there are some who just live, really, in hell, and they know it and they see what's happening and they go right on. I don't know." He sighed, dropped the notebook, folded his arms. "Some guys, you can tell from the way they play, they on something *all* the time. And you can see that, well, it makes something real for them. But of course," he picked up his beer from the floor and sipped it and put the can down again, "they *want* to, too, you've got to see that. Even some of them that say they don't—*some*, not all."

"And what about you?" I asked—I couldn't help it. "What about you? Do *you* want to?"

He stood up and walked to the window and remained silent for a long time. Then he sighed. "Me," he said. Then: "While I was downstairs before, on my way here, listening to that woman sing, it struck me all of a sudden how much suffering she must have had to go through—to sing like that. It's *repulsive* to think you have to suffer that much."

I said: "But there's no way not to suffer—is there, Sonny?"

"I believe not," he said, and smiled, "but that's never stopped anyone from trying." He looked at me. "Has it?" I realized, with this mocking look, that there stood between us, forever, beyond the power of time or forgiveness, the fact that I had held silence—so long!— when he had needed human speech to help him. He turned back to the window. "No, there's no way not to suffer. But you try all kinds of ways to keep from drowning in it, to keep on top of it, and to make it seem—well, like *you*. Like you did something, all right, and now you're suffering for it. You know?" I said nothing. "Well, you know," he said, impatiently, "why *do* people suffer? Maybe it's better to do something to give it a reason, *any* reason."

"But we just agreed," I said, "that there's no way not to suffer. Isn't it better, then, just to—take it?"

"But nobody just takes it," Sonny cried, "that's what I'm telling you! *Everybody* tries not to. You're just hung up on the *way* some people try—it's not *your* way!"

The hair on my face began to itch, my face felt wet. "That's not true," I said, "that's not true. I don't give a damn what other people do, I don't even care how they suffer. I just care how *you* suffer." And he looked at me. "Please believe me," I said, "I don't want to see you—die—trying not to suffer."

"I won't," he said, flatly, "die trying not to suffer. At least, not any faster than anybody else."

"But there's no need," I said, trying to laugh, "is there? in killing yourself."

I wanted to say more, but I couldn't. I wanted to talk about will power and how life could be—well, beautiful. I wanted to say that it was all within; but was it? Or, rather, wasn't that exactly the trouble? And I wanted to promise that I would never fail him again. But it would all have sounded—empty words and lies.

So I made the promise to myself and prayed that I would keep it.

"It's terrible sometimes, inside," he said, "that's what's the trouble. You walk these streets, black and funky and cold, and there's not really a living ass to talk to, and there's nothing shaking, and there's no way of getting it out—that storm inside. You can't talk it and you can't make love with it, and when you finally try to get with it and play it, you realize *nobody's* listening. So *you've* got to listen. You got to find a way to listen."

And then he walked away from the window and sat on the sofa again, as though all the wind had suddenly been knocked out of him. "Sometimes you'll do *anything* to play, even cut your mother's throat." He laughed and looked at me. "Or your brother's." Then he sobered. "Or your own." Then: "Don't worry. I'm all right now and I think I'll *be* all right. But I can't forget—where I've been. I don't mean just the physical place I've been, I mean where I've *been*. And *what* I've been."

"What have you been, Sonny?" I asked.

He smiled—but sat sideways on the sofa, his elbow resting on the back, his fingers playing with his mouth and chin, not looking at me. "I've been something I didn't recognize, didn't know I could be. Didn't know anybody could be." He stopped, looking inward, looking helplessly young, looking old. "I'm not talking about it now because I feel *guilty* or anything like that—maybe it would be better if I did, I don't know. Anyway, I can't really talk about it. Not to you, not to anybody," and now he turned and faced me. "Sometimes, you know, and it was actually when I was most *out* of the world, I felt that I was in it, and that I was *with* it, really, and I could play or I didn't really have to *play,* it just came out of me, it was there. And I don't know how I played, thinking about it now, but I know I did awful things, those times, sometimes, to people. Or it wasn't that I *did* anything to them—it was that they weren't real." He picked up the beer can; it was empty; he rolled it between his palms: "And other times—well, I needed a fix, I needed to find a place to lean, I needed to clear a space to *listen*—and I couldn't find it, and I—went crazy, I did terrible things to *me,* I was terrible *for* me." He began pressing the beer can between his hands, I watched the metal begin to give. It glittered, as he played with it, like a knife, and I was afraid he would cut himself, but I said nothing. "Oh well. I can never tell you. I was all by myself at the bottom of something, stinking and sweating and crying and shaking, and I smelled it, you know? *my* stink, and I thought I'd die if I couldn't get away from it and yet, all the same, I knew that everything I was doing was just locking me in with it. And I didn't know," he paused, still flattening the beer can, "I didn't know, I still *don't* know, something kept telling me that maybe it was good to smell your own stink, but I didn't think that *that* was what I'd been trying to do—and—who can stand it?" and he abruptly dropped the ruined beer can, looking at me with a small, still smile, and then rose, walking to the window as though it were the lodestone rock. I watched his face, he watched the avenue. "I couldn't tell you when Mama died—but the reason I wanted to leave Harlem so bad was to get away from drugs. And then, when I ran away, that's what I was running from—really. When I came back, nothing had changed, *I* hadn't changed, I was just—older." And he stopped, drumming with his fingers on the windowpane. The sun had vanished, soon darkness would fall. I watched his face. "It can come again," he said, almost as though speaking to himself. Then he turned to me. "It can come again," he repeated. "I just want you to know that."

"All right," I said, at last. "So it can come again. All right."

He smiled, but the smile was sorrowful. "I had to try to tell you," he said.

"Yes," I said. "I understand that."

"You're my brother," he said, looking straight at me, and not smiling at all.

"Yes," I repeated, "yes. I understand that."

He turned back to the window, looking out. "All that hatred down there," he said, "all that hatred and misery and love. It's a wonder it doesn't blow the avenue apart."

We went to the only night club on a short, dark street, downtown. We squeezed through the narrow, chattering, jam-packed bar to the entrance of the big room, where the bandstand was. And we stood there for a moment, for the lights were very dim in this room and we couldn't see. Then, "Hello, boy," said a voice and an enormous black man, much older than Sonny or myself, erupted out of all that atmospheric lighting and put an arm around Sonny's shoulder. "I been sitting right here," he said, "waiting for you."

He had a big voice, too, and heads in the darkness turned toward us.

Sonny grinned and pulled a little away, and said, "Creole, this is my brother. I told you about him."

Creole shook my hand. "I'm glad to meet you, son," he said, and it was clear that he was glad to meet me *there,* for Sonny's sake. And he smiled, "You got a real musician in *your* family," and he took his arm from Sonny's shoulder and slapped him, lightly, affectionately, with the back of his hand.

"Well. Now I've heard it all," said a voice behind us. This was another musician, and a friend of Sonny's, a coal-black, cheerful-looking man, built close to the ground. He immediately began confiding to me, at the top of his lungs, the most terrible things about Sonny, his teeth gleaming like a lighthouse and his laugh coming up out of him like the beginning of an earthquake. And it turned out that everyone at the bar knew Sonny, or almost everyone; some were musicians, working there, or nearby, or not working, some were simply hangers-on, and some were there to hear Sonny play. I was introduced to all of them and they were all very polite to me. Yet, it was clear that, for them, I was only Sonny's brother. Here, I was in Sonny's world. Or, rather: his kingdom. Here, it was not even a question that his veins bore royal blood.

They were going to play soon and Creole installed me, by myself, at a table in a dark corner. Then I watched them, Creole, and the little black man, and Sonny, and the others, while they horsed around, standing just below the bandstand. The light from the bandstand spilled just a little short of them and, watching them laughing and gesturing and moving about, I had the feeling that they, nevertheless, were being most careful not to step into that circle of light too suddenly: that if they moved into the light too suddenly, without thinking, they would perish in flame. Then, while I watched, one of them, the small, black man, moved into the light and crossed the bandstand and started fooling around with his drums. Then—being funny and being, also, extremely ceremonious—Creole took Sonny by the arm and led him to the piano. A woman's voice called Sonny's name and a few hands started clapping. And Sonny, also being funny and being ceremonious, and so touched, I think, that he could have cried, but neither hiding it nor showing it, riding it like a man, grinned, and put both hands to his heart and bowed from the waist.

Creole then went to the bass fiddle and a lean, very bright-skinned brown man jumped up on the bandstand and picked up his horn. So there they were, and the atmosphere on the bandstand and in the room began to change and tighten. Someone stepped up to the microphone and announced them. Then there were all kinds of murmurs. Some people at the bar shushed others. The waitress ran around, frantically getting in the last orders, guys and chicks got closer to each other, and the lights on the bandstand, on the quartet, turned to a kind of indigo. Then they all looked different there. Creole looked about him for the last time, as though he were making certain that all his chickens were in the coop, and then he jumped and struck the fiddle. And there they were.

All I know about music is that not many people ever really hear it. And even then, on the rare occasions when something opens within, and the music enters, what we mainly hear, or hear corroborated, are personal, private, vanishing evocations. But the man who creates the music is hearing something else, is dealing with the roar rising from the void and imposing order on it as it hits the air. What is evoked in him, then, is of another order, more terrible because it has no words, and triumphant, too, for that same reason. And his triumph, when he triumphs, is ours. I just watched Sonny's face. His face was troubled, he was working hard, but he wasn't with it. And I had the feeling that, in a way, everyone on the bandstand was waiting for him, both waiting for him and pushing him along. But as I began to watch Creole, I realized that it was Creole who held them all back. He had them on a short rein. Up there, keeping the beat with his whole body, wailing on the fiddle, with his eyes half closed, he was listening to everything, but he was listening to Sonny. He was having a dialogue with Sonny. He wanted Sonny to leave the shore line and strike out for the deep water. He was Sonny's witness that deep water and drowning were not the same thing—he had been there, and he knew. And he wanted Sonny to know. He was waiting for Sonny to do the things on the keys which would let Creole know that Sonny was in the water.

And, while Creole listened, Sonny moved, deep within, exactly like someone in torment. I had never before thought of how awful the relationship must be between the musician and his instrument. He has to fill it, this instrument, with the breath of life, his own. He has to make it do what he wants it to do. And a piano is just a piano. It's made out of so much wood and wires and little hammers and big ones, and ivory. While there's only so much you can do with it, the only way to find this out is to try and make it do everything.

And Sonny hadn't been near a piano for over a year. And he wasn't on much better terms with his life, not the life that stretched before him now. He and the piano stammered, started one way, got scared, stopped; started another way, panicked, marked time, started again; then seemed to have found a direction, panicked again, got stuck. And the face I saw on Sonny I'd never seen before. Everything had been burned out of it, and, at the same time, things usually hidden were being burned in, by the fire and fury of the battle which was occurring in him up there.

Yet, watching Creole's face as they neared the end of the first set, I had the feeling that something had happened, something I hadn't heard. Then they finished, there was scattered applause, and then, without an instant's warning, Creole started into something else, it was almost sardonic, it was *Am I Blue*. And, as though he commanded, Sonny began to play. Something began to happen. And Creole let out the reins. The dry, low, black man said something awful on the drums, Creole answered, and the drums talked back. Then the horn insisted, sweet and high, slightly detached perhaps, and Creole listened, commenting now and then, dry, and driving, beautiful and calm and old. Then they all came together again, and Sonny was part of the family again. I could tell this from his face. He seemed to have found, right there beneath his fingers, a damn brand-new piano. It seemed that he couldn't get over it. Then, for awhile, just being happy with Sonny, they seemed to be agreeing with him that brand-new pianos certainly were a gas.

Then Creole stepped forward to remind them that what they were playing was the blues. He hit something in all of them, he hit something in me, myself, and the music tightened and deepened, apprehension began to beat the air. Creole began to tell us what the blues were all about. They were not about anything very new. He and his boys up there were keeping it new, at the risk of ruin, destruction, madness, and death, in order to find new ways to make us listen. For, while the tale of how we suffer, and how we are delighted, and how we may triumph is never new, it always must be heard. There isn't any other tale to tell, it's the only light we've got in all this darkness.

And this tale, according to that face, that body, those strong hands on those strings, has another aspect in every country, and a new depth in every generation. Listen, Creole seemed to be saying, listen. Now these are Sonny's blues. He made the little black man on the drums know it, and the bright, brown man on the horn. Creole wasn't trying any longer to get Sonny in the water. He was wishing him Godspeed. Then he stepped back, very slowly, filling the air with the immense suggestion that Sonny speak for himself.

Then they all gathered around Sonny and Sonny played. Every now and again one of them seemed to say, Amen. Sonny's fingers filled the air with life, his life. But that life contained so many others. And Sonny went all the way back, he really began with the spare, flat statement of the opening phrase of the song. Then he began to make it his. It was very beautiful because it wasn't hurried and it was no longer a lament. I seemed to hear with what burning he had made it his, with what burning we had yet to make it ours, how we could cease lamenting. Freedom lurked around us and I understood, at last, that he could help us to be free if we would listen, that he would never be free until we did. Yet, there was no battle in his face now. I heard what he had gone through, and would continue to go through until he came to rest in earth. He had made it his: that long line, of which we knew only Mama and Daddy. And he was giving it back, as everything must be given back, so that, passing through death, it can live forever. I saw my mother's face again, and felt, for the first time, how the stones of the road she had walked on must have bruised her feet. I saw the moonlit road where my father's brother died. And it brought something else back to me, and carried me past it, I saw my little girl again and felt Isabel's tears again, and I felt my own tears begin to rise. And I was yet aware that this was only a moment, that the world waited outside, as hungry as a tiger, and that trouble stretched above us, longer than the sky.

Then it was over. Creole and Sonny let out their breath, both soaking wet, and grinning. There was a lot of applause and some of it was real. In the dark, the girl came by and I asked her to take drinks to the bandstand. There was a long pause, while they talked up there in the indigo light and after awhile I saw the girl put a Scotch and milk on top of the piano for Sonny. He didn't seem to notice it, but just before they started playing again, he sipped from it and looked toward me, and nodded. Then he put it back on top of the piano. For me, then, as they began to play again, it glowed and shook above my brother's head like the very cup of trembling.

# Jorge Luis Borges

### (1899–1986)

Born in Argentina and educated in Europe, Jorge Luis Borges spent a number of years working in the Argentinian National Library, eventually becoming its director but leaving the job after offending the dictator Juan Perón. Borges began his literary life as a member of the Spanish ultraisme movement, an antirealist style preferring image and metaphor to characterization or plot development. Borges greatly contributed to the advent of postmodernism in American fiction. Many of his best stories, including "Funes the Memorious," "The Garden of Forking Paths," and "The Library of Babel," are collected in *Ficciones* (1944) and *The Aleph and Other Stories* (1970). Of writing, he believed that nothing is truly original, declaring, "I don't think we're capable of creation in the way that God created the world." His chosen metaphor was the labyrinth, an object that fascinated him: "the very word labyrinth is a beautiful word [that] derives from the Greek labyrinthos, which initially denotes the shafts and corridors of a mine and . . . now denotes that strange construction especially built so that people would get lost." For Borges, the labyrinth symbolized a belief that the universe, however confusing, also has a center, and therefore a constructed order. Human life and human fiction, Borges believed, are much the same thing.

## Emma Zunz

1949

TRANSLATED BY DONALD A. YATES

On January 14, 1922, when Emma Zunz returned home from the Tarbuch & Loewenthal weaving mill, she found a letter at the far end of the entryway to her building; it had been sent from Brazil, and it informed her that her father had died. She was misled at first by the stamp and the envelope; then the unknown handwriting made her heart flutter. Nine or ten smudgy lines covered almost the entire piece of paper; Emma read that Sr. Maier had accidentally ingested an overdose of veronal and died on the third *inst.* in the hospital at Bagé. The letter was signed by a resident of the rooming house in which her father had lived, one Fein or Fain, in Rio Grande; he could not have known that he was writing to the dead man's daughter.

Emma dropped the letter. The first thing she felt was a sinking in her stomach and a trembling in her knees; then, a sense of blind guilt, of unreality, of cold, of fear; then, a desire for this day to be past. Then immediately she realized that such a wish was pointless, for her father's death was the only thing that had happened in the world, and it would go on happening, endlessly, forever after. She picked up the piece of paper and went to her room. Furtively, she put it away for safekeeping in a drawer, as though she somehow knew what was coming. She may already have begun to see the things that would happen next; she was already the person she was to become.

In the growing darkness, and until the end of that day, Emma wept over the suicide of Manuel Maier, who in happier days gone by had been Emanuel Zunz. She recalled summer outings to a small farm near Gualeguay, she recalled (or tried to recall) her mother, she recalled the family's little house in Lanús that had been sold at auction, she recalled the yellow lozenges of a window, recalled the verdict of prison, the disgrace, the anonymous letters with the newspaper article about the "Embezzlement of Funds by Teller," recalled (and this she would never forget) that on the last night, her father had sworn that the thief was Loewenthal—Loewenthal, Aaron

Loewenthal, formerly the manager of the mill and now one of its owners. Since 1916, Emma had kept the secret. She had revealed it to no one, not even to Elsa Urstein, her best friend. Perhaps she shrank from it out of profane incredulity; perhaps she thought that the secret was the link between herself and the absent man. Loewenthal didn't know she knew; Emma Zunz gleaned from that minuscule fact a sense of power.

She did not sleep that night, and by the time first light defined the rectangle of the window, she had perfected her plan. She tried to make that day (which seemed interminable to her) be like every other. In the mill, there were rumors of a strike; Emma declared, as she always did, that she was opposed to all forms of violence. At six, when her workday was done, she went with Elsa to a women's club that had a gymnasium and a swimming pool. They joined; she had to repeat and then spell her name; she had to applaud the vulgar jokes that accompanied the struggle to get it correct. She discussed with Elsa and the younger of the Kronfuss girls which moving picture they would see Sunday evening. And then there was talk of boyfriends; no one expected Emma to have anything to say. In April she would be nineteen, but men still inspired in her an almost pathological fear. . . . Home again, she made soup thickened with manioc flakes and some vegetables, ate early, went to bed, and forced herself to sleep. Thus passed Friday the fifteenth—a day of work, bustle, and trivia—the day before *the day.*

On Saturday, impatience wakened her. Impatience, not nervousness or second thoughts—and the remarkable sense of relief that she had reached this day at last. There was nothing else for her to plan or picture to herself; within a few hours she would have come to the simplicity of the *fait accompli.* She read in *La Prensa* that the *Nordstjärnan,* from Malmö, was to weigh anchor that night from Pier 3; she telephoned Loewenthal, insinuated that she had something to tell him, in confidence, about the strike, and promised to stop by his office at nightfall. Her voice quivered; the quiver befitted a snitch. No other memorable event took place that morning. Emma worked until noon and then settled with Perla Kronfuss and Elsa on the details of their outing on Sunday. She lay down after lunch and with her eyes closed went over the plan she had conceived. She reflected that the final step would be less horrible than the first, and would give her, she had no doubt of it, the taste of victory, and of justice. Suddenly, alarmed, she leaped out of bed and ran to the dressing table drawer. She opened it; under the portrait of Milton Sills, where she had left it night before last, she found Fain's letter. No one could have seen it; she began to read it, and then she tore it up.

To recount with some degree of reality the events of that evening would be difficult, and perhaps inappropriate. One characteristic of hell is its unreality, which might be thought to mitigate hell's terrors but perhaps makes them all the worse. How to make plausible an act in which even she who was to commit it scarcely believed? How to recover those brief hours of chaos that Emma Zunz's memory today repudiates and confuses? Emma lived in Amalgro, on Calle Liniers; we know that that evening she went down to the docks. On the infamous Paseo de Julio she may have seen herself multiplied in mirrors, made public by lights, and stripped naked by hungry eyes—but it is more reasonable to assume that at first she simply wandered, unnoticed, through the indifferent streets. . . . She stepped into two or three bars, observed the routine or the maneuvers of other women. Finally she ran into some men from the *Nordstjärnan*. One of them, who was quite young, she feared might inspire in her some hint of tenderness, so she chose a different one—perhaps a bit shorter than she, and foul-mouthed—so that there might be no mitigation of the purity of the horror. The man led her to a door and then down a gloomy entryway and then to a tortuous stairway and then into a vestibule (with lozenges identical to those of the house in Lanús) and then down a hallway and then to a door that closed behind them. The most solemn of events are outside time—whether because in the most solemn of events the immediate past is severed, as it were, from the future or because the elements that compose those events seem not to be consecutive.

In that time outside time, in that welter of disjointed and horrible sensations, did Emma Zunz think *even once* about the death that inspired the sacrifice? In my view, she thought about it once, and that was enough to endanger her desperate goal. She thought (she could not help thinking) that her father had done to her mother the horrible thing being done to her now. She thought it with weak-limbed astonishment, and then, immediately, took refuge in vertigo. The man—a Swede or Finn—did not speak Spanish; he was an instrument for Emma, as she was for him—but she was used for pleasure, while he was used for justice.

When she was alone, Emma did not open her eyes immediately. On the night table was the money the man had left. Emma sat up and tore it to shreds, as she had torn up the letter a short time before. Tearing up money is an act of impiety, like throwing away bread; the minute she did it, Emma wished she hadn't—an act of pride, and on *that* day. . . . Foreboding melted into the sadness of her body, into the revulsion. Sadness and revulsion lay upon Emma like chains, but slowly she got up and began to dress. The room had no bright colors; the last light of evening made it all the drearier. She managed to slip out without being seen. On the corner she mounted a westbound Lacroze and following her plan, she sat in the car's frontmost seat, so that no one would see her face. Perhaps she was comforted to see, in the banal bustle of the streets, that what had happened had not polluted everything. She rode through gloomy, shrinking neighborhoods, seeing them and forgetting them instantly, and got off at one of the stops on Warnes. Paradoxically, her weariness turned into a strength, for it forced her to concentrate on the details of her mission and masked from her its true nature and its final purpose.

Aaron Loewenthal was in the eyes of all an upright man; in those of his few closest acquaintances, a miser. He lived above the mill, alone. Living in the run-down slum, he feared thieves; in the courtyard of the mill there was a big dog, and in his desk drawer, as everyone knew, a revolver. The year before, he had decorously grieved the unexpected death of his wife—a Gauss! who'd brought him an excellent dowry!—but money was his true passion. With secret shame, he knew he was not as good at earning it as at holding on to it. He was quite religious; he believed he had a secret pact with the Lord—in return for prayers and devotions, he was exempted from doing good works. Bald, heavyset, dressed in mourning, with his dark-lensed pince-nez and blond beard, he was standing next to the window, awaiting the confidential report from operator Zunz.

He saw her push open the gate (which he had left ajar on purpose) and cross the gloomy courtyard. He saw her make a small detour when the dog (tied up on purpose) barked. Emma's lips were moving, like those of a person praying under her breath; weary, over and over they rehearsed the phrases that Sr. Loewenthal would hear before he died.

Things didn't happen the way Emma Zunz had foreseen. Since early the previous morning, many times she had dreamed that she would point the firm revolver, force the miserable wretch to confess his miserable guilt, explain to him the daring strata-gem that would allow God's justice to triumph over man's. (It was not out of fear, but because she was an instrument of that justice, that she herself intended not to be pun-ished.) Then, a single bullet in the center of his chest would put an end to Loewen-thal's life. But things didn't happen that way.

Sitting before Aaron Loewenthal, Emma felt (more than the urgency to avenge her father) the urgency to punish the outrage she herself had suffered. She could not *not* kill him, after being so fully and thoroughly dishonored. Nor did she have time to waste on theatrics. Sitting timidly in his office, she begged Loewenthal's pardon, in-voked (in her guise as snitch) the obligations entailed by loyalty, mentioned a few names, insinuated others, and stopped short, as though overcome by fearfulness. Her performance succeeded; Loewenthal went out to get her a glass of water. By the time he returned from the dining hall, incredulous at the woman's fluttering perturbation yet full of solicitude, Emma had found the heavy revolver in the drawer. She pulled the trigger twice. Loewenthal's considerable body crumpled as though crushed by the explosions and the smoke; the glass of water shattered; his face looked at her with as-tonishment and fury; the mouth in the face cursed her in Spanish and in Yiddish. The filthy words went on and on; Emma had to shoot him again. Down in the courtyard, the dog, chained to his post, began barking furiously, as a spurt of sudden blood gushed from the obscene lips and sullied the beard and clothes. Emma began the ac-cusation she had prepared ("I have avenged my father, and I shall not be pun-ished . . .") but she didn't finish it, because Sr. Loewenthal was dead. She never knew whether he had managed to understand.

The dog's tyrannical barking reminded her that she couldn't rest, not yet. She mussed up the couch, unbuttoned the dead man's suit coat, removed his spattered pince-nez and left them on the filing-cabinet. Then she picked up the telephone and repeated what she was to repeat so many times, in those and other words: *Something has happened, something unbelievable. . . . Sr. Loewenthal sent for me on the pretext of the strike. . . . He raped me. . . . I killed him. . . .*

The story was unbelievable, yes—and yet it convinced everyone, because in sub-stance it was true. Emma Zunz's tone of voice was real, her shame was real, her hatred was real. The outrage that had been done to her was real, as well; all that was false were the circumstances, the time, and one or two proper names.

# Willa Cather

## (1873–1947)

On the subject of good writing, Willa Cather observed, "It is just the thing . . . which escapes analysis that makes [a writer's work] first-rate." Cather worked as a journalist and teacher of high school English and Latin in Pittsburgh, Pennsylvania, after graduating from the University of Nebraska with a degree in classics. In 1903, she published her first book of poetry, *April Twilights*, and in 1905 she completed the first of four collections of short stories, entitled *The Troll Gardens*. Influenced by Sarah Orne Jewett, whom she met in Boston, she tried to follow that author's advice to "write to the human heart, the great consciousness that all humanity goes to make up." Her first novel was the 1913 *O Pioneers!*, which was followed by *The Song of the Lark* in 1918. Her most highly acclaimed novel, *My Antonia*, depicts the life of an American pioneer woman. Cather had begun writing novels after revisiting Red Cloud, the frontier town where she grew up and where she realized that her own experiences were worth writing about. She said, "Life began for me when I ceased to admire and began to remember."

## Paul's Case
1905

### A Study in Temperament

It was Paul's afternoon to appear before the faculty of the Pittsburgh High School to account for his various misdemeanours. He had been suspended a week ago, and his father had called at the Principal's office and confessed his perplexity about his son. Paul entered the faculty room suave and smiling. His clothes were a trifle outgrown and the tan velvet on the collar of his open overcoat was frayed and worn; but for all that there was something of the dandy about him, and he wore an opal pin in his neatly knotted black four-in-hand,[1] and a red carnation in his buttonhole. This latter adornment the faculty somehow felt was not properly significant of the contrite spirit befitting a boy under the ban of suspension.

Paul was tall for his age and very thin, with high, cramped shoulders and a narrow chest. His eyes were remarkable for a certain hysterical brilliancy and he continually used them in a conscious, theatrical sort of way, peculiarly offensive in a boy. The pupils were abnormally large, as though he were addicted to belladonna, but there was a glassy glitter about them which that drug does not produce.

---

1 **four-in-hand:** Necktie.

When questioned by the Principal as to why he was there, Paul stated, politely enough, that he wanted to come back to school. This was a lie, but Paul was quite accustomed to lying; found it, indeed, indispensable for overcoming friction. His teachers were asked to state their respective charges against him, which they did with such a rancour and aggrievedness as evinced that this was not a usual case. Disorder and impertinence were among the offences named, yet each of his instructors felt that it was scarcely possible to put into words the real cause of the trouble, which lay in a sort of hysterically defiant manner of the boy's; in the contempt which they all knew he felt for them, and which he seemingly made not the least effort to conceal. Once, when he had been making a synopsis of a paragraph at the blackboard, his English teacher had stepped to his side and attempted to guide his hand. Paul had started back with a shudder and thrust his hands violently behind him. The astonished woman could scarcely have been more hurt and embarrassed had he struck at her. The insult was so involuntary and definitely personal as to be unforgettable. In one way and another, he had made all his teachers, men and women alike, conscious of the same feeling of physical aversion. In one class he habitually sat with his hand shading his eyes; in another he always looked out of the window during the recitation; in another he made a running commentary on the lecture, with humorous intention.

His teachers felt this afternoon that his whole attitude was symbolized by his shrug and his flippantly red carnation flower, and they fell upon him without mercy, his English teacher leading the pack. He stood through it smiling, his pale lips parted over his white teeth. (His lips were continually twitching, and he had a habit of raising his eyebrows that was contemptuous and irritating to the last degree.) Older boys than Paul had broken down and shed tears under that baptism of fire, but his set smile did not once desert him, and his only sign of discomfort was the nervous trembling of the fingers that toyed with the buttons of his overcoat, and an occasional jerking of the other hand that held his hat. Paul was always smiling, always glancing about him, seeming to feel that people might be watching him and trying to detect something. This conscious expression, since it was as far as possible from boyish mirthfulness, was usually attributed to insolence or "smartness."

As the inquisition proceeded, one of his instructors repeated an impertinent remark of the boy's, and the Principal asked him whether he thought that a courteous speech to have made a woman. Paul shrugged his shoulders slightly and his eyebrows twitched.

"I don't know," he replied. "I didn't mean to be polite or impolite, either. I guess it's a sort of way I have of saying things regardless."

The Principal, who was a sympathetic man, asked him whether he didn't think that a way it would be well to get rid of. Paul grinned and said he guessed so. When he was told that he could go, he bowed gracefully and went out. His bow was but a repetition of the scandalous red carnation.

His teachers were in despair, and his drawing master voiced the feeling of them all when he declared there was something about the boy which none of them understood. He added: "I don't really believe that smile of his comes altogether from insolence; there's something sort of haunted about it. The boy is not strong, for one thing.

I happen to know that he was born in Colorado, only a few months before his mother died out there of a long illness. There is something wrong about the fellow."

The drawing master had come to realize that, in looking at Paul, one saw only his white teeth and the forced animation of his eyes. One warm afternoon the boy had gone to sleep at his drawing-board, and his master had noted with amazement what a white, blue-veined face it was; drawn and wrinkled like an old man's about the eyes, the lips twitching even in his sleep, and stiff with a nervous tension that drew them back from his teeth.

His teachers left the building dissatisfied and unhappy; humiliated to have felt so vindictive toward a mere boy, to have uttered this feeling in cutting terms, and to have set each other on, as it were, in the grewsome game of intemperate reproach. Some of them remembered having seen a miserable street cat set at bay by a ring of tormentors.

As for Paul, he ran down the hill whistling the Soldiers' Chorus from *Faust*, looking wildly behind him now and then to see whether some of his teachers were not there to writhe under his light-heartedness. As it was now late in the afternoon and Paul was on duty that evening as usher at Carnegie Hall, he decided that he would not go home to supper. When he reached the concert hall the doors were not yet open and, as it was chilly outside, he decided to go up into the picture gallery—always deserted at this hour—where there were some of Raffelli's[2] gay studies of Paris streets and an airy blue Venetian scene or two that always exhilarated him. He was delighted to find no one in the gallery but the old guard, who sat in one corner, a newspaper on his knee, a black patch over one eye and the other closed. Paul possessed himself of the place and walked confidently up and down, whistling under his breath. After a while he sat down before a blue Rico[3] and lost himself. When he bethought him to look at his watch, it was after seven o'clock, and he rose with a start and ran downstairs, making a face at Augustus, peering out from the castroom, and an evil gesture at the Venus of Milo as he passed her on the stairway.

When Paul reached the ushers' dressing-room half-a-dozen boys were there already, and he began excitedly to tumble into his uniform. It was one of the few that at all approached fitting, and Paul thought it very becoming—though he knew that the tight, straight coat accentuated his narrow chest, about which he was exceedingly sensitive. He was always considerably excited while he dressed, twanging all over to the tuning of the strings and the preliminary flourishes of the horns in the music-room; but to-night he seemed quite beside himself, and he teased and plagued the boys until, telling him that he was crazy, they put him down on the floor and sat on him.

Somewhat calmed by his suppression, Paul dashed out to the front of the house to seat the early comers. He was a model usher; gracious and smiling he ran up and down the aisles; nothing was too much trouble for him; he carried messages and brought programmes as though it were his greatest pleasure in life, and all the people in his section thought him a charming boy, feeling that he remembered and admired

---

2 **Raffelli:** Jean-François Raffaelli (1850–1924), French painter and sculptor.
3 **Rico:** Andreas Rico (1500–1550), Italian painter.

them. As the house filled, he grew more and more vivacious and animated, and the colour came to his cheeks and lips. It was very much as though this were a great reception and Paul were the host. Just as the musicians came out to take their places, his English teacher arrived with checks for the seats which a prominent manufacturer had taken for the season. She betrayed some embarrassment when she handed Paul the tickets, and a *hauteur* which subsequently made her feel very foolish. Paul was startled for a moment, and had the feeling of wanting to put her out; what business had she here among all these fine people and gay colours? He looked her over and decided that she was not appropriately dressed and must be a fool to sit downstairs in such togs. The tickets had probably been sent her out of kindness, he reflected as he put down a seat for her, and she had about as much right to sit there as he had.

When the symphony began Paul sank into one of the rear seats with a long sigh of relief, and lost himself as he had done before the Rico. It was not that symphonies, as such, meant anything in particular to Paul, but the first sigh of the instruments seemed to free some hilarious and potent spirit within him; something that struggled there like the Genie in the bottle[4] found by the Arab fisherman. He felt a sudden zest of life; the lights danced before his eyes and the concert hall blazed into unimaginable splendour. When the soprano soloist came on, Paul forgot even the nastiness of his teacher's being there and gave himself up to the peculiar stimulus such personages always had for him. The soloist chanced to be a German woman, by no means in her first youth, and the mother of many children; but she wore an elaborate gown and a tiara, and above all she had that indefinable air of achievement, that world-shine upon her which, in Paul's eyes, made her a veritable queen of Romance.

After a concert was over Paul was always irritable and wretched until he got to sleep, and to-night he was even more than usually restless. He had the feeling of not being able to let down, of its being impossible to give up this delicious excitement which was the only thing that could be called living at all. During the last number he withdrew and, after hastily changing his clothes in the dressing-room, slipped out to the side door where the soprano's carriage stood. Here he began pacing rapidly up and down the walk, waiting to see her come out.

Over yonder the Schenley, in its vacant stretch, loomed big and square through the fine rain, the windows of its twelve stories glowing like those of a lighted cardboard house under a Christmas tree. All the actors and singers of the better class stayed there when they were in the city, and a number of the big manufacturers of the place lived there in the winter. Paul had often hung about the hotel, watching the people go in and out, longing to enter and leave school-masters and dull care behind him forever.

At last the singer came out, accompanied by the conductor, who helped her into her carriage and closed the door with a cordial *auf wiedersehen* which set Paul to wondering whether she were not an old sweetheart of his. Paul followed the carriage over

4 **genie in the bottle:** An allusion to one of the tales in *Thousand and One Nights* (or *Arabian Nights*) in which Ali Baba discovers a genie in a bottle who will grant him wishes.

to the hotel, walking so rapidly as not to be far from the entrance when the singer alighted and disappeared behind the swinging glass doors that were opened by a negro in a tall hat and a long coat. In the moment that the door was ajar it seemed to Paul that he, too, entered. He seemed to feel himself go after her up the steps, into the warm, lighted building, into an exotic, a tropical world of shiny, glistening surfaces and basking ease. He reflected upon the mysterious dishes that were brought into the dining-room, the green bottles in buckets of ice, as he had seen them in the supper party pictures of the *Sunday World* supplement. A quick gust of wind brought the rain down with sudden vehemence, and Paul was startled to find that he was still outside in the slush of the gravel driveway; that his boots were letting in the water and his scanty overcoat was clinging wet about him; that the lights in front of the concert hall were out, and that the rain was driving in sheets between him and the orange glow of the windows above him. There it was, what he wanted—tangibly before him, like the fairy world of a Christmas pantomime, but mocking spirits stood guard at the doors, and, as the rain beat in his face, Paul wondered whether he were destined always to shiver in the black night outside, looking up at it.

He turned and walked reluctantly toward the car tracks. The end had to come sometime; his father in his night-clothes at the top of the stairs, explanations that did not explain, hastily improvised fictions that were forever tripping him up, his upstairs room and its horrible yellow wall-paper, the creaking bureau with the greasy plush collar-box, and over his painted wooden bed the pictures of George Washington and John Calvin,[5] and the framed motto, "Feed my Lambs," which had been worked in red worsted by his mother.

Half an hour later, Paul alighted from his car and went slowly down one of the side streets off the main thoroughfare. It was a highly respectable street, where all the houses were exactly alike, and where business men of moderate means begot and reared large families of children, all of whom went to Sabbath-school and learned the shorter catechism, and were interested in arithmetic; all of whom were as exactly alike as their homes, and of a piece with the monotony in which they lived. Paul never went up Cordelia Street without a shudder of loathing. His home was next to the house of the Cumberland minister. He approached it to-night with the nerveless sense of defeat, the hopeless feeling of sinking back forever into ugliness and commonness that he had always had when he came home. The moment he turned into Cordelia Street he felt the waters close above his head. After each of these orgies of living, he experienced all the physical depression which follows a debauch; the loathing of respectable beds, of common food, of a house penetrated by kitchen odours; a shuddering repulsion for the flavourless, colourless mass of every-day existence; a morbid desire for cool things and soft lights and fresh flowers.

The nearer he approached the house, the more absolutely unequal Paul felt to the sight of it all; his ugly sleeping chamber; the cold bathroom with the grimy zinc tub, the cracked mirror, the dripping spiggots; his father, at the top of the stairs, his hairy legs sticking out from his night-shirt, his feet thrust into carpet slippers. He was so

5 **John Calvin:** John Calvin (1509–1564), Protestant reformer.

much later than usual that there would certainly be inquiries and reproaches. Paul stopped short before the door. He felt that he could not be accosted by his father to-night; that he could not toss again on that miserable bed. He would not go in. He would tell his father that he had no car fare, and it was raining so hard he had gone home with one of the boys and stayed all night.

Meanwhile, he was wet and cold. He went around to the back of the house and tried one of the basement windows, found it open, raised it cautiously, and scrambled down the cellar wall to the floor. There he stood, holding his breath, terrified by the noise he had made, but the floor above him was silent, and there was no creak on the stairs. He found a soap-box, and carried it over to the soft ring of light that streamed from the furnace door, and sat down. He was horribly afraid of rats, so he did not try to sleep, but sat looking distrustfully at the dark, still terrified lest he might have awakened his father. In such reactions, after one of the experiences which made days and nights out of the dreary blanks of the calendar, when his senses were deadened, Paul's head was always singularly clear. Suppose his father had heard him getting in at the window and had come down and shot him for a burglar? Then, again, suppose his father had come down, pistol in hand, and he had cried out in time to save himself, and his father had been horrified to think how nearly he had killed him? Then, again, suppose a day should come when his father would remember that night, and wish there had been no warning cry to stay his hand? With this last supposition Paul entertained himself until daybreak.

The following Sunday was fine; the sodden November chill was broken by the last flash of autumnal summer. In the morning Paul had to go to church and Sabbath-school, as always. On seasonable Sunday afternoons the burghers of Cordelia Street always sat out on their front "stoops," and talked to their neighbours on the next stoop, or called to those across the street in neighbourly fashion. The men usually sat on gay cushions placed upon the steps that led down to the sidewalk, while the women, in their Sunday "waists,"[6] sat in rockers on the cramped porches, pretending to be greatly at their ease. The children played in the streets; there were so many of them that the place resembled the recreation grounds of a kindergarten. The men on the steps—all in their shirt sleeves, their vests unbuttoned—sat with their legs well apart, their stomachs comfortably protruding, and talked of the prices of things, or told anecdotes of the sagacity of their various chiefs and overlords. They occasionally looked over the multitude of squabbling children, listened affectionately to their high-pitched, nasal voices, smiling to see their own proclivities reproduced in their offspring, and interspersed their legends of the iron kings[7] with remarks about their sons' progress at school, their grades in arithmetic, and the amounts they had saved in their toy banks.

On this last Sunday of November, Paul sat all the afternoon on the lowest step of his "stoop," staring into the street, while his sisters, in their rockers, were talking to the minister's daughters next door about how many shirt-waists they had made in the last

6 **waists:** Blouses.
7 **iron kings:** An allusion to iron and steel tycoons.

week, and how many waffles some one had eaten at the last church supper. When the weather was warm, and his father was in a particularly jovial frame of mind, the girls made lemonade, which was always brought out in a red-glass pitcher, ornamented with forget-me-nots in blue enamel. This the girls thought very fine, and the neighbours always joked about the suspicious colour of the pitcher.

To-day Paul's father sat on the top step, talking to a young man who shifted a restless baby from knee to knee. He happened to be the young man who was daily held up to Paul as a model, and after whom it was his father's dearest hope that he would pattern. This young man was of a ruddy complexion, with a compressed, red mouth, and faded, near-sighted eyes, over which he wore thick spectacles, with gold bows that curved about his ears. He was clerk to one of the magnates of a great steel corporation, and was looked upon in Cordelia Street as a young man with a future. There was a story that, some five years ago—he was now barely twenty-six—he had been a trifle dissipated but in order to curb his appetites and save the loss of time and strength that a sowing of wild oats might have entailed, he had taken his chief's advice, oft reiterated to his employees, and at twenty-one had married the first woman whom he could persuade to share his fortunes. She happened to be an angular schoolmistress, much older than he, who also wore thick glasses, and who had now borne him four children, all near-sighted, like herself.

The young man was relating how his chief, now cruising in the Mediterranean, kept in touch with all the details of the business, arranging his office hours on his yacht just as though he were at home, and "knocking off work enough to keep two stenographers busy." His father told, in turn, the plan his corporation was considering, of putting in an electric railway plant at Cairo. Paul snapped his teeth; he had an awful apprehension that they might spoil it all before he got there. Yet he rather liked to hear these legends of the iron kings, that were told and retold on Sundays and holidays; these stories of palaces in Venice, yachts on the Mediterranean, and high play at Monte Carlo appealed to his fancy, and he was interested in the triumphs of these cash boys who had become famous, though he had no mind for the cash-boy stage.

After supper was over, and he had helped to dry the dishes, Paul nervously asked his father whether he could go to George's to get some help in his geometry, and still more nervously asked for car fare. This latter request he had to repeat, as his father, on principle, did not like to hear requests for money, whether much or little. He asked Paul whether he could not go to some boy who lived nearer, and told him that he ought not to leave his school work until Sunday; but he gave him the dime. He was not a poor man, but he had a worthy ambition to come up in the world. His only reason for allowing Paul to usher was, that he thought a boy ought to be earning a little.

Paul bounded upstairs, scrubbed the greasy odour of the dish-water from his hands with the ill-smelling soap he hated, and then shook over his fingers a few drops of violet water from the bottle he kept hidden in his drawer. He left the house with his geometry conspicuously under his arm, and the moment he got out of Cordelia Street and boarded a downtown car, he shook off the lethargy of two deadening days, and began to live again.

The leading juvenile of the permanent stock company which played at one of the downtown theatres was an acquaintance of Paul's, and the boy had been invited to drop in at the Sunday-night rehearsals whenever he could. For more than a year Paul had spent every available moment loitering about Charley Edwards's dressing-room. He had won a place among Edwards's following not only because the young actor, who could not afford to employ a dresser, often found him useful, but because he recognized in Paul something akin to what churchmen term "vocation."

It was at the theatre and at Carnegie Hall that Paul really lived; the rest was but a sleep and a forgetting. This was Paul's fairy tale, and it had for him all the allurement of a secret love. The moment he inhaled the gassy, painty, dusty odour behind the scenes, he breathed like a prisoner set free, and felt within him the possibility of doing or saying splendid, brilliant, poetic things. The moment the cracked orchestra beat out the overture from *Martha*, or jerked at the serenade from *Rigoletto*, all stupid and ugly things slid from him, and his senses were deliciously, yet delicately fired.

Perhaps it was because, in Paul's world, the natural nearly always wore the guise of ugliness, that a certain element of artificiality seemed to him necessary in beauty. Perhaps it was because his experience of life elsewhere was so full of Sabbath-school picnics, petty economies, wholesome advice as to how to succeed in life, and the unescapable odours of cooking, that he found this existence so alluring, these smartly-clad men and women so attractive, that he was so moved by these starry apple orchards that bloomed perennially under the lime-light.

It would be difficult to put it strongly enough how convincingly the stage entrance of that theatre was for Paul the actual portal of Romance. Certainly none of the company ever suspected it, least of all Charley Edwards. It was very like the old stories that used to float about London of fabulously rich Jews, who had subterranean halls there, with palms, and fountains, and soft lamps and richly apparelled women who never saw the disenchanting light of London day. So, in the midst of that smoke-palled city, enamoured of figures and grimy toil, Paul had his secret temple, his wishing carpet, his bit of blue-and-white Mediterranean shore bathed in perpetual sunshine.

Several of Paul's teachers had a theory that his imagination had been perverted by garish fiction, but the truth was that he scarcely ever read at all. The books at home were not such as would either tempt or corrupt a youthful mind, and as for reading the novels that some of his friends urged upon him—well, he got what he wanted much more quickly from music; any sort of music, from an orchestra to a barrel organ. He needed only the spark, the indescribable thrill that made his imagination master of his senses, and he could make plots and pictures enough of his own. It was equally true that he was not stage struck—not, at any rate, in the usual acceptation of that expression. He had no desire to become an actor, any more than he had to become a musician. He felt no necessity to do any of these things; what he wanted was to see, to be in the atmosphere, float on the wave of it, to be carried out, blue league after blue league, away from everything.

After a night behind the scenes, Paul found the school-room more than ever repulsive; the bare floors and naked walls; the prosy men who never wore frock coats, or violets in their buttonholes; the women with their dull gowns, shrill voices, and pitiful seriousness about prepositions that govern the dative. He could not bear to have the other pupils think, for a moment, that he took these people seriously; he must convey to them that he considered it all trivial, and was there only by way of a jest, anyway. He had autographed pictures of all the members of the stock company which he showed his classmates, telling them the most incredible stories of his familiarity with these people, of his acquaintance with the soloists who came to Carnegie Hall, his suppers with them and the flowers he sent them. When these stories lost their effect, and his audience grew listless, he became desperate and would bid all the boys good-bye, announcing that he was going to travel for a while; going to Naples, to Venice, to Egypt. Then, next Monday, he would slip back, conscious and nervously smiling; his sister was ill, and he should have to defer his voyage until spring.

Matters went steadily worse with Paul at school. In the itch to let his instructors know how heartily he despised them and their homilies, and how thoroughly he was appreciated elsewhere, he mentioned once or twice that he had no time to fool with theorems; adding—with a twitch of the eyebrows and a touch of that nervous bravado which so perplexed them—that he was helping the people down at the stock company; they were old friends of his.

The upshot of the matter was that the Principal went to Paul's father, and Paul was taken out of school and put to work. The manager at Carnegie Hall was told to get another usher in his stead; the doorkeeper at the theatre was warned not to admit him to the house; and Charley Edwards remorsefully promised the boy's father not to see him again.

The members of the stock company were vastly amused when some of Paul's stories reached them—especially the women. They were hardworking women, most of them supporting indigent husbands or brothers, and they laughed rather bitterly at having stirred the boy to such fervid and florid inventions. They agreed with the faculty and with his father that Paul's was a bad case.

The east-bound train was ploughing through a January snow-storm; the dull dawn was beginning to show grey when the engine whistled a mile out of Newark. Paul started up from the seat where he had lain curled in uneasy slumber, rubbed the breath-misted window glass with his hand, and peered out. The snow was whirling in curling eddies above the white bottom lands, and the drifts lay already deep in the fields and along the fences, while here and there the long dead grass and dried weed stalks protruded black above it. Lights shone from the scattered houses, and a gang of labourers who stood beside the track waved their lanterns.

Paul had slept very little, and he felt grimy and uncomfortable. He had made the all-night journey in a day coach, partly because he was ashamed, dressed as he was, to go into a Pullman, and partly because he was afraid of being seen there by some Pittsburgh business man, who might have noticed him in Denny & Carson's office. When the whistle awoke him, he clutched quickly at his breast pocket, glancing about him with an uncertain smile. But the little, clay-bespattered Italians were still sleeping, the slatternly women across the aisle were in open-mouthed oblivion, and even the crumby, crying babies were for the nonce stilled. Paul settled back to struggle with his impatience as best he could.

When he arrived at the Jersey City station, he hurried through his breakfast, manifestly ill at ease and keeping a sharp eye about him. After he reached the Twenty-third Street station, he consulted a cabman, and had himself driven to a men's furnishing establishment that was just opening for the day. He spent upward of two hours there, buying with endless reconsidering and great care. His new street suit he put on in the fitting-room; the frock coat and dress clothes he had bundled into the cab with his linen. Then he drove to a hatter's and a shoe house. His next errand was at Tiffany's, where he selected his silver and a new scarf-pin. He would not wait to have his silver marked, he said. Lastly, he stopped at a trunk shop on Broadway, and had his purchases packed into various travelling bags.

It was a little after one o'clock when he drove up to the Waldorf, and after settling with the cabman, went into the office. He registered from Washington; said his mother and father had been abroad, and that he had come down to await the arrival of their steamer. He told his story plausibly and had no trouble, since he volunteered to pay for them in advance, in engaging his rooms; a sleeping-room, sitting-room and bath.

Not once, but a hundred times Paul had planned this entry into New York. He had gone over every detail of it with Charley Edwards, and in his scrap book at home there were pages of description about New York hotels, cut from the Sunday papers. When he was shown to his sitting-room on the eighth floor, he saw at a glance that everything was as it should be; there was but one detail in his mental picture that the place did not realize, so he rang for the bell boy and sent him down for flowers. He moved about nervously until the boy returned, putting away his new linen and fingering it delightedly as he did so. When the flowers came, he put them hastily into water, and then tumbled into a hot bath. Presently he came out of his white bath-room, resplendent in his new silk underwear, and playing with the tassels of his red robe. The snow was whirling so fiercely outside his windows that he could scarcely see across the street, but within the air was deliciously soft and fragrant. He put the violets and jonquils on the taboret beside the couch, and threw himself down, with a long sigh, covering himself with a Roman blanket. He was thoroughly tired; he had been in such haste, he had stood up to such a strain, covered so much ground in the last twenty-four hours, that he wanted to think how it had all come about. Lulled by the sound of the wind, the warm air, and the cool fragrance of the flowers, he sank into deep, drowsy retrospection.

It had been wonderfully simple; when they had shut him out of the theatre and concert hall, when they had taken away his bone, the whole thing was virtually determined. The rest was a mere matter of opportunity. The only thing that at all surprised him was his own courage—for he realized well enough that he had always been tormented by fear, a sort of apprehensive dread that, of late years, as the meshes of the lies he had told closed about him, had been pulling the muscles of his body tighter and tighter. Until now, he could not remember the time when he had not been dreading something. Even when he was a little boy, it was always there—behind him, or before, or on either side. There had always been the shadowed corner, the dark place into which he dared not look, but from which something seemed always to be watching him—and Paul had done things that were not pretty to watch, he knew.

But now he had a curious sense of relief, as though he had at last thrown down the gauntlet to the thing in the corner.

Yet it was but a day since he had been sulking in the traces; but yesterday afternoon that he had been sent to the bank with Denny & Carson's deposit, as usual—but this time he was instructed to leave the book to be balanced. There was above two thousand dollars in checks, and nearly a thousand in the bank notes which he had taken from the book and quietly transferred to his pocket. At the bank he had made out a new deposit slip. His nerves had been steady enough to permit of his returning to the office, where he had finished his work and asked for a full day's holiday to-morrow, Saturday, giving a perfectly reasonable pretext. The bank book, he knew, would not be returned before Monday or Tuesday, and his father would be out of town for the next week. From the time he slipped the bank notes into his pocket until he boarded the night train for New York, he had not known a moment's hesitation. It was not the first time Paul had steered through treacherous waters.

How astonishingly easy it had all been; here he was, the thing done; and this time there would be no awakening, no figure at the top of the stairs. He watched the snow flakes whirling by his window until he fell asleep.

When he awoke, it was three o'clock in the afternoon. He bounded up with a start; half of one of his precious days gone already! He spent more than an hour in dressing, watching every stage of his toilet carefully in the mirror. Everything was quite perfect; he was exactly the kind of boy he had always wanted to be.

When he went downstairs, Paul took a carriage and drove up Fifth Avenue toward the Park. The snow had somewhat abated; carriages and tradesmen's wagons were hurrying soundlessly to and fro in the winter twilight; boys in woollen mufflers were shovelling off the doorsteps; the avenue stages[8] made fine spots of colour against the white street. Here and there on the corners were stands, with whole flower gardens blooming under glass cases, against the sides of which the snow flakes stuck and melted; violets, roses, carnations, lilies of the valley—somehow vastly more lovely and alluring that they blossomed thus unnaturally in the snow. The Park itself was a wonderful stage winterpiece.

When he returned, the pause of the twilight had ceased, and the tune of the streets had changed. The snow was falling faster, lights streamed from the hotels that reared their dozen stories fearlessly up into the storm, defying the raging Atlantic winds. A long, black stream of carriages poured down the avenue, intersected here and there by other streams, tending horizontally. There were a score of cabs about the entrance of his hotel, and his driver had to wait. Boys in livery were running in and out of the awning stretched across the sidewalk, up and down the red velvet carpet laid from the door to the street. Above, about, within it all was the rumble and roar, the hurry and toss of thousands of human beings as hot for pleasure as himself, and on every side of him towered the glaring affirmation of the omnipotence of wealth.

The boy set his teeth and drew his shoulders together in a spasm of realization;

8 **avenue stages:** Window displays.

the plot of all dramas, the text of all romances, the nerve-stuff of all sensations was whirling about him like the snow flakes. He burnt like a faggot in a tempest.

When Paul went down to dinner, the music of the orchestra came floating up the elevator shaft to greet him. His head whirled as he stepped into the thronged corridor, and he sank back into one of the chairs against the wall to get his breath. The lights, the chatter, the perfumes, the bewildering medley of colour—he had, for a moment, the feeling of not being able to stand it. But only for a moment; these were his own people, he told himself. He went slowly about the corridors, through the writing-rooms, smoking-rooms, reception-rooms, as though he were exploring the chambers of an enchanted palace, built and peopled for him alone.

When he reached the dining-room he sat down at a table near a window. The flowers, the white linen, the many-coloured wine glasses, the gay toilettes of the women, the low popping of corks, the undulating repetitions of the *Blue Danube* from the orchestra, all flooded Paul's dream with bewildering radiance. When the roseate tinge of his champagne was added—that cold, precious, bubbling stuff that creamed and foamed in his glass—Paul wondered that there were honest men in the world at all. This was what all the world was fighting for, he reflected; this was what all the struggle was about. He doubted the reality of his past. Had he ever known a place called Cordelia Street, a place where fagged-looking businessmen got on the early car; mere rivets in a machine they seemed to Paul,—sickening men, with combings of children's hair always hanging to their coats, and the smell of cooking in their clothes. Cordelia Street—Ah! that belonged to another time and country; had he not always been thus, had he not sat here night after night, from as far back as he could remember, looking pensively over just such shimmering textures, and slowly twirling the stem of a glass like this one between his thumb and middle finger? He rather thought he had.

He was not in the least abashed or lonely. He had no especial desire to meet or to know any of these people; all he demanded was the right to look on and conjecture, to watch the pageant. The mere stage properties were all he contended for. Nor was he lonely later in the evening, in his loge at the Metropolitan. He was now entirely rid of his nervous misgivings, of his forced aggressiveness, of the imperative desire to show himself different from his surroundings. He felt now that his surroundings explained him. Nobody questioned the purple; he had only to wear it passively. He had only to glance down at his attire to reassure himself that here it would be impossible for anyone to humiliate him.

He found it hard to leave his beautiful sitting-room to go to bed that night, and sat long watching the raging storm from his turret window. When he went to sleep it was with the lights turned on in his bedroom; partly because of his old timidity, and partly so that, if he should wake in the night, there would be no wretched moment of doubt, no horrible suspicion of yellow wall-paper, or of Washington and Calvin above his bed.

Sunday morning the city was practically snow-bound. Paul breakfasted late, and in the afternoon he fell in with a wild San Francisco boy, a freshman at Yale, who said he had run down for a "little flyer" over Sunday. The young man offered to show Paul the night side of the town, and the two boys went out together after dinner, not returning to the hotel until seven o'clock the next morning. They had started out in the confiding warmth of a champagne friendship, but their parting in the elevator was singularly cool. The freshman pulled himself together to make his train, and Paul went to bed. He awoke at two o'clock in the afternoon, very thirsty and dizzy, and rang for ice-water, coffee, and the Pittsburgh papers.

On the part of the hotel management, Paul excited no suspicion. There was this to be said for him, that he wore his spoils with dignity and in no way made himself conspicuous. Even under the glow of his wine he was never boisterous, though he found the stuff like a magician's wand for wonder-building. His chief greediness lay in his ears and eyes, and his excesses were not offensive ones. His dearest pleasures were the grey winter twilights in his sitting-room; his quiet enjoyment of his flowers, his clothes, his wide divan, his cigarette and his sense of power. He could not remember a time when he had felt so at peace with himself. The mere release from the necessity of petty lying, lying every day and every day, restored his self-respect. He had never lied for pleasure, even at school; but to be noticed and admired, to assert his difference from other Cordelia Street boys; and he felt a good deal more manly, more honest, even, now that he had no need for boastful pretensions, now that he could, as his actor friends used to say, "dress the part." It was characteristic that remorse did not occur to him. His golden days went by without a shadow, and he made each as perfect as he could.

On the eighth day after his arrival in New York, he found the whole affair exploited in the Pittsburgh papers, exploited with a wealth of detail which indicated that local news of a sensational nature was at a low ebb. The firm of Denny & Carson announced that the boy's father had refunded the full amount of the theft, and that they had no intention of prosecuting. The Cumberland minister had been interviewed, and expressed his hope of yet reclaiming the motherless lad, and his Sabbath-school teacher declared that she would spare no effort to that end. The rumour had reached Pittsburgh that the boy had been seen in a New York hotel, and his father had gone East to find him and bring him home.

Paul had just come in to dress for dinner; he sank into a chair, weak to the knees, and clasped his head in his hands. It was to be worse than jail, even; the tepid waters of Cordelia Street were to close over him finally and forever. The grey monotony stretched before him in hopeless, unrelieved years; Sabbath-school, Young People's Meeting, the yellow-papered room, the damp dish-towels; it all rushed back upon him with a sickening vividness. He had the old feeling that the orchestra had suddenly stopped, the sinking sensation that the play was over. The sweat broke out on his face, and he sprang to his feet, looked about him with his white, conscious smile, and winked at himself in the mirror. With something of the old childish belief in miracles with which he had so often gone to class, all his lessons unlearned, Paul dressed and dashed whistling down the corridor to the elevator.

He had no sooner entered the dining-room and caught the measure of the music than his remembrance was lightened by his old elastic power of claiming the moment, mounting with it, and finding it all sufficient. The glare and glitter about him, the mere scenic accessories had again, and for the last time, their old potency. He would show himself that he was game, he would finish the thing splendidly. He doubted, more than ever, the existence of Cordelia Street, and for the first time he drank his wine recklessly. Was he not, after all, one of those fortunate beings born to the purple, was he not still himself and in his own place? He drummed a nervous accompaniment to the Pagliacci music and looked about him, telling himself over and over that it had paid.

He reflected drowsily, to the swell of the music and the chill sweetness of his wine, that he might have done it more wisely. He might have caught an outbound steamer and been well out of their clutches before now. But the other side of the world had seemed too far away and too uncertain then; he could not have waited for it; his need had been too sharp. If he had to choose over again, he would do the same thing tomorrow. He looked affectionately about the dining-room, now gilded with a soft mist. Ah, it had paid indeed!

Paul was awakened next morning by a painful throbbing in his head and feet. He had thrown himself across the bed without undressing, and had slept with his shoes on. His limbs and hands were lead heavy, and his tongue and throat were parched and burnt. There came upon him one of those fateful attacks of clear-headedness that never occurred except when he was physically exhausted and his nerves hung loose. He lay still and closed his eyes and let the tide of things wash over him.

His father was in New York; "stopping at some joint or other," he told himself. The memory of successive summers on the front stoop fell upon him like a weight of black water. He had not a hundred dollars left; and he knew now, more than ever, that money was everything, the wall that stood between all he loathed and all he wanted. The thing was winding itself up; he had thought of that on his first glorious day in New York, and had even provided a way to snap the thread. It lay on his dressing-table now; he had got it out last night when he came blindly up from dinner, but the shiny metal hurt his eyes, and he disliked the looks of it.

He rose and moved about with a painful effort, succumbing now and again to attacks of nausea. It was the old depression exaggerated; all the world had become Cordelia Street. Yet somehow he was not afraid of anything, was absolutely calm; perhaps because he had looked into the dark corner at last and knew. It was bad enough, what he saw there, but somehow not so bad as his long fear of it had been. He saw everything clearly now. He had a feeling that he had made the best of it, that he had lived the sort of life he was meant to live, and for half an hour he sat staring at the revolver. But he told himself that was not the way, so he went downstairs and took a cab to the ferry.

When Paul arrived at Newark, he got off the train and took another cab, directing the driver to follow the Pennsylvania tracks out of the town. The snow lay heavy on the roadways and had drifted deep in the open fields. Only here and there the dead grass or dried weed stalks projected, singularly black, above it. Once well into the country, Paul dismissed the carriage and walked, floundering along the tracks, his mind a medley of irrelevant things. He seemed to hold in his brain an actual picture of everything he had seen that morning. He remembered every feature of both his drivers, of the toothless old woman from whom he had bought the red flowers in his coat, the agent from whom he had got his ticket, and all of his fellow-passengers on the ferry. His mind, unable to cope with vital matters near at hand, worked feverishly and deftly at sorting and grouping these images. They made for him a part of the ugliness of the world, of the ache in his head, and the bitter burning on his tongue. He stooped and put a handful of snow into his mouth as he walked, but that, too, seemed hot. When he reached a little hillside, where the tracks ran through a cut some twenty feet below him, he stopped and sat down.

The carnations in his coat were drooping with the cold, he noticed; their red glory all over. It occurred to him that all the flowers he had seen in the glass cases that first night must have gone the same way, long before this. It was only one splendid breath they had, in spite of their brave mockery at the winter outside the glass; and it was a losing game in the end, it seemed, this revolt against the homilies by which the world is run. Paul took one of the blossoms carefully from his coat and scooped a little hole in the snow, where he covered it up. Then he dozed a while, from his weak condition, seemingly insensible to the cold.

The sound of an approaching train awoke him, and he started to his feet, remembering only his resolution, and afraid lest he should be too late. He stood watching the approaching locomotive, his teeth chattering, his lips drawn away from them in a frightened smile; once or twice he glanced nervously sidewise, as though he were being watched. When the right moment came, he jumped. As he fell, the folly of his haste occurred to him with merciless clearness, the vastness of what he had left undone. There flashed through his brain, clearer than ever before, the blue of Adriatic water, the yellow of Algerian sands.

He felt something strike his chest, and that his body was being thrown swiftly through the air, on and on, immeasurably far and fast, while his limbs were gently relaxed. Then, because the picture making mechanism was crushed, the disturbing visions flashed into black, and Paul dropped back into the immense design of things.

# John Cheever

## (1912–1982)

The stories of John Cheever describe the manners and morals of middle-class, suburban America. Cheever drew largely on his own life for material. When he was expelled from Thayer Academy for smoking, he turned the incident into a short story, "Expelled." The story was published in 1930 in the *New Republic*. In 1932, Cheever moved to New York City and supported himself with a variety of writing jobs, including a position with the Works Progress Administration. He married May Winternitz in 1941 and enlisted in the United States Army a year later. His first book, *The Way Some People Live*, was published in 1943, and he was quickly transferred to the Signal Corps to work on public relations films. He and his family moved to Ossining, New York, in 1956. This region would become "Cheever country," a world of country clubs and commuter trains. In the following years, Cheever taught at several universities, including Barnard, the University of Iowa, and Boston University. He also taught at Sing Sing Prison in the early 1970s. *The Stories of John Cheever* (1978) won the Pulitzer Prize and the National Book Critics Circle award, and in 1979 Cheever received the Edwards MacDowell medal. His major works include *The Wapshot Scandal* (1963), *Bullet Park* (1969), and *Falconer* (1977). He died June 18, 1982, of kidney and bone cancer.

## The Enormous Radio                                               1953

Jim and Irene Westcott were the kind of people who seem to strike that satisfactory average of income, endeavor, and respectability that is reached by the statistical reports in college alumni bulletins. They were the parents of two young children, they had been married nine years, they lived on the twelfth floor of an apartment house near Sutton Place, they went to the theatre on an average of 10.3 times a year, and they hoped someday to live in Westchester.[1] Irene Westcott was a pleasant, rather plain girl with soft brown hair and a wide, fine forehead upon which nothing at all had been written, and in the cold weather she wore a coat of fitch skins dyed to resemble mink. You could not say that Jim Westcott looked younger than he was, but you could at least say of him that he seemed to feel younger. He wore his graying hair cut very short, he dressed in the kind of clothes his class had worn at Andover, and his manner was earnest, vehement, and intentionally naïve. The Westcotts differed from their friends, their classmates, and their neighbors only in an interest they shared in serious music. They went to a great many concerts—although they seldom mentioned this to anyone—and they spent a good deal of time listening to music on the radio.

Their radio was an old instrument, sensitive, unpredictable, and beyond repair. Neither of them understood the mechanics of radio—or of any of the other appliances that surrounded them—and when the instrument faltered, Jim would strike the side of the cabinet with his hand. This sometimes helped. One Sunday afternoon, in the middle of a Schubert quartet, the music faded away altogether. Jim struck the cabinet repeatedly, but there was no response; the Schubert was lost to them forever. He promised to buy Irene a new radio, and on Monday when he came home from work he told her that he had got one. He refused to describe it, and said it would be a surprise for her when it came.

The radio was delivered at the kitchen door the following afternoon, and with the assistance of her maid and the handyman Irene uncrated it and brought it into the living room. She was struck at once with the physical ugliness of the large gumwood cabinet. Irene was proud of her living room, she had chosen its furnishings and colors as carefully as she chose her clothes, and now it seemed to her that the new radio

1 **Sutton Place:** Fashionable area on New York City's East Side. **Westchester:** Affluent suburb of New York.

stood among her intimate possessions like an aggressive intruder. She was confounded by the number of dials and switches on the instrument panel, and she studied them thoroughly before she put the plug into a wall socket and turned the radio on. The dials flooded with a malevolent green light, and in the distance she heard the music of a piano quintet. The quintet was in the distance for only an instant; it bore down upon her with a speed greater than light and filled the apartment with the noise of music amplified so mightily that it knocked a china ornament from a table to the floor. She rushed to the instrument and reduced the volume. The violent forces that were snared in the ugly gumwood cabinet made her uneasy. Her children came home from school then, and she took them to the Park. It was not until later in the afternoon that she was able to return to the radio.

The maid had given the children their suppers and was supervising their baths when Irene turned on the radio, reduced the volume, and sat down to listen to a Mozart quintet that she knew and enjoyed. The music came through clearly. The new instrument had a much purer tone, she thought, than the old one. She decided that tone was most important and that she could conceal the cabinet behind a sofa. But as soon as she had made her peace with the radio, the interference began. A crackling sound like the noise of a burning powder fuse began to accompany the singing of the strings. Beyond the music, there was a rustling that reminded Irene unpleasantly of the sea, and as the quintet progressed, these noises were joined by many others. She tried all the dials and switches but nothing dimmed the interference, and she sat down, disappointed and bewildered, and tried to trace the flight of the melody. The elevator shaft in her building ran beside the living-room wall, and it was the noise of the elevator that gave her a clue to the character of the static. The rattling of the elevator cables and the opening and closing of the elevator doors were reproduced in her loudspeaker, and, realizing that the radio was sensitive to electrical currents of all sorts, she began to discern through the Mozart the ringing of telephone bells, the dialing of phones, and the lamentation of a vacuum cleaner. By listening more carefully, she was able to distinguish doorbells, elevator bells, electric razors, and Waring mixers, whose sounds had been picked up from the apartments that surrounded hers and transmitted through her loudspeaker. The powerful and ugly instrument, with its mistaken sensitivity to discord, was more than she could hope to master, so she turned the thing off and went into the nursery to see her children.

When Jim Westcott came home that night, he went to the radio confidently and worked the controls. He had the same sort of experience Irene had had. A man was speaking on the station Jim had chosen, and his voice swung instantly from the distance into a force so powerful that it shook the apartment. Jim turned the volume control and reduced the voice. Then, a minute or two later, the interference began. The ringing of telephones and doorbells set in, joined by the rasp of the elevator doors and the whir of cooking appliances. The character of the noise had changed since Irene had tried the radio earlier; the last of the electric razors was being unplugged, the vacuum cleaners had all been returned to their closets, and the static reflected that change in pace that overtakes the city after the sun goes down. He fiddled with the knobs but couldn't get rid of the noises, so he turned the radio off and told Irene that in the morning he'd call the people who had sold it to him and give them hell.

The following afternoon, when Irene returned to the apartment from a luncheon date, the maid told her that a man had come and fixed the radio. Irene went into the living room before she took off her hat or her furs and tried the instrument. From the loudspeaker came a recording of the "Missouri Waltz." It reminded her of the thin, scratchy music from an old-fashioned phonograph that she sometimes heard across the lake where she spent her summers. She waited until the waltz had finished, expecting an explanation of the recording, but there was none. The music was followed by silence, and then the plaintive and scratchy record was repeated. She turned the dial and got a satisfactory burst of Caucasian music—the thump of bare feet in the dust and the rattle of coin jewelry—but in the background she could hear the ringing of bells and a confusion of voices. Her children came home from school then, and she turned off the radio and went to the nursery.

When Jim came home that night, he was tired, and he took a bath and changed his clothes. Then he joined Irene in the living room. He had just turned on the radio when the maid announced dinner, so he left it on, and he and Irene went to the table.

Jim was too tired to make even a pretense of sociability, and there was nothing about the dinner to hold Irene's interest, so her attention wandered from the food to the deposits of silver polish on the candlesticks and from there to the music in the other room. She listened for a few moments to a Chopin prelude and then was surprised to hear a man's voice break in. "For Christ's sake, Kathy," he said, "do you always have to play the piano when I get home?" The music stopped abruptly. "It's the only chance I have," a woman said. "I'm at the office all day." "So am I," the man said. He added something obscene about an upright piano, and slammed a door. The passionate and melancholy music began again.

"Did you hear that?" Irene asked.

"What?" Jim was eating his dessert.

"The radio. A man said something while the music was still going on—something dirty."

"It's probably a play."

"I don't think it *is* a play," Irene said.

They left the table and took their coffee into the living room. Irene asked Jim to try another station. He turned the knob. "Have you seen my garters?" a man asked. "Button me up," a woman said. "Have you seen my garters?" the man said again. "Just button me up and I'll find your garters," the woman said. Jim shifted to another station. "I wish you wouldn't leave apple cores in the ashtrays," a man said. "I hate the smell."

"This is strange," Jim said.

"Isn't it?" Irene said.

Jim turned the knob again. " 'On the coast of Coromandel where the early pumpkins blow,' " a woman with a pronounced English accent said, " 'in the middle of the woods lived the Yonghy-Bonghy-Bò.[2] Two old chairs, and half a candle, one old jug without a handle . . .' "

"My God!" Irene cried. "That's the Sweeneys' nurse."

---

2 **Yonghy-Bonghy-Bò:** From the poem "The Courtship of the Yonghy-Bonghy-Bò" by Edward Lear (1812–1888).

"'These were all his worldly goods,'" the British voice continued.

"Turn that thing off," Irene said. "Maybe they can hear *us*." Jim switched the radio off. "That was Miss Armstrong, the Sweeneys' nurse," Irene said. "She must be reading to the little girl. They live in 17-B. I've talked with Miss Armstrong in the Park. I know her voice very well. We must be getting other people's apartments."

"That's impossible," Jim said.

"Well, that was the Sweeneys' nurse," Irene said hotly. "I know her voice. I know it very well. I'm wondering if they can hear us."

Jim turned the switch. First from a distance and then nearer, nearer, as if borne on the wind, came the pure accents of the Sweeneys' nurse again: "'*Lady Jingly! Lady Jingly!*'" she said, "'*Sitting where the pumpkins blow, will you come and be my wife,* said the Yonghy-Bonghy-Bò . . .'"

Jim went over to the radio and said "Hello" loudly into the speaker.

"'*I am tired of living singly,*'" the nurse went on, "'*on this coast so wild and shingly, I'm a-weary of my life; if you'll come and be my wife, quite serene would be my life . . .*'"

"I guess she can't hear us," Irene said. "Try something else."

Jim turned to another station, and the living room was filled with the uproar of a cocktail party that had overshot its mark. Someone was playing the piano and singing the Whiffenpoof Song,[3] and the voices that surrounded the piano were vehement and happy. "Eat some more sandwiches," a woman shrieked. There were screams of laughter and a dish of some sort crashed to the floor.

"Those must be the Fullers, in 11-E," Irene said. "I knew they were giving a party this afternoon. I saw her in the liquor store. Isn't this too divine? Try something else. See if you can get those people in 18-C."

The Westcotts overheard that evening a monologue on salmon fishing in Canada, a bridge game, running comments on home movies of what had apparently been a fortnight at Sea Island, and a bitter family quarrel about an overdraft at the bank. They turned off their radio at midnight and went to bed, weak with laughter. Sometime in the night, their son began to call for a glass of water and Irene got one and took it to his room. It was very early. All the lights in the neighborhood were extinguished, and from the boy's window she could see the empty street. She went into the living room and tried the radio. There was some faint coughing, a moan, and then a man spoke. "Are you all right, darling?" he asked. "Yes," a woman said wearily. "Yes, I'm all right, I guess," and then she added with great feeling, "but, you know, Charlie, I don't feel like myself any more. Sometimes there are about fifteen or twenty minutes in the week when I feel like myself. I don't like to go to another doctor, because the doctor's bills are so awful already, but I just don't feel like myself, Charlie. I just never feel like myself." They were not young, Irene thought. She guessed from the timbre of their voices that they were middle-aged. The restrained melancholy of the dialogue and the draft from the bedroom window made her shiver, and she went back to bed.

---

3 **Whiffenpoof Song:** Yale drinking song.

The following morning, Irene cooked breakfast for the family—the maid didn't come up from her room in the basement until ten—braided her daughter's hair, and waited at the door until her children and her husband had been carried away in the elevator. Then she went into the living room and tried the radio. "I don't want to go to school," a child screamed. "I hate school. I won't go to school. I hate school." "You will go to school," an enraged woman said. "We paid eight hundred dollars to get you into that school and you'll go if it kills you." The next number on the dial produced the worn record of the "Missouri Waltz." Irene shifted the control and invaded the privacy of several breakfast tables. She overheard demonstrations of indigestion, carnal love, abysmal vanity, faith, and despair. Irene's life was nearly as simple and sheltered as it appeared to be, and the forthright and sometimes brutal language that came from the loudspeaker that morning astonished and troubled her. She continued to listen until her maid came in. Then she turned off the radio quickly, since this insight, she realized, was a furtive one.

Irene had a luncheon date with a friend that day, and she left her apartment at a little after twelve. There were a number of women in the elevator when it stopped at her floor. She stared at their handsome and impassive faces, their furs, and the cloth flowers in their hats. Which one of them had been to Sea Island, she wondered. Which one had overdrawn her bank account? The elevator stopped at the tenth floor and a woman with a pair of Skye terriers joined them. Her hair was rigged high on her head and she wore a mink cape. She was humming the "Missouri Waltz."

Irene had two Martinis at lunch, and she looked searchingly at her friend and wondered what her secrets were. They had intended to go shopping after lunch, but Irene excused herself and went home. She told the maid that she was not to be disturbed; then she went into the living room, closed the doors, and switched on the radio. She heard, in the course of the afternoon, the halting conversation of a woman entertaining her aunt, the hysterical conclusion of a luncheon party, and a hostess briefing her maid about some cocktail guests. "Don't give the best Scotch to anyone who hasn't white hair," the hostess said. "See if you can get rid of that liver paste before you pass those hot things, and could you lend me five dollars? I want to tip the elevator man."

As the afternoon waned, the conversations increased in intensity. From where Irene sat, she could see the open sky above the East River. There were hundreds of clouds in the sky, as though the south wind had broken the winter into pieces and were blowing it north, and on her radio she could hear the arrival of cocktail guests and the return of children and businessmen from their schools and offices. "I found a good-sized diamond on the bathroom floor this morning," a woman said. "It must have fallen out of that bracelet Mrs. Dunston was wearing last night." "We'll sell it," a man said. "Take it down to the jeweller on Madison Avenue and sell it. Mrs. Dunston won't know the difference, and we could use a couple of hundred bucks . . ." "'Oranges and lemons, say the bells of St. Clement's,'" the Sweeneys' nurse sang. "'Halfpence and farthings, say the bells of St. Martin's. When will you pay me? say the bells at old Bailey . . .'" "It's not a hat," a woman cried, and at her back roared a cocktail party. "It's not a hat, it's a love affair. That's what Walter Florell said. He said it's not a hat, it's a love affair," and then, in a lower voice, the same woman added, "Talk to somebody, for Christ's sake, honey, talk to somebody. If she catches you standing here not talking to anybody, she'll take us off her invitation list, and I love these parties."

The Westcotts were going out for dinner that night, and when Jim came home, Irene was dressing. She seemed sad and vague, and he brought her a drink. They were dining with friends in the neighborhood, and they walked to where they were going. The sky was broad and filled with light. It was one of those splendid spring evenings that excite memory and desire, and the air that touched their hands and faces felt very soft. A Salvation Army band was on the corner playing "Jesus Is Sweeter." Irene drew on her husband's arm and held him there for a minute, to hear the music. "They're really such nice people, aren't they?" she said. "They have such nice faces. Actually, they're so much nicer than a lot of the people we know." She took a bill from her purse and walked over and dropped it into the tambourine. There was in her face, when she returned to her husband, a look of radiant melancholy that he was not familiar with. And her conduct at the dinner party that night seemed strange to him, too. She interrupted her hostess rudely and stared at the people across the table from her with an intensity for which she would have punished her children.

It was still mild when they walked home from the party, and Irene looked up at the spring stars. "'How far that little candle throws its beams,'" she exclaimed. "'So shines a good deed in a naughty world.'"[4] She waited that night until Jim had fallen asleep, and then went into the living room and turned on the radio.

Jim came home at about six the next night. Emma, the maid, let him in, and he had taken off his hat and was taking off his coat when Irene ran into the hall. Her face was shining with tears and her hair was disordered. "Go up to 16-C, Jim!" she screamed. "Don't take off your coat. Go up to 16-C. Mr. Osborn's beating his wife. They've been quarrelling since four o'clock, and now he's hitting her. Go up there and stop him."

From the radio in the living room, Jim heard screams, obscenities, and thuds. "You know you don't have to listen to this sort of thing," he said. He strode into the living room and turned the switch. "It's indecent," he said. "It's like looking in windows. You know you don't have to listen to this sort of thing. You can turn it off."

"Oh, it's so horrible, it's so dreadful," Irene was sobbing. "I've been listening all day, and it's so depressing."

"Well, if it's so depressing, why do you listen to it? I bought this damned radio to give you some pleasure," he said. "I paid a great deal of money for it. I thought it might make you happy. I wanted to make you happy."

"Don't, don't, don't, don't quarrel with me," she moaned, and laid her head on his shoulder. "All the others have been quarrelling all day. Everybody's been quarrelling. They're all worried about money. Mrs. Hutchinson's mother is dying of cancer in Florida and they don't have enough money to send her to the Mayo Clinic. At least, Mr. Hutchinson says they don't have enough money. And some woman in this building is having an affair with the handyman—with that hideous handyman. It's too dis-

---

4 **"How far . . . naughty world'":** From Shakespeare's *Merchant of Venice*, V.i.

gusting. And Mrs. Melville has heart trouble and Mr. Hendricks is going to lose his job in April and Mrs. Hendricks is horrid about the whole thing and that girl who plays the 'Missouri Waltz' is a whore, a common whore, and the elevator man has tuberculosis and Mr. Osborn has been beating Mrs. Osborn." She wailed, she trembled with grief and checked the stream of tears down her face with the heel of her palm.

"Well, why do you have to listen?" Jim asked again. "Why do you have to listen to this stuff if it makes you so miserable?"

"Oh, don't, don't, don't," she cried. "Life is too terrible, too sordid and awful. But we've never been like that, have we, darling? Have we? I mean we've always been good and decent and loving to one another, haven't we? And we have two children, two beautiful children. Our lives aren't sordid, are they, darling? Are they?" She flung her arms around his neck and drew his face down to hers. "We're happy, aren't we, darling? We are happy, aren't we?"

"Of course we're happy," he said tiredly. He began to surrender his resentment. "Of course we're happy. I'll have that damned radio fixed or taken away tomorrow." He stroked her soft hair. "My poor girl," he said.

"You love me, don't you?" she asked. "And we're not hypercritical or worried about money or dishonest, are we?"

"No, darling," he said.

A man came in the morning and fixed the radio. Irene turned it on cautiously and was happy to hear a California-wine commercial and a recording of Beethoven's Ninth Symphony, including Schiller's "Ode to Joy." She kept the radio on all day and nothing untoward came from the speaker.

A Spanish suite was being played when Jim came home. "Is everything all right?" he asked. His face was pale, she thought. They had some cocktails and went in to dinner to the "Anvil Chorus" from "Il Trovatore." This was followed by Debussy's "La Mer."

"I paid the bill for the radio today," Jim said. "It cost four hundred dollars. I hope you'll get some enjoyment out of it."

"Oh, I'm sure I will," Irene said.

"Four hundred dollars is a good deal more than I can afford," he went on. "I wanted to get something that you'd enjoy. It's the last extravagance we'll be able to indulge in this year. I see that you haven't paid your clothing bills yet. I saw them on your dressing table." He looked directly at her. "Why did you tell me you'd paid them? Why did you lie to me?"

"I just didn't want you to worry, Jim," she said. She drank some water. "I'll be able to pay my bills out of this month's allowance. There were the slipcovers last month, and that party."

"You've got to learn to handle the money I give you a little more intelligently, Irene," he said. "You've got to understand that we won't have as much money this year as we had last. I had a very sobering talk with Mitchell today. No one is buying anything. We're spending all our time promoting new issues, and you know how long that takes. I'm not getting any younger, you know. I'm thirty-seven. My hair will be gray next year. I haven't done as well as I'd hoped to do. And I don't suppose things will get any better."

"Yes, dear," she said.

"We've got to start cutting down," Jim said. "We've got to think of the children. To be perfectly frank with you, I worry about money a great deal. I'm not at all sure of the future. No one is. If anything should happen to me, there's the insurance, but that wouldn't go very far today. I've worked awfully hard to give you and the children a comfortable life," he said bitterly. "I don't like to see all of my energies, all of my youth, wasted in fur coats and radios and slipcovers and—"

"Please, Jim," she said. "Please. They'll hear us."

"*Who'll hear us?* Emma can't hear us."

"The radio."

"Oh, I'm sick!" he shouted. "I'm sick to death of your apprehensiveness. The radio can't hear us. Nobody can hear us. And what if they can hear us? Who cares?"

Irene got up from the table and went into the living room. Jim went to the door and shouted at her from there. "Why are you so Christly all of a sudden? What's turned you overnight into a convent girl? You stole your mother's jewelry before they probated her will. You never gave your sister a cent of that money that was intended for her—not even when she needed it. You made Grace Howland's life miserable, and where was all your piety and your virtue when you went to that abortionist? I'll never forget how cool you were. You packed your bag and went off to have that child murdered as if you were going to Nassau. If you'd had any reasons, if you'd had any good reasons—"

Irene stood for a minute before the hideous cabinet, disgraced and sickened, but she held her hand on the switch before she extinguished the music and the voices, hoping that the instrument might speak to her kindly, that she might hear the Sweeneys' nurse. Jim continued to shout at her from the door. The voice on the radio was suave and noncommittal. "An early-morning railroad disaster in Tokyo," the loudspeaker said, "killed twenty-nine people. A fire in a Catholic hospital near Buffalo for the care of blind children was extinguished early this morning by nuns. The temperature is forty-seven. The humidity is eighty-nine."

## The Swimmer

*1964*

It was one of those midsummer Sundays when everyone sits around saying, "I *drank* too much last night." You might have heard it whispered by the parishioners leaving church, heard it from the lips of the priest himself, struggling with his cassock in the *vestiarium,* heard it from the golf links and the tennis courts, heard it from the wild-life preserve where the leader of the Audubon group was suffering from a terrible hangover. "I *drank* too much," said Donald Westerhazy. "We all *drank* too much," said Lucinda Merrill. "It must have been the wine," said Helen Westerhazy. "I *drank* too much of that claret."

This was the edge of the Westerhazys' pool. The pool, fed by an artesian well with a high iron content, was a pale shade of green. It was a fine day. In the west there was a massive stand of cumulus cloud so like a city seen from a distance—from the bow of an approaching ship—that it might have had a name. Lisbon. Hackensack. The sun was hot. Neddy Merrill sat by the green water, one hand in it, one around a glass of gin. He was a slender man—he seemed to have the especial slenderness of youth— and while he was far from young he had slid down his banister that morning and given the bronze backside of Aphrodite on the hall table a smack, as he jogged toward the smell of coffee in his dining room. He might have been compared to a summer's day, particularly the last hours of one, and while he lacked a tennis racket or a sail bag the impression was definitely one of youth, sport, and clement weather. He had been swimming and now he was breathing deeply, stertorously as if he could gulp into his lungs the components of that moment, the heat of the sun, the intenseness of his pleasure. It all seemed to flow into his chest. His own house stood in Bullet Park, eight miles to the south, where his four beautiful daughters would have had their lunch and might be playing tennis. Then it occurred to him that by taking a dogleg to the south-west he could reach his home by water.

His life was not confining and the delight he took in this observation could not be explained by its suggestion of escape. He seemed to see, with a cartographer's eye, that string of swimming pools, that quasi-subterranean stream that curved across the county. He had made a discovery, a contribution to modern geography; he would name the stream Lucinda after his wife. He was not a practical joker nor was he a fool but he was determinedly original and had a vague and modest idea of himself as a leg-endary figure. The day was beautiful and it seemed to him that a long swim might en-large and celebrate its beauty.

He took off a sweater that was hung over his shoulders and dove in. He had an inexplicable contempt for men who did not hurl themselves into pools. He swam a choppy crawl, breathing either with every stroke or every fourth stroke and counting somewhere well in the back of his mind the one-two one-two of a flutter kick. It was not a serviceable stroke for long distances but the domestication of swimming had saddled the sport with some customs and in his part of the world a crawl was cus-tomary. To be embraced and sustained by the light green water was less a pleasure, it seemed, than the resumption of a natural condition, and he would have liked to swim without trunks, but this was not possible, considering his project. He hoisted himself up on the far curb—he never used the ladder—and started across the lawn. When Lu-cinda asked where he was going he said he was going to swim home.

The only maps and charts he had to go by were remembered or imaginary but these were clear enough. First there were the Grahams, the Hammers, the Lears, the Howlands, and the Crosscups. He would cross Ditmar Street to the Bunkers and come, after a short portage, to the Levys, the Welchers, and the public pool in Lan-caster. Then there were the Hallorans, the Sachses, the Biswangers, Shirley Adams, the Gilmartins, and the Clydes. The day was lovely, and that he lived in a world so gener-ously supplied with water seemed like a clemency, a beneficence. His heart was high and he ran across the grass. Making his way home by an uncommon route gave him the feeling that he was a pilgrim, an explorer, a man with a destiny, and he knew that he would find friends all along the way; friends would line the banks of the Lucinda River.

He went through a hedge that separated the Westerhazys' land from the Grahams', walked under some flowering apple trees, passed the shed that housed their pump and filter, and came out at the Grahams' pool. "Why, Neddy," Mrs. Graham said, "what a marvelous surprise. I've been trying to get you on the phone all morning. Here, let me get you a drink." He saw then, like any explorer, that the hospitable customs and traditions of the natives would have to be handled with diplomacy if he was ever going to reach his destination. He did not want to mystify or seem rude to the Grahams nor did he have the time to linger there. He swam the length of their pool and joined them in the sun and was rescued, a few minutes later, by the arrival of two carloads of friends from Connecticut. During the uproarious reunions he was able to slip away. He went down by the front of the Grahams' house, stepped over a thorny hedge, and crossed a vacant lot to the Hammers'. Mrs. Hammer, looking up from her roses, saw him swim by although she wasn't quite sure who it was. The Lears heard him splashing past the open windows of their living room. The Howlands and the Crosscups were away. After leaving the Howlands' he crossed Ditmar Street and started for the Bunkers', where he could hear, even at that distance, the noise of a party.

The water refracted the sound of voices and laughter and seemed to suspend it in midair. The Bunkers' pool was on a rise and he climbed some stairs to a terrace where twenty-five or thirty men and women were drinking. The only person in the water was Rusty Towers, who floated there on a rubber raft. Oh, how bonny and lush were the banks of the Lucinda River! Prosperous men and women gathered by the sapphire-colored waters while caterer's men in white coats passed them cold gin. Overhead a red de Haviland trainer was circling around and around and around in the sky with something like the glee of a child in a swing. Ned felt a passing affection for the scene, a tenderness for the gathering, as if it was something he might touch. In the distance he heard thunder. As soon as Enid Bunker saw him she began to scream: "Oh, look who's here! What a marvelous surprise! When Lucinda said you couldn't come I thought I'd *die*." She made her way to him through the crowd, and when they had finished kissing she led him to the bar, a progress that was slowed by the fact that he stopped to kiss eight or ten other women and shake the hands of as many men. A smiling bartender he had seen at a hundred parties gave him a gin and tonic and he stood by the bar for a moment, anxious not to get stuck in any conversation that would delay his voyage. When he seemed about to be surrounded he dove in and swam close to the side to avoid colliding with Rusty's raft. At the far end of the pool he bypassed the Tomlinsons with a broad smile and jogged up the garden path. The gravel cut his feet but this was only unpleasantness. The party was confined to the pool, and as he went toward the house he heard the brilliant, watery sound of voices fade, heard the noise of a radio from the Bunkers' kitchen, where someone was listening to a ball game. Sunday afternoon. He made his way through the parked cars and down the grassy border of their driveway to Alewives Lane. He did not want to be seen on the road in his bathing trunks but there was no traffic and he made the short distance to the Levys' driveway, marked with a PRIVATE PROPERTY sign and a green tube for *The New York Times.* All the doors and windows of the big house were open but there were no signs of life; not even a dog barked. He went around the side of the house to the pool and saw that the Levys had only recently left. Glasses and bottles and dishes of nuts were on a table at the deep end, where there was a bathhouse or gazebo, hung with Japanese lanterns. After swimming the pool he got himself a glass and poured a drink. It was his fourth or fifth drink and he had swum nearly half the length of the Lucinda River. He felt tired, clean, and pleased at that moment to be alone; pleased with everything.

It would storm. The stand of cumulus cloud—that city—had risen and darkened, and while he sat there he heard the percussiveness of thunder again. The de Haviland trainer was still circling overhead and it seemed to Ned that he could almost hear the pilot laugh with pleasure in the afternoon; but when there was another peal of thunder he took off for home. A train whistle blew and he wondered what time it had gotten to be. Four? Five? He thought of the provincial station at that hour, where a waiter, his tuxedo concealed by a raincoat, a dwarf with some flowers wrapped in newspaper, and a woman who had been crying would be waiting for the local. It was suddenly growing dark; it was that moment when the pin-headed birds seemed to organize their song into some acute and knowledgeable recognition of the storm's approach. Then there was a fine noise of rushing water from the crown of an oak at his back, as if a spigot there had been turned. Then the noise of fountains came from the crowns of all the tall trees. Why did he love storms, what was the meaning of his excitement when the door sprang open and the rain wind fled rudely up the stairs, why had the simple task of shutting the windows of an old house seemed fitting and urgent, why did the first watery notes of a storm wind have for him the unmistakable sound of good news, cheer, glad tidings? Then there was an explosion, a smell of cordite, and rain lashed the Japanese lanterns that Mrs. Levy had bought in Kyoto the year before last, or was it the year before that?

He stayed in the Levys' gazebo until the storm had passed. The rain had cooled the air and he shivered. The force of the wind had stripped a maple of its red and yellow leaves and scattered them over the grass and the water. Since it was midsummer the tree must be blighted, and yet he felt a peculiar sadness at this sign of autumn. He braced his shoulders, emptied his glass, and started for the Welchers' pool. This meant crossing the Lindleys' riding ring and he was surprised to find it overgrown with grass and all the jumps dismantled. He wondered if the Lindleys had sold their horses or gone away for the summer and put them out to board. He seemed to remember having heard something about the Lindleys and their horses but the memory was unclear. On he went, barefoot through the wet grass, to the Welchers', where he found their pool was dry.

This breach in his chain of water disappointed him absurdly, and he felt like some explorer who seeks a torrential headwater and finds a dead stream. He was disappointed and mystified. It was common enough to go away for the summer but no one ever drained his pool. The Welchers had definitely gone away. The pool furniture was folded, stacked, and covered with a tarpaulin. The bathhouse was locked. All the windows of the house were shut, and when he went around to the driveway in front he saw a FOR SALE sign nailed to a tree. When had he last heard from the Welchers—when, that is, had he and Lucinda last regretted an invitation to dine with them? It seemed only a week or so ago. Was his memory failing or had he so disciplined it in the repression of unpleasant facts that he had damaged his sense of the truth? Then in the distance he heard the sound of a tennis game. This cheered him, cleared away all his apprehensions and let him regard the overcast sky and the cold air with indifference. This was the day that Neddy Merrill swam across the county. That was the day! He started off then for his most difficult portage.

Had you gone for a Sunday afternoon ride that day you might have seen him, close to naked, standing on the shoulders of Route 424, waiting for a chance to cross. You might have wondered if he was the victim of foul play, had his car broken down, or was he merely a fool. Standing barefoot in the deposits of the highway—beer cans, rags, and blowout patches—exposed to all kinds of ridicule, he seemed pitiful. He had known when he started that this was a part of his journey—it had been on his maps—but confronted with the lines of traffic, worming through the summery light, he found himself unprepared. He was laughed at, jeered at, a beer can was thrown at him, and he had no dignity or humor to bring to the situation. He could have gone back, back to the Westerhazys', where Lucinda would still be sitting in the sun. He had signed nothing, vowed nothing, pledged nothing, not even to himself. Why, believing as he did, that all human obduracy was susceptible to common sense, was he unable to turn back? Why was he determined to complete his journey even if it meant putting his life in danger? At what point had this prank, this joke, this piece of horseplay become serious? He could not go back, he could not even recall with any clearness the green water at the Westerhazys', the sense of inhaling the day's components, the friendly and relaxed voices saying that they had *drunk* too much. In the space of an hour, more or less, he had covered a distance that made his return impossible.

An old man, tooling down the highway at fifteen miles an hour, let him get to the middle of the road, where there was a grass divider. Here he was exposed to the ridicule of the northbound traffic, but after ten or fifteen minutes he was able to cross. From here he had only a short walk to the Recreation Center at the edge of the village of Lancaster, where there were some handball courts and a public pool.

The effect of the water on voices, the illusion of brilliance and suspense, was the same here as it had been at the Bunkers' but the sounds here were louder, harsher, and more shrill, and as soon as he entered the crowded enclosure he was confronted with regimentation. "ALL SWIMMERS MUST TAKE A SHOWER BEFORE USING THE POOL. ALL SWIMMERS MUST USE THE FOOTBATH. ALL SWIMMERS MUST WEAR THEIR IDENTIFICATION DISKS." He took a shower, washed his feet in a cloudy and bitter solution, and made his way to the edge of the water. It stank of chlorine and looked to him like a sink. A pair of lifeguards in a pair of towers blew police whistles at what seemed to be regular intervals and abused the swimmers through a public address system. Neddy remembered the sapphire water at the Bunkers' with longing and thought that he might contaminate himself—damage his own prosperousness and charm—by swimming in this murk, but he reminded himself that he was an explorer, a pilgrim, and that this was merely a stagnant bend in the Lucinda River. He dove, scowling with distaste, into the chlorine and had to swim with his head above water to avoid collisions, but even so he was bumped into, splashed, and jostled. When he got to the shallow end both lifeguards were shouting at him: "Hey, you, you without the identification disk, get outa the water." He did, but they had no way of pursuing him and he went through the reek of suntan oil and chlorine out through the hurricane fence and passed the handball courts. By crossing the road he entered the wooded part of the Halloran estate. The woods were not cleared and the footing was treacherous and difficult until he reached the lawn and the clipped beech hedge that encircled their pool.

The Hallorans were friends, an elderly couple of enormous wealth who seemed to bask in the suspicion that they might be Communists. They were zealous reformers but they were not Communists, and yet when they were accused, as they sometimes were, of subversion, it seemed to gratify and excite them. Their beech hedge was yellow and he guessed this had been blighted like the Levys' maple. He called hullo, hullo, to warn the Hallorans of his approach, to palliate his invasion of their privacy. The Hallorans, for reasons that had never been explained to him, did not wear bathing suits. No explanations were in order, really. Their nakedness was a detail in their uncompromising zeal for reform and he stepped politely out of his trunks before he went through the opening in the hedge.

Mrs. Halloran, a stout woman with white hair and a serene face, was reading the *Times*. Mr. Halloran was taking beech leaves out of the water with a scoop. They seemed not surprised or displeased to see him. Their pool was perhaps the oldest in the country, a fieldstone rectangle, fed by a brook. It had no filter or pump and its waters were the opaque gold of the stream.

"I'm swimming across the county," Ned said.

"Why, I didn't know one could," exclaimed Mrs. Halloran.

"Well, I've made it from the Westerhazys'," Ned said. "That must be about four miles."

He left his trunks at the deep end, walked to the shallow end, and swam this stretch. As he was pulling himself out of the water he heard Mrs. Halloran say, "We've been *terribly* sorry to hear about all your misfortunes, Neddy."

"My misfortunes?" Ned asked. "I don't know what you mean."

"Why we heard that you'd sold the house and that your poor children. . . ."

"I don't recall having sold the house," Ned said, "and the girls are at home."

"Yes," Mrs. Halloran sighed. "Yes. . . ." Her voice filled the air with an unseasonable melancholy and Ned spoke briskly. "Thank you for the swim."

"Well, have a nice trip," said Mrs. Halloran.

Beyond the hedge he pulled on his trunks and fastened them. They were loose and he wondered if, during the space of an afternoon, he could have lost some weight. He was cold and he was tired and the naked Hallorans and their dark water had depressed him. The swim was too much for his strength but how could he have guessed this, sliding down the banister that morning and sitting in the Westerhazys' sun? His arms were lame. His legs felt rubbery and ached at the joints. The worst of it was the cold in his bones and the feeling that he might never be warm again. Leaves were falling down around him and he smelled wood smoke on the wind. Who would be burning wood at this time of the year?

He needed a drink. Whiskey would warm him, pick him up, carry him through the last of his journey, refresh his feeling that it was original and valorous to swim across the county. Channel swimmers took brandy. He needed a stimulant. He crossed the lawn in front of the Hallorans' house and went down a little path to where they had built a house for their only daughter, Helen, and her husband, Eric Sachs. The Sachses' pool was small and he found Helen and her husband there.

"Oh, *Neddy,*" Helen said. "Did you lunch at Mother's?"

"Not *really,*" Ned said. "I *did* stop to see your parents." This seemed to be explanation enough. "I'm terribly sorry to break in on you like this but I've taken a chill and I wonder if you'd give me a drink."

"Why, I'd *love* to," Helen said, "but there hasn't been anything in this house to drink since Eric's operation. That was three years ago."

Was he losing his memory, had his gift for concealing painful facts let him forget that he had sold his house, that his children were in trouble, and that his friend had been ill? His eyes slipped from Eric's face to his abdomen, where he saw three pale, sutured scars, two of them at least a foot long. Gone was his navel, and what, Neddy thought, would the roving hand, bed-checking one's gifts at 3 A.M., make of a belly with no navel, no link to birth, this breach in the succession?

"I'm sure you can get a drink at the Biswangers'," Helen said. "They're having an enormous do. You can hear it from here. Listen!"

She raised her head and from across the road, the lawns, the gardens, the woods, the fields, he heard again the brilliant noise of voices over water. "Well, I'll get wet," he said, still feeling that he had no freedom of choice about his means of travel. He dove into the Sachses' cold water, and gasping, close to drowning, made his way from one end of the pool to the other. "Lucinda and I want *terribly* to see you," he said over his shoulder, his face set toward the Biswangers'. "We're sorry it's been so long and we'll call you *very* soon."

He crossed some fields to the Biswangers' and the sounds of revelry there. They would be honored to give him a drink, they would be happy to give him a drink. The Biswangers invited him and Lucinda for dinner four times a year, six weeks in advance. They were always rebuffed and yet they continued to send out their invitations, unwilling to comprehend the rigid and undemocratic realities of their society. They were the sort of people who discussed the price of things at cocktails, exchanged market tips during dinner, and after dinner told dirty stories to mixed company. They did not belong to Neddy's set—they were not even on Lucinda's Christmas card list. He went toward their pool with feelings of indifference, charity, and some unease, since it seemed to be getting dark and these were the longest days of the year. The party when he joined it was noisy and large. Grace Biswanger was the kind of hostess who asked the optometrist, the veterinarian, the real-estate dealer, and the dentist. No one was swimming and the twilight, reflected on the water of the pool, had a wintry gleam. There was a bar and he started for this. When Grace Biswanger saw him she came toward him, not affectionately as he had every right to expect, but bellicosely.

"Why, this party has everything," she said loudly, "including a gate crasher."

She could not deal him a social blow—there was no question about this and he did not flinch. "As a gate crasher," he asked politely, "do I rate a drink?"

"Suit yourself," she said. "You don't seem to pay much attention to invitations."

She turned her back on him and joined some guests, and he went to the bar and ordered a whiskey. The bartender served him but he served him rudely. His was a world in which the caterer's men kept the social score, and to be rebuffed by a part-time barkeep meant that he had suffered some loss of social esteem. Or perhaps the man was new and uninformed. Then he heard Grace at his back say: "They went for broke overnight—nothing but income—and he showed up drunk one Sunday and asked us to loan him five thousand dollars. . . ." She was always talking about money. It was worse than eating your peas off a knife. He dove into the pool, swam its length, and went away.

The next pool on his list, the last but two, belonged to his old mistress, Shirley Adams. If he had suffered any injuries at the Biswangers', they would be cured here. Love—sexual roughhouse in fact—was the supreme elixir, the pain killer, the brightly colored pill that would put the spring back into his step, the joy of life in his heart. They had had an affair last week, last month, last year. He couldn't remember. It was he who had broken it off, his was the upper hand, and he stepped through the gate of the wall that surrounded her pool with nothing so considered as self-confidence. It seemed in a way to be his pool, as the lover, particularly the illicit lover, enjoys the possessions of his mistress with an authority unknown to holy matrimony. She was there, her hair the color of brass, but her figure, at the edge of the lighted, cerulean water, excited in him no profound memories. It had been, he thought, a lighthearted affair, although she had wept when he broke it off. She seemed confused to see him and he wondered if she was still wounded. Would she, God forbid, weep again?

"What do you want?" she asked.

"I'm swimming across the county."

"Good Christ. Will you ever grow up?"

"What's the matter?"

"If you've come here for money," she said, "I won't give you another cent."

"You could give me a drink."

"I could but I won't. I'm not alone."

"Well, I'm on my way."

He dove in and swam the pool, but when he tried to haul himself up onto the curb he found that the strength in his arms and shoulders had gone, and he paddled to the ladder and climbed out. Looking over his shoulder he saw, in the lighted bathhouse, a young man. Going out onto the dark lawn he smelled chrysanthemums or marigolds—some stubborn autumnal fragrance—on the night air, strong as gas. Looking overhead he saw that the stars had come out, but why should he seem to see Andromeda, Cepheus, and Cassiopeia? What had become of the constellations of midsummer? He began to cry.

It was probably the first time in his adult life that he had ever cried, certainly the first time in his life that he had ever felt so miserable, cold, tired, and bewildered. He could not understand the rudeness of the caterer's barkeep or the rudeness of a mistress who had come to him on her knees and showered his trousers with tears. He had swum too long, he had been immersed too long, and his nose and his throat were sore from the water. What he needed then was a drink, some company, and some clean, dry clothes, and while he could have cut directly across the road to his home he went on to the Gilmartins' pool. Here, for the first time in his life, he did not dive but went down the steps into the icy water and swam a hobbled sidestroke that he might have learned as a youth. He staggered with fatigue on his way to the Clydes' and paddled the length of their pool, stopping again and again with his hand on the curb to rest. He climbed up the ladder and wondered if he had the strength to get home. He had done what he wanted, he had swum the county, but he was so stupefied with exhaustion that his triumph seemed vague. Stooped, holding on to the gateposts for support, he turned up the driveway of his own house.

The place was dark. Was it so late that they had all gone to bed? Had Lucinda stayed at the Westerhazys' for supper? Had the girls joined her there or gone someplace else? Hadn't they agreed, as they usually did on Sunday, to regret all their invitations and stay at home? He tried the garage doors to see what cars were in but the doors were locked and rust came off the handles onto his hands. Going toward the house, he saw the force of the thunderstorm had knocked one of the rain gutters loose. It hung down over the front door like an umbrella rib, but it could be fixed in the morning. The house was locked, and he thought that the stupid cook or the stupid maid must have locked the place up until he remembered that it had been some time since they had employed a maid or a cook. He shouted, pounded on the door, tried to force it with his shoulder, and then, looking in at the windows, saw that the place was empty.

# Colette

## (1873–1954)

A contemporary of Marcel Proust, Paul Valéry, André Gide, and Paul Claudel, Colette was known for writing about the joy and pain of love and about female sexuality in a male-dominated world. In 1893 she married Henri Gauthier-Villars, whom critics have labeled a literary charlatan and degenerate. Her first four *Claudine* novels (1900–1903), published under her husband's penname, were an incredible success. It is said that Henri locked Colette in a room and would not release her until she had written enough pages. She divorced him in 1906 and went on to become a music-hall performer. She quickly gained fame as a writer, actress, and lesbian and was even managed by Napoleon III's niece. During World War I, she converted her husband's estate into a hospital for the wounded, and she was made a Chevalier of the Legion of Honor in 1920. Her works include *Chéri* (1920), *My Mother's House* (1922), *Sido* (1929), *Gigi* (1945), and *The Last of Chéri* (1951). In 1953 she became a Grand Officer of the Legion of Honor. She died in 1954; despite the refusal of Catholic rites on the grounds that she had been divorced, Colette was given a state funeral attended by thousands of mourners.

## The Other Wife

1924

TRANSLATED BY MATTHEW WARD

"Table for two? This way, Monsieur, Madame, there is still a table next to the window, if Madame and Monsieur would like a view of the bay."

Alice followed the maître d'.

"Oh, yes. Come on, Marc, it'll be like having lunch on a boat on the water . . ."

Her husband caught her by passing his arm under hers. "We'll be more comfortable over there."

"There? In the middle of all those people? I'd much rather . . ."

"Alice, please."

He tightened his grip in such a meaningful way that she turned around. "What's the matter?"

"Shh . . ." he said softly, looking at her intently, and led her toward the table in the middle.

"What is it, Marc?"

"I'll tell you, darling. Let me order lunch first. Would you like the shrimp? Or the eggs in aspic?"

"Whatever you like, you know that."

They smiled at one another, wasting the precious time of an overworked maître d', stricken with a kind of nervous dance, who was standing next to them, perspiring.

"The shrimp," said Marc. "Then the eggs and bacon. And the cold chicken with a romaine salad. *Fromage blanc?* The house specialty? We'll go with the specialty. Two strong coffees. My chauffeur will be having lunch also, we'll be leaving again at two o'clock. Some cider? No, I don't trust it . . . Dry champagne."

He sighed as if he had just moved an armoire, gazed at the colorless midday sea, at the pearly white sky, then at his wife, whom he found lovely in her little Mercury hat with its large, hanging veil.

"You're looking well, darling. And all this blue water makes your eyes look green, imagine that! And you've put on weight since you've been traveling . . . It's nice up to a point, but only up to a point!"

Her firm, round breasts rose proudly as she leaned over the table.

"Why did you keep me from taking that place next to the window?"

Marc Seguy never considered lying. "Because you were about to sit next to someone I know."

"Someone I don't know?"

"My ex-wife."

She couldn't think of anything to say and opened her blue eyes wider. "So what, darling? It'll happen again. It's not important."

The words came back to Alice and she asked, in order, the inevitable questions. "Did she see you? Could she see that you saw her? Will you point her out to me?"

"Don't look now, please, she must be watching us. . . . The lady with brown hair, no hat, she must be staying in this hotel. By herself, behind those children in red . . ."

"Yes, I see."

Hidden behind some broad-brimmed beach hats, Alice was able to look at the woman who, fifteen months ago, had still been her husband's wife.

"Incompatibility," Marc said. "Oh, I mean . . . total incompatibility! We divorced like well-bred people, almost like friends, quietly, quickly. And then I fell in love with you, and you really wanted to be happy with me. How lucky we are that our happiness doesn't involve any guilty parties or victims!"

The woman in white, whose smooth, lustrous hair reflected the light from the sea in azure patches, was smoking a cigarette with her eyes half closed. Alice turned back toward her husband, took some shrimp and butter, and ate calmly. After a moment's silence she asked: "Why didn't you ever tell me that she had blue eyes, too?"

"Well, I never thought about it!"

He kissed the hand she was extending toward the bread basket and she blushed with pleasure. Dusky and ample, she might have seemed somewhat coarse, but the changeable blue of her eyes and her wavy, golden hair made her look like a frail and sentimental blonde. She vowed overwhelming gratitude to her husband. Immodest without knowing it, everything about her bore the overly conspicuous marks of extreme happiness.

They ate and drank heartily, and each thought the other had forgotten the woman in white. Now and then, however, Alice laughed too loudly, and Marc was careful about his posture, holding his shoulders back, his head up. They waited quite a long time for their coffee, in silence. An incandescent river, the straggled reflection of the invisible sun overhead, shifted slowly across the sea and shone with a blinding brilliance.

"She's still there, you know," Alice whispered.

"Is she making you uncomfortable? Would you like to have coffee somewhere else?"

"No, not at all! She's the one who must be uncomfortable! Besides, she doesn't exactly seem to be having a wild time, if you could see her . . ."

"I don't have to. I know that look of hers."

"Oh, was she like that?"

He exhaled his cigarette smoke through his nostrils and knitted his eyebrows. "Like that? No. To tell you honestly, she wasn't happy with me."

"Oh, really now!"

"The way you indulge me is so charming, darling . . . It's crazy . . . You're an angel . . . You love me . . . I'm so proud when I see those eyes of yours. Yes, those eyes . . . She . . . I just didn't know how to make her happy, that's all, I didn't know how."

"She's just difficult!"

Alice fanned herself irritably, and cast brief glances at the woman in white, who was smoking, her head resting against the back of the cane chair, her eyes closed with an air of satisfied lassitude.

Marc shrugged his shoulders modestly.

"That's the right word," he admitted. "What can you do? You have to feel sorry for people who are never satisfied. But we're satisfied . . . Aren't we, darling?"

She did not answer. She was looking furtively, and closely, at her husband's face, ruddy and regular; at his thick hair, threaded here and there with white silk; at his short, well-cared-for hands; and doubtful for the first time, she asked herself, "What more did she want from him?"

And as they were leaving, while Marc was paying the bill and asking for the chauffeur and about the route, she kept looking, with envy and curiosity, at the woman in white, this dissatisfied, this difficult, this superior . . .

*[handwritten margin note: The wife envied the ex-wife.]*

# Haroldo Conti

## (1925–1976?)

Haroldo Conti was born in Chacabuco, a province of Buenos Aires. Conti was an author, actor, director, scriptwriter, and professor of philosophy. His list of published works includes *Examined* (1955), *The American Hunter* (1975), *All the Summers* (1965), *With Another People* (1967), and *The Ballad of the Carolina Poplar* (1975). Conti's stories revolve around questions of identity and social and political change. He was kidnapped at dawn on May 5, 1976, by an intelligence unit of the Argentine army and is still missing.

## Lost

*1967*

TRANSLATED BY NORMAN THOMAS DI GIOVANNI

The train was leaving at eight or eight thirty. The engine wouldn't be coupled up until ten minutes before, but somehow his uncle began fretting a whole hour ahead. That's the way country people were. They no sooner got somewhere than they thought about returning. His father had been the same. Half the time he'd be thinking about his chickens, which were fed at a certain time, or about his dog, which he had left with a neighbor. To Oreste, Buenos Aires was the English Clock Tower, the Avenida de Mayo, Alem, and, somewhat unusually, the statue of Garibaldi in Plaza Italia, because the first time he ever set foot in the city—he was with his mother—they got lost and that's where they ended up. They had their picture taken, and the man with the camera steered them to a tram that got them to Retiro Station. They managed to arrive in plenty of time, but all the same they were so flustered they almost boarded the wrong train.

Now, crossing Plaza Británica with its clock tower that somehow presided over his life and that he saw or glimpsed at some point every day year in and year out as he tramped about Buenos Aires, here was his old melancholy welling up, and Oreste pictured his uncle in a corner of the waiting room of the Pacific (they still called it the Pacific), collapsed into an overcoat that smelled of tobacco, with his imitation-leather cardboard suitcase on one side and a heap of packages on his knees, feeling in his pocket to make sure his second-class ticket was still there.

His uncle had phoned two or three times from the Hotel Universo, but Oreste had been out, and the girl had only half understood the message. After that the uncle tried to make his way to Oreste's house—on foot, of course, since the trolleys and buses terrified him. At some point along Leandro Alem he had gone wrong and, rather than lose sight of Plaza Británica, he thought it best to return to Retiro and wait for his train.

It had been several years since Oreste last saw his uncle, but he knew he'd have no trouble spotting him. The same spongy, white face peppered with blackheads and hairs, and those glaring eyes that grew smaller when he stared at something, the polka-dot bow tie, faded and grease stained, the same black overcoat with the velvet collar, the felt hat with the tall crown and wide brim that he put on with both hands, and the pair of elastic-sided spats.

The Pacific Station had grown smaller with the years. That's how it seemed, anyway. Actually it was a forlorn shed with a few poorly lighted platforms. A long time ago, however, Oreste had seen it all colored by a mysterious light. People themselves were steeped in that light then. It was wonderful, soft and gentle, as though it would never change or die out, and the station was lit up like a circus. But people had changed somehow and now the old Pacific Station was lit up like what it was—a forlorn corrugated-iron shed, filled with noise and the smell of frying.

Oreste saw his uncle on a bench under the schedule board. He seemed very small and unassuming. Hands in his pockets, legs close together, he held an umbrella across his knees, and his gaze was lost somewhere in front of him. He was looking Oreste's way but did not see him. He saw nothing, and only when Oreste stood in front of him did his uncle react.

"Oreste!"

They embraced and kissed in accordance with the old custom. Oreste let his uncle clap him on the back for a good long while. His uncle had that familiar smell, a masculine smell that reminded Oreste of those aloof, noncommittal men of his boyhood who smiled on him with brief indulgence—like Uncle Ernesto, who stood as big as a wardrobe and in whose presence Oreste always went dry in the mouth; or his great-uncle Agustín, on whom Oreste had laid eyes only once, the day Agustín had driven all the way from Bragado in that model-A Ford that spouted a cloud of steam from its radiator; or Uncle Bautista when he was really himself and not this mere shadow.

They separated, and his uncle asked, without letting go of Oreste's arms, "How are you?"

"Fine, fine."

They looked at each other, smiling, then embraced again.

"And how are things with you?"

"Fine, fine."

"And Auntie?"

"Fine . . . yes, fine."

His uncle put a hand on Oreste's shoulder and looked and looked at him. Oreste slowly smiled. He was used to this style.

"What time's your train leave?"

"Eight thirty."

"It's a quarter past seven. Why don't we have a drink?"

"No, we'd better stay here. Anyway, where can we go? By the time the train comes in and they hitch up the locomotive there won't be much time."

"Yes, but that's got nothing to do with us. Come on."

"But where? Don't feel obliged, my boy."

They bickered a while until at last Oreste prevailed and they went into the station bar, where they found a place from which it was just possible to keep an eye on a stretch of Platform 4.

Oreste asked for an aperitif, and his uncle, after much insisting on Oreste's part, a Cinzano with bitters.

"What brought you all this way?"

"Well, I'd been thinking about it for some time."

His uncle looked at the bar clock, and his face went suddenly white.

"It's not working," said Oreste, holding him back.

His uncle did not seem convinced. He took out and examined his old Tissot with its oriental hands.

"What was I saying? Oh, yes. I came to see my cousin Vicente. It's been six years since I last saw him. He's from Baigorrita, too. I don't know how long I've been promising him—today, tomorrow."

He took a small sip of his Cinzano.

"He's aged. I barely recognized him."

His uncle went silent for a moment or two with the same preoccupied air he'd had in the waiting room.

"How are you? How are things?" he asked again, this time less eager.

"Fine, fine."

"Getting on, then?"

"Getting on."

They looked at each other with fondness, smiled, and turned silent. His uncle had always been like this. His uncle and all of them.

"I came with a load of errands. Your aunt wanted a tin or two of Hunt's Salts. It's over a year she's been after some. Two months ago I had a good look around Junín without finding any. No, it was November—four months ago."

"What's it for?"

"The stomach. It's quite a thing. People take all sorts of rubbish nowadays, but this is really good."

A locomotive whistled, and his uncle gave a start.

"Still plenty of time."

His uncle looked at his watch again and took another sip of his Cinzano.

"So I went to the Franco-Inglesa and found all I wanted. I showed the clerk an empty tin, and he said, 'How many do you want?' He hardly even looked at it. How about that?"

In a short while his uncle was going to disappear into a second-class coach, and Oreste would not see him for another four or five years. It had been five years since he last saw him. Oreste's father disappeared like that one day, and Oreste never saw him again.

"And back there?" asked Oreste after a while.

Back there. It was a painful chafing, a crumbling away of years grown old, a question asked of himself in a black shadowy hole.

"The same."

"The boys?"

"Just the same."

Again neither spoke.

His uncle turned his glass in his fingers and sipped the last swallow.

"What time is it?"

"Quarter to eight."

His uncle took out his watch and looked at it, anxious.

"Nearly ten to. Shall we go?"

Oreste held back a moment.

"All right."

They were connecting the locomotive. His uncle picked up his packages and suitcase and hurriedly set off for Platform 4. He seemed to have forgotten Oreste.

Oreste tried to take the suitcase from him, and his uncle shot him a strange look.

"It's all right, my boy. I can manage."

"Greetings to Auntie—and everyone."

"Thanks, son. Thanks."

They rushed along the length of the train, bumping into other second-class passengers, themselves in a rush, as if the station were tumbling down around them. People were shoving children and suitcases in through the windows to secure themselves seats. His uncle boarded one of the coaches up by the engine and after a few moments stuck his head out of a window.

"When will you be making the trip?" he asked, his eyes on the people crowding the platform.

"Soon as I can."

"You must come, no two ways about it. When did you say?"

"When I can."

His uncle turned aside a moment to put up his suitcase. Then he sat at the end of the bench and said nothing more.

When again their eyes met, his uncle smiled and said, "Oreste . . ."

Oreste smiled, too, distantly, from the edge of the platform. There was a bell, and his uncle hurriedly shoved himself half out of the window.

"Bye, son, bye!" he said, and, as best he could, he kissed Oreste on the cheek. Oreste tried to kiss him, too, but his uncle had already taken his seat.

The train jolted from end to end. His uncle waved a hand and smiled, safe now. Oreste ran a few yards alongside the train. He ran along, his eyes on his uncle, who was smiling a smile of satisfaction like those men in Oreste's childhood.

Then the train got up steam, and Oreste lifted a hand, but there was no response.

# Julio Cortázar

## (1914–1984)

Julio Cortázar was born in Brussels and wrote his first novel when he was nine years old. He published his first collection of poems, *Presencia* (1938), under the pseudonym Julia Denis. In 1944, Cortázar moved to Cuyo, Mendoza, where he taught French literature. He was arrested in 1946 for demonstrating against Juan Perón, the soon-to-be president. After his release, Cortázar quit his teaching position and moved to Buenos Aires. In 1961, he visited Cuba for the first time and, while there, said that he felt "the great political void I had, my political uselessness." His writing is often filled with such angst in its exploration of identity and meaning in life. In 1979, after visiting Nicaragua, he decided to devote himself to the Sandinista revolution, and some of his texts were used in the country's literacy campaign. He eventually moved to Paris, where he became interested in surrealism and adopted French nationality in 1981. Cortázar's works include *Bestiario* (1951), *Hopscotch* (1963), *End of the Game* (1967), *62: A Model Kit* (1968), *We Love Glenda So Much* (1981), and *Paris: The Essence of an Image* (1981).

## Continuity of Parks

*1967*

TRANSLATED BY PAUL BLACKBURN

He had begun to read the novel a few days before. He had put it down because of some urgent business conferences, opened it again on his way back to the estate by train; he permitted himself a slowly growing interest in the plot, in the characterizations. That afternoon, after writing a letter giving his power of attorney and discussing a matter of joint ownership with the manager of his estate, he returned to the book in the tranquillity of his study which looked out upon the park with its oaks. Sprawled in his favorite armchair, its back toward the door—even the possibility of an intrusion would have irritated him, had he thought of it—he let his left hand caress repeatedly the green velvet upholstery and set to reading the final chapters. He remembered effortlessly the names and his mental image of the characters; the novel spread its glamour over him almost at once. He tasted the almost perverse pleasure of disengaging himself line by line from the things around him, and at the same time feeling his head rest comfortably on the green velvet of the chair with its high back, sensing that the cigarettes rested within reach of his hand, that beyond the great windows the air of afternoon danced under the oak trees in the park. Word by word, licked up by the sordid dilemma of the hero and heroine, letting himself be absorbed to the point where the images settled down and took on color and movement, he was witness to the final encounter in the mountain cabin.

The woman arrived first, apprehensive; now the lover came in, his face cut by the backlash of a branch. Admirably, she stanched the blood with her kisses, but he rebuffed her caresses, he had not come to perform again the ceremonies of a secret passion, protected by a world of dry leaves and furtive paths through the forest. The dagger warmed itself against his chest, and underneath liberty pounded, hidden close. A lustful, panting dialogue raced down the pages like a rivulet of snakes, and one felt it had all been decided from eternity. Even to those caresses which writhed about the lover's body, as though wishing to keep him there, to dissuade him from it; they sketched abominably the frame of that other body it was necessary to destroy. Nothing had been forgotten: alibis, unforeseen hazards, possible mistakes. From this hour on, each instant had its use minutely assigned. The cold-blooded, twice-gone-over reexamination of the details was barely broken off so that a hand could caress a cheek. It was beginning to get dark.

Not looking at one another now, rigidly fixed upon the task which awaited them, they separated at the cabin door. She was to follow the trail that led north. On the path leading in the opposite direction, he turned for a moment to watch her running, her hair loosened and flying. He ran in turn, crouching among the trees and hedges until, in the yellowish fog of dusk, he could distinguish the avenue of trees which led up to the house. The dogs were not supposed to bark, they did not bark. The estate manager would not be there at this hour, and he was not there. He went up the three porch steps and entered. The woman's words reached him over the thudding of blood in his ears: first a blue chamber, then a hall, then a carpeted stairway. At the top, two doors. No one in the first room, no one in the second. The door of the salon, and then, the knife in hand, the light from the great windows, the high back of an armchair covered in green velvet, the head of the man in the chair reading a novel.

# Ralph Ellison

## (1914–1994)

Named after American poet and philosopher Ralph Waldo Emerson, Ralph Ellison was born in Oklahoma City, Oklahoma, in 1914. He studied at the Tuskegee Institute after being awarded a music scholarship, but he dropped out in 1936 to pursue a career in the visual arts. Ellison moved to New York City to study sculpture, but after meeting Langston Hughes and Richard Wright, he joined the Federal Writers' Project. Ellison's stories were published in *New Masses*, and he worked as an editor of *Negro Quarterly*. From 1943 to 1945, he served as a cook in the Merchant Marines. His novel *Invisible Man*, published in 1952, is narrated by an unnamed young black man who encounters the political organizations and jazz music of Harlem. His story represents the cultural and geographical journeys of many African Americans in the first half of the twentieth century. After its publication and the release of a collection of essays titled *Shadow and Act* (1964), Ellison lectured at various colleges in the United States. He taught at New York University as the Albert Schweitzer Professor in the Humanities. Ellison received numerous awards and honors during his lifetime, including the Medal of Freedom (1969), the Chevalier de l'Ordre des Arts et Lettres (1970), and the National Medal of Arts for *Invisible Man* (1985). His second novel, *Juneteenth* (1999), planned as part of a trilogy, was left unfinished at his death.

## The Battle Royal                                                    1952

It goes a long way back, some twenty years. All my life I had been looking for something, and everywhere I turned someone tried to tell me what it was. I accepted their answers too, though they were often in contradiction and even self-contradictory. I was naïve. I was looking for myself and asking everyone except myself questions which I, and only I, could answer. It took me a long time and much painful boomeranging of my expectations to achieve a realization everyone else appears to have been born with: That I am nobody but myself. But first I had to discover that I am an invisible man!

*[handwritten margin note: He realizes he's nobody but himself.]*

And yet I am no freak of nature, nor of history. I was in the cards, other things having been equal (or unequal) eighty-five years ago. I am not ashamed of my grandparents for having been slaves. I am only ashamed of myself for having at one time been ashamed. About eighty-five years ago they were told that they were free, united with others of our country in everything pertaining to the common good, and, in everything social, separate like the fingers of the hand. And they believed it. They exulted in it. They stayed in their place, worked hard, and brought up my father to do the same. But my grandfather is the one. He was an odd old guy, my grandfather, and

I am told I take after him. It was he who caused the trouble. On his deathbed he called my father to him and said, "Son, after I'm gone I want you to keep up the good fight. I never told you, but our life is a war and I have been a traitor all my born days, a spy in the enemy's country ever since I give up my gun back in the Reconstruction. Live with your head in the lion's mouth. I want you to overcome 'em with yeses, undermine 'em with grins, agree 'em to death and destruction, let 'em swoller you till they vomit or bust wide open." They thought the old man had gone out of his mind. He had been the meekest of men. The younger children were rushed from the room, the shades drawn and the flame of the lamp turned so low that it sputtered on the wick like the old man's breathing. "Learn it to the younguns," he whispered fiercely; then he died.

But my folks were more alarmed over his last words than over his dying. It was as though he had not died at all, his words caused so much anxiety. I was warned emphatically to forget what he had said and, indeed, this is the first time it has been mentioned outside the family circle. It had a tremendous effect upon me, however. I could never be sure of what he meant. Grandfather had been a quiet old man who never made any trouble, yet on his deathbed he had called himself a traitor and a spy, and he had spoken of his meekness as a dangerous activity. It became a constant puzzle which lay unanswered in the back of my mind. And whenever things went well for me I remembered my grandfather and felt guilty and uncomfortable. It was as though I was carrying out his advice in spite of myself. And to make it worse, everyone loved me for it. I was praised by the most lily-white men of the town. I was considered an example of desirable conduct—just as my grandfather had been. And what puzzled me was that the old man had defined it as *treachery*. When I was praised for my conduct I felt a guilt that in some way I was doing something that was really against the wishes of the white folks, that if they had understood they would have desired me to act just the opposite, that I should have been sulky and mean, and that that really would have been what they wanted, even though they were fooled and thought they wanted me to act as I did. It made me afraid that some day they would look upon me as a traitor and I would be lost. Still I was more afraid to act any other way because they didn't like that at all. The old man's words were like a curse. On my graduation day I delivered an oration in which I showed that humility was the secret, indeed, the very essence of progress. (Not that I believed this—how could I, remembering my grandfather?—I only believed that it worked.) It was a great success. Everyone praised me and I was invited to give the speech at a gathering of the town's leading white citizens. It was a triumph for our whole community.

It was in the main ballroom of the leading hotel. When I got there I discovered that it was on the occasion of a smoker, and I was told that since I was to be there anyway I might as well take part in the battle royal to be fought by some of my schoolmates as part of the entertainment. The battle royal came first.

All of the town's big shots were there in their tuxedoes, wolfing down the buffet foods, drinking beer and whiskey and smoking black cigars. It was a large room with a high ceiling. Chairs were arranged in neat rows around three sides of a portable boxing ring. The fourth side was clear, revealing a gleaming space of polished floor. I had some misgivings over the battle royal, by the way. Not from a distaste for fighting, but because I didn't care too much for the other fellows who were to take part. They were tough guys who seemed to have no grandfather's curse worrying their minds. No one could mistake their toughness. And besides, I suspected that fighting a battle royal might detract from the dignity of my speech. In those pre-invisible days I visualized myself as a potential Booker T. Washington. But the other fellows didn't care too much for me either, and there were nine of them. I felt superior to them in my way, and I didn't like the manner in which we were all crowded together into the servants' elevator. Nor did they like my being there. In fact, as the warmly lighted floors flashed past the elevator we had words over the fact that I, by taking part in the fight, had knocked one of their friends out of a night's work.

We were led out of the elevator through a rococo hall into in anteroom and told to get into our fighting togs. Each of us was issued a pair of boxing gloves and ushered out into the big mirrored hall, which we entered looking cautiously about us and whispering, lest we might accidentally be heard above the noise of the room. It was foggy with cigar smoke. And already the whiskey was taking effect. I was shocked to see some of the most important men of the town quite tipsy. They were all there—bankers, lawyers, judges, doctors, fire chiefs, teachers, merchants. Even one of the more fashionable pastors. Something we could not see was going on up front. A clarinet was vibrating sensuously and the men were standing up and moving eagerly forward. We were a small tight group, clustered together, our bare upper bodies touching and shining with anticipatory sweat; while up front the big shots were becoming increasingly excited over something we still could not see. Suddenly I heard the school superintendent, who had told me to come, yell, "Bring up the shines, gentlemen! Bring up the little shines!"

We were rushed up to the front of the ballroom, where it smelled even more strongly of tobacco and whiskey. Then we were pushed into place. I almost wet my pants. A sea of faces, some hostile, some aroused, ringed around us, and in the center, facing us, stood a magnificent blonde—stark naked. There was dead silence. I felt a blast of cold air chill me. I tried to back away, but they were behind me and around me. Some of the boys stood with lowered heads, trembling. I felt a wave of irrational guilt and fear. My teeth chattered, my skin turned to goose flesh, my knees knocked. Yet I was strongly attracted and looked in spite of myself. Had the price of looking been blindness, I would have looked. The hair was yellow like that of a circus kewpie doll, the face heavily powdered and rouged, as though to form an abstract mask, the eyes hollow and smeared a cool blue, the color of a baboon's butt. I felt a desire to spit upon her as my eyes brushed slowly over her body. Her breasts were firm and round as the domes of East Indian temples, and I stood so close as to see the fine skin texture and beads of pearly perspiration glistening like dew around the pink and erected buds of her nipples. I wanted at one and the same time to run from the room, to sink through the floor, or go to her and cover her from my eyes and the eyes of the others with my body; to feel the soft thighs, to caress her and destroy her, to love her and murder her, to hide from her, and yet to stroke where below the small American flag tattooed upon her belly her thighs formed a capital V. I had a notion that of all in the room she saw only me with her impersonal eyes.

And then she began to dance, a slow sensuous movement; the smoke of a hundred cigars clinging to her like the thinnest of veils. She seemed like a fair bird-girl girdled in veils calling to me from the angry surface of some gray and threatening sea. I was transported. Then I became aware of the clarinet playing and the big shots yelling at us. Some threatened us if we looked and others if we did not. On my right I saw one boy faint. And now a man grabbed a silver pitcher from a table and stepped close as he dashed ice water upon him and stood him up and forced two of us to support him as his head hung and moans issued from his thick bluish lips. Another boy began to plead to go home. He was the largest of the group, wearing dark red fighting trunks much too small to conceal the erection which projected from him as though in answer to the insinuating low-registered moaning of the clarinet. He tried to hide himself with his boxing gloves.

And all the while the blonde continued dancing, smiling faintly at the big shots who watched her with fascination, and faintly smiling at our fear. I noticed a certain merchant who followed her hungrily, his lips loose and drooling. He was a large man who wore diamond studs in a shirtfront which swelled with the ample paunch underneath, and each time the blonde swayed her undulating hips he ran his hand through the thin hair of his bald head and, with his arms upheld, his posture clumsy like that of an intoxicated panda, wound his belly in a slow and obscene grind. This creature was completely hypnotized. The music had quickened. As the dancer flung herself about with a detached expression on her face, the men began reaching out to touch her. I could see their beefy fingers sink into the soft flesh. Some of the others tried to stop them and she began to move around the floor in graceful circles, as they gave chase, slipping and sliding over the polished floor. It was mad. Chairs went crashing, drinks were spilt, as they ran laughing and howling after her. They caught her just as she reached a door, raised her from the floor, and tossed her as college boys are tossed at a hazing, and above her red, fixed-smiling lips I saw the terror and disgust in her eyes, almost like my own terror and that which I saw in some of the other boys. As I watched, they tossed her twice and her soft breasts seemed to flatten against the air and her legs flung wildly as she spun. Some of the more sober ones helped her to escape. And I started off the floor, heading for the anteroom with the rest of the boys.

Some were still crying and in hysteria. But as we tried to leave we were stopped and ordered to get into the ring. There was nothing to do but what we were told. All ten of us climbed under the ropes and allowed ourselves to be blindfolded with broad bands of white cloth. One of the men seemed to feel a bit sympathetic and tried to cheer us up as we stood with our backs against the ropes. Some of us tried to grin. "See that boy over there?" one of the men said. "I want you to run across at the bell and give it to him right in the belly. If you don't get him, I'm going to get you. I don't like his looks." Each of us was told the same. The blindfolds were put on. Yet even then I had been going over my speech. In my mind each word was as bright as flame. I felt the cloth pressed into place, and frowned so that it would be loosened when I relaxed.

But now I felt a sudden fit of blind terror. I was unused to darkness. It was as though I had suddenly found myself in a dark room filled with poisonous cottonmouths. I could hear the bleary voices yelling insistently for the battle royal to begin.

"Get going in there!"

"Let me at that big nigger!"

I strained to pick up the school superintendent's voice, as though to squeeze some security out of that slightly more familiar sound.

"Let me at those black sonsabitches!" someone yelled.

"No, Jackson, no!" another voice yelled. "Here, somebody, help me hold Jack."

"I want to get at that ginger-colored nigger. Tear him limb from limb," the first voice yelled.

I stood against the ropes trembling. For in those days I was what they called ginger-colored, and he sounded as though he might crunch me between his teeth like a crisp ginger cookie.

Quite a struggle was going on. Chairs were being kicked about and I could hear voices grunting as with a terrific effort. I wanted to see, to see more desperately than ever before. But the blindfold was tight as a thick skin-puckering scab and when I raised my gloved hands to push the layers of white aside a voice yelled, "Oh, no you don't, black bastard! Leave that alone!"

"Ring the bell before Jackson kills him a coon!" someone boomed in the sudden silence. And I heard the bell clang and the sound of the feet scuffling forward.

A glove smacked against my head. I pivoted, striking out stiffly as someone went past, and felt the jar ripple along the length of my arm to my shoulder. Then it seemed as though all nine of the boys had turned upon me at once. Blows pounded me from all sides while I struck out as best I could. So many blows landed upon me that I wondered if I were not the only blindfolded fighter in the ring, or if the man called Jackson hadn't succeeded in getting me after all.

Blindfolded, I could no longer control my motions. I had no dignity. I stumbled about like a baby or a drunken man. The smoke had become thicker and with each new blow it seemed to sear and further restrict my lungs. My saliva became like hot bitter glue. A glove connected with my head, filling my mouth with warm blood. It was everywhere. I could not tell if the moisture I felt upon my body was sweat or blood. A blow landed hard against the nape of my neck. I felt myself going over, my head hitting the floor. Streaks of blue light filled the black world behind the blindfold. I lay prone, pretending that I was knocked out, but felt myself seized by hands and yanked to my feet. "Get going, black boy! Mix it up!" My arms were like lead, my head smarting from blows. I managed to feel my way to the ropes and held on, trying to catch my breath. A glove landed in my mid-section and I went over again, feeling as though the smoke had become a knife jabbed into my guts. Pushed this way and that by the legs milling around me, I finally pulled erect and discovered that I could see the black, sweat-washed forms weaving in the smoky-blue atmosphere like drunken dancers weaving to the rapid drum-like thuds of blows.

Everyone fought hysterically. It was complete anarchy. Everybody fought everybody else. No group fought together for long. Two, three, four, fought one, then turned to fight each other, were themselves attacked. Blows landed below the belt and in the kidney, with the gloves open as well as closed, and with my eye partly opened now there was not so much terror. I moved carefully, avoiding blows, although not too many to attract attention, fighting from group to group. The boys groped about like blind, cautious crabs crouching to protect their mid-sections, their heads pulled in short against their shoulders, their arms stretched nervously before them, with their fists testing the smoke-filled air like the knobbed feelers of hypersensitive snails. In one corner I glimpsed a boy violently punching the air and heard him scream in pain as he smashed his hand against a ring post. For a second I saw him bent over holding his hand, then going down as a blow caught his unprotected head. I played one group against the other, slipping in and throwing a punch then stepping out of range while pushing the others into the melee to take the blows blindly aimed at me. The smoke was agonizing and there were no rounds, no bells at three minute intervals to relieve our exhaustion. The room spun round me, a swirl of lights, smoke, sweating bodies surrounded by tense white faces. I bled from both nose and mouth, the blood spattering upon my chest.

The men kept yelling, "Slug him, black boy! Knock his guts out!"

"Uppercut him! Kill him! Kill that big boy!"

Taking a fake fall, I saw a boy going down heavily beside me as though we were felled by a single blow, saw a sneaker-clad foot shoot into his groin as the two who had knocked him down stumbled upon him. I rolled out of range, feeling a twinge of nausea.

The harder we fought the more threatening the men became. And yet, I had begun to worry about my speech again. How would it go? Would they recognize my ability? What would they give me?

I was fighting automatically when suddenly I noticed that one after another of the boys was leaving the ring. I was surprised, filled with panic, as though I had been left alone with an unknown danger. Then I understood. The boys had arranged it among themselves. It was the custom for the two men left in the ring to slug it out for the winner's prize. I discovered this too late. When the bell sounded two men in tuxedoes leaped into the ring and removed the blindfold. I found myself facing Tatlock, the biggest of the gang. I felt sick at my stomach. Hardly had the bell stopped ringing in my ears than it clanged again and I saw him moving swiftly toward me. Thinking of nothing else to do I hit him smash on the nose. He kept coming, bringing the rank sharp violence of stale sweat. His face was a black blank of a face, only his eyes alive— with hate of me and aglow with a feverish terror from what had happened to us all. I became anxious. I wanted to deliver my speech and he came at me as though he meant to beat it out of me. I smashed him again and again, taking his blows as they came. Then on a sudden impulse I struck him lightly and as we clinched, I whispered, "Fake like I knocked you out, you can have the prize."

"I'll break your behind," he whispered hoarsely.

"For *them?*"

"For *me*, sonofabitch!"

They were yelling for us to break it up and Tatlock spun me half around with a blow, and as a joggled camera sweeps in a reeling scene, I saw the howling red faces crouching tense beneath the cloud of blue-gray smoke. For a moment the world wavered, unraveled, flowed, then my head cleared and Tatlock bounced before me. That fluttering shadow before my eyes was his jabbing left hand. Then falling forward, my head against his damp shoulder, I whispered,

"I'll make it five dollars more."

"Go to hell!"

But his muscles relaxed a trifle beneath my pressure and I breathed, "Seven?"

"Give it to your ma," he said, ripping me beneath the heart.

And while I still held him I butted him and moved away. I felt myself bombarded with punches. I fought back with hopeless desperation. I wanted to deliver my speech more than anything else in the world, because I felt that only these men could judge truly my ability, and now this stupid clown was ruining my chances. I began fighting carefully now, moving in to punch him and out again with my greater speed. A lucky blow to his chin and I had him going too—until I heard a loud voice yell, "I got my money on the big boy."

Hearing this, I almost dropped my guard. I was confused: Should I try to win against the voice out there? Would not this go against my speech, and was not this a moment for humility, for nonresistance? A blow to my head as I danced about sent my right eye popping like a jack-in-the-box and settled my dilemma. The room went red as I fell. It was a dream fall, my body languid and fastidious as to where to land, until the floor became impatient and smashed up to meet me. A moment later I came to. An hypnotic voice said FIVE emphatically. And I lay there, hazily watching a dark red spot of my own blood shaping itself into a butterfly, glistening and soaking into the soiled gray world of the canvas.

When the voice drawled TEN I was lifted up and dragged to a chair. I sat dazed. My eye pained and swelled with each throb of my pounding heart and I wondered if now I would be allowed to speak. I was wringing wet, my mouth still bleeding. We were grouped along the wall now. The other boys ignored me as they congratulated Tatlock and speculated as to how much they would be paid. One boy whimpered over his smashed hand. Looking up front, I saw attendants in white jackets rolling the portable ring away and placing a small square rug in the vacant space surrounded by chairs. Perhaps, I thought, I will stand on the rug to deliver my speech.

Then the M.C. called to us, "Come on up here boys and get your money."

We ran forward to where the men laughed and talked in their chairs, waiting. Everyone seemed friendly now.

"There it is on the rug," the man said. I saw the rug covered with coins of all dimensions and a few crumpled bills. But what excited me, scattered here and there, were the gold pieces.

"Boys, it's all yours," the man said. "You get all you grab."

"That's right, Sambo," a blond man said, winking at me confidentially.

I trembled with excitement, forgetting my pain. I would get the gold and the bills, I thought. I would use both hands. I would throw my body against the boys nearest me to block them from the gold.

"Get down around the rug now," the man commanded, "and don't anyone touch it until I give the signal."

"This ought to be good," I heard.

As told, we got around the square rug on our knees. Slowly the man raised his freckled hand as we followed it upward with our eyes.

I heard, "These niggers look like they're about to pray!"

Then, "Ready," the man said. "Go!"

I lunged for a yellow coin lying on the blue design of the carpet, touching it and sending a surprised shriek to join those rising around me. I tried frantically to remove my hand but could not let go. A hot, violent force tore through my body, shaking me like a wet rat. The rug was electrified. The hair bristled up on my head as I shook myself free. My muscles jumped, my nerves jangled, writhed. But I saw that this was not stopping the other boys. Laughing in fear and embarrassment, some were holding back and scooping up the coins knocked off by the painful contortions of the others. The men roared above us as we struggled.

"Pick it up, goddamnit, pick it up!" someone called like a bass-voiced parrot. "Go on, get it!"

I crawled rapidly around the floor, picking up the coins, trying to avoid the coppers and to get greenbacks and the gold. Ignoring the shock by laughing, as I brushed the coins off quickly, I discovered that I could contain the electricity—a contradiction, but it works. Then the men began to push us onto the rug. Laughing embarrassedly, we struggled out of their hands and kept after the coins. We were all wet and slippery and hard to hold. Suddenly I saw a boy lifted into the air, glistening with sweat like a circus seal, and dropped, his wet back landing flush upon the charged rug, heard him yell and saw him literally dance upon his back, his elbows beating a frenzied tattoo upon the floor, his muscles twitching like the flesh of a horse stung by many flies. When he finally rolled off, his face was gray and no one stopped him when he ran from the floor amid booming laughter.

"Get the money," the M.C. called. "That's good hard American cash!"

And we snatched and grabbed, snatched and grabbed. I was careful not to come too close to the rug now, and when I felt the hot whiskey breath descend upon me like a cloud of foul air I reached out and grabbed the leg of a chair. It was occupied and I held on desperately.

"Leggo, nigger! Leggo!"

The huge face wavered down to mine as he tried to push me free. But my body was slippery and he was too drunk. It was Mr. Colcord, who owned a chain of movie houses and "entertainment palaces." Each time he grabbed me I slipped out of his hands. It became a real struggle. I feared the rug more than I did the drunk, so I held on, surprising myself for a moment by trying to topple *him* upon the rug. It was such an enormous idea that I found myself actually carrying it out. I tried not to be obvious, yet when I grabbed his leg, trying to tumble him out of the chair, he raised up roaring with laughter, and, looking at me with soberness dead in the eye, kicked me viciously in the chest. The chair leg flew out of my hand and I felt myself going and rolled. It was as though I had rolled through a bed of hot coals. It seemed a whole century would pass before I would roll free, a century in which I was seared through the deepest levels of my body to the fearful breath within me and the breath seared and heated to the point of explosion. It'll all be over in a flash, I thought as I rolled clear. It'll all be over in a flash.

But not yet, the men on the other side were waiting, red faces swollen as though from apoplexy as they bent forward in their chairs. Seeing their fingers coming toward me I rolled away as I fumbled football rolls off the receiver's fingertips, back into the coals. That time I luckily sent the rug sliding out of place and heard the coins ringing against the floor and the boys scuffling to pick them up and the M.C. calling, "All right, boys, that's all. Go get dressed and get your money."

I was limp as a dish rag. My back felt as though it had been beaten with wires.

When we had dressed the M.C. came in and gave us each five dollars, except Tatlock, who got ten for being last in the ring. Then he told us to leave. I was not to get a chance to deliver my speech, I thought. I was going out into the dim alley in despair when I was stopped and told to go back. I returned to the ballroom, where the men were pushing back their chairs and gathering in groups to talk.

The M.C. knocked on a table for quiet. "Gentlemen," he said , "we almost forgot an important part of the program. A most serious part, gentlemen. This boy was brought here to deliver a speech which he made at his graduation yesterday . . ."

"Bravo!"

"I'm told that he is the smartest boy we've got out there in Greenwood. I'm told that he knows more big words than a pocket-sized dictionary."

Much applause and laughter.

"So now, gentlemen, I want you to give him your attention."

There was still laughter as I faced them, my mouth dry, my eye throbbing. I began slowly, but evidently my throat was tense, because they began shouting, "Louder! Louder!"

"We of the younger generation extol the wisdom of that great leader and educator," I shouted, "who first spoke these flaming words of wisdom: 'A ship lost at sea for many days suddenly sighted a friendly vessel. From the mast of the unfortunate vessel was seen a signal: "Water, water; we die of thirst!" The answer from the friendly vessel came back: "Cast down your bucket where you are." The captain of the distressed vessel, at last heeding the injunction, cast down his bucket, and it came up full of fresh sparkling water from the mouth of the Amazon River.' And like him I say, and in his words, 'To those of my race who depend upon bettering their condition in a foreign land, or who underestimate the importance of cultivating friendly relations with the Southern white man, who is his next-door neighbor, I would say: "Cast down your bucket where you are"—cast it down in making friends in every manly way of the people of all races by whom we are surrounded . . .'"

I spoke automatically and with such fervor that I did not realize that the men were still talking and laughing until my dry mouth, filling up with blood from the cut, almost strangled me. I coughed, wanting to stop and go to one of the tall brass, sand-filled spittoons to relieve myself, but a few of the men, especially the superintendent, were listening and I was afraid. So I gulped it down, blood, saliva and all, and continued. (What powers of endurance I had during those days! What enthusiasm! What a belief in the rightness of things!) I spoke even louder in spite of the pain. But still they talked and still they laughed, as though deaf with cotton in dirty ears. So I spoke with greater emotional emphasis. I closed my ears and swallowed blood until I was nauseated. The speech seemed a hundred times as long as before, but I could not leave out a single word. All had to be said, each memorized nuance considered, rendered. Nor was that all. Whenever I uttered a word of three or more syllables a group of voices would yell for me to repeat it. I used the phrase "social responsibility" and they yelled:

"What's that word you say, boy?"

"Social responsibility," I said.

"What?"

"Social . . ."

"Louder."

". . . responsibility."

"More!"

"Respon—"

"Repeat!"

"—sibility."

The room filled with the uproar of laughter until, no doubt, distracted by having to gulp down my blood, I made a mistake and yelled a phrase I had often seen denounced in newspaper editorials, heard debated in private.

"Social . . ."

"What?" they yelled.

". . . equality—"

The laughter hung smokelike in the sudden stillness. I opened my eyes, puzzled. Sounds of displeasure filled the room. The M.C. rushed forward. They shouted hostile phrases at me. But I did not understand.

A small dry mustached man in the front row blared out, "Say that slowly, son!"

"What, sir?"

"What you just said!"

"Social responsibility, sir," I said.

"You weren't being smart, were you, boy?" he said, not unkindly.

"No, sir!"

"You sure that about 'equality' was a mistake?"

"Oh, yes, sir," I said. "I was swallowing blood."

"Well, you had better speak more slowly so we can understand. We mean to do right by you, but you've got to know your place at all times. All right, now, go on with your speech."

I was afraid. I wanted to leave but I wanted also to speak and I was afraid they'd snatch me down.

"Thank you, sir," I said, beginning where I had left off, and having them ignore me as before.

Yet when I finished there was a thunderous applause. I was surprised to see the superintendent come forth with a package wrapped in white tissue paper, and, gesturing for quiet, address the men.

"Gentlemen, you see that I did not overpraise this boy. He makes a good speech and some day he'll lead his people in the proper paths. And I don't have to tell you that that is important in these days and times. This is a good, smart boy, and so to encourage him in the right direction, in the name of the Board of Education I wish to present him a prize in the form of this . . ."

He paused, removing the tissue paper and revealing a gleaming calfskin brief case.

". . . in the form of this first-class article from Shad Whitmore's shop."

"Boy," he said, addressing me, "take this prize and keep it well. Consider it a badge of office. Prize it. Keep developing as you are and some day it will be filled with important papers that will help shape the destiny of your people."

I was so moved that I could hardly express my thanks. A rope of bloody saliva forming a shape like an undiscovered continent drooled upon the leather and I wiped it quickly away. I felt an importance that I had never dreamed.

"Open it and see what's inside," I was told.

My fingers a-tremble, I complied, smelling the fresh leather and finding an official-looking document inside. It was a scholarship to the state college for Negroes. My eyes filled with tears and I ran awkwardly off the floor.

I was overjoyed; I did not even mind when I discovered that the gold pieces I had scrambled for were brass pocket tokens advertising a certain make of automobile.

When I reached home everyone was excited. Next day the neighbors came to congratulate me. I even felt safe from grandfather, whose deathbed curse usually spoiled my triumphs. I stood beneath his photograph with my brief case in hand and smiled triumphantly into his stolid black peasant's face. It was a face that fascinated me. The eyes seemed to follow everywhere I went.

That night I dreamed I was at a circus with him and that he refused to laugh at the clowns no matter what they did. Then later he told me to open my brief case and read what was inside and I did, finding an official envelope stamped with the state seal; and inside the envelope I found another and another, endlessly, and I thought I would fall of weariness. "Them's years," he said. "Now open that one." And I did and in it I found an engraved document containing a short message in letters of gold. "Read it," my grandfather said. "Out loud!"

"To Whom It May Concern," I intoned. "Keep This Nigger-Boy Running."

I awoke with the old man's laughter ringing in my ears.

(It was a dream I was to remember and dream again for many years after. But at that time I had no insight into its meaning. First I had to attend college.)

# William Faulkner

## (1897–1962)

William Faulkner said that "the writer's only responsibility is to his art. He will be completely ruthless if he is a good one." Faulkner was born in New Albany, Mississippi, and began writing poetry at the age of thirteen. He served in the Royal Air Force during World War I, though he never saw any action. Faulkner studied at the University of Mississippi for a short time, where he wrote some poems and drew cartoons for the university's humor magazine, *The Scream*. He left without earning his degree and published his first collection of poems, *The Marble Faun*, in 1924 and his first novel, *Soldier's Pay*, in 1926. In 1929, Faulkner married Estelle Oldham Franklin, his childhood sweetheart, and purchased a southern pillared house in Oxford. He obsessively restored the house during his lifetime.

*Sartoris* (1929) was the first of fifteen novels set in Yoknapatawpha County, a fictional southern community shaped by a history of slavery and civil war, where the present is undeniably created by the past. Much of Faulkner's writing explores themes of time, memory, pride, and sacrifice with inventive and complex syntax influenced by Joycean stream of consciousness. *Sartoris* was followed by *The Sound and the Fury* (1929) and *As I Lay Dying* (1930), which Faulkner wrote while working the nightshift at an electrical power station. Over the next twenty years, Faulkner worked on screenplays in Hollywood to earn money. He became good friends with Howard Hawks and worked on several of his films, including *To Have and Have Not* (1944) and *The Big Sleep* (1946). Faulkner continued to publish during this time, producing such works as *Pylon* (1934), *Absalom, Absalom!* (1936), *The Portable Faulkner* (1946), *Requiem for a Nun* (1951), *The Town* (1957), *The Mansion* (1959), and *The Reivers* (1962). He was awarded the Nobel Prize for literature in 1949.

## A Rose for Emily                                                                1931

### I

When Miss Emily Grierson died, our whole town went to her funeral: the men through a sort of respectful affection for a fallen monument, the women mostly out of curiosity to see the inside of her house, which no one save an old man-servant—a combined gardener and cook—had seen in at least ten years.

It was a big, squarish frame house that had once been white, decorated with cupolas and spires, and scrolled balconies in the heavily lightsome style of the seventies, set on what had once been our most select street. But garages and cotton gins had encroached and obliterated even the august names of that neighborhood; only Miss Emily's house was left, lifting its stubborn and coquettish decay above the cotton wagons and the gasoline pumps—an eyesore among eyesores. And now Miss Emily had gone to join the representatives of those august names where they lay in the cedar-bemused cemetery among the ranked and anonymous graves of Union and Confederate soldiers who fell at the battle of Jefferson.

Alive, Miss Emily had been a tradition, a duty, and a care; a sort of hereditary obligation upon the town, dating from that day in 1894 when Colonel Sartoris, the mayor—he who fathered the edict that no Negro woman should appear on the street without an apron—remitted her taxes, the dispensation dating from the death of her father on into perpetuity. Not that Miss Emily would have accepted charity. Colonel Sartoris invented an involved tale to the effect that Miss Emily's father had loaned money to the town, which the town, as a matter of business, preferred this way of repaying. Only a man of Colonel Sartoris' generation and thought could have invented it, and only a woman could have believed it.

When the next generation, with its more modern ideas, became mayors and aldermen, this arrangement created some little dissatisfaction. On the first of the year they mailed her a tax notice. February came, and there was no reply. They wrote her a formal letter, asking her to call at the sheriff's office at her convenience. A week later the mayor wrote her himself, offering to call or to send his car for her, and received in reply a note on paper of an archaic shape, in a thin, flowing calligraphy in faded ink, to the effect that she no longer went out at all. The tax notice was also enclosed, without comment.

They called a special meeting of the Board of Aldermen. A deputation waited upon her, knocked at the door through which no visitor had passed since she ceased giving china-painting lessons eight or ten years earlier. They were admitted by the old Negro into a dim hall from which a stairway mounted into still more shadow. It smelled of dust and disuse—a close, dank smell. The Negro led them into the parlor. It was furnished in heavy, leather-covered furniture. When the Negro opened the blinds of one window, they could see that the leather was cracked; and when they sat down, a faint dust rose sluggishly about their thighs, spinning with slow motes in the single sun-ray. On a tarnished gilt easel before the fireplace stood a crayon portrait of Miss Emily's father.

They rose when she entered—a small, fat woman in black, with a thin gold chain descending to her waist and vanishing into her belt, leaning on an ebony cane with a tarnished gold head. Her skeleton was small and spare; perhaps that was why what would have been merely plumpness in another was obesity in her. She looked bloated, like a body long submerged in motionless water, and of that pallid hue. Her eyes, lost in the fatty ridges of her face, looked like two small pieces of coal pressed into a lump of dough as they moved from one face to another while the visitors stated their errand.

She did not ask them to sit. She just stood in the door and listened quietly until the spokesman came to a stumbling halt. Then they could hear the invisible watch ticking at the end of the gold chain.

Her voice was dry and cold. "I have no taxes in Jefferson. Colonel Sartoris explained it to me. Perhaps one of you can gain access to the city records and satisfy yourselves."

"But we have. We are the city authorities, Miss Emily. Didn't you get a notice from the sheriff, signed by him?"

"I received a paper, yes," Miss Emily said. "Perhaps he considers himself the sheriff . . . I have no taxes in Jefferson."

"But there is nothing on the books to show that, you see. We must go by the—"

"See Colonel Sartoris. I have no taxes in Jefferson."

"But Miss Emily—"

"See Colonel Sartoris." (Colonel Sartoris had been dead almost ten years.) "I have no taxes in Jefferson. Tobe!" The Negro appeared. "Show these gentlemen out."

## II

So she vanquished them, horse and foot,[1] just as she had vanquished their fathers thirty years before about the smell. That was two years after her father's death and a short time after her sweetheart—the one we believed would marry her—had deserted her. After her father's death she went out very little; after her sweetheart went away, people hardly saw her at all. A few of the ladies had the temerity to call, but were not received, and the only sign of life about the place was the Negro man—a young man then—going in and out with a market basket.

"Just as if a man—any man—could keep a kitchen properly," the ladies said; so they were not surprised when the smell developed. It was another link between the gross, teeming world and the high and mighty Griersons.

A neighbor, a woman, complained to the mayor, Judge Stevens, eighty years old.

"But what will you have me do about it, madam?" he said.

"Why, send her word to stop it," the woman said. "Isn't there a law?"

"I'm sure that won't be necessary," Judge Stevens said. "It's probably just a snake or a rat that nigger of hers killed in the yard. I'll speak to him about it."

The next day he received two more complaints, one from a man who came in diffident deprecation. "We really must do something about it, Judge. I'd be the last one in the world to bother Miss Emily, but we've got to do something." That night the Board of Aldermen met—three graybeards and one younger man, a member of the rising generation.

"It's simple enough," he said. "Send her word to have her place cleaned up. Give her a certain time do it in, and if she don't . . ."

"Dammit, sir," Judge Stevens said, "will you accuse a lady to her face of smelling bad?"

So the next night, after midnight, four men crossed Miss Emily's lawn and slunk about the house like burglars, sniffing along the base of the brickwork and at the cellar openings while one of them performed a regular sowing motion with his hand out of a sack slung from his shoulder. They broke open the cellar door and sprinkled

---

1 **horse and foot:** Completely, totally. Reference to victory over an army's cavalry and infantry.

lime there, and in all the outbuildings. As they recrossed the lawn, a window that had been dark was lighted and Miss Emily sat in it, the light behind her, and her upright torso motionless as that of an idol. They crept quietly across the lawn and into the shadow of the locusts that lined the street. After a week or two the smell went away.

That was when people had begun to feel really sorry for her. People in our town, remembering how old lady Wyatt, her great-aunt, had gone completely crazy at last, believed that the Griersons held themselves a little too high for what they really were. None of the young men were quite good enough for Miss Emily and such. We had long thought of them as a tableau, Miss Emily a slender figure in white in the background, her father a spraddled silhouette in the foreground, his back to her and clutching a horsewhip, the two of them framed by the backflung front door. When she got to be thirty and was still single, we were not pleased exactly, but vindicated; even with insanity in the family she wouldn't have turned down all of her chances if they had really materialized.

When her father died, it got about that the house was all that was left to her; and in a way, people were glad. At last they could pity Miss Emily. Being left alone, and a pauper, she had become humanized. Now she too would know the old thrill and the old despair of a penny more or less.

The day after his death all the ladies prepared to call at the house and offer condolence and aid, as is our custom. Miss Emily met them at the door, dressed as usual and with no trace of grief on her face. She told them that her father was not dead. She did that for three days, with the ministers calling on her, and the doctors, trying to persuade her to let them dispose of the body. Just as they were about to resort to law and force, she broke down, and they buried her father quickly.

We did not say she was crazy then. We believed she had to do that. We remembered all the young men her father had driven away, and we knew that with nothing left, she would have to cling to that which had robbed her, as people will.

### III

She was sick for a long time. When we saw her again, her hair was cut short, making her look like a girl, with a vague resemblance to those angels in colored church windows—sort of tragic and serene.

The town had just let the contracts for paving the sidewalks, and in the summer after her father's death they began the work. The construction company came with niggers and mules and machinery, and a foreman named Homer Barron, a Yankee—a big, dark, ready man, with a big voice and eyes lighter than his face. The little boys would follow in groups to hear him cuss the niggers, and the niggers singing in time to the rise and fall of picks. Pretty soon he knew everybody in town. Whenever you heard a lot of laughing anywhere about the square, Homer Barron would be in the center of the group. Presently we began to see him and Miss Emily on Sunday afternoons driving in the yellow-wheeled buggy and the matched team of bays from the livery stable.

At first we were glad that Miss Emily would have an interest, because the ladies all said, "Of course a Grierson would not think seriously of a Northerner, a day laborer." But there were still others, older people, who said that even grief could not cause a real lady to forget *noblesse oblige*[2]—without calling it *noblesse oblige*. They just said, "Poor Emily. Her kinsfolk should come to her." She had some kin in Alabama; but years ago her father had fallen out with them over the estate of old Lady Wyatt, the crazy woman, and there was no communication between the two families. They had not even been represented at the funeral.

And as soon as the old people said, "Poor Emily," the whispering began. "Do you suppose it's really so?" they said to one another. "Of course it is. What else could . . ." This behind their hands; rustling of craned silk and satin behind jalousies closed upon the sun of Sunday afternoon as the thin, swift clop-clop-clop of the matched team passed: "Poor Emily."

She carried her head high enough—even when we believed that she was fallen. It was as if she demanded more than ever the recognition of her dignity as the last Grierson; as if it had wanted that touch of earthiness to reaffirm her imperviousness. Like when she bought the rat poison, the arsenic. That was over a year after they had begun to say "Poor Emily," and while the two female cousins were visiting her.

"I want some poison," she said to the druggist. She was over thirty then, still a slight woman, though thinner than usual, with cold, haughty black eyes in a face the flesh of which was strained across the temples and about the eye-sockets as you imagine a lighthouse-keeper's face ought to look. "I want some poison," she said.

"Yes, Miss Emily. What kind? For rats and such? I'd recom—"

"I want the best you have. I don't care what kind."

The druggist named several. "They'll kill anything up to an elephant. But what you want is—"

"Arsenic," Miss Emily said. "Is that a good one?"

"Is . . . arsenic? Yes, ma'am. But what you want—"

"I want arsenic."

The druggist looked down at her. She looked back at him, erect, her face like a strained flag. "Why, of course," the druggist said. "If that's what you want. But the law requires you to tell what you are going to use it for."

Miss Emily just stared at him, her head tilted back in order to look him eye for eye, until he looked away and went and got the arsenic and wrapped it up. The Negro delivery boy brought her the package; the druggist didn't come back. When she opened the package at home there was written on the box, under the skull and bones: "For rats."

## IV

So the next day we all said, "She will kill herself"; and we said it would be the best thing. When she had first begun to be seen with Homer Barron, we had said, "She will

---

2 ***noblesse oblige:*** French. Benevolent, honorable behavior, considered the duty of persons of high birth or rank.

marry him." Then we said, "She will persuade him yet," because Homer himself had remarked—he liked men, and it was known that he drank with the younger men in the Elks' Club—that he was not a marrying man. Later we said, "Poor Emily" behind the jalousies as they passed on Sunday afternoon in the glittering buggy, Miss Emily with her head high and Homer Barron with his hat cocked and cigar in his teeth, reins and whip in a yellow glove.

Then some of the ladies began to say that it was a disgrace to the town and a bad example to the young people. The men did not want to interfere, but at last the ladies forced the Baptist minister—Miss Emily's people were Episcopal—to call upon her. He would never divulge what happened during that interview, but he refused to go back again. The next Sunday they again drove about the streets, and the following day the minister's wife wrote to Miss Emily's relations in Alabama.

So she had blood-kin under her roof again and we sat back to watch developments. At first nothing happened. Then we were sure that they were to be married. We learned that Miss Emily had been to the jeweler's and ordered a man's toilet set in silver, with the letters H. B. on each piece. Two days later we learned that she had bought a complete outfit of men's clothing, including a nightshirt, and we said, "They are married." We were really glad. We were glad because the two female cousins were even more Grierson than Miss Emily had ever been.

So we were not surprised when Homer Barron—the streets had been finished some time since—was gone. We were a little disappointed that there was not a public blowing-off, but we believed that he had gone on to prepare for Miss Emily's coming, or to give her a chance to get rid of the cousins. (By that time it was a cabal, and we were all Miss Emily's allies to help circumvent the cousins.) Sure enough, after another week they departed. And, as we had expected all along, within three days Homer Barron was back in town. A neighbor saw the Negro man admit him at the kitchen door at dusk one evening.

And that was the last we saw of Homer Barron. And of Miss Emily for some time. The Negro man went in and out with the market basket, but the front door remained closed. Now and then we would see her at a window for a moment, as the men did that night when they sprinkled the lime, but for almost six months she did not appear on the streets. Then we knew that this was to be expected too; as if that quality of her father which had thwarted her woman's life so many times had been too virulent and too furious to die.

When we next saw Miss Emily, she had grown fat and her hair was turning gray. During the next few years it grew grayer and grayer until it attained an even pepper-and-salt iron-gray, when it ceased turning. Up to the day of her death at seventy-four it was still that vigorous iron-gray, like the hair of an active man.

From that time on her front door remained closed, save for a period of six or seven years, when she was about forty, during which she gave lessons in china-painting. She fitted up a studio in one of the downstairs rooms, where the daughters and granddaughters of Colonel Sartoris' contemporaries were sent to her with the same regularity and in the same spirit that they were sent to church on Sunday with a twenty-five-cent piece for the collection plate. Meanwhile her taxes had been remitted.

Then the newer generation became the backbone and the spirit of the town, and the painting pupils grew up and fell away and did not send their children to her with boxes of color and tedious brushes and pictures cut from the ladies' magazines. The front door closed upon the last one and remained closed for good. When the town got free postal delivery, Miss Emily alone refused to let them fasten the metal numbers above her door and attach a mailbox to it. She would not listen to them.

Daily, monthly, yearly we watched the Negro grow grayer and more stooped, going in and out with the market basket. Each December we sent her a tax notice, which would be returned by the post office a week later, unclaimed. Now and then we would see her in one of the downstairs windows—she had evidently shut up the top floor of the house—like the carven torso of an idol in a niche, looking or not looking at us, we could never tell which. Thus she passed from generation to generation—dear, inescapable, impervious, tranquil, and perverse.

And so she died. Fell ill in the house filled with dust and shadows, with only a doddering Negro man to wait on her. We did not even know she was sick; we had long since given up trying to get any information from the Negro. He talked to no one, probably not even to her, for his voice had grown harsh and rusty, as if from disuse.

She died in one of the downstairs rooms, in a heavy walnut bed with a curtain, her gray head propped on a pillow yellow and moldy with age and lack of sunlight.

## V

The Negro met the first of the ladies at the front door and let them in, with their hushed, sibilant voices and their quick, curious glances, and then he disappeared. He walked right through the house and out the back and was not seen again.

The two female cousins came at once. They held the funeral on the second day, with the town coming to look at Miss Emily beneath a mass of bought flowers, with the crayon face of her father musing profoundly above the bier and the ladies sibilant and macabre; and the very old men—some in their brushed Confederate uniforms—on the porch and the lawn, talking of Miss Emily as if she had been a contemporary of theirs, believing that they had danced with her and courted her perhaps, confusing time with its mathematical progression, as the old do, to whom all the past is not a diminishing road but, instead, a huge meadow which no winter ever quite touches, divided from them now by the narrow bottle-neck of the most recent decade of years.

Already we knew that there was one room in that region above stairs which no one had seen in forty years, and which would have to be forced. They waited until Miss Emily was decently in the ground before they opened it.

The violence of breaking down the door seemed to fill this room with pervading dust. A thin, acrid pall of the tomb seemed to lie everywhere upon this room decked and furnished as for a bridal: upon the valance curtains of faded rose color, upon the rose-shaded lights, upon the dressing table, upon the delicate array of crystal and the man's toilet things backed with tarnished silver, silver so tarnished that the monogram was obscured. Among them lay a collar and tie, as if they had just been removed, which, lifted, left upon the surface a pale crescent in the dust. Upon a chair hung the suit, carefully folded; beneath it the two mute shoes and the discarded socks.

The man himself lay in the bed.

For a long while we just stood there, looking down at the profound and fleshless grin. The body had apparently once lain in the attitude of an embrace, but now the long sleep that outlasts love, that conquers even the grimace of love, had cuckolded him. What was left of him, rotted beneath what was left of the nightshirt, had become inextricable from the bed in which he lay; and upon him and upon the pillow beside him lay that even coating of the patient and biding dust.

Then we noticed that in the second pillow was the indentation of a head. One of us lifted something from it, and leaning forward, that faint and invisible dust dry and acrid in the nostrils, we saw a long strand of iron-gray hair.

# F. Scott Fitzgerald

## (1896–1940)

A descendant of Francis Scott Key, F. Scott Fitzgerald was considered the mouthpiece for the American "Lost Generation" after World War I, recording in his fiction its characteristic romanticization of and disappointment in the "American dream." Most of his writing was semiautobiographical and often resembled the conversational "magazine pieces" of the time. Born in Minnesota to poor but class-conscious parents, Fitzgerald left his northern home at age sixteen to attend Princeton University. His undergraduate experience with that wealth-driven society, though never culminating in a degree, supplied material for a first novel and provided a venue, in the college's *Nassau Literary Magazine*, for his first publications of fiction and poetry. In 1917, Fitzgerald left Princeton to enlist in the army and spent his time during World War I in a camp in Alabama, where he began working on *This Side of Paradise* (1920). Upon being discharged from the army, he moved to New York City, began working for an advertising agency, and married Zelda Sayre the following year. Because of the popularity of his first book, Fitzgerald easily published his first short story collection, *Flappers and Philosophers,* which, like most of his work, described the rebellious energy of World War I survivors. In 1922, he followed this with a novel, *The Beautiful and the Damned,* and two more story collections, *Tales of the Jazz Age* and *All the Sad Young Men.* In 1925, Fitzgerald produced his most successful and enduring novel, *The Great Gatsby,* which focuses on a man's desire to redeem the past.

Between 1924 and 1931, Fitzgerald and his wife lived an expatriate life in Europe. During the Great Depression, his popularity lessened, and Zelda's mental illness and alcoholism increasingly burdened both of their lives. After her final breakdown in 1930, Fitzgerald began his own downward spiral into alcoholism, depression, and Hollywood screenplay writing. During this period, he wrote *Tender Is the Night,* based on his experiences with Zelda, another short story collection called *Taps at Reveille,* and a never-completed novel entitled *The Last Tycoon.* Over the course of his life, he produced over 160 short stories. The critic Edmund Wilson said that F. Scott Fitzgerald belonged to the "school of fiction [of] the ironical-pessimistic." In a letter to his daughter, late in life, Fitzgerald himself remarked, "I guess I . . . really want to preach at people in some acceptable form." He admired Ernest Hemingway, Samuel Butler, Frank Norris, H. L. Mencken, and Joseph Conrad. Fitzgerald's simple, descriptive style, paired as it is with romantic irony and the rhetoric and dialect of 1920s America, has lasting appeal.

---

## Babylon Revisited

1935

### I

"And where's Mr. Campbell?" Charlie asked.

"Gone to Switzerland. Mr. Campbell's a pretty sick man, Mr. Wales."

"I'm sorry to hear that. And George Hardt?" Charlie inquired.

"Back in America, gone to work."

"And where is the Snow Bird?"

"He was in here last week. Anyway, his friend, Mr. Schaeffer, is in Paris."

Two familiar names from the long list of a year and a half ago. Charlie scribbled an address in his notebook and tore out the page.

"If you see Mr. Schaeffer, give him this," he said. "It's my brother-in-law's address. I haven't settled on a hotel yet."

He was not really disappointed to find Paris was so empty. But the stillness in the Ritz bar was strange and portentous. It was not an American bar any more—he felt polite in it, and not as if he owned it. It had gone back into France. He felt the stillness from the moment he got out of the taxi and saw the doorman, usually in a frenzy of activity at this hour, gossiping with a *chasseur*[1] by the servants' entrance.

Passing through the corridor, he heard only a single, bored voice in the once-clamorous women's room. When he turned into the bar he traveled the twenty feet of green carpet with his eyes fixed straight ahead by old habit; and then, with his foot firmly on the rail, he turned and surveyed the room, encountering only a single pair of eyes that fluttered up from a newspaper in the corner. Charlie asked for the head barman, Paul, who in the latter days of the bull market[2] had come to work in his own

---

1 *chasseur:* French. Hotel porter.
2 **bull market:** The stock market before the crash of 1929.

custom-built car—disembarking, however, with due nicety at the nearest corner. But Paul was at his country house today and Alix giving him information.

"No, no more," Charlie said, "I'm going slow these days."

Alix congratulated him: "You were going pretty strong a couple of years ago."

"I'll stick to it all right," Charlie assured him. "I've stuck to it for over a year and a half now."

"How do you find conditions in America?"

"I haven't been to America for months. I'm in business in Prague, representing a couple of concerns there. They don't know about me down there."

Alix smiled.

"Remember the night of George Hardt's bachelor dinner here?" said Charlie. "By the way, what's become of Claude Fessenden?"

Alix lowered his voice confidentially: "He's in Paris, but he doesn't come here any more. Paul doesn't allow it. He ran up a bill of thirty thousand francs, charging all his drinks and his lunches, and usually his dinner, for more than a year. And when Paul finally told him he had to pay, he gave him a bad check."

Alix shook his head sadly.

"I don't understand it, such a dandy fellow. Now he's all bloated up—" He made a plump apple of his hands.

Charlie watched a group of strident queens installing themselves in a corner.

"Nothing affects them," he thought. "Stocks rise and fall, people loaf or work, but they go on forever." The place oppressed him. He called for the dice and shook with Alix for the drink.

"Here for long, Mr. Wales?"

"I'm here for four or five days to see my little girl."

"Oh-h! You have a little girl?"

Outside, the fire-red, gas-blue, ghost-green signs shone smokily through the tranquil rain. It was late afternoon and the streets were in movement; the bistros gleamed. At the corner of the Boulevard des Capucines he took a taxi. The Place de la Concorde moved by in pink majesty; they crossed the logical Seine, and Charlie felt the sudden provincial quality of the Left Bank.[3]

Charlie directed his taxi to the Avenue de l'Opéra, which was out of his way. But he wanted to see the blue hour spread over the magnificent façade, and imagine that the cab horns, playing endlessly the first few bars of *Le Plus que Lent*,[4] were the trumpets of the Second Empire.[5] They were closing the iron grill in front of Brentano's Bookstore, and people were already at dinner behind the trim little bourgeois hedge of Duval's. He had never eaten at a really cheap restaurant in Paris. Five-course dinner, four francs fifty, eighteen cents, wine included. For some odd reason he wished that he had.

---

3 Fitzgerald deleted this paragraph in a marked copy of *Taps at Reveille* because it was "Used in *Tender*." The excision solves the problem of Charlie's puzzling Right Bank–Left Bank–Right Bank–Left Bank itinerary.

4 *La Plus que Lent*: Piano music by Claude Debussy.

5 **Second Empire**: The reign of Napoleon III (1851–1870), a time of great luxury and wealth.

As they rolled on to the Left Bank, and he felt its sudden provincialism, he thought, "I spoiled this city for myself. I didn't realize it, but the days came along one after another, and then two years were gone, and everything was gone, and I was gone."

He was thirty-five, and good to look at. The Irish mobility of his face was sobered by a deep wrinkle between his eyes. As he rang his brother-in-law's bell in the Rue Palatine, the wrinkle deepened till it pulled down his brows; he felt a cramping sensation in his belly. From behind the maid who opened the door darted a lovely little girl of nine who shrieked "Daddy!" and flew up, struggling like a fish, into his arms. She pulled his head around by one ear and set her cheek against his.

"My old pie," he said.

"Oh, daddy, daddy, daddy, daddy, dads, dads, dads!"

She drew him into the salon, where the family waited, a boy and a girl his daughter's age, his sister-in-law and her husband. He greeted Marion with his voice pitched carefully to avoid either feigned enthusiasm or dislike, but her response was more frankly tepid, though she minimized her expression of unalterable distrust by directing her regard toward his child. The two men clasped hands in a friendly way and Lincoln Peters rested his for a moment on Charlie's shoulder.

The room was warm and comfortably American. The three children moved intimately about, playing through the yellow oblongs that led to other rooms; the cheer of six o'clock spoke in the eager smacks of the fire and the sounds of French activity in the kitchen. But Charlie did not relax; his heart sat up rigidly in his body and he drew confidence from his daughter, who from time to time came close to him, holding in his arms the doll he had brought.

"Really extremely well," he declared in answer to Lincoln's question. "There's a lot of business there that isn't moving at all, but we're doing even better than ever. In fact, damn well. I'm bringing my sister over from America next month to keep house for me. My income last year was bigger than it was when I had money. You see, the Czechs——"

His boasting was for a specific purpose; but after a moment, seeing a faint restiveness in Lincoln's eye, he changed the subject:

"Those are fine children of yours, well brought up, good manners."

"We think Honoria's a great little girl too."

Marion Peters came back from the kitchen. She was a tall woman with worried eyes, who had once possessed a fresh American loveliness. Charlie had never been sensitive to it and was always surprised when people spoke of how pretty she had been. From the first there had been an instinctive antipathy between them.

"Well, how do you find Honoria?" she asked.

"Wonderful. I was astonished how much she's grown in ten months. All the children are looking well."

"We haven't had a doctor for a year. How do you like being back in Paris?"

"It seems very funny to see so few Americans around."

"I'm delighted," Marion said vehemently. "Now at least you can go into a store without their assuming you're a millionaire. We've suffered like everybody, but on the whole it's a good deal pleasanter."

"But it was nice while it lasted," Charlie said. "We were a sort of royalty, almost infallible, with a sort of magic around us. In the bar this afternoon"—he stumbled, seeing his mistake—"there wasn't a man I knew."

She looked at him keenly. "I should think you'd have had enough of bars."

"I only stayed a minute. I take one drink every afternoon, and no more."

"Don't you want a cocktail before dinner?" Lincoln asked.

"I take only one drink every afternoon, and I've had that."

"I hope you keep to it," said Marion.

Her dislike was evident in the coldness with which she spoke, but Charlie only smiled; he had larger plans. Her very aggressiveness gave him an advantage, and he knew enough to wait. He wanted them to initiate the discussion of what they knew had brought him to Paris.

At dinner he couldn't decide whether Honoria was most like him or her mother. Fortunate if she didn't combine the traits of both that had brought them to disaster. A great wave of protectiveness went over him. He thought he knew what to do for her. He believed in character; he wanted to jump back a whole generation and trust in character again as the eternally valuable element. Everything else wore out.

He left soon after dinner, but not to go home. He was curious to see Paris by night with clearer and more judicious eyes than those of other days. He bought a *strapontin*[6] for the Casino and watched Josephine Baker[7] go through her chocolate arabesques.

After an hour he left and strolled toward Montmartre, up the Rue Pigalle into the Place Blanche. The rain had stopped and there were a few people in evening clothes disembarking from taxis in front of cabarets, and *cocottes*[8] prowling singly or in pairs, and many Negroes. He passed a lighted door from which issued music, and stopped with the sense of familiarity; it was Bricktop's, where he had parted with so many hours and so much money. A few doors farther on he found another ancient rendezvous and incautiously put his head inside. Immediately an eager orchestra burst into sound, a pair of professional dancers leaped to their feet and a maitre d'hôtel swooped toward him, crying, "Crowd just arriving, sir!" But he withdrew quickly.

"You have to be damn drunk," he thought.

Zelli's was closed, the bleak and sinister cheap hotels surrounding it were dark; up in the Rue Blanche there was more light and a local, colloquial French crowd. The Poet's Cave had disappeared, but the two great mouths of the Café of Heaven and the Café of Hell still yawned—even devoured, as he watched, the meager contents of a tourist bus—a German, a Japanese, and an American couple who glanced at him with frightened eyes.

So much for the effort and ingenuity of Montmartre. All the catering to vice and waste was on an utterly childish scale, and he suddenly realized the meaning of the word "dissipate"—to dissipate into thin air; to make nothing out of something. In the

---

6 *strapontin:* French. A folding chair placed in a theater aisle.
7 **Josephine Baker:** African American entertainer who performed in Paris in the 1920s and 1930s.
8 *cocottes:* French. Prostitutes.

little hours of the night every move from place to place was an enormous human jump, an increase of paying for the privilege of slower and slower motion.

He remembered thousand-franc notes given to an orchestra for playing a single number, hundred-franc notes tossed to a doorman for calling a cab.

But it hadn't been given for nothing.

It had been given, even the most wildly squandered sum, as an offering to destiny that he might not remember the things most worth remembering, the things that now he would always remember—his child taken from his control, his wife escaped to a grave in Vermont.

In the glare of a *brasserie*[9] a woman spoke to him. He bought her some eggs and coffee, and then, eluding her encouraging stare, gave her a twenty-franc note and took a taxi to his hotel.

## II

He woke upon a fine fall day—football weather. The depression of yesterday was gone and he liked the people on the streets. At noon he sat opposite Honoria at Le Grand Vatel, the only restaurant he could think of not reminiscent of champagne dinners and long luncheons that began at two and ended in a blurred and vague twilight.

"Now, how about vegetables? Oughtn't you to have some vegetables?"

"Well, yes."

"Here's *épinards* and *chou-fleur* and carrots and *haricots*."[10]

"I'd like *chou-fleur*."

"Wouldn't you like to have two vegetables?"

"I usually only have one at lunch."

The waiter was pretending to be inordinately fond of children. *"Qu'elle est mignonne la petite! Elle parle exactement comme une française."*[11]

"How about dessert? Shall we wait and see?"

The waiter disappeared. Honoria looked at her father expectantly.

"What are we going to do?"

"First, we're going to that toy store in the Rue Saint-Honoré and buy you anything you like. And then we're going to the vaudeville at the Empire."

She hesitated. "I like it about the vaudeville, but not the toy store."

"Why not?"

"Well, you brought me this doll." She had it with her. "And I've got lots of things. And we're not rich any more, are we?"

"We never were. But today you are to have anything you want."

"All right," she agreed resignedly.

---

9  *brasserie:* French. Restaurant-bar.

10  *épinards . . . chou-fleur . . . haricots:* French. Spinach, cauliflower, beans.

11  *"Qu'elle est mignonne . . . comme une française":* French: What a darling little one. She speaks exactly like a French girl.

When there had been her mother and a French nurse he had been inclined to be strict; now he extended himself, reached out for a new tolerance; he must be both parents to her and not shut any of her out of communication.

"I want to get to know you," he said gravely. "First let me introduce myself. My name is Charles J. Wales, of Prague."

"Oh, daddy!" her voice cracked with laughter.

"And who are you, please?" he persisted, and she accepted a role immediately: "Honoria Wales, Rue Palatine, Paris."

"Married or single?"

"No, not married. Single."

He indicated the doll. "But I see you have a child, madame."

Unwilling to disinherit it, she took it to her heart and thought quickly: "Yes, I've been married, but I'm not married now. My husband is dead."

He went on quickly, "And the child's name?"

"Simone. That's after my best friend at school."

"I'm very pleased that you're doing so well at school."

"I'm third this month," she boasted. "Elsie"—that was her cousin—"is only about eighteenth, and Richard is about at the bottom."

"You like Richard and Elsie, don't you?"

"Oh, yes. I like Richard quite well and I like her all right."

Cautiously and casually he asked: "And Aunt Marion and Uncle Lincoln—which do you like best?"

"Oh, Uncle Lincoln, I guess."

He was increasingly aware of her presence. As they came in, a murmur of ". . . adorable" followed them, and now the people at the next table bent all their silences upon her, staring as if she were something no more conscious than a flower.

"Why don't I live with you?" she asked suddenly. "Because mamma's dead?"

"You must stay here and learn more French. It would have been hard for daddy to take care of you so well."

"I don't really need much taking care of any more. I do everything for myself."

Going out of the restaurant, a man and a woman unexpectedly hailed him. "Well, the old Wales!"

"Hello there, Lorraine. . . . Dunc."

Sudden ghosts out of the past: Duncan Schaeffer, a friend from college. Lorraine Quarrles, a lovely, pale blonde of thirty; one of a crowd who had helped him make months into days in the lavish times of three years ago.

"My husband couldn't come this year," she said, in answer to his question. "We're poor as hell. So he gave me two hundred a month and told me I could do my worst on that. . . . This your little girl?"

"What about coming back and sitting down?" Duncan asked.

"Can't do it." He was glad for an excuse. As always, he felt Lorraine's passionate, provocative attraction, but his own rhythm was different now.

"Well, how about dinner?" she asked.

"I'm not free. Give me your address and let me call you."

"Charlie, I believe you're sober," she said judicially. "I honestly believe he's sober, Dunc. Pinch him and see if he's sober."

Charlie indicated Honoria with his head. They both laughed.

"What's your address?" said Duncan skeptically.

He hesitated, unwilling to give the name of his hotel.

"I'm not settled yet. I'd better call you. We're going to see the vaudeville at the Empire."

"There! That's what I want to do," Lorraine said. "I want to see some clowns and acrobats and jugglers. That's just what we'll do, Dunc."

"We've got to do an errand first," said Charlie. "Perhaps we'll see you there."

"All right, you snob. . . . Good-by, beautiful little girl."

"Good-by."

Honoria bobbed politely.

Somehow, an unwelcome encounter. They liked him because he was functioning, because he was serious; they wanted to see him, because he was stronger than they were now, because they wanted to draw a certain sustenance from his strength.

At the Empire, Honoria proudly refused to sit upon her father's folded coat. She was already an individual with a code of her own, and Charlie was more and more absorbed by the desire of putting a little of himself into her before she crystallized utterly. It was hopeless to try to know her in so short a time.

Between the acts they came upon Duncan and Lorraine in the lobby where the band was playing.

"Have a drink?"

"All right, but not up at the bar. We'll take a table."

"The perfect father."

Listening abstractedly to Lorraine, Charlie watched Honoria's eyes leave their table, and he followed them wistfully about the room, wondering what they saw. He met her glance and she smiled.

"I liked that lemonade," she said.

What had she said? What had he expected? Going home in a taxi afterward, he pulled her over until her head rested against his chest.

"Darling, do you ever think about your mother?"

"Yes, sometimes," she answered vaguely.

"I don't want you to forget her. Have you got a picture of her?"

"Yes, I think so. Anyhow, Aunt Marion has. Why don't you want me to forget her?"

"She loved you very much."

"I loved her too."

They were silent for a moment.

"Daddy, I want to come and live with you," she said suddenly.

His heart leaped; he had wanted it to come like this.

"Aren't you perfectly happy?"

"Yes, but I love you better than anybody. And you love me better than anybody, don't you, now that mummy's dead?"

"Of course I do. But you won't always like me best, honey. You'll grow up and meet somebody your own age and go marry him and forget you ever had a daddy."

"Yes, that's true," she agreed tranquilly.

He didn't go in. He was coming back at nine o'clock and he wanted to keep himself fresh and new for the thing he must say then.

"When you're safe inside, just show yourself in that window."

"All right. Good-by, dads, dads, dads, dads."

He waited in the dark street until she appeared, all warm and glowing, in the window above and kissed her fingers out into the night.

### III

They were waiting. Marion sat behind the coffee service in a dignified black dinner dress that just faintly suggested mourning. Lincoln was walking up and down with the animation of one who had already been talking. They were as anxious as he was to get into the question. He opened it almost immediately:

"I suppose you know what I want to see you about—why I really came to Paris."

Marion played with the black stars on her necklace and frowned.

"I'm awfully anxious to have a home," he continued. "And I'm awfully anxious to have Honoria in it. I appreciate your taking in Honoria for her mother's sake, but things have changed now"—he hesitated and then continued more forcibly—"changed radically with me, and I want to ask you to reconsider the matter. It would be silly for me to deny that about three years ago I was acting badly—"

Marion looked up at him with hard eyes.

"—but all that's over. As I told you, I haven't had more than a drink a day for over a year, and I take that drink deliberately, so that the idea of alcohol won't get too big in my imagination. You see the idea?"

"No," said Marion succinctly.

"It's a sort of stunt I set myself. It keeps the matter in proportion."

"I get you," said Lincoln. "You don't want to admit it's got any attraction for you."

"Something like that. Sometimes I forget and don't take it. But I try to take it. Anyhow, I couldn't afford to drink in my position. The people I represent are more than satisfied with what I've done, and I'm bringing my sister over from Burlington to keep house for me, and I want awfully to have Honoria too. You know that even when her mother and I weren't getting along well we never let anything that happened touch Honoria. I know she's fond of me and I know I'm able to take care of her and—well, there you are. How do you feel about it?"

He knew that now he would have to take a beating. It would last an hour or two hours, and it would be difficult, but if he modulated his inevitable resentment to the chastened attitude of the reformed sinner, he might win his point in the end.

Keep your temper, he told himself. You don't want to be justified. You want Honoria.

Lincoln spoke first: "We've been talking it over ever since we got your letter last month. We're happy to have Honoria here. She's a dear little thing, and we're glad to be able to help her, but of course that isn't the question—"

Marion interrupted suddenly. "How long are you going to stay sober, Charlie?" she asked.

"Permanently, I hope."

"How can anybody count on that?"

"You know I never did drink heavily until I gave up business and came over here with nothing to do. Then Helen and I began to run around with—"

"Please leave Helen out of it. I can't bear to hear you talk about her like that."

He stared at her grimly; he had never been certain how fond of each other the sisters were in life.

"My drinking only lasted about a year and a half—from the time we came over until I—collapsed."

"It was time enough."

"It was time enough," he agreed.

"My duty is entirely to Helen," she said. "I try to think what she would have wanted me to do. Frankly, from the night you did that terrible thing you haven't really existed for me. I can't help that. She was my sister."

"Yes."

"When she was dying she asked me to look out for Honoria. If you hadn't been in a sanitarium then, it might have helped matters."

He had no answer.

"I'll never in my life be able to forget the morning when Helen knocked at my door, soaked to the skin and shivering, and said you'd locked her out."

Charlie gripped the sides of the chair. This was more difficult than he expected; he wanted to launch out into a long expostulation and explanation, but he only said: "The night I locked her out—" and she interrupted, "I don't feel up to going over that again."

After a moment's silence Lincoln said: "We're getting off the subject. You want Marion to set aside her legal guardianship and give you Honoria. I think the main point for her is whether she has confidence in you or not."

"I don't blame Marion," Charlie said slowly, "but I think she can have entire confidence in me. I had a good record up to three years ago. Of course, it's within human possibilities I might go wrong any time. But if we wait much longer I'll lose Honoria's childhood and my chance for a home." He shook his head. "I'll simply lose her, don't you see?"

"Yes, I see," said Lincoln.

"Why didn't you think of all this before?" Marion asked.

"I suppose I did, from time to time, but Helen and I were getting along badly. When I consented to the guardianship, I was flat on my back in a sanitarium and the market had cleaned me out. I knew I'd acted badly, and I thought if it would bring any peace to Helen, I'd agree to anything. But now it's different. I'm functioning, I'm behaving damn well, so far as——"

"Please don't swear at me," Marion said.

He looked at her, startled. With each remark the force of her dislike became more and more apparent. She had built up all her fear of life into one wall and faced it toward him. This trivial reproof was possibly the result of some trouble with the cook several hours before. Charlie became increasingly alarmed at leaving Honoria in this atmosphere of hostility against himself; sooner or later it would come out, in a word here, a shake of the head there, and some of that distrust would be irrevocably implanted in Honoria. But he pulled his temper down out of his face and shut it up inside him; he had won a point, for Lincoln realized the absurdity of Marion's remark and asked her lightly since when she had objected to the word "damn."

"Another thing," Charlie said: "I'm able to give her certain advantages now. I'm going to take a French governess to Prague with me. I've got a lease on a new apartment——"

He stopped, realizing that he was blundering. They couldn't be expected to accept with equanimity the fact that his income was again twice as large as their own.

"I suppose you can give her more luxuries than we can," said Marion. "When you were throwing away money we were living along watching every ten francs. . . . I suppose you'll start doing it again."

"Oh, no," he said. "I've learned. I worked hard for ten years, you know—until I got lucky in the market, like so many people. Terribly lucky. It won't happen again."

There was a long silence. All of them felt their nerves straining, and for the first time in a year Charlie wanted a drink. He was sure now that Lincoln Peters wanted him to have his child.

Marion shuddered suddenly; part of her saw that Charlie's feet were planted on the earth now, and her own maternal feeling recognized the naturalness of his desire; but she had lived for a long time with a prejudice—a prejudice founded on a curious disbelief in her sister's happiness, which, in the shock of one terrible night, had turned to hatred for him. It had all happened at a point in her life where the discouragement of ill health and adverse circumstances made it necessary for her to believe in tangible villainy and a tangible villain.

"I can't help what I think!" she cried out suddenly. "How much you were responsible for Helen's death, I don't know. It's something you'll have to square with your own conscience."

An electric current of agony surged through him; for a moment he was almost on his feet, an unuttered sound echoing in his throat. He hung on to himself for a moment, another moment.

"Hold on there," said Lincoln uncomfortably. "I never thought you were responsible for that."

"Helen died of heart trouble," Charlie said dully.

"Yes, heart trouble." Marion spoke as if the phrase had another meaning for her.

Then, in the flatness that followed her outburst, she saw him plainly and she knew he had somehow arrived at control over the situation. Glancing at her husband, she found no help from him, and as abruptly as if it were a matter of no importance, she threw up the sponge.

"Do what you like!" she cried, springing up from her chair. "She's your child. I'm

not the person to stand in your way. I think if it were my child I'd rather see her—"
She managed to check herself. "You two decide it. I can't stand this. I'm sick. I'm going to bed."

She hurried from the room; after a moment Lincoln said:

"This has been a hard day for her. You know how strongly she feels—" His voice was almost apologetic: "When a woman gets an idea in her head."

"Of course."

"It's going to be all right. I think she sees now that you—can provide for the child, and so we can't very well stand in your way or Honoria's way."

"Thank you, Lincoln."

"I'd better go along and see how she is."

"I'm going."

He was still trembling when he reached the street, but a walk down the Rue Bonaparte to the *quais*[12] set him up, and as he crossed the Seine, fresh and new by the *quai* lamps, he felt exultant. But back in his room he couldn't sleep. The image of Helen haunted him. Helen whom he had loved so until they had senselessly begun to abuse each other's love, tear it into shreds. On that terrible February night that Marion remembered so vividly, a slow quarrel had gone on for hours. There was a scene at the Florida, and then he attempted to take her home, and then she kissed young Webb at a table; after that there was what she had hysterically said. When he arrived home alone he turned the key in the lock in wild anger. How could he know she would arrive an hour later alone, that there would be a snow storm in which she wandered about in slippers, too confused to find a taxi? Then the aftermath, her escaping pneumonia by a miracle, and all the attendant horror. They were "reconciled," but that was the beginning of the end, and Marion, who had seen with her own eyes and who imagined it to be one of many scenes from her sister's martyrdom, never forgot.

Going over it again brought Helen nearer, and in the white, soft light that steals upon half sleep near morning he found himself talking to her again. She said that he was perfectly right about Honoria and that she wanted Honoria to be with him. She said she was glad he was being good and doing better. She said a lot of other things— very friendly things—but she was in a swing in a white dress, and swinging faster and faster all the time, so that at the end he could not hear clearly all that she said.

## IV

He woke up feeling happy. The door of the world was open again. He made plans, vistas, futures for Honoria and himself, but suddenly he grew sad, remembering all the plans he and Helen had made. She had not planned to die. The present was the thing—work to do and someone to love. But not to love too much, for he knew the injury that a father can do to a daughter or a mother to a son by attaching them too

12 *quais:* French. Paved riverbanks.

closely: afterward, out in the world, the child would seek in the marriage partner the same blind tenderness and, failing probably to find it, turn against love and life.

It was another bright, crisp day. He called Lincoln Peters at the bank where he worked and asked if he could count on taking Honoria when he left for Prague. Lincoln agreed that there was no reason for delay. One thing—the legal guardianship. Marion wanted to retain that awhile longer. She was upset by the whole matter, and it would oil things if she felt that the situation was still in her control for another year. Charlie agreed, wanting only the tangible, visible child.

Then the question of a governess. Charlie sat in a gloomy agency and talked to a cross Béarnaise and to a buxom Breton peasant, neither of whom he could have endured. There were others whom he would see tomorrow.

He lunched with Lincoln Peters at Griffons, trying to keep down his exultation.

"There's nothing quite like your own child," Lincoln said. "But you understand how Marion feels too."

"She's forgotten how hard I worked for seven years there," Charlie said. "She just remembers one night."

"There's another thing," Lincoln hesitated. "While you and Helen were tearing around Europe throwing money away, we were just getting along. I didn't touch any of the prosperity because I never got ahead enough to carry anything but my insurance. I think Marion felt there was some kind of injustice in it—you not even working toward the end, and getting richer and richer."

"It went just as quick as it came," said Charlie.

"Yes, a lot of it stayed in the hands of *chasseurs* and saxaphone players and maitres d'hôtel—well, the big party's over now. I just said that to explain Marion's feeling about those crazy years. If you drop in about six o'clock tonight before Marion's too tired, we'll settle the details on the spot."

Back at his hotel, Charlie found a *pneumatique*[13] that had been redirected from the Ritz bar, where Charlie had left his address for the purpose of a certain man.

> Dear Charlie:
>
> You were so strange when we saw you the other day that I wondered if I did something to offend you. If so, I'm not conscious of it. In fact, I have thought about you too much for the last year, and it's always been in the back of my mind that I might see you if I came over here. We *did* have such good times that crazy spring, like the night you and I stole the butcher's tricycle, and the time we tried to call on the president and you had the old derby rim and the wire cane. Everybody seems so old lately, but I don't feel old a bit. Couldn't we get together some time today for old time's sake? I've got a vile hangover for the moment, but will be feeling better this afternoon and will look for you about five in the sweatshop at the Ritz.
>
> Always devotedly,
> Lorraine

---

13 **pneumatique:** French. Message delivered through a system of pneumatic tubes, since the French phone system was unreliable in the 1920s and 1930s.

His first feeling was one of awe that he had actually, in his mature years, stolen a tricycle and pedaled Lorraine all over the Étoile between the small hours and dawn. In retrospect it was a nightmare. Locking out Helen didn't fit in with any other act of his life, but the tricycle incident did—it was one of many. How many weeks or months of dissipation to arrive at that condition of utter irresponsibility?

He tried to picture how Lorraine had appeared to him then—very attractive; Helen was unhappy about it, though she said nothing. Yesterday, in the restaurant, Lorraine had seemed trite, blurred, worn away. He emphatically did not want to see her, and he was glad Alix had not given away his hotel address. It was a relief to think, instead, of Honoria, to think of Sundays spent with her and of saying good morning to her and knowing she was there in his house at night, drawing her breath in the darkness.

At five he took a taxi and bought presents for all the Peterses—a piquant cloth doll, a box of Roman soldiers, flowers for Marion, big linen handkerchiefs for Lincoln.

He saw, when he arrived in the apartment, that Marion had accepted the inevitable. She greeted him now as though he were a recalcitrant member of the family, rather than a menacing outsider. Honoria had been told she was going; Charlie was glad to see that her tact made her conceal her excessive happiness. Only on his lap did she whisper her delight and the question "When?" before she slipped away with the other children.

He and Marion were alone for a minute in the room, and on an impulse he spoke out boldly:

"Family quarrels are bitter things. They don't go according to any rules. They're not like aches or wounds; they're more like splits in the skin that won't heal because there's not enough material. I wish you and I could be on better terms."

"Some things are hard to forget," she answered. "It's a question of confidence." There was no answer to this and presently she asked, "When do you propose to take her?"

"As soon as I can get a governess. I hoped the day after tomorrow."

"That's impossible. I've got to get her things in shape. Not before Saturday."

He yielded. Coming back into the room, Lincoln offered him a drink.

"I'll take my daily whisky," he said.

It was warm here, it was a home, people together by a fire. The children felt very safe and important; the mother and father were serious, watchful. They had things to do for the children more important than his visit here. A spoonful of medicine was, after all, more important than the strained relations between Marion and himself. They were not dull people, but they were very much in the grip of life and circumstances. He wondered if he couldn't do something to get Lincoln out of his rut at the bank.

A long peal at the doorbell; the *bonne à tout faire*[14] passed through and went down the corridor. The door opened upon another long ring, and then voices, and the three in the salon looked up expectantly; Lincoln moved to bring the corridor

---

14 *bonne à tout faire:* French. Maid of all work.

within his range of vision, and Marion rose. Then the maid came back along the corridor, closely followed by the voices, which developed under the light into Duncan Schaeffer and Lorraine Quarrles.

They were gay, they were hilarious, they were roaring with laughter. For a moment Charlie was astounded; unable to understand how they ferreted out the Peterses' address.

"Ah-h-h!" Duncan wagged his finger roguishly at Charlie. "Ah-h-h!"

They both slid down another cascade of laughter. Anxious and at a loss, Charlie shook hands with them quickly and presented them to Lincoln and Marion. Marion nodded, scarcely speaking. She had drawn back a step toward the fire; her little girl stood beside her, and Marion put an arm about her shoulder.

With growing annoyance at the intrusion, Charlie waited for them to explain themselves. After some concentration Duncan said:

"We came to invite you out to dinner. Lorraine and I insist that all this shishi, cagy business 'bout your address got to stop."

Charlie came closer to them, as if to force them backward down the corridor.

"Sorry, but I can't. Tell me where you'll be and I'll phone you in half an hour."

This made no impression. Lorraine sat down suddenly on the side of a chair, and focusing her eyes on Richard, cried, "Oh, what a nice little boy! Come here, little boy." Richard glanced at his mother, but did not move. With a perceptible shrug of her shoulder, Lorraine turned back to Charlie:

"Come and dine. Sure your cousins won' mine. See you so sel'om. Or solemn."

"I can't," said Charlie sharply. "You two have dinner and I'll phone you."

Her voice became suddenly unpleasant. "All right, we'll go. But I remember once when you hammered on my door at four A.M. I was enough of a good sport to give you a drink. Come on, Dunc."

Still in slow motion, with blurred, angry faces, with uncertain feet, they retired along the corridor.

"Good night," Charlie said.

"Good night!" responded Lorraine emphatically.

When he went back into the salon Marion had not moved, only now her son was standing in the circle of her other arm. Lincoln was still swinging Honoria back and forth like a pendulum from side to side.

"What an outrage!" Charlie broke out. "What an absolute outrage!"

Neither of them answered. Charlie dropped into an armchair, picked up his drink, set it down again and said:

"People I haven't seen for two years having the colossal nerve——"

He broke off. Marion had made the sound "Oh!" in one swift, furious breath, turned her body from him with a jerk and left the room.

Lincoln set down Honoria carefully.

"You children go in and start your soup," he said, and when they obeyed, he said to Charlie:

"Marion's not well and she can't stand shocks. That kind of people make her really physically sick."

"I didn't tell them to come here. They wormed your name out of somebody. They deliberately——"

"Well, it's too bad. It doesn't help matters. Excuse me a minute."

Left alone, Charlie sat tense in his chair. In the next room he could hear the children eating, talking in monosyllables, already oblivious to the scene between their elders. He heard a murmur of conversation from a farther room and then the ticking bell of a telephone receiver picked up, and in a panic he moved to the other side of the room and out of earshot.

In a minute Lincoln came back. "Look here, Charlie. I think we'd better call off dinner for tonight. Marion's in bad shape."

"Is she angry with me?"

"Sort of," he said, almost roughly. "She's not strong and——"

"You mean she's changed her mind about Honoria?"

"She's pretty bitter right now. I don't know. You phone me at the bank tomorrow."

"I wish you'd explain to her I never dreamed these people would come here. I'm just as sore as you are."

"I couldn't explain anything to her now."

Charlie got up. He took his coat and hat and started down the corridor. Then he opened the door of the dining room and said in a strange voice, "Good night, children."

Honoria rose and ran around the table to hug him.

"Good night, sweetheart," he said vaguely, and then trying to make his voice more tender, trying to conciliate something, "Good night, dear children."

## V

Charlie went directly to the Ritz bar with the furious idea of finding Lorraine and Duncan, but they were not there, and he realized that in any case there was nothing he could do. He had not touched his drink at the Peterses, and now he ordered a whisky-and-soda. Paul came over to say hello.

"It's a great change," he said sadly. "We do about half the business we did. So many fellows I hear about back in the States lost everything, maybe not in the first crash, but then in the second. Your friend George Hardt lost every cent, I hear. Are you back in the States?"

"No, I'm in business in Prague."

"I heard that you lost a lot in the crash."

"I did," and he added grimly, "but I lost everything I wanted in the boom."

"Selling short."

"Something like that."

Again the memory of those days swept over him like a nightmare—the people they had met traveling; then people who couldn't add a row of figures or speak a coherent sentence. The little man Helen had consented to dance with at the ship's party, who had insulted her ten feet from the table; the women and girls carried screaming with drink or drugs out of public places——

—The men who locked their wives out in the snow, because the snow of twenty-nine wasn't real snow. If you didn't want it to be snow, you just paid some money.

He went to the phone and called the Peterses' apartment; Lincoln answered.

"I called up because this thing is on my mind. Has Marion said anything definite?"

"Marion's sick," Lincoln answered shortly. "I know this thing isn't altogether your fault, but I can't have her go to pieces about it. I'm afraid we'll have to let it slide for six months; I can't take the chance of working her up to this state again."

"I see."

"I'm sorry, Charlie."

He went back to his table. His whisky glass was empty, but he shook his head when Alix looked at it questioningly. There wasn't much he could do now except send Honoria some things; he would send her a lot of things tomorrow. He thought rather angrily that this was just money—he had given so many people money. . . .

"No, no more," he said to another waiter. "What do I owe you?"

He would come back some day; they couldn't make him pay forever. But he wanted his child, and nothing was much good now, beside that fact. He wasn't young any more, with a lot of nice thoughts and dreams to have by himself. He was absolutely sure Helen wouldn't have wanted him to be so alone.

# Ernest Hemingway

## (1899–1961)

Known for his sparse dialogue and straightforward prose, Ernest Hemingway pitted tough and almost primitive individuals—soldiers, hunters, and bullfighters—against modern society. He was born in Oak Park, Illinois, in 1899 and began his career as a writer for a Kansas City newspaper at the age of seventeen. During World War I, he served in an ambulance unit in the Italian army. He was wounded while serving at the front and decorated by the Italian government. Hemingway returned to the United States and continued his work as a reporter, but in the 1920s he left the country and became a member of a group of expatriate Americans in Paris. *The Sun Also Rises* (1926) describes this group. Hemingway followed this novel with *A Farewell to Arms* (1929), *To Have and Have Not* (1937), *For Whom the Bell Tolls* (1940), and *The Old Man and the Sea* (1952), the last of which won him the Pulitzer Prize. In 1954, Hemingway survived two plane crashes while on safari in Africa. The second crash seriously injured him, though the extent of the damage was not immediately apparent. In the same year, Hemingway won the Nobel Prize for literature. Over a span of two years, he followed the bullfights of two of Spain's best matadors, publishing the resulting work, "The Dangerous Summer" (1960), in *Life* magazine. In the fall of 1960, Hemingway was admitted to the Mayo Clinic to treat severe depression. However, the treatment he received was electroshock therapy, which destroyed his memory. On July 2, 1961, Hemingway committed suicide. His memoir, *A Moveable Feast* (1964), was published posthumously.

## Hills Like White Elephants                    1927

The hills across the valley of the Ebro[1] were long and white. On this side there was no shade and no trees and the station was between two lines of rails in the sun. Close against the side of the station there was the warm shadow of the building and a curtain, made of strings of bamboo beads, hung across the open door into the bar, to keep out flies. The American and the girl with him sat at a table in the shade, outside the building. It was very hot and the express from Barcelona would come in forty minutes. It stopped at this junction for two minutes and went on to Madrid.

"What should we drink?" the girl asked. She had taken off her hat and put it on the table.

"It's pretty hot," the man said.

"Let's drink beer."

"Dos cervezas," the man said into the curtain.

"Big ones?" a woman asked from the doorway.

"Yes. Two big ones."

The woman brought two glasses of beer and two felt pads. She put the felt pads and the beer glasses on the table and looked at the man and the girl. The girl was looking off at the line of hills. They were white in the sun and the country was brown and dry.

"They look like white elephants," she said.

"I've never seen one," the man drank his beer.

"No, you wouldn't have."

"I might have," the man said. "Just because you say I wouldn't have doesn't prove anything."

The girl looked at the bead curtain. "They've painted something on it," she said. "What does it say?"

"Anis del Toro. It's a drink."

"Could we try it?"

The man called "Listen" through the curtain. The woman came out from the bar.

"Four reales."[2]

"We want two Anis del Toro."

"With water?"

"Do you want it with water?"

"I don't know," the girl said. "Is it good with water?"

"It's all right."

---

1 **Ebro:** River in northern Spain.
2 **reales:** Spanish coins.

"You want them with water?" asked the woman.

"Yes, with water."

"It tastes like licorice," the girl said and put the glass down.

"That's the way with everything."

"Yes," said the girl. "Everything tastes of licorice. Especially all the things you've waited so long for, like absinthe."

"Oh, cut it out."

"You started it," the girl said. "I was being amused. I was having a fine time."

"Well, let's try and have a fine time."

"All right. I was trying. I said the mountains looked like white elephants. Wasn't that bright?"

"That was bright."

"I wanted to try this new drink. That's all we do, isn't it—look at things and try new drinks?"

"I guess so."

The girl looked across at the hills.

"They're lovely hills," she said. "They don't really look like white elephants. I just meant the coloring of their skin through the trees."

"Should we have another drink?"

"All right."

The warm wind blew the bead curtain against the table.

"The beer's nice and cool," the man said.

"It's lovely," the girl said.

"It's really an awfully simple operation, Jig," the man said. "It's not really an operation at all."

The girl looked at the ground the table legs rested on.

"I know you wouldn't mind it, Jig. It's really not anything. It's just to let the air in."

The girl did not say anything.

"I'll go with you and I'll stay with you all the time. They just let the air in and then it's all perfectly natural."

"Then what will we do afterward?"

"We'll be fine afterward. Just like we were before."

"What makes you think so?"

"That's the only thing that bothers us. It's the only thing that's made us unhappy."

The girl looked at the bead curtain, put her hand out and took hold of two of the strings of beads.

"And you think then we'll be all right and be happy."

"I know we will. You don't have to be afraid. I've known lots of people that have done it."

"So have I," said the girl. "And afterward they were all so happy."

"Well," the man said, "if you don't want to you don't have to. I wouldn't have you do it if you didn't want to. But I know it's perfectly simple."

"And you really want to?"

"I think it's the best thing to do. But I don't want you to do it if you don't really want to."

"And if I do it you'll be happy and things will be like they were and you'll love me?"

"I love you now. You know I love you."

"I know. But if I do it, then it will be nice again if I say things are like white elephants, and you'll like it?"

"I'll love it. I love it now but I just can't think about it. You know how I get when I worry."

"If I do it you won't ever worry?"

"I won't worry about that because it's perfectly simple."

"Then I'll do it. Because I don't care about me."

"What do you mean?"

"I don't care about me."

"Well, I care about you."

"Oh, yes. But I don't care about me. And I'll do it and then everything will be fine."

"I don't want you to do it if you feel that way."

The girl stood up and walked to the end of the station. Across, on the other side, were fields of grain and trees along the banks of the Ebro. Far away, beyond the river, were mountains. The shadow of a cloud moved across the field of grain and she saw the river through the trees.

"And we could have all this," she said. "And we could have everything and every day we make it more impossible."

"What did you say?"

"I said we could have everything."

"We can have everything."

"No, we can't."

"We can have the whole world."

"No, we can't."

"We can go everywhere."

"No, we can't. It isn't ours any more."

"It's ours."

"No, it isn't. And once they take it away, you never get it back."

"But they haven't taken it away."

"We'll wait and see."

"Come on back in the shade," he said. "You mustn't feel that way."

"I don't feel any way," the girl said. "I just know things."

"I don't want you to do anything that you don't want to do—"

"Nor that isn't good for me," she said. "I know. Could we have another beer?"

"All right. But you've got to realize—"

"I realize," the girl said. "Can't we maybe stop talking?"

They sat down at the table and the girl looked across at the hills on the dry side of the valley and the man looked at her and at the table.

"You've got to realize," he said, "that I don't want you to do it if you don't want to. I'm perfectly willing to go through with it if it means anything to you."

"Doesn't it mean anything to you? We could get along."

"Of course it does. But I don't want anybody but you. I don't want any one else. And I know it's perfectly simple."

"Yes, you know it's perfectly simple."

"It's all right for you to say that, but I do know it."

"Would you do something for me now?"

"I'd do anything for you."

"Would you please please please please please please please stop talking?"

He did not say anything but looked at the bags against the wall of the station. There were labels on them from all the hotels where they had spent nights.

"But I don't want you to," he said, "I don't care anything about it."

"I'll scream," the girl said.

The woman came out through the curtains with two glasses of beer and put them down on the damp felt pads. "The train comes in five minutes," she said.

"What did she say?" asked the girl.

"That the train is coming in five minutes."

The girl smiled brightly at the woman, to thank her.

"I'd better take the bags over to the other side of the station," the man said. She smiled at him.

"All right. Then come back and we'll finish the beer."

He picked up the two heavy bags and carried them around the station to the other tracks. He looked up the tracks but could not see the train. Coming back, he walked through the barroom, where people waiting for the train were drinking. He drank an Anis at the bar and looked at the people. They were all waiting reasonably for the train. He went out through the bead curtain. She was sitting at the table and smiled at him.

"Do you feel better?" he asked.

"I feel fine," she said. "There's nothing wrong with me. I feel fine."

# Shirley Jackson

## (1919–1965)

Born in San Francisco, California, Shirley Jackson attended the University of Rochester but left after one year because of severe depression. Thereafter, she found it therapeutic to adhere to a daily writing regimen, religiously writing a thousand words a day while recuperating at home. In 1937, she made another attempt at college, this time attending Syracuse University, and earned her bachelor's degree in 1940. She married soon after, and the following year she published her first short story, "My Life with R. H. Macy," about working as a clerk in a department store. She continued to write on a strict schedule, raising four children and publishing three novels in addition to numerous short stories. Her most enduring and controversial work is "The Lottery," which she considered to be in the allegorical tradition of Nathaniel Hawthorne. After its publication in the *New Yorker* in 1948, the magazine received more mail than ever before in response to a work of fiction. Jackson herself received almost three hundred antagonistic letters. About this experience, Jackson wrote, "The general tone [of the letters] . . . was a kind of wide-eyed, shocked innocence. People at first were not so much concerned with what the story meant; what they wanted to know was where these lotteries were being held, and whether they could go there and watch."

## The Lottery                                                    1948

The morning of June 27th was clear and sunny, with the fresh warmth of a full-summer day; the flowers were blossoming profusely and the grass was richly green. The people of the village began to gather in the square, between the post office and the bank, around ten o'clock; in some towns there were so many people that the lottery took two days and had to be started on June 26th, but in this village, where there were only about three hundred people, the whole lottery took less than two hours, so it could begin at ten o'clock in the morning and still be through in time to allow the villagers to get home for noon dinner.

The children assembled first, of course. School was recently over for the summer, and the feeling of liberty sat uneasily on most of them; they tended to gather together quietly for a while before they broke into boisterous play, and their talk was still of the classroom and the teacher, of books and reprimands. Bobby Martin had already stuffed his pockets full of stones, and the other boys soon followed his example, selecting the smoothest and roundest stones; Bobby and Harry Jones and Dickie Delacroix—the villagers pronounced his name "Delacroy"—eventually made a great pile of stones in one corner of the square and guarded it against the raids of the other boys. The girls stood aside, talking among themselves, looking over their shoulders at the boys, and the very small children rolled in the dust or clung to the hands of their older brothers or sisters.

Soon the men began to gather, surveying their own children, speaking of planting and rain, tractors and taxes. They stood together, away from the pile of stones in the corner, and their jokes were quiet and they smiled rather than laughed. The women, wearing faded house dresses and sweaters, came shortly after their menfolk. They greeted one another and exchanged bits of gossip as they went to join their husbands. Soon the women, standing by their husbands, began to call to their children, and the children came reluctantly, having to be called four or five times. Bobby Martin ducked under his mother's grasping hand and ran, laughing, back to the pile of stones. His father spoke up sharply, and Bobby came quickly and took his place between his father and his oldest brother.

The lottery was conducted—as were the square dances, the teenage club, the Halloween program—by Mr. Summers, who had time and energy to devote to civic activities. He was a round-faced, jovial man and he ran the coal business, and people were sorry for him, because he had no children and his wife was a scold. When he arrived in the square, carrying the black wooden box, there was a murmur of conversation among the villagers, and he waved and called, "Little late today, folks." The postmaster, Mr. Graves, followed him, carrying a three-legged stool, and the stool was put in the center of the square and Mr. Summers set the black box down on it. The villagers kept their distance, leaving a space between themselves and the stool, and when Mr. Summers said, "Some of you fellows want to give me a hand?" there was a hesitation before two men, Mr. Martin and his oldest son, Baxter, came forward to hold the box steady on the stool while Mr. Summers stirred up the papers inside it.

The original paraphernalia for the lottery had been lost long ago, and the black box now resting on the stool had been put into use even before Old Man Warner, the oldest man in town, was born. Mr. Summers spoke frequently to the villagers about making a new box, but no one liked to upset even as much tradition as was represented by the black box. There was a story that the present box had been made with some pieces of the box that had preceded it, the one that had been constructed when the first people settled down to make a village here. Every year, after the lottery, Mr. Summers began talking again about a new box, but every year the subject was allowed to fade off without anything's being done. The black box grew shabbier each year; by now it was no longer completely black but splintered badly along one side to show the original wood color, and in some places faded or stained.

Mr. Martin and his oldest son, Baxter, held the black box securely on the stool until Mr. Summers had stirred the papers thoroughly with his hand. Because so much of the ritual had been forgotten or discarded, Mr. Summers had been successful in having slips of paper substituted for the chips of wood that had been used for generations. Chips of wood, Mr. Summers had argued, had been all very well when the village was tiny, but now that the population was more than three hundred and likely to keep on growing, it was necessary to use something that would fit more easily into the black box. The night before the lottery, Mr. Summers and Mr. Graves made up the slips of paper and put them in the box, and it was then taken to the safe of Mr. Summers's coal company and locked up until Mr. Summers was ready to take it to the square next morning. The rest of the year, the box was put away, sometimes one place, sometimes another; it had spent one year in Mr. Graves's barn and another year underfoot in the post office, and sometimes it was set on a shelf in the Martin grocery and left there.

There was a great deal of fussing to be done before Mr. Summers declared the lottery open. There were the lists to make up—of heads of families, heads of households in each family, members of each household in each family. There was the proper swearing-in of Mr. Summers by the postmaster, as the official of the lottery; at one time, some people remembered, there had been a recital of some sort, performed by the official of the lottery, a perfunctory, tuneless chant that had been rattled off duly each year; some people believed that the official of the lottery used to stand just so when he said or sang it, others believed that he was supposed to walk among the people, but years and years ago this part of the ritual had been allowed to lapse. There had been, also, a ritual salute, which the official of the lottery had had to use in addressing each person who came up to draw from the box, but this also had changed with time, until now it was felt necessary only for the official to speak to each person approaching. Mr. Summers was very good at all this; in his clean white shirt and blue jeans, with one hand resting carelessly on the black box, he seemed very proper and important as he talked interminably to Mr. Graves and the Martins.

Just as Mr. Summers finally left off talking and turned to the assembled villagers, Mrs. Hutchinson came hurriedly along the path to the square, her sweater thrown over her shoulders, and slid into place in the back of the crowd. "Clean forgot what day it was," she said to Mrs. Delacroix, who stood next to her, and they both laughed softly. "Thought my old man was out back stacking wood," Mrs. Hutchinson went on, "and then I looked out the window and the kids was gone, and then I remembered it was the twenty-seventh and came a-running." She dried her hands on her apron, and Mrs. Delacroix said, "You're in time, though. They're still talking away up there."

Mrs. Hutchinson craned her neck to see through the crowd and found her husband and children standing near the front. She tapped Mrs. Delacroix on the arm as a farewell and began to make her way through the crowd. The people separated good-humoredly to let her through; two or three people said, in voices just loud enough to be heard across the crowd, "Here comes your Missus, Hutchinson," and "Bill, she made it after all." Mrs. Hutchinson reached her husband, and Mr. Summers, who had been waiting, said cheerfully, "Thought we were going to have to get on without you, Tessie." Mrs. Hutchinson said, grinning, "Wouldn't have me leave m'dishes in the sink, now, would you, Joe?" and soft laughter ran through the crowd as the people stirred back into position after Mrs. Hutchinson's arrival.

"Well, now," Mr. Summers said soberly, "guess we better get started, get this over with, so's we can go back to work. Anybody ain't here?"

"Dunbar," several people said. "Dunbar, Dunbar."

Mr. Summers consulted his list. "Clyde Dunbar," he said. "That's right. He's broke his leg, hasn't he? Who's drawing for him?"

"Me, I guess," a woman said, and Mr. Summers turned to look at her. "Wife draws for her husband," Mr. Summers said. "Don't you have a grown boy to do it for you, Janey?" Although Mr. Summers and everyone else in the village knew the answer perfectly well, it was the business of the official of the lottery to ask such questions formally. Mr. Summers waited with an expression of polite interest while Mrs. Dunbar answered.

"Horace's not but sixteen yet," Mrs. Dunbar said regretfully. "Guess I gotta fill in for the old man this year."

"Right," Mr. Summers said. He made a note on the list he was holding. Then he asked, "Watson boy drawing this year?"

A tall boy in the crowd raised his hand. "Here," he said. "I'm drawing for m'mother and me." He blinked his eyes nervously and ducked his head as several voices in the crowd said things like "Good fellow, Jack," and "Glad to see your mother's got a man to do it."

"Well," Mr. Summers said, "guess that's everyone. Old Man Warner make it?"

"Here," a voice said, and Mr. Summers nodded.

A sudden hush fell on the crowd as Mr. Summers cleared his throat and looked at the list. "All ready?" he called. "Now, I'll read the names—heads of families first—and the men come up and take a paper out of the box. Keep the paper folded in your hand without looking at it until everyone has had a turn. Everything clear?"

The people had done it so many times that they only half-listened to the directions; most of them were quiet, wetting their lips, not looking around. Then Mr. Summers raised one hand high and said, "Adams." A man disengaged himself from the crowd and came forward. "Hi, Steve," Mr. Summers said, and Mr. Adams said, "Hi, Joe." They grinned at one another humorlessly and nervously. Then Mr. Adams reached into the black box and took out a folded paper. He held it firmly by one corner as he turned and went hastily back to his place in the crowd, where he stood a little apart from his family, not looking down at his hand.

"Allen," Mr. Summers said. "Anderson. . . . Bentham."

"Seems like there's no time at all between lotteries any more," Mrs. Delacroix said to Mrs. Graves in the back row. "Seems like we got through with the last one only last week."

"Time sure goes fast," Mrs. Graves said.

"Clark. . . . Delacroix."

"There goes my old man," Mrs. Delacroix said. She held her breath while her husband went forward.

"Dunbar," Mr. Summers said, and Mrs. Dunbar went steadily to the box while one of the women said, "Go on, Janey," and another said, "There she goes."

"We're next," Mrs. Graves said. She watched while Mr. Graves came around from the side of the box, greeted Mr. Summers gravely, and selected a slip of paper from the box. By now, all through the crowd there were men holding the small folded papers in their large hands, turning them over and over nervously. Mrs. Dunbar and her two sons stood together, Mrs. Dunbar holding the slip of paper.

"Harburt. . . . Hutchinson."

"Get up there, Bill," Mrs. Hutchinson said, and the people near her laughed.

"Jones."

"They do say," Mr. Adams said to Old Man Warner, who stood next to him, "that over in the north village they're talking of giving up the lottery."

Old Man Warner snorted. "Pack of crazy fools," he said. "Listening to the young folks, nothing's good enough for *them*. Next thing you know, they'll be wanting to go back to living in caves, nobody work any more, live *that* way for a while. Used to be a saying about 'Lottery in June, corn be heavy soon.' First thing you know, we'd all be eating stewed chickweed and acorns. There's *always* been a lottery," he added petulantly. "Bad enough to see young Joe Summers up there joking with everybody."

"Some places have already quit lotteries," Mrs. Adams said.

"Nothing but trouble in *that,*" Old Man Warner said stoutly. "Pack of young fools."

"Martin." And Bobby Martin watched his father go forward. "Overdyke. . . . Percy."

"I wish they'd hurry," Mrs. Dunbar said to her older son. "I wish they'd hurry."

"They're almost through," her son said.

"You get ready to run tell Dad," Mrs. Dunbar said.

Mr. Summers called his own name and then stepped forward precisely and selected a slip from the box. Then he called, "Warner."

"Seventy-seventh year I been in the lottery," Old Man Warner said as he went through the crowd. "Seventy-seventh time."

"Watson." The tall boy came awkwardly through the crowd. Someone said, "Don't be nervous, Jack," and Mr. Summers said, "Take your time, son."

"Zanini."

After that, there was a long pause, a breathless pause, until Mr. Summers, holding his slip of paper in the air, said, "All right, fellows." For a minute, no one moved, and then all the slips of paper were opened. Suddenly, all the women began to speak at once, saying, "Who is it?," "Who's got it?," "Is it the Dunbars?," "Is it the Watsons?" Then the voices began to say, "It's Hutchinson. It's Bill," "Bill Hutchinson's got it."

"Go tell your father," Mrs. Dunbar said to her older son.

People began to look around to see the Hutchinsons. Bill Hutchinson was standing quiet, staring down at the paper in his hand. Suddenly, Tessie Hutchinson shouted to Mr. Summers, "You didn't give him time enough to take any paper he wanted. I saw you. It wasn't fair!"

"Be a good sport, Tessie," Mrs. Delacroix called, and Mrs. Graves said, "All of us took the same chance."

"Shut up, Tessie," Bill Hutchinson said.

"Well, everyone," Mr. Summers said, "that was done pretty fast, and now we've got to be hurrying a little more to get done in time." He consulted his next list. "Bill," he said, "you draw for the Hutchinson family. You got any other households in the Hutchinsons?"

"There's Don and Eva," Mrs. Hutchinson yelled. "Make *them* take their chance!"

"Daughters draw with their husbands' families, Tessie," Mr. Summers said gently. "You know that as well as anyone else."

"It wasn't *fair,*" Tessie said.

"I guess not, Joe," Bill Hutchinson said regretfully. "My daughter draws with her husband's family, that's only fair. And I've got no other family except the kids."

"Then, as far as drawing for families is concerned, it's you," Mr. Summers said in explanation, "and as far as drawing for households is concerned, that's you, too. Right?"

"Right," Bill Hutchinson said.

"How many kids, Bill?" Mr. Summers asked formally.

"Three," Bill Hutchinson said. "There's Bill, Jr., and Nancy, and little Dave. And Tessie and me."

"All right, then," Mr. Summers said. "Harry, you got their tickets back?"

Mr. Graves nodded and held up the slips of paper. "Put them in the box, then," Mr. Summers directed. "Take Bill's and put it in."

"I think we ought to start over," Mrs. Hutchinson said, as quietly as she could. "I tell you it wasn't *fair*. You didn't give him time enough to choose. *Every*body saw that."

Mr. Graves had selected the five slips and put them in the box, and he dropped all the papers but those onto the ground, where the breeze caught them and lifted them off.

"Listen, everybody," Mrs. Hutchinson was saying to the people around her.

"Ready, Bill?" Mr. Summers asked, and Bill Hutchinson, with one quick glance around at his wife and children, nodded.

"Remember," Mr. Summers said, "take the slips and keep them folded until each person has taken one. Harry, you help little Dave." Mr. Graves took the hand of the little boy, who came willingly with him up to the box. "Take a paper out of the box, Davy," Mr. Summers said. Davy put his hand into the box and laughed. "Take just *one* paper," Mr. Summers said. "Harry, you hold it for him." Mr. Graves took the child's hand and removed the folded paper from the tight fist and held it while little Dave stood next to him and looked up at him wonderingly.

"Nancy next," Mr. Summers said. Nancy was twelve, and her school friends breathed heavily as she went forward, switching her skirt, and took a slip daintily from the box. "Bill, Jr.," Mr. Summers said, and Billy, his face red and his feet over-large, nearly knocked the box over as he got a paper out. "Tessie," Mr. Summers said. She hesitated for a minute, looking around defiantly, and then set her lips and went up to the box. She snatched a paper out and held it behind her.

"Bill," Mr. Summers said, and Bill Hutchinson reached into the box and felt around, bringing his hand out at last with the slip of paper in it.

The crowd was quiet. A girl whispered, "I hope it's not Nancy," and the sound of the whisper reached the edges of the crowd.

"It's not the way it used to be," Old Man Warner said clearly. "People ain't the way they used to be."

"All right," Mr. Summers said. "Open the papers. Harry, you open little Dave's."

Mr. Graves opened the slip of paper and there was a general sigh through the crowd as he held it up and everyone could see that it was blank. Nancy and Bill, Jr., opened theirs at the same time, and both beamed and laughed, turning around to the crowd and holding their slips of paper above their heads.

"Tessie," Mr. Summers said. There was a pause, and then Mr. Summers looked at Bill Hutchinson, and Bill unfolded his paper and showed it. It was blank.

"It's Tessie," Mr. Summers said, and his voice was hushed. "Show us her paper, Bill."

Bill Hutchinson went over to his wife and forced the slip of paper out of her hand. It had a black spot on it, the black spot Mr. Summers had made the night before with the heavy pencil in the coal-company office. Bill Hutchinson held it up, and there was a stir in the crowd.

"All right, folks," Mr. Summers said. "Let's finish quickly."

Although the villagers had forgotten the ritual and lost the original black box, they still remembered to use stones. The pile of stones the boys had made earlier was ready; there were stones on the ground with the blowing scraps of paper that had come out of the box. Mrs. Delacroix selected a stone so large she had to pick it up with both hands and turned to Mrs. Dunbar. "Come on," she said. "Hurry up."

Mrs. Dunbar had small stones in both hands, and she said, gasping for breath, "I can't run at all. You'll have to go ahead and I'll catch up with you."

The children had stones already, and someone gave little Davy Hutchinson a few pebbles.

Tessie Hutchinson was in the center of a cleared space by now, and she held her hands out desperately as the villagers moved in on her. "It isn't fair," she said. A stone hit her on the side of the head.

Old Man Warner was saying, "Come on, come on, everyone." Steve Adams was in the front of the crowd of villagers, with Mrs. Graves beside him.

"It ain't fair, it isn't right," Mrs. Hutchinson screamed, and then they were upon her.

# James Joyce

## (1882–1941)

Born during troubled times in Dublin, Ireland, James Joyce was the eldest child in an increasingly impoverished family of twelve. The family had many different homes during James's childhood; his father, who wanted his first son to be a lawyer, once tried to strangle his wife because of the frequent deaths of her infants and dangled his son upside down in a river just to give him character. As a child, Joyce equated his mother with the Virgin Mary and even wrote a hymn to her. He went to school first with the Jesuits, and he progressed to being a brilliant scholarship student who left for Paris soon after his graduation from University College. There he wrote "Epiphanies," a series of journal entries that he would later use in his fiction. Saddened by the state of religious and political affairs in Ireland and angered by protracted difficulties with publishing his first short story collection, *Dubliners* (finally printed in 1916), Joyce left for good or, as Edna O'Brien wrote, "for fear he might succumb to the national disease which was provincialness, wind-and-piss philosophizing, crookedness, vacuity and a verbal spouting that reserved sentiment for God and for the dead." Joyce thereafter made his home in Switzerland and in France; but the people of his native country remained the subject of his thoughts and work. Joyce himself said that the Dublin of his day, should it have vanished, could have been reconstructed out of his own writings.

As an expatriate, Joyce wrote the semiautobiographical *A Portrait of the Artist as a Young Man* in 1916, *Ulysses* in 1922, and *Finnegan's Wake* in 1939. He was greatly influenced by the work of Henrik Ibsen, to whom he wrote letters as a student of nineteen and whom he judged a better writer than Shakespeare because of the playwright's adherence to the uncomplicated truth. His stories, such as "Araby," are built around "a sudden spiritual manifestation" of change in the psychology of the character, rather than a constructed plot. After the publication of *Dubliners*, his writing departed from traditional narrative into an inventive, symbolic mode. This radical stylistic experiment produced fiction that is associative and dreamlike. Of the Joycean technique in fiction, Samuel Beckett commented, "To Joyce reality was a paradigm, an illustration of a possibly unstateable rule."

## *Araby*                                                                 *1904*

North Richmond Street, being blind, was a quiet street except at the hour when the Christian Brothers' School set the boys free. An uninhabited house of two storeys stood at the blind end, detached from its neighbours in a square ground. The other houses of the street, conscious of decent lives within them, gazed at one another with brown imperturbable faces.

The former tenant of our house, a priest, had died in the back drawing-room. Air, musty from having been long enclosed, hung in all the rooms, and the waste room behind the kitchen was littered with old useless papers. Among these I found a few paper-covered books, the pages of which were curled and damp: *The Abbot,* by Walter Scott,[1] *The Devout Communicant*[2] and *The Memoirs of Vidocq.*[3] I liked the last best because its leaves were yellow. The wild garden behind the house contained a central apple-tree and a few straggling bushes under one of which I found the late tenant's rusty bicycle-pump. He had been a very charitable priest; in his will he had left all his money to institutions and the furniture of his house to his sister.

When the short days of winter came dusk fell before we had well eaten our dinners. When we met in the street the houses had grown sombre. The space of sky above us was the colour of ever-changing violet and towards it the lamps of the street lifted their feeble lanterns. The cold air stung us and we played till our bodies glowed. Our shouts echoed in the silent street. The career of our play brought us through the dark muddy lanes behind the houses where we ran the gauntlet of the rough tribes from the cottages, to the back doors of the dark dripping gardens where odours arose from the ashpits, to the dark odorous stables where a coachman smoothed and combed the horse or shook music from the buckled harness. When we returned to the street light from the kitchen windows had filled the areas. If my uncle was seen turning the corner we hid in the shadow until we had seen him safely housed. Or if Mangan's sister

---

1 **Walter Scott:** Sir Walter Scott (1771–1832), an English romantic novelist.
2 *The Devout Communicant:* A religious tract by Franciscan Friar Pacificus Baker.
3 *The Memoirs of Vidocq:* The autobiography of a French police agent and soldier of fortune, Eugène François Vidocq (1775–1857).

came out on the doorstep to call her brother in to his tea we watched her from our shadow peer up and down the street. We waited to see whether she would remain or go in and, if she remained, we left our shadow and walked up to Mangan's steps resignedly. She was waiting for us, her figure defined by the light from the half-opened door. Her brother always teased her before he obeyed and I stood by the railings looking at her. Her dress swung as she moved her body and the soft rope of her hair tossed from side to side.

Every morning I lay on the floor in the front parlour watching her door. The blind was pulled down to within an inch of the sash so that I could not be seen. When she came out on the doorstep my heart leaped. I ran to the hall, seized my books and followed her. I kept her brown figure always in my eye and, when we came near the point at which our ways diverged, I quickened my pace and passed her. This happened morning after morning. I had never spoken to her, except for a few casual words, and yet her name was like a summons to all my foolish blood.

Her image accompanied me even in places the most hostile to romance. On Saturday evenings when my aunt went marketing I had to go to carry some of the parcels. We walked through the flaring streets, jostled by drunken men and bargaining women, amid the curses of labourers, the shrill litanies of shop-boys who stood on guard by the barrels of pigs' cheeks, the nasal chanting of street-singers, who sang a *come-all-you*[4] about O'Donovan Rossa,[5] or a ballad about the troubles in our native land. These noises converged in a single sensation of life for me: I imagined that I bore my chalice safely through a throng of foes. Her name sprang to my lips at moments in strange prayers and praises which I myself did not understand. My eyes were often full of tears (I could not tell why) and at times a flood from my heart seemed to pour itself out into my bosom. I thought little of the future. I did not know whether I would ever speak to her or not or, if I spoke to her, how I could tell her of my confused adoration. But my body was like a harp and her words and gestures were like fingers running upon the wires.

One evening I went into the back drawing-room in which the priest had died. It was a dark rainy evening and there was no sound in the house. Through one of the broken panes I heard the rain impinge upon the earth, the fine incessant needles of water playing in the sodden beds. Some distant lamp or lighted window gleamed below me. I was thankful that I could see so little. All my senses seemed to desire to veil themselves and, feeling that I was about to slip from them, I pressed the palms of my hands together until they trembled, murmuring: "*O love! O love!*" many times.

At last she spoke to me. When she addressed the first words to me I was so confused that I did not know what to answer. She asked me was I going to *Araby*. I forgot whether I answered yes or no. It would be a splendid bazaar, she said she would love to go.

4 **come-all-you:** A standard Irish song, beginning "Come all you Irishmen . . . ," that can be modified to accommodate any subject.
5 **O'Donovan Rossa:** Jeremiah O'Donovan (1831–1915), an Irish nationalist banished to the United States in 1870 for revolutionary activities.

"And why can't you?" I asked.

While she spoke she turned a silver bracelet round and round her wrist. She could not go, she said, because there would be a retreat that week in her convent. Her brother and two other boys were fighting for their caps and I was alone at the railings. She held one of the spikes, bowing her head towards me. The light from the lamp opposite our door caught the white curve of her neck, lit up her hair that rested there and, falling, lit up the hand upon the railing. It fell over one side of her dress and caught the white border of a petticoat, just visible as she stood at ease.

"It's well for you," she said.

"If I go," I said, "I will bring you something."

What innumerable follies laid waste my waking and sleeping thoughts after that evening! I wished to annihilate the tedious intervening days. I chafed against the work of school. At night in my bedroom and by day in the classroom her image came between me and the page I strove to read. The syllables of the word *Araby* were called to me through the silence in which my soul luxuriated and cast an Eastern enchantment over me. I asked for leave to go to the bazaar on Saturday night. My aunt was surprised and hoped it was not some Freemason[6] affair. I answered few questions in class. I watched my master's face pass from amiability to sternness; he hoped I was not beginning to idle. I could not call my wandering thoughts together. I had hardly any patience with the serious work of life which, now that it stood between me and my desire, seemed to me child's play, ugly monotonous child's play.

On Saturday morning I reminded my uncle that I wished to go to the bazaar in the evening. He was fussing at the hallstand, looking for the hat-brush, and answered me curtly:

"Yes, boy, I know."

As he was in the hall I could not go into the front parlour and lie at the window. I left the house in bad humour and walked slowly towards the school. The air was pitilessly raw and already my heart misgave me.

When I came home to dinner my uncle had not yet been home. Still it was early. I sat staring at the clock for some time and, when its ticking began to irritate me, I left the room. I mounted the staircase and gained the upper part of the house. The high cold empty gloomy rooms liberated me and I went from room to room singing. From the front window I saw my companions playing below in the street. Their cries reached me weakened and indistinct and, leaning my forehead against the cool glass, I looked over at the dark house where she lived. I may have stood there for an hour, seeing nothing but the brown-clad figure cast by my imagination, touched discreetly by the lamplight at the curved neck, at the hand upon the railings and at the border below the dress.

When I came downstairs again I found Mrs. Mercer sitting at the fire. She was an old garrulous woman, a pawnbroker's widow, who collected used stamps for some pious purpose. I had to endure the gossip of the tea-table. The meal was prolonged

---

6 **Freemason:** The Masonic order, an international fraternal charitable organization. Catholics felt Freemasons to be enemies of the Catholic Church.

beyond an hour and still my uncle did not come. Mrs. Mercer stood up to go: she was sorry she couldn't wait any longer, but it was after eight o'clock and she did not like to be out late, as the night air was bad for her. When she had gone I began to walk up and down the room, clenching my fists. My aunt said:

"I'm afraid you may put off your bazaar for this night of Our Lord."

At nine o'clock I heard my uncle's latchkey in the halldoor. I heard him talking to himself and heard the hallstand rocking when it had received the weight of his over-coat. I could interpret these signs. When he was midway through his dinner I asked him to give me the money to go to the bazaar. He had forgotten.

"The people are in bed and after their first sleep now," he said.

I did not smile. My aunt said to him energetically:

"Can't you give him the money and let him go? You've kept him late enough as it is."

My uncle said he was very sorry he had forgotten. He said he believed in the old saying: "All work and no play makes Jack a dull boy." He asked me where I was going and, when I had told him a second time he asked me did I know *The Arab's Farewell to his Steed.*[7] When I left the kitchen he was about to recite the opening lines of the piece to my aunt.

I held a florin[8] tightly in my hand as I strode down Buckingham Street towards the station. The sight of the streets thronged with buyers and glaring with gas recalled to me the purpose of my journey. I took my seat in a third-class carriage of a deserted train. After an intolerable delay the train moved out of the station slowly. It crept on-ward among ruinous houses and over the twinkling river. At Westland Row Station a crowd of people pressed to the carriage doors; but the porters moved them back, say-ing that it was a special train for the bazaar. I remained alone in the bare carriage. In a few minutes the train drew up beside an improvised wooden platform. I passed out on to the road and saw by the lighted dial of a clock that it was ten minutes to ten. In front of me was a large building which displayed the magical name.

I could not find any sixpenny entrance and, fearing that the bazaar would be closed, I passed in quickly through a turnstile, handing a shilling to a weary-looking man. I found myself in a big hall girdled at half its height by a gallery. Nearly all the stalls were closed and the greater part of the hall was in darkness. I recognised a si-lence like that which pervades a church after a service. I walked into the centre of the bazaar timidly. A few people were gathered about the stalls which were still open. Be-fore a curtain, over which the words *Café Chantant* were written in coloured lamps, two men were counting money on a salver. I listened to the fall of the coins.

Remembering with difficulty why I had come I went over to one of the stalls and examined porcelain vases and flowered tea-sets. At the door of the stall a young lady was talking and laughing with two young gentlemen. I remarked their English accents and listened vaguely to their conversation.

"O, I never said such a thing!"

7 **The Arab's Farewell to his Steed:** A poem by Caroline Norton (1808–1877). An Arab boy sells his horse for gold coins. However, as the horse is being led away, the boy changes his mind and rushes after the man to return the money and reclaim his love.
8 **florin:** A two-shilling coin.

"O, but you did!"

"O, but I didn't!"

"Didn't she say that?"

"Yes. I heard her."

"O, there's a . . . fib!"

Observing me the young lady came over and asked me did I wish to buy anything. The tone of her voice was not encouraging; she seemed to have spoken to me out of a sense of duty. I looked humbly at the great jars that stood like eastern guards at either side of the dark entrance to the stall and murmured:

"No, thank you."

The young lady changed the position of one of the vases and went back to the two young men. They began to talk of the same subject. Once or twice the young lady glanced at me over her shoulder.

I lingered before her stall, though I knew my stay was useless, to make my interest in her wares seem the more real. Then I turned away slowly and walked down the middle of the bazaar. I allowed the two pennies to fall against the sixpence in my pocket. I heard a voice call from one end of the gallery that the light was out. The upper part of the hall was now completely dark.

Gazing up into the darkness I saw myself as a creature driven and derided by vanity; and my eyes burned with anguish and anger.

# Franz Kafka

## (1883–1924)

Franz Kafka published only one book during his lifetime, and on his deathbed he requested that all of his manuscripts be destroyed. His close friend and biographer, Max Brod, disregarded Kafka's request and published his works. Kafka's stories express the alienation of the twentieth century as well as the struggle between father and son. His father, Hermann Kafka, was an overbearing, domestic tyrant who pushed Kafka to climb the social ladder by attending German schools instead of Czech ones. Kafka attended Ferdinand-Karls University, where he first met Brod. In 1906, he received his doctorate in law and a year later began working in the insurance business. He continued in this line of work for the next sixteen years. In 1910 Kafka began to keep notebooks in which he recorded his literary ideas, dreams, and everyday experiences, and in 1913, at the urging of Brod, he published a collection of his short stories called *Meditation*. In 1917, Kafka discovered that he had contracted tuberculosis. He spent several years in and out of hospitals and died on June 3, 1924. His works include "The Judgment" (1913), "The Metamorphosis" (1915), *Letter to His Father* (1919), *The Trial* (1925), and *Amerika* (1927).

## A Hunger Artist

1924

TRANSLATED BY WILLA AND EDWIN MUIR

During these last decades the interest in professional fasting has markedly diminished. It used to pay very well to stage such great performances under one's own management, but today that is quite impossible. We live in a different world now. At one time the whole town took a lively interest in the hunger artist; from day to day of his fast the excitement mounted; everybody wanted to see him at least once a day; there were people who bought season tickets for the last few days and sat from morning till night in front of his small barred cage; even in the nighttime there were visiting hours, when the whole effect was heightened by torch flares; on fine days the cage was set out in the open air, and then it was the children's special treat to see the hunger artist; for their elders he was often just a joke that happened to be in fashion, but the children stood open-mouthed, holding each other's hands for greater security, marvelling at him as he sat there pallid in black tights, with his ribs sticking out so prominently, not even on a seat but down among straw on the ground, sometimes giving a courteous nod, answering questions with a constrained smile, or perhaps stretching an arm through the bars so that one might feel how thin it was, and then again withdrawing deep into himself, paying no attention to anyone or anything, not even to the all-important striking of the clock that was the only piece of furniture in his cage, but merely staring into vacancy with half-shut eyes, now and then taking a sip from a tiny glass of water to moisten his lips.

Besides casual onlookers there were also relays of permanent watchers selected by the public, usually butchers, strangely enough, and it was their task to watch the hunger artist day and night, three of them at a time, in case he should have some secret recourse to nourishment. This was nothing but a formality, instituted to reassure the masses, for the initiates knew well enough that during his fast the artist would never in any circumstances, not even under forcible compulsion, swallow the smallest morsel of food; the honor of his profession forbade it. Not every watcher, of course, was capable of understanding this, there were often groups of night watchers who were very lax in carrying out their duties and deliberately huddled together in a retired corner to play cards with great absorption, obviously intending to give the hunger artist the chance of a little refreshment, which they supposed he could draw from some private hoard. Nothing annoyed the artist more than such watchers; they made him miserable; they made his fast seem unendurable; sometimes he mastered his feebleness sufficiently to sing during their watch for as long as he could keep going, to show them how unjust their suspicions were. But that was of little use; they only wondered at his cleverness in being able to fill his mouth even while singing. Much more to his taste were the watchers who sat close up to the bars, who were not content with the dim night lighting of the hall but focused him in the full glare of the electric pocket torch given them by the impresario. The harsh light did not trouble him at all. In any case he could never sleep properly, and he could always drowse a little, whatever the light, at any hour, even when the hall was thronged with noisy onlookers. He was quite happy at the prospect of spending a sleepless night with such watchers; he was ready to exchange jokes with them, to tell them stories out of his no-madic life, anything at all to keep them awake and demonstrate to them again that he had no eatables in his cage and that he was fasting as not one of them could fast. But his happiest moment was when the morning came and an enormous breakfast was brought them, at his expense, on which they flung themselves with the keen appetite of healthy men after a weary night of wakefulness. Of course there were people who argued that this breakfast was an unfair attempt to bribe the watchers, but that was going rather too far, and when they were invited to take on a night's vigil without a breakfast, merely for the sake of the cause, they made themselves scarce, although they stuck stubbornly to their suspicions.

Such suspicions, anyhow, were a necessary accompaniment to the profession of fasting. No one could possibly watch the hunger artist continuously, day and night, and so no one could produce first-hand evidence that the fast had really been rigor-ous and continuous; only the artist himself could know that; he was therefore bound to be the sole completely satisfied spectator of his own fast. Yet for other reasons he was never satisfied; it was not perhaps mere fasting that had brought him to such skeleton thinness that many people had regretfully to keep away from his exhibitions, because the sight of him was too much for them, perhaps it was dissatisfaction with himself that had worn him down. For he alone knew, what no other initiate knew, how easy it was to fast. It was the easiest thing in the world. He made no secret of this, yet people did not believe him; at the best they set him down as modest, most of them, however, thought he was out for publicity or else was some kind of cheat who found it easy to fast because he had discovered a way of making it easy, and then had the impudence to admit the fact, more or less. He had to put up with all that, and in the course of time had got used to it, but his inner dissatisfaction always rankled, and never yet, after any term of fasting—this must be granted to his credit—had he left the cage of his own free will. The longest period of fasting was fixed by his impresario at forty days, beyond that term he was not allowed to go, not even in great cities, and there was good reason for it, too. Experience had proved that for about forty days the interest of the public could be stimulated by a steadily increasing pressure of adver-tisement, but after that the town began to lose interest, sympathetic support began notably to fall off; there were of course local variations as between one town and an-other or one country and another, but as a general rule forty days marked the limit. So on the fortieth day the flower-bedecked cage was opened, enthusiastic spectators filled the hall, a military band played, two doctors entered the cage to measure the re-sults of the fast, which were announced through a megaphone, and finally two young ladies appeared, blissful at having been selected for the honor, to help the hunger artist down the few steps leading to a small table on which was spread a carefully cho-sen invalid repast. And at this very moment the artist always turned stubborn. True, he would entrust his bony arms to the outstretched helping hands of the ladies bend-ing over him, but stand up he would not. Why stop fasting at this particular moment, after forty days of it? He had held out for a long time, an illimitably long time; why stop now, when he was in his best fasting form, or rather, not yet quite in his best fasting form? Why should he be cheated of the fame he would get for fasting longer, for being not only the record hunger artist of all time, which presumably he was already, but for beating his own record by a performance beyond human imagination, since he felt that there were no limits to his capacity for fasting? His public pretended to admire him so much, why should it have so little patience with him; if he could endure fasting longer, why shouldn't the public endure it? Besides, he was tired, he was comfortable sitting in the straw, and now he was supposed to lift himself to his full height and go down to a meal the very thought of which gave him a nausea that only the presence of the ladies kept him from betraying, and even that with an effort. And he looked up into the eyes of the ladies who were apparently so friendly and in reality so cruel, and shook his head, which felt too heavy on its strengthless neck. But then there happened yet again what always happened. The impresario came forward, without a word—for the band made speech impossible—lifted his arms in the air above the artist, as if inviting Heaven to look down upon its creature here in the straw, this suffering martyr, which indeed he was, although in quite another sense; grasped him round the emaciated waist, with exaggerated caution, so that the frail condition he was in might be appreciated; and committed him to the care of the blenching ladies, not without secretly giving him a shaking so that his legs and body tottered and swayed. The artist now submitted completely; his head lolled on his breast as if it had landed there by chance; his body was hollowed out; his legs in a spasm of self-preservation clung close to each other at the knees, yet scraped on the ground as if it were not really solid ground, as if they were only trying to find solid ground; and the whole weight of his body, a featherweight after all, relapsed onto one of the ladies, who, looking round for help and panting a little—this post of honor was not at all what she had expected it to be—first stretched her neck as far as she could to keep her face at least free from contact with the artist, then finding this impossible, and her more fortunate companion not coming to her aid but merely holding extended on her own trembling hand the little bunch of knucklebones that was the artist's, to the great delight of the spectators burst into tears and had to be replaced by an attendant who had long been stationed in readiness. Then came the food, a little of which the impresario managed to get between the artist's lips, while he sat in a kind of half-fainting trance, to the accompaniment of cheerful patter designed to distract the public's attention from the artist's condition; after that, a toast was drunk to the public, supposedly prompted by a whisper from the artist in the impresario's ear; the band confirmed it with a mighty flourish, the spectators melted away, and no one had any cause to be dissatisfied with the proceedings, no one except the hunger artist himself, he only, as always.

So he lived for many years, with small regular intervals of recuperation, in visible glory, honored by the world, yet in spite of that troubled in spirit, and all the more troubled because no one would take his trouble seriously. What comfort could he possibly need? What more could he possibly wish for? And if some good-natured person, feeling sorry for him, tried to console him by pointing out that his melancholy was probably caused by fasting, it could happen, especially when he had been fasting for some time, that he reacted with an outburst of fury and to the general alarm began to shake the bars of his cage like a wild animal. Yet the impresario had a way of punishing these outbreaks which he rather enjoyed putting into operation. He would apologize publicly for the artist's behavior, which was only to be excused, he admitted, because of the irritability caused by fasting; a condition hardly to be understood by well-fed people; then by natural transition he went on to mention the artist's equally incomprehensible boast that he could fast for much longer than he was doing; he praised the high ambition, the good will, the great self-denial undoubtedly implicit in such a statement; and then quite simply countered it by bringing out photographs, which were also on sale to the public, showing the artist on the fortieth day of a fast lying in bed almost dead from exhaustion. This perversion of the truth, familiar to the artist though it was, always unnerved him afresh and proved too much for him. What was a consequence of the premature ending of his fast was here presented as the cause of it! To fight against this lack of understanding, against a whole world of non-understanding, was impossible. Time and again in good faith he stood by the bars listening to the impresario, but as soon as the photographs appeared he always let go and sank with a groan back on to his straw, and the reassured public could once more come close and gaze at him.

A few years later when the witnesses of such scenes called them to mind, they often failed to understand themselves at all. For meanwhile the aforementioned change in public interest had set in; it seemed to happen almost overnight; there may have been profound causes for it, but who was going to bother about that; at any rate the pampered hunger artist suddenly found himself deserted one fine day by the amusement seekers, who went streaming past him to other more favored attractions. For the last time the impresario hurried him over half Europe to discover whether the old interest might still survive here and there; all in vain; everywhere, as if by secret agreement, a positive revulsion from professional fasting was in evidence. Of course it could not really have sprung up so suddenly as all that, and many premonitory symptoms which had not been sufficiently remarked or suppressed during the rush and glitter of success now came retrospectively to mind, but it was now too late to take any countermeasures. Fasting would surely come into fashion again at some future date, yet that was no comfort for those living in the present. What, then, was the hunger artist to do? He had been applauded by thousands in his time and could hardly come down to showing himself in a street booth at village fairs, and as for adopting another profession, he was not only too old for that but too fanatically devoted to fasting. So he took leave of the impresario, his partner in an unparalleled career, and hired himself to a large circus; in order to spare his own feelings he avoided reading the conditions of his contract.

A large circus with its enormous traffic in replacing and recruiting men, animals and apparatus can always find a use for people at any time, even for a hunger artist, provided of course that he does not ask too much, and in this particular case anyhow it was not only the artist who was taken on but his famous and long-known name as well; indeed considering the peculiar nature of his performance, which was not impaired by advancing age, it could not be objected that here was an artist past his prime, no longer at the height of his professional skill, seeking a refuge in some quiet corner of a circus; on the contrary, the hunger artist averred that he could fast as well as ever, which was entirely credible; he even alleged that if he were allowed to fast as he liked, and this was at once promised him without more ado, he could astound the world by establishing a record never yet achieved, a statement which certainly provoked a smile among the other professionals, since it left out of account the change in public opinion, which the hunger artist in his zeal conveniently forgot.

He had not, however, actually lost his sense of the real situation and took it as a matter of course that he and his cage should be stationed, not in the middle of the ring as a main attraction, but outside, near the animal cages, on a site that was after all easily accessible. Large and gaily painted placards made a frame for the cage and announced what was to be seen inside it. When the public came thronging out in the intervals to see the animals, they could hardly avoid passing the hunger artist's cage and stopping there for a moment, perhaps they might even have stayed longer had not those pressing behind them in the narrow gangway, who did not understand why they should be held up on their way towards the excitements of the menagerie, made it impossible for anyone to stand gazing quietly for any length of time. And that was the reason why the hunger artist, who had of course been looking forward to these visiting hours as the main achievement of his life, began instead to shrink from them. At first he could hardly wait for the intervals; it was exhilarating to watch the crowds come streaming his way, until only too soon—not even the most obstinate self-deception, clung to almost consciously, could hold out against the fact—the conviction was borne in upon him that these people, most of them, to judge from their actions, again and again, without exception, were all on their way to the menagerie. And the first sight of them from the distance remained the best. For when they reached his cage he was at once deafened by the storm of shouting and abuse that arose from the two contending factions, which renewed themselves continuously, of those who wanted to stop and stare at him—he soon began to dislike them more than the others—not out of real interest but only out of obstinate self-assertiveness, and those who wanted to go straight on to the animals. When the first great rush was past, the stragglers came along, and these, whom nothing could have prevented from stopping to look at him as long as they had breath, raced past with long strides, hardly even glancing at him, in their haste to get to the menagerie in time. And all too rarely did it happen that he had a stroke of luck, when some father of a family fetched up before him with his children, pointed a finger at the hunger artist and explained at length what the phenomenon meant, telling stories of earlier years when he himself had watched similar but much more thrilling performances, and the children, still rather uncomprehending, since neither inside nor outside school had they been sufficiently prepared for this lesson—what did they care about fasting?—yet showed by the brightness of their intent eyes that new and better times might be coming. Perhaps, said the hunger artist to himself many a time, things would be a little better if his cage were set not quite so near the menagerie. That made it too easy for people to make their choice, to say nothing of what he suffered from the stench of the menagerie, the animals' restlessness by night, the carrying past of raw lumps of flesh for the beasts of prey, the roaring at feeding times, which depressed him continually.

But he did not dare to lodge a complaint with the management; after all, he had the animals to thank for the troops of people who passed his cage, among whom there might always be one here and there to take an interest in him, and who could tell where they might seclude him if he called attention to his existence and thereby to the fact that, strictly speaking, he was only an impediment on the way to the menagerie.

A small impediment, to be sure, one that grew steadily less. People grew familiar with the strange idea that they could be expected, in times like these, to take an interest in a hunger artist, and with this familiarity the verdict went out against him. He might fast as much as he could, and he did so; but nothing could save him now, people passed him by. Just try to explain to anyone the art of fasting! Anyone who has no feeling for it cannot be made to understand it. The fine placards grew dirty and illegible, they were torn down; the little notice board telling the number of fast days achieved, which at first was changed carefully every day, had long stayed at the same figure, for after the first few weeks even this small task seemed pointless to the staff; and so the artist simply fasted on and on, as he had once dreamed of doing, and it was no trouble to him, just as he had always foretold, but no one counted the days, no one, not even the artist himself, knew what records he was already breaking, and his heart grew heavy. And when once in a time some leisurely passer-by stopped, made merry over the old figure on the board and spoke of swindling, that was in its way the stupidest lie ever invented by indifference and inborn malice, since it was not the hunger artist who was cheating; he was working honestly, but the world was cheating him of his reward.

Many more days went by, however, and that too came to an end. An overseer's eye fell on the cage one day and he asked the attendants why this perfectly good stage should be left standing there unused with dirty straw inside it; nobody knew, until one man, helped out by the notice board, remembered about the hunger artist. They poked into the straw with sticks and found him in it. "Are you still fasting?" asked the overseer. "When on earth do you mean to stop?" "Forgive me, everybody," whispered the hunger artist; only the overseer, who had his ear to the bars, understood him. "Of course," said the overseer, and tapped his forehead with a finger to let the attendants know what state the man was in, "we forgive you." "I always wanted you to admire my fasting," said the hunger artist. "We do admire it," said the overseer, affably. "But you shouldn't admire it," said the hunger artist. "Well, then we don't admire it," said the overseer, "but why shouldn't we admire it?" "Because I have to fast, I can't help it," said the hunger artist. "What a fellow you are," said the overseer, "and why can't you help it?" "Because," said the hunger artist, lifting his head a little and speaking, with his lips pursed, as if for a kiss, right into the overseer's ear, so that no syllable might be lost, "because I couldn't find the food I liked. If I had found it, believe me, I should have made no fuss and stuffed myself like you or anyone else." These were his last words, but in his dimming eyes remained the firm though no longer proud persuasion that he was still continuing to fast.

"Well, clear this out now!" said the overseer, and they buried the hunger artist, straw and all. Into the cage they put a young panther. Even the most insensitive felt it refreshing to see this wild creature leaping around the cage that had so long been dreary. The panther was all right. The food he liked was brought him without hesitation by the attendants; he seemed not even to miss his freedom; his noble body, furnished almost to the bursting point with all that it needed, seemed to carry freedom around with it too; somewhere in his jaws it seemed to lurk; and the joy of life streamed with such ardent passion from his throat that for the onlookers it was not easy to stand the shock of it. But they braced themselves, crowded round the cage, and did not want ever to move away.

# D. H. Lawrence

## (1885–1930)

D. H. (David Herbert) Lawrence's vision was of a Dionysian utopia in which uninhibitedness should lead to social and personal harmony. Although he was an iconoclast in his choice of subject matter and frequently the victim of censorship for making sexuality and social criticism overtly his topics, his writing reflects a classic verbal efficiency and attention to form.

Lawrence was born in England the son of a coal miner, and he rejected the dreariness of industrialization in both his life and his art, traveling far away from his Nottingham home to Australia and New Mexico in search of surroundings conducive to the flourishing of mind and spirit and, later on, for relief from tuberculosis. As his mother was before him, Lawrence became a schoolteacher for a while, after a stint as a factory worker in a prosthetic limb plant. He began to paint and write poetry before leaving teaching in 1911 due to illness. The following year, he left for Germany with the wife of his former French teacher, and he married her after her official divorce in 1914. Like Henry James, Lawrence wrote about complex human relationships and the conundrums that lie in wait on the path of attempted psychological fulfillment.

Lawrence's first novel was *The White Peacock* (1911), followed by *The Trespasser* in 1912. Some of his most important works were written during World War I, while the British government harassed Lawrence and his wife about her German lineage and his lack of patriotism. *Sons and Lovers,* completed in 1913, was his first success. Other works include *The Rainbow* (1915), all copies of which were destroyed because of its obscene content; *Women in Love* (1921), whose heroine is based on the writer Katherine Mansfield; and the then scandalous *Lady Chatterley's Lover* (1928). He also wrote a 1929 novel about a prophet who comes back to life only to choose human love over divinity, called *The Man Who Died.* Lawrence was a prolific short story writer, poet, essayist, critic, and travel writer, who published the story collections *The Prussian Officer* and *The Woman Who Rode Away* and nonfiction works such as *Psychoanalysis* and the Unconscious, Pornography and Obscenity, Apocalypse,* and a number of travelogues, including *Mornings in Mexico* and *Etruscan Places.*

## The Rocking-Horse Winner                                      1926

There was a woman who was beautiful, who started with all the advantages, yet she had no luck. She married for love, and the love turned to dust. She had bonny children, yet she felt they had been thrust upon her, and she could not love them. They looked at her coldly, as if they were finding fault with her. And hurriedly she felt she must cover up some fault in herself. Yet what it was that she must cover up she never knew. Nevertheless, when her children were present, she always felt the centre of her heart go hard. This troubled her, and in her manner she was all the more gentle and anxious for her children, as if she loved them very much. Only she herself knew that at the centre of her heart was a hard little place that could not feel love, no, not for anybody. Everybody else said of her: "She is such a good mother. She adores her children." Only she herself, and her children themselves, knew it was not so. They read it in each other's eyes.

There were a boy and two little girls. They lived in a pleasant house, with a garden, and they had discreet servants, and felt themselves superior to anyone in the neighbourhood.

Although they lived in style, they felt always an anxiety in the house. There was never enough money. The mother had a small income, and the father had a small income, but not nearly enough for the social position which they had to keep up. The father went into town to some office. But though he had good prospects, these prospects never materialized. There was always the grinding sense of the shortage of money, though the style was always kept up.

At last the mother said: "I will see if I can't make something." But she did not know where to begin. She racked her brains, and tried this thing and the other, but could not find anything successful. The failure made deep lines come into her face. Her children were growing up, they would have to go to school. There must be more money, there must be more money. The father, who was always very handsome and expensive in his tastes, seemed as if he never would be able to do anything worth doing. And the mother, who had a great belief in herself, did not succeed any better, and her tastes were just as expensive.

And so the house came to be haunted by the unspoken phrase: There must be more money! There must be more money! The children could hear it all the time, though nobody said it aloud. They heard it at Christmas, when the expensive and splendid toys filled the nursery. Behind the shining modern rocking horse, behind the smart doll's-house, a voice would start whispering: "There must be more money! There must be more money!" And the children would stop playing, to listen for a moment. They would look into each other's eyes, to see if they had all heard. And each one saw in the eyes of the other two that they too had heard. "There must be more money! There must be more money!"

It came whispering from the springs of the still-swaying rocking horse, and even the horse, bending his wooden, champing head, heard it. The big doll, sitting so pink and smirking in her new pram,[1] could hear it quite plainly, and seemed to be smirking all the more self-consciously because of it. The foolish puppy, too, that took the place of the Teddy bear, he was looking so extraordinarily foolish for no other reason but that he heard the secret whisper all over the house: "There must be more money!"

Yet nobody ever said it aloud. The whisper was everywhere, and therefore no one spoke it. Just as no one ever says: "We are breathing!" in spite of the fact that breath is coming and going all the time.

"Mother," said the boy Paul one day, "why don't we keep a car of our own? Why do we always use uncle's, or else a taxi?"

"Because we're the poor members of the family," said the mother.

"But why are we, mother?"

"Well—I suppose," she said slowly and bitterly, "it's because your father has no luck."

The boy was silent for some time.

"Is luck money, mother?" he asked, rather timidly.

"No, Paul. Not quite. It's what causes you to have money."

"Oh!" said Paul vaguely. "I thought when Uncle Oscar said filthy lucker, it meant money."

"Filthy lucre does mean money," said the mother. "But it's lucre, not luck."

"Oh!" said the boy. "Then what is luck, mother?"

"It's what causes you to have money. If you're lucky you have money. That's why it's better to be born lucky than rich. If you're rich, you may lose your money. But if you're lucky, you will always get more money."

"Oh! Will you? And is father not lucky?"

"Very unlucky, I should say," she said bitterly.

The boy watched her with unsure eyes.

"Why?" he asked.

"I don't know. Nobody ever knows why one person is lucky and another unlucky."

"Don't they? Nobody at all? Does nobody know?"

"Perhaps God. But He never tells."

"He ought to, then. And aren't you lucky either, mother?"

"I can't be, if I married an unlucky husband."

"But by yourself, aren't you?"

"I used to think I was, before I married. Now I think I am very unlucky indeed."

"Why?"

"Well—never mind! Perhaps I'm not really," she said.

The child looked at her, to see if she meant it. But he saw, by the lines of her mouth, that she was only trying to hide something from him.

"Well, anyhow," he said stoutly, "I'm a lucky person."

---

1 **pram:** A baby carriage.

"Why?" said his mother, with a sudden laugh.

He stared at her. He didn't even know why he had said it.

"God told me," he asserted, brazening it out.

"I hope He did, dear!" she said, again with a laugh, but rather bitter.

"He did, mother!"

"Excellent!" said the mother, using one of her husband's exclamations.

The boy saw she did not believe him; or, rather, that she paid no attention to his assertion. This angered him somewhat, and made him want to compel her attention.

He went off by himself, vaguely, in a childish way, seeking for the clue to "luck." Absorbed, taking no heed of other people, he went about with a sort of stealth, seeking inwardly for luck. He wanted luck, he wanted it, he wanted it. When the two girls were playing dolls in the nursery, he would sit on his big rocking horse, charging madly into space, with a frenzy that made the little girls peer at him uneasily. Wildly the horse careered, the waving dark hair of the boy tossed, his eyes had a strange glare in them. The little girls dared not speak to him.

When he had ridden to the end of his mad little journey, he climbed down and stood in front of his rocking horse, staring fixedly into its lowered face. Its red mouth was slightly open, its big eye was wide and glassy-bright.

"Now!" he would silently command the snorting steed. "Now, take me to where there is luck! Now take me!"

And he would slash the horse on the neck with the little whip he had asked Uncle Oscar for. He knew the horse could take him to where there was luck, if only he forced it. So he would mount again, and start on his furious ride, hoping at last to get there. He knew he could get there.

"You'll break your horse, Paul!" said the nurse.

"He's always riding like that! I wish he'd leave off!" said his elder sister Joan.

But he only glared down on them in silence. Nurse gave him up. She could make nothing of him. Anyhow he was growing beyond her.

One day his mother and his Uncle Oscar came in when he was on one of his furious rides. He did not speak to them.

"Hallo, you young jockey! Riding a winner?" said his uncle.

"Aren't you growing too big for a rocking horse? You're not a very little boy any longer, you know," said his mother.

But Paul only gave a blue glare from his big, rather close-set eyes. He would speak to nobody when he was in full tilt. His mother watched him with an anxious expression on her face.

At last he suddenly stopped forcing his horse into the mechanical gallop, and slid down.

"Well, I got there!" he announced fiercely, his blue eyes still flaring, and his sturdy long legs straddling apart.

"Where did you get to?" asked his mother.

"Where I wanted to go," he flared back at her.

"That's right, son!" said Uncle Oscar. "Don't you stop till you get there. What's the horse's name?"

"He doesn't have a name," said the boy.

"Gets on without all right?" asked the uncle.

"Well, he has different names. He was called Sansovino last week."

"Sansovino, eh? Won the Ascot.[2] How did you know his name?"

"He always talks about horse races with Bassett," said Joan.

The uncle was delighted to find that his small nephew was posted with all the racing news. Bassett, the young gardener, who had been wounded in the left foot in the war and had got his present job through Oscar Cresswell, whose batman[3] he had been, was a perfect blade of the "turf."[4] He lived in the racing events, and the small boy lived with him.

Oscar Cresswell got it all from Bassett.

"Master Paul comes and asks me, so I can't do more than tell him, sir," said Bassett, his face terribly serious, as if he were speaking of religious matters.

"And does he ever put anything on a horse he fancies?"

"Well—I don't want to give him away—he's a young sport, a fine sport, sir. Would you mind asking him yourself? He sort of takes a pleasure in it, and perhaps he'd feel I was giving him away, sir, if you don't mind."

Bassett was serious as a church.

The uncle went back to his nephew, and took him off for a ride in the car.

"Say, Paul, old man, do you ever put anything on a horse?" the uncle asked.

The boy watched the handsome man closely.

"Why, do you think I oughtn't to?" he parried.

"Not a bit of it! I thought perhaps you might give me a tip for the Lincoln."

The car sped on into the country, going down to Uncle Oscar's place in Hampshire.

"Honour bright?" said the nephew.

"Honour bright, son!" said the uncle.

"Well, then, Daffodil."

"Daffodil! I doubt it, sonny. What about Mirza?"

"I only know the winner," said the boy. "That's Daffodil."

"Daffodil, eh?"

There was a pause. Daffodil was an obscure horse comparatively.

"Uncle!"

"Yes, son?"

"You won't let it go any further, will you? I promised Bassett."

"Bassett be damned, old man! What's he got to do with it?"

"We're partners. We've been partners from the first. Uncle, he lent me my first five shillings, which I lost. I promised him, honour bright, it was only between me and him; only you gave me that ten-shilling note I started winning with, so I thought you were lucky. You won't let it go any further, will you?"

---

2 **Ascot:** An annual horse race. The following, mentioned later, are annual horse races as well: Lincoln, Grand National, Derby, and Lincolnshire.

3 **batman:** A hospital orderly.

4 **blade of the "turf":** A fan of horse racing.

The boy gazed at his uncle from those big, hot, blue eyes, set rather close together. The uncle stirred and laughed uneasily.

"Right you are, son! I'll keep your tip private. Daffodil, eh? How much are you putting on him?"

"All except twenty pounds," said the boy. "I keep that in reserve."

The uncle thought it a good joke.

"You keep twenty pounds in reserve, do you, you young romancer? What are you betting, then?"

"I'm betting three hundred," said the boy gravely. "But it's between you and me, Uncle Oscar! Honour bright?"

The uncle burst into a roar of laughter.

"It's between you and me all right, you young Nat Gould,"[5] he said, laughing. "But where's your three hundred?"

"Bassett keeps it for me. We're partners."

"You are, are you! And what is Bassett putting on Daffodil?"

"He won't go quite as high as I do, I expect. Perhaps he'll go a hundred and fifty."

"What, pennies?" laughed the uncle.

"Pounds," said the child, with a surprised look at his uncle. "Bassett keeps a bigger reserve than I do."

Between wonder and amusement Uncle Oscar was silent. He pursued the matter no further, but he determined to take his nephew with him to the Lincoln races.

"Now, son," he said, "I'm putting twenty on Mirza, and I'll put five for you on any horse you fancy. What's your pick?"

"Daffodil, uncle."

"No, not the fiver on Daffodil!"

"I should if it was my own fiver," said the child.

"Good! Good! Right you are! A fiver for me and a fiver for you on Daffodil."

The child had never been to a race meeting before, and his eyes were blue fire. He pursed his mouth tight, and watched. A Frenchman just in front had put his money on Lancelot. Wild with excitement, he flayed his arms up and down, yelling "Lancelot! Lancelot!" in his French accent.

Daffodil came in first, Lancelot second, Mirza third. The child, flushed and with eyes blazing, was curiously serene. His uncle brought him four five-pound notes, four to one.

"What am I to do with these?" he cried, waving them before the boy's eyes.

"I suppose we'll talk to Bassett," said the boy. "I expect I have fifteen hundred now; and twenty in reserve; and this twenty."

His uncle studied him for some moments.

"Look here, son!" he said. "You're not serious about Bassett and that fifteen hundred, are you?"

"Yes, I am. But it's between you and me, uncle. Honour bright!"

"Honour bright all right, son! But I must talk to Bassett."

---

5 **Nat Gould:** English writer (1857–1919) who wrote many popular novels about horse racing.

"If you'd like to be a partner, uncle, with Bassett and me, we could all be partners. Only, you'd have to promise, honour bright, uncle, not to let it go beyond us three. Bassett and I are lucky, and you must be lucky, because it was your ten shillings I started winning with . . ."

Uncle Oscar took both Bassett and Paul into Richmond Park for an afternoon, and there they talked.

"It's like this, you see, sir," Bassett said. "Master Paul would get me talking about racing events, spinning yarns, you know, sir. And he was always keen on knowing if I'd made or if I'd lost. It's about a year since, now, that I put five shillings on Blush of Dawn for him—and we lost. Then the luck turned, with that ten shillings he had from you, that we put on Singhalese. And since that time, it's been pretty steady, all things considering. What do you say, Master Paul?"

"We're all right when we're sure," said Paul. "It's when we're not quite sure that we go down."

"Oh, but we're careful then," said Bassett.

"But when are you sure?" smiled Uncle Oscar.

"It's Master Paul, sir," said Bassett, in a secret, religious voice. "It's as if he had it from heaven. Like Daffodil, now, for the Lincoln. That was as sure as eggs."

"Did you put anything on Daffodil?" asked Oscar Cresswell.

"Yes, sir, I made my bit."

"And my nephew?"

Bassett was obstinately silent, looking at Paul.

"I made twelve hundred, didn't I, Bassett? I told uncle I was putting three hundred on Daffodil."

"That's right," said Bassett, nodding.

"But where's the money?" asked the uncle.

"I keep it safe locked up, sir. Master Paul he can have it any minute he likes to ask for it."

"What, fifteen hundred pounds?"

"And twenty! and forty, that is, with the twenty he made on the course."

"It's amazing!" said the uncle.

"If Master Paul offers you to be partners, sir, I would, if I were you; if you'll excuse me," said Bassett.

Oscar Cresswell thought about it.

"I'll see the money," he said.

They drove home again, and sure enough, Bassett came round to the garden-house with fifteen hundred pounds in notes. The twenty pounds reserve was left with Joe Glee, in the Turf Commission deposit.

"You see, it's all right, uncle, when I'm sure! Then we go strong, for all we're worth. Don't we, Bassett?"

"We do that, Master Paul."

"And when are you sure?" said the uncle, laughing.

"Oh, well, sometimes I'm absolutely sure, like about Daffodil," said the boy; "and sometimes I have an idea; and sometimes I haven't even an idea, have I, Bassett? Then we're careful, because we mostly go down."

"You do, do you! And when you're sure, like about Daffodil, what makes you sure, sonny?"

"Oh, well, I don't know," said the boy uneasily. "I'm sure, you know, uncle; that's all."

"It's as if he had it from heaven, sir," Bassett reiterated.

"I should say so!" said the uncle.

But he became a partner. And when the Leger was coming on, Paul was "sure" about Lively Spark, which was a quite inconsiderable horse. The boy insisted on putting a thousand on the horse, Bassett went for five hundred, and Oscar Cresswell two hundred. Lively Spark came in first, and the betting had been ten to one against him. Paul had made ten thousand.

"You see," he said, "I was absolutely sure of him."

Even Oscar Cresswell had cleared two thousand.

"Look here, son," he said, "this sort of thing makes me nervous."

"It needn't, uncle! Perhaps I shan't be sure again for a long time."

"But what are you going to do with your money?" asked the uncle.

"Of course," said the boy, "I started it for mother. She said she had no luck, because father is unlucky, so I thought if I was lucky, it might stop whispering."

"What might stop whispering?"

"Our house. I hate our house for whispering."

"What does it whisper?"

"Why—why"—the boy fidgeted—"why, I don't know. But it's always short of money, you know, uncle."

"I know it, son, I know it."

"You know people send mother writs,[6] don't you, uncle?"

"I'm afraid I do," said the uncle.

"And then the house whispers, like people laughing at you behind your back. It's awful, that is! I thought if I was lucky . . ."

"You might stop it," added the uncle.

The boy watched him with big blue eyes that had an uncanny cold fire in them, and he said never a word.

"Well, then!" said the uncle. "What are we doing?"

"I shouldn't like mother to know I was lucky," said the boy.

"Why not, son?"

"She'd stop me."

"I don't think she would."

"Oh!"—and the boy writhed in an odd way—"I don't want her to know, uncle."

"All right, son! We'll manage it without her knowing."

They managed it very easily. Paul, at the other's suggestion, handed over five

6 **writs:** Legal threats.

thousand pounds to his uncle, who deposited it with the family lawyer, who was then to inform Paul's mother that a relative had put five thousand pounds into his hands, which sum was to be paid out a thousand pounds at a time, on the mother's birthday, for the next five years.

"So she'll have a birthday present of a thousand pounds for five successive years," said Uncle Oscar. "I hope it won't make it all the harder for her later."

Paul's mother had her birthday in November. The house had been "whispering" worse than ever lately, and, even in spite of his luck, Paul could not bear up against it. He was very anxious to see the effect of the birthday letter, telling his mother about the thousand pounds.

When there were no visitors, Paul now took his meals with his parents, as he was beyond the nursery control. His mother went into town nearly every day. She had discovered that she had an odd knack of sketching furs and dress materials, so she worked secretly in the studio of a friend who was the chief "artist" for the leading drapers. She drew the figures of ladies in furs and ladies in silk and sequins for the newspaper advertisements. This young woman artist earned several thousand pounds a year, but Paul's mother only made several hundreds, and she was again dissatisfied. She so wanted to be first in something, and she did not succeed, even in making sketches for drapery advertisements.

She was down to breakfast on the morning of her birthday. Paul watched her face as she read her letters. He knew the lawyer's letter. As his mother read it, her face hardened and became more expressionless. Then a cold, determined look came on her mouth. She hid the letter under the pile of others, and said not a word about it.

"Didn't you have anything nice in the post for your birthday, mother?" said Paul.

"Quite moderately nice," she said, her voice cold and absent.

She went away to town without saying more.

But in the afternoon Uncle Oscar appeared. He said Paul's mother had had a long interview with the lawyer, asking if the whole five thousand could be advanced at once, as she was in debt.

"What do you think, uncle?" said the boy.

"I leave it to you, son."

"Oh, let her have it, then! We can get some more with the other," said the boy.

"A bird in the hand is worth two in the bush, laddie!" said Uncle Oscar.

"But I'm sure to know for the Grand National; or the Lincolnshire; or else the Derby. I'm sure to know for one of them," said Paul.

So Uncle Oscar signed the agreement, and Paul's mother touched the whole five thousand. Then something very curious happened. The voices in the house suddenly went mad, like a chorus of frogs on a spring evening. There were certain new furnishings, and Paul had a tutor. He was really going to Eton,[7] his father's school, in the following autumn. There were flowers in the winter, and a blossoming of the luxury Paul's mother had been used to. And yet the voices in the house, behind the sprays of mimosa and almond blossom, and from under the piles of iridescent cushions, sim-

---

7 **Eton:** A public (i.e., private) school where upper-class boys are prepared for college.

ply trilled and screamed in a sort of ecstasy: "There must be more money! Oh-h-h, there must be more money. Oh, now, now-w! Now-w-w—there must be more money—more than ever! More than ever!"

It frightened Paul terribly. He studied away at his Latin and Greek with his tutors. But his intense hours were spent with Bassett. The Grand National had gone by: he had not "known," and had lost a hundred pounds. Summer was at hand. He was in agony for the Lincoln. But even for the Lincoln he didn't "know" and he lost fifty pounds. He became wild-eyed and strange, as if something were going to explode in him.

"Let it alone, son! Don't you bother about it!" urged Uncle Oscar. But it was as if the boy couldn't really hear what his uncle was saying.

"I've got to know for the Derby! I've got to know for the Derby!" the child reiterated, his big blue eyes blazing with a sort of madness.

His mother noticed how overwrought he was.

"You'd better go to the seaside. Wouldn't you like to go now to the seaside, instead of waiting? I think you'd better," she said, looking down at him anxiously, her heart curiously heavy because of him.

But the child lifted his uncanny blue eyes.

"I couldn't possibly go before the Derby, mother!" he said. "I couldn't possibly!"

"Why not?" she said, her voice becoming heavy when she was opposed. "Why not? You can still go from the seaside to see the Derby with your Uncle Oscar, if that's what you wish. No need for you to wait here. Besides, I think you care too much about these races. It's a bad sign. My family has been a gambling family, and you won't know till you grow up how much damage it has done. But it has done damage. I shall have to send Bassett away, and ask Uncle Oscar not to talk racing to you, unless you promise to be reasonable about it; go away to the seaside and forget it. You're all nerves!"

"I'll do what you like, mother, so long as you don't send me away till after the Derby," the boy said.

"Send you away from where? Just from this house?"

"Yes," he said, gazing at her.

"Why, you curious child, what makes you care about this house so much, suddenly? I never knew you loved it."

He gazed at her without speaking. He had a secret within a secret, something he had not divulged, even to Bassett or to his Uncle Oscar.

But his mother, after standing undecided and a little bit sullen for some moments, said:

"Very well, then! Don't go to the seaside till after the Derby, if you don't wish it. But promise me you won't let your nerves go to pieces. Promise you won't think so much about horse racing and events, as you call them!"

"Oh, no," said the boy casually. "I won't think much about them, mother. You needn't worry. I wouldn't worry, mother, if I were you."

"If you were me and I were you," said his mother, "I wonder what we should do!"

"But you know you needn't worry, mother, don't you?" the boy repeated.

"I should be awfully glad to know it," she said wearily.

"Oh, well, you can, you know. I mean, you ought to know you needn't worry," he insisted.

"Ought I? Then I'll see about it," she said.

Paul's secret of secrets was his wooden horse, that which had no name. Since he was emancipated from a nurse and a nursery-governess, he had had his rocking horse removed to his own bedroom at the top of the house.

"Surely, you're too big for a rocking horse!" his mother had remonstrated.

"Well, you see, mother, till I can have a real horse, I like to have some sort of animal about," had been his quaint answer.

"Do you feel he keeps you company?" she laughed.

"Oh, yes! He's very good, he always keeps me company, when I'm there," said Paul.

So the horse, rather shabby, stood in an arrested prance in the boy's bedroom.

The Derby was drawing near, and the boy grew more and more tense. He hardly heard what was spoken to him, he was very frail, and his eyes were really uncanny. His mother had sudden seizures of uneasiness about him. Sometimes, for half-an-hour, she would feel a sudden anxiety about him that was almost anguish. She wanted to rush to him at once, and know he was safe.

Two nights before the Derby, she was at a big party in town, when one of her rushes of anxiety about her boy, her first-born, gripped her heart till she could hardly speak. She fought with the feeling, might and main, for she believed in common sense. But it was too strong. She had to leave the dance and go downstairs to telephone to the country. The children's nursery-governess was terribly surprised and startled at being rung up in the night.

"Are the children all right, Miss Wilmot?"

"Oh, yes, they are quite all right."

"Master Paul? Is he all right?"

"He went to bed as right as a trivet. Shall I run up and look at him?"

"No," said Paul's mother reluctantly. "No! Don't trouble. It's all right. Don't sit up. We shall be home fairly soon." She did not want her son's privacy intruded upon.

"Very good," said the governess.

It was about one o'clock when Paul's mother and father drove up to their house. All was still. Paul's mother went to her room and slipped off her white fur coat. She had told her maid not to wait up for her. She heard her husband downstairs, mixing a whisky-and-soda.

And then, because of the strange anxiety at her heart, she stole upstairs to her son's room. Noiselessly she went along the upper corridor. Was there a faint noise? What was it?

She stood, with arrested muscles, outside his door, listening. There was a strange, heavy, and yet not loud noise. Her heart stood still. It was a soundless noise, yet rushing and powerful. Something huge, in violent, hushed motion. What was it? What in God's name was it? She ought to know. She felt that she knew the noise. She knew what it was.

Yet she could not place it. She couldn't say what it was. And on and on it went, like a madness.

Softly, frozen with anxiety and fear, she turned the door handle.

The room was dark. Yet in the space near the window, she heard and saw something plunging to and fro. She gazed in fear and amazement.

Then suddenly she switched on the light, and saw her son, in his green pyjamas, madly surging on the rocking horse. The blaze of light suddenly lit him up, as he urged the wooden horse, and lit her up, as she stood, blonde, in her dress of pale green and crystal, in the doorway.

"Paul!" she cried. "Whatever are you doing?"

"It's Malabar!" he screamed, in a powerful, strange voice. "It's Malabar."

His eyes blazed at her for one strange and senseless second, as he ceased urging his wooden horse. Then he fell with a crash to the ground, and she, all her tormented motherhood flooding upon her, rushed to gather him up.

But he was unconscious, and unconscious he remained, with some brain-fever. He talked and tossed, and his mother sat stonily by his side.

"Malabar! It's Malabar! Bassett, Bassett, I know it! It's Malabar!"

So the child cried, trying to get up and urge the rocking horse that gave him his inspiration.

"What does he mean by Malabar?" asked the heart-frozen mother.

"I don't know," said the father stonily.

"What does he mean by Malabar?" she asked her brother Oscar.

"It's one of the horses running for the Derby," was the answer.

And, in spite of himself, Oscar Cresswell spoke to Bassett, and himself put a thousand on Malabar: at fourteen to one.

The third day of the illness was critical: they were waiting for a change. The boy, with his rather long, curly hair, was tossing ceaselessly on the pillow. He neither slept nor regained consciousness, and his eyes were like blue stones. His mother sat, feeling her heart had gone, turned actually into a stone.

In the evening, Oscar Cresswell did not come, but Bassett sent a message, saying could he come up for one moment, just one moment? Paul's mother was very angry at the intrusion, but on second thought she agreed. The boy was the same. Perhaps Bassett might bring him to consciousness.

The gardener, a shortish fellow with a little brown moustache, and sharp little brown eyes, tiptoed into the room, touched his imaginary cap to Paul's mother, and stole to the bedside, staring with glittering, smallish eyes, at the tossing, dying child.

"Master Paul!" he whispered. "Master Paul! Malabar come in first all right, a clean win. I did as you told me. You've made over seventy thousand pounds, you have; you've got over eighty thousand. Malabar came in all right, Master Paul."

"Malabar! Malabar! Did I say Malabar, mother? Did I say Malabar? Do you think I'm lucky, mother? I knew Malabar, didn't I? Over eighty thousand pounds! I call that lucky, don't you, mother? Over eighty thousand pounds! I knew, didn't I know I knew? Malabar came in all right. If I ride my horse till I'm sure, then I tell you, Bassett, you can go as high as you like. Did you go for all you were worth, Bassett?"

"I went a thousand on it, Master Paul."

"I never told you, mother that if I can ride my horse, and get there, then I'm absolutely sure—oh, absolutely! Mother, did I ever tell you? I'm lucky."

"No, you never did," said the mother.

But the boy died in the night.

And even as he lay dead, his mother heard her brother's voice saying to her: "My God, Hester, you're eighty-odd thousand to the good and a poor devil of a son to the bad. But, poor devil, poor devil, he's best gone out of a life where he rides his rocking horse to find a winner."

# Doris Lessing

## (b. 1919)

Doris Lessing's novels and short stories focus on the struggle among opposing elements within an individual's own personality and the conflict between the individual conscience and the collective good. Lessing was born in what is now Iran, and, in 1925, her family moved to the British colony in Southern Rhodesia (now Zimbabwe). Lessing's mother enforced a rigid system of rules and hygiene at home and sent her daughter to a convent school and, later, an all-girls high school in Salisbury. Lessing dropped out at the age of fourteen, ending her formal education. She was influenced at an early age by Charles Dickens, Robert Louis Stevenson, and Rudyard Kipling; later she discovered D. H. Lawrence, Stendhal, Tolstoy, and Dostoevsky. In 1934, Lessing left home and took a job as a nursemaid, and in 1937 she moved to Salisbury, where she worked as a telephone operator.

Lessing's first novel, *The Grass Is Singing*, was published in 1949; it was followed by the Children of Violence series (1951–1959). Her works include *The Golden Notebook* (1962), *Briefing for a Descent into Hell* (1971), *Memoirs of a Survivor* (1974), *The Good Terrorist* (1985), and *The Fifth Child* (1988). She also published *The Diary of a Good Neighbour* (1983) and *If the Old Could . . .* (1984) under the pseudonym Jane Somers. Lessing has been nominated for and received numerous awards, including a nomination for the Nobel Prize for literature (1996), an appointment as a Companion of Honour (1999), the Prince of Asturias Prize in Literature (2001), and the David Cohen British Literature Prize (2001). A collection of her essays, *Learning How to Read*, was recently published.

## *To Room Nineteen*                                                          1963

This is a story, I suppose, about a failure in intelligence: the Rawlings' marriage was grounded in intelligence.

They were older when they married than most of their married friends: in their well-seasoned late twenties. Both had had a number of affairs, sweet rather than bitter;

and when they fell in love—for they did fall in love—had known each other for some time. They joked that they had saved each other "for the real thing." That they had waited so long (but not too long) for this real thing was to them a proof of their sensible discrimination. A good many of their friends had married young, and now (they felt) probably regretted lost opportunities; while others, still unmarried, seemed to them arid, self-doubting, and likely to make desperate or romantic marriages.

Not only they, but others, felt they were well-matched: their friends' delight was an additional proof of their happiness. They had played the same roles, male and female, in this group or set, if such a wide, loosely connected, constantly changing constellation of people could be called a set. They had both become, by virtue of their moderation, their humour, and their abstinence from painful experience, people to whom others came for advice. They could be, and were, relied on. It was one of those cases of a man and a woman linking themselves whom no one else had ever thought of linking, probably because of their similarities. But then everyone exclaimed: Of course! How right! How was it we never thought of it before!

And so they married amid general rejoicing, and because of their foresight and their sense for what was probable, nothing was a surprise to them.

Both had well-paid jobs. Matthew was a subeditor on a large London newspaper, and Susan worked in an advertising firm. He was not the stuff of which editors or publicised journalists are made, but he was much more than "a subeditor," being one of the essential background people who in fact steady, inspire and make possible the people in the limelight. He was content with this position. Susan had a talent for commercial drawing. She was humorous about the advertisements she was responsible for, but she did not feel strongly about them one way or the other.

Both, before they married, had had pleasant flats, but they felt it unwise to base a marriage on either flat, because it might seem like a submission of personality on the part of the one whose flat it was not. They moved into a new flat in South Kensington on the clear understanding that when their marriage had settled down (a process they knew would not take long, and was in fact more a humorous concession to popular wisdom than what was due to themselves) they would buy a house and start a family.

And this is what happened. They lived in their charming flat for two years, giving parties and going to them, being a popular young married couple, and then Susan became pregnant, she gave up her job, and they bought a house in Richmond. It was typical of this couple that they had a son first, then a daughter, then twins, son and daughter. Everything right, appropriate, and what everyone would wish for, if they could choose. But people did feel these two had chosen; this balanced and sensible family was no more than what was due to them because of their infallible sense for *choosing* right.

And so they lived with their four children in their gardened house in Richmond and were happy. They had everything they had wanted and had planned for.

*And yet* . . .

Well, even this was expected, that there must be a certain flatness. . . .

Yes, yes, of course, it was natural they sometimes felt like this. Like what?

Their life seemed to be like a snake biting its tail. Matthew's job for the sake of

Susan, children, house, and garden—which caravanserai needed a well-paid job to maintain it. And Susan's practical intelligence for the sake of Matthew, the children, the house and the garden—which unit would have collapsed in a week without her.

But there was no point about which either could say: "For the sake of *this* is all the rest." Children? But children can't be a centre of life and a reason for being. They can be a thousand things that are delightful, interesting, satisfying, but they can't be a wellspring to live from. Or they shouldn't be. Susan and Matthew knew that well enough.

Matthew's job? Ridiculous. It was an interesting job, but scarcely a reason for living. Matthew took pride in doing it well, but he could hardly be expected to be proud of the newspaper; the newspaper he read, *his* newspaper, was not the one he worked for.

Their love for each other? Well, that was nearest it. If this wasn't a centre, what was? Yes, it was around this point, their love, that the whole extraordinary structure revolved. For extraordinary it certainly was. Both Susan and Matthew had moments of thinking so, of looking in secret disbelief at this thing they had created: marriage, four children, big house, garden, charwomen, friends, cars . . . and this *thing*, this entity, all of it had come into existence, been blown into being out of nowhere, because Susan loved Matthew and Matthew loved Susan. Extraordinary. So that was the central point, the wellspring.

And if one felt that it simply was not strong enough, important enough, to support it all, well whose fault was that? Certainly neither Susan's nor Matthew's. It was in the nature of things. And they sensibly blamed neither themselves nor each other.

On the contrary, they used their intelligence to preserve what they had created from a painful and explosive world: they looked around them, and took lessons. All around them, marriages collapsing, or breaking, or rubbing along (even worse, they felt). They must not make the same mistakes, they must not.

They had avoided the pitfall so many of their friends had fallen into—of buying a house in the country *for the sake of the children,* so that the husband became a weekend husband, a weekend father, and the wife always careful not to ask what went on in the town flat which they called (in joke) a bachelor flat. No, Matthew was a full-time husband, a full-time father, and at night, in the big married bed in the big married bedroom (which had an attractive view of the river), they lay beside each other talking and he told her about his day, and what he had done, and whom he had met; and she told him about her day (not as interesting, but that was not her fault), for both knew of the hidden resentments and deprivations of the woman who has lived her own life—and above all, has earned her own living—and is now dependent on a husband for outside interests and money.

Nor did Susan make the mistake of taking a job for the sake of her independence, which she might very well have done, since her old firm, missing her qualities of humour, balance, and sense, invited her often to go back. Children needed their mother to a certain age, that both parents knew and agreed on; and when these four healthy wisely brought up children were of the right age, Susan would work again, because she knew, and so did he, what happened to women of fifty at the height of their energy and ability, with grownup children who no longer needed their full devotion.

So here was this couple, testing their marriage, looking after it, treating it like a small boat full of helpless people in a very stormy sea. Well, of course, so it was. . . . The storms of the world were bad, but not too close—which is not to say they were selfishly felt: Susan and Matthew were both well-informed and responsible people. And the inner storms and quicksands were understood and charted. So everything was all right. Everything was in order. Yes, things were under control.

So what did it matter if they felt dry, flat? People like themselves, fed on a hundred books (psychological, anthropological, sociological), could scarcely be unprepared for the dry, controlled wistfulness which is the distinguishing mark of the intelligent marriage. Two people, endowed with education, with discrimination, with judgement, linked together voluntarily from their will to be happy together and to be of use to others—one sees them everywhere, one knows them, one even is that thing oneself: sadness because so much is after all so little. These two, unsurprised, turned towards each other with even more courtesy and gentle love: this was life, that two people, no matter how carefully chosen, could not be everything to each other. In fact, even to say so, to think in such a way, was banal; they were ashamed to do it.

It was banal, too, when one night Matthew came home late and confessed he had been to a party, taken a girl home and slept with her. Susan forgave him, of course. Except that forgiveness is hardly the word. Understanding, yes. But if you understand something, you don't forgive it, you are the thing itself: forgiveness is for what you *don't* understand. Nor had he *confessed*—what sort of word is that?

The whole thing was not important. After all, years ago they had joked: Of course I'm not going to be faithful to you, no one can be faithful to one other person for a whole lifetime. (And there was the word "faithful"—stupid, all these words, stupid, belonging to a savage old world.) But the incident left both of them irritable. Strange, but they were both bad-tempered, annoyed. There was something unassimilable about it.

Making love splendidly after he had come home that night, both had felt that the idea that Myra Jenkins, a pretty girl met at a party, could be even relevant was ridiculous. They had loved each other for over a decade, would love each other for years more. Who, then, was Myra Jenkins?

Except, thought Susan, unaccountably bad-tempered, she was (is?) the first. In ten years. So either the ten years' fidelity was not important, or she isn't. (No, no, there is something wrong with this way of thinking, there must be.) But if she isn't important, presumably it wasn't important either when Matthew and I first went to bed with each other that afternoon whose delight even now (like a very long shadow at sundown) lays a long, wandlike finger over us. (Why did I say sundown?) Well, if what we felt that afternoon was not important, nothing is important, because if it hadn't been for what we felt, we wouldn't be Mr. and Mrs. Rawlings with four children, et cetera, et cetera. The whole thing is *absurd*—for him to have come home and told me was absurd. For him not to have told me was absurd. For me to care or, for that matter, not to care, is absurd . . . and who is Myra Jenkins? Why, no one at all.

There was only one thing to do, and of course these sensible people did it; they put the thing behind them, and consciously, knowing what they were doing, moved forward into a different phase of their marriage, giving thanks for past good fortune as they did so.

For it was inevitable that the handsome, blond, attractive, manly man, Matthew Rawlings, should be at times tempted (oh, what a word!) by the attractive girls at parties she could not attend because of the four children; and that sometimes he would succumb (a word even more repulsive, if possible) and that she, a goodlooking woman in the big well-tended garden at Richmond, would sometimes be pierced as by an arrow from the sky with bitterness. Except that bitterness was not in order, it was out of court. Did the casual girls touch the marriage? They did not. Rather it was they who knew defeat because of the handsome Matthew Rawlings' marriage body and soul to Susan Rawlings.

In that case why did Susan feel (though luckily not for longer than a few seconds at a time) as if life had become a desert, and that nothing mattered, and that her children were not her own?

Meanwhile her intelligence continued to assert that all was well. What if her Matthew did have an occasional sweet afternoon, the odd affair? For she knew quite well, except in her moments of aridity, that they were very happy, that the affairs were not important.

Perhaps that was the trouble? It was in the nature of things that the adventures and delights could no longer be hers, because of the four children and the big house that needed so much attention. But perhaps she was secretly wishing, and even knowing that she did, that the wildness and the beauty could be his. But he was married to her. She was married to him. They were married inextricably. And therefore the gods could not strike him with the real magic, not really. Well, was it Susan's fault that after he came home from an adventure he looked harassed rather than fulfilled? (In fact, that was how she knew he had been *unfaithful,* because of his sullen air, and his glances at her, similar to hers at him: What is it that I share with this person that shields all delight from me? ) But none of it by anybody's fault. (But what did they feel ought to be somebody's fault?) Nobody's fault, nothing to be at fault, no one to blame, no one to offer or to take it . . . and nothing wrong, either, except that Matthew never was really struck, as he wanted to be, by joy; and that Susan was more and more often threatened by emptiness. (It was usually in the garden that she was invaded by this feeling: she was coming to avoid the garden, unless the children or Matthew were with her.) There was no need to use the dramatic words "unfaithful," "forgive," and the rest: intelligence forbade them. Intelligence barred, too, quarrelling, sulking, anger, silences of withdrawal, accusations and tears. Above all, intelligence forbids tears.

A high price has to be paid for the happy marriage with the four healthy children in the large white gardened house.

And they were paying it, willingly, knowing what they were doing. When they lay side by side or breast to breast in the big civilised bedroom overlooking the wild sullied river, they laughed, often, for no particular reason; but they knew it was really because of these two small people, Susan and Matthew, supporting such an edifice on their intelligent love. The laugh comforted them; it saved them both, though from what, they did not know.

They were now both fortyish. The older children, boy and girl, were ten and eight, at school. The twins, six, were still at home. Susan did not have nurses or girls to help her: childhood is short; and she did not regret the hard work. Often enough she was bored, since small children can be boring; she was often very tired; but she regretted nothing. In another decade, she would turn herself back into being a woman with a life of her own.

Soon the twins would go to school, and they would be away from home from nine until four. These hours, so Susan saw it, would be the preparation for her own slow emancipation away from the role of hub-of-the-family into woman-with-her-own-life. She was already planning for the hours of freedom when all the children would be "off her hands." That was the phrase used by Matthew and by Susan and by their friends, for the moment when the youngest child went off to school. "They'll be off your hands, darling Susan, and you'll have time to yourself." So said Matthew, the intelligent husband, who had often enough commended and consoled Susan, standing by her in spirit during the years when her soul was not her own, as she said, but her children's.

What it amounted to was that Susan saw herself as she had been at twenty-eight, unmarried; and then again somewhere about fifty, blossoming from the root of what she had been twenty years before. As if the essential Susan were in abeyance, as if she were in cold storage. Matthew said something like this to Susan one night: and she agreed that it was true—she did feel something like that. What, then, was this essential Susan? She did not know. Put like that it sounded ridiculous, and she did not really feel it. Anyway, they had a long discussion about the whole thing before going off to sleep in each other's arms.

So the twins went off to their school, two bright affectionate children who had no problems about it, since their older brother and sister had trodden this path so successfully before them. And now Susan was going to be alone in the big house, every day of the school term, except for the daily woman who came in to clean.

It was now, for the first time in this marriage, that something happened which neither of them had foreseen.

This is what happened. She returned, at nine-thirty, from taking the twins to the school by car, looking forward to seven blissful hours of freedom. On the first morning she was simply restless, worrying about the twins "naturally enough" since this was their first day away at school. She was hardly able to contain herself until they came back. Which they did happily, excited by the world of school, looking forward to the next day. And the next day Susan took them, dropped them, came back, and found herself reluctant to enter her big and beautiful home because it was as if something was waiting for her there that she did not wish to confront. Sensibly, however, she parked the car in the garage, entered the house, spoke to Mrs. Parkes, the daily woman, about her duties, and went up to her bedroom. She was possessed by a fever which drove her out again, downstairs, into the kitchen, where Mrs. Parkes was making cake and did not need her, and into the garden. There she sat on a bench and tried to calm herself looking at trees, at a brown glimpse of the river. But she was filled with tension, like a panic: as if an enemy was in the garden with her. She spoke to herself severely, thus: All this is quite natural. First, I spent twelve years of my adult life working, *living my own life*. Then I married, and from the moment I became pregnant for the first time I signed myself over, so to speak, to other people. To the children. Not for one moment in twelve years have I been alone, had time to myself. So now I have to learn to be myself again. That's all.

And she went indoors to help Mrs. Parkes cook and clean, and found some sewing to do for the children. She kept herself occupied every day. At the end of the first term she understood she felt two contrary emotions. First: secret astonishment and dismay that during those weeks when the house was empty of children she had in fact been more occupied (had been careful to keep herself occupied) than ever she had been when the children were around her needing her continual attention. Second: that now she knew the house would be full of them, and for five weeks, she resented the fact she would never be alone. She was already looking back at those hours of sewing, cooking (but by herself) as at a lost freedom which would not be hers for five long weeks. And the two months of term which would succeed the five weeks stretched alluringly open to her—freedom. But what freedom—when in fact she had been so careful *not* to be free of small duties during the last weeks? She looked at herself, Susan Rawlings, sitting in a big chair by the window in the bedroom, sewing shirts or dresses, which she might just as well have bought. She saw herself making cakes for hours at a time in the big family kitchen: yet usually she bought cakes. What she saw was a woman alone, that was true, but she had not felt alone. For instance, Mrs. Parkes was always somewhere in the house. And she did not like being in the garden at all, because of the closeness there of the enemy—irritation, restlessness, emptiness, whatever it was—which keeping her hands occupied made less dangerous for some reason.

Susan did not tell Matthew of these thoughts. They were not sensible. She did not recognise herself in them. What should she say to her dear friend and husband, Matthew? "When I go into the garden, that is, if the children are not there, I feel as if there is an enemy there waiting to invade me." "What enemy, Susan darling?" "Well I don't know, really. . . ." "Perhaps you should see a doctor?"

No, clearly this conversation should not take place. The holidays began and Susan welcomed them. Four children, lively, energetic, intelligent, demanding: she was never, not for a moment of her day, alone. If she was in a room, they would be in the next room, or waiting for her to do something for them; or it would soon be time for lunch or tea, or to take one of them to the dentist. Something to do: five weeks of it, thank goodness.

On the fourth day of these so welcome holidays, she found she was storming with anger at the twins; two shrinking beautiful children who (and this is what checked her) stood hand in hand looking at her with sheer dismayed disbelief. This was their calm mother, shouting at them. And for what? They had come to her with some game, some bit of nonsense. They looked at each other, moved closer for support, and went off hand in hand, leaving Susan holding on to the windowsill of the livingroom, breathing deep, feeling sick. She went to lie down, telling the older children she had a headache. She heard the boy Harry telling the little ones: "It's all right, Mother's got a headache." She heard that *It's all right* with pain.

That night she said to her husband: "Today I shouted at the twins, quite unfairly." She sounded miserable, and he said gently: "Well, what of it?"

"It's more of an adjustment than I thought, their going to school."

"But Susie, Susie darling. . . ." For she was crouched weeping on the bed. He comforted her: "Susan, what is all this about? You shouted at them? What of it? If you shouted at them fifty times a day it wouldn't be more than the little devils deserve." But she wouldn't laugh. She wept. Soon he comforted her with his body. She became calm. Calm, she wondered what was wrong with her, and why she should mind so much that she might, just once, have behaved unjustly with the children. What did it matter? They had forgotten it all long ago: Mother had a headache and everything was all right.

It was a long time later that Susan understood that that night, when she had wept and Matthew had driven the misery out of her with his big solid body, was the last time, ever in their married life, that they had been—to use their mutual language—with each other. And even that was a lie, because she had not told him of her real fears at all.

The five weeks passed, and Susan was in control of herself, and good and kind, and she looked forward to the holidays with a mixture of fear and longing. She did not know what to expect. She took the twins off to school (the elder children took themselves to school) and she returned to the house determined to face the enemy wherever he was, in the house, or the garden or—where?

She was again restless, she was possessed by restlessness. She cooked and sewed and worked as before, day after day, while Mrs. Parkes remonstrated: "Mrs. Rawlings, what's the need for it? I can do that, it's what you pay me for."

And it was so irrational that she checked herself. She would put the car into the garage, go up to her bedroom, and sit, hands in her lap, forcing herself to be quiet. She listened to Mrs. Parkes moving around the house. She looked out into the garden and saw the branches shake the trees. She sat defeating the enemy, restlessness. Emptiness. She ought to be thinking about her life, about herself. But she did not. Or perhaps she could not. As soon as she forced her mind to think about Susan (for what else did she want to be alone for?), it skipped off to thoughts of butter or school clothes. Or it thought of Mrs. Parkes. She realised that she sat listening for the movements of the cleaning woman, following her every turn, bend, thought. She followed her in her mind from kitchen to bathroom, from table to oven, and it was as if the duster, the cleaning cloth, the saucepan, were in her own hand. She would hear herself saying: No, not like that, don't put that there. . . . Yet she did not give a damn what Mrs. Parkes did, or if she did it at all. Yet she could not prevent herself from being conscious of her, every minute. Yes, this was what was wrong with her: she needed, when she was alone, to be really alone, with no one near. She could not endure the knowledge that in ten minutes or in half an hour Mrs. Parkes would call up the stairs: "Mrs. Rawlings, there's no silver polish. Madam, we're out of flour."

So she left the house and went to sit in the garden where she was screened from the house by trees. She waited for the demon to appear and claim her, but he did not.

She was keeping him off, because she had not, after all, come to an end of arranging herself.

She was planning how to be somewhere where Mrs. Parkes would not come after her with a cup of tea, or a demand to be allowed to telephone (always irritating, since Susan did not care who she telephoned or how often), or just a nice talk about something. Yes, she needed a place, or a state of affairs, where it would not be necessary to keep reminding herself: In ten minutes I must telephone Matthew about . . . and at half past three I must leave early for the children because the car needs cleaning. And at ten o'clock tomorrow I must remember. . . . She was possessed with resentment that the seven hours of freedom in every day (during weekdays in the school term) were not free, that never, not for one second, ever, was she free from the pressure of time, from having to remember this or that. She could never forget herself; never really let herself go into forgetfulness.

Resentment. It was poisoning her. (She looked at this emotion and thought it was absurd. Yet she felt it.) She was a prisoner. (She looked at this thought too, and it was no good telling herself it was a ridiculous one.) She must tell Matthew—but what? She was filled with emotions that were utterly ridiculous, that she despised, yet that nevertheless she was feeling so strongly she could not shake them off.

The school holidays came round, and this time they were for nearly two months, and she behaved with a conscious controlled decency that nearly drove her crazy. She would lock herself in the bathroom, and sit on the edge of the bath, breathing deep, trying to let go into some kind of calm. Or she went up into the spare room, usually empty, where no one would expect her to be. She heard the children calling "Mother, Mother," and kept silent, feeling guilty. Or she went to the very end of the garden, by herself, and looked at the slow-moving brown river; she looked at the river and closed her eyes and breathed slow and deep, taking it into her being, into her veins.

Then she returned to the family, wife and mother, smiling and responsible, feeling as if the pressure of these people—four lively children and her husband—were a painful pressure on the surface of her skin, a hand pressing on her brain. She did not once break down into irritation during these holidays, but it was like living out a prison sentence, and when the children went back to school, she sat on a white stone near the flowing river, and she thought: It is not even a year since the twins went to school, since *they were off my hands* (What on earth did I think I meant when I used that stupid phrase?), and yet I'm a different person. I'm simply not myself. I don't understand it.

Yet she had to understand it. For she knew that this structure—big white house, on which the mortgage still cost four hundred a year, a husband, so good and kind and insightful; four children, all doing so nicely; and the garden where she sat; and Mrs. Parkes, the cleaning woman—all this depended on her, and yet she could not understand why, or even what it was she contributed to it.

She said to Matthew in their bedroom: "I think there must be something wrong with me."

And he said: "Surely not, Susan? You look marvellous—you're as lovely as ever."

She looked at the handsome blond man, with his clear, intelligent, blue-eyed face, and thought: Why is it I can't tell him? Why not? And she said: "I need to be alone more than I am."

At which he swung his slow blue gaze at her, and she saw what she had been dreading: Incredulity. Disbelief. And fear. An incredulous blue stare from a stranger who was her husband, as close to her as her own breath.

He said: "But the children are at school and off your hands."

She said to herself: I've got to force myself to say: Yes, but do you realize that I never feel free? There's never a moment I can say to myself: There's nothing I have to remind myself about, nothing I have to do in half an hour, or an hour, or two hours. . . .

But she said: "I don't feel well."

He said: "Perhaps you need a holiday."

She said, appalled: "But not without you, surely?" For she could not imagine herself going off without him. Yet that was what he meant. Seeing her face, he laughed, and opened his arms, and she went into them, thinking: Yes, yes, but why can't I say it? And what is it I have to say?

She tried to tell him, about never being free. And he listened and said: "But Susan, what sort of freedom can you possibly want—short of being dead! Am I ever free? I go to the office, and I have to be there at ten—all right, half past ten, sometimes. And I have to do this or that, don't I? Then I've got to come home at a certain time—I don't mean it, you know I don't—but if I'm not going to be back home at six I telephone you. When can I ever say to myself: I have nothing to be responsible for in the next six hours?"

Susan, hearing this, was remorseful. Because it was true. The good marriage, the house, the children, depended just as much on his voluntary bondage as it did on hers. But why did he not feel bound? Why didn't he chafe and become restless? No, there was something really wrong with her and this proved it.

And that word "bondage"—why had she used it? She had never felt marriage, or the children, as bondage. Neither had he, or surely they wouldn't be together lying in each other's arms content after twelve years of marriage.

No, her state (whatever it was) was irrelevant, nothing to do with her real good life with her family. She had to accept the fact that, after all, she was an irrational person and to live with it. Some people had to live with crippled arms, or stammers, or being deaf. She would have to live knowing she was subject to a state of mind she could not own.

Nevertheless, as a result of this conversation with her husband, there was a new regime next holidays.

The spare room at the top of the house now had a cardboard sign saying: PRIVATE! DO NOT DISTURB! on it. (This sign had been drawn in coloured chalks by the children, after a discussion between the parents in which it was decided this was psychologically the right thing.) The family and Mrs. Parkes knew this was "Mother's Room" and that she was entitled to her privacy. Many serious conversations took place between Matthew and the children about not taking Mother for granted. Susan overheard the first, between father and Harry, the older boy, and was surprised at her irritation over it. Surely she could have a room somewhere in that big house and retire into it without such a fuss being made? Without it being so solemnly discussed?

Why couldn't she simply have announced: "I'm going to fit out the little top room for myself, and when I'm in it I'm not to be disturbed for anything short of fire"? Just that, and finished; instead of long earnest discussions. When she heard Harry and Matthew explaining it to the twins with Mrs. Parkes coming in—"Yes, well, a family sometimes gets on top of a woman"—she had to go right away to the bottom of the garden until the devils of exasperation had finished their dance in her blood.

But now there was a room, and she could go there when she liked, she used it seldom: she felt even more caged there than in her bedroom. One day she had gone up there after a lunch for ten children she had cooked and served because Mrs. Parkes was not there, and had sat alone for a while looking into the garden. She saw the children stream out from the kitchen and stand looking up at the window where she sat behind the curtains. They were all—her children and their friends—discussing Mother's Room. A few minutes later, the chase of children in some game came pounding up the stairs, but ended as abruptly as if they had fallen over a ravine, so sudden was the silence. They had remembered she was there, and had gone silent in a great gale of "Hush! Shhhhhh! Quiet, you'll disturb her. . . ." And they went tiptoeing downstairs like criminal conspirators. When she came down to make tea for them, they all apologised. The twins put their arms around her, from front and back, making a human cage of loving limbs, and promised it would never occur again. "We forgot, Mummy, we forgot all about it!"

What it amounted to was that Mother's Room, and her need for privacy, had become a valuable lesson in respect for other people's rights. Quite soon Susan was going up to the room only because it was a lesson it was a pity to drop. Then she took sewing up there, and the children and Mrs. Parkes came in and out: it had become another family room.

She sighed, and smiled, and resigned herself—she made jokes at her own expense with Matthew over the room. That is, she did from the self she liked, she respected. But at the same time, something inside her howled with impatience, with rage. . . . And she was frightened. One day she found herself kneeling by her bed and praying: "Dear God, keep it away from me, keep him away from me." She meant the devil, for she now thought of it, not caring if she was irrational, as some sort of demon. She imagined him, or it, as a youngish man, or perhaps a middleaged man pretending to be young. Or a man young-looking from immaturity? At any rate, she saw the young-looking face which, when she drew closer, had dry lines about mouth and eyes. He was thinnish, meagre in build. And he had a reddish complexion, and ginger hair. That was he—a gingery, energetic man, and he wore a reddish hairy jacket, unpleasant to the touch.

Well, one day she saw him. She was standing at the bottom of the garden, watching the river ebb past, when she raised her eyes and saw this person, or being, sitting on the white stone bench. He was looking at her, and grinning. In his hand was a long crooked stick, which he had picked off the ground, or broken off the tree above him. He was absent-mindedly, out of an absent-minded or freakish impulse of spite, using the stick to stir around in the coils of a blindworm or a grass snake (or some kind of snakelike creature: it was whitish and unhealthy to look at, unpleasant). The snake was twisting about, flinging its coils from side to side in a kind of dance of protest against the teasing prodding stick.

Susan looked at him, thinking: Who is the stranger? What is he doing in our garden? Then she recognised the man around whom her terrors had crystallised. As she did so, he vanished. She made herself walk over to the bench. A shadow from a branch lay across thin emerald grass, moving jerkily over its roughness, and she could see why she had taken it for a snake, lashing and twisting. She went back to the house thinking: Right, then, so I've seen him with my own eyes, so I'm not crazy after all— there *is* a danger because I've seen him. He is lurking in the garden and sometimes even in the house, and he wants to *get into me and to take me over.*

She dreamed of having a room or a place, anywhere, where she could go and sit, by herself, no one knowing where she was.

Once, near Victoria, she found herself outside a news agent that had Rooms to Let advertised. She decided to rent a room, telling no one. Sometimes she could take the train in to Richmond and sit alone in it for an hour or two. Yet how could she? A room would cost three or four pounds a week, and she earned no money, and how could she explain to Matthew that she needed such a sum? What for? It did not occur to her that she was taking it for granted she wasn't going to tell him about the room.

Well, it was out of the question, having a room; yet she knew she must.

One day, when a school term was well established, and none of the children had measles or other ailments, and everything seemed in order, she did the shopping early, explained to Mrs. Parkes she was meeting an old school friend, took the train to Victoria, searched until she found a small quiet hotel, and asked for a room for the day. They did not let rooms by the day, the manageress said, looking doubtful, since Susan so obviously was not the kind of woman who needed a room for unrespectable reasons. Susan made a long explanation about not being well, being unable to shop without frequent rests for lying down. At last she was allowed to rent the room provided she paid a full night's price for it. She was taken up by the manageress and a maid, both concerned over the state of her health . . . which must be pretty bad if, living at Richmond (she had signed her name and address in the register), she needed a shelter at Victoria.

The room was ordinary and anonymous, and was just what Susan needed. She put a shilling in the gas fire, and sat, eyes shut, in a dingy armchair with her back to a dingy window. She was alone. She was alone. She was alone. She could feel pressures lifting off her. First the sounds of traffic came very loud; then they seemed to vanish; she might even have slept a little. A knock on the door: it was Miss Townsend, the manageress, bringing her a cup of tea with her own hands, so concerned was she over Susan's long silence and possible illness.

Miss Townsend was a lonely woman of fifty, running this hotel with all the rectitude expected of her, and she sensed in Susan the possibility of understanding companionship. She stayed to talk. Susan found herself in the middle of a fantastic story about her illness, which got more and more impossible as she tried to make it tally with the large house at Richmond, well-off husband, and four children. Suppose she said instead: Miss Townsend, I'm here in your hotel because I need to be alone for a few hours, above all *alone and with no one knowing where I am.* She said it mentally, and saw, mentally, the look that would inevitably come on Miss Townsend's elderly maiden's face. "Miss Townsend, my four children and my husband are driving me insane, do you understand that? Yes, I can see from the gleam of hysteria in your eyes that comes from loneliness controlled but only just contained that I've got everything in the world you've ever longed for. Well, Miss Townsend, I don't want any of it. You can have it, Miss Townsend. I wish I was absolutely alone in the world, like you. Miss Townsend, I'm besieged by seven devils, Miss Townsend, Miss Townsend, let me stay here in your hotel where the devils can't get me. . . ." Instead of saying all this, she described her anaemia, agreed to try Miss Townsend's remedy for it, which was raw liver, minced, between whole-meal bread, and said yes, perhaps it would be better if she stayed at home and let a friend do shopping for her. She paid her bill and left the hotel, defeated.

At home Mrs. Parkes said she didn't really like it, no, not really, when Mrs. Rawlings was away from nine in the morning until five. The teacher had telephoned from school to say Joan's teeth were paining her, and she hadn't known what to say; and what was she to make for the children's tea, Mrs. Rawlings hadn't said.

All this was nonsense, of course. Mrs. Parkes's complaint was that Susan had withdrawn herself spiritually, leaving the burden of the big house on her.

Susan looked back at her day of "freedom" which had resulted in her becoming a friend of the lonely Miss Townsend, and in Mrs. Parkes's remonstrances. Yet she remembered the short blissful hour of being alone, really alone. She was determined to arrange her life, no matter what it cost, so that she could have that solitude more often. An absolute solitude, where no one knew her or cared about her.

But how? She thought of saying to her old employer: I want you to back me up in a story with Matthew that I am doing part-time work for you. The truth is that . . . But she would have to tell him a lie too, and which lie? She could not say: I want to sit by myself three or four times a week in a rented room. And besides, he knew Matthew, and she could not really ask him to tell lies on her behalf, apart from being bound to think it meant a lover.

Suppose she really took a part-time job, which she could get through fast and efficiently, leaving time for herself. What job? Addressing envelopes? Canvassing?

And there was Mrs. Parkes, working widow, who knew exactly what she was prepared to give to the house, who knew by instinct when her mistress withdrew in spirit from her responsibilities. Mrs. Parkes was one of the servers of this world, but she needed someone to serve. She had to have Mrs. Rawlings, her madam, at the top of the house or in the garden, so that she could come and get support from her: "Yes, the bread's not what it was when I was a girl. . . . Yes, Harry's got a wonderful appetite, I wonder where he puts it all. . . . Yes, it's lucky the twins are so much of a size, they can wear each other's shoes, that's a saving in these hard times. . . . Yes, the cherry jam from Switzerland is not a patch on the jam from Poland, and three times the price . . ." And so on. That sort of talk Mrs. Parkes must have, every day, or she would leave, not knowing herself why she left.

Susan Rawlings, thinking these thoughts, found that she was prowling through the great thicketed garden like a wild cat: she was walking up the stairs, down the stairs, through the rooms into the garden, along the brown running river, back, up through the house, down again. . . . It was a wonder Mrs. Parkes did not think it strange. But, on the contrary, Mrs. Rawlings could do what she liked, she could stand on her head if she wanted, provided she was *there*. Susan Rawlings prowled and muttered through her house, hating Mrs. Parkes, hating poor Miss Townsend, dreaming of her hour of solitude in the dingy respectability of Miss Townsend's hotel bedroom, and she knew quite well she was mad. Yes, she was mad.

She said to Matthew that she must have a holiday. Matthew agreed with her. This was not as things had been once—how they had talked in each other's arms in the marriage bed. He had, she knew, diagnosed her finally as *unreasonable*. She had become someone outside himself that he had to manage. They were living side by side in this house like two tolerably friendly strangers.

Having told Mrs. Parkes—or rather, asked for her permission—she went off on a walking holiday in Wales. She chose the remotest place she knew of. Every morning the children telephoned her before they went off to school, to encourage and support her, just as they had over Mother's Room. Every evening she telephoned them, spoke to each child in turn, and then to Matthew. Mrs. Parkes, given permission to telephone for instructions or advice, did so every day at lunchtime. When, as happened three times, Mrs. Rawlings was out on the mountainside, Mrs. Parkes asked that she should ring back at such-and-such a time, for she would not be happy in what she was doing without Mrs. Rawlings' blessing.

Susan prowled over wild country with the telephone wire holding her to her duty like a leash. The next time she must telephone, or wait to be telephoned, nailed her to her cross. The mountains themselves seemed trammelled by her unfreedom. Everywhere on the mountains, where she met no one at all, from breakfast time to dusk, excepting sheep, or a shepherd, she came face to face with her own craziness, which might attack her in the broadest valleys, so that they seemed too small, or on a mountain top from which she could see a hundred other mountains and valleys, so that they seemed too low, too small, with the sky pressing down too close. She would stand gazing at a hillside brilliant with ferns and bracken, jewelled with running water, and see nothing but her devil, who lifted inhuman eyes at her from where he leaned negligently on a rock, switching at his ugly yellow boots with a leafy twig.

She returned to her home and family, with the Welsh emptiness at the back of her mind like a promise of freedom.

She told her husband she wanted to have an *au pair* girl.

They were in their bedroom, it was late at night, the children slept. He sat, shirted and slippered, in a chair by the window, looking out. She sat brushing her hair and watching him in the mirror. A time-hallowed scene in the connubial bedroom. He said nothing, while she heard the arguments coming into his mind, only to be rejected because every one was *reasonable*.

"It seems strange to get one now; after all, the children are in school most of the day. Surely the time for you to have help was when you were stuck with them day and night. Why don't you ask Mrs. Parkes to cook for you? She's even offered to—I can understand if you are tired of cooking for six people. But you know that an *au pair* girl means all kinds of problems; it's not like having an ordinary char in during the day. . . ."

Finally he said carefully: "Are you thinking of going back to work?"

"No," she said, "no, not really." She made herself sound vague, rather stupid. She went on brushing her black hair and peering at herself so as to be oblivious of the short uneasy glances her Matthew kept giving her. "Do you think we can't afford it?" she went on vaguely, not at all the old efficient Susan who knew exactly what they could afford.

"It's not that," he said, looking out of the window at dark trees, so as not to look at her. Meanwhile she examined a round, candid, pleasant face with clear dark brows and clear grey eyes. A sensible face. She brushed thick healthy black hair and thought: Yet that's the reflection of a madwoman. How very strange! Much more to the point if what looked back at me was the gingery green-eyed demon with his dry meagre smile. . . . Why wasn't Matthew agreeing? After all, what else could he do? She was breaking her part of the bargain and there was no way of forcing her to keep it: that her spirit, her soul, should live in this house, so that the people in it could grow like plants in water, and Mrs. Parkes remain content in their service. In return for this, he would be a good loving husband, and responsible towards the children. Well, nothing like this had been true of either of them for a long time. He did his duty, perfunctorily; she did not even pretend to do hers. And he had become like other husbands, with his real life in his work and the people he met there, and very likely a serious affair. All this was her fault.

At last he drew heavy curtains, blotting out the trees, and turned to force her attention: "Susan, are you really sure we need a girl?" But she would not meet his appeal at all. She was running the brush over her hair again and again, lifting fine black clouds in a small hiss of electricity. She was peering in and smiling as if she were amused at the clinging hissing hair that followed the brush.

"Yes, I think it would be a good idea, on the whole," she said, with the cunning of a madwoman evading the real point.

In the mirror she could see her Matthew lying on his back, his hands behind his head, staring upwards, his face sad and hard. She felt her heart (the old heart of Susan Rawlings) soften and call out to him. But she set it to be indifferent.

He said: "Susan, the children?" It was an appeal that *almost* reached her. He opened his arms, lifting them palms up, empty. She had only to run across and fling herself into them, onto his hard, warm chest, and melt into herself, into Susan. But she could not. She would not see his lifted arms. She said vaguely: "Well, surely it'll be even better for them? We'll get a French or a German girl and they'll learn the language."

In the dark she lay beside him, feeling frozen, a stranger. She felt as if Susan had been spirited away. She disliked very much this woman who lay here, cold and indifferent beside a suffering man, but she could not change her.

Next morning she set about getting a girl, and very soon came Sophie Traub from Hamburg, a girl of twenty, laughing, healthy, blue-eyed, intending to learn English. Indeed, she already spoke a good deal. In return for a room—"Mother's Room"—and her food, she undertook to do some light cooking, and to be with the children when Mrs. Rawlings asked. She was an intelligent girl and understood perfectly what was needed. Susan said: "I go off sometimes, for the morning or for the day—well, sometimes the children run home from school, or they ring up, or a teacher rings up. I should be here, really. And there's the daily woman. . . ." And Sophie laughed her deep fruity *Fräulein's* laugh, showed her fine white teeth and her dimples, and said: "You want some person to play mistress of the house sometimes, not so?"

"Yes, that is just so," said Susan, a bit dry, despite herself, thinking in secret fear how easy it was, how much nearer to the end she was than she thought. Healthy Fräulein Traub's instant understanding of their position proved this to be true.

The *au pair* girl, because of her own commonsense, or (as Susan said to herself, with her new inward shudder) because she had been *chosen* so well by Susan, was a success with everyone, the children liking her, Mrs. Parkes forgetting almost at once that she was German, and Matthew finding her "nice to have around the house." For he was now taking things as they came, from the surface of life, withdrawn both as a husband and a father from the household.

One day Susan saw how Sophie and Mrs. Parkes were talking and laughing in the kitchen, and she announced that she would be away until tea time. She knew exactly where to go and what she must look for. She took the District Line to South Kensington, changed to the Circle, got off at Paddington, and walked around looking at the smaller hotels until she was satisfied with one which had FRED'S HOTEL painted on windowpanes that needed cleaning. The facade was a faded shiny yellow, like unhealthy skin. A door at the end of a passage said she must knock; she did, and Fred appeared. He was not at all attractive, not in any way, being fattish, and run-down, and wearing a tasteless striped suit. He had small sharp eyes in a white creased face, and was quite prepared to let Mrs. Jones (she chose the farcical name deliberately, staring him out) have a room three days a week from ten until six. Provided of course that she paid in advance each time she came? Susan produced fifteen shillings (no price had been set by him) and held it out, still fixing him with a bold unblinking challenge she had not known until then she could use at will. Looking at her still, he took up a ten-shilling note from her palm between thumb and forefinger, fingered it; then shuffled up two half-crowns, held out his own palm with these bits of money displayed thereon, and let his gaze lower broodingly at them. They were standing in the passage, a red-shaded light above, bare boards beneath, and a strong smell of floor polish rising about them. He shot his gaze up at her over the still-extended palm, and smiled as if to say: What do you take me for? "I shan't," said Susan, "be using this room for the purposes of making money." He still waited. She added another five shillings, at which he nodded and said: "You pay, and I ask no questions." "Good," said Susan. He now went past her to the stairs, and there waited a moment: the light from the street door being in her eyes, she lost sight of him momentarily. Then she saw a sober-suited, white-faced, white-balding little man trotting up the stairs like a waiter, and she went after him. They proceeded in utter silence up the stairs of this house where no questions were asked—Fred's Hotel, which could afford the freedom for its visitors that poor Miss Townsend's hotel could not. The room was hideous. It had a single window, with thin green brocade curtains, a three-quarter bed that had a cheap green satin bedspread on it, a fireplace with a gas fire and a shilling meter by it, a chest of drawers, and a green wicker armchair.

"Thank you," said Susan, knowing that Fred (if this was Fred, and not George, or Herbert or Charlie) was looking at her, not so much with curiosity, an emotion he would not own to, for professional reasons, but with a philosophical sense of what was appropriate. Having taken her money and shown her up and agreed to everything, he was clearly disapproving of her for coming here. She did not belong here at all, so his look said. (But she knew, already, how very much she did belong: the room had been waiting for her to join it.) "Would you have me called at five o'clock, please?" and he nodded and went downstairs.

It was twelve in the morning. She was free. She sat in the armchair, she simply sat, she closed her eyes and sat and let herself be alone. She was alone and no one knew where she was. When a knock came on the door she was annoyed, and prepared to show it: but it was Fred himself; it was five o'clock and he was calling her as ordered. He flicked his sharp little eyes over the room—bed, first. It was undisturbed. She might never have been in the room at all. She thanked him, said she would be returning the day after tomorrow, and left. She was back home in time to cook supper, to put the children to bed, to cook a second supper for her husband and herself later. And to welcome Sophie back from the pictures where she had gone with a friend. All these things she did cheerfully, willingly. But she was thinking all the time of the hotel room; she was longing for it with her whole being.

Three times a week. She arrived promptly at ten, looked Fred in the eyes, gave him twenty shillings, followed him up the stairs, went into the room, and shut the door on him with gentle firmness. For Fred, disapproving of her being here at all, was quite ready to let friendship, or at least acquaintanceship, follow his disapproval, if only she would let him. But he was content to go off on her dismissing nod, with the twenty shillings in his hand.

She sat in the armchair and shut her eyes.

What did she *do* in the room? Why, nothing at all. From the chair, when it had rested her, she went to the window, stretching her arms, smiling, treasuring her anonymity, to look out. She was no longer Susan Rawlings, mother of four, wife of Matthew, employer of Mrs. Parkes and of Sophie Traub, with these and those relations with friends, school-teachers, tradesmen. She no longer was mistress of the big white house and garden, owning clothes suitable for this and that activity or occasion. She was Mrs. Jones, and she was alone, and she had no past and no future. Here I am, she thought, after all these years of being married and having children and playing those roles of responsibility—and I'm just the same. Yet there have been times I thought that nothing existed of me except the roles that went with being Mrs. Matthew Rawlings. Yes, here I am, and if I never saw any of my family again, here I would still be . . . how very strange that is! And she leaned on the sill, and looked into the street, loving the men and women who passed, because she did not know them.

She looked at the downtrodden buildings over the street, and at the sky, wet and dingy, or sometimes blue, and she felt she had never seen buildings or sky before. And then she went back to the chair, empty, her mind a blank. Sometimes she talked aloud, saying nothing—an exclamation, meaningless, followed by a comment about the floral pattern on the thin rug, or a stain on the green satin coverlet. For the most part, she wool-gathered—what word is there for it?—brooded, wandered, simply went dark, feeling emptiness run deliciously through her veins like the movement of her blood.

This room had become more her own than the house she lived in. One morning she found Fred taking her a flight higher than usual. She stopped, refusing to go up, and demanded her usual room, Number 19. "Well, you'll have to wait half an hour, then," he said. Willingly she descended to the dark disinfectant-smelling hall, and sat waiting until the two, man and woman, came down the stairs, giving her swift indifferent glances before they hurried out into the street, separating at the door. She went up to the room, *her* room, which they had just vacated. It was no less hers, though the windows were set wide open, and a maid was straightening the bed as she came in.

After these days of solitude, it was both easy to play her part as mother and wife, and difficult—because it was so easy: she felt an imposter. She felt as if her shell moved here, with her family, answering to Mummy, Mother, Susan, Mrs. Rawlings. She was surprised no one saw through her, that she wasn't turned out of doors, as a fake. On the contrary, it seemed the children loved her more; Matthew and she "got on" pleasantly, and Mrs. Parkes was happy in her work under (for the most part, it must be confessed) Sophie Traub. At night she lay beside her husband, and they made love again, apparently just as they used to, when they were really married. But she, Susan, or the being who answered so readily and improbably to the name of Susan, was not there: she was in Fred's Hotel, in Paddington, waiting for the easing hours of solitude to begin.

Soon she made a new arrangement with Fred and with Sophie. It was for five days a week. As for the money, five pounds, she simply asked Matthew for it. She saw that she was not even frightened he might ask what for: he would give it to her, she knew that, and yet it was terrifying it could be so, for this close couple, these partners, had once known the destination of every shilling they must spend. He agreed to give her five pounds a week. She asked for just so much, not a penny more. He sounded indifferent about it. It was as if he were paying her, she thought: *paying her off*—yes, that was it. Terror came back for a moment when she understood this, but she stilled it: things had gone too far for that. Now, every week, on Sunday nights, he gave her five pounds, turning away from her before their eyes could meet on the transaction. As for Sophie Traub, she was to be somewhere in or near the house until six at night, after which she was free. She was not to cook, or to clean; she was simply to be there. So she gardened or sewed, and asked friends in, being a person who was bound to have a lot of friends. If the children were sick, she nursed them. If teachers telephoned, she answered them sensibly. For the five daytimes in the school week, she was altogether the mistress of the house.

One night in the bedroom, Matthew asked: "Susan, I don't want to interfere—don't think that, please—but are you sure you are well?"

She was brushing her hair at the mirror. She made two more strokes on either side of her head, before she replied: "Yes, dear, I am sure I am well."

He was again lying on his back, his blond head on his hands, his elbows angled up and part-concealing his face. He said: "Then Susan, I have to ask you this question, though you must understand, I'm not putting any sort of pressure on you." (Susan heard the word "pressure" with dismay, because this was inevitable; of course she could not go on like this.) "Are things going to go on like this?"

"Well," she said, going vague and bright and idiotic again, so as to escape: "Well, I don't see why not."

He was jerking his elbows up and down, in annoyance or in pain, and, looking at him, she saw he had got thin, even gaunt; and restless angry movements were not what she remembered of him. He said: "Do you want a divorce, is that it?"

At this, Susan only with the greatest difficulty stopped herself from laughing: she could hear the bright bubbling laughter she *would* have emitted, had she let herself. He could only mean one thing: she had a lover, and that was why she spent her days in London, as lost to him as if she had vanished to another continent.

Then the small panic set in again: she understood that he hoped she did have a lover, he was begging her to say so, because otherwise it would be too terrifying.

She thought this out as she brushed her hair, watching the fine black stuff fly up to make its little clouds of electricity, hiss, hiss, hiss. Behind her head, across the room, was a blue wall. She realised she was absorbed in watching the black hair making shapes against the blue. She should be answering him. "Do *you* want a divorce, Matthew?"

He said: "That surely isn't the point, is it?"

"You brought it up, I didn't," she said, brightly, suppressing meaningless tinkling laughter.

Next day she asked Fred: "Have enquiries been made for me?"

He hesitated, and she said: "I've been coming here a year now. I've made no trouble, and you've been paid every day. I have a right to be told."

"As a matter of fact, Mrs. Jones, a man did come asking."

"A man from a detective agency?"

"Well, he could have been, couldn't he?"

"I was asking you. . . . Well, what did you tell him?"

"I told him a Mrs. Jones came every weekday from ten until five or six and stayed in Number 19 by herself."

"Describing me?"

"Well, Mrs. Jones, I had no alternative. Put yourself in my place."

"By rights I should deduct what that man gave you for the information."

He raised shocked eyes: she was not the sort of person to make jokes like this! Then he chose to laugh: a pinkish wet slit appeared across his white crinkled face; his eyes positively begged her to laugh, otherwise he might lose some money. She remained grave, looking at him.

He stopped laughing and said: "You want to go up now?"—returning to the familiarity, the comradeship, of the country where no questions are asked, on which (and he knew it) she depended completely.

She went up to sit in her wicker chair. But it was not the same. Her husband had searched her out. (The world had searched her out.) The pressures were on her. She was here with his connivance. He might walk in at any moment, here, into Room 19. She imagined the report from the detective agency: "A woman calling herself Mrs. Jones, fitting the description of your wife (et cetera, et cetera, et cetera), stays alone all day in Room No. 19. She insists on this room, waits for it if it is engaged. As far as the proprietor knows, she receives no visitors there, male or female." A report something on these lines Matthew must have received.

Well, of course he was right: things couldn't go on like this. He had put an end to it all simply by sending the detective after her.

She tried to shrink herself back into the shelter of the room, a snail pecked out of its shell and trying to squirm back. But the peace of the room had gone. She was trying consciously to revive it, trying to let go into the dark creative trance (or whatever it was) that she had found there. It was no use, yet she craved for it, she was as ill as a suddenly deprived addict.

Several times she returned to the room, to look for herself there, but instead she found the unnamed spirit of restlessness, a pricking fevered hunger for movement, an irritable self-consciousness that made her brain feel as if it had coloured lights going on and off inside it. Instead of the soft dark that had been the room's air, were now waiting for her demons that made her dash blindly about, muttering words of hate; she was impelling herself from point to point like a moth dashing itself against a windowpane, sliding to the bottom, fluttering off on broken wings, then crashing into the invisible barrier again. And again and again. Soon she was exhausted, and she told Fred that for a while she would not be needing the room, she was going on holiday. Home she went, to the big white house by the river. The middle of a weekday, and she felt guilty at returning to her own home when not expected. She stood unseen, looking in at the kitchen window. Mrs. Parkes, wearing a discarded floral overall of Susan's, was stooping to slide something into the oven. Sophie, arms folded, was leaning her back against a cupboard and laughing at some joke made by a girl not seen before by Susan—a dark foreign girl, Sophie's visitor. In an armchair Molly, one of the twins, lay curled, sucking her thumb and watching the grownups. She must have some sickness, to be kept from school. The child's listless face, the dark circles under her eyes, hurt Susan: Molly was looking at the three grownups working and talking in exactly the same way Susan looked at the four through the kitchen window: she was remote, shut off from them.

But then, just as Susan imagined herself going in, picking up the little girl, and sitting in an armchair with her, stroking her probably heated forehead, Sophie did just that: she had been standing on one leg, the other knee flexed, its foot set against the wall. Now she let her foot in its ribbon-tied red shoe slide down the wall, stood solid on two feet, clapping her hands before and behind her, and sang a couple of lines in German, so that the child lifted her heavy eyes at her and began to smile. Then she walked, or rather skipped, over to the child, swung her up, and let her fall into her lap at the same moment she sat herself. She said "Hopla! Hopla! Molly . . ." and began stroking the dark untidy young head that Molly laid on her shoulder for comfort.

*Well*. . . . Susan blinked the tears of farewell out of her eyes, and went quietly up through the house to her bedroom. There she sat looking at the river through the trees. She felt at peace, but in a way that was new to her. She had no desire to move, to talk, to do anything at all. The devils that had haunted the house, the garden, were not there; but she knew it was because her soul was in Room 19 in Fred's Hotel; she was not really here at all. It was a sensation that should have been frightening: to sit at her own bedroom window, listening to Sophie's rich young voice sing German nursery songs to her child, listening to Mrs. Parkes clatter and move below, and to know that all this had nothing to do with her: she was already out of it.

Later, she made herself go down and say she was home: it was unfair to be here unannounced. She took lunch with Mrs. Parkes, Sophie, Sophie's Italian friend Maria, and her daughter Molly, and felt like a visitor.

A few days later, at bedtime, Matthew said: "Here's your five pounds," and pushed them over at her. Yet he must have known she had not been leaving the house at all.

She shook her head, gave it back to him, and said, in explanation, not in accusation: "As soon as you knew where I was, there was no point."

He nodded, not looking at her. He was turned away from her: thinking, she knew, how best to handle this wife who terrified him.

He said: "I wasn't trying to . . . It's just that I was worried."

"Yes, I know."

"I must confess that I was beginning to wonder . . ."

"You thought I had a lover?"

"Yes, I am afraid I did."

She knew that he wished she had. She sat wondering how to say: "For a year now I've been spending all my days in a very sordid hotel room. It's the place where I'm happy. In fact, without it I don't exist." She heard herself saying this, and understood how terrified he was that she might. So instead she said: "Well, perhaps you're not far wrong."

Probably Matthew would think the hotel proprietor lied: he would want to think so.

"Well," he said, and she could hear his voice spring up, so to speak, with relief, "in that case I must confess I've got a bit of an affair on myself."

She said, detached and interested: "Really? Who is she?" and saw Matthew's startled look because of this reaction.

"It's Phil. Phil Hunt."

She had known Phil Hunt well in the old unmarried days. She was thinking: No, she won't do, she's too neurotic and difficult. She's never been happy yet. Sophie's much better. Well, Matthew will see that himself, as sensible as he is.

This line of thought went on in silence, while she said aloud: "It's no point telling you about mine, because you don't know him."

Quick, quick, invent, she thought. Remember how you invented all that nonsense for Miss Townsend.

She began slowly, careful not to contradict herself: "His name is Michael" (*Michael What?*)—"Michael Plant." (What a silly name!) "He's rather like you— in looks, I mean." And indeed, she could imagine herself being touched by no one but Matthew himself. "He's a publisher." (Really? Why?) "He's got a wife already and two children."

She brought out this fantasy, proud of herself.

Matthew said: "Are you two thinking of marrying?"

She said, before she could stop herself: "Good God, *no!*"

She realised, if Matthew wanted to marry Phil Hunt, that this was too emphatic, but apparently it was all right, for his voice sounded relieved as he said: "It is a bit impossible to imagine oneself married to anyone else, isn't it?" With which he pulled her to him, so that her head lay on his shoulder. She turned her face into the dark of his flesh, and listened to the blood pounding through her ears saying: I am alone, I am alone, I am alone.

In the morning Susan lay in bed while he dressed.

He had been thinking things out in the night, because now he said: "Susan, why don't we make a foursome?"

Of course, she said to herself, of course he would be bound to say that. If one is sensible, if one is reasonable, if one never allows oneself a base thought or an envious emotion, naturally one says: Let's make a foursome!

"Why not?" she said.

"We could all meet for lunch. I mean, it's ridiculous, you sneaking off to filthy hotels, and me staying late at the office, and all the lies everyone has to tell."

What on earth did I say his name was?—she panicked, then said: "I think it's a good idea, but Michael is away at the moment. When he comes back, though—and I'm sure you two would like each other."

"He's away, is he? So that's why you've been . . ." Her husband put his hand to the knot of his tie in a gesture of male coquetry she would not before have associated with him; and he bent to kiss her cheek with the expression that goes with the words: Oh you naughty little puss! And she felt its answering look, naughty and coy, come onto her face.

Inside she was dissolving in horror at them both, at how far they had both sunk from honesty of emotion.

So now she was saddled with a lover, and he had a mistress! How ordinary, how reassuring, how jolly! And now they would make a foursome of it, and go about to theatres and restaurants. After all, the Rawlings could well afford that sort of thing, and presumably the publisher Michael Plant could afford to do himself and his mistress quite well. No, there was nothing to stop the four of them developing the most intricate relationship of civilised tolerance, all enveloped in a charming afterglow of autumnal passion. Perhaps they would all go off on holidays together? She had known people who did. Or perhaps Matthew would draw the line there? Why should he, though, if he was capable of talking about "foursomes" at all?

She lay in the empty bedroom, listening to the car drive off with Matthew in it, off to work. Then she heard the children clattering off to school to the accompaniment of Sophie's cheerfully ringing voice. She slid down into the hollow of the bed, for shelter against her own irrelevance. And she stretched out her hand to the hollow where her husband's body had lain, but found no comfort there: he was not her husband. She curled herself up in a small tight ball under the clothes: she could stay here all day, all week, indeed, all her life.

But in a few days she must produce Michael Plant, and—but how? She must presumably find some agreeable man prepared to impersonate a publisher called Michael Plant. And in return for which she would—what? Well, for one thing they would make love. The idea made her want to cry with sheer exhaustion. Oh no, she had finished with all that—the proof of it was that the words "make love," or even imagining it, trying hard to revive no more than the pleasures of sensuality, let alone affection, or love, made her want to run away and hide from the sheer effort of the thing. . . . Good Lord, why make love at all? Why make love with anyone? Or if you are going to make love, what does it matter who with? Why shouldn't she simply walk into the street, pick up a man and have a roaring sexual affair with him? Why not? Or even with Fred? What difference did it make?

But she had let herself in for it—an interminable stretch of time with a lover, called Michael, as part of a gallant civilised foursome. Well, she could not, and she would not.

She got up, dressed, went down to find Mrs. Parkes, and asked her for the loan of a pound, since Matthew, she said, had forgotten to leave her money. She exchanged with Mrs. Parkes variations on the theme that husbands are all the same, they don't think, and without saying a word to Sophie, whose voice could be heard upstairs from the telephone, walked to the underground, travelled to South Kensington, changed to the Inner Circle, got out at Paddington, and walked to Fred's Hotel. There she told Fred that she wasn't going on holiday after all, she needed the room. She would have to wait an hour, Fred said. She went to a busy tearoom-cum-restaurant around the corner, and sat watching the people flow in and out the door that kept swinging open and shut, watched them mingle and merge, and separate, felt her being flow into them, into their movement. When the hour was up, she left a half-crown for her pot of tea, and left the place without looking back at it, just as she had left her house, the big, beautiful white house, without another look, but silently dedicating it to Sophie. She returned to Fred, received the key of Number 19, now free, and ascended the grimy stairs slowly, letting floor after floor fall away below her, keeping her eyes lifted, so that floor after floor descended jerkily to her level of vision, and fell away out of sight.

Number 19 was the same. She saw everything with an acute, narrow, checking glance: the cheap shine of the satin spread, which had been replaced carelessly after the two bodies had finished their convulsions under it; a trace of powder on the glass that topped the chest of drawers; an intense green shade in a fold of the curtain. She stood at the window, looking down, watching people pass and pass and pass until her mind went dark from the constant movement. Then she sat in the wicker chair, letting herself go slack. But she had to be careful, because she did not want, today, to be surprised by Fred's knock at five o'clock.

The demons were not here. They had gone forever, because she was buying her freedom from them. She was slipping already into the dark fructifying dream that seemed to caress her inwardly, like the movement of her blood . . . but she had to think about Matthew first. Should she write a letter for the coroner? But what should she say? She would like to leave him with the look on his face she had seen this morning—banal, admittedly, but at least confidently healthy. Well, that was impossible, one did not look like that with a wife dead from suicide. But how to leave him believing she was dying because of a man—because of the fascinating publisher Michael Plant? Oh, how ridiculous! How absurd! How humiliating! But she decided not to trouble about it, simply not to think about the living. If he wanted to believe she had a lover, he would believe it. And he *did* want to believe it. Even when he had found out that there was no publisher in London called Michael Plant, he would think: Oh poor Susan, she was afraid to give me his real name.

And what did it matter whether he married Phil Hunt or Sophie? Though it ought to be Sophie, who was already the mother of those children . . . and what hypocrisy to sit here worrying about the children, when she was going to leave them because she had not got the energy to stay.

She had about four hours. She spent them delightfully, darkly, sweetly, letting herself slide gently, gently, to the edge of the river. Then, with hardly a break in her consciousness, she got up, pushed the thin rug against the door, made sure the windows were tight shut, put two shillings in the meter, and turned on the gas. For the first time since she had been in the room she lay on the hard bed that smelled stale, that smelled of sweat and sex.

She lay on her back on the green satin cover, but her legs were chilly. She got up, found a blanket folded in the bottom of the chest of drawers, and carefully covered her legs with it. She was quite content lying there, listening to the faint soft hiss of the gas that poured into the room, into her lungs, into her brain, as she drifted off into the dark river.

# Clarice Lispector

## (1920–1977)

Born in Tchetchelnik, Ukraine, in 1925, Clarice Lispector immigrated with her parents, Pedro and Marian Lispector, to Brazil when she just was two months old. After spending eleven years in Alagoas, Brazil, the family moved to the country's vibrant capital, Rio de Janeiro. In 1940, while studying for a degree in law, Lispector began working as an editor for the prestigious *Agência Nacional* newspaper. She met a number of emerging writers and intellectuals, including Antônio Callado, Lúcio Cardoso, Adonias Filho, Otávio de Faria, and Cornélio

Pena. These writers influenced Lispector to write creatively and to reinvigorate Brazilian literature. This experimentation is exemplified in Lispector's first novel, *Perto do coração selvagem* (1944; translated as *Near to the Wild Heart*, 1990), which was inspired by James Joyce's *Portrait of an Artist as a Young Man*. Lispector's novel is a symbolic and poetic exploration of a young woman's discovery of self. Though the novel was quite successful and initiated critical conversations about the trajectory of the Brazilian narrative, Lispector remained largely anonymous internationally until the publication of her short story collection, *Laços de família* (1960; translated as *Family Ties*, 1972). Lispector's great skill resides in her intricately developed plots and her ability to reveal characters as complex human beings. Her skill in creating experimental narratives that can still powerfully appeal to her readers brought Lispector fame beyond Brazil, in Europe, and throughout the Americas.

Lispector published numerous works, including the novels *A maçã no escuro* (1961; translated as *The Apple in the Dark*, 1967), *A paixão segundo G. H.* (1964; translated as *The Passion According to G. H.*, 1988), and *Agua viva* (1973; translated as *The Stream of Life*, 1989) and the short story collections *Onde estivestes de noite* (*Where Were You at Night*, 1974) and *A via crucis do corpo* (*The Cross Way of the Flesh*, 1974), both translated in *Soulstorm*, 1989. She revolutionized the Brazilian novel not only by making it more symbolic and psychological, but also by taking the narrative to the city and including liberated women as main characters. Lispector died of cancer in 1977, and her posthumous work, *Um sopro de vida* (*A Breath of Life*, 1978), written while she knew she was dying, is a tribute to Lispector's contribution to literature, exploring the mystical relationship between words and life, between narrative and the soul.

---

## The Smallest Woman in the World                    1960

TRANSLATED BY GIOVANNI PONTIERO

In the depths of equatorial Africa the French explorer, Marcel Pretre, hunter and man of the world, came across a tribe of pygmies of surprising minuteness. He was even more surprised, however, to learn that an even smaller race existed far beyond the forests. So he traveled more deeply into the jungle.

In the Central Congo he discovered, in fact, the smallest pygmies in the world. And—like a box inside another box, inside yet another box—among the smallest pygmies in the world, he found the smallest of the smallest pygmies in the world, answering, perhaps, to the need that Nature sometimes feels to surpass herself.

Among the mosquitoes and the trees moist with humidity, among the luxuriant vegetation of the most indolent green, Marcel Pretre came face to face with a woman no more than forty-five centimeters tall, mature, black, and silent. "As black as a monkey," he would inform the newspapers, and she lived at the top of a tree with her little mate. In the warm humidity of the forest, which matured the fruits quickly and gave them an unbearably sweet taste, she was pregnant. Meanwhile there she stood, the smallest woman in the world. For a second, in the drone of the jungle heat, it was as if the Frenchman had unexpectedly arrived at the end of the line. Certainly, it was only because he was sane that he managed to keep his head and not lose control. Sensing a sudden need to restore order, and to give a name to what exists, he called her Little Flower. And, in order to be able to classify her among the identifiable realities, he immediately began to gather data about her.

Her race is slowly being exterminated. Few human examples remain of their species which, were it not for the subtle dangers of Africa, would be a widely scattered race.

Excluding disease, the polluted air of its rivers, deficiencies of food, and wild beasts on the prowl, the greatest hazard for the few remaining Likoualas are the savage Bantus, a threat which surrounds them in the silent air as on the morning of battle. The Bantus pursue them with nets as they pursue monkeys. And they eat them. Just like that: they pursue them with nets and eat them. So this race of tiny people went on retreating and retreating until it finally settled in the heart of Africa where the fortunate explorer was to discover them. As a strategic defense, they live in the highest trees. The women come down in order to cook maize, grind mandioca, and gather green vegetables; the men to hunt. When a child is born, he is given his freedom almost at once. Often, one must concede, the child does not enjoy his freedom for long among the wild beasts of the jungle, but, at least, he cannot complain that for such a short life the labor had been long. Even the language that the child learns is short and simple, consisting only of the essentials. The Likoualas use few names and they refer to things by gestures and animal noises. As a spiritual enhancement, he possesses his drum. While they dance to the sound of the drum, a tiny male keeps watch for the Bantus, who appear from heaven knows where.

This, then, was how the explorer discovered at his feet the smallest human creature that exists. His heart pounded, for surely no emerald is so rare. Not even the teachings of the Indian sages are so rare, and even the richest man in the world has not witnessed such strange charm. There, before his eyes, stood a woman such as the delights of the most exquisite dream had never equaled. It was then that the explorer timidly pronounced with a delicacy of feeling of which even his wife would never have believed him capable, "You are Little Flower."

At that moment, Little Flower scratched herself where one never scratches oneself. The explorer—as if he were receiving the highest prize of chastity to which man, always so full of ideals, dare aspire—the explorer who has so much experience of life, turned away his eyes.

The photograph of Little Flower was published in the color supplement of the Sunday newspapers, where she was reproduced life size. She appeared wrapped in a shawl, with her belly in an advanced stage. Her nose was flat, her face black, her eyes deep-set, and her feet splayed. She looked just like a dog.

That same Sunday, in an apartment, a woman, glancing at the picture of Little Flower in the open newspaper, did not care to look a second time, "because it distresses me."

In another apartment, a woman felt such a perverse tenderness for the daintiness of the African woman that—prevention being better than cure—Little Flower should never be left alone with the tenderness of that woman. Who knows to what darkness of love her affection might extend. The woman passed a troubled day, overcome, one might say, by desire. Besides, it was spring and there was a dangerous longing in the air.

In another house, a little five-year-old girl, upon seeing Little Flower's picture and listening to the comments of her parents, became frightened. In that house of adults, this little girl had been, until now, the smallest of human beings. And, if this was the source of the nicest endearments, it was also the source of that first fear of tyrannical love. The existence of Little Flower caused the little girl to feel—with a vagueness which only many years later, and, for quite different reasons, she was to experience as a concrete thought—caused her to feel with premature awareness, that "misfortune knows no limits."

In another house, in the consecration of spring, a young girl about to be married burst out compassionately, "Mother, look at her picture, poor little thing! Just look at her sad expression!"

"Yes," replied the girl's mother—hard, defeated, and proud—"but that is the sadness of an animal, not of a human."

"Oh Mother!" the girl protested in despair.

It was in another house that a bright child had a bright idea.

"Mummy, what if I were to put this tiny woman in little Paul's bed while he is sleeping? When he wakes up, what a fright he'll get, eh? What a din he'll make when he finds her sitting up in bed beside him! And then we could play with her! We could make her our toy, eh!"

His mother, at that moment, was rolling her hair in front of the bathroom mirror, and she remembered what the cook had told her about her time as an orphan. Not having any dolls to play with, and maternal feelings already stirring furiously in their hearts, some deceitful girls in the orphanage had concealed from the nun in charge the death of one of their companions. They kept her body in a cupboard until Sister went out, and then they played with the dead girl, bathing her and feeding her little tidbits, and they punished her only to be able to kiss and comfort her afterward.

The mother recalled this in the bathroom and she lowered her awkward hands, full of hairpins. And she considered the cruel necessity of loving. She considered the malignity of our desire to be happy. She considered the ferocity with which we want to play. And the number of times when we murder for love. She then looked at her mischievous son as if she were looking at a dangerous stranger. And she was horrified at her own soul, which, more than her body, had engendered that being so apt for life and happiness. And thus she looked at him, attentively and with uneasy pride, her child already without two front teeth, his evolution, his evolution under way, his teeth falling out to make room for those which bite best. "I must buy him a new suit," she decided, looking at him intently. She obstinately dressed up her toothless child in fancy clothes, and obstinately insisted upon keeping him clean and tidy, as if cleanliness might give emphasis to a tranquilizing superficiality, obstinately perfecting the polite aspect of beauty. Obstinately removing herself, and removing him from something which must be as "black as a monkey." Then, looking into the bathroom mirror, the mother smiled, intentionally refined and polished, placing between that face of hers of abstract lines and the raw face of Little Flower, the insuperable distance of millennia. But with years of experience she knew that this would be a Sunday on which she would have to conceal from herself her anxiety, her dream, and the lost millennia.

In another house, against a wall, they set about the exciting business of calculating with a measuring tape the forty-five centimeters of Little Flower. And as they enjoyed themselves they made a startling discovery: she was even smaller than the most penetrating imagination could ever have invented. In the heart of each member of the family there arose the gnawing desire to possess that minute and indomitable thing for himself, that thing which had been saved from being devoured, that enduring fount of charity. The eager soul of that family was roused to dedication. And, indeed, who has not wanted to possess a human being just for himself? A thing, it is true, which would not always be convenient, for there are moments when one would choose not to have sentiments.

"I'll bet you if she lived here we would finish up quarreling," said the father, seated in his armchair, firmly turning the pages of the newspaper. "In this house everything finishes up with a quarrel."

"You are always such a pessimist, José," said the mother.

"Mother, can you imagine how tiny her little child will be?" their oldest girl, thirteen, asked intensely.

The father fidgeted behind his newspaper.

"It must be the smallest black baby in the world," replied the mother, melting with pleasure. "Just imagine her waiting on table here in the house! And with her swollen little belly."

"That's enough of that rubbish!" muttered the father, annoyed.

"You must admit," said the mother, unexpectedly peeved, "that the thing is unique. You are the one who is insensitive."

And what about the unique thing itself?

Meanwhile, in Africa, the unique thing itself felt in its heart—perhaps also black, because one can no longer have confidence in a Nature that had already blundered once—meanwhile the unique thing itself felt in its heart something still more rare, rather like the secret of its own secret: a minute child. Methodically, the explorer examined with his gaze the belly of the smallest mature human being. It was at that moment that the explorer, for the first time since he had known her—instead of experiencing curiosity, enthusiasm, a sense of triumph, or the excitement of discovery—felt distinctly ill at ease.

The fact is that the smallest woman in the world was smiling. She was smiling and warm, warm. Little Flower was enjoying herself. The unique thing itself was enjoying the ineffable sensation of not having been devoured yet. Not to have been devoured was something which at other times gave her the sudden impulse to leap from branch to branch. But at this tranquil moment, among the dense undergrowth of the Central Congo, she was not applying that impulse to an action—and the impulse concentrated itself completely in the very smallness of the unique thing itself. And suddenly she was smiling. It was a smile that only someone who does not speak can smile. A smile that the uncomfortable explorer did not succeed in classifying. And she went on enjoying her own gentle smile, she who was not being devoured. Not to be devoured is the most perfect sentiment. Not to be devoured is the secret objective of a whole existence. While she was not being devoured, her animal smile was as delicate as happiness. The explorer felt disconcerted.

In the second place, if the unique thing itself was smiling it was because, inside her minute body, a great darkness had started to stir.

It is that the unique thing itself felt her breast warm with that which might be called love. She loved that yellow explorer. If she knew how to speak and should say that she loved him, he would swell with pride. Pride that would diminish when she should add that she also adored the explorer's ring and his boots. And when he became deflated with disappointment, Little Flower would fail to understand. Because, not even remotely, would her love for the explorer—one can even say her "deep love," because without other resources she was reduced to depth—since not even remotely would her deep love for the explorer lose its value because she also loved his boots. There is an old misunderstanding about the word "love," and if many children are born on account of that mistake, many others have lost the unique instant of birth simply on account of a susceptibility which exacts that it should be me, me that should be loved and not my money. But in the humidity of the jungle, there do not exist these cruel refinements; love is not to be devoured, love is to find boots pretty, love is to like the strange color of a man who is not black, love is to smile out of love at a ring that shines. Little Flower blinked with love and smiled, warm, small, pregnant, and warm.

The explorer tried to smile back at her, without knowing exactly to which charm his smile was replying, and then became disturbed as only a full-grown man becomes disturbed. He tried to conceal his uneasiness, by adjusting his helmet on his head, and he blushed with embarrassment. He turned a pretty color, his own, greenish pink hue, like that of a lime in the morning light. He must be sour.

It was probably upon adjusting his symbolic helmet that the explorer called himself to order, returned severely to the discipline of work, and resumed taking notes. He had learned to understand some of the few words articulated by the tribe and to interpret their signs. He was already able to ask questions.

Little Flower answered "yes." That it was very nice to have a tree in which to live by herself, all by herself. Because—and this she did not say, but her eyes became so dark that they said it—because it is nice to possess, so nice to possess. The explorer blinked several times.

Marcel Pretre experienced a few difficult moments trying to control himself. But at least he was kept occupied in taking notes. Anyone not taking notes had to get along as best he could.

"Well, it just goes to show," an old woman suddenly exclaimed, folding her newspaper with determination, "it just goes to show. I'll say one thing though—God knows what He's about."

# Jack London

## (1876–1916)

The adventurer Jack London was the son of a wandering astrologer from Maine and an Ohioan woman. Boisterous and fearless in writing style and subject matter, the man who was known to address his wife as "Mate Woman" wrote fifty books that were so compelling to the imaginations of his readers that he continued to receive fan mail for sixty years after he died. London was the epitome of the saying "Live an interesting life and then write about it," except that he managed to live an interesting life and write about it at the same time.

Born in San Francisco, London spent his early childhood on California ranches, reading Washington Irving, Captain Cook, and Ouida's *Signa* for entertainment. He dropped out of college after one semester because of financial difficulties and went to work at various fishing trades based in San Francisco Bay. At seventeen, he sailed to Japan and Russia aboard a sealing schooner, and upon his return to the United States traveled north to Canada, Alaska, the Northwest Territory, and the Sierra Nevadas. At age eighteen, he decided to ride the rails east and was arrested for vagrancy in Niagara Falls; sentenced to one month in the Erie County Penitentiary, he would later recount this experience in the 1907 *The Road*. At age twenty-one, he joined the Socialist Labor Party, and at twenty-two he joined the Klondike gold rush, spending that winter in the Yukon and returning by boat down the Mississippi River after learning of the death of his father. These travels gave rise to London's first magazine article, "To the Man on the Trail," published in 1899, which brought him instant popularity and a contract for a book of short stories, *The Son of the Wolf*, completed in 1900. In 1902, after living for six weeks in a London ghetto, he published a sociological study entitled *The People of the Abyss* (the title credited to H. G. Wells). The same year, he published his first novel, *A Daughter of the Snows*, and in 1903 wrote the work he is probably most remembered for, *The Call of the Wild*.

A mostly self-educated man, London later cited his writing influences as Charles Dickens, Edgar Allan Poe, George Eliot, Stephen Crane, and especially Robert Louis Stevenson, whom he praised for putting "himself almost wholly into his work." London was also avidly devoted to Rudyard Kipling, partly because of what he identified as Kipling's admiration for "the English-speaking people of all the world." In his essay "On the Writer's Philosophy of Life," London advised young writers, "Read the best, and the best only. Don't finish a tale simply because you have commenced it. Remember that you are a writer, first, last and always."

## To Build a Fire

1908

Day had broken cold and gray, exceedingly cold and gray, when the man turned aside from the main Yukon trail and climbed the high earth-bank, where a dim and little-travelled trail led eastward through the fat spruce timberland. It was a steep bank, and he paused for breath at the top, excusing the act to himself by looking at his watch. It was nine o'clock. There was no sun nor hint of sun, though there was not a cloud in the sky. It was a clear day, and yet there seemed an intangible pall over the face of things, a subtle gloom that made the day dark, and that was due to the absence of sun. This fact did not worry the man. He was used to the lack of sun. It had been days since he had seen the sun, and he knew that a few more days must pass before that cheerful orb, due south, would just peep above the sky-line and dip immediately from view.

The man flung a look back along the way he had come. The Yukon lay a mile wide and hidden under three feet of ice. On top of this ice were as many feet of snow. It was all pure white, rolling in gentle undulations where the ice-jams of the freeze-up had formed. North and south, as far as his eye could see, it was unbroken white, save for a dark hair-line that curved and twisted from around the spruce-covered island to the south, and that curved and twisted away into the north, where it disappeared behind another spruce-covered island. This dark hair-line was the trail—the main trail—that led south five hundred miles to the Chilcoot Pass, Dyea, and salt water; and that led north seventy miles to Dawson, and still on to the north a thousand miles to Nulato, and finally to St. Michael on Bering Sea, a thousand miles and half a thousand more.

But all this—the mysterious, far-reaching hair-line trail, the absence of sun from the sky, the tremendous cold, and the strangeness and weirdness of it all—made no impression on the man. It was not because he was long used to it. He was a newcomer in the land, a *chechaquo*, and this was his first winter. The trouble with him was that he was without imagination. He was quick and alert in the things of life, but only in the things, and not in the significances. Fifty degrees below zero mean eighty-odd degrees of frost. Such fact impressed him as being cold and uncomfortable, and that was all. It did not lead him to meditate upon his frailty as a creature of temperature, and upon man's frailty in general, able only to live within certain narrow limits of heat and cold; and from there on it did not lead him to the conjectural field of immortality and man's place in the universe. Fifty degrees below zero stood for a bite of frost that hurt and that must be guarded against by the use of mittens, ear-flaps, warm moccasins, and thick socks. That there should be anything more to it than that was a thought that never entered his head.

As he turned to go on, he spat speculatively. There was a sharp, explosive crackle that startled him. He spat again. And again, in the air, before it could fall to the snow, the spittle crackled. He knew that at fifty below spittle crackled on the snow, but this spittle had crackled in the air. Undoubtedly it was colder than fifty below—how much colder he did not know. But the temperature did not matter. He was bound for the old claim on the left fork of Henderson Creek, where the boys were already. They had come over across the divide from the Indian Creek country, while he had come the roundabout way to take a look at the possibilities of getting out logs in the spring from the islands in the Yukon. He would be in to camp by six o'clock; a bit after dark, it was true, but the boys would be there, a fire would be going, and a hot supper would be ready. As for lunch, he pressed his hand against the protruding bundle under his jacket. It was also under his shirt, wrapped up in a handkerchief and lying against the naked skin. It was the only way to keep the biscuits from freezing. He smiled agreeably to himself as he thought of those biscuits, each cut open and sopped in bacon grease, and each enclosing a generous slice of fried bacon.

He plunged in among the big spruce trees. The trail was faint. A foot of snow had fallen since the last sled had passed over, and he was glad he was without a sled, travelling light. In fact, he carried nothing but the lunch wrapped in the handkerchief. He was surprised, however, at the cold. It certainly was cold, he concluded, as he rubbed his numb nose and cheek-bones with his mittened hand. He was a warm-whiskered man, but the hair on his face did not protect the high cheek-bones and the eager nose that thrust itself aggressively into the frosty air.

At the man's heels trotted a dog, a big native husky, the proper wolf-dog, gray-coated and without any visible or temperamental difference from its brother, the wild wolf. The animal was depressed by the tremendous cold. It knew that it was no time for travelling. Its instinct told it a truer tale than was told to the man by the man's judgment. In reality, it was not merely colder than fifty below zero; it was colder than sixty below, than seventy below. It was seventy-five below zero. Since the freezing-point is thirty-two above zero, it meant that one hundred and seven degrees of frost obtained. The dog did not know anything about thermometers. Possibly in its brain there was no sharp consciousness of a condition of very cold such as was in the man's brain. But the brute had its instinct. It experienced a vague but menacing apprehension that subdued it and made it slink along at the man's heels, and that made it question eagerly every unwonted movement of the man as if expecting him to go into camp or to seek shelter somewhere to build a fire. The dog had learned fire, and it wanted fire, or else to burrow under the snow and cuddle its warmth away from the air.

The frozen moisture of its breathing had settled on its fur in a fine powder of frost, and especially where its jowls, muzzle, and eyelashes whitened by its crystalled breath. The man's red beard and mustache were likewise frosted, but more solidly, the deposit taking the form of ice and increasing with every warm, moist breath he exhaled. Also, the man was chewing tobacco, and the muzzle of ice held his lips so rigidly that he was unable to clear his chin when he expelled the juice. The result was that a crystal beard of the color and solidity of amber was increasing its length on his chin. If he fell down it would shatter itself, like glass, into brittle fragments. But he did not mind the appendage. It was the penalty all tobacco-chewers paid in that country, and he had been out before in two cold snaps. They had not been so cold as this, he knew, but by the spirit thermometer at Sixty Mile he knew they had been registered at fifty below and at fifty-five.

He held on through the level stretch of woods for several miles, crossed a wide flat of niggerheads, and dropped down a bank to the frozen bed of a small stream.

This was Henderson Creek, and he knew he was ten miles from the forks. He looked at his watch. It was ten o'clock. He was making four miles an hour, and he calculated that he would arrive at the forks at half-past twelve. He decided to celebrate that event by eating his lunch there.

The dog dropped in again at his heels, with a tail drooping discouragement, as the man swung along the creek-bed. The furrow of the old sled-trail was plainly visible, but a dozen inches of snow covered the marks of the last runners. In a month no man had come up or down that silent creek. The man held steadily on. He was not much given to thinking, and just then particularly he had nothing to think about save that he would eat lunch at the forks and that at six o'clock he would be in camp with the boys. There was nobody to talk to, and, had there been, speech would have been impossible because of the ice-muzzle on his mouth. So he continued monotonously to chew tobacco and to increase the length of his amber beard.

Once in a while the thought reiterated itself that it was very cold and that he had never experienced such cold. As he walked along he rubbed his cheek-bones and nose with the back of his mittened hand. He did this automatically, now and again changing hands. But rub as he would, the instant he stopped his cheek-bones went numb. He was sure to frost his cheeks; he knew that, and experienced a pang of regret that he had not devised a nose-strap of the sort Bud wore in cold snaps. Such a strap passed across the cheeks, as well, and saved them. But it didn't matter much, after all. What were frosted cheeks? A bit painful, that was all; they were never serious.

Empty as the man's mind was of thoughts, he was keenly observant, and he noticed the changes in the creek, the curves and bends and timber-jams, and always he sharply noted where he placed his feet. Once, coming around a bend, he shied abruptly, like a startled horse, curved away from the place where he had been walking, and retreated several paces back along the trail. The creek he knew was frozen clear to the bottom,—no creek could contain water in that arctic winter,—but he knew also that there were springs that bubbled out from the hillsides and ran along under the snow and on top the ice of the creek. He knew that the coldest snaps never froze these springs, and he knew likewise their danger. They were traps. They hid pools of water under the snow that might be three inches deep, or three feet. Sometimes a skin of ice half an inch thick covered them, and in turn was covered by snow. Sometimes there were alternate layers of water and ice-skin, so that when one broke through he kept on breaking through for a while, sometimes wetting himself to the waist.

That was why he had shied in such panic. He had felt the give under his feet and heard the crackle of a snow-hidden ice-skin. And to get his feet wet in such a temperature meant trouble and danger. At the very least it meant delay, for he would be forced to stop and build a fire, and under its protection to bare his feet while he dried his socks and moccasins. He stood and studied the creek-bed and its banks, and decided that the flow of water came from the right. He reflected awhile, rubbing his nose and cheeks, then skirted to the left, stepping gingerly and testing the footing for each step. Once clear of the danger, he took a fresh chew of tobacco and swung along at his four-mile gait.

In the course of the next two hours he came upon several similar traps. Usually the snow above the hidden pools had a sunken, candied appearance that advertised the danger. Once again, however, he had a close call; and once, suspecting danger, he compelled the dog to go on in front. The dog did not want to go. It hung back while the man shoved it forward, and then it went quickly across the white, unbroken surface. Suddenly it broke through, floundered to one side, and got away to firmer footing. It had wet its forefeet and legs, and almost immediately the water that clung to it turned to ice. It made quick efforts to lick the ice off its legs, then dropped down in the snow and began to bite out the ice that had formed between the toes. This was a matter of instinct. To permit the ice to remain would mean sore feet. It did not know this. It merely obeyed the mysterious prompting that arose from the deep crypts of its being. But the man knew, having achieved a judgment on the subject, and he removed the mitten from his right hand and helped tear out the ice-particles. He did not expose his fingers for more than a minute, and was astonished at the swift numbness that smote them. It certainly was cold. He pulled on the mitten hastily, and beat the hand savagely across his chest.

At twelve o'clock the day was at its brightest. Yet the sun was too far south on its winter journey to clear the horizon. The bulge of the earth intervened between it and Henderson Creek, where the man walked under a clear sky at noon and cast no shadow. At half-past twelve, to the minute, he arrived at the forks of the creek. He was pleased at the speed he had made. If he kept it up, he would certainly be with the boys by six. He unbottoned his jacket and shirt and drew forth his lunch. The action consumed no more than a quarter of a minute, yet in that brief moment the numbness laid hold of the exposed fingers. He did not put the mitten on, but, instead, struck the fingers a dozen sharp smashes against his leg. Then he sat down on a snow-covered log to eat. The sting that followed upon the striking fingers against his leg ceased so quickly that he was startled. He had had no chance to take a bite of biscuit. He struck the fingers repeatedly and returned them to the mitten, baring the other hand for the purpose of eating. He tried to take a mouthful, but the ice-muzzle prevented. He had forgotten to build a fire and thaw out. He chuckled at his foolishness, and as he chuckled he noted the numbness creeping into the exposed fingers. Also, he noted that the stinging which had first come to his toes when he sat down was already passing away. He wondered whether the toes were warm or numb. He moved them inside the moccasins and decided that they were numb.

He pulled the mitten on hurriedly and stood up. He was a bit frightened. He stamped up and down until the stinging returned into the feet. It certainly was cold, was his thought. That man from Sulphur Creek had spoken the truth when telling how cold it sometimes got in the country. And he had laughed at him at the time! That showed one must not be too sure of things. There was no mistake about it, it was cold. He strode up and down, stamping his feet and threshing his arms, until reassured by the returning warmth. Then he got out matches and proceeded to make a fire. From the undergrowth, where high water of the previous spring had lodged a supply of seasoned twigs, he got his fire-wood. Working carefully from a small beginning, he soon had a roaring fire, over which he thawed the ice from his face and in the protection of which he ate his biscuits. For the moment the cold of the space was outwitted. The dog took satisfaction in the fire, stretching out close enough for warmth and far away enough to escape being singed.

When the man had finished, he filled his pipe and took his comfortable time over a smoke. Then he pulled on his mittens, settled the ear-flaps of his cap firmly about his ears, and took the creek trail up the left fork. The dog was disappointed and yearned back toward the fire. This man did not know cold. Possibly all the generations of his ancestry had been ignorant of cold, of cold one hundred and seven degrees below freezing-point. But the dog knew; all its ancestry knew, and it had inherited the knowledge. And it knew that it was not good to walk abroad in such fearful cold. It was time to lie snug in a hole in the snow and wait for a curtain of cloud to be drawn across the face of outer space whence this cold came. On the other hand, there was no keen intimacy between the dog and the man. The one was the toil-slave of the other, and the only caresses it had ever received were the caresses of the whip-lash and of harsh and menacing throat-sounds that threatened the whip-lash. So the dog made no effort to communicate its apprehension to the man. It was not concerned in the welfare of the man; it was for its own sake that it yearned back toward the fire. But the man whistled, spoke to it with the sound of whip-lashes, and the dog swung in at the man's heels and followed after.

The man took a chew of tobacco and proceeded to start a new amber beard. Also, his moist breath quickly powdered with white his mustache, eyebrows, and lashes. There did not seem to be so many springs on the left fork of the Henderson, and for half an hour the man saw no signs of any. And then it happened. At a place where there were no signs, where the soft, unbroken snow seemed to advertise solidity beneath, the man broke through. It was not deep. He wet himself halfway to his knees before he floundered out to the firm crust.

He was angry, and cursed his luck aloud. He had hoped to get into camp with the boys at six o'clock, and this would delay him for an hour, for he would have to build a fire and dry out his foot-gear. This was imperative at that low temperature—he knew that much; and he turned aside to the bank, which he climbed. On top, tangled in the underbrush about the trunks of several small spruce trees, was a high-water deposit of dry fire-wood—sticks and twigs, principally, but also larger portions of seasoned branches and fine, dry, last-year's grasses. He threw down several large pieces on top of the snow. This served for a foundation and prevented the young flame from drowning itself in the snow it otherwise would melt. The flame he got by touching a match to a small thread of birch-bark that he took from his pocket. This burned even more readily than paper. Placing it on the foundation, he fed the young flame with wisps of dry grass and with the tiniest dry twigs.

He worked slowly and carefully, keenly away of his danger. Gradually, as the flame grew stronger, he increased the size of the twigs with which he fed it. He squatted in the snow, pulling the twigs out from their entanglement in the brush and feeding directly to the flame. He knew there must be no failure. When it is seventy-five below zero, a man must not fail in his first attempt to build a fire—that is, if his feet are wet. If his feet are dry, and he fail, he can run along the trail for half a mile and restore his circulation. But the circulation of wet and freezing feet cannot be restored by running when it is seventy-five below. No matter how fast he runs, the wet feet will freeze the harder.

All this the man knew. The old-timer on Sulphur Creek had told him about it the previous fall, and now he was appreciating the advice. Already all sensation had gone out of his feet. To build a fire he had been forced to remove his mittens, and the fingers had quickly gone numb. His pace of four miles an hour had kept his heart pumping blood to the surface of his body and to all the extremities. But the instant he stopped, the action of the pump eased down. The cold of space smote the unprotected tip of the planet, and he, being on that unprotected tip, received the full force of the blow. The blood of his body recoiled before it. The blood was alive, like the dog, and like the dog it wanted to hide away and cover itself up from the fearful cold. So long as he walked four miles an hour, he pumped that blood, willy-nilly, to the surface; but now it ebbed away and sank down into the recesses of his body. The extremities were the first to feel its absence. His wet feet froze the faster, and his exposed fingers numbed the faster, though they had not yet begun to freeze. Nose and cheeks were already freezing, while the skin of all his body chilled as it lost its blood.

But he was safe. Toes and nose and cheeks would be only touched by the frost, for the fire was beginning to burn with strength. He was feeding it with twigs the size of his finger. In another minute he would be able to feed it with branches the size of his wrist, and then he could remove his wet foot-gear, and, while it dried, he could keep his naked feet warm by the fire, rubbing them at first, of course, with snow. The fire was a success. He was safe. He remembered the advice of the old-timer at Sulphur Creek, and smiled. The old-timer had been very serious in laying down the law that no man must travel alone in the Klondike after fifty below. Well, here he was; he had had an accident; he was alone; and he had saved himself. Those old-timers were rather womanish, some of them, he thought. All a man had to do was to keep his head, and he was all right. Any man who was a man could travel alone. But it was surprising, the rapidity with which his cheeks and nose were freezing. And he had not thought his fingers could go lifeless in so short a time. Lifeless they were, for he could scarcely make them move together to grip a twig, and they seemed remote from his body and from him. When he touched a twig, he had to look and see whether or not he had hold of it. The wires were pretty well down between him and his finger-ends.

All of which counted for little. There was the fire, snapping and crackling and promising life with every dancing flame. He started to untie his moccasins. They were coated with ice; the thick German socks were like sheaths of iron halfway to the knees; and the moccasin strings were like rods of steel all twisted and knotted as by some conflagration. For a moment he tugged with his numb fingers, then, realizing the folly of it, he drew his sheath-knife.

But before he could cut the strings, it happened. It was his own fault or, rather, his mistake. He should not have built the fire under the spruce tree. He should have built it in the open. But it had been easier to pull the twigs from the brush and drop them directly on the fire. Now the tree under which he had done this carried a weight of snow on its boughs. No wind had blown for weeks, and each bough was fully freighted. Each time he pulled a twig he had communicated a slight agitation to the tree—an imperceptible agitation, so far as he was concerned, but an agitation sufficient to bring about the disaster. High up in the tree one bough capsized its load of snow. This fell on the boughs beneath, capsizing them. This process continued, spreading out and involving the whole tree. It grew like an avalanche, and it descended without warning upon the man and the fire, and the fire was blotted out! Where it had burned was a mantle of fresh and disordered snow.

The man was shocked. It was as though he had just heard his own sentence of death. For a moment he sat and stared at the spot where the fire had been. Then he grew very calm. Perhaps the old-timer on Sulphur Creek was right. If he had only had a trail-mate he would have been in no danger now. The trail-mate could have built the fire. Well, it was up to him to build the fire all over again, and this second time there must be no failure. Even if he succeeded, he would most likely lose some toes. His feet must be badly frozen by now, and there would be some time before the second fire was ready.

Such were his thoughts, but he did not sit and think them. He was busy all the time they were passing through his mind. He made a new foundation for a fire, this time in the open, where no treacherous tree could blot it out. Next, he gathered dry grasses and tiny twigs from the high-water flotsam. He could not bring his fingers together to pull them out, but he was able to gather them by the handful. In this way he got many rotten twigs and bits of green moss that were undesirable, but it was the best he could do. He worked methodically, even collecting an armful of the larger branches to be used later when the fire gathered strength. And all the while the dog sat and watched him, a certain yearning wistfulness in its eyes, for it looked upon him as the fire-provider, and the fire was slow in coming.

When all was ready, the man reached in his pocket for a second piece of birch bark. He knew the bark was there, and, though he could not feel it with his fingers, he could hear its crisp rustling as he fumbled for it. Try as he would, he could not clutch hold of it. And all the time, in his consciousness, was the knowledge that each instant his feet were freezing. This thought tended to put him in a panic, but he fought against it and kept calm. He pulled on his mittens with his teeth, and threshed his arms back and forth, beating his hands with all his might against his sides. He did this sitting down, and he stood up to do it; and all the while the dog sat in the snow, its wolf-brush of a tail curled around warmly over its forefeet, its sharp wolf-ears pricked forward intently as it watched the man. And the man, as he beat and threshed with his arms and hands, felt a great surge of envy as he regarded the creature that was warm and secure in its natural covering.

After a time he was aware of the first faraway signals of sensation in his beaten fingers. The faint tingling grew stronger till it evolved into a stinging ache that was excruciating, but which the man hailed with satisfaction. He stripped the mitten from his right hand and fetched forth the birch-bark. The exposed fingers were quickly going numb again. Next he brought out his bunch of sulphur matches. But the tremendous cold had already driven the life out of his fingers. In his effort to separate one match from the others, the whole bunch fell in the snow. He tried to pick it out of the snow, but failed. The dead fingers could neither touch nor clutch. He was very careful. He drove the thought of his freezing feet, and nose, and cheeks, out of his mind, devoting his whole soul to the matches. He watched, using the sense of vision in place of that of his touch, and when he saw his fingers on each side the bunch, he closed them—that is, he willed to close them, for the wires were down, and the fingers did not obey. He pulled the mitten on the right hand, and beat it fiercely against his knee. Then, with both mittened hands, he scooped the bunch of matches, along with much snow, into his lap. Yet he was no better off.

After some manipulation he managed to get the bunch between the heels of his mittened hands. In this fashion he carried it to his mouth. The ice crackled and snapped when by a violent effort he opened his mouth. He drew the lower jaw in, curled the upper lip out of the way, and scraped the bunch with his upper teeth in order to separate a match. He succeeded in getting one, which he dropped on his lap. He was no better off. He could not pick it up. Then he devised a way. He picked it up in his teeth and scratched it on his leg. Twenty times he scratched before he succeeded in lighting it. As it flamed he held it with his teeth to the birch-bark. But the burning brimstone went up his nostrils and into his lungs, causing him to cough spasmodically. The match fell into the snow and went out.

The old timer on Sulphur Creek was right, he thought in the moment of controlled despair that ensued: after fifty below, a man should travel with a partner. He beat his hands, but failed in exciting any sensation. Suddenly he bared both hands, removing the mittens with his teeth. He caught the whole bunch between the heels of his hands. His arm-muscles not being frozen enabled him to press the hand-heels tightly against the matches. Then he scratched the bunch along his leg. It flared into flame, seventy sulphur matches at once! There was no wind to blow them out. He kept his head to one side to escape the strangling fumes, and he held the blazing bunch to the birch-bark. As he so held it, he became aware of sensation in his hand. His flesh was burning. He could smell it. Deep down below the surface he could feel it. The sensation developed into pain that grew acute. And still he endured it, holding the flame of the matches clumsily to the bark that would not light readily because his own burning hands were in the way, absorbing most of the flame.

At last, when he could endure no more, he jerked his hands apart. The blazing matches fell sizzling into the snow, but the birch-bark was alight. He began laying dry grasses and the tiniest twigs on the flame. He could not pick and choose, for he had to lift the fuel between the heels of his hands. Small pieces of rotten wood and green moss clung to the twigs, and he bit them off as well as he could with his teeth. He cherished the flame carefully and awkwardly. It meant life, and it must not perish. The withdrawal of blood from the surface of his body now made him begin to shiver, and he grew more awkward. A large piece of green moss fell squarely on the little fire. He tried to poke it out with his fingers, but his shivering frame made him poke too far, and he disrupted the nucleus of the little fire, the burning grasses and tiny twigs separating and scattering. He tried to poke them together again, but in spite of the tenseness of the effort, his shivering got away with him, and the twigs were hopelessly scattered. Each twig gushed in a puff of smoke and went out. The fire-provider had failed. As he looked apathetically about him, his eyes chanced on the dog, sitting across the ruins of the fire from him, in the snow, making restless, hunching movements, slightly lifting one forefoot and then the other, shifting its weight back and forth on them with wistful eagerness.

The sight of the dog put a wild idea into his head. He remembered the tale of the man, caught in a blizzard, who killed a steer and crawled inside the carcass, and so was saved. He would kill the dog and bury his hands in the warm body until the numbness went out of them. Then he could build another fire. He spoke to the dog, calling, calling it to him; but in his voice was a strange note of fear that frightened the animal, who had never know the man to speak in such way before. Something was the matter, and its suspicious nature sensed danger—it knew not what danger, but somewhere, somehow, in its brain arose an apprehension of the man. It flattened its ears down at the sound of the man's voice, and its restless, hunching movements and the liftings and shiftings of its forefeet became more pronounced; but it would not come to the man. He got on his hands and knees and crawled toward the dog. This unusual posture again excited suspicion, and the animal sidled mincingly away.

The man sat up in the snow for a moment and struggled for calmness. Then he pulled on his mittens, by means of his teeth, and got upon his feet. He glanced down at first in order to assure himself that he was really standing up, for the absence of sensation in his feet left him unrelated to the earth. His erect position in itself started to drive the webs of suspicion from the dog's mind; and when he spoke peremptorily, with the sound of whip-lashes in his voice, the dog rendered its customary allegiance and came to him. As it came within reaching distance, the man lost his control. His arms flashed out to the dog, and he experienced genuine surprise when he discovered that his hands could not clutch, that there was neither bend nor feeling in the fingers. He had forgotten for the moment that they were frozen and that they were freezing more and more. All this happened quickly, and before the animal could get away, he encircled its body with his arms. He sat down in the snow, and in this fashion held the dog, while it snarled and whined and struggled.

But it was all he could do, hold its body encircled in his arms and sit there. He realized that he could not kill the dog. There was no way to do it. With his helpless hands he could neither draw nor hold his sheath-knife nor throttle the animal. He released it, and it plunged wildly away, with tail between its legs, and still snarling. It halted forty feet away and surveyed him curiously, with ears sharply pricked forward. The man looked down at his hands in order to locate them, and found them hanging on the ends of his arms. It struck him as curious that one should have to use his eye in order to find out where his hands were. He began threshing his arms back and forth, beating the mittened hands against his sides. He did this for five minutes, violently, and his heart pumped enough blood up to the surface to put a stop to his shivering. But no sensation was aroused in the hands. He had an impression that they hung like weights on the ends of his arms, but when he tried to run the impression down, he could not find it.

A certain fear of death, dull and oppressive, came to him. This fear quickly became poignant as he realized that it was no longer a mere matter of freezing his fingers and toes, or of losing his hands and feet, but that it was a matter of life and death with the chances against him. This threw him into a panic, and he turned and ran up the creek-bed along the old, dim trail. The dog joined in behind and kept up with him. He ran blindly, without intention, in fear such as he had never known in his life. Slowly, as he ploughed and floundered through the snow, he began to see things again,—the banks of the creek, the old timber-jams, the leafless aspens, and the sky.

The running made him feel better. He did not shiver. Maybe, if he ran on, his feet would thaw out; and, anyway, if he ran far enough, he would reach camp and the boys. Without doubt he would lose some fingers and toes and some of his face; but the boys would take care of him, and save the rest of him when he got there. And at the same time there was another thought in his mind that said he would never get to the camp and the boys; that it was too many miles away, that the freezing had too great a start on him, and that he would soon be stiff and dead. This thought he kept in the background and refused to consider. Sometimes it pushed itself forward and demanded to be heard, but he thrust it back and strove to think of other things.

It struck him as curious that he could run at all on feet so frozen that he could not feel them when they struck the earth and took the weight of his body. He seemed to himself to skim along above the surface, and to have no connection with the earth. Somewhere he had once seen a winged Mercury, and he wondered if Mercury felt as he felt when skimming over the earth.

His theory of running until he reached camp and the boys had one flaw in it: he lacked the endurance. Several times he stumbled, and finally he tottered, crumpled up, and fell. When he tried to rise, he failed. He must sit and rest, he decided, and next time he would merely walk and keep on going. As he sat and regained his breath, he noted that he was feeling quite warm and comfortable. He was not shivering, and it even seemed that a warm glow had come to his chest and trunk. And yet, when he touched his nose or cheeks, there was no sensation. Running would not thaw them out. Nor would it thaw out his hands and feet. Then the thought came to him that the frozen portions of his body must be extending. He tried to keep this thought down, to forget it, to think of something else; he was aware of the panicky feeling that it caused, and he was afraid of the panic. But the thought asserted itself, and persisted, until it produced a vision of his body totally frozen. This was too much and he made another wild run along the trail. Once he slowed down to a walk, but the thought of the freezing extending itself made him run again.

And all the time the dog ran with him, at his heels. When he fell down a second time, it curled its tail over its forefeet and sat in front of him, facing him, curiously eager and intent. The warmth and security of the animal angered him, and he cursed it till it flattened down its ears appeasingly. This time the shivering came more quickly upon the man. He was losing in this battle with the frost. It was creeping into his body from all sides. The thought of it drove him on, but he ran no more than a hundred feet, when he staggered and pitched headlong. It was his last panic. When he recovered his breath and control, he sat up and entertained in his mind the conception of meeting death with dignity. However, the conception did not come to him in such terms. His idea of it was that he had been making a fool of himself, running around like a chicken with its head cut off—such was the simile that occurred to him. Well, he was bound to freeze anyway, and he might as well take it decently. With this newfound peace of mind came the first glimmerings of drowsiness. A good idea, he thought, to sleep off to death. It was like taking an anaesthetic. Freezing was not so bad as people thought. There were lots worse ways to die.

He pictured the boys finding his body next day. Suddenly he found himself with them, coming along the trail and looking for himself. And, still with them, he came around a turn in the trail and found himself lying in the snow. He did not belong with himself any more, for even then he was out of himself, standing with the boys and looking at himself in the snow. It certainly was cold, was his thought. When he got back to the States he could tell the folks what real cold was. He drifted on from this to a vision of the old-timer on Sulphur Creek. He could see him quite clearly, warm and comfortable, and smoking a pipe.

"You were right, old hoss; you were right," the man mumbled to the old-timer of Sulphur Creek.

Then the man drowsed off into what seemed to him the most comfortable and satisfying sleep he had ever known. The dog sat facing him and waiting. The brief day drew to a close in a long, slow twilight. There were no signs of a fire to be made, and, besides, never in the dog's experience had it known a man to sit like that in the snow and make no fire. As twilight drew on, its eager yearning for the fire mastered it, and with a great lifting and shifting of forefeet, it whined softly, then flattened its ears down in anticipation of being chidden by the man. But the man remained silent. Later, the dog whined loudly. And still late it crept close to the man and caught the scent of death. This made the animal bristle and back away. A little longer it delayed, howling under the stars that leaped and danced and shone brightly in the cold sky. Then it turned and trotted up the trail in the direction of the camp it knew, where were the other food-providers and fire-providers.

# Bernard Malamud

## (1914–1986)

Bernard Malamud's stories of Jewish immigrants in urban New York combine humor, suffering, and, above all, emotional honesty. Malamud was born in Brooklyn, New York, the son of Russian Jews. He received his B.A. from City College of New York in 1936 and taught at several high schools in New York City from 1940 until 1949. During that time, he attended Columbia University, where he received his M.A. in 1942. He also published his first short stories, "Benefit Performance" in *Threshold* and "The Place Is Different Now" in *American Preface*, in 1943. From 1949 to 1961, Malamud taught at Oregon State University. In 1952, he published his first book, *The Natural*, a fable about a baseball hero gifted with miraculous powers. He followed with *The Assistant* (1957). *The Magic Barrel* (1958), his first collection of stories, won the National Book Award in 1959. Malamud was a professor at Bennington College from 1961 to 1966 and 1968 to 1986. His works include *A New Life* (1961), *Idiots First* (1963), *The Fixer* (1966), *Pictures of Fidelman* (1969), *The Tenants* (1971), *Dubin's Lives* (1979), and *God's Grace* (1982). *The Fixer* won both the Pulitzer Prize and the National Book Award.

## The Magic Barrel                                             1958

Not long ago there lived in uptown New York, in a small, almost meager room, though crowded with books, Leo Finkle, a rabbinical student at the Yeshiva University. Finkle, after six years of study, was to be ordained in June and had been advised by an acquaintance that he might find it easier to win himself a congregation if he were married. Since he had no present prospects of marriage, after two tormented days of turning it over in his mind, he called in Pinye Salzman, a marriage broker whose two-line advertisement he had read in the *Forward.*[1]

The matchmaker appeared one night out of the dark fourth-floor hallway of the graystone rooming house where Finkle lived, grasping a black, strapped portfolio that had been worn thin with use. Salzman, who had been long in the business, was of slight but dignified build, wearing an old hat, and an overcoat too short and tight for him. He smelled frankly of fish, which he loved to eat, and although he was missing a few teeth, his presence was not displeasing, because of an amiable manner curiously contrasted with mournful eyes. His voice, his lips, his wisp of beard, his bony fingers were animated, but give him a moment of repose and his mild blue eyes revealed a depth of sadness, a characteristic that put Leo a little at ease although the situation, for him, was inherently tense.

He at once informed Salzman why he had asked him to come, explaining that but for his parents, who had married comparatively late in life, he was alone in the world. He had for six years devoted himself almost entirely to his studies, as a result of which, understandably, he had found himself without time for social life and the company of young women. Therefore he thought it the better part of trial and error—of embarrassing fumbling—to call in an experienced person to advise him on these matters. He remarked in passing that the function of the marriage broker was ancient and honorable, highly approved in the Jewish community, because it made practical the necessary without hindering joy. Moreover, his own parents had been brought together by a matchmaker. They had made, if not a financially profitable marriage—since neither had possessed any worldly goods to speak of—at least a successful one in the sense of their everlasting devotion to each other. Salzman listened in embarrassed surprise, sensing a sort of apology. Later, however, he experienced a glow of pride in his work, an emotion that had left him years ago, and he heartily approved of Finkle.

The two went to their business. Leo had led Salzman to the only clear place in the room, a table near a window that overlooked the lamp-lit city. He seated himself at the matchmaker's side but facing him, attempting by an act of will to suppress the unpleasant tickle in his throat. Salzman eagerly unstrapped his portfolio and removed a loose rubber band from a thin packet of much-handled cards. As he flipped through them, a gesture and sound that physically hurt Leo, the student pretended not to see and gazed steadfastly out the window. Although it was still February, winter was on its

---

1 **Forward:** *The Jewish Daily Forward,* a Yiddish-language newspaper.

last legs, signs of which he had for the first time in years begun to notice. He now observed the round white moon, moving high in the sky through a cloud menagerie, and watched with half-open mouth as it penetrated a huge hen, and dropped out of her like an egg laying itself. Salzman, though pretending through eyeglasses he had just slipped on to be engaged in scanning the writing on the cards, stole occasional glances at the young man's distinguished face, noting with pleasure the long, severe scholar's nose, brown eyes heavy with learning, sensitive yet ascetic lips, and a certain almost hollow quality of the dark cheeks. He gazed around at shelves upon shelves of books and let out a soft, contented sigh.

When Leo's eyes fell upon the cards, he counted six spread out in Salzman's hand. "So few?" he asked in disappointment.

"You wouldn't believe me how much cards I got in my office," Salzman replied. "The drawers are already filled to the top, so I keep them now in a barrel, but is every girl good for a new rabbi?"

Leo blushed at this, regretting all he had revealed of himself in a curriculum vitae he had sent to Salzman. He had thought it best to acquaint him with his strict standards and specifications, but in having done so, felt he had told the marriage broker more than was absolutely necessary.

He hesitantly inquired, "Do you keep photographs of your clients on file?"

"First comes family, amount of dowry, also what kind promises," Salzman replied, unbuttoning his tight coat and settling himself in the chair. "After comes pictures, rabbi."

"Call me Mr. Finkle. I'm not yet a rabbi."

Salzman said he would, but instead called him doctor, which he changed to rabbi when Leo was not listening too attentively.

Salzman adjusted his horn-rimmed spectacles, gently cleared his throat, and read in an eager voice the contents of the top card:

"Sophie P. Twenty-four years. Widow one year. No children. Educated high school and two years college. Father promises eight thousand dollars. Has wonderful wholesale business. Also real estate. On the mother's side comes teachers, also one actor. Well known on Second Avenue."

Leo gazed up in surprise. "Did you say a widow?"

"A widow don't mean spoiled, rabbi. She lived with her husband maybe four months. He was a sick boy she made a mistake to marry him."

"Marrying a widow has never entered my mind."

"This is because you have no experience. A widow, especially if she is young and healthy like this girl, is a wonderful person to marry. She will be thankful to you the rest of her life. Believe me, if I was looking now for a bride, I would marry a widow."

Leo reflected, then shook his head.

Salzman hunched his shoulders in an almost imperceptible gesture of disappointment. He placed the card down on the wooden table and began to read another:

"Lily H. High school teacher. Regular. Not a substitute. Has savings and new Dodge car. Lived in Paris one year. Father is successful dentist thirty-five years. Interested in professional man. Well-Americanized family. Wonderful opportunity.

"I know her personally," said Salzman. "I wish you could see this girl. She is a doll. Also very intelligent. All day you could talk to her about books and theyater and what not. She also knows current events."

"I don't believe you mentioned her age?"

"Her age?" Salzman said, raising his brows. "Her age is thirty-two years."

Leo said after a while, "I'm afraid that seems a little too old."

Salzman let out a laugh. "So how old are you, rabbi?"

"Twenty-seven."

"So what is the difference, tell me, between twenty-seven and thirty-two? My own wife is seven years older than me. So what did I suffer?—Nothing. If Roth-schild's[2] daughter wants to marry you, would you say on account her age, no?"

"Yes," Leo said dryly.

Salzman shook off the no in the yes. "Five years don't mean a thing. I give you my word that when you will live with her for one week you will forget her age. What does it mean five years—that she lived more and knows more than somebody who is younger? On this girl, God bless her, years are not wasted. Each one that it comes makes better the bargain."

"What subject does she teach in high school?"

"Languages. If you heard the way she speaks French, you will think it is music. I am in the business twenty-five years, and I recommend her with my whole heart. Believe me, I know what I'm talking, rabbi."

"What's on the next card?" Leo said abruptly.

Salzman reluctantly turned up the third card:

"Ruth K. Nineteen years. Honor student. Father offers thirteen thousand cash to the right bridegroom. He is a medical doctor. Stomach specialist with marvelous practice. Brother-in-law owns own garment business. Particular people."

Salzman looked as if he had read his trump card.

"Did you say nineteen?" Leo asked with interest.

"On the dot."

"Is she attractive?" He blushed. "Pretty?"

Salzman kissed his fingertips. "A little doll. On this I give you my word. Let me call the father tonight and you will see what means pretty."

But Leo was troubled. "You're sure she's that young?"

"This I am positive. The father will show you the birth certificate."

"Are you positive there isn't something wrong with her?" Leo insisted.

"Who says there is wrong?"

"I don't understand why an American girl her age should go to a marriage broker."

A smile spread over Salzman's face.

"So for the same reason you went, she comes."

Leo flushed. "I am pressed for time."

2 **Rothschild:** Jewish-German family of bankers, including Mayer Amschal (1743–1812), Salomon (1774–1855), and Nathan Mayer (1774–1836).

Salzman, realizing he had been tactless, quickly explained. "The father came, not her. He wants she should have the best, so he looks around himself. When we will locate the right boy he will introduce him and encourage. This makes a better marriage than if a young girl without experience takes for herself. I don't have to tell you this."

"But don't you think this young girl believes in love?" Leo spoke uneasily.

Salzman was about to guffaw but caught himself and said soberly, "Love comes with the right person, not before."

Leo parted dry lips but did not speak. Noticing that Salzman had snatched a glance at the next card, he cleverly asked, "How is her health?"

"Perfect," Salzman said, breathing with difficulty. "Of course, she is a little lame on her right foot from an auto accident that it happened to her when she was twelve years, but nobody notices on account she is so brilliant and also beautiful."

Leo got up heavily and went to the window. He felt curiously bitter and upbraided himself for having called in the marriage broker. Finally, he shook his head.

"Why not?" Salzman persisted, the pitch of his voice rising.

"Because I detest stomach specialists."

"So what do you care what is his business? After you marry her do you need him? Who says he must come every Friday night in your house?"

Ashamed of the way the talk was going, Leo dismissed Salzman, who went home with heavy, melancholy eyes.

Though he had felt only relief at the marriage broker's departure, Leo was in low spirits the next day. He explained it as arising from Salzman's failure to produce a suitable bride for him. He did not care for his type of clientele. But when Leo found himself hesitating whether to seek out another matchmaker, one more polished than Pinye, he wondered if it could be—his protestations to the contrary, and although he honored his father and mother—that he did not, in essence, care for the matchmaking institution? This thought he quickly put out of mind yet found himself still upset. All day he ran around in the woods—missed an important appointment, forgot to give out his laundry, walked out of a Broadway cafeteria without paying and had to run back with the ticket in his hand; had even not recognized his landlady in the street when she passed with a friend and courteously called out, "A good evening to you, Doctor Finkle." By nightfall, however, he had regained sufficient calm to sink his nose into a book and there found peace from his thoughts.

Almost at once there came a knock on the door. Before Leo could say enter, Salzman, commercial cupid, was standing in the room. His face was gray and meager, his expression hungry, and he looked as if he would expire on his feet. Yet the marriage broker managed, by some trick of the muscles, to display a broad smile.

"So good evening. I am invited?"

Leo nodded, disturbed to see him again, yet unwilling to ask the man to leave.

Beaming still, Salzman laid his portfolio on the table. "Rabbi, I got for you tonight good news."

"I've asked you not to call me rabbi. I'm still a student."

"Your worries are finished. I have for you a first-class bride."

"Leave me in peace concerning this subject." Leo pretended lack of interest.

"The world will dance at your wedding."

"Please, Mr. Salzman, no more."

"But first must come back my strength," Salzman said weakly. He fumbled with the portfolio straps and took out of the leather case an oily paper bag, from which he extracted a hard, seeded roll and a small smoked whitefish. With a quick motion of his hand he stripped the fish out of its skin and began ravenously to chew. "All day in a rush," he muttered.

Leo watched him eat.

"A sliced tomato you have maybe?" Salzman hesitantly inquired.

"No."

The marriage broker shut his eyes and ate. When he had finished he carefully cleaned up the crumbs and rolled up the remains of the fish, in the paper bag. His spectacled eyes roamed the room until he discovered, amid some piles of books, a one-burner gas stove. Lifting his hat he humbly asked, "A glass tea you got, rabbi?"

Conscience-stricken, Leo rose and brewed the tea. He served it with a chunk of lemon and two cubes of lump sugar, delighting Salzman.

After he had drunk his tea, Salzman's strength and good spirits were restored.

"So tell me, rabbi," he said amiably, "you considered some more the three clients I mentioned yesterday?"

"There was no need to consider."

"Why not?"

"None of them suits me."

"What then suits you?"

Leo let it pass because he could give only a confused answer.

Without waiting for a reply, Salzman asked, "You remember this girl I talked to you—the high school teacher?"

"Age thirty-two?"

But, surprisingly, Salzman's face lit in a smile. "Age twenty-nine."

Leo shot him a look. "Reduced from thirty-two?"

"A mistake," Salzman avowed. "I talked today with the dentist. He took me to his safety deposit box and showed me the birth certificate. She was twenty-nine years last August. They made her a party in the mountains where she went for her vacation. When her father spoke to me the first time I forgot to write the age and I told you thirty-two, but now I remember this was a different client, a widow."

"The same one you told me about, I thought she was twenty-four?"

"A different. Am I responsible that the world is filled with widows?"

"No, but I'm not interested in them, nor, for that matter, in schoolteachers."

Salzman pulled his clasped hands to his breast. Looking at the ceiling he devoutly exclaimed, "Yiddishe kinder,[3] what can I say to somebody that he is not interested in high school teachers? So what then you are interested?"

Leo flushed but controlled himself.

"In what else will you be interested," Salzman went on, "if you not interested in

---

3 **Yiddishe kinder:** Yiddish. Yiddish (Jewish) children.

this fine girl that she speaks four languages and has personally in the bank ten thousand dollars? Also her father guarantees further twelve thousand. Also she has a new car, wonderful clothes, talks on all subjects, and she will give you a first-class home and children. How near do we come in our life to paradise?"

"If she's so wonderful, why wasn't she married ten years ago?"

"Why?" said Salzman with a heavy laugh. "—Why? Because she is *partikiler*. This is why. She wants the *best*."

Leo was silent, amused at how he had entangled himself. But Salzman had aroused his interest in Lily H., and he began seriously to consider calling on her. When the marriage broker observed how intently Leo's mind was at work on the facts he had supplied, he felt certain they would soon come to an agreement.

Late Saturday afternoon, conscious of Salzman, Leo Finkle walked with Lily Hirschorn along Riverside Drive. He walked briskly and erectly, wearing with distinction the black fedora he had that morning taken with trepidation out of the dusty hat box on his closet shelf, and the heavy black Saturday coat he had thoroughly whisked clean. Leo also owned a walking stick, a present from a distant relative, but quickly put temptation aside and did not use it. Lily, petite and not unpretty, had on something signifying the approach of spring. She was au courant,[4] animatedly, with all sorts of subjects, and he weighed her words and found her surprisingly sound—score another for Salzman, whom he uneasily sensed to be somewhere around, hiding perhaps high in a tree along the street, flashing the lady signals with a pocket mirror; or perhaps a cloven-hoofed Pan, piping nuptial ditties as he danced his invisible way before them, strewing wild buds on the walk and purple grapes in their path, symbolizing fruit of a union, though there was of course still none.

Lily startled Leo by remarking, "I was thinking of Mr. Salzman, a curious figure, wouldn't you say?"

Not certain what to answer, he nodded.

She bravely went on, blushing, "I for one am grateful for his introducing us. Aren't you?"

He courteously replied, "I am."

"I mean," she said with a little laugh—and it was all in good taste, or at least gave the effect of being not in bad—"do you mind that we came together so?"

He was not displeased with her honesty, recognizing that she meant to set the relationship aright, and understanding that it took a certain amount of experience in life, and courage, to want to do it quite that way. One had to have some sort of past to make that kind of beginning.

He said that he did not mind. Salzman's function was traditional and honorable—valuable for what it might achieve, which, he pointed out, was frequently nothing.

Lily agreed with a sigh. They walked on for a while and she said after a long silence, again with a nervous laugh, "Would you mind if I asked you something a little bit personal? Frankly, I find the subject fascinating." Although Leo shrugged, she went

4 **au courant:** Up-to-date, knowledgeable.

on half embarrassedly, "How was it that you came to your calling? I mean, was it a sudden passionate inspiration?"

Leo, after a time, slowly replied, "I was always interested in the Law."

"You saw revealed in it the presence of the Highest?"

He nodded and changed the subject. "I understand that you spent a little time in Paris, Miss Hirschorn?"

"Oh, did Mr. Salzman tell you, Rabbi Finkle?" Leo winced but she went on, "It was ages ago and almost forgotten. I remember I had to return for my sister's wedding."

And Lily would not be put off. "When," she asked in a slightly trembly voice, "did you become enamored of God?"

He stared at her. Then it came to him that she was talking not about Leo Finkle but of a total stranger, some mystical figure, perhaps even passionate prophet that Salzman had dreamed up for her—no relation to the living or dead. Leo trembled with rage and weakness. The trickster had obviously sold her a bill of goods, just as he had him, who'd expected to become acquainted with a young lady of twenty-nine, only to behold, the moment he had laid eyes upon her strained and anxious face, a woman past thirty-five and aging rapidly. Only his self-control had kept him this long in her presence.

"I am not," he said gravely, "a talented religious person," and in seeking words to go on, found himself possessed by shame and fear. "I think," he said in a strained manner, "that I came to God not because I loved Him but because I did not."

This confession he spoke harshly because its unexpectedness shook him.

Lily wilted. Leo saw a profusion of loaves of bread go flying like ducks high over his head, not unlike the winged loaves by which he had counted himself to sleep last night. Mercifully, then, it snowed, which he would not put past Salzman's machinations.

He was infuriated with the marriage broker and swore he would throw him out of the room the moment he reappeared. But Salzman did not come that night, and when Leo's anger had subsided, an unaccountable despair grew in its place. At first he thought this was caused by his disappointment in Lily, but before long it became evident that he had involved himself with Salzman without a true knowledge of his own intent. He gradually realized—with an emptiness that seized him with six hands—that he had called in the broker to find him a bride because he was incapable of doing it himself. This terrifying insight he had derived as a result of his meeting and conversation with Lily Hirschorn. Her probing questions had somehow irritated him into revealing—to himself more than her—the true nature of his relationship to God, and from that it had come upon him, with shocking force, that apart from his parents, he had never loved anyone. Or perhaps it went the other way, that he did not love God so well as he might, because he had not loved man. It seemed to Leo that his whole life stood starkly revealed and he saw himself for the first time as he truly was— unloved and loveless. This bitter but somehow not fully unexpected revelation brought him to a point of panic, controlled only by extraordinary effort. He covered his face with his hands and cried.

The week that followed was the worst of his life. He did not eat and lost weight. His beard darkened and grew ragged. He stopped attending seminars and almost never opened a book. He seriously considered leaving the Yeshiva, although he was deeply troubled at the thought of the loss of all his years of study—saw them like pages torn from a book, strewn over the city—and at the devastating effect of this decision upon his parents. But he had lived without knowledge of himself, and never in the Five Books and all the Commentaries[5]—mea culpa[6]—had the truth been revealed to him. He did not know where to turn, and in all this desolating loneliness there was no *to whom,* although he often thought of Lily but not once could bring himself to go downstairs and make the call. He became touchy and irritable, especially with his landlady, who asked him all manner of personal questions; on the other hand, sensing his own disagreeableness, he waylaid her on the stairs and apologized abjectly, until, mortified, she ran from him. Out of this, however, he drew the consolation that he was a Jew and that a Jew suffered. But gradually, as the long and terrible week drew to a close, he regained his composure and some idea of purpose in life: to go on as planned. Although he was imperfect, the ideal was not. As for his quest of a bride, the thought of continuing afflicted him with anxiety and heartburn, yet perhaps with this new knowledge of himself he would be more successful than in the past. Perhaps love would now come to him and a bride to that love. And for this sanctified seeking who needed a Salzman?

The marriage broker, a skeleton with haunted eyes, returned that very night. He looked, withal, the picture of frustrated expectancy—as if he had steadfastly waited the week at Miss Lily Hirschorn's side for a telephone call that never came.

Casually coughing, Salzman came immediately to the point: "So how did you like her?"

Leo's anger rose and he could not refrain from chiding the matchmaker: "Why did you lie to me, Salzman?"

Salzman's pale face went dead white, the world had snowed on him.

"Did you not state that she was twenty-nine?" Leo insisted.

"I give you my word—"

"She was thirty-five, if a day. *At least* thirty-five."

"Of this don't be too sure. Her father told me—"

"Never mind. The worst of it is that you lied to her."

"How did I lie to her, tell me?"

"You told her things about me that weren't true. You made me out to be more, consequently less than I am. She had in mind a totally different person, a sort of semi-mystical Wonder Rabbi."

"All I said, you was a religious man."

"I can imagine."

Salzman sighed. "This is my weakness that I have," he confessed. "My wife says to

5 **Five Books and all the Commentaries:** The first five books of the Hebrew Bible are Genesis, Exodus, Leviticus, Numbers, and Deuteronomy.
6 **mea culpa:** Latin. Through my fault.

me I shouldn't be a salesman, but when I have two fine people that they would be wonderful to be married, I am so happy that I talk too much." He smiled wanly. "This is why Salzman is a poor man."

Leo's anger left him. "Well, Salzman, I'm afraid that's all."

The marriage broker fastened hungry eyes on him.

"You don't want any more a bride?"

"I do," said Leo, "but I have decided to seek her in another way. I am no longer interested in an arranged marriage. To be frank, I now admit the necessity of premarital love. That is, I want to be in love with the one I marry."

"Love?" said Salzman, astounded. After a moment he remarked, "For us, our love is our life, not for the ladies. In the ghetto they—"

"I know, I know," said Leo. "I've thought of it often. Love, I have said to myself, should be a product of living and worship rather than its own end. Yet for myself I find it necessary to establish the level of my need and fulfill it."

Salzman shrugged but answered, "Listen, rabbi, if you want love, this I can find for you also. I have such beautiful clients that you will love them the minute your eyes will see them."

Leo smiled unhappily. "I'm afraid you don't understand."

But Salzman hastily unstrapped his portfolio and withdrew a manila packet from it.

"Pictures," he said, quickly laying the envelope on the table.

Leo called after him to take the pictures away, but as if on the wings of the wind, Salzman had disappeared.

March came. Leo had returned to his regular routine. Although he felt not quite himself yet—lacked energy—he was making plans for a more active social life. Of course it would cost something, but he was an expert in cutting corners; and when there were no corners left he would make circles rounder. All the while Salzman's pictures had lain on the table, gathering dust. Occasionally as Leo sat studying, or enjoying a cup of tea, his eyes fell on the manila envelope, but he never opened it.

The days went by and no social life to speak of developed with a member of the opposite sex—it was difficult, given the circumstances of his situation. One morning Leo toiled up the stairs to his room and stared out the window at the city. Although the day was bright his view of it was dark. For some time he watched the people in the street below hurrying along and then turned with a heavy heart to his little room. On the table was the packet. With a sudden relentless gesture he tore it open. For a half hour he stood by the table in a state of excitement, examining the photographs of the ladies Salzman had included. Finally, with a deep sigh he put them down. There were six, of varying degrees of attractiveness, but look at them long enough and they all became Lily Hirschorn: all past their prime, all starved behind bright smiles, not a true personality in the lot. Life, despite their frantic yoohooings, had passed them by; they were pictures in a briefcase that stank of fish. After a while, however, as Leo attempted to return the photographs into the envelope, he found in it another, a snapshot of the type taken by a machine for a quarter. He gazed at it a moment and let out a low cry.

Her face deeply moved him. Why, he could at first not say. It gave him the impression of youth—spring flowers, yet age—a sense of having been used to the bone, wasted; this came from the eyes, which were hauntingly familiar, yet absolutely strange. He had a vivid impression that he had met her before, but try as he might he could not place her although he could almost recall her name, as if he had read it in her own handwriting. No, this couldn't be; he would have remembered her. It was not, he affirmed, that she had an extraordinary beauty—no, though her face was attractive enough; it was that *something* about her moved him. Feature for feature, even some of the ladies of the photographs could do better; but she leaped forth to his heart—had *lived,* or wanted to—more than just wanted, perhaps regretted how she had lived—had somehow deeply suffered: it could be seen in the depths of those reluctant eyes, and from the way the light enclosed and shone from her, and within her, opening realms of possibility: this was her own. Her he desired. His head ached and eyes narrowed with the intensity of his gazing, then as if an obscure fog had blown up in the mind, he experienced fear of her and was aware that he had received an impression, somehow, of evil. He shuddered, saying softly, it is thus with us all. Leo brewed some tea in a small pot and sat sipping it without sugar, to calm himself. But before he had finished drinking, again with excitement he examined the face and found it good: good for Leo Finkle. Only such a one could understand him and help him seek whatever he was seeking. She might, perhaps, love him. How she had happened to be among the discards in Salzman's barrel he could never guess, but he knew he must urgently go find her.

Leo rushed downstairs, grabbed up the Bronx telephone book, and searched for Salzman's home address. He was not listed, nor was his office. Neither was he in the Manhattan book. But Leo remembered having written down the address on a slip of paper after he had read Salzman's advertisement in the "personals" column of the *Forward.* He ran up to his room and tore through his papers, without luck. It was exasperating. Just when he needed the matchmaker he was nowhere to be found. Fortunately Leo remembered to look in his wallet. There on a card he found his name written and a Bronx address. No phone number was listed, the reason—Leo now recalled—he had originally communicated with Salzman by letter. He got on his coat, put a hat on over his skullcap and hurried to the subway station. All the way to the far end of the Bronx he sat on the edge of his seat. He was more than once tempted to take out the picture and see if the girl's face was as he remembered, but he refrained, allowing the snapshot to remain in his inside coat pocket, content to have her so close. When the train pulled into the station he was waiting at the door and bolted out. He quickly located the street Salzman had advertised.

The building he sought was less than a block from the subway, but it was not an office building, nor even a loft, nor a store in which one could rent office space. It was a very old tenement house. Leo found Salzman's name in pencil on a soiled tag under the bell and climbed three dark flights to his apartment. When he knocked, the door was opened by a thin, asthmatic, gray-haired woman, in felt slippers.

"Yes?" she said, expecting nothing. She listened without listening. He could have sworn he had seen her, too, before but knew it was an illusion.

"Salzman—does he live here? Pinye Salzman," he said, "the matchmaker?"

She stared at him a long minute. "Of course."

He felt embarrassed. "Is he in?"

"No." Her mouth, though left open, offered nothing more.

"The matter is urgent. Can you tell me where his office is?"

"In the air." She pointed upward.

"You mean he has no office?" Leo asked.

"In his socks."

He peered into the apartment. It was sunless and dingy, one large room divided by a half-open curtain, beyond which he could see a sagging metal bed. The near side of the room was crowded with rickety chairs, old bureaus, a three-legged table, racks of cooking utensils, and all the apparatus of a kitchen. But there was no sign of Salzman or his magic barrel, probably also a figment of the imagination. An odor of frying fish made Leo weak to the knees.

"Where is he?" he insisted. "I've got to see your husband."

At length she answered, "So who knows where he is? Every time he thinks a new thought he runs to a different place. Go home, he will find you."

"Tell him Leo Finkle."

She gave no sign she had heard.

He walked downstairs, depressed.

But Salzman, breathless, stood waiting at his door.

Leo was astounded and overjoyed. "How did you get here before me?"

"I rushed."

"Come inside."

They entered. Leo fixed tea, and a sardine sandwich for Salzman. As they were drinking he reached behind him for the packet of pictures and handed them to the marriage broker.

Salzman put down his glass and said expectantly, "You found somebody you like?"

"Not among these."

The marriage broker turned away.

"Here is the one I want." Leo held forth the snapshot.

Salzman slipped on his glasses and took the picture into his trembling hand. He turned ghastly and let out a groan.

"What's the matter?" cried Leo.

"Excuse me. Was an accident this picture. She isn't for you."

Salzman frantically shoved the manila packet into his portfolio. He thrust the snapshot into his pocket and fled down the stairs.

Leo, after momentary paralysis, gave chase and cornered the marriage broker in the vestibule. The landlady made hysterical outcries but neither of them listened.

"Give me back the picture, Salzman."

"No." The pain in his eyes was terrible.

"Tell me who she is then."

"This I can't tell you. Excuse me."

He made to depart, but Leo, forgetting himself, seized the matchmaker by his tight coat and shook him frenziedly.

"Please," sighed Salzman. "*Please.*"

Leo ashamedly let him go. "Tell me who she is," he begged. "It's very important for me to know."

"She is not for you. She is a wild one—wild, without shame. This is not a bride for a rabbi."

"What do you mean wild?"

"Like an animal. Like a dog. For her to be poor was a sin. This is why to me she is dead now."

"In God's name, what do you mean?"

"Her I can't introduce to you," Salzman cried.

"Why are you so excited?"

"Why, he asks," Salzman said, bursting into tears. "This is my baby, my Stella, she should burn in hell."

Leo hurried up to bed and hid under the covers. Under the covers he thought his life through. Although he soon fell asleep he could not sleep her out of his mind. He woke, beating his breast. Though he prayed to be rid of her, his prayers went unanswered. Through days of torment he endlessly struggled not to love her; fearing success, he escaped it. He then concluded to convert her to goodness, himself to God. The idea alternately nauseated and exalted him.

He perhaps did not know that he had come to a final decision until he encountered Salzman in a Broadway cafeteria. He was sitting alone at a rear table, sucking the bony remains of a fish. The marriage broker appeared haggard, and transparent to the point of vanishing.

Salzman looked up at first without recognizing him. Leo had grown a pointed beard and his eyes were weighted with wisdom.

"Salzman," he said, "love has at last come to my heart."

"Who can love from a picture?" mocked the marriage broker.

"It is not impossible."

"If you can love her, then you can love anybody. Let me show you some new clients that they just sent me their photographs. One is a little doll."

"Just her I want," Leo murmured.

"Don't be a fool, doctor. Don't bother with her."

"Put me in touch with her, Salzman," Leo said humbly. "Perhaps I can be of service."

Salzman had stopped eating and Leo understood with emotion that it was now arranged.

Leaving the cafeteria, he was, however, afflicted by a tormenting suspicion that Salzman had planned it all to happen this way.

Leo was informed by letter that she would meet him on a certain corner, and she was there one spring night, waiting under a street lamp. He appeared, carrying a small bouquet of violets and rosebuds. Stella stood by the lamp post, smoking. She wore white with red shoes, which fitted his expectations, although in a troubled moment he had imagined the dress red, and only the shoes white. She waited uneasily and shyly. From afar he saw that her eyes—clearly her father's—were filled with desperate innocence. He pictured, in her, his own redemption. Violins and lit candles revolved in the sky. Leo ran forward with flowers outthrust.

Around the corner, Salzman, leaning against a wall, chanted prayers for the dead.

# Katherine Mansfield

## (1888–1923)

Katherine Mansfield's writing reflects her feelings of loneliness, jealousy, alienation, and illness. She is known for her use of stream of consciousness and was greatly influenced by Anton Chekhov. Mansfield was born in Wellington, New Zealand, where she lived for six years in the rural village of Karori. In 1930, she went to London to study at Queen's College, and while there she joined the staff of the college magazine. She returned to New Zealand in 1906 and began to study music. During those years, Mansfield had several affairs with both men and women. In 1908, her lifelong friend Ida Baker convinced Mansfield's father to allow her to move back to England, with an allowance of 100 pounds a year. Mansfield never visited New Zealand again. In 1909, she toured Germany as an extra in an opera, and during that time she wrote *In a German Pension* (1911). She returned to London in 1910 but became ill from an untreated sexually transmitted disease. The condition weakened her health for the rest of her life.

In 1911, Mansfield met John Middleton Murray, a socialist and former literary critic, and the two became lovers. Her most famous story, "Prelude," was published in 1916. Murray and Mansfield married in 1918, the same year she discovered that she had tuberculosis. The couple became good friends with D. H. Lawrence and his wife Frieda, though Lawrence later turned against them. Mansfield published *Bliss* (1920), her family memoirs, and *Garden Party* (1922), a collection of short stories. In 1922, she underwent treatment for tuberculosis. The particular treatment consisted of spending a few hours every day on a platform suspended over a cow manger. Understandably, this did nothing to improve her health, and Mansfield died in 1923.

## *The Garden-Party*

*1922*

And after all the weather was ideal. They could not have had a more perfect day for a garden-party if they had ordered it. Windless, warm, the sky without a cloud. Only the blue was veiled with a haze of light gold, as it is sometimes in early summer. The gardener had been up since dawn, mowing the lawns and sweeping them, until the grass and the dark flat rosettes where the daisy plants had been seemed to shine. As for the roses, you could not help feeling they understood that roses are the only flowers that impress people at garden-parties; the only flowers that everybody is certain of knowing. Hundreds, yes, literally hundreds, had come out in a single night; the green bushes bowed down as though they had been visited by archangels.

Breakfast was not yet over before the men came to put up the marquee.[1]

"Where do you want the marquee put, mother?"

"My dear child, it's no use asking me. I'm determined to leave everything to you children this year. Forget I am your mother. Treat me as an honoured guest."

But Meg could not possibly go and supervise the men. She had washed her hair before breakfast, and she sat drinking her coffee in a green turban, with a dark wet curl stamped on each cheek. Jose, the butterfly, always came down in a silk petticoat and a kimono jacket.

"You'll have to go, Laura; you're the artistic one."

Away Laura flew, still holding her piece of bread-and-butter. It's so delicious to have an excuse for eating out of doors, and besides, she loved having to arrange things; she always felt she could do it so much better than anybody else.

Four men in their shirt-sleeves stood grouped together on the garden path. They carried staves covered with rolls of canvas, and they had big tool-bags slung on their backs. They looked impressive. Laura wished now that she had not got the bread-and-butter, but there was nowhere to put it, and she couldn't possibly throw it away. She blushed and tried to look severe and even a little bit short-sighted as she came up to them.

"Good morning," she said, copying her mother's voice. But that sounded so fearfully affected that she was ashamed, and stammered like a little girl, "Oh—er—have you come—is it about the marquee?"

"That's right, miss," said the tallest of the men, a lanky, freckled fellow, and he shifted his tool-bag, knocked back his straw hat and smiled down at her. "That's about it."

His smile was so easy, so friendly that Laura recovered. What nice eyes he had, small, but such a dark blue! And now she looked at the others, they were smiling too. "Cheer-up, we won't bite," their smile seemed to say. How very nice workmen were! And what a beautiful morning! She mustn't mention the morning; she must be business like. The marquee.

"Well, what about the lily-lawn? Would that do?"

And she pointed to the lily-lawn with the hand that didn't hold the bread-and-butter. They turned, they stared in the direction. A little fat chap thrust out his under-lip, and the tall fellow frowned.

"I don't fancy it," said he. "Not conspicuous enough. You see, with a thing like a

---

1 **marquee:** A canvas open-sided tent set up for outdoor parties.

marquee," and he turned to Laura in his easy way, "you want to put it somewhere where it'll give you a bang slap in the eye, if you follow me."

Laura's upbringing made her wonder for a moment whether it was quite respectful of a workman to talk to her of bangs slap in the eye. But she did quite follow him.

"A corner of the tennis-court," she suggested. "But the band's going to be in one corner."

"H'm, going to have a band, are you?" said another of the workmen. He was pale. He had a haggard look as his dark eyes scanned the tennis-court. What was he thinking?

"Only a very small band," said Laura gently. Perhaps he wouldn't mind so much if the band was quite small. But the tall fellow interrupted.

"Look here, miss, that's the place. Against those trees. Over there. That'll do fine."

Against the karakas. Then the karaka trees would be hidden. And they were so lovely, with their broad, gleaming leaves, and their clusters of yellow fruit. They were like trees you imagined growing on a desert island, proud, solitary, lifting their leaves and fruits to the sun in a kind of silent splendour. Must they be hidden by a marquee?

They must. Already the men had shouldered their staves and were making for the place. Only the tall fellow was left. He bent down, pinched a sprig of lavender, put his thumb and forefinger to his nose and snuffed up the smell. When Laura saw that gesture she forgot all about the karakas in her wonder at him caring for things like that— caring for the smell of lavender. How many men that she knew would have done such a thing? Oh, how extraordinarily nice workmen were, she thought. Why couldn't she have workmen for friends rather than the silly boys she danced with and who came to Sunday night supper? She would get on much better with men like these.

It's all the fault, she decided, as the tall fellow drew something on the back of an envelope, something that was to be looped up or left to hang, of these absurd class distinctions. Well, for her part, she didn't feel them. Not a bit, not an atom. . . . And now there came the chock-chock of wooden hammers. Some one whistled, some one sang out, "Are you right there, matey?" "Matey!" The friendliness of it, the—the— Just to prove how happy she was, just to show the tall fellow how at home she felt, and how she despised stupid conventions, Laura took a big bite of her bread-and-butter as she stared at the little drawing. She felt just like a work-girl.

"Laura, Laura, where are you? Telephone, Laura!" a voice cried from the house.

"Coming!" Away she skimmed, over the lawn, up the path, up the steps, across the verandah, and into the porch. In the hall her father and Laurie were brushing their hats ready to go to the office.

"I say, Laura," said Laurie very fast, "you might just give a squiz at my coat before this afternoon. See if it wants pressing."

"I will," she said. Suddenly she couldn't stop herself. She ran at Laurie and gave him a small, quick squeeze. "Oh, I do love parties, don't you?" gasped Laura.

"Rather," said Laurie's warm, boyish voice, and he squeezed his sister too, and gave her a gentle push. "Dash off to the telephone, old girl."

The telephone. "Yes; yes; oh yes. Kitty? Good morning, dear. Come to lunch? Do, dear. Delighted of course. It will only be a very scratch meal—just the sandwich crusts and broken meringue-shells and what's left over. Yes, isn't it a perfect morning? Your white? Oh, I certainly should. One moment—hold the line. Mother's calling." And Laura sat back. "What, mother? Can't hear."

Mrs. Sheridan's voice floated down the stairs. "Tell her to wear that sweet hat she had on last Sunday."

"Mother says you're to wear that *sweet* hat you had on last Sunday. Good. One o'clock. Bye-bye."

Laura put back the receiver, flung her arms over her head, took a deep breath, stretched and let them fall. "Huh," she sighed, and the moment after the sigh she sat up quickly. She was still, listening. All the doors in the house seemed to open. The house was alive with soft, quick steps and running voices. The green baize door that led to the kitchen regions swung open and shut with a muffled thud. And now there came a long, chuckling absurd sound. It was the heavy piano being moved on its stiff castors. But the air! If you stopped to notice, was the air always like this? Little faint winds were playing chase, in at the tops of the windows, out at the doors. And there were two tiny spots of sun, one on the inkpot, one on a silver photograph frame, playing too. Darling little spots. Especially the one on the inkpot lid. It was quite warm. A warm little silver star. She could have kissed it.

The front door bell pealed, and there sounded the rustle of Sadie's print skirt on the stairs. A man's voice murmured; Sadie answered, careless, "I'm sure I don't know. Wait. I'll ask Mrs. Sheridan."

"What is it, Sadie?" Laura came into the hall.

"It's the florist, Miss Laura."

It was, indeed. There, just inside the door, stood a wide, shallow tray full of pots of pink lilies. No other kind. Nothing but lilies—canna lilies, big pink flowers, wide open, radiant, almost frighteningly alive on bright crimson stems.

"O-oh, Sadie!" said Laura, and the sound was like a little moan. She crouched down as if to warm herself at that blaze of lilies; she felt they were in her fingers, on her lips, growing in her breast.

"It's some mistake," she said faintly. "Nobody ever ordered so many. Sadie, go and find mother."

But at that moment Mrs. Sheridan joined them.

"It's quite right," she said calmly. "Yes, I ordered them. Aren't they lovely?" She pressed Laura's arm. "I was passing the shop yesterday, and I saw them in the window. And I suddenly thought for once in my life I shall have enough canna lilies. The garden-party will be a good excuse."

"But I thought you said you didn't mean to interfere," said Laura. Sadie had gone. The florist's man was still outside at his van. She put her arm round her mother's neck and gently, very gently, she bit her mother's ear.

"My darling child, you wouldn't like a logical mother, would you? Don't do that. Here's the man."

He carried more lilies still, another whole tray.

"Bank them up, just inside the door, on both sides of the porch, please," said Mrs. Sheridan. "Don't you agree, Laura?"

"Oh, I *do* mother."

In the drawing-room, Meg, Jose and good little Hans had at last succeeded in moving the piano.

"Now, if we put this chesterfield against the wall and move everything out of the room except the chairs, don't you think?"

"Quite."

"Hans, move these tables into the smoking-room, and bring a sweeper to take these marks off the carpet and—one moment, Hans—" Jose loved giving orders to the servants, and they loved obeying her. She always made them feel they were taking part in some drama. "Tell mother and Miss Laura to come here at once."

"Very good, Miss Jose."

She turned to Meg. "I want to hear what the piano sounds like, just in case I'm asked to sing this afternoon. Let's try over 'This life is Weary.'"

*Pom!* Ta-ta-ta *Tee*-ta! The piano burst out so passionately that Jose's face changed. She clasped her hands. She looked mournfully and enigmatically at her mother and Laura as they came in.

> This Life is *Wee*-ary,
> A Tear—a Sigh.
> A Love that *Chan*-ges,
> > This life is *Wee*-ary,
> A Tear—a Sigh.
> A Love that *Chan*-ges,
> And then . . . Good-bye!

But at the word "Good-bye," and although the piano sounded more desperate than ever, her face broke into a brilliant, dreadfully unsympathetic smile.

"Aren't I in good voice, mummy?" she beamed.

> This Life is *Wee*-ary,
> Hope come to Die.
> A Dream—a *Wa*-kening.

But now Sadie interrupted them. "What is it, Sadie?"

"If you please, m'm, cook says have you got the flags[2] for the sandwiches?"

"The flags for the sandwiches, Sadie?" echoed Mrs. Sheridan dreamily. And the children knew by her face that she hadn't got them. "Let me see." And she said to Sadie firmly, "Tell cook I'll let her have them in ten minutes."

Sadie went.

"Now, Laura," said her mother quickly. "Come with me into the smoking-room. I've got the names somewhere on the back of an envelope. You'll have to write them out for me. Meg, go upstairs this minute and take that wet thing off your head. Jose, run and finish dressing this instant. Do you hear me, children, or shall I have to tell

2 **flags:** Toothpick and paper decorations placed on the top of sandwiches or hors d'oeuvres.

your father when he comes home to-night? And—and, Jose, pacify cook if you do go into the kitchen, will you? I'm terrified of her this morning."

The envelope was found at last behind the dining-room clock, though how it had got there Mrs. Sheridan could not imagine.

"One of you children must have stolen it out of my bag, because I remember vividly—cream cheese and lemon-curd. Have you done that?"

"Yes."

"Egg and—" Mrs. Sheridan held the envelope away from her. "It looks like mice. It can't be mice, can it?"

"Olive, pet," said Laura, looking over her shoulder.

"Yes, of course, olive. What a horrible combination it sounds. Egg and olive."

They were finished at last, and Laura took them off to the kitchen. She found Jose there pacifying the cook, who did not look at all terrifying.

"I have never seen such exquisite sandwiches," said Jose's rapturous voice. "How many kinds did you say there were, cook? Fifteen?"

"Fifteen, Miss Jose."

"Well, cook, I congratulate you."

Cook swept up crusts with the long sandwich knife, and smiled broadly.

"Godber's has come," announced Sadie, issuing out of the pantry. She had seen the man pass the window.

That meant the cream puffs had come. Godber's were famous for their cream puffs. Nobody ever thought of making them at home.

"Bring them in and put them on the table, my girl," ordered cook.

Sadie brought them in and went back to the door. Of course Laura and Jose were far too grown-up to really care about such things. All the same, they couldn't help agreeing that the puffs looked very attractive. Very. Cook began arranging them, shaking off the extra icing sugar.

"Don't they carry one back to all one's parties?" said Laura.

"I suppose they do," said practical Jose, who never liked to be carried back. "They look beautifully light and feathery, I must say."

"Have one each, my dears," said cook in her comfortable voice. "Yer ma won't know."

Oh, impossible. Fancy cream puffs so soon after breakfast. The very idea made one shudder. All the same, two minutes later Jose and Laura were licking their fingers with that absorbed inward look that only comes from whipped cream.

"Let's go into the garden, out by the back way," suggested Laura. "I want to see how the men are getting on with the marquee. They're such awfully nice men."

But the back door was blocked by cook, Sadie, Godber's man and Hans.

Something had happened.

"Tuk-tuk-tuk," clucked cook like an agitated hen. Sadie had her hand clapped to her cheek as though she had toothache. Hans' face was screwed up in the effort to understand. Only Godber's man seemed to be enjoying himself; it was his story.

"What's the matter? What's happened?"

"There's been a horrible accident," said cook. "A man killed."

"A man killed! Where? How? When?"

But Godber's man wasn't going to have his story snatched from under his very nose. "Know those little cottages just below here, miss?" Know them? Of course, she knew them. "Well, there's a young chap living there, name of Scott, a carter. His horse shied at a traction-engine, corner of Hawke Street this morning, and he was thrown out on the back of his head. Killed."

"Dead!" Laura stared at Godber's man.

"Dead when they picked him up," said Godber's man with relish. "They were taking the body home as I come up here." And he said to the cook, "He's left a wife and five little ones."

"Jose, come here." Laura caught hold of her sister's sleeve and dragged her through the kitchen to the other side of the green baize door. There she paused and leaned against it. "Jose!" she said, horrified, "however are we going to stop everything?"

"Stop everything, Laura!" cried Jose in astonishment. "What do you mean?"

"Stop the garden-party, of course." Why did Jose pretend?

But Jose was still more amazed. "Stop the garden-party? My dear Laura, don't be so absurd. Of course we can't do anything of the kind. Nobody expects us to. Don't be so extravagant."

"But we can't possibly have a garden-party with a man dead just outside the front gate."

That really was extravagant, for the little cottages were in a lane to themselves at the very bottom of a steep rise that led up to the house. A broad road ran between. True, they were far too near. They were the greatest possible eyesore, and they had no right to be in that neighbourhood at all. They were little mean dwellings painted a chocolate brown. In the garden patches there was nothing but cabbage stalks, sick hens and tomato cans. The very smoke coming out of their chimneys was poverty-stricken. Little rags and shreds of smoke, so unlike the great silvery plumes that uncurled from the Sheridans' chimneys. Washerwomen lived in the lane and sweeps and a cobbler, and a man whose house-front was studded all over with minute bird-cages. Children swarmed. When the Sheridans were little they were forbidden to set foot there because of the revolting language and of what they might catch. But since they were grown up, Laura and Laurie on their prowls sometimes walked through. It was disgusting and sordid. They came out with a shudder. But still one must go everywhere; one must see everything. So through they went.

"And just think of what the band would sound like to that poor woman," said Laura.

"Oh, Laura!" Jose began to be seriously annoyed. "If you're going to stop a band playing every time some one has an accident, you'll lead a very strenuous life. I'm every bit as sorry about it as you. I feel just as sympathetic." Her eyes hardened. She looked at her sister just as she used to when they were little and fighting together. "You won't bring a drunken workman back to life by being sentimental," she said softly.

"Drunk! Who said he was drunk?" Laura turned furiously on Jose. She said, just as they had used to say on those occasions, "I'm going straight up to tell mother."

"Do, dear," cooed Jose.

"Mother, can I come into your room?" Laura turned the big glass doorknob.

"Of course, child. Why, what's the matter? What's given you such a colour?" And Mrs. Sheridan turned round from her dressing table. She was trying on a new hat.

"Mother, a man's been killed," began Laura.

"*Not* in the garden?" interrupted her mother.

"No, no!"

"Oh, what a fright you gave me!" Mrs. Sheridan sighed with relief, and took off the big hat and held it on her knees.

"But listen, mother," said Laura. Breathless, half-choking, she told the dreadful story. "Of course, we can't have our party, can we?" she pleaded. "The band and everybody arriving. They'd hear us, mother, they're nearly neighbours!"

To Laura's astonishment her mother behaved just like Jose; it was harder to bear because she seemed amused. She refused to take Laura seriously.

"But, my dear child, use your common sense. It's only by accident we've heard of it. If some one had died there normally—and I can't understand how they keep alive in those poky little holes—we should still be having our party, shouldn't we?"

Laura had to say "yes" to that, but she felt it was all wrong. She sat down on her mother's sofa and pinched the cushion frill.

"Mother, isn't it really terribly heartless of us?" she asked.

"Darling!" Mrs. Sheridan got up and came over to her, carrying the hat. Before Laura could stop her she had popped it on. "My child," said her mother, "the hat is yours. It's made for you. It's much too young for me. I have never seen you look such a picture. Look at yourself!" And she held up her hand-mirror.

"But, mother," Laura began again. She couldn't look at herself; she turned aside.

This time Mrs. Sheridan lost patience just as Jose had done.

"You are being very absurd, Laura," she said coldly. "People like that don't expect sacrifices from us. And it's not very sympathetic to spoil everybody's enjoyment as you're doing now."

"I don't understand," said Laura, and she walked quickly out of the room into her own bedroom. There, quite by chance, the first thing she saw was this charming girl in the mirror, in her black hat trimmed with gold daisies, and a long black velvet ribbon. Never had she imagined she could look like that. Is mother right? she thought. And now she hoped her mother was right. Am I being extravagant? Perhaps it was extravagant. Just for a moment she had another glimpse of that poor woman and those little children, and the body being carried into the house. But it all seemed blurred, unreal, like a picture in the newspaper. I'll remember it again after the party's over, she decided. And somehow that seemed quite the best plan. . . .

Lunch was over by half past one. By half past two they were all ready for the fray. The green-coated band had arrived and was established in a corner of the tennis-court.

"My dear!" trilled Kitty Maitland, "aren't they too like frogs for words? You ought to have arranged them round the pond with the conductor in the middle on a leaf."

Laurie arrived and hailed them on his way to dress. At the sight of him Laura remembered the accident again. She wanted to tell him. If Laurie agreed with the others, then it was bound to be all right. And she followed him into the hall.

"Laurie!" "Hallo!" He was half-way upstairs, but when he turned around and saw Laura he suddenly puffed out his cheeks and goggled his eyes at her. "My word, Laura; you do look stunning," said Laurie. "What an absolutely topping hat!"

Laura said faintly "Is it?" and smiled up at Laurie, and didn't tell him after all.

Soon after that people began coming in streams. The band struck up; the hired waiters ran from the house to the marquee. Wherever you looked there were couples strolling, bending to the flowers, greeting, moving on over the lawn. They were like bright birds that had alighted in the Sheridans' garden for this one afternoon, on their way to—where? Ah, what happiness it is to be with people who all are happy, to press hands, press cheeks, smile into eyes.

"Darling Laura, how well you look!"

"What a becoming hat, child!"

"Laura, you look quite Spanish. I've never seen you look so striking."

And Laura, glowing, answered softly, "Have you had tea? Won't you have an ice? The passion-fruit ices really are rather special." She ran to her father and begged him. "Daddy darling, can't the band have something to drink?"

And the perfect afternoon slowly ripened, slowly faded, slowly its petals closed.

"Never a more delightful garden-party . . ." "The greatest success . . ." "Quite the most . . ."

Laura helped her mother with the good-byes. They stood side by side in the porch till it was all over.

"All over, all over, thank heaven," said Mrs. Sheridan. "Round in the others, Laura. Let's go and have some fresh coffee. I'm exhausted. Yes, it's been very successful. But oh, these parties, these parties! Why will you children insist on giving parties!" And they all of them sat down in the deserted marquee.

"Have a sandwich, daddy dear. I wrote the flag."

"Thanks." Mr. Sheridan took a bite and the sandwich was gone. He took another. "I suppose you didn't hear of a beastly accident that happened to-day?" he said.

"My dear," said Mrs. Sheridan, holding up her hand, "we did. It nearly ruined the party. Laura insisted we should put it off."

"Oh, mother!" Laura didn't want to be teased about it.

"It was a horrible affair all the same," said Mr. Sheridan. "The chap was married too. Lived just below in the lane, and leaves a wife and half a dozen kiddies, so they say."

An awkward little silence fell. Mrs. Sheridan fidgeted with her cup. Really, it was very tactless of father . . .

Suddenly she looked up. There on the table were all those sandwiches, cakes, puffs, all uneaten, all going to be wasted. She had one of her brilliant ideas.

"I know," she said. "Let's make up a basket. Let's send that poor creature some of this perfectly good food. At any rate, it will be the greatest treat for the children. Don't you agree? And she's sure to have neighbours calling in and so on. What a point to have it all ready prepared. Laura!" She jumped up. "Get me the big basket out of the stairs cupboard."

"But, mother, do you really think it's a good idea?" said Laura.

Again, how curious, she seemed to be different from them all. To take scraps from their party. Would the poor woman really like that?

"Of course! What's the matter with you to-day? An hour or two ago you were insisting on us being sympathetic, and now—"

Oh, well! Laura ran for the basket. It was filled, it was heaped by her mother.

"Take it yourself, darling," said she. "Run down just as you are. No, wait, take the arum lilies too. People of that class are so impressed by arum lilies."

"The stems will ruin her lace frock," said practical Jose.

So they would. Just in time. "Only the basket, then. And, Laura!"—her mother followed her out of the marquee—"don't on any account—"

"What, mother?"

No, better not put such ideas into the child's head! "Nothing! Run along."

It was just growing dusky as Laura shut their garden gates. A big dog ran by like a shadow. The road gleamed white, and down below in the hollow the little cottages were in deep shade. How quiet it seemed after the afternoon. Here she was going down the hill to somewhere where a man lay dead, and she couldn't realize it. Why couldn't she? She stopped a minute. And it seemed to her that kisses, voices, tinkling spoons, laughter, the smell of crushed grass were somehow inside her. She had no room for anything else. How strange! She looked up at the pale sky, and all she thought was, "Yes, it was the most successful party."

Now the broad road was crossed. The lane began, smoky and dark. Women in shawls and men's tweed caps hurried by. Men hung over the palings; the children played in the doorways. A low hum came from the mean little cottages. In some of them there was a flicker of light, and a shadow, crab-like, moved across the window. Laura bent her head and hurried on. She wished now she had put on a coat. How her frock shone! And the big hat with the velvet streamer—if only it was another hat! Were the people looking at her? They must be. It was a mistake to have come; she knew all along it was a mistake. Should she go back even now?

No, too late. This was the house. It must be. A dark knot of people stood outside. Beside the gate an old, old woman with a crutch sat in a chair, watching. She had her feet on a newspaper. The voices stopped as Laura drew near. The group parted. It was as though she was expected, as though they had known she was coming here.

Laura was terribly nervous. Tossing the velvet ribbon over her shoulder, she said to a woman standing by, "Is this Mrs. Scott's house?" and the woman, smiling queerly, said, "It is, my lass."

Oh, to be away from this! She actually said, "Help me, God," as she walked up the tiny path and knocked. To be away from those staring eyes, or to be covered up in anything, one of those women's shawls even. I'll just leave the basket and go, she decided. I shan't even wait for it to be emptied.

Then the door opened. A little woman in black showed in the gloom.

Laura said, "Are you Mrs. Scott?" But to her horror the woman answered, "Walk in please, miss," and she was shut in the passage.

"No," said Laura, "I don't want to come in. I only want to leave this basket. Mother sent—"

The little woman in the gloomy passage seemed not to have heard her. "Step this way, please, miss," she said in an oily voice, and Laura followed her.

She found herself in a wretched little low kitchen, lighted by a smoky lamp. There was a woman sitting before the fire.

"Em," said the little creature who had let her in. "Em! It's a young lady." She turned to Laura. She said meaningly, "I'm 'er sister, miss. You'll excuse 'er, won't you?"

"Oh, but of course!" said Laura. "Please, don't disturb her. I—I only want to leave—"

But at that moment the woman at the fire turned round. Her face, puffed up, red, with swollen eyes and swollen lips, looked terrible. She seemed as though she couldn't understand why Laura was there. What did it mean? Why was this stranger standing in the kitchen with a basket? What was it all about? And the poor face puckered up again.

"All right, my dear," said the other. "I'll thank the young lady."

And again she began, "You'll excuse her, miss, I'm sure," and her face, swollen too, tried an oily smile.

Laura only wanted to get out, to get away. She was back in the passage. The door opened. She walked straight through into the bedroom, where the dead was lying.

"You'd like a look at 'im, wouldn't you?" said Em's sister, and she brushed past Laura over to the bed. "Don't be afraid, my lass,—" and now her voice sounded fond and sly, and fondly she drew down the sheet—"'e looks a picture. There's nothing to show. Come along, my dear."

Laura came.

There lay a young man, fast asleep—sleeping so soundly, so deeply, that he was far, far away from them both. Oh, so remote, so peaceful. He was dreaming. Never wake him up again. His head was sunk in the pillow, his eyes were closed; they were blind under the closed eyelids. He was given up to his dream. What did garden-parties and baskets and lace frocks matter to him? He was far from all those things. He was wonderful, beautiful. While they were laughing and while the band was playing, this marvel had come to the lane. Happy . . . happy. . . . All is well, said that sleeping face. This is just as it should be. I am content.

But all the same you had to cry, and she couldn't go out of the room without saying something to him. Laura gave a loud childish sob.

"Forgive my hat," she said.

And this time she didn't wait for Em's sister. She found her way out of the door, down the path, past all those dark people. At the corner of the lane she met Laurie.

He stepped out of the shadow. "Is that you, Laura?"

"Yes."

"Mother was getting anxious. Was it all right?"

"Yes, quite. Oh, Laurie!" She took his arm, she pressed up against him.

"I say, you're not crying, are you?" asked her brother.

Laura shook her head. She was.

Laurie put his arm round her shoulder. "Don't cry," he said in his warm, loving voice. "Was it awful?"

"No," sobbed Laura. "It was simply marvelous. But. Laurie—" She stopped, she looked at her brother. "Isn't life," she stammered, "Isn't life—" But what life was she couldn't explain. No matter. He quite understood.

"*Isn't* it, darling?" said Laurie.

# Yukio Mishima

## (1925–1970)

Born as Kimatake Hiroaka, Yukio Mishima was raised by his grandmother, Natsuko Hiroaka, though his mother lived in the same household. Natsuko instilled in her grandson the spirit of her samurai ancestors and emphasized self-discipline and complete control over both mind and body. She also taught him to be proud and to carry that sense of pride with him at all times. Mishima returned to his mother in 1937, and Natsuko died in 1939. His first story, "The Forest in Full Bloom" (1941), was published in *Bungei Bunka* magazine. In 1943, Mishima entered Tokyo Imperial University, where he studied law. While there, his first collection of short stories, *The Forest in Full Bloom* (1944), was published, and the first print sold out in one week. This was considered a great achievement, particularly because of the paper shortage caused by World War II. Mishima graduated in 1947 and worked for a brief time at the Finance Ministry. In 1948, Mishima dedicated himself exclusively to his writing.

Mishima's works include *Confessions of a Mask* (1949), *Thirst for Love* (1950), *The Temple of the Golden Pavilion* (1956), and *The Sailor Who Fell from Grace with the Sea* (1963). Influenced by premodern Japanese literature, his writings pursue the varied themes of homosexuality, physical appearances, and Western influences on Japan's traditions. From 1964 to 1970, Mishima worked on the Sea of Fertility novels, a portrait of Japanese life from 1912 to 1970. On November 25, 1970, the same day he finished the last novel of the Sea of Fertility series, he and several members of his private army, "The Shield Society," took over a military base in Ichigaya and demanded the resignation of Japan's prime minister. When his actions failed to rouse the soldiers to revolt, he committed suicide.

---

*Patriotism*                                                                                            1961

TRANSLATED BY GEOFFREY W. SARGENT

## I

On the twenty-eighth of February, 1936[1] (on the third day, that is, of the February 26 Incident), Lieutenant Shinji Takeyama of the Konoe Transport Battalion—

---

1 **twenty-eighth of February, 1936:** Protesting corruption within the Japanese government, a number of Japanese officers staged a revolt and assassinated several government officials.

profoundly disturbed by the knowledge that his closest colleagues had been with the mutineers from the beginning, and indignant at the imminent prospect of Imperial troops attacking Imperial troops—took his officer's sword and ceremonially disemboweled himself in the eight-mat room[2] of his private residence in the sixth block of Aoba-chō, in Yotsuya Ward. His wife, Reiko, followed him, stabbing herself to death. The lieutenant's farewell note consisted of one sentence: "Long live the Imperial Forces." His wife, after apologies for her unfilial conduct in thus preceding her parents to the grave, concluded: "The day which, for a soldier's wife, had to come, has come. . . ." The last moments of this heroic and dedicated couple were such as to make the gods themselves weep. The lieutenant's age, it should be noted, was thirty-one, his wife's twenty-three; and it was not half a year since the celebration of their marriage.

## 2

Those who saw the bride and bridegroom in the commemorative photograph—perhaps no less than those actually present at the lieutenant's wedding—had exclaimed in wonder at the bearing of this handsome couple. The lieutenant, majestic in military uniform, stood protectively beside his bride, his right hand resting upon his sword, his officer's cap held at his left side. His expression was severe, and his dark brows and wide-gazing eyes well conveyed the clear integrity of youth. For the beauty of the bride in her white over-robe no comparisons were adequate. In the eyes, round beneath soft brows, in the slender, finely shaped nose, and in the full lips, there was both sensuousness and refinement. One hand, emerging shyly from a sleeve of the over-robe, held a fan, and the tips of the fingers, clustering delicately, were like the bud of a moonflower.

After the suicide, people would take out this photograph and examine it, and sadly reflect that too often there was a curse on these seemingly flawless unions. Perhaps it was no more than imagination, but looking at the picture after the tragedy it almost seemed as if the two young people before the gold-lacquered screen were gazing, each with equal clarity, at the deaths which lay before them.

Thanks to the good offices of their go-between, Lieutenant General Ozeki, they had been able to set themselves up in a new home at Aoba-chō in Yotsuya. "New home" is perhaps misleading. It was an old three-room rented house backing onto a small garden. As neither the six- nor the four-and-a-half-mat room downstairs was favored by the sun, they used the upstairs eight-mat room as both bedroom and guest room. There was no maid, so Reiko was left alone to guard the house in her husband's absence.

The honeymoon trip was dispensed with on the grounds that these were times of national emergency.[3] The two of them had spent the first night of their marriage at

2 **eight-mat room:** Japanese rooms are measured by the number of three-by-six-foot straw mats that are required to cover the floor.

3 **national emergency:** In the 1930s, Japan invaded China as a precursor to Japanese invasions in Southeast Asia.

this house. Before going to bed, Shinji, sitting erect on the floor with his sword laid before him, had bestowed upon his wife a soldierly lecture. A woman who had become the wife of a soldier should know and resolutely accept that her husband's death might come at any moment. It could be tomorrow. It could be the day after. But, no matter when it came—he asked—was she steadfast in her resolve to accept it? Reiko rose to her feet, pulled open a drawer of the cabinet, and took out what was the most prized of her new possessions, the dagger her mother had given her. Returning to her place, she laid the dagger without a word on the mat before her, just as her husband had laid his sword. A silent understanding was achieved at once, and the lieutenant never again sought to test his wife's resolve.

In the first few months of her marriage Reiko's beauty grew daily more radiant, shining serene like the moon after rain.

As both were possessed of young, vigorous bodies, their relationship was passionate. Nor was this merely a matter of the night. On more than one occasion, returning home straight from maneuvers, and begrudging even the time it took to remove his mud-splashed uniform, the lieutenant had pushed his wife to the floor almost as soon as he had entered the house. Reiko was equally ardent in her response. For a little more or a little less than a month, from the first night of their marriage Reiko knew happiness, and the lieutenant, seeing this, was happy too.

Reiko's body was white and pure, and her swelling breasts conveyed a firm and chaste refusal; but, upon consent, those breasts were lavish with their intimate, welcoming warmth. Even in bed these two were frighteningly and awesomely serious. In the very midst of wild, intoxicating passions, their hearts were sober and serious.

By day the lieutenant would think of his wife in the brief rest periods between training; and all day long, at home, Reiko would recall the image of her husband. Even when apart, however, they had only to look at the wedding photograph for their happiness to be once more confirmed. Reiko felt not the slightest surprise that a man who had been a complete stranger until a few months ago should now have become the sun about which her whole world revolved.

All these things had a moral basis, and were in accordance with the Education Rescript's[4] injunction that "husband and wife should be harmonious." Not once did Reiko contradict her husband, nor did the lieutenant ever find reason to scold his wife. On the god shelf[5] below the stairway, alongside the tablet from the Great Ise Shrine,[6] were set photographs of their Imperial Majesties, and regularly every morning, before leaving for duty, the lieutenant would stand with his wife at this hallowed place and together they would bow their heads low. The offering water was renewed each morning, and the sacred sprig of *sasaki*[7] was always green and fresh. Their lives were lived beneath the solemn protection of the gods and were filled with an intense happiness which set every fiber in their bodies trembling.

---

4 **Education Rescript:** A code of conduct.
5 **god shelf:** A small shrine in the home for burning incense and making offerings to ancestors.
6 **Great Ise Shrine:** A shrine in the city of Ise, where the Imperial family was first established as rulers of Japan.
7 *sasaki:* An evergreen plant used in Shinto ceremonies.

# 3

Although Lord Privy Seal Saitō's[8] house was in their neighborhood, neither of them heard any noise of gunfire on the morning of February 26. It was a bugle, sounding muster in the dim, snowy dawn, when the ten-minute tragedy had already ended, which first disrupted the lieutenant's slumbers. Leaping at once from his bed, and without speaking a word, the lieutenant donned his uniform, buckled on the sword held ready for him by his wife, and hurried swiftly out into the snow-covered streets of the still darkened morning. He did not return until the evening of the twenty-eighth.

Later, from the radio news, Reiko learned the full extent of this sudden eruption of violence. Her life throughout the subsequent two days was lived alone, in complete tranquillity, and behind locked doors.

In the lieutenant's face, as he hurried silently out into the snowy morning, Reiko had read the determination to die. If her husband did not return, her own decision was made: she too would die. Quietly she attended to the disposition of her personal possessions. She chose her sets of visiting kimonos as keepsakes for friends of her schooldays, and she wrote a name and address on the stiff paper wrapping in which each was folded. Constantly admonished by her husband never to think of the morrow, Reiko had not even kept a diary and was now denied the pleasure of assiduously rereading her record of the happiness of the past few months and consigning each page to the fire as she did so. Ranged across the top of the radio were a small china dog, a rabbit, a squirrel, a bear, and a fox. There were also a small vase and a water pitcher. These comprised Reiko's one and only collection. But it would hardly do, she imagined, to give such things as keepsakes. Nor again would it be quite proper to ask specifically for them to be included in the coffin. It seemed to Reiko, as these thoughts passed through her mind, that the expressions on the small animals' faces grew even more lost and forlorn.

Reiko took the squirrel in her hand and looked at it. And then, her thoughts turning to a realm far beyond these childlike affections, she gazed up into the distance at the great sunlike principle which her husband embodied. She was ready, and happy, to be hurtled along to her destruction in that gleaming sun chariot—but now, for these few moments of solitude, she allowed herself to luxuriate in this innocent attachment to trifles. The time when she had genuinely loved these things, however, was long past. Now she merely loved the memory of having once loved them, and their place in her heart had been filled by more intense passions, by a more frenzied happiness. . . . For Reiko had never, even to herself, thought of those soaring joys of the flesh as a mere pleasure. The February cold, and the icy touch of the china squirrel, and numbed Reiko's slender fingers; yet, even so, in her lower limbs, beneath the ordered repetition of the pattern which crossed the skirt of her trim *meisen* kimono,[9] she could feel now, as she thought of the lieutenant's powerful arms reaching out toward her, a hot moistness of the flesh which defied the snows.

---

8 **Lord Privy Seal Saitō:** A government official who was assassinated in the Japanese officer uprising.
9 ***meisen* kimono:** A kimono worn for everyday use.

She was not in the least afraid of the death hovering in her mind. Waiting alone at home, Reiko firmly believed that everything her husband was feeling or thinking now, his anguish and distress, was leading her—just as surely as the power in his flesh—to a welcome death. She felt as if her body could melt away with ease and be transformed to the merest fraction of her husband's thought.

Listening to the frequent announcements on the radio, she heard the names of several of her husband's colleagues mentioned among those of the insurgents. This was news of death. She followed the developments closely, wondering anxiously, as the situation became daily more irrevocable, why no Imperial ordinance was sent down, and watching what had at first been taken as a movement to restore the nation's honor come gradually to be branded with the infamous name of mutiny. There was no communication from the regiment. At any moment, it seemed, fighting might commence in the city streets, where the remains of the snow still lay.

Toward sundown on the twenty-eighth Reiko was startled by a furious pounding on the front door. She hurried downstairs. As she pulled with fumbling fingers at the bolt, the shape dimly outlined beyond the frosted-glass panel made no sound, but she knew it was her husband. Reiko had never known the bolt on the sliding door to be so stiff. Still it resisted. The door just would not open.

In a moment, almost before she knew she had succeeded, the lieutenant was standing before her on the cement floor inside the porch, muffled in a khaki greatcoat, his top boots heavy with slush from the street. Closing the door behind him, he returned the bolt once more to its socket. With what significance, Reiko did not understand.

"Welcome home."

Reiko bowed deeply, but her husband made no response. As he had already unfastened his sword and was about to remove his greatcoat, Reiko moved around behind to assist. The coat, which was cold and damp and had lost the odor of horse dung it normally exuded when exposed to the sun, weighed heavily upon her arm. Draping it across a hanger, and cradling the sword and leather belt in her sleeves, she waited while her husband removed his top boots and then followed behind him into the "living room." This was the six-mat room downstairs.

Seen in the clear light from the lamp, her husband's face, covered with a heavy growth of bristle, was almost unrecognizably wasted and thin. The cheeks were hollow, their luster and resilience gone. In his normal good spirits he would have changed into old clothes as soon as he was home and have pressed her to get supper at once, but now he sat before the table still in his uniform, his head drooping dejectedly. Reiko refrained from asking whether she should prepare the supper.

After an interval the lieutenant spoke.

"I knew nothing. They hadn't asked me to join. Perhaps out of consideration, because I was newly married. Kanō, and Homma too, and Yamaguchi."

Reiko recalled momentarily the faces of high-spirited young officers, friends of her husband, who had come to the house occasionally as guests.

"There may be an Imperial ordinance sent down tomorrow. They'll be posted as rebels, I imagine. I shall be in command of a unit with orders to attack them. . . . I can't do it. It's impossible to do a thing like that."

He spoke again.

"They've taken me off guard duty, and I have permission to return home for one night. Tomorrow morning, without question, I must leave to join the attack. I can't do it, Reiko."

Reiko sat erect with lowered eyes. She understood clearly that her husband had spoken of his death. The lieutenant was resolved. Each word, being rooted in death, emerged sharply and with powerful significance against this dark, unmovable background. Although the lieutenant was speaking of his dilemma, already there was no room in his mind for vacillation.

However, there was a clarity, like the clarity of a stream fed from melting snows, in the silence which rested between them. Sitting in his own home after the long two-day ordeal, and looking across at the face of his beautiful wife, the lieutenant was for the first time experiencing true peace of mind. For he had at once known, though she said nothing, that his wife divined the resolve which lay beneath his words.

"Well, then . . ." The lieutenant's eyes opened wide. Despite his exhaustion they were strong and clear, and now for the first time they looked straight into the eyes of his wife. "Tonight I shall cut my stomach."

Reiko did not flinch.

Her round eyes showed tension, as taut as the clang of a bell.

"I am ready," she said. "I ask permission to accompany you."

The lieutenant felt almost mesmerized by the strength in those eyes. His words flowed swiftly and easily, like the utterances of a man in delirium, and it was beyond his understanding how permission in a matter of such weight could be expressed so casually.

"Good. We'll go together. But I want you as a witness, first, for my own suicide. Agreed?"

When this was said a sudden release of abundant happiness welled up in both their hearts. Reiko was deeply affected by the greatness of her husband's trust in her. It was vital for the lieutenant, whatever else might happen, that there should be no irregularity in his death. For that reason there had to be a witness. The fact that he had chosen his wife for this was the first mark of his trust. The second, and even greater mark, was that though he had pledged that they should die together he did not intend to kill his wife first—he had deferred her death to a time when he would no longer be there to verify it. If the lieutenant had been a suspicious husband, he would doubtless, as in the usual suicide pact, have chosen to kill his wife first.

When Reiko said, "I ask permission to accompany you," the lieutenant felt these words to be the final fruit of the education which he had himself given his wife, starting on the first night of their marriage, and which had schooled her, when the moment came, to say what had to be said without a shadow of hesitation. This flattered the lieutenant's opinion of himself as a self-reliant man. He was not so romantic or conceited as to imagine that the words were spoken spontaneously, out of love for her husband.

With happiness welling almost too abundantly in their hearts, they could not help smiling at each other. Reiko felt as if she had returned to her wedding night.

Before her eyes was neither pain nor death. She seemed to see only a free and limitless expanse opening out into vast distances.

"The water is hot. Will you take your bath now?"

"Ah yes, of course."

"And supper . . . ?"

The words were delivered in such level, domestic tones that the lieutenant came near to thinking, for the fraction of a second, that everything had been a hallucination.

"I don't think we'll need supper. But perhaps you could warm some sake?"

"As you wish."

As Reiko rose and took a *tanzen* gown[10] from the cabinet for after the bath, she purposely directed her husband's attention to the opened drawer. The lieutenant rose, crossed to the cabinet, and looked inside. From the ordered array of paper wrappings he read, one by one, the addresses of the keepsakes. There was no grief in the lieutenant's response to this demonstration of heroic resolve. His heart was filled with tenderness. Like a husband who is proudly shown the childish purchases of a young wife, the lieutenant, overwhelmed by affection, lovingly embraced his wife from behind and implanted a kiss upon her neck.

Reiko felt the roughness of the lieutenant's unshaven skin against her neck. This sensation, more than being just a thing of this world, was for Reiko almost the world itself, but now—with the feeling that it was soon to be lost forever—it had freshness beyond all her experience. Each moment had its own vital strength, and the senses in every corner of her body were reawakened. Accepting her husband's caresses from behind, Reiko raised herself on the tips of her toes, letting the vitality seep through her entire body.

"First the bath, and then, after some sake . . . lay out the bedding upstairs, will you?"

The lieutenant whispered the words into his wife's ear. Reiko silently nodded.

Flinging off his uniform, the lieutenant went to the bath. To faint background noises of slopping water Reiko tended the charcoal brazier in the living room and began the preparations for warming the sake.

Taking the *tanzen,* a sash, and some underclothes, she went to the bathroom to ask how the water was. In the midst of a coiling cloud of steam the lieutenant was sitting cross-legged on the floor, shaving, and she could dimly discern the rippling movements of the muscles on his damp, powerful back as they responded to the movement of his arms.

There was nothing to suggest a time of any special significance. Reiko, going busily about her tasks, was preparing side dishes from odds and ends in stock. Her hands did not tremble. If anything, she managed even more efficiently and smoothly than usual. From time to time, it is true, there was a strange throbbing deep within her breast. Like distant lightning, it had a moment of sharp intensity and then vanished without trace. Apart from that, nothing was in any way out of the ordinary.

The lieutenant, shaving in the bathroom, felt his warmed body miraculously

---

10 *tanzen* gown: A heavy kimono worn for warmth.

healed at last of the desperate tiredness of the days of indecision and filled—in spite of the death which lay ahead—with pleasurable anticipation. The sound of his wife going about her work came to him faintly. A healthy physical craving, submerged for two days, reasserted itself.

The lieutenant was confident there had been no impurity in that joy they had experienced when resolving upon death. They had both sensed at that moment—though not, of course, in any clear and conscious way—that those permissible pleasures which they shared in private were once more beneath the protection of Righteousness and Divine Power, and of a complete and unassailable morality. On looking into each other's eyes and discovering there an honorable death, they had felt themselves safe once more behind steel walls which none could destroy, encased in an impenetrable armor of Beauty and Truth. Thus, so far from seeing any inconsistency or conflict between the urges of his flesh and the sincerity of his patriotism, the lieutenant was even able to regard the two as parts of the same thing.

Thrusting his face close to the dark, cracked, misted wall mirror, the lieutenant shaved himself with great care. This would be his death face. There must be no unsightly blemishes. The clean-shaven face gleamed once more with a youthful luster, seeming to brighten the darkness of the mirror. There was a certain elegance, he even felt, in the association of death with this radiantly healthy face.

Just as it looked now, this would become his death face! Already, in fact, it had half departed from the lieutenant's personal possession and had become the bust above a dead soldier's memorial. As an experiment he closed his eyes tight. Everything was wrapped in blackness, and he was no longer a living, seeing creature.

Returning from the bath, the traces of the shave glowing faintly blue beneath his smooth cheeks, he seated himself beside the now well-kindled charcoal brazier. Busy though Reiko was, he noticed, she had found time lightly to touch up her face. Her cheeks were gay and her lips moist. There was no shadow of sadness to be seen. Truly, the lieutenant felt, as he saw this mark of his young wife's passionate nature, he had chosen the wife he ought to have chosen.

As soon as the lieutenant had drained his sake cup he offered it to Reiko. Reiko had never before tasted sake, but she accepted without hesitation and sipped timidly.

"Come here," the lieutenant said.

Reiko moved to her husband's side and was embraced as she leaned backward across his lap. Her breast was in violent commotion, as if sadness, joy, and the potent sake were mingling and reacting within her. The lieutenant looked down into his wife's face. It was the last face he would see in this world, the last face he would see of his wife. The lieutenant scrutinized the face minutely, with the eyes of a traveler bidding farewell to splendid vistas which he will never revisit. It was a face he could not tire of looking at—the features regular yet not cold, the lips lightly closed with a soft strength. The lieutenant kissed those lips, unthinkingly. And suddenly, though there was not the slightest distortion of the face into the unsightliness of sobbing, he noticed that tears were welling slowly from beneath the long lashes of the closed eyes and brimming over into a glistening stream.

When, a little later, the lieutenant urged that they should move to the upstairs bedroom, his wife replied that she would follow after taking a bath. Climbing the stairs alone to the bedroom, where the air was already warmed by the gas heater, the lieutenant lay down on the bedding with arms outstretched and legs apart. Even the time at which he lay waiting for his wife to join him was no later and no earlier than usual.

He folded his hands beneath his head and gazed at the dark boards of the ceiling in the dimness beyond the range of the standard lamp. Was it death he was now waiting for? Or a wild ecstasy of the senses? The two seemed to overlap, almost as if the object of this bodily desire was death itself. But, however that might be, it was certain that never before had the lieutenant tasted such total freedom.

There was the sound of a car outside the window. He could hear the screech of its tires skidding in the snow piled at the side of the street. The sound of its horn re-echoed from near-by walls. . . . Listening to these noises he had the feeling that this house rose like a solitary island in the ocean of a society going as restlessly about its business as ever. All around, vastly and untidily, stretched the country for which he grieved. He was to give his life for it. But would that great country, with which he was prepared to remonstrate to the extent of destroying himself, take the slightest heed of his death? He did not know; and it did not matter. His was a battlefield without glory, a battlefield where none could display deeds of valor: it was the front line of the spirit.

Reiko's footsteps sounded on the stairway. The steep stairs in this old house creaked badly. There were fond memories in that creaking, and many a time, while waiting in bed, the lieutenant had listened to its welcome sound. At the thought that he would hear it no more he listened with intense concentration, striving for every corner of every moment of this precious time to be filled with the sound of those soft footfalls on the creaking stairway. The moments seemed transformed to jewels, sparkling with inner light.

Reiko wore a Nagoya sash about the waist of her *yukata*,[11] but as the lieutenant reached toward it, its redness sobered by the dimness of the light, Reiko's hand moved to his assistance and the sash fell away, slithering swiftly to the floor. As she stood before him, still in her *yukata*, the lieutenant inserted his hands through the side slits beneath each sleeve, intending to embrace her as she was; but at the touch of his finger tips upon the warm naked flesh, and as the armpits closed gently about his hands, his whole body was suddenly aflame.

In a few moments the two lay naked before the glowing gas heater.

Neither spoke the thought, but their hearts, their bodies, and their pounding breasts blazed with the knowledge that this was the very last time. It was as if the words "The Last Time" were spelled out, in invisible brushstrokes, across every inch of their bodies.

The lieutenant drew his wife close and kissed her vehemently. As their tongues explored each other's mouths, reaching out into the smooth, moist interior, they felt as if the still-unknown agonies of death had tempered their senses to the keenness of red-hot steel. The agonies they could not yet feel, the distant pains of death, had refined their awareness of pleasure.

---

11 *yukata:* A thin cotton kimono.

"This is the last time I shall see your body," said the lieutenant. "Let me look at it closely." And, tilting the shade on the lampstand to one side, he directed the rays along the full length of Reiko's outstretched form.

Reiko lay still with her eyes closed. The light from the low lamp clearly revealed the majestic sweep of her white flesh. The lieutenant, not without a touch of egocentricity, rejoiced that he would never see this beauty crumble in death.

At his leisure, the lieutenant allowed the unforgettable spectacle to engrave itself upon his mind. With one hand he fondled the hair, with the other he softly stroked the magnificent face, implanting kisses here and there where his eyes lingered. The quiet coldness of the high, tapering forehead, the closed eyes with their long lashes beneath faintly etched brows, the set of the finely shaped nose, the gleam of teeth glimpsed between full, regular lips, the soft cheeks and the small, wise chin . . . these things conjured up in the lieutenant's mind the vision of a truly radiant death face, and again and again he pressed his lips tight against the white throat—where Reiko's own hand was soon to strike—and the throat reddened faintly beneath his kisses. Returning to the mouth he laid his lips against it with the gentlest of pressures, and moved them rhythmically over Reiko's with the light rolling motion of a small boat. If he closed his eyes, the world became a rocking cradle.

Wherever the lieutenant's eyes moved his lips faithfully followed. The high, swelling breasts, surmounted by nipples like the buds of a wild cherry, hardened as the lieutenant's lips closed about them. The arms flowed smoothly downward from each side of the breast, tapering toward the wrists, yet losing nothing of their roundness or symmetry, and at their tips were those delicate fingers which had held the fan at the wedding ceremony. One by one, as the lieutenant kissed them, the fingers withdrew behind their neighbor as if in shame. . . . The natural hollow curving between the bosom and the stomach carried in its lines a suggestion not only of softness but of resilient strength, and while it gave forewarning of the rich curves spreading outward from here to the hips it had, in itself, an appearance only of restraint and proper discipline. The whiteness and richness of the stomach and hips was like milk brimming in a great bowl, and the sharply shadowed dip of the navel could have been the fresh impress of a raindrop, fallen there that very moment. Where the shadows gathered more thickly, hair clustered, gentle and sensitive, and as the agitation mounted in the now no longer passive body there hung over this region a scent like the smoldering of fragrant blossoms, growing steadily more pervasive.

At length, in a tremulous voice, Reiko spoke.

"Show me. . . . Let me look too, for the last time."

Never before had he heard from his wife's lips so strong and unequivocal a request. It was as if something which her modesty had wished to keep hidden to the end had suddenly burst its bonds of constraint. The lieutenant obediently lay back and surrendered himself to his wife. Lithely she raised her white, trembling body, and— burning with an innocent desire to return to her husband what he had done for her— placed two white fingers on the lieutenant's eyes, which gazed fixedly up at her, and gently stroked them shut.

Suddenly overwhelmed by tenderness, her cheeks flushed by a dizzying uprush of emotion, Reiko threw her arms about the lieutenant's close-cropped head. The bristly hairs rubbed painfully against her breast, the prominent nose was cold as it dug into her flesh, and his breath was hot. Relaxing her embrace, she gazed down at her husband's masculine face. The severe brows, the closed eyes, the splendid bridge of the nose, the shapely lips drawn firmly together . . . the blue, clean-shaven cheeks reflecting the light and gleaming smoothly. Reiko kissed each of these. She kissed the broad nape of the neck, the strong, erect shoulders, the powerful chest with its twin circles like shields and its russet nipples. In the armpits, deeply shadowed by the ample flesh of the shoulders and chest, a sweet and melancholy odor emanated from the growth of hair, and in the sweetness of this odor was contained, somehow, the essence of young death. The lieutenant's naked skin glowed like a field of barley, and everywhere the muscles showed in sharp relief, converging on the lower abdomen about the small, unassuming navel. Gazing at the youthful, firm stomach, modestly covered by a vigorous growth of hair, Reiko thought of it as it was soon to be, cruelly cut by the sword, and she laid her head upon it, sobbing in pity, and bathed it with kisses.

At the touch of his wife's tears upon his stomach the lieutenant felt ready to endure with courage the cruelest agonies of his suicide.

What ecstasies they experienced after these tender exchanges may well be imagined. The lieutenant raised himself and enfolded his wife in a powerful embrace, her body now limp with exhaustion after her grief and tears. Passionately they held their faces close, rubbing cheek against cheek. Reiko's body was trembling. Their breasts, moist with sweat, were tightly joined, and every inch of the young and beautiful bodies had become so much one with the other that it seemed impossible there should ever again be a separation. Reiko cried out. From the heights they plunged into the abyss, and from the abyss they took wing and soared once more to dizzying heights. The lieutenant panted like the regimental standard-bearer on a route march. . . . As one cycle ended, almost immediately a new wave of passion would be generated, and together—with no trace of fatigue—they would climb again in a single breathless movement to the very summit.

## 4

When the lieutenant at last turned away, it was not from weariness. For one thing, he was anxious not to undermine the considerable strength he would need in carrying out his suicide. For another, he would have been sorry to mar the sweetness of these last memories by overindulgence.

Since the lieutenant had clearly desisted, Reiko too, with her usual compliance, followed his example. The two lay naked on their backs, with fingers interlaced, staring fixedly at the dark ceiling. The room was warm from the heater, and even when the sweat had ceased to pour from their bodies they felt no cold. Outside, in the hushed night, the sounds of passing traffic had ceased. Even the noises of the trains and streetcars around Yotsuya station did not penetrate this far. After echoing through the region bounded by the moat, they were lost in the heavily wooded park fronting the broad driveway before Akasaka Palace.[12] It was hard to believe in the tension gripping this whole quarter, where the two factions of the bitterly divided Imperial Army now confronted each other, poised for battle.

Savoring the warmth glowing within themselves, they lay still and recalled the ecstasies they had just known. Each moment of the experience was relived. They remembered the taste of kisses which had never wearied, the touch of naked flesh, episode after episode of dizzying bliss. But already, from the dark boards of the ceiling, the face of death was peering down. These joys had been final, and their bodies would never know them again. Not that joy of this intensity—and the same thought had occurred to them both—was ever likely to be reexperienced, even if they should live on to old age.

The feel of their fingers intertwined—this too would soon be lost. Even the woodgrain patterns they now gazed at on the dark ceiling boards would be taken from them. They could feel death edging in, nearer and nearer. There could be no hesitation now. They must have the courage to reach out to death themselves, and to seize it.

"Well, let's make our preparations," said the lieutenant. The note of determination in the words was unmistakable, but at the same time Reiko had never heard her husband's voice so warm and tender.

After they had risen, a variety of tasks awaited them.

The lieutenant, who had never once before helped with the bedding, now cheerfully slid back the door of the closet, lifted the mattress across the room by himself, and stowed it away inside.

Reiko turned off the gas heater and put away the lamp standard. During the lieutenant's absence she had arranged this room carefully, sweeping and dusting it to a fresh cleanness, and now—if one overlooked the rosewood table drawn into one corner—the eight-mat room gave all the appearance of a reception room ready to welcome an important guest.

"We've seen some drinking here, haven't we? With Kanō and Homma and Noguchi . . ."

"Yes, they were great drinkers, all of them."

"We'll be meeting them before long, in the other world. They'll tease us, I imagine, when they find I've brought you with me."

Descending the stairs, the lieutenant turned to look back into this calm, clean room, now brightly illuminated by the ceiling lamp. There floated across his mind the faces of the young officers who had drunk there, and laughed, and innocently bragged. He had never dreamed then that he would one day cut open his stomach in this room.

In the two rooms downstairs husband and wife busied themselves smoothly and serenely with their respective preparations. The lieutenant went to the toilet, and then to the bathroom to wash. Meanwhile Reiko folded away her husband's padded robe, placed his uniform tunic, his trousers, and a newly cut bleached loincloth in the bathroom, and set out sheets of paper on the living-room table for the farewell notes.

12 **Akasaka Palace:** Located in the Imperial palace complex in Tokyo.

Then she removed the lid from the writing box and began rubbing ink from the ink tablet. She had already decided upon the wording of her own note.

Reiko's fingers pressed hard upon the cold gilt letters of the ink tablet, and the water in the shallow well at once darkened, as if a black cloud had spread across it. She stopped thinking that this repeated action, this pressure from her fingers, this rise and fall of faint sound, was all and solely for death. It was a routine domestic task, a simple paring away of time until death should finally stand before her. But somehow, in the increasingly smooth motion of the tablet rubbing on the stone, and in the scent from the thickening ink, there was unspeakable darkness.

Neat in his uniform, which he now wore next to his skin, the lieutenant emerged from the bathroom. Without a word he seated himself at the table, bolt upright, took a brush in his hand, and stared undecidedly at the paper before him.

Reiko took a white silk kimono with her and entered the bathroom. When she reappeared in the living room, clad in the white kimono and with her face lightly made up, the farewell note lay completed on the table beneath the lamp. The thick black brushstrokes said simply:

"Long Live the Imperial Forces—Army Lieutenant Takeyama Shinji."

While Reiko sat opposite him writing her own note, the lieutenant gazed in silence, intensely serious, at the controlled movement of his wife's pale fingers as they manipulated the brush.

With their respective notes in their hands—the lieutenant's sword strapped to his side, Reiko's small dagger thrust into the sash of her white kimono—the two of them stood before the god shelf and silently prayed. Then they put out all the downstairs lights. As he mounted the stairs the lieutenant turned his head and gazed back at the striking, white-clad figure of his wife, climbing behind him, with lowered eyes, from the darkness beneath.

The farewell notes were laid side by side in the alcove of the upstairs room. They wondered whether they ought not to remove the hanging scroll, but since it had been written by their go-between, Lieutenant General Ozeki, and consisted, moreover, of two Chinese characters signifying "Sincerity," they left it where it was. Even if it were to become stained with splashes of blood, they felt that the lieutenant general would understand.

The lieutenant, sitting erect with his back to the alcove, laid his sword on the floor before him.

Reiko sat facing him, a mat's width away. With the rest of her so severely white the touch of rouge on her lips seemed remarkably seductive.

Across the dividing mat they gazed intently into each other's eyes. The lieutenant's sword lay before his knees. Seeing it, Reiko recalled their first night and was overwhelmed with sadness. The lieutenant spoke, in a hoarse voice:

"As I have no second to help me I shall cut deep. It may look unpleasant, but please do not panic. Death of any sort is a fearful thing to watch. You must not be discouraged by what you see. Is that all right?"

"Yes."

Reiko nodded deeply.

Looking at the slender white figure of his wife the lieutenant experienced a bizarre excitement. What he was about to perform was an act in his public capacity as a soldier, something he had never previously shown his wife. It called for a resolution equal to the courage to enter battle; it was a death of no less degree and quality than death in the front line. It was his conduct on the battlefield that he was now to display.

Momentarily the thought led the lieutenant to a strange fantasy. A lonely death on the battlefield, a death beneath the eyes of his beautiful wife . . . in the sensation that he was now to die in these two dimensions, realizing an impossible union of them both, there was sweetness beyond words. This must be the very pinnacle of good fortune, he thought. To have every moment of his death observed by those beautiful eyes—it was like being borne to death on a gentle, fragrant breeze. There was some special favor here. He did not understand precisely what it was, but it was a domain unknown to others: a dispensation granted to no one else had been permitted to himself. In the radiant, bridelike figure of his white-robed wife the lieutenant seemed to see a vision of all those things he had loved and for which he was to lay down his life—the Imperial Household, the Nation, the Army Flag. All these, no less than the wife who sat before him, were presences observing him closely with clear and never-faltering eyes.

Reiko too was gazing intently at her husband, so soon to die, and she thought that never in this world had she seen anything so beautiful. The lieutenant always looked well in uniform, but now, as he contemplated death with severe brows and firmly closed lips, he revealed what was perhaps masculine beauty at its most superb.

"It's time to go," the lieutenant said at last.

Reiko bent her body low to the mat in a deep bow. She could not raise her face. She did not wish to spoil her make-up with tears, but the tears could not be held back.

When at length she looked up she saw hazily through the tears that her husband had wound a white bandage around the blade of his now unsheathed sword, leaving five or six inches of naked steel showing at the point.

Resting the sword in its cloth wrapping on the mat before him, the lieutenant rose from his knees, resettled himself cross-legged, and unfastened the hooks of his uniform collar. His eyes no longer saw his wife. Slowly, one by one, he undid the flat brass buttons. The dusky brown chest was revealed, and then the stomach. He unclasped his belt and undid the buttons of his trousers. The pure whiteness of the thickly coiled loincloth showed itself. The lieutenant pushed the cloth down with both hands, further to ease his stomach, and then reached for the white-bandaged blade of his sword. With his left hand he massaged his abdomen, glancing downward as he did so.

To reassure himself on the sharpness of his sword's cutting edge the lieutenant folded back the left trouser flap, exposing a little of his thigh, and lightly drew the blade across the skin. Blood welled up in the wound at once, and several streaks of red trickled downward, glistening in the strong light.

It was the first time Reiko had ever seen her husband's blood, and she felt a violent throbbing in her chest. She looked at her husband's face. The lieutenant was looking at the blood with calm appraisal. For a moment—though thinking at the same time that it was hollow comfort—Reiko experienced a sense of relief.

The lieutenant's eyes fixed his wife with an intense, hawklike stare. Moving the sword around to his front, he raised himself slightly on his hips and let the upper half of his body lean over the sword point. That he was mustering his whole strength was apparent from the angry tension of the uniform at his shoulders. The lieutenant aimed to strike deep into the left of his stomach. His sharp cry pierced the silence of the room.

Despite the effort he had himself put into the blow, the lieutenant had the impression that someone else had struck the side of his stomach agonizingly with a thick rod of iron. For a second or so his head reeled and he had no idea what had happened. The five or six inches of naked point had vanished completely into his flesh, and the white bandage, gripped in his clenched fist, pressed directly against his stomach.

He returned to consciousness. The blade had certainly pierced the wall of the stomach, he thought. His breathing was difficult, his chest thumped violently, and in some far deep region, which he could hardly believe was a part of himself, a fearful and excruciating pain came welling up as if the ground had split open to disgorge a boiling stream of molten rock. The pain came suddenly nearer, with terrifying speed. The lieutenant bit his lower lip and stifled an instinctive moan.

Was this *seppuku?*[13]—he was thinking. It was a sensation of utter chaos, as if the sky had fallen on his head and the world was reeling drunkenly. His will power and courage, which had seemed so robust before he made the incision, had now dwindled to something like a single hairlike thread of steel, and he was assailed by the uneasy feeling that he must advance along this thread, clinging to it with desperation. His clenched fist had grown moist. Looking down, he saw that both his hand and the cloth about the blade were drenched in blood. His loincloth too was dyed a deep red. It struck him as incredible that, amidst this terrible agony, things which could be seen could still be seen, and existing things existed still.

The moment the lieutenant thrust the sword into his left side and she saw the deathly pallor fall across his face, like an abruptly lowered curtain, Reiko had to struggle to prevent herself from rushing to his side. Whatever happened, she must watch. She must be a witness. That was the duty her husband had laid upon her. Opposite her, a mat's space away, she could clearly see her husband biting his lip to stifle the pain. The pain was there, with absolute certainty, before her eyes. And Reiko had no means of rescuing him from it.

The sweat glistened on her husband's forehead. The lieutenant closed his eyes, and then opened them again, as if experimenting. The eyes had lost their luster, and seemed innocent and empty like the eyes of a small animal.

The agony before Reiko's eyes burned as strong as the summer sun, utterly remote from the grief which seemed to be tearing herself apart within. The pain grew steadily in stature, stretching upward. Reiko felt that her husband had already become a man in a separate world, a man whose whole being had been resolved into pain, a prisoner in a cage of pain where no hand could reach out to him. But Reiko felt no pain at all. Her grief was not pain. As she thought about this, Reiko began to feel as if someone had raised a cruel wall of glass high between herself and her husband.

13  *seppuku:* Ritual suicide by disembowelment, the traditional form of suicide for military men.

Ever since her marriage her husband's existence had been her own existence, and every breath of his had been a breath drawn by herself. But now, while her husband's existence in pain was a vivid reality, Reiko could find in this grief of hers no certain proof at all of her own existence.

With only his right hand on the sword the lieutenant began to cut sideways across his stomach. But as the blade became entangled with the entrails it was pushed constantly outward by their soft resilience; and the lieutenant realized that it would be necessary, as he cut, to use both hands to keep the point pressed deep into his stomach. He pulled the blade across. It did not cut as easily as he had expected. He directed the strength of his whole body into his right hand and pulled again. There was a cut of three or four inches.

The pain spread slowly outward from the inner depths until the whole stomach reverberated. It was like the wild clanging of a bell. Or like a thousand bells which jangled simultaneously at every breath he breathed and every throb of his pulse, rocking his whole being. The lieutenant could no longer stop himself from moaning. But by now the blade had cut its way through to below the navel, and when he noticed this he felt a sense of satisfaction, and a renewal of courage.

The volume of blood had steadily increased, and now it spurted from the wound as if propelled by the beat of the pulse. The mat before the lieutenant was drenched red with splattered blood, and more blood overflowed onto it from pools which gathered in the folds of the lieutenant's khaki trousers. A spot, like a bird, came flying across to Reiko and settled on the lap of her white silk kimono.

By the time the lieutenant had at last drawn the sword across to the right side of his stomach, the blade was already cutting shallow and had revealed its naked tip, slippery with blood and grease. But, suddenly stricken by a fit of vomiting, the lieutenant cried out hoarsely. The vomiting made the fierce pain fiercer still, and the stomach, which had thus far remained firm and compact, now abruptly heaved, opening wide its wound, and the entrails burst through, as if the wound too were vomiting. Seemingly ignorant of their master's suffering, the entrails gave an impression of robust health and almost disagreeable vitality as they slipped smoothly out and spilled over into the crotch. The lieutenant's head drooped, his shoulders heaved, his eyes opened to narrow slits, and a thin trickle of saliva dribbled from his mouth. The gold markings on his epaulettes caught the light and glinted.

Blood was scattered everywhere. The lieutenant was soaked in it to his knees, and he sat now in a crumpled and listless posture, one hand on the floor. A raw smell filled the room. The lieutenant, his head drooping, retched repeatedly, and the movement showed vividly in his shoulders. The blade of the sword, now pushed back by the entrails and exposed to its tip, was still in the lieutenant's right hand.

It would be difficult to imagine a more heroic sight than that of the lieutenant at this moment, as he mustered his strength and flung back his head. The movement was performed with sudden violence, and the back of his head struck with a sharp crack against the alcove pillar. Reiko had been sitting until now with her face lowered, gazing in fascination at the tide of blood advancing toward her knees, but the sound took her by surprise and she looked up.

The lieutenant's face was not the face of a living man. The eyes were hollow, the skin parched, the once so lustrous cheeks and lips the color of dried mud. The right hand alone was moving. Laboriously gripping the sword, it hovered shakily in the air like the hand of a marionette and strove to direct the point at the base of the lieutenant's throat. Reiko watched her husband make this last, most heart-rending, futile exertion. Glistening with blood and grease, the point was thrust at the throat again and again. And each time it missed its aim. The strength to guide it was no longer there. The straying point struck the collar and the collar badges. Although its hooks had been unfastened, the stiff military collar had closed together again and was protecting the throat.

Reiko could bear the sight no longer. She tried to go to her husband's help, but she could not stand. She moved through the blood on her knees, and her white skirts grew deep red. Moving to the rear of her husband, she helped no more than by loosening the collar. The quivering blade at last contacted the naked flesh of the throat. At that moment Reiko's impression was that she herself had propelled her husband forward; but that was not the case. It was a movement planned by the lieutenant himself, his last exertion of strength. Abruptly he threw his body at the blade, and the blade pierced his neck, emerging at the nape. There was a tremendous spurt of blood and the lieutenant lay still, cold blue-tinged steel protruding from his neck at the back.

## 5

Slowly, her socks slippery with blood, Reiko descended the stairway. The upstairs room was now completely still.

Switching on the ground-floor lights, she checked the gas jet and the main gas plug and poured water over the smoldering, half-buried charcoal in the brazier. She stood before the upright mirror in the four-and-a-half-mat room and held up her skirts. The bloodstains made it seem as if a bold, vivid pattern was printed across the lower half of her white kimono. When she sat down before the mirror, she was conscious of the dampness and coldness of her husband's blood in the region of her thighs, and she shivered. Then, for a long while, she lingered over her toilet preparations. She applied the rouge generously to her cheeks, and her lips too she painted heavily. This was no longer make-up to please her husband. It was make-up for the world which she would leave behind, and there was a touch of the magnificent and the spectacular in her brushwork. When she rose, the mat before the mirror was wet with blood. Reiko was not concerned about this.

Returning from the toilet, Reiko stood finally on the cement floor of the porchway. When her husband had bolted the door here last night it had been in preparation for death. For a while she stood immersed in the consideration of a simple problem. Should she now leave the bolt drawn? If she were to lock the door, it could be that the neighbors might not notice their suicide for several days. Reiko did not relish the thought of their two corpses putrifying before discovery. After all, it seemed, it would be best to leave it open. . . . She released the bolt, and also drew open the frosted-glass door a fraction. . . .

At once, a chill wind blew in. There was no sign of anyone in the midnight streets, and stars glittered ice-cold through the trees in the large house opposite.

Leaving the door as it was, Reiko mounted the stairs. She had walked here and there for some time and her socks were no longer slippery. About halfway up, her nostrils were already assailed by a peculiar smell.

The lieutenant was lying on his face in a sea of blood. The point protruding from his neck seemed to have grown even more prominent than before. Reiko walked heedlessly across the blood. Sitting beside the lieutenant's corpse, she stared intently at the face, which lay on one cheek on the mat. The eyes were opened wide, as if the lieutenant's attention had been attracted by something. She raised the head, folding it in her sleeve, wiped the blood from the lips, and bestowed a last kiss.

Then she rose and took from the closet a new white blanket and a waist cord. To prevent any derangement of her skirts, she wrapped the blanket about her waist and bound it there firmly with the cord.

Reiko sat herself on a spot about one foot distant from the lieutenant's body. Drawing the dagger from her sash, she examined its dully gleaming blade intently, and held it to her tongue. The taste of the polished steel was slightly sweet.

Reiko did not linger. When she thought how the pain which had previously opened such a gulf between herself and her dying husband was now to become a part of her own experience, she saw before her only the joy of herself entering a realm her husband had already made his own. In her husband's agonized face there had been something inexplicable which she was seeing for the first time. Now she would solve that riddle. Reiko sensed that at last she too would be able to taste the true bitterness and sweetness of that great moral principle in which her husband believed. What had until now been tasted only faintly through her husband's example she was about to savor directly with her own tongue.

Reiko rested the point of the blade against the base of her throat. She thrust hard. The wound was only shallow. Her head blazed, and her hands shook uncontrollably. She gave the blade a strong pull sideways. A warm substance flooded into her mouth, and everything before her eyes reddened in a vision of spouting blood. She gathered her strength and plunged the point of the blade deep into her throat.

# Flannery O'Connor

## (1925–1964)

Flannery O'Connor is best known for her short stories, though she only published thirty-one during her lifetime. Her writing combines the comedic with the tragic and often brutal. Born into a Catholic family in Savannah, Georgia, O'Connor was greatly influenced by the Bible Belt, evident in her continual return to themes of sin, mercy, salvation, revelation, and redemption. She attended the Georgia State College for Women, where she edited the college magazine and received her A.B. in 1945. O'Connor then went on to the University of Iowa, where she studied with Paul Engle. She published her first short story, "The Geranium" (1946), in *Accent* magazine at the age of twenty-one, and in 1947 received her degree. O'Connor suffered her first attack from disseminated lupus, the disease that killed her father, in 1950. Afterward, she returned to her mother's dairy farm to live with her. Nevertheless, O'Connor continued to write and occasionally lecture to creative writing classes. Her first novel, *Wise Blood,* was published in 1952 and was followed by *A Good Man Is Hard to Find, and Other Stories* (1955), *The Violent Bear It Away* (1960), and *The Memoir of Mary Ann* (1962). O'Connor died in 1964 after an abdominal operation reactivated the lupus. Several collections of her writing were published posthumously, including *Everything That Rises Must Converge* (1965), *Mystery and Manners: Occasional Prose* (1969), and *The Complete Short Stories* (1971). *The Habit of Being* (1979) is a collection of O'Connor's personal letters.

## Good Country People
*1955*

Besides the neutral expression that she wore when she was alone, Mrs. Freeman had two others, forward and reverse, that she used for all her human dealings. Her forward expression was steady and driving like the advance of a heavy truck. Her eyes never swerved to left or right but turned as the story turned as if they followed a yellow line down the center of it. She seldom used the other expression because it was not often necessary for her to retract a statement, but when she did, her face came to a complete stop, there was an almost imperceptible movement of her black eyes, during which they seemed to be receding, and then the observer would see that Mrs. Freeman, though she might stand there as real as several grain sacks thrown on top of each other, was no longer there in spirit. As for getting anything across to her when this was the case, Mrs. Hopewell had given it up. She might talk her head off. Mrs. Freeman could never be brought to admit herself wrong on any point. She would stand there and if she could be brought to say anything, it was something like, "Well, I wouldn't of said it was and I wouldn't of said it wasn't," or letting her gaze range over the top kitchen shelf where there was an assortment of dusty bottles, she might remark, "I see you ain't ate many of them figs you put up last summer."

They carried on their most important business in the kitchen at breakfast. Every morning Mrs. Hopewell got up at seven o'clock and lit her gas heater and Joy's. Joy was her daughter, a large blonde girl who had an artificial leg. Mrs. Hopewell thought of her as a child though she was thirty-two years old and highly educated. Joy would get up while her mother was eating and lumber into the bathroom and slam the door, and before long, Mrs. Freeman would arrive at the back door. Joy would hear her mother call, "Come on in," and then they would talk for a while in low voices that were indistinguishable in the bathroom. By the time Joy came in, they had usually finished the weather report and were on one or the other of Mrs. Freeman's daughters, Glynese or

Carramae. Joy called them Glycerin and Caramel. Glynese, a redhead, was eighteen and had many admirers; Carramae, a blonde, was only fifteen but already married and pregnant. She could not keep anything on her stomach. Every morning Mrs. Freeman told Mrs. Hopewell how many times she had vomited since the last report.

Mrs. Hopewell liked to tell people that Glynese and Carramae were two of the finest girls she knew and that Mrs. Freeman was a *lady* and that she was never ashamed to take her anywhere or introduce her to anybody they might meet. Then she would tell how she had happened to hire the Freemans in the first place and how they were a godsend to her and how she had had them four years. The reason for her keeping them so long was that they were not trash. They were good country people. She had telephoned the man whose name they had given as a reference and he had told her that Mr. Freeman was a good farmer but that his wife was the nosiest woman ever to walk the earth. "She's got to be into everything," the man said. "If she don't get there before the dust settles, you can bet she's dead, that's all. She'll want to know all your business. I can stand him real good," he had said, "but me nor my wife neither could have stood that woman one more minute on this place." That had put Mrs. Hopewell off for a few days.

She had hired them in the end because there were no other applicants but she had made up her mind beforehand exactly how she would handle the woman. Since she was the type who had to be into everything, then, Mrs. Hopewell had decided, she would not only let her be into everything, she would *see to it* that she was into everything—she would give her the responsibility of everything, she would put her in charge. Mrs. Hopewell had no bad qualities of her own but she was able to use other people's in such a constructive way that she never felt the lack. She had hired the Freemans and she had kept them four years.

Nothing is perfect. This was one of Mrs. Hopewell's favorite sayings. Another was: that is life! And still another, the most important, was: well, other people have their opinions too. She would make these statements, usually at the table, in a tone of gentle insistence as if no one held them but her, and the large hulking Joy, whose constant outrage had obliterated every expression from her face, would stare just a little to the side of her, her eyes icy blue, with the look of someone who has achieved blindness by an act of will and means to keep it.

When Mrs. Hopewell said to Mrs. Freeman that life was like that, Mrs. Freeman would say, "I always said so myself." Nothing had been arrived at by anyone that had not first been arrived at by her. She was quicker than Mr. Freeman. When Mrs. Hopewell said to her after they had been on the place awhile, "You know, you're the wheel behind the wheel," and winked, Mrs. Freeman had said, "I know it. I've always been quick. It's some that are quicker than others."

"Everybody is different," Mrs. Hopewell said.

"Yes, most people is," Mrs. Freeman said.

"It takes all kinds to make the world."

"I always said it did myself."

The girl was used to this kind of dialogue for breakfast and more of it for dinner; sometimes they had it for supper too. When they had no guest they ate in the kitchen because that was easier. Mrs. Freeman always managed to arrive at some point during the meal and to watch them finish it. She would stand in the doorway if it were summer but in the winter she would stand with one elbow on top of the refrigerator and look down on them, or she would stand by the gas heater, lifting the back of her skirt slightly. Occasionally she would stand against the wall and roll her head from side to side. At no time was she in any hurry to leave. All this was very trying on Mrs. Hopewell but she was a woman of great patience. She realized that nothing is perfect and that in the Freemans she had good country people and that if, in this day and age, you get good country people, you had better hang onto them.

She had had plenty of experience with trash. Before the Freemans she had averaged one tenant family a year. The wives of these farmers were not the kind you would want to be around you for very long. Mrs. Hopewell, who had divorced her husband long ago, needed someone to walk over the fields with her; and when Joy had to be impressed for these services, her remarks were usually so ugly and her face so glum that Mrs. Hopewell would say, "If you can't come pleasantly, I don't want you at all," to which the girl, standing square and rigid-shouldered with her neck thrust slightly forward, would reply, "If you want me, here I am—LIKE I AM."

Mrs. Hopewell excused this attitude because of the leg (which had been shot off in a hunting accident when Joy was ten). It was hard for Mrs. Hopewell to realize that her child was thirty-two now and that for more than twenty years she had had only one leg. She thought of her still as a child because it tore her heart to think instead of the poor stout girl in her thirties who had never danced a step or had any *normal* good times. Her name was really Joy but as soon as she was twenty-one and away from home, she had had it legally changed. Mrs. Hopewell was certain that she had thought and thought until she had hit upon the ugliest name in any language. Then she had gone and had the beautiful name, Joy, changed without telling her mother until after she had done it. Her legal name was Hulga.

When Mrs. Hopewell thought the name, Hulga, she thought of the broad blank hull of a battleship. She would not use it. She continued to call her Joy to which the girl responded but in a purely mechanical way.

Hulga had learned to tolerate Mrs. Freeman, who saved her from taking walks with her mother. Even Glynese and Carramae were useful when they occupied attention that might otherwise have been directed at her. At first she had thought she could not stand Mrs. Freeman for she had found that it was not possible to be rude to her. Mrs. Freeman would take on strange resentments and for days together she would be sullen but the source of her displeasure was always obscure; a direct attack, a positive leer, blatant ugliness to her face—these never touched her. And without warning one day, she began calling her Hulga.

She did not call her that in front of Mrs. Hopewell who would have been incensed but when she and the girl happened to be out of the house together, she would say something and add the name Hulga to the end of it, and the big spectacled Joy-Hulga would scowl and redden as if her privacy had been intruded upon. She considered the name her personal affair. She had arrived at it first purely on the basis of its ugly sound and then the full genius of its fitness had struck her. She had a vision of the name working like the ugly sweating Vulcan[1] who stayed in the furnace and to whom, presumably, the goddess had to come when called. She saw it as the name of her highest creative act. One of her major triumphs was that her mother had not been able to turn her dust into Joy, but the greater one was that she had been able to turn it herself into Hulga. However, Mrs. Freeman's relish for using the name only irritated her. It was as if Mrs. Freeman's beady steel-pointed eyes had penetrated far enough behind her face to reach some secret fact. Something about her seemed to fascinate Mrs. Freeman and then one day Hulga realized that it was the artificial leg. Mrs. Freeman had a special fondness for the details of secret infections, hidden deformities, assaults upon children. Of diseases, she preferred the lingering or incurable. Hulga had heard Mrs. Hopewell give her the details of the hunting accident, how the leg had been literally blasted off, how she had never lost consciousness. Mrs. Freeman could listen to it any time as if it had happened an hour ago.

When Hulga stumped into the kitchen in the morning (she could walk without making the awful noise but she made it—Mrs. Hopewell was certain—because it was ugly-sounding), she glanced at them and did not speak. Mrs. Hopewell would be in her red kimono with her hair tied around her head in rags. She would be sitting at the table, finishing her breakfast and Mrs. Freeman would be hanging by her elbow outward from the refrigerator, looking down at the table. Hulga always put her eggs on the stove to boil and then stood over them with her arms folded, and Mrs. Hopewell would look at her—a kind of indirect gaze divided between her and Mrs. Freeman—and would think that if she would only keep herself up a little, she wouldn't be so bad looking. There was nothing wrong with her face that a pleasant expression wouldn't help. Mrs. Hopewell said that people who looked on the bright side of things would be beautiful even if they were not.

Whenever she looked at Joy this way, she could not help but feel that it would have been better if the child had not taken the Ph.D. It had certainly not brought her out any and now that she had it, there was no more excuse for her to go to school again. Mrs. Hopewell thought it was nice for girls to go to school to have a good time but Joy had "gone through." Anyhow, she would not have been strong enough to go again. The doctors had told Mrs. Hopewell that with the best of care, Joy might see forty-five. She had a weak heart. Joy had made it plain that if it had not been for this condition, she would be far from these red hills and good country people. She would be in a university lecturing to people who knew what she was talking about. And Mrs. Hopewell could very well picture her there, looking like a scarecrow and lecturing to more of the same. Here she went about all day in a six-year-old skirt and a yellow sweat shirt with a faded cowboy on a horse embossed on it. She thought this was funny; Mrs. Hopewell thought it was idiotic and showed simply that she was still a child. She was brilliant but she didn't have a grain of sense. It seemed to Mrs. Hopewell that every year she grew less like other people and more like herself—bloated, rude, and squint-eyed. And she said such strange things! To her own mother she had said—without warning, without excuse, standing up in the middle of a meal

---

1 **Vulcan:** The Greek god of fire. His wife was Venus, the goddess of love.

with her face purple and her mouth half full—"Woman! do you ever look inside? Do you ever look inside and see what you are *not*? God!" she had cried sinking down again and staring at her plate, "Malebranche[2] was right: we are not our own light. We are not our own light!" Mrs. Hopewell had no idea to this day what brought that on. She had only made the remark, hoping Joy would take it in, that a smile never hurt anyone.

The girl had taken the Ph.D. in philosophy and this left Mrs. Hopewell at a complete loss. You could say, "My daughter is a nurse," or "My daughter is a school teacher," or even, "My daughter is a chemical engineer." You could not say, "My daughter is a philosopher." That was something that had ended with the Greeks and Romans. All day Joy sat on her neck in a deep chair, reading. Sometimes she went for walks but she didn't like dogs or cats or birds or flowers or nature or nice young men. She looked at nice young men as if she could smell their stupidity.

One day Mrs. Hopewell had picked up one of the books the girl had just put down and opening it at random, she read, "Science, on the other hand, has to assert its soberness and seriousness afresh and declare that it is concerned solely with what-is. Nothing—how can it be for science anything but a horror and a phantasm? If science is right, then one thing stands firm: science wishes to know nothing of nothing. Such is after all the strictly scientific approach to Nothing. We know it by wishing to know nothing of Nothing." These words had been underlined with a blue pencil and they worked on Mrs. Hopewell like some evil incantation in gibberish. She shut the book quickly and went out of the room as if she were having a chill.

This morning when the girl came in, Mrs. Freeman was on Carramae. "She thrown up four times after supper," she said, "and was up twice in the night after three o'clock. Yesterday she didn't do nothing but ramble in the bureau drawer. All she did. Stand up there and see what she could run up on."

"She's got to eat," Mrs. Hopewell muttered, sipping her coffee, while she watched Joy's back at the stove. She was wondering what the child had said to the Bible salesman. She could not imagine what kind of a conversation she could possibly have had with him.

He was a tall gaunt hatless youth who had called yesterday to sell them a Bible. He had appeared at the door, carrying a large black suitcase that weighted him so heavily on one side that he had to brace himself against the door facing. He seemed on the point of collapse but he said in a cheerful voice, "Good morning, Mrs. Cedars!" and set the suitcase down on the mat. He was not a bad-looking young man though he had on a bright blue suit and yellow socks that were not pulled up far enough. He had prominent face bones and a streak of sticky-looking brown hair falling across his forehead.

"I'm Mrs. Hopewell," she said.

"Oh!" he said, pretending to look puzzled but with his eyes sparkling, "I saw it said 'The Cedars,' on the mailbox so I thought you was Mrs. Cedars!" and he burst out in a pleasant laugh. He picked up the satchel and under cover of a pant, he fell forward into her hall. It was rather as if the suitcase had moved first, jerking him after it.

---

2 **Malebranche:** Nicolas Malebranche (1638–1715), French philosopher.

"Mrs. Hopewell!" he said and grabbed her hand. "I hope you are well!" and he laughed again and then all at once his face sobered completely. He paused and gave her a straight earnest look and said, "Lady, I've come to speak of serious things."

"Well, come in," she muttered, none too pleased because her dinner was almost ready. He came into the parlor and sat down on the edge of a straight chair and put the suitcase between his feet and glanced around the room as if he were sizing her up by it. Her silver gleamed on the two sideboards; she decided he had never been in a room as elegant as this.

"Mrs. Hopewell," he began, using her name in a way that sounded almost intimate, "I know you believe in Christian service."

"Well yes," she murmured.

"I know," he said and paused, looking very wise with his head cocked on one side, "that you're a good woman. Friends have told me."

Mrs. Hopewell never liked to be taken for a fool. "What are you selling?" she asked.

"Bibles," the young man said and his eye raced around the room before he added, "I see you have no family Bible in your parlor, I see that is the one lack you got!"

Mrs. Hopewell could not say, "My daughter is an atheist and won't let me keep the Bible in the parlor." She said, stiffening slightly, "I keep my Bible by my bedside." This was not the truth. It was in the attic somewhere.

"Lady," he said, "the word of God ought to be in the parlor."

"Well, I think that's a matter of taste," she began. "I think . . ."

"Lady," he said, "for a Christian, the word of God ought to be in every room in the house besides in his heart. I know you're a Christian because I can see it in every line of your face."

She stood up and said, "Well, young man, I don't want to buy a Bible and I smell my dinner burning."

He didn't get up. He began to twist his hands and looking down at them, he said softly, "Well lady, I'll tell you the truth—not many people want to buy one nowadays and besides, I know I'm real simple. I don't know how to say a thing but to say it. I'm just a country boy." He glanced up into her unfriendly face. "People like you don't like to fool with country people like me!"

"Why!" she cried, "good country people are the salt of the earth! Besides, we all have different ways of doing, it takes all kinds to make the world go 'round. That's life!"

"You said a mouthful," he said.

"Why, I think there aren't enough good country people in the world!" she said, stirred. "I think that's what's wrong with it!"

His face had brightened. "I didn't inraduce myself," he said. "I'm Manley Pointer from out in the country around Willohobie, not even from a place, just from near a place."

"You wait a minute," she said. "I have to see about my dinner." She went out to the kitchen and found Joy standing near the door where she had been listening.

"Get rid of the salt of the earth," she said, "and let's eat."

Mrs. Hopewell gave her a pained look and turned the heat down under the vegetables. "*I* can't be rude to anybody," she murmured and went back into the parlor.

He had opened the suitcase and was sitting with a Bible on each knee.

"You might as well put those up," she told him. "I don't want one."

"I appreciate your honesty," he said. "You don't see any more real honest people unless you go way out in the country."

"I know," she said, "real genuine folks!" Through the crack in the door she heard a groan.

"I guess a lot of boys come telling you they're working their way through college," he said, "but I'm not going to tell you that. Somehow," he said, "I don't want to go to college. I want to devote my life to Christian service. See," he said, lowering his voice, "I got this heart condition. I may not live long. When you know it's something wrong with you and you may not live long, well, then, lady . . ." He paused, with his mouth open, and stared at her.

He and Joy had the same condition! She knew that her eyes were filling with tears but she collected herself quickly and murmured, "Won't you stay for dinner? We'd love to have you!" and was sorry the instant she heard herself say it.

"Yes mam," he said in an abashed voice, "I would sher love to do that!"

Joy had given him one look on being introduced to him and then throughout the meal had not glanced at him again. He had addressed several remarks to her, which she had pretended not to hear. Mrs. Hopewell could not understand deliberate rudeness, although she lived with it, and she felt she had always to overflow with hospitality to make up for Joy's lack of courtesy. She urged him to talk about himself and he did. He said he was the seventh child of twelve and that his father had been crushed under a tree when he himself was eight year old. He had been crushed very badly, in fact, almost cut in two and was practically not recognizable. His mother had got along the best she could by hard working and she had always seen that her children went to Sunday School and that they read the Bible every evening. He was now nineteen year old and he had been selling Bibles for four months. In that time he had sold seventy-seven Bibles and had the promise of two more sales. He wanted to become a missionary because he thought that was the way you could do the most for people. "He who losest his life shall find it," he said simply and he was so sincere, so genuine and earnest that Mrs. Hopewell would not for the world have smiled. He prevented his peas from sliding onto the table by blocking them with a piece of bread which he later cleaned his plate with. She could see Joy observing sidewise how he handled his knife and fork and she saw too that every few minutes, the boy would dart a keen appraising glance at the girl as if he were trying to attract her attention.

After dinner Joy cleared the dishes off the table and disappeared and Mrs. Hopewell was left to talk with him. He told her again about his childhood and his father's accident and about various things that had happened to him. Every five minutes or so she would stifle a yawn. He sat for two hours until finally she told him she must go because she had an appointment in town. He packed his Bibles and thanked her and prepared to leave, but in the doorway he stopped and wrung her hand and said that not on any of his trips had he met a lady as nice as her and he asked if he could come again. She had said she would always be happy to see him.

Joy had been standing in the road, apparently looking at something in the distance, when he came down the steps toward her, bent to the side with his heavy valise. He stopped where she was standing and confronted her directly. Mrs. Hopewell could not hear what he said but she trembled to think what Joy would say to him. She could see that after a minute Joy said something and that then the boy began to speak again, making an excited gesture with his free hand. After a minute Joy said something else at which the boy began to speak once more. Then to her amazement, Mrs. Hopewell saw the two of them walk off together, toward the gate. Joy had walked all the way to the gate with him and Mrs. Hopewell could not imagine what they had said to each other, and she had not yet dared to ask.

Mrs. Freeman was insisting upon her attention. She had moved from the refrigerator to the heater so that Mrs. Hopewell had to turn and face her in order to seem to be listening. "Glynese gone out with Harvey Hill again last night," she said. "She had this sty."

"Hill," Mrs. Hopewell said absently, "is that the one who works in the garage?"

"Nome, he's the one that goes to chiropracter school," Mrs. Freeman said. "She had this sty. Been had it two days. So she says when he brought her in the other night he says, 'Lemme get rid of that sty for you,' and she says, 'How?' and he says, 'You just lay yourself down across the seat of that car and I'll show you.' So she done it and he popped her neck. Kept on a-popping it several times until she made him quit. This morning," Mrs. Freeman said, "she ain't got no sty. She ain't got no traces of a sty."

"I never heard of that before," Mrs. Hopewell said.

"He ast her to marry him before the Ordinary,"[3] Mrs. Freeman went on, "and she told him she wasn't going to be married in no *office*."

"Well, Glynese is a fine girl," Mrs. Hopewell said. "Glynese and Carramae are both fine girls."

"Carramae said when her and Lyman was married Lyman said it sure felt sacred to him. She said he said he wouldn't take five hundred dollars for being married by a preacher."

"How much would he take?" the girl asked from the stove.

"He said he wouldn't take five hundred dollars," Mrs. Freeman repeated.

"Well we all have work to do," Mrs. Hopewell said.

"Lyman said it just felt more sacred to him," Mrs. Freeman said. "The doctor wants Carramae to eat prunes. Says instead of medicine. Says them cramps is coming from pressure. You know where I think it is?"

"She'll be better in a few weeks," Mrs. Hopewell said.

"In the tube," Mrs. Freeman said. "Else she wouldn't be as sick as she is."

Hulga had cracked her two eggs into a saucer and was bringing them to the table along with a cup of coffee that she had filled too full. She sat down carefully and began to eat, meaning to keep Mrs. Freeman there by questions if for any reason she showed an inclination to leave. She could perceive her mother's eye on her. The first roundabout question would be about the Bible salesman and she did not wish to bring it on. "How did he pop her neck?" she asked.

3 **Ordinary:** A judge who can perform the marriage ceremony in his chambers.

Mrs. Freeman went into a description of how he had popped her neck. She said he owned a '55 Mercury but that Glynese said she would rather marry a man with only a '36 Plymouth who would be married by a preacher. The girl asked what if he had a '32 Plymouth and Mrs. Freeman said what Glynese had said was a '36 Plymouth.

Mrs. Hopewell said there were not many girls with Glynese's common sense. She said what she admired in those girls was their common sense. She said that reminded her that they had a nice visitor yesterday, a young man selling Bibles. "Lord," she said, "he bored me to death but he was so sincere and genuine I couldn't be rude to him. He was just good country people, you know," she said, "—just the salt of the earth."

"I seen him walk up," Mrs. Freeman said, "and then later—I seen him walk off," and Hulga could feel the slight shift in her voice, the slight insinuation, that he had not walked off alone, had he? Her face remained expressionless but the color rose into her neck and she seemed to swallow it down with the next spoonful of egg. Mrs. Freeman was looking at her as if they had a secret together.

"Well, it takes all kinds of people to make the world go 'round," Mrs. Hopewell said. "It's very good we aren't all alike."

"Some people are more alike than others," Mrs. Freeman said.

Hulga got up and stumped, with about twice the noise that was necessary, into her room and locked the door. She was to meet the Bible salesman at ten o'clock at the gate. She had thought about it half the night. She had started thinking of it as a great joke and then she had begun to see profound implications in it. She had lain in bed imagining dialogues for them that were insane on the surface but that reached below to depths that no Bible salesman would be aware of. Their conversation yesterday had been of this kind.

He had stopped in front of her and had simply stood there. His face was bony and sweaty and bright, with a little pointed nose in the center of it, and his look was different from what it had been at the dinner table. He was gazing at her with open curiosity, with fascination, like a child watching a new fantastic animal at the zoo, and he was breathing as if he had run a great distance to reach her. His gaze seemed somehow familiar but she could not think where she had been regarded with it before. For almost a minute he didn't say anything. Then on what seemed an insuck of breath, he whispered, "You ever ate a chicken that was two days old?"

The girl looked at him stonily. He might have just put this question up for consideration at the meeting of a philosophical association. "Yes," she presently replied as if she had considered it from all angles.

"It must have been mighty small!" he said triumphantly and shook all over with little nervous giggles, getting very red in the face, and subsiding finally into his gaze of complete admiration, while the girl's expression remained exactly the same.

"How old are you?" he asked softly.

She waited some time before she answered. Then in a flat voice she said, "Seventeen."

His smiles came in succession like waves breaking on the surface of a little lake. "I see you got a wooden leg," he said. "I think you're real brave. I think you're real sweet."

The girl stood blank and solid and silent.

"Walk to the gate with me," he said. "You're a brave sweet little thing and I liked you the minute I seen you walk in the door."

Hulga began to move forward.

"What's your name?" he asked, smiling down on the top of her head.

"Hulga," she said.

"Hulga," he murmured, "Hulga. Hulga. I never heard of anybody name Hulga before. You're shy, aren't you, Hulga?" he asked.

She nodded, watching his large red hand on the handle of the giant valise.

"I like girls that wear glasses," he said. "I think a lot. I'm not like these people that a serious thought don't ever enter their heads. It's because I may die."

"I may die too," she said suddenly and looked up at him. His eyes were very small and brown, glittering feverishly.

"Listen," he said, "don't you think some people was meant to meet on account of what all they got in common and all? Like they both think serious thoughts and all?" He shifted the valise to his other hand so that the hand nearest her was free. He caught hold of her elbow and shook it a little. "I don't work on Saturday," he said. "I like to walk in the woods and see what Mother Nature is wearing. O'er the hills and far away. Pic-nics and things. Couldn't we go on a pic-nic tomorrow? Say yes, Hulga," he said and gave her a dying look as if he felt his insides about to drop out of him. He had even seemed to sway slightly toward her.

During the night she had imagined that she seduced him. She imagined that the two of them walked on the place until they came to the storage barn beyond the two back fields and there, she imagined, that things came to such a pass that she very easily seduced him and that then, of course, she had to reckon with his remorse. True genius can get an idea across even to an inferior mind. She imagined that she took his remorse in hand and changed it into a deeper understanding of life. She took all his shame away and turned it into something useful.

She set off for the gate at exactly ten o'clock, escaping without drawing Mrs. Hopewell's attention. She didn't take anything to eat, forgetting that food is usually taken on a picnic. She wore a pair of slacks and a dirty white shirt, and as an after-thought, she had put some Vapex on the collar of it since she did not own any perfume. When she reached the gate no one was there.

She looked up and down the empty highway and had the furious feeling that she had been tricked, that he had only meant to make her walk to the gate after the idea of him. Then suddenly he stood up, very tall, from behind a bush on the opposite embankment. Smiling, he lifted his hat which was new and wide-brimmed. He had not worn it yesterday and she wondered if he had bought it for the occasion. It was toast-colored with a red and white band around it and was slightly too large for him. He stepped from behind the bush still carrying the black valise. He had on the same suit and the same yellow socks sucked down in his shoes from walking. He crossed the highway and said, "I knew you'd come!"

The girl wondered acidly how he had known this. She pointed to the valise and asked, "Why did you bring your Bibles?"

He took her elbow, smiling down on her as if he could not stop. "You can never tell when you'll need the word of God, Hulga," he said. She had a moment in which she doubted that this was actually happening and then they began to climb the embankment. They went down into the pasture toward the woods. The boy walked lightly by her side, bouncing on his toes. The valise did not seem to be heavy today; he even swung it. They crossed half the pasture without saying anything and then, putting his hand easily on the small of her back, he asked softly, "Where does your wooden leg join on?"

She turned an ugly red and glared at him and for an instant the boy looked abashed. "I didn't mean you no harm," he said. "I only meant you're so brave and all. I guess God takes care of you."

"No," she said, looking forward and walking fast, "I don't even believe in God."

At this he stopped and whistled. "No!" he exclaimed as if he were too astonished to say anything else.

She walked on and in a second he was bouncing at her side, fanning with his hat. "That's very unusual for a girl," he remarked, watching her out of the corner of his eye. When they reached the edge of the wood, he put his hand on her back again and drew her against him without a word and kissed her heavily.

The kiss, which had more pressure than feeling behind it, produced that extra surge of adrenaline in the girl that enables one to carry a packed trunk out of a burning house, but in her, the power went at once to the brain. Even before he released her, her mind, clear and detached and ironic anyway, was regarding him from a great distance, with amusement but with pity. She had never been kissed before and she was pleased to discover that it was an unexceptional experience and all a matter of the mind's control. Some people might enjoy drain water if they were told it was vodka. When the boy, looking expectant but uncertain, pushed her gently away, she turned and walked on, saying nothing as if such business, for her, were common enough.

He came along panting at her side, trying to help her when he saw a root that she might trip over. He caught and held back the long swaying blades of thorn vine until she had passed beyond them. She led the way and he came breathing heavily behind her. Then they came out on a sunlit hillside, sloping softly into another one a little smaller. Beyond, they could see the rusted top of the old barn where the extra hay was stored.

The hill was sprinkled with small pink weeds. "Then you ain't saved?" he asked suddenly, stopping.

The girl smiled. It was the first time she had smiled at him at all. "In my economy," she said, "I'm saved and you are damned but I told you I didn't believe in God."

Nothing seemed to destroy the boy's look of admiration. He gazed at her now as if the fantastic animal at the zoo had put its paw through the bars and given him a loving poke. She thought he looked as if he wanted to kiss her again and she walked on before he had the chance.

"Ain't there somewheres we can sit down sometime?" he murmured, his voice softening toward the end of the sentence.

"In that barn," she said.

They made for it rapidly as if it might slide away like a train. It was a large two-story barn, cool and dark inside. The boy pointed up the ladder that led into the loft and said, "It's too bad we can't go up there."

"Why can't we?" she asked.

"Yer leg," he said reverently.

The girl gave him a contemptuous look and putting both hands on the ladder, she climbed it while he stood below, apparently awestruck. She pulled herself expertly through the opening and then looked down at him and said, "Well, come on if you're coming," and he began to climb the ladder, awkwardly bringing the suitcase with him.

"We won't need the Bible," she observed.

"You never can tell," he said, panting. After he had got into the loft, he was a few seconds catching his breath. She had sat down in a pile of straw. A wide sheath of sunlight, filled with dust particles, slanted over her. She lay back against a bale, her face turned away, looking out the front opening of the barn where hay was thrown from a wagon into the loft. The two pink-speckled hillsides lay back against a dark ridge of woods. The sky was cloudless and cold blue. The boy dropped down by her side and put one arm under her and the other over her and began methodically kissing her face, making little noises like a fish. He did not remove his hat but it was pushed far enough back not to interfere. When her glasses got in his way, he took them off of her and slipped them into his pocket.

The girl at first did not return any of the kisses but presently she began to and after she had put several on his cheek, she reached his lips and remained there, kissing him again and again as if she were trying to draw all the breath out of him. His breath was clear and sweet like a child's and the kisses were sticky like a child's. He mumbled about loving her and about knowing when he first seen her that he loved her, but the mumbling was like the sleepy fretting of a child being put to sleep by his mother. Her mind, throughout this, never stopped or lost itself for a second to her feelings. "You ain't said you love me none," he whispered finally, pulling back from her. "You got to say that."

She looked away from him off into the hollow sky and then down at a black ridge and then down farther into what appeared to be two green swelling lakes. She didn't realize he had taken her glasses but this landscape could not seem exceptional to her for she seldom paid any close attention to her surroundings.

"You got to say it," he repeated. "You got to say you love me."

She was always careful how she committed herself. "In a sense," she began, "if you use the word loosely, you might say that. But it's not a word I use. I don't have illusions. I'm one of those people who see *through* to nothing."

The boy was frowning. "You got to say it. I said it and you got to say it," he said.

The girl looked at him almost tenderly. "You poor baby," she murmured. "It's just as well you don't understand," and she pulled him by the neck, face-down, against her. "We are all damned," she said, "but some of us have taken off our blindfolds and see that there's nothing to see. It's a kind of salvation."

The boy's astonished eyes looked blankly through the ends of her hair. "Okay," he almost whined, "but do you love me or don'tcher?"

"Yes," she said and added, "in a sense. But I must tell you something. There mustn't be anything dishonest between us." She lifted his head and looked him in the eye. "I am thirty years old," she said. "I have a number of degrees."

The boy's look was irritated but dogged. "I don't care," he said. "I don't care a thing about what all you done. I just want to know if you love me or don'tcher?" and he caught her to him and wildly planted her face with kisses until she said, "Yes, yes."

"Okay then," he said, letting her go. "Prove it."

She smiled, looking dreamily out on the shifty landscape. She had seduced him without even making up her mind to try. "How?" she asked, feeling that he should be delayed a little.

He leaned over and put his lips to her ear. "Show me where your wooden leg joins on," he whispered.

The girl uttered a sharp little cry and her face instantly drained of color. The obscenity of the suggestion was not what shocked her. As a child she had sometimes been subject to feelings of shame but education had removed the last traces of that as a good surgeon scrapes for cancer; she would no more have felt it over what he was asking than she would have believed in his Bible. But she was as sensitive about the artificial leg as a peacock about his tail. No one ever touched it but her. She took care of it as someone else would his soul, in private and almost with her own eyes turned away. "No," she said.

"I known it," he muttered, sitting up. "You're just playing me for a sucker."

"Oh no no!" she cried. "It joins on at the knee. Only at the knee. Why do you want to see it?"

The boy gave her a long penetrating look. "Because," he said, "it's what makes you different. You ain't like anybody else."

She sat staring at him. There was nothing about her face or her round freezing-blue eyes to indicate that this had moved her; but she felt as if her heart had stopped and left her mind to pump her blood. She decided that for the first time in her life she was face to face with real innocence. This boy, with an instinct that came from beyond wisdom, had touched the truth about her. When after a minute, she said in a hoarse high voice, "All right," it was like surrendering to him completely. It was like losing her own life and finding it again, miraculously, in his.

Very gently he began to roll the slack leg up. The artificial limb, in a white sock and brown flat shoe, was bound in a heavy material like canvas and ended in an ugly jointure where it was attached to the stump. The boy's face and his voice were entirely reverent as he uncovered it and said, "Now show me how to take it off and on."

She took it off for him and put it back on again and then he took it off himself, handling it as tenderly as if it were a real one. "See!" he said with a delighted child's face. "Now I can do it myself!"

"Put it back on," she said. She was thinking that she would run away with him and that every night he would take the leg off and every morning put it back on again. "Put it back on," she said.

"Not yet," he murmured, setting it on its foot out of her reach. "Leave it off for a while. You got me instead."

She gave a little cry of alarm but he pushed her down and began to kiss her again.

Without the leg she felt entirely dependent on him. Her brain seemed to have stopped thinking altogether and to be about some other function that it was not very good at. Different expressions raced back and forth over her face. Every now and then the boy, his eyes like two steel spikes, would glance behind him where the leg stood. Finally she pushed him off and said, "Put it back on me now."

"Wait," he said. He leaned the other way and pulled the valise toward him and opened it. It had a pale blue spotted lining and there were only two Bibles in it. He took one of these out and opened the cover of it. It was hollow and contained a pocket flask of whiskey, a pack of cards, and a small blue box with printing on it. He laid these out in front of her one at a time in an evenly spaced row, like one presenting offerings at the shrine of a goddess. He put the blue box in her hand. THIS PRODUCT TO BE USED ONLY FOR THE PREVENTION OF DISEASE, she read, and dropped it. The boy was unscrewing the top of the flask. He stopped and pointed, with a smile, to the deck of cards. It was not an ordinary deck but one with an obscene picture on the back of each card. "Take a swig," he said, offering her the bottle first. He held it in front of her, but like one mesmerized, she did not move.

Her voice when she spoke had an almost pleading sound. "Aren't you," she murmured, "aren't you just good country people?"

The boy cocked his head. He looked as if he were just beginning to understand that she might be trying to insult him. "Yeah," he said, curling his lip slightly, "but it ain't held me back none. I'm as good as you any day in the week."

"Give me my leg," she said.

He pushed it farther away with his foot. "Come on now, let's begin to have us a good time," he said coaxingly. "We ain't got to know one another good yet."

"Give me my leg!" she screamed and tried to lunge for it but he pushed her down easily.

"What's the matter with you all of a sudden?" he asked, frowning as he screwed the top on the flask and put it quickly back inside the Bible. "You just a while ago said you didn't believe in nothing. I thought you was some girl!"

Her face was almost purple. "You're a Christian!" she hissed. "You're a fine Christian! You're just like them all—say one thing and do another. You're a perfect Christian, you're . . ."

The boy's mouth was set angrily. "I hope you don't think," he said in a lofty indignant tone, "that I believe in that crap! I may sell Bibles but I know which end is up and I wasn't born yesterday and I know where I'm going!"

"Give me my leg!" she screeched. He jumped up so quickly that she barely saw him sweep the cards and the blue box back into the Bible and throw the Bible into the valise. She saw him grab the leg and then she saw it for an instant slanted forlornly across the inside of the suitcase with a Bible at either side of its opposite ends. He slammed the lid shut and snatched up the valise and swung it down the hole and then stepped through himself.

When all of him had passed but his head, he turned and regarded her with a look that no longer had any admiration in it. "I've gotten a lot of interesting things," he said. "One time I got a woman's glass eye this way. And you needn't to think you'll catch me because Pointer ain't really my name. I use a different name at every house I call at and don't stay nowhere long. And I'll tell you another thing, Hulga," he said, using the name as if he didn't think much of it, "you ain't so smart. I been believing in nothing ever since I was born!" and then the toast-colored hat disappeared down the hole and the girl was left, sitting on the straw in the dusty sunlight. When she turned her churning face toward the opening, she saw his blue figure struggling successfully over the green speckled lake.

Mrs. Hopewell and Mrs. Freeman, who were in the back pasture, digging up onions, saw him emerge a little later from the woods and head across the meadow toward the highway. "Why, that looks like that nice dull young man that tried to sell me a Bible yesterday," Mrs. Hopewell said, squinting. "He must have been selling them to the Negroes back in there. He was so simple," she said, "but I guess the world would be better off if we were all that simple."

Mrs. Freeman's gaze drove forward and just touched him before he disappeared under the hill. Then she returned her attention to the evil-smelling onion shoot she was lifting from the ground. "Some can't be that simple," she said. "I know I never could."

## A Good Man Is Hard to Find                                      1953

The grandmother didn't want to go to Florida. She wanted to visit some of her connections in east Tennessee and she was seizing at every chance to change Bailey's mind. Bailey was the son she lived with, her only boy. He was sitting on the edge of his chair at the table, bent over the orange sports section of the *Journal*. "Now look here, Bailey," she said, "see here, read this," and she stood with one hand on her thin hip and the other rattling the newspaper at his bald head. "Here this fellow that calls himself The Misfit is aloose from the Federal Pen and headed toward Florida and you read here what it says he did to these people. Just you read it. I wouldn't take my children in any direction with a criminal like that aloose in it. I couldn't answer to my conscience if I did."

Bailey didn't look up from his reading so she wheeled around then and faced the children's mother, a young woman in slacks, whose face was as broad and innocent as a cabbage and was tied round with a green head-kerchief that had two points on the top like rabbit's ears. She was sitting on the sofa, feeding the baby his apricots out of a jar. "The children have been to Florida before," the old lady said. "You all ought to take them somewhere else for a change so they would see different parts of the world and be broad. They never have been to east Tennessee."

The children's mother didn't seem to hear her but the eight-year-old boy, John Wesley, a stocky child with glasses, said, "If you don't want to go to Florida, why dontcha stay at home?" He and the little girl, June Star, were reading the funny papers on the floor.

"She wouldn't stay at home to be queen for a day," June Star said without raising her yellow head.

"Yes and what would you do if this fellow, The Misfit, caught you?" the grandmother asked.

"I'd smack his face," John Wesley said.

"She wouldn't stay at home for a million bucks," June Star said. "Afraid she'd miss something. She has to go everywhere we go."

"All right, Miss," the grandmother said. "Just remember that the next time you want me to curl your hair."

June Star said her hair was naturally curly.

The next morning the grandmother was the first one in the car, ready to go. She had her big black valise that looked like the head of a hippopotamus in one corner, and underneath it she was hiding a basket with Pitty Sing,[1] the cat, in it. She didn't intend for the cat to be left alone in the house for three days because he would miss her too much and she was afraid he might brush against one of the gas burners and accidentally asphyxiate himself. Her son, Bailey, didn't like to arrive at a motel with a cat.

She sat in the middle of the back seat with John Wesley and June Star on either side of her. Bailey and the children's mother and the baby sat in the front and they left Atlanta at eight forty-five with the mileage on the car at 55890. The grandmother wrote this down because she thought it would be interesting to say how many miles they had been when they got back. It took them twenty minutes to reach the outskirts of the city.

The old lady settled herself comfortably, removing her white cotton gloves and putting them up with her purse on the shelf in front of the back window. The children's mother still had on slacks and still had her head tied up in a green kerchief, but the grandmother had on a navy blue straw sailor hat with a bunch of white violets on the brim and a navy blue dress with a small white dot in the print. Her collar and cuffs were white organdy trimmed with lace and at her neckline she had pinned a purple spray of cloth violets containing a sachet. In case of an accident, anyone seeing her dead on the highway would know at once that she was a lady.

She said she thought it was going to be a good day for driving, neither too hot nor too cold, and she cautioned Bailey that the speed limit was fifty-five miles an hour and that the patrolmen hid themselves behind billboards and small clumps of trees and sped out after you before you had a chance to slow down. She pointed out interesting details of the scenery: Stone Mountain; the blue granite that in some places came up to both sides of the highway; the brilliant red clay banks slightly streaked with purple; and the various crops that made rows of green lace-work on the ground. The trees were full of silver-white sunlight and the meanest of them sparkled. The children were reading comic magazines and their mother had gone back to sleep.

"Let's go through Georgia fast so we won't have to look at it much," John Wesley said.

"If I were a little boy," said the grandmother, "I wouldn't talk about my native state that way. Tennessee has the mountains and Georgia has the hills."

1 **Pitty Sing:** The name of a character in *The Mikado,* an operetta by Gilbert and Sullivan.

"Tennessee is just a hillbilly dumping ground," John Wesley said, "and Georgia is a lousy state too."

"You said it," June Star said.

"In my time," said the grandmother, folding her thin veined fingers, "children were more respectful of their native states and their parents and everything else. People did right then. Oh look at the cute little pickaninny!" she said and pointed to a Negro child standing in the door of a shack. "Wouldn't that make a picture, now?" she asked and they all turned and looked at the little Negro out of the back window. He waved.

"He didn't have any britches on," June said.

"He probably didn't have any," the grandmother explained. "Little niggers in the country don't have things like we do. If I could paint, I'd paint that picture," she said.

The children exchanged comic books.

The grandmother offered to hold the baby and the children's mother passed him over the front seat to her. She set him on her knee and bounced him and told him about the things they were passing. She rolled her eyes and screwed up her mouth and stuck her leathery thin face into his smooth bland one. Occasionally he gave her a far-away smile. They passed a large cotton field with five or six graves fenced in the middle of it, like a small island. "Look at the graveyard!" the grandmother said, pointing it out. "That was the old family burying ground. That belonged to the plantation."

"Where's the plantation?" John Wesley asked.

"Gone With the Wind," said the grandmother. "Ha. Ha."

When the children finished all the comic books they had brought, they opened the lunch and ate it. The grandmother ate a peanut butter sandwich and an olive and would not let the children throw the box and the paper napkins out the window. When there was nothing else to do they played a game by choosing a cloud and making the other two guess what shape it suggested. John Wesley took one the shape of a cow and June Star guessed a cow and John Wesley said, no, an automobile, and June Star said he didn't play fair, and they began to slap each other over the grandmother.

The grandmother said she would tell them a story if they would keep quiet. When she told a story, she rolled her eyes and waved her head and was very dramatic. She said once when she was a maiden lady she had been courted by a Mr. Edgar Atkins Teagarden from Jasper, Georgia. She said he was a very good-looking man and a gentleman and that he brought her a watermelon every Saturday afternoon with his initials cut in it, E. A. T. Well, one Saturday, she said, Mr. Teagarden brought the watermelon and there was nobody at home and he left it on the front porch and returned in his buggy to Jasper, but she never got the watermelon, she said, because a nigger boy ate it when he saw the initials, E. A. T.! This story tickled John Wesley's funny bone and he giggled and giggled but June Star didn't think it was any good. She said she wouldn't marry a man that just brought her a watermelon on Saturday. The grandmother said she would have done well to marry Mr. Teagarden because he was a gentleman and had bought Coca-Cola stock when it first came out and that he had died only a few years ago, a very wealthy man.

They stopped at The Tower for barbecued sandwiches. The Tower was a part stucco and part wood filling station and dance hall set in a clearing outside of Timothy. A fat man named Red Sammy Butts ran it and there were signs stuck here and there on the building and for miles up and down the highway saying, TRY RED SAMMY'S FAMOUS BARBECUE. NONE LIKE FAMOUS RED SAMMY'S! RED SAM! THE FAT BOY WITH THE HAPPY LAUGH. A VETERAN! SAMMY'S YOUR MAN!

Red Sammy was lying on the bare ground outside The Tower with his head under a truck while a gray monkey about a foot high, chained to a small chinaberry tree, chattered nearby. The monkey sprang back into the tree and got on the highest limb as soon as he saw the children jump out of the car and run toward him.

Inside, The Tower was a long dark room with a counter at one end and tables at the other and dancing space in the middle. They all sat down at a broad table next to the nickelodeon and Red Sam's wife, a tall burnt-brown woman with hair and eyes lighter than her skin, came and took their order. The children's mother put a dime in the machine and played "The Tennessee Waltz," and the grandmother said that tune always made her want to dance. She asked Bailey if he would like to dance but he only glared at her. He didn't have a naturally sunny disposition like she did and trips made him nervous. The grandmother's brown eyes were very bright. She swayed her head from side to side and pretended she was dancing in her chair. June Star said play something she could tap to so the children's mother put in another dime and played a fast number and June Star stepped out onto the dance floor and did her tap routine.

"Ain't she cute?" Red Sam's wife said, leaning over the counter. "Would you like to come be my little girl?"

"No I certainly wouldn't," June Star said. "I wouldn't live in a broken-down place like this for a million bucks!" and she ran back to the table.

"Ain't she cute?" the woman repeated, stretching her mouth politely.

"Aren't you ashamed?" hissed the grandmother.

Red Sam came in and told his wife to quit lounging on the counter and hurry with these people's order. His khaki trousers reached just to his hip bones and his stomach hung over them like a sack of meal swaying under his shirt. He came over and sat down at a table nearby and let out a combination sigh and yodel. "You can't win," he said. "You can't win," and he wiped his sweating red face off with a gray hand-kerchief. "These days you don't know who to trust," he said. "Ain't that the truth?"

"People are certainly not nice like they used to be," said the grandmother.

"Two fellers come in here last week," Red Sammy said, "driving a Chrysler. It was a old beat-up car but it was a good one and these boys looked all right to me. Said they worked at the mill and you know I let them fellers charge the gas they bought? Now why did I do that?"

"Because you're a good man!" the grandmother said at once.

"Yes'm, I suppose so," Red Sam said as if he were struck with the answer.

His wife brought the orders, carrying the five plates all at once without a tray, two in each hand and one balanced on her arm. "It isn't a soul in this green world of God's that you can trust," she said. "And I don't count anybody out of that, not nobody," she repeated, looking at Red Sammy.

"Did you read about that criminal, The Misfit, that's escaped?" asked the grandmother.

"I wouldn't be a bit surprised if he didn't attact this place right here," said the woman. "If he hears about it being here, I wouldn't be none surprised to see him. If he hears it's two cent in the cash register, I wouldn't be a tall surprised if he . . ."

"That'll do," Red Sam said. "Go bring these people their Co'Colas," and the woman went off to get the rest of the order.

"A good man is hard to find," Red Sammy said. "Everything is getting terrible. I remember the day you could go off and leave your screen door unlatched. Not no more."

He and the grandmother discussed better times. The old lady said that in her opinion Europe was entirely to blame for the way things were now. She said the way Europe acted you would think we were made of money and Red Sam said it was no use talking about it, she was exactly right. The children ran outside into the white sunlight and looked at the monkey in the lacy chinaberry tree. He was busy catching fleas on himself and biting each one carefully between his teeth as if it were a delicacy.

They drove off again into the hot afternoon. The grandmother took cat naps and woke up every few minutes with her own snoring. Outside of Toombsboro she woke up and recalled an old plantation that she had visited in this neighborhood once when she was a young lady. She said the house had six white columns across the front and that there was an avenue of oaks leading up to it and two little wooden trellis arbors on either side in front where you sat down with your suitor after a stroll in the garden. She recalled exactly which road to turn off to get to it. She knew that Bailey would not be willing to lose any time looking at an old house, but the more she talked about it, the more she wanted to see it once again and find out if the little twin arbors were still standing. "There was a secret panel in this house," she said craftily, not telling the truth but wishing that she were, "and the story went that all the family silver was hidden in it when Sherman[2] came through but it was never found . . ."

"Hey!" John Wesley said. "Let's go see it! We'll find it! We'll poke all the woodwork and find it! Who lives there? Where do you turn off at? Hey Pop, can't we turn off there?"

"We never have seen a house with a secret panel!" June Star shrieked. "Let's go to the house with the secret panel! Hey, Pop, can't we go see the house with the secret panel!"

"It's not far from here, I know," the grandmother said. "It wouldn't take over twenty minutes."

Bailey was looking straight ahead. His jaw was as rigid as a horseshoe. "No," he said.

The children began to yell and scream that they wanted to see the house with the secret panel. John Wesley kicked the back of the front seat and June Star hung over her mother's shoulder and whined desperately into her ear that they never had any fun even on their vacation, and that they could never do what THEY wanted to do. The baby began to scream and John Wesley kicked the back of the seat so hard that his father could feel the blows in his kidney.

"All right!" he shouted, and drew the car to a stop at the side of the road. "Will you all shut up? Will you all just shut up for one second? If you don't shut up, we won't go anywhere."

2 **Sherman:** General William Tecumseh Sherman (1820–1891), northern Civil War general who marched his army from Atlanta, Georgia, to the Atlantic coast, destroying houses and plantations on the way.

"It would be very educational for them," the grandmother murmured.

"All right," Bailey said, "but get this: this is the only time we're going to stop for anything like this. This is the one and only time."

"The dirt road that you have to turn down is about a mile back," the grandmother directed. "I marked it when we passed."

"A dirt road," Bailey groaned.

After they had turned around and were headed toward the dirt road, the grandmother recalled other points about the house, the beautiful glass over the front doorway and the candle-lamp in the hall. John Wesley said that the secret panel was probably in the fireplace.

"You can't go inside this house," Bailey said. "You don't know who lives there."

"While you all talk to the people in front, I'll run around behind and get in a window," John Wesley suggested.

"We'll all stay in the car," his mother said.

They turned onto the dirt road and the car raced roughly along in a swirl of pink dust. The grandmother recalled the times when there were no paved roads and thirty miles was a day's journey. The dirt road was hilly and there were sudden washes in it and sharp curves on dangerous embankments. All at once they would be on a hill, looking down over the blue tops of trees for miles around, then the next minute, they would be in a red depression with the dust-coated trees looking down on them.

"This place had better turn up in a minute," Bailey said, "or I'm going to turn around."

The road looked as if no one had traveled on it in months.

"It's not much farther," the grandmother said and just as she said it, a horrible thought came to her. The thought was so embarrassing that she turned red in the face and her eyes dilated and her feet jumped up, upsetting her valise in the corner. The instant the valise moved, the newspaper top she had over the basket under it rose with a snarl and Pitty Sing, the cat, sprang onto Bailey's shoulder.

The children were thrown to the floor and their mother, clutching the baby, was thrown out the door onto the ground, the old lady was thrown into the front seat. The car turned over once and landed right-side-up in a gulch on the side of the road. Bailey remained in the driver's seat with the cat—gray-striped with a broad white face and an orange nose—clinging to his neck like a caterpillar.

As soon as the children saw they could move their arms and legs, they scrambled out of the car, shouting, "We've had an ACCIDENT!" The grandmother was curled up under the dashboard, hoping she was injured so that Bailey's wrath would not come down on her all at once. The horrible thought she had had before the accident was that the house she had remembered so vividly was not in Georgia but in Tennessee.

Bailey removed the cat from his neck with both hands and flung it out the window against the side of a pine tree. Then he got out of the car and started looking for the children's mother. She was sitting against the side of the red gutted ditch, holding the screaming baby, but she only had a cut down her face and a broken shoulder. "We've had an ACCIDENT!" the children screamed in a frenzy of delight.

"But nobody's killed," June Star said with disappointment as the grandmother limped out of the car, her hat still pinned to her head but the broken front brim standing up at a jaunty angle and the violet spray hanging off the side. They all sat down in the ditch, except the children, to recover from the shock. They were all shaking.

"Maybe a car will come along," said the children's mother hoarsely.

"I believe I have injured an organ," said the grandmother, pressing her side, but no one answered her. Bailey's teeth were clattering. He had on a yellow sport shirt with bright blue parrots designed in it and his face was as yellow as the shirt. The grandmother decided that she would not mention that the house was in Tennessee.

The road was about ten feet above and they could see only the tops of the trees on the other side of it. Behind the ditch they were sitting in there were more woods, tall and dark and deep. In a few minutes they saw a car some distance away on top of a hill, coming slowly as if the occupants were watching them. The grandmother stood up and waved both arms dramatically to attract their attention. The car continued to come on slowly, disappeared around a bend and appeared again, moving even slower, on top of the hill they had gone over. It was a big black battered hearse-like automobile. There were three men in it.

It came to a stop just over them and for some minutes, the driver looked down with a steady expressionless gaze to where they were sitting, and didn't speak. Then he turned his head and muttered something to the other two and they got out. One was a fat boy in black trousers and a red sweat shirt with a silver stallion embossed on the front of it. He moved around on the right side of them and stood staring, his mouth partly open in a kind of loose grin. The other had on khaki pants and a blue striped coat and a gray hat pulled down very low, hiding most of his face. He came around slowly on the left side. Neither spoke.

The driver got out of the car and stood by the side of it, looking down at them. He was an older man than the other two. His hair was just beginning to gray and he wore silver-rimmed spectacles that gave him a scholarly look. He had a long creased face and didn't have on any shirt or undershirt. He had on blue jeans that were too tight for him and was holding a black hat and a gun. The two boys also had guns.

"We've had an ACCIDENT!" the children screamed.

The grandmother had the peculiar feeling that the bespectacled man was someone she knew. His face was as familiar to her as if she had known him all her life but she could not recall who he was. He moved away from the car and began to come down the embankment, placing his feet carefully so that he wouldn't slip. He had on tan and white shoes and no socks, and his ankles were red and thin. "Good afternoon," he said. "I see you all had you a little spill."

"We turned over twice!" said the grandmother.

"Oncet," he corrected. "We seen it happen. Try their car and see will it run, Hiram," he said quietly to the boy with the gray hat.

"What you got that gun for?" John Wesley asked. "Whatcha gonna do with that gun?"

"Lady," the man said to the children's mother, "would you mind calling them children to sit down by you? Children make me nervous. I want all you all to sit down right together there where you're at."

"What are you telling us what to do for?" June Star asked.

Behind them the line of woods gaped like a dark open mouth. "Come here," said their mother.

"Look here now," Bailey began suddenly, "we're in a predicament! We're in . . ."

The grandmother shrieked. She scrambled to her feet and stood staring. "You're The Misfit!" she said. "I recognized you at once."

"Yes'm," the man said, smiling slightly as if he were pleased in spite of himself to be known, "but it would have been better for all of you, lady, if you hadn't of reckernized me."

Bailey turned his head sharply and said something to his mother that shocked even the children. The old lady began to cry and The Misfit reddened.

"Lady," he said, "don't you get upset. Sometimes a man says things he don't mean. I don't reckon he meant to talk to you thataway."

"You wouldn't shoot a lady, would you?" the grandmother said and removed a clean handkerchief from her cuff and began to slap at her eyes with it.

The Misfit pointed the toe of his shoe into the ground and made a little hole and then covered it up again. "I would hate to have to," he said.

"Listen," the grandmother almost screamed, "I know you're a good man. You don't look a bit like you have common blood. I know you must come from nice people!"

"Yes mam," he said, "finest people in the world." When he smiled he showed a row of strong white teeth. "God never made a finer woman than my mother and my daddy's heart was pure gold," he said. The boy with the red sweat shirt had come around behind them and was standing with his gun at his hip. The Misfit squatted down on the ground. "Watch them children, Bobby Lee," he said. "You know they make me nervous." He looked at the six of them huddled together in front of him and he seemed to be embarrassed as if he couldn't think of anything to say. "Ain't a cloud in the sky," he remarked, looking up at it. "Don't see no sun but don't see no cloud neither."

"Yes, it's a beautiful day," said the grandmother. "Listen," she said, "you shouldn't call yourself The Misfit because I know you're a good man at heart. I can just look at you and tell."

"Hush!" Bailey yelled. "Hush! Everybody shut up and let me handle this." He was squatting in the position of a runner about to sprint forward but he didn't move.

"I pre-chate that, lady," The Misfit said and drew a little circle in the ground with the butt of his gun.

"It'll take a half a hour to fix this here car," Hiram called, looking over the raised hood of it.

"Well, first you and Bobby Lee get him and that little boy to step over yonder with you," The Misfit said, pointing to Bailey and John Wesley. "The boys want to ask you something," he said to Bailey. "Would you mind stepping back in them woods there with them?"

"Listen," Bailey began, "we're in a terrible predicament. Nobody realizes what this is," and his voice cracked. His eyes were as blue and intense as the parrots in his shirt and he remained perfectly still.

The grandmother reached up to adjust her hat brim as if she were going to the woods with him but it came off in her hand. She stood staring at it and after a second she let it fall on the ground. Hiram pulled Bailey up by the arm as if he were assisting an old man. John Wesley caught hold of his father's hand and Bobby Lee followed. They went off toward the woods and just as they reached the dark edge, Bailey turned and supporting himself against a gray naked pine trunk, he shouted, "I'll be back in a minute, Mamma, wait on me!"

"Come back this instant!" his mother shrilled but they all disappeared into the woods.

"Bailey Boy!" the grandmother called in a tragic voice but she found she was looking at The Misfit squatting on the ground in front of her. "I just know you're a good man," she said desperately. "You're not a bit common!"

"Nome, I ain't a good man," The Misfit said after a second as if he had considered her statement carefully, "but I ain't the worst in the world neither. My daddy said I was different breed of dog from my brothers and sisters. 'You know,' Daddy said, 'it's some that can live their whole life out without asking about it and it's others has to know why it is, and this boy is one of the latters. He's going to be into everything!' " He put on his black hat and looked up suddenly and then away deep into the woods as if he were embarrassed again. "I'm sorry I don't have on a shirt before you ladies," he said, hunching his shoulders slightly. "We buried our clothes that we had on when we escaped and we're just making do until we can get better. We borrowed these from some folks we met," he explained.

"That's perfectly all right," the grandmother said. "Maybe Bailey has an extra shirt in his suitcase."

"I'll look and see terrectly," The Misfit said.

"Where are they taking him?" the children's mother screamed.

"Daddy was a card himself," The Misfit said. "You couldn't put anything over on him. He never got in trouble with the Authorities though. Just had the knack of handling them."

"You could be honest too if you'd only try," said the grandmother. "Think how wonderful it would be to settle down and live a comfortable life and not have to think about somebody chasing you all the time."

The Misfit kept scratching in the ground with the butt of his gun as if he were thinking about it. "Yes'm, somebody is always after you," he murmured.

The grandmother noticed how thin his shoulder blades were just behind his hat because she was standing up looking down on him. "Do you ever pray?" she asked.

He shook his head. All she saw was the black hat wiggle between his shoulder blades. "Nome," he said.

There was a pistol shot from the woods, followed closely by another. Then silence. The old lady's head jerked around. She could hear the wind move through the tree tops like a long satisfied insuck of breath. "Bailey Boy!" she called.

"I was a gospel singer for a while," The Misfit said. "I been most everything. Been in the arm service, both land and sea, at home and abroad, been twict married, been an undertaker, been with the railroads, plowed Mother Earth, been in a tornado, seen a man burnt alive oncet," and he looked up at the children's mother and the little girl who were sitting close together, their faces white and their eyes glassy; "I even seen a woman flogged," he said.

"Pray, pray," the grandmother began, "pray, pray . . ."

"I never was a bad boy that I remember of," The Misfit said in an almost dreamy voice, "but somewheres along the line I done something wrong and got sent to the penitentiary. I was buried alive," and he looked up and held her attention to him by a steady stare.

"That's when you should have started to pray," she said. "What did you do to get sent to the penitentiary that first time?"

"Turn to the right, it was a wall," The Misfit said, looking up again at the cloud-less sky. "Turn to the left, it was a wall. Look up it was a ceiling, look down it was a floor. I forgot what I done, lady. I set there and set there, trying to remember what it was I done and I ain't recalled it to this day. Oncet in a while, I would think it was coming to me, but it never come."

"Maybe they put you in by mistake," the old lady said vaguely.

"Nome," he said. "It wasn't no mistake. They had the papers on me."

"You must have stolen something," she said.

The Misfit sneered slightly. "Nobody had nothing I wanted," he said. "It was a head-doctor at the penitentiary said what I had done was kill my daddy but I know that for a lie. My daddy died in nineteen ought nineteen of the epidemic flu and I never had a thing to do with it. He was buried in the Mount Hopewell Baptist church-yard and you can go there and see for yourself."

"If you would pray," the old lady said, "Jesus would help you."

"That's right," The Misfit said.

"Well then, why don't you pray?" she asked trembling with delight suddenly.

"I don't want no hep," he said. "I'm doing all right by myself."

Bobby Lee and Hiram came ambling back from the woods. Bobby Lee was drag-ging a yellow shirt with bright blue parrots in it.

"Throw me that shirt, Bobby Lee," The Misfit said. The shirt came flying at him and landed on his shoulder and he put it on. The grandmother couldn't name what the shirt reminded her of. "No, lady," The Misfit said while he was buttoning it up. "I found out the crime don't matter. You can do one thing or you can do another, kill a man or take a tire off his car, because sooner or later you're going to forget what it was you done and just be punished for it."

The children's mother had begun to make heaving noises as if she couldn't get her breath. "Lady," he asked, "would you and that little girl like to step off yonder with Bobby Lee and Hiram and join your husband?"

"Yes, thank you," the mother said faintly. Her left arm dangled helplessly and she was holding the baby, who had gone to sleep, in the other. "Hep that lady up, Hiram," The Misfit said as she struggled to climb out of the ditch, "and Bobby Lee, you hold onto that little girl's hand."

"I don't want to hold hands with him," June Star said. "He reminds me of a pig."

The fat boy blushed and laughed and caught her by the arm and pulled her off into the woods after Hiram and her mother.

Alone with The Misfit, the grandmother found that she had lost her voice. There was not a cloud in the sky nor any sun. There was nothing around her but woods. She wanted to tell him that he must pray. She opened and closed her mouth several times before anything came out. Finally she found herself saying, "Jesus, Jesus," meaning Jesus will help you, but the way she was saying it, it sounded as if she might be cursing.

"Yes'm," The Misfit said as if he agreed. "Jesus thown everything off balance. It was the same case with Him as with me except He hadn't committed any crime and they could prove I had committed one because they had the papers on me. Of course," he said, "they never shown me any papers. That's why I sign myself now. I said long ago, you get you a signature and sign everything you do and keep a copy of it. Then you'll know what you done and you can hold up the crime to the punishment and see do they match and in the end you'll have something to prove you ain't been treated right. I call myself The Misfit," he said, "because I can't make what all I done wrong fit what all I gone through in punishment."

There was a piercing scream from the woods, followed closely by a pistol report. "Does it seem right to you, lady, that one is punished a heap and another ain't punished at all?"

"Jesus!" the old lady cried. "You've got good blood! I know you wouldn't shoot a lady! I know you come from nice people! Pray! Jesus, you ought not to shoot a lady. I'll give you all the money I've got!"

"Lady," The Misfit said, looking beyond her far into the woods, "there never was a body that give the undertaker a tip."

There were two more pistol reports and the grandmother raised her head like a parched old turkey hen crying for water and called, "Bailey Boy, Bailey Boy!" as if her heart would break.

"Jesus was the only One that ever raised the dead," The Misfit continued, "and He shouldn't have done it. He thrown everything off balance. If He did what He said, then it's nothing for you to do but thow away everything and follow Him, and if He didn't, then it's nothing for you to do but enjoy the few minutes you got left the best way you can—by killing somebody or burning down his house or doing some other meanness to him. No pleasure but meanness," he said and his voice had become almost a snarl.

"Maybe He didn't raise the dead," the old lady mumbled, not knowing what she was saying and feeling so dizzy that she sank down in the ditch with her legs twisted under her.

"I wasn't there so I can't say He didn't," The Misfit said. "I wisht I had of been there," he said, hitting the ground with his fist. "It ain't right I wasn't there because if I had of been there I would of known. Listen lady," he said in a high voice, "if I had of been there I would of known and I wouldn't be like I am now." His voice seemed about to crack and the grandmother's head cleared for an instant. She saw the man's face twisted close to her own as if he were going to cry and she murmured, "Why you're one of my babies. You're one of my own children!" She reached out and touched him on the shoulder. The Misfit sprang back as if a snake had bitten him and shot her three times through the chest. Then he put his gun down on the ground and took off his glasses and began to clean them.

Hiram and Bobby Lee returned from the woods and stood over the ditch, looking down at the grandmother who half sat and half lay in a puddle of blood with her legs crossed under her like a child's and her face smiling up at the cloudless sky.

Without his glasses, The Misfit's eyes were red-rimmed and pale and defenseless-looking. "Take her off and throw her where you thrown the others," he said, picking up the cat that was rubbing itself against his leg.

"She was a talker, wasn't she?" Bobby Lee said, sliding down the ditch with a yodel.

"She would of been a good woman," The Misfit said, "if it had been somebody there to shoot her every minute of her life."

"Some fun!" Bobby Lee said.

"Shut up, Bobby Lee," The Misfit said. "It's no real pleasure in life."

# Frank O'Connor

## (1903–1966)

Frank O'Connor was born Michael O'Donovan in 1903 in Cork, Ireland. He was forced to leave school at the age of fourteen to help support his family and served in the Irish Republican Army (IRA) during the Irish civil war. The defeat of the IRA and the division of Ireland greatly disappointed O'Connor. He published his first collection of stories, *Guests of the Nation*, in 1931. In the 1930s, O'Connor became the director of the Abbey Theatre in Dublin. During this time, he wrote several plays and published works such as *Bones of Contention* (1936), *Three Old Brothers* (1936), *The Saint and Mary Kate* (1936), and *The Big Fellow* (1937), a biography of Michael Collins, the leader of the Irish rebellion against the British. He resigned from the Abbey board after William Butler Yeats's death in 1939. Several collections of O'Connor's work were published posthumously, including *Collected Stories* (1981), *The Collar: Stories of Irish Priests* (1993), and *A Frank O'Connor Reader* (1994). O'Connor's work speaks against repression and inhumanity in its depiction of the political strife in Irish history.

## Guests of the Nation                                          1931

I

At dusk the big Englishman, Belcher, would shift his long legs out of the ashes and say "Well, chums, what about it?" and Noble or me would say "All right, chum" (for we had picked up some of their curious expressions), and the little Englishman, Hawkins, would light the lamp and bring out the cards. Sometimes Jeremiah Donovan would come up and supervise the game and get excited over Hawkins's cards, which he always played badly, and shout at him as if he was one of our own "Ah, you divil, you, why didn't you play the tray?"

But ordinarily Jeremiah was a sober and contented poor devil like the big English-man, Belcher, and was looked up to only because he was a fair hand at documents, though he was slow enough even with them. He wore a small cloth hat and big gaiters over his long pants, and you seldom saw him with his hands out of his pockets. He reddened when you talked to him, tilting from toe to heel and back, and looking down all the time at his big farmer's feet. Noble and me used to make fun of his broad accent because we were from the town.

I couldn't at the time see the point of me and Noble guarding Belcher and Hawkins[1] at all, for it was my belief that you could have planted that pair down anywhere from this to Claregalway and they'd have taken root there like a native weed. I never in my short experience seen two men to take to the country as they did.

They were handed on to us by the Second Battalion when the search for them became too hot, and Noble and myself, being young, took over with a natural feeling of responsibility, but Hawkins made us look like fools when he showed that he knew the country better than we did.

"You're the bloke they calls Bonaparte," he says to me. "Mary Brigid O'Connell told me to ask you what you done with the pair of her brother's socks you borrowed."

For it seemed, as they explained it, that the Second used to have little evenings, and some of the girls of the neighborhood turned in, and, seeing they were such decent chaps, our fellows couldn't leave the two Englishmen out of them. Hawkins learned to dance "The Walls of Limerick," "The Siege of Ennis," and "The Waves of Tory"[2] as well as any of them, though, naturally, he couldn't return the compliment, because our lads at that time did not dance foreign dances on principle.

So whatever privileges Belcher and Hawkins had with the Second they just naturally took with us, and after the first day or two we gave up all pretense of keeping a close eye on them. Not that they could have got far, for they had accents you could cut with a knife and wore khaki tunics and overcoats with civilian pants and boots. But it's my belief that they never had any idea of escaping and were quite content to be where they were.

It was a treat to see how Belcher got off with the old woman of the house where we were staying. She was a great warrant to scold, and cranky even with us, but before ever she had a chance of giving our guests, as I may call them, a lick of her tongue, Belcher had made her his friend for life. She was breaking sticks, and Belcher, who hadn't been more than ten minutes in the house, jumped up from his seat and went over to her.

"Allow me, madam," he says, smiling his queer little smile, "please allow me"; and he takes the bloody hatchet. She was struck too paralytic to speak, and after that, Belcher would be at her heels, carrying a bucket, a basket, or a load of turf, as the case might be. As Noble said, he got into looking before she leapt, and hot water, or any little thing she wanted, Belcher would have it ready for her. For such a huge man

---

1 **Belcher and Hawkins:** These English soldiers were captured during Ireland's battle for independence in 1922.

2 **"The Walls of Limerick," "The Siege of Ennis," and "The Waves of Tory":** Traditional Irish dances.

(and though I am five foot ten myself I had to look up at him) he had an uncommon shortness—or should I say lack?—of speech. It took us some time to get used to him, walking in and out, like a ghost, without a word. Especially because Hawkins talked enough for a platoon, it was strange to hear big Belcher with his toes in the ashes come out with a solitary "Excuse me, chum" or "That's right, chum." His one and only passion was cards, and I will say for him that he was a good card-player. He could have fleeced myself and Noble, but whatever we lost to him Hawkins lost to us, and Hawkins played with the money Belcher gave him.

Hawkins lost to us because he had too much old gab, and we probably lost to Belcher for the same reason. Hawkins and Noble would spit at one another about religion into the early hours of the morning, and Hawkins worried the soul out of Noble, whose brother was a priest, with a string of questions that would puzzle a cardinal. To make it worse even in treating of holy subjects, Hawkins had a deplorable tongue. I never in all my career met a man who could mix such a variety of cursing and bad language into an argument. He was a terrible man, and a fright to argue. He never did a stroke of work, and when he had no one else to talk to, he got stuck in the old woman.

He met his match in her, for one day when he tried to get her to complain profanely of the drought, she gave him a great come-down by blaming it entirely on Jupiter Pluvius (a deity neither Hawkins nor I have ever heard of, though Noble said that among the pagans it was believed that he had something to do with the rain). Another day he was swearing at the capitalists for starting the German war[3] when the old lady laid down her iron, puckered up her little crab's mouth, and said: "Mr. Hawkins, you can say what you like about the war, and think you'll deceive me because I'm only a simple poor countrywoman, but I know what started the war. It was the Italian Count that stole the heathen divinity out of the temple in Japan. Believe me, Mr. Hawkins, nothing but sorrow and want can follow the people that disturb the hidden powers."

A queer old girl, all right.

## II

We had our tea one evening, and Hawkins lit the lamp and we all sat into cards. Jeremiah Donovan came in too, and sat down and watched us for a while, and it suddenly struck me that he had no great love for the two Englishmen. It came as a great surprise to me, because I hadn't noticed anything about him before.

Late in the evening a really terrible argument blew up between Hawkins and Noble, about capitalists and priests and love of your country.

"The capitalists," says Hawkins with an angry gulp, "pays the priests to tell you about the next world so as you won't notice what the bastards are up to in this."

"Nonsense, man!" says Noble, losing his temper. "Before ever a capitalist was thought of, people believed in the next world."

---

3 **German war:** World War I.

Hawkins stood up as though he was preaching a sermon.

"Oh, they did, did they?" he says with a sneer. "They believed all the things you believe, isn't that what you mean? And you believe that God created Adam, and Adam created Shem, and Shem created Jehoshophat. You believe all that silly old fairytale about Eve and Eden and the apple. Well, listen to me, chum. If you're entitled to hold a silly belief like that, I'm entitled to hold my silly belief—which is that the first thing your God created was a bleeding capitalist, with morality and Rolls-Royce complete. Am I right, chum?" he says to Belcher.

"You're right, chum," says Belcher with his amused smile, and got up from the table to stretch his long legs into the fire and stroke his moustache. So, seeing that Jeremiah Donovan was going, and that there was no knowing when the argument about religion would be over, I went out with him. We strolled down to the village together, and then he stopped and started blushing and mumbling and saying I ought to be behind, keeping guard on the prisoners. I didn't like the tone he took with me, and anyway I was bored with life in the cottage, so I replied by asking him what the hell we wanted guarding them at all for. I told him I'd talked it over with Noble, and that we'd both rather be out with a fighting column.

"What use are those fellows to us?" says I.

He looked at me in surprise and said: "I thought you knew we were keeping them as hostages."

"Hostages?" I said.

"The enemy have prisoners belonging to us," he says, "and now they're talking of shooting them. If they shoot our prisoners, we'll shoot theirs."

"Shoot them?" I said.

"What else did you think we were keeping them for?" he says.

"Wasn't it very unforeseen of you not to warn Noble and myself of that in the beginning?" I said.

"How was it?" says he. "You might have known it."

"We couldn't know it, Jeremiah Donovan," says I. "How could we when they were on our hands so long?"

"The enemy have our prisoners as long and longer," says he.

"That's not the same thing at all," says I.

"What difference is there?" says he.

I couldn't tell him, because I knew he wouldn't understand. If it was only an old dog that was going to the vet's, you'd try and not get too fond of him, but Jeremiah Donovan wasn't a man that would ever be in danger of that.

"And when is this thing going to be decided?" says I.

"We might hear tonight," he says. "Or tomorrow or the next day at latest. So if it's only hanging round here that's a trouble to you, you'll be free soon enough."

It wasn't the hanging round that was a trouble to me at all by this time. I had worse things to worry about. When I got back to the cottage the argument was still on. Hawkins was holding forth in his best style, maintaining that there was no next world, and Noble was maintaining that there was; but I could see that Hawkins had had the best of it.

"Do you know what, chum?" he was saying with a saucy smile. "I think you're just as big a bleeding unbeliever as I am. You say you believe in the next world, and you know just as much about the next world as I do, which is sweet damn-all. What's heaven? You don't know. Where's heaven? You don't know. You know sweet damn-all! I ask you again, do they wear wings?"

"Very well, then," says Noble, "they do. Is that enough for you? They do wear wings."

"Where do they get them, then? Who makes them? Have they a factory for wings? Have they a sort of store where you hands in your chit and takes your bleeding wings?"

"You're an impossible man to argue with," says Noble. "Now, listen to me—" And they were off again.

It was long after midnight when we locked up and went to bed. As I blew out the candle I told Noble what Jeremiah Donovan was after telling me. Noble took it very quietly. When we'd been in bed about an hour he asked me did I think we ought to tell the Englishmen. I didn't think we should, because it was more than likely that the English wouldn't shoot our men, and even if they did, the brigade officers, who were always up and down with the Second Battalion and knew the Englishmen well, wouldn't be likely to want them plugged. "I think so too," says Noble. "It would be great cruelty to put the wind up them now."

"It was very unforeseen of Jeremiah Donovan anyhow," says I.

It was next morning that we found it so hard to face Belcher and Hawkins. We went about the house all day scarcely saying a word. Belcher didn't seem to notice; he was stretched into the ashes as usual, with his usual look of waiting in quietness for something unforeseen to happen, but Hawkins noticed and put it down to Noble's being beaten in the argument of the night before.

"Why can't you take a discussion in the proper spirit?" he says severely. "You and your Adam and Eve! I'm a Communist, that's what I am. Communist or anarchist, it all comes to much the same thing." And for hours he went round the house, muttering when the fit took him. "Adam and Eve! Adam and Eve! Nothing better to do with their time than picking bleeding apples!"

## III

I don't know how we got through that day, but I was very glad when it was over, the tea things were cleared away, and Belcher said in his peaceable way: "Well, chums, what about it?" We sat round the table and Hawkins took out the cards, and just then I heard Jeremiah Donovan's footstep on the path and a dark presentiment crossed my mind. I rose from the table and caught him before he reached the door.

"What do you want?" I asked.

"I want those two soldier friends of yours," he says, getting red.

"Is that the way, Jeremiah Donovan?" I asked.

"That's the way. There were four of our lads shot this morning, one of them a boy of sixteen."

"That's bad," I said.

At that moment, Noble followed me out, and the three of us walked down the path together, talking in whispers. Feeney, the local intelligence officer, was standing by the gate.

"What are you going to do about it?" I asked Jeremiah Donovan.

"I want you and Noble to get them out; tell them they're being shifted again; that'll be the quietest way."

"Leave me out of that," says Noble under his breath.

Jeremiah Donovan looks at him hard.

"All right," he says. "You and Feeney get a few tools from the shed and dig a hole by the far end of the bog. Bonaparte and myself will be after you. Don't let anyone see you with the tools. I wouldn't like it to go beyond ourselves."

We saw Feeney and Noble go round to the shed and went in ourselves. I left Jeremiah Donovan to do the explanations. He told them that he had orders to send them back to the Second Battalion. Hawkins let out a mouthful of curses, and you could see that though Belcher didn't say anything, he was a bit upset too. The old woman was for having them stay in spite of us, and she didn't stop advising them until Jeremiah Donovan lost his temper and turned on her. He had a nasty temper, I noticed. It was pitch-dark in the cottage by this time, but no one thought of lighting the lamp, and in the darkness the two Englishmen fetched their topcoats and said good-bye to the old woman.

"Just as a man makes a home of a bleeding place, some bastard at headquarters thinks you're too cushy and shunts you off," says Hawkins, shaking her hand.

"A thousand thanks, madam," says Belcher. "A thousand thanks for everything"— as though he'd made it up.

We went round to the back of the house and down towards the bog. It was only then that Jeremiah Donovan told them. He was shaking with excitement.

"There were four of our fellows shot in Cork this morning and now you're to be shot as a reprisal."

"What are you talking about?" snaps Hawkins. "It's bad enough being mucked about as we are without having to put up with your funny jokes."

"It isn't a joke," says Donovan. "I'm sorry, Hawkins, but it's true," and begins on the usual rigmarole about duty and how unpleasant it is.

I never noticed that people who talk a lot about duty find it much of a trouble to them.

"Oh, cut it out!" says Hawkins.

"Ask Bonaparte," says Donovan, seeing that Hawkins isn't taking him seriously. "Isn't it true, Bonaparte?"

"It is," I say, and Hawkins stops.

"Ah, for Christ's sake, chum!"

"I mean it, chum," I say.

"You don't sound as if you mean it."

"If he doesn't mean it, I do," says Donovan, working himself up.

"What have you against me, Jeremiah Donovan?"

"I never said I had anything against you. But why did your people take out four of our prisoners and shoot them in cold blood?"

He took Hawkins by the arm and dragged him on, but it was impossible to make him understand that we were in earnest. I had the Smith and Wesson in my pocket and I kept fingering it and wondering what I'd do if they put up a fight for it or ran, and wishing to God they'd do one or the other. I knew if they did run for it, that I'd never fire on them. Hawkins wanted to know was Noble in it, and when we said yes, he asked us why Noble wanted to plug him. Why did any of us want to plug him? What had he done to us? Weren't we all chums? Didn't we understand him and didn't he understand us? Did we imagine for an instant that he'd shoot us for all the so-and-so officers in the so-and-so British Army?

By this time we'd reached the bog, and I was so sick I couldn't even answer him. We walked along the edge of it in the darkness, and every now and then Hawkins would call a halt and begin all over again, as if he was wound up, about our being chums, and I knew that nothing but the sight of the grave would convince him that we had to do it. And all the time I was hoping that something would happen; that they'd run for it or that Noble would take over the responsibility from me. I had the feeling that it was worse on Noble than on me.

## IV

At last we saw the lantern in the distance and made towards it. Noble was carrying it, and Feeney was standing somewhere in the darkness behind him, and the picture of them so still and silent in the bogland brought it home to me that we were in earnest, and banished the last bit of hope I had.

Belcher, on recognizing Noble, said: "Hallo, chum," in his quiet way, but Hawkins flew at him at once, and the argument began all over again, only this time Noble had nothing to say for himself and stood with his head down, holding the lantern between his legs.

It was Jeremiah Donovan who did the answering. For the twentieth time, as though it was haunting his mind, Hawkins asked if anybody thought he'd shoot Noble.

"Yes, you would," says Jeremiah Donovan.

"No, I wouldn't, damn you!"

"You would, because you'd know you'd be shot for not doing it."

"I wouldn't, not if I was to be shot twenty times over. I wouldn't shoot a pal. And Belcher wouldn't—isn't that right, Belcher?"

"That's right, chum," Belcher said, but more by way of answering the question than of joining in the argument. Belcher sounded as though whatever unforeseen thing he'd always been waiting for had come at last.

"Anyway, who says Noble would be shot if I wasn't? What do you think I'd do if I was in his place, out in the middle of a blasted bog?"

"What would you do?" asks Donovan.

"I'd go with him wherever he was going, of course. Share my last bob with him and stick by him through thick and thin. No one can ever say of me that I let down a pal."

"We had enough of this," says Jeremiah Donovan, cocking his revolver. "Is there any message you want to send?"

"No, there isn't."

"Do you want to say your prayers?"

Hawkins came out with a cold-blooded remark that even shocked me and turned on Noble again.

"Listen to me, Noble," he says. "You and me are chums. You can't come over to my side, so I'll come over to your side. That show you I mean what I say? Give me a rifle and I'll go along with you and the other lads."

Nobody answered him. We knew that was no way out.

"Hear what I'm saying?" he says. "I'm through with it. I'm a deserter or anything else you like. I don't believe in your stuff, but it's no worse than mine. That satisfy you?"

Noble raised his head, but Donovan began to speak and he lowered it again without replying.

"For the last time, have you any messages to send?" says Donovan in a cool, excited sort of voice.

"Shut up, Donovan! You don't understand me, but these lads do. They're not the sort to make a pal and kill a pal. They're not the tools of any capitalist."

I alone of the crowd saw Donovan raise his Webley to the back of Hawkins's neck, and as he did so I shut my eyes and tried to pray. Hawkins had begun to say something else when Donovan fired, and as I opened my eyes at the bang, I saw Hawkins stagger at the knees and lie out flat at Noble's feet, slowly and as quiet as a kid falling asleep, with the lantern-light on his lean legs and bright farmer's boots. We all stood very still, watching him settle out in the last agony.

Then Belcher took out a handkerchief and began to tie it about his own eyes (in our excitement we'd forgotten to do the same for Hawkins), and, seeing it wasn't big enough, turned and asked for the loan of mine. I gave it to him and he knotted the two together and pointed with his foot at Hawkins.

"He's not quite dead," he says. "Better give him another."

Sure enough, Hawkins's left knee is beginning to rise. I bend down and put my gun to his head; then, recollecting myself, I get up again. Belcher understands what's in my mind.

"Give him his first," he says. "I don't mind. Poor bastard, we don't know what's happening to him now."

I knelt and fired. By this time I didn't seem to know what I was doing. Belcher, who was fumbling a bit awkwardly with the handkerchiefs, came out with a laugh as he heard the shot. It was the first time I heard him laugh and it sent a shudder down my back; it sounded so unnatural.

"Poor bugger!" he said quietly. "And last night he was so curious about it all. It's very queer, chums, I always think. Now he knows as much about it as they'll ever let him know, and last night he was all in the dark."

Donovan helped him to tie the handkerchiefs about his eyes. "Thanks, chum," he said. Donovan asked if there were any messages he wanted sent.

"No, chum," he says, "Not for me. If any of you would like to write to Hawkins's mother, you'll find a letter from her in his pocket. He and his mother were great chums. But my missus left me eight years ago. Went away with another fellow and took the kid with her. I like the feeling of a home, as you may have noticed, but I couldn't start again after that."

It was an extraordinary thing, but in those few minutes Belcher said more than in all the weeks before. It was just as if the sound of the shot had started a flood of talk in him and he could go on the whole night like that, quite happily, talking about himself. We stood round like fools now that he couldn't see us any longer. Donovan looked at Noble, and Noble shook his head. Then Donovan raised his Webley, and at that moment Belcher gives his queer laugh again. He may have thought we were talking about him, or perhaps he noticed the same thing I'd noticed and couldn't understand it.

"Excuse me, chums," he says. "I feel I'm talking the hell of a lot, and so silly, about my being so handy about a house and things like that. But this thing came on me suddenly. You'll forgive me, I'm sure."

"You don't want to say a prayer?" asks Donovan.

"No, chum," he says. "I don't think it would help. I'm ready, and you boys want to get it over."

"You understand that we're only doing our duty?" says Donovan.

Belcher's head was raised like a blind man's, so that you could only see his chin and the tip of his nose in the lantern-light.

"I never could make out what duty was myself," he said. "I think you're all good lads, if that's what you mean. I'm not complaining."

Noble, just as if he couldn't bear any more of it, raised his fist at Donovan, and in a flash Donovan raised his gun and fired. The big man went over like a sack of meal, and this time there was no need of a second shot.

I don't remember much about the burying, but that it was worse than all the rest because we had to carry them to the grave. It was all mad lonely with nothing but a patch of lantern-light between ourselves and the dark, and birds hooting and screeching all round, disturbed by the guns. Noble went through Hawkins's belongings to find the letter from his mother, and then joined his hands together. He did the same with Belcher. Then, when we'd filled the grave, we separated from Jeremiah Donovan and Feeney and took our tools back to the shed. All the way we didn't speak a word. The kitchen was dark and cold as we'd left it, and the old woman was sitting over the hearth, saying her beads. We walked past her into the room, and Noble struck a match to light the lamp. She rose quietly and came to the doorway with all her cantankerousness gone.

"What did ye do with them?" she asked in a whisper, and Noble started so that the match went out in his hand.

"What's that?" he asked without turning around.

"I heard ye," she said.

"What did you hear?" asked Noble.

"I heard ye. Do ye think I didn't hear ye, putting the spade back in the houseen?"
Noble struck another match and this time the lamp lit for him.

"Was that what ye did to them?" she asked.

Then, by God, in the very doorway, she fell on her knees and began praying, and after looking at her for a minute or two Noble did the same by the fireplace. I pushed my way out past her and left them at it. I stood at the door, watching the stars and listening to the shrieking of the birds dying out over the bogs. It is so strange what you feel at times like that that you can't describe it. Noble says he saw everything ten times the size, as though there were nothing in the whole world but that little patch of bog with the two Englishmen stiffening into it, but with me it was as if the patch of bog where the Englishmen were was a million miles away, and even Noble and the old woman, mumbling behind me, and the birds and the bloody stars were all far away, and I was somehow very small and very lost and lonely like a child astray in the snow. And anything that happened to me afterwards, I never felt the same about again.

# Tillie Olsen

## (c. 1912– )

Born in Nebraska in 1912, Tillie Olsen was the daughter of politically active parents. Both her mother and father were socialists, and Olsen greatly admired Eugene Debs, a family friend. She was unable to regularly attend school for many years because she worked to support her family. Nevertheless, Olsen read as often as possible, receiving the opportunity most often when she was ill. Olsen read "old revolutionary pamphlets" and journals such as the *Liberator*, the *Comrade*, and *Modern Quarterly*. She also read the Haldeman-Julius *Little Blue Books*, which introduced her to author Thomas Hardy, a lifelong favorite. In 1931, Olsen joined the Young Communist League and in 1932 moved to Faribault, Minnesota, for health reasons. She took the opportunity to write, but she became pregnant and gave birth to a daughter, Karla. In the following years, Olsen was often forced to choose between supporting her family and writing. Her first short story, "The Iron Throat," was published in the *Partisan Review* in 1934.

In 1936, Olsen moved to San Francisco, and in 1944 she married Jack Olsen. From 1936 to 1959, she worked at a variety of jobs—waitress, shaker in a laundry, transcriber in a dairy equipment company, capper of mayonnaise jars, secretary, and "Kelly Girl." Olsen continued to write during this time, but she was often frustrated. In 1953, after her youngest child entered school, Olsen was able to enroll in a creative writing course at San Francisco State University. She won a Stanford University Creative Writing Fellowship in 1955 and a Ford Foundation grant in 1959. This grant allowed her to finish and publish "Tell Me a Riddle," which won the O. Henry Award for Best Short Story of the Year (1961). In 1974, she published *Yonnondio*, which she had begun in 1932. She has also worked to restore out-of-print women's writing, including Rebecca Harding Davis's *Life in the Iron Mills,* Charlotte Perkins Gilman's *The Yellow Wallpaper,* and Moa Martinson's *Women and Apple Trees.* Olsen sought to bring depictions of the underrepresented working class to the literary world. She uses the nonstandard English of immigrant communities to explore the difficulties of wage labor.

## *I Stand Here Ironing* 1961

I stand here ironing, and what you asked me moves tormented back and forth with the iron.

"I wish you would manage the time to come in and talk with me about your daughter. I'm sure you can help me understand her. She's a youngster who needs help and whom I'm deeply interested in helping."

"Who needs help." . . . Even if I came, what good would it do? You think because I am her mother I have a key, or that in some way you could use me as a key? She has lived for nineteen years. There is all that life that has happened outside of me, beyond me.

And when is there time to remember, to sift, to weigh, to estimate, to total? I will start and there will be an interruption and I will have to gather it all together again. Or I will become engulfed with all I did or did not do, with what should have been and what cannot be helped.

She was a beautiful baby. The first and only one of our five that was beautiful at birth. You do not guess how new and uneasy her tenancy in her now-loveliness. You did not know her all those years she was thought homely, or see her poring over her baby pictures, making me tell her over and over how beautiful she had been—and would be, I would tell her—and was now, to the seeing eye. But the seeing eyes were few or nonexistent. Including mine.

I nursed her. They feel that's important nowadays. I nursed all the children, but with her, with all the fierce rigidity of first motherhood, I did like the books then said. Though her cries battered me to trembling and my breasts ached with swollenness, I waited till the clock decreed.

Why do I put that first? I do not even know if it matters, or if it explains anything.

She was a beautiful baby. She blew shining bubbles of sound. She loved motion, loved light, loved color and music and textures. She would lie on the floor in her blue overalls patting the surface so hard in ecstasy her hands and feet would blur. She was a miracle to me, but when she was eight months old I had to leave her daytimes with the woman downstairs to whom she was no miracle at all, for I worked or looked for work and for Emily's father, who "could no longer endure" (he wrote in his good-bye note) "sharing want with us."

I was nineteen. It was the pre-relief, pre-WPA world of the depression. I would start running as soon as I got off the streetcar, running up the stairs, the place smelling sour, and awake or asleep to startle awake, when she saw me she would break into a clogged weeping that could not be comforted, a weeping I can hear yet.

After a while I found a job hashing at night so I could be with her days, and it was better. But it came to where I had to bring her to his family and leave her.

It took a long time to raise the money for her fare back. Then she got chicken pox and I had to wait longer. When she finally came, I hardly knew her, walking quick and nervous like her father, looking like her father, thin, and dressed in a shoddy red that yellowed her skin and glared at the pockmarks. All the baby loveliness gone.

She was two. Old enough for nursery school they said, and I did not know then what I know now—the fatigue of the long day, and the lacerations of group life in the kinds of nurseries that are only parking places for children.

Except that it would have made no difference if I had known. It was the only place there was. It was the only way we could be together, the only way I could hold a job.

And even without knowing, I knew. I knew the teacher that was evil because all these years it has curdled into my memory, the little boy hunched in the corner, her rasp, "why aren't you outside, because Alvin hits you? that's no reason, go out, scaredy." I knew Emily hated it even if she did not clutch and implore "don't go Mommy" like the other children, mornings.

She always had a reason why we should stay home. Momma, you look sick. Momma, I feel sick. Momma, the teachers aren't here today, they're sick. Momma, we can't go, there was a fire there last night. Momma, it's a holiday today, no school, they told me.

But never a direct protest, never rebellion. I think of our others in their three-, four-year-oldness—the explosions, tempers, the denunciations, the demands—and I feel suddenly ill. I put the iron down. What in me demanded that goodness in her? And what was the cost, the cost to her of such goodness?

The old man living in the back once said in his gentle way: "You should smile at Emily more when you look at her." What *was* in my face when I looked at her? I loved her. There were all the acts of love.

It was only with the others I remembered what he said, and it was the face of joy, and not of care or tightness or worry I turned to them—too late for Emily. She does not smile easily, let alone almost always as her brothers and sisters do. Her face is closed and sombre, but when she wants, how fluid. You must have seen it in her pantomimes, you spoke of her rare gift for comedy on the stage that rouses laughter out of the audience so dear they applaud and applaud and do not want to let her go.

Where does it come from, that comedy? There was none of it in her when she came back to me that second time, after I had to send her away again. She had a new daddy now to learn to love, and I think perhaps it was a better time.

Except when we left her alone nights, telling ourselves she was old enough.

"Can't you go some other time, Mommy, like tomorrow?" she would ask. "Will it be just a little while you'll be gone? Do you promise?"

The time we came back, the front door open, the clock on the floor in the hall. She rigid awake. "It wasn't just a little while. I didn't cry. Three times I called you, just three times, and then I ran downstairs to open the door so you could come faster. The clock talked loud. I threw it away, it scared me what it talked."

She said the clock talked loud again that night I went to the hospital to have Susan. She was delirious with the fever that comes before red measles, but she was fully conscious all the week I was gone and the week after we were home when she could not come near the new baby or me.

She did not get well. She stayed skeleton thin, not wanting to eat, and night after night she had nightmares. She would call for me, and I would rouse from exhaustion to sleepily call back: "You're all right, darling, go to sleep, it's just a dream," and if she still called, in a sterner voice, "now to go sleep, Emily, there's nothing to hurt you." Twice, only twice, when I had to get up for Susan anyhow, I went in to sit with her.

Now when it is too late (as if she would let me hold and comfort her like I do the others) I get up and go to her at once at her moan or restless stirring. "Are you awake, Emily? Can I get you something?" And the answer is always the same: "No, I'm all right, go back to sleep, Mother."

They persuaded me at the clinic to send her away to a convalescent home in the country where "she can have the kind of food and care you can't manage for her, and you'll be free to concentrate on the new baby." They still send children to that place. I see pictures on the society page of sleek young women planning affairs to raise money for it, or dancing at the affairs, or decorating Easter eggs or filling Christmas stockings for the children.

They never have a picture of the children so I do not know if the girls still wear those gigantic red bows and the ravaged looks on the every other Sunday when parents can come to visit "unless otherwise notified"—as we were notified the first six weeks.

Oh it is a handsome place, green lawns and tall trees and fluted flower beds. High up on the balconies of each cottage the children stand, the girls in their red bows and white dresses, the boys in white suits and giant red ties. The parents stand below shrieking up to be heard and the children shriek down to be heard, and between them the invisible wall "Not To Be Contaminated by Parental Germs or Physical Affection."

There was a tiny girl who always stood hand in hand with Emily. Her parents never came. One visit she was gone. "They moved her to Rose Cottage," Emily shouted in explanation. "They don't like you to love anybody here."

She wrote once a week, the labored writing of a seven-year-old. "I am fine. How is the baby. If I write my letter nicely I will have a star. Love." There never was a star. We wrote every other day, letters she could never hold or keep but only hear read— once. "We simply do not have room for children to keep any personal possessions," they patiently explained when we pieced one Sunday's shrieking together to plead how much it would mean to Emily, who loved so to keep things, to be allowed to keep her letters and cards.

Each visit she looked frailer. "She isn't eating," they told us.

(They had runny eggs for breakfast or mush with lumps, Emily said later, I'd hold it in my mouth and not swallow. Nothing ever tasted good, just when they had chicken.)

It took us eight months to get her released home, and only the fact that she gained back so little of her seven lost pounds convinced the social worker.

I used to try to hold and love her after she came back, but her body would stay stiff, and after a while she'd push away. She ate little. Food sickened her, and I think much of life too. Oh she had physical lightness and brightness, twinkling by on skates, bouncing like a ball up and down up and down over the jump rope, skimming over the hill; but these were momentary.

She fretted about her appearance, thin and dark and foreign-looking at a time when every little girl was supposed to look or thought she should look a chubby blonde replica of Shirley Temple. The doorbell sometimes rang for her, but no one seemed to come and play in the house or be a best friend. Maybe because we moved so much.

There was a boy she loved painfully through two school semesters. Months later she told me how she had taken pennies from my purse to buy him candy. "Licorice was his favorite and I brought him some every day, but he still liked Jennifer better'n me. Why, Mommy?" The kind of question for which there is no answer.

School was a worry to her. She was not glib or quick in a world where glibness and quickness were easily confused with ability to learn. To her overworked and exasperated teachers she was an overconscientious "slow learner" who kept trying to catch up and was absent entirely too often.

I let her be absent, though sometimes the illness was imaginary. How different from my now-strictness about attendance with the others. I wasn't working. We had a new baby, I was home anyhow. Sometimes, after Susan grew old enough, I would keep her home from school, too, to have them all together.

Mostly Emily had asthma, and her breathing, harsh and labored, would fill the house with a curiously tranquil sound. I would bring the two old dresser mirrors and her boxes of collections to her bed. She would select beads and single earrings, bottle tops and shells, dried flowers and pebbles, old postcards and scraps, all sorts of oddments; then she and Susan would play Kingdom, setting up landscapes and furniture, peopling them with action.

Those were the only times of peaceful companionship between her and Susan. I have edged away from it, that poisonous feeling between them, that terrible balancing of hurts and needs I had to do between the two, and did so badly, those earlier years.

Oh there are conflicts between the others too, each one human, needing, demanding, hurting, taking—but only between Emily and Susan, no, Emily toward Susan that corroding resentment. It seems so obvious on the surface, yet it is not obvious. Susan, the second child, Susan, golden- and curly-haired and chubby, quick and articulate and assured, everything in appearance and manner Emily was not; Susan, not able to resist Emily's precious things, losing or sometimes clumsily breaking them; Susan telling jokes and riddles to company for applause while Emily sat silent (to say to me later: that was *my* riddle, Mother, I told it to Susan); Susan, who for all the five years' difference in age was just a year behind Emily in developing physically.

I am glad for that slow physical development that widened the difference between her and her contemporaries, though she suffered over it. She was too vulnerable for that terrible world of youthful competition, of preening and parading, of constant measuring of yourself against every other, of envy, "If I had that copper hair," "If I had that skin. . . ." She tormented herself enough about not looking like the others, there was enough of the unsureness, the having to be conscious of words before you speak, the constant caring—what are they thinking of me? without having it all magnified by the merciless physical drives.

Ronnie is calling. He is wet and I change him. It is rare there is such a cry now. That time of motherhood is almost behind me when the ear is not one's own but must always be racked and listening for the child cry, the child call. We sit for a while and I hold him, looking out over the city spread in charcoal with its soft aisles of light. "*Shoogily*," he breathes and curls closer. I carry him back to bed, asleep. *Shoogily*. A funny word, a family word, inherited from Emily, invented by her to say: *comfort*.

In this and other ways she leaves her seal, I say aloud. And startle at my saying it. What do I mean? What did I start to gather together, to try and make coherent? I was at the terrible, growing years. War years. I do not remember them well. I was working, there were four smaller ones now, there was not time for her. She had to help be a mother, and housekeeper, and shopper. She had to set her seal. Mornings of crisis and near hysteria trying to get lunches packed, hair combed, coats and shoes found, everyone to school or Child Care on time, the baby ready for transportation. And always the paper scribbled on by a smaller one, the book looked at by Susan then mislaid, the homework not done. Running out to that huge school where she was one, she was lost, she was a drop; suffering over the unpreparedness, stammering and unsure in her classes.

There was so little time left at night after the kids were bedded down. She would struggle over books, always eating (it was in those years she developed her enormous appetite that is legendary in our family) and I would be ironing, or preparing food for the next day, or writing V-mail to Bill, or tending the baby. Sometimes, to make me laugh, or out of her despair, she would imitate happenings or types at school.

I think I said once: "Why don't you do something like this in the school amateur show?" One morning she phoned me at work, hardly understandable through the weeping: "Mother, I did it. I won, I won; they gave me first prize; they clapped and clapped and wouldn't let me go."

Now suddenly she was Somebody, and as imprisoned in her difference as she had been in anonymity.

She began to be asked to perform at other high schools, even in colleges, then at city and statewide affairs. The first one we went to, I only recognized her that first moment when thin, shy, she almost drowned herself into the curtains. Then: Was this Emily? The control, the command, the convulsing and deadly clowning, the spell, then the roaring, stamping audience, unwilling to let this rare and precious laughter out of their lives.

Afterwards: You ought to do something about her with a gift like that—but without money or knowing how, what does one do? We have left it all to her, and the gift has as often eddied inside, clogged and clotted, as been used and growing.

She is coming. She runs up the stairs two at a time with her light graceful step, and I know she is happy tonight. Whatever it was that occasioned your call did not happen today.

"Aren't you ever going to finish the ironing, Mother? Whistler painted his mother in a rocker. I'd have to paint mine standing over an ironing board." This is one of her communicative nights and she tells me everything and nothing as she fixes herself a plate of food out of the icebox.

She is so lovely. Why did you want me to come in at all? Why were you concerned? She will find her way.

She starts up the stairs to bed. "Don't get me up with the rest in the morning." "But I thought you were having midterms." "Oh, those," she comes back in, kisses me, and says quite lightly, "in a couple of years when we'll all be atom-dead they won't matter a bit."

She has said it before. She *believes* it. But because I have been dredging the past, and all that compounds a human being is so heavy and meaningful in me, I cannot endure it tonight.

I will never total it all. I will never come in to say: She was a child seldom smiled at. Her father left me before she was a year old. I had to work her first six years when there was work, or I sent her home and to his relatives. There were years she had care she hated. She was dark and thin and foreign-looking in a world where the prestige went to blondeness and curly hair and dimples, she was slow where glibness was prized. She was a child of anxious, not proud, love. We were poor and could not afford for her the soil of easy growth. I was a young mother, I was a distracted mother. There were other children pushing up, demanding. Her younger sister seemed all that she was not. There were years she did not want me to touch her. She kept too much in herself, her life was such she had to keep too much in herself. My wisdom came too late. She has much to her and probably little will come of it. She is a child of her age, of depression, of war, of fear.

Let her be. So all that is in her will not bloom—but in how many does it? There is still enough left to live by. Only help her to know—help make it so there is cause for her to know—that she is more than this dress on the ironing board, helpless before the iron.

# Anna Maria Ortese

## (1914–1998)

Italian writer Anna Maria Ortese was first praised as a magical realist, a phrase invented by writer Massimo Bontempelli, who is also credited with having discovered her. She was born in Rome and attended primary school in Libya. One of seven children in a family burdened by economic hardship, Ortese was forced to quit school at thirteen. She published her first story in 1931, when she was only seventeen and in 1937 published a collection of short stories, *Angelici Dolori*. Ortese was the recipient of several Italian literary awards, including the Strega, the Premio Viareggio, and the Fiuggi. Her novel *The Iguana* appeared in an English translation in 1986; it was followed by *A Music Behind the Wall* (1994) and *Alonso e i Visionari* (1996). Her stories depict the tragedies and illusions of the impoverished.

---

## A Pair of Glasses                                                   1967

TRANSLATED BY KATHRINE JASON

Don Peppino Quaglia stood near the threshold of the basement apartment, singing "Ce sta' o sole . . . 'o sole!"

"Leave the sun to God," his wife Rosa answered, her soft, vaguely cheerful voice rising from within where she was laid up in bed with arthritic pain, complicated by heart disease; and addressing her sister-in-law, who was in the bathroom, she added: "You know what I'm going to do, Nunziata? I'll get up later and take the soaking clothes out of the wash."

"Do as you please, but I think you're crazy," Nunziata answered from the little cubbyhole, in her dry, sad voice. "With the pains that you have, one more day in bed wouldn't hurt you!" A silence. "We have to put down that other poison, I found a cockroach in my sleeve this morning."

And then Eugenia's calm, quiet voice called from the bed in the rear of the room, a veritable grotto with its low ceiling vault strung with spider webs:

"Mama, today I get my glasses."

There was a kind of secret jubilation in the little girl's subdued tone; she was Don Peppino's third-born (the first two, Carmela and Luisella, were with the nuns, and would soon don the veil, convinced as they were that this life is a punishment; and the two small ones, Pasqualino and Teresella, still lay feet first, snoring in their mother's bed).

"And smash them too, I bet," her aunt insisted, even more irritated now, from behind the door. She made everybody pay for the displeasures of her life, most importantly the displeasure of being unmarried and of being subjected, as she saw it, to her sister-in-law's charity, although she never failed to mention that she offered this humiliation to God. She had put a little of her own savings aside, however, and since she was not really mean, she offered to buy glasses for Eugenia after the family had discovered that she couldn't see a thing. "And what they cost!" she added now. "Eight thousand lire in hard cash." Eugenia heard water running in the basin and pictured her washing her face, squinting, her eyes full of soap, and she didn't bother to answer.

Anyway, she was much too happy to bother.

A week ago she and her aunt had gone to an optometrist on Via Roma. There, in that elegant store full of shining tables and a marvelous green reflection that rained down from the curtains, the doctor had tested her eyes, making her read entire columns of letters printed on a card, some as big as boxes and others as tiny as pins, while he changed lenses. "This poor child is nearly blind," he finally said to her aunt, as if in commiseration. "She must never take these glasses off again." And then, while

Eugenia sat waiting anxiously on a stool, he quickly placed another pair of lenses in a white wire frame on her face and said to her: "Now look at the street." Eugenia stood, her legs trembling with excitement, and could not hold back a little shout of joy. Well-dressed people, so many of them, passed before her on the sidewalk, and they were crystal clear even if smaller than usual: ladies in silk suits and powdered faces, young men with long hair and colorful sweaters, an old man with a white beard and reddened hands clasping a cane with a silver handle; and in the street, beautiful automobiles that looked like toys, painted shiny red or light green; and green trolleys as big as houses. Across the street, the elegant stores whose windows shone like mirrors (sales clerks in black smocks were polishing them) were so full of fine things that Eugenia's heart swelled. There was a cafe with red and yellow tables outside, and young girls with golden hair sitting cross-legged laughed as they drank from tall, colored glasses. Above the cafe, balcony doors stood ajar, as it was already spring; the embroidered curtains blew, revealing blue and gold paintings, heavy gold and crystal chandeliers that glittered. Amazing! Enthralled by all that splendor, she had not followed the conversation between her aunt and the doctor. Her aunt, standing at some distance from the glass counter in her brown Sunday dress, now broached the subject of the price with a timidity that was unnatural for her. "Doctor, don't forget to give us a good price, we're poor people . . ." And when she had heard "eight thousand lire," she nearly fainted.

"For two pieces of glass? What are you saying? Jesus Christ!"

"You see, when people are ignorant, they never reason things out. But if you give this child two pieces of glass, tell me, won't she see better? She has nine diopters in one eye, and ten in the other. And if you want to know the truth, she's nearly blind."

While the doctor wrote down the child's first and last name, "Eugenia Quaglia, vicolo della Cupa, Santa Maria in Portico," Nunziata walked over to Eugenia, who still stood in the doorway of the store, adjusting the glasses with her damp hands and looking about eagerly. "Look, look, my lovely girl. You see what this luxury is costing us! Eight thousand lire, did you hear? Eight thousand in hard cash!" She could barely breathe. Eugenia had turned completely red, not so much at this reproach, but at the gaze of the cashier who had been looking at them while her aunt announced the family's poverty. She took off the glasses.

"But how can she be so young and so myopic already?" the cashier asked as Nunziata signed the receipt, adding "and wrinkled too?"

"My good lady, there's not a pair of bad eyes in our house, this is just a stroke of bad luck that came . . . along with all the others. God rubs salt in our wounds. . . ."

"Come back in a week," the doctor said. "The glasses will be ready."

Eugenia tripped on the stairs as she was leaving.

"Thank you, Aunt Nunzia," she said after a while. "I'm always so rude to you and you're so nice to buy me glasses."

Her voice was trembling.

"Listen, my dear, it's better not to see the world than to see it," Nunziata answered with sudden melancholy.

Eugenia did not even answer her this time. Aunt Nunzia was often strange; she cried and shouted over nothing and said so many ugly words. On the other hand, she went to mass conscientiously; she was a good Christian, and whenever some wretch needed help, she was always there, with a full heart. Eugenia didn't have to worry.

From that day on, Eugenia lived in a sort of rapture, waiting for those blessed glasses that would allow her to see every single person, every little thing in its minutest detail. Until now, she had been enveloped in a fog: the room where she lived, the courtyard that was always hung with clothes, the *vicolo*, spilling over with colors and noises—all of that for her was covered by a thick veil: the only faces she knew well were those of her intimates—her mother especially, and her brothers and sisters because they often slept together. Sometimes when she woke in the night, she would look at them in the gaslight. Her mother slept with her mouth open, and Eugenia could see her broken, yellowed teeth; and Pasqualino and Teresella were always dirty and covered with boils, their noses full of mucus: when they slept, they made a strange noise, as if they had beasts inside them. Once in a while, Eugenia caught herself staring without really knowing what she was thinking. She felt confusedly that beyond that room, forever filled with its dripping clothing, broken chairs and stinking toilet, there must be beautiful light, sounds, things; and the moment she had put the glasses on, the revelation struck her: the world outside was beautiful, quite beautiful.

"Respects, Marchesa. . . ."

It was her father speaking. She saw his tattered shirt, his back moving out of the doorframe.

"You must do me a favor, Don Peppino . . . ," the marchesa said now in a placid, indifferent voice.

"Whatever you want, tell me . . ."

Eugenia wriggled out of bed without a sound, slipped into a dress and went barefoot to the door. The sun, which entered the ugly courtyard early every morning through a fissure between the buildings, came towards her in all its purity and splendor, illuminating her little old woman's face, her strawlike, disheveled hair, her small, coarse wooden hands with their long, dirty fingernails. Oh, if only she had glasses now! The marchesa was standing there with that majestic and kindly air that so enchanted Eugenia, wearing a black silk suit, a little lace scarf, her white hands covered with jewels; but her face was not clear, it was an oval, a whitish stain. Two violet feathers quivered above it.

"Listen, you must do the child's mattress again . . . Can you come up at around ten-thirty?"

"Gladly, gladly, but I wouldn't be ready until this afternoon, Signora marchesa . . ."

"No, Don Peppino, it must be done in the morning. People are coming this afternoon. You can work out on the terrace. Don't make me beg you, do me this favor. They're ringing the bells for mass now. Call me at ten-thirty."

And without waiting for an answer, she walked away, carefully avoiding a yellow stream of water that was spilling down from one of the terraces into a puddle on the ground.

"Papa," Eugenia said, coming up behind her father as he headed back inside the basement apartment. "The marchesa is so good, isn't she! She treats you like a gentleman. God will reward her for it."

"A good Christian she certainly is," Don Peppino answered, implying another meaning beyond Eugenia's understanding. Exploiting the fact that she was the landlord, the Marchesa D'Avanzo made the people in the courtyard serve her continually; she would give Don Peppino a pittance for the mattress; and Rosa, who waited on the marchesa even when her bones burned, was always at her beck and call to bring clean sheets. It's true, the marchesa had cloistered the girls, saving two souls from the world's perils, which are numerous for the poor. But she charged three thousand lire, and not one less, for that basement space where everyone had gotten sick. She loved to repeat, with a certain cool tone, "I would do it with all my heart, I would, it's just the money that's missing. These days, Don Peppino, you're a gentleman, and you should be grateful that you have no worries, thankful that providence has given you such a situation, has saved you. . . ." Donna Rosa felt a sort of adoration for the marchesa and her religious sentiments: whenever they saw one another, they spoke continually of the other life. And though the marchesa didn't put much credence in it, she didn't say so; she exhorted the mother of the family to be patient and hope.

"Did you speak to her?" Donna Rosa asked anxiously from the bed.

"She wants me to make a bed for her nephew," said Don Peppino, annoyed. He had taken the tripod stove, a gift from the nuns, outside to heat some coffee and now came back in for water. "I won't do it for less than five hundred," he said.

"That's a fair price."

"And who's going to pick up Eugenia's glasses?" asked Aunt Nunzia, coming out of the bathroom. She was wearing a shirt, a skirt whose hem was down, and slippers. Her pointed shoulders, grey as rocks, poked through her shirt. She was drying her face with a napkin. "I can't go and Rosa is sick . . ."

Nobody noticed Eugenia's large, nearly blind eyes filling with tears. See, maybe she wouldn't have her glasses for another day now. She sidled up to her mother's bed and let her arms and forehead fall on the blanket with a pathetic gesture. Donna Rosa reached a hand out to caress her.

"I'll go, Nunzia, don't get worked up. In fact, it'll do me good to go out."

"Mama!" Eugenia kissed her hand.

At eight, there was a great commotion in the courtyard. Rosa had just stepped out; in the stained, too-short black coat without shoulder pads, she was a tall, gaunt figure whose legs stuck out like wooden sticks. She held a shopping bag on her arm for the bread she'd pick up on her way back from the optician. Don Peppino was sweeping the water out of the middle of the courtyard with a long broom, a useless effort because the tub leaked constantly, like a spring. The courtyard was hung with the clothes of the two families upstairs: the Greborio sisters on the first floor, and the cavaliere Amodio's wife, who'd had a baby two days early. In fact, the Greborio's maid, Lina Tarallo, was making a terrible racket as she shook out the carpets on the balcony. The dust, mixed with real filth, drifted down and gradually settled like a cloud over those poor people. But nobody paid it any attention. Then suddenly shrill screams, cries broke out: Aunt Nunzia was calling upon all the saints to be her witness: she was cursed, and all because Pasqualino was bawling and screeching like a devil to go with his mother. "Look at him, look at this demon!" screamed Aunt

Nunzia. "*Madonna bella*, have mercy on me, let me die, let me die now if you can, because only thieves and bad women are fit for this life." Teresella, who was smaller than her brother because she was born the year the king fled, sat in the doorway smiling; every now and then she would lick a crust of bread that she found under a chair.

Eugenia was sitting on the steps of the doorkeeper Mariuccia's apartment, looking at a page from a children's magazine which had fallen from the third floor. She had her nose to it because that was the only way she could read the words under the colored figures: a little blue river in the middle of an endless meadow, and a boat going . . . going . . . who knows where? It was not in dialect but in Italian, so she didn't understand much. But now and then she would laugh for no reason.

"So, today you're going to get your glasses?" said Mariuccia, leaning over her shoulder. Everybody in the courtyard knew because Eugenia could not resist telling, and also because Aunt Nunziata had found it necessary to announce that she was the one in the family who would spend her own money. . . .

"Your aunt is giving them to you, eh?" added Mariuccia, smiling good-naturedly. She was a small woman, almost a dwarf with a man's face, full of whiskers. Just then she was brushing the long black hair which reached her knees: one of the few attributes that attested to the fact that she was a woman too. She brushed slowly, her sly, kind, mousey eyes smiling.

"Mama went to Via Roma to get them," said Eugenia with a look of gratitude. "We paid eight thousand lire for them, you know, in hard cash. . . . My aunt is," she was adding, when Nunziata appeared in the doorway of the cubbyhole and screeched furiously: "Eugenia!"

Pasqualino stood behind her with a terrible grimace of disdain and surprise on his face, all red and dazed. "Go to the tobacconist and buy me two three-lire caramels from Don Vincenzo. And come back right away!"

"Yes, Aunt."

She took the money in her fist, without another thought of the magazine, and walked out of the courtyard swiftly.

As she entered the tobacconist's, she grazed by Rosaria Buonincontri's yellow basket. Rosaria, the Amodio's fat maid, was wearing black but her legs were white, and her face flushed, calm. "Tell your mama to come up for a moment today, Signora Amodio has a message for her."

Eugenia recognized the voice.

"She's not home. She went to Via Roma to pick up my glasses."

"I have to get a pair too, but my fiancé doesn't want me to."

Eugenia did not grasp the meaning of this prohibition. She answered ingenuously: "They really cost a lot, you have to take care of them."

They entered the hole that was Don Vincenzo's store. People were waiting and Eugenia was pushed backwards. "Move up . . . you really are blind," Amodio's maid commented, with a kindly smile.

"But now your Aunt Nunzia is giving you glasses," Don Vincenzo cut in, winking with a playful, complicitous air when he overheard. He wore glasses too.

"At your age," he said, handing her the candies, "I could see like a cat, my grandmother wanted me around all the time because I could thread needles at night . . . but now I'm old . . ."

Eugenia nodded vaguely.

"None of my friends wear glasses," she said. Then turning back to Buonincontri, but speaking for Don Vincenzo's benefit as well: "Only me . . . I have nine diopters in one eye and ten in the other . . . I'm practically blind!" she stressed gently.

"See how lucky you are," Don Vincenzo to her, laughing; and to Rosaria: "How much salt?"

"Poor thing!" said Amodio's maid after Eugenia had gone, all contented. "It's the damp that ruined her. It nails us down in that house. Now Donna Rosa has pains in her bones. Give me a kilo of coarse salt and a package of the fine type."

"You've got it."

"What a morning we have today, eh, Don Vincenzo? It seems like summer already."

Walking back more slowly than she had come, Eugenia began to unwrap one of the candies without thinking and stuck it in her mouth. It was lemon-flavored. "I'll tell Aunt Nunzia that I lost it on the street," she decided. She was happy, she didn't care if her nice aunt (who was so good to her) got angry.

What a great day! Maybe mama was returning now with the glasses all wrapped in a package. . . . Soon she would be wearing them, she would. . . . A fury of slaps pounded her head, a real avalanche. She felt as if she were crumbling; futilely, she raised her hands to defend herself. It was Aunt Nunzia—who else?—furious that she was late, and right behind her Pasqualino was throwing a tantrum because he didn't believe the line about the candies anymore. "I'm dying! Here, blind, ugly thing! . . . And I give you everything I have for this kind of gratitude! You'll end up a good-for-nothing, that's what you'll be! Eight thousand lire it cost me! These demons . . . they're killing me! . . ."

She let her hands drop to her sides only to burst out into tears. "Suffering virgin, Jesus, for the wounds you suffered, let me die."

Now Eugenia was crying hard too.

"Oh, Aunt, forgive me . . . Aunt . . ."

"Uh . . . uh . . . uh . . . ," Pasqualino grunted, his mouth gaping.

"Poor thing," said Donna Mariuccia walking over to Eugenia, who was trying to hide her blotched, tear-stained face from her aunt's anger. "She didn't do it on purpose, Nunzia . . . , calm down." And to Eugenia: "What did you do with the candies?"

Eugenia answered softly, hopelessly, holding out the remaining candy in a dirty hand. "I ate one. I was hungry."

Before her aunt could attack the child again, the marchesa's voice called down softly, calmly, from the third floor, where the sun was shining.

"Nunziata!"

Aunt Nunzia lifted her embittered face which resembled the one at the end of her bed, the Madonna of the seven afflictions.

"Today is the first Friday of the month. Offer your prayers to God."

"Marchesa, you are so kind! These children make me commit so many little sins,

I am losing my soul, I . . . ," and her head collapsed into her pawlike hands, the skin brown and scaly as a laborer's.

"Your brother isn't home?"

"Your poor aunt, she buys you a pair of glasses and this is how you thank her . . . ," Mariuccia said to Eugenia who was still trembling.

"Yes, signora, here I am," answered Don Peppino, emerging from behind the apartment door that had half-concealed him; he'd been fanning the fire under his lunch with a piece of cardboard.

"Can you come up now?"

"My wife went to get Eugenia's glasses. . . . I'm watching the beans . . . would you mind waiting?"

"Then send up the little girl. I have a dress for Nunziata. I want to give it to her."

"God will reward you. We're ever so grateful," answered Don Peppino with a sigh of relief, because this was the one thing that would calm his sister. But looking over at Nunziata, he realized that she was not cheered at all. She went on crying her heart out, and her lament had so stunned Pasqualino that the child had fallen into a silence of fascination, a small sweet smile on his face; he was licking the mucus that dripped from his nose.

"Did you hear? Go up to the marchesa's, she wants to give you a dress," Don Peppino said to his daughter.

Eugenia's eyes were fixed on something in the air, seeing nothing: opened wide, they focused and focused. She started and got up quickly, obediently.

"Tell her, 'God will reward you,' and stay outside the door."

"Yes, Papa."

"Believe me, Mariuccia," Aunt Nunziata said when Eugenia was out of earshot, "I adore that child, and afterwards I regret slapping her, God only knows. But believe me, when I have to struggle with kids the blood goes right to my head. I'm not young anymore, as you can see . . . ," and she touched her sunken cheeks. "Sometimes I feel like a mad woman. . . ."

"On the other hand, they also have to let off steam," answered Donna Mariuccia, "they're just innocent souls. They'll have plenty of time for tears. When I look at them and think they'll become like us . . ." She went to fetch a broom and pushed a cabbage leaf over the threshold, "I really wonder what God is up to."

"You're giving it away brand new!" said Eugenia, pressing her nose to the green dress, spread across the kitchen sofa while the marchesa went to look for an old newspaper to wrap it in.

Signora D'Avanzo was thinking that the child could not see at all if she didn't realize the dress was ancient and darned all over (it was her dead sister's), but she said nothing. Only when she returned with the newspaper did she finally ask after several seconds:

"And the glasses your aunt gave you? Are they new?"

"They have gold wires. And they cost eight thousand lire," Eugenia answered in a breath, moved again at the thought of the privilege that had touched her. "Because I'm nearly blind," she added bluntly.

"In my opinion," said the marchesa, wrapping the dress in the newspaper gently and then opening the package again because a sleeve was sticking out, "your aunt could've spent less. I've seen the best eyeglasses for only two thousand lire at a store on Ascenzione."

Eugenia blushed. She realized that the marchesa was displeased. "Each in his own range, we must all limit ourselves. . . ." She had heard her say so many times when Donna Rosa brought up the clean wash and lingered to lament the family's financial straits.

"Maybe they weren't any good. . . . I have nine diopters," Eugenia answered timidly.

The marchesa raised an eyebrow, but fortunately Eugenia didn't see.

"I'm telling you, they were good," Signora D'Avanzo insisted, her voice hardening slightly. Then regretting it, she said more gently, "My dear child, I'm saying this because I know your family's troubles. With that six thousand lire, you could buy bread for ten days, you could buy . . . why, why should you need to see well? With what is around you! . . ." There was a silence. "To read? Do you read?"

"No, Signora."

"But I've seen you with your nose in a book sometimes. So, you're a liar too, my child. . . . That's no good. . . ."

Eugenia did not answer this time. Feeling utterly hopeless, she fixed her nearly white eyes on the dress.

"Is it silk?" she asked stupidly.

The marchesa looked at her pensively.

"You don't deserve it, but I want to give you a little something," she said suddenly, and she walked toward an armoire of white wood. Just at that moment, the telephone, which was in the hall, began to ring, and instead of opening the armoire Signora D'Avanzo went to answer it. Eugenia was so discouraged by those words she had barely heard the old woman's consoling hint; and as soon as she was alone, she began looking—as best she could—all around her. There were so many beautiful, fine things, just like the store on Via Roma! And there, right before her eyes, was an open balcony covered with vases of flowers.

She went out on the balcony. So much space, so much blue! The houses seemed to be covered by a blue veil, and the vicolo below looked like a well with so many ants coming and going . . . like her family. . . . What were they doing, where were they going? They came out and went back inside little holes, carrying large crumbs of bread: that's what they were doing, they had done it yesterday, they would do it again tomorrow, and forever . . . forever. So many holes, so many ants. And all around, nearly invisible in the great light, was the world as God had made it, with wind and sun, and further away, the great, clear sea. . . . She stood there thoughtfully, resting her chin on the grating, with an expression of pain, of dismay that made her ugly. The marchesa's voice called out, calm, pious. In her hand, her smooth ivory hand, she held a little book covered with black pasteboard and gold letters.

"These are the saints' reflections, dear girl. You people today don't read anything, and that's why the world is changing. Take it, it's my gift. But you must promise me that you'll read a little every night. Now that you've got glasses."

"Yes, Signora," Eugenia replied quickly as she took the book, blushing once again because the marchesa had found her on the balcony. The signora gazed at her, pleased.

"The Lord wanted to save you, my child!" she said, going to get the package with the dress and handing it to her. "You're not pretty, quite the contrary, you already look like an old woman. The Lord chose you above others, precisely so that you wouldn't get into trouble. He wants you to be saintly, like your sisters!"

Because Eugenia had been long prepared for a life lacking in joy, albeit unconsciously, she was not really wounded by these words, but she was disturbed nevertheless. And it seemed to her, if only for a moment, that the sun was less bright: even the thought of the glasses failed to cheer her. She stared vaguely, her eyes nearly dark, at the faded green of Posillipo that stretched into the sea like a lizard.

"Tell your papa," the marchesa went on, "that we won't be doing anything about the child's mattress today. My cousin called, and I have to be down at Posillipo all day."

"I was once there too," Eugenia began, coming alive again at the sound of that name and gazing out toward it with a look of enchantment.

"Oh, really?" Signora D'Avanzo was indifferent; to her the name meant nothing. Then, moving with all the majesty of her person, she walked to the front door with the child, who lingered, turning back to stare at that luminous point until the door closed gently behind her.

It was as she was stepping off the last step into the courtyard that the shadow which had momentarily darkened her forehead lifted, and her mouth opened in a cry of joy as she caught sight of her mother returning. Her familiar shabby figure was easily recognizable. She threw the dress down on a chair and ran toward her.

"Mama, my glasses!"

"Slow down, child. You'll knock me down!"

Immediately a small crowd gathered around them. Donna Mariuccia, Don Peppino, one of the Geborios who had stopped to rest on a chair before tackling the stairs, Amodio's maid who had just come in, and of course, Pasqualino and Teresella who were screeching to see too, their hands outstretched. Nunziata was observing the unwrapped dress with a crestfallen expression.

"See Mariuccia, this looks like pretty old stuff to me. . . . It's all worn out under the arms," she said approaching the group. But nobody paid her any attention. Donna Rosa was taking the wrapped case from the collar of her dress, opening it with the utmost care. Like a sort of radiant insect with two big, big eyes and two curved antennae, it lay shining in a blurred ray of sunlight, as Donna Rosa extended her long, red hand into the circle of those poor admiring people.

"Eight thousand lire for a thing like this," said Donna Rosa, gazing religiously but with a sort of remorse at the glasses.

Then silently she placed them on Eugenia's face; ecstatic, the child raised her hands to push the antennae carefully behind her ears. "Well, do you see us?" she asked, nearly moved to tears.

Arranging them with her hands, as if she were afraid someone would grab them away, her eyes half-closed and her mouth half-open in an enraptured smile, Eugenia took two steps backward, stumbling into a chair.

"Congratulations," said Greborio's maid.

"Congratulations," said Signora Greborio.

"She looks like a teacher, doesn't she?" said Don Peppino, delighted.

"Not as much as a thank you," said Aunt Nunziata, looking bitterly at the dress. "Even after all this: Congratulations."

"She's afraid, my dear," murmured Donna Rosa, walking towards the door of the apartment to put down her things. "This is the first time she's ever worn glasses," she said, looking up at the first floor balcony where the other Greborio sister stood gazing down.

"Everybody looks so little," Eugenia said in a strange voice that sounded as if it were coming from under a chair. "And very, very black."

"Of course, it's a double lens. But do you see well?" asked Don Peppino. "That's the important thing. She's wearing her glasses for the first time," he repeated, turning to Sir Amodio who was passing by with an opened newspaper in his hand.

"I warn you," said Amodio, after having stared at Eugenia for a moment as if she were a cat, "the stairs have not been swept. . . . I found fish bones in front of the door!" And he walked off, all but hidden behind the newspaper, bent over an article about the proposed law for pensions that concerned him.

Eugenia walked to the front door to look out into the Vicolo della Cupa, her hands still on the glasses. Her legs were shaking, her head spinning, all the joy had gone out of her. She wanted to smile, but her whitened lips were turned down in an idiotic grimace. Suddenly, there were so many balconies—two thousand, one-hundred thousand; the vegetable carts rushed towards her, the voices filling the air, the cries, the sound of the whip, all filled her head at once as if she were sick. Staggering, she turned back towards the courtyard, and the terrible impression grew: the courtyard she saw now, a slimy funnel pointing up towards the sky, had leprous walls and decrepit balconies. There were black arches over the ground floor apartments and circles of bright bulbs around Our Lady of Sorrows; the pavement was white with soapy water and cauliflower leaves, scraps of paper, garbage; and in the middle of the courtyard, that group of tattered, deformed Christians, their faces pocked by poverty and resignation, turned their eyes toward her now, full of love. They began to twist, to blur, to grow. Through the two bewitched circles of her glasses, she saw them coming at her all at once. But it was Mariuccia who realized that the little girl was not well and pulled off her glasses. Whimpering, Eugenia had doubled over and vomited.

"They made her sick to her stomach!" yelled Mariuccia, feeling her forehead. "Go get a coffee bean, Nunziata!"

"Eight thousand lire in hard cash!" Aunt Nunziata cried with fury in her eyes, as she ran to the basement apartment to take a coffee bean from a bottle on the credenza; and she raised the new glasses into the air, as if to receive some explanation from God. "And now they're not even right!"

"It's always like this the first time," Amodio's maid said to Donna Rosa calmly. "You shouldn't be alarmed; she'll adjust to them with time."

"It's nothing, child, nothing, don't be afraid," but Donna Rosa's heart tightened at the thought of how unfortunate they were.

When Aunt Nunziata came back with the coffee, she was still screaming, "Eight thousand in hard cash!" while Eugenia, who had turned white as a ghost, gagged uselessly, for there was nothing left inside her. Her bulging eyes were nearly crossed from the strain, and her tear-stained, ancient face appeared stunned. She leaned against her mother and shook.

"Mama, where are we?"

"We're in the courtyard, that's where, child," Donna Rosa said patiently, and the flickering smile of pity and awe that shone in her eyes suddenly brightened the faces of all those wretched people.

"She's half-blind!"

"She's half-stupid is what she is!"

"Let her be, poor thing, she's just shocked," said Donna Mariuccia, her face grim with compassion as she walked back into her own apartment which looked darker than ever.

Only Aunt Nunziata was still wringing her hands:

"Eight thousand lire!"

# Dorothy Parker

## (1893–1967)

Dorothy Parker, essayist, short story writer, screenwriter, and poet, was ironically best known in New York literary circles in the 1930s not for her written work, but for her urbane wit. A member of the celebrated Algonquin Round Table, a group of (often out-of-work) writers in New York, she spent her days entertaining her colleagues, who listened ardently for her humorous perspective. Upon the death of Calvin Coolidge, Parker stated, "How could they tell?" A brilliant wordsmith, she was once asked at a party to use the word *horticulture* in a sentence. In a moment, she came up with this: "You can lead a horticulture, but you can't make her think." Her wit became so well known and she was so often quoted in magazines, in newspapers, and at social events that witticisms that were not hers were sometimes attributed to her.

Parker graduated from finishing school in 1911 and began writing for *Vanity Fair* in 1917. A rabble rouser from a young age, she was fired when she flouted a company policy against discussing wages by posting a sign around her neck bearing her salary. She went on to freelance and publish short, humorous pieces in the *Saturday Evening Post*, but after she spent a weekend at the editor's estate and made scathing remarks about his bourgeois lifestyle, her contributions were no longer welcome.

In 1927 Parker began writing book reviews for the *New Yorker*, and she worked there for two years as a regular contributor. In the early 1930s she moved to Los Angeles and began a successful career as a well-paid screenwriter.

This career drew to an unhappy close when she became blacklisted for her membership in the Communist Party. Becoming acutely aware of social problems and the serious nature of government corruption, she actively participated in the American Communist Party and openly stated her regret for having lived an empty life of cavalier socializing. Her poetry often conveyed a wry, humorous look at the life of women in New York social circles, and many of her short stories take a dim view of that life, such as "Big Blonde" (winner of the O. Henry Prize, 1929) and "Horsie." These short stories criticize the empty value system of the idle rich and the bon vivant crowd of which she was often a member. Parker's works include *Enough Rope* (1926), *Death and Taxes* (1931), *After Such Pleasures* (1933), *Not So Deep as a Well* (1936), and *Here Lies* (1940), a collection of all of her fiction published to that date.

## Big Blonde
*1929*

### I

Hazel Morse was a large, fair woman of the type that incites some men when they use the word "blonde" to click their tongues and wag their heads roguishly. She prided herself upon her small feet and suffered for her vanity, boxing them in snub-toed, high-heeled slippers of the shortest bearable size. The curious things about her were her hands, strange terminations to the flabby white arms splattered with pale tan spots—long, quivering hands with deep and convex nails. She should not have disfigured them with little jewels.

She was not a woman given to recollections. At her middle thirties, her old days were a blurred and flickering sequence, an imperfect film, dealing with the actions of strangers.

In her twenties, after the deferred death of a hazy widowed mother, she had been employed as a model in a wholesale dress establishment—it was still the day of the big woman, and she was then prettily colored and erect and high-breasted. Her job was not onerous, and she met numbers of men and spent numbers of evenings with them, laughing at their jokes and telling them she loved their neckties. Men liked her, and she took it for granted that the liking of many men was a desirable thing. Popularity seemed to her to be worth all the work that had to be put into its achievement. Men liked you because you were fun, and when they liked you they took you out, and there you were. So, and successfully, she was fun. She was a good sport. Men like a good sport.

No other form of diversion, simpler or more complicated, drew her attention. She never pondered if she might not be better occupied doing something else. Her ideas, or, better, her acceptances, ran right along with those of the other substantially built blondes in whom she found her friends.

When she had been working in the dress establishment some years she met Herbie Morse. He was thin, quick, attractive, with shifting lines about his shiny, brown eyes and a habit of fiercely biting at the skin around his finger nails. He drank largely; she found that entertaining. Her habitual greeting to him was an allusion to his state of the previous night.

"Oh, what a peach you had," she used to say, through her easy laugh. "I thought I'd die, the way you kept asking the waiter to dance with you."

She liked him immediately upon their meeting. She was enormously amused at his fast, slurred sentences, his interpolations of apt phrases from vaudeville acts and comic strips; she thrilled at the feel of his lean arm tucked firm beneath the sleeve of her coat; she wanted to touch the wet, flat surface of his hair. He was as promptly drawn to her. They were married six weeks after they had met.

She was delighted at the idea of being a bride; coquetted with it, played upon it. Other offers of marriage she had had, and not a few of them, but it happened that they were all from stout, serious men who had visited the dress establishment as buyers; men from Des Moines and Houston and Chicago and, in her phrase, even funnier places. There was always something immensely comic to her in the thought of living elsewhere than New York. She could not regard as serious proposals that she share a western residence.

She wanted to be married. She was nearing thirty now, and she did not take the years well. She spread and softened, and her darkening hair turned her to inexpert dabblings with peroxide. There were times when she had little flashes of fear about her job. And she had had a couple of thousand evenings of being a good sport among her male acquaintants. She had come to be more conscientious than spontaneous about it.

Herbie earned enough, and they took a little apartment far uptown. There was a Mission-furnished dining-room with a hanging central light globed in liver-colored glass; in the living-room were an "over-stuffed suite," a Boston fern, and a reproduction of the Henner "Magdalene" with the red hair and the blue draperies; the bedroom was in gray enamel and old rose, with Herbie's photograph on Hazel's dressing-table and Hazel's likeness on Herbie's chest of drawers.

She cooked—and she was a good cook—and marketed and chatted with the delivery boys and the colored laundress. She loved the flat, she loved her life, she loved Herbie. In the first months of their marriage, she gave him all the passion she was ever to know.

She had not realized how tired she was. It was a delight, a new game, a holiday, to give up being a good sport. If her head ached or her arches throbbed, she complained piteously, babyishly. If her mood was quiet, she did not talk. If tears came to her eyes, she let them fall.

She fell readily into the habit of tears during the first year of her marriage. Even in her good sport days, she had been known to weep lavishly and disinterestedly on occasion. Her behavior at the theater was a standing joke. She could weep at anything in a play—tiny garments, love both unrequited and mutual, seduction, purity, faithful servitors, wedlock, the triangle.

"There goes Haze," her friends would say, watching her. "She's off again."

Wedded and relaxed, she poured her tears freely. To her who had laughed so much, crying was delicious. All sorrows became her sorrows; she was Tenderness. She would cry long and softly over newspaper accounts of kidnaped babies, deserted wives, unemployed men, strayed cats, heroic dogs. Even when the paper was no longer before her, her mind revolved upon these things and the drops slipped rhythmically over her plump cheeks.

"Honestly," she would say to Herbie, "all the sadness there is in the world when you stop to think about it!"

"Yeah," Herbie would say.

She missed nobody. The old crowd, the people who had brought her and Herbie together, dropped from their lives, lingeringly at first. When she thought of this at all, it was only to consider it fitting. This was marriage. This was peace.

But the thing was that Herbie was not amused.

For a time, he had enjoyed being alone with her. He found the voluntary isolation novel and sweet. Then it palled with a ferocious suddenness. It was as if one night, sitting with her in the steam-heated living-room, he would ask no more; and the next night he was through and done with the whole thing.

He became annoyed by her misty melancholies. At first, when he came home to find her softly tired and moody, he kissed her neck and patted her shoulder and begged her to tell her Herbie what was wrong. She loved that. But time slid by, and he found that there was never anything really, personally, the matter.

"Ah, for God's sake," he would say. "Crabbing again. All right, sit here and crab your head off. I'm going out."

And he would slam out of the flat and come back late and drunk.

She was completely bewildered by what happened to their marriage. First they were lovers; and then, it seemed without transition, they were enemies. She never understood it.

There were longer and longer intervals between his leaving his office and his arrival at the apartment. She went through agonies of picturing him run over and bleeding, dead and covered with a sheet. Then she lost her fears for his safety and grew sullen and wounded. When a person wanted to be with a person, he came as soon as possible. She desperately wanted him to want to be with her; her own hours only marked the time till he would come. It was often nearly nine o'clock before he came home to dinner. Always he had had many drinks, and their effect would die in him, leaving him loud and querulous and bristling for affronts.

He was too nervous, he said, to sit and do nothing for an evening. He boasted, probably not in all truth, that he had never read a book in his life.

"What am I expected to do—sit around this dump on my tail all night?" he would ask, rhetorically. And again he would slam out.

She did not know what to do. She could not manage him. She could not meet him.

She fought him furiously. A terrific domesticity had come upon her, and she would bite and scratch to guard it. She wanted what she called "a nice home." She wanted a sober, tender husband, prompt at dinner, punctual at work. She wanted sweet, comforting evenings. The idea of intimacy with other men was terrible to her; the thought that Herbie might be seeking entertainment in other women set her frantic.

It seemed to her that almost everything she read—novels from the drug-store lending library, magazine stories, women's pages in the papers—dealt with wives who lost their husbands' love. She could bear those, at that, better than accounts of neat, companionable marriage and living happily ever after.

She was frightened. Several times when Herbie came home in the evening, he found her determinedly dressed—she had had to alter those of her clothes that were not new, to make them fasten—and rouged.

"Let's go wild tonight, what do you say?" she would hail him. "A person's got lots of time to hang around and do nothing when they're dead."

So they would go out, to chop houses and the less expensive cabarets. But it turned out badly. She could no longer find amusement in watching Herbie drink. She could not laugh at his whimsicalities, she was so tensely counting his indulgences. And she was unable to keep back her remonstrances—"Ah, come on, Herb, you've had enough, haven't you? You'll feel something terrible in the morning."

He would be immediately enraged. All right, crab; crab, crab, crab, crab, that was all she ever did. What a lousy sport *she* was! There would be scenes, and one or the other of them would rise and stalk out in fury.

She could not recall the definite day that she started drinking, herself. There was nothing separate about her days. Like drops upon a windowpane, they ran together and trickled away. She had been married six months; then a year; then three years.

She had never needed to drink, formerly. She could sit for most of a night at a table where the others were imbibing earnestly and never droop in looks or spirits, nor be bored by the doings of those about her. If she took a cocktail, it was so unusual as to cause twenty minutes or so of jocular comment. But now anguish was in her. Frequently, after a quarrel, Herbie would stay out for the night, and she could not learn from him where the time had been spent. Her heart felt tight and sore in her breast, and her mind turned like an electric fan.

She hated the taste of liquor. Gin, plain or in mixtures, made her promptly sick. After experiment, she found that Scotch whisky was best for her. She took it without water, because that was the quickest way to its effect.

Herbie pressed it on her. He was glad to see her drink. They both felt it might restore her high spirits, and their good times together might again be possible.

"'Atta girl," he would approve her. "Let's see you get boiled, baby."

But it brought them no nearer. When she drank with him, there would be a little while of gaiety and then, strangely without beginning, they would be in a wild quarrel. They would wake in the morning not sure what it had all been about, foggy as to what had been said and done, but each deeply injured and bitterly resentful. There would be days of vengeful silence.

There had been a time when they had made up their quarrels, usually in bed. There would be kisses and little names and assurances of fresh starts. . . . "Oh, it's going to be great now, Herb. We'll have swell times. I was a crab. I guess I must have been tired. But everything's going to be swell. You'll see."

Now there were no gentle reconciliations. They resumed friendly relations only in the brief magnanimity caused by liquor, before more liquor drew them into new battles. The scenes became more violent. There were shouted invectives and pushes, and sometimes sharp slaps. Once she had a black eye. Herbie was horrified next day at sight of it. He did not go to work; he followed her about, suggesting remedies and heaping dark blame on himself. But after they had had a few drinks—"to pull themselves together"—she made so many wistful references to her bruise that he shouted at her and rushed out and was gone for two days.

Each time he left the place in a rage, he threatened never to come back. She did not believe him, nor did she consider separation. Somewhere in her head or her heart was the lazy, nebulous hope that things would change and she and Herbie settle suddenly into soothing married life. Here were her home, her furniture, her husband, her station. She summoned no alternatives.

She could no longer bustle and potter. She had no more vicarious tears; the hot drops she shed were for herself. She walked ceaselessly about the rooms, her thoughts running mechanically round and round Herbie. In those days began the hatred of being alone that she was never to overcome. You could be by yourself when things were all right, but when you were blue you got the howling horrors.

She commenced drinking alone, little, short drinks all through the day. It was only with Herbie that alcohol made her nervous and quick in offense. Alone, it blurred sharp things for her. She lived in a haze of it. Her life took on a dream-like quality. Nothing was astonishing.

A Mrs. Martin moved into the flat across the hall. She was a great blonde woman of forty, a promise in looks of what Mrs. Morse was to be. They made acquaintance, quickly became inseparable. Mrs. Morse spent her days in the opposite apartment. They drank together, to brace themselves after the drinks of the nights before.

She never confided her troubles about Herbie to Mrs. Martin. The subject was too bewildering to her to find comfort in talk. She let it be assumed that her husband's business kept him much away. It was not regarded as important; husbands, as such, played but shadowy parts in Mrs. Martin's circle.

Mrs. Martin had no visible spouse; you were left to decide for yourself whether he was or was not dead. She had an admirer, Joe, who came to see her almost nightly. Often he brought several friends with him—"The Boys," they were called. The Boys were big, red, good-humored men, perhaps forty-five, perhaps fifty. Mrs. Morse was glad of invitations to join the parties—Herbie was scarcely ever at home at night now. If he did come home, she did not visit Mrs. Martin. An evening alone with Herbie meant inevitably a quarrel, yet she would stay with him. There was always her thin and wordless idea that, maybe, this night, things would begin to be all right.

The Boys brought plenty of liquor along with them whenever they came to Mrs. Martin's. Drinking with them, Mrs. Morse became lively and good-natured and audacious. She was quickly popular. When she had drunk enough to cloud her most recent battle with Herbie, she was excited by their approbation. Crab, was she? Rotten sport, was she? Well, there were some that thought different.

Ed was one of The Boys. He lived in Utica—had "his own business" there, was the awed report—but he came to New York almost every week. He was married. He showed Mrs. Morse the then current photographs of Junior and Sister, and she praised them abundantly and sincerely. Soon it was accepted by the others that Ed was her particular friend.

He staked her when they all played poker; sat next to her and occasionally rubbed his knee against hers during the game. She was rather lucky. Frequently she went home with a twenty-dollar bill or a ten-dollar bill or a handful of crumpled dollars. She was glad of them. Herbie was getting, in her words, something awful about money. To ask him for it brought an instant row.

"What the hell do you do with it?" he would say. "Shoot it all on Scotch?"

"I try to run this house half-way decent," she would retort. "Never thought of that, did you? Oh, no, his lordship couldn't be bothered with that."

Again, she could not find a definite day, to fix the beginning of Ed's proprietorship. It became his custom to kiss her on the mouth when he came in, as well as for farewell, and he gave her little quick kisses of approval all through the evening. She liked this rather more than she disliked it. She never thought of his kisses when she was not with him.

He would run his hand lingeringly over her back and shoulders.

"Some dizzy blonde, eh?" he would say. "Some doll."

One afternoon she came home from Mrs. Martin's to find Herbie in the bedroom. He had been away for several nights, evidently on a prolonged drinking bout. His face was gray, his hands jerked as if they were on wires. On the bed were two old suitcases, packed high. Only her photograph remained on his bureau, and the wide doors of his closet disclosed nothing but coat-hangers.

"I'm blowing," he said. "I'm through with the whole works. I got a job in Detroit."

She sat down on the edge of the bed. She had drunk much the night before, and the four Scotches she had had with Mrs. Martin had only increased her fogginess.

"Good job?" she said.

"Oh, yeah," he said. "Looks all right."

He closed a suitcase with difficulty, swearing at it in whispers.

"There's some dough in the bank," he said. "The bank book's in your top drawer. You can have the furniture and stuff."

He looked at her, and his forehead twitched.

"God damn it, I'm through, I'm telling you," he cried. "I'm through."

"All right, all right," she said. "I heard you, didn't I?"

She saw him as if he were at one end of a cannon and she at the other. Her head was beginning to ache bumpingly, and her voice had a dreary, tiresome tone. She could not have raised it.

"Like a drink before you go?" she asked.

Again he looked at her, and a corner of his mouth jerked up.

"Cockeyed again for a change, aren't you?" he said. "That's nice. Sure, get a couple of shots, will you?"

She went to the pantry, mixed him a stiff highball, poured herself a couple of inches of whisky and drank it. Then she gave herself another portion and brought the glasses into the bedroom. He had strapped both suitcases and had put on his hat and overcoat.

He took his highball.

"Well," he said, and he gave a sudden, uncertain laugh. "Here's mud in your eye."

"Mud in your eye," she said.

They drank. He put down his glass and took up the heavy suitcases.

"Got to get a train around six," he said.

She followed him down the hall. There was a song, a song that Mrs. Martin played doggedly on the phonograph, running loudly through her mind. She had never liked the thing.

> "Night and daytime,
> Always playtime.
> Ain't we got fun?"

At the door he put down the bags and faced her.

"Well," he said, "Well, take care of yourself. You'll be all right, will you?"

"Oh, sure," she said.

He opened the door, then came back to her, holding out his hand.

" 'By, Haze," he said. "Good luck to you."

She took his hand and shook it.

"Pardon my wet glove," she said.

When the door was closed behind him, she went back to the pantry.

She was flushed and lively when she went in to Mrs. Martin's that evening. The Boys were there, Ed among them. He was glad to be in town, frisky and loud and full of jokes. But she spoke quietly to him for a minute.

"Herbie blew today," she said. "Going to live out west."

"That so?" he said. He looked at her and played with the fountain pen clipped to his waistcoat pocket.

"Think he's gone for good, do you?" he asked.

"Yeah," she said. "I know he is. I know. Yeah."

"You going to live on across the hall just the same?" he said. "Know what you're going to do?"

"Gee, I don't know," she said. "I don't give much of a damn."

"Oh, come on, that's no way to talk," he told her. "What you need—you need a little snifter. How about it?"

"Yeah," she said. "Just straight."

She won forty-three dollars at poker. When the game broke up, Ed took her back to her apartment.

"Got a little kiss for me?" he asked.

He wrapped her in his big arms and kissed her violently. She was entirely passive. He held her away and looked at her.

"Little tight, honey?" he asked, anxiously. "Not going to be sick, are you?"

"Me?" she said. "I'm swell."

## II

When Ed left in the morning, he took her photograph with him. He said he wanted her picture to look at, up in Utica. "You can have that one on the bureau," she said.

She put Herbie's picture in a drawer, out of her sight. When she could look at it, she meant to tear it up. She was fairly successful in keeping her mind from racing around him. Whisky slowed it for her. She was almost peaceful, in her mist.

She accepted her relationship with Ed without question or enthusiasm. When he was away, she seldom thought definitely of him. He was good to her; he gave her frequent presents and a regular allowance. She was even able to save. She did not plan ahead of any day, but her wants were few, and you might as well put money in the bank as have it lying around.

When the lease of her apartment neared its end, it was Ed who suggested moving. His friendship with Mrs. Martin and Joe had become strained over a dispute at poker; a feud was impending.

"Let's get the hell out of here," Ed said. "What I want you to have is a place near the Grand Central. Make it easier for me."

So she took a little flat in the Forties. A colored maid came in every day to clean and to make coffee for her—she was "through with that housekeeping stuff," she said, and Ed, twenty years married to a passionately domestic woman, admired this romantic uselessness and felt doubly a man of the world in abetting it.

The coffee was all she had until she went out to dinner, but alcohol kept her fat. Prohibition she regarded only as a basis for jokes. You could always get all you wanted. She was never noticeably drunk and seldom nearly sober. It required a larger daily allowance to keep her misty-minded. Too little, and she was achingly melancholy.

Ed brought her to Jimmy's. He was proud, with the pride of the transient who would be mistaken for a native, in his knowledge of small, recent restaurants occupying the lower floors of shabby brownstone houses; places where, upon mentioning the name of an habitué friend, might be obtained strange whisky and fresh gin in many of their ramifications. Jimmy's place was the favorite of his acquaintances.

There, through Ed, Mrs. Morse met many men and women, formed quick friendships. The men often took her out when Ed was in Utica. He was proud of her popularity.

She fell into the habit of going to Jimmy's alone when she had no engagement. She was certain to meet some people she knew, and join them. It was a club for her friends, both men and women.

The women at Jimmy's looked remarkably alike, and this was curious, for, through feuds, removals, and opportunities of more profitable contacts, the personnel of the group changed constantly. Yet always the newcomers resembled those whom they replaced. They were all big women and stout, broad of shoulder and abundantly breasted, with faces thickly clothed in soft, high-colored flesh. They laughed loud and often, showing opaque and lusterless teeth like squares of crockery. There was about them the health of the big, yet a slight, unwholesome suggestion of stubborn preservation. They might have been thirty-six or forty-five or anywhere between.

They composed their titles of their own first names with their husbands' surnames—Mrs. Florence Miller, Mrs. Vera Riley, Mrs. Lilian Block. This gave at the same time the solidity of marriage and the glamour of freedom. Yet only one or two were actually divorced. Most of them never referred to their dimmed spouses; some, a shorter time separated, described them in terms of great biological interest. Several were mothers, each of an only child—a boy at school somewhere, or a girl being cared for by a grandmother. Often, well on towards morning, there would be displays of kodak portraits and of tears.

They were comfortable women, cordial and friendly and irrepressibly matronly. Theirs was the quality of ease. Become fatalistic, especially about money matters, they were unworried. Whenever their funds dropped alarmingly, a new donor appeared; this had always happened. The aim of each was to have one man, permanently, to pay all her bills, in return for which she would have immediately given up other admirers and probably would have become exceedingly fond of him; for the affections of all of them were, by now, unexacting, tranquil, and easily arranged. This end, however, grew increasingly difficult yearly. Mrs. Morse was regarded as fortunate.

Ed had a good year, increased her allowance and gave her a sealskin coat. But she had to be careful of her moods with him. He insisted upon gaiety. He would not listen to admissions of aches or weariness.

"Hey, listen," he would say, "I got worries of my own, and plenty. Nobody wants to hear other people's troubles, sweetie. What you got to do, you got to be a sport and forget it. See? Well, slip us a little smile, then. That's my girl."

She never had enough interest to quarrel with him as she had with Herbie, but she wanted the privilege of occasional admitted sadness. It was strange. The other women she saw did not have to fight their moods. There was Mrs. Florence Miller who got regular crying jags, and the men sought only to cheer and comfort her. The others spent whole evenings in grieved recitals of worries and ills; their escorts paid them deep sympathy. But she was instantly undesirable when she was low in spirits. Once, at Jimmy's, when she could not make herself lively, Ed had walked out and left her.

"Why the hell don't you stay home and not go spoiling everybody's evening?" he had roared.

Even her slightest acquaintances seemed irritated if she were not conspicuously light-hearted.

"What's the matter with you, anyway?" they would say. "Be your age, why don't you? Have a little drink and snap out of it."

When her relationship with Ed had continued nearly three years, he moved to Florida to live. He hated leaving her; he gave her a large check and some shares of a sound stock, and his pale eyes were wet when he said good-by. She did not miss him. He came to New York infrequently, perhaps two or three times a year, and hurried directly from the train to see her. She was always pleased to have him come and never sorry to see him go.

Charley, an acquaintance of Ed's that she had met at Jimmy's, had long admired her. He had always made opportunities of touching her and leaning close to talk to her. He asked repeatedly of all their friends if they had ever heard such a fine laugh as she had. After Ed left, Charley became the main figure in her life. She classified him and spoke of him as "not so bad." There was nearly a year of Charley; then she divided her time between him and Sydney, another frequenter of Jimmy's; then Charley slipped away altogether.

Sydney was a little, brightly dressed, clever Jew. She was perhaps nearest contentment with him. He amused her always; her laughter was not forced.

He admired her completely. Her softness and size delighted him. And he thought she was great, he often told her, because she kept gay and lively when she was drunk.

"Once I had a gal," he said, "used to try and throw herself out of the window every time she got a can on. Jee-*zuss,*" he added, feelingly.

Then Sydney married a rich and watchful bride, and then there was Billy. No— after Sydney came Ferd, then Billy. In her haze, she never recalled how men entered her life and left it. There were no surprises. She had no thrill at their advent, nor woe at their departure. She seemed to be always able to attract men. There was never another as rich as Ed, but they were all generous to her, in their means.

Once she had news of Herbie. She met Mrs. Martin dining at Jimmy's, and the old friendship was vigorously renewed. The still admiring Joe, while on a business trip, had seen Herbie. He had settled in Chicago, he looked fine, he was living with some woman—seemed to be crazy about her. Mrs. Morse had been drinking vastly that day. She took the news with mild interest, as one hearing of the sex peccadilloes of somebody whose name is, after a moment's groping, familiar.

"Must be damn near seven years since I saw him," she commented. "Gee. Seven years."

More and more, her days lost their individuality. She never knew dates, nor was sure of the day of the week.

"My God, was that a year ago!" she would exclaim, when an event was recalled in conversation.

She was tired so much of the time. Tired and blue. Almost everything could give her the blues. Those old horses she saw on Sixth Avenue—struggling and slipping along the car-tracks, or standing at the curb, their heads dropped level with their worn knees. The tightly stored tears would squeeze from her eyes as she teetered past on her aching feet in the stubby, champagne-colored slippers.

The thought of death came and stayed with her and lent her a sort of drowsy cheer. It would be nice, nice and restful, to be dead.

There was no settled, shocked moment when she first thought of killing herself; it seemed to her as if the idea had always been with her. She pounced upon all the accounts of suicides in the newspapers. There was an epidemic of self-killings—or maybe it was just that she searched for the stories of them so eagerly that she found many. To read of them roused reassurance in her; she felt a cozy solidarity with the big company of the voluntary dead.

She slept, aided by whisky, till deep into the afternoons, then lay abed, a bottle and glass at her hand, until it was time to dress to go out for dinner. She was beginning to feel towards alcohol a little puzzled distrust, as toward an old friend who has refused a simple favor. Whisky could still soothe her for most of the time, but there were sudden, inexplicable moments when the cloud fell treacherously away from her, and she was sawed by the sorrow and bewilderment and nuisance of all living. She played voluptuously with the thought of cool, sleepy retreat. She had never been troubled by religious belief and no vision of an after-life intimidated her. She dreamed by day of never again putting on tight shoes, of never having to laugh and listen and admire, of never more being a good sport. Never.

But how would you do it? It made her sick to think of jumping from heights. She could not stand a gun. At the theater, if one of the actors drew a revolver, she crammed her fingers into her ears and could not even look at the stage until after the shot had been fired. There was no gas in her flat. She looked long at the bright blue veins in her slim wrists—a cut with a razor blade, and there you'd be. But it would hurt, hurt like hell, and there would be blood to see. Poison—something tasteless and quick and painless—was the thing. But they wouldn't sell it to you in drugstores, because of the law.

She had few other thoughts.

There was a new man now—Art. He was short and fat and exacting and hard on her patience when he was drunk. But there had been only occasionals for some time before him, and she was glad of a little stability. Too, Art must be away for weeks at a stretch, selling silks, and that was restful. She was convincingly gay with him, though the effort shook her.

"The best sport in the world," he would murmur, deep in her neck. "The best sport in the world."

One night, when he had taken her to Jimmy's, she went into the dressing-room with Mrs. Florence Miller. There, while designing curly mouths on their faces with lip-rouge, they compared experiences of insomnia.

"Honestly," Mrs. Morse said, "I wouldn't close an eye if I didn't go to bed full of Scotch. I lie there and toss and turn and toss and turn. Blue! Does a person get blue lying awake that way!"

"Say, listen Hazel," Mrs. Miller said, impressively, "I'm telling you I'd be awake for a year if I didn't take veronal. That stuff makes you sleep like a fool."

"Isn't it poison, or something?" Mrs. Morse asked.

"Oh, you take too much and you're out for the count," said Mrs. Miller. "I just take five grains—they come in tablets. I'd be scared to fool around with it. But five grains, and you cork off pretty."

"Can you get it anywhere?" Mrs. Morse felt superbly Machiavellian.

"Get all you want in Jersey," said Mrs. Miller. "They won't give it to you here without you have a doctor's prescription. Finished? We'd better go back and see what the boys are doing."

That night, Art left Mrs. Morse at the door of her apartment; his mother was in town. Mrs. Morse was still sober, and it happened that there was no whisky left in her cupboard. She lay in bed, looking up at the black ceiling.

She rose early, for her, and went to New Jersey. She had never taken the tube, and did not understand it. So she went to the Pennsylvania Station and bought a railroad ticket to Newark. She thought of nothing in particular on the trip out. She looked at the uninspired hats of the women about her and gazed through the smeared window at the flat, gritty scene.

In Newark, in the first drug-store she came to, she asked for a tin of talcum powder, a nailbrush, and a box of veronal tablets. The powder and the brush were to make the hypnotic seem also a casual need. The clerk was entirely unconcerned. "We only keep them in bottles," he said, and wrapped up for her a little glass vial containing ten white tablets, stacked one on another.

She went to another drug-store and bought a face-cloth, an orangewood stick, and a bottle of veronal tablets. The clerk was also uninterested.

"Well, I guess I got enough to kill an ox," she thought, and went back to the station.

At home, she put the little vials in the drawer of her dressing-table and stood looking at them with a dreamy tenderness.

"There they are, God bless them," she said, and she kissed her fingertip and touched each bottle.

The colored maid was busy in the living-room.

"Hey, Nettie," Mrs. Morse called. "Be an angel, will you? Run around to Jimmy's and get me a quart of Scotch."

She hummed while she awaited the girl's return.

During the next few days, whisky ministered to her as tenderly as it had done when she first turned to its aid. Alone, she was soothed and vague, at Jimmy's she was the gayest of the groups. Art was delighted with her.

Then, one night, she had an appointment to meet Art at Jimmy's for an early dinner. He was to leave afterward on a business excursion, to be away for a week. Mrs. Morse had been drinking all the afternoon; while she dressed to go out, she felt herself rising pleasurably from drowsiness to high spirits. But as she came out into the street the effects of the whisky deserted her completely, and she was filled with a slow, grinding wretchedness so horrible that she stood swaying on the pavement, unable for a moment to move forward. It was a gray night with spurts of mean, thin snow, and the streets shone with dark ice. As she slowly crossed Sixth Avenue, consciously dragging one foot past the other, a big, scarred horse pulling a rickety express-wagon crashed to his knees before her. The driver swore and screamed and lashed the beast insanely, bringing the whip back over his shoulder for every blow, while the horse struggled to get a footing on the slippery asphalt. A group gathered and watched with interest.

Art was waiting, when Mrs. Morse reached Jimmy's.

"What's the matter with you, for God's sake?" was his greeting to her.

"I saw a horse," she said. "Gee, I—a person feels sorry for horses. I—it isn't just horses. Everything's kind of terrible, isn't it? I can't help getting sunk."

"Ah, sunk, me eye," he said. "What's the idea of all the bellyaching? What have you got to be sunk about?"

"I can't help it," she said.

"Ah, help it, me eye," he said. "Pull yourself together, will you? Come on and sit down, and take that face off you."

She drank industriously and she tried hard, but she could not overcome her melancholy. Others joined them and commented on her gloom, and she could do no more for them than smile weakly. She made little dabs at her eyes with her handkerchief, trying to time her movements so they would be unnoticed, but several times Art caught her and scowled and shifted impatiently in his chair.

When it was time for him to go to his train, she said she would leave, too, and go home.

"And not a bad idea, either," he said. "See if you can't sleep yourself out of it. I'll see you Thursday. For God's sake, try and cheer up by then, will you?"

"Yeah," she said. "I will."

In her bedroom, she undressed with a tense speed wholly unlike her usual slow uncertainty. She put on her nightgown, took off her hair-net and passed the comb quickly through her dry, vari-colored hair. Then she took the two little vials from the drawer and carried them into the bathroom. The splintering misery had gone from her, and she felt the quick excitement of one who is about to receive an anticipated gift.

She uncorked the vials, filled a glass with water and stood before the mirror, a tablet between her fingers. Suddenly she bowed graciously to her reflection, and raised the glass to it.

"Well, here's mud in your eye," she said.

The tablets were unpleasant to take, dry and powdery and sticking obstinately half-way down her throat. It took her a long time to swallow all twenty of them. She stood watching her reflection with deep, impersonal interest, studying the movements of the gulping throat. Once more she spoke aloud.

"For God's sake, try and cheer up by Thursday, will you?" she said. "Well, you know what he can do. He and the whole lot of them."

She had no idea how quickly to expect effect from the veronal. When she had taken the last tablet, she stood uncertainly, wondering, still with a courteous, vicarious interest, if death would strike her down then and there. She felt in no way strange, save for a slight stirring of sickness from the effort of swallowing the tablets, nor did her reflected face look at all different. It would not be immediate, then; it might even take an hour or so.

She stretched her arms high and gave a vast yawn.

"Guess I'll go to bed," she said. "Gee, I'm nearly dead."

That struck her as comic, and she turned out the bathroom light and went in and laid herself down in her bed, chuckling softly all the time.

"Gee, I'm nearly dead," she quoted. "That's a hot one!"

### III

Nettie, the colored maid, came in late the next afternoon to clean the apartment, and found Mrs. Morse in her bed. But then, that was not unusual. Usually, though, the sounds of cleaning waked her, and she did not like to wake up. Nettie, an agreeable girl, had learned to move softly about her work.

But when she had done the living-room and stolen in to tidy the little square bedroom, she could not avoid a tiny clatter as she arranged the objects on the dressing-table. Instinctively, she glanced over her shoulder at the sleeper, and without warning a sickly uneasiness crept over her. She came to the bed and stared down at the woman lying there.

Mrs. Morse lay on her back, one flabby, white arm flung up, the wrist against her forehead. Her stiff hair hung untenderly along her face. The bed covers were pushed down, exposing a deep square of soft neck and a pink nightgown, its fabric worn uneven by many launderings; her great breasts, freed from their tight confiner, sagged beneath her armpits. Now and then she made knotted, snoring sounds, and from the corner of her opened mouth to the blurred turn of her jaw ran a lane of crusted spittle.

"Mis' Morse," Nettie called. "Oh, Mis' Morse! It's terrible late."

Mrs. Morse made no move.

"Mis' Morse," said Nettie. "Look, Mis' Morse. How'm I goin' get this bed made?"

Panic sprang upon the girl. She shook the woman's hot shoulder.

"Ah, wake up, will yuh?" she whined. "Ah, please wake up."

Suddenly the girl turned and ran out in the hall to the elevator door, keeping her thumb firm on the black, shiny button until the elderly car and its Negro attendant stood before her. She poured a jumble of words over the boy, and led him back to the apartment. He tiptoed creakingly in to the bedside; first gingerly, then so lustily that he left marks in the soft flesh, he prodded the unconscious woman.

"Hey, there!" he cried, and listened intently, as for an echo.

"Jeez. Out like a light," he commented.

At his interest in the spectacle, Nettie's panic left her. Importance was big in both of them. They talked in quick, unfinished whispers, and it was the boy's suggestion that he fetch the young doctor who lived on the ground floor. Nettie hurried along with him. They looked forward to the limelit moment of breaking their news of something untoward, something pleasurably unpleasant. Mrs. Morse had become the medium of drama. With no ill wish to her, they hoped that her state was serious, that she would not let them down by being awake and normal on their return. A little fear of this determined them to make the most, to the doctor, of her present condition. "Matter of life and death," returned to Nettie from her thin store of reading. She considered startling the doctor with the phrase.

The doctor was in and none too pleased at interruption. He wore a yellow and blue striped dressing-gown, and he was lying on his sofa, laughing with a dark girl, her face scaly with inexpensive powder, who perched on the arm. Half-emptied highball glasses stood beside them, and her coat and hat were neatly hung up with the comfortable implication of a long stay.

Always something, the doctor grumbled. Couldn't let anybody alone after a hard day. But he put some bottles and instruments into a case, changed his dressing-gown for his coat and started out with the Negroes.

"Snap it up there, big boy," the girl called after him. "Don't be all night."

The doctor strode loudly into Mrs. Morse's flat and on to the bedroom, Nettie and the boy right behind him. Mrs. Morse had not moved; her sleep was as deep, but soundless, now. The doctor looked sharply at her, then plunged his thumbs into the lidded pits above her eyeballs and threw his weight upon them. A high, sickened cry broke from Nettie.

"Look like he tryin' to push her right on th'ough the bed," said the boy. He chuckled.

Mrs. Morse gave no sign under the pressure. Abruptly the doctor abandoned it, and with one quick movement swept the covers down to the foot of the bed. With another he flung her nightgown back and lifted the thick, white legs, cross-hatched with blocks of tiny, iris-colored veins. He pinched them repeatedly, with long, cruel nips, back of the knees. She did not awaken.

"What's she been drinking?" he asked Nettie, over his shoulder.

With the certain celerity of one who knows just where to lay hands on a thing, Nettie went into the bathroom, bound for the cupboard where Mrs. Morse kept her whisky. But she stopped at the sight of the two vials, with their red and white labels, lying before the mirror. She brought them to the doctor.

"Oh, for the Lord Almighty's sweet sake!" he said. He dropped Mrs. Morse's legs, and pushed them impatiently across the bed. "What did she want to go taking that tripe for? Rotten yellow trick, that's what a thing like that is. Now we'll have to pump her out, and all that stuff. Nuisance, a thing like that is; that's what it amounts to. Here, George, take me down in the elevator. You wait here, maid. She won't do anything."

"She won't die on me, will she?" cried Nettie.

"No," said the doctor. "God, no. You couldn't kill her with an ax."

## IV

After two days, Mrs. Morse came back to consciousness, dazed at first, then with a comprehension that brought with it the slow, saturating wretchedness.

"Oh, Lord, oh, Lord," she moaned, and tears for herself and for life striped her cheeks.

Nettie came in at the sound. For two days she had done the ugly, incessant tasks in the nursing of the unconscious, for two nights she had caught broken bits of sleep on the living-room couch. She looked coldly at the big, blown woman in the bed.

"What you been tryin' to do, Mis' Morse?" she said. "What kine o' work is that, takin' all that stuff?"

"Oh, Lord," moaned Mrs. Morse, again, and she tried to cover her eyes with her arms. But the joints felt stiff and brittle, and she cried out at their ache.

"Tha's no way to ack, takin' them pills," said Nettie. "You can thank you' stars you heah at all. How you feel now?"

"Oh, I feel great," said Mrs. Morse. "Swell, I feel."

Her hot, painful tears fell as if they would never stop.

"Tha's no way to take on, cryin' like that," Nettie said. "After what you done. The doctor, he says he could have you arrested, doin' a thing like that. He was fit to be tied, here."

"Why couldn't he let me alone?" wailed Mrs. Morse. "Why the hell couldn't he have?"

"Tha's terr'ble, Mis' Morse, swearin' an' talkin' like that," said Nettie, "after what people done for you. Here I ain' had no sleep at all for two nights, an' had to give up goin' out to my other ladies!"

"Oh, I'm sorry, Nettie," she said. "You're a peach. I'm sorry I've given you so much trouble. I couldn't help it. I just got sunk. Didn't you ever feel like doing it? When everything looks just lousy to you?"

"I wouldn' think o' no such thing," declared Nettie. "You got to cheer up. Tha's what you got to do. Everybody's got their troubles."

"Yeah," said Mrs. Morse. "I know."

"Come a pretty picture card for you," Nettie said. "Maybe that will cheer you up."

She handed Mrs. Morse a post-card. Mrs. Morse had to cover one eye with her hand, in order to read the message; her eyes were not yet focusing correctly.

It was from Art. On the back of a view of the Detroit Athletic Club he had written: "Greeting and salutations. Hope you have lost that gloom. Cheer up and don't take any rubber nickles. See you on Thursday."

She dropped the card to the floor. Misery crushed her as if she were between great smooth stones. There passed before her a slow, slow pageant of days spent lying in her flat, of evenings at Jimmy's being a good sport, making herself laugh and coo at Art and other Arts; she saw a long parade of weary horses and shivering beggars and all beaten, driven, stumbling things. Her feet throbbed as if she had crammed them into the stubby champagne-colored slippers. Her heart seemed to swell and harden.

"Nettie," she cried, "for heaven's sake pour me a drink, will you?"

The maid looked doubtful.

"Now you know, Mis' Morse," she said, "you been near daid. I don' know if the doctor he let you drink nothin' yet."

"Oh, never mind him," she said. "You get me one, and bring in the bottle. Take one yourself."

"Well," said Nettie.

She poured them each a drink, deferentially leaving hers in the bathroom to be taken in solitude, and brought Mrs. Morse's glass in to her.

Mrs. Morse looked into the liquor and shuddered back from its odor. Maybe it would help. Maybe, when you had been knocked cold for a few days, your very first drink would give you a lift. Maybe whisky would be her friend again. She prayed without addressing a God, without knowing a God. Oh, please, please, let her be able to get drunk, please keep her always drunk.

She lifted the glass.

"Thanks, Nettie," she said. "Here's mud in your eye."

The maid giggled. "Tha's the way, Mis' Morse," she said. "You cheer up, now."

"Yeah," said Mrs. Morse. "Sure."

# Luigi Pirandello

## (1867–1936)

Luigi Pirandello was born in Agrigento, Sicily, in 1867. Though his father wanted him to become a businessman, Pirandello attended the University of Bonn, Germany, where he received his doctoral degree in Roman philology in 1891. Upon returning to Rome, he began his career as a writer with the assistance of his family. His first novel, *The Outcast,* was published in 1893. The following year he published a collection of short stories, *Loves without Love* (1894), and agreed to marry Antonietta Portulano, whom he had never met. Pirandello's philosophical tales question the stability of reality and convey the unknowable, the illusive, and the unachievable. In 1898, Pirandello became a professor of Italian literature at a teacher's college for women, where he worked for the next twenty-four years. After the birth of their third child, Antonietta suffered a mental breakdown. Her condition worsened steadily, and she became insane with jealous paranoia. However, Pirandello refused to place her in an institution until 1919. His wife's illness greatly influenced his writing. In 1915, Pirandello concentrated on writing for the theater, and he wrote sixteen plays within a span of six years. His first notable critical success came in 1920 with *As Before, Better than Before.* He followed this with the plays *Six Characters in Search of an Author* and *Henry IV.* In 1923, Pirandello requested membership in the Fascist Party and obtained Mussolini's support in founding the National Art Theater of Rome, but his loyalty to the Fascist Party is subject to debate. Pirandello was awarded the Nobel Prize for literature in 1934.

## The Jar

1912

TRANSLATED BY ARTHUR AND HENRI MAYNE

The olive crop was a bumper one that year: the trees had flowered luxuriantly the year before, and, though there had been a long spell of misty weather at the time, the fruit had set well. Lollo Zirafa had a fine plantation on his farm at Primosole. Reckoning that the five old jars of glazed earthenware which he had in his wine-cellar would not suffice to hold all the oil of that harvest, he had placed an order well beforehand at Santo Stefano Di Camastra, where they are made. His new jar was to be of greater capacity—breast-high and pot-bellied; it would be the mother-superior to the little community of five other jars.

I need scarcely say that Don Lollo Zirafa had had a dispute with the potter concerning this jar. It would indeed be hard to name anyone with whom he had not picked a quarrel: for every trifle—be it merely a stone that had fallen from his boundary wall, or a handful of straw—he would shout out to the servants to saddle his mule, so that he could hurry to the town and file a suit. He had half-ruined himself, because of the large sums he had had to spend on court fees and lawyers' bills, bringing actions against one person after another, which always ended in his having to pay the costs of both sides. People said that his legal adviser grew so tired of seeing him appear two or three times a week that he tried to reduce the frequency of his visits by making him a present of a volume which looked like a prayer-book: it contained the judicial code—the idea being that he should take the trouble to see for himself what the rights and wrongs of the case were before hurrying to bring a suit.

Previously, when anyone had a difference with him, they would try to make him lose his temper by shouting out: "Saddle the mule!" but now they changed it to "Go and look up your pocket-code!" Don Lollo would reply: "That I will and I'll break the lot of you, you sons of bitches!"

In course of time, the new jar, for which he had paid the goodly sum of four florins, duly arrived; until room could be found for it in the wine-cellar, it was lodged in the crushing-shed for a few days. Never had there been a finer jar. It was quite distressing to see it lodged in that foul den, which reeked of stale grape-juice and had that musty smell of places deprived of light and air.

It was now two days since the harvesting of the olives had begun, and Don Lollo was almost beside himself, having to supervise not only the men who were beating down the fruit from the trees, but also a number of others who had come with mule-loads of manure to be deposited in heaps on the hill-side, where he had a field in which he was going to sow beans for the next crop. He felt that it was really more than one man could manage, he was at his wits' ends whom to attend to: cursing like a trooper, he vowed he would exterminate, first this man and then that, if an olive—one single olive—was missing: he almost talked as if he had counted them, one by one, on his trees; then he would turn to the muleteers and utter the direst threats as to what would happen, if any one heap of manure were not exactly the same size as the others. A little white cap on his head, his sleeves rolled up and his shirt open at the front, he rushed here, there and everywhere; his face was a bright red and poured with sweat, his eyes glared about him wolfishly, while his hands rubbed angrily at his shaven chin, where a fresh growth of beard always sprouted the moment the razor had left it.

At the close of the third day's work, three of the farm-hands—rough fellows with dirty, brutish faces—went to the crushing-shed; they had been beating the olive trees and went to replace their ladders and poles in the shed. They stood aghast at the sight of the fine new jar in two pieces, looking for all the world as if some one had caught hold of the bulging front and cut it off with a sharp sweep of the knife.

"Oh, my God! look! look!"

"How on earth has that happened?"

"My holy aunt! When Don Lollo hears of it! The new jar! What a pity, though!"

The first of the three, more frightened than his companions, proposed to shut the door again at once and to sneak away very quietly, leaving their ladders and poles outside leaning up against the wall; but the second took him up sharply.

"That's a stupid idea! You can't try that on Don Lollo. As like as not he'd believe we broke it ourselves. No, we all stay here!"

He went out of the shed and, using his hands as a trumpet, called out:—

"Don Lollo! Oh! Don LOLLOOOOO!"

When the farmer came up and saw the damage, he fell into a towering passion. First he vented his fury on the three men. He seized one of them by the throat, pinned him against the wall, and shouted:—

"By the Virgin's blood, you'll pay for that!"

The other two sprang forward in wild excitement, fell upon Don Lollo and pulled him away. Then his mad rage turned against himself: he stamped his feet, flung his cap on the ground, and slapped his cheeks, bewailing his loss with screams suited only for the death of a relation.

"The new jar! A four-florin jar! Brand new!"

Who could have broken it? Could it possibly have broken of itself? Certainly some one must have broken it, out of malice or from envy at his possession of such a beauty. But when? How? There was no sign of violence. Could it conceivably have come in a broken condition from the pottery? No, it rang like a bell on its arrival.

As soon as the farm-hands saw that their master's first outburst of rage was spent, they began to console him, saying that he should not take it so to heart, as the jar could be mended. After all, the break was not a bad one, for the front had come away all in one piece; a clever rivetter could repair it and make it as good as new. Zi' Dima Licasi was just the man for the job: he had invented a marvellous cement made of some composition which he kept a strict secret—miraculous stuff! Once it had set, you couldn't loosen it, even with a hammer. So they suggested that, if Don Lollo agreed, Zi' Dima Licasi should turn up at day-break and—as sure as eggs were eggs—the jar would be repaired and be even better than a new one.

For a long time Don Lollo turned a deaf ear to their advice—it was quite useless, there was no making good the damage—but in the end he allowed himself to be persuaded and punctually at day-break Zi' Dima Licasi arrived at Primosole, with his outfit in a basket slung on his back. He turned out to be a misshapen old man with swollen, crooked joints, like the stem of an ancient Saracen olive tree. To extract a word from him, it looked as if you would have to use a pair of forceps on his mouth. His ungraceful figure seemed to radiate discontent or gloom, due perhaps to his disappointment that no one had so far been found willing to do justice to his merits as an inventor. For Zi' Dima Licasi had not yet patented his discovery; he wanted to make a name for it first by its successful application. Meanwhile he felt it necessary to keep a sharp look-out, for fear lest some one steal the secret of his process.

"Let me see that cement of yours," began Don Lollo in a distrustful tone, after examining him from head to foot for several minutes.

Zi' Dima declined, with a dignified shake of the head.

"You'll see its results."

"But, will it hold?"

Zi' Dima put his basket on the ground and took out from it a red bundle composed of a large cotton handkerchief, much the worse for wear, wrapped round and round something. He began to unroll it very carefully, while they all stood round watching him with close attention. When at last, however, nothing came to light save a pair of spectacles with bridge and sides broken and tied up with string, there was a general laugh. Zi' Dima took no notice, but wiped his fingers before handling the spectacles, then put them on and, with much solemnity, began his examination of the jar, which had been brought outside on to the threshing-floor. Finally he said:

"It'll hold."

"But I can't trust cement alone," Don Lollo stipulated, "I must have rivets as well."

"I'm off," Zi' Dima promptly replied, standing up and replacing his basket on his back.

Don Lollo caught hold of his arm:—

"Off? Where to? You've got no more manners than a pig! . . . Just look at this pauper putting on an air of royalty! . . . Why! you wretched fool, I've got to put oil in that jar, and don't you know that oil oozes? Yards and yards to join together, and you talk of using cement alone! I want rivets—cement and rivets. It's for me to decide."

Zi' Dima shut his eyes, closed his lips tightly and shook his head. People were all like that—they refused to give him the satisfaction of turning out a neat bit of work, performed with artistic thoroughness and proving the wonderful virtues of his cement.

"If," he said, "the jar doesn't ring as true as a bell once more . . ."

"I won't listen to a word," Don Lollo broke in. "I want rivets! I'll pay you for cement and rivets. How much will it come to?"

"If I use cement only . . ."

"My God! what an obstinate fellow! What did I say? I told you I wanted rivets. We'll settle the terms after the work is done. I've no more time to waste on you."

And he went off to look after his men.

In a state of great indignation Zi' Dima started on the job and his temper continued to rise as he bored hole after hole in the jar and in its broken section—holes for his iron rivets. Along with the squeaking of his tool went a running accompaniment of grunts which grew steadily louder and more frequent; his fury made his eyes more piercing and bloodshot and his face became green with bile. When he had finished that first operation, he flung his borer angrily into the basket and held the detached portion up against the jar to satisfy himself that the holes were at equal distances and fitted one another; next he took his pliers and cut a length of iron wire into as many pieces as he needed rivets, and then called to one of the men who were beating the olive trees to come and help him.

"Cheer up, Zi' Dima!" said the labourer, seeing how upset the old man looked.

Zi' Dima raised his hand with a savage gesture. He opened the tin which contained the cement and held it up towards heaven, as if offering it to God, seeing that men refused to recognise its value. Then he began to spread it with his finger all round the detached portion and along the broken edge of the jar. Taking his pliers and the iron rivets he had prepared, he crept inside the open belly of the jar and instructed the farm-hand to hold the piece up, fitting it closely to the jar as he had himself done a short time previously. Before starting to put in the rivets, he spoke from inside the jar:—

"Pull! Pull! Tug at it with all your might! . . . You see it doesn't come loose. Curses on people who won't believe me! Knock it! Yes, knock it! . . . Doesn't it ring like a bell, even with me inside it? Go and tell your master that!"

"It's for the top-dog to give orders, Zi' Dima," said the man with a sigh, "and it's for the under-dog to carry them out. Put the rivets in. Put 'em in."

Zi' Dima began to pass the bits of iron through the adjacent holes, one on each side of the crack, twisting up the ends with his pliers. It took him an hour to put them all in, and he poured with sweat inside the jar. As he worked, he complained of his misfortune and the farm-hand stayed near, trying to console him.

"Now help me to get out," said Zi' Dima, when all was finished.

But large though its belly was, the jar had a distinctly narrow neck—a fact which Zi' Dima had overlooked, being so absorbed in his grievance. Now, try as he would, he could not manage to squeeze his way out. Instead of helping him, the farm-hand stood idly by, convulsed with laughter. So there was poor Zi' Dima, imprisoned in the jar which he had mended and—there was no use in blinking at the fact—in a jar which would have to be broken to let him out, and this time broken for good.

Hearing the laughter and shouts, Don Lollo came rushing up. Inside the jar Zi' Dima was spitting like an angry cat.

"Let me out," he screamed, "for God's sake! I want to get out! Be quick! Help!"

Don Lollo was quite taken aback and unable to believe his own ears.

"What? Inside there? He's rivetted himself up inside?"

Then he went up to the jar and shouted out to Zi' Dima:—

"Help you? What help do you think I can give you? You stupid old dodderer, what d'you mean by it? Why couldn't you measure it first? Come, have a try! Put an arm out . . . that's it! Now the head! Up you come! . . . No, no, gently! . . . Down again. . . . Wait a bit! . . . Not that way. . . . Down, get down. . . . How on earth could you do such a thing? . . . What about my jar now? . . .

"Keep calm! Keep calm!" he recommended to all the onlookers, as if it was they who were becoming excited and not himself. . . . "My head's going round! Keep calm! This is quite a new point! Get me my mule!"

He rapped the jar with his knuckles. Yes, it really rang like a bell once again.

"Fine! Repaired as good as new. . . . You wait a bit!" he said to the prisoner; then instructed his man to be off and saddle the mule. He rubbed his forehead vigorously with his fingers, and continued:—

"I wonder what's the best course. That's not a jar, it's a contrivance of the devil himself. . . . Keep still! Keep still!" he exclaimed, rushing up to steady the jar, in which Zi' Dima, now in a towering passion, was struggling like a wild animal in a trap.

"It's a new point, my good man, which the lawyer must settle. I can't rely on my own judgment. . . . Where's that mule? Hurry up with the mule! . . . I'll go straight there and back. You must wait patiently: it's in your own interest. . . . Meanwhile, keep quiet, be calm! I must look after my own rights. And, first of all, to put myself in the right, I fulfil my obligation. Here you are! I am paying you for your work, for a whole day's work. Here are your five lire. Is that enough?"

"I don't want anything," shouted Zi' Dima. "I want to get out!"

"You shall get out, but meanwhile I, for my part, am paying you. There they are—five lire."

He took the money out of his waistcoat pocket and tossed it into the jar, then enquired in a tone of great concern:—

"Have you had any lunch? . . . Bread and something to eat with it, at once! . . . What! You don't want it? Well, then, throw it to the dogs! I shall have done my duty when I've given it to you."

Having ordered the food, he mounted and set out for the town. His wild gesticulations made those who saw him galloping past think that he might well be hastening to shut himself up in a lunatic asylum.

As luck would have it, he did not have to spend much time in the ante-room before being admitted to the lawyer's study; he had, however, to wait a long while before the lawyer could finish laughing, after the matter had been related to him. Annoyed at the amusement he caused, Don Lollo said irritably:—

"Excuse me, but I don't see anything to laugh at. It's all very well for your Honour, who is not the sufferer, but the jar is my property."

The lawyer, however, continued to laugh and then made him tell the story all over again, just as it had happened, so that he could raise another laugh out of it.

"Inside, eh? So he'd rivetted himself inside?" And what did Don Lollo want to do? . . . "To ke . . . to ke . . . keep him there inside—ha! ha! ha! . . . keep him there inside, so as not to lose the jar?"

"Why should I lose it?" cried Don Lollo, clenching his fists. "Why should I put up with the loss of my money, and have people laughing at me?"

"But don't you know what that's called?" said the lawyer at last. "It's called 'wrongful confinement'."

"Confinement? Well, who's confined him? He's confined himself! What fault is that of mine?"

The lawyer then explained to him that the matter gave rise to two cases: on the one hand he, Don Lollo, must straightway liberate the prisoner, if he wished to escape from being prosecuted for wrongful confinement; while, on the other hand, the rivetter would be responsible for making good the loss resulting from his lack of skill or his stupidity.

"Ah!" said Don Lollo, with a sigh of relief. "So he'll have to pay me for my jar?"

"Wait a bit," remarked the lawyer. "Not as if it were a new jar, remember!"

"Why not?"

"Because it was a broken one, badly broken, too."

"Broken! No, Sir. Not broken. It's perfectly sound now and better than ever it was—he says so himself. And if I have to break it again, I shall not be able to have it mended. The jar will be ruined, Sir!"

The lawyer assured him that that point would be taken into account and that the rivetter would have to pay the value which the jar had in its present condition.

"Therefore," he counselled, "get the man himself to give you an estimate of its value first."

"I kiss your hands," Don Lollo murmured, and hurried away.

On his return home towards evening, he found all his labourers engaged in a celebration around the inhabited jar. The watch-dogs joined in the festivities with joyous barks and capers. Zi' Dima had not only calmed down, but had even come to
enjoy his curious adventure and was able to laugh at it, with the melancholy humour
of the unfortunate.

Don Lollo drove them all aside and bent down to look into the jar.

"Hallo! Getting along well?"

"Splendid! An open-air life for me!" replied the man. "It's better than in my
own house."

"I'm glad to hear it. Meanwhile I'd just like you to know that that jar cost me four
florins when it was new. How much do you think it is worth now?"

"With me inside it?" asked Zi' Dima.

The rustics laughed.

"Silence!" shouted Don Lollo. "Either your cement is of some use or it is of no
use. There is no third possibility. If it is of no use, you are a fraud. If it is of some use,
the jar, in its present condition, must have a value. What is that value? I ask for your
estimate."

After a space for reflection, Zi' Dima said:—

"Here is my answer: if you had let me mend it with cement only—as I wanted to
do—first of all I should not have been shut up inside it and the jar would have had
its original value, without any doubt. But spoilt by these rivets, which had to be
done from inside, it has lost most of its value. It's worth a third of its former price,
more or less."

"One-third? That's one florin, thirty-three cents."

"Maybe less, but not more than that."

"Well," said Don Lollo. "Promise me that you'll pay me one florin thirty-
three cents."

"What?" asked Zi' Dima, as if he did not grasp the point.

"I will break the jar to let you out," replied Don Lollo. "And—the lawyer tells
me—you are to pay me its value according to your own estimate—one florin
thirty-three."

"I? Pay?" laughed Zi' Dima, "I'd sooner stay here till I rot!"

With some difficulty he managed to extract from his pocket a short and peculiarly foul pipe and lighted it, puffing out the smoke through the neck of the jar.

Don Lollo stood there scowling: the possibility that Zi' Dima would no longer be
willing to leave the jar, had not been foreseen either by himself or by the lawyer. What
step should he take now? He was on the point of ordering them to saddle the mule,
but reflected that it was already evening.

"Oh ho!" he said. "So you want to take up your abode in my jar! I call upon all
you men as witnesses to his statement. He refuses to come out, in order to escape
from paying. I am quite prepared to break it. Well, as you insist on staying there, I
shall take proceedings against you tomorrow for unlawful occupancy of the jar and
for preventing me from my rightful use of it."

Zi' Dima blew out another puff of smoke and answered calmly:—

"No, your Honour. I don't want to prevent you at all. Do you think I am here because I like it? Let me out and I'll go away gladly enough. But as for paying, I wouldn't dream of it, your Honour."

In a sudden access of fury Don Lollo made to give a kick at the jar but stopped in time. Instead he seized it with both hands and shook it violently, uttering a hoarse growl.

"You see what fine cement it is," Zi' Dima remarked from inside.

"You rascal!" roared Don Lollo. "Whose fault is it, yours or mine? You expect me to pay for it, do you? You can starve to death inside first. We'll see who'll win."

He went away, forgetting all about the five lire which he had tossed into the jar that morning. But the first thing Zi' Dima thought of doing was to spend that money in having a festive evening, in company with the farm-hands, who had been delayed in their work by that strange accident, and had decided to spend the night at the farm, in the open air, sleeping on the threshing-floor. One of them went to a neighbouring tavern to make the necessary purchases. The moon was so bright that it seemed almost day—a splendid night for their carousal.

Many hours later Don Lollo was awakened by an infernal din. Looking out from the farm-house balcony, he could see in the moonlight what looked like a gang of devils on his threshing-floor: his men, all roaring drunk, were holding hands and performing a dance round the jar, while Zi' Dima, inside it, was singing at the top of his voice.

This time Don Lollo could not restrain himself, but rushed down like a mad bull and, before they could stop him, gave the jar a push which started it rolling down the slope. It continued on its course, to the delight of the intoxicated company, until it hit an olive tree and cracked in pieces, leaving Zi' Dima the winner in the dispute.

# Katherine Ann Porter

## (1890–1980)

Katherine Ann Porter called herself the "grandchild" of the Civil War. At the peak of her career, while living in Washington, D.C., she dined regularly with President Lyndon B. Johnson as the figurehead of the American literary world. She was born in Texas, the setting for her story "The Jilting of Granny Weatherall," and educated in Louisiana convent schools, from which she ran away to get married at age sixteen. She worked as a singer and bit player in the movies and made a foray into teaching. By age nineteen, Porter was divorced and living in Colorado, where she worked as a reporter for the *Rocky Mountain News* and almost died during the flu epidemic of 1918. This near-death experience gave her the idea for her pre–World War I story, "Pale Horse, Pale Rider," later published as a trilogy in 1939 along with "Noon Wine" and "Old Mortality." Porter continued to travel, writing "Flowering Judas" after becoming involved in the Mexican Obregon Revolution, and "The Leaning Tower" after observing firsthand the tensions of pre-Nazi Germany. A cruise Porter embarked upon from Vera Cruz, Mexico, to Germany was to serve as the partial basis for her 1962 novel, *Ship of Fools,* also inspired by the fifteenth-century allegory of the same name. During the 1930s, Porter lived in Paris with her third husband. Her anthology *The Collected Stories of Katherine Ann Porter* won the 1966 Pulitzer Prize. In 1977, she published *The Never-Ending Wrong,* an autobiographical record of her involvement in the 1927 protests of the Sacco-Vanzetti executions.

Porter continued the realist tradition of earlier American writers, creating mythologies of southern life and, as Jane Krause DeMouy writes, "offer[ing] feminine examples of the lone American Adam . . . facing adversity with grace and courage . . . alone." Porter believed art to be the enduring and redemptive ultimate reality of life. Her own art garnered the acclaim of such writers as Eudora Welty, Robert Penn Warren, and Cleanth Brooks; her writing was called "irony with a center."

---

# Theft                                                    1935

She had the purse in her hand when she came in. Standing in the middle of the floor, holding her bathrobe around her and trailing a damp towel in one hand, she surveyed the immediate past and remembered everything clearly. Yes, she had opened the flap and spread it out on the bench after she had dried the purse with her handkerchief.

She had intended to take the Elevated, and naturally she looked in her purse to make certain she had the fare, and was pleased to find forty cents in the coin envelope. She was going to pay her own fare, too, even if Camilo did have the habit of seeing her up the steps and dropping a nickel in the machine before he gave the turnstile a little push and sent her through it with a bow. Camilo by a series of compromises had managed to make effective a fairly complete set of small courtesies, ignoring the larger and more troublesome ones. She had walked with him to the station in a pouring rain, because she knew he was almost as poor as she was, and when he insisted on a taxi, she was firm and said, "You know it simply will not do." He was wearing a new hat of a pretty biscuit shade, for it never occurred to him to buy anything of a practical color; he had put it on for the first time and the rain was spoiling it. She kept thinking, "But this is dreadful, where will he get another?" She compared it with Eddie's hats that always seemed to be precisely seven years old and as if they had been quite purposely left out in the rain, and yet they sat with a careless and incidental rightness on Eddie. But Camilo was far different; if he wore a shabby hat it would be merely shabby on him, and he would lose his spirits over it. If she had not feared Camilo would take it badly, for he insisted on the practice of his little ceremonies up to the point he had fixed for them, she would have said to him as they left Thora's house, "Do go home. I can surely reach the station by myself."

"It is written that we must be rained upon tonight," said Camilo, "so let it be together."

At the foot of the platform stairway she staggered slightly—they were both nicely set up on Thora's cocktails—and said: "At least, Camilo, do me the favor not to climb these stairs in your present state, since for you it is only a matter of coming down again at once, and you'll certainly break your neck."

He made three quick bows, he was Spanish, and leaped off through the rainy darkness. She stood watching him, for he was a very graceful young man, thinking that tomorrow morning he would gaze soberly at his spoiled hat and soggy shoes and possibly associate her with his misery. As she watched, he stopped at the far corner and took off his hat and hid it under his overcoat. She felt she had betrayed him by seeing, because he would have been humiliated if he thought she even suspected him of trying to save his hat.

Roger's voice sounded over her shoulder above the clang of the rain falling on the stairway shed, wanting to know what she was doing out in the rain at this time of night, and did she take herself for a duck? His long, imperturbable face was streaming with water, and he tapped a bulging spot on the breast of his buttoned-up overcoat: "Hat," he said. "Come on, let's take a taxi."

She settled back against Roger's arm which he laid around her shoulders, and with the gesture they exchanged a glance full of long amiable associations, then she looked through the window at the rain changing the shapes of everything, and the colors. The taxi dodged in and out between the pillars of the Elevated, skidding slightly on every curve, and she said: "The more it skids the calmer I feel, so I really must be drunk."

"You must be," said Roger. "This bird is a homicidal maniac, and I could do with a cocktail myself this minute."

They waited on the traffic at Fortieth Street and Sixth Avenue, and three boys walked before the nose of the taxi. Under the globes of light they were cheerful scarecrows, all very thin and all wearing very seedy snappy-cut suits and gay neckties. They were not very sober either, and they stood for a moment wobbling in front of the car, and there was an argument going on among them. They leaned toward each other as if they were getting ready to sing, and the first one said: "When I get married it won't be jus' for getting married, I'm gonna marry for *love*, see?" and the second one said, "Aw, gwan and tell that stuff to *her*, why n't yuh?" and the third one gave a kind of hoot, and said, "Hell, dis guy? Wot the hell's he got?" and the first one said: "Aaah, shurrup yuh mush, I got plenty." Then they all squealed and scrambled across the street beating the first one on the back and pushing him around.

"Nuts," commented Roger, "pure nuts."

Two girls went skittering by in short transparent raincoats, one green, one red, their heads tucked against the drive of the rain. One of them was saying to the other, "Yes, I know all about *that*. But what about me? You're always so sorry for *him* . . ." and they ran on with their little pelican legs flashing back and forth.

The taxi backed up suddenly and leaped forward again, and after a while Roger said: "I had a letter from Stella today, and she'll be home on the twenty-sixth, so I suppose she's made up her mind and it's all settled."

"I had a sort of letter today too," she said, "making up my mind for me. I think it is time for you and Stella to do something definite."

When the taxi stopped on the corner of West Fifty-third Street, Roger said, "I've just enough if you'll add ten cents," so she opened her purse and gave him a dime, and he said, "That's beautiful, that purse."

"It's a birthday present," she told him, "and I like it. How's your show coming?"

"Oh, still hanging on, I guess. I don't go near the place. Nothing sold yet. I mean to keep right on the way I'm going and they can take it or leave it. I'm through with the argument."

"It's absolutely a matter of holding out, isn't it?"

"Holding out's the tough part."

"Good night, Roger."

"Good night, you should take aspirin and push yourself into a tub of hot water, you look as though you're catching cold."

"I will."

With the purse under her arm she went upstairs, and on the first landing Bill heard her step and poked his head out with his hair tumbled and his eyes red, and he said: "For Christ's sake, come in and have a drink with me. I've had some bad news."

"You're perfectly sopping," said Bill, looking at her drenched feet. They had two drinks, while Bill told her how the director had thrown his play out after the cast had been picked over twice, and had gone through three rehearsals. "I said to him, 'I didn't say it was a masterpiece, I said it would make a good show.' And he said, 'It just doesn't *play,* do you see? It needs a doctor.' So I'm stuck, absolutely stuck," said Bill, on the edge of weeping again. "I've been crying," he told her, "in my cups." And he went on to ask her if she realized his wife was ruining him with her extravagance. "I send her ten dollars every week of my unhappy life, and I don't really have to. She threatens to jail me if I don't, but she can't do it. God, let her try it after the way she treated me! She's no right to alimony and she knows it. She keeps on saying she's got to have it for the baby and I keep on sending it because I can't bear to see anybody suffer. So I'm way behind on the piano and the victrola, both—"

"Well, this is a pretty rug, anyhow," she said.

Bill stared at it and blew his nose. "I got it at Ricci's for ninety-five dollars," he said. "Ricci told me it once belonged to Marie Dressler, and cost fifteen hundred dollars, but there's a burnt place on it, under the divan. Can you beat that?"

"No," she said. She was thinking about her empty purse and that she could not possibly expect a check for her latest review for another three days, and her arrangement with the basement restaurant could not last much longer if she did not pay something on account. "It's no time to speak of it," she said, "but I've been hoping you would have by now that fifty dollars you promised for my scene in the third act. Even if it doesn't play. You were to pay me for the work anyhow out of your advance."

"Weeping Jesus," said Bill, "you, too?" He gave a loud sob, or hiccough, in his moist handkerchief. "Your stuff was no better than mine, after all. Think of that."

"But you got something for it," she said. "Seven hundred dollars."

Bill said, "Do me a favor, will you? Have another drink and forget about it. I can't, you know I can't, I would if I could, but you know the fix I'm in."

"Let it go, then," she found herself saying almost in spite of herself. She had meant to be quite firm about it. They drank again without speaking, and she went to her apartment on the floor above.

There, she now remembered distinctly, she had taken the letter out of the purse before she spread the purse out to dry.

She had sat down and read the letter over again: but there were phrases that insisted on being read many times, they had a life of their own separate from the others, and when she tried to read past and around them, they moved with the movement of her eyes, and she could not escape them . . . "thinking about you more than I mean to . . . yes, I even talk about you . . . why were you so anxious to destroy . . . even if I could see you now I would not . . . not worth all this abominable . . . the end . . ."

Carefully she tore the letter into narrow strips and touched a lighted match to them in the coal grate.

Early the next morning she was in the bathtub when the janitress knocked and then came in, calling out that she wished to examine the radiators before she started the furnace going for the winter. After moving about the room for a few minutes, the janitress went out, closing the door very sharply.

She came out of the bathroom to get a cigarette from the package in the purse. The purse was gone. She dressed and made coffee, and sat by the window while she drank it. Certainly the janitress had taken the purse, and certainly it would be impossible to get it back without a great deal of ridiculous excitement. Then let it go. With this decision of her mind, there rose coincidentally in her blood a deep almost murderous anger. She set the cup carefully in the center of the table, and walked steadily downstairs, three long flights and a short hall and a steep short flight into the basement, where the janitress, her face streaked with coal dust, was shaking up the furnace. "Will you please give me back my purse? There isn't any money in it. It was a present, and I don't want to lose it."

The janitress turned without straightening up and peered at her with hot flickering eyes, a red light from the furnace reflected in them. "What do you mean, your purse?"

"The gold cloth purse you took from the wooden bench in my room," she said. "I must have it back."

"Before God I never laid eyes on your purse, and that's the holy truth," said the janitress.

"Oh, well then, keep it," she said, but in a very bitter voice; "keep it if you want it so much." And she walked away.

She remembered how she had never locked a door in her life, on some principle of rejection in her that made her uncomfortable in the ownership of things, and her paradoxical boast before the warnings of her friends, that she had never lost a penny by theft; and she had been pleased with the bleak humility of this concrete example designed to illustrate and justify a certain fixed, otherwise baseless and general faith which ordered the movements of her life without regard to her will in the matter.

In this moment she felt that she had been robbed of an enormous number of valuable things, whether material or intangible: things lost or broken by her own fault, things she had forgotten and left in houses when she moved: books borrowed from her and not returned, journeys she had planned and had not made, words she had waited to hear spoken to her and had not heard, and the words she had meant to answer with; bitter alternatives and intolerable substitutes worse than nothing, and yet inescapable: the long patient suffering of dying friendships and the dark inexplicable death of love—all that she had had, and all that she had missed, were lost together, and were twice lost in this landslide of remembered losses.

The janitress was following her upstairs with the purse in her hand and the same deep red fire flickering in her eyes. The janitress thrust the purse towards her while they were still a half dozen steps apart, and said: "Don't never tell on me. I musta been crazy. I get crazy in the head sometimes, I swear I do. My son can tell you."

She took the purse after a moment, and the janitress went on: "I got a niece who is going on seventeen, and she's a nice girl and I thought I'd give it to her. She needs a pretty purse. I musta been crazy; I thought maybe you wouldn't mind, you leave things around and don't seem to notice much."

She said: "I missed this because it was a present to me from someone . . ."

The janitress said: "He'd get you another if you lost this one. My niece is young and needs pretty things, we oughta give the young ones a chance. She's got young men after her maybe will want to marry her. She oughta have nice things. She needs them bad right now. You're a grown woman, you've had your chance, you ought to know how it is!"

She held the purse out to the janitress saying: "You don't know what you're talking about. Here, take it, I've changed my mind. I really don't want it."

The janitress looked up at her with hatred and said: "I don't want it either now. My niece is young and pretty, she don't need fixin' up to be pretty, she's young and pretty anyhow! I guess you need it worse than she does!"

"It wasn't really yours in the first place," she said, turning away. "You mustn't talk as if I had stolen it from you."

"It's not from me, it's from her you're stealing it," said the janitress, and went back downstairs.

She laid the purse on the table and sat down with the cup of chilled coffee, and thought: I was right not to be afraid of any thief but myself, who will end by leaving me nothing.

# Jean-Paul Sartre

## (1905–1980)

French novelist Jean-Paul Sartre was born in Paris in 1905. His maternal grandfather, Charles Schweitzer, was the uncle of celebrated medical missionary Albert Schweitzer. Sartre's father died young, and his mother and grandfather raised him. He graduated from the École Normale Supérieure in 1929, where he studied philosophy. During his education, Sartre met author and philosopher Simone de Beauvoir, with whom he would have a lifelong relationship. He also became acquainted with Raymond Aron, Simone Weil, Maurice Merlasu-Ponty, and Claude Lévi-Strauss. In 1933 he traveled to Berlin to study phenomenology and attended lectures given by Edmund Husserl. His first novel, *Nausea*, was published in 1938. Sartre was a proponent of an existentialist philosophy based on a recognition of human freedom and thus responsibility for human actions. His stories embody this philosophy in characters burdened by questions of meaninglessness and infinite choices.

In 1939 Sartre was inducted into the French military, and in 1940 he was captured by Nazis and imprisoned. After his release in 1941, he became active in the French resistance and wrote the antiauthoritarian play *The Flies* (1943) and also published *Being and Nothingness* (1943). In 1945 he founded the political and literary magazine *Les Temps modernes*. After World War II, Sartre moved away from his own philosophy and more toward Marxism. He rejected the Nobel Prize in literature in 1964, explaining that to accept such an award would compromise his integrity as a writer. He died in 1980. Sartre's ashes were buried at the Montparnasse Cemetery. Later, Simone de Beauvoir's ashes were buried next to his.

---

## The Room                                                                      1938

TRANSLATED BY LLOYD ALEXANDER

## I

**M**me. Darbedat held a *rahat-loukoum* between her fingers. She brought it carefully to her lips and held her breath, afraid that the fine dust of sugar that powdered it would blow away. "Just right," she told herself. She bit quickly into its glassy flesh and a scent of stagnation filled her mouth. "Odd how illness sharpens the sensations." She began to think of mosques, of obsequious Orientals (she had been to Algeria for her honeymoon) and her pale lips started in a smile: the *rahat-loukoum* was obsequious too.

Several times she had to pass the palm of her hand over the pages of her book, for in spite of the precaution she had taken they were covered with a thin coat of white powder. Her hand made the little grains of sugar slide and roll, grating on the smooth paper: "That makes me think of Arcachon, when I used to read on the beach." She had spent the summer of 1907 at the seashore. Then she wore a big straw hat with a green ribbon; she sat close to the jetty, with a novel by Gyp or Colette Yver. The wind made swirls of sand rain down upon her knees, and from time to time she had to shake the book, holding it by the corners. It was the same sensation: only the grains of sand were dry while the small bits of sugar stuck a little to the ends of her fingers. Again she saw a band of pearl gray sky above a black sea. "Eve wasn't born yet." She felt herself all weighted down with memories and precious as a coffer of sandalwood. The name of the book she used to read suddenly came back to mind: it was called *Petite Madame,* not at all boring. But ever since an unknown illness had confined her to her room she preferred memories and historical works.

She hoped that suffering, heavy readings, a vigilant attention to her memories and the most exquisite sensations would ripen her as a lovely hothouse fruit.

She thought, with some annoyance, that her husband would soon be knocking at her door. On other days of the week he came only in the evening, kissed her brow in silence and read *Le Temps,* sitting in the armchair across from her. But Thursday was M. Darbedat's *day:* he spent an hour with his daughter, generally from three to four. Before going he stopped in to see his wife and both discussed their son-in-law with bitterness. These Thursday conversations, predictable to their slightest detail, exhausted Mme. Darbedat. M. Darbedat filled the quiet room with his presence. He never sat, but walked in circles about the room. Each of his outbursts wounded Mme. Darbedat like a glass splintering. This particular Thursday was worse than usual: at the thought that it would soon be necessary to repeat Eve's confessions to her husband, and to see his great terrifying body convulse with fury, Mme. Darbedat broke out in a sweat. She picked up a *loukoum* from the saucer, studied it for a while with hesitation, then sadly set it down: she did not like her husband to see her eating *loukoums.*

She heard a knock and started up. "Come in," she said weakly.

M. Darbedat entered on tiptoe. "I'm going to see Eve," he said, as he did every Thursday. Mme. Darbedat smiled at him. "Give her a kiss for me."

M. Darbedat did not answer and his forehead wrinkled worriedly: every Thursday at the same time a muffled irritation mingled with the load of his digestion. "I'll stop in and see Franchot after leaving her, I wish he'd talk to her seriously and try to convince her."

He made frequent visits to Dr. Franchot. But in vain. Mme. Darbedat raised her eyebrows. Before, when she was well, she shrugged her shoulders. But since sickness had weighted down her body, she replaced the gestures which would have tired her by plays of emotion in the face: she said *yes* with her eyes, *no* with the corners of her mouth: she raised her eyebrows instead of her shoulders.

"There should be some way to take him away from her by force."

"I told you already it was impossible. And besides, the law is very poorly drawn up. Only the other day Franchot was telling me that they have a tremendous amount of trouble with the families: people who can't make up their mind, who want to keep the patient at home; the doctors' hands are tied. They can give their advice, period. That's all. He would," he went on, "have to make a public scandal or else she would have to ask to have him put away herself."

"And that," said Mme. Darbedat, "isn't going to happen tomorrow."

"No." He turned to the mirror and began to comb his fingers through his beard. Mme. Darbedat looked at the powerful red neck of her husband without affection.

"If she keeps on," said M. Darbedat, "she'll be crazier than he is. It's terribly unhealthy. She doesn't leave his side, she only goes out to see you. She has no visitors.

The air in their room is simply unbreathable. She never opens the window because Pierre doesn't want it open. As if you should ask a sick man. I believe they burn incense, some rubbish in a little pan, you'd think it was a church. Really, sometimes I wonder . . . she's got a funny look in her eyes, you know."

"I haven't noticed," Mme. Darbedat said. "I find her quite normal. She looks sad, obviously."

"She has a face like an unburied corpse. Does she sleep? Does she eat? But we aren't supposed to ask her about those things. But I should think that with a fellow like Pierre next to her, she wouldn't sleep a wink all night." He shrugged his shoulders. "What I find amazing is that we, her parents, don't have the right to protect her against herself. Understand that Pierre would be much better cared for by Franchot. There's a big park. And besides, I think," he added, smiling a little, "he'd get along much better with people of his own type. People like that are children, you have to leave them alone with each other; they form a sort of freemasonry. That's where he should have been put the first day and for his own good, I'd say. Of course it's in his own best interest."

After a moment, he added, "I tell you I don't like to know she's alone with Pierre, especially at night. Suppose something happened. Pierre has a very sly way about him."

"I don't know," Mme. Darbedat said, "if there's any reason to worry. He always looked like that. He always seemed to be making fun of the world. Poor boy," she sighed, "to have had his pride and then come to that. He thought he was cleverer than all of us. He had a way of saying 'You're right' simply to end the argument. . . . It's a blessing for him that he can't see the state he's in."

She recalled with displeasure the long, ironic face, always turned a little to the side. During the first days of Eve's marriage, Mme. Darbedat asked nothing more than a little intimacy with her son-in-law. But he had discouraged her: he almost never spoke, he always agreed quickly and absent-mindedly.

M. Darbedat pursued his idea. "Franchot let me visit his place," he said. "It was magnificent. The patients have private rooms with leather armchairs, if you please, and day-beds. You know, they have a tennis court and they're going to build a swimming pool."

He was planted before the window, looking out, rocking a little on his bent legs. Suddenly he turned lithely on his heel, shoulders lowered, hands in his pockets. Mme. Darbedat felt she was going to start perspiring: it was the same thing every time: now he was pacing back and forth like a bear in a cage and his shoes squeaked at every step.

"Please, please won't you sit down. You're tiring me." Hesitating, she added, "I have something important to tell you."

M. Darbedat sat in the armchair and put his hands on his knees; a slight chill ran up Mme. Darbedat's spine: the time had come, she had to speak.

"You know," she said with an embarrassed cough, "I saw Eve on Tuesday."

"Yes."

"We talked about a lot of things, she was very nice, she hasn't been so confiding for a long time. Then I questioned her a little, I got her to talk about Pierre. Well, I found out," she added, again embarrassed, "that she is *very* attached to him."

"I know that too damned well," said M. Darbedat.

He irritated Mme. Darbedat a little: she always had to explain things in such detail. Mme. Darbedat dreamed of living in the company of fine and sensitive people who would understand her slightest word.

"But I mean," she went on, "that she is attached to him *differently* than we imagined."

M. Darbedat rolled furious, anxious eyes, as he always did when he never completely grasped the sense of an allusion or something new.

"What does that all mean?"

"Charles," said Mme. Darbedat, "don't tire me. You should understand a mother has difficulty in telling certain things."

"I don't understand a damned word of anything you say," M. Darbedat said with irritation. "You can't mean . . ."

"Yes," she said.

"They're still . . . now, still . . . ?"

"Yes! Yes! Yes!" she said, in three annoyed and dry little jolts.

M. Darbedat spread his arms, lowered his head and was silent.

"Charles," his wife said, worriedly, "I shouldn't have told you. But I couldn't keep it to myself."

"Our child," he said slowly. "With this madman! He doesn't even recognize her any more. He called her Agatha. She must have lost all sense of her own dignity."

He raised his head and looked at his wife severely. "You're sure you aren't mistaken?"

"No possible doubt. Like you," she added quickly, "I couldn't believe her and I still can't. The mere idea of being touched by that wretch . . . So . . ." she sighed, "I suppose that's how he holds on to her."

"Do you remember what I told you," M. Darbedat said, "when he came to ask for her hand? I told you I thought he pleased Eve *too much*. You wouldn't believe me." He struck the table suddenly, blushing violently. "It's perversity! He takes her in his arms, kisses her and calls her Agatha, selling her on a lot of nonsense about flying statues and God knows what else! Without a word from her! But what in heaven's name's between those two? Let her be sorry for him, let her put him in a sanitorium and see him every day—fine. But I never thought . . . I considered her a widow. Listen, Jeannette," he said gravely, "I'm going to speak frankly to you; if she had any sense, I'd rather see her take a lover!"

"Be quiet, Charles!" Mme. Darbedat cried.

M. Darbedat wearily took his hat and the cane he had left on the stool. "After what you've just told me," he concluded, "I don't have much hope left. In any case, I'll have a talk with her because it's my duty."

Mme. Darbedat wished he would go quickly.

"You know," she said to encourage him, "I think Eve is more headstrong than . . . than anything. She knows he's incurable but she's obstinate, she doesn't want to be in the wrong."

M. Darbedat stroked his beard absently.

"Headstrong? Maybe so. If you're right, she'll finally get tired of it. He's not always pleasant and he doesn't have much to say. When I say hello to him he gives me a flabby handshake and doesn't say a word. As soon as they're alone, I think they go back to his obsessions: she tells me sometimes he screams as though his throat were being cut because of his hallucinations. He sees statues. They frighten him because they buzz. He says they fly around and make fishy eyes at him."

He put on his gloves and continued, "She'll get tired of it, I'm not saying she won't. But suppose she goes crazy before that? I wish she'd go out a little, see the world: she'd meet some nice young man—well, someone like Schroeder, an engineer with Simplon, somebody with a future, she could see him a little here and there and she'd get used to the idea of making a new life for herself."

Mme. Darbedat did not answer, afraid of starting the conversation up again. Her husband bent over her.

"So," he said, "I've got to be on my way."

"Good-by, Papa," Mme. Darbedat said, lifting her forehead up to him. "Kiss her for me and tell her for me she's a poor dear."

Once her husband had gone, Mme. Darbedat let herself drift to the bottom of her armchair and closed her eyes, exhausted. "What vitality," she thought reproachfully. As soon as she got a little strength back, she quietly stretched out her pale hand and took a *loukoum* from the saucer, groping for it without opening her eyes.

Eve lived with her husband on the sixth floor of an old building on the Rue du Bac. M. Darbedat slowly climbed the 112 steps of the stairway. He was not even out of breath when he pushed the bell. He remembered with satisfaction the words of Mlle. Dormoy: "Charles, for your age, you're simply marvelous." Never did he feel himself stronger and healthier than on Thursday, especially after these invigorating climbs.

Eve opened the door: that's right, she doesn't have a maid. No girls *can* stay with her. I can put myself in their place. He kissed her. "Hello, poor darling."

Eve greeted him with a certain coldness.

"You look a little pale," M. Darbedat said, touching her cheek. "You don't get enough exercise."

There was a moment of silence.

"Is Mamma well?" Eve asked.

"Not good, not too bad. You saw her Tuesday? Well, she's just the same. Your Aunt Louise came to see her yesterday, that pleased her. She likes to have visitors, but they can't stay too long. Aunt Louise came to Paris for that mortgage business. I think I told you about it, a very odd sort of affair. She stopped in at the office to ask my advice. I told her there was only one thing to do: sell. She found a taker, by the way: Bretonnel. You remember Bretonnel. He's retired from business now."

He stopped suddenly: Eve was hardly listening. He thought sadly that nothing interested her any more. It's like the books. Before you had to tear them away from her. Now she doesn't even read any more.

"How is Pierre?"

"Well," Eve said. "Do you want to see him?"

"Of course," M. Darbedat said gaily, "I'd like to pay him a little call."

He was full of compassion for this poor young man, but he could not see him without repugnance. *I detest unhealthy people.* Obviously, it was not Pierre's fault: his heredity was terribly loaded down. M. Darbedat sighed: *All the precautions are taken in vain, you find out those things too late.* No, Pierre was not responsible. But still he had always carried that fault in him; it formed the base of his character; it wasn't like cancer or tuberculosis, something you could always put aside when you wanted to judge a man as he is. His nervous grace, the subtlety which pleased Eve so much when he was courting her were the flowers of madness. He was already mad when he married her only you couldn't tell.

*It makes you wonder,* thought M. Darbedat, *where responsibility begins, or rather, where it ends.* In any case, he was always analyzing himself too much, always turned in on himself. But was it the cause or effect of his sickness? He followed his daughter through a long, dim corridor.

"This apartment is too big for you," he said. "You ought to move out."

"You say that every time, Papa," Eve answered, "but I've already told you Pierre doesn't want to leave his room."

Eve was amazing. Enough to make you wonder if she realized her husband's state. He was insane enough to be in a strait-jacket and she respected his decisions and advice as if he still had good sense.

"What I'm saying is for your own good," M. Darbedat went on, somewhat annoyed, "It seems to me that if I were a woman I'd be afraid of these badly lighted old rooms. I'd like to see you in a bright apartment, the kind they're putting up near Auteuil, three airy little rooms. They lowered the rents because they couldn't find any tenants; this would be just the time."

Eve quietly turned the doorknob and they entered the room. M. Darbedat's throat tightened at the heavy odor of incense. The curtains were drawn. In the shadows he made out a thin neck above the back of an armchair: Pierre's back was turned. He was eating.

"Hello, Pierre," M. Darbedat said, raising his voice. "How are we today?" He drew near him: the sick man was seated in front of a small table; he looked sly.

"I see we had soft boiled eggs," M. Darbedat said, raising his voice higher. "That's good!"

"I'm not deaf," Pierre said quietly.

Irritated, M. Darbedat turned his eyes toward Eve as his witness. But Eve gave him a hard glance and was silent. M. Darbedat realized he had hurt her. Too bad for her. It was impossible to find just the right tone for this boy. He had less sense than a child of four and Eve wanted him treated like a man. M. Darbedat could not keep himself from waiting with impatience for the moment when all this ridiculous business would be finished. Sick people always annoyed him a little—especially madmen because they were wrong. Poor Pierre, for example, was wrong all along the line, he couldn't speak a reasonable word and yet it would be useless to expect the least humility from him, or even temporary recognition of his errors.

Eve cleared away the eggshells and the cup. She put a knife and fork in front of Pierre.

"What's he going to eat now," M. Darbedat said jovially.

"A steak."

Pierre had taken the fork and held it in the ends of his long, pale fingers. He inspected it minutely and then gave a slight laugh.

"I can't use it this time," he murmured, setting it down, "I was warned."

Eve came in and looked at the fork with passionate interest.

"Agatha," Pierre said, "give me another one."

Eve obeyed and Pierre began to eat. She had taken the suspect fork and held it tightly in her hands, her eyes never leaving it; she seemed to make a violent effort. How suspicious all their gestures and relationships are! thought M. Darbedat.

He was uneasy.

"Be careful, Pierre, take it by the middle because of the prongs."

Eve sighed and laid the fork on the serving table. M. Darbedat felt his gall rising. He did not think it well to give in to all this poor man's whims—even from Pierre's viewpoint it was pernicious. Franchot had said: "One must never enter the delirium of a madman." Instead of giving him another fork, it would have been better to have reasoned quietly and made him understand that the first was like all the others.

He went to the serving table, took the fork ostentatiously and tested the prongs with a light finger. Then he turned to Pierre. But the latter was cutting his meat peacefully: he gave his father-in-law a gentle, inexpressive glance.

"I'd like to have a little talk with you," M. Darbedat said to Eve.

She followed him docilely into the salon. Sitting on the couch, M. Darbedat realized he had kept the fork in his hand. He threw it on the table.

"It's much better here," he said.

"I never come here."

"All right to smoke?"

"Of course, Papa," Eve said hurriedly. "Do you want a cigar?"

M. Darbedat preferred to roll a cigarette. He thought eagerly of the discussion he was about to begin. Speaking to Pierre he felt as embarrassed about his reason as a giant about his strength when playing with a child. All his qualities of clarity, sharpness, precision, turned against him; *I must confess it's somewhat the same with my poor Jeannette.* Certainly Mme. Darbedat was not insane, but this illness had . . . stultified her. Eve, on the other hand, took after her father . . . a straight, logical nature; discussion with her was a pleasure; *that's why I don't want them to ruin her.* M. Darbedat raised his eyes. Once again he wanted to see the fine intelligent features of his daughter. He was disappointed with this face; once so reasonable and transparent, there was now something clouded and opaque in it. Eve had always been beautiful. M. Darbedat noticed she was made up with great care, almost with pomp. She had blued her eyelids and put mascara on her long lashes. This violent and perfect make-up made a painful impression on her father.

"You're green beneath your rouge," he told her. "I'm afraid you're getting sick. And the way you make yourself up now! You used to be so discreet."

Eve did not answer and for an embarrassed moment M. Darbedat considered this brilliant, worn-out face beneath the heavy mass of black hair. He thought she looked like a tragedian. *I even know who she looks like. That woman . . . That Romanian who played* Phèdre *in French at the Mur d'Orange.* He regretted having made so disagreeable a remark: *It escaped me! Better not worry her with little things.*

"Excuse me," he said smiling, "you know I'm an old purist. I don't like all these creams and paints women stick on their face today. But I'm in the wrong. You must live in your time."

Eve smiled amiably at him. M. Darbedat lit a cigarette and drew several puffs.

"My child," he began, "I wanted to talk with you: the two of us are going to talk the way we used to. Come, sit down and listen to me nicely; you must have confidence in your old Papa."

"I'd rather stand," Eve said. "What did you want to tell me?"

"I'm going to ask you a single question," M. Darbedat said a little more dryly. "Where will all this lead you?"

"All this?" Eve asked astonished.

"Yes . . . all this whole life you've made for yourself. Listen," he went on, "don't think I don't understand you [he had a sudden illumination] but what you want to do is beyond human strength. You want to live solely by imagination, isn't that it? You don't want to admit he's sick. You don't want to see the Pierre of today, do you? You have eyes only for the Pierre of before. My dear, my darling little girl, it's an impossible bet to win," M. Darbedat continued. "Now I'm going to tell you a story which perhaps you don't know. When we were at Sables-d'Olonne—you were three years old—your mother made the acquaintance of a charming young woman with a superb little boy. You played on the beach with this little boy, you were thick as thieves, you were engaged to marry him. A while later, in Paris, your mother wanted to see this young woman again; she was told she had had a terrible accident. That fine little boy's head was cut off by a car. They told your mother, 'Go and see her, but above all don't talk to her about the death of her child, she *will not* believe he is dead.' Your mother went, she found a half-mad creature: she lived as though her boy was still alive; she spoke to him, she set his place at the table. She lived in such a state of nervous tension that after six months they had to take her away by force to a sanitorium where she was obliged to stay three years. No, my child," M. Darbedat said, shaking his head, "these things are impossible. It would have been better if she had recognized the truth courageously. She would have suffered once, then time would have erased with its sponge. There is nothing like looking things in the face, believe me."

"You're wrong," Eve said with effort. "I know very well that Pierre is . . ."

The word did not escape. She held herself very straight and put her hands on the back of the armchair: there was something dry and ugly in the lower part of her face.

"So . . . ?" asked M. Darbedat, astonished.

"So . . . ?"

"You . . . ?"

"I love him as he is," said Eve rapidly and with an irritated look.

"Not true," M. Darbedat said forcefully. "It isn't true: you don't love him, you can't love him. You can only feel that way about a healthy, normal person. You pity Pierre, I don't doubt it, and surely you have the memory of three years of happiness he gave you. But don't tell me you love him. I won't believe you."

Eve remained wordless, staring at the carpet absently.

"You could at least answer me," M. Darbedat said coldly. "Don't think this conversation has been any less painful for me than it has for you."

"More than you think."

"Well then, if you love him," he cried, exasperated, "it is a great misfortune for you, for me and for your poor mother because I'm going to tell you something I would rather have hidden from you: before three years Pierre will be sunk in complete dementia, he'll be like a beast."

He watched his daughter with hard eyes: he was angry at her for having compelled him, by stubbornness, to make this painful revelation.

Eve was motionless; she did not so much as raise her eyes.

"I knew."

"Who told you?" he asked stupefied.

"Franchot. I knew six months ago."

"And I told him to be careful with you," said M. Darbedat with bitterness. "Maybe it's better. But under those circumstances you must understand that it would be unpardonable to keep Pierre with you. The struggle you have undertaken is doomed to failure, his illness won't spare him. If there were something to be done, if we could save him by care, I'd say yes. But look: you're pretty, intelligent, gay, you're destroying yourself willingly and without profit. I know you've been admirable, but now it's over . . . done, you've done your duty and more; now it would be immoral to continue. We also have duties to ourselves, child. And then you aren't thinking about us. You must," he repeated, hammering the words, "send Pierre to Franchot's clinic. Leave this apartment where you've had nothing but sorrow and come home to us. If you want to be useful and ease the sufferings of someone else, you have your mother. The poor woman is cared for by nurses, she needs someone closer to her, and *she*," he added, "can appreciate what you do for her and be grateful."

There was a long silence. M. Darbedat heard Pierre singing in the next room. It was hardly a song, rather a sort of sharp, hasty recitative. M. Darbedat raised his eyes to his daughter.

"It's no then?"

"Pierre will stay with me," she said quietly. "I get along well with him."

"By living like an animal all day long?"

Eve smiled and shot a glance at her father, strange, mocking and almost gay. *It's true,* M. Darbedat thought furiously, *that's not all they do; they sleep together.*

"You are completely mad," he said, rising.

Eve smiled sadly and murmured, as if to herself, "Not enough so."

"Not enough? I can only tell you one thing, my child. You frighten me."

He kissed her hastily and left. Going down the stairs he thought: *we should send out two strong-arm men who'd take the poor imbecile away and stick him under a shower without asking his advice on the matter.*

It was a fine autumn day, calm and without mystery; the sunlight gilded the faces of the passers-by. M. Darbedat was struck with the simplicity of the faces; some weather-beaten, others smooth, but they reflected all the happiness and care with which he was so familiar.

*I know exactly what I resent in Eve,* he told himself, entering the Boulevard St. Germain. *I resent her living outside the limits of human nature. Pierre is no longer a human being: in all the care and all the love she gives him she deprives human beings of a little. We don't have the right to refuse ourselves to the world; no matter what, we live in society.*

He watched the faces of the passers-by with sympathy; he loved their clear, serious looks. In these sunlit streets, in the midst of mankind, one felt secure, as in the midst of a large family.

A woman stopped in front of an open-air display counter. She was holding a little girl by the hand.

"What's that?" the little girl asked, pointing to a radio set.

"Mustn't touch," her mother said. "It's a radio; it plays music."

They stood for a moment without speaking, in ecstasy. Touched, M. Darbedat bent down to the little girl and smiled.

## II

"He's gone." The door closed with a dry snap. Eve was alone in the salon. *I wish he'd die.*

She twisted her hands around the back of the armchair: she had just remembered her father's eyes. M. Darbedat was bent over Pierre with a competent air; he had said "That's good!" the way someone says when they speak to invalids. He had looked and Pierre's face had been painted in the depths of his sharp, bulging eyes. *I hate him when he looks at him because I think he sees him.*

Eve's hands slid along the armchair and she turned to the window. She was dazzled. The room was filled with sunlight, it was everywhere, in pale splotches on the rug, in the air like a blinding dust. Eve was not accustomed to this diligent, indiscreet light which darted from everywhere, scouring all the corners, rubbing the furniture like a busy housewife and making it glisten. However, she went to the window and raised the muslin curtain which hung against the pane. Just at that moment M. Darbedat left the building; Eve suddenly caught sight of his broad shoulders. He raised his head and looked at the sky, blinking, then with the stride of a young man he walked away. *He's straining himself,* thought Eve, *soon he'll have a stitch in the side.* She hardly hated him any longer: there was so little in that head; only the tiny worry of appearing young. Yet rage took her again when she saw him turn the corner of the Boulevard St. Germain and disappear. *He's thinking about Pierre.* A little of their life had escaped from the closed room and was being dragged through the streets, in the sun, among the people. *Can they never forget about us?*

The Rue du Bac was almost deserted. An old lady crossed the street with mincing steps; three girls passed, laughing. Then men, strong, serious men carrying briefcases and talking among themselves. *Normal people,* thought Eve, astonished at finding such a powerful hatred in herself. A handsome, fleshy woman ran heavily toward an elegant gentleman. He took her in his arms and kissed her on the mouth. Eve gave a hard laugh and let the curtain fall.

Pierre sang no more but the woman on the fourth floor was playing the piano; she played a Chopin Etude. Eve felt calmer; she took a step toward Pierre's room but stopped almost immediately and leaned against the wall in anguish; each time she left the room, she was panic-stricken at the thought of going back. Yet she knew she could live nowhere else: she loved the room. She looked around it with cold curiosity as if to gain a little time: this shadowless, odorless room where she waited for her courage to return. *You'd think it was a dentist's waiting room.* Armchairs of pink silk, the divan, the tabourets were somber and discreet, a little fatherly; man's best friends. Eve imagined those grave gentlemen dressed in light suits, all like the ones she saw at the window, entering the room, continuing a conversation already begun. They did not even take time to reconnoiter, but advanced with firm step to the middle of the room; one of them, letting his hand drag behind him like a wake in passing knocked over cushions, objects on the table, and was never disturbed by their contact. And when a piece of furniture was in their way, these poised men, far from making a detour to avoid it, quietly changed its place. Finally they sat down, still plunged in their conversation, without even glancing behind them. *A living room for normal people,* thought Eve. She stared at the knob of the closed door and anguish clutched her throat: *I must go back. I never leave him alone so long.* She would have to open the door, then stand for a moment on the threshold, trying to accustom her eyes to the shadow and the room would push her back with all its strength. Eve would have to triumph over this resistance and enter all the way into the heart of the room. Suddenly she wanted violently to see Pierre; she would have liked to make fun of M. Darbedat with him. But Pierre had no need of her; Eve could not foresee the welcome he had in store for her. Suddenly she thought with a sort of pride that she had no place anywhere. *Normal people think I belong with them. But I couldn't stay an hour among them. I need to live out there, on the other side of the wall. But they don't want me out there.*

A profound change was taking place around her. The light had grown old and graying: it was heavy, like the water in a vase of flowers that hasn't been changed since the day before. In this aged light Eve found a melancholy she had long forgotten: the melancholy of an autumn afternoon that was ending. She looked around her, hesitant, almost timid: all that was so far away: there was neither day nor night nor season nor melancholy in the room. She vaguely recalled autumns long past, autumns of her childhood, then suddenly she stiffened: she was afraid of memories.

She heard Pierre's voice. "Agatha! Where are you?"

"Coming!" she cried.

She opened the door and entered the room.

The heavy odor of incense filled her mouth and nostrils as she opened her eyes and stretched out her hands—for a long time the perfume and the gloom had meant nothing more to her than a single element, acrid and heavy, as simple, as familiar as water, air or fire—and she prudently advanced toward a pale stain which seemed to float in the fog. It was Pierre's face: Pierre's clothing (he dressed in black ever since he had been sick) melted in obscurity. Pierre had thrown back his head and closed his eyes. He was handsome. Eve looked at his long, curved lashes, then sat close to him on the low chair. *He seems to be suffering,* she thought. Little by little her eyes grew used to the darkness. The bureau emerged first, then the bed, then Pierre's personal things: scissors, the pot of glue, books, the herbarium which shed its leaves onto the rug near the armchair.

"Agatha?"

Pierre had opened his eyes. He was watching her, smiling. "You know, that fork?" he said. "I did it to frighten that fellow. There was *almost* nothing the matter with it."

Eve's apprehensions faded and she gave a light laugh. "You succeeded," she said. "You drove him completely out of his mind."

Pierre smiled. "Did you see? He played with it a long time, he held it right in his hands. The trouble is," he said, "they don't know how to take hold of things; they grab them."

"That's right," Eve said.

Pierre tapped the palm of his left hand lightly with the index of his right.

"They take with that. They reach out their fingers and when they catch hold of something they crack down on it to knock it out."

He spoke rapidly and hardly moving his lips; he looked puzzled.

"I wonder what they want," he said at last, "that fellow has already been here. Why did they send him to me? If they want to know what I'm doing all they have to do is read it on the screen, they don't even need to leave the house. They make mistakes. They have the power but they make mistakes. I never make any, that's my trump card. *Hoffka!*" he said. He shook his long hands before his forehead. "The bitch Hoffka! Paffka! Suffka! Do you want any more?"

"Is it the bell?" asked Eve.

"Yes. It's gone." He went on severely. "This fellow, he's just a subordinate. You know him, you went into the living room with him."

Eve did not answer.

"What did he want?" asked Pierre. "He must have told you."

She hesitated an instant, then answered brutally. "He wanted you locked up."

When the truth was told quietly to Pierre he distrusted it. He had to be dealt with violently in order to daze and paralyze his suspicions. Eve preferred to brutalize him rather than lie: when she lied and he acted as if he believed it she could not avoid a very slight feeling of superiority which made her horrified at herself.

"Lock me up!" Pierre repeated ironically. "They're crazy. What can walls do to me. Maybe they think that's going to stop me. I sometimes wonder if there aren't two groups. The real one, the Negro—and then a bunch of fools trying to stick their noses in and making mistake after mistake."

He made his hand jump up from the arm of the chair and looked at it happily.

"I can get through walls. What did you tell them?" he asked, turning to Eve with curiosity.

"Not to lock you up."

He shrugged. "You shouldn't have said that. You made a mistake too . . . unless you did it on purpose. You've got to call their bluff."

He was silent. Eve lowered her head sadly: *"They grab things!" How scornfully he said that—and he was right. Do I grab things too? It doesn't do any good to watch myself, I think most of my movements annoy him. But he doesn't say anything.* Suddenly she felt as miserable as when she was fourteen and Mme. Darbedat told her "You don't know what to do with your hands." She didn't dare make a move and just at that time she had an irresistible desire to change her position. Quietly she put her feet under the chair, barely touching the rug. She watched the lamp on the table—the lamp whose base Pierre had painted black—and the chess set. Pierre had left only the black pawns on the board. Sometimes he would get up, go to the table and take the pawns in his hands one by one. He spoke to them, called them Robots and they seemed to stir with a mute life under his fingers. When he set them down, Eve went and touched them in her turn (she always felt somewhat ridiculous about it). They had become little bits of dead wood again but something vague and incomprehensible stayed in them, something like understanding. *These are* his *things,* she thought. *There is nothing of mine in the room.* She had had a few pieces of furniture before; the mirror and the little inlaid dresser handed down from her grandmother and which Pierre jokingly called *"your* dresser." Pierre had carried them away with him; things showed their true face to Pierre alone. Eve could watch them for hours: they were unflaggingly stubborn and determined to deceive her, offering her nothing but their appearance—as they did to Dr. Franchot and M. Darbedat. *Yet,* she told herself with anguish, *I don't see them quite like my father. It isn't possible for me to see them exactly like him.*

She moved her knees a little: her legs felt as though they were crawling with ants. Her body was stiff and taut and hurt her; she felt it too alive, too demanding. *I would like to be invisible and stay here seeing him without his seeing me. He doesn't need me; I am useless in this room.* She turned her head slightly and looked at the wall above Pierre. Threats were written on the wall. Eve knew it but she could not read them. She often watched the big red roses on the wallpaper until they began to dance before her eyes. The roses flamed in shadow. Most of the time the threat was written near the ceiling, a little to the left of the bed; but sometimes it moved. *I must get up. I can't . . . I can't sit down any longer.* There were also white disks on the wall that looked like slices of onion. The disks spun and Eve's hands began to tremble: *Sometimes I think I'm going mad. But no,* she thought, *I can't go mad. I get nervous, that's all.*

Suddenly she felt Pierre's hand on hers.

"Agatha," Pierre said tenderly.

He smiled at her but he held her hand by the ends of his fingers with a sort of revulsion, as though he had picked up a crab by the back and wanted to avoid its claws.

"Agatha," he said, "I would so much like to have confidence in you."

She closed her eyes and her breast heaved. *I mustn't answer anything, if I do he'll get angry, he won't say anything more.*

Pierre had dropped her hand. "I like you, Agatha," he said, "but I can't understand you. Why do you stay in the room all the time?"

Eve did not answer.

"Tell me why."

"You know I love you," she said dryly.

"I don't believe you," Pierre said. "Why should you love me? I must frighten you: I'm haunted." He smiled but suddenly became serious. "There is a wall between you and me. I see you, I speak to you, but you're on the other side. What keeps us from loving? I think it was easier before. In Hamburg."

"Yes," Eve said sadly. Always Hamburg. He never spoke of their real past. Neither Eve nor he had ever been to Hamburg.

"We used to walk along the canal. There was a barge, remember? The barge was black; there was a dog on the deck."

He made it up as he went along; it sounded false.

"I held your hand. You had another skin. I believed all you told me. Be quiet!" he shouted.

He listened for a moment. "They're coming," he said mournfully.

Eve jumped up. "They're coming? I thought they wouldn't ever come again."

Pierre had been calmer for the past three days; the statues did not come. Pierre was terribly afraid of the statues even though he would never admit it. Eve was not afraid: but when they began to fly, buzzing, around the room, she was afraid of Pierre.

"Give me the ziuthre," Pierre said.

Eve got up and took the ziuthre: it was a collection of pieces of cardboard Pierre had glued together; he used it to conjure the statues. The ziuthre looked like a spider. On one of the cardboards Pierre had written "Power over ambush" and on the other "Black." On a third he had drawn a laughing face with wrinkled eyes: it was Voltaire.

Pierre seized the ziuthre by one end and looked at it darkly.

"I can't use it any more," he said.

"Why?"

"They turned it upside down."

"Will you make another?"

He looked at her for a long while. "You'd like me to, wouldn't you," he said between his teeth.

Eve was angry at Pierre. *He's warned every time they come: how does he do it? He's never wrong.*

The ziuthre dangled pitifully from the ends of Pierre's fingers. *He always finds a good reason not to use it. Sunday when they came he pretended he'd lost it but I saw it behind the paste pot and he couldn't fail to see it. I wonder if he isn't the one who brings them.* One could never tell if he were completely sincere. Sometimes Eve had the impression that despite himself Pierre was surrounded by a swarm of unhealthy thoughts and visions. But at other times Pierre seemed to invent them. *He suffers. But how much does he* believe *in the statues and the Negro. Anyhow, I know he doesn't see the statues, he only hears them: when they pass he turns his head away; but he still says he sees them; he describes them.* She remembered the red face of Dr. Franchot: "But my dear madame, all mentally unbalanced persons are liars; you're wasting your time if you're trying to distinguish between what they really feel and what they pretend to feel." She gave a start. *What is Franchot doing here? I don't want to start thinking like him.*

Pierre had gotten up. He went to throw the ziuthre into the wastebasket: *I want to think like you,* she murmured. He walked with tiny steps, on tiptoe, pressing his elbows against his hips so as to take up the least possible space. He came back and sat down and looked at Eve with a closed expression.

"We'll have to put up black wallpaper," he said. "There isn't enough black in this room."

He was crouched in the armchair. Sadly Eve watched his meager body, always ready to withdraw, to shrink: the arms, legs and head looked like retractable organs. The clock struck six. The piano downstairs was silent. Eve sighed: the statues would not come right away; they had to wait for them.

"Do you want me to turn on the light?"

She would rather not wait for them in darkness.

"Do as you please," Pierre said.

Eve lit the small lamp on the bureau and a red mist filled the room. Pierre was waiting too.

He did not speak but his lips were moving, making two dark stains in the red mist. Eve loved Pierre's lips. Before, they had been moving and sensual; but they had lost their sensuality. They were wide apart, trembling a little, coming together incessantly, crushing against each other only to separate again. They were the only living things in this blank face; they looked like two frightened animals. Pierre could mutter like that for hours without a sound leaving his mouth and Eve often let herself be fascinated by this tiny, obstinate movement. *I love his mouth.* He never kissed her any more; he was horrified at contacts: at night they touched him—the hands of men, hard and dry, pinched him all over; the long-nailed hands of women caressed him. Often he went to bed with his clothes on but the hands slipped under the clothes and tugged at his shirt. Once he heard laughter and puffy lips were placed on his mouth. He never kissed Eve after that night.

"Agatha," Pierre said, "don't look at my mouth."

Eve lowered her eyes.

"I am not unaware that people can learn to read lips," he went on insolently.

His hand trembled on the arm of the chair. The index finger stretched out, tapped three times on the thumb and the other fingers curled: this was a spell. *It's going to start,* she thought. She wanted to take Pierre in her arms.

Pierre began to speak at the top of his voice in a very sophisticated tone.

"Do you remember Sao Paulo?"

No answer. Perhaps it was a trap.

"I met you there," he said, satisfied. "I took you away from a Danish sailor. We almost fought but I paid for a round of drinks and he let me take you away. All that was only a joke."

*He's lying, he doesn't believe a word of what he says. He knows my name isn't Agatha. I hate him when he lies.* But she saw his staring eyes and her rage melted. *He isn't lying,* she thought, *he can't stand it any more. He feels them coming; he's talking to keep from hearing them.* Pierre dug both hands into the arm of the chair. His face was pale; he was smiling.

"These meetings are often strange," he said, "but I don't believe it's by chance. I'm not asking who sent you. I know you wouldn't answer. Anyhow, you've been smart enough to bluff me."

He spoke with great difficulty, in a sharp, hurried voice. There were words he could not pronounce and which left his mouth like some soft and shapeless substance.

"You dragged me away right in the middle of the party, between the rows of black automobiles, but behind the cars there was an army with red eyes which glowed as soon as I turned my back. I think you made signs to them, all the time hanging on my arm, but I didn't see a thing. I was too absorbed by the great ceremonies of the Coronation."

He looked straight ahead, his eyes wide open. He passed his hand over his forehead very rapidly, in one spare gesture, without stopping his talking. He did not want to stop talking.

"It was the Coronation of the Republic," he said stridently, "an impressive spectacle of its kind because of all the species of animals that the colonies sent for the ceremony. You were afraid to get lost among the monkeys. I said among the monkeys," he repeated arrogantly, looking around him, "I could say *among the Negroes!* The abortions sliding under the tables, trying to pass unseen, are discovered and nailed to the spot by my Look. The password is silence. To be silent. Everything in place and attention for the entrance of the statues, that's the countersign. Tralala . . ." he shrieked and cupped his hands to his mouth. "Tralalala, tralalalala!"

He was silent and Eve knew that the statues had come into the room. He was stiff, pale and distrustful. Eve stiffened too and both waited in silence. Someone was walking in the corridor: it was Marie the housecleaner, she had undoubtedly just arrived. Eve thought, *I have to give her money for the gas.* And then the statues began to fly; they passed between Eve and Pierre.

Pierre went "Ah!" and sank down in the armchair, folding his legs beneath him. He turned his face away; sometimes he grinned, but drops of sweat pearled his forehead. Eve could stand the sight no longer, this pale cheek, this mouth deformed by a trembling grimace; she closed her eyes. Gold threads began to dance on the red background of her eyelids; she felt old and heavy. Not far from her Pierre was breathing violently. *They're flying, they're buzzing, they're bending over him.* She felt a slight tickling, a pain in the shoulder and right side. Instinctively her body bent to the left as if to avoid some disagreeable contact, as if to let a heavy, awkward object pass. Suddenly the floor creaked and she had an insane desire to open her eyes, to look to her right, sweeping the air with her hand.

She did nothing; she kept her eyes closed and a bitter joy made her tremble: *I am afraid too,* she thought. Her entire life had taken refuge in her right side. She leaned toward Pierre without opening her eyes. The slightest effort would be enough and she would enter this tragic world for the first time. *I'm afraid of the statues,* she thought. It was a violent, blind affirmation, an incantation. She wanted to believe in their presence with all her strength. She tried to make a new sense, a sense of touch out of the anguish which paralyzed her right side. She *felt* their passage in her arm, in her side and shoulder.

The statues flew low and gently; they buzzed. Eve knew that they had an evil look and that eyelashes stuck out from the stone around their eyes; but she pictured them badly. She knew, too, that they were not quite alive but that slabs of flesh, warm scales appeared on their great bodies; the stone peeled from the ends of their fingers and their palms were eaten away. Eve could not *see* all that: she simply thought of enormous women sliding against her, solemn and grotesque, with a human look and compact heads of stone. *They are bending over Pierre*—Eve made such a violent effort that her hands began trembling—*they are bending over me.* A horrible cry suddenly chilled her. They had touched him. She opened her eyes: Pierre's head was in his hands, he was breathing heavily. Eve felt exhausted: *a game,* she thought with remorse; *it was only a game. I didn't sincerely believe it for an instant. And all that time he suffered as if it were real.*

Pierre relaxed and breathed freely. But his pupils were strangely dilated and he was perspiring.

"Did you see them?" he asked.

"I can't see them."

"Better for you. They'd frighten you," he said. "I am used to them."

Eve's hands were still shaking and the blood had rushed to her head. Pierre took a cigarette from his pocket and brought it up to his mouth. But he did not light it.

"I don't care whether I see them or not," he said, "but I don't want them to touch me: I'm afraid they'll give me pimples."

He thought for an instant, then asked, "Did you hear them?"

"Yes," Eve said, "it's like an airplane engine." (Pierre had told her this the previous Sunday.)

Pierre smiled with condescension. "You exaggerate," he said. But he was still pale. He looked at Eve's hands. "Your hands are trembling. That made quite an impression on you, my poor Agatha. But don't worry. They won't come back again before tomorrow." Eve could not speak. Her teeth were chattering and she was afraid Pierre would notice it. Pierre watched her for a long time.

"You're tremendously beautiful," he said, nodding his head. "It's too bad, too bad."

He put out his hand quickly and toyed with her ear. "My lovely devil-woman. You disturb me a little, you are too beautiful: that distracts me. If it weren't a question of recapitulation . . ."

He stopped and looked at Eve with surprise.

"That's not the word . . . it came . . . it came," he said, smiling vaguely. "I had another on the tip of my tongue . . . but this one . . . came in its place. I forget what I was telling you."

He thought for a moment, then shook his head.

"Come," he said, "I want to sleep." He added in a childish voice, "You know, Agatha, I'm tired. I can't collect my thoughts any more."

He threw away his cigarette and looked at the rug anxiously. Eve slipped a pillow under his head.

"You can sleep too," he told her, "they won't be back."

*. . . Recapitulation . . .*

Pierre was asleep, a candid, half-smile on his face; his head was turned to one side: one might have thought he wanted to caress his cheek with his shoulder. Eve was not sleepy, she was thoughtful: *Recapitulation.* Pierre had suddenly looked stupid and the word had slipped out of his mouth, long and whitish. Pierre had stared ahead of him in astonishment, as if he had seen the word and didn't recognize it; his mouth was open, soft: something seemed broken in it. He stammered. *That's the first time it ever happened to him: he noticed it, too. He said he couldn't collect his thoughts any more.* Pierre gave a voluptuous little whimper and his hand made a vague movement. Eve watched him harshly: *how is he going to wake up.* It gnawed at her. As soon as Pierre was asleep she had to think about it. She was afraid he would wake up wild-eyed and stammering. *I'm stupid,* she thought, *it can't start before a year; Franchot said so.* But the anguish did not leave her; a year: a winter, a springtime, a summer, the beginning of another autumn. One day his features would grow confused, his jaw would hang loose, he would half open his weeping eyes. Eve bent over Pierre's hand and pressed her lips against it: *I'll kill you before that.*

# Delmore Schwartz

## (1913–1966)

The son of Romanian immigrants, Delmore Schwartz was born in Brooklyn in 1913. He was a gifted student and enrolled early at Columbia University. He also studied at the University of Wisconsin and, in 1935, received his degree in philosophy from New York University. In 1936, he won the Bowdoin Prize in the Humanities for his essay "Poetry as Imitation." His first short story, "In Dreams Begin Responsibilities" (1937), was published in the *Partisan Review.* In the following year he published his first book, *In Dreams Begin Responsibilities* (1938). In his stories, Schwartz examines the psychological effects of the Great Depression on the lives of Jewish, middle-class families. Though he never finished his advanced degree in philosophy at Harvard, he was hired by the school as the Briggs-Copeland Lecturer and was later given an Assistant Professorship. In 1947 he left Harvard and, in 1948, published his collection of short stories, *The World Is a Wedding.* He taught at several universities, including Syracuse, Princeton, Bennington College, Kenyon College, and the writer's colony Yaddo. In 1960, Schwartz won the Bollingen Prize. During his life, Schwartz frequently used barbiturates and amphetamines. This, along with his alcoholism, seriously compromised his health, and in the summer of 1966 he checked into the Times

Square Hotel to focus on writing. He worked continuously until July 11, when he died in the hotel lobby of a heart attack.

———————

## *"In Dreams Begin Responsibilities"* 1937

I think it is the year 1909. I feel as if I were in a moving-picture theatre, the long arm of light crossing the darkness and spinning, my eyes fixed upon the screen. It is a silent picture, as if an old Biograph one, in which the actors are dressed in ridiculously old-fashioned clothes, and one flash succeeds another with sudden jumps, and the actors, too, seem to jump about, walking too fast. The shots are full of rays and dots, as if it had been raining when the picture was photographed. The light is bad.

It is Sunday afternoon, June 12th, 1909, and my father is walking down the quiet streets of Brooklyn on his way to visit my mother. His clothes are newly pressed, and his tie is too tight in his high collar. He jingles the coins in his pocket, thinking of the witty things he will say. I feel as if I had by now relaxed entirely in the soft darkness of the theatre; the organist peals out the obvious approximate emotions on which the audience rocks unknowingly. I am anonymous. I have forgotten myself: it is always so when one goes to a movie, it is, as they say, a drug.

My father walks from street to street of trees, lawns and houses, once in a while coming to an avenue on which a street-car skates and gnaws, progressing slowly. The motorman, who has a handle-bar mustache, helps a young lady wearing a hat like a feathered bowl onto the car. He leisurely makes change and rings his bell as the passengers mount the car. It is obviously Sunday, for everyone is wearing Sunday clothes and the street-car's noises emphasize the quiet of the holiday (Brooklyn is said to be the city of churches). The shops are closed and their shades drawn but for an occasional stationery store or drugstore with great green balls in the window.

My father has chosen to take this long walk because he likes to walk and think. He thinks about himself in the future and so arrives at the place he is to visit in a mild state of exaltation. He pays no attention to the houses he is passing, in which the Sunday dinner is being eaten, nor to the many trees which line each street, now coming to their full green and the time when they will enclose the whole street in leafy shadow. An occasional carriage passes, the horses' hooves falling like stones in the quiet afternoon, and once in a while an automobile, looking like an enormous upholstered sofa, puffs and passes.

My father thinks of my mother, of how lady-like she is, and of the pride which will be his when he introduces her to his family. They are not yet engaged and he is not yet sure that he loves my mother, so that, once in a while, he becomes panicky about the bond already established. But then he reassures himself by thinking of the big men he admires who are married: William Randolph Hearst and William Howard Taft, who has just become the President of the United States.

My father arrives at my mother's house. He has come too early and so is suddenly embarrassed. My aunt, my mother's younger sister, answers the loud bell with her napkin in her hand, for the family is still at dinner. As my father enters, my grandfather rises from the table and shakes hands with him. My mother has run upstairs to tidy herself. My grandmother asks my father if he has had dinner and tells him that my mother will be down soon. My grandfather opens the conversation by remarking about the mild June weather. My father sits uncomfortably near the table, holding his hat in his hand. My grandmother tells my aunt to take my father's hat. My uncle, twelve years old, runs into the house, his hair tousled. He shouts a greeting to my father, who has often given him nickels, and then runs upstairs, as my grandmother shouts after him. It is evident that the respect in which my father is held in this house is tempered by a good deal of mirth. He is impressive, but also very awkward.

## II

Finally my mother comes downstairs and my father, being at the moment engaged in conversation with my grandfather, is made uneasy by her entrance, for he does not know whether to greet my mother or to continue the conversation. He gets up from his chair clumsily and says "Hello" gruffly. My grandfather watches this, examining their congruence, such as it is, with a critical eye, and meanwhile rubbing his bearded cheek roughly, as he always does when he reasons. He is worried; he is afraid that my father will not make a good husband for his oldest daughter. At this point something happens to the film, just as my father says something funny to my mother: I am awakened to myself and my unhappiness just as my interest has become most intense. The audience begins to clap impatiently. Then the trouble is attended to, but the film has been returned to a portion just shown, and once more I see my grandfather rubbing his bearded cheek, pondering my father's character. It is difficult to get back into the picture once more and forget myself, but as my mother giggles at my father's words, the darkness drowns me.

My father and mother depart from the house, my father shaking hands with my grandfather once more, out of some unknown uneasiness. I stir uneasily also, slouched in the hard chair of the theater. Where is the older uncle, my mother's older brother? He is studying in his bedroom upstairs, studying for his final examinations at the College of the City of New York, having been dead of double pneumonia for the last twenty-one years. My mother and father walk down the same quiet streets once more. My mother is holding my father's arm and telling him of the novel she has been reading and my father utters judgments of the characters as the plot is made clear to him. This is a habit which he very much enjoys, for he feels the utmost superiority and confidence when he is approving or condemning the behavior of other people. At times he feels moved to utter a brief "Ugh," whenever the story becomes what he would call sugary. This tribute is the assertion of his manliness. My mother feels satisfied by the interest she has awakened; and she is showing my father how intelligent she is and how interesting.

They reach the avenue, and the street-car leisurely arrives. They are going to Coney Island this afternoon, although my mother really considers such pleasures inferior. She has made up her mind to indulge only in a walk on the boardwalk and a pleasant dinner, avoiding the riotous amusements as being beneath the dignity of so dignified a couple.

My father tells my mother how much money he has made in the week just past, exaggerating an amount which need not have been exaggerated. But my father has always felt that actualities somehow fall short, no matter how fine they are. Suddenly I begin to weep. The determined old lady who sits next to me in the theatre is annoyed and looks at me with an angry face, and being intimidated, I stop. I drag out my handkerchief and dry my face, licking the drop which has fallen near my lips. Meanwhile I have missed something, for here are my father and mother alighting from the street-car at the last stop, Coney Island.

## III

They walk toward the boardwalk and my mother commands my father to inhale the pungent air from the sea. They both breathe in deeply, both of them laughing as they do so. They have in common a great interest in health, although my father is strong and husky, and my mother is frail. They are both full of theories about what is good to eat and not good to eat, and sometimes have heated discussions about it, the whole matter ending in my father's announcement, made with a scornful bluster, that you have to die sooner or later anyway. On the boardwalk's flagpole, the American flag is pulsing in an intermittent wind from the sea.

My father and mother go to the rail of the boardwalk and look down on the beach where a good many bathers are casually walking about. A few are in the surf. A peanut whistle pierces the air with its pleasant and active whine, and my father goes to buy peanuts. My mother remains at the rail and stares at the ocean. The ocean seems merry to her; it pointedly sparkles and again and again the pony waves are released. She notices the children digging in the wet sand, and the bathing costumes of the girls who are her own age. My father returns with the peanuts. Overhead the sun's lightning strikes and strikes, but neither of them are at all aware of it. The boardwalk is full of people dressed in their Sunday clothes and casually strolling. The tide does not reach as far as the boardwalk, and the strollers would feel no danger if it did. My father and mother lean on the rail of the boardwalk and absently stare at the ocean. The ocean is becoming rough; the waves come in slowly, tugging strength from far back. The moment before they somersault, the moment when they arch their backs so beautifully, showing white veins in the green and black, that moment is intolerable. They finally crack, dashing fiercely upon the sand, actually driving, full force downward, against it, bouncing upward and forward, and at last petering out into a small stream of bubbles which slides up the beach and then is recalled. The sun overhead does not disturb my father and my mother. They gaze idly at the ocean, scarcely interested in its harshness. But I stare at the terrible sun which breaks up sight, and the fatal merciless passionate ocean. I forget my parents. I stare fascinated, and finally, shocked by their indifference, I burst out weeping once more. The old lady next to me pats my shoulder and says "There, there, young man, all of this is only a movie, only a movie," but I look up once more at the terrifying sun and the terrifying ocean, and being unable to control my tears I get up and go to the men's room, stumbling over the feet of the other people seated in my row.

## IV

When I return, feeling as if I had just awakened in the morning sick for lack of sleep, several hours have apparently passed and my parents are riding on the merry-go-round. My father is on a black horse, my mother on a white one, and they seem to be making an eternal circuit for the single purpose of snatching the nickel rings which are attached to an arm of one of the posts. A hand organ is playing; it is inseparable from the ceaseless circling of the merry-go-round.

For a moment it seems that they will never get off the carousel, for it will never stop, and I feel as if I were looking down from the fiftieth story of a building. But at length they do get off; even the hand-organ has ceased for a moment. There is a sudden and sweet stillness, as if the achievement of so much motion. My mother has acquired only two rings, my father, however, ten of them, although it was my mother who really wanted them.

They walk on along the boardwalk as the afternoon descends by imperceptible degrees into the incredible violet of dusk. Everything fades into a relaxed glow, even the ceaseless murmuring from the beach. They look for a place to have dinner. My father suggests the best restaurant on the boardwalk and my mother demurs, according to her principles of economy and housewifeliness.

However they do go to the best place, asking for a table near the window so that they can look out upon the boardwalk and the mobile ocean. My father feels omnipotent as he places a quarter in the waiter's hand in asking for a table. The place is crowded and here too there is music, this time from a kind of string trio. My father orders with a fine confidence.

As their dinner goes on, my father tells of his plans for the future and my mother shows with expressive face how interested she is, and how impressed. My father becomes exultant, lifted up by the waltz that is being played and his own future begins to intoxicate him. My father tells my mother that he is going to expand his business, for there is a great deal of money to be made. He wants to settle down. After all, he is twenty-nine, he has lived by himself since his thirteenth year, he is making more and more money, and he is envious of his friends when he visits them in the security of their homes, surrounded, it seems, by the calm domestic pleasures, and by delightful children, and then as the waltz reaches the moment when the dancers all swing madly, then, then with awful daring, then he asks my mother to marry him, although awkwardly enough and puzzled as to how he had arrived at the question, and she, to make the whole business worse, begins to cry, and my father looks nervously about, not knowing at all what to do now, and my mother says: "It's all I've wanted from the first moment I saw you," sobbing, and he finds all of this very difficult, scarcely to his taste, scarcely as he thought it would be, on his long walks over Brooklyn Bridge in the revery of a fine cigar, and it was then, at that point, that I stood up in the theatre and shouted: "Don't do it! It's not too late to change your minds, both of you. Nothing good will come of it, only remorse, hatred, scandal, and two children whose characters are monstrous." The whole audience turned to look at me, annoyed, the usher came hurrying down the aisle flashing his searchlight, and the old lady next to me tugged me down into my seat, saying: "Be quiet. You'll be put out, and you paid thirty-five cents to come in." And so I shut my eyes because I could not bear to see what was happening. I sat there quietly.

## V

But after a while I begin to take brief glimpses and at length I watch again with thirsty interest, like a child who tries to maintain his sulk when he is offered the bribe of candy. My parents are now having their picture taken in a photographer's booth along the boardwalk. The place is shadowed in the mauve light which is apparently necessary. The camera is set to the side on its tripod and looks like a Martian man. The photographer is instructing my parents in how to pose. My father has his arm over my mother's shoulder, and both of them smile emphatically. The photographer brings my mother a bouquet of flowers to hold in her hand, but she holds it at the wrong angle. Then the photographer covers himself with the black cloth which drapes the camera and all that one sees of him is one protruding arm and his hand with which he holds tightly to the rubber ball which he squeezes when the picture is taken. But he is not satisfied with their appearance. He feels that somehow there is something wrong in their pose. Again and again he comes out from his hiding place with new directions. Each suggestion merely makes matters worse. My father is becoming impatient. They try a seated pose. The photographer explains that he has his pride, he wants to make beautiful pictures, he is not merely interested in all of this for the money. My father says: "Hurry up, will you? We haven't got all night." But the photographer only scurries about apologetically, issuing new directions. The photographer charms me, and I approve of him with all my heart, for I know exactly how he feels, and as he criticizes each revised pose according to some obscure idea of rightness, I become quite hopeful. But then my father says angrily: "Come on, you've had enough time, we're not going to wait any longer." And the photographer, sighing unhappily, goes back into the black covering, and holds out his hand, saying: "One, two, three, Now!", and the picture is taken, with my father's smile turned to a grimace and my mother's bright and false. It takes a few minutes for the picture to be developed and as my parents sit in the curious light they become depressed.

## VI

They have passed a fortune-teller's booth and my mother wishes to go in, but my father does not. They begin to argue about it. My mother becomes stubborn, my father once more impatient. What my father would like to do now is walk off and leave my mother there, but he knows that that would never do. My mother refuses to budge. She is near tears, but she feels an uncontrollable desire to hear what the palm-reader will say. My father consents angrily and they both go into the booth which is, in a way, like the photographer's, since it is draped in black cloth and its light is colored and shadowed. The place is too warm, and my father keeps saying that this is all nonsense, pointing to the crystal ball on the table. The fortune-teller, a short, fat woman garbed in robes supposedly exotic, comes into the room and greets them, speaking with an accent. But suddenly my father feels that the whole thing is intolerable; he tugs at my mother's arm but my mother refuses to budge. And then, in terrible anger, my father lets go of my mother's arm and strides out, leaving my mother stunned. She makes a movement as if to go after him, but the fortune-teller holds her and begs her not to do so, and I in my seat in the darkness am shocked and horrified. I feel as if I were walking a tightrope one hundred feet over a circus audience and suddenly the rope is showing signs of breaking, and I get up from my seat and begin to shout once more the first words I can think of to communicate my terrible fear, and once more the usher comes hurrying down the aisle flashing his searchlight, and the old lady pleads with me, and the shocked audience has turned to stare at me, and I keep shouting: "What are they doing? Don't they know what they are doing? Why doesn't my mother go after my father and beg him not to be angry? If she does not do that, what will she do? Doesn't my father know what he is doing?" But the usher has seized my arm, and is dragging me away, and as he does so, he says: "What are *you* doing? Don't you know you can't do things like this, you can't do whatever you want to do, even if other people aren't about? You will be sorry if you do not do what you should do. You can't carry on like this, it is not right, you will find that out soon enough, everything you do matters too much," and as he said that, dragging me through the lobby of the theatre, into the cold light, I woke up into the bleak winter morning of my twenty-first birthday, the window-sill shining with its lip of snow, and the morning already begun.

# John Steinbeck

## (1902–1968)

_____

Born in Salinas, California, John Steinbeck used the Monterey Bay region as a setting for most of his fiction. The majority of his novels concern the economic problems of rural labor. He studied marine biology at Stanford University but did not earn his degree. Instead, Steinbeck went to New York, where he tried for a few years to establish himself as a freelance writer. He was not successful, and eventually he returned to California. There he held a series of odd jobs, including working as an apprentice painter and fruit picker. He wrote *Cup of Gold* (1929) while working as a watchman in a house in the High Sierras, but the book did not even earn the $250 the publisher had given him in an advance. It was *Tortilla Flat* (1935), about a group of unconventional dreamers on the California coast, that made Steinbeck a well-known author. In the following years he published *In Dubious Battle* (1936), *The Red Pony* (1937), and *Of Mice and Men* (1937). *The Grapes of Wrath* (1939), his best-known book, was an instant success, and in 1940 Steinbeck fled to Mexico to avoid publicity. During World War II, he served as a war correspondent for the *New York Herald Tribune* in Great Britain, and in 1943 he moved to New York City. Steinbeck continued to publish throughout his life, writing books such as *Cannery Row* (1945), *The Pearl* (1947), *A Russian Journal* (1948), *East of Eden* (1952), *Sweet Thursday* (1954), and *The Winter of Our Discontent* (1961). He received the Nobel Prize for literature in 1962.

---

## The Chrysanthemums                                                    1938

The high gray-flannel fog of winter closed off the Salinas Valley from the sky and from all the rest of the world. On every side it sat like a lid on the mountains and made of the great valley a closed pot. On the broad, level land floor the gang plows bit deep and left the black earth shining like metal where the shares had cut. On the foothill ranches across the Salinas River, the yellow stubble fields seemed to be bathed in pale cold sunshine, but there was no sunshine in the valley now in December. The thick willow scrub along the river flamed with sharp and positive yellow leaves.

It was a time of quiet and of waiting. The air was cold and tender. A light wind blew up from the southwest so that the farmers were mildly hopeful of a good rain before long; but fog and rain do not go together.

Across the river, on Henry Allen's foothill ranch there was little work to be done, for the hay was cut and stored and the orchards were plowed up to receive the rain deeply when it should come. The cattle on the higher slopes were becoming shaggy and rough-coated.

Elisa Allen, working in her flower garden, looked down across the yard and saw Henry, her husband, talking to two men in business suits. The three of them stood by the tractor shed, each man with one foot on the side of the little Fordson. They smoked cigarettes and studied the machine as they talked.

Elisa watched them for a moment and then went back to her work. She was thirty-five. Her face was lean and strong and her eyes were as clear as water. Her figure looked blocked and heavy in her gardening costume, a man's black hat pulled down over her eyes, clodhopper shoes, a figured print dress almost completely covered by a big corduroy apron with four big pockets to hold the snips, the trowel and scratcher, the seeds and the knife she worked with. She wore heavy leather gloves to protect her hands while she worked.

She was cutting down the old year's chrysanthemum stalks with a pair of short and powerful scissors. She looked down toward the men by the tractor shed now and then. Her face was eager and mature and handsome; even her work with the scissors was over-eager, over-powerful. The chrysanthemum stems seemed too small and easy for her energy.

She brushed a cloud of hair out of her eyes with the back of her glove, and left a smudge of earth on her cheek in doing it. Behind her stood the neat white farm house with red geraniums close-banked around it as high as the windows. It was a hard-swept looking little house, with hard-polished windows, and a clean mud-mat on the front steps.

Elisa cast another glance toward the tractor shed. The strangers were getting into their Ford coupe. She took off a glove and put her strong fingers down into the forest of new green chrysanthemum sprouts that were growing around the old roots. She spread the leaves and looked down among the close-growing stems. No aphids were there, no sow-bugs or snails or cutworms. Her terrier fingers destroyed such pests before they could get started.

Elisa started at the sound of her husband's voice. He had come near quietly, and he leaned over the wire fence that protected her flower garden from cattle and dogs and chickens.

"At it again," he said. "You've got a strong new crop coming."

Elisa straightened her back and pulled on the gardening glove again. "Yes. They'll be strong this coming year." In her tone and on her face there was a little smugness.

"You've got a gift with things," Henry observed. "Some of those yellow chrysanthemums you had this year were ten inches across. I wish you'd work out in the orchard and raise some apples that big."

Her eyes sharpened. "Maybe I could do it, too. I've a gift with things, all right. My mother had it. She could stick anything in the ground and make it grow. She said it was having planters' hands that knew how to do it."

"Well, it sure works with flowers," he said.

"Henry, who were those men you were talking to?"

"Why, sure, that's what I came to tell you. They were from the Western Meat Company. I sold them those thirty head of three-year-old steers. Got nearly my own price, too."

"Good," she said. "Good for you."

"And I thought," he continued, "I thought how it's Saturday afternoon, and we might go into Salinas for dinner at a restaurant, and then to a picture show—to celebrate, you see."

"Good," she repeated. "Oh, yes. That will be good."

Henry put on his joking tone. "There's fights tonight. How'd you like to go to the fights?"

"Oh, no," she said breathlessly. "No, I wouldn't like fights."

"Just fooling, Elisa. We'll go to a movie. Let's see. It's two now. I'm going to take Scotty and bring down those steers from the hill. It'll take us maybe two hours. We'll go in town about five and have dinner at the Cominos Hotel. Like that?"

"Of course I'll like it. It's good to eat away from home."

"All right, then, I'll go get up a couple of horses."

She said, "I'll have plenty of time to transplant some of these sets, I guess."

She heard her husband calling Scotty down by the barn. And a little later she saw the two men ride up the pale yellow hillside in search of the steers.

There was a little square sandy bed kept for rooting the chrysanthemums. With her trowel she turned the soil over and over, and smoothed it and patted it firm. Then she dug ten parallel trenches to receive the sets. Back at the chrysanthemum bed she pulled out the little crisp shoots, trimmed off the leaves of each one with her scissors and laid it on a small orderly pile.

A squeak of wheels and plod of hoofs came from the road. Elisa looked up. The country road ran along the dense bank of willows and cottonwoods that bordered the river, and up this road came a curious vehicle, curiously drawn. It was an old spring-wagon, with a round canvas top on it like the cover of a prairie schooner. It was drawn by an old bay horse and a little gray-and-white burro. A big stubble-bearded man sat between the cover flaps and drove the crawling team. Underneath the wagon, between the hind wheels, a lean and rangy mongrel dog walked sedately. Words were painted on the canvas, in clumsy, crooked letters. "Pots, pans, knives, sisors, lawn mores, Fixed." Two rows of articles, and the triumphantly definitive "Fixed" below. The black paint had run down in little sharp points beneath each letter.

Elisa, squatting on the ground, watched to see the crazy, loose-jointed wagon pass by. But it didn't pass. It turned into the farm road in front of her house, crooked old wheels skirling and squeaking. The rangy dog darted from between the wheels and ran ahead. Instantly the two ranch shepherds flew out at him. Then all three stopped and with stiff and quivering tails, with taut straight legs, with ambassadorial dignity, they slowly circled, sniffing daintily. The caravan pulled up to Elisa's wire fence and stopped. Now the newcomer dog, feeling out-numbered, lowered his tail and retired under the wagon with raised hackles and bared teeth.

The man on the wagon seat called out, "That's a bad dog in a fight when he gets started."

Elisa laughed. "I see he is. How soon does he generally get started?"

The man caught up her laughter and echoed it heartily. "Sometimes not for weeks and weeks," he said. He climbed stiffly down, over the wheel. The horse and the donkey drooped like unwatered flowers.

Elisa saw that he was a very big man. Although his hair and beard were graying, he did not look old. His worn black suit was wrinkled and spotted with grease. The laughter had disappeared from his face and eyes the moment his laughing voice ceased. His eyes were dark, and they were full of the brooding that gets in the eyes of teamsters and of sailors. The calloused hands he rested on the wire fence were cracked, and every crack was a black line. He took off his battered hat.

"I'm off my general road, ma'am," he said. "Does this dirt road cut over across the river to the Los Angeles highway?"

Elisa stood up and shoved the thick scissors in her apron pocket. "Well, yes, it does, but it winds around and then fords the river. I don't think your team could pull through the sand."

He replied with some asperity, "It might surprise you what them beasts can pull through."

"When they get started?" she asked.

He smiled for a second. "Yes. When they get started."

"Well," said Elisa, "I think you'll save time if you go back to the Salinas road and pick up the highway there."

He drew a big finger down the chicken wire and made it sing. "I ain't in any hurry, ma'am. I go from Seattle to San Diego and back every year. Takes all my time. About six months each way. I aim to follow nice weather."

Elisa took off her gloves and stuffed them in the apron pocket with the scissors. She touched the under edge of her man's hat, searching for fugitive hairs. "That sounds like a nice kind of way to live," she said.

He leaned confidentially over the fence. "Maybe you noticed the writing on my wagon. I mend pots and sharpen knives and scissors. You got any of them things to do?"

"Oh, no," she said quickly. "Nothing like that." Her eyes hardened with resistance.

"Scissors is the worst thing," he explained. "Most people just ruin scissors trying to sharpen 'em, but I know how. I got a special tool. It's a little bobbit kind of thing, and patented. But it sure does the trick."

"No. My scissors are all sharp."

"All right, then. Take a pot," he continued earnestly, "a bent pot, or a pot with a hole. I can make it like new so you don't have to buy no new ones. That's a saving for you."

"No," she said shortly. "I tell you I have nothing like that for you to do."

His face fell to an exaggerated sadness. His voice took on a whining undertone. "I ain't had a thing to do today. Maybe I won't have no supper tonight. You see I'm off my regular road. I know folks on the highway clear from Seattle to San Diego. They save their things for me to sharpen up because they know I do it so good and save them money."

"I'm sorry," Elisa said irritably. "I haven't anything for you to do."

His eyes left her face and fell to searching the ground. They roamed about until they came to the chrysanthemum bed where she had been working. "What's them plants, ma'am?"

The irritation and resistance melted from Elisa's face. "Oh, those are chrysanthemums, giant whites and yellows. I raise them every year, bigger than anybody around here."

"Kind of a long-stemmed flower? Looks like a quick puff of colored smoke?" he asked.

"That's it. What a nice way to describe them."

"They smell kind of nasty till you get used to them," he said.

"It's a good bitter smell," she retorted, "not nasty at all."

He changed his tone quickly. "I like the smell myself."

"I had ten-inch blooms this year," she said.

The man leaned farther over the fence. "Look. I know a lady down the road a piece, has got the nicest garden you ever seen. Got nearly every kind of flower but no chrysanthemums. Last time I was mending a copper-bottom washtub for her (that's a hard job but I do it good), she said to me, 'If you ever run acrost some nice chrysanthemums I wish you'd try to get me a few seeds.' That's what she told me."

Elisa's eyes grew alert and eager. "She couldn't have known much about chrysanthemums. You *can* raise them from seed, but it's much easier to root the little sprouts you see there."

"Oh," he said, "I s'pose I can't take none to her, then."

"Why yes you can," Elisa cried. "I can put some in damp sand, and you can carry them right along with you. They'll take root in the pot if you keep them damp. And then she can transplant them."

"She'd sure like to have some, ma'am. You say they're nice ones?"

"Beautiful," she said. "Oh, beautiful." Her eyes shone. She tore off the battered hat and shook out her dark pretty hair. "I'll put them in a flower pot, and you can take them right with you. Come into the yard."

While the man came through the picket gate Elisa ran excitedly along the geranium-bordered path to the back of the house. And she returned carrying a big red flower pot. The gloves were forgotten now. She kneeled on the ground by the starting bed and dug up the sandy soil with her fingers and scooped it into the bright new flower pot. Then she picked up the little pile of shoots she had prepared. With her strong fingers she pressed them into the sand and tamped around them with her knuckles. The man stood over her. "I'll tell you what to do," she said. "You remember so you can tell the lady."

"Yes, I'll try to remember."

"Well, look. These will take root in about a month. Then she must set them out, about a foot apart in good rich earth like this, see?" She lifted a handful of dark soil for him to look at. "They'll grow fast and tall. Now remember this: In July tell her to cut them down, about eight inches from the ground."

"Before they bloom?" he asked.

"Yes, before they bloom." Her face was tight with eagerness. "They'll grow right up again. About the last of September the buds will start."

She stopped and seemed perplexed. "It's the budding that takes the most care," she said hesitantly. "I don't know how to tell you." She looked deep into his eyes, searchingly. Her mouth opened a little, and she seemed to be listening. "I'll try to tell you," she said. "Did you ever hear of planting hands?"

"Can't say I have, ma'am."

"Well, I can only tell you what it feels like. It's when you're picking off the buds you don't want. Everything goes right down into your fingertips. You watch your fingers work. They do it themselves. You can feel how it is. They pick and pick the buds.

They never make a mistake. They're with the plant. Do you see? Your fingers and the plant. You can feel that, right up your arm. They know. They never make a mistake. You can feel it. When you're like that you can't do anything wrong. Do you see that? Can you understand that?"

She was kneeling on the ground looking up at him. Her breast swelled passionately.

The man's eyes narrowed. He looked away self-consciously. "Maybe I know," he said. "Sometimes in the night in the wagon there—"

Elisa's voice grew husky. She broke in on him, "I've never lived as you do, but I know what you mean. When the night is dark—why, the stars are sharp-pointed, and there's quiet. Why, you rise up and up! Every pointed star gets driven into your body. It's like that. Hot and sharp and—lovely."

Kneeling there, her hand went out toward his legs in the greasy black trousers. Her hesitant fingers almost touched the cloth. Then her hand dropped to the ground. She crouched low like a fawning dog.

He said, "It's nice, just like you say. Only when you don't have no dinner, it ain't."

She stood up then, very straight, and her face was ashamed. She held the flower pot out to him and placed it gently in his arms. "Here. Put it in your wagon, on the seat, where you can watch it. Maybe I can find something for you to do."

At the back of the house she dug in the can pile and found two old and battered aluminum saucepans. She carried them back and gave them to him. "Here, maybe you can fix these."

His manner changed. He became professional. "Good as new I can fix them." At the back of his wagon he set a little anvil, and out of an oily tool box dug a small machine hammer. Elisa came through the gate to watch him while he pounded out the dents in the kettles. His mouth grew sure and knowing. At a difficult part of the work he sucked his underlip.

"You sleep right in the wagon?" Elisa asked.

"Right in the wagon, ma'am. Rain or shine I'm dry as a cow in there."

"It must be nice," she said. "It must be very nice. I wish women could do such things."

"It ain't the right kind of a life for a woman."

Her upper lip raised a little, showing her teeth. "How do you know? How can you tell?" she said.

"I don't know, ma'am," he protested. "Of course I don't know. Now here's your kettles, done. You don't have to buy no new ones."

"How much?"

"Oh, fifty cents'll do. I keep my prices down and my work good. That's why I have all them satisfied customers up and down the highway."

Elisa brought him a fifty-cent piece from the house and dropped it in his hand. "You might be surprised to have a rival some time. I can sharpen scissors, too. And I can beat the dents out of little pots. I could show you what a woman might do."

He put his hammer back in the oily box and shoved the little anvil out of sight. "It would be a lonely life for a woman, ma'am, and a scary life, too, with animals creeping under the wagon all night." He climbed over the singletree, steadying himself with a hand on the burro's white rump. He settled himself in the seat, picked up the lines. "Thank you kindly, ma'am," he said. "I'll do like you told me; I'll go back and catch the Salinas road."

"Mind," she called, "if you're long in getting there, keep the sand damp."

"Sand, ma'am? . . . Sand? Oh, sure. You mean around the chrysanthemums. Sure I will." He clucked his tongue. The beasts leaned luxuriously into their collars. The mongrel dog took his place between the back wheels. The wagon turned and crawled out the entrance road and back the way it had come, along the river.

Elisa stood in front of her wire fence watching the slow progress of the caravan. Her shoulders were straight, her head thrown back, her eyes half-closed, so that the scene came vaguely into them. Her lips moved silently, forming the words "Good-bye—good-bye." Then she whispered, "That's a bright direction. There's a glowing there." The sound of her whisper startled her. She shook herself free and looked about to see whether anyone had been listening. Only the dogs had heard. They lifted their heads toward her from their sleeping in the dust, and then stretched out their chins and settled asleep again. Elisa turned and ran hurriedly into the house.

In the kitchen she reached behind the stove and felt the water tank. It was full of hot water from the noonday cooking. In the bathroom she tore off her soiled clothes and flung them into the corner. And then she scrubbed herself with a little block of pumice, legs and thighs, loins and chest and arms, until her skin was scratched and red. When she had dried herself she stood in front of a mirror in her bedroom and looked at her body. She tightened her stomach and threw out her chest. She turned and looked over her shoulder at her back.

After a while she began to dress slowly. She put on her newest underclothing and her nicest stockings and the dress which was the symbol of her prettiness. She worked carefully on her hair, penciled her eyebrows and rouged her lips.

Before she was finished she heard the little thunder of hoofs and the shouts of Henry and his helper as they drove the red steers into the corral. She heard the gate bang shut and set herself for Henry's arrival.

His steps sounded on the porch. He entered the house calling, "Elisa, where are you?"

"In my room dressing. I'm not ready. There's hot water for your bath. Hurry up. It's getting late."

When she heard him splashing in the tub, Elisa laid his dark suit on the bed, and shirt and socks and tie beside it. She stood his polished shoes on the floor beside the bed. Then she went to the porch and sat primly and stiffly down. She looked toward the river road where the willow-line was still yellow with frosted leaves so that under the high gray fog they seemed a thin band of sunshine. This was the only color in the gray afternoon. She sat unmoved for a long time. Her eyes blinked rarely.

Henry came banging out of the door, shoving his tie inside his vest as he came. Elisa stiffened and her face grew tight. Henry stopped short and looked at her. "Why—why, Elisa. You look so nice!"

"Nice? You think I look nice? What do you mean by 'nice'?"

Henry blundered on. "I don't know. I mean you look different, strong and happy."

"I am strong? Yes, strong. What do you mean 'strong'?"

He looked bewildered. "You're playing some kind of a game," he said helplessly. "It's a kind of a play. You look strong enough to break a calf over your knee, happy enough to eat it like a watermelon."

For a second she lost her rigidity. "Henry! Don't talk like that. You didn't know what you said." She grew complete again. "I'm strong," she boasted. "I never knew before how strong."

Henry looked down toward the tractor shed, and when he brought his eyes back to her, they were his own again. "I'll get out the car. You can put on your coat while I'm starting."

Elisa went into the house. She heard him drive to the gate and idle down his motor, and then she took a long time to put on her hat. She pulled it here and pressed it there. When Henry turned the motor off she slipped into her coat and went out.

The little roadster bounced along on the dirt road by the river, raising the birds and driving the rabbits into the brush. Two cranes flapped heavily over the willow-line and dropped into the riverbed.

Far ahead on the road Elisa saw a dark speck. She knew.

She tried not to look as they passed it, but her eyes would not obey. She whispered to herself sadly, "He might have thrown them off the road. That wouldn't have been much trouble, not very much. But he kept the pot," she explained. "He had to keep the pot. That's why he couldn't get them off the road."

The roadster turned a bend and she saw the caravan ahead. She swung full around toward her husband so she could not see the little covered wagon and the mismatched team as the car passed them.

In a moment it was over. The thing was done. She did not look back.

She said loudly, to be heard above the motor, "It will be good, tonight, a good dinner."

"Now you're changed again," Henry complained. He took one hand from the wheel and patted her knee. "I ought to take you in to dinner oftener. It would be good for both of us. We get so heavy out on the ranch."

"Henry," she asked, "could we have wine at dinner?"

"Sure we could. Say! That will be fine."

She was silent for a while; then she said, "Henry, at those prize fights, do the men hurt each other very much?"

"Sometimes a little, not often. Why?"

"Well, I've read how they break noses, and blood runs down their chests. I've read how the fighting gloves get heavy and soggy with blood."

He looked around at her. "What's the matter, Elisa? I didn't know you read things like that." He brought the car to a stop, then turned to the right over the Salinas River bridge.

"Do any women ever go to the fights?" she asked.

"Oh, sure, some. What's the matter, Elisa? Do you want to go? I don't think you'd like it, but I'll take you if you really want to go."

She relaxed limply in the seat. "Oh, no. No. I don't want to go. I'm sure I don't." Her face was turned away from him. "It will be enough if we can have wine. It will be plenty." She turned up her coat collar so he could not see that she was crying weakly— like an old woman.

# John Updike

## (b. 1932)

John Updike views writing as a learning process, "for writing educates the writer as it goes along." He was born in Reading, Pennsylvania, and, as a child, read books by Erle Stanley Gardner, Ellery Queen, Agatha Christie, John Dickson Carr, and P. G. Wodehouse. He claimed that dead authors depressed him. Updike attended Harvard, where he majored in English and contributed to and edited the *Harvard Lampoon.* One year after graduating, Updike began working for the *New Yorker,* where he contributed editorials, poetry, stories, and criticism. He left the magazine in 1957 to become a full-time writer. His first book, *The Carpentered Hen and Other Tame Creatures* (1958), was a collection of poetry. *The Poorhouse Fair* (1959) was his first novel. Updike's works include *Rabbit, Run* (1960), *The Centaur* (1963), *Couples* (1968), *Rabbit Redux* (1971), *The Coup* (1979), and *Rabbit at Rest* (1990). Updike's work often takes a satirical view of small-town, middle-class life. His collection *Licks of Love* (2000) features a novella called "Rabbit Remembered," the final chapter of Harry "Rabbit" Angstrom's story. Updike has received several awards during his career, among them a Guggenheim Fellowship (1959), the National Book Award in Fiction (1964), the O. Henry Prize (1967–1968), and the National Medal of the Arts (1989). In 2003 Updike received the National Medal for Humanities.

## *A & P*
1961

In walks these three girls in nothing but bathing suits. I'm in the third checkout slot, with my back to the door, so I don't see them until they're over by the bread. The one that caught my eye first was the one in the plaid green two-piece. She was a chunky kid, with a good tan and a sweet broad soft-looking can with those two crescents of white just under it, where the sun never seems to hit, at the top of the backs of her legs. I stood there with my hand on a box of HiHo crackers trying to remember if I rang it up or not. I ring it up again and the customer starts giving me hell. She's one of these cash-register-watchers, a witch about fifty with rouge on her cheekbones and no eyebrows, and I know it made her day to trip me up. She'd been watching cash registers for fifty years and probably never seen a mistake before.

By the time I got her feathers smoothed and her goodies into a bag—she gives me a little snort in passing, if she'd been born at the right time they would have burned her over in Salem—by the time I get her on her way the girls had circled around the bread and were coming back, without a pushcart, back my way along the counters, in the aisle between the checkouts and the Special bins. They didn't even have shoes on. There was this chunky one, with the two-piece—it was bright green and all the seams on the bra were still sharp and her belly was still pretty pale so I guessed she just got it (the suit)—there was this one, with one of those chubby berry-faces, the lips all bunched together under her nose, this one, and a tall one, with black hair that hadn't quite frizzed right, and one of these sunburns right across under the eyes, and a chin that was too long—you know, the kind of girl other girls think is very "striking" and "attractive" but never quite makes it, as they very well know, which is why they like her so much—and then the third one, that wasn't quite so tall. She was the queen. She kind of led them, the other two peeking around and making their shoulders round. She didn't look around, not this queen, she just walked straight on slowly, on these long white primadonna legs. She came down a little hard on her heels, as if she didn't walk in bare feet that much, putting down her heels and then letting the weight move along to her toes as if she was testing the floor with every step, putting a little deliberate extra action into it. You never know for sure how girls' minds work (do you really think it's a mind in there or just a little buzz like a bee in a glass jar?) but you got the idea she had talked the other two into coming here with her, and now she was showing them how to do it, walk slow and hold yourself straight.

She had on a kind of dirty-pink—beige maybe, I don't know—bathing suit with a little nubble all over it and, what got me, the straps were down. They were off her shoulders looped loose around the cool tops of her arms, and I guess as a result the suit had slipped a little on her, so all around the top of the cloth there was this shining rim. If it hadn't been there you wouldn't have known there could have been anything whiter than those shoulders. With the straps pushed off, there was nothing between the top of the suit and the top of her head except just *her*, this clean bare plane of the top of her chest down from the shoulder bones like a dented sheet of metal tilted in the light. I mean, it was more than pretty.

She had a sort of oaky hair that the sun and salt had bleached, done up in a bun that was unravelling, and a kind of prim face. Walking into the A & P with your straps down, I suppose it's the only kind of face you *can* have. She held her head so high her neck, coming up out of those white shoulders, looked kind of stretched, but I didn't mind. The longer her neck was, the more of her there was.

She must have felt in the corner of her eye me and over my shoulder Stokesie in the second slot watching, but she didn't tip. Not this queen. She kept her eyes moving across the racks, and stopped, and turned so slow it made my stomach rub the inside of my apron, and buzzed to the other two, who kind of huddled against her for relief, and then they all three of them went up the cat-and-dog-food-breakfast-cereal-macaroni-rice-raisins-seasonings-spreads-spaghetti-soft-drinks-crackers-and-cookies aisle. From the third slot I look straight up this aisle to the meat counter, and I watched them all the way. The fat one with the tan sort of fumbled with the cookies, but on second thought she put the package back. The sheep pushing their carts down the aisle—the girls were walking against the usual traffic (not that we have one-way signs or anything)—were pretty hilarious. You could see them, when Queenie's white shoulders dawned on them, kind of jerk, or hop, or hiccup, but their eyes snapped back to their own baskets and on they pushed. I bet you could set off dynamite in an A & P and the people would by and large keep reaching and checking oatmeal off their lists and muttering "Let me see, there was a third thing, began with A, asparagus, no, ah, yes, applesauce!" or whatever it is they do mutter. But there was no doubt, this jiggled them. A few houseslaves in pin curlers even looked around after pushing their carts past to make sure what they had seen was correct.

You know, it's one thing to have a girl in a bathing suit down on the beach, where what with the glare nobody can look at each other much anyway, and another thing in the cool of the A & P, under the fluorescent lights, against all those stacked packages, with her feet paddling along naked over our checker-board green-and-cream rubber-tile floor.

"Oh Daddy," Stokesie said beside me. "I feel so faint."

"Darling," I said. "Hold me tight." Stokesie's married, with two babies chalked up on his fuselage already, but as far as I can tell that's the only difference. He's twenty-two, and I was nineteen this April.

"Is it done?" he asks, the responsible married man finding his voice. I forgot to say he thinks he's going to be manager some sunny day, maybe in 1990 when it's called the Great Alexandrov and Petrooshki Tea Company or something.

What he meant was, our town is five miles from a beach, with a big summer colony out on the Point, but we're right in the middle of town, and the women generally put on a shirt or shorts or something before they get out of the car into the street. And anyway these are usually women with six children and varicose veins mapping their legs and nobody, including them, could care less. As I say, we're right in the middle of town, and if you stand at our front doors you can see two banks and the Congregational church and the newspaper store and three real-estate offices and about twenty-seven old freeloaders tearing up Central Street because the sewer broke again. It's not as if we're on the Cape; we're north of Boston and there's people in this town haven't seen the ocean for twenty years.

The girls had reached the meat counter and were asking McMahon something. He pointed, they pointed, and they shuffled out of sight behind a pyramid of Diet Delight peaches. All that was left for us to see was old McMahon patting his mouth and looking after them sizing up their joints. Poor kids, I began to feel sorry for them, they couldn't help it.

Now here comes the sad part of the story, at least my family says it's sad, but I don't think it's so sad myself. The store's pretty empty, it being Thursday afternoon, so there was nothing much to do except lean on the register and wait for the girls to show up again. The whole store was like a pinball machine and I didn't know which tunnel they'd come out of. After a while they come around out of the far aisle, around the light bulbs, records at discount of the Caribbean Six or Tony Martin Sings or some such gunk you wonder they waste the wax on, six-packs of candy bars, and plastic toys done up in cellophane that fall apart when a kid looks at them anyway. Around they come, Queenie still leading the way, and holding a little gray jar in her hand. Slots Three through Seven are unmanned and I could see her wondering between Stokes and me, but Stokesie with his usual luck draws an old party in baggy gray pants who stumbles up with four giant cans of pineapple juice (what do these bums *do* with all that pineapple juice? I've often asked myself) so the girls come to me. Queenie puts down the jar and I take it into my fingers icy cold. Kingfish Fancy Herring Snacks in Pure Sour Cream: 49¢. Now her hands are empty, not a ring or a bracelet, bare as God made them, and I wonder where the money's coming from. Still with that prim look she lifts a folded dollar bill out of the hollow at the center of her nubbled pink top. The jar went heavy in my hand. Really, I thought that was so cute.

Then everybody's luck begins to run out. Lengel comes in from haggling with a truck full of cabbages on the lot and is about to scuttle into that door marked MAN-AGER behind which he hides all day when the girls touch his eye. Lengel's pretty dreary, teaches Sunday school and the rest, but he doesn't miss that much. He comes over and says, "Girls, this isn't the beach."

Queenie blushes, though maybe it's just a brush of sunburn I was noticing for the first time, now that she was so close. "My mother asked me to pick up a jar of herring snacks." Her voice kind of startled me, the way voices do when you see the people first, coming out so flat and dumb yet kind of tony, too, the way it ticked over "pick up" and "snacks." All of a sudden I slid right down her voice into her living room. Her father and the other men were standing around in ice-cream coats and bow ties and the women were in sandals picking up herring snacks on toothpicks off a big glass plate and they were all holding drinks the color of water with olives and springs of mint in them. When my parents have somebody over they get lemonade and if it's a real racy affair Schlitz in tall glasses with "They'll Do It Every Time" cartoons stencilled on.

"That's all right," Lengel said. "But this isn't the beach." His repeating this struck me as funny, as if it had just occurred to him, and he had been thinking all these years the A & P was a great big dune and he was the head lifeguard. He didn't like my smiling—as I say he doesn't miss much—but he concentrates on giving the girls that sad Sunday-school-superintendent stare.

Queenie's blush is no sunburn now, and the plump one in plaid, that I liked better from the back—a really sweet can—pipes up, "We weren't doing any shopping. We just came in for the one thing."

"That makes no difference," Lengel tells her, and I could see from the way his eyes went that he hadn't noticed she was wearing a two-piece before. "We want you decently dressed when you come in here."

"We *are* decent," Queenie says suddenly, her lower lip pushing, getting sore now that she remembers her place, a place from which the crowd that runs the A & P must look pretty crummy. Fancy Herring Snacks flashed in her very blue eyes.

"Girls, I don't want to argue with you. After this come in here with your shoulders covered. It's our policy." He turns his back. That's policy for you. Policy is what the kingpins want. What the others want is juvenile delinquency.

All this while, the customers had been showing up with their carts but, you know, sheep, seeing a scene, they had all bunched up on Stokesie, who shook open a paper bag as gently as peeling a peach, not wanting to miss a word. I could feel in the silence everybody getting nervous, most of all Lengel, who asks me, "Sammy, have you rung up their purchase?"

I thought and said "No" but it wasn't about that I was thinking. I go through the punches, 4, 9, GROC, TOT—it's more complicated than you think, and after you do it often enough, it begins to make a little song, that you hear words to, in my case "Hello (*bing*) there, you (*gung*) hap-py *pee*-pul (*splat*)!"—the *splat* being the drawer flying out. I uncrease the bill, tenderly as you may imagine, it just having come from between the two smoothest scoops of vanilla I had ever known there were, and pass a half and a penny into her narrow pink palm, and nestle the herrings in a bag and twist its neck and hand it over, all the time thinking.

The girls, and who'd blame them, are in a hurry to get out, so I say "I quit" to Lengel quick enough for them to hear, hoping they'll stop and watch me, their unsuspected hero. They keep right on going, into the electric eye; the door flies open and they flicker across the lot to their car, Queenie and Plaid and Big Tall Goony-Goony (not that as raw material she was so bad), leaving me with Lengel and a kink in his eyebrow.

"Did you say something, Sammy?"

"I said I quit."

"I thought you did."

"You didn't have to embarrass them."

"It was they who were embarrassing us."

I started to say something that came out "Fiddle-de-do." It's a saying of my grandmother's, and I know she would have been pleased.

"I don't think you know what you're saying," Lengel said.

"I know you don't," I said. "But I do." I pull the bow at the back of my apron and start shrugging it off my shoulders. A couple of customers that had been heading for my slot begin to knock against each other, like scared pigs in a chute.

Lengel sighs and begins to look very patient and old and gray. He's been a friend of my parents for years. "Sammy, you don't want to do this to your Mom and Dad," he tells me. It's true, I don't. But it seems to me that once you begin a gesture it's fatal not to go through with it. I folded the apron, "Sammy" stitched in red on the pocket, and put it on the counter, and drop the bow tie on top of it. The bow tie is theirs, if you've ever wondered. "You'll feel this for the rest of your life," Lengel says, and I know that's true, too, but remembering how he made that pretty girl blush makes me so scrunchy inside I punch the No Sale tab and the machine whirs "pee-pul" and the drawer splats out. One advantage to this scene taking place in summer, I can follow this up with a clean exit, there's no fumbling around getting your coat and galoshes, I just saunter into the electric eye in my white shirt that my mother ironed the night before, and the door heaves itself open, and outside the sunshine is skating around on the asphalt.

I look around for my girls, but they're gone, of course. There wasn't anybody but some young married screaming with her children about some candy they didn't get by the door of a powder-blue Falcon station wagon. Looking back in the big windows, over the bags of peat moss and aluminum lawn furniture stacked on the pavement, I could see Lengel in my place in the slot, checking the sheep through. His face was dark gray and his back stiff, as if he's just had an injection of iron, and my stomach kind of fell as I felt how hard the world was going to be to me hereafter.

# Luisa Valenzuela

## (1938– )

Luisa Valenzuela was born in Buenos Aires in 1938. She began writing as a journalist for *Crisis* magazine and the newspaper *The Nation*. In 1959 she went to Paris and from 1972 to 1974 visited Mexico, Paris, Barcelona, and New York. She began teaching in New York in 1979 and received a Guggenheim Fellowship in 1983. She has published several books, including *The Lizard's Tail* (1983), *He Who Searches* (1987), *The Censors* (1992), *Symmetries* (1993), and *Black Novel with Argentines* (2002). She writes about Argentinean culture and politics, the repressions of dictatorship, and the intricacies of exile, memory, language, and national identity.

## *A Family for Clotilde*                                                   1966

TRANSLATED BY HORTENSE CARPENTIER AND J. JORGE CASTELLO

Rolo spent that morning, like so many others, watching Rolando. For his father, taking a rest meant exhausting himself physically: long jogs down the deserted beach, racing, leaping, one exercise after another. He was forty-six and still physically fit. Rolo was about to turn seventeen; it was a serious age, and unlike his father, he felt sick and tired of the world.

Standing at the top of a dune, or drinking an orangeade, Rolo watched the sun glistening on his father's golden back as he conscientiously did his calisthenics. Rolando was a good athlete and he knew it. Rolo looked at his own pale body, narrow at the shoulders, and understood why he was ashamed to walk next to his father when they were both in bathing suits. Even so, as the season progressed, and they rented a cabana, Rolo preferred going to the beach with his father to sitting in a beach chair next to his mother all day long. She was unusually emphatic in her attitudes, and if in November and December she was busy in the house and didn't take a moment's rest, for the remainder of the vacation she would forget the house and family and dedicate herself entirely to sunbathing. She wanted to return to Buenos Aires looking as if she had had a good time.

That afternoon there was nothing to do, as usual, and Rolo sat on the fence and dreamed about dancing, about girls in bikinis, about friends he missed. At four o'clock Don Luis clambered up from the beach along the path between the dunes that led to Rolando's house. Don Luis's cart was massive, and corroded by the sea.

"Good afternoon," said the driver.

"Hi," said Rolo.

"You could make that sound more cheerful. I have the valises of the lady who's going to stay in the cottage in back of your house. Your family's lucky, I told your father, because at this time of year nobody rents or sells."

The horses pulling the cart rested after the hard trek. Only the pony was impatient and breathing hard.

"Uh huh," Rolo mumbled without enthusiasm, but he looked intently at the white leather bags and the enormous old-fashioned trunk.

"Looks like the lady's going to stay a long time, eh?"

"Uh huh."

"All summer?"

"All summer, part of autumn, the rest of her life. That goes for us, too; we'll never move away from here. Buried."

He dug his penknife into the trunk of a pine tree. He wanted to go away, anyplace. If only Pinamar were a port, then he could at least imagine trips. . . .

It was Sunday morning. With his jacket over his shoulder, Rolo walked through the trees surrounding the house, along the border of thickly clustered acacias, to the garden of the rear cottage. He had forgotten about the new tenant, but there she was to remind him, reclining on a deck chair in the shade, showing a great deal of white flesh and gleaming red hair. Rolo stopped short.

"Hi, darling. Where're you off to?" She had a warm, soft voice.

"To Mass," he answered grudgingly.

"To Mass?" Coming from her, the word sounded new and mysterious.

The sun was burning bright. Rolo wanted to stretch out in the cool air under the pines and simply listen to her. Instead he said, "Yes, to Mass. You may think our chapel small and ugly and unfinished, but that's not what counts if you want to go to Mass."

"Hmm. And if you were to stay here at my side and sip a gin and tonic, wouldn't that be nicer than going to church?"

"No."

"Well, your good father would prefer to sit here with me. He isn't like you. He doesn't go to Mass. Yesterday afternoon he passed by here on horseback five times. Just a little while ago I saw him in a bathing suit; he must be off for a swim. . . . Stay a bit."

She had deep-set dark-gray eyes. Rolo ran off without answering her.

I'll show that wild woman I'm not like my father, he thought. Who does the old man think he is, coming through here all hot and excited? I'll teach them. . . .

As the days passed, Rolando grew pensive. Rolo followed him all over the house, taunting him whenever he could. But Rolando didn't complain; in fact, it was practically impossible to drag a word out of him on any subject.

"Dear, don't put your feet on the sofa, you'll dirty the cretonne."

"Dear, move a little so I can open the windows and air the place a bit."

And the dear did as he was asked, without protest. Astonishing.

Rolo first became suspicious when he noticed that his father no longer got up at seven o'clock to take his early-morning swim. Then, one afternoon during siesta, he saw Rolando sneaking out through the kitchen door. Rolo raced upstairs to the attic and peered out of the small window just as Rolando entered Clotilde's house—without knocking, as if she were one of the family.

They're going to find out what I can do, and they'll have to learn the hard way, Rolo thought. They'll see. No one plays dirty with me. I was invited first.

Rolo had never thought of himself as patient, but sometimes virtues surface in time of need. Squatting on the dry, brittle leaves behind the bank of acacias, he waited two long hours for Rolando to abandon her body, the body that must be so white between the sheets, so soft to sink one's hands into. He thought of the other poor bodies he had known, withered and worn, smelling of his friends who had been there before him.

Clotilde must be different, he thought, and he had her in the palm of his hand. Now that he knew their secret and could denounce them. Soon he would show those two he also was a man. Rolo, little Rolo, would follow his father's footsteps to Clotilde's flesh. He would put his mouth where his father's had been, he would carefully imitate each of his gestures. The wait was long and torturous, but the compensation of Clotilde's hot, slippery body would come.

A blossoming azalea exuded a subtle smell that Rolo was not prepared to appreciate. Beyond the flowers, beyond the walls of the house, he imagined his naked father on the white Clotilde, and he knew his turn would come.

Rolando wouldn't take long. The door with the slightly flaky green paint would open just wide enough for him to slip out, and Rolo would only wait long enough to see Rolando recede in the distance. Then he would enter quickly and take Clotilde by force. She'd have no way to defend herself.

That wasn't how it happened at all, of course. Clotilde saw him, called to him, and he surrendered as meekly as a puppy. It was Clotilde who guided his hands along the trail of his father's hands.

"He asked me to swear not to say anything to you, and I swore and asked him to go on kissing me. . . . As if I cared . . ."

Rolando laughed a cold, empty laugh, but Clotilde went on chattering. When she tried to cuddle up against his body, however, the muscles of his back arched one by one, and he leaped up, smashing his fist on the night table. A little while later, though, he sauntered into the bathroom as if nothing had happened. He came back looking calm and lay down beside her, but then doubt assailed him again and he shook Clotilde violently, shouting, "I'm better than the kid, right? Tell me I'm better than the kid!"

"Yes, yes," she said, and she thought of the boy who had never dared to sigh, and she felt tender toward him.

The following afternoon, Rolando told his wife that he was going out to get some cigarettes, and she seemed to believe him.

Rolo, however, couldn't say, "I'm going out to get some cigarettes," because he wasn't allowed to smoke. But he was allowed to come and go as he pleased, so he didn't have to make up excuses in order to visit Clotilde and engage in something far more serious than smoking.

As soon as his father left, Rolo, as usual, ran upstairs to spy on him from the attic window. The scene was always the same: Rolando, hurrying, furtive, ran into her open arms, and he, Rolo, felt happy because he would soon be on the path his father had paved for him, thus proving that he was no less a man.

But any man is a man, given certain attributes. In a sense, Clotilde was as much a man as either of them: she manipulated them as she pleased, frustrating them, pitting one against the other, favoring one over the other. She was the real man there, and she knew it. She reaffirmed it every night in the bed that often bore the weight and heat of one of them before the weight and heat of the other had faded. Clotilde. She would look at herself in the mirror, caressing her full breasts, smiling and showing her teeth, white, even, indifferent. Thinking was a tremendous effort for her: she simply felt happy and at times nostalgic. She also enjoyed tantalizing those who had the good fortune to touch her. And she felt no remorse about it.

In the big house on the other side of the dense acacias and the soft rosy mattress of pine needles, Estela, Rolo's mother and Rolando's wife, was also in the habit of looking at herself in the bathroom mirror. Her image emerged from the cloud of foam she used to clean the mirror. She ran the rag back and forth furiously, sometimes allowing only her eyes to appear, sometimes an ear or a corner of her mouth that revealed a hurt expression. She would have loved to rub that image out altogether, but there it was, facing her, inexorable, and all she could do was wash the mirror and hope a little of the cleanliness would rub off on her soul.

She knew it: her two men were gone forever, gone to the other woman because Estela was soft and easy, not hard and strong like the other one.

Rolo crouched behind the thick maze of acacias. He knew that the door would open at any moment, and he curled up even more in his hiding place. But it was a false alarm, or, more accurately, a false hope. His father was lingering longer than usual on Clotilde's body; it wasn't fair; Rolo was restless. What if she was detaining him? Could she have asked his father not to leave her? Still, the one time he had asked her how Rolando caressed her, she had answered, "Not exactly out of this world . . ."

"Please tell me what he does with you. I don't want to be less of a man."

"No, I like the differences. He's a brute. He beats me. Sometimes he slaps me across the face and shouts while he's making love to me."

She had turned toward him and put his uncombed head on her belly. "But you are soft, almost like a girl. I like to stroke your face, your shoulders, your back."

"Have you ever done it with a woman?"

"Hmm," she had answered vaguely. Sometimes he interpreted the *hmm* as yes, sometimes as no, depending on his mood.

He had been hiding behind the acacias for over two hours. Soon his mother would wake up from her siesta; he was furious. Clotilde knew very well that he was there, but there wasn't even a sign from her. That whore. She was worse, devouring anything that came her way—men, women, old people, children; a sexual ostrich.

To calm himself, Rolo walked behind the cottage. Hidden behind the shutters, the father watched his son's every move.

He doesn't know yet Clotilde isn't here. What the hell, let him suffer. I'm suffering too, Rolando kept repeating to himself.

Rolo stopped abruptly. Behind the climbing jasmines, in front of the bedroom window, there was a mound of cigar butts, some crushed, some smoked down to a nub, some only half smoked, all with a cork tip. His father had been there many times, probably hoping his son would leave Clotilde's bed once and for all so he, Rolando, could go back to her and have the last laugh.

Rolando knew his secret, he knew his son had also been there, just as he had been before him, just as he would be again. Always Rolando had to have the last word, the last loud laugh, the last act of love. His father always bested him, always flattened him out. It was Clotilde's fault this time for telling him everything, for not keeping her mouth shut. Whore.

Behind the shutters, Rolando felt jealous of his son and happy to see him standing there confused. Clotilde had left him a note saying she would be gone until evening. She must be avoiding him; she knew he would be coming that afternoon. And that poor boy, standing there disconsolate, believing his father was performing Heaven knows what feats, not realizing that those feats are usually a young man's prerogative.

On either side of the closed shutters, father and son stood overcome, defeated. He'll stay in there all afternoon, Rolo thought, all night, forcing her to forget about me. Finally Rolo decided to leave. He walked slowly down the path, kicking pebbles and telling himself that, after all, Clotilde must prefer women anyway, the struggle wasn't worth it.

Rolando watched Rolo move in the distance. He may be too thin, thought Rolando, and his back may curve, but still and all, Rolo is young and strong and intense in the way women like.

Neither of them could guess that Clotilde was fed up with the whole affair, with Rolo hiding in the garden while Rolando was with her, and then Rolando pacing back and forth in the garden like a caged lion, although he would never admit it. As if she didn't know that they were searching for each other through her.

That night, Rolo helped his mother wash the dishes, a thing he seldom did.

"Mama," he said after a long silence, "do you know the woman who rents the cottage in the back?"

"No."

There was an uncomfortable pause.

"You should get to know her. Make friends with her. She's very nice."

"I don't need friends. Not the likes of her, anyway."

"Why not make friends with her, Mama? After all, she's our tenant." It was a bold statement to make to a mother who must have known quite well what was going on. "You could go see her tomorrow and bring her a piece of that delicious cake you make. . . ."

His mother wiped the burners of the stove furiously, then took off her apron and went into the bedroom.

Rolando was in bed. He had not gone for a walk in the woods, he was not reading in the living room. He was simply there, installed in bed as if he'd been waiting for her.

She spent a long time in the bathroom and came back into the bedroom in her nightgown.

"Estela," Rolando said, "Estela, you've been alone so much, too much lately. If we're going to stay here another two months, why not get to know people?"

"My friends are coming after Epiphany. . . ."

"That's a month away, Estela. Meanwhile what? Stay shut up in this house? The weather's nice now for the beach. You ought to have a friend to go with you."

"You have someone in mind?"

"In mind, no . . . the tenant, maybe. She seems pleasant enough."

It must be a conspiracy, she thought. They must be making fun of me. She was sick and tired of being treated like an idiot for trying to keep peace in the family. They wanted to see her act, well, she would act. The fight's on, she thought; let's see who wins. An inspection of the enemy camp can't hurt; that will give me an equal chance.

"Fine," she said, gently as usual. "If tomorrow's all right with you, I'll go visit her and bring some cake for tea."

Rolando was astonished at the ease with which he had convinced her.

The men in the family are sadder than ever. While they were enjoying themselves they could afford to overlook her pain. It had been a clean fight between men, altogether understandable. They had eaten with gusto, shown their happiness in an effort to make each other suffer. They had paid no attention to the woman who sat in front of them, doing her best not to burst into tears.

Now the situation is very different. Estela is exultant, she has turned into an eloquent conversationalist. She has acquired a new grandeur. She, Estela, now occupies an ample and warm place where the two men had once fit. Now Estela is alone and triumphant in Clotilde's bosom.

Listless, they never look at her or at each other. They only walk back and forth in the house that is no longer a home because Estela has neglected the floor, the meals. And she no longer bothers to put flowers on the table. She has other interests. From the last bite of lunch until sunset, she spends the day in Clotilde's cottage. A lightning friendship, one might say, blissful love at first sight, the reunion of queen bees, with the drones buzzing around like lost souls. Sometimes they circle around Estela, trying to get her back; at other times they attempt to get back to Clotilde. They haven't succeeded with either—no bread and no cake.

Finally, they were ready for a confrontation. But what could those two dispossessed beings say to each other, those two males who had learned that the only way they could reach each other was through silent competition?

The days went on until Rolo couldn't stand it any longer. He walked over to his old hiding place to spy on the cottage. He had hoped to set his mother against his father, but the wind had blown another way: good-by, Clotilde; good-by, love; good-by. Estela now took up all her time, all her gestures, all her words. She had shown herself to be the most astute: she had conquered Clotilde effortlessly. "You have a formidable mother," Clotilde had said to him the one time he saw her alone. And she hadn't said another word—no apologies, no gratitude for what had gone on before. About-face, march, and once again she was inside her cottage with the door firmly closed.

Huddled behind the acacias, Rolo is remembering the past with Clotilde. He knows that a few feet away, Rolando is taking his customary walk behind the climbing jasmines. Both are caught in the same trap, spying on the women who are devoted to one another and have no intention of parting.

Neither knows what he is waiting for, and each ignores the other's presence. They ignore everything except the world from which they have been excluded forever. They listen, and each in his hiding place receives on his face the lash of a kind of laugh, a submissive laugh, somewhat ashamed, that rises suddenly to cover up something and then lowers in tone, changing into a whisper that filters into the bones. Rolo leaps up and runs toward the bedroom window and, unexpectedly, collides with his father, who has also left his hiding place on hearing that laugh that threatens not to end. They look at each other accusingly, but neither says a word. They are both outside forever, and it is only because they had had the idea of putting Estela inside the cottage. Now Estela was never going to leave, for she had awakened Clotilde's laugh.

It is a well-tuned murmuring, like the pines, caressing, loving. Suddenly it begins to rain, softly at first, then with some fury. They remain in the garden, drenched, waiting until night falls.

Inside the cottage, Estela doesn't feel the cold, the rain, the night. She smiles with beatific happiness because her plan has succeeded. She makes Clotilde repeat once again the Act of Contrition and the Prayer to the Virgin. "Hail Mary, full of grace . . ." The prayer returns and undulates like a laugh that leaves Clotilde's contrite lips. And Estela, who doesn't really care about Clotilde's contrition, smiles because she knows that she has won back her men.

# Eudora Welty

## (1909–2001)

Writer and photographer Eudora Welty was born in 1909 in Jackson, Mississippi. With her parents' encouragement, Welty transferred to the University of Wisconsin in 1927 and began to focus on writing. In 1929, she earned a B.A. She also attended Columbia University Graduate School of Business in New York, studying advertising. During the Great Depression, Welty worked for the Works Progress Administration as a Junior Publicity Agent. Her duties were to write newspaper copy, take photographs of places after destruction, study troubled juveniles, put booths in county fairs, and interview various people. Her first story, "Death of a Traveling Salesman" (1936), was published in *Manuscript* magazine. She published *The Robber Bridegroom* (1942), *Delta Wedding* (1946), *The Golden Apples* (1949), and *The Ponder Heart* (1954) before setting aside her writing in 1955 to care for her two brothers, who were diagnosed with severe arthritis, and her mother, who was paralyzed by a stroke. Welty spent the next eleven years caring for her family. After her brothers and her mother died in 1966, she began writing again and, in 1969, published *The Optimist's Daughter.* With keen visual imagery and subtle humor, Welty's writings consider small-town life, non-conformity, and the passage of time. Welty received several awards throughout her life, including a Guggenheim fellowship (1942), the National Medal for Literature (1980), the National Medal of Arts (1987), and the French Legion of Honor (1996). In 1999, she became the first living writer ever to be included in the Library of America series.

---

## Why I Live at the P.O. 1941

**I** was getting along fine with Mama, Papa-Daddy and Uncle Rondo until my sister Stella-Rondo just separated from her husband and came back home again. Mr. Whitaker! Of course I went with Mr. Whitaker first, when he first appeared here in China Grove, taking "Pose Yourself" photos, and Stella-Rondo broke us up. Told him I was one-sided. Bigger on one side than the other, which is a deliberate, calculated falsehood: I'm the same. Stella-Rondo is exactly twelve months to the day younger than I am and for that reason she's spoiled.

She's always had anything in the world she wanted and then she'd throw it away. Papa-Daddy gave her this gorgeous Add-a-Pearl necklace when she was eight years old and she threw it away playing baseball when she was nine, with only two pearls.

So as soon as she got married and moved away from home the first thing she did was separate! From Mr. Whitaker! This photographer with the popeyes she said she trusted. Came home from one of those towns up in Illinois and to our complete surprise brought this child of two.

Mama said she like to made her drop dead for a second. "Here you had this marvelous blonde child and never so much as wrote your mother a word about it," says Mama. "I'm thoroughly ashamed of you." But of course she wasn't.

Stella-Rondo just calmly takes off this *hat,* I wish you could see it. She says, "Why, Mama, Shirley-T.'s adopted, I can prove it."

"How?" says Mama, but all I says was, "H'm!" There I was over the hot stove, trying to stretch two chickens over five people and a completely unexpected child into the bargain, without one moment's notice.

"What do you mean—'H'm!'?" says Stella-Rondo, and Mama says, "I heard that, Sister."

I said that oh, I didn't mean a thing, only that whoever Shirley-T. was, she was the spit-image of Papa-Daddy if he'd cut off his beard, which of course he'd never do in the world. Papa-Daddy's Mama's papa and sulks.

Stella-Rondo got furious! She said, "Sister, I don't need to tell you you got a lot of nerve and always did have and I'll thank you to make no future reference to my adopted child whatsoever."

"Very well," I said. "Very well, very well. Of course I noticed at once she looks like

Mr. Whitaker's side too. That frown. She looks like a cross between Mr. Whitaker and Papa-Daddy."

"Well, all I can say is she isn't."

"She looks exactly like Shirley Temple to me," says Mama, but Shirley-T. just ran away from her.

So the first thing Stella-Rondo did at the table was turn Papa-Daddy against me.

"Papa-Daddy," she says. He was trying to cut up his meat. "Papa-Daddy!" I was taken completely by surprise. Papa-Daddy is about a million years old, and's got this long-long beard. "Papa-Daddy, Sister said she fails to understand why you don't cut off your beard."

So Papa-Daddy l-a-y-s down his knife and fork! He's real rich. Mama says he is, he says he isn't. So he says, "Have I heard correctly? You don't understand why I don't cut off my beard?"

"Why," I says, "Papa-Daddy, of course I understand, I did not say any such of a thing, the idea!"

He says, "Hussy!"

I says, "Papa-Daddy, you know I wouldn't any more want you to cut off your beard than the man in the moon. It was the farthest thing from my mind! Stella-Rondo sat there and made that up while she was eating breast of chicken."

But he says, "So the postmistress fails to understand why I don't cut off my beard. Which job I got you through my influence with the government. 'Bird's nest'—is that what you call it?"

Not that it isn't the next to smallest P.O. in the entire state of Mississippi.

I says, "Oh, Papa-Daddy," I says, "I didn't say any such of a thing, I never dreamed it was a bird's nest, I have always been grateful though this is the next to smallest P.O. in the state of Mississippi, and I do enjoy being referred to as a hussy by my own grandfather."

But Stella-Rondo says, "Yes, you did say it too. Anybody in the world could of heard you, that had ears."

"Stop right there," says Mama, looking at *me*.

So I pulled my napkin straight back through the napkin ring and left the table.

As soon as I was out of the room, Mama says, "Call her back, or she'll starve to death," but Papa-Daddy says, "This is the beard I started growing on the Coast when I was fifteen years old." He would of gone on till nightfall if Shirley-T. hadn't lost the Milky Way she ate in Cairo.

So Papa-Daddy says,"I am going out and lie in the hammock, and you can sit here and remember my words: I'll never cut off my beard as long as I live, even one inch, and I don't appreciate it in you at all." Passed right by me in the hall and went straight out and got in the hammock.

It would be a holiday. It wasn't five minutes before Uncle Rondo suddenly appeared in the hall in one of Stella-Rondo's flesh-colored kimonos, all cut on the bias, like something Mr. Whitaker probably thought was gorgeous.

"Uncle Rondo!" I says, "I didn't know who that was! Where are you going?"

"Sister," he says, "get out of my way, I'm poisoned."

"If you're poisoned stay away from Papa-Daddy," I says. "Keep out of the hammock. Papa-Daddy will certainly beat you on the head if you come within forty miles of him. He thinks I deliberately said he ought to cut off his beard after he got me the P.O., and I've told him and told him and told him, and he acts like he just don't hear me. Papa-Daddy must of gone stone deaf."

"He picked a find day to do it then," says Uncle Rondo, and before you could say "Jack Robinson" flew out in the yard.

What he'd really done, he'd drunk another bottle of that prescription. He does it every single Fourth of July as sure as shooting, and it's horribly expensive. Then he falls over in the hammock and snores. So he insisted on zigzagging right out to the hammock, looking like a half-wit.

Papa-Daddy woke up with this horrible yell and right there without moving an inch he tried to turn Uncle Rondo against me. I heard every word he said. Oh, he told Uncle Rondo I didn't learn to read till I was eight years old and he didn't see how in the world I ever got the mail put up at the P.O., much less read it all, and he said if Uncle Rondo could only fathom the lengths he had gone to to get me that job! And he said on the other hand he thought Stella-Rondo had a brilliant mind and deserved credit for getting out of town. All the time he was just lying there swinging as pretty as you please and looping out his beard, and poor Uncle Rondo was *pleading* with him to slow down the hammock, it was making him as dizzy as a witch to watch it. But that's what Papa-Daddy likes about a hammock. So Uncle Rondo was too dizzy to get turned against me for the time being. He's Mama's only brother and is a good case of a one-track mind. Ask anybody. A certified pharmacist.

Just then I heard Stella-Rondo raising the upstairs window. While she was married she got this peculiar idea that it's cooler with the windows shut and locked. So she has to raise the window before she can make a soul hear her outdoors.

So she raises the window and says, "*Oh!*" You would have thought she was mortally wounded.

Uncle Rondo and Papa-Daddy didn't even look up, but kept right on with what they were doing. I had to laugh.

I flew up the stairs and threw the door open! I says, "What in the wide world's the matter, Stella-Rondo? You mortally wounded?"

"No," she says, "I am not mortally wounded but I wish you would do me the favor of looking out that window there and telling me what you see."

So I shade my eyes and look out the window.

"I see the front yard," I says.

"Don't you see any human beings?" she says.

"I see Uncle Rondo trying to run Papa-Daddy out of the hammock," I says. "Nothing more. Naturally, it's so suffocating-hot in the house, with all the windows shut and locked, everybody who cares to stay in their right mind will have to go out and get in the hammock before the Fourth of July is over."

"Don't you notice anything different about Uncle Rondo?" asks Stella-Rondo.

"Why, no, except he's got on some terrible looking flesh-colored contraption I wouldn't be found dead in, is all I can see," I says.

"Never mind, you won't be found dead in it, because it happens to be part of my trousseau, and Mr. Whitaker took several dozen photographs of me in it," says

Stella-Rondo. "What on earth could Uncle Rondo *mean* by wearing part of my trousseau out in the broad open daylight without saying so much as 'Kiss my foot,' *knowing* I only got home this morning after my separation and hung my negligee up on the bathroom door, just as nervous as I could be?"

"I'm sure I don't know, and what do you expect me to do about it?" I says. "Jump out the window?"

"No, I expect nothing of the kind. I simply declare that Uncle Rondo looks like a fool in it, that's all," she says. "It makes me sick to my stomach."

"Well, he looks as good as he can," I says. "As good as anybody in reason could." I stood up for Uncle Rondo, please remember. And I said to Stella-Rondo, "I think I would do well not to criticize so freely if I were you and came home with a two-year-old child I had never said a word about, and no explanation whatever about my separation."

"I asked you the instant I entered this house not to refer one more time to my adopted child, and you gave me your word of honor you would not," was all Stella-Rondo would say, and started pulling out every one of her eyebrows with some cheap Kress tweezers.

So I merely slammed the door behind me and went down to get some green-tomato pickle. Somebody had to do it. Of course Mama had turned both the niggers loose; she always said no earthly power could hold one anyway on the Fourth of July, so she wouldn't even try. It turned out that Jaypan fell in the lake and came within a very narrow limit of drowning.

So Mama trots in. Lifts up the lid and says, "H'm! Not very good for your Uncle Rondo in his precarious condition, I must say. Or poor little adopted Shirley-T. Shame on you!"

That made me tired. I says, "Well, Stella-Rondo had better thank her lucky stars it was her instead of me came trotting in with that very peculiar-looking child. Now if it had been me that trotted in from Illinois and brought a peculiar-looking child of two, I shudder to think of the reception I'd of got, much less controlled the diet of an entire family."

"But you must remember, Sister, that you were never married to Mr. Whitaker in the first place and didn't go up to Illinois to live," says Mama, shaking a spoon in my face. "If you had I would of been just as overjoyed to see you and your little adopted girl as I was to see Stella-Rondo, when you wound up with your separation and came on back home."

"You would not," I says.

"Don't contradict me, I would," says Mama.

But I said she couldn't convince me though she talked till she was blue in the face. Then I said, "Besides, you know as well as I do that child is not adopted."

"She most certainly is adopted," says Mama, stiff as a poker.

I says, "Why, Mama, Stella-Rondo had her just as sure as anything in this world, and just too stuck up to admit it."

"Why, Sister," said Mama. "Here I thought we were going to have a pleasant Fourth of July, and you start right out not believing a word your own baby sister tells you!"

"Just like Cousin Annie Flo. Went to her grave denying the facts of life," I remind Mama.

"I told you if you ever mentioned Annie Flo's name I'd slap your face," says Mama, and slaps my face.

"All right, you wait and see," I says.

"I," says Mama, "*I* prefer to take my children's word for anything when it's humanly possible." You ought to see Mama, she weighs two hundred pounds and has real tiny feet.

Just then something perfectly horrible occurred to me.

"Mama," I says, "can that child talk?" I simply had to whisper! "Mama, I wonder if that child can be—you know—in any way? Do you realize," I says, "that she hasn't spoken one single, solitary word to a human being up to this minute? This is the way she looks," I says, and I looked like this.

Well, Mama and I just stood there and stared at each other. It was horrible!

"I remember well that Joe Whitaker frequently drank like a fish," says Mama. "I believed to my soul he drank *chemicals*." And without another word she marches to the foot of the stairs and calls Stella-Rondo.

"Stella-Rondo? O-o-o-o-o! Stella-Rondo!"

"What?" says Stella-Rondo from upstairs. Not even the grace to get up off the bed.

"Can that child of yours talk?" asks Mama.

Stella-Rondo says, "Can she what?"

"Talk! Talk!" says Mama. "Burdyburdyburdyburdy!"

So Stella-Rondo yells back, "Who says she can't talk?"

"Sister says so," says Mama.

"You didn't have to tell me. I know whose word of honor don't mean a thing in this house," says Stella-Rondo.

And in a minute the loudest Yankee voice I ever heard in my life yells out, "OE'm Pop-OE the Sailor-r-r Ma-a-an!" and then somebody jumps up and down in the upstairs hall. In another second the house would of fallen down.

"Not only talks, she can tap-dance!" calls Stella-Rondo. "Which is more than some people I won't name can do."

"Why, the little precious darling thing!" Mama says, so surprised. "Just as smart as she can be!" Starts talking baby talk right there. Then she turns on me. "Sister, you ought to be thoroughly ashamed! Run upstairs this instant and apologize to Stella-Rondo and Shirley-T."

"Apologize for what?" I says. "I merely wondered if the child was normal, that's all. Now that she's proved she is, why, I have nothing further to say."

But Mama just turned on her heel and flew out, furious. She ran right upstairs and hugged the baby. She believed it was adopted. Stella-Rondo hadn't done a thing but turn her against me from upstairs while I stood there helpless over the hot stove. So that made Mama, Papa-Daddy and the baby all on Stella-Rondo's side.

Next, Uncle Rondo.

I must say that Uncle Rondo has been marvelous to me at various times in the past and I was completely unprepared to be made to jump out of my skin, the way it turned out. Once Stella-Rondo did something perfectly horrible to him—broke a chain letter from Flanders Field—and he took the radio back he had given her and gave it to me. Stella-Rondo was furious! For six months we all had to call her Stella instead of Stella-Rondo, or she wouldn't answer. I always thought Uncle Rondo had all the brains of the entire family. Another time he sent me to Mammoth Cave, with all expenses paid.

But this would be the day he was drinking that prescription, the Fourth of July.

So at supper Stella-Rondo speaks up and says she thinks Uncle Rondo ought to try to eat a little something. So finally Uncle Rondo said he would try a little cold biscuits and ketchup, but that was all. So *she* brought it to him.

"Do you think it wise to disport with ketchup in Stella-Rondo's flesh-colored kimono?" I says. Trying to be considerate! If Stella-Rondo couldn't watch out for her trousseau, somebody had to.

"Any objections?" asks Uncle Rondo, just about to pour out all the ketchup.

"Don't mind what she says, Uncle Rondo," says Stella-Rondo. "Sister has been devoting this solid afternoon to sneering out my bedroom window at the way you look."

"What's that?" says Uncle Rondo. Uncle Rondo has got the most terrible temper in the world. Anything is liable to make him tear the house down if it comes at the wrong time.

So Stella-Rondo says, "Sister says, 'Uncle Rondo certainly does look like a fool in that pink kimono!'"

Do you remember who it was really said that?

Uncle Rondo spills out all the ketchup and jumps out of his chair and tears off the kimono and throws it on the dirty floor and puts his foot on it. It had to be sent all the way to Jackson to the cleaners and re-pleated.

"So that's your opinion of your Uncle Rondo, is it?" he says. "I look like a fool, do I? Well, that's the last straw. A whole day in this house with nothing to do, and then to hear you come out with a remark like that behind my back!"

"I didn't say any such kind of a thing, Uncle Rondo," I says, "and I'm not saying who did, either. Why, I think you look all right. Just try to take care of yourself and not talk and eat at the same time," I says. "I think you better go lie down."

"Lie down my foot," says Uncle Rondo. I ought to of known by that he was fixing to do something perfectly horrible.

So he didn't do anything that night in the precarious state he was in—just played Casino with Mama and Stella-Rondo and Shirley-T. and gave Shirley-T. a nickel with a head on both sides. It tickled her nearly to death, and she called him "Papa." But at 6:30 A.M. the next morning, he threw a whole five-cent package of some unsold one-inch firecrackers from the store as hard as he could into my bedroom and they every one went off. Not one bad one in the string. Anybody else, there'd be one that wouldn't go off.

Well, I'm just terribly susceptible to noise of any kind, the doctor has always told me I was the most sensitive person he had ever seen in his whole life, and I was simply prostrated. I couldn't eat! People tell me they heard it as far as the cemetery, and old Aunt Jep Patterson, that had been holding her own so good, thought it was Judgment Day and she was going to meet her whole family. It's usually so quiet here.

And I'll tell you it didn't take me any longer than a minute to make up my mind what to do. There I was with the whole entire house on Stella-Rondo's side and turned against me. If I have anything at all I have pride.

So I just decided I'd go straight down to the P.O. There's plenty of room there in the back, I says to myself.

Well! I made no bones about letting the family catch on to what I was up to. I didn't try to conceal it.

The first thing they knew, I marched in where they were all playing Old Maid and pulled the electric oscillating fan out by the plug, and everything got real hot. Next I snatched the pillow I'd done the needlepoint on right off the davenport from behind Papa-Daddy. He went "Ugh!" I beat Stella-Rondo up the stairs and finally found my charm bracelet in her bureau drawer under a picture of Nelson Eddy.

"So that's the way the land lies," says Uncle Rondo. There he was, piecing on the ham. "Well, Sister, I'll be glad to donate my army cot if you got any place to set it up, providing you'll leave right this minute and let me get some peace." Uncle Rondo was in France.

"Thank you kindly for the cot and 'peace' is hardly the word I would select if I had to resort to firecrackers at 6:30 A.M. in a young girl's bedroom," I says back to him. "And as to where I intend to go, you seem to forget my position as postmistress of China Grove, Mississippi," I says. "I've always got the P.O."

Well, that made them all sit up and take notice.

I went out front and started digging up some four-o'-clocks to plant around the P.O.

"Ah-ah-ah!" says Mama, raising the window. "Those happen to be my four-o'-clocks. Everything planted in that star is mine. I've never known you to make anything grow in your life."

"Very well," I says. "But I'll take the fern. Even you, Mama, can't stand there and deny that I'm the one watered that fern. And I happen to know where I can send in a box top and get a packet of one thousand mixed seeds, no two the same kind, free."

"Oh, where?" Mama wants to know.

But I says, "Too late. You 'tend to your house, and I'll 'tend to mine. You hear things like that all the time if you know how to listen to the radio. Perfectly marvelous offers. Get anything you want free."

So I hope to tell you I marched in and got that radio, and they could of all bit a nail in two, especially Stella-Rondo, that it used to belong to, and she well knew she couldn't get it back, I'd sue for it like a shot. And I very politely took the sewing-machine motor I helped pay the most on to give Mama for Christmas back in 1929, and a good big calendar, with the first-aid remedies on it. The thermometer and the Hawaiian ukulele certainly were rightfully mine, and I stood on the step-ladder and got all my watermelon-rind preserves and every fruit and vegetable I'd put up, every jar. Then I began to pull the tacks out of the bluebird wall vases on the archway to the dining room.

"Who told you you could have those, Miss Priss?" says Mama, fanning as hard as she could.

"I bought 'em and I'll keep track of 'em," I says. "I'll tack 'em up one on each side the post-office window, and you can see 'em when you come to ask me for your mail, if you're so dead to see 'em."

"Not I! I'll never darken the door to that post office again if I live to be a hundred," Mama says. "Ungrateful child! After all the money we spent on you at the Normal."

"Me either," says Stella-Rondo. "You can just let my mail lie there and *rot,* for all I care. I'll never come and relieve you of a single, solitary piece."

"I should worry," I says. "And who you think's going to sit down and write you all those big fat letters and postcards, by the way? Mr. Whitaker? Just because he was the only man ever dropped down in China Grove and you got him—unfairly—is he going to sit down and write you a lengthy correspondence after you come home giving no rhyme nor reason whatsoever for your separation and no explanation for the presence of that child? I may not have your brilliant mind, but I fail to see it."

So Mama says, "Sister, I've told you a thousand times that Stella-Rondo simply got homesick, and this child is far too big to be hers," and she says, "Now, why don't you all just sit down and play Casino?"

Then Shirley-T. sticks out her tongue at me in this perfectly horrible way. She has no more manners than the man in the moon. I told her she was going to cross her eyes like that some day and they'd stick.

"It's too late to stop me now," I says. "You should have tried that yesterday. I'm going to the P.O. and the only way you can possibly see me is to visit me there."

So Papa-Daddy says, "You'll never catch me setting foot in that post office, even if I should take a notion into my head to write a letter some place." He says, "I won't have you reachin' out of that little old window with a pair of shears and cuttin' off any beard of mine. I'm too smart for you!"

"We all are," says Stella-Rondo.

But I said, "If you're so smart, where's Mr. Whitaker?"

So then Uncle Rondo says, "I'll thank you from now on to stop reading all the orders I get on postcards and telling everybody in China Grove what you think is the matter with them," but I says, "I draw my own conclusions and will continue in the future to draw them." I says, "If people want to write their inmost secrets on penny postcards, there's nothing in the wide world you can do about it, Uncle Rondo."

"And if you think we'll ever *write* another postcard you're sadly mistaken," says Mama.

"Cutting off your nose to spite your face then," I says. "But if you're all determined to have no more to do with the U. S. mail, think of this: What will Stella-Rondo do now, if she wants to tell Mr. Whitaker to come after her?"

"Wah!" says Stella-Rondo. I knew she'd cry. She had a conniption fit right there in the kitchen.

"It will be interesting to see how long she holds out," I says. "And now—I am leaving."

"Good-bye," says Uncle Rondo.

"Oh, I declare," says Mama, "to think that a family of mine should quarrel on the Fourth of July, or the day after, over Stella-Rondo leaving old Mr. Whitaker and having the sweetest little adopted child! It looks like we'd all be glad!"

"Wah!" says Stella-Rondo, and has a fresh conniption fit.

"*He* left *her*—you mark my words," I says. "That's Mr. Whitaker. I know Mr. Whitaker. After all, I knew him first. I said from the beginning he'd up and leave her. I foretold every single thing that's happened."

"Where did he go?" asks Mama.

"Probably to the North Pole, if he knows what's good for him," I says.

But Stella-Rondo just bawled and wouldn't say another word. She flew to her room and slammed the door.

"Now look what you've gone and done, Sister," says Mama. "You go apologize."

"I haven't got time, I'm leaving," I says.

"Well, what are you waiting around for?" asks Uncle Rondo.

So I just picked up the kitchen clock and marched off, without saying "Kiss my foot" or anything, and never did tell Stella-Rondo good-bye.

There was a nigger girl going along on a little wagon right in front.

"Girl," I says, "come help me haul these things down the hill. I'm going to live in the post office."

Took her nine trips in her express wagon. Uncle Rondo came out on the porch and threw her a nickel.

And that's the last I've laid eyes on any of my family or my family laid eyes on me for five solid days and nights. Stella-Rondo may be telling the most horrible tales in the world about Mr. Whitaker, but I haven't heard them. As I tell everybody, I draw my own conclusions.

But, oh, I like it here. It's ideal, as I've been saying. You see, I've got everything cater-cornered, the way I like it. Hear the radio? All the war news. Radio, sewing machine, book ends, ironing board and that great big piano lamp—peace, that's what I like. Butter-bean vines planted all along the front where the strings are.

Of course, there's not much mail. My family are naturally the main people in China Grove, and if they prefer to vanish from the face of the earth, for all the mail they write, why, I'm not going to open my mouth. Some of the folks here in town are taking up for me and some turned against me. I know which is which. There are always people who will quit buying stamps just to get on the right side of Papa-Daddy.

But here I am, and here I'll stay. I want the world to know I'm happy.

And if Stella-Rondo should come to me this minute, on bended knees, and *attempt* to explain the incidents of her life with Mr. Whitaker, I'd simply put my fingers in both my ears and refuse to listen.

# Edith Wharton

## (1862–1937)

Edith Wharton was born in 1862 into the socially elite class that she so often wrote about and criticized. She did not attend school but was tutored by a governess and educated herself by reading in her father's library. In 1885, she married Edward Robbins Wharton, a kind man but one who did not share Wharton's artistic interests. It was an unhappy marriage, and Wharton was treated for depression during the 1890s. It was recommended to her that she write and travel, so she escaped to France and Italy, where she became inspired to write about art, architecture, and gardens. Her first book, *The Decoration of Houses* (1897), was cowritten with her architect friend, Ogden Codman. The two denounced Victorian decorating practices and proposed creating rooms based on simple, classical designs and principles that stressed symmetry, proportion, and balance. The book was an immediate success. Wharton followed it with *The House of Mirth* (1905).

In 1906, she spent most of her time living in Europe, where she became friends with Henry James, Walter Berry, and Bernard Berenson. In 1908, Wharton met Morton Fullerton and the two became lovers. She divorced her husband in 1913. During World War I, Wharton became fiercely dedicated to the Allied cause and created hostels and schools for refugees. She also traveled to the front lines to observe the fighting and wrote stories and reports urging the United States to join the war effort. Wharton published numerous books, including *Ethan Frome* (1911), *The Reef* (1912), *The Custom of the Country* (1913), *The Age of Innocence* (1920), *The Glimpses of the Moon* (1922), *Twilight Sleep* (1927), and *The Gods Arrive* (1932). She received the Pulitzer Prize for *The Age of Innocence* (1921) and an honorary degree from Yale (1923). *The Letters of Edith Wharton* was published in 1988 and includes many of her letters to Fullerton.

## Roman Fever                                                                               1936

I

From the table at which they had been lunching two American ladies of ripe but well-cared-for middle age moved across the lofty terrace of the Roman restaurant and, leaning on its parapet, looked first at each other, and then down on the outspread glories of the Palatine[1] and the Forum,[2] with the same expression of vague but benevolent approval.

1 **Palatine:** One of the seven hills of Rome.
2 **Forum:** The ruins of the political, religious, and business center of ancient Rome.

As they leaned there a girlish voice echoed up gaily from the stairs leading to the court below. "Well, come along, then," it cried, not to them but to an invisible companion, "and let's leave the young things to their knitting"; and a voice as fresh laughed back: "Oh, look here, Babs, not actually *knitting*—" "Well, I mean figuratively," rejoined the first. "After all, we haven't left our poor parents much else to do. . . ." and at that point the turn of the stairs engulfed the dialogue.

The two ladies looked at each other again, this time with a tingle of smiling embarrassment, and the smaller and paler one shook her head and colored slightly.

"Barbara!" she murmured, sending an unheard rebuke after the mocking voice in the stairway.

The other lady, who was fuller, and higher in color, with a small determined nose supported by vigorous black eyebrows, gave a good-humored laugh. "That's what our daughters think of us!"

Her companion replied by a deprecating gesture. "Not of us individually. We must remember that. It's just the collective modern idea of Mothers. And you see—" Half-guiltily she drew from her handsomely mounted black handbag a twist of crimson silk run through by two fine knitting needles. "One never knows," she murmured. "The new system has certainly given us a good deal of time to kill; and sometimes I get tired just looking—even at this." Her gesture was now addressed to the stupendous scene at their feet.

The dark lady laughed again, and they both relapsed upon the view, contemplating it in silence, with a sort of diffused serenity which might have been borrowed from the spring effulgence of the Roman skies. The luncheon hour was long past, and the two had their end of the vast terrace to themselves. At its opposite extremity a few groups, detained by a lingering look at the outspread city, were gathering up guidebooks and fumbling for tips. The last of them scattered, and the two ladies were alone on the air-washed height.

"Well, I don't see why we shouldn't just stay here," said Mrs. Slade, the lady of the high color and energetic brows. Two derelict basket chairs stood near, and she pushed them into the angle of the parapet, and settled herself in one, her gaze upon the Palatine. "After all, it's still the most beautiful view in the world."

"It always will be, to me," assented her friend Mrs. Ansley, with so slight a stress on the "me" that Mrs. Slade, though she noticed it, wondered if it were not merely accidental, like the random underlinings of old-fashioned letter writers.

"Grace Ansley was always old-fashioned," she thought; and added aloud, with a retrospective smile: "It's a view we've both been familiar with for a good many years. When we first met here we were younger than our girls are now. You remember?"

"Oh, yes, I remember," murmured Mrs. Ansley, with the same undefinable stress. "There's that headwaiter wondering," she interpolated. She was evidently far less sure than her companion of herself and of her rights in the world.

"I'll cure him of wondering," said Mrs. Slade, stretching her hand toward a bag as discreetly opulent-looking as Mrs. Ansley's. Signing to the headwaiter, she explained that she and her friend were old lovers of Rome, and would like to spend the end of the afternoon looking down on the view—that is, if it did not disturb the service? The headwaiter, bowing over her gratuity, assured her that the ladies were most welcome, and would be still more so if they would condescend to remain for dinner. A full-moon night, they would remember. . . .

Mrs. Slade's black brows drew together, as though references to the moon were out of place and even unwelcome. But she smiled away her frown as the headwaiter retreated. "Well, why not? We might do worse. There's no knowing, I suppose, when the girls will be back. Do you even know back from *where*? I don't!"

Mrs. Ansley again colored slightly. "I think those young Italian aviators we met at the Embassy invited them to fly to Tarquinia for tea. I suppose they'll want to wait and fly back by moonlight."

"Moonlight—moonlight! What a part it still plays. Do you suppose they're as sentimental as we were?"

"I've come to the conclusion that I don't in the least know what they are," said Mrs. Ansley. "And perhaps we didn't know much more about each other."

"No; perhaps we didn't."

Her friend gave her a shy glance. "I never should have supposed you were sentimental, Alida."

"Well, perhaps I wasn't." Mrs. Slade drew her lids together in retrospect; and for a few moments the two ladies, who had been intimate since childhood, reflected how little they knew each other. Each one, of course, had a label ready to attach to the other's name; Mrs. Delphin Slade, for instance, would have told herself, or anyone who asked her, that Mrs. Horace Ansley, twenty-five years ago, had been exquisitely lovely—no, you wouldn't believe it, would you? . . . though, of course, still charming, distinguished. . . . Well, as a girl she had been exquisite; far more beautiful than her daughter Barbara, though certainly Babs, according to the new standards at any rate, was more effective—had more *edge,* as they say. Funny where she got it, with those two nullities as parents. Yes; Horace Ansley was—well, just the duplicate of his wife. Museum specimens of old New York. Good-looking, irreproachable, exemplary. Mrs. Slade and Mrs. Ansley had lived opposite each other—actually as well as figuratively—for years. When the drawing-room curtains in No. 20 East 73rd Street were renewed, No. 23, across the way, was always aware of it. And of all the movings, buyings, travels, anniversaries, illnesses—the tame chronicle of an estimable pair. Little of it escaped Mrs. Slade. But she had grown bored with it by the time her husband made his big *coup* in Wall Street, and when they bought in upper Park Avenue had already begun to think: "I'd rather live opposite a speakeasy for a change; at least one might see it raided." The idea of seeing Grace raided was so amusing that (before the move) she launched it at a woman's lunch. It made a hit, and went the rounds—she sometimes wondered if it had crossed the street, and reached Mrs. Ansley. She hoped not, but didn't much mind. Those were the days when respectability was at a discount, and it did the irreproachable no harm to laugh at them a little.

A few years later, and not many months apart, both ladies lost their husbands. There was an appropriate exchange of wreaths and condolences, and a brief renewal of intimacy in the half-shadow of their mourning; and now, after another interval, they had run across each other in Rome, at the same hotel, each of them the modest appendage of a salient daughter. The similarity of their lot had again drawn them together, lending itself to mild jokes, and the mutual confession that, if in old days it must have been tiring to "keep up" with daughters, it was now, at times, a little dull not to.

No doubt, Mrs. Slade reflected, she felt her unemployment more than poor Grace ever would. It was a big drop from being the wife of Delphin Slade to being his widow. She had always regarded herself (with a certain conjugal pride) as his equal in social gifts, as contributing her full share to the making of the exceptional couple they were: but the difference after his death was irremediable. As the wife of the famous corporation lawyer, always with an international case or two on hand, every day brought its exciting and unexpected obligation: the impromptu entertaining of eminent colleagues from abroad, the hurried dashes on legal business to London, Paris or Rome, where the entertaining was so handsomely reciprocated; the amusement of hearing in her wake: "What, that handsome woman with the good clothes and the eyes is Mrs. Slade—*the* Slade's wife? Really? Generally the wives of celebrities are such frumps."

Yes; being *the* Slade's widow was a dullish business after that. In living up to such a husband all her faculties had been engaged; now she had only her daughter to live up to, for the son who seemed to have inherited his father's gifts had died suddenly in boyhood. She had fought through that agony because her husband was there, to be helped and to help; now, after the father's death, the thought of the boy had become unbearable. There was nothing left but to mother her daughter; and dear Jenny was such a perfect daughter that she needed no excessive mothering. "Now with Babs Ansley I don't know that I *should* be so quiet," Mrs. Slade sometimes half-enviously reflected; but Jenny, who was younger than her brilliant friend, was that rare accident, an extremely pretty girl who somehow made youth and prettiness seem as safe as their absence. It was all perplexing—and to Mrs. Slade a little boring. She wished that Jenny would fall in love—with the wrong man, even; that she might have to be watched, out-maneuvered, rescued. And instead, it was Jenny who watched her mother, kept her out of drafts, made sure that she had taken her tonic. . . .

Mrs. Ansley was much less articulate than her friend, and her mental portrait of Mrs. Slade was slighter, and drawn with fainter touches. "Alida Slade's awfully brilliant; but not as brilliant as she thinks," would have summed it up; though she would have added, for the enlightenment of strangers, that Mrs. Slade had been an extremely dashing girl; much more so than her daughter, who was pretty, of course, and clever in a way, but had none of her mother's—well, "vividness," someone had once called it. Mrs. Ansley would take up current words like this, and cite them in quotation marks, as unheard-of audacities. No; Jenny was not like her mother. Sometimes Mrs. Ansley thought Alida Slade was disappointed; on the whole she had had a sad life. Full of failures and mistakes; Mrs. Ansley had always been rather sorry for her. . . .

So these two ladies visualized each other, each through the wrong end of her little telescope.

## II

For a long time they continued to sit side by side without speaking. It seemed as though, to both, there was a relief in laying down their somewhat futile activities in the presence of the vast Memento Mori[3] which faced them. Mrs. Slade sat quite still, her eyes fixed on the golden slope of the Palace of the Caesars, and after a while Mrs. Ansley ceased to fidget with her bag, and she too sank into meditation. Like many intimate friends, the two ladies had never before had occasion to be silent together, and Mrs. Ansley was slightly embarrassed by what seemed, after so many years, a new stage in their intimacy, and one with which she did not yet know how to deal.

Suddenly the air was full of that deep clangor of bells which periodically covers Rome with a roof of silver. Mrs. Slade glanced at her wristwatch. "Five o'clock already," she said, as though surprised.

Mrs. Ansley suggested interrogatively: "There's bridge at the Embassy at five." For a long time Mrs. Slade did not answer. She appeared to be lost in contemplation, and Mrs. Ansley thought the remark had escaped her. But after a while she said, as if speaking out of a dream: "Bridge, did you say? Not unless you want to. . . . But I don't think I will, you know."

"Oh, no," Mrs. Ansley hastened to assure her. "I don't care to at all. It's so lovely here; and so full of old memories, as you say." She settled herself in her chair, and almost furtively drew forth her knitting. Mrs. Slade took sideway note of this activity, but her own beautifully cared-for hands remained motionless on her knee.

"I was just thinking," she said slowly, "what different things Rome stands for to each generation of travelers. To our grandmothers, Roman fever[4]; to our mothers, sentimental dangers—how we used to be guarded!—to our daughters, no more dangers than the middle of Main Street. They don't know it—but how much they're missing!"

The long golden light was beginning to pale, and Mrs. Ansley lifted her knitting a little closer to her eyes. "Yes; how we were guarded!"

"I always used to think," Mrs. Slade continued, "that our mothers had a much more difficult job than our grandmothers. When Roman fever stalked the streets it must have been comparatively easy to gather in the girls at the danger hour;[5] but when you and I were young, with such beauty calling us, and the spice of disobedience thrown in, and no worse risk than catching cold during the cool hour after sunset, the mothers used to be put to it to keep us in—didn't they?"

She turned again toward Mrs. Ansley, but the latter had reached a delicate point in her knitting. "One, two, three—slip two; yes, they must have been," she assented, without looking up.

Mrs. Slade's eyes rested on her with a deepened attention. "She can knit—in the face of *this*! How like her. . . ."

3 **Memento Mori:** A reminder of mortality.
4 **Roman fever:** Malaria.
5 **danger hour:** At the time it was thought that malaria was contracted in the evening hours.

Mrs. Slade leaned back, brooding, her eyes ranging from the ruins which faced her to the long green hollow of the Forum, the fading glow of the church fronts beyond it, and the outlying immensity of the Colosseum.[6] Suddenly she thought: "It's all very well to say that our girls have done away with sentiment and moonlight. But if Babs Ansley isn't out to catch that young aviator—the one who's a Marchese—then I don't know anything. And Jenny has no chance beside her. I know that too. I wonder if that's why Grace Ansley likes the two girls to go everywhere together? My poor Jenny as a foil—!" Mrs. Slade gave a hardly audible laugh, and at the sound Mrs. Ansley dropped her knitting.

"Yes—?"

"I—oh, nothing. I was only thinking how your Babs carries everything before her. That Campolieri boy is one of the best matches in Rome. Don't look so innocent, my dear—you know he is. And I was wondering, ever so respectfully, you understand . . . wondering how two such exemplary characters as you and Horace had managed to produce anything quite so dynamic." Mrs. Slade laughed again, with a touch of asperity.

Mrs. Ansley's hands lay inert across her needles. She looked straight out at the great accumulated wreckage of passion and splendor at her feet. But her small profile was almost expressionless. At length she said: "I think you overrate Babs, my dear."

Mrs. Slade's tone grew easier. "No; I don't. I appreciate her. And perhaps envy you. Oh, my girl's perfect; if I were a chronic invalid I'd—well, I think I'd rather be in Jenny's hands. There must be times . . . but there! I always wanted a brilliant daughter . . . and never quite understood why I got an angel instead."

Mrs. Ansley echoed her laugh in a faint murmur. "Babs is an angel too."

"Of course—of course! But she's got rainbow wings. Well, they're wandering by the sea with their young men; and here we sit . . . and it all brings back the past a little too acutely."

Mrs. Ansley had resumed her knitting. One might almost have imagined (if one had known her less well, Mrs. Slade reflected) that, for her also, too many memories rose from the lengthening shadows of those august ruins. But no; she was simply absorbed in her work. What was there for her to worry about? She knew that Babs would almost certainly come back engaged to the extremely eligible Campolieri. "And she'll sell the New York house, and settle down near them in Rome, and never be in their way . . . she's much too tactful. But she'll have an excellent cook, and just the right people in for bridge and cocktails . . . and a perfectly peaceful old age among her grandchildren."

Mrs. Slade broke off this prophetic flight with a recoil of self-disgust. There was no one of whom she had less right to think unkindly than of Grace Ansley. Would she never cure herself of envying her? Perhaps she had begun too long ago.

She stood up and leaned against the parapet, filling her troubled eyes with the tranquilizing magic of the hour. But instead of tranquilizing her the sight seemed to increase her exasperation. Her gaze turned toward the Colosseum. Already its golden

---

6 **Colosseum:** The famous amphitheater of ancient Rome.

flank was drowned in purple shadow, and above it the sky curved crystal clear, without light or color. It was the moment when afternoon and evening hang balanced in mid-heaven.

Mrs. Slade turned back and laid her hand on her friend's arm. The gesture was so abrupt that Mrs. Ansley looked up, startled.

"The sun's set. You're not afraid, my dear?"

"Afraid—?"

"Of Roman fever or pneumonia? I remember how ill you were that winter. As a girl you had a very delicate throat, hadn't you?"

"Oh, we're all right up here. Down below, in the Forum, it does get deathly cold, all of a sudden . . . but not here."

"Ah, of course you know because you had to be so careful." Mrs. Slade turned back to the parapet. She thought: "I must make one more effort not to hate her." Aloud she said: "Whenever I look at the Forum from up here, I remember that story about a great-aunt of yours, wasn't she? A dreadfully wicked great-aunt?"

"Oh, yes; great-aunt Harriet. The one who was supposed to have sent her young sister out to the Forum after sunset to gather a night-blooming flower for her album. All our great-aunts and grandmothers used to have albums of dried flowers."

Mrs. Slade nodded. "But she really sent her because they were in love with the same man—"

"Well, that was the family tradition. They said Aunt Harriet confessed it years afterward. At any rate, the poor little sister caught the fever and died. Mother used to frighten us with the story when we were children."

"And you frightened *me* with it, that winter when you and I were here as girls. The winter I was engaged to Delphin."

Mrs. Ansley gave a faint laugh. "Oh, did I? Really frighten you? I don't believe you're easily frightened."

"Not often; but I was then. I was easily frightened because I was too happy. I wonder if you know what that means?"

"I—yes. . . ." Mrs. Ansley faltered.

"Well, I suppose that was why the story of your wicked aunt made such an impression on me. And I thought: 'There's no more Roman fever, but the Forum is deathly cold after sunset—especially after a hot day. And the Colosseum's even colder and damper.'"

"The Colosseum—?"

"Yes. It wasn't easy to get in, after the gates were locked for the night. Far from easy. Still, in those days it could be managed; it *was* managed, often. Lovers met there who couldn't meet elsewhere. You knew that?"

"I—I dare say. I don't remember."

"You don't remember? You don't remember going to visit some ruins or other one evening, just after dark, and catching a bad chill? You were supposed to have gone to see the moon rise. People always said that expedition was what caused your illness."

There was a moment's silence; then Mrs. Ansley rejoined: "Did they? It was all so long ago."

"Yes. And you got well again—so it didn't matter. But I suppose it struck your friends—the reason given for your illness, I mean—because everybody knew you were so prudent on account of your throat, and your mother took such care of you. . . . You *had* been out late sight-seeing, hadn't you, that night?"

"Perhaps I had. The most prudent girls aren't always prudent. What made you think of it now?"

Mrs. Slade seemed to have no answer ready. But after a moment she broke out: "Because I simply can't bear it any longer—!"

Mrs. Ansley lifted her head quickly. Her eyes were wide and very pale. "Can't bear what?"

"Why—your not knowing that I've always known why you went."

"Why I went—?"

"Yes. You think I'm bluffing, don't you? Well, you went to meet the man I was engaged to—and I can repeat every word of the letter that took you there."

While Mrs. Slade spoke Mrs. Ansley had risen unsteadily to her feet. Her bag, her knitting and gloves, slid in a panic-stricken heap to the ground. She looked at Mrs. Slade as though she were looking at a ghost.

"No, no—don't," she faltered out.

"Why not? Listen, if you don't believe me. 'My one darling, things can't go on like this. I must see you alone. Come to the Colosseum immediately after dark tomorrow. There will be somebody to let you in. No one whom you need fear will suspect'—but perhaps you've forgotten what the letter said?"

Mrs. Ansley met the challenge with an unexpected composure. Steadying herself against the chair she looked at her friend, and replied: "No; I know it by heart too."

"And the signature? 'Only *your* D.S.' Was that it? I'm right, am I? That was the letter that took you out that evening after dark?"

Mrs. Ansley was still looking at her. It seemed to Mrs. Slade that a slow struggle was going on behind the voluntarily controlled mask of her small quiet face. "I shouldn't have thought she had herself so well in hand," Mrs. Slade reflected, almost resentfully. But at this moment Mrs. Ansley spoke. "I don't know how you knew. I burnt that letter at once."

"Yes; you would, naturally—you're so prudent!" The sneer was open now. "And if you burnt the letter you're wondering how on earth I know what was in it. That's it, isn't it?"

Mrs. Slade waited, but Mrs. Ansley did not speak.

"Well, my dear, I know what was in that letter because I wrote it!"

"You wrote it?"

"Yes."

The two women stood for a minute staring at each other in the last golden light. Then Mrs. Ansley dropped back into her chair. "Oh," she murmured, and covered her face with her hands.

Mrs. Slade waited nervously for another word or movement. None came, and at length she broke out: "I horrify you."

Mrs. Ansley's hands dropped to her knee. The face they uncovered was streaked with tears. "I wasn't thinking of you. I was thinking—it was the only letter I ever had from him!"

"And I wrote it. Yes; I wrote it! But I was the girl he was engaged to. Did you happen to remember that?"

Mrs. Ansley's head dropped again. "I'm not trying to excuse myself . . . I remembered. . . ."

"And still you went?"

"Still I went."

Mrs. Slade stood looking down on the small bowed figure at her side. The flame of her wrath had already sunk, and she wondered why she had ever thought there would be any satisfaction in inflicting so purposeless a wound on her friend. But she had to justify herself.

"You do understand? I'd found out—and I hated you, hated you. I knew you were in love with Delphin—and I was afraid; afraid of you, of your quiet ways, your sweetness . . . your . . . well, I wanted you out of the way, that's all. Just for a few weeks; just till I was sure of him. So in a blind fury I wrote that letter . . . I don't know why I'm telling you now."

"I suppose," said Mrs. Ansley slowly, "it's because you've always gone on hating me."

"Perhaps. Or because I wanted to get the whole thing off my mind." She paused. "I'm glad you destroyed the letter. Of course I never thought you'd die."

Mrs. Ansley relapsed into silence, and Mrs. Slade, leaning above her, was conscious of a strange sense of isolation, of being cut off from the warm current of human communion. "You think me a monster!"

"I don't know. . . . It was the only letter I had, and you say he didn't write it?"

"Ah, how you care for him still!"

"I cared for that memory," said Mrs. Ansley.

Mrs. Slade continued to look down at her. She seemed physically reduced by the blow—as if, when she got up, the wind might scatter her like a puff of dust. Mrs. Slade's jealousy suddenly leapt up again at the sight. All these years the woman had been living on that letter. How she must have loved him, to treasure the mere memory of its ashes! The letter of the man her friend was engaged to. Wasn't it she who was the monster?

"You tried your best to get him away from me, didn't you? But you failed; and I kept him. That's all."

"Yes. That's all."

"I wish now I hadn't told you. I'd no idea you'd feel about it as you do; I thought you'd be amused. It all happened so long ago, as you say; and you must do me the justice to remember that I had no reason to think you'd ever taken it seriously. How could I, when you were married to Horace Ansley two months afterward? As soon as you could get out of bed your mother rushed you off to Florence and married you. People were rather surprised—they wondered at its being done so quickly; but I thought I knew. I had an idea you did it out of *pique*—to be able to say you'd got ahead of Delphin and me. Girls have such silly reasons for doing the most serious things. And your marrying so soon convinced me that you'd never really cared."

"Yes, I suppose it would," Mrs. Ansley assented.

The clear heaven overhead was emptied of all its gold. Dusk spread over it, abruptly darkening the Seven Hills. Here and there lights began to twinkle through the foliage at their feet. Steps were coming and going on the deserted terrace—waiters looking out of the doorway at the head of the stairs, then reappearing with trays and napkins and flasks of wine. Tables were moved, chairs straightened. A feeble string of electric lights flickered out. Some vases of faded flowers were carried away, and brought back replenished. A stout lady in a dust coat suddenly appeared, asking in broken Italian if anyone had seen the elastic band which held together her tattered Baedeker.[7] She poked with her stick under the table at which she had lunched, the waiters assisting.

The corner where Mrs. Slade and Mrs. Ansley sat was still shadowy and deserted. For a long time neither of them spoke. At length Mrs. Slade began again: "I suppose I did it as a sort of joke—"

"A joke?"

"Well, girls are ferocious sometimes, you know. Girls in love especially. And I remember laughing to myself all that evening at the idea that you were waiting around there in the dark, dodging out of sight, listening for every sound, trying to get in—. Of course I was upset when I heard you were so ill afterward."

Mrs. Ansley had not moved for a long time. But now she turned slowly toward her companion. "But I didn't wait. He'd arranged everything. He was there. We were let in at once," she said.

Mrs. Slade sprang up from her leaning position. "Delphin there? They let you in?—Ah, now you're lying!" she burst out with violence.

Mrs. Ansley's voice grew clearer, and full of surprise. "But of course he was there. Naturally he came—"

"Came? How did he know he'd find you there? You must be raving!"

Mrs. Ansley hesitated, as though reflecting. "But I answered the letter. I told him I'd be there. So he came."

Mrs. Slade flung her hands up to her face. "Oh, God—you answered! I never thought of your answering. . . ."

"It's odd you never thought of it, if you wrote the letter."

"Yes. I was blind with rage."

Mrs. Ansley rose, and drew her fur scarf about her. "It is cold here. We'd better go. . . . I'm sorry for you," she said, as she clasped the fur about her throat.

The unexpected words sent a pang through Mrs. Slade. "Yes; we'd better go." She gathered up her bag and cloak. "I don't know why you should be sorry for me," she muttered.

Mrs. Ansley stood looking away from her toward the dusky secret mass of the Colosseum. "Well—because I didn't have to wait that night."

7 **Baedeker:** A tourist guidebook.

Mrs. Slade gave an unquiet laugh. "Yes; I was beaten there. But I oughtn't to begrudge it to you, I suppose. At the end of all these years. After all, I had everything; I had him for twenty-five years. And you had nothing but that one letter that he didn't write."

Mrs. Ansley was again silent. At length she turned toward the door of the terrace. She took a step, and turned back, facing her companion.

"I had Barbara," she said, and began to move ahead of Mrs. Slade toward the stairway.

# Richard Wright

## (1908–1960)

Richard Wright was born in Roxie, Mississippi, in 1908, and his childhood was spent being shuffled between relatives in Arkansas and Mississippi. He went to school for a few months at a time and held a variety of jobs to support his family. During this time, Wright read pulp novels, magazines, and anything else he could get his hands on, including books from the whites-only library in Memphis. His first short story, "The Voodoo of Hell's Half-Acre," was published in 1924. In 1925, Wright graduated from junior high school in Jackson, Mississippi. He became a member of the Communist Party in 1932, and his poetry was published in journals such as *Left Front, Midland Left, Anvil, Partisan Review,* and *New Masses.* In 1937, he went to New York, where he became the Harlem editor of the *Daily Worker.* He also helped to launch the short-lived magazine *New Challenge.* His collection of stories, *Uncle Tom's Children,* was published in 1938, and because of it he was awarded a Guggenheim Fellowship. His story "Fire and Cloud" also won the O. Henry Memorial award in 1938.

Wright's best-known work, *Native Son,* was published in 1940. Through a story of poverty and violence in 1930s Chicago, it conveys the hopelessness created by a racist society. The book was an instant success, and, shortly after its release, Wright collaborated with Paul Green on a stage adaptation directed by Orson Welles. Wright left the Communist Party in 1944, and in the following year he and his family moved to France. There he became acquainted with, among others, Gertrude Stein, Jean-Paul Sartre, Albert Camus, James Baldwin, and Léopold Senghor. In the following years, Wright published several books, including *Black Boy: A Record of Childhood and Youth* (1945), *The Outsider* (1953), *Black Power* (1954), *Savage Holiday* (1954), and *White Man, Listen!* (1957). In Wright's last years, he suffered from aerobic dysentery and financial difficulties. During this time he wrote approximately 4,000 haikus and the novel *The Long Dream* (1958). He died November 28, 1960, and was cremated with a copy of *Black Boy.*

## The Man Who Was Almost a Man                                    1961

Dave struck out across the fields, looking homeward through paling light. Whut's the use talkin wid em niggers in the field? Anyhow, his mother was putting supper on the table. Them niggers can't understan nothing. One of these days he was going to get a gun and practice shooting, then they couldn't talk to him as though he were a little boy. He slowed, looking at the ground. Shucks, Ah ain scareda them even ef they are biggern me! Aw, Ah know whut Ahma do. Ahm going by ol Joe's sto n git that Sears Roebuck catlog n look at them guns. Mebbe Ma will lemme buy one when she gits mah pay from ol man Hawkins. Ahma beg her t gimme some money. Ahm ol ernough to hava gun. Ahm seventeen. Almost a man. He strode, feeling his long loose-jointed limbs. Shucks, a man oughta hava little gun aftah he done worked hard all day.

He came in sight of Joe's store. A yellow lantern glowed on the front porch. He mounted steps and went through the screen door, hearing it bang behind him. There was a strong smell of coal oil and mackerel fish. He felt very confident until he saw fat Joe walk in through the rear door, then his courage began to ooze.

"Howdy, Dave! Whutcha want?"

"How yuh, Mistah Joe? Aw, Ah don wanna buy nothing. Ah jus wanted t see ef yuhd lemme look at tha catlog erwhile."

"Sure! You wanna see it here?"

"Nawsuh. Ah wans t take it home wid me. Ah'll bring it back termorrow when Ah come in from the fiels."

"You plannin on buying something?"

"Yessuh."

"Your ma lettin you have your own money now?"

"Shucks. Mistah Joe, Ahm gittin t be a man like anybody else!"

Joe laughed and wiped his greasy white face with a red bandanna.

"Whut you plannin on buyin?"

Dave looked at the floor, scratched his head, scratched his thigh, and smiled. Then he looked up shyly.

"Ah'll tell yuh, Mistah Joe, ef yuh promise yuh won't tell."

"I promise."

"Waal, Ahma buy a gun."

"A gun? Whut you want with a gun?"

"Ah wanna keep it."

"You ain't nothing but a boy. You don't need a gun."

"Aw, lemme have the catlog, Mistah Joe. Ah'll bring it back."

Joe walked through the rear door. Dave was elated. He looked around at barrels of sugar and flour. He heard Joe coming back. He craned his neck to see if he were bringing the book. Yeah, he's got it. Gawddog, he's got it!

"Here, but be sure you bring it back. It's the only one I got."

"Sho, Mistah Joe."

"Say, if you wanna buy a gun, why don't you buy one from me? I gotta gun to sell."

"Will it shoot?"

"Sure it'll shoot."

"Whut kind is it?"

"Oh, it's kinda old . . . a left-hand Wheeler. A pistol. A big one."

"Is it got bullets in it?"

"It's loaded."

"Kin Ah see it?"

"Where's your money?"

"Whut yuh wan fer it?"

"I'll let you have it for two dollars."

"Just two dollahs? Shucks, Ah could buy tha when Ah git mah pay."

"I'll have it here when you want it."

"Awright, suh. Ah be in fer it."

He went through the door, hearing it slam again behind him. Ahma git some money from Ma n buy me a gun! Only two dollahs! He tucked the thick catalogue under his arm and hurried.

"Where yuh been, boy?" His mother held a steaming dish of black-eyed peas.

"Aw, Ma, Ah jus stopped down the road t talk wid the boys."

"Yuh know bettah t keep suppah waitin."

He sat down, resting the catalogue on the edge of the table.

"Yuh git up from there and git to the well n wash yoself! Ah ain feedin no hogs in mah house!"

She grabbed his shoulder and pushed him. He stumbled out of the room, then came back to get the catalogue.

"Whut this?"

"Aw, Ma, it's jusa catlog."

"Who yuh git it from?"

"From Joe, down at the sto."

"Waal, thas good. We kin use it in the outhouse."

"Naw, Ma." He grabbed for it. "Gimme ma catlog, Ma."

She held onto it and glared at him.

"Quit hollerin at me! Whut's wrong wid yuh? Yuh crazy?"

"But Ma, please. It ain mine! It's Joe's! He tol me t bring it back t im termorrow."

She gave up the book. He stumbled down the back steps, hugging the thick book under his arm. When he had splashed water on his face and hands, he groped back to the kitchen and fumbled in a corner for the towel. He bumped into a chair; it clattered to the floor. The catalogue sprawled at his feet. When he had dried his eyes he snatched up the book and held it again under his arm. His mother stood watching him.

"Now, ef yuh gonna act a fool over that ol book, Ah'll take it n burn it up."

"Naw, Ma, please."

"Waal, set down n be still!"

He sat down and drew the oil lamp close. He thumbed page after page, unaware of the food his mother set on the table. His father came in. Then his small brother.

"Whutcha got there, Dave?" his father asked.

"Jusa catlog," he answered, not looking up.

"Yeah, here they is!" His eyes glowed at blue-and-black revolvers. He glanced up, feeling sudden guilt. His father was watching him. He eased the book under the table and rested it on his knees. After the blessing was asked, he ate. He scooped up peas and swallowed fat meat without chewing. Buttermilk helped to wash it down. He did not want to mention money before his father. He would do much better by cornering his mother when she was alone. He looked at his father uneasily out of the edge of his eye.

"Boy, how come yuh don quit foolin wid tha book n eat yo suppah?"

"Yessuh."

"How you n ol man Hawkins gitten erlong?"

"Suh?"

"Can't yuh hear? Why don yuh lissen? Ah ast yu how wuz yuh n ol man Hawkins gittin erlong?"

"Oh, swell, Pa. Ah plows mo lan than anybody over there."

'Waal, yuh oughta keep yo mind on whut yuh doin."

"Yessuh."

He poured his plate full of molasses and sopped it up slowly with a chunk of cornbread. When his father and brother had left the kitchen, he still sat and looked again at the guns in the catalogue, longing to muster courage enough to present his case to his mother. Lawd, ef Ah only had tha pretty one! He could almost feel the slickness of the weapon with his fingers. If he had a gun like that he would polish it and keep it shining so it would never rust. N Ah'd keep it loaded, by Gawd!

"Ma?" His voice was hesitant.

"Hunh?"

"Ol man Hawkins give yuh mah money yit?"

"Yeah, but ain no usa yuh thinking bout throwin nona it erway. Ahm keepin tha money sos yuh kin have cloes t go to school this winter."

He rose and went to her side with the open catalogue in his palms. She was washing dishes, her head bent low over a pan. Shyly he raised the book. When he spoke, his voice was husky, faint.

"Ma, Gawd knows Ah wans one of these."

"One of whut?" she asked, not raising her eyes.

"One of these," he said again, not daring even to point. She glanced up at the page, then at him with wide eyes.

"Nigger, is yuh gone plumb crazy?"

"Aw, Ma—"

"Git outta here! Don yuh talk t me bout no gun! Yuh a fool!"

"Ma, Ah kin buy one fer two dollahs."

"Not ef Ah knows it, yuh ain!"

"But yuh promised me one—"

"Ah don care whut Ah promised! Yuh ain nothing but a boy yit!"

"Ma, ef yuh lemme buy one Ah'll *never* ast yuh fer nothing no mo."

"Ah tol yuh t git outta here! Yuh ain gonna toucha penny of tha money fer no gun! Thas how come Ah has Mistah Hawkins t pay yo wages t me, cause Ah knows yuh ain got no sense."

"But, Ma, we needa gun. Pa ain got no gun. We needa gun in the house. Yuh kin never tell whut might happen."

"Now don yuh try to maka fool outta me, boy! Ef we did hava gun, yuh wouldn't have it!"

He laid the catalogue down and slipped his arm around her waist.

"Aw, Ma, Ah done worked hard alla summer n ain ast yuh fer nothin, is Ah, now?"

"Thas whut yuh spose t do!"

"But Ma, Ah wans a gun. Yuh kin lemme have two dollahs outta mah money. Please, Ma. I kin give it to Pa . . . Please, Ma! Ah loves yuh, Ma."

When she spoke her voice came soft and low.

"Whut yu wan wida gun, Dave? Yuh don need no gun. You'll git in trouble. N ef yo pa jus thought Ah let yuh have money t buy a gun he'd hava fit."

"Ah'll hide it, Ma. It ain but two dollahs."

"Lawd, chil, whut's wrong wid yuh?"

"Ain nothin wrong, Ma. Ahm almos a man now. Ah wans a gun."

"Who gonna sell yuh a gun?"

"Ol Joe at the sto."

"N it don cos but two dollahs?"

"Thas all, Ma. Jus two dollahs. Please, Ma."

She was stacking the plates away; her hands moved slowly, reflectively. Dave kept an anxious silence. Finally, she turned to him.

"Ah'll let yuh git tha gun ef yuh promise me one thing."

"Whut's tha, Ma?"

"Yuh bring it straight back t me, yuh hear? It be fer Pa."

"Yessum! Lemme go now, Ma."

She stooped, turned slightly to one side, raised the hem of her dress, rolled down the top of her stocking, and came up with a slender wad of bills.

"Here," she said. "Lawd knows yuh don need no gun. But yer pa does. Yuh bring it right back t me, yuh hear? Ahma put it up. Now ef yuh don, Ahma have yuh pa lick yuh so hard yuh won fergit it."

"Yessum."

He took the money, ran down the steps, and across the yard.

"Dave! Yuuuuuh Daaaaave!"

He heard, but he was not going to stop now. "Naw, Lawd!"

The first movement he made the following morning was to reach under his pillow for the gun. In the gray light of dawn he held it loosely, feeling a sense of power. Could kill a man with a gun like this. Kill anybody, black or white. And if he were holding his gun in his hand, nobody could run over him; they would have to respect him. It was a big gun, with a long barrel and a heavy handle. He raised and lowered it in his hand, marveling at its weight.

He had not come straight home with it as his mother had asked; instead he had stayed out in the fields, holding the weapon in his hand, aiming it now and then at some imaginary foe. But he had not fired it; he had been afraid that his father might hear. Also he was not sure he knew how to fire it.

To avoid surrendering the pistol he had not come into the house until he knew that they were all asleep. When his mother had tiptoed to his bedside late that night and demanded the gun, he had first played possum; then he had told her that the gun was hidden outdoors, that he would bring it to her in the morning. Now he lay turning it slowly in his hands. He broke it, took out the cartridges, felt them, and then put them back.

He slid out of bed, got a long strip of old flannel from a trunk, wrapped the gun in it, and tied it to his naked thigh while it was still loaded. He did not go in to breakfast. Even though it was not yet daylight, he started for Jim Hawkins' plantation. Just as the sun was rising he reached the barns where the mules and plows were kept.

"Hey! That you, Dave?"

He turned. Jim Hawkins stood eying him suspiciously.

"What're yuh doing here so early?"

"Ah didn't know Ah wuz gittin up so early, Mistah Hawkins. Ah wuz fixin t hitch up ol Jenny n take her t the fiels."

"Good. Since you're so early, how about plowing that stretch down by the woods?"

"Suits me, Mistah Hawkins."

"O.K. Go to it!"

He hitched Jenny to a plow and started across the fields. Hot dog! This was just what he wanted. If he could get down by the woods, he could shoot his gun and nobody would hear. He walked behind the plow, hearing the traces creaking, feeling the gun tied tight to his thigh.

When he reached the woods, he plowed two whole rows before he decided to take out the gun. Finally, he stopped, looked in all directions, then untied the gun and held it in his hand. He turned to the mule and smiled.

"Know whut this is, Jenny? Naw, yuh wouldn know! Yuhs jusa ol mule! Anyhow, this is a gun, n it kin shoot, by Gawd!"

He held the gun at arm's length. Whut t hell, Ahma shoot this thing! He looked at Jenny again.

"Lissen here, Jenny! When Ah pull this ol trigger, Ah don wan yuh t run n acka fool now!"

Jenny stood with head down, her short ears pricked straight. Dave walked off about twenty feet, held the gun far out from him at arm's length, and turned his head. Hell, he told himself, Ah ain afraid. The gun felt loose in his fingers; he waved it wildly for a moment. Then he shut his eyes and tightened his forefinger. Bloom! A report half deafened him and he thought his right hand was torn from his arm. He heard Jenny whinnying and galloping over the field, and he found himself on his knees squeezing his fingers hard between his legs. His hand was numb; he jammed it into his mouth, trying to warm it, trying to stop the pain. The gun lay at his feet. He did not quite know what had happened. He stood up and stared at the gun as though it were a living thing. He gritted his teeth and kicked the gun. Yuh almos broke mah arm! He turned to look for Jenny; she was far over the fields, tossing her head and kicking wildly.

"Hol on there, ol mule!"

When he caught up with her she stood trembling, walling her big white eyes at him. The plow was far away; the traces had broken. Then Dave stopped short, looking, not believing. Jenny was bleeding. Her left side was red and wet with blood. He went closer. Lawd, have mercy! Wondah did Ah shoot this mule? He grabbed for Jenny's mane. She flinched, snorted, whirled, tossing her head.

"Hol on now! Hol on."

Then he saw the hole in Jenny's side, right between the ribs. It was round, wet, red. A crimson stream streaked down the front leg, flowing fast. Good Gawd! Ah wuzn't shootin at tha mule. He felt panic. He knew he had to stop that blood, or Jenny would bleed to death. He had never seen so much blood in all his life. He chased the mule for half a mile, trying to catch her. Finally she stopped, breathing hard, stumpy tail half arched. He caught her mane and led her back to where the plough and gun lay. Then he stooped and grabbed handfuls of damp black earth and tried to plug the bullet hole. Jenny shuddered, whinnied, and broke from him.

"Hol on! Hol on now!"

He tried to plug it again, but blood came anyhow. His fingers were hot and sticky. He rubbed dirt into his palms, trying to dry them. Then again he attempted to plug the bullet hole, but Jenny shied away, kicking her heels high. He stood helpless. He had to do something. He ran at Jenny; she dodged him. He watched a red stream of blood flow down Jenny's leg and form a bright pool at her feet.

"Jenny . . . Jenny," he called weakly.

His lips trembled. She's bleeding t death! He looked in the direction of home, wanting to go back, wanting to get help. But he saw the pistol lying in the damp black clay. He had a queer feeling that if he only did something, this would not be; Jenny would not be there bleeding to death.

When he went to her this time, she did not move. She stood with sleepy, dreamy eyes; and when he touched her she gave a low-pitched whinny and knelt to the ground, her front knees slopping in blood.

"Jenny . . . Jenny . . ." he whispered.

For a long time she held her neck erect; then her head sank, slowly. Her ribs swelled with a mighty heave and she went over.

Dave's stomach felt empty, very empty. He picked up the gun and held it gingerly between his thumb and forefinger. He buried it at the foot of a tree. He took a stick and tried to cover the pool of blood with dirt—but what was the use? There was Jenny lying with her mouth open and her eyes walled and glassy. He could not tell Jim Hawkins he had shot his mule. But he had to tell something. Yeah, Ah'll tell em Jenny started gittin wil n fell on the joint of the plow. . . . But that would hardly happen to a mule. He walked across the field slowly, head down.

It was sunset. Two of Jim Hawkins' men were over near the edge of the woods digging a hole in which to bury Jenny. Dave was surrounded by a knot of people, all of whom were looking down at the dead mule.

"I don't see how in the world it happened," said Jim Hawkins for the tenth time.

The crowd parted and Dave's mother, father, and small brother pushed into the center.

"Where Dave?" his mother called.

"There he is," said Jim Hawkins.

His mother grabbed him.

"Whut happened, Dave? Whut yuh done?"

"Nothin."

"C mon, boy, talk," his father said.

Dave took a deep breath and told the story he knew nobody believed.

"Waal," he drawled. "Ah brung ol Jenny down here sos Ah could do mah plowin. Ah plowed bout two rows, just like yuh see." He stopped and pointed at the long rows of upturned earth. "Then somethin musta been wrong wid ol Jenny. She wouldn ack right a-tall. She started snortin n kickin her heels. Ah tried t hol her, but she pulled er-way, rearin n goin in. Then when the point of the plow was stickin up in the air, she swung erroun n twisted herself back on it . . . She stuck herself n started t bleed. N fo Ah could do anything, she wuz dead."

"Did you ever hear of anything like that in all your life?" asked Jim Hawkins.

There were white and black standing in the crowd. They murmured. Dave's mother came close to him and looked hard into his face. "Tell the truth, Dave," she said.

"Looks like a bullet hole to me," said one man.

"Dave, whut yuh do wid the gun?" his mother asked.

The crowd surged in, looking at him. He jammed his hands into his pockets, shook his head slowly from left to right, and backed away. His eyes were wide and painful.

"Did he hava gun?" asked Jim Hawkins.

"By Gawd, Ah tol him tha wuz a gun wound," said a man, slapping his thigh.

His father caught his shoulders and shook him till his teeth rattled.

"Tell whut happened, yuh rascal! Tell whut . . ."

Dave looked at Jenny's stiff legs and began to cry.

"Whut yuh do wid tha gun?" his mother asked.

"Whut wuz he doin wida gun?" his father asked.

"Come on and tell the truth," said Hawkins. "Ain't nobody going to hurt you . . ."

His mother crowded close to him.

"Did yuh shoot tha mule, Dave?"

Dave cried, seeing blurred white and black faces.

"Ahh ddinn gggo tt sshooot hher . . . Ah ssswear ffo Gawd Ahh ddin . . . Ah wuz a-tryin t sssee ef the old gggun would sshoot—"

"Where yuh git the gun from?" his father asked.

"Ah got it from Joe, at the sto."

"Where yuh git the money?"

"Ma give it t me."

"He kept worryin me, Bob. Ah had t. Ah tol im t bring the gun right back t me . . . It was fer yuh, the gun."

"But how yuh happen to shoot that mule?" asked Jim Hawkins.

"Ah wuzn shootin at the mule, Mistah Hawkins. The gun jumped when Ah pulled the trigger . . . N for Ah knowed anythin Jenny was there a-bleedin."

Somebody in the crowd laughed. Jim Hawkins walked close to Dave and looked into his face.

"Well, looks like you have bought a mule, Dave."

"Ah swear to Gawd, Ah didn go t kill the mule, Mistah Hawkins!"

"But you killed her!"

All the crowd was laughing now. They stood on tiptoe and poked heads over one another's shoulders.

"Well, boy, looks like yuh done bought a dead mule! Hahaha!"

"Ain tha ershame."

"Hohohohoho."

Dave stood, head down, twisting his feet in the dirt.

"Well, you needn't worry about it, Bob," said Jim Hawkins to Dave's father. "Just let the boy keep on working and pay me two dollars a month."

"Whut yuh wan fer yo mule, Mistah Hawkins?"

Jim Hawkins screwed up his eyes.

"Fifty dollars."

"Whut yuh do wid tha gun?" Dave's father demanded.

Dave said nothing.

"Yuh wan me t take a tree n beat yuh till yuh talk!"

"Nawsuh!"

"Whut yuh do wid it?"

"Ah throwed it erway."

"Where?"

"Ah . . . Ah throwed it in the creek."

"Waal, c mon home. N firs thing in the mawnin git to tha creek n fin tha gun."

"Yessuh."

"Whut yuh pay fer it?"

"Two dollahs."

"Take tha gun n git yu money back n carry it t Mistah Hawkins, yuh hear? N don fergit Ahma lam you black bottom good fer this! Now march yosef on home, suh!"

Dave turned and walked slowly. He heard people laughing. Dave glared, his eyes welling with tears. Hot anger bubbled in him. Then he swallowed and stumbled on.

That night Dave did not sleep. He was glad that he had gotten out of killing the mule so easily, but he was hurt. Something hot seemed to turn over inside him each time he remembered how they had laughed. He tossed on his bed, feeling his hard pillow. N Pa says he's gonna beat me . . . He remembered other beatings, and his back quivered. Naw, naw. Ah sho don wan im t beat me tha way no mo. Dam em all! Nobody ever gave him anything. All he did was work. They treat me like a mule, n then they beat me. He gritted his teeth. N Ma had t tell on me.

Well, if he had to, he would take old man Hawkins that two dollars. But that meant selling the gun. And he wanted to keep that gun. Fifty dollars for a dead mule.

He turned over, thinking how he had fired the gun. He had an itch to fire it again. Ef other men kin shoota gun, by Gawd, Ah kin! He was still, listening. Mebbe they all sleepin now. The house was still. He heard the soft breathing of his brother. Yes, now! He would go down and get that gun and see if he could fire it! He eased out of bed and slipped into overalls.

The moon was bright. He ran almost all the way to the edge of the woods. He stumbled over the ground, looking for the spot where he had buried the gun. Yeah, here it is. Like a hungry dog scratching for a bone, he pawed it up. He puffed his black cheeks and blew dirt from the trigger and barrel. He broke it and found four cartridges unshot. He looked around; the fields were filled with silence and moonlight. He clutched the gun stiff and hard in his fingers. But, as soon as he wanted to pull the trigger, he shut his eyes and turned his head. Naw, Ah can't shoot wid mah eyes closed n mah head turned. With effort he held his eyes open; then he squeezed. *Blooooom!* He was stiff, not breathing. The gun was still in his hands. Dammit, he'd done it! He fired again. *Blooooom!* He smiled. *Blooooom! Blooooom! Click, click.* There! It was empty. If anybody could shoot a gun, he could. He put the gun into his hip pocket and started across the fields.

When he reached the top of a ridge he stood straight and proud in the moonlight, looking at Jim Hawkins' big white house, feeling the gun sagging in his pocket. Lawd, ef Ah had just one mo bullet Ah'd taka shot at tha house. Ah'd like t scare ol man Hawkins jusa little . . . Jusa enough t let im know Dave Saunders is a man.

To his left the road curved, running to the tracks of the Illinois Central. He jerked his head, listening. From far off came a faint *hoooof-hoooof; hoooof-hoooof; hoooof-hoooof.* . . . He stood rigid. Two dollahs a mont. Les see now . . . Tha means it'll take bout two years. Shucks! Ah'll be dam!

He started down the road, toward the tracks. Yeah, here she comes! He stood beside the track and held himself stiffly. Here she comes, erroun the ben . . . C mon, yuh slow poke! C mon! He had his hand on his gun; something quivered in his stomach. Then the train thundered past, the gray and brown box cars rumbling and clinking. He gripped the gun tightly; then he jerked his hand out of his pocket. Ah betcha Bill wouldn't do it! Ah-betcha . . . The cars slid past, steel grinding upon steel. Ahm ridin yuh ternight, so hep me Gawd! He was hot all over. He hesitated just a moment; then he grabbed, pulled atop of a car, and lay flat. He felt his pocket; the gun was still there. Ahead the long rails were glinting in the moonlight, stretching away, away to somewhere, somewhere where he could be a man . . .

# Modern Cluster

# The Harlem Renaissance

The Harlem Renaissance is the name given to a cultural, artistic, and intellectual movement that flourished in the African American community roughly between the years of 1919 and 1940. Although New York was not the only place where blacks gathered, organized, and worked creatively, New York, and specifically the community of Harlem, became a magnet for blacks escaping the South. After the Civil War, Reconstruction began as freed slaves tried to live "free" lives and the South set about rebuilding its social and economic base. However, after the landmark case *Plessy* v. *Ferguson* (1896) determined that African Americans and whites must travel separately, life in the South for free blacks became less tolerable: segregation spread to every aspect of life and the lynching of black men became an everyday occurrence.

Blacks saw migration north as the only means to live safe and productive lives. Increasing industrial innovation and the beginning of World War I also provided African Americans living in northern cities the chance for decent jobs and wages. Migrating blacks chose a number of northern cities—Chicago, Philadelphia, Cleveland—but New York City was the biggest draw in the East. Harlem became home to African Americans of all kinds, including artists, writers, and jazz musicians. Black-owned and -operated newspapers flourished, and political organizations such as the National Association for the Advancement of Colored People (NAACP) established headquarters in Harlem. Magazines like *Opportunity* (edited by Charles S. Johnson) and W. E. B. DuBois' *The Crisis* published stories, essays, and poems by

*Aaron Douglas, Cover,* Opportunity: A Journal of Negro Life, *June 1926*

up-and-coming black writers like Jessie Redmon Fauset, Langston Hughes, Arna Bontemps, Zora Neale Hurston, Claude McKay, and Nella Larsen.

The writing of the Harlem Renaissance revolved around many of the themes established in modernism, a literary genre developing alongside the Harlem movement, including alienation and disappointment with the trappings of the modern world. But black writers balked at the elitist overtones of the white-dominated modernist movement and chose to address issues of race and class while advocating that writers in this genre write for and to African Americans. Harlem Renaissance writers often employed folktales, black dialect, and African oral storytelling traditions to make their works relevant to the African American community. The writers and their advocates believed that this cultural renaissance would help strengthen the black community—in and out of the city—and enable it to grow and flourish.

Just as economic prosperity fostered the Harlem Renaissance, so the changing economic climate ushered the movement out. Many writers of the Harlem Renaissance relied on white patrons to help pay their way while writing, and the expansion of the movement depended on the prosperity of publishers, but the Great Depression signaled the end of these opportunities. The levity and enthusiasm of the Jazz Age gave way to hard times for Americans of every ethnicity, and supporting the arts moved far down the list of public priorities. However, the effects of the Harlem Renaissance did not diminish; black writers continue to articulate issues of race and self-definition in literature and beyond.

# Arna Bontemps

## (1902–1973)

A master of many genres, Arna Bontemps devoted most of his time to writing for children. He chose young readers because they were "not yet insensitive to man's inhumanity to man." Bontemps was born in Alexandria, Louisiana, and was the son of a skilled brick mason. The family moved to Los Angeles in 1905, and in 1923 Bontemps graduated from Pacific Union College in Angwin, California. He began publishing poetry in 1924 and received the Alexander Pushkin Prize from *Opportunity* magazine in 1926 and 1927, as well as the *Crisis* Poetry Prize in 1926. He then moved to New York City to teach at the Harlem Academy and during the next five years became close with Langston Hughes, Countée Cullen, W. E. B. DuBois, Zora Neale Hurston, James Weldon Johnson, Claude McKay, and Jean Toomer. His first book, *God Sends Sunday*, was published in 1931. In the same year he and his family moved to Huntsville, Alabama, and he began teaching at Oakwood Junior College.

It was during this time that Bontemps became frustrated in trying to reach his own generation. His works were not always well received, and he was unable to support his family with his royalties. *Popo and Fifina,* his first children's book, written in collaboration with Langston Hughes, was published in 1932. For the remaining forty years of his life, Bontemps wrote biographies, children's fiction, and African American history and compiled literary anthologies. His works include *Black Thunder* (1936), *Golden Slippers* (1941), *The Fast Sooner Hound* (1942), *The Story of the Negro* (1948), *Chariot in the Sky* (1951), and *Personals* (1963). In 1943 he obtained his master's degree in library science and served as the head librarian at Fisk University until his retirement. While there, he developed an archive of African American cultural material that is still a major resource for study.

---

## A Summary Tragedy
1933

Old Jeff Patton, the black share farmer, fumbled with his bow tie. His fingers trembled, and the high, stiff collar pinched his throat. A fellow loses his hand for such vanities after thirty or forty years of simple life. Once a year, or maybe twice if there's a wedding among his kin-folks, he may spruce up; but generally fancy clothes do nothing but adorn the wall of the big room and feed the moths. That had been Jeff Patton's experience. He had not worn his stiff-bosomed shirt more than a dozen times in all his married life. His swallowtailed coat lay on the bed beside him, freshly brushed and pressed, but it was as full of holes as the overalls in which he worked on week days. The moths had used it badly. Jeff twisted his mouth into a hideous toothless grimace as he contended with the obstinate bow. He stamped his good foot and decided to give up the struggle.

"Jennie," he called.

"What's that, Jeff?" His wife's shrunken voice came out of the adjoining room like an echo. It was hardly bigger than a whisper.

"I reckon you'll have to he'p me wid this heah bow tie, baby," he said meekly. "Dog if I can hitch it up."

Her answer was not strong enough to reach him, but presently the old woman came to the door, feeling her way with a stick. She had a wasted, dead-leaf appearance. Her body, as scrawny and gnarled as a stringbean, seemed less than nothing in the ocean of frayed and faded petticoats that surrounded her. These hung an inch or two above the tops of her heavy, unlaced shoes and showed little grotesque piles where the stockings had fallen down from her negligible legs.

"You oughta could do a heap mo' wid a thing like that 'n me—beingst as you got yo' good sight."

"Looks like I *oughta* could," he admitted. "But ma fingers is gone democrat on me. I get all mixed up in the looking glass an' can't tell whicha way to twist the devilish thing."

Jennie sat on the side of the bed and old Jeff Patton got down on one knee while she tied the bow knot. It was a slow and painful ordeal for each of them in this position. Jeff's bones cracked, his knee ached, and it was only after a half dozen attempts that Jennie worked a semblance of a bow into the tie.

"I got to dress maself now," the old woman whispered. "These is ma old shoes an' stockings, and I ain't so much as unwrapped ma dress."

"Well, don't worry 'bout me no mo', baby," Jeff said. "That 'bout finishes me. All I gotta do now is slip on that old coat 'n ves' an' I'll be fixed to leave."

Jennie disappeared again through the dim passage into the shed room. Being blind was no handicap to her in that black hole. Jeff heard the cane placed against the wall beside the door and knew that his wife was on easy ground. He put on his coat, took a battered top hat from the bed post, and hobbled to the front door. He was ready to travel. As soon as Jennie could get on her Sunday shoes and her old black silk dress, they would start.

Outside the tiny log house the day was warm and mellow with sunshine. A host of wasps was humming with busy excitement in the trunk of a dead sycamore. Gray squirrels were searching through the grass for hickory nuts and blue jays were in the trees, hopping from branch to branch. Pine woods stretched away to the left like a black sea. Among them were scattered scores of log houses like Jeff's, houses of black share farmers. Cows and pigs wandered freely among the trees. There was no danger of loss. Each farmer knew his own stock and knew his neighbor's as well as he knew his neighbor's children.

Down the slope to the right were the cultivated acres on which the colored folks worked. They extended to the river, more than two miles away, and they were today green with the unmade cotton crop. A tiny thread of a road, which passed directly in front of Jeff's place, ran through these green fields like a pencil mark.

Jeff, standing outside the door with his absurd hat in his left hand, surveyed the wide scene tenderly. He had been forty-five years on these acres. He loved them with the unexplained affection that others have for the countries to which they belong.

The sun was hot on his head, his collar still pinched his throat, and the Sunday clothes were intolerably hot. Jeff transferred the hat to his right hand and began fanning with it. Suddenly the whisper that was Jennie's voice came out of the shed room.

"You can bring the car round front whilst you's waitin'," it said feebly. There was a tired pause, then it added, "I'll soon be fixed to go."

"A'right, baby," Jeff answered. "I'll get it in a minute."

But he didn't move. A thought struck him that made his mouth fall open. The mention of the car brought to his mind, with new intensity, the trip he and Jennie were about to take. Fear came into his eyes; excitement took his breath. Lord, Jesus!

"Jeff . . . Oh Jeff," the old woman's whisper called.

He awakened with a jolt. "Hunh, baby?"

"What you doin'?"

"Nuthin. Jes studyin'. I jes been turnin' things round 'n round in ma mind."

"You could be gettin' the car," she said.

"Oh yes, right away, baby."

He started round to the shed, limping heavily on his bad leg. There were three frizzly chickens in the yard. All his other chickens had been killed or stolen recently. But the frizzly chickens had been saved somehow. That was fortunate indeed, for these curious creatures had a way of devouring "poison" from the yard and in that way protecting against conjure and bad luck and spells. But even the frizzly chickens seemed now to be in a stupor. Jeff thought they had some ailment; he expected all three of them to die shortly.

The shed in which the old model-T Ford stood was only a grass roof held up by four corner poles. It had been built by tremulous hands at a time when the little rattle-trap car had been regarded as a peculiar treasure. And, miraculously, despite wind and downpour, it still stood.

Jeff adjusted the crank and put his weight on it. The engine came to life with a sputter and bang that rattled the old car from radiator to tail light. Jeff hopped into the seat and put his foot on the accelerator. The sputtering and banging increased. The rattling became more violent. That was good. It was good banging, good sputtering and rattling, and it meant that the aged car was still in running condition. She could be depended on for this trip.

Again Jeff's thought halted as if paralyzed. The suggestion of the trip fell into the machinery of his mind like a wrench. He felt dazed and weak. He swung the car out into the yard, made a half turn, and drove around to the front door. When he took his hands off the wheel, he noticed that he was trembling violently. He cut off the motor and climbed to the ground to wait for Jennie.

A few moments later she was at the window, her voice rattling against the pane like a broken shutter.

"I'm ready, Jeff."

He did not answer, but limped into the house and took her by the arm. He led her slowly through the big room, down the step, and across the yard.

"You reckon I'd oughta lock the do'?" he asked softly.

They stopped and Jennie weighed the question. Finally she shook her head.

"Ne' mind the do'," she said. "I don't see no cause to lock up things."

"You right," Jeff agreed. "No cause to lock up."

Jeff opened the door and helped his wife into the car. A quick shudder passed over him. Jesus! Again he trembled.

"How come you shaking so?" Jennie whispered.

"I don't know," he said.

"You mus' be scairt, Jeff."

"No, baby, I ain't scairt."

He slammed the door after her and went around to crank up again. The motor started easily. Jeff wished that it had not been so responsive. He would have liked a few more minutes in which to turn things around in his head. As it was, with Jennie chiding him about being afraid, he had to keep going. He swung the car into the little pencilmark road and started off toward the river, driving very slowly, very cautiously.

Chugging across the green countryside, the small, battered Ford seemed tiny indeed. Jeff felt a familiar excitement, a thrill, as they came down the first slope to the immense levels on which the cotton was growing. He could not help reflecting that the crops were good. He knew what that meant, too; he had made forty-five of them with his own hands. It was true that he had worn out nearly a dozen mules, but that was the fault of old man Stevenson, the owner of the land. Major Stevenson had the odd notion that one mule was all a share farmer needed to work a thirty-acre plot. It was an expensive notion, the way it killed mules from overwork, but the old man held to it. Jeff thought it killed a good many share farmers as well as mules, but he had no sympathy for them. He had always been strong, and he had been taught to have no patience with weakness in men. Women or children might be tolerated if they were puny, but a weak man was a curse. Of course, his own children—

Jeff's thought halted there. He and Jennie never mentioned their dead children any more. And naturally he did not wish to dwell upon them in his mind. Before he knew it, some remark would slip out of his mouth and that would make Jennie feel blue. Perhaps she would cry. A woman like Jennie could not easily throw off the grief that comes from losing five grown children within two years. Even Jeff was still staggered by the blow. His memory had not been much good recently. He frequently talked to himself. And, although he had kept it a secret, he knew that his courage had left him. He was terrified by the least unfamiliar sound at night. He was reluctant to venture far from home in the daytime. And that habit of trembling when he felt fearful was now far beyond his control. Sometimes he became afraid and trembled without knowing what had frightened him. The feeling would just come over him like a chill.

The car rattled slowly over the dusty road. Jennie sat erect and silent, with a little absurd hat pinned to her hair. Her useless eyes seemed very large and very white in their deep sockets. Suddenly Jeff heard her voice, and he inclined his head to catch the words.

"Is we passed Delia Moore's house yet?" she asked.

"Not yet," he said.

"You must be drivin' mighty slow, Jeff."

"We jes as well take our time, baby."

There was a pause. A little puff of steam was coming out of the radiator of the car. Heat wavered above the hood. Delia Moore's house was nearly half a mile away. After a moment Jennie spoke again.

"You ain't really scairt, is you, Jeff?"

"Nah, baby, I ain't scairt."

"You know how we agreed—we gotta keep on goin'."

Jewels of perspiration appeared on Jeff's forehead. His eyes rounded, blinked, became fixed on the road.

"I don't know," he said with a shiver. "I reckon it's the only thing to do."

"Hm."

A flock of guinea fowls, pecking in the road, were scattered by the passing car. Some of them took to their wings; others hid under bushes. A blue jay, swaying on a leafy twig, was annoying a roadside squirrel. Jeff held an even speed till he came near Delia's place. Then he slowed down noticeably.

Delia's house was really no house at all, but an abandoned store building converted into a dwelling. It sat near a crossroads, beneath a single black cedar tree. There Delia, a catlike old creature of Jennie's age, lived alone. She had been there more years than anybody could remember, and long ago had won the disfavor of such women as Jennie. For in her young days Delia had been gayer, yellower, and saucier than seemed proper in those parts. Her ways with menfolks had been dark and suspicious. And the fact that she had had as many husbands as children did not help her reputation.

"Yonder's old Delia," Jeff said as they passed.

"What she doin'?"

"Jes sittin' in the do'," he said.

"She see us?"

"Hm," Jeff said. "Musta did."

That relieved Jennie. It strengthened her to know that her old enemy had seen her pass in her best clothes. That would give the old she-devil something to chew her gums and fret about, Jennie thought. Wouldn't she have a fit if she didn't find out? Old evil Delia! This would be just the thing for her. It would pay her back for being so evil. It would also pay her, Jennie thought, for the way she used to grin at Jeff—long ago when her teeth were good.

The road became smooth and red, and Jeff could tell by the smell of the air that they were nearing the river. He could see the rise where the road turned and ran along parallel to the stream. The car chugged on monotonously. After a long silent spell, Jennie leaned against Jeff and spoke.

"How many bale o' cotton you think we got standin'?" she said.

Jeff wrinkled his forehead as he calculated.

" 'Bout twenty-five, I reckon."

"How many you make las' year?"

"Twenty-eight," he said. "How come you ask that?"

"I's jes thinkin'," Jennie said quietly.

"It don't make a speck o' diff'ence though," Jeff reflected. "If we get much or if we get little, we still gonna be in debt to old man Stevenson when he gets through counting up agin us. It's took us a long time to learn that."

Jennie was not listening to these words. She had fallen into a trance-like meditation. Her lips twitched. She chewed her gums and rubbed her old gnarled hands nervously. Suddenly, she leaned forward, buried her face in the nervous hands, and burst into tears. She cried aloud in a dry, cracked voice that suggested the rattle of fodder on dead stalks. She cried aloud like a child, for she had never learned to suppress a genuine sob. Her slight old frame shook heavily and seemed hardly able to sustain such violent grief.

"What's the matter, baby?" Jeff asked awkwardly. "Why you cryin' like all that?"

"I's jes thinkin'," she said.

"So you the one what's scairt now, hunh?"

"I ain't scairt, Jeff. I's jes thinkin' 'bout leavin' eve'thing like this—eve'thing we been used to. It's right sad-like."

Jeff did not answer, and presently Jennie buried her face again and continued crying.

The sun was almost overhead. It beat down furiously on the dusty wagon path road, on the parched roadside grass, and the tiny battered car. Jeff's hands, gripping the wheel, became wet with perspiration; his forehead sparkled. Jeff's lips parted and his mouth shaped a hideous grimace. His face suggested the face of a man being burned. But the torture passed and his expression softened again.

"You mustn't cry, baby," he said to his wife. "We gotta be strong. We can't break down."

Jennie waited a few seconds, then said, "You reckon we oughta do it, Jeff? You reckon we oughta go 'head an' do it really?"

Jeff's voice choked; his eyes blurred. He was terrified to hear Jennie say the thing that had been in his mind all morning. She had egged him on when he had wanted more than anything in the world to wait, to reconsider, to think things over a little longer. Now *she* was getting cold feet. Actually, there was no need of thinking the question through again. It would only end in making the same painful decision once more. Jeff knew that. There was no need of fooling around longer.

"We jes as well to do like we planned," he said. "They ain't nuthin else for us now—it's the bes' thing."

Jeff thought of the handicaps, the near impossibility, of making another crop with his leg bothering him more and more each week. Then there was always the chance that he would have another stroke, like the one that had made him lame. Another one might kill him. The least it could do would be to leave him helpless. Jeff gasped . . . Lord, Jesus! He could not bear to think of being helpless, like a baby, on Jennie's hands. Frail, blind Jennie.

The little pounding motor of the car worked harder and harder. The puff of steam from the cracked radiator became larger. Jeff realized that they were climbing a little rise. A moment later the road turned abruptly and he looked down upon the face of the river.

"Jeff."

"Hunh?"

"Is that the water I hear?"

"Hm. Tha's it."

"Well, which way you goin' now?"

"Down this-a way," he answered. "The road runs 'longside o' the water a lil piece."

She waited a while calmly. Then she said, "Drive faster."

"A'right, baby," Jeff said.

The water roared in the bed of the river. It was fifty or sixty feet below the level of the road. Between the road and the water there was a long smooth slope, sharply inclined. The slope was dry; the clay had been hardened by prolonged summer heat. The water below, roaring in a narrow channel, was noisy and wild.

"Jeff."

"Hunh?"

"How far you goin'?"

"Jes a lil piece down the road."

"You ain't scairt is you, Jeff?"

"Nah, baby," he said trembling. "I ain't scairt."

"Remember how we planned it, Jeff. We gotta do it like we said. Brave-like."

"Hm."

Jeff's brain darkened. Things suddenly seemed unreal, like figures in a dream. Thoughts swam in his mind foolishly, hysterically, like little blind fish in a pool within a dense cave. They rushed, crossed one another, jostled, collided, retreated, and rushed again. Jeff soon became dizzy. He shuddered violently and turned to his wife.

"Jennie, I can't do it. I can't." His voice broke pitifully.

She did not appear to be listening. All the grief had gone from her face. She sat erect, her unseeing eyes wide open, strained and frightful. Her glossy black skin had become dull. She seemed as thin and as sharp and bony as a starved bird. Now, having suffered and endured the sadness of tearing herself away from beloved things, she showed no anguish. She was absorbed with her own thoughts, and she didn't even hear Jeff's voice shouting in her ear.

Jeff said nothing more. For an instant there was light in his cavernous brain. That chamber was, for less than a second, peopled by characters he knew and loved. They were simple, healthy creatures, and they behaved in a manner that he could understand. They had quality. But since he had already taken leave of them long ago, the remembrance did not break his heart again. Young Jeff Patton was among them, the Jeff Patton of fifty years ago who went down to New Orleans with a crowd of country boys to the Mardi Gras doings. The gay young crowd—boys with candy-striped shirts and rouged brown girls in noisy silks—was like a picture in his head. Yet it did not make him sad. On that very trip Slim Burns had killed Joe Beasley—the crowd had been broken up. Since then Jeff Patton's world had been the Greenbrier Plantation. If there had been other Mardi Gras carnivals, he had not heard of them. Since then there had been no time; the years had fallen on him like waves. Now he was old, worn out. Another paralytic stroke like the one he had already suffered would put him on his back for keeps. In that condition, with a frail blind woman to look after him, he would be worse off than if he were dead.

Suddenly Jeff's hands became steady. He actually felt brave. He slowed down the motor of the car and carefully pulled off the road. Below, the water of the stream boomed, a soft thunder in the deep channel. Jeff ran the car onto the clay slope, pointed it directly toward the stream, and put his foot heavily on the accelerator. The little car leaped furiously down the steep incline toward the water. The movement was nearly as swift and direct as a fall. The two old black folks, sitting quietly side by side, showed no excitement. In another instant the car hit the water and dropped immediately out of sight.

A little later it lodged in the mud of a shallow place. One wheel of the crushed and upturned little Ford became visible above the rushing water.

# Langston Hughes

## (1902–1967)

Born in Joplin, Missouri, Langston Hughes was a member of the "New Negro Renaissance" and was influenced as a youth by the poetry of Carl Sandburg and Paul Laurence Dunbar. His work was among the most unique and wide-ranging of black writers during the 1900s. After his graduation from high school, Hughes spent a year and a half in Mexico with his father; upon his return, he attended Columbia University for one year. He then, in 1923, joined a crew on a ship, the S.S. *Malone,* sailing for Africa, and thereafter traveled to Paris, Venice, and Genoa. After he returned to New York, he encountered the literary circle that would be the most artistically influential for his flowering as a writer, the Harlem Renaissance writers. In 1921, he published his first poem in the literary magazine *Crisis,* "The Negro Speaks of Rivers," dedicated to W. E. B. DuBois, and in 1923 he completed "The Weary Blues," published in New York's *Amsterdam News.* In 1925, Hughes's first collection of poetry, bearing the same name, proved to be a great success. In 1930, he published the novel *Not Without Laughter.*

Influenced by the Harlem writers Countée Cullen, Arna Bontemps, Wallace Thurman, Zora Neale Hurston, and Eric Walrond, among others, Hughes took his literary style from the music of African American tradition: spirituals, blues, and jazz. He wanted, he said, "to explain and illuminate the Negro condition in America." Hughes was concerned with preserving and celebrating African American experience and folk heritage, and his poetry found popularity internationally, especially among African and Caribbean poetic colleagues. In an essay written for the *Nation* in 1926, Hughes commented, "We younger Negro artists . . . now intend to express our individual dark skinned selves without fear or shame." Langston Hughes produced more than twelve volumes of poetry, in addition to essays and works of fiction, drama, and history. He gave readings and lectures throughout the world during the course of his career and was an inspiration to the emerging black writers of the 1960s.

## Cora Unashamed

1934

### I

Melton was one of those miserable in-between little places, not large enough to be a town, nor small enough to be a village—that is, a village in the rural, charming sense of the word. Melton had no charm about it. It was merely a nondescript collection of houses and buildings in a region of farms—one of those sad American places with sidewalks, but no paved streets; electric lights, but no sewage; a station, but no trains that stopped, save a jerky local, morning and evening. And it was 150 miles from any city at all—even Sioux City.

Cora Jenkins was one of the least of the citizens of Melton. She was what the people referred to when they wanted to be polite, as a Negress, and when they wanted to be rude, as a nigger—sometimes adding the word "wench" for no good reason, for Cora was usually an inoffensive soul, except that she sometimes cussed.

She had been in Melton for forty years. Born there. Would die there probably. She worked for the Studevants, who treated her like a dog. She stood it. Had to stand it; or work for poorer white folks who would treat her worse; or go jobless. Cora was like a tree—once rooted, she stood, in spite of storms and strife, wind, and rocks, in the earth.

She was the Studevants' maid of all work—washing, ironing, cooking, scrubbing, taking care of kids, nursing old folks, making fires, carrying water.

Cora, bake three cakes for Mary's birthday tomorrow night. You Cora, give Rover a bath in that tar soap I bought. Cora, take Ma some jello, and don't let her have even a taste of that raisin pie. She'll keep us up all night if you do. Cora, iron my stockings. Cora, come here . . . Cora, put . . . Cora . . . Cora . . . Cora! Cora!

And Cora would answer, "Yes, m'am."

The Studevants thought they owned her, and they were perfectly right: they did. There was something about the teeth in the trap of economic circumstance that kept her in their power practically all her life—in the Studevant kitchen, cooking; in the Studevant parlor, sweeping; in the Studevant backyard, hanging clothes.

You want to know how that could be? How a trap could close so tightly? Here is the outline:

Cora was the oldest of a family of eight children—the Jenkins niggers. The only Negroes in Melton, thank God! Where they came from originally—that is, the old folks—God knows. The kids were born there. The old folks are still there now: Pa drives a junk wagon. The old woman ails around the house, ails and quarrels. Seven kids are gone. Only Cora remains. Cora simply couldn't go, with nobody else to help take care of Ma. And before that she couldn't go, with nobody to see that her brothers and sisters got through school (she the oldest, and Ma ailing). And before that—well, somebody had to help Ma look after one baby behind another that kept on coming.

As a child Cora had no playtime. She always had a little brother, or a little sister in her arms. Bad, crying, bratty babies, hungry and mean. In the eighth grade she quit school and went to work with the Studevants.

After that, she ate better. Half day's work at first, helping Ma at home the rest of the time. Then full days, bringing home her pay to feed her father's children. The old man was rather a drunkard. What little money he made from closet-cleaning, ash-hauling, and junk-dealing he spent mostly on the stuff that makes you forget you have eight kids.

He passed the evenings telling long, comical lies to the white riff-raff of the town, and drinking licker. When his horse died, Cora's money went for a new one to haul her Pa and his rickety wagon around. When the mortgage money came due, Cora's wages kept the man from taking the roof from over their heads. When Pa got in jail, Cora borrowed ten dollars from Mrs. Studevant and got him out.

Cora stinted, and Cora saved, and wore the Studevants' old clothes, and ate the Studevants' leftover food, and brought her pay home. Brothers and sisters grew up. The boys, lonesome, went away, as far as they could from Melton. One by one, the girls left too, mostly in disgrace. "Ruinin' ma name," Pa Jenkins said, "ruinin' ma good name! They can't go out berryin' but what they come back in disgrace." There was something about the cream-and-tan Jenkins girls that attracted the white farm hands.

Even Cora, the humble, had a lover once. He came to town on a freight train (long ago now), and worked at the livery-stable. (That was before autos got to be so common.) Everybody said he was an I. W. W. Cora didn't care. He was the first man and the last she ever remembered wanting. She had never known a colored lover. There weren't any around. That was not her fault.

This white boy, Joe, he always smelt like the horses. He was some kind of foreigner. Had an accent, and yellow hair, big hands, and grey eyes.

It was summer. A few blocks beyond the Studevants' house, meadows and orchards and sweet fields stretched away to the far horizon. At night, stars in the velvet sky. Moon sometimes. Crickets and katydids and lightning bugs. The scent of grass. Cora waiting. That boy, Joe, a cigarette spark far off, whistling in the dark. Love didn't take long—Cora with the scent of Studevants' supper about her, and a cheap perfume. Joe, big and strong and careless as the horses he took care of, smelling like the stable.

Ma would quarrel because Cora came home late, or because none of the kids had written for three or four weeks, or because Pa was drunk again. Thus the summer passed, a dream of big hands and grey eyes.

Cora didn't go anywhere to have her child. Nor tried to hide it. When the baby grew big within her, she didn't feel that it was a disgrace. The Studevants told her to go home and stay there. Joe left town. Pa cussed. Ma cried. One April morning the kid was born. She had grey eyes, and Cora called her Josephine, after Joe.

Cora was humble and shameless before the fact of the child. There were no Negroes in Melton to gossip, and she didn't care what the white people said. They were in another world. Of course, she hadn't expected to marry Joe, or keep him. He was of that other world, too. But the child was hers—a living bridge between two worlds. Let people talk.

Cora went back to work at the Studevants'—coming home at night to nurse her kid, and quarrel with Ma. About that time, Mrs. Art Studevant had a child, too, and Cora nursed it. The Studevants' little girl was named Jessie. As the two children began to walk and talk, Cora sometimes brought Josephine to play with Jessie—until the Studevants objected, saying she could get her work done better if she left her child at home.

"Yes, m'am," said Cora.

But in a little while they didn't need to tell Cora to leave her child at home, for Josephine died of whooping-cough. One rosy afternoon, Cora saw the little body go down into the ground in a white casket that cost four weeks' wages.

Since Ma was ailing, Pa, smelling of licker, stood with her at the grave. The two of them alone. Cora was not humble before the fact of death. As she turned away from the hole, tears came—but at the same time a stream of curses so violent that they made the grave-tenders look up in startled horror.

She cussed out God for taking away the life that she herself had given. She screamed, "My baby! God damn it! My baby! I bear her and you take her away!" She looked at the sky where the sun was setting and yelled in defiance. Pa was amazed and scared. He pulled her up on his rickety wagon and drove off, clattering down the road between green fields and sweet meadows that stretched away to the far horizon. All through the ugly town Cora wept and cursed, using all the bad words she had learned from Pa in his drunkenness.

The next week she went back to the Studevants. She was gentle and humble in the face of life—she loved their baby. In the afternoons on the back porch, she would pick little Jessie up and rock her to sleep, burying her dark face in the milky smell of the white child's hair.

**II**

The years passed. Pa and Ma Jenkins only dried up a little. Old Man Studevant died. The old lady had two strokes. Mrs. Art Studevant and her husband began to look their age, greying hair and sagging stomachs. The children were grown, or nearly so. Kenneth took over the management of the hardware store that Grandpa had left. Jack went off to college. Mary was a teacher. Only Jessie remained a child—her last year in high-school. Jessie, nineteen now, and rather slow in her studies, graduating at last. In the Fall she would go to Normal.

Cora hated to think about her going away. In her heart she had adopted Jessie. In that big and careless household it was always Cora who stood like a calm and sheltering tree for Jessie to run to in her troubles. As a child, when Mrs. Art spanked her, as soon as she could, the tears still streaming, Jessie would find her way to the kitchen and Cora. At each school term's end, when Jessie had usually failed in some of her subjects (she quite often failed, being a dull child), it was Cora who saw the report-card first with the bad marks on it. Then Cora would devise some way of breaking the news gently to the old folks.

Her mother was always a little ashamed of stupid Jessie, for Mrs. Art was the civic and social leader of Melton, president of the Woman's Club three years straight, and one of the pillars of her church. Mary, the elder, the teacher, would follow with dignity in her footsteps, but Jessie! That child! Spankings in her youth, and scoldings now, did nothing to Jessie's inner being. She remained a plump, dull, freckled girl, placid and strange. Everybody found fault with her but Cora.

In the kitchen Jessie bloomed. She laughed. She talked. She was sometimes even witty. And she learned to cook wonderfully. With Cora, everything seemed so simple—not hard and involved like algebra, or Latin grammar, or the civic problems of Mama's club, or the sermons at church. Nowhere in Melton, nor with anyone, did Jessie feel so comfortable as with Cora in the kitchen. She knew her mother looked down on her as a stupid girl. And with her father there was no bond. He was always too busy buying and selling to bother with the kids. And often he was off in the city. Old doddering Grandma made Jessie sleepy and sick. Cousin Nora (Mother's cousin) was as stiff and prim as a minister's daughter. And Jessie's older brothers and sister went their ways, seeing Jessie hardly at all, except at the big table at mealtimes.

Like all the unpleasant things in the house, Jessie was left to Cora. And Cora was happy. To have a child to raise, a child the same age as her Josephine would have been, gave her a purpose in life, a warmth inside herself. It was Cora who nursed and mothered and petted and loved the dull little Jessie through the years. And now Jessie was a young woman, graduating (late) from high-school.

But something had happened to Jessie. Cora knew it before Mrs. Art did. Jessie was not too stupid to have a boy-friend. She told Cora about it like a mother. She was afraid to tell Mrs. Art. Afraid! Afraid! Afraid!

Cora said, "I'll tell her." So, humble and unashamed about her life, one afternoon she marched into Mrs. Art's sun-porch and announced quite simply, "Jessie's going to have a baby."

Cora smiled, but Mrs. Art stiffened like a bolt. Her mouth went dry. She rose like a soldier. Sat down. Rose again. Walked straight toward the door, turned around, and whispered, "What?"

"Yes, m'am, a baby. She told me. A little child. Its father is Willie Matsoulos, whose folks runs the ice-cream stand on Main. She told me. They want to get married, but Willie ain't here now. He don't know yet about the child."

Cora would have gone on humbly and shamelessly talking about the little unborn had not Mrs. Art fallen into uncontrollable hysterics. Cousin Nora came running from the library, her glasses on a chain. Old Lady Studevant's wheel-chair rolled up, doddering and shaking with excitement. Jessie came, when called, red and sweating, but had to go out, for when her mother looked up from the couch and saw her she yelled louder than ever. There was a rush for camphor bottles and water and ice. Crying and praying followed all over the house. Scandalization! Oh, my Lord! Jessie was in trouble.

"She ain't in trouble neither," Cora insisted. "No trouble having a baby you want. I had one."

"Shut up, Cora!"

"Yes, ma'm. . . . But I had one."

"Hush, I tell you."

"Yes, m'am."

### III

Then it was that Cora began to be shut out. Jessie was confined to her room. That afternoon, when Miss Mary came home from school, the four white women got together behind closed doors in Mrs. Art's bedroom. For once Cora cooked supper in the kitchen without being bothered by an interfering voice. Mr. Studevant was away in Des Moines. Somehow Cora wished he was home. Big and gruff as he was, he had more sense than the women. He'd probably make a shot-gun wedding out of it. But left to Mrs. Art, Jessie would never marry the Greek boy at all. This Cora knew. No man had been found yet good enough for sister Mary to mate with. Mrs. Art had ambitions which didn't include the likes of Greek ice-cream makers' sons.

Jessie was crying when Cora brought her supper up. The black woman sat down on the bed and lifted the white girl's head in her dark hands. "Don't you mind, honey," Cora said. "Just sit tight, and when the boy comes back I'll tell him how things are. If he loves you he'll want you. And there ain't no reason why you can't marry, neither—you both white. Even if he is a foreigner, he's a right nice boy."

"He loves me," Jessie said. "I know he does. He said so."

But before the boy came back (or Mr. Studevant either) Mrs. Art and Jessie went to Kansas City. "For an Easter shopping trip," the weekly paper said.

Then Spring came in full bloom, and the fields and orchards at the edge of Melton stretched green and beautiful to the far horizon. Cora remembered her own Spring, twenty years ago, and a great sympathy and pain welled up in her heart for Jessie, who was the same age that Josephine would have been, had she lived. Sitting on the kitchen porch shelling peas, Cora thought back over her own life—years and years of working for the Studevants; years and years of going home to nobody but Ma and Pa; little Josephine dead; only Jessie to keep her heart warm. And she knew that Jessie was the dearest thing she had in the world. All the time the girl was gone now, she worried.

After ten days, Mrs. Art and her daughter came back. But Jessie was thinner and paler than she'd ever been in her life. There was no light in her eyes at all. Mrs. Art looked a little scared as they got off the train.

"She had an awful attack of indigestion in Kansas City," she told the neighbors and club women. "That's why I stayed away so long, waiting for her to be able to travel. Poor Jessie! She looks healthy, but she's never been a strong child. She's one of the worries of my life." Mrs. Art talked a lot, explained a lot, about how Jessie had eaten the wrong things in Kansas City.

At home, Jessie went to bed. She wouldn't eat. When Cora brought her food up, she whispered, "The baby's gone."

Cora's face went dark. She bit her lips to keep from cursing. She put her arms about Jessie's neck. The girl cried. Her food went untouched.

A week passed. They tried to *make* Jessie eat then. But the food wouldn't stay in her stomach. Her eyes grew yellow, her tongue white, her heart acted crazy. They called in old Doctor Brown, but within a month (as quick as that) Jessie died.

She never saw the Greek boy any more. Indeed, his father had lost his license, "due to several complaints by the mothers of children, backed by the Woman's Club," that he was selling tainted ice-cream. Mrs. Art Studevant had started a campaign to rid the town of objectionable tradespeople and questionable characters. Greeks were bound to be one or the other. For a while they even closed up Pa Jenkins' favorite bootlegger. Mrs. Studevant thought this would please Cora, but Cora only said, "Pa's been drinkin' so long he just as well keep on." She refused further to remark on her employer's campaign of purity. In the midst of this clean-up Jessie died.

On the day of the funeral, the house was stacked with flowers. (They held the funeral, not at the church, but at home, on account of old Grandma Studevant's in-firmities.) All the family dressed in deep mourning. Mrs. Art was prostrate. As the hour for the services approached, she revived, however, and ate an omelette, "to help me go through the afternoon."

"And Cora," she said, "cook me a little piece of ham with it. I feel so weak."

"Yes, m'am."

The senior class from the high-school came in a body. The Woman's Club came with their badges. The Reverend Doctor McElroy had on his highest collar and longest coat. The choir sat behind the coffin, with a special soloist to sing "He Feedeth His Flocks Like a Shepherd." It was a beautiful Spring afternoon, and a beautiful funeral.

Except that Cora was there. Of course, her presence created no comment (she was the family servant), but it was what she did, and how she did it, that has remained the talk of Melton to this day—for Cora was not humble in the face of death.

When the Reverend Doctor McElroy had finished his eulogy, and the senior class had read their memorials, and the songs had been sung, and they were about to allow the relatives and friends to pass around for one last look at Jessie Studevant, Cora got up from her seat by the dining-room door. She said, "Honey, I want to say something." She spoke as if she were addressing Jessie. She approached the coffin and held out her brown hands over the white girl's body. Her face moved in agitation. People sat stone-still and there was a long pause. Suddenly she screamed. "They killed you! And for nothin'. . . . They killed your child. . . . They took you away from here in the Springtime of your life, and now you'se gone, gone, gone!"

Folks were paralyzed in their seats.

Cora went on: "They preaches you a pretty sermon and they don't say nothin'. They sings you a song, and they don't say nothin'. But Cora's here, honey, and she's gone tell 'em what they done to you. She's gonna tell 'em why they took you to Kansas City."

A loud scream rent the air. Mrs. Art fell back in her chair, stiff as a board. Cousin Nora and sister Mary sat like stones. The men of the family rushed forward to grab Cora. They stumbled over wreaths and garlands. Before they could reach her, Cora pointed her long fingers at the women in black and said, "They killed you, honey. They killed you and your child. I told 'em you loved it, but they didn't care. They killed it before it was . . ."

A strong hand went around Cora's waist. Another grabbed her arm. The Stude-vant males half pulled, half pushed her through the aisles of folding chairs, through the crowded dining-room, out into the empty kitchen, through the screen door into the backyard. She struggled against them all the way, accusing their women. At the door she sobbed, great tears coming for the love of Jessie.

She sat down on a wash-bench in the backyard, crying. In the parlor she could hear the choir singing weakly. In a few moments she gathered herself together, and went back into the house. Slowly, she picked up her few belongings from the kitchen and pantry, her aprons and her umbrella, and went off down the alley, home to Ma. Cora never came back to work for the Studevants.

Now she and Ma live from the little garden they raise, and from the junk Pa collects—when they can take by main force a part of his meager earnings before he buys his licker.

Anyhow, on the edge of Melton, the Jenkins niggers, Pa and Ma and Cora, somehow manage to get along.

# Zora Neale Hurston

## (C. 1901–1960)

Zora Neale Hurston was born in Florida in either 1901 or 1902, and she died there in 1960 in an ironically similar state of anonymity. During her lifetime, however, she was part of the Harlem Renaissance, coauthoring a comedy with Langston Hughes entitled *Mule Bone* and, after attending Howard University, studying anthropology at Barnard College under Franz Boas. She came from the town of Eatonville, the nation's first incorporated all-black community; her father was the town's minister and mayor and also, by trade, a carpenter. Hurston was to return to the region to collect its folklore, and the lives of the people among whom she had lived as a child served as material and inspiration for her writing. During these travels through the American South, she carried a gun in her purse and told anyone who asked that she was the fleeing mistress of a bootlegger. With a fellowship she attained on the recommendation of Boas, Hurston wrote *Jonah's Gourd Vine* in 1934, which was followed by *Their Eyes Were Watching God* in 1937 and a study in Floridian African American folklore, *Mules and Men* (1935), the first book of its kind. These were followed by a Caribbean travelogue, *Tell My Horse,* in 1938, and *Seraph on the Sewanee,* a novel published during that same year. In 1942, her autobiography *Dust Tracks on a Road* was nationally recognized, and her portrait appeared on the cover of the *Saturday Review.*

Hurston withdrew from public life following an accusation of "false morals" in 1948 and thereafter suffered great financial hardship, returning to work as a maid even while she continued to publish occasional works of fiction. She died in poverty and was buried in an unmarked grave in a segregated cemetery, which Alice Walker many years later visited to place a memorial in Hurston's honor. Hurston's reputation as a writer experienced a revival during the last two decades of the twentieth century, when more of her books returned to print than had been in print at any time during her life. She is now recognized for preserving a literary record of the culture of blacks in the rural South in the first few decades of the 1900s, as well as for creating regional fiction that explores the universal psychology of human relationships.

## Drenched in Light

"You Isie Watts! Git 'own offen dat gate post an' rake up dis yahd!"

The small brown girl perched upon the gate post looked yearningly up the gleaming shell road that led to Orlando. After a while, she shrugged her thin shoulders. This only seemed to heap still more kindling on Grandma Potts's already burning ire.

"Lawd a-mussy!" she screamed, enraged—"Heah Joel, gimme dat wash stick. Ah'll show dat limb of Satan she cain't shake herself at *me*. If she ain't down by the time Ah gets dere, Ah'll break huh down in de lines."

"Aw Gran'ma, Ah see Mist' George and Jim Robinson comin' and Ah wanted to wave at 'em," the child said impatiently.

"You jes' wave dat rake at dis heah yahd, madame, else Ah'll take you down a buttonhole lower. Youse too 'oomanish jumpin' up in everybody's face dat pass."

This struck the child sorely, for nothing pleased her so much as to sit atop of the gate post and hail the passing vehicles on their way south to Orlando, or north to Sanford. That white shell road was her great attraction. She raced up and down the stretch of it that lay before her gate, like a round-eyed puppy hailing gleefully all travelers. Everybody in the country, white and colored, knew little Isis Watts, Isis the Joyful. The Robinson brothers, white cattlemen, were particularly fond of her and always extended a stirrup for her to climb up behind one of them for a short ride, or let her try to crack the long bullwhips and *yee whoo* at the cows.

Grandma Potts went inside, and Isis literally waved the rake at the "chaws" of ribbon cane that lay so bountifully about the yard in company with the knots and peelings with a thick sprinkling of peanut hulls.

The herd of cattle in their envelope of gray dust came alongside, and Isis dashed out to the nearest stirrup and was lifted up.

"Hello theah, Snidlits, I was wonderin' wheah you was," said Jim Robinson as she snuggled down behind him in the saddle. They were almost out of the danger zone when Grandma emerged. "You Isie," she bawled.

The child slid down on the opposite side of the house and executed a flank movement through the corn patch that brought her into the yard from behind the privy.

"You li'l hasion you! Wheah you been?"

"Out in de back yahd," Isis lied and did a cartwheel and a few fancy steps on her way to the front again.

"If you doan git in dat yahd, Ah make a mommuk of you!" Isis observed that Grandma was cutting a fancy assortment of switches from peach, guana, and cherry trees.

She finished the yard by raking everything under the edge of the porch and began a romp with the dogs, those lean, floppy-eared hounds that all country folks keep. But Grandma vetoed this also.

"Isie, you set on dat porch! Uh great big 'leben yeah ole gal racin' an' rompin' lak dat—set 'own!"

Isis flung herself upon the steps.

"Git up offa dem steps, you aggravatin' limb, 'fore Ah git dem hick'ries tuh you, an' set yo'seff on a cheah."

Isis arose, and then sat down as violently as possible in the chair. She slid down, and down, until she all but sat on her own shoulder blades.

"Now look atcher," Grandma screamed. "Put yo' knees together, an' git up offen yo' backbone! Lawd, you know dis hellion is gwine make me stomp huh insides out."

Isis sat bolt upright as if she wore a ramrod down her back and began to whistle. Now there are certain things that Grandma Potts felt no one of this female persuasion should do—one was to sit with the knees separated, "settin' brazen" she called it; another was whistling, another playing with boys. Finally, a lady must never cross her legs.

Grandma jumped up from her seat to get the switches.

"So youse whistlin' in mah face, huh!" She glared till her eyes were beady and Isis bolted for safety. But the noon hour brought John Watts the widowed father, and this excused the child from sitting for criticism.

Being the only girl in the family, of course she must wash the dishes, which she did in intervals between frolics with the dogs. She even gave Jake, the puppy, a swim in the dishpan by holding him suspended above the water that reeked of "pot likker"—just high enough so that his feet would be immersed. The deluded puppy swam and swam without ever crossing the pan, much to his annoyance. Hearing Grandma, she hurriedly dropped him on the floor, which he tracked-up with feet wet with dishwater.

Grandma took her patching and settled down in the front room to sew. She did this every afternoon and invariably slept in the big red rocker with her head lolled back over the back, the sewing falling from her hand.

Isis had crawled under the center table with its red plush cover with little round balls for fringe. She was lying on her back imagining herself various personages. She wore trailing robes, golden slippers with blue bottoms. She rode white horses with flaring pink nostrils to the horizon, for she still believed that to be land's end. She was picturing herself gazing over the edge of the world into the abyss when the spool of cotton fell from Grandma's lap and rolled away under the whatnot. Isis drew back from her contemplation of the nothingness at the horizon and glanced up at the sleeping woman. Her head had fallen far back. She breathed with a regular "mark" intake and "poosah" exhaust. But Isis was a visual-minded child. She heard the snores only subconsciously, but she saw the straggling beard on Grandma's chin, trembling a little with every "mark" and "poosah." They were long gray hairs curled every here and there against the dark brown skin. Isis was moved with pity for her mother's mother.

"Poah Gran-ma needs a shave," she murmured, and set about it. Just then Joel, next older than Isis, entered with a can of bait.

"Come on, Isie, les' we all go fishin'. The Perch is bitin' fine in Blue Sink."

"Sh-sh—" cautioned his sister. "Ah got to shave Gran'ma."

"Who say so?" Joel asked, surprised.

"Nobody doan hafta tell me. Look at her chin. No ladies don't weah whiskers if they kin help it. But Gran-ma gittin' ole, an' she doan know how to shave lak *me*."

The conference adjourned to the back porch lest Grandma wake.

"Aw, Isie, you doan know nothin' 'bout shavin' a-tall—but a *man* lak *me*—"

"Ah do so know."

"You don't not. Ah'm goin' shave her mahseff."

"Naw, you won't neither, Smarty. Ah saw her first an' thought it all up first," Isis declared, and ran to the calico-covered box on the wall above the wash basin and seized her father's razor. Joel was quick and seized the mug and brush.

"Now!" Isis cried defiantly. "Ah got the razor."

"Goody, goody, goody, pussy cat, Ah got th' brush an' you can't shave 'thout lather—see! Ah know mo' than you," Joel retorted.

"Aw, who don't know dat?" Isis pretended to scorn. But seeing her progress blocked from lack of lather, she compromised.

"Ah know! Les' we all shave her. You lather, an' Ah shave."

This was agreeable to Joel. He made mountains of lather and anointed his own chin, and the chin of Isis and the dogs, splashed the wall, and at last was persuaded to lather Grandma's chin. Not that he was loath, but he wanted his new plaything to last as long as possible.

Isis stood on one side of the chair with the razor clutched cleaver fashion. The niceties of razor-handling had passed over her head. The thing with her was to *hold* the razor—sufficient in itself.

Joel splashed on the lather in great gobs, and Grandma awoke.

For one bewildered moment she stared at the grinning boy with the brush and mug, but sensing another presence, she turned to behold the business face of Isis and the razor-clutching hand. Her jaw dropped, and Grandma, forgetting years and rheumatism, bolted from the chair and fled the house, screaming.

"She's gone to tell Papa, Isie. You didn't have no business wid his razor, and he's gonna lick yo' hide," Joel cried, running to replace mug and brush.

"You too, chuckle-head, you too," retorted Isis. "You was playin' wid his brush and put it all over the dogs—Ah seen you put it on Ned an' Beulah." Isis shaved and replaced it in the box. Joel took his bait and pole and hurried to Blue Sink. Isis crawled under the house to brood over the whipping she knew would come. She had meant well.

But sounding brass and tinkling cymbal drew her forth. The local lodge of the Grand United Order of Odd Fellows, led by a braying, thudding band, was marching in full regalia down the road. She had forgotten the barbecue and log-rolling to be held today for the benefit of the new hall.

Music to Isis meant motion. In a minute razor and whipping forgotten, she was doing a fair imitation of a Spanish dancer she had seen in a medicine show sometime before. Isis's feet were gifted—she could dance most anything she saw.

Up, up, went her spirits, her small feet doing all sorts of intricate things and her body in rhythm, hand curving above her head. But the music was growing faint. Grandma was nowhere in sight. Isis stole out of the gate, running and dancing after the band.

Not far down the road, Isis stopped. She realized she couldn't dance at the carnival. Her dress was torn and dirty. She picked a long-stemmed daisy and placed it behind her ear, but her dress remained torn and dirty just the same. Then Isis had an idea. Her thoughts returned to the battered, round-topped trunk back in the bedroom. She raced back to the house; then, happier, she raced down the white dusty road to the picnic grove, gorgeously clad. People laughed good-naturedly at her, the band played, and Isis danced because she couldn't help it. A crowd of children gathered admiringly about her as she wheeled lightly about, hand on hip, flower between her teeth with the red and white fringe of the tablecloth—Grandma's new red tablecloth that she wore in lieu of a Spanish shawl—trailing in the dust. It was too ample for her meager form, but she wore it like a gypsy. Her brown feet twinkled in and out of the fringe. Some grown people joined the children about her. The Grand Exalted Ruler rose to speak; the band was hushed, but Isis danced on, the crowd clapping their hands for her. No one listened to the Exalted one, for little by little the multitude had surrounded the small brown dancer.

An automobile drove up to the Crown and halted. Two white men and a lady got out and pushed into the crowd, suppressing mirth discreetly behind gloved hands. Isis looked up and waved them a magnificent hail and went on dancing until—

Grandma had returned to the house and missed Isis. She straightaway sought her at the festivities, expecting to find her in her soiled dress, shoeless, standing at the far edge of the crowd. What she saw now drove her frantic. Here was her granddaughter dancing before a gaping crowd in her brand-new red tablecloth, and reeking of lemon extract. Isis had added the final touch to her costume. Of course she must also have perfume.

When Isis saw her grandma, she bolted. She heard her grandma cry—"Mah Gawd, mah brand-new tablecloth Ah just bought f'um O'landah!"—as Isis fled through the crowd and on into the woods.

Isis followed the little creek until she came to the ford in a rutty wagon road that led to Apopka and lay down on the cool grass at the roadside. The April sun was quite warm.

Misery, misery and woe, settled down upon her. The child wept. She knew another whipping was in store.

"Oh, Ah wish Ah could die, then Gran'ma an' Papa would be sorry they beat me so much. Ah b'leeve Ah'll run away and never go home no mo'. Ah'm goin' drown mahseff in th' creek!"

Isis got up and waded into the water. She routed out a tiny 'gator and a huge bullfrog. She splashed and sang. Soon she was enjoying herself immensely. The purr of a motor struck her ear, and she saw a large, powerful car jolting along the rutty road toward her. It stopped at the water's edge.

"Well, I declare, it's our little gypsy," exclaimed the man at the wheel. "What are you doing here, now?"

"Ah'm killin' mahseff," Isis declared dramatically, " 'Cause Gran'ma beats me too much."

There was a hearty burst of laughter from the machine.

"You'll last some time the way you are going about it. Is this the way to Maitland? We want to go to the Park Hotel."

Isis saw no longer any reason to die. She came up out of the water, holding up the dripping fringe of the tablecloth.

"Naw, indeedy. You go to Maitlan' by the shell road—it goes by mah house—an' turn off at Lake Sebelia to the clay road that takes you right to the do'."

"Well," went on the driver, smiling furtively, "could you quit dying long enough to go with us?"

"Yessuh," she said thoughtfully, "Ah wanta go wid you."

The door of the car swung open. She was invited to a seat beside the driver. She had often dreamed of riding in one of these heavenly chariots but never thought she would, actually.

"Jump in then, Madame Tragedy, and show us. We lost ourselves after we left your barbecue."

During the drive Isis explained to the kind lady who smelt faintly of violets and to the indifferent men that she was really a princess. She told them about her trips to the horizon, about the trailing gowns, the gold shoes with blue bottoms—she insisted on the blue bottoms—the white charger, the time when she was Hercules and had slain numerous dragons and sundry giants. At last the car approached her gate, over which stood the umbrella chinaberry tree. The car was abreast of the gate and had all but passed when Grandma spied her glorious tablecloth lying back against the up-holstery of the Packard.

"You Isie-e!" she bawled, "You li'l wretch you! Come heah *dis instant*."

"That's me," the child confessed, mortified, to the lady on the rear seat.

"Oh Sewell, stop the car. This is where the child lives. I hate to give her up though."

"Do you wanta keep me?" Isis brightened.

"Oh, I wish I could. Wait, I'll try to save you a whipping this time."

She dismounted with the gaudy lemon-flavored culprit and advanced to the gate where Grandma stood glowering, switches in hand.

"You're gointuh ketchit f'um yo' haid to yo' heels, m'lady. Jes' come in heah."

"Why, good afternoon," she accosted the furious grandparent. "You're not going to whip this poor little thing, are you?" the lady asked in conciliatory tones.

"Yes, ma'am. She's de wustest li'l limb dat ever drawed bref. Jes' look at mah new tablecloth, dat ain't never been washed. She done traipsed all over de woods, uh dancin' un' uh prancin' in it. She done took a razor to me t'day, an' Lawd knows whut mo'."

Isis clung to the stranger's hand fearfully.

"Ah wuzn't gointer hurt Gran'ma, miss—Ah wuz just gointer shave her whiskers fuh huh 'cause she's old an' can't."

The white hand closed tightly over the little brown one that was quite soiled. She could understand a voluntary act of love even though it miscarried.

"Now, Mrs. er—er—I didn't get the name—how much did your tablecloth cost?"

"One whole big silvah dollar down at O'landah—ain't had it a week yit."

"Now here's five dollars to get another one. I want her to go to the hotel and dance for me. I could stand a little light today—"

"Oh, yessum, yessum," Grandma cut in, "everything's alright, sho' she kin go, yessum."

Feeling that Grandma had been somewhat squelched did not detract from Isis's spirit at all. She pranced over to the waiting motor-car and this time seated herself on the rear seat between the sweet-smiling lady and the rather aloof man in gray.

"Ah'm gointer stay wid you all," she said with a great deal of warmth and snuggled up to her benefactress. "Want me tuh sing a song fuh you?"

"There, Helen, you've been adopted," said the man with a short, harsh laugh.

"Oh, I hope so, Harry." She put her arm about the red-draped figure at her side and drew it close until she felt the warm puffs of the child's breath against her side. She looked hungrily ahead of her and spoke into space rather than to anyone in the car. "I would like just a little of her sunshine to soak into my soul. I would like that a lot."

## Sweat                                                                            1926

It was eleven o'clock of a Spring night in Florida. It was Sunday. Any other night, Delia Jones would have been in bed for two hours by this time. But she was a washwoman, and Monday morning meant a great deal to her. So she collected the soiled clothes on Saturday when she returned the clean things. Sunday night after church, she sorted them and put the white things to soak. It saved her almost a half day's start. A great hamper in the bedroom held the clothes that she brought home. It was so much neater than a number of bundles lying around.

She squatted on the kitchen floor beside the great pile of clothes, sorting them into small heaps according to color, and humming a song in a mournful key, but wondering through it all where Sykes, her husband, had gone with her horse and buckboard.

Just then something long, round, limp and black fell upon her shoulders and slithered to the floor beside her. A great terror took hold of her. It softened her knees and dried her mouth so that it was a full minute before she could cry out or move. Then she saw that it was the big bull whip her husband liked to carry when he drove.

She lifted her eyes to the door and saw him standing there bent over with laughter at her fright. She screamed at him.

"Sykes, what you throw dat whip on me like dat? You know it would skeer me— looks just like a snake, an' you knows how skeered Ah is of snakes."

"Course Ah knowed it! That's how come Ah done it." He slapped his leg with his hand and almost rolled on the ground in his mirth. "If you such a big fool dat you got to have a fit over a earth worm or a string, Ah don't keer how bad Ah skeer you."

"You aint got no business doing it. Gawd knows it's a sin. Some day Ah'm gointuh drop dead from some of yo' foolishness. 'Nother thing, where you been wid mah rig? Ah feeds dat pony. He aint fuh you to be drivin' wid no bull whip."

"You sho is one aggravatin' nigger woman!" he declared and stepped into the room. She resumed her work and did not answer him at once. "Ah done tole you time and again to keep them white folks' clothes outa dis house."

He picked up the whip and glared down at her. Delia went on with her work. She went out into the yard and returned with a galvanized tub and set it on the wash-bench. She saw that Sykes kicked all of the clothes together again, and now stood in her way truculently, his whole manner hoping, *praying,* for an argument. But she walked calmly around him and commenced to re-sort the things.

"Next time, Ah'm gointer kick 'em outdoors," he threatened as he struck a match along the leg of his corduroy breeches.

Delia never looked up from her work, and her thin, stooped shoulders sagged further.

"Ah aint for no fuss t'night, Sykes. Ah just come from taking sacrament at the church house."

He snorted scornfully. "Yeah, you just come from de church house on a Sunday night, but heah you is gone to work on them clothes. You ain't nothing but a hyp-ocrite. One of them amen-corner Christians—sing, whoop, and shout, then come home and wash white folks clothes on the Sabbath."

He stepped roughly upon the whitest pile of things, kicking them helter-skelter as he crossed the room. His wife gave a scream of dismay, and quickly gathered them together again.

"Sykes, you quit grindin' dirt into those clothes! How can Ah git through by Sat'day if Ah don't start on Sunday?"

"Ah don't keer if you never git through. Anyhow, Ah done promised Gawd and a couple of other men, Ah ain't gointer have it in mah house. Don't gimme no lip nei-ther, else Ah'll throw 'em out and put mah fist up side yo' head to boot."

Delia's habitual meekness seemed to slip from her shoulders like a blown scarf. She was on her feet; her poor little body, her bare knuckly hands bravely defying the strapping hulk before her.

"Looka heah, Sykes, you done gone too fur. Ah been married to you fur fifteen years, and Ah been takin' in washin' for fifteen years. Sweat, sweat, sweat! Work and sweat, cry and sweat, pray and sweat!"

"What's that got to do with me?" he asked brutally.

"What's it got to do with you, Sykes? Mah tub if suds is filled yo' belly with vittles more times than yo' hands is filled it. Mah sweat is done paid for this house and Ah reckon Ah kin keep on sweatin' in it."

She seized the iron skillet from the stove and struck a defensive pose, which act surprised him greatly, coming from her. It cowed him and he did not strike her as he usually did.

"Naw you wont," she panted, "that ole snaggle-toothed black woman you runnin' with ain't comin' heah to pile up on mah sweat and blood. You ain't paid for nothin' on this place, and Ah'm gointer stay right heah till Ah'm toted out foot foremost."

"Well, you better quit gittin' me riled up, else they'll be totin' you out sooner than you expect. Ah'm so tired of you Ah don't know whut to do. Gawd! how Ah hates skinny wimmen!"

A little awed by this new Delia, he sidled out of the door and slammed the back gate after him. He did not say where he had gone, but she knew too well. She knew very well that he would not return until nearly daybreak also. Her work over, she went on to bed but not to sleep at once. Things had come to a pretty pass!

She lay awake, gazing upon the debris that cluttered their matrimonial trail. Not an image left standing along the way. Anything like flowers had long ago been drowned in the salty stream that had been pressed from her heart. Her tears, her sweat, her blood. She had brought love to the union and he had brought a longing after the flesh.

Two months after the wedding, he had given her the first brutal beating. She had the memory of his numerous trips to Orlando with all of his wages when he had returned to her penniless, even before the first year had passed. She was young and soft then, but now she thought of her knotty, muscled limbs, her harsh, knuckly hands, and drew herself up into an unhappy little ball in the middle of the big feather bed. Too late now to hope for love, even if it were not Bertha it could be someone else. This case differed from the others only in that she was bolder than the others. Too late for everything except her little home. She had built it for her old days, and planted one by one the trees and flowers there. It was lovely to her, lovely.

Somehow, before sleep came, she found herself saying aloud: "Oh well, whatever goes over the Devil's back, is got to come under his belly. Sometime or ruther, Sykes, like everybody else, is gointer reap his sowing." After that she was able to build a spiritual earthworks against her husband. His shells could no longer reach her. *Amen.* She went to sleep and slept until he announced his presence in bed by kicking her feet and rudely snatching the covers away.

"Gimme some kivah heah, an' git yo' damn foots over on yo' own side! Ah oughter mash you in yo' mouf fuh drawing dat skillet on me."

Delia went clear to the rail without answering him. A triumphant indifference to all that he was or did.

The week was as full of work for Delia as all other weeks, and Saturday found her behind her little pony, collecting and delivering clothes.

It was a hot, hot day near the end of July. The village men on Joe Clarke's porch even chewed cane listlessly. They did not hurl the caneknots[1] as usual. They let them dribble over the edge of the porch. Even conversation had collapsed under the heat.

"Heah come Delia Jones," Jim Merchant said, as the shaggy pony came 'round the bend of the road toward them. The rusty buckboard was heaped with baskets of crisp, clean laundry.

"Yep," Joe Lindsay agreed. "Hot or col', rain or shine, jes ez reg'lar ez de weeks roll roun' Delia carries 'em an' fetches 'em on Sat'day."

"She better if she wanter eat," said Moss. "Syke Jones aint wuth de shot an' powder hit would tek tuh kill 'em. Not to *huh* he aint."

"He sho' aint," Walter Thomas chimed in. "It's too bad, too, cause she wuz a right pritty lil trick when he got huh. Ah'd uh mah'ied huh mahseff if he hadnter beat me to it."

1 **caneknots:** Indigestible parts of the sugarcane stalk.

Delia nodded briefly at the men as she drove past.

"Too much knockin' will ruin *any* 'oman. He done beat huh 'nough tuh kill three women, let 'lone change they looks," said Elijah Moseley. "How Syke kin stommuck dat big black greasy Mogul he's layin' roun' wid, gits me. Ah swear dat eight-rock[2] couldn't kiss a sardine can Ah done throwed out de back do' 'way las' yeah."

"Aw, she's fat, thass how come. He's allus been crazy 'bout fat women," put in Merchant. "He'd a' been tied up wid one long time ago if he could a' found one tuh have him. Did Ah tell yuh 'bout him come sidlin' roun' *mah* wife—bringin' her a basket uh peecans outa his yard fuh a present? Yessir, mah wife! She tol' him tuh take em right straight back home, cause Delia works so hard ovah dat wash tub she reckon everything on de place taste lak sweat an' soapsuds. Ah jus' wisht Ah'd a caught 'im 'roun' dere! Ah'd a' made his hips ketch on fiah down dat shell road."

"Ah know he done it, too. Ah sees 'im grinnin' at every 'oman dat passes," Walter Thomas said. "But even so, he useter eat some mighty big hunks uh humble pie tuh git dat lil' 'oman he got. She wuz ez pritty ez a speckled pup! Dat wuz fifteen yeahs ago. He useter be so skeered uh losin' huh, she could make him do some parts of a husband's duty. Dey never wuz de same in de mind."

"There oughter be a law about him," said Lindsay. "He aint fit tuh carry guts tuh a bear."

Clarke spoke for the first time. "Taint no law on earth dat kin make a man be decent if it aint in 'im. There's plenty men dat takes a wife lak dey do a joint uh sugarcane. It's round, juicy an' sweet when dey gits it. But dey squeeze an' grind, squeeze an' grind an' wring tell dey wring every drop uh pleasure dat's in 'em out. When dey's satisfied dat dey is wrung dry, dey treats 'em jes lak dey do a cane-chew. Dey throws 'em away. Dey knows whut dey is doin' while dey is at it, an' hates theirselves fuh it but they keeps on hangin' after huh tell she's empty. Den dey hates huh fuh bein' a cane-chew an' in de way."

"We oughter take Syke an' dat stray 'oman uh his'n down in Lake Howell swamp an' lay on de rawhide till they cain't say Lawd a' mussy.' He allus wuz uh ovahbearin' niggah, but since dat white 'oman from up north done teached 'im how to run a automobile, he done got too biggety to live—an' we oughter kill 'im," Old Man Anderson advised.

A grunt of approval went around the porch. But the heat was melting their civic virtue and Elijah Moseley began to bait Joe Clarke.

"Come on, Joe, git a melon outa dere an' slice it up for yo' customers. We'se all sufferin' wid de heat. De bear's done got *me!*"

"Thass right, Joe, a watermelon is jes' whut Ah needs tuh cure de eppizudicks,"[3] Walter Thomas joined forces with Moseley. "Come on dere, Joe. We all is steady customers an' you aint set us up in a long time. Ah chooses dat long, bowlegged Floridy favorite."

---

2 **eight-rock:** The eight ball in pool, black.

3 **eppizudicks:** Epizootic; refers to an epidemic affecting a large number of animals within a particular region.

"A god, an' be dough. You all gimme twenty cents and slice way," Clarke retorted. "Ah needs a col' slice m'self. Heah, everybody chip in. Ah'll lend y'll mah meat knife."

The money was quickly subscribed and the huge melon brought forth. At that moment, Sykes and Bertha arrived. A determined silence fell on the porch and the melon was put away again.

Merchant snapped down the blade of his jacknife and moved toward the store door.

"Come on in, Joe, an' gimme a slab uh sow belly an' uh pound uh coffee—almost fuhgot 'twas Sat'day. Got to git on home." Most of the men left also.

Just then Delia drove past on her way home, as Sykes was ordering magnificently for Bertha. It pleased him for Delia to see.

"Git whutsoever yo' heart desires, Honey. Wait a minute, Joe. Give huh two bottles uh strawberry soda-water, uh quart uh parched ground-peas, an' a block uh chewin' gum."

With all this they left the store, with Sykes reminding Bertha that this was his town and she could have it if she wanted it.

The men returned soon after they left, and held their watermelon feast.

"Where did Syke Jones git da 'oman from nohow?" Lindsay asked.

"Ovah Apopka. Guess dey musta been cleanin' out de town when she lef'. She don't look lak a thing but a hunk uh liver wid hair on it."

"Well, she sho' kin squall," Dave Carter contributed. "When she gits ready tuh laff, she jes' opens huh mouf an' latches it back tuh de las' notch. No ole grandpa alligator down in Lake Bell ain't got nothin' on huh."

Bertha had been in town three months now. Sykes was still paying her room rent at Della Lewis'—the only house in town that would have taken her in. Sykes took her frequently to Winter Park to "stomps."[4] He still assured her that he was the swellest man in the state.

"Sho' you kin have dat lil' ole house soon's Ah kin git dat 'oman outa dere. Everything b'longs tuh me an' you sho' kin have it. Ah sho' 'bominates uh skinny 'oman. Lawdy, you sho' is got one portly shape on you! You kin git *anything* you wants. Dis is *mah* town an' you sho' kin have it."

Delia's work-worn knees crawled over the earth in Gethsemane[5] and up the rocks of Calvary many, many times during these months. She avoided the villagers and meeting places in her efforts to be blind and deaf. But Bertha nullified this to a degree, by coming to Delia's house to call Sykes out to her at the gate.

Delia and Sykes fought all the time now with no peaceful interludes. They slept and ate in silence. Two or three times Delia had attempted a timid friendliness, but she was repulsed each time. It was plain that the breaches must remain agape.

The sun had burned July to August. The heat streamed down like a million hot arrows, smiting all things living upon the earth. Grass withered, leaves browned, snakes went blind in shedding and men and dogs went mad. Dog days!

4 **stomps:** Dance parties.
5 **Gethsemane:** A garden in Jerusalem where Jesus was arrested.

Delia came home one day and found Sykes there before her. She wondered, but started to go on into the house without speaking, even though he was standing in the kitchen door and she must either stoop under his arm or ask him to move. He made no room for her. She noticed a soap box beside the steps, but paid no particular attention to it, knowing that he must have brought it there. As she was stooping to pass under his outstretched arm, he suddenly pushed her backward, laughingly.

"Look in de box dere Delia, Ah done brung yuh somethin'!"

She nearly fell upon the box in her stumbling, and when she saw what it held, she all but fainted outright.

"Syke! Syke, mah Gawd! You take dat rattlesnake 'way from heah! You *gottuh*. Oh, Jesus, have mussy!"

"Ah aint gut tuh do nuthin' uh de kin'—fact is Ah aint got tuh do nothin' but die. Taint no use uh you puttin' on airs makin' out lak you skeered uh dat snake—he's gointer stay right heah tell he die. He wouldn't bite me cause Ah knows how tuh handle 'im. Nohow he wouldn't risk breakin' out his fangs 'gin *yo'* skinny laigs."

"Naw, now Syke, don't keep dat thing 'roun' heah tuh skeer me tuh death. You knows Ah'm even feared uh earth worms. Thass de biggest snake Ah evah did see. Kill 'im Syke, please."

"Doan ast me tuh do nothin' fuh yuh. Goin' 'roun' tryin' tuh be so damn asterperious. Naw, Ah aint gonna kill it. Ah think uh damn sight mo' uh him dan you! Dat's a nice snake an' anybody doan lak 'im kin jes' hit de grit."

The village soon heard that Sykes had the snake, and came to see and ask questions.

"How de hen-fire did you ketch dat six-foot rattler, Syke?" Thomas asked.

"He's full uh frogs so he caint hardly move, thass how Ah eased up on 'm. But Ah'm a snake charmer an' knows how tuh handle 'em. Shux, dat aint nothin'. Ah could ketch one eve'y day if Ah so wanted tuh."

"Whut he needs is a heavy hick'ry club leaned real heavy on his head. Dat's de bes 'way tuh charm a rattlesnake."

"Naw, Walt, y'll jes' don't understand dese diamon' backs lak Ah do," said Sykes in a superior tone of voice.

The village agreed with Walter, but the snake stayed on. His box remained by the kitchen door with its screen wire covering. Two or three days later it had digested its meal of frogs and literally came to life. It rattled at every movement in the kitchen or the yard. One day as Delia came down the kitchen steps she saw his chalky-white fangs curved like scimitars hung in the wire meshes. This time she did not run away with averted eyes as usual. She stood for a long time in the doorway in a red fury that grew bloodier for every second that she regarded the creature that was her torment.

That night she broached the subject as soon as Sykes sat down to the table.

"Syke, Ah wants you tuh take dat snake 'way fum heah. You done starved me an' Ah put up widcher, you done beat me an Ah took dat, but you done kilt all mah insides bringin' dat varmint heah."

Sykes poured out a saucer full of coffee and drank it deliberately before he answered her.

"A whole lot Ah keer 'bout how you feels inside uh out. Dat snake aint goin' no damn wheah till Ah gits ready fuh 'im tuh go. So fur as beatin' is concerned, yuh aint took near all dat you gointer take ef you stay 'roun' *me.*"

Delia pushed back her plate and got up from the table. "Ah hates you, Sykes," she said calmly. "Ah hates you tuh de same degree dat Ah useter love yuh. Ah done took an' took till mah belly is full up tuh mah neck. Dat's de reason Ah got mah letter fum de church an' moved mah membership tuh Woodbridge—so Ah don't haftuh take no sacrament wid yuh. Ah don't wantuh see yuh 'roun' me atall. Lay 'roun' wid dat 'oman all yuh wants tuh, but gwan 'way fum me an' mah house. Ah hates yuh lak uh suck-egg dog."

Sykes almost let the huge wad of corn bread and collard greens he was chewing fall out of his mouth in amazement. He had a hard time whipping himself up to the proper fury to try to answer Delia.

"Well, Ah'm glad you does hate me. Ah'm sho' tiahed uh you hangin' ontuh me. Ah don't want yuh. Look at yuh stringey ole neck! Yo' rawbony laigs an' arms is enough tuh cut uh man tuh death. You looks jes' lak de devvul's doll-baby tuh *me.* You cain't hate me no worse dan Ah hates you. Ah been hatin' *you* fuh years."

"Yo' ole black hide don't look lak nothin' tuh me, but uh passle uh wrinkled up rubber, wid yo' big ole yeahs flappin' on each side lak uh paih uh buzzard wings. Don't think Ah'm gointuh be run 'way fum mah house neither. Ah'm goin' tuh de white folks bout *you,* mah young man, de very nex' time you lay yo' han's on me. Mah cup is done run ovah."

Delia said this with no signs of fear and Sykes departed from the house, threatening her, but made not the slightest move to carry out any of them.

That night he did not return at all, and the next day being Sunday, Delia was glad she did not have to quarrel before she hitched up her pony and drove the four miles to Woodbridge.

She stayed to the night service—"love feast"—which was very warm and full of spirit. In the emotional winds her domestic trials were borne far and wide so that she sang as she drove homeward,

> "Jurden water, black an' col'
> Chills de body, not de soul
> An' Ah wantah cross Jurden in uh calm time."

She came from the barn to the kitchen door and stopped.

"Whut's de mattah, ol' satan, you aint kickin' up yo' racket?" She addressed the snake's box. Complete silence. She went on into the house with a new hope in its birth struggles. Perhaps her threat to go to the white folks had frightened Sykes! Perhaps he was sorry! Fifteen years of misery and suppression had brought Delia to the place where she would hope *anything* that looked towards a way over or through her wall of inhibitions.

She felt in the match safe behind the stove at once for a match. There was only one there.

"Dat niggah wouldn't fetch nothin' heah tuh save his rotten neck, but he kin run thew whut Ah brings quick enough. Now he done toted off nigh on tuh haff uh box uh matches. He done had dat 'oman heah in mah house too."

Nobody but a woman could tell how she knew this even before she struck the match. But she did and it put her into a new fury.

Presently she brought in the tubs to put the white things to soak. This time she decided she need not bring the hamper out of the bedroom: she would go in there and do the sorting. She picked up the pot-bellied lamp and went in. The room was small and the hamper stood hard by the foot of the white iron bed. She could sit and reach through the bedposts—resting as she worked.

"Ah wantah cross Jurden in uh calm time." She was singing again. The mood of the "love feast" had returned. She threw back the lid of the basket almost gaily. Then, moved by both horror and terror, she sprang back toward the door. *There lay the snake in the basket!* He moved sluggishly at first, but even as she turned round and round, jumped up and down in an insanity of fear, he began to stir vigorously. She saw him pouring his awful beauty from the basket upon the bed, then she seized the lamp and ran as fast as she could to the kitchen. The wind from the open door blew out the light and the darkness added to her terror. She sped to the darkness of the yard, slamming the door after her before she thought to set down the lamp. She did not feel safe even on the ground, so she climbed up in the hay barn.

There for an hour or more she lay sprawled upon the hay a gibbering wreck.

Finally she grew quiet, and after that, coherent thought. With this, stalked through her a cold, bloody rage. Hours of this. A period of introspection, a space of retrospection, then a mixture of both. Out of this an awful calm.

"Well, Ah done de bes' Ah could. If things aint right, Gawd knows taint mah fault."

She went to sleep—a twitch sleep—and woke up to a faint gray sky. There was a loud hollow sound below. She peered out. Sykes was at the wood-pile, demolishing a wire-covered box.

He hurried to the kitchen door, but hung outside there some minutes before he entered, and stood some minutes more inside before he closed it after him.

The gray in the sky was spreading. Delia descended without fear now, and crouched beneath the low bedroom window. The drawn shade shut out the dawn, shut in the night. But the thin walls held back no sound.

"Dat ol' scratch is woke up now!" She mused at the tremendous whirr inside, which every woodsman knows, is one of the sound illusions. The rattler is a ventriloquist. His whirr sounds to the right, to the left, straight ahead, behind, close under foot—everywhere but where it is. Woe to him who guesses wrong unless he is prepared to hold up his end of the argument! Sometimes he strikes without rattling at all.

Inside, Sykes heard nothing until he knocked a pot lid off the stove while trying to reach the match safe in the dark. He had emptied his pockets at Bertha's.

The snake seemed to wake up under the stove and Sykes made a quick leap into the bedroom. In spite of the gin he had had, his head was clearing now.

"Mah Gawd!" he chattered, "ef Ah could on'y strack uh light!"

The rattling ceased for a moment as he stood paralyzed. He waited. It seemed that the snake waited also.

"Oh, fuh de light! Ah thought he'd be too sick"—Sykes was muttering to himself when the whirr began again, closer, right underfoot this time. Long before this, Sykes' ability to think had been flattened down to primitive instinct and he leaped—onto the bed.

Outside Delia heard a cry that might have come from a maddened chimpanzee, a stricken gorilla. All the terror, all the horror, all the rage that man possibly could express, without a recognizable human sound.

A tremendous stir inside there, another series of animal screams, the intermittent whirr of the reptile. The shade torn violently down from the window, letting in the red dawn, a huge brown hand seizing the window stick, great dull blows upon the wooden floor punctuating the gibberish of sound long after the rattle of the snake had abruptly subsided. All this Delia could see and hear from her place beneath the window, and it made her ill. She crept over to the four-o'clocks and stretched herself on the cool earth to recover.

She lay there. "Delia, Delia!" She could hear Sykes calling in a most despairing tone as one who expected no answer. The sun crept on up, and he called. Delia could not move—her legs were gone flabby. She never moved, he called, and the sun kept rising.

"Mah Gawd!" She heard him moan, "Mah Gawd fum Heben!" She heard him stumbling about and got up from her flower-bed. The sun was growing warm. As she approached the door she heard him call out hopefully, "Delia, is dat you Ah heah?"

She saw him on his hands and knees as soon as she reached the door. He crept an inch or two toward her—all that he was able, and she saw his horribly swollen neck and his one open eye shining with hope. A surge of pity too strong to support bore her away from that eye that must, could not, fail to see the tubs. He would see the lamp. Orlando with its doctors was too far. She could scarcely reach the Chinaberry tree, where she waited in the growing heat while inside she knew the cold river was creeping up and up to extinguish that eye which must know by now that she knew.

# Langston Hughes

from *The Big Sea*                                                           1940

## When the Negro Was in Vogue

The 1920's were the years of Manhattan's black Renaissance. It began with *Shuffle Along*,[1] *Running Wild*,[2] and the Charleston.[3] Perhaps some people would say even with *The Emperor Jones*, Charles Gilpin, and the tom-toms at the Provincetown.[4] But

1 *Shuffle Along:* A 1921 musical comedy created by Flournoy Miller, Aubrey Lyles, Eubie Blake, and Noble Sissle that was a tremendous success in New York.
2 *Runnin' Wild:* Another musical revue by Miller and Lyles that is often credited with introducing New York to the Charleston in 1923.
3 the Charleston: A popular dance that swept the nation in the 1920s.
4 the Provincetown: The Provincetown Playhouse in the Greenwich Village neighborhood of New York City.

certainly it was the musical revue, *Shuffle Along,* that gave a scintillating send-off to that Negro vogue in Manhattan, which reached its peak just before the crash of 1929,[5] the crash that sent Negroes, white folks, and all rolling down the hill toward the Works Progress Administration.[6]

*Shuffle Along* was a honey of a show. Swift, bright, funny, rollicking, and gay, with a dozen danceable, singable tunes. Besides, look who were in it: The now famous choir director, Hall Johnson, and the composer, William Grant Still, were a part of the orchestra. Eubie Blake and Noble Sissle wrote the music and played and acted in the show. Miller and Lyles were the comics. Florence Mills skyrocketed to fame in the second act. Trixie Smith sang "He May Be Your Man But He Comes to See Me Sometimes." And Caterina Jarboro, now a European prima donna, and the internationally celebrated Josephine Baker[7] were merely in the chorus. Everybody was in the audience—including me. People came back to see it innumerable times. It was always packed.

To see *Shuffle Along* was the main reason I wanted to go to Columbia.[8] When I saw it, I was thrilled and delighted. From then on I was in the gallery of the Cort Theatre every time I got a chance. That year, too, I saw Katharine Cornell in *A Bill of Divorcement,* Margaret Wycherly in *The Verge,* Maugham's *The Circle* with Mrs. Leslie Carter, and the Theatre Guild production of Kaiser's *From Morn Till Midnight.* But I remember *Shuffle Along*[9] best of all. It gave just the proper push—a pre-Charleston kick—to that Negro vogue of the 20's, that spread to books, African sculpture, music, and dancing.

Put down the 1920's for the rise of Roland Hayes, who packed Carnegie Hall, the rise of Paul Robeson in New York and London, of Florence Mills over two continents, of Rose McClendon in Broadway parts that never measured up to her, the booming voice of Bessie Smith and the low moan of Clara on thousands of records, and the rise of that grand comedienne of song, Ethel Waters, singing: "Charlie's elected now! He's in right for sure!" Put down the 1920's for Louis Armstrong and Gladys Bentley and Josephine Baker.[10]

White people began to come to Harlem in droves. For several years they packed the expensive Cotton Club on Lenox Avenue. But I was never there, because the Cotton Club was a Jim Crow club for gangsters and monied whites. They were not cordial to Negro patronage, unless you were a celebrity like Bojangles.[11] So Harlem Negroes did not like the Cotton Club and never appreciated its Jim Crow policy in the very heart of their dark community. Nor did ordinary Negroes like the growing influx of whites toward Harlem after sundown, flooding the little cabarets and bars where formerly only

5  **the crash of 1929:** The stock market crash that ushered in the Great Depression.
6  **the Works Progress Administration:** One of Franklin Roosevelt's programs for economic recovery from the Great Depression.
7  **Hall Johnson . . . Josephine Baker:** African Americans who were involved in music or theater and became famous in the 1920s.
8  **Columbia:** Hughes attended Columbia University in New York from 1921 to 1922.
9  *A Bill of Divorcement . . . Shuffle Along:* plays that were hits on Broadway during the 1921 to 1922 season.
10  **Roland Hayes . . . Josephine Baker:** African American singers, actors, or musicians who were famous in the 1920s.
11  **Bojangles:** Bill "Bojangles" Robinson (1876–1949), a dancer.

colored people laughed and sang, and where now the strangers were given the best ring-side tables to sit and stare at the Negro customers—like amusing animals in a zoo.

The Negroes said: "We can't go downtown and sit and stare at you in your clubs. You won't even let us in your clubs." But they didn't say it out loud—for Negroes are practically never rude to white people. So thousands of whites came to Harlem night after night, thinking the Negroes loved to have them there, and firmly believing that all Harlemites left their houses at sundown to sing and dance in cabarets, because most of the whites saw nothing but the cabarets, not the houses.

Some of the owners of Harlem clubs, delighted at the flood of white patronage, made the grievous error of barring their own race, after the manner of the famous Cotton Club. But most of these quickly lost business and folded up, because they failed to realize that a large part of the Harlem attraction for downtown New Yorkers lay in simply watching the colored customers amuse themselves. And the smaller clubs, of course, had no big floor shows or a name band like the Cotton Club, where Duke Ellington[12] usually held forth, so, without black patronage, they were not amusing at all.

Some of the small clubs, however, had people like Gladys Bentley, who was something worth discovering in those days, before she got famous, acquired an accompanist, specially written material, and conscious vulgarity. But for two or three amazing years, Miss Bentley sat, and played a big piano all night long, literally all night, without stopping—singing songs like "The St. James Infirmary,"[13] from ten in the evening until dawn, with scarcely a break between the notes, sliding from one song to another, with a powerful and continuous underbeat of jungle rhythm. Miss Bentley was an amazing exhibition of musical energy—a large, dark, masculine lady, whose feet pounded the floor while her fingers pounded the keyboard—a perfect piece of African sculpture, animated by her own rhythm.

But when the place where she played became too well known, she began to sing with an accompanist, became a star, moved to a larger place, then downtown, and is now in Hollywood. The old magic of the woman and the piano and the night and the rhythm being one is gone. But everything goes, one way or another. The '20's are gone and lots of fine things in Harlem night life have disappeared like snow in the sun—since it became utterly commercial, planned for the downtown tourist trade, and therefore dull.

The lindy-hoppers[14] at the Savoy even began to practise acrobatic routines, and to do absurd things for the entertainment of the whites, that probably never would have entered their heads to attempt merely for their own effortless amusement. Some of the lindy-hoppers had cards printed with their names on them and became dance professors teaching the tourists. Then Harlem nights became show nights for the Nordics.[15]

Some critics say that that is what happened to certain Negro writers, too—that they ceased to write to amuse themselves and began to write to amuse and entertain white people, and in so doing distorted and over-colored their material, and left out a

12 **Duke Ellington:** A composer, pianist, and bandleader (1899–1974).
13 **"The St. James Infirmary":** A song with words and music by Joe Primrose (1930) but possibly known in the 1890s as "Gambler's Blues."
14 **The lindy-hoppers:** Young men and women who danced the lindy-hop, a dance named after the celebrated 1927 transatlantic solo flight of Charles Lindbergh.
15 **Nordics:** Whites.

great many things they thought would offend their American brothers of a lighter complexion. Maybe—since Negroes have writer-racketeers, as has any other race. But I have known almost all of them, and most of the good ones have tried to be honest, write honestly, and express their world as they saw it.

All of us know that the gay and sparkling life of the so-called Negro Renaissance of the '20's was not so gay and sparkling beneath the surface as it looked. Carl Van Vechten, in the character of Byron in *Nigger Heaven*,[16] captured some of the bitterness and frustration of literary Harlem that Wallace Thurman later so effectively poured into his *Infants of the Spring*[17]—the only novel by a Negro about that fantastic period when Harlem was in vogue.

It was a period when, at almost every Harlem upper-crust dance or party, one would be introduced to various distinguished white celebrities there as guests. It was a period when almost any Harlem Negro of any social importance at all would be likely to say casually: "As I was remarking the other day to Heywood—," meaning Heywood Broun.[18] Or: "As I said to George—," referring to George Gershwin.[19] It was a period when local and visiting royalty were not at all uncommon in Harlem. And when the parties of A'Lelia Walker,[20] the Negro heiress, were filled with guests whose names would turn any Nordic social climber green with envy. It was a period when Harold Jackman,[21] a handsome young Harlem school teacher of modest means, calmly announced one day that he was sailing for the Riviera for a fortnight, to attend Princess Murat's[22] yachting party. It was a period when Charleston preachers opened up shouting churches as sideshows for white tourists. It was a period when at least one charming colored chorus girl, amber enough to pass for a Latin American, was living in a pent house, with all her bills paid by a gentleman whose name was banker's magic on Wall Street. It was a period when every season there was at least one hit play on Broadway acted by a Negro cast. And when books by Negro authors were being published with much greater frequency and much more publicity than ever before or since in history. It was a period when white writers wrote about Negroes more successfully (commercially speaking) than Negroes did about themselves. It was the period (God help us!) when Ethel Barrymore[23] appeared in blackface in *Scarlet Sister Mary!*[24] It was the period when the Negro was in vogue.

I was there. I had a swell time while it lasted. But I thought it wouldn't last long. (I remember the vogue for things Russian, the season the Chauve-Souris[25] first came to town.) For how could a large and enthusiastic number of people be crazy about

16 *Nigger Heaven:* Van Vechten's 1926 novel set in Harlem.
17 *Infants of the Spring:* A satirical novel of 1932.
18 **Heywood Broun:** A celebrated literary and dramatic critic for the *New York Tribune* (1888–1939).
19 **George Gershwin:** A U.S. composer (1898–1937).
20 **A'Lelia Walker:** A daughter (1885–1932) of Sarah Breedlove "Madame C. J." Walker, the first African American woman to become a millionaire. Through sales of her hair-straightening preparations, Sarah Walker left a fortune of at least $2 million to her daughter, who became the central socialite of Harlem.
21 **Harold Jackman:** A Harlem schoolteacher (1900–1960) and close friend of Countée Cullen.
22 **Princess Murat:** A Princess Violette Murat visited Harlem regularly around 1928.
23 **Ethel Barrymore:** A U.S. actress (1879–1959).
24 *Scarlet Sister Mary:* A 1928 folk comedy based on a novel by Julia Peterkin (1880–1961), a white writer.
25 **Chauve-Souris:** A Russian troupe that presented programs of dance, drama, songs, and tableaux in New York City from 1922 to 1923.

Negroes forever? But some Harlemites thought the millennium had come. They thought the race problem had at last been solved through Art plus Gladys Bentley. They were sure the New Negro would lead a new life from then on in green pastures of tolerance created by Countee Cullen, Ethel Waters, Claude McKay,[26] Duke Ellington, Bojangles, and Alain Locke.

I don't know what made any Negroes think that—except that they were mostly intellectuals doing the thinking. The ordinary Negroes hadn't heard of the Negro Renaissance. And if they had, it hadn't raised their wages any. As for all those white folks in the speakeasies and night clubs of Harlem—well, maybe a colored man could find *some* place to have a drink that the tourists hadn't yet discovered.

Then it was that house-rent parties began to flourish—and not always to raise the rent either. But, as often as not, to have a get-together of one's own, where you could do the black-bottom with no stranger behind you trying to do it, too. Non-theatrical, non-intellectual Harlem was an unwilling victim of its own vogue. It didn't like to be stared at by white folks. But perhaps the downtowners never knew this—for the cabaret owners, the entertainers, and the speakeasy proprietors treated them fine—as long as they paid.

The Saturday night rent parties that I attended were often more amusing than any night club, in small apartments where God knows who lived—because the guests seldom did—but where the piano would often be augmented by a guitar, or an odd cornet, or somebody with a pair of drums walking in off the street. And where awful bootleg whiskey and good fried fish or steaming chitterling were sold at very low prices. And the dancing and singing and impromptu entertaining went on until dawn came in at the windows.

These parties, often termed whist parties or dances, were usually announced by brightly colored cards stuck in the grille of apartment house elevators. Some of the cards were highly entertaining in themselves:

---

We got yellow girls, we've got black and tan
Will you have a good time? - YEAH MAN !

## 𝔄 𝔖𝔬𝔠𝔦𝔞𝔩 𝔚𝔥𝔦𝔰𝔱 𝔓𝔞𝔯𝔱𝔶
—GIVEN BY—
**MARY WINSTON**

147 West 145th Street                    Apt. 5

---

**SATURDAY EVE., MARCH 19th, 1932**

---

**GOOD MUSIC**                    **REFRESHMENTS**

---

26 **Gladys Bentley . . . Claude McKay:** Bentley (1886–1954) was the editor of *The New Negro* (1927). Cullen (1903–1946) was the author of *Color* (1925). McKay (1889–1948) was a Jamaican-born poet whose *Harlem Shadows* (1922) is sometimes considered the first major achievement of the Harlem Renaissance.

**HURRAY**

COME AND SEE WHAT IS IN STORE FOR YOU AT THE

# TEA CUP PARTY

GIVEN BY MRS. VANDERBILT SMITH

## at 409 EDGECOMBE AVENUE
## NEW YORK CITY

Apartment 10-A

## on Thursday evening, January 23rd, 1930

at 8:30 P. M.

### ORIENTAL - GYPSY - SOUTHERN MAMMY - STARLIGHT

and other readers will be present

Music and Talent — — Refreshments Served

Ribbons-Bows and Trotters A Specialty

---

Fall in line, and watch your step, For there'll be Lots of Browns with plenty of Pep At

# A Social Whist Party

### Given by

## Lucille & Minnie

149 West 117th Street, N. Y. Gr. floor, W,

### Saturday Evening, Nov. 2nd 1929

Refreshments Just It          Music Won't Quit

---

If Sweet Mamma is running wild, and you are looking for a Do-right child, just come around and linger awhile at a

# SOCIAL WHIST PARTY

### GIVEN BY

## PINKNEY & EPPS

260 West 129th Street          Apartment 10

## SATURDAY EVENING, JUNE 9, 1928

GOOD MUSIC          REFRESHMENTS

# Railroad Men's Ball

### AT CANDY'S PLACE

### FRIDAY, SATURDAY & SUNDAY,

## April 29-30, May 1, 1927

**Black Wax, says change your mind and say they
do and he will give you a hearing, while MEAT
HOUSE SLIM, laying in the bin
killing all good men.**

L. A. VAUGH, *President*

---

OH BOY            OH JOY

# The Eleven Brown Skins

### of the

# Evening Shadow Social Club

### are giving their

## Second Annual St. Valentine Dance

### Saturday evening. Feb. 18th, 1928

### At 129 West 136th Street, New York City

Good Music          Refreshments Served

## Subscription            25 Cents

---

*Some wear pajamas, some wear pants, what does it matter
just so you can dance, at*

# A Social Whist Party

### GIVEN BY

### MR. & MRS. BROWN

### AT 258 W. 115TH STREET, APT. 9

## SATURDAY EVE., SEPT. 14, 1929

*The music is sweet and everything good to eat!*

Almost every Saturday night when I was in Harlem I went to a house-rent party. I wrote lots of poems about house-rent parties, and ate thereat many a fried fish and pig's foot—with liquid refreshments on the side. I met ladies' maids and truck drivers, laundry workers and shoe shine boys, seamstresses and porters. I can still hear their laughter in my ears, hear the soft slow music, and feel the floor shaking as the dancers danced.

## Harlem Literati

The summer of 1926, I lived in a rooming house[27] on 137th Street, where Wallace Thurman and Harcourt Tynes[28] also lived. Thurman was then managing editor of the *Messenger,* a Negro magazine that had a curious career. It began by being very radical, racial, and socialist, just after the war. I believe it received a grant from the Garland Fund[29] in its early days. Then it later became a kind of Negro society magazine and a plugger for Negro business, with photographs of prominent colored ladies and their nice homes in it. A. Phillip Randolph, now President of the Brotherhood of Sleeping Car Porters, Chandler Owen,[30] and George S. Schuyler[31] were connected with it. Schuyler's editorials, à la Mencken,[32] were the most interesting things in the magazine, verbal brickbats that said sometimes one thing, sometimes another, but always vigorously. I asked Thurman what kind of magazine the *Messenger* was, and he said it reflected the policy of whoever paid off best at the time.

Anyway, the *Messenger* bought my first short stories. They paid me ten dollars a story. Wallace Thurman wrote me that they were very bad stories, but better than any others they could find, so he published them.

Thurman had recently come from California to New York. He was a strangely brilliant black boy, who had read everything, and whose critical mind could find something wrong with everything he read. I have no critical mind, so I usually either like a book or don't. But I am not capable of liking a book and then finding a million things wrong with it, too—as Thurman was capable of doing.

Thurman had read so many books because he could read eleven lines at a time. He would get from the library a great pile of volumes that would have taken me a year to read. But he would go through them in less than a week, and be able to discuss each one at great length with anybody. That was why, I suppose, he was later given a job as a reader at Macaulay's—the only Negro reader, so far as I know, to be employed by any of the larger publishing firms.

27  **a rooming house:** This rooming house appears in Thurman's *Infants of the Spring* as "Niggerati Manor."
28  **Harcourt Tynes:** A friend of Thurman.
29  **the Garland Fund:** The American Fund for Public Service, established in 1920 by Charles Garland.
30  **A. Philip Randolph . . . Chandler Owen:** Randolph (1889–1976) and Owen (1889–1967) were editors at the *Messenger* and hired Schuyler as a writer in 1923.
31  **George S. Schuyler:** A conservative black writer (1895–1977).
32  **Mencken:** Henry Louis Mencken (1880–1956) was a prominent Baltimore essayist, critic, and editor who was a friend of Schuyler.

Later Thurman became a ghost writer for *True Story,* and other publications, writing under all sorts of fantastic names, like Ethel Belle Mandrake or Patrick Casey. He did Irish and Jewish and Catholic "true confessions." He collaborated with William Jordan Rapp[33] on plays and novels. Later he ghosted books. In fact, this quite dark young Negro is said to have written *Men, Women, and Checks.*

Wallace Thurman wanted to be a great writer, but none of his own work ever made him happy. *The Blacker the Berry,*[34] his first book, was an important novel on a subject little dwelt upon in Negro fiction—the plight of the very dark Negro woman, who encounters in some communities a double wall of color prejudice within and without the race. His play, *Harlem,* considerably distorted for box office purposes, was, nevertheless, a compelling study—and the only one in the theater—of the impact of Harlem on a Negro family fresh from the South. And his *Infants of the Spring,* a superb and bitter study of the bohemian fringe of Harlem's literary and artistic life, is a compelling book.

But none of these things pleased Wallace Thurman. He wanted to be a *very* great writer, like Gorki or Thomas Mann,[35] and he felt that he was merely a journalistic writer. His critical mind, comparing his pages to the thousands of other pages he had read, by Proust, Melville, Tolstoy, Galsworthy, Dostoyevski, Henry James, Sainte-Beauve, Taine, Anatole France,[36] found his own pages vastly wanting. So he contented himself by writing a great deal for money, laughing bitterly at his fabulously concocted "true stories," creating two bad motion pictures[37] of the "Adults Only" type for Hollywood, drinking more and more gin, and then threatening to jump out of windows at people's parties and kill himself.

During the summer of 1926, Wallace Thurman, Zora Neale Hurston, Aaron Douglas, John P. Davis, Bruce Nugent, Gwendolyn Bennett,[38] and I decided to publish "a Negro quarterly of the arts" to be called *Fire*—the idea being that it would burn up a lot of the old, dead conventional Negro-white ideas of the past, *épater le bourgeois*[39] into a realization of the existence of the younger Negro writers and artists, and provide us with an outlet for publication not available in the limited pages of the small Negro magazines then existing, the *Crisis, Opportunity,* and the *Messenger*—the

---

33. **William Jordan Rapp:** A white playwright (1895–1942) who was editor of *True Story* magazine. The only work certain to be a collaboration of Thurman and Rapp is the play *Harlem* (1929).
34. *The Blacker the Berry:* Published in 1929.
35. **Gorki or Thomas Mann:** Maxim Gorki was the pen name of Russian writer Aleksey Maksimovich Pyeshkov (1868–1936). Thomas Mann (1875–1955) was a German novelist.
36. **Proust . . . Anatole France:** Marcel Proust (1871–1922) was a French novelist. Herman Melville (1819–1891) was a U.S. writer. Leo Tolstoy (1828–1910) was a Russian novelist and social critic. John Galsworthy (1867–1933) was an English novelist. Fyodor Dostoyevski (1821–1881) was a Russian critic and novelist. Charles Augustin Sainte-Beuve (1804–1869) was a French critic and poet. Hippolyte Adolphe Taine (1828–1893) was a French critic and historian.
37. **two bad motion pictures:** *Tomorrow's Children* (1934) and *High School Girl* (1935).
38. **Zora Neale Hurston . . . Gwendolyn Bennett:** Hurston (1891–1960) was a novelist and folklore collector. Douglas (1898–1979) was an artist. Davis (1905–1973) was a lawyer and prominent leftist. Nugent (1906–1987) was an illustrator and writer. Bennett (1902–1981) was a poet.
39. *épater le bourgeois:* French. To shock the middle class.

first two being house organs for inter-racial organizations, and the latter being God knows what.

Sweltering summer evenings we met to plan *Fire*. Each of the seven of us agreed to give fifty dollars to finance the first issue. Thurman was to edit it, John P. Davis to handle the business end, and Bruce Nugent to take charge of distribution. The rest of us were to serve as an editorial board to collect material, contribute our own work, and act in any useful way that we could. For artists and writers, we got along fine and there were no quarrels. But October came before we were ready to go to press. I had to return to Lincoln,[40] John Davis to Law School at Harvard, Zora Hurston to her studies at Barnard, from whence she went about Harlem with an anthropologist's ruler, measuring heads for Franz Boas.[41]

Only three of the seven had contributed their fifty dollars, but the others faithfully promised to send theirs out of tuition checks, wages, or begging. Thurman went on with the work of preparing the magazine. He got a printer. He planned the layout. It had to be on good paper, he said, worthy of the drawings of Aaron Douglas. It had to have beautiful type, worthy of the first Negro art quarterly. It had to be what we seven young Negroes dreamed our magazine would be—so in the end it cost almost a thousand dollars, and nobody could pay the bills.

I don't know how Thurman persuaded the printer to let us have all the copies to distribute, but he did. I think Alain Locke, among others, signed notes guaranteeing payments. But since Thurman was the only one of the seven of us with a regular job, for the next three or four years his checks were constantly being attached and his income seized to pay for *Fire*. And whenever I sold a poem, mine went there, too—to *Fire*.

None of the older Negro intellectuals would have anything to do with *Fire*. Dr. DuBois[42] in the *Crisis* roasted it. The Negro press called it all sorts of bad names, largely because of a green and purple story[43] by Bruce Nugent, in the Oscar Wilde[44] tradition, which we had included. Rean Graves, the critic for the *Baltimore Afro-American*, began his review by saying: "I have just tossed the first issue of *Fire* into the fire." Commenting upon various of our contributors, he said: "Aaron Douglas who, in spite of himself and the meaningless grotesqueness of his creations, has gained a reputation as an artist, is permitted to spoil three perfectly good pages and a cover with his pen and ink hudge pudge. Countee Cullen has written a beautiful poem in his 'From a Dark Tower,' but tries his best to obscure the thought in superfluous sentences. Langston Hughes displays his usual ability to say nothing in many words."

So *Fire* had plenty of cold water thrown on it by the colored critics. The white critics (except for an excellent editorial in the *Bookman* for November, 1926) scarcely noticed it at all. We had no way of getting it distributed to bookstands or news stands. Bruce Nugent took it around New York on foot and some of the Greenwich Village

---

40 **Lincoln:** Lincoln University in Pennsylvania.
41 **Franz Boas:** A German-born American anthropologist (1858–1942).
42 **Dr. DuBois:** W. E. B. DuBois (1868–1963) was an African American writer, the editor of *Crisis,* and a cofounder of the National Association for the Advancement of Colored People (NAACP).
43 **a green and purple story:** The first installment of a novel called *Smoke, Lilies and Jade.*
44 **Oscar Wilde:** An Irish playwright (1854–1900) who was a proponent of the art-for-art's-sake movement.

bookshops put it on display, and sold it for us. But then Bruce, who had no job, would collect the money and, on account of salary, eat it up before he got back to Harlem.

Finally, irony of ironies, several hundred copies of *Fire* were stored in the basement of an apartment where an actual fire occurred and the bulk of the whole issue was burned up. Even after that Thurman had to go on paying the printer.

Now *Fire* is a collector's item, and very difficult to get, being mostly ashes.

That taught me a lesson about little magazines. But since white folks had them, we Negroes thought we could have one, too. But we didn't have the money.

Wallace Thurman laughed a long bitter laugh. He was a strange kind of fellow, who liked to drink gin, but *didn't* like to drink gin; who liked being a Negro, but felt it a great handicap; who adored bohemianism, but thought it wrong to be a bohemian. He liked to waste a lot of time, but he always felt guilty wasting time. He loathed crowds, yet he hated to be alone. He almost always felt bad, yet he didn't write poetry.

Once I told him if I could feel as bad as he did *all* the time, I would surely produce wonderful books. But he said you had to know how to *write*, as well as how to feel bad. I said I didn't have to know how to feel bad, because, every so often, the blues just naturally overtook me, like a blind beggar with an old guitar:

> You don't know,
> You don't know my mind—
> When you see me laughin',
> I'm laughin' to keep from cryin'.[45]

About the future of Negro literature Thurman was very pessimistic. He thought the Negro vogue had made us all too conscious of ourselves, had flattered and spoiled us, and had provided too many easy opportunities for some of us to drink gin and more gin, on which he thought we would always be drunk. With his bitter sense of humor, he called the Harlem literati, the "niggerati."

Of this "niggerati," Zora Neale Hurston was certainly the most amusing. Only to reach a wider audience, need she ever write books—because she is a perfect book of entertainment in herself. In her youth she was always getting scholarships and things from wealthy white people, some of whom simply paid her just to sit around and represent the Negro race for them, she did it in such a racy fashion. She was full of side-splitting anecdotes, humorous tales, and tragicomic stories, remembered out of her life in the South as a daughter of a travelling minister of God. She could make you laugh one minute and cry the next. To many of her white friends, no doubt, she was a perfect "darkie," in the nice meaning they give the term—that is a naïve, childlike, sweet, humorous, and highly colored Negro.

But Miss Hurston was clever, too—a student who didn't let college give her a broad *a* and who had great scorn for all pretensions, academic or otherwise. That is why she was such a fine folk-lore collector,[46] able to go among the people and never

---

45  **I'm laughin' to keep from cryin':** Hughes later titled a collection of his short stories *Laughing to Keep from Crying.*

46  **folk-lore collector:** Hurston published two such collections.

act as if she had been to school at all. Almost nobody else could stop the average Harlemite on Lenox Avenue and measure his head with a strange-looking, anthropological device and not get bawled out for the attempt, except Zora, who used to stop anyone whose head looked interesting, and measure it.

When Miss Hurston graduated from Barnard she took an apartment in West 66th Street near the park, in that row of Negro houses there. She moved in with no furniture at all and no money, but in a few days friends had given her everything, from decorative silver birds, perched atop the linen cabinet, down to a footstool. And on Saturday night, to christen the place, she had a *hand*-chicken dinner, since she had forgotten to say she needed forks.

She seemed to know almost everybody in New York. She had been a secretary to Fannie Hurst,[47] and had met dozens of celebrities whose friendship she retained. Yet she was always having terrific ups-and-downs about money. She tells this story on herself, about needing a nickel to go downtown one day and wondering where on earth she would get it. As she approached the subway, she was stopped by a blind beggar holding out his cup.

"Please help the blind! Help the blind! A nickel for the blind!"

"I need money worse than you today," said Miss Hurston, taking five cents out of his cup. "Lend me this! Next time, I'll give it back." And she went on downtown.

Harlem was like a great magnet for the Negro intellectual, pulling him from everywhere. Or perhaps the magnet was New York—but once in New York, he had to live in Harlem, for rooms were hardly to be found elsewhere unless one could pass for white or Mexican or Eurasian and perhaps live in the Village—which always seemed to me a very arty locale, in spite of the many real artists and writers who lived there. Only a few of the New Negroes lived in the Village, Harlem being their real stamping ground.

The wittiest of these New Negroes of Harlem, whose tongue was flavored with the sharpest and saltiest humor, was Rudolph Fisher,[48] whose stories appeared in the *Atlantic Monthly.* His novel, *Walls of Jericho,*[49] captures but slightly the raciness of his own conversation. He was a young medical doctor and X-ray specialist, who always frightened me a little, because he could think of the most incisively clever things to say—and I could never think of anything to answer. He and Alain Locke together were great for intellectual wise-cracking. The two would fling big and witty words about with such swift and punning innuendo that an ordinary mortal just sat and looked wary for fear of being caught in a net of witticisms beyond his cultural ken. I used to wish I could talk like Rudolph Fisher. Besides being a good writer, he was an excellent singer, and had sung with Paul Robeson during their college days. But I guess Fisher was too brilliant and too talented to stay long on this earth. During the same week, in December, 1934, he and Wallace Thurman both died.

Thurman died of tuberculosis in the charity ward at Bellevue Hospital, having just flown back to New York from Hollywood.

47  **Fannie Hurst:** A U.S. fiction writer (1899–1968).
48  **Rudolph Fisher:** A short-story writer (1897–1934).
49  ***Walls of Jericho:*** Published in 1928.

# Downtown

Downtown there were many interesting parties in those days, too, to which I was sometimes bidden. I remember one at Florine Stettheimer's, another at V. F. Calverton's,[50] and another at Bob Chandler's, where the walls were hung with paintings and Louise Helstrom served the drinks. Paul Haakon, who was a kid then whom Louise had "discovered" somewhere, danced and everybody Oh'ed and Ah'ed, and said what a beautiful young artist! What an artist! But later when nobody was listening, Paul Haakon said to me: "Some baloney—I'm no artist. I'm in vaudeville!"

I remember also a party at Jake Baker's, somewhere on the lower East Side near the river, where I do not recall any whites being present except Mr. Baker himself. Jake Baker then had one of the largest erotic libraries in New York, ranging from the ancient to the modern, the classic to the vulgar, the *Kama Sutra*[51] to T. R. Smith's anthology of *Poetica Erotica*.[52] But since Harlemites are not very familiar with erotic books, Mr. Baker was never able to get the party started. His gathering took on the atmosphere of the main reading room at the public library with everybody hunched over a book—trying to find out what white folks say about love when they really come to the point.

I remember also a big cocktail party for Ernestine Evans at the Ritz, when she had got a new job with some publishing firm and they were celebrating her addition to the staff. Josephine Herbst[53] was there and we had a long talk near the hors-d'œuvres, and I liked Josephine Herbst very much. Also I recall a dinner party for Claire Spencer at Colin McPhee's and Jane Belo's in the village, where Claire Spencer told about a thrilling night flight over Manhattan Island in a monoplane and also another party in the Fifties for Rebecca West,[54] who knew a lot of highly amusing gossip about the Queen of Rumania. I remember well, too, my first party after a Broadway opening, the one Horace Liveright[55] gave for Paul Robeson and Fredi Washington,[56] following the premiere of Jim Tully's *Black Boy*.[57] And there was one grand New Year's Eve fête at the Alfred A. Knopf's[58] on Fifth Avenue, where I met Ethel Barrymore and Jascha Heifetz,[59] and everybody was in tails but me, and all I had on was a blue serge suit—which didn't seem to matter to anyone—for Fifth Avenue was not nearly so snooty about clothes as Washington's Negro society.[60]

50 **V. F. Calverton:** The left-oriented editor (1900–1940) of *The Anthology of American Negro Literature* (1929).

51 *Kama Sutra:* A Hindu text on love and marriage.

52 *Poetica Erotica:* Published in 1927.

53 **Josephine Herbst:** A proletarian novelist of the 1930s (1897–1969).

54 **Rebecca West:** The pen name of English novelist Cicily Andrews (1892–1983).

55 **Horace Liveright:** A New York publisher (1886–1933).

56 **Fredi Washington:** A prominent African American actress (1903–1994), who starred in the 1934 film *Imitation of Life*.

57 *Black Boy:* A play by Tully and Frank Dazey that opened in 1926.

58 **Alfred A. Knopf's:** The apartment of a prominent New York publisher.

59 **Jascha Heifetz:** A U.S. violinist (1901–1987).

60 **Washington's Negro society:** In *The Big Sea*, Hughes depicts black society in Washington, D.C., where he lived in 1925, as particularly snobbish.

Downtown at Charlie Studin's parties, at Arthur and Mrs. Springarn's,[61] Eddie Wasserman's, at Muriel Draper's, or Rita Romilly's, one would often meet almost as many Negro guests as in Harlem. But only Carl Van Vechten's parties were *so* Negro that they were reported as a matter of course in the colored society columns, just as though they occurred in Harlem instead of West 55th Street, where he and Fania Marinoff[62] then lived in a Peter Whiffle[63] apartment, full of silver fishes and colored glass balls and ceiling-high shelves of gaily-bound books.

Not only were there interesting Negroes at Carl Van Vechten's parties, ranging from famous writers to famous tap dancers, but there were always many other celebrities of various colors and kinds, old ones and new ones from Hollywood, Broadway, London, Paris or Harlem. I remember one party when Chief Long Lance of the cinema did an Indian war dance, while Adelaide Hall of *Blackbirds*[64] played the drums, and an international assemblage crowded around to cheer.

At another of Mr. Van Vechten's parties, Bessie Smith sang the blues. And when she finished, Margarita D'Alvarez of the Metropolitan Opera arose and sang an aria. Bessie Smith did not know D'Alvarez, but, liking her voice, she went up to her when she had ceased and cried: "Don't let nobody tell you you can't sing!"

Carl Van Vechten and A'Lelia Walker were great friends, and at each of their parties many of the same people were to be seen, but more writers were present at Carl Van Vechten's. At cocktail time, or in the evening, I first met at his house Somerset Maugham, Hugh Walpole, Fannie Hurst, Witter Bynner, Isa Glenn, Emily Clark, William Seabrook, Arthur Davison Ficke, Louis Untermeyer, and George Sylvester Viereck.[65]

Mr. Viereck cured me of a very bad habit I used to have of thinking I had to say something nice to every writer I met concerning his work. Upon being introduced to Mr. Viereck, I said, "I like your books."

He demanded: "Which one?"

And I couldn't think of a single one.

Of course, at Mr. Van Vechten's parties there were always many others who were not writers: Lawrence Langner and Armina Marshall of the Theatre Guild, Eugene Goossens, Jane Belo, who married Colin McPhee and went to Bali to live, beautiful Rose Rolanda, who married Miguel Covarrubias, Lilyan Tashman, who died, Horace Liveright, Blanche Dunn, Ruben Mamoulian, Marie Doro, Nicholas Muray, Madame Helena Rubinstein, Richmond Barthe, Salvador Dali, Waldo Frank, Dudley Murphy, and often Dorothy Peterson, a charming colored girl who had grown up mostly in Puerto Rico, and who moved with such poise among these colorful celebrities that I thought when I first met her she was a white girl of the grande monde, slightly sun-

61 **Arthur and Mrs. Springarn's:** Arthur (1878–1971), a lawyer, and his wife, Marian, were supporters of the NAACP.

62 **Fania Marinoff:** A Russian-born actress (1887–1971) who married Van Vechten.

63 **Peter Whiffle:** The title character in a 1922 novel by Van Vechten.

64 ***Blackbirds:*** A series of musical reviews between 1926 and 1939 arranged by Will Vodery and staged by Lew Leslie, often featuring singer Hall.

65 **Somerset Maugham . . . George Sylvester Viereck:** Prominent English and American writers.

tanned. But she was a Negro teacher of French and Spanish, who later got a leave of absence from her school work to play Cain's Gal in *The Green Pastures*.

Being interested in the Negro problem in various parts of the world, Dorothy Peterson once asked Dali if he knew anything about Negroes.

"Everything!" Dali answered. "I've met Nancy Cunard!"

Speaking of celebrities, one night as one of Carl Van Vechten's parties was drawing to a close, Rudolph Valentino[66] called, saying that he was on his way. That was the only time I have ever seen the genial Van Vechten hospitality waver. He told Mr. Valentino the party was over. It seems that our host was slightly perturbed at the thought of so celebrated a guest coming into a party that had passed its peak. Besides, he told the rest of us, movie stars usually expect a lot of attention—and it was too late in the evening for such extended solicitude now.

Carl Van Vechten once wrote a book called *Parties*. But it is not nearly so amusing as his own parties. Once he gave a gossip party, where everybody was at liberty to go around the room repeating the worst things they could make up or recall about each other to their friends on opposite sides of the room—who were sure to go right over and tell them all about it.

At another party of his (but this was incidental) the guests were kept in a constant state of frightful expectancy by a lady standing in the hall outside Mr. Van Vechten's door, who announced that she was waiting for her husband to emerge from the opposite apartment, where he was visiting another woman. When I came to the party, I saw her standing grimly there. It was her full intention to kill her husband, she said. And she displayed to Mrs. Van Vechten's maids the pistol in her handbag.

At intervals during the evening, the woman in the hall would receive coffee from the Van Vechten party to help her maintain her vigil. But the suspense was not pleasant. I kept feeling goose pimples on my body and hearing a gun in my mind. Finally someone suggested phoning the apartment across the way to inform the erring husband of the fate awaiting him if he came out. Perhaps this was done. I don't know. But I learned later that the woman waited until dawn and then went home. No husband emerged from the silent door, so her gun was not fired.

Once when Mr. Van Vechten gave a bon voyage party in the Prince of Wales suite aboard the Cunarder on which he was sailing, as the champagne flowed, Nora Holt, the scintillating Negro blonde entertainer de luxe from Nevada, sang a ribald ditty called, "My Daddy Rocks Me With One Steady Roll." As she ceased, a well-known New York matron cried ecstatically, with tears in her eyes: "My dear! Oh, my dear! How beautifully you sing Negro spirituals!"

Carl Van Vechten moved about filling glasses and playing host with the greatest of zest at his parties, while his tiny wife, Fania Marinoff, looking always very pretty and very gay, when the evening grew late would sometimes take Mr. Van Vechten severely to task for his drinking—before bidding the remaining guests good night and retiring to her bed.

Now, Mr. Van Vechten has entirely given up drinking (as well as writing books

---

66 **Rudolph Valentino:** A popular silent screen actor (1895–1926).

and smoking cigarettes) in favor of photography. Although his parties are still gaily liquid for those who wish it, he himself is sober as a judge, but not as solemn.

For several pleasant years, he gave an annual birthday party for James Weldon Johnson, young Alfred A. Knopf, Jr., and himself, for their birthdays fall on the same day. At the last of these parties the year before Mr. Johnson died, on the Van Vechten table there were three cakes, one red, one white, and one blue—the colors of our flag. They honored a Gentile, a Negro, and a Jew—friends and fellow-Americans. But the differences of race did not occur to me until days later, when I thought back about the three colors and the three men.

Carl Van Vechten is like that party. He never talks grandiloquently about democracy or Americanism. Nor makes a fetish of those qualities. But he lives them with sincerity—and humor.

Perhaps that is why *his* parties were reported in the Harlem press.

*Aaron Douglas,* **Aspects of Negro Life: From Slavery through Reconstruction,** *oil painting, 1934*

# David Kuperman

## *Dying: The Shape of Victory in "A Summer Tragedy"* 1978

The passion of "A Summer Tragedy," the widely anthologized short story by Arna Bontemps first published in *Opportunity: A Journal of Negro Life* in 1933,[1] is the passion of realism, not sentiment, not rage. Jeff Patton, lame and palsied, and his frail, blind wife Jennie drive their rickety Model T into the river rather than wait for another stroke that might kill Jeff or, worse, leave him "helpless, like a baby, on Jennie's hands." The couple are share farmers—old, poor, debilitated and Black. But Bontemps ensures we recognize that they are not broken in spirit; they love the land and each other, and have a rich emotional life to live for. Their suicide is a victory of love over death. The matter-of-fact but eloquent tone that seldom wavers, the sensuous, uncompromising detail focused through Jeff's eyes and ears, project the couple's pride and determination. Other writers in the tradition of the Harlem Renaissance might have had us indulge in pity for the old folks or bitterness at the socio-economic system that left them no recourse but death. Bontemps evokes informed compassion and respect.

Action and motivation in "A Summer Tragedy," then, are universal, though emerging specifically from the Black experience. The sequence of emotions and images that flash through Jeff's mind as he approaches death underscores this universality born of realism. Resistance, life review and transcendence, according to a comprehensive study undertaken by Dr. Russell Noyes, Jr. are three mental phases often experienced by those who become suddenly aware of their imminent and unavoidable death.[2] The experience of Bontemps' share farmer is just this "rapidly unfolding experience that terminates in a mystical state of consciousness" (p. 174) observed by Noyes in a variety of clinical and autobiographical accounts.

The initial phase of the model, resistance, "includes recognition of the danger, fear, struggle, and finally acceptance of death" (p. 175), and is likely to be "accompanied by marked anxiety" and a struggle "between urges for active mastery on the one hand and passive resignation on the other" (p. 177). Jeff's trembling and hesitation throughout the story illustrate how repelled and frightened he is by what he and Jennie have determined to do, despite his acknowledgment that no alternative is left them and that further deliberation would inevitably lead them to the same conclusion. But when he actually hears "the water below, roaring in a narrow channel," his wife's admonitions to be brave lose effect. His brain darkens; he begins to panic and turns to Jennie in an attempt to gain from her some sanction for his inability, his refusal to go through with their agreement. Without his wife's concurrence, however, he cannot resist the inevitable, and Jennie is too absorbed in her own thoughts to reply to him. At the point of surrender this phase ends. Jeff's fear subsides and he grows tranquil.

"Immediately, as fear is replaced by calm and as active mastery is replaced by passive surrender, a curious splitting of the self from its bodily representation may occur" (p. 178). Jeff experiences this "out-of-the-body" phenomenon as he enters the second stage of the approach to death, the life review. He "correctly view[s] his body as near death but, being outside of it, he witnesses the scene with detached interest" as "vivid scenes of . . . his life flash through his mind in rapid succession . . . typically . . . accompanied by pleasurable emotions appropriate to the memories" (p. 178):

> For an instant there was a light in his cavernous brain. That chamber was, for less than a second, peopled by characters he knew and loved. They were simple, healthy creatures, and they behaved in a manner that he could understand. They had quality. But since he had already taken leave of them long ago, the remembrance did not break his heart again. Young Jeff Patton was among them, the Jeff Patton of fifty years ago who went down to New Orleans with a crowd of country boys to the Mardi Gras doings. The gay young crowd—boys with candy-striped shirts and

rouged brown girls in noisy silks—was like a picture in his head. Yet it did not make him sad.

Characteristics of the third phase, transcendence, may include, according to Noyes, experiencing oneself in a new manner, a feeling that one is outside of or beyond time, a sense of truth, and/or a loss of control. This phase, as reported by those who survived the threat of imminent death, is invariably ineffable and rapturous. True to his realistic mode, Bontemps makes no attempt to describe Jeff's feeling of transcendence. We are told, however, that "suddenly Jeff's hands became steady," and that "he actually felt brave." In light of the numerous references throughout the story to Jeff's fear and trembling, we must recognize his attainment of calm and the restoration of the manly bravery he set such store on as evidence of surrender and ecstasy. At the climax of his story's action, Bontemps indulges us with no tonal posturing, no sentimentalizing:

> Jeff ran the car onto the clay slope, pointed it directly toward the stream, and put his foot heavily on the accelerator. The little car leaped furiously down the steep incline toward the water. The movement was nearly as swift and direct as a fall. The two old black folks, sitting quietly side by side, showed no excitement.

Jeff's approach to death, paralleling Noyes's three psychodynamic phases of dying, universalizes his experience. It is no discredit to Bontemps's realism, however, but rather a vindication of it, that the reader is likely to see in Jeff's attainment of calm and rapture reward for the strength of his love and the steadfastness of his self-respect.

## Notes

1.  Reprinted in Arna Bontemps, *The Old South* (New York, 1973), from which the quotations used here are drawn.
2.  Russell Noyes, Jr., "The Experience of Dying," *Psychiatry*, 35 (1972), 174–84. Page references for quotations will be cited parenthetically.

# The Contemporary Short Story

*1970 to the Present*

1. U.S. helicopter hovering over farmers and their cattle during the Vietnam War, photograph, 1968
2. Gabriel García Márquez, photograph, 1982
3. David Hockney, *A Bigger Splash*, acrylic painting, 1967
4. Oscar Running Bear, a member of the American Indian Movement, at Wounded Knee, South Dakota, photograph, 1973
5. Toni Morrison, photograph, 2004
6. Judy Chicago, A plate for first woman burned at the stake for witchcraft, from *The Dinner Party*, ceramic, 1975–1979

© 2005 Judy Chicago

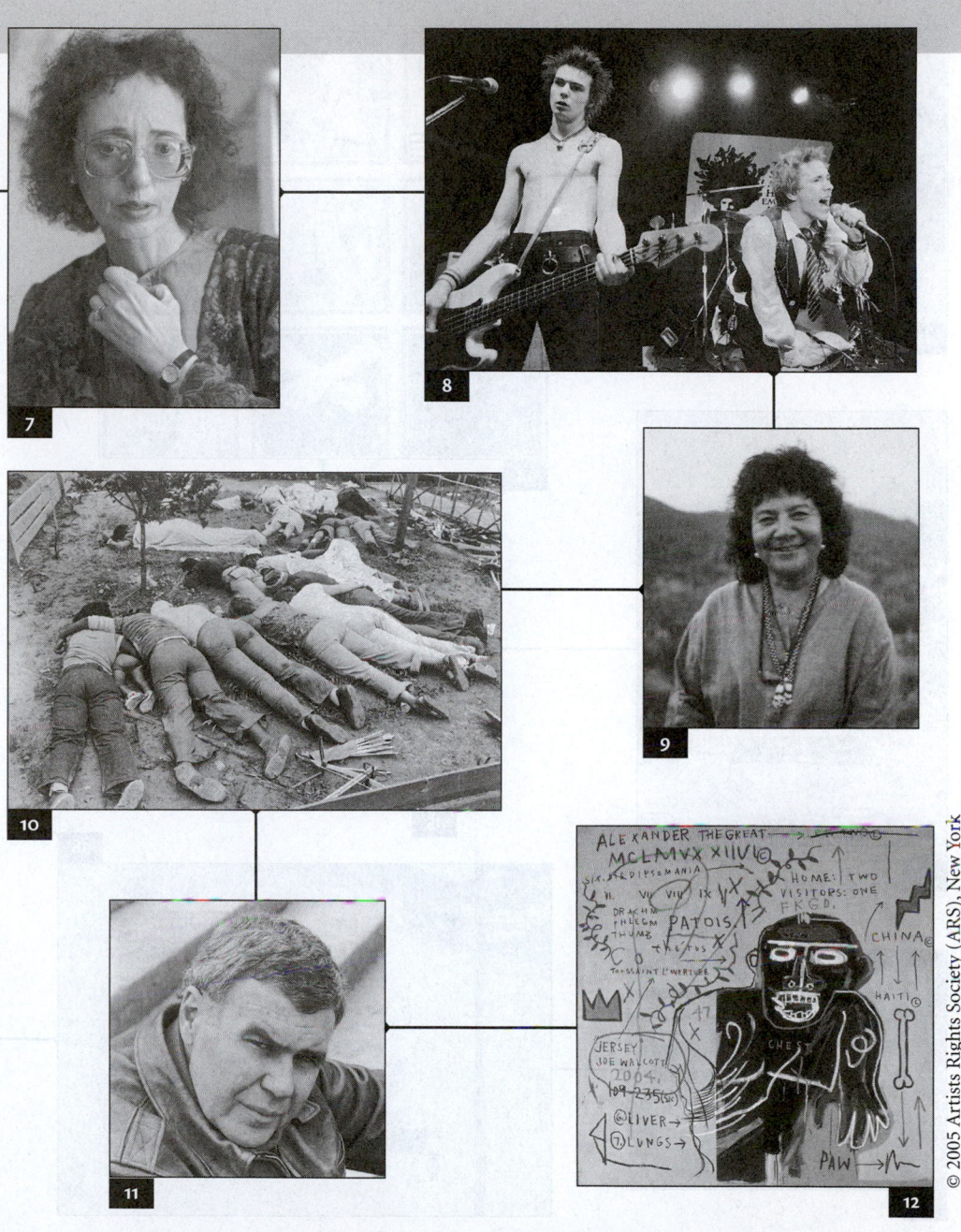

7. *Joyce Carol Oates, photograph, 2004*
8. *Sid Vicious and Johnny Rotten of the Sex Pistols, photograph, 1978*
9. *Leslie Marmon Silko, photograph*
10. *Mass suicide and executions at Jonestown, Guyana, photograph, 1978*
11. *Raymond Carver, photograph, 1987*
12. *Jean-Michel Basquiat, All Coloured Cast (Part II), acrylic, pencil, and collage, 1982*

13. *Salmon Rushdie, photograph, 2004*

14. *Barbara Kruger, Untitled (We will no longer be seen and not heard), 1985*

15. *Margaret Atwood, photograph*

16. *AIDS quilt on the Mall in Washington, D.C., photograph, 1996*

17. *Isabel Allende, photograph, 1994*

18. *Protester blocks tanks near Tiananmen Square, photograph, 1989*

19. *Hip-hop graffiti mural on wall, photograph, c. 1980s–1990s*
20. *Gish Jen and her daughter, photograph, 1999*
21. *Burning oil fields, Kuwait City, photograph, 1991*
22. *Hanif Kureishi, photograph, 2001*
23. *Nirvana, photograph, c. 1990*
24. *Jhumpa Lahiri, photograph*

The world broke open in the 1970s, giving birth to a global culture that in the last decades of the twentieth century forced people to reexamine notions of "them" and "us," redraw cultural and artistic boundaries, and redefine what it means to be a citizen of the world. In the last half of the twentieth century, the world's multicultural citizens announced their presence in a proliferation of voices surfacing from every corner of the globe in novels, short stories, essays, and poems readily available to the world's readers. Countries embroiled in changes throughout the 1960s and 1970s—wars, political coups, and the departure of colonial powers—made incredible strides in the last decades of the twentieth century.

As countries emerged from European colonialism, intellectual pursuit was no longer a simple repackaging of European ideas and artistic preferences but rather a reemergence of indigenous languages, cultures, and other traditional forms of expression. By the end of the twentieth century, short stories were being written by writers all over the world and were taking on particular literary and social significance. The short story—as a "bite" of textual information, a forum for telling smaller stories with larger import, and a genre of experimentation—was a perfect vehicle for expression in a world quickly dividing into a multitude of categories.

The short story as artistic expression, particularly for writers in newly "postcolonial" countries, continues to represent a middle ground between the colonial past and the modern present. Contemporary postcolonial literature often portrays characters who have learned, or must learn, how to adapt to living within and between two distinct cultures. Postcolonial theorist Homi Bhabha describes this effect of the colonial/postcolonial subject's "splitting and doubling" as cultural "hybridity"; that is, the colonized person desires both to "mimic" the colonizer's privileges and status and to reject oppression by the colonizer's hand. Indeed, much of the literature produced after 1970 reflects an attempt to preserve and understand ethnic identities, both in isolation and in conjunction with the majority, or colonizing, culture. Thus, contemporary literature, as it progressed through the last decades of the twentieth century, transformed the conventions of realism, naturalism, and modernism to create a new multivoiced literary tradition that expressed the diversity of contemporary culture.

## FEMINIST VOICES

Historically, the short story created a space for women of the world to express their desires, their unhappiness, and their dissatisfaction with life without branding themselves as political revolutionaries. The truth of women's lives could be effectively hidden beneath plot and character—available only to the most perceptive of readers. As women strode toward a greater sense of independence in the latter half of the twentieth century, the short story began to find new life as a space for them to engage in an open and honest expression of their lives. The postwar years brought about a rise in the legal status of women in most English-speaking countries. No-fault divorce laws, equal-pay acts, the Abortion Act (1967) in Great Britain, and *Roe v. Wade* (1973) in the United States signaled a revolutionary attitude toward women's control of their own bodies and destinies. Betty Friedan, author of *The Feminine Mystique* (1963), a groundbreaking text about the damage done to women through the cult of domesticity in the 1940s and 1950s, founded the National Organization for Women (NOW) in 1966. The emergence of NOW reflected not only a struggle for equality in contemporary America, but also the progressive politics of scores of women activists throughout the 1930s, 1940s, and 1950s. NOW attempted to unite women in an organized resistance to male-dominated American culture. In 1972, the year the Equal Rights Amendment was passed by Congress, Gloria Steinem founded *Ms.* magazine, thereby providing a forum for women's voices to be heard on a variety of political issues. This intense culmination of the women's rights movement led to a unique moment in literature. As African American activists recovered a long suppressed and forgotten (at least in mainstream culture) African American literary tradition, women writers like Adrienne Rich were calling for a recovery of "foremother" writers such as Virginia Woolf and Marianne Moore.

Breaking through the wall built by male literary predecessors presented a unique challenge to women writers of the 1970s. Writers like Tillie Olsen and Maya Angelou redefined women's literature as a vehicle for depicting women as complex beings who had sex, got angry, and moved vibrantly through the world at large. Additionally, Alice Walker's *In Search of Our Mothers' Gardens* sought to revive a relationship between contemporary women and the multitude of women writers and "mothers" who preceded them. Women also emerged as participants in intellectual life as Hannah Arendt, Susan Sontag, and Angela Davis rose to prominence in the United States while Helen Gardiner and Muriel Bradbrook held sway over Britain.

## POSTMODERN LITERATURE

As modernists sculpted a human landscape marked by an alienation and loneliness borne out of rapid industrialization and urbanization, writers in the 1970s grappled with an even more remarkable feeling of the separation of people from one another and, by extension, the individual from the self. Postmodern literature began not only as a period of literature "after" modernism, but also as a revolt against modernist sensibilities and as an attempt to more accurately express and reflect the rhythms of contemporary life. Postmodern writers took the modernist ethos of storytelling and fractured it beyond recognition. Writers such as Jorge Luis Borges, Thomas Pynchon, and Joan Didion reveal satiric, revisionary, and experimental impulses that deconstruct the form and subject of the novel or short story through spare prose, absurd situations, or unexpected characterizations. Postmodernism attempts to subvert established modes of thought and expression, revealing the void beneath an unthinking acceptance of the reality of the world. Thus, postmodern writers eschew modernism's adherence to the truth as a singular vision to create an imperfect and asymmetrical reflection of human experience.

Postmodern writing also requires a different kind of reading. Modernist authors often assumed a proprietary attitude toward their readers, guiding them toward the correct readerly response. The postmodernist author does not, in general, assume an authoritarian presence in the story. Instead, the reader is left to decode layers of meanings and symbols, and the open text invites the reader to create the story and its connotations as a coauthor. Contemporary literature as a whole often replaces the author as a trustworthy personality or "character" in the text with an anonymous or otherwise unstable narrative perspective. This destabilization of the narrative presence then encourages the reader to examine and understand the text not only on the merits of the plot points, but also on the way these plot points are delivered to the reader. The burden is placed on the reader to create and construct textual meaning, and the reading process becomes both technique and tool. The rejection of a stable center within the fictional text dovetailed with a movement in literary and critical theory called "poststructuralism." Contemporary thinkers such as Jacques Derrida, Michel Foucault, Jacques Lacan, and Roland Barthes all undermined the traditional understanding of the text as a stable document. For these theorists, the text is without a center or stabilizing force, and the writer, the writer's language, and the text all move toward a search for a center that can never be found. This deconstruction of the text as a complete unit, coupled with postmodernist writers' technique of presenting the reader with a number of complex ways of reading, directly reflects the contemporary thrust toward a global and diverse world.

## TEXTS WITHOUT CENTERS: THE MULTICULTURAL VOICE

Not all writing after modernism can be classified as "postmodern." Contemporary literature is made up of numerous kinds of textual experiments: some authors write stories that fold back upon themselves, while others opt for a more traditional narrative line; some evoke worlds that turn sharply away from reality, while many prefer approaches that mirror a documentary. Realism, abandoned by experimental writers in the 1960s, crept back in the 1980s, with authors using the form to explore contemporary concerns about cultural, ethnic, and sexual identity. Writers such as Raymond Carver and Gabriel García Márquez crafted stories that were as rooted in reality as they were in the absurd. The tension between these two states is precisely the aim of their writing: the text is not positioned to resolve the conflict, but instead illuminates conflict as its "destination." As realist fiction of the early twentieth century examined social concerns affecting readers and the world around them, contemporary realist fiction focuses on the diversity of the global world. The form of the short story, then, is also perfectly suited to this expression of diversity, since the abbreviated length allows for vast experimentation and each text serves as a tiny world, encapsulating one part of our frenetic, fractured contemporary life.

Though countless literary trends evolved in the latter half of the twentieth century, many could be collected under one umbrella: multiculturalism. In the 1960s, black writers joined together to form the Black Arts Movement, led by poet and political activist Amiri Baraka. The movement advocated literature and other writings that engaged in political rhetoric and ideas reflective of the African American community. Members of the Black Arts Movement attempted to break open the white literary, political, and historical traditions that ruled American thought and to infuse literature with the history and concerns of African Americans. However, some writers resisted the movement's implication that all African Americans thought the same way, and feminists like June Jordan rejected the seemingly male-centered construction of American blackness. Additionally, other black writers—gay, lesbian, and immigrant—were unsatisfied with definitions of blackness that did not include their experiences. Thus, African American literature in the 1970s became a way for black writers to redefine and remap the black experience. The proliferation of styles can be attributed, in part, to the African American community's interest in reframing black history and recovering long ignored traditions. African American writers chose to reactivate the painful ghost of slavery as a way to understand the contemporary configuration of black American life. The use of "Black English" allowed African American writers to shape a picture of black life that existed outside the boundaries of white language and experience.

The revolution in African American writing was also indicative of a literary renaissance in Africa. Though African nations were often divided against one another and subject to turbulent wars and repressive political regimes, all embraced art as a contributor to and carrier of culture. Africa's literary tradition grew out of oral and performative traditions, with contemporary novelists often drawing on specific stories and myths that reflect the beliefs and practices of particular tribes and villages. Contemporary African literature often explores oppositions: between the colonial world and the new world, the tension inherent in the existence of both Christianity and Islam, doubt about the importance of African culture in a modern world, and the disconnection between rural and city life. A tension is also present in the very language through which African writers craft their texts. A sense of what M. M. Bakhtin termed "multi-speechedness" is at play in the texts of Wole Soyinka, Chinua Achebe, Ngugi wa Thiong'o, and Nadine Gordimer. This linguistic tension represents not only the reality of a colonized world, but also the multiple identities such an occupation inevitably leaves behind.

A revolution in African and African American writing represents only one facet of the emergence of diverse voices throughout the 1970s, 1980s, and 1990s. As the civil rights era of the mid-1960s brought African Americans into the national spotlight, it drew Native American activists to the forefront as well. In 1968, the pan-Indian American Indian Movement (AIM) was founded to tackle problems such as unemployment, alienation, and poverty afflicting Native Americans throughout the United States. AIM's leaders used the media to focus attention on the plight of Native Americans, and protests were staged on college campuses, at Mount Rushmore, and at other historical sites throughout the country. In 1973, AIM leaders occupied Wounded Knee on the Pine Ridge reservation in South Dakota, the site of the 1890 massacre of over three hundred Lakota people. The standoff lasted seventy-one days, but the occupation was disastrous, leading to the deaths of both activists and FBI agents.

The occupation at Wounded Knee marked a watershed moment when Native Americans reentered the landscape of American intellectual and literary discourse and creation. Their novels, short stories, and plays explored Native American culture and the clash between traditional beliefs and practices and the contemporary world. By the 1980s, Leslie Marmon Silko and Louise Erdrich, among many other writers, further challenged assumptions about native peoples in narratives about Native American women who struggle in both white and Indian worlds. In the 1990s, Sherman Alexie again revitalized the voice of Native Americans by publishing stories that are at turns humorous, angry, and heartbreaking. In 1998, *Smoke Signals,* based on Alexie's collection of stories *The Lone Ranger and Tonto Fistfight in Heaven,* became one of the first movies to feature an all Native American cast, writer, director, and behind-the-scenes technicians.

Struggling to escape the shadow of mainstream American cultural dominance was a concern not only of ethnic groups within America, but also of America's "neighbors to the north." Canada was also a colonized nation, as its native peoples endured waves of English and French explorers and settlers throughout the seventeenth and eighteenth centuries. Initially, Canadian writers of the eighteenth and nineteenth centuries asserted their "Canadianness" by focusing on Canada's harsh climate and landscape—the very rawness of the earth and sky were indicative of an ability to simply *survive.* In contemporary Canadian writing, assertion of identity is centered on the instability of language itself as Canadian citizens vacillate between English and French, both in language and in culture. Writers like Alice Munro, Antonine Maillet, Roch Carrier, and Margaret Atwood reflect the multiplicity of the Canadian character.

Latinos also struggled for a place in mainstream American culture throughout the first half of the twentieth century. Their visibility increased in the mid-1960s when Chicano activists began to emerge on college campuses and city streets, protesting the invisibility of the Latino and demanding better education, resources, and treatment. Chicano literature became an important tool for reviving the Latino spirit and bringing awareness of Latino concerns to a wider audience. In his essay "Teaching Chicano Literature," Raymundo Paredes characterizes Chicano literature as one of America's youngest literatures, having begun only at the conclusion of the Mexican War in 1848. By the 1960s, presses like Quinto Sol were publishing the words of Rolando Hinojosa-Smith, Rodolfo Anaya, and Tomas Rivera, many of whom wrote in Spanish to underscore their reclamation of a culture and language many were forced to leave behind in the American push for acculturation.

Latina writers began publishing widely in the 1980s and 1990s with landmark texts like Gloria Anzaldúa's *Borderlands/La Frontera: The New Mestiza* (1987) and Sandra Cisneros's two collections of short stories, *The House on Mango Street* (1984) and *Woman Hollering Creek and Other Stories* (1991). Additionally, writers like Bernice Zamora and Pat Mora use Mexican myths about heroic and mystical women—

La Llorona, for example—to rewrite history and make it more inclusive of women and their experiences. Latina writers take on a number of oppressions, including gender, race, and class, and their texts, like Cisneros's story "Barbie-Q," excavate long buried feelings of anger and resentment.

Starting in the late 1880s, Latin America underwent an incredible process of modernization. Its intellectual life had been dominated by discourse generated from outsiders, namely, the Spanish, who had controlled and colonized Latin America. Before literary modernity, Latin American literature often reflected a narrow slice of reality through forms that had belonged to the Spanish long before Latin American writers utilized them. Most writers asserted that Latin Americans would not be independent until they established their own literary culture beyond the boundaries shown to them by their colonizers. Latin American literature, as an expression of a complex, postcolonial culture, began to become an independent force during a period called *modernismo.* As Latin America became modernized, writers gravitated toward a literature that exposed the complex problems modernity presented.

*Modernismo* literature soon developed into avant-garde experiments, commonly employing the technique known as magical realism. Writers such as Jorge Luis Borges, Gabriel García Márquez, and Julio Cortazar all flourished in this period, crafting novels and stories that seamlessly incorporated avant-garde techniques, magical realist situations, and a deft examination of the brutal politics that marred Latin American life. From the mid-1970s forward, however, Latin American literature has turned away from avant-garde aesthetics. Literary realism is again popular, as is the genre of the *testimonio,* or personal narrative. *Testimonios* often capture the rise of a person from the lower middle class to, if not the heights, then at least stable ground. This narrative plumbing of both the lows and the highs has contributed to the creation of the contemporary Latin American identity: that of survivor.

Asian American voices were always present in American life, but they truly entered the conversation with American literature only in the second half of the twentieth century. Maxine Hong Kingston's *The Woman Warrior* (1976) is, like the literature of Chicano writers, an integration of traditional myths and Chinese history with a story that spools out in the contemporary world. Amy Tan's *The Joy Luck Club* (1989) offers storytelling as the key for resistance against the homogenization of American culture. Indian subcontinental writers like Bharati Mukherjee, Jhumpa Lahiri, and Akhil Sharma have also become wildly popular on the American literary scene. Their stories of immigrant Indians struggling to understand the cultural divide between their world and the Western world speak beyond the boundaries of race. The story of a "fish out of water" is one to which everyone can relate, especially if the results are less than perfect.

China's tumultuous recent history—the bloody and repressive Cultural Revolution of 1966 to 1976 and the student protests in Tiananmen Square in 1989—left an indelible mark on contemporary Chinese fiction. Chinese writers, such as Ping Hsin, Lu Hsun, and Huang Ch'un-ming, walk a tenuous line between maintaining a sense of Chinese traditionalism and asserting the concerns of the Chinese people who must ultimately exist in a modern world. Contemporary Japanese literature, like that of Kawabata Yasunari, Hayashi Kyoko, and Banana Yoshimoto, also maintains a tension between the past and present. As Japan recovered from the devastation of World War II and rose to become an international economic and political power, its artistic products reflected the increasing complexity of Japanese identity. Japanese youths walk the streets in outrageous outfits that convey not only an outside-the-mainstream rebelliousness but also a reinvigorated sense of Japanese traditionalism combined with a fascination with Western culture. Japanese writing can be incredibly conventional or startlingly experimental, with texts that are pitched to be both highly realistic and fantastical while vacillating between pop cultural cheekiness and philosophical seriousness.

## Technology and the Contemporary Text

The magazines created by modernist adherents provided a space for alternative forms of literature not being published by mainstream publishing houses. Magazines like the *Masses* allowed modernists to make a dent in the wall of traditional literature that often obscured the view of alternative texts. The ability to establish small presses that published these revolutionary writings was a direct product of rapid industrialization throughout the United States and Europe. Technology, though often portrayed in modernist stories as an ominous monster threatening the sensitive human condition, provided non-mainstream writers with the ability to publish their own work.

Technological innovations rapidly reshaped the American landscape throughout the first sixty years of the twentieth century, but it is in the last thirty years that accelerating technological change has truly remapped the boundaries of literature. The computer revolution began to evolve long before the 1970s, but it reached into homes throughout the world in the subsequent three decades. The floppy disk appeared in 1970, and the next year Intel introduced the microprocessor, the "computer on a chip." By the 1980s, large numbers of people began using personal computers in their homes, offices, and schools. The World Wide Web was born in 1992, changing the way the world communicates, spends money, and conducts business. By 1994, 3 million people were online; by 1998, the number had risen to 100 million people; and by 2002, some 1 billion people were connected.

The Internet reopened the space for an alternative literature, much the way the aforementioned modernist magazine reopened spaces for Bohemian thought. Though alternative magazines have existed throughout history, their distribution was often limited and, thus, the audiences able to read works outside the mainstream were small. Additionally, the cost of magazines proved prohibitive for those living with stretched-to-the-limit budgets. The Internet offers a separate, free space where millions of people worldwide can put their ideas, stories, art, and politics online for anyone to access. The Internet has also revolutionized, though not conquered, the way in which books are created. In the late 1990s, author Stephen King published several books for exclusive access on the Internet, changing the very conception of what it means to own and to publish a "book."

## THE COMPLEX LEGACY OF CONTEMPORARY LITERATURE

In the 1970s, the rebellious spirit of the 1960s continued even as the Vietnam War came to a close. The Watergate scandal furthered the American public's growing disillusionment with government, while the women's movement and vocal African American, Native American, and Chicano political activists, along with their rebellious counterparts in other countries, agitated for a chance to live in a more inclusive world. The 1980s, however, saw a decrease in the mainstream rebelliousness that marked the 1960s and 1970s as political unrest gave way to a focus on conservative politics, and the infamous statement "greed is good" summarized the moneymaking thrust of business. The 1990s will surely be remembered as the decade in which the computer revolution truly touched most people living in developed nations. The World Wide Web, the Internet, chat rooms, and e-mail altered the shape of conversation and writing. As computer technology permanently reformulated the individual's relationship to what is public and what is private, people often perceived themselves to be living in a land of impermanence. The Internet has created a world within reach while also homogenizing individuality, as everyone can wear the same clothes, eat the same food, and watch the same TV shows and movies. Thus, contemporary writers are left to grapple with this loss of the individual by reasserting cultural origins and by recreating a language and literature exploring the loss and possible reclamation of a cohesive self.

The short story is an elastic genre, one perfectly suited to an exploration of the human spirit. During the nineteenth century, literature painted a number of smaller portraits, each particular to the nation from which it sprang; writers had little contact with a broad base of international literature, and readers even less so. However, as the twentieth century progressed, the ability to communicate and see beyond national borders increased, and literature began to reflect a deeply interconnected world. The short story provides a perfect lens through which to view this ever burgeoning human landscape, because it allows readers to completely immerse themselves within another culture for a brief moment. The process of reading and understanding literature is also an ambiguous project because readers bring to it their own viewpoints and experiences, which will temper their interpretation of the text. In forms such as the short story, then, we can contemplate our global citizenship and discover the bonds that link us across nations and cultures.

# Isabel Allende

### (B. 1942)

Isabel Allende writes in the style of magic realism, incorporating fantasy and myth in realistic fiction. She was born in Lima, Peru, and from 1959 to 1965 worked with the United Nations' Food and Agricultural Organization in Santiago

and Brussels. In 1973 her uncle, Chilean president Salvador Allende, was overthrown and assassinated. Allende and her family fled to Venezuela, where she
worked for the *El Naciona* newspaper in Caracas and as a teacher in a secondary
school. In 1981, when Allende learned that her grandfather was dying, she began writing him a letter that eventually evolved into the manuscript for *The
House of the Spirits* (1982), her first book. Her other works include *Of Love and
Shadows* (1984), *Eva Luna* (1985), *Paula* (1994), *Aphrodite* (1997), *Daughter of
Fortune* (1999), *Portrait in Sepia* (2000), and *My Invented Country* (2003). She
also published works for children and young adults, among them *The Porcelain
Fat Lady* (1984) and *City of the Beasts* (2002). Allende has taught literature at the
University of Virginia, Charlottesville; Montclair College, New Jersey; and the
University of California, Berkeley. She moved to California in 1988 and contin-
ues to live there.

## And of Clay Are We Created                    1989

TRANSLATED BY MARGARET SAYERS PEDEN

They discovered the girl's head protruding from the mudpit, eyes wide open, calling
soundlessly. She had a First Communion name, Azucena. Lily. In that vast cemetery
where the odor of death was already attracting vultures from far away, and where the
weeping of orphans and wails of the injured filled the air, the little girl obstinately
clinging to life became the symbol of the tragedy. The television cameras transmitted
so often the unbearable image of the head budding like a black squash from the clay
that there was no one who did not recognize her and know her name. And every time
we saw her on the screen, right behind her was Rolf Carlé, who had gone there on
assignment, never suspecting that he would find a fragment of his past, lost thirty
years before.

First a subterranean sob rocked the cotton fields, curling them like waves of
foam. Geologists had set up their seismographs weeks before and knew that the
mountain had awakened again. For some time they had predicted that the heat of the
eruption could detach the eternal ice from the slopes of the volcano, but no one
heeded their warnings; they sounded like the tales of frightened old women. The
towns in the valley went about their daily life, deaf to the moaning of the earth, until
that fateful Wednesday night in November when a prolonged roar announced the end
of the world, and walls of snow broke loose, rolling in an avalanche of clay, stones, and
water that descended on the villages and buried them beneath unfathomable meters
of telluric vomit. As soon as the survivors emerged from the paralysis of that first awful terror, they could see that houses, plazas, churches, white cotton plantations, dark
coffee forests, cattle pastures—all had disappeared. Much later, after soldiers and volunteers had arrived to rescue the living and try to assess the magnitude of the cataclysm, it was calculated that beneath the mud lay more than twenty thousand human
beings and an indefinite number of animals putrefying in a viscous soup. Forests and

rivers had also been swept away, and there was nothing to be seen but an immense desert of mire.

When the station called before dawn, Rolf Carlé and I were together. I crawled out of bed, dazed with sleep, and went to prepare coffee while he hurriedly dressed. He stuffed his gear in the green canvas backpack he always carried, and we said good-bye, as we had so many times before. I had no presentiments. I sat in the kitchen, sipping my coffee and planning the long hours without him, sure that he would be back the next day.

He was one of the first to reach the scene, because while other reporters were fighting their way to the edges of that morass in jeeps, bicycles, or on foot, each getting there however he could, Rolf Carlé had the advantage of the television helicopter, which flew him over the avalanche. We watched on our screens the footage captured by his assistant's camera, in which he was up to his knees in muck, a microphone in his hand, in the midst of a bedlam of lost children, wounded survivors, corpses, and devastation. The story came to us in his calm voice. For years he had been a familiar figure in newscasts, reporting live at the scene of battles and catastrophes with awesome tenacity. Nothing could stop him, and I was always amazed at his equanimity in the face of danger and suffering; it seemed as if nothing could shake his fortitude or deter his curiosity. Fear seemed never to touch him, although he had confessed to me that he was not a courageous man, far from it. I believe that the lens of the camera had a strange effect on him; it was as if it transported him to a different time from which he could watch events without actually participating in them. When I knew him better, I came to realize that this fictive distance seemed to protect him from his own emotions.

Rolf Carlé was in on the story of Azucena from the beginning. He filmed the volunteers who discovered her, and the first persons who tried to reach her; his camera zoomed in on the girl, her dark face, her large desolate eyes, the plastered-down tangle of her hair. The mud was like quicksand around her, and anyone attempting to reach her was in danger of sinking. They threw a rope to her that she made no effort to grasp until they shouted to her to catch it; then she pulled a hand from the mire and tried to move, but immediately sank a little deeper. Rolf threw down his knapsack and the rest of his equipment and waded into the quagmire, commenting for his assistant's microphone that it was cold and that one could begin to smell the stench of corpses.

"What's your name?" he asked the girl, and she told him her flower name. "Don't move, Azucena," Rolf Carlé directed, and kept talking to her, without a thought for what he was saying, just to distract her, while slowly he worked his way forward in mud up to his waist. The air around him seemed as murky as the mud.

It was impossible to reach her from the approach he was attempting, so he retreated and circled around where there seemed to be firmer footing. When finally he was close enough, he took the rope and tied it beneath her arms, so they could pull her out. He smiled at her with that smile that crinkles his eyes and makes him look like a little boy; he told her that everything was fine, that he was here with her now, that soon they would have her out. He signaled the others to pull, but as soon as the cord tensed, the girl screamed. They tried again, and her shoulders and arms appeared, but they could move her no farther; she was trapped. Someone suggested that her legs might be caught in the collapsed walls of her house, but she said it was not just rubble, that she was also held by the bodies of her brothers and sisters clinging to her legs.

"Don't worry, we'll get you out of here," Rolf promised. Despite the quality of the transmission, I could hear his voice break, and I loved him more than ever. Azucena looked at him, but said nothing.

During those first hours Rolf Carlé exhausted all the resources of his ingenuity to rescue her. He struggled with poles and ropes, but every tug was an intolerable torture for the imprisoned girl. It occurred to him to use one of the poles as a lever but got no result and had to abandon the idea. He talked a couple of soldiers into working with him for a while, but they had to leave because so many other victims were calling for help. The girl could not move, she barely could breathe, but she did not seem desperate, as if an ancestral resignation allowed her to accept her fate. The reporter, on the other hand, was determined to snatch her from death. Someone brought him a tire, which he placed beneath her arms like a life buoy, and then laid a plank near the hole to hold his weight and allow him to stay closer to her. As it was impossible to remove the rubble blindly, he tried once or twice to dive toward her feet, but emerged frustrated, covered with mud, and spitting gravel. He concluded that he would have to have a pump to drain the water, and radioed a request for one, but received in return a message that there was no available transport and it could not be sent until the next morning.

"We can't wait that long!" Rolf Carlé shouted, but in the pandemonium no one stopped to commiserate. Many more hours would go by before he accepted that time had stagnated and reality had been irreparably distorted.

A military doctor came to examine the girl, and observed that her heart was functioning well and that if she did not get too cold she could survive the night.

"Hang on, Azucena, we'll have the pump tomorrow," Rolf Carlé tried to console her.

"Don't leave me alone," she begged.

"No, of course I won't leave you."

Someone brought him coffee, and he helped the girl drink it, sip by sip. The warm liquid revived her and she began telling him about her small life, about her family and her school, about how things were in that little bit of world before the volcano had erupted. She was thirteen, and she had never been outside her village. Rolf Carlé, buoyed by a premature optimism, was convinced that everything would end well: the pump would arrive, they would drain the water, move the rubble, and Azucena would be transported by helicopter to a hospital where she would recover rapidly and where he could visit her and bring her gifts. He thought, She's already too old for dolls, and I don't know what would please her; maybe a dress. I don't know much about women, he concluded, amused, reflecting that although he had known many women in his lifetime, none had taught him these details. To pass the hours he began to tell Azucena about his travels and adventures as a newshound, and when he exhausted his memory, he called upon imagination, inventing things he thought might entertain her. From time to time she dozed, but he kept talking in the darkness, to assure her that he was still there and to overcome the menace of uncertainty.

That was a long night.

Many miles away, I watched Rolf Carlé and the girl on a television screen. I could not bear the wait at home, so I went to National Television, where I often spent entire nights with Rolf editing programs. There, I was near his world, and I could at least get a feeling of what he lived through during those three decisive days. I called all the important people in the city, senators, commanders of the armed forces, the North American ambassador, and the president of National Petroleum, begging them for a pump to remove the silt, but obtained only vague promises. I began to ask for urgent help on radio and television, to see if there wasn't *someone* who could help us. Between calls I would run to the newsroom to monitor the satellite transmissions that periodically brought new details of the catastrophe. While reporters selected scenes with most impact for the news report, I searched for footage that featured Azucena's mudpit. The screen reduced the disaster to a single plane and accentuated the tremendous distance that separated me from Rolf Carlé; nonetheless, I was there with him. The child's every suffering hurt me as it did him; I felt his frustration, his impotence. Faced with the impossibility of communicating with him, the fantastic idea came to me that if I tried, I could reach him by force of mind and in that way give him encouragement. I concentrated until I was dizzy—a frenzied and futile activity. At times I would be overcome with compassion and burst out crying; at other times, I was so drained I felt as if I were staring through a telescope at the light of a star dead for a million years.

I watched that hell on the first morning broadcast, cadavers of people and animals awash in the current of new rivers formed overnight from melted snow. Above the mud rose the tops of trees and the bell towers of a church where several people had taken refuge and were patiently awaiting rescue teams. Hundreds of soldiers and volunteers from the Civil Defense were clawing through rubble searching for survivors, while long rows of ragged specters awaited their turn for a cup of hot broth. Radio networks announced that their phones were jammed with calls from families offering shelter to orphaned children. Drinking water was in scarce supply, along with gasoline and food. Doctors, resigned to amputating arms and legs without anesthesia, pled that at least they be sent serum and painkillers and antibiotics; most of the roads, however, were impassable, and worse were the bureaucratic obstacles that stood in the way. To top it all, the clay contaminated by decomposing bodies threatened the living with an outbreak of epidemics.

Azucena was shivering inside the tire that held her above the surface. Immobility and tension had greatly weakened her, but she was conscious and could still be heard when a microphone was held out to her. Her tone was humble, as if apologizing for all the fuss. Rolf Carlé had a growth of beard, and dark circles beneath his eyes; he looked near exhaustion. Even from that enormous distance I could sense the quality of his weariness, so different from the fatigue of other adventures. He had completely forgotten the camera; he could not look at the girl through a lens any longer. The pictures we were receiving were not his assistant's but those of other reporters who had appropriated Azucena, bestowing on her the pathetic responsibility of embodying the horror of what had happened in that place. With the first light Rolf tried again to dislodge the obstacles that held the girl in her tomb, but he had only his hands to work with; he did not dare use a tool for fear of injuring her. He fed Azucena a cup of the cornmeal mush and bananas the Army was distributing, but she immediately vomited it up. A doctor stated that she had a fever, but added that there was little he could do: antibiotics were being reserved for cases of gangrene. A priest also passed by and blessed her, hanging a medal of the Virgin around her neck. By evening a gentle, persistent drizzle began to fall.

"The sky is weeping," Azucena murmured, and she, too, began to cry.

"Don't be afraid," Rolf begged. "You have to keep your strength up and be calm. Everything will be fine. I'm with you, and I'll get you out somehow."

Reporters returned to photograph Azucena and ask her the same questions, which she no longer tried to answer. In the meanwhile, more television and movie teams arrived with spools of cable, tapes, film, videos, precision lenses, recorders, sound consoles, lights, reflecting screens, auxiliary motors, cartons of supplies, electricians, sound technicians, and cameramen: Azucena's face was beamed to millions of screens around the world. And all the while Rolf Carlé kept pleading for a pump. The improved technical facilities bore results, and National Television began receiving sharper pictures and clearer sound; the distance seemed suddenly compressed, and I had the horrible sensation that Azucena and Rolf were by my side, separated from me by impenetrable glass. I was able to follow events hour by hour; I knew everything my love did to wrest the girl from her prison and help her endure her suffering; I overheard fragments of what they said to one another and could guess the rest; I was present when she taught Rolf to pray, and when he distracted her with the stories I had told him in a thousand and one nights beneath the white mosquito netting of our bed.

When darkness came on the second day, Rolf tried to sing Azucena to sleep with old Austrian folk songs he had learned from his mother, but she was far beyond sleep. They spent most of the night talking, each in a stupor of exhaustion and hunger, and shaking with cold. That night, imperceptibly, the unyielding floodgates that had contained Rolf Carlé's past for so many years began to open, and the torrent of all that had lain hidden in the deepest and most secret layers of memory poured out, leveling before it the obstacles that had blocked his consciousness for so long. He could not tell it all to Azucena; she perhaps did not know there was a world beyond the sea or time previous to her own; she was not capable of imagining Europe in the years of the war. So he could not tell her of defeat, nor of the afternoon the Russians had led them to the concentration camp to bury prisoners dead from starvation. Why should he describe to her how the naked bodies piled like a mountain of firewood resembled fragile china? How could he tell this dying child about ovens and gallows? Nor did he mention the night that he had seen his mother naked, shod in stiletto-heeled red boots, sobbing with humiliation. There was much he did not tell, but in those hours he relived for the first time all the things his mind had tried to erase. Azucena had surrendered her fear to him and so, without wishing it, had obliged Rolf to confront his own. There, beside that hellhole of mud, it was impossible for Rolf to flee from himself any longer, and the visceral terror he had lived as a boy suddenly invaded him. He reverted to the years when he was the age of Azucena, and younger, and, like her, found himself trapped in a pit without escape, buried in life, his head barely above ground; he saw before his eyes the boots and legs of his father, who had removed his belt and was whipping it in the air with the never-forgotten hiss of a viper coiled to strike. Sorrow flooded through him, intact and precise, as if it had lain always in his mind, waiting. He was once again in the armoire where his father locked him to punish him for imagined misbehavior, there where for eternal hours he had crouched with his eyes closed, not to see the darkness, with his hands over his ears, to shut out the beating of his heart, trembling, huddled like a cornered animal. Wandering in the mist of his memories he found his sister Katharina, a sweet, retarded child who spent her life hiding, with the hope that her father would forget the disgrace of her having been born. With Katharina, Rolf crawled beneath the dining room table, and with her hid there under the long white tablecloth, two children forever embraced, alert to footsteps and voices. Katharina's scent melded with his own sweat, with aromas of cooking, garlic, soup, freshly baked bread, and the unexpected odor of putrescent clay. His sister's hand in his, her frightened breathing, her silk hair against his cheek, the candid gaze of her eyes. Katharina . . . Katharina materialized before him, floating on the air like a flag, clothed in the white tablecloth, now a winding sheet, and at last he could weep for her death and for the guilt of having abandoned her. He understood then that all his exploits as a reporter, the feats that had won him such recognition and fame, were merely an attempt to keep his most ancient fears at bay, a stratagem for taking refuge behind a lens to test whether reality was more tolerable from that perspective. He took excessive risks as an exercise of courage, training by day to conquer the monsters that tormented him by night. But he had come face to face with the moment of truth; he could not continue to escape his past. He *was* Azucena; he was buried in the clayey mud; his terror was not the distant emotion of an almost forgotten childhood, it was a claw sunk in his throat. In the flush of his tears he saw his mother, dressed in black and clutching her imitation-crocodile pocketbook to her bosom, just as he had last seen her on the dock when she had come to put him on the boat to South America. She had not come to dry his tears, but to tell him to pick up a shovel: the war was over and now they must bury the dead.

"Don't cry. I don't hurt anymore. I'm fine," Azucena said when dawn came.

"I'm not crying for you," Rolf Carlé smiled. "I'm crying for myself. I hurt all over."

The third day in the valley of the cataclysm began with a pale light filtering through storm clouds. The President of the Republic visited the area in his tailored safari jacket to confirm that this was the worst catastrophe of the century; the country was in mourning; sister nations had offered aid; he had ordered a state of siege; the Armed Forces would be merciless, anyone caught stealing or committing other offenses would be shot on sight. He added that it was impossible to remove all the dead corpses or count the thousands who had disappeared; the entire valley would be declared holy ground, and bishops would come to celebrate a solemn mass for the souls of the victims.

He went to the Army field tents to offer relief in the form of vague promises to crowds of the rescued, then to the improvised hospital to offer a word of encouragement to doctors and nurses worn down from so many hours of tribulations. Then he asked to be taken to see Azucena, the little girl the whole world had seen. He waved to her with a limp statesman's hand, and microphones recorded his emotional voice and paternal tone as he told her that her courage had served as an example to the nation. Rolf Carlé interrupted to ask for a pump, and the President assured him that he personally would attend to the matter. I caught a glimpse of Rolf for a few seconds kneeling beside the mudpit. On the evening news broadcast, he was still in the same position; and I, glued to the screen like a fortuneteller to her crystal ball, could tell that something fundamental had changed in him. I knew somehow that during the night his defenses had crumbled and he had given in to grief; finally he was vulnerable. The girl had touched a part of him that he himself had no access to, a part he had never shared with me. Rolf had wanted to console her, but it was Azucena who had given him consolation.

I recognized the precise moment at which Rolf gave up the fight and surrendered to the torture of watching the girl die. I was with them, three days and two nights, spying on them from the other side of life. I was there when she told him that in all her thirteen years no boy had ever loved her and that it was a pity to leave this world without knowing love. Rolf assured her that he loved her more than he could ever love anyone, more than he loved his mother, more than his sister, more than all the women who had slept in his arms, more than he loved me, his life companion, who would have given anything to be trapped in that well in her place, who would have exchanged her life for Azucena's, and I watched as he leaned down to kiss her poor forehead, consumed by a sweet, sad emotion he could not name. I felt how in that instant both were saved from despair, how they were freed from the clay, how they rose above the vultures and helicopters, how together they flew above the vast swamp of corruption and laments. How, finally, they were able to accept death. Rolf Carlé prayed in silence that she would die quickly, because such pain cannot be borne.

By then I had obtained a pump and was in touch with a general who had agreed to ship it the next morning on a military cargo plane. But on the night of that third day, beneath the unblinking focus of quartz lamps and the lens of a hundred cameras, Azucena gave up, her eyes locked with those of the friend who had sustained her to the end. Rolf Carlé removed the life buoy, closed her eyelids, held her to his chest for a few moments, and then let her go. She sank slowly, a flower in the mud.

You are back with me, but you are not the same man. I often accompany you to the station and we watch the videos of Azucena again; you study them intently, looking for something you could have done to save her, something you did not think of in time. Or maybe you study them to see yourself as if in a mirror, naked. Your cameras lie forgotten in a closet; you do not write or sing; you sit long hours before the window, staring at the mountains. Beside you, I wait for you to complete the voyage into yourself, for the old wounds to heal. I know that when you return from your nightmares, we shall again walk hand in hand, as before.

# Margaret Atwood

## (B. 1939)

Poet, novelist, and critic Margaret Atwood was born in Ottawa, Ontario, Canada. She received her undergraduate degree from Victoria College at the University of Toronto and her master's degree from Radcliffe College. Atwood's contributions to Canadian literature extend beyond the boundaries of her own fiction. Her two critical studies of Canadian fiction, *Survival: A Thematic Guide to Canadian Literature* (1972) and *Strange Things: The Malevolent North in Canadian Literature* (1995), are both insightful examinations of Canadian identity. Atwood believes that the most omnipresent theme in Canadian life and letters is a love for a "good disaster." She also contributed greatly to feminist literature, particularly in her novels *The Edible Woman* (1969) and *The Handmaid's Tale* (1983), both of which use dystopia to explore women's position in the contemporary world. Her characters are often everyday people called upon to perform under the most extraordinary circumstances. Atwood's writing moves easily between real and imagined worlds, and she utilizes realism to sometimes surrealistic ends.

Atwood is the author of more than twenty-five volumes of poetry, fiction, and nonfiction. Her best-known works include *The Edible Woman* (1969), *The Handmaid's Tale* (1983), *The Robber Bride* (1994), *Alias Grace* (1996), and *The Blind Assassin* (2000), which won the prestigious Booker Prize. Her newest novel is *Oryx and Crake* (2003). Atwood's work has been translated into numerous languages and published in more than twenty-five countries. She has received many honors and awards for her writing.

## *Happy Endings*

1983

John and Mary meet.
What happens next?
If you want a happy ending, try A.

A.   John and Mary fall in love and get married. They both have worthwhile and remunerative jobs which they find stimulating and challenging. They buy a charming house. Real estate values go up. Eventually, when they can afford live-in help, they have two children, to whom they are devoted. The children turn out well. John and Mary have a stimulating and challenging sex life and worthwhile friends. They go on fun vacations together. They retire. They both have hobbies which they find stimulating and challenging. Eventually they die. This is the end of the story.

B.   Mary falls in love with John but John doesn't fall in love with Mary. He merely uses her body for selfish pleasure and ego gratification of a tepid kind. He comes to her apartment twice a week and she cooks him dinner, you'll notice that he doesn't even consider her worth the price of a dinner out, and after he's eaten the dinner he fucks her and after that he falls asleep, while she does the dishes so he won't think she's untidy, having all those dirty dishes lying around, and puts on fresh lipstick so she'll look good when he wakes up, but when he wakes up he doesn't even notice, he puts on his socks and his shorts and his pants and his shirt and his tie and his shoes, the reverse order from the one in which he took them off. He doesn't take off Mary's clothes, she takes them off herself, she acts as if she's dying for it every time, not be-cause she likes sex exactly, she doesn't, but she wants John to think she does because if they do it often enough surely he'll get used to her, he'll come to depend on her and they will get married, but John goes out the door with hardly so much as a good-night and three days later he turns up at six o'clock and they do the whole thing over again.

Mary gets run-down. Crying is bad for your face, everyone knows that and so does Mary but she can't stop. People at work notice. Her friends tell her John is a rat, a pig, a dog, he isn't good enough for her, but she can't believe it. Inside John, she thinks, is another John, who is much nicer. This other John will emerge like a butter-fly from a cocoon, a Jack from a box, a pit from a prune, if the first John is only squeezed enough.

One evening John complains about the food. He has never complained about the food before. Mary is hurt.

Her friends tell her they've seen him in a restaurant with another woman, whose name is Madge. It's not even Madge that finally gets to Mary: it's the restaurant. John has never taken Mary to a restaurant. Mary collects all the sleeping pills and aspirins she can find, and takes them and half a bottle of sherry. You can see what kind of a woman she is by the fact that it's not even whiskey. She leaves a note for John. She hopes he'll discover her and get her to the hospital in time and repent and then they can get married, but this fails to happen and she dies.

John marries Madge and everything continues as in A.

C.   John, who is an older man, falls in love with Mary, and Mary, who is only twenty-two, feels sorry for him because he's worried about his hair falling out. She sleeps with him even though she's not in love with him. She met him at work. She's in love with someone called James, who is twenty-two also and not yet ready to settle down.

John on the contrary settled down long ago: this is what is bothering him. John has a steady, respectable job and is getting ahead in his field, but Mary isn't impressed by him, she's impressed by James, who has a motorcycle and a fabulous record collec-tion. But James is often away on his motorcycle, being free. Freedom isn't the same for girls, so in the meantime Mary spends Thursday evenings with John. Thursdays are the only days John can get away.

John is married to a woman called Madge and they have two children, a charming house which they bought just before the real estate values went up, and hobbies which they find stimulating and challenging, when they have the time. John tells Mary how important she is to him, but of course he can't leave his wife because a commitment is a commitment. He goes on about this more than is necessary and Mary finds it boring, but older men can keep it up longer so on the whole she has a fairly good time.

One day James breezes in on his motorcycle with some top-grade California hybrid and James and Mary get higher than you'd believe possible and they climb into bed. Everything becomes very underwater, but along comes John, who has a key to Mary's apartment. He finds them stoned and entwined. He's hardly in any position to be jealous, considering Madge, but nevertheless he's overcome with despair. Finally he's middle-aged, in two years he'll be bald as an egg and he can't stand it. He purchases a handgun, saying he needs it for target practice—this is the thin part of the plot, but it can be dealt with later—and shoots the two of them and himself.

Madge, after a suitable period of mourning, marries an understanding man called Fred and everything continues as in A, but under different names.

D.   Fred and Madge have no problems. They get along exceptionally well and are good at working out any little difficulties that may arise. But their charming house is by the seashore and one day a giant tidal wave approaches. Real estate values go down. The rest of the story is about what caused the tidal wave and how they escape from it. They do, though thousands drown, but Fred and Madge are virtuous and lucky. Finally on high ground they clasp each other, wet and dripping and grateful, and continue as in A.

E.   Yes, but Fred has a bad heart. The rest of the story is about how kind and understanding they both are until Fred dies. Then Madge devotes herself to charity work until the end of A. If you like, it can be "Madge, " "cancer," "guilty and confused," and "bird watching."

F.   If you think this is all too bourgeois, make John a revolutionary and Mary a counterespionage agent and see how far that gets you. Remember, this is Canada. You'll still end up with A, though in between you may get a lustful brawling saga of passionate involvement, a chronicle of our times, sort of.

You'll have to face it, the endings are the same however you slice it. Don't be deluded by any other endings, they're all fake, either deliberately fake, with malicious intent to deceive, or just motivated by excessive optimism if not by downright sentimentality.

The only authentic ending is the one provided here:

John and Mary die. John and Mary die. John and Mary die.

So much for endings. Beginnings are always more fun. True connoisseurs, however, are known to favor the stretch in between, since it's the hardest to do anything with.

That's about all that can be said for plots, which anyway are just one thing after another, a what and a what and a what.

Now try How and Why.

# Toni Cade Bambara

## 1939–1995

Born Miltona Mirkin Cade on March 25, 1939, in New York City, Toni Cade Bambara was a writer, critic, filmmaker, activist, and feminist. She received her B.A. from Queens College and her master's degree from City College, New York, and continued to study subjects as diverse as mime and linguistics at institutions throughout Europe and America. She published her first short story, "Sweet Town," and received the John Golden Award for fiction in 1961. While teaching at City College from the mid- to late 1960s, Bambara was active in the civil rights movement and in local issues and community organizations. She also contributed to the Black Arts Movement, a group of African American activists, writers, and artists who dedicated themselves to creatively expressing the concerns of the African American community. In 1970, she edited *The Black Woman: An Anthology*, which featured work by Nikki Giovanni, Audre Lorde, Alice Walker, and Paule Marshall, among others. The anthology not only depicts African American lives but also advocates a change in the role of women in contemporary America. She edited a second anthology of African American stories entitled *Tales and Stories for Black Folks* in 1971.

Bambara released her first collection of short stories, *Gorilla, My Love*, in 1972. Much of her writing focuses on African American women who are, at times unwittingly, on a journey of self-discovery both within and outside the black community. She is also the author of *The Sea Birds Are Still Alive: Collected Stories* (1977) and two novels, *The Salt Eaters* (1980) and *If Blessing Comes* (1987). In 1986, Bambara's documentary, *The Bombing of Osage Avenue*, won an Academy Award for Best Documentary. The film focuses on the May 13, 1985, bombing of the headquarters of MOVE, a black activist organization. Diagnosed with colon cancer in 1993, Bambara continued to work on her next documentary, *W. E. B. DuBois: A Biography in Four Voices*. The film was released in 1995, the same year Bambara succumbed to cancer. Two publications were released after Bambara's death: *Deep Sightings and Rescue Missions: Fiction, Essays, and Conversations* in 1995, and *Those Bones Are Not My Child*, a novel about the Atlanta child murders of the early 1980s, edited by Toni Morrison and published in 1999.

---

## The Lesson                                                                                          1971

Back in the days when everyone was old and stupid or young and foolish and me and Sugar were the only ones just right, this lady moved on our block with nappy hair and proper speech and no makeup. And quite naturally we laughed at her, laughed the way we did at the junk man who went about his business like he was some big-time president and his sorry-ass horse his secretary. And we kinda hated her too, hated the way we did the winos who cluttered up our parks and pissed on our handball walls and stank up our hallways and stairs so you couldn't halfway play hide-and-seek without a goddamn gas mask. Miss Moore was her name. The only woman on the block with no first name. And she was black as hell, cept for her feet, which were fish-white and spooky. And she was always planning these boring-ass things for us to do, us being my cousins, mostly, who lived on the block cause we all moved North the same time and to the same apartment then spread out gradual to breathe. And our parents would yank our heads into some kinda shape and crisp up our clothes so we'd be presentable for travel with Miss Moore, who always looked like she was going to church, though she never did. Which is just one of the things the grownups talked about when they talked behind her back like a dog. But when she came calling with some sachet she'd sewed up or some gingerbread she'd made or some book, why then they'd all be too embarrassed to turn her down and we'd get handed over all spruced up. She'd been to college and said it was only right that she should take responsibility for the young ones' education, and she not even related by marriage or blood. So they'd go for it. Specially Aunt Gretchen. She was the main gofer in the family. You got some ole dumb shit foolishness you want somebody to go for, you send for Aunt Gretchen. She been screwed into the go-along for so long, it's a blood-deep natural thing with her. Which is how she got saddled with me and Sugar and Junior in the first place while our mothers were in a la-de-da apartment up the block having a good ole time.

So this one day, Miss Moore rounds us all up at the mailbox and it's purdee hot and she's knockin herself out about arithmetic. And school suppose to let up in summer I heard, but she don't never let up. And the starch in my pinafore scratching the shit outta me and I'm really hating this nappy-head bitch and her goddamn college degree. I'd much rather go to the pool or to the show where it's cool. So me and Sugar leaning on the mailbox being surly, which is a Miss Moore word. And Flyboy checking out what everybody brought for lunch. And Fat Butt already wasting his peanut-butter-and-jelly sandwich like the pig he is. And Junebug punchin on Q.T.'s arm for potato chips. And Rosie Giraffe shifting from one hip to the other waiting for somebody to step on her foot or ask her if she from Georgia so she can kick ass, preferably Mercedes'. And Miss Moore asking us do we know what money is, like we a bunch of retards. I mean real money, she say, like it's only poker chips or monopoly papers we lay on the grocer. So right away I'm tired of this and say so. And would much rather snatch Sugar and go to the Sunset and terrorize the West Indian kids and take their hair ribbons and their money too. And Miss Moore files that remark away for next week's lesson on brotherhood, I can tell. And finally I say we oughta get to the subway cause it's cooler and besides we might meet some cute boys. Sugar done swiped her mama's lipstick, so we ready.

So we heading down the street and she's boring us silly about what things cost and what our parents make and how much goes for rent and how money ain't divided up right in this country. And then she gets to the part about we all poor and live in the slums, which I don't feature. And I'm ready to speak on that, but she steps out in the street and hails two cabs just like that. Then she hustles half the crew in with her and hands me a five-dollar bill and tells me to calculate 10 percent tip for the driver. And we're off. Me and Sugar and Junebug and Flyboy hangin out the window and hollering to everybody, putting lipstick on each other cause Flyboy a faggot anyway, and making farts with our sweaty armpits. But I'm mostly trying to figure how to spend this money. But they all fascinated with the meter ticking and Junebug starts laying bets as to how much it'll read when Flyboy can't hold his breath no more. Then Sugar lays bets as to how much it'll be when we get there. So I'm stuck. Don't nobody want to go for my plan, which is to jump out at the next light and run off to the first bar-b-que we can find. Then the driver tells us to get the hell out cause we there already. And the meter reads eighty-five cents. And I'm stalling to figure out the tip and Sugar say give him a dime. And I decide he don't need it bad as I do, so later for him. But then he tries to take off with Junebug foot still in the door so we talk about his mamma something ferocious. Then we check out that we on Fifth Avenue and everybody dressed up in stockings. One lady in a fur coat, hot as it is. White folks crazy.

"This is the place," Miss Moore say, presenting it to us in the voice she uses at the museum. "Let's look in the windows before we go in."

"Can we steal?" Sugar asks very serious like she's getting the ground rules squared away before she plays. "I beg your pardon," say Miss Moore, and we fall out. So she leads us around the windows of the toy store and me and Sugar screamin, "This is mine, that's mine, I gotta have that, that was made for me, I was born for that," till Big Butt drowns us out.

"Hey, I'm goin to buy that there."

"That there? You don't even know what it is, stupid."

"I do so," he say punchin on Rosie Giraffe. "It's a microscope."

"Whatcha gonna do with a microscope, fool?"

"Look at things."

"Like what, Ronald?" ask Miss Moore. And Big Butt ain't got the first notion. So here go Miss Moore gabbing about the thousands of bacteria in a drop of water and the somethinorother in a speck of blood and the million and one living things in the air around us is invisible to the naked eye. And what she say that for? Junebug go to town on that "naked" and we rolling. Then Miss Moore ask what it cost. So we all jam into the window smudgin it up and the price tag say $300. So then she ask how long'd take for Big Butt and Junebug to save up their allowances. "Too long," I say. "Yeh," adds Sugar, "outgrown it by that time." And Miss Moore say no, you never outgrow learning instruments. "Why, even medical students and interns and," blah, blah, blah. And we ready to choke Big Butt for bringing it up in the first damn place.

"This here costs four hundred eighty dollars," say Rosie Giraffe. So we pile up all over her to see what she pointin out. My eyes tell me it's a chunk of glass cracked with something heavy, and different-color inks dripped into the splits, then the whole thing put into a oven or something. But for $480 it don't make sense.

"That's a paperweight made of semi-precious stones fused together under tremendous pressure," she explains slowly, with her hands doing the mining and all the factory work.

"So what's a paperweight?" ask Rosie Giraffe.

"To weigh paper with, dumbbell," say Flyboy, the wise man from the East.

"Not exactly," say Miss Moore, which is what she say when you warm or way off too. "It's to weigh paper down so it won't scatter and make your desk untidy." So right away me and Sugar curtsy to each other and then to Mercedes who is more the tidy type.

"We don't keep paper on top of the desk in my class," say Junebug, figuring Miss Moore crazy or lyin one.

"At home, then," she say. "Don't you have a calendar and a pencil case and blotter and a letter-opener on your desk at home where you do your homework?" And she know damn well what our homes look like cause she nosys around in them every chance she gets.

"I don't even have a desk," say Junebug. "Do we?"

"No. And I don't get no homework neither," says Big Butt.

"And I don't even have a home," says Flyboy like he do at school to keep the white folks off his back and sorry for him. Send this poor kid to camp posters, is his specialty.

"I do," says Mercedes. "I have a box of stationery on my desk and a picture of my cat. My godmother bought the stationery and the desk. There's a big rose on each sheet and the envelopes smell like roses."

"Who wants to know about your smelly-ass stationery," say Rosie Giraffe fore I can get my two cents in.

"It's important to have a work area all your own so that . . ."

"Will you look at this sailboat, please," say Flyboy, cutting her off and pointin to the thing like it was his. So once again we tumble all over each other to gaze at this magnificent thing in the toy store which is just big enough to maybe sail two kittens across the pond if you strap them to the posts tight. We all start reciting the price tag like we in assembly. "Handcrafted sailboat of fiberglass at one thousand one hundred ninety-five dollars."

"Unbelievable," I hear myself say and am really stunned. I read it again for myself just in case the group recitation put me in a trance. Same thing. For some reason this pisses me off. We look at Miss Moore and she lookin at us, waiting for I dunno what.

"Who'd pay all that when you can buy a sailboat set for a quarter at Pop's, a tube of glue for a dime, and a ball of string for eight cents? It must have a motor and a whole lot else besides," I say. "My sailboat cost me about fifty cents."

"But will it take water?" say Mercedes with her smart ass.

"Took mine to Alley Pond Park once," say Flyboy. "String broke. Lost it. Pity."

"Sailed mine in Central Park and it keeled over and sank. Had to ask my father for another dollar."

"And you got the strap," laugh Big Butt. "The jerk didn't even have a string on it. My old man wailed on his behind."

Little Q.T. was staring hard at the sailboat and you could see he wanted it bad. But he too little and somebody'd just take it from him. So what the hell. "This boat for kids, Miss Moore?"

"Parents silly to buy something like that just to get all broke up," say Rosie Giraffe.

"That much money it should last forever," I figure.

"My father'd buy it for me if I wanted it."

"Your father, my ass," say Rosie Giraffe getting a chance to finally push Mercedes.

"Must be rich people shop here," say Q.T.

"You are a very bright boy," say Flyboy. "What was your first clue?" And he rap him on the head with back of his knuckles, since Q.T. the only one he could get away with. Though Q.T. liable to come up behind you years later and get his licks in when you half expect it.

"What I want to know is," I says to Miss Moore though I never talk to her, I wouldn't give the bitch that satisfaction, "is how much a real boat costs? I figure a thousand'd get you a yacht any day."

"Why don't you check that out," she says, "and report back to the group?" Which really pains my ass. If you gonna mess up a perfectly good swim day least you could do is have some answers. "Let's go in," she say like she got something up her sleeve. Only she don't lead the way. So me and Sugar turn the corner to where the entrance is, but when we get there I kinda hang back. Not that I'm scared, what's there to be afraid of, just a toy store. But I feel funny, shame. But what I got to be shamed about? Got as much right to go in as anybody. But somehow I can't seem to get hold of the door, so I step away from Sugar to lead. But she hangs back too. And I look at her and she looks at me and this is ridiculous. I mean, damn, I have never ever been shy about doing nothing or going nowhere. But then Mercedes steps up and then Rosie Giraffe and Big Butt crowd in behind and shove, and next thing we all stuffed into the doorway with only Mercedes squeezing past us, smoothing out her jumper and walking right down the aisle. Then the rest of us tumble in like a glued-together jigsaw done all wrong. And people lookin at us. And it's like the time me and Sugar crashed into the Catholic church on a dare. But once we got in there and everything so hushed and holy and the candles and the bowin and the handkerchiefs on all the drooping heads, I just couldn't go through with the plan. Which was for me to run up to the altar and do a tap dance while Sugar played the nose flute and messed around in the holy water. And Sugar kept given me the elbow. Then later teased me so bad I tied her up in the shower and turned it on and locked her in. And she'd be there till this day if Aunt Gretchen hadn't finally figured I was lyin about the boarder takin a shower.

Same thing in the store. We all walkin on tiptoe and hardly touchin the games and puzzles and things. And I watched Miss Moore who is steady watchin us like she waitin for a sign. Like Mama Drewery watches the sky and sniffs the air and takes note of just how much slant is in the bird formation. Then me and Sugar bump smack into each other, so busy gazing at the toys, 'specially the sailboat. But we don't laugh and go into our fat-lady bump-stomach routine. We just stare at that price tag. Then Sugar run a finger over the whole boat. And I'm jealous and want to hit her. Maybe not her, but I sure want to punch somebody in the mouth.

"Watcha bring us here for, Miss Moore?"

"You sound angry, Sylvia. Are you mad about something?" Givin me one of them grins like she tellin a grown-up joke that never turns out to be funny. And she's lookin very closely at me like maybe she plannin to do my portrait from memory. I'm mad, but I won't give her that satisfaction. So I slouch around the store bein very bored and say, "Let's go."

Me and Sugar at the back of the train watchin the tracks whizzin by large then small then getting gobbled up in the dark. I'm thinkin about this tricky toy I saw in the store. A clown that somersaults on a bar then does chin-ups just cause you yank lightly at his leg. Cost $35. I could see me askin my mother for a $35 birthday clown. "You wanna who that costs what?" she'd say, cocking her head to the side to get a better view of the hole in my head. Thirty-five dollars could buy new bunk beds for Junior and Gretchen's boy. Thirty-five dollars and the whole household could go visit Granddaddy Nelson in the country. Thirty-five dollars would pay for the rent and the piano bill too. Who are these people that spend that much for performing clowns and $1000 for toy sailboats? What kinda work they do and how they live and how come we ain't in on it? Where we are is who we are, Miss Moore always pointin out. But it don't necessarily have to be that way, she always adds then waits for somebody to say that poor people have to wake up and demand their share of the pie and don't none of us know what kind of pie she talking about in the first damn place. But she ain't so smart cause I still got her four dollars from the taxi and she sure ain't gettin it. Messin up my day with this shit. Sugar nudges me in my pocket and winks.

Miss Moore lines us up in front of the mailbox where we started from, seem like years ago, and I got a headache for thinkin so hard. And we lean all over each other so we can hold up under the draggy-ass lecture she always finishes us off with at the end before we thank her for borin us to tears. But she just looks at us like she readin tea leaves. Finally she say, "Well, what did you think of F. A. O. Schwarz?"

Rosie Giraffe mumbles, "White folks crazy."

"I'd like to go there again when I get my birthday money," says Mercedes, and we shove her out the pack so she has to lean on the mailbox by herself.

"I'd like a shower. Tiring day," say Flyboy.

Then Sugar surprises me by sayin, "You know, Miss Moore, I don't think all of us here put together eat in a year what that sailboat costs." And Miss Moore lights up like somebody goosed her. "And?" she say, urging Sugar on. Only I'm standin on her foot so she don't continue.

"Imagine for a minute what kind of society it is in which some people can spend on a toy what it would cost to feed a family of six or seven. What do you think?"

"I think," say Sugar pushing me off her feet like she never done before, cause I whip her ass in a minute, "that this is not much of a democracy if you ask me. Equal chance to pursue happiness means an equal crack at the dough, don't it?" Miss Moore is besides herself and I am disgusted with Sugar's treachery. So I stand on her foot one more time to see if she'll shove me. She shuts up, and Miss Moore looks at me, sorrowfully I'm thinkin. And somethin weird is going on, I can feel it in my chest.

"Anybody else learn anything today?" lookin dead at me. I walk away and Sugar has to run to catch up and don't even seem to notice when I shrug her arm off my shoulder.

"Well, we got four dollars anyway," she says.

"Uh, hunh."

"We could go to Hascombs and get a half a chocolate layer and then go to the Sunset and still have plenty money for potato chips and ice cream sodas."

"Uh hunh."

"Race you to Hascombs," she say.

We start down the block and she gets ahead which is O.K. by me cause I'm going to the West End and then over to the Drive to think this day through. She can run if she want to and even run faster. But ain't nobody gonna beat me at nuthin.

# T. C. Boyle

## (B. 1948)

T. C. Boyle was first interested in becoming a musician, but a poor audition for his college's music program led him to writing. However, Boyle feels that music has become an integral part of his work: "Somehow, the sense of rhythm has infected my work. Anyone who hears me read aloud will understand the importance to me of rhythm." He received his M.F.A. from the University of Iowa Writers' Workshop in 1974 and married Karen Kvashay in the same year. In 1977, he received his Ph.D. in nineteenth-century British literature from Iowa University. His works include *Descent of Man* (1979), *Budding Prospects* (1984), *World's End* (1987), *If the River Was Whiskey* (1989), *The Tortilla Curtain* (1995), *Riven Rock* (1998), *A Friend of the Earth* (2000), *After the Plague* (2001), *Drop City* (2003), and *The Inner Circle* (2004). Boyle has received numerous awards and since 1986 has been a professor of English at the University of Southern California. He combines surrealism, satire, and wit in stories about pop culture, materialism, and the hopelessness of humanity.

## Sinking House                                                                                        1987

When Monty's last breath caught somewhere in the back of his throat with a sound like the tired wheeze of an old screen door, the first thing she did was turn on the water. She leaned over him a minute to make sure, then she wiped her hands on her dress and shuffled into the kitchen. Her fingers trembled as she jerked at the lever and felt the water surge against the porcelain. Steam rose in her face; a glitter of liquid leapt for the drain. Croak, that's what they called it. Now she knew why. She left the faucet running in the kitchen and crossed the gloomy expanse of the living room, swung down the hallway to the guest bedroom, and turned on both taps in the bathroom there. It was almost as an afterthought that she decided to fill the tub too.

For a long while she sat in the leather armchair in the living room. The sound of running water—pure, baptismal, as uncomplicated as the murmur of a brook in Vermont or a toilet at the Waldorf—soothed her. It trickled and trilled, burbling from either side of the house and driving down the terrible silence that crouched in the bedroom over the lifeless form of her husband.

The afternoon was gone and the sun plunging into the canopy of the big eucalyptus behind the Finkelsteins' when she finally pushed herself up from the chair. Head down, arms moving stiffly at her sides, she scuffed out the back door, crossed the patio, and bent to turn on the sprinklers. They sputtered and spat—not enough pressure, that much she understood—but finally came to life in halfhearted umbrellas of mist. She left the hose trickling in the rose garden, then went back into the house, passed through the living room, the kitchen, the master bedroom—not even a glance for Monty, no: she wouldn't look at him, not yet—and on into the master bath. The taps were weak, barely a trickle, but she left them on anyway, then flushed the toilet and pinned down the float with the brick Monty had used as a doorstop. And then finally, so weary she could barely lift her arms, she leaned into the stall and flipped on the shower.

Two weeks after the ambulance came for the old man next door, Meg Terwilliger was doing her stretching exercises on the prayer rug in the sunroom, a menthol cigarette glowing in the ashtray on the floor beside her, the new CD by Sandee and the Sharks thumping out of the big speakers in the corners. Meg was twenty-three, with the fine bones and haunted eyes of a poster child. She wore her black hair cut close at the temples, long in front, and she used a sheeny black eyeshadow to bring out the hunger in her eyes. In half an hour she'd have to pick up Tiffany at nursery school, drop off the dog at the veterinarian's, take Sonny's shirts to the cleaner's, buy a pound and a half of thresher shark, cilantro, and flour tortillas at the market, and start the burritos for supper. But now, she was stretching.

She took a deep drag on the cigarette, tugged at her right foot, and brought it up snug against her buttocks. After a moment she released it and drew back her left foot in its place. One palm flat on the floor, her head bobbing vaguely to the beat of the music, she did half a dozen repetitions, then paused to relight her cigarette. It wasn't until she turned over to do her straight-leg lifts that she noticed the dampness in the rug.

Puzzled, she rose to her knees and reached behind her to rub at the twin wet spots on the seat of her sweats. She lifted the corner of the rug, suspecting the dog, but there was no odor of urine. Looking closer, she saw that the concrete floor was a shade darker beneath the rug, as if it were bleeding moisture as it sometimes did in the winter. But this wasn't winter, this was high summer in Los Angeles and it hadn't rained for months. Cursing Sonny—he'd promised her ceramic tile and though she'd run all over town to get the best price on a nice Italian floral pattern, he still hadn't found the time to go look at it—she shot back the sliding door and stepped into the yard to investigate.

Immediately, she felt the Bermuda grass squelch beneath the soles of her aerobic shoes. She hadn't taken three strides—the sun in her face, Queenie yapping frantically from the fenced-in pool area—and her feet were wet. Had Sonny left the hose running? Or Tiffany? She slogged across the lawn, the pastel Reeboks spattered with wet, and checked the hose. It was innocently coiled on its tender, the tap firmly shut. Queenie's yapping went up an octave. The heat—it must have been ninety-five, a hundred—made her feel faint. She gazed up into the cloudless sky, then bent to check each of the sprinklers in succession.

She was poking around in the welter of bushes along the fence, looking for an errant sprinkler, when she thought of the old lady next door—Muriel, wasn't that her name? What with her husband dying and all, maybe she'd left the hose running and forgotten all about it. Meg rose on her tiptoes to peer over the redwood fence that separated her yard from the neighbors' and found herself looking into a glistening, sunstruck garden, with banks of impatiens, bird of paradise, oleander, and loquat, roses in half a dozen shades. The sprinklers were on and the hose was running. For a long moment Meg stood there, mesmerized by the play of light through the drifting fans of water; she was wondering what it would be like to be old, thinking of how it would be if Sonny died and Tiffany were grown up and gone. She'd probably forget to turn off the sprinklers too.

The moment passed. The heat was deadening, the dog hysterical. Meg knew she would have to do something about the sodden yard and wet floor in the sunroom, but she dreaded facing the old woman. What would she say—I'm sorry your husband died but could you turn off the sprinklers? She was thinking maybe she'd phone—or wait till Sonny got home and let him handle it—when she stepped back from the fence and sank to her ankles in mud.

When the doorbell rang, Muriel was staring absently at the cover of an old *National Geographic* which lay beneath a patina of dust on the coffee table. The cover photo showed the beige and yellow sands of some distant desert, rippled to the horizon with corrugations that might have been waves on a barren sea. Monty was dead and buried. She wasn't eating much. Or sleeping much either. The sympathy cards sat unopened on the table in the kitchen, where the tap overflowed the sink and water plunged to the floor with a pertinacity that was like a redemption. When it was quiet—in the early morning or late at night—she could distinguish the separate taps, each with its own voice and rhythm, as they dripped and trickled from the far corners of the house. In those suspended hours she could make out the comforting gurgle of the toilet in the guest room, the musical wash of the tub as water cascaded over the lip of its porcelain dam, the quickening rush of the stream in the hallway as it shot like a miniature Niagara down the chasm of the floor vent . . . she could hear the drip in the master bedroom, the distant hiss of a shower, and the sweet eternal sizzle of the sprinklers on the back lawn.

But now she heard the doorbell.

Wearily, gritting her teeth against the pain in her lower legs and the damp lingering ache of her feet, she pushed herself up from the chair and sloshed her way to the door. The carpet was black with water, soaked through like a sponge—and in a tidy corner of her mind she regretted it—but most of the runoff was finding its way to the heating vents and the gaps in the corners where Monty had miscalculated the angle of the baseboard. She heard it dripping somewhere beneath the house and for a moment pictured the water lying dark and still in a shadowy lagoon that held the leaking ship of the house poised on its trembling surface. The doorbell sounded again. "All right, all right," she muttered, "I'm coming."

A girl with dark circles round her eyes stood on the doorstep. She looked vaguely familiar, and for a moment Muriel thought she recognized her from a TV program about a streetwalker who rises up to kill her pimp and liberate all the other leather-clad, black-eyed streetwalkers of the neighborhood, but then the girl spoke and Muriel realized her mistake. "Hi," the girl said, and Muriel saw that her shoes were black with mud, "I'm your neighbor? Meg Terwilliger?"

Muriel was listening to the bathroom sink. She said nothing. The girl looked down at her muddy shoes. "I, uh, just wanted to tell you that we're, uh—Sonny and I, I mean—he's my husband?—we're sorry about your trouble and all, but I wondered if you knew your sprinklers were on out back?"

Muriel attempted a smile—surely a smile was appropriate at this juncture, wasn't it?—but managed only to lift her upper lip back from her teeth in a sort of wince or grimace.

The girl was noticing the rug now, and Muriel's sodden slippers. She looked baffled, perhaps even a little frightened. And young. So young. Muriel had had a young friend once, a girl from the community college who used to come to the house before Monty got sick. She had a tape recorder, and she would ask them questions about their childhood, about the days when the San Fernando Valley was dirt roads and orange groves. Oral history, she called it. "It's all right," Muriel said, trying to reassure her.

"I just—is it a plumbing problem?" the girl said, backing away from the door. "Sonny . . ." she said, but didn't finish the thought. She ducked her head and retreated down the steps but when she reached the walk she wheeled around. "I mean you really ought to see about the sprinklers," she blurted, "the whole place is soaked, my sunroom and everything—"

"It's all right," Muriel repeated, and then the girl was gone and she shut the door.

"She's nuts, she is. Really. I mean she's out of her gourd."

Meg was searing chunks of thresher shark in a pan with green chilies, sweet red pepper, onion, and cilantro. Sonny, who was twenty-eight and so intoxicated by real estate he had to forgo the morning paper till he got home at night, was slumped in the breakfast nook with a vodka tonic and the sports pages. His white-blond hair was cut fashionably, in what might once have been called a flattop, though it was thinning, and his open, appealing face, with its boyish look, had begun to show signs of wear, particularly around the eyes, where years of escrow had taken their toll. Tiffany was in her room, playing quietly with a pair of six-inch dolls that had cost sixty-five dollars each.

"Who?" Sonny murmured, tugging unconsciously at the gold chain he wore around his neck.

"Muriel. The old lady next door. Haven't you heard a thing I've been saying?" With an angry snap of her wrist, Meg cut the heat beneath the saucepan and clapped a lid over it. "The floor in the sunroom is flooded, for god's sake," she said, stalking across the kitchen in her bare feet till she stood poised over him. "The rug is ruined. Or almost is. And the yard—"

Sonny slapped the paper down on the table. "All right! Just let me relax a minute, will you?"

She put on her pleading look. It was a look compounded of pouty lips, tousled hair, and those inevitable eyes, and it always had its effect on him. "One minute," she murmured. "That's all it'll take. I just want you to see the backyard."

She took him by the hand and led him through the living room to the sunroom, where he stood a moment contemplating the damp spot on the concrete floor. She was surprised herself at how the spot had grown—it was three times what it had been that afternoon, and it seemed to have sprouted wings and legs like an enormous Rorshach. She pictured a butterfly. Or no, a hovering crow or bat. She wondered what Muriel would have made of it.

Outside, she let out a little yelp of disgust—all the earthworms in the yard had crawled up on the step to die. And the lawn wasn't merely spongy now, it was soaked through, puddled like a swamp. "Jesus Christ," Sonny muttered, sinking in his wing-tips. He cakewalked across the yard to where the fence had begun to sag, the post leaning drunkenly, the slats bowed. "Will you look at this?" he shouted over his shoulder. Squeamish about the worms, Meg stood at the door to the sunroom. "The goddamn fence is falling down!"

He stood there a moment, water seeping into his shoes, a look of stupefaction on his face. Meg recognized the look. It stole over his features in moments of extremity, as when he tore open the phone bill to discover mysterious twenty-dollar calls to Billings, Montana, and Greenleaf, Mississippi, or when his buyer called on the day escrow was to close to tell him he'd assaulted the seller and wondered if Sonny had five hundred dollars for bail. These occasions always took him by surprise. He was shocked anew each time the crisply surveyed, neatly kept world he so cherished rose up to confront him with all its essential sloppiness, irrationality, and bad business sense. Meg watched the look of disbelief turn to one of injured rage. She followed him through the house, up the walk, and into Muriel's yard, where he stalked up to the front door and pounded like the Gestapo.

There was no response.

"Son of a bitch," he spat, turning to glare over his shoulder at her as if it were her fault or something. From inside they could hear the drama of running water, a drip and gurgle, a sough and hiss. Sonny turned back to the door, hammering his fist against it till Meg swore she could see the panels jump.

It frightened her, this sudden rage. Sure, there was a problem here and she was glad he was taking care of it, but did he have to get violent, did he have to get crazy? "You don't have to beat her door down," she called, focusing on the swell of his shoulder and the hammer of his fist as it rose and fell in savage rhythm. "Sonny, come on. It's only water, for god's sake."

"Only?" he snarled, spinning round to face her. "You saw the fence—next thing you know the foundation'll shift on us. The whole damn house—" He never finished. The look on her face told him that Muriel had opened the door.

Muriel was wearing the same faded blue housecoat she'd had on earlier, and the same wet slippers. Short, heavyset, so big in front it seemed as if she were about to topple over, she clung to the doorframe and peered up at Sonny out of a stony face. Meg watched as Sonny jerked round to confront her and then stopped cold when he got a look at the interior of the house. The plaster walls were stained now, drinking up the wet in long jagged fingers that clawed toward the ceiling, and a dribble of coffee-colored liquid began to seep across the doorstep and puddle at Sonny's feet. The sound of rushing water was unmistakable, even from where Meg was standing. "Yes?" Muriel said, the voice withered in her throat. "Can I help you?"

It took Sonny a minute—Meg could see it in his eyes: this was more than he could handle, willful destruction of a domicile, every tap in the place on full, the floors warped, plaster ruined—but then he recovered himself. "The water," he said. "You—our fence—I mean you can't, you've got to stop this—"

The old woman drew herself up, clutching the belt of her housedress till her knuckles bulged with the tension. She looked first at Meg, still planted in the corner of the yard, and then turned to Sonny. "Water?" she said. "What water?"

The young man at the door reminded her, in a way, of Monty. Something about the eyes or the set of the ears—or maybe it was the crisp high cut of the sideburns . . . Of course, most young men reminded her of Monty. The Monty of fifty years ago, that is. The Monty who'd opened up the world to her over the shift lever of his Model-A Ford, not the crabbed and abrasive old man who called her bonehead and dildo and cuffed her like a dog. Monty. When the stroke brought him down, she was almost glad. She saw him pinned beneath his tubes in the hospital and something stirred in her; she brought him home and changed his bedpan, peered into the vaults of his eyes, fed him Gerber's like the baby she'd never had, and she knew it was over. Fifty years. No more drunken rages, no more pans flung against the wall, never again his sour flesh pressed to hers. She was on top now.

The second young man—he was a Mexican, short, stocky, with a mustache so thin it could have been penciled on and wicked little red-flecked eyes—also reminded her of Monty. Not so much in the way he looked as in the way he held himself, the way he swaggered and puffed out his chest. And the uniform too, of course. Monty had worn a uniform during the war.

"Mrs. Burgess?" the Mexican asked.

Muriel stood at the open door. It was dusk, the heat cut as if there was a thermostat in the sky. She'd been sitting in the dark. The electricity had gone out on her—something to do with the water and the wires. She nodded her head in response to the policeman's question.

"We've had a complaint," he said.

Little piggy eyes. A complaint. *We've had a complaint.* He wasn't fooling her, not for a minute. She knew what they wanted, the police, the girl next door, and the boy she was married to—they wanted to bring Monty back. Prop him up against the bed-frame, stick his legs back under him, put the bellow back in his voice. Oh, no, they weren't fooling her.

She followed the policeman around the darkened house as he went from faucet to faucet, sink to tub to shower. He firmly twisted each of the taps closed and drained the basins, then crossed to the patio to kill the sprinklers and the hose too. "Are you all right?" he kept asking. "Are you all right?"

She had to hold her chin in her palm to keep her lips from trembling. "If you mean am I in possession of my faculties, yes, I am, thank you. I am all right."

They were back at the front door now. He leaned nonchalantly against the door-frame and dropped his voice to a confidential whisper. "So what's this with the water then?"

She wouldn't answer him. She knew her rights. What business was it of his, or anybody's, what she did with her own taps and her own sprinklers? She could pay the water bill. Had paid it, in fact. Eleven hundred dollars' worth. She watched his eyes and shrugged.

"Next of kin?" he asked. "Daughter? Son? Anybody we can call?"

Now her lips held. She shook her head.

He gave it a moment, then let out a sigh. "Okay," he said, speaking slowly and with exaggerated emphasis, as if he were talking to a child, "I'm going now. You leave the water alone—wash your face, brush your teeth, do the dishes. But no more of this." He swaggered back from her, fingering his belt, his holster, the dead weight of his nightstick. "One more complaint and we'll have to take you into custody for your own good. You're endangering yourself and the neighbors too. Understand?"

Smile, she told herself, smile. "Oh yes," she said softly. "Yes, I understand."

He held her eyes a moment, threatening her—just like Monty used to do, just like Monty—and then he was gone.

She stood there on the doorstep a long while, the night deepening around her. She listened to the cowbirds, the wild parakeets that nested in the Murtaughs' palm, the whoosh of traffic from the distant freeway. After a while, she sat on the step. Be-hind her, the house was silent: no faucet dripped, no sprinkler hissed, no toilet gur-gled. It was horrible. Insupportable. In the pit of that dry silence she could hear him, Monty, treading the buckled floors, pouring himself another vodka, cursing her in a voice like sandpaper.

She couldn't go back in there. Not tonight. The place was deadly, contaminated, sick as the grave—after all was said and done, it just wasn't clean enough. If the rest of it was a mystery—oral history, fifty years of Monty, the girl with the blackened eyes—that much she understood.

Meg was watering the cane plant in the living room when the police cruiser came for the old lady next door. The police had been there the night before and Sonny had stood out front with his arms folded while the officer shut down Muriel's taps and sprinklers. "I guess that's that," he said, coming up the walk in the oversized Hawaiian shirt she'd given him for Father's Day. But in the morning, the sprinklers were on again and Sonny called the local substation three times before he left for work. She's crazy, he'd hollered into the phone, irresponsible, a threat to herself and the community. He had a four-year-old daughter to worry about, for christ's sake. A dog. A wife. His fence was falling down. Did they have any idea what that amount of water was going to do to the substrata beneath the house?

Now the police were back. The patrol car stretched across the window and slid silently into the driveway next door. Meg set down the watering can. She was wearing her Fila sweats and a new pair of Nikes and her hair was tied back in a red scarf. She'd dropped Tiffany off at nursery school, but she had the watering and her stretching exercises to do and a pasta salad to make before she picked up Queenie at the vet's. Still, she went directly to the front door and then out onto the walk.

The police—it took her a minute to realize that the shorter of the two was a woman—were on Muriel's front porch, looking stiff and uncertain in their razor-creased uniforms. The man knocked first—once, twice, three times. Nothing happened. Then the woman knocked. Still nothing. Meg folded her arms and waited. After a minute, the man went around to the side gate and let himself into the yard. Meg heard the sprinklers die with a wheeze, and then the officer was back, his shoes heavy with mud.

Again he thumped at the door, much more violently now, and Meg thought of Sonny. "Open up," the woman called in a breathy contralto she tried unsuccessfully to deepen, "police."

It was then that Meg saw her, Muriel, at the bay window on the near side of the door. "Look," she shouted before she knew what she was saying, "she's there, there in the window!"

The male officer—he had a mustache and pale, fine hair like Sonny's—leaned out over the railing and gestured impatiently at the figure behind the window. "Police," he growled. "Open the door." Muriel never moved. "All right," he grunted, cursing under his breath, "all right," and he put his shoulder to the door. There was nothing to it. The frame splintered, water dribbled out, and both officers disappeared into the house.

Meg waited. She had things to do, yes, but she waited anyway, bending to pull the odd dandelion the gardener had missed, trying to look busy. The police were in there an awful long time—twenty minutes, half an hour—and then the woman appeared in the doorway with Muriel.

Muriel seemed heavier than ever, her face pouchy, arms swollen. She was wearing white sandals on her old splayed feet, a shapeless print dress, and a white straw hat that looked as if it had been dug out of a box in the attic. The woman had her by the arm; the man loomed behind her with a suitcase. Down the steps and up the walk, she never turned her head. But then, just as the policewoman was helping her into the backseat of the patrol car, Muriel swung round as if to take one last look at her house. But it wasn't the house she was looking at: it was Meg.

The morning gave way to the heat of afternoon. Meg finished the watering, made the pasta salad—bow-tie twists, fresh salmon, black olives, and pine nuts—ran her errands, picked up Tiffany, and put her down for a nap. Somehow, though, she just couldn't get Muriel out of her head. The old lady had stared at her for five seconds maybe, and then the policewoman was coaxing her into the car. Meg had felt like sinking into the ground. But then she realized that Muriel's look wasn't vengeful at all—it was just sad. It was a look that said this is what it comes to. Fifty years and this is what it comes to.

The backyard was an inferno, the sun poised directly overhead. Queenie, defleaed, shampooed, and with her toenails clipped, was stretched out asleep in the shade beside the pool. It was quiet. Even the birds were still. Meg took off her Nikes and walked barefoot through the sopping grass to the fence, or what was left of it. The post had buckled overnight, canting the whole business into Muriel's yard. Meg never hesitated. She sprang up onto the plane of the slats and dropped to the grass on the other side.

Her feet sank in the mud, the earth like pudding, like chocolate pudding, and as she lifted her feet to move toward the house the tracks she left behind her slowly filled with water. The patio was an island. She crossed it, dodging potted plants and wicker furniture, and tried the back door; finding it locked, she moved to the window, shaded her face with her hands, and peered in. The sight made her catch her breath. The plaster was crumbling, wallpaper peeling, the rug and floors ruined: she knew it was bad, but this was crazy, this was suicide.

Grief, that's what it was. Or was it? And then she was thinking of Sonny again—what if he was dead and she was old like Muriel? She wouldn't be so fat, of course, but maybe like one of those thin and elegant old ladies in Palm Springs, the ones who'd done their stretching all their lives. Or what if she wasn't an old lady at all—the thought swooped down on her like a bird out of the sky—what if Sonny was in a car wreck or something? It could happen.

She stood there gazing in on the mess through her own wavering reflection. One moment she saw the wreckage of the old lady's life, the next the fine mouth and expressive eyes everyone commented on. After a while, she turned away from the window and looked out on the yard as Muriel must have seen it. There were the roses, gorged with water and flowering madly, the impatiens, rigid as sticks, oleander drowning in their own yellowed leaves—and there, poking innocuously from the bushes at the far corner of the patio, was the steel wand that controlled the sprinklers. Handle, neck, prongs: it was just like theirs.

And then it came to her. She'd turn them on—the sprinklers—just for a minute, to see what it felt like. She wouldn't leave them on long—it could threaten the whole foundation of her house.

That much she understood.

# Kate Braverman

(B. 1950)

A native of Los Angeles, Kate Braverman has published several collections of poetry and stories, such as *Milkrun* (1977), *Lullaby for Sinners* (1980), *Hurricane Warnings* (1987), *Postcards from August* (1990), and *Squandering the Blue* (1990). Her novels include *Lithium for Medea* (1979), *Palm Latitudes* (1988), and *Wonders of the West* (1993). Her female characters often confront both hope and self-destruction, both revelation and loss, in their meandering quests for truth and meaning. In 1992 she received the O. Henry Award for her short story "Tall Tales from the Mekong Delta" (1990). Her most recent book, *The Incantation of Frida K.*, was published in 2002.

## Hour of the Fathers                                                    1997

It was late spring, just after my twelfth birthday, when I discovered I had a father. It had never occurred to me to wonder about the specific configuration of who or what he might be. I assumed there had been some complicated natural phenomenon, like a lightning storm or a strange disruption at sea when everything glows. It had the sense of prehistoric ritual. But there had been no residue. My mother and I were always untouched, without tarnish, in the uninterrupted pale green state of grace that was my childhood.

Then it was May, and suddenly I had a father who had one leg, a father who was Jewish, who had been in the war in Vietnam. A father with a name. Jay. A name and no job.

"He never has a job," my mother said. She seemed cheerful. "He's what we call the walking wounded. It's become his profession."

We were driving to the Greyhound bus station to have dinner with my father. He had come down from Seattle, where it was too cold. He had a three-hour layover. Then he was going to Houston. It was part of the loop he was taking back to Miami.

Suddenly the world was littered with cities where I had never expected them. I repeated their names, Seattle and Miami. They glistened in the warm air like individual orbs, miniature artificial worlds that could be strung like beads. I had heard about the Wandering Jew. Perhaps this was why my father was roaming between cities. Perhaps it was genetic. It might be in my blood, too.

I wanted to remember everything about the drive to the bus station. I wanted to impart the images directly into my cells and fibers, into the molecular level I imagined then as being a kind of web, a mesh, a sort of tiny aviary where small stark birds flew. I wanted to chart the precise way I felt in the manner a fever is noted by points and a red graph. I wanted to measure my father-hours the way a river is drawn in a blue curve. I wanted to know the actual dimensions, to make calculations. It must have been in a slow spreading season when I believed, absolutely, in the power of miles and pints and decimal points, the ruler and protractor. It was when I believed in straight A's.

It already seemed, by the spring of my twelfth birthday, that the definitive moments of my life had come when I wasn't looking, when I wasn't entirely prepared. My first period had been like that, even though I felt it coming, a sort of turning of an invisible coil inside that felt like wire. I had been carrying pads in my backpack for months, but the actual onset of the flow, the trickle of blood that slid down my thigh and farther, streaking my leg to my thick white gym sock, had been a complete surprise, a paralyzing startlement. I had stood on the school-ground pavement, feeling confused by the afternoon sun, noticing, through a series of odd blisters like pinpoints of white explosions, how square and flat the playground was, how it was entirely surrounded by a high fence. It was curious that I had not observed it this way before.

That had happened the previous winter, when I had promised to be alert and somehow hadn't. I had missed the winter streets, how they seemed unusually greened, darkened, mossy, somehow bloated and rotting. There was a sense of the streets as so many wet amputations, stumps where there had been boulevards. And I realized later this was the first intuition I had of my father preparing to enter my life.

"There are the walking wounded," my mother said, as she drove, "and there are those that crawl and drool. Be prepared."

We were pointed inland on a sequence of purple boulevards and I knew it was a definitive moment. It was coming up on the horizon. It would have a name in neon and a parking lot. This time it wouldn't fail me the way the other events of my life had, like becoming a woman. And before that, leaving the apartment on Nightingale Lane and moving to the house in Santa Monica, how I had somehow forgotten to take a picture of my bedroom, even though I had a camera and months to pack. I had somehow failed to turn around as we left the driveway, missed my chance to imprint the building and the way my bedroom windows faced directly into a patch of eucalyptus and orange trees, how the air was always stinging with citrus. There must be a way to take a picture of that, the textures that reside without structure in air.

I sensed that something would intercede on the day we moved. There would be an inexplicable circumstance, a sudden blizzard, a message delivered in person, some astral aberration. There would be a reason why it was obvious that we should not go. But at precisely 9:30 the moving truck came, just as my mother had ordained. And I realized there was a rule of trucks and clocks. This was a kind of mesh, too, a secret aviary, a silent mechanism that also ran the world. The truck I had willed not to come drove up to the curb, we got in our car, and I forgot to look back.

Now, as we drove to meet my father for dinner, I could see there was a greasy quality to the sunlight. It was nearly June, the month of the cold mornings that spoiled every summer. It was always like that, the haze that didn't burn off until four in the afternoon and by then it was too late to go swimming. There were years when I only wore my bathing suit once or twice. That was before my mother began to take me to Maui and Kauai.

We were driving inland and the haze turned thick and heavy. It hung on the leaves that weren't glistening, really, as much as they were coated and dazed. Jacaranda was blossoming everywhere, with its uniformly excessive purple. It was a color I thought I could apply the word *tawdry* to. It was one of my special summer-project extra-credit words. And I realized that I had never really observed jacaranda before. The afternoon was thick with a vague fragrance I decided might be the way dog urine is in the tropics. It was an odor of decay and lamplight, of something getting tarnished on the inside where soap won't remove it.

I explained this to my mother, my sense of the afternoon rotting, and she laughed. "It's definitely spoiled," she agreed. "Ruined, all right. Bad to the bone. Jay will love it."

The jarcaranda was incredibly beautiful, especially when it spilled into the gutters like a kind of purple river, hardly moving, lazy and stalled. It seemed to be strangling on itself. I wondered if I had invented a paradox, how something could be exquisite and simultaneously torn and suffocating.

And it was slippery. It stained the cars, everyone complained, even Moe. He was eighty-three years old, and every May and June he stood on the sidewalk, sweeping petals, muttering. But I had forgotten to turn back that day on Nightingale Lane, and I knew even then, without asking my mother, that I would never see Moe again. He was too old, and Nightingale Lane was too far away. It was across the entire city, which was a sort of aviary of boulevards and cement, and I could never walk that far. My mother wasn't going back. My mother hated nostalgia, photographs from vacations, souvenirs of where we had once been. She called it Americana and said it made her nauseous. And the jarcaranda stained feet and carpets. I had learned to wear sandals on sidewalks where the petals had fallen. I had several times slipped and skinned my knees.

It is odd, but I believe this was the last day I saw jarcaranda for the rest of my childhood. I did not see it again until I was an adult, and it abruptly reappeared. My mother and I were walking across the parking lot, into the moment that was father, which opened like a soft wound. Spring vanished and the landscape was gone, and in their place was my father, Jay.

My mother introduced us, awkwardly. I reached out to shake hands and he stared at my arm. Everything was stalled and off balance. My father was wearing black sunglasses, a navy-blue coat that looked both wet and dusty, and he didn't smile. He was smoking a cigarette. We finally shook hands, and I understood why certain gestures are called wooden. My father, Jay, walked with a limp and a cane. His cane was fantastic, a reddish wood he said was mahogany. It had a silver band at the bottom and a snake that coiled, silver, along the side. The head of the snake formed the handle. It's mouth was open; a silver tongue protruded from it.

"I don't take that VA crap," my father said, following my gaze, explaining his cane. "That aluminum shit. What you see here is handcarved. This is a nine hundred dollar job."

I didn't know what to say. Everyone kept looking at their watches and the clock on the wall of the restaurant where my mother and I ordered salads. My father ordered soup and a well-done steak, and he ate everything on his plate including the garnish, which he called the best part. My mother went to pay the check.

"Did you really kill people?" I asked.

"Where?" My father looked around the restaurant.

"In Vietnam," I said.

My father lit a cigarette. His eyes were half-closed, as if something more than smoke were clawing at them. There were invisible wires strung in the air, camouflaged the color of dusk; a person could trip. "What you have to understand is this. It was very dark. There was lots of confusion. Everything happened so fast."

After that first appearance near my twelfth birthday, after that first furious passing, when we walked him across a parking lot to a bus that had the word *Dallas* printed in black block letters above the enormous windshield, my father would appear periodically. I thought he was like a comet with his erratic flash and dust. He would arrive in Los Angeles on the train or on a Greyhound bus. Sometimes he crossed the country in a sequence of trucks. He called this thumbing it. There were implications. His methods of transportation always seemed somehow obscene and hazardous.

"What does it mean to be Jewish?" I asked on that first ride home. This was something new and completely unexpected that I had become, like a woman who bled, like a woman with a one-legged father.

"I asked myself that once," my mother laughed. She had smoked a cigarette with Jay. Now she was smoking another. I had never seen her smoke before. "Standing in his mother's house. It was Malibu. On the ocean. A grand piano. A Miró. Minor, but I recognized it across the room. I took a deep breath. Imagine me, a girl from the projects. I couldn't breathe enough of that Jewish air."

"Then what?" I was also holding my breath.

"We got married. I got my degree. He enlisted, came back strung-out. A petty thief and part-time junky. You were born. They disinherited him. I filed for divorce. Then all the air went away." My mother shrugged. She had learned to breathe on her own.

My father, Jay, was a comet with a predictable orbit. You could plot his course. He existed in a sort of void, and we were a kind of gravity. I thought space was filled with the paths orbs made. I imagined them as a skater's blade marks left in ice. My father had a cutting arc. Space was cold and littered with the trails of what had passed, scars, indentures, lines like the mesh in aviaries. I thought of mathematics and music.

I began to understand that my father orbited around various race tracks across the country. He came to Southern California for the summer meet at Del Mar. Once he came for the winter meet at Santa Anita. But it is the summers in the rented apartments in San Diego that I most remember.

My mother made me visit him for long weekends. She often sent me with gift-wrapped packages on the bottom of Saks Fifth Avenue shopping bags with sandwiches on top. Sometimes she put the gift-wrapped objects—and I knew they were objects and not presents—inside my suitcase.

"I don't want to go," I would say.

"I know. He left his leg in Da Nang and now everybody pays. Even you," my mother said, lighting a cigarette, looking past me. Since that first evening at the bus station my mother had been smoking.

"You don't know how bad it is," I began.

I thought of the sounds I heard through the open windows of apartments in San Diego. The fathers yelling at their daughters. Calling them tramps and pieces of trash. The way I tried to read on the sofa while my father got drunk and the people across the courtyard shouted at each other. In the nights in San Diego I felt physically assaulted, as if the air had been driven from my lungs. There had been a puncture, a slap or a kick. There was the sense of being violated and betrayed.

"Don't I?" My mother smiled. She looked at me. "He was six months away from graduation. The biggest firm in Laguna Beach wanted him. So he quit school and enlisted."

"Why?" I had never understood this.

"He said deferments were unfair to blacks and Mexicans who couldn't go to architectural school. Christ," my mother shook her head. "He called himself a man of conscience."

"Was he?" I asked. We were in her bedroom in the new house. It was early summer. Outside was a wash of mockingbirds and jasmine, the citrus of lemons, leaves being brushed by the sea breeze. I could taste the eucalyptus, pale, medicinal. The avocados hung like dark green stones, like triangular Christmas ornaments.

"A man of conscience?" My mother looked into the night. "Absolutely," she said. "Now it's time to pack."

Throughout high school, I made my visits to one interchangeable apartment in the suburbs of San Diego or another. I took the bus or more often the train, carrying packages wrapped in birthday paper that I knew were filled with lies, pretenses, or something worse. I could remember my separate journeys by the wrappings my mother covered the packages with. She usually wrapped them in birthday paper, little boys playing baseball on a glossy green field with matching red caps and uniforms. Sometimes there were balloons or pages of antique cars. There were the birthday-cake motifs with candles and hats and purple-and-gold confetti. There were floral prints with delicate white or lavender bows. Once, a large box with a soft rubbed away looking blue that offered *Congratulations on your new baby.*

"Christ. He's moving lids," my mother said once. "I can't believe it. He's down to moving lids."

I didn't ask her what these lids were. I knew they had nothing to do with jars. It was obvious they were meager and flawed and evil, whatever they were. The pretty wrapping was a masquerade. It was camouflage. There was something decaying and rotting inside, brittle and turning brown. It was something I wouldn't want to touch.

"I don't want to go," I was saying, watching my mother place several wrapped gifts in my suitcase. It was time for a floral print. I touched the tip of a pink peony. The packages felt like cold meatloaves.

"We owe him," my mother said. It was another summer. My mother had managed to quit smoking. It was a year when she wore perfume that seemed tart and vaguely like ginger. She was writing advertisements for perfumes. She had just been promoted again. Now she had two secretaries.

"What do we owe him?" I demanded.

We owned our house. When he telephoned he called collect. He was in a phone booth in a rainstorm in Fresno or Portland or Austin. He had just pawned something. It was always a night that seemed to smell of vinegar and rusty metal and a wind with sulfur in it, old lightning, something hollowed out and burning quiet in the dark behind a packing plant and a trailer park.

Once when he came for the winter meet at Santa Anita, my mother dropped me off in front of the apartment he had rented in Hollywood. She gave me a bag for him that contained a new sweater, socks, underwear. She gave him a black cashmere scarf she had been saving for a special occasion. I wondered what we owed him.

"Karmically," my mother said. "He went to Nam so some Puerto Rican kid could stay home and OD. Now everybody has to pick up the slack."

I was sitting in the car with my mother. Hollywood was broken, shabby, even the trees gleamed rancid. It was a hot winter. The Santa Anas had been blowing. The air was charged. I was thinking of invisible cables, how if it got hot enough, the day could start buzzing, it could sound like a kind of song. I was thinking I would refuse to get out of the car.

"It's show time," my mother said. She seemed to be in a hurry. She found a Springsteen tape, pushed it into the cassette player.

"You know he only listens to music from bands that have at least one dead guy in them," I told her. "He says that makes it authentic."

"Authentic," my mother repeated. "That's a word you don't hear much about anymore. That man is a living museum."

"Listen. Are these visits with Dad going to continue indefinitely?" I was angry. We were parked by the curb of a red brick building that said ROOMS on it in a chipped gray paint.

"No," my mother decided. "He doesn't have the attention span. He'll get bored after awhile."

"How long will that take?" Outside was Hollywood in a strange hot winter when everything seemed singed. The stray air over the gutted shell.

"He'll find somebody. A nurse at the VA maybe. That VA he likes in Georgia where they give him morphine." My mother glanced out the window. She was wearing sunglasses. A man with a snarling dog passed close to her window, and the dog turned and barked. She didn't flinch.

"Is that it?" I wanted to know.

"He might get busted. There's always the hope of incarceration." Her voice was completely indifferent. For the first time, I realized she didn't care.

"Do you think he might die?" I tried. I felt, suddenly, as if I might smile.

"He's suicidal. That's obvious." My mother looked at her watch. She pointed at the car door. "I just heard your cue," she said.

Then it was summer, and I would begin to feel sick on the train. California lay outside the window, as if it had stumbled and fallen down. Maybe it tripped a mine.

A booby trap. It was convulsing under a thick greenish smog that called itself Irvine, Oceanside, and San Clemente. If I studied the air hard enough, I could see the architecture of individual strands of pollution. They were like so many sutures, fast stitches like the ones you get in makeshift hospitals near the front.

Then I was walking off the train. My father was leaning on his cane with the snake he claimed was sterling silver. I knew it was only plated. I could see where it was chipping and showing the bronze underneath. He was waving a white handkerchief at me like an emblem, a badge that admitted a wound. How could I possibly miss him, the one crippled man on the platform?

It was the Del Mar train station. It was near the ocean. And as I climbed down the steps, I knew what all condemned women know, what all refugees know. The game is lost. You walk down the steps, you enter the compound, one compound or another. There is barbed wire, real or symbolic, it doesn't matter. You know what the parameters are. It is simply a question of how much is going to be taken.

Then you are walking into the lost game. That's part of the ritual, how you enter of your own volition, how you don't run away. The man is sick. He spends part of each year in the VA, one VA or another. The man is missing a leg. He still gets infections, phantom pains. The man is dependent on a stick he pretends is encrusted with silver. He makes collect calls from gas stations on deserted night highways. He doesn't have a permanent mailing address. My mother gives him a credit card, just for emergencies, she says. This is a man who can't dance, climb a fence.

"He saw it as an existential moment," my mother said, her voice light. It was the night before I left for San Diego. "He made his statement."

I was sixteen. This would be my last summer. I was going to take a job next June, and after that I would go to the university. No one would ever again make me deliver fake wrapped presents to this man. He was my father by marginal technicality, a spasm and a shudder. As far as I could see, I didn't owe him the time of day.

"He's a downer," I complained. I was thinking of the train ride in the morning, how I knew California was ruined. It was limping along. It looked like it needed a cane. "He hates everybody."

"Not everybody. Just the old military-industrial-complex," my mother corrected.

It was a cool night. Blue jays and white star jasmine. The roses by the hedge. My mother had a new project at the advertising agency she now partially owned. She was vice-president in charge of creative work. She was designing a city. She had the scale model of the streets with mock cardboard houses on them, with grassy areas in green felt, with glued-on pine and palm trees. She was naming the streets, the entrance gates, the courtyard area by the swimming pool, the paths to the tennis courts. Marine Avenue. Dolphin Way. Canyon of the Coyotes. Driftwood Drive.

My mother put her pencil down. "He's terminally low-rent," she said. "But that's not a crime. You should learn to be cool."

My mother turned away. She was studying photographs of herself for the brochure that would describe the city by the ocean that did not yet have a name. She was looking at the photographs in an abstract way, as if they were the faces of strangers. Or perhaps they were people she had met once and briefly shared a train ride with, something had happened that she couldn't quite remember. My mother was holding a photograph of her face at a slight angle. It glistened as if it was covered with a kind of enamel paint containing preserving properties.

I wondered if my mother was cool, if it, too, was genetic. Something made me shiver. In the morning I was going to San Diego and she was going to Hawaii with somebody named Tony. She had already taken out her suitcase, made a pile of bathing suits and nightgowns.

Then I was walking off the train, and my father and I were riding a bus into San Diego. It was always a one-bedroom apartment that he rented. He let me have the bedroom while he slept on the sofa in the living room. The sofas were always a beige vinyl. The apartment smelled of him, of bourbon and cigars and what I had finally learned was marijuana. That's what was in the wrapped-with-ribbon birthday packages. My mother got him pounds of it, and he sold it in smaller units at the racetrack. He didn't have enough money to buy his own pounds. No one would give him credit.

"Even on his own diminished terms, he's a failure," my mother had observed. There was something flat in her tone that I did not quite understand.

I walked into the apartment and it smelled of some tangible despair, as if heartbreak could be opened like a sore. It was as if a certain emotional condition had an actual morphology, a size and a texture. There was a sour odor like a cold sweat that has only recently and partially dried, a sweat that comes from fear or a disorienting sickness, something like malaria. I thought it was a by-product of his psychiatric disturbance secreted through his pores. It was some eccentric biochemical poison that I could actually smell.

My father would remove his prosthetic device, push it under the table. He would hop and lean against walls, panting between lurches. His remaining leg was like a sausage. The skin was camellia pink. It looked glazed.

"History," my father drank his bourbon. "See my leg," he pointed at his stump. "My leg is history."

In the morning, we went to the racetrack at Del Mar. I found a bench in the shade. One summer visit I read *War and Peace* and *Madame Bovary* in one week. This time I had brought *The Brothers Karamazov* and *Crime and Punishment*. I chose books by their size. They were like bricks in the wall I built to protect myself.

My father was limping around Del Mar, making five dollar bets, selling quarter ounces. He would buy me the daily program. He asked if I had any hunches, if any of the names appealed to me, if I wanted to see the horses in the paddock, help him check for bandages. I said no.

"Your mother was like that. Sitting on the commons reading T. S. Eliot while they tear-gassed the town. I went to Nam and she got her degree on time. She didn't miss a beat. Not even one quarter late," he smiled. "Now she writes ads for hair spray. I'd never tell a lie that small. I wouldn't bother."

That night, it occurred to me that a kind of infection lay over these San Diego apartments. They were a sequence of Formica tabletops with views of fences embossed by singed red hibiscus and bitter oranges. There was a sense of flesh being severed and hospitals. It was there in the harsh overhead light bulbs, in the carpets that reeked of recent disinfectant and insecticide. It was as if transience was not simply a concept or a set of behaviors but an actual entity, and I could see it being preserved in a kind of formaldehyde.

"You college babes knock me out," my father said. He was drinking bourbon. He was smoking pot and cigarettes. "There's more history one morning at the track then you'll find in four years of college. This is the campus of life, baby."

It was an expectant air that seemed to demand something. My father sensed this. My father said the words. He trashed the night. He strung his own barbed wire wherever he went. He filled rooms with an aviary of sharp string.

We would eat a frozen dinner he microwaved. We ate it directly from the plastic container. Then the night came in with the sounds from other apartments. The fathers were calling their daughters whores, tramps, pigs. My father had taken off his artificial leg. His stump glistened red. We were playing poker using pills for chips. The yellow Percodan, the red Seconal, the blue Valium. We would ante with the codeine. They were white. I could hear the fathers in nearby bungalows yelling at their daughters, their Tracys and Darlenes, calling them sluts, calling them no good. I realized my father didn't hear this. It didn't register. It was beyond his perimeter. It didn't matter.

"I'll take you to Tijuana. That's being inside history, baby. That's where the books stop," my father said. "You could stay an extra day, maybe."

I didn't say anything. We were playing poker. His pills were the chips. They had different value. I studied my cards. I could hear the ice melting in his bourbon with the buzz of dying flies. I could see his cane with its chipped snake handle in the glare of the light that coated everything with a sort of plastic. It had nothing to do with illumination. The greasy light settled over my skin, stinging and numbing it. I thought of fossils trapped in amber and how the light was a sort of starch laminating this one particular moment.

I was considering the nature of this light as I boarded the train to Los Angeles in the morning. Soon I would be studying history at a college in New England in a city without a racetrack. As for next summer, I had a catalog of jobs for college students. There were listings for raft guides on the Arkansas River and dance instructors on cruise ships in the Caribbean. I could teach English in the South American jungle or in Japan or Korea. I could pass out blankets and vitamins in famine areas. I could clean up otters from oil spills. There were hundreds of possibilities and locations.

"I could ride up to L.A. with you," my father suddenly offered, quite unexpectedly. "It would give us a chance to talk."

"What would we talk about?" I asked.

I was boarding the train. I could spend the rest of my life boarding trains, following the tracks, the sutures in the earth, believing there was a destination, a depot of revelation. If you traveled far enough you could find the central mystery. I was going to leave this region that had so little to do with history as it had once been known. I was going to invent and map my own terrain, and this time I wouldn't miss a thing.

I realized that one could get trapped in moments, laminated by a certain lamplight, a sudden confluence of elements the color of brutally overripe lemons. It is always a summer evening strung with the accusation of slut and tramp sailing through the mesh of wide-open windows in rented bungalows in towns and cities near borders. It is always the hour of the fathers, when the mouth bruises and soils the night. There is the smell of rotting sun-sick camellias, bourbon and marijuana, shirts that should be washed. We are pinned there. Circumstances become dimensional and we are paralyzed, set in a sort of photograph we carry permanently like a kind of identification. When we are asked for our papers, this is what we are really reaching for. It is for this that we are frightened.

My father was on the platform. I could see him from my window so I looked away. The ocean was a slow, exhausted blue. I opened my book of summer jobs. I thought about rivers and mountains encrusted with columbine and larkspur, capitals with bridges and steeples and tiled domes. I could sense my father leaning on his cane, waving his white handkerchief that was like a flag of surrender below the decadent palms. I could have seen him this one last time if I had bothered to turn around.

# Robert Olen Butler

## (B. 1945)

Robert Olen Butler was born in Granite City, Illinois. In 1971 he served as a U.S. Army counterintelligence linguist in Saigon, Vietnam. Butler's training included a rigorous program in the Vietnamese language, which he eventually mastered. This facility with Vietnamese allowed Butler to interact with the local Vietnamese population, and his linguistic ability allowed him to break traditions in American literature. Literature about Vietnam written by Americans has traditionally been about the American male experience in the war. Butler's book of short stories, *A Good Scent from a Strange Mountain* (1992), is unique because he assumes the voices of immigrant Vietnamese. The characters in the fifteen connected stories have left war-torn Vietnam and now live in New Orleans, Louisiana, where they battle with cultural and social assimilation.

Butler is the author of numerous works, including the Vietnam trilogy, *The Alleys of Eden* (1981), *Sun Dogs* (1982), and *On Distant Ground* (1985), and the novels *Wabash* (1987), *With the Deuce* (1989), *They Whisper* (1994), *The Deep Green Sea* (1998), *Mr. Spaceman* (2000), and *Fair Warning* (2002). He is also the author of two collections of short stories, *A Good Scent from a Strange Mountain* (1992), already mentioned, and *Tabloid Dreams* (1996). Although Butler often returns to Vietnam for his setting and plot, his writing includes stories about Depression-era Illinois, contemporary New York City, and even outer space. He is the recipient of numerous awards, including the Pulitzer Prize. Butler is currently a professor of fiction writing at McNeese State University in Lake Charles, Louisiana.

# A Good Scent from a Strange Mountain
*1991*

Hô Chí Minh came to me again last night, his hands covered with confectioners' sugar. This was something of a surprise to me, the first time I saw him beside my bed, in the dim light from the open shade. My oldest daughter leaves my shades open, I think so that I will not forget that the sun has risen again in the morning. I am a very old man. She seems to expect that one morning I will simply forget to keep living. This is very foolish. I will one night rise up from my bed and slip into her room and open the shade there. Let her see the sun in the morning. She is sixty-four years old and she should worry for herself. I could never die from forgetting.

But the light from the street was enough to let me recognize Hô when I woke, and he said to me, "Đạo, my old friend, I have heard it is time to visit you." Already on that first night there was a sweet smell about him, very strong in the dark, even before I could see his hands. I said nothing, but I stretched to the nightstand beside me and I turned on the light to see if he would go away. And he did not. He stood there beside the bed—I could even see him reflected in the window—and I know it was real because he did not appear as he was when I'd known him but as he was when he'd died. This was Uncle Hô before me, the thin old man with the dewlap beard wearing the dark clothes of a peasant and the rubber sandals, just like in the news pictures I studied with such a strange feeling for all those years. Strange because when I knew him, he was not yet Hô Chí Minh. It was 1917 and he was Nguyễn Aí Quôc and we were both young men with clean-shaven faces, the best of friends, and we worked at the Carlton Hotel in London, where I was a dishwasher and he was a pastry cook under the great Escoffier. We were the best of friends and we saw snow for the first time together. This was before we began to work at the hotel. We shoveled snow and Hô would stop for a moment and blow his breath out before him and it would make him smile, to see what was inside him, as if it was the casting of bones to tell the future.

On that first night when he came to me in my house in New Orleans, I finally saw what it was that smelled so sweet and I said to him, "Your hands are covered with sugar."

He looked at them with a kind of sadness.

I have received that look myself in the past week. It is time now for me to see my family, and the friends I have made who are still alive. This is our custom from Vietnam. When you are very old, you put aside a week or two to receive the people of your life so that you can tell one another your feelings, or try at last to understand one another, or simply say good-bye. It is a formal leave-taking, and with good luck you can do this before you have your final illness. I have lived almost a century and perhaps I should have called them all to me sooner, but at last I felt a deep weariness and I said to my oldest daughter that it was time.

They look at me with sadness, some of them. Usually the dull-witted ones, or the insincere ones. But Hô's look was, of course, not dull-witted or insincere. He considered his hands and said, "The glaze. Maestro's glaze."

There was the soft edge of yearning in his voice and I had the thought that perhaps he had come to me for some sort of help. I said to him, "I don't remember. I only washed dishes." As soon as the words were out of my mouth, I decided it was foolish for me to think he had come to ask me about the glaze.

But Hô did not treat me as foolish. He looked at me and shook his head. "It's all right," he said. "I remember the temperature now. Two hundred and thirty degrees, when the sugar is between the large thread stage and the small orb stage. The Maestro was very clear about that and I remember." I knew from his eyes, however, that there was much more that still eluded him. His eyes did not seem to move at all from my face, but there was some little shifting of them, a restlessness that perhaps only I could see, since I was his close friend from the days when the world did not know him.

I am nearly one hundred years old, but I can still read a man's face. Perhaps better than I ever have. I sit in the overstuffed chair in my living room and I receive my visitors and I want these people, even the dull-witted and insincere ones—please excuse an old man's ill temper for calling them that—I want them all to be good with one another. A Vietnamese family is extended as far as the bloodline strings us together, like so many paper lanterns around a village square. And we all give off light together. That's the way it has always been in our culture. But these people who come to visit me have been in America for a long time and there are very strange things going on that I can see in their faces.

None stranger than this morning. I was in my overstuffed chair and with me there were four of the many members of my family: my son-in-law Thắng, a former colonel in the Army of the Republic of Vietnam and one of the insincere ones, sitting on my Castro convertible couch; his youngest son, Lợi, who had come in late, just a few minutes earlier, and had thrown himself down on the couch as well, youngest but a man old enough to have served as a lieutenant under his father as our country fell to the communists more than a decade ago; my daughter Lâm, who is Thắng's wife, hovering behind the both of them and refusing all invitations to sit down; and my oldest daughter, leaning against the door frame, having no doubt just returned from my room, where she had opened the shade that I had closed when I awoke.

It was Thắng who gave me the sad look I have grown accustomed to, and I perhaps seemed to him at that moment a little weak, a little distant. I had stopped listening to the small talk of these people and I had let my eyes half close, though I could still see them clearly and I was very alert. Thắng has a steady face and the quick eyes of a man who is ready to come under fire, but I have always read much more there, in spite of his efforts to show nothing. So after he thought I'd faded from the room, it was with slow eyes, not quick, that he moved to his son and began to speak of the killing.

You should understand that Mr. Nguyễn Bích Lê had been shot dead in our community here in New Orleans just last week. There are many of us Vietnamese living in New Orleans and one man, Mr. Lê, published a little newspaper for all of us. He had recently made the fatal error—though it should not be that in America—of writing that it was time to accept the reality of the communist government in Vietnam and begin to talk with them. We had to work now with those who controlled our country. He said that he remained a patriot to the Republic of Vietnam, and I believed him. If anyone had asked an old man's opinion on this whole matter, I would not have been afraid to say that Mr. Lê was right.

But he was shot dead last week. He was forty-five years old and he had a wife and three children and he was shot as he sat behind the wheel of his Chevrolet pickup truck. I find a detail like that especially moving, that this man was killed in his Chevrolet, which I understand is a strongly American thing. We knew this in Saigon. In Saigon it was very American to own a Chevrolet, just as it was French to own a Citroën.

And Mr. Lê had taken one more step in his trusting embrace of this new culture. He had bought not only a Chevrolet but a Chevrolet pickup truck, which made him not only American but also a man of Louisiana, where there are many pickup trucks. He did not, however, also purchase a gun rack for the back window, another sign of this place. Perhaps it would have been well if he had, for it was through the back window that the bullet was fired. Someone had hidden in the bed of his truck and had killed him from behind in his Chevrolet and the reason for this act was made very clear in a phone call to the newspaper office by a nameless representative of the Vietnamese Party for the Annihilation of Communism and for the National Restoration.

And Thắng, my son-in-law, said to his youngest son, Lợi, "There is no murder weapon." What I saw was a faint lift of his eyebrows as he said this, like he was inviting his son to listen beneath his words. Then he said it again, more slowly, like it was code. "There is no *weapon*." My grandson nodded his head once, a crisp little snap. Then my daughter Lâm said in a very loud voice, with her eyes on me, "That was a terrible thing, the death of Mr. Lê." She nudged her husband and son, and both men turned their faces sharply to me and they looked at me squarely and said, also in very loud voices, "Yes, it was terrible."

I am not deaf, and I closed my eyes further, having seen enough and wanting them to think that their loud talk had not only failed to awake me but had put me more completely to sleep. I did not like to deceive them, however, even though I have already spoken critically of these members of my family. I am a Hòa Hảo Buddhist and I believe in harmony among all living things, especially the members of a Vietnamese family.

After Hô had reassured me, on that first visit, about the temperature needed to heat Maestro Escoffier's glaze, he said, "Đạo, my old friend, do you still follow the path you chose in Paris?"

He meant by this my religion. It was in Paris that I embraced the Buddha and disappointed Hô. We went to France in early 1918, with the war still on, and we lived in the poorest street of the poorest part of the Seventeenth Arrondissement. Number nine, Impasse Compoint, a blind alley with a few crumbling Houses, all but ours rented out for storage. The cobblestones were littered with fallen roof tiles and Quốc and I each had a tiny single room with only an iron bedstead and a crate to sit on. I could see my friend Quốc in the light of the tallow candle and he was dressed in a dark suit and a bowler hat and he looked very foolish. I did not say so, but he knew it himself and he kept seating and reseating the hat and shaking his head very slowly, with a loudly silent anger. This was near the end of our time together, for I was visiting daily with a Buddhist monk and he was drawing me back to the religion of my father. I had run from my father, gone to sea, and that was where I had met Nguyễn Aí Quôc and we had gone to London and to Paris and now my father was calling me back, through a Vietnamese monk I met in the Tuileries.

Quôc, on the other hand, was being called not from his past but from his future. He had rented the dark suit and bowler and he would spend the following weeks in Versailles, walking up and down the mirrored corridors of the Palace trying to gain an audience with Woodrow Wilson. Quôc had eight requests for the Western world concerning Indochina. Simple things. Equal rights, freedom of assembly, freedom of the press. The essential things that he knew Wilson would understand, based as they were on Wilson's own Fourteen Points. And Quôc did not even intend to ask for independence. He wanted Vietnamese representatives in the French Parliament. That was all he would ask. But his bowler made him angry. He wrenched out of the puddle of candlelight, both his hands clutching the bowler, and I heard him muttering in the darkness and I felt that this was a bad sign already, even before he had set foot in Versailles. And as it turned out, he never saw Wilson, or Lloyd George either, or even Clemenceau. But somehow his frustration with his hat was what made me sad, even now, and I reached out from my bedside and said, "Uncle Hô, it's all right."

He was still beside me. This was not an awakening, as you might expect, this was not a dream ending with the bowler in Paris and I awaking to find that Hô was never there. He was still beside my bed, though he was just beyond my outstretched hand and he did not move to me. He smiled on one side of his mouth, a smile full of irony, as if he, too, was thinking about the night he'd tried on his rented clothes. He said, "Do you remember how I worked in Paris?"

I thought about this and I did remember, with the words of his advertisement in the newspaper "La Vie Ouvrière": "If you would like a lifelong memento of your family, have your photos retouched at Nguyễn Aí Quôc's." This was his work in Paris; he retouched photos with a very delicate hand, the same fine hand that Monsieur Escoffier had admired in London. I said, "Yes, I remember."

Hô nodded gravely. "I painted the blush into the cheeks of Frenchmen."

I said, "A lovely portrait in a lovely frame for forty francs," another phrase from his advertisement.

"Forty-five," Hô said.

I thought now of his question that I had not answered. I motioned to the far corner of the room where the prayer table stood. "I still follow the path."

He looked and said, "At least you became a Hòa Hảo."

He could tell this from the simplicity of the table. There was only a red cloth upon it and four Chinese characters: Bao Sơ'n Kỳ Hu'o'ng. This is the saying of the Hòa Hảos. We follow the teachings of a monk who broke away from the fancy rituals of the other Buddhists. We do not need elaborate pagodas or rituals. The Hòa Hảo believes that the maintenance of our spirits is very simple, and the mystery of joy is simple, too. The four characters mean "A good scent from a strange mountain."

I had always admired the sense of humor of my friend Quôc, so I said, "You never did stop painting the blush into the faces of Westerners."

Hô looked back to me but he did not smile. I was surprised at this but more surprised at my little joke seeming to remind him of his hands. He raised them and studied them and said, "After the heating, what was the surface for the glaze?"

"My old friend," I said, "you worry me now."

But Hô did not seem to hear. He turned away and crossed the room and I knew he was real because he did not vanish from my sight but opened the door and went out and closed the door behind him with a loud click.

I rang for my daughter. She had given me a porcelain bell, and after allowing Hô enough time to go down the stairs and out the front door, if that was where he was headed, I rang the bell, and my daughter, who is a very light sleeper, soon appeared.

"What is it, Father?" she asked with great patience in her voice. She is a good girl. She understands about Vietnamese families and she is a smart girl.

"Please feel the doorknob," I said.

She did so without the slightest hesitation and this was a lovely gesture on her part, a thing that made me wish to rise up and embrace her, though I was very tired and did not move.

"Yes?" she asked after touching the knob.

"Is it sticky?"

She touched it again. "Ever so slightly," she said. "Would you like for me to clean it?"

"In the morning," I said.

She smiled and crossed the room and kissed me on the forehead. She smelled of lavender and fresh bedclothes and there are so many who have gone on before me into the world of spirits and I yearn for them all, yearn to find them all together in a village square, my wife there smelling of lavender and our own sweat, like on a night in Saigon soon after the terrible fighting in 1968 when we finally opened the windows onto the night and there were sounds of bombs falling on the horizon and there was no breeze at all, just the heavy stillness of the time between the dry season and the wet, and Saigon smelled of tar and motorcycle exhaust and cordite but when I opened the window and turned to my wife, the room was full of a wonderful scent, a sweet smell that made her sit up, for she sensed it, too. This was a smell that had nothing to do with flowers but instead reminded us that flowers were always ready to fall into dust, while this smell was as if a gemstone had begun to give off a scent, as if a mountain of emerald had found its own scent. I crossed the room to my wife and we were already old, we had already buried children and grandchildren that we prayed waited for us in that village square at the foot of the strange mountain, but when I came near the bed, she lifted her silk gown and threw it aside and I pressed close to her and our own sweat smelled sweet on that night. I want to be with her in that square and with the rest of those we'd buried, the tiny limbs and the sullen eyes and the gray faces of the puzzled children and the surprised adults and the weary old people who have gone before us, who know the secrets now. And the sweet smell of the glaze on Hô's hands reminds me of others that I would want in the square, the people from the ship, too, the Vietnamese boy from a village near my own who died of a fever in the Indian Ocean and the natives in Dakar who were forced by colonial officials to swim out to our ship in shark-infested waters to secure the moorings and two were killed before our eyes without a French regret. Hô was very moved by this, and I want those men in our square and I want the Frenchman, too, who called Hô "monsieur" for the first time. A man on the dock in Marseilles. Hô spoke of him twice more during our years together and I want that Frenchman there. And, of course, Hô. Was he in the village square even now, waiting? Heating his glaze fondant? My daughter was smoothing my covers around me and the smell of lavender on her was still strong.

"He was in this room," I said to her to explain the sticky doorknob.

"Who was?"

But I was very sleepy and I could say no more, though perhaps she would not have understood anyway, in spite of being the smart girl that she is.

The next night I left my light on to watch for Hô's arrival, but I dozed off and he had to wake me. He was sitting in a chair that he'd brought from across the room. He said to me, "Đao. Wake up, my old friend."

I must have awakened when he pulled the chair near to me, for I heard each of these words. "I am awake," I said. "I was thinking of the poor men who had to swim out to our ship."

"They are already among those I have served," Hô said. "Before I forgot." And he raised his hands and they were still covered with sugar.

I said, "Wasn't it a marble slab?" I had a memory, strangely clear after these many years, as strange as my memory of Hô's Paris business card.

"A marble slab," Hô repeated, puzzled.

"That you poured the heated sugar on."

"Yes." Hô's sweet-smelling hands came forward but they did not quite touch me. I thought to reach out from beneath the covers and take them in my own hands, but Hô leaped up and paced about the room. "The marble slab, moderately oiled. Of course. I am to let the sugar half cool and then use the spatula to move it about in all directions, every bit of it, so that it doesn't harden and form lumps."

I asked, "Have you seen my wife?"

Hô had wandered to the far side of the room, but he turned and crossed back to me at this. "I'm sorry, my friend. I never knew her."

I must have shown some disappointment in my face, for Hô sat down and brought his own face near mine. "I'm sorry," he said. "There are many other people that I must find here."

"Are you very disappointed in me?" I asked. "For not having traveled the road with you?"

"It's very complicated," Hô said softly. "You felt that you'd taken action. I am no longer in a position to question another soul's choice."

"Are you at peace, where you are?" I asked this knowing of his worry over the recipe for the glaze, but I hoped that this was only a minor difficulty in the afterlife, like the natural anticipation of the good cook expecting guests when everything always turns out fine in the end.

But Hô said, "I am not at peace."

"Is Monsieur Escoffier over there?"

"I have not seen him. This has nothing to do with him, directly."

"What is it about?"

"I don't know."

"You won the country. You know that, don't you?"

Hô shrugged. "There are no countries here."

I should have remembered Hô's shrug when I began to see things in the faces of my son-in-law and grandson this morning. But something quickened in me, a suspicion. I kept my eyes shut and laid my head to the side, as if I was fast asleep, encouraging them to talk more.

My daughter said, "This is not the place to speak."

But the men did not regard her. "How?" Lợi asked his father, referring to the missing murder weapon.

It's best not to know too much," Thắng said.

Then there was a silence. For all the quickness I'd felt at the first suspicion, I was very slow now. In fact, I did think of Hô from that second night. Not his shrug. He had fallen silent for a long time and I had closed my eyes, for the light seemed very bright. I listened to his silence just as I listened to the silence of these two conspirators before me.

And then Hô said, "They were fools, but I can't bring myself to grow angry anymore."

I opened my eyes in the bedroom and the light was off. Hô had turned it off, knowing that it was bothering me. "Who were fools?" I asked.

"We had fought together to throw out the Japanese. I had very good friends among them. I smoked their lovely Salem cigarettes. They had been repressed by colonialists themselves. Did they not know their own history?"

"Do you mean the Americans?"

"There are a million souls here with me, the young men of our country, and they are all dressed in black suits and bowler hats. In the mirrors they are made ten million, a hundred million."

"I chose my path, my dear friend Quốc, so that there might be harmony."

And even with that yearning for harmony I could not overlook what my mind made of what my ears had heard this morning. Thắng was telling Lợi that the murder weapon had been disposed of. Thắng and Lợi both knew the killers, were in sympathy with them, perhaps were part of the killing. The father and son had been airborne rangers and I had several times heard them talk bitterly of the exile of our people. We were fools for trusting the Americans all along, they said. We should have taken matters forward and disposed of the infinitely corrupt Thieu and done what needed to be done. Whenever they spoke like this in front of me, there was soon a quick exchange of sideways glances at me and then a turn and an apology. "We're sorry, Grandfather. Old times often bring old anger. We are happy our family is living a new life."

I would wave my hand at this, glad to have the peace of the family restored. Glad to turn my face and smell the dogwood tree or even smell the coffee plant across the highway. These things had come to be the new smells of our family. But then a weakness often came upon me. The others would drift away, the men, and perhaps one of my daughters would come to me and stroke my head and not say a word and none of them ever would ask why I was weeping. I would smell the rich blood smells of the afterbirth and I would hold our first son, still slippery in my arms, and there was the smell of dust from the square and the smell of the South China Sea just over the rise of the hill and there was the smell of the blood and of the inner flesh from my wife as my son's own private sea flowed from this woman that I loved, flowed and carried him into the life that would disappear from him so soon. In the afterlife would he stand before me on unsteady child's legs? Would I have to bend low to greet him or would he be a man now?

My grandson said, after the silence had nearly carried me into real sleep, troubled sleep, my grandosn Lợi said to his father, "I would be a coward not to know."

Thắng laughed and said, "You have proved yourself no coward."

And I wished then to sleep, I wished to fall asleep and let go of life somewhere in my dreams and seek my village square. I have lived too long, I thought. My daughter was saying, "Are you both mad?" And then she changed her voice, making the words very precise. "Let Grandfather sleep."

So when Hô came tonight for the third time, I wanted to ask his advice. His hands were still covered with sugar and his mind was, as it had been for the past two nights, very much distracted. "There's something still wrong with the glaze," he said to me in the dark, and I pulled back the covers and swung my legs around to get up. He did not try to stop me, but he did draw back quietly into the shadows.

"I want to pace the room with you," I said. "As we did in Paris, those tiny rooms of ours. We would talk about Marx and about Buddha and I must pace with you now."

"Very well," he said. "Perhaps it will help me remember."

I slipped on my sandals and I stood up and Hô's shadow moved past me, through the spill of streetlight and into the dark near the door. I followed him, smelling the sugar on his hands, first before me and then moving past me as I went on into the darkness he'd just left. I stopped as I turned and I could see Hô outlined before the window and I said, "I believe my son-in-law and grandson are involved in the killing of a man. A political killing."

Hô stayed where he was, a dark shape against the light, and he said nothing and I could not smell his hands from across the room and I smelled only the sourness of Lợi as he laid his head on my shoulder. He was a baby and my daughter Lâm retreated to our balcony window after handing him to me and the boy turned his head and I turned mine to him and I could smell his mother's milk, sour on his breath, he had a sour smell and there was incense burning in the room, jasmine, the smoke of souls, and the boy sighed on my shoulder, and I turned my face away from the smell of him. Thắng was across the room and his eyes were quick to find his wife and he was waiting for her to take the child from me.

"You have never done the political thing," Hô said.

"Is this true?"

"Of course."

I asked, "Are there politics where you are now, my friend?"

I did not see him moving toward me, but the smell of the sugar on his hands grew stronger, very strong, and I felt Hô Chí Minh very close to me, though I could not see him. He was very close and the smell was strong and sweet and it was filling my lungs as if from the inside, as if Hô was passing through my very body, and I heard the door open behind me and then close softly shut.

I moved across the room to the bed. I turned to sit down but I was facing the window, the scattering of a streetlamp on the window like a nova in some far part of the universe. I stepped to the window and touched the reflected light there, wondering if there was a great smell when a star explodes, a great burning smell of gas and dust. Then I closed the shade and slipped into bed, quite gracefully, I felt, I was quite wonderfully graceful, and I lie here now waiting for sleep. Hô is right, of course. I will never say a word about my grandson. And perhaps I will be as restless as Hô when I join him. But that will be all right. He and I will be together again and perhaps we can help each other. I know now what it is that he has forgotten. He has used confectioners' sugar for his glaze fondant and he should be using granulated sugar. I was only a washer of dishes but I did listen carefully when Monsieur Escoffier spoke. I wanted to understand everything. His kitchen was full of such smells that you knew you had to understand everything or you would be incomplete forever.

# Ethan Canin

## (B. 1960)

Ethan Canin was born in Ann Arbor, Michigan. His family eventually settled in San Francisco, where Canin spent most of his childhood. He enrolled at Stanford University, where he first majored in engineering and finally earned his B.A. in English. In 1984, Canin earned his M.F.A. from the University of Iowa, but he felt like a failure. He entered Harvard Medical School, where he wrote a manuscript that would eventually be published as *Emperor of the Air* (1988). In these carefully crafted stories of family relationships, Canin reveals connections and disjunctions of communication and moments of self-recognition and discovery. Canin earned his medical degree in 1991 and began an internal medicine residency at the University of California, San Francisco. Though he divided his time between medicine and writing for several years, after the publication of *The Palace Thief* (1996), Canin decided to devote himself entirely to writing. He also cofounded the Writers' Grotto in San Francisco. In 1998, Canin joined the Iowa Writers' Workshop faculty. He has also published *For Kings and Planets* (1998) and *Carry Me across the Water* (2001).

## Emperor of the Air

1985

Let me tell you who I am. I'm sixty-nine years old, live in the same house I was raised in, and have been the high school biology and astronomy teacher in this town so long that I have taught the grandson of one of my former students. I wear my father's wristwatch, which tells me it is past four-thirty in the morning, and though I have thought otherwise, I now think that hope is the essence of all good men.

My wife, Vera, and I have no children. This has enabled us to do a great many things in our lives: we have stood on the Great Wall of China, toured the Pyramid of Cheops, sunned in Lapland at midnight. Vera, who is near my age, is off on the Appalachian Trail. She has been gone two weeks and expects to be gone one more, on a trip on which a group of men and women, some of them half her age, are walking all the way through three states. Age, it seems, has left my wife alone. She ice-skates and hikes and will swim nude in a mountain lake. She does these things without me, however, for now my life has slowed. Last fall, as I pushed a lawn-mower around our yard, I felt a squeezing in my chest and a burst of pain in my shoulder, and I spent a week in a semi-private hospital room. A heart attack. Myocardial infarction, minor. I will no longer run for a train, and in my shirt pocket I keep a small vial of nitroglycerine pills. In slow supermarket lines or traffic snarls I tell myself that impatience is not worth dying over, and last week, as I stood at the window and watched my neighbor, Mr. Pike, cross the yard toward our front door carrying a chain saw, I told myself that he was nothing but a doomed and hopeless man.

I had found the insects in my elm a couple of days before, the slim red line running from the ground up the long trunk and vanishing into the lower boughs. I brought out a magnifying glass to examine them—their shiny arthroderms, torsos elongated like drops of red liquid; their tiny legs, jointed and wiry, climbing the fissured bark. The morning I found them, Mr. Pike came over from next door and stood on our porch. "There's vermin in your elm," he said.

"I know," I said. "Come in."

"It's a shame, but I'll be frank: there's other trees on this block. I've got my own three elms to think of."

Mr. Pike is a builder, a thick and unpleasant man with whom I have rarely spoken. Though I had seen him at high school athletic events, the judgmental tilt to his jaw always suggested to me that he was merely watching for the players' mistakes. He is short, with thick arms and a thick neck and a son, Kurt, in whose bellicose shouts I can already begin to hear the thickness of his father. Mr. Pike owns or partly owns a construction company that erected a line of low prefabricated houses on the outskirts of town, on a plot I remember from my youth as having been razed by fire. Once, a plumber who was working on our basement pipes told me that Mr. Pike was a poor craftsman, a man who valued money over quality. The plumber, a man my age who kept his tools in a wooden chest, shook his head when he told me that Mr. Pike used plastic pipes in the houses he had built. "They'll last ten years," the plumber told me. "Then the seams will go and the walls and ceilings will start to fill with water." I myself had had little to do with Mr. Pike until he told me he wanted my elm cut down to protect the three saplings in his yard. Our houses are separated by a tall stand of rhododendron and ivy, so we don't see each other's private lives as most neighbors do. When we talked on the street, we spoke only about a football score or the incessant rain, and I had not been on his property since shortly after he moved in, when I had gone over to introduce myself and he had shown me the spot where, underneath his rolling back lawn, he planned to build a bomb shelter.

Last week he stood on my porch with the chain saw in his hands. "I've got young elms," he said. "I can't let them be infested."

"My tree is over two hundred years old."

"It's a shame," he said, showing me the saw, "but I'll be frank. I just wanted you to know I could have it cut down as soon as you give the word."

All week I had a hard time sleeping. I read Dickens in bed, heated cups of milk, but nothing worked. The elm was dying. Vera was gone, and I lay in bed thinking of the insects, of their miniature jaws carrying away heartwood. It was late summer, the nights were still warm, and sometimes I went outside in my nightclothes and looked up at the sky. I teach astronomy, as I have said, and though sometimes I try to see the stars as milky dots or pearls, they are forever arranged in my eye according to the astronomic charts. I stood by the elm and looked up at Ursa Minor and Lyra, at Cygnus and Corona Borealis. I went back inside, read, peeled an orange. I sat at the window and thought about the insects, and every morning at five a boy who had once taken my astronomy class rode by on his bicycle, whistling the national anthem, and threw the newspaper onto our porch.

Sometimes I heard them, chewing the heart of my splendid elm.

The day after I first found the insects I called a man at the tree nursery. He described them for me, the bodies like red droplets, the wiry legs; he told me their genus and species.

"Will they kill the tree?"

"They could."

"We can poison them, can't we?"

"Probably not," he said. He told me that once they were visible outside the bark they had already invaded the tree too thoroughly for pesticide. "To kill them," he said, "we would end up killing the tree."

"Does that mean the tree is dead?"

"No," he said. "It depends on the colony of insects. Sometimes they invade a tree but don't kill it, don't even weaken it. They eat the wood, but sometimes they eat it so slowly that the tree can replace it."

When Mr. Pike came over the next day, I told him this. "You're asking me to kill a two-hundred-and-fifty-year-old tree that otherwise wouldn't die for a long time."

"The tree's over eighty feet tall," he said.

"So?"

"It stands fifty-two feet from my house."

"Mr. Pike, it's older than the Liberty Bell."

"I don't want to be unpleasant," he said, "but a storm could blow twenty-eight feet of that tree through the wall of my house."

"How long have you lived in that house?"

He looked at me, picked at his tooth. "You know."

"Four years," I said. "I was living here when a czar ruled Russia. An elm grows one quarter inch in width each year, when it's still growing. That tree is four feet thick, and it has yet to chip the paint on either your house or mine."

"It's sick," he said. "It's a sick tree. It could fall."

"Could," I said. "It *could* fall."

"It very well *might* fall."

We looked at each other for a moment. Then he averted his eyes, and with his right hand adjusted something on his watch. I looked at his wrist. The watch had a shiny metal band, with the hours, minutes, seconds, blinking in the display.

The next day he was back on my porch.

"We can plant another one," he said.

"What?"

"We can plant another tree. After we cut the elm, we can plant a new one."

"Do you have any idea how long it would take to grow a tree like that one?"

"You can buy trees half-grown. They bring them in on a truck and replant them."

"Even a half-grown tree would take a century to reach the size of the elm. A century."

He looked at me. Then he shrugged, turned around, and went back down the steps. I sat down in the open doorway. A century. What would be left of the earth in a century? I didn't think I was a sentimental man, and I don't weep at plays or movies, but certain moments have always been peculiarly moving for me, and the mention of a century was one. There have been others. Standing out of the way on a fall evening, as couples and families converge on the concert hall from the radiating footpaths, has always filled me with a longing, though I don't know for what. I have taught the life of the simple hydra that is drawn, for no reasons it could ever understand, toward the bright surface of the water, and the spectacle of a thousand human beings organizing themselves into a single room to hear the quartets of Beethoven is as moving to me as birth or death. I feel the same way during the passage in an automobile across a cantilever span above the Mississippi, mother of rivers. These moments overwhelm me, and sitting on the porch that day as Mr. Pike retreated up the footpath, paused at the elm, and then went back into his house, I felt my life open up and present itself to me.

When he had gone back into his house I went out to the elm and studied the insects, which emerged from a spot in the grass and disappeared above my sight, in the lowest branches. Their line was dense and unbroken. I went inside and found yesterday's newspaper, which I rolled up and brought back out. With it I slapped up and down the trunk until the line was in chaos. I slapped until the newspaper was wet and tearing; with my fingernails I squashed stragglers between the narrow crags of bark. I stamped the sod where they emerged, dug my shoe tip into their underground tunnels. When my breathing became painful, I stopped and sat on the ground. I closed my eyes until the pulse in my neck was calm, and I sat there, mildly triumphant, master at last. After a while I looked up again at the tree and found the line perfectly restored.

That afternoon I mixed a strong insect poison, which I brought outside and painted around the bottom of the trunk. Mr. Pike came out onto his steps to watch. He walked down, stood on the sidewalk behind me, made little chuckling noises. "There's no poison that'll work," he whispered.

But that evening, when I came outside, the insects were gone. The trunk was bare. I ran my finger around the circumference. I rang Mr. Pike's doorbell and we went out and stood by the tree together. He felt in the notches of the bark, scratched bits of earth from the base. "I'll be damned," he said.

When I was a boy in this town, the summers were hot and the forest to the north and east often dried to the point where the undergrowth, not fit to compete with the deciduous trees for groundwater, turned crackling brown. The shrubbery became as fragile as straw, and the summer I was sixteen the forest ignited. A sheet of flame raced and bellowed day and night as loud as a fleet of propeller planes. Whole families gathered in the street and evacuation plans were made, street routes drawn out beneath the night sky, which, despite the ten miles' distance to the fire, shone with orange light. My father had a wireless with which he communicated to the fire lines. He stayed up all night and promised that he would wake the neighbors if the wind changed or the fire otherwise turned toward town. That night the wind held, and by morning a firebreak the width of a street had been cut. My father took me down to see it the next day, a ribbon of cleared land as bare as if it had been drawn with a razor. Trees had been felled, the underbrush sickled down and removed. We stood at the edge of the cleared land, the town behind us, and watched the fire. Then we got into my father's Plymouth and drove as close as we were allowed. A fireman near the flames had been asphyxiated, someone said, when the cone of fire had turned abruptly and sucked up all the oxygen in the air. My father explained to me how a flame breathed oxygen like a man. We got out of the car. The heat curled the hair on our arms and turned the ends of our eyelashes white.

My father was a pharmacist and had taken me to the fire out of curiosity. Anything scientific interested him. He kept tide tables and collected the details of nature— butterflies and moths, seeds, wildflowers—and stored them in glass-fronted cases, which he leaned against the stone wall of our cellar. One summer he taught me the constellations of the Northern Hemisphere. We went outside at night, and as the summer progressed he showed me how to find Perseus and Boötes and Andromeda, how some of the brightest stars illuminated Lyra and Aquila, how, though the constellations proceed with the seasons, Polaris remains most fixed and is thus the set point of a mariner's navigation. He taught me the night sky, and I find now that this is rare knowledge. Later, when I taught astronomy, my students rarely cared about the silicon or iron on the sun, but when I spoke of Cepheus or Lacerta, they were silent and attended my words. At a party now I can always find a drinking husband who will come outside with me and sip cognac while I point out the stars and say their names.

That day, as I stood and watched the fire, I thought the flames were as loud and powerful as the sea, and that evening, when we were home, I went out to the front yard and climbed the elm to watch the forest burn. Climbing the elm was forbidden me, because the lowest limbs even then were well above my reach and because my father believed that anybody lucky enough to make it up into the lower boughs would almost certainly fall on the way down. But I knew how to climb it anyway. I had done it before, when my parents were gone. I had never made it as far as the first limbs, but I had learned the knobs and handholds on which, with balance and strength, I could climb to within a single jump of the boughs. The jump frightened me, however, and I had never attempted it. To reach the boughs one had to gather strength and leap upward into the air, propelled only by the purchase of feet and hands on the small juttings of bark. It was a terrible risk. I could no more imagine myself making this leap than I could imagine diving headlong from a coastal cliff into the sea. I was an adventurous youth, as I was later an adventurous man, but all my adventures had a quality about them of safety and planned success. This is still true. In Ethiopia I have photographed a lioness with her cubs; along the Barrier Reef I have dived among barracuda and scorpion fish—but these things have never frightened me. In my life I have done few things that have frightened me.

That night, though, I made the leap into the lower boughs of the elm. My parents were inside the house, and I made my way upward until I crawled out of the leaves onto a narrow top branch and looked around me at a world that on two sides was entirely red and orange with flame. After a time I came back down and went inside to sleep, but that night the wind changed. My father woke us, and we gathered outside on the street with all the other families on our block. People carried blankets filled with the treasures of their lives. One woman wore a fur coat, though the air was suffused with ash and was as warm as an afternoon. My father stood on the hood of a car and spoke. He had heard through the radio that the fire had leaped the break, that a house on the eastern edge of town was in full flame, and, as we all could feel, that the wind was strong and blowing straight west. He told the families to finish loading their cars and leave as soon as possible. Though the fire was still across town, he said, the air was filling with smoke so rapidly that breathing would soon be difficult. He got down off the car and we went inside to gather things together. We had an RCA radio in our living room and a set of Swiss china in my mother's cupboard, but my father instead loaded a box with the *Encyclopaedia Britannica* and carried up from the basement the heavy glass cases that contained his species chart of the North American butterflies. We carried these things outside to the Plymouth. When we returned, my other was standing in the doorway.

"This is my home," she said.

"We're in a hurry," said my father.

"This is my home, this is my children's home. I'm not leaving."

My father stood on the porch looking at her. "Stay here," he said to me. Then he took my mother's arm and they went into the house. I stood on the steps outside, and when my father came out again in a few minutes, he was alone, just as when we drove west that night and slept with the rest of our neighborhood on army cots in the high school gym in the next town, we were alone. My mother had stayed behind.

Nothing important came of this. That night the wind calmed and the burning house was extinguished; the next day a heavy rain wet the fire and it was put out. Everybody came home, and the settled ash was swept from the houses and walkways into black piles in the street. I mention the incident now only because it points out, I think, what I have always lacked: I inherited none of my mother's moral stubbornness. In spite of my age, still, arriving on foot at a crosswalk where the light is red but no cars are in sight, I'm thrown into confusion. My decisions never seem to engage the certainty that I had hoped to enjoy late in my life. But I was adamant and angry when Mr. Pike came to my door. The elm was ancient and exquisite: we could not let it die.

Now, though, the tree was safe. I examined it in the morning, in the afternoon, in the evening, and with a lantern at night. The bark was clear. I slept.

The next morning Mr. Pike was at my door.

"Good morning, neighbor," I said.

"They're back."

"They can't be."

"They are. Look," he said, and walked out to the tree. He pointed up to the first bough.

"You probably can't see them," he said, "but I can. They're up there, a whole line of them."

"They couldn't be."

"They sure are. Listen," he said, "I don't want to be unpleasant, but I'll be frank."

That evening he left a note in our mail slot. It said that he had contacted the authorities, who had agreed to enforce the cutting of the tree if I didn't do it myself. I read the note in the kitchen. Vera had been cooking some Indian chicken before she left for the Appalachian Trail, and on the counter was a big jar filled with flour and spices that she shook pieces of chicken in. I read Mr. Pike's note again. Then I got a fishing knife and a flashlight from the closet, emptied Vera's jar, and went outside with these things to the elm. The street was quiet. I made a few calculations, and then with the knife cut the bark. Nothing. I had to do it only a couple more times, however, before I hit the mark and, sure enough, the tree sprouted insects. Tiny red bugs shot crazily from the slit in the bark. I touched my finger there and they spread in an instant all over my hand and up my arm. I had to shake them off. Then I opened the jar, laid the fishing knife out from the opening like a bridge, and touched the blade to the slit in the tree. They scrambled up the knife and began to fill the jar as fast as a trickling spring. After a few minutes I pulled out the knife, closed the lid, and went back into the house.

Mr. Pike is my neighbor, and so I felt a certain remorse. What I contemplated, however, was not going to kill the elms. It was going to save them. If Mr. Pike's trees were infested, they would still more than likely live, and he would no longer want mine chopped down. This is the nature of the world. In the dark house, feeling half like a criminal and half like a man of mercy, my heart arrhythmic in anticipation, I went upstairs to prepare. I put on black pants and a black shirt. I dabbed shoe polish on my cheeks, my neck, my wrists, the backs of my hands. Over my white hair I stretched a tight black cap. Then I walked downstairs. I picked up the jar and the flashlight and went outside into the night.

I have always enjoyed gestures—never failing to bow, for example, when I finished dancing with a woman—but one attribute I have acquired with age is the ability to predict when I am about to act foolishly. As I slid calmly into the shadowy cavern behind our side yard rhododendron and paused to catch my breath, I thought that perhaps I had better go back inside and get into my bed. But then I decided to go through with it. As I stood there in the shadow of the swaying rhododendron, waiting to pass into the back yard of my neighbor, I thought of Hannibal and Napoleon and MacArthur. I tested my flashlight and shook the jar, which made a soft colliding sound as if it were filled with rice. A light was on in the Pikes' living room, but the alley between our houses was dark. I passed through.

The Pikes' yard is large, larger than ours, and slopes twice within its length, so that the lawn that night seemed like a dark, furrowed flag stretching back to the three elms. I paused at the border of the driveway, where the grass began, and looked out at the young trees outlined by the lighted houses behind them. In what strange ways, I thought, do our lives turn. Then I got down on my hands and knees. Staying along the fence that separates our yards, I crawled toward the back of the Pikes' lawn. In my life I have not crawled a lot. With Vera I have gone spelunking in the limestone caves of southern Minnesota, but there the crawling was obligate, and as we made our way along the narrow, wet channel into the heart of the rock, I felt a strange grace in my knees and elbows. The channel was hideously narrow, and my life depended on the sureness of my limbs. Now, in the Pikes' yard, my knees felt arthritic and torn. I made my way along the driveway toward the young elms against the back fence. The grass was wet and the water dampened my trousers. I was hurrying as best I could across the open lawn, the insect-filled jar in my hand, the flashlight in my pocket, when I put my palm on something cement. I stopped and looked down. In the dim light I saw what looked like the hatch door on a submarine. Round, the size of a manhole, marked with a fluorescent cross—oh, Mr. Pike, I didn't think you'd do it. I put down the jar and felt for the handle in the dark, and when I found it I braced myself and turned. I certainly didn't expect it to give, but it did, circling once, twice, around in my grasp and loosening like the lid of a bottle. I pulled the hatch and up it came. Then I picked up the insects, felt with my feet for the ladder inside, and went down.

I still planned to deposit the insects on his trees, but something about crime is contagious. I knew that what I was doing was foolish and that it increased the risk of being caught, but as I descended the ladder into Mr. Pike's bomb shelter, I could barely distinguish fear from elation. At the bottom of the ladder I switched on the flashlight. The room was round, the ceiling and floor were concrete, and against the wall stood a cabinet of metal shelves filled with canned foods. On one shelf were a dictionary and some magazines. Oh, Mr. Pike. I thought of his sapling elms, of the roots making their steady, blind way through the earth; I thought of his house ten years from now, when the pipes cracked and the ceilings began to pool with water. What a hopeless man he seemed to me then, how small and afraid.

I stood thinking about him, and after a moment I heard a door close in the house. I climbed the ladder and peeked out under the hatch. There on the porch stood Kurt and Mr. Pike. As I watched, they came down off the steps, walked over and stood on the grass near me. I could see the watch blinking on Mr. Pike's wrist. I lowered my head. They were silent, and I wondered what Mr. Pike would do if he found me in his bomb shelter. He was thickly built, as I have said, but I didn't think he was a violent man. One afternoon I had watched as Kurt slammed the front door of their house and ran down the steps onto the lawn, where he stopped and threw an object— an ashtray, I think it was—right through the front window of the house. When the glass shattered, he ran, and Mr. Pike soon appeared on the front steps. The reason I say that he is not a violent man is that I saw something beyond anger, perhaps a certain doom, in his posture as he went back inside that afternoon and began cleaning up the glass with a broom. I watched him through the broken front window of their house.

How would I explain to him, though, the bottle of mad insects I now held? I could have run then, I suppose, made a break up and out of the shelter while their backs were turned. I could have been out the driveway and across the street without their recognizing me. But there was, of course, my heart. I moved back down the ladder. As I descended and began to think about a place to hide my insects, I heard Mr. Pike speak. I climbed back up the ladder. When I looked out under the hatch, I saw the two of them, backs toward me, pointing at the sky. Mr. Pike was sighting something with his finger, and Kurt followed. Then I realized that he was pointing out the constellations, but that he didn't know what they were and was making up their names as he spoke. His voice was not fanciful. It was direct and scientific, and he was lying to his son about what he knew. "These," he said, "these are the Mermaid's Tail, and south you can see the three peaks of Mount Olympus, and then the sword that belongs to the Emperor of the Air." I looked where he was pointing. It was late summer, near midnight, and what he had described was actually Cygnus's bright tail and the outstretched neck of Pegasus.

Presently he ceased speaking, and after a time they walked back across the lawn and went into the house. The light in the kitchen went on, then off. I stepped from my hiding place. I suppose I could have continued with my mission, but the air was calm, it was a perfect and still night, and my plan, I felt, had been interrupted. In my hand the jar felt large and dangerous. I crept back across the lawn, staying in the shadows of the ivy and rhododendron along the fence, until I was in the driveway between our two houses. In the side window of the Pikes' house a light was on. I paused at a point where the angle allowed me a view through the glass, down the hallway, and through an open door into the living room. Mr. Pike and Kurt were sitting together on a brown couch against the far wall of the room, watching television. I came up close to the window and peered through. Though I knew this was foolish, that any neighbor, any man walking his dog at night, would have thought me a burglar in my black clothing, I stayed and watched. The light was on inside, it was dark around me, and I knew I could look in without being seen. Mr. Pike had his hand on Kurt's shoulder. Every so often when they laughed at something on the screen, he moved his hand up and tousled Kurt's hair, and the sight of this suddenly made me feel the way I do on the bridge across the Mississippi River. When he put his hand on Kurt's hair again, I moved out of the shadows and went back to my own house.

I wanted to run, or kick a ball, or shout a soliloquy into the night. I could have stepped up on a car hood then and lured the Pikes, the paper boy, all the neighbors, out into the night. I could have spoken about the laboratory of a biology teacher, about the rows of specimen jars. How could one not hope here? At three weeks the human embryo has gill arches on its neck, like a fish; at six weeks, amphibians' webs still connect its blunt fingers. Miracles. This is true everywhere in nature. The evolution of five hundred million years is mimicked in each gestation: birds that in the egg look like fish; fish that emerge like their spineless, leaflike ancestors. What it is to study life! Anybody who had seen a cell divide could have invented religion.

I sat down on the porch steps and looked at the elm. After a while I stood up and went inside. With turpentine I cleaned the shoe polish from my face, and then I went upstairs. I got into bed. For an hour or two I lay there, sleepless, hot, my thoughts racing, before I gave up and went to the bedroom window. The jar, which I had brought up with me, stood on the sill, and I saw that the insects were either asleep or dead. I opened the window then and emptied them down onto the lawn, and at that moment, as they rained away into the night, glinting and cascading, I thought of asking Vera for a child. I knew it was not possible, but I considered it anyway. Standing there at the window, I thought of Vera, ageless, in forest boots and shorts, perspiring through a flannel blouse as she dipped drinking water from an Appalachian stream. What had we, she and I? The night was calm, dark. Above me Polaris blinked.

I tried going to sleep again. I lay in bed for a time, and then gave up and went downstairs. I ate some crackers. I drank two glasses of bourbon. I sat at the window and looked out at the front yard. Then I got up and went outside and looked up at the stars, and I tried to see them for their beauty and mystery. I thought of billions of tons of exploding gases, hydrogen and helium, red giants, supernovas. In places they were as dense as clouds. I thought of magnesium and silicon and iron. I tried to see them out of their constellatory order, but it was like trying to look at a word without reading it, and I stood there in the night unable to scramble the patterns. Some clouds had blown in and begun to cover Auriga and Taurus. I was watching them begin to spread and refract moonlight when I heard the paper boy whistling the national anthem. When he reached me, I was standing by the elm, still in my nightclothes, unshaven, a little drunk.

"I want you to do something for me," I said.

"Sir?"

"I'm an old man and I want you to do something for me. Put down your bicycle," I said. "Put down your bicycle and look up at the stars."

# Raymond Carver

## (1938–1988)

Raymond Carver's writing style has been compared to that of Franz Kafka, Stephen Crane, and Ernest Hemingway. He was born in Clatskanie, Oregon. His father, a sawmill worker, was an alcoholic, a trait that Carver shared in later years. After graduating high school, Carver married his girlfriend, Maryann Burk, who was sixteen and pregnant at the time. She had a second child when she was eighteen, and Carver supported his family by working odd jobs. They moved to California to be near Burk's family, and there Carver took his first creative writing course. He enrolled at Humboldt State College and received his B.A. in 1963.

While at Humboldt, Carver published his first story, "Pastoral," in the *Western Humanities Review* and his first poem, "The Brass Ring," in *Targets.* In the following years Carver published *Put Yourself in My Shoes* (1974), *Will You Please Be Quiet, Please?* (1976), *What We Talk about When We Talk about Love* (1981), *Where Water Comes Together with Other Water* (1985), and *Where I'm Calling From* (1988). Carver, who drank heavily for two decades, stopped drinking on June 2, 1977. He died of lung cancer in 1988. In his powerfully minimalist style, Carver tells stories of financial and emotional struggle, love, and unspoken and unresolved conflicts.

---

## Cathedral

1983

This blind man, an old friend of my wife's, he was on his way to spend the night. His wife had died. So he was visiting the dead wife's relatives in Connecticut. He called my wife from his in-laws'. Arrangements were made. He would come by train, a five-hour trip, and my wife would meet him at the station. She hadn't seen him since she worked for him one summer in Seattle ten years ago. But she and the blind man had kept in touch. They made tapes and mailed them back and forth. I wasn't enthusiastic about his visit. He was no one I knew. And his being blind bothered me. My idea of blindness came from the movies. In the movies, the blind moved slowly and never laughed. Sometimes they were led by seeing-eye dogs. A blind man in my house was not something I looked forward to.

That summer in Seattle she had needed a job. She didn't have any money. The man she was going to marry at the end of the summer was in officers' training school. He didn't have any money, either. But she was in love with the guy, and he was in love with her, etc. She'd seen something in the paper: HELP WANTED—*Reading to Blind Man,* and a telephone number. She phoned and went over, was hired on the spot. She'd worked with this blind man all summer. She read stuff to him, case studies, reports, that sort of thing. She helped him organize his little office in the county social-service department. They'd become good friends, my wife and the blind man. How do I know these things? She told me. And she told me something else. On her last day in the office, the blind man asked if he could touch her face. She agreed to this. She told me he touched his fingers to every part of her face, her nose—even her neck! She never forgot it. She even tried to write a poem about it. She was always trying to write a poem. She wrote a poem or two every year, usually after something really important had happened to her.

When we first started going out together, she showed me the poem. In the poem, she recalled his fingers and the way they had moved around over her face. In the poem, she talked about what she had felt at the time, about what went through her mind when the blind man touched her nose and lips. I can remember I didn't think much of the poem. Of course, I didn't tell her that. Maybe I just don't understand poetry. I admit it's not the first thing I reach for when I pick up something to read.

Anyway, this man who'd first enjoyed her favors, the officer-to-be, he'd been her childhood sweetheart. So okay. I'm saying that at the end of the summer she let the blind man run his hands over her face, said good-bye to him, married her childhood etc., who was now a commissioned officer, and she moved away from Seattle. But they'd kept in touch, she and the blind man. She made the first contact after a year or so. She called him up one night from an Air Force base in Alabama. She wanted to talk. They talked. He asked her to send him a tape and tell him about her life. She did this. She sent the tape. On the tape, she told the blind man about her husband and about their life together in the military. She told the blind man she loved her husband but she didn't like it where they lived and she didn't like it that he was a part of the military-industrial thing. She told the blind man she'd written a poem and he was in it. She told him that she was writing a poem about what it was like to be an Air Force officer's wife. The poem wasn't finished yet. She was still writing it. The blind man made a tape. He sent her the tape. She made a tape. This went on for years. My wife's officer was posted to one base and then another. She sent tapes from Moody AFB, McGuire, McConnell, and finally Travis, near Sacramento, where one night she got to feeling lonely and cut off from people she kept losing in that moving-around life. She got to feeling she couldn't go it another step. She went in and swallowed all the pills and capsules in the medicine chest and washed them down with a bottle of gin. Then she got into a hot bath and passed out.

But instead of dying, she got sick. She threw up. Her officer—why should he have a name? he was the childhood sweetheart, and what more does he want?—came home from somewhere, found her, and called the ambulance. In time, she put it all on a tape and sent the tape to the blind man. Over the years, she put all kinds of stuff on tapes and sent the tapes off lickety-split. Next to writing a poem every year, I think it was her chief means of recreation. On one tape, she told the blind man she'd decided to live away from her officer for a time. On another tape, she told him about her divorce. She and I began going out, and of course she told her blind man about it. She told him everything, or so it seemed to me. Once she asked me if I'd like to hear the latest tape from the blind man. This was a year ago. I was on the tape, she said. So I said okay, I'd listen to it. I got us drinks and we settled down in the living room. We made ready to listen. First she inserted the tape into the player and adjusted a couple of dials. Then she pushed a lever. The tape squeaked and someone began to talk in this loud voice. She lowered the volume. After a few minutes of harmless chitchat, I heard my own name in the mouth of this stranger, this blind man I didn't even know! And then this: "From all you've said about him, I can only conclude—" But we were interrupted, a knock at the door, something, and we didn't ever get back to the tape. Maybe it was just as well. I'd heard all I wanted to.

Now this same blind man was coming to sleep in my house.

"Maybe I could take him bowling," I said to my wife. She was at the draining board doing scalloped potatoes. She put down the knife she was using and turned around.

"If you love me," she said, "you can do this for me. If you don't love me, okay. But if you had a friend, any friend, and the friend came to visit, I'd make him feel comfortable." She wiped her hands with the dish towel.

"I don't have any blind friends," I said.

"You don't have *any* friends," she said. "Period. Besides," she said, "goddamn it, his wife's just died! Don't you understand that? The man's lost his wife!"

I didn't answer. She'd told me a little about the blind man's wife. Her name was Beulah. Beulah! That's a name for a colored woman.

"Was his wife a Negro?" I asked.

"Are you crazy?" my wife said. "Have you just flipped or something?" She picked up a potato. I saw it hit the floor, then roll under the stove. "What's wrong with you?" she said. "Are you drunk?"

"I'm just asking," I said.

Right then my wife filled me in with more detail than I cared to know. I made a drink and sat at the kitchen table to listen. Pieces of the story began to fall into place.

Beulah had gone to work for the blind man the summer after my wife had stopped working for him. Pretty soon Beulah and the blind man had themselves a church wedding. It was a little wedding—who'd want to go to such a wedding in the first place?—just the two of them, plus the minister and the minister's wife. But it was a church wedding just the same. It was what Beulah had wanted, he'd said. But even then Beulah must have been carrying the cancer in her glands. After they had been in-separable for eight years—my wife's word, *inseparable*—Beulah's health went into a rapid decline. She died in a Seattle hospital room, the blind man sitting beside the bed and holding on to her hand. They'd married, lived and worked together, slept together—had sex, sure—and then the blind man had to bury her. All this without his having ever seen what the goddamned woman looked like. It was beyond my under-standing. Hearing this, I felt sorry for the blind man for a little bit. And then I found myself thinking what a pitiful life this woman must have led. Imagine a woman who could never see herself as she was seen in the eyes of her loved one. A woman who could go on day after day and never receive the smallest compliment from her beloved. A woman whose husband could never read the expression on her face, be it misery or something better. Someone who could wear makeup or not—what difference to him? She could, if she wanted, wear green eye-shadow around one eye, a straight pin in her nostril, yellow slacks, and purple shoes, no matter. And then to slip off into death, the blind man's hand on her hand, his blind eyes streaming tears—I'm imagining now—her last thought maybe this: that he never even knew what she looked like, and she on an express to the grave. Robert was left with a small insurance policy and half of a twenty-peso Mexican coin. The other half of the coin went into the box with her. Pathetic.

So when the time rolled around, my wife went to the depot to pick him up. With nothing to do but wait—sure, I blamed him for that—I was having a drink and watching the TV when I heard the car pull into the drive. I got up from the sofa with my drink and went to the window to have a look.

I saw my wife laughing as she parked the car. I saw her get out of the car and shut the door. She was still wearing a smile. Just amazing. She went around to the other side of the car to where the blind man was already starting to get out. This blind man, feature this, he was wearing a full beard! A beard on a blind man! Too much, I say. The blind man reached into the backseat and dragged out a suitcase. My wife took his arm, shut the car door, and, talking all the way, moved him down the drive and then up the steps to the front porch. I turned off the TV. I finished my drink, rinsed the glass, dried my hands. Then I went to the door.

My wife said, "I want you to meet Robert. Robert, this is my husband. I've told you all about him." She was beaming. She had this blind man by his coat sleeve.

The blind man let go of his suitcase and up came his hand.

I took it. He squeezed hard, held my hand, and then he let it go.

"I feel like we've already met," he boomed.

"Likewise," I said. I didn't know what else to say. Then I said, "Welcome. I've heard a lot about you." We began to move then, a little group, from the porch into the living room, my wife guiding him by the arm. The blind man was carrying his suitcase in his other hand. My wife said things like, "To your left here, Robert. That's right. Now watch it, there's a chair. That's it. Sit down right here. This is the sofa. We just bought this sofa two weeks ago."

I started to say something about the old sofa. I'd liked that old sofa. But I didn't say anything. Then I wanted to say something else, small-talk, about the scenic ride along the Hudson. How going *to* New York, you should sit on the right-hand side of the train, and coming *from* New York, the left-hand side.

"Did you have a good train ride?" I said. "Which side of the train did you sit on, by the way?"

"What a question, which side!" my wife said. "What's it matter which side?" she said.

"I just asked," I said.

"Right side," the blind man said. "I hadn't been on a train in nearly forty years. Not since I was a kid. With my folks. That's been a long time. I'd nearly forgotten the sensation. I have winter in my beard now," he said. "So I've been told, anyway. Do I look distinguished, my dear?" the blind man said to my wife.

"You look distinguished, Robert," she said. "Robert," she said. "Robert, it's just so good to see you."

My wife finally took her eyes off the blind man and looked at me. I had the feeling she didn't like what she saw. I shrugged.

I've never met, or personally known, anyone who was blind. This blind man was late forties, a heavy-set, balding man with stooped shoulders, as if he carried a great weight there. He wore brown slacks, brown shoes, a light-brown shirt, a tie, a sports coat. Spiffy. He also had this full beard. But he didn't use a cane and he didn't wear dark glasses. I'd always thought dark glasses were a must for the blind. Fact was, I wished he had a pair. At first glance, his eyes looked like anyone else's eyes. But if you looked close, there was something different about them. Too much white in the iris, for one thing, and the pupils seemed to move around in the sockets without his knowing it or being able to stop it. Creepy. As I stared at his face, I saw the left pupil turn in toward his nose while the other made an effort to keep in one place. But it was only an effort, for that eye was on the roam without his knowing it or wanting it to be.

I said, "Let me get you a drink. What's your pleasure? We have a little of everything. It's one of our pastimes."

"Bub, I'm a Scotch man myself," he said fast enough in this big voice.

"Right," I said. Bub! "Sure you are. I knew it."

He let his fingers touch his suitcase, which was sitting alongside the sofa. He was taking his bearings. I didn't blame him for that.

"I'll move that up to your room," my wife said.

"No, that's fine," the blind man said loudly. "It can go up when I go up."

"A little water with the Scotch?" I said.

"Very little," he said.

"I knew it," I said.

He said, "Just a tad. The Irish actor, Barry Fitzgerald? I'm like that fellow. When I drink water, Fitzgerald said, I drink water. When I drink whiskey, I drink whiskey." My wife laughed. The blind man brought his hand up under his beard. He lifted his beard slowly and let it drop.

I did the drinks, three big glasses of Scotch with a splash of water in each. Then we made ourselves comfortable and talked about Robert's travels. First the long flight from the West Coast to Connecticut, we covered that. Then from Connecticut up here by train. We had another drink concerning that leg of the trip.

I remembered having read somewhere that the blind didn't smoke because, as speculation had it, they couldn't see the smoke they exhaled. I thought I knew that much and that much only about blind people. But this blind man smoked his cigarette down to the nubbin and then lit another one. This blind man filled his ashtray and my wife emptied it.

When we sat down at the table for dinner, we had another drink. My wife heaped Robert's plate with cube steak, scalloped potatoes, green beans. I buttered him up two slices of bread. I said, "Here's bread and butter for you." I swallowed some of my drink. "Now let us pray," I said, and the blind man lowered his head. My wife looked at me, her mouth agape. "Pray the phone won't ring and the food doesn't get cold," I said.

We dug in. We ate everything there was to eat on the table. We ate like there was no tomorrow. We didn't talk. We ate. We scarfed. We grazed that table. We were into serious eating. The blind man had right away located his foods, he knew just where everything was on his plate. I watched with admiration as he used his knife and fork on the meat. He'd cut two pieces of meat, fork the meat into his mouth, and then go all out for the scalloped potatoes, the beans next, and then he'd tear off a hunk of buttered bread and eat that. He'd follow this up with a big drink of milk. It didn't seem to bother him to use his fingers once in a while, either.

We finished everything, including half a strawberry pie. For a few moments, we sat as if stunned. Sweat beaded on our faces. Finally, we got up from the table and left the dirty plates. We didn't look back. We took ourselves into the living room and sank into our places again. Robert and my wife sat on the sofa. I took the big chair. We had us two or three more drinks while they talked about the major things that had come to pass for them in the past ten years. For the most part, I just listened. Now and then I joined in. I didn't want him to think I'd left the room, and I didn't want her to think I was feeling left out. They talked of things that had happened to them—to them!— these past ten years. I waited in vain to hear my name on my wife's sweet lips: "And then my dear husband came into my life"—something like that. But I heard nothing of the sort. More talk of Robert. Robert had done a little of everything, it seemed, a regular blind jack-of-all-trades. But most recently he and his wife had had an Amway distributorship, from which, I gathered, they'd earned a living, such as it was. The blind man was also a ham radio operator. He talked in his loud voice about conversations he'd had with fellow operators in Guam, in the Philippines, in Alaska, and even in Tahiti. He said he'd have a lot of friends there if he ever wanted to go visit those places. From time to time, he'd turn his blind face toward me, put his hand under his beard, ask me something. How long had I been in my present position? (Three years.) Did I like my work? (I didn't.) Was I going to stay with it? (What were the options?) Finally, when I thought he was beginning to run down, I got up and turned on the TV.

My wife looked at me with irritation. She was heading toward a boil. Then she looked at the blind man and said, "Robert, do you have a TV?"

The blind man said, "My dear, I have two TVs. I have a color set and a black-and-white thing, an old relic. It's funny, but if I turn the TV on, and I'm always turning it on, I turn on the color set. It's funny, don't you think?"

I didn't know what to say to that. I had absolutely nothing to say to that. No opinion. So I watched the news program and tried to listen to what the announcer was saying.

"This is a color TV," the blind man said. "Don't ask me how, but I can tell."

"We traded up a while ago," I said.

The blind man had another taste of his drink. He lifted his beard, sniffed it, and let it fall. He leaned forward on the sofa. He positioned his ashtray on the coffee table, then put the lighter to his cigarette. He leaned back on the sofa and crossed his legs at the ankles.

My wife covered her mouth, and then she yawned. She stretched. She said, "I think I'll go upstairs and put on my robe. I think I'll change into something else. Robert, you make yourself comfortable," she said.

"I'm comfortable," the blind man said.

"I want you to feel comfortable in this house," she said.

"I am comfortable," the blind man said.

After she'd left the room, he and I listened to the weather report and then to the sports roundup. By that time, she'd been gone so long I didn't know if she was going to come back. I thought she might have gone to bed. I wished she'd come back downstairs. I didn't want to be left alone with a blind man. I asked him if he wanted another drink, and he said sure. Then I asked if he wanted to smoke some dope with me. I said I'd just rolled a number. I hadn't, but I planned to do so in about two shakes.

"I'll try some with you," he said.

"Damn right," I said. "That's the stuff."

I got our drinks and sat down on the sofa with him. Then I rolled us two fat numbers. I lit one and passed it. I brought it to his fingers. He took it and inhaled.

"Hold it as long as you can," I said. I could tell he didn't know the first thing.

My wife came back downstairs wearing her pink robe and her pink slippers.

"What do I smell?" she said.

"We thought we'd have us some cannabis," I said.

My wife gave me a savage look. Then she looked at the blind man and said, "Robert, I didn't know you smoked."

He said, "I do now, my dear. There's a first time for everything. But I don't feel anything yet."

"This stuff is pretty mellow," I said. "This stuff is mild. It's dope you can reason with," I said. "It doesn't mess you up."

"Not much it doesn't, bub," he said, and laughed.

My wife sat on the sofa between the blind man and me. I passed her the number. She took it and toked and then passed it back to me. "Which way is this going?" she said. Then she said, "I shouldn't be smoking this. I can hardly keep my eyes open as it is. That dinner did me in. I shouldn't have eaten so much."

"It was the strawberry pie," the blind man said. "That's what did it," he said, and he laughed his big laugh. Then he shook his head.

"There's more strawberry pie," I said.

"Do you want some more, Robert?" my wife said.

"Maybe in a little while," he said.

We gave our attention to the TV. My wife yawned again. She said, "Your bed is made up when you feel like going to bed, Robert. I know you must have had a long day. When you're ready to go to bed, say so."

She pulled his arm. "Robert?"

He came to and said, "I've had a real nice time. This beats tapes, doesn't it?"

I said, "Coming at you," and I put the number between his fingers. He inhaled, held the smoke, and then let it go. It was like he'd been doing it since he was nine years old.

"Thanks, bub," he said. "But I think this is all for me. I think I'm beginning to feel it," he said. He held the burning roach out for my wife.

"Same here," she said. "Ditto. Me, too." She took the roach and passed it to me. "I may just sit here for a while between you two guys with my eyes closed. But don't let me bother you, okay? Either one of you. If it bothers you, say so. Otherwise, I may just sit here with my eyes closed until you're ready to go to bed," she said. "Your bed's made up, Robert, when you're ready. It's right next to our room at the top of the stairs. We'll show you up when you're ready. You wake me up now, you guys, if I fall asleep." She said that and then she closed her eyes and went to sleep.

The news program ended. I got up and changed the channel. I sat back down on the sofa. I wished my wife hadn't pooped out. Her head lay across the back of the sofa, her mouth open. She'd turned so that her robe had slipped away from her legs, exposing a juicy thigh. I reached to draw her robe back over her, and it was then that I glanced at the blind man. What the hell! I flipped the robe open again.

"You say when you want some strawberry pie," I said.

"I will," he said.

I said, "Are you tired? Do you want me to take you up to your bed? Are you ready to hit the hay?"

"Not yet," he said. "No, I'll stay up with you, bub. If that's all right. I'll stay up un-til you're ready to turn in. We haven't had a chance to talk. Know what I mean? I feel like me and her monopolized the evening." He lifted his beard and he let it fall. He picked up his cigarettes and his lighter.

"That's all right," I said. Then I said, "I'm glad for the company."

And I guess I was. Every night I smoked dope and stayed up as long as I could be-fore I fell asleep. My wife and I hardly ever went to bed at the same time. When I did go to sleep, I had these dreams. Sometimes I'd wake up from one of them, my heart going crazy.

Something about the church and the Middle Ages was on the TV. Not your run-of-the-mill TV fare. I wanted to watch something else. I turned to the other channels. But there was nothing on them, either. So I turned back to the first channel and apologized.

"Bub, it's all right," the blind man said. "It's fine with me. Whatever you want to watch is okay. I'm always learning something. Learning never ends. It won't hurt me to learn something tonight. I got ears," he said.

We didn't say anything for a time. He was leaning forward with his head turned at me, his right ear aimed in the direction of the set. Very disconcerting. Now and then his eyelids drooped and then they snapped open again. Now and then he put his fingers into his beard and tugged, like he was thinking about something he was hearing on the television.

On the screen, a group of men wearing cowls was being set upon and tormented by men dressed in skeleton costumes and men dressed as devils. The men dressed as devils wore devil masks, horns, and long tails. This pageant was part of a procession. The Englishman who was narrating the thing said it took place in Spain once a year. I tried to explain to the blind man what was happening.

"Skeletons," he said. "I know about skeletons," he said, and he nodded.

The TV showed this one cathedral. Then there was a long, slow look at another one. Finally, the picture switched to the famous one in Paris, with its flying buttresses and its spires reaching up to the clouds. The camera pulled away to show the whole of the cathedral rising above the skyline.

There were times when the Englishman who was telling the thing would shut up, would simply let the camera move around over the cathedrals. Or else the camera would tour the countryside, men in fields walking behind oxen. I waited as long as I could. Then I felt I had to say something. I said, "They're showing the outside of this cathedral now. Gargoyles. Little statues carved to look like monsters. Now I guess they're in Italy. Yeah, they're in Italy. There's paintings on the walls of this one church."

"Are those fresco paintings, bub?" he asked, and he sipped from his drink.

I reached for my glass. But it was empty. I tried to remember what I could remember. "You're asking me are those frescoes?" I said. "That's a good question. I don't know."

The camera moved to a cathedral outside Lisbon. The differences in the Por-tuguese cathedral compared with the French and Italian were not that great. But they were there. Mostly the interior stuff. Then something occurred to me, and I said, "Something has occurred to me. Do you have any idea what a cathedral is? What they look like, that is? Do you follow me? If somebody says cathedral to you, do you have any notion what they're talking about? Do you know the difference between that and a Baptist church, say?"

He let the smoke dribble from his mouth. "I know they took hundreds of workers fifty or a hundred years to build," he said. "I just heard the man say that, of course. I know generations of the same families worked on a cathedral. I heard him say that, too. The men who began their life's work on them, they never lived to see the completion of their work. In that wise, bub, they're no different from the rest of us, right?" He laughed. Then his eyelids drooped again. His head nodded. He seemed to be snoozing. Maybe he was imagining himself in Portugal. The TV was showing another cathedral now. This one was in Germany. The Englishman's voice droned on. "Cathedrals," the blind man said. He sat up and rolled his head back and forth. "If you want the truth, bub, that's about all I know. What I just said. What I heard him say. But maybe you could describe one to me? I wish you'd do it. I'd like that. If you want to know, I really don't have a good idea."

I stared hard at the shot of the cathedral on the TV. How could I even begin to describe it? But say my life depended on it. Say my life was being threatened by an insane guy who said I had to do it or else.

I stared some more at the cathedral before the picture flipped off into the countryside. There was no use. I turned to the blind man and said, "To begin with, they're very tall." I was looking around the room for clues. "They reach way up. Up and up. Toward the sky. They're so big, some of them, they have to have these supports. To help hold them up, so to speak. These supports are called buttresses. They remind me of viaducts, for some reason. But maybe you don't know viaducts, either? Sometimes the cathedrals have devils and such carved into the front. Sometimes lords and ladies. Don't ask me why this is," I said.

He was nodding. The whole upper part of his body seemed to be moving back and forth.

"I'm not doing so good, am I?" I said.

He stopped nodding and leaned forward on the edge of the sofa. As he listened to me, he was running his fingers through his beard. I wasn't getting through to him, I could see that. But he waited for me to go on just the same. He nodded, like he was trying to encourage me. I tried to think what else to say. "They're really big," I said. "They're massive. They're built of stone. Marble, too, sometimes. In those olden days, when they built cathedrals, men wanted to be close to God. In those olden days, God was an important part of everyone's life. You could tell this from their cathedral-building. I'm sorry," I said, "but it looks like that's the best I can do for you. I'm just no good at it."

"That's all right, bub," the blind man said. "Hey, listen. I hope you don't mind my asking you. Can I ask you something? Let me ask you a simple question, yes or no. I'm just curious and there's no offense. You're my host. But let me ask if you are in any way religious? You don't mind my asking?"

I shook my head. He couldn't see that, though. A wink is the same as a nod to a blind man. "I guess I don't believe in it. In anything. Sometimes it's hard. You know what I'm saying?"

"Sure, I do," he said.

"Right," I said.

The Englishman was still holding forth. My wife sighed in her sleep. She drew a long breath and went on with her sleeping.

"You'll have to forgive me," I said. "But I can't tell you what a cathedral looks like. It just isn't in me to do it. I can't do any more than I've done."

The blind man sat very still, his head down, as he listened to me.

I said, "The truth is, cathedrals don't mean anything special to me. Nothing. Cathedrals. They're something to look at on late-night TV. That's all they are."

It was then that the blind man cleared his throat. He brought something up. He took a handkerchief from his back pocket. Then he said, "I get it, bub. It's okay. It happens. Don't worry about it," he said. "Hey, listen to me. Will you do me a favor? I got an idea. Why don't you find us some heavy paper? And a pen. We'll do something. We'll draw one together. Get us a pen and some heavy paper. Go on, bub, get the stuff," he said.

So I went upstairs. My legs felt like they didn't have any strength in them. They felt like they did after I'd done some running. In my wife's room, I looked around. I found some ballpoints in a little basket on her table. And then I tried to think where to look for the kind of paper he was talking about.

Downstairs, in the kitchen, I found a shopping bag with onion skins in the bottom of the bag. I emptied the bag and shook it. I brought it into the living room and sat down with it near his legs. I moved some things, smoothed the wrinkles from the bag, spread it out on the coffee table.

The blind man got down from the sofa and sat next to me on the carpet.

He ran his fingers over the paper. He went up and down the sides of the paper. The edges, even the edges. He fingered the corners.

"All right," he said. "All right, let's do her."

He found my hand, the hand with the pen. He closed his hand over my hand. "Go ahead, bub, draw," he said. "Draw. You'll see. I'll follow along with you. It'll be okay. Just begin now like I'm telling you. You'll see. Draw," the blind man said.

So I began. First I drew a box that looked like a house. It could have been the house I lived in. Then I put a roof on it. At either end of the roof, I drew spires. Crazy.

"Swell," he said. "Terrific. You're doing fine," he said. "Never thought anything like this could happen in your lifetime, did you, bub? Well, it's a strange life, we all know that. Go on now. Keep it up."

I put in windows with arches. I drew flying buttresses. I hung great doors. I couldn't stop. The TV station went off the air. I put down the pen and closed and opened my fingers. The blind man felt around over the paper. He moved the tips of his fingers over the paper, all over what I had drawn, and he nodded.

"Doing fine," the blind man said.

I took up the pen again, and he found my hand. I kept at it. I'm no artist. But I kept drawing just the same.

My wife opened up her eyes and gazed at us. She sat up on the sofa, her robe hanging open. She said, "What are you doing? Tell me, I want to know."

I didn't answer her.

The blind man said, "We're drawing a cathedral. Me and him are working on it. Press hard," he said to me. "That's right. That's good," he said. "Sure. You got it, bub. I can tell. You didn't think you could. But you can, can't you? You're cooking with gas now. You know what I'm saying? We're going to really have us something here in a minute. How's the old arm?" he said. "Put some people in there now. What's a cathedral without people?"

My wife said, "What's going on? Robert, what are you doing? What's going on?"

"It's all right," he said to her. "Close your eyes now," the blind man said to me.

I did it. I closed them just like he said.

"Are they closed?" he said. "Don't fudge."

"They're closed," I said.

"Keep them that way," he said. He said, "Don't stop now. Draw."

So we kept on with it. His fingers rode my fingers as my hand went over the paper. It was like nothing else in my life up to now.

Then he said, "I think that's it. I think you got it," he said. "Take a look. What do you think?"

But I had my eyes closed. I thought I'd keep them that way for a little longer. I thought it was something I ought to do.

"Well?" he said. "Are you looking?"

My eyes were still closed. I was in my house. I knew that. But I didn't feel like I was inside anything.

"It's really something," I said.

## A Small, Good Thing                                                    *1983*

Saturday afternoon she drove to the bakery in the shopping center. After looking through a loose-leaf binder with photographs of cakes taped onto the pages, she ordered chocolate, the child's favorite. The cake she chose was decorated with a space ship and launching pad under a sprinkling of white stars, and a planet made of red frosting at the other end. His name, SCOTTY, would be in green letters beneath the planet. The baker, who was an older man with a thick neck, listened without saying anything when she told him the child would be eight years old next Monday. The baker wore a white apron that looked like a smock. Straps cut under his arms, went around in back and then to the front again, where they were secured under his heavy waist. He wiped his hands on his apron as he listened to her. He kept his eyes down on the photographs and let her talk. He let her take her time. He'd just come to work and he'd be there all night, baking, and he was in no real hurry.

She gave the baker her name, Ann Weiss, and her telephone number. The cake would be ready on Monday morning, just out of the oven, in plenty of time for the child's party that afternoon. The baker was not jolly. There were no pleasantries between them, just the minimum exchange of words, the necessary information. He made her feel uncomfortable, and she didn't like that. While he was bent over the counter with the pencil in his hand, she studied his coarse features and wondered if he'd ever done anything else with his life besides be a baker. She was a mother and thirty-three years old, and it seemed to her that everyone, especially someone the baker's age—a man old enough to be her father—must have children who'd gone through this special time of cakes and birthday parties. There must be that between them, she thought. But he was abrupt with her—not rude, just abrupt. She gave up trying to make friends with him. She looked into the back of the bakery and could see a long, heavy wooden table with aluminum pie pans stacked at one end; and beside the table a metal container filled with empty racks. There was an enormous oven. A radio was playing country-Western music.

The baker finished printing the information on the special order card and closed up the binder. He looked at her and said, "Monday morning." She thanked him and drove home.

On Monday morning, the birthday boy was walking to school with another boy. They were passing a bag of potato chips back and forth and the birthday boy was trying to find out what his friend intended to give him for his birthday that afternoon. Without looking, the birthday boy stepped off the curb at an intersection and was immediately knocked down by a car. He fell on his side with his head in the gutter and his legs out in the road. His eyes were closed, but his legs moved back and forth as if he were trying to climb over something. His friend dropped the potato chips and started to cry. The car had gone a hundred feet or so and stopped in the middle of the road. The man in the driver's seat looked back over his shoulder. He waited until the boy got unsteadily to his feet. The boy wobbled a little. He looked dazed, but okay. The driver put the car into gear and drove away.

The birthday boy didn't cry, but he didn't have anything to say about anything either. He wouldn't answer when his friend asked him what it felt like to be hit by a car. He walked home, and his friend went on to school. But after the birthday boy was inside his house and was telling his mother about it—she sitting beside him on the sofa, holding his hands in her lap, saying, "Scotty, honey, are you sure you feel all right, baby?" thinking she would call the doctor anyway—he suddenly lay back on the sofa, closed his eyes, and went limp. When she couldn't wake him up, she hurried to the telephone and called her husband at work. Howard told her to remain calm, remain calm, and then he called an ambulance for the child and left for the hospital himself.

Of course, the birthday party was canceled. The child was in the hospital with a mild concussion and suffering from shock. There'd been vomiting, and his lungs had taken in fluid which needed pumping out that afternoon. Now he simply seemed to be in a very deep sleep—but no coma, Dr. Francis had emphasized, no coma, when he saw the alarm in the parents' eyes. At eleven o'clock that night, when the boy seemed to be resting comfortably enough after the many X-rays and the lab work, and it was just a matter of his waking up and coming around, Howard left the hospital. He and Ann had been at the hospital with the child since that afternoon, and he was going home for a short while to bathe and change clothes. "I'll be back in an hour," he said. She nodded. "It's fine," she said. "I'll be right here." He kissed her on the forehead, and they touched hands. She sat in the chair beside the bed and looked at the child. She was waiting for him to wake up and be all right. Then she could begin to relax.

Howard drove home from the hospital. He took the wet, dark streets very fast, then caught himself and slowed down. Until now, his life had gone smoothly and to his satisfaction—college, marriage, another year of college for the advanced degree in business, a junior partnership in an investment firm. Fatherhood. He was happy and, so far, lucky—he knew that. His parents were still living, his brothers and his sister were established, his friends from college had gone out to take their places in the world. So far, he had kept away from any real harm, from those forces he knew existed and that could cripple or bring down a man if the luck went bad, if things suddenly turned. He pulled into the driveway and parked. His left leg began to tremble. He sat in the car for a minute and tried to deal with the present situation in a rational manner. Scotty had been hit by a car and was in the hospital, but he was going to be all right. Howard closed his eyes and ran his hand over his face. He got out of the car and went up to the front door. The dog was barking inside the house. The telephone rang and rang while he unlocked the door and fumbled for the light switch. He shouldn't have left the hospital, he shouldn't have. "Goddamn it!" he said. He picked up the receiver and said, "I just walked in the door!"

"There's a cake here that wasn't picked up," the voice on the other end of the line said.

"What are you saying?" Howard asked.

"A cake," the voice said. "A sixteen-dollar cake."

Howard held the receiver against his ear, trying to understand. "I don't know anything about a cake," he said. "Jesus, what are you talking about?"

"Don't hand me that," the voice said.

Howard hung up the telephone. He went into the kitchen and poured himself some whiskey. He called the hospital. But the child's condition remained the same; he was still sleeping and nothing had changed there. While water poured into the tub, Howard lathered his face and shaved. He'd just stretched out in the tub and closed his eyes when the telephone rang again. He hauled himself out, grabbed a towel, and hurried through the house, saying, "Stupid, stupid," for having left the hospital. But when he picked up the receiver and shouted, "Hello!" there was no sound at the other end of the line. Then the caller hung up.

He arrived back at the hospital a little after midnight. Ann still sat in the chair beside the bed. She looked up at Howard, and then she looked back at the child. The child's eyes stayed closed, the head was still wrapped in bandages. His breathing was quiet and regular. From an apparatus over the bed hung a bottle of glucose with a tube running from the bottle to the boy's arm.

"How is he?" Howard said. "What's all this?" waving at the glucose and the tube.

"Dr. Francis's orders," she said. "He needs nourishment. He needs to keep up his strength. Why doesn't he wake up, Howard? I don't understand, if he's all right."

Howard put his hand against the back of her head. He ran his fingers through her hair. "He's going to be all right. He'll wake up in a little while. Dr. Francis knows what's what."

After a time, he said, "Maybe you should go home and get some rest. I'll stay here. Just don't put up with this creep who keeps calling. Hang up right away."

"Who's calling?" she asked.

"I don't know who, just somebody with nothing better to do than call up people. You go on now."

She shook her head. "No," she said, "I'm fine."

"Really," he said. "Go home for a while, and then come back and spell me in the morning. It'll be all right. What did Dr. Francis say? He said Scotty's going to be all right. We don't have to worry. He's just sleeping now, that's all."

A nurse pushed the door open. She nodded at them as she went to the bedside. She took the left arm out from under the covers and put her fingers on the wrist, found the pulse, then consulted her watch. In a little while, she put the arm back under the covers and moved to the foot of the bed, where she wrote something on a clipboard attached to the bed.

"How is he?" Ann said. Howard's hand was a weight on her shoulder. She was aware of the pressure from his fingers.

"He's stable," the nurse said. Then she said, "Doctor will be in again shortly. Doctor's back in the hospital. He's making rounds right now."

"I was saying maybe she'd want to go home and get a little rest," Howard said. "After the doctor comes," he said.

"She could do that," the nurse said. "I think you should both feel free to do that, if you wish." The nurse was a big Scandinavian woman with blond hair. There was the trace of an accent in her speech.

"We'll see what the doctor says," Ann said. "I want to talk to the doctor. I don't think he should keep sleeping like this. I don't think that's a good sign." She brought her hand up to her eyes and let her head come forward a little. Howard's grip tightened on her shoulder, and then his hand moved up to her neck, where his fingers began to knead the muscles there.

"Dr. Francis will be here in a few minutes," the nurse said. Then she left the room.

Howard gazed at his son for a time, the small chest quietly rising and falling under the covers. For the first time since the terrible minutes after Ann's telephone call to him at his office, he felt a genuine fear starting in his limbs. He began shaking his head. Scotty was fine, but instead of sleeping at home in his own bed, he was in a hospital bed with bandages around his head and a tube in his arm. But this help was what he needed right now.

Dr. Francis came in and shook hands with Howard, though they'd just seen each other a few hours before. Ann got up from the chair. "Doctor?"

"Ann," he said and nodded. "Let's just first see how he's doing," the doctor said.

He moved to the side of the bed and took the boy's pulse. He peeled back one eyelid and then the other. Howard and Ann stood beside the doctor and watched. Then the doctor turned back the covers and listened to the boy's heart and lungs with his stethoscope. He pressed his fingers here and there on the abdomen. When he was finished, he went to the end of the bed and studied the chart. He noted the time, scribbled something on the chart, and then looked at Howard and Ann.

"Doctor, how is he?" Howard said. "What's the matter with him exactly?"

"Why doesn't he wake up?" Ann said.

The doctor was a handsome, big-shouldered man with a tanned face. He wore a three-piece blue suit, a striped tie, and ivory cufflinks. His gray hair was combed along the sides of his head, and he looked as if he had just come from a concert. "He's all right," the doctor said. "Nothing to shout about, he could be better, I think. But he's all right. Still, I wish he'd wake up. He should wake up pretty soon." The doctor looked at the boy again. "We'll know some more in a couple of hours, after the results of a few more tests are in. But he's all right, believe me, except for the hairline fracture of the skull. He does have that."

"Oh, no," Ann said.

"And a bit of a concussion, as I said before. Of course, you know he's in shock," the doctor said. "Sometimes you see this in shock cases. This sleeping."

"But he's out of any real danger?" Howard said. "You said before he's not in a coma. You wouldn't call this a coma, then—would you, doctor?" Howard waited. He looked at the doctor.

"No, I don't want to call it a coma," the doctor said and glanced over at the boy once more. "He's just in a very deep sleep. It's a restorative measure the body is taking on its own. He's out of any real danger, I'd say that for certain, yes. But we'll know more when he wakes up and the other tests are in," the doctor said.

"It's a coma," Ann said. "Of sorts."

"It's not a coma yet, not exactly," the doctor said. "I wouldn't want to call it coma. Not yet, anyway. He's suffered shock. In shock cases, this kind of reaction is common enough; it's a temporary reaction to bodily trauma. Coma. Well, coma is a deep, prolonged unconsciousness, something that could go on for days, or weeks even. Scotty's not in that area, not as far as we can tell. I'm certain his condition will show improvement by morning. I'm betting that it will. We'll know more when he wakes up, which shouldn't be long now. Of course, you may do as you like, stay here or go home for a time. But by all means feel free to leave the hospital for a while if you want. This is not easy, I know." The doctor gazed at the boy again, watching him, and then he turned to Ann and said, "You try not to worry, little mother. Believe me, we're doing all that can be done. It's just a question of a little more time now." He nodded at her, shook hands with Howard again, and then he left the room.

Ann put her hand over the child's forehead. "At least he doesn't have a fever," she said. Then she said, "My God, he feels so cold, though. Howard? Is he supposed to feel like this? Feel his head."

Howard touched the child's temples. His own breathing had slowed. "I think he's supposed to feel this way right now," he said. "He's in shock, remember? That's what the doctor said. The doctor was just in here. He would have said something if Scotty wasn't okay."

Ann stood there a while longer, working her lip with her teeth. Then she moved over to her chair and sat down.

Howard sat in the chair next to her chair. They looked at each other. He wanted to say something else and reassure her, but he was afraid, too. He took her hand and put it in his lap, and this made him feel better, her hand being there. He picked up her hand and squeezed it. Then he just held her hand. They sat like that for a while, watching the boy and not talking. From time to time, he squeezed her hand. Finally, she took her hand away.

"I've been praying," she said.

He nodded.

She said, "I almost thought I'd forgotten how, but it came back to me. All I had to do was close my eyes and say, 'Please God, help us—help Scotty,' and then the rest was easy. The words were right there. Maybe if you prayed, too," she said to him.

"I've already prayed," he said. "I prayed this afternoon—yesterday afternoon, I mean—after you called, while I was driving to the hospital. I've been praying," he said.

"That's good," she said. For the first time, she felt they were together in it, this trouble. She realized with a start that, until now, it had only been happening to her and to Scotty. She hadn't let Howard into it, though he was there and needed all along. She felt glad to be his wife.

The same nurse came in and took the boy's pulse again and checked the flow from the bottle hanging above the bed.

In an hour, another doctor came in. He said his name was Parsons, from Radiology. He had a bushy mustache. He was wearing loafers, a Western shirt, and a pair of jeans.

"We're going to take him downstairs for more pictures," he told them. "We need to do some more pictures, and we want to do a scan."

"What's that?" Ann said. "A scan?" She stood between this new doctor and the bed. "I thought you'd already taken all your X-rays."

"I'm afraid we need some more," he said. "Nothing to be alarmed about. We just need some more pictures, and we want to do a brain scan on him."

"My God," Ann said.

"It's perfectly normal procedure in cases like this," this new doctor said. "We just need to find out for sure why he isn't back awake yet. It's normal medical procedure, and nothing to be alarmed about. We'll be taking him down in a few minutes," this doctor said.

In a little while, two orderlies came into the room with a gurney. They were black-haired, dark-complexioned men in white uniforms, and they said a few words to each other in a foreign tongue as they unhooked the boy from the tube and moved him from his bed to the gurney. Then they wheeled him from the room. Howard and Ann got on the same elevator. Ann gazed at the child. She closed her eyes as the elevator began its descent. The orderlies stood at either end of the gurney without saying anything, though once one of the men made a comment to the other in their own language, and the other man nodded slowly in response.

Later that morning, just as the sun was beginning to lighten the windows in the waiting room outside the X-ray department, they brought the boy out and moved him back up to his room. Howard and Ann rode up on the elevator with him once more, and once more they took up their places beside the bed.

They waited all day, but still the boy did not wake up. Occasionally, one of them would leave the room to go downstairs to the cafeteria to drink coffee and then, as if suddenly remembering and feeling guilty, get up from the table and hurry back to the room. Dr. Francis came again that afternoon and examined the boy once more and then left after telling them he was coming along and could wake up at any minute now. Nurses, different nurses from the night before, came in from time to time. Then a young woman from the lab knocked and entered the room. She wore white slacks and a white blouse and carried a little tray of things which she put on the stand beside the bed. Without a word to them, she took blood from the boy's arm. Howard closed his eyes as the woman found the right place on the boy's arm and pushed the needle in.

"I don't understand this," Ann said to the woman.

"Doctor's orders," the young woman said. "I do what I'm told. They say draw that one, I draw. What's wrong with him, anyway?" she said. "He's a sweetie."

"He was hit by a car," Howard said. "A hit-and-run."

The young woman shook her head and looked again at the boy. Then she took her tray and left the room.

"Why won't he wake up?" Ann said. "Howard? I want some answers from these people."

Howard didn't say anything. He sat down again in the chair and crossed one leg over the other. He rubbed his face. He looked at his son and then he settled back in the chair, closed his eyes, and went to sleep.

Ann walked to the window and looked out at the parking lot. It was night, and cars were driving into and out of the parking lot with their lights on. She stood at the window with her hands gripping the sill, and knew in her heart that they were into something now, something hard. She was afraid, and her teeth began to chatter until she tightened her jaws. She saw a big car stop in front of the hospital and someone, a woman in a long coat, get into the car. She wished she were that woman and somebody, anybody, was driving her away from here to somewhere else, a place where she would find Scotty waiting for her when she stepped out of the car, ready to say *Mom* and let her gather him in her arms.

In a little while, Howard woke up. He looked at the boy again. Then he got up from the chair, stretched, and went over to stand beside her at the window. They both stared out at the parking lot. They didn't say anything. But they seemed to feel each other's insides now, as though the worry had made them transparent in a perfectly natural way.

The door opened and Dr. Francis came in. He was wearing a different suit and tie this time. His gray hair was combed along the sides of his head, and he looked as if he had just shaved. He went straight to the bed and examined the boy. "He ought to have come around by now. There's just no good reason for this," he said. "But I can tell you we're all convinced he's out of any danger. We'll just feel better when he wakes up. There's no reason, absolutely none, why he shouldn't come around. Very soon. Oh, he'll have himself a dilly of a headache when he does, you can count on that. But all of his signs are fine. They're as normal as can be."

"It is a coma, then?" Ann said.

The doctor rubbed his smooth cheek. "We'll call it that for the time being, until he wakes up. But you must be worn out. This is hard. I know this is hard. Feel free to go out for a bite," he said. "It would do you good. I'll put a nurse in here while you're gone if you'll feel better about going. Go and have yourselves something to eat."

"I couldn't eat anything," Ann said.

"Do what you need to do, of course," the doctor said. "Anyway, I wanted to tell you that all the signs are good, the tests are negative, nothing showed up at all, and just as soon as he wakes up he'll be over the hill."

"Thank you, doctor," Howard said. He shook hands with the doctor again. The doctor patted Howard's shoulder and went out.

"I suppose one of us should go home and check on things," Howard said. "Slug needs to be fed, for one thing."

"Call one of the neighbors," Ann said. "Call the Morgans. Anyone will feed a dog if you ask them to."

"All right," Howard said. After a while, he said, "Honey, why don't *you* do it? Why don't you go home and check on things, and then come back? It'll do you good. I'll be right here with him. Seriously," he said. "We need to keep up our strength on this. We'll want to be here for a while even after he wakes up."

"Why don't *you* go?" she said. "Feed Slug. Feed yourself."

"I already went," he said. "I was gone for exactly an hour and fifteen minutes. You go home for an hour and freshen up. Then come back."

She tried to think about it, but she was too tired. She closed her eyes and tried to think about it again. After a time, she said, "Maybe I *will* go home for a few minutes. Maybe if I'm not just sitting right here watching him every second, he'll wake up and be all right. You know? Maybe he'll wake up if I'm not here. I'll go home and take a bath and put on clean clothes. I'll feed Slug. Then I'll come back."

"I'll be right here," he said. "You go on home, honey. I'll keep an eye on things here." His eyes were bloodshot and small, as if he'd been drinking for a long time. His clothes were rumpled. His beard had come out again. She touched his face, and then she took her hand back. She understood he wanted to be by himself for a while, not have to talk or share his worry for a time. She picked her purse up from the nightstand, and he helped her into her coat.

"I won't be gone long," she said.

"Just sit and rest for a little while when you get home," he said. "Eat something. Take a bath. After you get out of the bath, just sit for a while and rest. It'll do you a world of good, you'll see. Then come back," he said. "Let's try not to worry. You heard what Dr. Francis said."

She stood in her coat for a minute trying to recall the doctor's exact words, looking for any nuances, any hint of something behind his words other than what he had said. She tried to remember if his expression had changed any when he bent over to examine the child. She remembered the way his features had composed themselves as he rolled back the child's eyelids and then listened to his breathing.

She went to the door, where she turned and looked back. She looked at the child, and then she looked at the father. Howard nodded. She stepped out of the room and pulled the door closed behind her.

She went past the nurses' station and down to the end of the corridor, looking for the elevator. At the end of the corridor, she turned to her right and entered a little waiting room where a Negro family sat in wicker chairs. There was a middle-aged man in a khaki shirt and pants, a baseball cap pushed back on his head. A large woman wearing a housedress and slippers was slumped in one of the chairs. A teenaged girl in jeans, hair done in dozens of little braids, lay stretched out in one of the chairs smoking a cigarette, her legs crossed at the ankles. The family swung their eyes to Ann as she entered the room. The little table was littered with hamburger wrappers and Styrofoam cups.

"Franklin," the large woman said as she roused herself. "Is it about Franklin?" Her eyes widened. "Tell me now, lady," the woman said. "Is it about Franklin?" She was trying to rise from her chair, but the man had closed his hand over her arm.

"Here, here," he said. "Evelyn."

"I'm sorry," Ann said. "I'm looking for the elevator. My son is in the hospital, and now I can't find the elevator."

"Elevator is down that way, turn left," the man said as he aimed a finger.

The girl drew on her cigarette and stared at Ann. Her eyes were narrowed to slits, and her broad lips parted slowly as she let the smoke escape. The Negro woman let her head fall on her shoulder and looked away from Ann, no longer interested.

"My son was hit by a car," Ann said to the man. She seemed to need to explain herself. "He has a concussion and a little skull fracture, but he's going to be all right. He's in shock now, but it might be some kind of coma, too. That's what really worries us, the coma part. I'm going out for a little while, but my husband is with him. Maybe he'll wake up while I'm gone."

"That's too bad," the man said and shifted in the chair. He shook his head. He looked down at the table, and then he looked back at Ann. She was still standing there. He said, "Our Franklin, he's on the operating table. Somebody cut him. Tried to kill him. There was a fight where he was at. At this party. They say he was just standing and watching. Not bothering nobody. But that don't mean nothing these days. Now he's on the operating table. We're just hoping and praying, that's all we can do now." He gazed at her steadily.

Ann looked at the girl again, who was still watching her, and at the older woman, who kept her head down, but whose eyes were now closed. Ann saw the lips moving silently, making words. She had an urge to ask what those words were. She wanted to talk more with these people who were in the same kind of waiting she was in. She was afraid, and they were afraid. They had that in common. She would have liked to have said something else about the accident, told them more about Scotty, that it had happened on the day of his birthday, Monday, and that he was still unconscious. Yet she didn't know how to begin. She stood looking at them without saying anything more.

She went down the corridor the man had indicated and found the elevator. She waited a minute in front of the closed doors, still wondering if she was doing the right thing. Then she put out her finger and touched the button.

She pulled into the driveway and cut the engine. She closed her eyes and leaned her head against the wheel for a minute. She listened to the ticking sounds the engine made as it began to cool. Then she got out of the car. She could hear the dog barking inside the house. She went to the front door, which was unlocked. She went inside and turned on lights and put on a kettle of water for tea. She opened some dogfood and fed Slug on the back porch. The dog ate in hungry little smacks. It kept running into the kitchen to see that she was going to stay. As she sat down on the sofa with her tea, the telephone rang.

"Yes!" she said as she answered. "Hello!"

"Mrs. Weiss," a man's voice said. It was five o'clock in the morning, and she thought she could hear machinery or equipment of some kind in the background.

"Yes, yes! What is it?" she said. "This is Mrs. Weiss. This is she. What is it, please?" She listened to whatever it was in the background. "Is it Scotty, for Christ's sake?"

"Scotty," the man's voice said. "It's about Scotty, yes. It has to do with Scotty, that problem. Have you forgotten about Scotty?" the man said. Then he hung up.

She dialed the hospital's number and asked for the third floor. She demanded information about her son from the nurse who answered the telephone. Then she asked to speak to her husband. It was, she said, an emergency.

She waited, turning the telephone cord in her fingers. She closed her eyes and felt sick at her stomach. She would have to make herself eat. Slug came in from the back porch and lay down near her feet. He wagged his tail. She pulled at his ear while he licked her fingers. Howard was on the line.

"Somebody just called here," she said. She twisted the telephone cord. "He said it was about Scotty," she cried.

"Scotty's fine," Howard told her. "I mean, he's still sleeping. There's been no change. The nurse has been in twice since you've been gone. A nurse or else a doctor. He's all right."

"This man called. He said it was about Scotty," she told him.

"Honey, you rest for a little while, you need the rest. It must be that same caller I had. Just forget it. Come back down here after you've rested. Then we'll have breakfast or something."

"Breakfast," she said. "I don't want any breakfast."

"You know what I mean," he said. "Juice, something. I don't know. I don't know anything, Ann. Jesus, I'm not hungry, either. Ann, it's hard to talk now. I'm standing here at the desk. Dr. Francis is coming again at eight o'clock this morning. He's going to have something to tell us then, something more definite. That's what one of the nurses said. She didn't know any more than that. Ann? Honey, maybe we'll know something more then. At eight o'clock. Come back here before eight. Meanwhile, I'm right here and Scotty's all right. He's still the same," he added.

"I was drinking a cup of tea," she said, "when the telephone rang. They said it was about Scotty. There was a noise in the background. Was there a noise in the background on that call you had, Howard?"

"I don't remember," he said. "Maybe the driver of the car, maybe he's a psychopath and found out about Scotty somehow. But I'm here with him. Just rest like you were going to do. Take a bath and come back by seven or so, and we'll talk to the doctor together when he gets here. It's going to be all right, honey. I'm here, and there are doctors and nurses around. They say his condition is stable."

"I'm scared to death," she said.

She ran water, undressed, and got into the tub. She washed and dried quickly, not taking the time to wash her hair. She put on clean underwear, wool slacks, and a sweater. She went into the living room, where the dog looked up at her and let its tail thump once against the floor. It was just starting to get light outside when she went out to the car.

She drove into the parking lot of the hospital and found a space close to the front door. She felt she was in some obscure way responsible for what had happened to the child. She let her thoughts move to the Negro family. She remembered the name Franklin and the table that was covered with hamburger papers, and the teenaged girl staring at her as she drew on her cigarette. "Don't have children," she told the girl's image as she entered the front door of the hospital. "For God's sake, don't."

She took the elevator up to the third floor with two nurses who were just going on duty. It was Wednesday morning, a few minutes before seven. There was a page for a Dr. Madison as the elevator doors slid open on the third floor. She got off behind the nurses, who turned in the other direction and continued the conversation she had interrupted when she'd gotten into the elevator. She walked down the corridor to the little alcove where the Negro family had been waiting. They were gone now, but the chairs were scattered in such a way that it looked as if people had just jumped up from them the minute before. The tabletop was cluttered with the same cups and papers, the ashtray was filled with cigarette butts.

She stopped at the nurses' station. A nurse was standing behind the counter, brushing her hair and yawning.

"There was a Negro boy in surgery last night," Ann said. "Franklin was his name. His family was in the waiting room. I'd like to inquire about his condition."

A nurse who was sitting at a desk behind the counter looked up from a chart in front of her. The telephone buzzed and she picked up the receiver, but she kept her eyes on Ann.

"He passed away," said the nurse at the counter. The nurse held the hairbrush and kept looking at her. "Are you a friend of the family or what?"

"I met the family last night," Ann said. "My own son is in the hospital. I guess he's in shock. We don't know for sure what's wrong. I just wondered about Franklin, that's all. Thank you." She moved down the corridor. Elevator doors the same color as the walls slid open and a gaunt, bald man in white pants and white canvas shoes pulled a heavy cart off the elevator. She hadn't noticed these doors last night. The man wheeled the cart out into the corridor and stopped in front of the room nearest the elevator and consulted a clipboard. Then he reached down and slid a tray out of the cart. He rapped lightly on the door and entered the room. She could smell the unpleasant odors of warm food as she passed the cart. She hurried on without looking at any of the nurses and pushed open the door to the child's room.

Howard was standing at the window with his hands behind his back. He turned around as she came in.

"How is he?" she said. She went over to the bed. She dropped her purse on the floor beside the nightstand. It seemed to her she had been gone a long time. She touched the child's face. "Howard?"

"Dr. Francis was here a little while ago," Howard said. She looked at him closely and thought his shoulders were bunched a little.

"I thought he wasn't coming until eight o'clock this morning," she said quickly.

"There was another doctor with him. A neurologist."

"A neurologist," she said.

Howard nodded. His shoulders were bunching, she could see that. "What'd they say, Howard? For Christ's sake, what'd they say? What is it?"

"They said they're going to take him down and run more tests on him, Ann. They think they're going to operate, honey. Honey, they *are* going to operate. They can't figure out why he won't wake up. It's more than just shock or concussion, they know that much now. It's in his skull, the fracture, it has something, something to do with that, they think. So they're going to operate. I tried to call you, but I guess you'd already left the house."

"Oh, God," she said. "Oh, please, Howard, please," she said, taking his arms.

"Look!" Howard said. "Scotty! Look, Ann!" He turned her toward the bed.

The boy had opened his eyes, then closed them. He opened them again now. The eyes stared straight ahead for a minute, then moved slowly in his head until they rested on Howard and Ann, then traveled away again.

"Scotty," his mother said, moving to the bed.

"Hey, Scott," his father said. "Hey, son."

They leaned over the bed. Howard took the child's hand in his hands and began to pat and squeeze the hand. Ann bent over the boy and kissed his forehead again and again. She put her hands on either side of his face. "Scotty, honey, it's Mommy and Daddy," she said. "Scotty?"

The boy looked at them, but without any sign of recognition. Then his mouth opened, his eyes scrunched closed, and he howled until he had no more air in his lungs. His face seemed to relax and soften then. His lips parted as his last breath was puffed through his throat and exhaled gently through the clenched teeth.

The doctors called it a hidden occlusion and said it was a one-in-a-million circumstance. Maybe if it could have been detected somehow and surgery undertaken immediately, they could have saved him. But more than likely not. In any case, what would they have been looking for? Nothing had shown up in the tests or in the X-rays.

Dr. Francis was shaken. "I can't tell you how badly I feel. I'm so very sorry, I can't tell you," he said as he led them into the doctors' lounge. There was a doctor sitting in a chair with his legs hooked over the back of another chair, watching an early-morning TV show. He was wearing a green delivery-room outfit, loose green pants and green blouse, and a green cap that covered his hair. He looked at Howard and Ann and then looked at Dr. Francis. He got to his feet and turned off the set and went out of the room. Dr. Francis guided Ann to the sofa, sat down beside her, and began to talk in a low, consoling voice. At one point, he leaned over and embraced her. She could feel his chest rising and falling evenly against her shoulder. She kept her eyes open and let him hold her. Howard went into the bathroom, but he left the door open. After a violent fit of weeping, he ran water and washed his face. Then he came out and sat down at the little table that held a telephone. He looked at the telephone as though deciding what to do first. He made some calls. After a time, Dr. Francis used the telephone.

"Is there anything else I can do for the moment?" he asked them.

Howard shook his head. Ann stared at Dr. Francis as if unable to comprehend his words.

The doctor walked them to the hospital's front door. People were entering and leaving the hospital. It was eleven o'clock in the morning. Ann was aware of how slowly, almost reluctantly, she moved her feet. It seemed to her that Dr. Francis was making them leave when she felt they should stay, when it would be more the right thing to do to stay. She gazed out into the parking lot and then turned around and looked back at the front of the hospital. She began shaking her head. "No, no," she said. "I can't leave him here, no." She heard herself say that and thought how unfair it was that the only words that came out were the sort of words used on TV shows where people were stunned by violent or sudden deaths. She wanted her words to be her own. "No," she said, and for some reason the memory of the Negro woman's head lolling on the woman's shoulder came to her. "No," she said again.

"I'll be talking to you later in the day," the doctor was saying to Howard. "There are still some things that have to be done, things that have to be cleared up to our satisfaction. Some things that need explaining."

"An autopsy," Howard said.

Dr. Francis nodded.

"I understand," Howard said. Then he said, "Oh, Jesus. No, I don't understand, doctor. I can't, I can't. I just can't."

Dr. Francis put his arm around Howard's shoulders. "I'm sorry. God, how I'm sorry." He let go of Howard's shoulders and held out his hand. Howard looked at the hand, and then he took it. Dr. Francis put his arms around Ann once more. He seemed full of some goodness she didn't understand. She let her head rest on his shoulder, but her eyes stayed open. She kept looking at the hospital. As they drove out of the parking lot, she looked back at the hospital.

At home, she sat on the sofa with her hands in her coat pockets. Howard closed the door to the child's room. He got the coffee-maker going and then he found an empty box. He had thought to pick up some of the child's things that were scattered around the living room. But instead he sat down beside her on the sofa, pushed the box to one side, and leaned forward, arms between his knees. He began to weep. She pulled his head over into her lap and patted his shoulder. "He's gone," she said. She kept patting his shoulder. Over his sobs, she could hear the coffee-maker hissing in the kitchen. "There, there," she said tenderly. "Howard, he's gone. He's gone and now we'll have to get used to that. To being alone."

In a little while, Howard got up and began moving aimlessly around the room with the box, not putting anything into it, but collecting some things together on the floor at one end of the sofa. She continued to sit with her hands in her coat pockets. Howard put the box down and brought coffee into the living room. Later, Ann made calls to relatives. After each call had been placed and the party had answered, Ann would blurt out a few words and cry for a minute. Then she would quietly explain, in a measured voice, what had happened and tell them about arrangements. Howard took the box out to the garage, where he saw the child's bicycle. He dropped the box and sat down on the pavement beside the bicycle. He took hold of the bicycle awkwardly so that it leaned against his chest. He held it, the rubber pedal sticking into his chest. He gave the wheel a turn.

Ann hung up the telephone after talking to her sister. She was looking up another number when the telephone rang. She picked it up on the first ring.

"Hello," she said, and she heard something in the background, a humming noise. "Hello!" she said. "For God's sake," she said. "Who is this? What is it you want?"

"Your Scotty, I got him ready for you," the man's voice said. "Did you forget him?"

"You evil bastard!" she shouted into the receiver. "How can you do this, you evil son of a bitch?"

"Scotty," the man said. "Have you forgotten about Scotty?" Then the man hung up on her.

Howard heard the shouting and came in to find her with her head on her arms over the table, weeping. He picked up the receiver and listened to the dial tone.

Much later, just before midnight, after they had dealt with many things, the telephone rang again.

"You answer it," she said. "Howard, it's him, I know." They were sitting at the kitchen table with coffee in front of them. Howard had a small glass of whiskey beside his cup. He answered on the third ring.

"Hello," he said. "Who is this? Hello! Hello!" The line went dead. "He hung up," Howard said. "Whoever it was."

"It was him," she said. "That bastard. I'd like to kill him," she said. "I'd like to shoot him and watch him kick," she said.

"Ann, my God," he said.

"Could you hear anything?" she said. "In the background? A noise, machinery, something humming?"

"Nothing, really. Nothing like that," he said. "There wasn't much time. I think there was some radio music. Yes, there was a radio going, that's all I could tell. I don't know what in God's name is going on," he said.

She shook her head. "If I could, could get my hands on him." It came to her then. She knew who it was. Scotty, the cake, the telephone number. She pushed the chair away from the table and got up. "Drive me down to the shopping center," she said. "Howard."

"What are you saying?"

"The shopping center. I know who it is who's calling. I know who it is. It's the baker, the son-of-a-bitching baker, Howard. I had him bake a cake for Scotty's birthday. That's who's calling. That's who has the number and keeps calling us. To harass us about that cake. The baker, that bastard."

They drove down to the shopping center. The sky was clear and stars were out. It was cold, and they ran the heater in the car. They parked in front of the bakery. All of the shops and stores were closed, but there were cars at the far end of the lot in front of the movie theater. The bakery windows were dark, but when they looked through the glass they could see a light in the back room and, now and then, a big man in an apron moving in and out of the white, even light. Through the glass, she could see the display cases and some little tables with chairs. She tried the door. She rapped on the glass. But if the baker heard them, he gave no sign. He didn't look in their direction.

They drove around behind the bakery and parked. They got out of the car. There was a lighted window too high up for them to see inside. A sign near the back door said THE PANTRY BAKERY, SPECIAL ORDERS. She could hear faintly a radio playing inside and something creak—an oven door as it was pulled down? She knocked on the door and waited. Then she knocked again, louder. The radio was turned down and there was a scraping sound now, the distinct sound of something, a drawer, being pulled open and then closed.

Someone unlocked the door and opened it. The baker stood in the light and peered out at them. "I'm closed for business," he said. "What do you want at this hour? It's midnight. Are you drunk or something?"

She stepped into the light that fell through the open door. He blinked his heavy eyelids as he recognized her. "It's you," he said.

"It's me," she said. "Scotty's mother. This is Scotty's father. We'd like to come in."

The baker said, "I'm busy now. I have work to do."

She had stepped inside the doorway anyway. Howard came in behind her. The baker moved back. "It smells like a bakery in here. Doesn't it smell like a bakery in here, Howard?"

"What do you want?" the baker said. "Maybe you want your cake? That's it, you decided you want your cake. You ordered a cake, didn't you?"

"You're pretty smart for a baker," she said. "Howard, this is the man who's been calling us." She clenched her fists. She stared at him fiercely. There was a deep burning inside her, an anger that made her feel larger than herself, larger than either of these men.

"Just a minute here," the baker said. "You want to pick up your three-day-old cake? That it? I don't want to argue with you, lady. There it sits over there, getting stale. I'll give it to you for half of what I quoted you. No. You want it? You can have it. It's no good to me, no good to anyone now. It cost me time and money to make that cake. If you want it, okay, if you don't, that's okay, too. I have to get back to work." He looked at them and rolled his tongue behind his teeth.

"More cakes," she said. She knew she was in control of it, of what was increasing in her. She was calm.

"Lady, I work sixteen hours a day in this place to earn a living," the baker said. He wiped his hands on his apron. "I work night and day in here, trying to make ends meet." A look crossed Ann's face that made the baker move back and say, "No trouble, now." He reached to the counter and picked up a rolling pin with his right hand and began to tap it against the palm of his other hand. "You want the cake or not? I have to get back to work. Bakers work at night," he said again. His eyes were small, mean-looking, she thought, nearly lost in the bristly flesh around his cheeks. His neck was thick with fat.

"I know bakers work at night," Ann said. "They make phone calls at night, too. You bastard," she said.

The baker continued to tap the rolling pin against his hand. He glanced at Howard. "Careful, careful," he said to Howard.

"My son's dead," she said with a cold, even finality. "He was hit by a car Monday morning. We've been waiting with him until he died. But, of course, you couldn't be expected to know that, could you? Bakers can't know everything—can they, Mr. Baker? But he's dead. He's dead, you bastard!" Just as suddenly as it had welled in her, the anger dwindled, gave way to something else, a dizzy feeling of nausea. She leaned against the wooden table that was sprinkled with flour, put her hands over her face, and began to cry, her shoulders rocking back and forth. "It isn't fair," she said. "It isn't, isn't fair."

Howard put his hand at the small of her back and looked at the baker. "Shame on you," Howard said to him. "Shame."

The baker put the rolling pin back on the counter. He undid his apron and threw it on the counter. He looked at them, and then he shook his head slowly. He pulled a chair out from under the card table that held papers and receipts, an adding machine, and a telephone directory. "Please sit down," he said. "Let me get you a chair," he said to Howard. "Sit down now, please." The baker went into the front of the shop and returned with two little wrought-iron chairs. "Please sit down, you people."

Ann wiped her eyes and looked at the baker. "I wanted to kill you," she said. "I wanted you dead."

The baker had cleared a space for them at the table. He shoved the adding machine to one side, along with the stacks of notepaper and receipts. He pushed the telephone directory onto the floor, where it landed with a thud. Howard and Ann sat down and pulled their chairs up to the table. The baker sat down, too.

"Let me say how sorry I am," the baker said, putting his elbows on the table. "God alone knows how sorry. Listen to me. I'm just a baker. I don't claim to be anything else. Maybe once, maybe years ago, I was a different kind of human being. I've forgotten, I don't know for sure. But I'm not any longer, if I ever was. Now I'm just a baker. That don't excuse my doing what I did, I know. But I'm deeply sorry. I'm sorry for your son, and sorry for my part in this," the baker said. He spread his hands out on the table and turned them over to reveal his palms. "I don't have any children myself, so I can only imagine what you must be feeling. All I can say to you now is that I'm sorry. Forgive me, if you can," the baker said. "I'm not an evil man, I don't think. Not evil, like you said on the phone. You got to understand what it comes down to is I don't know how to act anymore, it would seem. Please," the man said, "let me ask you if you can find it in your hearts to forgive me?"

It was warm inside the bakery. Howard stood up from the table and took off his coat. He helped Ann from her coat. The baker looked at them for a minute and then nodded and got up from the table. He went to the oven and turned off some switches. He found cups and poured coffee from an electric coffee-maker. He put a carton of cream on the table, and a bowl of sugar.

"You probably need to eat something," the baker said. "I hope you'll eat some of my hot rolls. You have to eat and keep going. Eating is a small, good thing in a time like this," he said.

He served them warm cinnamon rolls just out of the oven, the icing still runny. He put butter on the table and knives to spread the butter. Then the baker sat down at the table with them. He waited. He waited until they each took a roll from the platter and began to eat. "It's good to eat something," he said, watching them. "There's more. Eat up. Eat all you want. There's all the rolls in the world in here."

They ate rolls and drank coffee. Ann was suddenly hungry, and the rolls were warm and sweet. She ate three of them, which pleased the baker. Then he began to talk. They listened carefully. Although they were tired and in anguish, they listened to what the baker had to say. They nodded when the baker began to speak of loneliness, and of the sense of doubt and limitation that had come to him in his middle years. He told them what it was like to be childless all these years. To repeat the days with the ovens endlessly full and endlessly empty. The party food, the celebrations he'd worked over. Icing knuckle-deep. The tiny wedding couples stuck into cakes. Hundreds of them, no, thousands by now. Birthdays. Just imagine all those candles burning. He had a necessary trade. He was a baker. He was glad he wasn't a florist. It was better to be feeding people. This was a better smell anytime than flowers.

"Smell this," the baker said, breaking open a dark loaf. "It's a heavy bread, but rich." They smelled it, then he had them taste it. It had the taste of molasses and coarse grains. They listened to him. They ate what they could. They swallowed the dark bread. It was like daylight under the fluorescent trays of light. They talked on into the early morning, the high, pale cast of light in the windows, and they did not think of leaving.

# Sandra Cisneros

## (B. 1954)

Sandra Cisneros was born to a Mexican father and Chicana mother in Chicago, Illinois. Her childhood was marked by frequent household moves and family trips between the United States and Mexico. Cisneros combated loneliness with writing, becoming the editor of her high school literary magazine. She earned a B.A. in English from Loyola University of Chicago in 1976 and received a master's degree in writing from the University of Iowa Writer's Workshop. Her experience as the lone Chicana in her writing workshops led Cisneros to examine her relationship to her Mexican heritage and, by extension, the condition of being both Mexican and American.

Cisneros's first novel, a collection of interrelated short stories entitled *The House on Mango Street*, was published in 1984 and won the Before Columbus Foundation's American Book Award in 1985. In 1987, Cisneros published *My Wicked, Wicked Ways*, her first book of poetry, which took the spare storytelling style familiar to readers of *The House on Mango Street* and infused it with a sinuous rhythm born from the intermingling of English and Spanish—Spanglish. Her second collection of short stories, *Woman Hollering Creek*, was published in 1991 and won numerous awards. In 1995, Cisneros won a MacArthur Foundation fellowship while working at a local youth center in San Antonio, Texas. As one of the most visible Chicanas in contemporary literature, Cisneros continues to redefine Chicano literature. She takes Spanglish, traditional Mexican folktales and figures, and urban Latino culture and concerns and mixes them into deceptively simple stories that parse the struggles of everyday Americans. Her first novel, *Caramelo*, was published in 2002.

---

## *Barbie-Q*                                                                1991

*for Licha*

Yours is the one with mean eyes and a ponytail. Striped swimsuit, stilettos, sunglasses, and gold hoop earrings. Mine is the one with bubble hair. Red swimsuit, stilettos, pearl earrings, and a wire stand. But that's all we can afford, besides one extra outfit apiece. Yours, "Red Flair," sophisticated A-line coatdress with a Jackie Kennedy pillbox hat, white gloves, handbag, and heels included. Mine, "Solo in the Spotlight," evening elegance in black glitter strapless gown with a puffy skirt at the bottom like a mermaid tail, formal-length gloves, pink chiffon scarf, and mike included. From so much dressing and undressing, the black glitter wears off where her titties stick out. This and a dress invented from an old sock when we cut holes here and here and here, the cuff rolled over for the glamorous, fancy-free, off-the-shoulder look.

Every time the same story. Your Barbie is roommates with my Barbie, and my Barbie's boyfriend comes over and your Barbie steals him, okay? Kiss kiss kiss. Then the two Barbies fight. You dumbbell! He's mine. Oh no he's not, you stinky! Only Ken's invisible, right? Because we don't have money for a stupid-looking boy doll when we'd both rather ask for a new Barbie outfit next Christmas. We have to make do with your mean-eyed Barbie and my bubblehead Barbie and our one outfit apiece not including the sock dress.

Until next Sunday when we are walking through the flea market on Maxwell Street and *there!* Lying on the street next to some tool bits, and platform shoes with the heels all squashed, and a fluorescent green wicker wastebasket, and aluminum foil, and hubcaps, and a pink shag rug, and windshield wiper blades, and dusty mason jars, and a coffee can full of rusty nails. *There!* Where? Two Mattel boxes. One with the "Career Gal" ensemble, snappy black-and-white business suit, three-quarter-length sleeve jacket with kick-pleat skirt, red sleeveless shell, gloves, pumps, and matching hat included. The other, "Sweet Dreams," dreamy pink-and-white plaid nightgown and matching robe, lace-trimmed slippers, hair-brush and hand mirror included. How much? Please, please, please, please, please, please, please, until they say okay.

On the outside you and me skipping and humming but inside we are doing loopity-loops and pirouetting. Until at the next vendor's stand, next to boxed pies, and bright orange toilet brushes, and rubber gloves, and wrench sets, and bouquets of feather flowers, and glass towel racks, and steel wool, and Alvin and the Chipmunks records, *there!* And *there!* And *there!* And *there!* and *there!* and *there!* and *there!* Bendable Legs Barbie with her new page-boy hairdo, Midge, Barbie's best friend. Ken, Barbie's boyfriend. Skipper, Barbie's little sister. Tutti and Todd, Barbie and Skipper's tiny twin sister and brother. Skipper's friends, Scooter and Ricky. Alan, Ken's buddy. And Francie, Barbie's MOD'ern cousin.

Everybody today selling toys, all of them damaged with water and smelling of smoke. Because a big toy warehouse on Halsted Street burned down yesterday—see there?—the smoke still rising and drifting across the Dan Ryan expressway. And now there is a big fire sale at Maxwell Street, today only.

So what if we didn't get our new Bendable Legs Barbie and Midge and Ken and Skipper and Tutti and Todd and Scooter and Ricky and Alan and Francie in nice clean boxes and had to buy them on Maxwell Street, all water-soaked and sooty. So what if our Barbies smell like smoke when you hold them up to your nose even after you wash and wash and wash them. And if the prettiest doll, Barbie's MOD'ern cousin Francie with real eyelashes, eyelash brush included, has a left foot that's melted a little—so? If you dress her in her new "Prom Pinks" outfit, satin splendor with matching coat, gold belt, clutch, and hair bow included, so long as you don't lift her dress, right?—who's to know.

# Peter Ho Davies

## (B. 1966)

Peter Ho Davies's writing explores his multicultural identity. He was born to Welsh and Chinese parents, and his mother was raised in a Malaysian community. Davies was educated in England, and he received his B.A. in physics and English from the University of Manchester. He then moved to the United States, where he received his M.A. in creative writing from Boston University. His first collection of stories, *The Ugliest House in the World,* was published in 1998 and contains short stories set in Malaysia, South Africa, and Patagonia. It won the PEN/Macmillan Silver Pen Fiction Award and the Mail on Sunday/John Llewellyn Rhys Prize. *Equal Love* (2000) is his second collection of stories. Davies currently directs the M.F.A. program in creative writing at the University of Michigan.

## What You Know                                            2001

People suddenly want to know all about my students, what they're like. What do I know? I want to say. I'm just a writer, a writer-in-the-schools. All I see is their writing.

So what are they like as writers?

They're shocking. Appalling, in fact. Indescribably awful (and when a writer, even one of my low self-esteem, says that, you know it's serious). The good ones are bad, and the bad ones are tragic.

When at the start of each class I ask them their favorite books, their fifteen-year-old faces are as blank as paper. The better students struggle to offer a "right" answer: *Catcher, Gatsby,* the Bible(!). The honest ones, the stupid, arrogant honest ones, tell me, *For the Love of the Game* by Michael Jordan, or the latest Dean Koontz.

The most voracious readers among them are the science-fiction fans, the genre nerds, the heavy-duty bookworms (all those sequels and prequels, trilogies and tetralogies), but none of them are deterred for a nanosecond when I tell them that good science fiction is one of the hardest things to write. After all, they're thinking— I can see it in their eyes—it's just a matter of taste, isn't it?

As a matter of fact, no. I believe in the well-made story. Have your character want something, I tell them. Have a conflict. Have the character change. Learn these simple rules, and you can spend the rest of your life breaking them.

But most of the time I find myself telling them what not to write. All the narrative clichés. No stories about suicide. No flashbacks longer than a page. No narrators from beyond the grave. No "And then I woke up" endings. No "I woke up and then . . ." beginnings. No psychedelic dream sequences. The list of boringly bad stories ("But it's supposed to be boring, life is boring") goes on and on.

"No suicides?" they say in their flat, whiny voices, as if there is nothing else, nothing better. "How can suicide be boring?"

Maybe not in life, I explain quickly, but in fiction? Sure. It's a cruel world of readers out there—callous, heartless, *commuting* readers—who've been there, seen that, read it all before. "I'm not saying you can't try to write about suicide," I console them. "I'm just saying it's hard to do well, that you owe it to the material to do it justice, to find a way of making it real and raw for readers again."

Writers aren't godlike, I tell them, readers are. Writers only create, readers judge.

They nod in complete incomprehension. Yes, they're saying. Yes, we see now that there is absolutely no chance we'll understand a word you say. We're just here for the extra credit. It's the nod you give a crazy man, a lunatic with a gun.

What redeems it? My love of teaching? I do love teaching, but for all the wrong reasons. I love the sound of my own voice. I love to pontificate about writing, get excited about it, argue about it (and usually win) with people who have to listen to me, more or less (unlike my parents, my friends, my wife). But always, behind their acquiescence, behind the fact that however bad my taste I'm still the coolest teacher they have (the competition is not stiff), lie the awful, numbing questions: "What have you published? Why haven't we heard of you?"

What really redeems it are the laughs. The laughable badness of their prose. The moose frozen like a *dear* in the headlights. The cop slapping on the *cuff links*. The *viscous* criminal. The *escape* goat.

It's as if they're hard of hearing, snatching up half-heard, half-comprehended phrases, trusting blindly in their spell checkers to save them. (Think! Think who designs spell checkers for a moment. Were these people ever good spellers?)

I once had a heated argument with one student about the death knoll.

"Knell," I said.

"Knoll," he insisted with vehemence, until finally we determined that he was thinking of the *grassy* knoll. My way might be right, he conceded grudgingly, but his way made more sense. We took a vote in class (they love democracy) and the majority agreed. And perhaps this is the way that language, meaning, evolves before our very eyes and ears. "It's the death mole of literacy," I told them, but they didn't get it. Sometimes, I despair of language. If only there was some way for what I know to just appear, instantaneously, in their heads.

So *that,* if you really want to know, is what my students are like. Does any of it explain why one of them last week shot his father in the head across the breakfast nook, rode the bus to school with a pistol in his waistband, emptied it in his homeroom, killing two and wounding five, before putting the gun in his mouth and splashing his brains all over the whiteboard!

No stories about suicide?

No viscous criminals?

In the moments after the crisis no one thinks to call me—as the other staff, the *full-time* staff, are called—to warn me not to talk to the media. No one, in fact, calls me *apart* from the media. "It's CNN," my wife says, passing me the phone, then stepping back as if I hold a snake in my hands. But we're *watching* CNN, I want to say. I look at her and she mimes helplessness. It never occurs to me that all my fellow teachers have been asked to say nothing to the media, that this is why some bright spark in Atlanta after trying five or six names and getting the same response has slid his finger down the faxed list before him to "Other" and found me, not quite a teacher, but better than a janitor.

What he wants to know is if I had taught the killer, the dead boy, Clark, and when I admit, and it feels like an admission, nothing to be proud of, that yes I have, I have him—*had* him (watch those tense changes)—in a writing workshop, I can hear the reporter lean forward in his chair, cup his hand around the mouthpiece. I wonder for a second about him, this young journalist, probably around my age, looking for his big break. This could be it, I realize, and I feel an odd vertiginous jealousy, almost wanting to hold back. But later, listening to my voice over and over on national TV— a grainy photo from the latest yearbook and a caption identifying me as a writer floating over a live shot of the blank school buildings—I'm glad I talked to him, glad I didn't say anything stupid, that I come across as dignified and responsible. I answer all his questions in the first person plural. "We're shocked and appalled. We'll all be doing our best to help our students through this awful period. Our hearts go out to the families in the tragedy." Later my mother will call from Arizona, then my colleagues, even the principal with a warning not to say anything else, but an off-the-record pat on the back for "our unofficial spokesman." "A way with words," my mother will say. "You always had a way with words." Even though she's never read a single one of my stories. I tell her it was easy and it was. It comes naturally. For months now I've been talking in the first person plural. We're pregnant, my wife and I. We're expecting. We're about to be parents ourselves.

"CNN," my wife says, touching her stomach. "Something to tell the kid." It's not often she's proud of me, and I'm pleased, even though I despise the network, its incompetent staff. I heard one anchor a couple of years back talking about a first in the "anals" of country music. Another time I caught a piece in which the President was described as being "salt and peppered" with questions at a news conference. Someone wrote that, was paid to. "I suppose I should be grateful," I tell my wife. "My caption could have read 'waiter' not 'writer.'" And she smiles uncertainly, not sure who this particular joke is on.

What I tell no one, though, not even my wife, is the reporter's last question, off air, quietly into my ear after he has thanked me and double-checked the spelling of my name. Only the tone alerted me, otherwise this could have been the same as any of the previous questions—"Was he a good student? What was he like?" This final shot: "Do you have anything he wrote for you? A poem or a story?"

I said, "No," but something in my voice must have made him wonder because he added softly, "It could be worth a great deal." So I said, "No" again, more forcefully, and then, "I'm sorry," and hung up.

Why was I sorry? Easier to explain why I said, "No," with that catch of hesitation. Because I couldn't remember, that's why. I had work upstairs, ungraded stories, the response to an exercise: "Write about a moment of extreme emotion—fear, hate, love, joy, laughter." The idea is to have them write about a true emotion and use this as a benchmark against which to compare the emotions of their fictional characters. Something by Clark might be there, if he'd done the assignment. They often didn't. And, indeed, when I look there's nothing, just a note—brief—he'd been sick, and below his own signature, another—larger, flowing. It takes me a second to realize; it's his father's.

So why was I sorry? Because I'm a writer-in-the-schools. I earn $8,000 a year ($6,000 less than my wife's bookstore job pays) and we are pregnant. I am sorry I hadn't had the nerve to say: "How much?" He might have even been bullshitting me, the reporter. CNN would never do business like that, right? But something in his voice, the shift of register, made me think he might have just slipped into freelance mode. The phone was hot where I was pressing it against my head, but for a second I could have sworn it was his warm breath in my ear. Now I wondered—$1,000, $5,000, $10,000? Who knew? I was only sure it would be more than anything I'd ever gotten for my own work. And out of this irony, of course, came this idea. I could write a piece by Clark. *I* could write it and sell it. I could. His letter was typed, printed. He was a loner, without friends. His father was dead. He was dead. Who would know?

No narrators from beyond the grave?

Have your character want something.

Ten thousand big ones.

As a plan it seemed so simple at first, at least if you separate it from the issue of morality. And separating from that issue is something I teach my students. Don't stop yourselves writing something because it might hurt someone—your family, your friends. Don't stop yourself writing it because you think it's too personal, sexual, violent. Don't censor yourselves, I tell them, at least not alone when it's just you and the paper.

Oddly, they're prudish. Reluctant to write about feelings, except in the safest, most clichéd terms. Love, sex especially, makes them sneer with embarrassment, while violence is simply comic.

"But what's the point?" I remember one of them asking (I wish I could say it was Clark, but I can't picture him any more than I can bring to mind the faces of three or four other boys who sit in the back row with their baseball caps pulled low over their eyes), "what's the point writing it if you're not going to show it to someone?" And I have sympathy with this. I believe in writing for an audience. Writing fiction is an act of communication—not just facts or opinions like a newspaper, but emotions. I tell them this. And in truth once something is written, actually expressed, showing it to someone—the desire to do that—is hard to escape. It's the momentum of the act. So I tell myself that writing a piece as Clark isn't the same as passing it off to others as Clark's, but once you've got it—especially if it's good—what else is there to do with it? So perhaps the moral problem does lie behind this practical one: it should be easy to write this piece—it doesn't have to be *good*, after all; it needs, in fact, to be bad to be good—yet, after all the mockery I've heaped on their work, I can't do it. I can't imitate my students.

God help me, I'm blocked.

Here's the trouble. If I'm to write this and overcome the lie of it I need it to mean something, to explain something. I want to offer, coded, buried, subtly perhaps, an answer, a psychological, sociological subtext, that will explain these deaths, and in explaining offer some hope or comfort to us all. It may not be *the* meaning, but surely any meaning, even a sniff of meaning, is what we want. It is the writer's instinct to offer these things, and, beyond mere morality, I can't quite shrug off this duty to, of all things, art.

Which is why I find myself in my 1988 Subaru wagon, driving out to a gun range on the interstate called the Duke's Den. I have never fired a gun before and I decide that this—everything else notwithstanding—is the problem. If I want to understand Clark, take on his voice, I should at least try to understand how he expressed himself.

And this, too, is what I teach them. Show don't tell. Write what you know. Did Clark's baseball cap bob at that one? Did he take notes? Some of them do and it still amazes me, makes me think they're making fun, when in truth they only set down what they don't understand. "Show," they write carefully, "and Tell."

Write what you know is even worse. They look at me as if I've asked them to raise the dead, as if they know nothing or everything. Some I have to persuade that their lives are important enough; others that they're not quite as important as they think. But either way, what most of them know is deadly—not the stories themselves, or their lives as such, but how they live them, think about them. The best ones, they know this already. Know it like an instinct. Write what they know? Not yet. Not until they know what they know. But the worst ones? They don't even want to know what they know.

"So is that why we can't write about suicide? Because if you know it, you're, like dead?"

"Yeah, and there's no narrators from beyond the grave, right?"

They look at me, so pleased, so earnest, as if they figured it out, and I feel my heart clench. I think about explaining that the rule really ought to be: "Write whatever you know just a little more about than your reader." But truly what I want to tell them is that these rules aren't, after all, rules for writers; they're rules for people who are trying to be writers but won't ever make it.

So I don't get any suicide stories (though as one bright spark recently pointed out: "It's ironic, don't you think? Considering how many writers kill themselves"). Instead, I get first-kiss stories, first-joint stories, the death of pets, the death of grandparents, sad fat girls, thin sad girls. The tone is always the same—life is tragic; tragically small or epically tragic (the chasm, come to think of it, that suicide bridges).

Lighten up, I want to tell them. It's not the end of the world. You've got your whole life before you. All the lines my father taught me when I was their age and deciding to become a writer, all the lines I've taught them to recognize as clichés. Except, as they like to remind me, that doesn't mean they can't still be true. Some people do have apple cheeks or strawberry hair or cherry lips (the fruit-salad style of physical description). Don't clichés, in fact, have to be true to become clichés? No, I tell them, we just have to want them to be true.

What else do I teach them? Certainly not how to be creative. I'm not into breathing exercises, or free writing, or journaling. Sucking up to the muse. Nor even how to write correctly—I'm no grammar maven. "How to tell stories" is what I told CNN, though the line never aired, and that's closer to the truth.

I teach them what Forster says: that there are stories and there are plots. That stories are simple sequences of events (this happened and then this and then that), but that plots are about causes, motivation (this happened because of this, on account of that). Plots are what stories mean. And the truth is that life is all stories and fiction is all plots, and what we're looking for in Clark's story is the plot that makes sense of it. Which is why it has to be someone's fault—his, his father's, the NRA, Nintendo, Hollywood, all the escape goats—doesn't it? This happened because of that or that or that. Or all of them.

So I teach them how to tell stories, or (since we're all storytellers every time we open our mouths) how to tell them better, which is to say I try to teach them to make sense of their stories, to figure out what they mean if they mean anything. Because the way we tell stories explains them.

Write what they know? Mostly, I just try to help them know what they write.

So that's what I teach them: how to plot.

And if that's beyond them, what I try to leave them with is this: when in doubt, when stuck, blocked, or fucked, to always ask themselves, "What if?" (Even if their instinct is to ask, "So what?")

What if I pick up a gun and fire it?

The range is quiet. It's the weekend after the shooting, we're still in shock. I show my driver's license and join for $25, which entitles me to rent guns from behind the counter for $5 an hour. It seems so cheap—what can you get for five bucks?—but as I buy ammunition for my choice, a .38 caliber revolver (I just pointed to the first gun I recognized from TV), I realize that this is what costs. Guns are just game consoles, VCRs; it's what you put in them that costs. The man behind the counter is unfailingly polite and helpful. He reminds me of a hardware salesman, the kind of guy in a brown apron who'll show you how to use a tool, dig out exactly the right size of wrench or washer for your job. The kind of guy who'll tell you all about it if you're not careful. His name is Vern, and above his head, hanging up like so many hammers and saws on a workshop wall, are all manner of guns, not just pistols but rifles, even a replica tommy gun, the kind of thing Al Capone might have used. There's an air of fancy dress about the display; an air of the toy store, the magic trick. On a ledge at the very top of the display is a line of model railway rolling stock. Vern is a train enthusiast, a hobbyist.

After the gun and the shells—they come in a plastic rack, not the waxed paper box I expect—he hands over a pair of ear defenders and then asks, "Target?" I must look puzzled, because he repeats himself. "What kind of target."

"What kinds do you have?"

He grins, glad I asked, and starts to show me. There's a simple roundel, each ring marked with a score, a sheet covered in playing cards for "shooting poker," the "classic" silhouette, a double one—of a gunman and a woman, his hostage—and finally a set of caricature targets of everyone from Saddam Hussein to Barney. I take the classic silhouette, and Vern rolls it for me and secures it with a rubber band. He hands me the lot—gun, shells, target, ear defenders in an EZ-carry plastic tray—and points me back toward the range, which is separated from the shop by double glazing. Through the glass I can see one man, broad shouldered, graying, balding, firing. "You put your headset on in the booth," Vern tells me, indicating the double set of doors between the shop and the range. "Take lane three."

Inside, with the ear defenders pinching my skull, the shots from the other man in the range sound like a distant hammering pulse. I set up in the lane beside him. Place the gun on the counter and the shells beside it, work the toggle switch that brings the target toward me on a wire. All this is familiar from the movies. When the target board arrives I'm momentarily at a loss as to how to fix the silhouette to it. I look around and there's Vern on the other side of the glass pointing, and when I look again I see a tape dispenser mounted to the wall.

I run the target back about halfway to the rear concrete wall. It's ridged, corrugated, and it takes me a slow moment to realize that this is to prevent ricochets. The concrete makes the range cooler than the shop, like a bunker, and it smells, but only faintly, of the Fourth of July, fireworks. And this creeping nostalgia, the insulation of the ear defenders, the odd underground cool, give the experience an air of unreality.

The target jumps about on the wire for a few seconds like a puppet, and I wait until it's still before turning to the gun. Vern has taught me how to load it, flipping out the cylinder and dropping in the shells. It's a six-shooter, but he warned me to put five shots in and leave the chamber under the hammer empty, "to save your toes." The bullets go in very easily and quickly—the whole thing feels well made in a way that very few things do these days—and I slide the cylinder back into the gun. I hold it away from me and down and then slowly raise it. Vern has shown me how to cock the hammer and fire or how to pull the trigger all the way back. He has advised me to keep my trigger finger outside the guard until I'm ready to shoot. I'm frightened of it going off before I'm ready, of seeming dangerous. But once I have it in position cocking it is simple, and when I fire my first shot I'm surprised how easy it comes. (Vern is a good teacher.) There's a crack and a small flash from the gun, but the recoil is almost playful in the way it bats my hand up. I've hit serves that jarred worse. I look last at the target and see a small neat puncture in the shoulder of my silhouette. Almost too neat, but for the slight tearing of the paper. I fire again. And again and again and again. Because, after all, what else is there to do? By my fifth shot I'm not cocking but experimenting with pulling the trigger back. Two of my shots score tens in the target's chest. With my next set I take aim at the head and put all five on target. I feel like Dirty Harry or Steve McGarrett. Just not Clark.

Beside me as I'm loading again, the other shooter reels in his target, unrolls another, and tapes it up. He's old, grandfatherly, dressed in polyester, metallic-blue Sansabelt pants and a teal polo shirt. He nods and I nod back. He looks like a bowler, and I realize that's exactly what this experience is reminding me of, bowling. I'd laugh at him rather than nod back, that slightly too portentous nod, except that he has a loaded weapon on the counter before him, a tool with which he could kill me. It occurs to me that if he took that into his head the only thing stopping him would be the fact that I might shoot back.

I try to ask myself what this might have meant to Clark, but I can't guess. The experience isn't inspiring, just deadening, mechanical. I feel the panic rising again, the greed. We need the money. I think of my own son, my unborn son (I wanted to know the sex; not for me the surprise ending), for whom I'm doing this, and I wonder what might possibly ever drive him to kill me. I know I thought about killing him. We talked about it, about a termination, an abortion. We hadn't planned on this. I kept thinking something would come up—a new job, a major publication. I had a story with one of the slick magazines, and they had held it for weeks, months, so long my hopes were rising day by day. A score like that—thousands of dollars—could change our lives. I found myself putting my imaginative energy not into new work but into visualizing that moment, the letter in the mail, not in my own self-addressed envelope but the magazine's embossed one, telling me blah, blah, blah, *delighted.* I didn't say so, but I think I'd decided we'd keep the baby if I sold the story. When the rejection letter ("too familiar") finally came, with that sudden rushing inevitability they all have, I couldn't stop shaking. My wife, used to rages or resignation, was speechless. But later, lying in bed, I realized, *how insane.* In the morning we talked it through again and I told my wife I thought we should go ahead and she cried and held me and I felt saved.

So the thought that one day in some world this child might kill me, might shoot me in the face, who wants to imagine that? And yet, and yet, when I think of my own father, there have been . . . moments. If I'd had a gun, known how to use one. Oh yes. But petty reasons, anger over a grounding, over using the car, disappointing him. Not worth killing for. Not worth going out and buying a gun and laying in ambush for. But if the gun were at hand? Not worth running upstairs for, perhaps, not worth crossing the hall for, but if it were on the counter (what the fuck would it be doing on the counter? but just suppose), on the table, in my hand. I did punch my father once. I'd come in late and he waited up, barred the door to my room. We yelled at each other and I raised a fist. There was a moment when I could have lowered it, merely threatened, but having made it I couldn't stop. I hit him and he took a step back, out of surprise, I think. "Do that again," he told me when he'd recovered himself, and I did—bowing to that curious complicit male desire to make a bad thing worse, to transform an accident, a mistake, into a tragedy, to render ourselves not hapless, not foolish and vain, but heroic, grand, awesome. And he took the next shot too, and then he beat me unconscious (in fact, he only raised his own fist, and I took a step back, fell down the stairs, and knocked myself cold—so close is tragedy to farce—but the first version makes a better story). Except if it hadn't been a fist, if it had been a gun I'd raised, he wouldn't have had the chance, would he? And all over nothing.

He's dead now, my father, and as I empty the gun I'm thinking of naming my son after him.

Shooting is actually duller than bowling, I'm finding, duller and easier. I can daydream while doing it. There's something effortless and magical in the seemingly instantaneous bang and the appearance yards away of a small hole. I fire another twenty rounds. I move the target back, forward. I shoot to kill, I shoot to wound, I shoot from the hip. I suddenly understand why someone might rent a machine gun. What I want most in the world I realize is a moving target, a more interesting target. The idea on the range is marksmanship, but there's no real challenge here. I look down the barrel of my gun but watch the shots of the man next to me. He doesn't seem much better, and I've only been shooting for twenty minutes. I watch him cluster his shots in the high-scoring body of the target—one, two, three, four. Nothing. And something about the rhythm, my focus on his target, makes me swing my gun over and put a fifth shot into the face of his target. Perhaps because of the angle I'm firing from, the bullet makes a ragged hole, tearing loose a strip of paper that curls slightly, flaps like a tongue. I hold my breath, horrified. I keep the gun raised, keep sighting down it. I can't hear anything from my neighbor behind his screen. Perhaps he's reloading, hasn't noticed. The pause goes on, and eventually I empty my revolver, slowly and methodically into my target. When I'm done and my gun is down and I'm pushing out the shells, I feel a heavy tap on my shoulder. It's him. He's waited for me to empty.

Have some conflict.

He mouths something, and I shake my head, lift an ear cup.

"What the hell was that back there?" he asks again, gesturing toward the target without taking his eyes off me. His hand is huge and mottled red and white where he's been gripping his gun. His other hand is out of sight.

"Sorry," I tell him, and it sounds as if I'm speaking in slow motion. "A. Mis. Fire?"

He looks at me for a long moment, waits for my eyes to meet his, the dark muzzles of his pupils behind their yellow protective goggles. It occurs to me that they are the exact same shade as my computer screen, and I imagine my precious last words drifting across them, the letters springing into existence under the beating cursor: "like a dear in the headlights." Finally, he nods and says, "All right, then," vanishes back behind his booth.

I reload, pressing the shells home, letting their snug fit steady me, and wait for him to start firing again. And wait and wait and wait until my hand begins to tremble, and finally I can't not fire. The gap between thought and action is so fine. It's like standing on a cliff, the way the fear of falling makes you want to end the tension, take control, jump before you fall. I felt the death mole, if you like. I felt it burrowing forward, undermining me.

Only when I'm empty do I see my neighbor's target beside me jerk finally. He puts five rounds into the head of his target in a tight fist, then draws it toward him, packs up, and leaves. I still have ammo left. Unfinished business, like a chore. I pick the gun back up and fire round after round after round like hammering nails.

Sometime in there—after the fear wears off and then the elation, and the boredom sets in—I realize there's nothing to learn here. This won't tell me anything about Clark. And the thought of continuing failure fills me with sudden despair. I put the gun down for a moment, afraid of it. I have about one suicidal thought a year, but this isn't a good time to be having it. And then the moment passes, because I know with an adrenaline-fueled clarity that killing myself won't make any kind of difference. I know my wife will go on, my son will be born. My work won't suddenly be discovered. There's no point. And it's a crushing feeling. Knowing that the ultimate gesture, the very worst thing you can do, is nothing special, a failure of imagination.

I fire five more times, reel in my target, roll it up in a tight tube.

When I return my gun and pay, Vern gives my credit card a long look.

"I thought I knew you. You're the teacher from that school. You were on TV." He shakes his head sadly, and for a second I think it's a moment of contrition, and then he says, "What are you teaching those kids anyway?"

I pass behind school on my way home, and I have to stop, I'm shaking so much. It's in my bones now, the distant ringing shudder of the gun. My hands smell of powder, my hair, my shirt, and I clamber out of the car so I won't gag. There's an old pack of Marlboro Lights in the glove box from before my wife got pregnant, and I fumble for a cigarette, suck on it until all I can taste is tobacco smoke. The storm fence here has been festooned with tokens—flowers, cards, soft toys, hang from the wire. Damp from the dew, a little faded already, they ripple in the breeze, fluttering and twisting against the chain-link as if caught in a net. I lean on my hood, watching the twilight seep up out of the earth toward the still bright sky.

Have your character change.

What do I teach them? I teach them that telling stories is the easiest and hardest thing in the world, and among the looks of disbelief and confusion there's always one who nods, who gets it, like the teenage fatalist who asked me once, "Because there are only so many stories, right? Like seven or something." Seven, or ten, or a dozen, though no one can agree what they are and there are countless ways of telling them wrong. But the theory feels right. A finite number of stories, which writers try to tell over and over again. So suicide is boring? Then how do you make it not boring? How do you make it exciting? How do you make it new? So fresh, so vital, so original, that it speaks to an audience?

Before the light fades completely, I step up to the fence to read the messages. The first moves me close to tears, and I sag against the wire. It's such a relief. I read another and another, hungrily, but by the time I've read a dozen my eyes are dry as stone. I snatch at them, plucking them down, the ribbon and colored wool they dangle from gouging through the soft card. Taken together they're clichéd, mawkish, misspelled. There are hundreds of them stretching forty, fifty yards in each direction, as far as I can see in the gloom, like so much litter swept here by the wind. And I want to tear them all down, I want to rip them to shreds. Every awful word.

# Louise Erdrich

## (B. 1954)

Louise Erdrich was born in Little Falls, Minnesota, and is the oldest of seven children. Born to a French Ojibwe mother and a German American father, Erdrich is a member of the Turtle Mountain Band of Chippewa. She began attending Dartmouth in 1972 as part of the school's first coeducational class. While still a student at Dartmouth, Erdrich had a poem published in *Ms.* magazine, and she was awarded an American Academy of Poets prize during her junior year. After completing her undergraduate degree, Erdrich taught writing through a youth program and was awarded a Johns Hopkins University fellowship to be a part of its writing program in 1979. While giving a reading at Dartmouth, Erdrich reconnected with old friend and professor Michael Dorris, whom she married in 1981. Though the couple relied on each other intensively for creative support, Erdrich and Dorris separated in 1995 and Dorris subsequently committed suicide in March 1997.

Erdrich published two volumes of poetry, *Imagination* (1981) and *Jacklight* (1984), but it wasn't until the publication of her novel, *Love Medicine*, in 1984 that she was thrust into the literary limelight. *Love Medicine* is the first in a long line of interrelated and interconnected novels that deal with four Anishinaabe families: the Kashpaws, the Lamartines, the Pillagers, and the Morrisseys. All the novels in the series move from one character to another, equally privileging the stories of men and women, old and young, white and Native American.

Erdrich's family tetralogy appears in various forms in the novels *The Beet Queen* (1986), *Tracks* (1988), *The Bingo Palace* (1994), *Tales of Burning Love* (1996), *The Antelope Wife* (1998), and *Master Butchers Singing Club* (2003). Erdrich continues Native American oral storytelling traditions in her novels, but she also expands the tradition with her transformative use of the trickster character and with her sometimes comic approach to tragedy. The novels also reflect Erdrich's own stance as a woman of mixed-blood heritage and her navigation between native and white worlds. Her latest novel, *Four Souls*, was published in 2004.

---

## American Horse                                      *1986*

The woman sleeping on the cot in the woodshed was Albertine American Horse. The name was left over from her mother's short marriage. The boy was the son of the man she had loved and let go. Buddy was on the cot, too, sitting on the edge because he'd been awake three hours watching out for his mother and besides, she took up the whole cot. Her feet hung over the edge, limp and brown as two trout. Her long arms reached out and slapped at things she saw in her dreams.

Buddy had been knocked awake out of hiding in a washing machine while herds of policemen with dogs searched through a large building with many tiny rooms. When the arm came down, Buddy screamed because it had a blue cuff and sharp silver buttons. "Tss," his mother mumbled, half awake, "wasn't nothing." But Buddy sat up after her breathing went deep again, and he watched.

There was something coming and he knew it.

It was coming from very far off but he had a picture of it in his mind. It was a large thing made of metal with many barbed hooks, points, and drag chains on it, something like a giant potato peeler that rolled out of the sky, scraping clouds down with it and jabbing or crushing everything that lay in its path on the ground.

Buddy watched his mother. If he woke her up, she would know what to do about the thing, but he thought he'd wait until he saw it for sure before he shook her. She was pretty, sleeping, and he liked knowing he could look at her as long and close up as he wanted. He took a strand of her hair and held it in his hands as if it was the rein to a delicate beast. She was strong enough and could pull him along like the horse their name was.

Buddy had his mother's and his grandmother's name because his father had been a big mistake.

"They're all mistakes, even your father. But *you* are the best thing that ever happened to me."

That was what she said when he asked.

Even Kadie, the boyfriend crippled from being in a car wreck, was not as good a thing that had happened to his mother as Buddy was. "He was a medium-size mistake," she said. "He's hurt and I shouldn't even say that, but it's the truth." At the moment, Buddy knew that being the best thing in his mother's life, he was also the reason they were hiding from the cops.

He wanted to touch the satin roses sewed on her pink tee-shirt, but he knew he shouldn't do that even in her sleep. If she woke up and found him touching the roses, she would say, "Quit that, Buddy." Sometimes she told him to stop hugging her like a gorilla. She never said that in the mean voice she used when he oppressed her, but when she said that he loosened up anyway.

There were times he felt like hugging her so hard and in such a special way that she would say to him, "Let's get married." There were also times he closed his eyes and wished that she would die, only a few times, but still it haunted him that his wish might come true. He and Uncle Lawrence would be left alone. Buddy wasn't worried, though, about his mother getting married to somebody else. She had said to her friend, Madonna, "All men suck," when she thought Buddy wasn't listening. He had made an uncertain sound, and when they heard him they took him in their arms.

"Except for you, Buddy," his mother said. "All except for you and maybe Uncle Lawrence, although he's pushing it."

"The cops suck the worst though," Buddy whispered to his mother's sleeping face, "because they're after us." He felt tired again, slumped down, and put his legs beneath the blanket. He closed his eyes and got the feeling that the cot was lifting up beneath him, that it was arching its canvas back and then traveling, traveling very fast and in the wrong direction for when he looked up he saw the three of them were advancing to meet the great metal thing with hooks and barbs and all sorts of sharp equipment to catch their bodies and draw their blood. He heard its insides as it rushed toward them, purring softly like a powerful motor and then they were right in its shadow. He pulled the reins as hard as he could and the beast reared, lifting him. His mother clapped her hand across his mouth.

"Okay," she said. "Lay low. They're outside and they're gonna hunt."

She touched his shoulder and Buddy leaned over with her to look through a crack in the boards.

They were out there all right, Albertine saw them. Two officers and that social worker woman. Vicki Koob. There had been no whistle, no dream, no voice to warn her that they were coming. There was only the crunching sound of cinders in the yard, the engine purring, the dust sifting off their car in a fine light brownish cloud and settling around them.

The three people came to a halt in their husk of metal—the car emblazoned with the North Dakota State Highway Patrol emblem which is the glowing profile of the Sioux policeman, Red Tomahawk, the one who killed Sitting Bull. Albertine gave Buddy the blanket and told him that he might have to wrap it around him and hide underneath the cot.

"We're gonna wait and see what they do." She took him in her lap and hunched her arms around him. "Don't you worry," she whispered against his ear. "Lawrence knows how to fool them."

Buddy didn't want to look at the car and the people. He felt his mother's heart beating beneath his ear so fast it seemed to push the satin roses in and out. He put his face to them carefully and breathed the deep, soft powdery woman smell of her. That smell was also in her little face cream bottles, in her brushes, and around the wash-bowl after she used it. The satin felt so unbearably smooth against his cheek that he had to press closer. She didn't push him away, like he expected, but hugged him still tighter until he felt as close as he had ever been to back inside her again where she said he came from. Within the smells of her things, her soft skin and the satin of her roses, he closed his eyes then, and took his breaths softly and quickly with her heart.

They were out there, but they didn't dare get out of the car yet because of Lawrence's big, ragged dogs. Three of these dogs had loped up the dirt driveway with the car. They were rangy, alert, and bounced up and down on their cushioned paws like wolves. They didn't waste their energy barking, but positioned themselves quietly, one at either car door and the third in front of the bellied-out screen door to Uncle Lawrence's house. It was six in the morning but the wind was up already, blowing dust, ruffling their short moth-eaten coats. The big brown one on Vicki Koob's side had unusual black and white markings, stripes almost, like a hyena and he grinned at her, tongue out and teeth showing.

"Shoo!" Miss Koob opened her door with a quick jerk.

The brown dog sidestepped the door and jumped before her, tiptoeing. Its dirty white muzzle curled and its eyes crossed suddenly as it was zeroing its cross-hair sights in on the exact place it would bite her. She ducked back and slammed the door.

"It's mean," she told Officer Brackett. He was printing out some type of form. The other officer, Harmony, a slow man, had not yet reacted to the car's halt. He had been sitting quietly in the back seat, but now he rolled down his window and with no change in expression unsnapped his holster and drew his pistol out and pointed it at the dog on his side. The dog smacked down on its belly, wiggled under the car and was out and around the back of the house before Harmony drew his gun back. The other dogs vanished with him. From wherever they had disappeared to they began to yap and howl, and the door to the low shoebox-style house fell open.

"Heya, what's going on?"

Uncle Lawrence put his head out the door and opened wide the one eye he had in working order. The eye bulged impossibly wider in outrage when he saw the police car. But the eyes of the two officers and Miss Vicki Koob were wide open too because they had never seen Uncle Lawrence in his sleeping getup or, indeed, witnessed anything like it. For his ribs, which were cracked from a bad fall and still mending, Uncle Lawrence wore a thick white corset laced up the front with a striped sneakers lace. His glass eye and his set of dentures were still out for the night so his face puckered here and there, around its absences and scars, like a damaged but fierce little cake. Although he had a few gray streaks now, Uncle Lawrence's hair was still thick, and because he wore a special contraption of elastic straps around his head every night, two oiled waves always crested on either side of his middle part. All of this would have been sufficient to astonish, even without the most striking part of his outfit— the smoking jacket. It was made of black satin and hung open around his corset, dragging a tasseled belt. Gold thread dragons struggled up the lapels and blasted their furry red breath around his neck. As Lawrence walked down the steps, he put his arms up in surrender and the gold tassels in the inner seams of his sleeves dropped into view.

"My heavens, what a sight." Vicki Koob was impressed.

"A character," apologized Officer Harmony.

As a tribal police officer who could be counted on to help out the State Patrol, Harmony thought he always had to explain about Indians or get twice as tough to show he did not favor them. He was slow-moving and shy but two jumps ahead of other people all the same, and now, as he watched Uncle Lawrence's splendid approach, he gazed speculatively at the torn and bulging pocket of the smoking jacket. Harmony had been inside Uncle Lawrence's house before and knew that above his draped orange-crate shelf of war medals a blue-black German luger was hung carefully in a net of flat-headed nails and fishing line. Thinking of this deadly exhibition, he got out of the car and shambled toward Lawrence with a dreamy little smile of welcome on his face. But when he searched Lawrence, he found that the bulging pocket held only the lonesome-looking dentures from Lawrence's empty jaw. They were still dripping denture polish.

"I had been cleaning them when you arrived," Uncle Lawrence explained with acid dignity.

He took the toothbrush from his other pocket and aimed it like a rifle.

"Quit that, you old idiot." Harmony tossed the toothbrush away. "For once you ain't done nothing. We came for your nephew."

Lawrence looked at Harmony with a faint air of puzzlement.

"Ma Frere, listen," threatened Harmony amiably, "those two white people in the car came to get him for the welfare. They got papers on your nephew that give them the right to take him."

"Papers?" Uncle Lawrence puffed out his deeply pitted cheeks. "Let me see them papers."

The two of them walked over to Vicki's side of the car and she pulled a copy of the court order from her purse. Lawrence put his teeth back in and adjusted them with busy workings of his jaw.

"Just a minute," he reached into his breast pocket as he bent close to Miss Vicki Koob. "I can't read these without I have in my eye."

He took the eye from his breast pocket delicately, and as he popped it into his face the social worker's mouth fell open in a consternated O.

"What is this," she cried in a little voice.

Uncle Lawrence looked at her mildly. The white glass of the eye was cold as lard. The black iris was strangely charged and menacing.

"He's nuts," Brackett huffed along the side of Vicki's neck. "Never mind him."

Vicki's hair had sweated down her nape in tiny corkscrews and some of the hairs were so long and dangly now that they disappeared into the zippered back of her dress. Brackett noticed this as he spoke into her ear. His face grew red and the backs of his hands prickled. He slid under the steering wheel and got out of the car. He walked around the hood to stand with Leo Harmony.

"We could take you in too," said Brackett roughly. Lawrence eyed the officers in what was taken as defiance. "If you don't cooperate, we'll get out the handcuffs," they warned.

One of Lawrence's arms was stiff and would not move until he'd rubbed it with witch hazel in the morning. His other arm worked fine though, and he stuck it out in front of Brackett.

"Get them handcuffs," he urged them. "Put me in a welfare home."

Brackett snapped one side of the handcuffs on Lawrence's good arm and the other to the handle of the police car.

"That's to hold you," he said. "We're wasting our time. Harmony, you search that little shed over by the tall grass and Miss Koob and myself will search the house."

"My rights is violated!" Lawrence shrieked suddenly. They ignored him. He tugged at the handcuff and thought of the good heavy file he kept in his tool box and the German luger oiled and ready but never loaded, because of Buddy, over his shelf. He should have used it on these bad ones, even Harmony in his big-time white man job. He wouldn't last long in that job anyway before somebody gave him what for.

"It's a damn scheme," said Uncle Lawrence, rattling his chains against the car. He looked over at the shed and thought maybe Albertine and Buddy had sneaked away before the car pulled into the yard. But he sagged, seeing Albertine move like a shadow within the boards. "Oh, it's all a damn scheme," he muttered again.

"I want to find that boy and salvage him," Vicki Koob explained to Officer Brackett as they walked into the house. "Look at his family life—the old man crazy as a bedbug, the mother intoxicated somewhere."

Brackett nodded, energetic, eager. He was a short hopeful redhead who failed consistently to win the hearts of women. Vicki Koob intrigued him. Now, as he watched, she pulled a tiny pen out of an ornamental clip on her blouse. It was attached to a retractable line that would suck the pen back, like a child eating one strand of spaghetti. Something about the pen on its line excited Brackett to the point of discomfort. His hand shook as he opened the screendoor and stepped in, beckoning Miss Koob to follow.

They could see the house was empty at first glance. It was only one rectangular room with whitewashed walls and a little gas stove in the middle. They had already come through the cooking lean-to with the other stove and washstand and rusty old refrigerator. That refrigerator had nothing in it but some wrinkled potatoes and a package of turkey necks. Vicki Koob noted that in her perfect-bound notebook. The beds along the walls of the big room were covered with quilts that Albertine's mother, Sophie, had made from bits of old wool coats and pants that the Sisters sold in bundles at the mission. There was no one hiding beneath the beds. No one was under the little aluminum dinette table covered with a green oilcoth, or the soft brown wood chairs tucked up to it. One wall of the big room was filled with neatly stacked crates of things—old tools and springs and small half-dismantled appliances. Five or six television sets were stacked against the wall. Their control panels spewed colored wires and at least one was cracked all the way across. Only the topmost set, with coathanger antenna angled sensitively to catch the bounding signals around Little Shell, looked like it could possibly work.

Not one thing escaped Vicki Koob's trained and cataloguing gaze. She made note of the cupboard that held only commodity flour and sugar. The unsanitary tin oil drum beneath the kitchen window, full of empty surplus pork cans and beer bottles, caught her eye as did Uncle Lawrence's physical and mental deteriorations. She quickly described these "benchmarks of alcoholic dependency within the extended family of Woodrow (Buddy) American Horse" as she walked around the room with the little notebook open, pushed against her belly to steady it. Although Vicki had been there before, Albertine's presence had always made it difficult for her to take notes.

"Twice the maximum allowable space between door and threshold," she wrote now. "Probably no insulation. 2–3 inch cracks in walls inadequately sealed with whitewashed mud." She made a mental note but could see no point in describing Lawrence's stuffed reclining chair that only reclined, the shadeless lamp with its plastic orchid in the bubble glass base, or the three-dimensional picture of Jesus that Lawrence had once demonstrated to her. When plugged in, lights rolled behind the water the Lord stood on so that he seemed to be strolling although he never actually went forward, of course, but only pushed the glowing waves behind him forever like a poor tame rat in a treadmill.

Brackett cleared his throat with a nervous rasp and touched Vicki's shoulder.

"What are you writing?"

She moved away and continued to scribble as if thoroughly absorbed in her work. "Officer Brackett displays an undue amount of interest in my person," she wrote. "Perhaps?"

He snatched playfully at the book, but she hugged it to her chest and moved off smiling. More curls had fallen, wetted to the base of her neck. Looking out the window, she sighed long and loud.

"All night on brush rollers for this. What a joke."

Brackett shoved his hands in his pockets. His mouth opened slightly, then shut with a small throttled cluck.

When Albertine saw Harmony ambling across the yard with his big brown thumbs in his belt, his placid smile, and his tiny black eyes moving back and forth, she put Buddy under the cot. Harmony stopped at the shed and stood quietly. He spread his arms wide to show her he hadn't drawn his big police gun.

"Ma Cousin," he said in the Michif dialect that people used if they were relatives or sometimes if they needed gas or a couple of dollars, "why don't you come out here and stop this foolishness?"

"I ain't your cousin," Albertine said. Anger boiled up in her suddenly. "I ain't related to no pigs."

She bit her lip and watched him through the cracks, circling, a big tan punching dummy with his boots full of sand so he never stayed down once he fell. He was empty inside, all stale air. But he knew how to get to her so much better than a white cop could. And now he was circling because he wasn't sure she didn't have a weapon, maybe a knife or the German luger that was the only thing that her father, Albert American Horse, had left his wife and daughter besides his name. Harmony knew that Albertine was a tall strong woman who took two big men to subdue when she didn't want to go in the drunk tank. She had hard hips, broad shoulders, and stood tall like her Sioux father, the American Horse who was killed threshing in Belle Prairie.

"I feel bad to have to do this," Harmony said to Albertine. "But for godsakes, let's nobody get hurt. Come on out with the boy why don't you. I know you got him in there."

Albertine did not give herself away this time. She let him wonder. Slowly and quietly she pulled her belt through its loops and wrapped it around and around her hand until only the big oval buckle with turquoise chunks shaped into a butterfly stuck out over her knuckles. Harmony was talking but she wasn't listening to what he said. She was listening to the pitch of his voice, the tone of it that would tighten or tremble at a certain moment when he decided to rush the shed. He kept talking slowly and reasonably, flexing the dialect from time to time, even mentioning her father.

"He was a damn good man. I don't care what they say, Albertine, I knew him."

Albertine looked at the stone butterfly that spread its wings across her fist. The wings looked light and cool, not heavy. It almost looked like it was ready to fly. Harmony wanted to get to Albertine through her father but she would not think about American Horse. She concentrated on the sky-blue stone.

Yet the shape of the stone, the color, betrayed her.

She saw her father suddenly, bending at the grille of their old grey car. She was small then. The memory came from so long ago it seemed like a dream—narrowly focused, snapshot clear. He was bending by the grille in the sun. It was hot summer. Wings of sweat, dark blue, spread across the back of his work shirt. He always wore soft blue shirts, the color of shade cloudier than this stone. His stiff hair had grown out of its short haircut and flopped over his forehead. When he stood up and turned away from the car, Albertine saw that he had a butterfly.

"It's dead," he told her. "Broke its wings and died on the grille."

She must have been five, maybe six, wearing one of the boy's tee-shirts Mama bleached in hilex-water. American Horse took the butterfly, a black and yellow one, and rubbed it on Albertine's collarbone and chest and arms until the color and the powder of it were blended into her skin.

"For grace," he said.

And Albertine had felt a strange lightening in her arms, in her chest, when he did this and said, "For grace." The way he said it, grace meant everything the butterfly was. The sharp delicate wings. The way it floated over grass. The way its wings seemed to breathe fanning in the sun. The wisdom of the way it blended into flowers or changed into a leaf. In herself she felt the same kind of possibilities and closed her eyes almost in shock or pain, she felt so light and powerful at that moment.

Then her father had caught her and thrown her high into the air. She could not remember landing in his arms or landing at all. She only remembered the sun filling her eyes and the world tipping crazily behind her, out of sight.

"He was a damn good man," Harmony said again.

Albertine heard his starched uniform gathering before his boots hit the ground. Once, twice, three times. It took him four solid jumps to get right where she wanted him. She kicked the plank door open when he reached for the handle and the corner caught him on the jaw. He faltered, and Albertine hit him flat on the chin with the butterfly. She hit him so hard the shock of it went up her arm like a string pulled taut. Her fist opened, numb, and she let the belt unloop before she closed her hand on the tip end of it and sent the stone butterfly swooping out in a wide circle around her as if it was on the end of a leash. Harmony reeled backward as she walked toward him swinging the belt. She expected him to fall but he just stumbled. And then he took the gun from his hip.

Albertine let the belt go limp. She and Harmony stood within feet of each other, breathing. Each heard the human sound of air going in and out of the other person's lungs. Each read the face of the other as if deciphering letters carved into softly eroding veins of stone. Albertine saw the pattern of tiny arteries that age, drink, and hard living had blown to the surface of the man's face. She saw the spoked wheels of his iris and the arteries like tangled threads that sewed him up. She saw the living net of springs and tissue that held him together, and trapped him. She saw the random, intimate plan of his person.

She took a quick shallow breath and her face went strange and tight. She saw the black veins in the wings of the butterfly, roads burnt into a map, and then she was located somewhere in the net of veins and sinew that was the tragic complexity of the world so she did not see Officer Brackett and Vicki Koob rushing toward her, but felt them instead like flies caught in the same web, rocking it.

"Albertine!" Vicki Koob had stopped in the grass. Her voice was shrill and tight. "It's better this way, Albertine. We're going to help you."

Albertine straightened, threw her shoulders back. Her father's hand was on her chest and shoulders lightening her wonderfully. Then on wings of her father's hands, on dead butterfly wings, Albertine lifted into the air and flew toward the others. The light powerful feeling swept her up the way she had floated higher, seeing the grass below. It was her father throwing her up into the air and out of danger. Her arms opened for bullets but no bullets came. Harmony did not shoot. Instead, he raised his fist and brought it down hard on her head.

Albertine did not fall immediately, but stood in his arms a moment. Perhaps she gazed still farther back behind the covering of his face. Perhaps she was completely stunned and did not think as she sagged and fell. Her face rolled forward and hair covered her features, so it was impossible for Harmony to see with just what particular expression she gazed into the head-splitting wheel of light, or blackness, that overcame her.

Harmony turned the vehicle onto the gravel road that led back to town. He had convinced the other two that Albertine was more trouble than she was worth, and so they left her behind, and Lawrence too. He stood swearing in his cinder driveway as the car rolled out of sight. Buddy sat between the social worker and Officer Brackett. Vicki tried to hold Buddy fast and keep her arm down at the same time, for the words she'd screamed at Albertine had broken the seal of antiperspirant beneath her arms. She was sweating now as though she'd stored an ocean up inside of her. Sweat rolled down her back in a shallow river and pooled at her waist and between her breasts. A thin sheen of water came out on her forearms, her face. Vicki gave an irritated moan but Brackett seemed not to take notice, or take offense at least. Air-conditioned breezes were sweeping over the seat anyway, and very soon they would be comfortable. She smiled at Brackett over Buddy's head. The man grinned back. Buddy stirred. Vicki remembered the emergency chocolate bar she kept in her purse, fished it out, and offered it to Buddy. He did not react, so she closed his fingers over the package and peeled the paper off one end.

The car accelerated. Buddy felt the road and wheels pummeling each other and the rush of the heavy motor purring in high gear. Buddy knew that what he'd seen in his mind that morning, the thing coming out of the sky with barbs and chains, had hooked him. Somehow he was caught and held in the sour tin smell of the pale woman's armpit. Somehow he was pinned between their pounds of breathless flesh. He looked at the chocolate in his hand. He was squeezing the bar so hard that a thin brown trickle had melted down his arm. Automatically, he put the bar in his mouth.

As he bit down he saw his mother very clearly, just as she had been when she carried him from the shed. She was stretched flat on the ground, on her stomach, and her arms were curled around her head as if in sleep. One leg was drawn up and it looked for all the world like she was running full tilt into the ground, as though she had been trying to pass into the earth, to bury herself, but at the last moment something had stopped her.

There was no blood on Albertine, but Buddy tasted blood now at the sight of her, for he bit down hard and cut his own lip. He ate the chocolate, every bit of it, tasting his mother's blood. And when he had the chocolate down inside him and all licked off his hands, he opened his mouth to say thank you to the woman, as his mother had taught him. But instead of a thank you coming out he was astonished to hear a great rattling scream, and then another, rip out of him like pieces of his own body and whirl onto the sharp things all around him.

## The Red Convertible 1984

### Lyman Lamartine

I was the first one to drive a convertible on my reservation. And of course it was red, a red Olds. I owned that car along with my brother Henry Junior. We owned it together until his boots filled with water on a windy night and he bought out my share. Now Henry owns the whole car, and his younger brother Lyman (that's myself), Lyman walks everywhere he goes.

How did I earn enough money to buy my share in the first place? My one talent was I could always make money. I had a touch for it, unusual in a Chippewa. From the first I was different that way, and everyone recognized it. I was the only kid they let in the American Legion Hall to shine shoes, for example, and one Christmas I sold spiritual bouquets for the mission door to door. The nuns let me keep a percentage. Once I started, it seemed the more money I made the easier the money came. Everyone encouraged it. When I was fifteen I got a job washing dishes at the Joliet Café, and that was where my first big break happened.

It wasn't long before I was promoted to busing tables, and then the short-order cook quit and I was hired to take her place. No sooner than you know it I was managing the Joliet. The rest is history. I went on managing. I soon became part owner, and of course there was no stopping me then. It wasn't long before the whole thing was mine.

After I'd owned the Joliet for one year, it blew over in the worst tornado ever seen around here. The whole operation was smashed to bits. A total loss. The fryalator was up in a tree, the grill torn in half like it was paper. I was only sixteen. I had it all in my mother's name, and I lost it quick, but before I lost it I had every one of my relatives, and their relatives, to dinner, and I also bought that red Olds I mentioned, along with Henry.

The first time we saw it! I'll tell you when we first saw it. We had gotten a ride up to Winnipeg, and both of us had money. Don't ask me why, because we never mentioned a car or anything, we just had all our money. Mine was cash, a big bankroll from the Joliet's insurance. Henry had two checks—a week's extra pay for being laid off, and his regular check from the Jewel Bearing Plant.

We were walking down Portage anyway, seeing the sights, when we saw it. There it was, parked, large as life. Really, as *if* it was alive. I thought of the word *repose*, because the car wasn't simply stopped, parked, or whatever. That car reposed, calm and gleaming, a FOR SALE sign on its left front window. Then, before we had thought it over at all, the car belonged to us and our pockets were empty. We had just enough money for gas back home.

We went places in that car, me and Henry. We took off driving all one whole summer. We started off toward the Little Knife River and Mandaree in Fort Berthold and then we found ourselves down in Wakpala somehow, and then suddenly we were over in Montana on the Rocky Boy, and yet the summer was not even half over. Some people hang on to details when they travel, but we didn't let them bother us and just lived our everyday lives here to there.

I do remember this one place with willows. I remember I laid under those trees and it was comfortable. So comfortable. The branches bent down all around me like a tent or a stable. And quiet, it was quiet, even though there was a powwow close enough so I could see it going on. The air was not too still, not too windy either. When the dust rises up and hangs in the air around the dancers like that, I feel good. Henry was asleep with his arms thrown wide. Later on, he woke up and we started driving again. We were somewhere in Montana, or maybe on the Blood Reserve—it could have been anywhere. Anyway, it was where we met the girl.

All her hair was in buns around her ears, that's the first thing I noticed about her. She was posed alongside the road with her arm out so we stopped. That girl was short, so short her lumber shirt looked comical on her, like a nightgown. She had jeans on and fancy moccasins and she carried a little suitcase.

"Hop on in," says Henry. So she climbs in between us.

"We'll take you home," I says. "Where do you live?"

"Chicken," she says.

"Where the hell's that?" I ask her.

"Alaska."

"Okay," says Henry, and we drive.

We got up there and never wanted to leave. The sun doesn't truly set there in summer, and the night is more a soft dusk. You might doze off, sometimes, but before you know it you're up again, like an animal in nature. You never feel like you have to sleep hard or put away the world. And things would grow up there. One day just dirt or moss, the next day flowers and long grass. The girl's name was Susy. Her family really took to us. They fed us and put us up. We had our own tent to live in by their house, and the kids would be in and out of there all day and night. They couldn't get over me and Henry being brothers, we looked so different. We told them we knew we had the same mother, anyway.

One night Susy came in to visit us. We sat around in the tent talking of this and that. The season was changing. It was getting darker by that time, and the cold was even getting just a little mean. I told her it was time for us to go. She stood up on a chair.

"You never seen my hair," Susy said.

That was true. She was standing on a chair, but still, when she unclipped her buns the hair reached all the way to the ground. Our eyes opened. You couldn't tell how much hair she had when it was rolled up so neatly. Then my brother Henry did something funny. He went up to the chair and said, "Jump on my shoulders." So she did that, and her hair reached down past his waist, and he started twirling, this way and that, so her hair was flung out from side to side.

"I always wondered what it was like to have long pretty hair," Henry says. Well we laughed. It was a funny sight, the way he did it. The next morning we got up and took leave of those people.

On to greener pastures, as they say. It was down through Spokane and across Idaho then Montana and very soon we were racing the weather right along under the Canadian border through Columbus, Des Lacs, and then we were in Bottineau County and soon home. We'd made most of the trip that summer, without putting up the car hood at all. We got home just in time, it turned out, for the army to remember Henry had signed up to join it.

I don't wonder that the army was so glad to get my brother that they turned him into a Marine. He was built like a brick outhouse anyway. We liked to tease him that they really wanted him for his Indian nose. He had a nose big and sharp as a hatchet, like the nose on Red Tomahawk, the Indian who killed Sitting Bull, whose profile is on signs all along the North Dakota highways. Henry went off to training camp, came home once during Christmas, then the next thing you know we got an overseas letter from him. It was 1970, and he said he was stationed up in the northern hill country. Whereabouts I did not know. He wasn't such a hot letter writer, and only got off two before the enemy caught him. I could never keep it straight, which direction those good Vietnam soldiers were from.

I wrote him back several times, even though I didn't know if those letters would get through. I kept him informed all about the car. Most of the time I had it up on blocks in the yard or half taken apart, because that long trip did a hard job on it under the hood.

I always had good luck with numbers, and never worried about the draft myself. I never even had to think about what my number was. But Henry was never lucky in the same way as me. It was at least three years before Henry came home. By then I guess the whole war was solved in the government's mind, but for him it would keep on going. In those years, I'd put his car into almost perfect shape. I always thought of it as his car while he was gone, even though when he left he said, "Now it's yours," and threw me his key.

"Thanks for the extra key," I'd said. "I'll put it up in your drawer just in case I need it." He laughed.

When he came home, though, Henry was very different, and I'll say this: the change was no good. You could hardly expect him to change for the better, I know. But he was quiet, so quiet and never comfortable sitting still anywhere but always up and moving around. I thought back to times we'd sat still for whole afternoons, never moving a muscle, just shifting our weight along the ground, talking to whoever sat with us, watching things. He'd always had a joke, then, too, and now you couldn't get him to laugh, or when he did it was more the sound of a man choking, a sound that stopped up the throats of other people around him. They got to leaving him alone most of the time, and I didn't blame them. It was a fact: Henry was jumpy and mean.

I'd bought a color TV set for my mom and the rest of us while Henry was away. Money still came very easy. I was sorry I'd ever bought it though, because of Henry. I was also sorry I'd bought color, because with black-and-white the pictures seem older and farther away. But what are you going to do? He sat in front of it, watching it, and that was the only time he was completely still. But it was the kind of stillness that you see in a rabbit when it freezes and before it will bolt. He was not easy. He sat in his chair gripping the armrests with all his might, as if the chair itself was moving at a high speed and if he let go at all he would rocket forward and maybe crash right through the set.

Once I was in the room watching TV with Henry and I heard his teeth click at something. I looked over, and he'd bitten through his lip. Blood was going down his chin. I tell you right then I wanted to smash that tube to pieces. I went over to it but Henry must have known what I was up to. He rushed from his chair and shoved me out of the way, against the wall. I told myself he didn't know what he was doing.

My mom came in, turned the set off real quiet, and told us she had made something for supper. So we went and sat down. There was still blood going down Henry's chin, but he didn't notice it and no one said anything, even though every time he took a bite of his bread his blood fell onto it until he was eating his own blood mixed in with the food.

While Henry was not around we talked about what was going to happen to him. There were no Indian doctors on the reservation, and my mom couldn't come around to trusting the old man, Moses Pillager, because he courted her long ago and was jealous of her husbands. He might take revenge through her son. We were afraid that if we brought Henry to a regular hospital they would keep him.

"They don't fix them in those places," Mom said; "they just give them drugs."

"We wouldn't get him there in the first place," I agreed, "so let's just forget about it."

Then I thought about the car.

Henry had not even looked at the car since he'd gotten home, though like I said, it was in tip-top condition and ready to drive. I thought the car might bring the old Henry back somehow. So I bided my time and waited for my chance to interest him in the vehicle.

One night Henry was off somewhere. I took myself a hammer. I went out to that car and I did a number on its underside. Whacked it up. Bent the tail pipe double. Ripped the muffler loose. By the time I was done with the car it looked worse than any typical Indian car that has been driven all its life on reservation roads, which they always say are like government promises—full of holes. It just about hurt me, I'll tell you that! I threw dirt in the carburetor and I ripped all the electric tape off the seats. I made it look just as beat up as I could. Then I sat back and waited for Henry to find it.

Still, it took him over a month. That was all right, because it was just getting warm enough, not melting, but warm enough to work outside.

"Lyman," he says, walking in one day, "that red car looks like shit."

"Well, it's old," I says. "You got to expect that."

"No way!" says Henry. "That car's a classic! But you went and ran the piss right out of it, Lyman, and you know it don't deserve that. I kept that car in A-one shape. You don't remember. You're too young. But when I left, that car was running like a watch. Now I don't even know if I can get it to start again, let alone get it anywhere near its old condition."

"Well you try," I said, like I was getting mad, "but I say it's a piece of junk."

Then I walked out before he could realize I knew he'd strung together more than six words at once.

After that I thought he'd freeze himself to death working on that car. He was out there all day, and at night he rigged up a little lamp, ran a cord out the window, and had himself some light to see by while he worked. He was better than he had been before, but that's still not saying much. It was easier for him to do the things the rest of us did. He ate more slowly and didn't jump up and down during the meal to get this or that or look out the window. I put my hand in the back of the TV set, I admit, and fiddled around with it good, so that it was almost impossible now to get a clear picture. He didn't look at it very often anyway. He was always out with that car or going off to get parts for it. By the time it was really melting outside, he had it fixed.

I had been feeling down in the dumps about Henry around this time. We had always been together before. Henry and Lyman. But he was such a loner now that I didn't know how to take it. So I jumped at the chance one day when Henry seemed friendly. It's not that he smiled or anything. He just said, "Let's take that old shitbox for a spin." Just the way he said it made me think he could be coming around.

We went out to the car. It was spring. The sun was shining very bright. My only sister, Bonita, who was just eleven years old, came out and made us stand together for a picture. Henry leaned his elbow on the red car's windshield, and he took his other arm and put it over my shoulder, very carefully, as though it was heavy for him to lift and he didn't want to bring the weight down all at once.

"Smile," Bonita said, and he did.

That picture. I never look at it anymore. A few months ago, I don't know why, I got his picture out and tacked it on the wall. I felt good about Henry at the time, close to him. I felt good having his picture on the wall, until one night when I was looking at television. I was a little drunk and stoned. I looked up at the wall and Henry was staring at me. I don't know what it was, but his smile had changed, or maybe it was gone. All I know is I couldn't stay in the same room with that picture. I was shaking. I got up, closed the door, and went into the kitchen. A little later my friend Ray came over and we both went back into that room. We put the picture in a brown bag, folded the bag over and over tightly, then put it way back in a closet.

I still see that picture now, as it tugs at me, whenever I pass that closet door. The picture is very clear in my mind. It was so sunny that day Henry had to squint against the glare. Or maybe the camera Bonita held flashed like a mirror, blinding him, before she snapped the picture. My face is right out in the sun, big and round. But he might have drawn back, because the shadows on his face are deep as holes. There are two shadows curved like little hooks around the ends of his smile, as if to frame it and try to keep it there—that one, first smile that looked like it might have hurt his face. He has his field jacket on and the worn-in clothes he'd come back in and kept wearing ever since. After Bonita took the picture, she went into the house and we got into the car. There was a full cooler in the trunk. We started off, east, toward Pembina and the Red River because Henry said he wanted to see the high water.

The trip over there was beautiful. When everything starts changing, drying up, clearing off, you feel like your whole life is starting. Henry felt it, too. The top was down and the car hummed like a top. He'd really put it back in shape, even the tape on the seats was very carefully put down and glued back in layers. It's not that he smiled again or even joked, but his face looked to me as if it was clear, more peaceful. It looked as though he wasn't thinking of anything in particular except the bare fields and windbreaks and houses we were passing.

The river was high and full of winter trash when we got there. The sun was still out, but it was colder by the river. There were still little clumps of dirty snow here and there on the banks. The water hadn't gone over the banks yet, but it would, you could tell. It was just at its limit, hard swollen, glossy like an old gray scar. We made ourselves a fire, and we sat down and watched the current go. As I watched it I felt something squeezing inside me and tightening and trying to let go all at the same time. I knew I was not just feeling it myself; I knew I was feeling what Henry was going through at that moment. Except that I couldn't stand it, the closing and opening. I jumped to my feet. I took Henry by the shoulders and I started shaking him. "Wake up," I says, "wake up, wake up, wake up!" I didn't know what had come over me. I sat down beside him again.

His face was totally white and hard. Then it broke, like stones break all of a sudden when water boils up inside them.

"I know it," he says. "I know it. I can't help it. It's no use."

We start talking. He said he knew what I'd done with the car. It was obvious it had been whacked out of shape and not just neglected. He said he wanted to give the car to me for good now, it was no use. He said he'd fixed it just to give it back and I should take it.

"No way," I says. "I don't want it."

"That's okay," he says, "you take it."

"I don't want it, though," I says back to him, and then to emphasize, just to emphasize, you understand, I touch his shoulder. He slaps my hand off.

"Take that car," he says.

"No," I say. "Make me," I say, and then he grabs my jacket and rips the arm loose. That jacket is a class act, suede with tags and zippers. I push Henry backwards, off the log. He jumps up and bowls me over. We go down in a clinch and come up swinging hard, for all we're worth, with our fists. He socks my jaw so hard I feel like it swings loose. Then I'm at his rib cage and land a good one under his chin so his head snaps back. He's dazzled. He looks at me and I look at him and then his eyes are full of tears and blood and at first I think he's crying. But no, he's laughing. "Ha! Ha!" he says. "Ha! Ha! Take good care of it."

"Okay," I says. "Okay, no problem. Ha! Ha!"

I can't help it, and I start laughing, too. My face feels fat and strange, and after a while I get a beer from the cooler in the trunk, and when I hand it to Henry he takes his shirt and wipes my germs off. "Hoof-and-mouth disease," he says. For some reason this cracks me up, and so we're really laughing for a while, and then we drink all the rest of the beers one by one and throw them in the river and see how far, how fast, the current takes them before they fill up and sink.

"You want to go on back?" I ask after a while. "Maybe we could snag a couple nice Kashpaw girls."

He says nothing. But I can tell his mood is turning again.

"They're all crazy, the girls up here, every damn one of them."

"You're crazy too," I say, to jolly him up. "Crazy Lamartine boys!"

He looks as though he will take this wrong at first. His face twists, then clears, and he jumps up on his feet. "That's right!" he says. "Crazier 'n hell. Crazy Indians!"

I think it's the old Henry again. He throws off his jacket and starts springing his legs up from the knees like a fancy dancer. He's down doing something between a grass dance and a bunny hop, no kind of dance I ever saw before, but neither has anyone else on all this green growing earth. He's wild. He wants to pitch whoopee! He's up and at me and all over. All this time I'm laughing so hard, so hard my belly is getting tied up in a knot.

"Got to cool me off!" he shouts all of a sudden. Then he runs over to the river and jumps in.

There's boards and other things in the current. It's so high. No sound comes from the river after the splash he makes, so I run right over. I look around. It's getting dark. I see he's halfway across the water already, and I know he didn't swim there but the current took him. It's far. I hear his voice, though, very clearly across it.

"My boots are filling," he says.

He says this in a normal voice, like he just noticed and he doesn't know what to think of it. Then he's gone. A branch comes by. Another branch. And I go in.

By the time I get out of the river, off the snag I pulled myself onto, the sun is down. I walk back to the car, turn on the high beams, and drive it up the bank. I put it in first gear and then I take my foot off the clutch. I get out, close the door, and watch it plow softly into the water. The headlights reach in as they go down, searching, still lighted even after the water swirls over the back end. I wait. The wires short out. It is all finally dark. And then there is only the water, the sound of it going and running and going and running and running.

## The Shawl                                            2001

Among the Anishinaabeg on the road where I live, it is told how a woman loved a man other than her husband and went off into the bush and bore his child. Her name was Aanakwad, which means cloud, and like a cloud she was changeable. She was moody and sullen one moment, her lower lip jutting and her eyes flashing, filled with storms. The next, she would shake her hair over her face and blow it straight out in front of her to make her children scream with laughter. For she also had two children by her husband, one a yearning boy of five years and the other a capable daughter of nine.

When Aanakwad brought the new baby out of the trees that autumn, the older girl was like a second mother, even waking in the night to clean the baby and nudge it to her mother's breast. Aanakwad slept through its cries, hardly woke. It wasn't that she didn't love her baby; no, it was the opposite—she loved it too much, the way she loved its father, and not her husband. This passion ate away at her, and her feelings were unbearable. If she could have thrown off that wronghearted love, she would have, but the thought of the other man, who lived across the lake, was with her always. She became a gray sky, stared monotonously at the walls, sometimes wept into her hands for hours at a time. Soon, she couldn't rise to cook or keep the cabin neat, and it was too much for the girl, who curled up each night exhausted in her red-and-brown plaid shawl, and slept and slept, until the husband had to wake her to awaken her mother, for he was afraid of his wife's bad temper, and it was he who roused Aanakwad into anger by the sheer fact that he was himself and not the other.

At last, even though he loved Aanakwad, the husband had to admit that their life together was no good anymore. And it was he who sent for the other man's uncle. In those days, our people lived widely scattered, along the shores and in the islands, even out on the plains. There were no roads then, just trails, though we had horses and wagons and, for the winter, sleds. When the uncle came around to fetch Aanakwad, in his wagon fitted out with sled runners, it was very hard, for she and her husband had argued right up to the last about the children, argued fiercely until the husband had finally given in. He turned his face to the wall, and did not move to see the daughter, whom he treasured, sit down beside her mother, wrapped in her plaid robe in the wagon bed. They left right away, with their bundles and sacks, not bothering to heat up the stones to warm their feet. The father had stopped his ears, so he did not hear his son cry out when he suddenly understood that he would be left behind.

As the uncle slapped the reins and the horse lurched forward, the boy tried to jump into the wagon, but his mother pried his hands off the boards, crying, *Gego, gego,* and he fell down hard. But there was something in him that would not let her leave. He jumped up and, although he was wearing only light clothing, he ran behind the wagon over the packed drifts. The horses picked up speed. His chest was scorched with pain, and yet he pushed himself on. He'd never run so fast, so hard and furiously, but he was determined, and he refused to believe that the increasing distance between him and the wagon was real. He kept going until his throat closed, he saw red, and in the ice of the air his lungs shut. Then, as he fell onto the board-hard snow, he raised his head. He watched the back of the wagon and the tiny figures of his mother and sister disappear, and something failed in him. Something broke. At that moment he truly did not care if he was alive or dead. So when he saw the gray shapes, the shadows, bounding lightly from the trees to either side of the trail, far ahead, he was not afraid.

The next the boy knew, his father had him wrapped in a blanket and was carrying him home. His father's chest was broad and, although he already spat the tubercular blood that would write the end of his story, he was still a strong man. It would take him many years to die. In those years, the father would tell the boy, who had forgotten this part entirely, that at first when he talked about the shadows the father thought he'd been visited by *manidoog*. But then, as the boy described the shapes, his father had understood that they were not spirits. Uneasy, he had decided to take his gun back along the trail. He had built up the fire in the cabin, and settled his boy near it, and gone back out into the snow. Perhaps the story spread through our settlements because the father had to tell what he saw, again and again, in order to get rid of it. Perhaps as with all frightful dreams, *amaniso*, he had to talk about it to destroy its power—though in this case nothing could stop the dream from being real.

The shadow's tracks were the tracks of wolves, and in those days, when our guns had taken all their food for furs and hides to sell, the wolves were bold and had abandoned the old agreement between them and the first humans. For a time, until we understood and let the game increase, the wolves hunted us. The father bounded forward when he saw the tracks. He could see where the pack, desperate, had tried to slash the tendons of the horses' legs. Next, where they'd leaped for the back of the wagon. He hurried on to where the trail gave out at the broad empty ice of the lake. There, he saw what he saw, scattered, and the ravens, attending to the bitter small leavings of the wolves.

For a time, the boy had no understanding of what had happened. His father kept what he knew to himself, at least that first year and when his son asked about his sister's torn plaid shawl, and why it was kept in the house, his father said nothing. But he wept when the boy asked if his sister was cold. It was only after his father had been weakened by the disease that he began to tell the story, far too often and always the same way: he told how when the wolves closed in Aanakwad had thrown her daughter to them.

When his father said those words, the boy went still. What had his sister felt? What had thrust through her heart? Had something broken inside her, too, as it had in him? Even then, he knew that this broken place inside him would not be mended, except by some terrible means. For he kept seeing his mother put the baby down and grip his sister around the waist. He saw Aanakwad swing the girl lightly out over the side of the wagon. He saw the brown shawl with its red lines flying open. He saw the shadows, the wolves, rush together, quick and avid, as the wagon with sled runners disappeared into the distance—forever, for neither he nor his father saw Aanakwad again.

When I was little, my own father terrified us with his drinking. This was after we lost our mother, because before that the only time I was aware that he touched the *ishkode waaboo* was on an occasional weekend when they got home late, or sometimes during berry-picking gatherings when we went out to the bush and camped with others. Not until she died did he start the heavy sort of drinking, the continuous drinking, where we were left alone in the house for days. The kind where, when he came home, we'd jump out the window and hide in the woods while he barged around, shouting for us. We'd go back only after he had fallen dead asleep.

There were three of us: me, the oldest at ten, and my little sister and brother, twins, and only six years old. I was surprisingly good at taking care of them, I think, and because we learned to survive together during those drinking years we have always been close. Their names are Doris and Raymond, and they married a brother and sister. When we get together, which is often, for we live on the same road, there come times in the talking and card-playing, and maybe even in the light beer now and then, when we will bring up those days. Most people understand how it was. Our story isn't uncommon. But for us it helps to compare our points of view.

How else would I know, for instance, that Raymond saw me the first time I hid my father's belt? I pulled it from around his waist while he was passed out, and then I buried it in the woods. I kept doing it after that. Our father couldn't understand why his belt was always stolen when he went to town drinking. He even accused his *shkwebii* buddies of the theft. But I had good reasons. Not only was he embarrassed, afterward, to go out with his pants held up by rope, but he couldn't snake his belt out in anger and snap the hooked buckle end in the air. He couldn't hit us with it. Of course, being resourceful, he used other things. There was a board. A willow wand. And there was himself—his hands and fists and boots—and things he could throw. But eventually it became easy to evade him, and after a while we rarely suffered a bruise or a scratch. We had our own place in the woods, even a little campfire for the cold nights. And we'd take money from him every chance we got, slip it from his shoe, where he thought it well hidden. He became, for us, a thing to be avoided, outsmarted, and exploited. We survived off him as if he were a capricious and dangerous line of work. I suppose we stopped thinking of him as a human being, certainly as a father.

I got my growth earlier than some boys, and, one night when I was thirteen and Doris and Raymond and I were sitting around wishing for something besides the oatmeal and commodity canned milk I'd stashed so he couldn't sell them, I heard him coming down the road. He was shouting and making noise all the way to the house, and Doris and Raymond looked at me and headed for the back window. When they saw that I wasn't coming they stopped. C'mon, *ondaas*, get with it—they tried to pull me along. I shook them off and told them to get out quickly—I was staying. I think I can take him now is what I said.

He was big; he hadn't yet wasted away from the alcohol. His nose had been pushed to one side in a fight, then slammed back to the other side, so now it was straight. His teeth were half gone, and he smelled the way he had to smell, being five days drunk. When he came in the door, he paused for a moment, his eyes red and swollen, tiny slits. Then he saw that I was waiting for him, and he smiled in a bad way. My first punch surprised him. I had been practicing on a hay-stuffed bag, then on a padded board, toughening my fists, and I'd got so quick I flickered like fire. I still wasn't as strong as he was, and he had a good twenty pounds on me. Yet I'd do some damage, I was sure of it. I'd teach him not to mess with me. What I didn't foresee was how the fight itself would get right into me.

There is something terrible about fighting your father. It came on suddenly, with the second blow—a frightful kind of joy. A power surged up from the center of me, and I danced at him, light and giddy, full of a heady rightness. Here is the thing: I wanted to waste him, waste him good. I wanted to smack the living shit out of him. Kill him, if I must. A punch for Doris, a kick for Raymond. And all the while I was silent, then screaming, then silent again, in this rage of happiness that filled me with a simultaneous despair so that, I guess you could say, I stood apart from myself.

He came at me, crashed over a chair that was already broken, then threw the pieces. I grabbed one of the legs and whacked him on the ear so that his head spun and turned back to me, bloody. I watched myself striking him again and again. I knew what I was doing, but not really, not in the ordinary sense. It was as if I were standing calm, against the wall with my arms folded, pitying us both. I saw the boy, the chair leg, the man fold and fall, his hands held up in begging fashion. Then I also saw that, for a while now, the bigger man had not even bothered to fight back.

Suddenly, he was my father again. And when I knelt down next to him, I was his son. I reached for the closest rag, and picked up this piece of blanket that my father always kept with him for some reason. And as I picked it up and wiped the blood off his face, I said to him, Your nose is crooked again. He looked at me, steady and quizzical, as though he had never had a drink in his life, and I wiped his face again with that frayed piece of blanket. Well, it was a shawl, really, a kind of old-fashioned woman's blanket-shawl. Once, maybe, it had been plaid. You could still see lines, some red, the background a faded brown. He watched intently as my hand brought the rag to his face. I was pretty sure, then, that I'd clocked him too hard, that he'd really lost it now. Gently, though, he clasped one hand around my waist. With the other hand he took the shawl. He crumpled it and held it to the middle of his forehead. It was as if he were praying, as if he were having thoughts he wanted to collect in that piece of cloth. For a while he lay like that, and I, crouched over, let him be, hardly breathing. Something told me to sit there, still. And then at last he said to me, in the sober new voice I would hear from then on, *Did you know I had a sister once?*

There was a time when the government moved everybody off the farthest reaches of the reservation, onto roads, into towns, into housing. It looked good at first, and then it all went sour. Shortly afterward, it seemed that anyone who was someone was either drunk, killed, near suicide, or had just dusted himself. None of the old sort were left, it seemed—the old kind of people, the Gete-anishinaabeg, who are kind beyond kindness and would do anything for others. It was during that time that my mother died and my father hurt us, as I have said.

Now, gradually, that term of despair has lifted somewhat and yielded up its survivors. But we still have sorrows that are passed to us from early generations, sorrows to handle in addition to our own, and cruelties lodged where we cannot forget them. We have the need to forget. We are always walking on oblivion's edge.

Some get away, like my brother and sister, married now and living quietly down the road. And me, to some degree, though I prefer to live alone. And even my father, who recently found a woman. Once, when he brought up the old days, and we went over the story again, I told him at last the two things I had been thinking.

First, I told him that keeping his sister's shawl was wrong, because we never keep the clothing of the dead. Now's the time to burn it, I said. Send it off to cloak her spirit. And he agreed.

The other thing I said to him was in the form of a question. Have you ever considered, I asked him, given how tenderhearted your sister was, and how brave, that she looked at the whole situation? She saw that the wolves were only hungry. She knew that their need was only need. She knew that you were back there, alone in the snow. She understood that the baby she loved would not live without a mother, and that only the uncle knew the way. She saw clearly that one person on the wagon had to be offered up, or they all would die. And in that moment of knowledge, don't you think, being who she was, of the old sort of Anishinaabeg, who thinks of the good of the people first, she jumped, my father, n'dede, brother to that little girl? Don't you think she lifted her shawl and flew?

# Richard Ford

## (B. 1944)

Born in Jackson, Mississippi, Richard Ford developed a prose style that is straightforward and, at times, even spare. He received his B.A. from Michigan State University and his M.F.A. from the University of California at Irvine. In 1968 he married Kristina Hensley. After publishing *A Piece of My Heart* (1978) and *The Ultimate Good Luck* (1981), Ford began working for *Inside Sports* magazine. When the magazine was sold, he wrote a book entitled *The Sportswriter* (1986), which earned him a PEN/Faulkner citation for fiction in 1987. His other works include *Wildlife* (1990), *Independence Day* (1995), and *A Multitude of Sins: Stories* (2002). Ford has received numerous awards, including the Pulitzer Prize for his novel *Independence Day*. He has taught writing and literature at the University of Michigan at Ann Arbor, at Princeton University, and at Williams College. Richard Ford's graceful, taut prose evokes an America filled equally with the cautiously hopeful and the desperately lonely.

## Rock Springs

1987

Edna and I had started down from Kalispell, heading for Tampa–St. Pete where I still had some friends from the old glory days who wouldn't turn me in to the police. I had managed to scrape with the law in Kalispell over several bad checks—which is a prison crime in Montana. And I knew Edna was already looking at her cards and thinking about a move, since it wasn't the first time I'd been in law scrapes in my life. She herself had already had her troubles, losing her kids and keeping her ex-husband, Danny, from breaking in her house and stealing her things while she was at work, which was really why I had moved in in the first place, that and needing to give my little daughter, Cheryl, a better shake in things.

I don't know what was between Edna and me, just beached by the same tides when you got down to it. Though love has been built on frailer ground than that, as I well know. And when I came in the house that afternoon, I just asked her if she wanted to go to Florida with me, leave things where they sat, and she said, "Why not? My datebook's not that full."

Edna and I had been a pair eight months, more or less man and wife, some of which time I had been out of work, and some when I'd worked at the dog track as a lead-out and could help with the rent and talk sense to Danny when he came around. Danny was afraid of me because Edna had told him I'd been in prison in Florida for killing a man, though that wasn't true. I had once been in jail in Tallahassee for stealing tires and had gotten into a fight on the county farm where a man had lost his eye. But I hadn't done the hurting, and Edna just wanted the story worse than it was so Danny wouldn't act crazy and make her have to take her kids back, since she had made a good adjustment to not having them, and I already had Cheryl with me. I'm not a violent person and would never put a man's eye out, much less kill someone. My former wife, Helen, would come all the way from Waikiki Beach to testify to that. We never had violence, and I believe in crossing the street to stay out of trouble's way. Though Danny didn't know that.

But we were half down through Wyoming, going toward I-80 and feeling good about things, when the oil light flashed on in the car I'd stolen, a sign I knew to be a bad one.

I'd gotten us a good car, a cranberry Mercedes I'd stolen out of an ophthalmologist's lot in Whitefish, Montana. I stole it because I thought it would be comfortable over a long haul, because I thought it got good mileage, which it didn't, and because I'd never had a good car in my life, just old Chevy junkers and used trucks back from when I was a kid swamping citrus with Cubans.

The car made us all high that day. I ran the windows up and down, and Edna told us some jokes and made faces. She could be lively. Her features would light up like a beacon and you could see her beauty, which wasn't ordinary. It all made me giddy, and I drove clear down to Bozeman, then straight on through the park to Jackson Hole. I rented us the bridal suite in the Quality Court in Jackson and left Cheryl and her little dog, Duke, sleeping while Edna and I drove to a rib barn and drank beer and laughed till after midnight.

It felt like a whole new beginning for us, bad memories left behind and a new horizon to build on. I got so worked up, I had a tattoo done on my arm that said FAMOUS TIMES, and Edna bought a Bailey hat with an Indian feather band and a little turquoise-and-silver bracelet for Cheryl, and we made love on the seat of the car in the Quality Court parking lot just as the sun was burning up on the Snake River, and everything seemed then like the end of the rainbow.

It was that very enthusiasm, in fact, that made me keep the car one day longer instead of driving it into the river and stealing another one, like I should've done and *had* done before.

Where the car went bad there wasn't a town in sight or even a house, just some low mountains maybe fifty miles away or maybe a hundred, a barbed-wire fence in both directions, hardpan prairie, and some hawks riding the evening air seizing insects.

I got out to look at the motor, and Edna got out with Cheryl and the dog to let them have a pee by the car. I checked the water and checked the oil stick, and both of them said perfect.

"What's that light mean, Earl?" Edna said. She had come and stood by the car with her hat on. She was just sizing things up for herself.

"We shouldn't run it," I said. "Something's not right in the oil."

She looked around at Cheryl and Little Duke, who were peeing on the hardtop side-by-side like two little dolls, then out at the mountains, which were becoming black and lost in the distance. "What're we doing?" she said. She wasn't worried yet, but she wanted to know what I was thinking about.

"Let me try it again."

"That's a good idea," she said, and we all got back in the car.

When I turned the motor over, it started right away and the red light stayed off and there weren't any noises to make you think something was wrong. I let it idle a minute, then pushed the accelerator down and watched the red bulb. But there wasn't any light on, and I started wondering if maybe I hadn't dreamed I saw it, or that it had been the sun catching an angle off the window chrome, or maybe I was scared of something and didn't know it.

"What's the matter with it, Daddy?" Cheryl said from the back seat. I looked back at her, and she had on her turquoise bracelet and Edna's hat set back on the back of her head and that little black-and-white Heinz dog on her lap. She looked like a little cowgirl in the movies.

"Nothing, honey, everything's fine now," I said.

"Little Duke tinkled where I tinkled," Cheryl said, and laughed.

"You're two of a kind," Edna said, not looking back. Edna was usually good with Cheryl, but I knew she was tired now. We hadn't had much sleep, and she had a tendency to get cranky when she didn't sleep. "We oughta ditch this damn car first chance we get," she said.

"What's the first chance we got?" I asked, because I knew she'd been at the map.

"Rock Springs, Wyoming," Edna said with conviction. "Thirty miles down this road." She pointed out ahead.

I had wanted all along to drive the car into Florida like a big success story. But I knew Edna was right about it, that we shouldn't take crazy chances. I had kept thinking of it as my car, and not the ophthalmologist's, and that was how you got caught in these things.

"Then my belief is we ought to go to Rock Springs and negotiate ourselves a new car," I said. I wanted to stay upbeat, like everything was panning out right.

"That's a great idea," Edna said, and she leaned over and kissed me hard on the mouth.

"That's a great idea," Cheryl said. "Let's pull on out of here right now."

The sunset that day I remember as being the prettiest I'd ever seen. Just as it touched the rim of the horizon, it all at once fired the air into jewels and red sequins the precise likes of which I had never seen before and haven't seen since. The West has it all over everywhere for sunsets, even Florida, where it's supposedly flat but where half the time trees block your view.

"It's cocktail hour," Edna said after we'd driven awhile. "We ought to have a drink and celebrate something." She felt better thinking we were going to get rid of the car. It certainly had dark troubles and was something you'd want to put behind you.

Edna had out a whiskey bottle and some plastic cups and was measuring levels on the glove-box lid. She liked drinking, and she liked drinking in the car, which was something you got used to in Montana, where it wasn't against the law, but where, strangely enough, a bad check would land you in Deer Lodge Prison for a year.

"Did I ever tell you I once had a monkey?" Edna said, setting my drink on the dashboard where I could reach it when I was ready. Her spirits were already picked up. She was like that, up one minute and down the next.

"I don't think you ever did tell me that," I said. "Where were you then?"

"Missoula," she said. She put her bare feet on the dash and rested the cup on her breasts. "I was waitressing at the AmVets. This was before I met you. Some guy came in one day with a monkey. A spider monkey. And I said, just to be joking, 'I'll roll you for that monkey.' And the guy said, 'Just one roll?' And I said, 'Sure.' He put the monkey down on the bar, picked up the cup, and rolled out boxcars. I picked it up and rolled out three fives. And I just stood there looking at the guy. He was just some guy passing through, I guess a vet. He got a strange look on his face—I'm sure not as strange as the one I had—but he looked kind of sad and surprised and satisfied all at once. I said, 'We can roll again.' But he said, 'No, I never roll twice for anything.' And he sat and drank a beer and talked about one thing and another for a while, about nuclear war and building a stronghold somewhere up in the Bitterroot, whatever it was, while I just watched the monkey, wondering what I was going to do with it when the guy left. And pretty soon he got up and said, 'Well, good-bye, Chipper'—that was this monkey's name, of course. And then he left before I could say anything. And the monkey just sat on the bar all that night. I don't know what made me think of that, Earl. Just something weird. I'm letting my mind wander."

"That's perfectly fine," I said. I took a drink of my drink. "I'd never own a monkey," I said after a minute. "They're too nasty. I'm sure Cheryl would like a monkey, though, wouldn't you, honey?" Cheryl was down on the seat playing with Little Duke. She used to talk about monkeys all the time then. "What'd you ever do with that monkey?" I said, watching the speedometer. We were having to go slower now because the red light kept fluttering on. And all I could do to keep it off was go slower. We were going maybe thirty-five and it was an hour before dark, and I was hoping Rock Springs wasn't far away.

"You really want to know?" Edna said. She gave me a quick glance, then looked back at the empty desert as if she was brooding over it.

"Sure," I said. I was still upbeat. I figured I could worry about breaking down and let other people be happy for a change.

"I kept it a week." And she seemed gloomy all of a sudden, as if she saw some aspect of the story she had never seen before. "I took it home and back and forth to the AmVets on my shifts. And it didn't cause any trouble. I fixed a chair up for it to sit on, back of the bar, and people liked it. It made a nice little clicking noise. We changed its name to Mary because the bartender figured out it was a girl. Though I was never really comfortable with it at home. I felt like it watched me too much. Then one day a guy came in, some guy who'd been in Vietnam, still wore a fatigue coat. And he said to me, 'Don't you know that a monkey'll kill you? It's got more strength in its fingers than you got in your whole body.' He said people had been killed in Vietnam by monkeys, bunches of them marauding while you were asleep, killing you and covering you with leaves. I didn't believe a word of it, except that when I got home and got undressed I started looking over across the room at Mary on her chair in the dark watching me. And I got the creeps. And after a while I got up and went out to the car, got a length of clothesline wire, and came back in and wired her to the doorknob through her little silver collar, then went back and tried to sleep. And I guess I must've slept the sleep of the dead—though I don't remember it—because when I got up I found Mary had tipped off her chair-back and hanged herself on the wire line. I'd made it too short."

Edna seemed badly affected by that story and slid low in the seat so she couldn't see out over the dash. "Isn't that a shameful story, Earl, what happened to that poor little monkey?"

"I see a town! I see a town!" Cheryl started yelling from the backseat, and right up Little Duke started yapping and the whole car fell into a racket. And sure enough she had seen something I hadn't, which was Rock Springs, Wyoming, at the bottom of a long hill, a little glowing jewel in the desert with I-80 running on the north side and the black desert spread out behind.

"That's it, honey," I said. "That's where we're going. You saw it first."

"We're hungry," Cheryl said. "Little Duke wants some fish, and I want spaghetti." She put her arms around my neck and hugged me.

"Then you'll just get it," I said. "You can have anything you want. And so can Edna and so can Little Duke." I looked over at Edna, smiling, but she was staring at me with eyes that were fierce with anger. "What's wrong?" I said.

"Don't you care anything about that awful thing that happened to me?" Her mouth was drawn tight, and her eyes kept cutting back at Cheryl and Little Duke, as if they had been tormenting her.

"Of course I do," I said. "I thought that was an awful thing." I didn't want her to be unhappy. We were almost there, and pretty soon we could sit down and have a real meal without thinking somebody might be hurting us.

"You want to know what I did with that monkey?" Edna said.

"Sure I do," I said.

"I put her in a green garbage bag, put it in the trunk of my car, drove to the dump, and threw her in the trash." She was staring at me darkly, as if the story meant something to her that was real important but that only she could see and that the rest of the world was a fool for.

"Well, that's horrible," I said. "But I don't see what else you could do. You didn't mean to kill it. You'd have done it differently if you had. And then you had to get rid of it, and I don't know what else you could have done. Throwing it away might seem unsympathetic to somebody, probably, but not to me. Sometimes that's all you can do, and you can't worry about what somebody else thinks." I tried to smile at her, but the red light was staying on if I pushed the accelerator at all, and I was trying to gauge if we could coast to Rock Springs before the car gave out completely. I looked at Edna again. "What else can I say?" I said.

"Nothing," she said, and stared back at the dark highway. "I should've known that's what you'd think. You've got a character that leaves something out, Earl. I've known that a long time."

"And yet here you are," I said. "And you're not doing so bad. Things could be a lot worse. At least we're all together here."

"Things could always be worse," Edna said. "You could go to the electric chair tomorrow."

"That's right," I said. "And somewhere somebody probably will. Only it won't be you."

"I'm hungry," said Cheryl. "When're we gonna eat? Let's find a motel. I'm tired of this. Little Duke's tired of it too."

Where the car stopped rolling was some distance from the town, though you could see the clear outline of the interstate in the dark with Rock Springs lighting up the sky behind. You could hear the big tractors hitting the spacers in the overpass, revving up for the climb to the mountains.

I shut off the lights.

"What're we going to do now?" Edna said irritably, giving me a bitter look.

"I'm figuring it," I said. "It won't be hard, whatever it is. You won't have to do anything."

"I'd hope not," she said and looked the other way.

Across the road and across a dry wash a hundred yards was what looked like a huge mobile-home town, with a factory or a refinery of some kind lit up behind it and in full swing. There were lights on in a lot of the mobile homes, and there were cars moving along an access road that ended near the freeway overpass a mile the other way. The lights in the mobile homes seemed friendly to me, and I knew right then what I should do.

"Get out," I said, opening my door.

"Are we walking?" Edna said.

"We're pushing."

"I'm not pushing." Edna reached up and locked her door.

"All right," I said. "Then you just steer."

"You're pushing us to Rock Springs, are you, Earl? It doesn't look like it's more than about three miles."

"I'll push," Cheryl said from the back.

"No, hon. Daddy'll push. You just get out with Little Duke and move out of the way."

Edna gave me a threatening look, just as if I'd tried to hit her. But when I got out she slid into my seat and took the wheel, staring angrily ahead straight into the cottonwood scrub.

"Edna can't drive that car," Cheryl said from out in the dark. "She'll run it in the ditch."

"Yes, she can, hon. Edna can drive it as good as I can. Probably better."

"No she can't," Cheryl said. "No she can't either." And I thought she was about to cry, but she didn't.

I told Edna to keep the ignition on so it wouldn't lock up and to steer into the cottonwoods with the parking lights on so she could see. And when I started, she steered it straight off into the trees, and I kept pushing until we were twenty yards into the cover and the tires sank in the soft sand and nothing at all could be seen from the road.

"Now where are we?" she said, sitting at the wheel. Her voice was tired and hard, and I knew she could have put a good meal to use. She had a sweet nature, and I recognized that this wasn't her fault but mine. Only I wished she could be more hopeful.

"You stay right here, and I'll go over to that trailer park and call us a cab," I said.

"What cab?" Edna said, her mouth wrinkled as if she'd never heard anything like that in her life.

"There'll be cabs," I said, and tried to smile at her. "There's cabs everywhere."

"What're you going to tell him when he gets here? Our stolen car broke down and we need a ride to where we can steal another one? That'll be a big hit, Earl."

"I'll talk," I said. "You just listen to the radio for ten minutes and then walk on out to the shoulder like nothing was suspicious. And you and Cheryl act nice. She doesn't need to know about this car."

"Like we're not suspicious enough already, right?" Edna looked up at me out of the lighted car. "You don't think right, did you know that, Earl? You think the world's stupid and you're smart. But that's not how it is. I feel sorry for you. You might've *been* something, but things just went crazy someplace."

I had a thought about poor Danny. He was a vet and crazy as a shit-house mouse, and I was glad he wasn't in for all this. "Just get the baby in the car," I said, trying to be patient. "I'm hungry like you are."

"I'm tired of this," Edna said. "I wish I'd stayed in Montana."

"Then you can go back in the morning," I said. "I'll buy the ticket and put you on the bus. But not till then."

"Just get on with it, Earl." She slumped down in the seat, turning off the parking lights with one foot and the radio on with the other.

The mobile-home community was as big as any I'd ever seen. It was attached in some way to the plant that was lighted up behind it, because I could see a car once in a while leave one of the trailer streets, turn in the direction of the plant, then go slowly into it. Everything in the plant was white, and you could see that all the trailers were painted white and looked exactly alike. A deep hum came out of the plant, and I thought as I got closer that it wouldn't be a location I'd ever want to work in.

I went right to the first trailer where there was a light, and knocked on the metal door. Kids' toys were lying in the gravel around the little wood steps, and I could hear talking on TV that suddenly went off. I heard a woman's voice talking, and then the door opened wide.

A large Negro woman with a wide, friendly face stood in the doorway. She smiled at me and moved forward as if she was going to come out, but she stopped at the top step. There was a little Negro boy behind her peeping out from behind her legs, watching me with his eyes half closed. The trailer had that feeling that no one else was inside, which was a feeling I knew something about.

"I'm sorry to intrude," I said. "But I've run up on a little bad luck tonight. My name's Earl Middleton."

The woman looked at me, then out into the night toward the freeway as if what I had said was something she was going to be able to see. "What kind of bad luck?" she said, looking down at me again.

"My car broke down out on the highway," I said. "I can't fix it myself, and I wondered if I could use your phone to call for help."

The woman smiled down at me knowingly. "We can't live without cars, can we?"

"That's the honest truth," I said.

"They're like our hearts," she said, her face shining in the little bulb light that burned beside the door. "Where's your car situated?"

I turned and looked over into the dark, but I couldn't see anything because of where we'd put it. "It's over there," I said. "You can't see it in the dark."

"Who all's with you now?" the woman said. "Have you got your wife with you?"

"She's with my little girl and our dog in the car," I said. "My daughter's asleep or I would have brought them."

"They shouldn't be left in the dark by themselves," the woman said and frowned. "There's too much unsavoriness out there."

"The best I can do is hurry back." I tried to look sincere, since everything except Cheryl being asleep and Edna being my wife was the truth. The truth is meant to serve you if you'll let it, and I wanted it to serve me. "I'll pay for the phone call," I said. "If you'll bring the phone to the door I'll call from right here."

The woman looked at me again as if she was searching for a truth of her own, then back out into the night. She was maybe in her sixties, but I couldn't say for sure. "You're not going to rob me, are you, Mr. Middleton?" She smiled like it was a joke between us.

"Not tonight," I said, and smiled a genuine smile. "I'm not up to it tonight. Maybe another time."

"Then I guess Terrel and I can let you use our phone with Daddy not here, can't we, Terrel? This is my grandson, Terrel Junior, Mr. Middleton." She put her hand on the boy's head and looked down at him. "Terrel won't talk. Though if he did he'd tell you to use our phone. He's a sweet boy." She opened the screen for me to come in.

The trailer was a big one with a new rug and a new couch and a living room that expanded to give the space of a real house. Something good and sweet was cooking in the kitchen, and the trailer felt like it was somebody's new home instead of just temporary. I've lived in trailers, but they were just snail-backs with one room and no toilet, and they always felt cramped and unhappy—though I've thought maybe it might've been me that was unhappy in them.

There was a big Sony TV and a lot of kids' toys scattered on the floor. I recognized a Greyhound bus I'd gotten for Cheryl. The phone was beside a new leather recliner, and the Negro woman pointed for me to sit down and call and gave me the phone book. Terrel began fingering his toys and the woman sat on the couch while I called, watching me and smiling.

There were three listings for cab companies, all with one number different. I called the numbers in order and didn't get an answer until the last one, which answered with the name of the second company. I said I was on the highway beyond the interstate and that my wife and family needed to be taken to town and I would arrange for a tow later. While I was giving the location, I looked up the name of a tow service to tell the driver in case he asked.

When I hung up, the Negro woman was sitting looking at me with the same look she had been staring with into the dark, a look that seemed to want truth. She was smiling, though. Something pleased her and I reminded her of it.

"This is a very nice home," I said, resting in the recliner, which felt like the driver's seat of the Mercedes, and where I'd have been happy to stay.

"This isn't *our* house, Mr. Middleton," the Negro woman said. "The company owns these. They give them to us for nothing. We have our own home in Rockford, Illinois."

"That's wonderful," I said.

"It's never wonderful when you have to be away from home, Mr. Middleton, though we're only here three months, and it'll be easier when Terrel Junior begins his special school. You see, our son was killed in the war, and his wife ran off without Terrel Junior. Though you shouldn't worry. He can't understand us. His little feelings can't be hurt." The woman folded her hands in her lap and smiled in a satisfied way. She was an attractive woman, and had on a blue-and-pink floral dress that made her seem bigger than she could've been, just the right woman to sit on the couch she was sitting on. She was good nature's picture, and I was glad she could be, with her little brain-damaged boy, living in a place where no one in his right mind would want to live a minute. "Where do *you* live, Mr. Middleton?" she said politely, smiling in the same sympathetic way.

"My family and I are in transit," I said. "I'm an ophthalmologist, and we're moving back to Florida, where I'm from. I'm setting up practice in some little town where it's warm year-round. I haven't decided where."

"Florida's a wonderful place," the woman said. "I think Terrel would like it there."

"Could I ask you something?" I said.

"You certainly may," the woman said. Terrel had begun pushing his Greyhound across the front of the TV screen, making a scratch that no one watching the set could miss. "Stop that, Terrel Junior," the woman said quietly. But Terrel kept pushing his bus on the glass, and she smiled at me again as if we both understood something sad. Except I knew Cheryl would never damage a television set. She had respect for nice things, and I was sorry for the lady that Terrel didn't. "What did you want to ask?" the woman said.

"What goes on in that plant or whatever it is back there beyond these trailers, where all the lights are on?"

"Gold," the woman said and smiled.

"It's what?" I said.

"Gold," the Negro woman said, smiling as she had for almost all the time I'd been there. "It's a gold mine."

"They're mining gold back there?" I said, pointing.

"Every night and every day." She smiled in a pleased way.

"Does your husband work there?" I said.

"He's the assayer," she said. "He controls the quality. He works three months a year, and we live the rest of the time at home in Rockford. We've waited a long time for this. We've been happy to have our grandson, but I won't say I'll be sorry to have him go. We're ready to start our lives over." She smiled broadly at me and then at Terrel, who was giving her a spiteful look from the floor. "You said you had a daughter," the Negro woman said. "And what's her name?"

"Irma Cheryl," I said. "She's named for my mother."

"That's nice. And she's healthy, too. I can see it in your face." She looked at Terrel Junior with pity.

"I guess I'm lucky," I said.

"So far you are. But children bring you grief, the same way they bring you joy. We were unhappy for a long time before my husband got his job in the gold mine. Now, when Terrel starts to school, we'll be kids again." She stood up. "You might miss your cab, Mr. Middleton," she said, walking toward the door, though not to be forcing me out. She was too polite. "If *we* can't see your car, the cab surely won't be able to."

"That's true." I got up off the recliner, where I'd been so comfortable. "None of us have eaten yet, and your food makes me know how hungry we probably all are."

"There are fine restaurants in town, and you'll find them," the Negro woman said. "I'm sorry you didn't meet my husband. He's a wonderful man. He's everything to me."

"Tell him I appreciate the phone," I said. "You saved me."

"You weren't hard to save," the woman said. "Saving people is what we were all put on earth to do. I just passed you on to whatever's coming to you."

"Let's hope it's good," I said, stepping back into the dark.

"I'll be hoping, Mr. Middleton. Terrel and I will both be hoping."

I waved to her as I walked out into the darkness toward the car where it was hidden in the night.

The cab had already arrived when I got there. I could see its little red-and-green roof lights all the way across the dry wash, and it made me worry that Edna was already saying something to get us in trouble, something about the car or where we'd come from, something that would cast suspicion on us. I thought, then, how I never planned things well enough. There was always a gap between my plan and what happened, and I only responded to things as they came along and hoped I wouldn't get in trouble. I was an offender in the law's eyes. But I always *thought* differently, as if I weren't an offender and had no intention of being one, which was the truth. But as I read on a napkin once, between the idea and the act a whole kingdom lies. And I had a hard time with my acts, which were oftentimes offender's acts, and my ideas, which were as good as the gold they mined there where the bright lights were blazing.

"We're waiting for you, Daddy," Cheryl said when I crossed the road. "The taxicab's already here."

"I see, hon," I said, and gave Cheryl a big hug. The cabdriver was sitting in the driver's seat having a smoke with the lights on inside. Edna was leaning against the back of the cab between the taillights, wearing her Bailey hat. "What'd you tell him?" I said when I got close.

"Nothing," she said. "What's there to tell?"

"Did you see the car?"

She glanced over in the direction of the trees where we had hid the Mercedes. Nothing was visible in the darkness, though I could hear Little Duke combing around in the underbrush tracking something, his little collar tinkling. "Where're we going?" she said. "I'm so hungry I could pass out."

"Edna's in a terrible mood," Cheryl said. "She already snapped at me."

"We're tired, honey," I said. "So try to be nicer."

"She's never nice," Cheryl said.

"Run go get Little Duke," I said. "And hurry back."

"I guess *my* questions come last here, right?" Edna said.

I put my arm around her. "That's not true."

"Did you find somebody over there in the trailers you'd rather stay with? You were gone long enough."

"That's not a thing to say," I said. "I was just trying to make things look right, so we don't get put in jail."

"So *you* don't, you mean." Edna laughed a little laugh I didn't like hearing.

"That's right. So I don't," I said. "I'd be the one in Dutch." I stared out at the big, lighted assemblage of white buildings and white lights beyond the trailer community, plumes of white smoke escaping up into the heartless Wyoming sky, the whole company of buildings looking like some unbelievable castle, humming away in a distorted dream. "You know what all those buildings are there?" I said to Edna, who hadn't moved and who didn't really seem to care if she ever moved anymore ever.

"No. But I can't say it matters, because it isn't a motel and it isn't a restaurant."

"It's a gold mine," I said, staring at the gold mine, which, I knew now, was a greater distance from us than it seemed, though it seemed huge and near, up against the cold sky. I thought there should've been a wall around it with guards instead of just the lights and no fence. It seemed as if anyone could go in and take what they wanted, just the way I had gone up to that woman's trailer and used the telephone, though that obviously wasn't true.

Edna began to laugh then. Not the mean laugh I didn't like, but a laugh that had something caring behind it, a full laugh that enjoyed a joke, a laugh she was laughing the first time I laid eyes on her, in Missoula in the East Gate Bar in 1979, a laugh we used to laugh together when Cheryl was still with her mother and I was working steady at the track and not stealing cars or passing bogus checks to merchants. A better time all around. And for some reason it made me laugh just hearing her, and we both stood there behind the cab in the dark, laughing at the gold mine up in the desert, me with my arm around her and Cheryl out rustling up Little Duke and the cabdriver smoking in the cab and our stolen Mercedes-Benz, which I'd had such hopes for in Florida, stuck up to its axle in sand, where I'd never get to see it again.

"I always wondered what a gold mine would look like when I saw it," Edna said, still laughing, wiping a tear from her eye.

"Me too," I said. "I was always curious about it."

"We're a couple of fools, aren't we, Earl?" she said, unable to quit laughing completely. "We're two of a kind."

"It might be a good sign, though," I said.

"How could it be? It's not our gold mine. There aren't any drive-up windows." She was still laughing.

"We've seen it," I said, pointing. "That's it right there. It may mean we're getting closer. Some people never see it at all."

"In a pig's eye, Earl," she said. "You and me see it in a pig's eye."

And she turned and got in the cab to go.

The cabdriver didn't ask anything about our car or where it was, to mean he'd noticed something queer. All of which made me feel like we had made a clean break from the car and couldn't be connected with it until it was too late, if ever. The driver told us a lot about Rock Springs while he drove, that because of the gold mine a lot of people had moved there in just six months, people from all over, including New York, and that most of them lived out in the trailers. Prostitutes from New York City, who he called "B-girls," had come into town, he said, on the prosperity tide, and Cadillacs with New York plates cruised the little streets every night, full of Negroes with big hats who ran the women. He told us that everybody who got in his cab now wanted to know where the women were, and when he got our call he almost didn't come because some of the trailers were brothels operated by the mine for engineers and computer people away from home. He said he got tired of running back and forth out there just for vile business. He said that *60 Minutes* had even done a program about Rock Springs and that a blow-up had resulted in Cheyenne, though nothing could be done unless the boom left town. "It's prosperity's fruit," the driver said. "I'd rather be poor, which is lucky for me."

He said all the motels were sky-high, but since we were a family he could show us a nice one that was affordable. But I told him we wanted a first-rate place where they took animals, and the money didn't matter because we had had a hard day and wanted to finish on a high note. I also knew that it was in the little nowhere places that the police look for you and find you. People I'd known were always being arrested in cheap hotels and tourist courts with names you'd never heard of before. Never in Holiday Inns or TraveLodges.

I asked him to drive us to the middle of town and back out again so Cheryl could see the train station, and while we were there I saw a pink Cadillac with New York plates and a TV aerial being driven slowly by a Negro in a big hat down a narrow street where there were just bars and a Chinese restaurant. It was an odd sight, nothing you could ever expect.

"There's your pure criminal element," the cabdriver said and seemed sad. "I'm sorry for people like you to see a thing like that. We've got a nice town here, but there're some that want to ruin it for everybody. There used to be a way to deal with trash and criminals, but those days are gone forever."

"You said it," Edna said.

"You shouldn't let it get *you* down," I said to him. "There's more of you than them. And there always will be. You're the best advertisement this town has. I know Cheryl will remember you and not *that* man, won't you, honey?" But Cheryl was asleep by then, holding Little Duke in her arms on the taxi seat.

The driver took us to the Ramada Inn on the interstate, not far from where we'd broken down. I had a small pain of regret as we drove under the Ramada awning that we hadn't driven up in a cranberry-colored Mercedes but instead in a beat-up old Chrysler taxi driven by an old man full of complaints. Though I knew it was for the best. We were better off without that car; better, really, in any other car but that one, where the signs had turned bad.

I registered under another name and paid for the room in cash so there wouldn't be any questions. On the line where it said "Representing" I wrote "Ophthalmologist" and put "M.D." after the name. It had a nice look to it, even though it wasn't my name.

When we got to the room, which was in the back where I'd asked for it, I put Cheryl on one of the beds and Little Duke beside her so they'd sleep. She'd missed dinner, but it only meant she'd be hungry in the morning, when she could have anything she wanted. A few missed meals don't make a kid bad. I'd missed a lot of them myself and haven't turned out completely bad.

"Let's have some fried chicken," I said to Edna when she came out of the bathroom. "They have good fried chicken at Ramadas, and I noticed the buffet was still up. Cheryl can stay right here, where it's safe, till we're back."

"I guess I'm not hungry anymore," Edna said. She stood at the window staring out into the dark. I could see out the window past her some yellowish foggy glow in the sky. For a moment I thought it was the gold mine out in the distance lighting the night, though it was only the interstate.

"We could order up," I said. "Whatever you want. There's a menu on the phone book. You could just have a salad."

"You go ahead," she said. "I've lost my hungry spirit." She sat on the bed beside Cheryl and Little Duke and looked at them in a sweet way and put her hand on Cheryl's cheek just as if she'd had a fever. "Sweet little girl," she said. "Everybody loves you."

"What do you want to do?" I said. "I'd like to eat. Maybe *I'll* order up some chicken."

"Why don't you do that?" she said. "It's your favorite." And she smiled at me from the bed.

I sat on the other bed and dialed room service. I asked for chicken, garden salad, potato and a roll, plus a piece of hot apple pie and iced tea. I realized I hadn't eaten all day. When I put down the phone I saw that Edna was watching me, not in a hateful way or a loving way, just in a way that seemed to say she didn't understand something and was going to ask me about it.

"When did watching me get so entertaining?" I said and smiled at her. I was trying to be friendly. I knew how tired she must be. It was after nine o'clock.

"I was just thinking how much I hated being in a motel without a car that was mine to drive. Isn't that funny? I started feeling like that last night when that purple car wasn't mine. That purple car just gave me the willies, I guess, Earl."

"One of those cars *outside* is yours," I said. "Just stand right there and pick it out."

"I know," she said. "But that's different, isn't it?" She reached and got her blue Bailey hat, put it on her head, and set it way back like Dale Evans. She looked sweet. "I used to like to go to motels, you know," she said. "There's something secret about them and free—I was never paying, of course. But you felt safe from everything and free to do what you wanted because you'd made the decision to be there and paid that price, and all the rest was the good part. Fucking and everything, you know." She smiled at me in a good-natured way.

"Isn't that the way this is?" I was sitting on the bed, watching her, not knowing what to expect her to say next.

"I don't guess it is, Earl," she said and stared out the window. "I'm thirty-two and I'm going to have to give up on motels. I can't keep that fantasy going anymore."

"Don't you like this place?" I said and looked around at the room. I appreciated the modern paintings and the lowboy bureau and the big TV. It seemed like a plenty nice enough place to me, considering where we'd been.

"No, I don't," Edna said with real conviction. "There's no use in my getting mad at you about it. It isn't your fault. You do the best you can for everybody. But every trip teaches you something. And I've learned I need to give up on motels before some bad thing happens to me. I'm sorry."

"What does that mean?" I said, because I really didn't know what she had in mind to do, though I should've guessed.

"I guess I'll take that ticket you mentioned," she said, and got up and faced the window. "Tomorrow's soon enough. We haven't got a car to take me anyhow."

"Well, that's a fine thing," I said, sitting on the bed, feeling like I was in shock. I wanted to say something to her, to argue with her, but I couldn't think what to say that seemed right. I didn't want to be mad at her, but it made me mad.

"You've got a right to be mad at me, Earl," she said, "but I don't think you can really blame me." She turned around and faced me and sat on the windowsill, her hands on her knees. Someone knocked on the door, and I just yelled for them to set the tray down and put it on the bill.

"I guess I *do* blame you," I said, and I was angry. I thought about how I could've disappeared into that trailer community and hadn't, had come back to keep things going, had tried to take control of things for everybody when they looked bad.

"Don't. I wish you wouldn't," Edna said and smiled at me like she wanted me to hug her. "Anybody ought to have their choice in things if they can. Don't you believe that, Earl? Here I am out here in the desert where I don't know anything, in a stolen car, in a motel room under an assumed name, with no money of my own, a kid that's not mine, and the law after me. And I have a choice to get out of all of it by getting on a bus. What would you do? I know exactly what you'd do."

"You think you do," I said. But I didn't want to get into an argument about it and tell her all I could've done and didn't do. Because it wouldn't have done any good. When you get to the point of arguing, you're past the point of changing anybody's mind, even though it's supposed to be the other way, and maybe for some classes of people it is, just never mine.

Edna smiled at me and came across the room and put her arms around me where I was sitting on the bed. Cheryl rolled over and looked at us and smiled, then closed her eyes, and the room was quiet. I was beginning to think of Rock Springs in a way I knew I would always think of it, a lowdown city full of crimes and whores and disappointments, a place where a woman left me, instead of a place where I got things on the straight track once and for all, a place I saw a gold mine.

"Eat your chicken, Earl," Edna said. "Then we can go to bed. I'm tired, but I'd like to make love to you anyway. None of this is a matter of not loving you, you know that."

Sometime late in the night, after Edna was asleep, I got up and walked outside into the parking lot. It could've been anytime because there was still the light from the interstate frosting the low sky and the big red Ramada sign humming motionlessly in the night and no light at all in the east to indicate it might be morning. The lot was full of cars all nosed in, a couple of them with suitcases strapped to their roofs and their trunks weighed down with belongings the people were taking someplace, to a new home or a vacation resort in the mountains. I had laid in bed a long time after Edna was asleep, watching the Atlanta Braves on television, trying to get my mind off how I'd feel when I saw that bus pull away the next day, and how I'd feel when I turned around and there stood Cheryl and Little Duke and no one to see about them but me alone, and that the first thing I had to do was get hold of some automobile and get the plates switched, then get them some breakfast and get us all on the road to Florida, all in the space of probably two hours, since that Mercedes would certainly look less hid in the daytime than the night, and word travels fast. I've always taken care of Cheryl myself as long as I've had her with me. None of the women ever did. Most of them didn't even seem to like her, though they took care of me in a way so that I could take care of her. And I knew that once Edna left, all that was going to get harder. Though what I wanted most to do was not think about it just for a little while, try to let my mind go limp so it could be strong for the rest of what there was. I thought that the difference between a successful life and an unsuccessful one, between me at that moment and all the people who owned the cars that were nosed into their proper places in the lot, maybe between me and that woman out in the trailers by the gold mine, was how well you were able to put things like this out of your mind and not be bothered by them, and maybe, too, by how many troubles like this one you had to face in a lifetime. Through luck or design they had all faced fewer troubles, and by their own characters, they forgot them faster. And that's what I wanted for me. Fewer troubles, fewer memories of trouble.

I walked over to a car, a Pontiac with Ohio tags, one of the ones with bundles and suitcases strapped to the top and a lot more in the trunk, by the way it was riding. I looked inside the driver's window. There were maps and paperback books and sunglasses and the little plastic holders for cans that hang on the window wells. And in the back there were kids' toys and some pillows and a cat box with a cat sitting in it staring up at me like I was the face of the moon. It all looked familiar to me, the very same things I would have in my car if I had a car. Nothing seemed surprising, nothing different. Though I had a funny sensation at that moment and turned and looked up at the windows along the back of the motel. All were dark except two. Mine and another one. And I wondered, because it seemed funny, what would you think a man was doing if you saw him in the middle of the night looking in the windows of cars in the parking lot of the Ramada Inn? Would you think he was trying to get his head cleared? Would you think he was trying to get ready for a day when trouble would come down on him? Would you think his girlfriend was leaving him? Would you think he had a daughter? Would you think he was anybody like you?

# Mary Gaitskill

## (B. 1954)

Mary Gaitskill was born in Lexington, Kentucky. She graduated in 1981 from the University of Michigan, where she collected her short fiction into a volume entitled *The Woman Who Knew Judo and Other Stories*. Her first book of stories, *Bad Behavior*, was published in 1988. In 1991 Gaitskill published her first novel, *Two Girls Fat and Thin*. Gaitskill's own history as a troubled teen informs many of her stories, if not in subject, then in tone. Her work is dedicated to uncovering the beautiful in life's most difficult and seemingly untenable moments, and she crafts her stories around characters set on survival, even though survival might seem the furthest thing from their grasp. In 2002, the movie *Secretary*, based on Mary Gaitskill's story of the same name, was released to critical acclaim.

## Tiny, Smiling Daddy 1997

He lay in his reclining chair, barely awake enough to feel the dream moving just under his thoughts. It felt like one of those pure, beautiful dreams in which he was young again, and filled with the realization that the friends who had died, or gone away, or decided that they didn't like him anymore, had really been there all along, loving him. A piece of the dream flickered, and he made out the lips and cheekbones of a tender woman, smiling as she leaned toward him. The phone rang, and the sound rippled through his pliant wakefulness, into the pending dream. But his wife had turned the answering machine up too loud again, and it attacked him with a garbled, furred roar that turned into the voice of his friend Norm.

*[handwritten left margin: He was dreaming about old friends]*

Resentful at being waked and grateful that for once somebody had called him, he got up to answer. He picked up the phone, and the answering machine screeched at him through the receiver. He cursed as he fooled with it, hating his stiff fingers. Irritably, he exchanged greetings with his friend, and then Norm, his voice oddly weighted, said, "I saw the issue of *Self* with Kitty in it."

He waited for an explanation. None came, so he said, "What? Issue of *Self*? What's *Self*?"

"Good grief, Stew, I thought for sure you'd of seen it. Now I feel funny."

The dream pulsed forward and receded again. "Funny about what?"

"My daughter's got a subscription to this magazine, *Self*. And they printed an article that Kitty wrote about fathers and daughters talking to each other, and she, well, she wrote about you. Laurel showed it to me."

"My God."

"It's ridiculous that I'm the one to tell you. I just thought—"

"It was bad?"

"No, she didn't say anything bad. I just didn't understand the whole idea of it. And I wondered what you thought."

He got off the phone and walked back into the living room, now fully awake. His daughter, Kitty, was living in South Carolina, working in a used-record store and making animal statuettes, which she sold on commission. She had never written anything that he knew of, yet she'd apparently published an article in a national magazine about him. He lifted his arms and put them on the windowsill; the air from the open window cooled his underarms. Outside, the Starlings' tiny dog marched officiously up and down the pavement, looking for someone to bark at. Maybe she had written an article about how wonderful he was, and she was too shy to show him right away. This was doubtful. Kitty was quiet, but she wasn't shy. She was untactful and she could be aggressive. Uncertainty only made her doubly aggressive.

He turned the edge of one nostril over with his thumb and nervously stroked his nose hairs with one finger. He knew it was a nasty habit, but it soothed him. When Kitty was a little girl he would do it to make her laugh. "Well," he'd say, "do you think it's time we played with the hairs in our nose?" And she would giggle, holding her hands against her face, eyes sparkling over her knuckles.

Then she was fourteen, and as scornful and rejecting as any girl he had ever thrown a spitball at when he was that age. They didn't get along so well anymore. Once, they were sitting in the rec room watching TV, he on the couch, she on the footstool. There was a Charlie Chan movie on, but he was mostly watching her back and her long, thick brown hair, which she had just washed and was brushing. She dropped her head forward from the neck to let the hair fall between her spread legs and began slowly stroking it with a pink nylon brush.

"Say, don't you think it's time we played with the hairs in our nose?"

No reaction from bent back and hair.

"Who wants to play with the hairs in their nose?"

Nothing.

"Hairs in the nose, hairs in the nose," he sang.

She bolted violently up from the stool. "You are so gross you disgust me!" She stormed from the room, shoulders in a tailored jacket of indignation.

Sometimes he said it just to see her exasperation, to feel the adorable, futile outrage of her violated girl delicacy.

He wished that his wife would come home with the car, so that he could drive to the store and buy a copy of *Self.* His car was being repaired, and he could not walk to the little cluster of stores and parking lots that constituted "town" in this heat. It would take a good twenty minutes, and he would be completely worn out when he got there. He would find the magazine and stand there in the drugstore and read it, and if it was something bad, he might not have the strength to walk back.

He went into the kitchen, opened a beer, and brought it into the living room. His wife had been gone for over an hour, and God knew how much longer she would be. She could spend literally all day driving around the country, doing nothing but buying a jar of honey or a bag of apples. Of course, he could call Kitty, but he'd probably just get her answering machine, and besides, he didn't want to talk to her before he understood the situation. He felt helplessness move through his body the way a swimmer feels a large sea creature pass beneath him. How could she have done this to him? She knew how he dreaded exposure of any kind, she knew the way he guarded himself against strangers, the way he carefully drew all the curtains when twilight approached so that no one could see them walking through the house. She knew how ashamed he had been when, at sixteen, she announced that she was lesbian.

The Starling dog was now across the street, yapping at the heels of a bow-legged old lady in a blue dress who was trying to walk down the sidewalk. "Dammit," he said. He left the window and got the afternoon opera station on the radio. They were in the final act of *La Bohème.*

He did not remember precisely when it had happened, but Kitty, his beautiful, happy little girl, turned into a glum, weird teenager that other kids picked on. She got skinny and ugly. Her blue eyes, which had been so sensitive and bright, turned filmy, as if the real Kitty had retreated so far from the surface that her eyes existed to shield rather than reflect her. It was as if she deliberately held her beauty away from them, only showing glimpses of it during unavoidable lapses, like the time she sat before the TV, daydreaming and lazily brushing her hair. At moments like this, her dormant charm broke his heart. It also annoyed him. What did she have to retreat from? They had both loved her. When she was little and she couldn't sleep at night, Marsha would sit with her in bed for hours. She praised her stories and her drawings as if she were a genius. When Kitty was seven, she and her mother had special times, during which they went off together and talked about whatever Kitty wanted to talk about.

He tried to compare the sullen, morbid Kitty of sixteen with the slender, self-possessed twenty-eight-year-old lesbian who wrote articles for *Self*. He pictured himself in court, waving a copy of *Self* before a shocked jury. The case would be taken up by the press. He saw the headlines: Dad Sues Mag—Dyke Daughter Reveals . . . reveals what? What had Kitty found to say about him that was of interest to the entire country, that she didn't want him to know about?

Anger overrode his helplessness. Kitty could be vicious. He hadn't seen her vicious side in years, but he knew it was there. He remembered the time he'd stood behind the half-open front door when fifteen-year-old Kitty sat hunched on the front steps with one of her few friends, a homely blonde who wore white lipstick and a white leather jacket. He had come to the door to view the weather and say something to the girls, but they were muttering so intently that curiosity got the better of him, and he hung back a moment to listen. "Well, at least your mom's smart," said Kitty. "My mom's not only a bitch, she's stupid."

This after the lullabies and special times! It wasn't just an isolated incident, either; every time he'd come home from work, his wife had something bad to say about Kitty. She hadn't set the table until she had been asked four times. She'd gone to Lois's house instead of coming straight home like she'd been told to do. She'd worn a dress to school that was short enough to show the tops of her panty hose.

By the time Kitty came to dinner, looking as if she'd been doing slave labor all day, he would be mad at her. He couldn't help it. Here was his wife doing her damnedest to raise a family and cook dinner, and here was this awful kid looking ugly, acting mean, and not setting the table. It seemed unreasonable that she should turn out so badly after taking up so much of their time. Her afflicted expression made him angry too. What had anybody ever done to her?

He sat forward and gently gnawed the insides of his mouth as he listened to the dying girl in *La Bohème*. He saw his wife's car pull into the driveway. He walked to the back door, almost wringing his hands, and waited for her to come through the door. When she did, he snatched the grocery bag from her arms and said, "Give me the keys." She stood openmouthed in the stairwell, looking at him with idiotic consternation. "Give me the keys!"

"What is it, Stew? What's happened?"

"I'll tell you when I get back."

He got in the car and became part of it, this panting mobile case propelling him through the incredibly complex and fast-moving world of other people, their houses, their children, their dogs, their lives. He wasn't usually so aware of this unpleasant sense of disconnection between him and everyone else, but he had the feeling that it had been there all along, underneath what he thought about most of the time. It was ironic that it should rear up so visibly at a time when there was in fact a mundane yet invasive and horribly real connection between him and everyone else in Wayne County: the hundreds of copies of *Self* magazine sitting in countless drugstores, bookstores, groceries, and libraries. It was as if there were a tentacle plugged into the side of the car, linking him with the random humans who picked up the magazine, possibly his very neighbors. He stopped at a crowded intersection, feeling like an ant in an enemy swarm.

Kitty had projected herself out of the house and into this swarm very early, ostensibly because life with him and Marsha had been so awful. Well, it had been awful, but because of Kitty, not them. As if it weren't enough to be sullen and dull, she turned into a lesbian. Kids followed her down the street, jeering at her. Somebody dropped her books in a toilet. She got into a fistfight. Their neighbors gave them looks. This reaction seemed only to steel Kitty's grip on her new identity; it made her romanticize herself, like the kid she was. She wrote poems about heroic women warriors, she brought home strange books and magazines, which, among other things, seemed to glorify prostitutes. Marsha looked for them and threw them away. Kitty screamed at her, the tendons leaping out on her slender neck. He punched Kitty and knocked her down. Marsha tried to stop him, and he yelled at her. Kitty jumped up and leapt between them, as if to defend her mother. He grabbed her and shook her, but he could not shake the conviction off her face.

Most of the time, though, they continued as always, eating dinner together, watching TV, making jokes. That was the worst thing; he would look at Kitty and see his daughter, now familiar in her withdrawn sullenness, and feel comfort and affection. Then he would remember that she was a lesbian, and a morass of complication and wrongness would come down between them, making it impossible for him to see her. Then she would just be Kitty again. He hated it.

She ran away at sixteen, and the police found her in the apartment of an eighteen-year-old bodybuilder named Dolores, who had a naked woman tattooed on her sinister bicep. Marsha made them put her in a mental hospital so psychiatrists could observe her, but he hated the psychiatrists—mean, supercilious sons of bitches who delighted in the trick question—so he took her out. She finished school, and they told her if she wanted to leave it was all right with them. She didn't waste any time in getting out of the house.

She moved into an apartment near Detroit with a girl named George and took a job at a home for retarded kids. She would appear for visits with a huge bag of laundry every few weeks. She was thin and neurotically muscular, her body having the look of a fighting dog on a leash. She cut her hair like a boy's and wore black sunglasses, black leather half-gloves, and leather belts. The only remnant of her beauty was her erect, martial carriage and her efficient movements; she walked through a room like the commander of a guerrilla force. She would sit at the dining room table with Marsha, drinking tea and having a laconic verbal conversation, her body speaking its precise martial language while the washing machine droned from the utility room, and he wandered in and out, trying to make sense of what she said. Sometimes she would stay into the evening, to eat dinner and watch *All in the Family*. Then Marsha would send her home with a jar of homemade tapioca pudding or a bag of apples and oranges.

One day, instead of a visit they got a letter postmarked San Francisco. She had left George, she said. She listed strange details about her current environment and was vague about how she was supporting herself. He had nightmares about Kitty, with her brave, proudly muscular little body, lost among big fleshy women who danced naked in go-go bars and took drugs with needles, terrible women whom his confused, romantic daughter invested with oppressed heroism and intensely female glamour. He got up at night and stumbled into the bathroom for stomach medicine, the familiar darkness of the house heavy with menacing images that pressed about him, images he saw reflected in his own expression when he turned on the bathroom light over the mirror.

Then one year she came home for Christmas. She came into the house with her luggage and a shopping bag of gifts for them, and he saw that she was beautiful again. It was a beauty that both offended and titillated his senses. Her short, spiky hair was streaked with purple, her dainty mouth was lipsticked, her nose and ears were pierced with amethyst and dangling silver. Her face had opened in thousands of petals. Her eyes shone with quick perception as she put down her bag, and he knew that she had seen him see her beauty. She moved toward him with fluid hips; she embraced him for the first time in years. He felt her live, lithe body against his, and his heart pulsed a message of blood and love. "Merry Christmas, Daddy," she said.

Her voice was husky and coarse; it reeked of knowledge and confidence. Her T-shirt said "Chicks With Balls." She was twenty-two years old.

She stayed for a week, discharging her strange jangling beauty into the house and changing the molecules of its air. She talked about the girls she shared an apartment with, her job at a coffee shop, how Californians were different from Michiganders. She talked about her friends: Lorraine, who was so pretty men fell off their bicycles as they twisted their bodies for a better look at her; Judy, a martial arts expert; and Meredith, who was raising a child with her husband, Angela. She talked of poetry readings, ceramics classes, workshops on piercing.

He realized, as he watched her, that she was now doing things that were as bad as or worse than the things that had made him angry at her five years before, yet they didn't quarrel. It seemed that a large white space existed between him and her, and that it was impossible to enter this space or to argue across it. Besides, she might never come back if he yelled at her.

Instead, he watched her, puzzling at the metamorphosis she had undergone. First she had been a beautiful, happy child turned homely, snotty, miserable adolescent. From there she had become a martinet girl with the eyes of a stifled pervert. Now she was a vibrant imp, living, it seemed, in a world constructed of topsy-turvy junk pasted with rhinestones. Where had these three different people come from? Not even Marsha, who had spent so much time with her as a child, could trace the genesis of the new Kitty from the old one. Sometimes he bitterly reflected that he and Marsha weren't even real parents anymore but bereft old people rattling around in a house, connected not to a real child who was going to college, or who at least had some kind of understandable life, but to a changeling who was the product of only their most obscure quirks, a being who came from recesses that neither of them suspected they'd had.

There were only a few cars in the parking lot. He wheeled through it with pointless deliberation before parking near the drugstore. He spent irritating seconds searching for *Self*, until he realized that its air-brushed cover girl was grinning right at him. He stormed the table of contents, then headed for the back of the magazine. "Speak Easy" was written sideways across the top of the page in round turquoise letters. At the bottom was his daughter's name in a little box. "Kitty Thorne is a ceramic artist living in South Carolina." His hands were trembling.

It was hard for him to rationally ingest the beginning paragraphs, which seemed, incredibly, to be about a phone conversation they'd had some time ago about the emptiness and selfishness of people who have sex but don't get married and have children. A few phrases stood out clearly: ". . . my father may love me but he doesn't love the way I live." ". . . even more complicated because I'm gay." ". . . because it still hurts me."

For reasons he didn't understand, he felt a nervous smile tremble under his skin. He suppressed it.

"This hurt has its roots deep in our relationship, starting, I think, when I was a teenager."

He was horribly aware of being in public, so he paid for the thing and took it out to the car. He drove slowly to another spot in the lot, as far away from the drugstore as possible, picked up the magazine, and began again. She described the "terrible difficulties" between him and her. She recounted, briefly and with hieroglyphic politeness, the fighting, the running away, the return, the tacit reconciliation.

"There is an emotional distance that we have both accepted and chosen to work around, hoping the occasional contact—love, anger, something—will get through."

He put the magazine down and looked out the window. It was near dusk; most of the stores in the little mall were closed. There were only two other cars in the parking lot, and a big, slow, frowning woman with two grocery bags was getting ready to drive one away. He was parked before a weedy piece of land at the edge of the lot. In it were rough, picky weeds spread out like big green tarantulas, young yellow dandelions, frail old dandelions, and bunches of tough blue chickweed. Even in his distress he vaguely appreciated the beauty of the blue weeds against the cool white-and-gray sky. For a moment the sound of insects comforted him. Images of Kitty passed through his memory with terrible speed: her nine-year-old forehead bent over her dish of ice cream, her tiny nightgowned form ran up the stairs, her ringed hand brushed her face, the keys on her belt jiggled as she walked her slow blue-jeaned walk away from the house. Gone, all gone.

The article went on to describe how Kitty hung up the phone feeling frustrated and then listed all the things she could've said to him to let him know how hurt she was, paving the way for "real communication"; it was all in ghastly talk-show language. He was unable to put these words together with the Kitty he had last seen lounging around the house. She was twenty-eight now, and she no longer dyed her hair or wore jewels in her nose. Her demeanor was serious, bookish, almost old-maidish. Once, he'd overheard her saying to Marsha, "So then this Italian girl gives me the once-over and says to Joanne, 'You 'ang around with too many Wasp.' And I said, 'I'm not a Wasp, I'm white trash.'"

"Speak for yourself," he'd said.

"If the worst occurred and my father was unable to respond to me in kind, I still would have done a good thing. I would have acknowledged my own needs and created the possibility to connect with what therapists call 'the good parent' in myself."

Well, if that was the kind of thing she was going to say to him, he was relieved she hadn't said it. But if she hadn't said it to him, why was she saying it to the rest of the country?

He turned on the radio. It sang: "Try to remember, and if you remember, then follow, follow." He turned it off. The interrupted dream echoed faintly. He closed his eyes. When he was nine or ten, an uncle of his had told him, "Everybody makes his own world. You see what you want to see and hear what you want to hear. You can do it right now. If you blink ten times and then close your eyes real tight, you can see anything you want to see in front of you." He'd tried it, rather halfheartedly, and hadn't seen anything but the vague suggestion of a yellowish-white ball moving creepily through the dark. At the time, he'd thought it was perhaps because he hadn't tried hard enough.

He had told Kitty to do the same thing, or something like it, when she was eight or nine. They were sitting on the back porch in striped lawn chairs, holding hands and watching the fireflies turn on and off.

She closed her eyes for a long time. Then very seriously, she said, "I see big balls of color, like shaggy flowers. They're pink and red and turquoise. I see an island with palm trees and pink rocks. There's dolphins and mermaids swimming in the water around it." He'd been almost awed by her belief in this impossible vision. Then he was sad, because she would never see what she wanted to see. Then he thought she was sort of stupid, even for a kid.

His memory flashed back to his boyhood. He was walking down the middle of the street at dusk, sweating lightly after a basketball game. There were crickets and the muted barks of dogs and the low, affirming mumble of people on their front porches. Securely held by the warm night and its sounds, he felt an exquisite blend of happiness and sorrow that life could contain this perfect moment, and a sadness that he would soon arrive home, walk into bright light, and be on his way into the next day, with its loud noise and alarming possibility. He resolved to hold this evening walk in his mind forever, to imprint in a permanent place all the sensations that occurred to him as he walked by the Oatlanders' house, so that he could always take them out and look at them. He dimly recalled feeling that if he could successfully do that, he could stop time and hold it.

He knew he had to go home soon. He didn't want to talk about the article with Marsha, but the idea of sitting in the house with her and not talking about it was hard to bear. He imagined the conversation grinding into being, a future conversation with Kitty gestating within it. The conversation was a vast, complex machine like those that occasionally appeared in his dreams; if he could only pull the switch, everything would be all right, but he felt too stupefied by the weight and complexity of the thing to do so. Besides, in this case, everything might not be all right. He put the magazine under his seat and started the car.

Marsha was in her armchair, reading. She looked up, and the expression on her face seemed like the result of internal conflict as complicated and strong as his own, but cross-pulled in different directions, uncomprehending of him and what he knew. In his mind, he withdrew from her so quickly that for a moment the familiar room was fraught with the inexplicable horror of a banal nightmare. Then the ordinariness of the scene threw the extraordinary event of the day into relief, and he felt so angry and bewildered he could've howled.

"Everything all right, Stew?" asked Marsha.

"No, nothing is all right. I'm a tired old man in a shitty world I don't want to be in. I go out there, it's like walking on knives. Everything is an attack—the ugliness, the cheapness, the rudeness, everything." He sensed her withdrawing from him into her own world of disgruntlement, her lips drawn together in that look of exasperated perseverance she'd gotten from her mother. Like Kitty, like everyone else, she was leaving him. "I don't have a real daughter, and I don't have a real wife who's here with me, because she's too busy running around on some—"

"We've been through this before. We agreed I could—"

"That was different! That was when we had two cars!" His voice tore through his throat in a jagged whiplash and came out a cracked half scream. "I don't have a car, remember? That means I'm stranded, all alone for hours, and Norm Pisarro can call me up and casually tell me that my lesbian daughter has just betrayed me in a national magazine and what do I think about that?" He wanted to punch the wall until his hand was bloody. He wanted Kitty to see the blood. Marsha's expression broke into soft, openmouthed consternation. The helplessness of it made his anger seem huge and terrible, then impotent and helpless itself. He sat down on the couch and, instead of anger, felt pain.

"What did Kitty do? What happened? What does Norm have—"

"She wrote an article in *Self* magazine about being a lesbian and her problems and something to do with me. I don't know; I could barely read the crap."

Marsha looked down at her nails.

He looked at her and saw the aged beauty of her ivory skin, sagging under the weight of her years and her cockeyed bifocals, the emotional receptivity of her face, the dark down on her upper lip, the childish pearl buttons of her sweater, only the top button done.

"I'm surprised at Norm, that he would call you like that."

"Oh, who the hell knows what he thought." His heart was soothed and slowed by her words, even if they didn't address its real unhappiness.

"Here," she said. "Let me rub your shoulders."

He allowed her to approach him, and they sat sideways on the couch, his weight balanced on the edge by his awkwardly planted legs, she sitting primly on one hip with her legs tightly crossed. The discomfort of the position negated the practical value of the massage, but he welcomed her touch. Marsha had strong, intelligent hands that spoke to his muscles of deep safety and love and the delight of physical life. In her effort, she leaned close, and her sweatered breast touched him, releasing his tension almost against his will. Through half-closed eyes he observed her sneakers on the floor—he could not quite get over this phenomenon of adult women wearing what had been boys' shoes—in the dim light, one toe atop the other as though cuddling, their laces in pretty disorganization.

Poor Kitty. It hadn't really been so bad that she hadn't set the table on time. He couldn't remember why he and Marsha had been so angry over the table. Unless it was Kitty's coldness, her always turning away, her sarcastic voice. But she was a teenager, and that's what teenagers did. Well, it was too bad, but it couldn't be helped now.

He thought of his father. That was too bad too, and nobody was writing articles about that. There had been a distance between them, so great and so absolute that the word "distance" seemed inadequate to describe it. But that was probably because he had known his father only when he was a very young child; if his father had lived longer, perhaps they would've become closer. He could recall his father's face clearly only at the breakfast table, where it appeared silent and still except for lip and jaw motions, comforting in its constancy. His father ate his oatmeal with one hand working the spoon, one elbow on the table, eyes down, sometimes his other hand holding a cold rag to his head, which always hurt with what seemed to be a noble pain, willingly taken on with his duties as a husband and father. He had loved to stare at the big face with its deep lines and long earlobes, its thin lips and loose, loopily chewing jaws. Its almost godlike stillness and expressionlessness filled him with admiration and reassurance, until one day his father slowly looked up from his cereal, met his eye, and said, "Stop staring at me, you little shit."

In the other memories, his father was a large, heavy body with a vague oblong face. He saw him sleeping in the armchair in the living room, his large, hairy-knuckled hands grazing the floor. He saw him walking up the front walk with the quick, clipped steps that he always used coming home from work, the straight-backed choppy gait that gave the big body an awesome mechanicalness. His shirt was wet under the arms, his head was down, the eyes were abstracted but alert, as though keeping careful watch on the outside world in case something nasty came at him while he attended to the more important business inside.

"The good parent in yourself."

What did the well-meaning idiots who thought of these phrases mean by them? When a father dies, he is gone; there is no tiny, smiling daddy who appears, waving happily, in a secret pocket in your chest. Some kinds of loss are absolute. And no amount of self-realization or self-expression will change that.

As if she had heard him, Marsha urgently pressed her weight into her hands and applied all her strength to relaxing his muscles. Her sweat and scented deodorant filtered through her sweater, which added its muted woolliness to her smell. "All righty!" She rubbed his shoulders and briskly patted him. He reached back and touched her hand in thanks.

Across from where they sat had once been a red chair, and in it had once sat Kitty, looking away from him, her fist hiding her face.

"You're a lesbian? Fine," he said. "You mean nothing to me. You walk out that door, it doesn't matter. And if you come back in, I'm going to spit in your face. I don't care if I'm on my deathbed, I'll still have the energy to spit in your face."

She did not move when he said that. Tears ran over her fist and down her arm, but she didn't look at him.

Marsha's hands lingered on him for a moment. Then she moved and sat away from him on the couch.

# Gabriel García Márquez

### (B. 1928)

Gabriel García Márquez, a central figure in the magical realism, was influenced by Franz Kafka, Virginia Woolf, and Juan Rulfo. He was born in the small town of Aractaca, in northern Colombia, and was raised by his maternal grandparents. He studied law and journalism at the National University in Bogotá, and published his first short story, "The Third Resignation," in 1947. García Márquez worked in Rome and Paris as a journalist for the *El Espectador* in 1955, but the newspaper was shut down the following year. His novel *Leaf Storm* (1955) served as an introduction to the Colombian village of Macondo, an equivalent to Faulkner's fictional world, Yoknapatawpha. In the 1960s, García Márquez moved to Mexico City and worked as a screenwriter, journalist, and publicist. He has published numerous works, including *One Hundred Years of Solitude* (1967), *The Autumn of the Patriarch* (1975), *Chronicle of a Death Foretold* (1981), and *Love in the Time of Cholera* (1985). In 1982, García Márquez was awarded the Nobel Prize for literature. In 1999, he was hospitalized and diagnosed with lymphatic cancer. The first part of his autobiography, *Living to Tell the Tale*, was published in 2002.

## *"I Only Came to Use the Phone"*         1992

TRANSLATED BY EDITH GROSSMAN

One rainy spring afternoon, while María de la Luz Cervantes was driving alone back to Barcelona, her rented car broke down in the Monegros desert. She was twenty-seven years old, a thoughtful, pretty Mexican who had enjoyed a certain fame as a music hall performer a few years earlier. She was married to a cabaret magician, whom she was to meet later that day after visiting some relatives in Zaragoza. For an hour she made desperate signals to the cars and trucks that sped past her in the storm, until at last the driver of a ramshackle bus took pity on her. He did warn her, however, that he was not going very far.

"It doesn't matter," said María. "All I need is a telephone."

That was true, and she needed it only to let her husband know that she would not be home before seven. Wearing a student's coat and beach shoes in April, she looked like a bedraggled little bird, and she was so distraught after her mishap that she forgot to take the car keys. A woman with a military air was sitting next to the driver, and she gave María a towel and a blanket and made room for her on the seat. María wiped off the worst of the rain and then sat down, wrapped herself in the blanket, and tried to light a cigarette, but her matches were wet. The woman sharing the seat gave her a light and asked for one of the few cigarettes that were still dry. While they smoked, María gave in to a desire to vent her feelings and raised her voice over the noise of the rain and the clatter of the bus. The woman interrupted her by placing a forefinger to her lips.

"They're asleep," she whispered.

María looked over her shoulder and saw that the bus was full of women of uncertain ages and varying conditions who were sleeping in blankets just like hers. Their serenity was contagious, and María curled up in her seat and succumbed to the sound of the rain. When she awoke, it was dark and the storm had dissolved into an icy drizzle. She had no idea how long she had slept or what place in the world they had come to. Her neighbor looked watchful.

"Where are we?" María asked.

"We've arrived," answered the woman.

The bus was entering the cobbled courtyard of an enormous, gloomy building that seemed to be an old convent in a forest of colossal trees. The passengers, just visible in the dim light of a lamp in the courtyard, sat motionless until the woman with the military air ordered them out of the bus with the kind of primitive directions used in nursery school. They were all older women, and their movements were so lethargic in the half-light of the courtyard that they looked like images in a dream. María, the last to climb down, thought they were nuns. She was less certain when she saw several women in uniform who received them at the door of the bus, pulled the blankets over their heads to keep them dry, and lined them up single file, directing them not by speaking but with rhythmic, peremptory clapping. María said good-bye and tried to give the blanket to the woman whose seat she had shared, but the woman told her to use it to cover her head while she crossed the courtyard and then return it at the porter's office.

"Is there a telephone?" María asked.

"Of course," said the woman. "They'll show you where it is."

She asked for another cigarette, and María gave her the rest of the damp pack. "They'll dry on the way," she said. The woman waved good-bye from the running board, and called "Good luck" in a voice that was almost a shout. The bus pulled away without giving her time to say anything else.

María started running toward the doorway of the building. A matron tried to stop her with an energetic clap of the hands, but had to resort to an imperious shout: "Stop, I said!" María looked out from under the blanket and saw a pair of icy eyes and an inescapable forefinger pointing her into the line. She obeyed. Once inside the vestibule she separated from the group and asked the porter where the telephone was. One of the matrons returned her to the line with little pats on the shoulder while she said in a saccharine voice:

"This way, beautiful, the telephone's this way."

María walked with the other women down a dim corridor until they came to a communal dormitory, where the matrons collected the blankets and began to assign beds. Another matron, who seemed more humane and of higher rank to María, walked down the line comparing a list of names with those written on cardboard tags stitched to the bodices of the new arrivals. When she reached María, she was surprised to see that she was not wearing her identification.

"I only came to use the phone," María told her.

She explained with great urgency that her car had broken down on the highway. Her husband, who performed magic tricks at parties, was waiting for her in Barcelona because they had three engagements before midnight, and she wanted to let him know she would not be there in time to go with him. It was almost seven o'clock. He had to leave home in ten minutes, and she was afraid he would cancel everything because she was late. The matron appeared to listen to her with attention.

"What's your name?" she asked.

María said her name with a sigh of relief, but the woman did not find it after going over the list several times. With some alarm she questioned another matron, who had nothing to say and shrugged her shoulders.

"But I only came to use the phone," said María.

"Sure, honey," the supervisor told her, escorting her to her bed with a sweetness that was too patent to be real, "if you're good you can call anybody you want. But not now, tomorrow."

Then something clicked in María's mind, and she understood why the women on the bus moved as if they were on the bottom of an aquarium. They were, in fact, sedated with tranquilizers, and that dark palace with the thick stone walls and frozen stairways was really a hospital for female mental patients. She raced out of the dormitory in dismay, but before she could reach the main door a gigantic matron wearing mechanic's coveralls stopped her with a blow of her huge hand and held her immobile on the floor in an armlock. María, paralyzed with terror, looked at her sideways.

"For the love of God," she said. "I swear by my dead mother I only came to use the phone."

Just one glance at her face was enough for María to know that no amount of pleading would move that maniac in coveralls who was called Herculina because of her uncommon strength. She was in charge of difficult cases, and two inmates had been strangled to death by her polar bear arm skilled in the art of killing by mistake. It was established that the first case had been an accident. The second proved less clear, and Herculina was admonished and warned that the next time she would be subjected to a thorough investigation. The accepted story was that this black sheep of a fine old family had a dubious history of suspicious accidents in various mental hospitals throughout Spain.

They had to inject María with a sedative to make her sleep the first night. When a longing to smoke roused her before dawn, she was tied to the metal bars of the bed by her wrists and ankles. She shouted, but no one came. In the morning, while her husband could find no trace of her in Barcelona, she had to be taken to the infirmary, for they found her senseless in a swamp of her own misery.

When she regained consciousness she did not know how much time had passed. But now the world seemed a haven of love. Beside her bed, a monumental old man with a flat-footed walk and a calming smile gave her back her joy in being alive with two masterful passes of his hand. He was the director of the sanatorium.

Before saying anything to him, without even greeting him, María asked for a cigarette. He lit one and handed it to her, along with the pack, which was almost full. María could not hold back her tears.

"Now is the time to cry to your heart's content," the doctor said in a soporific voice. "Tears are the best medicine."

María unburdened herself without shame, as she had never been able to do with her casual lovers in the empty times that followed lovemaking. As he listened, the doctor smoothed her hair with his fingers, arranged her pillow to ease her breathing, guided her through the labyrinth of her uncertainty with a wisdom and a sweetness she never had dreamed possible. This was, for the first time in her life, the miracle of being understood by a man who listened to her with all his heart and did not expect to go to bed with her as a reward. At the end of a long hour, when she had bared the depths of her soul, she asked permission to speak to her husband on the telephone.

The doctor stood up with all the majesty of his position. "Not yet, princess," he said, patting her cheek with more tenderness than she ever had felt before. "Everything in due course." He gave her a bishop's blessing from the door, asked her to trust him, and disappeared forever.

That same afternoon María was admitted to the asylum with a serial number and a few superficial comments concerning the enigma of where she had come from and the doubts surrounding her identity. In the margin the director had written an assessment in his own hand: *agitated.*

Just as María had foreseen, her husband left their modest apartment in the Horta district half an hour behind schedule for his three engagements. It was the first time she had been late in the almost two years of their free and very harmonious union, and he assumed it was due to the heavy downpours that had devastated the entire province that weekend. Before he went out he pinned a note to the door with his itinerary for the night.

At the first party, where all the children were dressed in kangaroo costumes, he omitted his best illusion, the invisible fish, because he could not do it without her assistance. His second engagement was in the house of a ninety-three-year-old woman in a wheelchair, who prided herself on having celebrated each of her last thirty birthdays with a different magician. He was so troubled by María's absence that he could not concentrate on the simplest tricks. At his third engagement, the one he did every night at a café on the Ramblas, he gave an uninspired performance for a group of French tourists who could not believe what they saw because they refused to believe in magic. After each show he telephoned his house, and waited in despair for María to answer. After the last call he could no longer control his concern that something had happened to her.

On his way home, in the van adapted for public performances, he saw the splendor of spring in the palm trees along the Paseo de Gracia, and he shuddered at the ominous thought of what the city would be like without María. His last hope vanished when he found his note still pinned to the door. He was so troubled he forgot to feed the cat.

I realize now as I write this that I never learned his real name, because in Barcelona we knew him only by his professional name: Saturno the Magician. He was a man of odd character and irredeemable social awkwardness, but María had more than enough of the tact and charm he lacked. It was she who led him by the hand through this community of great mysteries, where no man would have dreamed of calling after midnight to look for his wife. Saturno had, soon after he arrived, and he preferred to forget the incident. And so that night he settled for calling Zaragoza, where a sleepy grandmother told him with no alarm that María had said goodbye after lunch. He slept for just an hour at dawn. He had a muddled dream in which he saw María wearing a ragged wedding dress spattered with blood, and he woke with the fearful certainty that this time she had left him forever, to face the vast world without her.

She had deserted three different men, including him, in the last five years. She had left him in Mexico City six months after they met, when they were in the throes of pleasure from their demented lovemaking in a maid's room in the Anzures district. One morning, after a night of unspeakable profligacy, María was gone. She left behind everything that was hers, even the ring from her previous marriage, along with a letter in which she said she was incapable of surviving the torment of that wild love. Saturno thought she had returned to her first husband, a high school classmate she had married in secret while still a minor and abandoned for another man after two loveless years. But no: She had gone to her parents' house, and Saturno followed to get her back regardless of the cost. His pleading was unconditional, he made many more promises than he was prepared to keep, but he came up against an invincible determination. "There are short loves and there are long ones," she told him. And she concluded with a merciless, "This was a short one." Her inflexibility forced him to admit defeat. But in the early hours of the morning of All Saints' Day, when he returned to his orphan's room after almost a year of deliberate forgetting, he found her asleep on the living room sofa with the crown of orange blossoms and long tulle train worn by virgin brides.

María told him the truth. Her new fiancé, a childless widower with a settled life and a mind to marry forever in the Catholic Church, had left her dressed and waiting at the altar. Her parents decided to hold the reception anyway, and she played along with them. She danced, sang with the mariachis, had too much to drink, and in a terrible state of belated remorse left at midnight to find Saturno.

He was not home, but she found the keys in the flower pot in the hall, where they always hid them. Now she was the one whose surrender was unconditional. "How long this time?" he asked. She answered with a line by Vinicius de Moraes: "Love is eternal for as long as it lasts." Two years later, it was still eternal.

María seemed to mature. She renounced her dreams of being an actress and dedicated herself to him, both in work and in bed. At the end of the previous year they had attended a magicians' convention in Perpignan, and on their way home they visited Barcelona for the first time. They liked it so much they had been living here for eight months, and it suited them so well they bought an apartment in the very Catalonian neighborhood of Horta. It was noisy, and they had no porter, but there was more than enough room for five children. Their happiness was all one could hope for, until the weekend when she rented a car and went to visit her relatives in Zaragoza, promising to be back by seven on Monday night. By dawn on Thursday there was still no word from her.

On Monday of the following week, the insurance company for the rented car called and asked for María. "I don't know anything," said Saturno. "Look for her in Zaragoza." He hung up. A week later a police officer came to the house to report that the car had been found, stripped bare, on a back road to Cádiz, nine hundred kilometers from the spot where María had abandoned it. The officer wanted to know if she had further details regarding the theft. Saturno was feeding the cat, and he did not look up when he told him straight out that the police shouldn't waste their time because his wife had left him and he didn't know where she had gone or with whom. His conviction was so great that the officer felt uncomfortable and apologized for his questions. They declared the case closed.

The suspicion that María might leave him again had assailed Saturno at Easter in Cadaqués, where Rosa Regás had invited them to go sailing. In the Marítim, the crowded, sordid bar of the *gauche divine* during the twilight of Francoism, twenty of us were squeezed together around one of those wrought-iron tables that had room only for six. After she smoked her second pack of cigarettes for the day, María ran out of matches. A thin, downy arm wearing a Roman bronze bracelet made its way through the noisy crowd at the table and gave her a light. She said thank you without looking at the person she was thanking, but Saturno the Magician saw him—a bony, clean-shaven adolescent as pale as death, with a very black ponytail that hung down to his waist. The windowpanes in the bar just managed to withstand the fury of the spring tramontana wind, but he wore a kind of street pajama made of raw cotton, and a pair of farmer's sandals.

They did not see him again until late autumn, in a seafood bar in La Barceloneta, wearing the same plain cotton outfit and a long braid instead of the ponytail. He greeted them both as if they were old friends, and the way he kissed María, and the way she kissed him back, struck Saturno with the suspicion that they had been seeing each other in secret. Days later he happened to come across a new name and phone number that María had written in their household address book, and the unmerciful lucidity of jealousy revealed to him whose they were. The intruder's background was the final proof: He was twenty-two years old, the only child of a wealthy family, and a decorator of fashionable shop windows, with a casual reputation as a bisexual and a well-founded notoriety as a paid comforter of married women. But Saturno managed to restrain himself until the night María did not come home. Then he began calling him every day, from six in the morning until just before the following dawn, every two or three hours at first, and then whenever he was near a telephone. The fact that no one answered intensified Saturno's martyrdom.

On the fourth day an Andalusian woman who was there just to clean picked up the phone. "The gentleman's gone away," she said, with enough vagueness to drive him mad. Saturno did not resist the temptation of asking if Señorita María was in by any chance.

"Nobody named María lives here," the woman told him. "The gentleman is a bachelor."

"I know," he said. "She doesn't live there, but sometimes she visits, right?"

The woman became annoyed.

"Who the hell is this, anyway?"

Saturno hung up. The woman's denial seemed one more confirmation of what for him was no longer a suspicion but a burning certainty. He lost control. In the days that followed he called everyone he knew in Barcelona, in alphabetical order. No one could tell him anything, but each call deepened his misery, because his jealous frenzies had become famous among the unrepentant night owls of the *gauche divine,* and they responded with any kind of joke that would make him suffer. Only then did he realize how alone he was in that beautiful, lunatic, impenetrable city, where he would never be happy. At dawn, after he fed the cat, he hardened his heart to keep from dying and resolved to forget María.

After two months María had not yet adjusted to life in the sanatorium. She survived by just picking at the prison rations with flatware chained to the long table of unfinished wood, her eyes fixed on the lithograph of General Francisco Franco that presided over the gloomy medieval dining room. At first she resisted the canonical hours with their mindless routine of matins, lauds, vespers, as well as the other church services that took up most of the time. She refused to play ball in the recreation yard, or to make artificial flowers in the workshop that a group of inmates attended with frenetic diligence. But after the third week she began, little by little, to join in the life of the cloister. After all, said the doctors, every one of them started out the same way, and sooner or later they became integrated into the community.

The lack of cigarettes, resolved in the first few days by a matron who sold them for the price of gold, returned to torment her again when she had spent the little money she had with her. Then she took comfort in the newspaper cigarettes that some inmates made with the butts they picked out of the trash, for her obsessive desire to smoke had become as intense as her fixation on the telephone. Later on, the few pesetas she earned making artificial flowers allowed her an ephemeral consolation.

Hardest of all was her loneliness at night. Many inmates lay awake in the semi-darkness, as she did, not daring to do anything because the night matron at the heavy door secured with a chain and padlock was awake too. One night, however, overcome with grief, María asked in a voice loud enough for the woman in the next bed to hear:

"Where are we?"

The grave, lucid voice of her neighbor answered:

"In the pit of hell."

"They say this is the country of the Moors," said another, distant voice that resounded throughout the dormitory. "And it must be true, because in the summer, when there's a moon, you can hear the dogs barking at the sea."

The chain running through the locks sounded like the anchor of a galleon, and the door opened. Their pitiless guardian, the only creature who seemed alive in the instantaneous silence, began walking from one end of the dormitory to the other. María was seized with terror, and only she knew why.

Since her first week in the sanatorium, the night matron had been proposing outright that María sleep with her in the guardroom. She began in a concrete, businesslike tone: an exchange of love for cigarettes, for chocolate, for whatever she wanted. "You'll have everything," the matron said, tremulous. "You'll be the queen." When María refused, she changed her tactics, leaving little love notes under her pillow, in the pockets of her robe, in the most unexpected places. They were messages of a heartbreaking urgency that could have moved a stone. On the night of the dormitory incident, it had been more than a month that she had seemed resigned to defeat.

When she was certain the other inmates were asleep, the matron approached María's bed and whispered all kinds of tender obscenities in her ear while she kissed her face, her neck tensed with terror, her rigid arms, her exhausted legs. Then, thinking perhaps that María's paralysis stemmed not from fear but from compliance, she dared to go further. That was when María hit her with the back of her hand and sent her crashing into the next bed. The enraged matron stood up in the midst of the uproar created by the agitated inmates.

"You bitch!" she shouted. "We'll rot together in this hellhole until you go crazy for me."

Summer arrived without warning on the first Sunday in June, requiring emergency measures because during Mass the sweltering inmates began taking off their shapeless serge gowns. With some amusement María watched the spectacle of naked patients being chased like blind chickens up and down the aisles by the matrons. In the confusion she tried to protect herself from wild blows, and she somehow found herself alone in an empty office, where the incessant ring of a telephone had a pleading tone. María answered without thinking and heard a distant, smiling voice that took great pleasure in imitating the telephone company's time service:

"The time is forty-five hours, ninety-two minutes, and one hundred seven seconds."

"Asshole," said María.

She hung up, amused. She was about to leave when she realized she was allowing a unique opportunity to slip away. She dialed six digits, with so much tension and so much haste she was not sure it was her home number. She waited, her heart racing, she heard the avid, sad sound of the familiar ring, once, twice, three times, and at last she heard the voice of the man she loved, in the house without her.

"Hello?"

She had to wait for the knot of tears that formed in her throat to dissolve.

"Baby, sweetheart," she sighed.

Her tears overcame her. On the other end of the line there was a brief, horrified silence, and a voice burning with jealousy spit out the word:

"Whore!"

And he slammed down the receiver.

That night, in an attack of rage, María pulled down the lithograph of the Generalissimo in the refectory, crashed it with all her strength into the stained-glass window that led to the garden, and threw herself to the floor, covered in blood. She still had enough fury left to resist the blows of the matrons who tried, with no success, to restrain her, until she saw Herculina standing in the doorway with her arms folded, staring at her. María gave up. Nevertheless, they dragged her to the ward for violent patients, subdued her with a hose spurting icy water, and injected turpentine into her legs. The swelling that resulted prevented her from walking, and María realized there was nothing in the world she would not do to escape that hell. The following week, when she was back in the dormitory, she tiptoed to the night matron's room and knocked at the door.

María's price, which she demanded in advance, was that the matron send a message to her husband. The matron agreed, on the condition that their dealings be kept an absolute secret. And she pointed an inexorable forefinger at her.

"If they ever find out, you die."

And so, on the following Saturday, Saturno the Magician drove to the asylum for women in the circus van, which he had prepared to celebrate María's return. The director himself received him in his office, which was as clean and well ordered as a battleship, and made an affectionate report on his wife's condition. No one had known where she came from, or how or when, since the first information regarding her arrival was the official admittance form he had dictated after interviewing her. An investigation begun that same day had proved inconclusive. In any event, what most intrigued the director was how Saturno had learned his wife's whereabouts. Saturno protected the matron.

"The insurance company told me," he said.

The director nodded, satisfied. "I don't know how insurance companies manage to find out everything," he said. He looked over the file lying on his ascetic's desk, and concluded:

"The only certainty is the seriousness of her condition."

He was prepared to authorize a visit with all the necessary precautions if Saturno the Magician would promise, for the good of his wife, to adhere without question to the rules of behavior that he would indicate. Above all with reference to how he treated her, in order to avoid a recurrence of the fits of rage that were becoming more and more frequent and dangerous.

"How strange," said Saturno. "She always was quick-tempered, but had a lot of self-control."

The doctor made a learned man's gesture. "There are behaviors that remain latent for many years, and then one day they erupt," he said. "All in all, it is fortunate she happened to come here, because we specialize in cases requiring a firm hand." Then he warned him about María's strange obsession with the telephone.

"Humor her," he said.

"Don't worry, Doctor," Saturno said with a cheerful air. "That's my specialty."

The visiting room, a combination of prison cell and confessional, was the former locutory of the convent. Saturno's entrance was not the explosion of joy they both might have expected. María stood in the middle of the room, next to a small table with two chairs and a vase empty of flowers. It was obvious she was ready to leave, with her lamentable strawberry-colored coat and a pair of disreputable shoes given to her out of charity. Herculina stood in a corner, almost invisible, her arms folded. María did not move when she saw her husband come in, and her face, still marked by the shattered window glass, showed no emotion. They exchanged routine kisses.

"How do you feel?" he asked her.

"Happy you're here at last, baby," she said. "This has been death."

They did not have time to sit down. Drowning in tears, María told him about the miseries of the cloister, the brutality of the matrons, the food not fit for dogs, the endless nights when terror kept her from closing her eyes.

"I don't even know how many days I've been here, or how many months or years, all I know is that each one has been worse than the last," and she sighed with all her soul. "I don't think I'll ever be the same."

"That's all over now," he said, caressing the recent scars on her face with his fingertips. "I'll come every Saturday. More often than that, if the director lets me. You'll see, everything will turn out just fine."

She fixed her terrified eyes on his. Saturno tried to use his performer's charm. He told her, in the puerile tone of all great lies, a sweetened version of the doctor's prognosis. "It means," he concluded, "that you still need a few more days to make a complete recovery." María understood the truth.

"For God's sake, baby," she said, stunned. "Don't tell me you think I'm crazy too!"

"The things you think of!" he said, trying to laugh. "But it really will be much better for everybody if you stay here a while. Under better conditions, of course."

"But I've already told you I only came to use the phone!" said María.

He did not know how to react to her dreadful obsession. He looked at Herculina. She took advantage of the opportunity to point at her wristwatch as a sign that it was time to end the visit. María intercepted the signal, glanced behind her, and saw Herculina tensing for an imminent attack. Then she clung to her husband's neck, screaming like a real madwoman. He freed himself with as much love as he could muster, and left her to the mercies of Herculina, who jumped her from behind. Without giving María time to react, she applied an armlock with her left hand, put her other iron arm around her throat, and shouted at Saturno the Magician:

"Leave!"

Saturno fled in terror.

But on the following Saturday, when he had recovered from the shock of the visit, he returned to the sanatorium with the cat, which he had dressed in an outfit identical to his: the red-and-yellow tights of the great Leotardo, a top hat, and a swirling cape that seemed made for flying. He drove the circus van into the courtyard of the cloister, and there he put on a prodigious show lasting almost three hours, which the inmates enjoyed from the balconies with discordant shouts and inopportune applause. They were all there except María, who not only refused to receive her husband but would not even watch him from the balconies. Saturno felt wounded to the quick.

"It is a typical reaction," the director consoled him. "It will pass."

But it never passed. After attempting many times to see María again, Saturno did all he could to have her accept a letter from him, but to no avail. She returned it four times, unopened and with no comments. Saturno gave up but continued leaving a supply of cigarettes at the porter's office without ever finding out if they reached María, until at last reality defeated him.

No one heard any more about him except that he married again and returned to his own country. Before leaving Barcelona he gave the half-starved cat to a casual girlfriend, who also promised to take cigarettes to María. But she disappeared too. Rosa Regás remembered seeing her in the Corte Inglés department store about twelve years ago, with the shaved head and orange robes of some Oriental sect, and very pregnant. She told Rosa she had taken cigarettes to María as often as she could, and settled some unforeseen emergencies for her, until one day she found only the ruins of the hospital, which had been demolished like a bad memory of those wretched times. María seemed very lucid on her last visit, a little overweight, and content with the peace of the cloister. That was the day she also brought María the cat, because she had spent all the money that Saturno had given her for its food.

## A Very Old Man with Enormous Wings · 1968

### A Tale for Children

TRANSLATED BY GREGORY RABASSA

On the third day of rain they had killed so many crabs inside the house that Pelayo had to cross his drenched courtyard and throw them into the sea, because the newborn child had a temperature all night and they thought it was due to the stench. The world had been sad since Tuesday. Sea and sky were a single ash-gray thing and the sands of the beach, which on March nights glimmered like powdered light, had become a stew of mud and rotten shellfish. The light was so weak at noon that when Pelayo was coming back to the house after throwing away the crabs, it was hard for him to see what it was that was moving and groaning in the rear of the courtyard. He had to go very close to see that it was an old man, a very old man, lying face down in the mud, who, in spite of his tremendous efforts, couldn't get up, impeded by his enormous wings.

Frightened by that nightmare, Pelayo ran to get Elisenda, his wife, who was putting compresses on the sick child, and he took her to the rear of the courtyard. They both looked at the fallen body with mute stupor. He was dressed like a ragpicker. There were only a few faded hairs left on his bald skull and very few teeth in his mouth, and his pitiful condition of a drenched great-grandfather had taken away any sense of grandeur he might have had. His huge buzzard wings, dirty and half-plucked, were forever entangled in the mud. They looked at him so long and so closely that Pelayo and Elisenda very soon overcame their surprise and in the end found him familiar. Then they dared speak to him, and he answered in an incomprehensible dialect with a strong sailor's voice. That was how they skipped over the inconvenience of the wings and quite intelligently concluded that he was a lonely castaway from some foreign ship wrecked by the storm. And yet, they called in a neighbor woman who knew everything about life and death to see him, and all she needed was one look to show them their mistake.

"He's an angel," she told them. "He must have been coming for the child, but the poor fellow is so old that the rain knocked him down."

On the following day everyone knew that a flesh-and-blood angel was held captive in Pelayo's house. Against the judgment of the wise neighbor woman, for whom angels in those times were the fugitive survivors of a celestial conspiracy, they did not have the heart to club him to death. Pelayo watched over him all afternoon from the kitchen, armed with his bailiff's club, and before going to bed dragged him out of the mud and locked him up with the hens in the wire chicken coop. In the middle of the night, when the rain stopped, Pelayo and Elisenda were still killing crabs. A short time afterward the child woke up without a fever and with a desire to eat. Then they felt magnanimous and decided to put the angel on a raft with fresh water and provisions for three days and leave him to his fate on the high seas. But when they went out into the courtyard with the first light of dawn, they found the whole neighborhood in front of the chicken coop having fun with the angel, without the slightest reverence, tossing him things to eat through the openings in the wire as if he weren't a supernatural creature but a circus animal.

Father Gonzaga arrived before seven o'clock, alarmed at the strange news. By that time onlookers less frivolous than those at dawn had already arrived and they were making all kinds of conjectures concerning the captive's future. The simplest among them thought that he should be named mayor of the world. Others of sterner mind felt that he should be promoted to the rank of five-star general in order to win all wars. Some visionaries hoped that he could be put to stud in order to implant on earth a race of winged wise men who could take charge of the universe. But Father Gonzaga, before becoming a priest, had been a robust woodcutter. Standing by the wire, he reviewed his catechism in an instant and asked them to open the door so that he could take a close look at that pitiful man who looked more like a huge decrepit hen among the fascinated chickens. He was lying in a corner drying his open wings in the sunlight among the fruit peels and breakfast leftovers that the early risers had thrown him. Alien to the impertinences of the world, he only lifted his antiquarian eyes and murmured something in his dialect when Father Gonzaga went into the chicken coop and said good morning to him in Latin. The parish priest had his first suspicion of an imposter when he saw that he did not understand the language of God or know how to greet His ministers. Then he noticed that seen close up he was much too human: he had an unbearable smell of outdoors, the back side of his wings was strewn with parasites and his main feathers had been mistreated by terrestrial winds, and nothing about him measured up to the proud dignity of angels. Then he came out of the chicken coop and in a brief sermon warned the curious against the risks of being ingenuous. He reminded them that the devil had the bad habit of making use of carnival tricks in order to confuse the unwary. He argued that if wings were not the essential element in determining the difference between a hawk and an airplane, they were even less so in the recognition of angels. Nevertheless, he promised to write a letter to his bishop so that the latter would write to his primate[1] so that the latter would write to the Supreme Pontiff[2] in order to get the final verdict from the highest courts.

His prudence fell on sterile hearts. The news of the captive angel spread with such rapidity that after a few hours the courtyard had the bustle of a marketplace and they had to call in troops with fixed bayonets to disperse the mob that was about to knock the house down. Elisenda, her spine all twisted from sweeping up so much marketplace trash, then got the idea of fencing in the yard and charging five cents admission to see the angel.

The curious came from far away. A traveling carnival arrived with a flying acrobat who buzzed over the crowd several times, but no one paid any attention to him because his wings were not those of an angel but, rather, those of a sidereal bat. The most unfortunate invalids on earth came in search of health: a poor woman who since childhood had been counting her heartbeats and had run out of numbers; a Portuguese man who couldn't sleep because the noise of the stars disturbed him; a sleepwalker who got up at night to undo the things he had done while awake; and many others with less serious ailments. In the midst of that shipwreck disorder that made the earth tremble, Pelayo and Elisenda were happy with fatigue, for in less than a week they had crammed their rooms with money and the line of pilgrims waiting their turn to enter still reached beyond the horizon.

The angel was the only one who took no part in his own act. He spent his time trying to get comfortable in his borrowed nest, befuddled by the hellish heat of the oil lamps and sacramental candles that had been placed along the wire. At first they tried to make him eat some mothballs, which, according to the wisdom of the wise neighbor woman, were the food prescribed for angels. But he turned them down, just as he turned down the papal lunches that the penitents brought him and they never found out whether it was because he was an angel or because he was an old man that in the end he ate nothing but eggplant mush. His only supernatural virtue seemed to be patience. Especially during the first days, when the hens pecked at him, searching for the stellar parasites that proliferated in his wings, and the cripples pulled out feathers to touch their defective parts with, and even the most merciful threw stones at him, trying to get him to rise so they could see him standing. The only time they succeeded in arousing him was when they burned his side with an iron for branding steers, for he

1 **primate:** A bishop or archbishop with authority over several provinces.
2 **Pontiff:** Usually the pope or a high bishop in the Catholic Church. Derives from the Latin *Pontifex* (bridge-maker).

had been motionless for so many hours that they thought he was dead. He awoke with a start, ranting in his hermetic language and with tears in his eyes, and he flapped his wings a couple of times, which brought on a whirlwind of chicken dung and lunar dust and a gale of panic that did not seem to be of this world. Although many thought that his reaction had been one not of rage but of pain, from then on they were careful not to annoy him, because the majority understood that his passivity was not that of a hero taking his ease but that of a cataclysm in repose.

Father Gonzaga held back the crowd's frivolity with formulas of maid-servant inspiration while awaiting the arrival of a final judgment on the nature of the captive. But the mail from Rome showed no sense of urgency. They spent their time finding out if the prisoner had a navel, if his dialect had any connection with Aramaic,[3] how many times he could fit on the head of a pin, or whether he wasn't just a Norwegian with wings. Those meager letters might have come and gone until the end of time if a providential event had not put an end to the priest's tribulations.

It so happened that during those days, among so many other carnival attractions, there arrived in town the traveling show of the woman who had been changed into a spider for having disobeyed her parents. The admission to see her was not only less than the admission to see the angel, but people were permitted to ask her all manner of questions about her absurd state and to examine her up and down so that no one would ever doubt the truth of her horror. She was a frightful tarantula the size of a ram and with the head of a sad maiden. What was most heart-rending, however, was not her outlandish shape but the sincere affliction with which she recounted the details of her misfortune. While still practically a child she had sneaked out of her parents' house to go to a dance, and while she was coming back through the woods after having danced all night without permission, a fearful thunderclap rent the sky in two and through the crack came the lightning bolt of brimstone that changed her into a spider. Her only nourishment came from the meatballs that charitable souls chose to toss into her mouth. A spectacle like that, full of so much human truth and with such a fearful lesson, was bound to defeat without even trying that of a haughty angel who scarcely deigned to look at mortals. Besides, the few miracles attributed to the angel showed a certain mental disorder, like the blind man who didn't recover his sight but grew three new teeth, or the paralytic who didn't get to walk but almost won the lottery, and the leper whose sores sprouted sunflowers. Those consolation miracles, which were more like mocking fun, had already ruined the angel's reputation when the woman who had been changed into a spider finally crushed him completely. That was how Father Gonzaga was cured forever of his insomnia and Pelayo's courtyard went back to being as empty as during the time it had rained for three days and crabs walked through the bedrooms.

The owners of the house had no reason to lament. With the money they saved they built a two-story mansion with balconies and gardens and high netting so that crabs wouldn't get in during the winter, and with iron bars on the windows so that

---

3 **Aramaic:** A Semitic language used in portions of the Bible. Some believe that this is the language Jesus spoke.

angels wouldn't get in. Pelayo also set up a rabbit warren close to town and gave up his job as bailiff for good, and Elisenda bought some satin pumps with high heels and many dresses of iridescent silk, the kind worn on Sunday by the most desirable women in those times. The chicken coop was the only thing that didn't receive any attention. If they washed it down with creolin and burned tears of myrrh inside it every so often, it was not in homage to the angel but to drive away the dungheap stench that still hung everywhere like a ghost and was turning the new house into an old one. At first, when the child learned to walk, they were careful that he not get too close to the chicken coop. But then they began to lose their fears and got used to the smell, and before the child got his second teeth he'd gone inside the chicken coop to play, where the wires were falling apart. The angel was no less standoffish with him than with other mortals, but he tolerated the most ingenious infamies with the patience of a dog who had no illusions. They both came down with chicken pox at the same time. The doctor who took care of the child couldn't resist the temptation to listen to the angel's heart, and he found so much whistling in the heart and so many sounds in his kidneys that it seemed impossible for him to be alive. What surprised him most, however, was the logic of his wings. They seemed so natural on that completely human organism that he couldn't understand why other men didn't have them too.

When the child began school it had been some time since the sun and rain had caused the collapse of the chicken coop. The angel went dragging himself about here and there like a stray dying man. They would drive him out of the bedroom with a broom and a moment later find him in the kitchen. He seemed to be in so many places at the same time that they grew to think that he'd been duplicated, that he was reproducing himself all through the house, and the exasperated and unhinged Elisenda shouted that it was awful living in that hell full of angels. He could scarcely eat and his antiquarian eyes had also become so foggy that he went about bumping into posts. All he had left were the bare cannulae of his last feathers. Pelayo threw a blanket over him and extended him the charity of letting him sleep in the shed, and only then did they notice that he had a temperature at night, and was delirious with the tongue twisters of an Old Norwegian. That was one of the few times they became alarmed, for they thought he was going to die and not even the wise neighbor woman had been able to tell them what to do with dead angels.

And yet he not only survived his worst winter, but seemed improved with the first sunny days. He remained motionless for several days in the farthest corner of the courtyard, where no one would see him, and at the beginning of December some large, stiff feathers began to grow on his wings, the feathers of a scarecrow, which looked more like another misfortune of decrepitude. But he must have known the reason for those changes, for he was quite careful that no one should notice them, that no one should hear the sea chanteys that he sometimes sang under the stars. One morning Elisenda was cutting some bunches of onions for lunch when a wind that seemed to come from the high seas blew into the kitchen. Then she went to the window and caught the angel in his first attempts at flight. They were so clumsy that his fingernails opened a furrow in the vegetable patch and he was on the point of knocking the shed down with the ungainly flapping that slipped on the light and couldn't get a grip on the air. But he did manage to gain altitude. Elisenda let out a sigh of relief, for herself and for him, when she saw him pass over the last houses, holding himself up in some way with the risky flapping of a senile vulture. She kept watching him even when she was through cutting the onions and she kept on watching until it was no longer possible for her to see him, because then he was no longer an annoyance in her life but an imaginary dot on the horizon of the sea.

# Alan Gurganus

## (B. 1947)

Born in Rocky Mount, North Carolina, Alan Gurganus was originally trained as a painter. Many of his paintings are represented in public and private collections, and he also illustrates his fiction. His first book, *Oldest Living Confederate Widow Tells All* (1989), won the Sue Kaufman Prize from the American Academy of Arts and Letters. His book *White People* (1991) won the *Los Angeles Times* book prize. His stories carefully balance humor and pathos and often explore characters who bring a sense of heroism to their battle with life's daily foibles. Gurganus has worked for many years to fight censorship and homophobia. His political editorials are often published in the *New York Times*.

## He's at the Office                                                              2000

Till the Japanese bombed Pearl Harbor, most American men wore hats to work. What happened? Did our guys—suddenly scouting overhead for worse Sunday raids—come to fear their hat brims' interference? My unsuspecting father wore his till yesterday. He owned three. A gray, a brown, and a summer straw one, whose maroon-striped rayon band could only have been woven in America in the 1940s.

Last month, I lured him from his self-imposed office hours for a walk around our block. My father insisted on bringing his briefcase. "You never know," he said. We soon passed a huge young hipster, creaking in black leather. The kid's pierced face flashed more silver than most bait shops sell. His jeans, half down, exposed hat racks of white hipbone; the haircut arched high over jug ears. He was scouting Father's shoes. Long before fashion joined him, Dad favored an under-evolved antique form of orthopedic Doc Martens. These impressed a punk now scanning the Sherman tank of a cowhide briefcase with chromium corner braces. The camel-hair overcoat was cut to resemble some boxy-backed 1947 Packard. And, of course, up top sat "the gray."

Pointing to it, the boy smiled. "Way bad look on you, guy."

My father, seeking interpretation, stared at me. I simply shook my head no. I could not explain Dad to himself in terms of tidal fashion trends. All I said was "I think he likes you."

Dad's face folded. "Uh-oh."

By the end, my father, the fifty-two-year veteran of Integrity Office Supplier, Unlimited, had become quite cool again, way.

We couldn't vacation for more than three full days. He'd veer our Plymouth toward some way-station pay phone. We soon laughed as Dad, in the glass booth, commenced to wave his arms, shake his head, shift his weight from foot to foot. We knew Miss Green must be telling him of botched orders, delivery mistakes. We were nearly to Gettysburg. I'd been studying battle maps. Now I knew we'd never make it.

My father bounded back to the car and smiled in. "Terrible mixup with the Wilmington school system's carbon paper for next year. Major goof, but typical. Guy's got to do it all himself. Young Green didn't insist I come back, but she sure hinted."

We U-turned southward, and my father briefly became the most charming man on earth. He now seemed to be selling something we needed, whatever we needed. Traveling north into a holiday—the very curse of leisure—he had kept as silent as some fellow with toothaches. Now he was our tour guide, interviewing us, telling and retelling his joke. Passing a cemetery, he said (over his family's dry carbon-paper unison), "I hear they're dying to get in there!" "Look on the bright side," I told myself: "we'll arrive home and escape him as he runs—literally runs—to the office."

Dad was, like me, an early riser. Six days a week, Mom sealed his single-sandwich lunch into its Tupperware jacket; this fit accidentally yet exactly within the lid compartment of his durable briefcase. He would then pull on his overcoat—bulky, war-efficient, strong-seamed, four buttons as big as silver dollars and carved from actual shell. He'd place the cake-sized hat in place, nod in our general direction, and set off hurrying. Dad faced each day as one more worthy enemy. If he had been Dwight Eisenhower saving the Western world, or Jonas Salk freeing kids our age from crutches, okay. But yellow Eagle pencils? Utility paperweights in park-bench green?

Once a year, Mom told my brother and me how much the war had darkened her young husband; he'd enlisted with three other guys from Falls; he alone came back alive with all his limbs. "Before that," she smiled, "your father was funnier, funny. And smarter. Great dancer. You can't blame mustard gas, not this time. It's more what Dick saw. He came home and he was all business. Before that, he'd been mischievous and talkative and strange. He was always playing around with words. Very entertaining. Eyelashes out to here. For years, I figured that in time he'd come back to being whole. But since June of forty-five it's been All Work and No Play Makes Jack."

Mom remembered their fourth anniversary. "I hired an overnight sitter for you two. We drove to an inn near Asheville. It had the state's best restaurant, candlelight, a real string quartet. I'd made myself a green velvet dress. I was twenty-eight and never in my whole life have I ever looked better. You just know it. Dick recognized some man who'd bought two adding machines. Dick invited him to join us. Then I saw how much his work was going to have to mean to him. Don't be too hard on him, please. He feeds us, he puts aside real savings for you boys' college. Dick pays our taxes. Dick has no secrets. He's not hurting anyone." Brother and I gave each other a look Mom recognized and understood but refused to return.

The office seemed to tap some part of him that was either off limits to us or simply did not otherwise exist. My brother and I griped that he'd never attended our Little League games (not that we ever made the starting lineup). He missed our father-son Cub Scout banquet; it conflicted with a major envelope convention in Newport News. Mother neutrally said he loved us as much as he could. She was a funny, energetic person—all that wasted good will. And even as kids, we knew not to blame her.

Ignored, Mom created a small sewing room. Economizing needlessly, she stayed busy stitching all our school clothes, cowboy motifs galore. For a while, each shirt pocket bristled with Mom-designed embroidered cacti. But Simplicity patterns were never going to engage a mind as complex as hers. Soon Mom was spending most mornings playing vicious duplicate bridge. Our toothbrush glasses briefly broke out in rashes of red hearts, black clubs. Mom's new pals were society ladies respectful of her brainy speed, her impenitent wit; she never bothered introducing them to her husband. She laughed more now. She started wearing rouge.

We lived a short walk from both our school and his wholesale office. Dad sometimes left the Plymouth parked all night outside the workplace, his desk lamp the last one burning on the whole third floor. Integrity's president, passing headquarters late, always fell for it. "Dick, what do you do up there all night, son?" My father's shrug became his finest boast. The raises kept pace; Integrity Office Supplier was still considered quite a comer. And R. Richard Markham, Sr.—as handsome as a collar ad, a hat ad, forever at the office—was the heir apparent.

Dad's was Integrity's flagship office: "Maker of World's Highest Quality Clerical Supplies." No other schoolboys had sturdier pastel subject dividers, more clip-in see-through three-ring pen caddies. The night before school started, Dad would be up late at our kitchen table, swilling coffee, "getting you boys set." Zippered leather cases, English slide rules, folders more suitable for treaties than for book reports ("*Skipper, A Dog of the Pyrenees,* by Marjorie Hopgood Purling"). Our notebooks soon proved too heavy to carry far; we secretly stripped them, swapping gear for lunchbox treats more exotic than Mom's hard-boiled eggs and Sun-Maid raisin packs.

Twenty years ago, Dad's Integrity got bought out by a German firm. The business's vitality proved somewhat hobbled by computers' onslaught. "A fad," my father called computers in 1976. "Let others retool. We'll stand firm with our yellow legals, erasers, Parker ink, fountain pens. Don't worry, our regulars'll come back. True vision always lets you act kind in the end, boys. Remember."

Yeah, right.

My father postponed his retirement. Mom encouraged that and felt relieved; she could not imagine him at home all day. As Integrity's market share dwindled, Dad spent more time at the office, as if to compensate with his own body for the course of modern life.

His secretary, the admired Miss Green, had once been what Pop still called "something of a bombshell." (He stuck with a Second World War terminology that had, like the hat, served him too well ever to leave behind.)

Still favoring shoulder pads, dressed in unyielding woolen Joan Crawford solids, Green wore an auburn pageboy that looked burned by decades of ungrateful dyes. She kicked off her shoes beneath her desk, revealing feet that told the tale of high heels' worthless weekday brutality. She'd quit college to tend an ailing mother, who proved demanding, then immortal. Brother and I teased Mom: poor Green appeared to worship her longtime boss, a guy whose face was as smooth and wedged and classic as his hat. Into Dick Markham's blunted constancy she read actual "moods."

He still viewed Green, now past sixty, as a promising virginal girl. In their small adjoining offices, these two thrived within a fond impersonality that permeated the ads of the period.

Integrity's flagship headquarters remained enameled a flavorless mint green, unaltered for five decades. The dark Mission coatrack was made by Limbert—quite a good piece. One ashtray—upright, floor model, brushed chromium—proved the size and shape of some landlocked torpedo. Moored to walls, dented metal desks were as gray as battleships. A series of forest green filing cabinets seemed banished, as patient as a family of trolls, to one shaming little closet all their own. Dad's office might've been decorated by a firm called Edward Hopper & Sam Spade, Unlimited.

For more than half a century, he walked in each day at seven-oh-nine sharp, as Miss Green forever said, "Morning, Mr. Markham. I left your appointments written on your desk pad, can I get you you coffee? Is now good, sir?" And Dad said, "Yes, why, thanks, Miss Green, how's your mother, don't mind if I do."

Four years ago, I received a panicked phone call: "You the junior to a guy about eighty, guy in a hat?"

"Probably." I was working at home. I pressed my computer's "Save" function. This, I sensed, might take a while. "Save."

"Exit? No? Yes?"

"Yes."

"Mister, your dad thinks we're camped out in his office and he's been banging against our door. He's convinced we've evicted his files and what he calls his Green. 'What have you done with young Green?' Get down here A.S.A.P. Get him out of our hair or it's nine-one-one in three minutes, swear to God."

From my car, I phoned home. Mom must have been off somewhere playing bridge with the mayor's blond wife and his blond ex-wife; they'd sensibly become excellent friends. The best women are the best people on earth; and the worst men the very worst. Mother, overlooked by Dad for years, had continued finding what she called "certain outlets."

When I arrived, Dad was still heaving himself against an office door, deadbolt-locked from within. Since its upper panel was frosted glass, I could make out the colors of the clothes of three or four people pressing from their side. They'd used masking tape to crosshatch the glass, as if bracing for a hurricane. The old man held his briefcase, wore his gray hat, the tan boxy coat.

"Dad?" He stopped with a mechanical cartoon verve, jumped my way, and smiled so hard it warmed my heart and scared me witless. My father had never acted so glad to see me—not when I graduated summa cum laude, not at my wedding, not after the birth of my son—and I felt joy in the presence of such joy from him.

"Reinforcements. Good man. We've got quite a hostage situation here. Let's put our shoulders to it, shall we?"

"Dad?" I grabbed the padded shoulders of his overcoat. These crumpled to reveal a man far sketchier hiding in there somewhere—a guy only twenty years from a hundred, after all.

"Dad? Dad. We have a good-news, bad-news setup here today. It's this. You found the right building, Dad. Wrong floor."

I led him back to the clattering, oil-smelling elevator. I thought to return, tap on the barricaded door, explain. But, in time, hey, they'd peek, they'd figure out the coast was clear. That they hadn't recognized him, after his fifty-two years of long days in this very building, said something. New people, everywhere.

I saw at once that Miss Green had been crying. Her face was caked with so much powder it looked like calamine. "Little mixup," I said.

"Mr. Markham? We got three calls about those gum erasers," she said, faking a frontal normality. "I think they're putting sawdust in them these days, sir. They leave skid marks, apparently. I put the information on your desk. With your day's appointments. Like your coffee? Like it now? Sir?"

I hung his hat on the hat tree; I slid his coat onto its one wooden Deco hanger that could, at any flea market today, bring thirty-five dollars easy, two tones of wood, inlaid.

I wanted to have a heart-to-heart. I was so disoriented as to feel half-sane myself. But I overheard Father already returning his calls. He ignored me, and that seemed, within this radically altered gravitational field, a good sign. I sneaked back to Miss Green's desk, and admitted, "I'll need to call his doctor. I want him seen today, Miss Green. He was up on four, trying to get into that new headhunting service. He told them his name. Mom was out. So they, clever, looked him up in the book and found his junior and phoned me to come help."

She sat forward, strenuously feigning surprise. She looked rigid, chained to this metal desk by both gnarled feet. "How long?" I somehow knew to ask.

Green appeared ecstatic, then relieved, then, suddenly, happily weeping, tears pouring down—small tears, lopsided, mascaraed grit. She blinked up at me with a spaniel's gratitude. Suddenly, if slowly, I began to understand. In mere seconds, she had caved about Dad's years-long caving-in. It was my turn now.

Miss Green now whispered certain of his mistakes. There were forgotten parking tickets by the dozen. There was his attempt to purchase a lake house on land already flooded for a dam. Quietly, she admitted years of covering.

From her purse, she lifted a page covered in Dad's stern Germanic cursive, blue ink fighting to stay isometrically between red lines.

"I found this one last week." Green's voice seemed steadied by the joy of having told. "I fear this is about the worst, to date, we've been."

If they say "Hot enough for you?," it means recent weather. "Yes indeed" still a good comeback. Order forms pink. Requisition yellow. Miss green's birthday June 12. She work with you fifty-one years. Is still unmarried. Mother now dead, since '76, so stop asking about Mother, health of. Home address, 712 Marigold Street: Left at Oak, can always walk there. After last week, never go near car again. Unfair to others. Take second left at biggest tree. Your new Butcher's name is: Al. Wife: Betty. Sons: Matthew and Dick Junior. Grandson Richie (your name with a III added on it). List of credit cards, licnse etc. below in case you lose walet agn, you big dope. Put copies somewhere safe, 3 places, write down, hide many. You are 80, yes, eighty.

And yet, as we now eavesdropped, Dick Markham dealt with a complaining customer. He sounded practiced, jokey, conversant, exact.

"Dad, you have an unexpected doctor's appointment." I handed Dad his hat. I'd phoned our family physician from Miss Green's extension.

For once, they were ready for us. The nurses kept calling him by name, smiling, overinsistent, as if hinting at answers for a kid about to take his make-or-break college exam. I could see they'd always liked him. In a town this small, they'd maybe heard about his trouble earlier today.

As Dad got ushered in for tests, he glowered accusations back at me as if I had just dragged him to a Nazi medical experiment. He finally reemerged, scarily pale, pressing a bit of gauze into the crook of his bare arm, its long veins the exact blue of Parker's washable ink. They directed him toward the lobby bathroom. They gave him a cup for his urine specimen. He held it before him with two hands like some Magus's treasure.

His hat, briefcase, and overcoat remained behind, resting on an orange plastic chair all their own. Toward these I could display a permissible tenderness. I lightly set my hand on each item. Call it superstition. I now lifted the hat and sniffed it. It smelled like Dad. It smelled like rope. Physical intimacy has never been a possibility. My brother and I, half-drunk, once tried to picture the improbable, the sexual conjunction of our parents. Brother said, "Well, he probably pretends he's at the office, unsealing her like a good manila envelope that requires a rubber stamp—legible, yes, keep it legible, *legible,* now speed-mail!"

I had flipped through four stale magazines before I saw the nurses peeking from their crudely cut window. "He has been quite a while, Mr. Markham. Going on thirty minutes."

"Shall I?" I rose and knocked. No answer. "Would you come stand behind me?" Cowardly, I signaled to an older nurse.

The door proved unlocked. I opened it. I saw one old man aimed the other way and trembling with hesitation. Before him, a white toilet, a white sink, and a white enamel trash can, the three aligned—each its own insistent invitation. In one hand, the old man held an empty specimen cup. In the other hand, his dick.

Turning my way, grateful, unashamed to be caught sobbing, he cried, "Which one, son? Fill which one?"

Forcibly retired, my father lived at home in his pajamas. Mom made him wear the slippers and robe to help with his morale. "Think *Thin Man.* Think William Powell."

But the poor guy literally hung his head with shame. That phrase took on new meaning now that his routine and dignity proved so reduced. Dad's mopey presence clogged every outlet she'd perfected to avoid him. The two of them were driving each other crazy.

Lacking the cash for live-in help, she was forced to cut way back on her bridge game and female company. She lost ten pounds—it showed in her neck and face—and then she gave up rouge. You could see Mom missed her fancy friends. I soon pitied her nearly as much as I pitied him—no, more. At least he allowed himself to be distracted. She couldn't forget.

Mom kept urging him to get dressed. She said they needed to go to the zoo. She had to get out and "do" something. One morning, she was trying to force Dad into his dress pants when he struck her. She fell right over the back of an armchair. The whole left side of her head stayed a rubber-stamp pad's blue-black for one whole week. Odd, this made it easier for both of them to stay home. Now two people hung their heads in shame.

At a window overlooking the busy street, Dad would stand staring out, one way. On the window glass, his forehead left a persistent oval of human oil. His pajama knees pressed against the radiator. He silently second-guessed parallel parkers. He studied westerly-moving traffic. Sometimes he'd stand guard there for six uninterrupted hours. Did he await some detained patriotic parade? I pictured poor Green on a passing float—hoisting his coffee mug and the black phone receiver, waving him back down to street level, reality, use.

One December morning, Mom—library book in lap, trying to reinterest herself in Daphne du Maurier, in anything—smelled scorching. Like Campbell's mushroom soup left far too long on simmer. Twice she checked their stove and toaster oven. Finally, around his nap time, she pulled Dad away from the radiator: his shins had cooked. "Didn't it hurt you, Dick? Darling, didn't you ever feel anything?"

Next morning at six-thirty, I got her call. Mom's husky tone sounded too jolly for the hour. She described bandaging both legs. "As you kids say, I don't think this is working for us. This might be beyond me. Integrity's fleabag insurance won't provide him with that good a home. We have just enough to go on living here as usual. Now, I'll maybe shock you and you might find me weak or, worse, disloyal. But would you consider someday checking out some nice retreats or facilities in driving distance? Even if it uses up the savings. Your father is the love of my life—one per customer. I just hate to get any more afraid of him!"

I said I'd phone all good local places, adding, giddy, "I hear they're dying to get in there."

This drew a silence as cold as his. "Your dad's been home from the office—what, seven months? Most men lean toward their leisure years, but who ever hated leisure more than Dick? When I think of everything he gave Integrity and how little he's getting back . . . I'm not strong enough to *keep* him, but I can't bear to *put* him anywhere. Still, at this rate, all I'll want for Christmas is a nice white padded cell for two."

I wished my mother belonged to our generation, where the women work. She could've done anything. And now to be saddled with a man who'd known nothing but enslavement to one so-so office. The workaholic, tabled. He still refused to dress; she focused on the sight of his pajamas. My folks now argued with the energy of newlyweds; then she felt ashamed of herself and he forgot to do whatever he'd just promised.

On Christmas Eve, she was determined to put up a tree for him. But Dad, somehow frightened by the ladder and all the unfamiliar boxes everywhere, got her into such a lethal headlock she had to scream for help. Now the neighbors were involved. People I barely knew interrupted my work hours, saying, "Something's got to be done. It took three of us to pull him off of her. He's still strong as a horse. It's getting dangerous over there. He could escape."

Sometimes, at two in the morning, she'd find him standing in their closet, wearing his p.j.s and the season's correct hat. He'd be looking at his business suits. The right hand would be filing, "walking," back and forth across creased pant legs, as if seeking the . . . exact . . . right . . . pair . . . for . . . the office . . . today.

I tried to keep Miss Green informed. She'd sold her duplex and moved into our town's most stylish old-age home. When she swept downstairs to greet me, I didn't recognize her. "God, you look fifteen years younger." I checked her smile for hints of a possible lift.

She just laughed, giving her torso one mild shimmy. "Look, Ma. No shoulder pads."

Her forties hairdo, with its banked, rolled edges, had softened into pretty little curls around her face. She'd let its color go her natural silvery blond. Green gave me a slow look. If I didn't know her better, I'd have sworn she was flirting.

She appeared shorter in flats. I now understood: her toes had been so mangled by wearing those forties Quonset-huts of high heels, ones she'd probably owned since age eighteen. Her feet had grown, but she'd stayed true to the old shoes, part of some illusion she felt my dad required.

Others in the lobby perked up at her fond greeting; I saw she'd already become the belle of this place. She let me admire her updated charms.

"No." She smiled simply. "It's that I tried to keep it all somewhat familiar for him. How I looked and all. We got to where Mr. Markham found any change a kind of danger, so . . . I mean, it wasn't as if a dozen other suitors were beating down my door. What with Mother being moody and sick that long. And so, day to day, well . . ." She shrugged.

Now, in my life I've had very few inspired ideas. Much of me, like Pop, is helplessly a company man. So forgive my boasting of this.

Leaving Miss Green's, I stopped by a huge Salvation Army store. It was a good one. Over the years, I've found a few fine Federal side chairs here and many a great tweed jacket. Browsing through the used-furniture room, I wandered beneath a cardboard placard hand-lettered "The World of Early American." Ladder-back deacon's chairs and plaid upholstered things rested knee to knee, like sad and separate families.

I chanced to notice a homeless man, asleep, a toothless white fellow. His overcoat looked filthy. His belongings were bunched around him in six rubber-banded shoeboxes. His feet, in paint-stained shoes, rested on an ordinary school administrator's putty-colored desk. "The Wonderful World of Work" hung over hand-me-down waiting rooms still waiting. Business furniture sat parlored—forlorn as any gray-green

Irish wake. There was something about the sight of this old guy's midday snoring in so safe a fluorescent make-work cubicle.

Mom now used her sewing room only for those few overnight third cousins willing to endure its lumpy foldout couch. The room had become a catchall, cold storage, since about 1970. We waited for Dad's longest nap of the day. Then, in a crazed burst of energy, we cleared her lair, purging it of boxes, photo albums, four unused exercise machines. I paint-rolled its walls in record time, the ugliest latex junior-high-school green that Sherwin-Williams sells (there's still quite a range). The Salvation Army delivers: within two days, I had arranged this new-used-junk to resemble Integrity's workspace, familiarly anonymous. A gray desk nuzzled one wall—the window wasted behind. Three green file cabinets made a glum herd. One swivel wooden chair rode squeaky casters. The hat rack antlered upright over a dented tin wastebasket. The ashtray looked big enough to serve an entire cancer ward. Wire shelves predicted a neutral "in," a far more optimistic "out." I stuffed desk drawers with Parker ink, cheap fountain pens, yellow legal pads, four dozen paper clips. I'd bought a big black rotary phone, and Mom got him his own line.

Against her wishes, I'd saved most of Dad's old account ledgers. Yellowed already, they could've come from a barrister's desk in a Dickens novel. I scattered "1959–62." In one corner I piled all Dad's boxed records, back taxes, old Christmas cards from customers. The man saved everything.

The evening before we planned introducing him to his new quarters, I disarranged the place a bit. I tossed a dozen pages on the floor near his chair. I left the desk lamp lit all night. It gave this small room a strange hot smell, overworked. The lamp was made of nubbly brown cast metal (recast war surplus?), its red button indicating "on." Black meant "off."

That morning I was there to help him dress. Mom made us a hearty oatmeal breakfast, packed his lunch, and snapped the Tupperware insert into his briefcase.

"And where am *I* going?" he asked us in a dead voice.

"To the office," I said. "Where else do you go this time of day?"

He appeared sour, puffy, skeptical. Soon as I could, I glanced at Mom. This was not going to be as easy as we'd hoped.

I got Dad's coat and hat. He looked gray and dubious. He would never believe in this new space if I simply squired him down the hall to it. So, after handing him his briefcase, I led Dad back along our corridor and out onto the street.

Some of the old-timers, recognizing him, called, "Looking good, Mr. Markham," or "Cold enough for you?" Arm in arm, we nodded past them.

My grammar school had been one block from his office. Forty years back, we'd set out on foot like this together. The nearer Dad drew to Integrity, the livelier he became; the closer I got to school, the more withdrawn I acted. But today I kept up a mindless overplentiful patter. My tone neither cheered nor deflected him. One block before his office building, I swerved back down an alley toward the house. As we approached, I saw that Mom had been imaginative enough to leave our front door wide open. She'd removed a bird print that had hung in our foyer hall unloved forever. A mere shape, it still always marked this as our hall, our home.

"*Here* we are!" I threw open his office door. I took his hat and placed it on its hook. I helped him free of his coat. Just as his face had grown bored, then irked, and finally enraged at our deception, the phone rang. From where I stood—half in the office, half in the hall—I could see Mom holding the white phone in the kitchen.

My father paused—since when did he answer the phone?—and, finally, flushed, reached for it himself. "Dick?" Mom said. "You'll hate me, I'm getting so absent-minded. But you did take your lunch along today, right? I mean, go check. Be patient with me, okay?" Phone cradled between his head and shoulder, he lifted his briefcase and snapped it open—his efficiency still water-clear, and scary. Dad then said to the receiver, "Lunch is definitely here, per usual. But, honey, haven't I told you about these personal calls at the office?"

Then I saw him bend to pick up scattered pages. I saw him touch one yellow legal pad and start to square all desktop pens at sharp right angles. As he pulled the chair two inches forward I slowly shut his door behind me. Then Mother and I, hidden in the kitchen, held each other and, not expecting it, cried, if very, very silently.

When we peeked in two hours later, he was filing.

Every morning, Sundays included, Dad walked to the office. Even our ruse of walking him around the block was relaxed. Mom simply set a straw hat atop him (after Labor Day, she knew to switch to his gray). With his packed lunch, he would stride nine paces from the kitchen table, step in, and pull the door shut, muttering complaints of overwork, no rest ever.

Dad spent a lot of time on the phone. Long-distance directory-assistance charges constituted a large part of his monthly bill. But he "came home" for supper with the weary sense of blurred accomplishment we recalled from olden times.

Once, having dinner with them, I asked Dad how he was. He sighed. "Well, July is peak for getting their school supplies ordered. So the pressure is on. My heart's not what it was, heart's not completely in it lately, I admit. They downsized Green. Terrible loss to me. With its being crunch season, I get a certain shortness of breath. Suppliers aren't where they were, the gear is often second-rate, little of it any longer American-made. But you keep going, because it's what you know and because your clients count on you. I may be beat, but, hey—it's still a job."

"Aha," I said.

Mom received a call on her own line. It was from some kindergarten owner. Dad—plundering his old red address book—had somehow made himself a go-between, arranging sales, but working freelance now. He appeared to be doing it unsalaried, not for whole school systems but for small local outfits like day care centers. This teacher had to let Mom know that he'd sent too much of the paste. No invoice with it, a pallet of free jarred white school paste waiting out under the swing sets. Whom to thank?

Once, I tiptoed in and saw a long list of figures he kept meaning to add up. I noticed that, in his desperate daily fight to keep his desktop clear, he'd placed seven separate five-inch piles of papers at evened intervals along the far wall. I found such ankle-level filing sad till slowly I recognized a pattern—oh, yeah, "The Pile System." It was my own technique for maintaining provisional emergency order, and one which I now rejudged to be quite sane.

Inked directly into the wooden bottom of his top desk drawer was this:

Check Green's sick leave ridic. long. Nazis still soundly defeated. Double enter all new receipts, nincompoop. Yes, you . . . eighty-one. Old Woman roommate is: "Betty."

Mom felt safe holding bridge parties at the house again, telling friends that Dad was in there writing letters and doing paperwork, and who could say he wasn't? Days, Mom could now shop or attend master-point tournaments at good-driving-distance hotels. In her own little kitchen-corner office, she entered bridge chat rooms, E-mailing game-theory arcana to well-known French and Russian players. She'd regained some weight and her face was fuller, and prettier for that. She bought herself a bottle-green velvet suit. "It's just a cheap Chanel knockoff, but these ol' legs still ain't that bad, hmm?" She looked more rested than I'd seen her in a year or two.

I cut a mail slot in Dad's office door, and around eleven Mom would slip in his today's *Wall Street Journal.* You'd hear him fall upon it like a zoo animal, fed.

Since Dad had tried to break down the headhunters' door I hadn't dared go on vacation myself. But Mother encouraged me to take my family to Hawaii. She laughed. "Go ahead, enjoy yourself, for Pete's sake. Everything under control. I'm playing what friends swear is my best bridge ever, and Dick's sure working good long hours again. By now I should know the drill, huh?"

I was just getting into my bathing suit when the hotel phone rang. I could see my wife and son down there on the white beach.

"Honey? Me. There's news about your father."

Mom's voice sounded vexed but contained. Her businesslike tone seemed assigned. It let me understand.

"When?"

"This afternoon around six-thirty our time. Maybe it happened earlier, I don't know. I found him. First I convinced myself he was just asleep. But I guess, even earlier, I knew."

I stood here against glass, on holiday. I pictured my father facedown at his desk. The tie still perfectly knotted, his hat yet safe on its hook. I imagined Dad's head at rest atop those forty pages of figures he kept meaning to add up.

I told Mom I was sorry; I said we'd fly right back.

"No, please," she said. "I've put everything off till next week. It's just us now. Why hurry? And, son? Along with the bad news, I think there's something good. He died at the office."

# Patricia Henley

(B. 1947)

Born into a large, working-class family, Patricia Henley decided at the age of nineteen that she would be a writer. She attended Johns Hopkins University, where she received her M.A. in poetry. She passionately loves the outdoors and often sets her stories in her native state, Indiana. She has published several collections of poems and short stories, among them *Friday Night at Silver Star* (1986), *Learning to Die* (1977), *The Secret of Cartwheels* (1992), *Back Roads* (1996), and *Worship of the Common Heart* (2000). Her two novels are *Hummingbird House* (1999) and *In the River Sweet* (2002). Henley is currently a professor of creative writing at Purdue University.

---

## The Secret of Cartwheels                                          1992

The winesap trees along the road were skeletal in the early evening light. I stared out the school bus window and cupped like a baby chick the news I looked forward to telling Mother: I'd decided on my confirmation name.

"What's nine times seven?" Jan Mary said.

"Sixty-three," I said. *Joan.* That was Mother's confirmation name, and I wanted it to be mine as well. She'd told me it was a name of strength, a name to carry you into battle.

"I tore my cords," Christopher said. He stood in the aisle, bracing himself with one hand on the chrome pole beside the driver, who wore a baseball cap and a big plaid mackinaw.

The bus driver sang, "Don't sit under the apple tree with anyone else but me." I knew we were nearing our stop, the end of the route, whenever the driver sang this song. We were the last ones on the bus. Although the heater was chuffing hard, frost in the shape of flames curled along the edges of the windows.

"Sweet dreams," the driver said, as we plodded down the slippery steps of the school bus.

Aunt Opal's pale green Cadillac was parked at an odd angle near the woodshed. I knew something was wrong—she never drove out from Wenatchee to visit in the winter. I remembered what our mother had told me the night before. Before bedtime we all lined up to kiss her good night, and when my turn came, she'd said, "There are signs in life. Signs that tell you what you have to do." Her voice had frightened me. I didn't want to hear what she had to say.

Jan Mary said, "Who's that?" Her knit gloves were soggy, her knees chapped above slipping down socks.

"Aunt Opal," Christopher said. His voice was dead and I knew he knew and understood.

Our breath came in blue blossoms in the cold, cutting air, and a light went on in the living room. I didn't want to go in, but I kept trudging through the snow.

Inside, everything was in its place, but our mother was gone, which made the house seem cold and empty. Four-year-old Suzanne stood on the heat register, her grubby chenille blanket a cape around her shoulders. Her hair had been recently brushed, and she wore plastic barrettes, a duck on one side, a bow on the other. When I remember those years at home, this is one of the things I focus on, how nothing ever matched, not sheets, not barrettes, not cups and saucers, not socks. And sometimes I think the sad and petty effort to have matching things has been one of the chief concerns of my adult life. Aunt Opal perched uneasily on a ladder-back chair with the baby, Laura Jean, on her lap. Laura Jean, eyes roving, held her own bottle of milk, and when she saw me, her looked latched on to me and she stopped sucking and squirmed and kicked. Her plastic bottle clunked onto the floor. Aunt Opal's white wool pantsuit stretched tightly across her fat thighs. Her teased hair stood hard and swirled. Ill-at-ease, she shifted her weight gingerly as though she might get dirty. I thought I saw pity in her eyes, and I looked away. Christopher and Jan Mary hung back by the kitchen door, Christopher banging his metal lunch box softly against his leg.

"Where's our mother?" I said, scooping Laura Jean away from Aunt Opal.

"Now I hate to have to be the bearer of bad tidings," she began. "I know this will be hard on you children. I don't know what your mother was thinking of." She got up and stalked over to Suzanne, her spike heels dragging on the linoleum.

"Just tell me where she is." The baby stiffened in my arms. This was the first time I'd ever issued a command to a grownup, and I felt both powerful and worried. Without our mother there, I was suddenly older.

Aunt Opal took a few seconds to adjust one of Suzanne's barrettes. "At the VA hospital," she said. "She's sick. Surely you must have known? She needs a rest. She's gone away and left you."

Christopher and Jan Mary went meek as old dogs into the living room and turned on the television. I snugged the baby into her high chair, wrapped a receiving blanket around her bare legs, and began peeling potatoes for supper. Suzanne sat in her miniature rocker, holding a Dr. Seuss book upside down and mouthing the words she knew by heart. I remember thinking if we could just have an ordinary supper, do our homework, fold the laundry, say our prayers, then it would be all right with mother away. We might feel as though she'd just gone through the orchard to visit a neighbor, and that she might return at any moment.

"You'll have places to go, of course," Aunt Opal said, lighting the gas under the stale morning coffee. The sulphurous smell of the match lingered.

"Places?"

"Christopher can stay with Grandma and Grandpa. Janice will take the baby."

"We'll stay here together," I said.

"Roxanne," she said, pouring coffee into a flowered teacup. "You can't stay here alone with all these children."

I remember feeling small and powerless then, and I saw that I still needed to be taken care of—in fact, wanted to be taken care of—but I did not think I would be. I had no trust in anyone, and when you are a child feeling this way, every day becomes a swim through white water with no life jacket. Many years went by before I allowed myself to wonder where my father was during this time.

"How long will we be gone?" I said.

"It's hard to say," Aunt Opal said, sighing. "It's really hard to say."

I was thirteen, Christopher twelve, and Jan Mary eight. We went to St. Martin's and rode the public school bus home, aware of our oddity—Christopher's salt-and-pepper cords instead of jeans, the scratchy scapulars against our chests, the memorization of saints' names and days and deeds. The week before our mother went away, I had stayed home from school twice, missing play auditions and report card day. She had written excuses on foolscap: *Please excuse Roxanne from school yesterday. I needed her at home.*

Our father worked in another state. The house was isolated, out in the country; our nearest neighbor lived a mile away. During the summer I loved where we lived—the ocean of apple blooms, the muted voices of the Spanish-speaking orchard workers, the wild berries, like deep black fleece along the railroad tracks. Winters were another story. We heated with wood, and the fine wood ash smudged our schoolbooks, our clothes and linens, our wrists and necks. The well was running dry, and we children shared our bathwater. By my turn the water was tepid and gray. Our mother fed the fire, waking sometimes twice in the night to keep it going, and her hands and fingers were cracked, swollen. I wanted to cry whenever I looked at them. The loneliness was like a bad smell in the house.

In the evening while the others, the younger ones, watched "I Love Lucy," she sipped Jack Daniel's from a jelly glass and told me her secrets, plucking me from childhood's shore. Very late, when the others had gone to bed, she'd curse our father in a whisper. One night, when she had filled that jelly glass for the third time, and wanted company, she told me about her true love, a woman she'd known in the WACS during the war when they worked together in the motor pool in Dayton, Ohio. You can learn too much too soon about your mother's past. The weight of her concerns made me turn from her and wish that something would save us from the life we shared with her. I couldn't make the wish while watching her split and bleeding hands light a cigarette. But later, lying confused and rigid in the double bed I shared with cuddling Jan Mary and Suzanne, I wished that our mother would go away.

All of the moving took place at night. Aunt Opal drove Suzanne, Jan Mary, and me up the Entiat River to Entiat Home, a place local people called the orphans' home, but in truth the children there were not orphans but children whose parents could not care for them. The frozen river glittered in the moonlight. The fir trees rode in dark procession along the far bank. I sat in the front seat, a privilege of the oldest. The car was vast and luxurious and foreign. Most of the way, no one spoke.

Finally, from the cavernous backseat, Suzanne said, "Where's the baby?"

Don't ask, I thought, don't ask. I tried to send this silent message to Suzanne, but she didn't get it. Blood beat in my head.

"Laura Jean might need us," she said.

"Laura will be fine. Fine, fine," Aunt Opal said. "She's with your cousin Janice, who has another baby for her to play with."

Her jolly voice made me feel as though someone was hugging me too hard, painfully. When we'd left Christopher at Grandma and Grandpa Swanson's I'd felt sick to my stomach, not because I would be separated from him—no—but because I wanted to stay there too. I wanted to cling to Grandma Swanson and say, Take me, keep me. But I was the oldest. I didn't cling and cry.

I would miss Christopher. We had fallen into the habit of sitting in the unfinished knotty-pine pantry, after our baths and the dishes were done, listening to the high-school basketball games on the staticky radio. We knew the players' names and numbers. Together we had anticipated the mystery of going to high school.

Aunt Opal turned slowly into the uphill drive, which was lined with billows of snow. The dark was my comfort—I didn't want to see everything at once. We parked in front of a red brick house with two wrought iron lamps beside the neatly shoveled steps. Silence leaped at us when Aunt Opal shut off the engine. The place seemed a last outpost before the black and convoluted mountains, the Cascades, which, I imagined, went slanted and ragged to the sea. Then quickly, nimbly, a man and woman came coatless down the steps and opened the car doors, greeting us as though we were their own children returning home. The woman was thin and wore pearls and a skirt and sweater. The man had hair as black as an eggplant. Their voices were cheerful, but they kept their hands to themselves, as though they knew we would not want to be touched by strangers.

One moment we were in the dark, the car, the winter mountain air; the next, all three of us were ushered into the blinding white room, which was like a hospital room, with white metal cupboards, white metal cots, and everything amazingly clean and shiny under the fluorescent lights, cleaner even than Grandma Swanson's house.

We sat on the edge of one cot without speaking to one another. Snow dripped in dirty puddles from our saddle oxfords. The floor was black and white like a checkerboard. In the hallway, out of sight, Aunt Opal spoke with the man and woman— "Well behaved," I heard her say—and then she departed with all the speed and indifference of a UPS driver. Through a tall window in the room I watched her headlights sweep across the cinnamon bark of a ponderosa pine. From someplace faraway in the house came Christmas carols, wreathed in pure recorded voices. My body played tricks on me; my head hurt; my stomach knotted in an acid snarl.

Suzanne growled in a baby way she had when she was tired or angry. I pulled her onto my lap and she sucked her thumb. Consoling her was my only source of reassurance.

Jan Mary stamped the dirty puddles with the toe of her shoe. "How will we get to school?" she said.

"We'll go to a different school."

"I don't want to."

"We don't always get to do what we want," I said, shocked at the way I parroted our mother.

The woman in the pearls came into the bright room and leaned over us, one arm around Jan Mary's back.

"I'm Mrs. Thompson," she said. Her words were stout with kindness, which seemed a warning to me, as though she could hurt me, and she smelled good, like flowery cologne. She's someone's perfect mother, I thought.

"You'll need baths before bedtime, girls," she said. She strode to the oak door across the room and opened it, then switched on the bathroom light. "You have your own pajamas?"

"Yes," I said, nodding in the direction of the cardboard *Cream of Wheat* carton, which held my clothes. Each of us had packed a carton with our best things.

"You can help your sisters bathe, Roxanne," she said. "Then I'll check your heads for lice."

"Our mother wouldn't allow that," I said.

"What did you say?"

"Our mother wouldn't allow us to have lice," I said. My voice seemed inordinately loud.

"It's just our policy," she said. "Now get moving. It's late."

We bedded down the first night in that same room, on the single cots made up with coarse cotton sheets and cream-colored wool blankets with a navy stripe around the edge. The light from the hallway bridged the high transom of the closed door, and I didn't sleep for a long time. Our presence there rebuked our mother, and I felt that humiliation as keenly as though I were she. I kept thinking, We'll be better when we go home—we'll work harder, knock down the cobwebs more often, check Jan Mary's homework, throw out the mismatched socks. Keeping domestic order was, inexplicably, bound up with being good, blessed. The fantasies that lulled me to sleep were of cupboards packed with thick folded towels, full cookie jars, an orderly abundance like perpetual fire against the night.

The next morning I lay there, warm but wet, with the covers up to my neck. Suzanne and Jan Mary were still asleep. A cat meowed urgently in the hallway. The windows were long and divided into panes of wavery old glass. Outside it was snowing; the dry, fine net of winter. There was an old cottonwood tree in the yard that had been struck by lightning some time ago. The split in the main trunk had been girdled with an iron band; it had healed, and now the scar tissue bloomed over the edge of the metal ring. I wondered what time it was and what would happen next. The procedure of moving, being dropped off like a litter of kittens, had been bad enough, and now I had to admit I'd wet the bed. I dreaded telling someone, but wanted to get it over with.

I thought of Mary in *The Secret Garden* and the way her spite protected her. I remembered the places I'd read the book: on the school steps at recess in second grade, under the cooling arms of a juniper tree when I was eleven. My own spite and anger could not protect me. They were repulsive thoughts I couldn't bear to admit to myself, because then I'd have to admit them to the priest. I'd told him once that I'd wished our mother would go away. I'd wished it for my birthday, which seemed to magnify the sin. He did not understand the power of wishes, and for penance he gave me a mere five Hail Marys. And now our mother *was* gone and I tried to imagine her inside the VA Hospital, but I could only picture the rusted iron bars, the flaking pink stucco walls. It was down by the Columbia River. The summer I was ten, a male patient people called *a crazy* had deliberately walked into the river and drowned.

The door opened, Mrs. Thompson peeked in, and Jan Mary and Suzanne sat up in their cots, their choppy hair all askew, eyes puffy with sleep.

"Time to get up, ladies," Mrs. Thompson said. She wore a robe of some soft peach fabric.

"Snow," Suzanne announced.

I threw back the covers, and the cool air sliced through my wet pajamas and chilled me. I forced myself to slither across the floor.

"Mrs. Thompson," I said officiously, as though I spoke of someone else, "I've wet the bed."

"Oh?"

"What shall I do?"

She stepped into the room and closed the door. "Does this happen often?" She walked to my cot, with me close behind.

"Roxie wet the bed, Roxie wet the bed," Jan Mary sang.

I flung her a murderous glare, which silenced her at once.

"Sometimes," I said vaguely. By this time I had no feelings in the matter. I'd killed them, the way you track down a mud dauber and squash him.

Mrs. Thompson quickly jerked the sheets from the bed and carried them into the bathroom, holding them at arm's length from her peachy robe.

"Please," I said. "Let me."

She dumped the sheets in the tub. "Run cold water on them. Add your pajamas. Rinse them good. Ask your sister to help you wring them out and then hang them over this shower curtain. When they dry, we'll put them in the dirty laundry." I felt I'd depleted whatever good will there'd been between us.

The entire six months at Entiat I followed this routine. I managed to keep from wetting the bed four times in that six months, by what miracle I could not tell. I tried prayers and wishes, not drinking water after six in the evening. Nothing worked. I lived in the Little Girls' House, though my age was borderline—they could have assigned me to the Big Girls' House. And every day all the little girls knew what I'd done when they saw my slick and gelid sheets hanging like Halloween ghosts in the bathroom.

Mrs. Hayes, the dorm mother of the Little Girls' House, had two immense tom-cats, Springer and Beau, whose claws had been removed. They lived like kings, always indoors. Everyone called the dorm mother Gabby Hayes behind her back. She was in her fifties and smelled of gardenias and cigarette smoke. Her lipstick was thick and cakey, the color of clay flower pots. She prided herself on her hair—it was coppery and resembled scrubbing pads we used in the kitchen. If someone broke the rules, she would announce to the group at large, "That's not allowed here." The chill in her voice always arrested the deviant.

Life in the Little Girls' House was orderly, neat, regulated. Before school in the morning we did our chores, young ones polishing the wooden stairs, older ones carting the laundry in duffle bags to the laundry building. Some were assigned kitchen duty, others bathrooms. Everyone, down to the four-year-olds, had work to do. I was impressed with the efficiency and equanimity with which work was accomplished. I wrote letters to our mother, in my experimental loopy left-hand slant, suggesting job charts on the refrigerator, new systems we could invent to relieve her of her crushing burden.

There were twenty-three of us. Jan Mary and Suzanne naturally gravitated toward others their age. They slept away from the oldest girls, in a drafty long hall near Mrs. Hayes's apartment. Our family ties were frayed, and I was genuinely surprised when I met Jan Mary's musing blue eyes in recognition across the dinner table. She seemed to be saying, How in the world did we arrive here?

The first day at the new school I was issued a faded blue cotton bloomer for PE. At St. Martin's, PE had meant softball on the playground. At the new school the locker room was my personal hell: the body smells, the safety-pinned bras, the stained slips, the hickeys, the pubic hair growing wild down our thighs. Sister Michael had always told us not to look at ourselves when we bathed, to be ashamed and vigilant. In the locker room we girls were elbow to elbow in the narrow aisle beside the dented pink lockers.

"What is your *problem*?"

"The F word. That's all he knows these days."

"My mother won't let me."

"Bud's getting a car for his birthday."

Their conversations shimmered around me like a beaded curtain. We couldn't help but see one another—our new breasts, our worn underwear—but the talk kept us on another plane, a place above the locker room, where we could pretend we weren't totally vulnerable, absolutely displayed.

Georgia Cowley, a squat freckled woman, ruled that class with a cruel hand. When I entered the gym for the first time, she waved sharply in my direction and I went over to her.

"Name?"

"Roxanne Miller."

"We're tumbling, Roxanne Miller," she said, writing something on her clipboard. "You ever tumbled?"

"No, ma'am." I looked at the girls casually turning cartwheels, blue blurs, on the hardwood floor. My hope of fading into the wrestling mats for the hour fluttered like a candle in a storm.

"Come out here with me," she said.

I followed her to the sweaty red mat in front of the stage.

"We start with forward rolls. Squat down."

I squatted, glancing desperately around to see if there was someone I could imitate. All motion had wound down, and the girls were gathered in gossip knots, chattering and watching me with slitted eyes. I remember staring at Miss Cowley's gym shoes; there were dried tomato seeds on the toes.

"Tuck your head. Now one foot forward, hands on the mat."

She gave me a little shove to propel me forward. I fell sideways, my pale thigh plopping fishlike on the floor. The girls giggled and hot tears swelled in my head. The seconds on the floor expanded, seemed to go on forever.

"Get up," she said. "Sit over there on the bleachers for a while and watch. You'll get the hang of it." Then she blew her chrome whistle, and the girls lined up to do their forward rolls.

On the bleachers, a Negro girl from Entiat, Nadine, slid next to me, sighing hard. "Got the curse," she said. "I'm sitting out."

"You can sit out?"

"Sure 'nough." She scratched her skinny calf. "You know the secret of cartwheels, Roxanne?"

"No," I said, interested, thinking there might be some secret I could learn from her, some intellectual knowledge that I could translate into body knowledge.

"Catch yourself before you kill yourself," she whispered, as she retied her sneaker. "Catch yo-*self*." And then she leaped up and turned a few, flinging herself into them with her own peculiar flick of her pink palms above her nappy head.

"Jefferson," Cowley barked. "Sit down and keep quiet."

For the rest of gym period, Nadine and I wrote messages on each other's backs, using our index fingers like pencils through the scratchy blue bloomer blouses.

At Christmas we were farmed out. I do not know how these decisions were made. Certainly I don't remember being asked where I would like to go for Christmas. Suzanne went with Mr. and Mrs. Thompson. Jan Mary was taken by Aunt Opal. I went to stay with the family of Darla Reamer, who had been our neighbor for five years. Darla was two years older than I was. When I'd been in fifth grade and Darla in seventh, we rode the school bus together and wrote love notes to one another using a special language we'd developed, a lispish baby talk in writing. Later that year she chose another girl as her best friend and left me miserable. Going to spend Christmas with her and her family, enduring their charity, was like an arduous school assignment I had to survive to attain the next grade. Her mother gave me a Shetland sweater and a jar of Pacquins hand cream. Her father took me out in the wind-crusted snowy field to see his apiary. We went to church, and those brief moments kneeling in the oak pew and at the altar, with its starlike poinsettias, were the only familiarity and peace I experienced. Darla spent many hours on the telephone with Julia, the one who'd taken my place. I was relieved when Mr. Reamer drove me back to Entiat on Christmas night. Many girls were still away and Mrs. Hayes let me stay up late. I drank hot chocolate alone in the dining room and wrote our mother a letter of false cheer and fantasy about the future.

In the older girls' sleeping quarters, after lights out, under cover of dark, some girls took turns revealing fears, shames, wishes expressed as truth. When this talk began, their voices shifted from the usual shrill razzmatazz repartee about hairstyles, boys at school, and who'd been caught smoking. They spoke in church whispers.

"My mother tore my lip once. I have five stitches."

"My father's coming to get me on my birthday."

I didn't participate in this round-robin, but instead lay on my stomach, my pillow buckled under my chest, and watched the occasional gossamer thread of headlights on the river road. It seemed there was so much freedom and purpose—a will at work—in night travel. Their talk was sad and low, and I, in my isolation, dreamed of going away, of having the power, the inestimable power, to say *I'm leaving*. Boys could somehow run away and make it, survive. But everyone knew that a girl's life was over if she ran away from home, or whatever had become home, whatever sheltered her from ruin.

Some nights, if we heard the rush of Mrs. Hayes's shower, we would sing in our thin voices a maudlin song that was popular at the time—"Teen Angel." One night the community of singing gave me courage, and after the song faded, I said, "I saw my mother hit my father with a belt."

As one they sucked in their breath. Then Nadine said, "No *wonder* your mama in the hospital, girl."

And the others laughed, a false, tentative snicker. I hated Nadine at that moment and felt heartbroken in my hate. I'd always tried to be nice to her, because our mother had said they were just like everyone else inside.

On Valentine's Day we received a crumpled package wrapped in a brown grocery sack and tied with butcher twine. Inside was a cellophane bag of hard candy hearts stamped BE MINE and I LOVE YOU. Our mother had enclosed three penny valentines and on mine she wrote, "I'm home now with Laura Jean and Christopher. See you soon." She was home! I'd given up on mail from her, but I'd kept writing. I tried to imagine her there with Christopher and the baby, without me to help her, and the thought made me feel invisible, unnecessary in the world. Don't think about it, I said to myself, and I began then the habit of blocking my thoughts with that simple chant. *Don't think about it.*

In April we were allowed to go home for a weekend.

"Your neighbor's here," Mrs. Hayes whispered in my ear, early that Saturday morning. "Help your sisters dress. I'll give him a tour while he's waiting."

I had a great deal to be excited about: seeing Christopher, going to our old church, being with our mother. Our mother. Her life without me was a puzzle, with crucial pieces missing. I had high hopes about going home. Our mother was well; everyone—Mrs. Hayes, Mr. Reamer—said so.

We met him by his pickup truck. His khakis were spattered with pastel paint; he said he'd been painting his bee boxes. We fell into silence on the drive home. The thought surfaced, like the devil's tempting forefinger, that though we were only an hour's drive from our mother, we hadn't seen her since that morning in December when we went to school not knowing life would be irrevocably changed by the time we returned home. Did she know that morning that she wouldn't see us for four months?

Spring was alive down in the valley. The daffodil leaves were up along the driveway, though the flowers were still just pale shadows of memory, curled tightly and green. Mr. Reamer parked his pickup truck and sat hunched, arms folded across the steering wheel, waiting for us to get out.

We were all shy, bashful, and I hung back, urging Jan Mary and Suzanne forward with little pushes on their shoulder blades.

Jan Mary flinched and said meanly, "Don't push."

"Don't spoil it now," I said.

And we three walked forward in a solemn row down the gravel drive toward the house. We wore our next-best-dresses. Mine was a taffeta plaid with a smocked bodice and a sash, and I'd worn my cream-colored knee highs, saving my one pair of nylons for Sunday morning. I hadn't wanted to go home in nylons—they were a new addition to my sock drawer and I was afraid our mother would say I was growing up too fast. The house looked the same, sagging at the roof corners, the gray paint blistering along the bottom of the door. It was a sunny day. Darla Reamer's cocker spaniel came yapping out the drive, flipping and bouncing the way cockers do. As we drew near the house, I saw that Darla was sitting with our mother in that small patch of grass in front of the house. Someone had put a wooden cable spool there for a table, and Darla and Mother sat near each other in lawn chairs. Darla was painting Mother's fingernails.

"Here come my girls," Mother said, waving her free hand.

Music was on inside the house and we could hear it through the open window: *you made me love you.* I didn't know what to do with Darla there. I'd imagined our mother embracing us, welcoming us, with significance. My heart sank in disappointment, a rancid feeling, everything going sour at once. Suzanne, being only four, went right up to our mother and slipped her little arms around her neck and kissed her cheek. Jan Mary said, "Will you do mine, too, Darla?"

Laura Jean started crying from somewhere in the house. Mother, startled, rose partway from her chair and then sank back, waving her wet fingernails and looking helplessly at Darla. There was a raw, clean smell about the yard, like cornsilk when you go outside to shuck corn in the summer dusk. Darla looked older, in a straight linen skirt with a kick pleat in the back. She had on slim flats and tan-tinted nylons. Her hair was in a French roll.

"I'll get her," Darla said, and she went in the house, letting the screen door slam. Suzanne was close on her heels.

Mother pulled me near, her arm around my waist. "How's my big girl?" she asked. She'd had her black hair frizzed in a permanent wave and her nails were painted fire-engine red. With one hand she shook a Lucky from the pack on the table. A glass of whiskey and melting ice was on the ground beside her chair. Her knuckles looked pink, but the cuts and splits were healed.

"Fine," I said.

"Darla's been helping me," she said.

I held my breath to keep from crying.

I felt exhausted, not the clean exhaustion of after-dark softball but a kind of weariness. I was worn out with the knowledge that life would be different, but not in the way I had imagined or hoped. I didn't want to forgive her for being the way she was, but you have to forgive your mother. She searched my eyes and tried to make some long-ago connection, sweet scrutiny, perhaps the way she'd looked at me when I was a new baby, her first baby. I looked away. Jan Mary gnawed delicately at her cuticles. Christopher came around the corner of the house swinging his Mickey Mantle bat, his leather mitt looped on his belt. The new spring leaves were so bright they hurt my eyes.

# Gish Jen

B. 1956

Gish Jen was born in Scarsdale, New York, as a second-generation Chinese American, whose parents emigrated from China during World War II. She earned a B.A. from Harvard University in 1977 and completed an M.F.A. at the University of Iowa in 1983. Jen's fiction is marked by a distinctively comic voice that beckons the reader to participate in the story at an intimate level. Although she writes about Chinese American characters, she is also interested in the cultural collisions that occur in African American, Jewish American, and Irish American families. Jen has published two novels, *Typical American* (1991) and *Mona in the Promised Land* (1996), both of which tell the story of the Chang family (first encountered in her short story "In the American Society"), Chinese immigrants who are forced to adapt to American society's behaviors and values in the hope of achieving the American dream. Jen's collection of short stories, *Who's Irish?* was published in 1999 and includes new and previously published works.

---

## In the American Society
1991

### I.  His Own Society

When my father took over the pancake house, it was to send my little sister Mona and me to college. We were only in junior high at the time, but my father believed in getting a jump on things. "Those Americans always saying it," he told us. "Smart guys thinking in advance." My mother elaborated, explaining that businesses took bringing up, like children. They could take years to get going, she said, years.

In this case, though, we got rich right away. At two months we were breaking even, and at four, those same hotcakes that could barely withstand the weight of butter and syrup were supporting our family with ease. My mother bought a station wagon with air conditioning, my father an oversized, red vinyl recliner for the back room; and as time went on and the business continued to thrive, my father started to talk about his grandfather and the village he had reigned over in China—things my father had never talked about when he worked for other people. He told us about the bags of rice his family would give out to the poor at New Year's, and about the people who came to beg, on their hands and knees, for his grandfather to intercede for the more wayward of their relatives. "Like that Godfather in the movie," he would tell us as, his feet up, he distributed paychecks. Sometimes an employee would get two green envelopes instead of one, which meant that Jimmy needed a tooth pulled, say, or that Tiffany's husband was in the clinker again.

"It's nothing, nothing," he would insist, sinking back into his chair. "Who else is going to take care of you people?"

My mother would mostly just sigh about it. "Your father thinks this is China," she would say, and then she would go back to her mending. Once in a while, though, when my father had given away a particularly large sum, she would exclaim, outraged, "But this here is the U—S—of—A!"—this apparently having been what she used to tell immigrant stock boys when they came in late.

She didn't work at the supermarket anymore; but she had made it to the rank of manager before she left, and this had given her not only new words and phrases, but new ideas about herself, and about America, and about what was what in general. She had opinions, now, on how downtown should be zoned; she could pump her own gas and check her own oil; and for all she used to chide Mona and me for being "copy-cats," she herself was now interested in espadrilles, and wallpaper, and most recently, the town country club.

"So join already," said Mona, flicking a fly off her knee.

My mother enumerated the problems as she sliced up a quarter round of water-melon: There was the cost. There was the waiting list. There was the fact that no one in our family played either tennis or golf.

"So what?" said Mona.

"It would be waste," said my mother.

"Me and Callie can swim in the pool."

"Plus you need that recommendation letter from a member."

"Come *on*," said Mona. "Annie's mom'd write you a letter in *sec.*"

My mother's knife glinted in the early summer sun. I spread some more newspa-per on the picnic table.

"*Plus* you have to eat there twice a month. You know what that means." My mother cut another, enormous slice of fruit.

"No, I *don't* know what that means," said Mona.

"It means Dad would have to wear a jacket, dummy," I said.

"Oh! Oh! Oh!" said Mona, clasping her hand to her breast. "Oh! Oh! Oh! Oh! Oh!"

We all laughed: my father had no use for nice clothes, and would wear only ten-year-old shirts, with grease-spotted pants, to show how little he cared what anyone thought.

"Your father doesn't believe in joining the American society," said my mother. "He wants to have his own society."

"So go to dinner without him." Mona shot her seeds out in long arcs over the lawn. "Who cares what he thinks?"

But of course we all did care, and knew my mother could not simply up and do as she pleased. For in my father's mind, a family owed its head a degree of loyalty that left no room for dissent. To embrace what he embraced was to love; and to embrace something else was to betray him.

He demanded a similar sort of loyalty of his workers, whom he treated more like servants than employees. Not in the beginning, of course. In the beginning all he wanted was for them to keep on doing what they used to do, and to that end he concentrated mostly on leaving them alone. As the months passed, though, he expected more and more of them, with the result that for all his largesse, he began to have trouble keeping help. The cooks and busboys complained that he asked them to fix radiators and trim hedges, not only at the restaurant, but at our house; the waitresses that he sent them on errands and made them chauffeur him around. Our head waitress, Gertrude, claimed that he once even asked her to scratch his back.

"It's not just the blacks don't believe in slavery," she said when she quit.

My father never quite registered her complaint, though, nor those of the others who left. Even after Eleanor quit, then Tiffany, then Gerald, and Jimmy, and even his best cook, Eureka Andy, for whom he had bought new glasses, he remained mostly convinced that the fault lay with them.

"All they understand is that assembly line," he lamented. "Robots, they are. They want to be robots."

There *were* occasions when the clear running truth seemed to eddy, when he would pinch the vinyl of his chair up into little peaks and wonder if he was doing things right. But with time he would always smooth the peaks back down; and when business started to slide in the spring, he kept on like a horse in his ways.

By the summer our dishboy was overwhelmed with scraping. It was no longer just the hashbrowns that people were leaving for trash, and the service was as bad as the food. The waitresses served up French pancakes instead of German, apple juice instead of orange, spilt things on laps, on coats. On the Fourth of July some greenhorn sent an entire side of fries slaloming down a lady's *massif centrale*.[1] Meanwhile in the back room, my father labored through articles on the economy.

"What is housing starts?" he puzzled. "What is GNP?"

Mona and I did what we could, filling in as busgirls and bookkeepers and, one afternoon, stuffing the comments box that hung by the cashier's desk. That was Mona's idea. We rustled up a variety of pens and pencils, checked boxes for an hour, smeared the cards up with coffee and grease, and waited. It took a few days for my father to notice that the box was full, and he didn't say anything about it for a few days more. Finally, though, he started to complain of fatigue; and then he began to complain that the staff was not what it could be. We encouraged him in this—pointing out, for instance, how many dishes got chipped—but in the end all that happened was that, for the first time since we took over the restaurant, my father got it into his head to fire someone. Skip, a skinny busboy who was saving up for a sportscar, said nothing as my father mumbled on about the price of dishes. My father's hands shook as he wrote out the severance check; and he spent the rest of the day napping in his chair once it was over.

As it was going on midsummer, Skip wasn't easy to replace. We hung a sign in the window and advertised in the paper, but no one called the first week, and the person

---

1 *massif centrale:* A mountainous plateau in the Auvergne region of France.

who called the second didn't show up for his interview. The third week, my father phoned Skip to see if he would come back, but a friend of his had already sold him a Corvette for cheap.

Finally a Chinese guy named Booker turned up. He couldn't have been more than thirty, and was wearing a lighthearted seersucker suit, but he looked as though life had him pinned: his eyes were bloodshot and his chest sunken, and the muscles of his neck seemed to strain with the effort of holding his head up. In a single dry breath he told us that he had never bussed tables but was willing to learn, and that he was on the lam from the deportation authorities.

"I do not want to lie to you," he kept saying. He had come to the United States on a student visa, had run out of money, and was now in a bind. He was loath to go back to Taiwan, as it happened—he looked up at this point, to be sure my father wasn't pro-KMT[2]—but all he had was a phony social security card and a willingness to absorb all blame, should anything untoward come to pass.

"I do not think, anyway, that it is against law to hire me, only to be me," he said, smiling faintly.

Anyone else would have examined him on this, but my father conceived of laws as speed bumps rather than curbs. He wiped the counter with his sleeve, and told Booker to report the next morning.

"I will be good worker," said Booker.

"Good," said my father.

"Anything you want me to do, I will do."

My father nodded.

Booker seemed to sink into himself for a moment. "Thank you," he said finally. "I am appreciate your help. I am very, very appreciate for everything." He reached out to shake my father's hand.

My father looked at him. "Did you eat today?" he asked in Mandarin.

Booker pulled at the hem of his jacket.

"Sit down," said my father. "Please, have a seat."

My father didn't tell my mother about Booker, and my mother didn't tell my father about the country club. She would never have applied, except that Mona, while over at Annie's, had let it drop that our mother wanted to join. Mrs. Lardner came by the very next day.

"Why, I'd be honored and delighted to write you people a letter," she said. Her skirt billowed around her.

"Thank you so much," said my mother. "But it's too much trouble for you, and also my husband is . . ."

"Oh, it's no trouble at all, no trouble at all. I tell you." She leaned forward so that her chest freckles showed. "I know just how it is. It's a secret of course, but you know, my natural father was Jewish. Can you see it? Just look at my skin."

2 KMT: Kuomintang, the Chinese "national people's party," a political party once dominant and often at war with the Communist Party in China and Taiwan.

"My husband," said my mother.

"I'd be honored and delighted," said Mrs. Lardner with a little wave of her hands. "Just honored and delighted."

Mona was triumphant. "See, Mom," she said, waltzing around the kitchen when Mrs. Lardner left. "What did I tell you? 'I'm just honored and delighted, just honored and delighted.'" She waved her hands in the air.

"You know, the Chinese have a saying," said my mother. "To do nothing is better than to overdo. You mean well, but you tell me now what will happen."

"I'll talk Dad into it," said Mona, still waltzing. "Or I bet Callie can. He'll do anything Callie says."

"I can try, anyway," I said.

"Did you hear what I said?" said my mother. Mona bumped into the broom closet door. "You're not going to talk anything; you've already made enough trouble." She started on the dishes with a clatter.

Mona poked diffidently at a mop.

I sponged off the counter. "Anyway," I ventured. "I bet our name'll never even come up."

"That's if we're lucky," said my mother.

"There's all these people waiting," I said.

"Good," she said. She started on a pot.

I looked over at Mona, who was still cowering in the broom closet. "In fact, there's some black family's been waiting so long, they're going to sue," I said.

My mother turned off the water. "Where'd you hear that?"

"Patty told me."

She turned the water back on, started to wash a dish, then put it back down and shut the faucet.

"I'm sorry," said Mona.

"Forget it," said my mother. "Just forget it."

Booker turned out to be a model worker, whose boundless gratitude translated into a willingness to do anything. As he also learned quickly, he soon knew not only how to bus, but how to cook, and how to wait table, and how to keep the books. He fixed the walk-in door so that it stayed shut, reupholstered the torn seats in the dining room, and devised a system for tracking inventory. The only stone in the rice was that he tended to be sickly; but, reliable even in illness, he would always send a friend to take his place. In this way we got to know Ronald, Lynn, Dirk, and Cedric, all of whom, like Booker, had problems with their legal status and were anxious to please. They weren't all as capable as Booker, though, with the exception of Cedric, whom my father often hired even when Booker was well. A round wag of a man who called Mona and me *shou hou*—skinny monkeys—he was a professed non-smoker who was nevertheless always begging drags off of other people's cigarettes. This last habit drove our head cook, Fernando, crazy, especially since, when refused a hit, Cedric would occasionally snitch one. Winking impishly at Mona and me, he would steal up to an ashtray, take a quick puff, and then break out laughing so that the smoke came rolling out of his

mouth in a great incriminatory cloud. Fernando accused him of stealing fresh cigarettes too, even whole packs.

"Why else do you think he's weaseling around in the back of the store all the
time," he said. His face was blotchy with anger. "The man is a frigging thief."

Other members of the staff supported him in this contention and joined in on an
"Operation Identification," which involved numbering and initialing their cigarettes—
even though what they seemed to fear for wasn't so much their cigarettes as their jobs.
Then one of the cooks quit; and rather than promote someone, my father hired
Cedric for the position. Rumors flew that he was taking only half the normal salary,
that Alex had been pressured to resign, and that my father was looking for a position
with which to placate Booker, who had been bypassed because of his health.

The result was that Fernando categorically refused to work with Cedric.

"The only way I'll cook with that piece of slime," he said, shaking his huge tattooed fist, "is if it's his ass frying on the grill."

My father cajoled and cajoled, to no avail, and in the end was simply forced to put
them on different schedules.

The next week Fernando got caught stealing a carton of minute steaks. My father
would not tell even Mona and me how he knew to be standing by the back door when
Fernando was on his way out, but everyone suspected Booker. Everyone but Fernando,
that is, who was sure Cedric had been the tip-off. My father held a staff meeting in which
he tried to reassure everyone that Alex had left on his own, and that he had no intention
of firing anyone. But though he was careful not to mention Fernando, everyone was
so amazed that he was being allowed to stay that Fernando was incensed nonetheless.

"Don't you all be putting your bug eyes on me," he said. "*He's* the frigging crook."
He grabbed Cedric by the collar.

Cedric raised an eyebrow. "Cook, you mean," he said.

At this Fernando punched Cedric in the mouth; and the words he had just uttered notwithstanding, my father fired him on the spot.

With everything that was happening, Mona and I were ready to be getting out of the
restaurant. It was almost time: the days were still stuffy with summer, but our window
shade had started flapping in the evening as if gearing up to go out. That year the
breezes were full of salt, as they sometimes were when they came in from the East, and
they blew anchors and docks through my mind like so many tumbleweeds, filling my
dreams with wherries and lobsters and grainy-faced men who squinted, day in and
day out, at the sky.

It was time for a change, you could feel it; and yet the pancake house was the
same as ever. The day before school started my father came home with bad news.

"Fernando called police," he said, wiping his hand on his pant leg.

My mother naturally wanted to know what police; and so with much coughing
and hawing, the long story began, the latest installment of which had the police calling immigration, and immigration sending an investigator. My mother sat stiff as
whalebone as my father described how the man summarily refused lunch on the
house and how my father had admitted, under pressure, that he knew there were
"things" about his workers.

"So now what happens?"

My father didn't know. "Booker and Cedric went with him to the jail," he said. "But me, here I am." He laughed uncomfortably.

The next day my father posted bail for "his boys" and waited apprehensively for something to happen. The day after that he waited again, and the day after that he called our neighbor's law student son, who suggested my father call the immigration department under an alias. My father took his advice; and it was thus that he discovered that Booker was right: it was illegal for aliens to work, but it wasn't to hire them.

In the happy interval that ensued, my father apologized to my mother, who in turn confessed about the country club, for which my father had no choice but to forgive her. Then he turned his attention back to "his boys."

My mother didn't see that there was anything to do.

"I like to talking to the judge," said my father.

"This is not China," said my mother.

"I'm only talking to him. I'm not give him money unless he wants it."

"You're going to land up in jail."

"So what else I should do?" My father threw up his hands. "Those are my boys."

"Your boys!" exploded my mother. "What about your family? What about your wife?"

My father took a long sip of tea. "You know," he said finally. "In the war my father sent our cook to the soldiers to use. He always said it—the province comes before the town, the town comes before the family."

"A restaurant is not a town," said my mother.

My father sipped at his tea again. "You know, when I first come to the United States, I also had to hide-and-seek with those deportation guys. If people did not helping me, I'm not here today."

My mother scrutinized her hem.

After a minute I volunteered that before seeing a judge, he might try a lawyer.

He turned. "Since when did you become so afraid like your mother?"

I started to say that it wasn't a matter of fear, but he cut me off.

"What I need today," he said, "is a son."

My father and I spent the better part of the next day standing in lines at the immigration office. He did not get to speak to a judge, but with much persistence he managed to speak to a judge's clerk, who tried to persuade him that it was not her place to extend him advice. My father, though, shamelessly plied her with compliments and offers of free pancakes until she finally conceded that she personally doubted anything would happen to either Cedric or Booker.

"Especially if they're 'needed workers,'" she said, rubbing at the red marks her glasses left on her nose. She yawned. "Have you thought about sponsoring them to become permanent residents?"

Could he do that? My father was overjoyed. And what if he saw to it right away? Would she perhaps put in a good word with the judge?

She yawned again, her nostrils flaring. "Don't worry," she said. "They'll get a fair hearing."

My father returned jubilant. Booker and Cedric hailed him as their savior, their Buddha incarnate. He was like a father to them, they said; and laughing and clapping, they made him tell the story over and over, sorting over the details like jewels. And how old was the assistant judge? And what did she say?

That evening my father tipped the paperboy a dollar and bought a pot of mums for my mother, who suffered them to be placed on the dining room table. The next night he took us all out to dinner. Then on Saturday, Mona found a letter on my father's chair at the restaurant.

> Dear Mr. Chang,
> You are the grat boss. But, we do not like to trial, so will runing away now. Plese to excus us. People saying the law in America is fears like dragon. Here is only $140. We hope some day we can pay back the rest bale. You will getting intrest, as you diserving, so grat a boss you are. Thank you for every thing. In next life you will be burn in rich family, with no more pancaks.
>
> Yours truley,
> Booker + Cedric

In the weeks that followed my father went to the pancake house for crises, but otherwise hung around our house, fiddling idly with the sump pump and boiler in an effort, he said, to get ready for winter. It was as though he had gone into retirement, except that instead of moving south, he had moved to the basement. He even took to showering my mother with little attentions, and to calling her "old girl," and when we finally heard that the club had entertained all the applications it could for the year, he was so sympathetic that he seemed more disappointed than my mother.

## II.   In the American Society

Mrs. Lardner tempered the bad news with an invitation to a bon voyage "bash" she was throwing for a friend of hers who was going to Greece for six months.

"Do come," she urged. "You'll meet everyone, and then, you know, if things open up in the spring . . ." She waved her hands.

My mother wondered if it would be appropriate to show up at a party for someone they didn't know, but "the honest truth" was that this was an annual affair. "If it's not Greece, it's Antibes," sighed Mrs. Lardner. "We really just do it because his wife left him and his daughter doesn't speak to him, and poor Jeremy just feels so *unloved.*"

She also invited Mona and me to the goings on, as "*demi*-guests" to keep Annie out of the champagne. I wasn't too keen on the idea, but before I could say anything, she had already thanked us for so generously agreeing to honor her with our presence.

"A pair of little princesses, you are!" she told us. "A pair of princesses!"

The party was that Sunday. On Saturday, my mother took my father out shopping for a suit. As it was the end of September, she insisted that he buy a worsted rather than a seersucker, even though it was only ten, rather than fifty percent off. My father protested that it was as hot out as ever, which was true—a thick Indian summer had cozied murderously up to us—but to no avail. Summer clothes, said my mother, were not properly worn after Labor Day.

The suit was unfortunately as extravagant in length as it was in price, which posed an additional quandary, since the tailor wouldn't be in until Monday. The salesgirl, though, found a way of tacking it up temporarily.

"Maybe this suit not fit me," fretted my father.

"Just don't take your jacket off," said the salesgirl.

He gave her a tip before they left, but when he got home refused to remove the price tag.

"I like to asking the tailor about the size," he insisted.

"You mean you're going to *wear* it and then *return* it?" Mona rolled her eyes.

"I didn't say I'm return it," said my father stiffly. "I like to asking the tailor, that's all."

The party started off swimmingly, except that most people were wearing bermudas or wrap skirts. Still, my parents carried on, sharing with great feeling the complaints about the heat. Of course my father tried to eat a cracker full of shallots and burnt himself in an attempt to help Mr. Lardner turn the coals of the barbeque; but on the whole he seemed to be doing all right. Not nearly so well as my mother, though, who had accepted an entire cupful of Mrs. Lardner's magic punch, and seemed indeed to be under some spell. As Mona and Annie skirmished over whether some boy in their class inhaled when he smoked, I watched my mother take off her shoes, laughing and laughing as a man with a beard regaled her with navy stories by the pool. Apparently he had been stationed in the Orient and remembered a few words of Chinese, which made my mother laugh still more. My father excused himself to go to the men's room then drifted back and weighed anchor at the hors d'oeuvres table, while my mother sailed on to a group of women, who tinkled at length over the clarity of her complexion. I dug out a book I had brought.

Just when I'd cracked the spine, though, Mrs. Lardner came by to bewail her shortage of servers. Her caterers were criminals, I agreed; and the next thing I knew I was handing out bits of marine life, making the rounds as amiably as I could.

"Here you go, Dad," I said when I got to the hors d'oeuvres table.

"Everything is fine," he said.

I hesitated to leave him alone; but then the man with the beard zeroed in on him, and though he talked of nothing but my mother, I thought it would be okay to get back to work. Just that moment, though, Jeremy Brothers lurched our way, an empty, albeit corked, wine bottle in hand. He was a slim, well-proportioned man, with a Roman nose and small eyes and a nice manly jaw that he allowed to hang agape.

"Hello," he said drunkenly. "Pleased to meet you."

"Pleased to meeting you," said my father.

"Right," said Jeremy. "Right. Listen. I have this bottle here, this most recalcitrant bottle. You see that it refuses to do my bidding. I bid it open sesame, please, and it does nothing." He pulled the cork out with his teeth, then turned the bottle upside down.

My father nodded.

"Would you have a word with it please?" said Jeremy. The man with the beard excused himself. "Would you please have a goddamned word with it?"

My father laughed uncomfortably.

"Ah!" Jeremy bowed a little. "Excuse me, excuse me, excuse me. You are not my man, not my man at all." He bowed again and started to leave, but then circled back. "Viticulture is not your forte, yes I can see that, see that plainly. But may I trouble you on another matter? Forget the damned bottle." He threw it into the pool, and winked at the people he splashed. "I have another matter. Do you speak Chinese?"

My father said he did not, but Jeremy pulled out a handkerchief with some characters on it anyway, saying that his daughter had sent it from Hong Kong and that he thought the characters might be some secret message.

"Long life," said my father.

"But you haven't looked at it yet."

"I know what it says without looking." My father winked at me.

"You do?"

"Yes, I do."

"You're making fun of me, aren't you?"

"No, no, no," said my father, winking again.

"Who are you anyway?" said Jeremy.

His smile fading, my father shrugged.

"*Who are you?*"

My father shrugged again.

Jeremy began to roar. "This is my party, *my party,* and I've never seen you before in my life." My father backed up as Jeremy came toward him. "*Who are you? WHO ARE YOU?*"

Just as my father was going to step back into the pool, Mrs. Lardner came running up. Jeremy informed her that there was a man crashing his party.

"Nonsense," said Mrs. Lardner. "This is Ralph Chang, who I invited extra especially so he could meet you." She straightened the collar of Jeremy's peach-colored polo shirt for him.

"Yes, well, we've had a chance to chat," said Jeremy.

She whispered in his ear; he mumbled something; she whispered something more.

"I do apologize," he said finally.

My father didn't say anything.

"I do." Jeremy seemed genuinely contrite. "Doubtless you've seen drunks before, haven't you? You must have them in China."

"Okay," said my father.

As Mrs. Lardner glided off, Jeremy clapped his arm over my father's shoulders. "You know, I really am quite sorry, quite sorry."

My father nodded.

"What can I do, how can I make it up to you?"

"No thank you."

"No, tell me, tell me," wheedled Jeremy. "Tickets to casino night?" My father shook his head. "You don't gamble. Dinner at Bartholomew's?" My father shook his head again. "You don't eat." Jeremy scratched his chin. "You know, my wife was like you. Old Annabelle could never let me make things up—never, never, never, never, never."

My father wriggled out from under his arm.

"How about sport clothes? You are rather overdressed, you know, excuse me for saying so. But here." He took off his polo shirt and folded it up. "You can have this with my most profound apologies." He ruffled his chest hairs with his free hand.

"No thank you," said my father.

"No, take it, take it. Accept my apologies." He thrust the shirt into my father's arms. "I'm so very sorry, so very sorry. Please, try it on."

Helplessly holding the shirt, my father searched the crowd for my mother.

"Here, I'll help you off with your coat."

My father froze.

Jeremy reached over and took his jacket off. "Milton's, one hundred twenty-five dollars reduced to one hundred twelve-fifty," he read. "What a bargain, what a bargain!"

"Please give it back," pleaded my father. "Please."

"Now for your shirt," ordered Jeremy.

Heads began to turn.

"Take off your shirt."

"I do not take orders like a servant," announced my father.

"Take off your shirt, or I'm going to throw this jacket right into the pool, just right into this little pool here." Jeremy held it over the water.

"Go ahead."

"One hundred twelve-fifty," taunted Jeremy. "One hundred twelve . . ."

My father flung the polo shirt into the water with such force that part of it bounced back up into the air like a fluorescent fountain. Then it settled into a soft heap on top of the water. My mother hurried up.

"You're a sport!" said Jeremy, suddenly breaking into a smile and slapping my father on the back. "You're a sport! I like that. A man with spirit, that's what you are. A man with panache. Allow me to return to you your jacket." He handed it back to my father. "Good value you got on that, good value."

My father hurled the coat into the pool too. "We're leaving," he said grimly. "Leaving!"

"Now, Ralphie," said Mrs. Lardner, bustling up; but my father was already stomping off.

"Get your sister," he told me. To my mother: "Get your shoes."

"That was *great*, Dad," said Mona as we walked down to the car. "You were *stupendous*."

"Way to show 'em," I said.

"What?" said my father offhandedly.

Although it was only just dusk, we were in a gulch, which made it hard to see anything except the gleam of his white shirt moving up the hill ahead of us.

"It was all my fault," began my mother.

"Forget it," said my father grandly. Then he said, "The only trouble is I left those keys in my jacket pocket."

"Oh *no*," said Mona.

"Oh no is right," said my mother.

"So we'll walk home," I said.

"But how're we going to get into the *house*," said Mona.

The noise of the party churned through the silence.

"Someone has to going back," said my father.

"Let's go to the pancake house first," suggested my mother. "We can wait there until the party is finished, and then call Mrs. Lardner."

Having all agreed that that was a good plan, we started walking again.

"God, just think," said Mona. "We're going to have to *dive* for them."

My father stopped a moment. We waited.

"You girls are good swimmers," he said finally. "Not like me."

Then his shirt started moving again, and we trooped up the hill after it, into the dark.

# Le Minh Khue

## (B. 1949)

A veteran of the Vietnam/American War, Le Minh Khue served as a member of the Youth Volunteers Brigade and as a war correspondent for Tien Phong and Giai Phong. She is one of the leading writers in Vietnam. Khue coedited *The Other Side of Heaven: Postwar Fiction by Vietnamese and American Writers* (1995) with Wayne Karlin and Truong Vu. Her collection of short stories, *The Stars, the Earth, the River* (1997) is heavily grounded in Khue's personal history. She currently serves as the chief fiction editor at the Vietnam Writers' Association Publishing House in Hanoi.

---

## *The Distant Stars*                                        1997

TRANSLATED BY BAC HOAI TRAN AND DANA SACHS

There were three of us. Three girls. We lived in a cavern at the foot of a strategic hill. The trail led past the front of the cave and on up the hillside somewhere, very far. It had been punctured by bombs, mixing the red and white soil together. Neither side of the trail had any sign of vegetation. There were only stripped and burned tree trunks, uprooted trees, boulders, and a few empty gas cans and twisted parts of vehicles, rusting in the earth.

Our job was to sit there. Whenever a bomb exploded, we had to run up, figure out how much earth was needed to fill the hole, count the unexploded bombs, and, if necessary, detonate them. They called us the Ground Reconnaissance Team. That title inspired in us a passion to do heroic deeds and therefore our work was not that simple. The bombs often buried us. Sometimes, when we came down from the hill we were so covered in dirt that only our gleaming eyes showed through. When we laughed, our teeth glowed out of our grimy faces. At those moments, we called each other the "Black-Eyed Demons."

Our unit took good care of us. When they had something to eat, they would say, "Leave some for the Recon Team, because they're up there."

It was easy to understand that. The unit often went out at sunset and sometimes they worked all night. But, as for us, we had to be up there even in the daylight. And being out on that hill in the daytime was no fun. Death was a serious guy. He hid himself inside the bombs. But every job has its own pleasures. Where else could you experience smoking earth, trembling air, or the roar of airplanes that only gradually fades away? Where else could you experience taut nerves, an erratic heartbeat and the knowledge that all around lay unexploded bombs. Maybe they'd explode now or maybe in another moment. But definitely they would explode.

When we finished, we'd go back and take one more look at the road, breathe with relief, and dash back into the cave. Outside, it was over 30 degrees celsius, so when we crawled into the cave, we entered a different world. The chill made our bodies suddenly begin to shiver. Then we'd turn our heads up to drink some sugared spring water from our canteens. After that, we'd stretch out on the damp ground and squint our eyes while listening to the music on our tiny radio, for which we always had batteries. Maybe we'd listen closely, maybe just think about things.

It seemed like we were about to start a big offensive. Every night, a stream of vehicles drove by on the trail. At night we usually could sleep. But for the past few nights it had been impossible. Two of us carried our spades up to the strategic hill, where we had fun joking with the drivers. Too bad for the one who had to stay in the cave to answer the two-way radio.

It was noon and very quiet. I sat leaning against the stone wall, humming a song. I loved to sing. Often I would memorize a certain melody and then make up my own words. My lyrics were so confused and silly that they sometimes surprised me and made me burst out laughing all by myself.

I was a Hanoi girl. To put it modestly, I was impressive. My ponytails were thick and relatively soft. My neck was graceful and I stood as proud as a lily. And as for my eyes, the drivers would say, "You have such a distant look in your eyes."

Regardless of how distant the look was, I liked to hold the mirror and gaze into my own eyes. They were long and narrow, brown, and were often squinted as if from a glare.

It puzzled me that the drivers and artillery men often asked about me. Either they asked about me or they sent me long letters as if we were thousands of kilometers apart, although we could greet each other in person every day. I never made an effort to please them. Whenever the girls grouped together to talk to some eloquent army man, I always stood aloof, looking elsewhere, my lips tightly sealed. But I was only striking a pose. The truth is that in my thoughts, the most handsome, intelligent, courageous and noble men were these, the men who wore military uniforms with stars on their caps.

I never said that to anyone, but the men who went by on the trail still sent me their greetings in a respectful and affectionate manner.

"You sing well, you look pretty decent, and you are an expert at detonating bombs," my friends explained. Though of course, that was not accurate.

Outside, it was still quiet. Ever since ten in the morning, no planes had flown past the strategic hill. They'd only dropped bombs further inland, as we could tell from the reverberations. It was precisely this low, seemingly fragile rumble, carried here on the wind, that made the quiet more tense, as if it were heralding something fierce. The sun burned. The wind was dry. But inside the cave, it was cool.

Each of us had her own hobby. Nho was embroidering a pillow. Thao was copying a song into a small journal balanced on her thigh. The two of them were talking, but I hadn't listened to the first part. Then, I suddenly began to pay attention.

"When will it be over?" Nho asked.

"When will what be over?" Thao didn't look up, but her voice betrayed some surprise.

Nho yawned. Then they were quiet. I knew what she meant. She would have said that when the war was over she wanted a job in a big hydroelectric plant. She would work as a welder and play on the plant's volleyball team. She would try to really slam the ball and—who knew?—with luck she might be selected for the Northern team.

As for Thao, she wanted to become a doctor. Her husband would be a captain in the military who would travel to distant places and sport a beard. She had no desire to live by his side every day because love would quickly become boring.

I also often talked about my own plans. I had many wishes, but I still didn't know my priorities. Perhaps to become an architect? How interesting! A voice-over artist in a children's movie theater? A freight driver on the wharf? Or a singer in a choir at a construction site? Any of those careers would mean happiness. I would be as enthusiastic and creative as I was now, out here at our strategic hill, where wishes and desires were born.

But these things were for later. After the war. When the trail we were protecting here was evenly paved with asphalt. Electricity would flow on wires deep into the forest and timber mills would run all day and all night. All three of us understood this. We understood and believed it with a fierce faith.

The pillow in Nho's hands was dainty and white. She embroidered careless and gaudy flowers. She made the borders thick as ropes. If anyone criticized her efforts, she would ignore the criticism and her hand would move ahead with the needle as if nothing had happened. When they really let her have it, she would bite her lips, tear the thread between her two even rows of teeth and raise her voice to a falsetto, saying, "I want it to be different!"

Nho was rather peculiar—on the one hand, affectionate and cheerful and, on the other, very stubborn. Those traits were not contradictory, but, rather, complementary, and they caused Nho to have a rather rare personality. She had lived with me ever since I first arrived at this strategic hill. At that time, everything was strange to me. I was shocked when people first ordered me to go and haul dirt.

"Young volunteers have to do this? Haul dirt?" (I couldn't have imagined it. I thought that we would be carrying guns, marching in force within a forest so deep we couldn't even see the moon or the stars. Our speech would be strong and terse, just like the slogans.)

But I just hauled dirt. And then I got used to it.

Many meals we had no broth, so we girls poured drinking water over our rice. We did this in public and we looked so miserable that some of the men cried out in pity. The first time we heard the sound of the bombs, some of us were so scared we lay down and hugged the earth.

But now we'd gotten used to it.

I joined the unit after Nho. That day, I looked lost as I set my knapsack down on a log behind the barracks. Nho walked up from the stream. Her hair was wet. Drops of water remained on her forehead and her nose. The water in the stream must have been abundant. Maybe people could swim in it, I thought. Nho paused for only a second, then approached me without saying a word, her hands busily wringing her wet washcloth. She tossed her head once, then swept her haughty eyes from the tip of my head to the mud-covered shoes that I was rubbing hard against each other.

"What unit sent you here? Where are you from? What's your name?"

I stopped rubbing my shoes together and stood ready. In my military training classes at school, I had studied martial arts. I set my arms akimbo, taking a guarded position and deliberated over whether I should punch her. Where should I punch her first? I would just hit lightly at one of her vital points. On her hand.

But at that moment, Nho turned around and stuck her hands into her trouser pockets.

"Go to headquarters," she motioned with her chin, taking off in front of me.

Of course, we'd paid a lot of attention to each other since then. Gradually, we got to know each other and at some point we became friends. Both of us had just turned seventeen. That a veteran bullied a newcomer a bit wasn't something worth resenting. It turned out that I liked her. She had a remarkable character. The boys had great respect for her, although they sometimes still managed to tease her.

Like me, Nho liked independence. We would say to each other, "From now until we're old, we'll have romance but we'll never marry. Marriage would mean too much work. Diapers. Blankets. Mosquito nets. Sawdust. Fish sauce. There would be no time left for fun. In love, he'll take you to the movies. He'll be sweet to you when you sulk. You'll have plenty of time to read books."

Nho had a guy who worked as an engineer in a machine shop. He diligently wrote to her and his letters were often so long that reading them wore your eyes out.

He justified himself, saying, "In Hanoi, people have more time than at the front." He kept a photo of Nho when she was two years old. She was wearing baby's pants, with their open rear end, and a wide-brimmed bonnet, and she was holding a bunch of wildflowers at the foot of some tall mustard greens. I had read many of the letters he sent to Nho. Once, he wrote, "I'm very well. I've been enjoying playing soccer and have two muscular forearms. I look at the picture of you at two years old and it's impossible for me to imagine you as you are now. I can only think: Here you are, so small, holding flowers in your hands. Do you want me to pick you up? Take you out? Buy you some candy? Where else should we go? I'll carry you there."

His ideas were pretty funny, but we didn't laugh when we read the letter. Gravely, we turned in the direction of the north, where Hanoi lay. We had been away for so long. We missed our green city. We treasured its tranquillity as a memory. This was the place where we were growing up, but we were always thinking of Hanoi.

In Hanoi, I had a small room on the second floor. My house was ancient and deep within an alleyway where many green trees grew. Those trees were so old that creeping mistletoe now covered them. At night, I would perch on the edge of the windowsill looking out over the uneven lines of the black roofs, and I would sing. I sang with passion, loudly. Next door lived a doctor who had trouble sleeping. He would switch on his light and politely tap three times against the wall. Twenty nights out of every month would be like that. I sat waiting for sleep to come back to the doctor, justifying myself by thinking, "Only I can know the vastness and freshness of the city night. How can the doctor experience anything like this in his disruptible dreams?" It was also because of my passionate singing that once I almost fell off the windowsill. Frantically grabbing the shutter, I dizzily glanced down into the bottomless abyss. Somewhere down there was a hose which ran all night to fill a cistern. The gushing of the water gave me the feeling that it was about to rise to the windowsill. I pulled myself up and carefully drew my legs inside. I resumed singing, but I sang more softly and listened for the sound of the tapping on the wall.

In the corner of the room sat a desk that my mother had made for me over the course of two afternoons. Every time I did anything that required paper and ink, I would pull all my books and notebooks out of my drawers and my satchel and spread them out across the desk and bed, although all of those things weren't necessary for what I was about to do. For a long time, I searched endlessly among those papers, unable to do anything and also unable to put them in order. So impatient that I could cry, I shouted for my mother. She left her sewing machine and ran in, and, while lightly grumbling, arranged all the papers.

She scolded me, but without determination. "What kind of girl are you?" she asked. "Your husband will beat you. Beat you!"

Therefore, even when I was still at home, I swore to myself that I'd never marry.

Nho said, "Hey. Hurry up."

"What?" She startled me. For the past few minutes, I'd been singing. Singing and thinking aimlessly.

Nho rolled up her pillow and quickly put it into her bag. Thao looked toward the entrance to the cave. It was a reconnaissance plane, alright. Life here had taught us the meaning of silence. It was abnormal that, ever since morning, the day had been so quiet. And now, the reason for that was on the way. The reconnaissance plane was buzzing overhead and the jets were roaring up behind it. Those two kinds of sounds mixed together in one's ears to create a feeling of unsettling tension.

"They're almost here!" Nho turned her back on us, putting her steel helmet on her head. Thao fished a biscuit out of her pocket and munched on it in a leisurely manner. Whenever she knew that something dangerous was about to happen, she would look so calm it was annoying. But whenever she saw blood or even a jungle leech, she would force her eyes shut and her face would turn white. All of her undershirts were embroidered with colored threads. She also plucked her eyebrows until they were as thin as toothpicks. But as far as work was concerned, everyone respected her. She showed determination and daring.

These things happened every day: airplanes screamed; bombs exploded. This time, they exploded on the strategic hill about 300 meters from our cave. The ground beneath our feet shook. Even the washcloths we'd hung out to dry shook. Everything became feverish. Smoke rose up and filled the entrance to the cave. We couldn't see the clouds or the sky any longer.

Thao took the yardstick from my hand and, with gusto, swallowed the last morsel of her biscuit.

"Dinh, you stay inside," she told me. "This time, they only dropped a few. Two of us can do it."

Pulling on the sleeve of Nho's shirt, she flung the shovel over her shoulder and walked out of the cave.

I didn't argue with her. She had the authority to give assignments. Time became tense. My mind was tense as well. Neither the things that had happened nor those about to happen mattered any more. If my friends didn't come back, would they make any difference? The two-way radio rang. The company commander wanted to know the situation.

I shouted into the machine. "The reconnaissance team hasn't come back yet!"

I didn't know why I was shouting. There was one more wave of bombs. The smoke filled the cave. I choked coughing and my chest burned. The hill was now deserted. There was only Nho and Thao. And the bomb. And here I was, sitting in the cave. And our anti-aircraft guns were on the other side of the hill. They now responded and the sound of these guns rising up from the ground was reassuring. There is nothing more lonely and terrifying than when bombs explode around you and nothing comes up from below. Even the sound of a single rifle can give you a feeling of some protection, an impression of solid self-defense.

Feeling restless, I ran outside for a moment. I couldn't see anything except the smoke from the bombs. I was worried. Suddenly, the strategic hill next to ours echoed with the sound of the 12.7s. Great! It was the battalion of military construction workers. They had been sent as reinforcement for the men on the anti-aircraft guns, and for us. Suddenly, I wanted to shout for joy. Now, that normally deserted hill was overrun with people. The anti-aircraft gunners, the liaison people, and the engineers were all very fond of us. It was only necessary to fire off a single rifle requesting help and they would get the message and immediately appear.

Half an hour later, Thao crawled into the cave. Calm, exhausted, and bad-tempered, she refused to look at me.

"We'll need more than a thousand cubic meters of dirt!" she said.

She sat down and drank some water from the canteen. Water fell continuously from her chin to her shirt, like raindrops. I radioed the headquarters to tell them.

The company commander said, "Is that so? Thank you all."

The commander often used polite phrases like, "thank you," "excuse me," and "good luck." He was young and thin, suffered from rheumatism, and often wrote popular rhymes for the newspapers posted on the walls. His house was somewhere near the end of Lo Duc Street.

Nho had just bathed in the stream and was walking back up. That section of the stream often had time-delayed bombs detonate in it. In her wet clothes, Nho sat down and asked for some candy. I dug into my pocket. Luckily, I still had two lemon candies, although they were covered with grains of sand and melting.

Nho said, "There were only four of those time-delayed bombs. Not so many."

She put her arms behind her and leaned all the way back. Her neck was round and her shirt had delicate buttons on it. I wanted to lift her in my arms. She looked as light and fresh as an ice cream bar. The company commander had asked if we needed any help. I said no. As always, we would do everything ourselves.

"Wonderful! Thank you, all!" The company commander thanked us again. "The whole unit is opening a road for the missile regiment to go through the forest. They haven't rested since morning. I also have to go now. Just do your best."

That night, too, we would have to work outside. As usual.

I began working on a bomb up on the hill. Nho did two that sat on the road. Thao had one by the old bunker.

It was so quiet it was scary. The remaining trees were twisted and broken. The earth was hot. The black smoke floated in clumps through the air, blocking our view of things in the distance. Could the anti-aircraft gunners see us? Perhaps they could. They had binoculars that could shrink the whole earth into their sights. I approached the time-delayed bomb. Feeling the soldiers' eyes upon me, I was no longer afraid. I would not bend down. They wouldn't like it. They liked the gait of someone standing straight and calmly stepping forward.

The bomb lay within a dry bush, its head stuck in the ground and its back end painted with two concentric yellow circles.

I used a small shovel to dig the dirt from under the bomb. The earth was hard. Pebbles flew out from under both sides of my hand. Sometimes, the edge of the shovel scraped the side of the bomb. It made a sound so sharp it cut into my skin. I shivered and suddenly realized I was working too slowly. Hurry up a little! The casing of the bomb was hot. That was a bad sign.

It might be the heat from inside the bomb. Or maybe it had retained the heat from the sun.

Thao whistled. That meant that twenty minutes had passed already. I carefully packed the sticks of dynamite into the hole that I had dug. The fuse was long, coiled and resilient. I poured the dirt into the hole, lit the fuse, and then ran for shelter.

Thao whistled again. I pressed myself against the wall of earth, looking at my watch. There was no wind. I couldn't hear my heart beat. The only calm thing, ignoring all the happenings around it, was the hand on my watch. It kept ticking, lively and softly, running past the eternal numbers, while over there, the fire burned along the fuse and entered the bomb.

I was used to it. We exploded bombs up to five times a day. Sometimes it was fewer: three times. I did think of death. But it was a vague death, not a concrete one. The chief thing was whether or not the bomb or the mine would explode at all. If not, then how would you light the fuse the second time? I considered that, and something else as well. If a bomb fragment hit my arm, that would be rather troublesome.

Salty sweat dripped down my lips and sand grated against my teeth.

The bomb did explode. It had a weird sound and it jarred me. I felt a pain in my chest. My eyes watered and it was a while before I could open them again. The smell of the explosives made me nauseated. Three explosions followed. Dirt rained down and silently disappeared into the bushes. Fragments of the bombs tore through the air with a whine, invisible over my head.

I brushed off my shirt. Straining my eyes to see through the smoke, I ran after Thao. Normally, wanting to meet Nho and me so that we could go back to the cave together, Thao would come by my place. This time, she was smiling, her white teeth shining and her scar looking glossy. She held a piece of parachute around her shoulders and ran ahead of me. The wind tried to snatch the parachute, but couldn't do it.

Thao tripped and fell and I tried to help her up but she pushed me away. Her eyes were open wide and I could see now that they were glazed over, as if there were no more life in them. I didn't understand. She grabbed my hand and pulled me down next to a mound of earth. It was a small mound, rather long, and covered with the gray explosives of a bomb.

"Nho! Where are you hurt?" Thao sobbed, but she had no tears.

I scraped at the earth, pulled out Nho, and lay her across my lap. Blood gushed out of her arm and was absorbed into the earth. She didn't look as light and fresh as an ice cream bar any longer. Her skin was pale, her eyes shut tight, and her clothes were covered with dirt. The bomb had leaped up and exploded in the air. Her underground shelter had collapsed, that was all.

I cleaned Nho with water I'd boiled over the coal stove. Using cotton wool bandages, I wrapped the wound, which wasn't deep enough to tear the muscle. But because the bomb had exploded so close to her, Nho was in shock. I gave her an injection. Her eyes fluttered and she looked comfortable; perhaps she wasn't in pain. Thao was pacing back and forth outside. She was restless because she didn't know what to do, and still she tried to do something. She was afraid of blood.

"Let me call headquarters, okay?" she asked.

Thao only approached once Nho was lying clean and tidy on the wooden plank bed.

"She won't die," I replied. "The unit is busy opening a road. We don't need to make so many people worry. Why are you in such a panic?"

"It's only normal. Those who aren't wounded often feel more pain than those who are." Thao turned her face to the entrance to the cave and drank some water from the canteen.

Nho put one arm over her eyes. She knew that she shouldn't drink any water so I mixed some milk for her in the steel mug.

Thao said, "Put a lot of sugar in and mix it so it's strong."

After she finished drinking the milk, Nho slept. The reconnaissance planes were still scraping away the silence of the mountains and forests. Thao leaned against the wall with her hands clasped behind her neck. She wouldn't look at me.

"Sing, Phuong Dinh. Sing your favorite song," she said.

I liked a lot of songs. I liked the marching songs the soldiers sometimes sang at the front. I liked the gentle folk duets. I liked the "Katyusha" of the Soviet Red Army and to hold my knees up to my chest and sing, "Return to Sorrento." Because it was a romantic Italian folk song, you had to start very low. I liked it a lot. But I didn't want to sing just then. I was mad at Thao, although I understood the feelings whirling inside her. She kept glancing at Nho, raising a hand to adjust her collar and then her lapel and her hair. She hadn't cried and she didn't even like tears. Anyone who shed a tear while we needed strength from each other would be seen as guilty of self-debasement.

Nobody said it, but we could read it in each other's eyes.

Thao sang, "Here is Thang Long. Here is Dong Do. Here is Hanoi." Her voice was both squeaky and out of tune, so she couldn't sing anything smoothly, but she had three thick notebooks that she'd filled with the lyrics of songs. Whenever she had a free moment, she would sit down and copy out a song. She'd even passionately copied out the words of songs that I'd made up.

A cloud floated by outside the cave. Then another. They were going by faster and faster. In front of the entrance to the cave, the open sky grew dark. A storm was coming in. Sand filled the air. The wind lifted up then tossed down the dry branches of the tress. Leaves flew in all directions. It was as sudden as a change in the human heart. In this season, unexpected rain often came down on the forest. But now it was hailing. At first, I didn't notice, but then I heard a tapping against the overhang of the cave. I stepped outside. Something sharp was pulverizing the air, tearing it into tiny fragments. The wind. I felt a pain and at the same time, my cheeks became wet.

"It's hailing. It's hailing!"

I ran inside, and put a few small hailstones into Nho's open palm. Then, I ran back outside, extremely thrilled.

The year I finished the tenth grade, we had also had hail. During the night, the hail had hit the walls with that same tapping sound.

I had flung open the door, run into the hallway, and pounded on the doors, shouting at the top of my lungs as if I had gone crazy.

"Heavens! Get up quick! It's hailing!"

Then, I complained to myself, "Only fools would stay in bed at a time like this."

The doctor was not a fool at all, but he proclaimed gravely, "If you continue with this noise, we will be forced to take the necessary measures."

And the woman teacher next door sighed inconsolably, "Why won't you let us sleep?"

Only the driver who lived downstairs stayed up with me throughout that miraculous night. After that, he joined the army and became a hero at destroying enemy vehicles. He wrote to me and often mentioned those hailstones of long ago as one of his "memories of the past."

Here, on this bomb-covered hill, we also got hail and my childish joy had bloomed again. Here there was no one to reproach me. Thao was busy scooping up something from the ground. Maybe it was hailstones. As for Nho, she sat up, her lips parting.

"Hey, give me some more of those hailstones," she said.

But it had stopped already, over as quickly as it had begun. Why so fast? I suddenly became dazed, filled with an unspeakable regret. Clearly, it wasn't regret for the hailstones. The storm had come and gone. But I missed something. Maybe it was my mother. Or the window. Or the big stars over the city. Right. Maybe it was those things. Or maybe it was the trees. Or the dome of the opera house. Or the woman pushing her cart filled with ice cream, surrounded by expectant children. The asphalt road at night after a summer rain seemed wider, longer, reflecting the lights, looking like a river of black water. The electric lights over the square glowed like the stars in the stories about fairylands. The flowers in the park. The soccer balls carelessly kicked by children from street corners. The hawking of the woman who sold sticky rice in the morning, carrying a bamboo basket on her head.

Maybe it was all those things. They were so far away and then, because of a hailstorm, they came in waves to flood my mind.

People asked if Hanoi women could bear three days away from home. But here we were, living on this hill for three years already. The drivers and artillery men called each of us in our unit by name, without ever making a mistake. As for us, we knew who, among those men, was in love, who had a first-born daughter, who was courageous, and who was irritable. During the night, while we were repairing the road, those men would toss us Ngoc Lan toothpaste, perfume-scented writing paper, and lemon candies. Often, we didn't even know who was throwing it because the trucks would go by so quickly. But we spread the news among ourselves.

"Those trucks were from Hanoi!" we'd say.

Because only Hanoi had those things.

In Hanoi, we'd never even paid attention to such things. But here we felt so happy to hold one thin sheet of fragrant paper, put it into an envelope, and send it to someone further toward the front.

"Get down!" Thao shouted.

As if I had just received a punch in the stomach, I doubled over and then threw myself on the ground. Bombs! It sounded like they thudded as they fell and then exploded. The surface of the earth was like a shaking giant.

It seemed like thousands of airplanes were turning somersaults over head. I dragged myself back into the cave and Thao dragged herself in behind me.

"Damn it. They don't give us a chance to breathe," she mumbled. Slender, well-proportioned, with hair down to her shoulders, her scar invisible in the dark, she stood with one hand clinging to the line where we hung our washcloths. If she had a good voice, she would have been better off in the theater. On the stage, she would have looked presentable. But her squeaky voice hurt people's ears. She herself admitted it.

"Bring the radio over here," Nho motioned.

I carried it over to Nho and then I picked up the yardstick and went back outside with Thao.

We had to run a lot and so the wound in my thigh began to hurt. I could still run, provided that the wound didn't make me limp. Thao was very determined. Of course, she wouldn't worry about going up the hill by herself.

There were so many bomb craters. We measured them and, doing some mental addition, shouted to each other the results. Thao recorded them in the logbook. There were no time-delayed bombs, but we would need a lot of dirt. The total came to two thousand cubic meters. Suddenly, as if something had shoved her in the back, Thao flew forward, grasped me against her chest, and together we fell to the ground. In a flash, an avalanche of earth came down on us. Big chunks of wet dirt mixed with the dry dirt from deeper underground. It was hot. Something pulled my head down. Thrusting my legs down for momentum, I pushed myself up, up, and up. Grains of dirt filled my nostrils. Shaking my head, I felt clods of earth fall off. All around me was the steely, ponderous gray of billowing smoke.

I couldn't see Thao anywhere. "Thao," I tried to scream but I choked. Dirt filled my mouth. Damn! I spat out a clump of earth. Groping around, my hand touched Thao's hair. I turned around and, pushing myself forward, used both hands to claw at the dirt. I found her, but I couldn't sense her breathing. Then, suddenly, she flung an arm around my neck and shakily stood up.

Back in the cave, Nho grimaced like a child. "That bad?" she asked.

Thao smiled strangely and slowly regained her composure. "A piece of bad luck," she said. "But it was really nothing."

It couldn't just be bad luck. Her body carried nine wounds, both big and small, already. Nho had five. I had the fewest, only four. I had one scar on my stomach that had been severe enough to consign me to a military hospital for three months. Being buried by an avalanche was normal.

I looked at my friends. Thao was very pale. She was exhausted. Nho brought her a mug of water and, using her pinkie, flicked the grains of dirt from her hair.

Suddenly, she philosophized, "That's life on a strategic hill!"

Thao burst into laugher, motioning with her head in my direction. "Log in the numbers before you forget," she said. As I cranked the two-way radio, Thao hurried over to my side. "Tell them everything, but let them know that we've stood our ground."

It wasn't the company commander but the liaison officer who answered the radio. He was a polite and hospitable guy who didn't smoke or flirt with the girls.

"Where did the commander go?"

"He's out giving orders where they're opening the road, because the trucks are coming through with the missiles soon. But it's late afternoon already. Nobody can sleep. What about you guys?"

"We're pretty exhausted. More than two thousand cubic meters of earth already and it's not even near dark yet. We're still standing our ground."

"If things get worse, fire off some shots immediately, you hear? The unit is always concerned about you up there. The assault troopers can get up there quickly."

That afternoon, Thao and I had to run up the strategic hill three more times. We detonated eight more bombs. And the amount of earth rose to three thousand two hundred cubic meters. Every time, I tried to find excuses to keep Thao at home. But she was smart and it was hard to trick her. As she ran, her breathing grew more and more labored. Small blue veins stood out on her temples and across the backs of her hands. I was afraid she would collapse. And every time we came back, Nho would step out of the cave again and scowl, repeating, "Thao! Thao!"

The last time, we nearly crawled back to the cave. Thao helped me lie down. I tried to open my eyes. They felt as if they were glued together. I didn't even know what I wanted now.

"I'm sleepy." I heard my voice floating by and then the coolness of the cave flowed in as I quickly fell asleep.

A squad of assault troopers came up from where they were building the road through the forest. They probably hadn't even eaten before they ran up our hill. I heard their voices as if they were coming from a distance. They asked about something and Thao answered them. They teased Nho. She got angry and then started laughing. Someone was singing softly.

Someone's hair brushed against my cheek, then the sound of breathing came down from above. It was warm and enveloped me. I felt as if I were lying in my mother's arms.

"She's a Hanoi girl!"

I recognized the voice of the liaison officer and woke up immediately. He was a Hanoi guy. His father was an electrical worker and his mother was a clothing worker. At home, he had often played hooky and gotten bad grades. One time he rolled five bombs over a precipice, forcing them to explode down there so that they wouldn't damage the road. He was polite, hospitable, didn't smoke, and didn't flirt with us girls. As for us, we wouldn't leave him alone.

"If you go out with your sweetheart, for sure you'll force her to cut her hair, wear a suit and black boots, won't you?"

He would look uncomfortable, scratch his head, and blush deeply. "In everything, there are always exceptions, dear ladies! Anyway, I've never been in love."

I opened my eyes. The cave had grown dark already. The small light had already been lit on top of the ammunition trunk. A picture of Uncle Ho was glued onto the middle of a piece of large white paper. Just beneath it, an empty explosives canister held a bunch of fresh flowers. We always had flowers there, but in the lamplight I couldn't tell their colors. Maybe someone had just brought us these. We were a priority.

The liaison officer was boiling some water, his back turned to us, solid as a bedboard. But when he stood up, I saw that his waist was as slender and attractive as a ping-pong player's.

Murmurs carried in from outside. The happiest moments were coming. I told myself I had to go outside, so I put my feet against the wall and, with my hands behind me, gave one hard push. As I jumped up, pain shot through my thigh. My head and my joints ached, but I managed to stand up anyway.

The liaison officer helped me. "Are you crazy?" he asked me. "If you're tired, then you should sleep."

"I'm going out now."

"Going out!" He smiled. His lips were thin, his teeth even, and his eyebrows thick. "You're not going anywhere. First of all, you've got to sleep."

"That's silly. No way," I mumbled and went toward the entrance to the cave, groping my way like a blind person. I wasn't the only one who was crazy because Nho had already disappeared. Thao was even crazier. I could hear her laughing up on the hill.

I saw Nho among a group of military construction workers. She told me that it was nearly midnight and the trucks were about to leave. While I was sleeping, many more bombs had exploded on the hill. But everything was alright because of the assault troops.

The top of the hill reverberated with the sounds of bulldozers, hoes, and talking and laughing. Occasionally, a mine would explode. Those explosions were even bigger than the sounds of the bombs. The stars seemed to move overhead. They were very far away, but as clear as drops of blue water, and they were scattered all across the sky. How vast was the sky! Suddenly, I remembered a poem written by a forward observer who tossed it to us when his group went by. He called us "the stars above the strategic hill." They were bright stars but for some reason he thought of them as "distant." We debated with each other and guessed that maybe he just wanted it to sound literary, because it was obvious that if they were stars they would be distant. I wanted so much to meet that artillery solider. But his group was long gone.

The trucks got on their way at midnight. The engines roared. The road became alive with noise. The driver in the cabin of the fifth truck saw us. "Hey, Hanoi girls!" he cried. "You must really miss your mothers!"

"I think that's Thang from the Quang Trung group," Nho said quietly.

The bandage on her arm glowed white. She was quiet, with a round face and straight nose. She leaned against me, looking light and fresh as a white ice cream bar.

"They said that I should go to a hospital in the rear," she said. "That's ridiculous. Shots every day. Pills. Also, meat porridge. And, please eat a lot. Yuck! Like a spoiled brat lying in a bed. It's naive of them to think that they can force me to go. How annoying!" She hissed, as if I were preparing to drag her onto the medical truck myself.

She had turned around to discuss the phenomenon of shooting stars with one of the construction workers when she saw at the edge of the forest a star fall, disappearing midway through its course.

I folded my arms across my chest and walked some distance away, not looking at that soldier but at one of the trucks approaching us. I had struck a pose and that was all. How could I help it? There was no way that I could, right at this moment, rush up and hold the hand of every soldier on this hill, bursting into tears because of the youthful joy that was rising inside of me. I loved everyone, with a passionate love, a love beyond words, that only someone who had stood on that hill in those moments, as I did, could understand fully.

The trucks followed each other without lights, forming a single mass on the road. The leaves that were used as camouflage made every truck seem double its size. To me, those convoys always looked limitless and countless. Long. Numerous. Gigantic.

"Probably the Hanoi men will come tonight!" Nho said, still quietly. She was in the same state of mind as me: loving everyone. That was the love of the people in smoke and fire, the people of war. It was a selfless, passionate, and carefree love, only found in the hearts of soldiers. I put my arm around Nho and squeezed her small, soft shoulder. We said nothing to each other. She was here, brave, gentle, from the same city as me and standing with me on this night on a hill covered by bomb craters near the front. We understood each other and felt completely happy.

# Jamaica Kincaid

## (B. 1949)

Jamaica Kincaid was born Elaine Potter Richardson in St. John's, Antigua. As a child, she felt isolated and alone, struggling as the only girl in her family and as a bright girl in a British colonial school system that did little to encourage her ambitions. Chafing against her loneliness and the Antiguan subjection to continuing British rule, Kincaid left St. John's for New York City at the age of seventeen. She began writing for a girls' magazine, *Ingénue*, and officially changed her name to Jamaica. Her work for *Ingénue* and the *Village Voice* drew the attention of William Shawn, the legendary editor of the *New Yorker*. In 1976, Kincaid became a featured columnist for the "Talk of the Town" section of the magazine, and in 1978 the *New Yorker* published Kincaid's first short story. Her first collection of stories, *At The Bottom of the River*, was published in 1983. The stories are constructed in Kincaid's spare and suggestive language, and all reflect not only her recurrent themes of girlhood and mother-daughter relationships, but also colonial oppression.

Kincaid's novel, *Annie John*, was published in 1985 and focuses on the crumbling relationship between an Antiguan mother and daughter. She also uses this relationship as a metaphor with which to explore the vexed bonds between a colonial power and those under the thumb of this power. Her next book, a nonfiction piece entitled *A Small Place* (1988), explicitly explores this difficult power dynamic through an examination of the effects of brutal colonial oppression on the Antiguan culture. Kincaid's other major works include *Lucy* (1990), *The Autobiography of My Mother* (1996), *My Brother* (1997), *My Garden*

(1999), *Talk Stories* (2001), and *Seed Gathering atop the World* (2002). Kincaid received a nomination for the 1997 National Book Award for *My Brother*, the story of her relationship with her youngest brother while he was dying from AIDS.

## Wingless 1978

The small children are reading from a book filled with simple words and sentences.

"'Once upon a time there was a little chimney-sweep, whose name was Tom.'"

"'He cried half his time, and laughed the other half.'"

"'You would have been giddy, perhaps, at looking down: but Tom was not.'"

"'You, of course, would have been very cold sitting there on a September night, without the least bit of clothes on your wet back; but Tom was a water-baby, and therefore felt cold no more than a fish.'"

The children have already learned to write their names in beautiful penmanship. They have already learned how many farthings make a penny, how many pennies make a shilling, how many shillings make a pound, how many days in April, how many stone in a ton. Now they singsong here and tumble there, tearing skirts with swift movements. Must Dulcie really cry after thirteen of her play chums have sat on her? There, Dulcie, there. I myself have been kissed by many rude boys with small, damp lips, on their way to boys' drill. I myself have humped girls under my mother's house. But I swim in a shaft of light, upside down, and I can see myself clearly, through and through, from every angle. Perhaps I stand on the brink of a great discovery, and perhaps after I have made my great discovery I will be sent home in chains. Then again, perhaps my life is as predictable as an insect's and I am in my pupa stage. How low can I sink, then? That woman over there, that large-bottomed woman, is important to me. It's for her that I save up my sixpences instead of spending for sweets. Is this a love like no other? And what pain have I caused her? And does she love me? My needs are great, I can see. But there are the children again (of which I am one), shrieking, whether in pain or pleasure I cannot tell. The children, who are beautiful in groupings of three, and who only last night pleaded with their mothers to sing softly to them, are today maiming each other. The children at the end of the day have sour necks, frayed hair, dirt under their fingernails, scuffed shoes, torn clothing. And why? First they must be children.

I shall grow up to be a tall, graceful, and altogether beautiful woman, and I shall impose on large numbers of people my will and also, for my own amusement, great pain. But now. I shall try to see clearly. I shall try to tell differences. I shall try to distinguish the subtle gradations of color in fine cloth, of fingernail length, of manners. That woman over there. Is she cruel? Does she love me? And if not, can I make her? I am not yet tall, beautiful, graceful, and able to impose my will. Now I swim in a shaft of light and can see myself clearly. The schoolhouse is yellow and stands among big green-leaved trees. Inside are our desks and a woman who wears spectacles, playing the piano. Is a girl who can sing "Gaily the troubadour plucked his guitar" in a pleasing way worthy of being my best friend? There is the same girl, unwashed and glistening, setting traps for talking birds. Is she to be one of my temptations? Oh, this must be a love like no other. But how can my limbs that hate be the same limbs that love? How can the same limbs that make me blind make me see? I am defenseless and small. I shall try to see clearly. I shall try to separate and divide things as if they were sums, as if they were drygoods on the grocer's shelves. Is this my mother? Is she here to embarrass me? What shall I say about her behind her back, when she isn't there, long after she has gone? In her smile lies her goodness. Will I always remember that? Am I horrid? And if so, will I always be that way? Not getting my own way causes me to fret so, I clench my fist. My charm is limited, and I haven't learned to smile yet. I have picked many flowers and then deliberately torn them to shreds, petal by petal. I am so unhappy, my face is so wet, and still I can stand up and walk and tell lies in the face of terrible punishments. I can see the great danger in what I am—a defenseless and pitiful child. Here is a list of what I must do. So is my life to be like an apprenticeship in dressmaking, a thorny path to carefully follow or avoid? Inside, standing around the spectacled woman playing the piano, the children are singing a song in harmony. The children's voices: pinks, blues, yellows, violets, all suspended. All is soft, all is embracing, all is comforting. And yet I myself, at my age, have suffered so. My tears, big, have run down my cheeks in uneven lines—my tears, big, and my hands too small to hold them. My tears have been the result of my disappointments. My disappointments stand up and grow ever taller. They will not be lost to me. There they are. Let them pin tags on them. Let me have them registered, like newly domesticated animals. Let me cherish my disappointments, fold them up, tuck them away, close to my breast, because they are so important to me.

But again I swim in a shaft of light, upside down, and I can see myself clearly, through and through, from every angle. Over there, I stand on the brink of a great discovery, and it is possible that like an ancient piece of history my presence will leave room for theories. But who will say? For days my body has been collecting water, but still I won't cry. What is that to me? I am not yet a woman with a terrible and unwanted burden. I am not yet a dog with a cruel and unloving master. I am not yet a tree growing on barren and bitter land. I am not yet the shape of darkness in a dungeon.

Where? What? Why? How then? Oh, that!

I am primitive and wingless.

"Don't eat the strings on bananas—they will wrap around your heart and kill you."

"Oh. Is that true?"

"No."

"Is that something to tell children?"

"No. But it's so funny. You should see how you look trying to remove all the strings from the bananas with your monkey fingernails. Frightened?"

"Frightened. Very frightened."

Today, keeping a safe distance, I followed the woman I love when she walked on a carpet of pond lilies. As she walked, she ate some black nuts, pond-lily black nuts. She walked for a long time, saying what must be wonderful things to herself. Then in the middle of the pond she stopped, because a man had stood up suddenly in front of her. I could see that he wore clothes made of tree bark and sticks in his ears. He said things to her and I couldn't make them out, but he said them to her so forcefully that drops of brown water sprang from his mouth. The woman I love put her hands over her ears, shielding herself from the things he said. Then he put wind in his cheeks and blew himself up until in the bright sun he looked like a boil, and the woman I love put her hands over her eyes, shielding herself from the way he looked. Then, instead of removing her cutlass from the folds of her big and beautiful skirt and cutting the man in two at the waist, she only smiled—a red, red smile—and like a fly he dropped dead.

The sea, the shimmering pink-colored sand, the swimmers with hats, two people walking arm in arm, talking in each other's face, dots of water landing on noses, the sea spray on ankles, on overdeveloped calves, the blue, the green, the black, so deep, so smooth, a great and swift undercurrent, glassy, the white wavelets, a storm so blinding that the salt got in our eyes, the sea turning inside out, shaking everything up like a bottle with sediment, a boat with two people heaving a brown package overboard, the mystery, the sharp teeth of that yellow spotted eel, the wriggle, the smooth lines, open mouths, families of great noisy birds, families of great noisy people, families of biting flies, the sea, following me home, snapping at my heels, all the way to the door, the sea, the woman.

"I have frightened you? Again, you are frightened of me?"

"You have frightened me. I am very frightened of you."

"Oh, you should see your face. I wish you could see your face. How you make me laugh."

And what are my fears? What large cows! When I see them coming, shall I run and hide face down in the gutter? Are they really cows? Can I stand in a field of tall grass and see nothing for miles and miles? On the other hand, the sky, which is big and blue as always, has its limits. This afternoon the wind is loud as in a hurricane. There isn't enough light. There is a noise—I can't tell where it is coming from. A big box has stamped on it, "Handle Carefully." I have been in a big white building with curving corridors. I have passed a dead person. There is the woman I love, who is so much bigger than me.

That mosquito . . . now a stain on the wall. That lizard, running up and down, up and down . . . now so still. That ant, bloated and sluggish, a purseful of eggs in its jaws . . . now so still. That blue-and-green bird, head held aloft, singing . . . now so still. That land crab, moving slowly, softly, even beautifully, sideways . . . but now so still. That cricket, standing on a tree stem, so ugly, so revolting, I am made so unhappy . . . now so still. That mongoose, now asleep in its hole, now stealing the sleeping chickens, moving so quickly, its eyes like two grains of light . . . now so still. That fly, moving so contentedly from tea bun to tea bun . . . now so still. That butterfly, moving contentedly from beautiful plant to beautiful plant in the early morning sun . . . now so still. That tadpole, swimming playfully in the shallow water . . . now so still.

I shall cast a shadow and I shall remain unaware.

My hands, brown on this side, pink on this side, now indiscriminately dangerous, now vagabond and prodigal, now cruel and careless, now without remorse or forgiveness, but now innocently slipping into a dress with braided sleeves, now holding an ice-cream cone, now reaching up with longing, now clasped in prayer, now feeling for reassurance, now pleading my desires, now pleasing, and now, even now, so still in bed, in sleep.

# Jhumpa Lahiri

## (B. 1967)

The daughter of Bengali parents, Jhumpa Lahiri was born in London and raised in Rhode Island. This multicultural existence is reflected in her fiction as often alienated and lonely immigrants navigate a path between two culturally different worlds. Lahiri received her B.A. from Barnard College and earned master's degrees in English, creative writing, and comparative studies in literature and the arts at Boston University. She obtained a Ph.D. in Renaissance studies from Boston University as well. After graduation, Lahiri found an agent and began work on her first book. She had three short stories published in the *New Yorker* in 1998. Her first collection of stories, *Interpreter of Maladies* (1999), won the 2000 Pulitzer Prize for fiction.

*Interpreter of Maladies* portrays first- and second-generation Indian immigrants who wage a battle against the common difficulty of contemporary culture: failed relationships, whether they be romantic relationships or the relationship between immigrants and a bewildering new world. Lahiri incorporates traditional Indian names, folktales, foods, and wardrobes into her fiction, creating a richly textured world of difference that nonetheless feels familiar to a reader sensitive to the daily struggles of average human beings. Her other work includes *India Holy Song* (2000) and her first novel, *The Namesake* (2004).

## *A Temporary Matter* 1998

The notice informed them that it was a temporary matter: for five days their electricity would be cut off for one hour, beginning at eight P.M. A line had gone down in the last snowstorm, and the repairmen were going to take advantage of the milder evenings to set it right. The work would affect only the houses on the quiet tree-lined

street, within walking distance of a row of brick-faced stores and a trolley stop, where
Shoba and Shukumar had lived for three years.

"It's good of them to warn us," Shoba conceded after reading the notice aloud,
more for her own benefit than Shukumar's. She let the strap of her leather satchel,
plump with files, slip from her shoulders, and left it in the hallway as she walked into
the kitchen. She wore a navy blue poplin raincoat over gray sweatpants and white
sneakers, looking, at thirty-three, like the type of woman she'd once claimed she
would never resemble.

She'd come from the gym. Her cranberry lipstick was visible only on the outer
reaches of her mouth, and her eyeliner had left charcoal patches beneath her lower
lashes. She used to look this way sometimes, Shukumar thought, on mornings after a
party or a night at a bar, when she'd been too lazy to wash her face, too eager to collapse into his arms. She dropped a sheaf of mail on the table without a glance. Her
eyes were still fixed on the notice in her other hand. "But they should do this sort of
thing during the day."

"When I'm here, you mean," Shukumar said. He put a glass lid on a pot of lamb,
adjusting it so only the slightest bit of steam could escape. Since January he'd been
working at home, trying to complete the final chapters of his dissertation on agrarian
revolts in India. "When do the repairs start?"

"It says March nineteenth. Is today the nineteenth?" Shoba walked over to the
framed corkboard that hung on the wall by the fridge, bare except for a calendar of
William Morris wallpaper patterns. She looked at it as if for the first time, studying
the wallpaper pattern carefully on the top half before allowing her eyes to fall to the
numbered grid on the bottom. A friend had sent the calendar in the mail as a Christmas gift, even though Shoba and Shukumar hadn't celebrated Christmas that year.

"Today then," Shoba announced. "You have a dentist appointment next Friday,
by the way."

He ran his tongue over the tops of his teeth; he'd forgotten to brush them that
morning. It wasn't the first time. He hadn't left the house at all that day, or the day before. The more Shoba stayed out, the more she began putting in extra hours at work
and taking on additional projects, the more he wanted to stay in, not even leaving to
get the mail, or to buy fruit or wine at the stores by the trolley stop.

Six months ago, in September, Shukumar was at an academic conference in Baltimore when Shoba went into labor, three weeks before her due date. He hadn't
wanted to go to the conference, but she had insisted; it was important to make contacts, and he would be entering the job market next year. She told him that she had his
number at the hotel, and a copy of his schedule and flight numbers, and she had
arranged with her friend Gillian for a ride to the hospital in the event of an emergency. When the cab pulled away that morning for the airport, Shoba stood waving
good-bye in her robe, with one arm resting on the mound of her belly as if it were a
perfectly natural part of her body.

Each time he thought of that moment, the last moment he saw Shoba pregnant,
it was the cab he remembered most, a station wagon, painted red with blue lettering.
It was cavernous compared to their own car. Although Shukumar was six feet tall,

with hands too big ever to rest comfortably in the pockets of his jeans, he felt dwarfed in the back seat. As the cab sped down Beacon Street, he imagined a day when he and Shoba might need to buy a station wagon of their own, to cart their children back and forth from music lessons and dentist appointments. He imagined himself gripping the wheel, as Shoba turned around to hand the children juice boxes. Once, these images of parenthood had troubled Shukumar, adding to his anxiety that he was still a student at thirty-five. But that early autumn morning, the trees still heavy with bronze leaves, he welcomed the image for the first time.

A member of the staff had found him somehow among the identical convention rooms and handed him a stiff square of stationery. It was only a telephone number, but Shukumar knew it was the hospital. When he returned to Boston it was over. The baby had been born dead. Shoba was lying on a bed, asleep, in a private room so small there was barely enough space to stand beside her, in a wing of the hospital they hadn't been to on the tour of expectant parents. Her placenta had weakened and she'd had a cesarean, though not quickly enough. The doctor explained that these things happen. He smiled in the kindest way it was possible to smile at people known only professionally. Shoba would be back on her feet in a few weeks. There was nothing to indicate that she would not be able to have children in the future.

These days Shoba was always gone by the time Shukumar woke up. He would open his eyes and see the long black hairs she shed on her pillow and think of her, dressed, sipping her third cup of coffee already, in her office downtown, where she searched for typographical errors in textbooks and marked them, in a code she had once explained to him, with an assortment of colored pencils. She would do the same for his dissertation, she promised, when it was ready. He envied her the specificity of her task, so unlike the elusive nature of his. He was a mediocre student who had a facility for absorbing details without curiosity. Until September he had been diligent if not dedicated, summarizing chapters, outlining arguments on pads of yellow lined paper. But now he would lie in their bed until he grew bored, gazing at his side of the closet which Shoba always left partly open, at a row of tweed jackets and corduroy trousers he would not have to choose from to teach his classes that semester. After the baby died it was too late to withdraw from his teaching duties. But his adviser had arranged things so that he had the spring semester to himself. Shukumar was in his sixth year of graduate school. "That and the summer should give you a good push," his adviser had said. "You should be able to wrap things up by next September."

But nothing was pushing Shukumar. Instead he thought of how he and Shoba had become experts at avoiding each other in their three-bedroom house, spending as much time on separate floors as possible. He thought of how he no longer looked forward to weekends, when she sat for hours on the sofa with her colored pencils and her files, so that he feared that putting on a record in his own house might be rude. He thought of how long it had been since she looked into his eyes and smiled, or whispered his name on those rare occasions they still reached for each other's bodies before sleeping.

In the beginning he had believed that it would pass, that he and Shoba would get through it all somehow. She was only thirty-three. She was strong, on her feet again.

But it wasn't a consolation. It was often nearly lunchtime when Shukumar would finally pull himself out of bed and head downstairs to the coffeepot, pouring out the extra bit Shoba left for him, along with an empty mug, on the countertop.

Shukumar gathered onion skins in his hands and let them drop into the garbage pail on top of the ribbons of fat he'd trimmed from the lamb. He ran the water in the sink, soaking the knife and the cutting board, and rubbed a lemon half along his fingertips to get rid of the garlic smell, a trick he'd learned from Shoba. It was seven-thirty. Through the window he saw the sky, like soft black pitch. Uneven banks of snow still lined the sidewalks, though it was warm enough for people to walk about without hats or gloves. Nearly three feet had fallen in the last storm, so that for a week people had to walk single file, in narrow trenches. For a week that was Shukumar's excuse for not leaving the house. But now the trenches were widening, and water drained steadily into grates in the pavement.

"The lamb won't be done by eight," Shukumar said. "We may have to eat in the dark."

"We can light candles," Shoba suggested. She unclipped her hair, coiled neatly at her nape during the days, and pried the sneakers from her feet without untying them. "I'm going to shower before the lights go," she said, heading for the staircase. "I'll be down."

Shukumar moved her satchel and her sneakers to the side of the fridge. She wasn't this way before. She used to put her coat on a hanger, her sneakers in the closet, and she paid bills as soon as they came. But now she treated the house as if it were a hotel. The fact that the yellow chintz armchair in the living room clashed with the blue-and-maroon Turkish carpet no longer bothered her. On the enclosed porch at the back of the house, a crisp white bag still sat on the wicker chaise, filled with lace she had once planned to turn into curtains.

While Shoba showered, Shukumar went into the downstairs bathroom and found a new toothbrush in its box beneath the sink. The cheap, stiff bristles hurt his gums, and he spit some blood into the basin. The spare brush was one of many stored in a metal basket. Shoba had bought them once when they were on sale, in the event that a visitor decided, at the last minute, to spend the night.

It was typical of her. She was the type to prepare for surprises, good and bad. If she found a skirt or a purse she liked she bought two. She kept the bonuses from her job in a separate bank account in her name. It hadn't bothered him. His own mother had fallen to pieces when his father died, abandoning the house he grew up in and moving back to Calcutta, leaving Shukumar to settle it all. He liked that Shoba was different. It astonished him, her capacity to think ahead. When she used to do the shopping, the pantry was always stocked with extra bottles of olive and corn oil, depending on whether they were cooking Italian or Indian. There were endless boxes of pasta in all shapes and colors, zippered sacks of basmati race, whole sides of lambs and goats from the Muslim butchers at Haymarket, chopped up and frozen in endless plastic bags. Every other Saturday they wound through the maze of stalls Shukumar eventually knew by heart. He watched in disbelief as she bought more food, trailing behind her with canvas bags as she pushed through the crowd, arguing under the morning sun with boys too young to shave but already missing teeth, who twisted up brown paper bags of artichokes, plums, gingerroot, and yams, and dropped them on their scales, and tossed them to Shoba one by one. She didn't mind being jostled, even when she was pregnant. She was tall, and broad-shouldered, with hips that her obstetrician assured her were made for childbearing. During the drive back home, as the car curved along the Charles, they invariably marveled at how much food they'd bought.

It never went to waste. When friends dropped by, Shoba would throw together meals that appeared to have taken half a day to prepare, from things she had frozen and bottled, not cheap things in tins but peppers she had marinated herself with rosemary, and chutneys that she cooked on Sundays, stirring boiling pots of tomatoes and prunes. Her labeled mason jars lined the shelves of the kitchen, in endless sealed pyramids, enough, they'd agreed, to last for their grandchildren to taste. They'd eaten it all by now. Shukumar had been going through their supplies steadily, preparing meals for the two of them, measuring out cupfuls of rice, defrosting bags of meat day after day. He combed through her cookbooks every afternoon, following her penciled instructions to use two teaspoons of ground coriander seeds instead of one, or red lentils instead of yellow. Each of the recipes was dated, telling the first time they had eaten the dish together. April 2, cauliflower with fennel. January 14, chicken with almonds and sultanas. He had no memory of eating those meals, yet there they were, recorded in her neat proofreader's hand. Shukumar enjoyed cooking now. It was the one thing that made him feel productive. If it weren't for him, he knew, Shoba would eat a bowl of cereal for her dinner.

Tonight, with no lights, they would have to eat together. For months now they'd served themselves from the stove, and he'd taken his plate into his study, letting the meal grow cold on his desk before shoving it into his mouth without pause, while Shoba took her plate to the living room and watched game shows, or proofread files with her arsenal of colored pencils at hand.

At some point in the evening she visited him. When he heard her approach he would put away his novel and begin typing sentences. She would rest her hands on his shoulders and stare with him into the blue glow of the computer screen. "Don't work too hard," she would say after a minute or two, and head off to bed. It was the one time in the day she sought him out, and yet he'd come to dread it. He knew it was something she forced herself to do. She would look around the walls of the room, which they had decorated together last summer with a border of marching ducks and rabbits playing trumpets and drums. By the end of August there was a cherry crib under the window, a white changing table with mint-green knobs, and a rocking chair with checkered cushions. Shukumar had disassembled it all before bringing Shoba back from the hospital, scraping off the rabbits and ducks with a spatula. For some reason the room did not haunt him the way it haunted Shoba. In January, when he stopped working at his carrel in the library, he set up his desk there deliberately, partly because the room soothed him, and partly because it was a place Shoba avoided.

Shukumar returned to the kitchen and began to open drawers. He tried to locate a candle among the scissors, the eggbeaters and whisks, and mortar and pestle she'd bought in a bazaar in Calcutta, and used to pound garlic cloves and cardamom pods, back when she used to cook. He found a flashlight, but no batteries, and a half-empty box of birthday candles. Shoba had thrown him a surprise birthday party last May. One hundred and twenty people had crammed into the house—all the friends and the friends of friends they now systematically avoided. Bottles of vinho verde had nested in a bed of ice in the bathtub. Shoba was in her fifth month, drinking ginger ale from a martini glass. She had made a vanilla cream cake with custard and spun sugar. All night she kept Shukumar's long fingers linked with hers as they walked among the guests at the party.

Since September their only guest had been Shoba's mother. She came from Arizona and stayed with them for two months after Shoba returned from the hospital. She cooked dinner every night, drove herself to the supermarket, washed their clothes, put them away. She was a religious woman. She set up a small shrine, a framed picture of a lavender-faced goddess and a plate of marigold petals, on the bedside table in the guest room, and prayed twice a day for healthy grandchildren in the future. She was polite to Shukumar without being friendly. She folded his sweaters with an expertise she had learned from her job in a department store. She replaced a missing button on his winter coat and knit him a beige and brown scarf, presenting it to him without the least bit of ceremony, as if he had only dropped it and hadn't noticed. She never talked to him about Shoba; once, when he mentioned the baby's death, she looked up from her knitting, and said, "But you weren't even there."

It struck him as odd that there were no real candles in the house. That Shoba hadn't prepared for such an ordinary emergency. He looked now for something to put the birthday candles in and settled on the soil of a potted ivy that normally sat on the windowsill over the sink. Even though the plant was inches from the tap, the soil was so dry that he had to water it first before the candles would stand straight. He pushed aside the things on the kitchen table, the piles of mail, the unread library books. He remembered their first meals there, when they were so thrilled to be married, to be living together in the same house at last, that they would just reach for each other foolishly, more eager to make love than to eat. He put down two embroidered place mats, a wedding gift from an uncle in Lucknow, and set out the plates and wineglasses they usually saved for guests. He put the ivy in the middle, the white-edged, star-shaped leaves girded by ten little candles. He switched on the digital clock radio and tuned it to a jazz station.

"What's all this?" Shoba said when she came downstairs. Her hair was wrapped in a thick white towel. She undid the towel and draped it over a chair, allowing her hair, damp and dark, to fall across her back. As she walked absently toward the stove she took out a few tangles with her fingers. She wore a clean pair of sweatpants, a T-shirt, an old flannel robe. Her stomach was flat again, her waist narrow before the flare of her hips, the belt of the robe tied in a floppy knot.

It was nearly eight. Shukumar put the rice on the table and the lentils from the night before into the microwave oven, punching the numbers on the timer.

"You made *rogan josh*," Shoba observed, looking through the glass lid at the bright paprika stew.

Shukumar took out a piece of lamb, pinching it quickly between his fingers so as not to scald himself. He prodded a larger piece with a serving spoon to make sure the meat slipped easily from the bone. "It's ready," he announced.

The microwave had just beeped when the lights went out, and the music disappeared.

"Perfect timing," Shoba said.

"All I could find were birthday candles." He lit up the ivy, keeping the rest of the candles and a book of matches by his plate.

"It doesn't matter," she said, running a finger along the stem of her wineglass. "It looks lovely."

In the dimness, he knew how she sat, a bit forward in her chair, ankles crossed against the lowest rung, left elbow on the table. During his search for candles, Shukumar had found a bottle of wine in a crate he had thought was empty. He clamped the bottle between his knees while he turned in the corkscrew. He worried about spilling, and so he picked up the glasses and held them close to his lap while he filled them. They served themselves, stirring the rice with their forks, squinting as they extracted bay leaves and cloves from the stew. Every few minutes Shukumar lit a few more birthday candles and drove them into the soil of the pot.

"It's like India," Shoba said, watching him tend his makeshift candelabra. "Sometimes the current disappears for hours at a stretch. I once had to attend an entire rice ceremony in the dark. The baby just cried and cried. It must have been so hot."

Their baby had never cried, Shukumar considered. Their baby would never have a rice ceremony, even though Shoba had already made the guest list, and decided on which of her three brothers she was going to ask to feed the child its first taste of solid food, at six months if it was a boy, seven if it was a girl.

"Are you hot?" he asked her. He pushed the blazing ivy pot to the other end of the table, closer to the piles of books and mail, making it even more difficult for them to see each other. He was suddenly irritated that he couldn't go upstairs and sit in front of the computer.

"No. It's delicious," she said, tapping her plate with her fork. "It really is."

He refilled the wine in her glass. She thanked him.

They weren't like this before. Now he had to struggle to say something that interested her, something that made her look up from her plate, or from her proofreading files. Eventually he gave up trying to amuse her. He learned not to mind the silences.

"I remember during power failures at my grandmother's house, we all had to say something," Shoba continued. He could barely see her face, but from her tone he knew her eyes were narrowed, as if trying to focus on a distant object. It was a habit of hers.

"Like what?"

"I don't know. A little poem. A joke. A fact about the world. For some reason my relatives always wanted me to tell them the names of my friends in America. I don't know why the information was so interesting to them. The last time I saw my aunt she asked after four girls I went to elementary school with in Tucson. I barely remember them now."

Shukumar hadn't spent as much time in India as Shoba had. His parents, who settled in New Hampshire, used to go back without him. The first time he'd gone as an infant he'd nearly died of amoebic dysentery. His father, a nervous type, was afraid to take him again, in case something were to happen, and left him with his aunt and uncle in Concord. As a teenager he preferred sailing camp or scooping ice cream during the summers to going to Calcutta. It wasn't until after his father died, in his last year of college, that the country began to interest him, and he studied its history from course books as if it were any other subject. He wished now that he had his own childhood story of India.

"Let's do that," she said suddenly.

"Do what?"

"Say something to each other in the dark."

"Like what? I don't know any jokes."

"No, no jokes." She thought for a minute. "How about telling each other something we've never told before."

"I used to play this game in high school," Shukumar recalled. "When I got drunk."

"You're thinking of truth or dare. This is different. Okay, I'll start." She took a sip of wine. "The first time I was alone in your apartment, I looked in your address book to see if you'd written me in. I think we'd known each other two weeks."

"Where was I?"

"You went to answer the telephone in the other room. It was your mother, and I figured it would be a long call. I wanted to know if you'd promoted me from the margins of your newspaper."

"Had I?"

"No. But I didn't give up on you. Now it's your turn."

He couldn't think of anything, but Shoba was waiting for him to speak. She hadn't appeared so determined in months. What was there left to say to her? He thought back to their first meeting, four years earlier at a lecture hall in Cambridge, where a group of Bengali poets were giving a recital. They'd ended up side by side, on folding wooden chairs. Shukumar was soon bored; he was unable to decipher the literary diction, and couldn't join the rest of the audience as they sighed and nodded solemnly after certain phrases. Peering at the newspaper folded in his lap, he studied the temperatures of cities around the world. Ninety-one degrees in Singapore yesterday, fifty-one in Stockholm. When he turned his head to the left, he saw a woman next to him making a grocery list on the back of a folder, and was startled to find that she was beautiful.

"Okay," he said, remembering. "The first time we went out to dinner, to the Portuguese place, I forgot to tip the waiter. I went back the next morning, found out his name, left money with the manager."

"You went all the way back to Somerville just to tip a waiter?"

"I took a cab."

"Why did you forget to tip the waiter?"

The birthday candles had burned out, but he pictured her face clearly in the dark, the wide tilting eyes, the full grape-toned lips, the fall at age two from her high chair still visible as a comma on her chin. Each day, Shukumar noticed, her beauty, which had once overwhelmed him, seemed to fade. The cosmetics that had seemed superfluous were necessary now, not to improve her but to define her somehow.

"By the end of the meal I had a funny feeling that I might marry you," he said, admitting it to himself as well as to her for the first time. "It must have distracted me."

The next night Shoba came home earlier than usual. There was lamb left over from the evening before, and Shukumar heated it up so that they were able to eat by seven. He'd gone out that day, through the melting snow, and bought a packet of taper candles from the corner store, and batteries to fit the flashlight. He had the candles ready on the countertop, standing in brass holders shaped like lotuses, but they ate under the glow of the copper-shaded ceiling lamp that hung over the table.

When they had finished eating, Shukumar was surprised to see that Shoba was stacking her plate on top of his, and then carrying them over to the sink. He had assumed she would retreat to the living room, behind her barricade of files.

"Don't worry about the dishes," he said, taking them from her hands.

"It seems silly not to," she replied, pouring a drop of detergent onto a sponge. "It's nearly eight o'clock."

His heart quickened. All day Shukumar had looked forward to the lights going out. He thought about what Shoba had said the night before, about looking in his address book. It felt good to remember her as she was then, how bold yet nervous she'd been when they first met, how hopeful. They stood side by side at the sink, their reflections fitting together in the frame of the window. It made him shy, the way he felt the first time they stood together in a mirror. He couldn't recall the last time they'd been photographed. They had stopped attending parties, went nowhere together. The film in his camera still contained pictures of Shoba, in the yard, when she was pregnant.

After finishing the dishes, they leaned against the counter, drying their hands on either end of a towel. At eight o'clock the house went black. Shukumar lit the wicks of the candles, impressed by their long, steady flames.

"Let's sit outside," Shoba said. "I think it's warm still."

They each took a candle and sat down on the steps. It seemed strange to be sitting outside with patches of snow still on the ground. But everyone was out of their houses tonight, the air fresh enough to make people restless. Screen doors opened and closed. A small parade of neighbors passed by with flashlights.

"We're going to the bookstore to browse," a silver-haired man called out. He was walking with his wife, a thin woman in a windbreaker, and holding a dog on a leash. They were the Bradfords, and they had tucked a sympathy card into Shoba and Shukumar's mailbox back in September. "I hear they've got their power."

"They'd better," Shukumar said. "Or you'll be browsing in the dark."

The woman laughed, slipping her arm through the crook of her husband's elbow. "Want to join us?"

"No thanks," Shoba and Shukumar called out together. It surprised Shukumar that his words matched hers.

He wondered what Shoba would tell him in the dark. The worst possibilities had already run through his head. That she'd had an affair. That she didn't respect him for being thirty-five and still a student. That she blamed him for being in Baltimore the way her mother did. But he knew those things weren't true. She'd been faithful, as had he. She believed in him. It was she who had insisted he go to Baltimore. What didn't they know about each other? He knew she curled her fingers tightly when she slept, that her body twitched during bad dreams. He knew it was honeydew she favored over cantaloupe. He knew that when they returned from the hospital the first thing she did when she walked into the house was pick out object of theirs and toss them into a pile in the hallway: books from the shelves, plants from the windowsills, paintings from walls, photos from tables, pots and pans that hung from the hooks over the stove. Shukumar had stepped out of her way, watching as she moved methodically from room to room. When she was satisfied, she stood there staring at the pile she'd made, her lips drawn back in such distaste that Shukumar had thought she would spit. Then she'd started to cry.

He began to feel cold as he sat there on the steps. He felt that he needed her to talk first, in order to reciprocate.

"That time when your mother came to visit us," she said finally. "When I said one night that I had to stay late at work, I went out with Gillian and had a martini."

He looked at her profile, the slender nose, the slightly masculine set of her jaw. He remembered that night well; eating with his mother, tired from teaching two classes back to back, wishing Shoba were there to say more of the right things because he came up with only the wrong ones. It had been twelve years since his father had died, and his mother had come to spend two weeks with him and Shoba, so they could honor his father's memory together. Each night his mother cooked something his father had liked, but she was too upset to eat the dishes herself, and her eyes would well up as Shoba stroked her hand. "It's so touching," Shoba had said to him at the time. Now he pictured Shoba with Gillian, in a bar with striped velvet sofas, the one they used to go to after the movies, making sure she got her extra olive, asking Gillian for a cigarette. He imagined her complaining, and Gillian sympathizing about visits from in-laws. It was Gillian who had driven Shoba to the hospital.

"Your turn," she said, stopping his thoughts.

At the end of their street Shukumar heard sounds of a drill and the electricians shouting over it. He looked at the darkened facades of the houses lining the street. Candles glowed in the windows of one. In spite of the warmth, smoke rose from the chimney.

"I cheated on my Oriental Civilization exam in college," he said. "It was my last semester, my last set of exams. My father had died a few months before. I could see the blue book of the guy next to me. He was an American guy, a maniac. He knew Urdu and Sanskrit. I couldn't remember if the verse we had to identify was an example of a *ghazal* or not. I looked at his answer and copied it down."

It had happened over fifteen years ago. He felt relief now, having told her.

She turned to him, looking not at his face, but at his shoes—old moccasins he wore as if they were slippers, the leather at the back permanently flattened. He wondered if it bothered her, what he'd said. She took his hand and pressed it. "You didn't have to tell me why you did it," she said, moving closer to him.

They sat together until nine o'clock, when the lights came on. They heard some people across the street clapping from their porch, and televisions being turned on. The Bradfords walked back down the street, eating ice-cream cones and waving. Shoba and Shukumar waved back. Then they stood up, his hand still in hers, and went inside.

Somehow, without saying anything, it had turned into this. Into an exchange of confessions—the little ways they'd hurt or disappointed each other, and themselves. The following day Shukumar thought for hours about what to say to her. He was torn between admitting that he once ripped out a photo of a woman in one of the fashion magazines she used to subscribe to and carried it in his books for a week, or saying that he really hadn't lost the sweater-vest she bought him for their third wedding anniversary but had exchanged it for cash at Filene's, and that he had gotten drunk alone in the middle of the day at a hotel bar. For their first anniversary, Shoba had cooked a ten-course dinner just for him. The vest depressed him. "My wife gave me a sweater-vest for our anniversary," he complained to the bartender, his head heavy with cognac. "What do you expect?" the bartender had replied. "You're married."

As for the picture of the woman, he didn't know why he'd ripped it out. She wasn't as pretty as Shoba. She wore a white sequined dress, and had a sullen face and lean, mannish legs. Her bare arms were raised, her fists around her head, as if she were about to punch herself in the ears. It was an advertisement for stockings. Shoba had been pregnant at the time, her stomach suddenly immense, to the point where Shukumar no longer wanted to touch her. The first time he saw the picture he was lying in bed next to her, watching her as she read. When he noticed the magazine in the recycling pile he found the woman and tore out the page as carefully as he could. For about a week he allowed himself a glimpse each day. He felt an intense desire for the woman, but it was a desire that turned to disgust after a minute or two. It was the closest he'd come to infidelity.

He told Shoba about the sweater on the third night, the picture on the fourth. She said nothing as he spoke, expressed no protest or reproach. She simply listened, and then she took his hand, pressing it as she had before. On the third night, she told him that once after a lecture they'd attended, she let him speak to the chairman of his department without telling him that he had a dab of pâté on his chin. She'd been irritated with him for some reason, and so she'd let him go on and on, about securing his fellowship for the following semester, without putting a finger to her own chin as a signal. The fourth night, she said that she never liked the one poem he'd ever published in his life, in a literary magazine in Utah. He'd written the poem after meeting Shoba. She added that she found the poem sentimental.

Something happened when the house was dark. They were able to talk to each other again. The third night after supper they'd sat together on the sofa, and once it was dark he began kissing her awkwardly on her forehead and her face, and though it was dark he closed his eyes, and knew that she did, too. The fourth night they walked carefully upstairs, to bed, feeling together for the final step with their feet before the landing, and making love with a desperation they had forgotten. She wept without sound, and whispered his name, and traced his eyebrows with her finger in the dark. As he made love to her he wondered what he would say to her the next night, and what she would say, the thought of it exciting him. "Hold me," he said, "hold me in your arms." By the time the lights came back on downstairs, they'd fallen asleep.

The morning of the fifth night Shukumar found another notice from the electric company in the mailbox. The line had been repaired ahead of schedule, it said. He was disappointed. He had planned on making shrimp *malai* for Shoba, but when he arrived at the store he didn't feel like cooking anymore. It wasn't the same, he thought, knowing that the lights wouldn't go out. In the store the shrimp looked gray and thin. The coconut milk tin was dusty and overpriced. Still, he bought them, along with a beeswax candle and two bottles of wine.

She came home at seven-thirty. "I suppose this is the end of our game," he said when he saw her reading the notice.

She looked at him. "You can still light candles if you want." She hadn't been to the gym tonight. She wore a suit beneath the raincoat. Her makeup had been retouched recently.

When she went upstairs to change, Shukumar poured himself some wine and put on a record, a Thelonius Monk album he knew she liked.

When she came downstairs they ate together. She didn't thank him or compliment him. They simply ate in a darkened room, in the glow of a beeswax candle. They had survived a difficult time. They finished off the shrimp. They finished off the first bottle of wine and moved on to the second. They sat together until the candle had nearly burned away. She shifted in her chair, and Shukumar thought that she was about to say something. But instead she blew out the candle, stood up, turned on the light switch, and sat down again.

"Shouldn't we keep the lights off?" Shukumar asked.

She set her plate aside and clasped her hands on the table. "I want you to see my face when I tell you this," she said gently.

His heart began to pound. The day she told him she was pregnant, she had used the very same words, saying them in the same gentle way, turning off the basketball game he'd been watching on television. He hadn't been prepared then. Now he was.

Only he didn't want her to be pregnant again. He didn't want to have to pretend to be happy.

"I've been looking for an apartment and I've found one," she said, narrowing her eyes on something, it seemed, behind his left shoulder. It was nobody's fault, she continued. They'd been through enough. She needed some time alone. She had money saved up from a security deposit. The apartment was on Beacon Hill, so she could walk to work. She had signed the lease that night before coming home.

She wouldn't look at him, but he stared at her. It was obvious that she'd rehearsed the lines. All this time she'd been looking for an apartment, testing the water pressure, asking a Realtor if heat and hot water were included in the rent. It sickened Shukumar, knowing that she had spent these past evenings preparing for a life without him. He was relieved and yet he was sickened. This was what she'd been trying to tell him for the past four evenings. This was the point of her game.

Now it was his turn to speak. There was something he'd sworn he would never tell her, and for six months he had done his best to block it from his mind. Before the ultrasound she had asked the doctor not to tell her the sex of their child, and Shukumar had agreed. She had wanted it to be a surprise.

Later, those few times they talked about what had happened, she said at least they'd been spared that knowledge. In a way she almost took pride in her decision, for it enabled her to seek refuge in a mystery. He knew that she assumed it was a mystery for him, too. He'd arrived too late from Baltimore—when it was all over and she was lying on the hospital bed. But he hadn't. He'd arrived early enough to see their baby, and to hold him before they cremated him. At first he had recoiled at the suggestion, but the doctor said holding the baby might help him with the process of grieving. Shoba was asleep. The baby had been cleaned off, his bulbous lids shut tight to the world.

"Our baby was a boy," he said. "His skin was more red than brown. He had black hair on his head. He weighed almost five pounds. His fingers were curled shut, just like yours in the night."

Shoba looked at him now, her face contorted with sorrow. He had cheated on a college exam, ripped a picture of a woman out of a magazine. He had returned a sweater and got drunk in the middle of the day instead. These were the things he had told her. He had held his son, who had known life only within her, against his chest in a darkened room in an unknown wing of the hospital. He had held him until a nurse knocked and took him away, and he promised himself that day that he would never tell Shoba, because he still loved her then, and it was the one thing in her life that she had wanted to be a surprise.

Shukumar stood up and stacked his plate on top of hers. He carried the plates to the sink, but instead of running the tap he looked out the window. Outside the evening was still warm, and the Bradfords were walking arm in arm. As he watched the couple the room went dark, and he spun around. Shoba had turned the lights off. She came back to the table and sat down, and after a moment Shukumar joined her. They wept together, for the things they now knew.

# Ursula K. Le Guin

## (B. 1929)

Known primarily as a science fiction and fantasy writer, Ursula K. Le Guin's writing reflects themes of interdependence and a search for ordered wholeness. She was born in Berkeley, California. Her mother wrote children's stories and her father was the head of the University of California, Berkeley's anthropology department. In 1951, Le Guin received her B.A. from Radcliffe College, and in 1952 she earned her master's degree in romantic languages from Columbia University. While studying in France on a Fulbright scholarship, she met Charles Le Guin, a historian, and they were married in 1953. Le Guin has taught throughout her career, working at Pacific University (1971), University of Washington (1971–1973), Portland State University (1974, 1977, 1979), the University of Reading (1976), and the University of California, San Diego (1979). In 1966, her first novel, *Rocannon's World,* was published. It was the first in a series of science fiction novels about the descendants from an ancient civilization, the Hain, who were seeded on habitable worlds. Other books in Le Guin's Hainish series include *Planet of Exile* (1966), *City of Illusions* (1967), *The Left Hand of Darkness* (1969), *The Dispossessed* (1974), *Four Ways to Forgiveness* (1997), and *The Telling* (2000). Le Guin was awarded the Hugo and the Nebula for *The Left Hand of Darkness.* She has also published a writing guide called *Steering the Craft* (1998).

---

## The Ones Who Walk Away from Omelas                    1976

*(Variations on a theme by William James)*[1]

With a clamor of bells that set the swallows soaring, the Festival of Summer came to the city Omelas, bright-towered by the sea. The rigging of the boats in harbor sparkled with flags. In the streets between houses with red roofs and painted walls, between old moss-grown gardens and under avenues of trees, past great parks and public buildings, processions moved. Some were decorous: old people in long stiff robes of mauve and grey, grave master workmen, quiet, merry women carrying their babies and chatting as they walked. In other streets the music beat faster, a shimmering of gong and tambourine, and the people went dancing, the procession was a dance. Children dodged in and out, their high calls rising like the swallows' crossing flights over the music and the singing. All the processions wound towards the north side of the city, where on the great water-meadow called the Green Fields boys and girls, naked in the bright air, with mud-stained feet and ankles and long, lithe arms,

---

1 **William James:** An American philosopher and psychologist (1842–1910), brother of novelist Henry James.

exercised their restive horses before the race. The horses wore no gear at all but a halter without bit. Their manes were braided with streamers of silver, gold, and green. They flared their nostrils and pranced and boasted to one another; they were vastly excited, the horse being the only animal who has adopted our ceremonies as his own. Far off to the north and west the mountains stood up half encircling Omelas on her bay. The air of morning was so clear that the snow still crowning the Eighteen Peaks burned with white-gold fire across the miles of sunlit air, under the dark blue of the sky. There was just enough wind to make the banners that marked the race-course snap and flutter now and then. In the silence of the broad green meadows one could hear the music winding through the city streets, farther and nearer and ever approaching, a cheerful faint sweetness of the air that from time to time trembled and gathered together and broke out into the great joyous clanging of the bells.

Joyous! How is one to tell about joy? How describe the citizens of Omelas?

They were not simple folk, you see, though they were happy. But we do not say the words of cheer much any more. All smiles have become archaic. Given a description such as this one tends to make certain assumptions. Given a description such as this one tends to look next for the King, mounted on a splendid stallion and surrounded by his noble knights, or perhaps in a golden litter borne by great-muscled slaves. But there was no king. They did not use swords, or keep slaves. They were not barbarians. I do not know the rules and laws of their society, but I suspect that they were singularly few. As they did without monarchy and slavery, so they also got on without the stock exchange, the advertisement, the secret police, and the bomb. Yet I repeat that these were not simple folk, not dulcent shepherds, noble savages, bland utopians. They were not less complex than us. The trouble is that we have a bad habit, encouraged by pedants and sophisticates, of considering happiness as something rather stupid. Only pain is intellectual, only evil interesting. This is the treason of the artist: a refusal to admit the banality of evil and the terrible boredom of pain. If you can't lick 'em, join 'em. If it hurts, repeat it. But to praise despair is to condemn delight, to embrace violence is to lose hold of everything else. We have almost lost hold; we can no longer describe a happy man, nor make any celebration of joy. How can I tell you about the people of Omelas? They were not naïve and happy children—though their children were, in fact, happy. They were mature, intelligent, passionate adults whose lives were not wretched. O miracle! but I wish I could describe it better. I wish I could convince you. Omelas sounds in my words like a city in a fairy tale, long ago and far away, once upon a time. Perhaps it would be best if you imagined it as your own fancy bids, assuming it will rise to the occasion, for certainly I cannot suit you all. For instance, how about technology? I think that there would be no cars or helicopters in and above the streets; this follows from the fact that the people of Omelas are happy people. Happiness is based on a just discrimination of what is necessary, what is neither necessary nor destructive, and what is destructive. In the middle category, however—that of the unnecessary but undestructive, that of comfort, luxury, exuberance, etc.—they could perfectly well have central heating, subway trains, washing machines, and all kinds of marvelous devices not yet invented here, floating light-sources, fuelless power, a cure for the common cold. Or they could have none of that:

it doesn't matter. As you like it. I incline to think that people from towns up and down the coast have been coming in to Omelas during the last days before the Festival on very fast little trains and double-decked trams, and that the train station of Omelas is actually the handsomest building in town, though plainer than the magnificent Farmers' Market. But even granted trains, I fear that Omelas so far strikes some of you as goody-goody. Smiles, bells, parades, horses, bleh. If so, please add an orgy. If an orgy would help, don't hesitate. Let us not, however, have temples from which issue beautiful nude priests and priestesses already half in ecstasy and ready to copulate with any man or woman, lover or stranger, who desires union with the deep godhead of the blood, although that was my first idea. But really it would be better not to have any temples in Omelas—at least, not manned temples. Religion yes, clergy no. Surely the beautiful nudes can just wander about, offering themselves like divine soufflés to the hunger of the needy and the rapture of the flesh. Let them join the processions. Let tambourines be struck above the copulations, and the glory of desire be proclaimed upon the gongs, and (a not unimportant point) let the offspring of these delightful rituals be beloved and looked after by all. One thing I know there is none of in Omelas is guilt. But what else should there be? I thought at first there were no drugs, but that is puritanical. For those who like it, the faint insistent sweetness of *drooz* may perfume the ways of the city, *drooz* which first brings a great lightness and brilliance to the mind and limbs, and then after some hours a dreamy languor, and wonderful visions at last of the very arcana and inmost secrets of the Universe, as well as exciting the pleasure of sex beyond all belief; and it is not habit-forming. For more modest tastes I think there ought to be beer. What else, what else belongs in the joyous city? The sense of victory, surely, the celebration of courage. But as we did without clergy, let us do without soldiers. The joy built upon successful slaughter is not the right kind of joy; it will not do; it is fearful and it is trivial. A boundless and generous contentment, a magnanimous triumph felt not against some outer enemy but in communion with the finest and fairest in the souls of all men everywhere and the splendor of the world's summer: this is what swells the hearts of the people of Omelas, and the victory they celebrate is that of life. I really don't think many of them need to take *drooz.*

Most of the processions have reached the Green Fields by now. A marvelous smell of cooking goes forth from the red and blue tents of the provisioners. The faces of small children are amiably sticky; in the benign grey beard of a man a couple of crumbs of rich pastry are entangled. The youths and girls have mounted their horses and are beginning to group around the startling line of the course. An old woman, small, fat, and laughing, is passing out flowers from a basket, and tall young men wear her flowers in their shining hair. A child of nine or ten sits at the edge of the crowd, alone, playing on a wooden flute. People pause to listen, and they smile, but they do not speak to him, for he never ceases playing and never sees them, his dark eyes wholly rapt in the sweet, thin magic of the tune.

He finishes, and slowly lowers his hands holding the wooden flute.

As if that little private silence were the signal, all at once a trumpet sounds from the pavilion near the starting line: imperious, melancholy, piercing. The horses rear on their slender legs, and some of them neigh in answer. Sober-faced, the young riders stroke the horses' necks and soothe them, whispering, "Quiet, quiet, there my beauty, my hope. . . ." They begin to form in rank along the starting line. The crowds along the racecourse are like a field of grass and flowers in the wind. The Festival of Summer has begun.

Do you believe? Do you accept the festival, the city, the joy? No? Then let me describe one more thing.

In a casement under one of the beautiful public buildings of Omelas, or perhaps in the cellar of one of its spacious private homes, there is a room. It has one locked door, and no window. A little light seeps in dustily between cracks in the boards, secondhand from a cobwebbed window somewhere across the cellar. In one corner of the little room a couple of mops, with stiff, clotted, foul-smelling heads, stand near a rusty bucket. The floor is dirt, a little damp to the touch, as cellar dirt usually is. The room is about three paces long and two wide: a mere broom closet or disused tool room. In the room a child is sitting. It could be a boy or a girl. It looks about six, but actually is nearly ten. It is feeble-minded. Perhaps it was born defective, or perhaps it has become imbecile through fear, malnutrition, and neglect. It picks its nose and occasionally fumbles vaguely with its toes or genitals, as it sits hunched in the corner farthest from the bucket and the two mops. It is afraid of the mops. It finds them horrible. It shuts its eyes, but it knows the mops are still standing there; and the door is locked; and nobody will come. The door is always locked; and nobody ever comes, except that sometimes—the child has no understanding of time or interval—sometimes the door rattles terribly and opens, and a person, or several people, are there. One of them may come in and kick the child to make it stand up. The others never come close, but peer in at it with frightened, disgusted eyes. The food bowl and the water jug are hastily filled, the door is locked, the eyes disappear. The people at the door never say anything, but the child, who has not always lived in the tool room, and can remember sunlight and its mother's voice, sometimes speaks. "I will be good," it says. "Please let me out. I will be good!" They never answer. The child used to scream for help at night, and cry a good deal, but now it only makes a kind of whining, "eh-haa, eh-haa," and it speaks less and less often. It is so thin there are no calves to its legs; its belly protrudes; it lives on a half-bowl of corn meal and grease a day. It is naked. Its buttocks and thighs are a mass of festered sores, as it sits in its own excrement continually.

They all know it is there, all the people of Omelas. Some of them have come to see it, others are content merely to know it is there. They all know that it has to be there. Some of them understand why, and some do not, but they all understand that their happiness, the beauty of their city, the tenderness of their friendships, the health of their children, the wisdom of their scholars, the skill of their makers, even the abundance of their harvest and the kindly weathers of their skies, depend wholly on this child's abominable misery.

This is usually explained to children when they are between eight and twelve, whenever they seem capable of understanding; and most of those who come to see the child are young people, though often enough an adult comes, or comes back, to see the child. No matter how well the matter has been explained to them, these young spectators are always shocked and sickened at the sight. They feel disgust, which they had thought themselves superior to. They feel anger, outrage, impotence, despite all the explanations. They would like to do something for the child. But there is nothing they can do. If the child were brought up into the sunlight out of that vile place, if it were cleaned and fed and comforted, that would be a good thing, indeed; but if it were done, in that day and hour all the prosperity and beauty and delight of Omelas would wither and be destroyed. Those are the terms. To exchange all the goodness and grace of every life in Omelas for that single, small improvement: to throw away the happiness of thousands for the chance of the happiness of one: that would be to let guilt within the walls indeed.

The terms are strict and absolute; there may not even be a kind word spoken to the child.

Often the young people go home in tears, or in a tearless rage, when they have seen the child and faced this terrible paradox. They may brood over it for weeks or years. But as time goes on they begin to realize that even if the child could be released, it would not get much good of its freedom: a little vague pleasure of warmth and food, no doubt, but little more. It is too degraded and imbecile to know any real joy. It has been afraid too long ever to be free of fear. Its habits are too uncouth for it to respond to humane treatment. Indeed, after so long it would probably be wretched without walls about to protect it, and darkness for its eyes, and its own excrement to sit in. Their tears at the bitter injustice dry when they begin to perceive the terrible justice of reality, and to accept it. Yet it is their tears and anger, the trying of their generosity and the acceptance of their helplessness, which are perhaps the true source of the splendor of their lives. Theirs is no vapid, irresponsible happiness. They know that they, like the child, are not free. They know compassion. It is the existence of the child, and their knowledge of its existence, that makes possible the nobility of their architecture, the poignancy of their music, the profundity of their science. It is because of the child that they are so gentle with children. They know that if the wretched one were not here snivelling in the dark, the other one, the flute-player, could make no joyful music as the young riders line up in their beauty for the race in the sunlight of the first morning of summer.

Now do you believe them? Are they not more credible? But there is one more thing to tell, and this is quite incredible.

At times one of the adolescent girls or boys who go to see the child does not go home to weep or rage, does not, in fact, go home at all. Sometimes also a man or a woman much older falls silent for a day or two, and then leaves home. These people go out into the street, and walk down the street alone. They keep walking, and walk straight out of the city of Omelas, through the beautiful gates. They keep walking across the farmlands of Omelas. Each one goes alone, youth or girl, man or woman. Night falls; the traveler must pass down village streets, between the houses with yellow-lit windows, and on out into the darkness of the fields. Each alone, they go west or north, towards the mountains. They go on. They leave Omelas, they walk ahead into the darkness, and they do not come back. The place they go towards is a place even less imaginable to most of us than the city of happiness. I cannot describe it at all. It is possible that it does not exist. But they seem to know where they are going, the ones who walk away from Omelas.

# David Leavitt

(B. 1961)

In 1982, while still an undergraduate at Yale, David Leavitt published his first short story in the *New Yorker*. It was the magazine's first openly gay piece of fiction. Leavitt graduated the following year, receiving a B.A. in English. His first book, *Family Dancing* (1985), was a finalist for the PEN/Faulkner Prize and the National Book Critics Circle Award. Leavitt has also published *The Lost Language of Cranes* (1986), *Equal Affections* (1989), *Arkansas* (1996), and *The Body of Jonah Boyd* (2004). He cowrote *Italian Pleasures* (1996) with his partner, Mark Mitchell. Leavitt currently teaches at the University of Florida. His stories confront difficult, taboo, and at times brutal subjects with bracing humor and elegantly crafted language.

---

## Houses
1990

When I arrived at my office that morning—the morning after Susan took me back—an old man and woman wearing wide-brimmed hats and sweatpants were peering at the little snapshots of houses pinned up in the window, discussing their prices in loud voices. There was nothing surprising in this, except that it was still spring, and the costume and demeanor of the couple emphatically suggested summer vacations. It was very early in the day as well as the season—not yet eight and not yet April. They had the look of people who never slept, people who propelled themselves through life on sheer adrenaline, and they also had the look of kindness and good intention gone awry which so often seems to motivate people like that.

I lingered for a few moments outside the office door before going in, so that I could hear their conversation. I had taken a lot of the snapshots myself, and written the descriptive tags underneath them, and I was curious which houses would pique their interest. At first, of course, they looked at the mansions—one of them, oceanfront with ten bathrooms and two pools, was listed for $10.5 million. "Can you imagine!" the wife said. "Mostly it's corporations that buy those," the husband answered. Then their attentions shifted to some more moderately priced, but still expensive, contemporaries. "I don't know, it's like living on the starship *Enterprise*, if you ask me," the wife said. "Personally, I never would get used to a house like that." The husband chuckled. Then the wife's mouth opened and she said, "Will you look at this, Ed? Just look!" and pointed to a snapshot of a small, cedar-shingled house which I happened to know stood not five hundred feet from the office—$165,000, price negotiable. "It's adorable!" the wife said. "It's just like the house in my dream!"

I wanted to tell her it was my dream house too, my dream house first, to beg her not to buy it. But I held back. I reminded myself I already had a house. I reminded myself I had a wife, a dog.

Ed took off his glasses and peered skeptically at the picture. "It doesn't look too bad," he said. "Still, something must be wrong with it. The price is just too low."

"It's the house in my dream, Ed! The one I dreamed about! I swear it is!"

"I told you, Grace-Anne, the last thing I need is a handyman's special. These are my retirement years."

"But how can you know it needs work? We haven't even seen it! Can't we just look at it? Please?"

"Let's have breakfast and talk it over."

"Okay, okay. No point in getting overeager right?" They headed toward the coffee shop across the street, and I leaned back against the window.

It was just an ordinary house, the plainest of houses. And yet, as I unlocked the office door to let myself in, I found myself swearing I'd burn it down before I'd let that couple take possession of it. Love can push you to all sorts of unlikely threats.

What had happened was this: The night before, I had gone back to my wife after three months of living with a man. I was thirty-two years old, and more than anything in the world, I wanted things to slow, slow down.

It was a quiet morning. We live year-round in a resort town, and except for the summer months, not a whole lot goes on here. Next week things would start gearing up for the Memorial Day closings—my wife Susan's law firm was already frantic with work—but for the moment I was in a lull. It was still early—not even the receptionists had come in yet—so I sat at my desk, and looked at the one picture I kept there, of Susan running on the beach with our golden retriever, Charlotte. Susan held out a tennis ball in the picture, toward which Charlotte, barely out of puppyhood, was inclining her head. And of course I remembered that even now Susan didn't know the extent to which Charlotte was wound up in all of it.

Around nine forty-five I called Ted at the Elegant Canine. I was halfway through dialing before I realized that it was probably improper for me to be doing this, now that I'd officially gone back to Susan, that Susan, if she knew I was calling him, would more than likely have sent me packing—our reconciliation was that fragile. One of her conditions for taking me back was that I not see, not even speak to Ted, and in my shame I'd agreed. Nonetheless, here I was, listening as the phone rang. His boss, Patricia, answered. In the background was the usual cacophony of yelps and barks.

"I don't have much time," Ted said, when he picked up a few seconds later. "I have Mrs. Morrison's poodle to blow-dry."

"I didn't mean to bother you," I said. "I just wondered how you were doing."

"Fine," Ted said. "How are you doing?"

"Oh, okay."

"How did things go with Susan last night?"

"Okay."

"Just okay?"

"Well—it felt so good to be home again—in my own bed, with Susan and Charlotte—" I closed my eyes and pressed the bridge of my nose with my fingers. "Anyway," I said, "it's not fair of me to impose all of this on you. Not fair at all. I mean, here I am, back with Susan, leaving you—"

"Don't worry about it."

"I do worry about it. I do."

There was a barely muffled canine scream in the background and then I could hear Patricia calling for Ted.

"I have to go, Paul—"

"I guess I just wanted to say I miss you. There, I've said it. There's nothing to do about it, but I wanted to say it, because it's what I feel."

"I miss you too, Paul, but listen, I have to go—"

"Wait, wait. There's something I have to tell you."

"What?"

"There was a couple today. Outside the office. They were looking at our house."

"Paul—"

"I don't know what I'd do if they bought it."

"Paul," Ted said, "it's not our house. It never was."

"No, I guess it wasn't." Again I squeezed the bridge of my nose. I could hear the barking in the background grow louder, but this time Ted didn't tell me he had to go.

"Ted?"

"What?"

"Would you mind if I called you tomorrow?"

"You can call me whenever you want."

"Thanks," I said, and then he said a quick good-bye, and all the dogs were gone.

There months before, things had been simpler. There was Susan, and me, and Charlotte. Charlotte was starting to smell, and the monthly ordeal of bathing her was getting to be too much for both of us, and anyway, Susan reasoned, now that she'd finally paid off the last of her law school loans, we really did have the right to hire someone to bathe our dog. (We were both raised in penny-pinching families; even in relative affluence, we had no cleaning woman, no gardener. I mowed our lawn.) And so, on a drab Wednesday morning before work, I bundled Charlotte into the car and drove her over to the Elegant Canine. There, among the fake emerald collars, the squeaky toys in the shape of mice and hamburgers, the rawhide bones and shoes and pizzas, was Ted. He had wheat-colored hair and green eyes, and he smiled at me in a frank and unwavering way I found difficult to turn away from. I smiled back, left Charlotte in his capable-seeming hands and headed off to work. The morning proceeded lazily. At noon I drove back to fetch Charlotte, and found her looking golden and glorious, leashed to a small post in a waiting area just to the side of the main desk. Through the door behind the desk I saw a very wet Pekingese being shampooed in a tub and a West Highland white terrier sitting alertly on a metal table, a chain around its neck. I rang a bell, and Ted emerged, waving to me with an arm around which a large bloody bandage had been carefully wrapped.

"My God," I said. "Was it—"

"I'm afraid so," Ted said. "You say she's never been to a groomer's?"

"I assure you, never in her entire life—we've left her alone with small children— our friends joke that she could be a babysitter—" I turned to Charlotte, who looked up at me, panting in that retriever way. "What got into you?" I said, rather hesitantly. And even more hesitantly: "Bad, bad dog—"

"Don't worry about it," Ted said, laughing. "It's happened before and it'll happen again."

"I am so sorry. I am just so—sorry. I had no idea, really."

"Look, it's an occupational hazard. Anyway we're great at first aid around here." He smiled again, and, calmed for the moment, I smiled back. "I just can't imagine what got into her. She's supposed to go to the vet next week, so I'll ask him what he thinks."

"Well, Charlotte's a sweetheart," Ted said. "After our initial hostilities, we got to be great friends, right, Charlotte?" He ruffled the top of her head, and she looked up at him adoringly. We were both looking at Charlotte. Then we were looking at each other. Ted raised his eyebrows. I flushed. The look went on just a beat too long, before I turned away, and he was totaling the bill.

Afterwards, at home, I told Susan about it, and she got into a state. "What if he sues?" she said, running her left hand nervously through her hair. She had taken her shoes off; the heels of her panty hose were black with the dye from her shoes.

"Susan, he's not going to sue. He's a very nice kid, very friendly."

I put my arms around her, but she pushed me away. "Was he the boss?" she said. "You said someone else was the boss."

"Yes, a woman."

"Oh, great. Women are much more vicious than men, Paul, believe me. Especially professional women. He's perfectly friendly and wants to forget it, but for all we know she's been dreaming about going on *People's Court* her whole life." She hit the palm of her hand against her forehead:

"Susan," I said, "I really don't think—"

"Did you give him anything?"

"Give him anything?"

"You know, a tip. Something."

"No."

"Jesus, hasn't being married to a lawyer all these years taught you anything?" She sat down and stood up again. "All right, all right, here's what we're going to do. I want you to have a bottle of champagne sent over to the guy. With an apology, a note. Marcia Grossman did that after she hit that tree, and it worked wonders." She blew out breath. "I don't see what else we *can* do at this point, except wait, and hope—"

"Susan, I really think you're making too much of all this. This isn't New York City, after all, and really, he didn't seem to mind at all—"

"Paul, honey, please trust me. You've always been very naive about these things. Just send the champagne, all right?"

Her voice had reached an unendurable pitch of annoyance. I stood up. She looked at me guardedly. It was the beginning of a familiar fight between us—in her anxiety, she'd say something to imply, not so subtly, how much more she understood about the world than I did, and in response I would stalk off, insulted and pouty. But this time I did not stalk off—I just stood there—and Susan, closing her eyes in a manner which suggested profound regret at having acted rashly, said in a very soft voice, "I don't mean to yell. It's just that you know how insecure I get about things like this, and really, it'll make me feel so much better to know we've done something. So send the champagne for my sake, okay?" Suddenly she was small and vulnerable, a little girl victimized by her own anxieties. It was a transformation she made easily, and often used to explain her entire life.

"Okay," I said, as I always said, and that was the end of it.

The next day I sent the champagne. The note read (according to Susan's instructions): "Dear Ted: Please accept this little gift as a token of thanks for your professionalism and good humor. Sincerely, Paul Hoover and Charlotte." I should add that at this point I believed I was leaving Susan's name off only because she hadn't been there.

The phone at my office rang the next morning at nine-thirty. "Listen," Ted said, "thanks for the champagne! That was so thoughtful of you."

"Oh, it was nothing."

"No, but it means a lot that you cared enough to send it." He was quiet for a moment. "So few clients do, you know. Care."

"Oh, well," I said. "My pleasure."

Then Ted asked me if I wanted to have dinner with him sometime during the week.

"Dinner? Um—well—"

"I know, you're probably thinking this is sudden and rash of me, but— Well, you seemed like such a nice guy, and—I don't know—I don't meet many people I can really even stand to be around—men, that is—so what's the point of pussyfooting around?"

"No, no, I understand," I said. "That sounds great. Dinner, that is—sounds great."

Ted made noises of relief. "Terrific, terrific. What night would be good for you?"

"Oh, I don't know. Thursday?" Thursday Susan was going to New York to sell her mother's apartment.

"Thursday's terrific," Ted said. "Do you like Dunes?"

"Sure." Dunes was a gay bar and restaurant I'd never been to.

"So I'll make a reservation. Eight o'clock? We'll meet there?"

"That's fine."

"I'm so glad," Ted said. "I'm really looking forward to it."

It may be hard to believe, but even then I still told myself I was doing it to make sure he didn't sue us.

Now, I should point out that not *all* of this was a new experience for me. It's true I'd never been to Dunes, but in my town, late at night, there is a beach, and not too far down the highway, a parking area. Those nights Susan and I fought, it was usually at one of these places that I ended up.

Still, nothing I'd done in the dark prepared me for Dunes, when I got there Thursday night. Not that it was so different from any other restaurant I'd gone to—it was your basic scrubbed-oak, piano-bar sort of place. Only everyone was a man. The maitre d', white-bearded and red-cheeked, a displaced Santa Claus, smiled at me and said, "Meeting someone?"

"Yes, in fact." I scanned the row of young and youngish men sitting at the bar, looking for Ted. "He doesn't seem to be here yet."

"Ted Potter, right?"

I didn't know Ted's last name. "Yes, I think so."

"The dog groomer?"

"Right."

The maitre d', I thought, smirked. "Well, I can seat you now, or you can wait at the bar."

"Oh, I think I'll just wait here, thanks, if that's okay."

"Whatever you want," the maitre d' said. He drifted off toward a large, familial-looking group of young men who'd just walked in the door. Guardedly I surveyed the restaurant for a familiar face which, thankfully, never materialized. I had two or three co-workers who I suspected ate here regularly.

I had to go to the bathroom, which was across the room. As far as I could tell there was no ladies' room at all. As for the men's room, it was small and cramped, with a long trough reminiscent of junior high school summer camp instead of urinals. Above the trough a mirror had been strategically tilted at a downward angle.

By the time I'd finished, and emerged once again into the restaurant, Ted had arrived. He looked breathless and a little worried and was consulting busily with the maitre d'. I waved; he waved back with his bandaged hand, said a few more words to the maitre d' and strode up briskly to greet me. "Hello," he said, clasping my hand with his unbandaged one. It was a large hand, cool and powdery. "Gosh, I'm sorry I'm late. I have to say, when I got here, and didn't see you, I was worried you might have left. Joey—that's the owner—said you'd been standing there one minute and the next you were gone."

"I was just in the bathroom."

"I'm glad you didn't leave." He exhaled what seemed an enormous quantity of breath. "Wow, it's great to see you! You look great!"

"Thanks," I said. "So do you." He did. He was wearing a white oxford shirt with the first couple of buttons unbuttoned, and a blazer the color of the beach.

"There you are," said Joey—the maitre d'. "We were wondering where you'd run off to. Well, your table's ready." He escorted us to the middle of the hubbub. "Let's order some wine," Ted said as we sat down. "What kind do you like?"

I wasn't a big wine expert—Susan had always done the ordering for us—so I deferred to Ted, who, after conferring for a few moments with Joey, mentioned something that sounded Italian. Then he leaned back and cracked his knuckles, bewildered, apparently, to be suddenly without tasks.

"So," he said.

"So," I said.

"I'm glad to see you."

"I'm glad to see you too."

We both blushed. "You're a real estate broker, right? At least, that's what I figured from your business card."

"That's right."

"How long have you been doing that?"

I dug back. "Oh, eight years or so."

"That's great. Have you been out here the whole time?"

"No, no, we moved out here six years ago."

"We?"

"Uh—Charlotte and I."

"Oh." Again Ted smiled. "So do you like it, living year-round in a resort town?"

"Sure. How about you?"

"I ended up out here by accident and just sort of stayed. A lot of people I've met have the same story. They'd like to leave, but you know—the climate is nice, life's not too difficult. It's hard to pull yourself away."

I nodded nervously.

"Is that your story too?"

"Oh—well, sort of," I said. "I was born in Queens, and then—I was living in Manhattan for a while—and then we decided to move out here—Charlotte and I—because I'd always loved the beach, and wanted to have a house, and here you could sell real estate and live all year round." I looked at Ted: Had I caught myself up in a lie or a contradiction? What I was telling him, essentially, was my history, but without Susan—and that was ridiculous, since my history was bound up with Susan's every step of the way. We'd started dating in high school, gone to the same college. The truth was I'd lived in Manhattan only while she was in law school, and had started selling real estate to help pay her tuition. No wonder the story sounded so strangely motiveless as I told it. I'd left out the reasons for everything. Susan was the reason for everything.

A waiter—a youngish blond man with a mustache so pale you could barely see it—gave us menus. He was wearing a white T-shirt and had a corkscrew outlined in the pocket of his jeans.

"Hello, Teddy," he said to Ted. Then he looked at me and said very fast, as if it were one sentence, "I'm Bobby and I'll be your waiter for the evening would you like something from the bar?"

"We've already ordered some wine," Ted said. "You want anything else, Paul?"

"I'm fine."

"Okay, would you like to hear the specials now?"

We both nodded, and Bobby rattled off a list of complex-sounding dishes. It was hard for me to separate one from the other. I had no appetite. He handed us our menus and moved on to another table.

I opened the menu. Everything I read sounded like it would make me sick.

"So do you like selling houses?" Ted asked.

"Oh yes, I love it—I love houses." I looked up, suddenly nervous that I was talking too much about myself. Shouldn't I ask him something about himself? I hadn't been on a date for fifteen years, after all, and even then the only girl I dated was Susan, whom I'd known forever. What was the etiquette in a situation like this? Probably I should ask Ted something about his life, but what kind of question would be appropriate?

Another waiter arrived with our bottle of wine, which Ted poured.

"How long have you been a dog groomer?" I asked rather tentatively.

"A couple of years. Of course I never intended to be a professional dog groomer. It was just something I did to make money. What I really wanted to be, just like about a million and a half other people, was an actor. Then I took a job out here for the summer, and like I said, I just stayed. I actually love the work. I love animals. When I was growing up my mom kept saying I should have been a veterinarian. She still says that to me sometimes, tells me it's not too late. I don't know. Frankly, I don't think I have what it takes to be a vet, and anyway, I don't want to be one. It's important work, but let's fact it, I'm not for it and it's not for me. So I'm content to be a dog groomer." He picked up his wineglass and shook it, so that the wine lapped the rim in little waves.

"I know what you mean," I said, and I did. For years Susan had been complaining that I should have been an architect, insisting that I would have been happier, when the truth was she was just the tiniest bit ashamed of being married to a real estate broker. In her fantasies, "My husband is an architect" sounded so much better.

"My mother always wanted me to be an architect," I said now. "But it was just so she could tell her friends. For some reason people think real estate is a slightly shameful profession, like prostitution or something. They just assume on some level you make your living ripping people off. There's no way around it. An occupational hazard, I guess."

"Like dog bites," said Ted. He poured more wine.

"Oh, about that—" But Bobby was back to take our orders. He was pulling a green pad from the pocket on the back of his apron when another waiter came up to him from behind and whispered something in his ear. Suddenly they were both giggling wildly.

"You going to fill us in?" Ted asked, after the second waiter had left.

"I'm really sorry about this," Bobby said, still giggling. "It's just—" He bent down close to us, and in a confiding voice said, "Jill over at the bar brought in some like really good Vanna, just before work, and like, everything seems really hysterical to me? You know, like it's five years ago and I'm this boy from Emporia, Kansas?" He cast his eyes to the ceiling. "God, I'm like a complete retard tonight. Anyway, what did you say you wanted?"

Ted ordered grilled paillard of chicken with shitake mushrooms in a papaya vinaigrette; I ordered a cheeseburger.

"Who's Jill?" I asked after Bobby had left.

"Everyone's Jill," Ted said. "They're all Jill."

"And Vanna?"

"Vanna White. It's what they call cocaine here." He leaned closer. "I'll bet you're thinking this place is really ridiculous, and you're right. The truth is, I kind of hate it. Only can you name me someplace else where two men can go on a date? I like the fact that you can act datish here, if you know what I mean." He smiled. Under the table our hands interlocked. We were acting very datish indeed.

It was all very unreal. I thought of Susan, in Queens, with her mother. She'd probably called the house two or three times already, was worrying where I was. It occurred to me, dimly and distantly, like something in another life, that Ted knew nothing about Susan. I wondered if I should tell him.

But I did not tell him. We finished dinner, and went to Ted's apartment. He lived in the attic of a rambling old house near the center of town.

We never drank more than a sip or two each of the cups of tea he made for us.

It was funny—when we began making love that first time, Ted and I, what I was thinking was that, like most sex between men, this was really a matter of exorcism, the expulsion of bedeviling lusts. Or exercise, if you will. Or horniness—a word that always makes me think of demons. So why was it, when we finished, there were tears in my eyes, and I was turning, putting my mouth against his hair, preparing to whisper something—who knows what?

Ted looked upset. "What's wrong?" he asked. "Did I hurt you?"

"No," I said. "No. You didn't hurt me."

"Then what is it?"

"I guess I'm just not used to— I didn't expect— I never expected—" Again I was crying.

"It's okay," he said. "I feel it too."

"I have a wife," I said.

At first he didn't answer.

I've always loved houses. Most people I know in real estate don't love houses; they love making money, or making deals, or making sales pitches. But Susan and I, from when we first knew each other, from when we were very young, we loved houses better than anything else. Perhaps this was because we'd both been raised by divorced parents in stuffy apartments in Queens—I can't be sure. All I know is that as early as senior year in high school we shared a desire to get as far out of that city we'd grown up in as we could; we wanted a green lawn, and a mailbox, and a garage. And that passion, as it turned out, was so strong in us that it determined everything. I needn't say more about myself, and as for Susan—well, name me one other first-in-her-class in law school who's chosen—*chosen*—basically to do house closings for a living.

Susan wishes I was an architect. It is her not-so-secret dream to be married to an architect. Truthfully, she wanted me to have a profession she wouldn't have to think was below her own. But the fact is, I never could have been a decent architect because I have no patience for the engineering, the inner workings, the slow layering of concrete slab and wood and Sheetrock. Real estate is a business of surfaces, of first impressions; you have to brush past the water stain in the bathroom, put a Kleenex box over the gouge in the Formica, stretch the life expectancy of the heater from three to six years. Tear off the tile and the paint, the crumbly wallboard and the crackly blanket of insulation, and you'll see what flimsy scarecrows our houses really are, stripped down to their bare beams. I hate the sight of houses in the midst of renovation, naked and exposed like that. But give me a finished house, a polished floor, a sunny day; then I will show you what I'm made of.

The house I loved best, however, the house where, in those mad months, I imagined I might actually live with Ted, was the sort that most brokers shrink from—pretty enough, but drab, undistinguished. No dishwasher, no cathedral ceilings. It would sell, if it sold at all, to a young couple short on cash, or a retiring widow. So don't ask me why I loved this house. My passion for it was inexplicable, yet intense. Somehow I was utterly convinced that this, much more than the sleek suburban one-story Susan and I shared, with its Garland stove and Sub-Zero fridge—this was the house of love.

The day I told Susan I was leaving her, she threw the Cuisinart at me. It bounced against the wall with a thud, and that vicious little blade, dislodged, rolled along the floor like a revolving saw, until it gouged the wall. I stared at it, held fast and suspended above the ground. "How can you just come home from work and tell me this?" Susan screamed. "No preparation, no warning—"

"I thought you'd be relieved," I said.

"Relieved!"

She threw the blender next. It hit me in the chest, then fell on my foot. Instantly I dove to the floor, buried my head in my knees and was weeping as hoarsely and furiously as a child.

"Stop throwing things!" I shouted weakly.

"I can't believe you," Susan said. "You tell me you're leaving me for a man and then you want me to mother you, take care of you? Is that all I've ever been to you? Fuck that! You're not a baby!"

I heard footsteps next, a car starting, Charlotte barking. I opened my eyes. Broken glass, destroyed machinery all over the tiles.

I got in my car and followed her. All the way to the beach. "Leave me alone!" she shouted, pulling off her shoes and running out onto the sand. "Leave me the fuck alone!" Charlotte romped after her, barking.

"Susan!" I screamed. "Susan!" I chased her. She picked up a bit piece of driftwood and hit me with it. I stopped, dropped once again to my knees. Susan kept running. Eventually she stopped. I saw her a few hundred feet up the beach, staring at the waves.

Charlotte kept running between us, licking our faces, in a panic of barks and wails.

Susan started walking back toward me. I saw her getting larger and larger as she strode down the beach. She strode right past me.

"Charlotte!" Susan called from the parking lot. "Charlotte!" But Charlotte stayed. Susan got back in her car and drove away.

At first I stayed at Ted's house. But Susan—we were seeing each other again, taking walks on the beach, negotiating—said that was too much, so I moved into the Dutch

Boy Motel. Still, every day, I went to see the house, either to eat my lunch or just stand in the yard, feeling the sun come down through the branches of the trees there. I was learning a lot about the house. It had been built in 1934 by Josiah Applegate, a local contractor, as a wedding present for his daughter, Julia, and her husband, Spencer Bledsoe. The Bledsoes occupied the house for six years before the birth of their fourth child forced them to move, at which point it was sold to another couple, Mr. and Mrs. Hubert White. They, in turn, sold the house to Mr. and Mrs. Salvatore Rinaldi, who sold it to Mrs. Barbara Adams, a widow, who died. The estate of Mrs. Adams then sold the house to Arthur and Penelope Hilliard, who lived in it until their deaths just last year at the ages of eighty-six and eighty-two. Mrs. Hilliard was the first to go, in her sleep; according to her niece, Mr. Hilliard then wasted away, eventually having to be transferred to Shady Manor Nursing Home, where a few months later a heart attack took him. They had no children. Mr. Hilliard was a retired postman. Mrs. Hilliard did not work, but was an active member of the Ladies' Village Improvement Society. She was famous for her apple cakes, which she sold every year at bake sales. Apparently she went through periods when she would write letters to the local paper every week, long diatribes about the insensitivity of the new houses and new people. I never met her. She had a reputation for being crotchety, but maternal. Her husband was regarded as docile and wicked at poker.

The house had three bedrooms—one pitifully small—and two and a half baths. The kitchen cabinets were made of knotty, dark wood which had grown sticky from fifty years of grease, and the ancient yellow Formica countertops were scarred with burns and knife scratches. The wallpaper was red roses in the kitchen, leafy green leaves in the living room, and was yellowing and peeling at the edges. The yard contained a dogwood, a cherry tree and a clump of gladiolas. Overgrown privet hedges fenced the front door, which was white with a beaten brass knocker. In the living room was a dusty pair of sofas, and dark wood shelves lined with Reader's Digest Condensed Books, and a big television from the early seventies. The shag carpeting—coffee brown—appeared to be a recent addition.

The quilts on the beds, the Hilliards' niece told me, were handmade, and might be for sale. They were old-fashioned patchwork quilts, no doubt stitched together over several winters in front of the television. "Of course," the niece said, "if the price was right, we might throw the quilts in—you know, as an extra."

I was a man with the keys to fifty houses in my pockets. Just that morning I had toured the ten bathrooms of the $10.5-million oceanfront. And I was smiling. I was smiling like someone in love.

I took Ted to see the house about a week after I left Susan. It was a strange time for both of us. I was promising him my undying love, but I was also waking up in the middle of every night crying for Susan and Charlotte. We walked from room to room, just as I'd imagined, and just as I'd planned, in the doorway to the master bedroom, I turned him around to face me, bent his head down (he was considerably taller than me) and kissed him. It was meant to be a moment of sealing, of confirmation, a moment that would make radiantly, abundantly clear the extent to which this house was meant for us, and we for it. But instead the kiss felt rehearsed, dispassionate. And Ted looked nervous. "It's a cute house, Paul," he said. "But God knows I don't have any money. And you already own a house. How can we just *buy* it?"

"As soon as the divorce is settled, I'll get my equity."

"You haven't even filed for divorce yet. And once you do, it could take years."

"Probably not *years*."

"So when *are* you filing for divorce?"

He had his hands in his pockets. He was leaning against a window draped with white flounces of cotton and powderpuffs.

"I need to take things slow," I said. "This is all new for me."

"It seems to me," Ted said, "that you need to take things slow and take things fast at the same time."

"Oh, Ted!" I said. "Why do you have to complicate everything? I just love this house, that's all. I feel like this is where I—where we—where we're meant to live. Our dream house, Ted. Our love nest. Our cottage."

Ted was looking at his feet. "Do you really think you'll be able to leave Susan? For good?"

"Well, of course, I— Of course."

"I don't believe you. Soon enough she's going to make an ultimatum. Come back, give up Ted, or that's it. And you know what you're going to do? You're going to go back to her."

"I'm not," I said. "I wouldn't."

"Mark my words," Ted said.

I lunged toward him, trying to pull him down on the sofa, but he pushed me away.

"I love you," I said.

"And Susan?"

I faltered. "Of course, I love Susan too."

"You can't love two people, Paul. It doesn't work that way."

"Susan said the same thing, last week."

"She's right."

"Why?"

"Because it isn't fair."

I considered this. I considered Ted, considered Susan. I had known Susan since Mrs. Polanski's homeroom in fourth grade. We played *Star Trek* on the playground together, and roamed the back streets of Bayside. We were children in love, and we sought out every movie or book we could find about children in love.

Ted I'd known only a few months, but we'd made love with a passion I'd never imagined possible, and the sight of him unbuttoning his shirt made my heart race.

It was at that moment that I realized that while it is possible to love two people at the same time, in different ways, in the heart, it is not possible to do so in the world.

I had to choose, so of course, I chose Susan.

That day—the day of Ed and Grace-Anne, the day that threatened to end with the loss of my beloved house—Susan did not call me at work. The morning progressed slowly. I was waiting for Ed and Grace-Anne to reappear at the window and walk in the office doors, and sure enough, around eleven-thirty, they did. The receptionist led them to my desk.

"I'm Ed Cavallaro," Ed said across my desk, as I stood to shake his hand. "This is my wife."

"How do you do?" Grace-Anne said. She smelled of some sort of fruity perfume or lipstick, the kind teenaged girls wear. We sat down.

"Well, I'll tell you, Mr. Hoover," Ed said, "we've been summering around here for years, and I've just retired—I worked over at Grumman, upisland?"

"Congratulations," I said.

"Ed was there thirty-seven years," Grace-Anne said. "They gave him a party like you wouldn't believe."

"So, you enjoying retired life?"

"Just between you and me, I'm climbing the walls."

"We're active people," Grace-Anne said.

"Anyway, we've always dreamed about having a house near the beach."

"Ed, let *me* tell about the dream."

"I didn't mean *that* dream."

"I had a dream," Grace-Anne said. "I saw the house we were meant to retire in, clear as day. And then, just this morning walking down the street, we look in your window, and what do we see? The very same house! The house from my dream!"

"How amazing," I said. "Which house was it?"

"That cute little one for one sixty-five," Grace-Anne said. "You know, with the cedar shingles?"

"I'm not sure."

"Oh, I'll show you."

We stood up and walked outside, to the window. "Oh, that house!" I said. "Sure, sure. Been on the market almost a year now. Not much interest in it, I'm afraid."

"Now why is that?" Ed asked, and I shrugged.

"It's a pleasant enough house. But it does have some problems. It'll require a lot of TLC."

"TLC we've got plenty of," Grace-Anne said.

"Grace-Anne, I told you," Ed said, "the last thing I want to do is waste my retirement fixing up."

"But it's my dream house!" Grace-Anne fingered the buttons of her blouse. "Anyway, what harm can it do to look at it?"

"I have a number of other houses in roughly the same price range which you might want to look at—"

"Fine, fine, but first, couldn't we look at that house? I'd be so grateful if you could arrange it."

I shrugged my shoulders. "It's not occupied. Why not?"

And Grace-Anne smiled.

Even though the house was only a few hundred feet away, we drove. One of the rules of real estate is: Drive the clients everywhere. This means your car has to be both commodious and spotlessly clean. I spent a lot—too much—of my life cleaning my car—especially difficult, considering Charlotte.

And so we piled in—Grace-Anne and I in front, Ed in back—and drove the block or so to Maple Street. I hadn't been by the house for a few weeks, and I was happy to see that the spring seemed to have treated it well. The rich greens of the grass and the big maple trees framed it, I thought, rather lushly.

I unlocked the door, and we headed into that musty interior odor which, I think, may well be the very essence of stagnation, cryogenics and bliss.

"Just like I dreamed," Grace-Anne said, and I could understand why. Probably the Hilliards had been very much like the Cavallaros.

"The kitchen's in bad shape," Ed said. "How's the boiler?"

"Old, but functional." We headed down into the spidery basement. Ed kicked things.

Grace-Anne was rapturously fingering the quilts. "Ed, I love this house," she said. "I love it."

Ed sighed laboriously.

"Now, there are several other nice homes you might want to see—"

"None of them was in my dream."

But Ed sounded hopeful. "Grace-Anne, it can't hurt to look. You said it yourself."

"But what if someone else snatches it from under us?" Grace-Anne asked, suddenly horrified.

"I tend to doubt that's going to happen," I said in as comforting a tone as I could muster. "As I mentioned earlier, the house has been on the market for over a year."

"All right," Grace-Anne said reluctantly, "I suppose we could look—*look*—at a few others."

"I'm sure you won't regret it."

"Yes, well."

I turned from them, breathing evenly.

Of course she had no idea I would sooner make sure the house burned down than see a contract for its purchase signed with her husband's name.

I fingered some matches in my pocket. I felt terrified. Terrified and powerful.

When I got home from work that afternoon, Susan's car was in the driveway and Charlotte, from her usual position of territorial inspection on the front stoop, was smiling up at me in her doggy way. I patted her head and went inside, but when I got there, there was a palpable silence which was far from ordinary, and soon enough I saw that its source was Susan, leaning over the kitchen counter in her sleek lawyer's suit, one leg tucked under, like a flamingo.

"Hi," I said.

I tried to kiss her, and she turned away.

"This isn't going to work, Paul," she said.

I was quiet a moment. "Why?" I asked.

"You sound relieved, grateful. You do. I knew you would."

"I'm neither of those things. Just tell me why you've changed your mind since last night."

"You tell me you're in love with a man, you up and leave for three months, then out of the blue you come back. I just don't know what you expect—do you want me to jump for joy and welcome you back like nothing's happened?"

"Susan, yesterday you said—"

"Yesterday," Susan said, "I hadn't thought about it enough. Yesterday I was confused, and grateful, and— God, I was so relieved. But now—now I just don't know. I mean, what the hell has this been for you, anyway?"

"Susan, honey," I said, "I love you. I've loved you my whole life. Remember what your mother used to say, when we were kids, and we'd come back from playing on Saturdays? 'You two are joined at the hip,' she'd say. And we still are."

"Have you ever loved me sexually?" Susan asked, suddenly turning to face me.

"Susan," I said.

"Have you?"

"Of course."

"I don't believe you. I think it's all been cuddling and hugging. Kid stuff. I think the sex only mattered to me. How do I know you weren't thinking about men all those times?"

"Susan, of course not—"

"What a mistake," Susan said. "If only I'd known back then, when I was a kid—"

"Doesn't it matter to you that I'm back?"

"It's not like you never left, for Christ's sake!" She put her hands on my cheeks. "You *left*," she said quietly. "For three months you *left*. And I don't know, maybe love *can* be killed."

She let go. I didn't say anything.

"I think you should leave for a while," Susan said. "I think I need some time alone—some time alone knowing you're alone too."

I looked at the floor. "Okay," I said. And I suppose I said it too eagerly, because Susan said, "If you go back to Ted, that's it. We're finished for good."

"I won't go back to Ted," I said.

We were both quiet for a few seconds.

"Should I go now?"

Susan nodded.

"Well, then, good-bye," I said. And I went.

This brings me to where I am now, which is, precisely, nowhere. I waited three hours in front of Ted's house that night, but when, at twelve-thirty, his car finally pulled into the driveway, someone else got out with him. It has been two weeks since that night. Each day I sit at my desk, and wait for one of them, or a lawyer, to call. I suppose I am homeless, although I think it is probably inaccurate to say that a man with fifty keys in his pocket is ever homeless. Say, then, that I am a man with no home, but many houses.

Of course I am careful. I never spend the night in the same house twice. I bring my own sheets, and in the morning I always remake the bed I've slept in as impeccably as I can. The fact that I'm an early riser helps as well—that way, if another broker arrives, or a cleaning woman, I can say I'm just checking the place out. And if the owners are coming back, I'm always the first one to be notified.

The other night I slept at the $10.5-million oceanfront. I used all the bathrooms; I swam in both the pools.

As for the Hilliards' house—well, so far I've allowed myself to stay there only once a week. Not because it's inconvenient—God knows, no one ever shows the place—but because to sleep there more frequently would bring me closer to a dream of unbearable pleasure than I feel I can safely go.

The Cavallaros, by the way, ended up buying a contemporary in the woods for a hundred and seventy-five, the superb kitchen of which turned out to be more persuasive than Grace-Anne's dream. The Hilliards' house remains empty, unsold. Their niece just lowered the price to one fifty—quilts included.

Funny: Even with all my other luxurious possibilities, I look forward to those nights I spend at the Hilliards' with greater anticipation than anything else in my life. When the key clicks, and the door opens onto that living room with its rows of Reader's Digest Condensed Books, a rare sense of relief runs through me. I feel as if I've come home.

One thing about the Hilliards' house is that the lighting is terrible. It seems there isn't a bulb in the house over twenty-five watts. And perhaps this isn't surprising— they were old people, after all, by no means readers. They spent their lives in front of the television. So when I arrive at night, I have to go around the house, turning on light after light, like ancient oil lamps. Not much to read by, but dim light, I've noticed, has a kind of warmth which bright light lacks. It casts a glow against the woodwork which is exactly, just exactly, like the reflection of raging fire.

# Bobbie Ann Mason

## (B. 1940)

Bobbie Ann Mason was born in Mayfield, Kentucky, where her family had a dairy farm. She received her B.A. in journalism in 1962 from the University of Kentucky, where she wrote for the school paper and published stories in the student literary magazine. After graduation, she worked for film and television magazines while living in New York City. After this, Mason returned to school to earn an M.A. in English from SUNY-Binghamton in 1966 and a Ph.D. in English from the University of Connecticut in 1972. Until 1979, she taught literature at Mansfield State College in Pennsylvania while also writing literary criticism and publishing short stories in the *New Yorker* and other popular magazines.

Mason's first collection of short stories, *Shiloh and Other Stories* (1982), contains lively references to pop culture—television shows, Top 40 music, and fast food restaurants—but it is also tempered by Mason's assured and quiet tone. The collection was awarded the Ernest Hemingway Award in 1983. In 1985 Mason published her first novel, *In Country,* which details a teenage girl's quest to understand the death of her father in Vietnam. The novel was made into a major motion picture. Mason's other works include the novels *Spence + Lila* (1988) and *Feather Crowns* (1993); another collection of short stories, *Love Life* (1989);

and a memoir, *Clear Springs: A Family Story* (1999), one of three finalists for the Pulitzer Prize in 2000.

## *Shiloh*                                                                    1982

Leroy Moffitt's wife, Norma Jean, is working on her pectorals. She lifts three-pound dumbbells to warm up, then progresses to a twenty-pound barbell. Standing with her legs apart, she reminds Leroy of Wonder Woman.

"I'd give anything if I could just get those muscles to where they're real hard," says Norma Jean. "Feel this arm. It's not as hard as the other one."

"That's 'cause you're right-handed," says Leroy, dodging as she swings the barbell in an arc.

"Do you think so?"

"Sure."

Leroy is a truckdriver. He injured his leg in a highway accident four months ago, and his physical therapy, which involves weights and a pulley, prompted Norma Jean to try building herself up. Now she is attending a body-building class. Leroy has been collecting temporary disability since his tractor-trailer jackknifed in Missouri, badly twisting his left leg in its socket. He has a steel pin in his hip. He will probably not be able to drive his rig again. It sits in the backyard, like a gigantic bird that has flown home to roost. Leroy has been home in Kentucky for three months, and his leg is almost healed, but the accident frightened him and he does not want to drive any more long hauls. He is not sure what to do next. In the meantime, he makes things from craft kits. He started by building a miniature log cabin from notched Popsicle sticks. He varnished it and placed it on the TV set, where it remains. It reminds him of a rustic Nativity scene. Then he tried string art (sailing ships on black velvet), a macramé owl kit, a snap-together B-17 Flying Fortress, and a lamp made out of a model truck, with a light fixture screwed in the top of the cab. At first the kits were diversions, something to kill time, but now he is thinking about building a full-scale log house from a kit. It would be considerably cheaper than building a regular house, and besides, Leroy has grown to appreciate how things are put together. He has begun to realize that in all the years he was on the road he never took time to examine anything. He was always flying past scenery.

"They won't let you build a log cabin in any of the new subdivisions," Norma Jean tells him.

"They will if I tell them it's for you," he says, teasing her. Ever since they were married, he has promised Norma Jean he would build her a new home one day. They have always rented, and the house they live in is small and nondescript. It does not even feel like a home. Leroy realizes now.

Norma Jean works at the Rexall drugstore, and she has acquired an amazing amount of information about cosmetics. When she explains to Leroy the three stages of complexion care, involving creams, toners, and moisturizers, he thinks happily of other petroleum products—axle grease, diesel fuel. This is a connection between him and Norma Jean. Since he has been home, he has felt unusually tender about his wife and guilty over his long absences. But he can tell what she feels about him. Norma Jean has never complained about his traveling; she has never made hurt remarks, like calling his truck a "widow-maker." He is reasonably certain she has been faithful to him, but he wishes she would celebrate his permanent homecoming more happily. Norma Jean is often startled to find Leroy at home, and he thinks she seems a little disappointed about it. Perhaps he reminds her too much of the early days of their marriage, before he went on the road. They had a child who died as an infant, years ago. They never speak about their memories of Randy, which have almost faded, but now that Leroy is home all the time, they sometimes feel awkward around each other, and Leroy wonders if one of them should mention the child. He has the feeling that they are waking up out of a dream together—that they must create a new marriage, start fresh. They are lucky they are still married. Leroy has read that for most people losing a child destroys the marriage—or else he heard this on *Donahue*. He can't always remember where he learns things anymore.

At Christmas, Leroy bought an electric organ for Norma Jean. She used to play the piano when she was in high school. "It don't leave you," she told him once. "It's like riding a bicycle."

The new instrument had so many keys and buttons that she was bewildered by it at first. She touched the keys tentatively, pushed some buttons, then pecked out "Chopsticks." It came out in an amplified fox-trot rhythm, with marimba sounds.

"It's an orchestra!" she cried.

The organ had a pecan-look finish and eighteen preset chords, with optional flute, violin, trumpet, clarinet, and banjo accompaniments. Norma Jean mastered the organ almost immediately. At first she played Christmas songs. Then she bought *The Sixties Songbook* and learned every tune in it, adding variations to each with the rows of brightly colored buttons.

"I didn't like these old songs back then," she said. "But I have this crazy feeling I missed something."

"You didn't miss a thing," said Leroy.

Leroy likes to lie on the couch and smoke a joint and listen to Norma Jean play "Can't Take My Eyes Off You" and "I'll Be Back." He is back again. After fifteen years on the road, he is finally settling down with the woman he loves. She is still pretty. Her skin is flawless. Her frosted curls resemble pencil trimmings.

Now that Leroy has come home to stay, he notices how much the town has changed. Subdivisions are spreading across western Kentucky like an oil slick. The sign at the edge of town says "Pop: 11,500"—only seven hundred more than it said twenty years before. Leroy can't figure out who is living in all the new houses. The farmers who used to gather around the courthouse square on Saturday afternoons to play checkers and spit tobacco juice have gone. It has been years since Leroy has thought about the farmers, and they have disappeared without his noticing.

Leroy meets a kid named Stevie Hamilton in the parking lot at the new shopping center. While they pretend to be strangers meeting over a stalled car, Stevie tosses an ounce of marijuana under the front seat of Leroy's car. Stevie is wearing orange jogging shoes and a T-shirt that says CHATTAHOOCHEE SUPER-RAT. His father is a prominent doctor who lives in one of the expensive subdivisions in a new white-columned brick house that looks like a funeral parlor. In the phone book under his name there is a separate number, with the listing "Teenagers."

"Where do you get this stuff?" asks Leroy. "From your pappy?"

"That's for me to know and you to find out," Stevie says. He is slit-eyed and skinny.

"What else you got?"

"What you interested in?"

"Nothing special. Just wondered."

Leroy used to take speed on the road. Now he has to go slowly. He needs to be mellow. He leans back against the car and says, "I'm aiming to build me a log house, soon as I get time. My wife, though, I don't think she likes the idea."

"Well, let me know when you want me again," Stevie says. He has a cigarette in his cupped palm, as though sheltering it from the wind. He takes a long drag, then stomps it on the asphalt and slouches away.

Stevie's father was two years ahead of Leroy in high school. Leroy is thirty-four. He married Norma Jean when they were both eighteen, and their child Randy was born a few months later, but he died at the age of four months and three days. He would be about Stevie's age now. Norma Jean and Leroy were at the drive-in, watching a double feature (*Dr. Strangelove* and *Lover Come Back*), and the baby was sleeping in the back seat. When the first movie ended, the baby was dead. It was the sudden infant death syndrome. Leroy remembers handing Randy to a nurse at the emergency room, as though he were offering her a large doll as a present. A dead baby feels like a sack of flour. "It just happens sometimes," said the doctor, in what Leroy always recalls as a nonchalant tone. Leroy can hardly remember the child anymore, but he still sees vividly a scene from *Dr. Strangelove* in which the President of the United States was talking in a folksy voice on the hot line to the Soviet premier about the bomber accidentally headed toward Russia. He was in the War Room, and the world map was lit up. Leroy remembers Norma Jean standing catatonically beside him in the hospital and himself thinking: Who is this strange girl? He had forgotten who she was. Now scientists are saying that crib death is caused by a virus. Nobody knows anything, Leroy thinks. The answers are always changing.

When Leroy gets home from the shopping center, Norma Jean's mother, Mabel Beasley, is there. Until this year, Leroy has not realized how much time she spends with Norma Jean. When she visits, she inspects the closets and then the plants, informing Norma Jean when a plant is droopy or yellow. Mabel calls the plants "flowers," although there are never any blooms. She always notices if Norma Jean's laundry is piling up. Mabel is a short, overweight woman whose tight, brown-dyed curls look more like a wig than the actual wig she sometimes wears. Today she has brought Norma Jean an off-white dust ruffle she made for the bed; Mabel works in a custom-upholstery shop.

"This is the tenth one I made this year," Mabel says. "I got started and couldn't stop."

"It's real pretty," says Norma Jean.

"Now we can hide things under the bed," says Leroy, who gets along with his mother-in-law primarily by joking with her. Mabel has never really forgiven him for disgracing her by getting Norma Jean pregnant. When the baby died, she said that fate was mocking her.

"What's that thing?" Mabel says to Leroy in a loud voice, pointing to a tangle of yarn on a piece of canvas.

Leroy holds it up for Mabel to see. "It's my needlepoint," he explains. "This is a *Star Trek* pillow cover."

"That's what a woman would do," says Mabel. "Great day in the morning!"

"All the big football players on TV do it," he says.

"Why, Leroy, you're always trying to fool me. I don't believe you for one minute. You don't know what to do with yourself—that's the whole trouble. Sewing!"

"I'm aiming to build us a log house," says Leroy. "Soon as my plans come."

"Like *heck* you are," says Norma Jean. She takes Leroy's needlepoint and shoves it into a drawer. "You have to find a job first. Nobody can afford to build now anyway."

Mabel straightens her girdle and says, "I still think before you get tied down y'all ought to take a little run to Shiloh."

"One of these days, Mama," Norma Jean says impatiently.

Mabel is talking about Shiloh, Tennessee. For the past few years, she has been urging Leroy and Norma Jean to visit the Civil War battleground there. Mabel went there on her honeymoon—the only real trip she ever took. Her husband died of a perforated ulcer when Norma Jean was ten, but Mabel, who was accepted into the United Daughters of the Confederacy in 1975, is still preoccupied with going back to Shiloh.

"I've been to kingdom come and back in that truck out yonder," Leroy says to Mabel, "but we never yet set foot in that battleground. Ain't that something? How did I miss it?"

"It's not even that far," Mabel says.

After Mabel leaves, Norma Jean reads to Leroy from a list she has made. "Things you could do," she announces. "You could get a job as a guard at Union Carbide, where they'd let you set on a stool. You could get on at the lumberyard. You could do a little carpenter work, if you want to build so bad. You could—"

"I can't do something where I'd have to stand up all day."

"You ought to try standing up all day behind a cosmetics counter. It's amazing that I have strong feet, coming from two parents that never had strong feet at all." At the moment Norma Jean is holding on to the kitchen counter, raising her knees one at a time as she talks. She is wearing two-pound ankle weights.

"Don't worry," says Leroy. "I'll do something."

"You could truck calves to slaughter for somebody. You wouldn't have to drive any big old truck for that."

"I'm going to build you this house," says Leroy. "I want to make you a real home."

"I don't want to live in any log cabin."

"It's not a cabin. It's a house."

"I don't care. It looks like a cabin."

"You and me together could lift those logs. It's just like lifting weights."

Norma Jean doesn't answer. Under her breath, she is counting. Now she is marching through the kitchen. She is doing goose steps.

Before his accident, when Leroy came home he used to stay in the house with Norma Jean, watching TV in bed and playing cards. She would cook fried chicken, picnic ham, chocolate pie—all his favorites. Now he is home alone much of the time. In the mornings, Norma Jean disappears, leaving a cooling place in the bed. She eats a cereal called Body Buddies, and she leaves the bowl on the table with soggy tan balls floating in a milk puddle. He sees things about Norma Jean that he never realized before. When she chops onions, she stares off into a corner, as if she can't bear to look. She puts on her house slippers almost precisely at nine o'clock every evening and nudges her jogging shoes under the couch. She saves bread heels for the birds. Leroy watches the birds at the feeder. He notices the peculiar way goldfinches fly past the window. They close their wings, then fall, then spread their wings to catch and lift themselves. He wonders if they close their eyes when they fall. Norma Jean closes her eyes when they are in bed. She wants the lights turned out. Even then, he is sure she closes her eyes.

He goes for long drives around town. He tends to drive a car rather carelessly. Power steering and an automatic shift make a car feel so small and inconsequential that his body is hardly involved in the driving process. His injured leg stretches out comfortably. Once or twice he has almost hit something, but even the prospect of an accident seems minor in a car. He cruises the new subdivisions, feeling like a criminal rehearsing for a robbery. Norma Jean is probably right about a log house being inappropriate here in the new subdivisions. All the houses look grand and complicated. They depress him.

One day when Leroy comes home from a drive he finds Norma Jean in tears. She is in the kitchen making a potato and mushroom-soup casserole, with grated-cheese topping. She is crying because her mother caught her smoking.

"I didn't hear her coming. I was standing here puffing away pretty as you please," Norma Jean says, wiping her eyes.

"I knew it would happen sooner or later," says Leroy, putting his arm around her.

"She don't know the meaning of the word 'knock,'" says Norma Jean. "It's a wonder she hadn't caught me years ago."

"Think of it this way," Leroy says. "What if she caught me with a joint?"

"You better not let her!" Norma Jean shrieks. "I'm warning you, Leroy Moffitt!"

"I'm just kidding. Here, play me a tune. That'll help you relax."

Norma Jean puts the casserole in the oven and sets the timer. Then she plays a ragtime tune, with horns and banjo, as Leroy lights up a joint and lies on the couch, laughing to himself about Mabel's catching him at it. He thinks of Stevie Hamilton— a doctor's son pushing grass. Everything is funny. The whole town seems crazy and small. He is reminded of Virgil Mathis, a boastful policeman Leroy used to shoot pool with. Virgil recently led a drug bust in a back room at a bowling alley, where he seized ten thousand dollars' worth of marijuana. The newspaper had a picture of him holding up the bags of grass and grinning widely. Right now, Leroy can imagine Virgil breaking down the door and arresting him with a lungful of smoke. Virgil would probably have been alerted to the scene because of all the racket Norma Jean is making. Now she sounds like a hard-rock band. Norma Jean is terrific. When she switches to a Latin-rhythm version of "Sunshine Superman," Leroy hums along. Norma Jean's foot goes up and down, up and down.

"Well, what do you think?" Leroy says, when Norma Jean pauses to search through her music.

"What do I think about what?"

His mind has gone blank. Then he says, "I'll sell my rig and build us a house." That wasn't what he wanted to say. He wanted to know what she thought—what she *really* thought—about them.

"Don't start in on that again," says Norma Jean. She begins playing "Who'll Be the Next in Line?"

Leroy used to tell hitchhikers his whole life story—about his travels, his hometown, the baby. He would end with a question: "Well, what do you think?" It was just a rhetorical question. In time, he had the feeling that he'd been telling the same story over and over to the same hitchhikers. He quit talking to hitchhikers when he realized how his voice sounded—whining and self-pitying, like some teenage-tragedy song. Now Leroy has the sudden impulse to tell Norma Jean about himself, as if he had just met her. They have known each other so long they have forgotten a lot about each other. They could become reacquainted. But when the oven timer goes off and she runs to the kitchen, he forgets why he wants to do this.

The next day, Mabel drops by. It is Saturday and Norma Jean is cleaning. Leroy is studying the plans of his log house, which have finally come in the mail. He has them spread out on the table—big sheets of stiff blue paper, with diagrams and numbers printed in white. While Norma Jean runs the vacuum, Mabel drinks coffee. She sets her coffee cup on a blueprint.

"I'm just waiting for time to pass," she says to Leroy drumming her fingers on the table.

As soon as Norma Jean switches off the vacuum, Mabel says in a loud voice, "Did you hear about the datsun dog that killed the baby?"

Norma Jean says, "The word is 'dachshund.'"

"They put the dog on trial. It chewed the baby's legs off. The mother was in the next room all the time." She raises her voice. "They thought it was neglect."

Norma Jean is holding her ears. Leroy manages to open the refrigerator and get some Diet Pepsi to offer Mabel. Mabel still has some coffee and she waves away the Pepsi.

"Datsuns are like that," Mabel says. "They're jealous dogs. They'll tear a place to pieces if you don't keep an eye on them."

"You better watch out what you're saying, Mabel," says Leroy.

"Well, facts is facts."

Leroy looks out the window at his rig. It is like a huge piece of furniture gathering dust in the backyard. Pretty soon it will be an antique. He hears the vacuum cleaner. Norma Jean seems to be cleaning the living room rug again.

Later, she says to Leroy. "She just said that about the baby because she caught me smoking. She's trying to pay me back."

"What are you talking about?" Leroy says, nervously shuffling blueprints.

"You know good and well," Norma Jean says. She is sitting in a kitchen chair with her feet up and her arms wrapped around her knees. She looks small and helpless. She says, "The very idea, her bringing up a subject like that! Saying it was neglect."

"She didn't meant that," Leroy says.

"She might not have *thought* she meant it. She always says things like that. You don't know how she goes on."

"But she didn't really mean it. She was just talking."

Leroy opens a king-sized bottle of beer and pours it into two glasses, dividing it carefully. He hands a glass to Norma Jean and she takes it from him mechanically. For a long time, they sit by the kitchen window watching the birds at the feeder.

Something is happening. Norma Jean is going to night school. She has graduated from her six-week body-building course and now she is taking an adult-education course in composition at Paducah Community College. She spends her evenings outlining paragraphs.

"First you have a topic sentence," she explains to Leroy. "Then you divide it up. Your secondary topic has to be connected to your primary topic."

To Leroy, this sounds intimidating. "I never was any good in English," he says.

"It makes a lot of sense."

"What are you doing this for, anyhow?"

She shrugs. "It's something to do." She stands up and lifts her dumbbells a few times.

"Driving a rig, nobody cared about my English."

"I'm not criticizing your English."

Norma Jean used to say, "If I lose ten minutes' sleep, I just drag all day." Now she stays up late, writing compositions. She got a B on her first paper—a how-to theme on soup-based casseroles. Recently Norma Jean has been cooking unusual foods— tacos, lasagna, Bombay chicken. She doesn't play the organ anymore, though her second paper was called "Why Music Is Important to Me." She sits at the kitchen table, concentrating on her outlines, while Leroy plays with his log house plans, practicing with a set of Lincoln Logs. The thought of getting a truckload of notched, numbered logs scares him, and he wants to be prepared. As he and Norma Jean work together at the kitchen table, Leroy has the hopeful thought that they are sharing something, but he knows he is a fool to think this. Norma Jean is miles away. He knows he is going to lose her. Like Mabel, he is just waiting for time to pass.

One day, Mabel is there before Norma Jean gets home from work, and Leroy finds himself confiding in her. Mabel, he realizes, must know Norma Jean better than he does.

"I don't know what's got into that girl," Mabel says. "She used to go to bed with the chickens. Now you say she's up all hours. Plus her a-smoking. I like to died."

"I want to make her this beautiful home," Leroy says, indicating the Lincoln Logs. "I don't think she even wants it. Maybe she was happier with me gone."

"She don't know what to make of you, coming home like this."

"Is that it?"

Mabel takes the roof off his Lincoln Log cabin. "You couldn't get *me* in a log cabin," she says. "I was raised in one. It's no picnic, let me tell you."

"They're different now," says Leroy.

"I tell you what," Mabel says, smiling oddly at Leroy.

"What?"

"Take her on down to Shiloh. Y'all need to get out together, stir a little. Her brain's all balled up over them books."

Leroy can see traces of Norma Jean's features in her mother's face. Mabel's worn face has the texture of crinkled cotton, but suddenly she looks pretty. It occurs to Leroy that Mabel has been hinting all along that she wants them to take her with them to Shiloh.

"Let's all go to Shiloh," he says. "You and me and her. Come Sunday."

Mabel throws up her hands in protest. "Oh, no, not me. Young folks want to be by themselves."

When Norma Jean comes in with groceries, Leroy says excitedly, "Your mama here's been dying to go to Shiloh for thirty-five years. It's about time we went, don't you think?"

"I'm not going to butt in on anybody's second honeymoon," Mabel says.

"Who's going on a honeymoon, for Christ sake?" Norma Jean says loudly.

"I never raised no daughter of mine to talk that-a-way," Mabel says.

"You ain't seen nothing yet," says Norma Jean. She starts putting away boxes and cans, slamming cabinet doors.

"There's a log cabin at Shiloh," Mabel says. "It was there during the battle. There's bullet holes in it."

"When are you going to *shut up* about Shiloh, Mama?" asks Norma Jean.

"I always thought Shiloh was the prettiest place, so full of history," Mabel goes on. "I just hoped y'all could see it once before I die, so you could tell me about it." Later, she whispers to Leroy, "You do what I said. A little change is what she needs."

"Your name means 'the king,'" Norma Jean says to Leroy that evening. He is trying to get her to go to Shiloh, and she is reading a book about another century.

"Well, I reckon I ought to be right proud."

"I guess so."

"Am I still king around here?"

Norma Jean flexes her biceps and feels them for hardness. "I'm not fooling around with anybody, if that's what you mean," she says.

"Would you tell me if you were?"

"I don't know."

"What does *your* name mean?"

"It was Marilyn Monroe's real name."

"No kidding!"

"Norma comes from the Normans. They were invaders," she says. She closes her book and looks hard at Leroy. "I'll go to Shiloh with you if you'll stop staring at me."

On Sunday, Norma Jean packs a picnic and they go to Shiloh. To Leroy's relief, Mabel says she does not want to come with them. Norma Jean drives, and Leroy, sitting beside her, feels like some boring hitchhiker she has picked up. He tries some conversation, but she answers him in monosyllables. At Shiloh, she drives aimlessly through the park, past bluffs and trails and steep ravines. Shiloh is an immense place, and Leroy cannot see it as a battleground. It is not what he expected. He thought it would look like a golf course. Monuments are everywhere, showing through the thick clusters of trees. Norma Jean passes the log cabin Mabel mentioned. It is surrounded by tourists looking for bullet holes.

"That's not the kind of log house I've got in mind," says Leroy apologetically.

"I know *that*."

"This is a pretty place. Your mama was right."

"It's O.K.," says Norma Jean. "Well, we've seen it. I hope she's satisfied."

They burst out laughing together.

At the park museum, a movie on Shiloh is shown every half hour, but they decide that they don't want to see it. They buy a souvenir Confederate flag for Mabel, and then they find a picnic spot near the cemetery. Norma Jean has brought a picnic cooler, with pimiento sandwiches, soft drinks, and Yodels. Leroy eats a sandwich and then smokes a joint, hiding it behind the picnic cooler. Norma Jean has quit smoking altogether. She is picking cake crumbs from the cellophane wrapper, like a fussy bird.

Leroy says, "So the boys in gray ended up in Corinth. The Union soldiers zapped 'em finally. April 7, 1862."

They both know that he doesn't know any history. He is just talking about some of the historical plaques they have read. He feels awkward, like a boy on a date with an older girl. They are still just making conversation.

"Corinth is where Mama eloped to," says Norma Jean.

They sit in silence and stare at the cemetery for the Union dead and, beyond, at a tall cluster of trees. Campers are parked nearby, bumper to bumper, and small children in bright clothing are cavorting and squealing. Norma Jean wads up the cake wrapper and squeezes it tightly in her hand. Without looking at Leroy, she says, "I want to leave you."

Leroy takes a bottle of Coke out of the cooler and flips off the cap. He holds the bottle poised near his mouth but cannot remember to take a drink. Finally he says, "No, you don't."

"Yes, I do."

"I won't let you."

"You can't stop me."

"Don't do me that way."

Leroy knows Norma Jean will have her own way. "Didn't I promise to be home from now on?" he says.

"In some ways, a woman prefers a man who wanders," says Norma Jean. "That sounds crazy, I know."

"You're not crazy."

Leroy remembers to drink from his Coke. Then he says, "Yes, you *are* crazy. You and me could start all over again. Right back at the beginning."

"We *have* started all over again," says Norma Jean. "And this is how it turned out."

"What did I do wrong?"

"Nothing."

"Is this one of those women's lib things?" Leroy asks.

"Don't be funny."

The cemetery, a green slope dotted with white markers, looks like a subdivision site. Leroy is trying to comprehend that his marriage is breaking up, but for some reason he is wondering about white slabs in a graveyard.

"Everything was fine till Mama caught me smoking," says Norma Jean, standing up. "That set something off."

"What are you talking about?"

"She won't leave me alone—*you* won't leave me alone." Norma Jean seems to be crying, but she is looking away from him. "I feel eighteen again. I can't face that all over again." She starts walking away. "No, it *wasn't* fine. I don't know what I'm saying. Forget it."

Leroy takes a lungful of smoke and closes his eyes as Norma Jean's words sink in. He tries to focus on the fact that thirty-five hundred soldiers died on the grounds around him. He can only think of that war as a board game with plastic soldiers. Leroy almost smiles, as he compares the Confederates' daring attack on the Union camps and Virgil Mathis's raid on the bowling alley. General Grant, drunk and furious, shoved the Southerners back to Corinth, where Mabel and Jet Beasley were married years later, when Mabel was still thin and good-looking. The next day, Mabel and Jet visited the battleground, and then Norma Jean was born, and then she married Leroy and they had a baby, which they lost, and now Leroy and Norma Jean are here at the same battleground. Leroy knows he is leaving out a lot. He is leaving out the insides of history. History was always just names and dates to him. It occurs to him that building a house out of logs is similarly empty—too simple. And the real inner workings of a marriage, like most of history, have escaped him. Now he sees that building a log house is the dumbest idea he could have had. It was clumsy of him to think Norma Jean would want a log house. It was a crazy idea. He'll have to think of something else, quickly. He will wad the blueprints into tight balls and fling them into the lake. Then he'll get moving again. He opens his eyes. Norma Jean has moved away and is walking through the cemetery, following a serpentine brick path.

Leroy gets up to follow his wife, but his good leg is asleep and his bad leg still hurts him. Norma Jean is far away, walking rapidly toward the bluff by the river, and he tries to hobble toward her. Some children run past him, screaming noisily. Norma Jean has reached the bluff, and she is looking out over the Tennessee River. Now she turns toward Leroy and waves her arms. Is she beckoning to him? She seems to be doing an exercise for her chest muscles. The sky is unusually pale—the color of the dust ruffle Mabel made for their bed.

# Toni Morrison

## (B. 1931)

Toni Morrison was born Chloe Anthony Wofford in Loraine, Ohio. An African American novelist, essayist, teacher, and critic, Morrison has contributed to the world of literature by portraying not only the lives of African Americans, but also the lives of women and girls and men and boys who struggle for a sense of self in the American landscape. Morrison joined a writing group in 1961, where each week group members brought a short story or poem for the group to review. She presented a story about a young black girl who prayed to God for blue eyes. Years later, Morrison used this story as the basis for her first novel, *The Bluest Eye* (1970). Her novels *Sula* (1973) and *Song of Solomon* (1977) won the National Book Critic Circle award. *Tar Baby* (1981) won many awards and led to her appearance on the cover of *Newsweek* magazine. While working as the Albert Schweitzer professor of the humanities at the State University of New York in Albany, Morrison wrote her first play, *Dreaming Emmett,* which premiered on January 4, 1986, at the Marketplace Theater in Albany. It is based on the life of Emmett Till, the black fourteen-year-old who was brutally killed in 1955 after he whistled at a white woman.

In 1987, Morrison's groundbreaking novel, *Beloved,* was published to critical accolades, receiving the Pulitzer Prize in fiction in 1988. *Beloved* is the story of Sethe, an escaped slave, who chooses to kill one of her children rather than return her to slavery. It is a complex and lyrically beautiful novel that embodies all of Morrison's creative strengths. While continuing to teach at Princeton University, Morrison completed her novel *Jazz* (1992) and received the Nobel Prize for literature in 1993. The Nobel Committee complimented Morrison for freeing language and American life from the confines of simple conversations about race. She was the eighth woman and the first black woman to win the prize. Morrison's recent work includes the novels *Paradise* (1998) and *Love* (2003). In addition to her novels, she has published a collection of essays, *Playing in the Dark* (1992). "Recitatif" is her only published short story.

## Recitatif                                                          1983

**M**y mother danced all night and Roberta's was sick. That's why we were taken to St. Bonny's. People want to put their arms around you when you tell them you were in a shelter, but it really wasn't bad. No big long room with one hundred beds like Bellevue. There were four to a room, and when Roberta and me came, there was a shortage of state kids, so we were the only ones assigned to 406 and could go from bed to bed if we wanted to. And we wanted to, too. We changed beds every night and for the whole four months we were there we never picked one out as our own permanent bed.

It didn't start out that way. The minute I walked in and the Big Bozo introduced us, I got sick to my stomach. It was one thing to be taken out of your own bed early in the morning—it was something else to be stuck in a strange place with a girl from a whole other race. And Mary, that's my mother, she was right. Every now and then she would stop dancing long enough to tell me something important and one of the things she said was that they never washed their hair and they smelled funny. Roberta sure did. Smell funny, I mean. So when the Big Bozo (nobody ever called her Mrs. Itkin, just like nobody ever said St. Bonaventure)—when she said, "Twyla, this is Roberta. Roberta, this is Twyla. Make each other welcome," I said. "My mother won't like you putting me in here."

"Good," said Bozo. "Maybe then she'll come and take you home."

How's that for mean? If Roberta had laughed I would have killed her, but she didn't. She just walked over to the window and stood with her back to us.

"Turn around," said Bozo. "Don't be rude. Now Twyla. Roberta. When you hear a loud buzzer, that's the call for dinner. Come down to the first floor. Any fights and no movie." And then, just to make sure we knew what we would be missing: *The Wizard of Oz.*

Roberta must have thought I meant that my mother would be mad about my being put in a shelter. Not about rooming with her, because as soon as Bozo left she came over to me and said, "Is your mother sick too?"

"No," I said. "She just likes to dance all night."

"Oh." She nodded her head and I liked the way she understood things so fast. So for the moment it didn't matter that we looked like salt and pepper standing there and that's what the other kids called us sometimes. We were eight years old and got F's all the time. Me because I couldn't remember what I read or what the teacher said. And Roberta because she couldn't read at all and didn't even listen to the teacher. She wasn't good at anything except jacks, at which she was a killer: pow scoop pow scoop pow scoop.

We didn't like each other all that much at first, but nobody else wanted to play with us because we weren't real orphans with beautiful dead parents in the sky. We were dumped. Even the New York City Puerto Ricans and the upstate Indians ignored us. All kinds of kids were in there, black ones, white ones, even two Koreans. The food was good, thought. At least I thought so. Roberta hated it and left whole pieces of things on her plate: Spam, Salisbury steak—even Jell-O with fruit cocktail in it, and she didn't care if I ate what she wouldn't. Mary's idea of supper was popcorn and a can of Yoo-Hoo. Hot mashed potatoes and two weenies was like Thanksgiving for me.

It really wasn't bad, St. Bonny's. The big girls on the second floor pushed us around now and then. But that was all. They wore lipstick and eyebrow pencil and wobbled their knees while they watched TV. Fifteen, sixteen, even, some of them were. They were put-out girls, scared runaways most of them. Poor little girls who fought their uncles off but looked tough to us, and mean. God, did they look mean. The staff tried to keep them separate from the younger children, but sometimes they caught us watching them in the orchard where they played radios and danced with each other. They'd light out after us and pull our hair or twist our arms. We were scared of them,

Roberta and me, but neither of us wanted the other one to know it. So we got a good list of dirty names we could shout back when we ran from them through the orchard. I used to dream a lot and almost always the orchard was there. Two acres, four maybe, of these little apple trees. Hundreds of them. Empty and crooked like beggar women when I first came to St. Bonny's but fat with flowers when I left. I don't know why I dreamt about that orchard so much. Nothing really happened there. Nothing all that important, I mean. Just the big girls dancing and playing the radio. Roberta and me watching. Maggie fell down there once. The kitchen woman with legs like parentheses. And the big girls laughed at her. We should have helped her up, I know, but we were scared of those girls with lipstick and eyebrow pencil. Maggie couldn't talk. The kids said she had her tongue cut out, but I think she was just born that way: mute. She was old and sandy-colored and she worked in the kitchen. I don't know if she was nice or not. I just remember her legs like parentheses and how she rocked when she walked. She worked from early in the morning till two o'clock, and if she was late, if she had too much cleaning and didn't get out till two-fifteen or so, she'd cut through the orchard so she wouldn't miss her bus and have to wait another hour. She wore this really stupid little hat—a kid's hat with ear flaps—and she wasn't much taller than we were. A really awful little hat. Even for a mute, it was dumb—dressing like a kid and never saying anything at all.

"But what about if somebody tries to kill her?" I used to wonder about that. "Or what if she wants to cry? Can she cry?"

"Sure," Roberta said. "But just tears. No sounds come out."

"She can't scream?"

"Nope. Nothing."

"Can she hear?"

"I guess."

"Let's call her," I said. And we did.

"Dummy! Dummy!" She never turned her head.

"Bow legs! Bow legs!" Nothing. She just rocked on, the chin straps of her baby-boy hat swaying from side to side. I think we were wrong. I think she could hear and didn't let on. And it shames me even now to think there was somebody in there after all who heard us call her those names and couldn't tell on us.

We got along all right, Roberta and me. Changed beds every night, got F's in civics and communication skills and gym. The Bozo was disappointed in us, she said. Out of 130 of us state cases, 90 were under twelve. Almost all were real orphans with beautiful dead parents in the sky. We were the only ones dumped and the only ones with F's in three classes including gym. So we got along—what with her leaving whole pieces of things on her plate and being nice about not asking questions.

I think it was the day before Maggie fell down that we found out our mothers were coming to visit us on the same Sunday. We had been at the shelter twenty-eight days (Roberta twenty-eight and a half) and this was their first visit with us. Our mothers would come at ten o'clock in time for chapel, then lunch with us in the teacher's lounge. I thought if my dancing mother met her sick mother it might be good for her. And Roberta thought her sick mother would get a bang out of a dancing one. We got excited about it and curled each other's hair. After breakfast we sat on the bed watching the road from the window. Roberta's socks were still wet. She washed them the night before and put them on the radiator to dry. They hadn't, but she put them on anyway because their tops were so pretty—scalloped in pink. Each of us had a purple construction-paper basket that we had made in craft class. Mine had a yellow crayon rabbit on it. Roberta's had eggs with wiggly lines of color. Inside were cellophane grass and just the jelly beans because I'd eaten the two marshmallow eggs they gave us. The Big Bozo came herself to get us. Smiling she told us we looked very nice and to come downstairs. We were so surprised by the smile we'd never seen before, neither of us moved.

"Don't you want to see your mommies?"

I stood up first and spilled the jelly beans all over the floor. Bozo's smile disappeared while we scrambled to get the candy up off the floor and put it back in the grass.

She escorted us downstairs to the first floor, where the other girls were lining up to file into the chapel. A bunch of grown-ups stood to one side. Viewers mostly. The old biddies who wanted servants and the fags who wanted company looking for children they might want to adopt. Once in a while a grandmother. Almost never anybody young or anybody whose face wouldn't scare you in the night. Because if any of the real orphans had young relatives they wouldn't be real orphans. I saw Mary right away. She had on those green slacks I hated and hated even more now because didn't she know we were going to chapel? And that fur jacket with the pocket linings so ripped she had to pull to get her hands out of them. But her face was pretty—like always—and she smiled and waved like she was the little girl looking for her mother, not me.

I walked slowly, trying not to drop the jelly beans and hoping the paper handle would hold. I had to use my last Chiclet because by the time I finished cutting everything out, all the Elmer's was gone. I am left-handed and the scissors never worked for me. It didn't matter, though; I might just as well have chewed the gum. Mary dropped to her knees and grabbed me, mashing the basket, the jelly beans, and the grass into her ratty fur jacket.

"Twyla, baby. Twyla, baby!"

I could have killed her. Already I heard the big girls in the orchard the next time saying, "Twyyyyla, baby!" But I couldn't stay mad at Mary while she was smiling and hugging me and smelling of Lady Esther dusting powder. I wanted to stay buried in her fur all day.

To tell the truth I forgot about Roberta. Mary and I got in line for the traipse into chapel and I was feeling proud because she looked so beautiful even in those ugly green slacks that made her behind stick out. A pretty mother on earth is better than a beautiful dead one in the sky even if she did leave you all alone to go dancing.

I felt a tap on my shoulder, turned, and saw Roberta smiling. I smiled back, but not too much lest somebody think this visit was the biggest thing that ever happened in my life. Then Roberta said, "Mother, I want you to meet my roommate, Twyla. And that's Twyla's mother."

I looked up it seemed for miles. She was big. Bigger than any man and on her chest was the biggest cross I'd ever seen. I swear it was six inches long each way. And in the crook of her arm was the biggest Bible ever made.

Mary, simpleminded as ever, grinned and tried to yank her hand out of the pocket with the raggedy lining—to shake hands, I guess. Roberta's mother looked down at me and then looked down at Mary too. She didn't say anything, just grabbed Roberta with her Bible-free hand and stepped out of line, walking quickly to the rear of it. Mary was still grinning because she's not too swift when it comes to what's really going on. Then this light bulb goes off in her head and she says "That bitch!" really loud and us almost in the chapel now. Organ music whining; the Bonny Angels singing sweetly. Everybody in the world turned around to look. And Mary would have kept it up—kept calling names if I hadn't squeezed her hand as hard as I could. That helped a little, but she still twitched and crossed and uncrossed her legs all through service. Even groaned a couple of times. Why did I think she would come there and act right? Slacks. No hat like the grandmothers and viewers, and groaning all the while. When we stood for hymns she kept her mouth shut. Wouldn't even look at the words on the page. She actually reached in her purse for a mirror to check her lipstick. All I could think of was that she really needed to be killed. The sermon lasted a year, and I knew the real orphans were looking smug again.

We were supposed to have lunch in the teachers' lounge, but Mary didn't bring anything, so we picked fur and cellophane grass off the mashed jelly beans and ate them. I could have killed her. I sneaked a look at Roberta. Her mother had brought chicken legs and ham sandwiches and oranges and a whole box of chocolate-covered grahams. Roberta drank milk from a thermos while her mother read the Bible to her.

Things are not right. The wrong food is always with the wrong people. Maybe that's why I got into waitress work later—to match up the right people with the right food. Roberta just let those chicken legs sit there, but she did bring a stack of grahams up to me later when the visit was over. I think she was sorry that her mother would not shake my mother's hand. And I liked that and I liked the fact that she didn't say a word about Mary groaning all the way through the service and not bringing any lunch.

Roberta left in May when the apple trees were heavy and white. On her last day we went to the orchard to watch the big girls smoke and dance by the radio. It didn't matter that they said, "Twyyyyla, baby." We sat on the ground and breathed. Lady Esther. Apple blossoms. I still go soft when I smell one or the other. Roberta was going home. The big cross and the big Bible was coming to get her and she seemed sort of glad and sort of not. I thought I would die in that room of four beds without her and I knew Bozo had plans to move some other dumped kid in there with me. Roberta promised to write every day, which was really sweet of her because she couldn't read a lick so how could she write anybody? I would have drawn pictures and sent them to her but she never gave me her address. Little by little she faded. Her wet socks with the pink scalloped tops and her big serious-looking eyes—that's all I could catch when I tried to bring her to mind.

I was working behind the counter at the Howard Johnson's on the Thruway just before the Kingston exit. Not a bad job. Kind of a long ride from Newburgh, but okay once I got there. Mine was the second shift, eleven to seven. Very light until a Greyhound checked in for breakfast around six-thirty. At that hour the sun was all the way clear of the hills behind the restaurant. The place looked better at night—more like shelter—but I loved it when the sun broke in, even if it did show all the cracks in the vinyl and the speckled floor looked dirty no matter what the mop boy did.

It was August and a bus crowd was just unloading. They would stand around a long while: going to the john, and looking at gifts and junk-for-sale machines, reluctant to sit down so soon. Even to eat. I was trying to fill the coffeepots and get them all situated on the electric burners when I saw her. She was sitting in a booth smoking a cigarette with two guys smothered in head and facial hair. Her own hair was so big and wild I could hardly see her face. But the eyes. I would know them anywhere. She had on a powder-blue halter and shorts outfit and earrings the size of bracelets. Talk about lipstick and eyebrow pencil. She made the big girls look like nuns. I couldn't get off the counter until seven o'clock but I kept watching the booth in case they got up to leave before that. My replacement was on time for a change, so I counted and stacked my receipts as fast as I could and signed off. I walked over to the booth, smiling and wondering if she would remember me. Or even if she wanted to remember me. Maybe she didn't want to be reminded of St. Bonny's or have anybody know she was ever there. I know I never talked about it to anybody.

I put my hands in my apron pockets and leaned against the back of the booth facing them.

"Roberta? Roberta Fisk?"

She looked up. "Yeah?"

"Twyla."

She squinted for a second and then said, "Wow."

"Remember me?"

"Sure. Hey. Wow."

"It's been awhile," I said, and gave a smile to the two hairy guys.

"Yeah. Wow. You work here?"

"Yeah," I said. "I live in Newburgh."

"Newburgh? No kidding?" She laughed then, a private laugh that included the guys, and they laughed with her. What could I do but laugh too and wonder why I was standing there with my knees showing out from under that uniform. Without looking I could see the blue-and-white triangle on my head, my hair shapeless in a net, my ankles thick in white oxfords. Nothing could have been less sheer than my stockings. There was this silence that came down right after I laughed. A silence it was her turn to fill up. With introductions, maybe, to her boyfriends or an invitation to sit down and have a Coke. Instead she lit a cigarette off the one she'd just finished and said, "We're on our way to the Coast. He's got an appointment with Hendrix." She gestured casually toward the boy next to her.

"Hendrix? Fantastic," I said. "Really fantastic. What's she doing now?"

Roberta coughed on her cigarette and the two guys rolled their eyes up at the ceiling.

"Hendrix. Jimi Hendrix, asshole. He's only the biggest—Oh, wow. Forget it."

I was dismissed without anyone saying good-bye, so I thought I would do it for her.

"How's your mother?" I asked. Her grin cracked her whole face. She swallowed. "Fine," she said. "How's yours?"

"Pretty as a picture," I said and turned away. The backs of my knees were damp. Howard Johnson's really was a dump in the sunlight.

James is as comfortable as a house slipper. He liked my cooking and I liked his big loud family. They have lived in Newburgh all of their lives and talk about it the way people do who have always known a home. His grandmother has a porch swing older than his father and when they talk about streets and avenues and buildings they call them names they no longer have. They still call the A&P Rico's because it stands on property once a mom-and-pop store owned by Mr. Rico. And they call the new community college Town Hall because it once was. My mother-in-law puts up jelly and cucumbers and buys butter wrapped in cloth from a dairy. James and his father talk about fishing and baseball and I can see them all together on the Hudson in a raggedy skiff. Half the population of Newburgh is on welfare now, but to my husband's family it was still some upstate paradise of a time long past. A time of ice houses and vegetable wagons, coal furnaces and children weeding gardens. When our son was born my mother-in-law gave me the crib blanket that had been hers.

But the town they remembered had changed. Something quick was in the air. Magnificent old houses, so ruined they had become shelter for squatters and rent risks, were bought and renovated. Smart IBM people moved out of their suburbs back into the city and put shutters up and herb gardens in their backyards. A brochure came in the mail announcing the opening of a Food Emporium. Gourmet food, it said—and listed items the rich IBM crowd would want. It was located in a new mall at the edge of town and I drove out to shop there one day—just to see. It was late in June. After the tulips were gone and the Queen Elizabeth roses were open everywhere. I trailed my cart along the aisle tossing in smoked oysters and Robert's sauce and things I knew would sit in my cupboard for years. Only when I found some Klondike ice cream bars did I feel less guilty about spending Jame's fireman's salary so foolishly. My father-in-law ate them with the same gusto little Joseph did.

Waiting in the checkout line I heard a voice say, "Twyla!"

The classical music piped over the aisles had affected me and the woman leaning toward me was dressed to kill. Diamonds on her hands, a smart white summer dress. "I'm Mrs. Benson," I said.

"Ho. Ho. The Big Bozo," she sang.

For a split second I didn't know what she was talking about. She had a bunch of asparagus and two cartons of fancy water.

"Roberta!"

"Right."

"For heaven's sake. Roberta."

"You look great," she said.

"So do you. Where are you? Here? In Newburgh?"

"Yes. Over in Annandale."

I was opening my mouth to say more when the cashier called my attention to her empty counter.

"Meet you outside." Roberta pointed her finger and went into the express line.

I placed the groceries and kept myself from glancing around to check Roberta's progress. I remembered Howard Johnson's and looking for a chance to speak only to be greeted with a stingy "wow." But she was waiting for me and her huge hair was sleek now, smooth around a small, nicely shaped head. Shoes, dress, everything lovely and summery and rich. I was dying to know what happened to her, how she got from Jimi Hendrix to Annandale, a neighborhood full of doctors and IBM executives. Easy, I thought. Everything is so easy for them. They think they own the world.

"How long," I asked her. "How long have you been here?"

"A year. I got married to a man who lives here. And you, you're married too, right? Benson, you said."

"Yeah. James Benson."

"And is he nice?"

"Oh, is he nice?"

"Well, is he?" Roberta's eyes were steady as though she really meant the question and wanted an answer.

"He's wonderful, Roberta. Wonderful."

"So you're happy."

"Very."

"That's good," she said and nodded her head. "I always hoped you'd be happy. Any kids? I know you have kids."

"One. A boy. How about you?"

"Four."

"Four?"

She laughed. "Step kids. He's a widower."

"Oh."

"Got a minute? Let's have coffee."

I thought about the Klondikes melting and the inconvenience of going all the way to my car and putting the bags in the trunk. Served me right for buying all that stuff I didn't need. Roberta was ahead of me.

"Put them in my car. It's right here."

And then I saw the dark blue limousine.

"You married a Chinaman?"

"No." She laughed. "He's the driver."

"Oh, my. If the Big Bozo could see you now."

We both giggled. Really giggled. Suddenly, in just a pulse beat, twenty years disappeared and all of it came rushing back. The big girls (whom we called gar girls—Roberta's misheard word for the evil stone faces described in a civics class) there dancing in the orchard, the ploppy mashed potatoes, the double weenies, the Spam with pineapple. We went into the coffee shop holding on to one another and I tried to think why we were glad to see each other this time and not before. Once, twelve years ago, we passed like strangers. A black girl and white girl meeting in a Howard Johnson's on the road and having nothing to say. One in a blue-and-white triangle waitress hat, the other on her way to see Hendrix. Now we were behaving like sisters separated for much too long. Those four short months were nothing in time. Maybe it was the thing itself. Just being there, together. Two little girls who knew what nobody else in the world knew—how not to ask questions. How to believe what had to be believed. There was politeness in that reluctance and generosity as well. Is your mother sick too? No, she dances all night. Oh—and an understanding nod.

We sat in a booth by the window and fell into recollection like veterans.

"Did you ever learn to read?"

"Watch." She picked up the menu. "Special of the day. Cream of corn soup. Entrées. Two dots and a wiggly line. Quiche. Chef salad, scallops. . . ."

I was laughing and applauding when the waitress came up.

"Remember the Easter baskets?"

"And how we tried to *introduce* them?"

"Your mother with that cross like two telephone poles."

"And yours with those tight slacks."

We laughed so loudly heads turned and made the laughter hard to suppress.

"What happened to the Jimi Hendrix date?"

Roberta made a blow-out sound with her lips.

"When he died I thought about you."

"Oh, you heard about him finally?"

"Finally. Come on. I was a small-town waitress."

"And I was a small-town country dropout. God, were we wild. I still don't know how I got out of there alive."

"But you did."

"I did. I really did. Now I'm Mrs. Kenneth Norton."

"Sounds like a mouthful."

"It is."

"Servants and all?"

Roberta held up two fingers.

"Ow! What does he do?"

"Computers and stuff. What do I know?"

"I don't remember a hell of a lot from those days, but Lord, St. Bonny's is as clear as daylight. Remember Maggie? The day she fell down and those gar girls laughed at her?"

Roberta looked up from her salad and stared at me. "Maggie didn't fall," she said.

"Yes, she did. You remember."

"No, Twyla. They knocked her down. Those girls pushed her down and tore her clothes. In the orchard."

"I don't—that's not what happened."

"Sure it is. In the orchard. Remember how scared we were?"

"Wait a minute. I don't remember any of that."

"And Bozo was fired."

"You're crazy. She was there when I left. You left before me."

"I went back. You weren't there when they fired Bozo."

"What?"

"Twice. Once for a year when I was about ten, another for two months when I was fourteen. That's when I ran away."

"You ran away from St. Bonny's?"

"I had to. What do you want? Me dancing in that orchard?"

"Are you sure about Maggie?"

"Of course I'm sure. You've blocked it, Twyla. It happened. Those girls had behavior problems, you know."

"Didn't they, though. But why can't I remember the Maggie thing?"

"Believe me. It happened. And we were there."

"Who did you room with when you went back?" I asked her as if I would know her. The Maggie thing was troubling me.

"Creeps. They tickled themselves in the night."

My ears were itching and I wanted to go home suddenly. This was all very well but she couldn't just comb her hair, wash her face, and pretend everything was hunky-dory. After the Howard Johnson's snub. And no apology. Nothing.

"Were you on dope or what that time at Howard Johnson's?" I tried to make my voice sound friendlier than I felt.

"Maybe, a little. I never did drugs much. Why?"

"I don't know, you acted sort of like you didn't want to know me then."

"Oh, Twyla, you know how it was in those days: black—white. You know how everything was."

But I didn't know. I thought it was just the opposite. Busloads of blacks and whites came into Howard Johnson's together. They roamed together then: students, musicians, lovers, protesters. You got to see everything at Howard Johnson's, and blacks were very friendly with whites in those days. But sitting there with nothing on my plate but two hard tomato wedges wondering about the melting Klondikes it seemed childish remembering the slight. We went to her car and, with the help of the driver, got my stuff into my station wagon.

"We'll keep in touch this time," she said.

"Sure," I said. "Sure. Give me a call."

"I will," she said, and then, just as I was sliding behind the wheel, she leaned into the window. "By the way. Your mother. Did she ever stop dancing?"

I shook my head. "No. Never."

Roberta nodded.

"And yours? Did she ever get well?"

She smiled a tiny sad smile. "No. She never did. Look, call me, okay?"

"Okay," I said, but I knew I wouldn't. Roberta had messed up my past somehow with that business about Maggie. I wouldn't forget a thing like that. Would I?

Strife came to us that fall. At least that's what the paper called it. Strife. Racial strife. The word made me think of a bird—a big shrieking bird out of 1,000,000,000 B.C. Flapping its wings and cawing. Its eye with no lid always bearing down on you. All day it screeched and at night it slept on the rooftops. It woke you in the morning, and from the *Today* show to the eleven o'clock news it kept you an awful company. I couldn't figure it out from one day to the next. I knew I was supposed to feel something strong, but I didn't know what, and James wasn't any help. Joseph was on the list of kids to be transferred from the junior high school to another one at some far-out-of-the-way place and I thought it was a good thing until I heard it was a bad thing. I mean I didn't know. All the schools seemed dumps to me, and the fact that one was nicer looking didn't hold much weight. But the papers were full of it and then the kids began to get jumpy. In August, mind you. Schools weren't even open yet. I thought Joseph might be frightened to go over there, but he didn't seem scared so I forgot about it, until I found myself driving along Hudson Street out there by the school they were trying to integrate and saw a line of women marching. And who do you suppose was in line, big as life, holding a sign in front of her bigger than her mother's cross. MOTHERS HAVE RIGHTS TOO! it said.

I drove on and then changed my mind. I circled the block, slowed down, and honked my horn.

Roberta looked over and when she saw me she waved. I didn't wave back, but I didn't move either. She handed her sign to another woman and came over to where I was parked.

"Hi."

"What are you doing?"

"Picketing. What's it look like?"

"What for?"

"What do you mean, 'What for?' They want to take my kids and send them out of the neighborhood. They don't want to go."

"So what if they go to another school? My boy's being bussed too, and I don't mind. Why should you?"

"It's not about us, Twyla. Me and you. It's about our kids."

"What's more *us* than that?"

"Well, it is a free country."

"Not yet, but it will be."

"What the hell does that mean? I'm not doing anything to you."

"You really think that?"

"I know it."

"I wonder what made me think you were different."

"I wonder what made me think you were different."

"Look at them," I said. "Just look. Who do they think they are? Swarming all over the place like they own it. And now they think they can decide where my child goes to school. Look at them, Roberta. They're Bozos."

Roberta turned around and looked at the women. Almost all of them were standing still now, waiting. Some were even edging toward us. Roberta looked at me out of some refrigerator behind her eyes. "No, they're not. They're just mothers."

"And what am I? Swiss cheese?"

"I used to curl your hair."

"I hated your hands in my hair."

The women were moving. Our faces looked mean to them of course and they looked as though they could not wait to throw themselves in front of a police car or, better yet, into my car and drage me away by my ankles. Now they surrounded my car and gently, gently began to rock it. I swayed back and forth like a sideways yo-yo. Automatically I reached for Roberta, like the old days in the orchard when they saw us watching them and we had to get out of there, and if one of us fell the other pulled her up and if one of us was caught the other stayed to kick and scratch, and neither would leave the other behind. My arm shot out of the car window but no receiving hand was there. Roberta was looking at me sway from side to side in the car and her face was still. My purse slid from the car seat down under the dashboard. The four policemen who had been drinking Tab in their car finally got the message and strolled over, forcing their way through the women. Quietly, firmly they spoke, "Okay, ladies. Back in line off the streets."

Some of them went away willingly; others had to be urged away from the car doors and the hood. Roberta didn't move. She was looking steadily at me. I was fumbling to turn on the ignition, which wouldn't catch because the gearshift was still in drive. The seats of the car were a mess because the swaying had thrown my grocery coupons all over and my purse was sprawled on the floor.

"Maybe I am different now, Twyla. But you're not. You're the same little state kid who kicked a poor old black lady when she was down on the ground. You kicked a black lady and you have the nerve to call me a bigot."

The coupons were everywhere and the guts of my purse were bunched under the dashboard. What was she saying? Black? Maggie wasn't black.

"She wasn't black," I said.

"Like hell she wasn't, and you kicked her. We both did. You kicked a black lady who couldn't even scream."

"Liar!"

"You're the liar! Why don't you just go on home and leave us alone, huh?"

She turned away and I skidded away from the curb.

The next morning I went into the garage and cut the side out of the carton our portable TV had come in. It wasn't nearly big enough, but after a while I had a decent sign: red spray-painted letters on a white background—AND SO DO CHILDREN****. I meant just to go down to the school and tack it up somewhere so those cows on the picket line across the street could see it, but when I got there, some ten or so others had assembled—protesting the cows across the street. Police permits and everything. I got in line and we strutted in time on our side while Roberta's group strutted on theirs. That first day we were all dignified, pretending the other side didn't exist. The second day there was name calling and finger gestures. But that was about all. People changed signs form time to time, but Roberta never did and neither did I. Actually my sign didn't make sense without Roberta's. "And so do children what?" one of the women on my side asked me. Have rights, I said, as though it was obvious.

Roberta didn't acknowledge my presence in any way, and I got to thinking maybe she didn't know I was there. I began to pace myself in line, jostling people one minute and lagging behind the next, so Roberta and I could reach the end of our respective lines at the same time and there would be a moment in our turn when we would face each other. Still, I couldn't tell whether she saw me and knew my sign was for her. The next day I went early before we were scheduled to assemble. I waited until she got there before I exposed my new creation. As soon as she hoisted her MOTHERS HAVE RIGHTS TOO I began to wave my new one, which said. HOW WOULD YOU KNOW? I know she saw that one, but I had gotten addicted now. My signs got crazier each day, and the women on my side decided that I was a kook. They couldn't make heads or tails out of my brilliant screaming posters.

I brought a painted sign in queenly red with huge black letters that said, IS YOUR MOTHER WELL? Roberta took her lunch break and didn't come back for the rest of the day or any day after. Two days later I stopped going too and couldn't have been missed because nobody understood my signs anyway.

It was a nasty six weeks. Classes were suspended and Joseph didn't go to anybody's school until October. The children—everybody's children—soon got bored with that extended vacation they thought was going to be so great. They looked at TV until their eyes flattened. I spent a couple of mornings tutoring my son, as the other mothers said we should. Twice I opened a text from last year that he had never turned in. Twice he yawned in my face. Other mothers organized living room sessions so the kids would keep up. None of the kids could concentrate, so they drifted back to *The Price Is Right* and *The Brady Bunch*. When the school finally opened there were fights once or twice and some sirens roared through the streets everyone once in a while. There were a lot of photographers from Albany. And just when ABC was about to send up a news crew, the kids settled down like nothing in the world had happened. Joseph hung my HOW WOULD YOU KNOW? sign in his bedroom. I don't know what became of AND SO DO CHILDREN****. I think my father-in-law cleaned some fish on it. He was always puttering around in our garage. Each of his five children lived in Newburgh, and he acted as though he had five extra homes.

I couldn't help looking for Roberta when Joseph graduated from high school, but I didn't see her. It didn't trouble me much what she had said to me in the car. I mean the kicking part. I know I didn't do that, I couldn't do that. But I was puzzled by her telling me Maggie was black. When I thought about it I actually couldn't be certain. She wasn't pitch-black, I knew, or I would have remembered that. What I remember was the kiddie hat and the semicircle legs. I tried to reassure myself about the race thing for a long time until it dawned on me that the truth was already there, and Roberta knew it. I didn't kick her; I didn't join in with the gar girls and kick that lady, but I sure did want to. We watched and never tried to help her and never called for help. Maggie was my dancing mother. Deaf, I thought, and dumb. Nobody inside. Nobody who would hear you if you cried in the night. Nobody who could tell you anything important that you could use. Rocking, dancing, swaying as she walked. And when the gar girls pushed her down and started roughhousing, I knew she wouldn't scream, couldn't—just like me—and I was glad about that.

We decided not to have a tree, because Christmas would be at my mother-in-law's house, so why have a tree at both places? Joseph was as SUNY New Palz and we had to economize, we said. But at the last minute, I changed my mind. Nothing could be that bad. So I rushed around town looking for a tree, something small but wide. By the time I found a place, it was snowing and very late. I dawdled like it was the most important purchase in the world and the tree man was fed up with me. Finally I chose one and had it tied onto the trunk of the car. I drove away slowly because the sand trucks were not out yet and the streets could be murder at the beginning of a snowfall. Downtown the streets were wide and rather empty except for a cluster of people coming out of the Newburgh Hotel. The one hotel in town that wasn't built out of cardboard and Plexiglas. A party, probably. The men huddled in the snow were dressed in tails and the women had on furs. Shiny things glittered from underneath their coats. It made me tired to look at them. Tired, tired, tired. On the next corner was a small diner with loops and loops of paper bells in the window. I stopped the car and went in. Just for a cup of coffee and twenty minutes of peace before I went home and tried to finish everything before Christmas Eve.

"Twyla?"

There she was. In a silvery evening gown and dark fur coat. A man and another woman were with her, the man fumbling for change to put in the cigarette machine. The woman was humming and tapping the counter with her fingernails. They all looked a little bit drunk.

"Well. It's you."

"How are you?"

I shrugged. "Pretty good. Frazzled. Christmas and all."

"Regular?" called the woman from the counter.

"Fine," Roberta called back and then, "Wait for me in the car."

She slipped into the booth beside me. "I have to tell you something, Twyla. I made up my mind if I ever saw you again, I'd tell you."

"I'd just as soon not hear anything, Roberta. It doesn't matter now, anyway."

"No," she said. "Not about that."

"Don't be long," said the woman. She carried two regulars to go and the man peeled his cigarette pack as they left.

"It's about St. Bonny's and Maggie."

"Oh, please."

"Listen to me. I really did think she was black. I didn't make that up. I really thought so. But now I can't be sure. I just remember her as old, so old. And because she couldn't talk—well, you know, I thought she was crazy. She'd been brought up in an institution like my mother was and like I thought I would be too. And you were right. We didn't kick her. It was the gar girls. Only them. But, well, I wanted to. I really wanted them to hurt her. I said we did it, too. You and me, but that's not true. And I don't want you to carry that around. It was just that I wanted to do it so bad that day—wanting to is doing it."

Her eyes were watery from the drinks she'd had, I guess. I know it's that way with me. One glass of wine and I start bawling over the littlest thing.

"We were kids, Roberta."

"Yeah. Yeah. I know, just kids."

"Eight."

"Eight."

"And lonely."

"Scared, too."

She wiped her cheeks with the heel of her hand and smiled. "Well, that's all I wanted to say."

I nodded and couldn't think of any way to fill the silence that went from the diner past the paper bells on out into the snow. It was heavy now. I thought I'd better wait for the sand trucks before starting home.

"Thanks, Roberta."

"Sure."

"Did I tell you? My mother, she never did stop dancing."

"Yes. You told me. And mine, she never got well." Roberta lifted her hands from the tabletop and covered her face with her palms. When she took them away she really was crying. "Oh, shit, Twyla. Shit, shit, shit. What the hell happened to Maggie?"

# Alice Munro

## (B. 1931)

Alice Munro was born in the small rural town of Wingham, in southwestern Ontario. She prefers to set her fiction within the borders of her native Canada, but her reputation as a writer of great complexity and sensitivity extends to an international audience. She published her first short story as a teen in 1950 and her first collection of stories, *Dance of the Happy Shades*, in 1968. The collection garnered Canada's highest literary prize, the Governor General's Award. Munro followed this success with *Lives of Girls and Women* (1971), a novel constructed from a series of interconnected short stories. Munro's remaining books are all short story collections: *Something I've Been Meaning to Tell You* (1974); *Who Do You Think You Are?* (titled *The Beggar Maid* in English and American editions, 1978); *The Moons of Jupiter* (1982); *The Progress of Love* (1986); *Friend of My Youth* (1990); *Open Secrets* (1994); *Selected Stories* (1996); *The Love of a Good Woman* (1998); and her newest publication, *Hateship, Friendship, Courtship, Loveship, Marriage* (2001).

Munro does not claim to write autobiographical fiction, but her stories set in rural Ontario contain an emotional truth that reflects her own experiences. Like regional writers of American fiction, such as William Faulkner or Eudora Welty, Munro's stories contain a landscape that informs and shapes the story, as well as the emotional lives of her characters. She has a sensitive ear for local speech patterns and expressions, and this particular attention to language creates an intense sense of intimacy between the reader and the character. Her later short story collections, including *Open Secrets* and *The Love of a Good*

*Woman,* were most responsible for the extension of Munro's fame outside Canada.

---

## Floating Bridge

*2001*

One time, she had left him. The immediate reason was fairly trivial. He had joined a couple of the Young Offenders ("Yo-yos" was what he called them) in gobbling up a gingerbread cake she had just made, and had been intending to serve after a meeting that evening. Unobserved—at least by Neal and the Yo-yos—she had left the house and gone to sit in a three-sided shelter on the main street, where the city bus stopped twice a day. She had never been in there before, and she had a couple of hours to wait. She sat and read everything that had been written on or cut into those wooden walls. Various initials loved each other 4 ever. Laurie G. sucked cock. Dunk Cultis was a fag. So was Mr. Garner (Math).

Eat Shit. H.W. Gange rules. God hates filth. Kevin S. Is Dead meat. Amanda W is beautiful and sweet and I wish they did not put her in jail because I miss her with all my heart. I want to fuck V.P. Ladies have to sit here and read this disgusting dirty things what you write. Fuck them.

Looking at this barrage of human messages—and puzzling in particular over the heartfelt, very neatly written sentence concerning Amanda W—Jinny wondered if people were alone when they wrote such things. And she went on to imagine herself sitting here or in some similar place, waiting for a bus, alone as she would surely be if she went ahead with the plan she was set on now. Would she be compelled to make statements on public walls?

She felt herself connected at present to those people who had had to write certain things down—connected by her feelings of anger and petty outrage (perhaps it was petty?), and by her excitement at what she was doing to Neal, to pay him back. It occurred to her that the life she was carrying herself into might not give her anybody to be effectively angry at, or anybody who owed her anything, who could possibly be rewarded or punished or truly affected by what she might do. She was not, after all, somebody people flocked to. And yet she was choosy, in her own way.

The bus was still not in sight when she got up and walked home. Neal was not there. He was returning the boys to the school, and by the time he got back, somebody had already arrived for the meeting. She told Neal what she'd done, but only when she was well over it and it could be turned into a joke. In fact, it became a joke she told in company—leaving out or just describing in a general way the things she'd read on the walls.

"Would you ever have thought to come after me?" she said to Neal.

"Of course. Given time."

The oncologist had a priestly demeanor and even wore a black turtleneck shirt under a white smock—an outfit that suggested he had just come from some ceremonial mixing and dosing. His skin was young and smooth—it looked like butterscotch. On the dome of his head, there was just a faint black growth of hair, a delicate sprouting, very like the fuzz Jinny was sporting herself, though hers was brownish-gray, like mouse fur. At first, Jinny had wondered if he could possibly be a patient as well as a doctor. Then, whether he had adopted this style to make the patients more comfortable. More likely it was a transplant. Or just the way he liked to wear his hair.

You couldn't ask him. He came from Syria or Jordan—someplace where doctors kept their dignity. His courtesies were frigid.

"Now," he said, "I do not wish to give a wrong impression."

She went out of the air-conditioned building into the stunning glare of a late afternoon, in August, in Ontario. Sometimes the sun burned through, sometimes it stayed behind thin clouds—it was just as hot either way. She saw the car detach itself from its place at the curb and make its way down the street to pick her up. It was a light-blue, shimmery, sickening color. Lighter blue where the rust spots had been painted over. Its stickers said, "I Know I Drive a Wreck But You Should See My House," and "Honor Thy Mother—Earth," and (this was more recent) "Use Pesticide—Kill Weeds, Promote Cancer."

Neal came around to help her.

"She's in the car," he said. There was an eager note in his voice which registered vaguely as a warning or a plea. A buzz around him, a tension, that told Jinny it wasn't time to give him her news, if "news" was what you'd call it. When Neal was around other people, even one person other than Jinny, his behavior changed, becoming more animated, enthusiastic, ingratiating. Jinny was not bothered by that anymore—they had been together for twenty-one years. And she herself changed—as a reaction, she used to think—becoming more reserved and slightly ironic. Some masquerades were necessary, or just too habitual to be dropped. Like Neal's antique appearance—the bandanna headband, the rough gray ponytail, the little gold earring that caught the light like the gold rims around his teeth, and his shaggy outlaw clothes.

While Jinny had been seeing the doctor, Neal had been picking up the girl who was going to help them with their life now. He knew her from the Correctional Institute for Young Offenders, where he was a teacher and she had worked in the kitchen. The Correctional Institute was just outside the town where they lived, about thirty miles away. The girl had quit her kitchen job a few months ago and taken a job looking after a farm household where the mother was sick. Luckily she was now free.

"What happened to the woman?" Jinny had said. "Did she die?"

Neal said, "She went into the hospital."

"Same deal."

Neal had spent nearly all his spare time, in the years Jinny had been with him, organizing and carrying out campaigns. Not just political campaigns (those, too) but efforts to preserve historic buildings and bridges and cemeteries, to keep trees from being cut down both along the town streets and in isolated patches of old forest, to save rivers from poisonous runoff and choice land from developers and the local population from casinos. Letters and petitions were always being written, government departments lobbied, posters distributed, protests organized. The front room of their house had been the scene of rages of indignation (which gave people a lot of satisfaction, Jinny thought) and of confused propositions and arguments, and Neal's nervy buoyancy. Now it was suddenly emptied. The front room would become the sickroom. It made her think of when she first walked into the house, straight from her parents' split-level with the swag curtains, and imagined all those shelves filled with books, wooden shutters on the windows, and those beautiful Middle Eastern rugs she always forgot the name of, on the varnished floor. On the one bare wall, the Canaletto print she had bought for her room at college—Lord Mayor's Day on the Thames. She had actually put that up, though she never noticed it anymore.

They rented a hospital bed—they didn't really need it yet, but it was better to get one while you could, because they were often in short supply. Neal thought of everything. He hung up some heavy curtains that were discards from a friend's family room. Jinny thought them very ugly, but she knew now that there comes a time when ugly and beautiful serve pretty much the same purpose, when anything you look at is just a peg to hang the unruly sensations of your body on.

Jinny was forty-two, and until recently she had looked younger than her age. Neal was sixteen years older than she was. So she had thought that in the natural course of things she would be in the position he was in now, and she had sometimes worried about how she would manage it. Once, when she was holding his hand in bed before they went to sleep, his warm and present hand, she had thought that she would hold or touch this hand, at least once, when he was dead. And no matter how long she had foreseen this, she would not be able to credit it. To think of his not having some knowledge of this moment and of her brought on a kind of emotional vertigo, the sense of a horrid drop.

And yet—an excitement. The unspeakable excitement you feel when a galloping disaster promises to release you from all responsibility for your own life. Then from shame you must compose yourself, and stay very quiet.

"Where are you going?" he had said, when she withdrew her hand.

"No place. Just turning over."

She didn't know if Neal had any such feeling, now that it had turned out to be her. She had asked him if he was used to the idea yet. He shook his head.

She said, "Me neither."

Then she said, "Just don't let the Grief Counsellors in. They could be hanging around already. Wanting to make a preëmptive strike."

"Don't harrow me," he said, in a voice of rare anger.

"Sorry."

"You don't always have to take the lighter view."

"I know," she said. But the fact was that, with so much going on and present events grabbing so much of her attention, she found it hard to take any view at all.

"This is Helen," Neal said. "This is who is going to look after us from now on. She won't stand for any nonsense, either."

"Good for her," said Jinny. She put out her hand, once she was settled in the car. But the girl might not have seen it, low down between the two front seats.

Or she might not have known what to do. Neal had said that she came from an unbelievable situation, an absolutely barbaric family. Things had gone on that you could not imagine going on in this day and age. An isolated farm, a widower—a tyrannical, deranged, incestuous old man—with a mentally deficient daughter and the two girl children. Helen, the older one, who had run away at the age of fourteen after beating up on the old man, had been sheltered by a neighbor, who phoned the police. And then the police had come and got the younger sister and made both children wards of the Children's Aid. The old man and his daughter—that is, the childrens' father and their mother—were both placed in a psychiatric hospital. Foster parents took Helen and her sister, who were mentally and physically normal. They were sent to school and had a miserable time there, having to start first grade in their teens. But they both learned enough to be employable.

When Neal had started the car up, the girl decided to speak.

"You picked a hot enough day to be out in," she said. It was the sort of thing she might have heard people say, to start a conversation. She spoke in a hard, flat tone of antagonism and distrust, but even that, Jinny knew by now, should not be taken personally. It was just the way some people sounded—particularly country people—in this part of the world.

"If you're hot, you can turn the air-conditioner on," Neal said. "We've got the old-fashioned kind—just roll down all the windows."

The turn they made at the next corner was one Jinny had not expected. "We have to go to the hospital," Neal said. "Helen's sister works there, and she's got something Helen wants to pick up. Isn't that right, Helen?"

Helen said, "Yeah. My good shoes."

"Helen's good shoes." Neal looked up at the mirror. "Miss Helen Rosie's good shoes."

"My name's not Helen Rosie," said Helen. It seemed as if it was not the first time she had said this.

"I just call you that because you have such a rosy face," Neal said.

"I have not."

"You do. Doesn't she, Jinny? Jinny agrees with me—you've got a rosy face. Miss Helen Rosie-Face."

The girl did have tender pink skin. Jinny had also noticed her nearly white lashes and eyebrows, her blood baby-wool hair, and her mouth, which had an oddly naked look, not just the normal look of a mouth without lipstick. A fresh-out-of-the-egg look was what she had, as if one layer of skin were still missing, one final growth of coarser, grown-up hair. She must be susceptible to rashes and infections, quick to show scrapes and bruises, to get sores around the mouth and sties between her white lashes, Jinny thought. Yet she didn't look frail. Her shoulders were broad, she was lean but big-boned. She didn't look stupid, either, though she had a head-on expression like a calf's or a deer's. Everything must be right on the surface with her, her attention and the whole of her personality coming straight at you, with an innocent and—to Jinny—a disagreeable power.

They drove up to the main doors of the hospital, then, following Helen's directions, swung around to the back. People in hospital dressing gowns, some trailing their I.V.s, had come outside to smoke.

"Helen's sister works in the laundry," Neal said. "What's her name, Helen? What's your sister's name?"

"Muriel," said Helen. "Stop here. O.K. Here."

They were in a parking lot at the back of a wing of the hospital. There were no doors on the ground floor except a loading door, shut tight. Helen was getting out of the car.

"You know how to find your way in?" Neal said.

"Easy."

The fire escape stopped four or five feet above the ground, but she was able to grab hold of the railing and swing herself up, maybe wedging a foot against a loose brick, in a matter of seconds. Neal was laughing.

"Go get 'em, girl!" he said.

"Isn't there any other way?" said Jinny.

Helen had run up to the third floor and disappeared.

"If there is, she ain't a-gonna use it," Neal said.

"Full of gumption," said Jinny, with an effort.

"Otherwise she'd never have broken out," he said. "She needed all the gumption she could get."

Jinny was wearing a wide-brimmed straw hat. She took it off and began to fan herself.

Neal said, "Sorry. There doesn't seem to be any shade to park in."

"Do I look too startling?" Jinny said. He was used to her asking that.

"You're fine. There's nobody around here anyway."

"The doctor I saw today wasn't the same one I'd seen before. I think this one was more important. The funny thing was he had a scalp that looked about like mine. Maybe he does it to put the patients at ease."

She meant to go on and tell him what the doctor had said, but the fanning took up most of her energy. He watched the building.

"I hope to Christ they didn't haul her up for getting in the wrong way," he said. "She is just not a gal for whom the rules were made."

After several minutes, he let out a whistle.

"Here she comes now. Here-she-comes. Headin' down the homestretch. Will she, will she, will she have enough sense to stop before she jumps? Look before she leaps? Will she, will she—nope. Nope. Unh-*unh*."

Helen had no shoes in her hands. She got into the car and banged the door shut and said, "Stupid idiots. First I get up there and this asshole gets in my way. Where's your tag? You gotta have a tag. I seen you come in off the fire escape, you can't do that. O.K., O.K., I gotta see my sister. You can't see her now, she's not on her break. I know that. That's why I come in off the fire escape. I just need to pick something up. I don't want to talk to her. I'm not goin' to take up her time. I just gotta pick something up. Well, you can't. Well, I can. Well, you can't. And then I start to holler *Muriel, Muriel.* All their machines goin'. It's two hundred degrees in there. I don't know where she is, can she hear me or not. But she comes tearing out and as soon as she sees me—Oh, shit. Oh, shit, she says, I went and forgot. She forgot. I phoned her up last night and reminded her, but there she is. Shit, she forgot. I could've beat her up. Now you get out, he says. Go downstairs and out. Not by the fire escape, because it's illegal. Piss on him."

Neal was laughing and laughing and shaking his head.

Jinny said, "Could we just start driving now and get some air? I don't think fanning is doing a lot of good."

"Fine," said Neal, and started the car and backed and turned around, and once more they were passing the familiar front of the hospital, with the same or different smokers parading by in their dreary hospital clothes with their I.V.s. "Helen will just have to tell us where to go."

He called into the back seat, "Helen."

"What?"

"Which way do we turn now to get to where your sister lives? Where your shoes are."

"We're not goin' to their place, so I'm not telling you. You done me one favor and that's enough." Helen sat as far forward as she could, pushing her head between Neal's seat and Jinny's.

They slowed down, turned into a side street. "That's silly," Neal said. "You're going thirty miles away, and you might not get back here for a while. You might need those shoes." No answer. He tried again. "Or don't you know the way? Don't you know the way from here?"

"I know it, but I'm not telling."

"So we're just going to have to drive around and around till you get ready to tell us."

They were driving through a part of town that Jinny had not seen before. They drove very slowly and made frequent turns, so that hardly any breeze went through the car. A boarded-up factory, discount stores, pawnshops. "Cash, Cash, Cash," said a flashing sign above barred windows. But there were houses, disreputable-looking old duplexes, and the sort of single wooden houses that were put up quickly, during the Second World War. In front of a corner store, some children were sucking on Popsicles. Helen spoke to Neal. "You're just wasting your gas."

"North of town?" Neal said. "South of town? North, south, east, west, Helen, tell us which is best." On Neal's face there was an expression of conscious, helpless silliness. His whole being was invaded. He was brimming with foolish bliss.

"You're just stubborn," Helen said.

"You'll see how stubborn."

"I am, too. I'm just as stubborn as what you are."

It seemed to Jinny that she could feel the blaze of Helen's cheek, which was so close to hers. And she could certainly hear the girl's breathing, hoarse and thick with excitement and showing some trace of asthma.

The sun had burned through the clouds again. It was still high and brassy in the sky. Neal swung the car onto a street lined with heavy old trees, and somewhat more respectable houses.

"Better here?" he said to Jinny. "More shade for you?" He spoke in a lowered, confidential tone, as if what was going on in the car could be set aside for a moment. It was all nonsense.

"Taking the scenic route," he said, pitching his voice again toward the back seat. "Taking the scenic route today, courtesy of Miss Helen Rosie-Face."

"Maybe we ought to just go on," Jinny said. "Maybe we ought to just go on home."

Helen broke in, almost shouting. "I don't want to stop nobody from getting home."

"Then you can just give me some directions," Neal said. He was trying hard to get his voice under control, to get some ordinary sobriety into it. And to banish the smile, which kept slipping back in place no matter how often he swallowed it.

Half a slow block more, and Helen groaned. "If I got to, I guess I got to," she said.

It was not very far that they had to go. They passed a subdivision, and Neal, speaking again to Jinny, said, "No creek that I can see. No estates either."

Jinny said, "What?"

"Amber Creek Estates. On the sign. They don't care what they say anymore. Nobody even expects them to explain it."

"Turn," said Helen.

"Left or right?"

"At the wrecker's."

They went past a wrecking yard, with the car bodies only partly hidden by a sagging tin fence. Then up a hill, and past the gates to a gravel pit, which was a great cavity in the center of the hill.

"That's them. That's their mailbox up ahead," Helen called out with some importance, and when they got close enough, she read out the name. "Matt and June Bergson. That's them."

A couple of dogs came barking down the short drive. One was large and black and one small and tan-colored, puppy-like. They bumbled around at the wheels and Neal sounded the horn. Then another dog—this one more sly and purposeful, with a slick coat and bluish spots—slid out of the long grass.

Helen called to them to shut up, to lie down, to piss off. "You don't need to bother about any of them but Pinto," she said. "Them other two's just cowards."

They stopped in a wide, ill-defined space, where some gravel had been laid down. On one side was a barn or implement shed, tin covered, and over to one side of it, on the edge of a cornfield, an abandoned farmhouse. The house inhabited nowadays was a trailer, nicely fixed up with a deck and an awning, and a flower garden behind what looked like a toy fence. The trailer and its garden looked proper and tidy, while the rest of the property was littered with things that might have a purpose or might just have been left around to rust or rot.

Helen had jumped out and was cuffing the dogs. But they kept on running past her, and jumping and barking at the car, until a man came out of the shed and called to them. The threats and names he called were not intelligible to Jinny, but the dogs quieted down.

Jinny put on her hat. All this time, she had been holding it in her hand.

"They just got to show off," said Helen. Neal had got out, too, and was negotiating with the dogs in a resolute way. The man from the shed came toward them. He wore a purple T-shirt that was wet with sweat, clinging to his chest and stomach. He was fat enough to have breasts, and you could see his navel pushing out like a pregnant woman's.

Neal went to meet him with his hand out. The man slapped his own hand on his work pants, laughed, and shook Neal's. Jinny could not hear what they said. A woman came out of the trailer and opened the toy gate and latched it behind her.

"Muriel went and forgot she was supposed to bring my shoes," Helen called to her. "I phoned her up and everything, but she went and forgot anyway, so Mr. Lockley brought me out to get them."

The woman was fat, too, though not as fat as her husband. She wore a pink muumuu with Aztec suns on it, and her hair was streaked with gold. She moved across the gravel with a composed and hospitable air. Neal turned and introduced himself, then brought her to the car and introduced Jinny.

"Glad to meet you," the woman said. "You're the lady that isn't very well?"

"I'm O.K.," said Jinny.

"Well, now you're here, you better come inside. Come in out of this heat."

The man had come closer. "We got the air-conditioning in there," he said. He was inspecting the car, and his expression was genial but disparaging.

"We just came to pick up the shoes," Jinny said.

"You got to do more than that, now you're here," said the woman, June, laughing as if the idea of their not coming in was a scandalous joke. "You come in and rest yourselves."

"We wouldn't like to disturb your supper," Neal said.

"We had it already," said Matt. "We eat early."

"But there's all kinds of chili left," said June. "You have to come in and help clean up that chili."

Jinny said, "Oh, thank you. But I don't think I could eat anything. I don't feel like eating anything when it's this hot."

"Then you better drink something, instead," June said. "We got ginger ale, Coke. We got peach schnapps."

"Beer," Matt said to Neal. "You like a Blue?"

Jinny waved at Neal, asking him to come close to her window. "I can't do it," she said. "Just tell them I can't."

"You know you'll hurt their feelings," he whispered. "They're trying to be nice."

"But I can't."

He bent closer. "You know what it looks like if you don't."

"You go."

"You'd be O.K. once you got inside. The air-conditioning really would do you good."

Jinny just shook her head.

Neal straightened up.

"Jinny thinks she better just stay in the car and rest here in the shade," Neal said. "But I wouldn't mind a Blue, actually."

He turned back to Jinny with a hard smile. He seemed to her desolate and angry. "You sure you'll be O.K.?" he said for the others to hear. "Sure? You don't mind if I go in for a little while?"

"I'll be fine," said Jinny.

He put one hand on Helen's shoulder and one on June's shoulder, walking them companionably toward the trailer. Matt smiled at Jinny curiously, and followed. This time, when he called the dogs to come after him, Jinny could make out their names.

Goober. Sally. Pinto.

The car was parked under a row of willow trees. These trees were big and old, but their leaves were thin and gave a wavering shade. Still, to be alone was a great relief.

Earlier today, driving along the highway from the town where they lived, they had stopped at a roadside stand and bought some early apples. Jinny got one out of the bag at her feet and took a small bite—more or less to see if she could taste and swallow it and hold it in her stomach. It was all right. The apple was firm and tart, but not too tart, and if she took small bites and chewed seriously she could manage it.

She'd seen Neal like this—or something like this—a few times before. It would be over some boy at the school. A mention of the name in an offhand, even belittling way. A mushy look, an apologetic yet somehow defiant bit of giggling. But that was never anybody she had to have around the house, and it could never come to anything. The boy's time would be up, he'd go away.

So would this time be up. It shouldn't matter. She had to wonder if it would have mattered less yesterday than it did today.

She got out of the car, leaving the door open so that she could hang on to the inside handle. Anything on the outside was too hot to hang on to for any length of time. She had to see if she was steady. Then she walked a little, in the shade. Some of the willow leaves were already going yellow. Some were already lying on the ground. She looked out from the shade at all the things in the yard.

A dented delivery van with both headlights gone and the name on the side painted out. A baby's stroller that the dogs had chewed the seat out of, a load of firewood dumped but not stacked, a pile of huge tires, a great number of plastic jugs and some oil cans and pieces of old lumber and a couple of orange plastic tarpaulins crumpled up by the wall of the shed. What a lot of things people could find themselves in charge of. As Jinny had been in charge of all those photographs, official letters, minutes of meetings, newspaper clippings, a thousand categories that she had devised and had been putting on disk when she had to go into chemo and everything got taken away. All those things might end up being thrown out. As all this might, if Matt died.

The cornfield was the place she wanted to get to. The corn was higher than her head now, maybe higher than Neal's head—she wanted to get into the shade of it. She made her way across the yard with this one thought in mind. The dogs, thank God, must have been taken inside.

There was no fence. The cornfield just petered out into the yard. She walked straight ahead into it, onto the narrow path between two rows. The leaves flapped in her face and against her arms like streamers of oilcloth. She had to remove her hat, so they would not knock it off. Each stalk had its cob, like a baby in a shroud. There was a strong, almost sickening smell of vegetable growth, of green starch and hot sap.

What she had intended to do, once she got in there, was lie down. Lie down in the shade of these large, coarse leaves and not come out till she heard Neal calling her. Perhaps not even then. But the rows were too close together to permit that, and she was too busy thinking to take the trouble. She was too angry.

It was not about anything that had happened recently. She was remembering how a group of people had been sitting around one evening on the floor of her living room—or meet room—playing one of those serious psychological games. One of those games that were supposed to make a person more honest and resilient. You had to say just what came into your mind as you looked at each of the others. And a white-haired woman named Addie Norton, a friend of Neal's, had said, "I hate to tell you this, Jinny, but whenever I look at you, all I can think of is—Nice Nelly."

Other people had said kinder things to her. "Flower child" or "Madonna of the Springs." She happened to know that whoever said that meant "Manon of the Springs," but she offered no correction. She was outraged at having to sit there and listen to people's opinions of her.

Everyone was wrong. She was not timid or acquiescent or natural or pure. When you died, of course, these wrong opinions were all that was left.

While this was going through her mind, she had done the easiest thing you can do in a cornfield—got lost. She had stepped over one row and then another, and probably got turned around. She tried going back the way she had come, but it obviously wasn't the right way. There were clouds over the sun again, so she couldn't tell where west was. And she had not checked which direction she was going when she entered the field, anyway, so that would not have helped. She stood still and heard nothing but the corn whispering away, and some distant traffic.

Her heart was pounding just like any heart that had years and years of life ahead of it.

Then a door opened, she heard the dogs barking and Matt yelling, and the door slammed shut. She pushed her way through stalks and leaves, in the direction of that noise. It turned out that she had not gone far at all. She had been stumbling around in one small corner of the field, the whole time.

Matt waved at her and warned off the dogs.

"Don't be scairt of them, don't be scairt," he called. He was going toward the car just as she was, though from another direction. As they got closer to each other, he spoke in a lower, perhaps more intimate, voice.

"You shoulda come and knocked on the door." He thought that she had gone into the corn to have a pee. "I just told your husband I'd come out and make sure you're O.K."

Jinny said, "I'm fine. Thank you." She got into the car but left the door open. He might be insulted if she closed it. Also, she felt too weak.

"He was sure hungry for that chili."

Who was he talking about?

Neal.

She was trembling and sweating and there was a hum in her head, as if a wire were strung between her ears.

"I could bring you some out if you'd like it."

She shook her head, smiling. He lifted up the bottle of beer in his hand—he seemed to be saluting her.

"Drink?"

She shook her head again, still smiling.

"Not even a drink of water? We got good water here."

"No, thanks." If she turned her head and looked at his purple navel, she would gag.

"You hear about this fellow going out the door with a jar of horseradish in his hand?" he said in a changed voice. "And his dad says to him, 'Where you goin' with that horseradish?'

"'Going to get a horse,' he says.

"Dad says, 'You're not goin' to catch a horse with no horseradish.'

"Fellow comes back next morning. Nice big horse on a halter. Puts it in the barn.

"Next day Dad sees him goin' out, bunch of branches in his hand.

"'What's them branches in your hand?'

"'Them's pussy willows—'"

"What are you telling me this for?" Jinny said, almost shaking. "I don't want to hear it. It's too much."

"What's the matter now?" Matt said. "All it is is a joke."

Jinny was shaking her head, squeezing her hand over her mouth.

"Never mind," he said. "I won't take no more of your time."

He turned his back on her, not even bothering to call to the dogs.

"I do not wish to give the wrong impression or get carried away with optimism." The doctor had spoken in a studious, almost mechanical way. "But it looks as if we have a significant shrinkage. What we hoped for, of course. But frankly, we did not expect it. I do not mean that the battle is over. But we can be to a certain extent optimistic and proceed with the next course of chemo and see how things look then."

*What are you telling me this for? I don't want to hear it. It's too much.*

Jinny had not said anything like that to the doctor. Why should she? Why should she behave in such an unsatisfactory and ungrateful way, turning his news on its head? Nothing was his fault. But it was true that what he had said made everything harder. It made her have to go back and start this year all over again. It removed a certain low-grade freedom. A dull, protecting membrane that she had not even known was there had been pulled away and left her raw.

Matt's thinking she had gone into the cornfield to pee had made her realize that she actually wanted to. Jinny got out of the car, stood cautiously, and spread her legs and lifted her wide cotton skirt. She had taken to wearing big skirts and no panties this summer, because her bladder was no longer under perfect control.

A dark stream trickled away from her through the gravel. The sun was down now. Evening was coming on, and there was a clear sky overhead. The clouds were gone.

One of the dogs barked halfheartedly, to say that somebody was coming but somebody they knew. They had not come over to bother her when she got out of the car—they were used to her now. They went running out to meet whoever it was, without any alarm or excitement.

It was a boy, or young man, riding a bicycle. He swerved toward the car and Jinny went round to meet him, a hand on the warm fender to support herself. When he spoke to her, she did not want it to be across her puddle. And maybe to distract him from even looking on the ground for such a thing, she spoke first. She said, "Hello. Are you delivering something?"

He laughed, springing off the bike and dropping it to the ground, all in one motion.

"I live here," he said. "I'm just getting home from work."

She thought that she should explain who she was, tell him how she came to be here and for how long. But all this was too difficult. Hanging on to the car like this, she must look like somebody who had just come out of a wreck.

"Yeah, I live here," he said. "But I work in a restaurant in town. I work at Sammy's."

A waiter. The bright-white shirt and black pants were waiters' clothes. And he had a waiter's air of patience and alertness.

"I'm Jinny Lockley," she said. "Helen. Helen is—"

"O.K., I know," he said. "You're who Helen's going to work for. Where's Helen?"

"In the house."

"Didn't nobody ask you in, then?"

He was about Helen's age, she thought. Seventeen or eighteen. Slim and graceful and cocky, with an ingenuous enthusiasm that would probably not get him as far as he hoped. Jinny had seen a few like that who ended up as Young Offenders. He seemed to understand things, though. He seemed to understand that she was exhausted and in some kind of muddle.

"June in there, too?" he said. "June's my mom."

His hair was colored like June's, gold streaks over dark. He wore it rather long, and parted in the middle, flopping off to either side.

"Matt, too?" he said.

"And my husband. Yes."

"That's a shame."

"Oh, no," she said. "They asked me. I said I'd rather wait out here."

Neal used sometimes to bring home a couple of Yo-yos, to be supervised doing lawn work or painting or basic carpentry. He thought it was good for them, to be accepted into somebody's home. Jinny had flirted with them occasionally, in a way that she could never be blamed for. Just a gentle tone, a way of making them aware of her soft skirts and her scent of apple soap. That wasn't why Neal had stopped bringing them. He had been told it was out of order.

"So how long have you been waiting?"

"I don't know," Jinny said. "I don't wear a watch."

"Is that right?" he said. "I don't, either. I don't hardly ever meet another person that doesn't wear a watch. Did you never wear one?"

She said, "No. Never."

"Me neither. Never, ever. I just never wanted to. I don't know why. Never, ever wanted to. Like, I always just seem to know what time it is anyway. Within a couple minutes. Five minutes at the most. Sometimes one of the diners asks me, 'Do you know the time,' and I just tell them. They don't even notice I'm not wearing a watch. I go and check as soon as I can, clock in the kitchen. But I never once had to go in there and tell them any different."

"I've been able to do that, too, once in a while," Jinny said. "I guess you do develop a sense, if you never wear a watch."

"Yeah, you really do."

"So what time do you think it is now?"

He laughed. He looked at the sky.

"Getting close to eight. Six, seven minutes to eight? I got an advantage, though. I know when I got off of work, and then I went to get some cigarettes at the 7-Eleven, and then I talked to some guys a couple of minutes, and then I biked home. You don't live in town, do you?"

Jinny said no.

"So, where do you live?"

She told him.

"You getting tired? You want to go home? You want me to go in and tell your husband you want to go home?"

"No. Don't do that," she said.

"O.K. O.K. I won't. June's probably telling their fortunes in there anyway. She can read hands."

"Can she?"

"Sure. She goes in the restaurant a couple of times a week. Tea, too. Tea leaves."

He picked up his bike and wheeled it out of the way of the car. Then he looked in, through the driver's window.

"Keys in the car," he said. "So—you want me to drive you home or what? Your husband can get Matt to drive him and Helen when they get ready. And he can bring me back from your place. Or if it don't look like Matt can, June can. June's my mom, but Matt's not my dad. You don't drive, do you?"

"No," said Jinny. She had not driven for months.

"No. I didn't think so. O.K. then? You want me to? O.K.?"

"This is just a road I know. It'll get you there as soon as the highway."

They had not driven past the subdivision. In fact, they had headed the other way, taking a road that seemed to circle the gravel pit. At least they were going west now, toward the brightest part of the sky. Ricky—that was what he'd told her his name was—had not yet turned the car lights on.

"No danger meeting anybody," he said. "I don't think I ever met a single car on this road, ever. See—not so many people even know this road is here. And if I was to turn the lights on, then the sky would go dark, and everything would go dark, and you wouldn't be able to see where you were. We just give it a little while more, so then when it gets dark, we can see the stars, that's when we turn the lights on."

The sky was like very faintly colored glass—red or yellow or green or blue glass, depending on which part of it you looked at. The bushes and trees would turn black, once the lights were on. There would just be black clumps along the road and the black mass of trees crowding in behind them, instead of, as now, the individual, still identifiable, spruce and cedar and feathery tamarack, and the jewelweed with its flowers like winking bits of fire. It seemed close enough to touch, and they were going slowly. She put her hand out.

Not quite. But close. The road seemed hardly wider than the car.

She thought she saw the gleam of a full ditch ahead. "Is there water down there?" she said.

"Down there?" said Ricky. "Down there and everywhere. There's water to both sides of us and lots of places, water underneath us. Want to see?"

He slowed the car down and stopped. "Look down your side," he said. "Open the door and look down."

When she did that, she saw that they were on a bridge. A little bridge, no more than ten feet long, of crosswise-laid planks. No railings. And motionless water.

"Bridges all along here," he said. "And where it's not bridges it's culverts. 'Cause it's always flowing back and forth under the road. Or just laying there and not flowing."

"How deep?" she said.

"Not deep. Not this time of year. Not till we get to the big pond—it's deeper. And then, in spring, it's all over the road, you can't drive here, it's deep then. This road goes flat for miles and miles, and it goes from one end to the other. There isn't even any road that cuts across it. This is the only road I know of through the Borneo Swamp."

Jinny said, "Borneo Swamp? There is an island called Borneo. It's halfway round the world."

"I don't know about that. All I ever heard of was just the Borneo Swamp."

There was a strip of dark grass now, growing down the middle of the road.

"Time for the lights," he said. He switched them on, and they were in a tunnel in the sudden night. "Once I turned the lights on like that, and there was this porcupine. It was just sitting there in the middle of the road, sitting up on its hind legs, and looking right at me. Like some little tiny old man. It was scared to death and it couldn't move. I could see its little old teeth chattering."

Jinny thought, This is where he brings his girls.

"So what do I do? I tried beeping the horn, and it still didn't do nothing. I didn't feel like getting out and chasing it. He was scared, but he still was a porcupine and he could let fly. So I just parked there. I had time. When I turned the lights on again, he was gone." Now the branches really did reach the car and brush against the door, but if there were flowers she could not see them.

"I am going to show you something," he said. "I'm going to show you something like I bet you never seen before."

If this had been happening back in her old, normal life, it's possible that she might now have begun to be frightened. If she were back in her old, normal life she would not be here at all.

"You're going to show me a porcupine," she said.

"Nope. Not that."

A few miles farther on, he turned off the lights. "See the stars?" he said. He stopped the car. Everywhere, there was at first a deep silence. Then this silence was filled in, at the edges, by some kind of humming that could have been faraway traffic, and little noises that passed before you properly heard them, that could have been made by birds or bats or night-feeding animals.

"Come in here in the springtime," he said, "you wouldn't hear nothing but the frogs. You'd think you were going deaf with the frogs." He opened the door on his side.

"Now. Get out and walk a ways with me."

She did as she was told. She walked in one of the wheel tracks, he in the other. The sky seemed to be lighter ahead, and there was a different sound—something like mild and rhythmical conversation. The road turned to wood and the trees on either side were gone.

"Walk out on it," he said. "Go on."

He came close and touched her waist, guiding her. Then he took his hand away, left her to walk on these planks, which were like the deck of a boat. Like the deck of a boat, they rose and fell. But it wasn't a movement of waves, it was their footsteps, his and hers, that caused this rising and falling of the boards beneath them. "Now do you know where you are?" he said.

"On a dock?" she said.

"On a bridge. This is a floating bridge."

Now she could make it out—the plank roadway just a few inches above the still water. He drew her over to the side, and they looked down. There were stars riding on the water.

"It's dark all the time," he said proudly. "That's because it's a swamp. It's got the same stuff in it tea has got, and it looks like black tea."

She could see the shoreline, and the reed beds. Water in the reeds, lapping water, was what was making that sound.

"Tannin," she said.

The slight movement of the bridge made her imagine that all the trees and the reed beds were set on saucers of earth and the road was a floating ribbon of earth and underneath it all was water.

It was at this moment that she realized she didn't have her hat. She not only didn't have it on, she hadn't had it with her in the car. She had not been wearing it when she got out of the car to pee and when she began to talk to Ricky. She had not been wearing it when she sat in the car with her head back against the seat and her eyes closed, when Matt was telling his joke. She must have dropped it in the cornfield, and in her panic left it there.

While she had been scared of seeing the mound of Matt's navel with the purple shirt plastered over it, he had been looking at her bleak knob.

"It's too bad the moon isn't up yet," Ricky said. "It's really nice here when the moon is up."

"It's nice now, too."

He slipped his arms around her as if there were no question at all about what he was doing and he could take all the time he wanted to do it. He kissed her mouth. It seemed to her that this was the first time that she had ever participated in a kiss that was an event in itself. The whole story, all by itself. A tender prologue, an efficient pressure, a wholehearted probing and receiving, a lingering thanks, and a drawing away satisfied.

"Oh," he said. "Oh."

He turned her around, and they walked back the way they had come.

"So was that the first you ever been on a floating bridge?"

She said yes, it was.

He took her hand and swung it as if he would like to toss it.

"And that's the first time I ever kissed a married woman."

"You'll probably kiss a lot more of them," she said. "Before you're done."

He sighed. "Yeah," he said. "Yeah, I probably will."

Amazed, sobered, by the thought of his future.

She had a sudden thought of Neal, back on dry land. Neal also startled by the thought of the future, giddy and besotted and disbelieving, as he opened his hand to the gaze of the woman with bright streaks in her hair.

Jinny felt a rain of compassion, almost like laughter. A swish of tender hilarity, getting the better of her sores and hollows, for the time given.

# R. K. Narayan

(1906–2001)

Narayan was born in Mysore, India, and is one of India's best-known and most prolific writers in English. Narayan created the town of Malgudi, a fictional backwater that serves as a setting for most of his novels, novellas, and short stories. Malgudi resembles Narayan's childhood village, though its varied citizens represent a cross section of India's larger society and its inhabitants. His fiction is populated with ordinary people who often accept disaster and misfortune, not just with a sense of the inevitable, but also with cheerful good humor. Narayan also infuses this ordinary world with the panapoly of Hindu gods, whose mythology and ethical principles lead his characters through the moral dilemmas of modern life. Though not overtly political, Narayan's early work does deal with tensions between Indian and Western cultures. Though he wrote in English, literary critics often see his work as echoing the rhythms and techniques of Indian oral storytelling traditions. His many publications include

*Swami and Friends* (1935), *The Bachelor of Arts* (1937), *The English Teacher* (1945; published in the United States as *Grateful to Life and Death*), *Mr. Sampath* (1949; published in the United States as *The Printer of Malgudi*), *Waiting for the Mahatma* (1955), *The Guide* (1958), *The Sweet-Vendor* (1967; published in the United States as *The Vendor of Sweets*), and his short story collections, *Gods, Demons and Others* (1965) and *The Grandmother's Tale* (1992).

---

## House Opposite                                                                                                1985

The hermit invariably shuddered when he looked out of his window. The house across the street was occupied by a shameless woman. Late in the evening, men kept coming and knocking on her door—afternoons, too, if there was a festival or holiday. Sometimes they lounged on the pyol of her house, smoking, chewing tobacco, and spitting into the gutter—committing all the sins of the world, according to the hermit who was striving to pursue a life of austerity, forswearing family, possessions, and all the comforts of life. He found this single-room tenement with a couple of coconut trees and a well at the backyard adequate, and the narrow street swarmed with children: sometimes he called in the children, seated them around, and taught them simple moral lessons and sacred verse. On the walls he had nailed a few pictures of gods cut out of old calendars, and made the children prostrate themselves in front of them before sending them away with a piece of sugar and candy each.

His daily life followed an unvarying pattern. Birdlike, he retired at dusk, lying on the bare floor with a wooden block under his head for a pillow. He woke up at four, ahead of the rooster at the street corner, bathed at the well, and sat down on a piece of deerskin to meditate. Later he lit the charcoal stove and baked a few chapattis for breakfast and lunch and cooked certain restricted vegetables and greens, avoiding potato, onion, okra, and such as might stimulate the baser impulses.

Even in the deepest state of meditation, he could not help hearing the creaking of the door across the street when a client left after a night of debauchery. He rigorously suppressed all cravings of the palate, and punished his body in a dozen ways. If you asked him why, he would have been at a loss to explain. He was the antithesis of the athlete who flexed his muscles and watched his expanding chest before a mirror. Our hermit, on the contrary, kept a minute check of his emaciation and felt a peculiar thrill out of such an achievement. He was only following without questioning his ancient guru's instructions, and hoped thus to attain spiritual liberation.

One afternoon, opening the window to sweep the dust on the sill, he noticed her standing on her doorstep, watching the street. His temples throbbed with the rush of blood. He studied her person—chiseled features, but sunk in fatty folds. She possessed, however, a seductive outline; her forearms were cushionlike and perhaps the feel of those encircling arms attracted men. His gaze, once it had begun to hover about her body, would not return to its anchor—which should normally be the tip of one's nose, as enjoined by his guru and the yoga shastras.

Her hips were large, thighs stout like banana stalks, on the whole a mattresslike creature on which a patron could loll all night without a scrap of covering—"Awful monster! Personification of evil." He felt suddenly angry. Why on earth should that creature stand there and ruin his tapas: all the merit he had so laboriously acquired was draining away like water through a sieve. Difficult to say whether it was those monstrous arms and breasts or thighs which tempted and ruined men . . . He hissed under his breath, "Get in, you devil, don't stand there!" She abruptly turned round and went in, shutting the door behind her. He felt triumphant, although his command and her compliance were coincidental. He bolted the window tight and retreated to the farthest corner of the room, settled down on the deerskin, and kept repeating, "Om, Om, Rama, Jayarama": the sound "Rama" had a potency all its own— and was reputed to check wandering thoughts and distractions. He had a profound knowledge of mantras and their efficacy. "Sri Rama . . . ," he repeated, but it was like a dilute and weak medicine for high fever. It didn't work. "Sri Rama, Jayarama . . . ," he repeated with a desperate fervor, but the effect lasted not even a second. Unnoticed his thoughts strayed, questioning: Who was that fellow in a check shirt and silk upper cloth over his shoulder descending the steps last evening when I went out to the market? Seen him somewhere . . . where? when? . . . ah, he was the big tailor on Market Road . . . with fashionable men and women clustering round him! Master-cutter who was a member of two or three clubs . . . Hobnobbed with officers and businessmen— and this was how he spent his evening, lounging on the human mattress! And yet fashionable persons allowed him to touch them with his measuring tape! Contamination, nothing but contamination; sinful life. He cried out in the lonely room, "Rama! Rama!" as if hailing someone hard of hearing. Presently he realized it was a futile exercise. Rama was a perfect incarnation, of course, but he was mild and gentle until provoked beyond limit, when he would storm and annihilate the evildoer without a trace, even if he was a monster like Ravana. Normally, however, he had forbearance, hence the repetition of his name only resulted in calmness and peace, but the present occasion demanded stern measures. God Siva's mantra should help. Did he not open his Third Eye and reduce the God of Love to ashes, when the latter slyly aimed his arrow at him while he was meditating? Our hermit pictured the god of matted locks and fiery eyes and recited aloud: "Om Namasivaya," that lonely hall resounding with his hoarse voice. His rambling, unwholesome thoughts were halted for a while, but presently regained their vigor and raced after the woman. She opened her door at least six times on an evening. Did she sleep with them all together at the same time? He paused to laugh at this notion, and also realized that his meditation on the austere god was gone. He banged his fist on his temples, which pained but improved his concentration. "Om Namasivaya . . ." Part of his mind noted the creaking of the door of the opposite house. She was a serpent in whose coils everyone was caught and destroyed—old and young and the middle-aged, tailors and students (he had noticed a couple of days ago a young B.Sc. student from Albert Mission Hostel at her door), lawyers and magistrates (why not?) . . . No wonder the world was getting overpopulated—with such pressure of the elemental urge within every individual! O God Siva, this woman must be eliminated. He would confront her some day and tell her to get out. He would tell her, "Oh, sinful wretch, who is spreading disease and filth like an open sewer: think of the contamination you have spread around—from middle-aged tailor to B.Sc. student. You are out to destroy mankind. Repent your sins, shave your head, cover your ample loins with sackcloth, sit at the temple gate and beg or drown yourself in sarayu after praying for a cleaner life at least in the next birth . . ."

Thus went his dialogue, the thought of the woman never leaving his mind, during all the wretched, ill-spent night; he lay tossing on the bare floor. He rose before dawn, his mind made up. He would clear out immediately, cross Nallappa's Grove, and reach the other side of the river. He did not need a permanent roof; he would drift and rest in any temple or mantap or in the shade of a banyan tree: he collected an ancient tale he had heard from his guru long ago . . . A harlot was sent to heaven when she died, while her detractor, a self-righteous reformer, found himself in hell. It was explained that while the harlot sinned only with her body, her detractor was corrupt mentally, as he was obsessed with the harlot and her activities, and could meditate on nothing else.

Our hermit packed his wicker box with his sparse possessions—a god's image in copper, a rosary, the deerskin, and a little brass bowl. Carrying his box in one hand, he stepped out of the house, closing the door gently behind him. In the dim hour of the dusk, shadowy figures were moving—a milkman driving his cow ahead, laborers bearing crowbars and spades, women with baskets on their way to the market. While he paused to take a final look at the shelter he was abandoning, he heard a plaintive cry, "Swamiji," from the opposite house, and saw the woman approach him with a tray, heaped with fruits and flowers. She placed it at his feet and said in a low reverential whisper: "Please accept my offering. This is a day of remembrance of my mother. On this day I pray and seek a saint's blessing. Forgive me . . ." All the lines he had rehearsed for a confrontation deserted him at this moment; looking at her flabby figure, the dark rings under her eyes, he felt pity. As she bent down to prostrate, he noticed that her hair was indifferently dyed and that the parting in the middle widened into a bald patch over which a string of jasmine dangled loosely. He touched her tray with the tip of his finger as a token of acceptance, and went down the street without a word.

# Joyce Carol Oates

### (B. 1938)

Joyce Carol Oates was born in Lockport, New York. She received a typewriter at the age of fourteen and began writing novels, training herself for her eventually prolific literary career. While she was attending Syracuse University, her short story "In The Old World" won the *Mademoiselle* college fiction award in 1959. She graduated with a B.A. in English and continued at the University of Wisconsin to pursue an M.A. in English. Oates settled in Detroit in 1962 with her husband, Raymond J. Smith, and there stumbled on one of her most enduring subjects: America's love affair with violence. In the 1960s, the city of Detroit was awash in social and racial tension, and Oates used her experience in the city as the basis for a number of novels and short stories. Her novel, *Them* (1969), was set against the volatile Detroit landscape and won the National Book Award in 1970. Oates taught at the University of Windsor, Canada, from 1968 to 1978, while publishing new books at a rate of two or three per year. Her constant productivity quickly made her one of the most respected writers in the United States—all by the time she was in her early thirties. In 1978, Oates moved to Princeton, New Jersey, where she continues to teach in Princeton University's creative writing program.

Oates has been able to maintain her prolific pace by constantly varying her writing style and subjects. She published a series of gothic novels in the early 1980s and has written pseudonymously a collection of suspense novels. However, Oates is best known for her realistic and psychologically penetrating novels and short collections. Recent publications include *Because It Is Bitter, and Because It Is My Heart* (1991), *We Were the Mulvaneys* (1996), *Man Crazy* (1998), and *You Must Remember This* (1998). Her novel *Black Water* (1992), based on the Kennedy-Chappaquiddick scandal, was nominated for a Pulitzer Prize, and her fictionalized account of the life of Marilyn Monroe, *Blonde* (2001), was a National Book Award finalist. Her most recent novel, *Tattooed Girl*, was published in 2004.

---

## How I Contemplated the World from the Detroit House of Correction and Began My Life Over Again                1970

*Notes for an Essay for an English Class at Baldwin Country Day School;*
*Poking Around in Debris; Disgust and Curiosity; A Revelation of the Meaning*
*of Life; A Happy Ending . . .*

## I. Events

The girl (myself) is walking through Branden's, that excellent store. Suburb of a large famous city that is a symbol for large famous American cities. The event sneaks up on the girl, who believes she is herding it along with a small fixed smile, a girl of fifteen, innocently experienced. She dawdles in a certain style by a counter of costume jewellery. Rings, earrings, necklaces. Prices from $5 to $50, all within reach. All ugly. She eases over to the glove counter, where everything is ugly too. In her close-fitted coat with its black fur collar she contemplates the luxury of Branden's, which she has known for many years: its many mild pale lights, easy on the eye and the soul, its elaborate tinkly decorations, its women shoppers with their excellent shoes and coats and hairdos, all dawdling gracefully, in no hurry.

Who was ever in a hurry here?

2. The girl seated at home. A small library, panelled walls of oak. Someone is talking to me. An earnest, husky, female voice drives itself against my ears, nervous, frightened, groping around my heart, saying, 'If you wanted gloves, why didn't you say so? Why didn't you ask for them?' That store, Branden's, is owned by Raymond Forrest who lives on Du Maurier Drive. We live on Sioux Drive. Raymond Forrest. A handsome man? An ugly man? A man of fifty or sixty, with grey hair, or a man of forty with earnest, courteous eyes, a good golf game; who is Raymond Forrest, this man who is my salvation? Father has been talking to him. Father is not his physician; Dr Berg is his physician. Father and Dr Berg refer patients to each other. There is a connection. Mother plays bridge with . . . On Mondays and Wednesdays our maid Billie works at . . . The strings draw together in a cat's cradle, making a net to save you when you fall. . . .

3. *Harriet Arnold's*. A small shop, better than Branden's. Mother in her black coat, I in my close-fitted blue coat. Shopping. Now look at this, isn't this cute, do you want this, why don't you want this, try this on, take this with you to the fitting room, take this also, what's wrong with you, what can I do for you, why are you so strange . . . ? 'I wanted to steal but not to buy,' I don't tell her. The girl droops along in her coat and gloves and leather boots, her eyes scan the horizon, which is pastel pink and decorated like Branden's, tasteful walls and modern ceilings with graceful glimmering lights.

4. Weeks later, the girl at a bus stop. Two o'clock in the afternoon, a Tuesday; obviously she has walked out of school.

5. The girl stepping down from a bus. Afternoon, weather changing to colder. Detroit. Pavement and closed-up stores; grill-work over the windows of a pawnshop. What is a pawnshop, exactly?

## II. Characters

1. The girl stands five feet five inches tall. An ordinary height. Baldwin Country Day School draws them up to that height. She dreams along the corridors and presses her face against the Thermoplex glass. No frost or steam can ever form on that glass. A smudge of grease from her forehead . . . could she be boiled down to grease? She wears her hair loose and long and straight in suburban teen-age style, 1968. Eyes smudged with pencil, dark brown. Brown hair. Vague green eyes. A pretty girl? An ugly girl? She sings to herself under her breath, idling in the corridor, thinking of her many secrets (the thirty dollars she once took from the purse of a friend's mother, just for fun, the basement window she smashed in her own house just for fun) and thinking of her brother who is at Susquehanna Boys' Academy, an excellent preparatory school in Maine, remembering him unclearly . . . he has long manic hair and a squeaking voice and he looks like one of the popular teen-age singers of 1968, one of

those in a group, *The Certain Forces, The Way Out, The Maniacs Responsible.* The girl in her turn looks like one of those fieldsful of girls who listen to the boys' singing, dreaming and mooning restlessly, breaking into high sullen laughter, innocently experienced.

2. The mother. A Midwestern woman of Detroit and suburbs. Belongs to the Detroit Athletic Club. Also the Detroit Golf Club. Also the Bloomfield Hills Country Club. The Village Women's Club at which lectures are given each winter on Genet and Sartre and James Baldwin, by the Director of the Adult Education Program at Wayne State University. . . . The Bloomfield Art Association. Also the Founders Society of the Detroit Institute of Arts. Also . . . Oh, she is in perpetual motion, this lady, hair like blown-up gold and finer than gold, hair and fingers and body of inestimable grace. Heavy weighs the gold on the back of her hairbrush and hand mirror. Heavy heavy the candlesticks in the dining room. Very heavy is the big car, a Lincoln, long and black, that on one cool autumn day split a squirrel's body in two unequal parts.

3. The father. Dr _____. He belongs to the same clubs as 2. A player of squash and golf; he has a golfer's umbrella of stripes. Candy stripes. In his mouth nothing turns to sugar, however; saliva works no miracles here. His doctoring is of the slightly sick. The sick are sent elsewhere (to Dr Berg?), the deathly sick are sent back for more tests and their bills are sent to their homes, the unsick are sent to Dr Coronet (Isabel, a lady), an excellent psychiatrist for unsick people who angrily believe they are sick and want to do something about it. If they demand a male psychiatrist, the unsick are sent by Dr _____ (my father) to Dr Lowenstein, a male psychiatrist, excellent and expensive, with a limited practice.

4. Clarita. She is twenty, twenty-five, she is thirty or more? Pretty, ugly, what? She is a woman lounging by the side of a road, in jeans and a sweater, hitchhiking, or she is slouched on a stool at a counter in some roadside diner. A hard line of jaw. Curious eyes. Amused eyes. Behind her eyes processions move, funeral pageants, cartoons. She says, 'I never can figure out why girls like you bum around down here. What are you looking for anyway?' An odour of tobacco about her. Unwashed underclothes, or no underclothes, unwashed skin, gritty toes, hair long and falling into strands, not recently washed.

5. Simon. In this city the weather changes abruptly, so Simon's weather changes abruptly. He sleeps through the afternoon. He sleeps through the morning. Rising, he gropes around for something to get him going, for a cigarette or a pill to drive him out to the street, where the temperature is hovering around 35°. Why doesn't it drop? Why, why doesn't the cold clean air come down from Canada; will he have to go up into Canada to get it? will he have to leave the Country of his Birth and sink into Canada's frosty fields . . . ? Will the F.B.I. (which he dreams about constantly) chase him over the Canadian border on foot, hounded out in a blizzard of broken glass and horns . . . ?

"Once I was Huckleberry Finn," Simon says, "but now I am Roderick Usher." Beset by frenzies and fears, this man who makes my spine go cold, he takes green pills, yellow pills, pills of white and capsules of dark blue and green . . . he takes other things I may not mention, for what if Simon seeks me out and climbs into my girl's bedroom here in Bloomfield Hills and strangles me, what then . . . ? (As I write this I begin to shiver. Why do I shiver? I am now sixteen and sixteen is not an age for shivering.) It comes from Simon, who is always cold.

## III. World Events

Nothing.

## IV. People & Circumstances Contributing to This Delinquency

Nothing.

## V. Sioux Drive

George, Clyde G. 240 Sioux. A manufacturer's representative; children, a dog, a wife. Georgian with the usual columns. You think of the White House, then of Thomas Jefferson, then your mind goes blank on the white pillars and you think of nothing. Norris, Ralph W. 246 Sioux. Public relations. Colonial. Bay window, brick, stone, concrete, wood, green shutters, sidewalk, lantern, grass, trees, blacktop drive, two children, one of them my classmate Esther (Esther Norris) at Baldwin. Wife, cars. Ramsey, Michael D. 250 Sioux. Colonial. Big living room, thirty by twenty-five, fireplaces in living room, library, recreation room, panelled walls wet bar five bathrooms five bedrooms two lavatories central air conditioning automatic sprinkler automatic garage door three children one wife two cars a breakfast room a patio a large fenced lot fourteen trees a front door with a brass knocker never knocked. Next is our house. Classic contemporary. Traditional modern. Attached garage, attached Florida room, attached patio, attached pool and cabana, attached roof. A front door mail slot through which pour *Time Magazine, Fortune, Life, Business Week,* the *Wall Street Journal,* the *New York Times,* the *New Yorker,* the *Saturday Review, M.D., Modern Medicine, Disease of the Month* . . . and also. . . . And in addition to all this, a quiet sealed letter from Baldwin saying: *Your daughter is not doing work compatible with her performance on the Stanford-Binet.* . . . And your son is not doing well, not well at all, very sad. Where is your son anyway? Once he stole trick-and-treat candy from some six-year-old kids, he himself being a robust ten. The beginning. Now your daughter steals. In the Village Pharmacy she made off with, yes she did, don't deny it, she made off with a copy of *Pageant Magazine* for no reason, she swiped a roll of Life Savers in a green wrapper and was in no need of saving her life or even in need of sucking candy; when she was no more than eight years old she stole, don't blush, she stole a package of Tums only because it was out on the counter and available, and the nice lady behind the counter (now dead) said nothing. . . . Sioux Drive. Maples, oaks, elms. Diseased elms cut down. Sioux Drive runs into Roosevelt Drive. Slow, turning lanes, not streets, all drives and lanes and ways and passes. A private police force. Quiet private police, in unmarked cars. Cruising on Saturday evenings with paternal smiles for the residents who are streaming in and out of houses, going to and from parties, a thousand parties, slightly staggering, the women in their furs alighting from automobiles bought of Ford and General Motors and Chrysler, very heavy automobiles. No foreign cars. Detroit. In 275 Sioux, down the block in that magnificent French-Normandy mansion, lives _____ himself, who has the C _____ account itself, imagine that! Look at where he lives and look at the enormous trees and chimneys, imagine his many fireplaces, imagine his wife and children, imagine his wife's hair, imagine her fingernails, imagine her bathtub of smooth clean glowing pink, imagine their embraces, his trouser pockets filled with odd coins and keys and dust and peanuts, imagine their ecstasy on Sioux Drive, imagine their income tax returns, imagine their little boy's pride in his experimental car, a scaled-down C _____, as he roars around the neighborhood on the sidewalks frightening dogs and Negro maids, oh imagine all these things, imagine everything, let your mind roar out all over Sioux Drive and Du Maurier Drive and Roosevelt Drive and Ticonderoga Pass and Burning Bush Way and Lincolnshire Pass and Lois Lane.

When spring comes, its winds blow nothing to Sioux Drive, no odours of hollyhocks or forsythia, nothing Sioux Drive doesn't already possess, everything is planted and performing. The weather vanes, had they weather vanes, don't have to turn with the wind, don't have to contend with the weather. There is no weather.

## VI. Detroit

There is always weather in Detroit. Detroit's temperature is always 32°. Fast-falling temperatures. Slow-rising temperatures. Wind from the north-northeast four to forty miles an hour, small-craft warnings, partly cloudy today and Wednesday changing to partly sunny through Thursday . . . small warnings of frost, soot warnings, traffic warnings, hazardous lake conditions for small craft and swimmers, restless Negro gangs, restless cloud formations, restless temperatures aching to fall out the very bottom of the thermometer or shoot up over the top and boil everything over in red mercury.

Detroit's temperature is 32°. Fast-falling temperatures. Slow-rising temperatures. Wind from the north-northeast four to forty miles an hour. . . .

## VII. Events

1. The girl's heart is pounding. In her pocket is a pair of gloves! In a plastic bag! Air-proof breathproof plastic bag, gloves selling for twenty-five dollars on Branden's

counter! In her pocket! Shoplifted! . . . In her purse is a blue comb, not very clean. In her purse is a leather billfold (a birthday present from her grandmother in Philadelphia) with snapshots of the family in clean plastic windows, in the billfold are bills, she doesn't know how many bills. . . . In her purse is an ominous note from her friend Tykie *What's this about Joe H. and the kids hanging around at Louise's Sat. night? You heard anything?* . . . passed in French class. In her purse is a lot of dirty yellow Kleenex, her mother's heart would break to see such very dirty Kleenex, and at the bottom of her purse are brown hairpins and safety pins and a broken pencil and a ballpoint pen (blue) stolen from somewhere forgotten and a purse-size compact of Cover Girl Make-Up, Ivory Rose. . . . Her lipstick is Broken Heart, a corrupt pink; her fingers are trembling like crazy; her teeth are beginning to chatter; her insides are alive; her eyes glow in her head; she is saying to her mother's astonished face *I want to steal but not to buy.*

2. At Clarita's. Day or night? What room is this? A bed, a regular bed, and a mattress on the floor nearby. Wallpaper hanging in strips. Clarita says she tore it like that with her teeth. She was fighting a barbaric tribe that night, high from some pills; she was battling for her life with men wearing helmets of heavy iron and their faces no more than Christian crosses to breathe through, every one of those bastards looking like her lover Simon, who seems to breathe with great difficulty through the slits of mouth and nostrils in his face. Clarita has never heard of Sioux Drive. Raymond Forrest cuts no ice with her, nor does the C_____ account and its millions; Harvard Business School could be at the corner of Vernor and 12th Street for all she cares, and Vietnam might have sunk by now into the Dead Sea under its ton of debris, for all the amazement she could show . . . her face is overworked, overwrought, at the age of twenty (thirty?) it is already exhausted but fanciful and ready for a laugh. Clarita says mournfully to me *Honey somebody is going to turn you out let me give you warning.* In a movie shown on late television Clarita is not a mess like this but a nurse, with short neat hair and a dedicated look, in love with her doctor and her doctor's patients and their diseases, enamoured of needles and sponges and rubbing alcohol. . . . Or no: she is a private secretary. Robert Cummings is her boss. She helps him with fantastic plots, the canned audience laughs, no, the audience doesn't laugh because nothing is funny, instead her boss is Robert Taylor and they are not boss and secretary but husband and wife, she is threatened by a young starlet, she is grim, handsome, wifely, a good companion for a good man. . . . She is Claudette Colbert. Her sister too is Claudette Colbert. They are twins, identical. Her husband Charles Boyer is a very rich handsome man and her sister, Claudette Colbert, is plotting her death in order to take her place as the rich man's wife, no one will know because they are *twins.* . . . All these marvellous lives Clarita might have lived, but she fell out the bottom at the age of thirteen. At the age when I was packing my overnight case for a slumber party at Toni Deshield's she was tearing filthy sheets off a bed and scratching up a rash on her arms. . . . Thirteen is uncommonly young for a white girl in Detroit, Miss Brock of the Detroit House of Correction said in a sad newspaper interview for the *Detroit News;* fifteen and sixteen are more likely. Eleven, twelve, thirteen are not surprising in coloured . . . they are more precocious. What can we do? Taxes are rising and the tax

base is falling. The temperature rises slowly but falls rapidly. Everything is falling out the bottom, Woodward Avenue is filthy, Livernois Avenue is filthy! Scraps of paper flutter in the air like pigeons, dirt flies up and hits you right in the eye, oh Detroit is breaking up into dangerous bits of newspaper and dirt, watch out. . . .

Clarita's apartment is over a restaurant. Simon her lover emerges from the cracks at dark. Mrs Olesko, a neighbour of Clarita's, an aged white wisp of a woman, doesn't complain but sniffs with contentment at Clarita's noisy life and doesn't tell the cops, hating cops, when the cops arrive. I should give more fake names, more blanks, instead of telling all these secrets. I myself am a secret; I am a minor.

3. My father reads a paper at a medical convention in Los Angeles. There he is, on the edge of the North American continent, when the unmarked detective put his hand so gently on my arm in the aisle of Branden's and said, "Miss, would you like to step over here for a minute?"

And where was he when Clarita put her hand on my arm, that wintry dark sulphurous aching day in Detroit, in the company of closed-down barber shops, closed-down diners, closed-down movie houses, homes, windows, basements, faces . . . she put her hand on my arm and said, "Honey, are you looking for somebody down here?"

And was he home worrying about me, gone for two weeks solid, when they carried me off . . . ? It took three of them to get me in the police cruiser, so they said, and they put more than their hands on my arm.

4. I work on this lesson. My English teacher is Mr Forest, who is from Michigan State. Not handsome, Mr Forest, and his name is plain, unlike Raymond Forrest's, but he is sweet and rodentlike, he has conferred with the principal and my parents, and everything is fixed . . . treat her as if nothing has happened, a new start, begin again, only sixteen years old, what a shame, how did it happen?—nothing happened, nothing could have happened, a slight physiological modification known only to a gynecologist or to Dr Coronet. I work on my lesson. I sit in my pink room. I look around the room with my sad pink eyes. I sigh, I dawdle, I pause, I eat up time, I am limp and happy to be home, I am sixteen years old suddenly, my head hangs heavy as a pumpkin on my shoulders, and my hair has just been cut by Mr Faye at the Crystal Salon and is said to be very becoming.

(Simon too put his hand on my arm and said, 'Honey, you have got to come with me,' and in his six-by-six room we got to know each other. Would I go back to Simon again? Would I lie down with him in all that filth and craziness? Over and over again. a Clarita is being betrayed as in front of a Cunningham Drug Store she is nervously eying a coloured man who may or may not have money, or a nervous white boy of twenty with sideburns and an Appalachian look, who may or may not have a knife hidden in his jacket pocket, or a husky red-faced man of friendly countenance who may or may not be a member of the Vice Squad out for an early twilight walk.)

I work on my lesson for Mr Forest. I have filled up eleven pages. Words pour out of me and won't stop. I want to tell everything . . . what was the song Simon was always humming, and who was Simon's friend in a very new trench coat with an old high school graduation ring on his finger . . . ? Simon's bearded friend? When I was down too low for him, Simon kicked me out and gave me to him for three days, I think, on Fourteenth Street in Detroit, an airy room of cold cruel drafts with newspapers on the floor. . . . Do I really remember that or am I piecing it together from what they told me? Did they tell the truth? Did they know much of the truth?

## VIII. Characters

1. Wednesdays after school, at four; Saturday mornings at ten. Mother drives me to Dr Coronet. Ferns in the office, plastic or real, they look the same. Dr Coronet is queenly, an elegant nicotine-stained lady who would have studied with Freud had circumstances not prevented it, a bit of a Catholic, ready to offer you some mystery if your teeth will ache too much without it. Highly recommended by Father! Forty dollars an hour, Father's forty dollars! Progress! Looking up! Looking better! That new haircut is so becoming, says Dr Coronet herself, showing how normal she is for a woman with an I.Q. of 180 and many advanced degrees.

2. Mother. A lady in a brown suede coat. Boots of shiny black material, black gloves, a black fur hat. She would be humiliated could she know that of all the people in the world it is my ex-lover Simon who walks most like her . . . self-conscious and unreal, listening to distant music, a little bowlegged with craftiness. . . .

3. Father. Tying a necktie. In a hurry. On my first evening home he put his hand on my arm and said, "Honey, we're going to forget all about this."

4. Simon. Outside, a plane is crossing the sky, in here we're in a hurry. Morning. It must be morning. The girl is half out of her mind, whimpering and vague; Simon her dear friend is wretched this morning . . . he is wretched with morning itself . . . he forces her to give him an injection with that needle she knows is filthy, she has a dread of needles and surgical instruments and the odour of things that are to be sent into the blood, thinking somehow of her father. . . . This is a bad morning, Simon says that his mind is being twisted out of shape, and so he submits to the needle that he usually scorns and bites his lip with his yellowish teeth, his face going very pale. *Ah baby!* he says in his soft mocking voice, which with all women is a mockery of love, *do it like this—Slowly—*And the girl, terrified, almost drops the precious needle but manages to turn it up to the light from the window . . . is it an extension of herself then? She can give him this gift then? *I wish you wouldn't do this to me,* she says, wise in her terror, because it seems to her that Simon's danger—in a few minutes he may be dead—is a way of pressing her against him that is more powerful than any other embrace. She has to work over his arm, the knotted corded veins of his arm, her fore-

head wet with perspiration as she pushes and releases the needle, staring at that mixture of liquid now stained with Simon's bright blood. . . . When the drug hits him she can feel it herself, she feels that magic that is more than any woman can give him, striking the back of his head and making his face stretch as if with the impact of a terrible sun. . . . She tries to embrace him but he pushes her aside and stumbles to his feet. *Jesus Christ,* he says. . . .

5. Princess, a Negro girl of eighteen. What is her charge? She is closed-mouthed about it, shrewd and silent, you know that no one had to wrestle her to the sidewalk to get her in here; she came with dignity. In the recreation room she sits reading *Nancy Drew and the Jewel Box Mystery,* which inspires in her face tiny wrinkles of alarm and interest: what a face! Light brown skin, heavy shaded eyes, heavy eyelashes, a serious sinister dark brow, graceful fingers, graceful wristbones, graceful legs, lips, tongue, a sugar-sweet voice, a leggy stride more masculine than Simon's and my mother's, decked out in a dirty white blouse and dirty white slacks; vaguely nautical is Princess' style. . . . At breakfast she is in charge of clearing the table and leans over me, saying, *Honey you sure you ate enough?*

6. The girl lies sleepless, wondering. Why here, why not there? Why Bloomfield Hills and not jail? Why jail and not her pink room? Why downtown Detroit and not Sioux Drive? What is the difference? Is Simon all the difference? The girl's head is a parade of wonders. She is nearly sixteen, her breath is marvellous with wonders, not long ago she was colouring with crayons and now she is smearing the landscape with paints that won't come off and won't come off her fingers either. She says to the matron *I am not talking about anything,* not because everyone has warned her not to talk but because, because she will not talk; because she won't say anything about Simon, who is her secret. And she says to the matron, *I won't go home,* up until that night in the lavatory when everything was changed. . . . "No, I won't go home I want to stay here," she says, listening to her own words with amazement, thinking that weeds might climb everywhere over that marvellous $180,000 house and dinosaurs might return to muddy the beige carpeting, but never never will she reconcile four o'clock in the morning in Detroit with eight o'clock breakfasts in Bloomfield Hills. . . . oh, she aches still for Simon's hands and his caressing breath, though he gave her little pleasure, he took everything from her (five-dollar bills, ten-dollar bills, passed into her numb hands by men and taken out of her hands by Simon) until she herself was passed into the hands of other men, police, when Simon evidently got tired of her and her hysteria. . . . *No, I won't go home, I don't want to be bailed out.* The girl thinks as a *Stubborn and Wayward Child* (one of several charges lodged against her), and the matron understands her crazy white-rimmed eyes that are seeking out some new violence that will keep her in jail, should someone threaten to let her out. Such children try to strangle the matrons, the attendants, or one another . . . they want the locks locked forever, the doors nailed shut . . . and this girl is no different up until that night her mind is changed for her. . . .

## IX. That Night

Princess and Dolly, a little white girl of maybe fifteen, hardy however as a sergeant and in the House of Correction for armed robbery, corner her in the lavatory at the farthest sink and the other girls look away and file out to bed, leaving her. God, how she is beaten up! Why is she beaten up? Why do they pound her, why such hatred? Princess vents all the hatred of a thousand silent Detroit winters on her body, this girl whose body belongs to me, fiercely she rides across the Midwestern plains on this girl's tender bruised body . . . revenge on the oppressed minorities of America! revenge on the slaughtered Indians! revenge on the female sex, on the male sex, revenge on Bloomfield Hills, revenge revenge. . . .

## X. Detroit

In Detroit, weather weighs heavily upon everyone. The sky looms large. The horizon shimmers in smoke. Downtown the buildings are imprecise in the haze. Perpetual haze. Perpetual motion inside the haze. Across the choppy river is the city of Windsor, in Canada. Part of the continent has bunched up here and is bulging outward, at the tip of Detroit; a cold hard rain is forever falling on the expressways. . . . Shoppers shop grimly, their cars are not parked in safe places, their windshields may be smashed and graceful ebony hands may drag them out through their shatterproof smashed windshields, crying, *Revenge for the Indians!* Ah, they all fear leaving Hudson's and being dragged to the very tip of the city and thrown off the parking roof of Cobo Hall, that expensive tomb, into the river. . . .

## XI. Characters We Are Forever Entwined With

1. Simon drew me into his tender rotting arms and breathed gravity into me. Then I came to earth, weighed down. He said, *You are such a little girl,* and he weighed me down with his delight. In the palms of his hands were teeth marks from his previous life experiences. He was thirty-five, they said. Imagine Simon in this room, in my pink room: he is about six feet tall and stoops slightly, in a feline cautious way, always thinking, always on guard, with his scuffed light suede shoes and his clothes that are anyone's clothes, slightly rumpled ordinary clothes that ordinary men might wear to not-bad jobs. Simon has fair long hair, curly hair, spent languid curls that are like . . . exactly like the curls of wood shavings to the touch, I am trying to be exact . . . and he smells of unheated mornings and coffee and too many pills coating his tongue with a faint green-white scum. . . . Dear Simon, who would be panicked in this room and in this house (right now Billie is vacuuming next door in my parents' room; a vacuum cleaner's roar is a sign of all good things), Simon who is said to have come from a home not much different from this, years ago, fleeing all the carpeting and the pol-

ished banisters . . . Simon has a deathly face, only desperate people fall in love with it. His face is bony and cautious, the bones of his cheeks prominent as if with the rigidity of his ceaseless thinking, plotting, for he has to make money out of girls to whom money means nothing, they're so far gone they can hardly count it, and in a sense money means nothing to him either except as a way of keeping on with his life. *Each Day's Proud Struggle*, the title of a novel we could read at jail. . . . Each day he needs a certain amount of money. He devours it. It wasn't love he uncoiled in me with his hollowed-out eyes and his courteous smile, that remnant of a prosperous past, but a dark terror that needed to press itself flat against him, or against another man . . . but he was the first, he came over to me and took my arm, a claim. We struggled on the stairs and I said, *Let me loose, you're hurting my neck, my face,* it was such a surprise that my skin hurt where he rubbed it, and afterward we lay face to face and he breathed everything into me. In the end I think he turned me in.

2. Raymond Forrest. I just read this morning that Raymond Forrest's father, the chairman of the board at_____, died of a heart attack on a plane bound for London. I would like to write Raymond Forrest a note of sympathy. I would like to thank him for not pressing charges against me one hundred years ago, saving me, being so generous . . . well, men like Raymond Forrest are generous men, not like Simon. I would like to write him a letter telling of my love, or of some other emotion that is positive and healthy. Not like Simon and his poetry, which he scrawled down when he was high and never changed a word . . . but when I try to think of something to say, it is Simon's language that comes back to me, caught in my head like a bad song, it is always Simon's language:

> There is no reality only dreams
> Your neck may get snapped when you wake
> My love is drawn to some violent end
> She keeps wanting to get away
> My love is heading downward
> And I am heading upward
> She is going to crash on the sidewalk
> And I am going to dissolve into the clouds

## XII. Events

1. Out of the hospital, bruised and saddened and converted, with Princess' grunts still tangled in my hair . . . and Father in his overcoat looking like a prince himself, come to carry me off. Up the expressway and out north to home. Jesus Christ, but the air is thinner and cleaner here. Monumental houses. Heartbreaking sidewalks, so clean.

2. Weeping in the living room. The ceiling is two stories high and two chandeliers hang from it. Weeping, weeping, though Billie the maid is *probably listening.* I will never leave home again. Never. Never leave home. Never leave this home again, never.

3. Sugar doughnuts for breakfast. The toaster is very shiny and my face is distorted in it. Is that my face?

4. The car is turning in the driveway. Father brings me home. Mother embraces me. Sunlight breaks in movieland patches on the roof of our traditional-contemporary home, which was designed for the famous automotive stylist whose identity, if I told you the name of the famous car he designed, you would all know, so I can't tell you because my teeth chatter at the thought of being sued . . . or having someone climb into my bedroom window with a rope to strangle me. . . . The car turns up the black-top drive. The house opens to me like a doll's house, so lovely in the sunlight, the big living room beckons to me with its walls falling away in a delirium of joy at my return, Billie the maid is *no doubt* listening from the kitchen as I burst into tears and the hysteria Simon got so sick of. Convulsed in Father's arms, I say I will never leave again, never, why did I leave, where did I go, what happened, my mind is gone wrong, my body is one big bruise, my backbone was sucked dry, it wasn't the men who hurt me and Simon never hurt me but only those girls . . . my God, how they hurt me . . . I will never leave home again. . . . The car is perpetually turning up the drive and I am perpetually taking the right exit from the expressway (Lahser Road) and the wall of the rest room is perpetually banging against my head and perpetually are Simon's hands moving across my body and adding everything up and so too are Father's hands on my shaking bruised back, far from the surface of my skin on the surface of my good blue cashmere coat (dry-cleaned for my release). . . . I weep for all the money here, for God in gold and beige carpeting, for the beauty of chandeliers and the miracle of a clean polished gleaming toaster and faucets that run both hot and cold water, and I tell them, *I will never leave home, this is my home, I love everything here, I am in love with everything here.* . . .

I am home.

## Where Are You Going, Where Have You Been? 1970

**H**er name was Connie. She was fifteen and she had a quick, nervous giggling habit of craning her neck to glance into mirrors or checking other people's faces to make sure her own was all right. Her mother, who noticed everything and knew everything and who hadn't much reason any longer to look at her own face, always scolded Connie about it. "Stop gawking at yourself. Who are you? You think you're so pretty?" she would say. Connie would raise her eyebrows at these familiar old complaints and look right through her mother, into a shadowy vision of herself as she was right at that moment: she knew she was pretty and that was everything. Her mother had been pretty once too, if you could believe those old snapshots in the album, but now her looks were gone and that was why she was always after Connie.

"Why don't you keep your room clean like your sister? How've you got your hair fixed—what the hell stinks? Hair spray? You don't see your sister using that junk."

Her sister June was twenty-four and still lived at home. She was a secretary in the high school Connie attended, and if that wasn't bad enough—with her in the same building—she was so plain and chunky and steady that Connie had to hear her praised all the time by her mother and her mother's sisters. June did this, June did that, she saved money and helped clean the house and cooked and Connie couldn't do a thing, her mind was all filled with trashy daydreams. Their father was away at work most of the time and when he came home he wanted supper and he read the newspaper at supper and after supper he went to bed. He didn't bother talking much to them, but around his bent head Connie's mother kept picking at her until Connie wished her mother was dead and she herself was dead and it was all over. "She makes me want to throw up sometimes," she complained to her friends. She had a high, breathless, amused voice that made everything she said sound a little forced, whether it was sincere or not.

There was one good thing: June went places with girl friends of hers, girls who were just as plain and steady as she, and so when Connie wanted to do that her mother had no objections. The father of Connie's best girl friend drove the girls the three miles to town and left them at a shopping plaza so they could walk through the stores or go to a movie, and when he came to pick them up again at eleven he never bothered to ask what they had done.

They must have been familiar sights, walking around the shopping plaza in their shorts and flat ballerina slippers that always scuffed the sidewalk, with charm bracelets jingling on their thin wrists; they would lean together to whisper and laugh secretly if someone passed who amused or interested them. Connie had long dark blond hair that drew anyone's eye to it, and she wore part of it pulled up on her head and puffed out; and the rest of it she let fall down her back. She wore a pull-over jersey blouse that looked one way when she was at home and another way when she was away from home. Everything about her had two sides to it, one for home and one for anywhere that was not home: her walk, which could be childlike and bobbing, or languid enough to make anyone think she was hearing music in her head; her mouth, which was pale and smirking most of the time, but bright and pink on these evenings out; her laugh, which was cynical and drawling at home—"Ha, ha, very funny,"—but high-pitched and nervous anywhere else, like the jingling of the charms on her bracelet.

Sometimes they did go shopping or to a movie, but sometimes they went across the highway, ducking fast across the busy road, to a drive-in restaurant where older kids hung out. The restaurant was shaped like a big bottle, though squatter than a real bottle, and on its cap was a revolving figure of a grinning boy holding a hamburger aloft. One night in midsummer they ran across, breathless with daring, and right away someone leaned out a car window and invited them over, but it was just a boy from high school they didn't like. It made them feel good to be able to ignore him. They went up through the maze of parked and cruising cars to the bright-lit, fly-infested restaurant, their faces pleased and expectant as if they were entering a sacred building that loomed up out of the night to give them what haven and blessing they yearned for. They sat at the counter and crossed their legs at the ankles, their thin shoulders rigid with excitement, and listened to the music that made everything so good: the music was always in the background, like music at a church service; it was something to depend upon.

A boy named Eddie came in to talk with them. He sat backwards on his stool, turning himself jerkily around in semicircles and then stopping and turning back again, and after a while he asked Connie if she would like something to eat. She said she would and so she tapped her friend's arm on her way out—her friend pulled her face up into a brave, droll look—and Connie said she would meet her at eleven, across the way. "I just hate to leave her like that," Connie said earnestly, but the boy said that she wouldn't be alone for long. So they went out to his car, and on the way Connie couldn't help but let her eyes wander over the windshields and faces all around her, her face gleaming with a joy that had nothing to do with Eddie or even this place; it might have been the music. She drew her shoulders up and sucked in her breath with the pure pleasure of being alive, and just at that moment she happened to glance at a face just a few feet from hers. It was a boy with shaggy black hair, in a convertible jalopy painted gold. He stared at her and then his lips widened into a grin. Connie slit her eyes at him and turned away, but she couldn't help glancing back and there he was, still watching her. He wagged a finger and laughed and said, "Gonna get you, baby," and Connie turned away again without Eddie noticing anything.

She spent three hours with him, at the restaurant where they ate hamburgers and drank Cokes in wax cups that were always sweating, and then down an alley a mile or so away, and when he left her off at five to eleven only the movie house was still open at the plaza. Her girl friend was there, talking with a boy. When Connie came up, the two girls smiled at each other and Connie said, "How was the movie?" and the girl said, "*You* should know." They rode off the with girl's father, sleepy and pleased, and Connie couldn't help but look back at the darkened shopping plaza with its big empty parking lot and its signs that were faded and ghostly now, and over at the drive-in restaurant where cars were still circling tirelessly. She couldn't hear the music at this distance.

Next morning June asked her how the movie was and Connie said, "So-so."

She and that girl and another girl went out several times a week, and the rest of the time Connie spent around the house—it was summer vacation—getting in her mother's way and thinking, dreaming about the boys she met. But all the boys fell back and dissolved into a single face that was not even a face but an idea, a feeling, mixed up with the urgent insistent pounding of the music and the humid night air of July. Connie's mother kept dragging her back to the daylight by finding things for her to do or saying suddenly, "What's this about the Pettinger girl?"

And Connie would say nervously, "Oh, her. That dope." She always drew thick clear lines between herself and such girls, and her mother was simple and kind enough to believe it. Her mother was so simple, Connie thought, that it was maybe cruel to fool her so much. Her mother went scuffling around the house in old bedroom slippers and complained over the telephone to one sister about the other, then the other called up and the two of them complained about the third one. If June's name was mentioned her mother's tone was approving, and if Connie's name was mentioned it was disapproving. This did not really mean she disliked Connie, and actually Connie thought that her mother preferred her to June just because she was prettier, but the two of them kept up a pretense of exasperation, a sense that they were tugging and struggling over something of little value to either of them. Sometimes, over coffee, they were almost friends, but something would come up—some vexation that was like a fly buzzing suddenly around their heads—and their faces went hard with contempt.

One Sunday Connie got up at eleven—none of them bothered with church—and washed her hair so that it could dry all day long in the sun. Her parents and sister were going to a barbeque at an aunt's house and Connie said no, she wasn't interested, rolling her eyes to let her mother know just what she thought of it. "Stay home alone then," her mother said sharply. Connie sat out back in a lawn chair and watched them drive away, her father quiet and bald, hunched around so that he could back the car out, her mother with a look that was still angry and not at all softened through the windshield, and in the back seat poor old June, all dressed up as if she didn't know what a barbeque was, with all the running yelling kids and the flies. Connie sat with her eyes closed in the sun, dreaming and dazed with the warmth about her as if this were a kind of love, the caresses of love, and her mind slipped over onto thoughts of the boy she had been with the night before and how nice he had been, how sweet it always was, not the way someone like June would suppose but sweet, gentle, the way it was in movies and promised in songs; and when she opened her eyes she hardly knew where she was, the back yard ran off into weeds and a fence-like line of trees and behind it the sky was perfectly blue and still. The asbestos "ranch house" that was now three years old startled her—it looked small. She shook her head as if to get awake.

It was too hot. She went inside the house and turned on the radio to drown out the quiet. She sat on the edge of her bed, barefoot, and listened for an hour and a half to a program called XYZ Sunday Jamboree, record after record of hard, fast, shrieking songs she sang along with, interspersed by exclamations from "Bobby King": "An' look here, you girls at Napoleon's—Son and Charley want you to pay real close attention to this song coming up."

And Connie paid close attention herself, bathed in a glow of slow-pulsed joy that seemed to rise mysteriously out of the music itself and lay languidly about the airless little room, breathed in and breathed out with each gentle rise and fall of her chest.

After a while she heard a car coming up the drive. She sat up at once, startled, because it couldn't be her father so soon. The gravel kept crunching all the way in from the road—the driveway was long—and Connie ran to the window. It was a car she didn't know. It was an open jalopy, painted a bright gold that caught the sunlight opaquely. Her heart began to pound and her fingers snatched at her hair, checking it, and she whispered, "Christ, Christ," wondering how bad she looked. The car came to a stop at the side door and the horn sounded four short taps, as if this were a signal Connie knew.

She went into the kitchen and approached the door slowly, then hung out the screen door, her bare toes curling down off the step. There were two boys in the car and now she recognized the driver: he had shaggy, shabby black hair that looked crazy as a wig and he was grinning at her.

"I ain't late, am I?" he said.

"Who the hell do you think you are?" Connie said.

"Toldja I'd be out, didn't I?"

"I don't even know who you are."

She spoke sullenly, careful to show no interest or pleasure, and he spoke in a fast, bright monotone. Connie looked past him to the other boy, taking her time. He had fair brown hair, with a lock that fell onto his forehead. His sideburns gave him a fierce, embarrassed look, but so far he hadn't even bothered to glance at her. Both boys wore sunglasses. The driver's glasses were metallic and mirrored everything in miniature.

"You wanta come for a ride?" he said.

Connie smirked and let her hair fall loose over one shoulder.

"Don'tcha like my car? New paint job," he said. "Hey."

"What?"

"You're cute."

She pretended to fidget, chasing flies away from the door.

"Don'tcha believe me, or what?" he said.

"Look, I don't even know who you are," Connie said in disgust.

"Hey, Ellie's got a radio, see. Mine broke down." He lifted his friend's arm and showed her the little transistor radio the boy was holding, and now Connie began to hear the music. It was the same program that was playing inside the house.

"Bobby King?" she said.

"I listen to him all the time. I think he's great."

"He's kind of great," Connie said reluctantly.

"Listen, that guy's *great*. He knows where the action is."

Connie blushed a little, because the glasses made it impossible for her to see just what this boy was looking at. She couldn't decide if she liked him or if he was a jerk, and so she dawdled in the doorway and wouldn't come down or go back inside. She said, "What's all that stuff painted on your car?"

"Can'tcha read it?" He opened the door very carefully, as if he were afraid it might fall off. He slid out just as carefully, planting his feet firmly on the ground, the tiny metallic world in his glasses slowing down like gelatine hardening, and in the midst of it Connie's bright green blouse. "This here is my name, to begin with," he said. ARNOLD FRIEND was written in tarlike black letters on the side, with a drawing of a round, grinning face that reminded Connie of a pumpkin, except it wore sunglasses. "I wanta introduce myself, I'm Arnold Friend and that's my real name and I'm gonna be your friend, honey, and inside the car's Ellie Oscar, he's kinda shy." Ellie brought his transistor radio up to his shoulder and balanced it there. "Now, these numbers are a secret code, honey," Arnold Friend explained. He read off the numbers 33, 19, 17 and raised his eyebrows at her to see what she thought of that, but she didn't think much of it. The left rear fender had been smashed and around it was written, on the gleaming gold background: DONE BY CRAZY WOMAN DRIVER. Connie had to laugh at that.

Arnold Friend was pleased at her laughter and looked up at her. "Around the other side's a lot more—you wanta come and see them?"

"No."

"Why not?"

"Why should I?"

"Don'tcha wanta see what's on the car? Don'tcha wanta go for a ride?"

"I don't know."

"Why not?"

"I got things to do."

"Like what?"

"Things."

He laughed as if she had said something funny. He slapped his thighs. He was standing in a strange way, leaning back against the car as if he were balancing himself. He wasn't tall, only an inch or so taller than she would be if she came down to him. Connie liked the way he was dressed, which was the way all of them dressed: tight faded jeans stuffed into black, scuffed boots, a belt that pulled his waist in and showed how lean he was, and a white pull-over shirt that was a little soiled and showed the hard small muscles of his arms and shoulders. He looked as if he probably did hard work, lifting and carrying things. Even his neck looked muscular. And his face was a familiar face, somehow: the jaw and chin and cheeks slightly darkened because he hadn't shaved for a day or two, and the nose long and hawklike, sniffing as if she were a treat he was going to gobble up and it was all a joke.

"Connie, you ain't telling the truth. This is your day set aside for a ride with me and you know it," he said, still laughing. The way he straightened and recovered from his fit of laughing showed that it had been all fake.

"How do you know what my name is?" she said suspiciously.

"It's Connie."

"Maybe and maybe not."

"I know my Connie," he said, wagging his finger. Now she remembered him even better, back at the restaurant, and her cheeks warmed at the thought of how she had sucked in her breath just at the moment she passed him—how she must have looked to him. And he had remembered her. "Ellie and I come here especially for you," he said. "Ellie can sit in back. How about it?"

"Where?"

"Where what?"

"Where're we going?"

He looked at her. He took off the sunglasses and she saw how pale the skin around his eyes was, like holes that were not in shadow but instead in light. His eyes were like chips of broken glass that catch the light in an amiable way. He smiled. It was as if the idea of going for a ride somewhere, to someplace, was a new idea to him.

"Just for a ride, Connie sweetheart."

"I never said my name was Connie," she said.

"But I know what it is. I know your name and all about you, lots of things,"

Arnold Friend said. He had not moved yet but stood still leaning back against the side of his jalopy. "I took a special interest in you, such a pretty girl, and found out all about you—like I know your parents and sister are gone somewheres and I know where and how long they're going to be gone, and I know who you were with last night, and your best girl friend's name is Betty. Right?"

He spoke in a simple lilting voice, exactly as if he were reciting the words to a song. His smile assured her that everything was fine. In the car Ellie turned up the volume on his radio and did not bother to look around at them.

"Ellie can sit in the back seat," Arnold Friend said. He indicated his friend with a casual jerk of his chin, as if Ellie did not count and she should not bother with him.

"How'd you find out all that stuff?" Connie said.

"Listen: Betty Schultz and Tony Fitch and Jimmy Pettinger and Nancy Pettinger," he said in a chant. "Raymond Stanley and Bob Hutter—"

"Do you know all those kids?"

"I know everybody."

"Look, you're kidding. You're not from around here."

"Sure."

"But—how come we never saw you before?"

"Sure you saw me before," he said. He looked down at his boots, as if he were a little offended. "You just don't remember."

"I guess I'd remember you," Connie said.

"Yeah?" He looked up at this beaming. He was pleased. He began to mark time with the music from Ellie's radio, tapping his fists lightly together. Connie looked away from his smile to the car, which was painted so bright it almost hurt her eyes to look at it. She looked at that name, ARNOLD FRIEND. And up at the front fender was an expression that was familiar—MAN THE FLYING SAUCERS. It was an expression kids had used the year before but didn't use this year. She looked at it for a while as if the words meant something to her that she did not yet know.

"What're you thinking about? Huh?" Arnold Friend demanded. "Not worried about your hair blowing around in the car, are you?"

"No."

"Think I maybe can't drive good?"

"How do I know?"

"You're a hard girl to handle. How come?" he said. "Don't you know I'm your friend? Didn't you see me put my sign in the air when you walked by?"

"What sign?"

"My sign." And he drew an X in the air, leaning out toward her. They were maybe ten feet apart. After his hand fell back to his side the X was still in the air, almost visible. Connie let the screen door close and stood perfectly still inside it, listening to the music from her radio and the boy's blend together. She stared at Arnold Friend. He stood there so stiffly relaxed, pretending to be relaxed, with one hand idly on the door handle as if he were keeping himself up that way and had no intention of ever moving again. She recognized most things about him, the tight jeans that showed his thighs and buttocks and the greasy leather boots and the tight shirt, and even that slippery friendly smile of his, that sleepy dreamy smile that all the boys used to get across ideas they didn't want to put into words. She recognized all this and also the singsong way he talked, slightly mocking, kidding, but serious and a little melancholy, and she recognized the way he tapped one fist against the other in homage to the perpetual music behind him. But all these things did not come together.

She said suddenly, "Hey, how old are you?"

His smile faded. She could see then that he wasn't a kid, he was much older—thirty, maybe more. At this knowledge her heart began to pound faster.

"That's a crazy thing to ask. Can'tcha see I'm your own age?"

"Like hell you are."

"Or maybe a coupla years older. I'm eighteen."

"Eighteen?" she said doubtfully.

He grinned to reassure her and lines appeared at the corners of his mouth. His teeth were big and white. He grinned so broadly his eyes became slits and she saw how thick the lashes were, thick and black as if painted with a black tarlike material. Then, abruptly, he seemed to become embarrassed and looked over his shoulder at Ellie. "*Him,* he's crazy," he said. "Ain't he a riot? He's a nut, a real character." Ellie was still listening to the music. His sunglasses told nothing about what he was thinking. He wore a bright orange shirt unbuttoned halfway to show his chest, which was a pale, bluish chest and not muscular like Arnold Friend's. His shirt collar was turned up all around and the very tips of the collar pointed out past his chin as if they were protecting him. He was pressing the transistor radio up against his ear and sat there in a kind of daze, right in the sun.

"He's kinda strange," Connie said.

"Hey, she says you're kinda strange! Kinda strange!" Arnold Friend cried. He pounded on the car to get Ellie's attention. Ellie turned for the first time and Connie saw with shock that he wasn't a kid either—he had a fair, hairless face, cheeks reddened slightly as if the veins grew too close to the surface of his skin, the face of a forty-year-old baby. Connie felt a wave of dizziness rise in her at this sight and she stared at him as if waiting for something to change the shock of the moment, make it all right again. Ellie's lips kept shaping words, mumbling along with the words blasting in his ear.

"Maybe you two better go away," Connie said faintly.

"What? How come?" Arnold Friend cried. "We come out here to take you for a ride. It's Sunday." He had the voice of the man on the radio now. It was the same voice, Connie thought. "Don'tcha know it's Sunday all day? And honey, no matter who you were with last night, today you're with Arnold Friend and don't you forget it! Maybe you better step out here," he said, and this last was in a different voice. It was a little flatter, as if the heat was finally getting to him.

"No. I got things to do."

"Hey."

"You two better leave."

"We ain't leaving until you come with us."

"Like hell I am—"

"Connie, don't fool around with me. I mean—I mean, don't fool *around*," he said, shaking his head. He laughed incredulously. He placed his sunglasses on top of his head, carefully, as if he were indeed wearing a wig, and brought the stems down behind his ears. Connie stared at him, another wave of dizziness and fear rising in her so that for a moment he wasn't even in focus but was just a blur standing there against his gold car, and she had the idea that he had driven up the driveway all right but had come from nowhere before that and belonged nowhere and that everything about him and even about the music that was so familiar to her was only half real.

"If my father comes and sees you—"

"He ain't coming. He's at a barbecue."

"How do you know that?"

"Aunt Tillie's. Right now they're—uh—they're drinking. Sitting around," he said vaguely, squinting as if he were staring all the way to town and over to Aunt Tillie's back yard. Then the vision seemed to get clear and he nodded energetically. "Yeah. Sitting around. There's your sister in a blue dress, huh? And high heels, the poor sad bitch—nothing like you, sweetheart! And your mother's helping some fat woman with the corn—they're cleaning the corn—husking the corn—"

"What fat woman?" Connie cried.

"How do I know what fat woman, I don't know every goddamn fat woman in the world!" Arnold Friend laughed.

"Oh, that's Mrs. Hornsby. . . . Who invited her?" Connie said. She felt a little lightheaded. Her breath was coming quickly.

"She's too fat. I don't like them fat. I like them the way you are, honey," he said, smiling sleepily at her. They stared at each other for a while through the screen door. He said softly, "Now, what you're going to do is this: you're going to come out that door. You're going to sit up front with me and Ellie's going to sit in the back, the hell with Ellie, right? This isn't Ellie's date. You're my date. I'm your lover, honey."

"What? You're crazy—"

"Yes, I'm your lover. You don't know what that is but you will," he said. "I know that too. I know all about you. But look: it's real nice and you couldn't ask for nobody better than me, or more polite. I always keep my word. I'll tell you how it is, I'm always nice at first, the first time. I'll hold you so tight you won't think you have to try to get away or pretend anything because you'll know you can't. And I'll come inside you where's it's all secret and you'll give in to me and you'll love me—"

"Shut up! You're crazy!" Connie said. She backed away from the door. She put her hands up against her ears as if she'd heard something terrible, something not meant for her. "People don't talk like that, you're crazy," she muttered. Her heart was almost too big now for her chest and its pumping made sweat break out all over her. She looked out to see Arnold Friend pause and then take a step toward the porch, lurching. He almost fell. But, like a clever drunken man, he managed to catch his balance. He wobbled in his high boots and grabbed hold of one of the porch posts.

"Honey?" he said. "You still listening?"

"Get the hell out of here!"

"Be nice, honey. Listen."

"I'm going to call the police—"

He wobbled again and out of the side of his mouth came a fast spat curse, an aside not meant for her to hear. But even this "Christ!" sounded forced. Then he began to smile again. She watched this smile come, awkward as if he were smiling from inside a mask. His whole face was a mask, she thought wildly, tanned down to his throat but then running out as if he had plastered make-up on his face but had forgotten about his throat.

"Honey—? Listen, here's how it is. I always tell the truth and I promise you this: I ain't coming in that house after you."

"You better not! I'm going to call the police if you—if you don't—"

"Honey," he said, talking right through her voice, "honey, I'm not coming in there but you are coming out here. You know why?"

She was panting. The kitchen looked like a place she had never seen before, some room she had run inside but that wasn't good enough, wasn't going to help her. The kitchen window had never had a curtain, after three years, and there were dishes in the sink for her to do—probably—and if you ran your hand across the table you'd probably feel something sticky there.

"You listening, honey? Hey?"

"—going to call the police—"

"Soon as you touch the phone I don't need to keep my promise and can come inside. You won't want that."

She rushed forward and tried to lock the door. Her fingers were shaking. "But why lock it," Arnold Friend said gently, talking right into her face. "It's just a screen door. It's just nothing." One of his boots was at a strange angle, as if his foot wasn't in it. It pointed out to the left, bent at the ankle. "I mean, anybody can break through a screen door and glass and wood and iron or anything else if he needs to, anybody at all, and specially Arnold Friend. If the place got lit up with fire, honey, you'd come runnin' out into my arms, right into my arms an' safe at home—like you knew I was your lover and'd stopped fooling around. I don't mind a nice shy girl but I don't like no fooling around." Part of those words were spoken with a slight rhythmic lilt, and Connie somehow recognized them—the echo of a song from last year, about a girl rushing into her boy friend's arms and coming home again—

Connie stood barefoot on the linoleum floor, staring at him. "What do you want?" she whispered.

"I want you," he said.

"What?"

"Seen you that night and thought, that's the one, yes sir. I never needed to look anymore."

"But my father's coming back. He's coming to get me. I had to wash my hair first—" She spoke in a dry, rapid voice, hardly raising it for him to hear.

"No, your daddy is not coming and yes, you had to wash your hair and you washed it for me. It's nice and shining and all for me. I thank you sweetheart," he said with a mock bow, but again he almost lost his balance. He had to bend and adjust his boots. Evidently his feet did not go all the way down; the boots must have been stuffed with something so that he would seem taller. Connie stared out at him and behind him at Ellie in the car, who seemed to be looking off toward Connie's right, into nothing. This Ellie said, pulling the words out of the air one after another as if he were just discovering them, "You want me to pull out the phone?"

"Shut your mouth and keep it shut," Arnold Friend said, his face red from bending over or maybe from embarrassment because Connie had seen his boots. "This ain't none of your business."

"What—what are you doing? What do you want?" Connie said. "If I call the police they'll get you, they'll arrest you—"

"Promise was not to come in unless you touch that phone, and I'll keep that promise," he said. He resumed his erect position and tried to force his shoulders back. He sounded like a hero in a movie, declaring something important. But he spoke too loudly and it was as if he were speaking to someone behind Connie. "I ain't made plans for coming in that house where I don't belong but just for you to come out to me, the way you should. Don't you know who I am?"

"You're crazy," she whispered. She backed away from the door but did not want to go into another part of the house, as if this would give him permission to come through the door. "What do you . . . you're crazy, you. . . ."

"Huh? What're you saying, honey?"

Her eyes darted everywhere in the kitchen. She could not remember what it was, this room.

"This is how it is, honey: you come out and we'll drive away, have a nice ride. But if you don't come out we're gonna wait till your people come home and then they're all going to get it."

"You want that telephone pulled out?" Ellie said. He held the radio away from his ear and grimaced, as if without the radio the air was too much for him.

"I toldja shut up, Ellie," Arnold Friend said, "you're deaf, get a hearing aid, right? Fix yourself up. This little girl's no trouble and's gonna be nice to me, so Ellie keep to yourself, this ain't your date—right? Don't hem in on me, don't hog, don't crush, don't bird dog, don't trail me," he said in a rapid, meaningless voice, as if he were running through all the expressions he'd learned but was no longer sure which of them was in style, then rushing on to new ones, making them up with his eyes closed. "Don't crawl under my fence, don't squeeze in my chipmunk hole, don't sniff my glue, suck my popsicle, keep your own greasy fingers on yourself!" He shaded his eyes and peered in at Connie, who was backed against the kitchen table. "Don't mind him, honey, he's just a creep. He's a dope. Right? I'm the boy for you and like I said, you come out here nice like a lady and give me your hand, and nobody else gets hurt, I mean, your nice old bald-headed daddy and your mummy and your sister in her high heels. Because listen: why bring them in this?"

"Leave me alone," Connie whispered.

"Hey, you know that old woman down the road, the one with the chickens and stuff—you know her?"

"She's dead!"

"Dead? What? You know her?" Arnold Friend said.

"She's dead—"

"Don't you like her?"

"She's dead—she's—she isn't here any more—"

"But don't you like her, I mean, you got something against her? Some grudge or something?" Then his voice dipped as if he were conscious of a rudeness. He touched the sunglasses perched up on top of his head as if to make sure they were still there. "Now, you be a good girl."

"What are you going to do?"

"Just two things, or maybe three," Arnold Friend said. "But I promise it won't last long and you'll like me the way you get to like people you're close to. You will. It's all over for you here, so come on out. You don't want your people in any trouble, do you?"

She turned and bumped against a chair or something, hurting her leg, but she ran into the back room and picked up the telephone. Something roared in her ear, a tiny roaring, and she was so sick with fear that she could do nothing but listen to it— the telephone was clammy and very heavy and her fingers groped down to the dial but were too weak to touch it. She began to scream into the phone, into the roaring. She cried out, she cried for her mother, she felt her breath start jerking back and forth in her lungs as if it were something Arnold Friend was stabbing her with again and again with no tenderness. A noisy sorrowful wailing rose all about her and she was locked inside it the way she was locked inside this house.

After a while she could hear again. She was sitting on the floor with her wet back against the wall.

Arnold Friend was saying from the door, "That's a good girl. Put the phone back."

She kicked the phone away from her.

"No, honey. Pick it up. Put it back right."

She picked it up and put it back. The dial tone stopped.

"That's a good girl. Now, you come outside."

She was hollow with what had been fear but what was now just an emptiness. All that screaming had blasted it out of her. She sat, one leg cramped under her, and deep inside her brain was something like a pinpoint of light that kept going and would not let her relax. She thought, I'm not going to see my mother again. She thought, I'm not going to sleep in my bed again. Her bright green blouse was all wet.

Arnold Friend said, in a gentle-loud voice that was like a stage voice, "The place where you came from ain't there any more, and where you had in mind to go is can-celled out. This place you are now—inside your daddy's house—is nothing but a cardboard box I can knock down any time. You know that and always did know it. You hear me?"

She thought, I have got to think. I have got to know what to do.

"We'll go out to a nice field, out in the country here where it smells so nice and it's sunny," Arnold Friend said. "I'll have my arms tight around you so you won't need to try to get away and I'll show you what love is like, what it does. The hell with this house! It looks solid all right," he said. He ran a fingernail down the screen and the noise did not make Connie shiver, as it would have the day before. "Now, put your hand on your heart, honey. Feel that? That feels solid too but we know better. Be nice to me, be sweet like you can because what else is there for a girl like you but to be sweet and pretty and give in?—and get away before her people come back?"

She felt her pounding heart. Her hand seemed to enclose it. She thought for the first time in her life that it was nothing that was hers, that belonged to her, but just a pounding, living thing inside this body that wasn't really hers either.

"You don't want them to get hurt," Arnold Friend went on. "Now, get up, honey. Get up all by yourself."

She stood.

"Now, turn this way. That's right. Come over here to me.—Ellie, put that away, didn't I tell you? You dope. You miserable creepy dope," Arnold Friend said. His words were not angry but only part of an incantation. The incantation was kindly. "Now, come out through the kitchen to me, honey, and let's see a smile, try it, you're a brave, sweet little girl and now they're eating corn and hot dogs cooked to bursting over an outdoor fire, and they don't know one thing about you and never did and honey, you're better than them because not a one of them would have done this for you."

Connie felt the linoleum under her feet; it was cool. She brushed her hair back out of her eyes. Arnold Friend let go of the post tentatively and opened his arms for her, his elbows pointing in toward each other and his wrists limp, to show that this was an embarrassed embrace and a little mocking, he didn't want to make her self-conscious.

She put out her hand against the screen. She watched herself push the door slowly open as if she were back safe somewhere in the other doorway, watching this body and this head of long hair moving out into the sunlight where Arnold Friend waited.

"My sweet little blue-eyed girl," he said in a half-sung sigh that had nothing to do with her brown eyes but was taken up just the same by the vast sunlit reaches of the land behind him and on all sides of him—so much land that Connie had never seen before and did not recognize except to know that she was going to it.

# Tim O'Brien

## (B. 1946)

Known for his stories about the Vietnam War, Tim O'Brien has said, "Stories are for joining the past to the future. . . . Stories are for eternity, when memory is erased, when there is nothing to remember except the story." After graduating from Macalester College in 1968, O'Brien was drafted, and he served in the U.S. Army's Fifth Battalion, Forty-Sixth Infantry from January 1969 to March 1970. He returned to the United States with a Purple Heart and entered the Ph.D. program at Harvard University. During the summers, he worked as a reporter for the *Washington Post*. O'Brien left the university in 1976 without a degree in order to write. His books include *If I Die in a Combat Zone, Box Me Up and Ship Me*

*Home* (1973), *Northern Lights* (1975), *Going after Cacciato* (1978), *The Nuclear Age* (1985), *In the Lake of the Woods* (1994), and *Tomcat in Love* (1998). He also has published a collection of thematically related short stories, *The Things They Carried* (1990). O'Brien is currently writer in residence at Southwest Texas State University, and his most recent book, *July, July,* was published in 2003.

## *Sweetheart of the Song Tra Bong* 1990

Vietnam was full of strange stories, some improbable, some well beyond that, but the stories that will last forever are those that swirl back and forth across the border between trivia and bedlam, the mad and the mundane. This one keeps returning to me. I heard it from Rat Kiley, who swore up and down to its truth, although in the end, I'll admit, that doesn't amount to much of a warranty. Among the men in Alpha Company, Rat had a reputation for exaggeration and overstatement, a compulsion to rev up the facts, and for most of us it was normal procedure to discount sixty or seventy percent of anything he had to say. If Rat told you, for example, that he'd slept with four girls one night, you could figure it was about a girl and a half. It wasn't a question of deceit. Just the opposite: he wanted to heat up the truth, to make it burn so hot that you would feel exactly what he felt. For Rat Kiley, I think, facts were formed by sensation, not the other way around, and when you listened to one of his stories, you'd find yourself performing rapid calculations in your head, subtracting superlatives, figuring the square root of an absolute and then multiplying by maybe.

Still, with this particular story, Rat never backed down. He claimed to have witnessed the incident with his own eyes, and I remember how upset he became one morning when Mitchell Sanders challenged him on its basic premise.

"It can't happen," Sanders said. "Nobody ships his honey over to Nam. It don't ring true. I mean, you just can't import your own personal poontang."

Rat shook his head. "I *saw* it, man. I was right there. This guy did it."

"His girlfriend?"

"Straight on. It's a fact." Rat's voice squeaked a little. He paused and looked at his hands. "Listen, the guy sends her the money. Flies her over. This cute blonde—just a kid, just barely out of high school—she shows up with a suitcase and one of those plastic cosmetic bags. Comes right out to the boonies. I swear to God, man, she's got on culottes. White culottes and this sexy pink sweater. There she *is.*"

I remember Mitchell Sanders folding his arms. He looked over at me for a second, not quite grinning, not saying a word, but I could read the amusement in his eyes.

Rat saw it, too.

"No lie," he muttered. "Culottes."

When he first arrived in-country, before joining Alpha Company, Rat had been assigned to a small medical detachment up in the mountains west of Chu Lai, near the village of Tra Bong, where along with eight other enlisted men he ran an aid station that provided basic emergency and trauma care. Casualties were flown in by helicopter, stabilized, then shipped out to hospitals in Chu Lai or Danang. It was gory work, Rat said, but predictable. Amputations, mostly—legs and feet. The area was heavily mined, thick with Bouncing Betties and homemade booby traps. For a medic, though, it was ideal duty, and Rat counted himself lucky. There was plenty of cold beer, three hot meals a day, a tin roof over his head. No humping at all. No officers, either. You could let your hair grow, he said, and you didn't have to polish your boots or snap off salutes or put up with the usual rear-echelon nonsense. The highest ranking NCO was an E-6 named Eddie Diamond, whose pleasures ran from dope to Darvon, and except for a rare field inspection there was no such thing as military discipline.

As Rat described it, the compound was situated at the top of a flat-crested hill along the northern outskirts of Tra Bong. At one end was a small dirt helipad; at the other end, in a rough semicircle, the mess hall and medical hootches overlooked a river called the Song Tra Bong. Surrounding the place were tangled rolls of concertina wire, with bunkers and reinforced firing positions at staggered intervals, and base security was provided by a mixed unit of RFs, PFs, and ARVN infantry. Which is to say virtually no security at all. As soldiers, the ARVNs were useless; the Ruff-and-Puffs were outright dangerous. And yet even with decent troops the place was clearly indefensible. To the north and west the country rose up in thick walls of wilderness, triple-canopied jungle, mountains unfolding into higher mountains, ravines and gorges and fast-moving rivers and waterfalls and exotic butterflies and steep cliffs and smoky little hamlets and great valleys of bamboo and elephant grass. Originally, in the early 1960s, the place had been set up as a Special Forces outpost, and when Rat Kiley arrived nearly a decade later, a squad of Six Green Berets still used the compound as a base of operations. The Greenies were not social animals. Animals, Rat said, but far from social. They had their own hootch at the edge of the perimeter, fortified with sandbags and a metal fence, and except for the bare essentials they avoided contact with the medical detachment. Secretive and suspicious, loners by nature, the six Greenies would sometimes vanish for days at a time, or even weeks, then late in the night they would just as magically reappear, moving like shadows through the moonlight, filing in silently from the dense rain forest off to the west. Among the medics there were jokes about this, but no one asked questions.

While the outpost was isolated and vulnerable, Rat said, he always felt a curious sense of safety there. Nothing much ever happened. The place was never mortared, never taken under fire, and the war seemed to be somewhere far away. On occasion, when casualties came in, there were quick spurts of activity, but otherwise the days flowed by without incident, a smooth and peaceful time. Most mornings were spent on the volleyball court. In the heat of midday the men would head for the shade, lazing away the long afternoons, and after sundown there were movies and card games and sometimes all-night drinking sessions.

It was during one of those late nights that Eddie Diamond first brought up the tantalizing possibility. It was an offhand comment. A joke, really. What they should do, Eddie said, was pool some bucks and bring in a few mama-sans from Saigon, spice things up, and after a moment one of the men laughed and said, "Our own little EM club," and somebody else said, "Hey, yeah, we pay our fuckin' dues, don't we?" It was nothing serious. Just passing time, playing with the possibilities, and so for a while they tossed the idea around, how you could actually get away with it, no officers or anything, nobody to clamp down, then they dropped the subject and moved on to cars and baseball.

Later in the night, though, a young medic named Mark Fossie kept coming back to the subject.

"Look, if you think about it," he said, "it's not that crazy. You could actually do it."

"Do what?" Rat said.

"You know. Bring in a girl. I mean, what's the problem?"

Rat shrugged. "Nothing. A war."

"Well, see, that's the thing," Mark Fossie said. "No war *here*. You could really do it. A pair of solid brass balls, that's all you'd need."

There was some laughter, and Eddie Diamond told him he'd best strap down his dick, but Fossie just frowned and looked at the ceiling for a while and then went off to write a letter.

Six weeks later his girlfriend showed up.

The way Rat told it, she came in by helicopter along with the daily resupply shipment out of Chu Lai. A tall, big-boned blonde. At best, Rat said, she was seventeen years old, fresh out of Cleveland Heights Senior High. She had long white legs and blue eyes and a complexion like strawberry ice cream. Very friendly, too.

At the helipad that morning, Mark Fossie grinned and put his arm around her and said, "Guys, this is Mary Anne."

The girl seemed tired and somewhat lost, but she smiled.

There was a heavy silence. Eddie Diamond, the ranking NCO, made a small motion with his hand, and some of the others murmured a word or two, then they watched Mark Fossie pick up her suitcase and lead her by the arm down to the hootches. For a long while the men were quiet.

"That fucker," somebody finally said.

At evening chow Mark Fossie explained how he'd set it up. It was expensive, he admitted, and the logistics were complicated, but it wasn't like going to the moon. Cleveland to Los Angeles, LA to Bangkok, Bangkok to Saigon. She'd hopped a C-130 up to Chu Lai and stayed overnight at the USO and the next morning hooked a ride west with the resupply chopper.

"A cinch," Fossie said, and gazed down at his pretty girlfriend. "Thing is, you just got to *want* it enough."

Mary Anne Bell and Mark Fossie had been sweethearts since grammar school From the sixth grade on they had known for a fact that someday they would be married, and live in a fine gingerbread house near Lake Erie, and have three healthy yellow-haired children, and grow old together, and no doubt die in each other's arms and be buried in the same walnut casket. That was the plan. They were very much in love, full of dreams, and in the ordinary flow of their lives the whole scenario might well have come true.

On the first night they set up house in one of the bunkers along the perimeter, near the Special Forces hootch, and over the next two weeks they stuck together like a pair of high school steadies. It was almost disgusting, Rat said, the way they mooned over each other. Always holding hands, always laughing over some private joke. All they needed, he said, were a couple of matching sweaters. But among the medics there was some envy. It was Vietnam, after all, and Mary Anne Bell was an attractive girl. Too wide in the shoulders, maybe, but she had terrific legs, a bubbly personality, a happy smile. The men genuinely liked her. Out on the volleyball court she wore cut-off blue jeans and a black swimsuit top, which the guys appreciated, and in the evenings she liked to dance to music from Rat's portable tape deck. There was a novelty to it; she was good for morale. At times she gave off a kind of come-get-me energy, coy and flirtatious, but apparently it never bothered Mark Fossie. In fact he seemed to enjoy it, just grinning at her, because he was so much in love, and because it was the sort of show that a girl will sometimes put on for her boyfriend's entertainment and education.

Though she was young, Rat said, Mary Anne Bell was no timid child. She was curious about things. During her first days in-country she liked to roam around the compound asking questions: What exactly was a trip flare? How did a Claymore work? What was behind those scary green mountains to the west? Then she'd squint and listen quietly while somebody filled her in. She had a good quick mind. She paid attention. Often, especially during the hot afternoons, she would spend time with the ARVNs out along the perimeter, picking up little phrases of Vietnamese, learning how to cook rice over a can of Sterno, how to eat with her hands. The guys sometimes liked to kid her about it—our own little native, they'd say—but Mary Anne would just smile and stick out her tongue. "I'm here," she'd say, "I might as well learn something."

The war intrigued her. The land, too, and the mystery. At the beginning of her second week she began pestering Mark Fossie to take her down to the village at the foot of the hill. In a quiet voice, very patiently, he tried to tell her that it was a bad idea, way too dangerous, but Mary Anne kept after him. She wanted to get a feel for how people lived, what the smells and customs were. It did not impress her that the VC owned the place.

"Listen, it can't be that bad," she said. "They're human beings, aren't they? Like everybody else?"

Fossie nodded. He loved her.

And so in the morning Rat Kiley and two other medics tagged along as security while Mark and Mary Anne strolled through the ville like a pair of tourists. If the girl was nervous, she didn't show it. She seemed comfortable and entirely at home; the hostile atmosphere did not seem to register. All morning Mary Anne chattered away about how quaint the place was, how she loved the thatched roofs and naked children, the wonderful simplicity of village life. A strange thing to watch, Rat said. This seventeen-year-old doll in her goddamn culottes, perky and fresh-faced, like a cheerleader visiting the opposing team's locker room. Her pretty blue eyes seemed to glow. She couldn't get enough of it. On their way back up to the compound she stopped for a swim in the Song Tra Bong, stripping down to her underwear, showing off her legs while Fossie tried to explain to her about things like ambushes and snipers and the stopping power of an AK-47.

The guys, though, were impressed.

"A real tiger," said Eddie Diamond. "D-cup guts, trainer-bra brains."

"She'll learn," somebody said.

Eddie Diamond gave a solemn nod. "There's the scary part. I promise you, this girl will most definitely learn."

In parts, at least, it was a funny story, and yet to hear Rat Kiley tell it you'd almost think it was intended as straight tragedy. He never smiled. Not even at the crazy stuff. There was always a dark, far-off look in his eyes, a kind of sadness, as if he were troubled by something sliding beneath the story's surface. Whenever we laughed, I remember, he'd sigh and wait it out, but the one thing he could not tolerate was disbelief. He'd get edgy if someone questioned one of the details. "She *wasn't* dumb," he'd snap. "I never said that. Young, that's all I said. Like you and me. A *girl*, that's the only difference, and I'll tell you something: it didn't amount to jack. I mean, when we first got here—all of us—we were real young and innocent, full of romantic bullshit, but we learned pretty damn quick. And so did Mary Anne."

Rat would peer down at his hands, silent and thoughtful. After a moment his voice would flatten out.

"You don't believe it?" he'd say. "Fine with me. But you don't know human nature. You don't know Nam."

Then he'd tell us to listen up.

A good sharp mind, Rat said. True, she could be silly sometimes, but she picked up on things fast. At the end of the second week, when four casualties came in, Mary Anne wasn't afraid to get her hands bloody. At times, in fact, she seemed fascinated by it. Not the gore so much, but the adrenaline buzz that went with the job, that quick hot rush in your veins when the choppers settled down and you had to do things fast and right. No time for sorting through options, no thinking at all; you just stuck your hands in and started plugging up holes. She was quiet and steady. She didn't back off from the ugly cases. Over the next day or two, as more casualties trickled in, she learned how to clip an artery and pump up a plastic splint and shoot in morphine. In times of action her face took on a sudden new composure, almost serene, the fuzzy blue eyes narrowing into a tight, intelligent focus. Mark Fossie would grin at this. He was proud, yes, but also amazed. A different person, it seemed, and he wasn't sure what to make of it.

Other things, too. The way she quickly fell into the habits of the bush. No cosmetics, no fingernail filing. She stopped wearing jewelry, cut her hair short and wrapped it in a dark green bandana. Hygiene became a matter of small consequence. In her second week Eddie Diamond taught her how to disassemble an M-16, how the various parts worked, and from there it was a natural progression to learning how to use the weapon. For hours at a time she plunked away at C-ration cans, a bit unsure of herself, but as it turned out she had a real knack for it. There was a new confidence in her voice, a new authority in the way she carried herself. In many ways she remained naive and immature, still a kid, but Cleveland Heights now seemed very far away.

Once or twice, gently, Mark Fossie suggested that it might be time to think about heading home, but Mary Anne laughed and told him to forget it. "Everything I want," she said, "is right here."

She stroked his arm, and then kissed him.

On one level things remained the same between them. They slept together. They held hands and made plans for after the war. But now there was a new impression in the way Mary Anne expressed her thoughts on certain subjects. Not necessarily three kids, she'd say. Not necessarily a house on Lake Erie. "Naturally we'll still get married," she'd tell him, "but it doesn't have to be right away. Maybe travel first. Maybe live together. Just test it out, you know?"

Mark Fossie would nod at this, even smile and agree, but it made him uncomfortable. He couldn't pin it down. Her body seemed foreign somehow—too stiff in places, too firm where the softness used to be. The bubbliness was gone. The nervous giggling, too. When she laughed now, which was rare, it was only when something struck her as truly funny. Her voice seemed to reorganize itself at a lower pitch. In the evenings, while the men played cards, she would sometimes fall into long elastic silences, her eyes fixed on the dark, her arms folded, her foot tapping out a coded message against the floor. When Fossie asked about it one evening, Mary Anne looked at him for a long moment and then shrugged. "It's nothing," she said. "Really nothing. To tell the truth, I've never been happier in my whole life. Never."

Twice, though, she came in late at night. Very late. And then finally she did not come in at all.

Rat Kiley heard about it from Fossie himself. Before dawn one morning, the kid shook him awake. He was in bad shape. His voice seemed hollow and stuffed up, nasal-sounding, as if he had a bad cold. He held a flashlight in his hand, clicking it on and off.

"Mary Anne," he whispered, "I can't *find* her."

Rat sat up and rubbed his face. Even in the dim light it was clear that the boy was in trouble. There were dark smudges under his eyes, the frayed edges of somebody who hadn't slept in a while.

"Gone," Fossie said. "Rat, listen, she's sleeping with somebody. Last night, she didn't even . . . I don't know what to *do*."

Abruptly then, Fossie seemed to collapse. He squatted down, rocking on his heels, still clutching the flashlight. Just a boy—eighteen years old. Tall and blond. A gifted athlete. A nice kid, too, polite and good-hearted, although for the moment none of it seemed to be serving him well.

He kept clicking the flashlight on and off.

"All right, start at the start," Rat said. "Nice and slow. Sleeping with who?"

"I don't know who. Eddie Diamond."

"Eddie?"

"Has to be. The guy's always there, always hanging on her."

Rat shook his head. "Man, I don't know. Can't say it strikes a right note, not with Eddie."

"Yes, but he's—"

"Easy does it," Rat said. He reached out and tapped the boy's shoulder. "Why not just check some bunks? We got nine guys. You and me, that's two, so there's seven possibles. Do a quick body count."

Fossie hesitated. "But I can't . . . If she's there, I mean, if she's with somebody—"

"Oh, Christ."

Rat pushed himself up. He took the flashlight, muttered something, and moved down to the far end of the hootch. For privacy, the men had rigged up curtained walls around their cots, small makeshift bedrooms, and in the dark Rat went quickly from room to room, using the flashlight to pluck out the faces. Eddie Diamond slept a hard deep sleep—the others, too. To be sure, though, Rat checked once more, very carefully, then he reported back to Fossie.

"All accounted for. No extras."

"Eddie?"

"Darvon dreams." Rat switched off the flashlight and tried to think it out. "Maybe she just—I don't know—maybe she camped out tonight. Under the stars or something. You search the compound?"

"Sure I did."

"Well, come on," Rat said. "One more time."

Outside, a soft violet light was spreading out across the eastern hillsides. Two or three ARVN soldiers had built their breakfast fires, but the place was mostly quiet and unmoving. They tried the helipad first, then the mess hall and supply hootches, then they walked the entire six hundred meters of perimeter.

"Okay," Rat finally said. "We got a problem."

When he first told the story, Rat stopped there and looked at Mitchell Sanders for a time.

"So what's your vote? Where was she?"

"The Greenies," Sanders said.

"Yeah?"

Sanders smiled. "No other option. That stuff about the Special Forces—how they used the place as a base of operations, how they'd glide in and out—all that had to be there for a *reason*. That's how stories work, man."

Rat thought about it, then shrugged.

"All right, sure, the Greenies. But it's not what Fossie thought. She wasn't sleeping with any of them. At least not exactly. I mean, in a way she was sleeping with *all* of them, more or less, except it wasn't sex or anything. They was just lying together, so to speak, Mary Anne and these six grungy weirded-out Green Berets."

"Lying down?" Sanders said.

"You got it."

"Lying down how?"

Rat smiled. "Ambush. All night long, man, Mary Anne's out on fuckin' *ambush*."

· · · · ·

Just after sunrise, Rat said, she came trooping in through the wire, tired-looking but cheerful as she dropped her gear and gave Mark Fossie a brisk hug. The six Green Berets did not speak. One of them nodded at her, and the others gave Fossie a long stare, then they filed off to their hootch at the edge of the compound.

"Please," she said. "Not a word."

Fossie took a half step forward and hesitated. It was as though he had trouble recognizing her. She wore a bush hat and filthy green fatigues; she carried the standard M-16 automatic assault rifle; her face was black with charcoal.

Mary Anne handed him the weapon. "I'm exhausted," she said. "We'll talk later."

She glance over at the Special Forces area, then turned and walked quickly across the compound toward her own bunker. Fossie stood still for a few seconds. A little dazed, it seemed. After a moment, though, he set his jaw and whispered something and went after her with a hard, fast stride.

"Not later!" he yelled. "Now!"

What happened between them, Rat said, nobody ever knew for sure. But in the mess hall that evening it was clear that an accommodation had been reached. Or more likely, he said, it was a case of setting down some new rules. Mary Anne's hair was freshly shampooed. She wore a white blouse, a navy blue skirt, a pair of plain black flats. Over dinner she kept her eyes down, poking at her food, subdued to the point of silence. Eddie Diamond and some of the others tried to nudge her into talking about the ambush—What was the feeling out there? What exactly did she see and hear?—but the questions seemed to give her trouble. Nervously, she'd look across the table at Fossie. She'd wait a moment, as if to receive some sort of clearance, then she'd bow her head and mumble out a vague word or two. There were no real answers.

Mark Fossie, too, had little to say.

"Nobody's business," he told Rat that night. Then he offered a brief smile. "One thing for sure, though, there won't be any more ambushes. No more late nights."

"You laid down the law?"

"Compromise," Fossie said. "I'll put it this way—we're officially engaged."

Rat nodded cautiously.

"Well hey, she'll make a sweet bride," he said. "Combat ready."

Over the next several days there was a strained, tightly wound quality to the way they treated each other, a rigid correctness that was enforced by repetitive acts of willpower. To look at them from a distance, Rat said, you would think they were the happiest two people on the planet. They spent the long afternoons sunbathing together, stretched out side by side on top of their bunker, or playing backgammon in the shade of a giant palm tree, or just sitting quietly. A model of togetherness, it seemed. And yet at close range their faces showed the tension. Too polite, too thoughtful. Mark Fossie tried hard to keep up a self-assured pose, as if nothing had ever come between them, or ever could, but there was a fragility to it, something tentative and false. If Mary Anne happened to move a few steps away from him, even briefly, he'd tighten up and force himself not to watch her. But then a moment later he'd be watching.

In the presence of others, at least, they kept on their masks. Over meals they talked about plans for a huge wedding in Cleveland Heights—a two-day bash, lots of flowers. And yet even then their smiles seemed too intense. They were too quick with their banter; they held hands as if afraid to let go.

It had to end, and eventually it did.

Near the end of the third week Fossie began making arrangements to send her home. At first, Rat said, Mary Anne seemed to accept it, but then after a day or two she fell into a restless gloom, sitting off by herself at the edge of the perimeter. She would not speak. Shoulders hunched, her blue eyes opaque, she seemed to disappear inside herself. A couple of times Fossie approached her and tried to talk it out, but Mary Anne just stared out at the dark green mountains to the west. The wilderness seemed to draw her in. A haunted look, Rat said—partly terror, partly rapture. It was as if she had come up on the edge of something, as if she were caught in that no-man's-land between Cleveland Heights and deep jungle. Seventeen years old. Just a child, blond and innocent, but then weren't they all?

The next morning she was gone. The six Greenies were gone, too.

In a way, Rat said, poor Fossie expected it, or something like it, but that did not help much with the pain. The kid couldn't function. The grief took him by the throat and squeezed and would not let go.

"Lost," he kept whispering.

It was nearly three weeks before she returned. But in a sense she never returned. Not entirely, not all of her.

By chance, Rat said, he was awake to see it. A damp misty night, he couldn't sleep, so he'd gone outside for a quick smoke. He was just standing there, he said, watching the moon, and then off to the west a column of silhouettes appeared as if by magic at the edge of the jungle. At first he didn't recognize her—a small, soft shadow among six other shadows. There was no sound. No real substance either. The seven silhouettes seemed to float across the surface of the earth, like spirits, vaporous and unreal. As he watched, Rat said, it made him think of some weird opium dream. The silhouettes moved without moving. Silently, one by one, they came up the hill, passed through the wire, and drifted in a loose file across the compound. It was then, Rat said, that he picked out Mary Anne's face. Her eyes seemed to shine in the dark—not blue, though, but a bright glowing jungle green. She did not pause at Fossie's bunker. She cradled her weapon and moved swiftly to the Special Forces hootch and followed the others inside.

Briefly, a light came on, and someone laughed, then the place went dark again.

Whenever he told the story, Rat had a tendency to stop now and then, interrupting the flow, inserting little clarifications or bits of analysis and personal opinion. It was a bad habit, Mitchell Sanders said, because all that matters is the raw material, the stuff itself, and you can clutter it up with your own half-baked commentary. That just breaks the spell. It destroys the magic. What you have to do, Sanders said, is trust your own story. Get the hell out of the way and let it tell itself.

But Rat Kiley couldn't help it. He wanted to bracket the full range of meaning.

"I know it sounds far-out," he'd tell us, "but it's not like *impossible* or anything. We all heard plenty of wackier stories. Some guy comes back from the bush, tells you he saw the Virgin Mary out there, she was riding a goddamn goose or something. Everybody buys it. Everybody smiles and asks how fast was they going, did she have spurs on. Well, it's not like that. This Mary Anne wasn't no virgin but at least she was real. I saw it. When she came in through the wire that night, I was right there, I saw those eyes of hers, I saw how she wasn't even the same person no more. What's so impossible about that? She was a girl, that's all. I mean, if it was a guy, everybody'd say, Hey, no big deal, he got caught up in the Nam shit, he got seduced by the Greenies. See what I mean? You got these blinders on about women. How gentle and peaceful they are. All that crap about how if we had a pussy for president there wouldn't be no more wars. Pure garbage. You got to get rid of that sexist attitude."

Rat would go on like that until Mitchell Sanders couldn't tolerate it any longer. It offended his inner ear.

"The story," Sanders would say. "The whole tone, man, you're wrecking it."

"Tone?"

"The *sound.* You need to get a consistent sound, like slow or fast, funny or sad. All these digressions, they just screw up your story's *sound.* Stick to what happened."

Frowning, Rat would close his eyes.

"Tone?" he'd say. "I didn't know it was all that complicated. The girl joined the zoo. One more animal—end of story."

"Yeah, fine. But tell it right."

At daybreak the next morning, when Mark Fossie heard she was back, he stationed himself outside the fenced-off Special Forces area. All morning he waited for her, and all afternoon. Around dusk Rat brought him something to eat.

"She has to come out," Fossie said. "Sooner or later, she has to."

"Or else what?" Rat said.

"I go get her. I bring her out."

Rat shook his head. "Your decision. I was you, though, no way I'd mess around with any Greenie types, not for nothing."

"It's Mary Anne in there."

"Sure, I know that. All the same, I'd knock real extra super polite."

Even with the cooling night air Fossie's face was slick with sweat. He looked sick. His eyes were bloodshot; his skin had a whitish, almost colorless cast. For a few minutes Rat waited with him, quietly watching the hootch, then he patted the kid's shoulder and left him alone.

It was after midnight when Rat and Eddie Diamond went out to check on him. The night had gone cold and steamy, a low fog sliding down from the mountains, and somewhere out in the dark they heard music playing. Not loud but not soft either. It had a chaotic, almost unmusical sound, without rhythm or form or progression, like the noise of nature. A synthesizer, it seemed, or maybe an electric organ. In the background, just audible, a woman's voice was half singing, half chanting, but the lyrics seemed to be in a foreign tongue.

They found Fossie squatting near the gate in front of the Special Forces area. Head bowed, he was swaying to the music, his face wet and shiny. As Eddie bent down beside him, the kid looked up with dull eyes, ashen and powdery, not quite in register.

"Hear that?" he whispered. "You *hear*? It's Mary Anne."

Eddie Diamond took his arm. "Let's get you inside. Somebody's radio, that's all it is. Move it now."

"Mary Anne. Just listen."

"Sure, but—"

"Listen!"

Fossie suddenly pulled away, twisting sideways, and fell back against the gate. He lay there with his eyes closed. The music—the noise, whatever it was—came from the hootch beyond the fence. The place was dark except for a small glowing window, which stood partly open, the panes dancing in bright reds and yellows as though the grass were on fire. The chanting seemed louder now. Fiercer, too, and higher pitched.

Fossie pushed himself up. He wavered for a moment then forced the gate open.

"That voice," he said. "Mary Anne."

Rat took a step forward, reaching out for him, but Fossie was already moving fast toward the hootch. He stumbled once, caught himself, and hit the door hard with both arms. There was a noise—a short screeching sound, like a cat—and the door swung in and Fossie was framed there for an instant, his arms stretched out, then he slipped inside. After a moment Rat and Eddie followed quietly. Just inside the door they found Fossie bent down on one knee. He wasn't moving.

Across the room a dozen candles were burning on the floor near the open window. The place seemed to echo with a weird deep-wilderness sound—tribal music—bamboo flutes and drums and chimes. But what hit you first, Rat said, was the smell. Two kinds of smells. There was a topmost scent of joss sticks and incense, like the fumes of some exotic smokehouse, but beneath the smoke lay a deeper and much more powerful stench. Impossible to describe, Rat said. It paralyzed your lungs. Thick and numbing, like an animal's den, a mix of blood and scorched hair and excrement and the sweet-sour odor of moldering flesh—the stink of the kill. But that wasn't all. On a post at the rear of the hootch was the decayed head of a large black leopard; strips of yellow-brown skin dangled from the overhead rafters. And bones. Stacks of bones— all kinds. To one side, propped up against a wall, stood a poster in neat black lettering: ASSEMBLE YOUR OWN GOOK!! FREE SAMPLE KIT!! The images came in a swirl, Rat said, and there was no way you could process it all. Off in the gloom a few dim figures lounged in hammocks, or on cots, but none of them moved or spoke. The background music came from a tape deck near the circle of candles, but the high voice was Mary Anne's.

After a second Mark Fossie made a soft moaning sound. He started to get up but then stiffened.

"Mary Anne?" he said.

Quietly then, she stepped out of the shadows. At least for a moment she seemed to be the same pretty young girl who had arrived a few weeks earlier. She was bare-foot. She wore her pink sweater and a white blouse and a simple cotton skirt.

For a long while the girl gazed down at Fossie, almost blankly, and in the candle-light her face had the composure of someone perfectly at peace with herself. It took a few seconds, Rat said, to appreciate the full change. In part it was her eyes: utterly flat and indifferent. There was no emotion in her stare, no sense of the person behind it. But the grotesque part, he said, was her jewelry. At the girl's throat was a necklace of human tongues. Elongated and narrow, like pieces of blackened leather, the tongues were threaded along a length of copper wire, one overlapping the next, the tips curled upward as if caught in a final shrill syllable.

Briefly, it seemed, the girl smiled at Mark Fossie.

"There's no sense talking," she said. "I know what you think, but it's not . . . it's not *bad*."

"Bad?" Fossie murmured.

"It's not."

In the shadows there was laughter.

One of the Greenies sat up and lighted a cigar. The others lay silent.

"You're in a place," Mary Anne said softly, "where you don't belong."

She moved her hand in a gesture that encompassed not just the hootch but everything around it, the entire war, the mountains, the mean little villages, the trails and trees and rivers and deep misted-over valleys.

"You just don't *know*," she said. "You hide in this little fortress, behind wire and sandbags, and you don't know what it's all about. Sometimes I want to *eat* this place. Vietnam. I want to swallow the whole country—the dirt, the death—I just want to eat it and have it there inside me. That's how I feel. It's like . . . this appetite. I get scared sometimes—lots of times—but it's not *bad*. You know? I feel close to myself. When I'm out there at night, I feel close to my own body, I can feel my blood moving, my skin and my fingernails, everything, it's like I'm full of electricity and I'm glowing in the dark—I'm on fire almost—I'm burning away into nothing—but it doesn't matter because I know exactly who I am. You can't feel like that anywhere else."

All this was said softly, as if to herself, her voice slow and impassive. She was not trying to persuade. For a few moments she looked at Mark Fossie, who seemed to shrink away, then she turned and moved back into the gloom.

There was nothing to be done.

Rat took Fossie's arm, helped him up, and led him outside. In the darkness there was that weird tribal music, which seemed to come from the earth itself, from the deep rain forest, and a woman's voice rising up in a language beyond translation.

Mark Fossie stood rigid.

"Do something," he whispered. "I can't just let her go like that."

Rat listened for a time, then shook his head.

"Man, you must be deaf. She's already gone."

Rat Riley stopped there, almost in midsentence, which drove Mitchell Sanders crazy.

"What next?" he said.

"Next?"

"The girl. What happened to her?"

Rat made a small, tired motion with his shoulders. "Hard to tell for sure. Maybe three, four days later I got orders to report here to Alpha Company. Jumped the first chopper out, that's the last I ever seen of the place. Mary Anne, too."

Mitchell Sanders stared at him.

"You can't do that."

"Do what?"

"Jesus Christ, it's against the *rules*," Sanders said. "Against human *nature*. This elaborate story, you can't say, Hey, by the way, I don't know the *ending*. I mean, you got certain obligations."

Rat gave a quick smile. "Patience, man. Up to now, everything I told you is from personal experience, the exact truth, but there's a few other things I heard secondhand. Thirdhand, actually. From here on it gets to be . . . I don't know what the word is."

"Speculation."

"Yeah, right." Rat looked off to the west, scanning the mountains, as if expecting something to appear on one of the high ridgelines. After a second he shrugged. "Anyhow, maybe two months later I ran into Eddie Diamond over in Bangkok—I was on R&R, just this fluke thing—and he told me some stuff I can't vouch for with my own eyes. Even Eddie didn't really see it. He heard it from one of the Greenies, so you got to take this with a whole shakerful of salt."

Once more, Rat searched the mountains, then he sat back and closed his eyes.

"You know," he said abruptly, "I loved her."

"Say again?"

"A lot. We all did, I guess. The way she looked, Mary Anne made you think about those girls back home, how clean and innocent they all are, how they'll never understand any of this, not in a billion years. Try to tell them about it, they'll just stare at you with those big round candy eyes. They won't understand zip. It's like trying to tell somebody what chocolate tastes like."

Mitchell Sanders nodded. "Or shit."

"There it is, you got to taste it, and that's the thing with Mary Anne. She was *there*. She was up to her eyeballs in it. After the war, man, I promise you, you won't find nobody like her."

Suddenly, Rat pushed up to his feet, moved a few steps away from us, then stopped and stood with his back turned. He was an emotional guy.

"Got hooked, I guess," he said. "I loved her. So when I heard from Eddie about what happened, it almost made me . . . Like you say, it's pure speculation."

"Go on," Mitchell Sanders said. "Finish up."

What happened to her, Rat said, was what happened to all of them. You come over clean and you get dirty and then afterward it's never the same. A question of degree. Some make it intact, some don't make it at all. For Mary Anne Bell, it seemed, Vietnam had the effect of a powerful drug: that mix of unnamed terror and unnamed pleasure that comes as the needle slips in and you know you're risking something. The endorphins start to flow, and the adrenaline, and you hold your breath and creep quietly through the moonlit nightscapes; you become intimate with danger; you're in touch with the far side of yourself, as though it's another hemisphere, and you want to string it out and go wherever the trip takes you and be host to all the possibilities inside yourself. Not *bad,* she'd said. Vietnam made her glow in the dark. She wanted more, she wanted to penetrate deeper into the mystery of herself, and after a time the wanting became needing, which turned then to craving.

According to Eddie Diamond, who heard it from one of the Greenies, she took a greedy pleasure in night patrols. She was good at it; she had the moves. All camouflaged up, her face smooth and vacant, she seemed to flow like water through the dark, like oil, without sound or center. She went barefoot. She stopped carrying a weapon. There were times, apparently, when she took crazy, death-wish chances— things that even the Greenies balked at. It was as if she were taunting some wild creature out in the bush, or in her head, inviting it to show itself, a curious game of hide-and-go-seek that was played out in the dense terrain of a nightmare. She was lost inside herself. On occasion, when they were taken under fire, Mary Anne would stand quietly and watch the tracer rounds snap by, a little smile at her lips, intent on some private transaction with the war. Other times she would simply vanish altogether— for hours, for days.

And then one morning, all alone, Mary Anne walked off into the mountains and did not come back.

No body was ever found. No equipment, no clothing. For all he knew, Rat said, the girl was still alive. Maybe up in one of the high mountain villas, maybe with the Montagnard tribes. But that was guesswork.

There was an inquiry, of course, and a week-long air search, and for a time the Tra Bong compound went crazy with MP and CID types. In the end, however, nothing came of it. It was a war and the war went on. Mark Fossie was busted to PFC, shipped back to a hospital in the States, and two months later received a medical discharge. Mary Anne Bell joined the missing.

But the story did not end there. If you believed the Greenies, Rat said, Mary Anne was still somewhere out there in the dark. Odd movements, odd shapes. Late at night, when the Greenies were out on ambush, the whole rain forest seemed to stare in at them—a watched feeling—and a couple of times they almost saw her sliding through the shadows. Not quite, but almost. She had crossed to the other side. She was part of the land. She was wearing her culottes, her pink sweater, and a necklace of human tongues. She was dangerous. She was ready for the kill.

## The Things They Carried                                          1986

First Lieutenant Jimmy Cross carried letters from a girl named Martha, a junior at Mount Sebastian College in New Jersey. They were not love letters, but Lieutenant Cross was hoping, so he kept them folded in plastic at the bottom of his rucksack. In the late afternoon, after a day's march, he would dig his foxhole, wash his hands under a canteen, unwrap the letters, hold them with the tips of his fingers, and spend the last hour of light pretending. He would imagine romantic camping trips into the White Mountains in New Hampshire. He would sometimes taste the envelope flaps, knowing her tongue had been there. More than anything, he wanted Martha to love him as he loved her, but the letters were mostly chatty, elusive on the matter of love. She was a virgin, he was almost sure. She was an English major at Mount Sebastian, and she wrote beautifully about her professors and roommates and midterm exams, about her respect for Chaucer and her great affection for Virginia Woolf. She often quoted lines of poetry; she never mentioned the war, except to say, Jimmy, take care of yourself. The letters weighed 10 ounces. They were signed Love, Martha, but Lieutenant Cross understood that Love was only a way of signing and did not mean what he sometimes pretended it meant. At dusk, he would carefully return the letters to his rucksack. Slowly, a bit distracted, he would get up and move among his men, checking the perimeter, then at full dark he would return to his hole and watch the night and wonder if Martha was a virgin.

The things they carried were largely determined by necessity. Among the necessities or near-necessities were P-38 can openers, pocket knives, heat tabs, wristwatches, dog tags, mosquito repellent, chewing gum, candy, cigarettes, salt tablets, packets of Kool-Aid, lighters, matches, sewing kits, Military Payment Certificates, C rations, and two or three canteens of water. Together, these items weighed between 15 and 20 pounds, depending upon a man's habits or rate of metabolism. Henry Dobbins, who was a big man, carried extra rations; he was especially fond of canned peaches in heavy syrup over pound cake. Dave Jensen, who practiced field hygiene, carried a toothbrush, dental floss, and several hotel-sized bars of soap he'd stolen on R&R in Sydney, Australia. Ted Lavender, who was scared, carried tranquilizers until he was shot in the head outside the village of Than Khe in mid-April. By necessity, and because it was SOP, they all carried steel helmets that weighed 5 pounds including the liner and camouflage cover. They carried the standard fatigue jackets and trousers. Very few carried underwear. On their feet they carried jungle boots—2.1 pounds—and Dave Jensen carried three pairs of socks and a can of Dr. Scholl's foot powder as a precaution against trench foot. Until he was shot, Ted Lavender carried six or seven ounces of premium dope, which for him was a necessity. Mitchell Sanders, the RTO, carried condoms. Norman Bowker carried a diary. Rat Kiley carried comic books. Kiowa, a devout Baptist, carried an illustrated New Testament that had been presented to him by his father, who taught Sunday school in Oklahoma City, Oklahoma. As a hedge against bad times, however, Kiowa also carried his grandmother's distrust of the white man, his grandfather's old hunting hatchet. Necessity dictated. Because the land was mined and booby-trapped, it was SOP for each man to carry a steel-centered, nylon-covered flak jacket, which weighed 6.7 pounds, but which on hot days seemed much heavier. Because you could die so quickly, each man carried at least one large compress bandage, usually in the helmet band for easy access. Because the nights were cold, and because the monsoons were wet, each carried a green plastic poncho that could be used as a raincoat or groundsheet or makeshift tent. With its quilted liner, the poncho weighed almost two pounds, but it was worth every ounce. In April, for instance, when Ted Lavender was shot, they used his poncho to wrap him up, then to carry him across the paddy, then to lift him into the chopper that took him away.

They were called legs or grunts.

To carry something was to hump it, as when Lieutenant Jimmy Cross humped his love for Martha up the hills and through the swamps. In its intransitive form, to hump meant to walk, or to march, but it implied burdens far beyond the intransitive.

Almost everyone humped photographs. In his wallet, Lieutenant Cross carried two photographs of Martha. The first was a Kodacolor snapshot signed Love, though he knew better. She stood against a brick wall. Her eyes were gray and neutral, her lips slightly open as she stared straight-on at the camera. At night, sometimes, Lieutenant Cross wondered who had taken the picture, because he knew she had boyfriends, because he loved her so much, and because he could see the shadow of the picture-taker spreading out against the brick wall. The second photograph had been clipped from the 1968 Mount Sebastian yearbook. It was an action shot—women's volleyball—and Martha was bent horizontal to the floor, reaching, the palms of her hands in sharp focus, the tongue taut, the expression frank and competitive. There was no visible sweat. She wore white gym shorts. Her legs, he thought, were almost certainly the legs of a virgin, dry and without hair, the left knee cocked and carrying her entire weight, which was just over one hundred pounds. Lieutenant Cross remembered touching that left knee. A dark theater, he remembered, and the movie was *Bonnie and Clyde,* and Martha wore a tweed skirt, and during the final scene, when he touched her knee, she turned and looked at him in a sad, sober way that made him pull his hand back, but he would always remember the feel of the tweed skirt and the knee beneath it and the sound of the gunfire that killed Bonnie and Clyde, how embarrassing it was, how slow and oppressive. He remembered kissing her good night at the dorm door. Right then, he thought, he should've done something brave. He should've carried her up the stairs to her room and tied her to the bed and touched that left knee all night long. He should've risked it. Whenever he looked at the photographs, he thought of new things he should've done.

What they carried was partly a function of rank, partly of field specialty.

As a first lieutenant and platoon leader, Jimmy Cross carried a compass, maps, code books, binoculars, and a .45-caliber pistol that weighed 2.9 pounds fully loaded. He carried a strobe light and the responsibility for the lives of his men.

As an RTO, Mitchell Sanders carried the PRC-25 radio, a killer, 26 pounds with its battery.

As a medic, Rat Kiley carried a canvas satchel filled with morphine and plasma and malaria tablets and surgical tape and comic books and all the things a medic must carry, including M&M's for especially bad wounds, for a total weight of nearly 20 pounds.

As a big man, therefore a machine gunner, Henry Dobbins carried the M-60, which weighed 23 pounds unloaded, but which was almost always loaded. In addition, Dobbins carried between 10 and 15 pounds of ammunition draped in belts across his chest and shoulders.

As PFCs or Spec 4s, most of them were common grunts and carried the standard M-16 gas-operated assault rifle. The weapon weighed 7.5 pounds unloaded, 8.2 pounds with its full 20-round magazine. Depending on numerous factors, such as topography and psychology, the riflemen carried anywhere from 12 to 20 magazines, usually in cloth bandoliers, adding on another 8.4 pounds at minimum, 14 pounds at maximum. When it was available, they also carried M-16 maintenance gear—rods and steel brushes and swabs and tubes of LSA oil—all of which weighed about a pound. Among the grunts, some carried the M-79 grenade launcher, 5.9 pounds unloaded, a reasonably light weapon except for the ammunition, which was heavy. A single round weighed 10 ounces. The typical load was 25 rounds. But Ted Lavender, who was scared, carried 34 rounds when he was shot and killed outside Than Khe, and he went down under an exceptional burden, more than 20 pounds of ammunition, plus the flak jacket and helmet and rations and water and toilet paper and tranquilizers and all the rest, plus the unweighed fear. He was dead weight. There was no twitching or flopping. Kiowa, who saw it happen, said it was like watching a rock fall, or a big sandbag or something—just boom, then down—not like the movies where the dead guy rolls around and does fancy spins and goes ass over teakettle—not like that, Kiowa said, the poor bastard just flat-fuck fell. Boom. Down. Nothing else. It was a bright morning in mid-April. Lieutenant Cross felt the pain. He blamed himself. They stripped off Lavender's canteens and ammo, all the heavy things, and Rat Kiley said the obvious, the guy's dead, and Mitchell Sanders used his radio to report one U.S. KIA and to request a chopper. Then they wrapped Lavender in his poncho. They carried him out to a dry paddy, established security, and sat smoking the dead man's dope until the chopper came. Lieutenant Cross kept to himself. He pictured Martha's smooth young face, thinking he loved her more than anything, more than his men, and now Ted Lavender was dead because he loved her so much and could not stop thinking about her. When the dustoff arrived, they carried Lavender aboard. Afterward they burned Than Khe. They marched until dusk, then dug their holes, and that night Kiowa kept explaining how you had to be there, how fast it was, how the poor guy just dropped like so much concrete. Boom-down, he said. Like cement.

In addition to the three standard weapons—the M-60, M-16, and M-79—they carried whatever presented itself, or whatever seemed appropriate as a means of killing or staying alive. They carried catch-as-catch-can. At various times, in various situations, they carried M-14s and CAR-15s and Swedish Ks and grease guns and captured AK-47s and Chi-Coms and RPGs and Simonov carbines and black market Uzis and .38-caliber Smith & Wesson handguns and 66 mm LAWs and shotguns and silencers and blackjacks and bayonets and C-4 plastic explosives. Lee Strunk carried a slingshot; a weapon of last resort, he called it. Mitchell Sanders carried brass knuckles. Kiowa carried his grandfather's feathered hatchet. Every third or fourth man carried a Claymore antipersonnel mine—3.5 pounds with its firing device. They all carried fragmentation grenades—14 ounces each. They all carried at least one M-18 colored smoke grenade—24 ounces. Some carried CS or tear gas grenades. Some carried white phosphorus grenades. They carried all they could bear, and then some, including a silent awe for the terrible power of the things they carried.

In the first week of April, before Lavender died, Lieutenant Jimmy Cross received a good-luck charm from Martha. It was a simple pebble, an ounce at most. Smooth to the touch, it was a milky white color with flecks of orange and violet, oval-shaped, like a miniature egg. In the accompanying letter, Martha wrote that she had found the pebble on the Jersey shoreline, precisely where the land touched water at high tide, where things came together but also separated. It was this separate-but-together quality, she wrote, that had inspired her to pick up the pebble and to carry it in her breast pocket for several days, where it seemed weightless, and then to send it through the mail, by air, as a token of her truest feelings for him. Lieutenant Cross found this romantic. But he wondered what her truest feelings were, exactly, and what she meant by separate-but-together. He wondered how the tides and waves had come into play that afternoon along the Jersey shoreline when Martha saw the pebble and bent down to rescue it from geology. He imagined bare feet. Martha was a poet, with the poet's sensibilities, and her feet would be brown and bare, the toenails unpainted, the eyes chilly and somber like the ocean in March, and though it was painful, he wondered who had been with her that afternoon. He imagined a pair of shadows moving along the strip of sand where things came together but also separated. It was phantom jealousy, he knew, but he couldn't help himself. He loved her so much. On the march, through the hot days of early April, he carried the pebble in his mouth, turning it with his tongue, tasting sea salt and moisture. His mind wandered. He had difficulty keeping his attention on the war. On occasion he would yell at his men to spread out the column, to keep their eyes open, but then he would slip away into daydreams, just pretending, walking barefoot along the Jersey shore, with Martha, carrying nothing. He would feel himself rising. Sun and waves and gentle winds, all love and lightness.

What they carried varied by mission.

When a mission took them to the mountains, they carried mosquito netting, machetes, canvas tarps, and extra bug juice.

If a mission seemed especially hazardous, or if it involved a place they knew to be bad, they carried everything they could. In certain heavily mined AOs, where the land was dense with Toe Poppers and Bouncing Betties, they took turns humping a 28-pound mine detector. With its headphones and big sensing plate, the equipment was a stress on the lower back and shoulders, awkward to handle, often useless because of the shrapnel in the earth, but they carried it anyway, partly for safety, partly for the illusion of safety.

On ambush, or other night missions, they carried peculiar little odds and ends. Kiowa always took along his New Testament and a pair of moccasins for silence. Dave Jensen carried night-sight vitamins high in carotene. Lee Strunk carried his slingshot;

ammo, he claimed, would never be a problem. Rat Kiley carried brandy and M&M's candy. Until he was shot, Ted Lavender carried the starlight scope, which weighed 6.3 pounds with its aluminum carrying case. Henry Dobbins carried his girlfriend's pantyhose wrapped around his neck as a comforter. They all carried ghosts. When dark came, they would move out single file across the meadows and paddies to their ambush coordinates, where they would quietly set up the Claymores and lie down and spend the night waiting.

Other missions were more complicated and required special equipment. In mid-April, it was their mission to search out and destroy the elaborate tunnel complexes in the Than Khe area south of Chu Lai. To blow the tunnels, they carried one-pound blocks of pentrite high explosives, four blocks to a man, 68 pounds in all. They carried wiring, detonators, and battery-powered clackers. Dave Jensen carried earplugs. Most often, before blowing the tunnels, they were ordered by higher command to search them, which was considered bad news, but by and large they just shrugged and carried out orders. Because he was a big man, Henry Dobbins was excused from tunnel duty. The others would draw numbers. Before Lavender died there were 17 men in the platoon, and whoever drew the number 17 would strip off his gear and crawl in headfirst with a flashlight and Lieutenant Cross's .45-caliber pistol. The rest of them would fan out as security. They would sit down or kneel, not facing the hole, listening to the ground beneath them, imagining cobwebs and ghosts, whatever was down there—the tunnel walls squeezing in—how the flashlight seemed impossibly heavy in the hand and how it was tunnel vision in the very strictest sense, compression in all ways, even time, and how you had to wiggle in—ass and elbows—a swallowed-up feeling—and how you found yourself worrying about odd things: Will your flashlight go dead? Do rats carry rabies? If you screamed, how far would the sound carry? Would your buddies hear it? Would they have the courage to drag you out? In some respects, though not many, the waiting was worse than the tunnel itself. Imagination was a killer.

On April 16, when Lee Strunk drew the number 17, he laughed and muttered something and went down quickly. The morning was hot and very still. Not good, Kiowa said. He looked at the tunnel opening, then out across a dry paddy toward the village of Than Khe. Nothing moved. No clouds or birds or people. As they waited, the men smoked and drank Kool-Aid, not talking much, feeling sympathy for Lee Strunk but also feeling the luck of the draw. You win some, you lose some, said Mitchell Sanders, and sometimes you settle for a rain check. It was a tired line and no one laughed.

Henry Dobbins ate a tropical chocolate bar. Ted Lavender popped a tranquilizer and went off to pee.

After five minutes, Lieutenant Jimmy Cross moved to the tunnel, leaned down, and examined the darkness. Trouble, he thought—a cave-in maybe. And then suddenly, without willing it, he was thinking about Martha. The stresses and fractures, the quick collapse, the two of them buried alive under all that weight. Dense, crushing love. Kneeling, watching the hole, he tried to concentrate on Lee Strunk and the war, all the dangers, but his love was too much for him, he felt paralyzed, he wanted to sleep inside her lungs and breathe her blood and be smothered. He wanted her to be a virgin and not a virgin, all at once. He wanted to know her. Intimate secrets: Why poetry? Why so sad? Why that grayness in her eyes? Why so alone? Not lonely, just alone—riding her bike across campus or sitting off by herself in the cafeteria—even dancing, she danced alone—and it was the aloneness that filled him with love. He remembered telling her that one evening. How she nodded and looked away. And how later, when he kissed her, she received the kiss without returning it, her eyes wide open, not afraid, not a virgin's eyes, just flat and uninvolved.

Lieutenant Cross gazed at the tunnel. But he was not there. He was buried with Martha under the white sand at the Jersey shore. They were pressed together, and the pebble in his mouth was her tongue. He was smiling. Vaguely, he was aware of how quiet the day was, the sullen paddies, yet he could not bring himself to worry about matters of security. He was beyond that. He was just a kid at war, in love. He was twenty-four years old. He couldn't help it.

A few moments later Lee Strunk crawled out of the tunnel. He came up grinning, filthy but alive. Lieutenant Cross nodded and closed his eyes while the others clapped Strunk on the back and made jokes about rising from the dead.

Worms, Rat Kiley said. Right out of the grave. Fuckin' zombie.

The men laughed. They all felt great relief.

Spook city, said Mitchell Sanders.

Lee Strunk made a funny ghost sound, a kind of moaning, yet very happy, and right then, when Strunk made that high happy moaning sound, when he went *Ahhooooo,* right then Ted Lavender was shot in the head on the way back from peeing. He lay with his mouth open. The teeth were broken. There was a swollen black bruise under his left eye. The cheekbone was gone. Oh shit, Rat Kiley said, the guy's dead. The guy's dead, he kept saying, which seemed very profound—the guy's dead. I mean really.

The things they carried were determined to some extent by superstition. Lieutenant Cross carried his good-luck pebble. Dave Jensen carried a rabbit's foot. Norman Bowker, otherwise a very gentle person, carried a thumb that had been presented to him as a gift by Mitchell Sanders. The thumb was dark brown, rubbery to the touch, and weighed four ounces at most. It had been cut from a VC corpse, a boy of fifteen or sixteen. They'd found him at the bottom of an irrigation ditch, badly burned, flies in his mouth and eyes. The boy wore black shorts and sandals. At the time of his death he had been carrying a pouch of rice, a rifle, and three magazines of ammunition.

You want my opinion, Mitchell Sanders said, there's a definite moral here.

He put his hand on the dead boy's wrist. He was quiet for a time, as if counting a pulse, then he patted the stomach, almost affectionately, and used Kiowa's hunting hatchet to remove the thumb.

Henry Dobbins asked what the moral was.

Moral?

You know. *Moral.*

Sanders wrapped the thumb in toilet paper and handed it across to Norman

Bowker. There was no blood. Smiling, he kicked the boy's head, watched the flies scatter, and said, It's like with that old TV show—Paladin. Have gun, will travel.

Henry Dobbins thought about it.

Yeah, well, he finally said. I don't see no moral.

There it *is*, man.

Fuck off.

They carried USO stationery and pencils and pens. They carried Sterno, safety pins, trip flares, signal flares, spools of wire, razor blades, chewing tobacco, liberated joss sticks and statuettes of the smiling Buddha, candles, grease pencils, *The Stars and Stripes*, fingernail clippers, Psy Ops leaflets, bush hats, bolos, and much more. Twice a week, when the resupply choppers came in, they carried hot chow in green mermite cans and large canvas bags filled with iced beer and soda pop. They carried plastic water containers, each with a two-gallon capacity. Mitchell Sanders carried a set of starched tiger fatigues for special occasions. Henry Dobbins carried Black Flag insecticide. Dave Jensen carried empty sandbags that could be filled at night for added protection. Lee Strunk carried tanning lotion. Some things they carried in common. Taking turns, they carried the big PRC-77 scrambler radio, which weighed 30 pounds with its battery. They shared the weight of memory. They took up what others could no longer bear. Often, they carried each other, the wounded or weak. They carried infections. They carried chess sets, basketballs, Vietnamese-English dictionaries, insignia of rank, Bronze Stars and Purple Hearts, plastic cards imprinted with the Code of Conduct. They carried diseases, among them malaria and dysentery. They carried lice and ringworm and leeches and paddy algae and various rots and molds. They carried the land itself—Vietnam, the place, the soil—a powdery orange-red dust that covered their boots and fatigues and faces. They carried the sky. The whole atmosphere, they carried it, the humidity, the monsoons, the stink of fungus and decay, all of it, they carried gravity. They moved like mules. By daylight they took sniper fire, at night they were mortared, but it was not battle, it was just the endless march, village to village, without purpose, nothing won or lost. They marched for the sake of the march. They plodded along slowly, dumbly, leaning forward against the heat, unthinking, all blood and bone, simple grunts, soldiering with their legs, toiling up the hills and down into the paddies and across the rivers and up again and down, just humping, one step and then the next and then another, but no volition, no will, because it was automatic, it was anatomy, and the war was entirely a matter of posture and carriage, the hump was everything, a kind of inertia, a kind of emptiness, a dullness of desire and intellect and conscience and hope and human sensibility. Their principles were in their feet. Their calculations were biological. They had no sense of strategy or mission. They searched the villages without knowing what to look for, not caring, kicking over jars of rice, frisking children and old men, blowing tunnels, sometimes setting fires and sometimes not, then forming up and moving on to the next village, then other villages, where it would always be the same. They carried their own lives. The pressures were enormous. In the heat of early afternoon, they would remove their helmets and flak jackets, walking bare, which was dangerous but which helped ease the strain. They would often discard things along the route of march. Purely for comfort, they would throw away rations, blow their Claymores and grenades, no matter, because by nightfall the resupply choppers would arrive with more of the same, then a day or two later still more, fresh watermelons and crates of ammunition and sunglasses and woolen sweaters—the resources were stunning—sparklers for the Fourth of July, colored eggs for Easter—it was the great American war chest—the fruits of science, the smokestacks, the canneries, the arsenals at Hartford, the Minnesota forests, the machine shops, the vast fields of corn and wheat—they carried like freight trains; they carried it on their backs and shoulders—and for all the ambiguities of Vietnam, all the mysteries and unknowns, there was at least the single abiding certainty that they would never be at a loss for things to carry.

After the chopper took Lavender away, Lieutenant Jimmy Cross led his men into the village of Than Khe. They burned everything. They shot chickens and dogs, they trashed the village well, they called in artillery and watched the wreckage, then they marched for several hours through the hot afternoon, and then at dusk, while Kiowa explained how Lavender died, Lieutenant Cross found himself trembling.

He tried not to cry. With his entrenching tool, which weighed five pounds, he began digging a hole in the earth.

He felt shame. He hated himself. He had loved Martha more than his men, and as a consequence Lavender was now dead, and this was something he would have to carry like a stone in his stomach for the rest of the war.

All he could do was dig. He used his entrenching tool like an ax, slashing, feeling both love and hate, and then later, when it was full dark, he sat at the bottom of his foxhole and wept. It went on for a long while. In part, he was grieving for Ted Lavender, but mostly it was for Martha, and for himself, because she belonged to another world, which was not quite real, and because she was a junior at Mount Sebastian College in New Jersey, a poet and a virgin and uninvolved, and because he realized she did not love him and never would.

Like cement, Kiowa whispered in the dark. I swear to God—boom, down. Not a word.

I've heard this, said Norman Bowker.

A pisser, you know? Still zipping himself up. Zapped while zipping.

All right, fine. That's enough.

Yeah, but you had to see it, the guy just—

I *heard,* man. Cement. So why not shut the fuck *up?*

Kiowa shook his head sadly and glanced over at the hole where Lieutenant Jimmy Cross sat watching the night. The air was thick and wet. A warm dense fog had settled over the paddies and there was the stillness that precedes rain.

After a time Kiowa sighed.

One thing for sure, he said. The lieutenant's in some deep hurt. I mean that crying jag—the way he was carrying on—it wasn't fake or anything, it was real heavy-duty hurt. The man cares.

Sure, Norman Bowker said.

Say what you want, the man does care.

We all got problems.

Not Lavender.

No, I guess not, Bowker said. Do me a favor, though.

Shut up?

That's a smart Indian. Shut up.

Shrugging, Kiowa pulled off his boots. He wanted to say more, just to lighten up his sleep, but instead he opened his New Testament and arranged it beneath his head as a pillow. The fog made things seem hollow and unattached. He tried not to think about Ted Lavender, but then he was thinking how fast it was, no drama, down and dead, and how it was hard to feel anything except surprise. It seemed unchristian. He wished he could find some great sadness, or even anger, but the emotion wasn't there and he couldn't make it happen. Mostly he felt pleased to be alive. He liked the smell of the New Testament under his cheek, the leather and ink and paper and glue, whatever the chemicals were. He liked hearing the sounds of the night. Even his fatigue, it felt fine, the stiff muscles and the prickly awareness of his own body, a floating feeling. He enjoyed not being dead. Lying there, Kiowa admired Lieutenant Jimmy Cross's capacity for grief. He wanted to share the man's pain, he wanted to care as Jimmy Cross cared. And yet when he closed his eyes, all he could think was Boom-down, and all he could feel was the pleasure of having his boots off and the fog curling in around him and the damp soil and the Bible smells and the plush comfort of the night.

After a moment Norman Bowker sat up in the dark.

What the hell, he said. You want to talk, *talk*. Tell it to me.

Forget it.

No, man, go on. One thing I hate, it's a silent Indian.

For the most part they carried themselves with poise, a kind of dignity. Now and then, however, there were times of panic, when they squealed or wanted to squeal but couldn't, when they twitched and made moaning sounds and covered their heads and said Dear Jesus and flopped around on the earth and fired their weapons blindly and cringed and sobbed and begged for the noise to stop and went wild and made stupid promises to themselves and to God and to their mothers and fathers, hoping not to die. In different ways, it happened to all of them. Afterward, when the firing ended, they would blink and peek up. They would touch their bodies, feeling shame, then quickly hiding it. They would force themselves to stand. As if in slow motion, frame by frame, the world would take on the old logic—absolute silence, then the wind, then sunlight, then voices. It was the burden of being alive. Awkwardly, the men would reassemble themselves, first in private, then in groups, becoming soldiers again. They would repair the leaks in their eyes. They would check for casualties, call in dustoffs, light cigarettes, try to smile, clear their throats and spit and begin cleaning their weapons. After a time someone would shake his head and say, No lie, I almost shit my pants, and someone else would laugh, which meant it was bad, yes, but the guy had obviously not shit his pants, it wasn't that bad, and in any case nobody would ever do such a thing and then go ahead and talk about it. They would squint into the dense, oppressive sunlight. For a few moments, perhaps, they would fall silent, lighting a joint and tracking its passage from man to man, inhaling, holding in the humiliation. Scary stuff, one of them might say. But then someone else would grin or flick his eyebrows and say, Roger-dodger, almost cut me a new asshole, *almost*.

There were numerous such poses. Some carried themselves with a sort of wistful resignation, others with pride or stiff soldierly discipline or good humor or macho zeal. They were afraid of dying but they were even more afraid to show it.

They found jokes to tell.

They used a hard vocabulary to contain the terrible softness. *Greased* they'd say. *Offed, lit up, zapped while zipping*. It wasn't cruelty, just stage presence. They were actors. When someone died, it wasn't quite dying, because in a curious way it seemed scripted, and because they had their lines mostly memorized, irony mixed with tragedy, and because they called it by other names, as if to encyst and destroy the reality of death itself. They kicked corpses. They cut off thumbs. They talked grunt lingo. They told stories about Ted Lavender's supply of tranquilizers, how the poor guy didn't feel a thing, how incredibly tranquil he was.

There's a moral here, said Mitchell Sanders.

They were waiting for Lavender's chopper, smoking the dead man's dope.

The moral's pretty obvious, Sanders said, and winked. Stay away from drugs. No joke, they'll ruin your day every time.

Cute, said Henry Dobbins.

Mind blower, get it? Talk about wiggy. Nothing left, just blood and brains.

They made themselves laugh.

There it is, they'd say. Over and over—there it is, my friend, there it is—as if the repetition itself were an act of poise, a balance between crazy and almost crazy, knowing without going, there it is, which meant be cool, let it ride, because Oh yeah, man, you can't change what can't be changed, there it is, there it absolutely and positively and fucking well *is*.

They were tough.

They carried all the emotional baggage of men who might die. Grief, terror, love, longing—these were intangibles, but the intangibles had their own mass and specific gravity, they had tangible weight. They carried shameful memories. They carried the common secret of cowardice barely restrained, the instinct to run or freeze or hide, and in many respects this was the heaviest burden of all, for it could never be put down, it required perfect balance and perfect posture. They carried their reputations. They carried the soldier's greatest fear, which was the fear of blushing. Men killed, and died, because they were embarrassed not to. It was what had brought them to the war in the first place, nothing positive, no dreams of glory or honor, just to avoid the blush of dishonor. They died so as not to die of embarrassment. They crawled into tunnels and walked point and advanced under fire. Each morning, despite the unknowns, they made their legs move. They endured. They kept humping. They did not submit to the obvious alternative, which was simply to close the eyes and fall. So easy, really. Go limp and tumble to the ground and let the muscles unwind and not speak and not budge until your buddies picked you up and lifted you into the chopper that would roar and dip its nose and carry you off to the world. A mere matter of falling, yet no one ever fell. It was not courage, exactly; the object was not valor. Rather, they were too frightened to be cowards.

By and large they carried these things inside, maintaining the masks of composure. They sneered at sick call. They spoke bitterly about guys who had found release by shooting off their own toes or fingers. Pussies, they'd say. Candy-asses. It was fierce, mocking talk, with only a trace of envy or awe, but even so the image played itself out behind their eyes.

They imagined the muzzle against flesh. So easy: squeeze the trigger and blow away a toe. They imagined it. They imagined the quick, sweet pain, then the evacuation to Japan, then a hospital with warm beds and cute geisha nurses.

And they dreamed of freedom birds.

At night, on guard, staring into the dark, they were carried away by jumbo jets. They felt the rush of takeoff. *Gone!* they yelled. And then velocity—wings and engines—a smiling stewardess—but it was more than a plane, it was a real bird, a big sleek silver bird with feathers and talons and high screeching. They were flying. The weights fell off; there was nothing to bear. They laughed and held on tight, feeling the cold slap of wind and altitude, soaring, thinking *It's over, I'm gone!*—they were naked, they were light and free— it was all lightness, bright and fast and buoyant, light as light, a helium buzz in the brain, a giddy bubbling in the lungs as they were taken up over the clouds and the war, beyond duty, beyond gravity and mortification and global entanglements—*Sin loi!* they yelled. *I'm sorry, motherfuckers, but I'm out of it, I'm goofed, I'm on a space cruise, I'm gone!*—and it was a restful, unencumbered sensation, just riding the light waves, sailing that big silver freedom bird over the mountains and oceans, over America, over the farms and great sleeping cities and cemeteries and highways and the golden arches of McDonald's, it was flight, a kind of fleeing, a kind of falling, falling higher and higher, spinning off the edge of the earth and beyond the sun and through the vast, silent vacuum where there were no burdens and where everything weighed exactly nothing—*Gone!* they screamed. *I'm sorry but I'm gone!*—and so at night, not quite dreaming, they gave themselves over to lightness, they were carried, they were purely borne.

On the morning after Ted Lavender died, First Lieutenant Jimmy Cross crouched at the bottom of his foxhole and burned Martha's letters. Then he burned the two photographs. There was a steady rain falling, which made it difficult, but he used heat tabs and Sterno to build a small fire, screening it with his body, holding the photographs over the tight blue flame with the tips of his fingers.

He realized it was only a gesture. Stupid, he thought. Sentimental, too, but mostly just stupid.

Lavender was dead. You couldn't burn the blame.

Besides, the letters were in his head. And even now, without photographs, Lieutenant Cross could see Martha playing volleyball in her white gym shorts and yellow T-shirt. He could see her moving in the rain.

When the fire died out, Lieutenant Cross pulled his poncho over his shoulders and ate breakfast from a can.

There was no great mystery, he decided.

In those burned letters Martha had never mentioned the war, except to say, Jimmy, take care of yourself. She wasn't involved. She signed the letters Love, but it wasn't love, and all the fine lines and technicalities did not matter. Virginity was no longer an issue. He hated her. Yes, he did. He hated her. Love, too, but it was a hard, hating kind of love.

The morning came up wet and blurry. Everything seemed part of everything else, the fog and Martha and the deepening rain.

He was a soldier, after all.

Half smiling Lieutenant Jimmy Cross took out his maps. He shook his head hard, as if to clear it, then bent forward and began planning the day's march. In ten minutes, or maybe twenty, he would rouse the men and they would pack up and head west, where the maps showed the country to be green and inviting. They would do what they had always done. The rain might add some weight, but otherwise it would be one more day layered upon all the other days.

He was realistic about it. There was that new hardness in his stomach. He loved her but he hated her.

No more fantasies, he told himself.

Henceforth, when he thought about Martha, it would be only to think that she belonged elsewhere. He would shut down the daydreams. This was not Mount Sebastian, it was another world, where there were no pretty poems or midterm exams, a place where men died because of carelessness and gross stupidity. Kiowa was right. Boom-down, and you were dead, never partly dead.

Briefly, in the rain, Lieutenant Cross saw Martha's gray eyes gazing back at him.

He understood.

It was very sad, he thought. The things men carried inside. The things men did or felt they had to do.

He almost nodded at her, but didn't.

Instead he went back to his maps. He was now determined to perform his duties firmly and without negligence. It wouldn't help Lavender, he knew that, but from this point on he would comport himself as an officer. He would dispose of his good-luck pebble. Swallow it, maybe, or use Lee Strunk's slingshot, or just drop it along the trail. On the march he would impose strict field discipline. He would be careful to send out flank security, to prevent straggling or bunching up, to keep his troops moving at the proper pace and at the proper interval. He would insist on clean weapons. He would confiscate the remainder of Lavender's dope. Later in the day, perhaps, he would call the men together and speak to them plainly. He would accept the blame for what had happened to Ted Lavender. He would be a man about it. He would look them in the eyes, keeping his chin level, and he would issue the new SOPs in a calm, impersonal tone of voice, a lieutenant's voice, leaving no room for argument or discussion. Commencing immediately, he'd tell them, they would no longer abandon equipment along the route of march. They would police up their acts. They would get their shit together, and keep it together, and maintain it neatly and in good working order.

He would not tolerate laxity. He would show strength, distancing himself.

Among the men there would be grumbling, of course, and maybe worse, because their days would seem longer and their loads heavier, but Lieutenant Jimmy Cross reminded himself that his obligation was not to be loved but to lead. He would dispense with love; it was not now a factor. And if anyone quarreled or complained, he would simply tighten his lips and arrange his shoulders in the correct command posture. He might give a curt little nod. Or he might not. He might just shrug and say, Carry on, then they would saddle up and form into a column and move out toward the villages west of Than Khe.

# ZZ Packer

## (B. 1973)

Zuwena (ZZ) Packer grew up in areas as diverse as Appalachia, Atlanta, and Baltimore. She graduated from Yale University and from the Iowa Writer's Workshop, and she received a master's degree from Johns Hopkins University. Her debut collection of short stories, *Drinking Coffee Elsewhere* (2003), was an instant sensation in the literary world, reaping praise from numerous reviewers and from fellow writers like John Updike, who chose Packer's book as the Today Book Club selection on the NBC network's *Today Show* in June 2003. The stories in *Drinking Coffee Elsewhere* examine the complexities of race, gender, and sexual identity within landscapes as disparate as a college campus, an inner-city classroom, a Brownie camp, and even Japan. Packer's greatest gift is her obvious love for her characters. Her stories are populated with finely drawn portraits of very real people, and it is the combination of classic storytelling craft and lively, often unexpected descriptions and language that brings her characters to life.

Packer is the recipient of a Whiting Writers' Award and a Rona Jaffe Foundation Writers' Award, and she has held Wallace Stegner and Truman Capote fellowships from Stanford University. Her stories have been published in the *New Yorker*, *Harper's*, and *Story*, and she was also included in *The Best American Short Stories of 2000*. She is currently at work on a novel about Buffalo Soldiers, the African American soldiers who helped to settle the West between 1866 and 1882.

## *Brownies*                                                    *1999*

By the end of our first day at Camp Crescendo, the girls in my Brownie troop had decided to kick the asses of each and every girl in Brownie Troop 909. Troop 909 was doomed from the first day of camp; they were white girls, their complexions like a blend of ice cream: strawberry, vanilla. They turtled out from their bus in pairs, their rolled-up sleeping bags chromatized with Disney characters—Sleeping Beauty, Snow White, Mickey Mouse—or the generic ones cheap parents bought—washed-out rainbows, unicorns, curly-eyelashed frogs. Some clutched Igloo coolers and still others held on to stuffed toys like pacifiers, looking all around them like tourists determined to be dazzled.

Our troop wended its way past their bus, past the ranger station, past the colorful trail guide drawn like a treasure map, locked behind glass.

"Man, did you smell them?" Arnetta said, giving the girls a slow once-over. "They smell like Chihuahuas. *Wet* Chihuahuas." Although we had passed their troop by yards, Arnetta raised her nose in the air and grimaced.

Arnetta said this from the very rear of the line, far away from Mrs. Margolin, who strung our troop behind her like a brood of obedient ducklings. Mrs. Margolin even looked like a mother duck—she had hair cropped close to a small ball of a head, almost no neck, and huge, miraculous breasts. She wore enormous belts that looked like the kind weight lifters wear, except hers were cheap metallic gold or rabbit fur or covered with gigantic fake sunflowers. Often these belts would become nature lessons in and of themselves. "See," Mrs. Margolin once said to us, pointing to her belt. "This one's made entirely from the feathers of baby pigeons."

The belt layered with feathers was uncanny enough, but I was more disturbed by the realization that I had never actually *seen* a baby pigeon. I searched for weeks for one, in vain—scampering after pigeons whenever I was downtown with my father.

But nature lessons were not Mrs. Margolin's top priority. She saw the position of troop leader as an evangelical post. Back at the A.M.E. church where our Brownie meetings were held, she was especially fond of imparting religious aphorisms by means of acrostics—Satan was the "Serpent Always Tempting And Noisome"; she'd refer to the Bible as "Basic Instructions Before Leaving the Earth." Whenever she occasionally quizzed us on these at the beginning of the Brownie meeting, expecting to hear the acrostics parroted back to her, only Arnetta's correct replies soared over our vague mumblings. "Jesus?" Mrs. Margolin might ask expectantly, and Arnetta alone would dutifully answer, "Jehovah's Example, Saving Us Sinners."

Arnetta made a point of listening to Mrs. Margolin's religious talk and giving her what she wanted to hear. Because of this, Arnetta could have blared through a megaphone that the white girls of Troop 909 were "wet Chihuahuas" without arousing so much as a blink from Mrs. Margolin. Once Arnetta killed the troop goldfish by feeding it a French fry covered in ketchup, and when Mrs. Margolin demanded an explanation, Arnetta claimed that the goldfish had been eyeing her meal for *hours,* until—giving in to temptation—it had leapt up and snatched the whole golden fry from her fingertips.

"*Serious* Chihuahua," Octavia added—though neither Arnetta nor Octavia could *spell* "Chihuahua" or had ever *seen* a Chihuahua. Trisyllabic words had gained a sort of exoticism within our fourth-grade set at Woodrow Wilson Elementary. Arnetta and Octavia, compelled to outdo each other, would flip through the dictionary, determined to work the vulgar-sounding ones like "Djibouti" and "asinine" into conversation.

"*Caucasian* Chihuahuas," Arnetta said.

That did it. Drema and Elise doubled up on each other like inextricably entwined kites; Octavia slapped the skin of her belly; Janice jumped straight up in the air, then did it again, just as hard, as if to slam-dunk her own head. No one had laughed so hard since a boy named Martez had stuck his pencil in the electric socket and spent the whole day with a strange grin on his face.

"Girls, girls," said our parent helper, Mrs. Hedy. Mrs. Hedy was Octavia's mother. She wagged her index finger perfunctorily, like a windshield wiper. "Stop it now. Be good." She said this loudly enough to be heard, but lazily, nasally, bereft of any feeling or indication that she meant to be obeyed, as though she would say these words again at the exact same pitch if a button somewhere on her were pressed.

But the girls didn't stop laughing; they only laughed louder. It was the word "Caucasian" that had got them all going. One day at school, about a month before the Brownie camping trip, Arnetta had turned to a boy wearing impossibly high-ankled floodwater jeans, and said "What are *you? Caucasian?*" The word took off from there, and soon everything was Caucasian. If you ate too fast, you ate like a Caucasian; if you ate too slow, you ate like a Caucasian. The biggest feat anyone at Woodrow Wilson could do was to jump off the swing in midair, at the highest point in its arc, and if you fell (like I had, more than once) instead of landing on your feet, knees bent Olympic-gymnast-style, Arnetta and Octavia were prepared to comment. They'd look at each other with the silence of passengers who'd narrowly escaped an accident, then nod their heads, and whisper with solemn horror and haughtiness, "*Caucasian.*"

Even the only white kid in our school, Dennis, got in on the Caucasian act. That time when Martez stuck his pencil in the socket, Dennis had pointed, and yelled, "That was *so* Caucasian!"

Living in the south suburbs of Atlanta, it was easy to forget about whites. Whites were like those baby pigeons: real and existing, but rarely thought about. Everyone had been to Rich's to go clothes shopping, everyone had seen white girls and their mothers coo-cooing over dresses; everyone had gone to the downtown library and seen white businessmen swish by importantly, wrists flexed in front of them to check the time on their watches as though they would change from Clark Kent into Superman any second. But those images were as fleeting as cards shuffled in a deck, whereas the ten white girls behind us—*invaders,* Arnetta would later call them—were instantly real and memorable, with their long shampoo-commercial hair, as straight as spaghetti from the box. This alone was reason for envy and hatred. The only black girl most of us had ever seen with hair that long was Octavia, whose hair hung past her butt like a Hawaiian hula dancer's. The sight of Octavia's mane prompted other girls to listen to her reverentially, as though whatever she had to say would somehow activate their own follicles. For example, when, on the first day of camp, Octavia made as if to speak, a silence began. "Nobody," Octavia said, "calls us niggers."

At the end of that first day, when half of our troop made its way back to the cabin after tag-team restroom visits, Arnetta said she'd heard one of the girls in Troop 909 call Daphne a nigger. The other half of the girls and I were helping Mrs. Margolin clean up the pots and pans from the ravioli dinner. When we made our way to the restrooms to wash up and brush our teeth, we met up with Arnetta midway.

"Man, I completely heard the girl," Arnetta reported. "Right, Daphne?"

Daphne hardly ever spoke, but when she did her voice was petite and tinkly, the voice one might expect from a shiny new earring. She'd written a poem once, for Langston Hughes Day, a poem brimming with all the teacher-winning ingredients— trees and oceans, sunsets and moons—but what cinched the poem for the grown-ups, snatching the win from Octavia's musical ode to Grandmaster Flash and the Furious Five, were Daphne's last lines:

> You are my father, the veteran
> When you cry in the dark
> It rains and rains and rains in my heart

She's worn clean, though faded, jumpers and dresses when Chic jeans were the fashion, but when she went up to the dais to receive her prize journal, pages trimmed in gold, she wore a new dress with a velveteen bodice and a taffeta skirt as wide as an umbrella. All the kids clapped, though none of them understood the poem. I'd read encyclopedias the way others read comics, and I didn't get it. But those last lines pricked me, they were so eerie, and as my father and I ate cereal, I'd whisper over my Froot Loops, like a mantra, "*You are my father, the veteran. You are my father, the veteran, the veteran, the veteran,*" until my father, who acted in plays as Caliban and Othello and was not a veteran, marched me up to my teacher one morning, and said, "Can you tell me what the hell's wrong with this kid?"

I had thought Daphne and I might become friends, but she seemed to grow spooked by me whispering those lines to her, begging her to tell me what they meant, and I had soon understood that two quiet people like us were better off quiet alone.

"Daphne? Didn't you hear them call you a nigger?" Arnetta asked, giving Daphne a nudge.

The sun was setting through the trees, and their leafy tops formed a canopy of black lace for the flame of the sun to pass through. Daphne shrugged her shoulders at first, then slowly nodded her head when Arnetta gave her a hard look.

Twenty minutes later, when my restroom group returned to the cabin, Arnetta was still talking about Troop 909. My restroom group had passed by some of the 909 girls. For the most part, they had deferred to us, waving us into the restrooms, letting us go even though they'd gotten there first.

We'd seen them, but from afar, never within their orbit enough to see whether their faces were the way all white girls appeared on TV—ponytailed and full of energy, bubbling over with love and money. All I could see was that some rapidly fanned their faces with their hands, though the heat of the day had long passed. A few seemed to be lolling their heads in slow circles, half-purposefully, as if exercising the muscles of their necks, half-ecstatically, rolling their heads about like Stevie Wonder.

"We can't let them get away with that," Arnetta said, dropping her voice to a laryngitic whisper. "We can't let them get away with calling us niggers. I say we teach them a lesson." She sat down cross-legged on a sleeping bag, an embittered Buddha, eyes glimmering acrylic black. "We can't go telling Mrs. Margolin, either. Mrs. Margolin'll say something about doing unto others and the path of righteousness and all. Forget that shit." She let her eyes flutter irreverently till they half closed, as though ignoring an insult not worth returning. We could all hear Mrs. Margolin outside, gathering the last of the metal campware.

Nobody said anything for a while. Arnetta's tone had an upholstered confidence that was somehow both regal and vulgar at once. It demanded a few moments of silence in its wake, like the ringing of a church bell or the playing of taps. Sometimes Octavia would ditto or dissent whatever Arnetta had said, and this was the signal that others could speak. But this time Octavia just swirled a long cord of hair into pretzel shapes.

"*Well?*" Arnetta said. She looked as if she had discerned the hidden severity of the situation and was waiting for the rest of us to catch up. Everyone looked from Arnetta to Daphne. It was, after all, Daphne who had supposedly been called the name, but Daphne sat on the bare cabin floor, flipping through the pages of the Girl Scout handbook, eyebrows arched in mock wonder, as if the handbook were a catalogue full of bright and startling foreign costumes. Janice broke the silence. She clapped her hands to broach her idea of a plan.

"They gone be sleeping," she whispered conspiratorially, "then we gone sneak into they cabin, then we gone put daddy longlegs in they sleeping bags. Then they'll wake up. Then we gone beat 'em up till they flat as frying pans!" She jammed her fist into the palm of her hand, then made a sizzling sound.

Janice's country accent was laughable, her looks homely, her jumpy acrobatics embarrassing to behold. Arnetta and Octavia volleyed amused, arrogant smiles whenever Janice opened her mouth, but Janice never caught the hint, spoke whenever she wanted, fluttered around Arnetta and Octavia futilely offering her opinions to their departing backs. Whenever Arnetta and Octavia shooed her away, Janice loitered until the two would finally sigh, "What *is* it, Miss Caucasoid? What do you want?"

"Oh shut up, Janice," Octavia said, letting a fingered loop of hair fall to her waist as though just the sound of Janice's voice had ruined the fun of her hair twisting.

"All right," Arnetta said, standing up. "We're going to have a secret meeting and talk about what we're going to do."

The word "secret" had a built-in importance. Everyone gravely nodded her head. The modifier form of the word had more clout than the noun. A secret meant nothing; it was like gossip: just a bit of unpleasant knowledge about someone who happened to be someone other than yourself. A secret *meeting*, or a secret *club*, was entirely different.

That was when Arnetta turned to me, as though she knew doing so was both a compliment and a charity.

"Snot, you're not going to be a bitch and tell Mrs. Margolin, are you?"

I had been called "Snot" ever since first grade, when I'd sneezed in class and two long ropes of mucus had splattered a nearby girl.

"Hey," I said. "Maybe you didn't hear them right—I mean—"

"Are you gonna tell on us or not?" was all Arnetta wanted to know, and by the time the question was asked, the rest of our Brownie troop looked at me as though they'd already decided their course of action, me being the only impediment. As though it were all a simple matter of patriotism.

Camp Crescendo used to double as a high school band and field hockey camp until an arching field hockey ball landed on the clasp of a girl's metal barrette, knifing a skull nerve, paralyzing the right side of her body. The camp closed down for a few years, and the girl's teammates built a memorial, filling the spot on which the girl fell with hockey balls, upon which they had painted—all in nail polish—get-well tidings, flowers, and hearts. The balls were still stacked there, like a shrine of ostrich eggs embedded in the ground.

On the second day of camp, Troop 909 was dancing around the mound of nail polish–decorated hockey balls, their limbs jangling awkwardly, their cries like the constant summer squeal of an amusement park. There was a stream that bordered the field hockey lawn, and the girls from my troop settled next to it, scarfing down the last of lunch: sandwiches made from salami and slices of tomato that had gotten waterlogged from the melting ice in the cooler. From the stream bank, Arnetta eyed the Troop 909 girls, scrutinizing their movements to glean inspiration for battle.

"Man," Arnetta said, "we could bum-rush them right now if that damn lady would *leave*."

The 909 troop leader was a white woman with the severe pageboy hairdo of an ancient Egyptian. She lay sprawled on a picnic blanket, Sphinxlike, eating a banana, sometimes holding it out in front of her like a microphone. Beside her sat a girl slowly flapping one hand like a bird with a broken wing. Occasionally, the leader would call out the names of girls who'd attempted leapfrogs and flips, or of girls who yelled too loudly or strayed far from the circle.

"I'm just glad Big Fat Mama's not following us here," Octavia said. "At least we don't have to worry about her." Mrs. Margolin, Octavia assured us, was having her Afternoon Devotional, shrouded in mosquito netting, in a clearing she'd found. Mrs. Hedy was cleaning mud from her espadrilles in the cabin.

"I handled them." Arnetta sucked on her teeth and proudly grinned. "I told her we was going to gather leaves."

"Gather leaves," Octavia said, nodding respectfully. "That's a good one. They're so mad-crazy about this camping thing." She looked from ground to sky, sky to ground. Her hair hung down her back in two braids like a squaw's. "I mean, I really don't know why it's even called *camping*—all we ever do with Nature is find some twigs and say something like, 'Wow, this fell from a tree.'" She then studied her sandwich. With two disdainful fingers, she picked out a slice of dripping tomato, the sections congealed with red slime. She pitched it into the stream embrowned with dead leaves and the murky effigies of other dead things, but in the opaque water a group of small silver-brown fish appeared. They surrounded the tomato and nibbled.

"Look!" Janice cried. "Fishes! Fishes!" As she scrambled to the edge of the stream to watch, a covey of insects threw up tantrums from the wheatgrass and nettle, a throng of tiny electric machines, all going at once. Octavia snuck up behind Janice as if to push her in. Daphne and I exchanged terrified looks. It seemed as though only we knew that Octavia was close enough—and bold enough—to actually push Janice into the stream. Janice turned around quickly, but Octavia was already staring serenely into the still water as though she were gathering some sort of courage from it. "What's so funny?" Janice said, eyeing them all suspiciously.

Elise began humming the tune to "Karma Chameleon," all the girls joining in, their hums light and facile. Janice began to hum, against everyone else, the high-octane opening chords of "Beat It."

"I love me some Michael Jackson," Janice said when she'd finished humming, smacking her lips as though Michael Jackson were a favorite meal. "I will marry Michael Jackson."

Before anyone had a chance to impress upon Janice the impossibility of this, Arnetta suddenly rose, made a sun visor of her hand, and watched Troop 909 leave the hockey lawn.

"Dammit!" she said. "We've got to get them *alone*."

"They won't ever be alone," I said. All the rest of the girls looked at me. If I spoke even a word, I could count on someone calling me Snot, but everyone seemed to think that we could beat up these girls; no one entertained the thought that they might fight *back*. "The only time they'll be unsupervised is in the bathroom."

"Oh shut up, Snot," Octavia said.

But Arnetta slowly nodded her head. "The bathroom," she said. "The bathroom," she said, again and again. "The bathroom! The bathroom!" She cheered so blissfully that I thought for a moment she was joking.

According to Octavia's watch, it took us five minutes to hike to the restrooms, which were midway between our cabin and Troop 909's. Inside, the mirrors above the sinks returned only the vaguest of reflections, as though someone had taken a scouring pad to their surfaces to obscure the shine. Pine needles, leaves, and dirty flattened wads of chewing gum covered the floor like a mosaic. Webs of hair matted the drain in the middle of the floor. Above the sinks and below the mirrors, stacks of folded white paper towels lay on a long metal counter. Shaggy white balls of paper towels sat on the sink tops in a line like corsages on display. A thread of floss snaked from a wad of tissues dotted with the faint red-pink of blood. One of those white girls, I thought, had just lost a tooth.

The restroom looked almost the same as it had the night before, but it somehow seemed stranger now. We had never noticed the wooden rafters before, coming together in great V's. We were, it seemed, inside a whale, viewing the ribs of the roof of its mouth.

"Wow. It's a mess," Elise said.

"You can say that again."

Arnetta leaned against the doorjamb of a restroom stall. "This is where they'll be again," she said. Just seeing the place, just having a plan, seemed to satisfy her. "We'll go in and talk to them. You know, 'How you doing? How long will you be here?' that sort of thing. Then Octavia and I are gonna tell them what happens when they call any one of us a nigger."

"I'm going to say something, too," Janice said.

Arnetta considered this. "Sure," she said. "Of course. Whatever you want."

Janice pointed her finger like a gun at Octavia and rehearsed the line she'd thought up, "We're gonna teach you a *lesson.*' That's what I'm going to say." She narrowed her eyes like a TV mobster. "'We're gonna teach you little girls a lesson!'"

With the back of her hand, Octavia brushed Janice's finger away. "You couldn't teach me to shit in a toilet."

"But," I said, "what if they say, 'We didn't say that. We didn't call anyone a N-I-G-G-E-R'?"

"Snot," Arnetta sighed. "Don't think. Just fight. If you even know how."

Everyone laughed while Daphne stood there. Arnetta gently laid her hand on Daphne's shoulder. "Daphne. You don't have to fight. We're doing this for you."

Daphne walked to the counter, took a clean paper towel, and carefully unfolded it like a map. With this, she began to pick up the trash all around. Everyone watched.

"C'mon," Arnetta said to everyone. "Let's beat it." We all ambled toward the restroom doorway, where the sunshine made one large white rectangle of light. We were immediately blinded and shielded our eyes with our hands, our forearms.

"Daphne?" Arnetta asked. "Are you coming?"

We all looked back at the girl, who was bending, the thin of her back hunched like a maid caught in stage limelight. Stray strands of her hair were lit nearly transparent, thin fiber-optic threads. She did not nod yes to the question, nor did she shake her head no. She abided, bent. Then she began again, picking up leaves, wads of paper, the cotton fluff innards from a torn stuffed toy. She did it so methodically, so exquisitely, so humbly, she must have been trained. I thought of those dresses she wore, faded and old, yet so pressed and clean; I then saw the poverty in them, I then could imagine her mother, cleaning the houses of others, returning home, weary.

"I guess she's not coming."

We left her, heading back to our cabin, over the pine needles and leaves, taking the path full of shade.

"What about our secret meeting?" Elise asked.

Arnetta enunciated in a way that defied contradiction: "We just had it."

Just as we caught sight of our cabin, Arnetta violently swerved away from Octavia. "You farted," she said.

Octavia began to sashay, as if on a catwalk, then proclaimed, in a Hollywood-starlet voice, "My farts smell like perfume."

It was nearing our bedtime, but in the lengthening days of spring, the sun had not yet set.

"Hey, your mama's coming," Arnetta said to Octavia when she saw Mrs. Hedy walk toward the cabin, sniffling. When Octavia's mother wasn't giving bored, parochial orders, she sniffled continuously, mourning an imminent divorce from her husband. She might begin a sentence, "I don't know what Robert will do when Octavia and I are gone. Who'll buy him cigarettes?" and Octavia would hotly whisper *Mama* in a way that meant: Please don't talk about our problems in front of everyone. Please shut up.

But when Mrs. Hedy began talking about her husband, thinking about her husband, seeing clouds shaped like the head of her husband, she couldn't be quiet, and no one could ever dislodge her from the comfort of her own woe. Only one thing could perk her up—Brownie songs. If the rest of the girls were quiet, and Mrs. Hedy was in her dopey sorrowful mood, she would say, "Y'all know I like those songs, girls. Why don't you sing one?" Everyone would groan except me and Daphne. I, for one, liked some of the songs.

"C'mon, everybody," Octavia said drearily. "She likes 'The Brownie Song' best."

We sang, loud enough to reach Mrs. Hedy:

> I've something in my pocket;
> It belongs across my face.
> And I keep it very close at hand in a most convenient place.
> I'm sure you couldn't guess it
> If you guessed a long, long while.
> So I'll take it out and put it on—
> It's a great big Brownie Smile!

"The Brownie Song" was supposed to be sung as though we were elves in a workshop, singing as we merrily cobbled shoes, but everyone except me hated the song and sang it like a maudlin record, played at the most sluggish of rpms.

"That was good," Mrs. Hedy said, closing the cabin door behind her. "Wasn't that nice, Linda?"

"Praise God," Mrs. Margolin answered without raising her head from the chore of counting out Popsicle sticks for the next day's session of crafts.

"Sing another one," Mrs. Hedy said, with a sort of joyful aggression, like a drunk I'd once seen who'd refused to leave a Korean grocery.

"God, Mama, get over it," Octavia whispered in a voice meant only for Arnetta, but Mrs. Hedy heard it and started to leave the cabin.

"Don't go," Arnetta said. She ran after Mrs. Hedy and held her by the arm. "We haven't finished singing." She nudged us with a single look. "Let's sing 'The Friends Song.' For Mrs. Hedy."

Although I liked some of the songs, I hated this one:

> Make new friends
> But keep the o-old,
> One is silver
> And the other gold.

If most of the girls in my troop could be any type of metal, they'd be bunched-up wads of tinfoil maybe, or rusty iron nails you had to get tetanus shots for.

"No, no, no," Mrs. Margolin said before anyone could start in on "The Friends Song." "An uplifting song. Something to lift her up and take her mind off all these earthly burdens."

Arnetta and Octavia rolled their eyes. Everyone knew what song Mrs. Margolin was talking about, and no one, no one, wanted to sing it.

"Please, no," a voice called out. "Not 'The Doughnut Song.'"

"Please not 'The Doughnut Song,'" Octavia pleaded.

"I'll brush my teeth twice if I don't have to sing 'The Doughnut—'"

"Sing!" Mrs. Margolin demanded.

We sang:

> Life without Jesus is like a do-ough-nut!
> Like a do-ooough-nut!
> Like a do-ooough-nut!
> Life without Jesus is like a do-ough-nut!
> There's a hole in the middle of my soul!

There were other verses, involving other pastries, but we stopped after the first one and cast glances toward Mrs. Margolin to see if we could gain a reprieve. Mrs. Margolin's eyes fluttered blissfully, half-asleep.

"Awww," Mrs. Hedy said, as though giant Mrs. Margolin were a cute baby. "Mrs. Margolin's had a long day."

"Yes indeed," Mrs. Margolin answered. "If you don't mind, I might just go to the lodge where the beds are. I haven't been the same since the operation."

I had not heard of this operation, or when it had occurred, since Mrs. Margolin had never missed the once-a-week Brownie meetings, and I could see from Daphne's face that she was concerned, and I could see that the other girls had decided that Mrs. Margolin's operation must have happened long ago in some remote time unconnected to our own. Nevertheless, they put on sad faces. We had all been taught that adulthood was full of sorrow and pain, taxes and bills, dreaded work and dealings with whites, sickness, and death.

"Go right ahead, Linda," Mrs. Hedy said. "I'll watch the girls." Mrs. Hedy seemed to forget about her divorce for a moment; she looked at us with dewy eyes, as if we were mysterious, furry creatures. Meanwhile, Mrs. Margolin walked through the maze of sleeping bags until she found her own. She gathered a neat stack of clothes and pajamas slowly, as though doing so were almost painful. She took her toothbrush, her toothpaste, her pillow. "All right!" Mrs. Margolin said, addressing us all from the threshold of the cabin. "Be in bed by nine." She said it with a twinkle in her voice, as though she were letting us know she was allowing us to be naughty and stay up till nine-fifteen.

"C'mon, everybody," Arnetta said after Mrs. Margolin left. "Time for us to wash up."

Everyone watched Mrs. Hedy closely, wondering whether she would insist on coming with us since it was night, making a fight with Troop 909 nearly impossible. Troop 909 would soon be in the bathroom, washing their faces, brushing their teeth—completely unsuspecting of our ambush.

"We won't be long," Arnetta said. "We're old enough to go to the restroom by ourselves."

Mrs. Hedy pursed her lips at this dilemma. "Well, I guess you Brownies are almost Girl Scouts, right?"

"Right!"

"Just one more badge," Drema said.

"And about," Octavia droned, "a million more cookies to sell." Octavia looked at all of us. *Now's our chance,* her face seemed to say, but our chance to do *what* I didn't exactly know.

Finally, Mrs. Hedy walked to the doorway where Octavia stood, dutifully waiting to say good-bye and looking bored doing it. Mrs. Hedy held Octavia's chin. "You'll be good?"

"Yes, Mama."

"And remember to pray for me and your father? If I'm asleep when you get back?"

"Yes, Mama."

When the other girls had finished getting their toothbrushes and washcloths and flashlights for the group restroom trip, I was drawing pictures of tiny birds with too many feathers. Daphne was sitting on her sleeping bag, reading.

"You're not going to come?" Octavia asked.

Daphne shook her head.

"I'm also gonna stay, too," I said. "I'll go to the restroom when Daphne and Mrs. Hedy go."

Arnetta leaned down toward me and whispered so that Mrs. Hedy, who had taken over Mrs. Margolin's task of counting Popsicle sticks, couldn't hear. "No, Snot. If we get in trouble, you're going to get in trouble with the rest of us."

We made our way through the darkness by flashlight. The tree branches that had shaded us just hours earlier, along the same path, now looked like arms sprouting menacing hands. The stars sprinkled the sky like spilled salt. They seemed fastened to the darkness, high up and holy, their places fixed and definite as we stirred beneath them.

Some, like me, were quiet because we were afraid of the dark; others were talking like crazy for some reason.

"Wow," Drema said, looking up. "Why are all the stars out here? I never see stars back on Oneida Street."

"It's a camping trip, that's why," Octavia said. "You're supposed to see stars on camping trips."

Janice said, "This place smells like the air freshener my mother uses."

"These woods are *pine*," Elise said. "Your mother probably uses pine air freshener."

Janice mouthed an exaggerated "Oh," nodding her head as though she just then understood one of the world's great secrets.

No one talked about fighting. Everyone was afraid enough just walking through the infinite deep of the woods. Even without seeing anyone's face, I could tell this wasn't about Daphne being called a nigger. The word that had started it all seemed melted now into some deeper, unnameable feeling. Even though I didn't want to fight, was afraid of fighting, I felt as though I were part of the rest of the troop, as though I were defending something. We trudged against the slight incline of the path, Arnetta leading the way. I wondered, looking at her back, what she could be thinking.

"You know," I said, "their leader will be there. Or they won't even be there. It's dark already. Last night the sun was still in the sky. I'm sure they're already finished."

"Whose flashlight is this?" Arnetta said, shaking the weakening beam of the light she was holding. "It's out of batteries."

Octavia handed Arnetta her flashlight. And that's when I saw it. The bathroom was just ahead.

But the girls were there. We could hear them before we could see them.

"Octavia and I will go in first so they'll think there's just two of us. Then wait till I say, 'We're gonna teach you a lesson,'" Arnetta said. "Then bust in. That'll surprise them."

"That's what I was supposed to say," Janice said.

Arnetta went inside, Octavia next to her. Janice followed, and the rest of us waited outside.

They were in there for what seemed like whole minutes, but something was wrong. Arnetta hadn't given the signal yet. I was with the girls outside when I heard one of the Troop 909 girls say, "NO. That did NOT happen!"

That was to be expected, that they'd deny the whole thing. What I hadn't expected was *the voice* in which the denial was said. The girl sounded as though her tongue were caught in her mouth. "That's a BAD word!" the girl continued. "We don't say BAD words!"

"Let's go in," Elise said.

"No," Drema said. "I don't want to. What if we get beat up?"

"Snot?" Elise turned to me, her flashlight blinding. It was the first time anyone had asked my opinion, though I knew they were just asking because they were afraid.

"I say we go inside, just to see what's going on."

"But Arnetta didn't give us the signal," Drema said. "She's supposed to say, 'We're going to teach you a lesson,' and I didn't hear her say it."

"C'mon," I said. "Let's just go in."

We went inside. There we found the white girls, but about five girls were huddled up next to one big girl. I instantly knew she was the owner of the voice we'd heard. Arnetta and Octavia inched toward us as soon as we entered.

"Where's Janice?" Elise asked, then we heard a flush. "Oh."

"I think," Octavia said, whispering to Elise, "they're retarded."

"We ARE NOT retarded!" the big girl said, though it was obvious that she was. That they all were. The girls around her began to whimper.

"They're just pretending," Arnetta said, trying to convince herself. "I know they are."

Octavia turned to Arnetta. "Arnetta. Let's just leave."

Janice came out of a stall, happy and relieved, then she suddenly remembered her line, pointed to the big girl, and said, "We're gonna teach you a lesson."

"Shut up, Janice," Octavia said, but her heart was not in it. Arnetta's face was set in a lost, deep scowl. Octavia turned to the big girl, and said loudly, slowly, as if they were all deaf, "We're going to leave. It was nice meeting you, okay? You don't have to tell anyone that we were here. Okay?"

"Why not?" said the big girl, like a taunt. When she spoke, her lips did not meet, her mouth did not close. Her tongue grazed the roof of her mouth, like a little pink fish. "You'll get in trouble. I know. I know."

Arnetta got back her old cunning. "If you said anything, then you'd be a tattletale."

The girl looked sad for a moment, then perked up quickly. A flash of genius crossed her face: "I *like* tattletale."

"It's all right, girls. It's gonna be all right!" the 909 troop leader said. It was as though someone had instructed all of Troop 909 to cry at once. The troop leader had girls under her arm, and all the rest of the girls crowded about her. It reminded me of a hog I'd seen on a field trip, where all the little hogs would gather about the mother at feeding time, latching on to her teats. The 909 troop leader had come into the bathroom shortly after the big girl threatened to tell. Then the ranger came, then, once the ranger had radioed the station, Mrs. Margolin arrived with Daphne in tow.

The ranger had left the restroom area, but everyone else was huddled just outside, swatting mosquitoes.

"Oh. They *will* apologize," Mrs. Margolin said to the 909 troop leader, but Mrs. Margolin said this so angrily, I knew she was speaking more to us than to the other troop leader. "When their parents find out, every one a them will be on punishment."

"It's all right. It's all right," the 909 troop leader reassured Mrs. Margolin. Her voice lilted in the same way it had when addressing the girls. She smiled the whole time she talked. She was like one of those TV cooking show women who talk and dice onions and smile all at the same time.

"See. It could have happened. I'm not calling your girls fibbers or anything." She shook her head ferociously from side to side, her Egyptian-style pageboy flapping against her cheeks like heavy drapes. "It *could* have happened, see. Our girls are *not* retarded. They are *delayed* learners." She said this in a syrupy instructional voice, as though our troop might be delayed learners as well. "We're from the Decatur Children's Academy. Many of them just have special needs."

"Now we won't be able to walk to the bathroom by ourselves!" the big girl said.

"Yes you will," the troop leader said, "but maybe we'll wait till we get back to Decatur—"

"I don't want to wait!" the girl said. "I want my Independence patch!"

The girls in my troop were entirely speechless. Arnetta looked as though she were soon to be tortured but was determined not to appear weak. Mrs. Margolin pursed her lips solemnly and said, "Bless them, Lord. Bless them."

In contrast, the Troop 909 leader was full of words and energy. "Some of our girls are echolalic—" She smiled and happily presented one of the girls hanging on to her, but the girl widened her eyes in horror and violently withdrew herself from the center of attention, as though she sensed she were being sacrificed for the village sins. "Echolalic," the troop leader continued. "That means they will say whatever they hear, like an echo—that's where the word comes from. It comes from 'echo.'" She ducked her head apologetically. "I mean, not all of them have the most *progressive* of parents, so if they heard a bad word they might have repeated it. But I guarantee it would not have been *intentional.*"

Arnetta spoke. "I saw her say the word. I heard her." She pointed to a small girl, smaller than any of us, wearing an oversized T-shirt that read: EAT BERTHA'S MUSSELS.

The troop leader shook her head and smiled. "That's impossible. She doesn't speak. She can, but she doesn't."

Arnetta furrowed her brow. "No. It wasn't her. That's right. It was *her.*"

The girl Arnetta pointed to grinned as though she'd been paid a compliment. She was the only one from either troop actually wearing a full uniform: the mocha-colored A-line shift, the orange ascot, the sash covered with patches, though all the same one—the Try-It patch. She took a few steps toward Arnetta and made a grand sweeping gesture toward the sash. "See," she said, full of self-importance, "I'm a Brownie." I had a hard time imagining this girl calling anyone "nigger"; the girl looked perpetually delighted, as though she would have cuddled up with a grizzly if someone had let her.

On the fourth morning, we boarded the bus to go home.

The previous day had been spent building miniature churches from Popsicle sticks. We hardly left the cabin. Mrs. Margolin and Mrs. Hedy guarded us so closely, almost no one talked for the entire day.

Even on the day of departure from Camp Crescendo, all was serious and silent. The bus ride began quietly enough. Arnetta had to sit beside Mrs. Margolin, Octavia had to sit beside her mother. I sat beside Daphne, who gave me her prize journal without a word of explanation.

"You don't want it?"

She shook her head no. It was empty.

Then Mrs. Hedy began to weep. "Octavia," Mrs. Hedy said to her daughter without looking at us. "I'm going to sit with Mrs. Margolin. All right?"

Arnetta exchanged seats with Mrs. Hedy. With the two women up front, Elise felt it safe to speak. "Hey," she said, then she set her face into a placid vacant stare, trying to imitate that of a Troop 909 girl. Emboldened, Arnetta made a gesture of mock pride toward an imaginary sash, the way the girl in full uniform had done. Then they all made a game of it, trying to do the most exaggerated imitations of the Troop 909 girls, all without speaking, all without laughing loud enough to catch the women's attention.

Daphne looked at her shoes, white with sneaker polish. I opened the journal she'd given me. I looked out the window, trying to decide what to write, searching for lines, but nothing could compare with the lines Daphne had written, *"My father, the veteran,"* my favorite line of all time. The line replayed itself in my head, and I gave up trying to write.

By then, it seemed as though the rest of the troop had given up making fun of the 909 girls. They were now quietly gossiping about who had passed notes to whom in school. For a moment the gossiping fell off, and all I heard was the hum of the bus as we sped down the road and the muffled sounds of Mrs. Hedy and Mrs. Margolin talking about serious things.

"You know," Octavia whispered, "why did *we* have to be stuck at a camp with re-tarded girls? You know?"

"*You* know why," Arnetta answered. She narrowed her eyes like a cat. "My mama and I were in the mall in Buckhead, and this white lady just kept looking at us. I mean, like we were foreign or something. Like we were from China."

"What did the woman say?" Elise asked.

"Nothing," Arnetta said. "She didn't say nothing."

A few girls quietly nodded their heads.

"There was this time," I said, "when my father and I were in the mall and—"

"Oh, shut up, Snot," Octavia said.

I stared at Octavia, then rolled my eyes from her to the window. As I watched the trees blur, I wanted nothing more than to be through with it all: the bus ride, the troop, school—all of it. But we were going home. I'd see the same girls in school the next day. We were on a bus, and there was nowhere else to go.

"Go on, Laurel," Daphne said to me. It was the first time she'd spoken the whole trip, and she'd said my name. I turned to her and smiled weakly so as not to cry, hop-ing she'd remember when I'd tried to be her friend, thinking maybe that her gift of the journal was an invitation of friendship. But she didn't smile back. All she said was, "What happened?"

I studied the girls, waiting for Octavia to tell me to "shut up" again before I even had a chance to utter another word, but everyone was amazed that Daphne had spo-ken. I gathered my voice. "Well," I said. "My father and I were in this mall, but *I* was the one doing the staring." I stopped and glanced from face to face. I continued. "There were these white people dressed like Puritans or something, but they weren't Puritans. They were Mennonites. They're these people who, if you ask them to do a favor, like paint your porch or something, they have to do it. It's in their rules."

"That sucks," someone said.

"C'mon," Arnetta said. "You're lying."

"I am not."

"How do you know that's not just some story someone made up?" Elise asked, her head cocked, full of daring. "I mean, who's gonna do whatever you ask?"

"It's not made up. I know because when I was looking at them, my father said, 'See those people. If you ask them to do something, they'll do it. Anything you want.'"

No one would call anyone's father a liar. Then they'd have to fight the person, but Drema parsed her words carefully. "How does your *father* know that's not just some story? Huh?"

"Because," I said, "he went up to the man and asked him would he paint our porch, and the man said, 'Yes.' It's their religion."

"Man, I'm glad I'm a Baptist," Elise said, shaking her head in sympathy for the Mennonites.

"So did the guy do it?" Drema asked, scooting closer to hear if the story got juicy.

"Yeah," I said. "His whole family was with him. My dad drove them to our house. They all painted our porch. The woman and girl were in bonnets and long, long skirts with buttons up to their necks. The guy wore this weird hat and these huge suspenders."

"Why," Arnetta asked archly, as though she didn't believe a word, "would someone pick a *porch*? If they'll do anything, why not make them paint the whole *house*? Why not ask for a hundred bucks?"

I thought about it, and I remembered the words my father had said about them painting our porch, though I had never seemed to think about his words after he'd said them.

"He said," I began, only then understanding the words as they uncoiled from my mouth, "it was the only time he'd have a white man on his knees doing something for a black man for free."

I remembered the Mennonites bending like Daphne had bent, cleaning the restroom. I remembered the dark blue of their bonnets, the black of their shoes. They painted the porch as though scrubbing a floor. I was already trembling before Daphne asked quietly, "Did he thank them?"

I looked out the window. I could not tell which were the thoughts and which were the trees. "No," I said, and suddenly knew there was something mean in the world that I could not stop.

Arnetta laughed. "If I asked them to take off their long skirts and bonnets and put on some jeans, they would do it?"

And Daphne's voice—quiet, steady: "Maybe they would. Just to be nice."

## Drinking Coffee Elsewhere                                              *2000*

Orientation games began the day I arrived at Yale from Baltimore. In my group we played heady, frustrating games for smart people. One game appeared to be charades reinterpreted by existentialists; another involved listening to rocks. Then a freshman counsellor made everyone play Trust. The idea was that if you had the faith to fall backward and wait for four scrawny former high-school geniuses to catch you, just before your head cracked on the slate sidewalk, then you might learn to trust your fellow-students. Russian roulette sounded like a better game.

"No way," I said. The white boys were waiting for me to fall, holding their arms out for me, sincerely, gallantly. "No fucking way."

"It's all cool, it's all cool," the counsellor said. Her hair was a shade of blond I'd seen only on *Playboy* covers, and she raised her hands as though backing away from a growling dog. "Sister," she said, in an I'm-down-with-the-struggle voice, "you don't have to play this game. As a person of color, you shouldn't have to fit into any white, patriarchal system."

I said, "It's a bit too late for that."

In the next game, all I had to do was wait in a circle until it was my turn to say what inanimate object I wanted to be. One guy said he'd like to be a gadfly, like

Socrates. "Stop me if I wax Platonic," he said. The girl next to him was eating a rice cake. She wanted to be the Earth, she said. Earth with a capital "E."

There was one other black person in the circle. He wore an Exeter T-shirt and his overly elastic expressions resembled a series of facial exercises. At the end of each person's turn, he smiled and bobbed his head with unfettered enthusiasm. "Oh, that was good," he said, as if the game were an experiment he'd set up and the results were turning out better than he'd expected. "Good, good, good!"

When it was my turn I said, "My name is Dina, and if I had to be any object, I guess I'd be a revolver." The sunlight dulled as if on cue. Clouds passed rapidly overhead, presaging rain. I don't know why I said it. Until that moment I'd been good in all the ways that were meant to matter. I was an honor-roll student—though I'd learned long ago not to mention it in the part of Baltimore where I lived. Suddenly I was hard-bitten and recalcitrant, the kind of kid who took pleasure in sticking pins into cats; the kind who chased down smart kids to spray them with mace.

"A revolver," the counsellor said, stroking his chin, as if it had grown a rabbinical beard. "Could you please elaborate?"

The black guy cocked his head and frowned, as if the beakers and Erlenmeyer flasks of his experiment had grown legs and scurried off.

"You were just kidding," the dean said, "about wiping out all of mankind. That, I suppose, was a joke." She squinted at me. One of her hands curved atop the other to form a pink, freckled molehill on her desk.

"Well," I said, "maybe I meant it at the time." I quickly saw that that was not the answer she wanted. "I don't know. I think it's the architecture."

Through the dimming light of the dean's-office window, I could see the fortress of the old campus. On my ride from the bus station to the campus, I'd barely glimpsed New Haven—a flash of crumpled building here, a trio of straggly kids there. A lot like Baltimore. But everything had changed when we reached those streets hooded by the Gothic buildings. I imagined how the college must have looked when it was founded, when most of the students owned slaves. I pictured men wearing tights and knickers, smoking pipes.

"The architecture," the dean repeated. She bit her lip and seemed to be making a calculation of some sort. I noticed that she blinked less often than most people. I sat there, waiting to see how long it would be before she blinked again.

My revolver comment won me a year's worth of psychiatric counselling, weekly meetings with Dean Guest, and—since the parents of the roommate I'd never met weren't too hip on the idea of their Amy sharing a bunk bed with a budding homicidal loony—my very own room.

Shortly after getting my first D, I also received the first knock on my door. The female counsellors never knocked. The dean had spoken to them; I was a priority. Every other day, right before dinnertime, they'd look in on me, unannounced. "Just checking up," a counsellor would say. It was the voice of a suburban mother in training. By the second week, I had made a point of sitting in a chair in front of the door, just when I expected a counsellor to pop her head around. This was intended to startle them. I also made a point of being naked. The unannounced visits ended.

The knocking persisted. Through the peephole I saw a white face, distorted and balloonish.

"Let me in." The person looked like a boy but sounded like a girl. "Let me in," the voice repeated.

"Not a chance," I said.

Then the person began to sob, and I heard a back slump against the door. If I hadn't known the person was white from the peephole, I'd have known it from a display like this. Black people didn't knock on strangers' doors, crying. Not that I understood the black people at Yale. There was something pitiful in how cool they were. Occasionally one would reach out to me with missionary zeal, but I'd rebuff that person with haughty silence.

"I don't have anyone to talk to!" the person on the other side of the door cried.

"That is correct."

"When I was a child," the person said, "I played by myself in a corner of the schoolyard all alone. I hated dolls and I hated games, animals were not friendly and birds flew away. If anyone was looking for me I hid behind a tree and cried out 'I am an orphan—'"

I opened the door. It was a she.

"Plagiarist!" I yelled. She had just recited a Frank O'Hara poem as though she'd thought it up herself. I knew the poem because it was one of the few things I'd been forced to read that I wished I'd written myself.

The girl turned to face me, smiling weakly, as though her triumph were not in getting me to open the door but in the fact that she was able to smile at all when she was so accustomed to crying. She was large but not obese, and crying had turned her face the color of raw chicken. She blew her nose into the waist end of her T-shirt, revealing a pale belly.

"How do you know that poem?"

She sniffed. "I'm in your Contemporary Poetry class."

She was Canadian and her name was Heidi, although she said she wanted people to call her Henrik. "That's a guy's name," I said. "What do you want? A sex change?"

She looked at me with so little surprise that I suspected she hadn't discounted this as an option. Then her story came out in teary, hiccup-like bursts. She had sucked some "cute guy's dick" and he'd told everybody and now people thought she was "a slut."

"Why'd you suck his dick? Aren't you a lesbian?"

She fit the bill. Short hair, hard, roach-stomping shoes. Dressed like an aspiring plumber. The lesbians I'd seen on TV were wiry, thin strips of muscle, but Heidi was round and soft and had a moonlike face. Drab mud-colored hair. And lesbians had cats. "Do you have a cat?" I asked.

Her eyes turned glossy with new tears. "No," she said, her voice wavering, "and I'm not a lesbian. Are you?"

"Do I look like one?" I said.

She didn't answer.

"O.K." I said. "I could suck a guy's dick, too, if I wanted. But I don't. The human penis is one of the most germ-ridden objects there is." Heidi looked at me, unconvinced. "What I meant to say," I began again, "is that I don't like anybody. Period. Guys or girls. I'm a misanthrope."

"I am, too."

"No," I said, guiding her back through my door and out into the hallway. "You're not."

"Have you had dinner?" she asked. "Let's go to Commons."

I pointed to a pyramid of ramen-noodle packages on my windowsill. "See that? That means I never have to go to Commons. Aside from class, I have contact with no one."

"I hate it here, too," she said. "I should have gone to McGill, eh."

"The way to feel better," I said, "is to get some ramen and lock yourself in your room. Everyone will forget about you and that guy's dick and you won't have to see anyone ever again. If anyone looks for you—"

"I'll hide behind a tree."

"A revolver?" Dr. Raeburn said, flipping through a manila folder. He looked up at me as if to ask another question, but he didn't.

Dr. Raeburn was the psychiatrist. He had the gray hair and whiskers of a Civil War general. He was also a chain smoker with beige teeth and a navy wool jacket smeared with ash. He asked about the revolver at the beginning of my first visit. When I was unable to explain myself he smiled, as if this were perfectly respectable.

"Tell me about your parents."

I wondered what he already had on file. The folder was thick, though I hadn't said a thing of significance since Day One.

"My father was a dick and my mother seemed to like him."

He patted his pockets for his cigarettes. "That's some heavy stuff," he said. "How do you feel about Dad?" The man couldn't say the word "father." "Is Dad someone you see often?"

"I hate my father almost as much as I hate the word 'Dad.'"

He started tapping his cigarette.

"You can't smoke in here."

"That's right," he said, and slipped the cigarette back into the packet. He smiled, widening his eyes brightly. "Don't ever start."

I thought that that first encounter would be the last of Heidi, but then her head appeared in a window of Linsly-Chit during my Chaucer class. Next, she swooped down a flight of stairs in Harkness. She hailed me from across Elm Street and found me in the Sterling Library stacks. After one of my meetings with Dr. Raeburn, she was waiting for me outside Health Services, legs crossed, cleaning her fingernails.

"You know," she said, as we walked through Old Campus, "you've got to stop eating ramen. Not only does it lack a single nutrient but it's full of MSG."

"I like eating chemicals," I said. "It keeps the skin radiant."

"There's also hepatitis." She already knew how to get my attention—mention a disease.

"You get hepatitis from unwashed lettuce," I said. "If there's anything safe from the perils of the food chain, it's ramen."

"But you refrigerate what you don't eat. Each time you reheat it, you're killing good bacteria, which then can't keep the bad bacteria in check. A guy got sick from re-heating Chinese noodles, and his son died from it. I read it in the *Times.*" With this, she put a jovial arm around my neck. I continued walking, a little stunned. Then, just as quickly, she dropped her arm and stopped walking. I stopped, too.

"Did you notice that I put my arm around you?"

"Yes," I said. "Next time, I'll have to chop it off."

"I don't want you to get sick," she said. "Let's eat at Commons."

In the cold air, her arm had felt good.

The problem with Commons was that it was too big; its ceiling was as high as a cathe-dral's, but below it there were no awestruck worshippers, only eighteen-year-olds at heavy wooden tables, chatting over veal patties and Jell-O.

We got our food, tacos stuffed with meat substitute, and made our way through the maze of tables. The Koreans had a table. Each singing group had a table. The crew team sat at a long table of its own. We passed the black table. The sheer quantity of Heidi's flesh accentuated just how white she was.

"How you doing, sista?" a guy asked, his voice full of accusation, eyeballing me as though I were clad in a Klansman's sheet and hood. "I guess we won't see you till graduation."

"If," I said, "you graduate."

The remark was not well received. As I walked past, I heard protests, angry and loud, as if they'd discovered a cheat at their poker game. Heidi and I found an unoc-cupied table along the periphery, which was isolated and dark. We sat down. Heidi prayed over her tacos.

"I thought you didn't believe in God," I said.

"Not in the God depicted in the Judeo-Christian Bible, but I do believe that na-ture's essence is a spirit that—"

"All right," I said. I had begun to eat, and cubes of diced tomato fell from my mouth when I spoke. "Stop right there. Tacos and spirits don't mix."

"You've always got to be so flip," she said. "I'm going to apply for another friend."

"There's always Mr. Dick," I said. "Slurp, slurp."

"You are so lame. So unbelievably lame. I'm going out with Mr. Dick. Thursday night at Atticus. His name is Keith."

Heidi hadn't mentioned Mr. Dick since the day I'd met her. That was more than a month ago and we'd spent a lot of that time together. I checked for signs that she was lying; her habit of smiling too much, her eyes bright and cheeks full, so that she looked like a chipmunk. But she looked normal. Pleased, even, to see me so flustered.

"You're insane! What are you going to do this time?" I asked. "Sleep with him?

Then when he makes fun of you, what? Come pound your head on my door reciting the 'Collected Poems of Sylvia Plath'?"

"He's going to apologize for before. And don't call me insane. You're the one going to the psychiatrist."

"Well, I'm not going to suck his dick, that's for sure."

She put her arm around me in mock comfort, but I pushed it off, and ignored her. She touched my shoulder again, and I turned, annoyed, but it wasn't Heidi after all; a sepia-toned boy dressed in khakis and a crisp plaid shirt was standing behind me. He handed me a hot-pink square of paper without a word, then briskly made his way toward the other end of Commons, where the crowds blossomed. Heidi leaned over and read it: "Wear Black Leather—the Less, the Better."

"It's a gay party," I said, crumpling the card. "He thinks we're fucking gay."

Heidi and I signed on to work at the Saybrook Dining Hall as dishwashers. The job consisted of dumping food from plates and trays into a vat of rushing water. It seemed straightforward, but then I learned better. You wouldn't believe what people could do with food until you worked in a dish room. Lettuce and crackers and soup would be bullied into a pulp in the bowl of some bored anorexic; ziti would be mixed with honey and granola; trays would appear heaped with mashed-potato snow women with melted chocolate ice cream for hair. Frat boys arrived at the dish-room window, en masse. They liked to fill glasses with food, then seal them, airtight, onto their trays. If you tried to prize them off, milk, Worcestershire sauce, peas, chunks of bread vomited onto your dish-room uniform.

When this happened one day in the middle of the lunch rush, for what seemed like the hundredth time, I tipped the tray toward one of the frat boys, popping the glasses off so that the mess spurted onto his Shetland sweater.

He looked down at his sweater. "Lesbo bitch!"

"No," I said, "that would be your mother."

Heidi, next to me, clenched my arm in support, but I remained motionless, waiting to see what the frat boy would do. He glared at me for a minute, then walked away.

"Let's take a smoke break," Heidi said.

I didn't smoke, but Heidi had begun to, because she thought it would help her lose weight. As I hefted a stack of glasses through the steamer, she lit up.

"Soft packs remind me of you," she said. "Just when you've smoked them all and you think there's none left, there's always one more, hiding in that little crushed corner." Before I could respond she said, "Oh, God. Not another mouse. You know whose job that is."

By the end of the rush, the floor mats got full and slippery with food. This was when mice tended to appear, scurrying over our shoes; more often than not, a mouse got caught in the grating that covered the drains in the floor. Sometimes the mouse was already dead by the time we noticed it. This one was alive.

"No way," I said. "This time you're going to help. Get some gloves and a trash bag."

"That's all I'm getting. I'm not getting that mouse out of there."

"Put on the gloves," I ordered. She winced, but put them on. "Reach down," I said. "At an angle, so you get at its middle. Otherwise, if you try to get it by its tail, the tail will break off."

"This is filthy, eh."

"That's why we're here," I said. "To clean up filth. Eh."

She reached down, but would not touch the mouse. I put my hand around her arm and pushed it till her hand made contact. The cries from the mouse were soft, songlike. "Oh, my God," she said. "Oh, my God, ohmigod." She wrestled it out of the grating and turned her head away.

"Don't you let it go," I said.

"Where's the food bag? It'll smother itself if I drop it in the food bag. Quick," she said, her head still turned away, her eyes closed. "Lead me to it."

"No. We are not going to smother this mouse. We've got to break its neck."

"You're one heartless bitch."

I wondered how to explain that if death is unavoidable it should be quick and painless. My mother had died slowly. At the hospital, they'd said it was kidney failure, but I knew that, in the end, it was my father. He made her scared to live in her own home, until she was finally driven away from it in an ambulance.

"Breaking its neck will save it the pain of smothering," I said. "Breaking its neck is more humane. Take the trash bag and cover it so you won't get any blood on you, then crush."

The loud jets of the steamer had shut off automatically and the dish room grew quiet. Heidi breathed in deeply, then crushed the mouse. She shuddered, disgusted. "Now what?"

"What do you mean, 'Now what?' Throw the little bastard in the trash."

At our third session, I told Dr. Raeburn I didn't mind if he smoked. He sat on the sill of his open window, smoking behind a jungle screen of office plants.

We spent the first ten minutes discussing the Iliad, and whether or not the text actually states that Achilles had been dipped in the River Styx. He said it did, and I said it didn't. After we'd finished with the Iliad, and with my new job in what he called "the scullery," he asked more questions about my parents. I told him nothing. It was none of his business. Instead, I talked about Heidi. I told him about the day in Commons, Heidi's plan to go on a date with Mr. Dick, and the invitation we'd been given to the gay party.

"You seem preoccupied by this soirée." He arched his eyebrows at the word "soirée."

"Wouldn't you be?"

"Dina," he said slowly, in a way that made my name seem like a song title, "have you ever had a romantic interest?"

"You want to know if I've ever had a boyfriend?" I said. "Just go ahead and ask if I've ever fucked anybody."

This appeared to surprise him. "I think that you are having a crisis of identity," he said.

"Oh, is that what this is?"

His profession had taught him not to roll his eyes. Instead, his exasperation revealed itself with a tiny pursing of his lips, as though he'd just tasted something awful and were trying very hard not to offend the cook.

"It doesn't have to be, as you say, someone you've fucked, it doesn't have to be a boyfriend," he said.

"Well, what are you trying to say? If it's not a boy, then you're saying it's a girl—"

"Calm down. It could be a crush, Dina." He lit one cigarette after another. "A crush on a male teacher, a crush on a dog, for heaven's sake. An interest. Not necessarily a relationship."

It was sacrifice time. If I could spend the next half hour talking about some boy, then I'd have given him what he wanted.

So I told him about the boy with the nice shoes.

I was sixteen and had spent the last few coins in my pocket on bus fare to buy groceries. I didn't like going to the Super Fresh two blocks away from my house, plunking government food stamps into the hands of the cashiers.

"There she go reading," one of them once said, even though I was only carrying a book. "Don't your eyes get tired?"

On Greenmount Avenue you could read schoolbooks—that was understandable. The government and your teachers forced you to read them. But anything else was anti-social. It meant you'd rather submit to the words of some white dude than shoot the breeze with your neighbors.

I hated those cashiers, and I hated them seeing me with food stamps, so I took the bus and shopped elsewhere. That day, I got off the bus at Govans, and though the neighborhood was black like my own—hair salon after hair salon of airbrushed signs promising arabesque hair styles and inch-long fingernails—the houses were neat and orderly, nothing at all like Greenmount, where every other house had at least one shattered window. The store was well swept, and people quietly checked long grocery lists—no screaming kids, no loud cashier-customer altercations. I got the groceries and left the store.

I decided to walk back. It was a fall day, and I walked for blocks. Then I sensed someone following me. I walked more quickly, my arms around the sack, the leafy lettuce tickling my nose. I didn't want to hold the sack so close that it would break the eggs or squash the hamburger buns, but it was slipping, and as I looked behind a boy my age, maybe older, rushed toward me.

"Let me help you," he said.

"That's all right." I set the bag on the sidewalk. Maybe I saw his face, maybe it was handsome enough, but what I noticed first, splayed on either side of the bag, were his shoes. They were nice shoes, real leather, a stitched design like a widow's peak on each one, or like birds' wings, and for the first time in my life I understood what people meant when they said "wing-tip shoes."

"I watched you carry them groceries out that store, then you look around, like you're lost, but like you liked being lost, then you walk down the sidewalk for blocks and blocks. Rearranging that bag, it almost gone to slip, then hefting it back up again."

"Huh, huh," I said.

"And then I passed my own house and was still following you. And then your bag really look like it was gone crash and everything. So I just thought I'd help." He sucked in his bottom lip, as if to keep it from making a smile. "What's your name?" When I told him, he said, "Dina, my name is Cecil." Then he said, "'D' comes right after 'C.'"

"Yes," I said, "it does, doesn't it?"

Then, half question, half statement, he said, "I could carry your groceries for you? And walk you home?"

I stopped the story there. Dr. Raeburn kept looking at me. "Then what happened?"

I couldn't tell him the rest: that I had not wanted the boy to walk me home, that I didn't want someone with such nice shoes to see where I lived.

Dr. Raeburn would only have pitied me if I'd told him that I ran down the sidewalk after I told the boy no, that I fell, the bag slipped, and the eggs cracked, their yolks running all over the lettuce. Clear amniotic fluid coated the can of cinnamon rolls. I left the bag there on the sidewalk, the groceries spilled out randomly like cards loosed from a deck. When I returned home, I told my mother I'd lost the food stamps.

"Lost?" she said. I'd expected her to get angry, I'd wanted her to get angry, but she hadn't. "Lost?" she repeated. Why had I been so clumsy and nervous around a harmless boy? I could have brought the groceries home and washed off the egg yolk, but, instead, I'd just left them there. "Come on," Mama said, snuffing her tears, pulling my arm, trying to get me to join her and start yanking cushions off the couch. "We'll find enough change here. We got to get something for dinner before your father gets back."

We'd already searched the couch for money the previous week, and I knew there'd be nothing now, but I began to push my fingers into the couch's boniest corners, pretending that it was only a matter of time before I'd find some change or a lost watch or an earring. Something pawnable, perhaps.

"What happened next?" Dr. Raeburn asked again. "Did you let the boy walk you home?"

"My house was far, so we went to his house instead." Though I was sure Dr. Raeburn knew that I was making this part up, I continued. "We made out on his sofa. He kissed me."

Dr. Raeburn lit his next cigarette like a detective. Cool, suspicious. "How did it feel?"

"You know," I said. "Like a kiss feels. It felt nice. The kiss felt very, very nice."

Raeburn smiled gently, though he seemed unconvinced. When he called time on our session his cigarette had become one long pole of ash. I left his office, walking quickly down the corridor, afraid to look back. It would be like him to trot after me, his navy blazer flapping, just to get the truth out of me. *You never kissed anyone.* The words slid from my brain, and knotted in my stomach.

When I reached my dorm, I found an old record player blocking my door and a Charles Mingus LP propped beside it. I carried them inside and then, lying on the floor, I played the Mingus over and over again until I fell asleep. I slept feeling as though Dr. Raeburn had attached electrodes to my head, willing into my mind a dream about my mother. I saw the lemon meringue of her skin, the long bone of her arm as she reached down to clip her toenails. I'd come home from a school trip to an aquarium, and I was explaining the differences between baleen and sperm whales according to the size of their heads, the range of their habitats, their feeding patterns.

I awoke remembering the expression on her face after I'd finished my dizzying whale lecture. She looked like a tourist who'd asked for directions to a place she thought was simple enough to get to only to hear a series of hypothetical turns, alleys, one-way streets. Her response was to nod politely at the perilous elaborateness of it all; to nod in the knowledge that she would never be able to get where she wanted to go.

The dishwashers always closed down the dining hall. One night, after everyone else had punched out, Heidi and I took a break, and though I wasn't a smoker, we set two milk crates upside down on the floor and smoked cigarettes.

The dishwashing machines were off, but steam still rose from them like a jungle mist. Outside in the winter air, students were singing carols in their groomed and tailored singing-group voices. The Whiffenpoofs were back in New Haven after a tour around the world, and I guess their return was a huge deal. Heidi and I craned our necks to watch the year's first snow through an open window.

"What are you going to do when you're finished?" Heidi asked. Sexy question marks of smoke drifted up to the windows before vanishing.

"Take a bath."

She swatted me with her free hand. "No, silly. Three years from now. When you leave Yale."

"I don't know. Open up a library. Somewhere where no one comes in for books. A library in a desert."

She looked at me as though she'd expected this sort of answer and didn't know why she'd asked in the first place.

"What are you going to do?" I asked her.

"Open up a psych clinic. In a desert. And my only patient will be some wacko who runs a library."

"Ha," I said. "Whatever you do, don't work in a dish room ever again. You're no good." I got up from the crate. "C'mon. Let's hose the place down."

We put out our cigarettes on the floor, since it was our job to clean it, anyway. We held squirt guns in one hand and used the other to douse the floors with the standard-issue, eye-burning cleaning solution. We hosed the dish room, the kitchen, the serving line, sending the water and crud and suds into the drains. Then we hosed them again so the solution wouldn't eat holes in our shoes as we left. Then I had an idea. I unbuckled my belt.

"What the hell are you doing?" Heidi said.

"Listen, it's too cold to go outside with our uniforms all wet. We could just take a shower right here. There's nobody but us."

"What the fuck, eh?"

I let my pants drop, then took off my shirt and panties. I didn't wear a bra, since

I didn't have much to fill one. I took off my shoes and hung my clothes on the stepladder.

"You've flipped," Heidi said. "I mean, really, psych-ward flipped."

I soaped up with the liquid hand soap until I felt as glazed as a ham. "Stand back and spray me."

"Oh, my God," she said. I didn't know whether she was confused or delighted, but she picked up the squirt gun and sprayed me. She was laughing. Then she got too close and the water started to sting.

"God damn it!" I said. "That hurt!"

"I was wondering what it would take to make you say that."

When all the soap had been rinsed off, I put on my regular clothes and said, "O.K. You're up next."

"No way," she said.

"Yes way."

She started to take off her uniform shirt, then stopped.

"What?"

"I'm too fat."

"You goddam right." She always said she was fat. One time, I'd told her that she should shut up about it, that large black women wore their fat like mink coats. "You're big as a house," I said now. "Frozen yogurt may be low in calories but not if you eat five tubs of it. Take your clothes off. I want to get out of here."

She began taking off her uniform, then stood there, hands cupped over her breasts, crouching at the pubic bone.

"Open up," I said, "or we'll never get done."

Her hands remained where they were. I threw the bottle of liquid soap at her, and she had to catch it, revealing herself as she did.

I turned on the squirt gun, and she stood there, stiff, arms at her sides, eyes closed, as though awaiting mummification. I began with the water on low, and she turned around in a full circle, hesitantly, letting the droplets from the spray fall on her as if she were submitting to a death by stoning.

When I increased the water pressure, she slipped and fell on the sudsy floor. She stood up and then slipped again. This time she laughed and remained on the floor, rolling around on it as I sprayed.

I think I began to love Heidi that night in the dish room, but who is to say that I hadn't begun to love her the first time I met her? I sprayed her and sprayed her, and she turned over and over like a large beautiful dolphin, lolling about in the sun.

Heidi started sleeping at my place. Sometimes she slept on the floor; sometimes we slept sardinelike, my feet at her head, until she complained that my feet were "taunting" her. When we finally slept head to head, she said, "Much better." She was so close I could smell her toothpaste. "I like your hair," she told me, touching it through the darkness. "You should wear it out more often."

"White people always say that about black people's hair. The worse it looks, the more they say they like it."

I'd expected her to disagree, but she kept touching my hair, her hands passing through it till my scalp tingled. When she began to touch the hair around the edge of my face, I felt myself quake. Her fingertips stopped for a moment, as if checking my pulse, then resumed.

"I like how it feels right here. See, mine just starts with the same old texture as the rest of my hair." She found my hand under the blanket and brought it to her hairline. "See," she said.

It was dark. As I touched her hair, it seemed as though I could smell it, too. Not a shampoo smell. Something richer, murkier. A bit dead, but sweet, like the decaying wood of a ship. She guided my hand.

"I see," I said. The record she'd given me was playing in my mind, and I kept trying to shut it off. I could also hear my mother saying that this is what happens when you've been around white people: things get weird. So weird I could hear the stylus etching its way into the flat vinyl of the record. "Listen," I said finally, when the bass and saxes started up. I heard Heidi breathe deeply, but she said nothing.

We spent the winter and some of the spring in my room—never hers—missing tests, listening to music, looking out my window to comment on people who wouldn't have given us a second thought. We read books related to none of our classes. I got riled up by "The Autobiography of Malcolm X" and "The Chomsky Reader"; Heidi read aloud passages from "The Anxiety of Influence." We guiltily read mysteries and "Clan of the Cave Bear," then immediately threw them away. Once, we looked up from our books at exactly the same moment, as though trapped at a dinner table with nothing to say. A pleasant trap of silence.

Then one weekend I went back to Baltimore. When I returned, to a sleepy, tree-scented spring, a group of students were holding what was called "Coming Out Day." I watched it from my room.

The m.c. was the sepia boy who'd invited us to that party months back. His speech was strident but still smooth, and peppered with jokes. There was a speech about AIDS, with lots of statistics: nothing that seemed to make "coming out" worth it. Then the women spoke. One girl pronounced herself "out" as casually as if she'd announced the time. Another said nothing at all: she appeared at the microphone accompanied by a woman who began cutting off her waist-length, bleached-blond hair. The woman doing the cutting tossed the shorn hair in every direction as she cut. People were clapping and cheering and catching the locks of hair.

And then there was Heidi. She was proud that she liked girls, she said when she reached the microphone. She loved them, wanted to sleep with them. She was a dyke, she said repeatedly, stabbing her finger to her chest in case anyone was unsure to whom she was referring. She could not have seen me. I was across the street, three stories up. And yet, when everyone clapped for her, she seemed to be looking straight at me.

Heidi knocked. "Let me in."

It was like the first time I met her. The tears, the raw pink of her face.

We hadn't spoken in weeks. Outside, pink-and-white blossoms hung from the

Old Campus trees. Students played hackeysack in T-shirts and shorts. Though I was the one who'd broken away after she went up to that podium, I still half expected her to poke her head out a window in Linsly-Chit, or tap on my back in Harkness, or even join me in the Commons dining hall, where I'd asked for my dish-room shift to be transferred. She did none of these.

"Well," I said, "what is it?"

She looked at me. "My mother," she said.

She continued to cry, but it seemed to have grown so silent in my room I wondered if I could hear the numbers change on my digital clock.

"When my parents were getting divorced," she said, "my mother bought a car. A used one. An El Dorado. It was filthy. It looked like a huge crushed can coming up the street. She kept trying to clean it out. I mean—"

I nodded and tried to think what to say in the pause she left behind. Finally I said, "We had one of those," though I was sure ours was an Impala.

She looked at me, eyes steely from trying not to cry. "Anyway, she'd drive me around in it and although she didn't like me to eat in it, I always did. One day, I was eating cantaloupe slices, spitting the seeds on the floor. Maybe a month later, I saw this little sprout, growing right up from the car floor. I just started laughing and she kept saying what, what? I was laughing and then I saw she was so—"

She didn't finish. So what? So sad? So awful? Heidi looked at me with what seemed to be a renewed vigor. "We could have gotten a better car, eh?"

"It's all right. It's not a big deal," I said.

Of course, that was the wrong thing to say. And I really didn't mean it to sound the way it had come out.

I told Dr. Raeburn about Heidi's mother having cancer and how I'd said it wasn't a big deal, though I'd wanted to say exactly the opposite. I meant that I knew what it was like to have a parent die. My mother had died. I knew how eventually one accustoms oneself to the physical world's lack of sympathy: the buses that still run on time, the kids who still play in the street, the clocks that won't stop ticking for the person who's gone.

"You're pretending," Dr. Raeburn said, not sage or professional but a little shocked by the discovery, as if I'd been trying to hide a pack of his cigarettes behind my back.

"I'm pretending?" I shook my head. "All those years of psych grad," I said. "And to tell me *that?*"

"You construct stories about yourself and dish them out—one for you, one for you—" Here he reënacted the process, showing me handing out lies as if they were apples.

"Pretending. I believe the professional name for it might be denial," I said. "Are you calling me gay?"

He pursed his lips noncommittally. "No, Dina. I don't think you're gay."

I checked his eyes. I couldn't read them.

"No. Not at all," he said, sounding as if he were telling a subtle joke. "But maybe you'll finally understand."

"Understand what?"

"That constantly saying what one doesn't mean accustoms the mouth to meaningless phrases." His eyes narrowed. "Maybe you'll understand that when you need to express something truly significant, your mouth will revert to the insignificant nonsense it knows so well." He looked at me, his hands sputtering in the air in a gesture of defeat. "Who knows?" he asked, with a glib, psychiatric smile I'd never seen before. "Maybe it's your survival mechanism. Black living in a white world."

I heard him, but only vaguely. I'd hooked on to that one word, pretending. What Dr. Raeburn would never understand was that pretending was what had got me this far. I remembered the morning of my mother's funeral. I'd been given milk to settle my stomach; I'd pretended it was coffee. I imagined I was drinking coffee elsewhere. Some Arabic-speaking country where the thick coffee served in little cups was so strong it could keep you awake for days. Some Arabic country where I'd sit in a tented café and be more than happy to don a veil.

Heidi wanted me to go with her to the funeral. She'd sent this message through the dean. "We'll pay for your ticket to Vancouver," the dean said.

"What about my ticket back?" I asked. "Maybe the shrink will pay for that."

The dean looked at me as though I were an insect she'd like to squash. "We'll pay for the whole thing. We might even pay for some lessons in manners."

So I packed my suitcase and walked from my suicide-single dorm to Heidi's room. A thin wispy girl in ragged cutoffs and a shirt that read "LSBN!" answered the door. A group of short-haired girls in thick black leather jackets, bundled up despite the summer heat, encircled Heidi in a protective fairy ring. They looked at me critically, clearly wondering if Heidi was too fragile for my company.

"You've got our numbers," one said, holding onto Heidi's shoulder. "And Vancouver's got a great gay community."

"Oh God," I said. "She's going to a funeral, not a 'Save the Dykes' rally."

One of the girls stepped in front of me.

"It's O.K., Cynthia," Heidi said. Then she ushered me into her bedroom and closed the door. A suitcase was on her bed, half packed. She folded a polka-dotted T-shirt that was wrong for any occasion. "Why haven't you talked to me?" she said. "Why haven't you talked to me in two months?"

"I don't know," I said.

"You don't know," she said, each syllable seeped in sarcasm. "You don't know. Well, I know. You thought I was going to try to sleep with you."

"Try to? We slept together all winter!"

"Smelling your feet is not 'sleeping together.' You've got a lot to learn." She seemed thinner and meaner.

"So tell me," I said. "What can you show me that I need to learn?" But as soon as I said it I somehow knew that she still hadn't slept with anyone.

"Am I supposed to come over there and sweep your enraged self into my arms?" I said. "Like in the movies? Is this the part where we're both so mad we kiss each other?"

She shook her head and smiled weakly. "You don't get it," she said. "My mother is dead." She closed her suitcase, clicking shut the old-fashioned locks. "My mother is dead," she said again, this time reminding herself. She set the suitcase upright on the floor and sat on it. She looked like someone waiting for a train.

"Fine," I said. "And she's going to be dead for a long time." Though it sounded stupid, I felt good saying it. As though I had my own locks to click shut.

Heidi went to Vancouver for her mother's funeral. I didn't go. Instead, I went back to Baltimore and moved in with an aunt I barely knew. Every day was the same: I read and smoked outside my aunt's apartment, studying the row of hair salons across the street, where girls in denim cut-offs and tank tops would troop in and come out hours later, a flash of neon nails, coifs the color and sheen of patent leather. And every day I imagined visiting Heidi in Vancouver. Her house would not be large, but it would be clean. Flowery shrubs would line the walks. The Canadian wind would whip us about like pennants. I'd be visiting her at some vague time in the future, deliberately vague, for people like me, who realign past events to suit themselves. In that future time, you always have a chance to catch the groceries before they fall, your words can always be rewound and erased, rewritten and revised.

But once I imagined Heidi visiting me. There would be no psychiatrists or deans. No boys with nice shoes or flip cashiers. Just me in my single room. She would knock on the door and say, "Open up."

# Grace Paley

## (B. 1922)

Grace Paley was born in New York City into a family of Russian immigrants. She began writing fiction in the 1950s, and her first collection of short stories, *Little Disturbances of Man* (1959), established her as a respected writer with a gift for naturalistic language and a keen sense of humor. Paley became active in the antiwar movement in the 1960s and 1970s, serving as secretary of the Greenwich Village Peace Center, spending time in jail for her antiwar activities, and visiting Hanoi and Moscow as a member of peace delegations. *Enormous Changes at the Last Minute*, Paley's second volume of mostly autobiographical short stories, was published in 1974. Her third book of stories, *Later the Same Day*, appeared in 1985. Paley is also the author of several poetry collections, including *16 Broadsides* (1980), *Goldenrod* (1982), and *Leaning Forward: Poems* (1985). In 1988 Paley was designated the first official New York State Author by an act of the state legislature.

Paley's participation in the feminist movement and the antiwar movement grew out of the socialist ideals of her Russian parents. This interest in the good of working people is reflected in her stories, which often describe the daily lives

of New York working-class men and women. Paley uses the rhythms and cadences of New York speech to create vignettes about extraordinary moments
in the ordinary world. She also uses her stories to liberate the American housewife, releasing her into the streets to have affairs, to protest nuclear wars, or to
simply climb trees in the middle of the day. Paley awards her characters, women
and men both, with moments of resistance often denied to the ordinary working-
class character in American fiction.

---

## A Conversation with My Father              1974

My father is eighty-six years old and in bed. His heart, that bloody motor, is equally
old and will not do certain jobs any more. It still floods his head with brainy light. But
it won't let his legs carry the weight of his body around the house. Despite my
metaphors, this muscle failure is not due to his old heart, he says, but to a potassium
shortage. Sitting on one pillow, leaning on three, he offers last-minute advice and
makes a request.

"I would like you to write a simple story just once more," he says, "the kind de
Maupassant wrote, or Chekhov, the kind you used to write. Just recognizable people
and then write down what happened to them next."

I say, "Yes, why not? That's possible." I want to please him, though I don't remember writing that way. I *would* like to try to tell such a story, if he means the kind
that begins: "There was a woman . . ." followed by plot, the absolute line between two
points which I've always despised. Not for literary reasons, but because it takes all
hope away. Everyone, real or invented, deserves the open destiny of life.

Finally I thought of a story that had been happening for a couple of years right
across the street. I wrote it down, then read it aloud. "Pa," I said, "how about this? Do
you mean something like this?"

> Once in my time there was a woman and she had a son. They lived nicely,
> in a small apartment in Manhattan. This boy at about fifteen became a
> junkie, which is not unusual in our neighborhood. In order to maintain
> her close friendship with him, she became a junkie too. She said it was part
> of the youth culture, with which she felt very much at home. After a while,
> for a number of reasons, the boy gave it all up and left the city and his
> mother in disgust. Hopeless and alone, she grieved. We all visit her.

"O.K., Pa, that's it," I said, "an unadorned and miserable tale."

"But that's not what I mean," my father said. "You misunderstood me on purpose.
You know there's a lot more to it. You know that. You left everything out. Turgenev
wouldn't do that. Chekhov wouldn't do that. There are in fact Russian writers you
never heard of, you don't have an inkling of, as good as anyone, who can write a plain
ordinary story, who would not leave out what you have left out. I object not to facts but
to people sitting in trees talking senselessly, voices from who knows where. . . ."

"Forget that one, Pa, what have I left out now? In this one?"

"Her looks, for instance."

"Oh. Quite handsome, I think. Yes."

"Her hair?"

"Dark, with heavy braids, as though she were a girl or a foreigner."

"What were her parents like, her stock? That she became such a person. It's interesting, you know."

"From out of town. Professional people. The first to be divorced in their county. How's that? Enough?" I asked.

"With you, it's all a joke," he said. "What about the boy's father? Why didn't you mention him? Who was he? Or was the boy born out of wedlock?"

"Yes," I said. "He was born out of wedlock."

"For Godsakes, doesn't anyone in your stories get married? Doesn't anyone have the time to run down to City Hall before they jump into bed?"

"No," I said. "In real life, yes. But in my stories, no."

"Why do you answer me like that?"

"Oh, Pa, this is a simple story about a smart woman who came to N.Y.C. full of interest love trust excitement very up to date, and about her son, what a hard time she had in this world. Married or not, it's of small consequence."

"It is of great consequence," he said.

"O.K.," I said.

"O.K. O.K. yourself," he said, "but listen. I believe you that she's good-looking, but I don't think she was so smart."

"That's true," I said. "Actually that's the trouble with stories. People start out fantastic. You think they're extraordinary, but it turns out as the work goes along, they're just average with a good education. Sometimes the other way around, the person's a kind of dumb innocent, but he outwits you and you can't even think of an ending good enough."

"What do you do then?" he asked. He had been a doctor for a couple of decades and then an artist for a couple of decades and he's still interested in details, craft, technique.

"Well, you just have to let the story lie around till some agreement can be reached between you and the stubborn hero."

"Aren't you talking silly now?" he asked. "Start again," he said. "It so happens I'm not going out this evening. Tell the story again. See what you can do this time."

"O.K.," I said. "But it's not a five-minute job." Second attempt:

> Once, across the street from us, there was a fine handsome woman, our neighbor. She had a son whom she loved because she'd known him since birth (in helpless chubby infancy, and in the wrestling, hugging ages, seven to ten, as well as earlier and later). This boy, when he fell into the first of adolescence, became a junkie. He was not a hopeless one. He was in fact hopeful, an ideologue and successful converter. With his busy brilliance, he wrote persuasive articles for his high-school newspaper. Seeking a wider

audience, using important connections, he drummed into Lower Manhattan newsstand distribution a periodical called *Oh! Golden Horse!*

In order to keep him from feeling guilty (because guilt is the stony heart of nine tenths of all clinically diagnosed cancers in America today, she said), and because she had always believed in giving bad habits room at home where one could keep an eye on them, she too became a junkie. Her kitchen was famous for a while—a center for intellectual addicts who knew what they were doing. A few felt artistic like Coleridge and others were scientific and revolutionary like Leary. Although she was often high herself, certain good mothering reflexes remained, and she saw to it that there was lots of orange juice around and honey and milk and vitamin pills. However, she never cooked anything but chili, and that no more than once a week. She explained, when we talked to her, seriously, with neighborly concern, that it was her part in the youth culture and she would rather be with the young, it was an honor, than with her own generation.

One week, while nodding through an Antonioni film, this boy was severely jabbed by the elbow of a stern and proselytizing girl, sitting beside him. She offered immediate apricots and nuts for his sugar level, spoke to him sharply, and took him home.

She had heard of him and his work and she herself published, edited, and wrote a competitive journal called *Man Does Live by Bread Alone.* In the organic heat of her continuous presence he could not help but become interested once more in his muscles, his arteries, and nerve connections. In fact he began to love them, treasure them, praise them with funny little songs in *Man Does Live. . . .*

> the fingers of my flesh transcend
> my transcendental soul
> the tightness in my shoulders end
> my teeth have made me whole

To the mouth of his head (that glory of will and determination) he brought hard apples, nuts, wheat germ, and soybean oil. He said to his old friends, From now on, I guess I'll keep my wits about me. I'm going on the natch. He said he was about to begin a spiritual deep-breathing journey. How about you too, Mom? he asked kindly.

His conversion was so radiant, splendid, that neighborhood kids his age began to say that he had never been a real addict at all, only a journalist along for the smell of the story. The mother tried several times to give up what had become without her son and his friends a lonely habit. This effort only brought it to supportable levels. The boy and his girl took their electronic mimeograph and moved to the bushy edge of another borough. They were very strict. They said they would not see her again until she had been off drugs for sixty days.

At home alone in the evening, weeping, the mother read and reread the seven issues of *Oh! Golden Horse!* They seemed to her as truthful as ever. We often crossed the street to visit and console. But if we mentioned any of our children who were at college or in the hospital or dropouts at home, she would cry out, My baby! My baby! and burst into terrible, face-scarring, time-consuming tears. The End.

First my father was silent, then he said, "Number One: You have a nice sense of humor. Number Two: I see you can't tell a plain story. So don't waste time." Then he said sadly, "Number Three: I suppose that means she was alone, she was left like that, his mother. Alone. Probably sick?"

I said, "Yes."

"Poor woman. Poor girl, to be born in a time of fools, to live among fools. The end. The end. You were right to put that down. The end."

I didn't want to argue, but I had to say, "Well, it is not necessarily the end, Pa."

"Yes," he said, "what a tragedy. The end of a person."

"No, Pa," I begged him. "It doesn't have to be. She's only about forty. She could be a hundred different things in this world as time goes on. A teacher or a social worker. An ex-junkie! Sometimes it's better than having a master's in education."

"Jokes," he said. "As a writer that's your main trouble. You don't want to recognize it. Tragedy! Plain tragedy! Historical tragedy! No hope. The end."

"Oh, Pa," I said. "She could change."

"In your own life, too, you have to look it in the face." He took a couple of nitro-glycerin. "Turn to five," he said, pointing to the dial on the oxygen tank. He inserted the tubes into his nostrils and breathed deep. He closed his eyes and said, "No."

I had promised the family to always let him have the last word when arguing, but in this case I had a different responsibility. That woman lives across the street. She's my knowledge and my invention. I'm sorry for her. I'm not going to leave her there in that house crying. (Actually neither would Life, which unlike me has no pity.)

Therefore: She did change. Of course her son never came home again. But right now, she's the receptionist in a storefront community clinic in the East Village. Most of the customers are young people, some old friends. The head doctor has said to her, "If we only had three people in this clinic with your experiences. . . ."

"The doctor said that?" My father took the oxygen tubes out of his nostrils and said, "Jokes. Jokes again."

"No, Pa, it could really happen that way, it's a funny world nowadays."

"No," he said. "Truth first. She will slide back. A person must have character. She does not."

"No, Pa," I said. "That's it. She's got a job. Forget it. She's in that storefront working."

"How long will it be?" he asked. "Tragedy! You too. When will you look it in the face?"

# Philip Roth

(B. 1933)

Philip Roth's grandparents were part of a wave of European Jews who immigrated to the United States in the nineteenth century. Roth grew up in New Jersey and taught English and creative writing until his retirement in 1992. His innovative stories and novels often depict middle-class Jewish Americans whose lives are carefully shaped by their historical and geographical milieus. He tackles controversial topics like sexuality and rebellion as he conveys the changes and defining characteristics of various periods of American history. Roth has said, "Sheer playfulness and deadly seriousness are my closest friends," and his writing embodies this combination of wit and gravity.

A prolific writer, Roth's writing career began with *Goodbye Columbus* (1959), a novella and five stories, and he followed this with three novels—*Letting Go* (1962), *When She Was Good* (1967), and *Portnoy's Complaint* (1969). His other works include *Our Gang* (1971), *The Breast* (1972), *The Great American Novel* (1973), *My Life as a Man* (1974), *The Ghost Writer* (1979), *Zuckerman Unbound* (1981), *The Anatomy Lesson* (1983), *The Counterlife* (1986), *The Facts* (1988), *Deception* (1990), *Patrimony* (1991), and *Operation Shylock* (1993). His most recent work includes *Sabbath's Theater* (1995), *American Pastoral* (1997), for which he won the Pulitzer Prize, *I Married a Communist* (1998), *The Human Stain* (2000), and *The Dying Animal* (2001). In 2002, Roth published *The Plot against America*, an alternative history in which Charles Lindbergh is elected president of the United States. He lives in Connecticut.

## Defender of the Faith
1959

In May of 1945, only a few weeks after the fighting had ended in Europe, I was rotated back to the States, where I spent the remainder of the war with a training company at Camp Crowder, Missouri. Along with the rest of the Ninth Army, I had been racing across Germany so swiftly during the late winter and spring that when I boarded the plane, I couldn't believe its destination lay to the west. My mind might inform me otherwise, but there was an inertia of the spirit that told me we were flying to a new front, where we would disembark and continue our push eastward—eastward until we'd circled the globe, marching through villages along whose twisting, cobbled streets crowds of the enemy would watch us take possession of what, up till then, they'd considered their own. I had changed enough in two years not to mind the trembling of old people, the crying of the very young, the uncertainty and fear in the eyes of the once arrogant. I had been fortunate enough to develop an infantryman's heart, which, like his feet, at first aches and swells but finally grows horny enough for him to travel the weirdest paths without feeling a thing.

Captain Paul Barrett was my C.O. in Camp Crowder. The day I reported for duty, he came out of his office to shake my hand. He was short, gruff, and fiery, and—indoors or out—he wore his polished helmet liner pulled down to his little eyes. In Europe, he had received a battlefield commission and a serious chest wound, and he'd been returned to the States only a few months before. He spoke easily to me, and at the evening formation he introduced me to the troops. "Gentlemen," he said, "Sergeant Thurston, as you know, is no longer with this company. Your new first sergeant is Sergeant Nathan Marx, here. He is a veteran of the European theater, and consequently will expect to find a company of soldiers here, and not a company of *boys*."

I sat up late in the orderly room that evening, trying half-heartedly to solve the riddle of duty rosters, personnel forms, and morning reports. The Charge of Quarters slept with his mouth open on a mattress on the floor. A trainee stood reading the next day's duty roster, which was posted on the bulletin board just inside the screen door. It was a warm evening, and I could hear radios playing dance music over in the barracks. The trainee, who had been staring at me whenever he thought I wouldn't notice, finally took a step in my direction.

"Hey, Sarge—we having a G.I. party tomorrow night?" he asked. A G.I. party is a barracks cleaning.

"You usually have them on Friday nights?" I asked him.

"Yes," he said, and then added, mysteriously, "that's the whole thing."

"Then you'll have a G.I. party."

He turned away, and I heard him mumbling. His shoulders were moving, and I wondered if he was crying.

"What's your name, soldier?" I asked.

He turned, not crying at all. Instead, his green-speckled eyes, long and narrow, flashed like fish in the sun. He walked over to me and sat on the edge of my desk. He reached out a hand. "Sheldon," he said.

"Stand on your feet, Sheldon."

Getting off the desk, he said, "Sheldon Grossbart." He smiled at the familiarity into which he'd led me.

"You against cleaning the barracks Friday night, Grossbart?" I said. "Maybe we shouldn't have G.I. parties. Maybe we should get a maid." My tone startled me. I felt I sounded like every top sergeant I had ever known.

"No, Sergeant." He grew serious, but with a seriousness that seemed to be only the stifling of a smile. "It's just—G.I. parties on Friday night, of all nights."

He slipped up onto the corner of the desk again—not quite sitting, but not quite standing, either. He looked at me with those speckled eyes flashing, and then made a gesture with his hand. It was very slight—no more than a movement back and forth of the wrist—and yet it managed to exclude from our affairs everything else in the orderly room, to make the two of us the center of the world. It seemed, in fact, to exclude everything even about the two of us except our hearts.

"Sergeant Thurston was one thing," he whispered, glancing at the sleeping C.Q., "but we thought that with you here things might be a little different."

"We?"

"The Jewish personnel."

"Why?" I asked, harshly. "What's on your mind?" Whether I was still angry at the "Sheldon" business, or now at something else, I hadn't time to tell, but clearly I was angry.

"We thought you—Marx, you know, like Karl Marx. The Marx Brothers. Those guys are well—M-a-r-x. Isn't that how *you* spell it, Sergeant?"

"M-a-r-x."

"Fishbein said—" He stopped. "What I mean to say, Sergeant—" His face and neck were red, and his mouth moved but no words came out. In a moment, he raised himself to attention, gazing down at me. It was as though he had suddenly decided he could expect no more sympathy from me than from Thurston, the reason being that I was of Thurston's faith, and not his. The young man had managed to confuse himself as to what my faith really was, but I felt no desire to straighten him out. Very simply, I didn't like him.

When I did nothing but return his gaze, he spoke, in an altered tone. "You see, Sergeant," he explained to me, "Friday nights, Jews are supposed to go to services."

"Did Sergeant Thurston tell you you couldn't go to them when there was a G.I. party?"

"No."

"Did he say you had to stay and scrub the floors?"

"No, Sergeant."

"Did the Captain say you had to stay and scrub the floors?"

"That isn't it, Sergeant. It's the other guys in the barracks." He leaned toward me. "They think we're goofing off. But we're not. That's when Jews go to services, Friday night. We have to."

"Then go."

"But the other guys make accusations. They have no right."

"That's not the Army's problem, Grossbart. It's a personal problem you'll have to work out yourself."

"But it's un*fair*."

I got up to leave. "There's nothing I can do about it," I said.

Grossbart stiffened and stood in front of me. "But this is a matter of *religion,* sir."

"Sergeant," I said.

"I mean 'Sergeant,'" he said, almost snarling.

"Look, go see the chaplain. You want to see Captain Barrett, I'll arrange an appointment."

"No, no. I don't want to make trouble, Sergeant. That's the first thing they throw up to you. I just want my rights!"

"Damn it, Grossbart, stop whining. You have your rights. You can stay and scrub floors or you can go to shul—"

The smile swam in again. Spittle gleamed at the corners of his mouth. "You mean church, Sergeant."

"I mean shul, Grossbart!"

I walked past him and went outside. Near me, I heard the scrunching of a guard's boots on gravel. Beyond the lighted windows of the barracks, young men in T shirts and fatigue pants were sitting on their bunks, polishing their rifles. Suddenly there was a light rustling behind me. I turned and saw Grossbart's dark frame fleeing back to the barracks, racing to tell his Jewish friends that they were right—that, like Karl and Harpo, I was one of them.

The next morning, while chatting with Captain Barrett, I recounted the incident of the previous evening. Somehow, in the telling, it must have seemed to the Captain that I was not so much explaining Grossbart's position as defending it. "Marx, I'd fight side by side with a nigger if the fella proved to me he was a man. I pride myself," he said, looking out the window, "that I've got an open mind. Consequently, Sergeant, nobody gets special treatment here, for the good *or* the bad. All a man's got to do is prove himself. A man fires well on the range, I give him a weekend pass. He scores high in P.T., he gets a weekend pass. He *earns* it." He turned from the window and pointed a finger at me. "You're a Jewish fella, am I right, Marx?"

"Yes, sir."

"And I admire you. I admire you because of the ribbons on your chest. I judge a man by what he shows me on the field of battle, Sergeant. It's what he's got *here*," he said, and then, though I expected he would point to his chest, he jerked a thumb toward the buttons straining to hold his blouse across his belly. "Guts," he said.

"O.K., sir. I only wanted to pass on to you how the men felt."

"Mr. Marx, you're going to be old before your time if you worry about how the men feel. Leave that stuff to the chaplain—that's his business, not yours. Let's us train these fellas to shoot straight. If the Jewish personnel feels the other men are accusing them of goldbricking—well, I just don't know. Seems awful funny that suddenly the Lord is calling so loud in Private Grossman's ear he's just got to run to church."

"Synagogue," I said.

"Synagogue is right, Sergeant. I'll write that down for handy reference. Thank you for stopping by."

That evening, a few minutes before the company gathered outside the orderly room for the chow formation, I called the C.Q., Corporal Robert LaHill, in to see me. LaHill was a dark, burly fellow whose hair curled out of his clothes wherever it could. He had a glaze in his eyes that made one think of caves and dinosaurs. "LaHill," I said, "when you take the formation, remind the men that they're free to attend church services *whenever* they are held, provided they report to the orderly room before they leave the area."

LaHill scratched his wrist, but gave no indication that he'd heard or understood.

"LaHill," I said, "*church*. You remember? Church, priest, Mass, confession."

He curled one lip into a kind of smile; I took it for a signal that for a second he had flickered back up into the human race.

"Jewish personnel who want to attend services this evening are to fall out in front of the orderly room at 1900," I said. Then, as an afterthought, I added, "By order of Captain Barrett."

A little while later, as the day's last light—softer than any I had seen that year—began to drop over Camp Crowder, I heard LaHill's thick, inflectionless voice outside my window: "Give me your ears, troopers. Toppie says for me to tell you that at 1900 hours all Jewish personnel is to fall out in front, here, if they want to attend the Jewish Mass."

At seven o'clock, I looked out the orderly-room window and saw three soldiers in starched khakis standing on the dusty quadrangle. They looked at their watches and fidgeted while they whispered back and forth. It was getting dimmer, and, alone on the otherwise deserted field, they looked tiny. When I opened the door, I heard the noises of the G.I. party coming from the surrounding barracks—bunks being pushed to the walls, faucets pounding water into buckets, brooms whisking at the wooden floors, cleaning the dirt away for Saturday's inspection. Big puffs of cloth moved round and round on the windowpanes. I walked outside, and the moment my foot hit the ground I thought I heard Grossbart call to the others, "'Ten-*hut!*" Or maybe, when they all three jumped to attention, I imagined I heard the command.

Grossbart stepped forward. "Thank you, sir," he said.

"'Sergeant,' Grossbart," I reminded him. "You call officers 'sir.' I'm not an officer. You've been in the Army three weeks—you know that."

He turned his palms out at his sides to indicate that, in truth, he and I lived beyond convention. "Thank you, anyway," he said.

"Yes," a tall boy behind him said. "Thanks a lot."

And the third boy whispered, "Thank you," but his mouth barely fluttered, so that he did not alter by more than a lip's movement his posture of attention.

"For what?" I asked.

Grossbart snorted happily. "For the announcement. The Corporal's announcement. It helped. It made it—"

"Fancier." The tall boy finished Grossbart's sentence.

Grossbart smiled. "He means formal, sir. Public," he said to me. "Now it won't seem as though we're just taking off—goldbricking because the work has begun."

"It was by order of Captain Barrett," I said.

"Aaah, but you pull a little weight," Grossbart said. "So we thank you." Then he turned to his companions. "Sergeant Marx, I want you to meet Larry Fishbein."

The tall boy stepped forward and extended his hand. I shook it. "You from New York?" he asked.

"Yes."

"Me, too." He had a cadaverous face that collapsed inward from his cheekbone to his jaw, and when he smiled—as he did at the news of our communal attachment—revealed a mouthful of bad teeth. He was blinking his eyes a good deal, as though he were fighting back tears. "What borough?" he asked.

I turned to Grossbart. "It's five after seven. What time are services?"

"Shul," he said, smiling, "is in ten minutes. I want you to meet Mickey Halpern. This is Nathan Marx, our sergeant."

The third boy hopped forward. "Private Michael Halpern." He saluted.

"Salute officers, Halpern," I said. The boy dropped his hand, and, on its way down, in his nervousness, checked to see if his shirt pockets were buttoned.

"Shall I march them over, sir?" Grossbart asked. "Or are you coming along?"

From behind Grossbart, Fishbein piped up. "Afterward, they're having refreshments. A ladies' auxiliary from St. Louis, the rabbi told us last week."

"The chaplain," Halpern whispered.

"You're welcome to come along," Grossbart said.

To avoid his plea, I looked away, and saw, in the windows of the barracks, a cloud of faces staring out at the four of us. "Hurry along, Grossbart," I said.

"O.K., then," he said. He turned to the others. "Double time, *march!*"

They started off, but ten feet away Grossbart spun around and, running backward, called to me, "Good *shabbus*, sir!" And then the three of them were swallowed into the alien Missouri dusk.

Even after they had disappeared over the parade ground, whose green was now a deep blue, I could hear Grossbart singing the double-time cadence, and as it grew dimmer and dimmer, it suddenly touched a deep memory—as did the slant of the light— and I was remembering the shrill sounds of a Bronx playground where, years ago, beside the Grand Concourse, I had played on long spring evenings such as this. It was a pleasant memory for a young man so far from peace and home, and it brought so many recollections with it that I began to grow exceedingly tender about myself. In fact, I indulged myself in a reverie so strong that I felt as though a hand were reaching down inside me. It had to reach so very far to touch me! It had to reach past those days in the forests of Belgium, and past the dying I'd refused to weep over; past the nights in German farmhouses whose books we'd burned to warm us; past endless stretches when I had shut off all softness I might feel for my fellows, and had managed even to deny myself the posture of a conqueror—the swagger that I, as a Jew, might well have worn as my boots whacked against the rubble of Wesel, Münster, and Braunschweig.

But now one night noise, one rumor of home and time past, and memory plunged down through all I had anesthetized, and came to what I suddenly remembered was myself. So it was not altogether curious that, in search of more of me, I found myself following Grossbart's tracks to Chapel No. 3, where the Jewish services were being held.

I took a seat in the last row, which was empty. Two rows in front of me sat Grossbart, Fishbein, and Halpern, holding little white Dixie cups. Each row of seats was raised higher than the one in front of it, and I could see clearly what was going on. Fishbein was pouring the contents of his cup into Grossbart's, and Grossbart looked mirthful as the liquid made a purple arc between Fishbein's hand and his. In the glaring yellow light, I saw the chaplain standing on the platform at the front; he was chanting the first line of the responsive reading. Grossbart's prayer book remained closed on his lap; he was swishing the cup around. Only Halpern responded to the chant by praying. The fingers of his right hand were spread wide across the cover of his open book. His cap was pulled down low onto his brow, which made it round, like a yarmulke. From time to time, Grossbart wet his lips at the cup's edge; Fishbein, his long yellow face a dying light bulb, looked from here to there, craning forward to catch sight of the faces down the row, then of those in front of him, then behind. He saw me, and his eyelids beat a tattoo. His elbow slid into Grossbart's side, his neck inclined toward his friend, he whispered something, and then, when the congregation next responded to the chant, Grossbart's voice was among the others. Fishbein looked into his book now, too; his lips, however, didn't move.

Finally, it was time to drink the wine. The chaplain smiled down at them as Grossbart swigged his in one long gulp, Halpern sipped, meditating, and Fishbein faked devotion with an empty cup. "As I look down amongst the congregation"—the chaplain grinned at the word—"this night, I see many new faces, and I want to welcome you to Friday-night services here at Camp Crowder. I am Major Leo Ben Ezra, your chaplain." Though an American, the chaplain spoke deliberately—syllable by syllable, almost— as though to communicate, above all, with the lip readers in his audience. "I have only a few words to say before we adjourn to the refreshment room, where the kind ladies of the Temple Sinai, St. Louis, Missouri, have a nice setting for you."

Applause and whistling broke out. After another momentary grin, the chaplain raised his hands, palms out, his eyes flicking upward a moment, as if to remind the troops where they were and Who Else might be in attendance. In the sudden silence that followed, I thought I heard Grossbart cackle, "Let the goyim clean the floors!" Were those the words? I wasn't sure, but Fishbein, grinning, nudged Halpern. Halpern looked dumbly at him, then went back to his prayer book, which had been occupying him all through the rabbi's talk. One hand tugged at the black kinky hair that stuck out under his cap. His lips moved.

The rabbi continued. "It is about the food that I want to speak to you for a moment. I know, I know, I know," he intoned, wearily, "how in the mouths of most of you the *trafe* food tastes like ashes. I know how you gag, some of you, and how your parents suffer to think of their children eating foods unclean and offensive to the palate. What can I tell you? I can only say, close your eyes and swallow as best you can. Eat what you must to live, and throw away the rest. I wish I could help more. For those of you who find this impossible, may I ask that you try and try, but then come to see me in private. If your revulsion is so great, we will have to seek aid from those higher up."

A round of chatter rose and subsided. Then everyone sang "Ain Kelohainu"; after all those years, I discovered I still knew the words. Then, suddenly, the service was over, Grossbart was upon me. "Higher up? He means the General?"

"Hey, Shelly," Fishbein said, "he means God." He smacked his face and looked at Halpern. "How high can you go!"

"Sh-h-h!" Grossbart said. "What do you think, Sergeant?"

"I don't know," I said. "You better ask the chaplain."

"I'm going to. I'm making an appointment to see him in private. So is Mickey."

Halpern shook his head. "No, no, Sheldon—"

"You have rights, Mickey," Grossbart said. "They can't push us around."

"It's O.K.," said Halpern. "It bothers my mother, not me."

Grossbart looked at me. "Yesterday he threw up. From the hash. It was all ham and God knows what else."

"I have a cold—that was why," Halpern said. He pushed his yarmulke back into a cap.

"What about you, Fishbein?" I asked. "You kosher, too?"

He flushed. "A little. But I'll let it ride. I have a very strong stomach, and I don't eat a lot anyway." I continued to look at him, and he held up his wrist to reinforce what he'd just said; his watch strap was tightened to the last hole, and he pointed that out to me.

"But services are important to you?" I asked him.

He looked at Grossbart. "Sure, sir."

"'Sergeant.'"

"Not so much at home," said Grossbart, stepping between us, "but away from home it gives one a sense of his Jewishness."

"We have to stick together," Fishbein said.

I started to walk toward the door; Halpern stepped back to make way for me.

"That's what happened in Germany," Grossbart was saying, loud enough for me to hear. "They didn't stick together. They let themselves get pushed around."

I turned. "Look, Grossbart. This is the Army, not summer camp."

He smiled. "So?"

Halpern tried to sneak off, but Grossbart held his arm.

"Grossbart, how old are you?" I asked.

"Nineteen."

"And you?" I said to Fishbein.

"The same. The same month, even."

"And what about him?" I pointed to Halpern, who had by now made it safely to the door.

"Eighteen," Grossbart whispered. "But like he can't tie his shoes or brush his teeth himself. I feel sorry for him."

"I feel sorry for all of us, Grossbart," I said, "but just act like a man. Just don't overdo it."

"Overdo what, sir?"

"The 'sir' business, for one thing. Don't overdo that," I said.

I left him standing there. I passed by Halpern, but he did not look at me. Then I was outside, but, behind, I heard Grossbart call, "Hey, Mickey, my *leben,* come on back. Refreshments!"

*"Leben!"* My grandmother's word for me!

One morning a week later, while I was working at my desk, Captain Barrett shouted for me to come into his office. When I entered, he had his helmet liner squashed down so far on his head that I couldn't even see his eyes. He was on the phone, and when he spoke to me, he cupped one hand over the mouthpiece. "Who the hell is Grossbart?"

"Third platoon, Captain," I said. "A trainee."

"What's all this stink about food? His mother called a goddam congressman about the food." He uncovered the mouthpiece and slid his helmet up until I could see his bottom eyelashes. "Yes, sir," he said into the phone. "Yes, sir. I'm still here, sir. I'm asking Marx, here, right now—"

He covered the mouthpiece again and turned his head back toward me. "Lightfoot Harry's on the phone," he said, between his teeth. "This congressman calls General Lyman, who calls Colonel Sousa, who calls the Major, who calls me. They're just dying to stick this thing on me. Whatsa matter?" He shook the phone at me. "I don't feed the troops? What is this?"

"Sir, Grossbart is strange—" Barrett greeted that with a mockingly indulgent smile. I altered my approach. "Captain, he's a very orthodox Jew, and so he's only allowed to eat certain foods."

"He throws up, the congressman said. Every time he eats something, his mother says, he throws up!"

"He's accustomed to observing the dietary laws, Captain."

"So why's his old lady have to call the White House?"

"Jewish parents, sir—they're apt to be more protective than you expect. I mean, Jews have a very close family life. A boy goes away from home, sometimes the mother is liable to get very upset. Probably the boy mentioned something in a letter, and his mother misinterpreted."

"I'd like to punch him one right in the mouth," the Captain said. "There's a war on, and he wants a silver platter!"

"I don't think the boy's to blame, sir. I'm sure we can straighten it out by just asking him. Jewish parents worry—"

"*All* parents worry, for Christ's sake. But they don't get on their high horse and start pulling strings—"

I interrupted, my voice higher, tighter than before. "The home life, Captain, is very important—but you're right, it may sometimes get out of hand. It's a very wonderful thing, Captain, but because it's so close, this kind of thing . . ."

He didn't listen any longer to my attempt to present both myself and Lightfoot Harry with an explanation for the letter. He turned back to the phone. "Sir?" he said. "Sir—Marx, here, tells me Jews have a tendency to be pushy. He says he thinks we can settle it right here in the company. . . . Yes, sir. . . . I *will* call back, sir, soon as I can." He hung up. "Where are the men, Sergeant?"

"On the range."

With a whack on the top of his helmet, he crushed it down over his eyes again, and charged out of his chair. "We're going for a ride," he said.

The Captain drove, and I sat beside him. It was a hot spring day, and under my newly starched fatigues I felt as though my armpits were melting down onto my sides and chest. The roads were dry, and by the time we reached the firing range, my teeth felt gritty with dust, though my mouth had been shut the whole trip. The Captain slammed the brakes on and told me to get the hell out and find Grossbart.

I found him on his belly, firing wildly at the five-hundred-feet target. Waiting their turns behind him were Halpern and Fishbein. Fishbein, wearing a pair of steel-rimmed G.I. glasses I hadn't seen on him before, had the appearance of an old peddler who would gladly have sold you his rifle and the cartridges that were slung all over him. I stood back by the ammo boxes, waiting for Grossbart to finish spraying the distant targets. Fishbein straggled back to stand near me.

"Hello, Sergeant Marx," he said.

"How are you?" I mumbled.

"Fine, thank you. Sheldon's really a good shot."

"I didn't notice."

"I'm not so good, but I think I'm getting the hang of it now. Sergeant, I don't mean to, you know, ask what I shouldn't—" The boy stopped. He was trying to speak intimately, but the noise of the shooting forced him to shout at me.

"What is it?" I asked. Down the range, I saw Captain Barrett standing up in the jeep, scanning the line for me and Grossbart.

"My parents keep asking and asking where we're going," Fishbein said. "Everybody says the Pacific. I don't care, but my parents— If I could relieve their minds, I think I could concentrate more on my shooting."

"I don't know where, Fishbein. Try to concentrate anyway."

"Sheldon says you might be able to find out."

"I don't know a thing, Fishbein. You just take it easy, and don't let Sheldon—"

"*I'm* taking it easy, Sergeant. It's at home—"

Grossbart had finished on the line, and was dusting his fatigues with one hand. I called to him. "Grossbart, the Captain wants to see you."

He came toward us. His eyes blazed and twinkled. "Hi!"

"Don't point that rifle!" I said.

"I wouldn't shoot you, Sarge." He gave me a smile as wide as a pumpkin, and turned the barrel aside.

"Damn you, Grossbart, this is no joke! Follow me."

I walked ahead of him, and had the awful suspicion that, behind me, Grossbart was *marching,* his rifle on his shoulder, as though he were a one-man detachment. At the jeep, he gave the Captain a rifle salute. "Private Sheldon Grossbart, sir."

"At ease, Grossman." The Captain sat down, slid over into the empty seat, and, crooking a finger, invited Grossbart closer.

"Bart, sir. Sheldon Gross*bart.* It's a common error." Grossbart nodded at me; *I* understood, he indicated. I looked away just as the mess truck pulled up to the range, disgorging a half-dozen K.P.s with rolled-up sleeves. The mess sergeant screamed at them while they set up the chow-line equipment.

"Grossbart, your mama wrote some congressman that we don't feed you right. Do you know that?" the Captain said.

"It was my father, sir. He wrote to Representative Franconi that my religion forbids me to eat certain foods."

"What religion is that, Grossbart?"

"Jewish."

"'Jewish, *sir,*'" I said to Grossbart.

"Excuse me, sir. Jewish, sir."

"What have you been living on?" the Captain asked. "You've been in the Army a month already. You don't look to me like you're falling to pieces."

"I eat because I have to, sir. But Sergeant Marx will testify to the fact that I don't eat one mouthful more than I need to in order to survive."

"Is that so, Marx?" Barrett asked.

"I've never seen Grossbart eat, sir," I said.

"But you heard the rabbi," Grossbart said. "He told us what to do, and I listened."

The Captain looked at me. "Well, Marx?"

"I still don't know what he eats and doesn't eat, sir."

Grossbart raised his arms to plead with me, and it looked for a moment as though he were going to hand me his weapon to hold. "But, Sergeant—"

"Look, Grossbart, just answer the Captain's questions," I said sharply.

Barrett smiled at me, and I resented it. "All right, Grossbart," he said. "What is it you want? The little piece of paper? You want out?"

"No, sir. Only to be allowed to live as a Jew. And for the others, too."

"What others?"

"Fishbein, sir, and Halpern."

"They don't like the way we serve, either?"

"Halpern throws up, sir. I've seen it."

"I thought *you* throw up."

"Just once, sir. I didn't know the sausage was sausage."

"We'll give menus, Grossbart. We'll show training films about the food, so you can identify when we're trying to poison you."

Grossbart did not answer. The men had been organized into two long chow lines. At the tail end of one, I spotted Fishbein—or, rather, his glasses spotted me. They winked sunlight back at me. Halpern stood next to him, patting the inside of his collar with a khaki handkerchief. They moved with the line as it began to edge up toward the food. The mess sergeant was still screaming at the K.P.s. For a moment, I was actually terrified by the thought that somehow the mess sergeant was going to become involved in Grossbart's problem.

"Marx," the Captain said, "you're a Jewish fella—am I right?"

I played straight man. "Yes, sir."

"How long you been in the Army? Tell this boy."

"Three years and two months."

"A year in combat, Grossbart. Twelve goddam months in combat all through Europe. I admire this man." The Captain snapped a wrist against my chest. "Do you hear him peeping about the food? Do you? I want an answer, Grossbart. Yes or no."

"No, sir."

"And why not? He's a Jewish fella."

"Some things are more important to some Jews than other things to other Jews."

Barrett blew up. "Look, Grossbart. Marx, here, is a good man—a goddam hero. When you were in high school, Sergeant Marx was killing Germans. Who does more for the Jews—you, by throwing up over a lousy piece of sausage, a piece of first-cut meat, or Marx, by killing those Nazi bastards? If I was a Jew, Grossbart, I'd kiss this man's feet. He's a goddam hero, and *he* eats what we give him. Why do you have to cause trouble is what I want to know! What is it you're buckin' for—a discharge?"

"No, sir."

"I'm talking to a wall! Sergeant, get him out of my way." Barrett swung himself back into the driver's seat. "I'm going to see the chaplain." The engine roared, the jeep spun around in a whirl of dust, and the Captain was headed back to camp.

For a moment, Grossbart and I stood side by side, watching the jeep. Then he looked at me and said, "I don't want to start trouble. That's the first thing they toss up to us."

When he spoke, I saw that his teeth were white and straight, and the sight of them suddenly made me understand that Grossbart actually did have parents—that once upon a time someone had taken little Sheldon to the dentist. He was their son. Despite all the talk about his parents, it was hard to believe in Grossbart as a child, an heir—as related by blood to anyone, mother, father, or, above all, to me. This realization led me to another.

"What does your father do, Grossbart?" I asked as we started to walk back toward the chow line.

"He's a tailor."

"An American?"

"Now, yes. A son in the Army," he said, jokingly.

"And your mother?" I asked.

He winked. "A *ballabusta*. She practically sleeps with a dustcloth in her hand."

"She's also an immigrant?"

"All she talks is Yiddish, still."

"And your father, too?"

"A little English. 'Clean,' 'Press,' 'Take the pants in.' That's the extent of it. But they're good to me."

"Then, Grossbart—" I reached out and stopped him. He turned toward me, and when our eyes met, his seemed to jump back, to shiver in their sockets. "Grossbart—you were the one who wrote that letter, weren't you?"

It took only a second or two for his eyes to flash happy again. "Yes." He walked on, and I kept pace. "It's what my father *would* have written if he had known how. It was his name, though. *He* signed it. He even mailed it. I sent it home. For the New York postmark."

I was astonished, and he saw it. With complete seriousness, he thrust his right arm in front of me. "Blood is blood, Sergeant," he said, pinching the blue vein in his wrist.

"What the hell *are* you trying to do, Grossbart?" I asked. "I've seen you eat. Do you know that? I told the Captain I don't know what you eat, but I've seen you eat like a hound at chow."

"We work hard, Sergeant. We're in training. For a furnace to work, you've got to feed it coal."

"Why did you say in the letter that you threw up all the time?"

"I was really talking about Mickey there. I was talking *for* him. He would never write, Sergeant, though I pleaded with him. He'll waste away to nothing if I don't help. Sergeant, I used my name—my father's name—but it's Mickey, and Fishbein, too, I'm watching out for."

"You're a regular Messiah, aren't you?"

We were at the chow line now.

"That's a good one, Sergeant," he said, smiling. "But who knows? Who can tell? Maybe you're the Messiah—a little bit. What Mickey says is the Messiah is a collective idea. He went to Yeshiva, Mickey, for a while. He says *together* we're the Messiah. Me a little bit, you a little bit. You should hear that kid talk, Sergeant, when he gets going."

"Me a little bit, you a little bit," I said. "You'd like to believe that, wouldn't you, Grossbart? That would make everything so clean for you."

"It doesn't seem too bad a thing to believe, Sergeant. It only means we should all *give* a little, is all."

I walked off to eat my rations with the other noncoms.

Two days later, a letter addressed to Captain Barrett passed over my desk. It had come through the chain of command—from the office of Congressman Franconi, where it had been received, to General Lyman, to Colonel Sousa, to Major Lamont, now to Captain Barrett. I read it over twice. It was dated May 14, the day Barrett had spoken with Grossbart on the rifle range.

> Dear Congressman:
>
> First let me thank you for your interest in behalf of my son, Private Sheldon Grossbart. Fortunately, I was able to speak with Sheldon on the phone the other night, and I think I've been able to solve our problem. He is, as I mentioned in my last letter, a very religious boy, and it was only with the greatest difficulty that I could persuade him that the religious thing to do—what God Himself would want Sheldon to do—would be to suffer the pangs of religious remorse for the good of his country and all mankind. It took some doing, Congressman, but finally he saw the light. In fact, what he said (and I wrote down the words on a scratch pad so as never to forget), what he said was "I guess you're right, Dad. So many millions of my fellow-Jews gave up their lives to the enemy, the least I can do is live for a while minus a bit of my heritage so as to help end this struggle and regain for all the children of God dignity and humanity." That, Congressman, would make any father proud.
>
> By the way, Sheldon wanted me to know—and to pass on to you—the name of a soldier who helped him reach this decision: SERGEANT NATHAN MARX. Sergeant Marx is a combat veteran who is Sheldon's first sergeant. This man has helped Sheldon over some of the first hurdles he's had to face in the Army, and is in part responsible for Sheldon's changing his mind about the dietary laws. I know Sheldon would appreciate any recognition Marx could receive.
>
> Thank you and good luck. I look forward to seeing your name on the next election ballot.
>
> Respectfully,
> Samuel E. Grossbart

Attached to Grossbart's communiqué was another, addressed to General Marshall Lyman, the post commander, and signed by Representative Charles E. Franconi, of the House of Representatives. The communiqué informed General Lyman that Sergeant Nathan Marx was a credit to the U.S. Army and the Jewish people.

What was Grossbart's motive in recanting? Did he feel he'd gone too far? Was the letter a strategic retreat—a crafty attempt to strengthen what he considered our alliance? Or had he actually changed his mind, via an imaginary dialogue between Grossbart *père* and Grossbart *fils?* I was puzzled, but only for a few days—that is, only until I realized that, whatever his reasons, he had actually decided to disappear from my life; he was going to allow himself to become just another trainee. I saw him at inspection, but he never winked; at chow formations, but he never flashed me a sign. On Sundays, with the other trainees, he would sit around watching the noncoms' softball team, for which I pitched, but not once did he speak an unnecessary word to me. Fishbein and Halpern retreated, too—at Grossbart's command, I was sure. Apparently he had seen that wisdom lay in turning back before he plunged over into the ugliness of privilege undeserved. Our separation allowed me to forgive him our past encounters, and, finally, to admire him for his good sense.

Meanwhile, free of Grossbart, I grew used to my job and my administrative tasks. I stepped on a scale one day, and discovered I had truly become a noncombatant; I had gained seven pounds. I found patience to get past the first three pages of a book. I thought about the future more and more, and wrote letters to girls I'd known before the war. I even got a few answers. I sent away to Columbia for a Law School catalogue. I continued to follow the war in the Pacific, but it was not my war. I thought I could see the end, and sometimes, at night, I dreamed that I was walking on the streets of Manhattan—Broadway, Third Avenue, 116th Street, where I had lived the three years I attended Columbia. I curled myself around these dreams and I began to be happy.

And then, one Sunday, when everybody was away and I was alone in the orderly room reading a month-old copy of the *Sporting News,* Grossbart reappeared.

"You a baseball fan, Sergeant?"

I looked up. "How are you?"

"Fine," Grossbart said. "They're making a soldier out of me."

"How are Fishbein and Halpern?"

"Coming along," he said. "We've got no training this afternoon. They're at the movies."

"How come you're not with them?"

"I wanted to come over and say hello."

He smiled—a shy, regular-guy smile, as though he and I well knew that our friendship drew its sustenance from unexpected visits, remembered birthdays, and borrowed lawnmowers. At first it offended me, and then the feeling was swallowed by the general uneasiness I felt at the thought that everyone on the post was locked away in a dark movie theater and I was here alone with Grossbart. I folded up my paper.

"Sergeant," he said, "I'd like to ask a favor. It is a favor, and I'm making no bones about it."

He stopped, allowing me to refuse him a hearing—which, of course, forced me into a courtesy I did not intend. "Go ahead."

"Well, actually it's two favors."

I said nothing.

"The first one's about these rumors. Everybody says we're going to the Pacific."

"As I told your friend Fishbein, I don't know," I said. "You'll just have to wait to find out. Like everybody else."

"You think there's a chance of any of us going East?"

"Germany?" I said. "Maybe."

"I meant New York."

"I don't think so, Grossbart. Offhand."

"Thanks for the information, Sergeant," he said.

"It's not information, Grossbart. Just what I surmise."

"It certainly would be good to be near home. My parents—you know." He took a step toward the door and then turned back. "Oh, the other thing. May I ask the other?"

"What is it?"

"The other thing is—I've got relatives in St. Louis, and they say they'll give me a whole Passover dinner if I can get down there. God, Sergeant, that'd mean an awful lot to me."

I stood up. "No passes during basic, Grossbart."

"But we're off from now till Monday morning, Sergeant. I could leave the post and no one would even know."

"I'd know. You'd know."

"But that's all. Just the two of us. Last night, I called my aunt, and you should have heard her. 'Come—come,' she said. 'I got gefilte fish, *chrain*—the works!' Just a day, Sergeant. I'd take the blame if anything happened."

"The Captain isn't here to sign a pass."

"You could sign."

"Look, Grossbart—"

"Sergeant, for two months, practically, I've been eating *trafe* till I want to die."

"I thought you'd made up your mind to live with it. To be minus a little bit of heritage."

He pointed a finger at me. "You!" he said. "That wasn't for you to read."

"I read it. So what?"

"That letter was addressed to a congressman."

"Grossbart, don't feed me any baloney. You *wanted* me to read it."

"Why are you persecuting me, Sergeant?"

"Are you kidding!"

"I've run into this before," he said, "but never from my own!"

"Get out of here, Grossbart! Get the hell out of my sight!"

He did not move. "Ashamed, that's what you are," he said. "So you take it out on the rest of us. They say Hitler himself was half a Jew. Hearing you, I wouldn't doubt it."

"What are you trying to do with me, Grossbart?" I asked him. "What are you after? You want me to give you special privileges, to change the food, to find out about your orders, to give you weekend passes."

"You even talk like a goy!" Grossbart shook his fist. "Is this just a weekend pass I'm asking for? Is a Seder sacred or not?"

Seder! It suddenly occurred to me that Passover had been celebrated weeks before. I said so.

"That's right," he replied. "Who says no? A month ago—and I was in the field eating hash! And now all I ask is a simple favor. A Jewish boy I thought would understand. My aunt's willing to go out of her way—to make a Seder a month later. . . ." He turned to go, mumbling.

"Come back here!" I called. He stopped and looked at me. "Grossbart, why can't you be like the rest? Why do you have to stick out like a sore thumb?"

"Because I'm a Jew, Sergeant. I *am* different. Better, maybe not. But different."

"This is a war, Grossbart. For the time being *be* the same."

"I refuse."

"What?"

"I refuse. I can't stop being me, that's all there is to it." Tears came to his eyes. "It's a hard thing to be a Jew. But now I understand what Mickey says—it's a harder thing to stay one." He raised a hand sadly toward me. "Look at *you*."

"Stop crying!"

"Stop this, stop that, stop the other thing! *You* stop, Sergeant. Stop closing your heart to your own!" And, wiping his face with his sleeve, he ran out the door. "The least we can do for one another—the least . . ."

An hour later, looking out of the window, I saw Grossbart headed across the field. He wore a pair of starched khakis and carried a little leather ditty bag. I went out into the heat of the day. It was quiet; not a soul was in sight except, over by the mess hall, four K.P.s sitting around a pan, sloped forward from their waists, gabbing and peeling potatoes in the sun.

"Grossbart!" I called.

He looked toward me and continued walking.

"Grossbart, get over here!"

He turned and came across the field. Finally, he stood before me.

"Where are you going?" I asked.

"St. Louis. I don't care."

"You'll get caught without a pass."

"So I'll get caught without a pass."

"You'll go to the stockade."

"I'm *in* the stockade." He made an about-face and headed off.

I let him go only a step or two. "Come back here," I said, and he followed me into the office, where I typed out a pass and signed the Captain's name, and my own initials after it.

He took the pass and then, a moment later, reached out and grabbed my hand. "Sergeant, you don't know how much this means to me."

"O.K.," I said. "Don't get in any trouble."

"I wish I could show you how much this means to me."

"Don't do me any favors. Don't write any more congressmen for citations."

He smiled. "You're right. I won't. But let me do something."

"Bring me a piece of that gefilte fish. Just get out of here."

"I will!" he said. "With a slice of carrot and a little horseradish. I won't forget."

"All right. Just show your pass at the gate. And don't tell *anybody*."

"I won't. It's a month late, but a good Yom Tov to you."

"Good Yom Tov, Grossbart," I said.

"You're a good Jew, Sergeant. You like to think you have a hard heart, but under- neath you're a fine, decent man. I mean that."

Those last three words touched me more than any words from Grossbart's mouth had the right to. "All right, Grossbart," I said. "Now call me 'sir,' and get the hell out of here."

He ran out the door and was gone. I felt very pleased with myself; it was a great relief to stop fighting Grossbart, and it had cost me nothing. Barrett would never find out, and if he did, I could manage to invent some excuse. For a while, I sat at my desk, comfortable in my decision. Then the screen door flew back and Grossbart burst in again. "Sergeant!" he said. Behind him I saw Fishbein and Halpern, both in starched khakis, both carrying ditty bags like Grossbart's.

"Sergeant, I caught Mickey and Larry coming out of the movies. I almost missed them."

"Grossbart—did I say tell no one?" I said.

"But my aunt said I could bring friends. That I should, in fact."

"*I'm* the Sergeant, Grossbart—not your aunt!"

Grossbart looked at me in disbelief. He pulled Halpern up by his sleeve. "Mickey, tell the Sergeant what this would mean to you."

Halpern looked at me and, shrugging, said, "A lot."

Fishbein stepped forward without prompting. "This would mean a great deal to me and my parents, Sergeant Marx."

"No!" I shouted.

Grossbart was shaking his head. "Sergeant, I could see you denying me, but how you can deny Mickey, a Yeshiva boy—that's beyond me."

"I'm not denying Mickey anything," I said. "You just pushed a little too hard, Grossbart. *You* denied him."

"I'll give him my pass, then," Grossbart said. "I'll give him my aunt's address and a little note. At least let him go."

In a second, he had crammed the pass into Halpern's pants pocket. Halpern looked at me, and so did Fishbein. Grossbart was at the door, pushing it open. "Mickey, bring me a piece of gefilte fish, at least," he said, and then he was outside again.

The three of us looked at one another, and then I said, "Halpern, hand that pass over."

He took it from his pocket and gave it to me. Fishbein had now moved to the doorway, where he lingered. He stood there for a moment with his mouth slightly open, and then he pointed to himself. "And me?" he asked.

His utter ridiculousness exhausted me. I slumped down in my seat and felt pulses knocking at the back of my eyes. "Fishbein," I said, "you understand I'm not trying to deny you anything, don't you? If it was my Army, I'd serve gefilte fish in the mess hall. I'd sell *kugel* in the PX, honest to God."

Halpern smiled.

"You understand, don't you, Halpern?"

"Yes, Sergeant."

"And you, Fishbein? I don't want enemies. I'm just like you—I want to serve my time and go home. I miss the same things you miss."

"Then, Sergeant," Fishbein said, "why don't you come, too?"

"Where?"

"To St. Louis. To Shelly's aunt. We'll have a regular Seder. Play hide-the-matzoh." He gave me a broad, black-toothed smile.

I saw Grossbart again, on the other side of the screen.

"Pst!" He waved a piece of paper. "Mickey, here's the address. Tell her I couldn't get away."

Halpern did not move. He looked at me, and I saw the shrug moving up his arms into his shoulders again. I took the cover off my typewriter and made out passes for him and Fishbein. "Go," I said. "The three of you."

I thought Halpern was going to kiss my hand.

That afternoon, in a bar in Joplin, I drank beer and listened with half an ear to the Cardinal game. I tried to look squarely at what I'd become involved in, and began to wonder if perhaps the struggle with Grossbart wasn't as much my fault as his. What was I that I had to *muster* generous feelings? Who was I to have been feeling so grudging, so tight-hearted? After all, I wasn't being asked to move the world. Had I a right, then, or a reason, to clamp down on Grossbart, when that meant clamping down on Halpern, too? And Fishbein—that ugly, agreeable soul? Out of many recollections of my childhood that had tumbled over me these past few days I heard my grandmother's voice: "What are you making a *tsimmes?*" It was what she would ask my mother when, say, I had cut myself while doing something I shouldn't have done, and her daughter was busy bawling me out. I needed a hug and a kiss, and my mother would moralize. But my grandmother knew—mercy overrides justice. I should have known it, too. Who was Nathan Marx to be such a penny pincher with kindness? Surely, I thought, the Messiah himself—if He should ever come—won't niggle over nickels and dimes. God willing, he'll hug and kiss.

The next day, while I was playing softball over on the parade ground, I decided to ask Bob Wright, who was noncom in charge of Classification and Assignment, where he thought our trainees would be sent when their cycle ended, in two weeks. I asked casually, between innings, and he said, "They're pushing them all into the Pacific. Shulman cut the orders on your boys the other day."

The news shocked me, as though I were the father of Halpern, Fishbein, and Grossbart.

. . .

That night, I was just sliding into sleep when someone tapped on my door. "Who is it?" I asked.

"Sheldon."

He opened the door and came in. For a moment, I felt his presence without being able to see him. "How was it?" I asked.

He popped into sight in the near-darkness before me. "Great, Sergeant." Then he was sitting on the edge of the bed. I sat up.

"How about you?" he asked. "Have a nice weekend?"

"Yes."

"The others went to sleep." He took a deep, paternal breath. We sat silent for a while, and a homey feeling invaded my ugly little cubicle; the door was locked, the cat was out, the children were safely in bed.

"Sergeant, can I tell you something? Personal?"

I did not answer, and he seemed to know why. "Not about me. About Mickey. Sergeant, I never felt for anybody like I feel for him. Last night I heard Mickey in the bed next to me. He was crying so, it could have broken your heart. Real sobs."

"I'm sorry to hear that."

"I had to talk to him to stop him. He held my hand, Sergeant—he wouldn't let it go. He was almost hysterical. He kept saying if he only knew where we were going. Even if he knew it *was* the Pacific, that would be better than nothing. Just to know."

Long ago, someone had taught Grossbart the sad rule that only lies can get the truth. Not that I couldn't believe in the fact of Halpern's crying; his eyes *always* seemed red-rimmed. But, fact or not, it became a lie when Grossbart uttered it. He was entirely strategic. But then—it came with the force of indictment—so was I! There are strategies of aggression, but there are strategies of retreat as well. And so, recognizing that I myself had not been without craft and guile, I told him what I knew. "It is the Pacific."

He let out a small gasp, which was not a lie. "I'll tell him. I wish it was otherwise."

"So do I."

He jumped on my words. "You mean you think you could do something? A change, maybe?"

"No, I couldn't do a thing."

"Don't you know anybody over at C. and A.?"

"Grossbart, there's nothing I can do," I said. "If your orders are for the Pacific, then it's the Pacific."

"But Mickey—"

"Mickey, you, me—everybody, Grossbart. There's nothing to be done. Maybe the war'll end before you go. Pray for a miracle."

"But—"

"Good night, Grossbart." I settled back, and was relieved to feel the springs unbend as Grossbart rose to leave. I could see him clearly now; his jaw had dropped, and he looked like a dazed prizefighter. I noticed for the first time a little paper bag in his hand.

"Grossbart." I smiled. "My gift?"

"Oh, yes, Sergeant. Here—from all of us." He handed me the bag. "It's egg roll."

"Egg roll?" I accepted the bag and felt a damp grease spot on the bottom. I opened it, sure that Grossbart was joking.

"We thought you'd probably like it. You know—Chinese egg roll. We thought you'd probably have a taste for—"

"Your aunt served egg roll?"

"She wasn't home."

"Grossbart, she invited you. You told me she invited you and your friends."

"I know," he said. "I just reread the letter. *Next* week."

I got out of bed and walked to the window. "Grossbart," I said. But I was not calling to him.

"What?"

"What are you, Grossbart? Honest to God, what are you?"

I think it was the first time I'd asked him a question for which he didn't have an immediate answer.

"How can you do this to people?" I went on.

"Sergeant, the day away did us all a world of good. Fishbein, you should see him, he *loves* Chinese food."

"But the Seder," I said.

"We took second best, Sergeant."

Rage came charging at me. I didn't sidestep. "Grossbart, you're a liar!" I said. "You're a schemer and a crook. You've got no respect for anything. Nothing at all. Not for me, for the truth—not even for poor Halpern! You use us all—"

"Sergeant, Sergeant, I feel for Mickey. Honest to God, I do. I *love* Mickey. I try—"

"You try! You feel!" I lurched toward him and grabbed his shirt front. I shook him furiously. "Grossbart, get out! Get out and stay the hell away from me. Because if I see you, I'll make your life miserable. *You understand that?*"

"Yes."

I let him free, and when he walked from the room, I wanted to spit on the floor where he had stood. I couldn't stop the fury. It engulfed me, owned me, till it seemed I could only rid myself of it with tears or an act of violence. I snatched from the bed the bag Grossbart had given me and, with all my strength, threw it out the window. And the next morning, as the men policed the area around the barracks, I heard a great cry go up from one of the trainees, who had been anticipating only his morning handful of cigarette butts and candy wrappers. "Egg roll!" he shouted. "Holy Christ, Chinese goddam egg roll!"

A week later, when I read the orders that had come down from C. and A., I couldn't believe my eyes. Every single trainee was to be shipped to Camp Stoneman, California, and from there to the Pacific—every trainee but one. Private Sheldon Grossbart. He was to be sent to Fort Monmouth, New Jersey. I read the mimeographed sheet several times. Dee, Farrell, Fishbein, Fuselli, Fylypowycz, Glinicki, Gromke, Gucwa, Halpern, Hardy, Helebrandt, right down to Anton Zygadlo—all were to be headed West before the month was out. All except Grossbart. He had pulled a string, and I wasn't it.

I lifted the phone and called C. and A.

The voice on the other end said smartly, "Corporal Shulman, sir."

"Let me speak to Sergeant Wright."

"Who is this calling, sir?"

"Sergeant Marx."

And, to my surprise, the voice said, *"Oh!"* Then, "Just a minute, Sergeant."

Shulman's *"Oh!"* stayed with me while I waited for Wright to come to the phone. Why *"Oh!"*? Who was Shulman? And then, so simply, I knew I'd discovered the string that Grossbart had pulled. In fact, I could hear Grossbart the day he'd discovered Shulman in the PX, or in the bowling alley, or maybe even at services. "Glad to meet you. Where you from? Bronx? Me, too. Do you know So-and-So? And So-and-So? Me, too! You work at C. and A.? Really? Hey, how's the chances of getting East? Could you do something? Change something? Swindle, cheat, lie? We gotta help each other, you know. If the Jews in Germany . . ."

Bob Wright answered the phone. "How are you, Nate? How's the pitching arm?"

"Good. Bob, I wonder if you could do me a favor." I heard clearly my own words, and they so reminded me of Grossbart that I dropped more easily than I could have imagined into what I had planned. "This may sound crazy, Bob, but I got a kid here on orders to Monmouth who wants them changed. He had a brother killed in Europe, and he's hot to go to the Pacific. Says he'd feel like a coward if he wound up Stateside. I don't know, Bob—can anything be done? Put somebody else in the Monmouth slot?"

"Who?" he asked cagily.

"Anybody. First guy in the alphabet. I don't care. The kid just asked if something could be done."

"What's his name?"

"Grossbart, Sheldon."

Wright didn't answer.

"Yeah," I said. "He's a Jewish kid, so he thought I could help him out. You know."

"I guess I can do something," he finally said. "The Major hasn't been around here for weeks. Temporary duty to the golf course. I'll try, Nate, that's all I can say."

"I'd appreciate it, Bob. See you Sunday." And I hung up, perspiring.

The following day, the corrected orders appeared: Fishbein, Fuselli, Fylypowycz, Glinicki, Gromke, Grossbart, Gucwa, Halpern, Hardy . . . Lucky Private Harley Alton was to go to Fort Monmouth, New Jersey, where, for some reason or other, they wanted an enlisted man with infantry training.

After chow that night, I stopped back at the orderly room to straighten out the guard-duty roster. Grossbart was waiting for me. He spoke first.

"You son of a bitch!"

I sat down at my desk, and while he glared at me, I began to make the necessary alterations in the duty roster.

"What do you have against me?" he cried. "Against my family? Would it kill you for me to be near my father, God knows how many months he has left to him?"

"Why so?"

"His heart," Grossbart said. "He hasn't had enough troubles in a lifetime, you've got to add to them. I curse the day I ever met you, Marx! Shulman told me what happened over there. There's no limit to your anti-Semitism, is there? The damage you've done here isn't enough. You have to make a special phone call! You really want me dead!"

I made the last few notations in the duty roster and got up to leave. "Good night, Grossbart."

"You owe me an explanation!" He stood in my path.

"Sheldon, you're the one who owes explanations."

He scowled. "To *you?*"

"To me, I think so—yes. Mostly to Fishbein and Halpern."

"That's right, twist things around. I owe nobody nothing, I've done all I could do for them. Now I think I've got the right to watch out for myself."

"For each other we have to learn to watch out, Sheldon. You told me yourself."

"You call this watching out for me—what you did?"

"No. For all of us."

I pushed him aside and started for the door. I heard his furious breathing behind me, and it sounded like steam rushing from an engine of terrible strength.

"*You'll* be all right," I said from the door. And, I thought, so would Fishbein and Halpern be all right, even in the Pacific, if only Grossbart continued to see—in the obsequiousness of the one, the soft spirituality of the other—some profit for himself.

I stood outside the orderly room, and I heard Grossbart weeping behind me. Over in the barracks, in the lighted windows, I could see the boys in their T shirts sitting on their bunks talking about their orders, as they'd been doing for the past two days. With a kind of quiet nervousness, they polished shoes, shined belt buckles, squared away underwear, trying as best they could to accept their fate. Behind me, Grossbart swallowed hard, accepting his. And then, resisting with all my will an impulse to turn and seek pardon for my vindictiveness, I accepted my own.

# Akhil Sharma

## (B. 1971)

Akhil Sharma was born in Delhi, India, but moved to Edison, New Jersey, when he was eight years old. He received his B.A. in public policy from Princeton and spent a year at Stanford after receiving a Stegner Fellowship in creative writing. His book, *An Obedient Father* (2000), focuses on Ram Karan, a corrupt civil servant who is overweight and self-loathing. Sharma's short stories have appeared in the *Best American Short Stories* anthology, the *O. Henry Award Winners* anthology, the *Atlantic Monthly,* and the *New Yorker.* He also won the Voice Literary Supplement's award for "Writers on the Verge" in 2000. He currently lives in New York City, where he is an investment banker at a major Wall Street firm. Sharma's stories tackle issues of cultural assimilation, the tension between men and women in both traditional and contemporary societies, and the basic human struggle for self-definition and fulfillment.

## *If You Sing Like That for Me*

1995

Late one June afternoon, seven months after my wedding, I woke from a short, deep sleep in love with my husband. I did not know then, lying in bed and looking out the window at the line of gray clouds, that my love would last only a few hours and that I would never again care for Rajinder with the same urgency—never again in the five homes we would share and through the two daughters and one son we would also share, though unevenly and with great bitterness. I did not know this then, suddenly awake and only twenty-six, with a husband not much older, nor did I know that the memory of the coming hours would periodically overwhelm me throughout my life.

We were living in a small flat on the roof of a three-story house in Defense Colony, in New Delhi. Rajinder had signed the lease a week before our wedding. Two days after we married, he took me to the flat. I had thought I would be frightened entering my new home for the first time, but I was not. I felt very still that morning, watching Rajinder in his gray sweater bend over and open the padlock. Although it was cold, I wore only a pink silk sari and blouse, because I knew that my thick eyebrows, broad nose, and thin lips made me homely, and to win his love I must try especially hard to be appealing, even though I did not want to be.

The sun filled the living room through a window that took up half a wall and looked out onto the concrete roof. Rajinder went in first, holding the heavy brass padlock in his right hand. In the center of the room was a low plywood table with a thistle broom on top, and in a corner three plastic folding chairs lay collapsed on the floor. I followed a few steps behind Rajinder. The room was a white rectangle. Looking at it, I felt nothing. I saw the table and broom, the window grille with its drooping iron flowers, the dust in which we left our footprints, and I thought I should be feeling something—some anxiety, or fear, or curiosity. Perhaps even joy.

"We can put the TV there," Rajinder said softly, standing before the window and pointing to the right corner of the living room. He was slightly overweight and wore sweaters that were a bit large for him. They made him appear humble, a small man aware of his smallness. The thick black frames of his glasses, his old-fashioned moustache, as thin as a scratch, and the fading hairline created an impression of thoughtfulness. "The sofa before the window." At that moment, and often that day, I would think of myself with his smallness forever, bearing his children, going where he went, having to open always to his touch, and whatever I was looking at would begin to waver, and I would want to run. Run down the curving dark stairs, fast, fast, through the colony's narrow streets, with my sandals loud and alone, until I got to the bus stand and the 52 came, and then at the ice factory I would change to the 10, and finally I would climb the wooden steps to my parents' flat and the door would be open and no one would have noticed that I had gone with some small man.

I followed Rajinder into the bedroom, and the terror was gone, an open door now shut, and again I felt nothing, as if I were marble inside. The two rooms were exactly alike, except the bedroom was empty. "And there, the bed," Rajinder said, placing it with a slight wave of his hand against the wall across from the window. He spoke slowly and firmly, as if he were describing what was already there. "The fridge we can put right there," at the foot of the bed. Both were part of my dowry. Whenever he looked at me, I either said yes or nodded my head in agreement. We went outside and he showed me the kitchen and the bathroom, which were connected to the flat but could be entered only through doors opening onto the roof.

From the roof, a little after eleven, I watched Rajinder drive away on his scooter. He was going to my parents' flat in the Old Vegetable Market, where my dowry and our wedding gifts were stored. I had nothing to do while he was gone, so I wandered in and out of the flat and around the roof. Defense Colony was composed of rows of pale two- or three-story buildings. A small park, edged with eucalyptus trees, was behind our house.

Rajinder returned two hours later with his elder brother, Ashok, and a yellow van. It took three trips to bring the TV, the sofa, the fridge, the mixer, the steel plates, and my clothes. Each time they left, I wanted them never to return. Whenever they pulled up outside, Ashok pressed the horn, which played "Jingle Bells." I was frightened by Ashok, because, with his handlebar moustache and muscular forearms, he reminded me of my father's brothers, who, my mother claimed, beat their wives. Listening to his curses drift out of the stairwell each time he bumped against a wall while maneuvering the sofa, TV, and fridge up the stairs, I felt ashamed, as if he were cursing the dowry and, through it, me.

On the first trip they brought back two suitcases that my mother had packed with my clothes. I was cold, and when they left, I changed in the bedroom. My hands were trembling by then, and each time I swallowed, I felt a sharp pain in my throat that made my eyes water. Standing there in the room gray with dust, the light like cold, clear water, I felt sad and lonely and excited at being naked in an empty room in a place where no one knew me. I put on a sylvar kamij, but even completely covered by the big shirt and pants, I was cold. I added a sweater and socks, but the cold had slipped under my skin and lingered beneath my fingernails.

Rajinder did not appear to notice I had changed. I swept the rooms while the men were gone, and stacked the kitchen shelves with the steel plates, saucers, and spoons that had come as gifts. Rajinder and Ashok brought all the gifts except the bed, which was too big for them. It was raised to the roof by pulleys the next day. They were able to bring up the mattress, though, and the sight of it made me happy, for I knew I would fall asleep easily and that another eight hours would pass.

We did not eat lunch, but in the evening I made rotis and lentils on a kerosene stove. The kitchen had no lightbulb, and I had only the stove's blue flame to see by.

The icy wind swirled around my feet. Nearly thirty years later I can still remember that wind. I could eat only one roti, while Rajinder and Ashok had six each. We sat in the living room, and they spoke loudly of their family's farm, gasoline prices, politics in Haryana, and Indira Gandhi's government. I spoke once, saying that I liked Indira Gandhi, and Ashok said that was because I was a Delhi woman who wanted to see women in power. My throat hurt and I felt as if I were breathing steam.

Ashok left after dinner, and Rajinder and I were truly alone for the first time since our marriage. Our voices were so respectful, we might have been in mourning. He took me silently in the bedroom, on the mattress beneath the window with the full moon peering in. When it was over and Rajinder was sleeping, I lifted myself on an elbow to look at him. I felt somehow that I could look at him more easily while he was asleep. I would not be nervous, trying to hide my scrutiny, and if the panic came, I could just hold on until it passed. I thought that if I could see him properly just once, I would no longer be frightened; I would know what kind of man he was and what the future held. But the narrow mouth and the stiff, straight way he slept, with his arms folded across his chest, said one thing, and the long, dark eyelashes denied it. I stared at him until he started flickering, and then I closed my eyes.

Three months earlier, when our parents introduced us, I did not think we would marry. The neutrality of Rajinder's features, across the restaurant table from me, reassured me that we would not meet after that dinner. It was not that I expected to marry someone particularly handsome. I was neither pretty nor talented, and my family was not rich. But I could not imagine spending my life with someone so anonymous. If asked, I would have been unable to tell what kind of man I wanted to marry, whether he should be handsome and funny. I was not even certain I wanted to marry, though at times I thought marriage would make me less lonely. What I wanted was to be with someone who could make me different, someone other than the person I was.

Rajinder did not appear to be such a man, and although the fact that we were meeting meant that our families approved of each other, I still felt safe. Twice before, my parents had sat on either side of me as I met men found through the matrimonial section of the Sunday *Times of India*. One received a job offer in Bombay, and Ma and Pitaji did not want to send me that far away with someone they could not be sure of. The other, who was very handsome and drove a motorcycle, had lied about his income. I was glad that he had lied, for what could such a handsome man find in me?

Those two introductions were also held in Vikrant, a two-story dosa restaurant across from the Amba cinema. I liked Vikrant, for I thought the place's obvious cheapness would be held against us. The evening that Rajinder and I met, Vikrant was crowded with people waiting for the six-to-nine show. We sat down and an adolescent waiter swept bits of sambhar and dosa from the table onto the floor. Footsteps upstairs caused flecks of blue paint to drift down.

As the dinner began, Rajinder's mother, a small, round woman with a pock-marked face, spoke of her sorrow that Rajinder's father had not lived to see his two sons reach manhood. Ashok, sitting on one side of Rajinder, nodded slowly and solemnly at this. Rajinder gave no indication of what he thought. After a moment of silence Pitaji, obese and bald, tilted slightly forward and said, "It's all in the stars. What can a man do?" The waiter returned with five glasses of water, his fingers dipped to the second joint in the water. Rajinder and I were supposed to speak, but I was nervous, despite my certainty that we would not marry, and could think of nothing to say. We did not open our mouths until we ordered our dosas. Pitaji, worried that we would spend the meal in silence, asked Rajinder, "Other than work, how do you like to spend your time?" Then, to impress Rajinder with his sophistication, he added in English, "What hobbies you have?" The door to the kitchen, a few tables from us, was open, and I saw a cow standing near the skillet.

"I like to read the newspaper. In college I played badminton," Rajinder answered in English. His voice was respectful, and he smoothed each word with his tongue before letting go.

"Anita sometimes reads the newspapers," Ma said, and then became quiet at the absurdity of her words.

The food came and we ate quickly and mostly in silence, though all of us made sure to leave a bit on the plate to show how full we were.

Rajinder's mother talked the most during the meal. She told us that Rajinder had always been favored over his elder brother—a beautiful, hardworking boy who obeyed his mother like God Ram—and how Rajinder had paid her back by being the first in the family to leave the farm in Bursa to attend college, where he got a master's, and by becoming a bank officer. To get to work from Bursa he had to commute two and a half hours every day. This was very strenuous, she said, and Rajinder had long ago reached the age for marriage, so he wished to set up a household in the city. "We want a city girl," his mother said loudly, as if boasting of her modernity. "With an education but a strong respect for tradition."

"Asha, Anita's younger sister, is finishing her Ph.D. in molecular biology and might be going to America in a year, for further studies," Ma said slowly, almost accidentally. She was a short, dark woman, so thin that her skin hung loose. "Two of my brothers are doctors; so is one sister. And I have one brother who is an engineer. I wanted Anita to be a doctor, but she was lazy and did not study." My mother and I loved each other, but sometimes something inside her would slip, and she would attack me, and she was so clever and I loved her so much that all I could do was feel helpless.

Dinner ended and I still had not spoken. When Rajinder said he did not want any dessert, I asked, "Do you like movies?" It was the only question I could think of, and I had felt pressured by Pitaji's stares.

"A little," Rajinder said seriously. After a pause he asked, "And you, do you like movies?"

"Yes," I said, and then, to be daring and to assert my personality, I added, "very much."

Two days after that Pitaji asked me if I would mind marrying Rajinder, and because I could not think of any reason not to, I said all right. Still, I did not think we would marry. Something would come up. His family might decide that my B.A. and B.Ed. were not enough, or Rajinder might suddenly announce that he was in love with his typist.

The engagement occurred a month later, and although I was not allowed to attend the ceremony, Asha was, and she described everything. Rajinder sat cross-legged before the pandit and the holy fire. Pitaji's pants were too tight for him to fold his legs, and he had to keep a foot on either side of the fire. Ashok and his mother were on either side of Rajinder. The small pink room was crowded with Rajinder's aunts and uncles. The uncles, Asha said, were unshaven and smelled faintly of manure. The pandit chanted in Sanskrit and at certain points motioned for Pitaji to tie a red thread around Rajinder's right wrist and to place a packet of one hundred five-rupee bills in his lap.

Only then, as Asha, grinning, described the ceremony, did I realize that I would actually marry Rajinder. I was shocked. I seemed to be standing outside myself, a stranger, looking at two women, Anita and Asha, sitting on a brown sofa in a wide, bright room. We were two women, both of whom would cry if slapped, laugh if tickled. But one was doing her Ph.D. and possibly going to America, and the other, her elder sister, who was slow in school, was now going to marry and have children and grow old. Why will she go to America and I stay here? I wanted to demand of someone, anyone. Why, when Pitaji took us out of school, saying what good was education for girls, did Asha, then only in third grade, go and re-enroll herself, while I waited for Pitaji to change his mind? I felt so sad I could not even hate Asha for her thoughtlessness.

As the days until the wedding evaporated, I had difficulty sleeping, and sometimes everything was lost in a sudden brightness. Often I woke at night and thought the engagement was a dream. Ma and Pitaji mentioned the marriage only in connection with the shopping involved. Once, Asha asked what I was feeling about the marriage, and I said, "What do you care?"

When I placed the necklace of marigolds around Rajinder's neck, to seal our marriage, I brushed my hand against his neck to confirm the reality of his presence. The pandit recited Sanskrit verses, occasionally pouring clarified butter into the holy fire, which we had just circled seven times. It is done, I thought. I am married now. I felt no different. I was wearing a bright-red silk sari and could smell the sourness of new cloth. People were surrounding us, many people. Movie songs blared over the loudspeakers. On the ground was a red-and-black-striped carpet. The tent above us had the same stripes. Rajinder draped a garland around my neck, and everyone began cheering. Their voices smothered the rumble of the night's traffic passing on the road outside the alley.

Although the celebration lasted another six hours, ending at about one in the morning, I did not remember most of it until many years later. I did not remember the two red thrones on which we sat and received the congratulations of women in pretty silk saris and men wearing handsome pants and shirts. I know about the cold only because of the photos showing vapor coming from people's mouths as they spoke. I still do not remember what I thought as I sat there. For nearly eight years I did not remember Ashok and his mother, Ma, Pitaji, and Asha getting in the car with us to go to the temple hostel where the people from Rajinder's side were housed. Nor did I remember walking through the long halls, with moisture on the once white walls, and seeing in rooms, long and wide, people sleeping on cots, mattresses without frames, blankets folded twice before being laid down. I did not remember all this until one evening eight years later, while wandering through Kamla Nagar market searching for a dress for Asha's first daughter. I was standing on the sidewalk looking at a stall display of hair bands and thinking of Asha's husband, a tall, yellow-haired American with a soft, open face, who I felt had made Asha happier and gentler. And then I began crying. People brushed past, trying to ignore me. I was so alone. I was thirty-three years old and so alone that I wanted to sit down on the sidewalk until someone came and picked me up.

I did remember Rajinder's opening the blue door to the room where we would spend our wedding night. Before we entered, we separated for a moment. Rajinder touched his mother's feet with his right hand and then touched his forehead with that hand. His mother embraced him. I did the same with each of my parents. As Ma held me, she whispered, "Earlier your father got drunk like the pig he is." Then Pitaji put his arms around me and said, "I love you," in English.

The English was what made me cry, even though everyone thought it was the grief of parting. The words reminded me of how Pitaji came home drunk after work once or twice a month and Ma, thin arms folded across her chest, stood in the doorway of his bedroom and watched him fumbling to undress. When I was young, he held me in his lap those nights, his arm tight around my waist, and spoke into my ear in English, as if to prove that he was sober. He would say, "No one loves me. You love me, don't you, my little sun-ripened mango? I try to be good. I work all day, but no one loves me." As he spoke, he rocked in place. He would be watching Ma to make sure she heard. Gradually his voice would become husky. He would cry slowly, gently, and when the tears began to come, he would let me go and continue rocking, lost gratefully in his own sadness. Sometimes he turned out the lights and cried silently in the dark for a half hour or more. Then he locked the door to his room and slept.

Those nights Ma offered dinner without speaking. Later she told her own story. But she did not cry, and although Ma knew how to let her voice falter as if the pain were too much to speak of, and her face crumpled with sorrow, I was more impressed by Pitaji's tears. Ma's story included some beautiful lines. Lines like "In higher secondary a teacher said, In seven years all the cells in our body change. So when Baby died, I thought, It will be all right. In seven years one of me will have touched Baby." Other lines were as fine, but this was Asha's favorite. It might have been what first interested her in microbiology. Ma would not eat dinner, but she sat with us on the floor and, leaning forward, told us how she had loved Pitaji once, but after Baby got sick and she kept sending telegrams to Beri for Pitaji to come home and he did not, she did not send a telegram about Baby's death. "What could he do," she would say, looking at the floor, "although he always cries so handsomely?" I was dazzled by her words—calling his tears handsome—in comparison with which Pitaji's ramblings appeared inept. But the grief of the tears seemed irrefutable. And because Ma loved Asha more than she did me, I was less compassionate toward her. When Pitaji awoke and asked for water to dissolve the herbs and medicines that he took to make himself vomit, I obeyed readily. When Pitaji spoke of love on my wedding night, the soft, wet vowels of his vomiting were what I remembered.

Rajinder closed and bolted the door. A double bed was in the center of the room, and near it a small table with a jug of water and two glasses. The room had yellow walls and smelled faintly of mildew. I stopped crying and suddenly felt very calm. I stood in the center of the room, a fold of the sari covering my head and falling before my eyes. I thought, I will just say this has been a terrible mistake. Rajinder lifted the sari's fold and, looking into my eyes, said he was very pleased to marry me. He was wearing a white silk kurta with tiny flowers embroidered around the neck and gold studs for buttons. He led me to the bed with his hand on my elbow and with a light squeeze let me know he wanted me to sit. He took off the loose shirt and suddenly looked small. *No, wait. I must tell you,* I said. His stomach drooped. What an ugly man, I thought. *No. Wait,* I said. He did not hear or I did not say. Louder. *You are a very nice man, I am sure.* The hard bed with the white sheet dotted with rose petals. The hands that undid the blouse and were disappointed by my small breasts. The ceiling was so far away. The moisture between my legs like breath on glass. Rajinder put his kurta back on and poured himself some water and then thought to offer me some.

Sleep was there, cool and dark, as soon as I closed my eyes. But around eight in the morning, when Rajinder shook me awake, I was exhausted. The door to our room was open, and I saw one of Rajinder's cousins, a fat, hairy man with a towel around his waist, walk past to the bathroom. He looked in and smiled broadly, and I felt ashamed. I was glad I had gotten up at some point in the night and wrapped the sari on again. I had not felt cold, but I had wanted to be completely covered.

Rajinder, Ashok, their mother, and I had breakfast in our room. We sat around the small table and ate rice and yogurt. I wanted to sleep. I wanted to tell them to go away, to stop talking about who had come last night and brought what, and who had not but might still be expected to send a gift—tell them they were boring, foolish people. Ashok and his mother spoke, while Rajinder just nodded. Their words were indistinct, as if coming from across a wide room, and I felt I was dreaming them. I wanted to close my eyes and rest my head on the table. "You eat like a bird," Rajinder's mother said, looking at me and smiling.

After breakfast we visited a widowed aunt of Rajinder's who had been unable to attend the wedding because of arthritis. She lived in a two-room flat covered with posters of gods and smelling of mothballs and old sweat. As she spoke of how carpenters and cobblers were moving in from the villages and passing themselves off as upper-castes, she drooled from the corners of her mouth. I was silent, except for when she asked me about my education and what dishes I liked to cook. As we left, she said, "A thousand years. A thousand children," and pressed fifty-one rupees in Rajinder's hands.

Then there was the long bus ride to Bursa. The roads were so bad that I kept being jolted awake, and my sleep became so fractured that I dreamed of the bus ride and being awakened. And in the village I saw grimy hens peering into the well, and women for whom I posed demurely in the courtyard. They sat in a circle around me and murmured compliments. My head and eyes were covered as they had been the night before, and as I stared at the floor, I fell asleep. I woke an hour later to their praise of my modesty. That night, in the dark room at the rear of the house, I was awakened by Rajinder's digging between my legs, and although he tried to be gentle, I just wished it over. His face, flat and distorted, was above me, and his hands raised my nipples cruelly, resentful of being cheated, even though I never heard anger in Rajinder's voice. He was always polite. Even in bed he was formal, "Could you get on all fours, please?"

So heavy and still did I feel on the first night in our new rooftop home, watching Rajinder sleep on the moonlight-soaked mattress, that I wanted the earth and sky to stop turning and for it always to be night. I did not want dawn to come and the day's activities to start again. I did not want to have to think and react to the world. I fell asleep then, only to wake in panic an hour later at the thought of the obscure life I would lead with Rajinder. Think slowly, I told myself, looking at Rajinder asleep with an arm thrown over his eyes. Slowly. I remembered the year between my B.A. and B.Ed., when, through influence, I got a job as a typist in a candle factory. For nearly a month, upon reaching home after work, I wanted to cry, for I was terrified at the idea of giving up eight hours a day, a third of my life, to typing letters concerning supplies of wax. And then one day I noticed that I no longer felt afraid. I had learned to stop thinking. I floated above the days.

In the morning I had a fever, and the stillness it brought with it spread into the coming days. It hardened around me, so that I did not feel as if I were the one making love or cooking dinner or going home to see Ma and Pitaji and behaving there as I always had. No one guessed it was not me. Nothing could break through the stillness, not even Rajinder's learning to caress me before parting my legs, or my growing to know all the turns of the colony's alleys, and the shopkeepers calling me by name.

Winter turned into spring, and the trees in the park swelled green. Rajinder was thoughtful and generous. Traveling for conferences to Baroda, Madras, Jaipur, Bangalore, he always brought back saris or other gifts. The week I had malaria, he came home every lunch hour and cooked gruel for me. On my twenty-sixth birthday he took me to the Taj Mahal, and arranged to have my family hidden in the flat when we returned in the evening. What a good man, I thought then, watching him standing proudly in a corner. What a good man, I thought, and was frightened, for that was not enough. I knew I needed something else, but I did not know what. Being his wife was not so bad. He did not make me do anything I did not want to, except make love, and even that was sometimes pleasant. I did not mind his being in the flat, and being alone is difficult. When he was away on his trips, I did not miss him, and he, I think, did not miss me, for he never mentioned it.

Summer came, and hot winds swept up from the Rajasthani deserts. The old cows that wander unattended on Delhi's streets began to die. The corpses lay untouched for a week sometimes; their tongues swelled and, cracking open the jaw, stuck out absurdly.

The heat was like a high-pitched buzzing that formed a film between flesh and bone, so that my skin felt thick and rubbery and I wished that I could just peel it off.

I woke at four every morning. to have an hour when breathing air would not be like inhaling liquid. By five the eastern edge of the sky was too bright to look at, even though the sun had yet to appear. I bathed both before and after breakfast and again after doing laundry but before lunch. As June progressed, and the very air seemed to whine under the heat's stress, I stopped eating lunch. Around two, before taking my nap, I would pour a few mugs of water on my head. I liked to lie on the bed imagining that the monsoon had come. Sometimes this made me sad, for the smell of the wet earth and the sound of the rain have always made me feel as if I have been waiting for someone all my life and that person has not yet come. I dreamed often of living near the sea, in a house with a sloping red roof and bright-blue window frames, and woke happy, hearing water on sand.

And so the summer passed, slowly and vengefully, until the last week of June, when the *Times of India* began its countdown to the monsoon, and I awoke one afternoon in love with my husband.

I had returned home that day after spending two weeks with my parents. Pitaji had had a mild heart attack, and I took turns with Ma and Asha being with him in Safdarjung Hospital. The heart attack was no surprise, for Pitaji had become so fat that even his largest shirts had to be worn unbuttoned. So when I opened the door late one night and saw Asha with her fist up, ready to start banging again, I did not have to be told that Pitaji had woken screaming that his heart was breaking.

While I hurried a sari and blouse into a plastic bag, Asha leaned against a wall of our bedroom, drinking water. It was three. Rajinder, in his undershirt and pajama pants, sat on the bed's edge and stared at the floor. I felt no fear, perhaps because Asha had said the heart attack was not so bad, or perhaps because I just did not care. The rushing and the banging on doors appeared to be the properly melodramatic behavior when one's father might be dying.

An auto-rickshaw was waiting for us downstairs, triangular, small, with plasticized cloth covering its frame. It seemed like a vehicle for desperate people. Before getting in, I looked up and saw Rajinder. He was leaning against the railing. The moon was yellow and uneven behind him. I waved and he waved back. Such formalities, I thought, and then we were off, racing through dark, abandoned streets.

"Ma's fine. He screamed so loud," Asha said. She is a few inches taller than I am, and although she, too, is not pretty, she uses makeup that gives angles to her round face. Asha sat slightly turned on the seat so that she could face me. "A thousand times we told him, Lose weight," she said, shaking her head impatiently. "When the doctor gave him that diet, he said, 'Is that before or after breakfast?'" She paused and added in a tight whisper, "He's laughing now."

I felt lonely sitting there while the city was silent and dark and we talked of our father without concern. "He wants to die," I said softly. I enjoyed saying such serious words. "He is so unhappy. I think our hopes are made when we are young, and we can never adjust them to the real world. He was nearly national champion in wrestling, and for the past thirty-seven years he has been examining government schools to see that they have the right PE equipment. He loves eating, and that is as fine a way to die as any."

"If he wants to die, wonderful; I don't like him. But why is he making it difficult for us?"

Her directness shocked me and made me feel that my sentimentality was dishonest. The night air was still bitter from the evening traffic. "He is a good man," I said unsteadily.

"The way he treated us all. Ma is like a slave."

"They are just not good together. It's no one's fault."

"How can it be no one's fault?"

"His father was an alcoholic."

"How long can you use your parents as an excuse?"

I did not respond at first, for I thought Asha might be saying this because I had always used Ma and Pitaji to explain away my failures. Then I said, "Look how good he is compared with his brothers. He must have had something good inside that let him be gentler than them. We should love him for that part alone."

"That's what he is relying on. It's a big world. A lot of people are worth loving. Why love someone mediocre?"

Broken glass was in the hallways of the hospital, and someone had urinated in the elevator. When we came into the yellow room that Pitaji shared with five other men, he was asleep. His face looked like a shiny brown stone. He was on the bed nearest the window. Ma sat at the foot of his bed, her back to us, looking out at the fading night.

"He will be all right," I said.

Turning toward us, Ma said, "When he goes, he wants to make sure we all hurt." She was crying. "I thought I did not love him, but you can't live this long with a person and not love just a bit. He knew that. When they were bringing him here, he said, 'See what you've done, demoness.'"

Asha took Ma away, still crying. I spent the rest of the night dozing in a chair next to his bed.

We fell into a pattern. Ma usually came in the morning, around eight, and I replaced her, hours later. Asha would take my place at three and stay until six, and then Ma's brother or his sons would stay until Ma returned.

I had thought I would be afraid of being in the hospital, but it was very peaceful. Pitaji slept most of the day and night because of the medicines, waking up every now and then to ask for water and quickly falling asleep again. A nice boy named Rajeeve, who also was staying with his father, told me funny stories about his family. At night Asha and I slept on adjacent cots on the roof. Before she went to bed, she read five pages of an English dictionary. She had been accepted into a postdoctoral program in America. She did not brag about it as I would have. Like Ma, Asha worked very hard, as if that were the only way to live and one needn't talk about it, and as if, like Ma, she assumed that we are all equally fortunate. But sometimes Asha would shout a word at me—"Alluvial!"—and then look at me as if she was waiting for a response. Once, Rajinder came to drop off some clothes, but I was away. I did not see him or talk with him for the two weeks.

Sometimes Pitaji could not sleep and he would tell me stories of his father, a schoolteacher, who would take Pitaji with him to the saloon, so that someone would be there to guide him home when he was drunk. Pitaji was eight or nine then. His mother beat him for accompanying Dadaji, but Pitaji, his breath sounding as if it were coming through a wet cloth, said that he was afraid Dadaji would be made fun of if he walked home alone. Pitaji told the story quietly, as if he were talking about someone else, and as soon as he finished, he changed the subject. I could not tell whether Pitaji was being modest or was manipulating me by pretending modesty.

He slept most of the day, and I sat beside him, listening to his little green transistor radio. The June sun filled half the sky, and the groundskeeper walked around the courtyard of the hospital in wide circles with a water bag as large as a man's body slung over one shoulder. He was sprinkling water to keep the dust settled. Sometimes I hummed along to Lata Mangeshkar or Mohammed Rafi singing that grief is no letter to be passed around to whoever wants to read.

There were afternoons when Pitaji became restless and whispered conspiratorially that he had always loved me most. Watching his face, puffy from the drugs, his nose broad and covered with blackheads, as he said again that Ma did not talk to him or that Asha was indifferent to his suffering, I felt exhausted. When he complained to Asha, "Your mother doesn't talk to me," she answered, "Maybe you aren't interesting."

Once, four or five days before we took him home, as he was complaining, I got up from the chair and went to look out the window. Beyond the courtyard was a string of yellow-and-black auto-rickshaws waiting under eucalyptus trees. I wanted desperately for Asha to come, so that I could leave, and bathe, and lie down to dream of a house with a red-tiled roof near the sea. "You must forgive me," Pitaji said as I looked out the window. I was surprised, for I could not remember his ever apologizing. "I sometimes forget that I will die soon and so act like a man who has many years left." I felt frightened, for I suddenly wanted to love him but could not trust him enough.

From then until we went home, Pitaji spoke little. Once, I forgot to bring his lunch from home and he did not complain, whereas before he would have screamed and tried to make me feel guilty. A few times he began crying to himself for no reason, and when I asked why, he did not answer.

Around eleven the day Pitaji was released, an ambulance carried Ma, Pitaji, and me to the Old Vegetable Market. Two orderlies, muscular men in white uniforms, carried him on a stretcher up three flights of stairs into the flat. The flat had four rooms and was part of a circle of dilapidated buildings that shared a courtyard. Fourteen or fifteen people turned out to watch Pitaji's return. Some of the very old women, sitting on cots in the courtyard, asked who Pitaji was, although he had lived there for twenty years. A few children climbed into the ambulance and played with the horn until they were chased out.

The orderlies laid Pitaji on the cot in his bedroom and left. The room was small and dark, smelling faintly of the kerosene with which the bookshelves were treated every other week to prevent termites. Traveling had tired him, and he fell asleep quickly. He woke as I was about to leave. Ma and I were speaking in whispers outside his bedroom.

"I am used to his screaming," Ma said. "He won't get any greasy food here. But once he can walk . . ."

"He seems to have changed."

"Right now he's afraid. Give him a few days and he'll return to normal. People can't change, even if they want to."

"What are you saying about me?" Pitaji tried to call out, but his voice was like wind on dry grass.

"You want something?" Ma asked.

"Water."

As I started toward the fridge, Ma said, "Nothing cold." The clay pot held only enough for one glass. I knelt beside the cot and helped Pitaji rise to a forty-five-degree angle. His heaviness and the weakness of his body moved me. Like a baby holding a bottle, Pitaji held the glass with both hands and made sucking noises as he drank. I lowered him when his shoulder muscles slackened. His eyes were red, and they moved about the room slowly. I wondered whether I could safely love him if I did not reveal my feelings.

"More?" he asked.

"Only fridge water," I said. Ma was clattering in the kitchen. "I am going home."

"Rajinder is good?" He looked at the ceiling while speaking.

"Yes," I said. A handkerchief of light covered his face, and faint blue veins, like delicate, almost translucent roots, showed through the skin of his forehead. "The results for his exam came," I told him. "He will be promoted. He was second in Delhi." Pitaji closed his eyes. "Are you hurting?" I asked.

"I feel tired."

I, too, felt tired. I did not know what to do with my new love or whether it would last. "That will pass, the doctor said. Why don't you sleep?"

"I don't want to," he said loudly, and my love drew back.

"I must go," I said, but made no move to.

"Forgive me," he said, and again I was surprised. "I am not worried usually, but I get frightened sometimes. Sometimes I dream that the heaviness is dirt. What an awful thing to be a Muslim or a Christian." He spoke slowly, and I felt my love returning. "Once, I dreamed of Baby's ghost."

"Oh."

"He was eight or nine and did not recognize me. He did not look like me. I was surprised, because he was my son and I had always expected him to look like me."

I felt exhausted. Something about the story was both awkward and polished, which indicated deceit. But Pitaji never lied completely, and the tiring part was not knowing. "God will forgive you," I said. But why should he? I thought. Why do people always think hurting others is all right, as long as they hurt themselves as well?

"Your mother has not."

I placed my hand on his, knowing that I was already in the trap. "Shhh."

"At your birthday, when she sang, I said, 'If you sing like that for me every day, I will love you forever.'"

"She loves you. She worries about you."

"That's not the same. When I tell Asha this, she tells me I'm sentimental. Ratha loved me once. But she cannot forgive. What happened so long ago, she cannot forgive." He was blinking rapidly, preparing to cry. "But that is a lie. She does not love me because," and he began crying without making a sound, "I did not love her for so long."

"Shhh. She loves you. She was just saying 'Oh, I love him so. I hope he gets better, for I love him so.'"

"Ratha could have loved me a little. She could have loved me twenty for my eleven." He was sobbing.

"Shhh. Shhh. Shhh." I wanted to run away, far away, and be someone else.

The sleep that afternoon was like falling. I lay down, closed my eyes, and plummeted. I woke as suddenly, without any half memories of dreams, into a silence that meant that the power was gone, and the ceiling fan was still, and the fridge was slowly warming.

It was cool, I noticed, unsurprised by the monsoon's approach—for I was in love. The window curtains stirred, revealing TV antennas and distant gray clouds and a few sparrows wheeling in the air. The sheet lay bunched at my feet. I felt gigantic. My legs stretched thousands of miles; my head rested in the Himalayas and my breath brought the world rain. If I stood up, I would scrape against the sky. But I was small and compact and distilled, too. I am in love, I thought, and a raspy voice echoed the words in my head, causing me to panic and lose my sense of omnipotence for a moment. I will love Rajinder slowly and carefully and cunningly, I thought, and suddenly felt peaceful again, as if I were a lake and the world could only form ripples on my surface, while the calm beneath continued in solitude. Time seemed endless, and I would surely have the minutes and seconds needed to plan a method of preserving this love, like the feeling in your stomach when you are in a car going swiftly down a hill. Don't worry, I thought, and I no longer did. My mind obeyed me limply, as if a terrible exhaustion had worn away all rebellion.

I got up and swung my legs off the bed. I was surprised that my love was not disturbed by my physical movements. I walked out onto the roof. The wind ruffled the treetops and small, gray clouds slid across the cool, pale sky. On the street eight or nine young boys played cricket. The school year had just started, and the children played desperately, as if they must run faster, leap higher, to recapture the hours spent indoors.

Tell me your stories, I would ask him. Pour them into me, so that I know everything you have ever loved or been scared of or laughed at. But thinking this, I became uneasy and feared that when I actually saw him, my love would fade and I would find my tongue thick and unresponsive. What should I say? I woke this afternoon in love with you. I love you too, he would answer. No, no, you see, I really love you. I love you so much that I think anything is possible, that I will live forever. Oh, he would say, and I would feel my love rush out of me.

I must say nothing at first, I decided. Slowly I will win his love. I will spoil him, and he will fall in love with me. And as long as he loves me, I will be able to love him. I will love him like a camera that closes at too much light and opens at too little, so his blemishes will never mar my love.

I watched the cricket game to the end. I felt very happy standing there, as if I had just discovered some profound secret. When the children dispersed, around five, I knew Rajinder would be home soon.

I bathed and changed into new clothes. I stood before the small mirror in the armoire as I dressed. Uneven brown aureoles, a flat stomach, the veins in my feet like pen marks. Will this be enough? I wondered. Once he loves me, I told myself. I lifted my arms and tried to smell the plantlike odor of my perspiration. I wore a bright-red cotton sari. What will I say first? *Namastay*—how was your day? With the informal "you." How was your day? The words felt strange, for I had never before used the informal with him. I had, as a show of modesty, never even used his name, except on the night before my wedding, when I said it over and over to myself to see how it felt— like nothing. Now when I said "Rajinder," the three syllables had too many edges, and again I doubted that he would love me. "Rajinder, Rajinder," I said rapidly several times, until it no longer felt strange. He will love me because to do otherwise would be too lonely, because I will love him so. I heard a scooter stopping outside the building and knew that he had come home.

My stomach was small and hard as I walked onto the roof. The dark clouds made it appear as if it were seven instead of five-thirty. I saw him roll the scooter into the courtyard and I felt happy. He parked the scooter and took off his gray helmet. He combed his hair carefully to hide the growing bald spot. The deliberateness of the way he tucked the comb into his back pocket overwhelmed me with tenderness. We will love each other gently and carefully, I thought.

I waited for him to rise out of the stairwell. The wind made my petticoat, drying on the clothesline, go *clap, clap*. I was smiling rigidly. How was your day? How *was* your day? Was your day good? Don't be so afraid, I told myself. What does it matter how you say hello? Tomorrow will come, and the day after, and the day after that.

His steps sounded like a shuffle. Leather rubbing against stone. Something forlorn and steady in the sound made me feel as if I were twenty years older and this were a game I should stop or I might get hurt. Rajinder, Rajinder, Rajinder, how are you?

First the head: oval, high forehead, handsome eyebrows. Then the not so broad but not so narrow shoulders. The top two buttons of the cream shirt were opened, revealing an undershirt and some hair. The two weeks had not changed him, yet seeing him, I felt as if he were somehow different, denser.

"How was your day?" I asked him, while he was still in the stairwell.

"All right," he said, stepping onto the balcony. He smiled, and I felt happy. His helmet was in his left hand and he had a plastic bag of mangoes in his right. "When did you get home?" The "you" was informal, and I felt a surge of relief. He will not resist, I thought.

" A little after three."

I followed him into the bedroom. He placed the helmet on the windowsill and the mangoes in the refrigerator. His careful way of folding the plastic bag before placing it in the basket on top of the refrigerator moved me. "Your father is fine?" I did not say anything.

Rajinder walked to the sink on the outside bathroom wall. I stood in the bedroom doorway and watched him wash his hands and face with soap. Before putting the chunk of soap down, he rinsed it of foam, and only then did he pour water on himself. He used a thin washcloth hanging on a nearby hook for drying.

"Yes," I said.

"What did the doctor say?" he asked, turning toward me. He is like a black diamond, I thought.

She said, I love you. "She said he must lose weight and watch what he eats. Nothing fattening. That he should rest at first and then start exercising. Walking would be best."

I watched Rajinder hang his shirt by the collar tips on the clothesline, and suddenly felt sad at the rigorous attention to detail necessary to preserve love. Perhaps love is different in other countries, I thought, where the climate is cooler, where a woman can say her husband's name, where the power does not go out every day, where not every clerk demands a bribe. That must be a different type of love, I thought, where one can be careless.

"It will rain tonight," he said, looking at the sky.

The eucalyptus trees shook their heads side to side. "The rain always makes me feel as if I am waiting for someone," I said, and then regretted saying it, for Rajinder was not paying attention, and perhaps it could have been said better. "Why don't you sit on the balcony, and I will make sherbet to drink?"

He took a chair and the newspaper with him. The fridge water was warm, and I felt sad again at the need for constant vigilance. I made the drink and gave him his glass. I placed mine on the floor and went to get a chair. A fruit seller passed by, calling out in a reedy voice, "Sweet, sweet mangoes. Sweeter than first love." On the roof directly across, a boy seven or eight years old was trying to fly a large purple kite. I sat down beside Rajinder and waited for him to look up so that I could interrupt his reading. When Rajinder looked away from the paper to take a sip of sherbet, I asked, "Did you fly kites?"

"A little," he answered, looking at the boy. "Ashok bought some with the money he earned, and he would let me fly them sometimes." The fact that his father had died when he was young made me hopeful, for I thought that one must suffer and be lonely before one can love.

"Do you like Ashok?"

"He is my brother," he answered, shrugging and looking at the newspaper. He took a sip of the sherbet. I felt hurt, as if he had reprimanded me.

I waited until seven for the power to return; then I gave up and started to prepare dinner in the dark. I sat beside Rajinder until then. I felt happy and excited and frightened being beside him. We spoke about Asha's going to America, though Rajinder did not want to talk about this. Rajinder had been the most educated member of his and my family and resented the idea that Asha would assume that position.

As I cooked in the kitchen, Rajinder sat on the balcony and listened to the radio. "This is Akashwani," the announcer said, and then music like horses racing played whenever a new program was about to start. It was very hot in the kitchen, and every now and then I stepped onto the roof to look at the curve of Rajinder's neck and confirm that the tenderness was still there.

We ate in the living room. Rajinder chewed slowly and was mostly silent. Once he complimented me on my cooking. "What are you thinking?" I asked. He appeared not to have heard. Tell me! Tell me! I thought, and was shocked by the urgency I felt.

A candle on the television made pillars of shadows rise and collapse on the walls. I searched for something to start a conversation with. "Pitaji began crying when I left."

"You could have stayed a few more days," he said.

"I did not want to." I thought of adding, "I missed you," but that would have been a lie, and I would have felt embarrassed saying it, when he had not missed me.

Rajinder mixed black pepper with his yogurt. "Did you tell him you would visit soon?"

"No. I think he was crying because he was lonely."

"He should have more courage." Rajinder did not like Pitaji, thought him weak-willed, although Rajinder had never told me that. He knew Pitaji drank, but Rajinder never referred to this, for which I was grateful. "He is old and must remember that shadows creep into one's heart at his age." The shutter of a bedroom window began slamming, and I got up to latch it shut.

I washed the dishes while Rajinder bathed. When he came out, dressed in his white kurta pajamas, with his hair slicked back, I was standing near the railing at the roof's edge, looking out beyond the darkness of our neighborhood at a distant ribbon of light. I was tired from the nervousness I had been feeling all evening. Rajinder came up behind me and asked, "Won't you bathe?" I suddenly doubted my ability to guard my love. Bathe so we can have sex. His words were too deliberately full of the unsaid, and so felt vulgar. I wondered if I had the courage to say no and realized I didn't. What kind of love can we have? I thought.

I said, "In a little while. Comedy hour is about to start." We sat down on our chairs with the radio between us and listened to Maurya's whiny voice. This week he had gotten involved with criminals who wanted to go to jail to collect the reward on themselves. The canned laughter gusted from several flats. When the music of the racing horses marked the close of the show, I felt hopeful again, and thought Rajinder looked very handsome in his kurta pajamas.

I bathed carefully, pouring mug after mug of cold water over myself until my fingertips were wrinkled and my nipples erect. The candlelight made the bathroom orange and my skin copper. I washed my pubis carefully to make sure no smell remained from urinating. Rubbing myself dry, I became aroused. I wore the red sari again, with a new blouse, and no bra, so that my nipples would show.

I came and stood beside Rajinder, my arm brushing against his kurta sleeve. Every now and then a raindrop fell, and I wondered if I were imagining it. On balconies and roofs all around us I could see the dim figures of men, women, and children waiting for the first rain. "You look pretty," he said. Somewhere Lata Mangeshkar sang with a static-induced huskiness. The street was silent. Even the children were hushed. As the wind picked up, Rajinder said, "Let's close the windows."

The wind coursed along the floor, upsetting newspapers and climbing the walls to swing on curtains. A candle stood on the refrigerator. As I leaned over to pull a window shut, Rajinder pressed against me and cupped my right breast. I felt a shock of desire pass through me. As I walked around the rooms shutting windows, he touched my buttocks, pubis, stomach.

When the last window was closed, I waited for a moment before turning around, because I knew he wanted me to turn around quickly. He pulled me close, with his hands on my buttocks. I took his tongue in my mouth. We kissed like this for a long time.

The rain began falling, and we heard a roar from the people on the roofs nearby. "The clothes," Rajinder said, and pulled away.

We ran out. We could barely see each other. Lightning bursts would illuminate an eye, an arm, some teeth, and then darkness would come again. We jerked the clothes off and let the pins fall to the ground. We deliberately rushed roughly against each other. The raindrops were like thorns, and we began laughing. Rajinder's shirt had wrapped itself around and around the clothesline. Wiping his face, he knocked his glasses off. As I saw him crouch and fumble around helplessly for them, I felt such tenderness that I knew I would never love him as much as I did at that moment. "The wind in the trees," I cried out, "it sounds like the sea."

We slowly wandered back inside, kissing all the while. He entered me like a sigh. He suckled on me and moved back and forth and side to side, and I felt myself growing warm and loose. He sucked on my nipples and held my waist with both hands. We made love gently at first, but as we both neared climax, Rajinder began stabbing me with his penis and I came in waves so strong that I felt myself vanishing. When Rajinder sank on top of me, I kept saying, "I love you. I love you."

"I love you too," he answered. Outside, the rain came in sheets and the thunder was like explosions in caverns.

The candle had gone out while we made love, and Rajinder got up to light it. He drank some water and then lay down beside me. I wanted some water too, but did not want to say anything that would make him feel bad about his thoughtlessness. "I'll be getting promoted soon. Minaji loves me," Rajinder said. I rolled onto my side to look at him. He had his arms folded across his chest. "Yesterday," he said, 'Come, Rajinderji, let us go write your confidential report.'" I put my hand on his stomach, and Rajinder said, "Don't," and pushed it away. "I said, 'Oh, I don't know whether that would be good, sir.' He laughed and patted me on the back. What a nincompoop. If it weren't for the quotas, he would never be manager." Rajinder chuckled. "I'll be the youngest bank manager in Delhi." I felt cold and tugged a sheet over our legs. "In college I had a schedule for where I wanted to be by the time I was thirty. By twenty-two I became an officer; soon I'll be a manager. I wanted a car, and we'll have that in a year. I wanted a wife, and I have that."

"You are so smart."

"Some people in college were smarter. But I knew exactly what I wanted. A life is like a house. One has to plan carefully where all the furniture will go."

"Did you plan me as your wife?" I asked, smiling.

"No. I had wanted at least an M.A., and someone who worked, but Mummy didn't approve of a daughter-in-law who worked. I was willing to change my requirements. Because I believe in moderation, I was successful. Everything in its place. And pay for everything. Other people got caught up in love and friendship. I've always felt that these things only became a big deal because of the movies."

"What do you mean? You love me and your mother, don't you?"

"There are so many people in the world that it is hard not to think that there are others you could love more."

Seeing the shock on my face, he quickly added, "Of course I love you. I just try not to be too emotional about it." The candle's shadows on the wall were like the wavery bands formed by light reflected off water. "We might even be able to get a foreign car."

The second time he took me that night, it was from behind. He pressed down heavily on my back and grabbed my breasts.

I woke at four or five. The rain scratched against the windows and a light like blue milk shone along the edges of the door. I was cold and tried to wrap myself in the sheet, but it was not large enough.

# Leslie Marmon Silko

## (B. 1948)

Leslie Marmon Silko's mix of Laguna Pueblo, Mexican, and Anglo ancestry has given her unique insight into the art of storytelling. She believes that story-telling is more than a form of entertainment or a way to pass on values and tra-ditions; it is a ritual ceremony that links people with the mystical. These beliefs are particularly evident in Silko's Yellow Woman stories. She grew up at the Pueblo of Laguna, where she learned cultural folklore through stories passed down by her grandmother Lilly and Aunt Susie. She attended the University of New Mexico and, in 1969, published her first short story, "The Man to Send Rain Clouds," which led to a National Endowment for the Humanities Discovery Grant. After graduating with a degree in English, Silko chose to pursue a law de-gree so that she could assist Native Americans. However, she soon left law school and devoted herself to her writing. Silko has published such works as *La-guna Woman* (1974), *Ceremony* (1977), *Storyteller* (1981), *Almanac of the Dead* (1991), *Yellow Women* (1993), and *Gardens in the Dunes* (1999).

## *Yellow Woman*                                    1974

### I

My thigh clung to his with dampness, and I watched the sun rising up through the tamaracks and willows. The small brown water birds came to the river and hopped across the mud, leaving brown scratches in the alkali-white crust. They bathed in the river silently. I could hear the water, almost at our feet where the narrow fast channel bubbled and washed green ragged moss and fern leaves. I looked at him beside me, rolled in the red blanket on the white river sand. I cleaned the sand out of the cracks between my toes, squinting because the sun was above the willow trees. I looked at him for the last time, sleeping on the white river sand.

I felt hungry and followed the river south the way we had come the afternoon before, following our footprints that were already blurred by the lizard tracks and bug trails. The horses were still lying down, and the black one whinnied when he saw me but he did not get up—maybe it was because the corral was made out of thick cedar branches and the horses had not yet felt the sun like I had. I tried to look beyond the pale red mesas to the pueblo. I knew it was there, even if I could not see it, on the sand rock hill above the river, the same river that moved past me now and had reflected the moon last night.

The horse felt warm underneath me. He shook his head and pawed the sand. The bay whinnied and leaned up against the gate trying to follow, and I remembered him asleep in the red blanket beside the river. I slid off the horse and tied him close to the other horse. I walked north with the river again, and the white sand broke loose in footprints over footprints.

"Wake up."

He moved in the blanket and turned his face to me with his eyes still closed. I knelt down to touch him.

"I'm leaving."

He smiled now, eyes still closed. "You are coming with me, remember?" He sat up now with his bare dark chest and belly in the sun.

"Where?"

"To my place."

"And will I come back?"

He pulled his pants on. I walked away from him, feeling him behind me and smelling the willows.

"Yellow Woman," he said.

I turned to face him. "Who are you?" I asked.

He laughed and knelt on the low, sandy bank, washing his face in the river. "Last night you guessed my name, and you knew why I had come."

I stared past him at the shallow moving water and tried to remember the night, but I could only see the moon in the water and remember his warmth around me.

"But I only said that you were him and that I was Yellow Woman—I'm not really her—I have my own name and I come from the pueblo on the other side of the mesa. Your name is Silva and you are a stranger I met by the river yesterday afternoon."

He laughed softly. "What happened yesterday has nothing to do with what you will do today, Yellow Woman."

"I know—that's what I'm saying—the old stories about the ka'tsina spirit and Yellow Woman can't mean us."

My old grandpa liked to tell those stories best. There is one about Badger and Coyote who went hunting and were gone all day, and when the sun was going down they found a house. There was a girl living there alone, and she had light hair and eyes and she told them that they could sleep with her. Coyote wanted to be with her all night so he sent Badger into a prairie-dog hole, telling him he thought he saw something in it. As soon as Badger crawled in, Coyote blocked up the entrance with rocks and hurried back to Yellow Woman.

"Come here," he said gently.

He touched my neck and I moved close to him to feel his breathing and to hear his heart. I was wondering if Yellow Woman had known who she was—if she knew that she would become part of the stories. Maybe she'd had another name that her husband and relatives called her so that only the ka'tsina from the north and the storytellers would know her as Yellow Woman. But I didn't go on; I felt him all around me, pushing me down into the white river sand.

Yellow Woman went away with the spirit from the north and lived with him and his relatives. She was gone for a long time, but then one day she came back and she brought twin boys.

"Do you know the story?"

"What story?" He smiled and pulled me close to him as he said this. I was afraid lying there on the red blanket. All I could know was the way he felt, warm, damp, his body beside me. This is the way it happens in the stories, I was thinking, with no thought beyond the moment she meets the ka'tsina spirit and they go.

"I don't have to go. What they tell in stories was real only then, back in time immemorial, like they say."

He stood up and pointed at my clothes tangled in the blanket. "Let's go," he said.

I walked beside him, breathing hard because he walked fast, his hand around my wrist. I had stopped trying to pull away from him, because his hand felt cool and the sun was high, drying the river bed into alkali. I will see someone, eventually I will see someone, and then I will be certain that he is only a man—some man from nearby—and I will be sure that I am not Yellow Woman. Because she is from out of time past and I live now and I've been to school and there are highways and pickup trucks that Yellow Woman never saw.

It was an easy ride north on horseback. I watched the change from the cottonwood trees along the river to the junipers that brushed past us in the foothills, and finally there were only piñons, and when I looked up at the rim of the mountain plateau I could see pine trees growing on the edge. Once I stopped to look down, but the pale sandstone had disappeared and the river was gone and the dark lava hills were all around. He touched my hand, not speaking, but always singing softly a mountain song and looking into my eyes.

I felt hungry and wondered what they were doing at home now—my mother, my grandmother, my husband, and the baby. Cooking breakfast, saying. "Where did she go?—maybe kidnapped," and Al going to the tribal police with the details: "She went walking along the river."

The house was made with black lava rock and red mud. It was high above the spreading miles of arroyos and long mesas. I smelled a mountain smell of pitch and buck brush. I stood there beside the black horse, looking down on the small, dim country we had passed, and I shivered.

"Yellow Woman, come inside where it's warm."

## II

He lit a fire in the stove. It was an old stove with a round belly and an enamel coffeepot on top. There was only the stove, some faded Navajo blankets, and a bedroll and cardboard box. The floor was made of smooth adobe plaster, and there was one small window facing east. He pointed at the box.

"There's some potatoes and the frying pan." He sat on the floor with his arms around his knees pulling them close to his chest and he watched me fry the potatoes. I didn't mind him watching me because he was always watching me—he had been watching me since I came upon him sitting on the river bank trimming leaves from a willow twig with his knife. We ate from the pan and he wiped the grease from his fingers on his Levis.

"Have you brought women here before?" He smiled and kept chewing, so I said, "Do you always use the same tricks?"

"What tricks?" He looked at me like he didn't understand.

"The story about being a ka'tsina from the mountains. The story about Yellow Woman."

Silva was silent; his face was calm.

"I don't believe it. Those stories couldn't happen now," I said.

He shook his head and said softly, "But someday they will talk about us, and they will say, 'Those two lived long ago when things like that happened.'"

He stood up and went out. I ate the rest of the potatoes and thought about things—about the noise the stove was making and the sound of the mountain wind outside. I remembered yesterday and the day before, and then I went outside.

I walked past the corral to the edge where the narrow trail cut through the black rim rock. I was standing in the sky with nothing around me but the wind that came down from the blue mountain peak behind me. I could see faint mountain images in the distance miles across the vast spread of mesas and valleys and plains. I wondered who was over there to feel the mountain wind on those sheer blue edges—who walks on the pine needles in those blue mountains.

"Can you see the pueblo?" Silva was standing behind me.

I shook my head. "We're too far away."

"From here I can see the world." He stepped out on the edge. "The Navajo reservation begins over there." He pointed to the east. "The Pueblo boundaries are over here." He looked below us to the south, where the narrow trail seemed to come from. "The Texans have their ranches over there, starting with that valley, the Concho Valley. The Mexicans run some cattle over there too."

"Do you ever work for them?"

"I steal from them," Silva answered. The sun was dropping behind us and shadows were filling the land below. I turned away from the edge that dropped forever into the valleys below.

"I'm cold," I said; "I'm going inside." I started wondering about this man who could speak the Pueblo language so well but who lived on a mountain and rustled cattle. I decided that this man Silva must be Navajo, because Pueblo men didn't do things like that.

"You must be a Navajo."

Silva shook his head gently. "Little Yellow Woman," he said, "you never give up, do you? I have told you who I am. The Navajo people know me, too." He knelt down and unrolled the bedroll and spread the extra blankets out on a piece of canvas. The sun was down, and the only light in the house came from outside—the dim orange light from sundown.

I stood there and waited for him to crawl under the blankets.

"What are you waiting for?" he said, and I lay down beside him. He undressed me slowly like the night before beside the river—kissing my face gently and running his hands up and down my belly and legs. He took off my pants and then he laughed.

"Why are you laughing?"

"You are breathing so hard."

I pulled away from him and turned my back to him.

He puled me around and pinned me down with his arms and chest. "You don't understand, do you, little Yellow Woman? You will do what I want."

And again he was all around me with his skin slippery against mine, and I was afraid because I understood that his strength could hurt me. I lay underneath him and I knew that he could destroy me. But later, while he slept beside me, I touched his face and I had a feeling—the kind of feeling for him that overcame me that morning along the river. I kissed him on the forehead and he reached out for me.

When I woke up in the morning he was gone. It gave me a strange feeling because for a long time I sat there on the blankets and looked around the little house for some object of his—some proof that he had been there or maybe that he was coming back. Only the blankets and the cardboard box remained. The .30–30 that had been leaning in the corner was gone, and so was the knife I had used the night before. He was gone, and I had my chance to go now. But first I had to eat, because I knew it would be a long walk home.

I found some dried apricots in the cardboard box, and I sat down on a rock at the edge of the plateau rim. There was no wind and the sun warmed me. I was surrounded by silence. I drowsed with apricots in my mouth, and I didn't believe that there were highways or railroads or cattle to steal.

When I woke up, I stared down at my feet in the black mountain dirt. Little black ants were swarming over the pine needles around my foot. They must have smelled the apricots. I thought about my family far below me. They would be wondering about me, because this had never happened to me before. The tribal police would file a report. But if old Grandpa weren't dead he would tell them what happened—he would laugh and say, "Stolen by a ka'tsina, a mountain spirit. She'll come home—they usually do." There are enough of them to handle things. My mother and grandmother will raise the baby like they raised me. Al will find someone else, and they will go on like before, except that there will be a story about the day I disappeared while I was walking along the river. Silva had come for me; he said he had. I did not decide to go. I just went. Moonflowers blossom in the sand hills before dawn, just as I followed him. That's what I was thinking as I wandered along the trail through the pine trees.

It was noon when I got back. When I saw the stone house I remembered that I had meant to go home. But that didn't seem important any more, maybe because there were little blue flowers growing in the meadow behind the stone house and the gray squirrels were playing in the pines next to the house. The horses were standing in the corral, and there was a beef carcass hanging on the shady side of a big pine in front of the house. Flies buzzed around the clotted blood that hung from the carcass. Silva was washing his hands in a bucket full of water. He must have heard me coming because he spoke to me without turning to face me.

"I've been waiting for you."

"I went walking in the big pine trees."

I looked into the bucket full of bloody water with brown-and-white animal hairs floating in it. Silva stood there letting his hand drip, examining me intently.

"Are you coming with me?"

"Where?" I asked him.

"To sell the meat at Marquez."

"If you're sure it's O.K."

"I wouldn't ask you if it wasn't," he answered.

He sloshed the water around in the bucket before he dumped it out and set the bucket upside down near the door. I followed him to the corral and watched him saddle the horses. Even beside the horses he looked tall, and I asked him again if he wasn't Navajo. He didn't say anything; he just shook his head and kept cinching up the saddle.

"But Navajos are tall."

"Get on the horse," he said, "and let's go."

The last thing he did before we started down the steep trail was to grab the .30–30 from the corner. He slid the rifle into the scabbard that hung from his saddle.

"Do they ever try to catch you?" I asked.

"They don't know who I am."

"Then why did you bring the rifle?"

"Because we are going to Marquez where the Mexicans live."

**III**

The trail leveled out on a narrow ridge that was steep on both sides like an animal spine. On one side I could see where the trail went around the rocky gray hills and disappeared into the southeast where the pale sandrock mesas stood in the distance near my home. On the other side was a trail that went west, and as I looked far into the distance I thought I saw the little town. But Silva said no, that I was looking in the wrong place, that I just thought I saw houses. After that I quit looking off into the distance; it was hot and the wildflowers were closing up their deep-yellow petals. Only the waxy cactus flowers bloomed in the bright sun, and I saw every color that a cactus blossom can be; the white ones and the red ones were still buds, but the purple and the yellow were blossoms, open full and the most beautiful of all.

Silva saw him before I did. The white man was riding a big gray horse, coming up the trail toward us. He was traveling fast and the gray horse's feet sent rocks rolling off the trail into the dry tumbleweeds. Silva motioned for me to stop and we watched the white man. He didn't see us right away, but finally his horse whinnied at our horses and he stopped. He looked at us briefly before he loped the gray horse across the three hundred yards that separated us. He stopped his horse in front of Silva, and his young fat face was shadowed by the brim of his hat. He didn't look mad, but his small, pale eyes moved from the blood-soaked gunny sacks hanging from my saddle to Silva's face and then back to my face.

"Where did you get the fresh meat?" the white man asked.

"I've been hunting," Silva said, and when he shifted his weight in the saddle the leather creaked.

"The hell you have, Indian. You've been rustling cattle. We've been looking for the thief for a long time."

The rancher was fat, and sweat began to soak through his white cowboy shirt and the wet cloth stuck to the thick rolls of belly fat. He almost seemed to be panting from the exertion of talking, and he smelled rancid, maybe because Silva scared him.

Silva turned to me and smiled. "Go back up the mountain, Yellow Woman."

The white man got angry when he heard Silva speak in a language he couldn't understand. "Don't try anything, Indian. Just keep riding to Marquez. We'll call the state police from there."

The rancher must have been unarmed because he was very frightened and if he had a gun he would have pulled it out then. I turned my horse around and the rancher yelled, "Stop!" I looked at Silva for an instant and there was something ancient and dark—something I could feel in my stomach—in his eyes, and when I glanced at his hand I saw his finger on the trigger of the .30–30 that was still in the saddle scabbard. I slapped my horse across the flank and the sacks of raw meat swung against my knees as the horse leaped up the trail. It was hard to keep my balance, and once I thought I felt the saddle slipping backward; it was because of this that I could not look back.

I didn't stop until I reached the ridge where the trail forked. The horse was breathing deep gasps and there was a dark film of sweat on its neck. I looked down in the direction I had come from, but I couldn't see the place. I waited. The wind came up and pushed warm air past me. I looked up at the sky, pale blue and full of thin clouds and fading vapor trails left by jets.

I think four shots were fired—I remember hearing four hollow explosions that reminded me of deer hunting. There could have been more shots after that, but I couldn't have heard them because my horse was running again and the loose rocks were making too much noise as they scattered around his feet.

Horses have a hard time running downhill, but I went that way instead of uphill to the mountain because I thought it was safer. I felt better with the horse running southeast past the round gray hills that were covered with cedar trees and black lava rock. When I got to the plain in the distance I could see the dark green patches of tamaracks that grew along the river; and beyond the river I could see the beginning of the pale sandrock mesas. I stopped the horse and looked back to see if anyone was coming; then I got off the horse and turned the horse around, wondering if it would go back to its corral under the pines on the mountain. It looked back at me for a moment and then plucked a mouthful of green tumbleweeds before it trotted back up the trail with its ears pointed forward, carrying its head daintily to one side to avoid stepping on the dragging reins. When the horse disappeared over the last hill, the gunny sacks full of meat were still swinging and bouncing.

## IV

I walked toward the river on a wood-hauler's road that I knew would eventually lead to the paved road. I was thinking about waiting beside the road for someone to drive by, but by the time I got to the pavement I had decided it wasn't very far to walk if I followed the river back the way Silva and I had come.

The river water tasted good, and I sat in the shade under a cluster of silvery willows. I thought about Silva, and I felt sad at leaving him; still, there was something strange about him, and I tried to figure it out all the way back home.

I came back to the place on the river bank where he had been sitting the first time I saw him. The green willow leaves that he had trimmed from the branch were still lying there, wilted in the sand. I saw the leaves and I wanted to go back to him—to kiss him and to touch him—but the mountains were too far away now. And I told myself, because I believe it, he will come back sometime and be waiting again by the river.

I followed the path up from the river into the village. The sun was getting low, and I could smell supper cooking when I got to the screen door of my house. I could hear their voices inside—my mother as telling my grandmother how to fix the Jell-o and my husband, Al, was playing with the baby. I decided to tell them that some Navajo had kidnapped me, but I was sorry that old Grandpa wasn't alive to hear my story because it was the Yellow Woman stories he liked to tell best.

# Helena Maria Viramontes

## (B. 1954)

Born in East Los Angeles, California, Helena Maria Viramontes is the daughter of a construction worker and a Chicana housewife. She received her B.A. from Immaculate Heart College in 1975, where she was one of five Chicanas in her class. In 1977, Viramontes won first prize in a literary contest sponsored by *Statement* magazine for her story "Requiem for the Poor." She also won a fiction prize, for her story "Birthday," in the University of California, Irvine's Chicano Literary Contest. In 1981, Viramontes entered the graduate program at U.C. Irvine as a creative writing student but left early, completing the requirements for the M.F.A. degree after the publication of her stories. Her works include *The Moths* and Other Stories (1985), Paris Rats in E.L.A. (1993), and Under the Feet of Jesus (1995). In 1985, Viramontes helped to organize the first national conference on Mexican American women writers, held at U.C. Irvine. The result was Beyond Stereotypes: A Critical Analysis of Chicana Literature (1985), which Viramontes coedited. Viramontes writes about the cultural, social, and economic tensions that inform, complicate, and define women's lives.

## The Moths                                                           1985

I was fourteen years old when Abuelita requested my help. And it seemed only fair. Abuelita had pulled me through the rages of scarlet fever by placing, removing and replacing potato slices on the temples of my forehead; she had seen me through several whippings, an arm broken by a dare jump off Tío Enrique's toolshed, puberty, and my first lie. Really, I told Amá, it was only fair.

Not that I was her favorite granddaughter or anything special. I wasn't even pretty or nice like my older sisters and I just couldn't do the girl things they could do. My hands were too big to handle the fineries of crocheting or embroidery and I always pricked my fingers or knotted my colored threads time and time again while my sisters laughed and called me bull hands with their cute waterlike voices. So I began keeping a piece of jagged brick in my sock to bash my sisters or anyone who called me bull hands. Once, while we all sat in the bedroom, I hit Teresa on the forehead, right above her eyebrow and she ran to Amá with her mouth open, her hand over her eye while blood seeped between her fingers. I was used to the whippings by then.

I wasn't respectful either. I even went so far as to doubt the power of Abuelita's slices, the slices she said absorbed my fever. "You're still alive, aren't you?" Abuelita snapped back, her pasty gray eye beaming at me and burning holes in my suspicions. Regretful that I had let secret questions drop out of my mouth, I couldn't look into her eyes. My hands began to fan out, grow like a liar's nose until they hung by my side like low weights. Abuelita made a balm out of dried moth wings and Vicks and rubbed my hands, shaped them back to size and it was the strangest feeling. Like bones melting. Like sun shining through the darkness of your eyelids. I didn't mind helping Abuelita after that, so Amá would always send me over to her.

In the early afternoon Amá would push her hair back, hand me my sweater and shoes, and tell me to go to Mama Luna's. This was to avoid another fight and another whipping, I knew. I would deliver one last direct shot on Marisela's arm and jump out of our house, the slam of the screen door burying her cries of anger, and I'd gladly go help Abuelita plant her wild lilies or jasmine or heliotrope or cilantro or hierbabuena in red Hills Brothers coffee cans. Abuelita would wait for me at the top step of her porch holding a hammer and nail and empty coffee cans. And although we hardly spoke, hardly looked at each other as we worked over root transplants, I always felt her gray eye on me. It made me feel, in a strange sort of way, safe and guarded and not alone. Like God was supposed to make you feel.

On Abuelita's porch, I would puncture holes in the bottom of the coffee cans with a nail and a precise hit of a hammer. This completed, my job was to fill them with red clay mud from beneath her rose bushes, packing it softly, then making a perfect hole, four fingers round, to nest a sprouting avocado pit, or the spidery sweet potatoes that Abuelita rooted in mayonnaise jars with toothpicks and daily water, or prickly chayotes that produced vines that twisted and wound all over her porch pillars, crawling to the roof, up and over the roof, and down the other side, making her small brick house look like it was cradled within the vines that grew pear-shaped squashes ready for the pick, ready to be steamed with onions and cheese and butter. The roots would burst out of the rusted coffee cans and search for a place to connect. I would then feed the seedlings with water.

But this was a different kind of help, Amá said, because Abuelita was dying. Looking into her gray eye, then into her brown one, the doctor said it was just a matter of days. And so it seemed only fair that these hands she had melted and formed found use in rubbing her caving body with alcohol and marihuana, rubbing her arms and legs, turning her face to the window so that she could watch the Bird of Paradise blooming or smell the scent of clove in the air. I toweled her face frequently and held her hand for hours. Her gray wiry hair hung over the mattress. Since I could remember, she'd kept her long hair in braids. Her mouth was vacant and when she slept, her eyelids never closed all the way. Up close, you could see her gray eye beaming out the window, staring hard as if to remember everything. I never kissed her. I left the window open when I went to the market.

Across the street from Jay's Market there was a chapel. I never knew its denomination, but I went in just the same to search for candles. I sat down on one of the pews because there were none. After I cleaned my fingernails, I looked up at the high ceiling. I had forgotten the vastness of these places, the coolness of the marble pillars and the frozen statues with blank eyes. I was alone. I knew why I had never returned.

That was one of Apá's biggest complaints. He would pound his hands on the table, rocking the sugar dish or spilling a cup of coffee and scream that if I didn't go to mass every Sunday to save my goddamn sinning soul, then I had no reason to go out of the house, period. Punto final. He would grab my arm and dig his nails into me to make sure I understood the importance of catechism. Did he make himself clear? Then he strategically directed his anger at Amá for her lousy ways of bringing up daughters, being disrespectful and unbelieving, and my older sisters would pull me aside and tell me if I didn't get to mass right this minute, they were all going to kick the holy shit out of me. Why am I so selfish? Can't you see what it's doing to Amá, you idiot? So I would wash my feet and stuff them in my black Easter shoes that shone with Vaseline, grab a missal and veil, and wave good-bye to Amá.

I would walk slowly down Lorena to First to Evergreen, counting the cracks on the cement. On Evergreen I would turn left and walk to Abuelita's. I liked her porch because it was shielded by the vines of the chayotes and I could get a good look at the people and car traffic on Evergreen without them knowing. I would jump up the porch steps, knock on the screen door as I wiped my feet and call Abuelita? mi

Abuelita? As I opened the door and stuck my head in, I would catch the gagging scent of toasting chile on the placa.[1] When I entered the sala,[2] she would greet me from the kitchen, wringing her hands in her apron. I'd sit at the corner of the table to keep from being in her way. The chiles made my eyes water. Am I crying? No, Mama Luna, I'm sure not crying. I don't like going to mass, but my eyes watered anyway, the tears dropping on the tablecloth like candle wax. Abuelita lifted the burnt chiles from the fire and sprinkled water on them until the skins began to separate. Placing them in front of me, she turned to check the menudo. I peeled the skins off and put the flimsy, limp looking green and yellow chiles in the molcajete[3] and began to crush and crush and twist and crush the heart out of the tomato, the clove of garlic, the stupid chiles that made me cry, crushed them until they turned into liquid under my bull hand. With a wooden spoon, I scraped hard to destroy the guilt, and my tears were gone. I put the bowl of chile next to a vase filled with freshly cut roses. Abuelita touched my hand and pointed to the bowl of menudo that steamed in front of me. I spooned some chile into the menudo and rolled a corn tortilla thin with the palms of my hands. As I ate, a fine Sunday breeze entered the kitchen and a rose petal calmly feathered down to the table.

I left the chapel without blessing myself and walked to Jay's. Most of the time Jay didn't have much of anything. The tomatoes were always soft and the cans of Campbell soups had rusted spots on them. There was dust on the tops of cereal boxes. I picked up what I needed: rubbing alcohol, five cans of chicken broth, a big bottle of Pine Sol. At first Jay got mad because I thought I had forgotten the money. But it was there all the time, in my back pocket.

When I returned from the market, I heard Amá crying in Abuelita's kitchen. She looked up at me with puffy eyes. I placed the bags of groceries on the table and began putting the cans of soup away. Amá sobbed quietly. I never kissed her. After a while, I patted her on the back for comfort. Finally: "¿Y mi Amá?" she asked in a whisper, then choked again and cried into her apron.

Abuelita fell off the bed twice yesterday, I said, knowing that I shouldn't have said it and wondering why I wanted to say it because it only made Amá cry harder. I guess I became angry and just so tired of the quarrels and beatings and unanswered prayers and my hands just there hanging helplessly by my side. Amá looked at me again, confused, angry, and her eyes were filled with sorrow. I went outside and sat on the porch swing and watched the people pass. I sat there until she left. I dozed off repeating the words to myself like rosary prayers: when do you stop giving when do you start giving when do you . . . and when my hands fell from my lap, I awoke to catch them. The sun was setting, an orange glow, and I knew Abuelita was hungry.

There comes a time when the sun is defiant. Just about the time when moods change, inevitable seasons of a day, transitions from one color to another, that hour or minute or second when the sun is finally defeated, finally sinks into the realization

---

1 **placa:** Spanish. A plate or board.
2 **sala:** Spanish. A living room.
3 **molcajete:** Spanish. A mortar, the small bowl used for grinding spices.

that it cannot with all its power to heal or burn, exist forever, there comes an illumination where the sun and earth meet, a final burst of burning red orange fury reminding us that although endings are inevitable, they are necessary for rebirths, and when that time came, just when I switched on the light in the kitchen to open Abuelita's can of soup, it was probably then that she died.

The room smelled of Pine Sol and vomit and Abuelita had defecated the remains of her cancerous stomach. She had turned to the window and tried to speak, but her mouth remained open and speechless. I heard you, Abuelita, I said, stroking her cheek, I heard you. I opened the windows of the house and let the soup simmer and overboil on the stove. I turned the stove off and poured the soup down the sink. From the cabinet I got a tin basin, filed it with lukewarm water and carried it carefully to the room. I went to the linen closet and took out some modest bleached white towels. With the sacredness of a priest preparing his vestments, I unfolded the towels one by one on my shoulders. I removed the sheets and blankets from her bed and peeled off her thick flannel nightgown. I toweled her puzzled face, stretching out the wrinkles, removing the coils of her neck, toweled her shoulders and breasts. Then I changed the water. I returned to towel the creases of her stretch-marked stomach, her sporadic vaginal hairs, and her sagging thighs. I removed the lint from between her toes and noticed a mapped birthmark on the fold of her buttock. The scars on her back which were as thin as the life lines on the palms of her hands made me realize how little I really knew of Abuelita. I covered her with a thin blanket and went into the bathroom. I washed my hands, and turned on the tub faucets and watched the water pour into the tub with vitality and steam. When it was full, I turned off the water and undressed. Then, I went to get Abuelita.

She was not as heavy as I thought and when I carried her in my arms, her body fell into a V, and yet my legs were tired, shaky, and I felt as if the distance between the bedroom and bathroom was miles and years away. Amá, where are you?

I stepped into the bathtub one leg first, then the other. I bent my knees slowly to descend into the water slowly so I wouldn't scald her skin. There, there, Abuelita, I said, cradling her, smoothing her as we descended, I heard you. Her hair fell back and spread across the water like eagle's wings. The water in the tub overflowed and poured onto the tile of the floor. Then the moths came. Small, gray ones that came from her soul and out through her mouth fluttering to light, circling the single dull light bulb of the bathroom. Dying is lonely and I wanted to go to where the moths were, stay with her and plant chayotes whose vines would crawl up her fingers and into the clouds; I wanted to rest my head on her chest with her stroking my hair, telling me about the moths that lay within the soul and slowly eat the spirit up; I wanted to return to the waters of the womb with her so that we would never be alone again. I wanted. I wanted my Amá. I removed a few strands of hair from Abuelita's face and held her small light head within the hollow of my neck. The bathroom was filled with moths, and for the first time in a long time I cried, rocking us, crying for her, for me, for Amá, the sobs emerging from the depths of anguish, the misery of feeling half born, sobbing until finally the sobs rippled into circles and circles of sadness and relief. There, there, I said to Abuelita, rocking us gently, there, there.

# Alice Walker

## (B. 1944)

Alice Walker, the youngest of eight children, was blinded and scarred in one eye in a childhood accident. This was partially corrected a year later, but Walker says that the experience had a profound influence on her. She attended Sarah Lawrence College, where she received her B.A. in 1965 and became active in the civil rights movement. She published her first book of poems, *Once* (1968), while she was a senior. After college, Walker returned to the South and worked to register voters and teach black history. She received a McDowell Fellowship in 1967 and completed her first novel, *The Third Life of Grange Copeland* in 1970. Walker continued to grow in fame as she published *In Love and Trouble* (1973), *Meridian* (1976), and *You Can't Keep a Good Woman Down* (1981). She won both the Pulitzer Prize and the American Book Award for *The Color Purple* (1982), one of her best-known works. Walker has also published *In Search of Our Mothers' Gardens* (1983), *The Temple of My Familiar* (1989), *Possessing the Secret of Joy* (1992), *By the Light of My Father's Smile* (1998), and *Now Is the Time to Open Your Heart* (2004). Alice Walker does not approach the project of unearthing the truth of women's lives lightly, but she does infuse her stories with a rich sense of humor and an indelible tone of hopefulness.

## *Everyday Use*                                                                      1973

### *For Your Grandmama*

I will wait for her in the yard that Maggie and I made so clean and wavy yesterday afternoon. A yard like this is more comfortable than most people know. It is not just a yard. It is like an extended living room. When the hard clay is swept clean as a floor and the fine sand around the edges lined with tiny, irregular grooves, anyone can come and sit and look up into the elm tree and wait for the breezes that never come inside the house.

Maggie will be nervous until after her sister goes: she will stand hopelessly in corners, homely and ashamed of the burn scars down her arms and legs, eying her sister with a mixture of envy and awe. She thinks her sister has held life always in the palm of one hand, that "no" is a word the world never learned to say to her.

You've no doubt seen those TV shows where the child who has "made it" is confronted, as a surprise, by her own mother and father, tottering in weakly from backstage. (A pleasant surprise, of course: What would they do if parent and child came on the show only to curse out and insult each other?) On TV mother and child embrace and smile into each other's faces. Sometimes the mother and father weep, the child wraps them in her arms and leans across the table to tell how she would not have made it without their help. I have seen these programs.

Sometimes I dream a dream in which Dee and I are suddenly brought together on a TV program of this sort. Out of a dark and soft-seated limousine I am ushered into a bright room filled with many people. There I meet a smiling, gray, sporty man like Johnny Carson who shakes my hand and tells me what a fine girl I have. Then we are on the stage and Dee is embracing me with tears in her eyes. She pins on my dress a large orchid, even though she has told me once that she thinks orchids are tacky flowers.

In real life I am a large, big-boned woman with rough, man-working hands. In the winter I wear flannel nightgowns to bed and overalls during the day. I can kill and clean a hog as mercilessly as a man. My fat keeps me hot in zero weather. I can work outside all day, breaking ice to get water for washing; I can eat pork liver cooked over the open fire minutes after it comes steaming from the hog. One winter I knocked a bull calf straight in the brain between the eyes with a sledge hammer and had the meat hung up to chill before nightfall. But of course all this does not show on television. I am the way my daughter would want me to be: a hundred pounds lighter, my skin like an uncooked barley pancake. My hair glistens in the hot bright lights. Johnny Carson has much to do to keep up with my quick and witty tongue.

But that is a mistake. I know even before I wake up. Who ever knew a Johnson with a quick tongue? Who can even imagine me looking a strange white man in the eye? It seems to me I have talked to them always with one foot raised in flight, with my head turned in whichever way is farthest from them. Dee, though. She would always look anyone in the eye. Hesitation was no part of her nature.

"How do I look, Mama?" Maggie says, showing just enough of her thin body enveloped in pink skirt and red blouse for me to know she's there, almost hidden by the door.

"Come out into the yard," I say.

Have you ever seen a lame animal, perhaps a dog run over by some careless person rich enough to own a car, sidle up to someone who is ignorant enough to be kind to him? That is the way my Maggie walks. She has been like this, chin on chest, eyes on ground, feet in shuffle, ever since the fire that burned the other house to the ground.

Dee is lighter than Maggie, with nicer hair and a fuller figure. She's a woman now, though sometimes I forget. How long ago was it that the other house burned? Ten, twelve years? Sometimes I can still hear the flames and feel Maggie's arms sticking to me, her hair smoking and her dress falling off her in little black papery flakes. Her eyes seemed stretched open, blazed open by the flames reflected in them. And Dee. I see her standing off under the sweet gum tree she used to dig gum out of; a look of concentration on her face as she watched the last dingy gray board of the house fall in toward the red-hot brick chimney. Why don't you do a dance around the ashes? I'd want to ask her. She had hated the house that much.

I used to think she hated Maggie, too. But that was before we raised the money, the church and me, to send her to Augusta to school. She used to read to us without pity; forcing words, lies, other folks' habits, whole lives upon us two, sitting trapped and ignorant underneath her voice. She washed us in a river of make-believe, burned us with a lot of knowledge we didn't necessarily need to know. Pressed us to her with the serious way she read, to shove us away at just the moment, like dimwits, we seemed about to understand.

Dee wanted nice things. A yellow organdy dress to wear to her graduation from high school; black pumps to match a green suit she'd made from an old suit somebody gave me. She was determined to stare down any disaster in her efforts. Her eyelids would not flicker for minutes at a time. Often I fought off the temptation to shake her. At sixteen she had a style of her own: and knew what style was.

I never had an education myself. After second grade the school was closed down. Don't ask me why: in 1927 colored asked fewer questions than they do now. Sometimes Maggie reads to me. She stumbles along good-naturedly but can't see well. She knows she is not bright. Like good looks and money, quickness passed her by. She will marry John Thomas (who has mossy teeth in an earnest face) and then I'll be free to sit here and I guess just sing church songs to myself. Although I never was a good singer. Never could carry a tune. I was always better at a man's job. I used to love to milk till I was hooked in the side in '49. Cows are soothing and slow and don't bother you, unless you try to milk them the wrong way.

I have deliberately turned my back on the house. It is three rooms, just like the one that burned, except the roof is tin; they don't make shingle roofs any more. There are no real windows, just some holes cut in the sides, like the portholes in a ship, but not round and not square, with rawhide holding the shutters up on the outside. This house is in a pasture, too, like the other one. No doubt when Dee sees it she will want to tear it down. She wrote me once that no matter where we "choose" to live, she will manage to come see us. But she will never bring her friends. Maggie and I thought about this and Maggie asked me, "Mama, when did Dee ever *have* any friends?"

She had a few. Furtive boys in pink shirts hanging about on washday after school. Nervous girls who never laughed. Impressed with her they worshipped the well-turned phrase, the cute shape, the scalding humor that erupted like bubbles in lye. She read to them.

When she was courting Jimmy T she didn't have much time to pay to us, but turned all her faultfinding power on him. He *flew* to marry a cheap city girl from a family of ignorant flashy people. She hardly had time to recompose herself.

When she comes I will meet—but there they are!

Maggie attempts to make a dash for the house, in her shuffling way, but I stay her with my hand. "Come back here," I say. And she stops and tries to dig a well in the sand with her toe.

It is hard to see them clearly through the strong sun. But even the first glimpse of leg out of the car tells me it is Dee. Her feet were always neat-looking, as if God himself had shaped them with a certain style. From the other side of the car comes a short, stocky man. Hair is all over his head a foot long and hanging from his chin like a kinky mule tail. I hear Maggie suck in her breath. "Uhnnnh," is what it sounds like. Like when you see the wriggling end of a snake just in front of your foot on the road. "Uhnnnh."

Dee next. A dress down to the ground, in this hot weather. A dress so loud it hurts my eyes. There are yellows and oranges enough to throw back the light of the sun. I feel my whole face warming from the heat waves it throws out. Earrings gold, too, and hanging down to her shoulders. Bracelets dangling and making noises when she moves her arm up to shake the folds of the dress out of her armpits. The dress is loose and flows, and as she walks closer, I like it. I hear Maggie go "Uhnnnh" again. It is her sister's hair. It stands straight up like the wool on a sheep. It is black as night and around the edges are two long pigtails that rope about like small lizards disappearing behind her ears.

"Wa-su-zo-Tean-o!" she says, coming on in that gliding way the dress makes her move. The short stocky fellow with the hair to his navel is all grinning and he follows up with "Asalamalakim, my mother and sister!" He moves to hug Maggie but she falls back, right up against the back of my chair. I feel her trembling there and when I look up I see the perspiration falling off her chin.

"Don't get up," says Dee. Since I am stout it takes something of a push. You can see me trying to move a second or two before I make it. She turns, showing white heels through her sandals, and goes back to the car. Out she peeks next with a Polaroid. She stoops down quickly and lines up picture after picture of me sitting there in front of the house with Maggie cowering behind me. She never takes a shot without making sure the house is included. When a cow comes nibbling around the edge of the yard she snaps it and me and Maggie *and* the house. Then she puts the Polaroid in the back seat of the car, and comes up and kisses me on the forehead.

Meanwhile Asalamalakim is going through motions with Maggie's hand. Maggie's hand is as limp as a fish, and probably as cold, despite the sweat, and she keeps trying to pull it back. It looks like Asalamalakim wants to shake hands but wants to do it fancy. Or maybe he don't know how people shake hands. Anyhow, he soon gives up on Maggie.

"Well," I say. "Dee."

"No, Mama," she says. "Not 'Dee,' Wangero Leewanika Kemanjo!"

"What happened to 'Dee'?" I wanted to know.

"She's dead," Wangero said. "I couldn't bear it any longer, being named after the people who oppress me."

"You know as well as me you was named after your aunt Dicie," I said. Dicie is my sister. She named Dee. We called her "Big Dee" after Dee was born.

"But who was *she* named after?" asked Wangero.

"I guess after Grandma Dee," I said.

"And who was she named after?" asked Wangero.

"Her mother," I said, and saw Wangero was getting tired. "That's about as far back as I can trace it," I said. Though, in fact, I probably could have carried it back beyond the Civil War through the branches.

"Well," said Asalamalakim, "there you are."

"Uhnnnh," I heard Maggie say.

"There I was not," I said, "before 'Dicie' cropped up in our family, so why should I try to trace it that far back?"

He just stood there grinning, looking down on me like somebody inspecting a Model A car. Every once in a while he and Wangero sent eye signals over my head.

"How do you pronounce this name?" I asked.

"You don't have to call me by it if you don't want to," said Wangero.

"Why shouldn't I?" I asked. "If that's what you want us to call you, we'll call you."

"I know it might sound awkward at first," said Wangero.

"I'll get used to it," I said. "Ream it out again."

Well, soon we got the name out of the way. Asalamalakim had a name twice as long and three times as hard. After I tripped over it two or three times he told me to just call him Hakim-a-barber. I wanted to ask him was he a barber, but I didn't really think he was, so I didn't ask.

"You must belong to those beef-cattle peoples down the road," I said. They said "Asalamalakim" when they met you, too, but they didn't shake hands. Always too busy: feeding the cattle, fixing the fences, putting up salt-lick shelters, throwing down hay. When the white folks poisoned some of the herd the men stayed up all night with rifles in their hands. I walked a mile and a half just to see the sight.

Hakim-a-barber said, "I accept some of their doctrines, but farming and raising cattle is not my style." (They didn't tell me, and I didn't ask, whether Wangero [Dee] had really gone and married him.)

We sat down to eat and right away he said he didn't eat collards and pork was unclean. Wangero, though, went on through the chitlins and corn bread, the greens and everything else. She talked a blue streak over the sweet potatoes. Everything delighted her. Even the fact that we still used the benches her daddy made for the table when we couldn't afford to buy chairs.

"Oh, Mama!" she cried. Then turned to Hakim-a-barber. "I never knew how lovely these benches are. You can feel the rump prints," she said, running her hands underneath her and long the bench. Then she gave a sigh and her hand closed over Grandma Dee's butter dish. "That's it!" she said. "I knew there was something I wanted to ask you if I could have." She jumped up from the table and went over in the corner where the churn stood, the milk in it clabber by now. She looked at the churn and looked at it.

"This churn top is what I need," she said. "Didn't Uncle Buddy whittle it out of a tree you all used to have?"

"Yes," I said.

"Uh huh," she said happily. "And I want the dasher, too."

"Uncle Buddy whittle that, too?" asked the barber.

Dee (Wangero) looked up at me.

"Aunt Dee's first husband whittled the dash," said Maggie so low you almost couldn't hear her. "His name was Henry, but they called him Stash."

"Maggie's brain is like an elephant's," Wangero said, laughing. "I can use the churn top as a centerpiece for the alcove table," she said, sliding a plate over the churn, "and I'll think of something artistic to do with the dasher."

When she finished wrapping the dasher the handle stuck out. I took it for a moment in my hands. You didn't even have to look close to see where hands pushing the dasher up and down to make butter had left a kind of sink in the wood. In fact, there were a lot of small sinks; you could see where thumbs and fingers had sunk into the wood. It was beautiful light yellow wood, from a tree that grew in the yard where Big Dee and Stash had lived.

After dinner Dee (Wangero) went to the trunk at the foot of my bed and started rifling through it. Maggie hung back in the kitchen over the dishpan. Out came Wangero with two quilts. They had been pieced by Grandma Dee and then Big Dee and me had hung them on the quilt frames on the front porch and quilted them. One was in the Lone Star pattern. The other was Walk Around the Mountain. In both of them were scraps of dresses Grandma Dee had worn fifty and more years ago. Bits and pieces of Grandpa Jarrell's Paisley shirts. And one teeny faded blue piece, about the size of a penny matchbox, that was from Great Grandpa Ezra's uniform that he wore in the Civil War.

"Mama," Wangero said sweet as a bird. "Can I have these old quilts?"

I heard something fall in the kitchen, and a minute later the kitchen door slammed.

"Why don't you take one or two of the others?" I asked. "These old things was just done by me and Big Dee from some tops your grandma pieced before she died."

"No," said Wangero. "I don't want those. They are stitched around the borders by machine."

"That'll make them last better," I said.

"That's not the point," said Wangero. "These are all pieces of dresses Grandma used to wear. She did all this stitching by hand. Imagine!" She held the quilts securely in her arms, stroking them.

"Some of the pieces, like those lavender ones, come from old clothes her mother handed down to her," I said, moving up to touch the quilts. Dee (Wangero) moved back just enough so that I couldn't reach the quilts. They already belonged to her.

"Imagine!" she breathed again, clutching them closely to her bosom.

"The truth is," I said, "I promised to give them quilts to Maggie, for when she marries John Thomas."

She gasped like a bee had stung her.

"Maggie can't appreciate these quilts!" she said. "She'd probably be backward enough to put them to everyday use."

"I reckon she would," I said. "God knows I been saving 'em for long enough with nobody using 'em. I hope she will!" I didn't want to bring up how I had offered Dee (Wangero) a quilt when she went away to college. Then she had told me they were old-fashioned, out of style.

"But they're *priceless!*" she was saying now, furiously; for she has a temper. "Maggie would put them on the bed and in five years they'd be in rags. Less than that!"

"She can always make some more," I said. "Maggie knows how to quilt."

Dee (Wangero) looked at me with hatred. "You just will not understand. The point is these quilts, *these* quilts!"

"Well," I said, stumped. "What would *you* do with them?"

"Hang them," she said. As if that was the only thing you *could* do with quilts.

Maggie by now was standing in the door. I could almost hear the sound her feet made as they scraped over each other.

"She can have them, Mama," she said, like somebody used to never winning anything, or having anything reserved for her. "I can 'member Grandma Dee without the quilts."

I looked at her hard. She had filled her bottom lip with checkerberry snuff and it gave her face a kind of dopey, hangdog look. It was Grandma Dee and Big Dee who taught her how to quilt herself. She stood there with her scarred hands hidden in the folds of her skirt. She looked at her sister with something like fear but she wasn't mad at her. This was Maggie's portion. This was the way she knew God to work.

When I looked at her like that something hit me in the top of my head and ran down to the soles of my feet. Just like when I'm in church and the spirit of God touches me and I get happy and shout. I did something I never had done before: hugged Maggie to me, then dragged her on into the room, snatched the quilts out of Miss Wangero's hands and dumped them into Maggie's lap. Maggie just sat there on my bed with her mouth open.

"Take one or two of the others," I said to Dee.

But she turned without a word and went out to Hakim-a-barber.

"You just don't understand," she said, as Maggie and I came out to the car.

"What don't I understand?" I wanted to know.

"Your heritage," she said. And then she turned to Maggie, kissed her, and said, "You ought to try to make something of yourself, too, Maggie. It's really a new day for us. But from the way you and Mama still live you'd never know it."

She put on some sunglasses that hid everything above the tip of her nose and her chin.

Maggie smiled; maybe at the sunglasses. But a real smile, not scared. After we watched the car dust settle I asked Maggie to bring me a dip of snuff. And then the two of us sat there just enjoying, until it was time to go in the house and go to bed.

# Tobias Wolff

### (B. 1945)

Tobias Wolff is best known for his memoir *This Boy's Life* (1989), which tells of his childhood and his relationship with his mother and abusive stepfather. Wolff has worked as a teacher as well as a writer and has won many awards for his writing. After completing his Stegner Fellowship, he served as the Jones Lecturer in creative writing at Stanford University (1975–1978). In 1980, Wolff became a part of the creative writing program at Syracuse University and worked there until 1997. He is currently teaching. Wolff's works include *In the Garden of the North American Martyrs* (1981), *The Barracks Thief* (1984), *Back in the World* (1985), *In Pharaoh's Army: Memories of the Lost War* (1994), and *The Night in Question* (1996). His first novel, *Old School,* was published in 2003. Wolff's characters are less than perfect, and he gets to the heart of American lives without sentimentality by means of evocative, spare prose.

## Bullet in the Brain                                                      1995

Anders couldn't get to the bank until just before it closed, so of course the line was endless and he got stuck behind two women whose loud, stupid conversation put him in a murderous temper. He was never in the best of tempers anyway, Anders—a book critic known for the weary, elegant savagery with which he dispatched almost everything he reviewed.

*Anders was always in bad mood.*

With the line still doubled around the rope, one of the tellers stuck a "POSITION CLOSED" sign in her window and walked to the back of the bank, where she leaned against a desk and began to pass the time with a man shuffling papers. The women in front of Anders broke off their conversation and watched the teller with hatred. "Oh, that's nice," one of them said. She turned to Anders and added, confident of his accord, "One of those little human touches that keep us coming back for more."

Anders had conceived his own towering hatred of the teller, but he immediately turned it on the presumptuous crybaby in front of him. "Damned unfair," he said. "Tragic, really. If they're not chopping off the wrong leg, or bombing your ancestral village, they're closing their positions."

She stood her ground. "I didn't say it was tragic," she said. "I just think it's a pretty lousy way to treat your customers."

"Unforgivable," Anders said. "Heaven will take note."

She sucked in her cheeks but stared past him and said nothing. Anders saw that the other woman, her friend, was looking in the same direction. And then the tellers stopped what they were doing, and the customers slowly turned, and silence came over the bank. Two men wearing black ski masks and blue business suits were standing to the side of the door. One of them had a pistol pressed against the guard's neck. The guard's eyes were closed, and his lips were moving. The other man had a sawed-off shotgun. "Keep your big mouth shut!" the man with the pistol said, though no one had spoken a word. "One of you tellers hits the alarm, you're all dead meat. Got it?"

*Bank was Robbed*

The tellers nodded.

"Oh, bravo," Anders said. "*Dead meat.*" He turned to the woman in front of him. "Great script, eh? The stern, brass-knuckled poetry of the dangerous classes."

She looked at him with drowning eyes.

The man with the shotgun pushed the guard to his knees. He handed the shotgun to his partner and yanked the guard's wrists up behind his back and locked them together with a pair of handcuffs. He toppled him onto the floor with a kick between the shoulder blades. Then he took his shotgun back and went over to the security gate at the end of the counter. He was short and heavy and moved with peculiar slowness, even torpor. "Buzz him in," his partner said. The man with the shotgun opened the gate and sauntered along the line of tellers, handing each of them a Hefty bag. When he came to the empty position he looked over at the man with the pistol, who said, "Whose slot is that?"

Anders watched the teller. She put her hand to her throat and turned to the man she'd been talking to. He nodded. "Mine," she said.

"Then get your ugly ass in gear and fill that bag."

"There you go," Anders said to the woman in front of him. "Justice is done."

"Hey! Bright boy! Did I tell you to talk?"

"No," Anders said.

"Then shut your trap."

"Did you hear that?" Anders said. "'Bright boy.' Right out of 'The Killers.'"

"Please be quiet," the woman said.

"Hey, you deaf or what?" The man with the pistol walked over to Anders. He poked the weapon into Anders' gut. "You think I'm playing games?"

"No," Anders said, but the barrel tickled like a stiff finger and he had to fight back the titters. He did this by making himself stare into the man's eyes, which were clearly visible behind the holes in the mask: pale blue and rawly red-rimmed. The man's left eyelid kept twitching. He breathed out a piercing, ammoniac smell that shocked Anders more than anything that had happened, and he was beginning to develop a sense of unease when the man prodded him again with the pistol.

"You like me, bright boy?" he said. "You want to suck my dick?"

"No," Anders said.

"Then stop looking at me."

Anders fixed his gaze on the man's shiny wing-tip shoes.

"Not down there. Up there." He stuck the pistol under Anders' chin and pushed it upward until Anders was looking at the ceiling.

Anders had never paid much attention to that part of the bank, a pompous old building with marble floors and counters and pillars, and gilt scrollwork over the tellers' cages. The domed ceiling had been decorated with mythological figures whose fleshy, toga-draped ugliness Anders had taken in at a glance many years earlier and afterward declined to notice. Now he had no choice but to scrutinize the painter's work. It was even worse than he remembered, and all of it executed with the utmost gravity. The artist had a few tricks up his sleeve and used them again and again—a certain rosy blush on the underside of the clouds, a coy backward glance on the faces of the cupids and fauns. The ceiling was crowded with various dramas, but the one that caught Anders' eye was Zeus and Europa—portrayed, in this rendition, as a bull ogling a cow from behind a haystack. To make the cow sexy, the painter had canted her hips suggestively and given her long, droopy eyelashes through which she gazed back at the bull with sultry welcome. The bull wore a smirk and his eyebrows were arched. If there'd been a bubble coming out of his mouth, it would have said, "Hubba hubba."

"What's so funny, bright boy?"

"Nothing."

"You think I'm comical? You think I'm some kind of clown?"

"No."

"You think you can fuck with me?"

"No."

"Fuck with me again, you're history. *Capiche?*"

Anders burst out laughing. He covered his mouth with both hands and said, "I'm sorry, I'm sorry," then snorted helplessly through his fingers and said, "*Capiche*—oh, God, *capiche*," and at that the man with the pistol raised the pistol and shot Anders right in the head.

The bullet smashed Anders' skull and ploughed through his brain and exited behind his right ear, scattering shards of bone into the cerebral cortex, the corpus callosum, back toward the basal ganglia, and down into the thalamus. But before all this occurred, the first appearance of the bullet in the cerebrum set off a crackling chain of ion transports and neuro-transmissions. Because of their peculiar origin these traced a peculiar pattern, flukishly calling to life a summer afternoon some forty years past, and long since lost to memory. After striking the cranium the bullet was moving at 900 feet per second, a pathetically sluggish, glacial pace compared to the synaptic lightning that flashed around it. Once in the brain, that is, the bullet came under the mediation of brain time, which gave Anders plenty of leisure to contemplate the scene that, in a phrase he would have abhorred, "passed before his eyes."

It is worth noting what Anders did not remember, given what he did remember. He did not remember his first lover, Sherry, or what he had most madly loved about her, before it came to irritate him—her unembarrassed carnality, and especially the cordial way she had with his unit, which she called Mr. Mole, as in, "Uh-oh, looks like Mr. Mole wants to play," and, "Let's hide Mr. Mole!" Anders did not remember his wife, whom he had also loved before she exhausted him with her predictability, or his daughter, now a sullen professor of economics at Dartmouth. He did not remember standing just outside his daughter's door as she lectured her bear about his naughtiness and described the truly appalling punishments Paws would receive unless he changed his ways. He did not remember a single line of the hundreds of poems he had committed to memory in his youth so that he could give himself the shivers at will— not "Silent, upon a peak in Darien," or "My God, I heard this day," or "All my pretty ones? Did you say all? O hell-kite! All?" None of these did he remember; not one. Anders did not remember his dying mother saying of his father, "I should have stabbed him in his sleep."

He did not remember Professor Josephs telling his class how Athenian prisoners in Sicily had been released if they could recite Aeschylus, and then reciting Aeschylus himself, right there, in the Greek. Anders did not remember how his eyes had burned at those sounds. He did not remember the surprise of seeing a college classmate's name on the jacket of a novel not long after they graduated, or the respect he had felt after reading the book. He did not remember the pleasure of giving respect.

1346 • The Contemporary Short Story

Nor did Anders remember seeing a woman leap to her death from the building opposite his own just days after his daughter was born. He did not remember shouting, "Lord have mercy!" He did not remember deliberately crashing his father's car into a tree, or having his ribs kicked in by three policemen at an anti-war rally, or waking himself up with laughter. He did not remember when he began to regard the heap of books on his desk with boredom and dread, or when he grew angry at writers for writing them. He did not remember when everything began to remind him of something else.

This is what he remembered. Heat. A baseball field. Yellow grass, the whirr of insects, himself leaning against a tree as the boys of the neighborhood gather for a pickup game. He looks on as the others argue the relative genius of Mantle and Mays. They have been worrying this subject all summer, and it has become tedious to Anders: an oppression, like the heat.

Then the last two boys arrive, Coyle and a cousin of his from Mississippi. Anders has never met Coyle's cousin before and will never see him again. He says hi with the rest but takes no further notice of him until they've chosen sides and someone asks the cousin what position he wants to play. "Shortstop," the boy says. "Short's the best position they is." Anders turns and looks at him. He wants to hear Coyle's cousin repeat what he's just said, but he knows better than to ask. The others will think he's being a jerk, ragging the kid for his grammar. But that isn't it, not at all—it's that Anders is strangely roused, elated, by those final two words, their pure unexpectedness and their music. He takes the field in a trance, repeating them to himself.

The bullet is already in the brain; it won't be outrun forever, or charmed to a halt. In the end it will do its work and leave the troubled skull behind, dragging its comet's tail of memory and hope and talent and love into the marble hall of commerce. That can't be helped. But for now Anders can still make time. Time for the shadows to lengthen on the grass, time for the tethered dog to bark at the flying ball, time for the boy in right field to smack his sweat-blackened mitt and softly chant, *They is, they is, they is.* — *everything was too ordinary for him.*

# Monica Wood

## (B. 1953)

Monica Wood was born in Mexico, Maine, to a family of devout Irish Catholics. She learned from her father that "stories had to be told in a certain way. . . . My grandfather used to sing long, melodramatic, novelistic ballads, another island tradition." She worked as a guidance counselor at Westbrook High School for eight years and began her writing career in her late twenties. Her works include *Secret Language* (1993), *My Only Story* (2000), and *Ernie's Ark: Stories* (2002). Wood has also published two books to help aspiring writers, *Description* (1999) and *The Pocket Muse* (2002). She infuses her works with the theme of family, saying that "any combination of people can fit into a family as long as they have some shared experience."

_____

## Disappearing

When he starts in, I don't look anymore, I know what it looks like, what he looks like, tobacco on his teeth. I just lie in the deep sheets and shut my eyes. I make noises that make it go faster and when he's done he's as far from me as he gets. He could be dead he's so far away.

Lettie says leave then stupid but who would want me. Three hundred pounds anyway but I never check. Skin like tapioca pudding, I wouldn't show anyone. A man.

So we go to the pool at the junior high, swimming lessons. First it's blow bubbles and breathe, blow and breathe. Awful, hot nosefuls of chlorine. My eyes stinging red and patches on my skin. I look worse. We'll get caps and goggles and earplugs and body cream Lettie says. It's better.

There are girls there, what bodies. Looking at me and Lettie out the side of their eyes. Gold hair, skin like milk, chlorine or no.

They thought when I first lowered into the pool, that fat one parting the Red Sea. I didn't care. Something happened when I floated. Good said the little instructor. A little redhead in an emerald suit, no stomach, a depression almost, and white wet skin. Good she said you float just great. Now we're getting somewhere. The whistle around her neck blinded my eyes. And the water under the fluorescent lights. I got scared and couldn't float again. The bottom of the pool was scarred, drops of gray shadow rippling. Without the water I would crack open my head, my dry flesh would sound like a splash on the tiles.

At home I ate a cake and a bottle of milk. No wonder you look like that he said. How can you stand yourself. You're no Cary Grant I told him and he laughed and laughed until I threw up.

When this happens I want to throw up again and again until my heart flops out wet and writhing on the kitchen floor. Then he would know I have one and it moves.

So I went back. And floated again. My arms came around and the groan of the water made the tight blondes smirk but I heard Good that's the crawl that's it in fragments from the redhead when I lifted my face. Through the earplugs I heard her skinny voice. She was happy that I was floating and moving too.

Lettie stopped the lessons and read to me things out of magazines. You have to swim a lot to lose weight. You have to stop eating too. Forget cake and ice cream. Doritos are out. I'm not doing it for that I told her but she wouldn't believe me. She couldn't imagine.

Looking down that shaft of water I know I won't fall. The water shimmers and eases up and down, the heft of me doesn't matter I float anyway.

He says it makes no difference I look the same. But I'm not the same. I can hold myself up in deep water. I can move my arms and feet and the water goes behind me, the wall comes closer. I can look down twelve feet to a cold slab of tile and not be afraid. It makes a difference I tell him. Better believe it mister.

Then this other part happens. Other men interest me. I look at them, real ones, not the ones on TV that's something else entirely. These are real. The one with the white milkweed hair who delivers the mail. The meter man from the light company, heavy thick feet in boots. A smile. Teeth. I drop something out of the cart in the supermarket to see who will pick it up. Sometimes a man. One had yellow short hair and called me ma'am. Young. Thin legs and an accent. One was older. Looked me in the eyes. Heavy, but not like me. My eyes are nice. I color the lids. In the pool it runs off in blue tears. When I come out my face is naked.

The lessons are over, I'm certified. A little certificate signed by the redhead. She says I can swim and I can. I'd do better with her body, thin calves hard as granite.

I get a lane to myself, no one shares. The blondes ignore me now that I don't splash the water, know how to lower myself silently. And when I swim I cut the water cleanly.

For one hour every day I am thin, thin as water, transparent, invisible, steam or smoke.

The redhead is gone, they put her at a different pool and I miss the glare of the whistle dangling between her emerald breasts. Lettie won't come over at all now that she is fatter than me. You're so uppity she says. All this talk about water and who do you think you are.

He says I'm looking all right, so at night it is worse but sometimes now when he starts in I say no. On Sundays the pool is closed I can't say no. I haven't been invisible. Even on days when I don't say no it's all right, he's better.

One night he says it won't last, what about the freezer full of low-cal dinners and that machine in the basement. I'm not doing it for that and he doesn't believe me either. But this time there is another part. There are other men in the water I tell him. Fish he says. Fish in the sea. Good luck.

Ma you've lost says my daughter-in-law, the one who didn't want me in the wedding pictures. One with the whole family, she couldn't help that. I learned how to swim I tell her. You should try it, it might help your ugly disposition.

They closed the pool for two weeks and I went crazy. Repairing the tiles. I went there anyway, drove by in the car. I drank water all day.

Then they opened again and I went every day, sometimes four times until the green paint and new stripes looked familiar as a face. At first the water was heavy as blood but I kept on until it was thinner and thinner, just enough to hold me up. That was when I stopped with the goggles and cap and plugs, things that kept the water out of me.

There was a time I went the day before a holiday and no one was there. It was echoey silence just me and the soundless empty pool and a lifeguard behind the glass. I lowered myself so slow it hurt every muscle but not a blip of water not a ripple not one sound and I was under in that other quiet, so quiet some tears got out, I saw their blue trail swirling.

The redhead is back and nods, she has seen me somewhere. I tell her I took lessons and she still doesn't remember.

This has gone too far he says I'm putting you in the hospital. He calls them at the pool and they pay no attention. He doesn't touch me and I smile into my pillow, a secret smile in my own square of the dark.

Oh my God Lettie says what the hell are you doing what the hell do you think you're doing. I'm disappearing I tell her and what can you do about it not a blessed thing.

For a long time in the middle of it people looked at me. Men. And I thought about it. Believe it, I thought. And now they don't look at me again. And it's better.

I'm almost there. Almost water.

The redhead taught me how to dive, how to tuck my head and vanish like a needle into skin, and every time it happens, my feet leaving the board, I think, this will be the time.

# Contemporary Cluster

# Postcolonial Literature

The term *postcolonial literature* arose out of linguistic necessity; literary critics and theorists needed a phrase capable of expressing the totality of literature written in English by nations once colonized by countries within the European empire, particularly England. The period of colonization varies by country, but it is relatively safe to say that the end of World War II also signaled the end of formal colonization. As writers from emerging nations such as India, Pakistan, and countries within Africa began publishing literature in English, the world of literature expanded exponentially. Therefore, the term *postcolonial literature* was needed, as Salman Rushdie explains in *Imaginary Homelands* (1983), because "the world language now also possesses a world literature."

But why not say, "Australian literature" or "Nigerian literature"? Although understanding and evaluating literature on a continent-by-continent or country-by-country basis is important and relevant, advocates of postcolonial studies feel it is also instructive to understand the general cultural and artistic tensions that are produced when a nation has both its own cultural life and cultural ideas and practices imposed by a colonizing nation. Thus the colonized nation emerges after the withdrawal of the colonizer as a country with three cultures: its own culture, an imposed culture, and a culture that reflects the two. Postcolonial literature is then one expression of this cultural amalgamation that can help readers understand the common themes and problems that arise in a postcolonial world.

The term *postcolonial literature,* however, also has its detractors. The list of formerly colonized nations is long and encompasses a variety of situations, including settler countries where much of the population now consists of individuals from the colonizing nation (such as Canada, Australia, New Zealand, and parts of South Africa and Zimbabwe), and nonsettler nations where the population was colonized but not necessarily displaced by European settlers (like India, Jamaica, and Nigeria). The term *postcolonial* does not account for the differences between those who settle a country and those who continue to live amidst settlement. Additionally, countries like Canada

*Women pouring drinking water into jars, Tamil Nadu, India, photograph*

and Australia enjoyed a different relationship with their "mother country" than did the citizens of India or Africa, and racial strife affects these nations differently. The term *postcolonial* can also apply to countries that may not be entirely independent or that in the twenty-first century find themselves at the mercy of globalization and expanding capitalism. Thus, the term *postcolonial* has had to become elastic, much like the world it tries to define.

# Ama Ata Aidoo

## (B. 1942)

Aidoo was born to Maame Abba Abasema and Chief Yaw Fama of the Fanti town of Abeadzi Kyiakor. Her royal upbringing exposed her to African oral storytelling traditions and to Western literature. She began writing plays in the 1960s while attending the University of Ghana. Although the 1965 publication of *The Dilemma of a Ghost* and *Anowa* established Aidoo as a notable playwright, she quickly turned to other forms of writing. She published a collection of short stories, *No Sweetness Here* (1970), and a novel, *Our Sister Killjoy, or Reflections from a Black-Eyed Squint* (1977), before the political climate in Ghana became hostile for intellectuals and artists. Aidoo then turned to teaching English literature at the University of Ghana, Cape Coast, from 1970 to 1983 and was a consulting professor in the ethnic studies program of the Phelps-Stokes Fund from 1974 to 1975. Since 1983, she has lived in Zimbabwe, where she has served as minister of education, worked on curriculum development, and become active in the Zimbabwe Women Writers Group.

Aidoo is the author of two collections of poetry, *Someone Talking to Sometime* (1985), and *An Angry Letter in January and Other Poems* (1992). With language both humorous and conversational, Aidoo questions definitions of identity, exile, and belonging. In 1992 she was awarded the Commonwealth Writers Prize for African Literature for *Changes: A Love Story* (1991). Her second short story collection, *The Girl Who Can and Other Stories* (1997), features young female characters who are trying to define themselves within patriarchal African society. This struggle against patriarchy dovetails with another recurrent theme in Aidoo's work: the link between Africa's social problems and the decline of its oral tradition because of European colonial rule. Thus, the marginalized African woman in Aidoo's stories is often a stand-in for an Africa marginalized on the world stage.

---

## The Message

"Look here my sister, it should not be said but they say they opened her up."

"They opened her up?"

"Yes, opened her up."

"And the baby removed?"

"Yes, the baby removed."

"Yes the baby removed."

"I say. . . ."

"They do not say, my sister."

"Have you heard it?"

"What?"

"This and this and that. . . ."

"A-a-ah! that is it. . . ."

"*Meewuo!*"[1]

---

1 *Meewuo:* Ghanaian. "I'm going to die."

"They don't say *meewuo*. . . ."

"And how is she?"

"Am I not here with you? Do I know the highway which leads to Cape Coast?"

"Hmmm. . . ."

"And anyway how can she live? What is it like even giving birth with a stomach which is whole . . . eh? . . . I am asking you. And if you are always standing on the brink of death who go to war with a stomach that is whole, then how would she do whose stomach is open to the winds?"

"Oh, *poo*, pity. . . ."

"I say. . . ."

My little bundle, come. You and I are going to Cape Coast today.

I am taking one of her own cloths with me, just in case. These people on the coast do not know how to do a thing and I am not going to have anybody mishandling my child's body. I hope they give it to me. Horrible things I have heard done to people's bodies. Cutting them up and using them for instructions. Whereas even murderers still have decent burials.

I see Mensima coming. . . . And there is Nkama too . . . and Adwoa Meenu. . . . Now they are coming to . . . "*poo* pity" me. Witches, witches, witches . . . they have picked mine up while theirs prosper around them, children, grandchildren and great-grandchildren—theirs shoot up like mushrooms.

"Esi, we have heard of your misfortune. . . ."

"That our little lady's womb has been opened up. . . ."

"And her baby removed. . . ."

Thank you very much.

"Has she lived through it?"

I do not know.

"Esi, bring her here, back home whatever happens."

*Yoo,*[2] thank you. If the government's people allow it, I shall bring her home.

"And have you got ready your things?"

Yes. . . . No.

I cannot even think well.

It feels so noisy in my head. . . . Oh my little child. . . . I am wasting time. . . . And so I am going. . . .

Yes, to Cape Coast.

No, I do not know anyone there now but do you think no one would show me the way to this big hospital . . . if I asked around?

Hmmm . . . it's me has ended up like this. I was thinking that everything was alright now. . . . *Yoo.* And thank you too. Shut the door for me when you are leaving. You may stay too long outside if you wait for me, so go home and be about your business. I will let you know when I bring her in.

"Maami Amfoa, where are you going?"

My daughter, I am going to Cape Coast.

---

2 *Yoo:* Ghanaina. Yes.

"And what is our old mother going to do with such swift steps? Is it serious?"

My daughter, it is very serious.

"Mother, may God go with you."

*Yoo,* my daughter.

"Eno, and what calls at this hour of the day?"

They want me at Cape Coast.

"Does my friend want to go and see how much the city has changed since we went there to meet the new Wesleyan Chairman,[3] twenty years ago?"

My sister, do you think I have knees to go parading on the streets of Cape Coast?

"Is it heavy?"

Yes, very heavy indeed. They have opened up my grandchild at the hospital, *hi, hi, hi....*

"Eno, *due, due, due.*[4] . . . I did not know. May God go with you. . . ."

Thank you *Yaa.*

"O, the world!"

"It's her grandchild. The only daughter of her only son. So you remember Kojo Amisa who went to sodja[5] and fell in the great war, overseas?"

"Yes, it's his daughter. . . ."

. . . O, *poo,* pity.

"Kobina, run to the street, tell Draba Anan to wait for Nana Amfoa."

". . . Draba Aran, Draba, my mother says I must come and tell you to wait for Nana Amfoa."

"And where is she?"

"There she comes."

"Just look at how she hops like a bird . . . does she think we are going to be here all day? And anyway we are full already. . . ."

O, you drivers!

"What have drivers done?"

"And do you think it shows respect when you speak in this way? It is only that things have not gone right; but she could, at least have been your mother. . . ."

"But what have I said? I have not insulted her. I just think that only Youth must be permitted to see Cape Coast, the town of the Dear and Expensive. . . ."

"And do you think she is going on a peaceful journey? The only daughter of her only son has been opened up and her baby removed from her womb."

O . . . God.

O

O

O

*Poo,* pity.

"Me . . . *poo*—pity, I am right about our modern wives. I always say they are useless as compared with our mothers."

---

3 **Wesleyan Chairman:** An official in the Wesleyan mission, a representative body of the Methodist Church.
4 *due, due, due:* Ghanaian. Similar to "tsk, tsk, tsk," a sound of pity.
5 **sodja:** A soldier.

"You drivers!"

"Now what have your modern wives done?"

"Am I not right what I always say about them?"

"You go and watch them in the big towns. All so thin and dry as sticks—you can literally blow them away with your breath. No decent flesh anywhere. Wooden chairs groan when they meet with their hard exteriors."

"O you drivers. . . ."

"But of course all drivers. . . ."

"What have I done? Don't all my male passengers agree with me? These modern girls. . . . Now here is one who cannot even have a baby in a decent way. But must have the baby removed from her stomach. *Tchiaa!*"

"What. . . ."

"Here is the old woman."

"Whose grandchild. . . . ?"

"Yes."

"Nana, I hear you are coming to Cape Coast with us."

Yes my master.

"We nearly left you behind but we heard it was you and that it is a heavy journey you are making."

Yes my master . . . thank you my master.

"Push up please . . . push up. Won't you push up? Why do you all sit looking at me with such eyes as if I was a block of wood?"

"It is not that there is nowhere to push up to. Five fat women should go on that seat, but look at you!"

"And our own grandmother here is none too plump herself. . . . Nana, if they won't push, come to the front seat with me."

". . . Hei, scholar, go to the back. . . ."

". . . And do not scowl on me. I know your sort too well. Something tells me you do not have any job at all. As for that suit you are wearing and looking so grand in, you hired or borrowed it. . . ."

"Oh you drivers!"

Oh you drivers. . . .

The scholar who read this tengram[6] thing, said it was made about three days ago. My lady's husband sent it. . . . Three days. . . . God—that is too long ago. Have they buried her . . . where? Or did they cut her up. . . . I should not think about it . . . or something will happen to me. Eleven or twelve . . . Efua Panyin, Okuma, Kwame Gyasi and who else? But they should not have left me here. Sometimes . . . ah, I hate this nausea. But it is this smell of petrol. Now I have remembered I never could travel in a lorry. I always was so sick. But now I hope at least that will not happen. These young people will think it is because I am old and they will laugh. At least if I knew the child of my child was alive, it would have been good. And the little things she sent me. . . . Sometimes some people like Mensima and Nkansa make me feel as if I had

---

6 **tengram:** A telegram.

been a barren woman instead of only one with whom infant-mortality pledged friendship. . . .

I will give her that set of earrings, bracelet and chain which Odwumfo Ata made for me. It is the most beautiful and the most expensive thing I have. . . . It does not hurt me to think that I am going to die very soon and have them and their children gloating over my things. After all what did they swallow my children for? It does not hurt me at all. If I had been someone else, I would have given them all away before I died. But it does not matter. They can share their own curse. Now, that is the end of me and my roots. . . . Eternal death has worked like a warrior rat, with diabolical sense of duty, to gnaw my bottom. Everything is finished now. The vacant lot is swept and the scraps of old sugar-cane pulp, dry sticks and bunches of hair burnt . . . how it reeks, the smoke!

"O, Nana do not weep. . . ."

"Is the old woman weeping?"

"If the only child of your only child died, won't you weep?"

"Why do you ask me? Did I know your grandchild is dead?"

"Where have you been, not in this lorry? Where were your ears when we were dis cussing it?"

"I do not go putting my mouth in other people's affairs. . . ."

"So what?"

"So go and die."

"*Hei, hei,* it is prohibited to quarrel in my lorry."

"Draba, here is me, sitting quiet and this lady of muscles and bones being cheeky to me."

"Look, I can beat you."

"Beat me . . . beat me . . . let's see."

"*Hei,* you are not civilised, eh?"

"Keep quiet and let us think, both of you, or I will put you down."

"Nana, do not weep. There is God above."

Thank you my master.

"But we are in Cape Coast already."

*Meewuo!* My God, hold me tight or something will happen to me.

My master, I will come down here.

"O Nana, I thought you said you were going to the hospital. . . . We are not there yet."

I am saying maybe I will get down here and ask my way around.

"Nana, you do not know these people, eh? They are very impudent here. They have no use for old age. So they do not respect it. Sit down, I will take you there."

Are you going there, my master?

"No, but I will take you there."

Ah, my master, your old mother thanks you. Do not shed a tear when you hear of my death . . . my master, your old mother thanks you.

I hear there is somewhere where they keep corpses until their owners claim them . . . if she has been buried, then I must find her husband . . . Esi Amfoa, what did I come to do under this sky? I have buried all my children and now I am going to bury my only grandchild!

"Nana we are there."

Is this the hospital?

"Yes, Nana. What is your child's name?"

Esi Amfoa. His father named her after me.

"Do you know her European name?"

No, my master.

"What shall we do?"

". . . Ei lady, Lady Nurse, we are looking for somebody."

"You are looking for somebody and can you read? If you cannot, you must ask someone what the rules in the hospital are. You can only come and visit people at three o'clock."

Lady, please. She was my only grandchild. . . .

"Who? And anyway, it is none of our business."

Nana, you must be patient . . . and not cry. . . .

"Old woman, why are you crying, it is not allowed here. No one must make any noise. . . ."

My lady, I am sorry but she was all I had.

"Who? Oh, you are the old woman who is looking for somebody?'

Yes.

"Who is he?"

She was my granddaughter—the only child of my only son.

"I mean, what was her name?"

Esi Amfoa.

"Esi Amfoa . . . Esi Amfoa. I am sorry, we do not have anyone whom they call like that here."

Is that it?

"Nana, I told you they may know only her European name here."

My master, what shall we do then?

"What is she ill with?"

She came here to have a child. . . .

". . . And they say, they opened her stomach and removed the baby. Oh . . . oh, I see."

My Lord, hold me tight so that nothing will happen to me now.

"I see. It is the Caesarean case."

"Nurse, you know her?"

And when I take her back, Anona Ebusuafo will say what I did not wait for them to come with me. . . .

"Yes. Are you her brother?"

"No. I am only the driver who brought the old woman."

"Did she bring all her clan?"

"No. She came alone."

"Strange thing for a villager to do."

I hope they have not cut her up already.

"Did she bring a whole bag full of cassava and plantain and kenkey?"[7]

"No. She has only her little bundle."

"Follow me. But you must not make any noise. This is not the hour for coming here. . . ."

My master, does she know her?

"Yes."

I hear it is very cold where they put them. . . .

It was feeding time for new babies. When old Esi Amfoa saw young Esi Amfoa, the latter was all neat and nice. White sheets and all. She did not see the beautiful stitches under the sheets. "This woman is a tough bundle," Dr. Gyamfi had declared after the identical twins had been removed, the last stitches had been threaded off and Mary Koomson, alias Esi Amfoa, had come to.

The old woman somersaulted into the room and lay groaning, not screaming, by the bed. For was not her last pot broken? So they lay them in state even in hospitals and not always cut them up for instruction?

The Nursing Sister was furious. Young Esi Amfoa spoke. And this time old Esi Amfoa wept loud and hard—wept all her tears.

Scrappy nurse-under-training, Jessy Treeson, second-generation-Cape Coaster-her-grandmother still-remembered-at-Egyaa No. 7 said, "As for these villagers," and giggled.

Draba Anan looked hard at Jessy Treeson, looked hard at her, all of her: her starched uniform, apron and cap . . . and then dismissed them all. . . . "Such a cassava stick . . . but maybe I will break my toe if I kicked at her buttocks," he thought.

And by the bed the old woman was trying hard to rise and look at the only pot which had refused to get broken.

# Peter Carey

## (B. 1943)

Born in Bacchus Marsh, Victoria, Australia, Carey has forged a reputation as one of Australia's most successful contemporary authors, winning two Booker Prizes and virtually every other Australian literary award. His novels and short stories feature the fantastic fused with the realistic, most often through a lens of humor, and he often emphasizes issues of postcolonialism as he points out the strangeness and failings of contemporary Australia. The short story collection *War Crimes* was awarded the New South Wales Premier's Literary Award in

---

7 **cassava and plantain and kenkey:** Cassava is a plant with a tuberous starchy root, a staple food and source of tapioca. Plantain is a banana-like fruit. Kenkey is food made from fermented corn.

1980, and his novel *Bliss* received the Miles Franklin Award, the New South Wales Premier's Literary Award, and the National Book Council Award. Carey's novel *Illywhacker* (1985) won the Victorian Premier's Literary Award and the National Book Council Award and was nominated for the Booker Prize in 1985. Carey won the Booker Prize twice for *Oscar and Lucinda* (1988) and *True History of the Kelly Gang* (2000).

Many of Carey's short stories offer characters in surrealistic moments within ordinary circumstances. He uses these moments to examine Australia's cultural legacy and the difficulties of a formerly colonized nation seeking to establish a true sense of self in the shadow of a colonizer that once totally informed its behavior, interests, and choices. Carey often dismisses a linear narrative and instead forces the reader to piece together the story's order, time, and sequence. By thus disordering the narrative, and by extension the reader, Carey forces the reader into the place of his characters, creating an intricate conversation in which the text and the reader need each other to forge the meaning of the story. After living in London and New York, Carey returned to his native Australia in 2000 to write *Thirty Days in Sydney: A Wildly Distorted Account*. The book is a raucous report on the city that he often observed, like James Joyce and Ireland, from a bemused position far away. His surreal and meaningful glance at the city depicts an Australia that has emerged from colonialism both damaged and triumphant. Carey currently lives in New York and teaches creative writing at New York University.

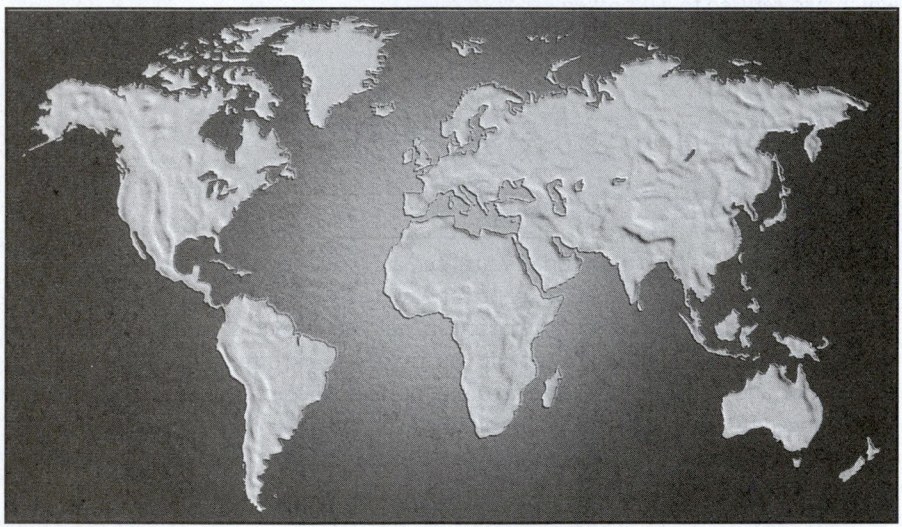

*World map*

## *"Do You Love Me?"*

### 1. The Role of the Cartographers

Perhaps a few words about the role of the Cartographers in our present society are warranted.

To begin with one must understand the nature of the yearly census, a manifestation of our desire to know, always, exactly where we stand. The census, originally a count of the population, has gradually extended until it has become a total inventory of the contents of the nation, a mammoth task which is continuing all the time—no sooner has one census been announced than work on another begins.

The results of the census play an important part in our national life and have, for many years, been the pivot point for the yearly "Festival of the Corn" (an ancient festival, related to the wealth of the earth).

We have a passion for lists. And nowhere is this more clearly illustrated than in the Festival of the Corn which takes place in midsummer, the weather always being fine and warm. On the night of the festival, the householders move their goods and possessions, all furniture, electrical goods, clothing, rugs, kitchen utensils, bathrobes, slippers, cushions, lawnmowers, curtains, doorstops, heirlooms, cameras, and anything else that can be moved into the street so that the census officials may the more easily check the inventory of each household.

The Festival of the Corn is, however, much more than a clerical affair. And, the day over and the night come, the householders invite each other to view their possessions which they refer to, on this night, as gifts. It is like nothing more than a wedding feast—there is much cooking, all sorts of traditional dishes, fine wines, strong liquors, music is played loudly in quiet neighborhoods, strangers copulate with strangers, men dance together, and maidens in yellow robes distribute small barley sugar corn-cobs to young and old alike.

And in all this the role of the Cartographers is perhaps the most important, for our people crave, more than anything else, to know the extent of the nation, to know, exactly, the shape of the coastline, to hear what land may have been lost to the sea, to know what has been reclaimed and what is still in doubt. If the Cartographers' report is good the Festival of the Corn will be a good festival. If the report is bad, one can always sense, for all the dancing and drinking, a feeling of nervousness and apprehension in the revelers, a certain desperation. In the year of a bad Cartographers' report there will always be fights and, occasionally, some property will be stolen as citizens attempt to compensate themselves for their sense of loss.

Because of the importance of their job the Cartographers have become an elite—well-paid, admired, envied, and having no small opinion of themselves. It is said by some that they are overproud, immoral, vain and footloose, and it is perhaps the last charge (by necessity true) that brings about the others. For the Cartographers spend their years traveling up and down the coast, along the great rivers, traversing great mountains and vast deserts. They travel in small parties of three, four, sometimes five, making their own time, working as they please, because eventually it is their own responsibility to see that their team's task is completed in time.

My father, a Cartographer himself, often told me stories about himself or his colleagues and the adventures they had in the wilderness.

There were other stories, however, that always remained in my mind and, as a child, caused me considerable anxiety. These were the stories of the nether regions and I doubt if they were known outside a very small circle of Cartographers and government officials. As a child in a house frequented by Cartographers, I often heard these tales which invariably made me cling closely to my mother's skirts.

It appears that for some time certain regions of the country had become less and less real and these regions were regarded fearfully even by the Cartographers, who prided themselves on their courage. The regions in question were invariably uninhabited, unused for agriculture or industry. There were certain sections of the Halverson Ranges, vast stretches of the Greater Desert, and long pieces of coastline which had begun to slowly disappear like the image on an improperly fixed photograph.

It was because of the nebulous areas that the Fischerscope was introduced. The Fischerscope is not unlike radar in its principle and is able to detect the presence of any object, no matter how dematerialized or insubstantial. In this way the Cartographers were still able to map the questionable pairs of the nether regions. To have returned with blanks on the maps would have created such public anxiety that no one dared think what it might do to the stability of our society. I now have reason to believe that certain areas of the country disappeared so completely that even the Fischerscope could not detect them and the Cartographers, acting under political pressure, used old maps to fake-in the missing sections. If my theory is grounded in fact, and I am sure it is, it would explain my father's cynicism about the Festival of the Corn.

## 2. The Archetypal Cartographer

My father was in his fifties but he had kept himself in good shape. His skin was brown and his muscles still firm. He was a tall man with a thick head of gray hair, a slightly less gray mustache and a long aquiline nose. Sitting on a horse he looked as proud and cruel as Genghis Khan. Lying on the beach clad only in bathers and sunglasses he still managed to retain his authoritative air.

Beside him I always felt as if I had betrayed him. I was slightly built, more like my mother.

It was the day before the festival and we lay on the beach, my father, my mother, my girlfriend and I. As was usual in these circumstances my father addressed all his remarks to Karen. He never considered the members of his own family worth talking to. I always had the uncomfortable feeling that he was flirting with my girlfriends and I never knew what to do about it.

People were lying in groups up and down the beach. Near us a family of five were playing with a large beach ball.

"Look at those fools," my father said to Karen.

"Why are they fools?" Karen asked.

"They're fools," said my father. "They were born fools and they'll die fools. Tomorrow they'll dance in the streets and drink too much."

"So," said Karen triumphantly, in the manner of one who has become privy to secret information. "It will be a good Cartographers' report?"

My father roared with laughter.

Karen looked hurt and pouted. "Am I a fool?"

"No," my father said, "you're really quite splendid."

## 3. The Most Famous Festival

The festival, as it turned out, was the greatest disaster in living memory.

The Cartographers' report was excellent, the weather was fine, but somewhere something had gone wrong.

The news was confusing. The television said that, in spite of the good report, various items had been stolen very early in the night. Later there was a news flash to say that a large house had completely disappeared in Howie Street.

Later still we looked out the window to see a huge band of people carrying lighted torches. There was a lot of shouting. The same image, exactly, was on the television and a reporter was explaining that bands of vigilantes were out looking for thieves.

My father stood at the window, a martini in his hand, and watched the vigilantes set alight a house opposite.

My mother wanted to know what we should do.

"Come and watch the fools," my father said, "they're incredible."

## 4. The I.C.I. Incident

The next day the I.C.I. building disappeared in front of a crowd of two thousand people. It took two hours. The crowd stood silently as the great steel and glass structure slowly faded before them.

The staff who were evacuated looked pale and shaken. The caretaker who was amongst the last to leave looked almost translucent. In the days that followed he made some name for himself as a mystic, claiming that he had been able to see other worlds, layer upon layer, through the fabric of the here and now.

## 5. Behavior When Confronted with Dematerialization

The anger of our people when confronted with acts of theft has always been legendary and was certainly highlighted by the incidents which occurred on the night of the festival.

But the fury exhibited on this famous night could not compare with the intensity of emotion displayed by those who witnessed the earliest scenes of dematerialization.

The silent crowd who watched the I.C.I. building erupted into hysteria when they realized that it had finally gone and wasn't likely to come back.

It was like some monstrous theft for which punishment must be meted out.

They stormed into the Shell building next door and smashed desks and ripped down office partitions. Reporters who attended the scene were rarely impartial observers, but one of the cooler headed members of the press remarked on the great number of weeping men and women who hurled typewriters from windows and scattered files through crowds of frightened office workers.

Five days later they displayed similar anger when the Shell building itself disappeared.

## 6. Behavior of Those Dematerializing

The first reports of dematerializing people were not generally believed and were suppressed by the media. But these things were soon common knowledge and few families were untouched by them. Such incidents were obviously not all the same but in many victims there was a tendency to exhibit extreme aggression towards those around them. Murders and assaults committed by these unfortunates were not uncommon and in most cases they exhibited an almost unbelievable rage, as if they were the victims of a shocking betrayal.

My friend James Bray was once stopped in the street by a very beautiful woman who clawed and scratched at his face and said: "You did this to me, you bastard, you did this to me."

He had never seen her before but he confessed that, in some irrational way, he felt responsible and didn't defend himself. Fortunately she disappeared before she could do him much damage.

## 7. Some Theories That Arose at the Time

1   The world is merely a dream dreamt by god who is waking after a long sleep. When he is properly awake the world will disappear completely. When the world disappears we will disappear with it and be happy.

2   The world has become sensitive to light. In the same way that prolonged use of say penicillin can suddenly result in a dangerous allergy, prolonged exposure of the world to the sun has made it sensitive to light.

    The advocates of this theory could be seen bustling through the city crowds in their long, hooded black robes.

3   The fact that the world is disappearing has been caused by the sloppy work of the Cartographers and census takers. Those who filled out their census forms incorrectly would lose those items they had neglected to describe. People overlooked in the census by impatient officials would also disappear. A strong pressure group demanded that a new census be taken quickly before matters got worse.

## 8. My Father's Theory

The world, according to my father, was exactly like the human body and had its own defense mechanisms with which it defended itself against anything that either threatened it or was unnecessary to it. The I.C.I. building and the I.C.I. company had obviously constituted some threat to the world or had simply been irrelevant. That's why it had disappeared and not because some damn fool god was waking up and rubbing his eyes.

"I don't believe in god," my father said. "Humanity is god. Humanity is the only god I know. If humanity doesn't need something it will disappear. People who are not loved will disappear. Everything that is not loved will disappear from the face of the earth. We only exist through the love of others and that's what it's all about."

## 9. A Contradiction

"Look at those fools," my father said, "they wouldn't know if they were up themselves."

## 10. An Unpleasant Scene

The world at this time was full of unpleasant and disturbing scenes. One that I recall vividly took place in the middle of the city on a hot, sultry Tuesday afternoon. It was about one-thirty and I was waiting for Karen by the post office when a man of forty or so ran past me. He was dematerializing rapidly. Everybody seemed to be deliberately looking the other way, which seemed to me to make him dematerialize faster. I stared at him hard, hoping that I could do something to keep him there until help arrived. I tried to love him, because I believe in my father's theory. I thought, I must love that man. But his face irritated me. It is not so easy to love a stranger and I'm ashamed to say that he had the small mouth and close-together eyes that I have always disliked in a person. I tried to love him but I'm afraid I failed.

While I watched he tried to hail taxi after taxi. But the taxi drivers were only too well aware of what was happening and had no wish to spend their time driving a passenger who, at any moment, might cease to exist. They looked the other way or put up their NOT FOR HIRE signs.

Finally he managed to way-lay a taxi at some traffic lights. By this time he was so insubstantial that I could see right through him. He was beginning to shout. A terrible thin noise, but penetrating nonetheless. He tried to open the cab door, but the driver had already locked it. I could hear the man's voice, high and piercing: "I want to go home." He repeated it over and over again. "I want to go home to my wife."

The taxi drove off when the lights changed. There was a lull in the traffic. People had fled the corner and left it deserted and it was I alone who saw the man finally disappear.

I felt sick.

Karen arrived five minutes later and found me pale and shaken. "Are you alright?" she said.

"Do you love me?" I said.

## 11. The Nether Regions

My father had an irritating way of explaining things to me I already understood, refusing to stop no matter how much I said "I know" or "You told me before."

Thus he expounded on the significance of the nether regions, adopting the tone of a lecturer speaking to a class of particularly backward children.

"As you know," he said, "the nether regions were amongst the first to disappear and this in itself is significant. These regions, I'm sure you know, are seldom visited by men and only then by people like me whose sole job is to make sure that they're still there. We had no use for these areas, these deserts, swamps, and coastlines which is why, of course, they disappeared. They were merely possessions of ours and if they had any use at all it was as symbols for our poets, writers and film makers. They were used as symbols of lovelessness, loneliness, uselessness and so on. Do you get what I mean?"

"Yes," I said, "I get what you mean."

"But do you?" my father insisted. "But do you really, I wonder." He examined me seriously, musing on the possibilities of my understanding him. "How old are you?"

"Twenty," I said.

"I knew, of course," he said. "Do you understand the significance of the nether regions?"

I sighed, a little too loudly and my father narrowed his eyes. Quickly I said: "They are like everything else. They're like the cities. The cities are deserts where people are alone and lonely. They don't love one another."

"Don't love one another," intoned my father, also sighing. "We no longer love one another. When we realize that we need one another we will stop disappearing. This is a lesson to us. A hard lesson, but, I hope, an effective one."

My father continued to speak, but I watched him without listening. After a few minutes he stopped abruptly: "Are you listening to me?" he said. I was surprised to detect real concern in his voice. He looked at me questioningly. "I've always looked after you," he said, "ever since you were little."

## 12. The Cartographers' Fall

I don't know when it was that I noticed my father had become depressed. It probably happened quite gradually without either my mother or me noticing it.

Even when I did become aware of it I attributed it to a woman. My father had a number of lovers and his moods usually reflected the success or failure of these relationships.

But I know now that he had heard already of Hurst and Jamov, the first two Cartographers to disappear. The news was suppressed for several weeks and then, some-how or other, leaked to the press. Certainly the Cartographers had enemies amongst the civil servants who regarded them as overproud and overpaid, and it was probably from one of these civil servants that the press heard the news.

When the news finally broke I understood my father's depression and felt sorry for him.

I didn't know how to help him. I wanted, badly, to make him happy. I had never been able to give him anything or do anything for him that he couldn't do better him-self. Now I wanted to help him, to show him I understood.

I found him sitting in front of the television one night when I returned from my office and I sat quietly beside him. he seemed more kindly now and he placed his hand on my knee and patted it.

I sat there for a while, overcome with the new warmth of this relationship and then, unable to contain my emotion any more, I blurted out. "You could change your job."

My father stiffened and sat bolt upright. The pressure of his hand on my knee in-creased until I yelped with pain, and still he held on, hurting me terribly.

"You are a fool," he said, "you wouldn't know if you were up yourself."

Through the pain in my leg, I felt the intensity of my father's fear.

## 13. Why the World Needs Cartographers

My father woke me at 3.00 a.m. to tell me why the world needed Cartographers. He smelled of whisky and seemed, once again, to be very gentle.

"The world needs Cartographers," he said softly, "because if they didn't have Cartographers the fools wouldn't know where they were. They wouldn't know if they were up themselves if they didn't have a Cartographer to tell them what's hap-pening. The world needs Cartographers," my father said, "it fucking well needs Cartographers."

## 14. One Final Scene

Let me describe a final scene to you: I am sitting on the sofa my father brought home when I was five years old. I am watching television. My father is sitting in a leather armchair that once belonged to his father and which has always been exclusively his. My mother is sitting in the dining alcove with her cards spread across the table, play-ing one more interminable game of patience.

I glance casually across at my father to see if he is doing anything more than stare into space, and notice, with a terrible shock that he is showing the first signs of dematerializing.

"What are you staring at?" My father, in fact, has been staring at me.

"Nothing."

"Well, don't."

Nervously I return my eyes to the inanity of the television. I don't know what to do. Should I tell my father that he is dematerializing? If I don't tell him will he notice? I feel I should do something but I can feel, already, the anger in his voice. His anger is nothing new. But this is possibly the beginning of a tide of uncontrollable rage. If he knows he is dematerializing, he will think I don't love him. He will blame me. He will attack me. Old as he is, he is still considerably stronger than I am and he could hurt me badly. I stare determinedly at the television and feel my father's eyes on me.

I try to feel love for my father. I try very, very hard.

I attempt to remember how I felt about him when I was little, in the days when he was still occasionally tender towards me.

But it's no good.

Because I can only remember how he has hit me, hurt me, humiliated me and flirted with my girlfriends. I realize, with a flush of panic and guilt, that I don't love him. In spite of which I say: "I love you."

My mother looks up sharply from her cards and lets out a surprised cry.

I turn to my father. He has almost disappeared. I can see the leather of the chair through his stomach.

I don't know whether it is my unconvincing declaration of love or my mother's exclamation that makes my father laugh. For whatever reason, he begins to laugh uncontrollably: "You bloody fools," he gasps, "I wish you could see the looks on your bloody silly faces."

And then he is gone.

My mother looks across at me nervously, a card still in her hand. "Do you love me?" she asks.

# Hanif Kureishi

## (B. 1954)

Hanif Kureishi was born in Bromley, England, to an English mother and a Pakistani father. Kureishi is not only a leading contemporary novelist but also a prominent playwright, essayist, and screenwriter. His work often depicts the immigrant experience in England, and he draws on his youthful experiences as an outsider in all-white schools. Kureishi eventually studied philosophy at King's College, London, where he received a B.A. While attending school, he worked at the Royal Court Theatre, where his first play was performed when he was only nineteen years old. Kureishi's breakthrough came in 1985, when his play, *My Beautiful Laundrette*, was produced on British television and subsequently released as a film that gained an Academy Award nomination for best original screenplay. *My Beautiful Laundrette* is primarily a story about two men who are lovers and who open a Laundromat. However, one man is Pakistani and one is white, and thus the story also offers a distinctive picture of the culture clash between South Asians and British on the streets of London.

Kureishi published his first novel, *The Buddha of Suburbia*, in 1990. The bizarre transformation of the protagonist's Indian father into an actual "Buddha of Suburbia" constitutes a humorous but profound exploration of how immigrant communities from colonized nations position themselves within the borders of the nation that colonized them. Kureishi has enjoyed great success in England, but he has also been the target of criticism within the Anglo-Pakistani community. Novels like *The Black Album* (1995) and his short story collection, *Love in a Blue Time* (1997), were condemned as negative portrayals of Pakistanis. However, Kureishi's use of flawed characters demystifies the immigrant community to reveal foibles, exploits, triumphs, and tragedies that are understandable in any language or cultural context.

---

# My Son the Fanatic
1997

Surreptitiously the father began going into his son's bedroom. He would sit there for hours, rousing himself only to seek clues. What bewildered him was that Ali was getting tidier. Instead of the usual tangle of clothes, books, cricket bats, video games, the room was becoming neat and ordered; spaces began appearing where before there had been only mess.

Initially Parvez had been pleased; his son was outgrowing his teenage attitudes. But one day, beside the dustbin, Parvez found a torn bag which contained not only old toys, but computer discs, video tapes, new books and fashionable clothes the boy had bought just a few months before. Also without explanation, Ali had parted from the English girlfriend who used to come often to the house. His old friends had stopped ringing.

For reasons he didn't himself understand, Parvez wasn't able to bring up the subject of Ali's unusual behavior. He was aware that he had become slightly afraid of his son, who, alongside his silences, was developing a sharp tongue. One remark Parvez did make, "You don't play your guitar any more," elicited the mysterious but conclusive reply. "There are more important things to be done."

Yet Parvez felt his son's eccentricity as an injustice. He had always been aware of the pitfalls which other men's sons had fallen into in England. And so, for Ali, he had worked long hours and spent a lot of money paying for his education as an accountant. He had bought him good suits, all the books he required and a computer. And now the boy was throwing his possessions out!

The TV, video and sound system followed the guitar. Soon the room was practically bare. Even the unhappy walls bore marks were Ali's pictures had been removed.

Parvez couldn't sleep; he went more to the whisky bottle, even when he was at work. He realized it was imperative to discuss the matter with someone sympathetic.

Parvez had been a taxi driver for twenty years. Half that time he'd worked for the same firm. Like him, most of the other drivers were Punjabis.[1] They preferred to work at night, the roads were clearer and the money better. They slept during the day, avoiding their wives. Together they led almost a boy's life in the cabbies' office, playing cards and practical jokes, exchanging lewd stories, eating together and discussing politics and their problems.

But Parvez had been unable to bring this subject up with his friends. He was too ashamed. And he was afraid, too, that they would blame him for the wrong turning his boy had taken, just as he had blamed other fathers whose sons had taken to running around with bad girls, truanting from school and joining gangs.

For years Parvez had boasted to the other men about how Ali excelled at cricket, swimming and football, and how attentive a scholar he was, getting straight "A's" in most subjects. Was it asking too much for Ali to get a good job now, marry the right girl and start a family? Once this happened, Parvez would be happy. His dreams of doing well in England would have come true. Where had he gone wrong?

But one night, sitting in the taxi office on busted chairs with his two closest friends watching a Sylvester Stallone film, he broke his silence.

"I can't understand it!" he burst out. "Everything is going from his room. And I can't talk to him any more. We were not father and son—we were brothers! Where has he gone? Why is he torturing me!"

And Parvez put his head in his hands.

Even as he poured out his account the men shook their heads and gave one another knowing glances. From their grave looks Parvez realized they understood the situation.

"Tell me what is happening!" he demanded.

The reply was almost triumphant. They had guessed something was going wrong. Now it was clear. Ali was taking drugs and selling his possessions to pay for them. That was why his bedroom was emptying.

"What must I do then?"

Parvez's friends instructed him to watch Ali scrupulously and then be severe with him, before the boy went mad, overdosed or murdered someone.

Parvez staggered out into the early morning air, terrified they were right. His boy—the drug addict killer!

To his relief he found Bettina sitting in his car.

Usually the last customers of the night were local "brasses" or prostitutes. The taxi drivers knew them well, often driving them to liaisons. At the end of the girls' shifts, the men would ferry them home, though sometimes the women would join them for a drinking session in the office. Occasionally the drivers would go with the girls. "A ride in exchange for a ride," it was called.

Bettina had known Parvez for three years. She lived outside the town and on the long drive home, where she sat not in the passenger seat but beside him, Parvez had talked to her about his life and hopes, just as she talked about hers. They saw each other most nights.

1 **Punjabis:** People from northwestern India or Pakistan.

He could talk to her about things he'd never be able to discuss with his own wife. Bettina, in turn, always reported on her night's activities. He liked to know where she was and with whom. Once he had rescued her from a violent client, and since then they had come to care for one another.

Though Bettina had never met the boy, she heard about Ali continually. That late night, when he told Bettina that he suspected Ali was on drugs, she judged neither the boy nor his father, but became businesslike and told him what to watch for.

"It's all in the eyes," she said. They might be bloodshot; the pupils might be dilated; he might look tired. He could be liable to sweats, or sudden mood changes. "Okay?"

Parvez began his vigil gratefully. Now he knew what the problem might be, he felt better. And surely, he figured, things couldn't have gone too far? With Bettina's help he would soon sort it out.

He watched each mouthful the boy took. He sat beside him at every opportunity and looked into his eyes. When he could he took the boy's hand, checking his temperature. If the boy wasn't at home Parvez was active, looking under the carpet, in his drawers, behind the empty wardrobe, sniffing, inspecting, probing. He knew what to look for: Bettina had drawn pictures of capsules, syringes, pills, powders, rocks.

Every night she waited to hear news of what he'd witnessed.

After a few days of constant observation, Parvez was able to report that although the boy had given up sports, he seemed healthy, with clear eyes. He didn't, as his father expected, flinch guiltily from his gaze. In fact the boy's mood was alert and steady in this sense: as well as being sullen, he was very watchful. He returned his father's long looks with more than a hint of criticism, of reproach even, so much so that Parvez began to feel that it was he who was in the wrong, and not the boy!

"And there's nothing else physically different?" Bettina asked.

"No!" Parvez thought for a moment. "But he is growing a beard."

One night after sitting with Bettina in an all-night coffee shop, Parvez came home particularly late. Reluctantly he and Bettina had abandoned their only explanation, the drug theory, for Parvez had found nothing resembling any drug in Ali's room. Besides, Ali wasn't selling his belongings. He threw them out, gave them away or donated them to charity shops.

Standing in the hall, Parvez heard his boy's alarm clock go off. Parvez hurried into his bedroom where his wife was still awake, sewing in bed. He ordered her to sit down and keep quiet, though she had neither stood up nor said a word. From this post, and with her watching him curiously, he observed his son through the crack in the door.

The boy went into the bathroom to wash. When he returned to his room Parvez sprang across the hall and set his ear at Ali's door. A muttering sound came from within. Parvez was puzzled but relieved.

Once this clue had been established, Parvez watched him at other times. The boy was praying. Without fail, when he was at home, he prayed five times a day.

Parvez had grown up in Lahore where all the boys had been taught the Koran. To stop him falling asleep when he studied, the Moulvi had attached a piece of string to the ceiling and tied it to Parvez's hair, so that if his head fell forward, he would instantly awake. After this indignity Parvez had avoided all religions. Not that the other taxi drivers had more respect. In fact they made jokes about the local mullahs[2] walking around with their caps and beards, thinking they could tell people how to live, while their eyes roved over the boys and girls in their care.

Parvez described to Bettina what he had discovered. He informed the men in the taxi office. The friends, who had been so curious before, now became oddly silent. They could hardly condemn the boy for his devotions.

Parvez decided to take a night off and go out with the boy. They could talk things over. He wanted to hear how things were going at college; he wanted to tell him stories about their family in Pakistan. More than anything he yearned to understand how Ali had discovered the "spiritual dimension," as Bettina described it.

To Parvez's surprise, the boy refused to accompany him. He claimed he had an appointment. Parvez had to insist that no appointment could be more important than that of a son with his father.

The next day, Parvez went immediately to the street where Bettina stood in the rain wearing high heels, a short skirt and a long mac on top, which she would open hopefully at passing cars.

"Get in, get in!" he said.

They drove out across the moors and parked at the spot where on better days, with a view unimpeded for many miles by nothing but wild deer and horses, they'd lie back, with their eyes half closed, saying "This is the life." This time Parvez was trembling. Bettina put her arms around him.

"What's happened?"

"I've just had the worst experience of my life."

As Bettina robbed his head Parvez told her that the previous evening he and Ali had gone to a restaurant. As they studied the menu, the waiter, whom Parvez knew, brought him his usual whisky and water. Parvez had been so nervous he had even prepared a question. He was going to ask Ali if he was worried about his imminent exams. But first, wanting to relax, he loosened his tie, crunched a popadom[3] and took a long drink.

Before Parvez could speak, Ali made a face.

"Don't you know it's wrong to drink alcohol?" he said.

"He spoke to me very harshly," Parvez told Bettina. "I was about to castigate the boy for being insolent, but managed to control myself."

He had explained patiently to Ali that for years he had worked more than ten hours a day, that he had few enjoyments or hobbies and never went on holiday. Surely it wasn't a crime to have a drink when he wanted one?

"But it is forbidden," the boy said.

Parvez shrugged, "I know."

"And so is gambling, isn't it?"

2 **mullahs:** Muslims who have studied Islamic theology.
3 **popadom:** Thin, flat, circular Indian bread.

"Yes. But surely we are only human?"

Each time Parvez took a drink, the boy winced, or made a fastidious face as an accompaniment. This made Parvez drink more quickly. The waiter, wanting to please his friend, brought another glass of whisky. Parvez knew he was getting drunk, but he couldn't stop himself. Ali had a horrible look on his face, full of disgust and censure. It was as if he hated his father.

Halfway through the meal Parvez suddenly lost his temper and threw a plate on the floor. He had felt like ripping the cloth from the table, but the waiters and other customers were staring at him. Yet he wouldn't stand for his own son telling him the difference between right and wrong. He knew he wasn't a bad man. He had a conscience. There were a few things of which he was ashamed, but on the whole he had lived a decent life.

"When have I had time to be wicked?" he asked Ali.

In a low monotonous voice the boy explained that Parvez had not, in fact, lived a good life. He had broken countless rules of the Koran.

"For instance?" Parvez demanded.

Ali hadn't needed time to think. As if he had been waiting for this moment, he asked his father if he didn't relish pork pies?

"Well . . ."

Parvez couldn't deny that he loved crispy bacon smothered with mushrooms and mustard and sandwiched between slices of fried bread. In fact he ate this for breakfast every morning.

Ali then reminded Parvez that he had ordered his own wife to cook pork sausages, saying to her, "You're not in the village now, this is England. We have to fit in!"

Parvez was so annoyed and perplexed by this attack that he called for more drink.

"The problem is this," the boy said. He leaned across the table. For the first time that night his eyes were alive. "You are too implicated in Western civilization."

Parvez burped; he thought he was going to choke. "Implicated!" he said. "But we live here!"

"The Western materialists hate us," Ali said. "Papa, how can you love something which hates you?"

"What is the answer then?" Parvez said miserably. "According to you."

Ali addressed his father fluently, as if Parvez were a rowdy crowd that had to be quelled and convinced. The Law of Islam would rule the world; the skin of the infidel would burn off again and again; the Jews and Christians would be routed. The West was a sink of hypocrites, adulterers, homosexuals, drug takers and prostitutes.

As Ali talked, Parvez looked out of the window as if to check that they were still in London.

"My people have taken enough. If the persecution doesn't stop there will be *jihad*.[4] I, and millions of others, will gladly give our lives for the cause."

"But why, why?" Parvez said.

---

4 *jihad:* Muslim holy war against nonbelievers.

"For us the reward will be in paradise."

"Paradise!"

Finally, as Parvez's eyes filled with tears, the boy urged him to mend his ways.

"How is that possible?" Parvez asked.

"Pray," Ali said. "Pray beside me."

Parvez called for the bill and ushered his boy out of the restaurant as soon as he was able. He couldn't take any more. Ali sounded as if he'd swallowed someone else's voice.

On the way home the boy sat in the back of the taxi, as if he were a customer.

"What has made you like this?" Parvez asked him, afraid that somehow he was to blame for all this. "Is there a particular event which has influenced you?"

"Living in this country."

"But I love England," Parvez said, watching his boy in the mirror. "They let you do almost anything here."

"That is the problem," he replied.

For the first time in years Parvez couldn't see straight. He knocked the side of the car against a lorry, ripping off the wing mirror. They were lucky not to have been stopped by the police. Parvez would have lost his license and therefore his job.

Getting out of the car back at the house, Parvez stumbled and fell in the road, scraping his hands and ripping his trousers. He managed to haul himself up. The boy didn't even offer him his hand.

Parvez told Bettina he was now willing to pray, if that was what the boy wanted, if that would dislodge the pitiless look from his eyes.

"But what I object to," he said, "is being told by my own son that I am going to hell!"

What finished Parvez off was that the boy had said he was giving up accountancy. When Parvez had asked why, Ali had said sarcastically that it was obvious.

"Western education cultivates an anti-religious attitude."

And, according to Ali, in the world of accountants it was usual to meet women, drink alcohol and practice usury.

"But it's well-paid work," Parvez argued. "For years you've been preparing!"

Ali said he was going to begin to work in prisons, with poor Muslims who were struggling to maintain their purity in the face of corruption. Finally, at the end of the evening, as Ali was going to bed, he had asked his father why he didn't have a beard, or at least a moustache.

"I feel as if I've lost my son," Parvez told Bettina. "I can't bear to be looked at as if I'm a criminal. I've decided what to do."

"What is it?"

"I'm going to tell him to pick up his prayer mat and get out of my house. It will be the hardest thing I've ever done, but tonight I'm going to do it."

"But you mustn't give up on him," said Bettina. "Many young people fall into cults and superstitious groups. It doesn't mean they'll always feel the same way."

She said Parvez had to stick by his boy, giving him support, until he came through.

Parvez was persuaded that she was right, even though he didn't feel like giving his son more love when he had hardly been thanked for all he had already given.

Nevertheless, Parvez tried to endure his son's looks and reproaches. He attempted to make conversation about his beliefs. But if Parvez ventured any criticism, Ali always had a brusque reply. On one occasion, Ali accused Parvez of "groveling" to the whites; in contrast, he explained, he was not "inferior"; there was more to the world than the West, though the West always thought it was best.

"How is it you know that?" Parvez said, "seeing as you've never left England?"

Ali replied with a look of contempt.

One night, having ensured there was no alcohol on his breath, Parvez sat down at the kitchen table with Ali. He hoped Ali would compliment him on the beard he was growing but Ali didn't appear to notice.

The previous day Parvez had been telling Bettina that he thought people in the West sometimes felt inwardly empty and that people needed a philosophy to live by.

"Yes," said Bettina. "That's the answer. You must tell him what your philosophy of life is. Then he will understand that there are other beliefs."

After some fatiguing consideration, Parvez was ready to begin. The boy watched him as if he expected nothing.

Haltingly Parvez said that people had to treat one another with respect, particularly children their parents. This did seem, for a moment, to affect the boy. Heartened, Parvez continued. In his view this life was all there was and when you died you rotted in the earth. "Grass and flowers will grow out of me, but something of me will live on—"

"How?"

"In other people. I will continue—in you." At this the boy appeared a little distressed. And your grandchildren," Parvez added for good measure. "But while I am here on earth I want to make the best of it. And I want you to, as well!"

"What d'you mean by 'make the best of it'?" asked the boy.

"Well," said Parvez. "For a start . . . you should enjoy yourself. Yes. Enjoy yourself without hurting others."

Ali said that enjoyment was a "bottomless pit."

"But I don't mean enjoyment like that!" said Parvez. "I mean the beauty of living!"

"All over the world our people are oppressed," was the boy's reply.

"I know," Parvez replied, not entirely sure who "our people" were, "but still—life is for living!"

Ali said, "Real morality has existed for hundreds of years. Around the world millions and millions of people share my beliefs. Are you saying you are right and they are all wrong?"

Ali looked at his father with such aggressive confidence that Parvez could say no more.

One evening Bettina was sitting in Parvez's car, after visiting a client, when they passed a boy on the street.

"That's my son," Parvez said suddenly. They were on the other side of town, in a poor district, where there were two mosques.

Parvez set his face hard.

Bettina turned to watch him. "Slow down then, slow down!" She said, "He's good-looking. Reminds me of you. But with a more determined face. Please, can't we stop?"

"What for?"

"I'd like to talk to him."

Parvez turned the cab round and stopped beside the boy.

"Coming home?" Parvez asked. "It's quite a way."

The sullen boy shrugged and got into the back seat. Bettina sat in the front. Parvez became aware of Bettina's short skirt, gaudy rings and ice-blue eyeshadow. He became conscious that the smell of her perfume, which he loved, filled the cab. He opened the window.

While Parvez drove as fast as he could, Bettina said gently to Ali, "Where have you been?"

"The mosque," he said.

"And how are you getting on at college? Are you working hard?"

"Who are you to ask me these question?" he said, looking out of the window. Then they hit bad traffic and the car came to a standstill.

By now Bettina had inadvertently laid her hand on Parvez's shoulder. She said, "Your father, who is a good man, is very worried about you. You know he loves you more than his own life."

"You say he loves me," the boy said.

"Yes!" said Bettina.

"Then why is he letting a woman like you touch him like that?"

If Bettina looked at the boy in anger, he looked back at her with twice as much cold fury.

She said, "What kind of woman am I that deserves to be spoken to like that?"

"You know," he said. "Now let me out."

"Never," Parvez replied.

"Don't worry, I'm getting out," Bettina said.

"No, don't!" said Parvez. But even as the car moved she opened the door, threw herself out and ran away across the road. Parvez shouted after her several times, but she had gone.

Parvez took Ali back to the house, saying nothing more to him. Ali went straight to his room. Parvez was unable to read the paper, watch television or even sit down. He kept pouring himself drinks.

At last he went upstairs and paced up and down outside Ali's room. When, finally, he opened the door, Ali was praying. The boy didn't even glance his way.

Parvez kicked him over. Then he dragged the boy up by his shirt and hit him. The boy fell back. Parvez hit him again. The boy's face was bloody. Parvez was panting. He knew that the boy was unreachable, but he struck him nonetheless. The boy neither covered himself nor retaliated; there was no fear in his eyes. He only said, through his split lip: "So who's the fanatic now?"

# Salman Rushdie

## (B. 1947)

An Anglo-Indian writer, Salman Rushdie incorporates fantasy, mythology, and religion in his stories, following in the style of magic realism. Rushdie was born in Bombay, India, to a middle-class Moslem family. In 1964, his parents moved to Karachi, Pakistan, reluctantly joining the Muslim exodus during the war between India and Pakistan. Rushdie graduated from King's College in Cambridge in 1968 and worked as a freelance advertising copywriter from 1971 to 1981. *Grimus* (1975) was his first novel. *Midnight's Children* (1981) won the Booker Prize and also made him internationally famous.

Rushdie's fourth novel, *The Satanic Verses* (1988), was banned in India and South Africa because it was considered blasphemous. The novel's plot involves a hijacked jetliner and the unlikely survival of two of its passengers: Gibreel Farishta, an Indian movie star, and Saladin Chamcha, an Indian expatriate returning to his homeland after fifteen years abroad. A fatwa—effectively a death sentence—was issued by Iran against Rushdie in 1989. He went into hiding but continued to write and publish. *In Good Faith* (1990) was published to appease Rushdie's critics and was issued as an apology in which he reaffirmed his respect for Islam. However, the fatwa was not withdrawn. Rushdie's other books include *Haroun and the Sea of Stories* (1990), *Moors Last Sight* (1995), *The Ground beneath Her Feet* (1999), *Fury* (2001), and *Step across This Line* (2003). In September of 1998 the Iranian government announced that the state would not be putting into effect the fatwa or encouraging anybody to do so. However, a political organization in Iran lined up more than five hundred men to make a donation of one kidney apiece to bankroll an assassination plot against Rushdie. He is no longer in hiding; Rushdie lives in both New York and London, where he continues to write.

## *Good Advice Is Rarer Than Rubies*                    1994

On the last Tuesday of the month, the dawn bus, its headlamps still shining, brought Miss Rehana to the gates of the British Consulate. It arrived pushing a cloud of dust, veiling her beauty from the eyes of strangers until she descended. The bus was brightly painted in multicolored arabesques, and on the front it said "MOVE OVER DARLING" in green and gold letters; on the back it added "Tata-Bata"[1] and also "O.K. GOOD-LIFE." Miss Rehana told the driver it was a beautiful bus, and he jumped down and held the door open for her, bowing theatrically as she descended.

---

1 **Tata-Bata:** Tata and Bata are both private Indian companies that, among other things, manufacture buses.

· · ·

Miss Rehana's eyes were large and black and bright enough not to need the help of antimony, and when the advice expert Muhammad Ali saw them he felt himself becoming young again. He watched her approaching the Consulate gates as the light strengthened, and asking the bearded lala[2] who guarded them in a gold-buttoned khaki uniform with a cockaded[3] turban when they would open. The lala, usually so rude to the Consulate's Tuesday women, answered Miss Rehana with something like courtesy.

"Half an hour," he said gruffly. "Maybe two hours. Who knows? The sahibs[4] are eating their breakfast."

The dusty compound between the bus stop and the Consulate was already full of Tuesday women, some veiled, a few barefaced like Miss Rehana. They all looked frightened, and leaned heavily on the arms of uncles or brothers, who were trying to look confident. But Miss Rehana had come on her own, and did not seem at all alarmed.

Muhammad Ali, who specialised in advising the most vulnerable-looking of these weekly supplicants, found his feet leading him towards the strange, big-eyed independent girl.

"Miss," he began. "You have come for a permit to London, I think so?"

She was standing at a hot-snack stall in the little shanty-town by the edge of the compound, munching chilli-pakoras[5] contentedly. She turned to look at him, and at close range those eyes did bad things to his digestive tract.

"Yes, I have."

"Then, please, you allow me to give some advice? Small cost only."

Miss Rehana smiled. "Good advice is rarer than rubies," she said, "But alas, I cannot pay. I am an orphan, not one of your wealthy ladies."

"Trust my grey hairs," Muhammad Ali urged her. "My advice is well tempered by experience. You will certainly find it good."

She shook her head. "I tell you I am a poor potato. There are women here with male family members, all earning good wages. Go to them. Good advice should find good money."

*I am going crazy,* Muhammad Ali thought, because he heard his voice telling her of its own volition, "Miss, I have been drawn to you by Fate. What to do? Our meeting was written. I also am a poor man only, but for you my advice comes free."

She smiled again. "Then I must surely listen. When Fate sends a gift, one receives good fortune."

He led her to the low wooden desk in his own special corner of the shanty-town. She followed, continuing to eat pakoras from a little newspaper packet. She did not offer him any.

Muhammad Ali put a cushion on the dusty ground. "Please to sit." She did as he

2 **lala:** A young gentleman.
3 **cockaded:** Decorated with a rosette or knot of ribbons.
4 **sahib:** A term of respect for European men in colonial India.
5 **pakoras:** Vegetable fritters.

asked. He sat cross-legged across the desk from her, conscious that two or three dozen pairs of male eyes were watching him enviously, that all the other shanty-town men were ogling the latest young lovely to be charmed by the old grey-hair fraud. He took a deep breath to settle himself.

"Name, please."

"Miss Rehana," she told him. "Fiancée of Mustafa Dar of Bradford, London."

"Bradford, England," he corrected her gently. "London is a town only, like Multan or Bahawalpur. England is a great nation full of the coldest fish in the world."

"I see. Thank you," she responded gravely, so that he was unsure if she was making fun of him.

"You have filled application form? Then let me see, please."

She passed him a neatly folded document in a brown envelope.

"Is it OK?" For the first time there was a note of anxiety in her voice.

He patted the desk quite near the place where her hand rested. "I am certain," he said. "Wait on and I will check."

She finished the pakoras while he scanned her papers.

"Tip-top," he pronounced at length. "All in order."

"Thank you for your advice," she said, making as if to rise. "I'll go now and wait by the gate."

"What are you thinking?" he cried loudly, smiting his forehead. "You consider this is easy business? Just give the form and proof, with a big smile they hand over the permit? Miss Rehana, I tell you, you are entering a worse place than any police station."

"Is it to, truly?" His oratory had done the trick. She was a captive audience now, and he would be able to look at her for a few moments longer.

Drawing another calming breath, he launched into his set speech. He told her that the sahibs thought that all the women who came on Tuesdays, claiming to be dependents of bus drivers in Luton or chartered accountants in Manchester, were crooks and liars and cheats.

She protested, "But then I will simply tell them that I, for one, am no such thing!"

Her innocence made him shiver with fear for her. She was a sparrow, he told her, and they were men with hooded eyes, like hawks. He explained that they would ask her questions, personal questions, questions such as a lady's own brother would be too shy to ask. They would ask if she was virgin, and, if not, what her fiancé's love-making habits were, and what secret nicknames they had invented for one another.

Muhammad Ali spoke brutally, on purpose, to lessen the shock she would feel when it, or something like it, actually happened. Her eyes remained steady, but her hands began to flutter at the edges of the desk.

He went on:

"They will ask you how many rooms are in your family home, and what colour are the walls, and what days do you empty the rubbish. They will ask your man's mother's third cousin's aunt's step-daughter's middle name. And all these things they have already asked your Mustafa Dar in his Bradford. And if you make one mistake, you are finished."

"Yes," she said, and he could hear her disciplining her voice. "And what is your advice, old man?"

It was at this point that Muhammad Ali usually began to whisper urgently, to mention that he knew a man, a very good type, who worked in the Consulate, and through him, for a fee, the necessary papers could be delivered, with all the proper authenticating seals. Business was good, because the women would often pay him five hundred rupees or give him a gold bracelet for his pains, and go away happy.

They came from hundreds of miles away—he normally made sure of this before beginning to trick them—so even when they discovered they had been swindled they were unlikely to return. They went away to Sargodha or Lalukhet and began to pack, and who knows at what point they found out they had been gulled, but it was a too-late point, anyway.

Life is hard, and an old man must live by his wits. It was not up to Muhammad Ali to have compassion for these Tuesday women.

But once again his voice betrayed him, and instead of starting his customary speech it began to reveal to her his greatest secret.

"Miss Rehana," his voice said, and he listened to it in amazement, "you are a rare person, a jewel, and for you I will do what I would not do for my own daughter, perhaps. One document has come into my possession that can solve all your worries at one stroke."

"And what is this sorcerer's paper?" she asked, her eyes unquestionably laughing at him now.

His voice fell low-as-low.

"Miss Rehana, it is a British passport. Completely genuine and pukka[6] goods. I have a good friend who will put your name and photo, and then, hey-presto, England there you come!"

He had said it!

Anything was possible now, on this day of his insanity. Probably he would give her the thing free-gratis, and then kick himself for a year afterwards.

*Old fool,* he berated himself. *The oldest fools are bewitched by the youngest girls.*

"Let me understand you," she was saying. "You are proposing I should commit a crime . . ."

"Not crime," he interposed. "Facilitation."

" . . . and go to Bradford, London, illegally, and therefore justify the low opinion the Consulate sahibs have of us all. Old babuji, this not good advice."

"Bradford, *England,*" he corrected her mournfully. "You should not take my gift in such a spirit."

"Then how?"

6 pukka: Substantial, genuine, or first class.

"Bibi, I am a poor fellow, and I have offered this prize because you are so beautiful. Do not spit on my generosity. Take the thing. Or else don't take, go home, forget England, only do not go into that building and lose your dignity."

But she was on her feet, turning away from him, walking towards the gates, where the women had begun to cluster and the lala was swearing at them to be patient or none of them would be admitted at all.

"So be a fool," Muhammad Ali shouted after her. "What goes of my father's if you are?" (Meaning, what was it to him.)

She did not turn.

"It is the curse of our people," he yelled. "We are poor, we are ignorant, and we completely refuse to learn."

"Hey, Muhammad Ali," the woman at the betel-nut stall called across to him. "Too bad, she likes them young."

That day Muhammad Ali did nothing but stand around near the Consulate gates. Many times he scolded himself, *Go from here, old goof, lady does not desire to speak with you any further.* But when she came out, she found him waiting.

"Salaam,[7] advice wallah," she greeted him.

She seemed calm, and at peace with him again, and he thought, *My God, ya Allah, she has pulled it off. The British sahibs also have been drowning in her eyes and she has got her passage to England.*

He smiled at her hopefully. She smiled back with no trouble at all.

"Miss Rehana Begum," he said, "felicitations, daughter, on what is obviously you're hour of triumph."

Impulsively, she took his forearm in her hand.

"Come," she said. "Let me buy you a pakora to thank you for your advice and to apologise for my rudeness, too."

The stood in the dust of the afternoon compound near the bus, which was getting ready to leave. Coolies[8] were tying bedding rolls to the roof. A hawker shouted at the passengers, trying to sell them love stories and green medicines, both of which cured unhappiness. Miss Rehana and a happy Muhammad Ali ate their pakoras sitting on the bus's "front mud-guard," that is, the bumper. The old advice expert began softly to hum a tune from a movie soundtrack. The day's heat was gone.

"It was an arranged engagement," Miss Rehana said all at once. "I was nine years old when my parents fixed it. Mustafa Dar was already thirty at that time, but my father wanted someone who could look after me as he had done himself and Mustafa was a man known to Daddyji as a solid type. Then my parents died and Mustafa Dar went to England and said he would send for me. That was many years ago. I have his photo, but he is like a stranger to me. Even his voice, I do not recognise it on the phone."

---

7 "**Salaam**": A ceremonial greeting, usually including a low bow.
8 **coolies**: Laborers from the East Indies, China, or Japan. Derogatory term.

· · ·

The confession took Muhammad Ali by surprise, but he nodded with what he hoped looked like wisdom.

"Still and after all," he said, "one's parents act in one's best interests. They found you a good and honest man who has kept his word and sent for you. And now you have a lifetime to get to know him, and to love."

He was puzzled, now, by the bitterness that had infected her smile.

"But, old man," she asked him, "why have you already packed me and posted me off to England?"

He stood up, shocked.

"You looked happy—so I just assumed . . . excuse me, but they turned you down or what?"

"I got all their questions wrong," she replied. "Distinguishing marks I put on the wrong cheeks, bathroom decor I completely redecorated, all absolutely topsy-turvy, you see."

"But what to do? How will you go?"

"Now I will go back to Lahore and my job. I work in a great house, as ayah⁹ to three good boys. They would have been sad to see me leave."

"But this is tragedy!" Muhammad Ali lamented. "Oh, how I pray that you had taken up my offer! Now, but, it is not possible, I regret to inform. Now they have your form on file, cross-check can be made, even the passport will not suffice.

"It is spoilt, all spoilt, and it could have been so easy if advice had been accepted in good time."

"I do not think," she told him, "I truly do not think you should be sad."

Her last smile, which he watched from the compound until the bus concealed it in a dust-cloud, was the happiest thing he had ever seen in his long, hot, hard, unloving life.

# John McLeod

## From "Commonwealth" to "Postcolonial"                    2000

### Introduction

The purpose of this [selection] is to approach a flexible but solid definition of the word "postcolonialism." In order to think about the range and variety of the term, we need to place it in two contexts. The first regards the historical experiences of de-

---

9 ayah: An Indian governess.

colonisation that have occurred chiefly in the twentieth century. The second concerns relevant intellectual developments in the latter part of the twentieth century, especially the shift from the study of "Commonwealth literature" to "postcolonialism." After looking at each, we will be in a position at the end of this [selection] to make some statements about how we might define "postcolonialism."

## Colonialism and Decolonisation

At the turn of the twentieth century, the British Empire covered a vast area of the earth that included parts of Africa, Asia, Australasia, Canada, the Caribbean and Ireland. At the turn of the twenty-first century, there remains a small number of British colonies. The phrase "the British Empire" is most commonly used these days in the past tense, signifying a historical period and set of relationships which are no longer current. In short, the twentieth century has been the century of colonial demise, and of decolonisation for millions of people who were once subject to the authority of the British crown.

Yet, at the start of the twenty-first century Britain remains a colonial power, with several possessions in (for example) the Caribbean and the South Atlantic. In addition, the material and imaginative legacies of both colonialism and decolonisation remain fundamentally important constitutive elements in a variety of contemporary domains, such as anthropology, economics, art, global politics, international capitalism, the mass-media and . . . literature.

Colonialism has taken many different forms and has engendered diverse effects around the world, but we must be as precise as we can when defining its meaning. This can be gauged by thinking first about its relationship with two other terms: "capitalism" and "imperialism." Let us take each in turn. As Denis Judd argues in his book *Empire: The British Imperial Experience from 1765 to the Present* (HarperCollins, 1996), "[n]o one can doubt that the desire for profitable trade, plunder and enrichment was the primary force that led to the establishment of the imperial structure" (p. 3). Judd argues that colonialism was first and foremost part of the commercial venture of the Western nations that developed from the late seventeenth and early eighteenth centuries (although others date its origins to the European "voyages of discovery" in the fifteenth and sixteenth centuries, such as those of Christopher Columbus). The seizing of "foreign" lands for government and settlement was in part motivated by the desire to create and control markets abroad for Western goods, as well as securing the natural resources and labour-power of different lands and peoples at the lowest possible cost. Colonialism was a lucrative commercial operation, bringing wealth and riches to Western nations through the economic exploitation of others. It was pursued for economic profit, reward and riches. Hence, colonialism and capitalism share a mutually supportive relationship with each other.

"Colonialism" is sometimes used interchangeably with "imperialism," but in truth the terms mean different things. As Peter Childs and Patrick Williams argue, imperialism is an ideological concept which upholds the legitimacy of the economic and military control of one nation by another. Colonialism, however, is only *one form of practice* which results from the ideology of imperialism, and specifically concerns the *settlement* of one group of people in a new location. Imperialism is not strictly concerned with the issue of settlement; it does not demand the settlement of different places in order to work. Childs and Williams define imperialism as "the extension and expansion of trade and commerce under the protection of political, legal, and military controls" (*An Introduction to Post-Colonial Theory,* Harvester Wheatsheaf, 1997, p. 227). Note how imperialism does *not* require the settling of communities from the imperial nation in another location. In these terms, colonialism is one historically specific experience of how imperialism can work through the act of settlement, but it is not the only way of pursuing imperialist ideals. Hence, it could be argued that while *colonialism* is virtually over today, *imperialism* continues apace as Western nations such as America are still engaged in imperial acts, securing wealth and power through the continuing economic exploitation of other nations. Thus, as Benita Parry puts it, colonialism is "a specific, and the most spectacular, mode of imperialism's many and mutable states, one which preceded the rule of international finance capitalism and whose formal ending imperialism has survived" ("Problems in Current Theories of Colonial Discourse," *Oxford Literary Review,* 9 (1–2), 1987, p. 34).

To recap: colonialism is a particular historical manifestation of imperialism, specific to certain places and times. Similarly, we can regard the British Empire as one form of an imperial economic and political structure. Thus, we can endorse Elleke Boehmer's judicious definition of colonialism in her book *Colonial and Postcolonial Literature* (Oxford University Press, 1995) as the "settlement of territory, the exploitation or development of resources, and the attempt to govern the indigenous inhabitants of occupied lands" (p. 2). Note in this definition (a) the emphasis on the *settlement* of land, (b) the *economic* relationship at the heart of colonialism, and (c) *the unequal relations of power* which colonialism constructs.

Boehmer's phrase "the attempt to govern" hints at the ways in which British colonialism was not always fully successful in securing its aims, and met with acts of resistance from the outset by indigenous inhabitants of colonized lands, as well as members of the European communities who had settled overseas and no longer wished to defer power and authority to the imperial "motherland." As regards the imperial venture of the British Empire, there are three distinct periods of *decolonisation* when the colonised nations won the right to govern their own affairs. The first was the loss of the American colonies and declaration of American independence in the late eighteenth century. The second period spans the end of the nineteenth century to the first decade of the twentieth century, and concerns the creation of the "dominions." This was the term used to describe the nations of Canada, Australia, New Zealand and South Africa. These nations (today referred to as "settler" nations) consisted of large European populations that had settled overseas, often violently displacing or destroying the indigenous peoples of these lands—Native Indians in Canada, Aboriginal communities in Australia and New Zealand, black African peoples in South Africa. The "settler" peoples of these nations agitated for forms of self-government which they achieved as dominions of the British Empire. Yet, as a "dominion" each still recognised and pledged allegiance to the ultimate authority of Britain as the "mother country."

Canada was the first to achieve a form of political autonomy in 1867; Australia followed suit in 1900, New Zealand similarly in 1907, and South Africa in 1909. Slightly after this period, Ireland won self-rule in 1922, although the country was partitioned and six counties in the North East remained under British control. In 1931 the Statute of Westminster removed the obligation for the dominions to defer ultimate authority to the British crown and gave them full governmental control.

The third period of decolonisation occurred in the decades immediately following the end of the Second World War. Unlike the self-governing settler dominions, the colonized lands in South Asia, Africa and the Caribbean did not become sites of mass European migration, and tended to feature larger dispossessed populations settled by small British colonial elites. The achievement of independence in these locations occurred mainly after the Second World War, often as a consequence of indigenous anti-colonial nationalism and military struggle. India and Pakistan gained independence in 1947, Ceylon (now Sri Lanka) in 1948. In 1957 Ghana became the first "majority-rule" independent African country, followed by Nigeria in 1960. In 1962, Jamaica and Trinidad and Tobago in the Caribbean followed suit. The decades of the 1960s and 1970s saw busy decolonisation throughout the declining Empire. So, with the passing of Hong Kong from Britain to China on 1 July 1997, the numbers of those living overseas under British rule fell below one million for the first time in centuries—a far cry from the days when British colonialism subjected millions around the globe.

There were, of course, as many reasons for decolonisation as there were once-colonised nations. One fundamental reason was due in many ways to the growth of various nationalist movements in both the "settler" and "settled" colonies which mounted resistance to British colonial authority. In addition, particularly after the Second World War, Britain's status as a world economic power rapidly declined, while America and the Soviet Union became the military superpowers of the post-war era. The British Empire was becoming increasingly expensive to administer, and it made economic sense to hand over the costly administration of colonial affairs to its people, whether or not the colonised peoples were prepared (economically or otherwise) for the shift of power.

## The Emergence of "Commonwealth Literature"

Let us move from this very brief history of colonialism and decolonisation to the intellectual contexts of postcolonialism. In particular, we need to look at two areas of intellectual study that have come to influence its emergence: "Commonwealth literature" and "theories of colonial discourses." This will equip us with a useful historical understanding of how postcolonialism has developed in recent years, while indicating its particular, if wide-ranging, scope. Of course, I do not wish to imply that the narrative which follows is a full account or representative of all the work that has occurred in the field; far from it. But in pointing to a few key developments we can begin to understand the intellectual scope and focus of postcolonialism as it is understood today.

One important antecedent for postcolonialism was the growth of the study of Commonwealth literature. "Commonwealth literature" was a term literary critics began to use from the 1950s to describe literatures in English emerging from a selection of countries with a history of colonialism. It incorporated the study of writers from the predominantly European settler communities, as well as writers belonging to those countries which were in the process of gaining independence from British rule, such as those from the African, Caribbean and South Asian nations. Literary critics began to distinguish a fast-growing body of literature written in English which included work by such figures as R. K. Narayan (India), George Lamming (Barbados), Katherine Mansfield (New Zealand) and Chinua Achebe (Nigeria). The creation of the category of "Commonwealth literature" as a special area of study was an attempt to identify and locate this vigorous literary activity, and to consider via a comparative approach the common concerns and attributes that these manifold literary voices might have. Significantly, neither American nor Irish literature were included in early formulations of the field. "Commonwealth literature," then, was associated exclusively with *selected* countries with a history of colonialism.

The term "Commonwealth literature" is important in the associations it beckons, and these associations have historical roots. One consequence of the decline of the British Empire in the twentieth century was the establishment of—to use its original title—the British Commonwealth of Nations. At first, this term was used to refer collectively to the special status of the dominions within the Empire and their continuing allegiance to Britain. However, as the relationship between Britain and the dominions changed in the first half of the century (with the term "dominions" being gradually dropped) a different meaning of "Commonwealth" emerged. In the early decades, Britain hosted frequent "colonial conferences" which gathered together the Governors of the colonies and heads of the dominions. In 1907 these meetings were re-named "imperial conferences" in recognition of the fact that the dominions were no longer strictly British colonies. After the Second World War, these meetings became "Commonwealth conferences" and featured the Heads of State of the newly independent nations. The British monarch was recognised as the head of the Commonwealth *in symbolic terms only;* the British crown held no political authority over other Commonwealth nations, and the word "British" was abandoned altogether. Thus, "Commonwealth" became redefined after the war in more equitable terms, as meaning an association of sovereign nations without deference to a single authority. Today, the Commonwealth of Nations as a body exists in name only. It has no constitution nor any legal authority, and its membership—although based on the old map of Empire—is not compulsory for the independent nations (Ireland and Burma elected to leave the Commonwealth in 1948).

This shift from "colonial" to "Commonwealth" perhaps suggests a particular version of history in which the status of the colonised countries happily changes from subservience to equality. But we must avoid subscribing to this selective view, not least because the economic and political relations between Britain and the commonwealth nations have remained far from equal. The identification and study of "Commonwealth literature" certainly echoed the tenor of the specifically benign usage of "Commonwealth," but it also had its own problems. In general the term suggested a shared, valuable literary inheritance between disparate and variable nations. It distinctly promoted unity in diversity—revealingly, the plural term "Commonwealth *literatures*" was rarely used. However, that common inheritance arguably served to reinforce the primacy of Britain among the Commonwealth nations. As A. Norman Jeffares declared in 1964, addressing the first conference of Commonwealth literature at the University of Leeds in England, "one reads [Commonwealth writers] because they bring new ideas, new interpretations of life to us" (*Commonwealth Literature: Unity and Diversity in a Common Culture,* ed. John Press, Heinemann, 1965, p. xiv). It is not clear whether the "us" in this sentence referred to the diverse audience at the conference comprising writers and academics from many Commonwealth nations, or specifically British (or, more widely, Western) readers in particular. "Commonwealth literature" may well have been created in an attempt to bring together writings from around the world on an equal footing, yet the assumption remained that these texts were addressed primarily to a Western English-speaking readership. The "Commonwealth" in "Commonwealth literature" was never fully free from the older, more imperious connotations of the term.

One of the fundamental assumptions held by the first Western critics of Commonwealth literature concerned the relationship between literature and the nation. In the introduction to a collection of essays *The Commonwealth Pen: An Introduction to the Literature of the British Commonwealth* (Cornell, 1961), the editor A. L. McLeod (no relation!) proposed that "[t]he genesis of a local literature in the Commonwealth countries has almost always been contemporaneous with the development of a truly nationalist sentiment: the larger British colonies such as Fiji, Hong Kong and Malta, where there are relatively large English-speaking populations, have produced no literature, even in the broadest sense of the term. The reason probably lies in the fact that they have, as yet, no sense of national identity, no cause to follow, no common goal" (p. 8). Many agreed that the "novel" ideas and new "interpretations of life" in Commonwealth literature owed much to the ways that writers were forging their own sense of national and cultural identity. This was certainly one of the functions of the texts regarded as "Commonwealth literature." . . .

However, the attention to the alleged nationalist purposes of much Commonwealth literature often played second fiddle to more abstract concerns which distracted attention away from specific national contexts. Many critics were primarily preoccupied with identifying a common goal shared among writers from many different nations that went beyond more "local" affairs. Just as the idea of a Commonwealth of nations suggested a diverse community with a common set of concerns, Commonwealth literature—whether produced in India, Australia or the Caribbean—was assumed to reach across national borders and deal with universal concerns. Commonwealth literature certainly dealt with national and cultural issues, but the best writing possessed the mysterious power to transcend them too.

Witness the editorial to the first edition of the *Journal of Commonwealth Literature* published in September 1965. The editorial saw the need to recognise the important cultural differences between writers from divergent locations. But it also revealed the ways in which literature from Commonwealth countries was unified through the category of "Commonwealth literature."

> The name of the journal is simply a piece of convenient shorthand, which should on no account be construed as a perverse underwriting of any concept of a single, culturally homogeneous body of writings to be thought of as "Commonwealth Literature." . . . Clearly, all writing . . . takes its place within the body of English literature, and becomes subject to the *criteria of excellence by which literary works in English are judged,* but the *pressures* that act upon a Canadian writing in English differ significantly from those operating upon an Indian using a language not his mother tongue, just as both kinds differ from those that affect an Englishman. (*Journal of Commonwealth Literature,* 1 (1), 1965, p. v—my emphasis)

Such "pressures" were presumably the historical and cultural influences of each writer that differed across time and space. How, then, could one account for the *common wealth* of these writings? As the editorial claims, because the texts studied as Commonwealth literature were written ostensibly in English, they were to be evaluated *in relation to* English literature, with the same criteria used to account for the literary value of the age-old English "classics." Commonwealth literature at its best was comparable with the English literary canon which functioned as the means of measuring its value. It was able to transcend its regional affiliations and produce work of *permanent* and *universal* relevance. As A. Norman Jeffares put it, a Commonwealth writer of value "wants ultimately to be judged not because he *[sic]* gives us a picture of life in a particular place, in a particular situation, but by the universal, lasting quality of his writings, judged by neither local nor yet national standards. Good writing is something which transcends borders, whether local or national, whether of the mind or of the spirit" (*Commonwealth Literature,* p. vxiii).

Commonwealth literature, then, was really a sub-set of canonical English literature, evaluated in terms derived from the conventional study of English that stressed the values of timelessness and universality. For example, consider the following moment from William Walsh's book *Commonwealth Literature* (Oxford University Press, 1973), when Walsh is discussing a novel by George Lamming. Lamming is from Barbados in the Caribbean and has African ancestry. This is what Walsh made of Lamming's novel *Season of Adventure* (1960):

> In this novel the African theme and connection become stronger and more positive, although it is never allowed to puff into a merely abstract existence. Indeed, Lamming's achievement is to make us hear the scream of the humiliated and persecuted and to make it simultaneously a metaphor for the damage *universal in mankind.* (p. 53—my emphasis)

Walsh identifies "African" elements in the novel that bear witness to the context of Lamming's position as a writer. But Africa is only a "theme" and not allowed to be the *primary* focus of the work, which is the novel's attention to the "damage universal in mankind." Later in his book Walsh reads the Australian Patrick White's novel *Voss* (1957) in similar terms, as "a powerful and humane work coloured with the light and soaked with the sweat and personality of Australia" (p. 134). So, for critics like Walsh, Commonwealth literature dealt fundamentally with the same preoccupations with the human condition as did Jane Austen or George Eliot. National differences were certainly important, adding the novelty of "personality," "light" and "colour"; but ultimately these "national" specifics were secondary to the fundamental universal meaning of the work.

Today this kind of critical approach that makes secondary the historical contexts that inform a work of literature is often described as "liberal humanist" (for a discussion of this term, see Peter Barry, *Beginning Theory*, Manchester University Press, 1995, pp. 11–38). For liberal humanists the most "literary" texts always transcend the provincial contexts of their initial production and deal with moral preoccupations relevant to people of all times and places. In retrospect, many critics of Commonwealth literature appear very much like liberal humanists. Unlike later critics, they did not always think how the texts they read so enthusiastically might resist their reading practices and challenge the assumptions of universality and timelessness that legitimated the criteria of "good writing." Indeed, one of the fundamental differences that many postcolonial critics today have from their Commonwealth predecessors is their insistence that historical, geographical and cultural specifics are *vital* to both the writing and the reading of a text, and cannot be so easily bracketed as secondary colouring or background. But for many critics of Commonwealth literature, these texts conformed to a critical *status quo*. They were not considered especially radical or oppositional; nor were they seen to challenge the Western criteria of excellence used to read them. Their experimental elements, their novelty and local focus made them exciting to read and helped depict the nation with which they were concerned. But their potential differences were contained by the identification within them of universal themes that bound texts safely inside the aesthetic criteria of the West. For postcolonial critics the *different* preoccupations and contexts of texts were to become more important than their alleged *similar* abstract qualities.

However, it would be a travesty to condemn or dismiss the work of a previous generation of critics of Commonwealth literature, on the grounds that it does not fit the current critical climate. True, critics like Jeffares and Walsh belong to an earlier phase of literary criticism that was soon to be radically challenged in the latter decades of the century. But they and others were instrumental in securing Commonwealth literature as an important category of artistic endeavour and as a viable area of academic study. In isolating the liberal assumptions of these critics' reading practices it can be too easily forgotten that the attention they gave to Commonwealth literature, and the space they cleared for it on university English courses in the West, constituted a fundamentally important political act. Such critics assisted in ensuring that these literatures were not a minor area of curiosity but a major field that merited serious attention on the same terms as the "classics" of English literature. What might today look like a liberal humanist enterprise was at the time also an important political investment in these new literatures as significant, despite the limitations we have considered. The patient, detailed and enthusiastic readings of Commonwealth literature laid the foundations for the various postcolonial criticisms that were to follow, and to which much postcolonial critical activity remains indebted.

As Shirley Chew has explained, "a paradox sits at the heart of the Commonwealth: described as a free association of equal and mutually cooperating nations, it is nevertheless drawn together by a shared history of colonial exploitation, dependence and interchange" ("The Commonwealth:" Pedestal or Pyre?," *New Statesman and Society,* 21 July 1995, p. 32). If the study of Commonwealth literature was pursued in the philanthropic spirit of the first side of this paradox, the critical activity of postcolonialism was to concentrate more on the other, darker side of exploitation and dependence. In the late 1970s and 1980s many critics endeavoured to discard the liberal humanist bias perceived in critics of Commonwealth literature, and to read the literature in new ways. In order to understand how and why this happened we need to look briefly at the second chief antecedent to postcolonialism: theories of "colonial discourses."

## Theories of Colonial Discourses: Frantz Fanon and Edward Said

Theories of colonial discourses have been hugely influential in the development of postcolonialism. In general, they explore the ways that *representations* and *modes of perception* are used as fundamental weapons of colonial power to keep colonised peoples subservient to colonial rule. Colonial discourses have been rigorously explored in recent years by critics working with developments in critical theory . . . .

A good introduction to the issues involved in the identification and study of colonial discourses can be made by considering the following statement by the Trinidadian writer Sam Selvon. At the beginning of his 1979 lecture, "Three Into One Can't Go—East Indian, Trinidadian, West Indian," Selvon recalls an Indian fisherman who used to visit his street in San Fernando, Trinidad, when he was a child. The fisherman, Sammy, was partly paralysed and was often a figure of ridicule by the children. One day Sammy brought a white assistant on his round with him, apparently an escaped convict. Selvon records his utter fury at Sammy for employing the white man as an assistant. This, it seemed to the young Selvon, was not the way life was organised: the white man should be the master, not Sammy. Selvon admits he felt sympathy and dismay for the white assistant, feelings he never had for the lame Sammy. He uses this anecdote to exemplify how as a child he had learned always to regard non-Westerners an inferior: the idea of a white assistant to the Indian Sammy was an affront to his sense of order. This example of the *internalising* of certain expectations about human relationships speaks volumes about how colonialism operates, as Selvon notes:

> When one talks of colonial indoctrination, it is usually about oppression
> or subjugation, or waving little Union Jacks on Empire Day and singing
> "God Save the King." But this gut feeling I had as a child, that the Indian
> was just a piece of cane trash while the white man was to be honoured and
> respected—where had it come from? I don't consciously remember being
> brainwashed to hold this view either at home or at school. (In *Foreday
> Morning: Selected Prose,* Longman, 1989, p. 211)

Where indeed? Much work has been done in recent years that could provide an answer to Selvon's question. Many writers have striven to demonstrate how colonialism suggests certain ways of seeing, specific modes of understanding the world and one's place in it that assist in justifying the subservience of colonised peoples to the (oft-assumed) "superior," civilised order of the British colonisers. These ways of seeing are at the root of the study of colonial discourses.

Colonialism is perpetuated in part by justifying to those in the colonising nation the idea that it is right and proper to rule over other peoples, and by getting colonised people to accept their lower ranking in the colonial order of things—a process we can call "colonising the mind." It operates by persuading people to internalise its logic and speak its language; to perpetuate the values and assumptions of the colonisers as regards the ways they perceive and represent the world. Theories of colonial discourses call attention to the role language plays in getting people to succumb to a particular way of seeing that results in the kind of situation Selvon describes. Although the term is often used in the singular, it is more accurate to talk of colonial *discourses* rather than "colonial discourse" due to its multifarious varieties and operations which differ in time and space. We shall use the plural term throughout this [selection] to keep this fact firmly in mind.

Colonial discourses form the intersections where language and power meet. Language, let us remember, is more than simply a means of communication; it constitutes our world-view by cutting up and ordering reality into meaningful units. The meanings we attach to things tell us which values we consider are important, and how we learn or choose to differentiate between superior or inferior qualities. Listen to Kenyan novelist Ngugi wa Thiong'o on this point:

> Language carries culture, and culture carries, particularly through orature and literature, the entire body of values by which we come to perceive ourselves and our place in the world. How people perceive themselves affects how they look at their culture, at their politics and at the social production of wealth, at their entire relationship to nature and to other human beings. Language is thus inseparable from ourselves as a community of human beings with a specific form and character, a specific history, a specific relationship to the world. (*Decolonising the Mind: The Politics of Language in African Literature*, James Currey, 1986, p. 16)

As Ngugi stresses, language does not just passively reflect reality; it also goes a long way towards creating a person's understanding of their world, and it houses the values by which we (either willingly or through force) live our lives. Under colonialism, a colonised people are made subservient to ways of regarding the world which reflect and support colonialist values. A particular value-system is taught as the best, truest world-view. The cultural values of the colonised peoples are deemed as lacking in value, or even as being "uncivilised," from which they must be rescued. To be blunt, the British Empire did not rule by military and physical force alone. It endured by getting *both colonising and colonised people* to see their world and themselves in a particular way, internalising the language of Empire as representing the natural, true order of life. Selvon's anecdote reveals just how far-reaching the invidious effects of internalising colonial assumptions about the "inferiority" of certain peoples can be.

If the internalisation of colonial sets of values was to a degree, as Selvon's example shows, an effective way of disempowering people, it was also the source of trauma for colonised peoples who were taught to look negatively upon their people, their culture and themselves. In the 1950s there emerged much important work that attempted to record the psychological damage suffered by colonised peoples who internalised these colonial discourses. Prominent was the psychologist Frantz Fanon, who wrote widely and passionately about the damage French colonialism had wreaked upon millions of people who suffered its power. Fanon is an important figure in the field of post-colonialism . . . . He was born in the French Antilles in 1925 and educated in Martinique and France. His experience of racism while being educated by and working for the French affected him deeply; in Algeria in 1954 he resigned his post as head of the Psychiatric Department in Blida-Joinville Hospital and joined with the Algerian rebels fighting against the French occupation of the country. Influenced by contemporary philosophers and poets such as Jean-Paul Sartre and Aimé Césaire, Fanon's publications include two polemical books—*Black Skin, White Masks* (trans. Charles Lam Markmann, Pluto [1952] 1986) and *The Wretched of the Earth* (trans. Constance Farrington, Penguin [1961] 1967)—that deal angrily with the mechanics of colonialism and its effects on those it ensnared. *Black Skin, White Masks* examined in the main the psychological effects of colonialism, drawing upon Fanon's experience as a psychoanalyst. In a narrative both inspiring and distressing, Fanon looked at the cost to the individual who lives in a world where due to the colour of his or her skin, he or she is rendered peculiar, an object of derision, an aberration. In the chapter "The Fact of Blackness" he remembers how he felt when in France white strangers pointed out his blackness, his difference with derogatory phrases such as "dirty nigger!" or "look, Negro!":

> On that day, completely dislocated, unable to be abroad with the other, the white man, who unmercifully imprisoned me, I took myself far off from my own presence, far indeed, and made myself an object. What else could it be for me but an amputation, an excision, a hemorrhage that spattered my whole body with black blood? But I did not want this revision, this thematisation. All I wanted was to be a man among other men. I wanted to come lithe and young into a world that was ours and to help to build it together. (*Black Skin, White Masks*, pp. 112–13)

In this scenario, Fanon's identity is defined in negative terms by those in a position of power. He is forced to see himself not as a human *subject,* with his own wants and needs as indicated at the end of the quotation, but an *object,* a peculiarity at the mercy of a group that identifies him as inferior, less than fully-human, placed at the mercy of their definitions and representations. The violence of this "revision" of his identity is conveyed powerfully in the image of amputation. Fanon feels abbreviated, violated, imprisoned by a way of seeing him that denies him the right to define his own identity as a subject. Identity is something that the French *make for him,* and in so doing they commit a violence that splits his very sense of self. The power of description, of naming, is not to be underestimated. The relationship between language and power is far-reaching and fundamental.

*Black Skin, White Masks* explains the consequences of identity formation for the colonised subject who is forced into the internalisation of the self as an "other." The "Negro" is deemed to epitomise everything that the colonising French are not. The colonisers are civilised, rational, intelligent: the "Negro" remains "other" to all these qualities against which colonising peoples derive their sense of superiority and normality. *Black Skin, White Masks* depicts those colonised by French imperialism doomed to hold a traumatic belief in their own inferiority. One response to such trauma is to strive to escape it by embracing the "civilised" ideals of the French "mother-land." But however hard the colonised try to accept the education, values and language of France—to don the white mask of civilisation that will cover up the "uncivilised" nature indexed by their black skins—they are never accepted on equal terms. "The white world," writes Fanon, "the only honourable one, barred me from all participation. A man was expected to behave like a man. I was expected to behave like a black man" (*Black Skin, White Masks*, p. 114). That imaginative distinction that differentiates between "man" (self) with "black man" (other) is an important, devastating part of the armoury of colonial domination, one that imprisons the mind as securely as chains imprison the body. For Fanon, the end of colonialism meant not just political and economic change, but psychological change too. Colonialism is destroyed only once this way of thinking about identity is successfully challenged.

In 1978 Edward W. Said's *Orientalism* was published. *Orientalism* is considered to be one of the most influential books of the late twentieth century. Said also looked at the divisive relationship between the coloniser and the colonised, but from a different angle. He, like Fanon, explored the extent to which colonialism created a way of seeing the world, an order of things that was to be learned as true and proper; but Said paid attention more to the colonisers than the colonised. *Orientalism* draws upon developments in Marxist theories of power, especially the political philosophy of the Italian intellectual Antonio Gramsci and France's Michel Foucault. . . . Briefly, Said examined how the knowledge that the Western imperial powers formed about their colonies helped continually to justify their subjugation. Western nations like France and Britain, he argued, spent an immense amount of time producing knowledge about the locations they dominated. Looking in particular at representations of Egypt and the Middle East in a variety of written materials, Said pointed out that rarely did Western travellers in these regions ever try to learn much about, or from, the native peoples they encountered. Instead, they recorded their observations based upon commonly-held *assumptions* about "the Orient" as a mythic place of exoticism, moral laxity, sexual degeneracy and so forth. These observations (which were not really observations at all) were presented as scientific truths that, in their turn, functioned to justify the very propriety of colonial domination. Thus colonialism continuously perpetuated itself. Colonial power was buttressed by the production of knowledge about colonised cultures which endlessly produced a degenerate image of the Orient for those in the West, or Occident.

This is a cursory summary of Said's work. . . . But at this stage we need to note that the work of Fanon and Said inspired a new generation of literary critics in the 1980s keen to apply their ideas to the reading of literary texts. What critics learned from the work of people like Fanon and Said was the simultaneously candid and complex fact that Empires colonise imaginations. Fanon shows how this works at a psychological level for the oppressed, while Said demonstrates the legitimation of Empire for the oppressor. Overturning colonialism, then, is not just about handing land back to its dispossessed peoples, returning power to those who were once ruled by Empire. It is also a process of overturning the dominant ways of seeing the world, and representing reality in ways which do *not* replicate colonialist values. If colonialism involves colonising the mind, then resistance to it requires, in Ngugi's phrase, "decolonising the mind." This is very much an issue of language. The Indian novelist Salman Rushdie puts it this way: "The language, like so much else in the colonies, needs to be decolonised, to be remade in other images, if those of us who use it from positions outside Anglo-Saxon culture are to be more than artistic Uncle Toms" (*The Times* 3 July 1982, p. 8).

So, freedom from colonialism comes not just from the signing of declarations of independence and the lowering and raising of flags. There must also be a change in the minds, a challenge to the dominant ways of seeing. This is a challenge to those from both the *colonised* and *colonising* nations. People from all parts of the Empire need to refuse the dominant languages of power that have divided them into master and slave, the ruler and the ruled, if progressive and lasting change is to be achieved. As Fanon wrote, "[a] man who has a language consequently possesses the world expressed and implied by that language" (*Black Skin, White Masks*, p. 18). The ability to read and write *otherwise*, to rethink our understanding of the order of things, contributes to the possibility of change. Indeed, in order to challenge the colonial order of things, some of us may need to re-examine our received assumptions of what we have been taught as "natural" or "true."

## The Turn to "Theory" in the 1980s

It would be grossly reductive to assert that Edward Said is the instigator of postcolonialism, not least because this would ignore the important anti-colonial critiques prior to 1978 of Fanon, Ngugi and others . . . . However, it is perhaps reasonable to suggest that, institutionally, the success of *Orientalism* did much to encourage new kinds of study. Sensitised by the work of Said and others to the operations of colonial discourses, a new generation of critics turned to more "theoretical" materials in their work. This was probably the beginning of postcolonialism as we understand it today and marked a major departure from the earlier, humanist approaches which characterised criticism of Commonwealth literature. Emerging in the 1980s were dynamic, excitingly new forms of textual analysis notable for their eclecticism and interdisciplinarity, combining the insights of feminism, philosophy, psychology, politics, anthropology and literary theory in provocative and energetic ways.

Three forms of textual analysis in particular became popular in the wake of *Orientalism*. One involved *re-reading canonical English literature* in order to examine if past texts perpetuated or questioned the latent assumptions of colonial discourses. This form of textual analysis proceeded along two avenues. In one direction, critics looked at writers who dealt manifestly with colonial themes and argued about whether their work was supportive or critical of colonial discourses. One example is Joseph Conrad's novel about colonialism in Africa, *Heart of Darkness* (1899). Critics debated whether Conrad's novel perpetuated colonialist views of the alleged inferiority of other peoples, or if it questioned the entire colonial project, dissenting from colonial discourses. In another direction, texts that seemingly had little to do with colonialism, such as Jane Austen's *Mansfield Park* (1814) or Charlotte Brontë's *Jane Eyre* (1847), were also re-read provocatively in terms of colonial discourses. . . .

Second, a group of critics who worked in the main with the poststructuralist thought of Jacques Derrida, Michel Foucault and Jacques Lacan began to enquire in particular into *the representation of colonised subjects* in a variety of colonial texts, not just literary ones. If, as Said claimed, the West produced knowledge about other peoples in order to prove the "truth" of their "inferiority," was it possible to read these texts *against the grain* and discover in them moments when the colonised subject *resisted* being represented with recourse to colonial values? This issue was pursued in different ways during the 1980s by two of the leading and most controversial postcolonial theorists, Homi K. Bhabha and Gayatri Chakravorty Spivak, as well as the *Subaltern Studies* scholars based in India. In his work on "mimicry," Bhabha explored the possibility of reading colonialist discourses as endlessly ambivalent, split and unstable, never able to install securely the colonial values they seemed to support. In her influential essays "Subaltern Studies: Deconstructing Historiography" (in *In Other Worlds: Essays in Cultural Politics,* Routledge, 1988) and "Can the Subaltern Speak?" (in Patrick Williams and Laura Chrisman (eds), *Colonial Discourse and Post-Colonial Theory,* Harvester Wheatsheaf, 1993), Spivak explored the problem of whether or not it was possible to recover the voices of those who had been made subjects of colonial representations, particularly women, and read them as potentially disruptive and subversive. Since the 1980s, Said, Bhabha and Spivak have opened a wide variety of theoretical issues central to postcolonialism. . . . They have also, for better or worse, emerged (in Robert Young's unfortunate phrase) as the "Holy Trinity" of critics working in the field (*Colonial Desire,* Routledge, 1995, p. 163) and their predominance can sometimes be at the expense of other equally important voices. . . .

## Postcolonialism at the Millennium

In the 1990s, postcolonialism has become increasingly busy and academically fashionable. In a literary context, a peculiar splitting of the field has been in danger of occurring between critical work which explores postcolonial theory, and textual criticism of postcolonial literatures. . . . However, in recent years the "Holy Trinity" of Said, Spivak and Bhabha has become the focus for much commentary and debate in postcolonialism, not least because several aspects of the work of Spivak and Bhabha can seem pretty impenetrable at first sight. Collectively, this has helped create "postcolonial theory" almost as a separate discipline in its own right, sometimes at the expense of criticism of postcolonial literature. (For a more detailed version of this argument, see Bart Moore-Gilbert, *Postcolonial Theory: Contexts, Practices, Politics,* Verso, 1997.)

The most useful surveys of postcolonial theory, not least because they go beyond the Said-Spivak-Bhabha triad, tend to be collections of essays rather than critical texts. *Colonial Discourse and Post-Colonial Theory,* edited by Patrick Williams and Laura Chrisman (Harvester, 1993) features extracts from the work of the "Holy Trinity" as well as many other important voices. By including some excellent introductory sections, the editors give a full and wide-ranging sense of the variety and excitement of postcolonial theory. There is a sense of this too in *The Post-Colonial Studies Reader,* edited by Ashcroft, Griffiths and Tiffin (Routledge, 1995), although the editors choose to give short extracts from longer pieces and little commentary, making this book seem rather threadbare. Another collection, *Colonial Discourse/Postcolonial Theory,* edited by Francis Barker, Peter Hulme and Margaret Iversen includes several essays which question many of the key assumptions of postcolonial theory, although the complexity of the criticism it includes makes it a text to be approached once you have made your beginnings in postcolonialism. We shall be referring to material in each of these useful collections throughout. . . .

As for prolonged critiques of Said, Bhabha and Spivak, the two most useful are Robert Young's *White Mythologies: Writing History and the West* (Routledge, 1990) and Bart Moore-Gilbert's *Postcolonial Theory,* mentioned above. Robert Young offers useful explanations of the work of the "Holy Trinity" and situates their work within a wider exploration of poststructuralist approaches to history. Bart Moore-Gilbert's book gives perhaps the fullest and richest work to date on postcolonial theory, and usefully situates it in relation both to "Commonwealth literature" and the work of other postcolonial writers (although Said, Spivak and Bhabha remain his primary subject-matter). Moore-Gilbert's prolonged attention to the nuances of postcolonial theory is highly impressive and extremely useful, although once again this means his is not really an introductory text.

There are specifically introductory guides to postcolonial theory, but they often struggle to deal adequately with postcolonial literatures; a surprising fact, perhaps, when one considers that their authors tend to work primarily in literary studies. Peter Childs and Patrick Williams's *An Introduction to Post-Colonial Theory* (Harvester Wheatsheaf, 1997) is certainly the most stimulating in that it deals with much more than Said, Spivak and Bhabha, and in clear and helpful terms, although once again the "Holy Trinity" remains paramount. Ania Loomba's *Colonialism/Postcolonialism* (Routledge, 1998) is detailed yet rather too often concerned with colonial rather than postcolonial representations. Leela Gandhi's *Postcolonial Theory: A Critical Introduction* (Edinburgh, 1998) is less successful, rendering the work of postcolonial theorists in an often synoptic and disorganised fashion; but at least she devotes a chapter to the problems and possibilities of reading postcolonial literatures with recourse to theoretical developments. But too few texts which deal with postcolonial theory pay this kind of attention to literature. Hence, postcolonialism can appear from one perspective as inward-looking and theoretically preoccupied with the privileged work of

Said, Spivak and Bhabha. In its less sophisticated versions, narratives of postcolonial theory can sensitise readers to the Derridean influences in Spivak's work or Bhabha's use of Lacanian psychoanalysis, but not much else.

Readings of postcolonial literatures in terms of new theoretical insights might not always be found in fashionable discussions of postcolonial theory, but they certainly *do* exist. It is fair to say that the many critics who do produce such readings have remained wary of producing the kind of wide-ranging and homogenising works of criticism that characterised critical texts on Commonwealth literature. Instead, more recent critical activity has attended more closely to the cultural and historical specifics of literature from particular locations in the light of important theoretical developments. Some randomly chosen examples would include Michael Chapman's *Southern African Literatures* (Longman, 1996) and Ato Quayson's *Strategic Transformations in Nigerian Writing* (James Currey, 1997). This kind of attention to the specifics of location is, as we have seen, vital to postcolonialism.

But there is also the risk that a more *comparative* approach to postcolonial literatures is lost, as well as a sense of how intellectual and artistic activity in one part of the world has been influential in others. However, several good comparative texts do exist. The best example is Edward Said's *Culture and Imperialism* (Vintage, 1993). . . . Two further books also attempt a wide-ranging and comparative approach in a strictly literary context. Elleke Boehmer's *Colonial and Postcolonial Literature* surveys a wealth of writing in a variety of locations both during and after colonialism. Boehmer skilfully identifies the salient literary themes and preconceptions that have crossed both time and space, without sacrificing an awareness of local and historical contests. However, although she creates a sophisticated and critical comparative account of the variety of postcolonial literatures, some of the theoretical questions concerning *how* we read them do not always inflect Boehmer's authoritative scholarship. Dennis Walder also attempts to bring the two together in his *Post-Colonial Literatures in English* (Blackwell, 1998), which looks in particular at "Indo-Anglian fiction," Caribbean and Black British Poetry, and recent South African literature. His attention to these "case studies" exemplifies the necessity and rewards of reading texts closely in context, although he cannot always offer the range of Boehmer's study.

## "Postcolonialism": Definitions and Dangers

Having looked at the historical and intellectual contexts for postcolonialism, we are now in a position to make some definitions.

First and foremost, we need to be very precise in how we understand the relationship between "colonialism" and "postcolonialism." As theories of colonial discourses argue, colonialism fundamentally affects modes of *representation*. Language carries with it a set of assumptions about the "proper order of things" that is taught as "truth" or "reality." It is by no means safe to assume that colonialism conveniently stops when a colony formally achieves its independence. The hoisting of a newly independent colony's flag might promise a crucial moment when governmental power shifts to those in the newly independent nation, yet it is crucial to realise that colonial values do not simply evaporate on the first day of independence. As Stuart Hall argues in his essay "When Was 'the Post-Colonial'?: Thinking at the Limit" (in *The Post-Colonial Question: Common Skies, Divided Horizons,* ed. Iain Chambers and Lidia Curti, Routledge, 1996, pp. 242–60), life after independence in many ways "is characterised by the persistence of many of the effects of colonisation" (p. 248). Colonialism's *representations, reading practices* and *values* are not so easily dislodged. Is it possible to speak about a "postcolonial" era if colonialism's various assumptions, opinions and knowledges remain unchallenged?

Postcolonialism, as we have seen, in part involves the *challenge* to colonial ways of knowing, "writing back" in opposition to such views. But colonial ways of knowing still circulate and have agency in the present; unfortunately, they have not magically disappeared as the Empire has declined. Thus, one of Carole Boyce Davies's reservations about "postcolonialism" is the impression it may give that colonial relationships no longer exist. In her book *Black Women, Writing and Identity* (Routledge, 1994) she argues that we must remember the "numerous peoples that are still existing in a colonial relationship" around the world, as well as those "people within certain nations who have been colonised with the former/colonies (Native Americans, African-Americans, South Africans, Palestinians, Aboriginal Australians)" (p. 83). This comment raises the issue of *internal colonialism* which persists in many once-colonised countries; for such peoples, colonial oppression is far from over. This is why we should beware using "postcolonialism" strictly as marking a historical moment or period . . . and reserve it for talking about aesthetic practices.

So, the term "postcolonialism" is *not* the same as "after colonialism," as if colonial values are no longer to be reckoned with. It does *not* define a radically new historical era, nor does it herald a brave new world where all the ills of the colonial past have been cured. Rather, "postcolonialism" recognises both historical *continuity* and *change.* On the one hand, it acknowledges that the material realities and modes of representation common to colonialism are still very much with us today, even if the political map of the world has changed through decolonisation. But on the other hand, it asserts the promise, the possibility, and the continuing necessity of change, while also recognising that important challenges and changes have already been achieved.

So, with this firmly in our minds, we can proceed to make some decisions about what is gathered under our umbrella-term "postcolonialism." Keeping in mind the disquiet with the range that the term often covers, we can identify at least three salient areas that fall within its remit. Very basically, and in a literary context, postcolonialism involves one or more of the following:

- Reading texts produced by writers from countries with a history of colonialism, primarily those texts concerned with the workings and legacy of colonialism in either the past or the present.

- Reading texts produced by those that have migrated from countries with a history of colonialism, or those descended from migrant families, which deal in the main with diaspora experience and its many consequences.

- In the light of theories of colonial discourses, re-reading texts produced during colonialism; both those that directly address the experiences of Empire, and those that seem not to.

A central term in each is "reading." The act of reading in postcolonial contexts is by no means a neutral activity. *How* we read is just as important as *what* we read. . . . The ideas we encounter within postcolonialism and the issues they raise demand that conventional reading methods and models of interpretation need to be rethought if our reading practices are to contribute to the contestation of colonial discourses to which postcolonialism aspires. Rethinking conventional modes of reading is fundamental to postcolonialism.

Of course, making distinctions like the ones above always involves a certain degree of generalisation. It would be impossible, as well as wrong, to unify these three areas into a single coherent "postcolonialism" with a common manifesto. Single-sentence definitions are impossible and unwise. In addition, we must be aware that each area *is itself* diverse and heterogeneous. For example, colonial discourses can function in particular ways for different peoples at different times. We should not presume consensus and totality where there is instead heterogeneity. . . .

One last word of warning, Postcolonialism may well *aim* to oppose colonial representation and values, but whether it *fulfils* these aims remains a hotly debated issue in the field. Postcolonialism may bring new possibilities, but, as we shall see, it is not free from problems of its own. So, in beginning postcolonialism, it is important that we maintain an element of suspicion too.

# Anne McClintock

## *The Angel of Progress: Pitfalls of the Term "Postcolonialism"*

*1992*

In 1855, the year of the first imperial Paris Exposition, Victor Hugo announced: "Progress is the footsteps of God himself." "Post-colonial Studies" has set itself against this imperial idea of linear time—the "grand idea of Progress and Perfectability," as Baudelaire called it. Yet the term "post-colonial," like the exhibition itself, is haunted by the very figure of linear "development" that it sets out to dismantle. Metaphorically, the term "post-colonialism" marks history as a series of stages along an epochal road from "the precolonial" to "the colonial" to "the post-colonial"—an unbidden, if disavowed, commitment to linear time and the idea of "development." If a theoretical tendency to envisage "Third World" literature as progressing from "protest literature" to "resistance literature" to "national literature" has been criticised as rehearsing the Enlightenment trope of sequential, "linear" progress, the term "post-colonialism" is questionable for the same reason. Metaphorically poised on the border between old and new, end and beginning, the term heralds the end of a world era, but within the same trope of linear progress that animated that era.

If "post-colonial" *theory* has sought to challenge the grand march of western historicism with its entourage of binaries (self–other, metropolis–colony, centre–periphery, etc.), the *term* "post colonialism" none the less re-orients the globe once more around a single, binary opposition: colonial/post-colonial. Moreover, theory is thereby shifted from the binary axis of *power* (coloniser/colonised—itself inadequately nuanced, as in the case of women) to the binary axis of *time*, an axis even less productive of political nuance since it does not distinguish between the beneficiaries of colonialism (the ex-colonisers) and the casualties of colonialism (the ex-colonised). The "post-colonial scene" occurs in an entranced suspension of history, as if the definitive historical events have preceded us, and are not now in the making. If the theory promises a decentring of history in hybridity, syncreticism, multi-dimensional time and so forth, the singularity of the term effects a re-centering of global history around the single rubric of European time. Colonialism returns at the moment of its disappearance.

The word "post," moreover, reduces the cultures of peoples beyond colonialism to *prepositional time.* The term confers on colonialism the prestige of history proper; colonialism is the determining marker of history. Other cultures share only a chronological, prepositional relation to a Eurocentred epoch that is over (post-), or not yet begun (pre-). In other words, the world's multitudinous cultures are marked not positively by what distinguishes them but by a subordinate, retrospective relation to linear, European time.

The term also signals a reluctance to surrender the privilege of seeing the world in terms of a singular and ahistorical abstraction. Rifling through the recent flurry of articles and books on "post-colonialism," I am struck by how seldom the term is used to denote *multiplicity.* The following proliferate: "*the* post-colonial condition," "*the* post-colonial scene," "*the* post-colonial intellectual," "*the* emerging disciplinary space of post-colonialism," "post-coloniality," "*the* post-colonial situation," "post-colonial space," "*the* practice of post-coloniality," "post-colonial discourse," and that most tedious, generic hold-all: "*the* post-colonial Other."

I am not convinced that one of the most important emerging areas of intellectual and political enquiry is best served by inscribing history as a single issue. Just as the singular category "Woman" has been discredited as a bogus universal for feminism, incapable of distinguishing between the varied histories and imbalances in power among women, so the singular category "post-colonial" may license too readily a panoptic tendency to view the globe within generic abstractions voided of political nuance. Must post-structural theory, with its insistence on infinite textuality, has disavowed the idea of "history," while none the less charting its own theory in very broad historical sweeps: the Enlightenment, modernity, postmodernity, postcolonialism and so forth. The arcing panorama of the horizon, however, becomes thereby so expansive that international imbalances in power remain effectively blurred. Historically voided categories such as "the other," "the signifier," "the signified," "the subject," "the phallus," "the postcolonial," while having academic clout and professional marketability, run the risk of telescoping crucial geopolitical distinctions into invisibility.

The authors of the recent book *The empire writes back,* for example, defend the term "post-colonial literature" on three grounds: it "focuses on that relationship which has provided the most important creative and psychological impetus in the writing"; it expresses the "rationale of the grouping in a common past," and it "hints at the vision of a more liberated and positive future" (Ashcroft, Griffiths and Tiffin 1989, p. 24). Yet the inscription of history around a single "continuity of preoccupations" and "a common past" runs the risk of a fetishistic disavowal of crucial international distinctions that are barely understood and inadequately theorised. Moreover, the authors decided, idiosyncratically to say the least, that the term "post-colonialism" should not be understood as everything that has happened since European colonialism but rather "all the culture affected by the imperial process from the moment of colonization to the present day" (p. 2). Which means turning back the clocks and unrolling the maps of "post-colonialism" to 1492, and earlier. Whereupon, at a stroke, Henry James and Charles Brockden Brown, to name only two on their list, are awakened from their *tête-à-tête* with time, and ushered into "the postcolonial scene" alongside more regular members like Ngugi Wa Thiong'o and Salman Rushdie.

Most problematically, the historical rupture suggested by the preposition "post" belies both the continuities and discontinuities of power that have shaped the legacies of the formal European and British colonial empires (not to mention the Islamic, Japanese, Chinese and other imperial powers). Political differences *between* cultures are thereby subordinated to their temporal distance *from* European colonialism. But "post-colonialism" (like postmodernism) is unevenly developed globally. Argentina, formally independent of imperial Spain for over a century and a half, is not "post-colonial" in the same way as Hong Kong (destined to be independent of Britain only in 1997). Nor is Brazil "post-colonial" in the same way as Zimbabwe. Can most of the world's countries be said, in any meaningful or theoretically rigorous sense, to share a single "common past," or a single common "condition," called "the post-colonial condition," or "post-coloniality"? The histories of African colonisation are certainly, in part, the histories of the collisions between European and Arab empires, and the myriad African lineage states and cultures. Can these countries now best be understood as shaped exclusively around the "common" experience of European colonisation? Indeed, many contemporary African, Latin American, Caribbean and Asian cultures, while profoundly affected by colonisation, are not necessarily primarily preoccupied with their erstwhile contact with European colonialism.

On the other hand, the term "post-colonialism" is, in many cases, prematurely celebratory. Ireland may, at a pinch, be "post-colonial," but for the inhabitants of British-occupied Northern Ireland, not to mention the Palestinian inhabitants of the Israeli Occupied Territories and the West Bank, there may be nothing "post" about colonialism at all. Is South Africa "post-colonial"? East Timor? Australia? By what fiat of historical amnesia can the United States of America, in particular, qualify as "post-colonial"—a term which can only be a monumental affront to the Native American peoples who opposed the confetti triumphalism of 1992. One can also ask whether the emergence of Fortress Europe in 1992 may not also signal the emergence of a new empire, as yet uncertain about the frontiers of its boundaries and global reach.

My misgivings, therefore, are not about the theoretical substance of "post-colonial theory," much of which I greatly admire. Rather, I wish to question the orientation of the emerging discipline and its concomitant theories and curricula changes, around a singular, monolithic term, used ahistorically, and haunted by the very image of linear "progress" that much of that same work challenges theoretically. Nor do I want to banish the term to some chilly, verbal Gulag; there seems no reason why it should not be used judiciously in appropriate circumstances, in the context of other terms, if in a less grandiose and global role.

One might distinguish theoretically between a variety of forms of global domination. Colonisation involves direct territorial appropriation of another geopolitical entity, combined with forthright exploitation of its resources and labour, and systematic interference in the capacity of the appropriated culture (itself not necessarily a homogenous entity) to organise its dispensations of power. Internal colonisation occurs where the dominant part of a country treats a group or region as it might a foreign colony. Imperial colonisation, by extension, involves large-scale, territorial domination of the kind that gave Britain and the European "lords of humankind" control over 85 per cent of the earth in the nineteenth century, and the USSR totalitarian rule over Hungary, Poland and Czechoslovakia in the twentieth century.

Colonisation, however, may involve only one country. Currently, China keeps its colonial grip on Tibet's throat, as does Indonesia on East Timor, Israel on the Occupied Territories and the West Bank, and Britain on Northern Ireland. Since 1966 South Africa, in defiance of a UN General Assembly Resolution and a 1971 World Court Order, kept its colonial boot on Namibia's soil. Only in 1990, having stripped Namibia of its last diamond resources, was South Africa content to hand back the economically empty shell to the Namibians. Israel remains in partial occupation of Lebanon and Syria, as does Turkey in Cyprus. None of these countries can, with justice, be called "post-colonial."

Different forms of colonisation have, moreover, given rise to different forms of decolonisation. Where *deep settler colonisation* prevailed, as in Algeria, Kenya, Zimbabwe and Vietnam, colonial powers clung on with particular brutality.[1] Decolonisation itself, moreover, has been unevenly won. In Zimbabwe, after a seven-year civil war of such ferocity that at the height of the war five hundred people were killed every month, and 40 per cent of the country's budget was spent on the military, the Lancaster House Agreement choreographed by Britain in 1979 ensured that one-third of Zimbabwe's arable land (12 million hectares) was to remain in white hands, a minute fraction of the population (Meldrum 1991, p. 13). In other words, while Zimbabwe gained formal political independence in 1980 (holding the chair of the 103-nation Non-Aligned Movement from 1986 to 1989) it has, economically, undergone only *partial decolonisation.*

*Breakaway settler colonies* can, moreover, be distinguished by their formal independence from the founding metropolitan country, along with continued control over the appropriated colony (thus displacing colonial control from the metropolis to the colony itself). The United States, South Africa, Australia and New Zealand remain, in my view, breakaway settler colonies that have not undergone decolonisation, nor, with the exception of South Africa, are they likely to in the near future.

Most importantly, orienting theory around the temporal axis colonial/postcolonial makes it easier not to see, and therefore harder to theorise, the continuities in international imbalances in imperial power. Since the 1940s, the United States' imperialism-without-colonies has taken a number of distinct forms (military, political, economic and cultural), some concealed, some half-concealed. The power of US finance capital and huge multinationals to direct the flows of capital, commodities, armaments and media information around the world can have an impact as massive as any colonial regime. It is precisely the greater subtlety, innovation and variety of these forms of imperialism that makes the historical rupture implied by the term "post-colonial" especially unwarranted.

"Post-colonial" Latin America has been invaded by the United States over a hundred times in the twentieth century alone. Each time, the USA has acted to install a dictatorship, prop up a puppet regime or wreck a democracy. In the 1940s, when the climate for gunboat diplomacy chilled, United States' relations with Latin America were warmed by an economic imperialist policy euphemistically dubbed "good Neighbourliness," primarily designed to make Latin America a safer backyard for the United States' virile agribusiness. The giant cold-storage ships of the United Fruit Company circled the world, taking bananas from poor agrarian countries dominated by monocultures and the marines to the tables of affluent US housewives (Enloe 1989, pp. 124–50). And while Latin America hand-picked bananas for the United States, the United States hand-picked dictators for Latin America. In Chile, Allende's elected socialist government was overthrown by a US-sponsored military coup. In Africa, more covert operations such as the CIA assassination of Patrice Lumumba in Zaire had consequences as far-reaching.

In the Cold War climate of the 1980s, the USA, still hampered by the Vietnam syndrome, fostered the more covert military policy of "low intensity" conflicts (in El Salvador and the Philippines), spawning death squads and proxy armies (Unita in Angola, and the Contras in Nicaragua) and training and aiding totalitarian military regimes in anti-democratic, "counter-insurgency" tactics (El Salvador, Honduras, South Africa, Israel and so forth). In Nicaragua in February 1990 the "vote of fear" of continuing, covert war with the USA brought down the Sandinistas.

The United States' recent fits of thuggery in Libya, Grenada and Panama, and most calamitously in Iraq, have every characteristic of renewed military imperialism, and a renewed determination to revamp military hegemony in a world in which it is rapidly losing economic hegemony. The attacks on Libya, Granada and Panama (where victory was assured) were practice runs for the new imperialism, testing both the USSR's will to protest and the US public's willingness to throw off the Vietnam syndrome, permitting thereby a more blatant era of intervening in Third World affairs. At the same time, having helped stoke the first Gulf War, the USA had no intention of letting a new boy on the block assert colonial dominance in the region.

For three years before the Gulf War, the US arms trade had been suffering a slump.

After what one military industrialist gloatingly called the Gulf War's "giant commercial-in-the-sky," US arms sales have soared. None the less, if the USA had the political muscle to resuscitate a nearly defunct Security Council and strong-arm a consensus through the UN, and the military capacity to make short shrift of 150,000 Iraqi soldiers and an estimated 200,000 civilians in one month, it did not have the economic means to pay for the war. Saddled with its own vast debts, the USA has been massively paid off in reimbursements (an estimated $50 billion) by Saudi Arabia, Kuwait, Japan and Germany, so that it now appears in fact to have profited from the war to the tune of $4–5 billion. At the same time, most of the estimated $20 billion necessary to restore Kuwait will go to western, largely US, companies. The war has thus made ever more likely a global security system based on military muscle, not political co-operation, policed by the United States' mercenary army (and perhaps NATO), moving rapidly and lightly around the world, paid for by Germany and Japan, and designed to prevent regional, Third World consensuses from emerging. Far from heralding the end of imperial intervention, the second Gulf War simply marks a new kind of interventionism. Not only is the term "postcolonial" inadequate to theorise these dynamics, it actively obscures the continuities and discontinuities of US power around the globe.

While some countries may be "post-colonial" with respect to their erstwhile European masters, they may not be "post-colonial" with respect to their new colonising neighbours. Both Mozambique and East Timor, for example, became "post-colonial" at much the same time, when the Portuguese Empire decamped in the mid-1970s, and both remain cautionary tales against the utopian promise and global sweep of the preposition "post." In East Timor, the beds of the Portuguese were scarcely cold before the Indonesians invaded, in an especially violent colonial occupation that has lasted nearly two decades. The colonial travail of the East Timoreans has gone largely unprotected by the UN—the familiar plight of countries whose pockets aren't deep, and whose voices don't carry.

In Mozambique, on the other hand, after three centuries of colonial drubbing, the Portuguese were ousted in 1975 by Frelimo, Mozambique's socialist independence movement. But across the border, white Rhodesians, resentful of Mozambique's independence and socialist promise, spawned the Mozambique National Resistance (MNR), a bandit army bent only on sowing ruin. After Zimbabwe itself became politically independent of Britain in 1980, the MNR has continued to be sponsored by South Africa. A decade of the MNR's killing-raids and South Africa's predations has subjected the country to a fatal blood-letting and displaced nearly two million people, in a war so catastrophic that Frelimo has been forced to renounce Marxism and consider shaking hands with the bandits. Now Mozambique is in every sense a country on its knees. What might have been a "post-colonial" showpiece has instead become the killing fields of Southern Africa.

Yet neither the term "post-colonial" nor "neocolonial" is truly adequate to account for the MNR. Neocolonialism is not simply a repeat performance of colonialism, nor is it a slightly more complicated, Hegelian merging of "tradition" and "colonialism" into some new, historic hybrid. In recent years, the MNR has become inextricably shaped around local inter-ethnic rivalries, distinct religious beliefs and notions of time and causality (especially ancestral intervention) which cannot be reduced to a western schema of linear time. More complex terms and analyses, of alternative times, histories and causalities, are required to deal with complexities that cannot be served under the single rubric "post-colonialism."

Singular universals such as "the postcolonial intellectual" obscure international disparities in cultural power, electronic technology and media information. The role of "Africa" in "post-colonial theory" is different from the role of "post-colonial theory" in Africa. In 1975 the entire continent had only 180 daily newspapers, compared with 1,900 for the USA, out of a world total of 7,970. By 1984, the number of African dailies dropped to 150, then staggered back to 180 in 1987 (the same figure as in 1955). In 1980, the annual production of films in the continent was seventy. In contrast, the production of long films in Asia was 2,300 in 1965, and 2,100 in 1987 (Kinfe 1990, pp. 47–9). The film industry in India remains the largest in the world, while Africa's share of television receivers, radio transmitters and electronic hardware is minuscule.

The term "post-colonialism" is prematurely celebratory and obfuscatory in more ways than one. The term becomes especially unstable with respect to women. In a world where women do two-thirds of the world's work, earn 10 percent of the world's income and own less than 1 per cent of the world's property, the promise of "post-colonialism" has been a history of hopes postponed. It has generally gone unremarked that the national bourgeoisies and kleptocracies that stepped into the shoes of "post-colonial" "progress" and industrial "modernisation" have been overwhelmingly and violently male. No "post-colonial" state anywhere has granted women and men equal access to the rights and resources of the nation state. Not only have the needs of "post-colonial nations" been largely identified with male conflicts, male aspirations and male interests, but the very representation of "national" power rests on prior constructions of gender power. Thus even for Fanon, who at other moments knew better, both "coloniser" and "colonised" are unthinkingly male: "The look that the native turns on the settler is a look of lust . . . to sit at the settlers' table, to sleep in the settler's bed, with his wife, if possible. The colonized man is an envious man" (Fanon 1968, p. 30). Despite most anti-colonial nationalisms' investment in the rhetoric of popular unity, most have served more properly to institutionalise gender power. Marital laws, in particular have served to ensure that for women citizenship in the nation state is mediated by the marriage relation, so that a woman's political relation to the nation is submerged in, and subordinated to, her social relation to a man through marriage.

The global militarisation of masculinity, and the feminisation of poverty have thus ensured that women and men do not live "post-coloniality" in the same way, or share the same singular "post-colonial condition." In most countries, IMF and World Bank policy favoured cash-cropping and capital surplus in the systematic interests of men, and formed a predictable pattern where men were given the training, the international aid, the machinery, the loans and cash. In Africa, women farmers produce 65–80 per cent of all agricultural produce, yet do not own the land they work, and are consistently bypassed by aid programmes and "development" projects.

The blame for women's continuing plight cannot be laid only at the door of colonialism, or footnoted and forgotten as a passing "neocolonial" dilemma. The continuing weight of male economic self-interest and the varied undertows of patriarchal

Christianity, Confucianism and Islamic fundamentalism continue to legitimise women's barred access to the corridors of political and economic power, their persistent educational disadvantage, the bad infinity of the domestic double day, unequal childcare, gendered malnutrition, sexual violence, genital mutilation and domestic battery. The histories of these male policies, while deeply implicated in colonialism, are not reducible to colonialism, and cannot be understood without distinct theories of gender power.

Finally, bogus universals such as "the post-colonial woman," or "the post-colonial other" obscure relations not only between men and women but among women. Relations between a French tourist and the Haitian woman who washes her bed linen are not the same as the relations between their husbands. Films like *Out of Africa,* clothing chains like Banana Republic and perfumes like "Safari" all peddle neocolonial nostalgia for an era when European women in brisk white shirts and safari green supposedly found freedom in empire: running coffee plantations, killing lions and zipping about the colonial skies in aeroplanes—an entirely misbegotten commercialisation of white women's "liberation" that has not made it any easier for women of colour to form alliances with white women anywhere, let alone parry criticisms by male nationalists already hostile to feminism.

How, then, does one account for the curious ubiquity of the preposition "post" in contemporary intellectual life, not only in the universities but in newspaper columns and on the lips of media moguls? In the case of "post-colonialism," at least, part of the reason is its academic marketability. While admittedly another PC word, "post-colonialism" is arguably more palatable and less foreign-sounding to skeptical deans than "Third World Studies." It also has a less accusatory ring than "Studies In Neocolonialism," say, or "Fighting Two Colonialisms." It is more global, and less fuddy-duddy, than "Commonwealth Studies." The term borrows, moreover, on the dazzling marketing success of the term "postmodernism." As the organising rubric of an emerging field of disciplinary studies and an archive of knowledge, the term "post-colonialism" makes possible the marketing of a whole new generation of panels, articles, books and courses.

The enthusiasm for "post-" words, however, ramifies beyond the corridors of the university. The recurrent, almost ritualistic incantation of the pre-position "post-" is a symptom, I believe, of a global crisis in ideologies of the future, particularly the ideology of "progress."

The first seismic shift in the idea of "progress" came with the abrupt shift in US Third World policy in the 1980s. Emboldened in the 1950s by its economic "great leap forward" (space, again, is time), the USA was empowered to insist globally that other countries could "progress" only if they followed the US road to mass-consumption prosperity. W. W. Rostow's "Non-communist manifesto" envisaged the so-called "developing" nations as passing through similar stages of development, out of tradition-bound poverty, through an industrialised modernisation overseen by the USA, the World Bank and the IMF, to mass-consumer prosperity. None the less, except for the Japanese "miracle" and the Four Tigers (Taiwan, Singapore, Hong Kong and South Korea), the vast majority of the world's populations have, since the 1940s, come to lag even further behind the consumer standards set by the west (Arrighi 1991, p. 40).

Then, between 1979 (the second oil shock) and 1982 (the Mexican default), the world economy began to creak. Increasingly, it became clear that the USA was no longer destined to be the only economic power of the future. Hobbled by its phenomenal debts, and increasingly diminished by the twin shadows of Japan and Germany, the USA summarily abandoned the doctrine of global "progress" and "development." During the Reagan era, the USA instituted instead a bullying debt-servicing policy towards poorer countries, bolstered by aggressive competition with them on the market, and defended by sporadic fits of military gangsterism, as in Grenada and Panama. The cataclysmic war in the Gulf served only to underscore the point.

For many poorer countries, the shift in US policy meant abandoning overnight the *fata Morgana* of capitalist "progress," and settling for chronically stricken positions in the global hierarchy. Henceforth, they could aspire only to tighten their belts, service their debts and maintain some credit. In 1974, Africa's debt-service ratio was a manageable 4.6 per cent. Thirteen years later it had rocketed to 25 per cent. But the collapse of the US model of "progress" has also meant the collapse, for many regimes, of the legitimacy of their national policies, in the panicky context of worldwide economic crisis, ecological calamity and spiraling popular desperation. Indeed, perhaps one reason, at least, for the burgeoning populist appeal of Islamic fundamentalism is the failure of other models of capitalist or communist "progress." As a senior Libyan aide, Major Abdel-Salaam Jalloud, has said of the destiny of the FIS in Algeria: "It's impossible to turn back. The FIS has an appointment with history; it will not miss it."

A monotonously simple pattern has emerged. Despite the hauling down of colonial flags in the 1950s, revamped economic imperialism has ensured that America and the former European colonial powers have become richer, while, with a tiny scattering of exceptions, their ex-colonies have become poorer (Payer 1974, 1982).[2] In Africa before decolonisation, World Bank projects were consistently supportive of the colonial economies. Since formal decolonisation, contrary to the World Bank's vaunted technical "neutrality" and myth of expertise, projects have aggressively favoured the refinement and streamlining of surplus extraction, cash crop exports, and large-scale projects going to the highest bidders, fostering thereby cartels and foreign operators, and ensuring that profits tumble into the coffers of the multinationals. During 1986, Africa lost $19 billion through collapsed export prices alone. In 1988 and 1989, debt service payments from the Third World to the USA were $100 billion. At the same time, as Fanon predicted, Third World kleptocracies, military oligarchies and warlords have scrambled over each other to plunder the system. To protect these interests, the tiny, male elites of "developing" countries have spent almost $2.4 trillion on the military between 1960 and 1987, almost twice the size of the entire Third World debt (Broad, Cavanagh and Bello 1992, p. 100).[3] Now, after the 1980s "desperate decade" of debt, drought and destabilisation, the majority of Third World countries are poorer than they were a decade ago. The World Bank has concluded that "fifteen African countries were worse off in a number of economic categories after structural adjustment programs" (Broad, Cavanagh, and Bello, p. 96). In Africa 28 millions face famine, and in countries like Mozambique, Ethiopia, Zaire and the Sudan the economies have simply collapsed.

The United States' "development" myth has had a catastrophic impact on global ecologies. By 1989, the World Bank had $225 billion in commitments to poorer countries, on condition that they, in turn, endure the purgatory of "structural adjustment," export their way to "progress," cut government spending on education and social services (with the axe falling most cruelly on women), devalue their currencies, remove trade barriers and raze their forests to pay their debts (George 1988, 1990). Under the financial spell of the USA (and now Japan), and in the name of the fairy-tale of unlimited technological and capital "growth," the World Bank engineered one ecological disaster after another: the Indonesian Transmigrasi programme, the Amazonian Grande Carajas iron-ore and strip-mining project, and Tucurui Dam deforestation project, and so on. The Polonoroeste scheme in Brazil carved a paved highway through Amazonia, luring timber, mining and cattle ranching interests into the region with such calamitous impact that in May 1987 even the President of the World Bank, Mr. Barber Conable, confessed he found the devastation "sobering" (Hancock 1989, p. 131).

The Four "miracle" Tigers have paid for progress with landscapes pitted with poisoned water, toxic soil, denuded mountains and dead coral seas. In "miracle" Taiwan, an estimated 20 per cent of the country's farmland is polluted by industrial waste, and 30 per cent of the rice crops contain unsafe levels of heavy metals, mercury and cadmium (Broad, Cavanagh, and Bello 1992, p. 91) A World Bank report in 1989 concluded gloomily that "adjustment programs" carry the by-product that "people below the poverty line will probably suffer irreparable damage in health, nutrition and education" (Broad, Cavanagh, and Bello 1992, p. 95). Now Japan, insatiably hungry for timber and raw resources, is the major foreign aid donor, to the tune of $10 billion. In short, the World Bank and IMF "road to progress" has proved a short road to what Susan George has called "a fate worse than debt."

To compound matters, the collapse of the US myth of "progress" was swiftly followed by the collapse of the Soviet Union, which dragged down with it an entire master narrative of communist "progress." The zigzag of Hegelian–Marxist "progress," managed by a bureaucratic, command economy, had been destined to arrive inevitably at its own utopian destination. The toppling of the Soviet Empire has meant, for many, the loss of a certain privileged relation to history as the epic unfolding of linear, if spasmodic progress, and with it the promise that the bureaucratic, communist economy could one day outstrip the USA in providing consumer abundance for all. As a result, there has also been some loss of political certitude in the inevitable role of the male (and, as it turns out, white) industrial working class as the privileged agent of history. If the bureaucracy of the Soviet Union fell, it was not under the weight of popular, industrial mobilisation, but rather under the double weight of its economic corruption and manic military spending. The irony is not lost that the ascendant economies of Japan and Germany were historically denied the unsupportable burden of the arms race. Thus, despite the fact that men are slaughtering each other around the globe with increased dedication, there has been a certain loss of faith in masculined militarism as the inevitable guarantee of historical "progress." For the first time in history, moreover, the idea of industrial "progress" impelled by technocratic "development" is meeting the limits of the world's natural resources.

Ironically, the last zone on earth to embrace the Enlightenment ideology of capitalist "development" may be the one now controlled by Mr. Yeltsin and his allies. The world has watched awestruck as Yeltsin and his fellow travellers swerved dizzyingly off the iron road of the centralised, communist, command economy and lurched bumpily on to the capitalist road of decentralisation, powered no longer by the dialectic as the motor and guarantee of "progress" but by tearaway competition and mad marketeering. Never mind that this swerve is likely to unleash a disaster on a scale comparable to the famines that followed the original Bolshevik revolution, nor that the rough beast that slouches out of the chaos may, indeed, not be western capitalism at all but a particularly grisly form of fascism.

For both communism and capitalism, "progress" was both a journey forward and the beginning of a return; for, as in all narratives of "progress," to travel the "road of progress" was to cover, once again, a road already travelled. The metaphor of the "road" or "railway" guaranteed that "progress" was a *fait accompli*. The journey was possible because the road had already been made (by God, the Dialectic, the *Weltgeist*, the Cunning of History, the Law of the Market, Scientific Materialism). As Hegel decreed, "progress" in the realm of history was possible because it has already been accomplished in the realm of "truth." But now, if the owl of Minerva has taken flight, there is widespread uncertainty whether it will return.

The collapse of both capitalist and communist teleologies of "progress" has resulted in a doubled and overdetermined crisis in images of future time.[4] The uncertain global situation has spawned a widespread sense of historic abandonment, of which the apocalyptic, time-stopped prevalence of "post-" words is only one symptom. The storm of "progress" had blown for both communism and capitalism alike. Now the wind is stilled, and the angel with hunched wings broods over the wreckage at its feet. In this calm at "the end of history," the millennium has come too soon, and the air seems thick with omen.

Francis Fukuyama has declared history dead. Capitalism, he claims, has won the grand Hegelian agon with communism, and is now "post-historic." Third World countries lag behind in the zone of the "historic," where matters are decided by force (Fukuyama 1990, p. 3). Far from the "end of history" and the triumph of US consumer capitalism, however, the new order of the day is most likely to be multi-polar competition between the four currently decisive regions of the world: Japan, the United States, Fortress Europe and the Middle East, with new power centres emerging in India, Brazil, Nigeria and the Pacific rim. The arms trade will continue, as the military industrial wizards of Armageddon turn their attention from Cold War scenarios to multiple dispersed wars of attrition, fought by the US mercenary army and other proxies, and paid for by Japan and Germany. Within the USA, with the vanishing of international communism as a rationale for militarism, new enemies will be found: the drug war, international "terrorism," lesbians and gays, feminists, the PC hordes and "tenured radicals," and any number of international "ethnic" targets.

For this reason, there is some urgency in the need for innovative theories of history and popular memory. Asking what single term might adequately replace "postcolonialism," for example, begs the question of rethinking the global situation as a multiplicity of powers and histories, which cannot be marshaled obediently under the flag of a single theoretical term, be that feminism, Marxism or post-colonialism. Nor does intervening in history mean lifting, again, the mantle of "progress" or the quill-pen of empiricism. "For the native," as Fanon said, "objectivity is always directed against him." Rather, a *proliferation* of historically nuanced theories and strategies is called for, which may enable us to engage more effectively in the politics of affiliation, and the currently catastrophic dispensations of power. Without a renewed will to intervene in the unacceptable, we face being becalmed in an historically empty space in which our sole direction is found by gazing back, spellbound, at the epoch behind us, in a perpetual present marked only as "post."

## Notes

This article expands on comments I made during the Symposium at Essex in 1991. The article first appeared in *Social text*, 31/32 (1992), pp. 84–98.

1   During the Algerian war of resistance, over a million Algerians died out of about nine million.
2   The international monetary system set up at the Bretton Woods Conference in 1944 excluded Africa (still colonised) and most of what is now called the Third World, and was designed to achieve two explicit objectives: the reconstruction of Europe after the Second World War and the expansion and maintenance (especially after decolonisation) of international trade in the interests of the colonial powers and America. The President of the World Bank and the deputy managing director are always American, while by tradition the managing director is European.
3   A few African socialist states, like Angola and Mozambique, tried to dodge the IMF and World Bank's blandishments, until national economic mismanagement and South Africa's regional maulings forced them to bend the knee.
4   Ironically, following the swift jettisoning of the doctrine of "progress" by the captains of capital in the 1980s, the "hybridity" and "syncreticism" celebrated by much postcolonial theory has become increasingly celebrated by the mass-consumption media-market.

# Part 2

# Reading, Writing, Discussing

# Reading

## *The Critical Essays*

Edgar Allan Poe's influential review of Nathaniel Hawthorne's *Twice-Told Tales* not only directed readers to important themes in Hawthorne's stories but also helped to define and shape the short story as a genre. Literary critics since Poe have greatly influenced the way short stories are defined, written, and understood. The following essays all encourage readers to explore particular stories more deeply, to develop their own readings, and to ask larger questions about the short story and society.

The essays represent a wide variety of literary approaches: essays like Pancho Savery's "Baldwin, Bebop, and 'Sonny's Blues'" assert the necessity of understanding a story's historical context to interpret its meaning. Other essays, like "A Rose for 'A Rose for Emily'" and "Edith Wharton's 'Roman Fever': A Rune of History," include feminist analysis, an examination of themes of power, gender, and the subordination of women. Biographical analyses like Sharon O'Brien's work on Willa Cather consider the meaning of stories within the context of an author's life, and most of the selections, notably the excerpt from *Friendly Fire,* use close reading practices to examine the details of language in specific passages of a story. Most critical essays, however, do not confine their analysis to one way of looking at a story. Savery's article, for example, includes biographical information and close reading as well as historical contextualization.

Each author argues persuasively for a particular interpretation, but the essays as a group demonstrate the remarkably varied ways of reading and understanding short fiction.

# Elizabeth Abel

## *Black Writing, White Reading: Race and the Politics of Feminist Interpretation* — 1993

**1**

> *I realize that the set of feelings that I used to have about French men I now have about African-American women. Those are the people I feel inadequate in relation to and try to please in my writing. It strikes me that this is not just idiosyncratic.*
>
> —JANE GALLOP,
> "CRITICIZING FEMINIST CRITICISM"

Twyla opens the narrative of Toni Morrison's provocative story "Recitatif" (1982) by recalling her placement as an eight-year-old child in St. Bonaventure, a shelter for neglected children, and her reaction to Roberta Fisk, the roommate she is assigned: "The minute I walked in . . . I got sick to my stomach. It was one thing to be taken out of your own bed early in the morning—it was something else to be stuck in a strange place with a girl from a whole other race. And Mary, that's my mother, she was right. Every now and then she would stop dancing long enough to tell me something important and one of the things she said was that they never washed their hair and they smelled funny. Roberta sure did. Smell funny, I mean." The racial ambiguity so deftly installed at the narrative's origin through codes that function symmetrically for black women and for white women ("they never washed their hair and they smelled funny") intensifies as the story tracks the encounters of its two female protagonists over approximately thirty years. Unmediated by the sexual triangulations (the predations of white men on black women, the susceptibility of black men to white women) that have dominated black women's narrative representations of women's fraught connections across racial lines, the relationship of Twyla and Roberta discloses the operations of race in the feminine. This is a story about a black woman and a white woman; but which is which?

I was introduced to "Recitatif" by a black feminist critic, Lula Fragd. Lula was certain that Twyla was black; I was equally convinced that she was white; most of the readers we summoned to resolve the dispute divided similarly along racial lines. By replacing the conventional signifiers of racial difference (such as skin color) with radically relativistic ones (such as who smells funny to whom) and by substituting for the racialized body a series of disaggregated cultural parts—pink-scalloped socks, tight green slacks, large hoop earrings, expertise at playing jacks, a taste for Jimi Hendrix or for bottled water and asparagus—the story renders race a contested terrain variously mapped from diverse positions in the social landscape. By forcing us to construct racial categories from highly ambiguous social cues, "Recitatif" elicits and exposes the unarticulated racial codes that operate at the boundaries of consciousness. To underscore the cultural specificity of these codes, Morrison writes into the text a figure of racial undecidability: Maggie, the mute kitchen worker at St. Bonaventure, who occasions the text's only mention of skin color, an explicitly ambiguous sandy color, and who walks through the text with her little kid's hat and her bowed legs "like parentheses," her silent self a blank parenthesis, a floating signifier ("R," p. 245). For both girls a hated reminder of their unresponsive mothers, Maggie is not "raced" to Twyla (that is, she is by default white); to Roberta, she is black. The two girls' readings of Maggie become in turn clues for our readings of them, readings that emanate similarly from our own cultural locations.

My own reading derived in part from Roberta's perception of Maggie as black; Roberta's more finely discriminating gaze ("she wasn't pitch-black, I knew," is all Twyla can summon to defend her assumption that Maggie is white) seemed to me to testify to the firsthand knowledge of discrimination ("R," p. 259). Similarly, Roberta is sceptical about racial harmony. When she and Twyla retrospectively discuss their tense encounter at a Howard Johnson's where Twyla was a waitress in the early 1960s, they read the historical context differently: "'Oh, Twyla, you know how it was in those days: black—white. You know how everything was.' But I didn't know. I thought it was just the opposite. Busloads of blacks and whites came into Howard Johnson's together. They roamed together then: students, musicians, lovers, protesters. You got to see everything at Howard Johnson's and blacks were very friendly with whites in those days" ("R," p. 255). In the civil rights movement that Twyla sees as a common struggle against racial barriers, Roberta sees the distrust of white intervention and the impulse toward a separatist Black Power movement: she has the insider's perspective on power and race relations.

It was a more pervasive asymmetry in authority, however, that secured my construction of race in the text, a construction I recount with considerable embarrassment for its possible usefulness in fleshing out the impulse within contemporary white feminism signalled by the "not just idiosyncratic" confession that stands as this paper's epigraph. As Gallop both wittily acknowledges the force of African-American women's political critique of white academic feminism's seduction by "French men" and, by simply transferring the transference, reenacts the process of idealization that unwittingly obscures more complex social relations, I singled out the power relations of the girls from the broader network of cultural signs. Roberta seemed to me consistently the more sophisticated reader of the social scene, the subject presumed by Twyla to know, the teller of the better (although not necessarily more truthful) stories, the adventurer whose casual mention of an appointment with Jimi Hendrix exposes the depths of Twyla's social ignorance ("'Hendrix? Fantastic,' I said. 'Really fantastic. What's she doing now?'" ["R," p. 250]). From the girls' first meeting at St. Bonaventure, Twyla feels vulnerable to Roberta's judgment and perceives Roberta (despite her anxiety about their differences) as possessing something she lacks and craves: a more acceptably negligent mother (a sick one rather than a dancing one) and, partially as a consequence, a more compelling physical presence that fortifies her cultural authority. Twyla is chronically hungry; Roberta seems to her replete, a daughter who has been adequately fed and thus can disdain the institutional Spam and Jell-O that Twyla devours as a contrast to the popcorn and Yoo-Hoo that had been her customary fare. The difference in maternal stature, linked in the text with nurture, structures Twyla's account of visiting day at St. Bonaventure. Twyla's mother, smiling and waving "like she was the little girl," arrives wearing tight green buttocks-hugging slacks and a ratty fur jacket for the chapel service, and bringing no food for the lunch that Twyla consequently improvises out of fur-covered jelly beans from her Easter basket ("R," p. 246). "Bigger than any man," Roberta's mother arrives bearing a huge cross on her chest, a Bible in the crook of her arm, and a basket of chicken, ham, oranges, and chocolate-covered graham crackers ("R," p. 247). In the subsequent Howard Johnson scene that Twyla's retrospective analysis links with the frustrations of visiting day ("The wrong food is always with the wrong people. Maybe that's why I got into waitress work later—to match up the right people with the right food" ["R," p. 248]) the difference in stature is replayed between the two daughters. Roberta, sitting in a booth with "two guys smothered in head and facial hair," her own hair "so big and wild I could hardly see her face," wearing a "powder-blue halter and shorts outfit and earrings the size of bracelets," rebuffs Twyla, clad in her waitress outfit, her knees rather than her midriff showing, her hair in a net, her legs in thick stockings and sturdy white shoes ("R," p. 249). Although the two bodies are never directly represented, the power of metonymy generates a contrast between the amplitude of the sexualized body and the skimpiness and pallor of the socially harnessed body. Twyla's sense of social and physical inadequacy vis-à-vis Roberta, like her representation of her mother's inferiority to Roberta's, signalled Twyla's whiteness to me by articulating a white woman's fantasy (my own) about black women's potency. This fantasy's tenaciousness is indicated by its persistence in the face of contrary evidence. Roberta's mother, the story strongly implies, is mentally rather than physically ill, her capacity to nurture largely fictional; Roberta, who is never actually represented eating, is more lastingly damaged than Twyla by maternal neglect, more vulnerable as an adult to its memory, a weakness on which Twyla capitalizes during their political conflicts as adults; the tenuousness of the adult Roberta's own maternal status (she acquires stepchildren, rather than biological children, through her marriage to an older man) may also testify figuratively to a lack created by insufficient mothering.

Pivoting not on skin color, but on size, sexuality, and the imagined capacity to nurture and be nurtured, on the construction of embodiedness itself as a symptom and source of cultural authority, my reading installs the (racialized) body at the center of a text that deliberately withholds conventional racial iconography. Even in her reading of this first half of the story, Lula's interpretation differed from mine by emphasizing cultural practices more historically nuanced than my categorical distinctions in body types, degrees of social cool, or modes of mothering. Instead of reading Twyla's body psychologically as white, Lula read Twyla's name as culturally black; and she placed greater emphasis on Roberta's language in the Howard Johnson scene—her primary locution being a decidedly white hippie "Oh, wow"—than on the image of her body gleaned by reading envy in the narrative gaze and by assigning racial meaning to such cultural accessories as the Afro, hoop earrings, and a passion for Jimi Hendrix that actually circulated independently of race throughout the counterculture of the 1960s; as Lula knew and I did not, Jimi Hendrix appealed more to white than to black audiences. Roberta's coldness in this scene—she barely acknowledges her childhood friend—becomes, in Lula's reading, a case of straightforward white racism, and Twyla's surprise at the rebuff reflects her naivete about the power of personal loyalties and social movements to undo racial hierarchies.

More importantly, however, this scene was not critical for Lula's reading. Instead of the historical locus that was salient for me—not coincidentally, I believe, since the particular aura of (some) black women for (some) white women during the civil rights movement is being recapitulated in contemporary feminism (as I will discuss later)—what was central to her were scenes from the less culturally exceptional 1970s, which disclosed the enduring systems of racism rather than the occasional moments of heightened black cultural prestige. In general, Lula focussed less on cultural than on economic status, and she was less concerned with daughters and their feelings toward their mothers than with these daughters' politics after they are mothers.

When Twyla and Roberta meet in a food emporium twelve years after the Howard Johnson scene, Twyla has married a fireman and has one child and limited income; Roberta has married an IBM executive and lives in luxury in the wealthy part of town with her husband, her four stepchildren, and her Chinese chauffeur. Twyla concludes in a voice of seemingly racial resentment: "Everything is so easy for them. They think they own the world" ("R," p. 252). A short time later the women find themselves on opposite sides of a school integration struggle in which both their children are faced with bussing: Twyla's to the school that Roberta's stepchildren now attend, and Roberta's to a school in a less affluent neighborhood. After Twyla challenges Roberta's opposition to the bussing, Roberta tries to defuse the conflict: "'Well, it is a free country.' 'Not yet, but it will be,'" Twyla responds ("R," p. 256). Twyla's support of bussing, and of social change generally, and Roberta's self-interested resistance to them position the women along the bitter racial lines that split the fraying fabric of feminism in the late 1970s and early 1980s.

Privileging psychology over politics, my reading disintegrates in the story's second half. Lula's reading succeeds more consistently, yet by constructing the black woman (in her account, Twyla) as the politically correct but politically naive and morally conventional foil to the more socially adventurous, if politically conservative, white woman (Roberta), it problematically racializes the moral (op)positions Morrison opens to revaluation in her extended (and in many ways parallel) narrative of female friendship, *Sula*. Neither reading can account adequately for the text's contradictory linguistic evidence, for if Twyla's name is more characteristically black than white, it is perhaps best known as the name of a white dancer, Twyla Tharp, whereas Roberta shares her last name, Fisk, with a celebrated black (now integrated) university. The text's heterogeneous inscriptions of race resist a totalizing reading.

Propelled by this irresolution to suspend my commitment to the intentional fallacy, I wrote to Toni Morrison. Her response raised as many questions as it resolved. Morrison explained that her project in this story was to substitute class for racial codes in order to drive a wedge between these typically elided categories. Both eliciting and foiling our assumption that Roberta's middle-class marriage and politics, and Twyla's working-class perspective, are reliable racial clues, Morrison incorporated details about their husbands' occupations that encourage an alternative conclusion. If we are familiar (as I was not) with IBM's efforts to recruit black executives and with the racial exclusiveness of the firemen's union in upstate New York, where the story is set, we read Roberta as middle-class black and Twyla as working-class white. Roberta's resistance to bussing, then, is based on class rather than racial loyalties: she doesn't want her (middle-class black) stepchildren bussed to a school in a (white) working-class neighborhood; Twyla, conversely, wants her (white) working-class child bussed to a middle-class school (regardless of that school's racial composition). What we hear, from this perspective, in Twyla's envy of Roberta, "Everything is so easy for them," and in her challenge to the status quo—it's not a free country "but it will be"—is class rather than (or perhaps compounded by) racial resentment, the adult economic counterpart to Twyla's childhood fantasy of Roberta's plenitude.

By underscoring the class-based evidence for reading Twyla as white, Morrison confirms at once my own conclusion and its fantasmatic basis. Morrison's weighting of social detail, her insistence on the intersections, however constructed, between race and class, are more closely aligned with Lula's political perspective than with my psychological reading, fueled by racially specific investments that the text deliberately solicits and exposes. By both inviting and challenging racialized readings that are either "right" for the "wrong" reasons or "wrong" for the "right" ones, "Recitatif" focusses some questions to address to the massive, asymmetrical crossing of racial boundaries in recent feminist criticism. If white feminist readings of black women's texts disclose white critical fantasies, what (if any) value do these readings have—and for whom? How do white women's readings of black women's biological bodies inform our readings of black women's textual bodies? How do different critical discourses both inflect and inscribe racial fantasies? What rhetorical strategies do these discourses produce, and (how) do these strategies bear on the value of the readings they ostensibly legitimate?

Black feminists have debated the politics and potential of white feminists' critical intervention, but they have not compared or critiqued specific reading strategies, which is perhaps more properly a task of white self-criticism. This essay attempts to contribute to this task by examining signal moments, across a range of discourses, in the white critical texts emerging with such volume and intensity within contemporary feminism. By "contemporary" I mean since 1985, a watershed year that marked the simultaneous emergence of what has been called postfeminism and, not coincidentally, of pervasive white feminist attention to texts by women of color. This new attentiveness was overdetermined: by the sheer brilliance and power of this writing and its escalating status in the literary marketplace and, consequently, the academy; by white feminist restlessness with an already well-mined white female literary tradition; and by the internal logic of white feminism's trajectory through theoretical discourses that, by evacuating the referent from the signifier's play, fostered a turn to texts that reassert the authority of experience, that reinstate political agency, and that rearticulate the body and its passions. The end of the most confident and ethnocentric period of the second wave (roughly 1970–1985) has interestingly collapsed postfeminism and prefeminism as the ideological frameworks in which white women turn to black women to articulate a politics and to embody a discursive authority that are either lost or not yet found. Like Frances D. Gage's perception of Sojourner Truth rescuing the faltering 1851 Women's Rights conference in Akron through the power of her physical presence and resounding question, "A'n't I a woman?" which took "us up in her strong arms and carried us safely over the slough of difficulty turning the whole tide in our favor"; or, in one of the generative contexts for the second wave of feminism, like Jane Stembridge's discovery of a miraculously unashamed mode of female speech in Fanny Lou Hamer's proud bearing and voice at a 1964 SNCC rally—"Mrs. Hamer . . . knows that she is good. . . . If she didn't know that . . . she wouldn't stand there, with her head back and sing! She couldn't speak the *way* that she speaks and the way she speaks is this: she announces. I do not announce. I apologize"; the postfeminist turn to black women novelists enacts an anxious transference onto black women's speech.

As Valerie Smith has eloquently argued, the attempt to rematerialize an attenuated white feminism by routing it through black women's texts reproduces in the textual realm white women's historical relation to the black female bodies that have nurtured them. This relation unfolds along a spectrum of materiality. More complex than its prefeminist analogue, contemporary white feminism invokes black women's texts not only to relegitimate the feminist agenda called into question by post-structuralism but also, paradoxically, to relegitimate post-structuralism by finding its prefiguration in black women's texts. Yet whether as a corrective difference or a confirming similarity, as a sanction for a renewed or a resuspended referentiality, black women writers are enlisted to bestow a cultural authority that derives in part from their enforced experience of embodiment.

To attempt to do justice to the spectrum of white feminist approaches, I have organized this study through three case studies that, although far from exhaustive, nevertheless offer a range of influential discourses: deconstruction, psychoanalysis, and cultural criticism. This sequence traces a trajectory from a strategy that seems able to escape my own fantasmatic production of an embodied other to one that unexpectedly reproduces it. My conclusion will turn to the conclusion of "Recitatif" to reopen the question of reading and race.

## 2

> The nonblack feminist critic/theorist who honestly engages his or her own
> autobiographical implication in a brutal past is likely to provide nuances
> such as that of the black feminist critic. What, however, are the precondi-
> tions and precautions for the nonblack feminist critic/theorist who dares
> to undertake such a project?
>
> —MAE G. HENDERSON, RESPONSE TO HOUSTON A. BAKER, JR.,
> "THERE IS NO MORE BEAUTIFUL WAY"

Through the exchanges between Derrida and Lacan, we have become familiar with the debate between deconstruction and psychoanalysis over the discursive construction of subjectivity. Recent work by two prominent white feminist theorists, Barbara Johnson and Margaret Homans, suggests how this debate plays out in the related question of the discursive construction of race: a question especially urgent for critics reading and writing across racial lines.

Because it directly poses the question of the white reader's relation to the African-American text and because it has widely influenced readings of Zora Neale Hurston in particular, and of race in general, "Thresholds of Difference: Structures of Address in Zora Neale Hurston" is an apt focus for a study of Barbara Johnson's textual strategies. "Thresholds" mounts an enormously complex and brilliant critique of the belief in essential racial differences that for Johnson is the substance of racism. (Arguing that black representations of a black essence always operate within a "specific interlocutionary situation" and are "matters of strategy rather than truth," Johnson brackets the question of a possible black belief in, or desire for belief in, a black identity ["I," p. 285].) Through a reading of three Hurston texts—"How It Feels to Be Colored Me" (1928); "What White Publishers Won't Print" (1950); and *Mules and Men* (1935)—Johnson maps the interlocutionary situations that generate Hurston's ambiguous and contradictory representations of racial identity and difference. Rather than a constant, color (which figures race for both Hurston and Johnson) varies with positions in discursive exchanges whose subversion of the difference between inside and outside, self and other, is detailed in Johnson's reading of Hurston's complex relation as a northern anthropologist to the southern black communities whose folklore (or "lies") she represents in *Mules and Men.* By anticipating and legitimating the project of dereferentializing race, and by relocating differences between the races as internal differences (as in her celebrated figure of resemblances among the heterogeneous contents of differently colored bags), Hurston—or the Hurston represented by these particular texts—is a deconstructive critic's dream.

In the body of the essay, Johnson and Hurston seem to speak in a single voice, but the two voices occasionally diverge, and through their divergence the essay interrogates the politics of interracial reading. Paralleling the "multilayered envelope of address" with which Hurston frames the folktales of *Mules and Men,* Johnson frames her own readings with an analysis of her position as a "white deconstructor" interpreting a "black novelist and anthropologist" ("T," p. 278). As her language indicates, the frame deploys the rhetoric of racial essences the rest of the essay deconstructs. In addressing (as does Hurston's frame) the politics of a discourse on race, the frame also demonstrates their effects: the interlocutory situation of a white reading of a black text demands some acknowledgement of racial differences. The essay thus deploys a schizophrenic discourse, split between a first-person discourse on the politics of discourse across race and a third-person discourse on the discursive (de)construction of race. The discursive position of a "white deconstructor" of race is self-different, embracing both the assertion and the deconstruction of difference, positions the text constructs as white and black, respectively.

These positions, however, are themselves unstable. Through what becomes an excess of politicized rhetoric in the frame, read retrospectively against the text's interior, the differences between outside and inside, first person and third person, white and black, collapse and with them the tension between politics and deconstruction. If the questioning of motive and audience in the frame's opening paragraph are to be taken straight, the response the next paragraph offers is far more problematic: "It was as though I were asking her [Hurston] for answers to questions I did not even know I was unable to formulate. I had a lot to learn, then, from Hurston's way of dealing with multiple agendas and heterogeneous implied readers" ("T," p. 278). The deference to Hurston seems as disingenuous as Hurston's comparably located and requisite expressions of gratitude to her white patron, Mrs. Osgood Mason; for as much as Johnson has to learn from Hurston about strategic discursive constructions of race, she has little to learn from her about strategies of discourse generally; far from a humble student or innocent reader with no anterior agendas of her own, she constitutes Hurston as much in her own deconstructive image as she is herself reconstituted by Hurston's texts. Yet read in the context of Johnson's reading of *Mules and Men,* the dissembling rhetoric of the frame becomes a deliberate imitation of Hurston's imitation of the strategy of "lying" that she learns from the Eatonville residents who, weary of white folks prying into their ways, set verbal "'toy(s)'" "'outside the door[s]'" of their minds to distract and deceive their white investigators ("T," p. 286). If, as Johnson argues, "it is impossible to tell whether Hurston the narrator is *describing* a strategy [of lying] or *employing* one" since "Hurston's very ability to fool us—or to fool us into *thinking* we have been fooled—is itself the only effective way of conveying the rhetoric of the 'lie,'" Johnson's ability to fool us functions analogously as a rhetorical tool that, once we have understood its calculated impact, transports us along with both Hurston and Johnson from the outside to the inside of Eatonville's discursive universe ("T," pp. 286, 289).

The fluidity of this boundary transgression, however, conceals an important difference between Hurston crossing the boundaries between subject and object, North and South, literate and oral communities, and Johnson or her white readers crossing a racial boundary. In the course of Johnson's essay, a discourse on positionality comes to displace, as well as to produce, a discourse on race. As the frame slides into the interior, the questions it raises disappear. There is no further problem about a white deconstructor writing about, or writing as, a black novelist and anthropologist, since position has come to stand for race. This erasure of conflict is clear when the frame briefly returns at the end, merging Johnson's and Hurston's voices in the single conclusion that "the terms 'black' and 'white,' 'inside' and 'outside,' continue to matter" only as diversely inhabited and mutually constitutive positions on a signifying chain ("T," p. 289). By dislocating race from historically accreted differences in power, Johnson's deconstructive reading dovetails with Hurston's libertarian politics.

In Johnson's discourse on gender, by contrast, her feminist politics enforce a distinction, political rather than metaphysical, between the positions inhabited by men and women: "Jacques Derrida may sometimes see himself as *philosophically* positioned as a woman, but he is not *politically* positioned as a woman. Being positioned as a woman is not something that is entirely voluntary." The shift from gender to race in the next sentence—"Or, to put it another way, if you tell a member of the Ku Klux Klan that racism is a repression of self-difference, you are likely to learn a thing or two about repression"—bypasses the racial analogy to the problematic masculine (= white) assumption of a figuratively feminine (= black) position to insinuate the reaction of the racist that places the white deconstructor in a position of vulnerability akin to (rather than politically distinct from) the black person's position. Similarly, Johnson distinguishes more firmly between the figurative and the literal in relation to gender than to race: "the revaluation of the *figure* of the woman by a male author cannot substitute for the actual participation of women in the literary conversation. Mallarmé may be able to speak from the place of the silenced woman, but as long as *he* is occupying it, the silence that is broken in theory is maintained in reality." Johnson's relentlessly deconstructive discourse on race subverts the equivalent gestures that would subject her own role as a white deconstructor to her critique of masculine deconstructions of gender. This difference within her practice of deconstruction, the undoing of a counterpart for race to the feminist resistance to deconstruction, facilitates the project of writing across race. The interlocutory situation that requires the white critic to acknowledge racial difference also requires her to dissolve the tension between literal and figurative, political and philosophical, voluntary and involuntary modes of sameness and difference.

Johnson's essay first appeared in the 1985 special issue of *Critical Inquiry* entitled "'*Race,*' *Writing, and Difference,*" edited by Henry Louis Gates, Jr., whose position on the figurative status of race is signalled by the quotation marks with which he encloses the word; Johnson's essay conforms clearly to that volume's ideology. Gates has been criticized for the politics of his deconstruction of race, and some of the most passionate criticism has been launched by black feminists. Following one of these women, Joyce A. Joyce, Margaret Homans argues compellingly in a recent essay, "'Racial Composition': Metaphor and the Body in the Writing of Race," that Gates's, and thus by extension Johnson's, deliteralization of race is effectively a masculinist position. The difference between Johnson and Homans derives to a significant degree from the shift from deconstruction to psychoanalysis and the consequent shift from the inside/outside opposition privileged by deconstruction to that between body and language, or the literal and the figurative, which psychoanalysis genders oppositely from deconstruction. Whereas for Johnson, playing primarily off Derrida, figuration enacts an emancipatory feminine displacement of phallogocentric reference, for Homans, playing off Lacan and Chodorow, figuration enacts a masculine displacement of the specifically female (maternal) body whose exclusion founds the symbolic register. Whereas for Johnson the figurativeness of race is enabling for all races, for Homans it enables only men, since women across race accede to figuration only by devaluing the femaleness that is culturally conflated with the body. Paradoxically, however, both positions serve to legitimate white feminist readings of black women's texts: privileging the figurative enables the white reader to achieve figurative blackness; privileging the literal enables the white *woman* reader to forge a gender alliance that outweighs (without negating) both racial differences within gender and racial alliances across gender.

"'Racial Composition'" takes as its starting point the debate on black literary criticism carried out in four texts in a 1987 issue of *New Literary History:* the original essay by Joyce A. Joyce, "The Black Canon: Reconstructing Black American Literary Criticism," criticizing the deliteralization of race in Gates and Houston A. Baker, Jr.; the responses by Gates and Baker; and Joyce's response to them. Building on her premises that "the position Gates inherits from post-structuralism identifies and celebrates the abstract as masculine and devalues embodiment as female," and that Gates "substitute(s), in the undesirable position of the referent or ground from which language differentiates itself, female for black," Homans deftly teases out a gendered subtext in the exchange ("RC," pp. 3–4). In Joyce's critique of the assimilation of black literary criticism to the elite discourse of post-structuralism that, through its esoteric terminology and representation of race as a metaphor, severs its connections with the black reading community, with literary traditions rooted in the lived experience of black people, and with the concrete, sensuous features of black literary language, Homans sees a defense of the "body that is troped as female in post-structuralist theory and whose absence that theory requires" ("RC," p. 7). In the high-handed and patronizing responses by Gates and Baker, she uncovers these critics' sexualized self-representations as the saviors of a feminized black literary body in danger of a retrograde sensualization at the hands of black feminists. Homans then proceeds, via an analysis of the more egalitarian tone and terms of the debate on essentialism within black feminism, to a powerful analysis of the rhetoric of critical scenes in narratives by Alice Walker, Toni Morrison, and Maya Angelou, where the tension between (relatively) literal and figurative language constitutes the "rhetorical form in which the debate over racial and gendered 'essence' is worked out. The use or representation of a relatively literal language corresponds to and puts into practice a belief in the embodiedness of race and of gender . . . while the view that race is figurative coincides with and is performed as a celebration of language as figuration and a tendency to use conspicuous metaphors" ("RC," p. 5). While insisting on the necessity of maintaining, at different times, both positions, Homans calls attention to black women writers' continuing and complex commitment "to the body and to the literal," a commitment that contrasts in both its substance and its ambivalence with Gates's and Baker's unequivocal endorsement of the figurative, and that reiterates, within a different context, Homans's own perspective in *Bearing the Word* ("RC," p. 19). As Johnson extends and reauthorizes deconstruction through Hurston, Homans extends and reauthorizes, primarily through Walker, a revaluation of the literal.

Like Johnson, Homans frames her argument by positioning herself in relation to black women's texts. Both frames incorporate acknowledgements of racial difference; but whereas Johnson becomes, in the course of her argument, figuratively black, Homans becomes more emphatically white: "Neither literally nor figuratively a black feminist, then (nor even figuratively literally), I would prefer, following bell hooks' recommendation, to identify my perspective clearly as that of a white feminist" ("RC," p. 38). Homans's feminist critique of the overvaluation of the figurative demands that, in direct opposition to Johnson, she affirm the literalness of (at least her own) race.

This is a necessary conclusion, in the context of Homans's argument, and also a brave and problematic one. By embodying her own whiteness, Homans contests the racialization that coexists with the more overt gendering of the symbolic register. In a white feminist counterpart to Gates's strategy of making blackness figurative and figuration black ("figuration is the nigger's occupation"), Homans insistently pinions (female) whiteness to literality, resisting through a different route the dominant culture's splitting of a white symbolic realm from a black materiality. Homans affirms solidarity with black women by asserting a literal difference that is ultimately overridden by the sameness of literality: by the shared association with embodiment.

In resisting white patriarchal culture's dissociation from the body, however, Homans also implicitly resists a recurrent construction of whiteness by black women writers such as Walker who, in one of the scenes from *The Temple of My Familiar* that Homans analyzes from a different perspective, represents whiteness as the "hideous personal deficiency" of having no skin, of being "a ghost," the quintessence of lack, not only of color, but also of body itself. The occasional and moving alliances between black and white women that Homans analyzes in texts by Walker and Morrison do not necessarily produce or reflect a shared experience of embodiment. Six months pregnant, beaten, "sweating" milk for the eighteen-month-old baby from whom she has been separated, torn between "the fire in her feet and the fire on her back," Sethe hears Amy Denver's "young white voice . . . like a sixteen-year-old boy's" before she sees the scrawny body with its "arms like cane stalks" (*B*, pp. 79, 31, 34, 32). Although she has been "'bleeding for four years,'" Amy "'ain't having nobody's baby'": the carmine velvet that constitutes the goal of *her* escape sublimates the reproductive female body into cloth (*B*, p. 83). As the midwife whose *last* name is conferred on Sethe's baby, Amy is affiliated as closely with the absent (and literate) father (with whom the baby will strongly identify) as with the birthing mother. By "reading" the scar inscribed on Sethe's back, Amy is positioned on the side of figuration vis-à-vis the massively embodied Sethe. By implying that the embodiment black and white women share is weightier than differences of color, Homans proposes a commonality often called into question by black women's texts.

More problematically, however, literalizing whiteness logically entails reliteralizing blackness as well, and an argument for the literalness of race (or sex) can be safely made only from the position of the subordinated race (or sex), which can define and revalue its own distinctiveness. Speaking for the literal from a position of dominance risks reinscribing the position of the dominated. Homans's position on figuration leads her to an impasse: as a woman she can't ally herself with a (masculine) position on the figurativeness of race; as a *white* woman she can't ally herself with black women writers' (ambivalent) adherence to the embodiedness of race without potentially reproducing the structure of dominance she wants to subvert. There are as serious, although very different, problems with revaluing the literalness of race as with asserting its figurativeness.

## 3

> I began to wonder whether there was any position from which a white
> middle-class feminist could say anything on the subject [of race] without
> sounding exactly like [a white middle-class feminist]. . . . The rhetorical
> predictability of it all. The political correctness. . . . In which case it might
> be better not to say anything.
>
> —NANCY K. MILLER, "CRITICIZING FEMINIST CRITICISM"

Different as are their consequences for the reading of race, deconstruction and psychoanalysis are both subjectivist critical ideologies that mandate a high degree of self-reflexiveness. Materialist feminisms, by contrast, which have always had priority within black feminist discourse, emphasize the political objectives (and objectivity) of the reading over the question of positionality. Designed to disclose systematically (and ultimately to change) the intersecting axes of race, class, gender, and sexuality through which women are multiply and differentially oppressed, materialist feminisms, both black and white, have de-emphasized the reader's racial location. White readers within this discourse have paid only perfunctory (if any) attention to the problem of their own positionality, and black materialists have generally been hospitable to white women's readings of black texts. It is not coincidental that Valerie Smith, who insists on the materialist orientation of black feminist theory, also redefines this theory to "refer not only to theory written (or practiced) by black feminists, but also to a way of reading inscriptions of race (particularly but not exclusively blackness), gender (particularly but not exclusively womanhood), and class in modes of cultural expression"; or that Hazel Carby, writing within the discourse of cultural studies, has become one of the most resolutely antiessentialist and politically exacting black feminist voices, calling into question simultaneously the presumption of interracial sisterhood and the presumption of seamless continuity between racial experience, discourse, and interpretation. The de-essentialization of race among black feminists (in contrast to both white feminists and male Afro-Americanists) has occurred primarily through the intervention of material rather than textual differences, and under the aegis of Marxism and cultural studies rather than deconstruction.

Materialist feminism would appear to be the approach through which white critics could write about black women's texts with the least self-consciousness about racial difference and perhaps with the least difference. Yet white investments in some form of black cultural or social specificity, investments exempted from analysis under the banner of an interracial socialist feminist sisterhood, tend to intervene in white readings of black texts, substituting racial for class specificity rather than disrupting each with the other. Racial differences are visibly played out in the critical response to *The Color Purple*. Both black and white feminists from diverse critical schools have celebrated the text's subversive stance toward the narrative and rhetorical conventions of epistolary, sentimental, and realist fiction, and toward the sexual, domestic, and spiritual institutions of patriarchy. But among materialist feminists race has made a difference in the assessment of the novel's politics. For example, bell hooks criticizes the novel for isolating individual quests and transformative private relationships from collective political effort, for celebrating the "ethics of a narcissistic new-age spirituality wherein economic prosperity indicates that one is chosen," and for breaking with the revolutionary impulse of the African-American literary tradition epitomized by the slave narrative; Cora Kaplan, in an essay entitled "Keeping the Color in *The Color Purple*," defends the novel from accusations of bourgeois liberalism by British socialists who, she feels, have "bleached" the text into "an uncontentious, sentimental, harmless piece of international libertarianism" by failing to understand its relation to "a specifically racial set of discourses about the family and femininity." Kaplan revalues the novel through a black cultural context that hooks claims the novel has repudiated. And whereas Hazel Carby criticizes the critics who, through their celebration of *The Color Purple* (and its line of descent from *Their Eyes Were Watching God*), indulge in a romantic vision of rural black culture that enables them to avoid confronting the complex social crises in the urban black community, Susan Willis praises the novel for contesting industrial capitalism by resurrecting the homestead and cottage industry. The representation of black social relations as utopian alternatives to industrial capitalism or to patriarchal nationalism has appealed more to white than to black materialist feminists.

This appeal, and its problems, surface clearly in the work of Willis, who deserves special attention as the only white feminist author of a book on black women novelists and of an essay in Cheryl A. Wall's recent anthology of black feminist criticism, *Changing Our Own Words* (1989). In *Specifying: Black Women Writing the American*

*Experience* (1987), Willis maps the ways that twentieth-century black women novelists record through their narrative strategies and subjects the shift from a southern agrarian to a northern industrial economy. Suffused with nostalgia for an agrarian culture that in Willis's opinion supported a "noncommodified relationship" between an author, her language, and her audience, the book insists that "one of the major problems facing black writers today is how to preserve the black cultural heritage in the face of the homogenizing function of bourgeois society." This romanticization of "the" black cultural heritage, whose truth resides in an uncontaminated past to which these novels' protagonists repeatedly return, becomes apparent through the contrast between Willis's study and Hazel Carby's *Reconstructing Womanhood: The Emergence of the Afro-American Woman Novelist,* published the same year, which situates nineteenth-century black women's cultural discourses in relation to hegemonic ideologies. In her essay "I Shop Therefore I Am: Is There a Place for Afro-American Culture in Commodity Culture?" however, Willis begins to engage this relation by shifting from a strict economic reading of a discrete literary tradition to a more variegated account of African-American participation in the cultural arena produced by commodity capitalism. The essay, more than the book, positions Willis in a relation to Fredric Jameson analogous to that between Johnson and Derrida, and even more to that between Homans and Lacan, since Willis, like Homans, prioritizes what is unincorporated by a master system. "I Shop Therefore I Am" opens up the third term that Jameson brackets in "Reification and Utopia in Mass Culture," the term representing the possibility of "authentic cultural production" by marginal social groups that inhabit a position outside the dialectic of high culture and mass culture. More committed than Jameson to criticizing mass culture from a position of estrangement that tends in her work to devolve into a place of authenticity, Willis both racializes and genders a cultural exterior, relinquishing black men to an ambiguous dance of subversion and assimilation with mass culture while retaining black women as unambivalent voices of resistance.

Willis answers her central question—whether it is possible for African Americans to participate in commodity culture without being assimilated to it—in gendered terms. The essay plays Toni Morrison, whose Claudia in *The Bluest Eye* represents for Willis "the radical potential inherent in the position of being 'other' to dominant society" by repudiating the white-dominated culture industry epitomized by a Shirley Temple doll, against Michael Jackson, who "states himself as a commodity" through the vertiginous display of self-transformations and imitations that undo the possibility of authenticity ("I," pp. 174, 187). "*Moonwalker* suggests a split between contemporary black women's fiction, which strives to create images of social wholeness based on the rejection of commodity capitalism, and what seems to be a black male position which sees the commodity as something that can be played with and enjoyed or subverted" ("I," p. 195). Although Willis reluctantly admits the subversive possibilities of parody, represented in her essay by Jackson and by the black film and art critic Kobena Mercer, who argues that commodity culture heightens the radical potential of artifice, she clearly prefers the authenticity represented for her by Morrison and Walker, with whom the essay begins and ends. This preference incurs two penalties. First, Willis's analytical inventiveness and subtlety are most impressively released by untangling the contradictions of mass cultural figures: Michael Jackson and his conservative antitype Mickey Mouse, on whose genealogical descent from the tradition of black minstrelsy she brilliantly speculates in an epilogue to a slightly different version of this essay that was published in *New Formations.* The utopian pressures Willis levies on black women writers, by contrast, simplifies her interpretation. Moreover, by pitting black women novelists against black male cultural critics and performers, Willis sidesteps an encounter with the black feminist critics who have endorsed the position she characterizes as "black male." Although there is more of an encounter with black feminist criticism in the essay, where Willis acknowledges her differences from Carby, for example, but doesn't theorize them, than in the book, where she lists black feminists in a general bibliography rather than engaging with them individually, Willis still doesn't interrogate what fuels her own investment in black women writers' representation of "social wholeness," "the autonomous subject," and "fullness of . . . humanity" ("I," pp. 195, 174).

The essay, however, does offer clues. In contrast to Homans, who invokes black women's representations of alliances with white women to underscore the prospects of reciprocity and commonality, Willis enlists black women's representations of white women to suggest women's socially constructed differences. In *The Bluest Eye*'s characterization of "frozen faced white baby dolls" and in *Meridian*'s account of the mummified white female body exhibited for profit by her husband, Willis finds images of the reification white women suffer through immersion (both longer and deeper than black women's) in the culture of commodities. Haunting the white female consumer's version of the cogito, "I shop therefore I am" (parody is apparently a strategy available to white feminists if not to black), the spectre of the self's mortification as commodity drives the commitment to the difference of black women's texts, as the title of the other version of this essay indicates: "I Want the Black One: Is There a Place for Afro-American Culture in Commodity Culture?" Overtly, this title replaces the voice of the white female consumer whose identity is shopping with the voice of the black female consumer manipulated into buying black replicants of white commodities, Christie dolls instead of Barbies. Yet the overdetermined referent of the first-person pronoun betrays as well (and this is presumably why this title was not used for the version of this essay in Wall's anthology) the desire of the white feminist critic who also wants "the black one"—the text that promises resistance and integrity, the utopian supplement to her own "deconstruction of commodities." White feminists, like the frozen or mummified white women represented in some black women's texts, seem in Willis's discourse to be corpses finding political energy through the corpus of black women.

Willis's essay brings us back, through a different route, to my reading of Roberta as a site of authority and plenitude figured as a vital, integrated body. In contrast to Johnson and Homans, who locate black and white women on the same (although opposite) sides of the symbolic register's divide, Willis and I operate from a model of difference rather than similarity. The claim for sameness is enabled by, and in turn reauthorizes, belief in a subversive feminine position in language (whether the subversion operates through figuration or literality); the argument for an idealized (biological, social, or literary) difference is fueled by the perception of an increasingly compromised white feminist social position drained by success of oppositionality. But whether argued in terms of sameness or of difference, or in terms of the symbolic or the social domains, these theorizations of reading across race are marked by white desires.

## 4

> The first thing you do is to forget that i'm Black. Second, you must never forget that i'm Black.
>
> —PAT PARKER, "FOR THE WHITE PERSON WHO
> WANTS TO KNOW HOW TO BE MY FRIEND"

How, then, should we evaluate this critical undertaking? The question incorporates two complexly interwoven ones, a hermeneutic question about difference and a political question about legitimacy, that I wish to (re)open briefly in my conclusion by returning to my starting point: reading "Recitatif."

To produce an allegory about reading and race, I omitted aspects of the story—most importantly, its own conclusion—that complicate the division between the characters and, consequently, between their readers. "Recitatif" ends with parallel recognitions by Twyla and Roberta that each perceived the mute Maggie as her own unresponsive, rejecting mother, and therefore hated and wanted to harm her. After dramatizing the differences produced by race and class, the story concludes with the shared experience of abandoned little girls who, in some strange twist of the oedipal story, discover that they killed (wanted to kill), as well as loved (wanted to love), their mothers (see "R," p. 261). Sameness coexists with difference, psychology with politics. Race enforces no absolute distinctions between either characters or readers, all of whom occupy diverse subject positions, some shared, some antithetical. By concluding with a psychological narrative that crosses differences (indeed, with a variant of *the* universalizing psychological narrative), "Recitatif" complicates, without cancelling, both its narrative of difference and the differences in reading that this narrative provokes.

Race enters complexly into feminist reading. The three case studies examined in this essay do indicate certain pervasive tendencies among white feminists, who have tended to read black women's texts through critical lenses that filter out the texts' embeddedness in black political and cultural traditions and that foreground instead their relation to the agendas of white feminism, which the texts alter, or prefigure, but ultimately reconfirm. For despite Jane Gallop's account of the displacement of French men by African-American women as figures of authority for white feminists, the discourses produced by French (and German and American) men continue to shape the reading habits of white feminists, who are usually better trained in literary theory than in African-American cultural studies. There has been little in white feminism comparable to the detailed reconstructions of black women's literary traditions produced by Barbara Christian, Mary Helen Washington, Deborah E. McDowell, Gloria T.

Hull, Nellie Y. McKay, or Margaret B. Wilkerson; or to the mapping of this literature's social and discursive contexts produced by Hazel Carby, Barbara Smith, Valerie Smith, bell hooks, Michele Wallace, Audre Lorde, or June Jordan. Instead, we have tended to focus our readings on the "celebrity" texts—preeminently those by Hurston, Walker, and Morrison—rather than on "thick" descriptions of discursive contexts, and have typically written articles or chapters (rather than books) representing black women's texts as literary and social paradigms for white readers and writers. In these texts we have found alternative family structures, narrative strategies, and constructions of subjectivity: alternative, that is, to the cultural practices of white patriarchy, with which literature by white women has come to seem uncomfortably complicit. The implied audience for this critical venture has been white.

The critical picture is not, however, entirely black and white. As the work of Hortense J. Spillers demonstrates especially well, black feminists draw from, as well as criticize, a range of "high" theoretical discourses, including the psychoanalytic discourses that have functioned more prominently within white feminism. As Deborah E. McDowell has powerfully argued, moreover, white feminist tendencies to construct black feminism as "high" theory's political "other" reinscribe, rather than rework, the theory/politics opposition. White feminist criticism is itself fractured by class and generational differences that partially undo the racial divide. Some still-unpublished essays, particularly those by a new and differently educated generation of graduate students, and some essays that are published less visibly than those analyzed in this paper, more closely approximate the historical and political concerns of black feminist criticism. Yet however interwoven with and ruptured by other differences, race remains a salient source of the fantasies and allegiances that shape our ways of reading.

Difference, however, paradoxically increases the value of crossing racial boundaries in reading. Our inability to avoid inscribing racially inflected investments and agendas limits white feminism's capacity either to impersonate black feminism, and potentially to render it expendable, or to counter its specific credibility. More important, white feminist readings contribute, however inadvertently, to a project many black feminists endorse: the racialization of whiteness. As masculinity takes shape in part through its constructions of femininity, whiteness—that elusive color that seems not to be one—gains materiality through the desires and fantasies played out in its interpretations of blackness, interpretations that, by making the unconscious conscious, supplement articulated ideologies of whiteness with less accessible assumptions. Reading black women's texts, and reading our readings of them, is one (although certainly not the only) strategy for changing our habitual perception that "race is always an issue of Otherness that is not white: it is black, brown, yellow, red, purple even."

Articulating the whiteness implied through the construction of blackness approaches, through a different route, the goal of Toni Morrison's recent critical project: "to avert the critical gaze from the racial object to the racial subject; from the described and imagined to the describers and imaginers; from the serving to the served." There is a significant political difference, of course, between Morrison analyzing European-American texts and white feminist theorists staking critical claims to the African-American texts that constitute a privileged and endangered terrain of black feminist inquiry. The risks of this intervention have been circumscribed, however, by the effectiveness of black feminists in establishing the authority of their own positions and by the failure of "high" theory to secure some unproblematic grounding for white feminists by either resolving or displacing the politics of reading and race. If we produce our readings cautiously and locate them in a self-conscious and self-critical relation to black feminist criticism, these risks, I hope, would be counterbalanced by the benefits of broadening the spectrum of interpretation, illuminating the social determinants of reading, and deepening our recognition of our racial selves and the "others" we fantasmatically construct—and thereby expanding the possibilities of dialogue across as well as about racial boundaries.

# Chinua Achebe

## The Novelist as Teacher

1975

Writing of the kind I do is relatively new in my part of the world and it is too soon to try and describe in detail the complex of relationships between us and our readers. However, I think I can safely deal with one aspect of these relationships which is rarely mentioned. Because of our largely European education, our writers may be pardoned if they begin by thinking that the relationship between European writers and their audience will automatically reproduce itself in Africa. We have learned from Europe that a writer or an artist lives on the fringe of society—wearing a beard and a peculiar dress and generally behaving in a strange, unpredictable way. He is in revolt against society, which in turn looks on him with suspicion if not hostility. The last thing society would dream of doing is to put him in charge of anything.

All that is well known, which is why some of us seem too eager for our society to treat us with the same hostility or even behave as though it already does. I am not interested now in what writers expect of society; that is generally contained in their books, or should be. What is not so well documented is what society expects of its writers.

I am assuming, of course, that our writer and his society live in the same place. I realize that a lot has been made of the allegation that African writers have to write for European and American readers because African readers, where they exist at all, are only interested in reading textbooks. I don't know if African writers always have a foreign audience in mind. What I do know is that they don't have to. At least I know that I don't have to. Last year the pattern of sales of *Things Fall Apart* in the cheap paperback edition was as follows: about 800 copies in Britain; 20,000 in Nigeria; and about 2,500 in all other places. The same pattern was true also of *No Longer at Ease*.

Most of my readers are young. They are either in school or college or have only recently left. And many of them look at me as a kind of teacher. Only the other day I received this letter from Northern Nigeria:

Dear C. Achebe, I do not usually write to authors, no matter how interesting their work is, but I feel I must tell you how much I enjoyed your editions of *Things Fall Apart* and *No Longer at Ease.* I look forward to reading your new edition of *Arrow of God.* Your novels serve as advice to us young. I trust that you will continue to produce as many of this type of book. With friendly greetings and best wishes.

Yours sincerely,
I. Buba Yero Mafindi

It is quite clear what this particular reader expects of me. Nor is there much doubt about another reader in Ghana who wrote me a rather pathetic letter to say that I had neglected to include questions and answers at the end of *Things Fall Apart* and could I make these available to him to insure his success at next year's school certificate examinations. This is what I would call in Nigerian pidgin "a how-for-do" reader and I hope there are not very many like him. But also in Ghana I met a young woman teacher who immediately took me to task for not making the hero of my *No Longer at Ease* marry the girl he is in love with. I made the kind of vague noises I usually make whenever a wise critic comes along to tell me I should have written a different book to the one I wrote. But my woman teacher was not going to be shaken off so easily. She was in deadly earnest. Did I know, she said, that there were many women in the kind of situation I had described and that I could have served them well if I had shown that it was possible to find one man with enough guts to go against custom?

I don't agree, of course. But this young woman spoke with so much feeling that I couldn't help being a little uneasy at the accusation (for it was indeed a serious accusation) that I had squandered a rare opportunity for education on a whimsical and frivolous exercise. It is important to say at this point that no self-respecting writer will take dictation from his audience. He must remain free to disagree with his society and go into rebellion against it if need be. But I am for choosing my cause very carefully. Why should I start waging war as a Nigerian newspaper editor was doing the other day on the "soulless efficiency" of Europe's industrial and technological civilization when the very thing my society needs may well be a little technical efficiency?

My thinking on the peculiar needs of different societies was sharpened when not long ago I heard an English pop song, which I think was entitled "I Ain't Gonna Wash for a Week." At first I wondered why it should occur to anyone to take such a vow when there were so many much more worthwhile resolutions to make. But later it dawned on me that this singer belonged to the same culture which, in an earlier age of self-satisfaction, had blasphemed and said that cleanliness was next to godliness. So I saw him in a new light—as a kind of divine administrator of vengeance. I make bold to say, however, that his particular offices would not be required in my society because we did not commit the sin of turning hygiene into a god.

Needless to say, we do have our own sins and blasphemies recorded against our name. If I were God, I would regard as the very worst our acceptance—for whatever reason—of racial inferiority. It is too late in the day to get worked up about it or to blame others, much as they may deserve such blame and condemnation. What we need to do is to look back and try to find out where we went wrong, where the rain began to beat us.

Let me give one or two examples of the result of the disaster brought upon the African psyche in the period of subjection to alien races. I remember the shock felt by Christians of my father's generation in my village in the early forties when, for the first time, the local girls' school performed Nigerian dances at the anniversary of the coming of the gospel. Hitherto they had always put on something Christian and civilized which I believe was called the Maypole dance. In those days—when I was growing up—I also remember that it was only the poor benighted heathen who had any use for our local handcraft, e.g., our pottery. Christians and the well-to-do (and they were usually the same people) displayed their tins and other metalware. We never carried waterpots to the stream. I had a small cylindrical biscuit tin suitable to my years, while the older members of our household carried four-gallon kerosene tins.

Today, things have changed a lot, but it would be foolish to pretend that we have fully recovered from the traumatic effects of our first confrontation with Europe. Three or four weeks ago, my wife, who teaches English in a boys' school, asked a pupil why he wrote about winter when he meant the harmattan. He said the other boys would call him a bushman if he did such a thing! Now, you wouldn't have thought, would you, that there was something shameful in your weather? But apparently we do. How can this great blasphemy be purged? I think it is part of my business as a writer to teach that boy that there is nothing disgraceful about the African weather, that the palm tree is a fit subject for poetry.

Here then is an adequate revolution for me to espouse—to help my society regain belief in itself and put away the complexes of the years of denigration and self-abasement. And it is essentially a question of education, in the best sense of the word. Here, I think, my aims and the deepest aspirations of my society meet. For no thinking African can escape the pain of the wound in our soul. You have all heard of the African personality, of African democracy, of the African way to socialism, of negritude, and so on. They are all props we have fashioned at different times to help us get on our feet again. Once we are up, we shan't need any of them any more. But for the moment it is in the nature of things that we may need to counter racism with what Jean-Paul Sartre has called an anti-racist racism, to announce not just that we are as good as the next man but that we are much better.

The writer cannot expect to be excused from the task of re-education and regeneration that must be done. In fact he should march right in front. For he is after all—as Ezekiel Mphahlele says in his *African Image*—the sensitive point of his community. The Ghanaian professor of philosophy, William Abraham, put it this way:

> Just as African scientists undertake to solve some of the scientific problems of Africa, African historians go into the history of Africa, African political scientists concern themselves with the politics of Africa; why should African literary creators be exempted from the services that they themselves recognize as genuine?

I, for one, would not wish to be excused. I would be quite satisfied if my novels (especially the ones I set in the past) did no more than teach my readers that their past—with all its imperfections—was not one long night of savagery from which the first Europeans acting on God's behalf delivered them. Perhaps what I write is applied art as distinct from pure. But who cares? Art is important, but so is education of the kind I have in mind. And I don't see that the two need be mutually antagonistic. In a recent anthology, a Hausa folk tale, having recounted the usual fabulous incidents, ends with these words:

> They all came and they lived happily together. He had several sons and
> daughters who grew up and helped in raising the standard of education in
> the country.

As I said elsewhere, if you consider this ending a naive anticlimax, then you cannot know very much about Africa.

# Margaret Atwood

## Reading Blind                                                          1989

**W**henever I'm asked to talk about what constitutes a "good" story, or what makes one well-written story "better" than another, I begin to feel very uncomfortable. Once you start making lists or devising rules for stories, or for any other kind of writing, some writer will be sure to happen along and casually break every abstract rule you or anyone else has ever thought up, and take your breath away in the process. The word *should* is a dangerous one to use when speaking of writing. It's a kind of challenge to the deviousness and inventiveness and audacity and perversity of the creative spirit. Sooner or later, anyone who has been too free with it will be liable to end up wearing it like a dunce's cap. We don't judge good stories by the application to them of some set of external measurements, as we judge giant pumpkins at the Fall Fair. We judge them by the way they strike us. And that will depend on a great many subjective imponderables, which we lump together under the general heading of taste. . . .

I've spoken of "the voice of the story," which has become a sort of catchall phrase; but by it I intend something more specific: a speaking voice, like the singing voice in music, that moves not across space, across the page, but through time. Surely every written story is, in the final analysis, a score for voice. Those little black marks on the page mean nothing without their retranslation into sound. Even when we read silently, we read with the ear, unless we are reading bank statements.

Perhaps, by abolishing the Victorian practice of family reading and by removing from our school curricula those old standbys, the set memory piece and the recitation, we've deprived both writers and readers of something essential to stories. We've led them to believe that prose comes in visual blocks, not in rhythms and cadences; that its texture should be flat because a page is flat; that written emotion should not be immediate, like a drumbeat, but more remote, like a painted landscape: something to be contemplated. But understatement can be overdone, plainsong can get too plain. When I asked a group of young writers, earlier this year, how many of them ever read their own work aloud, not one of them said she did.

I'm not arguing for the abolition of the eye, merely for the reinstatement of the voice, and for an appreciation of the way it carries the listener along with it at the pace of the story. (Incidentally, reading aloud disallows cheating; when you're reading aloud, you can't skip ahead.)

Our first stories come to us through the air. We hear voices.

Children in oral societies grow up within a web of stories; but so do all children. We listen before we can read. Some of our listening is more like listening in, to the calamitous or seductive voices of the adult world, on the radio or the television or in our daily lives. Often it's an overhearing of things we aren't supposed to hear, eavesdropping on scandalous gossip or family secrets. From all these scraps of voices, from the whispers and shouts that surround us, even from the ominous silences, the unfilled gaps in meaning, we patch together for ourselves an order of events, a plot or plots; these, then, are the things that happen, these are the people they happen to, this is the forbidden knowledge.

We have all been little pitchers with big ears, shooed out of the kitchen when the unspoken is being spoken, and we have probably all been tale-bearers, blurters at the dinner table, unwitting violators of adult rules of censorship. Perhaps this is what writers are: those who never kicked the habit. We remained tale-bearers. We learned to keep our eyes open, but not to keep our mouths shut.

If we're lucky, we may also be given stories meant for our ears, stories intended for us. These may be children's Bible stories, tidied up and simplified and with the vicious bits left out. They may be fairy tales, similarly sugared, although if we are very lucky it will be the straight stuff in both instances, with the slaughters, thunderbolts, and red-hot shoes left in. In any case, these tales will have deliberate, molded shapes, unlike the stories we have patched together for ourselves. They will contain mountains, deserts, talking donkeys, dragons; and, unlike the kitchen stories, they will have definite endings. We are likely to accept these stories as being on the same level of reality as the kitchen stories. It's only when we are older that we are taught to regard one kind of story as real and the other kind as mere invention. This is about the same time we're taught to believe that dentists are useful, and writers are not.

Traditionally, both the kitchen gossips and the readers-out-loud have been mothers or grandmothers, native languages have been mother tongues, and the kinds of stories that are told to children have been called nursery tales or old wives' tales. It struck me as no great coincidence when I learned recently that, when a great number of prominent writers were asked to write about the family member who had had the greatest influence on their literary careers, almost all of them, male as well as female, had picked their mothers. Perhaps this reflects the extent to which North American children have been deprived of their grandfathers, those other great repositories of story; perhaps it will come to change if men come to share in early child care, and we will have old husbands' tales. But as things are, language, including the language of our earliest-learned stories, is a verbal matrix, not a verbal patrix. . . .

Two kinds of stories we first encounter—the shaped tale, the overheard impromptu narrative we piece together—form our idea of what a story is and color the expectations we bring to stories later. Perhaps it's from the collisions between these two kinds of stories—what is often called "real life" (and which writers greedily think of as their "material") and what is sometimes dismissed as "mere literature" or "the kinds of things that happen only in stories"—that original and living writing is generated. A writer with nothing but a formal sense will produce dead work, but so will one whose only excuse for what is on the page is that it really happened. Anyone who has been trapped in a bus beside a nonstop talker graced with no narrative skill or sense of timing can testify to that. Or, as Raymond Chandler says in "The Simple Art of Murder": "All language beings with speech, and the speech of common men at that, but when it develops to the point of becoming a literary medium it only looks like speech."

Expressing yourself is not nearly enough. You must express the story. . . .

Perhaps all I want from a good story is what children want when they listen to tales both told and overheard—which turns out to be a good deal.

They want their attention held, and so do I. I always read to the end, out of some puritanical, and adult, sense of duty owed; but if I start to fidget and skip pages, and wonder if conscience demands I go back and read the middle, it's a sign that the story has lost me, or I have lost it.

They want to feel they are in safe hands, that they can trust the teller. With children this may mean simply that they know the speaker will not betray them by closing the book in the middle, or mixing up the heroes and the villains. With adult readers it's more complicated than that, and involves many dimensions, but there's the same element of keeping faith. Faith must be kept with the language—even if the story is funny, its language must be taken seriously—with the concrete details of locale, mannerism, clothing; with the shape of the story itself. A good story may tease, as long as this activity is foreplay and not used as an end in itself. If there's a promise held out, it must be honored. Whatever is hidden behind the curtain must be revealed at last, and it must be at one and the same time completely unexpected and inevitable. It's in this last respect that the story (as distinct from the novel) comes closest to resembling two of its oral predecessors, the riddle and the joke. Both, or all three, require the same mystifying buildup, the same surprising twist, the same impeccable sense of timing. If we guess the riddle at once, or if we can't guess it because the answer makes no sense—if we see the joke coming, or if the point is lost because the teller gets it muddled—there is failure. Stories can fail in the same way.

But anyone who has ever told, or tried to tell, a story to children will know that there is one thing without which none of the rest is any good. Young children have little sense of dutifulness or of delaying anticipation. They are longing to hear a story, but only if you are longing to tell one. They will not put up with your lassitude or boredom: If you want their full attention, you must give them yours. You must hold them with your glittering eye or suffer the pinches and whispering. You need the Ancient Mariner element, the Scheherazade element: a sense of urgency. *This is the story I must tell; this is the story you must hear.*

Urgency does not mean frenzy. The story can be a quiet story, a story about dismay or missed chances or a wordless revelation. But it must be urgently told. It must be told with as much intentness as if the teller's life depended on it. And, if you are a writer, so it does, because your life as the writer of each particular story is only as long, and as good, as the story itself. Most of those who hear it or read it will never know you, but they will know the story. Their act of listening is its reincarnation. . . .

From listening to the stories of others, we learn to tell our own.

# Dale M. Bauer

## *Edith Wharton's "Roman Fever": A Rune of History*                1988

R.W.B. Lewis' biography of Edith Wharton mentions with her other late works the 1934 short story "Roman Fever" as a masterpiece of "rhetorical coherence," but insists that in writing the piece Wharton was "unperturbed" by news from Europe of a "terrible revolution . . . at hand" (*Biography* 527). He suggests that the pervading tone of calm and repose in the story underscores her virtual mastery of history, of the past—both Wharton's own past and, in particular, the question of her paternity—as well as the past of the species represented by the Roman ruins. Yet her "Roman Fever" questions origins, persecution, and sexual violence—Rome itself being a powerful site of primal violence. Her story interrogates society's periodic demand for an ultimate return to origins: whether it be racial purification or sexual housekeeping. Lewis writes that the possibility of Wharton's illegitimacy "must have edged its way into Mrs. Wharton's mind over the years that followed [1908–09: the years in which the rumor began]. . . . The situation of Grace Ansley's whole lifetime is revealed in a single phrase, and just possibly, with all obliqueness, one phase of Edith Wharton's situation as well" (*Collected Stories* xxv). The question of race and origin, which is central to "Roman Fever," also centers the moment of history—the "terrible revolution" brewing in Europe.

Many critics would agree with Lewis about Wharton's apolitical, "serene," and "new state of being" in the thirties (*Biography* 524). Cynthia Griffin Wolff does not deal with Wharton's politics at all, while, at worst, other critics label Wharton an anti-Semite. Cynthia Ozick writes that Edith Wharton was compliant in the face of her friend Paul Bourget's openly-declared anti-Semitism (293). Sol Liptzin's *The Jew in American Literature* cites Wharton's caricature of the "bounder Jew" as an example of her anti-Semitism (154); Wharton's name also appears as evidence of a general cultural anti-Semitism in Florence Kiper Frank's 1930 *Bookman* essay, "The Presentment of the Jew in American Fiction" (274; see Dobkowski 177–80). At best, Wharton is considered a social critic with her own ideological blindspots, racism and anti-Semitism among them. (She condemns Carl Van Vechten's "Nigger Heaven," along with all "nigger society in Harlem," in an April 1, 1927 letter to Gaillard Lapsley.)

Perhaps the most quoted example of her anti-Semitism is figured in Simon Rosedale, the "glossy Jew" in *The House of Mirth*. Nevertheless, in Chapter VI of Book Two, Wharton has Rosedale take on the "paternal *rôle*" with Carry Fisher's child: Lily "could not but notice a quality of homely goodness in his advances to the child" (249–50). The same chapter casts Carry in the maternal rôle, providing a counterpart to Lily's new view of Rosedale. Rosedale not only becomes more like Carry, the most solicitous figure for Lily's welfare besides Gerty, but he also serves as Lily's foil: ". . . little by little, circumstances were breaking down her dislike for Rosedale. The dislike, indeed, still subsisted, but it was penetrated here and there by the perception of mitigating qualities in him: of a certain gross kindliness, a rather helpless fidelity of sentiment, which seemed to be struggling through the hard surface of his material ambitions" (299–300). Lily's view of Rosedale changes when she recognizes his sensitivity, his "gross kindliness." Her "old standard of values" has changed, as has her anti-Semitism. Whether Lily's change in attitude here mitigates for us the charge of anti-Semitism against Wharton is not the crucial issue. What is at issue is the tendency to read characters as the embodiment of an author's attitude; this tendency has proven to be a dangerous one in Wharton criticism. For one, it has led many to reject Wharton's late fictions as conservative, but Wharton's views—on cultural and racial politics and "race hygiene," as eugenics was called—do not necessarily coincide with her characters' views. And in at least one late novel—*Twilight Sleep*—Wharton refuses us the vantage point of one character's perspective. In fact, she denies us the narcissistic pleasure of identification by forcing us to see subjectivity as fragmented, to see as subjects without the grounding of "selves." As I see it, Wharton does not align her authorial voice with her characters', but orchestrates the cultural contradictions she foregrounds through narrative voices. In order to illuminate Wharton's politics, we need to look in other, less stereotypical places.

Charting the ideological shift in her work shows that "Roman Fever," for instance, responds to a reactionary political climate, demonstrating an antireactionary thrust to Wharton's fiction that counters the critical conception of her as apolitical or politically naive.

In the thirties' political climate, she notices the authoritarian powers at work, and her fiction addresses this political trajectory—just as she had earlier addressed "Fordian culture" in *Twilight Sleep* (1927). The stakes in such a critical endeavor are high: Wharton attempts to interpret for the popular audience a reactionary social climate and, therefore, teach her readers to be skeptical of the rhetoric of racial and cultural purity. I am not attempting to trace cultural or historical references, but to theorize the cultural impact of the air-wave and journalistic rhetoric upon the imagination of Wharton as social critic. The marks of a changing and horrifying political climate are etched in Wharton's fiction. Highlighting those marks brings the trace to the surface.

Before I turn to "Roman Fever" (written in the midst of Hitler's rise to power), I want to provide some sense of what Wharton would have been hearing about social politics in the thirties. Lewis claims that she listened to Hitler's rhetoric over her wireless; in her own words, she was appalled by his "'angry screams and accusations of cowardice against any one who loves peace and beauty better than a general massacre,'" no less than she was appalled by Italy's acceptance of fascism and the earlier rise of Mussolini (*Biography* 505). Lewis writes that Wharton "reserved her harshest words for Hitler." These are, however, Lewis' only references to the politics that inform Wharton's time.

Early 1933 seemed to be a turning point in anti-Semitic attacks, when, in fact, the European middle-class objected to "visible" attacks on Jews in their neighborhoods (Koonz 3–17). April 1, 1933 saw a "legal" boycott on Jewish businesses (called off after twenty-four hours). Shortly after this highly publicized incident, Edith Wharton wrote to her friend Gaillard Lapsley with the exclamation: "Oh, & how I want to talk to you about Roosevelt, Hitler, & that awful [Moscow] business, which I no longer find myself able to read.—" (April 15, 1933). Wharton has ostensibly turned her face to the wall when it comes to politics, but here (and elsewhere) the political situation appears to have been much on her mind. I read with irony her claims on June 3, 1935, to Royal Cortissoz, her friend and the art critic for the *New York Herald Tribune*:

> I have not met anyone in France who is alarmed for the future, as far as
> one's own personal welfare is concerned; but politically, it does not look
> brilliant at present; nor does ours at home, either. So perhaps we had bet-
> ter turn to the Titians and the Giorgione, and try to forget it all.

But she does not forget the present: her act of remembering is inscribed in her late fictions.

## The Law of the Father and Racial Purity

Wharton's story investigates a general force—call it fascism or patriarchy or discipline and repression—operating in culture. Wharton sees cultural origins as fictive rather than as mythic and pursues the danger of ignoring the difference. As Frank Kermode writes, "We have to distinguish between myths and fictions. Fictions can degenerate into myths whenever they are not consciously held to be fictive. In this sense anti-Semitism is a degenerate fiction, a myth. . . . Myths are the agents of stability, fictions the agents of change" (39). Wharton's "Roman Fever" acts as an agent of change. Her late fictions—from *The Mother's Recompense* to *Twilight Sleep* to "Roman Fever"—concern sexual violence, perhaps the only "form" which her more general preoccupation with culture and civilization could take.

Wharton's story is about procreation and history, two discourses which she finds perversely intertwined. Her story goes as follows: Two middle-aged women meet again, accidentally, in Rome, after many years, after much personal history, in a place where they had a shared history. They contemplate vaguely the Roman vista and the numerous ironies that emerge at their having been brought together once again at the scene of destruction—the Roman Forum—leaning as if at the limit of some terrible drama threatening to take both of them into its oblivion. Both had been teenagers here, and both had found husbands here. Both women have daughters, both of whom are marriageable and on a double-date. Their conversation leads to a reopening of old wounds, rivalry, renewed violence, and a series of revelations. Twenty-five years before, Alida Slade had forged a letter to Grace Ansley in the name of Alida's future husband, Delphin Slade, in order to get rid of Grace, who she knew was also in love with her husband-to-be. The letter sets up a rendezvous between Grace and Delphin in the Colosseum, though of course Delphin, according to Alida's plan, would not be there. That Alida says she knew Grace would not die of "Roman fever," even though Alida sends her to the Colosseum in the cold night air, does not diminish the essential violence of that letter. In a moment of forced contrition, Alida is willing to grant Grace this one possession—a memory—since Alida eventually married the man both of them loved and bore Delphin's legitimate child. Alida says Grace had nothing but a phony letter, while she herself had Delphin, his money, his name, and his child for twenty-five years. Grace retorts with the most effective comeback possible: the fact that she had Delphin's child, Barbara.

Thus, the story has a surprise ending: a specific hierarchical relation is reestablished between the two women in a story that begins, in the first paragraph, in a vague darkness: "From the table at which they had been lunching two American ladies of ripe but well-cared-for middle age moved across the lofty terrace of the Roman restaurant and, leaning on its parapet, looked first at each other, and then down on the outspread glories of the Palatine and the Forum, with the same expression of vague but benevolent approval" (9). As this opening suggests, the women remain content in their ignorance of events. The story, then, like a Greek ritual tragedy, moves gradually toward *anagnoresis*. What has brought these women here to battle for social position and authority?

The first paragraph, again, helps to suggest an answer. As they survey the Palatine Hill, these women have "a vague and benevolent approval" of these ruins, a site that not only represents great triumph but also vast decay, death, and destruction (9). If their mien is "vague," they must have temporarily forgotten whatever it is that might prevent their look of benevolence. And since they look benevolently at each other, then that forgetting also includes the repression of their shared history. The task of the narrative is to remember in an explicit way. What Eric Sundquist suggests in *Home as Found* about Hawthorne is true as well of Wharton: " 'remembrance' is often literally that: one re-members what has been dis-membered, reconstructs what has been shattered, and atones for what has been ruined or murdered" (91). In the act of writing, we re-member what has been dis-membered through experience; Wharton's storytelling here is an act of piecing together the histories of these women competing for Delphin Slade and for authority. Wharton's task is to remember the function of these Roman ruins both as a symbol of Western civilization's origins and as a place where young American women go to make love. The history of Roman treachery is repeated in a pale and humorous parody.

Consider the story of Great Aunt Harriet, a story that Grace Ansley first told to Alida when they were girls: Great Aunt Harriet seems to have committed "fratricide," as it were, by sending her rival—her sister—to her death of Roman fever. Now we also see that the story itself—a cautionary tale—has a specific function for different sets of women. As Mrs. Slade explains,

> "what different things Rome stands for to each generation of travellers. To our grandmothers, Roman fever; to our mothers, sentimental dangers— and how we used to be guarded!—to our daughters, no more dangers than the middle of Main Street. They don't know it—but how much they're missing!" (15)

For the mothers of Grace Ansley and Alida Slade, the tale functions to frighten the girls, to prevent them from going out and catching Roman fever or, what might be worse, going out and catching a Roman—or being caught by one. Grace Ansley uses this story in another way: since Roman fever no longer exists, the ruins seem to have been overrun with tenacious lovers. In other words, when Grace narrated the story of Aunt Harriet to Alida, she was attempting to warn her symbolically; the story, thus, is an apotropaic, a curse, a warning. However, when Alida reminds Grace that Grace had used the same warning against her, Alida is invoking that dangerous, destructive situation again. Alida means this memory to be a taunt since she believes Grace had been cheated, thwarted. Thwarted from what? From exercising her will in the only way women are allowed: reproductive choice.

The letter that Alida forges, too, has a similar place and function in the story, precisely because Alida seems to have cleverly turned the story against Grace. The same story has several different narrative uses depending on the situation: in the first case, the story is intended to discipline daughters. In the second instance, the story is used as a vehicle for Grace's aggression against her rival, Alida. In the third instance, the story is reappropriated by Alida in order to thwart—if not kill—her rival. In fact, the very act of storytelling on the terrace after dusk recalls the various levels of treachery that belong to their shared history. In any case, Alida writes fiction, the letter, which, given its context, has a powerful effect. She usurps Delphin's voice—that, too, is a kind of violence against herself and Grace—in order to trick her rival. And the trick would have been perfect had Grace not answered the letter to a willing Delphin. But that is precisely what a rival cannot imagine, the reciprocity of the act, a reply or counterthrust, the ultimate act of re-membering what had been dis-membered by the letter. Alida was too clever, perhaps. The counterthrust comes, then, years later when Grace has found a context within which to reply: "'I had Barbara'" (24). And at this point, we understand the nature of the displaced rivalry between the daughters, Babs and Jenny, who engage in the same kind of rivalry for a suitor in Europe.

Why women are moved to behave in this way is a question Wharton seems to be asking in her late fiction. Since the entirety of the story plays itself out against the backdrop of "the great accumulated wreckage of passion and splendour" in Rome, I am suggesting that Wharton means to put into some relation the fortunes of civilizations and the fortunes of these two families, the Slades and the Ansleys (17). The story insists, first of all, that our own myth of origins—from which we get all of our founding or inaugurating force, our authority—is inherently arbitrary. Like the stories we tell about ourselves, the foundations of civilization are always at risk, unsettled, in transition. Wharton's fiction, therefore, participates in a kind of demystification (destructive) process: both women believe their own inaugural myths about their daughters. Alida believes that her daughter is the only offspring of the man she loved. Grace believes that Delphin initiated the events that would result in the birth of Babs, that he "loved" Grace. Both are wrong about the order of things, and Wharton uncovers a profound emptiness at the heart of history since chance seems to rule. This makes Wharton's art not only profoundly disturbing, but also strictly in opposition to the patriarchal powers that benefit from the disorder of civilization by insisting on their names as a conservative force. The rub is that patriarchal powers sustain themselves in the very events that threaten them.

When the two women stare down at the Palatine, Mrs. Slade claims it to be the "most beautiful view in the world" (10). Mrs. Ansley replies that it will always be "'to me' . . . with so slight a stress on the 'me' that Mrs. Slade, though she noticed it, wondered if it were not merely accidental, like the random underlinings of old-fashioned letters" (10). That she wonders but dismisses Mrs. Ansley's stress or emphasis on "me" suggests that she does not really read their situation accurately. She is far more interested in her own pronouncements than in dialogue. What is more, Mrs. Ansley recognizes that there is an essential ignorance about each other, about their own daughters in fact: "'I've come to the conclusion that I don't in the least know what [our daughters] are. . . . And perhaps we didn't know much more about each other'" (11).

In fact, they "reflected how little they knew each other," but those reflections do not stop them from creating necessary fictions about the other:

> Each one, of course, had a label ready to attach to the other's name; Mrs. Delphin Slade, for instance, would have told herself, or any one who asked her, that Mrs. Horace Ansley, twenty-five years ago, had been exquisitely lovely—no, you wouldn't believe it, would you? . . . Good-looking, irreproachable, exemplary. (12)

That respectability, however, conceals the very disorder that gives respectability rational motivation. Mrs. Ansley manipulates appearances so that no one suspects that her exemplary marriage conceals an illegitimate child. Until the moment of the story's events, Mrs. Ansley behaves as a sort of sexual fugitive, which demonstrates the degree that she has internalized the social norms she eventually renounces. Even a moment of confession such as the last line in the story does not correct Grace's pretense for twenty-five years.

Indeed, after the deaths of Horace Ansley and Delphin Slade, Mrs. Slade especially feels the loss of her social status: "being *the* Slade's widow was a dullish business. . . . In the living up to such a husband all her faculties had been engaged" (13). From the time Mrs. Slade appropriates Delphin's voice in the letter she writes to Grace, she does not escape inscription into a world that makes her a social appendage to her husband. Such a state of affairs virtually assures that Alida's social and mental development would remain profoundly limited. In fact, what Mrs. Slade intimates, and is infuriated by, is Mrs. Ansley's pity for her: "Mrs. Ansley had always been rather sorry for her . . ." (14). Hence, the women continue in this round of petty suspicion and judgment: "So these two ladies visualized each other, each through the wrong end of her little telescope" (14). Which is to say, both Mrs. Slade and Mrs. Ansley see a reduced version of the other and of their social situations. In this limited vision, then, they do not see that their violence to each other belongs, as Wharton suggests, to the violence women have engaged in to force a place for themselves in society, a violence resident at the center of Western civilization. The surprise of the story demonstrates how hopelessly enmeshed they are in the fictions about women's place, the fictions their mothers told, for instance the one that Great Aunt Harriet enacted when she arranged for the death of her sister, her rival.

The "Memento Mori" which they face in Rome is not some abstract, historical ruin for these women, but the "rune," the sign, of their own deaths—acted out so long ago when they each warned the other about Roman fever (15). Right now, however, Alida Slade is consumed with envy because she imagines that Babs, Grace's daughter, is "out to catch that young aviator—the one who's a Marchese. . . . And Jenny has no chance beside her. I know that too. I wonder if that's why Grace Ansley likes the two girls to go everywhere together?" (16). In other words, Mrs. Slade still continues to think of marriage in terms of social hierarchy, just as she had thought about her own marriage to Delphin as the mark of social superiority over her rival. Although she notices that Roman fever has changed over the years, and the girls are no longer in danger of catching malaria, she does not notice that her account of Babs and Jenny—as rivals for the same man—dooms her to a repetition of her own history. In fact, the widows are in competition once again in marrying their daughters off; Mrs. Slade, however, envies Grace Ansley her brilliant daughter. "Mrs. Slade broke off this prophetic flight with a recoil of self-disgust. There was no one of whom she had less right to think unkindly of than Grace Ansley. Would she never cure herself of envying her? Perhaps she had begun too long ago" (17). History does not change for either Mrs. Slade or Mrs. Ansley. Why envy? Mrs. Ansley had posed a sexual threat to Mrs. Slade. And sexual threats for Wharton's characters invite violent retributions.

What is strange about the story is that Mrs. Slade realizes she hates and envies Mrs. Ansley, but she cannot pinpoint the source of her "exasperation" (18). She badgers Grace Ansley with reminders of her sight-seeing in the Colosseum, the sight-seeing she believes resulted in her "illness." All that Mrs. Ansley can gracefully reply is that "prudent girls aren't always prudent" (19). Once again, Mrs. Slade fails as a successful reader of the runes of her own personal history. She does not interpret any of Grace Ansley's statements, but merely takes them at face value, just as she had—years ago—failed to anticipate Grace's response to Delphin's letter. Mrs. Slade explains her part in the scheme to get rid of Mrs. Ansley, but her wrath and exasperation disappear immediately; ". . . she wondered why she had ever thought there would be any satisfaction in inflicting so purposeless a wound on her friend. But she had to justify herself" (21). Neither Mrs. Slade nor Mrs. Ansley can keep herself in check any longer after twenty-five years of silence. Hence, in their discussion, they let loose with what Wharton herself calls "violence." Although Alida realizes somehow that her aggression is misdirected, she is powerless to control it.

After Grace "recovers" from Roman Fever, her mother quickly marries her off to Horace Ansley, a move Alida Slade interprets as pique, "to be able to say you got ahead of Delphin and me. Girls have such silly reasons for doing the most serious things" (23). Here, above all, Alida trivializes Grace's quick marriage to Horace. This passage underscores the sense of fragility and emptiness of human institutions, since Alida interprets marriage as just another mode of competition. She can only see the competition as an instance of jealousy; passion does not even come into the picture for her because her rivalry drowns out all other emotions.

What Mrs. Slade suspects is the dissolution of distinctions between Mrs. Ansley and herself—a fearful symmetry between the women, making each one socially interchangeable as a prospective wife for Delphin Slade. Alida must get rid of Grace for a while in order to secure Delphin's affection. Her fear is that Delphin does not see a difference between them, and what difference he does see is in Grace's favor. Ironically, both women see their origins in Delphin—the originator of the rivalry. For Delphin, it seems, one woman is as good as another; it depends on the rivalry between the women, therefore, to determine who gets the community "prize"—the husband.

Significantly, during those years of marital comfort, Alida stares out the window in surveillance of her rival. "When the drawing-room curtains in No. 20 East 73rd Street were renewed, No. 23, across the way, was always aware of it. And of all the movings, buyings, travels, anniversaries, illnesses—the tame chronicle of an estimable pair. Little of it escaped Mrs. Slade" (12). She even jokes about Mrs. Ansley, when the Slades are about to move to Wall Street: "'I'd rather live opposite a speakeasy for a change; at least one might see it raided'" (12). This joke reveals Alida's fear of what is hidden, repressed in her opposition to Mrs. Ansley.

And it is this repressed joke that these women must confront in the restaurant looking over the Palatine. The joke results from Grace Ansley's uncanny ability to manipulate signs, to "signify herself" as an utterly respectable woman when we come to know that this respectability is a sham. When Alida finally confronts Grace with the forgery of the letter, Grace retaliates by rejecting her role as representation of the respectable. Alida has always existed as sign, as wife and widow to Delphin Slade. Grace Ansley now forces her to see the tension between herself as sign and as a subject responsible for her own determination. She makes Alida feel other to herself by tearing away the veil over Babs' paternity. Alida had always wondered "'how two such exemplary characters as [Grace] and Horace had managed to produce'" an offspring as "dynamic" as Babs (16–17). Once Alida discovers that Babs is the product of Grace's and Delphin's union in Rome, she realizes that Grace has become a mysterious quantity, not the other—the woman as sign—that she had so long believed. Ironically, Alida's usurpation of Delphin's power—his voice—is a ruse, a result of the competition forced upon women as a means of escaping their identical status as signs.

Elizabeth Allen writes that, in the nineteenth century,

> women represent the culture of America, its social relations, its customs, its manners, its forms. They carry on the appearances of life which can flourish only when some civilisation has been attained. As American

> women, they must both signify the degree to which America is different
> and changing (free and easy, democratic, spontaneous, young, rich, etc.)
> and the very constants of life, the customs and forms. (19)

If women as signs represent American culture, then Grace Ansley's gesture can only mean that this character rejects the domestic harmony and opts, instead, for the scene of destruction, the scene of confrontation with the other (Alida Slade) who represents the repressions of a patriarchal culture that has infected them (like the fever itself). By throwing the whole notion of paternity in doubt, and therefore throwing up her daughter's name for grabs, she displaces herself as sign of American culture and becomes the signifier of the disruption of the proper name, of paternity, of patriarchal order in general. History as Wharton plays it out becomes a scene of destruction of the patriarchal codes by which women are conventionally signified. If the proper name, the Name-of-the-Father, is an attempt to introduce order into an inherently unstable field of social relations, then Grace Ansley's final gesture in the story invites the whirl-wind. The setting of the story itself—the site of Roman dissolution—bequeaths, as it were, the legacy of corruption against which social law is meant to legislate.

The law of culture—in this case, the father's law to which Alida clings—Grace shows to be suspect and arbitrary, but all the more powerful because it is enforced. Grace refuses to signify the "truth" of American culture (whatever that truth happens to be): its moral rectitude, its vague link with a superior cultural heritage. Instead, her confession opens up the question of the patriarchal law, forcing us to see the Roman ruins as more than just an occasion for unreflective congeniality. As Jane Gallop, after Lacan, explains,

> The legal assignation of a Father's Name to a child is meant to call a halt to
> uncertainty about the identity of the father. If the mother's femininity
> (both her sexuality and her untrustworthiness) were affirmed, the Name-
> of-the-Father would always be in doubt, always be subject to the question
> of the mother's morality. Thus the Name-of-the-Father must be arbitrar-
> ily and absolutely imposed, thereby instituting the reign of the patriarchal
> law. (39)

In her claim that she "'had Barbara,'" then, Grace threatens the symbolic order of society by exposing the arbitrary assumption Alida makes about Babs' father, not to mention the assumption about Grace's respectability.

Here is Wharton's strongest doubt about origins and respectability. The Other must be invented in order to establish the boundaries of the self as subject. This is how Mrs. Slade imagines Mrs. Ansley—as the other who poses a threat to and at the same time constitutes self-consciousness. But her triumph is only made possible by entering the conflict in the first place and defeating her "friend," another woman—the husbands dead, rest in peace.

Grace undermines the Name-of-the-Father with her claim to "immorality" in which she authors a notion of herself for Alida, even though this gesture merely follows a long conformity to patriarchal law. In this way, she disrupts the dream of power Alida has had. "Paternity cannot be perceived, proven, known with certainty; it must be instituted by judgement of the mother's word" (Gallop 47). Even the suggestion of a mother's infidelity, Gallop goes on to argue, calls into question the Name-of-the-Father since "the imaginary of chivalry, the woman's presumed honour" is the most reinforced cultural assumption (48). In this case, Alida reproduces the chivalry of Grace's honour, thereby reproducing the law of culture, the father's law.

Grace and Horace "produce" in Babs a sign that does not signify the sexual union of Grace and Horace: it can be no representation or reproduction of their union. Rather, it is a misrepresentation, a simulacrum, the reading of which threatens Alida's own comprehension of herself as social sign. Grace does not cause Alida's lifetime anxiety; rather, Alida's assumptions about her place in the social hierarchy produce her anxiety, an anxiety that in any case does not end with marriage to the man she desires, which is the purported end to the sexual-social exchange. Alida doubts the mark of privilege that marriage (the proper name) has given her as Mr. Slade's wife. She has taken this privilege up to now as "natural" rather than as an ambiguous sign of her own uncertain status. And with these doubts, Wharton calls the "ruins of history" into question and unveils history as a "rune"—a sign of doubt—which demands reinterpretation.

Wharton's short story reproduces, at the level of form, the metaphor of the inverted telescope that describes the vision of the two women: it reduces the social landscape many times over and thereby participates in the scene of destruction. As Lewis suggests, the story assiduously forgets the rancorous events of its history—the European wars—in order to focus on a specific micro-conflict taking place between two well-to-do women at the end of their active social lives (their husbands' deaths, in effect, kill them as well in the social context). But even in this forgetting, the destructive character emerges, for forgetting clears the way for new orders and new possibilities. Grace Ansley appears to represent, against the life-denying investment in conventional norms that Alida has made, a kind of life principle. She condemns the past—the tradition that has imprisoned her under the Name-of-the-Father—in order to live, to assert her own life-making principle: "I had Barbara." Just so, Wharton attempts to write a past after the fact from which culture might originate, against that origin which has given it form in traditional culture.

All along, Alida has assumed Grace to be an exemplary figure, even boring in her moral rectitude. However, Grace's final speech dashes this assumption on at least two levels. First, it proves Alida to be wrong, factually. It proves wrong, in essence, the reduction Alida has made of Grace's character, a reduction in fact sanctioned by the norms of culture that would reward such exemplary behavior. Second, it reveals the grounds of this assumption—the unwavering belief in patriarchal authority and feminine complaisance—to be empty, as fragmented as the Roman ruins themselves.

Despite Grace's transgression early in life, and despite the eventual emergence of this secret after a long silence, her society's capacity to conserve itself in the face of dissolution remains powerful. However, at the very least, Wharton's story accounts for the pragmatic costs of the conservation of a surface structure in social relations that ultimately conceals an unstable ground. Cultural origins prove to be the stuff of fiction.

## Elements of Social Change

I want to open up a new discourse on Wharton's politics about which Wharton herself (and her critics) has ostensibly been silent. Wharton's silence in the face of Hitler's rise to power drives violence—as it does in Alida Slade's case—into the unconscious. In short, Wharton deserves much more credit as an acute observer and ironist in her contemporary scene than we have yet given. On the question of Edith Wharton's social politics a few words from Horkheimer and Adorno's "Elements of Anti-Semitism" in the *Dialectic of Enlightenment* seem enlightening. Written in 1944, Horkheimer and Adorno's work can illuminate Wharton's story and the culture in which "Roman Fever" was produced.

Horkheimer and Adorno write that race

> is not a naturally specific characteristic, as the folk mystics would have it. It is a reduction to the natural, to sheer force, to that stubborn particularity which in the status quo constitutes the generality. Today race has become the self-assertion of the bourgeois individual integrated within a barbaric collective. . . . The persecution of the Jews, like any other form of persecution, is inseparable from that system of order. However successfully it may at times be concealed, force is the essential nature of this order— and we are witnessing its naked truth today. (169–70)

Horkheimer and Adorno propose that the general symbolic order cannot be separated into pieces, such as anti-Semitism, anti-feminism, racism. These prejudices are all of a piece called force. And it is this force—the negative or destructive character, as Walter Benjamin called it—which Wharton isolates in her story.

Horkheimer and Adorno speculate on the social schema necessary to produce what looks to them like ritual murder, a powerful structure against which men and women have no resources for resistance. The opportunity to express repressed anger "does not help men but panders to their urge to destroy" (170). This anger leads to a ritual sacrifice of the other, not because the other is guilty, but because of his or her sacrificial vulnerability. Horkheimer and Adorno detail a rhetoric of motives for force and violence:

> Attacking or defending blindly, the persecutor and his victim belong to the same sphere of evil. . . . Anti-Semitism is a deeply imprinted schema, a ritual of civilization; the pogroms are the true ritual murders. They demonstrate the impotence of sense, significance, and ultimately of truth—which might hold them within bounds. The idle occupation of killing confirms the stubbornness of the life to which one has to conform, and to resign oneself. (171)

This ritual of hatred is played out in "Roman Fever": Mrs. Slade resigns herself to the law of culture; Mrs. Ansley, already a transgressor against the law of morality dominant at the time, pretends invisibility and respectability. But Mrs. Slade's hatred of the life she leads is translated into her competition and hatred of Mrs. Ansley—a deflected anger from their profound (if also repressed) discomfort with the reactionary force against them. Wharton's story turns on the hatred Mrs. Slade feels for Mrs. Ansley. As Horkheimer and Adorno have it in general terms:

> the hatred felt by the led, who can never be satisfied economically or sexually, knows no bounds. Their hatred cannot be worked off because it can never be fulfilled. . . . True, personal anger in the civilized man is roused by the constraining situation: by the anger of the tormentor and of the tormented, who are indistinguishable in their grimace. (171, 182)

In other terms, Mrs. Slade's long-repressed anger is roused by being Delphin Slade's widow (a dull, confining business); the anger of the tormented—Mrs. Ansley's anger—is roused by her rival's underestimation of her resistance.

Mrs. Slade's problem is a false projection onto the other—her victim—whom she wants to reduce to an object of hatred (a hatred of a bourgeois respectability that has kept her dominated by Delphin Slade and the social world he represents). In Horkheimer and Adorno's words, she clings to her "own paranoia by participating in the collective form, and clings passionately to the objectivized, collective and confirmed forms of delusion" (197). As Martin Jay explains, paranoia is no longer personal but politicized, part of a cultural and political unconscious. Jay notes: "For Horkheimer and Adorno, then, perhaps the ultimate source of anti-Semitism and its functional equivalents is the rage against the nonidentical that characterizes the totalistic dominating impulse of western civilization" (98–99). Mrs. Slade refuses to think through to the source of her hatred for Mrs. Ansley; she does not want to acknowledge that her paranoia about Mrs. Ansley's smile or offhand comments emerges from her dis-ease with the social law she is compelled to follow. Wharton demonstrates the lack of self-examination at the heart of all social relations—between the anti-Semites and the Jews, and between these two little women here—Mrs. Slade and Mrs. Ansley, looking at each other through the wrong end of their telescopes.

For Wharton, Alida Slade's attack on difference amounts to an attack on the cultural ideology (of difference) she values. "The anger against all that is different" is at the root of Wharton's story, just as it is at the root of anti-Semitism (Horkheimer and Adorno 207).

Grace's attack on Alida's shabby morality does not change either the morality or its products in the social relations articulated by Wharton's story. We might assume, without confirmation from the narrative, that Babs will get her mate and the rigid hierarchical relations that produced the mothers' histories will continue for another generation to come. Still, life outside the text—the only life that counts—is always open to question, and we can see the dangerous, destructive potential of Wharton's fiction if we understand the text to be a kind of symbolic hand-grenade. The text does not disrupt social relations themselves so much as it undermines the supposed ground of those relations without investing in some purely imaginary space of freedom.

In "Theses on Feuerbach: XI," Marx created a practical philosophy with the imperative to change, not merely interpret, the world. Wharton's fictions suggest this imperative to change. I suggest that we cannot take at face value Wharton's pronouncements about her turning her back on politics. She was elated that Aldous Huxley recognized in *Twilight Sleep* a sharp criticism of Fordian culture and the America of fads and cults. Wharton deserves the same credit for articulating the destructive character of a cultural misogyny that led all too quickly to what she saw in 1933, as she writes in a September 20 letter to Gaillard Lapsley, as "a world . . . whizzing down so crazily to the everlasting abyss."

## Works Cited

Allen, Elizabeth. *A Woman's Place in the Novels of Henry James.* New York: St. Martin's, 1984.

Benjamin, Walter. "The Destructive Character." *One-Way Street.* Trans. Edmund Jephcott and Kingsley Shorter. London: NLB, 1979. 157–59.

Dobkowski, Michael N. "American Anti-Semitism: A Reinterpretation." *American Quarterly* 29.2 (1977): 166–81.

Frank, Florence Kiper. "The Presentment of the Jew in American Fiction." *Bookman* LXXI (1930): 270–75.

Gallop, Jane. *The Daughter's Seduction: Feminism and Psychoanalysis.* Ithaca: Cornell UP, 1982.

Horkheimer, Max, and Theodor Adorno. "Elements of Anti-Semitism." *Dialectic of Enlightenment.* Trans. John Cumming. New York: Continuum, 1982. 168–208.

Jay, Martin. *Permanent Exiles: Essays on the Intellectual Migration from Germany to America.* New York: Columbia UP, 1985.

Kermode, Frank. *The Sense of an Ending.* New York: Oxford UP, 1967.

Koonz, Claudia. *Mothers in the Fatherland.* New York: St. Martin's, 1987.

Lewis, R.W.B. *Edith Wharton: A Biography.* New York: Harper, 1975.

———. "Introduction" to *The Collected Short Stories of Edith Wharton.* Vol. I. New York: Scribner, 1968. vii–xxv.

Liptzin, Solomon. *The Jew in American Literature.* New York: Bloch, 1966.

Marx, Karl, and Frederick Engels. *The German Ideology.* 1846. Ed. C. J. Arthur. New York: International, 1978.

Ozick, Cynthia. "The Lesson of the Master." *Art & Ardor.* New York: Dutton, 1984. 291–97.

Sundquist, Eric. *Home as Found: Authority and Genealogy in Nineteenth-Century American Literature.* Baltimore: Johns Hopkins UP, 1979.

Wharton, Edith. *The House of Mirth.* 1905. New York: Berkley, 1981.

———. Manuscript and letter collection in Beinecke Library, Yale University, New Haven.

———. *Foman Fever and Other Stories.* New York: Scribner, 1964.

Wolff, Cynthia Griffin. *A Feast of Words.* New York: Oxford UP, 1977.

# Steven Carter

## Tolstoy's "The Death of Ivan Ilyich" 2003

In Leo Tolstoy's "The Death of Ivan Ilyich," the narrator uses threadbare French phrases to define the lifestyle of the cozy, conforming, bourgeois protagonist Ivan.

Like many of his well-to-do fellows, Ivan is a *bon enfant* ("jolly good fellow"); his young manhood is summed up in a phrase that applies to everyone: *il faut que jeunesse se passe* ("youth must pass"); his wife's aberrations he attributes vaguely to *gaite de coeur* ("lightheartedness"); for his house, he chooses only antiques *comme il faut* ("as it should be"); and so on. Just when things seem to be going particularly well in Ivan's life, he slips off a ladder and bumps his left side on a doorknob, incurring an injury that will eventually kill him. From this moment on—from the moment that Ivan begins to suffer—all clichés suddenly disappear from the text. Why?

When the narrator observes that "Ivan Ilyich's life had been most simple and most ordinary and therefore most terrible," he indicates that not only can Ivan's life be classified as a tissue of clichés, but also that Ivan *is* a cliché, a human cipher dutifully plodding through a miasma of works and days (833). Until he begins to die, in fact, Ivan thinks of death itself in generalized terms:

> The syllogism he has learned from Kiesewetter's Logic: "Caius is a man, men are mortal, therefore Caius is mortal," had always seemed to him correct as applied to Caius, but certainly not as applied to himself. [ . . .] Caius really was mortal, and it was right for him to die; but for me, little Vanya, Ivan Ilyich, with all my thoughts and emotions, it's altogether a different matter. It cannot be that I ought to die. That would be too terrible. (854–55)

As long as he thinks of death in this way, it never occurs to Ivan that it is his entire life, not simply his dying, that is "most terrible." But then, in the story's supreme moment of irony, death, the syllogistic cliché that this callow *bon enfant* cannot apply to himself, miraculously transforms him into a unique individual. On his deathbed, Ivan becomes a person, not a cipher *malgre lui* ("in spite of himself"). For the act of dying suddenly puts him in mind of a host of fevered memories, which concretizes him as an individual:

> He had been little Vanya, with a mama and a papa, with Mitya and Voldya, and with all the joys, grief and delights of childhood. What did Caius know of the smell of that striped leather ball Vanya had been so fond of? Had Caius kissed his mother's hand? [ . . .] Had he rioted [ . . .] at school when the pastry was bad? (855)

As he physically weakens, Ivan's self-awakening—"Yes, it [his lifestyle] was not all the right thing"—alienates him from his family, which continues to treat him indifferently to the end (872). On the other hand, the nearer to death Ivan gets—and the more tedious his sufferings become to his wife and children—the more interesting he becomes to the reader. No longer a human cliché, Ivan achieves selfhood in the last few seconds of his life. For the transformed Ivan, death is a blessed event: "What joy!" (873)

# Judith Fetterley

## *A Rose for "A Rose for Emily"* 1978

In "A Rose for Emily" the grotesque reality implicit in Aylmer's idealization of Georgiana becomes explicit. Justifying Faulkner's use of the grotesque has been a major concern of critics who have written on the story. If, however, one approaches "A Rose for Emily" from a feminist perspective, one notices that the grotesque aspects of the story are a result of its violation of the expectations generated by the conventions of sexual politics. The ending shocks us not simply by its hint of necrophilia; more shocking is the fact that it is a woman who provides the hint. It is one thing for Poe to spend his nights in the tomb of Annabel Lee and another thing for Miss Emily Grierson to deposit a strand of iron-gray hair on the pillow beside the rotted corpse of Homer Barron. Further, we do not expect to discover that a woman has murdered a man. The conventions of sexual politics have familiarized us with the image of Georgiana nobly accepting death at her husband's hand. To reverse this "natural" pattern inevitably produces the grotesque.

Faulkner, however, is not interested in invoking the kind of grotesque which is the consequence of reversing the clichés of sexism for the sake of a cheap thrill; that is left to writers like Mickey Spillane. (Indeed, Spillane's ready willingness to capitalize on the shock value provided by the image of woman as killer in *I, the Jury* suggests, by contrast, how little such a sexist gambit is Faulkner's intent.) Rather, Faulkner invokes the grotesque in order to illuminate and define the true nature of the conventions on which it depends. "A Rose for Emily" is a story not of a conflict between the South and the North or between the old order and the new; it is a story of the patriarchy North and South, new and old, and of the sexual conflict within it. As Faulkner himself has implied, it is a story of a woman victimized and betrayed by the system of sexual politics, who nevertheless has discovered, within the structures that victimize her, sources of power for herself. If "The Birthmark" is the story of how to murder your wife and get away with it, "A Rose for Emily" is the story of how to murder your gentleman caller and get away with it. Faulkner's story is an analysis of how men's attitudes toward women turn back upon themselves; it is a demonstration of the thesis that it is impossible to oppress without in turn being oppressed, it is impossible to kill without creating the conditions for your own murder. "A Rose for Emily" is the story of a *lady* and of her revenge for that grotesque identity.

"When Miss Emily Grierson died, our whole town went to her funeral." The public and communal nature of Emily's funeral, a festival that brings the town together, clarifying its social relationships and revitalizing its sense of the past, indicates her central role in Jefferson. Alive, Emily is town property and the subject of shared speculation; dead, she is town history and the subject of legend. It is her value as a symbol, however obscure and however ambivalent, of something that is of central significance to the identity of Jefferson and to the meaning of its history that compels the narrator to assume a communal voice to tell her story. For Emily, like Georgiana, is a man-made object, a cultural artifact, and what she is reflects and defines the culture that has produced her.

The history the narrator relates to us reveals Jefferson's continuous emotional involvement with Emily. Indeed, though she shuts herself up in a house which she rarely leaves and which no one enters, her furious isolation is in direct proportion to the town's obsession with her. Like Georgiana, she is the object of incessant attention; her every act is immediately consumed by the town for gossip and seized on to justify their interference in her affairs. Her private life becomes a public document that the town folk feel free to interpret at will, and they are alternately curious, jealous, spiteful, pitying, partisan, proud, disapproving, admiring, and vindicated. Her funeral is not simply a communal ceremony; it is also the climax of their invasion of her private life and the logical extension of their voyeuristic attitude toward her. Despite the narrator's demurral, getting inside Emily's house is the all-consuming desire of the town's population, both male and female; while the men may wait a little longer, their motive is still prurient curiosity: "Already we knew that there was one room in that region above stairs which no one had seen in forty years, and which would have to be forced. They waited until Miss Emily was decently in the ground before they opened it."

In a context in which the overtones of violation and invasion are so palpable, the word "decently" has that ironic ring which gives the game away. When the men finally do break down the door, they find that Emily has satisfied their prurience with a vengeance and in doing so has created for them a mirror image of themselves. The true nature of Emily's relation to Jefferson is contained in the analogies between what those who break open that room see in it and what has brought them there to see it. The perverse, violent, and grotesque aspects of the sight of Homer Barron's rotted corpse in a room decked out for a bridal and now faded and covered in dust reflects back to them the perverseness of their own prurient interest in Emily, the violence implicit in their continued invasions of her life, and the grotesqueness of the symbolic artifact they have made of her—their monument, their idol, their lady. Thus, the figure that Jefferson places at the center of its legendary history does indeed contain the clue to the meaning of that history—a history which began long before Emily's funeral and long before Homer Barron's disappearance or appearance and long before Colonel Sartoris' fathering of edicts and remittances. It is recorded in that emblem which lies at the heart of the town's memory and at the heart of patriarchal culture: "We had long thought of them as a tableau, Miss Emily a slender figure in white in the background, her father a spraddled silhouette in the foreground, his back to her and clutching a horsewhip, the two of them framed by the back-flung front door."

The importance of Emily's father in shaping the quality of her life is insistent throughout the story. Even in her death the force of his presence is felt; above her dead body sits "the crayon face of her father musing profoundly," symbolic of the degree to which he has dominated and shadowed her life, "as if that quality of her father which had thwarted her woman's life so many times had been too virulent and too furious to die." The violence of this consuming relationship is made explicit in the imagery of the tableau. Although the violence is apparently directed outward—the upraised horsewhip against the would-be suitor—the real object of it is the woman–daughter, forced into the background and dominated by the phallic figure of the spraddled father whose back is turned on her and who prevents her from getting out at the same time that he prevents them from getting in. Like Georgiana's spatial confinement in "The Birthmark," Emily's is a metaphor for her psychic confinement: her identity is determined by the constructs of her father's mind, and she can no more escape from his creation of her as "a slender figure in white" than she can escape his house.

What is true for Emily in relation to her father is equally true for her in relation to Jefferson: her status as a lady is a cage from which she cannot escape. To them she is always *Miss* Emily; she is never referred to and never thought of as otherwise. In omitting her title from his, Faulkner emphasizes the point that the real violence done to Emily is in making her a "Miss"; the omission is one of his roses for her. Because she is *Miss* Emily *Grierson*, Emily's father dresses her in white, places her in the background, and drives away her suitors. Because she is Miss Emily Grierson, the town invests her with that communal significance which makes her the object of their obsession and the subject of their incessant scrutiny. And because she is a lady, the town is able to impose a particular code of behavior on her ("But there were still others, older people, who said that even grief could not cause a real lady to forget *noblesse oblige*") and to see in her failure to live up to that code an excuse for interfering in her life. As a lady, Emily is venerated, but veneration results in the more telling emotions of envy and spite: "It was another link between the gross, teeming world and the high and mighty Griersons"; "People . . . believed that the Griersons held themselves a little too high for what they really were." The violence implicit in the desire to see the monument fall and reveal itself for clay suggests the violence inherent in the original impulse to venerate.

The violence behind veneration is emphasized through another telling emblem in the story. Emily's position as an hereditary obligation upon the town dates from "that day in 1894 when Colonel Sartoris, the mayor—he who fathered the edict that no Negro woman should appear on the streets without an apron on—remitted her taxes, the dispensation dating from the death of her father on into perpetuity." The conjunction of these two actions in the same syntactic unit is crucial, for it insists on their essential similarity. It indicates that the impulse to exempt is analogous to the desire to restrict, and that what appears to be a kindness or an act of veneration is in fact an insult. Sartoris' remission of Emily's taxes is a public declaration of the fact that a lady is not considered to be, and hence not allowed or enabled to be, economically independent (consider, in this connection, Emily's lessons in china painting; they are a latter-day version of Sartoris' "charity" and a brilliant image of Emily's economic uselessness). His act is a public statement of the fact that a lady, if she is to survive, must have either husband or father, and that, because Emily has neither, the town must assume responsibility for her. The remission of taxes that defines Emily's status dates from the death of her father, and she is handed over from one patron to the next, the town instead of husband taking on the role of father. Indeed, the use of the word "fathered" in describing Sartoris' behavior as mayor underlines the fact that his chivalric attitude toward Emily is simply a subtler and more dishonest version of her father's horsewhip.

The narrator is the last of the patriarchs who take upon themselves the burden of defining Emily's life, and his violence toward her is the most subtle of all. His tone of incantatory reminiscence and nostalgic veneration seems free of the taint of horse-whip and edict. Yet a thoroughgoing contempt for the "ladies" who spy and pry and gossip out of their petty jealousy and curiosity is one of the clearest strands in the narrator's consciousness. Emily is exempted from the general indictment because she is a *real* lady—that is, eccentric, slightly crazy, obsolete, a "stubborn and coquettish decay," absurd but indulged; "dear, inescapable, impervious, tranquil, and perverse"; indeed, anything and everything but human.

Not only does "A Rose for Emily" expose the violence done to a woman by mak-ing her a lady; it also explores the particular form of power the victim gains from this position and can use on those who enact this violence. "A Rose for Emily" is con-cerned with the consequences of violence for both the violated and the violators. One of the most striking aspects of the story is the disparity between Miss Emily Grierson and the Emily to whom Faulkner gives his rose in ironic imitation of the chivalric be-havior the story exposes. The form of Faulkner's title establishes a camaraderie be-tween author and protagonist and signals that a distinction must be made between the story Faulkner is telling and the story the narrator is telling. This distinction is of major importance because it suggests, of course, that the narrator, looking through a patriarchal lens, does not see Emily at all but rather a figment of his own imagination created in conjunction with the cumulative imagination of the town. Like Ellison's in-visible man, nobody sees *Emily*. And because nobody sees *her*, she can literally get away with murder. Emily is characterized by her ability to understand and utilize the power that accrues to her from the fact that men do not see her but rather their con-cept of her: "'I have no taxes in Jefferson. Colonel Sartoris explained it to me. . . . Tobe! . . . Show these gentlemen out.'" Relying on the conventional assumptions about ladies who are expected to be neither reasonable nor in touch with reality, Emily presents an impregnable front that vanquishes the men "horse and foot, just as she had vanquished their fathers thirty years before." In spite of their "modern" ideas, this new generation, when faced with Miss Emily, are as much bound by the code of gentlemanly behavior as their fathers were ("They rose when she entered"). This code gives Emily a power that renders the gentlemen unable to function in a situation in which a lady neither sits down herself nor asks them to. They are brought to a "stumbling halt" and can do nothing when confronted with her refusal to engage in rational discourse. Their only recourse in the face of such eccentricity is to engage in behavior unbecoming to gentlemen, and Emily can count on their continuing to see themselves as gentlemen and her as a lady and on their returning a verdict of helpless noninterference.

It is in relation to Emily's disposal of Homer Barron, however, that Faulkner demonstrates most clearly the power of conventional assumptions about the nature of ladies to blind the town to what is going on and to allow Emily to murder with im-punity. When Emily buys the poison, it never occurs to anyone that she intends to use it on Homer, so strong is the presumption that ladies when jilted commit suicide, not murder. And when her house begins to smell, the women blame it on the eccentricity of having a man servant rather than a woman, "as if a man—any man—could keep a kitchen properly." And then they hint that her eccentricity may have shaded over into madness, "remembering how old lady Wyatt, her great aunt, had gone completely crazy at last." The presumption of madness, that preeminently female response to be- reavement, can be used to explain away much in the behavior of ladies whose activi- ties seem a bit odd.

But even more pointed is what happens when the men try not to explain but to do something about the smell: "'Dammit, sir,' Judge Stevens said, 'will you accuse a lady to her face of smelling bad?'" But if a lady cannot be told that she smells, then the cause of the smell cannot be discovered and so her crime is "perfect." Clearly, the as- sumptions behind the Judge's outraged retort go beyond the myth that ladies are out of touch with reality. His outburst insists that it is the responsibility of gentlemen to make them so. Ladies must not be confronted with facts; they must be shielded from all that is unpleasant. Thus Colonel Sartoris remits Emily's taxes with a palpably ab- surd story, designed to protect her from an awareness of her poverty and her depen- dence on charity, and to protect him from having to confront her with it. And thus Judge Stevens will not confront Emily with the fact that her house stinks, though she is living in it and can hardly be unaware of the odor. Committed as they are to the myth that ladies and bad smells cannot coexist, these gentlemen insulate themselves from reality. And by defining a lady as a subhuman and hence sublegal entity, they have created a situation their laws can't touch. They have made it possible for Emily to be extra-legal. "'Why, of course,' the druggist said, 'If that's what you want. But the law requires you to tell what you are going to use it for.' Miss Emily just stared at him, her head tilted back in order to look him eye for eye, until he looked away and went and got the arsenic and wrapped it up." And, finally, they have created a situation in which they become the criminals: "So the next night, after midnight, four men crossed Miss Emily's lawn and slunk about the house like burglars." Above them, "her upright torso motionless as that of an idol," sits Emily, observing them act out their charade of chivalry. As they leave, she confronts them with the reality they are trying to protect her from: she turns on the light so that they may see her watching them. One can only wonder at the fact, and regret, that she didn't call the sheriff and have them arrested for trespassing.

Not only is "A Rose for Emily" a supreme analysis of what men do to women by making them ladies; it is also an exposure of how this act in turn defines and recoils upon men. This is the significance of the dynamic that Faulkner establishes between Emily and Jefferson. And it is equally the point of the dynamic implied between the tableau of Emily and her father and the tableau which greets the men who break down the door of that room in the region above the stairs. When the would-be "suit- ors" finally get into her father's house, they discover the consequences of his oppres- sion of her, for the violence contained in the rotted corpse of Homer Barron is the mirror image of the violence represented in the tableau, the back-flung front door flung back with a vengeance. Having been consumed by her father, Emily in turn feeds off Homer Barron, becoming, after his death, suspiciously fat. Or, to put it an- other way, it is as if, after her father's death, she has reversed his act of incorporating her by incorporating and becoming him, metamorphosed from the slender figure in white to the obese figure in black whose hair is "a vigorous iron-gray, like the hair of an active man." She has taken into herself the violence in him which thwarted her and has reenacted it upon Homer Barron.

That final encounter, however, is not simply an image of the reciprocity of violence. Its power of definition also derives from its grotesqueness, which makes finally explicit the grotesqueness that has been latent in the description of Emily throughout the story: "Her skeleton was small and spare; perhaps that was why what would have been merely plumpness in another was obesity in her. She looked bloated, like a body long submerged in motionless water, and of that pallid hue. Her eyes, lost in the fatty ridges of her face, looked like two small pieces of coal pressed into a lump of dough." The impact of this description depends on the contrast it establishes between Emily's reality as a fat, bloated figure in black and the conventional image of a lady—expectations that are fostered in the town by its emblematic memory of Emily as a slender figure in white and in us by the narrator's tone of romantic invocation and by the passage itself. Were she not expected to look so different, were her skeleton not small and spare, Emily would not be so grotesque. Thus, the focus is on the grotesqueness that results when stereotypes are imposed upon reality. And the implication of this focus is that the real grotesque is the stereotype itself. If Emily is both lady and grotesque, then the syllogism must be completed thus: the idea of a lady is grotesque. So Emily is metaphor and mirror for the town of Jefferson; and when, at the end, the town folk finally discover who and what she is, they have in fact encountered who and what they are.

Despite similarities of focus and vision, "A Rose for Emily" is more implicitly feminist than "The Birthmark." For one thing, Faulkner does not have Hawthorne's compulsive ambivalence; one is not invited to misread "A Rose for Emily" as one is invited to misread "The Birthmark." Thus, the interpretation of "The Birthmark" that sees it as a story of misguided idealism, despite its massive oversights, nevertheless *works*; while the efforts to read "A Rose for Emily" as a parable of the relations between North and South, or as a conflict between an old order and a new, or as a story about the human relation to Time, don't work because the attempt to make Emily representative of such concepts stumbles over the fact that woman's condition is not the "human" condition. To understand Emily's experience requires a primary awareness of the fact that she is a woman.

But, more important, Faulkner provides us with an image of retaliation. Unlike Georgiana, Emily does not simply acquiesce; she prefers to murder rather than to die. In this respect she is a welcome change from the image of woman as willing victim that fills the pages of our literature, and whose other face is the ineffective fulminations of Dame Van Winkle. Nevertheless, Emily's action is still reaction. "A Rose for Emily" exposes the poverty of a situation in which turnabout is the only possibility and in which one's acts are neither self-generated nor self-determined but are simply a response to and a reflection of forces outside oneself. Though Emily may be proud, strong, and indomitable, her murder of Homer Barron is finally an indication of the severely limited nature of the power women can wrest from the system that oppresses them. Aylmer's murder of Georgiana is an indication of men's absolute power over women; it is an act performed in the complete security of his ability to legitimize it as a noble and human pursuit. Emily's act has no such context. It is possible only because it can be kept secret; and it can be kept secret only at the cost of exploiting her image as a lady. Furthermore, Aylmer murders Georgiana in order to get rid of her; Emily murders Homer Barron in order to have him.

Patriarchal culture is based to a considerable extent on the argument that men and women are made for each other and on the conviction that "masculinity" and "femininity" are the natural reflection of that divinely ordained complement. Yet, if one reads "The Birthmark" and "A Rose for Emily" as analyses of the consequences of a massive differentiation of everything according to sex, one sees that in reality a sexist culture is one in which men and women are not simply incompatible but murderously so. Aylmer murders Georgiana because he must at any cost get rid of the woman; Emily murders Homer Barron because she must at any cost get a man. The two stories define the disparity between cultural myth and cultural reality, and they suggest that in this disparity is the ultimate grotesque.

# Elizabeth Hardwick

## Bartleby in Manhattan                                1981

While preparing some lectures on the subject of New York City, that is, the present landscape in which an astonishing number of people still live, sustaining as they do the numerical sensationalism that qualifies New York as *one* of the great cities of the world, if not the *greatest,* the orotund *greatest* being reserved with an almost Biblical authority for our country as a whole; and also on "old New York," with its intimidating claim to vanished manners and social dominion, its hereditary furnishings of aggressive simplicity and shy opulence which would prove an unsteady bulwark against the flooding of the *nouveau riche*—during this reading I thought to look again at Melville's story "Bartleby, the Scrivener," because it carried the subtitle "A Story of Wall Street."

There did not appear to be much of Wall Street in this troubling composition of 1853 about a peculiar "copyist" who is hired by a "snug" little legal firm in the Wall Street district. No, nothing of the daunting, hungry "Manhattanism" of Whitman: "O an intense life, full to repletion and varied! / The life of the theatre, bar-room, huge hotel, for me!" Nothing of railroad schemes, cornering the gold market, or of that tense exclusion to be brought about by mistakes and follies in the private life which were to be the drama of "old New York" in Edith Wharton's novels. Bartleby seemed to me to be not its subtitle, but most of all an example of the superior uses of dialogue in fiction, here a strange, bone-thin dialogue that nevertheless serves to reveal a profoundly moving tragedy.

(Melville's brothers were lawyers, with offices at 10 Wall Street; a close friend was employed in a law office and seems to have been worn down by "incessant writing." About the story itself, some critics have thought of "Bartleby" as a masterly presentation of schizophrenic deterioration; others have seen the story as coming out of the rejection of Melville by the reading public and his own inability to be a popular "copyist." Some have found in the story the life of Wall Street, "walling in" the creative American spirit. All of these ideas are convincing and important. "Bartleby" may be one or all of these. My own reading is largely concerned with the nature of Bartleby's short sentences.)

Out of some sixteen thousand words, Bartleby, the cadaverous and yet blazing center of all our attention, speaks only thirty-seven short lines, more than a third of which are a repetition of a single line, the celebrated, the "famous," I think one might call it, retort: *I would prefer not to.* No, "retort" will not do, representing as it does too great a degree of active mutuality for Bartleby—*reply* perhaps.

Bartleby's reduction of language is of an expressiveness literally limitless. Few characters in fiction, if indeed any exist, have been able to say all they wish in so striking, so nearly speechless a manner. The work is, of course, a sort of fable of inanition, and returning to it, as I did, mindful of the old stone historical downtown and the new, insatiable necropolis of steel and glass, lying on the vegetation of the participial *declining* this and that, I found it possible to wish that "Bartleby, the Scrivener" was just itself, a masterpiece without the challenge of its setting, Wall Street. Still, the setting does not flee the mind, even if it does not quite bind itself either, the way unloaded furniture seems immediately bound to its doors and floors.

Melville has written his story in a cheerful, confident, rather optimistic, Dickensian manner. Or at least that is the manner in which it begins. In the law office, for instance, the copyists and errand-boy are introduced with their Dickensian *tics* and their tic-names: Nippers, Turkey, and Ginger Nut. An atmosphere of comedy, of small, amusing, busy particulars, surrounds Bartleby and his large, unofficial (not suited to an office) articulations, which are nevertheless clerkly and even, perhaps, clerical.

The narrator, a mild man of the law with a mild Wall Street business, is a "rather elderly man," as he says of himself at the time of putting down his remembrances of Bartleby. On the edge of retirement, the lawyer begins to think about that "singular set of men," the law-copyists or scriveners he has known in his thirty years of practice. He notes that he has seen nothing of these men in print and, were it not for the dominating memory of Bartleby, he might have told lighthearted professional anecdotes, something perhaps like the anecdotes of servants come and gone, such as we find in the letters of Jane Carlyle, girls from the country who are not always unlike the Turkeys, Nippers, and Ginger Nuts.

The lawyer understands that no biography of Bartleby is possible because "no materials exist," and indeed the work is not a character sketch and not a section of a "life," even though it ends in death. Yet the device of memory is not quite the way it works out, because each of Bartleby's thirty-seven lines, with their riveting variations, so slight as to be almost painful to the mind taking note of them, must be produced at the right pace and accompanied by the requests that occasion them. At a certain point, Bartleby must "gently disappear behind the screen," which, in a way, is a present rather than a past. In the end, Melville's structure is magical because the lawyer creates Bartleby by *allowing* him to be, a decision of nicely unprofessional impracticality. The competent, but scarcely strenuous, office allows Bartleby, although truly the allowance arises out of the fact that the lawyer is a far better man than he knows himself to be. And he is taken by surprise to learn of his tireless curiosity about the incurious ghost, Bartleby.

The lawyer has a "snug business among rich men's bonds and mortgages and title deeds," rather than the more dramatic actions before juries (a choice that would not be defining today). He has his public sinecures and when they are officially abolished he feels a bit of chagrin, but no vehemence. He recognizes the little vanities he has accumulated along the way, one of which is that he has done business with John Jacob Astor. And he likes to utter the name "for it hath a rounded and orbicular sound to it and rings like unto bullion." These are the thoughts of a man touched by the comic spirit, the one who will be touched for the first time in his life, and by way of his dealings with Bartleby, by "overpowering, stinging melancholy . . . a fraternal melancholy."

A flurry of copying demand had led the lawyer to run an advertisement which brought to his door a young man, Bartleby, a person sedate, "pallidly neat, pitiably respectable." Bartleby is taken on and placed at a desk which "originally had afforded a lateral view of certain grimy backyards and bricks, but which owing to subsequent erections, commanded at present no view at all." This is a suitable place for Bartleby, who does not require views of the outside world and who has no "views" of the other kind, that is, no opinions beyond his adamantine assertion of his own feelings, if feelings they are; he has, as soon becomes clear, his hard pebbles of response with their sumptuous, taciturn resonance.

Bartleby begins to copy without pause, as if "long famishing for something to copy." This is observed by the lawyer, who also observes that he himself feels no pleasure in it since it is done "silently, palely, mechanically." On the third day of employment, Bartleby appears, the genuine Bartleby, the one who gives utterance. His first utterance is like the soul escaping from the body, as in medieval drawings.

The tedious proofreading of the clerk's copy is for accuracy done in collaboration with another person, and it is the lawyer himself who calls out to Bartleby for assistance in the task. The laconic, implacable signature is at hand, the mysterious signature that cannot be interpreted and cannot be misunderstood. Bartleby replies, *I would prefer not to.*

The pretense of disbelief provides the occasion for *I would prefer not to* soon to be repeated three times and "with no uneasiness, anger, impatience or impertinence." By the singularity of refusal, the absence of "because" or of the opening up of some possibly alternating circumstance, this negative domination seizes the story like a sudden ambush in the streets.

Bartleby's "I" is of such a completeness that it does not require support. He possesses his "I" as if it were a visible part of the body, the way ordinary men possess a thumb. In his sentence he encloses his past, present, and future, himself, all there is.

His statement is positive indeed and the *not* is less important than the "I," because the "not" refers to the presence of others, to the world, inevitably making suggestions the "I" does not encompass.

Bartleby would prefer not to read proof with his employer; a little later he would prefer not to examine his own quadruplicate copyings with the help of the other clerks; he would prefer not to answer or to consider that this communal proof-reading is labor-saving and customary. About his "mulish vagary"—no answer.

As we read the story we are certain that, insofar as Bartleby himself is concerned, there is nothing to be thought of as "interesting" in his statement. There is no co-quetry; it is merely candid, final, inflexible. Above all it is not "personal"; that is, his objection is not to the collaborators themselves and not to the activity of proofread-ing, indeed no more repetitive than daylong copying. The reply is not personal and it is not invested with "personality." And this the kind and now violently curious and enduring lawyer cannot believe. He will struggle throughout the tale to fill up the hole, to wonder greatly, to prod as he can, in search of "personality." And the hole, the chasm, or better the "cistern," one of the lawyer's words for the view outside Bartleby's desk, will not be filled.

What began as a comedy, a bit of genre actually, ends as tragedy. But like Bartleby himself it is difficult for the reader to supply adjectives. Is Bartleby mysterious; is his nature dark, angular, subterranean? You are deterred by Bartleby's mastery from competing with him by your command of the adjective. He is overwhelmingly affect-ing to the emotions of the lawyer and the reader, but there is no hint that he is occu-pied with lack, disuse, failure, inadequacy. If one tries to imagine Bartleby alone, without the office, what is to be imagined? True, he is always alone, in an utter loneli-ness that pierces the lawyer's heart when he soon finds that Bartleby has no home at all but is living in the office at night.

No home, living in the office day and night. Here, having exempted this story from my study of Manhattanism because of its inspired occupation with an ultimate condition and its stepping aside from the garbage and shards of Manhattan history, I was stopped by this turn in the exposition. Yes, the undomesticity of a great city like New York, undomestic in the ways other cities are not—then, and still now. Bartleby, the extreme, the icon of the extreme, is not exactly living in the office. Instead he just does not leave it at the end of the day. But it is very easy to imagine from history where the clerks, Nippers and Turkey, are of an evening. They are living in lodging houses, where half of New York's population lived as late as 1841: newlyweds, families, single persons. Whitman did a lot of "boarding round," as he called it, and observed, with-out rebuke, or mostly without rebuke, that the boarding house led the unfamilied men to rush out after dinner to the saloon or brothel, away from the unprivate pri-vate, to the streets which are the spirit of the city, which are the lively blackmail that makes city citizens abide.

Lodgings then, and later the "divided space" of the apartment house, both ex-pressing Manhattanism as a life lived in transition. And lived in a space that is not bi-ography, but is to be fluent and changeable, an escape from the hometown and the homestead, an escape from the given. The rotting tenements of today are only metaphysical apartments and in deterioration take on the burdensome aspect of "homes" because they remind, in the absence of purchased maintenance, that something "homelike" may be asked of oneself and at the same time denied by the devastations coming from above, below, and next door. Manhattan, the release from the home, which is the leaking roof, the flooded basement, the garbage, and most of all the grounds, that is, surrounding nature. "After I learned about electricity I lost interest in nature. Not up-to-date enough." Mayakovsky, the poet of urbanism.

So Bartleby is found to be living in the office day and night. But Bartleby is not a true creature of Manhattan because he shuns the streets and is unmoved by the moral, religious, acute, obsessive, beautiful ideal of Consumption. Consumption is what one leaves one's "divided space" to honor, as the Muslim stops in his standing and moving to say his prayers five times a day, or is it six? But Bartleby eats only ginger-nuts and is starving himself to death. In that way he passes across one's mind like a feather, calling forth the vague Hinduism of Thoreau and the outer-world meditations of Emerson. (Thoreau, who disliked the city, any city, thought deeply about it, so deeply that in *Walden* he composed the city's most startling consummations, one of which is: "Of a life of luxury, the fruit is luxury.")

To return, what is Bartleby "thinking" about when he is alone? It is part of the perfect completeness of his presentation of himself, although he does not present himself, that one would be foolhardy to give him thoughts. They would dishonor him. So, Bartleby is not "thinking" or experiencing or longing or remembering. All one can say is that he is a master of language, of perfect expressiveness. He is style. This is shown when the lawyer tries to revise him.

On an occasion, the lawyer asks Bartleby to go on an errand to the post office. Bartleby replies that he would prefer not to. The lawyer, seeing a possibility for an entropic, involuntary movement in this mastery of meaning, proposes an italicized emendation. He is answered with an italicized insistence.

"You *will* not?"

"I *prefer* not."

What is the difference between *will* not and *prefer* not? There is no difference insofar as Bartleby's actions will be altered, but he seems to be pointing out by the italics that his preference is not under the rule of the conditional or the future tense. He does not mean to say that he prefers not, but will if he must, or if it is wished. His "I" that prefers not, will not. I do not think he has chosen the verb "prefer" in some emblematic way. That is his language and his language is what he is.

*Prefer* has its power, however. The nipping clerks who have been muttering that they would like to "black his eyes" or "kick him out of the office" begin, without sarcasm or mimicry, involuntarily, as it were, to say to the lawyer, "If you would prefer, Sir," and so on.

Bartleby's language reveals the all of him, but what is revealed? Character? Bartleby is not a character in the manner of the usual, imaginative, fictional construction. And he is not a character as we know them in life, with their bundling bustle of details, their suits and ties and felt hats, their love affairs surreptitious or binding, family albums, psychological justifications dragging like a little wagon along the highway of experience. We might say he is a destiny, without interruptions, revisions, second chances. But what is a destiny that is not endured by a "character"? Bartleby has no plot in his present existence, and we would not wish to imagine subplots for his already lived years. He is indeed only words, wonderful words, and very few of them. One might for a moment sink into the abyss and imagine that instead of *prefer not* he had said, "I don't want to" or "I don't feel like it." No, it is unthinkable, a vulgarization, adding truculence, idleness, foolishness, adding indeed "character" and altering a sublimity of definition.

Bartleby, the scrivener, "standing at the dead-wall window" announces that he will do no more copying. *No more.* The lawyer, marooned in the law of cause and effect, notices the appearance of eyestrain and that there is a possibility Bartleby is going blind. This is never clearly established—Melville's genius would not want at any part of the story to enter the region of sure reasons and causality.

In the midst of these peculiar colloquies, the lawyer asks Bartleby if he cannot indeed be a little reasonable here and there.

"'At present I would prefer not to be a little reasonable,' was his mildly cadaverous reply."

There is no imagining what the sudden intrusion of "at present" may signify and it seems to be just an appendage to the "I," without calling up the nonpresent, the future. From the moment of first refusal it had passed through the lawyer's mind that he might calmly and without resentment dismiss Bartleby, but he cannot, not even after "no more copying." He thinks: "I should have as soon thought of turning my pale, plaster-of-paris bust of Cicero out of doors." Ah. The "wondrous ascendancy" perhaps begins at that point, with the notion that Bartleby is a representation of life, a visage, but not the life itself.

The lawyer, overcome by pity, by troubling thoughts of human diversity, by self-analysis, goes so far as to take down from the shelf certain theological works which give him the idea that he is predestined to "have Bartleby." But as a cheerful, merely social visitor to Trinity Church, this idea does not last and indeed is too abstract because the lawyer has slowly been moving into a therapeutic role, a role in which he persists in the notion of "personality" that may be modified by patience, by suggestion, by reason.

Still, at last, it is clear that Bartleby must go, must be offered a generous bonus, every sort of accommodation and good wish. This done, the lawyer leaves in a pleasant agitation of mind, thinking of the laws of chance represented by his overhearing some betting going on in the street. Will Bartleby be there in the morning or will he at last be gone? Of course, he has remained and the offered money has not been picked up.

"Will you not quit me?"

"I would prefer *not* to quit you."

The "quitting" is to be accomplished by the lawyer's decision to "quit" himself, that is, to quit his offices for larger quarters. A new tenant is found, the boxes are packed and sent off, and Bartleby is bid good-bye. But no, the new tenants, who are not therapists, rush around to complain that he is still there and that he is not a part of their lease. They turn him out of the offices.

The lawyer goes back to the building and finds Bartleby still present, that is, sitting on the banister of the stairway in the entrance hallway.

"What are you doing here, Bartleby?"

"Sitting upon the banister."

The lawyer had meant to ask what will you do with your life, where will you go, and not, where is your body at this moment. But with Bartleby body and statement are one. Indeed the bewitching qualities, the concentrated seriousness, the genius of Bartleby's "dialogue" had long ago affected the style of the lawyer, but in the opposite direction, that is, to metaphor, arrived at by feeling. His head is full of images about the clerk and he thinks of him as "the last column of some ruined temple" and "a bit of wreck in the mid-Atlantic." And from these metaphors there can be no severance.

There with Bartleby sitting on the banister for life, as it were, the lawyer soars into the kindest of deliriums. The therapeutic wish, the beating of the wings of angels above the heads of the harassed and affectionate, unhinge his sense of the possible, the suitable, the imaginable. He begins to think of new occupations for Bartleby and it is so like the frenzied and loving moments in family life: would the pudgy, homely daughter like to comb her hair, neaten up a bit, and apply for a position as a model?— and why not, others have, and so on and so on.

The angel wings tremble and the lawyer says: "Would you like a clerkship in a dry-goods store?"

Bartleby, the unimaginable promoter of goods for sale, replies with his rapid deliberation. Slow deliberation is not necessary for one who knows the interior of his mind, as if that mind were the interior of a small, square box containing a single pair of cuff links.

To the idea of clerking in a store Bartleby at last appends a reason, one indeed of great opacity.

"There is too much confinement about that. No, I would not like a clerkship; but I am not particular."

Agitated rebuttal of "too much confinement" for one who keeps himself "confined all the time"!

Now, in gentle, coaxing hysteria, the lawyer wonders if the bartender's business would suit Bartleby and adds that "there is no trying of the eye-sight in that."

No, Bartleby would not like that at all, even though he repeats that he is not particular.

Would Bartleby like to go about collecting bills for merchants? It would take him outdoors and be good for his health. The answer: "No, I would prefer to be doing something else."

*Doing something else?* That is, sitting on the banister, rather than selling dry goods, bartending, and bill collecting.

Here the lawyer seems to experience a sudden blindness, the blindness of a bright light from an oncoming car on a dark road. The bright light is the terrible clarity of Bartleby.

So, in a blind panic: "How then would be going as a companion to Europe, to entertain some young gentleman with your conversation—how would that suit you?"

"Not at all. It does not strike me that there is anything definite about that. I like to be stationary. But I am not particular."

*Definite?* Conversation is not definite owing to its details of style, opinion, observation, humor, pause, and resumption; and it would not be at all pleasing to Bartleby's mathematical candor. Bartleby is *definite;* conversation is not. He has said it all.

*But I am not particular?* This slight addition has entered Bartleby at the moment the lawyer opens his fantastical employment agency. The phrase wishes to extend the lawyer's knowledge of his client, Bartleby, and to keep him from the tedium of error. Bartleby himself is particular, in that he is indeed a thing distinguished from another. But he is not particular in being fastidious, choosey. He would like the lawyer to understand that he is not concerned with the congenial. It is not suitability he pursues; it is essence, essence beyond detail.

The new tenants have Bartleby arrested as a vagrant and sent to the Tombs. The same idea had previously occurred to the lawyer in a moment of despair, but he could not see that the immobile, unbegging Bartleby could logically be declared a vagrant. "What! He a vagrant, a wanderer that refuses to budge?"

No matter, the lawyer cannot surrender this "case," this recalcitrant object of social service, this demand made upon his heart to provide benefit, this being now in an institution, the Tombs, but not yet locked away from the salvaging sentiments of one who remembers. A prison visit is made and in his ineffable therapeutic endurance the lawyer insists there is no reason to despair, the charge is not a disgrace, and even in prison one may sometimes see the sky and a patch of green.

Bartleby, with the final sigh of one who would instruct the uninstructable, says: *I know where I am.*

In a last urging, on his knees as it were, the lawyer desires to purchase extra food to add to the prison fare.

Bartleby: "I would prefer not to dine today. It would disagree with me; I am unused to dinners." And thus he dies.

Not quite the end for the lawyer with his compassion, his need to unearth some scrap of buried "personality," or private history. We have the beautiful coda Melville has written, a marvelous moment of composition, but perhaps too symbolical, too poetically signifying to be the epitaph of Bartleby. Yet he must be run down, if only to honor the graceful curiosity and the insatiable charity of the lawyer. He reports a rumor:

> The report was this: that Bartleby had been a subordinate clerk in the Dead Letter Office at Washington, from which he had been suddenly removed by a change in administration. . . . Dead letters! Does it not sound like dead men? Conceive a man by nature and misfortune prone to a pallid hopelessness, can any business seem more fitted to heighten it than that of continually handling these dead letters, and assorting them for the flames? . . . On errands of life, these letters sped to death. . . . Ah, Bartleby! Ah, humanity!

Bartleby in a sense is the underside of Billy Budd, but they are not opposites. Billy, the Handsome Sailor, the "Apollo with a portmanteau," the angel, "our beauty," the sunny day, and the unaccountable goodness, which is with him a sort of beautiful "innate disorder," such as the "innate, incurable disorder" represented by Bartleby. Neither of these curious creations knows resentment or grievance; they know nothing of pride, envy, or greed. There is a transcendent harmony in Billy Budd, and a terrifying, pure harmony in the tides of negation that define Bartleby. Billy, the lovely product of nature and, of course, not a perfection of ongoing citizen life, has a "vocal defect," the tendency to stutter at times of stress. By way of this defect, he goes to his death by hanging. Bartleby in no way has a vocal defect; indeed the claim this remarkable creation of American literature makes on our feelings lies entirely in his incomparable self-expression.

So, this bit of old New York, the sepia, horsecar Manhattan, Wall Street. Bartleby and the god-blessed lawyer. They were created by Melville before the Civil War and were coeval with John Jacob Astor's old age and the prime of Cornelius Vanderbilt. And yet here they are, strange apparitions in the metonymic Wall Street district where the exertions, as described by Mark Twain, were, "A year ago I didn't have a penny, and now I owe you a million dollars."

Looking down, or looking up, today at the sulky twin towers of the World Trade Center, "all shaft," the architects say, thinking of those towers as great sightless Brahmins brooding upon the absolute and the all-embracing spirit, it seemed to me that down below there is something of Manhattan in Bartleby and especially in his resistance to amelioration. His being stirs the water of pity, and we can imagine that the little boats that row about him throwing out ropes of personal charity or bureaucratic provision for his "case" may grow weary and move back to the shore in a mood of frustration and, finally, forgetfulness.

There is Manhattanism in the bafflement Bartleby represents to the alive and steady conscience of the lawyer who keeps going on and on in his old democratic, consecrated endurance—going on, even down to the Tombs, and at last to the tomb. If Bartleby is unsaveable, at least the lawyer's soul may be said to have been saved by the freeze of "fraternal melancholy" that swept over him from the fate he had placed at the desk beside him in a little corner of Wall Street. It is not thought that many "downtown" today would wish to profit from, oh, such a chill.

# Shirley Jackson

## *Biography of a Story* 1960

On the morning of June 28, 1948, I walked down to the post office in our little Vermont town to pick up the mail. I was quite casual about it, as I recall—I opened the box, took out a couple of bills and a letter or two, talked to the postmaster for a few minutes, and left, never supposing that it was the last time for months that I was to pick up the mail without an active feeling of panic. By the next week I had had to change my mailbox to the largest one in the post office, and casual conversation with the postmaster was out of the question, because he wasn't speaking to me. June 28, 1948 was the day *The New Yorker* came out with a story of mine in it. It was not my first published story, nor my last, but I have been assured over and over that if it had been the only story I ever wrote or published, there would be people who would not forget my name.

I had written the story three weeks before, on a bright June morning when summer seemed to have come at last, with blue skies and warm sun and no heavenly signs to warn me that my morning's work was anything but just another story. The idea had come to me while I was pushing my daughter up the hill in her stroller—it was, as I say, a warm morning, and the hill was steep, and beside my daughter the stroller held the day's groceries—and perhaps the effort of that last fifty yards up the hill put an edge to the story; at any rate, I had the idea fairly clearly in my mind when I put my daughter in her playpen and the frozen vegetables in the refrigerator, and, writing the story, I found that it went quickly and easily, moving from beginning to end without pause. As a matter of fact, when I read it over later I decided that except for one or two minor corrections, it needed no changes, and the story I finally typed up and sent off to my agent the next day was almost word for word the original draft. This, as any writer of stories can tell you, is not a usual thing. All I know is that when I came to read the story over I felt strongly that I didn't want to fuss with it. I didn't think it was perfect, but I didn't want to fuss with it. It was, I thought, a serious, straightforward story, and I was pleased and a little surprised at the ease with which it had been written; I was reasonably proud of it, and hoped that my agent would sell it to some magazine and I would have the gratification of seeing it in print.

My agent did not care for the story, but—as she said in her note at the time—her job was to sell it, not to like it. She sent it at once to *The New Yorker*, and about a week after the story had been written I received a telephone call from the fiction editor of *The New Yorker*; it was quite clear that he did not really care for the story, either, but *The New Yorker* was going to buy it. He asked for one change—that the date mentioned in the story be changed to coincide with the date of the issue of the magazine in which the story would appear, and I said of course. He then asked, hesitantly, if I had any particular interpretation of my own for the story; Mr. Harold Ross, then the editor of *The New Yorker*, was not altogether sure that he understood the story, and wondered if I cared to enlarge upon its meaning. I said no. Mr. Ross, he said, thought that the story might be puzzling to some people, and in case anyone telephoned the magazine, as sometimes happened, or wrote in asking about the story, was there anything in particular I wanted them to say? No, I said, nothing in particular; it was just a story I wrote.

I had no more preparation than that. I went on picking up the mail every morning, pushing my daughter up and down the hill in her stroller, anticipating pleasurably the check from *The New Yorker*, and shopping for groceries. The weather stayed nice and it looked as though it was going to be a good summer. Then, on June 28, *The New Yorker* came out with my story.

Things began mildly enough with a note from a friend at *The New Yorker:* "Your story has kicked up quite a fuss around the office," he wrote. I was flattered; it's nice to think that your friends notice what you write. Later that day there was a call from one of the magazine's editors; they had had a couple of people phone in about my story, he said, and was there anything I particularly wanted him to say if there were any more calls? No, I said, nothing particular; anything he chose to say was perfectly all right with me; it was just a story.

I was further puzzled by a cryptic note from another friend: "Heard a man talking about a story of yours on the bus this morning," she wrote. "Very exciting. I wanted to tell him I knew the author, but after I heard what he was saying I decided I'd better not."

One of the most terrifying aspects of publishing stories and books is the realization that they are going to be read, and read by strangers. I had never fully realized this before, although I had of course in my imagination dwelt lovingly upon the thought of the millions and millions of people who were going to be uplifted and enriched and delighted by the stories I wrote. It had simply never occurred to me that these millions and millions of people might be so far from being uplifted that they would sit down and write me letters I was downright scared to open; of the three-hundred-odd letters that I received that summer I can count only thirteen that spoke kindly to me, and they were mostly from friends. Even my mother scolded me: "Dad and I did not care at all for your story in *The New Yorker,*" she wrote sternly; "it does seem, dear, that this gloomy kind of story is what all you young people think about these days. Why don't you write something to cheer people up?"

By mid-July I had begun to perceive that I was very lucky indeed to be safely in Vermont, where no one in our small town had ever heard of *The New Yorker,* much less read my story. Millions of people, and my mother, had taken a pronounced dislike to me.

The magazine kept no track of telephone calls, but all letters addressed to me care of the magazine were forwarded directly to me for answering, and all letters addressed to the magazine—some of them addressed to Harold Ross personally; these were the most vehement—were answered at the magazine and then the letters were sent me in great batches, along with carbons of the answers written at the magazine. I have all the letters still, and if they could be considered to give any accurate cross section of the reading public, or the reading public of *The New Yorker,* or even the reading public of one issue of *The New Yorker,* I would stop writing now.

Judging from these letters, people who read stories are gullible, rude, frequently illiterate, and horribly afraid of being laughed at. Many of the writers were positive that *The New Yorker* was going to ridicule them in print, and the most cautious letters were headed, in capital letters: NOT FOR PUBLICATION or PLEASE DO NOT PRINT THIS LETTER or, at best, THIS LETTER MAY BE PUBLISHED AT YOUR USUAL RATES OF PAYMENT. Anonymous letters, of which there were a few, were destroyed. *The New Yorker* never published any comment of any kind about the story in the magazine, but did issue one publicity release saying that the story had received more mail than any piece of fiction they had ever published; this was after the newspapers had gotten into the act, in midsummer, with a front-page story in the San Francisco *Chronicle* begging to know what the story meant, and a series of columns in New York and Chicago papers pointing out that *New Yorker* subscriptions were being canceled right and left.

Curiously, there are three main themes which dominate the letters of that first summer—three themes which might be identified as bewilderment, speculation, and plain old-fashioned abuse. In the years since then, during which the story has been anthologized, dramatized, televised, and even—in one completely mystifying transformation—made into a ballet, the tenor of letters I receive has changed. I am addressed more politely, as a rule, and the letters largely confine themselves to questions like what does this story mean? The general tone of the early letters, however, was a kind of wide-eyed, shocked innocence. People at first were not so much concerned with what the story meant; what they wanted to know was where these lotteries were held, and whether they could go there and watch. Listen to these quotations:

(Kansas)  Will you please tell me the locale and the year of the custom?

(Oregon)  Where in heaven's name does there exist such barbarity as described in the story?

(New York)  Do such tribunal rituals still exist and if so where?

(New York)  To a reader who has only a fleeting knowledge of traditional rites in various parts of the country (I presume the plot was laid in the United States) I found the cruelty of the ceremony outrageous, if not unbelievable. It may be just a custom or ritual which I am not familiar with.

(New York)  Would you please explain whether such improbable rituals occur in our Middle Western states, and what their origin and purpose are?

(Nevada)  Although we recognize the story to be fiction is it possible that it is based on fact?

(Maryland)  Please let me know if the custom of which you wrote actually exists.

(New York)  To satisfy my curiosity would you please tell me if such rites are still practiced and if so where?

(California)  If it is based on fact would you please tell me the date and place of its origin?

(Texas)  What I would like to know, if you don't mind enlightening me, is in what part of the United States this organized, apparently legal lynching is practiced? Could it be that in New England or in equally enlightened regions, mass sadism is still part and parcel of the ordinary citizen's life?

(Georgia)  I'm hoping you'll find time to give me further details about the bizarre custom the story describes, where it occurs, who practices it, and why.

(Brooklyn, N.Y.)  I am interested in learning if there is any particular source or group of sources of fact or legend on which and from which this story is based? This story has caused me to be particularly disturbed by my lack of knowledge of such rites or lotteries in the United States.

(California)  If it actually occurred, it should be documented.

(New York)   We have not read about it in *In Fact*.

(New York)   Is it based on reality? Do these practices still continue in back-country England, the human sacrifice for the rich harvest? It's a frightening thought.

(Ohio)   I think your story is based on fact. Am I right? As a psychiatrist I am fascinated by the psychodynamic possibilities suggested by this anachronistic ritual.

(Mississippi)   You seem to describe a custom of which I am totally ignorant.

(California)   It seems like I remember reading somewhere a long time ago that that was the custom in a certain part of France some time ago. However I have never heard of it being practiced here in the United States. However would you please inform me where you got your information and whether or not anything of this nature has been perpetrated in modern times?

(Pennsylvania)   Are you describing a current custom?

(New York)   Is there some timeless community existing in New England where human sacrifices are made for the fertility of the crops?

(Boston)   Apparently this tale involves an English custom or tradition of which we in this country know nothing.

(Canada)   Can the lottery be some barbaric event, a hangover from the Middle Ages perhaps, which is still carried on in the States? In what part of the country does it take place?

(Los Angeles)   I have read of some queer cults in my time, but this one bothers me.

(Texas)   Was this group of people perhaps a settlement descended from early English colonists? And were they continuing a Druid rite to assure good crops?

(Quebec)   Is this a custom which is carried on somewhere in America?

(A London psychologist)   I have received requests for elucidation from English friends and patients. They would like to know if the barbarity of stoning still exists in the U.S.A. and in general what the tale is all about and where does the action take place.

(Oregon)   Is there a witchcraft hangover somewhere in these United States that we Far Westerners have missed?

(Madras, India)   We have been wondering whether the story was based on fact and if so whether the custom described therein of selecting one family by lot jointly to be stoned by the remainder of the villagers still persists anywhere in the United States. *The New Yorker* is read here in our United States information library and while we have had no inquiries about this particular article as yet, it is possible we shall have and I would be glad to be in a position to answer them.

(England)   I am sorry that I cannot find out the state in which this piece of annual propitiatory sacrifice takes place. Now I just frankly don't believe that even in the United States such things happen—at least not without being sponsored by Lynching Inc. or the All-American Morticians Group or some such high-powered organization. I was once offered a baby by a primitive tribe in the center of Laos (Indochina) which my interpreter (Chinese) informed me I had to kill so that my blood lust was satiated and I would leave the rest of the tribe alone. But NOT in the United States, PLEASE.

(Connecticut)    Other strange old things happen in the Appalachian mountain villages, I'm told.

As I say, if I thought this was a valid cross section of the reading public, I would give up writing. During this time, when I was carrying home some ten or twelve letters a day, and receiving a weekly package from *The New Yorker*, I got one letter which troubled me a good deal. It was from California, short, pleasant, and very informal. The man who wrote it clearly expected that I would recognize his name and his reputation, which I didn't. I puzzled over this letter for a day or two before I answered it, because of course it is always irritating to be on the edge of recognizing a name and have it escape you. I was pretty sure that it was someone who had written a book I had read or a book whose review I had read or a story in a recent magazine or possibly even—since I come originally from California—someone with whom I had gone to high school. Finally, since I had to answer the letter, I decided that something carefully complimentary and noncommittal would be best. One day, after I had mailed him my letter, some friends also from California stopped in and asked—as everyone was asking then— what new letters had come. I showed them the letter from my mysterious not-quite-remembered correspondent. Good heavens, they said, was this really a letter from *him*? Tell me who he is, I said desperately, just tell me who he is. Why, how could anyone forget? It had been all over the California papers for weeks, and in the New York papers, too; he had just been barely acquitted of murdering his wife with an ax. With a kind of awful realization creeping over me I went and looked up the carbon of the letter I had written him, my noncommittal letter. "Thank you very much for your kind letter about my story," I had written. "I admire *your* work, too."

The second major theme which dominates the letters is what I call speculation. These letters were from the people who sat down and figured out a meaning for the story, or a reason for writing it, and wrote in proudly to explain, or else wrote in to explain why they could not possibly believe the story had any meaning at all.

(New Jersey)    Surely it is only a bad dream the author had?
(New York)    Was it meant to be taken seriously?
(New York)    Was the sole purpose just to give the reader a nasty impact?
(California)    The main idea which has been evolved is that the author has tried to challenge the logic of our society's releasing its aggressions through the channel of minority prejudice by presenting an equally logical (or possibly more logical) method of selecting a scapegoat. The complete horror of the cold-blooded method of choosing a victim parallels our own culture's devices for handling deep-seated hostilities.

(Virginia)   I would list my questions about the story but it would be like trying to talk in an unknown language so far as I am concerned. The only thing that occurs to me is that perhaps the author meant we should not be too hard on our presidential nominees.

(Connecticut)   Is *The New Yorker* only maintaining further its policy of intellectual leg-pulling?

(New York)   Is it a publicity stunt?

(New Orleans)   I wish Mrs. Hutchinson had been queen for a day or something nice like that before they stoned the poor frightened creature.

(New York)   Anyone who seeks to communicate with the public should be at least lucid.

(New Jersey)   Please tell me if the feeling I have of having dreamed it once is just part of the hypnotic effect of the story.

(Massachusetts)   I earnestly grabbed my young nephew's encyclopedia and searched under "stoning" or "punishment" for some key to the mystery; to no avail.

(California)   Is it just a story? Why was it published? Is it a parable? Have you received other letters asking for some explanation?

(Illinois)   If it is simply a fictitious example of man's innate cruelty, it isn't a very good one. Man, stupid and cruel as he is, has always had sense enough to imagine or invent a charge against the objects of his persecution: the Christian martyrs, the New England witches, the Jews and Negroes. But nobody had anything against Mrs. Hutchinson, and they only wanted to get through quickly so they could go home for lunch.

(California)   Is it an allegory?

(California)   Please tell us it was all in fun.

(Los Angeles *Daily News*)   Was Tessie a witch? No, witches weren't selected by lottery. Anyway, these are present-day people. Is it the post-atomic age, in which there is insufficient food to sustain the population and one person is eliminated each year? Hardly. Is it just an old custom, difficult to break? Probably. But there is also the uncomfortable feeling that maybe the story wasn't supposed to make sense. The magazines have been straining in this direction for some time and *The New Yorker*, which we like very much, seems to have made it.

(Missouri)   In this story you show the perversion of democracy.

(California)   It seems obscure.

(California)   I caught myself dreaming about what I would do if my wife and I were in such a predicament. I think I would back out.

(Illinois)   A symbol of how village gossip destroys a victim?

(Puerto Rico)   You people print any story you get, just throwing the last paragraph into the wastebasket before it appears in the magazine.

(New York)   Were you saying that people will accept any evil as long as it doesn't touch them personally?

(Massachusetts)   I am approaching middle age; has senility set in at this rather early age, or is it that I am not so acute mentally as I have had reason to assume?

(Canada)  My only comment is what the hell?

(Maine)  I suppose that about once every so often a magazine may decide to print something that hasn't any point just to get people talking.

(California)  I don't know how there could be any confusion in anyone's mind as to what you were saying; nothing could possibly be clearer.

(Switzerland)  What does it mean? Does it hide some subtle allegory?

(Indiana)  What happened to the paragraph that tells what the devil is going on?

(California)  I missed something here. Perhaps there was some facet of the victim's character which made her unpopular with the other villagers. I expected the people to evince a feeling of dread and terror, or else sadistic pleasure, but perhaps they were laconic, unemotional New Englanders.

(Ohio)  A friend darkly suspects you people of having turned a bright editorial red, and that is how he construed the story. Please give me something to go on when I next try to placate my friend, who is now certain that you are tools of Stalin. If you *are* subversive, for goodness sake I don't blame you for not wanting to discuss the matter and of course you have every constitutional right in back of you. But at least please explain that damned story.

(Venezuela)  I have read the story twice and from what I can gather all a man gets for his winnings are rocks in his head, which seems rather futile.

(Virginia)  The printers left out three lines of type somewhere.

(Missouri)  You printed it. Now give with the explanations.

(New York)  To several of us there seemed to be a rather sinister symbolism in the cruelty of the people.

(Indiana)  When I first read the story in my issue, I felt that there was no moral significance present, that the story was just terrifying, and that was all. However, there has to be a reason why it is so alarming to so many people. I feel that the only solution, the only reason it bothered so many people is that it shows the power of society over the individual. We saw the ease with which society can crush any single one of us. At the same time, we saw that society need have no rational reason for crushing the one, or the few, or sometimes the many.

(Connecticut)  I thought that it might have been a small-scale representation of the sort of thing involved in the lottery which started the functioning of the selective-service system at the start of the last war.

Far and away the most emphatic letter writers were those who took this opportunity of indulging themselves in good old-fashioned name-calling. Since I am making no attempt whatsoever to interpret the motives of my correspondents, and would not if I could, I will not try now to say what I think of people who write nasty letters to other people who just write stories. I will only read some of their comments.

(Canada)  Tell Miss Jackson to stay out of Canada.

(New York)  I expect a personal apology from the author.

(Massachusetts)  I think I had better switch to the *Saturday Evening Post.*

(Massachusetts)  I will never buy *The New Yorker* again. I resent being tricked into reading perverted stories like "The Lottery."

(Connecticut)  Who is Shirley Jackson? Cannot decide whether she is a genius or a female and more subtle version of Orson Welles.

(New York)  We are fairly well educated and sophisticated people, but we feel that we have lost all faith in the truth of literature.

(Minnesota)  Never in the world did I think I'd protest a story in *The New Yorker,* but really, gentlemen, "The Lottery" seems to me to be in incredibly bad taste. I read it while soaking in the tub and was tempted to put my head under water and end it all.

(California; this from a world-famous anthropologist)  If the author's intent was to symbolize into complete mystification and at the same time be gratuitously disagreeable, she certainly succeeded.

(Georgia)  Couldn't the story have been a trifle esoteric, even for *The New Yorker* circulation?

(California)  "The Lottery" interested some of us and made the rest plain mad.

(Michigan)  It certainly is modern.

(California)  I am glad that your magazine does not have the popular and foreign-language circulation of the *Reader's Digest.* Such a story might make German, Russian, and Japanese realists feel lily-white in comparison with the American. The old saying about washing dirty linen in public has gone out of fashion with us. At any rate this story has reconciled me to not receiving your magazine next year.

(Illinois)  Even to be polite I can't say that I liked "The Lottery."

(Missouri)  When the author sent in this story, she undoubtedly included some explanation of place or some evidence that such a situation could exist. Then isn't the reader entitled to some such evidence? Otherwise the reader has a right to indict you as editor of willfully misrepresenting the human race. Perhaps you as editor are proud of publishing a story that reached a new low in human viciousness. The burden of proof is up to you when your own preoccupation with evil leads you into such evil ways. A few more such stories and you will alienate your most devoted readers, in which class I—until now—have been included.

(New Hampshire)  It was with great disappointment that I read the story "The Lottery." Stories such as this belong to *Esquire,* etc., but most assuredly not to *The New Yorker.*

(Massachusetts)  The ending of this story came as quite a jolt to my wife and, as a matter of fact, she was very upset by the whole thing for a day or two after.

(New York)  I read the story quite thoroughly and confess that I could make neither head nor tail out of it. The story was so horrible and grue-some in its effect that I could hardly see the point of your publishing it.

Now, a complete letter, from Illinois.

> Editor:
>
> Never has it been my lot to read so cunningly vicious a story as that published in your last issue for June. I tremble to think of the fate of American letters if that piece indicated the taste of the editors of a magazine I had considered distinguished. It has made me wonder what you had in mind when accepting it for publication. Certainly not the entertainment of the reader and if not entertainment, what? The strokes of genius were of course apparent in the story mentioned, but of a perverted genius whose efforts achieved a terrible malformation. You have betrayed a trust with your readers by giving them such a bestial selection. Unaware, the reader was led into a casual tale of the village folk, becoming conscious only gradually of the rising tension, till the shock of the unwholesome conclusion, skillful though it was wrought, left him with total disgust for the story and with disillusionment in the magazine publishing it.
>
> I speak of my own reaction. If that is not the reaction of the majority of your readers I miss my guess. Ethics and uplift are apparently not in your repertoire, nor are they expected, but as editors it is your responsibility to have a sounder and saner criterion for stories than the one which passed on "The Lottery."
>
> Heretofore mine has been almost a stockholder's pride in *The New Yorker.* I shared my copy with friends as I do the other possessions which I most enjoy. When your latest issue arrived, my new distaste kept me from removing the brown paper wrapping, and into the wastebasket it went. Since I can't conceive that I'll develop interest in it again, save the results of your efforts that indignity every week and cancel my subscription immediately.

Another letter, this one from Indiana.

> Sir:
>
> Thanks for letting us take a look at the nauseating and fiction-less bit of print which appeared in a recent issue. I gather that we read the literal translation.
>
> The process of moving set us back a few weeks, but unfortunately your magazine and Miss Jackson's consistently correct spelling and punctuation caught up with us.
>
> We are pleased to think that perhaps her story recalled happier days for you; days when you were able to hurl flat skipping stones at your aged grandmother. Not for any particular reason, of course, but because the village postmaster good-naturedly placed them in your hands, or because your chubby fingers felt good as they gripped the stone.

Our quarrel is not with Miss Jackson's amazingly clear style or reportorial observation. It is not with the strong motives exhibited by the native stone-throwers, or with the undertones and overtones which apparently we missed along the way.

It is simply that we read the piece before and not after supper. We are hammering together a few paragraphs on running the head of our kindly neighbor through the electric eggbeater, and will mail same when we have untangled her top-piece. This should give your many readers a low chuckle or at least provide the sophisticates with an inner glow. Also it might interest you to know that my wife and I are gathering up the smoothest, roundest stones in our yard and piling them up on the corner in small, neat pyramids. We're sentimentalists that way.

I have frequently wondered if this last letter is a practical joke; it is certainly not impossible, although I hope not, because it is quite my favorite letter of all "Lottery" correspondence. It was mailed to *The New Yorker,* from Los Angeles, of course, and written in pencil, on a sheet of lined paper torn from a pad; the spelling is atrocious.

Dear Sir:

The June 26 copy of your magazine fell into my hands in the Los Angeles railroad station yesterday. Although I donnot read your magazine very often I took this copy home to my folks and they had to agree with me that you speak straitforward to your readers.

My Aunt Ellise before she became priestess of the Exalted Rollers used to tell us a story just like "The Lottery" by Shirley Jackson. I don't know if Miss Jackson is a member of the Exhalted Rollers but with her round stones sure ought to be. There is a few points in her prophecy on which Aunt Ellise and me don't agree.

The Exalted Rollers donnot believe in the ballot box but believe that the true gospel of the redeeming light will become accepted by all when the prophecy comes true. It does seem likely to me that our sins will bring us punishment though a great scouraging war with the devil's toy (the atomic bomb). I don't think we will have to sacrifice humin beings fore atonement.

Our brothers feel that Miss Jackson is a true prophet and disciple of the true gospel of the redeeming light. When will the next revelations be published?

Yours in the spirit.

Of all the questions ever asked me about "Lottery," I feel that there is only one which I can answer fearlessly and honestly, and that is the question which closes this gentleman's letter. When will the next revelations be published, he wants to know, and I answer roundly, never. I am out of the lottery business for good.

# Roy Morris Junior

## from *Ambrose Bierce: Alone in Bad Company* 1995

Between visits from admirers and columns for the *Examiner,* Bierce continued working on his growing pile of stories. The great Civil War stories—"Chickamauga," "A Son of the Gods," "Killed at Resaca," "A Horseman in the Sky," "An Affair of Outposts," "One of the Missing"—alternated with such skin-crawling tales of the supernatural as "A Watcher by the Dead," "The Man and the Snake," "The Eyes of the Panther," and "The Suitable Surroundings." In mid-July 1890, he hit his peak with a story that masterfully combined the two genres, "An Occurrence at Owl Creek Bridge." More than any other work, this is the story for which Bierce is most remembered—and with good reason. "An Occurrence at Owl Creek" is, within its brilliantly controlled parameters, a perfect work of art. ("That story has everything. Nothing better exists," a young Stephen Crane gushed to a friend a few years later.) It is Bierce's most widely anthologized piece, appearing in virtually every college-level survey of American literature and numerous collections of great short stories. In 1963, a French screen version of the story won an Academy Award for best short film, and the film was later shown to millions of American viewers on the popular television series *The Twilight Zone.* Bierce may have surpassed the story in a few random passages here and there—the procession of wounded soldiers in "Chickamauga," the nighttime river crossing and the ravine of death in "What I Saw of Shiloh," the concluding paragraphs of "A Son of the Gods," the Faulkner-like drolleries of "Jupiter Doke, Brigadier-General"—but taken as a whole, "An Occurrence at Owl Creek Bridge" is Bierce at his best.

The plot of the story is deceptively simple: a pro-Confederate civilian named Peyton Farquhar is about to be hanged from the railroad trestle over Owl Creek Bridge for attempted sabotage. Waiting wordlessly for the execution to take place, the condemned man feels his senses heighten preternaturally; the ticking of his pocket watch sounds like a blacksmith's thunderous anvil strokes. As the Union sergeant steps off the wooden plank on which Farquhar is standing, a flashback shows us how the "well-to-do planter" was tricked into attempting to burn the bridge by a disguised Union scout. (Farquhar's own highly romantic and unrealistic views of war contribute as well to his fatal decision.) The hanging takes place as planned, but the rope breaks, and Farquhar plunges to the bottom of Owl Creek, where he frees himself from his bonds and resurfaces with a shout. Desperately, he swims away as Union marksmen pepper the stream with rifle fire. He makes good his escape, emerging downstream into the thick woods alongside the creek, and eventually finds his way home, where his wife stands waiting for him on the steps of their veranda. He springs forward to embrace her, but then "he feels a stunning blow upon the back of the neck; a blinding white light blazes all about him with a sound like the shock of a cannon— then all is darkness and silence." The story concludes with one of the most famous sentences in American literature: "Peyton Farquhar was dead; his body, with a broken neck, swung gently from side to side beneath the timbers of the Owl Creek bridge." The escape had been an illusive dream.

Careless readers (including, surprisingly, Cleanth Brooks and Robert Penn Warren, who no doubt disliked Bierce for being a former Union soldier) have misinterpreted the story as a bit of reverse O. Henry legerdemain. The so-called trick ending throws them off. A more careful reading of this most carefully written story reveals that the ending is no trick—except on the unfortunate and dull-witted Farquhar. Everywhere along the way, Bierce prepares the reader for the story's only possible conclusion. It is, after all, an *occurrence*—something that occurs—*at* Owl Creek Bridge— on or near the bridge, not downstream, miles away, at Farquhar's home. Given the circumstances, carefully spelled out in the precise militaristic language of the story's opening passage, the only event that could possibly have occurred that morning at Owl Creek Bridge is a hanging. Moreover, in the frequently misread second section of the story, Farquhar is revealed to be just the sort of self-deluding fool who would most likely imagine such a preposterous escape. As a wealthy civilian who somehow had managed to avoid military service, probably through the "Twenty Negro Law" that exempted from active duty any slave owners with more than twenty slaves on their property, Farquhar had "chafed under the inglorious restraint, longing for the release of his energies, the larger life of the soldier, the opportunity for distinction [t]hat he felt would come, as it comes to all in war time." It would come all right, but it would be the *it* of e. e. cummings's "Plato Told Him," the "nipponized bit of the old sixth avenue el in the top of his head," that teaches another obtuse war-lover the ultimate price of his naïve flirtation with war. The story, and Farquhar's story within a story, end with a jolt but not a surprise.

Actually, "An Occurrence at Owl Creek Bridge" ends twice, and both times the same way. The third and final section of the story opens with a remarkably graphic and convincing account of Farquhar's death by hanging. "A sharp pressure upon his throat, followed by a sense of suffocation," is accompanied by "keen poignant agonies [that] seemed to shoot from his neck downward through every fibre of his body and limbs." These, in turn, are followed by "a feeling of fulness—of congestion" in his head, and a sense of motion as "he swung through unthinkable arcs of oscillation, like a vast pendulum." Finally, he feels himself shoot upward—the rope has reached its limit and he is being jerked upward again in reverse—with "a frightful roaring in his ears," until "all was cold and dark." At this point, Farquhar is dead and the story is over, but it is Bierce's brilliant achievement to show how a dying man might, in the split second of life remaining to him, mistake the sensation of falling, being strangled, and being yanked skyward again for a saving plunge into deep water. No one knows if death by hanging really mimics death by drowning (probably it does not), but the similarity of the two is beside the point: It is Farquhar's dream we are experiencing, and since he is being hanged from a bridge over water, it is only natural that he would imagine himself falling into the water to escape and that he would confuse the congestion of suffocation with the sensation of drowning.

The rest of the story occurs not in real time but in the instant that Farquhar is dropping through space to the literal end of his rope. He is conscious of trying to free his hands, which anyone in his position would attempt to do, and his puzzling cry, "Put it back, put it back!" may indicate that he has freed one of his hands and that the Union captain is shouting at the guard to put the hand back behind him; or it might be his last, despairing wish that his executioners put back the board they have just yanked out from under him. Again he experiences the sensation of hanging: "His neck ached horribly; his brain was on fire; his heart, which had been fluttering faintly, gave a great leap, trying to force itself out of his mouth. His whole body was racked and wrenched by insupportable anguish." His senses, however, are unnaturally sharp (one thinks inevitably of Dr. Johnson's remark about how the knowledge that one is about to be hanged wonderfully concentrates the mind). Impossible feats of hearing and seeing are combined with equally marvelous physical feats—"What magnificent, what superhuman strength"—as he frees himself and effects his escape. Several critics have pointed out that Farquhar's emergence from the water—first head, then shoulders, then chest, and finally an astonished cry as he gulps the air—mimics the act of being born (defined by Bierce as "the first and direst of all disasters"). One critic goes so far as to suggest that the cry "Put it back!" is simply the baby's Freudian wish to have its mother's umbilical cord reattached, in which case the hangman's rope is an ironic substitute, bringing death, not life, in its wake.

Ongoing studies of near-death experiences have revealed a consistent pattern of similar sensations, of falling (or rising) through corridors of darkness toward a distant, finally all-encompassing light, which some have suggested are simply repressed memories of birth. And while Bierce could not have been exposed to such studies in his lifetime, it is significant that a "blinding white light" does blaze around Farquhar at the moment he hears "a sound like the shock of a cannon"—his own neck breaking. Since Bierce never described his own near-death experience at Kennesaw Mountain in 1864, it is impossible to say whether he was relying on personal knowledge in describing Farquhar's fate or was simply using the artist's creative prerogative. Certainly he used other personal experiences in writing the story: the real Owl Creek, which borders the battlefield at Shiloh; his regiment's railroad-guarding service in northern Alabama, which exactly corresponds to the time of the story; the hangings he witnessed as a soldier in the army and a reporter in San Francisco; even the miraculous "escape" from hanging that is the basic plot contrivance of the play *Ambrose Gwinett; or A Sea-Side Story.* The accretion of realistic details gives added weight to the unreal instant at the heart of the story. We believe it because, like Farquhar, we want to believe it.

# Katherine Kinney

## from *Friendly Fire*                                                     *2000*

Tim O'Brien's story "Sweetheart of the Song Tra Bong" offers a brilliant gloss of the gendered cultural logic of war stories. Framed as a tale told by a highly unreliable narrator, Rat Kiley, "Sweetheart" tells the impossible story of a girl who succeeds in "humping the boonies." A young medic at a small station in a remote mountain location of Vietnam sends his girlfriend a ticket to come visit him. Seventeen years old, fresh out of high school, Mary Ann Bell arrives on a chopper in white culottes and a "sexy pink sweater" full of innocent curiosity and good cheer (102). The story presses two conflicting points of impossibility: whether a girl could get to "the boonies" and what would happen if she did. Getting her there, the resourceful young medic, Mark Fossie, explains was expensive and "the logistics were complicated, but it wasn't like getting to the moon" (105). Mary Ann Bell becomes another of O'Brien's travelers, like Paul Berlin in *Going After Cacciato,* who embarks on an improbable but eminently mappable journey. It is the issue of what happens when she arrives in country that far more seriously strains not simply the imagination but the gendered narrative boundaries of war itself.

Mary Ann Bell's trip to Vietnam violates every operative assumption regarding how and when and where and why women enter war stories. At first she plays the traditional role, mooning over her boyfriend, flirting just enough with the seven other medics and playing volleyball in "cut-off blue jeans and a black swimsuit top, which the guys appreciated" (106). In short, "she was good for morale" (106). The guys like her but also come to respect her; she asks good questions, "paid attention," and when casualties come in "Mary Ann wasn't afraid to get her hands bloody" (108). She comes to feel "at home" in Vietnam (107). Besides her good-natured flirting and showing off her long legs, however, Mary Ann does nothing to make the camp seem more "like home." She does not cook or clean or offer any little domestic touches. Instead, her attention is drawn out of the camp, away from her boyfriend and his comfortably limited engagement with combat, and toward "those scary green mountains to the west" (106). From the ARVN soldiers camped at the perimeter she learns some Vietnamese, "how to cook rice over a can of Sterno, and how to eat with her fingers" (107). The men tease her about going "native." She badgers Fossie into taking her to the nearby village over his objection that the Viet Cong control it. She seems to know no fear.

"A real tiger," said Eddie Diamond. "D-cup guts, trainer bra brains."

"She'll learn," somebody said.

Eddie Diamond gave a solemn nod. "That's the scary part. I promise you. This girl will most definitely learn." (108)

Eddie's comic bra-size metaphor speaks to the heart of the story's improbability and its power. Mary Ann moves deeper into the war without moving out of her gender identity as a woman. When the wounded come in, "she learned how to clip an artery and pump up a plastic splint, and shoot in morphine," fascinated by the "adrenalin buzz that went with the job . . . [when] you have to do things fast and right" (109). Mary Ann gains confidence and focus; she seemed like a "different person." She learns to shoot and "Cleveland Heights seemed very far away" (109). This difference intrudes into her relationship with Mark. They still sleep together and plan for the future but "her body seemed foreign somehow—too stiff in places, too firm where the softness used to be" (110). At an obvious level, this hardening of her body suggests masculinization, but Mary Ann remains very much a desirable woman to Mark and to all the men. The more telling change is a narrative one—her new uncertainty in the story she had shared with Mark since grammar school: "that they would be married some day, and live in a fine gingerbread house near Lake Erie, and have three healthy yellow-haired children, and grow old and no doubt die in each others' arms and be buried in the same walnut casket" (106). After three weeks in country Mary Ann begins to qualify: "Not necessarily three kids, she'd say. Not necessarily a house on Lake Erie. 'Naturally we'll still get married,' she'd tell him, 'but it doesn't have to be right away. Maybe travel first. Maybe live together. Just test it out, you know?" (110). This change, associated in the story with the war, also speaks to the social transformation in traditional mores associated with the sexual revolution and women's liberation movements of the 1960s. Mary Ann has begun to question the inevitable logic of domesticity.

In very subtle and provocative ways, "Sweetheart of the Song Tra Bong" is a story of the women's movement: of one woman's move beyond naturalized gender roles which brings to light deeper assumptions about gender relations and the larger sense of reality. As narrator, Rat is furiously defensive of the story's veracity:

> [T]he one thing [Rat] could not tolerate was disbelief. . . . "She wasn't *dumb*," he'd snap. "Young, that's all I said. Like you and me. A *girl*, that's the only difference, and I'll tell you something: it didn't amount to jack. I mean, when we first got here—all of us—we were young and innocent, full of romantic bullshit, but we learned pretty damn quick. And so did Mary Ann." (108)

"You've got to get rid of that sexist attitude," Rat later chides his listeners, knowing that it is their assumptions about women and not their experience of the war which condition their sense of the possible or the real, their ability to believe the story (117). Like all the stories in *The Things They Carried*, "Sweetheart" is as much about the nature of stories as about the nature of war. At the crucial dramatic moment, Rat plays on his listeners' assumptions. Mark wakes Rat late at night; Mary Ann is gone and he assumes that she must be sleeping with someone else. Rat does a "body count" but all the men are sleeping alone. Rat interrupts his narration to ask his listeners, "Where is she?" One connoisseur of stories immediately knows: she's with the Green Berets that Rat had mentioned at the beginning of his tale who operate out of a hootch at the edge of the camp but generally ignore the medics: "all that's got to be there for a *reason*. That's how stories work, man" (112).

Allegiance to narrative form temporarily overrides gender assumptions, and, in any case, Mark's narrative, "she's sleeping with somebody," stands ready to recuperate more familiar patterns of possibility. But this assumption, too, proves wrong. "She wasn't sleeping with any of them," Rat explains. "At least not exactly. I mean, she was sleeping with *all* of them, more or less, except it wasn't sex or anything. They was just lying together, so to speak, Mary Ann and these six grungy weirded out Green Berets" (112). "Lying down how?" the skeptical and confused listeners ask. "Ambush. All night long. Mary Ann's out on fuckin' *ambush*" (113). That Rat stumbles over the sexual metaphor here is less a mark of his "bad habit" of interrupting the flow of his stories with "little clarifications or bits of analysis and personal opinions" than a measure of how deeply Mary Ann's actions have compromised narrative expectations and even possibility (116). Mary Ann has transgressed the boundaries of common sense in the deepest meaning of the term, the shared assumptions that create a sense of reality.

For common sense would surely suggest that whatever experience Mary Ann gains in Vietnam will necessarily be sexual. Going to Vietnam expands her horizons, her sense of herself and the world. Throughout the 1960s and beyond, sexual freedom has served as both the metaphor and the substance of all too many stories of women's liberation. The narrative that most directly maps the intersection of the Vietnam War and the contemporary shift in gender roles, the film *Coming Home,* plots Sally (Jane Fonda)'s personal growth as the move from the bed of her traditional soldier husband to that of the countercultural antiwar veteran. Sleeping with one of the "Greenies" is the expected way for Mary Ann to move beyond Eddie and escape the home he represents by acting out her fascination with the landscape of Vietnam. Moreover, "fucking ambush" encodes the violent sexual threat of war for women: rape. Common sense would dictate that Mary Ann would need to take one lover as protector from the sexual voraciousness depicted in most representations of the war. In an all-male society women are expected to serve as objects of sexual barter.

But O'Brien plots Mary Ann's move to the Greenies with even more care than her plausible if improbable journey to Vietnam. Crucial here is the emphasis on learning, on acquiring competence and with it respect. Rat's insistence that they were all innocent once but "learned pretty damn quick" in country speaks to the authorial heart of war stories which traces the soldier's journey from innocence to experience, from home to war. By constructing a plausible fiction which takes Mary Ann to Vietnam, O'Brien undoes the narrative presumption that identifies home as the realm of the female and war as the domain of the male. Once in country, she is taken through the deeply familiar routines of learning about the land and the war, its rhythms and demands. The men listening to Rat's story cannot disavow her story without disavowing the terms that authorize their own telling of war stories—how they acquired their own knowledge.

Mary Ann's interest in the land becomes desire and her knowledge translates into narrative possibility, moving ultimately to the story's radical denouement in which Mary Ann humps the boonies. Tellingly, however, the term is never used directly. Rat underlines the weirdness of her arrival by saying, "She shows up with a suitcase and one of those plastic cosmetic bags. Comes right out to the boonies" (102). By implication, the boonies are exactly that place where American women are not. But one of the things that makes her appearance at this remote base possible is that being stationed there involves "no humping at all" (103). In practical terms it is light duty with no officers, but the break in the metaphorical association of "boonies" and "humping" at the beginning of the story is literally and figuratively what makes its narration of the impossible possible. This unhooking of the sexual metaphor is generally characteristic of O'Brien's style which, almost uniquely among veterans writing fiction about the war, does not rely on the hypersexual vernacular of the grunt. If, according to Michael Herr, the feeling of being in a firefight is most closely akin to "the feeling you'd had when you were much, much younger and undressing a girl for the first time," then for Mary Ann to be out on "fucking ambush" is, to say the least, highly ironic (136). But the incongruity in "Sweetheart" rebounds on the male listeners (Herr's "you" literalized in Rat's audience) rather than violently back onto her body. Compare the violent fate of women caught playing soldier in the war zone in *The Short-Timers* or, as we shall see, in Larry Heinemann's *Paco's Story,* novels that contain some of the war literature's most brilliant linguistic plays on and with obscenity.

Within the story both Mary Ann and Rat scrupulously avoid using overt sexual metaphors to explain the desire she feels for the war. Mary Ann uses the term "appetite." "Sometimes I want to *eat* this place, Vietnam," she explains. "I want to swallow this whole country—the dirt, the death—I just want to eat it and have it there inside of me" (121). Certainly there are sexual inferences in this desire to consume; there very well may have to be sexual entendres for her experience to register as a war story. But she cannot respond to the land with the kind of explicit language used by Michael Herr, "kiss it, eat it, fuck it, plow it with your whole body" or even "pucker and submit," without reopening the barely suspended disbelief regarding what women can do in war (Herr 63). Women are typically assumed to be literally, rather than, like Herr, symbolically ravished by war. Rat's metaphor is similar: "Vietnam had the effect of a powerful drug," that is illicit, pleasurable, and dangerous, again like sex, but not quite sex (123).

Rat's ultimate metaphor for Mary Ann's experience echoes across the 1960s' language of sex, drugs, self-discovery, and the war alike; Vietnam becomes her "trip."

> The endorphins start to flow, and the adrenaline, and you hold your breath and creep quietly through the moonlit nightscapes; you become intimate with danger; you're in touch with the far side of yourself, as though it's another hemisphere, and you want to string it out and go where ever the trip takes you and be host to all the possibilities inside yourself. . . . She wanted more, she wanted to penetrate into the mystery of herself. . . . (124)

In a perverse way Mary Ann's trip answers directly Virginia Woolf's call—she moves away from domestic space, away from the future husband who presents himself as her identity and discovers herself in relation to the landscape and within herself. While Woolf would hardly endorse Mary Ann's claim to the masculine art of war and its colonial context, the story presses the textual and material implications of women's liberation. Mary Ann moves quite literally beyond Rat or, by implication, any man's narration. Rat infuriates his listeners by claiming he doesn't know what happened to her, but he finally presents an ending to his story based on rumor and conjecture. Like Sean Flynn in *Dispatches*, "Mary Ann Bell joined the missing" (125).

The story's end makes her absence radically active and thus powerfully denies any nostalgic recuperation of her character.

> But the story did not end there. If you believed the Greenies, Rat said, Mary Ann was still somewhere out there in the dark. Odd movements, odd shapes. Late at night, when the Greenies were out on ambush, the whole rain forest would seem to stare in at them—a watched feeling—and a couple of times they almost saw her sliding through the shadows. Not quite but almost. She had crossed over to the other side. She was a part of the land. She was wearing her culottes, her pink sweater, and a necklace of human tongues. She was dangerous. She was ready for the kill. (125)

Mary Ann's defection marks her as the enemy, but the story refuses to enact the familiar terms which connect women's liberation and the soldier's betrayal. "Sweetheart" is insistently about Mary Ann's self-discovery and its effect on the masculine activity of telling war stories rather than on the lives of the men she leaves behind. The story works directly against the deeply misogynist assumptions that make Jane Fonda such a familiar icon of veterans' feelings of betrayal. Rather than hatred, Rat confesses his love for Mary Ann, because she has ceased to be like "those girls back home . . . clean and innocent" who will never understand what he has been through. "After the war, man, I promise you, you won't find nobody like her" (123). Rat brings to the surface the contradictory structures of war narrative that ask women to heal and absolve men of experiences they are not allowed to know. The Greenies' haunting feeling of being watched asserts Mary Ann's subversive claim to knowledge and experience, just as her necklace of tongues testifies to her violently earned right to tell war stories. Mary Ann has passed Herr's "moment of initiation where you get down and bite the tongue off the corpse" and now sings in a language "beyond translation" (121).

But if gender is denaturalized as a system of absolute difference, Mary Ann's trip to the "far side of herself," especially as likened to "another hemisphere," also suggests more traditional patterns of imperial and racial otherness (123–124). The scene in which Mark and Rat confront Mary Ann in the Greenies' hootch is an orgy of hyperbolic imagery that parodies Kurtz's compound in *Apocalypse Now*: "tribal music," the "exotic" scent of incense mingling with the "stench of the kill," a decayed leopard's head, "strips of yellow brown skin" hanging from the rafters, and a poster that declares "in neat black lettering: ASSEMBLE YOUR OWN GOOK!! FREE SAMPLE KIT!!" (119). Mary Ann emerges out of the gloom, wearing "her pink sweater and a white blouse and a simple cotton skirt" (120). She is the same but clearly not the same. Her eyes are "utterly flat and indifferent," the mark of the proverbial thousand-yard stare.

> But the grotesque part, [Rat] said, was her jewelry. At the girl's throat was a necklace of human tongues. Elongated and narrow, like pieces of blackened leather, the tongues were threaded along a copper wire, one overlapping the next, the tips curled upward as if caught in some horrified final syllable. (120)

If this scene is the clearest display of Rat's "reputation for exaggeration and overstatement," it also presents a deeply familiar pattern of horror, of, in fact, *the* horror, Kurtz's vision of the heart of darkness (101).

Mary Ann's desire to "penetrate deeper into the mystery of herself" rebounds ironically on a Modernist legacy that projects the bourgeois unconscious onto the colonized landscapes of Asia and Africa. In a deeply canny revision of Conrad's *Heart of Darkness,* Mary Ann is both Kurtz and the Intended, liberating the woman from the drawing room where she is made to embody the hypocrisy of the imperial project. Mary Ann's "crossing over to the other side," which Rat describes not as joining the enemy's army but as "becoming part of the land," deconstructs the gendering of the boonies as both feminized landscape to be humped and the furthest distance from the home where the woman waits. But Mary Ann's identification with the land displaces the Vietnamese even as it makes manifest the gendered construction of the imperial landscape. The Vietnamese are literally dismembered, figured only as pieces of skin and the tongues Mary Ann has appropriated to voice her own experience. In particular, Mary Ann's claim to the landscape of the war displaces Vietnamese women, whose bodies stereotypically in American representations negotiate the relationship between war and sexuality, material and narrative violence in country. The exclusion of Vietnamese women from the story is a necessary condition of its narratability: their absence underwrites the construction of the boonies as the place where women are not and enables the gap between "humping" and "boonies." The "problem" that racial, national, and cultural difference poses in Mary Ann's liberation from the gendered conventions of war narrative is, not coincidentally, the problem of the women's movement itself floundered on in the 1970s.

# Sharon O'Brien

## from *Willa Cather: The Emerging Voice*                           1987

In "Paul's Case," however, Cather found a momentary and happy resolution to the tension between disclosure and concealment, life and art. Placed last (and seventh) in *The Troll Garden,* the story eludes categorization. Although set in the East, it does not romanticize Eastern culture and denigrate Western; a psychological study of a romantic temperament—a subject dear to Henry James—it is not Jamesian. In this beautifully crafted story, the high-water mark of her early fiction, Cather draws upon her observations of Presbyteria and Bohemia, her memories of a gifted and unhappy student in her Latin class, and her own adolescent rebellion. The result is neither unmediated self-disclosure nor protective imitation, but a controlled work of art that does seem, as she said of Sarah Orne Jewett's Maine stories, to resemble "life itself" (*CPF,* p. 6). Long the favorite of critics, this was Cather's first choice as well, and in later years the only short story she allowed to be anthologized.

"Paul's Case" demonstrates several literary advances. Cather manages to deal with the regressive components of the creative process—the unassimilated material that weakened earlier stories—by distancing herself from the character whose regressiveness becomes self-destructive; her continuing separation from male identification paradoxically allows her to project herself sympathetically into a male character who is not an unconvincing mask; and she integrates psychological and social worlds so subtly that the main character's rebellion and disintegration becomes a social commentary that is not intrusively polemical. Although the story stands beautifully on its own, it brilliantly synthesizes the themes, images, and metaphors of *The Troll Garden*, referring back to the other stories and to the epigraphs from Kingsley and Rossetti without paying undue deference to literary predecessors. Cather would not match this achievement until "The Bohemian Girl" (1912) and *O Pioneers!* (1913).

Cather looks back at an earlier self in "Paul's Case"—William Cather, Jr.—as she portrays another imaginative, sensitive youth at odds with a repressive society. Paul's enemy is the emotionally and aesthetically bankrupt middle-class world devoted to the gods of money and respectability. Cordelia Street, his dreary home where the ugliness of petty-bourgeois life is symbolized by the "horrible yellow wallpaper," the bathroom's grimy zinc tub and dripping spigots, and his father's hairy legs and carpet slippers, is Cather's Presbyteria. Paul's alternative world of fairy-tale allure—his troll garden—is the concert hall and theater where he feasts on delicious sensations, a version of Cather's Bohemia. Repulsed by the sordid vulgarity he sees around him, Paul plays the dandy's role to signify his citizenship in Bohemia, sporting an opal pin in his frayed coat and wearing a red carnation as his badge of defiance and kinship with the fin-de-siècle aesthetes and decadents.

In many ways Paul is a male version of Willa Cather. In addition to the adolescent rebellion, she grants him her love for music and theater; her distaste for the mundane and the conventional; and her repudiation of the expected gender role, expressed in the story by Paul's distaste for the Horatio Alger values. Another resemblance may be Paul's probable homosexuality, hinted by his similarity to Oscar Wilde and later by his ambiguous night on the town with a "wild" freshman from Yale. And yet Paul is a separate fictional creation whom Cather regards critically as well as sympathetically, as when she suggests that there is something unhealthy in his nature. His eyes have a "hysterical brilliancy," the pupils "abnormally large, as though he were addicted to belladonna." Paul is addicted, we discover, although not to belladonna. He is wedded to the artificial world of the theater and concert hall where he indulges in "orgies of living" and "debauches" of sensation, like the voracious Laura in "Goblin Market."

Paul has to be a glutton in Bohemia because he is famished for spiritual, aesthetic, and emotional food in Presbyteria. The portraits of John Calvin and George Washington over his bed embody the grim, repressive patriarchal values of the national religion of financial success, the Protestant ethic allied with a patriotic capitalism. These beliefs—Paul's paternal inheritance—offer him no sustenance, while the one legacy from his dead mother (the framed motto "Feed my Lambs" embroidered in red worsted) offers him only the inadequate nurturance of a feminized Christianity. The nourishment he absorbs during his other life as usher at Carnegie Hall and hanger-on at the local repertory company is evident in the transformation he undergoes in these magical realms: he becomes more "vivacious and animated," and the "colour came to his cheeks and lips." Like Katherine Gaylord, however, Paul is the parasite-vampire greedily drawing life from an external source, and his physical appearance reveals that such food is not wholesome. Like the "thirsty, cankered, goblin-ridden" Laura in Rossetti's poem or the dying Katherine, Paul is emaciated, with "high, cramped shoulders and a narrow chest," and despite his youth his "white blue-veined face" is "drawn and wrinkled like an old man's."

The story is subtitled "A Study in Temperament," and as Cather progressively makes clear, Paul's is not the artistic temperament. Delicately and consistently, she separates her point of view from his. She demonstrates the distorting power of Paul's excitable, greedy imagination, as when she shows us the discrepancy between his vision of an opera singer as a "veritable queen of Romance" and the mundane reality: the singer is a tired woman well past her first youth, and singing is just another job for her. In addition, Paul is no connoisseur of music; he can derive the escape he desires from anything from an "orchestra to a barrel organ." Symphonies and operas mean nothing to him as art forms. What he wants is to "lose himself," to "float on the wave of [music], to be carried out, blue league after blue league, away from everything."

Although Cather associated such loss of self with the creative process, Paul's self-dissolution is not the artist's desire to create, but the child's regressive yearning to regain the preoedipal union with the mother. He uses music to enter a solipsistic realm where he passively absorbs the sensations he craves. Cather creates parallels to the regressive William of "The Burglar's Christmas," who also sought the infant's gratifications, when she has Paul follow the opera singer to her hotel. As he shivers outside in the cold (as did William in "The Burglar's Christmas"), the singer enters the elegant, welcoming building. Paul accompanies her in his imagination:

> He seemed to feel himself go after her up the steps, into the warm, lighted building, into an exotic, a tropical world of shiny glistening surfaces and basking ease. He reflected upon the mysterious dishes that were brought into the dining room, the green bottles in buckets of ice, as he had seen them in the supper party pictures of the Sunday World supplement.

Like William, Paul gains this idyllic space when he becomes a thief: he steals money from his employers to finance his trip to New York, desperate to enter the world of "basking ease" into which the opera singer has vanished. His week-long orgy of gratification further demonstrates Cather's intention to portray his temperament as regressive rather than artistic. Entering his own expensive hotel, Paul gains the house of his dreams, a protected, expensive world where the air is "deliciously soft and fragrant," magically safe from the winter storm outside. Cather connects the hotel's "enchanted palace" both with the fairy palace of the Trolls and with the tempting, seductive garden of "Goblin Market." Commenting on the artificiality and precariousness of Paul's hothouse world through her use of space and metaphor, Cather connects his womblike hotel room—seemingly a refuge from the howling January blizzard—with a flower stand where "flower gardens [were] blooming under glass cases, against the sides of which the snow flakes stuck and melted; violets, roses, carnations, lilies of the valley—somehow vastly more lovely and alluring that they blossomed thus unnaturally in the snow."

The pleasures Paul seeks during his brief stay in the luxurious hotel also reveal the regressiveness of his journey. Despite his love for music he attends the opera only once, since he can attain his real goal—passive gratification—without music's aid. He spends most of his time sleeping, eating, and drinking. His most enjoyable waking moments are those passed in the sitting room, where he drowsily contemplates his delicate flowers, elegant new clothes, and gracious surroundings, or in the hotel dining room where he tastes unfamiliar delicacies and savors champagne.

When the theft is discovered and his money runs out, Paul envisions returning to Pittsburgh—its Sabbath schools, yellowing wallpaper, and cooking smells—in images of drowning, as he senses the "tepid waters of Cordelia Street" about to "close over him finally and forever." He finds this loss of self as terrifying as his floating "blue league after blue league" on the billows of gratification had been delectable. So he chooses to lose himself in death, a decision Cather links metaphorically and psychologically with all the forms of self-dissolution he has pursued. After the artificial garden disappears, Paul's quest for annihilation leads him to a snow-covered wasteland beside the train tracks. He throws himself in front of the train—as had Anna Karenina, whose romanticism Cather also criticized—and "dropped back into the immense design of things" (*CSF*, pp. 243–61).

The differences between "The Burglar's Christmas" and "Paul's Case," both stories where the protagonists seek a seductive, self-destructive nurturance, reveal the growth in Cather's art in the intervening decade. The first is a dreamlike fantasy, the second a rich and complex work of fiction. Cather's narrative technique reveals her psychological and aesthetic distance from her character, an impressive achievement since, as she acknowledged, Paul represented part of herself. Whereas "The Burglar's Christmas" suggests that the author shares William's blissful, self-annihilating desire to return to his mother, the omniscient narrator in "Paul's Case" has sufficient detachment to expose the limitations of his fantasies, while also possessing enough sympathy with them to suggest their appeal.

Although "Paul's Case" does not comment directly on the woman artist's plight, as do several of the other stories, it does show Cather's condemnation of conventional gender arrangements. Paul's alienation is connected with the polarized sex roles that Willa Cather had also confronted in adolescence; he is William Cather, Jr.'s opposite and double, as much in conflict with the male role as she had been with the female. Cather's sympathetic portrayal of this "girl-boy" who resembles Ethelbert Nevin reveals how far she was moving from male identification. Even though Cather was still subordinating herself to the male literary tradition, she had rejected the cult of virility once exemplified by Kipling and football. Androgynous or feminine men could be oppressive to women, too, as in "'A Death in the Desert'" where Adriance Hilgarde consumes Katharine Gaylord's life and imagination. And yet Cather's ability to create Paul, who is destroyed by the male world she had once wanted to enter, shows her awareness that men as well as women could be victims of masculine—and heterosexual—roles and values.

# Edgar Allan Poe

## *Hawthorne's "Twice-Told Tales"* *1842*

W e said a few hurried words about Mr. Hawthorne in our last number, with the design of speaking more fully in the present. We are still, however, pressed for room, and must necessarily discuss his volumes more briefly and more at random than their high merits deserve.

The book professes to be a collection of *tales,* yet is, in two respects, misnamed. These pieces are now in their third republication, and, of course, are thrice-told. Moreover, they are by no means *all* tales, either in the ordinary or in the legitimate understanding of the term. Many of them are pure essays, for example, "Sights from a Steeple," "Sunday at Home," "Little Annie's Ramble," "A Rill from the Town Pump," "The Toll-Gatherer's Day," "The Haunted Mind," "The Sister Years," "Snow-Flakes," "Night Sketches," and "Foot-Prints on the Sea-Shore." We mention these matters chiefly on account of their discrepancy with that marked precision and finish by which the body of the work is distinguished.

Of the essays just named, we must be content to speak in brief. They are each and all beautiful, without being characterised by the polish and adaptation so visible in the tales proper. A painter would at once note their leading or predominant feature, and style it *repose.* There is no attempt at effect. All is quiet, thoughtful, subdued. Yet this repose may exist simultaneously with high originality of thought; and Mr. Hawthorne has demonstrated the fact. At every turn we meet with novel combinations; yet these combinations never surpass the limits of the quiet. We are soothed as we read; and withal is a calm astonishment that ideas so apparently obvious have never occurred or been presented to us before. Herein our author differs materially from Lamb or Hunt or Hazlitt—who, with vivid originality of manner and expression, have less of the true novelty of thought than is generally supposed, and whose originality, at best, has an uneasy and meretricious quaintness, replete with startling effects unfounded in nature, and inducing trains of reflection which lead to no satisfactory result. The Essays of Hawthorne have much of the character of Irving, with more of originality, and less of finish; while compared with the Spectator, they have a vast superiority at all points. The Spectator, Mr. Irving, and Mr. Hawthorne have in common that tranquil and subdued manner which we have chosen to denominate *repose;* but, in the case of the two former, this repose is attained rather by the absence of novel combination, or of originality, than otherwise, and consists chiefly in the calm, quiet, unostentatious expression of commonplace thoughts, in an unambitious, unadulterated Saxon. In them, by strong effort, we are made to conceive the absence of all. In the essays before us the absence of effort is too obvious to be mistaken, and a strong under-current of *suggestion* runs continuously beneath the upper stream of the tranquil thesis. In short, these effusions of Mr. Hawthorne are the product of a truly imaginative intellect, restrained, and in some measure repressed, by fastidiousness of taste, by constitutional melancholy and by indolence.

But it is of his tales that we desire principally to speak. The tale proper, in our opinion, affords unquestionably the fairest field for the exercise of the loftiest talent, which can be afforded by the wide domains of mere prose. Were we bidden to say how the highest genius could be most advantageously employed for the best display of its own powers, we should answer, without hesitation—in the composition of a rhymed poem, not to exceed in length what might be perused in an hour. Within this limit alone can the highest order of true poetry exist. We need only here say, upon this topic, that, in almost all classes of composition, the unity of effect or impression is a point of the greatest importance. It is clear, moreover, that this unity cannot be thoroughly preserved in productions whose perusal cannot be completed at one sitting. We may continue the reading of a prose composition, from the very nature of prose itself, much longer than we can persevere, to any good purpose, in the perusal of a poem. This latter, if truly fulfilling the demands of the poetic sentiment, induces an exaltation of the soul which cannot be long sustained. All high excitements are necessarily transient. Thus a long poem is a paradox. And, without unity of impression, the deepest effects cannot be brought about. Epics were the offspring of an imperfect sense of Art, and their reign is no more. A poem *too* brief may produce a vivid, but never an intense or enduring impression. Without a certain continuity of effort—without a certain duration or repetition of purpose—the soul is never deeply moved. There must be the dropping of the water upon the rock. De Béranger has wrought brilliant things—pungent and spirit-stirring—but, like all immassive bodies, they lack *momentum*, and thus fail to satisfy the Poetic Sentiment. They sparkle and excite, but, from want of continuity, fail deeply to impress. Extreme brevity will degenerate into epigrammatism; but the sin of extreme length is even more unpardonable. *In medio tutissimus ibis* [you will go most safely in the middle path].

Were we called upon, however, to designate that class of composition which, next to such a poem as we have suggested, should best fulfil the demands of high genius—should offer it the most advantageous field of exertion—we should unhesitatingly speak of the prose tale, as Mr. Hawthorne has here exemplified it. We allude to the short prose narrative, requiring from a half-hour to one or two hours in its perusal. The ordinary novel is objectionable, from its length, for reasons already stated in substance. As it cannot be read at one sitting, it deprives itself, of course, of the immense force derivable from *totality.* Worldly interests intervening during the pauses of perusal, modify, annul, or counteract, in a greater or less degree, the impressions of the book. But simple cessation in reading, would, of itself, be sufficient to destroy the true unity. In the brief tale, however, the author is enabled to carry out the fulness of his intention, be it what it may. During the hour of perusal the soul of the reader is at the writer's control. There are no external or extrinsic influences—resulting from weariness or interruption.

A skilful literary artist has constructed a tale. If wise, he has not fashioned his thoughts to accommodate his incidents; but having conceived, with deliberate care, a certain unique or single *effect* to be wrought out, he then invents such incidents—he then combines such events as may best aid him in establishing this preconceived effect. If his very initial sentence tend not to the outbringing of this effect, then he has failed in his first step. In the whole composition there should be no word written, of which the tendency, direct or indirect, is not to the one pre-established design. And by such means, with such care and skill, a picture is at length painted which leaves in the mind of him who contemplates it with a kindred art, a sense of the fullest satisfaction. The idea of the tale has been presented unblemished, because undisturbed; and this is an end unattainable by the novel. Undue brevity is just as exceptionable here as in the poem; but undue length is yet more to be avoided.

We have said that the tale has a point of superiority even over the poem. In fact, while the *rhythm* of this latter is an essential aid in the development of the poet's highest idea—the idea of the Beautiful—the artificialities of this rhythm are an inseparable bar to the development of all points of thought or expression which have their basis in *Truth*. But Truth is often, and in very great degree, the aim of the tale. Some of the finest tales are tales of ratiocination. Thus the field of this species of composition, if not in so elevated a region on the mountain of Mind, is a table-land of far vaster extent than the domain of the mere poem. Its products are never so rich, but infinitely more numerous, and more appreciable by the mass of mankind. The writer of the prose tale, in short, may bring to his theme a vast variety of modes or inflections of thought and expression—(the ratiocinative, for example, the sarcastic, or the humorous) which are not only antagonistical to the nature of the poem, but absolutely forbidden by one of its most peculiar and indispensable adjuncts; we allude, of course, to rhythm. It may be added here, *par parenthèse,* that the author who aims at the purely beautiful in a prose tale is laboring at great disadvantage. For Beauty can be better treated in the poem. Not so with terror, or passion, or horror, or a multitude of such other points. And here it will be seen how full of prejudice are the usual animadversions against those *tales of effect,* many fine examples of which were found in the earlier numbers of Blackwood. The impressions produced were wrought in a legitimate sphere of action, and constituted a legitimate although sometimes an exaggerated interest. They were relished by every man of genius: although there were found many men of genius who condemned them without just ground. The true critic will but demand that the design intended be accomplished, to the fullest extent, by the means most advantageously applicable.

We have very few American tales of real merit—we may say, indeed, none, with the exception of "The Tales of a Traveller" of Washington Irving, and these "Twice-Told Tales" of Mr. Hawthorne. Some of the pieces of Mr. John Neal abound in vigor and originality; but in general, his compositions of this class are excessively diffuse, extravagant, and indicative of an imperfect sentiment of Art. Articles at random are, now and then, met with in our periodicals which might be advantageously compared with the best effusions of the British Magazines; but, upon the whole, we are far behind our progenitors in this department of literature.

Of Mr. Hawthorne's Tales we would say, emphatically, that they belong to the highest region of Art—an Art subservient to genius of a very lofty order. We had supposed, with good reason for so supposing, that he had been thrust into his present position by one of the impudent *cliques* which beset our literature, and whose pretensions it is our full purpose to expose at the earliest opportunity; but we have been most agreeably mistaken. We know of few compositions which the critic can more honestly commend than these "Twice-Told Tales." As Americans, we feel proud of the book.

Mr. Hawthorne's distinctive trait is invention, creation, imagination, originality—a trait which, in the literature of fiction, is positively worth all the rest. But the nature of originality, so far as regards its manifestation in letters, is but imperfectly understood. The inventive or original mind as frequently displays itself in novelty of *tone* as in novelty of matter. Mr. Hawthorne is original at *all* points.

It would be a matter of some difficulty to designate the best of these tales; we repeat that, without exception, they are beautiful. "Wakefield" is remarkable for the skill with which an old idea—a well-known incident—is worked up or discussed. A man of whims conceives the purpose of quitting his wife and residing *incognito*, for twenty years, in her immediate neighborhood. Something of this kind actually happened in London. The force of Mr. Hawthorne's tale lies in the analysis of the motives which must or might have impelled the husband to such folly, in the first instance, with the possible causes of his perseverance. Upon this thesis a sketch of singular power has been constructed.

"The Wedding Knell" is full of the boldest imagination—an imagination fully controlled by taste. The most captious critic could find no flaw in this production.

"The Minister's Black Veil" is a masterly composition of which the sole defect is that to the rabble its exquisite skill will be *caviare*. The *obvious* meaning of this article will be found to smother its insinuated one. The *moral* put into the mouth of the dying minister will be supposed to convey the *true* import of the narrative; and that a crime of dark dye, (having reference to the "young lady") has been committed, is a point which only minds congenial with that of the author will perceive.

"Mr. Higginbotham's Catastrophe" is vividly original and managed most dexterously.

"Dr. Heidegger's Experiment" is exceedingly well imagined, and executed with surpassing ability. The artist breathes in every line of it.

"The White Old Maid" is objectionable, even more than the "Minister's Black Veil," on the score of its mysticism. Even with the thoughtful and analytic, there will be much trouble in penetrating its entire import.

"The Hollow of the Three Hills" we would quote in full, had we space;—not as evincing higher talent than any of the other pieces, but as affording an excellent example of the author's peculiar ability. The subject is commonplace. A witch subjects the Distant and the Past to the view of a mourner. It has been the fashion to describe, in such cases, a mirror in which the images of the absent appear; or a cloud of smoke is made to arise, and thence the figures are gradually unfolded. Mr. Hawthorne has wonderfully heightened his effect by making the ear, in place of the eye, the medium by which the fantasy is conveyed. The head of the mourner is enveloped in the cloak of the witch, and within its magic folds there arise sounds which have an all-sufficient intelligence. Throughout this article also, the artist is conspicuous—not more in positive than in negative merits. Not only is all done that should be done, but (what perhaps is an end with more difficulty attained) there is nothing done which should not be. Every word *tells,* and there is not a word which does *not* tell.

In "Howe's Masquerade" we observe something which resembles plagiarism—but which *may be* a very flattering coincidence of thought. We quote the passage in question.

> With a dark flush of wrath upon his brow they saw the general *draw his sword* and *advance to meet* the figure *in the cloak* before the latter had stepped one pace upon the floor.
>
> "*Villain, unmuffle yourself,*" cried he, "you pass no farther!"
>
> The figure, without blenching a hair's breadth from the sword which was pointed at his breast, made a solemn pause, and *lowered the cape of the cloak* from his face, yet not sufficiently for the spectators to catch a glimpse of it. But Sir William Howe had evidently seen enough. The sternness of his countenance gave place to a look of wild amazement, if not horror, while he recoiled several steps from the figure, *and let fall his sword upon the floor.*—See Vol. 2, p. 20.

The idea here is, that the figure in the cloak is the phantom or reduplication of Sir William Howe; but in an article called "William Wilson," one of the "Tales of the Grotesque and Arabesque," we have not only the same idea, but the same idea similarly presented in several respects. We quote two paragraphs, which our readers may compare with what has been already given. We have italicized, above, the immediate particulars of resemblance.

> The brief moment in which I averted my eyes had been sufficient to produce, apparently, a material change in the arrangement at the upper or farther end of the room. A large mirror, it appeared to me, now stood where none had been perceptible before; and as I stepped up to it in extremity of terror, mine own image, but with features all pale and dabbled in blood, *advanced* with a feeble and tottering gait to meet me.
>
> Thus it appeared I say, but was not. It was Wilson, who then stood before me in the agonies of dissolution. Not a line in all the marked and singular lineaments of that face which was not even identically mine own. *His mask and cloak lay where he had thrown them, upon the floor.* Vol. 2, p. 57.

Here it will be observed that, not only are the two general conceptions identical, but there are various *points* of similarity. In each case the figure seen is the wraith of duplication of the beholder. In each case the scene is a masquerade. In each case the figure is cloaked. In each, there is a quarrel—that is to say, angry words pass between the parties. In each the beholder is enraged. In each the cloak and sword fall upon the floor. The "villain, unmuffle yourself," of Mr. H. is precisely paralleled by a passage at page 56 of "William Wilson."

In the way of objection we have scarcely a word to say of these tales. There is, perhaps, a somewhat too general or prevalent *tone*—a tone of melancholy and mysticism. The subjects are insufficiently varied. There is not so much of *versatility* evinced as we might well be warranted in expecting from the high powers of Mr. Hawthorne. But beyond these trivial exceptions we have really none to make. The style is purity itself. Force abounds. High imagination gleams from every page. Mr. Hawthorne is a man of the truest genius. We only regret that the limits of our Magazine will not permit us to pay him that full tribute of commendation, which, under other circumstances, we should be so eager to pay.

# Dana Sachs

## Small Tragedies and Distant Stars                                      1999

### Le Minh Khue's Language of Lost Ideals

In Le Minh Khue's short story "The Distant Stars," three teenage North Vietnamese girls detonate unexploded bombs and fill craters along the Ho Chi Minh Trail during the American War. Theirs is an uncertain existence. Explosions bury them in rubble. Bombs drop dangerously close to their hideout. But the young women approach their duty with good humor and a love that is "selfless, passionate, and carefree, only found in the hearts of soldiers."[1] War, as seen through the eyes of these young women, becomes the noble struggle of people who fervently believe in its goals.

In both its physical detail and ideological enthusiasm, "The Distant Stars" mirrors the early years of the author's life. Khue wrote the story in 1968, when she was 19 years old and living, like the young women in the story, as a soldier at the front. Just as the circumstances of the story resemble what Khue experienced in her own life, so, too, do the mood and tone of the writing directly parallel the feelings of the young women. One of the characters says, "I loved everyone, with a passionate love, a love beyond words, that only someone who had stood on that hill in those moments, as I did, could understand fully."[2] It's not hard to imagine an authorial voice which would cynically contradict such hopeful passion, but this story is narrated by one of these young women herself. Without any distance between the narrator and her implied audience, the story becomes imbued with the idealism of its characters.

The patriotic zeal of "The Distant Stars" contrasts markedly with the tone of a later story, "A Small Tragedy," published in 1990 when the author was 41 years of age. Once again, Khue presents an image of three girls at war, but this image is not a positive one. An important political official orders thousands of young people to fill bomb craters along a riverbank during the middle of the day. Although precautions

---

1 Le Minh Khue, *The Stars, The Earth, The River: Short Fiction by Le Minh Khue*. Translated by Bac Hoai Tran and Dana Sachs. Wayne Karlin, ed. (Willimantic, CT: Curbstone Press, 1997), 20.
2 Le Minh Khue, *The Stars*, 20.

might have been taken, none were, and when American AD6s fly over and drop bombs on the young people, many are killed. As one witness describes the scene, "I've never seen so many people die like that. They were empty-handed, puny, running like ants on the naked riverbank. . . . I tried to dig into one depression to pull out three young girls but they died in such a tight embrace I couldn't even untangle them."[3] Although this description sounds horrifying, its language is devoid of emotion. The closest the witness comes to articulating his horror is that same statement "I've never seen so many people die like that," which seems almost clinically detached in comparison with the passionate engagement of the earlier story. The effect of this understatement, however, is to increase the story's emotive power. By refusing to describe an emotional reaction, the author forces us to imagine the scene for ourselves.

A comparison of these images of young women in "The Distant Stars" and "A Small Tragedy" demonstrates a marked change in Khue's writing in the years since the war's end. Like a call and response across decades, the earlier, optimistic tale of three girls engaged in a heroic struggle is answered by a brutal depiction of three girls martyred for no reason whatsoever. In thematic terms, war, which once seemed like a valiant fight for freedom and self-determination, becomes an enterprise in which the powerful rule over the lives—and the deaths—of the powerless. In terms of Khue's prose style, a mature voice full of muted anger has come to replace the optimism and naiveté that marks the writing of her youth. Thus, Le Minh Khue, who once expressed the idealism and hopefulness of her nation, emerges as a severe critic of that society in which she once saw such promise. As we shall see, this social criticism is seldom explicit. Indeed, one of the great strengths of Khue's work lies in the ways she uses various literary techniques to subtly yet forcefully make her points. Through manipulations of narrative voice, contrasts between past and present, complex characterizations, and highly precise descriptions, she creates what I call her "language of lost ideals."

Before looking more closely at Khue's work, however, it is useful to reflect in a more general way on the literary milieu in which she has pursued her career. It is not unusual for a writer of Khue's generation to show disenchantment with Vietnam's government and Vietnamese society. In fact, an argument could be made that lost idealism has become the major literary theme in postwar Vietnam. From the perspective of the North Vietnamese, the war against South Vietnam and the United States was a continuation of the revolutionary struggle to drive the French colonizers out of their country. The ideals of this revolution promoted high expectations for a postcolonial society in which the lives of the formerly colonized people would become greatly improved. After the war, however, the greater goals of revolution were quickly subsumed by totalitarian policies and the grim struggles of everyday existence.

For many Vietnamese, the hollowness of revolutionary victory brought tragic disappointment, particularly in light of how much they had sacrificed in order to achieve that victory. In the mid-1980s, Vietnamese literature began to reflect that disappointment. This was the period during which the Vietnamese government introduced a series of economic and political reforms known as *Doi Moi*, or "renovation."

3 Le Minh Khue, *The Stars*, 186.

After years of promoting Socialist-Realist fiction, which placed the propaganda needs of the revolution above a writer's personal interests or style, the government began to allow a wider range of artistic expression. Communist Party Secretary General Nguyen Van Linh proclaimed to his nation's writers: "Speak the truth. No matter what happens, Comrades, don't curb your pen."[4]

The writers' response to this new freedom was to begin producing what has come to be known as *Doi Moi* literature, which led to the publication of numerous distinctive voices and authorial styles, many of which were critical of postwar Vietnamese society. University of California at Berkeley historian Peter Zinoman finds in the fiction of author Nguyen Huy Thiep, for example, "an implicit indictment of contemporary political culture."[5] And Harvard University critic Hue Tam Ho Tai, whose writing on Duong Thu Huong helped inspire this paper, notes that that novelist's "evolution as a writer is also the story of her transformation from war heroine to political dissident."[6] These authors, who came of age during what Vietnamese call "the American War," correspond to the "Vietnam Generation" of writers in the States. Like their American counterparts, they marked their transition into adulthood with an increasing awareness of the hypocrisies of the society in which they lived. No longer compelled to present their country as a unified nation of hardy citizens struggling for the greater good, *Doi Moi* writers portrayed Vietnam as, in the words of poet and editor Linh Dinh, "a backward, rundown and corrupt society."[7]

The transition from producing pro-government propaganda to writing severe critiques of their society has often caused problems for Vietnamese authors. Despite the secretary-general's urging that writers not curb their pens, criticism of the status quo has not always gone unpunished. When Duong Thu Huong became particularly outspoken in her condemnation of the Vietnamese government, she was arrested and held for seven months. Nguyen Huy Thiep, one of the most talented writers of his generation, has had trouble even getting his fiction published. And, over the past several years, Le Minh Khue has endured so much subtle harassment that she now hesitates before publishing anything at all.

This climate is, in part, responsible for the tendency among *Doi Moi* writers to keep their political criticism indirect. Nguyen Huy Thiep's short story "Fired Gold," for example, has three different more and less politically controversial conclusions, and the narrator exhorts the reader to pick the one that "he or she feels is most suitable."[8] Ho Anh Thai, on the other hand, writes folktale-like parables which astute readers will recognize as veiled comments on contemporary society.

Le Minh Khue's most scathing attacks center, first, on the transgressions that, in the name of revolution, took place in years past and, second, on the crimes of

4 Linh Dinh, ed. *Night Again: Contemporary Fiction from Vietnam* (New York: Seven Stories Press, 1996), xii.
5 Peter Zinoman, "Nguyen Huy Thiep's '*Vang Lua*' and the Nature of Intellectual Dissent in Contemporary Vietnam," *The Vietnam Forum* 14:37 (1994).
6 Hue Tam Ho Tai, "Duong Thu Huong and the Literature of Disenchantment," *The Vietnam Forum* 14:82 (1994).
7 Linh Dinh, *Night*, xiv.
8 Nguyen Huy Thiep, "*Vang Lua*" [Fired Gold], *The Vietnam Forum* 14:24 (1994).

pettiness and greed that occur at present. Because they don't explicitly criticize contemporary political culture, such attacks might serve to keep sharp-eyed authorities at bay, but political pressure is not the sole reason an author like Khue chooses to be indirect. Renewed artistic freedom has compelled the country's writers not only to express their political views but also to experiment with language in complex and original ways. In Khue's language of lost ideals, dry, understated commentary becomes even more powerful than explicit critiques. In "A Small Tragedy," for example, someone asks what happened to the government official responsible for sending all those young people to their deaths by ordering them to fill bomb craters in broad daylight. The witness replies, "Nothing happened to him. There was only this report in the newspapers: At the G Bridge we shot down an AD6. The soldiers and people put on a magnificently heroic struggle."[9] Rather than resorting to straightforward criticism, Khue appropriates the vocabulary of revolution—"magnificent," "heroic," "struggle," words in whose name these young people died—in order to expose the hypocrisy of an ideology that could so casually martyr its youth.

To best understand Khue's ideological, intellectual, and artistic development away from a story like "The Distant Stars" and toward "A Small Tragedy," one needs to recognize that to Vietnamese of Khue's generation in particular the crimes depicted in "A Small Tragedy" are signs of the degeneration of society. In his introduction to Le Minh Khue's collection of stories, *The Stars, The Earth, The River*, editor Wayne Karlin notes that

> "[Khue] grew up as part of a generation of young people to whom the justice of their cause was as clear as the fact of the American bombs falling on their cities; they were fervent not only with a belief in liberation from foreign domination and national unification, but also in the faith that a socially just and humane society would grow from the roots of victory."[10]

The distance between this idealistic clarity of purpose and subsequent social decay, between the hopefulness of "The Distant Stars" and the hopelessness of "A Small Tragedy," is the terrain that Le Minh Khue explores.

If one notable trait of Khue's language of lost ideals is a certain detached authorial voice, another is the complexity of her characterizations. For comparison, we should first look at the characters in the early story, "The Distant Stars," people who are almost uniformly heroic. Not only are the young women models of self-sacrifice and revolutionary zeal, but all the men are as well. The narrator describes one male officer as "a polite and hospitable guy who didn't smoke or flirt with girls."[11] Other soldiers, driving by in their trucks, toss the young women "Ngoc Lan toothpaste, perfume scented writing paper, and lemon candies."[12] Such characterizations have several effects on the story. The details, contrasting with the images of rubbled land-

9  Le Minh Khue, *The Stars*, 187.
10  Wayne Karlin, "Introduction," in *The Stars, The Earth, The River: Short Fiction by Le Minh Khue* (Willimantic, CT: Curbstone Press, 1997), vii.
11  Le Minh Khue, *The Stars*, 16.
12  Le Minh Khue, *The Stars*, 15.

scape, heat, and unexploded bombs, offer the reader exactly what they offer the young women—a respite from the bleakness of the war. But, more importantly, the images of beauty combine with the heroic characterizations of soldiers to imbue the story with a sense that something pure and good exists beyond the grueling struggles of war. Clearly, it's not just the girls who believe that their own sacrifices have meaning, but the author of the story as well.

As we will see from Khue's later work, these convictions did not long survive the war. It is impossible to judge exactly when Khue began to question her nationalist idealism, but the stories she published after the introduction of *Doi Moi* in 1986 show a marked shift from the patriotic zeal of "The Distant Stars." An interesting contrast to that earlier story is "The Blue Sky," first published in 1986. Like the young women in "The Distant Stars," the young journalist Ninh in "The Blue Sky" has a passionate belief in the revolutionary cause. But this story's omniscient, third-person point of view places a distance between the reader and the protagonist that the first-person narrative of "The Distant Stars" didn't have. As a result, Ninh's passion seems more ridiculous than admirable. She is so infatuated by the idea of heroism that she falls in love with every soldier she interviews. According to the narrator, "The quality of her emotion made it difficult for her to distinguish between love for an individual soldier and love for all of them."[13] To complement the passion of her news articles, Ninh wants as her editor a dashing man who wears "white sports clothes, [whistles] often, and [takes] the stairs three steps at a time."[14] In fact, however, she has to answer to Tuan Khang, a balding bureaucrat who beats his wife for losing the family's meat ration tickets and takes the stairs one step at a time. Worse, he's an experienced editor who questions the truth of the dramatic tales she brings back from the front. The sarcasm of this characterization makes it obvious that the author has a different goal in mind than inspiring revolutionary passion among her readers.

The exaggerated personality differences between Ninh and Tuan Khang set the stage for their ideological conflict. Whereas Ninh's belief in the cause leads her to accept as true every word she hears, Tuan Khang knows when to be suspicious. And though their arguments focus ostensibly on whether Ninh is too gullible or not, at the heart of their relationship rages a battle between idealism and cynicism. At story's end, Tuan Khang has succeeded in getting Ninh to share some of his indifference, and as a result Ninh's articles are now "accurate, temperate, and no longer as full of fire as before."[15] Ninh's conversion does not signal merely the triumph of clear-sightedness over gullibility, however; the characterizations are too complex to allow us such simple satisfactions. As readers, we have to respect Tuan Khang's motives in questioning the accuracy of Ninh's stories, but the change he effects in Ninh nevertheless disappoints us, because along with her naiveté, Ninh loses her passion. The birth of skepticism, Khue seems to say, marks the death of hope and high ideals.

In "The Blue Sky," opposing personalities demonstrate the clash of cynicism and

---

13  Le Minh Khue, *The Stars*, 26.
14  Le Minh Khue, *The Stars*, 29.
15  Le Minh Khue, *The Stars*, 35.

idealism that has so deeply marked twentieth-century life in Vietnam. The story "An Evening Away from the City"—which was written in 1982, foreshadowing the *Doi Moi* literary movement of four years later—also explores this clash, but here the author creates her oppositions by moving backwards and forwards in time. Following the fortunes of two friends during and after the war, the narrative moves back and forth between a noble past and a more self-involved and superficial present. As she did in "The Distant Stars," Khue fills this story's scenes of war with contrasting images of beauty and ugliness. Thus, Tan and Vien, the two friends, find happiness at the front, where "even their wishes [were] lighthearted," where young female soldiers "[embroidered] little flowers on white scarves, which they [tied] into their hair to make themselves even more charming."[16] At the same time, these two young women "always said goodbye as if they were offering each other their final testaments. Life and death were very close together. Who could know?"[17] By contrasting descriptions of embroidered scarves with those of wrenching goodbyes, Khue uses her characters' love of life to make their willingness to sacrifice themselves seem even more heroic.

These images of beauty and heroism recall those of the earlier story "The Distant Stars," but in "An Evening Away From the City" Khue adds a layer of contrasts that forces the reader to question the endurance of those heroic ideals. Within a few years of the war's end, the two friends, who had once meant so much to each other, begin to grow apart. They each marry, but while Tan lives in luxury in the city, Vien moves to the countryside, where she struggles to survive with too many children, an abusive husband, and almost no money. Vien writes Tan a letter describing her misery, but Tan barely takes the time to read it. When they do finally meet again, Tan promises to help Vien but never does, being too busy with her fashionable social life in the city to make good on her promise. Here, the selflessness that the young Khue had idealized in "The Distant Stars" becomes, under the pen of the more mature writer, a relic of a past as fleeting and impossible to maintain as youth.

Khue's Vietnam has not merely lost its ideological bearings (if it ever truly had them); it has also become so emotionally empty that friendship and love barely survive. The backdrop to the romance in the 1991 story "The Last Rain of the Monsoon," for example, is a dingy construction site where the industrial fumes are so powerful that even the water in the shower smells like diesel fuel. Here, Mi and Binh fall in love. Both are married, but marriage is not the barrier that ultimately keeps them apart. Rather, their lives are too miserable to admit the possibility of anything better. At first, after Mi says goodbye to Binh, she struggles against her situation. "If things are like this forever and ever," she says, "then there's nothing left for me."[18] A day later, though still broken hearted, she's already resigned herself to her fate. Through Mi's friend, the story's narrator, the author reveals the bitter irony of the situation: "These days, tears only flow when people play the wrong [lottery] number. And yet here she was, crying over love, over the trivial things of life, over extravagant wishes."[19] These tiny, telling

---

16  Le Minh Khue, *The Stars*, 159.
17  Le Minh Khue, *The Stars*, 160.
18  Le Minh Khue, *The Stars*, 110.
19  Le Minh Khue, *The Stars*, 116.

details build upon each other, enriching Khue's writing with irony and pathos. By focusing subtly on the smallest details—a shower that smells like diesel fuel, people's obsession with the lottery, the off-hand trivialization of love—Khue deftly implies larger points about the degeneration of her society.

As we have seen, narrative detachment, complex characterizations, contrasts between past and present, and precise, extremely telling details are a few of the qualities that contribute to Khue's language of lost ideals. Such qualities mark a shift away from the simple, naive exuberance of "The Distant Stars." "The Blue Sky," which, like "The Distant Stars," is about a young woman at war, describes the protagonist's development from a wide-eyed idealist into a clear-eyed skeptic, with regretful statements, like "[Ninh] didn't fall in love as easily," calling attention to the losses that come with greater awareness. Similarly, "An Evening Away from the City" unfolds with stark precision, and the relentless comparisons between the past and the present make the story of Tan's betrayal of Vien sound like the argument of a prosecutor outlining the chronology of a crime. In "A Small Tragedy," as in the love story "The Last Rain of the Monsoon," Khue relies on the understated power of realistic detail. Here, the image of young people callously mutilated by bombs dispels any romantic notions of war, forcing us to ask whether war is heroic after all, and whether the sacrifices people make in the name of revolution ultimately have any purpose. American writers have long been asking such questions, but in the political climate of Vietnam, military service is all but deified, and dissenting voices have been relatively few. In suggesting the questions they do, therefore, Le Minh Khue's stories force a reexamination of Vietnamese society's most fundamental ideals.

## References

Hue, Tam Ho Tai. "Duong Thu Huong and the Literature of Disenchantment." *The Vietnam Forum* 14 (1994): 82–91.

Karlin, Wayne. "Introduction." In *The Stars, The Earth, The River: Short Fiction by Le Minh Khue*. Wayne Karlin, ed. vii–xviii. Willimantic, CT: Curbstone Press, 1997.

Khue, Le Minh. *The Stars, the Earth, the River: Short Fiction by Le Minh Khue*. Trans. Bac Hoai Tran and Dana Sachs. Ed. Wayne Karlin. Willimantic, CT: Curbstone Press, 1997.

Linh, Dinh (ed.). *Night, Again: Contemporary Fiction from Vietnam*. New York: Seven Stories Press, 1996.

Nguyen, Huy Thiep. "*Vang Lua*" [Fired Gold]. Trans. Peter Zinoman. *The Vietnam Forum* 14 (1994): 18–25.

Zinoman, Peter. "Nguyen Huy Thiep's 'Vang Lua' and the Nature of Intellectual Dissent in Contemporary Vietnam." *The Vietnam Forum* 14 (1994): 36–44.

# Pancho Savery

## Baldwin, Bebop, and "Sonny's Blues" 1992

**W**ell before James Baldwin died in 1987, the literary critical establishment had made up its mind about him. Thus, there was hardly any surprise when Lee A. Daniels's front page *New York Times* obituary lauded, "James Baldwin, Eloquent Essayist In Behalf of Civil Rights, Is Dead." Equally unsurprising was Mark Feeney's *Boston Globe* "Appreciation" entitled "A Forceful Voice on the Issue of Race." What James Baldwin had become was, to a large extent, black America's interpreter of black America to and for white America. As such, Baldwin was essentially mummified into the "Voice of the Civil Rights Movement," a historical relic of the 1950s through the 1970s. But even in this position, Baldwin was not always on solid ground. In 1963, the same year Baldwin published *The Fire Next Time,* considered by many his quintessential work, Amiri Baraka called Baldwin, in "Brief Reflections on Two Hot Shots," the "Joan of Arc of the cocktail party" and characterized his work as "the *cry,* the spavined whine and plea" (later published in 1966, 117). Three years later, Larry Neal would declare that "Baldwin has missed the point by a wide margin," because his "uncertainty over identity and his failure to utilize, to its fullest extent, traditional aspects of Afro-American culture has tended to dull the intensity of his work" (later published in 1989a, 61). And although Baraka would change by the time of Baldwin's death, calling him in "Jimmy!" "this glorious, elegant griot of our oppressed African-American nation" (1989, 127) who "made us feel . . . that we could defend ourselves and define ourselves" (129), it still seems that Baldwin will go down in literary history primarily as the witness to and conscience of America's years of racial confrontation. But is this accurate? What of the eight books of fiction Baldwin published? Not only do I want to suggest that we need to reevaluate the fiction, but I want to do so by looking at Baldwin's most celebrated short story and suggest that, even here, there is more to be seen than has been previously, and that "Sonny's Blues" demonstrates a full use of "traditional aspects of Afro-American culture."

In his 1937 Emersonial manifesto "Blueprint for Negro Writing," Richard Wright asserted the existence of "a culture of the Negro" whose main sources were "(1) the Negro church; and (2) the folklore of the Negro people" (39). For Wright, this folklore expressed itself in "Blues, spirituals, and folk tales recounted from mouth to mouth." Wright criticized writers for not making more use of the folk tradition in their work, because in folklore "the Negro achieved his most indigenous and complete expression" (1978, 40). Two years later, Saunders Redding published the first in-depth, full-length work of African American literary criticism, *To Make a Poet Black* (1987 [1939]). There, Redding, following up on Wright, read African American literature from the beginning to the end of the Harlem Renaissance, and found that only two writers had escaped the two traps he found continually lurking. These were the traps of writing from a "very practical desire to adjust himself to the American environment" (1987, 3), and the trap of having to simultaneously write for two audiences in order to succeed. The two writers Redding found to be most successful, Sterling Brown and Zora Neale Hurston, were successful because of their works' immersion in "folk material" (122).

The most successful African American writers have continued to mine this vein, but the critics have often been behind. I would like to suggest that Baldwin is a case in point. Although there have been interesting analyses of "Sonny's Blues," none of them has gotten to the specificities of the music and the wider cultural implications.[1] Music is not simply the bridge the narrator crosses to get closer to Sonny, nor is it sufficient to point out that the music in the climactic scene is labeled as blues. What kind and form of these particular blues make all the difference.

An interesting way to begin thinking about "Sonny's Blues" is to think about when the story is supposed to be taking place. We know from the acknowledgments that it was first published in the summer of 1957, but can we be more precise? Part of the story takes place during "the war," but which one is it, Korea or World War II, and does it matter?

Baldwin tells us that Sonny's father "died suddenly, during a drunken weekend in the middle of the war, when Sonny was fifteen" (1966, 97). "[J]ust after Daddy died" (97), Sonny's brother, whom we know is seven years older (93), is "home on leave from the army" (97) and has his final conversation with his mother. In the passage, which begins with that wonderful evocation of the coming of the darkness on Sunday afternoon with the old and young together in the living room, "Mama" admonishes her older son to watch out for Sonny "and don't let him fall, no matter what it looks like is happening to him and no matter how evil you gets with him" (101). But the narrator tells us that he did not listen, got married, and went back to war. The next time he comes home is "on a special furlough" for his mother's funeral. The war is still going on. The narrator reminds Sonny that Sonny must "finish school," "And you only got another year" (106). The school that Sonny must finish is obviously high school. Thus, no more than a year or so has passed since the death of the father, who died "in the middle of the war." The United States was in World War II from December of 1941 until August of 1945. "The middle of the war" would have been approximately 1943, or 1942 if you start from the beginning of the war in Europe. Thus, the crucial conversation between Sonny and his brother, in which Sonny first says he wants to be a jazz musician, takes place about 1944. If, on the other hand, the war being fought is the Korean War (June 1950 to July 1953), the conversation takes place about 1952.

When Sonny reveals to his brother that first he wants to be a musician, and then a jazz musician, and then not a jazz musician like Louis Armstrong but one like Charlie Parker, the brother, after asking "Who's this Parker character," says, "I'll go out and buy all the cat's records right away, all right?" (104). From 1942 to 1944, there was a ban on recordings, at least in part due to a scarcity of materials because of the war. In 1944, Sonny's brother would not have been able to go out and buy new material by Bird (Parker) because there wasn't any. Bird's seminal recordings were made between 1945 and 1948.[2] It is, thus, reasonable to conclude that the war is the Korean.

By 1952, Bird had already revolutionized music. And so when Sonny's brother asks Sonny to name a musician he admires and Sonny says "Bird" and his brother says "Who?," Sonny is justified with his, "Bird! Charlie Parker! Don't they teach you nothing in the goddamn army?" (103).[3] Sonny's brother, at age twenty-four in 1952, can certainly be expected to have heard of Bird. After all, he has heard of Louis Armstrong.

But it is in Sonny's response to Armstrong that one of the keys to the story lies. Sonny's brother admits that, to him, the term "jazz musician" is synonymous with "hanging around nightclubs, clowning around on bandstands," and is, thus, "beneath him, somehow" (103). When, from this perspective, jazz musicians are "in a class with . . . 'good-time people'," his mentioning of Louis Armstrong needs to be looked at.

From one perspective, Louis Armstrong is one of the true titans of jazz.[4] On the other hand, to many of the Bebop era, Armstrong was considered part of the old guard who needed to be swept out with the new musical revolution, and Armstrong himself was not positively disposed towards Bop. One turning point came in February of 1949 when Armstrong was chosen King of the Zulus of the Mardi Gras parade in New Orleans. To many, he seemed to be donning the minstrel mask of acceptability to the larger white world, and this seemed confirmed when, the same week, he appeared on the cover of *Time* (February 21, 1949).[5] It would be "natural" that Sonny's brother, the future algebra teacher, would have heard of Armstrong, here the symbol of the old conservative, but not of Parker, not only the new and the revolutionary, but the "had been a revolutionary" for seven years. Sonny's response to Armstrong makes this clear:

> I suggested helpfully: "You mean—like Louis Armstrong?"
> His face closed as though I'd struck him. "No. I'm not talking about none of that old-time, down home crap."(103)

But the differences between Armstrong and Parker represent something much larger. Throughout history, African Americans have been engaged in intramural debate about the nature of identity. Du Bois, of course, put it best when he defined "double-consciousness" in *The Souls of Black Folk* and concluded:

> One ever feels his twoness,—an American, a Negro; two souls, two thoughts, two unreconciled strivings; two warring ideals in one dark body, whose dogged strength alone keeps it from being torn asunder. (1969, 45)

Du Bois's battles with Booker T. Washington and later with Marcus Garvey are one of the major moments in African American history when this debate was articulated. But there have also been many others; for example, Frederick Douglass and Martin Delany debating whether Africa or America was the place for blacks, and King and Malcolm on the issue of integration. But in order to look at African American culture fully, we cannot limit ourselves to the study of politics and history. As numerous commentators have pointed out, music is the key to much of the African American dispute over this issue of culture; and, therefore, knowledge of it is essential. For example:

> The complexities of the collective Black experience have always had their most valid and moving expression in Black music; music is the chief artifact created out of that experience. (William 1972, 136)

> To reiterate, the key to where the black people have to go is in the music. Our music has always been the most dominant manifestation of what we are and feel. . . . The best of it has always operated at the core of our lives, forcing itself upon us as in a ritual. It has always, somehow, represented the collective psyche. (Neal 1989b, 21–22)

> I think that it is not fantastic to say that only in music has there been any significant Negro contribution to a *formal* American culture. (Baraka 1963, 130–31)

> The tenor is a rhythm instrument, and the best statements Negroes have made, of what their soul is, have been on tenor saxophone. (Ornette Coleman, quoted in Spellman 1970, 102)

> There has never been an equivalent to Duke Ellington or Louis Armstrong in Negro writing, and even the best of contemporary literature written by Negroes cannot yet be compared to the fantastic beauty of the music of Charlie Parker. (Baraka, "Myth," 1966, 107)

Houston Baker has gone as far as suggesting that there is a "blues matrix" at the center of African American culture and that "a vernacular theory" of African American literature can be developed from this idea.

What I am arguing in general is that music is the cornerstone of African American culture; and that, further, Bebop was an absolute key moment. In African American culture, Bebop is as significant as the Harlem Renaissance, and Armstrong and Parker's roles somewhat resemble those of Washington and Du Bois, and Du Bois and Garvey. Armstrong, Washington, and Du Bois (to Garvey) represented the known, the old, and the traditional whose accomplishments were noted but who were considered somewhat passé by the younger, more radical Parker, Du Bois (to Washington), and Garvey.

Musically, Bebop was to a large extent a revolt against swing and the way African American music had been taken over, and diluted, by whites. Perhaps no more emblematic of this is that the aptly named Paul Whiteman and Benny Goodman were dubbed respectively "The King of Jazz" and "The King of Swing." As Gary Giddins succinctly puts it:

> Jazz in the Swing Era was so frequently compromised by chuckle-headed bandleaders, most of them white, who diluted and undermined the triumphs of serious musicians that a new virtuosity was essential. The modernists brandished it like a weapon. They confronted social and musical complacency in a spirit of arrogant romanticism. (1987, 78)

Ortiz Walton describes the musical revolution as "a major challenge to European standards of musical excellence and the beginning of a conscious black aesthetic in music" (1972, 104) because of Bebop's challenge to the European aesthetic emphasis on vibrato. This emphasis produced music that was easily imitable, and thus open to commercialization and co-optation. By revolting against this direction the music had taken and reclaiming it, "Afro-American musicians gained a measure of control over their product, a situation that had not existed since the expansion of the music industry in the Twenties" (106).

Another aspect of this Bop reclamation was a renewed emphasis on the blues. Although some people seem to think there is a dispute over this issue, it is clear from listening to Parker's first session as a leader that "Billie's Bounce" and "Now's the Time" are blues pieces. In his autobiography, Dizzy Gillespie asserts:

> Beboppers couldn't destroy the blues without seriously injuring themselves. The modern jazz musicians always remained very close to the blues musician. That was a characteristic of the bopper. (1979, 294)

To this we could add the following from Baraka:

> Bebop also re-established blues as the most important Afro-American form in Negro music by its astonishingly contemporary restatement of the basic blues impulse. The boppers returned to this basic form, reacting against the all but stifling advance artificial melody had made into jazz during the swing era. (1963, 194)

We could also look at Bebop in terms of the movement from the diatonic to the chromatic, from a more closed to an open form, a movement in the direction of a greater concern with structure, the beginning of jazz postmodernism that would reach its zenith in the work of Ornette Coleman. In "The Poetics of Jazz," Ajay Heble concludes, "Whereas diatonic jazz attempts to posit musical language as a way of thinking about things in the real world, chromaticism begins to foreground *form* rather than *substance*" (1988, 62).

What becomes clear in most of the above is that Bebop must be viewed from two perspectives, the sociopolitical as well as the musical. In Gary Giddins's words, "The Second World War severely altered the texture and tempo of American life, and jazz reflected those changes with greater acuteness by far than the other arts" (1987, 77). When Bebop began in the 1940s, America was in a similar position to what it had been in the 1920s. A war had been fought to free the world (again) for democracy; and once again, African Americans had participated and had assumed that this "loyal" participation would result in new rights and new levels of respect. When, once again, this did not appear to be happening, a new militancy developed in the African American community. Bebop was part of this new attitude. The militancy in the African American community that manifested itself in the 1941 strike of black Ford workers and the 1943 Harlem riot also manifested itself in Bebop. As Eric Lott notes:

> Brilliantly outside, bebop was intimately if indirectly related to the militancy of its moment. Militancy and music were undergirded by the same social facts; the music attempted to resolve at the level of style what the militancy combatted in the streets. (1988, 599)

Of course, this made Bebop dangerous and threatening to some, who saw it as (or potentially as) "too militant," and perhaps even un-American. And in response to this, Dizzy Gillespie retorts:

> Damn right! We refused to accept racism, poverty, or economic exploitation, nor would we live out uncreative humdrum lives merely for the sake of survival. But there was nothing unpatriotic about it. If America wouldn't honor its Constitution and respect us as men, we couldn't give a shit about the American way. And they made it damn near un-American to appreciate our music. (1979, 287)

The threat represented by Bebop was not only felt by the white world, but by the assimilationist black middle class as well. Baraka offers these perspectives:

> When the moderns, the beboppers, showed up to restore jazz, in some sense, to its original separateness, to drag it outside the mainstream of American culture again, most middle-class Negroes (as most Americans) were stuck; they had passed, for the most part, completely into the Platonic citizenship. The willfully harsh, *anti-assimilationist* sound of bebop fell on deaf or horrified ears, just as it did in white America. (1963, 181–82)
>
> Bebop rebelled against the absorption into garbage, monopoly music; it also signified a rebellion by the people who played the music, because it was not just the music that rebelled, as if the music had fallen out of the sky! But even more, dig it, it signified a rebellion rising out of the masses themselves, since that is the source of social movement—the people themselves! (1979, 236)
>
> What made bop strong is that no matter its pretensions, it was hooked up solidly and directly to the Afro-American blues tradition, and therefore was largely based in the experience and struggle of the black sector of the working class. (1979, 241)

In light of this historical context, Sonny's brother's never having heard of Bird is not just a rejection of the music of Bebop; it is also a rejection of the new political direction Bebop was representative of in the African American community.

When the story picks up several years later, some things have changed. Sonny has dropped out of high school, illegally enlisted in the navy and been shipped to Greece, returned to America, and moved to Greenwich Village. Other things have not changed: his brother has become an algebra teacher and a respected member of the black bourgeoisie. After Sonny has been released from prison, he invites his brother to watch him sit in "in a joint in the Village" (1966, 113).

What is usually discussed concerning this final scene is that the brother enters Sonny's world, recognizes that he is only a visitor to that world tolerated because of Sonny, that here Sonny is respected and taken care of, and that here is Sonny's true family:

> I was introduced to all of them and they were all very polite to me. Yet, it was clear that, for them, I was only Sonny's brother. Here, I was in Sonny's

world. Or, rather: his kingdom. Here, it was not even a question that his
veins bore royal blood. (118)

When the music Sonny plays is discussed, it is usually done either abstractly, music as the bridge that allows Sonny and his brother to become reunited and Sonny to find his identity, or simply in terms of the blues. It is, of course, totally legitimate to discuss the music in either of these ways. After all, music does function as a bridge between Sonny and his brother; and twice we are reminded in the same page that "what they were playing was the blues," and "Now these are Sonny's blues" (121).

At the climactic moment of the story, when Sonny finally feels so comfortable that his "fingers filled the air with life" (122), he is playing "Am I Blue." It is the first song of the second set, after a tentative performance by Sonny in the first set. Baldwin presents the moment of transition between sets by simply noting, "Then they finished, there was scattered applause, and then, without an instant's warning, Creole started into something else, it was almost sardonic, it was *Am I Blue*" (121). The word "sardonic," it seems to me, is key here. One of the characteristics of Bebop is taking an old standard and making it new. As Leonard Feather explains:

> In recent years it has been an increasingly common practice to take some
> definite chord sequence of a well-known song (usually a standard old
> favorite) and build a new melody around it. Since there is no copyright on
> a chord sequence, the musician is entitled to use this method to create an
> original composition and copyright it in his own name, regardless of who
> wrote the first composition that used the same chord pattern. (1977,
> 55–56)

This practice results in a song with a completely different title. Thus, "Back Home Again in Indiana" becomes Parker's "Donna Lee"; "Honeysuckle Rose" becomes "Scrapple from the Apple"; "I Got Rhythm" becomes "Dexterity," "Confirmation," and "Thriving on a Riff"; "How High the Moon" becomes "Bird Lore"; "Lover Come Back to Me" becomes "Bird Gets the Worm"; and "Cherokee" becomes "Warming Up a Riff" and "Ko-Ko." But it is also characteristic of Bebop to take the entire song, not simply a chord sequence, and play it in an entirely different way. Thus, for example, Bird's catalogue is filled with versions of tunes like "White Christmas," "Slow Boat to China," "East of the Sun and West of the Moon," "April in Paris," and "Embraceable You."[6] As Baraka notes:

> Bebop was a much more open rebellion in the sense that the musicians
> openly talked of the square, hopeless, corny rubbish put forth by the bour-
> geoisie. They made fun of it, refused to play it except in a mocking fashion.
> (1979, 237)

Baldwin's use of the word "sardonic," therefore, is clearly intended to tell us that something more is going on than simply playing a standard tune or playing the blues. "Am I Blue" is exactly the type of song that by itself wouldn't do much for anyone, but which could become rich and meaningful after being heated in the crucible of Bebop.

The point of all this is that, through his playing, Sonny becomes "part of the family again" (121), his family with the other musicians; likewise, Sonny's brother also becomes part of the family again, his family with Sonny. But in both cases, Baldwin wants us to view the idea of family through the musical and social revolution of Bebop. Note the brother's language as Sonny plays:

> Then he began to make it his. It was very beautiful because it wasn't hurried and it was no longer a lament. I seemed to hear with what burning we had yet to make it ours, how we could cease lamenting. Freedom lurked around us and I understood, at last, that he could help us to be free if we would listen, that he would never be free until we did. (122)

In the mid to late 1950s, the word "freedom" is obviously a highly charged one. Not only does it speak to the politics of the Civil Rights Movement, but it also points forward to the "Free Jazz" movement of the late 1950s and 1960s, the music of Ornette Coleman, Cecil Taylor, Albert Ayler, and Eric Dolphy. Baldwin's concept of family is, therefore, a highly political one, and one that has cultural implications.

In *Black Talk,* Ben Sidran concludes about Bebop:

> The importance of the bop musician was that he had achieved this confrontation—in terms of aesthetics and value structures as well as social action—well before organized legal or political action. Further, unlike the arguments of the NAACP, his music and his hip ethic were not subject to the kind of rationalization and verbal qualification that had all too often compromised out of existence all middle-class Negro gains. (1971, 115)

In "Sonny's Blues," Baldwin makes clear that, contrary to many opinions, he is in fact a major fiction writer; and that, Larry Neal notwithstanding, he *has* used to its fullest extent "traditional aspects of Afro-American culture." The implications are clear. Not only does Baldwin's fiction need to be looked at again, but when we are looking at it, writing about it, and teaching it, we need to be conversant with the specific cultural context he is writing in and from. And when we are, new things are there to be seen and heard.

## Notes

1. The two best treatments of "Sonny's Blues" are by Sherley Anne Williams and John Reilly. While Williams discusses music, she sees the musician in Baldwin as "an archetypal figure" (1972, 145). Reilly's 1974 "'Sonny's Blues': James Baldwin's Image of the Black Community," the single best essay on the story, actually does mention Bebop, but only in one paragraph, and then concentrates more on the importance of the blues.
2. For a description of Parker's first session as a leader, recorded on November 26, 1945, see Giddins 1987, 87–90.
3. Interestingly, Baraka notes that "Trane first heard Bird and Diz in the Navy, as the first records were beginning to get released" (1979, 234).
4. On the connection between Armstrong and Parker, see Williams, 1971, 108–9.

5. On Armstrong and the Mardi Gras see Murray, 1976, 190–91; and Albertson, 1978, 24 and 29.
6. It seems to me that this characteristic activity of Bebop is similar to Henry Louis Gates's theory of signifying, although Gates limits the concept to African American writers signifying on each other. On this issue, see both Gates (1988) and Cain (1990).

## Works Cited

Albertson, Chris. 1978. *Louis Armstrong.* Alexandria: Time-Life Records.

Baker, Houston A., Jr. 1984. *Blues, Ideology, and Afro-American Literature: A Vernacular Theory.* Chicago: University of Chicago Press.

Baldwin, James. 1966. *The Fire Next Time.* New York: Dial.

———. 1965. "Sonny's Blues." In *Going to Meet the Man,* 86–122. New York: Dial Press.

Baraka, Amiri. 1963. *Blues People: Negro Music in White America.* New York: Morrow.

———. 1966. "Brief Reflections on Two Hot Shots." In *Home: Social Essays,* 116–20. New York: Morrow.

———. 1966. "The Myth of a 'Negro Literature.'" In *Home: Social Essays,* 105–15.

———. 1979. "War/Philly Blues/Deeper Bop." In *Selected Plays and Prose of Amiri Baraka/ LeRoi Jones,* 228–41. New York: Morrow.

———. 1989. "Jimmy!" In *James Baldwin: The Legacy,* edited by Quincy Troupe, 127–34. New York: Simon and Schuster/Touchstone.

Cain, William E. 1990. "New Directions in Afro-American Literary Criticism." *American Quarterly* 42: 657–63.

Daniels, Lee A. 1987, December 2. "James Baldwin, Eloquent Essayist in Behalf of Civil Rights, Is Dead." *New York Times,* A1.

Du Bois, W. E. B. 1969 [1903]. *The Souls of Black Folk.* New York: Signet-NAL.

Feather, Leonard. 1977 [1949]. *Inside Jazz (Inside Be-bop).* New York: Da Capo.

Feeney, Mark. 1987, December 2. "James Baldwin Dies: A Forceful Voice on Issue of Race." *The Boston Globe,* 1.

Gates, Henry Louis, Jr. 1988. *The Signifying Monkey: A Theory of Afro-American Literary Criticism.* New York: Oxford University Press.

Giddins, Gary. 1987. *Celebrating Bird: The Triumph of Charlie Parker.* New York: Beech Tree Books/Morrow.

Gillespie, Dizzy, with Al Fraser. 1979. *To Be Or Not . . . To BOP: Memoirs.* Garden City: Doubleday.

Heble, Ajay. 1988. "The Poetics of Jazz: From Symbolic to Semiotic." *Textual Practice* 2: 51–68.

Lott, Eric. 1988. "Double V, Double-Time: Bebop's Politics of Style." *Callaloo* 11: 597–605.

Murray, Albert. 1976. *Stomping the Blues.* New York: McGraw-Hill.

Neal, Larry. 1989a. "The Black Writer's Role, III: James Baldwin." In *Visions of a Liberated Future: Black Arts Movement Writings,* edited by Michael Schwartz, 57–61. New York: Thunder's Mouth.

———. 1989b. "And Shine Swam On." In *Visions of a Liberated Future: Black Arts Movement Writings,* edited by Michael Schwartz, 7–23. New York: Thunder's Mouth Press.

Parker, Charlie. 1976. *Bird/The Savoy Recordings (Master Takes).* Savoy, SJL 2201.

Redding, J. Saunders. 1987 [1939]. *To Make a Poet Black.* Ithaca, NY: Cornell University Press.

Reilly, John M. 1974. "'Sonny's Blues': James Baldwin's Image of Black Community." In *James Baldwin: A Collection of Critical Essays,* edited by Keneth Kinnamon, 139–46. Englewood Cliffs, NJ: Prentice-Hall.

Sidran, Ben. 1971. *Black Talk.* New York: Holt, Rinehart, and Winston.

Spellman, A. B. 1970. *Black Music: Four Lives (Four Lives in the Bebop Business).* New York: Schocken.

Walton, Ortiz M. 1972. *Music: Black, White & Blue: A Sociological Survey of the Use and Misuse of Afro-American Music.* New York: Morrow.

Williams, Martin. 1971. *The Jazz Tradition.* New York: Mentor-NAL.

Williams, Sherley Anne. 1972. *Give Birth to Brightness: A Thematic Study in Neo-Black Literature.* New York: Dial.

Wright, Richard. 1978. "Blueprint for Negro Writing." In *Richard Wright Reader,* edited by Ellen Wright and Michel Fabre, 36–49. New York: Harper & Row.

# Sam Whitsitt

## In Spite of It All: A Reading of Alice Walker's "Everyday Use"

2000

> Perhaps the most resonant quality of quiltmaking is the promise of creating unity amongst disparate elements, of establishing connections in the midst of fragmentation.  —KELLEY 176

> Walker's peculiar sound, the specific mode through which her deepening of self-knowledge and self-love comes, seems to have much to do with her contrariness, her willingness at all turns to challenge the fashionable belief of the day. . . . —CHRISTIAN 124

Since its publication in 1973 in the collection of stories *In Love and Trouble,* Alice Walker's short story "Everyday Use" has become very popular—probably the most anthologized of her stories (Winchell 80)—and it clearly merits such critical acclaim. In 1994, the story was honored by a critical edition published in the Rutgers University Press series "Women Writers: Texts and Contexts." Paralleling the success of Walker's story has been that of another cultural artefact, the quilt, which since the Sixties has undergone a rather spectacular revaluation, moving from the marginalized position it held as a symbol of gossipy women's sewing circles, to becoming by the Seventies the "central metaphor of American cultural identity" (Showalter 215). One of the intentions of the Rutgers critical edition is to indicate a link between these two success stories. As Barbara Christian writes in the first paragraph of her introduction, it is in "Everyday Use" (1973) and "in her classic essay 'In Search of Our Mothers' Gardens' (1974) that Walker first articulates the metaphor of quilting to represent the creative legacy that African Americans have inherited from their maternal ancestors" (3). While Walker was not the first to write about quilts, she was one of the first to write of the value of the quilt in the Afro-American experience, and she has certainly been one of the most influential writers in rearticulating the value of the quilt and in contributing to its success in the collective imagination at large.

If it seems clear that the popularity of the quilt owes much to writers like Walker, one needs to ask, in turn, whether Walker's story would enjoy its current status if the quilt itself had not become such a privileged symbol. And yet another way of formulating this kind of question would be to ask whether we are to read the quilt as a figure in a story, or whether the story is, as it were, a figure of the quilt. Is the quilt, in other words, to be seen as one sign of women's creative activity among many, or as the very ground of a specifically woman's world?

How such questions might be answered is largely dependent on whether another significant characteristic of Walker's work is taken into consideration. As the epigraph above from Barbara Christian notes, central to Walker's work is a certain kind of "contrariness," a "willingness at all turns to challenge the fashionable belief of the day." And if the symbolic value attributed to the quilt can be taken as a "fashionable belief of the day," we might have a dilemma, since the very story which surely contributed to the success of such a belief could likewise be questioning it, and this would produce a dilemma, as well, for those critics who want to ensure that Walker holds an honored place in the history of quilting and who likewise feel that any questioning of that history would be dishonoring it. If there were any hint that such contrary questioning were coming from Walker's work itself, then perhaps a critic would be tempted to avoid a close reading of her text in order to avoid risking having to deal with such a disruption.

This very dilemma seems to be reflected in the Rutgers critical edition. While the short story "Everyday Use" is clearly central to the edition entitled *Everyday Use,* the story is not clearly central to each of the six articles which make up the section "Critical Essays." While Mary Helen Washington goes on to offer in her three-page, 1994 postscript some of the most insightful comments which have been made on the story, her original article, written in 1979, to which she appends the postscript, makes no reference whatsoever to "Everyday Use." Thadious Davis makes only a glancing reference to the story in noting how a character in "Everyday Use" whom she does not name (Maggie) serves as a predecessor for Celie of *The Color Purple.* Barbara Christian, as editor of the edition, deals directly with the story in both her introduction and article, but neither exclusively nor extensively. The title of Margot Anne Kelley's article, "Sisters' Choices: Quilting Aesthetics in Contemporary African-American Women's Fiction" (1994), would inspire anyone to wager that she mentions "Everyday Use" at least once—only to lose, since she doesn't. Elaine Showalter, in "Common Threads" (1991), mentions the story, but her comments seem more like an obligatory one-page stop before moving on, and her comments draw on what is the only article in the edition dealing exclusively with Walker's story, that by Houston Baker and Charlotte Pierce-Baker entitled "Patches: Quilts and Community in Alice Walker's 'Everyday Use.'" My point is not that these articles are uninteresting, but that in an edition dedicated to Walker's short story "Everyday Use," few critics put the story to the everyday use of criticism. It seems that Walker's "patch" of a story doesn't really fit very well in most of the critics' "quilts." If Walker's story is included in an article, it typically is not so much treated in and of itself, but as a fragment in a larger framework. The composition of the edition reflects a kind of quilting in which it is not

Walker's "piece" that receives a careful study of its textual fabric, but rather how that patch is pieced in and stitched to a larger whole.

It could of course be argued that what deflects the critics' attention away from the "patch" of a story is not the contrariness of the story, but rather that this edition simply reflects the sign of the times under which criticism tends to be written. The close reading of the text itself has been displaced by a reading which attempts to follow a series of threads leading outside the text: to author, biography, culture, politics, economies, and heritage. In this case, it is the heritage and culture of quilting among Southern, Afro-American women which figures largely, and Barbara Christian's introduction to the edition carefully situates both Walker and her story in that culture and its history.[1] But while in both her fiction and non-fiction Walker has courageously pointed to a set of specific historical, cultural, and political references outside and beyond her work, the question still remains of what the relationship is between her art and these references.

Among some critics there is a tendency, which finds encouragement in Walker's writing itself, to claim a strong analogy between quilting and storytelling, which allows one in turn to see Walker's storytelling as metaphorically subsumable to quilting, which in this scenario "precedes" her story. The violence of the metaphor is that it tends to cover over the very differences that make it possible, and the quilt seems to lend itself to this metaphoric violence since its figure tends to be taken literally. If "the most resonant quality of [real] quiltmaking," as Kelley writes, "is the promise of creating unity amongst disparate elements," it is not difficult to understand how a metaphoric slide creates an identity between the disparate elements of quilting, writing, and a world of womanly activity. The quilt is a trope whose analogue (the quilt itself) provides the stitch that untropes the trope; it is a trope stitched to a reality, and the tightness of the stitching depends on the tightness of the identity of any group which claims the quilt as its sign. Even if today, as Showalter notes, the quilt has "transcended the stigma of its sources in women's culture" and become the "central metaphor of American cultural identity" (215), that generalizing drift away from a certain womanly specificity has not diminished its appeal as a kind of ground for certain groups, particularly women's. Quilting can still be taken as a woman's activity which makes use of a woman's material; it can yet be deemed a woman's social, economic, and political activity which also produces an object of beauty which, moreover, does not drift into the domain of pure art, or the "institutional theories of aesthetics" (Baker and Pierce-Baker 161); just as disparate pieces of cloth get stitched together, the quilt itself is stitched to the world that produces it. The quilt "represents" herstory, history, and tradition, binding women, and men, to the past and the past to the present. And it has been powerful in providing a ground for women, particularly women writers. Precisely because "the writing of fiction," as Mary Helen Washington notes, can still be perceived as "done under the shadow of men" (103), the metaphor of the quilt and its world can take women out of that shadow and ground them in an open place of their own.

Moving out of the shadow of men, however, can lead to entanglements in the threads of women. In her article "The Needle or the Pen: The Literary Rediscovery of Women's Textile Work," Elaine Hedges shows how women writers prior to the mid-1900s sought to protect themselves and allay the fears of the male-dominated literary establishment by implying that what appeared to be writing was really only sewing—the pen was really only a needle. Today, many women writers who are neither forced to nor supposed to sew also invoke this metaphor. While the considerable power of the metaphor today is no doubt linked to an attempt to establish for women a ground of their own, this leads to a problem, which is also linked to the problem of grounding in general. The very identity and security a ground might give creates a problem for the writer insofar as writing is an activity which is transgressive, or contrary. For women writers prior to the mid-1900s, taking up the pen rather than the needle was a transgressive act which the metaphor of the needle facilitated. Today, however, this same metaphor runs the risk not only of being quite conservative but also of establishing a ground which can make a woman writer who does not "quilt" or use the metaphoric "needle" appear a transgressor or betrayer of that community. If the metaphor once helped women to get out of line, that same metaphor today runs the danger of working to keep women in line. To push the point, no one either yesterday or today seems to want to *think* of women as writing. Men wanted women literally to sew only figures; and many critics today, both male and female, literally want women to sew figuratively—which is to say, they want women to write as if they were really sewing, and all the better if about literally sewn things—like quilts, for example. Alice Walker writes a short story in which quilts are an important figure, but today it would seem that the story itself is but a figure for quilts.

Both Elaine Hedges and Elaine Showalter acknowledge the critical significance of quilting, but have reservations about how the quilt as a figure is employed. Hedges asks "whether the needle doesn't at times move too magically to dispel conflict, to solve complex issues of gender and male power" (359), and Elaine Showalter convincingly argues that, "while quilting does have crucial meaning for American women's texts, it can't be taken as a transhistorical and essential form of female expression, but rather as a gendered practice that change[s] from one generation to the next . . ." (197–98). While there is much in Alice Walker's short story which allows for a reading which would see it as a story which grounds itself in the figure of the quilt, the figurality of the ground itself always threatens to undo its grounding. As Diana Fuss notes, with regard to Irigaray, while "two lips" seem to be ever so literal, it is also a metaphor for metonymy (66).

In the highly politicized world of literary criticism, however, the space for the ungrounded, or the "wayward," to borrow Barbara Christian's term, is given little quarter. Identity politics and its polarizations, which seem to appear unproblematically alongside a discourse of difference, eclipse the space of a difference. What Fuss says of the use of metaphors borrowed from modern physics can also be said of how the quilt as a figure is often employed: "By locating difference *outside identity,* in the spaces *between* identities . . . the radicality of the poststructuralist view which locates differences *within* identities" comes to be ignored (103). When the Bakers write that "the sorority of quiltmakers, fragment weavers, holy patchers, possesses a sacred wisdom that it hands down from generation to generation of those who refuse the center for the ludic and unconfined spaces of the margins" (156), the ludic and unconfined space along the margins becomes carefully controlled to the limited extent that quilting takes place on holy ground; there is little space for the ludic at the heart of such a sorority when it comes down to the hand that hands something down and the hand that receives. That the Bakers close down differences within this identity and accentuate the difference between this identity and what does not belong to it becomes clear in their analysis of Dee, the wayward daughter, the figure who plays on the margins. That Dee does indeed *leave* at the end of the story does not coincide with the idea that Dee is being *excluded* from what Nancy Tuten calls "the establishment of a sisterhood between mother and daughter" (125), which is to say, the sisterhood between Mama and her daughter Maggie, but not the other daughter/sister, Dee. Both the Bakers and Tuten, as well as other critics, see Dee as being "narrated . . . out of the story altogether" (Tuten 127). What never seems to be noted is that what makes possible the sisterhood they value is *their* exclusion of a sister. The story out of which Dee gets narrated is not Walker's, but the critics' story of identity, which shuts down any room for a ludic play of differences. The aim of this article is to propose a reading which respects a play of difference, which keeps "things" like Dee, in play.

> Our mothers and grandmothers, some of them: moving to music not yet written. And they waited.
>     They waited for a day when the unknown thing that was in them would be made known; but they guessed, somehow in their darkness, that on the day of their revelation they would be long dead. Therefore to Toomer they walked, and even ran, in slow motion. (Walker, "In Search of Our Mothers' Gardens" 40)

"Everyday Use" begins with women waiting: Mama Johnson and her daughter Maggie, waiting at home, in the deep rural South, a place they had never left, for a visit from Dee, the daughter who had not waited, the daughter who could not wait to leave home. "I will wait for her in the yard that Maggie and I made so clean and wavy yesterday afternoon" (23), says Mama. But Mama and Maggie are not just waiting for Dee. They are waiting for redemption. Mama tells us that she has dreamed of a certain kind of redemption. In her dream, Dee, the daughter who has style, wits, and a cold determination to "get out," has made it big in the world out there; she is on some kind of Johnny Carson talk show, and Mama, having arrived backstage in a "soft-seated limousine," is ushered in, met by the Johnny Carson–type host, told "what a fine girl" she has, and brought on stage to be joined with her daughter Dee, who "is embracing me with tears in her eyes." In the dream, Mama is "the way my daughter would want me to be: a hundred pounds lighter, my skin like an uncooked barley pancake. My hair glistening . . . [and] Johnny Carson has much to do to keep up with my quick and witty tongue." But Mama is well aware that she isn't like that at all, and that the dream "is a mistake" (24). That she sometimes dreams this dream speaks, however, not merely of "her desire to be respected by her daughter" (Tuten 126), and her misdirected wish to measure up to standards of a White world, of the "Other"; it speaks more significantly of that desire to know, no matter how misdirected, some "unknown thing" inside her. But unlike the women Walker describes in the quote that prefaces this section of the essay, Mama is not moving toward someone like Toomer: Only in her dream does she move out of her place; in real life, as it were, she is waiting for her daughter in her yard, which is "like an extended living room" (23). She is at home. And it is at home, for Walker, that the unknown thing is finally to be found.

In Walker's writing, redemption will take one away and bring one back, in a perhaps humbling but empowering way, to something close to home. This form of redemption takes place as an epiphany: You realize that what can save you isn't out there, but has been nearby all along, beside you, even in you, but never noticed, never heard, or never given a second thought. Walker's well-known essay "In Search of Our Mothers' Gardens" turns on the idea of epiphany. It is here that she mentions the oft-cited epiphanic moment in the Smithsonian Institution when she saw an exquisite quilt on exhibit "made by an anonymous Black woman in Alabama, a hundred years ago" (46). In her essay, however, as the title suggests, it is not the quilt itself, or not only the quilt, to which Walker attends, but rather her mother's quilts, flower gardens, storytelling, cooking, and the skilled and careful handling of everyday life, all of which represent a creative dimension that had been there all along, at home, nearby, but to which Walker had not given that second thought.

Epiphany is like a "second thought." There is a difference, a lapse, between the two moments. To give or have a second thought, as it were, there must have been a first, distanced in time and space, but which comes to be first only secondarily. And for this to occur, there must be a certain detour, a departure; one must leave home in order to become aware of home, even though this departure holds no guarantee of a return. Epiphany would seem to necessitate this departure, this turning one's back on something. As Mama tells us as she waits for Dee, "I have deliberately turned my back on the house" (26), and on Maggie, too, her younger daughter, scarred by a fire which burned down the first house and which has left her ever since with "chin on chest, eyes on ground, feet in shuffle" (27). But this turning away does not eclipse or erase a link to what one leaves behind. As one turns the gaze of expectation away from what is then left behind, there is something which snags. And Maggie is there, right behind Mama's back.

Dee, however, does not seem to be one who is snagged by anything. "She would always look anyone in the eye," even strange white men, and "hesitation was no part of her nature." Unlike Maggie, with her eyes on the ground, and unlike Mama, who looks up but cannot imagine "looking a strange white man in the eye" (25), Dee would never lower her eyes under the gaze of Whites. As Mama says, Dee "was determined to stare down any disaster. . . . Her eyelids would not flicker for minutes at a time" (26). And Dee made it out, and seems to have made it in the South of the Sixties where, if the gaze itself of the Whites wasn't successful in making a Black lower his or her eyes and get back in place, there was no hesitation in using whatever means necessary. But making it, for Dee, and no doubt many others, had a price. The force required to stare the white world down was equaled by the intensity of a gaze, which burned her links to her past. If Dee didn't actually start the fire which burned down their first house, the "look of concentration" (25) on her face as she watched it burn could have "stared" it down. And having burned that ground which she saw as suffocating, she sought a new ground in the burgeoning Islamic and Back-to-Africa movements of the time. When the flashy Dee finally does return, greeting her mother in Arabic and declaring that she no longer bears the name "Dee," but the African name "Wangero," and that "Dee," "'She's dead'" (29)—it's as if there is not even a tombstone to mark the presence of her absence. Her return seems less a return than a passing by; she appears a curious visitor who has momentarily stopped off a road which began and ends elsewhere.

Yet Dee has returned. And Mama is mistaken about how Dee will react when she arrives. She believes that Dee still has an aversion for her home, and that when she sees the house, "she will want to tear it down" (27). But this is not what happens. She arrives, gets out of the car, approaches her mother and sister, but then stops short. While Dee's male friend attempts to hug Maggie, who shrinks back, Dee makes no physical contact; she touches no one and no thing. Not yet. She tells her mother just to stay put. Then she turns, goes back to the car, gets her camera, returns, and begins taking pictures: "She stoops down quickly and lines up picture after picture of me sitting there in front of the house with Maggie cowering behind me. She never takes a shot without making sure the house is included. When a cow comes nibbling around the edge of the yard she snaps it and me and Maggie *and* the house" (28–29). Then Dee goes back to the car, leaves the camera, and only then does she return, once again, this time to step into that world she has just framed, to greet her mother—not however with a dream-like hug, but with a kiss on the forehead.

Dee returns, but delays her arrival. Only after a series of photos, of carefully lined up frames, of pictures which do not include her, does she then include herself in the scene. It's as if before entering that scene Dee wants to make sure that she has a picture of herself not being in the picture. She wants to frame that world, define its borders, give it a wholeness which then allows her to handle it without being a part of it. This is what the Bakers call Dee's "fashionably 'aesthetic' distance from southern expediencies," her "'framed' experience." The Bakers speak contemptuously of Dee's "world of pretended wholeness," of "framed and institutionalized art"—her "Polaroid" world. In what seems to be an afterthought, however, they indirectly acknowledge that framing is not in itself pejorative, since even quilters need frames, and quilters too bring to their work a "completeness" (161). The Bakers do not ask how one differentiates between good and bad, or authentic and inauthentic frames; they seem to assume that, since quilting is authentic, the very authenticity of its frame unframes it—that the authentic frame of a quilter is not really a frame at all, and what one can call the narrative frame of the story cannot be a frame since Mama, who narrates the story, is incapable of framing: "The mother's cognition contains no categories for framed art" (163–64). The Bakers polarize this world into one of good and bad framing: "aesthetic" wholes, which are false and inauthentic, and represented by Dee; and wholes which emerge from "social activity," like quilting, which are authentic and true, unframed, and represented by Mama and Maggie. In this argument, the politics of identity and wholeness seem to tighten the threads, as it were, of the quilt of true community, and it is not surprising that Dee, a wayward daughter, gets hounded out of the picture. Patricia Kane sees Dee as the prodigal daughter who, in what for her is Walker's parody of the prodigal son story, gets just the opposite of a welcome; Nancy Tuten claims that Mama has a "distaste for Dee's egotism" (126), that Maggie has only "disgust with her sister," and that, "in the end, Dee's oppressive voice is mute, for Mama has narrated her out of the story altogether." The Bakers are more vitriolic: Dee is evil, a "serpent" in Mama's "calm pasture" (159); inauthentic ("Dee is not an example of the indigenous rapping and styling out of Afro-America" [160]); and a traitor ("Individualism and a flouting of convention in order to achieve 'aesthetic' success constitute acts of treachery in 'Everyday Use'" [163]). Dee, however, is not to be repressed.

There are several compelling arguments for why the reader must attend to Dee more carefully. In an interview in 1974, a year after "Everyday Use" was published, Walker expanded on a poem she had written entitled "The Girl Who Died #2." It is about a girl who attended the same college as did Walker and who committed suicide. "I learned," writes Walker, "from the dead girl's rather guilty-sounding 'brothers and sisters' that she had been hounded constantly because she was so 'incorrect' she thought she could be a black hippie. To top that, they tried to make her feel like a traitor because she refused to limit her interest to black men" (81). It takes no great leap to see that the Bakers' reading of Dee is not dissimilar to how the "brothers and sisters" read this girl, and it seems likewise clear that Walker has little sympathy for identity politics whose logic turns the contrary and the wayward into traitors. The stakes are, of course, raised as soon as one makes a link between Walker and the wayward, a link she herself does not shy away from. When referring to Dee, Walker calls her an *"autonomous person,"* and she tells us that she, like Dee, has an "African name . . . and I love it and use it when I want to, and I love my Kenyan gowns and my Ugandan gowns—the whole bit—it's part of me" (Washington 102). Moreover, the name Dee is given, "Wangero," is the same name Walker herself was given when she went to Africa (Christian 13).

Mary Helen Washington doesn't hesitate to make several acute observations: "Walker is most closely aligned in the story with the 'bad daughter,' Dee . . . the one who goes out in the world and returns with African clothes and an African name. Like Dee, Walker leaves the community, appropriating the oral tradition in order to turn it into a written artefact, which will no longer be available for 'everyday use' by its originators. . . . The story ends with Mama choosing Maggie and rejecting Dee, but Dee, who represents Walker herself as an artist who returns home, at least imaginatively, in order to collect the material for her art, certainly cannot be repressed." Washington cites Susan Willis in noting that, "when the black writer takes the materials of folk culture and subjects them to fiction[,] . . . she is engaged in 'an enterprise fraught with contradiction'" (102). Looking at what happens to Dee in the hands of the critics, we can add that she or he risks being branded as a traitor and excluded, or shunned. Of course, as Diana Fuss continually and convincingly argues in her book *Essentially Speaking,* it is infinitely wiser to keep chaos in play rather than attempt to eliminate it, which is what happens when Dee is muted and driven out as a traitor.

Dee must be kept within the picture, and there are structural and thematic reasons related to the question of framing for doing so. It is not problematic that Dee "frames" her experience; what *is* important is what it tells us about her, and what is revealed when we compare her framing to other frames in the story—most importantly, the narrative frames of both Mama and Walker herself. That Dee constructs a whole from which she excludes herself is no doubt Dee's way of maintaining a relation to a world that she does not want to be a part of. Dee has not returned to fill a place held for her while she was absent. What Dee doesn't want to see, cannot afford to see, refuses to see, is a link between herself and that place she came from. She is not a part of that whole. She does not stand in a metaphoric, or synecdochal, relation to that whole. Her framing of a whole before entering that frame seems, then, to be a way to deny a metaphoric relationship of herself as a part of that whole, yet maintain a relationship with it as a whole—as if the frame around a whole compensates for her absence within it, or as part of it. Had Dee seen herself as part of that whole, her relationship with those parts of that whole she eventually does take—the churn handle and churn lid, and the quilts she wants to take but can't—would have been metaphorically justified. The four-term metaphor which would have authorized this acquisition goes: The churn handle stands to the churn/home as Dee stands to home; therefore, Dee and the churn handle have a familiar, analogical link. It is because Dee refuses to see herself as part of that whole that her relationship to the churn handle comes to be metonymic, which is what then allows the reading which sees Dee as turning those parts of the whole into mere things, or aestheticized objects. A less severe judgment of Dee would leave open the possibility of seeing that between Dee and those "things" she lays her hands on is a different metaphoric relationship. One could say that what Dee sees in these parts of a whole is that they, like her, are not, nor have they ever been, recognized for what they are worth. When Dee claims that her sister Maggie "can't appreciate these quilts" (33), she is also claiming that Maggie cannot appreciate her; she is talking about herself and the inability of those at home to appreciate the daughter who, as a part of that whole, went away, changed, returned, and cannot find/does not want to find a reflection of herself in that whole. Dee's violent, metaphoric claim, then, is that her right to those parts of the whole comes from the whole's failure to appreciate the parts. Dee is both right and wrong; and, in that particularly ironic mode of Walker's world, she will, "in spite of herself" (131), which is how Barbara Christian so aptly captures the ironic doubleness which characterizes so many of Walker's characters, be the very agent that gets the whole, which is to say Mama and Maggie, to come to a revaluation of those parts.[2]

Dee returns, but constructs a frame around a picture in which there is no risk of her appearing. She makes a picture of her not being in the picture. Mama, however, is in the picture—but it is Dee's picture of her; and getting out of Dee's frame around her, getting out of being framed by others, as it were, will be the drama of the way Mama narrates the story. What is unusual about what Nancy Tuten calls Walker's "unusual narrative structure" (126) is its double nature. The story is told by Mama, in the first person, but in two different tenses: It begins in the present tense, only to subtly shift to the past tense about midway through the story. As Tuten notes, Mama changes to the past tense right after Dee has announced that "Dee" is dead. Tuten writes, ". . . when Dee goes so far as to disown her family identity, Mama reaches a watershed," and drawing on Marianne Hirsch's article ("Clytemnestra's Children: Writing (Out) the Mother's Anger"), Tuten goes on to note how Mama, who has previously been unable to express her anger at Dee, has now been pushed too far—or far enough so that Mama is finally "able to objectify the situation, to distance herself from it." Tuten continues, "The use of the present-tense verbs in the first half of the story suggests less

narrative authority: if Mama is telling the events as they happen, she is merely reacting. By shifting to the past tense, Walker strengthens Mama's voice, giving her more
control" (127).

If framing a narrative allows Mama to gain more control, which also results in
her "increasing emotional distance from Dee" (128), we can consider more acutely
what is at stake in Dee's emotions, since she feels a need to frame the "story" from the
outset. It would seem that Dee's emotions are indeed much more precarious than are
those of Mama, who, beginning without a frame, as it were, risks from the outset. A
significant difference between Mama and Dee is that Mama has this capacity to risk.
I agree with Hirsch when she mentions Mama's "ability to take pleasure in her daughter's difference without conceding any of her own choices and values," and her ability
to maintain a distance from Dee "without visibly rejecting her" (203). While critics
often point to Dee's aggressiveness, which intrudes into the pastoral calm of Mama's
home, by quoting Mama's comment that the dress Dee wears is "so loud it hurts my
eyes," they fail to note that Mama says shortly after, "I like it" (28). Mama has held a
place for "Dee," and if "Dee" is no longer there, she will try to accommodate
"Wangero." But in trying to find a place for Dee/Wangero, a figure of both presence
and absence, it is Mama who is slowly being displaced.

While a certain distance may result from anger, it seems more important to take
into account what Mama says when she does shift to the past tense. After Dee indicates that she no longer bears the name of "Dee," Mama responds with, "'What happened to "Dee"? *I wanted to know*'" (29; emphasis mine). It's not so evident that
Mama expresses her anger here (something like anger, or perhaps frustration, comes
later in the story), but it is evident that she expresses her desire "to know," and when
the narrative shifts to the past tense, we are being told that Mama knows that she
wants to know. If the narrative had remained in the present tense, as in "'What happened to "Dee"? I want to know,'" it would imply that Mama is not only "merely reacting" (Tuten 127) but remaining in the immediacy of the present, where there is no
distance for knowing that one knows; it would not be a recognition of what one is doing, but only the doing. It's as if there would be the claim that the linguistic representation of feeling and desire is not only identical to that feeling, but that there is no
difference between representation and presentation. It is, however, precisely such a
claim which seems to be at stake in the use of the present tense.

We can say that the story begins with the claim that it is not a story. Hearing
Mama speak in the first person, in the present, about the present, suggests that there
is no aesthetic frame, no fictionalization. It's as if, in order to hear this story, we must
be there with Mama, in her presence and present tense, listening to her voice. We are
as close to Mama and her voice as she is to her world. We are not only close to home,
whose proximity might lead us to think that we are in the realm of the authentic, but
too close. While such an immediacy might tempt us to feel we are near truth, it is that
kind of truth that is so true that we would never give it a second thought. The shift to
the past tense, however, shifts this non-story into a story, into something moving
toward art and representation. To shift from "I want to know" to "I wanted to know,"
is moving from speech to reported speech, and between the first moment and the second there is a temporal/spatial distance. When Mama shifts to the past tense, she is no

longer inside, immediately stitched into that world; she is in a narrating "present" which is not identical to the moment she is writing about. A frame begins to emerge, with Mama outside, yet inside, separated by a critical difference. At this moment, in the space marked by the shift to the past tense, a spatio-temporal dimension opens up which makes possible reflection, knowledge, representation, epiphany, manipulation, and power. And it is in such a space that we can begin to see how Mama, Dee, and Walker are linked.

In this story, unlike in Toomer's fiction, it is not the women who run to the artist, offering to the artist their stories, or stories they don't know are stories, but the artist, who in the figure of Dee, has come to the women who have stayed at home. What does the artist do with this world? It seems that the artist can take a story away, either by stealing it or by carrying it away in the name of giving voice to those who have never had a voice, or the artist can really try to give a voice to those who are at home. But if the artist, rather than taking a story away, attempts to get those at home to tell their own stories, or take their stories back, the artist would cease to be an artist. He or she would have shifted from art to a form of socio-political activity. This is one of the contradictions Susan Willis mentions: What does it really mean to give voice to someone, or some group of people? How can the artist avoid, in the name of speaking for a people, even if they are his or her "own" people, silencing them? Barbara Christian writes that "Toomer's women are silent, their sense of themselves and their condition interpreted by a male narrator" (9). But does the situation change with a woman narrator? Doesn't a problem of silencing remain as long as there is a narrator—one who speaks for and in the place of someone else? Moreover, who are the readers of the fiction whose subject are the people down home? The blunt fact, as Washington notes, is that the story of "Everyday Use," which is claimed by many to give voice to people in and outside of the story, circulates in a market far beyond them. They never hear their voices being heard.

This problem is very much at the heart of "Everyday Use." Part of what makes Walker such a powerful writer is her willingness to face such enormous problems straight on and, like Dee, not blink. And one of her attempts to work with this enterprise so fraught with contradictions is the narrative strategy she develops in "Everyday Use." One way into the problem is to begin with a narration that appears not to narrate at all. This is the significance of the present tense with which the story begins. This is Mama's voice and thoughts with no narrative frame. It is not the artist giving voice to Mama, but Mama's voice. It is not the artist telling the story of those at home, but those at home telling their own stories in their own words. This is what some would call authenticity; this is what some would call the true voice of true art; and this is what the Bakers hear: Mama represents that authentic art which is not "defined by social institutions such as museums, book reviews, and art dealers" (161). But what they don't attend to is the subtle, quiet, perhaps even reluctant, perhaps even guilty shift to the past tense, which is finally the mark, no matter how subtle, of the museum, book reviews, and art dealers. More importantly, however, is that this shift to the past tense is likewise the subtle mark of empowerment and control; for the possibility to frame, to represent one's own world, empowers. And while this may also be taken as the mark of a loss, one must ask—a loss for whom? The problem with those who desire to keep the voice "authentic" is that, to do so, they end up insisting that the voice stay at home, in its place, or her place, as happens to Mama when the Bakers say that she has "no categories for framed art" (163–64). Because Mama cannot frame her art, she must rely on those who, in the name of her best interest of course, will either tell it for her, or tell others that she isn't really doing what it seems she's doing. If she appears to be "writing," she's really only sewing. No matter how sacred the Bakers make the "sorority of quiltmakers," the "holy patchers" (156), that very appeal to sacredness would keep Mama in her place.

But Mama herself is a wayward artist. She drifts away from the present, not into a dream this time of distant fantasies far from home, but into a past tense, a narrative frame which creates distance at the same time that it makes possible a closeness, a coming home. This shift to the past tense allows for a present, as if the present, to be present, must be re-presented, re-proposed. It is likewise the condition necessary for a second thought. Mama's "epiphanic moment of recognition" (Baker and Pierce-Baker 161) is a re-cognition, made possible by the spatio-temporal difference that opens up with her wandering out from the present tense of home, out of that immediacy. These are not oppositional structures; or, rather, they are not the bipolar oppositions which work within a logic or politics of identity. What Barbara Christian has called Walker's "contrariness," and her creation of characters who act in spite of themselves, involves a doubling of each of the terms; and such a doubling opens up "differences *within* identities" (Fuss 103), within what for identity politics would be the two mutually exclusive terms of an opposition. But the past tense is not opposed to the present. If the past tense indicates distance and control, it is also the moment when distances collapse and control is lost. It is in the past tense that Mama has her epiphanic moment, wherein "something hit me in the top of my head and ran down to the soles of my feet," which in turn propels her to do something "I never had done before: hugged Maggie to me . . ." (34). But if the story ends with the embrace of this new intimacy between a mother and daughter, present to one another as never before, it is given in the past tense, and the story ends in that tense. And this leads one to reconsider the presentness of the present tense in which the story begins.

Fractured by dreams, by absences, by violent scars which mark Maggie's body and the memories of both Maggie and her mother, the present is not quite present. While the name "Dee/Wangero," most obviously indicates what appears to be an opposition, with "Wangero" insisting that "Dee" no longer exists, we see that both are "present," and traced each by the other. We can say the same about the relationship between the present/past, burnt house/new house, Mama in the present/Mama in the past, Maggie in the past/Maggie in the present, and framed/unframed narrative. One might say that what is being noted here is simply Walker's emphasis on change. All of the main characters, in fact, do change in the course of the story. More significant, however, is that Walker's contrariness provides delicate attention to the spatio-temporal dimension within "identities," which is what makes change possible and allows her characters to act in spite of themselves, in spite of their best and worst intentions. And this analysis can be extended to the question of what it means to give voice to those whose voice has not been heard.

Walker recognizes that art, or the artist, cannot do it—not that the answer would be to become a political activist who would with the best intentions go to the people and try to get them to have a voice. It might require, as in "Everyday Use," something of an anti-artist, or someone like Dee, whose insensitive intrusion, who *in spite of herself*, brings Mama to claim a voice. But when Mama takes over her own story, as symbolized in her refusal to let Dee take the quilts away, Mama herself becomes an artist. She will frame her story, and that frame, which marks a boundary of her being both inside and outside the frame, is the mark which marks the end of the "authentic" voice from "inside" yet makes possible having a voice of her "own." Walker does not allow Mama to remain in the present, in a world which is deemed more authentic just to the extent that she is seen as having no cognitive faculty for framed art. To have left Mama in the present tense would have left Walker in the position of an artist denying her own art, and would have suggested that Walker might be claiming that she is truly letting another speak in his or her own unframed voice, or that she is an artist who can genuinely speak for the other in the other's voice, with no frame, no distance, no loss. By having Mama shift to the past tense, however, Walker will have it appear that Mama cannot present herself without re-presenting herself.

Walker, as an artist, tells a story in which she explores the limits of both art and the authentic. She plays with the problem by knowing that art cannot simply or purely give voice to the voiceless, and that if the voiceless are to have a voice, and in particular their own, they can only have it through art's appropriation. It is not the artist who returns who can give voice to the voiceless, but art can give voice to how the voiceless come to have a voice; the fiction of "Everyday Use," in which Mama comes to have a voice, is an art which would on the one hand deny the role of the artist, but only insofar as the one who comes to have a voice becomes an artist. And once the voiceless give voice to themselves, they too are implicated in the very problem Walker articulates: To have a voice, to be able to represent one's own, means that one has drifted just that far away, as subtle as a shift from the present to the past tense, from one's own. Representation, in order to be representation, drifts away, must drift away, from one's own, which also translates the idea of "own" and "owning" into a different register that here can perhaps best be conceptualized in economic terms:

> . . . many African-American quilters employ large, often abstract designs. In the earliest days of the Freedom Quilting Bee in Alabama, this design preference contributed to the group's success. Francis Xavier Walter, a priest involved in the civil rights movement, bought quilts from women in Gee's Bend and its environs, sent them to New York to be auctioned, and gave the money to the women to support themselves and to re-invest into quilting—thus beginning one of the most successful, longest enduring quilting collectives in the nation. (Kelley 172)

As Elaine Showalter writes in her article "Common Threads," the quilt itself has drifted away from being specifically tied to woman's culture: "The patchwork quilt came to replace the melting-pot as the central metaphor of American cultural identity.

In a very unusual pattern, it transcended the stigma of its sources in women's culture and has been remade as a universal sign of American identity" (215). That the quilt drifted away from its ties to a particular origin attests to its power to function as a sign that circulates in an economy. Ironically, the marketing success of the quilt no doubt has much to do with its being seen as a commodity that denies that it is a commodity—which is to say, the quilt represents those values of things which do not circulate, do not wander, do not get traded or sold but, rather, stay at home. One might surely have misgivings about this commodification of the quilt, but then we have to ask whether our misgivings are linked to a kind of romantic, idealized desire of hearth and home which always keeps things and people at home and in their place. We overlook the empowerment of women when they send such items as quilts out on the market, as did the Freedom Quilting Bee group, or when women writers send out their stories, far from the home they write about.

The climax of the story, when Mama snatches the quilts out of Dee's arms and plops them in Maggie's lap, is most often read as saving the quilts from drifting away and circulating out there in an economy too far from home; in Maggie's arms, the quilts will be kept at home. When Dee threatens to take the quilts away and hang them on her wall, critics see Dee as representing "'institutionalized theories of aesthetics'" (212), as Showalter notes, quoting the Bakers. A polarization is established: Maggie and her mother represent "'everyday use'" (Showalter 212) and keeping things at home, whereas Dee represents a false aesthetics which put things out of use, out of place, and out of the home. Maggie, writes Showalter, "understands the quilt as a process rather than as commodity" (212), and Dee sees the quilt as a "thing" which could conceivably circulate as a commodity. Functional use is opposed to no use and the uselessness of that class of people who like to have art hanging around, as it were. But there seems to be some confusion as to how this climactic scene of the quilts has been interpreted.

Before "rifling" through the "trunk at the foot of [Mama's] bed" (32) and getting out the quilts, Dee has already removed all the items of everyday use that she will lay her hands on. The quilts she gets out of Mama's trunk are quite clearly in a trunk, which is to say not in everyday use. These quilts, which had been pieced by Mama's mother, and then quilted by her and her sister, had been tucked away, put in reserve, and not because they were being temporarily stored for the summer. When a horrified Dee claims that, if the quilts are given to Maggie, she would use and consequently ruin them, Mama responds, "'I reckon she would. . . . God knows I been saving 'em for long enough *with nobody using 'em*'" (33; emphasis mine). Nor is it the case that they had gone unused because they had been overlooked, or considered of little value. As Patricia Mainardi notes, "'The women who made quilts knew and valued what they were doing: frequently quilts were signed and dated by the maker, listed in her will with specific instructions as to who should inherit them, and treated with all the care that a fine piece of art deserves'" (qtd. in Showalter 200–01). The quilts in Mama's house had been placed in reserve because they held a certain value. That Mama had promised them to Maggie "for when she marries" (33), as a kind of wedding present or dowry, attests to their recognized value, and this value is being protected precisely in their not being put to everyday use. The contrast, then, is not one between use and disuse, between putting the quilts to daily use as opposed to putting them out of use by hanging them on a wall. That Dee wants to hang the quilts on a wall is not the issue. The quilts by Harriet Powers hanging on the wall of the Smithsonian Institution did not go unappreciated by Alice Walker; perhaps they even got there through the hands of someone like Dee.

The problem of Dee's relation to the quilts can be thought of in economic terms. When Dee first appears with the quilts in arm, she asks her mother, "'Can I have these *old* quilts?'" (32; emphasis mine), and when Mama says that they have already been promised to Maggie, Dee claims that they are *"priceless"* (33). In both cases, Dee has put the quilts not out of everyday use, but out of the economic order altogether. The quilts are either useless, like rags, and therefore something that can be tossed aside, outside of the economy of the home; or priceless, which is to say, outside of any economic system inasmuch as something without a price cannot circulate. That which is priceless generally "circulates" in two ways: by theft or by gift. These two modes are similar in that no price is involved, at least not immediately (a thief can pay with time or life; the recipient of a gift can pay whenever the never absent strings get tugged); the item "passed on," since it does not have to be represented in terms of something other than itself, as in a price, has that value of appearing to be even more itself; and the stolen or bequeathed thing does not get represented by something other, but represents itself, which, of course, *can* include, but doesn't have to, other symbolic values it may possess. The major difference between a gift and a theft is that of handing something down as opposed to underhandedly taking something away; in giving, the act itself creates links, whereas in taking all links are denied. And if the gift assumes an economic dimension, it is because the gift indebts the receiver. In this sense Dee is like a thief. While she wants "things" of the home, she does not want to feel any obligation, any link, any indebtedness. So in an underhanded way—denigrating the quilts, then claiming they are priceless—she seeks to steal them away. But what Dee also does is to denigrate in a more general sense the economic order of Mama's home and its system of values. What brings about the climactic moment in the story, however, which comes just before Mama's epiphanic moment, and contributes to her having that second thought, is Mama's own collusion with Dee in denigrating her own economic order.

When Dee hears that Mama had promised the quilts to Maggie, she explodes, "'Maggie can't appreciate these quilts! . . . She'd probably be backward enough to put them to everyday use.'" Mama responds: "'I reckon she would. . . . God knows I been saving 'em long enough with nobody using 'em. I hope she will!'" (33). When Dee accuses Maggie of being too backward to know the difference between things of value and of no value, she indirectly also includes Mama. And Mama's retort is in spite of, or spites, both herself and Maggie. It's as close as Mama comes to anger, and it seems that Mama is thrown off guard by Dee's comment. Indeed, what Dee does and says is enough to throw anyone off guard. She gets the quilts out of a trunk where they have been set aside, removed from everyday use, saved because of a certain value, and then accuses Maggie, and indirectly Mama, of being too backward to set them aside, save them, or know the value they have. Mama is not left without words, but she is left without the "right" words. She goes along with Dee's accusation that Maggie just might be backward enough to put the quilts to everyday use ("'I reckon she would'"), and in agreeing with Dee, she not only turns on Maggie, but also on herself and a system of values which she herself doesn't yet quite know how to value. It seems that it is in this turn away, however, this siding briefly and in spite of herself with Dee, that Mama moves away just far enough to be able to return, just far enough to be able to have her epiphany. It's as if Mama is not just talking at this moment, but hearing herself talk. So when Dee goes on to claim that, if an ignorant Maggie puts the quilts to everyday use they would be "'in rags'" in "'five years,'" which is no doubt true, Mama comes back with: "'She can always make some more. . . . Maggie *knows how to* quilt'" (33; emphasis mine). Mama raises the issue of knowing, and because of that knowledge of knowing how, the possibility to not be tied to a sign, or a metaphor, because one knows how to make a sign, a representation. Through knowing that one controls the means of production, one is released from being tied to a particular thing. And Mama is coming to know this, and she knows that Maggie knows.

While Dee, as happens in theft, keeps pointing to the value of "'these quilts, *these* quilts!'" (33), as she says, Mama understands that it is not at all a question of *these* quilts, but the ability to make others. And when, following close on this moment, Maggie says that Dee can have the quilts because, "'I can 'member Grandma Dee without the quilts'" (34), it is not just Mama's guilt for having sided with Dee against Maggie, her having "turned" on Maggie, that brings Mama to her epiphany which immediately follows Maggie's statement, but a recognition of an eco-nomos whose strength lies in not being bound to "*these* quilts."[3] To take the quilts out of Dee's hands and to put them into Maggie's is not putting the quilts to everyday use, nor is it putting them back *in their place*. Rather, they are being re-placed, not only as potentially replaceable, but placed in an economy where they can be used, saved, or even exchanged—where they can circulate. To return the quilts into the hands of a Maggie who does not need them in order to remember, and who can make more, is to remark not only their use value, or their exchange value, but the question of value itself. They can, in fact, at this point, even hang on a wall, be sold to the Smithsonian museum, be used as a dowry, or be auctioned in New York. For at this point, at this epiphanic moment, what has been realized is not the value of the quilts' representative dimension—which Mama and Maggie know already—but the power of representation. It is not a problem that Dee would have the quilts, even hang them on the wall—though it would be better if they were hung on a museum's wall perhaps; the problem is that Dee, by stealing them away, would take them out of an economy. A critical step is missed. The quilts might leave the home, but how they do so is significant. They must move through and out of the hands of Mama and Maggie. Of course Mama "sees" this only because they have passed into Dee's hands. It is as if Mama, like Walker herself, has an epiphany in seeing the quilts out of place. Mama, however, unlike Walker, snatches the quilts off the museum's wall—which is to say, out of Dee's hands—not because they might not eventually go there, but because they got there in the wrong way. Putting the quilts in Maggie's lap is not to bring them back home to be used at home, even if they could be used that way too. Rather, they are put in a place, which allows them to circulate. But what has re-marked the sign of the quilt as something that can circulate is its having passed through Dee's hands. In spite of herself, Dee provokes the question of value, of economy, of representation.

Barbara Christian's insight that Walker's characters often act in spite of themselves is critical. All the characters involved in this scene act in spite of themselves and others, but "in spite" seems to lead to insight. Maggie spites herself by offering to give up the quilts, but in doing so announces her freedom, through knowledge and memory, from the sign of that memory. Mama spites herself and Maggie by agreeing that they would probably be ignorant enough to ruin things of value, only to be led to see that their knowledge of quilting is where value lies. Dee, in trying to steal the quilts away, ends up losing them in spite of herself, but is also brought closer to home. And it is no doubt because of this appreciation of how sightless blundering can lead to insight that Walker does not reject Dee. If Mama, in her epiphanic moment, hugs Maggie for the first time, it must be noted that, before leaving, Dee, likewise, does something that we can assume she had never done before: If Dee, just before leaving, stings the family once again by telling them that they don't understand their heritage, she also "turn[s] to Maggie," and "kiss[es] her" (34). If Dee's desire has been rebuffed, she has been brought closer through that very distance. It is not only the "doubleness of the narrative voice" which is "key" to what Hirsch calls the story's "unusual and seemingly incongruous quality" (207), but a doubleness that works throughout the fabric of the story. Even Hirsch, whose reading is admirable in its attentiveness to this doubleness, limits that reading when it comes to both the quilt and to Dee. How one defines Dee is how one defines the quilt, and not to see a doubleness in Dee is not to see a doubleness in the quilt itself. So when Hirsch has Maggie "planning to use the quilts on her bed" (202–03), she slips into a polarization she elsewhere attempts to avoid, and it is not surprising then that, with regard to the climactic scene, Hirsch writes that "mother chooses Maggie and *rejects Dee*" (204; emphasis mine). To keep a doubleness in play, we would have to think that neither is Dee rejected nor does Maggie plan to use the quilts on her bed. As soon as we see the quilts as freed, as it were, from their use value only, which ends up keeping not only the quilts but everything else at home and in its place, Dee can no longer be seen as rejected from that home. Just to the extent that the quilts are seen in both their use and exchange value, seen as items that can leave home, Dee touches home.

Of course one might feel inclined to recall that the title of the story is, after all, "Everyday Use," which would seem to indicate that the idea here is that Maggie and Mama really ought to keep these quilts at home and on their beds. But I think it would be well to note that Walker, too, writes in spite of herself, and one of her remarkable powers is not to let the insights gained through blindness reject or repress that blindness—in spite of what some might consider are the better interests for her self and her writings.

## Notes

1. ". . . before the rise of Cultural Studies," Christian writes, "Walker celebrates the creative legacy, symbolized by the quilt that women like her mother had bestowed on her and other

contemporary black women writers" (4), and with the publication of Walker's first collection of short stories, *In Love and Trouble,* in which "Everyday Use" first appeared, we have "perhaps for the first time in contemporary United States literary history, a writer [who] feature[s] a variety of *Southern* black women's perspectives" (9).

2. This is the theme of Walker's poem "For My Sister Molly Who in the Fifties," written in 1972, the same period in which "Everyday Use" was being written, and by an Alice Walker who, like her sister Molly, had left home, changed, and returned. If Walker's sister Molly was "A light / A thousand watts / Bright and also blinding" (53), and if Dee, as Mama puts it, "burned us with a lot of knowledge we didn't necessarily need to know" (26), that is because those at home had no means to deflect or reflect that light, on the one hand, and because that light, on the other, becomes all the more intense in trying to find itself reflected—as if in not being reflected by those whose acknowledgment is desperately desired, the light might extinguish itself. Such a light, of course, blinds not only those at home, but the one who returns, too. Not to appreciate Dee's return is to dismiss the drama of what it means to return home which, as Hirsch notes, was a "vital" issue for that whole generation of black writers of which Walker is a part (201).

3. The association of *quilt* with *guilt* is not simple wordplay. Walker's generation in some ways marks a break between two "worlds." The quilt, which was handed down to Walker's world, was likewise handed over an abyss. Sons and daughters who no longer knew how to quilt, or were even interested in knowing, were given quilts with a double injunction: Put them to use but don't use them up (since you can't make any more). The impossibility of following that advice often led to packing the quilts away, guiltily. The subsequent expansion of the quilt market in the Seventies, which is to say their increased availability, no doubt contributed much to easing many people's conscience: If we use them up, we can always buy more. The commodification of this "non-commodity" has probably allowed many to feel more at home.

## Works Cited

Baker, Houston A., Jr., and Charlotte Pierce-Baker. "Patches: Quilts and Community in Alice Walker's *Everyday Use.*" Christian, ed., *Everyday* 149–65.

Bauer, Margaret D. "Alice Walker: Another Southern Writer Criticizing Codes Not Put To 'Everyday Use.'" *Studies in Short Fiction* 29 (Spring 1992): 143–51.

Christian, Barbara. "Alice Walker: The Black Woman Artist as Wayward." Christian, ed., *Everyday* 123–47.

———. "Introduction." Christian, ed., *Everyday* 3–17.

Christian, Barbara, ed. *Everyday Use.* New Brunswick: Rutgers UP, 1994.

Davis, Thadious M. "Alice Walker's Celebration of Self in Southern Generations." Christian, ed., *Everyday* 105–21.

Fuss, Diana. *Essentially Speaking: Feminism, Nature & Difference.* New York: Routledge, 1989.

Hedges, Elaine. "The Needle or the Pen: The Literary Rediscovery of Women's Textile Work." *Traditions and the Talents of Women.* Ed. Florence Howe. Urbana: U of Illinois P, 1991. 339–63.

Hirsch, Marianne. "Clytemnestra's Children: Writing (Out) the Mother's Anger." *Alice Walker: Modern Critical Views.* Ed. Harold Bloom. New York: Chelsea House, 1989. 195–213.

Kane, Patricia. "The Prodigal Daughter in Alice Walker's *Everyday Use.*" *Notes on Contemporary Literature* 15 (Mar. 1985): 7.

Kelley, Margot Anne. "Sisters' Choices: Quilting Aesthetics in Contemporary African-American Women's Fiction." Christian, ed., *Everyday* 167–94.

Showalter, Elaine. "Common Threads." Christian, ed., *Everyday* 195–224.

Tuten, Nancy. "Alice Walker's *Everyday Use.*" *Explicator* 51 (Winter 1993): 125–28.

Walker, Alice. "Everyday Use." 1973. Christian, ed., *Everyday* 23–35.

———. "For My Sister Molly Who in the Fifties." 1972. Christian, ed., *Everyday* 51–54.

———. "In Search of Our Mothers' Gardens." 1974. Christian, ed., *Everyday* 39–49.

Washington, Mary Helen. "An Essay on Alice Walker." Christian, ed., *Everyday* 85–104.

Winchell, Donna Haisty. *Alice Walker.* New York: Twayne, 1992.

# Writing

## *Crafting the Short Story*

Writers make themselves known through their work, weaving their concerns about the world into their texts. A good short story is intently crafted, its words carefully chosen, but each writer arrives at these words through a unique process that can be as planned as careful outlines or as unformed as simple sketches; Maxine Hong Kingston writes, "What I have at the beginning of a book is not an outline. . . . Sometimes I draw pictures. I draw a blob and then I have a little arrow and it goes to this other blob. . . . Then when it turns into words, I find the words lead me to various scenes and stories which I don't know about until I get there. I don't see the order until very late in the writing and sometimes the ending just comes. I just run up against it."

Writers are conscious not only of plot points but also of word choice, pacing, and character description and development. In the following essays, a few of the writers whose stories appear in this anthology talk not just about their own work, but also about the craft of writing itself. Each author has his or her own approach to the development and execution of a story, but all agree that a good story has the power to move a reader.

Thus, understanding the construction of a good story can help readers to thoroughly enjoy the text and confidently interpret its meaning. These essays also underscore the timelessness of good storytelling, as voices as diverse as Henry James (from the early twentieth century) and Jhumpa Lahiri (from the early twenty-first century) discuss the methods and means of telling engaging and purposeful stories.

# Raymond Carver

## On Writing                                                                1968

Back in the mid-1960s, I found I was having trouble concentrating my attention on long narrative fiction. For a time I experienced difficulty in trying to read it as well as in attempting to write it. My attention span had gone out on me; I no longer had the patience to try to write novels. It's an involved story, too tedious to talk about here. But I know it has much to do now with why I write poems and short stories. Get in, get out. Don't linger. Go on. It could be that I lost any great ambitions at about the same time, in my late twenties. If I did, I think it was good it happened. Ambition and a little luck are good things for a writer to have going for him. Too much ambition and bad luck, or no luck at all, can be killing. There has to be talent.

Some writers have a bunch of talent; I don't know any writers who are without it. But a unique and exact way of looking at things, and finding the right context for expressing that way of looking, that's something else. *The World According to Garp* is, of course, the marvelous world according to John Irving. There is another world according to Flannery O'Connor, and others according to William Faulkner and Ernest Hemingway. There are worlds according to Cheever, Updike, Singer, Stanley Elkin, Anne Beattie, Cynthia Ozick, Donald Barthelme, Mary Robison, William Kittredge, Barry Hannah, Ursula K. LeGuin. Every great or even every very good writer makes the world over according to his own specifications.

It's akin to style, what I'm talking about, but it isn't style alone. It is the writer's particular and unmistakable signature on everything he writes. It is his world and no other. This is one of the things that distinguishes one writer from another. Not talent. There's plenty of that around. But a writer who has some special way of looking at things and who gives artistic expression to that way of looking: that writer may be around for a time.

Isak Dinesen said that she wrote a little every day, without hope and without despair. Someday I'll put that on a three-by-five card and tape it to the wall beside my desk. I have some three-by-five cards on the wall now. "Fundamental accuracy of statement is the ONE sole morality of writing." Ezra Pound. It is not everything by ANY means, but if a writer has "fundamental accuracy of statement" going for him, he's at least on the right track.

I have a three-by-five up there with this fragment of a sentence from a story by Chekov: ". . . and suddenly everything became clear to him." I find these words filled with wonder and possibility. I love their simple clarity, and the hint of revelation that's implied. There is mystery, too. What has been unclear before? Why is it just now becoming clear? What's happened? Most of all—what now? There are consequences as a result of such sudden awakenings. I feel a sharp sense of relief—and anticipation.

I overheard the writer Geoffrey Wolff say "No cheap tricks" to a group of writing students. That should go on a three-by-five card. I'd amend it a little to "No tricks." Period. I hate tricks. At the first sign of a trick or a gimmick in a piece of fiction, a cheap trick or even an elaborate trick, I tend to look for cover. Tricks are ultimately boring, and I get bored easily, which may go along with my not having much of an attention span. But extremely clever chi-chi writing, or just plain tomfoolery writing, puts me to sleep. Writers don't need tricks or gimmicks or even necessarily need to be the smartest fellows on the block. At the risk of appearing foolish, a writer sometimes needs to be able to just stand and gape at this or that thing—a sunset or an old shoe—in absolute and simple amazement.

Some months back, in the *New York Times Book Review,* John Barth said that ten years ago most of the students in his fiction writing seminar were interested in "formal innovation," and this no longer seems to be the case. He's a little worried that writers are going to start writing mom and pop novels in the 1980s. He worries that experimentation may be on the way out, along with liberalism. I get a little nervous if I find myself within earshot of somber discussions about "formal innovation" in fiction writing. Too often "experimentation" is a license to be careless, silly or imitative in the writing. Even worse, a license to try to brutalize or alienate the reader. Too often such writing gives us no news of the world, or else describes a desert landscape and that's all—a few dunes and lizards here and there, but no people; a place uninhabited by anything recognizably human, a place of interest only to a few scientific specialists.

It should be noted that real experiment in fiction is original, hard-earned and cause for rejoicing. But someone else's way of looking at things—Barthelme's, for instance—should not be chased after by other writers. It won't work. There is only one Barthelme, and for another writer to try to appropriate Barthelme's peculiar sensibility or *mise en scene* under the rubric of innovation is for that writer to mess around with chaos and disaster and, worse, self-deception. The real experimenters have to Make It New, as Pound urged, and in the process have to find things out for themselves. But if writers haven't taken leave of their senses, they also want to stay in touch with us, they want to carry news from their world to ours.

It's possible, in a poem or a short story, to write about commonplace things and objects using commonplace but precise language, and to endow those things—a chair, a window curtain, a fork, a stone, a woman's earring—with immense, even startling power. It is possible to write a line of seemingly innocuous dialogue and have it send a chill along the reader's spine—the source of artistic delight, as Nabokov would have it. That's the kind of writing that most interests me. I hate sloppy or haphazard writing whether it flies under the banner of experimentation or else is just clumsily rendered realism. In Isaac Babel's wonderful short story, "Guy de Maupassant," the narrator has this to say about the writing of fiction: "No iron can pierce the heart with such force as a period put just at the right place." This too ought to go on a three-by-five.

Evan Connell said once that he knew he was finished with a short story when he found himself going through it and taking out commas and then going through the story again and putting commas back in the same places. I like that way of working on something. I respect that kind of care for what is being done. That's all we have, finally, the words, and they had better be the right ones, with the punctuation in the right places so that they can best say what they are meant to say. If the words are heavy with the writer's own unbridled emotions, or if they are imprecise and inaccurate for some other reason—if the words are in any way blurred—the reader's eyes will slide right over them and nothing will be achieved. The reader's own artistic sense will simply not be engaged. Henry James called this sort of hapless writing "weak specification."

I have friends who've told me they had to hurry a book because they needed the money, their editor or their wife was leaning on them or leaving them—something, some apology for the writing not being very good. "It would have been better if I'd taken the time." I was dumbfounded when I heard a novelist friend say this. I still am, if I think about it, which I don't. It's none of my business. But if the writing can't be made as good as it is within us to make it, then why do it? In the end, the satisfaction of having done our best, and the proof of that labor, is the one thing we can take into the grave. I wanted to say to my friend, for heaven's sake go do something else. There have to be easier and maybe more honest ways to try and earn a living. Or else just do it to the best of your abilities, your talents, and then don't justify or make excuses. Don't complain, don't explain.

In an essay called, simply enough, "Writing Short Stories," Flannery O'Connor talks about writing as an act of discovery. O'Connor says she most often did not know where she was going when she sat down to work on a short story. She says she doubts that many writers know where they are going when they begin something. She uses

"Good Country People" as an example of how she put together a short story whose ending she could not even guess at until she was nearly there:

> When I started writing that story, I didn't know there was going to be a Ph.D. with a wooden leg in it. I merely found myself one morning writing a description of two women I knew something about, and before I realized it, I had equipped one of them with a daughter with a wooden leg. I brought in the Bible salesman, but I had no idea what I was going to do with him. I didn't know he was going to steal that wooden leg until ten or twelve lines before he did it, but when I found out that this was what was going to happen, I realized it was inevitable.

When I read this some years ago it came as a shock that she, or anyone for that matter, wrote stories in this fashion. I thought this was my uncomfortable secret, and I was a little uneasy with it. For sure I thought this way of working on a short story somehow revealed my own shortcomings. I remember being tremendously heartened by reading what she had to say on the subject.

I once sat down to write what turned out to be a pretty good story, though only the first sentence of the story had offered itself to me when I began it. For several days I'd been going around with this sentence in my head: "He was running the vacuum cleaner when the telephone rang." I knew a story was there and that it wanted telling. I felt it in my bones, that a story belonged with that beginning, if I could just have the time to write it. I found the time, an entire day—twelve, fifteen hours even—if I wanted to make use of it. I did, and I sat down in the morning and wrote the first sentence, and other sentences promptly began to attach themselves. I made the story just as I'd make a poem; one line and then the next, and the next. Pretty soon I could see a story, and I knew it was my story, the one I'd been wanting to write.

I like it when there is some feeling of threat or sense of menace in short stories. I think a little menace is fine to have in a story. For one thing, it's good for the circulation. There has to be tension, a sense that something is imminent, that certain things are in relentless motion, or else, most often, there simply won't be a story. What creates tension in a piece of fiction is partly the way the concrete words are linked together to make up the visible action of the story. But it's also the things that are left out, that are implied, the landscape just under the smooth (but sometimes broken and unsettled) surface of things.

V.S. Pritchett's definition of a short story is "something glimpsed from the corner of the eye, in passing." Notice the "glimpse" part of this. First the glimpse. Then the glimpse given life, turned into something that illuminates the moment and may, if we're lucky—that word again—have even further-ranging consequences and meaning. The short story writer's task is to invest the glimpse with all that is in his power. He'll bring his intelligence and literary skill to bear (his talent), his sense of proportion and sense of the fitness of things: of how things out there really are and how he sees those things—like no one else sees them. And this is done through the use of clear and specific language, language used so as to bring to life the details that will light up the story for the reader. For the details to be concrete and convey meaning, the language must be accurate and precisely given. The words can be so precise they may even sound flat, but they can still carry; if used right, they can hit all the notes.

# Henry James

## The Art of Fiction

1884, 1888

I should not have affixed so comprehensive a title to these few remarks, necessarily wanting in any completeness upon a subject the full consideration of which would carry us far, did I not seem to discover a pretext for my temerity in the interesting pamphlet lately published under this name by Mr. Walter Besant. Mr Besant's lecture at the Royal Institution—the original form of his pamphlet—appears to indicate that many persons are interested in the art of fiction, and are not indifferent to such remarks, as those who practise it may attempt to make about it. I am therefore anxious not to lose the benefit of this favourable association, and to edge in a few words under cover of the attention which Mr. Besant is sure to have excited. There is something very encouraging in his having put into form certain of his ideas on the mystery of story-telling.

It is a proof of life and curiosity—curiosity on the part of the brotherhood of novelists as well as on the part of their readers. Only a short time ago it might have been supposed that the English novel was not what the French call *discutable*. It had no air of having a theory, a conviction, a consciousness of itself behind it—of being the expression of an artistic faith, the result of choice and comparison. I do not say it was necessarily the worse for that: it would take much more courage than I possess to intimate that the form of the novel as Dickens and Thackeray (for instance) saw it had any taint of incompleteness. It was, however, *naïf* (if I may help myself out with another French word); and evidently if it be destined to suffer in any way for having lost its *naïveté* it has now an idea of making sure of the corresponding advantages. During the period I have alluded to there was a comfortable, good-humoured feeling abroad that a novel is a novel, as a pudding is a pudding, and that our only business with it could be to swallow it. But within a year or two, for some reason or other, there have been signs of returning animation—the era of discussion would appear to have been to a certain extent opened. Art lives upon discussion, upon experiment, upon curiosity, upon variety of attempt, upon the exchange of views and the comparison of standpoints; and there is a presumption that those times when no one has anything particular to say about it, and has no reason to give for practice or preference, though they may be times of honour, are not times of development—are times, possibly even, a little of dulness. The successful application of any art is a delightful spectacle, but the theory too is interesting; and though there is a great deal of the latter without the former I suspect there has never been a genuine success that has not had a latent core of conviction. Discussion, suggestion, formulation, these things are fertilising when they are frank and sincere. Mr. Besant has set an excellent example in saying what he thinks, for his part, about the way in which fiction should be written, as well as about the way in which it should be published; for his view of the "art," carried on into an appendix, covers that too. Other labourers in the same field will doubtless take up the argument, they will give it the light of their experience, and the effect will surely be to make our interest in the novel a little more what it had for some time threatened to fail to be—a serious, active, inquiring interest, under protection of which this delightful study may, in moments of confidence, venture to say a little more what it thinks of itself.

It must take itself seriously for the public to take it so. The old superstition about fiction being "wicked" has doubtless died out in England; but the spirit of it lingers in a certain oblique regard directed toward any story which does not more or less admit that it is only a joke. Even the most jocular novel feels in some degree the weight of the proscription that was formerly directed against literary levity: the jocularity does not always succeed in passing for orthodoxy. It is still expected, though perhaps people are ashamed to say it, that a production which is after all only a "make-believe" (for what else is a "story"?) shall be in some degree apologetic—shall renounce the pretension of attempting really to represent life. This, of course, any sensible, wide-awake story declines to do, for it quickly perceives that the tolerance granted to it on such a condition is only an attempt to stifle it disguised in the form of generosity. The old evangelical hostility to the novel, which was as explicit as it was narrow, and which regarded it as little less favourable to our immortal part than a stage-play, was in reality far less insulting. The only reason for the existence of a novel is that it does attempt to represent life. When it relinquishes this attempt, the same attempt that we see on the canvas of the painter, it will have arrived at a very strange pass. It is not expected of the picture that it will make itself humble in order to be forgiven; and the analogy between the art of the painter and the art of the novelist is, so far as I am able to see, complete. Their inspiration is the same, their process (allowing for the different quality of the vehicle), is the same, their success is the same. They may learn from each other, they may explain and sustain each other. Their cause is the same, and the honour of one is the honour of another. The Mahometans think a picture an unholy thing, but it is a long time since any Christian did, and it is therefore the more odd that in the Christian mind the traces (dissimulated though they may be) of a suspicion of the sister art should linger to this day. The only effectual way to lay it to rest is to emphasise the analogy to which I just alluded—to insist on the fact that as the picture is reality, so the novel is history. That is the only general description (which does it justice) that we may give of the novel. But history also is allowed to represent life; it is not, any more than painting, expected to apologise. The subject-matter of fiction is stored up likewise in documents and records, and if it will not give itself away, as they say in California, it must speak with assurance, with the tone of the historian. Certain accomplished novelists have a habit of giving themselves away which must often bring tears to the eyes of people who take their fiction seriously. I was lately struck, in reading over many pages of Anthony Trollope, with his want of discretion in this particular. In a digression, a parenthesis or an aside, he concedes to the reader that he and this trusting friend are only "making believe." He admits that the events he narrates have not really happened, and that he can give his narrative any turn the reader may like best. Such a betrayal of a sacred office seems to me, I confess, a terrible crime; it is what I mean by the attitude of apology, and it shocks me every whit as much in Trollope as it would have shocked me in Gibbon or Macaulay. It implies that the novelist is less occupied in looking for the truth (the truth, of course I mean, that he assumes, the premises that we must grant him, whatever they may be), than the historian, and in doing so it deprives him at a stroke of all his standing-room. To represent and illustrate the past, the actions of men, is the task of either writer, and the only difference that I can see is, in proportion as he succeeds, to the honour of the novelist, consisting as it does in his having more difficulty in collecting his evidence, which is so far from being purely literary. It seems to me to give him a great character, the fact that he has at once so much in common with the philosopher and the painter; this double analogy is a magnificent heritage.

It is of all this evidently that Mr. Besant is full when he insists upon the fact that fiction is one of the *fine* arts, deserving in its turn of all the honours and emoluments that have hitherto been reserved for the successful profession of music, poetry, painting, architecture. It is impossible to insist too much on so important a truth, and the place that Mr. Besant demands for the work of the novelist may be represented, a trifle less abstractly, by saying that he demands not only that it shall be reputed artistic, but that it shall be reputed very artistic indeed. It is excellent that he should have struck this note, for his doing so indicates that there was need of it, that his proposition may be to many people a novelty. One rubs one's eyes at the thought; but the rest of Mr. Besant's essay confirms the revelation. I suspect in truth that it would be possible to confirm it still further, and that one would not be far wrong in saying that in addition to the people to whom it has never occurred that a novel ought to be artistic, there are a great many others who, if this principle were urged upon them, would be filled with an indefinable mistrust. They would find it difficult to explain their repugnance, but it would operate strongly to put them on their guard. "Art," in our Protestant communities, where so many things have got so strangely twisted about, is supposed in certain circles to have some vaguely injurious effect upon those who make it an important consideration, who let it weigh in the balance. It is assumed to be opposed in some mysterious manner to morality, to amusement, to instruction. When it is embodied in the work of the painter (the sculptor is another affair!) you know what it is: it stands there before you, in the honesty of pink and green and a gilt frame; you can see the worst of it at a glance, and you can be on your guard. But when it is introduced into literature it becomes more insidious—there is danger of its hurting you before you know it. Literature should be either instructive or amusing, and there is in many minds an impression that these artistic preoccupations, the search for form, contribute to neither end, interfere indeed with both. They are too frivolous to be edifying, and too serious to be diverting; and they are moreover priggish and paradoxical and superfluous. That, I think, represents the manner in which the latent thought of many people who read novels as an exercise in skipping would explain itself if it were to become articulate. They would argue, of course, that a novel ought to be "good," but they would interpret this term in a fashion of their own, which indeed would vary considerably from one critic to another. One would say that being good means representing virtuous and aspiring characters, placed in prominent positions; another would say that it depends on a "happy ending," on a distribution at the last of prizes, pensions, husbands, wives, babies, millions, appended paragraphs, and cheerful remarks. Another still would say that it means being full of incident and movement, so that we shall wish to jump ahead, to see who was the mysterious stranger, and if the stolen will was ever found, and shall not be distracted from this pleasure by any tiresome analysis or "description." But they would all agree that the "artistic" idea would spoil some of their fun. One would hold it accountable for all the description, another would see it revealed in the absence of sympathy. Its hostility to a happy ending would be evident, and it might even in some cases render any ending at all impossible. The "ending" of a novel is, for many persons, like that of a good dinner, a course of dessert and ices, and the artist in fiction is regarded as a sort of meddlesome doctor who forbids agreeable aftertastes. It is therefore true that this conception of Mr. Besant's of the novel as a superior form encounters not only a negative but a positive indifference. It matters little that as a work of art it should really be as little or as much of its essence to supply happy endings, sympathetic characters, and an objective tone, as if it were a work of mechanics: the association of ideas, however incongruous, might easily be too much for it if an eloquent voice were not sometimes raised to call attention to the fact that it is at once as free and as serious a branch of literature as any other.

Certainly this might sometimes be doubted in presence of the enormous number of works of fiction that appeal to the credulity of our generation, for it might easily seem that there could be no great character in a commodity so quickly and easily produced. It must be admitted that good novels are much compromised by bad ones, and that the field at large suffers discredit from overcrowding. I think, however, that this injury is only superficial, and that the superabundance of written fiction proves nothing against the principle itself. It has been vulgarised, like all other kinds of literature, like everything else to-day, and it has proved more than some kinds accessible to vulgarisation. But there is as much difference as there ever was between a good novel and a bad one: the bad is swept with all the daubed canvases and spoiled marble into some unvisited limbo, or infinite rubbish-yard beneath the back-windows of the world, and the good subsists and emits its light and stimulates our desire for perfection. As I shall take the liberty of making but a single criticism of Mr. Besant, whose tone is so full of the love of his art, I may as well have done with it at once. He seems to me to mistake in attempting to say so definitely beforehand what sort of an affair the good novel will be. To indicate the danger of such an error as that has been the purpose of these few pages; to suggest that certain traditions on the subject, applied *a priori*, have already had much to answer for, and that the good health of an art which undertakes so immediately to reproduce life must demand that it be perfectly free. It lives upon exercise, and the very meaning of exercise is freedom. The only obligation to which in advance we may hold a novel, without incurring the accusation of being arbitrary, is that it be interesting. That general responsibility rests upon it, but it is the only one I can think of. The ways in which it is at liberty to accomplish this result (of interesting us) strike me as innumerable, and such as can only suffer from being marked out or fenced in by prescription. They are as various as the temperament of man, and they are successful in proportion as they reveal a particular mind, different from others. A novel is in its broadest definition a personal, a direct impression of life; that, to begin with, constitutes its value, which is greater or less according to the intensity of the impression. But there will be no intensity at all, and therefore no value, unless there is freedom to feel and say. The tracing of a line to be followed, of a tone to be taken, of a form to be filled out, is a limitation of that freedom and a suppression of the very thing that we are most curious about. The form, it seems to me, is to be appreciated after the fact: then the author's choice has been made, his standard has been indicated; then we can follow lines and directions and compare tones and resemblances. Then in a word we can enjoy one of the most charming of pleasures, we can estimate quality, we can apply the test of execution. The execution belongs to the author alone; it is what is most personal to him, and we measure him by that. The advantage, the luxury, as well as the torment and responsibility of the novelist, is that there is no limit to what he may attempt as an executant— no limit to his possible experiments, efforts, discoveries, successes. Here it is especially that he works, step by step, like his brother of the brush, of whom we may always say that he has painted his picture in a manner best known to himself. His manner is his secret, not necessarily a jealous one. He cannot disclose it as a general thing if he would; he would be at a loss to teach it to others. I say this with a due recollection of having insisted on the community of method of the artist who paints a picture and the artist who writes a novel. The painter *is* able to teach the rudiments of his practice, and it is possible, from the study of good work (granted the aptitude), both to learn how to paint and to learn how to write. Yet it remains true, without injury to the *rapprochement,* that the literary artist would be obliged to say to his pupil much more than the other, "Ah, well, you must do it as you can!" It is a question of degree, a matter of delicacy. If there are exact sciences, there are also exact arts, and the grammar of painting is so much more definite that it makes the difference.

I ought to add, however, that if Mr. Besant says at the beginning of his essay that the "laws of fiction may be laid down and taught with as much precision and exactness as the laws of harmony, perspective, and proportion," he mitigates what might appear to be an extravagance by applying his remark to "general" laws, and by expressing most of these rules in a manner with which it would certainly be unaccommodating to disagree. That the novelist must write from his experience, that his "characters must be real and such as might be met with in actual life;" that "a young lady brought up in a quiet country village should avoid descriptions of garrison life," and "a writer whose friends and personal experiences belong to the lower middle-class should carefully avoid introducing his characters into society," that one should enter one's notes in a common-place book; that one's figures should be clear in outline; that making them clear by some trick of speech or of carriage is a bad method, and "describing them at length" is a worse one; that English Fiction should have a "conscious moral purpose;" that "it is almost impossible to estimate too highly the value of careful workmanship—

that is, of style;" that "the most important point of all is the story," that "the story is everything": these are principles with most of which it is surely impossible not to sympathise. That remark about the lower middle-class writer and his knowing his place is perhaps rather chilling; but for the rest I should find it difficult to dissent from any one of these recommendations. At the same time, I should find it difficult positively to assent to them, with the exception, perhaps, of the injunction as to entering one's notes in a common-place book. They scarcely seem to me to have the quality that Mr. Besant attributes to the rules of the novelist—the "precision and exactness" of "the laws of harmony, perspective, and proportion." They are suggestive, they are even inspiring, but they are not exact, though they are doubtless as much so as the case admits of: which is a proof of that liberty of interpretation for which I just contended. For the value of these different injunctions—so beautiful and so vague—is wholly in the meaning one attaches to them. The characters, the situation, which strike one as real will be those that touch and interest one most, but the measure of reality is very difficult to fix. The reality of Don Quixote or of Mr. Micawber is a very delicate shade; it is a reality so coloured by the author's vision that, vivid as it may be, one would hesitate to propose it as a model: one would expose one's self to some very embarrassing questions on the part of a pupil. It goes without saying that you will not write a good novel unless you possess the sense of reality; but it will be difficult to give you a recipe for calling that sense into being. Humanity is immense, and reality has a myriad forms; the most one can affirm is that some of the flowers of fiction have the odour of it, and others have not; as for telling you in advance how your nosegay should be composed, that is another affair. It is equally excellent and inconclusive to say that one must write from experience; to our supposititious aspirant such a declaration might savour of mockery. What kind of experience is intended, and where does it begin and end? Experience is never limited, and it is never complete; it is an immense sensibility, a kind of huge spider-web of the finest silken threads suspended in the chamber of consciousness, and catching every air-borne particle in its tissue. It is the very atmosphere of the mind; and when the mind is imaginative—much more when it happens to be that of a man of genius—it takes to itself the faintest hints of life, it converts the very pulses of the air into revelations. The young lady living in a village has only to be a damsel upon whom nothing is lost to make it quite unfair (as it seems to me) to declare to her that she shall have nothing to say about the military. Greater miracles have been seen than that, imagination assisting, she should speak the truth about some of these gentlemen. I remember an English novelist, a woman of genius, telling me that she was much commended for the impression she had managed to give in one of her tales of the nature and way of life of the French Protestant youth. She had been asked where she learned so much about this recondite being, she had been congratulated on her peculiar opportunities. These opportunities consisted in her having once, in Paris, as she ascended a staircase, passed an open door where, in the household of a *pasteur,* some of the young Protestants were seated at table round a finished meal. The glimpse made a picture; it lasted only a moment, but that moment was experience. She had got her direct personal impression, and she turned out her type. She knew what youth was, and what Protestantism; she also had the advantage of having seen what it was to be

French, so that she converted these ideas into a concrete image and produced a reality. Above all, however, she was blessed with the faculty which when you give it an inch takes an ell, and which for the artist is a much greater source of strength than any accident of residence or of place in the social scale. The power to guess the unseen from the seen, to trace the implication of things, to judge the whole piece by the pattern, the condition of feeling life in general so completely that you are well on your way to knowing any particular corner of it—this cluster of gifts may almost be said to constitute experience, and they occur in country and in town, and in the most differing stages of education. If experience consists of impressions, it may be said that impressions *are* experience, just as (have we not seen it?) they are the very air we breathe. Therefore, if I should certainly say to a novice, "Write from experience and experience only," I should feel that this was rather a tantalising monition if I were not careful immediately to add, "Try to be one of the people on whom nothing is lost!"

I am far from intending by this to minimise the importance of exactness—of truth of detail. One can speak best from one's own taste, and I may therefore venture to say that the air of reality (solidity of specification) seems to me to be the supreme virtue of a novel—the merit on which all its other merits (including that conscious moral purpose of which Mr. Besant speaks) helplessly and submissively depend. If it be not there they are all as nothing, and if these be there, they owe their effect to the success with which the author has produced the illusions of life. The cultivation of this success, the study of this exquisite process, form, to my taste, the beginning and the end of the art of the novelist. They are his inspiration, his despair, his reward, his torment, his delight. It is here in very truth that he competes with life; it is here that he competes with his brother the painter in *his* attempt to render the look of things, the look that conveys their meaning, to catch the colour, the relief, the expression, the surface, the substance of the human spectacle. It is in regard to this that Mr. Besant is well inspired when he bids him take notes. He cannot possibly take too many, he cannot possibly take enough. All life solicits him, and to "render" the simplest surface, to produce the most momentary illusion, is a very complicated business. His case would be easier, and the rule would be more exact, if Mr. Besant had been able to tell him what notes to take. But this, I fear, he can never learn in any manual; it is the business of his life. He has to take a great many in order to select a few, he has to work them up as he can, and even the guides and philosophers who might have most to say to him must leave him alone when it comes to the application of precepts, as we leave the painter in communion with his palette. That his characters "must be clear in outline," as Mr. Besant says—he feels that down to his boots; but how he shall make them so is a secret between his good angel and himself. It would be absurdly simple if he could be taught that a great deal of "description" would make them so, or that on the contrary the absence of description and the cultivation of dialogue, or the absence of dialogue and the multiplication of "incident," would rescue him from his difficulties. Nothing, for instance, is more possible than that he be of a turn of mind for which this odd, literal opposition of description and dialogue, incident and description, has little meaning and light. People often talk of these things as if they had a kind of internecine distinctness, instead of melting into each other at every breath, and being intimately associated parts of one general effort of expression. I cannot imagine composition existing in a series of blocks, nor conceive, in any novel worth discussing at all, of a passage of dialogue that is not in its intention descriptive, a touch of truth of any sort that does not partake of the nature of incident, or an incident that derives its interest from any other source than the general and only source of the success of a work of art—that of being illustrative. A novel is a living thing, all one and continuous, like any other organism, and in proportion as it lives will it be found, I think, that in each of the parts there is something of each of the other parts. The critic who over the close texture of a finished work shall pretend to trace a geography of items will mark some frontiers as artificial, I fear, as any that have been known to history. There is an old-fashioned distinction betwen the novel of character and the novel of incident which must have cost many a smile to the intending fabulist who was keen about his work. It appears to me as little to the point as the equally celebrated distinction between the novel and the romance—to answer as little to any reality. There are bad novels and good novels, as there are bad pictures and good pictures; but that is the only distinction in which I see any meaning, and I can as little imagine speaking of a novel of character as I can imagine speaking of a picture of character. When one says picture one says of character, when one says novel one says of incident, and the terms may be transposed at will. What is character but the determination of incident? What is incident but the illustration of character? What is either a picture or a novel that is *not* of character? What else do we seek in it and find in it? It is an incident for a woman to stand up with her hand resting on a table and look out at you in a certain way; or if it be not an incident I think it will be hard to say what it is. At the same time it is an expression of character. If you say you don't see it (character in *that—allons donc!*), this is exactly what the artist who has reasons of his own for thinking he *does* see it undertakes to show you. When a young man makes up his mind that he has not faith enough after all to enter the church as he intended, that is an incident, though you may not hurry to the end of the chapter to see whether perhaps he doesn't change once more. I do not say that these are extraordinary or startling incidents. I do not pretend to estimate the degree of interest proceeding from them, for this will depend upon the skill of the painter. It sounds almost puerile to say that some incidents are intrinsically much more important than others, and I need not take this precaution after having professed my sympathy for the major ones in remarking that the only classification of the novel that I can understand is into that which has life and that which has it not.

The novel and the romance, the novel of incident and that of character—these clumsy separations appear to me to have been made by critics and readers for their own convenience, and to help them out of some of their occasional queer predicaments, but to have little reality or interest for the producer, from whose point of view it is of course that we are attempting to consider the art of fiction. The case is the same with another shadowy category which Mr. Besant apparently is disposed to set up— that of the "modern English novel"; unless indeed it be that in this matter he has fallen into an accidental confusion of standpoints. It is not quite clear whether he intends the remarks in which he alludes to it to be didactic or historical. It is as difficult to suppose a person intending to write a modern English as to suppose him writing an ancient English novel: that is a label which begs the question. One writes the novel, one paints the picture, of one's language and of one's time, and calling it modern English will not, alas! make the difficult task any easier. No more, unfortunately, will calling this or that work of one's fellow-artist a romance—unless it be, of course, simply for the pleasantness of the thing, as for instance when Hawthorne gave this heading to his story of *Blithedale.* The French, who have brought the theory of fiction to remarkable completeness, have but one name for the novel, and have not attempted smaller things in it, that I can see, for that. I can think of no obligation to which the "romancer" would not be held equally with the novelist; the standard of execution is equally high for each. Of course it is of execution that we are talking—that being the only point of a novel that is open to contention. This is perhaps too often lost sight of, only to produce interminable confusions and cross-purposes. We must grant the artist his subject, his idea, his *donnée:* our criticism is applied only to what he makes of it. Naturally I do not mean that we are bound to like it or find it interesting: in case we do not our course is perfectly simple—to let it alone. We may believe that of a certain idea even the most sincere novelist can make nothing at all, and the event may perfectly justify our belief; but the failure will have been a failure to execute, and it is in the execution that the fatal weakness is recorded. If we pretend to respect the artist at all, we must allow him his freedom of choice, in the face, in particular cases, of innumerable presumptions that the choice will not fructify. Art derives a considerable part of its beneficial exercise from flying in the face of presumptions, and some of the most interesting experiments of which it is capable are hidden in the bosom of common things. Gustave Flaubert has written a story about the devotion of a servant-girl to a parrot, and the production, highly finished as it is, cannot on the whole be called a success. We are perfectly free to find it flat, but I think it might have been interesting; and I, for my part, am extremely glad he should have written it; it is a contribution to our knowledge of what can be done—or what cannot. Ivan Turgénieff has written a tale about a deaf and dumb serf and a lap-dog, and the thing is touching, loving, a little masterpiece. He struck the note of life where Gustave Flaubert missed it—he flew in the face of a presumption and achieved a victory.

Nothing, of course, will ever take the place of the good old fashion of "liking" a work of art or not liking it: the most improved criticism will not abolish that primitive, that ultimate test. I mention this to guard myself from the accusation of intimating that the idea, the subject, of a novel or a picture, does not matter. It matters, to my sense, in the highest degree, and if I might put up a prayer it would be that artists should select none but the richest. Some, as I have already hastened to admit, are much more remunerative than others, and it would be a world happily arranged in which persons intending to treat them should be exempt from confusions and mistakes. This fortunate condition will arrive only, I fear, on the same day that critics become purged from error. Meanwhile, I repeat, we do not judge the artist with fairness unless we say to him, "Oh, I grant you your starting-point, because if I did not I should seem to prescribe to you, and heaven forbid I should take that responsibility. If I pretend to tell you what you must not take, you will call upon me to tell you then what you must take; in which case I shall be prettily caught. Moreover, it isn't till I have accepted your data that I can begin to measure you. I have the standard, the pitch; I have no right to tamper with your flute and then criticise your music. Of course I may not care for your idea at all; I may think it silly, or stale, or unclean; in which case I wash my hands of you altogether. I may content myself with believing that you will not have succeeded in being interesting, but I shall, of course, not attempt to demonstrate it, and you will be as indifferent to me as I am to you. I needn't remind you that there are all sorts of tastes: who can know it better? Some people, for excellent reasons, don't like to read about carpenters; others, for reasons even better, don't like to read about courtesans. Many object to Americans. Others (I believe they are mainly editors and publishers) won't look at Italians. Some readers don't like quiet subjects; others don't like bustling ones. Some enjoy a complete illusion, others the consciousness of large concessions. They choose their novels accordingly, and if they don't care about your idea they won't, *a fortiori,* care about your treatment."

So that it comes back very quickly, as I have said, to the liking: in spite of M. Zola, who reasons less powerfully than he represents, and who will not reconcile himself to this absoluteness of taste, thinking that there are certain things that people ought to like, and that they can be made to like. I am quite at a loss to imagine anything (at any rate in this matter of fiction) that people *ought* to like or to dislike. Selection will be sure to take care of itself, for it has a constant motive behind it. That motive is simply experience. As people feel life, so they will feel the art that is most closely related to it. This closeness of relation is what we should never forget in talking of the effort of the novel. Many people speak of it as a factitious, artificial form, a product of ingenuity, the business of which is to alter and arrange the things that surround us, to translate them into conventional, traditional moulds. This, however, is a view of the matter which carries us but a very short way, condemns the art to an eternal repetition of a few familiar *clichés,* cuts short its development, and leads us straight up to a dead wall. Catching the very note and trick, the strange irregular rhythm of life, that is the attempt whose strenuous force keeps Fiction upon her feet. In proportion as in what she offers us we see life *without* rearrangement do we feel that we are touching the truth; in proportion as we see it *with* rearrangement do we feel that we are being put off with a substitute, a compromise and convention. It is not uncommon to hear an extraordinary assurance of remark in regard to this matter of rearranging, which is often spoken of as if it were the last word of art. Mr. Besant seems to me in danger of falling into the great error with his rather unguarded talk about "selection." Art is essentially selection, but it is a selection whose main care is to be typical, to be inclusive. For many people art means rose-coloured window-panes and selection means picking a bouquet for Mrs. Grundy. They will tell you glibly that artistic considerations have nothing to do with the disagreeable, with the ugly; they will rattle off shallow commonplaces about the province of art and the limits of art till you are moved to some wonder in return as to the province and the limits of ignorance. It appears to me that no one can ever have made a seriously artistic attempt without becoming conscious of an immense increase—a kind of revelation—of freedom. One perceives in that case—by the light of a heavenly ray—that the province of art is all life, all feeling, all observation, all vision. As Mr. Besant so justly intimates, it is all experience. That is a sufficient answer to those who maintain that it must not touch the sad things of life, who stick into its divine unconscious bosom little prohibitory inscriptions on the end of sticks, such as we see in public gardens—"It is forbidden to walk on the grass; it is forbidden to touch the flowers; it is not allowed to introduce dogs or to remain after dark; it is requested to keep to the right." The young aspirant in the line of fiction whom we continue to imagine will do nothing without taste, for in that case his freedom would be of little use to him; but the first advantage of his taste will be to reveal to him the absurdity of the little sticks and tickets. If he have taste, I must add, of course he will have ingenuity, and my disrespectful reference to that quality just now was not meant to imply that it is useless in fiction. But it is only a secondary aid; the first is a capacity for receiving straight impressions.

Mr. Besant has some remarks on the question of "the story" which I shall not attempt to criticise, though they seem to me to contain a singular ambiguity, because I do not think I understand them. I cannot see what is meant by talking as if there were a part of a novel which is the story and part of it which for mystical reasons is not—unless indeed the distinction be made in a sense in which it is difficult to suppose that any one should attempt to convey anything. "The story," if it represents anything, represents the subject, the idea, the *donnée* of the novel; and there is surely no "school"—Mr. Besant speaks of a school—which urges that a novel should be all treatment and no subject. There must assuredly be something to treat; every school is intimately conscious of that. This sense of the story being the idea, the starting-point, of the novel, is the only one that I see in which it can be spoken of as something different from its organic whole; and since in proportion as the work is successful the idea permeates and penetrates it, informs and animates it, so that every word and every punctuation-point contribute directly to the expression, in that proportion do we lose our sense of the story being a blade which may be drawn more or less out of its sheath. The story and the novel, the idea and the form, are the needle and thread, and I never heard of a guild of tailors who recommended the use of the thread without the needle, or the needle without the thread. Mr. Besant is not the only critic who may be observed to have spoken as if there were certain things in life which constitute stories, and certain others which do not. I find the same odd implication in an entertaining article in the *Pall Mall Gazette* devoted, as it happens, to Mr. Besant's lecture. "The story is the thing!" says this graceful writer, as if with a tone of opposition to some other idea. I should think it was, as every painter who, as the time for "sending in" his picture looms in the distance, finds himself still in quest of a subject—as every belated artist not fixed about his theme will heartily agree. There are some subjects which speak to us and others which do not, but he would be a clever man who should undertake to give a rule—an index expurgatorius—by which the story and the no-story should be known apart. It is impossible (to me at least) to imagine any such rule which shall not be altogether arbitrary. The writer in the *Pall Mall* opposes the delightful (as I suppose) novel of *Margot la Balafrée* to certain tales in which "Bostonian nymphs" appear to have "rejected English dukes for psychological reasons." I am not acquainted with the romance just designated, and can scarcely forgive the *Pall Mall* critic for not mentioning the name of the author, but the title appears to refer to a lady who may have received a scar in some heroic adventure. I am inconsolable at not being acquainted with this episode, but am utterly at a loss to see why it is a story when the rejection (or acceptance) of a duke is not, and why a reason, psychological or other, is not a subject when a cicatrix is. They are all particles of the multitudinous life with which the novel deals, and surely no dogma which pretends to make it lawful to touch the one and unlawful to touch the other will stand for a moment on its feet. It is the special picture that must stand or fall, according as it seem to possess truth or to lack it. Mr. Besant does not, to my sense, light up the subject by intimating that a story must, under penalty of not being a story, consist of "adventures." Why of adventures more than of green spectacles? He mentions a category of impossible things, and among them he places "fiction without adventure." Why without adventure, more than without matrimony, or celibacy, or parturition, or cholera, or hydropathy, or Jansenism? This seems to me to bring the novel back to the hapless little *rôle* of being an artificial, ingenious thing—bring it down from its large, free character of an immense and exquisite correspondence with life. And what *is* adventure, when it comes to that, and by what sign is the listening pupil to recognize it? It is an adventure—an immense one—for me to write this little article; and for a Bostonian nymph to reject an English duke is an adventure only less stirring, I should say, than for an English duke to be rejected by a Bostonian nymph. I see dramas within dramas in that, and innumerable points of view. A psychological reason is, to my imagination, an object adorably pictorial; to catch the tint of its complexion—I feel as if that idea might inspire one to Titianesque efforts. There are few things more exciting to me, in short, than a psychological reason, and yet, I protest, the novel seems to me the most magnificent form of art. I have just been reading, at the same time, the delightful story of *Treasure Island*, by Mr. Robert Louis Stevenson and, in a manner less consecutive, the last tale from M. Edmond de Goncourt, which is entitled *Chérie.* One of these works treats of murders, mysteries, islands of dreadful renown, hairbreadth escapes, miraculous coincidences and buried doubloons. The other treats of a little French girl who lived in a fine house in Paris, and died of wounded sensibility because no one would marry her. I call *Treasure Island* delightful, because it appears to me to have succeeded wonderfully in what it attempts; and I venture to bestow no epithet upon *Chérie,* which strikes me as having failed deplorably in what it attempts—that is in tracing the development of the moral consciousness of a child. But one of these productions strikes me as exactly as much of a novel as the other, and as having a "story" quite as much. The moral consciousness of a child is as much a part of life as the islands of the Spanish Main, and the one sort of geography seems to me to have those "surprises" of which Mr. Besant speaks quite as much as the other. For myself (since it comes back in the last resort, as I say, to the preference of the individual), the picture of the child's experience has the advantage that I can at successive steps (an immense luxury, near to the "sensual pleasure" of which Mr. Besant's critic in the *Pall Mall* speaks) say Yes or No, as it may be, to what the artist puts before me. I have been a child in fact, but I have been on a quest for a buried treasure only in supposition, and it is a simple accident that with M. de Goncourt I should have for the most part to say No. With George Eliot, when she painted that country with a far other intelligence, I always said Yes.

The most interesting part of Mr. Besant's lecture is unfortunately the briefest passage—his very cursory allusion to the "conscious moral purpose" of the novel. Here again it is not very clear whether he be recording a fact or laying down a principle; it is a great pity that in the latter case he should not have developed his idea. This branch of the subject is of immense importance, and Mr. Besant's few words point to considerations of the widest reach, not to be lightly disposed of. He will have treated the art of fiction but superficially who is not prepared to go every inch of the way that these considerations will carry him. It is for this reason that at the beginning of these remarks I was careful to notify the reader that my reflections on so large a theme have no pretension to be exhaustive. Like Mr. Besant, I have left the question of the morality of the novel till the last, and at the last I find I have used up my space. It is a question surrounded with difficulties, as witness the very first that meets us, in the form of a definite question, on the threshold. Vagueness, in such a discussion, is fatal, and what is the meaning of your morality and your conscious moral purpose? Will you not define your terms and explain how (a novel being a picture) a picture can be either moral or immoral? You wish to paint a moral picture or carve a moral statue: will you not tell us how you would set about it? We are discussing the Art of Fiction; questions of art are questions (in the widest sense) of execution; questions of morality are quite another affair, and will you not let us see how it is that you find it so easy to mix them up? These things are so clear to Mr. Besant that he has deduced from them a law which he sees embodied in English Fiction, and which is "a truly admirable thing and a great cause for congratulation." It is a great cause for congratulation indeed when such thorny problems become as smooth as silk. I may add that in so far as Mr. Besant perceives that in point of fact English Fiction has addressed itself preponderantly to these delicate questions he will appear to many people to have made a vain discovery. They will have been positively struck, on the contrary, with the moral timidity of the usual English novelist; with his (or with her) aversion to face the difficulties with which on every side the treatment of reality bristles. He is apt to be extremely shy (whereas the picture that Mr. Besant draws is a picture of boldness), and the sign of his work, for the most part, is a cautious silence on certain subjects. In the English novel (by which of course I mean the American as well), more than in any other, there is a traditional difference between that which people know and that which they agree to admit that they know, that which they see and that which they speak of, that which they feel to be a part of life and that which they allow to enter into literature. There is the great difference, in short, between what they talk of in conversation and what they talk of in print. The essence of moral energy is to survey the whole field, and I should directly reverse Mr. Besant's remark and say not that the English novel has a purpose, but that it has a diffidence. To what degree a purpose in a work of art is a source of corruption I shall not attempt to inquire; the one that seems to me least dangerous is the purpose of making a perfect work. As for our novel, I may say lastly on this score that as we find it in England to-day it strikes me as addressed in a large degree to "young people," and that this in itself constitutes a presumption that it will be rather shy. There are certain things which it is generally agreed not to discuss, not even to mention, before young people. That is very well, but the absence of discussion is not a symptom of the moral passion. The purpose of the English novel—"a truly admirable thing, and a great cause for congratulation"—strikes me therefore as rather negative.

There is one point at which the moral sense and the artistic sense lie very near together; that is in the light of the very obvious truth that the deepest quality of a work of art will always be the quality of the mind of the producer. In proportion as that intelligence is fine will the novel, the picture, the statue partake of the substance of beauty and truth. To be constituted of such elements is, to my vision, to have purpose enough. No good novel will ever proceed from a superficial mind; that seems to me an axiom which, for the artist in fiction, will cover all needful moral ground: if the youthful aspirant take it to heart it will illuminate for him many of the mysteries of "purpose." There are many other useful things that might be said to him, but I have come to the end of my article, and can only touch them as I pass. The critic in the *Pall Mall Gazette,* whom I have already quoted, draws attention to the danger, in speaking of the art of fiction, of generalising. The danger that he has in mind is rather, I imagine, that of particularising, for there are some comprehensive remarks which, in addition to those embodied in Mr. Besant's suggestive lecture, might without fear of misleading him be addressed to the ingenuous student. I should remind him first of the magnificence of the form that is open to him, which offers to sight so few restrictions and such innumerable opportunities. The other arts, in comparison, appear confined and hampered; the various conditions under which they are exercised are so rigid and definite. But the only condition that I can think of attaching to the composition of the novel is, as I have already said, that it be sincere. This freedom is a splendid privilege, and the first lesson of the young novelist is to learn to be worthy of it. "Enjoy it as it deserves," I should say to him; "take possession of it, explore it to its utmost extent, publish it, rejoice in it. All life belongs to you, and do not listen either to those who would shut you up into corners of it and tell you that it is only here and there that art inhabits, or to those who would persuade you that this heavenly messenger wings her way outside of life altogether, breathing a superfine air, and turning away her head from the truth of things. There is no impression of life, no manner of seeing it and feeling it, to which the plan of the novelist may not offer a place; you have only to remember that talents so dissimilar as those of Alexandre Dumas and Jane Austen, Charles Dickens and Gustave Flaubert have worked in this field with equal glory. Do not think too much about optimism and pessimism; try and catch the colour of life itself. In France to-day we see a prodigious effort (that of Emile Zola, to whose solid and serious work no explorer of the capacity of the novel can allude without respect), we see an extraordinary effort vitiated by a spirit of pessimism on a narrow basis. M. Zola is magnificent, but he strikes an English reader as ignorant; he has an air of working in the dark; if he had as much light as energy, his results would be of the highest value. As for the aberrations of a shallow optimism, the ground (of English fiction especially) is strewn with their brittle particles as with broken glass. If you must indulge in conclusions, let them have the taste of a wide knowledge.

Remember that your first duty is to be as complete as possible—to make as perfect a work. Be generous and delicate and pursue the prize."

# Jhumpa Lahiri

## *The Author of "Interpreter of Maladies" Interprets Herself* 2000

A letter came recently to my father's office from a Bengali gentleman in Calcutta. The author of the letter, unknown to my family, explained that he was a lifelong writer of fiction, adding that his "pen was never still." This prolific gentleman, impressed with the fact that I, with my recognizably Bengali name, had won the Pulitzer Prize, wanted to know how he himself might apply for the honor. On the phone from New York, I explained to my parents that it hadn't been a matter of applying, that it had actually been the single greatest surprise of my life, something like winning the lottery without ever having bought a ticket. When my father asked whether Indian nationals were eligible for the Pulitzer, I told him what I knew: that the book had to be by an American citizen, and deal, preferably, with "American life." At this point my mother interjected that the judges had made an exception in my case. I might have been naturalized as an American citizen when I was eighteen (I was born in London), but in her eyes I am first and forever Indian. Furthermore, my book, in her opinion, wasn't about American life. It was about people like herself and myself—Indians. I suppose I should be grateful that my mother wasn't on the Pulitzer committee.

I draw attention to this anecdote because it exemplifies the perplexing bicultural universe I inhabit, the expectations and assumptions I have always shuttled between. My mother has lived outside India for nearly thirty-five years; my father, nearly forty. Since 1969 they've made their home in the United States. But there were invisible walls erected around our home, walls intended to keep American influence at bay. Growing up, I was admonished not to "behave" like an American, or worse, to "think" of myself as one. Actually "being" an American was not an option. I believe what first drove me to write fiction was to escape the pitfalls of being viewed as one thing or the other. As an author, I could embody any individual my imagination enabled me to, of any origin. This sense of freedom is one of the greatest thrills of writing fiction, and for a person like me, who has never been confident of what to call herself or of where to say she is from, it is a solace. But what I have discovered upon publishing my book— *Interpreter of Maladies*—is that authorial freedom is limited to the process of writing itself, in the private sphere of creation. Once made public, both my book and myself were immediately and copiously categorized. Take, for instance, the various ways I am described: as an American author, as an Indian-American author, as a British-born author, as an Anglo-Indian author, as an NRI (non-resident Indian) author, as an ABCD author (ABCD stands for American born confused "desi"—"desi" meaning Indian—and is an acronym coined by Indian nationals to describe culturally challenged second-generation Indians raised in the U.S.). According to Indian academics, I've written something known as "Diaspora fiction"; in the U.S., it's "immigrant fiction." In a way, all of this amuses me. The book is what it is, and has been received in ways I have no desire or ability to control. The fact that I am described in two ways or twenty is of no consequence; as it turns out, each of those labels is accurate.

I have always lived under the pressure to be bilingual, bicultural, at ease on either side of the Lahiri family map. The first words I learned to utter and understand were in my parents' native tongue, Bengali. Until I was old enough to go to school, and my linguistic world split in two, I spoke Bengali exclusively and fluently. Though I still speak Bengali, I have lost this extreme fluency. I was stunned, listening a few years ago to a cassette tape that had recorded the wedding of one of my parents' friends, in 1970. There I was, three years old, prattling confidently on in a way I no longer can. Still, my ability to speak the language made me feel less foreign during visits to Calcutta every few years. It also made me feel less foreign in the expatriate Bengali community my parents socialize with in the United States and, on a more quotidian level, in my own home.

While English was not technically my first language, it has become so. My knowledge of Bengali is spoken, colloquial—above all, familial. It's hard for me to understand the formal elocution of a Bengali television newscast or the literary diction of a poem. I read with the humble prowess of a struggling young child. (Standard typeset letters are easier for me than penmanship.) My writing is at about the same level. Putting these skills to use was an isolated, occasional need: "Write a letter to your grandfather," my father would say. And then, "Try to read his reply." Still, my basic aptitude allowed me, in graduate school, to translate six short stories by a Bengali writer named Ashapurna Devi. The process was as follows: My mother would read the story aloud in Bengali, and I would simultaneously write a rough translation in English. Then I would go back and read the story to myself, at a snail's pace. The painstaking process made me realize that while I'd always liked to consider myself bilingual, this was hardly the case.

When it came to my own writing, English was, from the beginning, my only language. The very first stories I wrote, in the second grade during recess, were imitations of what I'd learned to read in the classroom. I proceeded to write throughout my childhood, always in English, never about anything to do with India. If writing may be seen, in part, as an impulse on the author's behalf to control the world, then this was my youthful attempt to maintain order: to write about one sort of life without letting the other sort seep in and complicate things. In my twenties, I began to complicate things. My first "adult" attempt at a story took place in India, as did a few others that followed. I had come to regard India as a place both in which and about which to write fiction. During visits there I was idle, unmoored, intensely curious about what I saw: an alternate life, which, had my parents chosen not to live their lives abroad, would have been mine. The main resource for any writer was suddenly, abundantly available to me—uninterrupted by time and relative isolation. (I say relative because in fact I was always literally surrounded by my relatives.) It was in India that I discovered the following: that given a stretch of time in which I had nothing to do, and given pen and paper, I would write something.

The earliest story in my book, "A Real Durwan," was written soon after returning from a visit to India in 1992, in my bedroom in my parents' house in Rhode Island. This story and another, "The Treatment of Bibi Haldar," have been attacked by Indian reviewers as having a "tunnel vision" of India. My only defense is that my own experience of India was largely that of a tunnel—the tunnel imposed by the single city we ever visited, by the handful of homes we stayed in, by the fact that I was not allowed to explore this city on my own. Still, within these narrow confines, I felt that I had seen enough of life, enough details and drama, to set stories on Indian soil. An Indian man I met at a dinner party in New York, speaking of "A Real Durwan," disagreed with me. He felt I had misrepresented the plumbing technologies of Calcutta. "All houses in Calcutta have sinks," he informed me, indignantly, assuming that I had never been there myself, or at best had been there once or twice as a child. I did not argue to the contrary, in spite of the fact that my maternal grandparents' house—the house the story was based on—had no sinks but rather a series of plastic and metal buckets from which we washed our hands and bathed. I realized that, according to this man I had carelessly construed the city from which he originally hailed. Mistranslated it, if you will.

What this gentleman was suggesting is something that has been stated more explicitly in certain reviews of my book in the Indian press. And that is that I, being an ABCD, lack the cultural ambidexterity to write about Indian life and characters in an authentic way. I have been accused of setting stories in India as a device in order to woo Western audiences with exotica. Non-Bengali reviewers make noises about the fact that I only write about Bengalis, only one of India's numerous regional populations. Even after I won the Pulitzer, *India Today,* a national news magazine, wrote that my setting stories in Calcutta was "an unwise decision." Most disturbing of all was a review in an Indian paper called *Business Standard,* in which the reviewer, discussing "Interpreter of Maladies," comments upon the infatuation of Mr. Kapasi, a part-time Indian tour guide, with the Indian-American Mrs. Das. In this story, Mr. Kapasi is intoxicated by the sight of Mrs. Das's bare legs and short skirt, things I had safely assumed many of the world's men found arousing. But Mr. Kapasi's intoxication was not universal in the reviewer's mind; it was "appalling[ly]" stereotypical, severe condemnation for a fiction writer. The review continues: "This could be understandable if the writer were a complete foreigner, but not from someone who flaunts her Indian lineage." In other words, had I no hereditary connection to India, the story's "stereotypical" premise would be an excusable offense. But given my family tree, and given the fact that I chose India as a subject matter, different rules apply: I should know better. And yet, given the fact that I was raised in the U.S., the review also implies that I cannot know better.

To avoid this sort of review in the future, I suppose I could decide to play it safe and never write about India or nonimmigrant Indians again. I am the first person to admit that my knowledge of India is limited, the way in which all translations are. I am impeded not only by my own lack of proximity but by the fact that my parents' impressions—one of my main resources when writing about India—are also arrested in time; the country they left in the sixties is, in many respects, unrecognizable to them today. Still, my translation of India has evoked, for some readers and reviewers here and there, the illusion of cultural accuracy, and resonance. One of my mother's cousins, now living in West Virginia, even went so far as to thank me for taking her back to the Calcutta of her childhood, all its requisite details, in her opinion, intact.

Rendering an Indian landscape into English, with or without sinks, is one thing. Dialogue is wholly another. Because Bengali is essentially a spoken language for me, because it occupies such an aural presence in my mind, forcing my Bengali characters to speak a tongue they either can't or wouldn't speak in a given scene is one of my most daunting challenges. It is a disorienting and at times highly dissatisfying thing to do. I must abandon a certain sense of verisimilitude in the process, a certain fidelity. It is something of a betrayal, for example, to have the family in "When Mr. Pirzada Came to Dine" speaking English when they are at home. For in my imagination, these characters are conversing in Bengali. Were I to tell this story to myself, I think I would narrate the expository passages in English while preserving all the dialogue, where appropriate, in Bengali. Such tactics aren't feasible for a general audience, except in very short doses. In some instances I do retain Bengali words in my stories. The *durwan* of "A Real Durwan" is one example. I liked the sound of the word in Bengali, and the full phrase, with the two English words in front of it, sounded perfectly normal, just as it is normal for me and even for my parents to slip the occasional English word into Bengali conversation. (Even the coinage ABCD betrays a similar linguistic hybridization.) The phrase *bechareh,* an epithet used to designate a pitiable person, also appears in "A Real Durwan." I included it not out of any need to be culturally accurate, but due to the whims of my own quasi-bilingual brain.

Incorporating Bengali words into my stories is something I have stopped doing. This may be attributed, in part, to a healthy artistic impulse: My writing, these days, is less a response to my parents' cultural nostalgia, and more an attempt to forge my own amalgamated domain. Writing "When Mr. Pirzada Came to Dine" was a turning point. I say turning point not because it was the first time I set a story on American soil or because it was the first time I had an Indian-American protagonist. Both of these things I had already done. But in this story I felt I was, for the first time, conveying that intimate Bengali of my upbringing, both spoken and otherwise, into English. Here I incorporated no foreign words or expressions. What concerned me more was the precise explanation of certain gestures and details—the manner in which the family eats, for example, and their preoccupation, while living in a small New England town, with the Pakistani civil war. My focus in this story wasn't the unilateral translation of a place or a language. Instead it was a simultaneous translation in both directions, of characters who literally dwell in two separate worlds. This story was recently translated and published in a Bengali literary magazine. While I can easily comprehend the dialogue, much of the story's vocabulary is inaccessible to me. At the same time, because the English "translation" is something I've already written and largely committed to memory, it's relatively easy to guess what an otherwise foreign word means.

Looking at my stories as a whole, I am aware that I am preoccupied with language, as if this concept, this fact of human life, were itself an element of drama. I seem especially preoccupied with the presence in any given character's life of two languages and sometimes more, in different sorts of equations. Almost all of my characters are translators, insofar as they must make sense of the foreign in order to survive. The failed linguist in the title story literally makes his living off his knowledge of English and other languages. In "Sexy," Miranda's curiosity about Bengali is a way for her to gain access to her married and increasingly unavailable lover. In "The Third and Final Continent," the last story in the book to be written, the protagonist notes that when his wife arrives in Boston, he speaks Bengali in America for the first time. Yet there is no discernible change in the style of his dialogue; he speaks to his wife in the same manner that he speaks in English to Mrs. Croft. For the ancient Mrs. Croft, meanwhile, modern life has itself become a baffling foreign language, one she neither participates in nor understands. The protagonist in this story also fears that his son will no longer speak in Bengali after he and his wife die. This is displaced anxiety on my part—my own fear of my parents' death. For if I am to survive them, it is I who will suffer the linguistic loss.

In my dictionary, the biblical definition of *translate* is "to convey to heaven without death." I am struck by the extent to which this decidedly Western, nonsecular definition sheds light on my own personal background of Eastern origin. For in my observation, translation is not only a finite linguistic act but an ongoing cultural one. It is the continuous struggle, on my parents' behalf, to preserve what it means to them to be first and forever Indian, to keep afloat certain familial and communal traditions in a foreign and at times indifferent world. The life my parents have made for themselves here has required a great movement, a long voyage, an uprooting of all things familiar in exchange for an immersion into all things strange. It has required, moreover, an endless going back and forth, repeated traveling, urgent telephone calls, decades of sending and receiving letters. Somehow they have conveyed the spirit of their former world to the here and now, where it exists for them, still thriving, still meaningful.

Unlike my parents, I translate not so much to survive in the world around me as to create and illuminate a nonexistent one. Fiction is the foreign land of my choosing, the place where I strive to convey and preserve the meaningful. And whether I write as an American or an Indian, about things American or Indian or otherwise, one thing remains constant: I translate, therefore I am.

# Alice Munro

## What Is Real?                                                              1982

Whenever people get an opportunity to ask me questions about my writing, I can be sure that some of the questions asked will be these:

"Do you write about real people?"

"Did those things really happen?"

"When you write about a small town are you really writing about Wingham?" (Wingham is the small town in Ontario where I was born and grew up, and it has often been assumed, by people who should know better, that I have simply "fictionalized" this place in my work. Indeed, the local newspaper has taken me to task for making it the "butt of a soured and cruel introspection.")

The usual thing, for writers, is to regard these either as very naïve questions, asked by people who really don't understand the difference between autobiography and fiction, who can't recognize the device of the first-person narrator, or else as catch-you-out questions posed by journalists who hope to stir up exactly the sort of dreary (and to outsiders, slightly comic) indignation voiced by my home-town paper. Writers answer such questions patiently or crossly according to temperament and the mood they're in. They say, no, you must understand, my characters are composites; no, those things didn't happen the way I wrote about them; no, of course not, that isn't Wingham (or whatever other place it may be that has had the queer unsought-after distinction of hatching a writer). Or the writer may, riskily, ask the questioners what is real, anyway? None of this seems to be very satisfactory. People go on asking these same questions because the subject really does interest and bewilder them. It would seem to be quite true that they don't actually know what fiction is.

And how could they know, when what it is, is changing all the time, and we differ among ourselves, and we don't really try to explain because it is too difficult?

What I would like to do here is what I can't do in two or three sentences at the end of a reading. I won't try to explain what fiction is, and what short stories are (assuming, which we can't, that there is any fixed thing that it is and they are), but what short stories are to me, and how I write them, and how I use things that are "real." I will start by explaining how I read stories written by other people. For one thing, I can start reading them anywhere; from beginning to end, from end to beginning, from any point in between in either direction. So obviously I don't take up a story and follow it as if it were a road, taking me somewhere, with views and neat diversions along the way. I go into it, and move back and forth and settle here and there, and stay in it for a while. It's more like a house. Everybody knows what a house does, how it encloses space and makes connections between one enclosed space and another and presents what is outside in a new way. This is the nearest I can come to explaining what a story does for me, and what I want my stories to do for other people.

So when I write a story I want to make a certain kind of structure, and I know the feeling I want to get from being inside that structure. This is the hard part of the explanation, where I have to use a word like "feeling," which is not very precise, because if I attempt to be more intellectually respectable I will have to be dishonest. "Feeling" will have to do.

There is no blueprint for the structure. It's not a question of, "I'll make this kind of house because if I do it right it will have this effect." I've got to make, I've got to build up, a house, a story, to fit around the indescribable "feeling" that is like the soul of the story, and which I must insist upon in a dogged, embarrassed way, as being no more definable than that. And I don't know where it comes from. It seems to be already there, and some unlikely clue, such as a shop window or a bit of conversation, makes me aware of it. Then I start accumulating the material and putting it together. Some of the material I may have lying around already, in memories and observations, and some I invent, and some I have to go diligently looking for (factual details), while some is dumped in my lap (anecdotes, bits of speech). I see how this material might go together to make the shape I need, and I try it. I keep trying and seeing where I went wrong and trying again.

I suppose this is the place where I should talk about technical problems and how I solve them. The main reason I can't is that I'm never sure I do solve anything. Even when I say that I see where I went wrong, I'm being misleading. I never figure out how I'm going to change things. I never say to myself, "That page is heavy going, that paragraph's clumsy, I need some dialogue and shorter sentences." I feel a part that's wrong, like a soggy weight; then I pay attention to the story, as if it were really happening somewhere, not just in my head, and in its own way, not mine. As a result, the sentences may indeed get shorter, there may be more dialogue, and so on. But though I've tried to pay attention to the story, I may not have got it right; those shorter sentences may be an evasion, a mistake. Every final draft, every published story, is still only an attempt, an approach, to the story.

I did promise to talk about using reality. "Why, if Jubilee isn't Wingham, has it got Shuter Street in it?" people want to know. Why have I described somebody's real ceramic elephant sitting on the mantelpiece? I could say I get momentum from doing things like this. The fictional room, town, world, needs a bit of starter dough from the real world. It's a device to help the writer—at least it helps me—but it arouses a certain baulked fury in the people who really do live on Shuter Street and the lady who owns the ceramic elephant. "Why do you put in something true and then go and tell lies?" they say, and anybody who has been on the receiving end of this kind of thing knows how they feel.

"I do it for the sake of my art and to make this structure that encloses the soul of my story, which I've been telling you about," says the writer. "That is more important than anything."

Not to everybody, it isn't.

So I can see there might be a case, once you've written the story and got the momentum, for going back and changing the elephant to a camel (though there's always a chance the lady might complain that you made a nasty camel out of a beautiful elephant), and changing Shuter Street to Blank Street. But what about the big chunks of reality, without which your story can't exist? In the story "Royal Beatings," I use a big chunk of reality: the story of the butcher, and of the young men who may have been egged on to "get" him. This is a story out of an old newspaper; it really did happen in a town I know. There is no legal difficulty about using it because it has been printed in a newspaper, and besides, the people who figure in it are all long dead. But there is a difficulty about offending people in that town who would feel that use of this story is a deliberate exposure, taunt, and insult. Other people who have no connection with the real happening would say, "Why write about anything so hideous?" And lest you think that such an objection could only be raised by simple folk who read nothing but Harlequin Romances, let me tell you that one of the questions most frequently asked at universities is, "Why do you write about things that are so depressing?" People can accept almost any amount of ugliness if it is contained in a familiar formula, as it is on television, but when they come closer to their own place, their own lives, they are much offended by a lack of editing.

There are ways I can defend myself against such objections. I can say, "I do it in the interests of historical reality. That is what the old days were really like." Or, "I do it to show the dark side of human nature, the beast let loose, the evil we can run up against in communities and families." In certain countries I could say, "I do it to show how bad things were under the old system when there were prosperous butchers and young fellows hanging around livery stables and nobody thought about building a new society." But the fact is, the minute I say *to show* I am telling a lie. I don't do it to show anything. I put this story at the heart of my story because I need it there and it belongs there. It is the black room at the centre of the house with all other rooms leading to and away from it. That is all. A strange defence. Who told me to write this story? Who feels any need of it before it is written? I do. I do, so that I might grab off this piece of horrid reality and install it where I see fit, even if Hat Nettleton and his friends were still around to make me sorry.

The answer seems to be as confusing as ever. Lots of true answers are. Yes and no. Yes, I use bits of what is real, in the sense of being really there and really happening, in the world, as most people see it, and I transform it into something that is really there and really happening, in my story. No, I am not concerned with using what is real to make any sort of record or prove any sort of point, and I am not concerned with any methods of selection but my own, which I can't fully explain. This is quite presumptuous, and if writers are not allowed to be so—and quite often, in many places, they are not—I see no point in the writing of fiction.

# Flannery O'Connor

## *Writing Short Stories* 1961

I have heard people say that the short story was one of the most difficult literary forms, and I've always tried to decide why people feel this way about what seems to me to be one of the most natural and fundamental ways of human expression. After all, you begin to hear and tell stories when you're a child, and there doesn't seem to be anything very complicated about it. I suspect that most of you have been telling stories all your lives, and yet here you sit—come to find out how to do it.

Then last week, after I had written down some of these serene thoughts to use here today, my calm was shattered when I was sent seven of your manuscripts to read.

After this experience, I found myself ready to admit, if not that the short story is one of the most difficult literary forms, at least that it is more difficult for some than for others.

I still suspect that most people start out with some kind of ability to tell a story but that it gets lost along the way. Of course, the ability to create life with words is essentially a gift. If you have it in the first place, you can develop it; if you don't have it, you might as well forget it.

But I have found that the people who don't have it are frequently the ones hell-bent on writing stories. I'm sure anyway that they are the ones who write the books and the magazine articles on how-to-write-short-stories. I have a friend who is taking a correspondence course in this subject, and she has passed a few of the chapter headings on to me—such as, "The Story Formula for Writers," "How to Create Characters," "Let's Plot!" This form of corruption is costing her twenty-seven dollars.

I feel that discussing story-writing in terms of plot, character, and theme is like trying to describe the expression on a face by saying where the eyes, nose, and mouth are. I've heard students say, "I'm very good with plot, but I can't do a thing with character," or, "I have this theme but I don't have a plot for it," and once I heard one say, "I've got the story but I don't have any technique."

Technique is a word they all trot out. I talked to a writers' club once, and during the question time, one good soul said, "Will you give me the technique for the frame-within-a-frame short story?" I had to admit I was so ignorant I didn't even know what that was, but she assured me there was such a thing because she had entered a contest to write one and the prize was fifty dollars.

But setting aside the people who have no talent for it, there are others who do have the talent but who flounder around because they don't really know what a story is.

I suppose that obvious things are the hardest to define. Everybody thinks he knows what a story is. But if you ask a beginning student to write a story, you're liable to get almost anything—a reminiscence, an episode, an opinion, an anecdote, anything under the sun but a story. A story is a complete dramatic action—and in good stories, the characters are shown through the action and the action is controlled through the characters, and the result of this is meaning that derives from the whole presented experience. I myself prefer to say that a story is a dramatic event that involves a person because he is a person, and a particular person—that is, because he shares in the general human condition and in some specific human situation. A story always involves, in a dramatic way, the mystery of personality. I lent some stories to a country lady who lives down the road from me, and when she returned them, she said, "Well, them stories just gone and shown you how some folks *would* do," and I thought to myself that that was right; when you write stories, you have to be content to start exactly there—showing how some specific folks *will* do, *will* do in spite of everything.

Now this is a very humble level to have to begin on, and most people who think they want to write stories are not willing to start there. They want to write about problems, not people; or about abstract issues, not concrete situations. They have an idea, or a feeling, or an overflowing ego, or they want to Be A Writer, or they want to give their wisdom to the world in a simple-enough way for the world to be able to absorb it. In any case, they don't have a story and they wouldn't be willing to write it if they did; and in the absence of a story, they set out to find a theory or a formula or a technique.

Now none of this is to say that when you write a story, you are supposed to forget or give up any moral position that you hold. Your beliefs will be the light by which you see, but they will not be what you see and they will not be a substitute for seeing. For the writer of fiction, everything has its testing point in the eye, and the eye is an organ that eventually involves the whole personality, and as much of the world as can be got into it. It involves judgment. Judgment is something that begins in the act of vision, and when it does not, or when it becomes separated from vision, then a confusion exists in the mind which transfers itself to the story.

Fiction operates through the senses, and I think one reason that people find it so difficult to write stories is that they forget how much time and patience is required to convince through the senses. No reader who doesn't actually experience, who isn't made to feel, the story is going to believe anything the fiction writer merely tells him. The first and most obvious characteristic of fiction is that it deals with reality through what can be seen, heard, smelt, tasted, and touched.

Now this is something that can't be learned only in the head; it has to be learned in the habits. It has to become a way that you habitually look at things. The fiction writer has to realize that he can't create compassion with compassion, or emotion with emotion, or thought with thought. He has to provide all these things with a body; he has to create a world with weight and extension.

I have found that the stories of beginning writers usually bristle with emotion, but *whose* emotion is often very hard to determine. Dialogue frequently proceeds without the assistance of any characters that you can actually see, and uncontained thought leaks out of every corner of the story. The reason is usually that the student is wholly interested in his thoughts and his emotions and not in his dramatic action, and that he is too lazy or highfalutin to descend to the concrete where fiction operates. He thinks that judgment exists in one place and sense-impression in another. But for the fiction writer, judgment begins in the details he sees and how he sees them.

Fiction writers who are not concerned with these concrete details are guilty of what Henry James called "weak specification." The eye will glide over their words while the attention goes to sleep. Ford Madox Ford taught that you couldn't have a man appear long enough to sell a newspaper in a story unless you put him there with enough detail to make the reader see him.

I have a friend who is taking acting classes in New York from a Russian lady who is supposed to be very good at teaching actors. My friend wrote me that the first month they didn't speak a line, they only learned to see. Now learning to see is the basis for learning all the arts except music. I know a good many fiction writers who paint, not because they're any good at painting, but because it helps their writing. It forces them to look at things. Fiction writing is very seldom a matter of saying things; it is a matter of showing things.

However, to say that fiction proceeds by the use of detail does not mean the simple, mechanical piling-up of detail. Detail has to be controlled by some overall purpose, and every detail has to be put to work for you. Art is selective. What is there is essential and creates movement.

Now all this requires time. A good short story should not have less meaning than a novel, nor should its action be less complete. Nothing essential to the main experience can be left out of a short story. All the action has to be satisfactorily accounted for in terms of motivation, and there has to be a beginning, a middle, and an end, though not necessarily in that order. I think many people decide that they want to write short stories because they're short, and by short, they mean short in every way. They think that a short story is an incomplete action in which a very little is shown and a great deal suggested, and they think you suggest something by leaving it out. It's very hard to disabuse a student of this notion, because he thinks that when he leaves something out, he's being subtle; and when you tell him that he has to put something in before anything can be there, he thinks you're an insensitive idiot.

Perhaps the central question to be considered in any discussion of the short story is what do we mean by short. Being short does not mean being slight. A short story should be long in depth and should give us an experience of meaning. I have an aunt who thinks that nothing happens in a story unless somebody gets married or shot at the end of it. I wrote a story about a tramp who marries an old woman's idiot daughter in order to acquire the old woman's automobile. After the marriage, he takes the daughter off on a wedding trip in the automobile and abandons her in an eating place and drives on by himself. Now that is a complete story. There is nothing more relating to the mystery of that man's personality that could be shown through that particular dramatization. But I've never been able to convince my aunt that it's a complete story. She wants to know what happened to the idiot daughter after that.

Not long ago that story was adapted for a television play, and the adapter, knowing his business, had the tramp have a change of heart and go back and pick up the idiot daughter and the two of them ride away, grinning madly. My aunt believes that the story is complete at last, but I have other sentiments about it—which are not suitable for public utterance. When you write a story, you only have to write one story, but there will always be people who will refuse to read the story you have written.

And this naturally brings up the awful question of what kind of a reader you are writing for when you write fiction. Perhaps we each think we have a personal solution for this problem. For my own part, I have a very high opinion of the art of fiction and a very low opinion of what is called the "average" reader. I tell myself that I can't escape him, that this is the personality I am supposed to keep awake, but that at the same time, I am also supposed to provide the intelligent reader with the deeper experience that he looks for in fiction. Now actually, both of these readers are just aspects of the writer's own personality, and in the last analysis, the only reader he can know anything about is himself. We all write at our own level of understanding, but it is the peculiar characteristic of fiction that its literal surface can be made to yield entertainment on an obvious physical plane to one sort of reader while the selfsame surface can be made to yield meaning to the person equipped to experience it there.

Meaning is what keeps the short story from being short. I prefer to talk about the meaning in a story rather than the theme of a story. People talk about the theme of a story as if the theme were like the string that a sack of chicken feed is tied with. They think that if you can pick out the theme, the way you pick the right thread in the chicken-feed sack, you can rip the story open and feed the chickens. But this is not the way meaning works in fiction.

When you can state the theme of a story, when you can separate it from the story itself, then you can be sure the story is not a very good one. The meaning of a story has to be embodied in it, has to be made concrete in it. A story is a way to say something that can't be said any other way, and it takes every word in the story to say what the meaning is. You tell a story because a statement would be inadequate. When anybody asks what a story is about, the only proper thing is to tell him to read the story. The meaning of fiction is not abstract meaning but experienced meaning, and the purpose of making statements about the meaning of a story is only to help you to experience that meaning more fully.

Fiction is an art that calls for the strictest attention to the real—whether the writer is writing a naturalistic story or a fantasy. I mean that we always begin with what is or with what has an eminent possibility of truth about it. Even when one writes a fantasy, reality is the proper basis of it. A thing is fantastic because it is so real, so real that it is fantastic. Graham Greene has said that he can't write, "I stood over a bottomless pit," because that couldn't be true, or "Running down the stairs I jumped into a taxi," because that couldn't be true either. But Elizabeth Bowen can write about one of her characters that "she snatched at her hair as if she heard something in it," because that is eminently possible.

I would even go so far as to say that the person writing a fantasy has to be even more strictly attentive to the concrete detail than someone writing in a naturalistic vein—because the greater the story's strain on the credulity, the more convincing the properties in it have to be.

A good example of this is a story called "The Metamorphosis" by Franz Kafka. This is a story about a man who wakes up one morning to find that he has turned into a cockroach overnight, while not discarding his human nature. The rest of the story concerns his life and feelings and eventual death as an insect with human nature, and this situation is accepted by the reader because the concrete detail of the story is absolutely convincing. The fact is that this story describes the dual nature of man in such a realistic fashion that it is almost unbearable. The truth is not distorted here, but rather, a certain distortion is used to get at the truth. If we admit, as we must, that appearance is not the same thing as reality, then we must give the artist the liberty to make certain rearrangements of nature if these will lead to greater depths of vision. The artist himself always has to remember that what he is rearranging *is* nature, and that he has to know it and be able to describe it accurately in order to have the authority to rearrange it at all.

The peculiar problem of the short-story writer is how to make the action he describes reveal as much of the mystery of existence as possible. He has only a short space to do it in and he can't do it by statement. He has to do it by showing, not by saying, and by showing the concrete—so that his problem is really how to make the concrete work double time for him.

In good fiction, certain of the details will tend to accumulate meaning from the action of the story itself, and when this happens they become symbolic in the way they work. I once wrote a story called "Good Country People," in which a lady Ph.D. has her wooden leg stolen by a Bible salesman whom she has tried to seduce. Now I'll admit that, paraphrased this way, the situation is simply a low joke. The average reader is pleased to observe anybody's wooden leg being stolen. But without ceasing to appeal to him and without making any statements of high intention, this story does manage to operate at another level of experience, by letting the wooden leg accumulate meaning. Early in the story, we're presented with the fact that the Ph.D. is spiritually as well as physically crippled. She believes in nothing but her own belief in nothing, and we perceive that there is a wooden part of her soul that corresponds to her wooden leg. Now of course this is never stated. The fiction writer states as little as possible. The reader makes this connection from things he is shown. He may not even know that he makes the connection, but the connection is there nevertheless and it has its effect on him. As the story goes on, the wooden leg continues to accumulate meaning. The reader learns how the girl feels about her leg, how her mother feels about it, and how the country woman on the place feels about it; and finally, by the time the Bible salesman comes along, the leg has accumulated so much meaning that it is, as the saying goes, loaded. And when the Bible salesman steals it, the reader realizes that he has taken away part of the girl's personality and has revealed her deeper affliction to her for the first time.

If you want to say that the wooden leg is a symbol, you can say that. But it is a wooden leg first, and as a wooden leg it is absolutely necessary to the story. It has its place on the literal level of the story, but it operates in depth as well as on the surface. It increases the story in every direction, and this is essentially the way a story escapes being short.

Now a little might be said about the way in which this happens. I wouldn't want you to think that in that story I sat down and said, "I am now going to write a story about a Ph.D. with a wooden leg, using the wooden leg as a symbol for another kind of affliction." I doubt myself if many writers know what they are going to do when they start out. When I started writing that story, I didn't know there was going to be a Ph.D. with a wooden leg in it. I merely found myself one morning writing a description of two women that I knew something about, and before I realized it, I had equipped one of them with a daughter with a wooden leg. As the story progressed, I brought in the Bible salesman, but I had no idea what I was going to do with him. I didn't know he was going to steal that wooden leg until ten or twelve lines before he did it, but when I found out that this was what was going to happen, I realized that it was inevitable. This is a story that produces a shock for the reader, and I think one reason for this is that it produced a shock for the writer.

Now despite the fact that this story came about in this seemingly mindless fashion, it is a story that almost no rewriting was done on. It is a story that was under control throughout the writing of it, and it might be asked how this kind of control comes about, since it is not entirely conscious.

I think the answer to this is what Maritain calls "the habit of art." It is a fact that fiction writing is something in which the whole personality takes part—the conscious as well as the unconscious mind. Art is the habit of the artist; and habits have to be rooted deep in the whole personality. They have to be cultivated like any other habit, over a long period of time, by experience; and teaching any kind of writing is largely a matter of helping the student develop the habit of art. I think this is more than just a discipline, although it is that; I think it is a way of looking at the created world and of using the senses so as to make them find as much meaning as possible in things.

Now I am not so naïve as to suppose that most people come to writers' conferences in order to hear what kind of vision is necessary to write stories that will become a permanent part of our literature. Even if you do wish to hear this, your greatest concerns are immediately practical. You want to know how you can actually write a good story, and further, how you can tell when you've done it; and so you want to know what the form of a short story is, as if the form were something that existed outside of each story and could be applied or imposed on the material. Of course, the more you write, the more you will realize that the form is organic, that it is something that grows out of the material, that the form of each story is unique. A story that is any good can't be reduced, it can only be expanded. A story is good when you continue to see more and more in it, and when it continues to escape you. In fiction two and two is always more than four.

The only way, I think, to learn to write short stories is to write them, and then to try to discover what you have done. The time to think of technique is when you've actually got the story in front of you. The teacher can help the student by looking at his individual work and trying to help him decide if he has written a complete story, one in which the action fully illuminates the meaning.

Perhaps the most profitable thing I can do is to tell you about some of the general observations I made about these seven stories I read of yours. All of these observations will not fit any one of the stories exactly, but they are points nevertheless that it won't hurt anyone interested in writing to think about.

The first thing that any professional writer is conscious of in reading anything is, naturally, the use of language. Now the use of language in these stories was such that, with one exception, it would be difficult to distinguish one story from another. While I can recall running into several clichés, I can't remember one image or one metaphor from the seven stories. I don't mean there weren't images in them; I just mean that there weren't any that were effective enough to take away with you.

In connection with this, I made another observation that startled me considerably. With the exception of one story, there was practically no use made of the local idiom. Now this is a Southern Writers' Conference. All the addresses on these stories were from Georgia or Tennessee, yet there was no distinctive sense of Southern life in them. A few place-names were dropped, Savannah or Atlanta or Jacksonville, but these could just as easily have been changed to Pittsburgh or Passaic without calling for any other alteration in the story. The characters spoke as if they had never heard any kind of language except what came out of a television set. This indicates that something is way out of focus.

There are two qualities that make fiction. One is the sense of mystery and the other is the sense of manners. You get the manners from the texture of existence that surrounds you. The great advantage of being a Southern writer is that we don't have to go anywhere to look for manners; bad or good, we've got them in abundance. We in the South live in a society that is rich in contradiction, rich in irony, rich in contrast, and particularly rich in its speech. And yet here are six stories by Southerners in which almost no use is made of the gifts of the region.

Of course the reason for this may be that you have seen these gifts abused so often that you have become self-conscious about using them. There is nothing worse than the writer who doesn't *use* the gifts of the region, but wallows in them. Everything becomes so Southern that it's sickening, so local that it is unintelligible, so literally reproduced that it conveys nothing. The general gets lost in the particular instead of being shown through it.

However, when the life that actually surrounds us is totally ignored, when our patterns of speech are absolutely overlooked, then something is out of kilter. The writer should then ask himself if he is not reaching out for a kind of life that is artificial to him.

An idiom characterizes a society, and when you ignore the idiom, you are very likely ignoring the whole social fabric that could make a meaningful character. You can't cut characters off from their society and say much about them as individuals. You can't say anything meaningful about the mystery of a personality unless you put that personality in a believable and significant social context. And the best way to do this is through the character's own language. When the old lady in one of Andrew Lytle's stories says contemptuously that she has a mule that is older than Birmingham, we get in that one sentence a sense of a society and its history. A great deal of the Southern writer's work is done for him before he begins, because our history lives in our talk. In one of Eudora Welty's stories a character says, "Where I come from, we use fox for yard dogs and owls for chickens, but we sing true." Now there is a whole book in that one sentence; and when the people of your section can talk like that, and you ignore it, you're just not taking advantage of what's yours. The sound of our talk is too definite to be discarded with impunity, and if the writer tries to get rid of it, he is liable to destroy the better part of his creative power.

Another thing I observed about these stories is that most of them don't go very far inside a character, don't reveal very much of the character. I don't mean that they don't enter the character's mind, but they simply don't show that he has a personality. Again this goes back partly to speech. These characters have no distinctive speech to reveal themselves with; and sometimes they have no really distinctive features. You feel in the end that no personality is revealed because no personality is there. In most good stories it is the character's personality that creates the action of the story. In most of these stories, I feel that the writer has thought of some action and then scrounged up a character to perform it. You will usually be more successful if you start the other way around. If you start with a real personality, a real character, then something is bound to happen; and you don't have to know what before you begin. In fact it may be better if you don't know what before you begin. You ought to be able to discover something from your stories. If you don't, probably nobody else will.

# Joyce Carol Oates

## Beginnings: The Origins and Art of the Short Story　　　1998

> Not that the story need be long, but it will take a long while to make it short.
>
> —HENRY DAVID THOREAU

Formal definitions of the short story are commonplace, yet there is none quite democratic enough to accommodate an art that includes so much variety and an art that so readily lends itself to experimentation and idiosyncratic voices. Perhaps length alone should be the sole criterion? Whenever critics try to impose other, more subjective strictures on the genre (as on any genre) too much work is excluded.

Yet length itself is problematic. No more than 10,000 words? Why not then 10,500? 11,000? Where, in fact, does a short story end and a novella begin? (Tolstoy's "The Death of Ivan Ilych" can be classified as both.) And there is the reverse problem, for, as short stories condense, they are equally difficult to define. What is the short-short story, precisely? What is that most teasing of prose works, the prose-poem? We can be guided by critical intuition in distinguishing between a newspaper article or an anecdote and a fully realized story, but intuition is notoriously difficult to define (or depend upon). Since the cultivation of the aesthetically subtle, minimally resolved short story by such masters as Chekhov, Lawrence, Joyce, and Hemingway, the definition of the "fully realized" story has become problematic as well.

My personal definition of the form is that it represents a concentration of imagination, and not an expansion; it *is* no more than 10,000 words; and, no matter its mysteries or experimental properties, it achieves closure—meaning that, when it ends, the attentive reader understands why.

That is to say, the short story is a prose piece that is not a mere concatenation of events, as in a news account or an anecdote, but an intensification of meaning by way of events. Its "plot" may be wholly interior, seemingly static, a matter of the progression of a character's thought. Its resolution need not be a formally articulated statement, as in many of Hawthorne's more didactic tales or in William Austin's once-famous cautionary tale, "Peter Rugg, the Missing Man," but it signals a tangible change of some sort, a distinct shift in consciousness; a deepening of insight. In the most elliptical of stories, a characteristic of the modern and contemporary story, the actual resolution frequently occurs in the reader's, and not the fictional characters', consciousness. To read stories as disparate as Katherine Anne Porter's "He," Paul Bowles's "A Distant Episode," Ray Bradbury's "There Will Come Soft Rains," Raymond Carver's "Are These Actual Miles?," and Tobias Wolff's "Hunters in the Snow" is to read stories so structured as to provide the reader, and not the characters themselves, with insight. Because the meaning of the story does not lie on its surface, visible and self-defining, does not mean that meaning does not exist. Indeed, the ambiguity of meaning, its inner, private quality, may well be part of the writer's vision.

In addition to these qualities, most short stories (but hardly all) are restricted in time and place; concentrate upon a very small number of characters; and move toward a single ascending dramatic scene or revelation. And all are generated by conflict.

The artist *is* the focal point of conflict. Lovers of pristine harmony, those who dislike being upset, shocked, made to think and to feel, are not naturally suited to appreciate art, at least not serious art; which, unlike television dramas and situation comedies, for instance, does not evoke conflict merely to solve it within a brief space of time. Rather, conflict is the implicit subject, itself; as conflict, the establishment of disequilibrium, is the impetus for the evolution of life, so is conflict the genesis, the prime mover, the secret heart of all art.

Discord, then, and not harmony, is the subject our writers share in common, although the quelling of discord and the reestablishment of harmony may well be the point of the art.

The "literary" short story, the meticulously constructed short story, descends to us by way of the phenomenon of magazine publication, beginning in the nineteenth century, but has as its ancestor the oral tale.

We must assume that storytelling is as old as mankind, at least as old as spoken language. Reality is not enough for us—we crave the imagination's embellishments upon it. *In the beginning. Once upon a time. A long time ago there lived a princess who.* How the pulse quickens, hearing such beginnings: such promises of something new, strange, unexpected! The epic poem, the ballad, the parable, the beast-fable, sacred narratives, visionary prophecies—the fabulous mythopoetic "histories" of ancient cultures—the "divinely inspired" books of the Old and New Testament: all are forms of storytelling, expressions of the human imagination.

Like a river fed by countless small streams, the modern short story derives from a multiplicity of sources. Historically, the earliest literary documents of which we have knowledge are Egyptian papyri dating from 4000–3000 B.C., containing a work called, most intriguingly, *Tales of the Magicians.* The Middle Ages revered such secular works as fabliaux, ballads, and verse romances; the Arabian *Thousand and One Nights* and the Latin tales and anecdotes of the *Gesta Romanorum,* collected before the end of the thirteenth century, as well as the one hundred tales of Boccaccio's *The Decameron* and Chaucer's *Canterbury Tales,* were enormously popular for centuries. Storytelling as an oral art, like the folk ballad, was, or is, characteristic of nonliterate cultures, for obvious reasons. Even the prolongation of light (by artificial means) had an effect upon the storytelling tradition of our ancestors. The rise in literacy marked the ebbing of interest in old fairy tales and ballads, as did the gradual stabilization of languages and the cessation of local dialects in which the tales and ballads had been told most effectively. (The Brothers Grimm noted this phenomenon: if, in High German, a fairy tale gained in superficial clarity, it "lost in flavor, and no longer had such a firm hold of the kernel of meaning.")

One of the signal accomplishments of American literature, most famously exemplified by the great commercial and critical success of Samuel Clemens, is the reclamation of that "lost" flavor—the use, as style, of dialect, regional, and strongly (often comically) vernacular language. Of course, before Samuel Clemens cultivated the ingenuous-ironic persona of "Mark Twain," there were dialect writers and tale-tellers in America (for instance, Joel Chandler Harris, creator of the popular "Uncle Remus" stories); but Mark Twain was a phenomenon of a kind previously unknown here— our first American writer to be avidly read, coast to coast, by all classes of Americans, from the most highborn to the least cultured and minimally literate. The development of mass-market newspapers and subscription book sales made this success possible, but it was the brilliant reclamation of the vernacular in Twain's work (the early "The Celebrated Jumping Frog of Calaveras County," for instance) that made him into so uniquely *American* a writer, our counterpart to Dickens.

Twain's rapid ascent was by way of popular newspapers, which syndicated features coast to coast, and his crowd-pleasing public performances, but the more typical outlet for a short story writer, particularly of self-consciously "literary" work, was the magazine. Writers from Washington Irving and Nathaniel Hawthorne onward began their careers by publishing short fiction in magazines before moving on to book publication; in the nineteenth century, such highly regarded, and, in some cases, high-paying magazines as *The North American Review, Harper's Monthly, Atlantic Monthly, Scribner's Monthly* (later *The Century*), *The Dial,* and *Graham's Magazine* (briefly edited by Edgar Allan Poe) advanced the careers of writers who would otherwise have had financial difficulties in establishing themselves. In post–World War II America, the majority of short story writers publish in small-circulation "literary" magazines throughout their careers. It is all but unknown for a writer to publish a book of short stories without having published most of them in magazines beforehand.

Edgar Allan Poe's famous review-essay of Hawthorne's *Twice-Told Tales* (*Graham's Magazine,* 1842) is justly celebrated as one of the crucial documents in the establishment of the short story as a distinct literary genre. Poe's aesthetic is a curious admixture of the romantic and the classic: the intention of the artwork is to move the reader's soul deeply, but the means to this intention is coolly, if not chillingly, cerebral. Poe in his philosophy as in his practice is both visionary and manipulator:

> A skillful literary artist has constructed his tale. If wise, he has not fashioned his thoughts to accommodate his incidents; but having conceived, with deliberate care, a certain unique or single *effect* to be wrought out, he then invents such incidents—he then combines such events as may best aid him in establishing this preconceived effect.

Magazine publication is the ideal outlet for Poe's hypothesized tale, where works "requiring from a half-hour to one or two hours in [their] perusal" appeared. Indeed, the emphasis in Poe's review-essay is on the reader's experience of the work, and not upon the work itself, as if—can this be genius speaking? in the very language of the hack?—it scarcely matters *what* has been written, only *that* it has been written with a certain preconceived effect. (It should be noted too, and not incidentally, that Poe was a man of vast literary ambitions, and not simply, or not exclusively, a tormented Romantic driven to the composition of uncanny poetry and prose: he wrote for magazines, and he edited magazines, and it was his professional obsession from 1836 to his death in 1849 to found and edit a magazine, to be called *Penn Magazine.*)

As the literary short story derives from the oral tale, so, in Poe's aesthetic, the meticulously constructed short story relates to the poem. While the highest genius, arguably, is best employed in poetry ("not to exceed in length what might be perused in an hour"), the "loftiest talent" may turn to the prose tale, as exemplified by Nathaniel Hawthorne. Poe elevates the prose tale above much of poetry, in fact, and above the novel, for poetry brings the reader to too high a pitch of excitement to be sustained, and the novel is objectionable because of its "undue" length. By contrast, the brief tale enables the writer "to carry out the fullness of his intention. . . . During the hour of perusal the soul of the reader is at the writer's control. There are no external or extrinsic influences—resulting from weariness or interruption."

In Poe's somewhat Aristotelian terms, the secret of the short story's composition is its unity. Yet, within this, as within a well-made play, a multiplicity of modes or inflections of thought and expression—"the ratiocinative, for example, the sarcastic, or the humourous"—are available to the writer, as they are not available, apparently, to the poet. This concept, dogmatic even for its time, relates only incidentally to the stories Poe himself wrote, but it provides an aesthetic anticipating the work of such masters of the genre as Chekhov, Joyce, Henry James, and Hemingway, in which everything is excluded that does not contribute to the general effect, or design, of the story. (Like most critics who are also artists, Poe was formulating an aesthetic to accommodate his own practice and his own limitations. Temperamentally, Poe was probably incapable of the sustained effort of the novelist; this helps to explain his envious disparagement of Charles Dickens, who, for all his apparent flaws in Poe's judgment, enjoyed the enormous popular success denied to Poe during his own lifetime.)

The American short story, however, has had no more thoughtful, visionary, and influential an early critic than Poe; just as the history of the short story itself in America is bound up with the unique work Poe published in 1840, *Tales of the Grotesque and Arabesque.*

A predominant vein connecting many American short stories, from Washington Irving and William Austin through to our contemporaries, is the quest, in some cases a distinctly *American* quest, for one's place in the world—one's cultural and spiritual identity, in terms of self and others.

For ours is the nation, so rare in human history, of self-determination—a theoretical experiment in newness, exploration, discovery. In theory, at least, who our ancestors have been, what languages they have spoken, in what religions they believed—these factors cannot really help to define *us*. And it has been often noted that, in the New World, history itself has moved with extraordinary rapidity. Each generation constitutes a beginning-again, a new discovery, sometimes of language itself.

In our contemporaries, the burden of history and politics as *personal* fate, weighing, at times, almost physically upon the shoulders of survivors and descendants, is dramatized in stories encompassing a wide range of subject matter, style, and vision—from Flannery O'Connor's mordant "A Late Encounter with the Enemy" (an aged Civil War veteran's hallucinatory descent into death, and into his identity) to Bernard Malamud's "My Son the Murderer" (generational conflict in the radicalized, despairing 1960s), Louise Erdrich's "Fleur" (a Native American "witch" resists the fate that would make her a victim), and Bharati Mukherjee's "The Management of Grief" (the surviving member of a Hindu family killed in a terrorist bombing detaches herself, through pain, from the paralysis of grief). The elliptical, poetic tales of Sandra Cisneros and the seemingly forthright, conversational "Two Kinds" by Amy Tan take for granted a dominant Caucasian world outside the family—here, such abstractions as history and politics are realized in the experience of sensitive, yet representative, adolescent girls.

Meticulous chroniclers of lives less dramatically touched by history, though yet distinctly, often disturbingly American, are such writers as John Cheever, John Updike, Alice Adams, Ursula LeGuin, and Raymond Carver, among others, who have taken for their subjects the lives (and what radically differing lives, told in what radically differing voices) of what might be called mainstream Americans of the Caucasian middle class. What these writers share is their artistry, their commitment to the short story, and their faith in the imaginative reconstruction of reality that constitutes literature.

As Tolstoy said, talent is the capacity to direct concentrated attention upon the subject: "the gift of seeing what others have not seen."

# Discussing

## *Writers Talk about Their Work*

When readers asked her about the theme of one of her short stories, Flannery O'Connor had a brief reply: "A story is a way to say something that can't be said in any other way, and it takes every word in the story to say what the meaning is. You tell a story because a statement would be inadequate. When anybody asks what a story is about, the only proper thing is to tell him to read the story" (from "The Nature and Aim of Fiction").

Stories entertain, teach, and provoke interest and curiosity because they produce multiple and interconnected interpretations, and authors generally do not simplify their ideas by endorsing a single reading. Nevertheless, talking with authors provides a great deal of insight into the background and interests that shape a story's characters and themes and, importantly, helps us to understand how authors work and imagine their narratives. Reading a group of interviews with various writers showcases the diversity of approaches to short fiction. Each interview provides a different angle of insight, from Hemingway's discussion of the autobiographical event that sparked "Hills like White Elephants," to Richard Ford's comments on how writing a short story differs from writing a novel, to Luisa Valenzuela's remarks on how Argentina's history shapes her themes and characters.

As Hemingway says, "The fun of talk is to explore." These interviews will help you to explore the stories in this anthology and to create your own questions about stories and their authors.

# Isabel Allende:
# Interviewed by Farhat Iftekharuddin

Isabel Allende, a Chilean, was born in Lima, Peru, in 1942. Her career covers a wide range of experiences including journalism and teaching. She has taught at the University of Virginia, Charlottesville, Montclair College, New Jersey, and as late as 1989, she taught creative writing at the University of California, Berkeley. She is the author of the international bestsellers *The House of the Spirits* (1981), *The Infinite Plan* (1991), *Of Love and Shadows* (1984), *Eva Luna* (1987), and *The Stories of Eva Luna* (1990). Her latest book is *Paula* (1994), a memoir of her heartbreaking experience watching her daughter die a prolonged death. Her novels *The House of the Spirits* and *Of Love and Shadows* have been adapted into motion pictures. Her works have been translated into more than 27 languages and have been bestsellers in Latin America, Australia, and the USA. She has won numerous literary awards including Books to Remember Award, American Library Association (1996), Critics' Choice Award (1996), Author the Year, Germany (1994), Book of the Year, Germany (1994), and Panorama Literario Award, Chile (1983). She currently resides with her husband in California.

---

**Iftekharuddin:** Critics have drawn comparisons between your works and other Latin American writers. They readily compare Gabriel García Márquez's *One Hundred Years of Solitude* with your novel *The House of the Spirits*. Some feel that it is a remake of Márquez's novel replacing patriarchal authority with emphasis on matrilineal strength. How do you respond?

**Allende:** I belong to the first generation of writers of my continent who have been brought up reading other writers from Latin America. The previous generation, which we have called the "boom" generation, included such writers as García Márquez, José Donoso, and Carlos Fuentes. The phenomenon of the "boom" started in Barcelona. I was very privileged to be a part of the readers of the writers of that time. I grew up reading them, and when I started writing, I think that all those wonderful words, those images, that tone to narrate our continent was so deeply rooted in me that it just came right out in a very natural way. It was not my intention at all to create anything ironic about *One Hundred Years of Solitude* because I really admire that novel very much. I have read it a long time ago, and I don't remember it very well. But comparing *The House of the Spirits* with *One Hundred Years of Solitude* in the way that it is compared is totally unfair.

**Iftekharuddin:** What were the compelling reasons for writing *The Stories of Eva Luna* after the novel *Eva Luna?*

**Allende:** Well, several reasons. The first one was that many people questioned, when I finished the book, that Eva Luna is a storyteller, this is her story, but where are the stories she tells? I had never considered the short story genre because I think it is very difficult. At the time, after I finished *Eva Luna,* I divorced my husband in Venezuela and went on a crazy lecturing tour that brought me to the United States. I ended up in northern California where I met a man and fell madly in love, so that's the reason too. I had to move to this country following a passionate heart; it was a very hectic time. The only advantage of short stories is that you work in fragments. I thought that since I had to go on working, the only thing I could do then was something brief. So, I thought that writing short stories that Eva Luna didn't tell in the book was a good idea.

**Iftekharuddin:** Almost every story in *The Stories of Eva Luna* has an epiphanic ending. Is this sudden awareness simply an awakening on the part of the character, or is there an imbedded socio-political message?

**Allende:** I don't try to give a message in anything I write. Sometimes there is a sort of surprise for me too because the characters come out with these endings; they come out with these things that happen to them in spite of myself. In some stories, I seem to know from the very beginning what the ending will be, but I know it at a gut level;

I don't know it intellectually. If I would have to tell you the story before writing, I wouldn't know, but when I start writing, everything seems to flow in a very natural way and ends up in a surprise for me, except in one of the stories. It's called "The Little Heidelberg." When I finished that story, my mother read it and said "I like the story, but this is a crappy ending." I thought she is right; there is something wrong with this ending. She couldn't tell me what was wrong, but I realized that I had not followed the instincts of the characters; I had tried to impose a happy ending, and it didn't work. So I just let the characters talk for themselves, and I got a very strange ending that is difficult to explain, but that's what they wanted.

**Iftekharuddin:** Was that the only story where you felt that you were being an intrusive author?

**Allende:** Yes, except for one other. The last story in this collection, which is the most elaborate story in the book, is called "And of Clay Are We Created"; and it is based on a real story. In 1985, there was a volcano eruption in Colombia and a little girl was trapped in the mud, and she died there after four days of terrible agony. I saw her on television in Venezuela, and I wrote this story. When I finished the story, I realized that I had tried to tell the story from an intellectual point of view, very passionate but it was my mind working. And then I realized that it wasn't the story of the little girl; it was the story of the man who was holding the little girl. So I rewrote the story once more, and when it was finished, I realized that there was something phony about it too. It wasn't the story of the man who was holding the girl; it was the story of the woman who is watching through a screen the man who holds the girl. This filter of the screen creates an artificial distance but also a terrible proximity because you see details that you would not see if you were actually there. And so, the story is about the change in the woman who watches the man holding the girl who is dying.

**Iftekharuddin:** Do you feel that aspiring short story authors should attempt to create that kind of a screen in order not only to distance themselves but also give themselves the ability to be introspective without being intrusive?

**Allende:** I think each author has a different approach. You cannot give a formula or a recipe because it won't work. What works for one story may not work for the other story. I think that in a short story the most important thing is to get the tone right in the first six lines. The tone determines the characters. In long fiction, it's plot, it's character, it's work, it's discipline—a lot of stuff that goes there. But in short stories, it's tone, language, suggestions—it's inspiration. So I don't have a recipe. That's why I don't like to write short stories; I hate them. I like to read them, but I don't like to write them. I would much rather write a thousand pages of a long novel than a short story. The shorter, the more difficult it is.

**Iftekharuddin:** Why don't you elaborate on what it is exactly that you find difficult about writing short stories?

**Allende:** The fact is that everything shows. In a novel, you can have a lot of knots and bad stitches, and if you are lucky, the charm of the tale will carry the book, and the reader will be trapped in the plot and in everything that happens there; it's like a party, an orgy. A short story is not; a short story has very brief time, very condensed concentrated plot, if there is a plot. The subtleties are important; the suggestion is important. You work with the reader's imagination, and your only tool is language, and there is no space or time for anything else. Everything shows. This is how I compare these genres: the novel being a very elaborate tapestry that has a lot of details, and you embroider it with threads of many colors without even knowing what the finished design is. A short story is like an arrow; you have only one shot, and you need the precision, the direction, the speed, the firm wrist of the archer to get it right. So, you do it right from the very beginning or just abandon it. Get it right the first time. How does one do it? I think that's where inspiration comes in, the muse. That's why I feel so uncomfortable with short story writing because I am not an inspired person; I am a hard working person. I don't mind spending twelve hours a day for a year writing fiction, but if I need the inspiration and I don't have it, I feel very distressed.

**Iftekharuddin:** Do you feel the impulse that it is time to write another short story?

**Allende:** I have not felt the impulse since 1987. But it may happen again in my life, depending on the circumstances. People are always asking me for short stories for some reason. The publishers don't like short stories. They think that they won't sell. However, the students seem to like them a lot. I get a lot of letters from them, and they always ask me for short stories. And you know what? The movie people want short stories because it is much easier to create a movie from a short story than from a novel.

**Iftekharuddin:** In the short story titled "Interminable Life," you write:

> There are all kinds of stories. Some are born with the telling; their substance is language, and before someone puts them into words they are but a hint of an emotion, a caprice of mind, an image, or an intangible recollection. Others are manifest whole, like an apple, and can be repeated infinitely without risk of altering their meaning. Some are taken from reality and processed through inspiration, while others rise up from an instant of inspiration and become real after being told. And then there are secret stories that remain hidden in the shadows of the mind; they are like living organisms, they grow roots and tentacles, they become covered with excrescences and parasites, and with time are transformed into the matter of nightmares. To exorcise the demons of memory, it is sometimes necessary to tell them as a story.

Is this your definition of short story and also your process of writing short stories?

**Allende:** This is how I feel about fiction writing. I have had a tormented and long life, and many things are hidden in the secret compartments of my heart and my mind. Sometimes, I don't even know that they are there, but I have the pain—I can feel the pain; I can feel this load of stories that I am carrying around. And then one day I write a story, and I realize that I have delivered something, that a demon has come out and has been exorcised. It's not something that I do consciously, except in very few occasions, but when it happens, it's such a relief. That's how I feel about fiction. Some people do this in therapy, some people do it in meditation, some people do it drinking. My way of getting rid of the pain, my way of exorcising and understanding the world is writing fiction. Maybe that paragraph is about that; it's about all the demons and the angels that I have inside that I don't know that I have, and I have to bring them out into the light and talk to them and see them in the light.

**Iftekharuddin:** What are the sources of the experiences that you describe in your stories?

**Allende:** Most of them come from things that have really happened. Newspapers, television, radios, those are the great sources of inspiration for me. For example, that story we were talking about "And of Clay Are We Created" is something that I saw on television. Sometimes, it is something that I see very briefly in the news, and I start asking myself questions about it. In *The Stories of Eva Luna,* there is the story—I don't remember the title ["If You Touched My Heart"]—of a woman who is kidnapped by a man and put in a cellar where she spends fifty years. She never talks to anybody and becomes like an animal in the darkness. When she is finally rescued, she is transformed, sort of, into a horrible beast that has spent all her life in that cellar. I got this from a spot on television (in the news) in Venezuela. A jealous man had kidnapped a young woman and put her in a cellar where she spent fifty years. I saw her on television when they brought her out wrapped in a blanket. That was it; she was never again in the news. So, I started asking myself, why did it happen? Why didn't she scream? Why didn't she try to get out? How did she survive? By asking myself those questions over and over again, the story came out; the motivations of the story were in those questions. Other times, it's people who tell me things, and I look behind whatever they have told me. They tell me something that they think is a story, and I realize that that is not the story. The story is something that lies behind that or beyond that. Often, it's something that I guess. I have one story called "Our Secret." It is a story of two young people who meet, make love, and in the lovemaking they discover that both have been tortured in the same way. The experience of torture has marked them so profoundly that they can't completely make love and cannot relate to the world; they have been destroyed. This came from something that I saw once. I had just met a couple of young people, Chileans, in Venezuela. I saw that both had similar marks on their wrists. At the beginning, I thought that they had tried to commit suicide. Then I realized that they were both from Chile, both were exiles, and both were from the same generation: I started asking myself more and more questions about them. Finally, when I came up with the story, I thought this is just pathological. I am imagining these awful things; this can't be true. Later, I confronted my theory with the reality of their lives, and it was true.

**Iftekharuddin:** How do you then cloak fiction with truth or truth with fiction?

**Allende:** I can't trace the boundary. I think that everything is true, that fiction is just a way of saying something that is truthful from the very beginning. What is fiction? A bunch of lies, but it wouldn't work if those lies didn't come from a very honest truthful place inside you. Why do you want to write that story? Why do you want those characters and no other characters? That plot and no other plot? Because you are tapping into something that is your own experience, your own sentiments, your own emotions, your past, your biography, or a collective soul. And because you tap into that, the story is true and it works. When you don't, you have created this artificial fiction that is reassuring—the romance novels, the thrillers, and the mysteries—which are genres that don't work with truth, but they are also categorized as fiction, entertainment. But we are not talking about that; we are talking about something that is much deeper.

**Iftekharuddin:** Is Agua Santa your mythical town like William Faulkner's Yoknapatawpha or Sherwood Anderson's Winesburg, Ohio?

**Allende:** No, I feel much better with an undetermined place and undetermined time. I like the ambiguity when the story happens in a landscape that the reader can invent. If you think about it, the only thing that you know about Agua Santa is that it's hot. You don't know anything else about it; you don't know where it is; you don't know how it looks or how many people live there because I want that place to be not my mythical place, but the reader's mythical place. And that's the same treatment that I give my characters. Very seldom is there a physical description of a character in my writing because I want the reader to create the character. So I only describe what is absolutely essential for the story. The fact that a person is retarded, or has a harelip, or is very tall is told because, in a way, that is important to the story; otherwise, I wouldn't even say that. I don't even mention the age; you don't know whether they are young or old.

**Iftekharuddin:** How about those characters who are highly sensuous. There is overt sexuality in stories such as "Wicked Girl" or "Toad's Mouth." Are you asserting the notion of female body as text in these stories?

**Allende:** I wouldn't say that my stories are sexual; I wish they were. I really would like to write erotic novels. Unfortunately, I was raised as a Catholic, and my mother is still alive, so it's difficult. However, I feel that there is a part of me as a person that is extremely sensuous and sexual. Through that part of me, I can express certain truths that I cannot express otherwise. When I say sensuous, I don't mean sexual: for me sensuous includes food, texture, and smells. In all my stories and novels you will find smells because that is extremely important to me. A few days ago, I was given a doctorate in Maine, and the person who was putting the hood on me smelled wonderful. I got totally distracted; I couldn't think of the fact that I was receiving this doctorate, only of his smell. I would have followed that man to the end of the world because he smelled a certain way. Smell is very important to me; it's like nature, like sounds.

**Iftekharuddin:** In your stories the real and the hyperbolic blend. That puts you into the field of magic realism. You also have an acute female sensibility that we can detect. Some have observed the parodying of perhaps Pablo Neruda and Marquis de Sade. If you were to characterize yourself, would you call yourself a feminist writer?

**Allende:** Yes. First of all we should agree on the term feminist. Right now it is loaded with negative meanings for a lot of people. Because I am a woman and because I am an intelligent woman, excuse my arrogance, I have to be a feminist. I am aware of my gender; I am aware of the fact that being born a woman is a handicap in most parts of the world. In only very privileged societies, very privileged groups, have women achieved enough freedom and enough awareness to be able to fight for their rights. But in any circumstance, a woman has to exert double the effort of any man to get half the recognition. I want my daughter, my granddaughters, and my great granddaughters to live in a more gentle world. In a world where my son, my grandsons, and my great grandsons will also live in a much better place and where people can be companions and partners, where sex can be something that we will both enjoy greatly, and where love for ourselves, love for each other, and love for this planet will prevail. I think that is what being a feminist means, the awareness and the strength to fight for what you believe.

**Iftekharuddin:** The epigraph to your novel *The House of the Spirits* is a poem by Pablo Neruda where the poet raises the questions, "How long does a man spend dying?" Addie's father in Faulkner's *As I Lay Dying* may have already responded to that when he said that "the reason for living was to get ready to stay dead a long time." How would Alba, Eva Luna, or even you, respond?

**Allende:** I don't know about Alba or Eva Luna, but I know what I would respond. I think that the reason to live is to learn. We come here to experience through the body things that the spirit could not experience otherwise. So we need this body, and we have to transform this body into a temple of learning. It is difficult because our culture does not promote that at all. But I try to use my senses, my imagination, my body, my mind, and all the things that I have in this life to make the spirit grow. That's what we come for. If you think about it, there is silence before we are born and silence after death; life is just a lot of noise.

**Iftekharuddin:** Elvira in *Eva Luna* tells Eva, "Your mother must have had a liquid womb to have given you that inventiveness you have to tell stories, little bird." Is that the secret of writing short stories?

**Allende:** That's one of the many dirty tricks. It's amazing. Sometimes these things just occur to me, and I write them down without ever thinking that anybody will even notice. For example, I write a food recipe. I just make it up and then people call me and say it didn't work. If I provide a beauty recipe saying that if you do this or that, it will make your hair blond, people believe it, but it's not true. It's just part of the tricks, and after all, all wombs are liquid when you are pregnant.

**Iftekharuddin:** Going back to the issue of asserting yourself as feminist, what is it that you don't want readers to view your work as? I hope it's never negative in the sense of not reading a piece of literature simply because it is viewed as feminist—that would destroy the essence of literature.

**Allende:** I don't know. Each reader has a different approach. I want my readers to be entertained. I want to grab them and seduce them into the reading. I want to invite them to this wonderful place where we can share a story, and I only give him or her half the story; the other half has to be recreated or created by the reader, and that is the space we are going to share. Sometimes in the stories there are political elements, social elements, feminist issues, or environmental issues. All the things I believe in come out, but I don't want to deliver messages. I don't have answers; I just have the questions, and I want to share the questions. On the other hand, labels are unavoidable when you have critics. Critics are terrible people. They will label you no matter what, and you have to be classified. I don't want to be called a feminist writer, a political writer, a social writer, a magic realism writer, or a Latin American writer. I am just a writer; I am a storyteller.

**Iftekharuddin:** Scheherazade not only saved her life through her stories, but also received the recognition of the Sultan. In essence, she brings herself into existence with words. Is Eva Luna your protagonist who brings "the female" into existence through words?

**Allende:** Yes. I also think that in a weird way Eva Luna is me or I am Eva Luna. She is a storyteller, and she creates herself; the reader doesn't know if he or she is reading Eva Luna's biography, what Eva Luna invents about herself, or the soap opera that she is writing. So there are three levels of writing and understanding this novel. I believe that in a certain way that's how my life has been. If you ask me to tell you my life, I will try, and it will probably be a bag of lies because I am inventing myself all the time, and at the same time I am inventing fiction, and through this fiction I am revealing myself. So these are the three levels through which my life happens. I can't say who I am because the boundaries, as I said before, between reality and fantasy are totally blurred.

**Iftekharuddin:** Are those the three levels that readers must also keep in mind when they read the collection of stories, *The Stories of Eva Luna?*

**Allende:** Don't keep in mind anything, just enjoy it.

**Iftekharuddin:** I think you are looking at a critic here.

**Allende:** Critic, just enjoy it.

**Iftekharuddin:** What do you think your narratives lose in translation?

**Allende:** My books have been translated into twenty-seven languages that I know of, but I also know of other translations that have not been authorized, for example Vietnamese and Chinese. I have no control over the official translations, let alone the ones that are not authorized. In English, French, and German, the translations I know are very good. Now, every time that I read aloud in English my own stories, I feel very uncomfortable. I think the translation is great; sometimes it sounds much better than in Spanish, but it's another story. I can only be myself in my own language. It's like making love, you know; I would feel ridiculous panting in English. I really need to express it in my own language. When I play with my grandchildren, it's always in Spanish. There is something that is playful and sensuous; it happens at a gut level, a very organic level that can only happen in your own language; it's like dreams.

**Iftekharuddin:** Is there something you cannot write about, a "demon of memory" that you cannot "exorcise?"

**Allende:** I don't know because I have been trying to exorcise them all and in the long run, I may achieve that if I have enough time, if I live long enough. I have a lot of demons. There are certain things that appear over and over in my writing that I can't avoid: they seem to be love and violence—two very strong issues in my life.

**Iftekharuddin:** You have written four novels and a collection of short stories. You have reached fame with these works. Is it time for another collection of short stories, you think?

**Allende:** You know, I have just finished another book that will be published soon. Now it's being translated. It's a sort of memoir. I think it's non-fiction; however, it reads like fiction. After finishing this book, I felt so exhausted, so drained, that I thought, well, I will spend six months without doing anything, and let's see what happens next. And there is a certain voice inside me saying why don't you just spend these six months thinking about short stories? But as I told you before, I really need inspiration and if it doesn't come . . .

**Iftekharuddin:** What's the title of this new work?

**Allende:** It's called *Paula*.

**Iftekharuddin:** What would you tell aspiring short story writers about writing short stories?

**Allende:** Don't. Write a novel; it's much easier—the longer the better. You will get a publisher, you will get an agent, and it will be much easier. It's much easier to write. Short stories are closer to poetry, to dreams than they are to long narratives. And I think that you need a very skilled writer. How many short stories can you remember? How many are memorable: How many have been transcendent? How many short story writers are really important writers only for their stories? It's because it's a very difficult genre, very difficult. So I would tell them, try with a novel first and when you have the skills, then you can write a short story. But people think it's the other way around. People think that if they can write a short story then eventually they will be able to write a novel. It's actually the other way around. If you are able to write a novel, someday with a lot of work and good luck you may be able to write a good short story.

**Iftekharuddin:** You started off your career as a journalist. Has that made writing fiction easier for you, particularly the short story?

**Allende:** Yes, because I still use many of the techniques that I used as a journalist: for example interviewing people. As a writer of fiction, I believe that it is much better to research with interviews of real people who have experienced the event, whatever that event may be, than going to a library and looking at books. Through interviews you can come up with things that you will never find in a book. Journalists are in the streets hand in hand with people talking, participating, and sharing. Writers are very isolated people. They usually live protected under the big umbrella of a university or some institution, and they are disconnected from real life in the world. They end up writing for professors, students, and critics and forget that there is the world out there. So, my background as a journalist helps me in that way. And there is something else that helps enormously. As a journalist, you know, you have a few sentences with which to grab your reader, and you are competing with other media; you are competing with other articles in the same newspaper or whatever media you are using. So you have to be very efficient with language, and you have to remember that the first important thing is to have a reader. Without a reader, there is no text. Writers forget that; writers write for themselves. I am in that sense much more of a journalist. I will not write something that is just for myself except the last book which I recently wrote, a book that I wrote out of extreme pain. I could not have written anything else. When I wrote it, I was not thinking of publishing it. My daughter died recently; she was in a coma for a year, and I took care of her. During that year, everything stopped in my life. I had a year to revise my life, to ask myself the questions that I had been avoiding and go through the most excruciating pain. I think that I am still in that tunnel of pain, but the fact that I finished the book has been like a catharsis in many ways. So, when I started writing *Paula,* my only goal was to survive; that is the only time that I have written something without thinking of a reader.

# Ernest Hemingway: Interviewed by George Plimpton

*Hemingway: You go to the races?*
*Interviewer: Yes, occasionally.*
*Hemingway: Then you read the* Racing Form
*. . . there you have the true Art of* Fiction.

—CONVERSATION IN A MADRID CAFE, MAY, 1954

_____

Ernest Hemingway writes in the bedroom of his home in the Havana suburb of San Francisco de Paula. He has a special workroom prepared for him in a square tower at the south-west corner of the house, but prefers to work in his bedroom, climbing to the tower-room only when "characters" drive him up there.

The bedroom is on the ground floor and connects with the main room of the house. The door between the two is kept ajar by a heavy volume listing and describing *The World's Aircraft Engines.* The bedroom is large, sunny, the windows facing east and south letting in the day's light on white walls and a yellow-tinged tile floor.

The room is divided into two alcoves by a pair of chest-high bookcases that stand out into the room at right angles from opposite walls. A large and low double-bed dominates one section, over-sized slippers and loafers neatly arranged at the foot, the two bedside tables at the head piled seven-high with books. In the other alcove stands a massive flat-top desk with two chairs at either side, its surface an ordered clutter of papers and mementos. Beyond it, at the far end of the room, is an armoire with a leopard skin draped across the top. The other walls are lined with white-painted bookcases from which books overflow to the floor, and are piled on top amongst old newspapers, bullfight journals, and stacks of letters bound together by rubber bands.

It is on the top of one of these cluttered bookcases—the one against the wall by the east window and three feet or so from his bed—that Hemingway has his "work-desk"—a square foot of cramped area hemmed in by books on one side and on the other by a newspaper-covered heap of papers, manuscripts, and pamphlets. There is just enough space left on top of the bookcase for a typewriter, surmounted by a wooden reading-board, five or six pencils, and a chunk of copper ore to weight down papers when the wind blows in from the east window.

A working habit he has had from the beginning, Hemingway stands when he writes. He stands in a pair of his oversized loafers on the worn skin of a Lesser Kudu—the typewriter and the reading-board chest-high opposite him.

When Hemingway starts on a project he always begins with a pencil, using the reading-board to write on onion-skin typewriter paper. He keeps a sheaf of the blank paper on a clipboard to the left of the typewriter, extracting the paper a sheet at a time from under a metal clip which reads "These Must Be Paid." He places the paper slantwise on the reading-board, leans against the board with his left arm, steadying the paper with his hand, and fills the paper with handwriting which in the years has become larger, more boyish, with a paucity of punctuation, very few capitals, and often the period marked with an x. The page completed, he clips it face-down on another clipboard which he places off to the right of the typewriter.

Hemingway shifts to the typewriter, lifting off the reading-board, only when the writing is going fast and well, or when the writing is, for him at least, simple: dialogue, for instance.

He keeps track of his daily progress—"so as not to kid myself"—on a large chart made out of the side of a cardboard packing case and set up against the wall under the nose of a mounted gazelle head. The numbers on the chart showing the daily output of words differ from 450, 575, 462, 1250, to 512, the higher figures on days Hemingway puts in extra work so he won't feel guilty spending the following day fishing on the Gulf Stream.

A man of habit, Hemingway does not use the perfectly suitable desk in the other alcove. Though it allows more space for writing, it too has its miscellany: stacks of letters, a stuffed toy lion of the type sold in Broadway nighteries, a small burlap bag full of carnivore teeth, shotgun shells, a shoe-horn, wood carvings of lion, rhino, two zebras, and a wart-hog—these last set in a neat row across the surface of the desk—and, of course, books. You remember books of the room, piled on the desk, bedside tables, jamming the shelves in indiscriminate order—novels, histories, collections of poetry, drama, essays. A look at their titles shows their variety. On the shelf opposite Hemingway's knees as he stands up to his "work-desk" are Virginia Woolf's *The Common Reader,* Ben Ames Williams' *House Divided, The Partisan Reader,* Charles A. Beard's *The Republic,* Tarle's *Napoleon's Invasion of Russia, How Young You Look* by one Peggy Wood, Alden Brook's *Shakespeare and the Dyer's Hand,* Baldwin's *African Hunting,* T. S. Eliot's *Collected Poems,* and two books on General Custer's fall at the battle of the Little Big Horn.

The room, however, for all the disorder sensed at first sight, indicates on inspection an owner who is basically neat but cannot bear to throw anything away—especially if sentimental value is attached. One bookcase top has an odd assortment of mementos: a giraffe made of wood beads, a little cast-iron turtle, tiny models of a locomotive, two jeeps and a Venetian gondola, a toy bear with a key in its back, a monkey carrying a pair of cymbals, a miniature guitar, and a little tin model of a U.S. Navy biplane (one wheel missing) resting awry on a circular straw placemat—the quality of the collection that of the odds-and-ends which turn up in a shoebox at the back of a small boy's closet. It is evident, though, that these tokens have their value, just as three buffalo horns Hemingway keeps in his bedroom have a value dependent not on size but because during the acquiring of them things went badly in the bush which ultimately turned out well. "It cheers me up to look at them," Hemingway says.

Hemingway may admit superstitions of this sort, but he prefers not to talk about them, feeling that whatever value they may have can be talked away. He has much the same attitude about writing. Many times during the making of this interview he stressed that the craft of writing should not be tampered with by an excess of scrutiny—"that though there is one part of writing that is solid and you do it no harm by talking about it, the other side is fragile, and if you talk about it, the structure cracks and you have nothing."

As a result, though a wonderful raconteur, a man of rich humor, and possessed of an amazing fund of knowledge on subjects which interest him, Hemingway finds it difficult to talk about writing—not because he has few ideas on the subject, but rather that he feels so strongly that such ideas should remain unexpressed, that to be asked questions on them "spooks" him (to use one of his favorite expressions) to the point where he is almost inarticulate. Many of the replies in this interview he preferred to work out on his reading-board. The occasional waspish tone of the answers is also part of this strong feeling that writing is a private, lonely occupation with no need for witnesses until the final work is done.

This dedication to his art may suggest a personality at odds with the rambunctious, carefree, world-wheeling Hemingway-at-play of popular conception. The point is, though, that Hemingway, while obviously enjoying life, brings an equivalent dedication to everything he does—an outlook that is essentially serious, with a horror of the inaccurate, the fraudulent, the deceptive, the half-baked.

Nowhere is the dedication he gives his art more evident than in the yellow-tiled bedroom—where early in the morning Hemingway gets up to stand in absolute concentration in front of his reading-board, moving only to shift weight from one foot to another, perspiring heavily when the work is going well, excited as a boy, fretful, miserable when the artistic touch momentarily vanishes—slave of a self-imposed discipline which lasts until about noon when he takes a knotted walking stick and leaves the house for the swimming pool where he takes his daily half-mile swim.

**Interviewer:** Are these hours during the actual process of writing pleasurable?

**Hemingway:** Very.

**Interviewer:** Could you say something of this process? When do you work? Do you keep to a strict schedule?

**Hemingway:** When I am working on a book or a story I write every morning as soon after first light as possible. There is no one to disturb you and it is cool or cold and you come to your work and warm as you write. You read what you have written and, as you always stop when you know what is going to happen next, you go on from there. You write until you come to a place where you still have your juice and know what will happen next and you stop and try to live through until the next day when you hit it again. You have started at six in the morning, say, and may go on until noon or be through before that. When you stop you are as empty, and at the same time never empty but filling, as when you have made love to someone you love. Nothing can hurt you, nothing can happen, nothing means anything until the next day when you do it again. It is the wait until the next day that is hard to get through.

**Interviewer:** Can you dismiss from your mind whatever project you're on when you're away from the typewriter?

**Hemingway:** Of course. But it takes discipline to do it and this discipline is acquired. It has to be.

**Interviewer:** Do you do any re-writing as you read up to the place you left off the day before? Or does that come later, when the whole is finished?

**Hemingway:** I always re-write each day up to the point where I stopped. When it is all finished, naturally you go over it. You get another chance to correct and re-write when someone else types it, and you see it clean in type. The last chance is in the proofs. You're grateful for these different chances.

**Interviewer:** How much re-writing do you do?

**Hemingway:** It depends. I re-wrote the ending to *Farewell to Arms*, the last page of it, thirty-nine times before I was satisfied.

**Interviewer:** Was there some technical problem there? What was it that had stumped you?

**Hemingway:** Getting the words right.

**Interviewer:** Is it the re-reading that gets the "juice" up?

**Hemingway:** Re-reading places you at the point where it *has* to go on, knowing it is as good as you can get it up to there. There is always juice somewhere.

**Interviewer:** But are there times when the inspiration isn't there at all?

**Hemingway:** Naturally. But if you stopped when you knew what would happen next, you can go on. As long as you can start, you are all right. The juice will come.

**Interviewer:** Thornton Wilder speaks of mnemonic devices that get the writer going on his day's work. He says you once told him you sharpened twenty pencils.

**Hemingway:** I don't think I ever owned twenty pencils at one time. Wearing down seven No. 2 pencils is a good day's work.

**Interviewer:** Where are some of the places you have found most advantageous to work? The Ambos Mundos hotel must have been one, judging from the number of books you did there. Or do surroundings have little effect on the work?

**Hemingway:** The Ambos Mundos in Havana was a very good place to work in. This Finca is a splendid place, or was. But I have worked well everywhere. I mean I have been able to work as well as I can under varied circumstances. The telephone and visitors are the work destroyers.

**Interviewer:** Is emotional stability necessary to write well? You told me once that you could only write well when you were in love. Could you expound on that a bit more?

**Hemingway:** What a question. But full marks for trying. You can write any time people will leave you alone and not interrupt you. Or rather you can if you will be ruthless enough about it. But the best writing is certainly when you are in love. If it is all the same to you I would rather not expound on that.

**Interviewer:** How about financial security? Can that be a detriment to good writing?

**Hemingway:** If it came early enough and you loved life as much as you loved your work it would take much character to resist the temptations. Once writing has become your major vice and greatest pleasure only death can stop it. Financial security then is a great help as it keeps you from worrying. Worry destroys the ability to write. Ill health is bad in the ratio that it produces worry which attacks your subconscious and destroys your reserves.

**Interviewer:** Can you recall an exact moment when you decided to become a writer?

**Hemingway:** No, I always wanted to be a writer.

**Interviewer:** Philip Young in his book on you suggests that the traumatic shock of your severe 1918 mortar wound had a great influence on you as a writer. I remember in Madrid you talked briefly about his thesis, finding little in it, and going on to say that you thought the artist's equipment was not an acquired characteristic, but inherited, in the Mendelian sense.

**Hemingway:** Evidently in Madrid that year my mind could not be called very sound.

The only thing to recommend it would be that I spoke only briefly about Mr. Young's book and his trauma theory of literature. Perhaps the two concussions and a skull fracture of that year had made me irresponsible in my statements. I do remember telling you that I believed imagination could be the result of inherited racial experience. It sounds all right in good jolly post-concussion talk, but I think that is more or less where it belongs. So until the next liberation trauma, let's leave it there. Do you agree? But thanks for leaving out the names of any relatives I might have implicated. The fun of talk is to explore, but much of it and all that is irresponsible should not be written. Once written you have to stand by it. You may have said it to see whether you believed it or not. On the question you raised, the effects of wounds vary greatly. Simple wounds which do not break bone are of little account. They sometimes give confidence. Wounds which do extensive bone and nerve damage are not good for writers, nor anybody else.

**Interviewer:** What would you consider the best intellectual training for the would-be writer?

**Hemingway:** Let's say that he should go out and hang himself because he finds that writing well is impossibly difficult. Then he should be cut down without mercy and forced by his own self to write as well as he can for the rest of his life. At least he will have the story of the hanging to commence with.

**Interviewer:** How about people who've gone into the academic career? Do you think the large number of writers who hold teaching positions have compromised their literary careers?

**Hemingway:** It depends on what you call compromise. Is the usage that of a woman who has been compromised? Or is it the compromise of the statesman? Or the compromise made with your grocer or your tailor that you will pay a little more but will pay it later? A writer who can both write and teach should be able to do both. Many competent writers have proved it could be done. I could not do it, I know, and I admire those who have been able to. I would think though that the academic life could put a period to outside experience which might possibly limit the growth of knowledge of the world. Knowledge, however, demands more responsibility of a writer and makes writing more difficult. Trying to write something of permanent value is a full-time job even though only a few hours a day are spent on the actual writing. A writer can be compared to a well. There are as many kinds of wells as there are writers. The important thing is to have good water in the well and it is better to take a regular amount out than to pump the well dry and wait for it to re-fill. I see I am getting away from the question, but the question was not very interesting.

**Interviewer:** Would you suggest newspaper work for the young writer? How helpful was the training you had with the *Kansas City Star*?

**Hemingway:** On the *Star* you were forced to learn to write a simple, declarative sentence. This is useful to anyone. Newspaper work will not harm a young writer and could help him if he gets out of it in time. This is one of the dustiest cliches there is and I apologize for it. But when you ask someone old tired questions you are apt to receive old tired answers.

**Interviewer:** You once wrote in the *Transatlantic Review* that the only reason for writing journalism was to be well-paid. You said: "And when you destroy the valuable things you have by writing about them, you want to get big money for it." Do you think of writing as a type of self-destruction?

**Hemingway:** I do not remember ever writing that. But it sounds silly and violent enough for me to have said it to avoid having to bite on the nail and make a sensible statement. I certainly do not think of writing as a type of self-destruction though journalism, after a point has been reached, can be a daily self-destruction for a serious creative writer.

**Interviewer:** Do you think the intellectual stimulus of the company of other writers is of any value to an author?

**Hemingway:** Certainly.

**Interviewer:** In the Paris of the twenties did you have any sense of "group feeling" with other writers and artists?

**Hemingway:** No. There was no group feeling. We had respect for each other. I respected a lot of painters, some of my own age, others older—Gris, Picasso, Braque, Monet, who was still alive then—and a few writers: Joyce, Ezra, the good of Stein . . .

**Interviewer:** When you are writing, do you ever find yourself influenced by what you're reading at the time?

**Hemingway:** Not since Joyce was writing *Ulysses*. His was not a direct influence. But in those days when words we knew were barred to us, and we had to fight for a single word, the influence of his work was what changed everything, and made it possible for us to break away from the restrictions.

**Interviewer:** Could you learn anything about writing from the writers? You were telling me yesterday that Joyce, for example, couldn't bear to talk about writing.

**Hemingway:** In company with people of your own trade you ordinarily speak of other writers' books. The better the writers the less they will speak about what they have written themselves. Joyce was a very great writer and he would only explain what he was doing to jerks. Other writers that he respected were supposed to be able to know what he was doing by reading it.

**Interviewer:** You seem to have avoided the company of writers in late years. Why?

**Hemingway:** That is more complicated. The further you go in writing the more alone you are. Most of your best and oldest friends die. Others move away. You do not see them except rarely, but you write and have much the same contact with them as though you were together at the cafe in the old days. You exchange comic, sometimes cheerfully obscene and irresponsible letters, and it is almost as good as talking. But you are more alone because that is how you must work and the time to work is shorter all the time and if you waste it you feel you have committed a sin for which there is no forgiveness.

**Interviewer:** What about the influence of these people—your contemporaries—on your work? What was Gertrude Stein's contribution, if any? Or Ezra Pound's? Or Max Perkins'?

**Hemingway:** I'm sorry but I am no good at these post-mortems. There are coroners literary and non-literary provided to deal with such matters. Miss Stein wrote at some length and with considerable inaccuracy about her influence on my work. It was necessary for her to do this after she had learned to write dialogue from a book called *The Sun Also Rises*. I was very fond of her and thought it was splendid she had learned to write conversation. It was no new thing to me to learn from everyone I could, living or dead, and I had no idea it would affect Gertrude so violently. She already wrote very well in other ways. Ezra was extremely intelligent on the subjects he really knew. Doesn't this sort of talk bore you? This backyard literary gossip while washing out the dirty clothes of thirty-five years ago is disgusting to me. It would be different if one had tried to tell the whole truth. That would have some value. Here it is simpler and better to thank Gertrude for everything I learned from her about the abstract relationship of words, say how fond I was of her, re-affirm my loyalty to Ezra as a great poet and a loyal friend, and say that I cared so much for Max Perkins that I have never been able to accept that he is dead. He never asked me to change anything I wrote except to remove certain words which were not then publishable. Blanks were left, and anyone who knew the words would know what they were. For me he was not an editor. He was a wise friend and a wonderful companion. I liked the way he wore his hat and the strange way his lips moved.

**Interviewer:** Who would you say are your literary forebears—those you have learned the most from?

**Hemingway:** Mark Twain, Flaubert, Stendhal, Bach, Turgeniev, Tolstoi, Dostoevsky, Chekhov, Andrew Marvell, John Donne, Maupassant, the good Kipling, Thoreau, Captain Marryat, Shakespeare, Mozart, Quevedo, Dante, Virgil, Tintoretto, Hieronymus Bosch, Breughel, Patinier, Goya, Giotto, Cézanne, Van Gogh, Gaughuin, San Juan de la Cruz, Gongora—it would take a day to remember everyone. Then it would sound as though I were claiming an erudition I did not possess instead of trying to remember all the people who have had an influence on my life and work. This isn't an old dull question. It is a very good but a solemn question and requires an examination of conscience. I put in painters, or started to, because I learn as much from painters about how to write as from writers. You ask how this is done? It would take another day of explaining. I should think what one learns from composers and from the study of harmony and counterpoint would be obvious.

**Interviewer:** Did you ever play a musical instrument?

**Hemingway:** I used to play cello. My mother kept me out of school a whole year to study music and counterpoint. She thought I had ability, but I was absolutely without talent. We played chamber music—someone came in to play the violin; my sister played the viola, and mother the piano. That cello—I played it worse than anyone on earth. Of course, that year I was out doing other things too.

**Interviewer:** Do you re-read the authors of your list—Twain, for instance?

**Hemingway:** You have to wait two or three years with Twain. You remember too well. I read some Shakespeare every year, *Lear* always. Cheers you up if you read that.

**Interviewer:** Reading, then, is a constant occupation and pleasure.

**Hemingway:** I'm always reading books—as many as there are. I ration myself on them so that I'll always be in supply.

**Interviewer:** Do you ever read manuscripts?

**Hemingway:** You can get into trouble doing that unless you know the author personally. Some years ago I was sued for plagiarism by a man who claimed that I'd lifted *For Whom the Bell Tolls* from an unpublished screen scenario he'd written. He'd read this scenario at some Hollywood party. I was there, he said, at least there was a fellow called "Ernie" there listening to the reading, and that was enough for him to sue for a million dollars. At the same time he sued the producers of the motion-pictures *North-West Mounted Police* and the *Cisco Kid*, claiming that these, as well, had been stolen from that same unpublished scenario. We went to court and, of course, won the case. The man turned out to be insolvent.

**Interviewer:** Well, could we go back to that list and take one of the painters—Hieronymus Bosch, for instance? The nightmare symbolic quality of his work seems so far removed from your own.

**Hemingway:** I have the nightmares and know about the ones other people have. But you do not have to write them down. Anything you can omit that you know you still have in the writing and its quality will show. When a writer omits things he does not know, they show like holes in his writing.

**Interviewer:** Does that mean that a close knowledge of the works of the people on your list helps fill the "well" you were speaking of a while back? Or were they consciously a help in developing the techniques of writing?

**Hemingway:** They were a part of learning to see, to hear, to think, to feel and not feel, and to write. The well is where your "juice" is. Nobody knows what it is made of, least of all yourself. What you know is if you have it, or you have to wait for it to come back.

**Interviewer:** Would you admit to there being symbolism in your novels?

**Hemingway:** I suppose there are symbols since critics keep finding them. If you do not mind I dislike talking about them and being questioned about them. It is hard enough to write books and stories without being asked to explain them as well. Also it deprives the explainers of work. If five or six or more good explainers can keep going why should I interfere with them? Read anything I write for the pleasure of reading it. Whatever else you find will be the measure of what you brought to the reading.

**Interviewer:** Continuing with just one question on this line: One of the advisory staff editors wonders about a parallel he feels he's found in *The Sun Also Rises* between the dramatis personae of the bull ring and the characters of the novel itself. He points out that the first sentence of the book tells us Robert Cohn is a boxer; later, during the des-encajonada, the bull is described as using his horns like a boxer, hooking and jabbing. And just as the bull is attracted and pacified by the presence of a steer, Robert Cohn defers to Jake who is emasculated precisely as is a steer. He sees Mike as the picador, baiting Cohn repeatedly. The editor's thesis goes on, but he wondered if it was your conscious intention to inform the novel with the tragic structure of the bullfight ritual.

**Hemingway:** It sounds as though the advisory staff editor was a little bit screwy. Who ever said Jake was "emasculated precisely as a steer?" Actually he had been wounded in quite a different way and his testicles were intact and not damaged. Thus he was capable of all normal feelings as a *man* but incapable of consummating them. The important distinction is that his wound was physical and not psychological and that he was not emasculated.

**Interviewer:** These questions which inquire into craftsmanship really are an annoyance.

**Hemingway:** A sensible question is neither a delight nor an annoyance. I still believe though that it is very bad for a writer to talk about how he writes. He writes to be read by the eye and no explanations nor dissertations should be necessary. You can be sure that there is much more than will be read at any first reading and having made this it is not the writer's province to explain it or run guided tours through the more difficult country of his work.

**Interviewer:** In connection with this, I remember you have also warned that it is dangerous for a writer to talk about a work-in-progress, that he can "talk it out" so to speak. Why should this be so? I only ask because there are so many writers—Twain, Wilde, Thurber, Steffens come to mind—who would seem to have polished their material by testing it on listeners.

**Hemingway:** I cannot believe Twain ever "tested out" *Huckleberry Finn* on listeners. If he did they probably had him cut out good things and put in the bad parts. Wilde was said by people who knew him to have been a better talker than a writer. Steffens talked better than he wrote. Both his writing and his talking were sometimes hard to believe, and I heard many stories change as he grew older. If Thurber can talk as well as he writes he must be one of the greatest and least boring talkers. The man I know who talks best about his own trade and has the pleasantest and most wicked tongue is Juan Belmonte, the matador.

**Interviewer:** Could you say how much thought-out effort went into the evolvement of your distinctive style?

**Hemingway:** That is a long-term tiring question and if you spent a couple of days answering it you would be so self-conscious that you could not write. I might say that what amateurs call a style is usually only the unavoidable awkwardness in first trying to make something that has not heretofore been made. Almost no new classics resemble other previous classics. At first people can only see the awkwardness. Then they are not so perceptible. When they show so very awkwardly people think these awkwardnesses are the style and many copy them. This is regrettable.

**Interviewer:** You once wrote me that the simple circumstances under which various pieces of fiction were written could be instructive. Could you apply this to "The Killers"—you said that you had written it, "Ten Indians" and "Today is Friday" in one day—and perhaps to your first novel *The Sun Also Rises?*

**Hemingway:** Let's see. *The Sun Also Rises* I started in Valencia on my birthday, July 21st. Hadley, my wife, and I had gone to Valencia early to get good tickets for the Feria there which started the 24th of July. Everybody my age had written a novel and I was still having a difficult time writing a paragraph. So I started the book on my birthday, wrote all through the Feria, in bed in the morning, went on to Madrid and wrote there. There was no Feria there, so we had a room with a table and I wrote in great luxury on the table and around the corner from the hotel in a beer place in the Pasaje Alvarez where it was cool. It finally got too hot to write and we went to Hendaye. There was a small cheap hotel there on the big long lovely beach and I worked very well there and then went up to Paris and finished the first draft in the apartment over the sawmill at 113 rue Notre-Dame-des-Champs six weeks from the day I started it. I showed the first draft to Nathan Asch, the novelist, who then had quite a strong accent and he said, "Hem, vaht do you mean saying you wrote a novel? A novel huh. Hem you are riding a travhel büch." I was not too discouraged by Nathan and rewrote the book, keeping in the travel (that was the part about the fishing trip and Pamplona) at Schruns in the Vorarlberg at the Hotel Taube.

The stories you mention I wrote in one day in Madrid on May 16 when it snowed out the San Isidro bullfights. First I wrote "The Killers" which I'd tried to write before and failed. Then after lunch I got in bed to keep warm and wrote "Today is Friday." I had so much juice I thought maybe I was going crazy and I had about six other stories to write. So I got dressed and walked to Fornos, the old bull fighter's cafe, and drank coffee and then came back and wrote *Ten Indians*. This made me very sad and I drank some brandy and went to sleep. I'd forgotten to eat and one of the waiters brought me up some Bacalao and a small steak and fried potatoes and a bottle of Valdepeñas.

The woman who ran the Pension was always worried that I did not eat enough and she had sent the waiter. I remember sitting up in bed and eating, and drinking the Valdepeñas. The waiter said he would bring up another bottle. He said the Señora wanted to know if I was going to write all night. I said no, I thought I would lay off for a while. Why don't you try to write just one more, the waiter asked. I'm only supposed to write one, I said. Nonsense, he said. You could write six. I'll try tomorrow, I said. Try it tonight, he said. What do you think the old woman sent the food up for?

I'm tired, I told him. Nonsense, he said (the word was not nonsense). You tired after three miserable little stories. Translate me one.

Leave me alone, I said. How am I going to write it if you don't leave me alone. So I sat up in bed and drank the Valdepeñas and thought what a hell of a writer I was if the first story was as good as I'd hoped.

**Interviewer:** How complete in your own mind is the conception of a short story? Does the theme, or the plot, or a character change as you go along?

**Hemingway:** Sometimes you know the story. Sometimes you make it up as you go along and have no idea how it will come out. Everything changes as it moves. That is what makes the movement which makes the story. Sometimes the movement is so slow it does not seem to be moving. But there is always change and always movement.

**Interviewer:** It is the same with the novel, or do you work out the whole plan before you start and adhere to it rigorously?

**Hemingway:** *For Whom the Bell Tolls* was a problem which I carried on each day. I knew what was going to happen in principle. But I invented what happened each day as I wrote.

**Interviewer:** Were the *Green Hills of Africa, To Have and Have Not,* and *Across the River and Into the Trees* all started as short stories and developed into novels? If so, are the two forms so similar that the writer can pass from one to the other without completely revamping his approach?

**Hemingway:** No, that is not true. The *Green Hills of Africa* is not a novel but was written in an attempt to write an absolutely true book to see whether the shape of a country and the pattern of a month's action could, if truly presented, compete with a work of the imagination. After I had written it I wrote two short stories, "The Snows of Kilimanjaro" and "The Short Happy Life of Francis Macomber." These were stories which I invented from the knowledge and experience acquired on the same long hunting trip one month of which I had tried to write a truthful account of in *The Green Hills. To Have and Have Not* and *Across the River and Into the Trees* were both started as short stories.

**Interviewer:** Do you find it easy to shift from one literary project to another or do you continue through to finish what you start?

**Hemingway:** The fact that I am interrupting serious work to answer these questions proves that I am so stupid that I should be penalized severely. I will be. Don't worry.

**Interviewer:** Do you think of yourself in competition with other writers?

**Hemingway:** Never. I used to try to write better than certain dead writers of whose value I was certain. For a long time now I have tried simply to write the best I can. Sometimes I have good luck and write better than I can.

**Interviewer:** Do you think a writer's power diminishes as he grows older? In the *Green*

*Hills of Africa* you mention that American writers at a certain age change into Old Mother Hubbards.

**Hemingway:** I don't know about that. People who know what they are doing should last as long as their heads last. In that book you mention, if you look it up, you'll see I was sounding off about American literature with a humorless Austrian character who was forcing me to talk when I wanted to do something else. I wrote an accurate account of the conversation. Not to make deathless pronouncements. A fair percent of the pronouncements are good enough.

**Interviewer:** We've not discussed character. Are the characters of your work taken without exception from real life?

**Hemingway:** Of course they are not. *Some* come from real life. Mostly you invent people from a knowledge and understanding and experience of people.

**Interviewer:** Could you say something about the process of turning a real-life character into a fictional one?

**Hemingway:** If I explained how that is sometimes done, it would be a handbook for libel lawyers.

**Interviewer:** Do you make a distinction—as E. M. Forster does—between "flat" and "round" characters?

**Hemingway:** If you describe someone, it is flat, as a photograph is, and from my standpoint a failure. If you make him up from what you know, there should be all the dimensions.

**Interviewer:** Which of your characters do you look back on with particular affection?

**Hemingway:** That would make too long a list.

**Interviewer:** Then you enjoy reading over your own books—without feeling there are changes you would like to make?

**Hemingway:** I read them sometimes to cheer me up when it is hard to write and then I remember that it was always difficult and how nearly impossible it was sometimes.

**Interviewer:** How do you name your characters?

**Hemingway:** The best I can.

**Interviewer:** Do the titles come to you while you're in the process of doing the story?

**Hemingway:** No. I make a list of titles *after* I've finished the story or the book—sometimes as many as 100. Then I start eliminating them, sometimes all of them.

**Interviewer:** And you do this even with a story whose title is supplied from the text—"Hills Like White Elephants," for example?

**Hemingway:** Yes. The title comes afterwards. I met a girl in Prunier where I'd gone to eat oysters before lunch. I knew she'd had an abortion. I went over and we talked, not about that, but on the way home I thought of the story, skipped lunch, and spent that afternoon writing it.

**Interviewer:** So when you're not writing, you remain constantly the observer, looking for something which can be of use.

**Hemingway:** Surely. If a writer stops observing he is finished. But he does not have to observe consciously nor think how it will be useful. Perhaps that would be true at the beginning. But later everything he sees goes into the great reserve of things he knew or has seen. If it is any use to know it, I always try to write on the principle of the iceberg. There is seven-eighths of it underwater for every part that shows. Anything you know you can eliminate and it only strengthens your iceberg. It is the part that doesn't show. If a writer omits something because he does not know it then there is a hole in the story.

*The Old Man and the Sea* could have been over a thousand pages long and had every character in the village in it and all the processes of how they made their living, were born, educated, bore children, etc. That is done excellently and well by other writers. In writing you are limited by what has already been done satisfactorily. So I have tried to learn to do something else. First I have tried to eliminate everything unnecessary to conveying experience to the reader so that after he or she has read something it will become a part of his or her experience and seem actually to have happened. This is very hard to do and I've worked at it very hard.

Anyway, to skip how it is done, I had unbelievable luck this time and could convey the experience completely and have it be one that no one had ever conveyed. The luck was that I had a good man and a good boy and lately writers have forgotten there still are such things. Then the ocean is worth writing about just as man is. So I was lucky there. I've seen the marlin mate and know about that. So I leave that out. I've seen a school (or pod) of more than fifty sperm whales in that same stretch of water and once harpooned one nearly sixty feet in length and lost him. So I left that out. All the stories I know from the fishing village I leave out. But the knowledge is what makes the underwater part of the iceberg.

**Interviewer:** Archibald MacLeish has spoken of a technical device you discovered which would seem to do with conveying experience to a reader. He said you developed it while covering baseball games back in those *Kansas City Star* days. It was simply that a writer should concentrate during moments of apparent inactivity—that what he described of those moments had an effect, and a powerful one, of making the reader conscious of what he had been aware of only subconsciously . . .

**Hemingway:** The anecdote is apocryphal. I never wrote baseball for the *Star*. What Archie was trying to remember was how I was trying to learn in Chicago in around 1920 and was searching for the unnoticed things that made emotions such as the way an outfielder tossed his glove without looking back to where it fell, the squeak of resin on canvas under a fighter's flat-soled gym-shoes, the gray colour of Jack Blackburn's skin when he had just come out of stir and other things I noted as a painter sketches. You saw Blackburn's strange colour and the old razor cuts and the way he spun a man before you knew his history. These were the things which moved you before you knew the story.

**Interviewer:** Have you ever described any type of situation of which you had no personal knowledge?

**Hemingway:** That is a strange question. By personal knowledge do you mean carnal knowledge? In that case the answer is positive. A writer, if he is any good, does not describe. He invents or *makes* out of knowledge personal and impersonal and sometimes he seems to have unexplained knowledge which could come from forgotten racial or family experience. Who teaches the homing pigeon to fly as he does; where does a fighting bull get his bravery, or a hunting-dog his nose? This is an elaboration or a condensation on that stuff we were talking in Madrid that time when my head was not to be trusted.

**Interviewer:** How detached must you be from an experience before you can write about it in fictional terms? The African air-crashes, for instance?

**Hemingway:** It depends on the experience. One part of you sees it with complete detachment from the start. Another part is very involved. I think there is no rule about how soon one should write about it. It would depend on how well adjusted the individual was and on his or her recuperative powers. Certainly it is valuable to a trained writer to crash in an aircraft which burns. He learns several important things very quickly. Whether they will be of use to him is conditioned by survival. Survival, with honor, that outmoded and all-important word, is as difficult as ever and as all important to a writer. Those who do not last are always more beloved since no one has to see them in their long, dull, unrelenting, no quarter given and no quarter received, fights that they make to do something as they believe it should be done before they die. Those who die or quit early and easy and with every good reason are preferred because they are understandable and human. Failure and well-disguised cowardice are more human and more beloved.

**Interviewer:** Could I ask you to what extent you think the writer should concern himself with the socio-political problems of his times?

**Hemingway:** Everyone has his own conscience and there should be no rules about how a conscience should function. All you can be sure about in a political-minded writer is that if his work should last you will have to skip the politics when you read it. Many of the so-called politically enlisted writers change their politics frequently. This is very exciting to them and to their political-literary reviews. Sometimes they even have to rewrite their view-points . . . and in a hurry. Perhaps it can be respected as a form of the pursuit of happiness.

**Interviewer:** Has the political influence of Ezra Pound on the segregationalist Kasper had any effect on your belief that the poet ought to be released from St. Elizabeth's Hospital?*

**Hemingway:** No. None at all. I believe that Ezra should be released and allowed to

---

*As this issue went to press a Federal Court in Washington, D.C. dismissed all charges against Pound, clearing the way for his release from St. Elizabeth's.

write poetry in Italy on an undertaking by him to abstain from any politics. I would be happy to see Kasper jailed as soon as possible. Great poets are not necessarily girl guides nor scoutmasters nor splendid influences on youth. To name a few: Verlaine, Rimbaud, Shelley, Byron, Baudelaire, Proust, Gide should not have been confined to prevent them from being aped in their thinking, their manners or their morals by local Kaspers. I am sure that it will take a footnote to this paragraph in ten years to explain who Kasper was.*

**Interviewer:** Would you say, ever, that there is any didactic intention in your work?

**Hemingway:** Didactic is a word that has been misused and has spoiled. *Death in the Afternoon* is an instructive book.

**Interviewer:** It has been said that a writer only deals with one or two ideas throughout his work. Would you say your work reflects one or two ideas?

**Hemingway:** Who said that? It sounds much too simple. The man who said it possibly *had* only one or two ideas.

**Interviewer:** Well, perhaps it would be better put this way: Graham Greene said in one of these interviews that a ruling passion gives to a shelf of novels the unity of a system. You yourself have said, I believe, that great writing comes out of a sense of injustice. Do you consider it important that a novelist be dominated in this way—by some such compelling sense?

**Hemingway:** Mr. Greene has a facility for making statements that I do not possess. It would be impossible for me to make generalizations about a shelf of novels or a wisp of snipe or a gaggle of geese. I'll try a generalization though. A writer without a sense of justice and of injustice would be better off editing the Year Book of a school for exceptional children than writing novels. Another generalization. You see; they are not so difficult when they are sufficiently obvious. The most essential gift for a good writer is a built-in, shock-proof, shit detector. This is the writer's radar and all great writers have had it.

**Interviewer:** Finally, a fundamental question: namely, as a creative writer what do you think is the function of your art? Why a representation of fact, rather than fact itself?

**Hemingway:** Why be puzzled by that? From things that have happened and from things as they exist and from all things that you know and all those you cannot know, you make something through your invention that is not a representation but a whole new thing truer than anything true and alive, and you make it alive, and if you make it well enough, you give it immortality. That is why you write and for no other reason that you know of. But what about all the reasons that no one knows?

*1958*

---

*John Kasper, organizer of the Seaboard White Citizens Council, had been found guilty of contempt of federal court in 1956—MJB.

# Louise Erdrich:
# Interviewed by Robert Spillman

---

"How is that we all, constantly, apologize for that womanizing, weak-spirited, failed contractor, our husband?" gripes Eleanor to the other three ex-wives of Jack, an irresistible lout around whom Louise Erdrich spins her latest multi-voiced novel, *Tales of Burning Love*. Driving away from Jack's funeral the wives are caught in a sudden squall that strands them under an overpass outside of Fargo, North Dakota. As the snow buries their car, the women stave off the bitter cold and fatal sleep by telling each other very different tales of Jack's ever-changing financial and amorous arrangements.

Like many of her characters, Jack included, Erdrich is of mixed Native American descent; her mother is French Ojibwa, while her father, who according to family legend was born in a tornado, is German American. Erdrich's parents worked for the Bureau of Indian Affairs as teachers on a nearby North Dakota reservation and she recalls that her father regularly recited memorized poetry—Frost and Byron—to her and her six siblings. Erdrich started her literary career as a poet, supporting herself by working at a Kentucky Fried Chicken and on road construction crews.

At 28, Erdrich published her first novel *Love Medicine*—which had been rejected by numerous publishing houses—when her husband, the author Michael Dorris, resubmitted it, posing as her literary agent. Despite a modest first print run, *Love Medicine* was a phenomenal word-of-mouth success, selling 400,000 copies in hardback and winning the 1984 National Book Critics Circle Award.

She followed with three bestsellers: *The Beet Queen*, *Tracks*, and *The Bingo Palace*, as well as *The Crown of Columbus*, another bestseller she co-authored with her husband, Michael Dorris. This spring, Hyperion is releasing her first children's book, *Grandmother's Pigeon*. She and Dorris have five children, two of whom are adopted.

Erdrich spoke with *Salon* at a plush midtown Manhattan hotel, where she was staying during her current book tour. At 41, Erdrich looks ten years younger, yet carries herself with the regal elegance of an elderly matriarch, speaking proprietarily of her characters, as if they were neighbors in the small town where she grew up.

---

**With *Tales of Burning Love*, did you set out to create a whole new cast of characters?**
Well, I thought they would be. I was kind of hoping I'd have an entire new cast, but they were indeed connected right into the beginning of *Love Medicine*, and that was a surprise for me.

**Your characters really linger in the mind. Do you ever feel like your characters get away from you or do you, as Nabokov has said, feel that your characters are "galley**

slaves"? They're certainly not galley slaves. I cannot call them up at will. When I was younger I used to take it for granted that they would be there when I needed to write about them. That's not true anymore. I've used up a lot of the emotional weight of my childhood experiences. I have to keep replenishing. I don't know where it comes from, but whatever it is, I find I need a lot more solitude than I used to, that I have to make a conscious decision to be reclusive and barricade myself. I find I have to make certain commitments to writing that I used to take for granted.

**Jack is a wonderfully flawed character. Was it fun writing about a scoundrel?** Yes. I identified with this person so thoroughly. I wanted in a way to make him a woman, and yet I wanted the women to have the center of the book. There's a character, Lulu Lammertine, in an earlier book, who has the same sort of scoundrelly way with the opposite gender, but for this one I wanted the core of women.

**The harsh landscape of the Great Plains has always played a prominent role in your work. Is it ingrained in your fictive sensibility?** It probably is. I don't feel at home in the writing—I don't know where I am setting down my feet or where the characters are—unless I have this visual backdrop for them.

**Could you ever see yourself writing a novel set in New England and populated with Puritans?** I have a character who's an Indian agent who starts off in New Hampshire. I've spent enough time in New England that I feel I can understand to some degree the landscape, but not the people. I don't understand the people. I really love the day-to-day stuff, but I don't know their moms, their connections. I don't know where they're coming from. I didn't leave home until I was 18, so I really grew up with one set of people in a small town, still know those people, what's happened to them. I keep in very close contact with them.

**Your novels have a spoken, storytelling quality. Did you grow up having stories told to you?** My mother read, my father told them to me. Lots of stories. That's the way they are. They're always making stories out of things—"This happened today and he is connected to so and so." It's a small town thing. There are certain characters that come in and out of the stories that you know instantly—the town gossip, the town drunk. We know when those characters come in what the story's going to be like.

**Do you read your own work aloud as you are composing?** Not really. I write things out by hand, then I put it on the computer. I started out as a poet. I think slowly. I may write it several times by hand. I write all my changes by hand. I rarely read it out loud, although I do like to do readings and I do my own recordings.

**With a household of children, especially small children, how do you create space to work?** They go to school now. That makes a big difference. I just work during school hours. I set limits. I don't work while they're around; I can't do that now. When they were younger, I had an office set up for them with a small desk so they could do coloring while I wrote.

**How has being a mother changed you as an artist?** I find myself emotionally engaged in ways I wouldn't have been otherwise. I wouldn't understand certain things that I'm starting to get now. In the book there's a part where a child, a girl who is 12, really has to figure out deception in order to cross over the threshold of becoming an adult. I wouldn't have understood that kind of change if I didn't have a daughter. It really takes the character consciously lying to grow her up. She becomes a woman when she does that. She loses her innocence and expressiveness. She takes on this woman's mask. She learns how to mask her emotions. She really cries for the first time and she understands what she has to do. I think that's definitely a mother's perspective.

**Some authors worry about what their parents will think of their work. Do you ever worry about your parents' or children's reactions to your novels?** I don't worry about my daughters reading my work at all. I do worry about my father. I don't worry about my mother, but my dad and I have this thing because there's a lot of sexuality in my work. So with this book, I gave him the reading copy with paper clips. I censored it. It's like ritual avoidance in traditional native cultures. He reported back that Mom was watching him so that he wouldn't take out the paper clips. He went through it with no problems. He was still a little horrified about some scenes that weren't clipped. There was a conversation about Jack's masculine dimensions and his wives were uncertain about his size since they had all had different experiences. Dad said, "This should've been clipped." It worked very well otherwise.

**Toni Morrison talks about finding a writer who gives one "permission" to write, someone who breaks down the barriers and allows you the self-confidence to write. Did you have any "permission-giving" writers when you first started to write?** Morrison was one of mine. She spoke about being a mother, and she always spoke about it as a great boon to her as a writer. Previous to that I don't think I'd read anything positive. There were few mothers writing, very few mothers who would talk about the benefits. Kay Boyle was one person for whom being a mother and a writer were passionately integral. Grace Paley, she's very funny about it. She claims to have neglected her children, because it was the only way she could get things done.

Toni Morrison's work always astounds me, that she's able to be both a mother and also admit to the cruelties of the world. It's a very hard thing for a mother to do because one almost protects the imagination against that kind of intrusion, protecting the children's imagination. She's so valiant, she doesn't do that. Otherwise, imaginative inspirations were Faulkner, Flannery O'Connor, and then I've got contemporaries whom I admire: Amy Tan and Michael.

**How do you feel about the new generation of Native American writers?** I think of Susan Power—she's my favorite—and Sherman Alexie. I think what's happening is that they're establishing different tribal traditions and it's exciting. Linda Hogan is a writer I particularly like, and Jim Welch, although he's not new.

**Morrison has stated that she dislikes being labeled a "black writer." Do you feel pigeonholed or limited by being called a "Native American" writer?** It's an academic distinction. It's made to attract people to courses where you can lump authors together. There's a mixture of people and characters in native fiction. I'm mixed. There's no other way I would have the artistic truth and veracity to write about all those characters. Labels make a good headline. I don't dislike it, but I find it tedious.

**On the other hand, do you feel pressure being one of the best known Native American writers in the country?** I really don't feel pressure to write a certain way. That's because I'm a very stubborn writer and I insist on writing whatever has to be written. The background of the characters doesn't matter. I feel that if I started thinking about all the things that other people tell you to write about or do, I would've never written in the first place. I was in a small town and I was supposed to write nice little romantic stories that always ended up happy. Having not done that, nothing will bother me. I'm so glad to talk about being a native writer because the other pressure I get is being talked about as a "commercial" writer versus a "literary" writer. The fact is, you write what you can write. I don't have a lot of choice. I still write in the same way. I curl up in my chair and just write it like I'm writing a poem.

*1996*

# Richard Ford:
# Interviewed by Ned Stuckey-French

**Stuckey-French:** A few years back in your introduction to the *Pushcart Anthology*, you said that when you were first starting out you wrote many short stories and sent them out, but had to face the rejection time after time and decided to heck with this, I'm going to start a longer project so I can get some more sustained time to write.

**Ford:** That's right. That's exactly right. I began writing *A Piece of My Heart.*

**Stuckey-French:** What finally led you back to short stories and when did you start writing them again?

**Ford:** I started writing short stories again in 1979. I was teaching at Williams College, and Ray Carver and I were great friends. He and I were kicking around and went to the dog track down on the Vermont-Massachusetts line, with Kristina. I had been thinking the dog track was sort of intriguing; but Ray really loved to gamble. He'd gamble on most anything—in a kind of sporting way. Nothing serious. I remember the three of us in the stands at the dog track, and Ray was continually going off to make a bet. And of course he knew nothing about dogs. We'd bought these little tout books they sold when you came in.

**Stuckey-French:** Which don't tell you much anyway.

**Ford:** They don't tell you *very* much. They tell you about the history of an individual dog, and its weight and age and where it was from. But that was all the inside dope he needed. And I'll never forget; he went down and made his bet, and he won. Then he went back down to get his money. This was in 1978, I guess, '78, '79. But when he came back up those concrete stairs, I saw a look in his eye of, sort of, wonderful, low-grade fury and frenzy. He had not been long from drinking at that time, and he still had a sort of wildness about him. But seeing that look made me think I'd like to write a story where somebody had that look. It was so vivid. I didn't really have an idea for a story, because I was at the time working on *The Ultimate Good Luck* and had pretty much put story-writing out of my mind, thinking that what I was was a novelist and not a story writer. But here was some little spark to seeing that look in Ray's eyes. God knows what its components were: avarice, pleasure, surprise, a glimpse at a life in which you were routinely a big winner. He liked thoughts of being a big winner—and he was one. But I went home to this big converted barn I was living in, and I thought to myself that I hadn't written a short story now in probably five or six years, or even tried. But I thought I'd try to write one, my first, all in a day. And so I sat down and I wrote it all in a day. It's a pretty short little story called "Going to the Dogs." It's about a man and it's not really about Ray, but a man who hatches a petty scheme to make a lot of money, and then doesn't. Ray's look, I guess, inclined me to that man.

**Stuckey-French:** So what was his anger about?

**Ford:** Oh, it wasn't anger. It was an ecstasy. He'd been having a few years of losses then, and this was different, and he liked it very, very much. It was sweet, really, and also funny. He pissed all the money away eventually that night.

**Stuckey-French:** By the sixth race it was gone.

**Ford:** By the sixth race, right. But anyway, I wrote that story and then didn't write another story till 1981. The stories all came one at a time. All the stories in *Rock Springs,* except for maybe the last two, were written one and two years apart. I wrote several of them during the time I was writing *The Sportswriter,* when I'd come to a patch of time when I wanted to stop and didn't know what else to do but wanted to keep writing. Kristina and I were living in Montana by then. And I would write one more story. And over time I began to think, as the stories accumulated, well maybe I can do this, whereas before I didn't think I could. And I thought it was natural in the life of a writer: that you at some point can do some things and at some other point you can't. Now, since 1987, I've written two stories, one of which is a novella-length piece and the other is a long story called *Jealous.* And I thought in each instance that those were going to be short stories, of some short story length. But they weren't. They were longer. So, short stories weren't available to me at first, and then they came, and then they went away again. It's not mystical, at all. But I don't really want to belabor the point. Maybe they'll become available again. Who knows?

**Stuckey-French:** So the most recent stories outgrew themselves?

**Ford:** Well, I'd like to write stories again. At the tag end of a long novel, novels seem like such a long thing to do. I'd like to do something that is somewhat less hard. And stories—for me—are less hard.

**Stuckey-French:** A novel is such a long project, such a big commitment of yourself and your time that it seems you must believe in it, believe that it's really going to hit, that this one's really going to work. But, with a short story, is it easier to believe that you have a little more leeway?

**Ford:** Well, if stories fail, then they don't make a short story. It's like bread. Either it's a loaf of bread or it's doughy goo. And you can put it away and not think to yourself you've just pissed away two years of your life, or lost your whole purchase on your vocation. I've never written a story I didn't finish though.

**Stuckey-French:** They always feel like a loaf of bread?

**Ford:** Yeah. I haven't written many, though.

**Stuckey-French:** Each one at the end, it feels like a winner?

**Ford:** Well, it's a finished story, anyway. I've really only written twelve short or slightly longer stories in my life—that is since I decided I might could write them at all. And what I do, which in a sense addresses what you just said, is try to compensate for the lesser status of a short story by overpreparing, by considering it at the time I write it as the most important thing in the world. I don't think other people are like that necessarily. Some probably are. But some can write stories perfectly well from one side of their desk, or one side of their mind. But I've found it most expeditious to really clear my decks completely and concentrate only on the story at hand, which makes it as important as I can make it.

**Stuckey-French:** That sounds in a way like what I've read about the way Ray Carver worked too. I remember reading about his desk one time and that he kept a very neat desk and that each story was in a folder and that he only had the one folder on the desk at a time.

**Ford:** Maybe. I don't know. I saw Ray's desk a few times. It didn't make a big impression on me. It was just where he wrote.

**Stuckey-French:** Not that neat?

**Ford:** I don't remember. That's the side of a writer's life that doesn't much interest me. This business of how you go about writing—your desk, etc.—doesn't seem to reveal anything very interesting. And when it does seem to reveal something interesting, I finally think it's trivial. It's the stories that are interesting. The other, I suppose, is an amateur fascination whose implication is that the "magic" of literature can somehow be penetrated by examining the rather inert artifacts of its making. Of course, maybe I'm wrong. That's always possible. Maybe you can get at something that way.

**Stuckey-French:** So in the generation of a short story you say you really prepare. Yet, you say that first one, the first one when you started again, "Going to the Dogs," came in a day. Do you usually feel that they just come in a rush now, once you're ready to write?

**Ford:** No. It took me about five days to write "Rock Springs." It took me thirty days to write "Empire." One of my continual wrestling matches with myself is to work harder, longer, have more concentration—the Protestant virtues of selflessness. And I'd like to get back to the point that in writing stories I *could* write them in a day, or write them, you know, in four days—some succinct time. But, I probably overprepare, which makes writing them a longer proposition. I habitually want to ward off a day when in the course of writing a story or a novel, I suddenly don't have anything else to write about and I'm only two-thirds through. That's more concern to me than writing a story quickly. It's hard completely to explain but I think it's me trying to be better, me trying to take my work more seriously, to prepare more, to get more into stories. But it's possible, I suppose, to reach a point of diminishing returns where your preparation and your wish to be serious begin to turn on you slightly.

**Stuckey-French:** I remember talking to Scott Russell Sanders—I don't know if you know his work, but he's written both stories and essays—and he said that the difference for him between an essay and a story is that for an essay he takes a lot of notes. He's an ex-scientist so he even numbers the notes; whereas for a story, it is more likely to grow out of an image, like the image you mentioned of Ray Carver coming back with the money from the window. Sanders said that for him a story almost writes itself, it comes in a rush, it comes at once, whereas an essay is more assembled. Is that some of what you're talking about when you say you want to guard against over-preparing? Do you want to move your stories away from being assembled and back toward the image?

**Ford:** The idea of an assembling is not foreign to the way I write essays, or to the way I write anything—stories included. I think of stories as constructions, and their logical, sequential nature is an achieved quality: the process of first putting one thing next to one thing, then putting the next; all of which creates, if you're lucky, the illusion of a cohesive story. You create the illusion of a told tale, and you create the illusion of naturally occurring linearness. I think I know what he means by things coming in a rush, as though they came to him and found their existence on the page in an already cohesive shape. That might be good if the story was full enough. My way at least lets me put whatever I want into a story and work at making it fit; instead of becoming, early on, submissive to a wholly formed, "naturally occurring" story whose structure is difficult to fiddle with.

**Stuckey-French:** Another example of this phenomenon is that Faulkner said that when he sat down to start *The Sound and the Fury,* all he had was the image of a little girl crawling out of a window and he could see her drawers . . .

**Ford:** If that's true, I guess he said that. Who knows if it was true. Why would he tell the truth?

**Stuckey-French:** Isn't it pretty to think so?

**Ford:** Well, to fit myself into that idea, it's possible that my recollection of what provoked "Going to the Dogs" is just a convenience of my memory. I'm sure I had other things circulating in my notebook, or so to speak, in my thinking, and I'm sure I wanted to work them into the story. That's certainly typical of me, and it's truthfully and fundamentally the way stories come into being for me. There are all these things that are accumulating in my head or my notebook, things I like or am interested in, and what I want to do is get them into stories. That's my use for them, and that's my understanding of what literary art is. I want to find or make a context in language and logic into which this detail, this line of dialogue, this concept will fit, and which context will, by making them contiguous and interactive, develop in all into something unforeseen, something that is actually new, larger than the sum of parts, and useful and perhaps pretty. And so, for me, it does slightly belie how stories occur when I say they originate in an image. Beyond that, stories originate in my life because of the inherited form of the short story into which I fit my practices. If that makes any sense.

**Stuckey-French:** Sure.

**Ford:** So that first there was a thing called the short story, and I work, and I find a way to inhabit it.

**Stuckey-French:** It makes lots of sense, and I guess, thinking about that, in looking for that linearity that the short story as a form has or is supposed to have, or does have.

**Ford:** Sometimes.

**Stuckey-French:** Right. It seems to me that in your stories often one of the things that kickstarts that line is an allusion to violence, or the threat of violence. That is often there and then the story unfolds.

**Ford:** I suppose.

**Stuckey-French:** Claude's father yanking him by the hair out of the car, that kind of thing. And then we wonder how bad can this get? Or how do we keep this from getting so bad it's just too awful?

**Ford:** My notion about what I guess you could call the ontogeny of fiction is that fiction is about (it is, anyway, when I write it) what we do as a consequence to dramatic acts. Much of our lives is spent dealing with the consequences of our own and others' important acts; trying to make virtues out of vices, trying to make normal things that have happened against our will and against all logic, seem normal, survivable. And so, for me, at least up to now, it has seemed that what stories can be about is how people put their lives in order after rather dramatic, sometimes violent, percussive events. And because I know those things happen to all of us—or if they don't happen to us literally, they happen to us in our ambient life—I know we're curious about them as determinants. We're natively curious about events that change even small personal histories. So, insofar as a story of mine might be instructive, it's that it is about what people do when bad things happen. For me, what's mostly threatened in the stories I've written is the fabric of affection that holds people close enough together to survive.

**Stuckey-French:** And that there might at least be the hope then at the end that that fabric of affection can be regained somehow?

**Ford:** In some fashion. At least it can be glimpsed by the reader, if not always the characters.

**Stuckey-French:** Or at least we can see some understanding of how it was lost?

**Ford:** That's right, and in that understanding achieve some kind of reconnection. I mean I know you can't ever put things back how they were. But maybe you can put them together in some way that they could never have been otherwise. There's a little moment at the end of "Optimists" when a man whose family has gone completely kaflooey sees his mother in a convenience store. She goes over to him and kisses him on the cheek and basically, implicitly, tells him that she loves him. And people have said to me, "God that's such a bleak view of the world. That's such a small grain of solace to have." But I think, well no it's not, because if in the midst of your hectic life you can unexpectedly see your mother, and she comes over and says, "You know, I loved your father and by extension loved you," well, gee, that's a lot to me.

**Stuckey-French:** Right, and if that's all there is, then that has to be enough. Certainly, it's a memory you could hold onto, that could help carry you through life from then on.

**Ford:** I'll tell you one part of the origin of that story too. I was once in a convenience store in Billings, and I was getting some Cokes for Kristina and me. We were, as usual, driving somewhere, I don't know where, and I saw a woman, who was clearly an Indian woman. But, she was quite done up in the way that you sometimes see Indian women. That is to say, she had on very tight jeans, and she had on very shiny boots, and she had on a lovely Western belt and brocaded white shirt. She had her hair done very slick and pulled way back strictly off her forehead, and she looked very, very sleek. But she was also pretty drunk, because she was reeling a bit in the aisles. I looked at her and it was only a couple, three years after my mother had died, and I thought to myself as I looked at her—she was a woman of about sixty—I thought, that's somebody's mother, even though she seemed utterly independent of anybody around.

**Stuckey-French:** The outfit had served to make her not a mother?

**Ford:** That's right, but maybe she was. At any rate, I went back and I sat down in the car and wrote out some notes on that story just sitting there in the car.

**Stuckey-French:** You talk about the preparation you do for your stories. In that case it seems like maybe you had been preparing for that story, but you needed that image of her to bring those things together. The convenience store gave you something.

**Ford:** Yeah, you gotta pay attention.

**Stuckey-French:** I wanted to ask you about the end of another story, "Rock Springs," and how its final moment of understanding is arrived at. It seems to me to be the same kind of moment of understanding and recognition, but it also seems to work a little differently because of the move into direct address at the very end. I guess direct address is always implicit in a first person narrator. I mean, there is always a "you," but . . .

**Ford:** Yes, but it had only been implicit up to then.

**Stuckey-French:** Right, and there it becomes explicit, and it's a way to summarize those understandings such as they are at that moment. They are there in a list of questions.

**Ford:** I think it comes less into that story as a rhetorical strategy than as a gesture of sympathy; the story trying to find a way to connect itself with whomever might be reading. It's saying, "we're alike."

**Stuckey-French:** Exactly, and that's the way I read it from the get-go. I just think it's a wonderful ending and that it really works that way.

**Ford:** It was just an act of God, with me doing God's bidding. I wrote that story sitting in a little loft in New York in February of 1981, with no heat and with construction going on. Kristina and I were living in this illegal loft on Greene Street, and the Streets People came and said, "You're using PVC to conduct gas into your apartment and we're going to cut you off." And they did. They cut us off. We had rented this apartment, and we had no place to go, and I had to sit with a little space heater in just the most remote place you could be from Rock Springs and I wrote that story then. In some ways, I think, if that story has any intensity in it at all, it has the intensity of wanting very much not to be where I was. In a way, empathizing with myself for being in a really bad situation in which a guy was in a bad situation which he doesn't see any way of getting out of.

**Stuckey-French:** My wife has taught that story and occasionally, she'll run into a student who just . . .

**Ford:** . . . hates him.

**Stuckey-French:** . . . just doesn't like the . . .

**Ford:** I know.

**Stuckey-French:** . . . who says, "Don't say 'you.' I'm not like you."

**Ford:** "I don't steal cars."

**Stuckey-French:** Exactly. I don't know the source of such a mis-reading. Well, I hate to call it a mis-reading . . .

**Ford:** Well, they're youngsters for one thing, and that is definitely not a youngsters' story. You know, I remember when I read *The Moviegoer* by Walker Percy I was living in New Orleans, on leave from the University of Michigan, and I couldn't wait to get back to Michigan and get other people to read it. Joe Blotner and I taught it, and the graduate students at Michigan could not understand why anybody in the world would be the way Binx was in that novel. They were just too young.

**Stuckey-French:** It's a wonderful book.

**Ford:** Oh, one of the great American books, I think. But, here is a guy turning thirty at Mardi Gras, and these graduate kids were smart, but they were not thirty and they weren't melancholy and it wasn't the '50s, and they had no purchase on that story whatsoever and it doesn't denigrate it in any way as a story. And I think that in "Rock Springs" you may have to have a few miles on you for that story to have the resonance that it could conceivably have.

**Stuckey-French:** And I wonder too if you have to have, in some way, stepped into that class, or have been in that class. Not that you have to have stolen cars, you know, but that you somehow need to have felt that desperation, that need to get out. In that story, it seems to me, a lot of it is not just getting out of that place, but getting out of that . . .

**Ford:** . . . mentality . . .

**Stuckey-French:** Right, or that economic situation.

**Ford:** Well, the story would, if it could, establish a sympathy for a person like that. And I've had that same sentiment expressed to me about my stories: "I don't like these people. These people are marginal and they're crooks and they're sort of lowlifes." And I think to myself . . .

**Stuckey-French:** Try to have some heart?

**Ford:** Yeah. This story says you have to have some sympathy for these people, and maybe it strains the point to say that you have to have some sympathy because you are like them. But, basically it says you have to have sympathy because they are on the earth here beside you. And if you don't have that sympathy, in my view . . . you ought to.

**Stuckey-French:** I agree. Somewhere, perhaps it was in your introduction to the Granta collection of American short stories, you mentioned that there could be such a thing as a Republican story . . .

**Ford:** (laughter)

**Stuckey-French:** . . . a story that tells you what it's like to be a Republican and why one should be a Republican, and thankfully, I think, you shuddered at such a thought, but do you write democratic short stories with a small *d?*

**Ford:** Yeah, I do. I think my playing field is broad and level. Though not everybody agrees with me about that. I don't think that's the only way to write stories. People have said to me, "Well, you didn't grow up lower middle class. You didn't grow up in those circumstances." Though I did grow up in circumstances of life in which my family had grappled themselves up out of that other stratum into one where there was some clear air to breathe. And I think one of the things that I grew up realizing was that they were terrifically fearful that something was going to happen that was going to drop them back down into worse circumstances. That's dramatic, I think.

**Stuckey-French:** I remember reading somewhere the adage that in our society every woman is just one man away from welfare.

**Ford:** And I believe that, and I think it about myself, about being a writer. Nothing's promised. I know my father felt that way. Maybe I inherited it from him.

**Stuckey-French:** He was a salesman. I thought of that in *A Piece of My Heart* where I guess it's Hewes who is talking about what that work can do to you, which I think a lot of people aren't aware of. Even those who've read *Death of a Salesman,* maybe they don't think about the hemorrhoids and . . .

**Ford:** . . . closing your hand up in the door and all those nights alone in motels and years and years of that. The thing I couldn't figure out was why he loved his work so much. He just loved it. I would think about all the particulars—loneliness, drive, drive, drive, hot, hot, hot. It was before the days of air-conditioning. I couldn't figure that out. Still, really, in a way can't. It's a fit subject for art, I think; to investigate that unknown.

**Stuckey-French:** So what did he love about it, do you think? The independence?

**Ford:** I don't know. He loved my mother desperately, and they had had this wonderful life together for years before I was born . . . fifteen years . . . and my mother was a really interesting person and compelling in a way, and I can't imagine what it would have been like to have had all those years together with her and then suddenly for me to have come along and for his life then to start out in a slightly different tack, which is being mostly alone. Maybe it is just that he wasn't a very sophisticated man, or maybe he just liked new beginnings every week, and the end of the week was the beginning of the weekend, and the beginning of the following week was the beginning of another week in which he didn't know exactly how things would go. And maybe, it was on that low level of satisfaction. Or maybe it was something entirely unknown to me. But really, when in a piece of fiction a writer says he "investigates" something, he is really just inventing possible answers—obvious ones and less obvious, fanciful ones.

**Stuckey-French:** And I guess part of those new beginnings is that you are just constantly meeting new people and you have that opportunity to talk.

**Ford:** That's right, and he did. A kind of endless, almost unhierarchical diversity. Once again, you go along this flat plain and you're constantly like a pinball being baffled back and forth among people, and maybe he just liked that. I don't know. I'm going to write an essay about him next year.

**Stuckey-French:** Are you?

**Ford:** I wrote a long essay about my mother. And I'd like to write something about my father. But the problem is that he wasn't around after I was sixteen, because he died, and I don't want to write the absent father essay. I'll have to figure out something different.

**Stuckey-French:** I noticed that *Wildlife* and "Great Falls" and, I don't know, a couple of other things that you've written are all about 1960–61 and a seventeen-year-old narrator. Is it important for you in some way to return to that moment when your father died?

**Ford:** Probably, but not I think in an autobiographical way. One of the things writers do is contend that their life is just like everybody else's life, and if something happened to me when I was sixteen that changed my life forever . . .

**Stuckey-French:** . . . everybody had something that did?

**Ford:** At least it is possible they did. Women and men too. Obviously there are limits to that contention, but I think it is true that when boys, and girls too, reach that age, they're beginning to leave adolescence or childhood and heading into adulthood, and all kinds of important things happen. And I thought for me it was crucial, and I thought all kinds of other things happened to kids all over the country that were crucial. So it was just the natural kind of writerly participation in the lives of others, which originates in my participation in my own life. But I didn't write anything in those stories there about fathers dying, because I didn't want to write about that.

**Stuckey-French:** Right, they're not about that.

**Ford:** I was interested, as I said before, in what happens beyond some crucial event, which even though it changes life it also lets it come back together, maybe in a more interesting way. I wished to have as many participants survive the event as can be. So death of the father didn't figure in.

**Stuckey-French:** Those stories, it seems to me, are more about the relationship between the boy and the mother, and how they're both at some turning point and have to get to what's next.

**Ford:** That's right. I guess I'm just interested in the whole configuration; from one permutation to the next at a particular age, or at least I was. I don't know if I'll write about it anymore.

**Stuckey-French:** The whole country turned at that moment too, I guess.

**Ford:** Well, the fifties officially ended. But I'm not sure the fifties ended until Kennedy was killed, really. But at least if you set something on the cusp of '59–'60, the reader now can look back at that time, and, through the focus of a story, history can be made to seem more intelligible, or at least seem to have implications that weren't immediately apparent then.

**Stuckey-French:** So, do you feel a responsibility or a desire not only to try to understand what happened on a personal level, but also . . .

**Ford:** In a historical way? No, I don't think so. I think history for me is a convenience, which is of the same kind of convenience as time-setting *The Sportswriter* on Easter was or time-setting other stories of mine: that is, they're set on days or years that are recognizable by the reader—on holidays or Halloween or Thanksgiving, or precise years. I like to set events at a time that the reader has some memory of. The reader then is more easily convinced to participate in the story's illusion, and the story then begins to inform that time for the reader through the agency of his memory. But I don't myself pretend to have any particular purchase on that time. I'm using it just as a mnemonic. Somebody asked me when I was in France a couple of weeks ago, what I took to be a theoretical question . . .

**Stuckey-French:** Well, you were in France.

**Ford:** . . . which had to do with my sense of history, and my view of it. And if I hadn't been respectful of the guy, I would have laughed, because I have almost no sense of history. But, in a way that the French might appreciate, I have a kind of existential freedom regarding history. I convert it. Traduce it. Change it. Maybe that means I have a sense, after all.

**Stuckey-French:** A sense of moment?

**Ford:** Yeah, or a willingness to change it, a willingness to say, "History's like this. For me, history's like this. I'll bet it was like that for you." And all I have to do is get you to agree that it was, because that's basically the nature of literary truth. If you and I can posit an important possibility and agree to it and live in accordance to it, I'm afraid it's on the way to becoming truth.

**Stuckey-French:** So, for instance, it can be Thanksgiving [in the story "Going to the Dogs"], but also on this other vector coming in it's the time I had to move out and stiff this guy on his lease?

**Ford:** That's right.

**Stuckey-French:** By bringing those two things together it's that much more memorable or believable?

**Ford:** You get a whole package of memories and a whole package of responses, which you otherwise weren't going to get if you had it be the 5th of November. We story writers need all the help we can get. And yet, when people say about *The Sportswriter* "You set it on Easter because it's a story about redemption, isn't it?" I think to myself, yeah, maybe that's right, maybe that's right. But the *real* reason I set it on Easter was that's the day I began writing it. Easter Day in 1982. And I think I began it then because Easter just struck me as a very memorable holiday—one anybody in America had some vivid associates with. Plus, I was looking for a short period of time in which a novel could take place and I thought "Well, Good Friday to Easter. That's a nice short little course that you can set a novel in." So that's what it was. That it became interested in redemptive issues was really after the fact.

**Stuckey-French:** So, it wasn't a question of trying to resurrect Ralph?

**Ford:** No, but I'll tell you, as I've said before, if you start monkeying around with these Judeo-Christian myths, you're in over your boot tops in a hurry. You better be up to it. They have remarkable potency, whether you're acquainted with them or just are a novice, as I was.

**Stuckey-French:** You better be ready for some readers who know it better than you?

**Ford:** R. Z. Sheppard in *Time*, when that book was reviewed (and he liked it), said he thought I had made it have fourteen chapters because there are fourteen stations to the Cross. But that was the first time I'd heard there were fourteen stations to the Cross.

**Stuckey-French:** I remember reading an interview where Bill Gass talking about how his story "In the Heart of the Heart of the Country," which opens with the allusion to "Sailing to Byzantium," "And so I have sailed the seas and come . . . / to B . . . / a small town fastened to a field in Indiana." Then it's written in those sections, you know "People," "Weather," whatever, and some critic counted the sections and said, "Ah ha, 32 and 32 lines in 'Sailing to Byzantium.'" And he [Gass] said the same thing you just said, "I'd never thought of that."

**Ford:** On the other hand, it's sometimes nice to think that you plugged your finger into a hot current, even if by accident. Only a fool would argue much.

**Stuckey-French:** What about some things that I wondered if you do put in a little more consciously? For instance, humor. It seems like you really enjoy writing something funny.

**Ford:** I'm actually quite bereft if I write a story which doesn't have any humor in it; and for various reasons: one, that humor finds its way into any piece of literature as a relief, and also because I think often people actually say important, serious things under the guise of not being serious about it. One of the purposes of any story is to ask the reader to pay attention to this which she or he might not have paid attention before, and indeed, pay attention to it in this degree of particularity, whereas in ordinary life things flow by and we don't pay much attention to them. So, I want stories to draw the reader's attention to something and say, "This is important." And humans always make jokes when they aren't joking at all. So, it has at least two sides to it and maybe it has other sides too—one of which is that writing something funny pleases *me*. Nothing makes me happier than when I can be writing a story and make myself laugh. I call that a triumph, even if I later throw it out, and I often do throw it out.

**Stuckey-French:** So what are some of the funniest moments for you?

**Ford:** I can't remember.

**Stuckey-French:** Well, I was thinking when you were saying that humor can instruct . . . that in "Winterkill" when the woman . . . ah, is it Nola?

**Ford:** Yeah, Nola, who just came out of the song, you know, "Walking along a thoroughfare." Do you know that song, "Nola"? That's the only reason I used the name. I have a friend in Chicago who can play "Nola"—the song—*on his head*, by hitting the top of his head with his knuckles and moving his open mouth in and out. Possibly you'd have to see it to think it was funny. In fact, I'm sure you would. But I thought it was very funny.

**Stuckey-French:** I would love to see and hear that. In the story, Nola's talking about when her husband knew he was going to die and he spontaneously decided that he wanted flank steak, and Troy connects right with it. He says, "I know. I thought of lobster when I was lying there dying." And I laughed there.

**Ford:** I wanted you to. I thought Troy was a comic character. But, in that story anyway, Troy seems comic in spite of being wrecked physically. Ultimately, too, of course, he isn't comic, but rather noble.

**Stuckey-French:** He's sad, and yet he's such a wonderful audience to her.

**Ford:** He's so thrilled to get to talk to a woman, whereas ordinarily he might've just been cast aside. I remember when I wrote *The Ultimate Good Luck* and Walter Clemons, who I'm sorry to say just died this summer, reviewed it in *Newsweek*. One of the things he said about it was that he liked the book, but he said I'd managed to write a book that short-circuited something I could do—which was to be funny. He'd liked another book of mine, *A Piece of My Heart,* which had comic parts. And that made an impression on me, and I just thought that I wasn't going to write anything else that short-circuited humor. (I've since broken that promise a time or two.) But one of the things that you want to do as a writer is to get everything you know and are capable of as a writer onto the page so that you can exceed it in the act of writing; gain access to something you couldn't otherwise ever have gotten access to. That's a problem for many young writers; they tap into only part of their abilities. It's something you can overcome with hard work, of course.

**Stuckey-French:** I'm thinking a little more about the humor in your stories. It seems like one of the agents for bringing the humor into your stories is children.

**Ford:** Oh, yeah, because I sometimes see them as such malevolent little creatures who rule (and often not benignly) the lives of adults.

**Stuckey-French:** Yeah, like Cherry imitating Paul Harvey. There's something wicked about that.

**Ford:** Yeah, well I think kids can be wicked by not knowing wicked.

**Stuckey-French:** They're not expected yet to have a conscience, or manners, or something.

**Ford:** That's a very Victorian idea. If you read Hardy and you read kids in Hardy. Or, if you remember in *Wuthering Heights,* there's a scene which occurs in a kitchen, and the children hanging puppies by a string off the back of a chair. And Father Time in *Jude the Obscure* comes into the book as a child but ages unnaturally fast and speaks only as an adult, speaks runically, speaks rivetingly to Jude. I think that's where I determined how to use children. You use them as extremely potent characters, rather than as bothersome non-entities (which they mostly are in life); little oracles who speak as adults or who affect events in large ways yet remain deceptively "innocent." You know, if you have to have children speak as children, they won't say anything very interesting. They don't know anything.

**Stuckey-French:** It's when they're imitating adults or trying to horn in on the adults' conversation that they get spooky, because there are these adult voices coming out of their mouths.

**Ford:** Truthfully, though, I'm only interested in adults. I think that's the only time when life begins to make any difference; when you can take responsibility for your actions and your actions can have a consequence which you can oversee. So, children are, for me, little condiments in stories. You know, you shake them in to spice it up, but the real events take place in the lives of people who are responsible, who bear the consequences of action as fully as it can be borne. I think that would probably get me in trouble with the Pope. [laughter] But he probably doesn't read my stories in Italian—or, really, know much about real life. I mean, he's a priest.

**Stuckey-French:** I don't know. He's laid up now with that broken leg. Maybe he has the time to read some fiction.

**Ford:** I want to know how he broke his hip. I want to know how he got down on the floor in that bathroom. That's what I want to know.

*1994*

# Leslie Marmon Silko: Interviewed by Florence Boos

**Boos:** Do you consider yourself primarily a writer of stories or a novelist?

**Silko:** I've never tried to categorize what I do according to generic labels. I'm a writer, and I love language and story. I started out loving stories that were told to me. Growing up at Laguna Pueblo, one is immersed in story telling, because the Laguna people did not use written language to keep track of history and philosophy and other aspects of their lives.

Imagine an entire culture that is passed down for thousands and thousands of years through the spoken word and narrative, so the whole of experience is put into narrative form—this is how the people know who they are as a people, and how individuals learn who they are. They hear stories about "the family," about grandma and grandpa and others.

When I started out at the University of New Mexico, I took a folklore class, and began to think about the differences between the story that's told and the literary short story. I started writing the "literary" short story, and tried to write it as closely as I could according to the "classical" rules which seemed to manifest themselves in my reading. I wanted to show that I could do it. But I've turned away from this since and haven't really written a short story in the usual sense since 1981. From 1981 to 1989 I worked on *Almanac of the Dead,* and so I don't think of myself as short story writer. Yet stories are at the basis of everything I do, even non-fiction, because a lot of non-fiction reminiscences or memories come to me in the form of narrative, since that's the way people at home organize all experience and information.

I found the rules of the "classical" short story confining. I think you can see why the post-modernist narrative and the contemporary short story went off in another direction. They're trying to escape the strictures of the formal story form.

I've now tasted the freedom one has with a novel, so I wonder if I'll turn back to more structured forms. I've written one short story, "Personal Property," which I'm going to read tonight, and which purposely breaks some of the rules of the classical short story. Maybe I'm not done with making trouble with the short story form!

**Boos:** How are your poems related to your stories?

**Silko:** For me a poem is a very mysterious event . . . my poems came to me mysteriously. I started out to write a narrative, fiction or non-fiction, and something would happen so that the story would organize itself in the form of a narrative poem rather than a short story.

In fact, that happened with "A Story from Bear Country," in *Storyteller.* I intended to make a note about a conversation I had had with Benjamin Barney, a Navajo friend, about the different ways our respective Navajo and Pueblo cultures viewed bears. I started a narrative of our conversation, but something shifted abruptly, and before I knew it, I was writing something that looked more like a poem. At the very end of that poem a voice comes in and says, "Whose voice is this? You may wonder, for after all you were here alone, but you have been listening to me for some time now." That voice is the seductive voice of the bears. Benjamin Barney and I had been discussing the notion that if humans venture too close to the bear people and their territory, the people are somehow seduced or enchanted. They're not mauled or killed, but they are seduced and taken away to live with the bears forever.

So I don't have control [over whether my tale becomes a tale or a poem]. I set out to narrate something—either something which actually happened or a story I was told—and after I begin the piece sorts itself into whether it will be a poem or a short story. I find a mixing of the two in "The Sacred Water," a piece that I wrote a couple of years ago—a wanting to have the two together—so that there's really no distinct genre. This story also contained a bit of "non-fiction." I wanted to blend fiction and non-fiction together in one narrative voice.

So I am never far away from oral narrative, storytelling and narration, and the use of narrative to order experience. The people at home believe that there is one big story going on made up of many little stories, and the story goes on and on. The stories are alive and they outlive us, and storytellers are only caretakers of the story. Storytellers can be anonymous. Their names don't matter because the stories live on. I think that's what people mean when they say that there are no new stories under the sun. It's true—the old stories live on, but with new caretakers.

**Boos:** You present yourself as a narrative writer, but it struck me as I read *Storyteller* that you also think visually. How do you decide where to put the words on the page?

**Silko:** I'm a very aural person. On the other hand, my father was a photographer, and when I was a child, I would go in the darkroom, sit quietly on the stool, and watch as the images of the photographs would develop. As I've written in *Storyteller,* there was this old Hopi basket full of snapshots. One of us kids would pull a photograph and say, "Grandma, who's this," or "what's this?" A photograph would be tied to narration. And when I was a child walking in the countryside, I'd see a certain sandstone formation of a certain shape, or a certain mesa, and someone would say, "Look, see that hill over there? Well, let me tell you . . ."

Through the years I've done a lot of thinking about the similarities and differences between the "literary" story and the story that's told. I began to realize that landscape could not be separated from narration and storytelling. One of the features of the written or old-fashioned short story was the careful, detailed description of its setting. By contrast, in Laguna oral stories, tellers and audience shared the same assumptions, a collective knowledge of the terrain and landscape which didn't need to be retold. That's why something an anthropologist or folklorist has collected may seem sparser than a literary short story; sometimes the oral short story can seem "too sparse." I realized that all communities have shared knowledge, and that the "literary" short story resulted when all over Europe—and all over the world—human populations started to move. People didn't have this common shared ground anymore.

**Boos:** *Storyteller* seemed to evoke a whole context related to your deep kinship with your family. Even the shapes of the stories seemed to arise from your identification with those telling the stories.

**Silko:** Right. One of the reasons that *Storyteller* contains photographs was my desire to convey that kinship and the whole context or field on which these episodes of my writing occurred. The photographs include not only those of my family, but of the old folks in the village and places in the village. I started to think of translation [from Laguna]. I realized that if one just works with the word on the page or the word in the air, something's left out. That's why I insisted on having photographs in *Storyteller*. I wanted to give the reader a sense of place, because here place is a character. For example, in the title story, "Storyteller," the main character is the weather and the free, frozen land itself. Or in the story I'm going to read tonight, "Private Property," the community itself is a character—although places and communities are not ordinarily characters in the "classical" literary short story. I felt a need to add in these other [visual] components which before were supposed to be extraneous to the narrative, but which existed at Laguna Pueblo as visual cues—a mountain or a tree or a photograph.

**Boos:** When you advise your creative writing students, what suggestions do you give about choosing topics or about technique?

**Silko:** Usually I tell them just to think about a good story, not to think consciously about topic or theme. I tell them that their stories should contain something that they don't know, something mysterious. It's better not to know too much, but to have just the bare bones of an idea, and let the writing be a process of enlightenment for them.

I often say, "Well, you can tell me the idea for the story, so why can't you write it down?" There's a large difference between speaking and writing. But when I'm writing, it's as natural to me as if I were speaking, though the results are different. The most difficult element of writing to teach the student is that ease—writing as if you were talking to yourself or to the wall.

Students are traumatized by the writing process. I've noticed the traumatization begins right from the first grade. Usually kids withstand it till around the seventh or eighth grade, and then they experience a real terror of failure and scolding. People who can talk, who can tell you things, freeze when they sit down in front of a blank piece and a pencil. It shouldn't be difficult to make the transition from speaking to writing, and I blame the United States educational system for the fact that it is.

**Boos:** Though you speak of an oral narrative tradition, you also remark that you speak and write differently. What's different about the writing process for you, and why do you value that?

**Silko:** I was conscious that I wasn't as good a storyteller as the storytellers at home, for the people at home are so good at this. An oral performance is just that, so I needed to go off in a room by myself to evoke that same sense of wholeness and excitement and perfection that I seemed to hear all around me [during their performances].

Also, when I'm writing I'm alone. When I'm speaking to an audience, by contrast, I'm very sensitive to what people want from me or expect from me, whether the audience are becoming restless or whatever, and I'm anxious to please and to serve, putting the comfort of others ahead of my own. When I write I'm alone with the voices . . . with the people in my memory. Some of the voices that I'm alone with might even be those of people still living, so that I could go and talk to them outside that door, but when I'm alone in the room writing, a connection with the older voices occurs, which cannot happen for me when I'm storytelling.

**Boos:** Writing isn't just inscription of stories, then, but something that requires solitude as well?

**Silko:** Being alone allows me to hear those voices. I think it's aloneness to be able to hear Aunt Susie's voice, for example. If I were in a room with her I would only listen, not write or speak, but solitude enables me to hear [and transcribe] her very distinctive voice. I think it was meant to be distinctive so that I could never forget it.

I've thought a lot about this distinction between oral narration and writing. Storytelling was done in a group so that the audience and teller would respond to each other, and be grounded in the present. As I said, I'm not as good at that, but I learned that it's also dangerous to go into the room alone and hear the voices alone, because those are voices from spirit beings who have real presence . . . and bring dangers . . . There's a real danger of being seduced by them, of wanting to join them and remain with them. I'm forty-six, and things are becoming clearer to me, things that before I had only heard about and hadn't experienced, so I couldn't judge.

But now I'm beginning to understand. Old Aunt Susie used to say that when she and her siblings were children, her grandmother started storytelling by bidding the youngest child to go open the door "so that our esteemed ancestors may bring in their gifts for us." But when we tell the stories of those past folks telling stories, they are actually here again in the room. It's therefore dangerous for a storyteller to write in a room alone without others, because those old ancestors are really coming in.

In writing *Almanac of the Dead,* I was forced to listen . . . I was visited by so many ancestors . . . it was very hard. It changed me as a human being. I came to love solitude almost too much, and it was very frightening.

**Boos:** Don't you ever fear that the presences of the dead might view critically something you wrote?

**Silko:** No, I've never been afraid. I know the voices of the storytellers, and I know that if you tell their truth and don't try to be self-serving, they aren't dangerous—in fact, they bring great protective power—*great protective power.*

**Boos:** How do you know what is true rather than self-serving?

**Silko:** I can tell. One method to avoid self-serving is to use a male protagonist, as in *Ceremony.* I wrote two stillborn versions of *Ceremony* now in the [Beinecke] Library at Yale—though I suspect that the rest of the university may have thought I was the Anti-Christ, so maybe they're not even catalogued! If anyone is interested, they can read the two stillborn drafts—each about sixty pages long—that lead up to *Ceremony.* "Stillborn" is of course such a grim term, but before I sold them to Yale University I looked at them again and saw that they're not really "stillborns" at all, but a necessary part of writing the novel. This gave me new confidence in the process of writing, and all young writers should understand that even those things that we throw in the trash can are necessary to get us to where we want to be. The first two stillborns had *female* protagonists.

**Boos:** Why would changing to a male protagonist have enabled you to transcend yourself?

**Silko:** When the characters were females, I identified too closely with them and wouldn't let them do things that I hadn't done or wouldn't do. It's not good to identify too closely with [one's own characters]. All this happened when I was very young; I started writing the "stillborn" versions of *Ceremony* when I was twenty-three.

**Boos:** Did you start to write short stories before you published poems? You published the poems of *Laguna Woman* quite early.

**Silko:** I wrote stories before I wrote poems, but the poems were easier to get out. That was because in writing stories I found myself too connected to the main character. Even though I wanted [her] to be a separate character, [she] wouldn't be. When on the third draft of *Ceremony,* I created Tayo, and I was so liberated by working with a male protagonist.

Also, in a matriarchy the young *man* symbolizes purity and virginity—and also the intellectual, the sterile, and the orderly. The female principle was the chaotic, the creative, the fertile, the powerful.

**Boos:** *Ceremony* struck me as a book about the bonds between men, very deep bonds. Why would it be liberating for you to deal with male bonding and the recovery of a man's sense of himself?

**Silko:** When I was a little girl, I hung around adults. I was always the kid who wouldn't go off and play with the other kids, but liked to watch and eavesdrop on adults. I come from a culture in which men and women are not segregated, and so I had a great deal of opportunity to listen to the men talking. When I was really small, I listened to World War II and Korean War veterans. They had drinking problems and lacked regular jobs, but they had good souls and good spirits. Perhaps tragedy and anguish and trouble attracted me right away as a little girl, more than the easier parts of life.

Also, the Laguna people lived in a matriarchy, and in a matriarchy one is more afraid of what women may say and think about oneself. Children feel less powerful than their mothers, and men seemed more interesting to them because they too had less power and were more like themselves.

Needless to say, women are a lot happier in a matriarchy than in a patriarchal society. Also those elements that had given women their strength and continuity were not nearly as shaken by outside pressures as were those reserved for men. I think this was mainly because when outsiders came in, they didn't realize the women's power, and so they left them alone. They stopped more of the things that men did traditionally than those that women did. So you see the men were more broken apart by the invasion. The government imprisoned men for practicing the Pueblo religion. Then of course war came, and the Second World War and the Korean War were devastating for men.

The Pueblo world is the reverse of Anglo-American and mainstream culture, where the final word is the man's word. In the Pueblo world, women have the final word in practical matters. This is a simplification, but women own all the property, children belong to their mother's clan, and all the mundane business—quarrels, problems—are handled by women. The female deity is the main deity, and in the Kiva ceremonies, men dress as women. But formerly the matriarchy was more evenly balanced, for the men were responsible for the hunting and religious ceremonies.

**Boos:** On the other hand, I've heard the theory that because the Euro-American legal system was so patriarchal, it destroyed certain aspects of Indian life that favored or protected women (by enforcing nineteenth-century laws, for example, which gave a married woman's property to her husband). If so, imposition of foreign laws sometimes diminished women's authority.

**Silko:** Well, we're only seeing that starting with my generation. It's taken that long for western European misogyny to arrive in the Pueblo. It's true that the conquerors negotiated only with Pueblo men, ignoring the clan mothers, but in the long run, when they destroyed what they thought was important, they left behind the authority of women.

Yet it's true that women are sometimes disadvantaged. A lot of tribal councils were established which didn't give women the right to vote, even though tribal organization was matriarchal. But that's a superficial level of damage, when you think that if the Conquistadors had really understood how important women were, they might have tried to [undermine their power]. Patriarchal attitudes have touched the Pueblo people only in a superficial way.

**Boos:** Does your identification with Tayo perhaps suggest that an author should try to identify with someone of the opposite sex as a way of moving towards a full presentation of reality?

**Silko:** Totally. When I was growing up, for a long time I felt that I was "just me." That was easy to be in a matriarchal culture, where women have access to the wide world. Women are everywhere and men are everywhere women are. There isn't this awful segregation that you find even now in the Anglo-American world . . .

**Boos:** In university life!

**Silko:** Yes, in university life. In the Pueblo, women crack dirty jokes to men who aren't their husbands or close relatives. There's a lot of banter, and a real feeling of equality and strength within the community. There weren't places where a little girl was told, "Oh, you can't go there!," or things of which a little boy was told, "Oh, you shouldn't do that!" I wasn't told that because I was a little girl, I had to dress or act a certain way. So for a long time, although I didn't think I was *really* a boy, I kind of . . .

**Boos:** . . . didn't learn *not* to identify with men.

**Silko:** Yes, I didn't learn not to identify with men. I had a horse and was kind of a tomboy, and I was glad of it. Although I was intensely attracted to men and males, I saw that as a part of being interested in them and watching their activities.

I finished writing *Ceremony* in 1977, when it was still not politically correct for a woman novelist to write from a man's point of view. Feminism in America was still so new that feminists wanted women to write of their own experiences, not those of men. Perhaps too, because my name is Leslie, which is kind of androgynous, they may not have realized that I was a woman author. For awhile I didn't hear anything from the feminists. I felt I was punished for using a male protagonist, but that was the only way I could write.

**Boos:** I'd like to ask you about some of your fellow contemporary women writers who have written novels about their own cultures –Michelle Cliff, Toni Morrison, and Maxine Hong Kingston among them. Are there contemporary women writers whose works you've read a great deal, or whose works you believe resemble yours in any way?

**Silko:** Of course Toni Morrison's work has been important to me, and that of Maxine Hong Kingston. Both women have encouraged me to believe that I'm on the right track, and that we share something—that it's not so lonely, for there are other women and other people thinking and writing about the same sorts of things.

**Boos:** It seemed to me that you portrayed discrimination profoundly from within, not preaching about it, but analyzing its different layers and guises. Might I ask you to comment on contemporary Native American political issues and conflicts?

**Silko:** I'll tell you what's happening in terms of history. The largest city in the world is Mexico City, and officials don't really know its population. The uncounted ones are the *Indios,* the Indian people. A huge, huge change is on the horizon, indeed it's already underway—and there's nothing you can do.

A couple months ago at sundown, a freight train came up from Nogales through Tucson, covered, crawling with human beings. People were sitting on top, people were hanging on the side—and so the great return to Aztlan which the Chicano people talk about is coming to pass in a big way. The Zapatista uprising on January 1st, 1994, was one of the most important signalings of what is to come. After that small demonstrations were held all over Mexico and the United States and Canada, showing the solidarity of Native American people throughout the Americas. We sense that the rising on January 1st was a sign of this awakening.

The most important thing right now which people must watch out for is jingoism and hysteria about immigrants and immigration. [The U.S. government] is building an iron curtain, a steel wall—Rudolfo Ortiz calls it the Tortilla Curtain—but it's ugly. They're trying to seal off Mexico from the United States. But [those they are sealing off] are Indians, Native-Americans, American Indians, original possessors of this continent, and [those who hate them] want to create a hysteria here so that it will justify U.S. troops opening fire and shooting and killing. The future could be a horrendous blood bath and upheaval not seen since the Civil War.

Right now the border patrol stops [Indian] people. I've been stopped three or four times, and have had dogs put on me.

**Boos:** Oh!?

**Silko:** This happened to me on my way from Albuquerque to Tucson. Many people in the rest of the United States don't understand that the U.S. government is destroying the civil rights of *all* citizens living near the border. Something terrible is developing, and it's being sold to the American people, or shoved down their throats through this hysteria over immigrants and the fear that their jobs will be taken. But I see a frightening collision on the horizon! I'll tell you something—the powers that be, those greedy corrupt white men like Rostenkowski and all those criminals in the United States Congress—their time is running out very soon! The forces from the south have spiritual power and legitimacy that'll blast those thieves and murderers right out of Washington, D.C.

**Boos:** Are there particular Native-American groups that you see working effectively against government wrongs?

**Silko:** Ah, ah, this change that's coming will not have leaders. People will wake up and know in their hearts that it's beginning. It's already happening across the United States. The change isn't just limited to Native Americans. It can come to Anglo-Americans, Chicanos, African-Americans as well. Every day people wake up to the inhumanity and violence this government perpetrates on its own citizens, and on citizens all over the world. That's why the change will not be stopped, for it will be a change of consciousness, a change of heart.

We don't need leaders. They can't stop [this revolution]. They can shoot some, they can kill some—like they have already—but this is a change that rises out of the earth's very being—a Hurricane Andrew, a Hurricane Hugo, an earthquake of consciousness. This earth itself is rebelling against what's been done to it in the name of greed and capitalism. No, there are no groups which bring change. They aren't needed. This change that's coming is much deeper and much larger. Think of it as a natural force—human beings massed into a natural force like a hurricane or a tidal wave. It will happen when the people come from the south, and when the people here [in the North and Midwest] understand.

One morning people will just wake up, and we'll all be different. That's why the greedy powerful white men will not be able to stop what happens, because there will be nothing to grab onto. There are no Martin Luther Kings to shoot, so the F.B.I. can give up on that!

There's no one that can stop us, because [the return of Aztlan] will be a change inside of *you!* It will happen without your knowing it. And this won't happen because someone preached at you, threatened you with prison, put a gun to your head. No, you'll wake up [yourself]. It will come to you through dreams!

**Boos:** No Martin Luther King will have helped bring about change, but what about Leslie Marmon Silko? How do you see yourself contributing to this movement?

**Silko:** Just by telling people—"Look, this is happening!" As I tried to make clear in *Almanac of the Dead,* you don't have to do anything, for the great change is already happening. But you maybe might want to be aware of what was coming, and you might want to think about the future choices that you might have to make. Though as I said, in your heart, you will already know.

**Boos:** Amen, and thank you.

*1997*

# Luisa Valenzuela:
# Interviewed by Marie-Lise Gazarian Gautier

**Interviewer:** Borges said that he worked with a few themes which he carried over from work to work. Do you find that each novel or short story that you write is a total break from the previous work, or is each new book a modified version of the same theme?

**Valenzuela:** I think it is both. The style, I feel, usually changes. I am always looking for different things to say and new ways of saying them. But there are small, or perhaps big obsessions, that come back again and again in a writer's work. One of my obsessions is with heresies, that very subtle point where any religion falls into heresy. Practically all living religions are heresies of the original dogma, and I find them marvelous because a human being should not be dogmatic at all. And there is also the theme of a search that comes back again and again in many of my works. I am still waiting to know what I am searching for.

**Interviewer:** Many of your characters are searching for identity. Will you explain why?

**Valenzuela:** The Argentines are searching for an identity. We have a very undefined identity, which is also part of our charm, in a way. Because we are half European and did not have a great Indian culture from our past to support us, we do not believe in the past so much. But I do not know whether we even believe in the present, that is the trouble. At the same time, we are very literary people.

**Interviewer:** Do you think of yourself as a novelist or a short-story writer?

**Valenzuela:** I think of myself as a writer. I don't like to put labels on things. I would just say that writing is a hard way of life. I don't like it too much. I do not think I like it too much.

**Interviewer:** Then why do you write?

**Valenzuela :** It is a necessity and it is a great joy when writing is going on very well. When you are really doing fine, writing is fabulous, but there is all this inner struggle, and the inner fight of knowing you are not writing enough, and you are not doing it well enough. So, sometimes short stories come to me and sometimes a novel grows on its own.

**Interviewer:** When you start writing do you know whether it will be a short story or a novel?

**Valenzuela:** Yes, although my first novel started out as a short story and turned into a novel, which surprised me very much. But now I know perfectly well what it is going to be at the outset, because the rhythm of a story is far different from that of a novel.

**Interviewer:** Could you describe your style, or is that difficult for you?

**Valenzuela:** My style changes, it is a search for my own voice. The trouble is that the search never ends because one's voice is always changing. Voice is everything, language is everything, so I think the only way we can express ourselves is through this voice. It can be exterior or interior, but what is really important for me is language. I usually play with it a lot and mostly let it play with me.

**Interviewer:** You have said that your novels are "an active dialogue with the reader." Do you think of the reader when you write?

**Valenzuela:** When writing, I think of myself as a reader. I enjoy it and surprise myself. I cannot write when I am not surprised, so I hope to do the same to the reader. I am always trying to present different possibilities and sufficient ambiguity in writing, so that the reader can add his own level of reading to the work.

**Interviewer:** Are your characters figments of your imagination or are they derived from your personal experiences?

**Valenzuela:** It is a cross between both. The experience might trigger an imaginative character. I seldom use myself as a character, although now I am trying to. But it is very hard because stories derived from my real life have no element of surprise for me. I am trying to be very much in touch with what we call reality, so I can allow it to grow on its own and not limit it to what I know for sure.

**Interviewer:** You have given seminars on the art of writing in many universities and also in Hispanic communities. Have you learned from your students?

**Valenzuela:** You always learn a lot. Borges used to say that parents learn from their children, and as he never had children he learned from Bioy Casares. I learn a lot from my students. I do not think you can teach anybody to be a good writer. That is not only a natural gift but also a great struggle in which you have to look and fight all the time. But you can teach people this act of freedom, which writing is all about. And you receive that freedom at the same time as you give it. More than anything else, I would tell young people to say everything, to be very courageous about it and not to censor themselves.

**Interviewer:** Could you discuss the importance of disguise, mask, and change of identity in your works?

**Valenzuela:** They are especially important in *Strange Things Happen Here.* I think that we are always using masks, we are never ourselves. You were laughing at me when I was trying to fix my hair before we started the interview, but that is my mask and I was trying to show a good face. The knowledge of our masks and the possibility of interrelating with others through these masks and disguises is very important. We are wearing them because we never have real access to our unconscious desire. The minute we become conscious of it, we lose it. So, the only way to reach certain strings of that desire is by wearing a mask.

**Interviewer:** Did you start writing because of your mother, Luisa Mercedes Levinson, who was an author in her own right?

**Valenzuela:** I started writing in spite of my mother's career. There were many writers who came to our home, so I wanted to be a painter or a mathematician or something completely different. One day, I decided it would be very easy to write a short story which could be as good as any written by my mother's friends. I then wrote my first story and everything started growing on its own.

**Interviewer:** Are you a feminist writer?

**Valenzuela:** I am against labels. I am a feminist in the sense that I am fighting for women to have all opportunities and freedom. What we women writers are looking for is a woman's language. We were never allowed to express ourselves in a very free way. So when women started writing they used an everyday pattern of speech which had been imposed on them by men. And I know there is a woman's language, which is very visceral and very strong, and not at all this nice, rhythmic sort of thing which men tried to make us believe is women's speech.

**Interviewer:** So you think women write differently from men?

**Valenzuela:** The difference is very subtle. It is not a different way of writing, it is a different approach to language. Language is sex, an idea which we never want to recognize.

**Interviewer:** What is women's place in Latin American literature today?

**Valenzuela:** Women's place is unfortunately the place society will allow us to have, for the time being. There are very fine women writers such as Clarice Lispector, who was an extraordinary writer and should have been part of the Boom. She belonged to the same generation as Cabrera Infante, so why was she not included in the Boom? Because she was a woman.

**Interviewer:** Can you explain how rebellion and freedom are vital parts of your works?

**Valenzuela:** I hope they are. Freedom is a search. We do not usually have it, but we are looking for it. We try to express it by showing our own inner freedom whenever we can. And the rebellion must be there constantly. If we forget to be rebels we are no longer writing, we are not being artists. If we repeat what has already been done or said, it is worthless.

**Interviewer:** Has censorship affected your writing?

**Valenzuela:** When I wrote *Strange Things Happen Here,* it was a moment of great violence in Argentina, and I was fighting to be able to say what was going on without being censored. That was a rather unconscious challenge, but it was there. So I managed to do something very positive for my style of writing, because that book became a metaphor for everything that was going on at the time. I was really playing my game then.

**Interviewer:** Why did you write *El gato eficaz,* which deals with death?

**Valenzuela:** Before I started writing that book I made a very serious statement. I said, "I never think about death, death does not worry me at all. It is something that is there, of course, but I believe I am immortal, I do not care about death." But then I wrote a whole book about it because I do care, as everyone does. Life and death are like a game, with the deadly things being sort of lifelike and the living things as if they were dead—not deadly, not dangerous, but sleepy.

**Interviewer:** You said in *He Who Searches,* "It is like nighttime, night is another country, a chest of mirrors, a nest of sparrows, night is the possibility of entering through the other door." Would you say that this quotation is symbolic of all your writing?

**Valenzuela:** It is symbolic of all writing in general. I had not thought about it, but now that you suggest it, "the possibility of entering through the other door" could be a definition of writing. I was thinking of night all the time I was writing that book. I had to write it at night, although I usually write during the day.

**Interviewer:** Carol Cook said, "There is something more to Valenzuela's art than just mastery. I think she may be divinely inspired." Are you religious? Do you believe in divine inspiration?

**Valenzuela:** I am religious in a very strange way, so I do not know very well whether this divine inspiration comes from above or below.

**Interviewer:** And what is below?

**Valenzuela:** Who knows? And what is above? I do not believe in inspiration at all. I believe in something much more reasonable: the unconscious mind of the writer and of everyone else. That conscious or unconscious possibility of writing is what I call inspiration.

**Interviewer:** Who are the writers who have influenced you the most?

**Valenzuela:** I think everyone has influenced me. Every writer influences all the others. Even the most horrible things I have read have influenced me. It would be a cliché to list the writers I care for most. However, I will mention Borges, Cortázar, and Bioy Casares. But I greatly enjoy other writers. I loved Carlos Fuentes's *Terra Nostra*. I started using it as a puzzle of time and space. We are all discoverers. That is why I also love the last of Carpentier's books, *El arpa y la sombra* (The Harp and the Shadow), which is the story of Christopher Columbus. He really did not discover a new world because he already knew there was a world there. Writers are like that. We feel as if we were discovering new lands, but we have in fact already heard of them from other writers. We are just making our humble explorations. Nevertheless, the trip can be full of risks, and we have to create our lies and our deceptions well so as to make the story worthwhile.

*1980*

# Part 3

# Appendixes

# Glossary of Literary Terms

**allegory** A narrative used to teach a moral, ethical, or religious lesson. In an allegory, characters and their situations not only tell the story but also represent abstract ideas that convey the message or lesson of the story.

**allusion** A reference to a literary or historical person, place, thing, or event that clarifies or adds depth and dimension to a character, plot point, or the story as a whole.

**analepsis** Also known as a "flashback." A narrative device in which the story's narrative line is interrupted by a glimpse of what has already happened in the story or to the character(s) in the past.

**analogy** A comparison in which the unfamiliar is explained in terms of the familiar. Similes and metaphors are types of analogies.

**antagonist** A major character in a narrative who functions as a counterpoint or challenge to the hero or protagonist.

**antihero** A character who lacks traditional heroic qualities such as courage, physical ability, and compassion. Antiheroes are often positioned as social outcasts and usually represent unconventional values or ideals.

**archetype** An original pattern or model from which all other things of similar kind are made. In literature, they appear as incidents, plots, or stereotyped characters that follow consistent patterns.

**audience** The people for whom a piece of literature is written.

**black humor** Writing that includes grotesque and humorous elements, thus forcing the reader to laugh at something normally thought to be horrific.

**climax** A turning point or moment of resolution, after which the action of the story subsides.

**colloquial style** A style that imitates casual or informal speech. Authors who want to convey regional or ethnic speech or dialect patterns sometimes use the colloquial style.

**conclusion** The ending of the story.

**conflict** The issue to be resolved in the story. The conflict of a story provides the obstacles the protagonist must conquer to reach his or her goal.

**convention** A literary device, style, or form established by repeated usage.

**deus ex machina** A Latin term meaning "god out of a machine." In Greek drama, a god was sometimes lowered onto the stage to rescue the hero or resolve the plot conflict. In literature, the term refers to any artificial device, coincidence, character, or action used to bring about a convenient and simple solution to a plot.

**diction** The selection and arrangement of words. There are four general types of

**diction:** *formal*, used in scholarly writing; *informal*, used in relaxed conversation; *colloquial*, used in everyday speech; and *slang*, words and other terms not accepted in formal usage.

**didactic** A work of literature is didactic if its aim is to teach a moral, religious, political, or practical lesson.

**dynamic character** A character who changes during the course of a story, usually as a result of the narrated events.

**empathy** The ability of the reader to experience the emotions of a character or to put himself or herself in the character's position.

**exposition** In literature, introductory material that informs readers about the characters and their situation before the action of the story begins.

**falling action** After the climax, various narrative threads are brought together to prepare the reader for the conclusion.

**figurative language** A technique in writing in which the author temporarily goes beyond literal meaning for a particular effect, often employing one or more figures of speech, such as hyperbole, irony, or simile.

**first-person narration** A story told by a single character who identifies himself or herself in the first person, or as "I."

**foreshadowing** A device used to hint at something to come later in the story.

**genre** A category of literary work, such as fiction, poetry, or drama.

**hyperbole** Deliberate exaggeration.

**image** A concrete representation of an object or sensory experience.

**intrusive narrator** A narrator who comments on the characters or plot of the story.

**irony** The use of language in which the literal meaning is the opposite of what is intended.

**limited third-person narration** A narrative perspective in which the narrator does not participate in the action and tells only the experiences of a single character.

**literal language** Writing that does not exaggerate or embellish the subject matter.

**magical realism** A Latin American style of narrative that contains both supernatural and realistic occurrences.

**metaphor** An implicit comparison between two seemingly different things.

**metonymy** A figure of speech in which the literal name of a thing is replaced by the name of another thing with which it is closely associated.

**mood** The prevailing feeling of a fictional work, which is not always based on the story's subject matter. Mood can be generated by language, setting, action, and characterization.

**narration** The telling of a series of events, real or invented.

**narrator** The teller of a story. The narrator may be the author or a character in the story through whom the author speaks.

**omniscient third-person narration** A narrative perspective in which the narrator does not participate in the action and is capable of relating what happens in all of the characters' minds.

**oxymoron** A phrase that combines two contradictory terms.

**parable** A story intended to teach a moral lesson or impart an ethical message.

**paradox** A statement that appears illogical, contradictory, or inconsistent with common sense but that might ultimately be true.

**parody** An often exaggerated imitation of a literary work or style of a particular author. A typical parody adopts the style of the original but applies it to an inappropriate subject for humorous effect.

**personification** A figure of speech that gives human qualities to abstract ideas, animals, or inanimate objects.

**prolepsis** Also known as a "flash forward." A narrative device in which the story's narrative line is interrupted by a glimpse of what will happen in the story or to the character(s) in the future.

**protagonist** The main character of a story who is the focus of the action and is central to the development of the story's plot.

**regional literature** Writing that emphasizes the dialect, customs, geography, and other features particular to a specific region.

**reliable narrator** A narrator trusted to tell a story objectively, without favoring particular characters or ideas.

**resolution** The point in a story at which the conflict is resolved.

**rising action** A deepening of complication and drama in the story.

**satire** A work of fiction that uses ridicule, humor, and wit to criticize and provoke change in people and institutions.

**simile** A comparison, usually using *like* or *as*.

**static character** A character who shows only one side, is not fully developed, and does not generally change throughout the story.

**stock character** A character with stereotypical traits who fills a conventional role in the story.

**stream of consciousness** A narrative technique that gives the reader the feeling of being inside a character's or narrator's mind and that expresses a constantly changing series of thoughts, emotions, images, and memories that mirror the spontaneity of the real world.

**style** A writer's unique manner of arranging words to correspond to his or her purpose or point in the story. Style includes the arrangement of narrative ideas through diction, sentence structure, rhythm, punctuation, and other formal elements of composition.

**subplot** The secondary story of a narrative. Subplots complicate, complement, or provide relief from the main plot.

**suspense** An author creates a mood of suspense or anticipation by writing that something will happen, without telling readers precisely what it is or when it will take place.

**symbol** A word, object, action, or event that suggests or stands for something more than its literal self.

**synecdoche** A metaphorical technique of naming a specific part when referring to the whole or using the whole to indicate a part.

**theme** The main point of a work of literature.

**tone** The author's attitude toward the narrative and its underlying themes. The tone not only affects the meaning of the written work but also has an impact on the audience's reception of the work.

**unintrusive narrator** A narrator who relates a story without comment or judgment.

**unity** The shape and consistency of a story. Unity of action in a story means that all events are linked purposefully together with each being essential to the others and to the resolution of the plot.

**Zeitgeist** A German term meaning "spirit of the time." It refers to the moral and intellectual trends of a given era.

# MLA
# Documentation

As you write about short fiction, you will often need to quote from or refer to ideas in short stories, books, critical essays, interviews, or Internet sources. Writers commonly use several different systems to cite sources in a clear and consistent way. Psychology professors might require APA style, the preferred system of documentation published by the American Psychological Association, whereas in the social sciences, your professors might ask you to use *The Chicago Manual of Style*. Each of these documentation styles differs from others to suit the needs of specific disciplines. In most of your literature and humanities courses, you will be asked to use MLA documentation, guidelines published by the Modern Language Association. It is important to follow these guidelines carefully for two reasons:

1.  Writing is an act of creativity and work, and authors deserve credit for their ideas and words. Neglecting to properly cite sources means failing to give credit to the writer for his or her work. Failing to clearly distinguish the ideas of other writers also makes it difficult for your reader to recognize your own unique words and ideas.
2.  Many readers will become interested in new topics or ideas by reading your paper. They might want to read more on the subject, and they will want to know how to find your sources. It is important for you to include all of the information necessary for your readers to locate the sources that they would like to investigate more fully.

## THE BASICS

Below you will find specific examples of how to cite material from various sources. The most important information for you to know, however, is that each source must be cited both within the text of your paper and on a Works Cited page at the end of your essay. In the text of your paper, it is necessary to include the name of the author and the page number of the relevant words or ideas. On your Works Cited page, you will include more detailed information, such as the title of the work, publisher, and year of publication.

## TAKING NOTES

Particularly if you are using sources outside your textbook, it is crucial to take careful notes so that you can avoid unintentional plagiarism and save valuable writing time. If you take notes as you read, be sure to place quotation marks around any words that you copy from the text. At the top of your page or note card, write down the author, title, publisher, and date of your source. Next to each note, whether a quotation, summary, or paraphrase, record the corresponding page number. Although you will need to be more organized and careful as you read, following these steps will save valuable time as you write. Nothing is more frustrating for a writer than including an important quotation and having to go back to the library or through a stack of books to find the citation information.

## QUOTATION MARKS OR ITALICS?

Use quotation marks around the titles of short stories, poems, newspaper articles, and essays. Use italics for books, films, plays, and newspapers.

## PARENTHETICAL CITATION

When you provide a quotation or paraphrase within your paper, include the author's name and page number in your text. The standard guideline is to include the author's name and page number in parentheses after the quote, like this:

(Hemingway 164)

Notice that there is no comma between the author's last name and the page number. If, however, you mention the name of the author in your sentence, you may include only the page number in parentheses, like this:

(164)

The positioning of parentheses in your sentence will depend on the length of your quotation. If your quotation is less than four lines in length, include the parenthetical reference as a part of your own sentence:

"Hills like White Elephants" begins with an image of blankness: "The hills across the valley of the Ebro were long and white" (Hemingway 164).

Notice that there is no period within the quotation marks. Instead, the period appears after the parenthetical reference. If your quotation exceeds four lines, use block format to set the quotation off from the rest of the text, like this:

"Hills like White Elephants" begins with an image of blankness and vulnerability characterized by exposure to the sun, to flies, and to scrutiny:

> The hills across the valley of the Ebro were long and white. On this side
> there was no shade and no trees and the station was between two lines
> of rails in the sun. Close against the side of the station there was the
> warm shadow of the building and a curtain, made of strings of bam-
> boo beads, hung across the open door into the bar, to keep out the flies.
> (Hemingway 164)

Note the differences between the previous example and the parenthetical citation in block format. The passage is indented 10 spaces (or 2 tabs) from the left margin of the essay. Because the indentation signals that this is a quotation, no quotation marks are necessary. In addition, the period appears at the end of the quotation and not after the parenthetical citation. Your instructor will likely ask you to double-space your paper, and the block quotation should be double-spaced as well unless your instructor tells you otherwise.

## How to Alter Quotations

It is possible, and often advisable, to omit unnecessary words from long quotations or to change the tense or subject position of a quote in order to integrate it into your own sentence. It is important, though, not to alter the meaning of the quotation. Change words only when necessary and when the changes do not modify content. Indicate altered words by enclosing them in square brackets. In the following quotation, "hung" has been changed to "hangs" to suit the tense of the author's sentence:

> In "Hills like White Elephants," a thin veil of beads "[hangs] across the open
> door into the bar, to keep out the flies" (Hemingway 164).

Indicate omitted words with an ellipsis enclosed in brackets. The brackets let the reader know that the ellipsis is not in the original text. For example, in the following quotation, the author omits part of a sentence:

> "Hills like White Elephants" begins with an image of blankness and vulnera-
> bility characterized by exposure to the sun, to flies, and to scrutiny:

> > The hills across the valley of the Ebro were long and white. On this side
> > there was no shade and no trees and the station was between two lines of
> > rails in the sun. Close against the side of the station [. . .] a curtain, made
> > of strings of bamboo beads, hung across the open door into the bar, to
> > keep out the flies. (Hemingway 164)

## Works Cited Page

Whether you reference just one work or many, you should include a Works Cited page that provides important details about your sources. Your instructor may request a

Works Cited page or a bibliography. A bibliography is formatted the same way as a Works Cited page, but it includes all of the books and articles you read for the project, not just the ones cited in your paper. Your citation page should be a separate page at the end of your document. Center the title at the top of the page, like this:

Works Cited

Notice that this title is not underlined and does not appear in any special font. Your next step is to list each of the sources used in your essay. Double-space the entire document and follow the format below for each type of source. In each entry, all lines after the first should be indented.

## Book

Kincaid, Jamaica. *At the Bottom of the River*. New York: Penguin Books, 1992.

## Story or Essay in an Anthology

Achebe, Chinua. "Dead Men's Path." *Fiction: A Pocket Anthology*. Ed. R. S. Gwynn. New York: Longman, 2002. 267–70.

## Article in a Periodical

Joseph, Philip. "The Verdict from the Porch: Zora Neale Hurston and Reparative Justice." *American Literature* 25 (2002): 455–83.

## Article in a Newspaper

Hendawi, Hamza. "U.N. Tackles Issue of Iraqi Election: Factions Disagree on Force of Its Findings." *New York Times* 8 February 2004: A9.

If the article continues on another page of the newspaper, include the first page of the article followed by a plus sign.

Hendawi, Hamza. "U.N. Tackles Issue of Iraqi Election: Factions Disagree on Force of Its Findings." *New York Times* 8 February 2004: A9+.

## Film

*The Swimmer*. Dir. Sydney Pollack and Frank Perry. Perf. Burt Lancaster. Columbia/Tristar, 1968.

## Online Article

Johnson, Marie. "Chekhov's Life in Letters." Online posting. 8 May 2001. Accessed 12 February 2004 <http://www.chekhov.com/Johnson>.

# FORMATTING YOUR DOCUMENT

Your instructor will likely provide guidelines on how to format your essay. If you do not receive formatting instructions, consult the checklist below for the most common rules:

- In the upper left corner of your essay, include your name, your instructor's name, the title of the class, the title of the assignment, and the date.

- Center your title above the text of your essay. Do not underline your title, and do not use any special color or font.

- Use a readable 12-point font and include 1-inch margins.

- Double-space your essay (including block quotations) and indent the first sentence of each paragraph.

- Number your pages.

## A NOTE ON PLAGIARISM

Most students know about the most egregious forms of intentional plagiarism, such as turning in an essay written by another student or copying or purchasing a paper from the Internet. Students often turn to this type of plagiarism out of desperation, lack of time, and anxiety. Take steps to eliminate this kind of anxiety by beginning your assignments early and by talking to your instructor about your writing process. Most instructors are very willing to help you overcome writing blocks and to give you suggestions about how to begin writing. It is always better to discuss your difficulties with your instructor than to risk the increasingly severe penalties for plagiarism. Software is now available to faculty members that can detect any text copied from an Internet source, and the penalties for plagiarism can range from a failed assignment to expulsion from the college. Make sure you know the academic honesty policy at your institution and seek help from your instructor, writing center, and advisor to reduce writing-related anxiety.

Unintentional plagiarism is a lesser known form of plagiarism that happens when students do not know the rules of documenting sources or take notes haphazardly. The penalties for unintentional plagiarism can be as severe as those for intentional plagiarism, so avoid this danger by adhering to the following rules:

1. Provide citation information for summaries and paraphrases as well as direct quotations. It is not enough to change a few words in a sentence to make it your own. If you repeat an idea from one of your sources, you must give credit even if you don't use the author's exact words.
2. Never copy words into your notebook without placing quotation marks around them. When you begin writing your paper, you might forget that a note was a direct quote rather than your own response.
3. Use quotation marks around unique phrases used by your source as well as around entire sentences.
4. You must provide a citation for any information not known by the general population or that could not be easily found in a dictionary or encyclopedia.
5. Emphasize the distinction between your source's ideas and your own by quoting

your source and then explaining your response to the quote. Do you agree with your source, disagree, or agree in part? How does the quotation relate to or support your own unique argument in the essay?

6. If you're not sure whether or not to cite a source, cite it. It is better to cite sources too often than to leave sources undocumented.

# Film Bibliography

## Films Based on Short Stories

*Almos' a Man.* Adaptation of Richard Wright's "The Man Who Was Almost a Man." Dir. Stan Lathan. Perf. Christopher Brooks, LeVar Burton, Robert DoQui, Henry Fonda, Gary Goodrow, and Madge Sinclair. Monterey Home Video, 1976. 39 min.

*Bartleby.* Adaptation of Herman Melville's "Bartleby, the Scrivener." Dir. Jonathan Parker. Perf. Crispin Glover, David Paymen, and Glenne Heady. Outrider Pictures, 2002. 82 min.

*Bartleby.* Adaptation of Herman Melville's "Bartleby, the Scrivener." Dir. Anthony Friedman. White Star, 1970.

*Big Blonde.* Dir. Kirk Browning. Perf. Sally Kellerman and John Lithgow. Kultur, 1980.

*Cora Unashamed.* Dir. Deborah Pratt. Perf. Regina Taylor and Cherry Jones. Warner Home Video, 2000.

*Daisy Miller.* Dir. Peter Bogdanovich. Perf. Cybill Shepherd and Barry Brown. Paramount Studios, 1974.

*The Dead.* Dir. John Huston. Perf. Anjelica Huston and Donal McCann. Vestron, 1987.

*Face to Face.* Includes an adaptation of "The Bride Comes to Yellow Sky." Dir. John Brahm and Bretaigne Windust. Perf. Robert Preston, Marjorie Steele, and Minor Watson. 1952.

*Faerie Tale Theatre: Rip Van Winkle.* Dir. Francis Ford Coppola. Perf. Harry Dean Stanton and Talia Shire. Hallmark Entertainment, 1984. 48 min.

*Good Country People.* Dir. Jeff Jackson. Perf. Johnnie Collins III, Shirley Slater, June Whitley Taylor, and Sue Marrow. 1997. 32 min.

*Guests of the Nation.* Perf. Estelle Parsons and Frank Converse. Kultur, 1981. 60 min.

*Kaos.* Includes an adaptation of Luigi Pirandello's "The Jar." Dir. Paolo and Vittorio Taviani. Perf. Margarita Lozano, Claudio Bigagli, Omero Antonutti, Franco Franchi, and Ciccio Ingrassia. 1984. 188 min.

*The Lady with the Dog.* Dir. Iosif Khejfits. White Star Studio, 1990.

*My Son the Fanatic.* Dir. Udayan Prasad. Perf. Om Puri and Rachel Griffiths. 1997. 87 min.

*The Notorious Jumping Frog of Calaveras County.* Anchor Bay Entertainment, 1999.

*The Notorious Jumping Frog of Calaveras County.* Dir. Robert Chenault. Perf. Billy Jayne, Steven Spencer, and Mara Alexander. 1981. 23 min.

*An Occurrence at Owl Creek Bridge.* Dir. Robert Enrico. Perf. Roger Jacquet, Anne Comaly, and Anker Larson. 1962. 28 min.

*An Occurrence at Owl Creek Bridge.* Dir. Brian James Egen. Perf. Bradley M. Egen and Aaron Jackson. Owl Creek Productions, 2003.

*The Overcoat.* Dir. Aleksei Batalov. Perf. Rolan Bykov and Yuri Tolubeyev. Hen's Tooth Video, 1959. 75 min.

*Paul's Case.* Dir. Lamont Johnson. Perf. Eric Roberts and Michael Higgins. Monterey Home Video, 1980. 55 min.

*Rappaccini's Daughter.* Dir. Dezso Magyar. Perf. Kristoffer Tabori and Kathleen Beller. Monterey Home Video, 1980. 55 min.

*The Revolt of Mother.* Dir. Victor Lobol. Perf. Amy Madigan and Jay O. Sanders. Monterey Home Video, 1986. 47 min.

*Rip Van Winkle.* Dir. Will Vinton. Fast Forward Marketing, 1978.

*The Rocking-Horse Winner.* Dir. Anthony Pelissier. Perf. Valerie Hobson and John Howard Davies. Home Vision Entertainment, 1950. 91 min.

*The Rocking-Horse Winner.* Dir. Michael Almereyda. Perf. Paula Malcomson and Eric Stoltz. 1997. 23 min.

*The Rocking-Horse Winner.* Dir. Robert Biernam. Perf. Eleanor David, Charles Keating, and Charles Hawthorne. 1983. 33 min.

*A Rose for Emily.* Dir. Lyndon Chubbuck. Perf. Anjelica Huston. Pyramid Home Video, 1982. 27 min.

*The Royal Scandal.* Adaptation of Arthur Conan Doyle's "A Scandal in Bohemia." Dir. Rodney Gibbons. Perf. Matt Frewer and Kenneth Welsh. 2001. 120 min.

*A Scandal in Bohemia.* Dir. David Carson and Derek Marlowe. Mpi Home Video, 1985.

*A Scandal in Bohemia.* Dir. Maurice Elvey. Perf. Eille Norwood and Hubert Willis. 1921.

*Short Cuts.* Based on the stories of Raymond Carver. Dir. Robert Altman. Perf. Andie MacDowell and Julianne Moore. New Line Studios Video, 1996.

*The Swimmer.* Dir. Sydney Pollack and Frank Perry. Perf. Burt Lancaster. Columbia/Tristar Studios, 1968.

*To Build a Fire.* Dir. Luca Armenia. Perf. Olivier Pages. 2003. 20 min.

*To Build a Fire.* With Ian Hogg and Orson Welles. Vci Home Video, 1969.

*A Very Old Man with Enormous Wings.* Dir. Fernando Birri. Perf. Marcia Barreto, Fernando Birri, and Daisy Asrubal Melendez. Fox Lorber Studio, 1988.

*The Yellow Wallpaper.* Dir. John Clive. Perf. Stephen Dillane, Julia Watson, Carolyn Pickles, and James Faulkner. 1989.

## Essays and Books about Film Adaptations of Short Stories

Archer, Jane Elizabeth. "'This Is My Place': The Short Films Made from Flannery O'Connor's Short Fiction." *Studies in American Humor* 1.1 (1982): 52–65.

Bailey, Ted. "From Fiction to Film: Two Versions of Ambrose Bierce's 'An Occurrence at Owl Creek Bridge.'" *BAS: British and American Studies* 7 (2001): 166–73.

Barolsky, Paul. "Joyce's Distant Music." *Virginia Quarterly Review: A National Journal of Literature and Discussion* 65.1 (1989): 111–18.

Barrett, Gerald R., and Thomas L. Erskine. *From Fiction to Film: "The Rocking Horse Winner."* Encino: Dickenson, 1974.

Becker, Henry III. "'The Rocking Horse Winner': Film as Parable." *Literature/Film Quarterly* 1 (1973): 55–63.

Birdsall, Eric. "Interpreting Henry James: Bogdanovich's *Daisy Miller.*" *Literature/Film Quarterly* 22.4 (1994): 272–77.

Bluestone, George. "Bartleby: The Tale, the Film." *A Symposium: Bartleby the Scrivener.* Ed. Howard P. Vincent. Kent: Kent State UP, 1966.

Carson, John F. "John Huston's *The Dead*: An Irish Encomium." *Proteus: A Journal of Ideas* 7.2 (1990): 26–29.

Cremona, Laetitia. "The City of Dublin and Its Symbols." Dubliners, *James Joyce;* The Dead, *John Huston.* Ed. Pascal Bataillard and Dominique Sipiere. Paris: Ellipses, 2000. 158–63.

Cross, David. "Framing the 'Sketch': Bogdanovich's *Daisy Miller.*" *Henry James on Stage and Screen.* Ed. John R. Bradley. New York: Palgrave, 2000. 127–42.

de Cacquery, Elizabeth, and Raphaelle Costa de Beauregard. "Polyphony in *The Dead* by John Huston." *Dubliners, James Joyce; The Dead, John Huston.* Ed. Pascal Bataillard and Dominique Sipiere. Paris: Ellipses, 2000. 183–200.

Demory, Pamela H. "Violence and Transcendence in Pulp Fiction and Flannery O'Connor." *The Image of Violence in Literature, the Media, and Society.* Ed. Will Wright and Steven Kaplan. Pueblo: Society for the Interdisciplinary Study of Social Imagery, U of Colorado, 1995.

Edwards, Paul C. "Transforming Cheever: Three Failures in Reimagination." *Literature in Performance: A Journal of Literary and Performing Art* 5.2 (1985): 14–26.

Frizler, Paul. "John Huston's Film of James Joyce's 'The Dead.'" *Proteus: A Journal of Ideas* 7.2 (1990): 22–25.

Fultz, James R. "High Jinks at Yellow Sky: James Agee and Stephen Crane." *Literature/Film Quarterly* 11.1 (1983): 46–54.

Geduld, Harry M. "Literature into Film: 'An Occurrence at Owl Creek Bridge.'" *Yearbook of Comparative and General Literature* 27 (1978): 56–58.

Gentry, Ric. "Coppola's Faerie Tale Theatre." *Post-Script: Essays in Film and the Humanities* 8.1 (1988): 43–63.

Gibbons, Luke. "'The Cracked Looking Glass' of Cinema: James Joyce, John Huston, and the Memory of 'The Dead.'" *Yale Journal of Criticism: Interpretation in the Humanities* 15.1 (2002): 127–48.

Goebel, Robert O. "Film Versions of Hawthorne's 'Rappaccini's Daughter.'" *West Virginia Philological Papers* 47 (2001): 63–68.

Hanne, Michael. "New Wine in a Very Old Jar: Adaptations of a Pirandello Story from Agrigento to Kakheti." *Journal of the Society for Pirandello Studies* 21 (2001): 66–99.

Howes, Marjorie. "Tradition, Gender, and Migration in 'The Dead,' or: How Many People Has Gretta Conroy Killed?" *Yale Journal of Criticism: Interpretation in the Humanities* 15.1 (2002): 149–71.

Huang, Guiyou. "The Use of Audiovisual Material as an Aid in Teaching 'The Yellow Wallpaper.'" *Approaches to Teaching Gilman's "The Yellow Wall-Paper" and Herland.* Ed. Denise D. Knight and Cynthia J. Davis. New York: Modern Language Association of America, 2003. 67–74.

Hughes, Rebecca, and Kieron O'Hara. "Filmmaker as Critic: Huston's *Under the Volcano* and *The Dead.*" *Joyce/Lowry: Critical Perspectives.* Ed. Patrick A. McCarthy and Paul Tiessen. Lexington: UP of Kentucky, 1997. 177–96.

Johnson, Stephen. "Evaluating Early Film as a Document of Theatre History: The 1896 Footage of Joseph Jefferson's *Rip Van Winkle.*" *Nineteenth-Century Theater* 20.2 (1992): 101–22.

Liggera, J. J. "'She Would Have Appreciated One's Esteem': Peter Bogdanovich's *Daisy Miller.*" *Literature/Film Quarterly* 9.1 (1981): 15–21.

Marcus, Fred H. "Film and Fiction: 'An Occurrence at Owl Creek Bridge.'" *California English Journal* 7 (1971): 14–23.

Moore, Gene M. "A Film for Emily." *Faulkner Journal* 16.1–2 (2001–2002): 87–94.

Oates, Joyce Carol. "'Where Are You Going, Where Have You Been?' and 'Smooth Talk': Short Story into Film." *New York Times* 23 March 1986.

O'Shea, Michael J. "'Raiders and Cinemen Too': Joyce and Video." *James Joyce Literary Supplement* 4.1 (1990): 21–23.

Palmer, James W. "From Owl Creek to La Riviere du Hibou: The Film Adaptation of Bierce's 'An Occurrence at Owl Creek Bridge.'" *Southern Humanities Review* 11 (1977): 363–71.

Paquet, Dyris. "Experiences of Epiphany: John Huston's *The Dead.*" *Dubliners, James Joyce; The Dead, John Huston.* Ed. Pascal Bataillard and Dominique Sipiere. Paris: Ellipses, 2000. 201–8.

Pederson, Ann. "Uncovering the Dead: A Study of Adaptation." *Literature/Film Quarterly* 21.1 (1993): 69–70.

Philipp, Frank. "Narrative Devices and Aesthetic Perception in Joyce and Huston's *The Dead.*" *Literature/Film Quarterly* 21.1 (1993): 61–68.

Shields, John C. "*Daisy Miller:* Bogdanovich's Film and James's Nouvelle." *Literature/Film Quarterly* 11.2 (1983): 105–11.

Shout, John D. "Joyce at Twenty-Five, Huston at Eighty-One: *The Dead.*" *Literature/Film Quarterly* 17.2 (1989): 91–94.

Siemens, Elena. "A Tempest in a Tea Cup: Mikalkov's 'Dark Eyes' and Chekhov's 'The Lady with the Dog.'" *Chekhov Then and Now: The Reception of Chekhov in World Culture.* Ed. J. Douglas Clayton. New York: Peter Lang, 1997. 259–67.

Silverman, Kaja. "Splits: Changing the Fantasmatic Scene." *Revista de Estudios Hispanicos* 22.3 (1988): 65–86.

Skaggs, Merrill. "Submission and Fidelity, Assertion and Surprise: Two 'Southern Women' Films." *The Southern Quarterly: A Journal of the Arts in the South* 24.3 (1986): 5–13.

Stocking, Fred, and Leslie Lee. "On Richard Wright and 'Almos' a Man.'" *The American Short Story.* Ed. Calvin Skaggs and Robert Geller. New York: Dell, 1977. 275–81.

Ulrich, Ursula. "'An Occurrence at Owl Creek Bridge': The Short Story and Its Cinema Adaptation." *Proceedings of the International Comparative Literature Association.* Ed. Eva Kushner, Roman Struc, and Milan V. Dimac. Stuttgart: Bieber, 1979.

Walz, Lawrence. "Mary Henry's Journey from Owl Creek Bridge." *Literature/Film Quarterly* 23.4 (1995): 262–65.

Wheatley-Lovoy, Cynthia D. "Mirrors, Echoes, and Music: Narcissus and Nietzsche in James Joyce's 'A Painful Case' and 'The Dead.'" *Authority and Transgression in Literature and Film.* Ed. Bonnie Braendlin and Hans Braendlin. Gainsville: UP of Florida, 1996. 177–96.

Young, Jane Jaffe. *D. H. Lawrence on Screen: Re-Visioning Prose Style in the Films of "The Rocking-Horse Winner,"* Sons and Lovers, *and* Women in Love. New York: Peter Lang, 1999.

# Chronological Contents

# Thematic Contents

## Gender

## Culture and Violence

## War

# Credits

**Text Credits**

Abel, Elizabeth, "Black Writing, White Reading: Race and the Politics of Feminist Interpretation," *Critical Inquiry* 19 (Spring 1993). Copyright © 1993 by The University of Chicago Press. This is an excerpt from the fully annotated longer essay.

Achebe, Chinua, "Dead Men's Path" from *Girls at War and Other Stories* by Chinua Achebe. Copyright © 1972, 1973 by Chinua Achebe. Used by permission of Doubleday, a division of Random House, Inc. "The Novelist as Teacher" from *Morning Yet on Creation Day* by Chinua Achebe. Copyright © 1975 by Chinua Achebe. Used by permission of Doubleday, a division of Random House, Inc.

Allende, Isabel, "And of Clay Are We Created" is reprinted with the permission of Scribner, an imprint of Simon & Schuster Adult Publishing Group, from *The Stories of Eva Luna* by Isabel Allende, translated from the Spanish by Margaret Sayers Peden. Copyright © 1989 by Isabel Allende. English translation copyright © 1991 by Macmillan Publishing Company. "An Interview with Isabel Allende by Farhat Iftekharuddin" from *Speaking of the Short Story: Interviews with Contemporary Writers* edited by Farhat Iftekharuddin, Mary Rohrberger, and Maurice Lee. Copyright 1997 by University Press of Mississippi. Reprinted with permission of University Press of Mississippi.

Atwood, Margaret, "Happy Endings" from *Good Bones and Simple Murders* by Margaret Atwood, copyright © 1983, 1992, 1994, by O. W. Toad, Ltd. A Nan A. Talese Book. Used by permission of Doubleday, a division of Random House, Inc. "Reading Blind" by Margaret Atwood, © 1989, O. W. Toad, Ltd. First appeared in the collection *Best American Short Stories 1989*, published in the United States by Houghton Mifflin.

Baldwin, James, "Sonny's Blues" copyright © 1957 by James Baldwin was originally published in *Partisan Review*. Copyright renewed. Collected in *Going to Meet the Man*, published by Vintage Books. Reprinted by arrangement with the James Baldwin Estate.

Bambara, Toni Cade, "The Lesson" copyright © 1972 by Toni Cade Bambara from *Gorilla, My Love* by Toni Cade Bambara. Used by permission of Random House, Inc.

Bauer, Dale M., "Edith Wharton's 'Roman Fever': A Rune of History," *College English*, Vol. 50, no. 6 (Oct., 1988), 681–693. Copyright 1988 by the National Council of Teachers of English. Reprinted with permission.

Bazan, Emilia Pardo, "The Heart Lover," translated by Edward and Elizabeth Huberman, from *Great Spanish Short Stories* edited by Angel Flores (New York: Dell, 1962). Copyright © 1962 and renewed 1990 by Dell Publishing. Reprinted with the permission of the Estate of Angel Flores, c/o The Permissions Company, Mount Pocono, Pennsylvania.

Bontemps, Arna, "A Summer Tragedy." Reprinted by permission of Harold Ober Associates Incorporated. First published in *Opportunity*. Copyright 1933 by Arna Bontemps.

**Kafka, Franz,** "A Hunger Artist" from *Franz Kafka: The Complete Stories* by Franz Kafka, edited by Nahum N. Glatzer, translated by Willa and Edwin Muir. Copyright 1946, 1947, 1948, 1949, 1954, 1958, 1971 by Schocken Books. Used by permission of Schocken Books, a division of Random House, Inc.

**Khue, Le Minh,** "The Distant Stars" from *The Stars, the Earth, the River* by Le Minh Khue, translated by Bac Hoai Tran and Dana Sachs (Curbstone Press, 1997). Reprinted with permission of Curbstone Press. Distributed by Consortium.

**Kincaid, Jamaica,** "Wingless" from *At the Bottom of the River* by Jamaica Kincaid. Copyright © 1983 by Jamaica Kincaid. Reprinted by permission of Farrar, Straus and Giroux, LLC.

**Kinney, Katherine,** from *Friendly Fire: American Images of the Vietnam War* by Katherine Kinney, pp. 150–156. Copyright © 2000 by Oxford University Press, Inc. Used by permission of Oxford University Press, Inc.

**Kuperman, David,** "Dying: The Shape of Victory in 'A Summer Tragedy'" from *Melus*, vol. 5, no. 1, *Critical Approaches to Ethnic Literature* (Spring 1978), 66–68. Reprinted with permission.

**Kureishi, Hanif,** "My Son the Fanatic" is reprinted with the permission of Scribner, an imprint of Simon & Schuster Adult Publishing Group, from *Love in a Blue Time* by Hanif Kureishi. Copyright © 1997 by Hanif Kureishi.

**Lahiri, Jhumpa,** "A Temporary Matter" from *The Interpreter of Maladies* by Jhumpa Lahiri. Copyright © 1999 by Jhumpa Lahiri. Reprinted by permission of Houghton Mifflin Company. All rights reserved. "The Author of *Interpreter of Maladies* Interprets Herself" from *Newsweek*, September 20, 1999. Copyright © 1999 Newsweek, Inc. All rights reserved. Reprinted by permission.

**Lawrence, D. H.,** "The Rocking-Horse Winner" from *Complete Short Stories of D. H. Lawrence* by D. H. Lawrence. Copyright 1933 by the Estate of D. H. Lawrence, renewed © 1961 by Angelo Ravagli and C. M. Weekley, executors of the Estate of Frieda Lawrence. Used by permission of Viking Penguin, a division of Penguin Group (USA) Inc.

**Leavitt, David,** "Houses" from *A Place I've Never Been.* Copyright © 2003 by David Leavitt, reprinted with the permission of the Wylie Agency Inc.

**Le Guin, Ursula K.,** "The Ones Who Walk Away from Omelas." Copyright © 1973, 2001 by Ursula K. Le Guin; first appeared in *The Wind's Twelve Quarters.* Reprinted by permission of the author and the author's agents, the Virginia Kidd Agency, Inc.

**Lessing, Doris,** "To Room Nineteen" from *A Man and Two Women.* Copyright © 1963 by Doris Lessing. Reprinted by kind permission of Jonathan Clowes Ltd., London, on behalf of Doris Lessing.

**Lispector, Clarice,** "The Smallest Woman in the World" from *Family Ties* by Clarice Lispector, translated by Giovanni Pontiero. Copyright © 1972. By permission of the University of Texas Press.

**Malamud, Bernard,** "The Magic Barrel" from *The Magic Barrel* by Bernard Malamud. Copyright © 1950, 1958, renewed 1977, 1986 by Bernard Malamud. Reprinted by permission of Farrar, Straus and Giroux, LLC.

**Márquez, Gabriel García,** "I Only Came to Use the Phone" from *Strange Pilgrims: Twelve Stories* by Gabriel García Márquez, translated by Edith Grossman. Copyright © 1993 by Gabriel García Márquez. Used by permission of Alfred A. Knopf, a division of Random House, Inc. All pages from "A Very Old Man with Enormous Wings" from *Leaf Storm and*

## Photo Credits

### Precursors to the Short Story

*Page 14:* 1, Frontispiece depicting the Creation, "Genesis," from the Luther Bible, 1st edition, 1534. Colored woodcut. Private Collection. Art Resource, NY.

2, Hellenistic Bust of Plato, Sala delle Muse. Museo Pio Clementino, Vatican Museum, Vatican State. Scala / Art Resource, NY.

3, © Bettmann/CORBIS.

4, Letter written on a snowy day, 4th century CE. Chinese calligraphy, Sixteen Kingdoms period, 321–379. National Palace Museum, Taipei, Taiwan. Lee & Lee Communications / Art Resource, NY.

5, The Mausoleum at Halicarnassus (Reconstruction after Adler), 353 BCE (one of the Seven Wonders of the World). Foto Marburg / Art Resource, NY.

6, Han Kan (8th century), *Painting of Two Horses and a Groom.* Tang dynasty. National Palace Museum, Taipei, Taiwan. Werner Forman / Art Resource, NY.

*Page 15:* 7, © Archivo Iconografico, S.A./CORBIS.

8, Chacomy white ware pitcher decorated with a spiral design, ca. 1100 CE. Mogollon/Anasazi Culture (U.S. A. H.: 20 cm). Maxwell Museum of Anthropology, Albuquerque, New Mexico, U.S.A. Werner Forman / Art Resource, NY.

9, © Bettmann/CORBIS.

10, Bath scene in the courtyard of a castle, 15th century CE. Roman des Chevaliers Galaad, Tristan and Lancelot (Ms. 48/404, fol. 415v). France, 1400–50. Musée Condé, Chantilly, France. Bridgeman-Giraudon / Art Resource, NY.

11, Anna Maria Elizabeth Jerichau-Baumann (1819–1881), *Jacob and Wilhelm Grimm,* 1855. Oil on canvas, 63 x 54 cm. Inv. NG 757. Andreas Kilger. Nationalgalerie, Staatliche Museen zu Berlin, Berlin, Germany. Bildarchiv Preussischer Kulturbesitz / Art Resource, NY.

12, © AINACO/CORBIS.

### The Nineteenth-Century Short Story: 1800 to 1899

*Page 52:* 1, © Bettmann/CORBIS.

2, © Bettmann/CORBIS.

3, © CORBIS.

4, Francisco de Goya y Lucientes (1746–1828), *The Clothed Maja,* c. 1800. Oil on canvas, 95 x 190 cm. Museo del Prado, Madrid, Spain. Erich Lessing / Art Resource, NY.

5, © Bettmann/CORBIS.

6, George Catlin (1796–1872), *Six, Chief of the Plains Ojibwa,* 1832. Oil on canvas, 29 x 24 in. Smithsonian American Art Museum, Washington, DC, U.S.A. Smithsonian American Art Museum, Washington, DC / Art Resource, NY.

*Page 53:* 7, © CORBIS.

8, © Bettmann/CORBIS.

9, Ilya Repin (1844–1930), *The Boatmen of the Volga,* 1873. Oil on canvas, 131.5 x 381 cm. Russian State Museum, St. Petersburg, Russia. Scala / Art Resource, NY.

10, © Bettmann/CORBIS.

11, © Bettmann/CORBIS.

12, © Bettmann/CORBIS.

## Nineteenth-Century Cluster: Domestic Fictions

## The Modern Short Story: 1900 to 1969

12, © Bettmann/CORBIS.

*Page 468:* 13, Georgia O'Keeffe (1887–1986), *Jimson Weed,* 1932. Oil on canvas. 48 x 40".
1996.01.01. Gift of The Burnett Foundation, The Georgia O'Keeffe Museum, Santa Fe,
New Mexico, U.S.A. Copyright © 2005 The Georgia O'Keeffe Foundation / Artists Rights
Society (ARS), New York. Malcolm Varon 2001 / Art Resource, NY.

14, © CORBIS.

15, © Getty Images.

16, © Bettmann/CORBIS.

17, © Sophie Bassouls/CORBIS SYGMA.

18, © CORBIS.

*Page 469:* 19, Frida Kahlo (1907–1954), *Self-Portrait with Cropped Hair,* 1940. Oil on canvas,
15 3/4 x 11". Gift of Edgar Kaufmann, Jr. (00003.1943), The Museum of Modern Art, New
York, NY, U.S.A. Copyright © Banco de Mexico Trust. Copyright © The Museum of Modern Art / Licensed by SCALA / Art Resource, NY

20, AP/Wide World Photos.

21, © PBNJ Productions/CORBIS.

22, Sophie Bassouls/CORBIS SYGMA.

23, Andy Warhol (1928–1987), *Campbell's Soup Can (Tomato),* 1965, Synthetic polymer paint
and silkscreen ink on canvas, 36" x 24". Copyright © 2005 The Andy Warhol Foundation
for the Visual Arts / Artists Rights Society (ARS), New York / TM licensed by Campbell's
Soup Co. / Art Resource, NY. All rights reserved.

24, © Hulton-Deutsch Collection/CORBIS.

## Modern Cluster: The Harlem Renaissance

*Page 861:* Cover of Opportunity Magazine, June 1926, by Aaron Douglas (1899–1979). ©
Copyright. Schomburg Center for Research in Black Culture, The New York Public Library, New York, NY, U.S.A. Photo credit: SCHOMBURG CENTER / Art Resource, NY.

*Page 905:* Aaron Douglas (1899–1979), *Aspects of Negro Life: From Slavery through Reconstruction,* 1934. Oil on canvas, 60 x 139". Art Resource, NY.

## The Contemporary Short Story: 1970 to the Present

*Page 910:* 1, © Tim Page/CORBIS.

2, © Bettmann/CORBIS.

3, David Hockney (b. 1937), *A Bigger Splash,* 1967, acrylic on canvas, 96 x 96". Copyright ©
David Hockney. Tate Gallery, London / Art Resource, NY.

4, © Bettmann/CORBIS.

5, © Colin McPherson/CORBIS.

6, Judy Chicago (b. 1939), Plate for first woman burned at the stake for witchcraft, from *The
Dinner Party,* 1975–1979. Copyright © 2005 Judy Chicago / Artists Rights Society (ARS),
New York. Melnik / Art Resource, NY.

*Page 911:* 7, AP/Wide World Photos.

8, © Bettmann/CORBIS.

9, © Robyn McDaniels.

10, © Bettmann/CORBIS.

11, © Sophie Bassouls/CORBIS SYGMA.

12, Jean-Michel Basquiat (1960–1988), *All Coloured Cast (Part II), 1982*. Acrylic and pencil and collage on wood support, 152.5 x 252.5 cm. Private collection. Copyright © 2005 Artists Rights Society (ARS), New York / ADAGP, Paris. Banque d'Images, ADAGP / Art Resource, NY.

*Page 912:* 13, © Nancy Kaszerman/ZUMA/CORBIS.

14, Barbara Kruger (b. 1945), *Untitled (We will no longer be seen and not heard)*, 1985, Nine color lithographs, 20 1/2" by 20 1/2" each. Courtesy Mary Boone Gallery, New York, Tate Gallery, London / Art Resource, NY.

15, AP/Wide World Photos.

16, © Lee Snider/Photo Images/CORBIS.

17, © Ed Kashi/CORBIS.

18, © Bettmann/CORBIS.

*Page 913:* 19, © Henry Diltz/CORBIS.

20, AP/Wide World Photos.

21, © Peter Turnley/CORBIS.

22, © McPherson Colin/CORBIS SYGMA.

23, © S.I.N./CORBIS.

24, © AP/Wide World Photos.

**Contemporary Cluster: Postcolonial Literature**
*Page 1352:* © Caroline Penn/Panos Pictures.
*Page 1360:* © Denis Scott/CORBIS.

# Index of Terms

# Index of Authors and Titles